Handbook for Achieving Gender Equity through Education

Second Edition

EDITORS

Susan S. Klein, General Editor

Barbara Richardson, Part I

Dolores A. Grayson, Part II

Lynn H. Fox, Part III

Cheris Kramarae, Part IV

Diane S. Pollard, Part V

Carol Anne Dwyer, Part VI

LAWRENCE ERLBAUM ASSOCIATES, PUBLISHERS
2007   Mahwah, New Jersey   London

Director of Editorial: Lane Akers
Editorial Assistant: Anthony Messina
Cover Art: Patricia E. Ortman
Cover Design: Tomai Maridou
Full-Service Compositor: MidAtlantic Books and Journals, Inc.

This book was typeset in 9/11 pt. Garamond ITC BT, Italic, Bold, and Bold Italic with
Novarese BT Book, Italic.

Lawrence Erlbaum Associates, Inc., Publishers
10 Industrial Avenue
Mahwah, New Jersey 07430
www.erlbaum.com

Handbook for achieving gender equity through education / Susan Klein ... [et al.].—
2nd ed.

Rev. ed. of: Handbook for achieving sex equity through education, c1985.
ISBN 978-0-8058-5453-4 (case: alk. paper) — ISBN 978-0-8058-5454-1 (pbk. : alk. paper)
— ISBN 978-1-4106-1763-7 (e book)

1. Educational equalization—United States. 2. Sex discrimination in education—United
States. 3. Sexism—United States.   I. Klein, Susan S. II. Handbook for achieving sex
equity through education. LC213.2.H36 2007
379.2'6—dc22

2007006401

Books published by Lawrence Erlbaum Associates are printed on
acid-free paper, and their bindings are chosen for strength and durability.

Printed in the United States of America

10 9 8 7 6 5 4 3 2 1

Handbook for Achieving Gender Equity through Education

www.feminist.org/education

Editors

Susan S. Klein, General Editor; Barbara Richardson, Part I; Dolores A. Grayson, Part II; Lynn H. Fox, Part III; Cheris Kramarae, Part IV; Diane S. Pollard, Part V; Carol Ann Dwyer, Part VI

CONTENTS

*The bold face names are the Lead Authors.

CONTRIBUTORS*

―――――――――――――――――――――― *Editors* ――――――――――――――――――――――

Susan S. Klein, General Editor
Feminist Majority Foundation, Arlington, Virginia
sklein@feminist.org

Sue Klein, Education Equity Director of the Feminist Majority Foundation since 2003, is the general editor of this *Handbook for Achieving Gender Equity through Education* and served the same role in the 1985 *Handbook for Achieving Sex Equity through Education*. She also developed the Title IX Action Network and a Web site to accompany the *Handbook*. She has an Ed.D. and a B.S. in Education from Temple University and a M.Ed. from the University of Pennsylvania. During 34 years in the research offices in the U.S. Department of Education (and its predecessors) she focused on gender equity, evaluation, and dissemination. During this time she: established the Gender Equity Expert Panel to identify promising and exemplary replicable gender equity programs, edited *Sex Equity and Sexuality in Education,* and received awards for her writing and leadership in education equity and dissemination.

Barbara Richardson, Part I—Facts and Assumptions about the Nature and Value of Gender Equity
Eastern Michigan University, Ypsilanti, Michigan
brichards@emich.edu

Barbara Richardson is a professor at Eastern Michigan University, Department of Sociology, Anthropology, and Criminology. Her degrees are from Harvard University (B.A. cum laude), Columbia University (M.A.), and Cornell University (Ph.D.). She helped found their early Women's Studies program and was a member of the "Cornell 11" activists. She then joined the Women's Research Team in the National Institute of Education in the U.S. Department of Education, followed by serving as academic vice president at West Virginia Wesleyan College. Her best known publications are two coauthored books: *Achievement and Women: Challenging the Assumptions* and *Sex Role Research: Measuring Social Change*.

Dolores A. Grayson, Part II—Administrative Strategies for Implementing Gender Equity
Executive Director, GrayMill Consulting, Tehachapi, California
dgrayson@iinet.com

Dolores A. Grayson is the founder and co-owner of GrayMill Consulting. She has been an educational equity professional for over 30 years. She has a B.S. from the University of North Carolina, Greensboro; a M.S. in Educational Administration from California State University, Fullerton; and, an interdisciplinary PhD in Educational Leadership from the Union

Institute and University, Cincinnati, Ohio. Her best known work includes the award-winning Generating Expectations for Student Achievement (GESA) program and numerous other training materials. In addition to helping found the Association for Gender Equity Leadership in Education (AGELE) formerly the National Coalition for Sex Equity in Education, she served as its chair and later received their first Grayson Award for scholarship related to gender equity in education.

Lynn H. Fox, Part III—A General Educational Practices for Promoting Gender Equity
American University, Washington, D.C.
lynn.fox@american.edu & drlynnfox@msn.com

Lynn H. Fox is an educational psychologist and former dean of the School of Education at American University where she taught courses in educational psychology, testing and measurement, quantitative research methods and math for elementary school teachers. Her Ph.D. is in psychology from the Johns Hopkins University where she was the director of the Intellectually Gifted Child Study Group from 1974 to 1985. She was also the general editor of "*Women in the Mathematical Mystique*" and many other publications on gifted girls. Throughout her career her focus has been on gender analysis, gifted and at-risk learners; and program evaluation. She is the author of numerous books, book chapters and journal articles and served on and wrote about the U.S. Department of Education's Gender Equity Expert Panel. She was a lead author of chapters 8 and 27 on testing and gifted students in this Handbook.

Cheris Kramarae, Part IV—Gender Equity Strategies in the Content Areas
Center for the Study of Women in Society, University of Oregon, Eugene, Oregon
cheris@uoregon.edu

Cheris Kramarae is the author or co-author of 75 articles; and author, editor, or co-editor of 12 books and editor of many articles and books on gender and language, education, technology, communication, history, and women's and gender studies. While a Jubilee Professor at the University of Illinois at Urbana-Champaign, she helped organize a faculty and student working colloquium "Women, Information Technology, and Scholarship," and served as a director of Gender and Women's Studies. She was an international dean of the experimental and innovative International Women's University held in Germany in 2000. With Dale Spender, she edited *The Routledge International Encyclopedia of Women: Global Women's Issues and Knowledge*.

―――

*The boldface names are the Lead authors.

Diane S. Pollard, Part V—Gender Equity Strategies
for Diverse Populations
Professor Emerita, University of Wisconsin-Milwaukee,
Milwaukee, Wisconsin
dpollard@uwm.edu

Diane S. Pollard is Professor Emerita, Department of Educational Psychology at the University of Wisconsin-Milwaukee. She received a B.A. in Psychology from Wellesley College, Wellesley, MA and an M.A. and Ph.D. in Education from the University of Chicago. She was the 1996 recipient of the Willystine Goodsel Award (AERA) and the 2000 recipient of the School of Education Research Award, University of Wisconsin-Milwaukee. Recent publications include: *From Center to Margins: The Importance of Self-Definition in Research* (with O. M. Welch); *Who will Socialize African American Students in Contemporary Public Schools?* (in Allen, W. A. et al.); *African American Education: Race, Community, Inequality and Achievement*; *A Tribute to Edgar G. Epps* (JAI); and *Feminist Perspectives on Education* (with S. K. Biklen), *Handbook or Research on Teaching*, AERA. In addition

to her research, she serves as program evaluator for several agencies in Milwaukee.

Carol Anne Dwyer, Part VI—Gender Equity From Early
Through Postsecondary Education
Educational Testing Service, Princeton, New Jersey
cdwyer@ets.org

Carol Anne Dwyer is Distinguished Presidential Appointee at Educational Testing Service, where she has also directed major test development, research, policy, and administrative units. Her work has been concerned with assessment and equity as they relate to teaching and learning in both higher education and K–12 settings. She has published extensively in the field of test validity, emphasizing uses of construct validity theory to promote test fairness and appropriate test design and use. She has also written about fairness and gender issues in communication skills, mathematical reasoning, grading practices, educational competitions, and other non-test achievement indicators. She served as editor of this Part of the Handbook for both the 1985 and 2007 versions.

Authors

Chapter 1—Examining the Achievement of Gender Equity in and through Education

Susan S. Klein
Feminist Majority Foundation, Arlington, Virginia
sklein@feminist.org
(*See editor information*).

With assistance of:

Cheris Kramarae
University of Oregon, Eugene, Oregon
cheris@uoregon.edu

Barbara Richardson
Eastern Michigan University, Ypsilanti, Michigan
brichards@emich.edu

Chapter 2—Facts and Assumptions about the Nature of Gender Differences and the Implications for Gender Equity

Janet Shibley-Hyde
University of Wisconsin, Madison, Wisconsin
jshyde@wisc.edu

Janet Shibley Hyde is the Helen Thompson Woolley Professor of Psychology and Women's Studies at the University of Wisconsin. The author of two undergraduate textbooks, *Half the Human Experience: The Psychology of Women* and *Understanding Human Sexuality*, she is best known for her meta-analyses of research on psychological gender differences. She is the winner of the Sherif Award from the Society for the Psychology of Women (APA Division 35) for career contributions to research on women and gender.

Sara M. Lindberg
University of Wisconsin, Madison, Wisconsin
smlindberg@wisc.edu

Sara Lindberg is currently a doctoral student in the Psychology Department at the University of Wisconsin. Her research examines how gender roles affect adolescent development. She developed a scale to measure objectified body consciousness in youth (*Psychology of Women*

Quarterly, 2006) and has examined ways in which pubertal development and other factors contribute to the development of objectified body consciousness. Sara is currently studying how gender differentiation in parent-child interactions affects children's academic and career aspirations, and she is conducting a meta-analysis of pubertal effects on internalizing, externalizing, and sexual behaviors.

Chapter 3—Gender Equity Education Globally

Nelly P. Stromquist
University of Southern California
stromqui@bcf.usc.edu

Nelly P. Stromquist (Ph.D., Stanford University) is a professor of comparative and development education at the Rossier School of Education, University of Southern California. Her recent books include: *Feminist Organizations in the Process of Social Change in Latin America* (2006), *Género, educación y política en América Latina* (2004), and *Education in a Globalized World. The Connectivity of Economic Power, Technology, and Knowledge* (2002). As a current Fulbright New Century Scholar, she is investigating modifications in the identity and practice of the professoriate as a consequence of globalization trends.

Chapter 4—Impact of Education on Gender Equity in Employment and Its Outcomes

Barbara Richardson
Eastern Michigan University, Ypsilanti, Michigan
brichards@emich.edu
(*See editor information*).

Pamela A. Sandoval
State University of New York System Administration,
Albany, New York
pamela.sandoval@suny.edu

Pamela A. Sandoval is assistant provost for P–16 education at the State University of New York System Administration. She has a B.A. in art from Mt. Mary College in Milwaukee and a M.S. in educational psychology and an interdisciplinary Ph.D. in Urban Sociology and History from University of Wisconsin-Milwaukee. She has numerous publications in

---

*The boldface names are the Lead authors.

the areas of assessment and evaluation with a focus on the areas of race, class, and gender. These articles have been published by journals such as *Urban Education* and *Urban Review*.

Chapter 5—The Role of Government in Advancing Gender Equity in Education

Margaret A. Nash
Assistant Professor, Graduate School of Education,
University of California at Riverside
margaret.nash@ucr.edu

Margaret A. Nash is an educational historian at the University of California, Riverside. She is the author of the book *Women's Education in the United States, 1780–1840* (Palgrave Press, 2005) and of articles in *Teachers College Record*, *History of Education Quarterly*, *History of Higher Education Annual*, and the *Journal of the Early Republic*. She was awarded a National Academy of Education/Spencer Foundation postdoctoral fellowship. She has a Ph.D. and M.A. in Educational Policy Studies from the University of Wisconsin-Madison, and a B.Ph. in Interdisciplinary Studies from Miami University of Ohio.

Susan S. Klein
Feminist Majority Foundation, Arlington, Virginia
sklein@feminist.org
(See editor information).

Barbara Bitters
Wisconsin Department of Public Instruction,
Madison, Wisconsin
barbara.bitters@dpi.state.wi.us

Barbara Bitters is the current chair of the Association for Gender Equity Leadership in Education (AGELE). Her educational equity leadership at the WDPI includes staffing a first-year WEEA grant 1976); Assistant Director of the Equal Educational Opportunities Office for Sex Equity (Title IV CRA-1977–78); Sex Equity Administrator in Career and Technical Education (1978–1990); Founder of the Wisconsin Vocational Equity Leadership Cadre (1987); Director of the Equity Mission Team (1990–2003); Title IX Coordinator for the DPI (1990 to the present); and MOA Coordinator 2003 to the present). She also served as the Special Assistant on Women's Issues in the OVAE at the U.S. Department of Education from 1979–1980.

Sharon F. Hobbs
Associate Professor, Dept. of Educational Theory & Practice,
Montana State University-Billings
shobbs@msubillings.edu

Sharon F. Hobbs teaches courses in the philosophy and sociology of education as well as school law. She is also the Assessment Coordinator for the College of Education. She has published articles on professional development school partnerships, collaboration, and school law, and is currently working on a longitudinal study of learning communities in online teacher preparation cohorts. She has a Ph.D. and M.Ed. in Education, Culture and Society from the University of Utah.

William A. Howe
Connecticut State Department of Education, Hartford, Connecticut
william.howe@ct.gov

Dr. William A. Howe is the Connecticut State Title IX Coordinator and the education consultant for multicultural education, gender equity, and civil rights in the Bureau of Educational Equity at the Connecticut State Department of Education. Dr. Howe has Bachelor's Degree from McMaster University and the University of Western Ontario, a Master's Degree from Lesley University School of Management, and a Master's Degree and a Doctorate in Education from Teachers College/Columbia University. He was President of the National Association for Multicultural Education (NAME). He serves on the boards of: *Multicultural Perspectives*, Native Village, Yale University Programs in International Educational Resources, University of Connecticut Asian American Studies Institute, Democracy Works and the Connecticut Center for the Book.

Linda Shevitz
Maryland State Department of Education,
Baltimore, Maryland
lshevitz@msde.state.md.us

Linda Shevitz is an Educational Equity Specialist at the Maryland State Department of Education, where she has worked as the statewide Title IX/Gender Equity Coordinator since 1982. She is the past chair of the Association for Gender Equity Leadership in Education (formerly the National Coalition for Sex Equity in Education), and past vice chair of the National Coalition for Women and Girls in Education. She was a Women's Educational Equity Act Associate and served on the Gender Equity Expert Panel for the U.S. Department of Education.

Linda Wharton
Richard Stockton College of New Jersey
linda.wharton@stockton.edu

Linda J. Wharton, Associate Professor of Political Science, Richard Stockton College of New Jersey. Professor Wharton has a J.D. from Rutgers School of Law and a B.A. from Bryn Mawr College. She was a law clerk to the Hon. Dolores K. Sloviter, Judge of the U.S. Court of Appeals for the Third Circuit. She is also the former managing attorney of the Women's Law Project in Philadelphia, PA and a lecturer-in-law at the University of Pennsylvania School of Law. She currently serves on the board of directors of the National Women's History Project.

With assistance of:

Eleanor Smeal
President, Feminist Majority Foundation and Publisher
of Ms. magazine, Arlington, Virginia
ellie@feminist.org

Chapter 6—Increasing Gender Equity in Educational Leadership

Charol Shakeshaft
Hofstra University
charolshakeshaft@aol.com

Charol Shakeshaft is a professor in the Department of Foundations, Leadership, and Policy Studies at Hofstra University and author of *Women in Educational Administration*. Her most recent book, *Educator Sexual Misconduct,* will be published in 2007. Dr. Shakeshaft was the principal investigator on a National Science Foundation project to promote interest in science careers, a U.S. Department of Education grant documenting peer relationships, and two U.S. Department of Education funded research projects on educator sexual misconduct. Since 1988, when Dr. Shakeshaft was appointed to the first National Policy Board for Educational Administration (NCBEA) Study Group, she has been involved in reform and improvement of preparation programs for educational leaders and administrations. Dr. Shakeshaft was the first female AERA Division A vice-president and a recipient of the AERA-RWE Willystine Goodsell Award.

Genevieve Brown
Sam Houston State University
brown@shsu.edu

Genevieve Brown is professor and dean of the College of Education at Sam Houston State University. She served as assistant superintendent

---

*The boldface names are the Lead authors.

for 10 years. Coauthor and coeditor of numerous articles and books on leadership, she is the codeveloper of *The Synergistic Leadership Theory*, the first leadership theory particularly inclusive of women's voices and reflective of women's experiences. Additionally, she is cofounder and coeditor of *Advancing Women in Leadership Journal*, the first international, online refereed journal for professional women, and a corecipient of the 2005 AERA-RWE Willystine Goodsell Award.

Beverly Irby
Sam Houston State University
edu_bid@exchange.shsu.edu
Beverly Irby is professor and chair, Department of Educational Leadership and Counseling at Sam Houston State University. She authored numerous grants funded by the U.S. Department of Education and the Institute for Education Science and related to social justice issues. She has served as the Director of Student Teaching and Field Experiences at SHSU and as director of the Doctoral Program in Educational Leadership. She is widely published with books and papers and is codeveloper of *The Synergistic Leadership Theory* and the *Advancing Women in Leadership Journal*. She is corecipient of the AERA-RWE Willystine Goodsell Award, 2005 and received the Margaret Montgomery Leadership Award from the Texas Council of Women School Executives.

Margaret Grogan
University of Missouri
groganm@missouri.edu
Margaret Grogan is currently professor and chair, Department of Educational Leadership and Policy Analysis, University of Missouri-Columbia. She is a past president of the University Council for Educational Administration. She edits a series on Women in Leadership for SUNY Press. Prior to Missouri, she was at the University of Virginia teaching in the principal and superintendent preparation programs there. Along with Cryss Brunner, Grogan was recently recognized by the American Association of School Administrators for her 10-year research on women in the superintendency.

Julia Ballenger
Stephen F. Austin State University
jnballenger@sfasu.edu
Julia Ballenger is currently associate professor and coordinator, Principal Preparation Program, in the Department of Secondary Education and Educational Leadership, Stephen F. Austin State University. Julia is president-elect of the Texas Council of Professors of Educational Administration (TCPEA) and serves on the editorial review board of TCPEA's *Journal of School Leadership Review*. She is also Membership-elect of Research on Women and Education. Her current research focuses on the principalship, women of color in leadership, and leadership for social justice.

Chapter 7—The Treatment of Gender Equity in Teacher Education

David Sadker
The American University, Washington, D.C.
dsadker@american.edu
David Sadker a professor at The American University has degrees from CCNY, Harvard, and the University of Massachusetts. With his late wife Myra Sadker, he coauthored *Failing at Fairness* (1995), *Teachers, Schools and Society* (McGraw Hill), now in its 8th edition, and he is coeditor of *Gender in the Classroom: Foundations, Skills, Methods and Strategies across the Curriculum* (Lawrence Erlbaum, 2006). The Sadkers' work has been recognized by the American Educational Research Association, The American Association of University Women, and the

American Association of Colleges of Teacher Education. David Sadker has received two honorary doctorates.

Karen Zittleman
The American University, Washington, D.C.
kz@american.edu
Karen Zittleman is coauthor of *Teachers, Schools, and Society: A Brief Introduction to Education* (McGraw-Hill, 2007). Her articles about teacher education, gender, and Title IX appear in the *Journal of Teacher Education, Educational Leadership, Phi Delta Kappan,* and *Principal* magazine. Karen is a contributing author to *Gender in the Classroom: Foundations, Skills, Methods and Strategies Across the Curriculum* (Lawrence Erlbaum, 2006), has taught several Title IX online courses through the Women's Educational Equity Act, and is project manager for the Myra Sadker Foundation.

Penelope M. Earley
George Mason University, Fairfax, Virginia
pearly@gmu.edu
Dr. Earley is founding Director of the Center for Education Policy and a professor in the Graduate School of Education at George Mason University. Before joining the GMU faculty, Earley was a vice president with the American Association of Colleges for Teachers Education. At AACTE she directed federal and state governmental relations, issue analysis, policy studies, and public relations. Dr. Earley's areas of research include federal and state education policy and governance, public policy regarding teacher education, and gender equity issues. She received her B.A. from the University of Michigan, MA, from the University of Virginia and Ph.D. from Virginia Tech.

Theresa McCormick
Consultant, Seattle, Washington
theresamcco@comcast.net
Theresa McCormick is Professor Emeritus, Iowa State University, where she wrote *"Creating the Nonsexist Classroom—A Multicultural Approach"* and numerous other publications. Her specializations are in multicultural/gender teacher education and gender studies. Now, living in Seattle, she is a consultant on multicultural/gender issues, a peace activist, writer and artist. She serves on the Board of the National Women's Studies Association Journal and on the Board of the United Nations Association of Seattle. Dr. McCormick is the 2006 winner of the AERA/RWE Willystine Goodsell Award. She has an Ed.D. and a M.A. from West Virginia University and a B.S. in Art Education from Oklahoma State University.

Candace A. Strawn
George Mason University, Fairfax, Virginia
cstrawn@gmu.edu
Dr. Strawn is the Coordinator of Secondary Education at George Mason University (GMU) in Fairfax, VA. She has been a high school teacher and a community college instructor. In addition to her George Mason duties, Dr. Strawn is the Membership Chair of the AERA:SIG, Research on Women and Education, and treasurer of the George Mason chapter of the Kappa Delta Pi educational honorary. She received her Ph.D. from Iowa State University.

Jo Anne Preston
Tufts University, Medford, Massachusetts
joanne.Preston@tufts.edu
Dr. Preston, a professor in the Department of Sociology is a historical sociologist who is finishing a book on the feminization of school teaching. Her published work examines occupational gender segregation, the influence of gender ideology on the social construction of teaching, the social dynamis of the nineteenth-century classroom, and teacher education in early female academies. She served on the edito-

---

*The boldface names are the Lead authors.

rial board of The History of Education Quarterly. She received her Ph.D. from Brandeis University and she is currently visiting the Department of Sociology, Tufs University.

Chapter 8—Gender Equity in Testing and Assessment

Dianne Reed
Sam Houston State University, Huntsville, Texas
edu_dxr@shsu.edu

Dr. Reed is an assistant professor and Principal Preparation Program Coordinator in the Educational Leadership Program. Her research interests include issues in education regarding gender, race and ethnicity, and impact of socioeconomic status; development of educational leadership programs to assist school districts in development, enhancement, and expansion of innovative programs to recruit, train, and mentor minority principals and assistant principals; literacy programs for migrant families and other students at risk of school failure; and training and information for parents of children with disabilities. She is the author of several publications in educational journals and books.

Lynn H. Fox
American University, Washington, D.C.
lynn.fox@american.edu & drlynnfox@msn.com
    (*See editor information*).

Mary Lou Andrews
University of Dayton, Dayton, Ohio
mary.andrews@notes.udayton.edu

Dr. Mary Lou Andrews is Administrative Faculty and Licensure Officer in the Department of Teacher Education at the University of Dayton. She teaches educational psychology and has published in the *Journal of Educational Research.* Her specializations are gender issues in schools, in particular, how gender issues are addressed in educational leadership programs. Currently, she is conducting a follow-up study of participants who took part in a gender-awareness program.

Nancy Betz
Ohio State University, Columbus, Ohio
betz.3@osu.edu

Dr. Nancy E. Betz is professor of psychology. She has authored or coauthored over 150 articles and chapters. She is the author of *Tests and Assessment*, with Bruce Walsh, and the *Career Psychology of Women,* with Louise Fitzgerald. Dr. Betz served as editor of the *Journal of Vocational Behavior* and has served on the Department of Defense Advisory Committee on Military Testing and the Research Advisory Board for Consulting Psychologists' Press (CPP, Inc.). Dr. Betz has received numerous awards for her research and scholarship.

Jan Perry Evenstad
Colorado State University, Denver, Colorado
evenstad@cahs.colostate.edu

Dr. Jan Perry Evenstad is a senior research associate at Colorado State University for the Interwest Equity Assistance Center. Dr. Perry Evenstad's expertise has been in effective teacher training practices that focus on areas of gender, race, and national origin. She is a national trainer for Generating Expectations for Student Achievement (GESA) and is a senior associate director of the GESA Educational Alliance.

Anthony J. Harris
Sam Houston State University, Huntsville, Texas
edu_ajh@shsu.edu

Dr. Harris is associate professor, Department of Educational Leadership and Counseling, Sam Houston State University. His master's and doctoral degrees are in counseling. He was a fellow with the Kellogg National Leadership Program; founded a mentoring program for African American boys; was vice president of the National African American Male Collaboration; a school board member; a mentor for the Rockefeller Brothers Fund for Educational Leadership; and a member of the Standards Writing Committee for School Counselor Certification for the National Board for Professional Teaching Standards.

Judy A. Johnson
University of Arkansas at Little Rock, Little Rock, Arkansas
jajohnson1@ualr.edu

Dr. Judy A. Johnson is a 25-year veteran educator with professional experience spanning early childhood through university and postgraduate education. Dr. Johnson has traveled nationally and internationally, writing and speaking in the area of leadership, organizational development, and school improvement. Currently an associate professor of educational leadership at the University of Arkansas–Little Rock, Dr. Johnson is working concurrently in the fields of urban and rural educational improvement and leadership.

Shirley Johnson
Sam Houston State University, Huntsville, Texas
elc_saj@shsu.edu

Dr. Shirley Johnson currently serves as an assistant professor training principals and superintendents in the graduate program at Sam Houston State University. She has served as an assistant superintendent in the Houston Independent School District and 17 years as a high school principal in urban and suburban communities. As a monitor for the Texas Education Agency for many years, she has remained current in the development of change and reform strategies for K–12 education.

Carol Hightower-Parker
Sam Houston State University, Huntsville, Texas
elc_cah@shsu.edu

Dr. Carol Parker is an associate professor in the Counseling Program at Sam Houston State University. Dr. Parker's expertise is school counseling, leadership, counselor supervision, and student learning and achievement, especially for minority students. She is a national trainer for the Center for Reforming School Counselor Initiative at the Education Trust in Washington, D.C. Dr. Parker serves on the Texas School Counselor Committee appointed by the State Board of Educator Certification (SBEC) to write new standards and assessments for school counselors.

Barbara Polnick
Sam Houston State University, Huntsville, Texas
elc_bep@shsu.edu

Dr. Barbara Polnick is an assistant professor in the Educational Leadership and Counseling Department at Sam Houston State University, Huntsville, TX. She earned her Ed.D. in Educational Administration from Texas A&M University, College Station, TX and holds a Master's degree in Reading. Dr. Polnick's research interests include social justice issues, teacher leadership, assessment, and evaluation of instructional programs. She has over 30 years of experience in the public schools as a reading and mathematics teacher, regional curriculum and mathematics specialist, instructional supervisor, assistant principal, and district curriculum director and school improvement consultant.

Phyllis Rosser
The Equality in Testing Project, New York, New York
wrosser@aol.com

Phyllis Rosser is director and owner of The Equality in Testing Project. In 1989, the Center for Women Policy Studies published her major research report, *The SAT Gender Gap: Identifying the Causes*, sup-

---

*The boldface names are the Lead authors.

ported by a grant from the Department of Education's Women's Educational Equity Act. She has testified before Congress and, in 1990, conducted a study on "Gender and Testing" for the National Commission on Testing and Public Policy that identifies differences in problem-solving styles between males and females, Whites and African Americans. Her recent work has focused on the college gender gap, which was the subject of "Too Many Women in College," published in the Fall 2005 issue of *Ms.* magazine.

Chapter 9—Gender Equity in Coeducational and Single Sex Educational Environments

Emily Arms
Loyola Marymount University, Los Angeles, California
earms@lmu.edu

A former high school English teacher and curriculum director, Emily Arms is currently an assistant professor at Loyola Marymount University where she teaches graduate courses in the School of Education. Prior to that, she taught courses in women's studies and education at UCLA, where she earned her Ph.D. in 2002. Her dissertation research was a case study of one large, urban public school experimenting with all single-sex classroom instruction. Her most recent publication on the topic is "Accountability and Single-Sex Schooling: A Collision of Reform Agendas" in *The American Educational Research Journal* (2004), with Kathryn Herr.

Chapter 10—Gender Equity in the Use of Educational Technology

Gypsy Abbott
School of Education, University of Alabama at Birmingham, Birmingham, Alabama
gabbott@uab.edu

Professor Gypsy Abbott, director of the NSF-funded UAP ADVANCE Institutional Transformation grant has conducted research and evaluation in gender education in math, science and technology for the past 20 years. She has been a Co-PI and program evaluator for numerous federally funded projects from NSF and the U.S. Department of Education. Division H of AERA has recognized two of the evaluation reports that she wrote as "Outstanding Evaluation Report" of the year. She was the Society for Information Technology & Teacher Education (SITE) recipient of the *2006 Outstanding Service in Digital Equity Award* and was recognized as the *Outstanding Contributor to Supercomputing in Alabama* in 2001.

Lisa Bievenue
University of Illinois at Urbana-Champaign, Urbana, Illinois
bievenue@uiuc.edu

Ms. Bievenue coordinates K–12 education outreach programs at the University of Illinois at Urbana-Champaign. She has led education projects that promote gender equity in the use of advanced computational and visualization technologies, and coordinates national teacher education programs in the use of advanced technologies in science and mathematics. She earned a B.S. in Computer Science and a M.A. in speech communication, both from the University of Illinois.

Suzanne Damarin
School of Educational Policy and Leadership, Ohio State University, Columbus, Ohio
damarin.1@osu.edu

Professor Suzanne Damarin works in the area of social and cultural foundations of education. Throughout her career, her teaching, research, and scholarship has been at the intersections of issues related to social diversity with issues in the fields of mathematics and technology. She is currently working on three projects concerned with: (a) how women who leave "the pipeline" get back in, (b) the unintended consequences of information and communications technologies on academic practice, and (c) the radical intra-actions of gender, mathematics, and technology.

Cheris Kramarae
Center for the Study of Women in Society, University of Oregon, Eugene, Oregon
cheris@uoregon.edu
(*See editor information*).

With assistance of:

Candace A. Strawn
Coordinator of Secondary Education at George Mason University (GMU) in Fairfax, Virginia
cstrawn@gmu.edu

Grace Jepkemboi
Ddoctoral student in the School of Education, University of Alabama, Birmingham, Alabama
memoi@uab.edu

Chapter 11—Sexual Harassment: The Hidden Gender Equity Problem

Michele A. Paludi
Union Graduate College and Human Resources Management Solutions, Schenectady, New York
mpaludi@aol.com

Michele Paludi has published extensively on sexual harassment, psychology of women, gender, and sexual harassment and victimization. Her book, *Ivory Power: Sexual Harassment on Campus*, (1990, SUNY Press), received the 1992 Myers Center Award for Outstanding Book on Human Rights in the United States. She was a consultant and a member of former New York State Governor Mario Cuomo's Task Force on Sexual Harassment. Dr. Paludi serves as an expert witness for court proceedings and administrative hearings on sexual harassment. She conducts training programs and investigations of sexual harassment and other EEO issues for businesses and educational institutions

Jennifer Martin
Oakland University, Rochester, Michigan
jenm999@twmi.rr.com

Jennifer Martin is department head of English at a public alternative high school for at-risk students in Michigan and holds a Ph.D. in Educational Leadership. She sought to reduce the high rate of peer sexual harassment that was occurring within her school by devising an intervention strategy to combat it; this became her dissertation research and it is how her interest in sexual harassment began. Dr. Martin is also an adjunct lecturer at Oakland University where she teaches graduate research methods. Her research interests include peer sexual harassment, feminist identification, teaching for social justice, service learning, and the at-risk student.

Carmen A. Paludi, Jr.
Human Resources Management Solutions, Niskayuna, New York
cpaludi@comcast.net

Ms. Paludi brings nearly 26 years of technical and program-management experience to human-resource management and its related fields. He provides guidance and direction on risk management, and out-of-the-box thought processes for complex systems and scenarios

---

*The boldface names are the Lead authors.

such that policies and procedures developed can be executed. He has been the motivating force behind integrating technology into the development of Web-based training services Human Resources Management Solutions provide.

Chapter 12—Gender Equity in Mathematics

Carole B. Lacampagne
George Washington University, Washington, D.C.
clacampagne@earthlink.net

Carole Lacampagne served as an Associate Professor of Mathematics at Northern Illinois University. In Washington, she has been engaged in a variety of mathematics education policy issues at the National Science Foundation, the U.S. Department of Education, RAND, and the National Academies of Science where she served as Director of the Mathematical Sciences Education Board. Throughout her career, Dr. Lacampagne has been active in encouraging women to enter mathematics. She chaired the Mathematical Association of America's Women and Mathematics program and won national awards for this program. She is now semi-retired and serving as an Adjunct Professor of Mathematics at George Washington University.

Patricia B. Campbell
Campbell-Kibler Associates, Groton, Massachusetts
campbell@campbell-kibler.com

Patricia B. Campbell, Ph.D., President of Campbell-Kibler Associates, Inc, has been involved in educational research and evaluation in science and mathematics education and race/ethnicity and gender since the mid 1970's. Dr. Campbell authored more than 90 publications including *Engagement, Capacity and Continuity: A Trilogy for Student Success* and *Upping the Numbers: Using Research-Based Decision Making to Increase Diversity in the Quantitative Sciences* with Eric Jolly and Lesley Perlman and *What Do We Know?: Seeking Effective Math and Science* with Beatriz Chu Clewell. She received the WEPAN Betty Vetter Research Award and the American Educational Research Association Willystine Goodsell Award.

Suzanne Damarin
Ohio State University, Columbus, Ohio
damarin.1@osu.edu

(*See author information, chapter 10*).

Abbe H. Herzig
University at Albany, State University of New York, Albany, New York
aherzig@uamail.albany.edu

Abbe Herzig is an assistant professor of mathematics education at the University at Albany, State University of New York, with appointments in the School of Education and the Department of Women's Studies. Her research focuses on equity, diversity, and social justice in mathematics and science education at all levels. Through her current research, she is investigating factors supporting the success of women and people of color in post-graduate mathematics. She is working with mathematics departments around the country to help them develop their graduate programs to allow talented students of all races and genders to develop into well-trained mathematical scientists. She has developed courses and programs to help diverse populations of young students discover the relevance of mathematics to their lives and has implemented professional development programs for K–12 teachers to support a view of mathematics education as a vehicle for social justice. As a professional statistician, she has consulted on diversity-related projects for the United Nations, the Legal Defense Fund of the NAACP, and others.

Christina Vogt
National, Academy of Engineering, Washington, D.C.
cvogt@nae.edu

Christina Vogt is currently a resident scholar at the National Academies in Washington, DC. In her current post, she is part of team to implement a program to attract more young women into engineering and retain those at the postsecondary level in mechanical and electrical engineering majors. As a past senior technical manager for a subsidiary of Lockheed, she well understands the challenges for women and girls in engineering and related scientific fields. Her current research focuses on classroom and institutional dynamics, which either help or hinder women in engineering programs. Her current activism work revolves around using human rights frameworks to advance women's rights in the U.S.

Chapter 13—Gender Equity in Science, Engineering, and Technology

Carol J. Burger
Virginia Polytechnic Institute and State University, Blacksburg, Virginia
cjburger@vt.edu

Carol J. Burger is Associate Professor, Interdisciplinary Studies, and founder and editor of the *Journal of Women and Minorities in Science and Engineering*, now in its 12th year of publication. She received a B.A. in chemistry from Dominican University and a Ph.D. in immunology from Virginia Tech. She has published over 50 immunology and SET equity research papers, book chapters, including *Cybergrrrl Education and Virtual Feminism: Using the Internet to Teach Introductory Women's Studies* which discusses the authors' experiences teaching a web-enhanced women's studies course, and three monographs. She is the co-investigator on several NSF-funded projects.

Gypsy Abbott
University of Alabama at Birmingham, Alabama
gabbott@uab.edu

(*See author information, chapter 10*).

Sheila Tobias
Independent Researcher, Tucson, Arizona
sheilat@sheilatobias.com

Sheila Tobias was trained in history and literature at Harvard-Radcliffe and Columbia Universities and pioneered women's studies in the late 1960s. In 1974, she studied women's avoidance of college-level mathematics and the physical sciences. She created a number of projects, 9 books, and contributed to the launching of a new professional science master's degree that is especially appealing to women. Her most recent books include: *They're not dumb, they're different: Stalking the second tier* (1990), *Breaking the Science Barrier* (1992), *Revitalizing Undergraduate Science: Why Some Things Work and Most Don't* (1992), *Rethinking Science as a Career* (1995), and *The Hidden Curriculum: Faculty Made Tests in Science* (1997), and Faces of Feminism: An Activists's Reflections on the Women's Movement, (1997).

Janice Koch
Hofstra University, Hempstead, New York
janice.koch@hofstra.edu

Janice Koch, is Professor of Science Education at Hofstra University and teaches courses in elementary and middle school science methods, gender issues in the classroom, and techniques of classroom research. Her science methods textbook is in third edition *Science Stories: Science methods for elementary and middle school teachers*

---

*The boldface names are the Lead authors.

(2005). She is the Director of IDEAS, the Institute for the Development of Education in the Advanced Sciences at Hofstra University. This outreach institute fosters the public understanding of science as well as furthering professional development in science and technology.

Christina M. Vogt
National Academy of Engineering, Washington, D.C.
cvogt@nae.edu
    (*See author information, chapter 12*).

Teri Sosa
St. Joseph University, Philadelphia, Pennsylvania
tsosa@sju.edu
    Teri Sosa is an Assistant Professor of Education, St. Joseph's University, Philadelphia. Her research explores ways to empower those who are underserved by society and the educational systems. She teaches Educational Technology. Her dissertation, Voices of Women Computer Programmers: Perspectives on Achievement, won the 2005 Selma Greenberg Dissertation Award. Prior to becoming a professor, Dr. Sosa was a computer programmer and computer system designer, a K–12 technology coordinator, and a coordinator of graduate Instructional Technology programs. Her degrees include an Ed.D. in Instructional Technology, Northern Illinois University, M.B.A. from Loyola University Chicago, and B.A., Shimer College.

With assistance of:

Lisa Bievenue
University of Illinois at Urbana-Champaign, Urbana, Illinois
bievenue@uiuc.edu

Candace A. Strawn
George Mason University, Fairfax, Virginia
cstrawn@gmu.edu

Chapter 14—Gender Equity in Communication Skills

Anita Taylor
Professor Emerita in Communication and Women's Studies,
George Mason University, Fairfax, Virginia
ataylor@gmu.edu
    Anita Taylor is long time editor of the research periodical, *Women and Language*, that is affiliated with the Organization for the Study of Communication Language and Gender. She has written or co-edited several books dealing with communication and gender, most recently *Hearing Many Voices*. Her work focuses on the intersections of language, communication and gender. She has taught at the post-secondary level for more than 40 years, and served in administrative roles at George Mason University and at the St. Louis Community College.

Alison L. Bailey
University of California, Los Angeles, California
abailey@gseis.ucla.edu
    Alison Bailey is associate professor in the Psychological Studies in Education Division of the Department of Education, UCLA, and a faculty associate researcher at the National Center for Research on Evaluation, Standards, and Student Testing (CRESST). A graduate of Harvard University, she focuses her research on language and literacy development and assessment of young second language learners. She directs the Academic English Language Proficiency project at CRESST which has conducted research to provide an empirical basis for the construct of academic language. She is editor of *The Language Demands of School: Putting Academic English to the Test* (Yale University Press).

Pamela Cooper
University of South Carolina Beaufort, Bluffton, South Carolina
hoelp@gwm.sc.edu
    Dr. Pamela Cooper is professor of communication and area coordinator for the Humanities Division at the University of South Carolina Beaufort. Dr. Cooper has authored textbooks and articles in the areas of classroom communication, gender communication, storytelling, intercultural communication, public communication, and interpersonal communication. She has received numerous teaching awards, the most recent, the National Communication Association's award for scholarship and teaching. She is a Past President of the Central States Communication Association. Her most recent work, *Bound for Beauty*, documents her work in China interviewing women with bound feet.

Carol Anne Dwyer
Educational Testing Service, Princeton, New Jersey
cdwyer@ets.org
    (*See editor information*).

Cheris Kramarae
Center for the Study of Women in Society, University of Oregon,
Eugene, Oregon
cheris@uoregon.edu
    (*See editor information*).

Barbara Lieb
Independent scholar in communication and education
in metropolitan Washington, D.C.
liebcom@comcast.net
    Barbara Lieb teaches communication courses at George Mason University, Fairfax, Virginia, and has published and presented extensively on a broad range of issues in communication education, including gender, diversity and teacher communication. She has held positions as Senior Research Analyst and Director of the Policy Institute in the Institute for Education Sciences, U.S. Dept. of Education; Associate Executive Director for Education and Research, National Communication Association; and Associate Professor, communication and teacher education, University of Nebraska. She earned a Ph.D. in speech communication and psychology from the Pennsylvania University.

Chapter 15—Gender Equity in Foreign and Second Language Learning

Cindy Brantmeier
Washington University, St. Louis, Missouri
cbrantme@wustl.edu
    Cindy Brantmeier is an Assistant Professor of Applied Linguistics and Spanish at Washington University in St. Louis. She is Co-Director of the Graduate Certificate in Language Instruction and Director of Advanced Spanish. She has given invited presentations of her research in Malaysia, Argentina, Costa Rica, Amsterdam, The Republic of Georgia, and more. This year she was selected to be an Oxford Roundtable Scholar at Oxford University, UK. She was recently nominated to the *College Board's World Language Advisory Committee*. She received her Ph.D. from Indiana University in 2000.

Jeanne Schueller
University of Wisconsin—Milwaukee, Milwaukee, Wisconsin
jeannems@uwm.edu
    Jeanne Schueller is an Assistant Professor of German in the Department of Foreign Languages and Linguistics at the University of Wisconsin—Milwaukee where she directs the first- and second-year German

---

*The boldface names are the Lead authors.

language program and supervises teaching assistants. She has published articles on international e-mail exchanges, foreign language reading strategies, including gender as a learner variable, and cooperation and collaboration between secondary and postsecondary language programs. She is currently working on a book titled *Cinema for German Conversation.* She earned a Ph.D. in German with an emphasis in second language acquisition from the University of Wisconsin-Madison.

Judith Wilde

βETA GROUP, Albuquerque, New Mexico and Arlington, Virginia

judithwilde@gmail.com

Much of Judith Wilde's career has been at federally-funded technical assistance centers focused on linguistically and culturally diverse (LCD) students. Dr. Wilde currently is the principal in βETA GROUP, a consulting firm working with schools, districts, states, and national organizations to develop and evaluate programs serving the needs of students at risk of educational failure, particularly the LCD. She also serves as Associate Director for Research and Accountability at the federally-funded National Clearinghouse for English Language Acquisition and Language Instruction Educational Programs (NCELA).

Celeste Kinginger

Pennsylvania State University, University Park, Pennsylvania

cxk37@psu.edu

Celeste Kinginger is an Associate Professor of French and Applied Linguistics at The Pennsylvania State University. Dr. Kinginger has published widely in leading journals on topics including sociocultural approaches to second language acquisition and teaching, narrative study in second language acquisition, site independent language learning, and language learning in education abroad. She is the recipient of numerous grants for improving language instruction, and she has given numerous invited talks around the United States.

Chapter 16—Gender Equity in Social Studies

Carole L. Hahn

Emory University, Atlanta, Georgia

chahn@emory.edu

Carole L. Hahn is the Charles Howard Candler Professor of Educational Studies at Emory University. She teaches courses in social studies education and comparative education and she is an associated faculty member of Women's Studies. She is a lead author of "Gender Equity in Social Studies" (1985). She has been writing about gender and social studies since 1973 and also writes broadly on citizenship and civic education. She has an Ed.D. from Indiana University, an M.A. from Stanford University, and a B.A. from the University of California, Davis.

Jane Bernard-Powers

San Francisco State University, San Francisco, California

jbp@sfsu.edu

Jane Bernard-Powers is Professor of Education at San Francisco State University. She is a lead author of "Gender Equity in Social Studies" and co-author of "Sex-Equity and Social Studies" (1985). She coordinates the M.A. program in Elementary Education, and she facilitates student research related to gender, curriculum and social studies. Gender, social studies and women's history have been the centerpieces of her academic work for the past 25 years. She has a Ph.D. and an M.A. from Stanford University and a B.A. from the University of Michigan.

Margaret Smith Crocco

Teachers College, Columbia University, New York

crocco@tc.edu

Margaret Smith Crocco is Professor and Coordinator of the Program in Social Studies at Teachers College, Columbia University and a major author of the chapter "Gender Equity in Social Studies." She has an A.B. from Georgetown University and an M.A. and Ph.D. from the University of Pennsylvania. She has been on the faculty of Teachers College since 1993. She publishes widely on gender, sexuality, and social studies and on the history of women working in citizenship education, among other topics.

Christine Woyshner

Temple University, Philadelphia, Pennsylvania

cwoyshne@temple.edu

Christine Woyshner is Associate Professor of Education and Coordinator of the Social Studies Program at Temple University, where she also is an affiliated faculty member in Women's Studies and Urban Education. She has an Ed.D. from Harvard University. She is a major author of the chapter "Gender Equity in Social Studies." Her research interests include gender in the social studies curriculum and women's volunteerism in the history of education. She is currently working on a book on the history of the PTA and civic engagement.

Chapter 17—Gender Equity in Visual Arts and Dance Education

Elizabeth Garber

University of Arizona, Tucson, Arizona

egarber@email.arizona.edu

Elizabeth Garber, Ph.D., M.F.A., is Professor of Art at the University of Arizona and Chair of the Division of Art and Visual Culture Education. Her research revolves around how art and visual culture education can contribute to social justice, and is concentrated on feminist and cultural theory, craft, and public and community arts. Published widely in journals and anthologies, she was a Fulbright scholar and professor at the University of Art and Design, Helsinki, during Fall 2000. Garber is a past president of the National Art Education Association's Women's Caucus and has been recognized with numerous national awards and membership on editorial boards and community organizations.

Renee Sandell

George Mason University, Fairfax, Virginia

rsandell@gmu.edu

Renee Sandell, Ph.D., M.A., is Professor and Director of M.A.T. in Art Education at George Mason University. She is Past Director of the Higher Education Division of the National Art Education Association and a member of the College Art Associations Education Committee. Sandell's research and teaching interests include visual literacy, gender issues, museum education, studio pedagogy, art and healing, technology and learning, and the professional development of teachers. Recipient of numerous honors and awards.

Mary Ann Stankiewicz

Pennsylvania State University, University Park, Pennsylvania

mas53@psu.edu

Mary Ann Stankiewicz, Ph.D., M.F.A., Professor of Art Education and Professor in Charge of the Art Education Program, Penn State, is a past president of the National Art Education Association. Her research on art education history and policy is published in major professional journals and presented nationally and internationally. *Roots of Art Education Practice*, a history of art education for art teachers, was published in 2001. A past president of NAEA's Women's Caucus, she edited *Art*

---

*The boldface names are the Lead authors.

Education, the NAEA journal (1996–1998) and serves on several editorial boards. In 2003 she received the June King McFee award from the NAEA Women's Caucus.

Doug Risner
Wayne State University, Detroit, Michigan
drisner@wayne.edu

Doug Risner, Ph.D., M.F.A., Chair and Associate Professor, Maggie Allesee Department of Dance, Wayne State University is Editor-in-Chief of the *Journal of Dance Education* and serves the National Dance Education Organization as Secretary and member of the Board of Directors. Risner holds a Ph.D. in Curriculum and Teaching and an M.F.A. in Choreography and Dance Performance from the University of North Carolina at Greensboro. Forthcoming book chapters focus on critical social issues in dance.

With assistance of:

Georgia C. Collins
University of Kentucky, Lexington, Kentucky
georgiaccollins@earthlink.net

Enid Zimmerman
Indiana University, Bloomington, Indiana
zimmerm@indiana.edu

Kristin Congdon
University of Central Florida, Orlando, Florida
kcongdon@pegasus.cc.ucf.edu

Minuette B. Floyd
University of South Carolina, Columbia, South Carolina
mbfloyd0@gwm.sc.edu

Marla Jaksch
Pennsylvania State University, University Park, Pennsylvania
marla@psu.edu

Peg Speirs
Kutztown University, Kutztown, Pennsylvania
speirs@kutztown.edu

Stephanie Springgay
Pennsylvania State University, University Park, Pennsylvania
sss23@psu.edu

Rita L. Irwin
University of British Columbia, Vancouver, BC, Canada
rita.irwin@ubc.ca

Chapter 18—Gender Equity in Physical Education and Athletics

Ellen J. Staurowsky
Ithaca College, Ithaca, New York
staurows@ithaca.edu

Staurowsky is Professor and Graduate Chair in the Department of Sport Management and Media at Ithaca College. She received her doctorate from Temple University. She is a scholar of international reputation, recognized for her work on social justice issues including the American Indian mascot controversy, athletes' rights, hazing, Title IX, and workplace equity. Staurowsky co-authored *College Athletes for Hire: The Evolution and Legacy of the NCAA Amateur Myth.* She currently serves as president of the AAHPERD Research Consortium, is past president of the North American Society for the Sociology of Sport, and is a founding member of the Drake Group.

Nancy Hogshead-Makar
Florida Coastal School of Law, Jacksonville, Florida
nhogshead@fcsl.edu

Hogshead-Makar is a Professor at the Florida Coastal School of Law. She is a former President of the Women's Sports Foundation (1992–1994) and currently serves as its legal advisor. She has testified in Congress numerous times on the topic of gender equity in athletics, written numerous scholarly and lay articles, and has been a frequent guest on national news programs on the topic. She serves as an expert witness in Title IX cases and has written amicus briefs representing athletic organizations in the U.S. Supreme Court. Her law degree is from Georgetown University and she is a graduate of Duke University.

Mary Jo Kane
University of Minnesota, Minneapolis, Minnesota
maryjo@umn.edu

Kane is Professor and Director of the School of Kinesiology at the University of Minnesota. She also serves as the Director of the Tucker Center for Research on Girls & Women in Sport. Professor Kane received her Ph.D. from the University of Illinois with an emphasis in sport sociology. She was recently elected as a Fellow in the American Academy of Kinesiology and Physical Education, the highest honor in her field. In 2004, she received the Scholar of the Year Award from the Women's Sports Foundation.

Phyllis K. Lerner
Education Consultant (Bethesda, MD); Faculty Associate,
Johns Hopkins University
phylliskLerner@aol.com

Lerner's background includes decades of work at the California State Department of Education Title IX Office and the Los Angeles Educational Equity Center with a special focus on physical education and athletics. She developed and appeared in a Master of Arts in Teaching series and produced, directed, and presented a gender equity program for The Educational Channel, in Baltimore followed by similar segments for Public Broadcasting in Massachusetts and Virginia. Phyllis was asked to develop, deliver, and now coordinate ASCD's Hurricane Relief: A Call to Action.

Emily H. Wughalter
San Jose State University, San Jose, California
emily.wughalter@sjsu.edu

Wughalter is a Professor of Kinesiology at San Jose State University. She has an earned B.A. (Lehman College), M.S. (University of Colorado), and EdD (University of Georgia). Dr. Wughalter is passionate about topics on motor learning and women's sport, and has published manuscripts on these topics. She has provided leadership in national and regional professional organizations: in particular, two separate term memberships on the Executive Board of the National Association for Girls and Women in Sport, President of the AAHPERD Research Consortium, and President of Western Society for Physical Education of College Women.

Athena Yiamouyiannis
Ohio University, Athens, Ohio
athenayiamouyiannis@msn.com

Yiamouyiannis is the former Executive Director of the National Association for Girls and Women in Sport (NAGWS) and is currently on the Ohio University Sport Management faculty. Previously, Yiamouyiannis worked at the National Collegiate Athletics Association (NCAA) where she served as Director of Membership Services and as a spokesperson on Title IX and gender equity issues. Recently, Yiamouyiannis worked with the National Coalition for Women and Girls in Education on the fight to save Title IX and has spoken on behalf of NAGWS and the Coalition

---

*The boldface names are the Lead authors.

including during the hearings of the Commission on Opportunity in Athletics.

Chapter 19—Gender Equity in Formal Sexuality Education

John DeLamater
University of Wisconsin

Professor of Sociology, University of Wisconsin–Madison, earned his Ph.D. in Social Psychology at the University of Michigan in 1969. He has been teaching the undergraduate course in human sexuality at Wisconsin since 1976, and is co-author of *Understanding Human Sexuality* (9th ed., 2006) with Janet Shibley Hyde. He has been writing and speaking about sex education since 2002. His research and writing are focused on the effects of life-course transitions on sexuality. He has published papers on the effects of having a child, of dual career couples, of divorce, and influences on sexual desire among men and women over 45.

Chapter 20—Gender Equity in Career and Technical Education

Mary E. Lufkin
National Alliance for Partnerships in Equity, Cochranville, Pennsylvania
mimilufkin@napequity.org

Mary (Mimi) Lufkin began her career teaching agriculture education at a California high school. She later joined the faculty of the Department of Agriculture Education at California Polytechnic State University, San Luis Obispo. She became a consultant to the California Department of Education, developing special projects in agriculture education and providing technical assistance and professional development to recipients of Perkins gender equity grants. In 1994, she became the Executive Director of the National Alliance for Partnerships in Equity in Pennsylvania. In this capacity she reviews and analyzes federal legislation, conducts professional development activities, and provides technical assistance to state and local educational agencies focused on best practices for serving special population students. She has a B.S. from the University of California, Davis, a M.S. from California Polytechnic University, San Luis Obipso, and a M.Ed. from St. Mary's College.

Mary M. Wiberg
California Commission on the Status of Women, Sacramento, California
mwiberg@women.ca.gov, mkwiberg@yahoo.com

Prior to becoming Executive Director of the State of California Commission on the Status of Women, Wiberg served for 17 years as Gender Equity Administrator for the State of Iowa Department of Education. She also worked extensively on welfare reform and workforce development issues. Wiberg has served as a member of Iowa Commission on the Status of Women, the Board of the National Association of Commissions for Women, and the Federal Committee on Registered Apprenticeship, advisory to the U.S. Secretary of Labor. She also served as Co-Chair of the Gender Equity Expert Panel, advisory to the U.S. Department of Education. She has a B.A. Augustana College, Rock Island, IL and a M.A., Illinois State University.

Courtney Reed Jenkins
Wisconsin Department of Public Instruction, Madison, Wisconsin
courtney.jenkins@dpi.state.wi.us

Courtney Reed Jenkins has nearly two decades of experience working in the public and not-for-profit sector on equity and diversity issues. Through her current service at the Wisconsin Department of Public Instruction, she has facilitated more than 100 trainings regarding equity in education and published articles on, among other topics, recruiting and retaining young women in math, science, and technology. She sits on several national and state boards and committees that focus on gender equity in education. Courtney has a Juris Doctor, Magna Cum Laude, and a Bachelor of Arts, with honors, from University of Iowa.

Stefanie L. Lee Berardi
Illinois State University, Normal, Illinois
slleebe@ilstu.edu

Stefanie L. Lee Berardi, Co-Director of the Illinois Center for Specialized Professional Support (ICSPS) at Illinois State University, provides leadership to Perkins-funded educational organizations. As a 2006 "Programs That Work" award recipient, Ms. Berardi has been involved with the Nontraditonal Look Project since its inception in 2002. She has experience working with persons with disabilities and other populations with specialized workforce needs and has created a number of technical assistance publications and websites. Ms. Berardi has a B.A. in Speech Pathology/Audiology from Illinois State University and a M.A. in Child, Family, and Community Services from University of Illinois at Springfield.

Teresa M. Boyer
Rutgers, The State University of New Jersey, New Brunswick, New Jersey
terri.boyer@rutgers.edu & drterriboyer@msn.com

Terri Boyer is an author of the Root Causes section of the chapter on Career and Technical Education. As Director of Education and Career Development Research and Programs at the Center for Women and Work at Rutgers, she oversees initiatives such as the Nontraditional Career Resource Center and staffs the New Jersey Council on Gender Parity. She holds an Ed.D. and M.A. from the University of Alabama, and a B.S. from Villanova University. She has also worked as the director of technical assistance for the WEEA Equity Resource Center, and Research Associate at the Gender, Diversities and Technology Institute at EDC, Inc.

Ellen Eardley
Woodley & McGillivary, a labor and employment law firm, Washington, D.C.
ele@wmlaborlaw.com & eeardley@hotmail.com

Ellen Eardley advocated for gender equity in education as a legal fellow at the National Women's Law Center (NWLC). In partnership with several organizations, she helped the NWLC coordinate the *Programs and Practices that Work Project* to recognize educational agencies that improve gender equity in vocational education. She also co-authored the NWLC's report: *Tools of the Trade: Using the Law to Address Sex Segregation in High School Career and Technical Education*. Currently, she represents employees who have experienced discrimination and harassment in the workplace. She holds a J.D. and M.A. in Women's Studies from the University of Cincinnati and a B.A. from Eastern Illinois University.

Janet K. Huss
Educational Equity Consultant, St. Joseph, Missouri
janeth@stjoelive.com

Jan Huss has spent most of her career working with equity and diversity issues. Jan developed and implemented support services programs for Des Moines Area Community College and Iowa State University. She served as an equity consultant for the Iowa Department of Education for over ten years where she coordinated the civil right compliance monitoring and equity leadership for Perkins grant recipients. Now retired, Jan does private consulting and continues her affiliation with the National Alliance for Partnerships in Equity and the American Association of University Women to continue her work with equity. Jan has a B.S.E. and MSE in education from Drake University in Des Moines, Iowa.

---

*The boldface names are the Lead authors.

Chapter 21—The Role of Women's and Gender Studies in Advancing Gender Equity

Betsy Eudey
California State University Stanislaus, Turlock, California
beudey@csustan.edu

Betsy Eudey has taught in Women's and Gender Studies since 1998, and is currently an Assistant Professor and Director of the Gender Studies program at California State University Stanislaus. She has a Ph.D. in Cultural Studies in Education from The Ohio State University, with an emphasis in Women's Studies, and an M.Ed. in Higher Education and Student Affairs Administration from the University of Vermont. Her research interests include gender and education, feminist activism, transnational feminism, and the impacts of the fields of Women's and Gender Studies. She is actively involved in the National Women's Studies Association, and currently serves as Co-Chair of the Pacific Southwest Women's Studies Association. She has previously worked as a campus women's center director, and is active in feminist and queer-focused activist projects.

With assistance of:

Scott Lukas
Lake Tahoe Community College, Lake Tahoe, California
Lukas@ltcc.edu

Elaine Correa
McGill University, Montreal, Canada
efrmc@yahoo.com

Chapter 22—Gender Equity for African Americans

Olga M. Welch
Duesquesne University, Pittsburgh, Pennsylvania
welcho@duq.edu

Olga Welch, Dean, School of Education, Dusquesne University, was Professor Emerita in the College of Education, Health, and Human Services, University of Tennessee. Her research focuses on achievement motivation for educationally disadvantaged African American high-school-age males and females. She has coauthored *Standing Outside on the Inside: Black Adolescents and the Construction of Academic Identity* and *Making Schools Work: Negotiating Meaning and Transforming the Margins*. With Diane S. Pollard, she examined the construction of research epistemologies by women of color in *From Center to Margins: The Importance of Self-Definition in Research*.

Faye E. Patterson
University of Tennessee, Knoxville, Tennessee
fpatter1@utk.edu

Faye Patterson, assistant professor, University of Tennessee, Knoxville, is Director of the School Administrator Certification Program. She received a B.S. degree in Elementary Education from Memphis State University; a M.A. in School Administration and Supervision from Hampton Institute, VA; and an Ed.D. Degree from the UT, Knoxville. Before joining the UT faculty, Dr. Patterson enjoyed public-school teaching and administration in Texas, VA, and the Department of Defense Schools, Germany. She spent 19 years in administration in Prince William County Public Schools, VA, including 10 years as an Associate Superintendent.

Diane S. Pollard
Professor Emerita, University of Wisconsin-Milwaukee, Milwaukee, Wisconsin
dpollard@uwm.edu
    (*See editor information*).

Kimberly A. Scott
Arizona State University, Tempe, Arizona
kimberly.a.scott@asu.edu

When she worked on the *Handbook* chapter, Kimberly A. Scott, Ed.D., was an Associate Professor in Hofstra University's Foundations, Leadership, and Policy Studies department. She recently coauthored a Rowman and Littlefield book, *Kids in Context*, and is working on another manuscript describing the lives of African American girls attending school in a state-operated district. Dr. Scott is currently on the faculty in Educational Leadership and Policy Studies in the College of Education, Arizona State University.

Chapter 23—Gender Equity for Latina/os

Angela B. Ginorio
University of Washington, Seattle, Washington
ginorio@u.washington.edu

Angela B. Ginorio is associate professor in the Department of Women Studies, and adjunct associate professor in the Departments of Psychology and American Ethnic Studies at the University of Washington-Seattle. She is co-author of *¡Sí se puede! Yes, we can! Latinas in schools* (2001). Her scholarship focuses on access issues in education for Latino/as and first-generation college students, feminist science studies, and violence against women. She is a fellow of the American Psychological Association (APA) and a former chair of the APA's Committee on Women in Psychology. She received her B.A. and M.A. in psychology from the University of Puerto Rico and her Ph.D. in psychology from Fordham University in New York City.

Yvette V. Lapayese
Loyola Marymount University, Los Angeles, California
ylapayese@lmu.edu

Yvette V. Lapayese is an assistant professor in the School of Education at Loyola Marymount University, Los Angeles, where she teaches courses on social foundations of education and Latino/Chicano issues in education. Her research focuses on revolutionary critical pedagogy, race and feminist methodologies, and bilingual/bicultural issues in education. She is author of several chapters and articles on the topic of teacher resistance to racist and classist educational policies and practices.

Melba Vasquez
Psychologist in Independent Practice, Austin, Texas
melvavasquez@aol.com

Melba Vásquez, psychologist in independent practice in Austin, Texas, obtained her Ph.D. in counseling psychology from the University of Texas at Austin. She publishes in the areas of ethnic minority psychology, psychology of women, and ethics. She is co-author, with Ken Pope, of *Ethics in Psychotherapy & Counseling* (3rd edition, 2007) and of *How to Survive and Thrive as a Therapist* (2005). She has served as president of the Texas Psychological Association, of APA Divisions 35 (Society of Psychology of Women) and 17 (Society of Counseling Psychology) and as a member-at-large of the APA's Board of Directors (2007–2009). She is a Fellow of APA and holds the Diplomate of the American Board of Professional Psychology (ABPP).

Chapter 24—Gender Equity for Asian and Pacific Island Americans

Mary L. Spencer
College of Liberal Arts and Social Sciences, University of Guam, Mangilao, Guam
class_uog@yahoo.com

Mary Spencer, Professor of Psychology, has been the Dean of the College of Liberal Arts and Social Sciences (formerly the College of

---

*The boldface names are the Lead authors.

Arts and Sciences) of the University of Guam since 1996. Prior to that she was Director of the University's Micronesian Language Institute. Her B.A., M.A., and Ph.D. in Psychology are from the University of New Mexico. Her research and writing encompasses bilingual education, language assessment, program evaluation, educational equity, and women's issues, particularly with ethnic and linguistic minority groups in California, Hawaii, and the U.S.-affiliated Western Pacific. She has worked in Micronesia for over 22 years.

Yukiko Inoue
School of Education, College of Professional Studies,
University of Guam, Mangilao, Guam
yinoue@uog9.uog.edu

Yukiko Inoue, Professor of Foundations and Educational Research in the School of Education, College of Professional Studies, University of Guam. She teaches educational and psychological research methods, qualitative inquiry and quantitative analysis. Her Ph.D. in Educational Psychology and Research is from the University of Memphis, Tennessee. She has an M.S. in Business Administration, Tokyo Keizai University, Japan, and a B.A. in Humanities and Sciences, Nihon University, Tokyo, Japan. She is a licensed Hawaii Teacher and is certified to teach English in junior and senior high schools in Japan. Her publications include Japanese poetry and a book on educational technology.

Grace Park McField
College of Education, California State University,
San Marcos, California
gmcfield@csusm.edu

Grace Park McField, Assistant Professor of Education, California State University, San Marcos, teaches and conducts research in the following areas: meta-analyses on bilingual education and English language development programs, effective educational practices with linguistically and culturally diverse students, and the role of social justice and equity in teacher preparation programs. She received her B.A. in Rhetoric with a minor in Education from the University of California, Berkeley, her M.Ed. and elementary teaching credential from the University of California, Los Angeles, and her Ph.D. in Learning and Instruction from the University of Southern California.

Chapter 25—Gender Equity for American Indians

J. Anne Calhoun, (Cherokee)
Department of Language, Literacy, and Sociocultural Studies,
University of New Mexico, Albuquerque, New Mexico
acalhoon@unm.edu

Anne Calhoun is an assistant professor at the University of New Mexico. She holds a Ph.D. in Educational Psychology from Marquette University in Milwaukee, Wisconsin. She teaches graduate courses in American Indian Education and in Literacy Education. Her research interests focus on the improvement of educational services, opportunities, and equity for American Indian students at all levels of education. She has been a program coordinator of the American Indian Education Program within the department of Language, Literacy, and Sociocultural Studies. She is one of seven affiliated faculty with the Institute for American Indian Education.

Mishuana Goeman, (Tonawada Seneca)
English and Native American Studies, Dartmouth College,
Hanover, New Hampshire
mishuana.goeman@Dartmouth.edu

Dr. Goeman is an Assistant Professor who currently teaches in Native American Studies, English, and Women and Gender Studies at Dartmouth College. She obtained her Ph.D. in Stanford University's Modern Thought and Literature program where she began her interdisciplinary

manuscript that incorporates literature, geography, gender and cultural studies into the field of Native American Studies from which she centers her work. Her research examines the way Western concepts of place and space and Native concepts of place and space collide producing tensions in social, political, economical and cultural narrations. She is also a contributor to the anthology/Native Feminisms Without Apology. She has been awarded a U.C. Presidential Post-doctoral Fellowship at Berkeley (2003), a Fellowship at the Institute of Women and Gender Studies at Stanford, and a Fellowship at the Research Institute on Comparative Studies in Race and Ethnicity at Stanford.

Monica Tsethlikai, (Zuni)
Psychology Department, University of Utah,
Salt Lake City, Utah
monicats@ucsc.edu & monica.tsethlikai@psych.utah.edu

Dr. Monica Tsethlikai is an Assistant Professor at the University of Utah in the Psychology Department. She has been a postdoctoral fellow at the University of California at Santa Cruz in the psychology department. She is a developmental psychologist who studies how cultural practices influence cognitive and social development. Dr. Tsethlikai was a Ford pre-doctoral fellow will soon become a post-doctoral fellow. Her dissertation, *Children's Memory for Conflicting Perspectives of an Event: Linking Cognitive Ability and Social Competence,* won an American Psychological Association award.

Chapter 26—Gender Equity and Lesbian, Gay, Bisexual, and Transgender Issues in Education

Joseph G. Kosciw
GLSEN (Gay, Lesbian and Straight Education Network),
New York, New York
jkosciw@glsen.org

Joseph G. Kosciw is Research Director at GLSEN (Gay, Lesbian and Straight Education Network), where he oversees the organization's research on LGBT issues in education and evaluation research on GLSEN's programs. Dr. Kosciw has a Ph.D. in psychology from New York University and a B.A. in Psychology and M.S.Ed. in Counseling from the University of Pennsylvania. Dr. Kosciw has been conducting community-based research for over 15 years, including program evaluations for non-profit social service organizations and for local government.

Eliza S. Byard
GLSEN (Gay, Lesbian and Straight Education Network),
New York, New York
ebyard@glsen.org

Eliza S. Byard is the Deputy Executive Director of GLSEN. She directs GLSEN's work in policy advocacy, student and community organizing, education, communications, and research. Dr. Byard frequently represents GLSEN as a spokesperson with print and broadcast media, and has made numerous presentations on GLSEN's work and LGBT issues in education to a variety of audiences. Dr. Byard joined GLSEN in 2001, after a varied career in non-profit administration, film and television production, and academia. She holds a Ph.D. in United States History from Columbia University, where she was a Presidential Fellow of the Faculty.

Sean N. Fischer
New York University, New York, New York
sean.fischer@nyu.edu

Sean N. Fischer is a doctoral candidate in New York University's Community Psychology program. He received his B.S. in Psychology from Loyola University Chicago and M.A. in Psychology from New York University. His dissertation focuses on the educational and psychologi-

---

*The boldface names are the Lead authors.

cal well being of lesbian, gay, bisexual, and transgender students. He has also conducted research in the area of homelessness.

Courtney Joslin
University of California, Berkeley &
Santa Clara University School of Law,
Santa Clara, California
courtneyjoslin@gmail.com

Courtney Joslin is an Adjunct Professor at Boalt Hall School of Law, University of California, Berkeley and Santa Clara University School of Law. She was formerly a Senior Staff Attorney at the National Center for Lesbian Rights (NCLR). At NCLR, Ms. Joslin focused on expanding the work of NCLR's Youth Project and was actively involved in litigation and advocacy work on behalf of lesbian, gay, bisexual, and transgender youth. Ms. Joslin has a B.A. from Brown University and received her law degree from Harvard Law School.

Chapter 27—Gender Equity for Gifted Students

Lynn H. Fox
American University, Washington, D.C.
lynnfox@american.edu & drlynnfox@msn.com
   (*See editor information*).

Janet F. Soller
American Psychological Association, Washington, D.C.
jsoller@apa.org

Janet F. Soller, Ph.D., is Director of Governance Affairs for the American Psychological Association's Publications and Databases. She received her doctorate in education from American University. Her research interests include the intersections of gifted women, talent development, higher education, and motivation. Former Assistant Director for APA's Center for Gifted Education Policy, she is a published author and classical musician.

Chapter 28—Gender Equity for People with Disabilities

Donna M. Mertens
Gallaudet University, Washington, D.C.
donna.mertens@gallaudet.edu

Donna Mertens is a Professor in the Department of Educational Foundations and Research where she teaches research design and program evaluation to deaf and hearing Ph.D. students. She is a past president and board member of the American Evaluation Association and has focused her service work in the area of diversity and international cooperation. She authored *Research and Evaluation in Education and Psychology: Integrating Diversity with Quantitative, Qualitative, and Mixed Methods* (2nd ed.) She obtained her Ph.D. from the University of Kentucky in the Department of Educational Psychology.

Amy T. Wilson
Gallaudet University, Washington, D.C.
amy.wilson@gallaudet.edu

Amy Wilson received her doctorate from Gallaudet University where she is the Program Director for International Development Programs in the Graduate School of Professional Programs, and teaches courses in international development with people with disabilities in developing countries, multicultural education, and research methods. Before teaching at Gallaudet, she spent 12 years teaching the sciences to deaf high school students, and then volunteered four years in northeast Brazil as a community development worker with the Mennonite Central Committee. Dr. Wilson's research in Africa, the Caribbean, Asia, and South America has been centered of after empowerment people with disabilities in developing countries.

Judith L. Mounty
Gallaudet University, Washington, D.C.
judith.mounty@gallaudet.edu

Judith Mounty (Ed.D, M.S.W.) directs the Center for American Sign Language Literacy at Gallaudet University and is also social worker and educational consultant with a small group practice in Maryland. Before coming to Gallaudet in 1996, she was a Research Scientist at Educational Testing Service addressing equity and access issues individuals with disabilities in education and testing and previously worked for many years as a teacher, teacher educator, and program administrator in the field of deaf education. Dr. Mounty was involved with the adaptation of a sexual abuse prevention curriculum for use with deaf and hard of hearing children.

Chapter 29—Gender Equity in Early Learning Environments

Barbara Polnick
Sam Houston State University, Huntsville, Texas
elc_bep@shsu.edu
   (*See author information, chapter 8*).

Carol Anne Dwyer
cdwyer@ets.org
Educational Testing Service, Princeton, New Jersey
   (*See editor information*).

Carol Funk Haynie
cjudge@tconline.net
Sam Houston State University, Huntsville, Texas

Professor Carole Funk Haynie is in the Educational Leadership program at Sam Houston State University. Carole's contributions throughout her 39 years in education have been recognized by several Texas state organizations, including the Texas Council of Women School Executives for the Margaret Montgomery Leadership Award. She is also the recipient of the cherished Piper Award given annually to professors from accredited Texas colleges and universities who demonstrate outstanding devotion to education and influence in their community. She received her Ed.D. and M.Ed. from Northeast Louisiana University (now University of Louisiana at Monroe).

Merle Froschl
Educational Equity Change Concepts to Center for both Froschl
and Sprung at the Academy for Educational Development,
New York, New York
mfroschl@aed.org

Merle Froschl is Cofounder and Codirector of the Educational Equity Center at the Academy for Educational Development (EEC/AED). Previously, she and Barbara Sprung cofounded and codirected Educational Equity Concepts, Inc. Merle has over 35 years of experience in education and publishing. She has authored and edited a number of articles, teacher's guides, and books including *Quit it! A teacher's guide on teasing and bullying for use with students in Grades K–3*, which she coauthored with Barbara Sprung and Nancy Mullin-Rindler. She has a B.S. from Syracuse University and is a graduate of the Institute for Not-for-Profit Management, Columbia University.

Barbara Sprung
Educational Equity Change Concepts to Center for both Froschl
and Sprung at the Academy for Educational Development,
New York, New York
bsprung@aed.org

Barbara Sprung is Codirector of the Educational Equity Center at the Academy for Educational Development (EEC/AED). Previously, she and

---

*The boldface names are the Lead authors.

Merle Froschl cofounded and codirected Educational Equity Concepts, Inc. Barbara is a well-known speaker, and the author of numerous articles and 10 books related to gender equity, early childhood, and learning science in the early years. Her most recent book was *The anti-bullying and teasing book for preschool classrooms,* which she coauthored with Merle Froschl. She has a B.A. from Sarah Lawrence College, an M.S. from Bank Street College of Education, and is a graduate of the Institute for Not-for-Profit Management, Columbia University.

Doris Fromberg
Hofstra Univ. Hempstead, New York
doris.p.fromberg@hofstra.edu

Doris Fromberg is an education professor at Hofstra University and a former president of the National Association of Early Childhood Teacher Educators Foundation. She is the author of *Play and meaning in early childhood education, Play from birth to twelve*, and a chapter in *Gender and schooling in the early years,* in addition to many other related publications. She received her B.A. from Brooklyn College-City University of New York and M.A. and Ed.D from Teachers College, Columbia University.

Chapter 30—Improving Gender Equity in Postsecondary Education

Joanne Cooper
University of Hawaii, Honolulu, Hawaii
jcooper@hawaii.edu

Joanne Cooper is a professor of higher education in department of Educational Administration at the University of Hawaii. She is lead author of *Tenure in the Sacred Grove: Issues and Strategies for Women and Minority Daculty* and is currently working on a new book entitled *Journal Writing for Teaching and Learning: The Power of Reflection in College Classrooms and Professional Life* with Stylus Press. Cooper serves on the editorial boards of the *American Educational Research Journal/SIA*, the *Journal of Research on Leadership Education, Advancing Women in Leadership,* and the *Journal of General Education.*

Pamela Eddy
Central Michigan University, Mount Pleasant, Michigan
eddy1pl@cmich.edu

Pamela Eddy is an associate professor of higher education and doctoral program coordinator in the department of Educational Leadership at Central Michigan University. Her research interests include community colleges, leadership development, gender roles in higher education, and faculty development. She is a co-author of *Creating the Future of Faculty Development: Learning from the Past, Understanding the Present*. Eddy serves as the coeditor for book reviews for the *Community College Journal of Research and Practice* and serves on the editorial board for *Community College Enterprise*. She received the 2006 emerging scholar award by the Council for the Study of Community Colleges.

Jeni Hart
University of Missouri-Columbia, Columbia, Missouri
hartjl@missouri.edu

Jeni Hart is an assistant professor in the Higher Education and Continuing Education emphasis in the department of Educational Leadership and Policy Analysis at the University of Missouri-Columbia. Hart has conducted research on activism among feminist faculty and on diversity and campus climate issues. Broadly, her agenda centers on gender issues, the professions, and organizational transformation within academe.

Jaime Lester
Old Dominion University, Norfolk, Virginia
jlester@odu.edu

Jaime Lester, Assistant Professor, Department of Leadership and Counseling, Old Dominion University, received her Ph.D. in Education with a focus on community colleges in the Rossier School of Education at the University of Southern California. She has a M.A. in Student Affairs at USC and a B.A. in English and Women's Studies from the University of Michigan. As a research assistant in the Center for Higher Education and Policy Analysis, she worked on the Transfer and Retention and Urban Community College Students Project and completed an ethnographic study that applied feminist performance theories to gender equity among faculty at an urban community college.

Scott Lukas
Lake Tahoe College, South Lake Tahoe, California
lukas@ltcc.edu

Scott Lukas is Chair of Anthropology and Sociology at Lake Tahoe College. His book, *The Themed Space: Locating Culture, Nation, and Self* is forthcoming with Lexington Books in 2007. He is the founder of the Gender Ads Project (http://www.genderads.com) In 2005, he was selected winner of the McGraw-Hill Award for Excellence in Undergraduate Teaching of Anthropology by the American Anthropological Association.

Betsy Eudey
California State University Stanislaus, Turlock, California
beudey@csustan.edu

(See author information, chapter 21).

Judith Glazer-Raymo
Teachers College, Columbia University, New York, New York
jg2377@columbia.edu

Judith Glazer-Raymo is Lecturer and Fellow of the Higher and Postsecondary Education Program at Teachers College, Columbia University, and Professor Emerita of Education at Long Island University. She also chairs Scholars and Advocates for Gender Equity (SAGE), a standing committee of the American Educational Research Association. Her research and scholarship focus on gender and ethnic diversity in higher education, innovations in graduate education, and critical approaches to higher education policy analysis. Judith is the author of *Shattering the Myths: Women in Academe* (1999, 2001) and *Professionalizing Graduate Education: The Master's Degree in the Marketplace* (2005).

Mary Madden
University of Maine, Orono, Maine
mary_madden@umit.maine.edu

Mary Madden, Ph.D. is an assistant research professor at the University of Maine in the College of Education and Human Development. She conducts research and evaluation studies on education programs and issues including girls' sexuality, girlfighting, gender equity and youth suicide. She teaches courses on girls' development and educational research and evaluation. Dr. Madden is the project director for the National Study of Student Hazing, a research initiative designed to examine hazing at postsecondary institutions. She received her doctorate at the University of Maine in 2000.

---

*The boldface names are the Lead authors.

**Chapter 31—Summary and Recommendations
for Achieving Gender Equity in and through Education**

Susan S. Klein
Feminist Majority Foundation, Arlington, Virginia
sklein@feminist.org
(See editor information).

Elizabeth Ann Homer
Chair, Michigan NOW Education Task Force, Lansing, Michigan
lizhomer@sbcglobal.net

Elizabeth Ann Homer was the first Education Director of the Michigan Women's Studies Association and curator of the Michigan Women's Historical Center and Hall of Fame. She was director of the Michigan Project on Equal Educational Rights, NOWLDEF, in the 1980s and a Consultant to the Michigan Department of Education and Michigan Department of Labor and served on the State Board for Community Colleges. She holds a B.S. in Elementary Education from the University of Michigan and a M.A. in Occupational Education Administration from Ferris State University. She is currently the Curator of the Turner-Dodge House and Historical Center in Lansing, Michigan and has been Chair of the Michigan NOW Education Task Force since 1989.

With assistance of:

Cheris Kramarae
University of Oregon, Eugene, Oregon
cheris@uoregon.edu

Margaret A. Nash
Graduate School of Education, University of California at Riverside, Riverside, California
margaret.nash@ucr.edu

Carol Burger
Virginia Polytechnic Institute and State University, Blacksburg, Virginia
cjburger@vt.edu

Linda Shevitz
Maryland State Department of Education, Baltimore, Maryland
lshevitz@msde.state.md.us

---

*The boldface names are the Lead authors.

FOREWORD: *HANDBOOK FOR ACHIEVING GENDER EQUITY THROUGH EDUCATION*

Eleanor Smeal

When the history of the feminist movement over the last forty years is recorded, one of its most remarkable achievements will surely be the increase in educational opportunity for women and girls. In the 1950s and 1960s, women were a minority of college students and just a very minute fraction of the student body in professional schools. Women were not admitted to most of the Ivy League schools or the military academies. Quota systems and stereotyped expectations limited the number of women students at many coeducational institutions of higher education.

At the secondary level, the education system channeled girls into a narrow range of occupations. Girls were required to take home economics, while boys were required to take shop and mechanical drawing. Whole high school systems provided no interscholastic athletic opportunities for girls.

Today, women are now the majority of college students and are well represented in the student bodies of most professional schools. About half of the medical and law students and over 75% of veterinary students are women. As we go to print, Harvard, our nation's oldest and one of the world's most prestigious universities, has appointed Drew Gilpin Faust as its first woman president. Dr. Faust is a former women's studies department chair and current Dean of the Radcliffe Institute for Advanced Study, a member center of the National Council for Research on Women.

None of this just *happened*. Feminists spent energy and resources to understand and fight sex discrimination in education. Many of the feminist activists in the late 1960s and early 1970s were academicians. The leading feminist organizations of the time, the National Organization for Women (NOW) and the Women's Equity Action League (WEAL) sued institutions of education. At one time, WEAL sued almost every medical and law school for sex discrimination in student admissions. NOW members collected information on discrimination at all levels of education and successfully fought to enforce the equality provisions in national and state constitutions and laws.

As a trained political scientist I saw the value of using research to fight for women's rights and civil rights in education, employment, political leadership, and much more using legal, legislative, and electoral strategies as well as educating the public and building support through the media and demonstrations.

I'm proud to say as a feminist activist and leader, I have fought on all levels—from nursery school to high school to college to graduate and professional schools—for the advancement of women and girls. I have personally demonstrated, picketed, led lawsuits, advocated for state and federal legislation, and negotiated for these advancements. Believe me, none of these advancements have come easily. Many courageous women have taken on the system and, although they may not have personally succeeded, they did open the doors—and eventually the floodgates—for countless numbers of women and girls to come.

As a young feminist activist in Pittsburgh, my colleagues and I not only fought for more opportunities for girls and women as students, teachers, and professors, but we also challenged sexist and racist curricula, textbooks, and testing. Moreover, we sued school districts to increase girls' athletic opportunities. One of NOW's early cases was to prevent the firing of pregnant teachers once they began to "show."

Contrary to conventional wisdom, the feminist struggle for women and girls' educational opportunities was also mindful of the importance of eliminating sexism in education not only for the sake of women and girls, but also for men and boys. The principal NOW work challenging sexism in books spoke to *both* Dick and Jane as victims. When girls and boys are stereotyped, both lose. When my son was young, we bought a second set of books for him to keep at home because boys who were studious and brought books home from school were ridiculed—that was okay only for girls. Boys were encouraged to be "rough and tumble," to play sports. Girls were not. Sexism cheats boys as well as girls from reaching their full potential.

When my local NOW chapter in the suburbs of Pittsburgh opened a full day nursery school in the early 1970s, we had to interview over 200 teachers to find one who would eagerly embrace a non-sexist and non-racist educational program and would gladly avoid "Prince Charming to the rescue" fairy tales. In fact, it proved difficult just finding an instructor who would teach democratic principles. Moreover, we were astounded to find in the alphabet cards of the time most frequently that "P" stood for "prince," not "president;" "Q" for "queen," not "quart;" and so on. So we learned sex stereotyping in education begins very early.

In our work to eliminate sex discrimination in education, feminists repeatedly turned to enacting and enforcing legal protections and to obtaining evidence to show the great need for ending gender inequities. Our fights for the passage and enforcement of the federal Equal Rights Amendment, state ERA's, Title IX in 1972, its regulations in 1975, its restoration from 1984 to 1988, and for state "Title IX's" was crucial to the current advancement of women and girls in the United States.

The struggle for the educational advancement of women and girls is, of course, not just in the United States, but worldwide. It is an especially critical concern for minority or less advantaged populations in all countries. Today, women and girls still constitute the majority of the illiterate and unschooled population. Even the United Nations has recognized that the empowerment of women and girls through education is essential for democracy, sustainable development, and meeting the Millennium Development Goals for developing nations.

But reactionary forces continue to suppress women and girls' opportunities. The most extreme, the Taliban militia in Afghanistan, is destroying girls' and coeducational schools, killing teachers of girls, and threatening to kill parents who send their girls to school. The women and girls in Afghanistan are the canaries in the mine. If women's rights are human rights, as the United Nation's 4th World Conference in Beijing on Women proclaimed, we must help Afghan women and girls end this oppression. That's why the Feminist Majority Foundation has led a campaign to help Afghan women and girls and to ensure their educational opportunities are not trampled, but expanded.

Afghan women, before the takeover by the Taliban in 1996, were about 70 percent of the country's school teachers and 40 percent of its doctors. Schools in Afghanistan were co-educational. The horrific treatment of Afghan women and girls in the past decade indicates how fragile women's equality and educational rights are. For women and girls' rights to be realized, feminists must remain vigilant, because nowhere on this great planet have women and girls yet achieved full equality with men and boys. Everywhere the struggle for gender equity is ongoing. Educational equity is imperative if we are ever to end discrimination that denies the reaching of full human potential.

The Feminist Majority Foundation, which is dedicated to advancing women's rights through research, education, and action, is committed to gender equity in education and to increasing our knowledge of how to do this. I believe the Feminist Majority Foundation's participation in this massive undertaking and this research based *Handbook for Achieving Gender Equity through Education* is a perfect way to commemorate the 20th anniversary of our Foundation and the 35th anniversaries of Title IX and *Ms.* Magazine. We salute the dedication and commitment of the over 200 authors and reviewers of the 31 chapters in this *Handbook*, its heroic co-editors, and especially our Educational Equity Director, Dr. Sue Klein, without whom such a monumental collaborative project would not have been possible.

Eleanor Smeal
President, Feminist Majority Foundation; Publisher, Ms. Magazine

For more than 30 years, Eleanor Smeal has been on the frontlines fighting for women's equality as a political analyst, strategist, and grassroots organizer. As president of the Feminist Majority Foundation (FMF) and former president of the National Organization for Women (NOW), she has played a pivotal role leading the fight for the Equal Rights Amendment, the full implementation and safeguarding of Title IX, and developing strategies which have charted the direction of the modern women's movement. She was the first to identify the "gender gap" and popularized its usage in election and polling analyses to enhance women's voting clout. Smeal's vision led to the FMF establishing the largest network of pro-choice groups on college campuses, fighting gender apartheid in Afghanistan and globally, and spearheading the struggle to bring mifepristone to American women as both an early abortion option and a drug to treat a variety of serious illnesses principally affecting women. She is publisher of Ms. magazine, on the executive committee of the National Council of Women's Organizations, a board member of the National Council for Research on Women, and chair of NOW National's Advisory Board. She is a Phi Beta Kappa graduate of Duke University and holds an M.A. degree from the University of Florida. She received an honorary Doctor of Law from Duke University in 1991 and an honorary Doctor of Science from the University of Florida in 2003.

PREFACE

This 2007 *Handbook for Achieving Gender Equity through Education* is a major update and expansion of the 1985 American Educational Research Association (AERA) sponsored *Handbook for Achieving Sex Equity through Education*. Both *Handbooks* were guided by similar purposes and strategies. The 1985 *Handbook* served as a definitive and guiding source of information on many aspects of sex or gender equity for 20 years and was used in education courses as far away as Taiwan. It is hoped that this more comprehensive, updated 2007 *Handbook* will have an even greater positive role in helping educators and all others who care about education equity continue activities designed not only to treat students and staff fairly, but to use education as a vehicle to decrease sex discrimination and gender stereotyping in society in the U.S., and also globally, to the extent possible.

The purposes for both *Handbooks* related to their substance, intended users, and goals of serving as a long-term, definitive resource and tool for building the capacity of researchers and educators concerned with achieving gender equity are quite similar. Additionally, many of the strategies used to develop the 1985 *Handbook* were adapted for this second edition of the *Handbook*.

The substantive purposes are so similar, except for a word change from *sex* equity to *gender* equity, that the following 1985 *Handbook* Preface statement remains perfect for this 2007 *Handbook*:

The long-range purpose is to aid in the achievement of sex equity *through* education by helping individuals use educational strategies to attain sex equity in society. The second (related and often prerequisite) purpose is to aid in the achievement of sex equity *in* educational activities and settings, whether or not the instructional content is dealing with sex equity issues. To accomplish these purposes, we have described key sex equity issues in our respective areas of expertise and have come to an agreement on some answers about how sex equity may be achieved in and through education.

The achievement of sex equity goals in society by the reduction of sex discrimination and sex stereotyping is valued for a wide variety of personal, political, economic, and philosophic reasons. Some personal and societal reasons for supporting sex equity are to optimize human development potential so that all females and males are able to develop themselves as individuals without limitations of gender-prescribed roles. For example, males as well as females should be encouraged to play nurturing roles toward their families and others. Key political reasons favoring sex equity focus on the need to provide basic human rights essential for a democracy and to eliminate discrimination against groups of people based on stereotypes. Some historians have also noted that less sex-stereotyped societies have had fewer wars than more sex-stereotyped societies. Economic reasons for advocating sex equity are based on concerns for adequate resource use. When certain groups are relegated to limited production responsibilities regardless of their qualifications, output is reduced. Philosophic reasons for sex equity are based on a variety of principles, including those that focus on justice, ethics, human dignity, and an accurate portrayal of the world as it is or can be, without the continuing neglect of the contributions of the 51% of the world's population that is female.

The possibility that sex equity goals can be at least partially achieved through education is a basic assumption of this handbook. (Klein et al. [Eds.], 1985, pp. xi and xii).[1]

Chapter 1, *Examining the achievement of gender equity in and through education*, addresses the purposes and assumptions used by the authors of this 2007 *Handbook* in more detail and also discusses why *gender* equity was substituted for *sex* equity in the title.

In addition to having similar purposes, we used similar strategies in developing both the 1985 and the 2007 *Handbooks*:

- Over 200 gender equity experts served as editors, authors, and reviewers for each *Handbook*. They did this as part of their voluntary professional contributions and without any extra financial remuneration. Some of the participants in the 1985 *Handbook* played leading roles in the 2007 *Handbook*.

- Both *Handbooks* were organized into six similar parts, and most of the content and chapters covered in the 1985 *Handbook* were also covered in the 2007 *Handbook*. Changes such as the omission of the philosophy and adult and rural women chapters and the addition of many new chapters, especially in the sections on diverse populations and content areas, are explained in chapter 1 of this new *Handbook*.

- The 2007 authors were asked to use a format or structure for their chapters that was similar to the 1985 *Handbook* chap-

---

[1]Much of the rest of this 1985 *Handbook* preface is also appropriate for this 2007 *Handbook* preface. The full 1985 preface and other key chapters will be posted on the Web site accompanying this 2007 *Handbook*.

ters, with recommendations at the end of each chapter for policy, practice, and future research. Like in the 1985 *Handbook*, these recommendations were compiled in a table in the summary chapter. Additionally, the authors of the 2007 *Handbook* were asked to:

– Use the same definitions and concepts as in chapter 1.
– Describe key changes in the patterns of equities and inequities in various topics covered by their chapter since what was reported in the 1985 *Handbook*. (Six of the 2007 chapters have many of the same authors as the 1985 *Handbook*).
– Explain contextual issues such as the nature of support or opposition to efforts in their specific area of gender equity.
– Explain methodology used to select and report evidence on progress toward gender equity. Authors were encouraged to briefly discuss the methods used in particular studies for the benefit of the critical researcher as well as educating nonresearchers about the veracity of the claims.
– Make every effort to report on disaggregated data regarding race/ethnicity, international comparisons, or socioeconomic status differences throughout the chapter.

• Despite concerns from our current publisher and others about efficiency, we used an extensive collaborative process to develop both *Handbooks*. This collaborative style was relatively new for the 1985 *Handbook*. The participants in the 2007 *Handbook* were more aware of the strengths and weaknesses, rewards and constraints of collaboration. The collaborative strategy has helped to create two authoritative research syntheses *Handbooks* with wide appeal and utility and also has helped to increase the viability of the field of gender equity in education. However, the chapters using collaborative teams of authors usually took longer to complete than the chapters with only one or two authors. As discussed in more detail in chapter 1, although we had substantial use of the Internet and *Blackboard* interactive web software to facilitate the exchange of information among the authors and reviewers for the 2007 *Handbook*, we also found that there were more disincentives for many authors to collaborate than there were in the early 1980s. Most of these constraints were related to stronger expectations for academics to publish their own research studies rather than to synthesize the work of others or to work in teams.

Although the two *Handbooks* had similar goals and strategies, here are some of the unique purposes and strategies for this new 2007 *Handbook*.

The 1985 *Handbook* has often been referred to as the "bible" of information on gender equity, and even many scholars or researchers working in the field of gender equity found it particularly useful, especially in topic areas where their personal expertise was limited. We hope that the 2007 *Handbook* will be even more valuable to the increased numbers of researchers, educators, and educational activists interested in gender equity. It should also become a key reference tool for the required Title IX gender equity coordinators and others who care about advancing gender equity at all educational levels and who are a key focus of our Feminist Majority Foundation's work with the Title IX Action Network. This new *Handbook* should also be a very useful reference for education equity trainers at the pre-service and in-service levels, whether or not

their primary area of expertise has been diversity issues in general or gender, race, language, disability, or sexual identity equity issues. In addition to schools of education, it will be a valuable reference book for women's and gender studies faculty and students, and for professional organizations concerned with educational equity. This new *Handbook* will also serve as an important reference for reporters and journalists as they work on stories, such as the release of National Assessment of Education Progress (NAEP) scores, or discuss equity aspects of education legislation at federal and state levels. It will be of high interest to public and organizational libraries as a key reference book especially if they have collections related to education or gender issues. International use should also increase since unlike the 1985 *Handbook*, the 2007 *Handbook* incorporates relevant research from outside the U.S., and it contains a new global gender equity education chapter.

While there is more U.S. media and politically influenced coverage of gender equity issues in education than in the early 1980s, there have also been inaccuracies and distortions particularly in some of the popular advice-type books about gender issues. This new *Handbook* helps refute some of these inaccurate and biased sources of frequently repeated misinformation. For example, the summary chapter shows how despite the media's tendency to highlight gender differences in educational achievement, a key success story has been the increase in gender similarities especially in areas such as mathematics course taking and achievement. The summary and many of the other chapters will also describe conundrums in understanding and measuring gender equity in educational processes, as well as in strategies to decrease the still extensive sex discrimination and stereotyping in society.

As previously discussed, most of the strategies used in the 1985 *Handbook* were repeated, with some modifications for this 2007 second edition. The modifications were related to changes in the context and opportunities. For example:

• The gender equity knowledge base is more extensive than it was 20 years ago, but it is also easier to access and synthesize using Internet and electronic access to national public databases such as from the Census Bureau and the U.S. Department of Education's National Center for Education Statistics.

• To increase consistency and coherence among the chapters in both *Handbooks*, we asked the authors to use the definitions and the conceptual framework provided in their respective first chapters. But for this 2007 *Handbook*, we also encouraged the authors to read and comment on any chapters of interest by posting the draft chapters on an author accessible *Blackboard* site.

• Assuming that most focus would be on the impact of the inequities on women rather than men, and that there might be limited attention to diverse populations relating to race, disability, and sexual orientation, we asked all the authors and reviewers to make sure that their chapters reported on the gender equity challenges of women and girls and men and boys of all the diverse populations represented in part V of the *Handbook*. We also encouraged men and women authors with diverse backgrounds to participate and to serve as lead authors. While most of the editors and authors came from universities, some of them worked in education, governmental organizations, or the private sector.

- We had a more deliberate process to involve outside experts as reviewers for each of the near final chapters to help ensure accuracy, clarity, and comprehensiveness. These reviewers are acknowledged in the beginning of each chapter. Additionally the responsible part editor and the general editor reviewed and commented on multiple versions of the draft chapters.

- While continuing the tradition from the 1985 *Handbook* to build a broad and diverse network of gender equity experts who are interested in research and practice and documenting what works to advance gender equity, we also encouraged the next generation of gender equity researchers and practitioners to participate.

- Another strategic change has been a switch of publishers and key sponsors for this 2007 *Handbook*. The 1985 *Handbook* was started under the auspices of the National Advisory Council on Women's Educational Programs (NACWEP), then administered by the U.S. Department of Education where the editor, Susan Klein, worked. However, this assignment ended soon after the Reagan administration changed leadership of the NACWEP and before the 1985 *Handbook* was finished. Thus, Klein and the others completed the *Handbook* without government support and gave the royalties to AERA. In October 2003, Klein retired from the U.S. Department of Education and became Education Equity Director of the Feminist Majority Foundation (FMF), with updating the *Handbook* as a major assignment. The Feminist Majority Foundation, founded in 1987, is the nation's largest feminist research and action organization dedicated to women's equality, reproductive rights and health, and nonviolence. Led by FMF President Eleanor Smeal, our efforts focus on advancing the legal, social, and political equality of women with men such as countering the backlash to women's advancement and achieving gender equity both in and through education. Eleanor Smeal is also publisher of *Ms.* magazine.

In 2004, Lawrence Erlbaum Associates, which specializes in publishing state-of-the-art research handbooks in education and the social sciences, was anxious to publish this new *Handbook,* and the 1985 *Handbook* publisher, Johns Hopkins University Press, had narrowed its focus to higher education. After we arranged the contract with the Feminist Majority Foundation and Lawrence Erlbaum Associates, Erlbaum arranged to publish a series of AERA *Handbooks*. This, and the fact that the Feminist Majority Foundation is working informally with AERA groups such as the Special Interest Group: Research on Women and Education and the Committee on Scholars and Advocates for Gender Equity in Education, should help maintain these helpful links. Another 1985 *Handbook* sponsor, the Association for Gender Equity Leadership in Education (AGELE), formerly called the National Coalition for Sex Equity in Education, has also helped publicize the *Handbook* in its newsletters and conferences. Lawrence Erlbaum Associates is making the *Handbook* available in hard and soft cover and electronically.

- Finally, a key difference in strategy for this 2007 *Handbook* will be the development of a web page to accompany the *Handbook* and provide updated and additional information for each chapter and even other new areas. Many of the chapters have already referenced materials that will be available on this web page including tables containing details on evidence and some of the chapters from the 1985 *Handbook*.

As with any reference book, we don't expect readers to read it from cover to cover, but we hope you will find plenty of information to interest and help you join with the authors and many others in continuing to develop and use knowledge about how to increase gender and other types of equity in our global society. As you do so, feel free to share information and insights through the Web site that will be linked to www.feminist.org/education and also directly with the authors whose e-mail addresses are listed at the end of their respective chapters.

Susan Shurberg Klein, Education Equity Director, Feminist Majority Foundation, and Eleanor Smeal, President, Feminist Majority Foundation, and Publisher of Ms. magazine.

February 2007

ACKNOWLEDGMENTS

As described in the preface, this *Handbook for Achieving Gender Equity through Education* builds on the experience and hard work of all involved in its predecessor, the inspirational 1985 *Handbook for Achieving Sex Equity through Education*.

Like the 1985 *Handbook*, this 2007 *Handbook* was developed through a collaborative process and the hard work of the editors and authors who were able to stick with us through the whole publication process. But we also want to thank our first Part IV editor, Helen Farmer, who helped the content authors get started, and Rosalind Hale who established the *Handbook's* first sophisticated *Blackboard* site and was the first lead author of the education technology chapter before she had to leave Xavier University in New Orleans due to the extensive damage from Hurricane Katrina in 2004. We also want to thank the many others who have supported this work including initial authors who had to drop out of active participation, but who helped us get the chapters going in the right direction. Thanks also to Beverly Irby and her colleagues at Sam Houston State University for helping us transfer the *Handbook* information to their *Blackboard* site when Xavier University had to close, and for having the largest number of their faculty contribute to the chapters.

While all who contributed to this *Handbook* were essential, our wonderful team of six distinguished coeditors deserve extra praise. In addition to writing the insightful overviews for each of their parts of the *Handbook*, they served as continual advisers on all phases of this *Handbook* development, made the chapters in their parts of the *Handbook* shine by helping the authors with numerous revisions, and often even participated in the research and writing of the chapters.

The more than 50 lead authors had especially demanding roles. It was exciting to watch many of them work in teams, sharing expertise, bringing out the best in all their contributors, and mentoring their less experienced colleagues. Additionally, we thank the more than 80 major authors and other authors who provided assistance with some of the information. We also thank everyone for contributions that had to be condensed or omitted from the final *Handbook*. Finally, we are especially grateful to the close to 100 distinguished reviewers who are acknowledged at the beginning of each chapter. In particular we want to thank Dr. Bernice Sandler, "godmother" of Title IX, who carefully reviewed several chapters, sometimes multiple times, to ensure that the information was accurate. A massive writing project like this is also beholden to the Feminist Majority Foundation interns, and the research assistants, librarians, and others who helped the authors in various ways.

We are especially grateful to Lane Akers, vice president-editorial of Lawrence Erlbaum Associates, who has always been an enthusiastic, supportive, and patient advisor. In addition to allowing us to use the more time consuming collaborative writing process, he met with the authors at the AERA meetings in San Diego and Montreal and arranged for the beautiful colorful *Handbook* cover. It is an art print "Equity Rules (Be Fair, Be Fair, Be Fair)" created by former women's studies professor and artist, Patricia E. Ortman, for the Feminist Majority Foundation Education Equity Program. We also thank copy editors and production and marketing staff at Lawrence Erlbaum Associates.

Our next thanks go to supportive organizations. The top of this list is the Feminist Majority Foundation (FMF) and its president, Eleanor Smeal, who has sponsored this *Handbook* since its inception, and to former FMF legal advisor, Sharyn Tejani and current FMF vice president, Diane Cutri, who helped with business and financial aspects. We thank the W. K. Kellogg Foundation for their initial grant from their former vice president, Anne Petersen, to help with the initial *Handbook* planning as well as with the start of the Title IX Action Network. We also thank organizations that have helped sponsor sessions at their conferences and reported on *Handbook* progress in their newsletters: the American Educational Research Association, especially the Special Interest Group: Research on Women and Education and the Committee on Scholars and Advocates for Gender Equity in Education; the Association for Gender Equity Leadership in Education; and the National Women's Studies Association.

Finally, our personal thanks go to the wonderful understanding and patient spouses, partners, other family members, and colleagues of the editors (Perry Klein, Pamela Miller, Harrison Fox, Jr., Dale Kramer, Scott Pollard and Miles McPeek), and of the over 200 authors and reviewers. All of these partners and colleagues did without the contributors' help and companionship while we spent countless volunteer hours working on many aspects of this *Handbook*.

Susan Shurberg Klein, Education Equity Director, Feminist Majority Foundation.

EXAMINING THE ACHIEVEMENT OF GENDER EQUITY IN AND THROUGH EDUCATION

Susan S. Klein* with Cheris Kramarae, Barbara Richardson

INTRODUCTION

Our empirical research and experience make clear that gender continues to be an important organizing and disempowering principle in the school system. Equity in education is not only a matter of numbers. While this *Handbook* provides many figures and statistics, the authors do not reduce equity issues to a series of variables, or to handicaps to be overcome. Instead, the authors detail the systematic, persistent, and group-based power and subordination problems in education. They also describe promising gender innovations needed throughout our educational systems to foster change and achieve equity. The material in these chapters challenges many current policies and practices, by reporting on empirical research, by noting serious gaps in the research, by describing programs that have and have not been successful, and by offering perspectives that can alter our current understanding of equity in education. The *Handbook* includes facts, assumptions, strategies, practices, and content related to curriculum, governance, socialization, psychology, working with diverse populations and multiple educational levels. It is a landmark and definitive piece of work for anyone studying, teaching, or interested in gender equity in education.

This chapter covers key purposes and understandings that have guided the development of this 22-year update of the *Handbook for Achieving Sex Equity through Education* (Klein, 1985). The first section explains the title and the underlying concepts of achieving gender equity in and through education along with key terms like *equality*, *sex equity*, and *gender analysis*. Section two shows how gender equity goals and values are supported by international and U.S. laws and policies. The final section compares four aspects of the 1985 and the 2007

Handbooks ranging from influences due to key changes in society, to expectations for gender equity research, to changes in the chapters covered. The *Handbook's* summary chapter highlights key findings, recommendations, and conundrums.

KEY WORDS AND CONCEPTS

Handbook for this volume means a research- and evidence-based summary analysis of a fairly comprehensive set of gender equity issues in 29 chapter topic areas related to education. Each chapter summarizes what is known about gender equity issues and solutions, with recommendations to guide future efforts to advance the field and practice of gender equitable education. Supplemental web pages will provide new research, recommendations, and related sources. Our publisher, Lawrence Erlbaum Associates, specializes in research-based *Handbooks* in a variety of fields inside and outside education.[1] According to Lane Akers, vice president-editorial of Lawrence Erlbaum Associates, these *Handbooks* "provide a broad, comprehensive snapshot of the theory, concepts, research, and methodologies that define a particular field of study. Most of them are interdisciplinary to some extent thereby introducing people in adjacent (but often isolated) fields to one another. In short, these comprehensive research *Handbooks* tend to bring integration to some loosely coupled fields of study."

Gender equity in and through education follows the common research and evaluation framework by examining education processes *in* education as well as outcomes *through* education to help make a more gender equitable, productive, and peaceful society. (This in and through distinction was also used

---

*The bold face names are the Lead Authors.
[1]After we made our publishing arrangements, the American Educational Research Association (AERA), a sponsor of our 1985 *Handbook for Achieving Sex Equity through Education,* agreed to have Lawrence Erlbaum Associates publish AERA Handbooks.

in the 1985 *Handbook*.) A key theme of this *Handbook* is that education is an important tool in creating gender equity in society. This in and through distinction helps explain the continuum of gender equity process and outcome goals, as it helps us think about the wide variety of process and outcome goals that are valued by society, clarifies how some people distinguish between equity and equality, and explains some contradictions such as why sex segregation in education processes may at times be justified if it leads to increased gender equity in outcomes.

Process and outcome goals fall on a continuum of education accomplishments and lifetime outcomes. In a continuum, sometimes indicators (such as high self-esteem or school attendance) are seen as part of the process and sometimes as the desired outcomes. There are variations among individuals and populations on what is most valued in the U.S. as well as around the world in terms of education processes and outcome goals. Sometimes there are also conflicting public laws and policies that support these values with sanctions or rewards. Conflicts between public secular policies and some religious policies, especially related to gender equity and the roles and constraints on women and men, create challenges in establishing consensus goals. As the *Handbook* authors point out, often values associated with men's stereotypical achievements have been favored over achievements more typically associated with women, and men have traditionally been expected to obtain more of the desired *gender equity goals*. If the outcomes are judged valuable for girls and women (such as empathy and cooperation), or for men (such as strength and earning ability), they should be equally valued by society and equally attainable by all population groups.

In discussing *efforts to achieve gender equity "in" formal and informal aspects of education*, *Handbook* authors address gender equity process goals that focus on fairness, following equity laws and policies, and the decrease of inappropriate sex or gender stereotyping or segregation. Using these process goals, it may be justifiable to treat specified girls and boys, women and men differently[2] if there is evidence that this treatment will increase gender equity in the desired quality of life outcomes for the individuals and for the larger society. As discussed in chapter 9 on "Coeducation and Single-Sex Environments" and chapter 5 on the role of government, some different treatment of boys and girls even in sex-segregated classes or schools is allowed under the 1975 Title IX Regulations (OCR, 1975). Title IX is the landmark 1972 U.S. federal education law that prohibits discrimination on the basis of sex by organizations receiving federal financial assistance for education programs or activities. Under the 1975 Title IX Regulations this temporary sex discrimination (or compensatory or affirmative action) is allowed if it contributes to ending sex discrimination or de-

creasing gender gaps in other outcomes. However some of the chapters in this *Handbook* were quickly updated when the Office for Civil Rights in the U.S. Department of Education issued new Title IX Regulations on October 25, 2006, (OCR, 2006) which said that single-sex education activities are permitted for a much broader array of purposes than ending sex discrimination. (See especially chapter 9 and the summary chapter 31 for the details.).

In discussing *achieving gender equity outcome goals through education*, the authors focus on all that is of value to individuals and society, including frequently neglected strengths and roles traditionally associated with women. The following 1994 gender equity outcome goals are based on the 1985 *Handbook for Achieving Sex Equity through Education* goals.

Gender equity outcomes are attained when:
- Both women and men acquire, or are given equitable opportunity to acquire, the most socially valued characteristics and skills (even if they have been generally attributed to only one gender), so that fewer jobs, roles, activities, expectations, and achievements are differentiated by gender.
- There is decreased use of gender stereotyping in decision making by or about individuals.
- Sex segregation in education and society caused by gender stereotyping and other inappropriate discriminatory factors is reduced and eventually eliminated. (Klein & Ortman, 1994, p. 13).

The concept of *gender equity outcomes valued by our society* means that women and men, girls and boys should have full access to the same personal aspirations, rights, and responsibilities related to basic indicators of quality of life such as health, productivity, knowledge, happiness, freedom, safety, economic self-sufficiency, etc. *Our society* refers to the diverse populations in the U.S. and the world. Our focus on what is valued by society will be the goals described in international agreements, such as the 1948 United Nations Universal Declaration of Human Rights, national constitutions and other detailed public laws and policies, such as the United States Title IX of the 1972 Education Amendments. These are discussed in part 2 of this chapter.

Gender equity and *gender equality*. Gender equity means attaining parity between women and men in the quality of life, academic, and work outcomes valued by our society, without limitations associated with gender stereotypes, gender roles, or prejudices. Although many who work toward these goals have their own definitions of equity and equality, there is no consensus on what these distinctions are. Thus, in this *Handbook* unless noted otherwise, the terms *gender equity*, *gender equitable*, and *gender equality*[3] are used interchangeably.

---

[2]Sometimes this differential treatment is called compensatory or affirmative action. Under the 1975 Regulations for Title IX, some sex segregation and related sex-differential instruction may be justifiable if it leads to decreased sex discrimination in outcomes.

[3]Some define gender *equality* as insuring that "different behaviour, aspirations and needs of women and men are considered, valued and favoured equally. It does not mean that women and men have to become the same but that their rights, responsibilities and opportunities should be the same and not depend on whether they are born" with a more male or female anatomy. Some define gender *equity* as meaning "fairness of treatment for women and men, according to their respective needs. This may include equal treatment or treatment that is different but which is considered equivalent in terms of rights, benefits, obligations and opportunities." Some chapters provide examples to show how deliberately different educational treatment for girls and boys may be used to increase desired gender equitable outcomes or decrease gender gaps in achievement. (Adapted from ABC of Women Workers' Rights And Gender Equality, ILO, Geneva, 2000, p. 48 as set forth on page 5 of *Gender Equality and Equity: A Summary review of UNESCO's accomplishments since the Fourth World Conference on Women (Beijing, 1995)* http://unesdoc.unesco.org/images/0012/001211/121145e.pdf

We have used gender equity instead of gender equality in the *Handbook* title to be consistent with the title of the 1985 *Handbook for Achieving Sex Equity through Education* and because equity is generally preferred and used by educators. Most authors would agree, however, that the word equality, meaning the same treatment and outcome, is especially appropriate when talking about equal rights, responsibilities, and opportunities (the process dimensions), as well as receiving the same equally valued outcomes desired by society. This includes equal pay for work of comparable value, for example when men and women athletic coaches or student newspaper advisors are equally qualified and are paid the same.

Educators use the term equity to talk about a wide variety of populations related to gender, race, poverty, disability, etc. (Klein, Ortman, & Friedman, 2002). Many also consider equity to be more comprehensive and flexible than equality because it implies the concept of *fairness* or some differences in education processes rather than the concept of *sameness* when dealing with a diverse student population. When educators make fine distinctions between equality and equity, they often define gender equity as:

- Providing an equal opportunity for access to education *even if it involves extra efforts to recruit the under-represented men and boys or women and girls.*

- Ensuring fair, just, and comparable *but not always identical* treatment during the education process. The differential treatment is based on gender differences in needs, or evidence that it will be more effective in contributing to the desired outcomes. For example, male and female athletic uniforms may be different if designed to protect different parts of the body such as the inclusion of a penis cup. Another example is *potty parity* with different types of facilities provided for women and men.[4]

- Reducing gender gaps by obtaining equal outcomes desired by society. In defining equity processes and outcomes, others say attaining equity means there are no systematic differences in the distribution of conditions, practices, and results related to gender, race/ethnicity, socioeconomic status, English language proficiency, or other relevant characteristics.

Some argue that in many cases, equality, or appropriate identical treatment, is preferred; however, others prefer the flexibility of the concept of equity. Both equality and equity are used in important legislation related to nondiscrimination on the basis of sex. For example, equality is key to equal rights protections in constitutions, and equity is allowed under the 1975 Title IX Regulations in education processes to allow different treatment of girls and boys (such as sex segregation) if this different treatment will result in more equal valued outcomes.

Gender equity and ***sex equity***. The title of the *Handbook* was changed from sex equity to gender equity to reflect the change in the use of these terms in the field over the past 20 years. For example, in a 2006 search of the Educational Resources Information System (ERIC), Sue Klein found 487 documents using the key words *sex equity* from pre 1966 to 1984, but only 9 documents using the key words *gender equity* during those years. During the time frame of the current *Handbook* (1985–2006), this ERIC search showed 709 documents using gender equity but only 397 documents using sex equity. During 2000 to 2006 when there were only 4 documents using sex equity and 163 using gender equity. For more on this trend see chapters by Klein, Ortman, and Friedman (2002) and Koch, Irby, and Brown (2002) in *Defining and Redefining Gender Equity in Education* (Koch & Irby, 2002). The large drop in the use of sex equity after 1998 is related to the drastic decrease in documents about vocational education sex equity coordinators and programs when the Perkins Vocational Education Act stopped requiring funding for these activities.

The use of gender rather than sex also reflects the importance of focusing on roles and gender identity, as well as female and male categories commonly associated with the biological sex continuum. Despite the general switch to gender to provide emphasis to the social construction of the behaviors and attitudes that a society considers generally associated with males and females (or masculinity or femininity), when the authors report on gender analyses, especially similarities and differences or gender gaps, their evidence is almost always based on the traditional sex or biological primary and secondary sex characteristics used to distinguish females and males. Social sciences make the distinction between the sex of their respondents or subjects in terms of sex differences or observations about boys compared to girls or men compared to women. They use the terms *gender indicator* or *gender role* when referring to research on the culturally defined stereotypes of masculinity or femininity. It is also common for there to be a difference between the sexes (sex differences between men and women) with regard to gender-related behaviors and expressions, e.g., masculine or feminine scripts for the expression of emotions. Gender-related expectations for what it means to be masculine or feminine in social roles can vary widely across cultures, times, and places. The definitions of what constitutes appropriate behavior can vary so widely that many feel it is best to speak of gender roles in the plural, e.g., masculinities and femininities. The authors have also used the word sex when talking about legal protections since sex discrimination is prohibited by Title IX and other international, federal, and state civil rights laws.

Advocates of this change in terminology—from sex to gender equity—also argued that the sexual behavior connections

---

[4]For those who make distinctions between equality and equity, most would agree that equality is needed in most circumstances such as equal pay for comparable work of women and men teachers. *Potty parity* rules can be analyzed in terms of gender equality or gender equity. Gender equality would occur when the same number and type of privacy stalls and facilities are provided in bathrooms for men and women. Gender equity would occur if there are different women's and men's bathrooms for multiple users, with each room designed to maximize the satisfaction and effectiveness for their respective users. Thus, if there are equal numbers of women and men using the bathrooms and if women need more time, to avoid longer lines they would require more stalls than the rooms for the men. Many agree that the gender equity definition of potty parity is preferred. Further, critics point out the common practice of providing boys less bathroom and shower privacy than girls is not fair.

associated with the word *sex* would limit popular support for important activities to end sex discrimination in education. Ironically, despite the change from sex equity to gender equity, this new *Handbook* covers much more information related to sexuality than did the 1985 "Sex Equity" *Handbook*. After the 1985 *Handbook* was published, the editor and her colleagues realized that there was practically no attention to sexuality-related issues that are often a key component of sex discrimination. For example, the only brief mention of sexual harassment in the 1985 *Handbook* was in the chapter on postsecondary education. Thus, they prepared an edited journal (Klein, 1989) and subsequent book on *Sex Equity and Sexuality in Education* (Klein, 1992). In contrast, this *Handbook* has a separate chapter on "Sexual Harassment: The Hidden Gender Equity Problem," and it is mentioned in many other chapters as well. Additionally there is a chapter on "Gender Equity in Formal Sexuality Education."

Gender equity and **women's equity.** For two reasons, the term *gender equity* is used instead of the terms *women's equity*, *women's equality*, or *women's advancement*. Although sex equity has frequently been used interchangeably with women's equity, most thought that like *manpower*, which often refers to men, women's equity was just for women. They didn't realize that legislation such as the Women's Educational Equity Act was also intended to benefit boys and men if they were the group facing sex discrimination under Title IX. The term gender equity focuses more attention on men and boys. This is appropriate when boys and men need to improve their achievement and other valued outcomes so that they will do as well as their female peers. Also, sex stereotyping and discrimination may be just as detrimental to boys and men as it is to girls and women. However, in documenting progress toward gender equity, the authors often show how men and boys have generally been favored over women and girls in the attainment of valued resources and outcomes in the U.S. and many other societies. Some chapters also show how gender gaps, even on similar indicators, may reverse direction over time and as we look at education outcomes and subsequent outcomes related to quality of life in society. For example, U.S. boys typically score lower than girls on writing tests, and yet, in careers such as writing and journalism, a large proportion of men are paid more than their women counterparts. (See the "Gender Equity in Communications Skills" chapter for more details.) Similarly, in many less developed nations, boys are more likely than girls to repeat grade levels. Yet, in many of these countries, boys complete elementary school and secondary school at higher rates than girls. Global research shows that the education of girls even more than boys in developing countries is associated with national improvements in economic conditions, health, and reductions in births. (See the "Gender Equity Education Globally" chapter).

The second reason to switch from women's equity to the more inclusive focus on gender equity is because this is congruent with governmental changes. For example the National Science Foundation has switched from programs for women and minorities to gender equity programs and, in the international area, the previous *Women in Development* programs are now generally called *gender equity* programs. Gender equity and gender analysis emphasize both male and female input, process, and outcome variables.

Gender Analysis and the **New Scholarship on Women.** In this 2007 *Handbook*, the approach used to understand, evaluate, and advance gender equity education is now called *gender analysis* or *using a gender lens* rather than "The New Scholarship on Women," which was the title of chapter 4 in the 1985 *Handbook*. Both "The New Scholarship on Women" chapter and gender analyses used by authors of this *Handbook* use concepts based on the feminist and equal rights principle that women and men should have equal access to all social, educational, political, and economic domains and that internalized gender stereotyping perpetuates the unequal nature of these institutions. The switch to *gender analysis* is often seen as broader than new scholarship on women. It is typically used in global gender equity work and in a wide variety of analyses that focus on the gender-related indicators. However, there are similarities in purposes. For example, the authors of the "New Scholarship on Women" chapter concluded that "The particular goal of sex equity in education is part of this larger agenda to shape a future in which gender is not the basis for discrimination, where one sex is not valued more highly than another and where what we know about human beings is based on the study of women's and girls' as well as men's and boys' lives." (Biklen & Shakeshaft, 1985, p. 45).[5]

LEGAL JUSTIFICATION FOR GENDER EQUITY IN AND THROUGH EDUCATION

As previously discussed, what is officially valued by institutions is usually documented in goals, policies, or laws intended to help people attain these outcomes. The following chart shows how these laws range from general principles, such as the U.N. Universal Declaration of Human Rights, to more specific gender equity education laws, such as the Title IX Regulations that guide many aspects about how the laws are implemented. The shaded boxes depict rights or goals specifically associated with gender, education, or both gender and education.

INTERNATIONAL AND U.S. EXAMPLES OF TYPES AND LEVELS OF EQUITY POLICIES

I. General protections against human rights discrimination or guarantees of equal rights. Some of these documents specifically mention principles such as nondiscrimination in education or on the basis of sex.
- U.N. Universal Declaration of Human Rights, 1948 http://www.un.org/Overview/rights.html (U.N., 1948).
- U.N. Covenants on Civil and Political Rights and Economic, Social & Cultural Rights, 1966 (U.N., 1966)

---

[5]The web page accompanying this chapter 1 contains "The New Scholarship on Women" chapter from the 1985 *Handbook*.

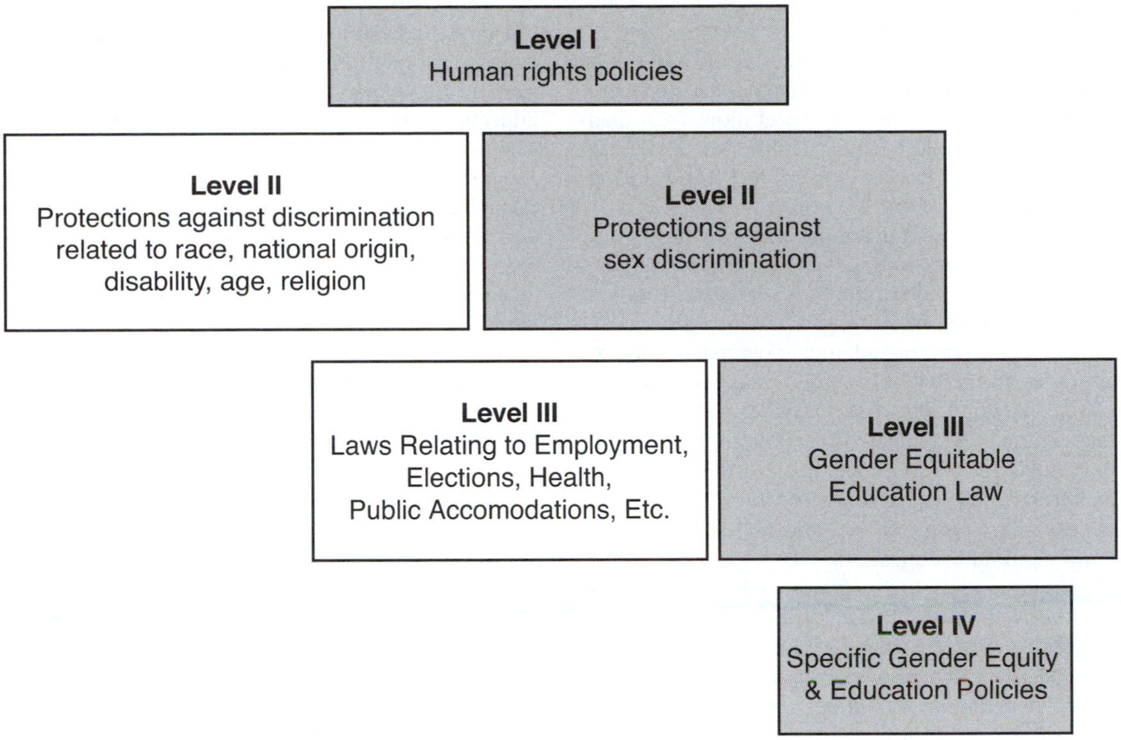

FIGURE 1.1. Types and levels of public equity policies.

- Equal protection statements in national constitutions for citizens and others. (U.S. equal protection clause in the 14th Amendment to the Constitution.)
II. Additional protections for specific populations against discrimination on the basis of sex, race, national origin, religion, age, disability, etc., for example, U.N. Conventions on Race Discrimination, 1966 and the Rights of the Child, 1979. Examples of U.N. and national protections against discrimination on the basis of sex/gender include:
  - The Convention on the Elimination of All Forms of Discrimination Against Women (CEDAW), 1997. www.cedaw.org (U.N., 1979).
  - The Platform for Action from the Beijing 4th World Conference on Women, 1995. It was reaffirmed in Beijing + 10 U.N. Meetings in NY, March, 2005 http://www.un.org/womenwatch/daw/beijing/platform/index.html (See education and training, girl child, and mechanisms sections in particular.) (U.N., 1995).
  - The 2000 U.N. Millennium Development Goals www.un.org/millenniumgoals. However, *Beijing Betrayed* (WEDO, 2005) describes global examples of limited implementation of these Millennium Goals and the Beijing Platform, based on reports from 150 countries (U.N., 2000).
  - National protections for specific populations. (Including equal rights on the basis of sex provisions in national constitutions. Gender equity advocates in the U.S. are still trying to obtain ratification of the Equal Rights Amendment (ERA) and CEDAW.)

III. Protections related to nondiscrimination in benefits and rights in specific areas such as education, employment, voting and political activity, public accommodations, and family rights. Examples related to sex/gender and education include:
  - U.N. Convention against Discrimination in Education, 1960, http://ww.unhchr.ch/html/menu3/b/d_c_educ.htm (U.N., 1960).
  - Education and Training and the Girl Child Provisions in Beijing Platform, U.N. (U.N., 1995)
  - UNESCO's Education for All, including the Development Index, and request for national plans of action based in Dakar Global 2000 Forum and follow-up. http://www.un.org/womenwatch/daw/index.html
  - The guarantees in many countries of free and compulsory education in their constitutions. In the U.S., this guarantee is in state constitutions.
  - U.S. and other nations' Title IX-type laws that prohibit sex discrimination in education in specified circumstances. In the U.S., complaints about sex discrimination in education may be accompanied by related complaints of race, handicap, or other types of discrimination by the same person. www.feminist.org/education. Taiwan has an extensive Title IX-type law and regulations that even include explicit prohibitions against discrimination related to sexual orientation (Klein, 2004, Taiwan Government).
  - U.S state and local laws that provide protection against sex discrimination and sex stereotyping in education. As of 2006, "twenty-two states have some form of explicit pro-

tection against sex discrimination in their state constitutions" (Wharton, 2006, p. 1202). At least 13 states have Title IX-type laws covering the same areas as the federal Title IX, and 18 other states have laws that provide some, but fewer protections. Some state laws cover more areas than Title IX, such as curriculum (Cheng, 1988). See the *Handbook* chapter on "The Role of Government in Advancing Gender Equity in Education" for more information.

IV. Protections against sex discrimination within specific aspects of education, such as admissions, sexual harassment, elimination of sex stereotypes in curriculum, sex segregation, athletics, and vocational education. Some laws also provide money and other types of support to implement governance mechanisms, programs, and activities designed to increase gender and other types of equity outcomes. Examples with a detailed focus on specific gender equity issues in education include:

- U.N. Beijing Platform and *Education for All* cover areas such as illiteracy, access to free and compulsory education, access to training, science and technology, vocational, and continuing education.
- The U.S. Title IX and its 1975 implementation regulations prohibit sex discrimination in facilities, access to courses, career guidance, student financial aid, health and insurance benefits, employment in educational institutions, athletics, sexual harassment, and other types of overt and subtle sex discrimination. States and local education agencies or institutions can also add additional protections against sex discrimination that cover areas such as sex stereotypes in curriculum that are not covered by the federal Title IX.
- There is also national support of specific gender equity programs. For example, the U.S. federal government has provided funding for gender equity in vocational and career education to help displaced homemakers and to encourage girls and boys to learn skills that will help them succeed in occupations that were previously segregated by sex. The U.S. government also provides support for girls' education programs in developing countries where girls have little access to schooling.

Implementation of Gender Equity Policies by the U.S. and Other Countries.

Having good comprehensive gender equity laws is the first step, but implementing and enforcing them adequately are essential to advance gender equity. Widespread public awareness and agreement with the law increases its chances for implementation. Additionally, easily accessible mechanisms should be in place to ensure that the laws are being used and that transparency, accountability, and appropriate sanctions are being enforced. [6]

National governments can increase gender equity by funding research, development, and assistance activities particularly when projects are based on participatory approaches that enable women and other subordinate groups to have greater access to agendas and decision making. [7] These insights can help

document the inequities as well as solutions to enable educators to further advance gender equity. Since 1976, the U.S. federal government has supported gender equity programs authorized by the Women's Educational Equity Act, Perkins Vocational Education Acts, Fund for the Improvement of Postsecondary Education, and the National Science Foundation (NSF). Additional programs were also added, including U.S. Agency for International Development efforts to advance girls' education internationally. However, this financial support has been declining. Most funding from the U.S. Department of Education (ED) was for sex equity and displaced homemaker activities in the Perkins Vocational Education Acts. From 1984 to 1998, this vocational sex equity funding was about $100 million annually. As of 2006 there was no specific funding for vocational education activities to advance gender equity. In contrast, funding for these NSF gender equity-related programs increased from $2.5 million annually in 1984, to over $40 million in 2006. (For more details on U.S. funding for gender equity education, see the *Handbook* chapter on "The Role of Government in Advancing Gender Equity in Education.")

COMPARING THE 1985 HANDBOOK FOR ACHIEVING SEX EQUITY THROUGH EDUCATION WITH THE NEW HANDBOOK FOR ACHIEVING GENDER EQUITY THROUGH EDUCATION

The following questions will be used to highlight some differences between the 1985 *Handbook* and this new 2007 *Handbook*.

1. What changes in U.S. society have influenced this *Handbook*?
2. How have the expectations for reporting on acceptable evidence to understand and achieve gender equity changed since the 1985 *Handbook*?
3. How has the process of developing this *Handbook* differed from the collaborative process used in developing the 1985 *Handbook*?
4. How have the chapter topics and organization of the *Handbook* changed as a result of the social changes since the 1985 *Handbook*?

1. **How changes in U.S. society from 1985 to now have influenced this *Handbook*.**
   - ***Continued growth in the field of gender equity education***. Much in the new *Handbook* focuses on the progress as well as the continued inequities facing girls and women, but authors also document progress and continuing challenges for boys and men.
   - The **mass media** have helped sustain attention on various aspects of gender equity. The media often focus on issues

---

[6]Many of the *Handbook* chapters discuss challenges in implementing Title IX, the key gender equity education law in the U.S.
[7]Subordinate or marginal groups are often marginal at all levels of the system. Their alternative viewpoints and value systems need to be involved throughout.

that generate controversy. They have done so in both negative ways such as writing about the "gender wars," and in more positive and responsible ways. For example, on January 14, 2005, Harvard President Lawrence Summers angered attendees at a conference[8] when he talked about "innate aptitudes" favoring men in high-level science performance. Media coverage and articulate rebuttals from experts, including those who were attendees at the conference, helped inform the public about research on gender equity that refuted much of what Summers said and implied. It also led to the creation of two Harvard task forces to address sex and race discrimination at Harvard, and the subsequent Harvard pledge of $50 million over 10 years to address the task force recommendations to end sex and race discrimination (Harvard President pledges $50 million for Women's Programs, 2005, and Harvard Task Forces on Women Release Findings and Recommendations, 2005). One of the conference participants and a leading researcher on sex discrimination facing academic faculty in the sciences said that this media reaction even contributed to positive action in Switzerland related to increased hiring of women science faculty in universities there (Donna Nelson, personal communication, March 5, 2005). It also appears that the negative publicity related to Summers' disparaging comments about women in science contributed to his resignation from the Harvard presidency about a year later (Harvard's Summers to Resign, 2006). This debunking of myths related to inherent sex differences in abilities is also supported by the evidence used in this *Handbook*.

There have also been **shifts in emphases** as the press and others focus on educational topics deemed newsworthy. Sometimes these shifts address a real need, such as the elimination of sexual harassment and discrimination related to sexual orientation. Sometimes issues related to gender are pushed by the media because they support other agendas, such as focusing attention on single sex education because it is likely to help justify private or charter schools or more recently because it is pushed by conservative groups. Some issues, such as attention to gender equity for boys, seem to wax and wane perennially. Some of the early attention to sex equity was intended to help boys in reading (Sexton, 1969; Best, 1983). The communications skills chapter reminds us that both boys and girls in the U.S. have made progress in reading and writing, but there is still a gap favoring girls. In particular, many low-income African American and Hispanic boys do poorly on these and other education achievement indicators. In the 2005 State of the Union message, President Bush heralded a new initiative to help boys to be led by First Lady Laura Bush. Her nine-agency project and White House Conference on Helping America's Youth resulted in a web-based best practices community guide that addresses risk and protective factors for both boys and girls (White House Of-

fice of the First Lady, 2005). But it was not included in the U.S. Department of Education budget requests for 2006 or 2007. In 2006, however, the gender equity needs of boys, especially minority boys, continued to receive substantial media and academic attention. These inequities were also the focus of conferences by two of the U.S. Department of Education's Equity Assistance Centers in 2006. A report by Sara Mead from the Education Sector on "The Evidence Suggests Otherwise: The Truth About Boys and Girls," while documenting gaps for low-income minority boys, pointed out that many media reports on boys in crisis were inaccurate because "The real story is not bad news about boys doing worse; it's good news about girls doing better" (Mead, 2006, p. 3). With the increased focus on gender equity rather than women's equity, the current *Handbook* authors have been asked to address male gender equity issues, but similar to this report by Mead, the 2007 *Handbook* authors generally found little evidence of gender inequities in educational processes that have a negative impact on boys and men in general, although this is not so true for many minority or lower SES males.

- As can be seen by the many valuable **research packed chapters** with extensive lists of references, there has been substantial work on the gender equity issues over the past 20 plus years. While the authors report on large gaps in what they would like to know and what they do know, readers will find much new information and insights, and researchers will learn about productive directions for future work. The authors and reviewers have also tried to make their chapters as definitive and accurate as possible—a large job when some of the popular literature and media accounts have been inaccurate and misleading.

- ***Increased use of technology***. Another major change in society that is also reflected in this 2007 *Handbook* is the change in the use of technology, especially in the use of computers and easier information access. It is also reflected in the increased focus on technology in the chapter topics. Two chapters in this *Handbook* have technology in their titles: chapter 10, "Gender Equity in the Use of Educational Technology," addresses many aspects of computer use in educational activities at all education levels, from preschool to distance education; chapter 13, "Gender Equity in Science, Engineering and Technology," focuses on preparing for careers in technology from computer science to information science. In addition, chapter 20, "Gender Equity in Career and Technical Education," focuses on computer careers as well as many other types of related technological activities and industries from aviation to telecommunications. Although none of the 1985 *Handbook* chapter titles included the word *technology,* the 1985 chapter on "Sex Equity and Sex Bias in Instructional Materials," discussed the need for both nonbiased and "sex-affirmative" changes in print and AV materials of that time. These gender equity goals remain prevalent in the technology education options

---

[8]Diversifying the Science & Engineering Workforce: Women, Underrepresented Minorities, and Their S&E Careers, organized by the National Bureau of Economic Research.

today. Additionally, the Internet, satellites, fiber-optic cables and cell phones, along with other media, bring new questions of power, access, and equity in education as well as in the broader society.

- ***More global focus and learning from other countries.*** In the past two decades, questions of education, knowledge, history, gender, class, and race have become profoundly complicated as we try to sort out relationships across borders. Globalization has become a key, if seldom defined, concept in public discourse.

This *Handbook* pays more attention to the global gender equity education context than did the 1985 *Handbook*. A previous part of this chapter described the legal framework for gender equity in the context of international policies and laws such as the United Nations Universal Declaration of Human Rights. And, unlike the 1985 *Handbook*, this 2007 *Handbook* has a chapter devoted to "Gender Equity Education Globally" as well as information in the chapter on "The role of government in advancing gender equity in education" on U.S. federal funding of gender equity education efforts in developing countries. The new "Gender Equity in Foreign and Second Language Learning" chapter also reports on gender equity challenges for the increasingly large numbers of students learning a language outside the U.S.

Like the 1985 *Handbook*, however, the focus of most chapters in this *Handbook* is on the U.S. patterns of gender inequities and contexts that contribute to these inequities and their potential solutions, such as implementing our federal Title IX law prohibiting sex discrimination in many education environments. Where feasible, the authors also reported on relevant evidence from other countries. For example, authors of several chapters helped explain gender similarities or differences in the U.S. by showing similar patterns in international studies of achievement. This type of international comparative information was not as widely available to the authors when they wrote the 1985 *Handbook*.

Compared to the 1985 authors, the current *Handbook* authors had easier access to research studies from other countries and were able to use them or exclude them as appropriate. Some chapter authors looked for gender equity solutions from other countries that were potentially feasible to the U.S. Even as we continue to learn from the work of researchers in other countries, the authors also hope that although the primary *Handbook* audience is the U.S., many of the U.S. strategies may be valuable for advancing gender equity in other countries as well.

- ***More attention to intersections of gender and other equity concerns.*** Authors of most chapters in this new *Handbook* have paid more attention to gender and race and some other equity concerns, especially sexual identity and sexual orientation issues than in the previous *Handbook*. Additionally, the four chapter section in the 1985 *Handbook* on "Sex Equity Strategies for Specific Populations" has been expanded to a seven chapter section on "Gender Equity Strategies for Diverse Populations" in this 2007 *Handbook*. A little more information on gender inequities based on race, national origin, socioeconomic status, sexual orientation, and disability has become available since the early 1980s, but not as much as gender equity experts would like. For example, in the meta-analyses related to assumptions about gender differences and in the international data on gender differences in access to education, disaggregated data on various cross-cutting populations were rarely available. It has even been difficult for our authors to obtain national test data on most subpopulations by gender, and our requests to NCES to provide these data and analysis in their reports such as "Trends in the Educational Equity of Girls and Women" (National Center for Education Statistics, 2004) have not resulted in much improvement.

While the chapter on "The Impact of Education on Gender Equity in Employment and Its Outcomes" discusses income inequities related to gender and other aspects of discrimination, most of the chapter authors found even less research on this important and still pervasive aspect of discrimination than on race and gender discrimination. The authors wanted to include more analyses related to family income differences and general economic inequities within student populations since the production and distribution of wealth practices are highly *genderized* and *racialized*, and have a huge impact on students. Following are some reasons for having limited information on interactions related to class: In the U.S., class inequities are more legitimized (that is, supported by laws or their absence) than are either race or gender inequalities (which, we should note, were also once strongly supported by laws). Also, for dependent children, distribution of wealth is primarily family based rather than society based, leading to large differences in access to food, shelter, clothing, health care, and educational resources. Even after childhood, the financial situation of a prospective student's family and kinship networks often determines whether attending college seems possible. In sum, class divisions/inequities, partially based on educational degrees and success, are major factors in the continuing inequality of education opportunities, are genderized and racialized, and should be the focus of more research, analysis, and change. (See Acker, 2006, for a discussion of gendered and racialized class.)

2. **How have the standards for reporting on acceptable evidence to understand and achieve gender equity changed since the 1985 *Handbook*?**

- ***Authors' aspirations for reporting on ample rigorous research results have not been met as well as they anticipated. They often found few sources of quality research and evaluation related to gender equity education and little disaggregation of information by sex, race, economic status, etc.*** Since 1985, there has been much rhetoric about good causal evidence to guide education decisions, but minimal U.S. government resources have been devoted to gender equity research, evaluation, and development, especially when compared with research focused on other populations such as people with disabilities.

While trying to make their chapters as accurate and definitive as possible, the current *Handbook* authors were generally frustrated by the lack of current and consistent high quality gender analysis evidence. So they presented the best evidence they could find. They were also careful not to make causal statements when the evidence at best was based only on correlational studies. Different chapters summarized different types of evidence. Most used some descriptive information from national databases as well as a wide variety of small scale studies. Some authors developed research summary charts so the readers would be able to have some information about the nature of the cited studies. Others provided a brief description of the study when they described the evidence. The evidence ranged from a summary of high quality research reviews using meta-analyses in chapter 2 on "Facts and Assumptions About the Nature of Gender Differences and the Implications for Gender Equity" to very small scale studies generally based on dissertation research in chapter 6 on "Increasing Gender Equity in Educational Leadership" since the bulk of the research on gender and education leadership is from dissertations.

As previously, there is more gender equity research and development in areas such as mathematics and science, because there has been more federal support as well as substantial research and evaluation requirements from the major funder, the National Science Foundation. Other areas, such as vocational and technical education (now called career and technical education), received substantial funding for gender equity programs and services until 1998, but much of this support went to providing direct services to students. Very little federal guidance or assistance was provided for replicating or scaling up programs or for evaluating them.

Except for chapter 2 authors Janet Hyde and Sara Lindberg who reviewed meta-analyses on gender differences and similarities, there were very few meta-analyses available to chapter authors and there was also a lack of other comprehensive high quality research syntheses or reviews focusing on gender in their topic areas. In most cases meta-analyses would have been impossible because there were insufficient quality studies in their chapter topic areas with the required effect size information.

There have been accountability requirements for data to be disaggregated by sex, race, disability, and family income in the 1998 Perkins vocational and technical education reauthorization, the 2002 No Child Left Behind federal legislation, and the authorization of the Institute of Education Sciences. But the authors of this *Handbook* found that it was difficult to obtain information on these population categories, or well-evaluated, replicable gender equity programs that would be judged exemplary by the standards set by the Gender Equity Expert Panel (Fox, 2000). Although there is increased sophistication in our understanding of how to examine different populations for evidence of sex discrimination and sex stereotyping,[9] it is still difficult to obtain important disaggregated input, process, and outcome data. As shown in chapter 2, "Facts and As-

sumptions About the Nature of Gender Differences and the Implications for Gender Equity," it is very complicated to examine gender equity among population groups, since the differences within groups are greater than the differences between groups. Authors of this *Handbook* also have an increased understanding of the dilemmas in measuring gender roles, and even biological sex.

• *The authors found that the 1985* Handbook *goals framework for analyzing gender equity continues to be useful.* The 1985 *Handbook* definition of sex equity and the related goals framework is robust and still appropriate for this 2007 *Handbook* despite changing terminology (from sex equity to gender equity). In chapter 1 of the 1985 *Handbook*, pages 4 and 5, Table 1.1 "Measuring Sex Equity in Education" shows initial input, process, and outcomes columns (Klein, Russo, Campbell, & Harvey, 1985). The top and bottom halves of this table provide examples of how to use the framework to assess the attainment of process and outcome goals. The top rows suggest analyses of sex discrimination by comparing females and males, and the bottom rows suggest analyzing changes in sex stereotyping on all genders. In this 2007 *Handbook*, the focus on process outcomes (such as inequities in classroom interactions) and subsequent education and societal outcomes related to quality of life (such as equal pay) remain useful distinctions.[10]

The most extensive use of this framework to learn if interventions designed to increase gender equity did so was by the now defunct Gender Equity Expert Panel (Fox, 2000; Fox, Klein, Ortman, & Wiberg, 2000; U.S. Department of Education, 2001). This panel demonstrated that some programs designed to increase gender equity did not consistently accomplish the intended goals of decreasing gender gaps in the outcomes or reducing sex stereotyping during the education process. However, the panel also found some programs developed to accomplish other goals such as increasing interest in computer skills for all also helped increase gender equity. This led to the understanding that gender analysis should be done routinely on all programs and not be limited to the few programs specifically intended to advance gender equity. Thus, 22 years after this framework was published, its usefulness can be reaffirmed and augmented.

• *The authors understand that the previous* Handbook *goals relating to decreasing sex stereotyping and sex segregation are still appropriate, but now see increased complexities.* This 2007 *Handbook* reaffirms the goal of the 1985 *Handbook*, which stated that decreasing, rather than attempting to eliminate, sex and gender stereotypes "in decision making by and about individuals" (ch. 1, p. 8) is a reasonable and obtainable goal. Recent research has shown, however, that information provided to students on gender stereotypes can be used to perpetuate stereotypes rather than to effectively counteract them. In *Same Difference: How Gender Myths Are Hurt-*

---

[9]See Seigart & Brisolara (2002) for many approaches to feminist evaluation.
[10]Chapter 1 from the 1985 *Handbook* can be found on the web page accompanying this chapter 1.

ing Our Relationships, Our Children, and Our Jobs (2004), authors Rosalind Barnett and Caryl Rivers describe how stereotypes, even if they are derived from research, may perpetuate gender inequities. For example, they explain how theories about natural selection have been used inappropriately to make policies that limit the roles of women and men in society. They also describe how patterns of behavior commonly associated with men or women can become inaccurate stereotypes when over generalized and used to predict individuals' behavior. They point out that some public interpretations of Deborah Tannen's research on female and male communication perpetuate gender stereotypes that may have a negative impact (Barnett & Rivers, 2004). Several *Handbook* chapters discuss the powerful influence of stereotypes on behavior such as research on stereotyped threat by Claude Steele and others. Chapter 2 of this *Handbook* on "Facts and Assumptions About the Nature of Gender Differences and the Implications for Gender Equity" describes research on patterns of gender differences, as well as the hypothesized sociocultural explanations/theories for these differences. The unconscious biases that keep operating even when we try to reject stereotypes may mean that ensuring an equal-opportunity education system may require gender-conscious recruiting and hiring, and proactive efforts to reduce bias. Various *Handbook* chapters discuss the importance of gender consciousness rather than gender blindness.

Another complexity relates to the challenges to assess both the intent and the impact of laws and policies as they relate to gender equity process and outcome goals. For example, although Title IX has been used to identify disparities in many process and outcome aspects of athletics, there have been few related efforts to use Title IX or other laws to decrease sex stereotyping and sex discrimination in other areas. One encouraging sign is recent attention to use Title IX to help end sex discrimination in mathematics and science education and employment outcomes. In the spring of 2006, the U.S. Department of Education said it would start to investigate compliance with Title IX related to the underrepresentation of women in mathematics and science departments in universities (Postsecondary Science and Math Programs Face Title IX Review, 2006). There has, however, been little discussion of applying Title IX or more extensive state laws to identify and similarly address gender inequities in other areas such as encouraging women in music composition, where there are few female faculty role models and where the canon of what is valued and taught is based mainly on the work of male composers.[11] The new chapter on the "Role of Government in Advancing Gender Equity in Education" provides recommendations on using required Title IX coordinators to col-

lect and report on data on gender gaps in many areas where schools are measuring accountability. As they do this, they should find the distinctions between process and outcome measures helpful in explaining patterns of gender gaps.

Another complexity (introduced in part 1 in this chapter) involves some careful justifications for sex segregation in specific (education process) situations only if there is a good chance that these gender conscious interventions will help end sex discrimination in the outcomes. This complexity was acknowledged in the 1985 conceptual framework where "special kinds of sex differential treatment in the short term" were allowed "to reach longer-term [gender equity outcome] goals" in some instances (ch. 1, 1985, p. 8). This principle is also included in the 1975 Title IX Regulations that allow some single-sex interventions for remedial or affirmative purposes. However, this sex differential treatment, especially in sex-segregated settings, should be implemented with caution and carefully evaluated to learn if it actually results in the desired gender equity outcomes. If it does not produce convincing evidence that it increases gender equity outcomes better than comparable mixed sex alternatives, this sex-differentiated instruction should be stopped.[12] Similar careful attention should be given when providing different advantages to either male or female students or educators in mixed-sex education opportunities to increase parity in desired outcomes. Are these affirmative or compensatory potential solutions legal and fair? Are they effective in reducing inequities in desired outcomes? For example, is it legal or fair to encourage women and men to pursue careers nontraditional to their gender by offering sex-specific scholarships such as nursing scholarships for men and physics scholarships for women? The *Handbook* chapters provide insights on these questions and in some cases may provide some recommendations to address them.

3. **How has the process of developing this *Handbook* differed from the collaborative process used in developing the 1985 *Handbook*?**
   • ***The ability to easily share and obtain documents and information was easier for the current authors because of improved technology.*** The 1985 *Handbook* authors were using some word processing machines, but had to rely on the U.S. mail and copy machines to send draft chapters and to create the manuscript; they also had to do manual searches of libraries and microfiche. Current authors and reviewers were able to easily e-mail chapter drafts and information to each other and use computer editing tools and a *Blackboard* system to access drafts of other chapters. However, they did not have sufficient time or facility to take full advantage of the *Blackboard* capabilities, such as discussion lists, as was envisioned by the original *Blackboard* manager.[13]

---

[11]Thanks to Dr. Shelley Olson for identifying some of these key aspects of discrimination in music education.

[12]As previously mentioned, the October 25, 2006 Title IX Regulations that expand the exceptions allowing single-sex education cause additional concern that sex segregation will increase sex discrimination in education.

[13]Dr. Rosalind Hale established and managed a sophisticated *Blackboard* interactive web site system at Xavier University in New Orleans in 2003 where all participants could e-mail each other and use their own password as they downloaded and discussed each other's documents. However, we did not re-establish all the sophisticated procedures after Hurricane Katrina hit New Orleans in Sept. 2005 and Xavier closed. Another *Handbook* author, Dr. Beverly Irby, helped us quickly change to a simpler use of her *Blackboard* system at Sam Houston State University.

Although the increased availability of computer technology from basic word processing and editing tools, to e-mail and the use of the World Wide Web for information, has been a great boon to learning and access to the most current available information, new technologies have not speeded up the writing and production process as much as the editors and authors of this *Handbook* had hoped. But it and telephone conference calls have made it easier for people in different institutions and locations to work together productively.

Because the authors know that it is difficult to write a definitive treatment of what is known about advancing gender equity in and through education, they plan to contribute to a supplemental Web site that will include many of the chapters from the 1985 *Handbook*, as well as supplemental materials and links too extensive or detailed to include in the *Handbook* itself. They also plan to update information related to each chapter to keep the *Handbook* current and to provide many practical links to related resources and organizations with relevant expertise.

- ***About the same numbers of gender equity experts worked together as editors, authors, and reviewers for both* Handbooks.** The collaborative process was relatively novel for authors of the 1985 Handbook and was used by many as a way to increase interaction with peers with related expertise and often to build collegial networks and lasting friendships. As previously, some of the current *Handbook* contributors work primarily in research institutions, while others combine academic and activist interests, or work in gender equity positions in a variety of educational contexts. While authors for specific chapters may have known each other's work, most hadn't worked closely together.

Much of the burden of organizing the collaboration and creating a well written chapter fell on the more than 50 lead authors and their editors. In some cases, the lead authors were able to work together like a relay team. When one was especially busy with other responsibilities, another lead author was able to carry on. The collaborative approach helped increase comprehensive coverage of the chapter topics and consensus recommendations. However, collaborative work is process as well as product oriented, and such work always requires extra time, whatever the technological aids available.

Despite the advantages from technology and excellent lead authors, external pressures on the current *Handbook* authors have made collaborative chapter writing especially challenging. Although participation was voluntary and unpaid for both *Handbooks*, authors of the current *Handbook* often had to give priority to their very demanding paid work. Thus, many ended up spending their weekends and holidays working on the *Handbook*, and others who originally wanted to help, dropped out. Some chapter authors were reluctant to participate in collaborative writing and research synthesis activities because their university faculty promotion criteria favored single author contributions and original research over research synthesis work even on major national projects. Other authors had participated in collaborative writing and concluded that they could do a better, more efficient job working alone or with only a few colleagues. Thus, although there was initially great interest and over 200 gender equity experts signed up to contribute, the final count of authors and editors is around 130, with many additional experts serving as reviewers or providing other assistance with the 31 chapters. In some cases authors contributed to more than one chapter, but they are only counted once. However, despite changes in circumstances and pressures on authors, about the same number of authors and reviewers participated in the development of both the 1985 and the 2007 *Handbooks*. Some of them were even the same devoted scholars.

4. **Have the chapter topics and organization of the *Handbook* changed in any basic ways?** At first glace it might seem that there was little change. This new *Handbook* follows the same general organization used in the 1985 *Handbook*, with the chapters organized into the same six interrelated parts. However the new *Handbook* has 31 chapters, instead of the 25 chapters in the 1985 *Handbook*, and most are much longer.

While we considered adding a specific chapter focusing on male gender equity issues, we decided instead to ask the authors to attend to this important aspect of gender equity in all chapters as appropriate. Unlike the 1985 *Handbook*, none of the chapters in the 2007 *Handbook* specifically focuses on girls and women, but due to the nature of the gender equity concerns in some areas, the primary discussions in some chapters, such as "Increasing Gender Equity in Educational Leadership," "Impact of Education on Gender Equity in Employment and Its Outcomes," and "Gender Equity in Science, Engineering, and Technology," emphasize equity needs of women.

In parts I, II, and III, which cover assumptions, administrative strategies, and general educational practices relating to gender equity education, new chapters include: "Gender Equity Education Globally," "Gender Equity in the Use of Educational Technology," and "Sexual Harassment: The Hidden Gender Equity Problem." The new "Gender Equity in Coeducational and Single Sex Educational Environments" chapter includes more focus on the research on single-sex education than did the 1985 "Classroom Organization and Climate" chapter. There is also a great deal more attention to Title IX in many of the current chapters than in the 1985 *Handbook*, which was written when the coverage of Title IX was temporarily diminished because of the 1984 Grove City College Supreme Court Decision limiting the scope of Title IX until it was overturned by the Civil Rights Restoration Act of 1987. (See the chapter on "The Role of Government in Advancing Gender Equity in Education" for more background.)

In the content area we have now split mathematics, science, engineering and technology into two chapters, and have added "Gender Equity in Foreign and Second Language Learning," "Gender Equity in Formal Sexuality Education," and "The Role of Women's and Gender Studies in Advancing Gender Equity." The previous chapter on "Sex Equity in Visual Arts" has now been expanded to cover dance.

Part V, examining gender equity for diverse populations, has greatly expanded. Instead of one chapter focusing on minority women, we now have chapters on "Gender Equity for

African Americans," "Gender Equity for Latina/os," "Gender Equity for Asian and Pacific Island Americans," and "Gender Equity for American Indians." We have also added chapters on "Lesbian, Gay, Bisexual, and Transgender Issues in Education" and "Gender Equity for People with Disabilities." We no longer have a chapter on "Rural Women and Girls," but instead have asked the authors to address urban and rural issues as appropriate. Similarly, we do not have a chapter on "Educational Programs for Adult Women," but have attended to gender equity issues for adult learners in the postsecondary education and other chapters. For example, in the "Gender Equity in the Use of Education Technologies" chapter, gender equity issues in distance education are especially relevant for many rural students and adult learners.

SUMMARY

As you read chapters of interest in this *Handbook*, you may want to think about underlying challenges to gender equity. First, the sociological significance of gender is that it is the device by which society controls its members. It opens and closes doors to power, property, and even prestige. Like social class it is a structural feature of society. This stratification is often referred to as the *sex/gender system*, or patriarchy, a system in which men dominate, and are more highly valued than women in most areas. This kind of differentiation occurs not only on an interpersonal level between individuals, but also on a structural level within a given society. The shape and form of these systems can vary historically and cross culturally, as well as across populations and topics (Renzetti & Curran, 2002). This is illustrated by differences in issues and solutions in the 31 chapters in this *Handbook*.

Second, gender stratification is associated with a wide range of gender inequities in the education process and in the outcomes. It is visible through gender stereotypes or simplistic sociocultural definitions of what it means to be ideally masculine or feminine. Gender stratification is embedded in the institutions of society, prescribing traits, behaviors and patterns of social interaction for men and women, boys and girls. These prescriptions influence the economy, political system, educational system, religion, family forms, and more. They are visible through institutional discrimination, defined as the denial of opportunities and equal rights to individuals or groups that result from the normal operations of a society (Schaefer, 2001, p. 310) unless they are counteracted by well implemented laws such as constitutional equal rights guarantees and Title IX-type laws prohibiting sex discrimination in education. Women and girls, men and boys often suffer from both individual acts of sexism and from institutional sexism. The authors hope that you will continue to learn with them how to combat this strong gender system and to work effectively to achieve gender equity in and through education!

ACKNOWLEDGMENTS

Thanks to reviewers Joan Korenman, University of Maryland Baltimore County, Jane Schubert, American Institutes for Research, Washington, DC, Carol Dwyer and Evelyn Fisch, Educational Testing Service, Princeton, NJ, for their improvements and suggestions, to Feminist Majority Foundation interns Marie Poling for her editorial suggestions on an earlier draft and Kamaria Campbell for her suggestions on the current version, and to Sharon Hobbs, Montana State University, Billings, MT, for help with the references.

References

Acker, J. (2006). *Class questions: Feminist answers.* Lanham, MD: Rowman & Littlefield.

Best, R. (1983). *We've All Got Scars: What boys and girls learn in elementary school.* Bloomington, IN: Indiana University Press.

Barnett, R., & Rivers, C. (2004). *Same difference: How gender myths are hurting our relationships, our children, and our jobs.* New York: Basic Books.

Biklen, S. K., & Shakeshaft, C. (1985). The new scholarship on women. In S. Klein (Ed.), *Handbook for achieving sex equity through education* (ch. 4). Baltimore: Johns Hopkins Press

Cheng, P. (1988). *The new federalism and women's educational equity: How the states respond.* Paper presented at the annual meeting of the Association of American Geographers, Phoenix, AZ.

Fox, L. (Ed.). (2000). *The Gender Equity Expert Panel: History and rationale.* Washington, DC: U.S. Department of Education.

Fox, L., Klein, S., Ortman, P., & Wiberg, M. (2000). Lessons learned by the Gender Equity Expert Panel. In L. Fox (Ed.), *The Gender Equity Expert Panel: History and Rationale.* Washington, DC: US Department of Education.

Harvard President Pledges $50 Million for Women's Programs. (2005, May 17) *Feminist Daily News Wire.* Retrieved March 11, 2006, from http://www.feminist.org/news/newsbyte/uswirestory.asp?id=9045

Harvard Task Forces on Women release findings and recommendations (2005, May 16) *Harvard University Gazette.* Retrieved March 11, 2006, from http://www.news.harvard.edu/gazette/daily/2005/05/16-wtaskforce_release.html

Harvard's Summers to Resign (2006, February 22). *Feminist Daily News Wire.* Retrieved April 30, 2006, from http://www.feminist.org/news/newsbyte/uswirestory.asp?id59529

Klein, S. (Ed.). (1985). *Handbook for achieving sex equity through education.* Baltimore: Johns Hopkins Press.

Klein, S. (Guest Ed.). (1989). Sex equity and sexuality in education [Special Issue]. *The Peabody Journal of Education, 64*(4). Summer 1987, published September 1989, Vanderbilt Univ., Nashville, TN.

Klein, S. (Ed.). (1992). *Sex equity and sexuality in education.* New York: SUNY Press.

Klein, S. (2003, April). Introduction to symposium on research and evaluation options to learn about the value of single-sex education interventions. Paper presented at the Annual Meeting of the American Educational Research Association, Chicago.

Klein, S. (2004, November). The role of public policy in advancing gender equity in education based on recent experience in the U.S.A. Paper presented at the First International Conference on Gender Equity Education in the Asia-Pacific Region, Taipei, Taiwan.

Klein, S., & Ortman, P. (1994). Continuing the journey toward gender equity. *Educational Researcher*, 23(8), 13–21.

Klein, S., Ortman, P., & Friedman, E. (2002). What is the field of gender equity in education? Questions and answers. In J. Koch and B. Irby (Eds.), *Defining and redefining gender equity in education,* (pp. 3–27). Greenwich, CT: Information Age Publishing.

Klein, S., Russo, L. N., Campbell, P. B., & Harvey, G. (1985). Examining the achievement of sex equity in and through education. In S. Klein (Ed.), *Handbook for achieving sex equity through education* (ch. 1). Baltimore: Johns Hopkins Press.

Koch, J., & Irby, B. (Eds.). (2002). Defining and redefining gender equity in education. Greenwich, CT: Information Age Publishing.

Koch, J., Irby, B., & Brown, G. (2002). Epilogue: Redefining gender equity. In B. Irby & J. Koch, (Eds.), *Defining and redefining gender equity in education* (pp. 181–192). Greenwich, CT: Information Age Publishing.

Mead, S. (2006, June) . The evidence suggests otherwise: The truth about boys and girls Washinghton, DC, The Education Sector, Retrieved June 26, 2006, from www.educationsector.org

National Center for Education Statistics (2004). *Trends in educational equity of girls and women*. Washington, DC: Institute of Education Sciences, U.S. Department of Education.

Postsecondary science and math programs face Title IX review. (2006, April 3). *Feminist Daily News Wire*. Retrieved April 30, 2006, from http://www.feminist.org/news/newsbyte/uswirestory.asp?id=9596

Office for Civil Rights. (1975, June). *Final Title IX regulation implementing education amendments of 1972 prohibiting sex discrimination in education*. Washington, DC: U.S. Department of Health, Education and Welfare/Office for Civil Rights.

Office for Civil Rights. (2006, October 25). *Final regulations. Nondiscrimination on the basis of sex in education programs or activities receiving federal financial assistance*. Washington, DC: U.S. Department of Education/Office for Civil Rights. Federal Register/Vol. 71, No. 206/Wednesday, October 25, 2006, pp. 62529–62543. Retrieved October 30, 2006, from www.ed.gov/legislation/FedRegister/finrule/2006-4/102506a.html

Renzetti, C., & Curran, D. (2002). *Women, men and society*. NY: Allyn & Bacon.

Schaefer, R. (2001). *Sociology*. New York: McGraw-Hill.

Seigart, D., & Brisolara, S. (Eds.). (2002). Feminist evaluation explorations and experiences. *New Directions for Evaluation*, 96, San Francisco: Jossey-Bass.

Sexton, P. (1969). *The feminized male: Classrooms, white collars and the decline of manliness*. New York: Random House.

Taiwan Government. (2004). Gender equity education act. Retrieved May 8, 2006, from http:law.moj.gov.tw/Eng/Fnews/brows.asp

Taiwan Government. (2005, June 13). Enforcement rules for the Gender Equity Education Act. Retrieved May 8, 2006, from http:law.moj.gov.tw/Eng/Fnews/brows.asp

United Nations. (1948). *Universal declaration of human rights, Article 26, Sections 1& 2*. Retrieved July 18, 2006, from www.un.org/rights/HRToday/

United Nations. (1960). *Convention against discrimination in education*.

United Nations. (1979.) *Convention on the elimination of all forms of discrimination against women, Part 3, Article 10*. Retrieved July 18, 2006, from www/un.org/womenwathch/daw/cedaw/frame.htm

United Nations. (1966). *Covenants on civil and political rights and economic, social & cultural rights*.

United Nations. (2000). *Millennium development goals*. Retrieved July 25, 2006, from www.un.org/millenniumgoals

United Nations. (1995). *Summary of the Beijing Declaration and Platform for Action adopted by the United Nations Fourth World Conference on Women*. Retrieved July 16, 2006, from www.feminist.org/other/beijing3.html

UNESCO Unit for the Promotion of the Status of Women and Gender Equality. (2000). *Gender equality and equity: A summary review of UNESCO's accomplishments since the Fourth World Conference on Women (Beijing, 1995)*. Retrieved July 18, 2006, from http://unesdoc.unesco.org/images/0012/001211/121145e.pdf

U.S. Department of Education. (2001). *U.S. Department of Education's Gender Equity Expert Panel exemplary and promising gender equity programs, 2000*. Washington, DC: Office of Reform Assistance and Dissemination. (ORAD 2001-1000) Retrieved July 18, 2006, from http://www.ed.gov/pubs/genderequity/index.html

WEDO (Women's Environment and Development Organization). (2005). *Beijing betrayed*. Retrieved May 20, 2006, from http://www.wedo.org/files/gmr2005english.html

Wharton, L. J. (2006). State equal rights amendments revisited: Evaluating their effectiveness in advancing protection against sex discrimination. *Rutgers Law Journal, 36*(4), (entire issue).

White House Office of the First Lady. (2005, October 27). Fact sheet: A commitment to helping America's youth. Retrieved March 13, 2006, from http://www.whitehouse.gov/news/releases/2005/10/20051027.html

OVERVIEW: FACTS AND ASSUMPTIONS ABOUT THE NATURE AND VALUE OF GENDER EQUITY

Barbara Richardson

Chapters 2, 3, and 4 in this section examine many of the assumptions underpinning the psychological, economic, and global social justice arguments for achieving gender equity through education. They provide an interdisciplinary context for the definitions and conceptual frameworks developed in chapter 1. The chapter authors remind us that while there are many important generalizations about the needs and accomplishments of the sexes, there is also great diversity in the contexts addressed. For example, one of the most consistent crosscutting issues in these foundation chapters is the need to pay attention to variations among subgroups related to age, race, social class, parental values and level of schooling.

THE NATURE OF GENDER DIFFERENCES

Janet Hyde and Sara Lindberg's chapter 2, "Facts and Assumptions About the Nature of Gender Differences and the Implications for Gender Equity" provides a comprehensive review of high quality meta-analyses that help to make sense of numerous research findings. They shed light on one of the most persistent arguments confronting gender equity advocates today—that is, that girls and women, and sometimes boys and men, are hindered in their educational achievement by deeply rooted sex differences in aspirations, skills, and abilities. In the previous 1985 *Handbook for Achieving Sex Equity through Education*, the related chapter by Marcia Linn and Anne Petersen systematically reviewed the pre-1985 evidence on gender differences: biological, cognitive, and psychosocial (Linn & Petersen, 1985). Their summary of the data 20 years ago was less definitive than that in Hyde and Lindberg's chapter 2, but the 1985 chapter still focused on the potential of children of both sexes for equal education outcomes (Klein, 1985). Linn and Petersen concluded that where there were sex differences in styles and abilities in learning, they could be readily remedied by instruction.

Today, the research on many of these issues is clearer, more consistent, and significant (Hyde, 2005). Hyde and Lindberg find that girls and boys are quite similar and should not be constrained in their curricula by gender. They find that even in areas where there have been persistent gender differences such as spatial abilities, these gender differences are related to experience and can be reduced by instruction. They arrive at this recommendation after an extensive review of a wide range of meta-analyses of learning styles and aptitudes. These include such personality factors as aggression and independence, and abilities such as verbal and mathematical skills. They conclude that there is a significant overlap between the distributions for males and females and that within-gender variability is substantial. In short, with few exceptions, the capacity for learning is essentially the same for both boys and girls, regardless of their transient (and sometimes gender stereotypical) educational preferences. Based on understandings of gender similarities and sex stereotyping, Hyde and Lindberg urge educators to avoid the constraints of single-sex schools or classrooms. Rather, they encourage girls and boys to learn together as they develop nontraditional skills commonly associated with each other. In short, given the essential similarities between the sexes, the decision to educate them together is better than in gender-segregated classes or schools. They argue that the strategies for maximizing girls' and boys' education achievement should not be guided by children's gender stereotypical educational preferences such as instruction in competitive or cooperative classrooms or sex-typed pacing of teacher student interactions.

GENDER EQUITY IN EDUCATION GLOBALLY

It is not surprising that there was no equivalent of chapter 3, "Gender Equity Education Globally" by Nelly Stromquist in the 1985 *Handbook*. At the time of the 1985 *Handbook*, considerably less systematic research was available on global gender equity in education than now. In the last several decades, there has been a burgeoning of international research funded by governments and a variety of international Non Governmental Organizations (NGOs) and substantial attention to gender analysis for education and other purposes. These analyses, such as *The Global Gender Gap Report 2006* (Hausmann, Tyson, & Zahidi, 2006) show that since the U.S. was only ranked 22 out of 115 countries in the relative size of its gender gaps on four composite indicators, it has much to learn from other countries especially in the areas of educational attainment where it ranked 65 and political empowerment where it ranked 66. In contrast, the overall ranks of Sweden, Norway, and Finland (1, 2, 3) indicate that they are the most advanced in eliminating gender gaps based on an examination of gender outcomes in economic participation and opportunity, educational attainment, health and survival, and political empowerment.

Stromquist's chapter 3 focuses on gender equity in developing nations, which is also a focus of U.S. federal support for international gender equity programs described in chapter 5 on "The Role of Government in Advancing Gender Equity in Education" in part II of this *Handbook.* Many other chapters in this 2007 *Handbook* pay attention to international education comparisons and to learning from the experiences of other countries.

Chapter 3 reviews the substantial evidence that increased gender parity in education is critical to the prosperity of developing nations. In doing so, Stromquist provides international gender comparisons related to literacy, school attendance, and children's general well-being. She also discusses some of the methodological challenges in making comparisons among countries due to differing levels and types of education, as well as different ways of defining and measuring the goals. She describes slow progress in achieving gender parity, even in primary and secondary school attendance in many developing nations. She also documents substantial diversity in the attainment of gender equity within global regions such as South America and Africa as well as diversity within many countries. She shows that in many countries girls receive fewer opportunities at all levels of their education despite major improvements in providing them with access to primary and secondary education. While boys suffer educational disadvantages in some cases, invariably girls are on the lower end of the scales of educational benefits. Similar patterns of education inequities are common in the United States where, like in many other countries, the consequence of sex-typed occupational segregation is associated with debilitating economic deprivation for women and their children (UNESCO, 2003). There is a growing global subculture of very poor and relatively uneducated women who have had children early in their lives and find it difficult to make a living for themselves and their families. This pattern can be found here in the United States, as well as worldwide (Richardson and Sandoval, 2007, Stromquist, 2002).

Stromquist suggests a series of practical measures for advancing gender equity that would foster the global empowerment of women and girls while enhancing the well-being of the nation as a whole—for men, women, and children alike. One area that echoes other recommendations in the *Handbook* is the importance of protecting both sexes, but especially girls,

from sexual harassment. Sexual harassment is covered in chapter 11 in this 2007 *Handbook*, as well as in numerous other chapters. Cultural- and religious-based practices of single-sex schools are another threat to gender equity in many countries, but especially to girls in Afghanistan where many girls' schools have been attacked and female teachers and students have been killed. These attacks and threats of more have greatly limited education opportunities since 2002 when girls started to be allowed to return to school. The boys and mixed sex schools are less often the targets of this violence. (Tribal elders, 2006)

GENDER EQUITY IN EMPLOYMENT AND ITS OUTCOMES

In their chapter 4 analysis of the "Impact of Education on Gender Equity in Employment and its Outcomes," Barbara Richardson and Pamela Sandoval review data on changing trends in today's labor market in the United States as they relate to gender equity and education. In the 1985 *Handbook*, the findings were more discouraging. Harvey and Noble wrote, "On balance, increased sex equity in education has not been as successful as many had hoped in reducing gender-related economic inequities" (Harvey & Noble, 1985, p. 25). Some of the same issues Harvey and Noble found discouraging 20 years ago have become less of an equity challenge today. Richardson and Sandoval provide evidence of how education, at any level, contributes to the abilities of both sexes to compete successfully in today's labor market. Thanks to increased education, raised expectations, and peer network resources, newly credentialed generations of young women, especially from the middle class, are forging ahead in nontraditional career territory. Nonetheless, despite the increased education of today's young women, there is slow progress in modifying most young women's gender traditional career choices. Young girls and boys still direct their aspirations primarily toward gender-typed occupations. In turn, we find that well over half of adult women find themselves working in occupations that are primarily occupied by other women—too often part-time, at minimum wage, and without health care or retirement benefits.

In 1985, Harvey and Noble also reported that wages could be predicted pretty well by knowing the person's sex, regardless of their educational attainment. Although Title VII of the Civil Rights Act and other federal and state laws to prohibit sex discrimination in employment have helped decrease the gender gap in wages, substantial sex discrimination in employment persists. For example, there is substantial sex-segregated employment with women dominated work receiving less pay than men's work of comparable value to society. After the recession in the 1990s, the gains women had started to experience declined (U.S. Department of Labor, Women's Bureau, 2000). Advocates for gender equity have called for the use of comparable worth strategies in the courts. This approach establishes standards comparing the skills and social value of the different occupations traditionally held by men and women. At least 20 states and 1,700 local jurisdictions have used this antidiscrimination strategy. For example, one court case compared the salaries of male car park attendants and female day care workers. This strategy moves beyond the simple pay equity arguments to comparable pay for comparable worth.

At the time of their review, Harvey and Noble also found it difficult to even determine a clear relationship between gender equity, education, and their economic "pay off" in the marketplace. While education is a critical resource in the labor market for both sexes, it is not always a hedge against poverty. Despite educated women's overall progress, and the general increase in equity in women's wages, women and children in poverty have lost ground. Low racial, gender, and ethnic status are associated with depressed wages (Feiner, 1994, and Richardson and Sandoval, 2007). In 2001, African American women earned 84.4% of White women's earning and Hispanic women earned just 74.7% of what White women earned. Those most vulnerable of all are women with the lowest educational resources—very young mothers and older retired women suffering from the results of lifelong discrimination. On a more positive note, Richardson and Sandoval describe a growing support for gender equity in career retraining. Increasingly, programs for adult learners assume that both sexes have the talent, ability, and motivation for learning later in life.

CONCLUSION

Chapters 2, 3, and 4 all focus on identifying social indicators useful in charting progress toward educational equity. Together, they provide new arguments and evidence for the importance of gender equity both as a means and end goal for education. The chapters to follow will often refer back to these foundational chapters rather than re-summarizing the same evidence and justifications for gender equity. The editors of the subsequent parts of the *Handbook* and their chapter authors were asked to make sure that what they said was congruent with these foundation chapters.[1]

In summary, these foundational chapters:

- dispel the myth that there are basic differences between the sexes that impact students' capacity to learn,
- remind us to be aware of the educational diversities within the sexes by age, level of education, race, ethnicity, sexual preference, and social class,
- provide an international perspective on key gender equity trends both in and out of the United States, cautioning us not to be too ethnocentric when looking at our own data, and

- show the important relationships of education to gender equality in employment among subgroups.

All three chapters reemphasize the importance of gender equity to the growth of a country's economy, including the United States. Much of the progress internationally is, in turn, due to the pressures for gender equity from both within the nation as well as to compete with others and to comply with international policies and U.N. Millennium Goals.

The policy recommendations in this first section remind us to consider the relationship between the achievement of gender equity and the nature of a nation's economy and social ideology. Hyde and Lindberg, for instance, make the point that even in western industrial countries, the magnitude of the gender differences in math performance correlates significantly with indicators of gender equality in the country, such as the percentage of women in the country's work force. They conclude ". . . the more equitable the country, the smaller the gender difference in math achievement" (p. 29). Richardson and Sandoval argue that the nature of the social structure has a powerful influence on the challenges girls face in translating their educational achievements into success in their chosen careers. They observe that young women's career preferences and educational achievements play a relatively small part in the sector they ultimately end up in in today's marketplace. Persistent gender inequities in economic achievement are profoundly influenced by factors like inflation that tend to negatively impact women's job stability or girls' access to entry-level jobs. This occurs because they are affected by the "last hired, first fired effect." or by employment in jobs without full benefits. This is especially true of part-time workers, a classification characteristically over represented by women. Another example of sociocultural factors, found especially in developing nations, might be influence of a controlling political party implementing economic policies that discriminated against women, for example, access to reproductive services or sex-segregated education. In poorer nations, in which women's educational potential is devalued, gender inequities are visible at every level of education. Stromquist points out that in times of a competitive global economy for instance, a secondary education that offers studies in math and science becomes increasingly valued as girls are recognized as an asset to the economy. In conclusion, the variability in the sexes' relative accomplishments may say as much about political and cultural change in societies as motivational changes among children.

---

[1]If the authors of the later *Handbook* chapters had evidence that was incongruent with chapters 2, 3, 4 (or any other chapter), they were expected to inform the part editors and authors of these early chapters about the discrepancies so that all could be corrected and made congruent.

References

Feiner, S. (1994). *Race and Gender in the American Economy* . NJ: Prentice Hall.

Harvey, G., & Noble, E. (1985). Economic considerations for achieving gender equity through education. In S. Klein, *Handbook for achieving gender equity through education* (pp. 17–28). Baltimore: Johns Hopkins Press.

Hausmann, R., Tyson, L. D., & Zahidi, S. (2006). *The Global Gender Gap Report 2006,* Geneva, Switzerland: World Economic Forum. Retrieved November 22, 2006, from http://www.weforum.org/pdf/gendergap/report2006.pdf

Hyde, J. S. (1984). How large are gender differences in aggression? A developmental meta-analysis. *Developmental Psychology, 20,* 722–736.

Hyde, J. S. (2005). The gender similarities hypothesis. *American Psychologist, 60,* 581–592.

Klein, S. (Ed.). (1985). *Handbook for achieving gender equity through education.* Baltimore: Johns Hopkins Press.

Linn, M., & Petersen, A. (1985). Facts and assumptions about the nature of sex differences. In Klein, *Handbook for achieving gender equity through education* (pp. 53–77). Baltimore: Johns Hopkins Press.

Richardson, B. and Sandoval, P. (2007) Impact of education on gender equity in employment and its outcomes, in *Handbook for Achieving Gender Equality Through Education.* NY: Lawrence Erlbaum Associates. (Handbook title should be italicized. Double check publisher city ref.)

Stromquist, N. (2002). Education as a means for empowering women. In J. Parpart, S. Rai, & K. Staudt (Eds.), *Rethinking empowerment. Gender and development in a global/local world.* London: Routledge.

Tribal elders work to reopen schools in southern Afghanistan. (November 14, 2006). *Feminist Daily News Wire.* Retrieved November 22, 2006, from http://www.feminist.org/news/newsbyte/uswirestory.asp?id=10007 and http://www.feminist.org/afghan/taliban_women.asp

UNESCO. (2003). *EFA global monitoring report. Gender and education for all. The leap to equality.* Paris: UNESCO.

U.S. Department of Labor, Women's Bureau. (2000). Earnings differences between men and women. In P. Dubeck & D. Dunn, D. (Eds.),*Workplace/women's place.* Los Angeles: Roxbury Publishing.

FACTS AND ASSUMPTIONS ABOUT
THE NATURE OF GENDER DIFFERENCES AND
THE IMPLICATIONS FOR GENDER EQUITY

Janet Shibley Hyde* and Sara M. Lindberg
University of Wisconsin

As we tackle the challenge of achieving gender equity in education, an immediate question arises: What about gender differences? Are boys more aggressive than girls and does that have an impact on interactions in the classroom and on the playground? Do girls lack mathematical ability and should we therefore kindly allow them to pursue less demanding mathematics courses? Are girls better able to control their motor activity, and, if so, does this give them an advantage in the classroom? In this chapter we review large bodies of evidence regarding whether there are gender differences in domains such as abilities and psychosocial characteristics (e.g., aggression, self-esteem). Then we consider the possible biological and sociocultural forces that may shape existing gender differences. First, though, we consider some overarching methodological issues in research on gender differences.

METHODOLOGICAL ISSUES

Research on psychological gender differences has been marred by a number of methodological issues that contribute to confused conclusions and reification of inaccurate assumptions. They include a focus on significance testing with neglect of effect sizes; over-reliance on individual studies while ignoring whether the findings replicate, particularly as assessed by meta-analysis, sex bias in measurement; causal inferences incorrectly based on correlational or quasi-experimental data; and researchers' beliefs.

Significance Testing versus Effect Sizes

Research in psychology and in education has traditionally relied on significance tests, for example, Analysis of Variance (ANOVA), as the gold standard for decision making. Amid mounting criticisms of this approach, alternatives have been suggested, including especially the reporting of effect sizes and confidence intervals (Wilkinson and the Task Force on Statistical Inference, 1999). A major problem with significance testing is that it is highly sensitive to the size of the sample. With a large enough sample, even a tiny, trivial difference can be significant.

Applied to research on gender differences, researchers have faithfully carried out significance tests but have rarely reported the corresponding effect sizes, that is, the magnitude of the gender difference. Many of these differences turn out to be small—sometimes so small as to be meaningless—when additional computations are conducted. For example, the Project Talent data set included 73,425 15 year olds at the time of testing (Hedges & Nowell, 1995). The gender difference in mathematics performance in this large sample is highly significant, but the magnitude of the difference is negligible, $d = 0.12$ (effect sizes are explained in the next section).

Meta-Analysis versus Individual Studies

Meta-analysis is a technique that allows the researcher to statistically combine the results from all previous studies of the question of interest—for example, gender differences in mathe-

---

*The bold face name is the Lead Author.

matics performance—to determine what the studies say when taken together. Meta-analyses generally proceed in four steps:

- the researcher locates all previous studies on the question under investigation, typically by using databases such as PsycINFO;
- for each study, the researcher computes a statistic that measures the magnitude of the difference between males and females. In research on gender differences, the common statistic is

$$d = \frac{M_M - M_F}{s}$$

where M_M is the mean or average score for males, M_F is the mean for females, and s is the average within-gender standard deviation; and

- the researcher averages all the values of d over all the studies. This average d reflects the magnitude and direction of the gender difference averaged across all studies.
- The researcher examines variability in the values of d across all studies. If there is substantial, significant variability, the researcher performs moderator analyses to determine what factors moderate the magnitude of the gender difference. For example, is the gender difference larger in some subgroups and smaller in others?

Although there is some disagreement among experts, a general guide is that an effect size d of 0.20 is a small difference, a d of 0.50 is moderate, and a d of 0.80 is a large difference (Cohen, 1988).

Conclusions based on meta-analyses are almost always more powerful than conclusions based on an individual study, for two reasons. First, because meta-analysis aggregates numerous studies, a meta-analysis typically represents the testing of tens of thousands, sometimes even millions, of participants. As such, the results should be far more reliable than those from any individual study. Second, findings from gender differences research are notoriously inconsistent across studies. For example, in the meta-analysis of gender differences in mathematics performance discussed later in this chapter, 51% of the studies showed males scoring higher, 6% showed exactly no difference between males and females, and 43% showed females scoring higher (Hyde, Fennema, & Lamon, 1990a). This makes it very easy to find a study that supports one's prejudices. The meta-analysis overcomes this problem by synthesizing all available studies.

Of course, not all meta-analyses are created equal. They differ in methodological quality. A complete consideration of these issues is beyond the scope of this chapter (for more detail, see Lipsey & Wilson, 2001). In brief, three criteria should be used in evaluation of meta-analyses. First, it is important that a large number of studies be included. A meta-analysis of five studies is not truly a meta-analysis. It is also important that unpublished data be included as much as possible, given the bias to publish significant findings and to relegate nonsignificant ones to the file drawer (Rosenthal, 1979). Third, the meta-analysis must deal with the issue of the quality of studies. Some meta-analyses select only studies of acceptable quality, which is one reasonable strategy. Other meta-analyses include all studies but then rate them on quality and present results separately for high quality and for other studies, which is also a reasonable strategy. The undesirable method is to include all studies and not sort them by quality.

In this chapter and throughout this handbook, we strive to use recent, high-quality meta-analyses as evidence whenever possible. Unfortunately, such studies are not available for every topic pertaining to gender differences and gender equity. Therefore, as necessary, we provide additional evidence from individual studies. In all cases, we strive to provide the most accurate, current, and nationally or internationally representative evidence possible.

Measurement

If girls score lower than boys on a particular ability or achievement test, two interpretations are possible: (a) girls are not as skilled at the ability being measured; or (b) girls are as skilled as boys but the test contains gender-biased items that do not accurately assess girls' skills. Equity in assessment is discussed in detail in the chapter on testing and assessment in this handbook, so we will not elaborate on it here. The issue must be kept in mind, though, as we review research on gender differences in tested abilities.

Causal Inferences from Correlational Data

Reaching conclusions about causality based on nonexperimental studies is considered to be poor scientific practice, for good reason. When a correlation between variables A and B is demonstrated and the researchers want to conclude that A influences B, it may just as well be the case that B influences A or that some third variable, C, influences both and creates the correlation.

This problem of scientific inference occurs particularly in research aimed at documenting the causes, whether biological or sociocultural, of psychological gender differences. A cautionary tale comes from research on gender differences in the brain region known as the corpus callosum. The original, much-publicized study appeared in the prestigious journal *Science* in 1982 (de Lacoste-Utamsing & Holloway, 1982; see also Holloway, Anderson, Defendini, & Harper, 1993). Based on anatomical analysis of 14 brains from cadavers (9 from males, 5 from females), the authors concluded that there was a sexual dimorphism (i.e., sex difference) in the corpus callosum, in particular in one region of it, called the splenium. Women had, on average, a larger splenium. Because the corpus callosum contains fibers connecting the two hemispheres of the brain, the researchers speculated that females' larger splenium accounted for the lesser cerebral lateralization of females, which had been proposed as an explanation for gender differences in verbal and mathematical abilities. As of February 2007, according to the Web of Science data base, the original article had been cited an astonishing 303 times, a testimony to its legendary status.

Methodologically, though, the quality of the evidence is flimsy at best. The conclusions and their notoriety are totally out of proportion to the five brains of deceased women that were studied. The original study included no measures of abilities of the persons in the sample, so the researchers did not even report a correlation between splenium size and performance on ability measures. A later meta-analysis of relevant studies concluded that there was no significant gender difference in the size of the splenium (Bishop & Wahlsten, 1997). And a meta-analysis of studies of lateralization of verbal functions concluded that there was no gender difference in lateralization (Sommer, Aleman, Bouma, & Kahn, 2004).

In sum, the research literature is littered with studies that show a biological gender difference and claim that it is the biological basis for some psychological gender difference. At most, studies of this type demonstrate a correlation between biology and psychology, not a causal chain. Frequently, such studies do not even test the correlation. Frequently, they do not replicate. Nonetheless, they attract widespread attention and often are accepted as well-established findings.

The alternative to the correlational study is *experimental research*, in which people are randomly assigned to an experimental group or control group. The experimental group is given some treatment, such as a particular kind of new training, and the control group either receives nothing or receives some other treatment, such as the old, traditional training. Studies such as this do permit inferences about what caused what. If the group that received the experimental training then performs better than the group that did not receive this training, we can conclude that the experimental training caused the improved performance. On many gender questions, experimental designs are not possible, but they are in some cases, such as evaluating the effects of new curricula designed to close the gender gap.

Gender Differences versus Individual Differences

It is easy for people to make a leap from the statement "Boys are more aggressive than girls" to the conclusion "All boys are more aggressive than all girls." Nothing could be farther from the truth. Even when research documents an average gender difference in a behavior such as aggression, within-gender variability is enormous and the overlap between the distributions for males and females is substantial. For example, for an effect size $d = .20$, there is 85% overlap between the distribution for males and the distribution for females (Cohen, 1988). And for an effect size of .20 on a measure favoring males, 45% of females and 55% of males would score above the overall mean (Hyde, 2005). For almost all psychological traits, including abilities and psychosocial factors, individual differences are enormous compared with gender differences (Hyde, 2005).

Researchers' Beliefs

Researchers' beliefs shape their research in numerous ways, including the choice of questions to ask, the ways that they choose to measure a construct, the design they choose, their observations of behavior, and their interpretation of the results (Hyde, 2006). For example, in regard to the choice of research question, researchers have devoted themselves to investigating gender differences in mathematics performance—what Caplan and Caplan (2005) have called *the perseverative search for sex differences in mathematics ability*. Very, very few researchers have investigated gender similarities in mathematics performance and their implications for education. Most researchers, then, hold a profound and unquestioned belief in gender differences in mathematics performance, and devote their efforts to documenting and elucidating the purported difference.

With these methodological caveats in mind, we turn to a consideration of the evidence regarding gender differences.

GENDER DIFFERENCES IN MOTOR BEHAVIORS

Activity Level

Folk knowledge has long maintained that boys are more active than girls; meta-analysis confirms that belief. In their meta-analysis of 127 studies of motor activity, Eaton and Enns (1986) found an overall effect size of 0.49, indicating a moderate effect in which boys were more active than girls by half a standard deviation. This effect was moderated by age and context, however. Gender differences were smaller among infants ($d = .29$) and increased through preschool ($d = .44$) and into childhood ($d = .64$). Gender differences were also accentuated when peers were present ($d = .62$), over when no peers were present ($d = .44$). Nonetheless, it is clear that a gender difference in activity level appears early and is robust across situations and studies.

Other Motor Behaviors

A meta-analysis of studies of gender differences in motor performance in children identified 20 different behaviors that had been investigated, including agility, reaction time, dash speed, sit-ups, and throwing distance (Thomas & French, 1985). Some of these gender differences were very large and put the magnitude of gender differences in cognitive abilities into perspective. For example, the effect size for throwing velocity was $d = 2.18$, averaged over all ages. That gender difference is even larger after puberty. For other motor behaviors, the gender difference was small. For example, $d = 0.18$ for reaction time and -0.21 for fine eye-motor coordination. It is worth noting that this meta-analysis was conducted on studies published before 1985. With the massive and successful entrance of girls into athletics, it would be interesting to know how large these gender differences are today.

COGNITIVE GENDER DIFFERENCES

Historically, research in psychology and education has supported the stereotype that girls and women excel on tests of verbal ability and that boys and men excel in mathematical and spatial abilities (Maccoby & Jacklin, 1974). The statistical technique of meta-analysis, however, has led to far better understanding of the evidence relating to these beliefs. In the sections that follow, we will base our conclusions, whenever possible, on the results of well-conducted meta-analyses.

Verbal Ability

A meta-analysis of studies of gender differences in verbal ability indicated that, overall, the difference was so small as to be negligible, $d = -0.11$ (Hyde & Linn, 1988). The negative value indicates better performance by females, but the magnitude of the difference is nonetheless quite small. There are many aspects to verbal ability, of course. When analyzed according to type of verbal ability, the results were as follows: for vocabulary, $d = -0.02$; for analogies, $d = 0.16$ (slightly better performance by males); for reading comprehension, $d = -0.03$; for speech production, $d = -0.33$; for essay writing, $d = -0.09$; for anagrams, $d = -0.22$; and for tests of general verbal ability, $d = -0.20$. The gender difference in speech production favoring females is the largest and confirms females' better performance on measures of verbal fluency (not to be confused with measures of talking time). The remaining effects range from small to zero. Moreover, the magnitude of the effect was consistently small at all ages.

A second meta-analysis confirmed these findings using somewhat different methods. Hedges and Nowell (1995) computed effect sizes from major well-sampled national studies, including Project Talent, NLS-72, NLSY, HS&B, and NELS:88. Effect sizes for gender differences in reading comprehension ranged between -0.15 and 0.00 across the various samples. For gender differences in vocabulary, effect sizes ranged between -0.06 and 0.07 for NLS-72, NLSY, and HS&B. Project Talent, at 0.25, was apparently an outlier. All other gender differences were small and close to 0.

Mathematical Performance

A major meta-analysis of studies of gender differences in mathematics performance surveyed 100 studies, representing the testing of more than 3 million persons (Hyde, Fennema, & Lamon, 1990a). Averaged over all samples of the general population, $d = -0.05$, a negligible difference favoring females.

An independent meta-analysis by Hedges and Nowell (1995), described earlier, confirmed the results of the meta-analysis by Hyde and colleagues. Hedges and Nowell found effect sizes for gender differences in mathematics performance ranging between 0.03 and 0.26 across samples—all differences in the negligible to small range. Results from the International Assessment of Educational Progress also confirm that gender differences in mathematics performance are small across numerous countries including Hungary, Ireland, Israel, and Spain (Beller & Gafni, 1996; see also Trends in International Mathematics and Science Study, 2003).

For issues of gender equity in education, however, this broad assessment of the magnitude of gender differences is probably less useful than an analysis by both age and cognitive level tapped by the mathematics test. These results from the Hyde et al. meta-analysis are shown in Table 2.1. Ages were grouped roughly into elementary school (ages 5–10 years), middle school (11–14), high school (15–18), and college age (19–25). Insufficient studies were available to compute mean effect sizes for older ages. Cognitive level of the test was coded as assessing either simple computation (requires the use of only algorithmic procedures to find a single numerical answer), conceptual (involves analysis or comprehension of mathematical ideas), problem solving (involves extending knowledge or ap-

TABLE 2.1 The Magnitude of Gender Differences in Mathematics Performance as a Function of Age and Cognitive Level of the Test

Age group	Cognitive Level		
	Computation	Concepts	Problem Solving
5–10	−0.20	−0.02	0.00
11–14	−0.22	−0.06	−0.02
15–18	0.00	0.07	0.29
19–25	NA	NA	0.32

Source: Hyde et al. (1990a).

plying it to new situations), or mixed. The results indicated that girls outperform boys by a small margin in computation in elementary school and middle school and that there is no gender difference in high school. For understanding of mathematical concepts, there is no gender difference at any age level. For problem solving there is no gender difference in elementary or middle school, but a small gender difference favoring males emerges in high school and the college years. There are no gender differences, then, or girls perform better, in all areas except problem solving beginning in the high school years.

This gender difference in problem solving favoring males deserves attention because problem solving is essential to success in occupations in engineering and the sciences, in which women are seriously underrepresented. Some have connected these two facts to suggest that lower problem solving ability in women accounts for some part of the gender difference in representation. Perhaps the best explanation for this gender difference, in view of the absence of a gender difference at earlier ages, is that it is a result of gender differences in course choice, that is, the tendency of girls not to select optional advanced mathematics courses and science courses in high school. The failure to take advanced science courses may be particularly crucial because traditional mathematics curricula often do not teach problem solving, whereas it typically is taught in chemistry and physics.

Current data indicate that the gender gap in taking advanced math courses is closing, but remains for some areas of science. In 1998, male and female high school graduates were equally likely to have taken advanced mathematics courses (beyond algebra II and geometry) during high school (National Science Foundation, 2004a). Girls were more likely than boys to have taken advanced biology or chemistry, whereas boys were more likely than girls to have taken physics. In many ways, this narrowing of the gender gap in course choice is a major victory for gender equity. We do not have definitive data on what caused the trend, but it seems likely that it resulted from parents, educators, and policymakers who encouraged greater educational aspirations for girls and the opening up to women of many traditionally male-dominated occupations. See the chapters on mathematics and science and engineering for further consideration of these issues.

If the real issue for gender differences in mathematical problem solving is not ability but rather courses taken, then research efforts should be directed at understanding gender and students' choice of courses. Eccles and her colleagues have conducted an extensive program of research on just this question (e.g., Anderman et al., 2001; Eccles, 1994; Meece, Eccles-Parsons, Kaczala, Goff, & Futterman, 1982; Wigfield & Eccles, 2000). In brief, Eccles proposed an expectancy value model, in which students choose to take on a challenging academic achievement task, such as taking calculus in high school, only if they have an expectation of success at the task and if they also value the task. That is, they must think that they have a reasonable chance of succeeding in the course and they must believe that the course has value for them. Both expectations and values are shaped by numerous forces, many of them in the schools. Girls' expectations for success are shaped by important socializers such as teachers and peers. The value attached to taking a math or science course is influenced by factors such as cultural stereotypes about the subject matter (math and science are both stereotyped as male domains), children's perceptions of teachers' attitudes, and the intrinsic value of the course (whether math and science are taught in ways that are interesting to girls). All of these factors provide opportunities for intervention.

The other possible explanation for gender differences in complex problem solving in high school—as well as for the gender gap on the mathematics portion of the SAT—is that the content of the word problems is gender biased, thereby lowering girls' performance (Chipman, Marshall, & Scott, 1991). For a more complete discussion of these issues see the chapter on testing and assessment in this volume.

The question of the gender difference favoring males on the mathematics portion of the SAT is complex. Why do girls continue to score lower than boys, even though girls are now taking as many math courses as boys? The most probable answer lies in the fact that more young women than men today are entering college, and, therefore, a higher percentage of women than men are taking the SAT. Essentially, then, the SAT-taking sample—and it is not at all a random sample of high school seniors—dips down further into the pool of female talent than it does in the pool of male talent. Confirming this explanation, boys taking the SAT are more advantaged than girls on measures such as family income and parents' education (Hyde et al., 1990a; Willingham & Cole, 1997).

Finally, it is important to consider an alternative measure of mathematics performance: grades in math courses. Girls earn better grades in mathematics at all grade levels (Kimball, 1989).

Spatial Performance

Spatial ability tests may tap any of several distinct skills: spatial visualization (finding a figure in a more complex one, like hidden-figures tests), spatial perception (identifying the true vertical or true horizontal when there is distracting information, such as the rod-and-frame task), and mental rotation (mentally rotating an object in three dimensions). Two meta-analyses are available on the question of gender differences in spatial performance. Linn and Petersen (1985) found that the magnitude of gender differences varied substantially across the three different types of spatial performance: $d = 0.13$ for spatial visualization, 0.44 for spatial perception, and 0.73 for mental rotation, all effects favoring males. The last difference is large and potentially influential. The other meta-analysis found $d = 0.56$ for mental rota-

tion (Voyer, Voyer, & Bryden, 1995), a somewhat smaller effect but nonetheless a substantial one.

Gender differences in spatial performance—specifically, mental rotation—are important for two reasons. First, some have hypothesized that gender differences in mental rotation ability are the source of gender differences in mathematics achievement, particularly in areas such as geometry and trigonometry (e.g., Friedman, 1995). Empirical research indicates that in fact math performance tends to correlate more highly with verbal ability than with spatial ability. A meta-analysis found that the correlation between mental rotation and performance in higher-level math is 0.31 for girls and 0.34 for boys ages 14 and older, whereas the correlations of mental rotation with verbal ability were 0.39 for both genders (Friedman, 1995). The spatial skill of mental rotation, then, may be a factor in math performance in high school, but it is certainly not the only factor, or even the strongest factor.

Second, mental rotation is crucial to some occupations in which women are substantially underrepresented, including engineering and physics. In 2003, women obtained 45% of all doctorates in the sciences (National Science Foundation, 2004b). However, only 17% of doctorates in engineering and 18% of doctorates in physics went to women. Mental rotation skills are essential in both areas. This points to the importance of including training in spatial skills as a serious part of any pre-college curriculum that aims at gender equity.

Innate Differences & Training Studies

Because research and stereotypes have so often been framed as gender differences in *ability*, the differences have too often been viewed as innate and fixed. However, if gender differences were truly innate and fixed, research would find differences present from birth or early childhood, and the differences could not be reduced with training. Research refutes each of these conditions.

For example, gender differences in math and science cannot be explained by innate differences in cognitive abilities (Spelke, 2005). Rather, most studies show no difference in the ways that male and female infants perceive and process information about objects in their environment, nor do most studies show any difference between boys and girls in the basic systems that support mathematical thinking during childhood (Spelke, 2005).

Furthermore, many training studies have been conducted, which provide direct training in the skills of concern to determine whether the gender gap can be closed with training. For example, scores on spatial tests can be improved by training (Baenninger & Newcombe, 1989; Newcombe, Mathason, & Terlecki, 2002; Vasta, Knott, & Gaze, 1996). Vasta and colleagues (1996), for example, were able to eliminate gender differences in performance on the water-level task (a measure of spatial perception) with a carefully designed training program for college students. The results, however, did not generalize to another, related task. The most recent development is multimedia software that provides training in 3-dimensional spatial visualization skills (Gerson, Sorby, Wysocki, & Baartmans, 2001). It has been used successfully with first-year engineering students. Importantly, there were improvements in the retention of women engineering students who took the course that included this training. A crucial issue is that schools currently offer little training in spatial skills in the curriculum. It would be an important addition to a truly gender-fair curriculum.

PSYCHOSOCIAL GENDER DIFFERENCES

Aggression

Studies consistently show a gender difference in children's physical and verbal aggression, where aggression refers to behavior intended to harm another person. Meta-analysis of aggression research demonstrates that boys are somewhat more aggressive than girls. Hyde (1984) reported an overall effect size of .50, a moderate effect, across 143 studies. In that analysis, the gender difference in aggression peaked during preschool and declined thereafter. Boys were more aggressive than girls in terms of both physical aggression and verbal aggression, but differences were largest and most consistent in physical aggression. Regarding aggression in adulthood, Eagly and Steffen (1986) meta-analyzed laboratory experimental studies of gender differences in aggression, most of them conducted with college students. The overall effect size was 0.29. Archer's (2004) meta-analysis of studies of aggression in real-world settings obtained results similar to Hyde's. The effect size for gender differences in aggression ranged from .30 to .63, depending on whether measurement was by self-report, observations, peer reports, or teacher reports. Gender differences were larger for physical than for verbal aggression. Gender differences in indirect aggression (purposely hurting another person by damaging their relationship with their peers, e.g., by spreading rumors) were small and favored females.

The gender difference in aggression is robust cross-culturally, having been found in nearly every culture that has been studied (Maccoby & Jacklin, 1974; Munroe, Hulefeld, Rodgers, Tomeo, & Yamazaki, 2000).

Helping Behavior

Studies of helping behavior reveal a somewhat surprising effect. Because nurturing is a part of the female role, we might expect to find more helping behavior among females than among males. Instead, meta-analysis of research studying gender differences in helping behavior revealed an overall effect size of 0.34, a small to moderate effect indicating more helping behavior by males than by females (Eagly & Crowley, 1986). However, the finding is elucidated when we examine the type of helping considered in each study. The gender difference favoring males was greatest in settings where helping could be deemed heroic or chivalrous, such as when others were present to witness the act or when the act was potentially dangerous. Without surveillance and in innocuous settings, such as on campus or in a psychology laboratory, there were either no gender differences in helping behavior or slight differences favoring females.

Self-Esteem

Researchers define self-esteem as a person's global level of self-regard, whether positive or negative. Popular culture has created the notion that self-esteem problems are rampant among girls and women. However, meta-analyses of studies of gender differences in self-esteem reveal a more tempered conclusion. A meta-analysis of 216 samples and almost 100,000 people found only a small overall gender difference of $d = 0.21$, with males reporting slightly greater self-esteem than females (Kling, Hyde, Showers, & Buswell, 1999; see also Major, Barr, Zubek, & Babey, 1999, for similar results). There was only a very small gender difference in self-esteem for elementary school children ($d = .16$), a slightly larger difference for middle-schoolers ($d = .23$), and a small to moderate difference for high-schoolers ($d = .33$). Among adults, gender differences in self-esteem were negligible. This trend of gender differences was found only among Whites, however. Blacks showed no gender difference in self-esteem. There were insufficient studies to test the gender difference in other minority groups.

Self-Confidence

A related question is whether there are gender differences in self-confidence. Whereas self-esteem refers to a person's global level of positive self-regard, self-confidence refers to a person's conviction that he or she can be successful at a specific task. Research shows that gender differences in self-confidence are not global; instead, they depend on the task in question. For example, a person might be very confident in mathematics but not at all confident in her ability to give an effective speech. That said, some research does show a gap between males' and females' self-confidence. When students are asked to estimate their expected score after taking a 100-point test, females tend to slightly underestimate their score by a few points. In contrast, males tend to slightly overestimate their score by the same margin (Beyer, 1999). The difference disappears, however, when women believe the task is gender appropriate, when they are given clear feedback about their performance, and in situations that do not encourage social comparison (Lenney, 1977, 1981).

Self-Discipline & Impulsivity

Recent meta-analysis suggests that there may be gender differences in self-discipline. Stated another way, males tend to be more impulsive than females. Silverman (2003) analyzed data from 33 studies that used delay-of-gratification tasks to measure impulsivity. In a delay-of-gratification task, research participants are given a choice between a small, immediate reward and a larger, delayed reward. Willingness to wait for the larger, delayed reward is thought to represent greater self-discipline and impulse control. Silverman found that males were more likely than females to take the immediate reward, and males were not willing to wait as long as women were in order to receive the larger reward.

Evidence is emerging that this gender difference in self-discipline or impulsivity may have important implications for classroom performance. For example, Duckworth and Seligman (2006) studied two groups of eighth graders at a charter school. They found that girls were more self-disciplined than boys (according to ratings by parents and teachers, self-report measures, and a delay-of-gratification task). In turn, self-discipline was related to school attendance, report card grades, and standardized test scores, such that girls' greater self-discipline accounted for their superior GPAs and test scores.

Learning Styles

A popular belief is that girls and boys differ in their learning styles and therefore require different kinds of instruction (Gurian & Ballew, 2003). The title of one helpful book is, *The Boys and Girls Learn Differently Action Guide for Teachers* (Gurian & Ballew, 2003). This approach, and many others like it, reflects an assumption that differences between boys and girls are categorical—that all girls will learn best under one condition and all boys under another—when in fact the distributions for boys and girls overlap considerably on almost every relevant outcome. Numerous learning style differences between boys and girls have been proposed. A particularly important one is the belief that girls perform better in a cooperative learning environment and boys perform better in a competitive one (e.g., Peterson & Fennema, 1985). No meta-analysis has assessed the effect of cooperative environments versus competitive environments for girls compared with boys. Individual studies, however, often provide evidence of gender similarities in performance in each of these environments (e.g., Gardunŏ, 2001). Indeed, many educators call for the incorporation of collaborative learning into all courses because such skills are valuable in the workplace.

HYPOTHESIZED BIOLOGICAL SOURCES OF GENDER DIFFERENCES

We have reviewed research on a wide array of purported gender differences. The evidence, often based on meta-analysis, indicates generally small gender differences for most abilities and behaviors, even those commonly said to show large differences. Nonetheless, there are notable exceptions: the gender difference in mathematical problem solving beginning in high school; the gender difference in spatial performance, specifically mental rotation; and the gender differences in aggression and in activity level. Here we review hypothesized biological sources of these gender differences.

Genes

Normal humans possess a set of 46 chromosomes in each cell of the body. Because chromosomes occur in pairs, there are 23 pairs, classified as 22 pairs of autosomes (nonsex chromosomes) and one pair of sex chromosomes (XX in females and XY in males). The autosomes pass back and forth between males and females across generations; that is, for a given pair,

the person received one from her mother and one from her father. Thus, in general, the autosomes should not be a source of psychological gender differences. The exception is when the expression of a gene is moderated by a factor such as sex hormones. Hormones' effects are discussed later in this chapter.

The sex chromosomes could hypothetically be a source of psychological gender differences. As of this writing, no gene has been identified on the X or Y chromosome that produces psychological gender differences, with the exception of the gene for color blindness, which is located on the X chromosome. Color blindness is manifested more frequently in males than females, as expected for X-linked traits (Dobyns et al., 2004).

Hormones

The sex hormones include the androgens (e.g., testosterone), estrogen, and progesterone. It is a misnomer to call testosterone a *male* hormone and estrogen and progesterone *female* hormones, because all are found in both women and men. Sex hormone effects are generally classified as either organizing effects, which occur prenatally or early in postnatal development and involve the differentiation of some structure such as the genitals or the hypothalamus in a male or female direction; or activating effects, which occur in adulthood, and activate particular behaviors.

Data across a wide variety of species indicate that the presence or absence of testosterone prenatally affects later aggressive behavior (Beatty, 1992). Whether these organizing effects hold for humans is controversial, although there is some supporting evidence (Collaer & Hines, 1995). Activating effects of testosterone on aggressive behavior in adults have also been documented across a wide variety of species and may be present in humans as well (Adkins-Regan, 1999; Albert, Jonik, & Walsh, 1992). One study of androgen administration to female-to-male transsexuals indicated that their aggression proneness increased with the influx of testosterone (Van Goozen, Cohen-Kettenis, Gooren, Frijda, & Van de Poll, 1995). Generally, human behavior is less affected by hormones than the behavior of other species is. It seems likely, however, that testosterone has both organizing and activating effects on humans, making males slightly more prone to aggressiveness than females. These small biological differences may then be magnified by socialization.

Today, the notion that hormones directly cause specific behaviors is considered too simple. Recent evidence indicates that hormones have bidirectional effects on both behavior and experience. For example, if women engage in resistance exercise, it raises their testosterone levels (Nindl et al., 2001).

Brain Structure and Function

During the process of prenatal sexual differentiation, gender differences are created in a few regions of the brain, although most regions display gender similarities. The chief structure that is gender-differentiated is the hypothalamus, a small region of the lower brain (Collaer & Hines, 1995; Fitch & Bimonte, 2002). The hypothalamus is important because it regulates vital functions and because it interacts closely with the pituitary gland, which is located just below the hypothalamus. The pituitary gland is often called the master gland of the endocrine system because of its far-reaching effects. In particular, it plays a crucial role in regulating levels of sex hormones. If testosterone is plentiful prenatally, the estrogen-sensitivity of certain cells in the hypothalamus is low; they are relatively insensitive. If estrogen is plentiful, these same cells are highly sensitive to estrogen (Choi et al., 2001; McEwen, 2001). A female-differentiated hypothalamus will then direct the cycling of hormones that creates the menstrual cycle beginning at puberty. Other consequences of the gender-differentiated hypothalamus are unclear, although it seems likely that aggressive behavior is affected.

Another hypothesized gender difference in the brain is in laterality. The right and left hemispheres of the brain are specialized for somewhat different functions, the left hemisphere being more specialized for language and the right for spatial tasks. The term lateralization refers to the extent to which a particular function, say spatial performance, is handled entirely by one hemisphere or is handled by both. Theories from several decades ago proposed that gender differences in lateralization explained gender differences in verbal, mathematical, and spatial abilities (e.g., Levy, 1976). However, a meta-analysis of empirical studies found that gender differences in lateralization for verbal or nonverbal tasks were close to zero, $d = 0.06$ (Voyer, 1996). Lateralization is therefore not a likely explanation for gender differences in abilities.

Evolution

Sociobiologists and evolutionary psychologists have proposed that evolution created many gender differences in behavior, including aggression (e.g., Buss, 1995; Buss & Schmitt, 1993; Geary, 1998; Tooby & Cosmides, 1992; Trivers, 1972). A thorough discussion of these theories, the evidence provided in support of them, and criticisms of them, is beyond the scope of this chapter. Several excellent criticisms are available elsewhere (e.g., Hrdy, 1981; Travis, 2003). Evolutionary psychology is a biological theory that specifies no exact biological mechanisms (e.g., the action of sex hormones or particular brain regions), and research in support of it typically includes no biological measures. Moreover, it cannot account for differences across nations in patterns of gender differences. Table 2.2 shows effect sizes for gender differences in the mathematics performance of eighth graders in eight nations, based on a large-scale

TABLE 2.2   Gender Differences in Mathematics Performance of Eighth-Graders Across Nations, 2003

Country	Effect Size, d
Chile	.09
Hungary	.05
Italy	.03
Japan	.01
Norway	−.02
Philippines	−.05
Singapore	−.05
United States	.02

Source: Trends in International Mathematics and Science Study (2003).

international study. In some countries boys score higher than girls and in others the reverse is true. In all cases, the gender difference is small.

HYPOTHESIZED SOCIOCULTURAL SOURCES OF GENDER DIFFERENCES

Gender Stereotypes and Socialization

Gender stereotypes are a culture's shared beliefs about the roles, behaviors, and personality traits of males and females. One possible explanation for gender differences is that they are caused, or at least perpetuated, by gender stereotypes. This hypothesis is supported by evidence that children learn gender stereotypes very early in development, and knowledge of gender stereotypes shapes their goals and behavior. For example, studies show that by 24 to 26 months of age, children are aware of gender-based toy categories (Levy, 1999). By age 3, children disapprove of peers who play with sex-inappropriate toys; by age 4, they choose to play with toys that are gender appropriate and anticipate positive self-evaluations for doing so (Bussey & Bandura, 1992).

Gender stereotypes operate in the academic domain, as well. For example, research by Eccles and colleagues showed that parents' beliefs about the gender appropriateness of math/science, reading, and sports influence their children's beliefs about and aspirations in each domain (Fredricks & Eccles, 2002). Other research documents the role of parents' gender stereotypes in their daughters' career development. Specifically, parents' gender-stereotyped attitudes are associated with adolescent girls' career choices. Daughters of traditional parents tend to pursue gender-traditional careers, whereas daughters of egalitarian parents are more likely to pursue nontraditional careers (Rainey & Borders, 1997).

Another important way that stereotypes operate to maintain gender differences is through stereotype threat. Stereotype threat occurs when a person feels at risk of confirming a negative stereotype about his or her group (Steele, 1997). For example, if males and females with equivalent math preparation and achievement are told that males typically outperform females on the test they are about to take, then their performance confirms the stereotype and males outperform females on the test. Alternatively, if they are told that there are typically no gender differences in how well students perform on the test, then there are no gender differences in their performance on the test (Spencer, Steele, & Quinn, 1999). Thus, stereotypes seem to influence attitudes and behavior in a variety of domains and may be one reason underlying gender differences.

Gender Schema Theory

A second account of gender differentiation has grown out of cognitive psychology and the notion that schemas, or knowledge structures, organize and shape thought and perception. Gender schema theory (e.g., Bem, 1981; Martin & Halverson, 1981; Tenenbaum & Leaper, 2002) is primarily concerned with the process of sex typing (i.e., how initial small anatomical differences between males and females are translated into culturally sanctioned, differentiated masculine and feminine roles, behaviors, and expectations). Gender schema theory posits that humans perceive and process information in terms of "organized networks of mental associations representing information about themselves and the sexes," called *gender schemas* (Martin, Ruble, & Szkrybalo, 2002, p. 911). Sex-typed behavior is enacted and preserved through these culturally transmitted gender schemas (Martin et al., 2002).

More specifically, humans have a natural propensity to classify and organize information; it aids their ability to make sense of the world (Martin et al., 2002). Because gender categories are perceptually and culturally salient, babies quickly learn to distinguish male from female. For example, at 6–8 months, babies can discriminate male and female voices (Miller, 1983); at 9–11 months, they can discriminate male and female faces (Leinbach & Fagot, 1993). Children's understanding soon proceeds beyond real, tangible differences between the sexes, however. Over time, children form coherent representations of what it means to be male or female, or—more accurately—what it means to be masculine or feminine (Martin & Halverson, 1981). Their ideas about gender are organized into gender schemas: salient networks of gender-related associations, stereotypes, metaphors, and scripts.

Importantly, gender schemas are not simply the product of gender-related experiences. They also *shape* experience. Gender schemas influence what information is attended to and how that information is perceived, processed, and utilized. For example, Bem (1981) showed that people who were highly sex-typed were most likely to remember words in gender-related clusters (e.g., bikini, butterfly, dress) rather than in category-related clusters (bikini, trousers, nylons), supporting the idea that highly sex-typed individuals engage in more gender-schematic processing than others. Furthermore, people change gender-role-inconsistent information to fit within their gender schemas. For example, Martin and Halverson (1983) showed that children have better memory of pictures showing models engaged in gender-role-consistent activities (e.g., boy playing with a train) than of pictures showing gender-role-inconsistent activities (e.g., girl sawing wood). Children's mistakes reveal that they incorrectly remember the inconsistent events as having been performed by gender-role-consistent models (e.g., boy sawing wood). Together, these studies show that individuals' cognitions about gender influence their perceptions about the world and themselves. Gender schemas influence attention, perception, and behavior, and they can be self-reinforced through selective memory.

Social Cognitive Theory

Social cognitive theory (Bandura, 1986; Bussey & Bandura, 1999) presents an alternative model of gender differentiation. Social cognitive theory acknowledges three sources of influence on gender development: individual factors (e.g., biology, personal attitudes, and preferences), the environment (e.g., societal pressures, role models), and behavior (e.g., experience). Social cognitive theory traditionally has paid little attention to biological and genetic factors that may underlie gender differences. Physical anatomy and genetic factors are seen as "biological potentialities, not behavioral dictates" (Bussey & Bandura, 1999, p. 684). Instead, social cognitive theory emphasizes the psychological and sociostructural determinants of gender role development. Humans' unique capacity for symbolization, observational learning, self-regulation, and self-reflection facilitate gender differentiation. According to social cognitive theory, "gender conceptions and role behavior are the products of a broad network of social influences operating both familially and in the many societal systems encountered in daily life" (Bussey & Bandura, 1999, p. 676).

Social cognitive theory outlines three processes by which gender roles and behaviors are learned: modeling, enactive experience, and direct tuition. In modeling, individuals see others in their environment (e.g., parents, peers, mass media) displaying gender-typed behavior. They attend to the behavior, assign it meaning, remember it, and later produce the gender-typed behaviors themselves. For example, a little girl might observe her mother performing childcare or household tasks and later mimic those behaviors when playing house. In enactive experience, individuals learn from the outcomes of their behavior. If a behavior is endorsed and rewarded, the individual learns that it is gender-appropriate and she or he is more likely to repeat it; whereas if a behavior is disapproved or punished, the individual learns that the behavior is probably not gender-appropriate and she or he is unlikely to repeat it. For example, a little boy might be praised by his peers for fighting another child on the playground and therefore continue to use aggression in future conflicts. Finally, in direct tuition, culturally competent others inform the individual about behaviors that are gender-appropriate and how to enact them. For example, a mother might tell her daughter that "nice little girls sit quietly and listen while Grandpa talks." In each of these ways, social cognitive theory says, individuals learn what roles and behaviors are appropriate for their own and the opposite gender.

Social cognitive theory argues that, once learned, gendered behavior is maintained through a combination of social sanctions and self-regulation (Bussey & Bandura, 1999). Especially for young children, socially-based consequences are powerful enforcers of gender development. Children (and adults) receive approval, praise, and reward for activities linked to their own gender, and they receive disapproval or even punishment for activities linked to the other gender. These social outcomes function as informational and motivational influences on their behavior. Over time, children internalize external mandates and begin to regulate their own behavior. They monitor their behavior, judge it against personal standards of what is gender-appropriate and what is not, and alter their behavior accordingly. Individuals are presumed to choose to behave in ways that give them self-satisfaction and boost their self-worth. Therefore, social sanctions and self-regulation serve as powerful motivators, ensuring that individuals enact gender-appropriate roles and behaviors.

Social-Structural Theory

An alternative psychosocial explanation for gender differences is that they are a product of the structure of the society (Eagly &

Wood, 1999). Social-structural theory emphasizes that there is significant variability in gender differences across cultures. In societies with large differences between the status of males and females, there tend to be substantial psychological gender differences. In societies that are more equitable, there are relatively few psychological gender differences. Social-structural theory argues that the gendered division of labor underlies most other gender differences.

In support of this claim, Eagly and Wood (1999) re-analyzed data that evolutionary psychologist David Buss had used to support his theory that psychological gender differences, such as mate preferences, are universal. Buss (1989) had collected data from 37 cultures and found support of his theory that men have evolved to prefer short-term, young, attractive partners whereas women prefer long-term, older mates with wealth and ambition. Eagly and Wood compared Buss's findings to United Nations data about gender equality in each of the 37 cultures. They found a strong connection between a society's gender inequity and its members' gender differences in mate preferences. That is, inequitable societies showed the pattern described by Buss, whereas more equitable societies showed minimal differences between the sexes.

Another example of the link between social structure and gender differentiation can be seen in students' math achievement. Just as the effect size for gender differences in math performance varies across studies, as mentioned previously, it also varies across countries. International studies show that, while gender differences in math achievement are small in all countries, there are differences in the size and direction of the difference. In some countries, males outperform females; in others, there is no gender difference; in still others, females outperform males (Baker & Jones, 1993). Importantly, the magnitude of the gender difference in math performance correlates significantly with indicators of gender equality in the country, such as the percentage of women in the country's workforce ($r = -.55$). That is, the more equitable the country, the smaller the gender difference in math achievement. Thus, social-structural theory argues that gender differences in psychological measures, such as mate selection and math achievement, are not evolved universals, but instead are a product of societal structure and gender equality.

Expectancy-Value Theory

A final psychosocial model of gender differentiation was posited explicitly to explain gender differences in achievement (e.g., Eccles et al., 1983). As discussed previously in the section on mathematics performance, expectancy-value theory proposes that gender differences in achievement stem from the different achievement-related choices that males and females make, such as which classes to take or which activities to engage in. Specifically, the theory posits that males and females hold different expectations for success and different beliefs about the value of achievement in certain domains (e.g., mathematics, athletics). These expectations and values guide achievement-related choices, and thus expectations and values underlie gender differences.

The expectancy-value model has received extensive empirical support. For example, there is considerable evidence that boys and girls hold different expectations about math, perhaps linked to the culturally based notion that math is a male domain (Benbow & Stanley, 1980). Across cultures and as early as first grade, boys believe that they are better at math than girls (Lummis & Stevenson, 1990). In addition, according to a meta-analysis, boys report more positive attitudes toward math than do girls, and they are more confident in their math abilities (Hyde, Fennema, Ryan, Frost, & Hopp, 1990b). These important differences in males' and females' attitudes toward math have been shown to underlie plans for future course enrollment and career choice (e.g., Eccles, 1984).

Another important finding that has emerged from this line of research is that parents play a major role in shaping their children's attitudes toward and subsequent success in mathematics and other domains. In one representative study, Frome and Eccles (1998) examined parents' and their adolescents' perceptions about math and reading. They found that parents' perceptions of their child's ability had a stronger influence on the child's self-perceptions than did the child's own grades. That is, if a child's parents thought that they were good/bad in math or that math was easy/hard, then the child was likely to perceive himself or herself in the same way. In fact, children were likely to hold views consistent with their parents' views, regardless of how well they were actually doing in math class. Notably, parents held more positive perceptions of boys' math ability than girls, controlling for actual ability (see also Lummis & Stevenson, 1990), and those perceptions were related to children's math self-concept and to children's expectations for future success in math.

Expectancy-value theory provides a cohesive structure for integrating the influences of important others, such as parents and teachers, with individual children's cognitions related to their abilities and the achievement-related choices they make.

IMPLICATIONS AND RECOMMENDATIONS FOR GENDER EQUITY

What are the implications of the findings reported in this chapter for gender equity in education? Here we consider three areas: findings of gender similarities, the importance of training in spatial skills, and the importance of the beliefs of important socializers.

Gender Similarities

Strong evidence exists, based on meta-analyses, in support of gender similarities in a number of abilities that have long been stereotyped as gender differentiated (Hyde, 2005). Table 2.3 summarizes findings from all of the meta-analyses discussed in this chapter. Notable among these are gender similarities in verbal ability and mathematical performance. These findings argue against placing any constraints on students' course of study or occupational aspirations based on gender.

These findings of similarity also argue against the practice of gender-based modes of instructions, that is, different methods of instruction for boys and girls. In regard to learning styles, for example, some have argued that boys thrive in a competitive

TABLE 2.3 Meta-Analyses Discussed in this Chapter

Study	Variable	Age	Reports (*n*)	*d*
Eaton and Enns (1986)	Activity level	All ages	205	+0.49
Thomas and French (1985)	Throwing velocity	All ages	12	+2.18
	Reaction time	All ages	42	+0.18
	Eye-motor coordination	All ages	30	−0.21
Hyde and Linn (1988)	Verbal ability	All ages	120	−0.14
Hyde et al. (1990a)	Mathematics computation	All ages	45	−0.14
	Mathematics concepts	All ages	41	−0.03
	Mathematics problem solving	All ages	48	+0.08
Hyde et al. (1990b)	Confidence in math ability	All ages	41	+0.15
Hedges and Nowell (1995)	Reading comprehension	Adolescents	5*	−0.09
	Vocabulary	Adolescents	4*	+0.06
	Mathematics	Adolescents	6*	+0.16
	Perceptual speed	Adolescents	4*	−0.28
	Science	Adolescents	4*	+0.32
	Spatial ability	Adolescents	2*	+0.19
Linn and Peterson (1985)	Spatial perception	All ages	62	+0.44
	Mental rotation	All ages	29	+0.73
	Spatial visualization	All ages	81	+0.13
Voyer et al. (1995)	Spatial perception	All ages	92	+0.44
	Mental rotation	All ages	78	+0.56
	Spatial visualization	All ages	116	+0.19
Hyde (1984)	Aggression (all types)	All ages	69	+0.50
	Physical aggression	All ages	26	+0.60
	Verbal aggression	All ages	6	+0.43
Eagly and Crowley (1986)	Helping behavior	Adults	99	+0.13
	Helping: Surveillance	Adults	16	+0.74
	Helping: No surveillance	Adults	41	0.02
Kling et al. (1999) Analysis I	Self-esteem	All ages	216	+0.21
Kling et al. (1999) Analysis II	Self-esteem	Adolescents	15*	+0.04 to +0.16
Major et al. (1999)	Self-esteem	All ages	226	+0.14
Silverman (2003)	Delay of gratification	All ages	38	+0.11

Note. Positive values of *d* represent higher scores for males; negative values of *d* represent higher scores for females. Asterisks denote that data were from major, large national samples.

math classroom whereas girls thrive in a cooperative math classroom. Even if it were true that girls on average preferred or learned more in a cooperative context, that would not mean that *all* girls prefer or learn more in a cooperative setting. Certainly it is good practice to offer instruction in multiple modes, but children should be assigned to these modes based on their learning styles, not based on their gender. Alternatively, we may want to encourage students to adopt multiple learning styles so that they have the flexibility to respond most effectively in different situations.

Recommendation. Because the best evidence indicates that boys and girls are quite similar in both their verbal and mathematical aptitude, students should not be constrained in their curriculum by gender. In particular, school personnel should not use gender stereotypes—for example, girls cannot succeed as scientists—in advising students.

The Importance of a Spatial Curriculum in the Schools

According to meta-analyses, females perform less well than males on one particular type of spatial ability, mental rotation. The gender difference is moderate, not large, but it requires at-

tention because it may be linked to the under-representation of women in some occupations requiring high levels of spatial performance (e.g., engineering), and because mental rotation is necessary for outstanding performance in some forms of advanced mathematics.

Most schools provide little or no explicit instruction in mental rotation (Matthewson, 1999). Training studies indicate that girls could be brought to the same average performance as boys with explicit spatial instruction. This increased competence could then be expected to have multiplier effects in girls' mathematics and science performance. They also might become more interested in physics and engineering if they felt more competent at one of the building blocks for success in those fields.

Recommendation. Gender equity in education requires an explicit curriculum in spatial skills.

The Importance of Socializers

The beliefs of important socializers, especially parents and teachers, about gender differences in abilities have a strong and potentially devastating impact on children's sense of their own competence. Studies by the Eccles group, reviewed earlier, indicate, for example, that children's self-perceptions of their abilities are more strongly influenced by their parents' perceptions of their children's abilities than by the children's actual grades in the subject. Therefore, an important task for educators is to get the word out to parents and teachers that gender differences, especially in mathematics performance, are small or nonexistent. Until we change parents' and teachers' beliefs, girls' belief in their own competence will continue to be undermined.

Recommendation. Educators should convey to parents that gender differences, especially in mathematics performance, are small or nonexistent so that girls' self-efficacy beliefs will not be undermined by parents' stereotyped beliefs.

Recommendation. Educators should be aware that they are socializers and should recognize the costs of over-inflated claims of psychological gender differences, which can discourage talented girls and boys from certain courses and occupations.

Single-Sex Education

Most arguments for single-sex schools or classrooms are based on assumptions of enormous psychological gender differences, when in fact boys and girls are quite similar on most relevant variables.

Recommendation. Educators should be wary of arguments for single-sex education that rest on assumptions of large psychological differences between boys and girls. These assumptions are not supported by the data.

Research

Research in both psychology and education has been characterized by a perseverative search for gender differences (Caplan & Caplan, 2005).

Recommendation. Researchers should be aware of the bias toward finding gender differences and ignoring gender similarities. They should strive for balanced reporting of differences and similarities.

ACKNOWLEDGMENTS

The authors would like to thank Marcia C. Linn, University of California, Berkeley, and Anne C. Petersen, University of Minnesota, Minneapolis, authors of the 1985 *Handbook for Achieving Sex Equity through Education* chapter on "Facts and Assumptions About the Nature of Sex Differences" for their helpful review of the draft of this chapter.

References

Adkins-Regan, E. (1999). Testosterone increases singing and aggression but not male-typical sexual partner preference in early estrogen treated female zebra finches. *Hormones & Behavior, 35,* 63–70.

Albert, D. J., Jonik, R. H., & Walsh, M. L. (1992). Hormone-dependent aggression in male and female rats: Experiential, hormonal, and neural foundations. *Neuroscience & Biobehavioral Reviews, 16,* 177–192.

Anderman, E. M., Eccles, J. S., Yoon, K. S., Roeser, R., Wigfield, A., & Blumenfeld, P. (2001). Learning to value mathematics and reading: Relations to mastery and performance-oriented instructional practices. *Contemporary Educational Psychology, 26,* 76–95.

*Archer, J. (2004). Sex differences in aggression in real-world settings: A meta-analytic review. *Review of General Psychology, 8,* 291–322.

*Baenninger, M., & Newcombe, N. (1989). The role of experience in spatial test performance: A meta-analysis. *Sex Roles, 20,* 327–344.

Baker, D. P., & Jones, D. P. (1993). Creating gender equality: Cross-national gender stratification and mathematical performance. *Sociology of Education, 66,* 91–103.

Bandura, A. (1986). *Social foundations of thought and action: A social cognitive theory.* Englewood Cliffs, NJ: Prentice Hall.

Beatty, W. (1992). Gonadal hormones and sex differences in nonreproductive behaviors. In A. A. Gerall, H. Moltz, & I. L. Ward (Eds.), *Handbook of behavioral neurobiology* (Vol. 11, pp. 85–128). New York: Plenum.

Beller, M., & Gafni, N. (1996). The 1991 International Assessment of Educational Progress in Mathematics and Sciences: The gender differences perspective. *Journal of Educational Psychology, 88,* 365–377.

Bem, S. L. (1981). Gender schema theory: A cognitive account of sex typing. *Psychological Review, 88,* 354–364.

Benbow, C. P., & Stanley, J. C. (1980). Sex differences in mathematical ability: Fact or artifact? *Science, 210,* 1262–1264.

Beyer, S. (1999). Gender differences in the accuracy of grade expectancies and evaluations. *Sex Roles, 41,* 279–296.

Bishop, K. M., & Wahlsten, D. (1997). Sex differences in the human corpus callosum: Myth or reality? *Neuroscience and Biobehavioral Reviews, 21,* 581–601.

Buss, D. M. (1989). Sex differences in mate preferences: Evolutionary hypotheses tested in 37 cultures. *Behavioral and Brain Sciences, 12,* 1–14.

Buss, D. M. (1995). Evolutionary psychology: A new paradigm for psychological science. *Psychological Inquiry, 6,* 1–30.

Buss, D. M., & Schmitt, D. P. (1993). Sexual strategies theory: An evolutionary perspective on human mating. *Psychological Review, 100,* 204–232.

Bussey, K., & Bandura, A. (1992). Self-regulatory mechanisms governing gender development. *Child Development, 63,* 1236–1250.

*Denotes a reference in which a meta-analysis is reported.

Bussey, K., & Bandura, A. (1999). Social cognitive theory of gender development and differentiation. *Psychological Review, 106*, 676–713.

Caplan, J. B., & Caplan, P. J. (2005). The perseverative search for sex differences in mathematics ability. In A. Gallagher & J. Kaufman (Eds.), *Gender differences in mathematics: An integrative psychological approach* (pp. 25–47). New York: Cambridge University Press.

Chipman, S. F., Marshall, S. P., & Scott, P. A. (1991). Content effects on word problem performance: A possible source of test bias? *American Educational Research Journal, 28*, 897–915.

Choi, E. J., Ha, C. M., Choi, J. G., Kang, S. S., Choi, W. S., Park, S. K., et al. (2001). Low-density cDNA array-coupled to PCT differential display identifies new estrogen-responsive genes during the postnatal differentiation of the rat hypothalamus. *Molecular Brain Research, 97*, 115–128.

Cohen, J. (1988). *Statistical power analysis for the behavioral sciences* (2nd ed.). Hillsdale, NJ: Lawrence Erlbaum Associates.

Collaer, M. L., & Hines, M. (1995). Human behavioral sex differences: A role for gonadal hormones during early development? *Psychological Bulletin, 118*, 55–107.

de Lacoste-Utamsing, C., & Holloway, R. L. (1982). Sexual dimorphism in the human corpus callosum. *Science, 216*, 1431–1432.

Dobyns, W. B., Filauro, A., Tomson, B., Chan, A., Ho, A., Ting, N., et al. (2004). Inheritance of most X-linked traits is not dominant or recessive, just X-linked. *American Journal of Medical Genetics, 129A*, 136–143.

Duckworth, A. L., & Seligman, M. E. P. (2006). Self-discipline gives girls the edge: Gender in self-discipline, grades, and achievement test scores. *Journal of Educational Psychology, 98*, 198–208.

*Eagly, A. H., & Crowley, M. (1986). Gender and helping behavior: A meta-analytic review of the social psychological literature. *Psychological Bulletin, 100*, 283–308.

*Eagly, A. H., & Steffen, V. (1986). Gender and aggressive behavior: A meta-analytic review of the social psychological literature. *Psychological Bulletin, 100*, 309–330.

Eagly, A. H., & Wood, W. (1999). The origins of sex differences in human behavior: Evolved dispositions versus social roles. *American Psychologist, 54*, 408–423.

*Eaton, W. O., & Enns, L. R. (1986). Sex differences in human motor activity level. *Psychological Bulletin, 100*, 19–28.

Eccles, J. E. (1994). Understanding women's educational and occupational choices: Applying the Eccles et al. Model of achievement-related choices. *Psychology of Women Quarterly, 18*, 585–610.

Eccles (Parsons), J. (1984). Sex differences in achievement patterns. In T. Sonderegger (Ed.), *Nebraska Symposium on Motivation* (Vol. 32, pp. 97–132). Lincoln: University of Nebraska Press.

Eccles, J. E., Adler, T. F., Futterman, R., Goff, S. B., Kaczala, C. M., Meece, J. L., et al. (1983). Expectations, values, and academic behaviors. In J. T. Spence (Ed.), *Achievement and achievement motives* (pp. 75–145). San Francisco: W. H. Freeman.

Fitch, R. H., & Bimonte, H. A. (2002). Hormones, brain, and behavior: Putative biological contributions to cognitive sex differences. In A. McGillicuddy-De Lisi & R. De Lisi (Eds.), *Biology, society, and behavior: The development of sex differences in cognition* (pp. 55–92). Westport, CT: Ablex.

Fredricks, J. A., & Eccles, J. S. (2002). Children's competence and value beliefs from childhood through adolescence: Growth trajectories in two male-sex-typed domains. *Developmental Psychology, 38*, 519–533.

Friedman, L. (1995). The space factor in mathematics: Gender differences. *Review of Educational Research, 65*, 22–50.

Frome, P. M., & Eccles, J. S. (1998). Parents' influence on children's achievement related perceptions. *Journal of Personality and Social Psychology, 74*, 435–452.

Garduño, E. L. H. (2001). The influence of cooperative problem solving on gender differences in achievement, self-efficacy, and attitudes toward mathematics in gifted students. *Gifted Child Quarterly, 45*, 269–282.

Geary, D. C. (1998). *Male, female: The evolution of human sex differences.* Washington, DC: American Psychological Association.

Gerson, H., Sorby, S. A., Wysocki, A., & Baartmans, B. J. (2001). The development and assessment of multimedia software for improving 3-D spatial visualization skills. *Computer Applications in Engineering Education, 9*, 105–113.

Gurian, M., & Ballew, A. C. (2003). *The boys and girls learn differently action guide for teachers.* San Francisco: Jossey-Bass.

*Hedges, L. V., & Nowell, A. (1995). Sex differences in mental test scores, variability, and numbers of high-scoring individuals. *Science, 269*, 41–45.

Holloway, R. L., Anderson, P., Defendini, R., & Harper, C. (1993). Sexual dimorphism of the human corpus callosum from 3 independent samples. *American Journal of Physical Anthropology, 92*, 481–498.

Hrdy, S. B. (1981). *The woman that never evolved.* Cambridge: Harvard University Press.

*Hyde, J. S. (1984). How large are gender differences in aggression? A developmental meta-analysis. *Developmental Psychology, 20*, 722–736.

*Hyde, J. S. (2005). The gender similarities hypothesis. *American Psychologist, 60*, 581–592.

*Hyde, J. S. (2006). *Half the human experience: The psychology of women* (7th ed.). Boston: Houghton-Mifflin.

*Hyde, J. S., Fennema, E., & Lamon, S. J. (1990a). Gender differences in mathematics performance: A meta-analysis. *Psychological Bulletin, 107*, 139–155.

*Hyde, J. S., Fennema, E., Ryan, M., Frost, L. A., & Hopp, C. (1990b). Gender comparisons of mathematics attitudes and affect. *Psychology of Women Quarterly, 14*, 299–324.

* Hyde, J. S., & Linn, M. C. (1988). Gender differences in verbal ability: A meta-analysis. *Psychological Bulletin, 104*, 53–69.

Kimball, M. M. (1989). A new perspective on women's math achievement. *Psychological Bulletin, 105*, 198–214.

*Kling, K. C., Hyde, J., Showers, C., & Buswell, B. (1999). Gender differences in self-esteem: A meta-analysis. *Psychological Bulletin, 125*, 470–500.

Leinbach, M., & Fagot, B. (1993). Categorical habituation to male and female faces: Gender schematic processing in infancy. *Infant Behavior and Development, 16*, 317–332.

Lenney, E. (1977). Women's self-confidence in achievement settings. *Psychological Bulletin, 84*, 1–13.

Lenney, E. (1981). What's fine for the gander isn't always good for the goose: Sex differences in self-confidence as a function of ability area and comparison with others. *Sex Roles, 7*, 905–924.

Levy, G. D. (1999). Gender-typed and non-gender-typed category awareness in toddlers. *Sex Roles, 41*, 851–874.

Levy, J. (1976). Cerebral lateralization and spatial ability. *Behavior Genetics, 6*, 171–188.

*Linn, M. C., & Petersen, A. C. (1985). Emergence and characterization of sex differences in spatial ability: A meta-analysis. *Child Development, 56*, 1479–1498.

Lipsey, M. W. & Wilson, D. B. (2001). *Practical meta-analysis.* Thousand Oaks, CA: Sage.

Lummis, M., & Stevenson, H. W. (1990). Gender differences in beliefs and achievement: A cross-cultural study. *Developmental Psychology, 26*, 254–263.

Maccoby, E. E., & Jacklin, C. N. (1974). *The psychology of sex differences.* Palo Alto, CA: Stanford University Press.

Major, B., Barr, L., Zubek, J., & Babey, S. H. (1999). Gender and self-esteem: A meta-analysis. In W. Swann, J. Langlois, & L. Gilbert (Eds.), *Sexism and stereotypes in modern society: The gender science of Janet Taylor Spence* (pp. 223–254). Washington, DC: American Psychological Association.

Martin, C. L., & Halverson, C. (1981). A schematic processing model of sex typing and stereotyping in children. *Child Development, 52,* 1119–1134.

Martin, C. L., & Halverson, C. (1983). The effects of sex-typing schemas on young children's memory. *Child Development, 54,* 563–574.

Martin, C., Ruble, D., & Szkrybalo, J. (2002). Cognitive theories of early gender development. *Psychological Bulletin, 128,* 903–933.

Matthewson, J. H. (1999). Visual-spatial thinking: An aspect of science overlooked by educators. *Science Education, 83,* 333–354.

McEwen, B. S. (2001). Estrogen effects on the brain: Multiple sites and molecular mechanisms. *Journal of Applied Physiology, 91,* 2785–2801.

Meece, J. L., Eccles-Parsons, J., Kaczala, C. M., Goff, S. B., & Futterman, R. (1982). Sex differences in math achievement: Toward a model of academic choice. *Psychological Bulletin, 91,* 324–348.

Miller, C. L. (1983). Developmental changes in male/female voice classifications by infants. *Infant Behavior and Development, 6,* 313–330.

Munroe, R. L., Hulefeld, R., Rodgers, J. M., Tomeo, D. L., & Yamazaki, S. (2000). Aggression among children in four cultures. *Cross-Cultural Research, 34,* 3–25.

National Science Foundation, Division of Science Resources Statistics (2004a). *Science and engineering indicators 2004.* NSF 04-01. Arlington, VA: Author.

National Science Foundation, Division of Science Resources Statistics (2004b). *Science and engineering doctorate awards: 2003.* NSF 05-300. Arlington, VA: Author.

Newcombe, N. S., Mathason, L., & Terlecki, M. (2002). Maximization of spatial competence: More important than finding the cause of sex differences. In A. McGillicuddy-De Lisi & R. De Lisi (Eds.), *Biology, society, and behavior: The development of sex differences in cognition.* (pp. 183–206). Westport, CT: Ablex.

Nindl, B. C., Kraemer, W. J., Gotschalk, L. A., Marx, J. O., Volek, J. S., Bush, J. A., et al. (2001). Testosterone responses after resistance exercise in women: Influence of regional fat distribution. *International Journal of Sport Nutrition and Exercise Metabolism, 11,* 451–465.

Peterson, P. L., & Fennema, E. (1985). Effective teaching, student engagement in classroom activities, and sex-related differences in learning mathematics. *American Educational Research Journal, 22,* 309–335.

Rainey, L. M., & Borders, L. D. (1997). Influential factor in career orientation and career aspiration of early adolescent girls. *Journal of Counseling Psychology, 44,* 160–172.

Rosenthal, R. (1979). The "file drawer problem" and tolerance for null results. *Psychological Bulletin, 86,* 638–661.

*Silverman, I. W. (2003). Gender differences in delay of gratification: A meta-analysis. *Sex Roles, 49,* 451–463.

*Sommer, I. E. C., Aleman, A., Bouma, A., & Kahn, R. S. (2004). Do women really have more bilateral language representation than men? A meta-analysis of functional imaging studies. *Brain, 127,* 1845–1852.

Spelke, E. S. (2005). Sex differences in intrinsic aptitude for mathematics and science? A critical review. *American Psychologist, 60,* 950–958.

Spencer, S. J., Steele, C. M., & Quinn, D. M., (1999). Stereotype threat and women's math performance. *Journal of Experimental Social Psychology, 35,* 4–28.

Steele, C. M. (1997). A threat in the air: How stereotypes shape intellectual identity and performance. *American Psychologist, 52,* 613–629.

*Tenenbaum, H. R., & Leaper, C. (2002). Are parents' gender schemas related to their children's gender-related cognitions? A meta-analysis. *Developmental Psychology, 38,* 615–630.

*Thomas, J. R., & French, K. E. (1985). Gender differences across age in motor performance: A meta-analysis. *Psychological Bulletin, 98,* 260–282.

Tooby, J., & Cosmides, L. (1992). The psychological foundations of culture. In J. Barkow, L. Cosmides, & J. Tooby (Eds.), *The adapted mind: Evolutionary psychology and the generation of culture* (pp. 19–136). New York: Oxford University Press.

Travis, C. B. (Ed.). (2003). *Evolution, gender, and rape.* Cambridge, MA: MIT Press.

Trends in International Mathematics and Science Study. (2003). Retrieved June 21, 2005, from http://nces.ed.gov/pubs2005/timss03

Trivers, R. (1972). Parental investment and sexual selection. In B. Campbell (Ed.), *Sexual selection and the descent of man.* Chicago: Aldine.

Van Goozen, S., Cohen-Kettenis, P., Gooren, L., Frijda, N., & Van de Poll, N. (1995). Gender differences in behaviour: Activating effects of cross-sex hormones. *Psychoneuroendocrinology, 20,* 343–363.

Vasta, R., Knott, J. A., & Gaze, C. E. (1996). Can spatial training erase the gender differences on the water-level task? *Psychology of Women Quarterly, 20,* 549–568.

Voyer, D. (1996). On the magnitude of laterality effects and sex differences in functional laterality. *Laterality, 1,* 51–83.

Voyer, D., Nolan, C., & Voyer, S. (2000). The relation between experience and spatial performance in men and women. *Sex Roles, 43,* 891–916.

*Voyer, D., Voyer, S., & Bryden, M. P. (1995). Magnitude of sex differences in spatial abilities: A meta-analysis and consideration of critical variables. *Psychological Bulletin, 117,* 250–270.

Wigfield, A., & Eccles, J. S. (2000). Expectancy-value theory of achievement motivation. *Contemporary Educational Psychology, 25,* 68–81.

Wilkinson, L., & the Task Force on Statistical Inference. (1999). Statistical methods in psychology journals: Guidelines and explanations. *American Psychologist, 54,* 594–604.

Willingham, W. W., & Cole, N. S. (1997) *Gender and fair assessment.* Mahwah, NJ: Lawrence Erlbaum Associates.

·3·

GENDER EQUITY EDUCATION GLOBALLY

Nelly P. Stromquist

This chapter reviews gender-related educational conditions, policy initiatives, and challenges throughout the world, with special emphasis on developing countries. It attempts to present a very concise picture and relies on the most recent and authoritative educational statistics and studies.

From a human capital perspective, education is related positively to individual, community, and national benefits. The education of women, in particular, has been found to have a major impact on social development indicators such as maternal and child health and nutrition, life expectancy, fertility, and resources for families in developing countries. Women's education is also associated with lower early marriage rates and positive outcomes for society such as lower petty crime rates, greater support for democratic practices, decreased school dropouts, and reduced domestic violence. Even low levels of education—as would be basic literacy (defined as the ability to read and write a simple sentence)—are linked to knowledge and skills essential to national development, although some outcomes, such as significantly decreased fertility rates, seem to need secondary education. What is more, in a number of dimensions, the education of mothers has a greater positive effect than the education of fathers. A comparative study of 41 countries (Filmer, 1999) found that the mother's education has a greater impact than the father's on student enrollment in some countries. (For comprehensive reviews of studies examining the impact of women's education on a long list of outcomes, see Herz & Sperling, 2003, and King & Hill, 1993.) Educating girls and women (and boys and men) in democratic values also helps to decrease sex stereotypes and promote social justice and peace.

PATTERNS IN EDUCATIONAL ACCESS AND COMPLETION

Access to and completion of education can be measured both in absolute and relative (proportional) terms for a given age or grade group.[1] They can also be measured by comparing one population group against another. The comparison of girls' and boys' access to schooling is usually done through the use of the gender parity index (GPI), a coefficient that at value 1.0 signals perfect numerical equality between both sexes. Fractions below 1.0 indicate inequality to the disadvantage of women. From a practical standpoint, UNESCO (2003, p. 109) recommends considering GPI coefficients of 0.97 and 1.03 as indicating parity.

Access to Schooling

There is great variability in access to schooling. In general, industrialized countries show higher levels of school enrollment and success in completing various levels of schooling than less industrialized countries; industrialized countries also show GPIs close to 1.0. Less industrialized countries are characterized by significant diversity. Regions with major problems in access and completion are sub-Saharan Africa and South and West Asia, while these problems are relatively minor in Latin America and East Asia. Developing countries also have considerable internal diversity, as is particularly the case for India.

---

[1]A note on methodology: Educational statistics gathered by governments and reported by UNESCO are based solely on administrative data, which contain only educational information pertaining to enrollment, completion, repetition, and dropping out. Crucial data combining sex, social class, ethnicity, and residence variables—that enable researchers to examine the impact on schooling due to economic and cultural factors—are recent additions from household surveys, and demographic and health surveys (DHS). However, DHS measures of attendance ask for school attendance the current or the previous week to the survey and should not be considered as indicators of "average daily attendance." Enrollment data depend on census data for their calculation; if population is underestimated, school enrollment will be overestimated. On the question of out-of-school children, these figures are probably slightly overestimated because the estimates include children of primary age who are enrolled either in preprimary or secondary schools.

Preschool. Access to early childhood and care education (ECCE) has indirect gender implications as it releases the mother to do productive work, frees the elder sister to attend school, enables the professional development of the mother as a preschool aide or teacher, and facilitates the empowering of the mother through her increased participation in the community (UNESCO, 2003). Coverage at this level is still very weak as 56 of 152 countries enroll fewer than 30% of the pertinent age group. There are very small gender disparities at this level, caused by two opposing forces: wealthy parents do not discriminate between sons' and daughters' preschool education, and poor children are benefiting through less formal educational approaches that seek to empower women and girls (UNESCO, 2006).

Primary Education. Girls have been improving their access to schooling faster than boys over the past 20 years, yet girls in low-income countries continue to have lower participation rates than boys, particularly in sub-Saharan Africa, the Arab States, and South and West Asia. On the other hand, in eastern and southern Africa boys have been affected by worsening economic conditions, internal conflict, and the persistent spread of HIV/AIDS, which have reduced their enrollment and completion of primary schooling by pushing them into the informal labor market or domestic armies.

In one third of the sub-Saharan countries, the female gross enrollment ratios are about three quarters of the male ratio or less (a GPI less than 0.76). Only Lesotho shows a GPI in favor of girls. In some countries in eastern and southern Africa (Madagascar, Malawi, Namibia, Rwanda, South Africa, Zambia, and Zimbabwe), girls' *attendance* (actually going to school) rates equal or exceed those of boys (Lloyd, 2005). Some Arab countries have the lowest girls' enrollment in the world (Djibouti and Sudan) and the largest gender disparities (Yemen and Djibouti). Among the 25 Arab states, one finds great diversity. As a whole, they have low levels of schooling and great disparities between men and women. In 2000, adult men averaged about 5 years of schooling while women had about 3.5. Thirteen countries in this region (over half of them) have no available data for primary enrollment (UNDP, 2003). In most of Latin America and the Caribbean, gender parity in primary education has been reached, and while there are instances of greater female enrollment, "disparities to the disadvantage of boys appear to be a much less significant feature in primary education as the GPI in no case exceeds 1.04" (UNESCO, 2003, p. 47).

In 2002 about 104 million children of primary school age were not enrolled in school, of which 57% are girls. Most of these children reside in sub-Saharan Africa, South and West Asia, which suggests that gender disparities in those regions will persist in the near future. In sub-Saharan Africa as a whole, the schooling expansion has been weak while the population growth has been strong; therefore, the number of African children out of school increased by 17% during 1990–2000 (UNESCO, 2003).

Secondary Education. In these times of competitive global economy, it is very important to have access to secondary schooling if one expects to get a good job, especially for women, given the statistical discrimination in the labor force. Women's gross secondary school enrollment rate presents a very strong correlation with GNP per capita (.65) and with an increased presence of women in political office (.41; Grown, Gupta, & Khan, 2003). This suggests that women's education contributes both to national wealth and to more representative governance.

Universal access to primary education may still produce weak coverage at the secondary school level. Access to secondary school continues to be very limited in the developing world. Only 20% of the appropriate age group (both boys and girls) are enrolled in secondary school in sub-Saharan Africa; Latin America has the highest secondary school enrollment, with about 54% of the relevant age group compared to industrialized countries whose average is 91%.

By 2002, only 57 of 172 countries reported gender parity at the secondary school level (UNESCO, 2006). However, gender disparities in secondary education are less pronounced than those at the primary education level, which suggests that once the student remains in school for several years, their chances of withdrawing from it are lessened (perhaps because some parents become committed to a longer investment regardless of income). These statistics also suggest that the association between access to school and social class becomes stronger at the secondary school level.

In terms of gender parity at the secondary school level, Latin America and the Caribbean have equal or greater enrollment of girls and boys in 24 of 37 countries. In some countries there are fewer boys than girls in secondary schools because boys tend to participate in programs that are shorter and do not lead to tertiary education (UNESCO, 2006). This is not the situation in other developing regions; the extreme case is sub-Saharan Africa, where only 6 of 26 countries for which data are available report equal or greater proportions of girls' enrollment (UNESCO, 2003). Of 75 countries examined by UNICEF by the end of 2004 using health and demographic survey data (and thus a different calculation based on attendance), only 22 of 75 countries would be able to reach the goal of gender parity in secondary schooling by 2015, 21 needed to make additional efforts, and 25 were far from the stated goal (UNICEF, 2004). Only a few countries compile information on specific fields of study at the secondary school level by sex; the available data indicate that in all developing regions women represent less than half of the enrollment in vocational and technical training.

Tertiary Education. At a global level, women and men show very slight differences in their tertiary education enrollment. On a country level, gender disparities tend to favor women. At present, women have higher enrollment ratios than men in 47 of 93 countries (UNESCO, 2006). Men constitute the majority enrollment in 24 of 28 sub-Saharan countries, in 7 of 12 Arab States, in 7 of 11 East Asian developing countries, but in only 2 of 17 Latin American countries for which data are available (UNESCO, 2003). In Arab countries the preponderance of women is the result of men's going for university study abroad; in the case of Latin America, the picture is more complex. To some extent, more women go to university in order to be able to compete with men in the labor force; also, men can get satisfactory paying jobs in masculine jobs such as construction, transportation, and serving in the security forces.

The category "tertiary education" comprises different types and levels. UNESCO classifies tertiary education into three levels:

5A (programs that are theory based and prepare one for entry into advanced research programs and professions with high skill requirements), 5B (programs that offer practical, technical, or occupational skills), and 6 (programs focusing on advanced studies and original research, leading to masters and doctoral degrees). There are more women than men enrolled in level 5B, whereas at level 6 "women are much more often in the minority—even in more industrialized countries," except in a few such as Argentina, Uruguay, Jamaica, and Portugal (UNESCO, 2003, p. 81). Further, women tend to be overrepresented in fields of study such as education, social sciences, and the humanities and to be underrepresented in the natural sciences such as mathematics, engineering, and agriculture. This distribution by field of study has shown to be quite persistent over time and is a major source of income differentials when women and men join the labor force.

Between 1990 and 2000, the participation of women in the teaching profession continued to increase in almost all countries. However, in only one country (Bangladesh) is this the product of deliberate policies to foster the formal education of women teachers (UNESCO, 2003).

Literacy.   The acquisition of literacy is crucial for both sexes because it provides fundamental skills for the exercise of citizenship, and the education of parents has a strong and positive impact both on school enrollment and schooling attainment of their children. A key predictor of educational success is parental income and wealth, which in turn is associated with parental levels of schooling. For women, literacy stimulates an indispensable (though not by itself sufficient) ingredient for their political, social, and economic empowerment. In the past four decades, there have been decreases in the illiteracy rate; worldwide, 18% of adults are illiterate at present. Women account for 64% of the world's illiterates in all developing regions, a proportion that has changed only between 1990 and 2002 (UNESCO, 2006). China and India together comprise about 50% of the world's illiterates. China registered an important decrease of illiteracy between 1990 and 2000, mostly due to increased access in primary education. India is the country with the greatest literacy gender gap. During the same period, the numbers of illiterates increased in Bangladesh, Egypt, Ethiopia, India, and Pakistan—all countries with very large populations, but declined considerably in Brazil, Indonesia, and Nigeria. Literacy projections indicate that the gender distribution will continue to be stable, but that the disparity will increase in East Asia and the Pacific (due to population growth), where women are projected to comprise up to three quarters of the total illiterates by 2015 (UNESCO, 2003, p. 89).

School Completion

In most countries boys tend to repeat more than girls. Gender gaps in repetition are particularly large in some sub-Saharan African countries, some Arab states, and in Latin America and the Caribbean (UNESCO, 2003). It is unclear whether this happens because parents keep boys in school even though they may not perform well or girls take their studies more seriously and thus make better progress. Despite their higher repetition rates (i.e., the proposition of students who fail a grade), boys complete primary and secondary school at greater rates than girls in many parts of the world, including in sub-Saharan Africa.

There is no cross-national data about dropouts, but the reasons for dropping out seem to differ by sex. Boys are leaving more for economic reasons and girls for family reasons. Commonly young women leave school to take positions as household help, or in response to an early pregnancy and subsequent motherhood. Girls tend to drop out at higher rates than boys throughout sub-Saharan Africa because of the intensive domestic work demands (which include fuel and water procurement) and consequently have greater absenteeism than boys; they also leave due to early pregnancy. In Kenya, which has achieved nearly universal enrollment at the primary school level (with about 96% enrollment for both girls and boys), girls drop out a greater rate than boys at the secondary school level (UNESCO, 2003). Boys tend to repeat more frequently than girls at this level. In other regions, such as the former Soviet Asia and Latin America and the Caribbean, fourth-grade completion rates are equal or slightly higher for girls than for boys, which suggests that different cultural and economic rationales are at work, with poor boys entering manual work outside the home more easily than girls in those parts of the world. In Latin America and the Caribbean, girls have higher rates of secondary school completion than boys, a phenomenon also detected in some industrialized countries such as the U.S. and the U.K. This outcome has been attributed to: (a) the lower need for boys to graduate from school to obtain manual work, and (b) girls' perception that higher levels of education are needed to compete in the labor market. Still, because of the historical disadvantage of women in most societies, women have fewer years of education than men. South America has presently attained secondary enrollment parity (and even slightly surpassed it in favor of girls); it now reports a mean achievement for girls in the 20–24 age group of 8 years of schooling for girls and 7.4 years for boys. The school attainment of women in this age group is as low as 4.8 years in Western and Middle Africa and as high as 10.8 in former Soviet Asia (Lloyd, 2005).

Factors that affect educational access and completion are similar across the world: poverty, rural residence, and affiliation with a minority group. In developing countries, both poor and non-poor households have greater enrollments in urban compared to rural areas. When school fees are charged, this has a substantial impact on the poor, as they represent about 20–30% of household income in poor families (Herz & Sperling, 2003). Gender disparities interact with social class, ethnicity, and urban/rural residence; for instance, in Guatemala only 46% of indigenous girls at age 13 attend school in contrast to 75% of their nonindigenous peers. In India, every day girls conduct three major household tasks (fetching water and fuel, and caring for children) that consume considerable time and energy, leaving little opportunity for study. Moreover, many parents tend to enroll their daughters in state-run schools and their sons in private or English-speaking schools, which enables sons to gain a better education and a greater possibility of better remunerated jobs (Shukla & Nischint, 2004). An important data set combining sex, social class, and level of education (proxied by age group) was collected between 1991 and 2001 in 45 developing countries. Analysis of such data showed that social class has a stronger effect on educational achievement than gender—an effect that increases as poor girls reach puberty (Lloyd, 2005). Within each social class segment and age group, being a woman produces greater disadvantage than being a man, and this disadvantage increases dramatically at the tertiary level of education. A recent regional study for Latin America (OREALC/UNESCO, 2004), focusing on youth 15–19 years of age and based on household surveys, estimates that 26% of the population in that age group, or about 6 million youth, do not complete primary education. The same study finds that educational disparities are most severe by income and then by residence (although the two overlap), rather than by sex. This finding had lead institutions such as the UNESCO Regional Office for Latin America and the Caribbean (OREALC/UNESCO, 2004) to assert that the existing disparities are a problem of *equity*, meaning that they require focalized action on the most needed groups, and, by implication, not on women or girls. This perspective is being adopted by a number of national governments and represents a limited understanding of the impacts of gender (Lewis & Lockheed, 2006).

BEYOND ACCESS

Access to schooling is unquestionably crucial. The content of knowledge gained—both explicit and implicit—while attending school is *equally* important. If content and the lived experience of learning were not important, there would be no gender problems in industrialized countries, including the United States, where the differences in enrollment rates between boys and girls at the primary level have been nil for many decades now and where girls slightly surpass boys at the secondary and tertiary levels of education (Bae et al., 2000).

Education participation statistics are easier to collect than are changes in perceptions and practices regarding the roles and possibilities of women and men in society. Educational access and attainment alone do not indicate that gender problems no longer exist; in most societies one can still document an asymmetrical distribution of political and economic power. On the average women earn 77% of what men earn in industrial countries and 73% of what men earn in developing countries. In most developing countries, except notably for Latin America and the former Soviet Asia, women do not have access to equality in terms of inheritance rights, property rights, and divorce rights (Lloyd, 2005).

In extreme cases, girls do not even have right to life, as reflected in the female infanticide rates that are reported in such countries as India and the abortion of female fetuses in China. In fact, China presents the worst case of "missing girls": while the world has an average of 105 boys for 100 girls, China had 119 boys for 100 girls in 2004, and one province, Anxi, had 134 boys for 100 girls ("In a Decade," 2005). As the country with the world's largest population—1.3 billion—China's absolute numbers of "missing women" are staggering.

Educational indicators cannot be adequately assessed independent of the cultural, social, economic, and political conditions of men and women in their respective countries. A question of fundamental importance should be: How is the education system contributing to securing the benefits of gender equality in society?

Some useful indicators of gender equity in society would include decreases of gender stereotypes in educational materials, and the questioning of gender ideologies underlying the curriculum. It would also include analyzing data related to the school and classroom climate such as gender equitable instruction and resources, gender fair teacher/student interaction styles without sexual harassment, non-sex biased teacher expectations of student academic and occupational performance, and actively counteracting gender stereotypes in sports and related extracurricular activities. There are few studies in developing countries that explore the socialization process in schools, and how gender relations are produced and reproduced on an everyday basis. Most evidence from developing regions comes from content analysis of textbooks. The majority of these studies indicates that there have in fact been efforts to remove sexual stereotypes from textbooks and that significant changes have occurred in the use of illustrations and a sex-neutral language; less progress has occurred in the funding and development of content favorable to the creation of positive identities among women and in the introduction of sex education programs in the curriculum. Nordic countries have been successful in decreasing male stereotypes and improving male parenting skills through various schools interventions—an effort that has taken place over close to four decades.

Research from the U.K., Australia, Canada, and the U.S. are the strongest sources of data about classroom changes. One of the few studies in developing countries explored the relationship between teacher attitudes about the teachability of boys and girls and their respective academic performance in Kenya. It found that girls were affected by negative teacher attitudes toward them but boys were not (Lloyd, 2005, citing Appleton, 1995). Another study, also in Kenya, found that various indicators of gender treatment by teachers, controlling for family and several indicators of school quality, were associated with the probability of dropout for girls but not for boys (Lloyd et al., 2000, cited in Lloyd 2005). Both studies suggest greater vulnerability of girls than boys to negative treatment and expectations. Qualitative studies from schools in different parts of sub-Saharan Africa (Guinea, Kenya, Malawi, and Togo) indicate that both male and female teachers display negative attitudes toward girls in their verbal comments and their behavior. In other parts of the world, such as Egypt and Pakistan, boys are more often than girls targets of physical punishment. About the Arab world, a recent UNDP report asserts, "hopes that Arab educational systems would overturn the influence of patriarchal upbringing on individuals have been frustrated" for lack of political will to act upon this issue (2003, p. 151). In the case of sub-Saharan Africa, though based on anecdotal data, there appears to exist a pervasive sexual harassment and exploitation of girls by teachers using the threat of poor grades in many African schools. This suggests the urgency of working on improving the school environment to make it more girl-friendly (Quist-Arcton, 2003). Girls are especially vulnerable to sexual harassment in countries undergoing interstate or internal conflict, which affects one fourth of all African countries (Mazunrana, 2004). In rural areas, particularly in several African countries, the lack of access to sanitary facilities affects adolescent girls during their menstrual period, causing absences that make girls fall behind in their academic subjects.

STUDENT PERFORMANCE

International comparisons of student learning, which center mostly on math and reading, are relatively recent, since the 1960s, and they often include comparisons by sex. The First International Mathematics Study (Husen, 1967), centering on 13-year-old students, found that boys did better than girls in verbal and computational skills for all 12 countries in the study, but it found no statistically significant differences among countries. Twenty-two years later, the Second International Mathematics Study examined two age groups: age 8 and age 14. Among the 8-year-old group, Robitaille (1989) found changes in gender performance as statistical differences in favor of boys were detected in only 3 countries and in favor of girls in 4 of the 12 countries in the study. Focusing on the 14-year-old students, Garden (1989) found boys did better than girls in a small number of the 15 countries in the study. A decade later, the Third International Mathematics and Science Study (TIMSS) also found gender differences in math and science: few differences were found at grades 4 and 8, but by the end of secondary school, 18 of 21 countries showed greater achievements by boys in math and science (Mullis, Martin, Fierros, Goldberg, & Stemler, 2000).

On the other hand, more recent international comparisons show that girls do better in reading. The Progress in International Reading Literacy Study (popularly known as PIRLS 2001), involving 35 countries and focusing on fourth-grade students, found that girls did better than boys in reading literacy in all countries in the study (Mullis, Martin, Gonzalez, & Kennedy, 2003). Similar results favoring girls in reading have also been found in the PISA (Programme for International Student Assessment) 2000 study, which examined performance in reading, math, and science of students age 15. It found that girls performed better in reading than boys in all of the 42 countries in the study, and in most countries the differences were substantial. PISA found more boys than girls performing at the lowest level of reading in all countries. In contrast, boys did better than girls in math in 34 of the 42 countries, but the differences were smaller than those registered by girls for reading. In science, the performance of both sexes was similar (UNESCO Institute for Statistics/OECD, 2003). TIMMS and PISA coincide regarding the outcomes in math by sex, but girls were found to reach better scores in the PISA study, which has been attributed to the different natures of the tests, with PISA having more open-ended and contextualized items that may have favored girls, while TIMMS had more multiple-choice items that may have favored boys.

The fact that girls' progress in mathematics has been improving over time, even though boys still perform better, suggests that math ability is not innate but susceptible to social influences and instruction. Far from reflecting differences in intellectual ability, this differential performance by sex—with girls improving their performance over time—has been attributed to the fact that girls "see education more consciously as an opportunity to break their family's cycle of poverty or to further improve the quality of their lives" (UNESCO, 2003, p. 105). PISA found that girls have a higher interest in reading than boys and spend more time reading, while boys show a greater interest in mathematics than girls. PISA also found that in 40 out of 42 countries girls had higher expectations toward their perceived occupations at age 30 than boys. Noting that in poor countries women do not have high representations in higher education, UNESCO (2003) observes that some girls "never have a chance to demonstrate their motivation and ability to learn. This is not only unjust. It represents a vast waste of talent for the girls concerned and for society at large" (p. 107). It is also important to remember that better performance on an academic test alone will not benefit women. In the U.K. girls have been performing better than boys in the secondary school completion certification (GCSE) since 1975, something that occurs because girls have been able to keep their advantage in English and to register improvements in math and science. Yet, women continue to experience subordinate positions in the labor force in that country (Arnot, David, & Weiner, 1990), in part due to insufficient attempts to use schools to question social stereotypes regarding masculinity and femininity. No comparable data exist for developing countries.

EDUCATIONAL POLICIES

A key mechanism to promote and accelerate change in the social relations of gender is through public policies. In the area of education in developing countries, it is difficult to find specific policies to help girls and women, like the U.S. Title IX, which prohibits discrimination of the basis on sex in education programs and activities (see the "Governance" chapter and chapter 1, this volume). One notable exception seems to be Taiwan, which in 2004 adopted a Gender Equity Act (covering educational institutions from kindergarten to the university level) against sexual discrimination and sexual harassment, and to foster gender-fair learning environments and materials. Much of the progress in female enrollment is due to the expansion of schooling rather than to measures focusing on ending discrimination against girls. Women's participation in tertiary education does not seem related to a country's level of economic development, although very poor countries do show very low enrollment rates for women at the tertiary level of education.

While basic education is a universal right and is protected by many national constitutions, some 43 countries (most of them in sub-Saharan Africa) do not offer such guarantees and many do not enforce compulsory attendance laws. School fees are still in effect in many sub-Saharan countries, a condition that affects girls more than boys because poor parents are less willing to pay fees for their daughters. It has been estimated that at least 101 developing countries charge school fees at the primary level (Tomasevski, 2003, cited in UNESCO, 2003, p. 132). This practice of charging fees has become necessary in recent years because of the low budgets allocated for public education, caused in turn by structural adjustment programs, which have severely reduced government investment in public education (UNESCO, 2003, Reimers, 1994). Rendering even more serious an already negative situation is the failure of a large number of countries to gather complete educational statistics. In 2003, gross enrollment rates for primary education, the most basic of statistics, were missing from 36% of the countries, and repetition data were missing for 53%.

It is difficult to find developing countries that have enacted, much less implemented, specific education policies to enhance women's participation in a widened definition of social and economic life. Policies to expand access to schooling are not sufficient to alter conceptions of masculinity and femininity; measures to attract and retain girls and women in formal education are needed. Such measures are necessary to counter the social attitudes of domesticity and exclusive dedication to motherhood held by peers, family, and prevailing women role models. Measures to encourage female students have been designed to reduce costs of schooling, give guidance to promote the choice of nonconventional fields of study, provide part-time programs for women, and launch public awareness campaigns. Compensatory programs (i.e., those targeted on very poor populations) focusing on girls' education are very limited. Exceptions to this pattern are: (a) PROGRESA (now *Oportunidades*), a sustained program for rural families in Mexico, which gives grants conditioned on the children's school attendance to grades 3–9 and provides slightly greater stipends for girls in the first three years of secondary schooling, and (b) the Female Secondary School Stipend Program in Bangladesh. By 2001, PROGRESA was covering 2.5 million families in over 2,000 municipalities and its successor, *Oportunidades*, was reaching about 5 million families by 2005. Evaluations of the program showed it had produced modest gains in girls' enrollment, permanence in schooling, and transition from primary to secondary schooling (Murphy-Graham, 2003).

The Bangladeshi program—also of large magnitude, reaching over 500,000 girls by 1995 and providing free tuition and a monthly stipend—has succeeded in increasing girls' enrollment, sometimes fivefold and promoting good attendance for both girls and boys (UNESCO, 2003; Khandker, Pitt, & Fuwa, 2003). Measures that have promoted girls' success in schooling also include the provision of nonformal education, such as those of Bangladesh BRAC schools in small rural communities, which attempt to enroll at least 70% girls, and the Quetta Girls' Fellowship program in Balochistan, Pakistan, that provides subsidies for private schools to offer basic education for low-income students. The BRAC schools, in existence since 1985, now number 40,000 and have served close to 8% of the primary school population in the country. The Quetta program is small, reaching some 10,000 students in schools that comprise about 30% girls. Both programs have succeeded in increasing the educational enrollment and completion of girls. Another form of compensatory programs aimed at girls has been the use of lowered selection criteria for the admission of girls relative to boys into secondary schools in Malawi and Ethiopia. This intervention seems limited to some schools and it is not clear whether and how effectively it has been operating, or whether it is even still functioning.

Other compensatory programs worth citing are those in India (the District Primary Education Program, DPEP), Brazil (*Bolsa Escola*, now termed *Bolsa Familia*), and Nicaragua (*Red de Protección Social*), all three for primary education students, and Colombia (PACES) for secondary school students. All aim at low-income groups and do not provide differential support by sex since educational authorities do not recognize a gender problem. Action focusing on the education of girls and women can be found in a handful of countries and comprises mostly timid and pilot-level interventions. An exception to this seems to be India, which reports a new plan Sarva Shiksha Abhiyan (SSA) to have all children complete fifth grade by 2007 and will invest $1 billion to that effect. India also has a nonformal education program (Mahila Samakya), now implemented in 9,000 villages in 10 states, and residential colleges for girls, some 750, centering on scheduled castes, scheduled tribes, and other *backward classes* (as disadvantaged groups are termed). The government has instituted a 2% tax to generate $1 billion per year to provide universal education for all children ages 6–14, while its National Policy for Empowerment of Women 2001 seeks to provide comprehensive services to adolescent girls. In India by law since 2001, free meals are to be given in all state-run schools to children ages 6–10. This policy has raised attendance but is not being evenly applied (Shukla and Nischint, 2004). Although the Indian DPEP is targeted at districts where female literacy is below the national average, it is difficult to assess its success. Overall, India reports an improved gender parity index for basic education from .38 in 1950 to .85 in 2002 (India, 2005; EPA Global Monitoring Report 2003/04, 2003).

A number of small-scale gender equity measures have been implemented in several developing countries. These include empowerment programs under the name *Tuseme* (meaning *speaking out* in Swahili), tried in a number of schools in six African countries to combat the sexual harassment of girls (Quist-Arcton, 2003). Since the lack of sanitary facilities has such a detrimental effect on girls, Uganda now has a pilot project to discuss sexual maturation within communities and to explore the possibility of removing taxes on sanitary materials and manufacturing them locally (Kanyka, Akankwasa, & Karungi, 2004). In Brazil, a program in place since 1987 provides information on reproductive health, sexually transmitted diseases and AIDS, human rights, and advocacy. It provides brochures and materials for students, parents, and teachers and seeks to reach 1,000 schools by 2005. In higher education, the World Bank has engaged in measures such as scholarships, creation of new residences for young women attending university, vocational or technical education programs, reserving a small number of places for women in nonconventional fields of study, particularly engineering and agriculture (DePietro-Jurand, 1993); these initiatives are mostly pilot studies with little follow-up.

Deserving special mention is a five-year effort (1996–2001) undertaken by the U.S. Agency for International Development in Guatemala, Guinea, Mali, Morocco, and Peru, with the objectives of increasing girls' primary school enrollment, retention, and completion. The project involved the host country's government, the private sector, and nongovernmental organizations (NGOs). Most of the activities centered on social awareness initiatives, the provision of scholarships, and the expansion of schools; little effort went to curriculum development and teacher training. The results indicate gains in girls' enrollment and retention in three of the five countries, but increases in completion in only two countries (Juarez & Associates, 2002), which highlights the need for deeper and longer interventions.

Most developing countries have no policies to introduce gender issues in the pre-service training of teachers. Several countries have engaged in gender training of in-service teachers and such efforts have covered small numbers of the teaching staffs and been sporadic. Even less frequent has been the gender training of educational administrators and key decision-makers. Taiwan emerges as an exception, since its gender equity policy (cited previously) explicitly requires the introduction of gender issues in the pre-service training of teachers. The Taiwanese policy calls for a decision-making committee at the institutional levels (schools or universities), calling for no less than one third of the members to be of either sex (Taiwan Government, 2004). At present, however, university presidents from three major national universities in Taiwan have expressed opposition to the 16 regulations mandated by the equity law. The absence of effective gender training programs has been a major source of difficulty in the implementation of gender as a crosscutting theme in the curriculum.

Global Policy Efforts

Since 1990, through a series of international conferences and agreements, women's education has been identified as being crucial to national development and a more democratic world. Especially important among the policies resulting from these meetings are the Education for All (EFA) objectives internationally approved in Dakar in 2000, and the Millennium Development Goals (MDGs) enacted by the United Nations in the same year (United Nations, 2000). These policies were drafted with little input from women's groups, which protested that the new goals dealt superficially with agreements made in previous world forums, particularly the International Conference on Population and Development (Cairo, 1994) and the Fourth Women's World Conference (Beijing, 1995).

Education for All. EFA lists six goals that comprise the whole range of educational levels, from early childhood education to adult literacy. It seeks gender parity in basic education by 2005 and at all levels of education by 2015. Most importantly, it seeks universal access to basic education for both girls and boys by 2015.

EFA policies have been described as "target-setting exercises," namely centrally identified benchmarks, with little recognition of the characteristics of the problem nor any formulation of actual steps to accomplish and evaluate the benchmarks (Goldstein, 2004). Countries are to respond to EFA policies by developing national plans of action. Although all signatory nations were committed to developing plans by 2002, a review of such plans in 2003 found that a large number of countries had failed to comply, with EFA plan completion rates going from a high of 80% for countries in South Asia to a low of 20% of the countries for Latin America. The available evidence indicates that over 70 countries failed to reach gender parity in primary education by the target date of 2005 and that the elimination of illiteracy by half will not be reached by 2015 by many African countries. To put it differently, of the 100 countries that had not achieved gender parity in either primary or secondary education or both levels by 2002, only 14 were judged likely to achieve gender parity by 2015 (UNESCO, 2006). Further, 86 countries were considered "at risk of not achieving" parity in primary education, 55 in secondary education, and 24 in both (UNESCO, 2006, p. 71). Facing this situation, the UNESCO Monitoring report concluded, "Gender disparities in enrollment remain the rule rather than the exception and present trends are insufficient for the Dakar goals to be met" (UNESCO, 2006, p. 71).

To promote girls' education within the EFA framework, the United Girls' Education Initiative (UNGEI) was established under the leadership of UNICEF. UNGEI detected a number of promising equity strategies being attempted in a handful of developing countries. These included such things as reducing distance between home and school; school expansion in Egypt, India, and Indonesia; serving hard-to-reach outlying groups in Bangladesh, Burkina Faso, and India; developing leadership skills for girls in South Africa and Uganda) . One of the biggest problems observed was in extending the implementation from pilot projects to nationwide interventions. UNGEI also noted that substantial obstacles reside in the scarcity of technically skilled personnel but even more, the lack of political will and commitment (Subrahmanian, 2005).

MDGs. This global policy recognizes two of the EFA goals: universal access to basic education by 2015, and gender parity in primary education by 2005 and at all levels by 2015. While the MDGs continue to recognize the importance of education, they reduce the EFA goals by not paying attention to early childhood education, by failing to include the goal of improving the quality of education, and by limiting the efforts in favor of literacy to the population ages 15–24 only, thus missing important demographic bands among women, such as the 25–45-age group, which would seem crucial in intergenerational, social, and political processes. The measurement of basic education in the MDGs reduces it to the completion of four years of school. This measurement is high for some countries, but for several others, it is a very modest indicator and in some cases, notably Latin America, it represents a step backward. (Regression analyses of the progress toward meeting all six EFA goals find that the best predictor is gender parity in basic education, closely followed by adult literacy (UNESCO, 2003). Similar influences of parental literacy on children's education have been found in industrialized countries). This evidence indicates that while it is correct to focus on formal education, it is also important to address the parents' literacy—something that current MDG indicators do not consider.

The MDGs constitute an endorsement of the goals expressed and approved at previous global forums: in Copenhagen (1993, human rights), Cairo (1994, population and development), Beijing (1995, women and development); and Dakar (2000, education for all). However, the plans for implementing these MDGs has not been accompanied by an adequate examination of the effectiveness of previous policies. This raises questions about the seriousness of global policies, which are unanimously agreed upon by government delegates, occasionally enacted into law, and rarely adequately funded and executed. An evaluation by women's groups of the achievement of objectives set forward at the Beijing conference came to the conclusion that the current nature of the global economy, dominated by a reduced participation by the state in social investment (including education), had resulted in increased poverty and deepened inequalities. The evaluation acknowledged that girls' primary education enrollment had improved, except in sub-Saharan Africa and West Asia. It also observed that dropout and illiteracy rates remained higher for girls than boys, and that inequalities in secondary and higher education as well as gender stereotypes in textbooks persist (WEDO, 2005).

The issue of the education of adult women is critical, especially in the context of developing countries, and deserves more consideration. From a gender perspective, the MDGs seem responsive to women, as their Goal No. 3 explicitly addresses their empowerment. It proposes four indicators to measure empowerment: the girls/boys enrollment ratio in primary schooling, the ratio of literate females to males ages 15–24, gender parity in labor force participation, and the proportion of seats held by women in national parliaments.

The tying of empowerment to education is warranted, yet it is clear that not all education automatically empowers. Focusing on the literacy acquisition of only the 15–24-age group ignores the social reproduction effect that the older generations may have on the younger. By looking at employment, while disregarding additional factors linked to participation in the labor force, the definition of empowerment ignores issues of occupational clustering and salary differential. The proportion of seats held by women in national parliaments is left undefined. How much is adequate? The indicator also disregards the need for gender-sensitive training among female (and male) politicians. One needs to think of empowerment as multidimensional. It is achieved not only through an understanding of gender relations and the ways in which these can be changed, but also through the set of learning mechanisms in ongoing socialization experiences. In order to develop a sense of self-worth among women, they need to develop the ability to generate choices, exercise bargaining power, and foster the ability to organize and influence the direction of social change (as proposed in the definition of empowerment developed by UNIFEM (2004; see also Stromquist, 2002).

The main mechanism by which to assess how countries comply with the MDGs is through their submission of annual reports to the United Nations Development Programme (UNDP), the agency in charge of monitoring progress in the implementation. By 2007, more than 140 countries had produced such annual reports. An examination of these plans by UNIFEM (2003) found that the discussion of women "continues to be instrumental rather than rights-based" (p. 25). Moreover, a very important MDG regional report for Latin America, produced by OREAL/UNESCO (2004), presents recent statistics on educational access and completion for the respective countries but fails to discuss what measures (if any) governments are putting in place to attain the MDG indicators in education.

Rarely do governments establish contact with women's groups who advocate gender-sensitive education. One exception is the Forum for African Women Educationalists (FAWE). In existence since 1991, this group's core membership comprises women who are or have been ministers of education, vice chancellors, or similar educational authorities, and men in similar positions, who serve as FAWE associate members. This group has succeeded in establishing effective alliances with donor agencies and in securing funds not only to advocate girls' access to schooling, but also to conduct campaigns to raise public awareness of the importance of girls' education and to implement interventions that introduce gender-sensitive teaching methodologies into the classroom (Mlama, 2005). There is no counterpart organization in the other developing regions.

In all, both national and global educational policies have learned to recognize the importance of women's education. Unfortunately, the participation of groups concerned with women's rights has seldom been an element in policy formulation, and the level of rhetorical appreciation is much greater than actual investment and action on this matter. Surprisingly, international donor agencies' support for education in developing countries declined in 2000 to $3.5 billion, which represented 30% less than that allocated in 1990 (UNICEF, 2004).

CONCLUSIONS

In recent decades, the enrollment of girls at all levels of schooling has been increasing rapidly and faster than that of boys, except in very poor countries. Nonetheless, significant gender gaps remain, particularly at the primary and secondary school levels, conditions that reduce the pool of girls moving to higher levels of education. Despite the extensive literature documenting the positive and substantial impacts of women's education on a number of demographic, economic, and political indicators, weak public investments are made to promote girls' school access and attainment.

When noticing that girls' enrollment surpasses that of boys in primary and secondary education, preoccupation with "the reverse gender gap" has been generated in industrialized countries such as the U.S., the U.K., and Australia. It does appear that in some cases, notions of masculinity negatively affect the participation and even performance of boys in schooling, as reflected in their higher rates of repetition, primary and secondary school completion, and academic performance in reading (UNESCO, 2006). This phenomenon highlights the urgency of working on the content of schooling to alter gender mentalities in girls and boys, as well as the importance of working with the society at large in order to modify pervasive constructions of the function and place of men and women in society.

The evidence suggests that insufficient work is occurring in most national educational systems to modify curriculum content, textbooks, and teachers' skills and understanding of gender issues. As long as the work conducted to change these mentalities remains limited, the differential power between men and women in society will continue. Formal school systems resist change when it is not properly acknowledged. This resistance is also present among state bureaucracies and cultural institutions (such as the Catholic Church in Latin America and fundamentalist religions and norms in other developing regions that reinforce sex stereotypes), which, while endorsing the need for education that advances women's conditions, are reluctant to alter curriculum and practices so that they are designed to support more equitable gender ideologies. Despite the weak attention to gender equity in schooling, it may represent the strongest source of counter messages to traditional norms learned in the family, community, and national media. Literacy may also serve as a powerful means to access more progressive international sources such as those afforded by the Internet.

An understanding of gender theory and the growing empirical evidence show that it is most unlikely that government programs will foster gender empowerment. Given the large number of illiterates who are women, the education of adult women must be a critical policy objective. The MDGs are failing to consider the organized groups most likely to promote empowerment of women. By so doing, they miss a crucial step in the realization of their own goal of improving women's status in society. In addition to government policies and laws stemming from the Convention on the Elimination of All Forms of Discrimination Against Women (CEDAW) and the Universal Declaration of Human rights, it is important for feminist groups and related progressive groups to continue to question the status quo that maintains gender asymmetries. The creation of a new culture of modified gender relations, admittedly a tall order, is essential, but is an issue that the MDG indicators do not touch. They simplify the notion of empowerment, co-opting the term, but not recognizing its full meaning.

It should be observed with some alarm that educational gaps between the developing and the industrialized countries are increasing considerably. Since 1985, the years of educational attainment have remained stable in developing countries—at about 5 years of schooling on average—while the educational attainment rate in industrialized countries has moved to 15 years (Orivel, 2004). With such dramatic contrasts as Canada with 17 years of schooling and Mali or Niger with less than 2, one must not lose sight that inequalities should be faced not only along gender lines, but also globally across countries. A discussion of debt relief to all developing countries—distant as it may seem at first face from specific gender concerns—would open the possibility to increase national allocations for expenditures on EFA. At the present time, about $100 billion per year goes to countries in the north as the developing countries repay their external debt. Global equity seems to be a necessary ingredient in efforts to reduce gender inequalities throughout the world.

SPECIFIC RECOMMENDATIONS FOR POLICY, PRACTICE AND RESEARCH

In the area of policy decision-making, the following measures are advisable:

- involving institutions of civil society, especially women-led NGOs, that support the education of girls and women
- addressing problems of structural adjustment and conditionality facing national governments to make more funds from national budgets available to education (see Marphatia and Archer, 2005, for a detailed examination of how international financial institutions forced budget rigidities on developing countries)
- working to create stronger links between education, gender objectives, and health in global policies, proposed in the MDGs
- providing more funding and trained staff for the women's offices now established in the national government machinery of most countries
- develop and implement school policies that do not expel pregnant girls, but rather enable them to complete their studies
- working with NGOs that promote women's rights so that education programs that foster empowerment are both developed and put into effect
- applying innovations (such as that proposed by Unterhalter, Kioko-Echessa, Pattman, Rajagopalan, & N'Jai, 2004) to measure not only girls' attendance and retention at the primary

and secondary school levels, but also to monitor national progress over time.

Practical measures to be expanded would include:

- providing recurrent gender training to teachers, administrators, and policy-makers
- creating safe school environments to protect children, girls and young from sexual harassment by adults and peers, both in school and university settings
- producing appealing and nonsexist educational materials
- offering increased and sustained training to parents and communities on gender issues, including the importance of girls' and women's education
- providing accelerated programs for girls who have been out of school for several years
- designing and implementing general practices to welcome adolescent mothers and pregnant girls in school settings
- providing or improving sanitary supplies and facilities for girls so they don't have to worry about absences due to menstruation
- supplying meals to poor students attending primary schools, thus diminishing economic expenditures for poor families
- providing adult education and especially literacy programs linking literacy to the development of democratic social relations.

In the area of research, useful initiatives would be:

- collecting comparable education data from all countries using high-quality and sex-disaggregated statistics
- conducting cross-national analysis of the presentation of gender issues in curriculum content and educational materials
- tracking girls receiving stipends over time to examine family dynamics that such support creates to enable girls to attend and remain in school
- understanding how teacher training programs deal (or fail to deal) with gender issues
- carrying out case studies to identify obstacles to the implementation of progressive educational policies that seek to promote girl-friendly environments and to change the social relations of gender
- conducting rigorous evaluations to identify effective gender-sensitive and gender-transformative interventions.

Some of these measures will require a redeployment of current funding and efforts to achieve greater efficiency and creative management; it is imperative that allocation of more funds to public education be the crucial first step.

ACKNOWLEDGMENT

Review comments made by the editors of this *Handbook* and by Jane Schubert (American Institutes for Research, Washington, DC) and Marlaine Lockheed (former World Bank official and currently a visiting fellow at the Center for Global Development, Washington, DC.) are greatly acknowledged.

References

Arnot, M., David, M., & Weiner, G. (1999). *Closing the gender gap in education.* Cambridge, UK: Polity Press.

Bae, Y., Choy S., Geddes, C, Sable, J. & Snyder, T. (2002). *Trends in educational equity of girls and women.* Washington, D.C.: Office of Educational Research and Improvement, U.S. Department of Education

DePietro-Jurand, R. (1993).*Women's access to higher education. A review of the literature.* Washington, DC: The World Bank.

EFA Global Monitoring Report 2003/04. (2003). *Gender and education for all. The leap to quality.* Paris: UNESCO.

Filmer, D. (1999). *The structure of social disparities in education. gender and wealth.* Washington, DC: The World Bank.

Garden, R. (1989). Students' achievement: Population B. In D. Robitaille & R. Garden (Eds.), *The IEA Study of Mathematics II. Contexts and outcomes of school mathematics.* Oxford: Pergamon.

Goldstein, H. (2004). The globalization of learning targets. *Comparative Education, 40*(1), 7–14.

Grown, C., Gupta, G. R., & Khan, Z. (2003, April). *Promises to keep: Achieving gender equality and the empowerment of women.* Background Paper of the Task Force on Education and Gender Equality. New York: Millennium Project.

Herz, B., & Sperling, G. What Works in Girls Education. Working draft, July 2003. Retrieved February 18, 2005, from http://www.savethe children.net/nepal.key_issues/girls_education.doc

Husen, T. (1967). International study of achievement in mathematics: A comparison of twelve countries. Stockholm: Almqvist and Wiksell.

In a decade 40 million bachelors without mates. (2005, January 31). *San Francisco Chronicle*, p. A6.

India. National Plan of Action. Retrieved June 5, 2005, from http://portal.unesco.org/education/en/ev.php

Juarez & Associates. (2002, May 31). *USAID Girls' Education Initiatives in Guatemala, Guinea, Mali, Morocco, and Peru: A performance review.* Washington, DC: Girls' Education Monitoring System.

Kanyke, F., Akankwasa, D., & Karungi, C. (2004, September). Menstruation as a barrier to gender equality in Uganda. *Insights Education, 3.* Retrieved November 20, 2005, from www.id21.org/insights/insights-ed03/insights-issed03-art 03.html.

Khandker, S, Pitt, M., & Fuwa, N. (2003, March). *Subsidy to promote girls' secondary education. The Female Stipend Program in Bangladesh.* Washington, DC: The World Bank.

King, E., & Hill, A. (Eds.). (1993). *Women's education in developing countries: Barriers, benefits, and policies.* Baltimore: Johns Hopkins Press.

Lewis, M., & Lockheed, M. (2006). *Inexcusable absence.* Washington, D.C.: Center for Global Development.

Lloyd, C. (Ed.). (2005). *Growing up global: The changing transitions to adulthood in developing countries.* Washington, DC: The National Academic Press.

Marphatia, A., & Archer, D. (2005, September). *Contradicting commitments. How the achievement of education for all is being undermined by the International Monetary Fund.* London: ActionAid. International.

Mazunrana, D. (2004, September). Reintegrating girls from fighting forces in Africa. *Insights Education, 3.* Retrieved November 20, 2005, from www.id21.org/insights/insights-ed03/insights-issed03-art 06.html

Mlama, P. (2005). Pressure from within: The Forum for African Women Educationalists. In N. Rao & I. Smyth (Eds.), *Partnerships for girls' education* (pp. 49–63). Dorset, UK: Oxfam.

Mullis, I., Martin, M., Fierros, E., Goldberg, A., & Stemler, S. (2000). *Gender differences in achievement. IEA's Third International Mathe-*

matics and Science Study (TIMMS). Chestnut Hill, MA: TIMMS International Study Center, Boston College.

Mullis, I, Martin, M., Gonzalez, E., & Kennedy, A. (2003). *PIRLS 2001. International report: IEA's study of reading literacy achievement in primary schools.* Chestnut Hill, MA: Boston College.

Murphy-Graham, E. (2003, February). PROGRESA/*Oportunidades* case study. Cambridge: Graduate School of Education, Harvard University. (Draft)

OREALC/UNESCO. (2004, October). *Informe Regional sobre los Objetivos de Desarrollo del Milenio Vinculados a la Educación. La Conclusión Universal de la Educación Primaria en América Latina. ¿Estamos Realmente Tan Cerca?* Santiago: OREALC/UNESCO.

Orivel, F. (2004, March). *Atteindre l'éducation pour tous en 2014 est-il un objectif réalisable?* Paper presented at the annual conference of the Comparative and International Education Society, Salt Lake City, Utah.

Quist-Arcton, O. (2003, June). Fighting prejudice and sexual harassment of girls in Schools. *All Africa, 12.* Retrieved November 20, 2005, from http://www.globalpolicy.org/socecon/unequal/2003/0512girls.htm

Reimers, F. (1994). Education and structural adjustment in Latin America and sub-Saharan Africa. *International Journal of Educational Development, 14*(2), 119–129.

Robitaille, D. (1989). Students' achievement: Population A. In D. Robitaille & R. Garden (Eds.). *The IEA Study of Mathematics II. Contexts and outcomes of school mathematics.* Oxford: Pergamon.

Shukla, S., & Nischint, H. (2004, September). Providing for pre-adolescent girls in India. September 2004. *Insights Education, 3.* Retrieved November 20, 2005, from www.id21.org/insights/insights-ed03/insights-issed02-art 06.html

Stromquist, N. (2002). Education as a means for empowering women. In J. Parpart, S. Rai, & K. Staudt (Eds.). *Rethinking empowerment. Gender and development in a global/local world.* London: Routledge.

Subrahmanian, R. (2005). *"Scaling Up" good practices in girls' education.* Paris: UNESCO.

Taiwan Government. (2004, June 25). Gender Equity Education Act. Taipei: Taiwan Government.

UNDP. (2003). *Arab human development report 2003. Building a knowledge society.* New York: United Nations Development Program.

UNESCO. (2003). *EFA Global Monitoring Report. Gender and education for all. The leap to equality.* Paris: UNESCO.

UNESCO. (2006). *EFA Global Monitoring Report. Gender and education for all. Literacy for life.* Paris: UNESCO.

UNESCO Institute for Statistics/OECD. (2003). *Literacy skills for the world of tomorrow—Further results from PISA 2000.* Montreal/Paris: UNESCO-UIS/OECD.

UNICEF. (2004). *The state of the world's children. Girls, education and development.* New York: UNICEF.

UNIFEM. (2004). *Pathway to gender equality. CEDAW, Beijing and the MDGs.* New York: UNIFEM.

UNIFEM. (2003). *Millenium development goals. A look through a gender lens.* New York: UNDP.

United Nations. (2000). *U.N. Millennium Development Goals.* New York: U.N. General Assembly.

Unterhalter, E., Kioko-Echessa, E., Pattman, R., Rajagopalan, R., & N'Jai, F. (c2004). *Scaling up girls' education: Towards a scorecard on girls' education in the Commonwealth.* Institute of Education, University of London and Oxfam GB.

WEDO. (2005). *Beijing betrayed: The women of the world are watching.* New York: Women's Environment and Development Organization.

·4·

IMPACT OF EDUCATION ON GENDER EQUITY IN EMPLOYMENT AND ITS OUTCOMES

Barbara Richardson and Pamela Sandoval

INTRODUCTION

This chapter focuses on the impact of education on women's status and employment in today's global labor market. Educational credentials are necessary but not always sufficient to assure fair rewards and recognition in girls' and women's jobs and careers. While educational skills prepare young women for work, they rarely provide them with all the tools needed to combat the gender inequities that pervade the job market. The degree to which education is gender fair determines how well women can support themselves and their families. In this chapter, we analyze the relationship between education and lifetime economic outcomes. Without intergenerational understanding of discrimination beyond the schools, little change or constructive remedies can occur. We must continue to seek equity so that boys and girls are treated fairly in schools and are equally prepared for a wide range of careers.

We also need to prepare our daughters and sons to anticipate the economic consequences of their vocational choices. They need to understand that regardless of social class or educational level achieved, gender roles shape the wages men and women receive and the nature of the workplace they will experience. Schools need to expand gender role perceptions so that women no longer limit themselves in the kinds of jobs they choose. We need to expand thinking about the family so new patterns of thinking and behavior will redefine cultural expectations as to who is expected to take time off from work to care for sick children or elders. Education is a critical force in changing the traditional scenarios that have led to the inequal labor market we describe in this chapter.

An educated labor force is of immeasurable benefit to a nation and community. Internationally, for instance, women's education and employment have a major impact on recognized social development indicators, such as capital resources to promote an educated workforce and to promote purveyors of new tech-

nologies. These benefits include such critical outcomes as improved maternal and child health and nutrition, life expectancy, fertility and families' economic well-being (Chen, Vanek, Lund, & Heintz, 2005). While there is growing national and international recognition that women's work, both paid and unpaid, has far-reaching effects on the economy, environmental sustainability and the implementation of domestic policies, their work in the labor market remains undervalued. In short, there are profound rewards for engaging educated women in the work of the economy. When women's contributions to the labor force are treated with the value they deserve, the nation as a whole will benefit as well as women's families.

This chapter focuses on women to a greater extent than men, because men continue to receive greater economic rewards vis-à-vis their education than do women. The link between education and economic security is two fold. On one hand, education leads to higher wages (U.S. Department of Labor, 2002b). On the other hand, gender inequities greatly modify this relationship so that women, on average, must have higher levels of education to successfully receive wages similar to men with less education. For example, women with college degrees made only slightly more ($36,901) than men with high school diplomas ($32,689; U.S. Department of Labor, 2002a). Thus, a woman with a college degree makes $139 more per week than a man with a high school diploma and $246 less than a man with a college degree. In 2004, women earned, on average, 80.4% as much as men (U.S. Department of Labor, 2004). As we will show later in the chapter, women of color earn even less money relative to white men. These comparisons between men's wages and women's wages vary slightly depending upon the specific year and how differences were counted. They do, however, show a pattern toward growing equity, but at a snail's pace, and while these differences may seem small, they compound dramatically over the course of a woman's lifetime.

Throughout this chapter, we emphasize that education at any level contributes to women's abilities to compete successfully in the labor market. It is important to examine the status of women of all educational backgrounds and all levels of employment. For each woman with a PhD in academia, there are many more women with high school diplomas working on a computer assembly line or taking orders in a fast food restaurant. For example, in 2002 there were 51,000 women in economics and 58,000 women in biology and life sciences as compared to 619,000 women janitors and 564,000 women assemblers (Bergmann, 2005). Some of these women are unionized and have made great progress parlaying their educational resources into a leadership role in their union. Most women however, are not covered by unions and are more likely to be in the vulnerable, marginal labor force, last hired and first fired. Most commonly, they are relegated to part-time work and subject to layoffs. Few holding these types of jobs can count on health benefits or retirement contributions. Even though many of these women may have done well in high school, without a college degree, it is difficult for women to earn the kinds of wages needed to support their families.

Men and women remain quite segregated in today's labor force. Most women remain confined to low-paying, often entry-level positions in what is known as the pink-collar ghetto. This sector of the labor force represents a highly segregated set of positions primarily populated by women, for example, waitress, secretary, and beautician, and after some recent turnover in composition, even school bus driver. Unfortunately, state and federal funding for continuing education and job training focused on getting degrees has been essentially cut, especially for women on public assistance. There is far more media coverage for those few who have pressed the boundaries of gender in traditionally male and elite occupations. These high-achieving women represent a small minority of working women who have done well. Regardless of the educational levels they've come from and their hopes for where they're going, many women are working the third shift—balancing the roles of mother, employee, and student. Further, the familiar term *Feminization of Poverty* reminds us that workplace inequities accumulate over the lifetime, resulting in much higher rates of poverty among older women than older men.

This chapter is divided into two major sections. The first is titled *Socioeconomic Factors in Employment Outcomes*. The second half of the chapter, is titled *Cost and Remedies of Gender Inequity in the Labor Market*. After a preliminary review of the historical links between education and employment, the remainder of this chapter examines the returns of an education for women in the contemporary labor market. It concentrates on documenting the gender inequities in today's job market. We take a special look at women's participation in the sex-typed occupational strata and the links to wage inequities across the spectrum of women's educational achievements. In addition to looking at the short-term costs of discrimination to women, we examine the longer-term costs of a lifetime of part-time, low-paying jobs in the pink-collar ghetto. These jobs are generally without the benefits that characterize many of the better-educated women in the labor market. We go on to make the point that in today's economy an education can serve as a hedge against unemployment; yet, women remain especially vulnerable to cutbacks if they are in the marginal sectors of the labor force. The result for too many is poverty,

with women and children the largest portion of that population at the present time

The closing section of this chapter analyzes the many remedies, from pragmatic to theoretical, that have been proposed to improve women's status in the economy. Many of these recommendations are familiar to all, such as, calling for more relevant changes in vocational counseling, job training, and adult education. Another, more challenging set of policy requests comes from those working with existing job retraining for unemployed workers or those on public assistance. More recently, social "reform" efforts have led to cuts in the very budgets that might have provided for continuing education as a vehicle for social mobility. Feminists call for a reassessment of wages that women receive in traditional jobs as well as the value of women's labors in the home as wives and mothers. Their focus on reevaluating their occupational contributions to the larger social good is a radical one, but an idea that is gradually making its way through the courts (National Women's Law Center, 2000). We conclude with a reminder that as more women enter the nontraditional domains of the economy, they will also learn to devise the kinds of reforms that will foster greater gender equity for generations to come.

SOCIOECONOMIC FACTORS IN EMPLOYMENT OUTCOMES

Historical Impact of Education on Employment

During the past century, with the rise of technology, and the move away from farming and manual labor toward service occupations, the link between formal education and employment has changed dramatically for both men and women. The 19th century movement of women into education and the workplace was strongly related to the industrial revolution or the move from *Gemeinschaft* communities to those known as *Gesellschaft* societies. During this transition, large numbers of men and women moved from self-employment on farms or small businesses to employment for wages. Middle- and upper-class women were more likely to be educated and become housewives after marriage. In contrast, working-class, immigrant and poor women were not likely to be educated and had to work whether they were married with children or not (Baxandall & Gordon, 1995). The focus on waged labor too often negates the reality that virtually all 18th- and 19th-century women worked— some for individual wages and others as part of the vast exchange economy that operated outside of the traditional capitalist market-economy. These women often carried heavier loads (in all senses of the term) than men. Farming was common, as was street vending, taking in boarders, doing laundry, serving as a factory girl, prostitute, or a domestic. Even middle- and upper-class women worked in the home and their *pay* came only through their husbands' incomes.

Initially, remuneration was paid as a family wage. Soon, however, in the absence of child labor laws and any restrictions on the capitalist owners of most enterprises, working men, women, and children were all paid as individual wage earners at a rate that could barely cover subsistence. This move to the individual wage, as well as access to education, represented a watershed in women's ability to support themselves or their children without a formal connection to a father or husband. Thus, despite the commonality of the sole breadwinner ideology, the reality was far different for most turn-of-the-century women. A common social belief sometimes still found in contemporary public assistance ideologies is that a husband is the sole breadwinner who will support women and their children. In the past, few viable, public safety-net systems were available for women who were their own self-support. Historically, most "virtuous" single women were forced to rely on private charity in their communities. In the early years of public welfare, spinsters and widows were recognized as "deserving poor" in financial need and provision was made by the state for such indigents. Today, although the media portrays women on welfare as young, unwed, and African American, larger numbers are older and white. The welfare system of today draws from two conflicting ideals— the Victorian and the modern—with a large dash of sexism and racism. Both philosophical (and political) approaches confound women's place in the labor market and at home. As the number of unwed mothers has increased, so have hostilities to those on public assistance, including deprivation of job-training opportunities (Solinger, 1992).

Coupled by the resurrection of the feminist movement, society has steadily redefined the ways in which women have made their livings. On one hand, conservative forces idealize a mother at home with a family-wage father. On the other, they have designated welfare mothers as "undeserving" and have pushed them to get a job. The old model of the breadwinning male is available only to those who are most well off. Today's families commonly rely on two incomes to maintain a preferred standard of living or simply to keep up. Still, however, the notion of a family breadwinner with a pin money wife permeates every level of the labor market from entry-level wages through to retirement benefits. As we proceed to examine the impact of education on gender inequities in the labor force, one ideology stands out. Underpinning the chief forms of institutional sexism is the latent assumption that education serves little purpose for women's vocations and women's salaries are economically secondary in the support of their families.

Gender Stereotypes, Traditional Career Choices, Occupational Choices

Schools prepare individuals for careers. What used to be handled mostly in the family and the workplace, now takes place in the primary, secondary, and for some, it also includes postsecondary classrooms. This preparation includes the basic skills that all persons should have, but it also includes vocational and career preparation. Although there is counseling in most school systems, the influence of peers and the media is profound. Children are immersed in a culture that continues to stereotype careers despite the efforts of some parents to present a more androgynous world of work opportunities to their children. Because considerable discussion of career choice has also been provided in other sections of this *Handbook*, we have only chosen a few examples here to illustrate the research linking

youths' career preferences to long-term financial success and mobility in employment. It is important to note that we do not mean to imply that financial success is, in any way, the same as social value or personal success.

As long as women's contributions to the economy are devalued financially in comparison to men's, young girls' aspirations will inevitably be compromised. If they look at traditionally gender-typed careers, the implicit message is that the contributions of workers in these fields are less valuable to the labor market. If they aspire to the most prestigious and highly paid positions, there is quickly the recognition that their presence would represent an exception to the rule. Few at this stage, however, can anticipate the paths their careers will lead them on in the future. Few school teachers or parents can help these young women anticipate that the careers they choose may be blocked by hurdles of discrimination, and the risks they take will be closely intertwined with their future family's economic and social well-being. Regardless of childhood choices, the forces of institutional discrimination remain as solid barriers to women translating their educational accomplishments into rewards in the labor force (Reskin & Roos, 1990; Robinson & McIlwee, 1989). The explanations for this situation are multiple, both at the individual and institutional levels. Here we examine those that are more psychologically focused on theories at the individual level.

Labor market inequities forcefully shape young women's anticipations about the role they will play in the labor force. Even today, with greater access to education, youth of all social classes are immersed in cultural gender role expectations. Young men and women alike still tend to develop differential educational aspirations. More than 30 years after Title IX, which prohibits sex discrimination in education, there continues to be a gender gap in technical education careers. High school girls are the vast majority of those enrolled in traditionally female courses such as cosmetology and child care. Auto mechanics and construction continue to remain the domains of boys (National Women's Law Center, 2005; Silverberg, Warner, Fong, & Goodwin, 2004). These differences are dramatically reflected in future salary expectations. Boys in these fields can expect to earn twice as much or more than girls working in child care or health professions. In cosmetology, for instance, in 2002, female workers earn a median weekly wage of $372; by comparison, electricians earn $730, almost twice as much (U.S. Department of Labor, 2004). One popular explanation for women's lower status in the job market is that psychological problems, often presumed to be rooted in early childhood development, contribute to ineffectiveness in competing in the adult job market. Some decades ago, explanations of sex differences in salaries, for instance, were rationalized on the basis of women's posited fear of success, low self-esteem, lack of internal locus of control, inadequate delay of gratification and attributions of luck for one's achievements. This level of analysis often stressed fears of taking risks and the overwhelming forces of the chilly climate of the labor market (Horner, 1972). Were these the main obstacles to change? Yes, we believe that social change in the labor market would have occurred more rapidly than it has to date were these obstacles not present. However, critics, such as Kaufman and Richardson (1986), suggest that these types of behaviors are highly situational and should not be used as though they measure long-term personality traits. Too often these types of theories emphasize the anxieties of achievement rather than their instrumentality in future careers. Perhaps most importantly, these models are based on the assumption that youth cannot learn from experience and will not want to modify their preferences for long-term goals with the greater maturity of time.

In much of the career aspiration literature, gender socialization is viewed as being the critical force in shaping young women's choices for future occupations. We do not wish to minimize the lasting impact of a child's immersion in a culture with strong prescriptions for gender roles. After systematic investigations, Curran and Renzetti (2003) reported that girls' underrepresentation in nontraditional courses could not be attributed to a lack of participation or interest. Rather, they found problematic practices that included gender-differential treatment by teachers and retaliation and sexual harassment by peers. Although there is some evidence that this pattern is gradually changing, their report concludes with detailed recommendations on how schools and federal and state agencies can take steps to encourage girls' untapped interests and improve their enrollment in nontraditional courses. Although change has occurred with more women pursuing traditionally male careers, there is other evidence that little change has occurred in the more traditional working class or technical career choices that girls and boys, men and woman pursue. (For a far more extended discussion of this research literature, we refer the reader to other chapters in this *Handbook*).

But, even these explanations of youthful educational abilities and career preferences underestimate the relatively negligibility educational achievement has in explaining the gender wage gap in the labor market after graduation. Research summarized by Curran and Renzetti (2003) indicates that sex differences in education have little to do with the wage gap. Robinson and McIlwee (1989) for instance found that educational attainment, as well as experience in the work force and job tenure, failed to explain the lower status of the female engineers in their sample relative to male engineers. The men and women in their study entered their professions with comparable education and females outperformed the men in their classes, earning slightly higher grade point averages. The same held true for Kay and Hagen's (1995) studies of graduates of law schools. Having attended an elite school acted as a bonus for men and not for women. Reskin and Roos (1990) state the familiar observation that women need to be twice as good to compete with their professional peers (see also Couric, 1998; Fuller & Schoenberger, 1991; Kay & Hagen, 1995; Maume & Hurling, 1999).

We have just reviewed some of the theoretical explanations attempting to attribute sex-typed occupational segregation to children's naïve career choices. Women's sex-stereotypical choices are also commonly related to daily culture pressures of gender. These explanations operate at the psychological level and focus on the purported fear individual women may experience over their conflicting social roles.

Controversies over the wisdom of educated women pursuing careers take place in an environment with serious fiscal realities. For most families wives are in the workforce because they need to be. Whether it is to support a family or to keep up with a standard of living established earlier, two paychecks have increasingly become a necessity. In order to keep up with the cost of inflation in daily living, increasingly, two partners are necessary to play the joint role of breadwinner. Women who are single heads of household are especially vulnerable in today's economy. Contemporary calls for a return to family values occur in the context of many immediately pressing concerns such as a family's economic survival. There are pressing issues on many women's minds, related to genuinely helpful job preparation, scholarships for educational degrees, children's day care and seniors' eldercare. In the national agenda these women's issues remain ignored and under funded.

Consequences of Careers Choices: Occupational Segregation

The traditional career choices that women have made have put them at a disadvantage in the labor market and ultimately in their pocketbooks. The kind of job a person enters greatly affects the pay that he or she will receive (Heyman, 2000). It is not just that women on average receive lower wages, but that these wages are generally associated with the kind of gender-linked jobs that women have traditionally held (U.S. Department of Labor, 2002a, 2002b). Women have traditionally been in the helping professions, whether that be as a nurse, secretary, or teacher. Women's potential and actual status as mothers often limits their job potential and depresses their wages (Sokoloff, 1980 Andronici & Katz, 2007). It also appears that the closer the job is to mothering young children, the lower the pay. For example, mothers, children's earliest teachers, receive no pay (Kaufman & Richardson, 1986). Early child care workers receive minimal wages. Teachers, mostly female, are college educated but receive lower wages than many other college majors and even many occupations that require less education. For example, teachers receive $46,597 on average per year, while engineers receive $78,023 (Muir & Nelson, 2005). In contrast, men dominate the upper ranks of academia, particularly in math and the sciences, the more prestigious educational occupations (U.S. Department of Education, 2003). The American Association of University Women (2004) points out that women make up about one half of instructors and lecturers. Among university professors, women are nearly one half of the assistant professors, but they are only one third of associate professors, and one fifth of full professors (American Association of University Women, 2004). Overall, women earn less, are more likely to hold lower ranking positions, and are less likely to have tenure.

Women are making headway in nontraditional occupations. Not since the days of Rosie the Riveter in World War II have so many women knocked on the doors of male-dominated jobs and insisted on admission. From the 1960s on, newly educated women have gone on to enter nontraditional jobs at every occupational strata in the labor force—from school bus drivers to lawyers, from welders to veterinarians. However, women are still underrepresented in many of these fields. For example, women comprise 11% of engineers, 4% of airline pilots, and 5% of mechanics and repairers (U.S. Department of Labor, 2004).

Traditionally, men have dominated majors and careers that require higher levels of mathematics, whereas, women have dominated in majors that require less mathematics. The size of these differences is narrowing rapidly. In 1984–85, the number of women receiving a degree in predominantly male majors included 15% in engineering, 25% in physical science, and 37% in computer and information science (Levin, 2001). In contrast, the number of women receiving a degree in predominantly female majors included 76% in education and 85% in health professions. In 2000 and 2001, the figures for women receiving degrees in predominantly male majors included 19.9% in engineering, 41.2% in physical sciences, and 27.7% in computer and information science (National Center for Education Statistics, 2003). Thus, since 1984 and 1985 a moderate gain was made in engineering, a greater gain in physical sciences, and a decrease in computer science.

During the past three decades, women have made significant gains in some nontraditional fields including biology, physical sciences, business, and mathematics. For example, women now earn more than 60% of undergraduate degrees in biology and nearly half (47%) of undergraduate degrees in mathematics (American Association of University Women, 2006). In spite of some gains toward equity, a majority of women are still majoring in predominantly female occupations.

There have been impressive shifts in the proportion of women moving into some sectors of the nontraditional economy (MacPherson & Hirsh, 1995). They are now completing more law and medical degrees; for example, in 2002 women comprised 29% of lawyers and 31% of physicians (U.S. Department of Labor, 2004). In turn, more men are entering nursing and becoming flight attendants; however, men are still less likely to participate in occupations working with young children (National Women's Law Center, 2005; U.S. Department of Labor, 2004).

Internationally, this same pattern of sex segregation in subjects studied and careers pursued is reflected in United Nations Educational, Scientific, and Cultural Organization (UNESCO; 2003) data. Globally, women also tend to be overrepresented in fields of study such as education, social sciences, and the humanities and to be underrepresented in the natural sciences such as mathematics, engineering, and agriculture. Similarly, this global pattern of distribution by field of study has shown to be quite persistent over time and is a major source of income differentials when women and men join the labor force.

While these shifts in the gendered composition of jobs help to challenge long-held beliefs about the limits of the sexes to perform in nontraditional roles, the story does not end with women's entry into new careers. What happens once women enter a career also matters. The disparity between men's and women's pay by profession is presented in Table 4.1. A number of professions provide telling indicators about that gap. For example, women lawyers make 76.8% less than men, women engineers make 85.7% less than men, and women physicians make 58.2% less than men. The pay gap among physicians was the largest gap among any of the jobs listed among the U.S. Department of Labor's 2004 reports. Among executives, administrators, and managers, women make 68.1% less than men.

Wage discrimination does not just occur in nontraditional occupations. The difference in pay holds whether it is within jobs or between traditional or nontraditional jobs. Even in traditionally female-dominated professions, men make more than women. For example, female elementary teachers earn 89.7% of men's salaries, and female registered nurses earn 90.9% compared to men (U.S. Department of Labor, 2004). Differences in pay are frequently attributed to the rigid occupational segregation that persists in the labor market (King, 1992). The gender inequity evident when educational credentials are similar even when an occupation is female typed is important because it highlights the degree to which sexism is pervasive throughout the labor market.

Gender inequity continues at every stage of the occupational ladder. Whether it is sexual harassment or the *glass ceiling* each represents the types of gender inequities women face regardless of their educational achievements. Institutional sexism exists in every strata of the labor force, whether in various nontraditional jobs and professions or more gender-typed careers (U.S. Department of Labor, 2004, 2005). For women of all educational levels, this differentiation by career choice is cumulative over a professional lifetime. It begins with their first job and follows them through to retirement.

Having a college degree is important, but only one of many factors that affect a woman's ability to support herself and use her full potential to the benefit of today's economy. Even if she is in a high-status career in medicine or law, a high-tech or a traditional high-skilled or apprenticed trade such as plumber, carpenter, or sheet-metal worker—occupations that few women currently enter—she will inevitably encounter a lifetime of gender-based wage discrimination.

TABLE 4.1   Median Usual Weekly Earning of Full-Time Wage and Salary Workers by Detailed Occupation and Sex, 2002 Annual Averages
(*total employed in thousands*)

Occupation	Both Sexes		Women		Men		Women's Earnings as a Percent of Men's
	Total Employed	Median Weekly Earnings	Total Employed	Median Weekly Earnings	Total Employed	Median Weekly Earnings	
Prof. Lawyers	605	$1,492	205	$1,237	400	$1,160	76.8
Engineers	1,889	$1,161	206	$1,011	1,683	$1,180	85.7
Physicians	538	$1,475	169	$947	370	$1,626	58.2
Exe./Adm. & Mgr.	16,065	$890	7,633	$763	8,432	$1,081	68.1
Elem. Teachers	2,039	$764	1,677	$750	362	$836	89.7
Reg. Nurses	1,737	$876	1,597	$870	140	$957	90.9

Table derived from Table 15 in Bureau of Labor Statistics, Women in the Labor Force: A Databook, U.S. Department of Labor, February 2004, Report 973, 40–47.

Gender Equity in Job Training and Adult Education

Education holds out the opportunity for upward mobility, especially when it provides for more highly paid, nontraditional occupations. Whether it is the retraining of union stewards from an assembly line, displaced homemakers, mothers on public assistance, or corporate executives retooling for reentry in a new location in the job market, it typically means going back to school. Elsewhere we have focused on educational credentials as an asset in finding and keeping a job, especially one with good benefits. In this section and those to follow, we also discuss the liabilities and hardships of women of all ages who may have dropped out of school or are ill equipped for occupations that provide security and offer mobility. While many fields certainly rely on a person's accumulation of knowledge from their early years, more knowledge and skills can be learned later in a lifetime. In short, the evidence of lifelong learning is that the mature worker has great potential to learn the skills necessary to work in a nontraditional occupation later in life. No longer can anyone presume continuity in his or her career, regardless of educational level. On average, most adults today can plan on multiple moves over the course of their professional lives. Whether Americans are on the job or off, they will need formal training over their lifetime to expand their skills (Hess, 2001; Vannoy & Dubeck, 1998).

Large numbers of mature or older students have returned to formal education to improve their status on the job or to fulfill personal goals for enrichment and advancement. Most of these returning students are driven by financial concerns. Those with union help or the corporate support of a golden parachute have had provisions made on their behalf. Others have had to figure out how to pay for their education mostly on their own.

Increasingly, women and men alike are engaged in the *triple shift*. This status characterizes individuals who are employed full-time, go to school part-time in search of a new degree for promotions, and support a family financially and emotionally. Nearly all of these triple-shift students are going to school at their own expense. Today, the options are scarce for obtaining formal educational credentials without large and costly loans.

Today, there are few resources for mature workers displaced from their original niche in the labor force (Tallichet, 1995). In years past, veterans received educational benefits as repayment from a grateful nation. In addition, they demonstrated their capabilities as adult learners. The benefits the nation received from these educated veterans have not been used as a model for the education of others who might, in turn, benefit the nation and themselves. There is a growing pool of disaffected workers, women first among them, eager to acquire new skills, but finding the education they need financially out of reach. Opportunities for these women and men to obtain financial backing have become increasingly difficult. Although this is true for those displaced, it is especially true for those suffering from poor educations and living under the current government welfare guidelines (Ashburn, 2006; Jones-DeWeever & Gault, 2006).

There is ample evidence of why employment and the search for job training represent a losing battle for most women on public assistance. There is clear documentation that when women work on the margins of the economy they are near or below above the poverty line. Meaningful career-based education is seriously neglected in current forms of job training (Tenny & Zahradnik, 2001). As a result, women hovering on the threshold of the poverty line only find minimum wage jobs open to them. With the passage of the Personal Responsibility and Work Opportunity Reconciliation Act of 1996 (PRWORA), women with children are being told to get jobs after only brief job preparation. Policies oriented to employment rather than job training have also placed social workers under pressure to place a larger proportion of their caseloads directly into low-paying jobs. Beginning in 2000, single mothers have been required to work at least 30 hours a week to be counted as engaging in employment. Federal and State programs like Temporary Assistance for Needy Families (TANF) increasingly limit the time for receiving benefits and mandate employment without adequate provision of transportation, childcare, further education, or job training (Tenny & Zahadranik, 2001).

One of the biggest losses in the latest policies on public assistance is the elimination of opportunities to pursue formal education and/or obtaining the skills necessary to obtain advanced credentials. The latest guidelines provide little provision for training for employment that provides educational skills with potential for mobility or portability across economic sectors. Prior to the passage of PRWORA, single mothers on welfare could pursue a college education while they cared for their children. Since federal and state welfare reforms, the use of education as a step toward economic independence has been greatly curtailed (Kemp, 1990; Yelowitz, 2000). Within three years after the passage of this act, the number of women requesting financial aid for further schooling and job training declined. The U.S. Department of Health and Human Services (1999) reported that about 47.6 % fewer women receiving assistance relied on postsecondary financial aid after welfare reform. Further evidence demonstrated that the number of welfare students enrolled in college dropped from 172,176 in 1996 to 58,055 in 1998 (Greenberg, Strawn, & Plimpton, 2000). Evidence from individual states and programs have shown similar reductions in the number of welfare students in college (Jones-DeWeever & Gault, 2006)

In the past, some states, such as Iowa, Massachusetts, Michigan, and South Dakota, used provisions of the federal law to use state funds earmarked to help mothers on public assistance to go to college or complete degree programs. Many other states stopped allowing for further postsecondary education for potential or current college welfare recipients (Jones-DeWeever & Gault, 2006). In 2006, additional U.S. Department of Health and Human Services guidelines were proposed that would reduce even further the number of those on welfare who might study at colleges. Ashley (June 29, 2006) reports:

Under the rules, up to a year of vocational training at a college would still count as work, but in the past states were allowed to define "vocational" broadly. The new rules narrow the definition, stating explicitly that baccalaureate and advanced-degree programs cannot count. (p. 1)

In nearly all cases however, the end result is that women are expected to look for jobs, regardless of their educational qualifications and job experience.

Welfare mothers need to be given the opportunity to complete their high school diplomas or to receive the kind of job training that will give them long-term promise in the labor market. This type of intervention can offer a significant resource in breaking the poverty cycle in the United States today (Gornick & Meyers, 2003).

COSTS AND REMEDIES FOR GENDER INEQUITIES IN THE LABOR MARKET

Income, Education, Gendered Wage Gaps

The historic rise in women's education with newly emerging opportunities in the job market has not led to the economic security and social justice women need and deserve. As we will see in the sections that follow, continuing gender discrimination in employment, regardless of individual women's educational credentials, is pervasive, deeply embedded, and often hard to document (Heyman, 2000). Given the same educational credentials and training, the issue of how much money women make compared to men is a persistent source of feminist concern. Women's economic well-being has improved to some degree as compared to men, but gender equity is still elusive when it comes to the pocketbook.

In the previous sections we focused on some of the critical factors in socialization into gender roles that contributed to the wage inequities and unequal pay-offs for young women in today's labor force, regardless of their educational level. In this section we will concentrate on identifying some of the systematic factors that transform and reinforce gender-based preferences. Our focus will be on the institutionalized barriers to financially rewarding career success. As discussed, earlier historical conditions interact with gender expectations in education and employment. Over the past few decades, vast demographic and economic forces have reshaped the pressures on families as well as the needs of the labor market. Shifts in the needs of the economy from farming and manual labor to the service sector, and the dissemination of new technologies have led to the largest number of women working for wages today than ever before (Cherlin, 2005). This trend is often referred to as the *Silent Revolution* (MacDonald & Siriani, 1996). More families today need greater participation in the labor force simply to maintain their economic status. Although there is no simple causal relationship, worldwide, as women's education continues to increase and their fertility declines, their labor force participation, in turn, accelerates (United Nations, 1995). Additionally, increased lifespan, mandatory public education, and increased access to postsecondary education have contributed to women's move into the labor force.

Employment rates for men and women in 1970 and 2002 are presented in Table 4.2, and rates for men and women with children are presented in Table 4.3. There are systematic patterns of participation, within these rates, depending upon whether women have children and their ages (U.S. Department of Labor, 2004). We note this for three reasons. First, women with young children account for some of the most dramatic increases in employment among women over the last few decades. Second, regardless of educational level, the divorce rates in the United States are some of the highest in the world (Henslin, 2006). An

TABLE 4.2 Employment Status of the Civilian Noninstitutional Population by Gender and Methnicity in 1970 and 2002 (*numbers in thousands*)

16 and older	Civilian Non-institutional Population	Employed		Unemployed	
		Total	Percent	Total	Percent
1970					
Women	72,782	29,688	40.8	1,855	5.9
All Men	64,304	48,990	76.2	2.238	4.4
2002					
All Women	112,985	63,582	56.3	3,781	5.6
Asian	5,136	2,866	55.8	172	5.7
Af-Am.	14,187	7,914	55.8	853	9.8
Hispanic	12,742	6,744	52.9	590	8
White	92,422	52,164	56.4	2,678	4.9
All Men	104,585	72,903	69.7	4,597	5.9
Asian	4,697	3,349	71.3	217	6.1
Af-Am.	11,391	6,959	61.1	835	10.7
Hispanic	13,221	9,845	74.5	764	7.2
White	87,361	61,849	70.8	3,459	5.3

Table derived from Tables 1, 3 & 4 in Bureau of Labor Statistics, Women in the Labor Force: A Databook, U.S. Department of Labor, February 2004, Report 973, 6–15.

TABLE 4.3 Employment Status of the Civilian Noninstitutional Population with Children by Gender and Major Ethnicity in 2002 (*numbers in thousands; asian women not included in table*)

16 and older	Civilian Non-institutional Population	Employed		Unemployed	
		Total	Percent	Total	Percent
With children under 18					
Women	36,187	24,642	68	1,529	5.8
Af-Am.	5,160	3,609	69.9	418	10.4
Hispanic	5,738	3,272	57	322	9
White	28,702	19,584	68.2	1,001	4.9
Men	28,042	25,301	90.2	1,182	4.5
Af-Am.	2,578	2,151	83.4	200	8.5
Hispanic	4,307	3,753	87.1	233	5.8
White	23,769	21,696	91.3	894	4
With children under 3					
Women	9,258	5,160	55.7	440	7.9
Af-Am.	1,255	726	57.8	135	15.7
Hispanic	1,821	836	45.9	89	9.6
White	7,375	4,136	59.1	269	6.1
Men	7,449	6,766	90.8	380	5.3
Af-Am.	650	563	86.7	60	9.6
Hispanic	1,464	1,279	87.4	102	7.4
White	6,330	5,788	91.4	293	4.8

Table derived from Table 5 in Bureau of Labor Statistics, Women in the Labor Force: A Databook, U.S. Department of Labor, February 2004, Report 973, 6–15. (Asian women not included in table.)

analysis of the 2005 U.S. census data shows that "more American women are living without a spouse than with one." In 1950 this was true for only 35% (51 percent of American women are single, 2007). Third, in a country lacking in so many forms of social support for young mothers, whether married or as single heads of household, mothers of young children have high rates of employment compared to the past, because of their need to support themselves out of sheer economic necessity (Steinberg & Cook, 1988). These changes have brought with them new opportunities, accompanied by ambiguous and often contradictory messages regarding definitions of contemporary gender roles.

There is little doubt that educational attainment improves one's earnings and that educated women's gap with men has gradually been narrowing. In 1985, women made $68.1 dollars for every $100 a man made (U.S. Department of Labor, 2004). The U.S. Department of Labor (2004) reported on the median weekly earnings of full-time workers (controlled for inflation, 2002 dollars). Women's median earnings as compared to men are shown in Table 4.4. Women who have dropped out of high school earn, on average, 40% as much as women who have graduated from college. Although the average size of the gender gap in pay has lessened, women still make less than men even when level of education attained is controlled for (Arnott & Matthei, 1996). In 2002, women made $77.9 for every $100 a man made (U.S. Department of Labor, 2004). Although improvement has occurred, it is not yet equitable.

Researchers have systematically analyzed possible sources of discrimination. They have checked such factors as hours on the job, educational backgrounds, and seniority and found that these combined account for about half the pay received. The researchers concluded that the balance is due to gender discrimination (Kemp, 1990). This conclusion is reinforced by additional research by Fuller and Schoenberger (1991). They examined the starting salaries of business graduates from a prestigious university. More than half of these graduates were women. They found that women's starting salaries averaged 11% ($1,737) less than the men's. They compared grades, internship experience, and details of college records. They found the women had higher grades and had completed more professional internships. In short, as we found in the earlier studies, the college women with better academic records, who were offered lower salaries than their male counterparts, had higher academic qualifica-

tions than their male counterparts. Had these young women's outstanding skills been rewarded as they continued on in their new jobs? Not at all! In fact, the gender gap grew. In four years, the women were earning 14% less than the men ($3,615; Fuller & Schoenberger, 1991).

Women's strides toward equity are not comparable for all women. Poor women and less-educated, working-class women and women of color have not experienced the same gains as white women (Grodsky & Pager, 2001). White women now earn more than African American men and African American women earn more than Hispanic men.

In spite of this overall progress, women and children in poverty have lost ground despite the general increase in women's wages. For example, in 1983 about 66% of unmarried mothers were in the labor force, yet 22% of these women were below the poverty line. In 2003, 73% of unmarried mothers had jobs, yet the proportion of those women below the poverty line had increased to 31% (Bergmann, 2005). Marked discrimination in pay by sex has been well documented historically and globally (See chapter on "Gender Equity Education Globally."). The persistence of these practices highlights the importance of education to assist all women to achieve equity in women's pay.

Unemployment, Education and Gender Inequity

Employment rates from 1970 to 2002 are shown in Table 4.5. These data have not been controlled for education, but it is fair to say that those most vulnerable to unemployment are those with the lowest educational resources and the most likely to be in the marginal sector of the labor force, that is, last hired, first fired. This is sometimes referred to as the *dual labor force*, one for women and another for men (Reskin, 1993). The likelihood of being unemployed has remained fairly steady for women since 1970.

Minority women are more likely to be unemployed and seeking work than white women (U.S. Department of Labor, 2004). In 2002, the unemployment rate for African American women was 9.8%, for Hispanic women 8.0%, and for Asian women 5.7%. The rates for men are similar within each ethnic group. The highest unemployment rate for women was among African American women with children under age 3. An alarming 16% of African American women with children under 3 were seeking employment. African American men also had the highest rate of unemployment at 9.6% among fathers with children under 3. The marginal sector is also almost always char-

TABLE 4.4 Median Usual Weekly Earning of Full-Time Wage and Salary Workers in Constant (2002) Dollars by Race, Hispanic Origin, and Sex for 1985 and 2002

	Weekly Earnings	Men's Earnings as a Percent of White Men	Weekly Earnings	Women's Earnings as a Percent of White Men	Women's Earning as a Percent of Men's Within Race
1985					
Af-Am.	$486	73	$402	60.4	82.6
Hispanic	$472	70.9	$367	5.1	77.7
White	$666	100	$448	67.2	67.2
Total	$649		$442		68.1
2002					
Af-Am.	$523	74.5	$474	67.5	90.6
Hispanic	$449	63.9	$396	56.4	88.2
White	$702	100	$549	78.2	78.2
Total	$680		$530		77.9

Table derived from Tables 13 & 14 in Bureau of Labor Statistics, Women in the Labor Force: A Databook, U.S. Department of Labor, February 2004, Report 973, 36–37. (Asian women not included in table.)

TABLE 4.5 Unemployment Rates for the Years 1970, 1976, 1982, 1989, 1996, and 2002 by Sex

Year	Female	Male
1970	5.9	4.4
1976	8.6	7.1
1982	9.4	9.9
1989	5.4	5.2
1996	5.4	5.4
2002	5.6	5.9

Table derived from Tables 2 & 3 in Bureau of Labor Statistics, Women in the Labor Force: A Databook, U.S. Department of Labor, February 2004, Report 973.

acterized by part-time jobs and no benefits. In general, poor women are the most likely to be unemployed and their families are most likely to feel the economic pinch. Baker and Boushey (2004) point out that although the unemployment rate is lower than it has been for the past 30 years, the number of adults who hold jobs has declined mainly due to decreases in male employment. The point we would draw from this review of women's vulnerability in today's labor market is that women workers are increasingly subject to the sudden economic hardships in the U.S. economy as are men. In an ironic sense, in this area, the gap between women and men is narrowing! Contemporary women's increased education certainly acts as a buffer against unemployment, but gender inequities cut across all social class and educational levels (Reskin, 1993).

In this global economy, even the most well-paid, well-educated professionals are caught off guard by downsizing (Wallace, 1998). A good education cannot always protect a woman from joining the ranks of the unemployed. The more senior the person, the greater the credentials, the higher the salary they are accustomed to commanding, the lower their desirability as an employee in a tight economy. Today's market is increasingly looking for eager, less experienced, less well paid employees, rather than older, experienced workers who command much higher salaries. As a result, those who find themselves downsized and unemployed, if they can afford it, are increasingly turning to continuing education and job training for new skills (Wallace, 1998). When one needs a job, being unemployed is stressful and affects the whole family. When an unemployed parent is single, this emotional turmoil is aggravated by the total loss of family income. When the unemployed person is a woman, the probability is that she was in a lower-paid job with little seniority and few, if any, benefits. If she does find work in the marginal sector of the economy, her wages may keep her barely hovering on the poverty line. If she is on public assistance, she will also have the threat of automatic deductions from her welfare check if she earns more than the prescribed allotment.

There is also the category of discouraged worker, which reflects a population who has run out of unemployment benefits and has, in essence, given up on job hunting in a serious way. Getting at the numbers who are in this category is difficult because discouraged workers are confounded with stay-at-home-moms, displaced homemakers, and retired persons. As discussed earlier, poor single mothers who once relied on public assistance to study to improve their job skills are now expected to get jobs. Jobs are not always available, or what is available is low-waged work with few benefits.

Educational Liabilities and the Feminization of Poverty

Generally, poverty rates are associated with unemployment. There is no doubt that minority rates of unemployment are nearly double those of whites (U.S. Department of Labor, 2002a), and that minority heads of household are also disproportionately in poverty. However, what the unemployment rates also tell us is that the majority of those women are employed even while living in poverty, often serving as heads of their households (Bane & Ellwood, 1994). While many work sporad-

ically, others who work full-time find their take-home pay insufficient to raise them above the poverty threshold.

An education provides both men and women tremendous resources for shifting gears and developing new skills that are often the legacy of enriching liberal arts training. Not all are so fortunate. While education is a hedge against poverty, it cannot alone protect an individual from the economic ravages of joblessness, serious illnesses of family members, or terrible natural disasters. This is even truer when we examine the situation of gender equity and poverty internationally. Julie Andrejewski cites Noleen Heyzer, UNIFEM Director, on the intransigence of these same problems globally. In her Plenary Address to the Fourth World Conference on Women in Beijing, Heyzer argued:

It is not acceptable for women to constitute 70 percent of the world's 1.3 billion absolute poor. Nor is it acceptable for women to work two-thirds of the world's working hours, but earn only one-tenth of the world's income and own less than one-tenth of the world's property. Many fundamental changes must be made. (Seager, 2003, p. 102)

Even in a climate of increased education for the majority of women, there is a growing subculture of very poor and relatively uneducated single mothers trying to make a living for themselves and their children (Bane & Ellwood, 1994; Blank & Haskins, 2001). Women who drop out of high school to marry, women who divorce, or have children early in their lives are more likely to live in poverty. In the 1980s, the higher a family's educational and occupational status, the later a daughter married, and the less likely she would live in poverty (Spitze & Waite, 1981). Rindfuss and St. John (1983) suggested that women from lower socioeconomic backgrounds are more likely to have lower levels of education, and reciprocally, those with lower levels of education have earlier births and higher fertility. This is true today worldwide (United Nations, 1995).

In the United States and globally, minority women have historically had lower levels of educational attainment than white men or women and minority men (Furstenberg, Brooks-Gunn, & Morgan, 1987; U.S. Bureau of the Census, 1987). This continues to be true today. In the United States, women heads of household and their families are generally poorer than men (Bergmann, 2005; U.S. Department of Labor, 2004, 2005). It is not surprising then, that unmarried women (especially African American unmarried women) are most needy in terms of economic support in their motherhood role (Solinger, 1992; Waring, 1988). So, despite women's steady improvement in levels of education, occupational segregation remains an important feature of the U.S. labor market. This two-tiered, sex-segregated model generally holds throughout the world (Jacobs & Lim, 1995, Reskin, 1993).

Of all the groups in the United States today, American children, especially those in families headed by single mothers, are the likeliest to be living in hunger, substandard housing and punishing economic deprivation (Cherlin, 2005; Cochran & Malone, 1999; Schiller, 2004). Eighteen percent of America's children are currently living in poverty, a statistic that is even more staggering for minority children. For example, the rates for African American children are 29.3% and Hispanics 30.3% (Cherlin, 2005). Taken together, the costs of not reaching out to provide educational intervention for these mothers both before and after a pregnancy is to condemn another generation to a loss of economic potential. To add insult to injury, poor children are more likely to have poor educational outcomes and to reproduce poverty among their own children. Thus, women from families who do not have the necessary cultural capital, for example, lower education, are at the greatest risk.

Given the cutbacks in affirmative action and welfare reform, with women expected to get jobs after only brief training. The current outlook is bleak for mothers seeking the skills provided by an education and/or meaningful job training. As Curran and Renzetti (2003) calculate it: if one holds a minimum-wage job paying $5.15 per hour, even if one works 40 hours per week, 52 weeks a year, the income before deductions ($10,712) for Social Security and employment-related expenses (e.g. child care, transportation, clothing) is still significantly below the poverty threshold of $14,122 for a family of three.

As part of an in-depth investigation, a feminist researcher left her privileged job and took on women's low wage labor, $6 or $10 per hour, for a year. She found that women in these jobs rarely earned sufficient income to pay for rent in low-income housing and still have enough to buy food, clothing, and transportation to and from work. Women in these positions might not technically be classified as poor but are technically referred to as the *near poor*, which is defined as having an income 200% of the poverty threshold (Ehrenrich, 2001; Manpower Demonstration Research Corporation, 2001). There is little by way of a security net at this time for those women and their families with the largest problems and the fewest resources.

Education, Work Benefits, and Aging

Regardless of education, most women are also shortchanged over the long term in their wages and benefits (Harrington, 1996). Although some economic disparities have been lessening, inflation has been cutting into the real pay of all workers. On top of this, job security and benefits packages have each become increasingly unstable (Henslin, 2006). For older workers, the cumulative result of discrimination is starkly written in the size of the paychecks they'll be living on as they enter retirement (Hess, 2001). A recent comprehensive study examines the long-term cost of gender discrimination over a woman's lifetime. Their findings should be of relevance to women of all educational levels. Rose and Hartman (2004) point out that even though the wage gap between men and women has lessened over time, it is still with us. Women suffer the greatest loss in their long-term accumulation of net worth (Burkhauser & Salisbury, 1993; Calasanti & Selvin, 2001). Due to lower wages and reduced benefits, women are less able to increase their net worth over time.

The focus of most research has been on single years, rather than on cumulative lifetime earnings (Mitchell, Levine, & Phillips, 1999; Scott, 2001). In their research, Rose and Hartman (2004) examined a 15-year time frame from 1983 to 1998. They found that prime age working women earned only $273,592, while men earned $722,693, a gap of 62%. The wage gap continued to hold even when controls were introduced for average education (Kemp, 1990). Those who have labored longest in the pink-collar ghetto are the most likely to have the greatest long-term economic disadvantage. In their later years, these same older women are frequently among the working poor who hover on the borderline of poverty (Ehrenrich, 2001).

Because of women's long periods in the marginal labor market, they are less likely than men to be in jobs that provide high levels of cumulative benefits. Traditionally, gender-based occupations like waitress, sales clerk, beautician, and domestic accumulate few health or retirement benefits. When men or women work in low-wage, part-time, nonunionized jobs, or when they work with short-term tenure at small firms, in sales, or the service sector, they are less likely to receive health benefits (Dewar, 2000; Seccombe & Amey, 1995). Taking a low-wage job means poor men and women (and their dependents) often do not have health insurance. Yet they may make too much money to remain eligible for Medicaid (Yelowitz, 2000). The cumulative effect of this lack of benefits is the serious neglect of preventative care for all family members.

In a related area of employment benefits, women are customarily facing gender inequities when they retire and seek Social Security benefits. Again, this is a condition that women at all educational levels are likely to confront. Resources for retirement overall are scarce except for a very minimum from whatever earned income was declared on income taxes that were paid earlier in life (Hess, 2001).

Among older cohorts, many women, even with educational advantages, are unemployed or working at home during the prime years of their earning lives (Farkas & O'Rand, 1998). If married, they depended on their husband's benefits, savings, and Social Security. These women stopped out of their careers to raise young children or care for sick and elderly relatives (Waldfogel, 1997). During these periods of nonemployment, women lose wages, their accumulation of net worth, and benefits (Budig & England, 2001). When women take time off to care for children or to tend sick family members, they do not accumulate Social Security benefits. If they work part-time they may accrue some benefits, but it is considerably lower than if they work full-time. Regardless, women in their later years, living alone and on their own, are likely to receive far fewer Social Security benefits than a single man (Traver, 2005). When we look at the full range of income among women who are retired, they have lower overall incomes compared to men (Lee, 2005). Once again, these findings generally hold across the educational continuum.

The cumulative result of inequities in all forms of employment-related benefits is a serious deprivation in the later years. This is also a serious problem for those who have lived in single-parent households or worked in the pink-collar ghetto during their most productive work years. Seventy percent of older adults who live in poverty are women.

The risk for poverty is especially high for widows, divorcees, displaced homemakers, and minorities. Once again women's vulnerability in the later years cuts across education and socioeconomic status.

As Calasanti and Selvin put it:

Putting women's lives at the center of analysis reveals the wide range of productive activities which men and women perform that have economic value, including paid labor, unpaid labor and services provided to others. When we define work this way, we see that, at all ages, women perform more productive activities than do men and that retirement (for women) does not mean leisure or freedom from labor. (2001, p. 371).

Whether women are well educated and actively employed or not, they are at a high risk of having to retire on meager benefits. Their rewards from a life of work may still lead to meager benefits, due to a lifetime of accumulated gender inequities.

Reconsidering the Value of Women's Public and Private Work

One type of legal challenge now in the courts is referred to as *comparable worth*. This argument makes the radical proposal that individuals should be paid for the value of their contribution to the greater social good, regardless of their occupational classification (Gold, 1983). Feminist economists attempt to bring into focus the value attributed to women's work in both the public and private domestic spheres (Acker, 1989; England, 1992). As an alternative proposal for addressing the gender-based inequality of pay, it is both imaginative and challenging to some of the very basic assumptions in the U.S. capitalist economy. Comparable worth arguments, as they are called, point to the relative influence of sex-stereotypical discrimination in explaining the cause for women's lower wages in the job market. This is in direct contrast to the theories reviewed earlier in this chapter that explained away labor market inequities as due to poor childhood career decisions adult personality conflicts, or choices about having children.

In most of the social sciences, especially economics, the concepts of equality and equity are not the same. Equality deals with income, for instance in terms of the same amount. Equity, on the other hand refers to fairness. Equality compares incomes against a specified standard. As we review the move from advocating equal pay, to comparable worth, the distinction between the two terms will become clearer. The Equal Pay Act of 1963 required employers to pay men and women equal pay for equal work. The Civil Rights Act of 1991 added provisions for compensatory damages to women whose pay was below that of men performing identical work in similar conditions. While this was a step in the right direction, feminist critics realized that these types of cases only represented a small portion of the female labor force, and that the equal pay concept was too restrictive. Because of occupational discrimination, few women even hold jobs identical to men's. The terms of the argument changed when the Supreme Court ruled in the case of the County of Washington versus Gunther, 1981. They held that female prison guards had the right to sue over pay discrimination even though they were not performing tasks identical to those performed by males. This ruling moved the compensation debate to an assessment of what constituted fair wages over and above equal wages. Arguments now compared comparable jobs, not just identical ones.

The remedies feminists propose would involve a major restructuring of today's capitalist economy (Acker, 1989; Heyman, 2000; Remick, 1984). The values of the labor market enter into wage calculations when engineers make dramatically more than teachers, despite the unique contributions each group makes to society. A proposed solution to this gap has often been to encourage more women to seek jobs in nontraditional occupations that pay better. Thus, women would be encouraged to go into engineering rather than teaching. Comparable worth arguments, however, suggest that men's and women's incomes should be on the basis of the skill and the worth of their labors in a more broadly defined societal sense. Comparability is measured in various ways, including skills, responsibility, mental and physical effort, importance and the extent of training required. By this standard, women should get equal pay for jobs that are comparable to men's jobs, not necessarily identical to them. (For further information on this topic, see the chapters on "Teacher Education" and "Postsecondary Education" in this *Handbook*).

Comparable worth argues that occupations that require equal education and equal requirements would pay about the same. There is one additional caveat. Proponents argue for taking into consideration the *social* value of both careers in the labor market and labor in the home. Rewards and wages would vary in terms of their jobs' value to the greater society. In this scenario, a child care worker or teacher might be ranked as having greater value than a middle-level bureaucrat in an auto factory. The social value is of course distinct from the market value, in which a premium is placed on which type of positions that are revenue generating (Acker, 1989). Similarly, professional socialization agents who serve as mentors, tutors, and significant others who remain relatively undervalued in today's labor market, would receive more recognition and greater compensation. This far-reaching call for a reexamination of the fairness in the value attached to sectors of the labor force challenges the most fundamental assumptions made by economists. In the section that follows, we raise an issue that most economists would find even more startling—reappraisal of the economic value of women's family roles in maintaining the business of the American economy.

As we have seen, the common solution to gender inequities in the economy has too often been to encourage women to pursue education for higher degrees and train for higher paying, nontraditional jobs. If this were to be carried out in the extreme, traditionally female professions (nursing, teaching, social worker, and day care worker. to name but a few) would be neglected in the work of our society. If these are central to the social welfare of a nation, why should these jobs be devalued (Hewitson, 1989; Waring, 1999)? Feminists have asked this question for many years (Bevier, 1918; Gilman, 1913). These issues reach beyond simple wage inequities or equal pay for equal worth.

A new set of legal and ethical analyses has moved feminists into a different type of paradigm—one of social justice and gender equity. When these concepts are tied to the economy, it suggests a radical departure from market economics, a daunting issue to confront. With the discussion of the value attached to women's labors, it was inevitable that a related issue, first raised by feminist decades ago, resurfaced. What were the costs to women for their many hours in the care of dependents, and what were the benefits to society (Ferber & Nelson, 1993; Folbre, 2001)? Does one's educational achievement help to reduce one's vulnerability to inequities? Ironically, as we shall see, the higher a woman's professional accomplishments, the greater her *mommy tax* is likely to be. Crittenden (2001), a feminist who studies the economics of family life, uses the term *mommy tax* to refer to the reduced earnings of any employed person who cares for any other dependent family member.

The next step in the feminist argument is not a new one. Many 19th century feminists argued that women's contributions in the home were both undervalued and/or should be compensated with real wages (Bevier, 1918). Few contemporary feminists have gone on to actively develop proposals for compensation, but they are calculating the costs. They have argued that women are not recognized for their contribution to society when they provide care and education for their children, parents, and husbands (Crittenden, 2001; Sokoloff, 1980; Waring, 1988).

Much of this critique is leveled at Human Capital theorists (Becker, 1975, 1995). Nancy Sokoloff (1980) for instance, charges that human capitalists assume that women's lower wages are caused by their grounding in gender role behavior and personality traits. Such choices might include having a child, leaving the labor market to care for a child or a parent, or changing careers and working part-time (Porter, 2006). From a human capitalist view, when mothers stay home with their children, they do not earn a wage and they are not recognized as increasing their on-the-job experience or contributing to the economy (Mincer & Polachek, 1974). Thus, human capital theorists would suggest that women's lower wages are a result of their motherhood role. The sooner a woman bears a child, the less opportunity she has to increase her human capital through education and work experience. Gary Becker (1995) argues that a mother is investing her time in the development of her children's human capital, not her own.

In the context of this theory, feminists argue that this model overlooks women's contributions (not rewarded economically) in the reproduction and production of a generation of future workers and managers. As Crittenden (2001) calculates it, the mommy tax is highest for well-educated, high-income individuals and lowest for poorly educated people who have less potential income to lose. Shirley Burggraf (1997) has calculated that a husband and wife who earn a combined income of $81,500 per year and who are capable of being equally employed will lose $1.35 million over their lifetime if the wife leaves the labor force to care for a child. She uses the term *feminine economy* to describe the total value of the work of caring for dependents.

Increasingly, family members are struggling to deal with the demands of ailing elders. Crittenden (2001) also reports on a survey of individuals who provided informal, unpaid care for family members and found it cost them an average of $659,139 in lost wages, Social Security, and pension benefits over their lifetimes. The subjects reported having to pass up promotions and training opportunities, use up their sick days and vacations, reduce their workload to part-time, and in many cases even quit their paid jobs altogether.

With this critique by feminist economists, questions are being asked that go beyond theoretical abstractions (Remick, 1984; Welch, 2001). Returning to issues of comparable worth, new generations of women are challenging the relative absence of economic value, monetary or otherwise, paid for women's unpaid labor (Gold, 1983). They are reconceptualizing the rewards and cost to society as well as themselves of bearing and raising children and maintaining a home for family members (Wharton, 2000). For that matter, does a highly educated mother impact more on their children than less educated moth-

ers? Or, as an economist might put it: what impact do educated women have on the quality of the production of future citizens? What is the opportunity cost of the loss of an educated mother's contribution to the productivity in the labor market? Neither male nor female parents are compensated or given recognizable exchange value for their contributions to the domestic sphere. In contrast, Bergmann (2005) discourages the notion of pay for homemaking. She claims that any pay would encourage more women to stay at home and would contribute to the already existing economic gender divide. Either way, the costs of this studied blindness to the value of work in the domestic sphere results in dramatically different costs for men and women. It is the cumulative costs of these gender inequities that this chapter has been reviewing.

Conclusion: A Call for Reforms

In this chapter, we have focused on the broadest of pictures to explain why some people with equal educational resources receive less compensation for their labors in the labor market. Although there are racial and age inequities, the most continuous and startling inequities are between men and women. Education does not lead to equal economic outcomes between men and women. Economic rewards are stratified by a person's place in the gender, education, class, and ethnic hierarchies. In the American meritocratic system, there is a cherished belief that a person's wage is determined by education, experience, level of hard work, and skilled knowledge (e.g., computer science) (Becker, 1975, 1995; Schultz, 1960; Mincer & Polachek, 1974). As we have shown, each of these determinants is linked to higher wages on average, but each includes the drawback of gender inequities for women.

Old explanations for the gender inequities in employment were fueled on assumptions that women's bodies determined their destinies. These models also presumed that individual choices determined economic outcomes. For example, women choose to stay at home with their children or choose to enter the labor market. Studies of career aspirations, wage gaps, and social mobility rarely critique the structural barriers that women face as mothers or as workers. Too often, the dynamics of sexist behavior on the job are treated as random acts rather than as systematic patterns of institutional behavior. Generations of women workers resonated to the naming and ultimately legislating against biased behavior when it manifests itself as sexual harassment, tokenism, or the glass ceiling (Maume & Hurling, 1999).

Contemporary feminists remind policymakers that the lack of support for parenting and other forms of child care are not the only aspects of women's work that are undervalued. For example, Waring (1988) points out how the costs of war and weapons are calculated into the gross national product, but the costs of sustenance and caring for children in homes are not. When we look at how jobs are valued, it seems clear that technology is valued more than caring. Similarly, war and entertainment are often valued over basic human needs. Although a great deal of lip service is paid to children and their care, when it comes to actual dollars (especially for poor children) our society does not value this work as much as it values forms of productive service.

As today's men and women enter the workplace, there is hopefully a legacy and higher consciousness of the value of social justice in the labor market. New generations of women will have studied the workings of institutional discrimination as they themselves have passed through the barriers of the glass ceiling. They will have taken a closer examination of the mechanisms of gender bias and will be better equipped to challenge encrusted discriminatory practices. It is important to educate a new generation to discuss and critique these traditional models of gender role contributions to the labor market. The employment indicators we have reviewed in this chapter are best understood in their cultural, social, economic, and political context. Most of the data we have discussed are derived from contemporary research in the United States. Many of the problems we have identified here show similarities to those currently experienced in other countries. We have much to learn from them, especially their efforts to bring about change. Conversations are continuing among feminists as well as policymakers with regard to the political and social methods available for fighting racist, ageist and sexist institutional discrimination in the labor market.

RECOMMENDATIONS

It is clear that gender, race, class, and other social determinants affect individual success in our society. Over the past 100 years, there have been large-scale improvements in the lives of women. It is also clear that true equity has not yet been achieved and that social barriers prevent many people from being full participants in the economic life of our society.

Although education cannot be a panacea for all social ills, it can be an instrument of positive change to make social justice more the norm than an idealized idiosyncrasy. Education continues to be viewed as the great equalizer and has served that purpose in our society, but is far from perfected because issues of race, class, gender, and other forms of stereotypical beliefs continue to pervade our society and our schools. Ameliorating long-lasting social constraints that limit women's economic success is not easy. Although many women have demanded and fought for equality, other women are trapped in cycles of poverty or have internalized beliefs about what is possible. How then do we create a social structure that provides greater equity and builds self-efficacy and knowledgeable decision-making among women and girls as well as among men and boys?

Breaking these patterns of inequity requires a great deal of concerted effort on the part of parents, teachers, and political advocates. Although some psychological and sociological research has been used to blame the victim, it is also clear that other research suggests avenues for individual and social change. Carol Dweck (1986, 2000, 2002, 2006) found a strong relationship between students' beliefs that ability is innate and a decrease in their actual performance especially when they believed their ability was low. In contrast, those who believe in hard work rather than ability persevere and overcome barriers to learning. Similarly, she found that this perseverance also applied to beliefs regarding personal or political change. From this, we can simply conclude that to create change, one must first believe that it is possible.

To accomplish these goals, educators must work on two levels. The first level inculcates boys and girls into the belief that they can understand knowledge and will learn the skills they need to be successful. For example, girls would gain confidence in their ability to be successful in mathematics and technology, and boys would believe that they could be successful caretakers as nurses and teachers. The second level means providing people in all life stages with a belief that they can engage in positive political change that increases equity. For example, more women would gather the support necessary to run for office. Both levels are critical for education.

Policy Recommendations

To create equitable change requires working on several levels of analysis and activism: These levels include:

- Implementing gender equitable career and economic education within schools.
- Preparing teachers to teach in gender-free ways that support increases in the number of women and girls in mathematical, technical, and scientific careers, and men and boys in caring professions.
- Preparing teachers to teach students self-efficacy and to teach them the how and why of political action so that students learn to fully participate in democracy.
- Advocating for continued funding for curriculum innovations at the primary and secondary levels, exposing children of both sexes to a wide range of careers than are traditionally associated with one gender or another.
- Advocating for gender-free policy and legislation that supports equitable wages within occupations and comparable worth between historically gendered occupations. Further examination and support for court cases testing arguments for both pay equality and equity or comparable worth.

There also is a need for more comprehensive data detailing women's status in the labor force. These include:

- Continuing funding of large-scale longitudinal surveys essential to tracking historical and demographic changes in women's status in the labor force.
- Funding to allow gathering and analysis of data to document details on subgroup populations in the labor force, for example, analysis by age, race, ethnicity, age and number of children, educational attainment, etc.
- Information on comparative international data.
- More specific data on the links between educational achievement at all levels and status in the labor force.
- More longitudinal data on career aspirations and actual choices as they change over a lifetime. Career path data are now extremely limited, concentrated on males, and narrow in the time band studied.
- More sophisticated occupational within-comparison studies comparing the wage gap by gender with intervening factors controlled, including educational accomplishments and status,

experience, relative seniority, parental status, and other demographic characteristics.

- More coordination in the data collected on entry into non-traditional occupations and types of obstacles encountered through institutional discrimination—for example, sexual harassment or the glass ceiling.
- More longitudinal data on the life course of macro age cohorts of gender differences in unemployment, benefits, retirement, and likely predictions for upcoming generations.
- Analysis of the Feminization of Poverty. Documentation of women's participation in the marginal economy.

The development of gender-free education requires that policies and practices cut across class and race and provide avenues for women to pursue education more lucrative careers even though they may be older than typical postsecondary students. This means that women advocate for a reexamination of recent policies that deprive women (and others) receiving public assistance the opportunity to obtain meaningful job training or further education to improve their status in the job market.

An expanded belief in the power of education also requires that advocates make clear that the responsibilities that parents share are the core of the entire production and reproduction of our society. Without children, our society has no future. Without a shared commitment to the caring and nurturing of our children, our society has little future. Advocates must call for more systematic challenges to cultural stereotypes heightening perceived conflicts between maternal and employment roles for both sexes, but especially among men. This means that all citizens share the burden of adequate day care and after school care, including high-quality teachers paid a living wage for their work with babies and small children. This also means improved labor market policies that support rather than jeopardize responsibilities for the care of dependents—ill family members or elders. It means educating all so that the progress of society is shared equally and that women and men will be equal economic partners.

ACKNOWLEDGMENTS

The authors are listed alphabetically and both contributed equally. The authors wish to thank the following people for their help with the chapter: Julie Andrejewski, Carrie Cate-Clements, and Karen Venditti who wrote several pages for an early draft that were not used because they overlapped with other chapters of the book. A few of the references they provided were used in this chapter. We give special thanks to Catherine Hill, American Association of University Women, Washington, DC, Barbara Gault, Institute for Women's Policy Research, Washington, DC, and Bernice Sandler, Women's Research and Education Institute, Washington, DC, who provided excellent critiques of the chapter. We also have a special place in our hearts for Sue Klein, our most tenacious, gender-equity colleague.

References

51% of American women are single. (2007, January 16). *Feminist Daily News Wire*. Retrieved February 9, 2007 from http://www.feminist.org/news/newsbyte/uswirestory.asp?id=10095

Acker, J. (1989). *Doing comparable worth: Gender, class and pay equity*. Philadelphia: Temple University Press.

Ashburn, E. (2006, June 29). New welfare rules may reduce poor Americans' access to higher education. *The Chronicle of Higher Education Daily News*. Retrieved June 29, 2006, from http://chronicle.com/daily2006/06/2006062901n.htm

American Association of University Women. (2004). *Tenure denied: Cases of sex discrimination in Academia*. Washington, DC: Author.

Andronici, J. F. & Katz, D. S. (2007). "Scaling the Maternal Wall: Recent court cases give moms hope against a common job bias" *Ms. magazine*. Winter 2007, 63–64.

Association of University Women. (2006). *Five frequently asked questions about university and college women*. Washington, DC: Author. Retrieved August 10, 2006, from http://www.aauw.org/print_page.cfml?Path_Info=F:\web\aauw\research tatedata\faq.cfm

Arnott, T., & Matthei, J. (1996). *Race, gender and work: A multicultural history of women in the United States* (Rev. ed.). Boston: South End Press.

Baker, D., & Boushey, H. (2004, June 2). *Plunging employment: Blame mom*. Washington, DC: Center for Economic and Policy Research.

Bane, M., & Ellwood, D. (1994). *Welfare realities*. Cambridge, MA: Harvard University Press.

Baxandall, R., & Gordon, L. (1995). America's working women: A documentary history, 1600 to the present. New York: Norton.

Becker, G. S. (1975). *Human capital: A theoretical and empirical analysis with special reference to education* (2nd ed.). Chicago: University of Chicago Press.

Becker, G. S. (1995). A *treatise on the family*. Cambridge, MA: Harvard University Press.

Bergmann, B. R. (2005). *The economic emergence of women* (2nd ed.). New York: Palgrave MacMillan.

Bevier, I. (1918). *The home economics movement*. Boston: Whitcomb & Barrows.

Blank, R., & Haskins, R. (2001). *The new world of welfare*. Washington, DC: Brookings Institute.

Budig, M., & England, P. (2001). The wage penalty for motherhood. *The American Sociological Review, 66,* 204–225.

Burggraf, S. P. (1997). *The feminine economy and economic man*. Boston: Addison-Wesley.

Burkhauser, R., & Salisbury, D. (1993). *Pensions in a changing economy* Washington, DC: Employee Benefit Research Institute, Education and Research Fund.

Calasanti, T., & Selvin, K. (2001). Gender, social inequalities and retirement Income. In T. Calasanti & K. Selvin (Eds.), *Gender, Social Inequalities and Aging* (pp. 93–120).

Chen, M., Vanek, J., Lund, F., & Heintz. (2005). *Progress of the world's women 2005: Women, work & poverty*. New York: United Nations.

Cherlin, A. (2005). *Public and private families*. New York: McGraw-Hill.

Cochran, S., & Malone, E. (1999). *Public policy: Perspectives and choices*. New York: McGraw-Hill.

Couric, E. (1998). An NJL/West survey, women in the law: Awaiting their turn. *National Law Journal*, S1, S12.

Crittenden, A. (2001). *The price of motherhood: Why the most important job in the world is still the least valued*. New York: Metropolitan Books.

Curran, M., & Renzetti, D. (2003). *Women, men and society*. New York: Allyn and Bacon.

Dewar, D. M. (2000). Gender impacts on health insurance coverage: Findings for unmarried full-time employees. *Women's Health Issues, 10*(5), 268–277.

Dweck, C. (1986). Motivational processes affecting learning. *American Psychologist, 41*, 1040–1047.

Dweck, C. (2000). *Self-theories: Their role in motivation, personality and development*. Philadelphia: Routledge Press.

Dweck, C. (2002). The development of ability conceptions. In A. Wigfield & J. S. Eccles (Eds.), *The development of achievement motivation* (pp. 57–91). San Diego, CA: Academic Press.

Dweck, C. (2006). *Mindset*. New York: Random House.

Ehrenrich, B. (2001). *Nickel and dimed: Or (not) getting by in America*. New York: Metropolitan Books/Henry Holt.

England, P. (1992). *Comparable worth: Theory and evidence*. New York: Aldine de Gruyter.

Farkas, J., & O'Rand, J. (1998). The pension mix for women in middle and later life: The changing employment relationship. *Social Forces, 76*(3), 1007–32.

Ferber, M., & Nelson J. (1993). *Beyond economic man*. Chicago: University of Chicago Press.

Folbre, N. (2001). *The invisible heart: Economics and family values*. New York: The New Press.

Fuller, R., & Schoenberger, R. (1991). The gender salary gap: Do academic achievement, internship experience & college major make a difference? *Social Science Quarterly, 72*(4), 715–726.

Furstenburg, F., Brooks-Gunn, J., & Morgan, S. (1987). *Adolescent mothers in later life*. Cambridge: Cambridge University Press.

Gilman, C. P. (1913). *The waste of public and private housekeeping, Annals of the American Academy of Political Social Sciences, 48*(July), 91–95.

Gold, M. (1983). *A dialogue on comparable worth*. Ithaca: ILR Press.

Gornick, J., & Meyers, M. (2003). *Families that work: Policies for reconciling parenthood and employment*. New York: Russell Sage Foundation.

Greenberg, M., Strawn, J., & Plimpton, L. (Revised February 2000). State opportunities to provide access to postsecondary education under TANF. Washington, DC: Center for Law and Social Policy.

Grodsky, E., & Pager, D. (2001). The structure of disadvantage: Individual and occupational determinants of the African American-white wage gap. *American Sociological Review, 66*, 542–567.

Harrington, M. (1996). Family status and poverty among older women: The gendered distribution of retirement income in the U.S. In B. Hess (Ed.), *Aging for the twenty-first century* (pp. 464–479). New York: St. Martin's Press.

Henslin, J. (2006). *Social problems*. New York: Prentice Hall.

Hess, B. (2001). Two-thousand indicators of well-being. *Federal Interagency Forum on Aging Related Statistics*. Retrieved June 2006, from http://www.agingstats.gov/

Hewitson, G. (1989). *Feminist economics: Interrogating the masculinity of rational economic man*. Northhampton, MA: Edwin Elgar Press.

Heyman, J. (2000). *The Widening Gap*. New York: Basic Books.

Horner, M. (1972). Toward an understanding of achievement related conflicts in women. *Journal of Social Issues, 28*(2), 242–265.

Jacobs, J., & Lim, S. (1995). Trends in occupational and industrial sex segregation in fifty-six countries. In J. Jacobs (Ed.), *Gender inequality at work* (pp. 259–293). Thousand Oaks, CA, Sage.

Jones-DeWeever, A. A., & Gault, B. (2006). *Resilient and reaching for more: Challenges and benefits for higher education for welfare participants and their children*. Washington, DC: Institute for Women's Policy Research.

Kay, F., & Hagen, J. (1995). The persistent glass ceiling: Inequalities in the earnings of lawyers. *British Journal of Sociology, 46*, 279–310.

Kaufman, D., & Richardson, B. (1986). *Achievement and women: Challenging the assumptions*. New York: The Free Press.

Kemp, J. (1990). Tackling poverty: Market-based policies to empower the poor. *Policy Review, 51*(Winter), 2–5.

King, M. (1992). Occupational segregation by race and sex, 1940–1988. *Monthly Labor Review, 114*(7), 30–36.

Lee, S. (2005, June). Women and social security: Benefit types and eligibility. IWPR #D463. Washington, DC: Institute for Women's Policy Research.

Levin, P. (2001). Gendering the market: Temporality, work and gender on the national future exchange. *Work and Occupations, 28*(1), 112–130.

MacDonald, C., & Siriani, C. (1996). *Working in the service society*. Philadelphia: Temple University Press.

MacPherson, D., & Hirsh, B. (1995). Wage and gender composition: Why do women's jobs pay less? *Journal of Labor Economics, 13*, 426–471.

Manpower Research Demonstration Corporation. (MRDC Report, 2001). *Is work enough: The experiences of current and former welfare mothers who work*. Available from, http//www.mdrev.org/ Reports 2001/UC-Is Work Enough/Overview- Is work enough .htm

Maume, M., & Hurling, T. (1999). Glass ceilings and glass elevators: Occupational segregation and race and sex differences in managerial promotions. *Work and Occupations, 26*, 483–509.

Mincer, J., & Polachek, S. W. (1974). Family investment in human capital: Earnings of women. *Journal of Political Economy, 82*, S76–S108.

Mitchell, O. S., Levine, P. B., & Phillips, J. W. (1999, September). *The impact of pay inequality, occupational segregation, and lifetime work experience on the retirement income of women and minorities*. Washington, DC: American Association of Retired Persons, Policy and Research.

Muir, E., & Nelson, F. H. (2005). *Survey and analysis of teacher salary trends 2004*. Washington, DC: American Federation of Teachers.

National Center for Education Statistics. (2003). *Total fall enrollment in degree-granting institutions, by level, sex, age & attendance status of students: 2001*. Washington, DC: U.S. Department of Education.

National Women's Law Center. (2000, June). Testimony of Judith C. Appelbaum, Vice President and Director of Employment Opportunities before the Committee on Health Education, Labor and Pensions, United States Senate. Washington, DC: Author. Retrieved August 10, 2006, from http://www.nwlc.org/details.cfm?id=227& section=employment

National Women's Law Center. (2005). *Tools of the trade: Using the law to address sex segregation in high school career and technical education*. Washington, DC: Author.

Porter, E. (2006, March 2). Stretched to the limit, women still march to work. *New York Times*, New York.

Remick, H. (1984). *Comparable worth and wage discrimination: Technical possibilities and political realities*. Philadelphia: Temple University Press.

Reskin, B. (1993). Sex segregation in the workplace. *Annual Review of Sociology, 19*, 241–270.

Reskin, B., & Roos, P. (1990). *Job queues, gender queues: Explaining women's inroads into male occupations*. Philadelphia: Temple University Press.

Rindfuss, R., & St. John, C. (1983). Social determinants of age at first birth. *Journal of Marriage and the Family, 45*, 553–565.

Robinson, J., & McIlwee, J. (1989). Women in engineering: A promise unfulfilled? *Social Problems. 36*, 455–472.

Rose, S. J., & Hartman, H. I. (2004). Still a man's labor market: The long-term earnings gap. Washington, DC: Institute for Women's Policy Research. Retrieved November 20, 2004, from www.iwpr.org

Schiller, B. (2004). *The economics of poverty and discrimination.* New York: Prentice Hall.

Schultz, T. W. (1960). Investment in human capital. *American Economic Review 51*(1), 1–17.

Scott, C. (2001). Aged SSI recipients: Income, work history & social security benefits. *Social Security Bulletin, 54*(8), 2–11.

Seager, J. (2003). *The Penguin atlas of women in the world.* Brighton: Penguin Books.

Seccombe, K., & Amey, C. (1995). Playing by the rules and losing: Health insurance and the working poor. *Journal of Health and Social Behavior, 36,* 168–181.

Silverberg, M., Warner, E., Fong, M., & Goodwin, D. (2004). *National assessment of vocational education: Final report to Congress.* Washington, DC: U.S. Department of Education.

Sokoloff, N. J. (1980). *Between money and love: The dialectics of women's home and market work.* Westport, CT: Praeger.

Solinger, R. (1992). *Wake up little Suzie: Single pregnancy and race before Roe V. Wade.* New York: Routledge.

Spitze, G. D., & Waite, L. J. (1981). 'Wives' employment: The role of husbands' perceived attitudes. *Journal of Marriage and the Family, 43,* 117–125.

Steinberg, R., & Cook, A. (1988). Policies affecting women's employment in industrial countries. In A. H. Stromberg & S. Harkess (Eds.), *Women Working* (pp. 307–328). Mountainview, CA: Mayfield.

Tallichet, S. (1995). Gendered relations in the mines and the division of labor underground. *Gender and Society, 9,* 697–711.

Tenny, D., & Zahradnik, B. (2001). *The poverty despite work handbook.* Washington DC: Center on Budget and Policy Priorities.

Traver, N. (2005, January 26). High stakes. *Chicago Tribune.*

United Nations. (1995). *Women's education and fertility behavior: Recent evidence from demographic and health surveys.* New York: United Nations, Department for Economic and Social Information and Policy Analysis.

United Nations Educational, Scientific and Cultural Organization. (2003). Why are girls still held back? *Education for all global monitoring report.* Retrieved August 29, 2005, from http://www.unesco.org/education/efa_report/2003_pdf/chapter3.pdf

U.S. Bureau of National Affairs. (1979). FEP Summary of Latest Developments. (No. 383).

U.S. Bureau of the Census. (1987). Current population reports series P-70, No. 11. What is it Worth? Education background and economic status: Spring 1984. Washington, DC: U.S. Government Printing Office.

U.S. Department of Education. (2003). Number of full time faulty members by sex, rank & racial and ethnic groups. Washington, DC: U.S. Government Printing Office.

U.S. Department of Health and Human Services. Administration for Children and Families, Office of Planning, Research and Evaluation. (1999). *Second annual report to Congress on the Temporary Assistance for Needy Families (TANF) program.* Washington, DC: U.S. Government Printing Office.

U.S. Department of Labor, Bureau of Labor Statistics. (2002a). *Employment status of the civilian population by sex and age*, January 2001. Retrieved September, 2004, from http://www.dol.gov

U.S. Department of Labor, Bureau of Labor Statistics. (2002b). *Current population survey, 2001: Employed persons by detailed occupations, sex, race & Hispanic origin.* Retrieved September, 2004, from http://www.dol.gov

U.S. Department of Labor, Bureau of Labor Statistics. (2004, February). *Women in the labor force: A databook* (Report 973). Washington, DC: U.S. Government Printing Office.

U.S. Department of Labor, Bureau of Labor Statistics. (2005, September). *Highlight of women's earning in 2004* (Report 987). Washington, DC: U.S. Government Printing Office.

Vannoy, D., & Dubeck, P. (1998). *Challenges for work and family in the twenty-first century.* New York: Aldine de Gruyter.

Waldfogel, J. (1997). The effect of children on women's wages. *American Sociological Review, 62,* 209–217.

Wallace, M. (1998). Downsizing the American dream. In C. Vannoy, & P. Dubeck (Eds.). *Challenges of work and family in the twentieth century* (pp. 23–39). New York: Walter de Gruyere.

Waring, M. (1988). *If women counted.* New York: Harper Collins.

Waring, M. (1999). *Counting for nothing: What men value and what women are worth.* Toronto: University of Toronto Press.

Welch, F. (2001). *The causes and consequences of increasing inequality.* Chicago: University of Chicago Press.

Wharton, A. S. (2000). Feminism at work. *Annals of the American Academy. 471,* 167–182.

Yelowitz, A. S. (2000). *Evaluating the effects of Medicaid on welfare and work: Evidence from the past decade.* Washington, DC: Employment Policies Institute.

Part

· II ·

OVERVIEW: ADMINISTRATIVE STRATEGIES FOR IMPLEMENTING GENDER EQUITY

Dolores A. Grayson

This section contains three chapters that focus on the roles of policymakers, administrators, teachers, teacher educators, and other educational leaders in implementing the legal mandates pertaining to gender equity in education, as well as the spirit of those mandates. As Patricia Schmuck said in the overview to this section for the 1985 *Handbook*, "Strategies for achieving sex equity involve many different approaches to change: they range from formulating new educational policy to the formation of active community pressure groups, from training teachers in methods of changing sex-stereotyped attitudes and behaviors to rewriting curriculum materials, from providing technical assistance to providing information on how to sue. Even though students and employees are guaranteed by law that sex cannot be used as a discriminatory attribute, the literature on school change makes it very clear that individuals or institutions do not change behavior or practice by administrative fiat alone" (p. 91).

After highlighting some of the important findings in each of the chapters, I will share my perspectives on the importance of using education to end gender stereotyping and then discuss some commonalities among the three chapters in addressing this challenge.

Chapter 5, "The Role of Government in Advancing Gender Equity in Education," describes the linkages between the federal and state mandates and educational policies and practices. The seven authors, Margaret Nash, Susan Klein, Barbara Bitters, Sharon Hobbs, William Howe, Linda Shevitz, and Linda Wharton, have had extensive experience fighting for gender equity at the federal and state levels or studying key aspects of the responsibilities of governments related to gender equity and education. This chapter is a must read for many educators who are unlikely to know much about Title IX and other laws that provide protections against sex discrimination at the federal and state levels. It also provides guidance on the current and potential roles of nongovernmental civil rights and education organizations in influencing or working with governmental agencies to advance gender equity. The chapter authors describe

weaknesses in the full implementation of the laws, such as decreased federal funding for most areas of gender equity assistance, and minimal attention to the work of required Title IX gender equity coordinators in organizations that receive federal financial assistance for education purposes. Although this is a long chapter, it doesn't cover much about local gender equity policies and procedures because there are few studies of the impact of successful organizations and strategies. This is in part because of the lack of funding for this research, and because it is difficult to show causality when the contexts for the policies and administrative strategies are so varied. The authors have many recommendations for how all of these entities can better advance gender equity. I hope you will read them and work with others to carry them out.

Chapter 6, "Increasing Gender Equity in Educational Leadership," led by Charol Shakeshaft, (the author of the related chapter in the 1985 *Handbook*) and four other professors of Educational Leadership, Genevieve Brown, Beverly Irby, Margaret Grogan, and Julia Ballenger, focuses on increasing the participation of women in K–12 educational leadership positions such as principals, central office staff, and superintendents. It also addresses persistent and emerging barriers to that goal.

The authors found that many of the studies in the past 20 years have been by women and on women. However, they are mainly dissertations by education leadership graduate students, not systematic large-scale studies. For example, while there is some evidence that the proportion of women with education leadership credentials and degrees is substantial, there were no national studies to show this. This national data is important, as it would help prove that there is a substantial disparity between the numbers of qualified women administrative leaders and the percent that are actually hired. Such patterns help provide evidence of sex discrimination.[1] Chapter 30 on "Improving Gender Equity in Postsecondary Education" provides related information on women administrators in community colleges as well as various other types of colleges and universities. The pattern of having a higher percentage of women in the less prestigious (lower paying) positions or institutions, (e.g., elementary school principals or community college presidents), is documented in both chapters. Chapter 6 also points out that the curriculum for educational leaders needs to reflect a diversity in leadership attributes, rather than assuming that one model works for everyone. However, a concern of Patricia Schmuck in the overview to this section of the 1985 *Handbook* is still relevant. She notes that "it remains unclear whether the increased employment of women administrators will alter the educational system enough to be an effective tool to implement and diffuse other sex equity practices in schools". (p. 93). Chapter 6 does not claim that having more women administrators will improve their organization's effectiveness in advancing gender equity. Instead, the current authors have started to address the role of all education leaders in effectively advancing social justice and gender equality in their educational institutions, and in the university courses that prepare them for their administration careers. However, more work is needed to develop effective models for both preservice and inservice training and credentialing to more fully engage educational administrators in the implementation of gender equitable policies.

David Sadker and Karen Zittleman were the lead authors for chapter 7 on the "Treatment of Gender Equity in Teacher Education." David and his late wife, Myra Sadker, authored the related chapter in the 1985 *Handbook*. The chapter also benefited from contributions by professors Penelope Earley, Theresa McCormick, Candace Strawn, and JoAnne Preston. This new chapter reports that during the past two decades, there has been remarkably little progress in preparing teachers to be more equitable in their instruction. Research on textbooks and teacher education programs reveals little information and few strategies to assist teachers in understanding how gender bias influences teaching and learning. Chapter 7 also discusses how the more conservative political environment has moved the national dialogue away from gender equity issues. The authors indicate that equity progress will rely on the research and teaching of individuals committed to this goal, as well as the reemergence of organizational and political support. They offer specific examples of updated and revised strategies for weaving gender issues throughout a teacher education curriculum, such as helping all teachers and prospective teachers detect and correct gender bias in curricula and classrooms, including addressing bias in instructional materials. A new aspect of this chapter is the documentation of the gendered devaluation of teaching and salary scales even for education professors. Sadly, this analysis holds true for many other topics covered in the *Handbook*, including educators in visual arts and dance as described in chapter 17.

It would appear from the wealth of information, studies, and strategies that have been written and developed in the more than two decades since the 1985 Handbook that researchers and advocates are less optimistic regarding actualizing systemic change to create equity, than in the '70s and '80s. Over the past 20 plus years, the general public has been exposed to a great deal of superficial information about gender equity in the popular press and other media, with little regard for attention to the legal aspects, Title IX requirements, and/or substantive, longitudinal research. In this section, it is obvious that those of us in it for the long haul are all part of a knowledge continuum, building on the previous work, much of which continues to inspire, motivate, and challenge all of us as scholars and members of society. The evidence in this section indicates that there is still a need for some of the previously identified best practices, programs, professional development, technical assistance, and equity accountability reviews, most of which are no longer available through federal funding.

This section provides a justification for why policy makers, educational leaders, teachers, students, and others should attend to gender equity, to nondiscrimination, to avoiding gender bias and stereotyping. As an education equity consultant and trainer, working with literally thousands of practitioners, many of whom have been consciously or unconsciously resistant to gender equity, some of the following contributions have helped provide a rationale for my belief that gender equity in education and other forms of human equity are issues of mental, emotional, physical, and spiritual health for our society and for the world as a whole. To perpetuate a world of roles and stereotypes based on gender, race, ethnicity, language, developmental or physical challenge, perceived ability, sexuality, socioeconomic class, religious beliefs, or any other perceived label or characteristic is to perpetuate an unhealthy world. Gender equity can bridge the gaps within and between these parallel human equity issues and help identify commonalities, as well as build respect for mutual differences.

The research and development work with which I've been involved for over 3 decades was rooted in concepts, theories, patterns, practices, and strategies first explored, developed, and tested from a gender equity knowledge base (Grayson & Martin, 1984, 1985, 1990, 1997, 1998 and 2003; Grayson, 2004). For example, Sandra Bem's instrument to measure psychological androgyny, the Bem Sex Role Inventory, has been a key influence. Bem states that her instrument allows individuals to be both feminine and masculine, unlike other tests prior to that time, which were restrictive to only one. If one scored high on both, one was seen as possessing both masculine and feminine traits and considered to be androgynous (psychologically), applying appropriate characteristics when necessary. Her research showed that androgynous individuals who possessed both sets of traits were "truly effective and well functioning" (Bem, 1974, 1993). Many equity professionals have modified and adapted these ideas and agree that a combination of emotional and psychological traits and skills is the most beneficial and that either extreme is unhealthy. When young girls and young boys are socialized to "score high" only on traditional feminine and masculine stereotypes, we are programming them toward psychological and emotional difficulties in life. For the girls, we've seen that result in repressed aggression, eating disorders, and victimiza-

---

[1]Chapter 13 on "Gender Equity in Science, Engineering, and Technology" uses similar logic in providing data from national studies that suggest women academic scientists are facing sex discrimination because a higher proportion of women are graduating with advanced science degrees than are being hired for academic science positions.

tion. For the boys at the other extreme, we've seen it predict uncontrolled rage, hostility, violence and criminal behavior, and a macho interest in sports and power. This is just one example of the many types of justifications that may help some education policymakers, administrators, and teachers realize the importance of using systematic strategies to advance gender equity. A variety of related justifications are included in the chapters in this section as well as in many other *Handbook* chapters.

The answers on how to use administrative strategies to advance gender equity involve all of us working together in our own spheres of influence for healthier people in a healthier world. The authors who have written the chapters in this section are committed, dedicated, and passionate scholars and researchers who have spent many years identifying problems and contributing to solutions for these issues. While each of the chapters in this section makes a unique contribution to the *Handbook* as a whole, there are some themes and commonalities in all three:

1. Since the chapters in this section were so similar to the 1985 chapters and in all cases involved at least one of the 1985 authors, it was easy to compare and contrast the information and examine the changes in positive and negative directions.
2. All of the chapters indicate how progress and known best practices have been interrupted by decreased funding, changes in

government policies and priorities, and societal backlash. Sadly, the conclusion of Patricia Schmuck in the 1985 Handbook overview is still true, "The weakness of evaluation is evident in all the chapters and suggest a future research need" (p. 93)
3. The multiple authors of each of the chapters in this section developed consensus recommendations and strategies for practitioners, policymakers, teachers and teacher educators, and other educational leaders to implement gender equity in education.
4. The chapters in this section are written in a way that will appeal to and are extremely relevant for practitioners, as well as other researchers and scholars.

This section recognizes that when injustice is institutionalized in a civilized society, the solutions must be institutionalized, and laws, policies, and procedures are essential first steps, as spelled out in chapter 5. Chapter 6 on "Increasing Gender Equity in Educational Leadership" reinforces that administrators and their training continue to be the gatekeepers to successful gender equity implementation in educational agencies and schools. Chapter 7 on "The Treatment of Gender Equity in Teacher Education" teaching reminds us that gender equitable practices need to happen behind the closed doors of classrooms and academia, in order to promote richer lives for all.

References

Bem, S. L. (1974). The measurement of psychological androgyny. *Journal of Consulting and Clinical Psychology, 42*, 155–162.

Bem, S. L. (1993). *The lenses of gender: Transforming the debate on sexual inequality.* New Haven, CT: Yale University Press.

Grayson, D. A., & Martin, M. D. (1997). *Generating expectations for student achievement, (GESA): An equitable approach to educational excellence.* Teacher handbook (3rd ed.) Canyon Lake, CA: GrayMill.

Grayson, D. A., & Martin, M. D. (1998). *Generating expectations for student achievement, (GESA): An equitable approach to educational excellence.* Participant booklet. (Rev. 2003, Tehachapi, CA). Canyon Lake, CA: GrayMill.

Grayson, D. A., & Martin, M. D. (1990) *Gender/ethnic expectations for student achievement (GESA)* (2nd ed.). Des Moines, IA: GrayMill Publications.

Grayson, D. A., & Martin, M. D. (1985–88). *Gender expectations and student achievement (GESA).* Downey, CA: Los Angeles County Office of Education.

Grayson, D. A., & Martin, M. D. (1984). *GESA: A teacher training program addressing gender disparity in the classroom.* Paper presented at the annual meeting of the American Educational Research Association, New Orleans. ERIC Document Reproduction Service, Bethesda, MD, ED 243-829, 1984.

Grayson, D. A. (2004). *Student Achievement Grounded in Equity.* Tehachapi, CA: GrayMill.

·5·

THE ROLE OF GOVERNMENT IN ADVANCING GENDER EQUITY IN EDUCATION

Margaret A. Nash, Susan S. Klein, Barbara Bitters, and *William Howe,*
Sharon Hobbs, Linda Shevitz, Linda Wharton with Eleanor Smeal

INTRODUCTION

This chapter discusses the critical role of government, especially at the federal and state levels, in institutionalizing gender equity policies and practices in K–12 and postsecondary education in the United States. Themes include:

- The passage of the federal Title IX and efforts to weaken its protections.
- Legislation and procedures used by federal, state, and local government agencies to implement laws to increase gender equity. Implementation includes funding gender focused programs and research as well as the enforcement of Title IX and other statutes.
- Implementation of state constitutional provisions and statutes prohibiting sex discrimination in education.
- The roles of states, education, civil rights, women's rights, and other organizations in creating and implementing gender/sex equity laws and programs and the mechanisms found to be helpful in these endeavors.

Finally, the authors provide recommendations for additional policy, programs or practice and research to maximize the role government can play in advancing gender equity education goals as described in chapter 1.

HISTORY OF TITLE IX AND RELATED CIVIL RIGHTS LAWS

In 1972, the United States Congress passed the first legislation ever to prohibit sex discrimination in educational programs and activities in institutions that receive federal financial assistance. Title IX of the Education Amendments of 1972 (Title IX) banned sex discrimination in a wide range of institutions with education programs and activities, from prisons to schools to museums, and in many activities, from admissions to athletics to employment. Title IX was renamed "The Patsy T. Mink Equal Opportunity in Education Act" in October 2002 to honor one of the law's foremost advocates.[1] As described in chapter 1 and in some of the following information on the history of Title IX, the Equal Protection Clause of the 14th Amendment to the U.S. Constitution has been used by the Supreme Court to provide protections against sex discrimination in many aspects of our society, including education. Other legislation has provided parallel protections. For instance, Title VI of the Civil Rights Act of 1964, which provides protection against discrimination on the basis of race, color, or national origin in all federally funded programs, was used as a model for Title IX. But unlike Title VI, Title IX coverage is limited to education.[2] Although Title IX covers education broadly, it does not cover sex bias in instructional materials.[3]

---

[1]Patsy Mink and many other supporters of Title IX suffered sex discrimination first hand. For example, she was denied admission to medical school and then only used her first initial with her subsequently successful law school application.

[2]Other U.S. civil rights laws such as Title VII of the 1964 Civil Rights Act (prohibiting discrimination in employment) and the Americans with Disabilities Act of 1990 apply to many organizations in addition to those receiving federal financial assistance.

[3]Although women's rights groups wanted to retain these prohibitions, arguments for omitting them were based on possible interference with Constitutional guarantees of freedom of speech and states' rights and responsibilities to make decisions about education.

The June 1975 House of Representatives hearings on the Title IX regulations reported that before Title IX, differential admission, treatment, and hiring of students, staff, and faculty were commonplace. Vocational education programs and career interest tests were segregated by gender. Programs open to girls included training for low-paying occupations in clerical fields and in homemaking programs that did not train students for wage-earning occupations at all. Girls often were discouraged or excluded from advanced science and math courses and related clubs. Programs open to boys included industrial arts and production agriculture. Boys were excluded from home economics and business courses and the clubs associated with those program areas. Guidance counselors routinely gave students interest inventories that were gender-coded; a boy and girl with similar interests were directed into gender-specific careers. Some schools had sex-segregated lunch tables, closets, toys, lines, reading lists, and even water fountains. School sports, at both the secondary and postsecondary levels, offered few if any programs and opportunities for girls and women. As late as 1975 in high schools across the country, the average budget for boys' sports was five times more than the budget for girls' sports. At the college level, the proportion rose to 30 times more money for men's athletics than for women's athletics (*Sex Discrimination Regulations*, 1975).

Many scholarships to colleges could be awarded only to men, and financial aid, including loans, could be denied to women who were married, pregnant, or had children. Colleges and universities had quota systems limiting the number of women who could attend and had different standards for admission based on sex. For example, in the 1970s Cornell admitted women only if they had SAT scores 30–40 points higher than the male average, and at Pennsylvania State University men were five times more likely to be admitted than women. High schools and colleges generally expelled pregnant students, married or not, or required pregnant students to accept home instruction. Many elementary and secondary school systems fired pregnant teachers, including married ones, or required them to resign at the end of the semester. School systems routinely paid women less and invested less in pension programs for women employees than for men (National Advisory Council on Women's Educational Programs, 1981). Clearly, sex discrimination was rampant in school systems and institutions of higher education. The need for equal rights legislation was great.

Title IX has been critical in eliminating substantial sex discrimination in education in the U.S. Many of the *Handbook* chapters describe progress toward gender equity associated with Title IX (as well as parallel civil rights laws, and social or political pressures). They show that opportunities expanded for both girls and boys in elementary and secondary education especially in sports and athletics, mathematics achievement scores for girls and boys became more similar as they took more of the same courses, the number and proportion of women enrolled in postsecondary institutions increased, and educational and employment opportunities for females and males expanded and in some cases became more equitable.

Congress Passes Title IX

During the 1950s and 1960s Congress passed a number of laws providing financial aid to institutions of higher education and their students. Many of these laws were set to expire in 1971, and in 1970 members of Congress introduced various bills to extend and expand these programs. Several key events led Congress to discuss legislation prohibiting sex discrimination in education in conjunction with the extension of these financial aid laws. In 1963, the U.S. Commission on the Status of Women issued a report documenting the secondary status of women in the U.S., with a special focus on women's economic disadvantages. This helped justify the passage of the Equal Pay Act of 1963. The Federation of Business and Professional Women worked quickly to establish state-level commissions on the status of women that would parallel the U.S. Commission. This created a network of women and men on the state level who researched and documented discrimination against women across the country, and therefore helped to build grassroots support for legislation aimed at gender equity (Threinen & Weck, 1983). In 1970, Dr. Bernice Sandler, under the auspices of the Women's Equity Action League (WEAL), filed a class action administrative complaint against hundreds of colleges and universities that had contracts with the federal government and charged them with violating President Johnson's 1965 Executive Order 11246, which was amended in 1968 to prohibit sex discrimination in federal contracts (Sandler, 1997).

Also in 1970, a presidential task force on women's rights and responsibilities issued its report that documented the existence of sex bias in American society and recommended legislative changes to ban sex discrimination in education and other areas (Fishel & Pottker, 1977; Threinen & Weck, 1983). The key proposed legislative change addressing this broad challenge to protect against sex discrimination was the Equal Rights Amendment (ERA), a proposed amendment to the U.S. Constitution, first introduced in Congress in 1923 and every year thereafter until it was was approved by the House of Representatives in 1971 and by the Senate in March 1972. Section 1 of the ERA states that "Equality of Rights under the law shall not be denied or abridged by the United States or by any state on account of sex." However, the ERA fell just three states short of the necessary 38 states needed to gain ratification, and it has not yet been ratified by enough states to become law. Section III of this chapter describes how many states use wording similar to the ERA to provide their own constitutional protections.

Various education bills, such as the omnibus higher education bill, were up for extension in 1970. As part of this higher education legislation, Representative Edith Green (OR) sponsored a bill to outlaw sex discrimination in education despite the general belief that sex discrimination was not a big education issue. Documentation of the need for such a law was not hard to find, and at the summer 1970 hearings held by Green with the assistance of Dr. Bernice Sandler, 75 different statements documenting the problems related to sex-role stereotyping and discrimination in education were made by educators and various women's groups. Representative Green hired Dr. Sandler to compile two volumes of testimony about sex discrimination in education from the hearings (Fishel & Pottker, 1977; Nash, 2002; Sandler, 1997; Threinen & Weck, 1983).

The following year, however, the House again was working on an omnibus higher education bill. The subcommittee, headed by Edith Green, again included a special provision banning sex discrimination in any program or activity receiving federal financial assistance, including education, housing, and public accomodations, modeled on Title VI of the Civil Rights Act of 1964, which prohibits discrimination on the basis of race, color, and national origin. Various members wanted the prohibition of sex discrimination to have limited coverage related to admissions policies; finally they agreed to exempt all undergraduate college admissions policies from coverage. The bill next went to the Education and Labor Committee, where Green, with help from women's groups, lobbied to have that exemption deleted and replaced with one that would exempt schools that were 90% or more of one sex. That version passed the committee and was sent to the House, with an attached note from nine Republican members who objected to the prohibitions against sex discrimination. The stated basis of their objection was federal restrictions and controls of higher education (Fishel & Pottker, 1977).

When the Education bill was sent to the House, once again the amendment exempting all undergraduate admissions was introduced, and passed. The House inserted this language in the Senate's bill and sent it back. In November 1971, with the bill in the Senate's Committee on Labor and Public Welfare, Senator Birch Bayh (IN) introduced an amended version of his earlier proposal. On the Senate floor, Bayh proposed a new amendment; it required protection against sex discrimination in services available to students within an institution or in employment within an institution; in the area of admissions, it exempted academic elementary and secondary schools, military and religious schools, and private undergraduate colleges. This amendment was passed and sent to Senate-House conference (Fishel & Pottker, 1977).

The conference committee took three months to resolve all the differences between the bills—250 in all, only 11 of which dealt with sex discrimination. Most of the higher education community spent their time trying to influence the outcome of other sections of the bill that they considered more important. Without this opposition, the Conference Committee adopted Title IX. President Nixon signed the Education Amendments of 1972 in June, and they became effective July 1, 1972. The first and key sentence of Title IX said simply and straightforwardly:

No person in the United States shall, on the basis of sex, be excluded from participation in, be denied the benefits of, or be subjected to discrimination under any education program or activity receiving federal financial assistance.

It is worth noting that this included educational agencies serving K–12 populations, as well as higher education and many other recipients of federal funds such as museums and prisons. Although Congress did not pass Title IX easily, there was relatively little debate about it. Court-ordered busing was both more visible and more controversial than banning sex discrimination in schools. To a large extent, Title IX did not garner attention from the media, the public, or from Congress until it already was law. When some representatives realized what they had done, they immediately started efforts to weaken Title IX (Salomone, 1986). When the hearings were held, the American Council on Education (ACE; higher education's lobbying arm) was asked to testify. They refused, stating that there was no sex discrimination, and besides, it was no problem. Thus they were not watching the bill at all and were not aware of its implications

for sports and other areas, except the admissions problems for single-sex schools and private undergraduate institutions.

Hot debates over busing and the March 1972 passage of the Equal Rights Amendment in Congress and its early state ratifications, and the Supreme Court's 1973 decision in *Roe v. Wade*, may have overshadowed Title IX initially, but soon opponents of Title IX created sensationalistic press coverage of their own. The main targets of criticism were coeducational physical education classes, intercollegiate athletics, and traditional single sex organizations such as fraternities and sororities. In 1974, Congress passed amendments that limited Title IX by excluding from coverage social fraternities and sororities, Boy Scouts, Girl Scouts, YMCA, YWCA, Camp Fire Girls, and other voluntary youth service organizations. In 1976, Congress passed several other amendments limiting Title IX. These amendments allowed scholarships to be awarded as prizes for beauty contests, and allowed single-sex events, such as Boys' State and Girls' State programs and father-son and mother-daughter events, to continue to be sponsored by schools (Fishel & Pottker, 1977; Salomone, 1986).

The National Collegiate Athletic Association (NCAA), which had administered only male athletic programs since 1910, conducted the biggest lobbying campaign against Title IX. The NCAA argued that if colleges had to fund women's athletics more than they already did, implementation of Title IX would "destroy major college football and basketball programs" (*Sex Discrimination Regulations*, 1975, p. 101). The NCAA continued to make this argument even after Congress passed the Javits Amendment in 1974, which stipulated, not that there should be immediate or total equality of expenditures in athletics (Title IX never called for such a plan), but simply required that there should be "reasonable provisions" concerning participation in intercollegiate athletic activities (Fishel & Pottker, 1977). While the NCAA was worrying about the destruction of football and basketball, women's athletics were in disastrous shape. In 1975, three years after Title IX became law, women's programs accounted for about 2% of total collegiate athletic budgets (*Sex Discrimination Regulations*, 1975, p. 70).

The Association for Intercollegiate Athletics for Women (AIAW) was created in 1971 (prior to the passage of Title IX). The AIAW organized and ran sport opportunities for college women. It advocated equality in sport and successfully provided competitive sports opportunities for collegiate women until 1982 when the NCAA, recognizing the monetary potential in women's sports related to Title IX, voted to administer competitive opportunities for women. The quest for gender equity in education has meant the loss of some organizations that pioneered support for girls and women until more mainstream organizations began to address the needs of all. Chapter 18 on "Gender Equity in Physical Education and Athletics" provides examples of how the NCAA has been more supportive of Title IX in recent years.

Title IX's Implementing Regulations

Once Congress passed Title IX, the next step was for the Department of Health, Education, and Welfare (HEW) to write the implementing regulation. In late July of 1972, Office for Civil Rights (OCR) staff and lawyers from HEW's General Counsel's office began discussing the regulation. In August 1972, a letter was sent to all public education institutions affected by Title IX. The memo merely stated the law, offering no guidance on what would be required of schools. As a result, few schools or colleges initiated policy changes (Fishel & Pottker, 1977; Nash, 2002).

In November 1972, OCR and General Counsel staff circulated a first draft of the regulation to various offices within HEW for review and comment. The regulation was criticized for being extremely general and vague and thus likely to result in enforcement disputes. OCR and the General Counsel staffs went back to work. There was a limited amount of case law on sex discrimination in education from which legal precedents could be drawn. The staff turned to precedents established in enforcing Title VI, which prohibits discrimination on the basis of race, color, and national origin for recipients of federal financial assistance (Fishel & Pottker, 1977).

Despite pressure from women's rights groups to develop strong regulations to guide the implementation of Title IX, the Department of Health, Education and Welfare did not make drafting the regulation a high priority. Only two lawyers in the General Counsel's office were assigned to work on Title IX, and this assignment was given to them in addition to their other responsibilities. During early 1973, there was no permanent director of OCR. The OCR and General Counsel staff working on Title IX were unsure who had the real decision-making authority. As a result, issues of policy and procedure often were left unraised and unresolved for long periods of time.

In June 1974, HEW released the proposed regulation, 2 years after Title IX became law.[4] The regulation covered three general areas: admissions, treatment, and employment. Regarding admissions, the regulation covered vocational education schools, professional education institutions, graduate schools of higher education, and public undergraduate colleges and universities. The regulation required that comparable efforts be made to recruit students of each sex, and that people not be treated differently because of sex in the admissions process.

Regarding treatment, the regulation covered guidance on nondiscrimination in access to and participation in courses and extracurriculars, including athletics; eligibility and receipt of benefits, services and financial aid; use of school facilities; and rules governing student housing and appearance codes. Essentially, the regulation required that once admitted to school, all students should be treated in a nondiscriminatory manner. Finally, the regulation stated that Title IX covered all full- and part-time employees. Like Title VII of the Civil Rights Act, Title IX prohibited discrimination in recruiting, hiring, promotion, tenure, termination, pay, job assignments, granting of leaves, fringe benefits, selection and support for training, sabbaticals, leaves of absence, employer-sponsored activities, and all other terms and conditions of employment (Fishel & Pottker, 1977). The Title IX regulation also contained three important requirements to help implement the law: the (one-time) institutional self-assessment, the development of a Title IX policy statement and supporting grievance procedure, and the designation of at least one Title IX Coordinator.

In developing the Title IX regulation, HEW met several times with college groups, sports groups, and women's rights groups. Many of the implementation suggestions such as the self-assessment, a grievance procedure and the Title IX coordinator came from the women's groups which testified on the proposed regulation in several states. In 1975, these women's rights groups established the National Coalition for Women and Girls in Education, a more formal group to support strong Title IX regulations.

Health Education and Welfare Secretary Caspar Weinberger allowed public comments on the regulation to be submitted for 4 months, rather than the more standard 30 days, in order to provide ample time for public consideration of the issues. The Project on the Status and Education of Women headed by Dr. Bernice Sandler, at the Association of American Colleges and Universities, sent to every college and university president as well as another 10,000 or more persons an analysis of the regulation, in great detail, showing what each section said, and why it was bad or good for women's equity, and if needed, what the language should state. This analysis played a role in the large number of comments received. Individuals and representatives of various organizations submitted an unprecedented 10,000 written comments to HEW. There was no consensus. Organizations representing women's, teachers', students', and civil rights groups advocated stronger national policies than did organizations representing elementary, secondary and higher education administrators and officials. With no consensus, HEW policymakers felt free to decide the issues themselves (Fishel & Pottker, 1977).

The most controversial issues were sent to Secretary Weinberger who modified the requirement of coeducational physical education to exclude contact sports and to allow for separation during sex education classes. In athletics, the final regulation deleted the requirement to take affirmative recruitment efforts for women in traditionally male sports and vice versa. The final regulation concurred with the proposed regulation that curriculum and textbooks are not covered in Title IX.[5] The proposed regulation exempted from compliance single-sex scholarships; the final regulation permitted schools to administer single-sex scholarships if the school made similar opportunities available for the other sex (Office for Civil Rights, 1975). Most often the position the Secretary took was the most conservative. The final regulation was considerably weaker than the proposed regulation (Fishel & Pottker, 1977).

In February 1975, Secretary Weinberger sent the final draft of the regulation to President Gerald Ford for his approval. The regulation was supposed to be secret at this point, but someone leaked a copy to a women's group leader, who distributed copies to other leaders. The women's groups were distressed with what they considered to be weakened regulation. In particular, they were upset by a requirement that individuals complaining about sex discrimination use an internal grievance procedure

---

[4]The Nixon Administration was by this time embroiled in proceedings that resulted in Nixon's July 27, 1974 impeachment for actions that started on or before June 17, 1972.

[5]Women's rights groups, led by the National Organization for Women, testified against this omission because both curriculum and textbooks not only omitted women's history and experience, but engaged in gross sex stereotyping.

established by a school before HEW would act on a complaint. This had not been in the proposed regulation, and the women's groups had not been aware that HEW was even considering such a requirement. The National Coalition for Women and Girls in Education (NCWGE) immediately sent a telegram to the president asking to meet with him, with no response. After numerous other efforts to reach the president, the White House finally told them to contact a member of the president's Domestic Council. Efforts to meet with that staff member also were unsuccessful. The women met with prominent Republicans who were interested in women's rights, asking them to use their influence to help arrange a meeting. Finally the Domestic Council staff agreed to meet with the women's groups, which proposed that schools be required to make a self-evaluation of their policies to determine the existence of sex discrimination; the Council and HEW eventually agreed to this. The Department of Health, Education and Welfare also agreed to drop the requirement that internal grievance procedures be used prior to filing a complaint, although it decided that the regulation would require schools to establish an internal grievance process. The Domestic Council staff and HEW disagreed on whether foreign scholarships should be covered; this was left to the president to resolve, who sided with HEW to allow schools to continue to nominate only male students for Rhodes scholarships. In a compromise, the final regulation required that schools participating in the Rhodes program had to provide comparable scholarships for women (Fishel & Pottker, 1977).

On May 27, 1975, President Ford signed the final regulation and forwarded it to Congress for review. Congress had 45 days to review the regulation, at the end of which it could pass a resolution by a majority vote of both Houses, or disapprove the regulation and order HEW to redraft. Women's groups were dissatisfied with a regulation they saw as being too weak and flawed to be effective, and considered supporting a Congressional resolution disapproving the regulation. In the end they chose not to oppose the regulation for fear that rewritten regulation might be even weaker. They also were concerned that school and college administrators would interpret a Congressional rejection of the regulation as a sign that schools could continue to discriminate. They began a massive lobbying effort to keep Congress from voting to disapprove the regulation or to amend the law (Fishel & Pottker, 1977). At the hearings in June, the most vocal opponents of the regulation were members of the NCAA (*Sex Discrimination Regulation*, 1975). Finally, on July 21, 1975, the regulation became effective. The National Coalition for Women and Girls in Education also met with Secretary Weinberger and convinced him to send a letter to every college president and superintendent of schools enclosing the regulation. This was and is unprecedented since regulations generally appear in the Federal Register and are not sent to those who might be affected by it. This action by Weinberger made many schools at all levels far more aware of Title IX and their obligations than had it only been printed in the Federal Register.

Enforcement of Title IX

Although enforcement of Title IX could have begun immediately after Congress voted it into law in 1972, the Office for Civil Rights did not actively pursue complaints for the first 3 years, citing the lack of regulation to provide guidance to OCR in evaluating compliance with the law. While there was some justification for not pursuing complaints of subtle bias without having the regulation, there was no legal necessity for not pursuing complaints of overt bias and discrimination.

Annoyed that so much time had passed without any apparent effort on the part of OCR to enforce Title IX, several women's groups banded together to file suit. In November 1974, the Women's Equity Action League (WEAL) and four other women's rights groups charged that the Department of Health, Education and Welfare and the Department of Labor (DOL) had failed to enforce anti-sex discrimination laws. The suit (originally referred to as *WEAL v. Weinberger*, it later became part of a larger case known as the Adams case) asked the U.S. District Court in D.C. to order HEW and DOL to begin concentrated enforcement programs. The suit also asked that the Departments cut off federal funds from institutions that refused to come into compliance with Title IX. The suit specifically charged that HEW had failed to take even initial steps to begin enforcing Title IX (Fishel & Pottker, 1977).

Certainly, OCR had plenty of complaints to investigate. In the calendar year of 1974, individuals and groups filed 127 higher education Title IX complaints with OCR. Of these, OCR resolved only 20. As of April, 1975, 250 student and employment complaints in higher education were filed under Title IX. During FY 75, OCR conducted only 38 compliance reviews in higher education institutions. In elementary and secondary education, individuals and groups filed 154 complaints in FY 74, and 196 in FY 75. During FY 75, OCR conducted only two Title IX onsite investigations; Title IX was included in 31 other investigations that primarily focused on Title VI (Raffel, 1975).

Officially, OCR listed Title IX as a low priority in its plans for FY 76. OCR ranked Title IX complaints eighth, Title IX investigations ninth, and combined Title VI and IX investigations twelfth out of 12 established priorities. OCR acknowledged that some regions would be able to deal only with the first three priorities, effectively ruling out any enforcement or investigation of sex discrimination in those regions (Raffel, 1975). In short, although individuals continued to be guaranteed the right to have their complaints investigated by OCR, in reality few complaints by individuals or groups were investigated at all. Only one out of five Title IX complaints filed against elementary and secondary schools between June 1972 and October 1976 were resolved by OCR. The Project on Equal Education Rights (PEER) of the National Organization for Women, Legal Defense and Education Fund (NOWLDEF) reported that 96% of complaints filed in 1973 were still pending in 1976 without either findings or negotiated remedies. Cases that were resolved took an average of 14 months (PEER, 1977; Salomone, 1986).

In 1976, the National Coalition for Women and Girls in Education charged that HEW had minimized the impact of Title IX in two major ways. First, HEW failed to take any "highly visible, aggressive enforcement action" that might "lend credibility to the threat of aid cutoff." Without such a threat, schools could choose not to obey the regulations without suffering any consequences. Second, the Coalition charged that HEW had contributed to negative views of Title IX by drawing publicity to unpopular and largely irrelevant issues, such as father/son banquets. They argued that because there had been only limited publicity covering Title

IX's impact on more important issues, Title IX "has become a symbol of bureaucratic intrusion" into "frivolous and purely local concerns" (Dunkle & Richards, 1977, pp. 3–4).

Reports issued by the Office of Education in 1978 and 1979 concluded that schools had not done much to comply with Title IX. One study found that efforts to increase enrollment of students in programs nontraditional for their gender had been "slow" or "mixed," and that while some states and schools had made progress, some "seem to have moved not at all." A second study concluded that most schools were not in compliance and "were exerting only minimal efforts to comply." In part, schools were not complying because administrators didn't have enough information; but where administrators were aware of the law, they saw sanctions for noncompliance as "no serious threat" (*Enforcing Title IX*, 1980, pp. 2, 28). In 1977, the American Friends Service Committee (AFSC) published a report on implementation and enforcement of Title IX regulations in six southern states. The Committee had done similar monitoring in these states regarding racial desegregation, and hoped that "the years of delay, evasion and defiance" experienced in regard to racial desegregation would not be repeated with Title IX. They concluded, however, that "identical patterns are being set and reinforced" (SPEP, 1977, p. i). The AFSC conducted its study 1 year after the final Title IX regulations (June 1975) were published, 4 years after Title IX became law. What they found caused them to issue a formal complaint to OCR and to request an immediate compliance review of each district in the six states.

The AFSC charged HEW with failure to disseminate clear regulations for Title IX. Even when school district administrators wanted to obey the law, they did not know how to do so. For instance, the city schools in Oxford, MS had not taken any initial steps toward compliance because the superintendent had "no idea" what the law required (SPEP, 1977, p. 10). Sometimes administrators conducted the required self-evaluation without remedying—or even seeing—existing problems. A guidance counselor in a Sumter, SC middle school reported that the principal said the self-evaluation had "not produced any vestiges of sex discrimination," yet parents told monitors that they had to fight to get their daughters enrolled in certain vocational education classes. At the high school in that same city, the principal said that as a result of the self-evaluation, the school added two sports for girls. He was not concerned that the athletic director requested more funds for boys' football equipment alone than for the entire girls' athletic budget (SPEP, 1977, p. 12).

More often than ignorance, however, the AFSC monitors found administrators who simply refused to follow the law. The superintendent of a Fairview, AR school district declared that he would not meet the Title IX regulations until "the last minute of the last day." A Title IX coordinator in South Carolina saw no need to conduct a Title IX evaluation, even though it was required by law; he felt that failure to conduct the evaluation posed "no danger" to the school from HEW. An attorney for the Starkville, MS school board told board members that they didn't need to do anything about Title IX "until people in the community got wind of it," adding that the board should take no steps to inform the community. In the same district, a teacher who read an article about Title IX in a National Education Association publication asked a school official about its application to her school. She was told, "It really doesn't make any difference here.

We have our laws and they [the NEA] have their laws" (SPEP, 1977, pp. 10, 15).

In the area of employment, AFSC monitors found many problems. The Oxford, MS school district included in its published criteria for employment the notice that men would be considered over women for all jobs. Once hired, the Sumter, SC school district helped male teachers financially to earn their master's degrees; women who requested such help were refused. In Greenville, SC, male teachers were given supplemental pay for the extra duties assigned to them, such as coaching. Female teachers were not paid for the extra duties assigned to them, which included drama coach, yearbook advisor, department chair, cheerleader coach, and class sponsors. In Arkansas, an elementary school principal stated that there were no women principals because "we need big tough men to deal with older students." He added that if women were hired on an equal basis with men, "spouses would have to be considered" and that such employment "might strain a home relationship." As late as 1976, teachers and secretaries in South Carolina were required to quit their jobs when their pregnancy became visible (SPEP, 1977, pp. 70, 73, 74, 76).

School system refusal to comply with Title IX continued well into the 1980s and beyond. As late as 1981 an OCR survey showed that there were still 86 all-male high schools, most of which were vocational-technical (Salomone, 1986). Not until 1983 was the Philadelphia school district obligated by a court decision that found the district in violation of the equal protection clause of the 14th Amendment and the Equal Rights Amendment to the Pennsylvania Constitution to admit girls to its prestigious Central High School. The school district argued that it offered comparable education at Girls High. However, when the schools were compared on the basis of campus size in proportion to student body, size of school library, faculty members with PhDs, course offerings in mathematics, and extracurricular programs, Girls High clearly came up short. A 1980 survey in one state concluded that 99% of the local education agencies in that state were not in compliance with Title IX. The same survey found 39 instances of course catalogs that listed sex-restricted courses (CCSSO, 1980).

HEW found that compliance reviews—independent of a complaint—were more effective in implementing the requirements of Title IX than individual complaint investigations. Compliance reviews resulted in change twice as often, and affected an average of six times as many people as complaint investigations. Yet in 1978, OCR planned only 14 Title IX compliance reviews and completed only 5. In 1979, OCR planned 77 reviews and completed only 24. The U.S. Commission on Civil Rights reported that OCR staff settled for compromise positions rather than full compliance when OCR staff and educational institutions knew that sanctions would not be imposed (*Enforcing Title IX*, 1980).

In the mid-1970s, the federal government (HEW) started funding training institutes through higher education agencies and state education agencies (SEA) to provide training and technical assistance to school districts on Title IX. Soon after, the Regional Desegregation Assistance Centers (DAC) funding expanded to provide training and technical assistance for race, sex and national origin desegregation. Some local educational agencies (LEAs) also received funding for assistance with compliance and implementation of Title IX. All of this was under the CRA

Title IV funds. In 1976, the federal Vocational Education Act created state sex equity coordinators and referenced the terms *sex equity*, *sex bias*. as well as *sex discrimination*. In 1978, the training provided to SEA personnel by Shirley McCune, and later Susan Bailey through the Council of Chief State School Officers (CCSSO), laid the groundwork for much of the technical assistance and training that would be provided to schools and districts throughout the 1980s and into the 1990s. Many of these projects were instumental in moving OCR along in their enforcement efforts. In 1978, OCR acknowledged that it had failed to inform administrators adequately. The director promised to publish interpretations and guidelines and send them to administrators. Instead, OCR published small digests of case memoranda, and did so only for 2 months. OCR sent these digests to 700 addresses, only 3.5% of the possible 20,000 institutions receiving federal funds (*Enforcing Title IX*, 1980).

The Reagan Administration slowed even further any enforcement of Title IX. In 1982, it rescinded the Title IX regulation prohibiting discrimination in dress codes. Girls had used this important regulation to protest school policies that did not allow them to wear pants, and boys, especially Native American boys, had used it to protest policies that required them to wear short hair. The Reagan Administration also sought to narrow the definition of "federal financial assistance," change the definition of discrimination, and restrict the meaning of "program and activity." It also switched many discretionary funding programs into block grants to states so that a specific funding trail could not be established for a specific program. The Civil Rights Leadership Conference Fund documented the Administration's dislike of Title IX in a 1983 report, *An Oath Betrayed*. The Fund's report quoted Secretary of Education Terrel Bell as saying, "It seems that we have some laws we should not have and my obligation to enforce them is against my own philosophy" (*An Oath Betrayed*, 1983, p. 1). Beginning at least as early as the spring of 1982, the Department's General Counsel and Secretary Bell sought exemptions from civil rights compliance (including Title VI, Title IX, and Section 504) for educational institutions that received federal aid only in the form of student financial assistance. Even though the Civil Rights Division of the Justice Department determined that this position could not be legally defended, the General Counsel advised Secretary Bell to appeal directly to the Attorney General, arguing that their job was "to curtail the interference of the federal government" (*An Oath Betrayed*, 1983).

Additionally, the Reagan Administration worked to make it harder to prove a violation of civil rights. Previously, a claimant needed only to prove that an action had a discriminatory effect or result. Under the Reagan Administration, however, the definition of discrimination changed so that a claimant had to prove that the institution intended to discriminate (*An Oath Betrayed*, 1983). Further, the Reagan Administration used the *pinpoint* theory to limit the coverage of civil rights laws. Under this theory, enforcement would apply only to the specific programs or activities receiving federal funds, and not to the entire institution.

The Grove City Supreme Court (*Grove City College v. Bell* 465 U.S. 555, 1984) decision dramatically limited the impact of Title IX. The case began in 1977 when Grove City College refused to sign the assurance of compliance with Title IX form, arguing that it received no direct federal aid and therefore was not subject to Title IX. When threatened with termination of federal student aid funds, the college sued HEW.[6] The Third Circuit, in August, 1982, ruled that private educational institutions such as Grove City College are covered as a whole when they or any of their students receive federal scholarship loans or grants (Salomone, 1986). But the Reagan Administration didn't agree. When the Grove City case came before the Supreme Court in 1984, this Reagan Administration position was presented to the Court in support of Grove City by the Solicitor General. In upholding the U.S. Supreme Court *Grove City College v. Bell* case, the Court ruled that *program or activity* could be defined narrowly meaning that only the particular program, not the entire institution, receiving federal financial assistance must comply.

The Grove City decision substantially gutted Title IX and similar civil rights provisions. The Supreme Court's ruling essentially allowed schools to discriminate in all areas that did not receive direct federal funding. Thus, athletic programs or particular academic programs of universities—for example, engineering schools—could discriminate based on sex so long as those specific programs did not directly receive federal funds. Within days, the Assistant Attorney General for Civil Rights told reporters that the Administration also would apply this "program specific" standard not only to Title IX, but to Title VI of the Civil Rights Act of 1964 and Section 504 of the Rehabilitation Act of 1973 (which provides nondiscrimination protections for individuals with disabilities).[7] Within a year, the Department of Education had closed, limited or suspended at least 63 discrimination cases: 44 Title IX, 5 Title VI, and 14 Section 504, based on the Grove City decision (Salomone, 1986). This provided the motivation for Eleanor Smeal as president of the National Organization for Women, and other supporters of Title IX to work closely with leaders of other civil rights organizations to convince Congress to counteract the Grove City College decision and the Federal government's curtailment of civil rights protections.

In April, 1984 Senators Edward Kennedy (MA) and Paul Simon (IL) introduced the Civil Rights Act of 1984, replacing Title IX's phrase *program or activity* with the term *recipient*. This passed overwhelmingly in the House, but Orrin Hatch (UT) argued that *recipient* was overly broad and beyond the scope of the law's original intent. The bill died in the Senate. In the next session, Kennedy and Gus Hawkins (CA) introduced the Civil Rights Restoration Act of 1985, amending Title IX, Title VI, Section 504, and the 1975 Age Discrimination Act to include an interpretation of *program or activity* that expressly covered all operations. Fund termination, however, would be limited to the specific program or activity that was discriminatory.

Opposition to this was strong and swift. The Assistant Attorney General for Civil Rights called it "one of the most far-reaching

---

[6]The U.S. Department of Education was created in 1980, but the Grove City case against HEW was earlier.
[7]All three civil rights provisions applied to recipients of federal financial assistance. Title IX and Section 504 were modeled after the language in Title VI of the 1964 Civil Rights Act.

legislative efforts in memory to stretch the tentacles of the federal government to every crevice of public and private-sector activity" (Salomone, 1986, pp. 132–133). In March of 1988, Congress voted in favor of the Civil Rights Restoration Act of 1987, passing it into law over President Reagan's veto, who called the Act "vague and sweeping," subjecting "nearly every facet of American life" to government interference (Suggs, 2005, p. 91). Thanks to the Civil Rights Restoration Act, the broad Title IX coverage in place before 1984 (but suspended from 1984–1987 by the Grove City Supreme Court decision) again applies to the entire institution receiving federal funds (Project on the Status and Education of Women, 1989).

The reach of Title IX has continued to be challenged and refined around several key issues. In the area of sexual harassment, the 1979 U.S. Supreme Court decision, *Cannon v. University of Chicago,* established that an individual can sue an educational institution for injunctive relief for violating Title IX. The following year, the United States Court of Appeals for the Second Circuit held in *Alexander v. Yale University* (2d Cir. 1980) that sexual harassment is included in Title IX's definition of sex discrimination. In 1992, in *Franklin v. Gwinnett County Public Schools*, the Supreme Court unanimously held that Title IX allows private individuals to bring claims for money damages. In 1998, in *Gebser v. Lago Vista Independent School District* case and again in 1999, in *Davis v. Monroe County Board of Education*, the Supreme Court further established that schools are required to take action to stop harassment. For more on issues of harassment, see the chapter on "Sexual Harassment: The Hidden Gender Equity Problem" in this *Handbook*. There have also been challenges to the Title IX regulation related to intercollegiate athletics. These are described in the "Gender Equity in Physical Education and Athletics" chapter so they will not be repeated here.

Another issue raised by Title IX and the Equal Protection Clause of the 14th Amendment to the U.S. Constitution is the legality of single-sex education. Based on the legal precedents set in the 1954 *Brown v. Board of Education of Topeka et al.* (347 U.S. 483) and the 1996 Virginia Military Institute Supreme Court (*U.S. v. Virginia et al.* (1996) decisions, separate is viewed as not equal. The 1975 Title IX regulation allows some single-sex education for limited purposes, such as using remedial or affirmative activities to overcome the effects of past sex discrimination, and for specific exceptions such as sexuality education or previously established single-sex schools or colleges. In May 2002, the Department of Education issued guidelines on these complicated sections of the Title IX regulation as required by provisions in the No Child Left Behind Act, which said that some Department funds could be used for single-sex schools or classes consistent with current applicable law. However, at that time the Department also issued a notice of proposed rulemaking and asked for public comment on how to change the Title IX regulations relating to single-sex schools and classes. Despite many objections to changes in the regulation, in March 2004 the Department issued the proposed new regulation to make it easier to establish single-sex schools or classes without regard to the current justifications in the Title IX regulation such as allowing

single-sex interventions only if there was evidence that it would decrease sex discrimination in the outcomes or reduce the gender gaps in what is desired for all students (OCR, 2004). Despite the short time (less than 40 working days) period allowed for public response to the proposed changes, the Department received over 5,000 comments against this change, and only around 100 supporting the proposed changes, and even some of these comments expressed concerns with the full set of proposed changes.[8] On October 25, 2006, the Department issued its final single-sex regulations, which were similar to the 2004 Proposed Regulations, in decreasing protections against sex discrimination while increasing the allowable types of single-sex education (OCR, 2006). The chapter on "Gender Equity in Coeducational and Single Sex Educational Environments" provides more information on this new regulation and summarizes research on sex segregation.

Congressional Actions to Strengthen the Implementation of Title IX

Recognizing the need for further efforts to achieve gender equity in education, in the fall of 1993 Senators Barbara Mikulski (MD), Paul Simon (IL), Carol Moseley-Braun (IL), Tom Harkin (IA) and Edward Kennedy (MA) introduced new federal gender equity in education legislative initiatives. Part of the reauthorization of the Elementary and Secondary Education Act, the bill included the creation of a Gender Equity Office with a full-time coordinator in the U.S. Department of Education, expansion of gender equity research and training in all areas of education, additional resources set aside for gender equity in mathematics and science, sexual harassment prevention and elimination training programs, and disclosure of data related to equity in athletics ("Federal 'Gender Equity in Education' Legislation," 1993). Only some of these ideas were actually included, often in a weakened form, in subsequent legislation. The next section will provide details on how these additional federal laws have been used to increase federal leadership, technical assistance, and program support to advance gender equity in education.

FEDERAL GENDER EQUITY LEADERSHIP, TECHNICAL ASSISTANCE, AND FUNDING

Supporters of educational equity did not stop working for legislative change once Congress passed Title IX. Inspired by Title IX, advocates of equity worked to pass additional federal legislation to provide funding and other types of support to implement Title IX and address other gender equity challenges in the years immediately following the authorization of Title IX. Together, Title IX (which sets out policy, procedures, and prohibitions, but no funding), and programmatic laws with funding provisions such as Title IV of the Civil Rights Act (1964), the Women's Educational Equity Act (1974) and the Vocational Education Act (1976) provided the initial implementation infra-

---

[8]Key objections to these regulations from the Feminist Majority Foundation and other members of the National Coalition for Women and Girls in Education (NCWGE) are posted on their respective Web sites www.feminist.org/education and www.ncwge.org, etc. (See Feminist Majority Foundation, 2006.)

structure for achieving gender equity at all levels of education. The infrastructure was largely constructed in the 1970s and enhanced in the 1980s. By the middle of the 1980s some programs and funding began to be cut as the Reagan Administration pushed consolidating national programs and giving block funding to the states. By the end of the 1990s, little remained of the federally supported gender equity assistance infrastructure. By 2006, federal support was reduced even more in the areas of leadership, technical assistance to educators and the public, as well as in funding local gender equity work.

Since the mid 1960s, both the "carrot and stick" were used to enable the federal government to implement civil rights laws such as Title IX. The Office for Civil Rights has responsibility for enforcing the laws by using compliance investigations, resolution agreements, and compliance reviews. Possible negative consequences for discrimination include withdrawing federal funding and large monetary settlements related to lawsuits. However, these negative consequences are rare. Other offices in the Department of Education (ED) use positive incentives for compliance with civil rights laws by providing technical assistance to help implement the laws and program funds for gender equity research, development, evaluation, and dissemination. Unlike other important federal programs such as special education receiving billions of federal dollars, almost no funding was provided for direct services to people facing sex discrimination. Even in comparably favorable years for funding gender equity, the federal financial support of Title IX and other activities to advance gender equity has been miniscule (less than .02% of the annual education agency budgets). It has also been much smaller than for other specific population groups such as individuals with disabilities, American Indians, or English Language Learners. These groups had their own offices within ED to administer funding for various types of education research, development, and services to their unique populations, but addressing gender inequities within their own populations has been a lower priority.

The federal role in protecting civil rights has been acknowledged for the past 4 decades. The first part of the mission statement in the Department of Education Organization Act (1979) is "to Strengthen the Federal commitment to assuring access to equal educational opportunity for every individual." States and local governments provide over 93% of the education funding and are responsible for decisions on curriculum content such as reading, mathematics, and social studies. Civil rights laws such as Title VI, Section 504, ADA, and Title IX must be followed by all recipients of federal financial assistance. Thus, despite providing only a 7% financial contribution to education across the nation, the federal government's role in enforcing civil rights related to education covers most educational institutions in the U.S. This includes approximately 15,000 school districts, 4,000 colleges and universities, 5,000 proprietary organizations, as well as libraries, museums, scientific research laboratories, vocational rehabilitation organizations, recreation departments, and correctional facilities (*OCR Annual Report*, 2000, U.S. GAO, 2004). Additionally, the Office for Civil Rights in the U.S. Department of Education is just one of the many civil rights offices in federal agencies with responsibility for implementing Title IX for recipients of federal financial assistance.

The federal leadership role in implementing civil rights laws and collecting national statistics was sustained even in the early 1980s when there were extensive efforts to substantially decrease the federal role in education by abolishing the newly created Department of Education and block granting (consolidating and cutting overall levels of previously restricted funding for specific purposes and allowing states to decide what to fund) most of the federal funds to the states. But over the years there have been numerous efforts to narrow interpretations of the protections provided by Title IX and other civil rights laws and to even decrease the collection of statistics by sex. There have also been substantial decreases in the federal *carrot* programs to help implement Title IX. The Reagan Administration recommended that competitive grant programs such as the 1974 Women's Educational Equity Act (WEEA) and the 1964 Civil Rights Act (CRA) Title IV receive no FY 1982 funds (Klein, 1981, 1984). Attempts to reduce federal support for these gender equity programs were repeated over the next decades, but Congress generally maintained a minimal funding level for them. Even when the dollar amounts remained stable, such as the fairly constant annual appropriation for the CRA Title IV activities (currently funded at a paltry $7 million for the entire nation), the actual resources to do the work decreased because of inflation.

Although investment in identifiable federally sponsored activities to advance gender equity has been a miniscule proportion of the education agencies' budgets, it has had some influence especially since it is tied to Title IX, which applies to all federal programs dealing with education, not just those focused on specific populations such as women or low income students. For example, NACWEP's report on *Sex Bias: Education Legislation and Regulations,* recommended ways the 1965 Higher Education Act should be changed to ensure that the federal funds for student financial assistance and programs become gender fair (Mastelli, 1977).

As previously mentioned, Title IX and the other federal civil rights laws also apply to agencies outside the Department of Education. If these agencies do not have their own Title IX regulation, they use the Final Common Rule (U.S. Department of Justice, 2000) which is modeled on the 1975 Title IX regulation used by the Department of Education (see www.feminist.org/education, Title IX Defined). Due to Title IX, all education programs in the Department of Education and other federal agencies should be paying attention to guaranteeing gender equitable treatment by organizations that receive funds from their agencies. Executive Order 13160 prohibits discrimination in federally conducted education and training programs. In addition to the Department of Education, key agencies with programs to provide funds to advance gender equity in education and training are the Women's Bureau in the U.S. Department of Labor, the Human Resources Development programs, especially the Gender Equity Program in the National Science Foundation (NSF) and the Women in Development, Girls Education programs in the U.S. Agency for International Development, now in the Department of State.

In recent years the usefulness of the federal *carrot and stick* analogy has decreased since funding laws such as the Elementary and Secondary Education Act, also known as No Child Left Behind Act (NCLB) of 2002 focus heavily on outcomes such as achievement scores and since funding for specific gender equity research, development, and service programs (such as programs to help displaced homemakers) has declined. Additionally, the federal use of the stick to provide penalties for noncompliance has often been seen as less of a threat than private law suits. Since there are few strong carrots or sticks, the Civil Rights laws are seen by those concerned with social justice as essential elements of many educational policies from athletics to testing to educating students about their rights and opportunities to achieve equality. Discussions of federal leadership in gender equity, technical assistance, and program funding to advance gender equity follow.

Federal Agency Gender Equity Leadership: Past, Current, and Future

Federal agencies have helped advance gender equity by using positive incentive strategies and some enforcement activities in both their internal staff management and training activities and in their administration of a wide variety of education programs carried out by recipients of agency financial assistance. This has and could be done by rigorous attention to existing gender equality laws and provisions such as helping educators and others know about and enforce Title IX and related policies. For example, one of the continuing leadership challenges in ED is to collect, report, and analyze data by sex as well as race, age, family income, disability status, etc. Gender equity leadership may also involve identifying specific gender equity challenges in education, and giving priority attention to addressing them in funding programs, data collection and in using the public bully pulpit to publicize problems such as sexual harassment as well as strategies to address these inequities. It can be accomplished through legally mandated job responsibilities such as the work of the required Title IX Coordinators, and to some extent, by proactive actions of employees at all levels of responsibility who pay special attention to gender equity needs and opportunities. For example, the 20-member National Advisory Council on Women's Educational Programs (NACWEP) under the direction of executive director, Joy Simonson, from 1975 to 1982, did this effectively until Simonson was replaced by the Illinois state director of the anti-ERA Eagle Forum during the Reagan Administration (Simonson, undated). Instead of working on improving gender equity, the new Council and staff members traveled around the country to help outreach to women voters for Reagan's reelection. When gender equity advocacy groups observed this misuse of federal funds, they no longer saw value in asking Congress to preserve this Council, and it ended in 1984. Another example of integrating gender equity throughout the agency has been the work of the USAID in incorporating gender analysis and technical assistance in all of its sector programs and giving attention to gender considerations in cross-cutting activities, as well, in its small Women in Development program. Similarly, the Women's Bureau has had coordinating and leadership responsibilites on gender issues in the Department of Labor.

High-level agency officials who are most visible in providing gender equity leadership can also rely on staff with expertise and designated responsibilities for gender equity. In 1994, the U.S. Department of Education Organization Act was changed to include a Special Assistant for Gender Equity (SAGE) to advise the Secretary and Deputy Secretary of Education. The SAGE is to promote, coordinate, and evaluate gender equity programs

and provide technical assistance. While it remains in the law, the position has not been filled since the end of the Clinton Administration. Deputy Secretary Kunin appointed an Equity Task Force that worked on gender equity and other issues with staff from across the agency and the help of the SAGE. Also, in 1994, section 427 was added to the General Education Provisions Act (GEPA). It was designed to insure that all recipients of federal funds describe how they will address barriers to equality for specific population groups. For example, would the grantee need to provide transportation for low-income single parents to get to their job training programs? However, this GEPA 427 provision lacked key guidance and incentives to make it more than additional equity intentions and assurances to add to funding proposals. Further, there was no analysis of the types of gender or other equity barriers described by the potential grantees for most of the ED programs.

Starting in 1995 until the end of the Clinton Administration, the ED also participated in the president's Interagency Council on Women (PICW), which among other things contributed to the reports on the U.S. follow-up to the Platform for Action from the 1995 4th World Conference on Women in Beijing. Both this Council and the NACWEP had active outreach activities such as hearings and meetings in various parts of the country to work with constituents across the nation interested in advancing gender equity. Table I shows how some of these education agency leadership activities were related to legislation and administration policies. Other agencies such as the National Science Foundation (NSF) had some similar patterns. NSF equity leadership benefitted from Congressionally mandated commissions that focused on increasing the participation of women and minorities in science, mathematics, and engineering.

Table 5.1 shows that many previous gender equity leadership structures in the ED and its predecessor federal agencies have disappeared, although some, such the Federal Women's Program and SAGE, remain in the laws even if they are not being implemented by current ED leaders.

Federal Technical Assistance Related to Gender Equity

A key aspect of federal technical assistance related to gender equity involves educating and helping the agency staff attend to these important civil rights responsibilities so that they can also help their constituents in elementary, secondary, and postsecondary education. A focus on advancing gender equity should be part of the responsibilities of all agency staff who manage programs since all of these programs must complete assurances that they comply with Title IX and other Civil Rights laws. For example, the National Advisory Council on Women's Educational Programs published documents such as Efforts Toward Sex Fairness in the Use of Education Division Funds (Steiger & Szanton, 1977), Sex Bias: Education Legislation and Regulations (Mastelli, 1977), *The Unenforced Law: Title IX Activity by Federal Agencies other Than HEW* (Balles, 1978), Sex Fairness in Education Division Publications (National Advisory Council, 1979) and Title IX: The Half Full, Half Empty Glass (National Advisory Council, 1981) while the Federal Women's Program Coordinator helped educate staff about nondiscrimination policies. But since this Council and the Federal Women's Program Coordinator positions ended, there has been almost no attention to educating ED staff about

TABLE 5.1   Federal Education Agency Leadership Activities to Advance Gender Equity in Education

Federal Law/Program	National Annual Budget & Activities	Multi-State	State	Local Education Level
OCR staff operations started in the Department of Health, Education and Welfare (HEW) and continue in the ED and other agencies	Develop policy & manage work	10 OCR Regional Offices are started in ED. (They do compliance reviews, review complaints, provide technical assistance.)	OCR provides annual training to SEA MOA Coordinators re 1979 Voc Ed Guidelines	All Ed Levels Pre K to postsec
Federal Women's Program, created in 1967 by Exec. Order 11375. Each Agency is supposed to have at least one Federal Women's Program Manager to advise the agency head. The Education Agency had an active Office on Women's Concerns in 1970s. Office of Education, Women's Program Office created 1974.	Identifies barriers to the hiring and advancement of women in federal gov. Now a responsibility of the EEOC. Requested Program Offices to report data collected by sex. (Steiger, 1977)			
NACWEP a 20-member council established by WEEA in 1975 ended in 1984.	NACWEP operated 1975–82 under Executive Director, Joy Simonson. It advised federal officials on a variety of activities to advance women's educational equity, held public hearings, and published influential reports.			
Special Assistant for Gender Equity (SAGE) required by The Improving America's Schools Act of 1994. Also in 8-03-05 Title 20, chap. 48 Subchapter 3412 Principal officers in the law establishing ED.	SAGE (if appointed) promotes, coordinates and evaluates gender equity programs and provides technical assistance, coordination and dissemination in addition to advising the Secretary and Deputy Secretary in all matters relating to gender equity.			
GEPA 427, General Education Provisions Act. Passed as part of IASA of 1994	Applicants for all federal financial assistance required to provide information on ensuring equitable access and participation in proposed activity.			
Equity Task Forces have been used in 1974 and then again in 1993 with senior officers and designated representatives	Intra-agency Equity Task Force under Deputy Sec. Kunin coordinated policy and management initiatives to promote equity practices in ED			
President's Interagency Council on Women, (PICW) 1995 2004 U.S. rejoins UNESCO (See chap. 1 for gender equity in UNESCO goals)	Coordinated U.S. implementation of the Platform for Action from the 4th World Conference on Women in Beijing in 1995.			

civil rights laws and responsibilities. About the only activity was an occasional program for women's history month with other agencies in the SW Washington, DC area, and a few mandated employee training sessions to discourage sexual harassment.

Even specific gender equity technical assistance activities to educators across the nation have decreased dramatically. In 1984 there were 12 Sex Desegregation Assistance Centers funded under CRA IV, and until 1996 there was competitive funding for at least a part-time gender equity/Title IX Coordinator and program funds in each participating state. The professionals working in these Title IV funded projects and others concerned about gender equity formed the Association for Gender Equity Leadership in Education (AGELE) (www.agele.org) in 1979 (formerly named NCSEE-National Coalition for Sex Equity in Education). By 1997, there was only $7 million for 10 multistate Equity Assistance Centers (EACS; formerly called Desegregation Assistance Centers [DAC]). These Centers provided assistance to states and K–12 school districts in their regions in preventing sex, race, and national origin discrimination. By 2001, only two states (Washington and Florida) maintained full-time Title IX Coordinators, and only seven maintained part-time staff specifically designated to provide Title IX technical assistance as well as assistance with their own state-level equity laws. Many states closed down their equity offices completely, impacting negatively not only on Title IX services, but on race and national-origin equity services as well. In 2006, only one of the remaining 10 Equity Assistance Centers (The Mid-Atlantic Equity Assistance Center) had specific information on sex equity resources on their web page. The total annual funding of $7 million for all 10 of these Equity Assistance Centers has also decreased from 1996–2007 because of inflation and because of broader responsibilities to assist with the goals of NCLB and with more customers like charter schools. Due to this and the few staff members with special responsibility for gender equity, it is probable that less than $2 million of the EAC resources focus on technical assistance related to sex discrimination. The OCR *Annual Report to Congress FY 2004* indicates that only 6% of the 5,044 complaints received by OCR focused on sex discrimination; most focused on special education and race discrimination issues. The OCR annual reports indicated that 7% of the OCR complaints in 2001, 2002, and 2003 focused on sex discrimination (Office for Civil Rights annual reports 2001–2004). However, it is possible that there are many serious violations that do not get pursued as OCR complaints.

The U.S. Department of Education's OCR sent "Dear Colleague" letters to state and local school superintendents and college presidents in 1997, 2004, and 2006 reminding them to pay attention to regulations requiring Title IX coordinators, grievance procedures, and reaffirming the OCR policy guidance on intercollegiate althletics as well as the 2001 sexual harassment guidance. However, OCR has done little to provide meaningful technical assistance or follow up. Technical assistance is necessary to both encourage educators, students, and others to know about their civil rights, and to be able to apply the detailed guidelines in appropriate and sensible ways. Instead of helping with the full implementaton of Title IX, some of the ED actions have resulted in confusion and even backtracking on full implementation of Title IX. Examples of this ED created confusion include: the previously discussed federal government role in the Supreme Court Grove City College decision (1984), the creation of the Secretary's Commission on Intercollegiate Athletics and its resulting "majority" report which would have limited Title IX protections, the U.S. Department of Education changes in the rules related to single-sex education (Office for Civil Rights, 2006), and the inappropriate 2005 "clarification" guidance on using an e-mail survey as a sufficient only way to assess the interest of female students in intercollegiate athletics. These threats to full

and appropriate use of Title IX are discussed in more detail in other parts of this chapter and in other chapters in this *Handbook*. Additionally, the key federally funded national provider of technical assistance and resources related to gender equity to both equity professionals and the public was the WEEA Equity Resource Center funded under a contract using some of the WEEA Program funds. ED decided not to recompete this contract despite the requests of many for its continued services. It ceased operation in early 2003. Education Development Center, Inc., its host organization, has maintained its archived Web site, which was still listed as a resource on the OCR Web site as of February 20, 2006. The WEEA Equity Resource Center also helped launch another important leadership activity, the Gender Equity Expert Panel, which will be discussed in the later section on federal education programs focusing on gender equity.

While many of the *Handbook* chapters show progress in decreasing some types of sex discrimination in education, it is possible that the relatively small percent of sex discrimination complaints to OCR may be related to ignorance of rights under Title IX. Reinstatement of support for previous federal technical assistance mechanisms such as State Title IX grants and a national Gender Equity Resource Center Web site and electronic mailing list may contribute substantially to rebuilding an effective gender equity infrastructure.

Federal Programs Supporting Gender Equity Research, Development, Dissemination, and Technical Assistance

Federal gender equity program funding generally means providing specified amounts of federal money appropriated by Congress for legislatively authorized discretionary competitive funding programs. However, most Department of Education and Department of Labor federal education funds go directly to states through formula funding to be distributed to districts in their states or to student grants and loans for postsecondary education. Agencies do not track how these block or multipurpose state or local funds are used to support gender-related activities. For example, when asked, ED staff said they could not provide information on whether any of the No Child Left Behind Local Innovative Program funds, which allowed for "Programs to provide same-gender schools and classrooms (consistent with applicable law)," were being used for this purpose or for any of the 26 other activities allowed in this section of the law (Klein, 2005).

National discretionary funding is usually through competitive grants for model programs or research or by contracts to accomplish specific technical assistance or dissemination services such as the Civil Rights Act Title IV Equity Assistance Centers. Most education funding programs authorized by Congress contain general mandates to improve education by addressing education equity needs. However, sometimes the separate annual Congressional funding appropriations also have specific provisions or priorities related to the authorized program. For example, in the 1978 reauthorization of the Women's Educational Equity Act Program, in addition to developing model programs, WEEA was authorized to use funds to help school districts implement Title IX and other sex-equity activities after the first $15 million, but the appropriation was always too small to do so. Similarly, in recent years while programs like the Fund for

TABLE 5.2   Federal Education Agency Technical Assistance Activities to Advance Gender Equity in Education

Federal Law/Program	National Annual Budget & Activities	Multi-state/ Regional	State	Local Education Level
OCR staff operations started in the Department of Health, Education and Welfare and continue in ED and other agencies.	ED OCR Staff provide consultations, training and materials. In FY 89 OCR received a little over $40 million for staffing and budget. In FY 95 it was over $58 million. In 1995 OCR had 778 FTE staff. OCR data collection ended 2002.	10 OCR Regional Offices. ED staff do compliance & complaint reviews, provide technical assistance &training if requested.	Using the 1979 Voc Ed Guidelines, OCR provides TA to state MOA staff who conduct civil rights reviews of their subrecipients.	All Ed Levels Pre-K to postsec
Title IV Civil Rights Act of 1964. Provide Technical Assistance for SEAs, K–12 school districts and others to combat race, national origin and sex discrimination. (Less than 1/3 of the total funds were used for sex equity although some EACS spend more than others.)	In FY 77 only $1.5 million of the $34.7 million went to projects specifically focusing on sex discrimination (Mastelli, 1977). In the 1990s, the funding for the CRA IV program was $21–24 million with 2/3 going to SEAs and 1/3 to EACs. In FY 96 it was reduced to $7 million only for EACs. In 2005 the Office of Elementary and Secondary Ed awarded 3 yr. contracts for 10 EACs.	12 regional Sex Desegregation Centers were funded from 1978–1987. Since 1987 multi-focus EACS have served states in their regions.	Title IV SEA grant program competition started in 1978 and ended 1996. Until 1987 SEAs could apply for sex desegregation grants separately.	Grants to local education agencies ended in 1982 Grants for training institutes run by higher ed. institutions ended by 1985.
WEEA Program contracts for technical assistance and dissemination	Over its 26-year existence, the WEEA Equity Resource Center worked with grantees to develop and disseminate products that captured the learning from local grants, provided technical assistance to the field on Title IX compliance and gender equitable education, developed and operated the EdEquity electronic discussion list, created a popular Web site with gender equity resources and information (now archived at http://www2.edc.org), and published periodicals addressing aspects of educational equity.			

the Improvement of Postsecondary Education (FIPSE) and the Fund for the Improvement of Education (FIE) were authorized to have competitions that addressed equity as well as other needs, most of their funding was reserved for Congressionally specified *earmarks* or projects to be given to a grantee specified by Congress without a federal merit-based competition. Very few of these earmark grants have gone to programs designed to advance gender equity. Information on each of the key programs that supported gender-equity education work is summarized in the following section, and additional details are provided in Table 5.2.

The Women's Educational Equity Act (WEEA). WEEA has been created in 1974 and the only legislatively authorized program in the U.S. Department of Education and its predecessor

agencies specifically focused on gender equity. It promotes educational equity for girls and women and pays special attention to populations likely to suffer from multiple types of discrimination based on gender, as well as race, ethnicity, limited English proficiency, disability, or age. The wide range of activities authorized include: assistance to educational agencies and institutions in Title IX compliance and training in gender-equitable practices. Since its initial operation in 1976, WEEA has funded over 800 projects through highly competitive grant competitions. However, many were short term and minimally evaluated. The highest annual appropriation was $10 million, in FY 1980. The five multi-state demonstration projects funded at this time are described in the 1985 *Handbook*. From 2000 through 2007, the Administration requested no funding for WEEA, but Congress appropriated approximately $3 million annually through

FY06. Because of limited funding, the program did not hold its annual competition during several of these years, when it only funded continuing grants.

Since the 1994 WEEA reauthorization, at least two thirds of the funds were to be used for grants that implement gender equitable programs in educational institutions including the evaluation of model programs. Up to one third of the appropriation was allowed for research and development grants, but when appropriations were low, this area of activity suffered. Research-and-development funding was designed to support such activities as development of strategies and model programs to promote equity in education; development of equitable assessment tools; evaluation, dissemination, and replication of promising or exemplary programs; and development and evaluation of model curricula, textbooks, software, and other educational materials. The federal contract for the national WEEA technical assistance center—designed to provide technical assistance to schools and broaden the impact of the grants program—was discontinued by the Department of Education in early 2003. Since 1978, the contract had been awarded to Education Development Center, Inc.. As described in the previous technical assistance section, it involved working with grantees to develop and disseminate materials about effective programs, providing technical assistance to states and local entities on Title IX compliance, and generally acting as a resource center to individuals and organizations on gender equitable education.

In 1996, the WEEA Equity Resource Center helped design and initiate the work of the Gender Equity Expert Panel, which was established to identify replicable policies, products, and programs that could provide evidence that they were effective in advancing gender equity. However, when Administrative support for gender equity was lowered, WEEA efforts to increase and share knowledge were curtailed. For example, in 1991 and again in 1999, reports coordinated by the WEEA Center on efforts to promote and assess the status of educational equity, both initially requested by the Department, were halted. Beginning in 2001, the Department's approval process for grantee products and informational materials slowed drastically, and very few materials were allowed to be printed and disseminated. Electronic products and dissemination, which were not then thoroughly covered by the ED regulations, became the principal means by which new publications and information were made available. In FY 2003, in spite of public support for the work and consistent increases in requests to the WEEA Center for its resources and services, the funding that had been utilized for 26 years to provide national technical assistance and dissemination was transferred out from oversight of the WEEA Program to fund a portion of a $1.5 million review of the research on single-sex education, a policy interest of the Administration. Worthy projects continue to be funded through WEEA, but without the WEEA Center or a federal entity committed to collecting and disseminating information nationally about project effectiveness, the potential impact of the projects is likely to remain limited in scope.

The Career and Technical Education.   This programs supporting gender equity were previously primarily supported by federal vocational education acts and called sex equity rather than gender equity programs. Starting in 1976 and 1977, there were two related Congressional laws which specifically ad-dressed gender inequities in career and vocational education. The 1976 Amendments to the Vocational Education Act of 1963 required a state sex equity coordinator in each state to be supported by a minimum of $50,000 of the state's vocational education funds. Each sex equity coordinator was to peform seven key functions, such as to create awareness of programs to reduce sex bias and stereotyping in vocational education, gather and analyze data on men and women in state vocational education programs, and assist local education agencies and others in improving vocational education opportunities for women. (More details are provided in the "Gender Equity in Career and Technical Education" chapter in this *Handbook*.) This amendment also required local applicants to promote sex equity in all career and vocational programs. Second, the Career Incentive Education Act of 1977 specifically provided for funding of career education activities designed to eliminate sex discrimination and stereotyping as part of the overall federal Career Education program. The Career Education program disappeared when it was put in the state block grants in 1981.

From 1984 to 1998 Perkins Vocational Education Act programs provided more funding and support for gender equity for students and adults in education than any other federal program. About $100 million annually was designated for gender equity activities during 1984–1998 when the Perkins Act I and II required percentage set-asides for sex equity and displaced homemakers from the overall vocational education appropriations to the states. Much attention was given to encouraging males and females in nontraditional occupations. Some of these funds that flowed through states were designated primarily for services to specified populations such as displaced homemakers, individuals who had been underserved, or individuals who had special educational needs relating to disabilities, poverty or limited English proficiency. These funds and requirements for state sex equity personnel to administer federal funds for sex equity programs in their states led to the important leadership roles of state career and technical education (CTE) sex equity coordinators. The federal vocational education staff also helped organize some initial meetings and networking of these coordinators who soon formed their own organizations, including the Vocational Education Equity Council (VEEC), which continues now as the Career and Technical Education Equity Council (CTEEC), and the Sex Equity Leadership Development Conference, which continues now as the National Alliance for Partnerships in Equity (NAPE; www.napeequity.org).

The Carl D. Perkins Vocational and Applied Technology Act of 1998 eliminated the set-asides of a percent of the overall funding for special needs such as gender equity, but included requirements for both states and participating districts to make progress on Non Traditional Occupations core performance indicators by sex, and race. Support for the sex equity coordinators and their gender equity programs decreased from $107 million in FY 98 to $5.6 million in FY 99. In the following years few states continued to support full-time sex equity coordinators although they were allowed, but not mandated, to use federal funds for these positions (Klein, Ortman, & Friedman, 2002).

The U.S. Department of Labor employment training programs and some provisions in the welfare and work programs also pay attention to various gender equity concerns as part of the requirements to provide services. In 2006, the Congress reauthorized the Perkins Act despite efforts by the Bush Administration to eliminate this funding. The Act retained the nontraditional core indicators and provisions to help special populations including displaced homemakers, single parents and students training for nontraditional employment.

Fund for the Improvement of Postsecondary Education (FIPSE).   This program to fund and evaluate innovative models was created in the same set of 1972 Amendments to the Education Act as Title IX. Since 1974, FIPSE has supported some very useful projects to address gender equity needs. For example, in 1975 it supported a grant to Sheila Tobias for a Math Anxiety Clinic at Wesleyan University, and later, various women's studies projects including a project on evaluating women's studies programs. A 1984 project by David and the late Myra Sadker helped postsecondary faculty teach in ways that don't discriminate against women or men in the classroom. FIPSE supported the National Center for Curriculum Transformation Resources on Women from 1994–1998 and two MentorNet Projects from 1998 to 2002. There have been 11 grants focusing to some extent on women's issues since 2000, including a grant to study women's human rights in North America and a dissemination grant for a women's health curriculum (U.S. Department of Education FIPSE Grant Database, 2006). In FY 06 FIPSE had about $22 million for competitive projects without the earmarks that consumed its whole budget in FY 05.

Education Agency Research Office Support for Gender Equity R&D.   The National Institute of Education (NIE) was created in 1972 as the major research component of the federal education agency then part of the Department of Health, Education and Welfare and later the Department of Education. As seen in Table III, NIE did more to advance research on gender equity than its successors, the Office of Educational Research and Improvement (OERI) and the Institute of Education Sciences (IES). Its earliest large investment in 1977 was in creating a well evaluated "Freestyle" career awareness TV program. One of the shows was about a girl who fought discrimination to learn how to become a "grease monkey" or car mechanic. As of 1981, NIE funded about 200 research-and-development projects related to gender equity issues (Klein and Thomas, 1981). The Women's Research team also organized research colloquia and NIE staff and grantees created numerous publications. NIE research-supported national studies of sex equity in classroom interactions have had a broad impact. (See *Handbook* chapter on Gender Equity in Coeducational and Single Sex Environments.) When the political climate changed, these important multi-year classroom interaction studies almost ended before they could be finished, but a compromise was made to continue them by changing their titles so they no longer said "sex equity." In 2000, the OERI group studying high-risk students sponsored a conference on African American boys, but they didn't consider this a gender equity issue although many of the conference participants did.

OERI's major contribution to gender equity was the leadership role of its Gender Equity Expert Panel (GEEP). The GEEP was created by Sue Klein, a staff member[9] who was committed to good evaluations and to gender equity. Klein admired the model program strategy used by WEEA and later the NSF gender equity program (NSF, 2002), but felt that it was hard for most users to know which programs were most likely to help them address the types of gender inequities they were facing. As other expert panels were created in areas of mathematics and science, safe and drug-free schools, and technology, Klein and the GEEP members encouraged them to use gender equity criteria such as making sure that the quality of the materials they reviewed avoided sex stereotyping and that when they analyzed evidence of effectiveness, they would check to see if the results were equally positive for males and females. The new OERI director who became the IES director ended all the expert panels and substituted a new *What Works Clearinghouse*, which focuses on rigorous evidence of effectiveness criteria, but has no provisions to search for, review, and prepare a comparative report on the relative merits of replicable programs that may advance gender equity. However, Clearinghouse instructions do ask if the program was differentially effective with different populations. While IES no longer has a plan like GEEP to learn about comparative replicable programs to advance gender equity, it funded a four-year, $2.2 million evaluation of "Replication and Outcomes of the Teaching SMART® Program in Elementary Science Classroooms," which is designed in part to help girls and minority students. However, the control groups in this study have no comparable focus on gender equity. As previously noted, the National Center for Education Statistics often reports results by sex and published *Trends in Educational Equity of Girls & Women: 2004.* The legislation creating IES and its National Center for Education Statistics contains requirements for disaggregation of research information by sex, race, and disability, but to date no analysis has been provided on the extent of compliance with these provisions.

National Science Foundation (NSF).   NSF has been focusing on increasing the participation of women in science since the 1981 Equal Opportunities for Women and Minorities in Science and Technology Act (NSF, 2002). Over the years the program has changed names and broadened its focus to include many aspects of gender equity, including new programs for women in computer science and technology as well as helping women succeed in academic science careers via the ADVANCE program started in 2003. By 2006, NSF was the largest supporter of gender equity programs in the government with over $40 million going to four programs. The core Program on Gender in Science and Engineering, has distributed over $9 million each year since 1999 for work at all levels of education. The other NSF funding programs include ADVANCE, Women in Engineering & Computer Science, and IT Workforce Research. The Program on Gender in Science and Engineering has supported experimental projects, model projects, and dissemination. In fact, the Department of Education's Gender Eq-

---

[9]Dr. Sue Klein, who worked in the federal education agency for 34 years before joining the Feminist Majority Foundation in 2003.

uity Expert Panel found that the NSF-funded model gender equity programs had better evaluation evidence than the gender equity programs funded by ED. There have also been a few smaller programs in other agencies such as a Women's Program at NASA and some programs in the Departments of Defense and Energy that provided some additional support for women.

U.S. Department of Labor (DOL), Women's Bureau.

Created in 1920, the Women's Bureau has responsibility for ensuring that all DOL programs pay attention to the needs of women in the workforce and for coordinating activities across the agency to accomplish these goals. For example it co-administered the Women in Apprenticeship and Nontraditional Occupations Grant Program (WANTO) until 2003. The DOL employment and Training Administration is managing WANTO grants from the 2006 appropriation. Women's Bureau staff provide assistance and leadership in regional offices as well as in policy activities in the Washington, DC headquarters. They also fund some replicable demonstration projects that serve working women and young girls. Many of these projects, such as Girls' E-Mentoring in Science, Engineering, and Technology (GEM-SET) developed partnerships with companies, universities, and community-based organizations. GEM-SET is being continued in the private sector. Protests by Women's groups helped stop the plans to close many of the Women's Bureau Regional Offices. But as of 2007, three of the 10 Regional Office Directors had responsibility for two regions. An additional threat to the effectiveness of the Women's Bureau is making the career staff, including staff in policy positions in headquarters, compete with contractors for their own jobs. In 2006, the budget for the whole Women's Bureau including the regional offices and the supported demonstration programs was $9 million, but it is difficult to judge the percentage of this that is focused on education and training to advance gender equity.

US AID, Office of Women in Development Program (WID).

The Office of Women in Development was established in 1974 to integrate gender considerations throughout USAID programs and to contribute to certain areas such as girls' education or later gender equality in education as well. Activities in this area focus on instituting gender equitable policies and practices in basic education, especially for girls, and addressing barriers such as sex discrimination in teaching, stereotypes in learning materials, and unsafe school environments. For example, the Girls Education Mentoring System (GEMS) project from 1999 to 2003 helped countries develop appropriate indicators to monitor and measure girls' education initiatives. A related Strategies to Advance Girls' Education (SAGE) project used a multisectorial approach to learn how to foster partnerships to increase girls' completion of primary school. The 1997–2002 Equity in the Classroom project trained educators, policy makers, and curriculum developers in eight countries. An influential conference in 1998 brought delegations of high-level education officials from many developing countries including India, Egypt, and China to Washington, DC to plan strategies to advance girls' education in their own countries. More recent 2003–2006 projects focus on implementing pilot initiatives on issues such as safe schools and providing technical assistance to strengthen institutional capacity to implement gender equitable practices and policies. From FY 03–05 the WID budget has been about $11 million with about 21% for Girls and Women's Education.

The Millennium Challenge Corporation (MCC).

A U.S. government corporation created by Congress in 2004, has distributed about $6 billion to eligible countries to reduce poverty through sustainable economic growth. To be eligible for funding, countries must do well on performance indicators such as governing justly, investing in people, and encouraging economic freedom. The MCC Threshold Program helps countries improve their performance so that they can later apply for the larger grants. One of the Threshold Programs in Burkina Faso is designed to increase girls' primary school completion rates by constructing schools, funding day care centers by providing materials, furniture, books, and even dry rations to female students who maintain an 80% attendance level, and by supporting adult literacy training for the mothers of students and a girls' mentoring program. (See www.mcc.gov.)

Department of Health and Human Services (HHS) Programs and Activities to Support Adolescent Pregnancy Prevention.

These programs, funded by different federal legislation, are administered in various parts of the HHS, including some activities in the Centers for Disease Control and Prevention and the Office of Women's Health. The more education specific programs focused on gender include demonstration programs in the Office of Adolescent Pregnancy Prevention at $30.7 million in FY 06, State Abstinence Education Program (Section 510) Title V Social Security Act Programs at $50 million in FY 06 (allocated on a formula basis to states), and the most restrictive of all, the abstinenceonly until marriage grant programs, the Community-Based Abstinence Education/Special Programs of National and Regional Significance (CBAE/SPRANS) for Adolescents at $115 million in FY 06.

HHS probably spent more than $200 million in FY 06 on adsolescent health programs that contain some requirements for abstinence only education. Many of these programs have been criticized for using curricula that are scientifically inaccurate and lack evidence that they prevent either sexual activity or adolescent pregnancy (It gets worse: A revamped federal abstinence-only program goes extreme, 2006). As of 2006, four states have rejected some federal abstinence education funding because government restrictions such as limiting discussions of contraception are too strict (Samuels, 2006; A brief history of abstinence-only-until-marriage education, 2006). The *Handbook* chapter on Gender Equity in Formal Sexuality Education concludes that while abstinence only programs do not work, there is evidence that many comprehensive sexuality education programs, which may not be able to receive HHS funding, do reduce adolescent pregnancy. The estimate of over $200 million in FY 06 for adolescent pregnancy prevention programs with abstinence only restrictions is probably low. For example, it doesn't include funding that may go to these activities via the Title X Family Planning Grants, or HIV/AIDS and STD prevention programs, or special earmark grants (A brief history of abstinence-only-until-marriage education, 2006).

TABLE 5.3 Key Federal Programs to Address Gender Equity in Education

Federal Law/Program	National Annual Budget & Activities	Multi-State/ Regional	State	Local Education Level
The Women's Educational Equity Act (WEEA) Promote educational equity for girls and boys, women and men, while paying special attention to those who suffer multiple discrimination based on gender and on race, ethnicity, national origin, disability, or age, and to provide funds to help education agencies and institutions meet the requirements of Title IX. Reauthorized or amended in 1978, 1984, and in 1994 as part of the Improving America's Schools Act. The Women's Educational Equity Act of 2001 was included in the No Child Left Behind Act. http://www.ed.gov/policy/elsec/leg/esea02/pg86.html	It was funded at $6.27 million in 1976; $10 million in FY 1980. From 1982 to 1986 it had about 5.7 million annually. From 1987–89 it had around $3 million annually. From 1990 to 1994 it was $2 million or less each year. This funding has continued at $3 million or less annually to 2006. WEEA funded over 800 projects from 1976 to 2006. Much of the focus has been on model replicable programs.	Five demonstration site contractors each worked with several states 1980–1983.	States have been occasional recipients of WEEA grant funds. However, during the period 1999–2003 no awards were made to state education agencies.	During the period 1999–2003, 7 grants went to local education agencies, representing approximately a quarter of all implementation grants. Local education agencies were frequent users of WEEA products and technical assistance.
Career and Technical Education Acts The 1976 amendments to the Vocational Education Act (VEA) of 1963.	Administered by Bureau for Occupational and Adult Education, then Office for Adult and Vocational Education (OVAE) FY 80 $5,634,243 for national projects and state funds.		'76 Required State plan and a full time State Sex Equity Coordinator to implement 7 functions. Had minimum of $50,000 for each state sex equity coordinator.	Required Local applicants to promote sex equity in all career and vocational programs.
Carl D. Perkins Vocational Education Act of 1984.	Allocated funds to consumer and homemaking education and provided for a National Advisory Council on Vocational Education. Provided model policies & programs for non-traditional careers that are effective. Network of Required State Sex Equity Coordinators who administered distribution of federal funds in states for sex equity programs. There was at least $3 million to cover $60,000 for each state sex equity coordinator.		'84 Expanded to 10 Functions, 3.5% Sex Equity Set-Aside and 7.5% Single Parent/Displaced Homemaker Set-Aside.	
The Carl D. Perkins Vocational and Applied Technology Act of 1990.	State sex equity coordinators allowed but not required. Many joined NAPE. Focus on Nontraditional Occupations, and Special Populations		'90 Required State Plan, State Sex Equity Coordinator, implement 10 Functions. Sex Equity and Single Parent & Displaced Homemaker Set-Asides of 12.5%.	
The Carl D. Perkins Vocational and Applied Technology Act of 1998.			'98 Required State Plan, Eliminated Set-Asides but included an NTO Performance Indicator.	
The Carl D. Perkins Career & Technical Education Improvement Act of 2006	Increases programs to address the needs of special populations such as displaced homemakers, single parents and students training for non-traditional employment.			

(continued)

TABLE 5.3   (Continued)

Federal Law/Program	National Annual Budget & Activities	Multi-state/Regional	State	Local Education Level
Career Incentive Education Act of 1977 (repealed in 1981) Career education program for elementary and secondary schools with post-secondary demonstration projects.	Some of the funding was for activities designed to eliminate sex discrimination and sex role stereotyping.		State career education leaders.	
Fund for the Improvement of Postsecondary Education (FIPSE) Part of the 1965 Higher Education Act Amendments of 1972 with funding for innovative projects starting in 1973.	Total 1980 appropriation $13.5 million with $1,579,725 for gender equity projects. 1984 was $11.71 with $1,053,900 for gender equity projects. 2004 supported 2 new multiyear projects with less than $200,000 supporting women's issues. In 2006 the FIPSE total is about $22 million with no earmarks.			
Research Programs in Education Agency *National Institute of Education* (NIE) was created in 1972 as key federal agency for educational research and development. Its mission was to promote educational equity and improve the quality of educational practice. When NIE was reauthorized in 1976 and 1980, educational equity was a mandated funding priority. In 1980, there was a Social/Process/Women's Research Team, a Women's Studies Team, a National Commission on Working Women, studies on teen pregnancy, a Congressionally mandated vocational education study focusing on eliminating sex stereotyping, etc., and a Minorities and Women's R& D Training Program (Klein, 1980). By 1982, the Women's teams and the Minorities' and Women's Program were dissolved. Some of the regional labs continued small programs for minorities and women, but they were no longer coordinated by federal staff.	The following are estimates of funding for sex equity research in NIE. The higher amounts in FY 79 include $3 million for the Minorities and Women's Program. $5,100,000 in FY 79 $3,180,000 in FY 80 $774,628 in FY 81 $513,240 in FY 82 and also FY83 $100,000 In FY 85 (Levy, 1985) There are compilations describing about 200 NIE sex equity research projects up to 1981 (Klein, 1980; Klein & Thomas, 1981) In 1981, the Women's research team funded 2 multiyear research projects on sex equity in classroom interactions.			
Office of Educational Research and Improvement (OERI) 1985–2002. OERI was reauthorized in 1994. The Institute of Education Sciences (IES) was created by the Education Sciences Reform Act of 2002. The National Center for Education Statistics was a part of each of these offices in the U.S. ED. All the legislation for these research offices specified the need to pay attention to equity and to disaggregate information by sex, race, and other appropriate categories, but there was little organizational attention to gender equity research until the Gender Equity Expert Panel 1996–2002.	There was no formal crosscutting or other group in OERI with a focus on gender equity. However, OERI supported a few gender equity projects some focusing on single-sex schools and colleges. There were also some small unsolicited research projects on gender equity topics. NCES prepared *Trends in Educational Equity for Girls and Women* (NCES, 2000, 2004). The first was for a Congressional requirement in the 1994 WEEA reauthorization.			

(continued)

The 1994 OERI reauthorization requested the establishment of panels of experts to identify promising and exemplary programs, products, practices, policies and research findings to increase gender and other aspects of equity, and the 1994 reauthorization of WEEA called for new evaluation and dissemination responsibilities so WEEA and OERI worked together on the GEEP.

While the 2002 legislation establishing IES continued some gender equity provisions, much IES work focuses on rigourous evaluation to determine what works, but little attention has been given to learning if it works differently for different populations on the basis of gender, race, etc. But, there is no focus on advancing gender equity.

The 11 GEEP promising and exemplary programs were announced after developing criteria to describe: effectiveness in promoting gender equity, the quality of the program, its educational significance, and usefulness to others or replicability. (Fox, 2000; OERI, 2001).

In 2005, one of the IES teacher quality studies was designed in part to learn if the replicable teacher training program was especially effective for girls and minority students, but it was not to be compared with other programs with similar goals.

National Science Foundation (NSF) was established in 1950. The Women in Science Program, created in 1976, provided experimental grants to learn how to address the underrepresentation of women in science and technical careers.

The Equal Opportunities for Women and Minorities in Science and Technology Act created the Committee on Equal Opportunities in Science and Technology and started activities such as Visiting Professorships for Women. A 1999 Congressionally created Commission on the Advancement of Women was influential in publicizing barriers faced by women and minority scientists and engineers.

The 2006 Research on Gender in Science and Engineering Program has been funding research, development, and dissemination projects since 1993 under different names. However it added funding for extension service projects to help educators implement the research-based practices that increase participation of women in science and engineering.

Funded model, research, and dissemination projects, elementary through college level

FY 84 $2,500,00
FY 93 $7,000,000 called Program for Gender Equity
FY 99 $9,750,000
FY 02 $9,700,000

FY 06 $40,300,000 for gender-based programs include ADVANCE (R&RA) $19,630,000 Women in Engineering & Computer Science $7,990,000 IT Workforce Research $3,000,000 Program for Gender Equity $9,680,000. (The annual budget totals include continuations for multi-year projects.)

U.S. Department of Labor
Women's Bureau and Job Training
Women's Bureau. created in 1920, has encouraged people to seek gender equity R&D and other funding from the 1978 Comprehensive Employment and Training Act and the Work Incentive Program and their successors (JTPA and WIA).

FY 05, $9 million for entire Bureau and regional offices

Used to have regional administrator for each of 10 offices. In 2006, 2 administrators manage more than one region.

Funds for clinics, etc via 10 regional offices.

TABLE 5.3 (Continued)

Federal Law/Program	National Annual Budget & Activities	Multi-state/ Regional	State	Local Education Level
Over the years the Women's Bureau has supported demonstration projects and it co-administered the Women in Apprenticeship and Nontraditional Occupations Grant Program until 2003.				
U.S. AID, Women in Development, Girls' Education 1973 Percy Amendment for USAID to integrate women into national economies of foreign countries to increase their status and the country's development.	Focuses on improving basic education of girls in developing countries From FY 03–5 WID budget has been about $11 million with about 21% for education of girls and women.			
Millennium Challenge Corporation (MCC) Established by Congress in 2004. MCC provides funds to help countries doing well on 16 indicators to to reduce poverty through large grants to qualifying countries, as well as a smaller Threshold program for countries who need help to reach all indicators such as creating parity in girls' education rates.	In FY 06, $13 million is going to Burkina Fasso to help build girl-friendly coed schools, which also includes providing day care to relieve older daughters from sibling-care responsibilities. Other projects also provide some help to gender equity education such as school construction or training both boys and girls in better agricultural practices.			
Dept. of Health and Human Services Office of Adolescent Pregnancy Programs (OAPP) created in 1981 as Title XX of the Public Health Service Act the Adolescent Family Life Program that supports research and demonstration projects for: abstinence education and care programs for parenting teens and their family members to decrease effects of too-early childbearing for teen parents.	OAPP FY 82 $11.4 for grants in Adolescent Family Life program FY 06 $30.7 million. Supported 58 abstinence education multiyear projects and 43 care projects		States must match $3 for every $4 in federal funding they receive.	Sexuality ed programs provided by public agencies, faith-based groups and other subcontractors
Title X Family Planning Grants created in 1970 to provide a wide range of acceptable and effective family planning methods and services.	FY 05 $288 million in HRSA	Funds for clinics, etc via 10 regional offices		
State Abstinence Education Program (Section 510 of Title V of the Social Security Act) Personal Responsibility and Work Opportunity Act of 1996 (the so-called Welfare Reform bill or TANF) to support abstinence-only programs.	$50 million total in block grants per year to participating states from 1998–2006 to teach abstinence only. (Participating states provide $3 for every $4 in federal funds.)		Participating states get money according to formula tied to low-income children and have an Abstinence Education Coordinator.	
Community-Based Abstinence Education/Special Programs of National and Regional Significance (CBAE/SPRANS) for adolescents 12–18, the Administration for Children and Families, under 1110 of the Social Security Act.	Public or private recipients of these implementation grants must agree not to provide any information that is inconsistent with the abstinence-until-marriage message. FY 05 $103.7 million FY 06 $115 million			CBAE funds go directly to public and private program suppliers

82

The Department of HHS has funded other types of worthwhile and hopefully effective gender equity health education activities such as the Girls Neighborhood Power initiative and the ongoing Office of Women's Health activities such as the 4girls.gov Web site and the National Bone Health Campaign, which especially focuses on helping girls combat osteoporosis, or the BodyWise Eating Disorder Educational Campaign.

Summary. Federal leadership, technical assistance, and funding to support sex or gender equity work have always been miniscule compared to federal funding for other specific population groups where there has been a history of stereotyping and discrimination such as for special education or English Language Learners. "For example, in FY 80 at $33.9 million, its highest level of support, the Office of Education spent only .2% of its budget on sex equity" (Levy, 1985). This proportion would be even smaller today as the total ED budget has grown substantially, but the only programs and activities to specifically support gender equity that remain as of FY 06 are: WEEA with less than $3 million, Gender Equity Assistance work by the CRA Title IV Equity Assistance Centers with less than $2 million (out of the total of $7 million for race, gender, and national origin), some competitive awards in FIPSE and IES, some ongoing staff work in OCR and the production of occasional descriptive reports in NCES.

At over $40 million, the NSF is the largest positive supporter of gender equity programs with its four FY 06 programs to increase the participation of women in science, mathematics, engineering, and technology. HHS spends more (over $200 million in FY 06) on education programs with a focus on gender, but most of these programs are required to emphasize HHS approved abstinence-only-until-marriage messages. Given that many of these abstinence-only programs are not gender equitable, and since they perpetuate gender stereotypes and misinformation, and since there is no evidence that they are effective in reducing pregnancies, many equity advocates recommend that this federal money be used instead for other worthwhile gender equity programs.

There is much room for enhancing the federal role in advancing gender equity. In addition to limited enforcement of Title IX, the U.S. Department of Education played a minimal role in supporting technical assistance and even the relatively inexpensive development and dissemination of high-quality gender equity resources. Starting in the early 1970s, ED collected some resources for the ERIC system and helped publish and share WEEA and other products via the WEEA Equity Resource Center. Additionally, the OCR in ED published a few brochures and guidelines on civil rights. The CRA IV-funded Equity Assistance Centers (http://www.ed.gov/about/contacts/gen/othersites/equity.html) published some information, increasingly Web-based, on gender equity such as the Mid-Atlantic Equity Center (MAEC) report cards and have also held training sessions and conferences on gender equity topics. However, with the exception of some work by NSF related to gender equity in mathematics and the sciences, most of this federal assistance with gender equity resources ended by 2003 when ED decided to discontinue the WEEA Equity Resource Center and the Gender Equity Expert Panel, which was designed to encourage the production and evaluation of replicable high quality and effective gender equity programs.

HOW STATES AND LOCAL GOVERNMENTS SUPPORT GENDER EQUITY IN EDUCATION

States and local governments can support gender equity in education through their leadership, technical assistance, budgets, and through their influence on how federal funds that flow through their agencies are used. Morever, many states have state laws and constitutional provisions prohibiting discrimination. Therefore, this section will focus on state- and local-government responsibilities to implement federal and state laws intended to protect all types of students and employees from discrimination based on sex.

In the majority of states, the State Education Agency (SEA) for public K–12 schools is separate from the state higher education agency. Generally state education agencies (SEAs) provide funds, assistance, and some regulatory functions for local school districts, educator preparation programs, and much more. Since SEAs and institutions of higher education (IHE) and local education agencies (LEA) receive federal financial assistance, they must comply with federal civil rights laws.

Additionally, many states have their own gender equity laws such as state constitutional equal rights amendments or Title IX-type statutory laws to protect against sex discrimination in education. Often these state equity laws are broader than the federal equal protection clause of the U.S. Constitution or the federal Title IX. Sexual orientation is a protected class in 13 states, but is not protected directly under federal law.

Summary of State Laws that Advance Gender Equity in Education

In addition to federal statutory and constitutional protection from sex discrimination in education, a variety of state antidiscrimination laws bar sex discrimination in schools. Since primary responsibility for education rests with each state, it is critical that nondiscrimination in education be included in state laws and regulations. State laws can be explicitly written or judicially interpreted to provide students with far greater protection against sex discrimination than federal laws. Especially when the federal and administrative branches and the United States Supreme Court are conservative, state laws are an especially important source of protection against sex discrimination in education. They may also provide enforcement mechanisms that supplement those available under federal law (National Women's Law Center, 2005).[10] State protection from sex discrimination comes from a variety of sources within state law; the

---

[10]For an overview of state law remedies for sex discrimination in education, see National Women's Law Center, *Tools of the Trade: Using the Law to Address Sex Segregation in High School Career and Technical Education* 17–22 (2005).

scope and breadth of protection varies considerably from state to state. The main sources of state law protection are: state constitutions, state statutes, and administrative regulations. However, even state guidelines that do not have the force of law can be a powerful tool to support equity in education.

State constitutions can be a strong source of protection from sex discrimination in education. This protection may come from general "equal protection" clauses within state constitutions or from provisions that specifically mandate gender equality. Some state constitutions have specific provisions that bar sex discrimination in education. Hawaii's constitution, for example, provides that "There shall be no discrimination in public education institutions because of race, religion, sex or ancestry. . . ."[11] Other states have more general sex-equality provisions. These so-called state Equal Rights Amendments can be an especially powerful source of protection.[12] Today, 22 states have some form of explicit protection against sex discrimination in their state constitutions.[13] Some of these state provisions have been interpreted under judicial review as being quite weak e.g., Virginia, Utah, and Illinois. In some noteworthy instances, however, these state equality guarantees have been interpreted to provide greater protection against sex discrimination than may be available under federal law. In *Commonwealth v. Pennsylvania Interscholastic Athletic Ass'n*, 334 A.2d 839 (Pa. 1975), the Pennsylvania Supreme Court used the Pennsylvania ERA to strike down a rule excluding girls from practice or competition with boys in all interscholastic sports, emphasizing that "even where separate teams are offered for boys and girls in the same sport, the most talented girls may still be denied the right to play at that level of competition which their ability might otherwise permit them."[14] In *Newberg v. Board of Public Education*, 26 Pa. D. & C.3d 682 (1983), a Pennsylvania Court held that Philadelphia's Central High School's all-male admissions policy violated both the federal constitution and the Pennsylvania ERA. The federal violation of the Constitution was based on the Equal Protection Clause of the Fourteenth Amendment.

Other important sources of state law protection for sex equity in schools are statutes and administrative regulations. Many states with statutes that specifically prohibit sex discrimination in education have language that is similar to Title IX. Most states have antidiscrimination statutes prohibiting sex discrimination in employment, housing, and places of public accommodation. Some states explicitly classify education as a place of public accommodation. These antidiscrimination laws may explicitly extend protection beyond Title IX. California,

New Jersey, and Wisconsin's laws against discrimination, for example, provide that schools may not discriminate based on sexual orientation.[15] These statutes are often implemented and clarified through administrative regulations issued by state departments of education or state civil rights agencies and approved by the legislature. Local ordinances and board of education policies may provide additional protection. Statutory protection may also be found in a variety of other state statutes not directed at education or civil rights, including those addressing hate crimes, bullying, and sexual assault.

Even where the language of these state statutes does not explicitly extend beyond Title IX, judges and administrative agencies have interpreted them as providing broader protection than Title IX based on their legislative history or state public policy.[16] For example, in *E.B. v. North Hunterdon Regional School District*, 12 N.J.A.R. 232 (1986), the New Jersey Commissioner of Education held that a female student must be allowed to try out for the boys' high school football team. Courts have extended broader protection than that afforded at the federal level in cases involving sexual harassment, pregnancy discrimination, and other sex equality issues.

Implementation of Federal and State Gender Equity Laws and Policies

States vary widely in the structure and organization of their state education agencies (SEAs), in the roles of the State Superintendent (or Commissioner) of Education and other agency heads, and in the relationships of SEAs with other state agencies and with local education agencies. In all but a handful of states, the governance of education lies with several agencies. Primary through secondary education often is under the authority of one state agency, while colleges and universities and two-year colleges may be under the jurisdiction of other entities. Many states also have a human rights agency to oversee federal and state civil rights laws. Whether elected or appointed, state superintendents or agency heads and state boards of education with a strong commitment to equity play an important part in providing leadership in support of Title IX, and state gender equity laws and in collaborating with other state agencies on gender equity issues.

With or without budgets for gender equity programs, one of the key ways states can provide leadership and oversight on gender and other aspects of equity is to employ experts with specific responsibilities for implementing these laws. The Ca-

---

[11]HAW. CONST. art. X, § 1. See also CAL. CONST. art. I, § 31(a); WYO. CONST. art. VII, §10; MONT. CONST. art. 10 § 7.

[12]For a thorough discussion of the impact of state equal rights amendments in advancing sex equality, see Linda J. Wharton, (2005), State Equal Rights Amendments Revisited: Evaluating Their Effectiveness in Advancing Protection Against Sex Discrimination, *Rutgers Law Journal, 36*, 1201.

[13]ALASKA CONST. art I, § 3; CAL. CONST. art. I, § 8; COLO. CONST. art. II, § 29; CONN. CONST. art. I, § 20; FLA. CONST. art. I, § 1; HAW. CONST. art. I, § 21; ILL. CONST. art. I, § 18; IOWA CONST. art. I, § 1; LA. CONST. art. I, § 3; MD. CONST. art. I, § 3; MASS. CONST. pt. I, art. 1; MONT. CONST. art. II, § 4; N.H. CONST. pt. I, art. 2; N.J. CONST. art. I, para. 1 & art. X, para. 4; N.M. CONST. art. II, § 1; PA. CONST. art. I, § 28 ; R.I. CONST. art. I, § 2; TEX. CONST. art. I, § 3a; VA. CONST. art. I, § 11;; UTAH CONST., art. IV, § 1; WASH. CONST. XXXI, § 1; WYO. CONST. art. I, § 2

[14]This case was initiated by Pennsylvania National Organization for Women, under the leadership of its president, Eleanor Smeal.

[15]N.J. Stat. Ann. § § 10:5-1 et. Seq. (2005).

[16]Some state courts might be more favorable to implementing anti sex discrimination laws than federal courts, which are dominated by conservative judicial appointments. It is wise to be aware of the chances for success when choosing a legal approach.

reer and Technical Education chapter describes the state sex equity coordinators who were required from 1976 until 1990 to administer sex equity programs under the federal Perkins Vocational Education Acts. However, when this requirement was eliminated, only a few of these coordinators, their budgets, and staffs were maintained by the states even though states were allowed to continue to use federal vocational education funds to do so. The remaining federal requirements for gender equity personnel in the state education agencies are for Title IX coordinators and administrators of the Memorandum of Agreement (MOA) developed to implement the 1979 vocational education guidelines to assure that subrecipients of federal funds comply with the civil rights laws related to race, color, national origin, sex, and handicap. However, it is common for individuals with these MOA assignments to have additional responsibilities as well.

Title IX Coordinators in the State Education Agencies

In 2004, the National Coalition for Women and Girls in Education (NCWGE) surveyed state education agencies to obtain information about their Title IX coordinators. They found that it was difficult to identify more than the 20 state coordinators who responded, and that even those who did respond to the survey were "undervalued, underutilized, and under funded" (Baulch, 2004). At the state level, Title IX coordinators often have multiple responsibilities. For example, one state Title IX coordinator is also the personnel director for her SEA and some are also MOA administrators. But more typically, the state Title IX coordinator also handles multicultural education programs, sexual harassment issues, bullying, and discrimination based on sexual orientation and other protected classes. In some states the designated state Title IX coordinator is only responsible for addressing sex discrimination related to SEA staff and a few SEA run schools, while in some states they have both an internal and external role. In some states individuals in affirmative action or human resources offices serve in the internal SEA role and another state Title IX Coordinator has responsibility for implementing gender equity laws in LEAs throughout the state. The previously discussed 2004 survey of state Title IX coordinators found that:

Even at the SEA level, the majority of Title IX coordinators report spending 10% or less of their time on their Title IX coordinator responsibilities. From 1976 to 1997, Title IV of the Civil Rights Act of 1964 provided funds to SEAs to administer race, national origin, and gender equity (Title IX coordinator) programs. At that time there were many states that had full-time Title IX coordinators. With the elimination of these funds for SEAs by Congress in 1996, no SEA now has a full-time Title IX coordinator. (Baulch, 2004, p. 3)

In June–July 2006, a survey of state Title IX coordinators was conducted by William A. Howe of the Connecticut State Department of Education. Forty-seven states responded to an e-mail and telephone survey. Of the 47 states, only 13 states permit the state Title IX coordinator to conduct investigations of Title IX violations although more may conduct investigations under their state civil rights laws. The average state Title IX coordinator reported only 15% of their work assignments were related to Title

IX. The range is from 1–40%. The median was 10%. Connecticut and Tennessee have the highest FTE percentage at 40. Several states indicated less than 3–5% of their work log was devoted to Title IX.

Under urging from NCWGE members, in 2004 the Office for Civil Rights within the U.S. Department of Education sent "Dear Colleague" letters to heads of state and local education agencies and institutions of higher education, reminding them of their obligation to have a Title IX coordinator. The Feminist Majority Foundation (FMF), with help from NCWGE members and the Equity Assistance Centers (EAC), identified Title IX coordinators for each state and the District of Columbia and made their contact information available on their Web site: www.feminist.org/education. This public listing of state Title IX coordinators led some states (that had previously neglected to make or renew such appointments) to appoint Title IX coordinators. But it took 18 months of extensive calls and e-mails, as well as reminders that compliance with the Title IX regulation required a public posting of information on how to contact each organization's Title IX coordinators, to complete this list. The FMF Education Equity Program tries to keep this list of state Title IX coordinators updated, but finds that sometimes when the Title IX coordinators leave their position, they are not replaced. A state Title IX coordinator working with the Title IX Action Network has established an electronic mailing list to facilitate communication among the state Title IX coordinators, and FMF is working with the Association for Gender Equity Leadership in Education (AGELE) and others to provide Web resources on Title IX such as training materials and descriptions of the roles of Title IX coordinators in state education agencies, school districts, postsecondary institutions, and other organizations. Coordination and collaboration among state Title IX coordinators is needed to build support and visibility for their work.

Although the 1975 federal Title IX regulations require recipients to provide public information on their grievance procedures and contact information on Title IX coordinators, it is a challenge to find them in school handbooks, telephone directories, or bulletin boards. Although Web sites did not exist in 1975, they are now a logical place for institutions to provide information on Title IX, Title IX coordinators, and grievance procedures. However, a 2005 FMF survey of SEA Web sites revealed that only 16 had contact information on their state Title IX coordinators clearly posted on their Web site. Some of these state education agency Web sites provide helpful information about Title IX and state gender equity laws and policies, as well as information on state Section 504 Handicapped coordinators, Civil Rights Act Title VI diversity or multicultural coordinators, and other civil rights laws (Walker, 2005).

In 2001, the U.S. Department of Justice prepared "Questions and Answers Regarding Title IX Procedural Requirements," which contains some guidance on the responsibilities and competencies needed by Title IX coordinators and on grievance procedures. Similarly, some regional Department of Education OCR offices have provided similar guidance. Various state and local agencies assign different responsibilities to their designated Title IX coordinators. Some state Title IX coordinators have had responsibility for training and assisting Title IX coordinators in local education agencies and other recipients of federal financial assistance in their states. Sometimes these coordinators have also worked closely with the Perkins sex equity coordinators as described in the Career and Technical Education chapter in this *Handbook* and in the next section of this chapter.

Most state Title IX coordinators have little or no funding to provide training activities, develop resources, or fund local district initiatives. Only two of the twenty 2004 survey respondents said that they received at least some minimal funds for their Title IX program (Baulch, 2004). Thus, they must rely on other departments in their agencies to provide financial support for their activities or infuse equity within their activities. Within SEAs, gender equity/Title IX issues are often addressed by offices that manage programs in the areas of career and technical education, athletics/physical education/health, science, technology, engineering and mathematics or other instructional discipline areas, as well as offices that address sexual harassment and bullying prevention. Outreach to colleges and universities by these Title IX coordinators and their SEA colleagues often focuses on preservice teacher education, counselor and administrator education, and nontraditional career awareness, exploration and preparation.

Relationship of State Education Agencies and the U.S. Department of Education

The federal government has provided the key impetus for most state education agency attention to gender equity and Title IX requirements. States vary in how closely they work with either the regional or federal level offices of the U.S. Department of Education, Office for Civil Rights. In some cases the relationship is virtually nonexistent. Part of the limited interaction is related to the lack of staff, budget, expertise, perceived conflicts of interest, and limited outreach or initiative on the part of regional OCR offices. Other times SEAs make little, if any effort to collaborate with OCR on Title IX issues. However, all recipients of federal financial assistance, including the various education agencies in each state, are required to have a designated Title IX coordinator (and they may have more than one). Key gender equity support to states from the federal government includes limited support from the 2006 Perkins Act[17] and the contractors for the Civil Rights Title IV Equity Assistance Centers for K–12 equity issues related to sex, race, and national origin.

The SEA Title IX coordinators have no formal relationship with the Office for Civil Rights and receive no direct or specialized information, support, or contact. The Office for Civil Rights has provided limited technical assistance (phone, e-mail), and through OCR, staff participation in an annual training conference to which MOA administrators from every state are strongly encouraged (by OCR) to attend. The likely reason for this federal support of the state MOA coordinators is because MOA coordinators have specified duties for which OCR has oversight responsibility as established by federal regulation. Although some assistance is available to state Title IX coordinators through regional OCR offices and Equity Assistance Centers, there is no designated Title IX official in OCR headquarters, nor is there OCR sponsored annual Title IX coordinator training or a formal mechanism for technical assistance or communication from the federal Department of Education. Since, there is a lack of federal coordination of Title IX implementation. Instead, efforts to urge the Department to act on Title IX issues come from external nongovernmental organizations like the National Women's Law Center (NWLC) or the National Coalition for Women and Girls in Education (NCWGE).

Relationships of the SEA Title IX Coordinators, LEAs, and Other State Entities Covered by Title IX

There should be between 50,000 and 150,000 active Title IX coordinators in the public and private educational institutions in the U.S. that receive federal financial assistance. This includes the 50 plus Title IX coordinators in all state education agencies for postsecondary and career and technical education as well as the state agency with K–12 responsibilities. This estimate of required Title IX coordinators is based on estimates for numbers of school districts and public and private schools and postsecondary institutions receiving federal financial assistance. It does not include other covered institutions such as scientific laboratories, prisons, recreation departments, museums, and various health and labor training programs that might receive federal financial assistance from agencies such as the Departments of Agriculture, Defense, Labor, and Health and Human Services.

While it is not explicit in the Title IX regulations, many SEA Title IX coordinators have taken an active role in providing assistance to the local Title IX coordinators in a wide variety of institutions in their state. In some states these resources are focused on the largest LEAs. State staff have often combined this with guidance on their own state gender and other equity laws and policies. Some states even list LEA or Community College Title IX coordinators on their SEA web page and have formal procedures for state Title IX coordinators to work with them.

The technical assistance provided by SEAs to others in their states usually consists of interpreting Title IX regulations and requirements, helping develop policies and procedures, providing consultation on sexual harassment and gender equity issues, and training. Some states do some data collection and conduct surveys, but less than two dozen do compliance investigations since this is generally the responsibility of the ED OCR and may not be part of state agency policy even in states with their own gender equity laws. Since most state Title IX coordinators are located in the K–12 part of the SEA, little attention is provided on assisting Title IX coordinators in public and private postsecondary institutions, which is surprising since almost all are covered by Title IX as their students receive federal financial assistance. Similarly, state Title IX coordinators rarely provide assistance to other types of entities covered by Title IX, such as museums, recreation departments, or prisons. Figure 5.1 "Title IX Coordinator Roles and Responsibilities for Local School Districts" was developed by state Title IX coordinators based on

---

[17]For many of the years each state had a minimum of $60,000 for the sex equity coordinator, plus program funds under the Perkins Vocational Education Acts.

"No person in the United States shall, on the basis of sex, be excluded from participation in, be denied the benefits of, or be subjected to discrimination under any education program or activity receiving Federal financial assistance."

Legal Citation: *Title IX of the Education Amendments of 1972, and its implementing regulation at 34 C.F.R. Part 106 (Title IX)*

Designation of a Coordinator

A. School systems or other recipients of federal funds (including all public schools, charter schools and magnet schools) must designate at least one professional employee as the Title IX coordinator to oversee compliance efforts and investigate any complaints of sex discrimination.

B. All students, applicants, employees, parents/guardians, and residents must be notified of the names, office address(es), and telephone number(s) of the designated coordinator(s) of Title IX.

Dissemination of Policy

The school district's policy of nondiscrimination must be prominently included in each student handbook, bulletin, catalog, booklet, announcement, brochure, student application form or other publication distributed to students, potential students, parents, and any other persons benefiting from the school district's activities and programs. The name and contact information (office address, telephone number, fax number, email address) of the Title IX Coordinator must also be included in this announcement. (*Although Internet was not available in 1975 when this policy was developed, all this Title IX information should now be made easily accessible on the institution's Web site.*)

Monitoring Compliance

The Title IX Coordinator is responsible for monitoring the overall implementation of Title IX for the school district and coordinating the institution's compliance with Title IX in all areas covered by the implementing regulations. The overall responsibility is the prevention of sex discrimination. Major monitoring duties include, but are not limited to, the following:

Admissions: Admissions and Recruitment

Education Programs and Activities: Housing, Comparable Facilities, Access to Course Offerings, Access to Schools operated by the School District, Counseling and Related Materials, participation in extra-curricular activities, Financial Assistance, Employment Assistance, Health Services and Insurance, Marital/Parental Status, Athletics and Physical Education.

Employment in Education Programs and Activities: Employment Criteria, Recruitment, Compensation, Job Classification, Fringe Benefits, Marital or Parental Status, Advertising, Pre-employment Activities

Sexual Harassment

Other areas of consideration include:

- Developing a committee to assist in meeting Title IX obligations is highly recommended.
- Arranging to have a Title IX/Equity coordinator in each school building enables better monitoring of Title IX in individual schools leaving the District Title IX Coordinator to take care of the district as a whole.
- Participating in the development and implementation of the school system's sexual harassment policy. Be aware of new needs which may dictate changes or revisions in existing policies or practices. For example, since sexual harassment is a violation of Title IX, the school district's list of disciplinary infractions should include prohibition of sexual harassment.
- Assisting faculty, counselors and administrators in complying with Title IX, and when a need arises, planning remedial actions. For example, if females are under-represented in advanced mathematics, science or computer programming courses, ask the faculty to plan for several workshops, student tutorial services, or other ways to increase enrollment of females in these advanced courses.
- Making the Title IX Coordinator known in the community by disseminating civil rights information or by speaking at parent-teacher group meetings, social or professional organization meetings, and other community functions and by providing contact and other information on the institution's Web-site.
- Serving as a resource to the local superintendent of schools on Title IX/Gender issues, and submitting annual reports on Title IX compliance activities to the district superintendent.

FIGURE 5.1   Title IX Coordinator Roles and Responsibilities for Local School Districts

- Monitoring and evaluating the district's Title IX compliance efforts and making recommendations for any appropriate changes.
- Providing updated information to schools on Title IX implementation and issues.
- Maintaining contact with the state education agency Title IX coordinator and with the federal regional equity assistance center
- Identifying and disseminating information about Title IX educational resources (organizations, individuals, print, Internet, and audio-visual)

Grievance Procedures

Adoption and publication of procedures providing prompt and equitable resolution of complaints is critical. Nondiscrimination policy notices and their attendant Grievance Procedures must be made public and disseminated throughout the educational community. Develop Title IX grievance procedures for students and teachers in cooperation with local student service and human resources staff; give public notice of the procedures and the name and contact information of the school system Title IX coordinator.

Have copies of the grievance procedure and any related forms available in schools and libraries to students, parents or school personnel alleging sexual harassment or discrimination. Assist them in filing their grievance and oversee the step-by-step procedure to be sure that time frames are met. Assist administrative personnel who need a better understanding of the grievance based on Title IX. Keep records of all grievances filed.

In carrying out this responsibility, the Title IX coordinator may actually investigate any complaint filed under the institution's grievance procedures. If the Title IX coordinator does not conduct the investigation of complaints, she or he should receive information about any grievance filed and the resolution. This will allow the institution to identify any patterns, and repeat offenders that may be missed when grievances are handled by several individuals. The coordinator should receive sufficient information throughout the process so that she or he can provide guidance or information to ensure that the institution carries out its responsibilities under Title IX. The Title IX coordinator should also be sufficiently knowledgeable about the requirements of the regulations to advise the institution about policies and practices, which may violate Title IX.

Core Responsibilities of Title IX Coordinators

- Develop a working knowledge of the federal Title IX (of the Education Amendments of 1972) law and its implementation regulations. Have a copy of Title IX readily available and understand the requirements and the intent of the law. Keep informed of current research and legal and judicial decisions related to Title IX and gender equity.
- Be informed about state laws, regulations and policies on all equity issues, including bullying and harassment and child abuse laws.
- Be knowledgeable of federal and state laws (e.g. ADA, Section 504, IDEA) prohibiting discrimination against all protected classes (including race, national origin, religion, disability, and sexual orientation) and assist whenever possible.
- Be sure female and male students participating in work-based learning programs are guaranteed equal treatment by their employers.
- Coordinate with other staff and document an internal self-evaluation of practices and policies with respect to treatment of female and male students, if this responsibility was never completed. If the evaluation was completed by a previous Title IX coordinator, check if the evaluation's remedies for eliminating segregation and discrimination were carried out.
- Provide program development, including in-service training, to eliminate sex discrimination in the district. Consider conducting a school-wide in-service or assembly on sexual harassment. For another example, continued gender-segregated classes in workforce development education courses should prompt quick remediation and activities to decrease students' gender role .
- Attend state and national conferences specifically for Title IX coordinators and/or on gender equity issues generally, and share the information with local administrators, staff and faculty.
- Provide updated resources on Title IX and gender equity to local school districts
- Keep all relevant records.

Adapted from the US Department of Education/Office for Civil Rights/Boston Regional Office, North Carolina State Board of Education, the New Hampshire Department of Education, the Connecticut State Department of Education and the Equity Assistance Center/NYU at Rutgers University, and the Maryland State Department of Education.

Minor update 6-24-06.
Barbara Bitters, Wisconsin Department of Public Instruction
William A. Howe, Connecticut State Department of Education
Marilyn Hulme, Equity Assistance Center/NYU at Rutgers University
Susan McKevitt, New Hampshire Department of Education
Linda Shevitz, Maryland State Department of Education

FIGURE 5.1 (Continued).

previous guidance from OCR and Title IX coordinator job descriptions from several states. It provides a good overview of LEA Title IX coordinator responsibilities that can be adapted for other organizations such as postsecondary institutions.

Background and Potential for LEA Title IX Coordinators

After the 1975 Title IX regulations were issued, Title IX coordinators at all levels were active in instituting change toward gender equality in their institutions. This was spurred by the requirement that recipient organizations conduct by July 21, 1976 an institution-wide, self-assessment to learn where they were and were not in compliance with Title IX. Public reports on these assessments were shared at the district level, and in some cases states or related entities such as Commissions on Women conducted periodic updates of these initially required self-assessments. Some state Title IX coordinators also organized state networks, conducted site visits to review compliance with Title IX, and provided training programs, often supported by federal funding. However, in recent years in many states, Title IX coordinators, where still present, have received little attention or support from public officials, and many institutions have been failing to appoint a Title IX coordinator altogether. Increasingly, educators who benefited from gender equity training in the 1975–1995 era are retiring, and educators stepping into leadership positions are completely unaware of the requirements.

Even when Title IX coordinators in local education agencies are designated, none are full-time and few receive funds for gender equity programs. In many cases, the person designated as the Title IX coordinator has other unrelated primary assignments, ranging from superintendent to football coach, and may not be very knowledgeable or interested in full implementation of Title IX. Few Title IX coordinators receive the support, training, technical assistance, and recognition that they need to perform even the minimum complaint-related aspects of their jobs. Thus, their Title IX responsibilities are often ignored or given short shrift. After the ED OCR sent letters to state and local education agencies in 1997 reminding them to designate and train a Title IX coordinator, evidence of noncompliance persisted. For example, in 2001 the *Pittsburgh Tribune* reported finding that Title IX coordinators in its area were unaware they were the coordinators, had not been trained to be coordinators, and were rarely consulted when the school made decisions concerning Title IX. Similarly in 2002, "the Chicago *Daily Herald* revealed that only six of 17 suburban districts contacted by the paper could direct the caller to the Title IX coordinator. When OCR conducted its own compliance investigations in areas such as sex discrimination in career and technical (formerly vocational) education or sexual harassment, it often found that the recipient institution facing these other charges also lacked a Title IX coordinator" (Baulch, 2004, p. 4). In 2005, when FMF called various offices on campus in two states to ask for contact information on the institution's Title IX coordinators, they had practically no success.

Importance of Title IX Coordinators at All Levels

Well-informed Title IX gender equity coordinators are needed to counteract the neglect of Title IX and help all educators and students learn about their rights and responsibilities to treat and be treated in a non sex discriminatory way. Without the essential Title IX gender equity coordinators in place, educators, parents, and students are frequently left unable to effectively solve or prevent problems. A recent study suggests that fewer than 50% of educators understand what Title IX covers, and that only a miniscule percentage of students and parents are aware of their rights under Title IX (Zittleman, 2005).

Perhaps more than entreaties to follow the law, negative consequences related to complaint investigations or litigation seem to encourage districts to appoint Title IX coordinators. For example, Title IX coordinators are often appointed after a complaint is advanced, instead of having a system in place to prevent the initial sex discrimination, or they are appointed after the district has had to settle by paying a large fine as was the case when Hawaii (in its school district capacity) had to pay $900,000 on a sexual harassment case. Filing complaints, the slowest and least cost-effective way to handle issues, is the only recourse left to many students and employees when the Title IX regulation provisions to prevent sex discrimination are ignored. (See www.feminist.org/education for information on some Title IX cases and settlements.)

Importance of Multiple Supporters for State, Local and Other Efforts to Advance Gender Equity in Education

Title IX coordinators often work with other state agencies or nonprofit organizations on gender equity issues. State and local Commissions for Women and nongovernmental organizations (NGOs) such as the National Organization for Women (NOW) and the American Association of University Women (AAUW) will often be involved with sexual harassment or sex equity claims in schools. Sexual Assault Crisis Centers provide training to schools and counseling on sexual assault. The American Civil Liberties Union (ACLU) is often invloved with free speech and other civil rights matters. Local affiliates of national advocacy groups for gay and lesbian students, such as the Gay Lesbian & Straight Education Network (GLSEN) or Parents, Families & Friends of Lesbians & Gays (PFLAG), will seek out the Title IX coordinators in SEAs and LEAs for assistance. National human rights groups such as the organizations participating in the Leadership Conference on Civil Rights and the National Council of Women's Organizations often are active at all levels of government. The next section of this chapter describes the role of many of these gender equity allies.

ROLE OF NONGOVERNMENTAL GENDER EQUITY EDUCATION ALLIES AND KEY STRATEGIES THEY EMPLOY

In the U.S., the government is supposed to be responsive to the will of the majority while protecting the rights of the minority. Government executive department employees at all levels are responsible for implementing the laws and policies in their agencies. The chapter so far has focused on the role of the federal and state governments in establishing and using policies specifically designed to advance gender equity in education contexts. This section will highlight key strategies nongovernmental organizations have used to help government agencies attend to gender equity. The NGOs have been critical in getting these laws passed and in sustaining them even when the administration, some congressional leaders, or the courts have tried to weaken or eliminate them. However, the NGOs have been less successful in maintaining federal funding and federal staff to provide leadership for gender equity in education programs. Several key types of NGOs have a special focus on gender equity education issues and include: professional and advocacy organizations such as members of the National Coalition for Women and Girls in Education (NCWGE), public interest law firms such as the National Women's Law Center, recipients of government funding for gender equity work, foundations and corporations that support this work, and media groups. There have also been a few national NGO organizations that fight against gender equity. Some of these forces are described in other parts of the *Handbook* and will not be covered in this chapter. In making their anti-gender equity arguments, they frequently use misguided or inaccurate information.

NGO Gender Equity Allies or Support Groups

NGO membership and advocacy organizations supporting gender equity in education are quite diverse.
Some have grass roots chapters in many areas of the country. Others are national organizations that are primarily supported by external grants. There are two major national umbrella organizations in the U.S. that are expressly focused on many aspects of gender equity education. They are the NCWGE (www.ncwge. org) and the Association for Gender Equity Leadership in Education (AGELE; www.agele.org), which was originally called the National Coalition for Sex Equity in Education (NCSEE). NCSEE was formed in 1979 by and for CRA Title IV-funded gender equity professionals and their allies. It is the only U.S. organization that hosts an annual conference focusing specifically on gender equity in education at every level and discipline. NCWGE formed in 1975 to push for good regulations to implement Title IX, and many other useful laws and regulations, and has national organization members including AGELE and 50 other organizations. NCWGE members such as the American Association of University Women (AAUW), the Feminist Majority Foundation (FMF), Girls Incorporated, National Organization for Women (NOW), and the National Women's Law Center (NWLC), and Legal Momentum focus on many women's rights issues from education to employment to ending violence against women. Members such as the Association for Women in Science (AWIS), National Alliance for Partnerships in Equity (NAPE), the National Women's History Project, the Women's Sports Foundation, and Women Work! focus on women's education issues in specific areas. Additional NCWGE members include education organizations that also care about gender equity such as the American Federation of Teachers (AFT), the National Education Association (NEA), the American Educational Research Association, the American Psychological Association, and the U.S. Student Association (USSA). Additionally

there are good alliances with other civil rights organizations. Many members of the NCWGE are also participants in the National Council of Women's Organizations, the National Council for Research on Women, the National Association for Multicultural Education, and the Leadership Conference on Civil Rights. Often NCWGE members work closely with organizations concerned with race, disability, and Lesbian, Gay, Bisexual, or Transgender (LGBT) rights at both the national and grass roots or local levels. Some previously influential organizations such as Women's Equity Action League (WEAL), the Federation of Organizations for Professional Women (FOPW), and the Project on Equal Education Rights (PEER) of the NOW Legal Defense and Education Fund have disbanded, but many of their activist members continue to work for gender equity in other organizations. A more extensive analysis of gender equity ally organizations is included in "What is the Field of Gender Equity in Education" by Klein, Ortman, and Friedman, 2002.

NCWGE monitors and influences Congress and federal agencies related to Title IX and other laws that fund gender equity programs and activities, as well as mainstream provisions that could help or harm women's rights related to education, such as provisions to allow parents on welfare to go to college or requirements to collect and report data by participants' sex, race, and disability. NCWGE helped sponsor a Gender Equity and Educational Achievement Conference in April 2004 and has prepared various publications such as *Title IX at 30: Report Card on Gender Equity* (2002) and *Title IX at 25: Report Card on Gender Equity* (1997).

Recipients of federal government funding for gender equity work include organizations that were awarded contracts or grants often to do development, dissemination, or coordination work for the federal programs. For example, the Education Development Center won the contracts for the WEEA Equity Resource Center (1977 to 2003), the Academy for Education Development works primarily in the areas of global gender equity and domestically with issues such as gender equity for young children. Many of the recipients of federal gender equity awards (especially from NSF) have been universities. Often individuals at these organizations and universities who obtain external federal and other funding for gender equity education work are able to institutionalize long-term projects or centers to maintain work in this area for many years and to bring in additional colleagues interested in advancing gender equity. The research component of the federal education agency has supported many specialized research centers, but none have focused on gender equity.

A wide variety of foundations and corporations also support gender equity research, model development and action projects. But their support has been minimal and infinitesimal compared to their overall investments on other education issues. A 2006 report by the Foundation Center found that 23% of the $15.5 billion foundation grant funds went to education, with health second highest at 22%. The fastest increases to beneficiary groups went to gays, lesbians, and people with AIDS (Foundation Center, 2006). The most well-known foundation supporter of gender equity education has been the Ford Foundation, which helped establish many of the university-based women's research centers. In 1979, a Ford Foundation program officer estimated that about 10% of the Ford Foundation projects from 1970–78 focused on women (Hunter & Marzone, 1980). University women's research centers have joined with other organizations with gender research activities, such as FMF and the Institute for Women's Policy Research (IWPR), to form the National Council for Research on Women (NCRW). Many other large and small foundations fund local, national, and international gender equity projects. For example, the W.K. Kellogg Foundation supported some of the initial Feminist Majority Foundation work related to this *Handbook* and the Title IX Action Network.

The mainstream and education media and more recently electronic media services have been important disseminators of gender equity information. For example, *Education Week* and *Inside Higher Education,* an electronic news service, provide information on gender equity challenges and sometimes the solutions. Mainstream media, such as TV and movies such as *North Country* that portrayed sexual harassment starting with high school and continuing in the iron ore mines in northern Minnesota (see Bingham & Gansler, 2005) and news articles (often by women reporters) help inform the public about gender equity issues in education. However, the most consistent coverage is by women's media. For example, "To the Contrary," a public television show on women's issues, mentions the importance of Title IX in a high percentage of its half hour shows and it is even distributed outside the U.S. by the Voice of America. Similarly, *Ms. magazine* covers important issues such *Handbook* author Phyllis Rosser's article on "Too Many Women in College?" (Fall 2005). Since 2000, an excellent source of information on gender equity education issues in the U.S., including many reports by previously mentioned gender equity organizations, is through the women's electronic news sources such as the *Feminist Daily News* from the Feminist Majority Foundation www.feminist.org and www.msmagazine.com and Women's eNews www.womensenews.com. Additionally, many organizations focusing on gender equity and education such as AAUW, AGELE, NAPE, NWLC, NOW have electronic alerts, newsletters, and blogs, and maintain well-organized information on their Web pages. The Feminist Majority Foundation Web site www.feminist.org contains the "Feminist Internet Gateway" with many types of reviewed links that are useful for gender equity and the "Feminist Research Center" with information on feminist journals, magazines, and even feminist Internet search utilities. Its sister site www.FeministCampus.org lists global women's studies programs with Web sites in English. Additionally, the Women's Studies Online Resources lists "Women's Studies Online Resources" http://research.umbc.edu/~korenman/wmst lists over 700 women's studies programs and research centers,[18] women and gender related e-mail lists, the file collection for the popular Academic Women's Studies List (WMST-L) electronic mailing list, and resources for women's studies students on financial aid and job opportunities.

Key Strategies Used by NGOs to Institutionalize Gender Equity Education Activities

From the history of Title IX in the first part of this chapter, it is clear that NGOs with a commitment to advancing gender and other types of education equity have been key players in developing and defending federal and state gender equity laws and policies, as well as in helping people pay attention to them. However, as this and other *Handbook* chapters show, while there has been some progress, there has been some backlash, and some slowing of the national momentum to support gender equity laws and programs since Title IX was passed in 1972, so the active and coordinated roles of the NGO equity allies is increasingly important:

NGOs help establish, maintain, refine, and implement gender equity laws and policies. Civil rights laws, include program authorizations and appropriations for research, development, evaluation, and technical assistance to support gender equity activities. The early part of this chapter and the parallel chapter (Schmuck et al., 1985) on the role of government in the 1985 *Handbook* describe how gender equity advocates in NGOs helped create Title IX and its regulations, as well as how they helped save Title IX from various threats to limit its coverage. The second part of this chapter shows less NGO success in saving federal funds for technical assistance and other types of research, development, and evaluation activities to advance gender equity. In recent years, NGOs have been supporting the use of Title IX and state equity laws by monitoring governmental activities and by working with other organizations in coalitions to influence government decision makers within the Executive Branch and Congress and the states. NGOs have also helped with litigation to both remedy individual grievances and establish precedent that will advance gender equity in future cases at the state and national level.

To assure adequate implementation of the gender equity policies, NGOs and independent consulting agencies play a major accountability role in making sure that the laws and policies designed to decrease sex discrimination are known and enforced. In addition to educating students, parents, and educators about their civil rights, they have helped develop and use accountability procedures and laws such as institutional self-assessments, checklists, and *gender equity report cards*. NGOs have also encouraged Congress to pass new accountability laws such as the Athletics Disclosure Act and other procedures to provide information on the sex of participants in various education situations.

NGOs focus on supporting individuals with gender equity responsibilities and interests. The role of government chapter in the 1985 *Handbook* and the previous section of this chapter on state and local governments show the importance of employing a person with gender equity responsibilities, such as a Title IX coordinator or a career and technical education Perkins Act sex equity coordinator. These agency employees and leaders are most likely to be effective in advancing gender equity if they see their role as advocates, have well-defined gender equity responsibilities, can devote a substantial

---

[18]This is up from 600 in the same data base in 2002, as reported in Klein, Ortman and Friedman, 2002, page 17.

amount of time to their gender equity work, have expertise in the federal and state laws related to gender equity, and if they have sufficient authority or support to carry out their responsibilities from the frequently changing agency leaders or legislators. Many of these gender equity leaders found it critical to participate in networks with their peers, independent equity consultants, and NGOs who have expertise in various aspects of gender equity. The NCWGE has played a strong role in supporting both full-time state sex equity CTE coordinators and Title IX Coordinators (Baulch, 2004; NAPE, 2004).

NGOs develop and share information and other resources to advance gender equity. This research, development, evaluation, and dissemination work has been both proactive and responsive to the needs of the gender equity professionals and those they serve. It has been supported by federal and private funds and by volunteers. Gender equity information, tools, and training resources are needed by students, educators, administrators, parents, employees, and community members. If well done and accurate, these resources can help potential users understand what is known and not known about gender issues, as well as legal rights related to discrimination. As described in the second section of this chapter, ED played a minimal role in supporting the development of or making high-quality gender equity resources available. With the exception of ongoing work at NSF, most of the support for gender equity resource disappeared by 2003 with the ending of the WEEA Equity Resource Center and the substitution of the What Works Clearinghouse for the Gender Equity and other Expert Panels.

Thus, this important gender equity resource development and dissemination work has fallen to the NGO community and some independent consulting agencies. AAUW has been especially productive in this area over the years. The AAUW report, *How Schools Shortchange Girls* (AAUW, 1992), prepared by Susan Bailey and her colleagues at the Wellesley College Center for Research on Women, was influential in informing the public about gender equity challenges for girls with the help of the national media and by forums involving AAUW members and gender equity experts. AAUW provided leadership in later years by helping the public understand that gender equity was also important for males and that the characterization of "gender wars" was inaccurate and inappropriate. With the advent of widespread use of the Internet, Web pages, and electronic mailing lists, NGOs have played an efficient role in developing and sharing gender equity resources. In general these NGOs and independent consultants have more freedom to do this than government agencies, which are increasingly concerned with making sure that the information they share fits the political agenda of the administration in power. (See National Council for Research on Women "Misinformation Clearinghouse" on www.ncrw.org) Some members of the NGO gender equity community are cooperating on providing complementary Web-based resources for different audiences and also doing more to share each others' good work. For example, the Title IX info Web site associated with the National Women's Law Center focuses on providing information for the general public, while the Feminist Majority Foundation Education Equity Program Web pages are more focused on serving the needs of gender equity professionals such as Title IX coordinators. The National Women's History Project Web site (www.nwhp.org) and other resources focus on assisting educators in incorporating women's history into curricula.

RECOMMENDATIONS

This chapter has shown how the federal, state, and nongovernmental organizations in the U.S. have played roles in developing and using laws and policies designed to advance gender equity. The laws prohibit sex discrimination and encourage activities that might result in more desirable gender equitable outcomes. However, having laws "on the books" is not enough to attain the desired equity goals. Using our democratic process, citizens and experts in gender equity have been responsible for obtaining the laws in the first place and later in trying to ensure they are used. The following recommendations for public policies, effective practices and programs, and for important research to advance gender equity in and through education related to the role of government in institutionalizing gender equity are based on understandings from this chapter, as well as related insights from other chapters in this *Handbook*.

Policy Recommendations to Institutionalize Gender Equity in Education

At this period in our history we need to take full advantage of the role of government, especially at the federal and state levels, in institutionalizing gender equity in education. The governments can contribute to this by having comprehensive clear laws prohibiting sex discrimination, laws that support positive actions to advance gender equity, and educated and helpful employees who make sure that these laws and policies are fully implemented to attain the gender equity goals. We also realize that this proactive role of government is most likely if citizens monitor and support the government commitments. Thus we should:

Maintain Full Federal Coverage of Title IX and Other Current Civil Rights Laws and Regulations

There have been a variety of threats to maintaining the full protections of Title IX and other civil rights laws. The chapter describes the challenges in limiting these continuing threats. Some strategies to support this recommendation include:

- All supporters of gender equity in education must stay connected and vigilant to save Title IX and other civil rights laws from ongoing challenges, as well as atrophy. They should know about the threats to Title IX and other governmental equity assistance so these challenges can be counteracted as quickly and effectively as possible (See www.feminist.org/education).
- Elect federal, state, and local representatives who will support and defend these laws and not approve judicial or other nominees who would weaken them.
- Make sure candidates and applicants for educational leadership positions are aware of and supportive of gender equity education. Ask candidates questions specifically related to Title IX.

- Insure that the Office for Civil Rights in the federal agencies work together to provide helpful interpretations of Title IX and other civil rights regulations as they did with the 2001 Sexual Harassment Guidelines. Insure that OCR initiatives avoid any weakening provision to the Title IX regulation or guidance documents.
- Increase funding for the Civil Rights Act Title IV Equity Assistance Centers (EACs) for them to actively advance gender equity along with race and national origin equity. They should be funded to support more entities than are covered by Title IX, including Bureau of Indian Affairs (BIA) schools, museums, and recreation departments. These Centers should help build and maintain the gender equity infrastrucures such as networks of Title IX and other equity coordinators, and they should help collect and share research and evaluation information on what works as they provide technical assistance to their constituents. These EACs should also work with NGOs and others to insure the training and full use of education employees and community members who are interested in knowing how to advance gender equity in their regions. For example, EACs could co-sponsor annual national and regional conferences on gender equity in connection with organizations such as AGELE.

Work for Full Implementation of Title IX and Other Civil Rights Laws, Regulations, and Policies.

One of the threats to Title IX is that it is often ignored because most educators do not know what it covers and how it can be used to help eliminate sex discrimination. (See research on lack of knowledge in the teacher education and the coeducation and single sex chapters.) Also see information on how the Title IX Action Network composed of Title IX coordinators and others who care about gender equity can work together to remedy this situation by visiting www.feminist.org/education. It is important for governments to develop and use both *carrots* (incentives) and *sticks* (punishments) in new and better ways.

Carrot strategies. To increase the implementation of these laws may include new legislation and funding that builds on models that work, funding mechanisms such as an expanded Women's Educational Equity Act program to provide support for development, technical assistance and dissemination, and the improvement of governmental and NGO infrastructures such as networks of Title IX coordinators and their gender equity partners. Both governmental employees and NGO experts should receive government resources to help provide these incentives and assistance to reach equity goals. Funding for these incentive strategies should come from all levels of government, but mostly from the federal government as civil rights protections are one of the key overarching federal education responsibiities. Most states do little to support their staff in these activities and it has been extremely rare for states to use state funds to support others in their states to do important gender equity work.

Some specific recommendations at the federal level include:
- Encourage federal agency leaders to actively support civil rights laws such as Title IX by their public statements and actions in providing implementation guidance within and out-

side their agency. Mitigate the effects of weakening Title IX, such as the October 25, 2006 regulation changes by withdrawing this regulation and also by educating the public about the costs and dangers of increasing single-sex education unless it is specifically designed to decrease sex discrimination as allowed under the 1975 Title IX regulation. If single-sex education is instituted, insist on safeguards such as reports of external evaluations that provide evidence of the presence or absence of sex stereotyping and sex discrimination in the classrooms and schools, as well as evidence that the single-sex intervention decreases sex discrimination in the outcomes better than mixed sex alternatives. We recommend that each school post an annual evaluation report on gender equity in their school on their Web site, that each report be reviewed and approved by the Title IX coordinator, and that it provide comparable information on gender equity results for any single sex-education activity.

- Fully implement the provisions to support the federal leadership and coordination role in gender equity such as appointing a full-time, well-qualified civil servant to serve as the Special Assistant for Gender Equity. Support and give prestige to intra- and interagency permanent committees on advancing gender equity to maximize benefit from implementing gender and related civil rights laws. Also improve on the model of coordination and assistance used by OCR in working with the state administrators of the Memorandum of Understanding provisions to implement the 1979 vocational education guidelines to avoid discrimination. Special effort should be made by OCR to work with NGOs with gender equity expertise, and to communicate with and provide training and assistance to Title IX coordinators at the state education agencies, and in postsecondary institutions.
- Establish an advisory group of national gender equity education experts recommended by gender equity organizations like the National Coalition for Women and Girls in Education, the Association for Gender Equity Leadership in Education, and the National Council for Research on Women to help increase the scope and effectiveness of activities within ED and with other agencies supporting gender equity education.
- Provide federal funding for gender analyses of gender-specific programs, as well as all other federally financially assisted programs, to identify any gender differences in outcomes. All federal funding and quality control should be based on scientific evidence and the responsibility of the contractor/grantees and their advisors, rather than direction and censorship by the federal staff as has been reported for the What Works Clearinghouse (Schoenfeld, 2006) and the employees and advisors at the Food and Drug Administration (FDA) on issues such a the approval of over-the-counter sales of emergency contraceptives (FDA Controversy, February, 2006).
- Expand and revise WEEA, the only ED legislation specifically focused on implementing Title IX and advancing gender equity. The new WEEA should have an appropriation of $100 million annually. It should focus on effective replicable models and supporting networks of NGOs and Title IX coordinators, as well as technical assistance and national dissemination of high-quality gender equity information. Key aspects of the Gender Equity Expert Panel should be in-

cluded in this plan to support the ongoing development, evaluation, and refinement of replicable gender equity education programs in a wide variety of topic areas. It should also be tied to networks of gender equity specialists in various topic areas.

- Reinstate the Title IV CRA SEA funding that was eliminated in 1996. Specify that gender, race, and national origin issues must all be addressed. Funding should be provided to support full-time staff including a full time Title IX coordinator in each state education agency and programs in all states, with more funding going to states with larger populations.
- Allocate substantial federal funding for building networks for gender equity professionals and allies such as Title IX coordinators. Most of the funding should be prioritized for gender equity NGOs to provide expertise and services to their constituents as well as the larger interested public.
- Reinstitute the state career and technical education leadership offices (former sex equity administrators), including $100 million annual funding for state career and technical gender equity coordinators, and have them work with Title IX coordinators. Continue building on the MOA activities to assure compliance with court orders and Title IX. Provide more national leadership support for their coordination work with NAPE. Coordinate with related programs to help women in the work force in partnership with DOL.
- Continue support for the NSF gender equity programs and learn from them about other effective support mechanisms for other types of gender equity education programs.
- Increase specific support for gender equity program development and assistance in other parts of ED such as FIPSE, Indian Education, Special Education, and the Institute for Education Sciences work.
- Transfer all funding from Health and Human Services abstinence education programs to comprehensive sexuality programs and gender equity programs, supported by evidence that they will decrease unwanted pregnancy and sexual diseases and increase attention to health challenges that may impact one sex more than the other.
- Increase funding and support for gender equity education in developing countries via the U.S. Agency for International Development. Build on the good research base established by previous funding, and support international conferences and electronic information exchanges on gender equity education.

Some specific recommendations at the state level include:

- Provide funding and adequate budgets for state Title IX coordinators so they can work with and provide leadership and education within their state as well as outside their state to others nationally and internationally.
- Help state Title IX coordinators lead and develop networks of Title IX coordinators at all levels of their state so that these individuals as well as their interested colleagues can work together. Develop and use state and local Web sites that include information to advance gender equity.
- Promote and implement additional state laws and policies that advance gender equity. Publicize especially effective policies and strategies to implement them so that other states can use them as models for their own laws as they strengthen implementation of federal civil rights laws.

Stick or enforcement strategies. Should be much more thorough and effective. Many of the Title IX regulations are ignored—including the use of Title IX coordinators to help implement the laws in the recipient organization. There have been few cases where federal financial assistance was withheld for noncompliance. It is difficult for the federal or state level officials to stop the many infractions of Title IX without substantial systematic technical assistance, monitoring, and actual rewards and penalties. Although it can be costly for both the responsible parties (generally the educational institution) and the recipient of discrimination, law suits and legal settlements may be increasingly effective deterrents, especially if they are well publicized. Some specific recommendations include:

- The Office for Civil Rights must be more proactive in monitoring schools, responding to complaints, and bringing enforcement actions for noncompliance with Title IX. This will be especially important if the October 2006 Regulations are not rescinded since sex-segregated environments are likely to be unequal and perpetuate sex stereotypes.
- Publicize OCR decisions and cases as exemplars to show why law suits and settlements may be more powerful than withdrawal of federal funds.
- Encourage the filing and public posting of Title IX complaints, including complaints about nonexistent or inadequate Title IX coordinators and guidance policies. Dr. Bernice Sandler, who frequently serves as an expert witness on Title IX cases, noted that soon after any type of Title IX complaint is filed the recipient organization often appoints a Title IX coordinator. With a well-informed Title IX coordinator in the first place, they may have avoided the complaint (B. R. Sandler personal communication with Sue Klein, Washington, DC, April 19, 2006).
- Publicize complaint resolutions and compliance reviews and require OCR to make a public Web listing of institutions found out of compliance with Title IX, their infractions and the remedies. One of the remedies may be a required Title IX self-assessment. This remedy should be applied to all recipients who don't have an appropriately qualified Title IX coordinator because it can be assumed that they weren't paying adequate attention to implementing Title IX.
- Remind recipients covered by Title IX that institutions should be interested in complying not only to provide each student with the best education possible, but also so they won't be sued if they implement the laws fairly based on the 1975 Title IX regulations and the 14th Amendment to the U.S. Constitution.
- Help educators and the public learn what is legal or illegal under federal and related state laws providing protections against sex discrimination.

Expand the Coverage, Guidance, and Support for Gender Equity

When students or others feel that they are being treated unfairly, they often assume that there is a law that will protect them against sex discrimination. Depending on where they live, this is not necessarily true in part because we don't have a national ERA and because Title IX is limited to education programs and activities of recipients of federal financial assistance. However, as described earlier, 22 states have some form of constitutional protection for sex discrimination in their state constitutions, and many states have their own Title IX-type state gender equity laws, regulations, and policies (which need to be defended as well). As previously noted, there is only a miniscule amount of federal or state support for research, development, and dissemination of related activities to implement gender equity laws. Although there is more federal support to help other populations in need of equitable treatment on the basis of race, disability, and poverty, the critical role of gender is rarely considered in these programs. Additionally, just as there are laws prohibiting discrimination on the basis of sex, there should be equally comprehensive laws prohibiting discrimination on the basis of sexual orientation or gender identity. Thus the U.S needs:

- Passage and enforcement of a national Equal Rights Amendment, state ERAs, and state Title IX-type laws.
- Passage and enforcement of national and state laws prohibiting discrimination on the basis of sexual orientation and gender identity.
- More funding and other federal and state government support for gender equity research, development, evaluation and technical assistance in many areas such as those recommended in this *Handbook*.
- Supporting proactive Title IX coordinators, and including their contact information and activities on behalf of gender equity on their insitution Web sites.
- Encouraging more institutional self-assessment reports and their publication on Web sites
- Ensuring that recipient institutions appoint legally required Title IX coordinators and Section 504 (disability) coordinators, and encouraging these experts to work with each other and others in their institutions who address equity issues such as race and national origin.
- Supporting greater collaboration among gender equity organizations such as members of the National Coalition for Women and Girls in Education

Assure Extensive Use of Monitoring and Accountability Practices to Help Implement equity Laws and Policies and to Judge Progress Toward Gender Equitable Education Goals.

There is a continuing trend to assess federal and state laws and programs to learn if they should be retained, eliminated, changed or implemented in different ways. However, gender equity analysis is often neglected.

- Gender equity goals need to be assessed in two ways:
  a. There should be a gender analysis of all government-supported programs to learn if they increase or decrease gender equity, and if possible, if this is true in specific sub-populations such as Hispanic/Latino males or females with mental disabilities. USAID has provided much guidance to various programs on how to do this type of gender analysis. Currently, there is little gender analysis in the performance reports from U.S. Department of Education pro-grams. For example, the analysis of scores on standardized tests of student performance used to judge schools' Adequate Yearly Progress (AYP) under the No Child Left Behind legislation does not require gender analysis (But it does require reporting on students according to their race, disability, LEP, and poverty status).

  b. All laws intended to advance gender equity and to avoid discrimination on the basis of sex should require a full gender analysis of the *inputs* as well as the *outcomes*. The educational inputs would require a careful analysis of the resources used for implementation, and the outcomes would be meaningful indicators of attainment that are likely to be associated with the use of the law or policy. Increases in sex stereotyping and sex discrimination would be considered undesirable inputs and outcomes.

- Examples of needed monitoring and accountability related to increasing the effectiveness of Title IX include:
  a. Implementation of the Title IX regulation requiring Title IX coordinators needs to be monitored more thoroughly. There is substantial evidence that this regulation is regularly neglected. This is especially important when paying attention to gender and accountability because the Title IX coordinators bring a critical perspective and assistance to an agency's requirements to collect and report on gender analyses, hopefully on the institution's Web site.
     – Request that baseline data be collected on compliance with Title IX coordinators and obtain other information on how they do their jobs, such as what kind of accountability gender analysis information they provide on their institution's Web site.
     – Request that GAO do this as an initial study of Title IX compliance with an additional purpose of finding examples of Title IX coordinators' effective use of accountability information to advance gender equity in their institution.
  b. Examine the equitable allocation of institutional resources for student activities and courses where there is less than one-third participation of either males or females. This could get at the gender disparities for both students and employees related to specific courses and majors especially in postsecondary eduation and also in programs such as athletics. Often faculty of female-dominant schools or departments such as education and art are paid less and supported less than more male-dominated departments such as physics. See chapters on teacher education and postsecondary education in the *Handbook* as well as chapters in the ten content areas.
  c. Governments should require more extensive use of checklists and other types of assessments related to compliance with Title IX as well as Web postings of the results. The initial regulation required a Title IX self-assessment within the first 3 years, but it did not require any periodic assessments. Some states have encouraged site visits and other monitoring to insure compliance with Title IX. This valuable process is still used in implementing the Methods of Administration requirements in career and technical education, however only 2.5% of subrecipients are visited each year.

Practice and Program Recommendations to Institutionalize Gender Equity

As described in this chapter and suggested by many of the policy recommendations, there is a great need for improving the quality and availability of gender equity professionals, resources, and an increased demand by educators and the public to advance gender equity in systematic ways. In implementing these recommendations it is feasible to build on past examples of government support, but it is also important to adapt them to maximize current resources such as the Internet, and to minimize current restraints such as the lack of support from some education and government officials and others in fully implementing the letter and spirit of gender equity laws and policies. Key recommendations include:

Increase Demand for Gender Equity in Education

Education of people in the U.S. about their gender equality rights is vital. Understanding of why stereotypes, biases and apathy are likely to contribute to harmful sex discrimination is also essential. Many of the chapters in this Handbook describe both subtle and overt types of discrimination, as well as long-standing patterns of inequities that limit the quality of life of both females and males and deprive society of benefiting from the quality contributions from all. Research shows that even educators who are advocates of gender equity have little knowledge of laws such as Title IX. They don't know what it covers or doesn't cover and have vague ideas that it is good because it might help us elect a woman as president of the U.S. or that it has something to do with athletics (Zittleman, 2005). Similarly, they know nothing about Title IX coordinators in their own school or where to go for resources on gender equity.

The general public knows even less about these civil rights protections and is often misinformed by news stories as well as research articles that provide inaccurate information. This is especially a problem related to the more complicated or unclear protections of Title IX. The same legal analysis is not used across the board. For example, Title IX allows certain types of single-sex classes for some aspects of sexuality education but not for most physical education classes. Some recommendations to address this challenge include:

- Increase awareness of the value of gender equity in and through education for individuals and groups. This is needed at all levels of sophistication and across many topic areas.
  - Education and training about sex discrimination should cover what it is, why it is illegal, and how it can be ended. Some good education models such as training developed for sexual harassment could be adapted to address other common types of gender inequities.
  - The media should commit to increasing public interest in and understanding of gender equity and Title IX. This can be done in fictional TV stories as well as news and opinion programs.
- Help people understand how full implementation of Title IX and other civil rights laws will improve society, and that there

are various threats to Title IX from opponents of gender equity and from lack of knowledge of its value.
- Increase the numbers and types of Title IX advocates ranging from parents and community members to student organizations and university presidents. This will be augmented by the full use of Title IX coordinators as recommended in the following section.

Improve Educators' and Students' Knowledge and Commitment to Attaining Gender Equity

Recommended strategies to do this include:

- Increase numbers of and the knowledge and skills of all gender equity professionals and educators working in governmental and nongovernmental organizations.
  - All educators including administrators, teachers, and counselors should know about and help implement Title IX and related civil rights laws and policies.
  - Schools of education should review teacher education programs to ensure that gender equity, including attention to Title IX, is a topic that is addressed and discussed throughout their programs to prepare new teachers.
  - Students should learn about their rights to equality and nondiscrimination and also how to ensure that they treat others fairly.
  - All recipients of federal financial assistance, including schools, should have at least one fully trained and highly accessible Title IX coordinator.
- Clarify and enhance the roles of Title IX coordinators and assure that they have adequate resources for their work within their own institution, as well as to work with peers and allies outside their institution. For example, Title IX coordinators should have:
  - Adequate resources, such as a budget for their work, including staff gender equity training, time to do their Title IX work, and a role in contributing to overall institutional policies.
  - Responsibilities for providing supportive leadership and accountability roles by managing permanent gender equity committees, advisory groups, commissions, or task forces, and using effective accountability, assessment, and public reporting strategies to keep their constituents informed of gender equity challenges and progress.
  - A focus on prevention first and foremost as well as responsive complaint resolution.
- NGOs can help develop effective networks of Title IX coordinators and their allies. (Expand the national Title IX network of SEA Title IX coordinators to include local school system K–12 Title IX Coordinators and institutions of higher education.)
  - Use electronic mailing lists and voluntary mailing lists.
  - Have national NGOs help with the development of public listings of Title IX coordinators.
  - Encourage Title IX coordinators to develop extensive helpful Web sites in their own institutions, which would include gender analyses and guidance.

- Facilitate the sharing of information and meetings of Title IX coordinators with gender equity allies locally, regionally, and nationally, and arrange for them to meet physically as well as virtually.
- Expand relationships with other educational equity organizations such as the National Association for Multicultural Education, Leadership Conference on Civil Rights, etc. to make connections between gender equity and other equity issues (e.g., race, ethnicity, national origin, sexual orientation, disability).

• Develop and share resources and models to help Title IX coordinators work with each other as well as other gender equity advocates. Suggestions include horizontal (peer) and vertical technical assistance and training networks. Use and adapt past gender equity education practices, training models, and guidance policies that are still likely to have good results in the current climate.

Improve and Make High Quality and Effective Gender Equity Resources and Information Easily Available to Constituents

When the 1985 *Handbook* was produced, the authors were optimistic that many model training materials based on the latest accurate information about gender equity would be developed, found to be effective, and replicated across the country. However, with the exception of some materials in the areas of mathematics and science this expectation was not met. Also, there were no systematic procedures to identify and revise effective programs or to easily and inexpensively get them to users for inservice, preservice, or informal training. This expectation was further thwarted when the Women's Eduational Equity Act Resource Center, the major federal publication and dissemination service, was discontinued by the Department of Education in 2003, when the Perkins Vocational Education Act funding for sex equity was eliminated in 1998, and when the Gender Equity Expert Panel in the ED Office of Educational Research and Improvement ended after one cycle in 2000. If this Panel and related federal dissemination support had been allowed to continue, it would have been able to serve as a quality control and motivator for high-quality, replicable gender equity training programs. In recent years, with the exception of the gender equity work in the National Science Foundation there has been little federal help in developing and sharing high-quality, effective programs and stategies to advance gender equity. Recommended strategies include:

• Restore and expand federal support for development, evaluation, dissemination, and implementation of high-quality, replicable gender equity materials for students, educators, and equity professionals.
• Establish a federally supported advisory board composed of nationally recognized gender equity experts to facilitate distribution and coordination of federal support across all the topic areas.
• Use the World Wide Web and Internet to share detailed information on gender equity resources including those un-

der revision or development. Provide evidence on their quality and ongoing user feedback on their usefulness and effectiveness in various contexts.

Research Recommendations to Institutionalize Gender Equity

Research is essential in guiding the implementation of effective gender equity policies, practices, and programs recommended here. However, federally supported research and evaluation should address a cumulative development of knowledge instead of small studies that aren't worth replication. To the extent possible, all information should be disaggregated by gender, race, ethnicity, disability, socioeconomic status (SES), and age. Gender analysis involving comparisons of males and females, as well as examining indicators of gender stereotyping, is important when studying diverse populations such as lesbian, gay, bisexual or transgender (LGBT) or American Indians.

Research to Improve Governmental Policies

• Have the U.S. Government Accountability Office (GAO) study the roles and responsibilities of Title IX coordinators with a specific focus on obtaining baseline information on compliance with Title IX regulation as well as learning about and publicizing exemplary Title IX coordinator activities.
• Help identify effective ways to build the gender equity education infrastructure with a focus on Title IX gender equity coordinators. This research should focus on strategies and campaigns, developing helpful liasons with other gender equity experts and advocates and with governmental peers with responsibility for other populations that face discrimination (race, ethnicity, disability, poverty, or sexual orientation).
• Develop effective education strategies or best practices to help people get fair treatment using Title IX and other laws. For example,
  - Title IX and related gender equity assessments and progress performance reports should be posted on the Web sites of recipient organizations using comparable information within and among states to make it easier to assess national trends and challenges.
  - Gender equity researchers may be able to develop guidelines for schools considering implementing single-sex education that would help them identify research-based interventions that have a track record of increasing gender equitable outcomes. The guidelines would describe evaluation and accountability standards that need to be met to learn if the approved implementation of the single-sex intervention was followed and whether or not it had the desired results in decreasing gender inequities in outcomes.
  - Gender equity researchers can recommend fair and practical ways to assess and report on athletic interests and opportunities using multiple measures.
  - State laws should be studied to learn how they differ or could be adapted to work in other states.

Research and Development on Practices to Eliminate Detrimental Sex Stereotyping and Discrimination

- The federal government should fund an improved Gender Equity Expert Panel (GEEP) that would build on the recommendations from the previous Panel (Fox, 2000) and assure full independence of the gender equity experts.
- The federal government should fund the development and evaluation of gender equity solutions in needed areas. This funding should be based on knowledge of effective approaches and what is learned from the GEEP.[19] As described in previous recommendations, much of this funding could come from an expanded WEEA or Gender Equity Education Act (GEEA) by including gender issues in national competitions for other programs such as FIPSE and special education in the U.S. Department of Education, as well as related increases in attention to gender equity in other agencies such as DOL, NSF, and USAID in the Department of State. Similarly, the government should focus on supporting funding for programs where there is evidence that they will result in desirable outcomes related to decreased sex discrimination.
- The federal government should work closely with national gender equity education experts in supporting research and evaluation on gender equity and education. If the Special Assistant for Gender Equity in ED is reinstated as recommended in policy recommendation #2, this individual should not only facilitate coordination of gender equity work among the Department offices, but with external gender equity groups.

The Federal Agencies Should Provide Routine Periodic Analysis and Reporting on What's Learned from Accountability Research and Gender Analysis (including subpopulations) on All Education Programs

- The National Center for Education Statistics (NCES) trends reports on *Education Equity for Girls and Women* should be expanded to include trends for boys and men and should (with input from nongovernmental gender equity experts) be issued every other year. Increased information should be provided on trends within subgroups such as low income Latinas.
- States and other recipients of federal financial assistance should report consistently on key indicators of populations served and outcomes by gender, race, national origin, disability, and income at the minimum. If decisions are based on comparisons within or among specific populations such as the Adequate Yearly Progress (AYP) requirements in the No Child Left Behind Act, gender analysis should be required. (For more details, see the testing chapter in this *Handbook*.) Additionally, evaluation and accountability requirements should be tied to compliance with important aspects of Title IX such as athletics and physical education, single-sex education, career and technical education and sexual harassment.

- The Department of Education-sponsored What Works Clearinghouse and related evaluation activities should consistently report on results by gender and other populations since it is possible that the intervention may have a differential impact with different categories of users.

CONCLUSION

Educational institutions have changed, and Title IX played an essential role in changes related to increased gender equality. Federal legislation prohibiting sex discrimination in education was necessary as a foundation for change. However, the movement toward gender equity in education has not been a clear linear progression. There have been setbacks along the way. For instance, immediately after passing Title IX and continuing through 2006, some members of Congress and leaders of the administration in power used numerous strategies to whittle away at Title IX's scope of coverage. Except for some science and technology programs, federal grant and assistance programs designed to advance gender equality in education, and those designed to open up careers to all, have been diminished. Sadly, there has been little systematic federal leadership in advancing gender equity in education even when there was specific legislation directing them to do so. For example,

- The U.S. Department of Education has not filled the legislated position of Special Assistant for Gender Equity in the Office of the Secretary to coordinate activities throughout the Department of Education since the Clinton Administration.
- There have been few Title IX investigations or formal threats to cut off federal funds as required by enforcement responsibilities in the Office for Civil Rights. Less than 1% of the nation's schools and colleges have ever seen—or are likely to see—a federal investigator (Sandler, 1981).
- There were no provisions to encourage any kind of periodic self-assessment for compliance with Title IX even though some states and districts did this voluntarily for a while.
- There were no organized federal efforts to assist, train, and publicize the required Title IX coordinators. Although it was common for federal programs to sponsor regional or national meetings for coordinators for various federal programs such as Title I, there were no similar meetings or communication networks developed for the Title IX coordinators. However, a successful related model was used for the vocational education legislatively mandated state sex equity coordinators, and although federal leadership and Congressional support for these important gender equity leaders ended in 1998, it can be reinstated in more powerful ways for all with gender equity responsibilities.

At the same time, Title IX provided "hope and a tool." Students, faculty, and staff for the first time had the means to amend or abolish sex discriminatory practices and policies. Once the 1975 Title IX regulation was in place, schools that took

---

[19]Training materials recommended by GEEP generally combined materials for teacher training and use by their students. (See Fox, 2000.)

it seriously learned a great deal about sex discrimination as they conducted the required institutional self-assessment to identify the initial inequities that they should address. Some states also provided guidance and training to Title IX coordinators and others, often by conducting site visits using well-structured observation checklists. In addition to education and assistance activities, successful lawsuits helped people understand the importance and power of Title IX and helped clarify its scope. Some law suits even used state laws such as Pennsylvania's ERA or the 14th Amendment to the Constitution, which provide broader protections against sex discrimination than Title IX.

To counteract the especially limited federal support for achieving gender equity, this chapter shows the power and effectiveness of women's rights groups and other nongovernmental organizations especially when they work together. With the major change in the mid-term elections in November 2006, many of these gender equity supporters should be encouraged to reactivate their efforts to reverse recent federal activities to weaken Title IX and instead develop strong legislative and action agendas to advance gender equity at the federal, state, and local levels.

ACKNOWLEDGMENTS

Major chapter reviewers include: Bernice Sandler, Women's Research and Education Institute, Washington, DC; Mary Gallet, CA State Department of Education, Sacramento, CA; Kathy Rigsby and Ramon Villarreal, Interwest Equity Assistance Center, Denver, CO; Darcy Lees, former Title IX Coordinator, Washington State; and Section editor, Dolores Grayson, GrayMill Consulting, Tehachapi, CA.

Thanks to Sundra Flansburg, Oklahoma City for WEEA information.

References

A brief history of abstinence-only-until-marriage education. (2006). No more money for abstinence-only-until-marriage programs. Retrieved November 10, 2006, from www.nonewmoney.org/history.html

Alexander v. Yale University, 631 F. 2d 178 (2d Cir. 1980).

American Association of University Women. (1992). *How schools short-change girls.* Washington, DC: AAUW Educational Foundation.

An oath betrayed: The Reagan Administration's civil rights enforcement record in education. (1983). Washington, DC: Civil Rights Leadership Conference Fund.

Balles, N. J. (1978). *The unenforced law: Title IX activity by federal agencies other than HEW.* Washington, DC: National Advisory Council on Women's Educational Programs.

Baulch, C. (2004). *History, status, and future roles of Title IX Gender Equity Coordinators.* Feminist Majority Foundation. Retrieved June 12, 2006, from http://www.feminist.org/education/TitleIX_Coordinators.pdf

Bingham, C., & Gansler, L. L. (2005). Tough as iron: How the courageous women depicted in North Country made legal history—and helped protect all of us against sexual harassment. *Ms. magazine,* (Fall), 38–41.

Brown v. Board of Education of Topeka et. al., 347 U.S. 483 (1954).

Cannon v. University of Chicago, 441 U.S. 677 (1979).

Commonwealth v. Pennsylvania Interscholastic Athletic Ass'n., 334 A.2d 839 (1975).

Council of Chief State School Officers (CCSSO). (1980). *Facing the future: Education and equity for females and males.* Washington, DC: Council of Chief State School Officers.

Davis v. Monroe County Board of Education, 526 U.S. 629 (1999).

Dunkle, M., & Richards, C. (1977). *Sex discrimination in education: A policy handbook.* Washington, DC: National Coalition for Women and Girls in Education.

E. B. v. North Hunterdon Regional School District, 12 NJ. Admin 232 (1986).

Enforcing Title IX. (1980). Washington, DC: U.S. Commission on Civil Rights.

FDA Controversy Over Plan B Continues. (February 22, 2006). *Feminist Daily News Wire.* Retrieved February 1, 2007 from http://www.feminist.org/news/newsyte/uswirestory.asp?id=9530

Federal 'gender equity in education' legislation. (1993). *NCSEE News,* 93–94(1), 14.

Feminist Majority Foundation. *Education equality: Sex segregation.* Retrieved June 12, 2006, from http://www.feminist.org/education/SexSegregation.asp

Final Title IX regulation implementing education amendments of 1972 prohibiting sex discrimination in education. (June 1975). Washington, DC: U.S. Department of Health, Education and Welfare/Office for Civil Rights.

Fishel, A., & Pottker, J. (1977). *National politics and sex discrimination in education.* Lexington, MA: Lexington Books.

Foundation Center. (2006). *Highlights of foundation giving trends.* Retrieved March, 6, 2006, from http://fdncenter.org/research/trends_analysis/pdf/fgt06highlights.pdf

Fox, L. (Ed.). (2000). *The gender equity expert panel: History and rationale.* Report to OERI, U.S. Department of Education, Washington, DC.

Franklin v. Gwinnett County Public Schools, 503 U.S. 60 (1992).

Gebser v. Lago Vista Independent School Dist., 524 U.S. 274 (1998).

Grove City College v. Bell, 465 U.S. 555 (1984).

Hunter, L., & Marzone, J. (Eds.). (1980). *Funding for women's educational equity: Papers presented at the 1979 AERA Symposium: Funding for women with a special emphasis on sources for women's educational equity.* San Francisco, CA.: Women's Educational Equity Communications Network, Far West Laboratory for Educational R&D. S. S. Klein (Compiler). (Feb. 1980) *Sex equity in education: NIE-sponsored projects and publications.* Washington, DC: National Institute of Education, U.S. Department of Health, Education and Welfare.

It gets worse: A revamped federal abstinence-only program goes extreme. (2006). Special Report. Sexuality Information and Education Council of the United States. Retrieved November 10, 2006, from www.nomoremoney.org/

Klein, S. S. (1981). *Summary of recent U.S. Department of Education activities to increase equal access and equal opportunities for women.* Washington, DC: National Advisory Council on Women's Educational Programs.

Klein, S. S. (1984). Education. In S. M. Pritchard (Ed.), *The women's annual, 4* (pp. 9–30). Boston, MA: G. K. Hall Women's Studies Publications.

Klein, S. (2005, October) *Title IX and single sex education.* Adapted from a presentation at the American Educational Research Association, Special Interest Group: Research on Women and Education Conference, Oct. 20, 2005 Opening Plenary. Available on http://www.feminist.org/education/SexSegregation.asp

Klein, S., Ortman, P., & Friedman, E. (2002). What is the field of gender equity in education? Questions and answers. In J. Koch & B. Irby (Eds.). *Defining and redefining gender equity in education*. Greenwich, CT: Information Age Publishing.

Klein, S. S., & Thomas, V. (Compilers). (1981, May). *Sex equity in education: NIE-sponsored projects and publications 1981*. Washington, DC: National Institute of Education, U.S. Department of Education.

Levy, K. E. (1985). *What's left of federal funding for sex equity in education and social science research?* Washington, DC: Federation of Organizations for Professional Women and Others.

Mastelli, G. L. (1977). *Sex bias: Education legislation and regulations*. Washington, DC: National Advisory Council on Women's Educational Programs.

Nash, M. A. (2002). *A history of Title IX. NCSEE/AGELE News*, 01-02(3): 5–7.

National Advisory Council on Women's Educational Programs. (1979). *Efforts toward sex fairness in education division publications*. Washington, DC: Department of Health, Education and Welfare.

National Advisory Council on Women's Educational Programs. (1981, Fall). *Title IX: The half full, half empty glass*. Washington, DC: U.S. Department of Education.

National Alliance for Partnerships in Equity (NAPE). (2004). *Equity pioneers: The sex equity coordinators: 1976–1998*. Retrieved June 12, 2006, from www.napequity.org

National Center for Education Statistics. (2000). *Trends in educational equity of girls and women* (NCES 2000–30). Washington, DC: Office of Educational Research and Improvement, U.S. Department of Education.

National Center for Education Statistics. (2004). *Trends in educational equity of girls and women: 2004* (NCES 2005-016). Washington, DC: Institute of Education Sciences, U.S. Department of Education.

National Coalition for Women and Girls in Education (NCWGE). (2002). *Title IX at 30: Report card on gender equity*. Washington, DC: Author.

National Coalition for Women and Girls in Education website. Retrieved March 2, 2006, from www.ncwge.org

National Council for Research on Women. (2006). *The misinformation clearinghouse*. Retrieved March 15, 2006, from http://www.ncrw.org/misinfo/index.htm

National Science Foundation (NSF). (2002). *NSF's program for gender equity in science, technology, engineering and mathematics: A brief retrospective 1993–2001*. Arlington, VA: National Science Foundation.

National Women's Law Center. (2005). *Tools of the trade: Using the law to address sex segregation in high school career and technical education*. Retrieved June 12, 2006, from www.nwlc.org

Newberg v. Board of Public Education, 26 Pa. D. & C. 3d 682 (pa. Ct. of Com. Please 1983).

Office for Civil Rights. (1975, June). *Final Title IX regulation implementing education amendments of 1972 prohibiting sex discrimination in education*. Washington, DC: U.S. Department of Health, Education and Welfare/Office for Civil Rights.

Office for Civil Rights (2004, March 9). Proposed Rules. *Nondiscrimination on the basis of sex in education programs or activities receiving federal financial assistance*. Washington, DC: U.S. Department of Education/Office for Civil Rights. *Federal Register*/Vol. 69, No. 46/Tuesday, March 9, 2004. Pages 11276. Retrieved February 1, 2007 from www.ed.gov/legislation/FedRegister/proprule/2004-1/030904a.pdf)

Office for Civil Rights. (2006, October 25). *Final regulations. Nondiscrimination on the basis of sex in education programs or activities receiving federal financial assistance*. Washington, DC: U.S. Department of Education/Office for Civil Rights. Federal Register/Vol. 71, No. 206/Wednesday, October 25, 2006 Pages 62529–62543. Re-

trieved October 30, 2006, from www.ed.gov/legislation/FedRegister/finrule/2006-4/102506a.html

Office for Civil Rights Annual Reports to Congress. (2000, 2001, 2002, 2003, 2004). Washington, DC: U.S. Department of Education.

Office of Educational Research and Improvement. (2001). *The U.S. Department of Educaton's Gender Equity Expert Panel, exemplary and promising gender equity programs, 2000*. Washington, DC: U.S. Department of Education.

Project on Equal Education Rights (PEER). (1977). *Stalled at the start: Government action on sex bias in the schools*. Washington, DC: Project on Equal Education Rights.

Project on the Status and Education of Women. (1989). *The restoration of Title IX: Implications for higher education*. Washington, DC: Association of American Colleges.

Raffel, N. K. (1975). *The enforcement of federal laws and regulations prohibiting sex discrimination in education*. Washington, DC: Women's Equity Action League.

Rosser, P. (2006). Too Many Women in College? *Ms.*, (Fall), 42–45.

Salomone, R. C. (1986). *Equal education under law*. NY: St. Martin's Press.

Samuels, C. A. (2006). GAO Opinion Renews Debate on Abstinence-Only Programs. November 1, 2006. *Education Week*, *26*(10), 7. Retrieved November 2, 2006, from Edweek.org

Sandler, B. (1981). Happy birthday Title IX! *On Campus with Women 12*, 1–2.

Sandler, B. (1997). "Too strong for a woman"—The five words that created Title IX. *About Women on Campus*. Retrieved June 12, 2006, from http://bernicesandler.com/id44.htm

Schmuck, P. A., Adkison, J. A., Peterson, B., Bailey, S., Glick, G. S., Klein, S. S., et al. (1985). Administrative strategies for institutionalizing sex equity in education and the role of government. In S. Klein (Ed.), *Handbook for achieving sex equity through education* (pp. 95–123). Baltimore: Johns Hopkins Press.

Schoenfeld, A. H. (March 2006). What doesn't work: The challenge and failure of the What Works Clearinghouse to conduct meaningful reviews of studies of mathematics curricula. *Educational Researcher*, *35*(2), 13–21.

Sex discrimination regulations. (June 1975). Hearings before the Subcommittee on Postsecondary Education of the Committee on Education and Labor. Washington, DC: House of Representatives Committee on Education and Labor.

Simonson, J. R. (undated, around 2002). *The rise and decline of the Advisory Council on Women's Educational Equity*. Archived on Women's Educational Equity Act Archived Web site www.edc.or/WomensEquity/resource/title9/article.htm

Southeastern Public Education Program (SPEP). (1977). *Almost as fairly: The first year of Title IX implementation in six Southern states*. Atlanta, GA: American Friends Service Committee.

Steiger, J. M., & Szanton, E. (1977). *Efforts toward sex fairness in the use of education division funds*. Washington, DC: National Advisory Council on Women's Educational Programs.

Suggs, W. (2005). *A place on the team: The triumph and tragedy of Title IX*. Princeton, NJ: Princeton University Press.

Threinen, C., & Weck, A. (1983). *Ten Years of Title IX*. Madison, WI: Wisconsin Department of Public Instruction.

U.S. Department of Education. (2006). FIPSE grant database. Retrieved March 9, 2006, from http://www.fipse.aed.org/search.cfm

U.S. Department of Justice. (2000). *Final common rule. Nondiscrimination on the basis of sex in education programs or activities receiving federal financial assistance*. Retrieved June 12, 2006 from http://www.usdoj.gov/crt/cor/coord/t9final.htm

U.S. Department of Justice. (2001). *Questions and answers regarding Title IX procedural requirements*. Retrieved June 12, 2006, from http://www.usdoj.gov/crt/cor/coord/TitleIXQandA.htm

U.S. General Accountability Office. (July 2004). Report to Congressional requesters, Gender issues: Women's participation in the sciences has increased, but agencies need to do more to ensure compliance with Title IX, Washington DC. Retrieved June 12, 2006 from http://www.gao.gov/new.items/d04639.pdf

United States v. Virginia et. al., 518 U.S. 515 (1996).

Walker, J. (2005, July). Title IX on State Education Agency (SEA) websites. Arlington, VA: Feminist Majority Foundation. Retrieved June 28, 2006, from http://www.feminist.org/education/StateEducationAgency Sites.pdf

Wharton, L. J. (2005). State equal rights amendments revisited: Evaluating their effectiveness in advancing protection against sex discrimination. *Rutgers Law Journal,* 36(4).

Zittleman, K. R. (2005). Gender and Title IX: A study of the knowledge, perceptions, and experiences of middle and junior high school teachers and students. Unpublished doctoral dissertation, American University, Washington, DC.

·6·

INCREASING GENDER EQUITY
IN EDUCATIONAL LEADERSHIP

Charol Shakeshaft, Genevieve Brown, Beverly J. Irby,
Margaret Grogan, and Julia Ballenger

INTRODUCTION

This chapter examines the research on gender equity in educational leadership published since 1985. Since the numbers of women in educational administration have remained very small compared to the numbers of men in educational administration, the research on gender equity has focused on women. There have been some gains at the central office level and in the elementary principalship, but the majority of educational leaders in schools and districts are still White men. Many of the studies investigating this problem over the past two decades have contributed knowledge of women's experiences as principals and superintendents to the existing literature on educational administration, which was largely written about and by men. In particular, scholars have targeted the barriers to women in school administration, career paths of women administrators, and women's leadership styles. These categories are little changed from the literature reviewed in the previous chapter on "Strategies for Overcoming the Barriers to Women in Educational Administration" (Shakeshaft, 1985c) in the *Handbook for Achieving Sex Equity through Education.*[1] Women still dominate the teaching forces from which leaders are recruited, and, as the following studies confirm, women prepare for leadership in degree programs, and aspire to the positions. This research has tried to understand better what it will take for leadership positions in preK–12 settings to become more equitably distributed. The postsecondary chapter addresses administrative gender equity issues in higher education.

The studies reviewed in this chapter include all empirically based dissertations and research published since 1985 that we were able to locate. Studies included range from samples of one to samples of thousands and include quantitative, qualitative, and historical inquiries. The organization of this chapter was guided by the previous *Handbook for Achieving Sex Equity through Education* chapter on women in leadership.

Representation of Women in School Administration

Comparing the representation of women in school administration "20 years later" is not as easy as looking up the numbers. As was true in the mid 1980s, documenting women's representation in formal leadership positions in schools continues to be difficult because of the absence of reliable and comparable data either nationally or within and across states. Because no federal or national organization, including the National Center for Education Statistics, collects or reports annual administrative data by gender—let alone by gender and ethnicity combined—there is no easy way to compare the representation of women in administration by position from year to year. Currently, the field relies upon membership counts in administrative organizations, occasional surveys by these organizations, or occasional surveys by the National Center for Education Statistics to report the percentage of women in administrative positions in public and private schools.[2]

---

*The bold face names are the Lead Authors.

[1] A full copy of this chapter will be posted on the web page accompanying this new 2007 *Handbook*.

[2] The most recent Schools and Staffing Survey (SASS) from the National Center for Education Statistics in the U.S. Department of Education reports on data collected in 2003–2004. The report does not indicate the percentage of females in the principalship, although this question was included on the survey. To find the percentage of women in the principalship, it is necessary to analyze the public use data sets for SASS. The latest data set available to the public reports 1999–2000 SASS results.

As Tyack and Hansot reported in 1982, the absence of data has historical precedent:

Amid proliferation of other kinds of statistical reporting is an age enamored of numbers—reports so detailed that one could give the precise salary of staff in every community across country and exact information in all sorts of other variables—data by sex became strangely inaccessible. A conspiracy of silence could hardly have been unintentional. (p. 13)

What these sources indicate is that although the representation of women in school leadership has increased in the past 20 years, women still do not fill administrative positions in proportion to their numbers in teaching or in proportion to those who are now trained and certified to become administrators.

The latest comparable data across job types from the U.S. Department of Education were collected in the Schools and Staff Survey in 1999–2000 and show that, despite gains, women are still not proportionately represented in elementary and secondary levels or in the superintendency.

Women constitute approximately 75% of the teaching force, the pool from which superintendents begin their career journey, but they are disproportionately underrepresented in the top positions in schools. Skrla (1999) concluded that men are 40 times more likely than women to advance from teaching to the superintendency.

Montenegro (1993) reported that in 1990 10.5% of superintendents were women. By 2000, the proportion increased to 13.2% (Glass, Björk, & Brunner, 2000). Three years later, for a study of women superintendents commissioned by the American Association of School Administrators (AASA), Grogan and Brunner (2005a–c) mailed surveys to all of the 2,500 female superintendents identified from the AASA membership and a Market Data Retrieval database. This list of 2,500 showed female leadership in 18.2% of all 13,728 districts nationwide. A study reported at about the same time by the *Scholastic Administrator* (2004) puts the number at closer to 14%. Whatever the exact proportion, two things are clear: documenting female representation in the superintendency continues to be imprecise, and at the current rate (.59% a year), women will not be proportionately represented in the superintendency until the 22nd century.

The proportion of women by ethnicity in the superintendency is even more difficult to determine. When statistics are available, they are often reported by sex or by ethnicity, but not by both sex and ethnicity. For instance, the 2003–2004 Schools and Staffing Survey (Strizek, Pittonsberger, Riordan, Lyter, & Orlofsky, 2006) reported only the racial/ethnic distribution of principals. The proportion of teachers and principals by racial/ethnic group is

more balanced, with Black principals being slightly overrepresented and Hispanic principals slightly underrepresented in relation to their distribution in the teaching ranks.

Grogan and Brunner reported 7% women of color superintendents and 10% women of color assistant/associate/deputy superintendents in their 2003 data (2005a). An earlier study by Glass, Björk, and Brunner (2000, p. 104) found 12% of superintendents are White women, 1.1% are women of color, 81.7% are White men, and 5.1% are men of color. Figure 6.1 indicates the changes from 2000 to 2003 by sex and ethnicity in the superintendency.

Despite disparities in hiring, women do aspire to the superintendency, and they prepare to fulfill their aspirations. According to the Grogan and Brunner study, 40% of the women in central office administration identified themselves as aspiring to the superintendency. Toward that end, 74% had either earned their superintendent credential or were working toward certification. Women of color were more likely to be prepared to assume the top job; 85% of women of color assistant/associate/deputy superintendents already have or are working on their superintendency certificate compared to 73% of White women (Brunner & Grogan, in press).

The number of women earning certification in educational administration is not available at the national level, although anecdotal information from preparation programs indicates that the majority of the students are women. Identifying the proportion of educators who are licensed or certified in school administration is difficult because the data are held at the state level and are not comparable across states. However, examining the percentage of degrees in education by sex shows female dominance at all levels in 2003–2004, the most recent data available (Rooney et al., 2006). Women earned 76.5% of bachelor's, 76.7% of master's, and 66.1% of doctoral degrees in education. In nearly a quarter century, there was a small increase in the percentage of women who earned bachelor's and master's degrees (3% and 5% increases), but the female proportion of doctoral degrees increased by nearly 19%. While these figures do not indicate the percentages by field in education or by certifi-

TABLE 6.1 Percent Public School Females by Job Title and Level, 1999–2000

	Elementary	Secondary	All
Teachers	84.9	55.8	74.9
Principals	51.8	21.6	43.8
Superintendents	N/A	N/A	18.0

Source: U.S Department of Education, National Center for Education Statistics, Schools and Staffing Survey, 1999–2000.

TABLE 6.2 Percent Public School Teachers and Principals by Race/Ethnicity, 2003–2004

	Elementary Teachers	Elementary Principals	Secondary Teachers	Secondary Principals	All Teachers	All Principals
White	82.1	81.0	84.3	84.8	83.1	82.4
Black	8.4	11.4	7.5	9.4	7.9	10.6
Hispanic	6.8	6.0	5.5	4.4	6.2	5.3
Other	2.7	1.6	2.7	1.4	2.8	1.7

Source: Strizek, Pittonsberger, Riordan, Lyter, and Orlofsky, 2006.

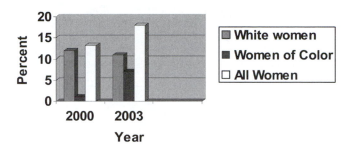

FIGURE 6.1   Percent of women in superintendency by sex and ethnicity.
Source: Glass, Björk, and Brunner (2000); Grogan and Brunner (2005a)

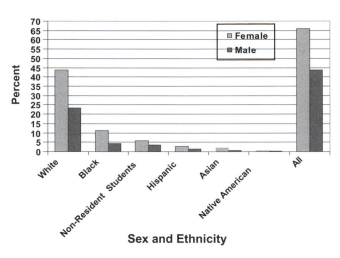

FIGURE 6.2   Percent education doctorates by sex and ethnicity.

cation, they do provide a framework for understanding educational attainment by sex.

An examination of doctoral degrees in education by sex and ethnicity indicates that for every ethnic group females earn more doctoral degrees than males. Figure 6.2 illustrates the dominance of females in attainment of doctorates in education in 2003–2004.

Looking at the pools from which administrators are selected—teachers, those administratively certified, or those with master's and doctoral degrees—the data indicate that both White and women of color are underrepresented in school administration.

History of Gender and School Leadership Research

In the field of school administration, the literature that identifies as *gender* research is almost entirely research on women in administration. The studies that include only males are not labeled gender research. Critics of the traditional research on education administration suggest that the literature of the field is really the study of male administrative behavior. Gender research in school administration, then, is generally thought to be studies of women, or studies which compare women and men.

Like the field itself, women are underrepresented in the administrative research. For instance, in the most recent analysis of the content of articles published in the *Educational Administration Quarterly*, Jones (1988) found that of the 187 empirical articles published, 41 or 21.9% included a gender mention, and only 18 (0.6%) provided sufficient information for a gender analysis. More than twice as many studies (*n* = 94) could have examined gender but did not. Of review or synthesis articles,

3.2% examined gender (7 out of 213). Of all types of articles, 25 (6.3%) reported or discussed gender.

The majority of empirical research in educational administration is found in the dissertation. Within dissertation research, women are similarly underrepresented as targets of study. Brown and Irby (2005) noted that dissertations that specifically include the study of women make up only about 9% of all leadership dissertations completed between 1985 and 2005 (Table 6.4).

The history of research on gender and administration is one that began with a social change agenda. Early research focused on documenting the numbers of women and men in administrative positions. Those studies prompted research on why there were fewer women than men in administrative positions. Barrier research opened the question of female approaches to leadership and to seeing the world from a female lens, as opposed to comparing male and female behaviors within a previously identified male paradigm. Many of the earlier studies compared female and male administrative styles and behavior and were undertaken in an effort to accumulate a knowledge base that would document female capability as equal to or better than male capability (Gross & Trask, 1964; Lyon & Saario, 1973; Schmuck, 1976).

As women became the focus of study, research began to move away from comparisons of women and men toward understanding the world of women. To understand women's worlds, it has been necessary to learn about them from women, not measured against male experiences. This perspective has influenced the research in the field so that 20 years after the publication of the *Handbook for Achieving Sex Equity through Education*, the prominent paradigm is the study of women, not women in comparison to men.

As early as 1987, Schmuck asserted, "the inclusion of women within the domain of inquiry must change the nature of the inquiry" (p. 9). Brown and Irby (2005) indicated that the more we know about women in leadership roles, how they obtain their positions, and how they have become successful, the greater the likelihood of increasing the numbers in the field. Blount (1995) stated that "As long as silences exist in data describing superintendents by sex, the phenomenon of the under representation of women in the superintendency will receive

TABLE 6.3   Female Degrees in Education 1980–81 to 2003–04

	Bachelor's Degrees	Master's Degrees	Doctoral Degrees
Percent female 1979–80	73.8	70.2	43.9
Percent female 1989–90	75.0	75.9	57.3
Percent female 2003–04	78.5	76.7	66.1

Source: U.S. Department of Education, National Center for Education Statistics, *Earned Degrees Conferred*, 1949–50 and 1959–60; Higher Education General Information Survey (HEGIS), Degrees and Other Formal Awards Conferred surveys, 1967–68 through 1985–86; and 1986–87 through 2003–04 Integrated Postsecondary Education Data System, Completions Survey (IPEDS-C:87–99), and Fall 2000 through Fall 2004.

TABLE 6.4 Dissertation Research Related to Female Superintendents and Principals

Level of Administrator (Descriptor)	# of Dissertations Related to the Generic Descriptor	# of Dissertations Related Specifically to the Generic Descriptor Including the Descriptor of Females/Women	Percentage of Studies that Included the Descriptor, Female/Women
Superintendents/Superintendency	3,323	292	8.8
Secondary/High School Principals	2,938	238	8.1
Elementary Principals	3,440	321	10.7
Total	9,701	851	8.8

TABLE 6.5 Research on Women by Methodological Approach, 1985–2005

	Qualitative		Quantitative		Mixed method		Historical	
	n	Percent	n	Percent	n	Percent	n	Percent
1985–1990	11	55	8	40	1	5	0	
1991–1995	20	53	13	34	4	11	1	2
1996–2000	32	53	17	28	11	18	0	0
2001–2005	49	61	18	23	10	13	3	3
Total	112	57	56	28	26	13	4	2

limited critical examination, a condition that obscures the need for remedies for systematic discriminatory hiring practices" (p. 4). Gupton (1998) further indicated a need to have objective gender data if women are to be dealt with fairly, in particular, in the superintendency. Skrla, Reyes, and Scheurich (2000) noted the lack of empathetic research methods that would record the voices of women. They also argued that as research is conducted with females in administrative positions, it is important that the research context encourage an empathetic dialogue that provides a comfortable place where women can tell stories of successful professional work interwoven with acknowledgments of their own silence. In this context, women are more likely to be able to relay candid accounts of their experiences with sexism and discriminatory treatment, which may make it possible to "learn how women leaders construct their identities in inherently inequitable circumstances such [as] those found in the superintendency" (Skrla et al., 2000, p. 71).

Although the number of studies from a woman's perspective has increased, Christman (2003) argued that qualitative, feminist research is trivialized and viewed as a threat to the stakeholders of the status quo because it challenges basic assumptions through alternative paradigms (Kelly, 1993).

Others pointed out that most findings are over or under generalized. For instance, Brown and Irby (2005) cautioned that a study that generalizes to all principals from a sample that is predominantly male is likely to misrepresent women's experiences. Similarly, generalizing to all administrators from studies that include primarily White administrators results in inaccurate assumptions and conclusions.

In 1999, Tallerico noted that "in virtually all cases, it is women and persons of color who are studying women superintendents and superintendents of color," and she further noted that there

is a "meager distribution of women and persons of color in the superintendency" (p. 43). Tallerico stated, "we need more than just a handful of researchers working toward this end in the future" (p. 43). The research on women and school leadership has begun to provide an additional perspective and to inform practice for both women and men.

In summary, the majority of studies on women leaders are reported in dissertations, few White men study women and/or people of color, and studies have shifted from comparisons by gender to examining the world as experienced by women.

Description of Research Reviewed

For this chapter, we include all empirical research on women in preK–12 administration that we were able to identify, either in the published literature or in dissertations.[3] We have limited the review to studies of administrative leaders. It does not include studies of teachers, school board members, unions, or parent associations.

Appendix A in the web page accompanying this chapter lists the primary empirical studies reviewed in this chapter by topic and research method.[4] As illustrated in Table 6.5, over the past 20 years, there has been a slight increase in the percentage of studies of women in leadership that use qualitative methods— from 55 to 61% of all studies—and a decrease in quantitative approaches—from 40 to 28% of all studies.

Mirroring all research in the field of educational administration, the research on women leaders is primarily reported in the dissertation. Of those studies identified for review in this chapter, 51% are dissertations or reports of research originally examined in a dissertation. One disadvantage of dissertation

[3]When the dissertation was not available, abstracted methods and results were reviewed.

[4]Although simplistic, we have coded studies into four categories, recognizing that these labels have descriptive limits.

research is that it is seldom reviewed for juried journal publications since the majority of dissertation research, whether about women or men, is not published. Therefore, many studies on gender and leadership reach a limited audience and do not add to the theoretical or practice foundation of the discipline. Not surprisingly, there was a scarcity of published research that grew out of the nearly 900 dissertations addressing women and leadership identified by Brown and Irby (2005). As a result, the majority of studies inclusive of women in educational leadership can only be read in dissertations

An additional limitation of the reports of research is that not all studies distinguish women administrators by role or disaggregate findings by role. Therefore, it is sometimes difficult to determine whether the finding represents assistant superintendents, superintendents, or principals.

Barriers to Women in Educational Leadership

The largest body of research related to women has examined barriers to women in entering the leadership hierarchy or in moving up that hierarchy. These studies focus on a number of challenges for women and largely expand or repeat the research conducted through 1985. The question that was asked over two decades ago in the *Handbook for Achieving Sex Equity through Education* continues to be appropriate. Why the "higher you go, the fewer you see" syndrome for women in school administration (Shakeshaft, 1985c, p. 125)? The research on barriers reviewed in this section responds to the categories identified in the 1985 *Handbook*.

The majority of the studies on barriers are self-report surveys or interviews in which women identify the barriers they experienced either obtaining an administrative position or keeping it. Although much has been written on the career paths of males, there is no distinct literature on barriers to White heterosexual males; where barriers are examined as part of male career advancement, race and sexual identity have been the focus.

In 1985, the barriers to women were described as either internally imposed or externally imposed. Since that time, the interaction of the two has been examined. The most recent research synthesized for this chapter indicates that more barriers previously identified as internal have been overcome than have barriers previously identified as external.

Poor Self-Image or Lack of Confidence

The barrier of poor self-image or lack of confidence was introduced by Schmuck in 1976, almost 10 years prior to the 1985 production of the first *Handbook for Achieving Sex Equity through Education* (Klein, 1985). Twenty years after the original Schmuck citation, several studies have been added to the literature that relates to self-image of women administrators (Brown & Irby, 1995; Gupton, 1998, Hewitt, 1989, Lutz, 1990, Scherr, 1995; Walker, 1995). The results of these studies are not disaggregated by race/ethnicity.

Women who aspire to become administrators are more likely to report lowered aspiration or lack of confidence than women who have become administrators. In studies of females aspiring to become administrators, Brown and Irby (1995) found a marked lack of self-confidence. On the other hand, 20 female elementary teachers who had been tapped for the principalship but who didn't want to become administrators exhibited no signs of low self-esteem or lack of confidence according to Hewitt (1989).

Although Walker (1995) and Gupton (1998) both noted that female administrators rarely see themselves as experts, often expressing a lack of confidence about seeing themselves at the top, women superintendents studied by Lutz (1990) reported no internal barrier of poor self-image or lack of confidence. Grogan (1996) found the superintendent aspirants in her study to be very confident of their abilities and qualifications to lead school districts. Similarly, Grogan and Brunner (2005a, b) report that 40% of women in senior central office positions feel competent to take on district leadership positions.

Low self-esteem and lack of self-confidence may be different than leadership identity, which is the feeling of belonging to a group of leaders or to a specific level of leadership and of feeling significant within that circle (Brown & Irby, 1996). Lack of a leadership identity can lead to a feeling of isolation and the feeling of being an outsider (Christman, 2003). In their findings related to superintendents and aspiring superintendents, Walker (1995) and Scherr (1995) indicated that women lack a sense of themselves as leaders and perceive that they have further to go in developing this leadership identity than do men.

Perhaps it is this lack of leadership identity, rather than low self-esteem that also perpetuates the perception of women that they must get more information, more education, and more experience in the classroom prior to seeking an administrative position (Grogan & Brunner, 2005a,b; Young & McLeod, 2001). Or perhaps it is the reality that for a woman to be considered equal, she must be better prepared than the man with whom she is competing for a job.

Lack of Aspiration or Motivation

Shakeshaft (1985) argued that women's lack of success in obtaining administrative positions was not due to lowered aspiration or lack of motivation on the part of women. Findings since 1985 document a healthy level of aspiration among women. For instance, a 1991 study of 488 central office administrators in New York found that 13.2% of the female respondents aspired to the superintendency. As stated in the previous section, a little over a decade later, Grogan and Brunner (2005a–c) found that 40% of women in central office positions plan on pursuing the superintendency.

Family and Home Responsibilities

Family and home responsibilities, place-bound circumstances, moves with spouses, or misalignment of personal and organizational goals were early contributors to women's lack of administrative success, either because the demands of family on women aspirants restricted them or because those who hired believed that women would be hindered by family commitments. According to Shakeshaft (1985), a direct impediment for females in attaining administrative positions is the reality-based factor of family responsibility; she continued to voice this concern some seven years later from data obtained in 1993 (Kamler & Shakeshaft, 1999).

A 1989 study of Kansas teachers documented family responsibilities as one reason why women teachers were not choosing to enter administration (Hewitt, 1989). Native American women in Montana also identified family responsibilities as a barrier to entering administration (Brown, 2004). Other researchers in the PK–12 field that have found similar tensions between the personal and the professional include Hill and Ragland (1995) and Tonnsen and Pigford (1998). In 2003, Lacey explored 1,344 female teachers' decisions in making or not making application to elementary or secondary principalships. Among her findings was that females were likely to be influenced in their decisions by family care responsibilities; however, these women did have conscious aspirations for leadership careers. Grogan (1996), Gupton (1998), Watkins, Herrin and McDonald (1993) and Wynn (2003) also noted that family responsibilities were considered by women in their decisions to apply for and maintain administrative positions. Balancing the personal and professional shapes the ways that some women structure their lives once they move into administration and is discussed later in this chapter.

Working Conditions and Sex Discrimination

The components of administrative work, as well as the perceived and real male-defined environments in which many women administrators must work, shape women's perceptions of the desirability of administration. The women teachers studied by Hewitt (1989) were discouraged from applying for administrative positions because of their understanding of the definition of the job of the principal. They did not perceive this definition as flexible or open for social construction. Principals studied by Clemens (1989) and McGovern-Robinett (2002) noted that supportive work environments were essential in choosing to become principals. Fourteen years later, Wynn's (2003) study of teachers with leadership skills determined that these women chose to stay in the classroom, rather than move into administration, partly because of their negative perception of the job of the principal. These women identified student discipline as one of the negative dimensions of the principalship.

Relatedly, the perceptions of lack of aspiration may also result when teachers fail to apply for leadership positions because their personal values are not aligned with those of the organization (Lacey, 2003). Scherr (1995) determined that women's failure to aspire to the superintendency might be a result of their experiences working with male superintendents, role models whose leadership behaviors may not be compatible with women's preferred ways of leading. The perceptions that women hold of what leaders do are largely based upon what they see administrators doing, rather than on imagining a different role.

Gardiner and Tiggemann (1999) found that the job stress of women was higher than that of men when working in a predominantly or traditionally male environment. Skrla, Reyes, and Scheurich (2000) described organizational contexts in which men used intimidation and silence to discourage women. Intimidating tactics and behaviors of board and community members included name-calling, rumors, and overt lies. Additionally, women reported that male subordinates were intimidating, at times indicating directly that they did not want to work for a woman. Logan (1999) also supported this finding in a study of 54 educational leadership department chairs. Lange (1995) in a survey of 561 women administrators found that 78% of women reported they had been sexually harassed by a higher status male and that sexual bribery by higher status male coworkers was a problem. Silence as a form of sexism was represented in personal silence about gender issues while in the superintendency and in the feelings of not being heard.

Lack of Support, Encouragement, and Counseling

Shakeshaft (1985) noted research studies from the late 1970s (Baughman, 1977; Schmuck, 1976) that pointed out that women traditionally had little support, encouragement, or counseling from family, peers, superordinates, or educational institutions to pursue careers in administration. At this time, even a little support from a few people such as a spouse or an administrator within the school district encouraged women to enter administration or stick with administration.

Support has continued to be an important factor for women moving into administration. Most researchers found that family endorsements and support and mentoring made the difference in encouraging women into principalships, the superintendency, community college presidencies, and other high-level executive positions in education (Alston, 1999; Brunner, 2000, 2003; Edson, 1988; Enomoto, Gardiner & Grogan, 2000; Gardiner, Enomoto, & Grogan, 2000; Grogan, 1996, 2000b, 2002; Grogan & Brunner, 2005a,b; Hill & Ragland, 1995; Jackson, 1999; Mendez-Morse, 1999, 2004; Scherr, 1995; Smulyan, 2000; Young & McLeod, 2001). Hewitt (1989) found lack of encouragement and support one of the reasons female elementary teachers in Kansas reported not entering administration. Several studies of women of color noted their lack of encouragement and support, as did a study of native women in Montana (Brown, 2004).

As late as 2000, Skrla, Reyes, and Scheurich found that silence on gender issues in educational administration preparation programs, state education agencies, professional organizations, and among school board members and associations was still characteristic, and that women equated silence with lack of support.

Pounder (1987) suggested that women should be encouraged to be on search teams for administrators and that professors of educational administration could encourage women by assuring school boards that women can be competent administrators. The National Policy Board for Educational Administration (1989) suggested that women can be encouraged toward administrative careers through the adoption of rigorous recruitment strategies by departments of educational administration to seek women in administrator training programs.

In the absence of attention to women's needs within traditional organizations and preparation programs, support systems specifically for women were developed. In 1998, Irby and Brown indicated that women's support organizations should serve as vehicles for the growth of women at initial administration career stages as well as for women in top level positions. While some women administrators' organizations, such as Northwest Women in Educational Administration in Oregon, which celebrated its 30th year of operation in 2006, or the Women's Caucus of the Pennsylvania Association of School Administrators, have continued to be strong influences in women's career path other organizations have been discontinued (Irby & Brown, 1998). For instance, the 25th anniversary of the American Association of School Administrators' (AASA) women's leadership conference was celebrated in 2005 with the announcement that the conference would no longer be sponsored by AASA.

Socialization and Sex Role Stereotyping

Organizational socialization is the process by which new leaders become integrated into the formal and informal norms, as well as the unspoken assumptions of a school or a district. Because traditional stereotypes cast women and minorities as socially incongruent as leaders, they face greater challenges becoming integrated into the organization (Hart, 1995). The 1985 *Handbook for Achieving Sex Equity through Education* reported, "socialization and sex role stereotyping have been potent obstacles to increasing women's participation in the management of schools" (Shakeshaft, 1985c, p. 127). Brathwaite (1986) attributed women's failure to advance to upper-level leadership positions in schools to oversaturation with the "cultural message of female inferiority within white male systems" (p. 16). This marginalization results in women not only being expected to "behave like men," but also on being judged on how "womanly" they are.

Since the mid 1980s, studies have continued to report that women believe that negative stereotypes of women by superintendents and school board members are a barrier. Reportedly, some persistent stereotypical and inaccurate views held by gatekeepers about women are their perceived inability to discipline students, supervise other adults, criticize constructively, manage finances, and function in a political frame (Folmar, 1989; Johnson, 2003; Lutz, 1990; Rossman, 2000). Young and McLeod (2001) stated, "many school board members, search consultants, search committee members, practicing administrators, and private citizens continue to believe old myths that have prevented women from becoming educational leaders in the past" (p. 494). Assumptions about appropriate activities relate to concerns about whether or not a woman can do the job. For example, the school board may lack confidence in a female superintendent's competency to oversee the construction of a new building, and when she completes the task successfully the board is surprised. Logan (1999) also found that women were still perceived as lacking the ability to handle discipline at a secondary school.

Skrla et al. (2000) reported that school boards and other administrators believe that women are malleable. The authors described malleable personalities as referring to school board perceptions of women superintendents as easy to direct just because they are female. If women turn out not to be malleable, the reaction is much more negative for women than for men

because women are violating expected norms. Thus, women are penalized not only when they don't act like men, since they are seen as incompetent, but also when they do act like men, because they are perceived a cold. Skrla et al. (2000) noted that these expectations of feminine behavior result in negative perceptions of assertive actions of women.

Bell (1995) and Skrla et al. (2000), suggested that in the superintendency, males have set the standard for what is valued, and, consequentially, women who do obtain superintendencies have pressure to de-feminize, or even to disaffiliate from other women, just so that they can prove themselves. Brown, Irby, and Smith (1993), in a study of 40 aspiring female administrators, also found this gender prejudice in that colleagues interpret negatively women's intelligence and assertiveness. Brunner (2000) reported that women must be aware of their leadership style because directness or assertiveness is unacceptable. Furthermore, Hill and Ragland (1995) indicated that colleagues might say such things as "the man is firm, but the female is stubborn," and school boards are more likely to negatively evaluate women superintendents who portray decisiveness, assertiveness, and directness (Bell, 1995).

Hill and Ragland (1995) pointed out the perpetuation of gender bias in media images of women leaders in which they are scheming, gold digging, seducing their way to the top, devious, immoral, and running over everyone in their way. Negative examples of women leaders in books, television, and movies also influence society's expectations of appropriate female leader behavior.

Another form of sex stereotyping reported by Irby and Brown (1995) related to societal perceptions that women work on an emotional level. Langford (1995) indicated that it is perceived that because women are intuitive (akin to the emotional work response), they cannot be natural, logical decision makers. Kamler and Shakeshaft (1999) supported these findings, pointing out the existence of the myth that "women are too emotional and can't see things rationally and so that affects their decision making" (p. 56).

Christman (2003) indicated that there exists a societal climate of unexpectation for women who hold administrative positions. Perhaps due to this "unexpectation," a more difficult socialization process into the profession occurs with women as opposed to men. Carr (1995), Reese (1993), and Christman (2003) indicated one of the reasons for the difficult socialization process is male dominance of the profession.

Studies of women of color found the double whammy of negative stereotypes, first about being female and then about ethnic background (Prescott-Hutchins, 2002; Trujillo-Ball, 2003).

Preparation Programs and Curriculum Materials

In the 1985 *Handbook*, Shakeshaft reported that there were fewer females than males participating in certification, doctoral, or internship programs in administration, and that women were less experienced and less prepared for administration than were men. She indicated, however, that this barrier could be overcome with more women receiving internships, administrative certifications, and doctoral degrees. As described earlier in this chapter, in the 20 years since the last *Handbook*, women have achieved parity and, in some instances dominance, in the student populations in preparation and doctoral programs. While data are not available nationwide on the proportion of females who are certified in school administration each year, the majority (66.1%) of doctoral degrees in education are earned by women (Rooney et al., 2006).

The increase in the proportion of women is not reflected in the curricular materials in these programs, however. Criticisms of educational administration programs, particularly superintendency training programs, have been consistent since the mid 1980s and include:

- Lack of attention to equity issues (Shakeshaft, 1993, 1995, 1999)
- Underrepresentation of women in curricular materials and case studies (Shakeshaft, 1993, 1995, 1999)
- Curriculum that is based upon gender deficit theories (Brown & Irby, 2005)
- Insufficient information regarding female relationships with local school boards (Douglas, 1992)
- Failure to address the gender knowledge and skill base needed for the superintendency (American Association of School Administrators, 1993).

While more administrators are prepared at local and small colleges, the University Council for Educational Administration (UCEA) has been central to reform in preparation programs. In operation since the mid fifties, UCEA is a consortium of major research universities with doctoral programs in educational leadership and policy. The dual mission of UCEA is to improve the preparation of educational leaders and promote the development of professional knowledge in school improvement and administration. UCEA is a strong supporter of social justice issues as evidenced by its conferences, and there have been 13 women presidents out of 45. At present there are more than 75 institutional members.

However, Logan (1999) indicated that in general University Council for Educational Administration (UCEA) universities are doing little to address the traditional deterrents to hiring women. She stated, "the historically androcentric paradigm is still present in UCEA educational administration programs; little, if anything, is being done to change that reality at the structural and cultural level." (p. 5). She suggested that it was time for educational administration departments to "reassess, adjust, and activate gender equity strategies that will bring about an equitable hiring context for all . . . graduates." (p. 6)

Skrla et al. (2000) found that women considered their superintendency preparation programs noninclusive of the experiences and voices of all women, including women of color. According to Iselt, Brown, and Irby (2001), recent research offers evidence that traditional paradigms and the university continue to perpetuate barriers encountered by women who seek the superintendency.

According to Iselt et al. (2001), 76 female superintendents in Texas found their programs less relevant than did 76 male superintendents. Male and female superintendents indicated that 21 of 30 leadership knowledge and skills topics were relevant to their job performance but were not emphasized suffi-

ciently for them in their programs. Female superintendents noted an additional eight topics among the 30 as more relevant to job performance than did males, pointing out that the following were not emphasized in their programs; (a) legal issues, (b) organizational culture/climate, (c) ethics, (d) working with the cultural/political system, (e) collaboration, (f) networking, (g) use of mentors, and (h) interviewing practice.

In 1987, Murphy and Hallinger criticized university preparation programs for their failure to connect theory and practice; more recently, programs have been criticized for the biased knowledge base, which does not include experiences of women administrators (Skrla et al., 2000). Superintendents have continued to insist that course time should be spent on field-based learning rather than on outdated gender-impoverished theoretical lectures (American Association of School Administrators, 1993; Iselt, 1999) in which the theory espoused comes from the male perspective and the assumption has been that male experiences can be generalized to explain all human behaviors (Brown & Irby, 1995; Irby, Brown, Duffy, & Trautman, 2002; McKay & Grady, 1994; Schmitt, 1995; Shakeshaft, 1989). Brown and Irby (1995) indicated that "the current theories taught in administrative preparation programs are negatively impacting the field because they (a) do not reflect currently advocated leadership practice; (b) do not address the concerns, needs, or realities of women; (c) perpetuate the barriers that women encounter; and (d) do not prepare women or men to create and work effectively in inclusive systems" (pp. 42–43).

This void of leadership theory inclusive of women's voices results in sexist curricular material. Since the publication of the 1985 *Handbook*, Papalewis (1994) examined 13 educational administration textbooks published after 1990 and determined that only one made any reference to the presence of women in the field of administration, and that single reference evoked negative connotations. Lunenburg and Ornstein (2004), co-authors of one of the most widely used educational administration texts (Monument, 2006), are the only scholars in educational leadership who include a deliberate, gender-inclusive leadership theory, the Synergistic Leadership Theory (Irby et al., 2002).

Brown and Irby (1996) argued that women in educational administrative programs have particular and unique needs, concerns, and challenges which should be addressed in leadership preparation programs. They presented a model for preparation considerations including 26 broad categories from research of women's needs that should be addressed in programs educating teachers who will be entering administrative ranks. In general, programs should assist women candidates in:

- learning how to alter negative perceptions of female leaders
- enhancing decision-making skills, while also encouraging their intuitive nature
- learning how to effectively select and work with role models, mentors, networks, and sponsors
- working successfully within the cultural and political system
- developing an understanding of language differences between men and women
- learning how to handle conflict
- managing legal issues

- learning stress management and time management techniques
- practicing fiscal management of various budgets
- learning how to present qualifications in a positive light
- learning techniques for creating inclusive environments
- learning how to reflect on experiences and project new goals
- examining theory and practice critically for gender bias
- developing career plans, résumés, portfolios, and interviewing skills. (p. 10)

Although a number of universities offered women in administration courses in the 1980s and 1990s, anecdotal reports indicate that these are no longer being widely offered, either because the need is not identified or because university faculty report that they have integrated gender issues into programs and courses. However, there is no study that focuses specifically on this issue.

Finances for Continuing Training

According to Shakeshaft (1985), women, more than men, referred to a lack of finances as a reason for being unable to continue administrative training. She cited Databank (1982), stating that women in public schools earn less than their male counterparts. She further noted that women have tended to sacrifice financially for their families and, therefore, cut short their educational opportunities. She suggested that women, more than men, are expected to give up their education or needs to shore up family resources.

Although there were no studies that directly examined this issue since 1982, Sokorosh (2004) in a study of 773 educational administration doctoral students in 69 programs found no differences by gender in the awarding of financial support.

Too Few Role Models, Sponsors, Mentors, and Networks

More than three decades ago the literature cited a lack of role models, lack of networks, and lack of support, sponsorship, and mentoring as barriers to women's entry into and advancement in educational leadership (Baughman, 1977; Lovelady-Dawson, 1980; Poll, 1978; Schmuck, 1976). Currently, the literature reveals similar barriers for women.

Professional socialization and growth continues to be enhanced by positive role models, sponsors, mentors, and networks. Role models are people who serve as examples of success, often because the role model is similar in characteristics and background. A mentor is someone who takes an active and focused role in developing another person, often shaping that person in the image of the mentor. A sponsor fills a similar role, but is much more a support than someone to be copied.

Role models. Role models provide standards and patterns to copy or modify. In 1985, Shakeshaft reported that research suggested that same-sex role models were the most effective for females, but not necessarily for males. Since that time, several researchers have reinforced the need for role models in the education administration profession (Brown & Merchant, 1993;

Hinkson, 2004; Irby & Brown, 1995; Slick & Gupton, 1993; Wesson & Grady, 1995).

In the Young and McLeod (2001) study, a purposive sample of 20 female administrators and educational administration students were interviewed. The researchers found that elementary school principals—more than any other administrative role—identify with their administrative role models. While there is a greater likelihood of having a role model of the same sex at the elementary level, this does not hold true of role models of the same ethnicity.

Mentors and sponsors. These two terms are often used interchangeably in the literature, although there are some important distinctions. Sponsors help others, providing advice and networking. They may or may not be role models, but they do provide access for aspiring administrators or for those wishing to make moves. Mentors take this a step farther and try to mold the mentee into the image of the mentor. Mentors may provide a number of functions. First, mentors may provide career development functions, which involve coaching, sponsoring, and advancement. Second, mentors may serve psychosocial support and increase the mentor self-confidence by serving as a friend, counselor, or role model (Kram, 1985, Ragins, 1989).

Shakeshaft (1985) noted that sponsors and mentors of either sex, unlike role models, were effective for women. However, Hinkson (2004) identified the importance of strong Black female role models for African descent women. Similarly, Gardiner et al. (2000) found that while male mentors were sometimes very helpful for women aspiring to educational leadership positions, the best mentors for women were female and of the same ethnicity. Until the cycle is broken, little hope exists for major breakthroughs in advancement of females and persons of color.

Because White males are still the majority of superintendents and principals, they provide not only the largest number of possible sponsors for women, but also the highest likelihood of supporting others like themselves. Research that examines the sexual tensions between male mentors and female mentees concludes that these tensions, which are seldom addressed directly, result in a less open and productive relationship for the mentee. Without a sponsor or mentor, only 17% of women who aspire to be principals are able to advance, according to Edson (1995, p. 42). In the original *Handbook* it was recounted that most women who *had* been successful in acquiring administrative titles had sponsors or mentors (Poll, 1978; Shakeshaft, 1985c). While family support is important for women to be able to gain the time and the approval of those immediately impacted by a decision to work longer hours, professional mentoring is vital to gain the knowledge and political information necessary for a woman to position herself as a viable top-level candidate.

Research has demonstrated that in general women lack mentoring since it has been more often associated with the male model of grooming the next generation of leaders. Women of color, in particular, have found great difficulties finding appropriate mentoring (Alston, 1999; Enomoto et al., 2000; Grogan & Brunner, 2005a; Jackson, 1999; Mendez-Morse, 1999, 2004; Ortiz, 1999; Salleh-Barone, 2004; Walker, 2003). Not only are there fewer individuals of color in executive positions in education, but women of color, even more conspicuously than White women, are outside the norm of those usually tapped for leadership positions. Salleh-Barone (2004) reported that only one of ten Asian descent women administrators she studied had experience with a mentor. Walker evaluated a mentoring program for African descent women administrators and found that the group who received mentoring ended with higher self-images than those women who did not receive mentoring.

In a recent AASA study of women superintendents and women in central office positions, Grogan and Brunner (2005a, b) found that central office administrators received less mentoring than superintendents (60% compared to 72%). One conclusion that might be inferred from this finding is that it takes additional mentoring to make the jump from a central office support position to the superintendency than it does to make it to the central office. Thus, a woman needs more mentoring to become a superintendent than to be appointed to the central office. Despite the fact that the majority of women in the study were mentored, it is important to note that nearly a third of women superintendents report that they were not mentored. In addition, 25% of women of color in that study reported waiting five or more years to gain a superintendency compared to only 8% of White women and 9% of men who wait that long.

Mentors and sponsors are critical to the socialization of women to the profession. This importance was stressed by Hill and Ragland (1995) in their study of 35 female educational leaders: "From the mentor in one's work setting, the novice learns political realities, secrets of moving a project through the chain of command, techniques for dealing with the bureaucracy, ways to creatively budget, contacts throughout the narrow and broader community, and other survival techniques not written in any employee handbook" (pp. 73–74).

The importance of sponsorship and mentoring for both females and males who are seeking academic advancement has been documented earlier in the research reviewed (Haynes, 1989; Noe, 1988; Ragins, 1989). Dreher and Cox (1996) found that women who have been mentored have greater opportunities for career advancement. Thus, while mentoring relationships are important for all organization members, they may be particularly important for women (Burke & McKeen, 1990; Noe, 1988; Ragins, 1989). The important sponsoring and mentoring experiences, which include both career and psychosocial aspects, continue to be addressed in the literature. Catalyst's 1999 study of women of color in all types of management documented that women of color surveyed placed greater emphasis on the importance of mentoring now than in the past. In fact, over the three-year period of the study, "69% of the women with mentors had received a promotion [compared to 49% of the women without mentors]" (p. 42).

The limited research that is available on women of color reveals similar important findings. Mentors were found to be extremely important for women of color in higher education (Ramey, 1993; however, professional women of color indicated a need for increased availability of same-sex and same-race mentors (Hite, 1998). Byrd-Blake (2004) examined a sample of female administrators serving in upper administrative ranks in the public school system to determine any similarities and differences among African American, Hispanic, and White female administrators related to their perception of barriers to career advancement. The survey responses from 175 women revealed that African American female administrators perceived more barriers as hindering their career advancement than Hispanic and White respondents, including lack of access to professional networks, a need for more training, and the feeling of exclusion from the informal socialization process.

However, Ragins (1997) noted a problem for both White women and women of color to be a lack of access to mentors. Many mentoring programs fail. Dunn and Moody (1995) found that adequate funding and cooperation of participants mean the difference between a successful or failed mentoring program. Trust can be a barrier of mentoring when programs suffer from a shortage of mentors, ill-matched partnerships, and an unreliable chain of command. The Cullen and Luna (1993) study included a total of 24 women in executive or administrative positions (e.g. provost, vice president, dean, director, or chair) also confirmed that the lack of senior women served as a barrier to mentoring. This study also noted that institutional environment and organization culture served as barriers to mentoring for women. Dunn and Moody's (1995) qualitative study comprised of 228 selected U.S. colleges found that gender continued to be an issue when matching participants for mentoring.

In Bova's (1995) qualitative study of Hispanic women, mentoring was found to be crucial to their career development; however, these women cited concerns regarding mentoring in the following areas: (a) limited opportunities for informal contact, (b) stereotypes of Hispanic women compounded by stereotypes of women in general, and (c) cultural conflicts" (as cited in Bova, 2000, p. 8). In addition to culture conflicts facing women of color, Kalbfleisch and Davies' (1991) study on the availability of mentors for Black professionals found "race to be a significant factor in the mentoring relationship" (as cited in Bova, 2000, p. 8). A more recent study of Bova (2000), using an exploratory research design and a primary data collection technique of in-depth interviews with 14 Black women, concluded, "mentoring was very important to their career development, however, stereotypes and racism were themes that emerged from the data" (p. 10). Clearly, mentoring relationships have the potential for enhancing the career advancement of women and particularly women of color. Hansman (1998) confirmed Bova's findings that the challenges of women of color are "compounded by the intersection of race and gender" (p. 67). Additional research is recommended related to mentoring and the intersection of race, culture, and gender.

Lack of networks. Networks are less formal connections than are sponsor or mentor relationships. In 1985, Shakeshaft noted a lack of established networks as a barrier for women. Related to sponsors and mentorships is the need to have access to a network that provides information on job openings and administrative strategies as well as promotes visibility and functions as a support group. Thirty years ago, Schmuck (1976) noted that women traditionally had been excluded from networks, had been unaware of administrative positions, had been unknown by others, and had few people to approach for support. Several studies postdating Schmuck have indicated that although women are gaining access to more networks, they still experience exclusion (Howell, 1989; Sherman, 2002; Washington, 2002).

In a study of formal and informal leadership programs and networks, Sherman (2002) found informal networking crucial to women aspiring to an administrative position and a factor that moves the aspirants into formal leadership positions. Brown and Irby (1998), in a study of 69 aspiring women administrators, reported that while the workplace is the most obvious arena for creating a network for career advancement, contacts in other settings can also be of great assistance to women. They suggested that women create a variety of networks—neighborhood, community, church—and, further, that they consider each person with whom an aspiring female would come into contact a member of her network. Additionally, they noted that the more people the aspirant knows and the more others know about the aspirants' capabilities and career goals, the greater the chances of learning about a position or having someone put in a "good word." Irby and Brown (1998), in a study regarding women's administrative support organizations, determined that state and regional organizations need to publicize information about networking opportunities and to actively promote activities that would allow women administrators networking opportunities and career advancement techniques. In summary, it appears from the literature these 20 years later that women still need assistance in establishing and effectively using networks, which include not only men who are in positions of power, but also other women; and, further, that organizations, single-sex or coed, should find ways to support networking.

Sex Discrimination in Hiring and Promotion

By 1985, a number of studies documented overt sex discrimination by school boards, departments of educational administration, and educational administrators, which prevented women from becoming school administrators. Shakeshaft (1985) indicated that people tend to hire those like themselves; thus, White males hire White males (Kanter, 1977; Ortiz, 1981). Marshall (1981) pointed out that affirmative action policies were often misused. In almost a quarter of a century since Marshall's assertion and despite the enormous gains made by the civil rights and women's rights movements, women and people of color still face unfair obstacles in education in general.

While sex discrimination occurs in hiring and in treatment once on the job, there is some evidence that discrimination in the principalship and in staff positions is decreasing. For instance, Goldberg (1991), in an experimental study of 598 superintendents who rated applicants for a position as an "assistant to" based upon identical resumes that differed only by female or male name of applicant, found no differences in the ratings by sex of applicant.

Shepard (1998) noted that women receive less than half as many interviews for the superintendency as men, indicating that women are not considered as serious candidates by school board presidents as are men. Logan (1999) found that some boards were reluctant to consider women for leadership based upon local cultural beliefs and the reluctance to change traditional hiring patterns. Both administrators and school board members identified covert sex discrimination as a barrier to women in Kentucky (Washington, 2002). The gatekeepers to the superintendency, school boards or search consultants, are in a position to give access to the superintendency. Marietti and Stout (1994) reported in their study of 114 school boards in 19 states that female-majority boards hired female superintendents more frequently than did male-majority boards; however, such boards are more likely to be governing K–8 districts. Chase and Bell (1990, p. 174) described subtle forms of sex discrimination by explaining how school board members and superintendent search consultants "may be helpful to individual women and at the same time participate in the processes that reproduce men's dominance." Kamler and Shakeshaft (1999) documented the filtering process of search consultants and the reluctance of headhunters to increase contacts with women. On the other hand, 23% of women superintendents nationwide reported they were hired by districts that used professional search firms compared to 17% of men. In addition, more women of color were hired by districts that used professional search firms (36% compared to 22%; Brunner & Grogan, in press). Men were more successful than women when the search was managed locally.

The most recent nationwide data on teacher salaries disaggregated by gender indicated that, with comparable backgrounds, years of experience, and school type, female teachers earned 95% of what their male counterparts were paid, not counting extra pay for after school or advising activities. In real terms, however, male elementary teacher salaries were 9.85% higher than female elementary salaries and male secondary teachers 12.97% more than female secondary teacher salaries (Chambers & Bobbitt, 1996). Hewitt (1989) reported lack of financial support and fear of losing job security as reasons women elementary teachers in Kansas gave for not pursuing administrative careers.

There are very little data on gender differences in administrative salaries. Goldberg (1991), in a survey of 588 administrative assistants in central office positions in New York, found that women reported earning half the salaries of men in similar positions. A *Scholastic Administrator* report in October 2004, which included a nationwide sample of all superintendents, found that "overall, female superintendents made slightly more than their male peers, averaging $128,349 versus $125,697 in base pay. Only the largest public school systems paid their female leaders less than their male head honchos." However, these data do not take into account school district size or urbanicity. A 2004 study of 127 superintendents on Long Island found that time in the superintendency was related to gender differences in earnings. There were no meaningful sexy differences in salary for superintendents in the first three years of the superintendency. However, males with four or more years in the superintendency earned more than females with similar experience. These differences were both statistically and practically significant (Shakeshaft, 2004).

Finally, the title that women use may affect the way they are perceived. In an experimental study, Griffith-Bullock (2005) randomly assigned 315 elementary students to one of four video presentations. Three of the four presentations were identical except for the title given to the female presenter (Ms, Mrs., Miss). The fourth video was a male who delivered the same presentation as the females. Students watched one of the four videos and then rated the presenter. Griffith-Bullock (2005) found that teachers and administrators who use "Ms" were significantly more likely to be rated as caring, friendly, honest, strong, and gentle than those educators who used the titles Miss, Mrs., or Mr. This acceptance of the gender-neutral Ms by elementary school children may signify a change in the ways women are evaluated by children. Many women in school administration still believe that using Ms is detrimental, which may help to explain why many women look forward to being able to use the gender-neutral title, Dr.

SUMMARY

Most of the barriers to women in administration that existed in the mid 1980s are still in evidence today. However, there have been gains in every category. Women no longer lack confidence, aspiration, or motivation. Family and home responsibilities are still more likely to affect the career patterns of women than of men, but women have received increased encouragement to enter administrative careers. Sex role stereotyping and overt discrimination still exist and impede women's career progress, but women are no longer underrepresented in preparation programs or in doctoral classes. Administrative preparation programs have not kept the faith with their women students or their students of color, still offering inadequate curriculum and materials. Sex discrimination is evident in hiring decisions, particularly at the superintendent level, and salaries are not yet equal. Finally, women continue to experience hostile workplaces that discourage participation and leadership

Career Paths of Women in Educational Leadership

Since the 1985 *Handbook* was published, research has continued to document women's career paths. The majority of these studies are descriptive, telling the story of women's choices as they move through administration. Some studies (Blount, 2003; 2005; Triggs, 2002) provide historical evidence of women's leadership contributions in education. Most of the studies on career paths report women's recollections of the obstacles the women face and their career decision-making process they employed. These studies tend not to be built on any theoretical foundation. Grogan's 1996 study grounded in feminist poststructuralism is an exception.

Qualitative studies of women are representative of research on career paths. The following dissertations are typical examples of case studies of women's careers. They include studies of five women administrators at a state agency (Black, 2003), ten Asian American administrators (Salleh-Barone, 2004), three Anglo high school principals (McGovern-Robinett, 2002), one Texas superintendent (McAndrew, 2002), nine women superintendents in California (Schuler, 2002), four Mexican American principals in Texas (Trujillo-Ball, 2003), six superintendents in Iowa (Montz, 2004), and four high school principals in Virginia (Robinson, 2004).

The meaning of family responsibilities and the impact on women's careers is not fully developed. Most studies that do examine the issue do so only for women. While the role of males may be changing, the impact of family responsibilities on male

education administration careers has not been documented. Nevertheless, research continues to document the tensions resulting from women being positioned in the conflicting discourses of leadership and family management.

In a comprehensive look at women's career development patterns, Schreiber (1998) contended that women's career choices must be understood in the context of current social norms and beliefs about women's capabilities and acceptable roles. Hawkins (1999) reported that for women administrators the traditional roles of mother, wife, and homemaker still weighed considerably in their everyday lives, and although many women have support, such as a partner or spouse, pursuing career goals can be very difficult in comparison with the norm established by their male counterparts.

In a study of 15 male and 15 female superintendents in California, Lutz (1990) reported anxieties of women superintendents in California. This finding was repeated by Rossman (2000) in New York. The women superintendents studied by Barbie (2004) described how their professional lives dominated their personal lives.

Family obligations often include geographic immobility due to spousal commitments (Brown & Irby, 1998; Gupton, 1998; Hill & Ragland, 1995; Irby & Brown, 1994; Walker, 1995; Watkins et al., 1993 from NCPEA 1995) which is more likely to restrict women than men.

In Grogan's (1996) study of women superintendents, women expressed fear of failing as a mother, responsibility for the maintenance of relationships, and the difficulties of coping with household labor. Unlike men who were in similar high-level central office positions, women experienced daily contradictions having to balance work and family. Ironically, some of the women in this study found themselves relying on husbands and partners to take up some of the slack in the management of the household, only to find themselves later separated or divorced.

Yet, divorce and separation are not always projected in a negative light. Smulyan's (2000) study of women principals highlighted the freedom and career changing opportunities presented to women aspiring to the principalship. Just as in Brunner (2000a) and Grogan (1996), some women gained mobility from the dissolution of a restrictive relationship, and a subsequent sense of self and confidence that propelled them to be successful in reaching career goals. Smulyan (2000) and Brunner (2000a) argued for the need of a more complex approach to understanding women's career trajectories. The interactions between gender, age, experience and context must be thoroughly analyzed, and space must be provided for the individual whose situation places her outside the stereotypical.

Descriptions of female career choices often relate to efforts to achieve a balance between work and family, career interruptions, and alternative career patterns (Amey, VanDerLinden & Brown, 2002; Hawkins, 1999; McKenney & Cejda, 2000; Schreiber, 1998). The world of work has historically been set in the traditional model, with little accommodation to the necessary combining of both work and family. For women who commonly interrupt their careers to care for young children or older parents, the challenges are getting back on track in terms of preparation, advancement, promotions, informal networking, and participation in special projects or committee work that bring career enhancing opportunities.

The eight New York superintendents studied by Guptill (2003) stressed the necessity of pre-planning to prepare for both the professional and the personal demands of the job. Other researchers have found a similar interaction between personal and professional needs (Hill & Ragland, 1995).

At the same time, there is growing evidence of women taking different career paths than typically followed by men (Amey et al., 2002; Grogan & Brunner, 2005a–c; McKenney & Cejdar, 2000; Schreiber, 1998; Young & McLeod, 2001). Women's careers are believed to be less well planned than men's, so what might be described as a career path for a man may not be as helpful to a woman who may choose to or be forced to take detours and come into the ladder of advancement from the side. Many of the studies of women describe what Mary Catherine Bateson (1990) has called "composing" a life. On their way to leadership positions, many women engage in part-time or project work. Many take staff positions as opposed to the more linear "line" positions that situate them on the ladder. Many women have no choice in the matter as contract work replaces full-time work in schools and universities all over the world (Blackmore, 1999).

The research still documents some differences in background and preparation of women and men. Warren (1990) in a study of Massachusetts administrators found that women were more likely than men to have doctorates and to be more interested in continuing professional development than their male counterparts. Women traditionally enter administration later in life and with more years of classroom experience. More recent research of a sample of all women superintendents in the U.S. (Grogan & Brunner, 2005a) found women are entering the superintendency at earlier ages than has previously been reported, indicating shorter periods of time in the principalship and in central office. Most women in their national study had gained a superintendency by the time they were 50, and 36% became superintendent before or by the time they were 45.

When career paths and family issues are researched, they are almost always based upon a heterosexual model of family. Conspicuously absent from the literature on career development of school administrators is research into gay, lesbian, and bisexual individuals' experiences. A January 2003 special issue of the *Journal of School Leadership* contained four articles (Blount, Lugg, Koschoreck, Fraynd, & Capper) that analyzed the history and experiences of gay and lesbian school administrators. These articles pointed out that given societal bias, there is understandable reluctance on the part of lesbian or gay administrators to identify themselves. Many still risk immediate termination based on the belief that lesbian, gay, and transgender administrators pose a threat to the stability of the school community if identified as homosexual. Thus, we know little about the educational leadership career aspirations or paths of identified lesbian or bisexual women or men.

Boatwright, Gilbert, Forrest, and Ketzenberger (1996) argued that the formation of a lesbian identity might disrupt the career process. They found that career development often delayed in deference to the more pressing matter of identity exploration. In addition, because many lesbians face fear of discovery, efforts to hide their identity may consume much of their time and place them outside the regular channels for advancement.

Lowell (2000), in a study of gay and lesbian educators, found that those who had broken the code of silence through disclosure perceive less heterosexist bias as a result. The presence of a supportive gay and lesbian community can help develop leadership and communication skills, give courage, and provide a network of caring individuals.

In summary, most career and family balance research is informed by a heterosexual paradigm as well as a traditional male roadmap. Within those contexts, male administrators tend to have more linear career paths than females, while women are more likely to have more education and more experience in the classroom than men.

Leadership Behavior and Gender Inclusive Leadership Theory

A number of researchers have noted that leadership theory is based primarily upon studies of males, which is not very useful for females nor for males trying to understand females. Gender-accurate leadership theory offers an understanding of leadership from all perspectives. In 1995, Brown and Irby echoed a 1984 challenge issued by Shakeshaft and Nowell (1984) and "averred that true reform in administrative preparation programs will not occur unless current theory is reevaluated and revaluated. The term 'reevaluated,' deals with the technical examination of the subject; while the term, 'revaluated,' refers to an examination of deep, personal value systems" (Brown & Irby, 1995, p. 41). They indicated that "the current theories taught in administrative preparation programs are negatively impacting the field because they (a) do not reflect currently advocated leadership practice; (b) do not address the concerns, needs, or realities of women; (c) perpetuate the barriers that women encounter; and (d) do not prepare women or men to create and work effectively in inclusive systems" (pp. 42–43). Grogan (1999) suggested that new conceptions of leadership theories are needed because current leadership theories have contributed to gender inequities. She stated, "it is reasonable to imagine that because women's lived experiences as leaders are different from men's, new theoretical understanding of a leadership that is premised on social justice might emerge" (pp. 533). McCarthy (1999) noted that educational administration programs have focused the study of leadership on traditional theories and understandings of how schools should be led and that the ways that women might lead are not included.

Young and McLeod (2001) warned, "exposing our students solely to traditional leadership literature [including leadership theories] essentially legitimizes traditionally male behavior and perspectives and delegitimizes the behavior and perspectives of women" (p. 491). Irby et al. (2002) stated, "male-based leadership theories advanced in coursework, texts, and discussion perpetuate barriers that women leaders encounter" (p. 306). Additionally, Young and McLeod found that "exposure to nontraditional leadership styles is a key element in facilitating women's paths into administration" (p. 491).

Although not always acknowledged by those doing the research, many of the early studies of leadership style compared females to males in an attempt to provide documentation that either there were no differences between the two groups or that women were better school administrators than men. This research was conducted in the larger context of few women being hired as administrators partly because women were believed to be "unfit" for administrative jobs due to their supposed inability to discipline, to work with men, to "command" respect, and to possess rational and logical approaches to leadership. In these early years, studies that did not compare women to men were deemed "inadequate." Critics argued that research on women was only valid if linked to research on men. Male behavior was the measuring stick against which all studies of women were to be compared.

As more women moved into school administration and as scholars argued that women's styles should be researched in their own right, more leadership studies that observed, interviewed, and surveyed only women administrators emerged. These studies sought to identify the ways in which women lead, as well as to describe best practice, regardless of whether or not there were differences in the ways that men administer schools. Comparison studies by gender have continued to be published, but the bulk of the studies from 1985 to 2005 are single-sex inquiries. These studies add to the literature on the many approaches to effective leadership and now provide a base for examining leadership through a number of perspectives.

Since the publication of the 1985 *Handbook*, several leadership concepts and/or leadership or organizational theories have either addressed female styles directly or have described leadership approaches that are consistent with research on women: (a) interactive leadership (Rosener, 1990), (b) caring leadership (Grogan, 1998, 2000b), (c) relational leadership (Reagan & Brooks, 1995), (d) power-shared leadership (Brunner, 1999c), (e) learning focused leadership (Beck & Murphy, 1996), (f) authentic, moral, servant, or value-added leadership (Sergiovanni, 1991, 1992, 1994), and (g) synergistic leadership (Irby et al., 2002).

Female Leadership Behaviors

The body of research that examines leadership behaviors suggests several components of female leadership, although the gender comparative studies do not support that only women employ these approaches. These components are similar to the leadership concepts theories previously mentioned.

Social justice. Interviews with four female African descent superintendents (Sanders-Lawson, 2001), a dozen administrators across the K–12 spectrum (Shapiro, 2004), six female African descent middle school principals (Smith-Campbell, 2002), and three female secondary school principals in New Zealand (Strachan, 1999) document commitment to social justice as a thread that runs across descriptions of what motivates women to enter administration and what keeps them focused. These studies describe behaviors that are compatible with moral leadership (Sergiovanni, 1999), servant leadership (Sergiovanni, 1992; Schlosberg, 2003), value added leadership (Covey, 1990; Sergiovanni, 1994), and the synergistic leadership theory (Brown & Irby, 2006; Irby et al., 2002).

Women of all ethnicities and males of color discuss their desire to "make things better," right social wrongs, and increase support for underserved groups (Alston, 2005; Dantley, 2005; Foster, 2005; Murtadha & Watts, 2005). Several studies cast women's approach as "servant leadership" (Alston, 1999; Brunner, 1999c) in which women seek to serve others by being the

facilitator of the organization, bringing groups together, motivating students and staff, and connecting with outside groups. In these studies, women *minister* to others in the spirit of the Latin roots of *administer*. For instance, the 10 African descent women superintendents in Collins' (2002) study described their jobs as "a mission." Although not specifically identified as striving for or achieving a social justice mission, responses to surveys from 58 female superintendents (Hines, 1999) categorized women administrators as transformative leaders on the Leadership Practices Inventory, and Burdick (2004) found that the 64 elementary teachers she surveyed were more likely to rate women principals, as opposed to men, as reform leaders.

Spiritual. Several studies document an additional dimension that some women add to their social justice, moral, or servant leadership approach. For instance, studies of African descent women who are principals and superintendents describe leaders who extend the ministerial aspect of their leadership and include a spiritual dimension (Bloom, 2001; Collins, 2002; Jones, 2003; Logan, 1989; Sanders-Lawson, 2001). Donaldson (2000), Stiernberg (2003), and Millar (2000) noted the spiritual dimensions of White women administrators.

Both women of color and White women administrators discuss the relationship between spirituality and the ways they model behavior and inspire others. Further, these women acknowledge the importance of their spirituality to their success and ability to push forward, often in conflicting and difficult situations.

Relational. A number of researchers document the importance of relationships for women leaders that prioritizes communication, teamwork, collaboration, and community connections. Several studies document women's propensity to listen to others whether in teamwork or one-on-one. Researchers have explored the themes of nurturing, emotional connections, and interpersonal relationships among women administrators, similar to the previously mentioned interactive, connected, and relationship concepts or theories.

Formisano (1987), Carnevale (1994), and Smith (1996) noted women's discomfort with being described as powerful or as having power in their studies of women assistant principals, principals, assistant superintendents, and superintendents. Women often describe power as something that increases as it is shared. In order for many women to be comfortable with the notion of holding power, power needs to be conceptualized as something that is shared with others and that is not power over, but rather, power with. The connection of power issues and the importance of relationships to women are crucial. Power used to help others strengthens relationships, while power used to control damages relationships (Brunner, 2000a; 2000c).

Instructional focus. Similar to learning focused leadership recommended by Beck and Murphy (1996), a number of studies noted that instruction is central to women. Women administrators are likely to introduce and support strong programs in staff development, encourage innovation, and experiment with instructional approaches. Women are likely to stress the importance of instructional competence in teachers and be attentive to task completion in terms of instructional programs. The importance of instruction overlaps with the social justice agenda of many women administrators. Both men and women superintendents believe that women are advantaged by their instructional and interpersonal strengths (Grogan & Brunner, 2005c, February).

Striving for balance. Women's leadership styles are developed within a framework of balancing personal and professional needs and responsibilities. Women administrators often report that it is difficult for them to determine the line between personal and professional.

GENDER DIFFERENCES IN LEADERSHIP

Documentation of leadership behaviors that predominate among women is not the same as saying that women lead differently than men. More than 50 studies, which compare female and male approaches to leadership, are mixed, with 100% of the qualitative studies and 14% of the quantitative studies identifying differences.

Where differences are reported, women are more likely than men to be rated by both those who work with them and by themselves as instructional, task oriented leaders. Nogay's (1995) study of teacher and superintendent evaluations of 76 high school principals (38 women and 38 men) using the Principal Instructional Management Rating Scale found that women principals were rated more highly than men principals. Spencer and Kochan's (2000) survey of 42% of male and female principals in Alabama found that women rate themselves higher in skill level and also access the importance of student, relational, and learning skills higher than do males.

In both qualitative and quantitative studies of principals and superintendents, women are identified as more relational and interpersonal, logging in more one-on-one contacts with staff (Counts, 1987; Nogay, 1995; Perry, 1992). However, men send more memos and write longer memos to staff than women (Rodgers, 1986). Genge's (2000) interviews with male and female secondary principals found that women are more likely to use humor as part of their leadership style and especially to diffuse conflict. Garfinkel (1988) reported differences in the ways in which the five women and five men superintendents he studied define loyal staff members. For women, a loyal staff member is one who is competent. For men, the most loyal staff members are the ones who agree with them publicly.

According to Gardiner et al. (2000), Gardiner and Tiggeman (1999), and Eagley and Johnson (1990), the gender context of the workplace makes a difference in leadership styles. Women are more likely to be more interpersonal than males in female dominated workplaces, but equally interpersonal in male-dominated workplaces. Women are equally task oriented in female dominated organizations, but more task oriented than men in male-dominated organizations. Among the 12 female secondary principals that Applewhite (2001) studied, leadership approaches were strategically chosen based upon the context, with women sometimes using more female-identified strategies and sometimes using more male-identified strategies. Barbie (2004) and Rottler (1996) both described a mix of traditionally male and female styles among the women superintendents they studied.

International Perspectives

There is increasing interest globally in women's educational leadership opportunities and in the conditions under which they serve in leadership positions. As in the United States, the issues for women in leadership include: the invisibility of women in positions of power in education; cultural tensions between professional careers and family obligations; and the values and priorities women in leadership positions indicate. The available literature written in or translated into English does not indicate that gender equity issues are different in other countries, though there could be much research that is not available in English.

Studies of women in educational leadership in Hong Kong, South Africa, Canada, New Zealand, Australia, the United Kingdom, Malaysia, Singapore, Thailand, Costa Rica, and Nigeria highlight the cultural interpretations of the *glass ceiling* effect (Blackmore & Sachs, 2000; Blackmore, 1999; Chisholm, 2001; Coleman, 2000; Court, 1998; Gill, 1997; Hall, 2001; Luke, 1998, 2001; McKay & Brown, 2000; Reynolds, 2002; Strachan, 1999; Twombly, 1998). Most authors caution that the western notion of a glass ceiling or set of barriers to leadership advancement cannot be assumed in all countries although similar challenges exist—women are generally underrepresented in positions of power. Despite the fact that women everywhere are investing in education more than ever before, and although equity legislation has found its way into most countries, there are no "significant breakthroughs into executive ranks . . . women in every country remain only a tiny fraction of those in senior positions" (Adler & Izraeli, 1994, p. 104).

In western countries like Australia, Canada, the United Kingdom, and New Zealand, findings are similar to those in the United States: women do not always have access to the "traditional" job preparation experiences on the way to advanced leadership positions; women work harder but their work is often less valued; women report conflicts between work and family responsibilities; women experience limited mentoring and role model experiences; lack of mobility; and hierarchical organizational structures repulse women who desire to work in more flattened, collaborative organizational structures.

In Asian countries, domestic, child care, and family responsibilities, as well as cultural beliefs about women, are powerful deterrents to success. Luke (2001) found that a lack of girls' success in schooling had a pipeline effect. She also talked of the *double-day* effect of Asian women having to take care of all the domestic duties after the workday is completed. Despite the cultural and class opportunities to employ household help, many of these women were expected to fulfill traditional mothering and partnering roles. Contrasting the somewhat negative western image of housewife, Luke (1998) pointed out that in most Asian countries, staying home with one's family and children is considered to be a luxury. In these countries only the poor and working class women must work to support their families.

Race intersects with gender in South Africa and Nigeria as many women fight the challenges of penetrating a largely male-dominated administrative force (Aladejana & Aldejana, 2005; Chisholm, 2001). The women in both studies indicated their struggle to have their authority accepted and respected once they were appointed to leadership positions. Chisholm reported that many were expected to do favors or were given extra responsibilities that would not have been asked of their male counterparts. Black and White women felt unsupported and virtually invisible as if their ideas or input simply did not matter. In Nigeria, while women leaders were viewed as managing schools better than men, teachers preferred working in schools with male leaders because men would be less likely to discipline them. In addition, the South African women, like the Asian women, reported that men take even less responsibility at home than men in the West. Nevertheless, the African women expressed a deep and passionate belief in the strength and capability of women.

A seeming anomaly to the conditions cited herein is a study of Costa Rican university women leaders by Twombly (1998). In 1993 when the study was conducted, women were widely represented in the faculty and administrative ranks. Many were department directors, four were deans (including a dean of engineering,) and three held positions in the highest university ranks. Twombly believed that the "percentage of women faculty and administrators [was] relatively higher than in countries thought to be more 'enlightened' with respect to gender equality" (p. 368, quotation marks in the original). One factor that seemed to account for this outlier is that, unlike women leaders in other countries, these women did not see themselves in comparison to male leaders. They "located themselves as a subculture of the larger machista society: and compared to women in general, they clearly viewed themselves as privileged" (p. 393). In addition, the women did not make a clear distinction between work and family life. They talked of having power in the family unit and, like the Black South African women mentioned earlier, viewed themselves as strong-willed, capable women overcoming obstacles to their success.

These international perspectives also include beliefs about what women put their leadership energies into. Like many of the studies of U.S. women leaders in this chapter, these women spoke of what they value and what they prioritize in their work. Women in many of these settings were viewed as change agents and representatives of diversity (Blackmore & Sachs, 2000; Coleman, 2000; Hall, 2001) and of preferring collaborative modes of leadership where students come first (Court, 1998; Gill, 1997). A theme of determination runs through these works. Women have fought hard to reach leadership positions, sometimes at great cost to family and self, but the rewards are in seeing what can be achieved once in the position.

Summary and Recommendations

The research that has consciously examined gender and leadership has been primarily about women and has evolved from studies that compare women and men to studies on women from their own perspectives. The bulk of the research has concentrated on barriers to women as well as descriptions of career paths. The examinations of female specific leadership styles are mixed, with qualitative studies describing a female approach and quantitative studies finding no differences between women and men. More research is conducted on women in the United States than in other countries.

The research on gender equity in educational leadership since the 1985 *Handbook* publication indicates that although some gaps have closed in the area of equity issues, there is yet work to be done in the areas of leadership practice, leadership preparation, and professional development programs, research, and policy.

RECOMMENDATIONS FOR LEADERSHIP PRACTICE

1. Women in positions of leadership need to communicate the feeling of efficacy they derive from their work. Emphasizing their joy in the work they do might motivate other women to seek positions of leadership, particularly at the level of the superintendent and counter perceptions of stress related to the superintendency that discourage those who have potential (Grogan, 2005).
2. Women serving in key leadership roles must talk about and think creatively with other women about ways to successfully balance family responsibilities and job demands (Grogan, 2005).
3. Women and men in positions of power in educational systems must deliberately mentor more women and especially more women of color.
4. Leaders need to be thoughtful about social justice and be strategic in promoting equity. Conducting equity audits is one tool for gathering evidence related to a socially just school, particularly in the area of gender.[5]
5. Leaders must acknowledge and endeavor to equalize power.
6. Preservice women teachers must be directed toward leadership and assured that administrators can focus on children and curriculum (Grogan, 2005).
7. Gender and equity must become institutionalized in schools.
8. Education leaders at all levels should ensure that all applicable equity laws are fully implemented and that they appoint and support Title IX coordinators as one of their strategies to institutionalize and monitor gender equity in their schools.
9. Professional associations should institutionalize gender and equity research efforts, awards, programs, and presentations on an ongoing basis, rather than reflect the personal preferences of ever-changing staff and elected officials.

RECOMMENDATIONS FOR LEADERSHIP PREPARATION AND PROFESSIONAL DEVELOPMENT PROGRAMS

The result of this chapter's synthesis holds a variety of implications for educational leadership preparation programs and pro-

---

[5]Equity audits are inclusive surveys used originally by Civil Rights Act Title IV-funded state equity offices and Regional Equity Assistance Centers to review districts for compliance and later for data-based decision making for planning. Many equity professionals who work with practitioners have continued to use them as needs assessments, when doing strategic planning for technical assistance and training. The Observation/Commentary/Visitation (OCV), developed by Barb Landers in the 1980s was revised and expanded by Grayson (1999) and again in GESA for Administrators (Grayson, 2004). Other equity audits exist including those created by Brown and Irby (2002) and Shakeshaft (1995).

fessional development for leaders on campuses, in districts, or on school boards

1. Preparation programs must deliberately focus on social justice, making sure equity is emphasized; these programs will produce graduates that are a new generation of leaders that are more sensitive to specifically gender equity issues, as well as equity in general. This movement should change perceptions and help future administrators learn behaviors that will advance equity.

2. Leadership preparation programs need to conduct follow-up studies of graduates and their job placement and success in leadership positions. Sharing examples of successful women leaders via newsletters or the Internet may be encouraging to those women who are considering educational administration as a career.

3. Preparation programs should take the lead in teaching how to search and hire school administrators, including the superintendent, in ways that are gender appropriate. Departments are well situated to offer such training to school boards

4. A coalition of leadership preparation organizations such as University Council for Educational Administration (UCEA), National Council of Professors of Educational Administration (NCPEA), Division A of the American Education Research Association (AERA), and American Association of School Administrators (AASA) should provide an equity curriculum clearinghouse for leadership preparation that offers materials, ideas, models, and suggestions using the Internet and other strategies.

5. Gender equity knowledge, dispositions and skills, and related research efforts should be clearly articulated and promoted in administrative preparation programs and used in accreditation visits and reviews by these agencies. Visitation teams should receive training in gender equity issues.

6. Ongoing professional development on gender and social justice must be provided to graduates of administrative programs and those already in administrative positions.

RECOMMENDATIONS FOR RESEARCH

To address the striking imbalance in the numbers of women and men in the highest position of educational leadership, as well as to continue to develop successful administrative approaches, research is needed.

1. State and federal agencies and foundations must fund more research on the topic. For example, NCES and others should collect and report information on the characteristics (sex, race, age, etc.) of education leadership/administration degree and certification enrollees and recipients.

2. In addition to major national studies, Education Administration Departments should encourage and support dissertation research on gender and social justice.

3. Studies of how women in educational leadership have engaged the legal system to counter gender discrimination in relation to hiring practices will increase the knowledge of employment policy and activism. For example, the strategy suggested for using Title IX compliance to obtain more gen-

der equitable hiring of chemistry professors to match the available supply of graduates in the "Gender Equity in Science, Engineering and Technology" chapter in this *Handbook* might serve as a overall model to increase the hiring of more women administrators, now that it is clear that the supply of qualified women is plentiful.

4. Research that examines how reorganizations at the central office and school levels related to a woman's sense of self, salaries, and compensation will focus on the gender aspects of organizational decisions.

5. Studies that examine curriculum in educational leadership programs nationally should be conducted to determine the extent of the integration of gender equity and other social justice issues.

6. Research on leaders must talk and think creatively about ways to combine administrative careers with family and personal lives.

7. Best administrative practices in advancing gender equity should be examined. Studies that document administrative behaviors and policies that promote equity will provide valuable practical examples of model administrative behavior and the effects of equitable leadership. Currently, there is very little available that provides evidence not only of administrators who engage in gender equity, but also of the benefits to their organizations.

8. Regional comparisons of school district equity audits would be beneficial. Annual equity audits by researchers that provide a way for school districts to see where they are strong and where they still need to focus attention can help to encourage schools to increase equity practices.

9. Studies of successful women and minority administrators would provide models of career choices.

10. Critical examinations of textbooks and other curriculum materials used in leadership preparation courses could provide administrator preparation programs with information on what is available, as well as what is missing related to addressing gender equitable leadership theory as well as special needs and interests of the many women students.

11. Comparable national statistics must be available to track representation by race and gender in administrative positions. Continued documentation of the distribution of senior administrative positions in relation to gender, race, ethnicity, and gender intersections in staffing positions, and examination of whether prestigious, higher paying, and influential positions are more common among one gender, race and ethnicity is vital.

12. Research related to mentoring and the intersection of race, culture, and gender is essential.

ACKNOWLEDGMENTS

Thanks to external reviewer Patricia A. Schmuck, Professor Emeritus, Lewis and Clark College, Portland, OR, and to team reviewers: C. Cryss Brunner, University of Minnesota; P. J. Ford, Catherine Hackney, Ursuline University; Jill Sperandio, Lehigh University; Kara Sweeney, Interactive, Inc.; Rachelle Wolosoff, Hofstra University.

References

Acker, S., & Armenti, C. (2004, March). Sleepless in academia. *Gender and Education, 16*(1).

Adler, N. J., & Izraeli, D. N. (1994). *Competitive frontiers: Women managers in a global economy.* Cambridge, MA: Blackwell Publishers.

Agars, M. D. (2004). Reconsidering the impact of gender stereotypes on the advancement of women in organizations. *Psychology of Women Quarterly, 28*(2), 103–112.

Aladejana, F., & Aladejana, T. I. (2005). Leadership in education: The place of Nigerian women. *International Studies in Educational Administration, 33*(2), 69–75.

Allen, K., Jacobson, S., & Lomotey, K. (1995). African American women in educational administration: The importance of mentors and sponsors. *The Journal of Negro Education, 64*(4), 409–22.

Alston, J. A. (2005, October). Tempered radicals and servant leaders: Black females persevering in the superintendency. *Educational Administration Quarterly, 41*(4), 675–688.

Alston, J. A. (1999). Climbing Hills and Mountains: Black Females Making It to the Superintendency. In C. C. Brunner (Ed.), *Sacred dreams: Women and the superintendency* (pp. 79–90). Albany: State University of New York Press.

American Association of School Administrators. (1993a). *Professional standards for the superintendency.* Arlington, VA: AASA.

American Association of School Administrators (1993b). *Women and Racial Minority Representation in School Administration. Office of Minority Affairs Reports.* Arlington, VA: AASA.

American Association of University Women. (2002). *Pathways to educational leadership: Advancing women as principals and superintendents.* Retrieved from http://www.aauw.org/7000/ef/pathways bd.html

Amey, M. J., VanDerLinden, K. E., & Brown, D. F. (2002). Career mobility and administrative issues: A twenty year comparison of the changing face of community colleges. *Community College Journal of Research and Practice, 26*(7–8), 573–589.

Anatole, M. J. (1997). *The characteristics of female secondary principals.* Doctoral dissertation. University of Southern California.

Apfelbaum, A. (1993). Norwegian and French women in high leadership positions. *Psychology of Women Quarterly, 17,* 409–429.

Applewhite, A. S. (2001). *Factors influencing Colorado female secondary principals' leadership practices.* Doctoral dissertation. Colorado State University.

Armenti, C. (2004, March). Women faculty seeking tenure and parenthood: lessons from previous generations. *Cambridge Journal of Education, 34*(1), 65–83.

Bailey, S. M. (1993). The current status of gender equity research in American schools. *Educational Psychologist, 28*(4), 321–340.

Baker, A. M. (2004). *Women education leaders: Beliefs, practices, and leadership characteristics for school improvement.* Doctoral dissertation. State University of West Georgia.

Barbie, J. A. (2004). *Narratives of women's life experiences and how it informs their practice as school district superintendents.* Doctoral dissertation. University of Denver.

Bateson, M. C. (1990). *Composing a Life.* New York: Grove Press.

Baughman, M. K. (1977). Attitudes and perceptions of a selected sample of women senior high teachers toward becoming school administrators in Detroit public schools. Doctoral dissertation, The University of Michigan, 1977. *Dissertation Abstracts International, 38,* 6420A.

Beaty, D. M. (2001). *Vital experiences of successful female high school principals: Adversities as they relate to success.* Doctoral dissertation. Texas A&M University–Commerce.

Beck, L., & Murphy, J. (1996). *The four imperatives of a successful school.* Thousand Oaks, CA: Corwin Press.

Begley, L. M. (2001). *Choices, decisions, and dilemmas of women and the superintendency: A qualitative study.* Doctoral dissertation. Hofstra University.

Bell, C. (1995). If I weren't involved in schools, I might be radical: Gender consciousness in context. In D. Dunlap & P. Schmuck (Eds.), *Women leading education* (pp. 288–312). Albany, NY: State University of New York Press.

Black, B. S. (2003). *Women who lead at a state education agency: Five lives.* Doctoral dissertation. North Carolina State University.

Black, A. E., & Rothman, S. (1998). Have you really come a long way? Women's access to power in the United States. *Gender Issues, 16,* 1–2.

Blackman, M. C., & Fenwick, L. (2000, March 29). The principalship. *Education Week on the Web.* Retrieved from http://www.edweek.org

Blackmore, J. (1999). Troubling women: Feminism, leadership and educational change: The upsides and downsides of leadership and the new managerialism. In C. Reynolds (Ed.). *Women and school leadership: International perspectives.* Albany, NY: SUNY Press.

Blackmore, J., & Sachs, J. (2000). Paradoxes of leadership and management in higher education in times of change: Some Australian reflections. *Leadership in Education, 3*(1), 1–16.

Bloom, C. M. (2001). *Critical race theory and the African-American woman principal: Alternative portrayals of effective leadership practice in urban schools.* Doctoral dissertation, Texas A&M University.

Blount, J. M. (1999). Manliness and the gendered construction of school administration in the USA. *International Journal of Leadership in Education: Theory and Practice, 2*(2), 55–68.

Blount, J. (1995). The politics of sex as a category of analysis in the history of educational administration. In B. J. Irby and G. Brown (Eds.), *Women as school executives: Voices and visions* (pp. 1–5). Huntsville, TX: Sam Houston Press.

Blount, J. M. (2003). Homosexuality and the school superintendents: A brief history. *Journal of School Leadership, 13*(1), 7–26.

Blount, J. M. (2005). *Fit to teach: Same-sex desire, gender, and school work in the Twentieth Century.* Albany, NY: SUNY Press

Boardman, M. (2001). The value of shared leadership: Tasmanian teachers and leaders differing views. *International Studies in Educational Administration, 29*(3), 2–9.

Boatwright, K. J., Gilbert, M. S., Forrest, L., & Ketzenberger, K. (1996). Impact of identity development upon career trajectory: Listening to the voices of lesbian women. *Journal of Vocational Behavior, 48,* 210–228.

Bolman, L., & Deal, T. (1991). Leadership and management effectiveness: A multi-frame, multi-sector analysis. *Human Resource Management, 30,* 509–534.

Bost, L. C. (2000). *Secrets of sisters: Understanding women administrators' existing feminist theories through personal narratives.* Doctoral dissertation, University of North Carolina–Greensboro.

Boudreau, C. A. (1994). *Professional challenges and coping strategies of women superintendents from selected school districts in Illinois.* Doctoral dissertation, Loyola University of Chicago.

Bova, B. M. (1995). Mentoring revisited: The hispanic women's experience, *The Journal of Adult Education* 236, pp. 8–18

Bova, B. M. (2000). Mentoring revisited: The Black women's experience. *Mentoring & Tutoring, 8*(1), 1–16.

Bowen, L. (1999). Beyond the degree: Men and women at the decision-making levels in British higher education, *Gender & Education, 11*(1).

Bowers, A. G. (1985). Mentoring and protégés in male-dominated corporate cultures: The experience of top-level women executives. *Dissertation Abstracts International, 45*:3103B.

Brathwaite, F. (1986). *The challenge for female educational leaders: An examination of the problem and proposed solutions through educational and social change strategies.* Synthesis paper for doctor of philosophy. Minneapolis, MN: Walden University Press. (ERIC Document Reproduction Service No. ED280129).

Brown, L. E. H. (2004). *Barriers to women in educational leadership roles in Montana.* Doctoral dissertation, Montana State University.

Brown, G., & Irby, B. J. (Eds.). (1995). *Women as school executives: Voices and Visions.* Huntsville, TX: Texas Council of Women School Executives, Sam Houston Press (ERIC Document Reproduction Service No. ED401252).

Brown, G. & Irby, B. J. (1996). Women in educational leadership: A research based model for course design. In J. Burdin (Ed.), *Prioritizing Instruction,* (pp. 131–138). Lancaster, PA: Technomic Publishing Co.

Brown, G., & Irby, B. J. (1998). Getting the first school executive position. In B. J. Irby & G. Brown (Eds.), *Women leaders: Structuring success* (pp. 98–111). Dubuque, IA: Kendall/Hunt.

Brown, G., & Irby, B. J. (2002). Women leaders: Creating inclusive school environments. In J. Koch & B. J. Irby (Eds.), *Women and education series: Defining and redefining gender equity* (Chap. 4). New York: Infoage Publishing.

Brown, G., & Irby, B. J. (2005). *Increasing gender equity in educational leadership.* Paper presented at the annual meeting of the American Educational Research Association, Montreal, Canada.

Brown, G., & Irby, B. J. (2006). Expanding the knowledge base: Socially just theory in educational leadership programs. In Fred Dembowski (Ed.), *Unbridled spirit* (pp. 7–13). Lancaster, PA: Proactive Publications.

Brown, G., Irby, B. J., & Iselt, C. C. (2001, January). Superintendency preparation programs: Gendered perspectives. *Joint Center for the Study of the Superintendency Newsletter.*

Brown, G., Irby, B. J., & Lara-Alecio, R. (2004, August). *Social justice in leadership theory: Research related to the synergistic leadership theory.* Paper presented at the National Council of Professors of Educational Administration, Branson, MO.

Brown, G., Irby, B. J., & Smith, C. (1993). Transforming the system: Women in educational leadership. In G. Brown & B. J. Irby (Eds.), *Women as school executives: A powerful paradigm* (pp. 71–74). Huntsville, TX: Sam Houston Press & Texas Council of Women School Executives.

Brown, G., & Merchant, J. (1993). Women in leadership: A support system for success. In G. Brown & B. J. Irby (Eds.), *Women as school executives: A powerful paradigm* (pp. 87–92). Huntsville, TX: Sam Houston Press & Texas Council of Women School Executives.

Brunner, C. C. (1995). By power defined: Women in the superintendency. *Educational Considerations, 22*(2), 21–27.

Brunner, C. C. (1997). Working through the 'riddle of the heart': Perspectives from women superintendents. *Journal of School Leadership, 7*(2), 138–164.

Brunner, C. C. (1998). Can power support an ethic of care? An examination of the professional practices of women superintendents. *Journal for a Just and Caring Education, 4*(2), 142–175.

Brunner, C. C. (1998). Women superintendents: Strategies for success. *The Journal of Educational Administration, 36*(2), 160–182.

Brunner, C. C. (1999a). "Back talk" from a woman superintendent: Just how useful is research? In Brunner, C. C. (Ed.), *Sacred dreams: Women and the superintendency* (pp. 179–198). New York: State University of New York Press.

Brunner, C. C. (1999b). Power, gender and superintendent selection. In C.C. Brunner (Ed.), *Sacred dreams: Women and the superintendency* (pp. 63–78). Albany, NY: State University of New York Press.

Brunner, C. C. (Ed.). (1999c). *Sacred dreams: Women and the superintendency.* New York: State University of New York Press.

Brunner, C. C. (1999d). Taking risks: A requirement of the new superintendency. *The Journal of School Leadership, 9*(4), 290–310.

Brunner, C. C. (2000a). *Principles of power: Women superintendents and the riddle of the heart.* New York: State University of New York Press.

Brunner, C. C. (2000b). Faced with a hostile press. In P. Short, P., & J. P. Scribner (Eds.), *Case studies on the superintendency* (pp. 61–80). Lancaster, PA: Technomic Publishing Co.

Brunner, C. C. (2000c). Unsettled moments in settled discourse: Women superintendents talk about inequality. *Educational Administration Quarterly, 36*(1), 76–116.

Brunner, C. C. (2002). Bane or benefit? Considering the usefulness of research focused on women superintendents. In B. Cooper & L. Fuscerilla (Eds.), *The promise and perils facing today's school superintendent* (pp. 221–246). Lanham, MA: Scarecrow Press.

Brunner, C. C. (2002). A proposition for re-conceptualizing the superintendency: Reconsidering traditional and nontraditional discourse. *Educational Administration Quarterly, 38*(3), 402–431.

Brunner, C. C. (2003). Invisible, limited, and emerging discourse: Research practices that restrict and/or increase access for women and people of color to the superintendency. *Journal of School Leadership, 13,* 428–450.

Brunner, C. C. (2004, April). *Women superintendents as gender benders: Toward a fuller understanding of power in leadership.* Paper presented at the annual meeting of the American Education Research Association, San Diego, CA.

Brunner, C. C. (2005). Women performing the superintendency: Problematizing the normative alignment of conceptions of power and constructions of gender. In J. Collard & C. Reynolds (Eds.), *Leadership, gender and culture: Male and female perspectives* (pp. 121–135). Two Penn Plaza, NY: Open University Press.

Brunner, C. C., & Duncan, P. (1998). Constructed collaborative leaders: In the company of women administrators. In G. Brown & B. J. Irby (Eds.), *Women leaders: Structuring success* (pp. 50–64). Dubuque, IA: Kendall Hunt.

Brunner, C. C., & Grogan, M. (in press). *Women leading school systems: Uncommon roads to fulfillment.* Lanham, MD: Rowman & Littlefield Education.

Brunner, C. C., Miller, M., & Hammel, K. (2004, April). *Leadership preparation, pedagogy, and technology.* Paper presented at the American Educational Research Association annual conference, San Diego, CA.

Brunner, C. C., & Peyton-Caire, L. M. (2000). Seeking representation: Supporting Black female graduate students who aspire to the superintendency. *Urban Education, 31*(5), 532–548.

Brunner, C. C., & Schumaker, P. (1998). Power and gender in "New View" public schools. *Policy Studies Journal, 26*(1), 30–45.

Burdick, D. C. (2004). *"Women hold up half the sky": Is principal selection based on gender and leadership style?* Doctoral dissertation, Arizona State University.

Burke, R. J., & McKeen, C. A. (1990). Mentoring in organizations: Implications for women. *Journal of Business Ethics, 9,* 317–332.

Bush, M. L. (2000). *An analysis of the barriers and career paths of women superintendents in the Council of Great City Schools.* Doctoral dissertation, University of Toledo.

Bynum, V. (2000). *An investigation of female leadership characteristics.* Doctoral dissertation, Capella University.

Byrd-Blake, M. (2004). *Female perspectives on career advancement.* Retrieved April 5, 2005, from http://www.advancingwomen.com/awl/spring2004/BYR

Cadenhead, J. K. (2004). *The tripartite self: Gender, identity, and power.* Doctoral dissertation, The University of Texas at Austin.

Campbell, A. M. (2003). *Through their eyes: Five Maine principals explore their learning about leadership.* Doctoral dissertation, University of Maine.

Carnevale, P. (1994). *An examination of the ways women in school administration conceptualize power.* Doctoral dissertation, Hofstra University.

Carr, C. S. (1995). How female principals communicate: Verbal and non-verbal micropolitical communication behaviors of female Anglo and Hispanic school principals. *Educational Considerations, 22*, 53–62.

Catalyst. (1999). *Catalyst study tells the stories of six women of color executives.* Retrieved March 9, 2005, from http://www.wib-i.com/org_catalyst.html

Celestin, C. A. (2003). *Role that professional positioning and professional socialization play in the career path of African-American women superintendents.* Doctoral dissertation, Western Michigan University.

Chambers, J., & Bobbitt, S. A. (1996). *The patterns of teacher compensation: National center for Educational Statistics statistical analysis report.* Retrieved March 12, 2005, from http://nces.ed.gov/pubs95/95829.pdf

Chase, S., & Bell, C. (1990). Ideology, discourse, and gender: How gatekeepers talk about women school superintendents. *Social Problems, 37*(2), 163–177.

Chen, M. (2003). *Contemporary women warriors: Ethnic, gender, and leadership development among Chinese-American females.* Doctoral dissertation, University of Washington.

Chisholm, L. (2001). Gender and leadership in South African educational administration. *Gender and Education, 13*(4), 387–399.

Christman, D. E. (2003, Winter). Women faculty in higher education: Impeded by academe. *Journal of Advancing Women.* Retrieved March 6, 2005, from www.advancingwomen.com/awl/winter2003/CHRIST~1.html

Clarke, S. J. (2003). Frances Lucas-Tauchar: A portrait of leadership (Mississippi). Doctoral dissertation, University of Nebraska–Lincoln.

Clemens, J. B. B. (1989). *The influence of mentors on career development of women in educational administration in Leon County, Florida.* Doctoral dissertation, Florida State University.

Clinch, L. W. (1996). *Women superintendents' forecast of critical leadership roles and responsibilities of the 21st century superintendent.* Doctoral dissertation, Texas A&M University.

Cline, K. R. (1996). *Pressing the ceiling: Stories of women executives in higher education.* Doctoral dissertation, Hofstra University.

Clisbee, M. A. (2004). *Leadership style: Do male and female school superintendents lead differently?* Doctoral dissertation, University of Massachusetts-Lowell.

Cobb-Clarke, D. A., & Dunlap, Y. (1999). The role of gender in job promotions. *Monthly Labor Review, 12*, 32–38.

Coleman, M. (2000). The female secondary head teacher in England and Wales: Leadership and management styles. *Journal of Educational Research, 42*(1), 13–28.

Collins, P. L. (2002). *Females of color who have served as superintendent: Their journeys to the superintendency and perceptions of the office.* Doctoral dissertation, Seton Hall University, College of Education and Human Services.

Conley, V. M. (2005, Summer). Career paths for women faculty: Evidence from NSOPF:99. *New Directions for Higher Education, 130.* Wiley Periodicals, Inc.

Cooke, L. H. (2004). *Finding the self who leads: From one woman's perspective.* Doctoral dissertation, University of North Carolina at Greensboro.

Counts, C. D. (1987). *Toward a relational managerial model for schools: A study of women and men as superintendents and principals.* Doctoral dissertation, Harvard University.

Court, M. (1998). Women challenging managerialism: Devolution dilemmas in the establishment of co-principalships in primary schools in New Zealand. *Journal of School Leadership & Management, 18*(1), 35–58.

Covey, S. (1990). *The 7 habits of highly effective people.* New York, NY: Simon & Schuster.

Crabb, S. A. (1997). *Women's perceptions of vertical career mobility in educational administrative positions in selected provinces in Canada.* Doctoral dissertation, University of Southern Mississippi.

Crane, E. (1992). *A Study of the relationship between level of education, career paths, and earnings for graduates of advanced programs in educational administration.* Doctoral dissertation, Hofstra University.

Cullen, D. L., & Luna, G. (1993). Women mentoring in academe: Addressing the gender gap in higher education. *Gender & Education, 5*(2), 125–137.

Cwick, E. D. (1999). *An investigation into the career paths and leadership experiences of three female high school principals.* Doctoral dissertation, Northern Illinois University.

Dabney, D. W. (2003). *Leadership styles of African-American female presidents at 4-year comprehensive institutions of higher education.* Doctoral dissertation, Walden University.

Dantley, M. E. (2005). African American spirituality and Cornel West's notions of prophetic pragmatism: Restructuring educational leadership in American urban schools. *Educational Administration Quarterly, 41*(4), 651–674.

Databank. (1982, March). *Education Week,* 12–13.

DeFrank-Cole, L. M. (2003). *An exploration of the differences in female and male self-perceptions of presidential leadership styles at colleges and universities in West Virginia.* Doctoral dissertation, University of Pittsburgh.

Dennis, M. R., & Kunkel, A. D. (2004). Perceptions of men, women, and CEOs: The effects of gender identity. *Social Behavior and Personality, 32*(2), 155–172.

Dias, S. L. (1975). A study of personal, perceptual, and motivational factors influential in predicting the aspiration level of women and men toward the administrative roles in education. Doctoral dissertation, Boston University, 1975. *Dissertation Abstracts International, 36,* 1202A.

Donaldson, C. A. M. (2000). *Together and alone: Women seeking the principalship.* Doctoral dissertation, University of Calgary (Canada).

Doty, K. L. (2001). *Women in public middle school administration in Georgia: A feminist analysis of the perceptions of women in power.* Doctoral dissertation, Georgia Southern University.

Douglas, D. C. (1992). Challenging the conventional assumptions about the preparation programs for aspiring superintendents. In F. C. Wendel (Ed.), *Reforming administrator preparation programs* (pp. 45–56). University Park, PA: University Council for Educational Administration.

Dreher, G. F., & Cox, T. H. (1996). Race, gender and opportunity: A study of compensation attainment and the establishment of mentoring relationships. *Journal of Applied Psychology, 81*(3), 297–308.

Dunn, R. E., & Moody, J. R. (1995). Mentoring In the Academy: A survey of existing programs. *Report–Evaluative/Feasibility, 142,* EDRS: 396 599.

Eagly, A. H., & Carli, L. L. (2003). The female leadership advantage: An evaluation of the evidence. *Leadership Quarterly, 14*(6), 807–835.

Eagly, A. H., & Carli, L. L. (2003). Finding gender advantage and disadvantage: Systematic research integration is the solution. *Leadership Quarterly, 14*(6), 851–860.

Eagly, A. H., & Johnson, B. T. (1990). Gender and Leadership Style: A Meta-analysis. *Psychological Bulletin, 106*(2), 233–256.

Ecarius, P. K. (2003). *Educational leadership in the 21st century: Female elementary principals and appreciative leadership attributes.* Doctoral dissertation, Central Michigan University.

Edson, S. K. (1988). *Pushing the limits: The Female administrative aspirant.* New York: State University of New York Press.

Edson, S. K. (1995). Ten years later: Too little, too late? In D. Dunlap & P. Schmuck (Eds.), *Women leading education* (pp. 36–48). Albany, NY: State University of New York Press.

Edwards, A. T. (1993). *The female high school principal in Fairfield County, Connecticut.* Doctoral dissertation, Columbia University, Teachers College.

Enomoto, E., Gardiner, M., & Grogan, M. (2000). Notes to Athene: Mentoring relationships for women of color. *Urban Education, 35*(5), 567–583.

Everett, L. W. (1989). *Perspectives on leadership from women in school administration.* Doctoral dissertation, University of Oklahoma.

Fairbairn, L. E. (1989). *A survey of superintendent/board of education relationships: Does sex of the superintendent make a difference?* Doctoral dissertation, Hofstra University.

Folmar, N. A. (1989). *Female applicants and the elementary school principalship: An analysis of the perceptions of selection personnel toward female applicants for the elementary principalship.* Doctoral dissertation, Texas A&M University.

Formisano J. M. (1987). *The approaches of female public school principals toward conflict management: A qualitative study.* Doctoral dissertation, Hofstra University.

Foster, L. (2005). The practice of educational leadership in African American communities of learning: Context, scope, and meaning. *Educational Administration Quarterly, 41*(4), 689–700.

Foster, W. R., Poole, J. H., & Coulson-Clark, M. M. (2001). Faculty mentoring in higher education: Hype or help. *School of Leadership Studies: Regent University.* Retrieved from http://www.regent.edu/acad/sls/publications/journals/leadershipadvance/pdf_2000-2001/foster_faculty_mentoring/pdf

Fox, M. F. (2001). Women, science, and academia: Graduate education and careers. *Gender & Society, 15*(5), 654–666.

Franklin, R. N. (2001). *North Carolina women superintendents and the boards that select them.* Doctoral dissertation, University of North Carolina-Chapel Hill.

Fraynd, D. J., & Capper C. (2003). Do You Have Any Idea Who You Just Hired?!?" A Study of Open and Closeted Sexual Minority K–12 Administrators. *Journal of School Leadership, 13*(1), 86–94.

Fries, E. (2001). *Leadership skills possessed and attitudes toward individual or group-centered leadership as perceived by Hispanic women with limited resources in the lower Rio Grande Valley of Texas.* Doctoral dissertation, Texas A&M University.

Fullerton, M. (2001). *Women's leadership in the public schools: Towards a feminist educational leadership model.* Doctoral dissertation, Washington State University.

Gardiner, M. E., Enomoto, E., & Grogan, M. (2000). *Coloring outside the lines: Mentoring women into school leadership.* New York: State University of New York Press.

Gardiner, M., & Tiggemann, M. (1999). Gender differences in leadership style, job stress and mental health in male- and female-dominated industries. *Journal of Occupational & Organizational Psychology, 72*(3), 301.

Garfinkel, E. Z. (1988). *An examination of the ways men and women in school administration conceptualize the administrative team.* Doctoral dissertation, Hofstra University.

Genge, M. C. (2000). *The development of transformational leaders: The journeys of female and male secondary school principals, alike or different?* Doctoral dissertation, University of Toronto (Canada).

Gentry, C. A. B. (1996). *Women in educational leadership: The issue of under-representation of women as secondary principals.* Doctoral dissertation, University of Mississippi.

Gieselman, S. R. (2004). *Predicting elementary school student achievement: The impact of principal gender and principal leadership skills.* Doctoral dissertation, University of Louisville.

Gill, B. A. (1997). *Becoming a leader: Strategies for women in educational administration.* Paper presented at the 25th Annual Learned Societies Conference of the Canadian Association for the Study of Women in Education, Newfoundland, Canada.

Glass, T., Bjork, L., & Brunner, C. C. (2000). *The study of the American superintendency: 2000.* Arlington, VA: American Association of School Administrators.

Goldberg, C. (1991). *A study of the career paths of administrators in central office positions in New York State public school districts.* Doctoral dissertation, Hofstra University.

Grace-Odeleye, B. E. (2003). *An examination of the role of forgiveness in the leadership practices of women leaders in higher education.* Doctoral dissertation, Regent University.

Graysan, D. A. (2004). Gene rating Expectations for Grayson, D.

Greenleaf, R. K. (1977). *Servant leadership.* New York: Paulist Press.

Gregory, C. L. (2003). *Leadership and resiliency characteristics of female community college presidents.* Doctoral dissertation, Baylor University.

Grewal, B. K. (2002). *Women superintendents in California: Characteristics, barriers, career paths and successes.* Doctoral dissertation, University of the Pacific.

Grimes, M. L. (2003). *The efficacy of using an integrated leadership model to assess the leadership styles of African-American women in the college presidency.* Doctoral dissertation, University of South Carolina.

Griffith-Bullock, B. (2005). *Early elementary students' perceptions of teachers in relation to teachers' titles of address.* Doctoral dissertation, Hofstra University.

Grogan, M. (1994, April). *Aspiring to the superintendency in the public school systems: Women's perspectives.* Paper presented at the annual meeting of the American Research Association, New Orleans, LA.

Grogan, M. (1996). *Voices of women aspiring to the superintendency.* Albany, NY: State University of New York Press.

Grogan, M. (1998). Feminist approaches to educational leadership. In B. J. Irby & G. Brown (Eds.), *Women leaders: Structuring success* (pp. 21–29). Dubuque, IA: Kendall/Hunt.

Grogan, M. (1999). Equity/equality issues of gender, race and class. *Educational Administration Quarterly, 35*(4), 518–536.

Grogan, M. (2000a). The short tenure of a woman superintendent: A clash of gender and politics. *Journal of School Leadership, 10*(2), 104–130.

Grogan, M. (2000b). Laying the Groundwork for a re-conception of the superintendency from feminist postmodern perspectives. *Education Administration Quarterly, 36*(1), 117–142.

Grogan, M. (2002). Influences of the discourse of globalisation on mentoring for gender equity and social justice in educational leadership. *Leading and Managing, 8*(2), 124–135. (Reprinted in *Leadership, gender and culture*, pp. 90–102, by J. Collard & C. Reynolds (Eds.), 2004, London: Open University Press.)

Grogan, M. (2005). Echoing their ancestors, women lead school districts in the United States. *International Studies in Educational Administration, 33*(2), 21–30.

Grogan, M., & Brunner, C. (2005a, February). Women leading systems. *The School Administrator, 62*(2), 46–50.

Grogan, M., & Brunner, C. C. (2005b, February). *What the latest facts and figures say about women in the superintendency today.* Retrieved March 12, 2005, from The American Association of School Administrator Web site: http://www.aaswherea.org/publications/sa/2005_02/grogan.htm

Grogan, M., & Brunner, C. C. (2005c). Women superintendents and role conception: (Un)troubling the norms. In L. G. Bjork & T. J. Kowalski (Eds.), *The contemporary superintendent: Preparation, practice, and development* (pp. 227–250). CA: Corwin Press.

Grogan, M., & Smith, F. (1998). A feminist perspective of women superintendents' approaches to moral dilemmas. *Just and Caring Education, 4*(2), 176–192. (Reprinted in *Values and educational leadership*, pp. 273–288, by P. Begley (Ed.), 1999, Albany, NY: SUNY Press).

Gross, N., & Trask, A. (1964). *Men and women as elementary school principals.* Cooperative research project #853. Graduate School of Education: Harvard University.

Gross, N., & Trask, A. (1976). *The sex factor and the management of schools.* NY: John Wiley.

Guptill, A. M. (2003). *Succeeding with support: Female superintendents in New York State.* Doctoral dissertation, State University of New York at Albany.

Gupton, S. L. (1998). Women as successful school superintendents. In B. J. Irby & G. Brown (Eds.), *Women leaders: Structuring success* (pp. 180–189). Dubuque, IA: Kendall/Hunt.

Hajinlian, N. J. (2000). *An examination of gender bias attitudes and behaviors of middle school educators within a suburban community.* Doctoral dissertation, Seton Hall University, College of Education and Human Services.

Hall, L. M. (2001). *A regional study of gender differential perceptions of mentoring functions in accessing the superintendency.* Doctoral dissertation, University of Southern Mississippi.

Hamilton, M. H. (2001). *The personal and professional backgrounds of Georgia's female high school principals.* Doctoral dissertation, Georgia Southern University.

Hansman, C. A. (1998). Mentoring and women's career development. *New Directions for Adults and Continuing Education, 80.* Jossey-Bass Publishers.

Harris, P. B. (1991). *Profiles in excellence—Leadership styles of female principals in high schools of excellence.* Doctoral dissertation, University of North Carolina—Greensboro.

Harris, B. J., Rhoads, T. R., Walden, S. E. Murphy, T. J., Meissler, R., & Reynolds, A. (2004). Gender equity in industrial engineering: A pilot study, *NWSA Journal, 16*(1).

Hart, A. (1995). Women Ascending to Leadership. In D. Dunlap & P. Schmuck (Eds.), *Women leading education* (pp. 36–48). Albany, NY: State University of New York Press.

Hawkins, A.D. (1999). Career Paths of Women Administrators in the California and North Carolina Community College System. Doctoral Dissertation, North Carolina State University, 1999.

Hawkins, L. G. (1991). *Barriers associated with the limited number of females in public school leadership positions in South Carolina.* Doctoral dissertation, University of South Carolina.

Haynes, K. (1989). *Women managers in human services.* New York: Springer.

Heward, C., & Taylor, P. (1995). What is behind Saturn's rings? Methodological problems in the investigation of gender and race in the academic profession. *British Educational Research Journal, 21*(2).

Hewitt, J. M. (1989). *Determinants of career choice: Women elementary teachers' perspective on the elementary principalship.* Doctoral dissertation, Kansas State University.

Higgins, C., & Kram, K. E. (2001). Re-conceptualizing mentoring at work: A developmental network perspective. *Academy of Management Review, 2,* 264–288.

Hill, M. S., & Ragland, J. C. (1995). *Women as educational leaders: Opening windows, pushing ceilings.* Thousand Oaks, CA: Corwin Press, Inc.

Hines, J. A. (1999). *A case study of women superintendents in the state of Ohio in their roles as transformational leaders in creating school district climate.* Doctoral dissertation, University of Akron.

Hinkson, A. E. (2004). *Leadership development in African-American graduates of a predominantly white women's college: A case study of Barnard College (New York).* Doctoral dissertation, University of Pennsylvania.

Hite, L. (1998). Race, gender, and mentoring Patterns. In *1998 Proceedings of the Academy of Human Resource Development Conference.* Oak Brooks, IL.

Hobson-Horton, L. D. (2000). *African-American women principals: Examples of urban educational leadership.* Doctoral dissertation, University of Wisconsin-Madison.

Holland, L. J. (2003). *Comparison by gender of school board presidents' perceptions of leadership practices relating to superintendents in selected school districts in Texas.* Doctoral dissertation, Texas A&M University-Corpus Christi.

Hopson, E. T. (1986). *An evaluation of the activities of a non-profit organization: Northwest women in educational administration.* Doctoral dissertation, University of Oregon.

Howell, R. W. (1989). *Commonalities among women superintendents in Texas.* Doctoral dissertation, University of North Texas.

Hubbard, L., & Datnow, A. (2000). A gendered look at educational reform. *Gender and Education, 12*(1), 115–129.

Hudak, J. M. (2000). *Perceptions of female school administrators of how legislative action, female leadership characteristics, and recent employment opportunities relate to obtainment of a leadership position.* Doctoral dissertation, Widener University.

Hutchinson, S. L. (2001). *A profile of women superintendents and women aspiring to the superintendency in the state of Missouri.* Doctoral dissertation, University of Missouri-Columbia.

Hyde, J. S., & Kling, K. C. (2001). Women, motivation, and achievement. *Psychology of Women Quarterly, 25,* 364–378.

Ignacio, M. (1995). *Lay women as principals of Catholic coeducational secondary schools.* Doctoral dissertation, University of San Francisco.

International Labor Organization. (2002). *World of Work Magazine.* Retrieved March 9, 2005, from http://www.ilo.org/public/english/bureau/inf/magazine/5

International Labor Organization. (2002). *International women's day 2004.* Retrieved March 9, 2005, from http://www.ilo.org/public/english/bureau/inf/magizine/5

Irby, B., & Brown, G. (1998). Exploratory study regarding the status of women's educational administrative support organizations. *Advancing Women in Leadership Journal* (Winter). Retrieved from http://www.advancing women.com/awl/winter98

Irby B. J., & Brown, G. (Eds.). (1995). *Women as school executives: Voices and visions.* Huntsville, TX: Sam Houston Press.

Irby, B. J., & Brown, G. (1994). Establishing partnerships among women executives in rural schools districts. In D. Montgomery (Ed.). *Conference proceedings of rural partnerships: Working together.* Austin, TX: The American Council on Rural Special Education.

Irby, B. J., Brown, G., Duffy, J., & Trautman, D. (2002). The synergistic leadership theory. *Journal of Educational Administration. 40*(4), 304–322.

Iselt, C. C. (1999). *Gender differences in Texas superintendents' perceptions of their superintendent preparation programs.* Doctoral dissertation, Sam Houston State University. *Dissertation Abstracts International, 60,* 4264A.

Iselt, C. C., Brown, G., & Irby, B. (2001). Gender differences in superintendents' perceptions of superintendent preparation programs. In C. C. Brunner & L. G. Bjork (Ed.), *Advances in research and theories of school management and educational policy* (Vol. 6, The new superintendency; pp. 55–75). New York: JAI Elsevier Science.

Jackson, B. L. (1999). Getting inside History–Against All Odds: African-American Women School Superintendents. In C. C. Brunner (Ed.), *Sacred Dreams: Women and the Superintendency* (pp. 144–160). Albany: State University of New York.

Jackson, J. (2002). *The absence of African American male superintendents in White suburban school districts.* Doctoral dissertation, Hofstra University.

Jenson, J., & Brushwood Rose, C. (2003). Women@Work: Listening to gendered relations of power in teachers' talk about new technologies. *Gender and Education, 15*(2), 169–181.

Johnson, C. L. C. (1995). *Career paths, barriers and strategies of female school superintendents in the Rocky Mountain region.* Doctoral dissertation, Colorado State University.

Johnson, L. M. (2003). *A study of women in leadership and the next glass ceiling.* Doctoral dissertation, University of Phoenix.

Johnson, S. M. (2003). *Missouri superintendents' perceptions of factors influencing the inequitable gender distribution of women in the high school principalship or superintendency.* Doctoral dissertation, Saint Louis University.

Jones, S. N. (2003). *The praxis of black female educational leadership from a systems thinking perspective*. Doctoral dissertation, Bowling Green State University.

Jones, B. K. (1988). *The gender difference hypothesis: A synthesis of research in the* Educational Administration Quarterly. Doctoral dissertation, Texas A&M University.

Kamler, E. (1995). *Gatekeeping: The Relationship between the search consultant, women, and the superintendency*. Doctoral dissertation, Hofstra University.

Kamler, E., & Shakeshaft, C. (1999). The role of search consultants in the career paths of women superintendents. In C. C. Brunner (Ed.), *Sacred dreams: Women and the superintendency* (pp. 51–62). Albany: State University of New York Press.

Kanter, R. M. (1977). *Men and women of the corporation*. New York: Basic Books.

Katz, S. J. (2001). *The perceptions of women superintendents regarding their leadership practices and uses of power*. Doctoral dissertation, Indiana State University.

Keller, B. (1999, November). Women superintendents: Few and far between. *Education Week, 19*(11), 1.

Kelly, J. W. (1993). *Women in academe: Historical and sociological perspectives*. Paper presented at the annual convention of the Eastern Communication Association, New Haven, CT.

Kinkade, K. (2003). *The association of self-leadership and coping style for urban, economically disadvantaged women*. Doctoral dissertation, University of Louisville.

Klein, S. (Ed.). (1985). *Handbook for achieving sex equity through education*. Baltimore: Johns Hopkins Press.

Knisely, B. (2003, February 23). *AASA study focuses on male-female disparities in superintendency*. Retrieved April 11, 2005, from American Association of School Administrators Web site: http://www.aasa.org/publications/conference/2003/sun_cryss.htm

Koschoreck, J. W. (2003). Easing the Violence: Transgressing Heteronormativity in Educational Administration. *Journal of School Leadership, 13*(1), 27–50.

Kowalski, T., & Brunner, C C. (2005). The school district superintendent. In F. English (Ed.), *The handbook of educational leadership* (pp. 142–67). Thousand Oaks, CA: Corwin Press.

Kram, K. E. (1985). Improving the mentoring process. *Training and Development Journal, 39*(4), 40–43.

Lacey, K. (2003, August). Factors that influence teachers' principal class leadership aspirations. *Post-Script, 4*(1), 22–33. Retrieved March 13, 2005, from www.edfac.unimelb.edu.au/student/insight/postscript files/vol4/vol4_1_lacey.pdf

Lambert, L., Walker, D., Zimmerman, D., Copper, J., Lambert, M., Gardner, M., & Ford Slack, P. J. (1995). *The Constructivist Leader*. New York: Teacher's College Press.

Lange, J. K. (1995). *An investigation of the dimension and extent of sexual harassment for women in administration in New York State's public schools*. Doctoral dissertation, Hofstra University.

Langford, T. (1995). The feminine agenda: Transformational and creative leadership. In B. J. Irby & G. Brown (Eds.), *Women as school executives: Voices and visions* (pp. 99–106). Huntsville, TX: Sam Houston Press.

LaPointe, B. N. (1994). *Women in public school administration: Factors that facilitate attainment*. Doctoral dissertation, Western Michigan University.

Leggett, A. R. (2002). *Emerging leadership among African-American female educators*. Doctoral dissertation, University of Oklahoma.

Lips, H. M. (2000). College students' vision of power and possibility as moderated by gender. *Psychology of Women Quarterly*, (24), 39–43.

Logan, C. B. M. (1989). *Black and white leader perception of school culture*. Doctoral dissertation, Hofstra University.

Logan, J. P. (1999, summer). *An educational leadership challenge: Refocusing gender equity strategies*. Retrieved March 12, 2005, from American Association of School Administrators Web site: http://www.aasa.org/publications/tap/2000summer/logan/htm

Lovelady-Dawson, F. (1981, September). No room at the top. *Principal, 37–40*.

Lowell, C. P. (2000). *Out of the classroom closet: A qualitative study of the social construction of professional identity among sexually marginalized educators*. Doctoral dissertation, Hofstra University.

Lugg, C. A. (2003, January). Our straight-laced administrators: The law, lesbian, gay, bisexual, and trans-gendered educational administrators and the assimilationist imperative. *Journal of School Leadership, 13*(1), 51–79.

Lugg, C. A. (2003). Sissies, faggots, lezzies, and dykes: Gender, sexual orientation, and a new politics of education? *Educational Administration Quarterly, 39*(1), 95–134.

Luke, C. (1998). "I got where I am by own strength": Women in Hong Kong higher education management. *Educational Journal (Hong Kong), 26*(1), 31–58.

Luke, C. (2001). *Globalization and women in academia: North/South/East/West*. Mahwah, NJ: Lawrence Erlbaum Associates.

Lunenburg, F. C., & Ornstein, A. C. (2004). *Educational administration: Concepts and practices* (4th ed.). Belmont, CA: Wadsworth/Thomson Learning.

Lutz, J. G. (1990). *A comparative analysis of the demographic characteristics, internal and external barriers, attitudes towards women in administration, and leadership behavior of California public school male and female superintendents hired during 1988*. Doctoral dissertation, University of San Francisco,

Lyon, C., & Saario, T. (1973). Women in public education: Sexual discrimination in promotions. *Phi Delta Kappan, 2*(55), 120–124.

Mack, N. H. (2003). *A study of the elements and events that influence leadership among women of color administrators at Oklahoma technology centers*. Doctoral dissertation, Oklahoma State University.

Madsden, K. E. (2000). *Women in the high school principalship: Leadership, gender, and mentorship*. Doctoral dissertation, University of Colorado at Denver, Graduate School of Public Affairs.

Malone, R. J. (2001, July). Principal mentoring. *Eric Digest, 149*.

Marcoux, J. S. (2002). Applying the portfolio process in principal evaluation: A case study. Doctoral dissertation, Sam Houston State University, 2002. *Dissertation Abstracts International, 63*, 2427.

Marietti, M., & Stout, R. (1994). School boards that hire female superintendents. *Urban Education, 8*(4), 373–385.

Marshall, C. (1981). Organizational policy and women's socialization in administration. *Urban Education, 16*(2), 205–231.

Matthews, E. N. (1986). *Women in educational administration: Support systems, career patterns, and job competencies*. Doctoral dissertation, University of Oregon.

McAndrew, S. B. (2002). *A woman's way of leading: The story of a successful female school superintendent*. Doctoral dissertation, University of Texas at Austin.

McCall, A. (1995). The bureaucratic restraints to caring in school. In D. Dunlap & P. Schmuck (Eds.), *Women leading education* (pp. 180–194). Albany, NY: State University of New York Press.

McCarthy, M. M. (1999). The evolution of educational leadership preparation programs. In J. Murphy & K. S. Louis (Eds.), *Handbook of research on educational administration* (2nd ed.; pp. 119–139). San Francisco, CA: Jossey-Bass.

McConnell, D. F. (2002). *Women's perceptions of themselves as leaders: A relationship study of undergraduate upper-class women in a women's college and a co-educational college*. Doctoral dissertation, George Mason University.

McDonald, V. S. (1997). *Six high school principals and their superintendents: A case study of the hiring of females as high school principals in Western Pennsylvania*. Doctoral dissertation, University of Pittsburgh.

McGovern-Robinett, D. E. (2002). *The other leadership: The nature of the leadership experiences of Anglo female high school principals in a male-defined arena.* Doctoral dissertation, The University of Texas at Austin.

McGuire, G. M. (2002). Gender, race, and the shadow structure a study of informal networks and inequality in a work organization. *Gender & Society, 16*(3), 303–322.

McKay, J., & Grady, M. (1994). Turnover at the top: Why the superintendency is becoming a revolving door. *Executive Educator, 16*, 37–38.

McKay, M., & Brown, M. (2000). The under-representation of women in senior management in UK independent secondary school. *The International Journal of Educational Management, 14*(3), 101–106.

McKenney, C. B., & Cejda, B. D. (2000). Profiling chief academic officers in public, community colleges. *Community College J. of Research and Practice. 24*(9), 745–758.

Mendez-Morse, S. E. (1999). Redefinition of self: Mexican-American women becoming superintendents. In C. C. Brunner (Ed.), *Sacred dreams: Women and the superintendency* (pp. 125–140). Albany: State University of New York.

Mendez-Morse, S. E. (2004). Constructing mentors: Latina educational leaders: Role models and mentors. *Education Administration Quarterly, 4*(40), 561–590.

Millar, V. J. (2000). The organizational entry and socialization of women in educational leadership positions: A case study. Doctoral dissertation, Eastern Michigan University.

Montenegro, X. (1993). Women and racial minority Representation in School Administration. Arlington, VA: AASA.

Montgomery, J. M. (1995). The impact of mentoring on leadership among young African American females, a dissertation submitted to the faculty at Western Michigan University, Ann Arbor, MI: UBI Dissertation Services.

Montz, C. B. (2004). *A case study of female superintendents from one mid-western state: Characteristics, skills, and barriers for female candidates aspiring to the superintendency.* Doctoral dissertation, University of Iowa.

Monument Information Resource. (2006). College Textbook National Market Report, Education Administration Introductory.

Morgan, C. (2001). The effects of negative managerial feedback on student motivation: Implications for gender differences in teacher/student relations. Statistical data included. *Sex Roles: A Journal of Research, 5*(1)

Morgen, S. (1994). Personalizing personnel decisions in feminist organizational theory and practice, *Human Relations, 47*(6), 665–684.

Mosley-Anderson, J. M. (2001). *Their perceptions of how others perceive them. Black women administrators internalize others' perceptions of them as leaders.* Doctoral dissertation, Miami University.

Muna, J. D. (1996). *Leadership style profiles of women and men in Utah superintendencies.* Doctoral dissertation, Brigham Young University.

Murphy, J., & Hallinger, P. (Eds.). (1987). *Approaches to administrative training in education.* Albany, NY: State University of New York Press.

Murphy, J., & Vriesenga, M. (2004) *Research on preparation programs in educational administration: An analysis. UCEA Monograph Series.* Columbia, MO: University Council for Educational Administration.

Murry, W. D. (2001). Supervisory support, social exchange relationships, and sexual harassment consequences: A test of competing models, *Leadership Quarterly, 12*(1), 1–29.

Murtadha, K., & Watts, D. M. (2005). Linking the struggle for education and social justice: Historical perspectives of African American leadership in schools. *Educational Administration Quarterly, 41*(4), 591–608.

Musick, C. F. (1995). *Analysis of the barriers affecting selected women school administrators in Ohio for successful school administration careers.* Doctoral dissertation, Ohio University.

National Center for Education Statistics (NCES). (June 2004). *The condition of education: Contexts of elementary and secondary education.* Washington, DC: U.S. Department of Education.

National Center for Education Statistics (NCES). (2004). *The digest of education statistics, 2004. Chapter 2: Elementary and secondary education.* Retrieved on March 6, 2005, from NCES Web site http://nces.ed.gov/programs/digest/d03/ch_2.asp

National Center for Education Statistics (NCES). (2002). Digest of education statistics: Chapter 3—Post-secondary education. *U.S. Department of Education.* Retrieved October 11, 2003, from http://nces.ed.gov/pubs2003/digest02/ch_3.asp

National Organization for Women. (2005). *Talking about affirmative action.* Retrieved February 26, 2005, from http://www.now.org/issues/affirm/talking.html

National Policy Board for Educational Administration. (1989). *Improving the preparation of school administrators: An agenda for reform.* Charlottesville, VA: Author.

Newberg, C. A. (1998). *A study of maverick teachers in educational organizations.* Doctoral dissertation, Hofstra University.

Nilsen, A. R. (2004). *The tenacious women of La Verne: A case study of factors that enabled resilient doctoral students from non-traditional backgrounds to overcome adversity and meet their goals.* Doctoral dissertation, University of La Verne, CA.

Noddings, N. (1984). *A feminist perspective.* Berkeley, CA: University of California Press.

Noe, R. A. (1988). Women and mentoring: A review and research agenda. *Academy of Management Review, 13*, 65–78.

Nogay, K. H. (1995). *The relationship of the superordinate and subordinate gender to the perceptions of leadership behaviors of female secondary principals.* Doctoral dissertation, Youngstown State University.

Nogay, K. H., & Beebe, R. J. (1997). Gender and perceptions: Females as secondary principals. *Journal of School Leadership, 7*, 246–65.

Obeng-Darko, E. (2003). *Navigating the four dimensional space of higher education: Storied narratives of women full professors as scholars and leaders in educational administration.* Doctoral dissertation, University of Cincinnati.

Obermeyer, L. E. (1996). *Profiles of women superintendents and women aspiring to the superintendency in California and barriers encountered during their careers.* Doctoral dissertation, University of La Verne, CA.

O'Donnell, E. (2001). *Women in the superintendency: A research synthesis and biographical case study (Ella Flagg Young, Mildred E. Doyle, Tennessee; Annie Webb Blanton, Texas; Julia Richman, New York City; Helen Ira Jarrell, Georgia).* Doctoral dissertation, State University of New York at Binghamton.

Olzendam, A. M. (1999). *Four women superintendents: The story of their success.* Doctoral dissertation, Gonzaga University.

Ortiz, F. I. (1981). *Career patterns in education: Men, women and minorities in public school administration.* New York: Praeger.

Ortiz, F. I. (1999). Seeking and selecting Hispanic female superintendents. In *Sacred Dreams: Women and the Superintendency* (pp. 91–102). Albany: State University of New York.

Panico, S. H. (2003). *Women who supervise women: The experience of women leaders in higher education.* Doctoral dissertation, Colorado State University.

Pankake, A., Schroth, G., & Funk, C. (Eds.). (2000). *Women as school executives: The complete picture.* Austin, TX: The Texas Council of Women Executives.

Papalewis, R. (1994). *Women in educational leadership: A review of mainstream literature.* Paper presented at annual conference of the American Educational Research Association Special Interest Group on Research on Women and Education, St. Paul, MN.

Partenheimer, P. R. (2002). *Assistant principal recruitment: The effects of job attributes, job assignment, gender, and administrator program status.* Doctoral dissertation, University of Louisville.

Patton, L. D., & Harper, S. R. (2003). Mentoring relationships among African-American women in graduate and professional schools. *New Directions for Student Services, 104*, 67–78.

Perna, L. W. (2001). Sex and Race Differences in Faculty Tenure and Promotion. *Research in Higher Education, 42*(5), 541–567.

Perry, A. B. (1992). *A comparison of the ways that women and men principals supervise teachers.* Doctoral dissertation, Hofstra University

Perz, S. M. (2002). *Contributions of women's embodied knowing to education for leadership and peacemaking.* Doctoral dissertation, School of Theology at Claremont.

Poll, C. (1978). *No room at the top: A study of the social processes that contribute to the underrepresentation of women on the administrative levels of the New York City school system.* Doctoral dissertation, City University of New York, 1978. *Dissertation Abstracts International, 39,* 3165A.

Pollard, D. S. (Fall 1993). Gender, achievement, and African-American students' perceptions of their school experience. *Educational Psychologist, 28*(4), 341–357, 2 charts (AN 9409010053).

Pounder, D. G. (1987, October 30–November 1). *Placement of women and minority graduates in educational administration.* Paper presented at the annual meeting of the University Council for Educational Administration, Charlottesville, VA.

Prescott-Hutchins, S. R. (2002). *The challenges and successes of African-American women principals in Georgia: A qualitative profile of lived experiences.* Doctoral dissertation, Georgia Southern University.

Quilantan, M. C. (2002). *Mexican American women: Unique superintendents in Texas.* Doctoral dissertation, University of Texas-Pan American.

Ragins, B. R. (1997). Diversified mentoring relationships in organizations: A power perspective. *Academy of Management Review, 22,* 482–521.

Ragins, B. R. (1989). Barriers to mentoring: The female manager's dilemma. *Human Relations, 42,* 1–22.

Ramey, F. H. (1993). Mentoring: Its Role in the Advancement of Women Administrators in Higher Education. *Black Issues in Higher Education, 10*(17), 116.

Randall, P. (1993). *Weaving A Tapestry: Stories Women Tell.* Doctoral dissertation, Hofstra University.

Randell, S. (1994, December). *Not Advancing Equally: Women in Educational Management in Australia.* Paper presented at the Annual Council of Europe International Conference on equal Advances in Educational Management, Vienna, Austria.

Reese, M. (1993). Rethinking the paradigm: The potential effect on women administrators. In G. Brown & B. J. Irby (Eds.), *Women as school executives: A powerful paradigm* (pp. 29–33). Huntsville, TX: Sam Houston Press.

Regan, B. J. (2001). *Professional socialization of women of color into the role of school district superintendent: Intrinsic indicators of independent success.* Doctoral dissertation, Northern Illinois University.

Regan, H. (1990). Not for women only: School administration as a feminist activity. *Teachers College Record, 91*(4), 565–577.

Regan, H., & Brooks, G. (1995). *Out of women's experiences: Creating relational leadership.* Thousand Oaks, CA: Corwin Press.

Remondini, B. J. (2001). *Leadership style and school climate: A comparison between Hispanic and non-Hispanic women principals in southern New Mexico.* Doctoral dissertation, New Mexico State University.

Reynolds, C. (2002). Changing gender scripts and moral dilemmas for women and men in education, 1940–1970. In C. Reynolds (Ed.), *Women and school leadership: International perspectives* (pp. 29–48). Albany, NY: SUNY Press.

Rhodes, P. W. (2001). *Women in the high school principalship: A multicase study.* Doctoral dissertation, University of Nebraska-Lincoln.

Ries, K. A. (2003). *A history of teachers as leaders in a suburban school district, 1955–1990.* Doctoral dissertation, University of St. Thomas, MN.

Ritter, B. A., & Yoder, J. D. (2004). Gender differences in leader emergence persist even for dominant women: An updated confirmation of role congruity theory. *Psychology of Women Quarterly, 28*(3), 187–194.

Robinson, C. C. (2004). *Women in high school principalships: A comparison of four case studies from a Virginia public school district from 1970–2000.* Doctoral dissertation, Virginia Polytechnic Institute and State University.

Robinson, R. W. J. (1991). *Through their eyes: Reflections of Pennsylvania female school administrators regarding career paths, mentoring and external barriers.* Doctoral dissertation, Temple University.

Robinson-Hornbuckle, M. L. (1991). *Female administrators in rural schools: Who are they? What are their leadership styles?* Doctoral dissertation, University of Oklahoma.

Rogers, E. J. (1986). *An examination of the written communications of male and female elementary school principals.* Doctoral dissertation, Hofstra University.

Rooney, P., Hussar, W., Planty, M., Choy, S., Hampden-Thompson, G. Provasnik, S., & Fox, M.A (June 2006). *The Condition of Education 2006.* U.S. Department of Education, National Center for Education Statistics. Washington, D.C.: U.S. Government Printing Office.

Rosener, J. (1990). Ways women lead. *Harvard Business Review, 68*(4), 28–49.

Rossman, E. (2000). *A study of barriers affecting women in educational administration.* Doctoral dissertation, Dowling College.

Rottler, J. M. (1996). *The women superintendents of Iowa: A 1990's analysis.* Doctoral dissertation, University of Northern Iowa.

Saffer, S. (1983). *A synthesis of dissertation research on stress in educational administration.* Doctoral dissertation, Hofstra University.

Salleh-Barone, N. (2004). *Asian American women educators: Narrations of their career paths to leadership.* Doctoral dissertation, State University of New York-Buffalo.

Sanders-Lawson, E. R. (2001). *Black women school superintendents leading for social justice.* Doctoral dissertation, Michigan State University.

Sandler, B. R. (1993). *Women as mentors: Myths and commandments.* Retrieved March 9, 2005, from http://www.bernicesandler.com/id30_m.htm

Savage, H. E., Karp, R. S., & Logue, R. (2004). Faculty mentorship at colleges and universities. *College Teaching, 52*(4). Retrieved March 18, 2005, from http://steenproxy.sfasu.edu:2091/itw/informark/81/270/64

Scherr, M. W. (1995). The glass ceiling reconsidered: Views from below. In P. M. Dunlap & P. A. Schmuck (Eds.), *Women leading education* (pp. 313–323). Albany, NY: State University of New York Press.

Schlosberg, T. V. (2003). Synergistic leadership: An international case study: The transportability of the synergistic leadership theory to selected educational leaders in Mexico. Doctoral dissertation, Sam Houston State University, 2003. *Dissertation Abstracts International, 64, 07A.*

Schmitt, D. M. (1995, October). *Women in leadership: Enacting a new curriculum in educational administration.* Paper presented at the annual conference on Gender Issues in Higher Education, Burlington, VT.

Schmuck, P. A. H. (1976). Sex differentiation in public school administration. Doctoral dissertation, University of Oregon, 1975. *Dissertation Abstracts International, 36,* 5719A.

Schmuck, P. A. (1987). Introduction. In P. A. Schmuck (Ed.), *Woman educators* (pp. 1–8). Albany, NY: State University of New York Press.

Schmuck, P. A. (1995). Advocacy organizations for women school administrators 1977–1993. In D. M. Dunlap & P. A. Schmuck (Eds.), *Women leading in education* (pp. 199–224). Albany, NY: State University of New York Press.

Schmuck, P. A., & Schubert, J. (1995). Women principals' views on sex equity: Exploring issues of integration and information. In

D. M. Dunlop & P. A. Schmuck (Eds.), *Women leading education* (pp. 274–287). Albany, NY: State University of New York Press.

Schreiber, P. J. (Winter,1998). Women's Career Development Patterns. *New Directions for Adult and Continuing Education, 80,* 5–13.

Scholastic Administrator (2004, October/November). *Race Debate: Q&A with Elaine Farris superintendent of Shelby County (KY) public schools.* Retrieved April 7, 2005, from *Scholastic Administrator* Web site: http://www.scholastic.com/administrator/octnov04/articles.asp?article=newsmaker

Schuler, M. A. B. (2002). *Women and the superintendency: The stealth career paradox.* Doctoral dissertation, Harvard University.

Scott, E. S. (2000). *The leadership stories of two women public school administrators.* Doctoral dissertation, University of Nebraska-Lincoln.

Scott, J. (1999). *Constructing, negotiating, and surviving gender in the public school superintendency: A study of exemplary women superintendents.* Doctoral dissertation, University of Texas at Austin.

Seelinger, K. L. (2000). *"I'm right there": Central Appalachian women in public schools leadership.* Doctoral dissertation, West Virginia University.

Senge, P. (1990). *The fifth discipline.* New York, NY: Doubleday/Currency.

Sergiovanni, T. J. (1991, March). Constructing and changing theories of practice: The key to preparing school administrators. *The Urban Review, 23*(1), 39–49.

Sergiovanni, T. J. (1992). *Moral leadership: Getting to the heart of school reform.* San Francisco, CA: Jossey-Bass.

Sergiovanni, T. J. (1994). *Building community in schools.* San Francisco, CA: Jossey-Bass.

Sergiovanni, T .J. (1999). Rethinking Leadership: A collection of articles. Arlington Heights, IL: SkyLight Training and Pub.

Shakeshaft, C. (1985a). The new scholarship on women in education. *Handbook for Achieving Sex Equity Through Education.* Baltimore. MD: John Hopkins Press.

Shakeshaft, C. (Committee) (1985b). Guidelines for eliminating race and sex bias in educational research. *Educational Researcher,* July 1985.

Shakeshaft, C., & Biklen, S. (1985c). Strategies for overcoming barriers to women administrators. *Handbook for Achieving Sex Equity through Education.* Baltimore: Johns Hopkins Press.

Shakeshaft, C. (1989). *Women in educational administration.* Newbury Park, CA: Corwin Press.

Shakeshaft, C. (1995). *School District Gender Audit.* Huntington, New York: Interactive, Inc.

Shakeshaft, C. (1999). The struggle to create a more gender-inclusive profession. *Handbook of Research on Educational Administration* (2nd ed.). San Francisco: Jossey-Bass.

Shakeshaft, C. (2004). Superintendents on Long Island. http://people.hofstra.edu/faculty/charol_s_shakeshaft/

Shakeshaft, C., & Nowell, I. (1984). Research on theories, concepts, and models of organizational behavior: The influence of gender. *Issues in Education, 2*(3), 186–200.

Shapiro, L. (2004). *Disrupting what is going on: Women educational leaders make art together to transform themselves and their schools.* Doctoral dissertation, Union Institute and University.

Shepard, I. S. (1998). Perception is reality: Perceptions of employment characteristics of women in administration. *Advancing Women in Leadership* (Summer). http://www.advancingwomen.com/awl/summer98/Shep.html.

Shepard, I. S. (2000). Barriers to women entering administration: Do they still exist? Is there the will to overcome? In C. Funk, A. Pankake, & G. Scroth (Eds.), *Women as school executives: The compete picture.* Commerce, TX: Texas A&M University-Commerce Press.

Sherman, W. H. (2002). *Women's experiences with a formal leadership program for aspiring administrators.* Doctoral dissertation, University of Virginia.

Shockley, L.S., & McKerrow, K. (2005, Fall). Advancing social justice: Women's work. *Advancing Women in Leadership, 19.* Retrieved March 25, 2006, from http://www.advancingwomen.com/awl/awl.html

Shuell, T. (1993). Toward an integrated theory of teaching and learning. *Educational Psychologist, 28*(4), 291–312.

Siebler, K. A. (2002). *Teacherly acts of transgression: How feminist educators are changing composition.* Doctoral dissertation, Miami University.

Simms, M. L. (2002). *Native American women's views of school leadership.* Doctoral dissertation, University of Wisconsin-Madison.

Simmons, J. C., Grogan, M., & Brunner, C. C. (2004, April 15). *Superintendents of color: Perspectives on racial and ethnic diversity and implications for professional preparation and practice.* Paper presented at the American Educational Research Association, San Diego, CA.

Skrla, L. (1999, April). *Femininity/masculinity: Hegemonic normalizations in the public school superintendency.* Paper presented at the annual conference of the American Educational Research Association, Montreal, Canada.

Skrla, L. (2000). Mourning silence: Women superintendents (and a researcher) rethink speaking up and speaking out. *International Journal of Qualitative Studies in Education, 13*(6), 611–628.

Skrla, L., Reyes, P., & Scheurich, J. J. (2000). Sexism, silence, and solutions: Women superintendents speak up and speak out. *Educational Administration Quarterly, 36*(1), 44–75.

Slamet, D. (2003, Spring). Women eligible for principal positions are often dealing with the demands of ageing parents and their own children and partner: Access to opportunities. *Australian Educator, 39,* 23–24. Retrieved February 27, 2005, from www.aeufederal.org.au/Publications/AE/GendAg/html

Slick, G. A., & Gupton, S. L. (1993). Voices of experience: Best advice to prospective and practicing women administrators from education's top female executives. In G. Brown & B. J. Irby (Eds.), *Women as school executives: A powerful paradigm* (pp. 75–85). Huntsville, TX: Sam Houston Press & Texas Council of Women School Executives.

Smith, K. (2003). *Ascension to the presidency: A descriptive study of female presidents in the North Carolina community college system.* Doctoral dissertation, North Carolina State University.

Smith, S. J. (1996). *Women administrators: Concepts of leadership, power and ethics.* Doctoral dissertation, University of Wyoming.

Smith-Campbell, S. I. (2002). *Exploring the world of Black women middle school principals.* Doctoral dissertation, Michigan State University.

Smulyan, L. (2000). *Balancing acts: Women principals at work.* Albany, NY: State University of New York Press.

Sorokosh, A. (2004). *Program factors that affect doctoral student retention and attrition: The development and initial validation of a program assessment instrument.* Doctoral dissertation, Hofstra University.

Spencer, W. A., & Kochan, F. K. (2000, January 24). Gender related differences in career patterns of principals in Alabama: A statewide study. *Education Policy Analysis Archives, 8*(9), ISSN 1068-2341.

Steele, J., James, J. B., & Barnett, R. C. (2002). Learning in a man's world: Examining the perceptions of undergraduate women in male-dominated academic areas. *Psychology of Women Quarterly, 26*(1), 46–51.

Stiernberg, P. W. (2003). *The relationship between spirituality and leadership practices of female administrators in K–12 schools.* Doctoral dissertation, Baylor University.

Strachan, J. (1999). Feminist educational leadership: Locating the concepts in practice. *Gender & Education, 11*(3), 309–323.

Student Achievement: An Equitable Approach to Educational Excellence for Administrators. Tehachapi, CA. Gray, M.

Strauss, S. (1993). Teachers' pedagogical content knowledge about children's minds and learning: Implications for teacher education. *Educational Psychologist, 28*(3), 279–291.

Strizek, G. A., Pittsonberger, J. L., Riordan, K. E., Lyter, D. M., & Orlofsky, G. F. (2006). *Characteristics of schools, districts, teachers, principals, and school libraries in the United States: 2003–2004. Schools and education staffing survey* (NCES 2006-313 Revised. U.S. Department of Education, National Center for Education Statistics. Washington, DC: U.S. Government Printing Office.

Swain, M. R. (2003). *Building a template of electoral strategies for women who aspire to the superintendency in appointed school districts within the southern United States.* Doctoral dissertation, Florida Atlantic University.

Tallerico, M. (1999). Women and the superintendency: What do we really know? In C. C. Brunner (Ed.), *Sacred Dreams: Women and the superintendency* (pp. 29–48). Albany, NY: State University of New York Press.

Taylor, A. (1995). Glass ceilings and stone walls: Employment equity for women in Ontario school boards, *Gender & Education, 7*(2), 123–143.

Theoharis, G. T. (2004). *Toward a theory of social justice educational leadership.* Paper presented at the annual meeting of the University Council of Educational Administration, Kansas City, MO.

Tobin, D. M. (2003). *The meaning of leadership for mid-level women administrators in higher education.* Doctoral dissertation, Pennsylvania State University,

Tong, R. (1989). *Feminist Thought.* San Francisco, CA: Westview Press.

Tonnsen, S., & Pigford, A. (1998). Balance between the professional and personal life. In B. J. Irby & G. Brown (Eds.), *Women leaders: Structuring success* (pp. 124–133). Dubuque, IA: Kendall-Hunt.

Triggs, S. A. (2002). *Our silent mentors: Kansas female county superintendents, 1872–1912.* Doctoral dissertation, Kansas State University.

Trujillo-Ball, L. A. (2003). *Mexican American female principals and their chameleon identity: Working against a socially constructed identity in a predominantly white school district.* Doctoral dissertation, University of Texas at Austin.

Twombly, S. (1998). Women academic leaders in a Latin American university: Reconciling the paradoxes of professional lives. *Higher Education, 35,* 367–397.

Tyack, D., & Hansot, E. (1982). *Managers of virtue: public school leadership in America.* NY: Basic Books.

U.S. Department of Education. National Center for Education Statistics (NCES). Schools and Staffing Survey, 1999–2000. *Public School Teacher Questionnaire* and *Public Charter School Teacher Questionnaire.*

U.S. Department of Education. (2005). National Center for Education Statistics (NCES). *Digest of Education Statistics, 2005.*

Valdez, S. M. (2003). *Looking forward, looking back, looking inward: Lessons from vital women leaders in old age.* Doctoral dissertation, University of San Diego.

Vandiver, J. L. (2002). *An investigation into understanding how work requirements of principals affect their quality of life: A case study of five women principals in the Piedmont of North Carolina.* Doctoral dissertation, University of North Carolina at Greensboro.

Vecchio, R. P. (2003). In search of gender advantage, *Leadership Quarterly, 14*(6), 835–851.

Walder, B. (2000). *Career perspectives of female superintendents in the state of Arizona.* Doctoral dissertation, Northern Arizona University.

Walker, B. J. (2003). *Building self-esteem through mentoring among African-American women for future leadership success.* Doctoral dissertation, University of Phoenix.

Walker, D. (1995). Patterns in women's emerging leadership. *Educational Consideration,*

Walker, K. (October 1995). *Ethical grounds for superintendents' decision making.* Paper presented at the annual meeting of the University Council for Educational Administration, Salt Lake City, Utah.

Warren, P. B. (1990). *Massachusetts female public school administrators and their professional development.* Doctoral dissertation, Boston University.

Washington, Y. O. C. (2002). Women in school leadership: A study of female superintendents in Kentucky. Doctoral dissertation, University of Louisville.

Watkins, P. M., Herrin, M., & McDonald, L. R. (1993). The juxtaposition of career and family: A dilemma for professional women. In G. Brown & B. J. Irby (Eds.), *Women as school executives: A powerful paradigm* (pp. 21–25). Huntsville, TX: Sam Houston Press.

Webster, J. R. (1985). *Case studies of women superintendents, assistant superintendents, secondary principals, and secondary assistant principals in the sate of Maine.* Doctoral dissertation, Peabody College for Teachers, Vanderbilt University.

Wesson, L. H., & Grady, M. (1995). A leadership perspective from women superintendents. In B. J. Irby & G. Brown (Eds.), *Women as school executives: Voices and visions* (pp. 35–41). Huntsville, TX: Sam Houston Press.

Wolverton, M., & MacDonald, R. T. (2004, January). Women in the superintendency: Opting in or opting out? *Journal of Women in Educational Leadership, 2*(1), 3–11.

Wood, K. B. (2004). *The effects of patriarchy on three women leaders in Catholic schools: A case study.* Doctoral dissertation, Georgia State University.

Wyatt, L. D. (1996). *A comparison of the leadership characteristics of practicing male and female public school administrators.* Doctoral dissertation, University of Nebraska.

Wynn, S. R. (2003). *Leadership-skilled women teachers who choose the classroom over administration: A case of career choice or career constraint?* Doctoral dissertation, University of North Carolina at Chapel Hill.

Young, M. D., & McLeod, S. (2001, October). Flukes, opportunities, and planned interventions: Factors affecting women's decisions to become school administrators. *Educational Administration Quarterly, 37*(4). 462–502.

Zekster, J. L. (1996). *Identification of the critical skills, attitudes, and experiences which would increase the probability of women being hired as a middle school principal.* Doctoral dissertation, University of La Verne, CA.

If not already indicated please note that references not cited in the text are in a table of studies on the Handbook web page—www.feminist.org/education.

·7·

THE TREATMENT OF GENDER EQUITY
IN TEACHER EDUCATION

David Sadker,* **Karen Zittleman,*** *Penelope Earley,*
Theresa McCormick, Candace Strawn, and Jo Anne Preston

INTRODUCTION

Every day new and experienced teachers face a myriad of gender-related decisions, decisions they are typically ill-prepared to make. Although gender bias characterizes classroom interactions, persists in the curriculum, is reflected in status, staffing patterns and wages, and influences how and what students learn, today's teachers are taught little if anything about these issues. If gender bias and discrimination are to be confronted and resolved, then teacher education programs are the logical place to begin. Unfortunately, current teacher education programs are unlikely to prepare teachers to "see" these problems, much less resolve them. In too many cases, today's teachers continue to reinforce gender biases.

More than three decades ago, the gender issue was new in our professional consciousness. *Sexism in School and Society* (1973) by Frazier and Sadker, documented how sexism impacted students and teachers, but teacher educators were slow to respond. McCune and Matthews (1975) surveyed teacher education programs and discovered that most preservice teacher education faculties were unaware of sex equity concerns. In the 1,200 teacher education programs that they surveyed, only 104 even offered a course related to women's issues. There were approximately 43 times more women's studies courses offered in nonteacher education departments, and Florence Howe (1979) concluded that schools of education "were among the most resistant to the impact of the women's movement." Lather (1981) found limited political awareness and aspirations in teacher education students and placed the responsibility for alerting future teachers to these issues "squarely on the shoulders of teacher education faculty" (p. 3).

In the earlier edition of this *Handbook,* Sadker and Sadker (1985) characterized gender equity efforts in teacher education as minimal and fragmented. They went on to report that "through omission and stereotyping these programs may be reinforcing or even creating biased teacher attitudes and behaviors" (p. 145). Although today's teacher education landscape is dramatically different from the one described more than two decades ago, in many ways, today's landscape is alarmingly similar. We now can analyze and evaluate a wealth of studies documenting gender bias at all levels of education. We have rich resources of programs, curricular material and training that neutralize gender bias and expand opportunities for both girls and boys. And certainly, the awareness of gender as an issue has grown among both faculty and students. Yet, teacher education continues to give gender issues short shrift, and many teacher education programs ignore both gender-related research and materials. Although gender-related topics are somewhat more likely to be mentioned in today's teacher education programs than they were in 1985, they likely will only be mentioned, and not always favorably. Equitable teaching behaviors are seldom promoted in student teaching or methods classes, and in some cases, conventional gender stereotypes emerge in teacher education curricular materials. The political backlash against gender equity, as well as the re-emergence of concern about boys' performance and behavior in school, has slowed if not stopped the drive to include gender equity preparation in schools of education.

In this chapter, the authors will explore the persistent institutional bias that relegates teacher education generally, and gender issues in particular, to a second class status in higher education. We will explore the gendered nature of teaching and salary scales, topics that were not included in the 1985 *Handbook*. We will provide an update of the textbook analysis that

---

*The bold face names are the Lead Authors.

was addressed in 1985, and then go on to discuss how gender priorities rise and fall in professional associations, another issue new to this edition. And finally, the chapter explores the political ramifications of the backlash against gender equity, and offers recommendations for more optimistic path to the future.

THE GENDERED PROFESSION

While the university offers a home to teacher education, teacher education is typically an ill-treated stepchild. Inadequate funding and low status characterize the teacher education enterprise in colleges and universities, as it is more often tolerated than nourished (Apple, 1990; McCormick, 1994). The historical, social, cultural, political, economic, and institutional contexts of higher education nurture academic hubris and sexism. "The entrenched sexism and classism of university culture may well account for part of the devaluation of teacher education and the generally low status of the profession" (Britzman, 1991, p. 40).

Britzman (1991) described three influential dynamics: (a) Academic, theoretical knowledge that is valued as more important than the practical domain: "From the perspective of the larger university, the work of the teacher is viewed as technical rather than intellectual." (b) . . . schools of education are not thought of as capable of producing scientific knowledge unencumbered by values and beliefs. (Britzman, 1991, p. 39) This notion belies the dominant idealized convention in universities where knowledge is valued when it is "unencumbered by interests and investments (Britzman, 1991, p. 39)." (c) In the reward system of the university, teaching is secondary to academic research. This dualism between academic knowledge and pedagogy . . . "works to dismiss the efforts of those learning to teach" (Britzman, 1991, p. 40). What results from this kind of thinking? Maher and Ward (2002) state one result is that "Education courses are looked down on by other faculty, students, and departments, and degrees in education are seen as second-class degrees" (p. 112). In fact, politicians supported by many in the general public, have limited the number of hours that can be taken in education, emphasizing content knowledge over teaching insights and skills.

Of course, the not-so-subtle irony is that those who denigrate teaching are in fact teachers themselves. University faculty members teach without training, so why would they value the training they themselves never had nor apparently needed? The truth, of course, is somewhat different: many knowledgeable, gifted academics are ineffective teachers, a fact both accepted and ignored by most faculties.

The gendered devaluation of teaching became part of the unspoken culture of higher education, a phenomenon that some have referred to as *gender blindness* (Bailey, Scantlebury, & Letts, 1997). Gender blindness describes the often unrecognized impact of gender. For example, the domination of women in the teaching profession, and their greater presence on teacher education faculties, contribute to the historic and continuing devaluation of the teaching profession. Research by Maher and Ward (2002) indicates that around 80% of elementary teachers are women; more than 50% of secondary teachers are women, yet a far smaller percentage are administrators, and fewer than 20% are superintendents. Sadker and Sadker (2005) place the history of

the low status of teachers within the context of the cultural, social, and economic milieu of the 19th century. During the early 19th century, a common attitude was that teachers were odd or weird men who could not hold a regular job, or were women who had nothing else to do. Men continued to dominate the teaching profession until the middle of the 19th century. "Teaching was a gendered career, and it was gendered 'male.' Although a few women taught at home in *dame schools,* the first women to become teachers in regular school settings and earning a public salary, were viewed as gender trespassers . . . and considered masculine" (Sadker & Sadker, 2005, pp. 293–294). More insight into how teaching came to be gendered female is provided by Webb, Metha, and Jordan (2000), including the story of Catherine Beecher (1800–1878) who saw her task as focusing the attention of the nation on the need for a corps of female teachers to staff the common schools, and her work on behalf of women pointed to a new American consensus concerning female roles.

A 19th century ideology of rigid male and female sex roles in the traditional family became the model for teaching and later, similarly influenced teacher education programs. Smith and Vaughn (2000) say, "Although women took over the nation's classrooms, males were increasingly in charge of the ever bureaucratized schools, seen as too complex to be run by a woman whose mission was to tend the nation's youth" (p. 8). When feminization of teaching became institutionalized with lower salaries for female teachers than males (even though they did basically the same work), the status of the teaching profession plummeted. This background of gender inequality in schools forecasted a gendered model that would be reproduced in teacher education, influencing its low status in the hierarchy of universities.

The historically low pay for teachers is one way the gendered model affected teacher education in universities. Even today when education policy makers are stressing the importance of funding high-quality teacher education, educators of teachers continue to receive salaries inferior to their university colleagues. The National Center for Educational Statistics reports that in 2003 education faculty members in 4-year, degree-granting institutions earn on average $12,500 less a year than the average wage for all faculty members. Despite public concern about increasing the quality of teacher education, the salary difference had increased by $2,500 over the preceding 5 years. In 2003, faculty teaching education students earned even less when compared to faculty in other professional programs. Teachers of students pursuing professional degrees in engineering and business receive more than $20,000 more in annual pay than teacher educators. Other sources of income, such as consulting, only widen the wage gap between educators of teachers and other faculty (United States Department of Education, National Center for Educational Statistics, 1999 & 2004b; Preston, 2003). Whatever significance educational policy makers now give to the strengthening of teacher preparation, it has not translated into higher wages for faculty teaching future teachers.

The gender-role stereotypes that function in schools (males are strong and make the best leaders (i.e., administrators; females are caregivers, nurturers, and make natural teachers) are the same ones that function in universities. Given the institutionalized traditional sex roles and gender inequality embedded in schools (Montecinos & Nielsen, 2004), there is a seamless fit between that culture and the culture of teacher education programs. Therefore, when teacher education programs joined the academy, it was natural to take on the existing notions of hegemonic masculinity (Montecinos & Nielsen, 2004) in order to be included in the *sacred grove* (see Aisenberg & Harrington, 1988).

Academia historically was designed and administered by and for White men of privilege. The criteria for success in an academic career, its time line, as well as the social structure and norms were engineered by males who had wives (Aisenberg & Harrington, 1988; Caplan, 1995; Cooper & Stevens, 2002). The overwhelming maleness of the academy is documented and analyzed by numerous scholars from Hall and Sandler (1984) in their report of the chilly climate for women in academia to Cooper and Stevens (2002) in their exploration of the pitfalls of tenure for women and individuals from diverse ethnic and racial backgrounds in the sacred grove of academia.

These notions of hegemonic masculinity not only affected salaries of teacher educators compared to those received by faculty in other disciplines, but also the salaries between women and men teacher educators. While full-time male education faculty in 4-year, degree-granting institutions earned $65,517 in 2003, full-time women teacher educators only earned $52,265. The gender gap in salaries in teacher education is very similar to that of the faculty as a whole. While women faculty teaching education students earn only 80% of what men teaching education students earn, for the faculty as a whole, women earn 78%. Women faculty in programs that train students for predominantly male fields do somewhat better. In 2003, for example, women faculty in engineering programs earned 85% of what men faculty earned.[1]

As noted earlier, gender bias in faculty salaries could have grown from the practice of paying women teachers less than men teachers in public schools. At the turn of the 20th century, the practice of offering women lower wages became institutionalized by gender-based salary regulations known as *double salary scales*. The word *double* was well-chosen. For job categories in which both women and men teachers were hired, school officials created a second category, gender, in which women were assigned the lower salaries. The most frequent use of the double salary scale was in high school teaching. Because women then comprised almost all teachers in elementary schools, towns tended to focus their efforts to differentially reward men on high school teaching, to which men were already attracted. At first most prevalent in New England, where the feminization of teaching (i.e., treating teaching as a female vocation meriting lower pay and status) was most advanced, double salary scales rapidly became adopted in other parts of the country (Preston, 2004). Newly instituted discriminatory wage scales encountered stiff opposition. Arguments for the double salary scales were firmly rejected by teachers' organizations, who opposed them at every level. In the 1930s, the National Education Association (NEA) and the state teachers' organizations lobbied for "equal pay for equal work." In its 1932 platform, the NEA placed a resolution declaring that teachers of equivalent training and experience doing the same kind of work should receive equal pay regardless of sex. Citing budgetary problems, school

administrators (especially school superintendents), became the strongest opponents to the NEA proposal. Despite such formidable opposition, states began to pass legislation forbidding the practice of assigning pay by gender. By 1937, 10 states had outlawed formal gender discrimination in the form of separate wage schedules (Chamberlain & Meece, 1937).

The movement to abolish the double salary scales inspired a parallel effort to eliminate institutionalized wage differences between elementary school teachers (who were almost all women) and high school teachers (who were about 50% men). The movement crystallized in the Single Salary Campaign led by the National League of Teachers' Associations. It defined the single salary as "one salary for all teachers of equal professional training and experience irrespective of the grade in which the service is rendered." Aimed at elevating the position of the predominantly female job of elementary school teacher, proponents of the system argued that "Elementary teachers provide the foundation for all higher education." By 1924, 152 cities (most west of the Mississippi), reported that they had adopted single salary scales (National League of Teachers Associations, 1925).

The effort to eliminate the double salary scale took decades, but the effects linger on. Today, women teachers continue to earn less then male teachers. According to NEA (one of the few organizations to collect teacher wage data by gender), from 1977 to 2001 the wage gap hovered around 10%, virtually unaffected by equal pay legislation (NEA, August, 2003). With gender-neutral salary schedules that give school committees little discretion in assigning wages, one wonders how women could earn less than men. The NEA, postulating that gender differences in teachers with advanced degrees might account for a part of this wage gap, reports that larger percentages of men teachers than women teachers held advanced degrees for all years of its 1961–2001 survey, yet in those same years women increasingly earned advanced degrees at the same rate as men and the wage differential stayed the same. In other words, the salary gap did not narrow with the decrease in the degree gap. A study by Lee and Smith (1990) suggests that gender bias might cause small differences in starting pay, which become magnified over time with pay raises given as percent increases of beginning salaries. This hidden yet persistent gender gap in salaries deserves closer scrutiny, more comprehensive data gathering, more objective and uniform collection efforts, and more affirmative action to remediate gaps based on subtle gender bias.

Other evidence suggests that gender discrimination in extra compensation pay for teachers may contribute to a gender gap in annual income. Those additional duties that school administrators assign to men, such as coaching athletic teams, pay more than those assigned to women who may direct the drama club (NEA, 2003). The wage data compiled by the NEA did not include these additional earnings, so the wage gap could be significantly greater.

The lingering salary differences at the elementary and secondary levels are mirrored in higher education, where many argue that a less-rigid salary scale has created even greater gender disparities. On a broader scale, the second class status of

---

[1]The wage data was calculated from raw data collected by the *2004 National Study of Postsecondary Faculty* with the assistance of Dr. Linda Zimber, National Center of Educational Statistics.

women in society has impacted teaching itself. According to Britzman (1991), "Historically, elite participation has meant the participation of upper- and middle-class white males who were educated to manage the society they studied. Juxtaposed to this is the fact that teachers work in mass institutions, and that for women, education constitutes a 'universal job ghetto'" (p. 40). Since the time that teaching became known as *women's work* (also referred to as *the feminization of teaching*), the status of the field dropped as did the status of teacher preparation programs in universities originally intended for White males:

Many people believe without even realizing that they hold this belief [teaching is a women's profession, like nursing and . . ., mothering], that teaching is easy and comes naturally to women because of their inborn capacities for caretaking and nurturance. Therefore, the training that they need is minimal. . . . Indeed, the only real kind of training teachers *need* is in their subject matter (the rest is innate). So college professors, who are of course teachers as well (and are mostly male) are respected for what they know, not for how well they convey. (Maher & Ward, 2002, pp. 111–112)

Teacher education programs adhered to the cultural hegemony (Beyer, 2001) embedded in universities, including a clearly proscribed and defined knowledge. This cultural hegemony means that the benchmarks for success and achievement, as well as important social values and perspectives, are those of White, heterosexual upper- or middle-class males (Giroux & McLaren, 1986). This hegemony influences ". . . ways in which the 'hidden' curriculum embodies some groups' interests rather than others" (Weis, 1986, p. 45). She writes, "The largely white male faculty . . ., encourages students to think that college knowledge, especially of the most prestigious sort, is possessed most 'naturally' by white men" (p. 45). The work by Cooper and Stevens (2002) reveals that "Despite efforts to increase the visibility of women scholars in academe . . ., women make up only 31% of full-time faculty in American higher education today, an increase of only 5% in the past 75 years . . ." (p. 6)

The histories of schooling and teacher education have tended to stress a functionalist orientation, to be highly prescriptive and regulated, and grounded in a technological mindset. All of these attributes help maintain the *status quo* and limit cross-fertilization with other fields and perspectives (e.g., women's studies, multicultural studies, and feminist pedagogy), which have the potential to enable schooling and teacher education to see and grow beyond the current restrictions of gender and color blindness.

In conforming to the university culture, teacher education ignores its own history. The contributions and experiences of women are to a great extent part of the null curriculum in teacher preparation. It is ironic that although teacher education programs are strongly affected by gender issues and taught to a majority female student body, females remain all but invisible in the curriculum. Teacher education programs typically offer very little information to their own students about the role of gender in education (Pryor & Mader, 1998). A study of the histories of 29 U.S. teacher education programs revealed almost no reference to women faculty or students (Goodlad, Soder, & Sirotnik, 1990). The history of women in shaping teaching practices, in creating more humane classrooms, despite their economic exploitation, are topics rarely discussed. Even the civil

rights struggle girls and women fought to be educated in the early seminaries and normal schools is often omitted Eisenmann (1991) says, ". . . the history of normal schools, when it was written at all, barely acknowledged that women were the largest group of students . . . most . . . histories simply ignored the fact and the impact of their female students . . . the history of teacher training has consistently ignored issues surrounding women's choices and experiences as students and professors" (p. 216). By ignoring the historic discrimination and exploitation of females in school and university teaching, such programs not only dishonor those who preceded us in the profession, but contribute to the continuation of gender blindness, and continuing exploitation. Such gender blindness and curricular omissions feed into the low status of teacher education in the academia, and beyond.

TEACHER EDUCATION CURRICULUM

Several studies confirm that teacher education practices and curriculum offer shallow, superficial, and even inaccurate treatment of the role of gender in teaching and learning. In 1994, Cynthia Mader surveyed 30 administrators and 247 faculty members in 30 Michigan preservice teacher education programs regarding gender equity. Although many agreed with the importance of the topic, only 11% self-reported extensive coverage of the topic, and 38% reported minimal coverage. Campbell and Sanders (1997) surveyed 353 math, science, and technology methods instructors nationwide and while three fourths reported that they considered gender equity an important topic, most taught the topic in less than 2 hours. Few reported spending time exploring positive responses to the issue, such as gender equitable teaching strategies. Pryor and Mader (1998) surveyed preservice students and their faculty and concluded that once again, faculty members viewed gender equity as important, but did not teach much about it. Students reported that if they learned about gender issues at all, it would most likely be in a teacher education course. Yet, this rarely happened.

Textbooks have the potential to help future teachers decrease gender bias in teacher attitudes and behaviors, or, through omission and stereotyping, they can reinforce or create biased attitudes and behaviors. Their content is critical. What do teacher education texts tell future teachers about gender?

The question is not new. It is the same question that Myra and David Sadker (1980) asked more than 2 decades ago when they analyzed 24 leading teacher education texts to assess their treatment of women, sex differences, and gender-related issues. Their study found that teacher education texts were as likely to promote sex bias as to reduce or eliminate it: less than 1% of content was devoted to the contributions and experiences of women, and discussions of Title IX and gender were rare. Jordan Titus (1993) also studied gender issues in eight introductory/foundation teacher education texts. Titus concluded that the treatment of gender issues in the most widely used foundation textbooks "was still cursory or nonexistent" in the early 1990s (p. 39).

Zittleman and Sadker (2002) completed the most recent content analysis of 23 leading teacher education texts to determine what they had to say about gender and education. All texts were published between 1998 and 2001, and included five areas: introductory/foundations in education, and the methods texts in reading, social studies, science and math. The line-by-line analysis (co-rater reliability was at 90% or higher) evaluated the inclusion and treatment of gender issues ranging from the experiences and contributions of women (even mentioning a woman's name) to exploring strategies to eliminate sex-role stereotyping.

Despite decades of research documenting gender bias in education, and the creation of resources to respond to such bias, Zittleman and Sadker found that these 23 teacher education texts devoted only about 3% of their space to gender. Although these textbooks were less offensive than those published 10 and 20 years earlier, they were far from equitable (see Figure 7.1). These texts often ignored or minimized the contributions and experiences of women, omitted critical gender topics, and lacked curricular and teaching strategies needed to respond to gender issues in the classroom. For example, reading these texts, teachers rarely, if ever, learned that boys faced special problems in reading, or that girls encountered similar challenges in physics and technology.

Foundations of education. Introductory texts chronicle key events and figures in education. In 1980, Sadker and Sadker found that gender-related content in foundations books ranged from a high of 3% to a low of 0.3% of coverage. More than twenty years later, Zittleman and Sadker (2002) discovered some improvement compared to such earlier studies. In the seven introductory/foundation books they analyzed, gender issues (including even the mention of a female name) comprised 7.4% of content. Unfortunately, this coverage too often continues to provide limited, fragmented, and even inaccurate information on gender in education. For example, *Becoming a Teacher* (Parkay & Stanford, 2001) included a chapter entitled "Ideas and Events that Shaped Education in the United States." While the chapter noted female educators Emma Willard, Margarethe Schurz, Elizabeth Palmer Peabody, Susan Blow, Ella Flagg Young, Catherine Goggin, Margaret Haley, and Jane Addams, it managed to discuss the work of all these women in only three sentences. Such cursory treatment was in stark contrast to the rest of this chapter, where 26 pages were required to detail the

contributions of male educators. The philosophy chapter of *Foundations of Education: The Challenge of Professional Practice* (McNergney & Herbert, 2001) opened with a photograph of Maria Montessori, suggesting the ideas of both genders would be presented. In fact, she was the only woman mentioned as a prominent, pioneering philosopher. The chapter discussed 37 males. Furthermore, Montessori was not included in the main text, but relegated to two lines in a box titled "Benchmarks: Developments in Western Intellect Thought and Their Influences on American Education" (p. 161).

These introductory texts often included interesting boxed-off inserts that reflect gender dimensions of schooling. For example, *Introduction to the Foundations of American Education* (Johnson, Dupuis, Musial, Hall, & Gollnick, 1999) included a Professional Dilemma insert "What If There Are Only a Few Girls in the Calculus Class?" (p. 88). Readers are encouraged to confront their assumptions regarding the math and science abilities of females and males. In *Teaching in America* (Morrison, 2000), one such special feature profiles "Emma Hart Willard's Plan for the Education of Women" and her pioneering vision to establish the Troy School (p. 381). These inserts provide valuable information, but they do so at a cost, since they separate gender issues from the main text. Such isolation teaches the subtle lesson that these topics are outside the mainstream, and of less importance.

Unfortunately, Title IX coverage in teacher education texts was typically quite superficial, stressing the sports implications at the expense of other provisions. In fact, the law protects students and faculty, both female and male, from sex discrimination in health benefits, counseling, admission, employment rights, scholarships, and a host of educational activities, although future teachers reading these texts would likely conclude that the law concerns only athletics.

Are attempts to level the educational playing field for girls harmful to boys? Is education a *zero sum game* where helping one group must come at the expense of another? This polarizing political ideology—known as the *backlash*—blames the academic problems of boys on efforts to ensure equal educational opportunities for girls. Remarkably, several recent teacher education textbooks now include backlash arguments that challenge Title IX and gender equity efforts, suggesting that equal educational opportunities for females comes at the expense of males, and that feminists are conducting a "war against boys" in America's schools (Sommers, 2000).

Missing methods: Strategies and skills for promoting equity. Teacher education programs include courses on teaching strategies and methods. These courses typically comprise practical skills of the craft, ranging from effective questioning techniques to classroom management, from offering constructive feedback to key components in writing a lesson plan. These skills are taught within a general methods course (e.g., Generic Methods of Teaching) as well as in specific subject matter methods courses (e.g., Teaching Secondary Mathematics). One of the major organizing mechanisms of classroom dynamics is gender—both the gender of the teacher, the students, and the "gender" of the formal and informal curriculum. Many students report that they prefer active participation to passive listening (Good & Brophy, 2000). Such direct, precise, and frequent

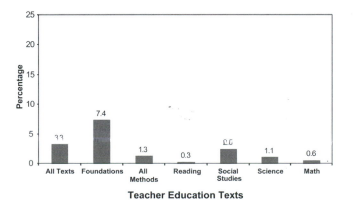

FIGURE 7.1 Coverage of gender as percentage of text content.

teacher attention is positively associated with student achievement (Johnson & Johnson, 1999; Sadker & Sadker, 1995). As a result, many teacher education programs consider the active and reflective engagement of teachers with students to be a critical goal in a teacher's education.

However, research findings also suggest that active engagement is not distributed to all students equitably. Instead, behavioral and demographic factors often guide where the teacher invests her or his resources. One of these factors influencing classroom dynamics is gender. Teachers give boys, especially more active boys, more questions, more higher-order, as well as lower-order questions (Jones & Gerig, 1994; Montague & Rinaldi, 2001; Sadker & Sadker, 1995). They direct more precise and helpful feedback to boys, including praise, criticism, and remediation. Although teachers are involved in as many as a thousand interactions with students a day, teachers are generally unaware of this gender dynamic, a situation that has been documented for decades (Jackson, 1968).

While teacher education programs frequently ignore such gender differences, there are constructive (and reflective) strategies available to remedy this situation and promote more equitable and thoughtful classroom dialogue. For example, organizing students into smaller groups encourages student participation. In one such approach, cooperative learning, active student collaboration is encouraged and students work together on tasks. For students from African American or Native American background, for many females, and even for shy males, this may be a more attractive and productive learning environment than large group instruction directed by the teacher. But even smaller student grouping is not problem-free, and inequities emerge. For instance, in cooperative learning groups, girls tend to assist both other girls and boys, while boys are more likely to help only other boys. In addition, boys often dominate the group, while girls are more reticent. These challenges suggest the need for active teacher involvement in managing small group learning, and a purposeful teacher education effort to promote such behaviors (Sadker & Sadker, 2005). It may be helpful to consider these differences not as indications of gender-different learning styles, but as socially constructed gender behaviors, predictable roles socially endorsed for girls, boys, and teachers.

The current use of wait time is another dynamic that detracts from equitable instruction. Research suggests that White male students, particularly high achievers, are more likely to be given adequate wait time—quiet time to respond to questions and to critically think about their answers—than are females and students of color (Rowe, 1986). Not only do teachers give different amounts of wait time to different students, they also give themselves inadequate time to consider student answers. Teachers who wait 3 to 5 seconds before calling on a student— known as wait time 1—can thoughtfully choose which students to call on, sending high-expectation messages that all students are expected to participate and that all students will receive enough time to develop thoughtful answers. Wait time 2 follows a student's answer, and is also only about one second long. If teachers extend this to 3–5 seconds, then students are likely to receive more careful and thoughtful responses. In fact, one benefit of extended wait times is an increase in the quality of student participation, even from students who were less

likely to participate, a group that includes females (Altermatt, Jovanovic, & Perry, 1998; Sadker & Sadker, 1995).

Current methods textbooks are also unlikely to prepare teachers for the gender issues involved in these and other instructional skills. The 16 methods texts analyzed by Zittleman and Sadker (2002) devoted just 1.3% of their content to gender issues. One math and two reading texts offer no gender coverage at all.

Although gender has been a central reading issue for both girls and boys, the four reading texts analyzed devote only 0.3% of content space to gender, the lowest percentage of any category in the study. For decades, males have consistently lagged behind females in reading and writing performance. Some have argued that reading is seen in society as feminine, or put another way, as "anti-boy" (Flesch, 1955; Gates, 1961; U.S. Department of Education, 2004a). Why do boys perform poorly in reading? What can teachers do to close this gender gap? These texts do not raise much less answer, these questions. (See the "Communication Skills" chapter)

While significant research exists concerning gender bias in basal readers and children's literature, you would not learn it from these reading methods texts. In current basal readers, male characters outnumber females two to one (Witt, 1996), and Caldecott books tell more male-centered stories (61%) than female (39%), (Davis & McDaniel, 1999). Although female characters do appear in newer roles such as doctors, lawyers, and scientists, stereotypes persist. Females are often the passive observers, watching their active brothers at work and at play, and focused on domestic life (Davis & McDaniel, 1999; Witt, 1996). Boys remain in the traditional role as well, unlikely to nurture or stray from typical male careers (Evans & Davies, 2000). Not one reading methods text analyzed offers a strategy for confronting such stereotypes.

The six social studies texts provide more space on the topic of gender than any other methods area (2.5% of their content space). Yet, serious problems persist, for future teachers are given few solid strategies to "rediscover" women in history. For example, in *Elementary and Middle School Social Studies: An Interdisciplinary Instruction Approach* (Farris, 2001), 10 group-project ideas are suggested for a unit on the Civil War. Only one includes females, and linguistic bias and stereotypes compromise even that suggestion: "Have a Civil War re-enactor come to class in uniform and discuss the segment of the Civil War with which *he* (italics added) is most familiar. Women often followed the troops" (p. 337). In this excerpt, *he* sends the message that the period was about men, while confirming a second class role for women, an afterthought even in the choice of actors. This era in American history involved serious social and economic reforms, with important female voices on and beyond the battlefield. However, these voices are silenced, with the result that both boys and girls will likely lower their opinions about the contributions of women in America's story. Such one-gendered accounts help explain why high school students have no problem naming important men in American history, but find it difficult to name even five important women. (Sadker & Sadker, 1995, p. 71).

Back in 1978, Mary Budd Rowe's *Teaching Science as Continuous Inquiry* discussed how being female was "A Special Handicap" in science. The text informed readers that girls "know less, do less, explore less, and are prone to be more superstitious than boys" (p. 68). Today, Zittleman and Sadker (2002) found that science and math methods texts avoid such overt and harmful stereotypes, yet give minimal coverage to gender issues (1.1% in science, and 0.6% in math). None of the science texts mention female scientists. Only one math text includes a female pioneer, whose contributions are given passing mention: "*Incidentally*, (italics added) the first woman mathematician we hear of in ancient time is Hypatia (ca. 410), who wrote commentaries on the work of Diophantus" (Posamentier & Stepelman, 1999, p. 201). This one-line acknowledgement is prefaced by a detailed analysis of the work of 17 male mathematicians.

In the math methods texts, word problems provide both positive and negative gender messages. For example, this problem depicts females as both physically active and using technology:

Sarah and Janice rode their bicycles to school one morning, and when they saw each other at the bicycle rack, they both checked their bike computers to see what their average speeds were. Sarah's computer said she averaged 12.6 miles per hour. Janice's said she averaged 20.5 kilometers per hour. If a kilometer equals about .6 miles, who rode faster? (Riedesel & Schwartz, 1999, p. 81)

But another text reinforces gender role stereotypes:

Linda has $4\frac{2}{3}$ yards of material. She is making baby clothes for the bazaar. Each dress pattern requires $1\frac{1}{6}$ yards of material. How many dresses will she be able to make from the material she has? (Van De Walle, 2001, p. 238)

John is building a patio. Each section requires $\frac{2}{3}$ of a cubic yard of concrete. The concrete truck holds $2\frac{1}{4}$ cubic yards of concrete. If there is not enough for a full section at the end, John can put in a divider and make a partial section. How many sections can John make with the concrete in the truck? (Van De Walle, 2001, p. 239)

Teacher education textbooks connect students to their future lives as classroom teachers, but in terms of gender equity, it is a fragile connection indeed. If future teachers are to end gender bias in schools, they will need to understand how sexism operates and how it harms all children. Every day they will confront bias in classroom interactions, harassment in the hallways, stereotypes in the curriculum, imbalance in school staffing, and a whole host of educational and political challenges. Current college textbooks are unlikely to prepare teachers to respond to these challenges.

HOW POLICY INFLUENCES GENDER ISSUES IN TEACHER EDUCATION ASSOCIATIONS

Professional societies and organizations serve a variety of purposes. Some set and enforce professional standards; most offer programs such as workshops or training sessions, and publish journals, monographs, or books; and a number attempt to influence professional or public policy agendas. All of these are deliberate acts and serve a public purpose for the organization's membership. That is, an organization through a governing body and/or central office staff will allocate funds and other resources—such as staff time—to specific activities and then makes their decision to do so known to members of the organization, interested publics,

and in certain cases to decision makers. This generally is a very transparent process. However, organizations also have private behaviors that are less transparent. By private behaviors we suggest that while an organization may appear to support a particular agenda—for example, gender equity—in practice, attention to that agenda may be minimal. Given this tension between public and private organizational behavior, we suggest that professional organizations can play a different and potentially more powerful role. That purpose is to be a catalyst for the creation of networks of people who share common characteristics, roles, or belief systems. This is a coincidental purpose that exists independently of an organization's agenda and programs. Tarule, Applegate, Earley, and Blackwell (2006) describe this phenomenon as nonproximate networks, meaning that the members of the networks do not need to live or work together, but meet and renew support systems through the opportunity to attend conferences sponsored by the professional organizations to which they belong. Ultimately the power of the network becomes greater than the organization's agenda, and attending a professional meeting is primarily a mechanism for gatherings of network members.

Even though teaching is often described as a pink collar profession because most PK-12 educators are women, as noted elsewhere in this chapter faculty in education schools and colleges are predominately male. Moreover, when looking at senior tenured faculty in all fields, men are represented in much greater numbers than women and typically at a higher salary (Wilson, 2004). One might surmise from this that in professional organizations that have as their members teacher education administrators, faculty, and education researchers, programs and activities designed to address inequities or negative climates on some campuses for women would be prominent and ongoing. After all, these issues impact the clientele these organizations serve and the ultimate quality of the teachers being trained. We selected three influential, prominent, and well-known professional teacher education organizations to study in terms of gender issues. All three involve teacher educators, education researchers, and teacher education administrators, and each exists to promote teacher education quality or research on education issues. (We note that technically AERA is not a teacher education association, however its largest division, Division K, is Teaching and Teacher Education and it is the primary membership organization for those who study teacher education.) But on closer look, the history of gender issues in these organizations raises some disturbing questions.

NCATE.   The National Council for the Accreditation of Teacher Education (NCATE) is a national, voluntary, organization that sets standards for teacher education programs and operates a system to evaluate institutions' compliance with them. In 2006, professional education units in over 600 colleges and universities held NCATE accreditation (NCATE, 2006). NCATE also offers training sessions for individuals who serve on teams that visit campuses as part of the accreditation process. Gender equity falls under the broad standard of attention to diversity. References appear in NCATE Standard 3, Element 3, which addresses teacher candidates' ability to teach all children and to have field experiences with diverse children; and Standard 4, which evaluates how diversity is integrated into the curriculum and clinical experiences, candidate diversity, faculty diversity, and teaching candidates' ability to work in diverse settings. Standard 4, in particular, is commonly viewed as the number of people in different categories (race, ethnicity, and gender) rather than issues of salary or the more nuanced consideration of campus climate.

In preparing this chapter, seven people who are at NCATE accredited institutions were sent e-mail communications and asked to characterize the nature of attention to gender equity as part of the accreditation process. All were assured that their responses would be kept anonymous, and for that reason they are referred to only by respondent number. Of the seven, six responded. Four individuals are women and two are men. Five of the individuals are experienced NCATE team members and three have been team chairs multiple times. One of the five individuals forwarded a copy of the standards with an accompanying note that gender equity falls under diversity (Respondent 1). Respondent 2 also forwarded the standards but added that [her] "gut feeling is that NCATE is more focused on racial, ethnic, and economic diversity [than on gender equity]." In terms of gender issues she concluded that other national organizations have been more up front in the area of gender equity, particularly as it relates to improving mathematics and science opportunities for girls and young women. Another individual noted that although "things are not perfect, they are considerably better than when David and Myra [Sadker] called attention to the issue 25 years ago" (respondent 3). Comments from Respondents 4, 5, and 6 were somewhat more pointed. One person (Respondent 4) replied that during the accreditation team's campus visit, "[gender equity] never came up, they showed no interest, and it was totally off the page." This respondent concluded, "gender equity and NCATE is an oxymoron." Respondent 5 referenced Standard 4 with the caveat that measuring it is ". . . really only in terms of numbers. She felt that attention to gender equity and rank would only show up if the institution decided to present the information and salary inequities that are not on the radar screen. It should be noted, that NCATE only requires evidence that resources devoted to the education unit are adequate, not salary data by gender, race, or ethnicity. A woman who serves on NCATE's Board of Examiners (Respondent 6) offered the following:

From my perspective as a Board of Examiner [member] for NCATE, the issue of gender equity doesn't come up in discussions of the diversity standard. Considerations around diversity still deal predominately with race. I don't hear comments about the gender balance in faculty nor do I hear comments about the gender balance in the student body of education schools which are predominately female. When I chair NCATE visits, I bring up the question of gender when we discuss the standard but that is because it is part of my consciousness.

A Google search using the words *gender equity*, *NCATE* resulted in 8,270 hits. The majority of these were references to institutional reports (data reported by gender) or faculty vita prepared for accreditation visits (citations for faculty who have published in the field of gender equity). Thus, it would appear that gender equity is considered as part of the teacher education accreditation process when the matter is raised by the institution itself or if it is an issue of importance to the team.

AACTE.   The American Association of Colleges for Teacher Education (AACTE) is a national organization with a membership made up of colleges and universities that have teacher education programs. The current AACTE membership is approximately 770 institutions (AACTE, 2004). Policies of the organization are reflected in resolutions of the membership and six resolutions relate specifically to gender. They are:

Resolution 2: Denounces discrimination by race, gender, and disability generally and in test construction.
Resolution 23: Calls for the elimination of sexism in society and in teacher education specifically.
Resolution 27: Deplores sexual harassment and suggests that AACTE help member institutions promote supportive environments for all students.
Resolution 28: Calls for the inclusion of gender equity in all PK–16 education reform efforts.
Resolution 29: Calls for efforts to support preparing more women to teach in mathematics and science fields
Resolution 45: Calls for the use of gender appropriate curricula and materials in teacher preparation programs (AACTE, 2004).

According to AACTE Bylaws (AACTE, 2004), resolutions of the membership govern actions of the board of directors and the central office staff. With these six resolutions in place, it is reasonable to expect that the organization would have a program or programs with a gender equity focus. Although attempts were made over time to create and sustain gender equity activities and to recognize outstanding achievements in gender equity, these efforts faced resistance and by 2006 all were abandoned.

AACTE's public attention to gender equity began in the late 1970s when a group of women education deans and directors petitioned the organization to create an opportunity for women from AACTE member institutions to meet and connect with one another in a systematic manner. That request led to the establishment of the Women's Breakfast held during the organization's annual conference. The breakfast began as a networking device, and within a few years added a speaker, either a well known woman, such as then Colorado Representative Pat Schroder or a man who had written about or studied issues of interest to women. Although the breakfast was a ticketed event— and priced to generate income—attendance generally was high.

Perhaps as a result of the Women's Breakfast, interest in more programs for women began to grow. It took over 15 years, but in 1992 AACTE's board of directors established a new standing committee, the Committee on Women's Issues (CWI). This group designed and offered mentoring workshops for women faculty interested in moving into higher education administration in conjunction with AACTE's annual conference. Because initially the committee had no organizational funds to support its work, members wrote proposals and received grant support for a symposium on the lack of conversations about gender equity as part of the debates on teacher education reform (Blackwell, with Applegate, Earley, & Tarule, 2000).

As noted previously, an organization's stated commitment to a particular agenda may be more symbolic than real. The Committee on Women's Issues struggled from the outset. Members of AACTE's board of directors (female and male) objected to creating a new committee. Critics noted that more women were now education deans—essentially asserting that gender equity is merely an issue of numbers—and suggested that gender equity should be covered through the work of the Multicultural Education Committee. Members of the Multicultural Education Committee voiced concern that expanding their charge to include gender equity would change, and possibly dilute, the focus of their work. In addition, there were several advocates for the new committee within the AACTE leadership who spoke in favor of it and that, together with the observations from the Multicultural Committee, tipped the balance in favor of the new CWI.

Membership on AACTE's board of directors and its standing committees is limited to three years. Consequently, in the decade following the creation of the Committee on Women's Issues all of the original advocates for it as well as the staff who championed the group either left AACTE or were not active in a leadership capacity. In 2005, the registration materials for the AACTE conference mentioned a breakfast session, featuring a woman speaker, but the designation Women's Breakfast was gone. An AACTE staff member offered the rationale that while the breakfast would still be sponsored by the CWI, the name was changed so that men would feel they could attend (men never were excluded from the previous breakfasts, and although they were few in number, men always attended). It is likely that a number of women will still choose to attend the breakfast session at AACTE—although the concomitant increase in cost may deter some junior faculty and administrators who find the $40 price a bit steep. The year 2006 brought additional changes when the Committee on Women's Issues was disbanded and replaced by a new Committee on Global Diversity and Inclusion. The charge to this new committee is: ". . . to foster the development of quality teaching and professional education practices that promote diversity, equity, and global perspectives that advance the preparation of world-class educators responsive to all learners. The Committee should endeavor to strengthen professional education programs and capacity by providing expertise and leadership resulting in the creation, promotion and/or dissemination of deliverables via AACTE or other approved venues (AACTE, 2006). The rationale for combining global education and diversity in all of its forms is to align committee work with AACTE's strategic goals (AACTE, 2006a). Yet in doing so, the organization implies that, resolutions of the membership notwithstanding, gender equity is on neither the organization's public nor private agendas.

Most organizations find ways to recognize the work of their members and AACTE is no exception. During the 1990s, the awards and recognitions system was reviewed and a number of new awards were established. One category was for best practices teacher education programs subdivided into eight fields, such as collaboration with community colleges, technology, diversity, and gender equity. In 1997, the Multicultural Education Committee created the Advocates for Justice Award to recognize individuals who were acknowledged leaders in promoting diversity. That award was first presented in 1998. The Committee on Women's Issues then established the Gender Equity Architect Award to recognize women and men who have publicly and privately promoted a gender equity agenda. That award was first presented in 1999 but abolished in 2003, along with the Advocate for Justice Award. Moreover, the call for nominations for awards in 2007 did not include a Best Practice Award for gender equity, folding it into the broader category of Best Practice in Global Diversity and Inclusion (AACTE, 2006b).

Even though a series of symbolic and very visible commitments to gender equity were lost, AACTE may not have abandoned its public commitment to social justice and gender equity entirely. Resolutions of the membership on these issues remain—even though there is no dedicated organizational structure to address them—and on April 23, 2004, AACTE submitted comments to the U.S. Department of Education objecting to proposed changes to the Title IX regulations, arguing that if this happens it will have an adverse impact on gender-fair treatment for girls by making it easier to sex segregate students without providing evidence that this temporary sex segregation will result in less sex discrimination in the outcomes as required by the current provisions in the Title IX regulations. (B. A. Albert, personal communication July 05, 2006). Despite their opposition, the proposed changes to Title IX were implemented in 2006.

AERA. The American Educational Research Association is an individual membership organization with most members holding faculty positions in institutions of higher education. AERA is composed of divisions and special interest groups such as the Special Interest Group: Research on Women and Education, which has been hosting its own separate annual fall meetings since the 1970s. The largest AERA division is devoted to teaching and teacher education. Like other professional organizations, AERA gives awards for high-quality work. Examples of this highly public behavior are awards for equity leadership, the 1992 Research Review Award to Sadker, Sadker, and Klein for a chapter on "The Issue of Gender in Elementary and Secondary Education," and the 1995 Research into Practice Award to Sadker and Sadker for their popular book *Failing at Fairness: How America's Schools Cheat Girls.*

Authority for policy decisions is vested in the AERA Council, which is made up of 20 elected individuals and two ex-officio staff members. The Committee on Scholars and Advocates for Gender Equity (SAGE; formerly the Committee on the Role and Status of Women) is one of the organization's 19 standing committees, and as reported on AERA's Web site, "AERA members serve as representatives, liaisons, and/or delegates of the Association to the following coalitions, associations and affiliated groups. Involvement and interaction with the larger educational community is a high priority for the Association in accordance with its mission and goals" (AERA, 2006). One of these coalitions is the National Coalition of Women and Girls in Education (NCWGE). With these public structures in place, it might be assumed that AERA would, like AACTE, submit comments to the U.S. Department of Education on proposed changes to Title IX. In fact, at a meeting of all AERA Committees in October 2004, the Governmental Relations Committee and SAGE drafted a joint statement recommending just that. However, after submitting this recommendation, members of the two committees were advised that the AERA Council must approve every policy decision, irrelevant of previous organizational history. That, coupled with the belief of some in the AERA leadership that the Department of Education's draft regulations were on target, stalled the issue and no comments were submitted.

AACTE and AERA in particular illustrate the tension between organizations' public and private faces and behaviors. In the case of AACTE, gender equity struggled for space on its agenda, and while resolutions of the membership supporting gender equity exist, there is to framework to support them. For AERA the governance structure creates a system where every decision is made and evaluated in the moment and past policy resolutions are neglected. The disconnect between recommendations of SAGE and GRC on the Title IX regulations and the action of the AERA Council led to drafting a policy on when and how decisions are made in response to federal regulations and similar acts, but these policies have not yet been tested (and, coincidently, cannot be found on the AERA web site).

Perhaps we expect more from professional organizations then they are prepared or able to deliver. There may be an assumption that organizational decisions are made by professional consensus: What are the needs of the members and how can the organization best meet those needs? In reality most organizations function through a process of building political consensus. Even organizations that on the surface seem highly homogeneous have factions within them. At AERA there are differences among researchers by field of concentration, and in some instances by preferred research methodologies. At AACTE there is an on-going tension between large universities, small colleges, public institutions, private institutions, programs accredited by NCATE, and those that are not. Thus, organizations attempt to satisfy the largest number of members while generating the least amount of friction. A more subtle factor is the composition of the organization's staff. An executive director, president, or vice president can help influence outcomes on an issue, and by the same token when staff leave or are replaced organizational priorities change.

We return to the work by Tarule et al. (2006) and the suggestion that irrespective of an organization's formal agenda, the meetings or conferences it sponsors create an opportunity for individuals who share a common perspective or set of values to construct supportive and reinforcing networks of colleagues. In the case of the network described by Tarule et al., groups of women devoted to issues of gender and leadership and to supporting other women have functioned well for over a decade. It is important to recognize that gender equity networks exist in spite of and independent from organizational agendas. Consequently, they function without organizational support and thus are highly dependent on the commitment of the individual members. Nevertheless, when professional organizations are not devoting their energy to gender equity—or if they do their resources are limited to tracking the number of women and men in particular roles—these networks are a way to provide a support system and address the much more complex issues of gender equity, campus climate, gender in education, and gendered leadership.

THE BACKLASH AND ITS IMPACT ON TEACHER EDUCATION

The attrition of gender activities and priorities detailed earlier is not isolated to teacher associations. In the 1985 edition of this *Handbook*, Sadker and Sadker (1985) reported on a number of promising projects. Some of these were directly linked to the professional associations like the American Association of Colleges for Teacher Education (AACTE) and National Association of State Directors of Teacher Education and Certification (NASDTEC) as they worked to include gender standards in teacher licensure responsibilities, although these efforts were not always successful (Sadker & Sadker, 1985, pp. 150–152, 153). Associations like the NEA and the AFT organized conferences and published materials to educate tomorrow's teachers (now yesterday's teachers) on the power and prevalence of sexism in education. Government agencies were also working to identify and eliminate sexism in education. The Women's Educational Equity Act (WEEA), although funded at a Lilliputian rate compared to most federal education programs (rarely above $3 million annually and typically below that figure), helped disseminate research and creative curricular development. (See Role of Government chapter). For example, working with the National Institute for Education, Sadker, Bauchner, Sadker, and Hergert (1984) as well as Lockheed (1985) studied the gender dynamics of classrooms, precisely the gender differences in teacher interactions with males and females. With support from the Fund for the Improvement of Post Secondary Education (FIPSE), a number of similar studies and training efforts were undertaken. For example, gender differences in classroom interaction and training of faculty was undertaken at the university level by Sadker and Sadker. These studies, from K–16, documented gender differences in teacher-student interaction and also showed that a well-designed training program could create more equitable interactions. Numerous articles were written in both professional journals and popular print and TV media about these efforts. The limited amount of government funds used to support these research and development efforts nevertheless yielded a rich crop of findings and materials, a productive but underutilized investment in public dollars. Few teacher education programs incorporated these findings or materials in their instructions, and by 2003 the government closed the WEEA Equity Resource Center. The result: a generation of carefully developed gender equity materials, and research resources were no longer available to the public.

Such efforts provide a foundation, a marker for future research. For example, the 1970s WEEA teacher education textbook study (Sadker & Sadker, 1980) provided a benchmark for future research, for replication (Zittleman & Sadker, 2002), and for remediation. Such benchmarks provide objective evidence of where we were, where we are, how far we have come, and how far we have yet to go to achieve equity. In a politically charged climate, such evidence is valuable indeed. The limited but productive government funding of the 1970s and 1980s provided several of these important benchmarks, as well as future direction.

For example, based on the lack of gender coverage in teacher education textbooks uncovered in the late 1970s and early 1980s, a Non-Sexist Teacher Education Project (N-STEP) was funded by WEEA in the 1980s, a project to infuse gender issues into teacher education. That project was described in detail in the previous *Handbook* (Sadker & Sadker, 1985), and is a prime example of the idealistic goals and practical materials that marked that decade. Materials like N-STEP were made available free or at cost to educators interested in and committed to gender fairness in schools. But as the Reagan era led to the Bush administration, the increasing influence of ultraconservatives became evident. The Heritage, Cathage, Bradley and Olin foundations, for example, funneled monies into numerous projects meant to discourage gender equity, impugn the credibility of the researchers, and reaffirm the traditional gender roles of the past. This effort became known as the backlash (Sommers, 1994; Sadker, July 2000, November, 2002), and this backlash probably contributed to reduced federal funding, including important dissemination activities like the WEEA Equity Resource Center.

Let's take a closer look at the backlash which has dramatically slowed much of the progression toward gender equity. The social context of the backlash offers us a keener understanding of how and why gender issues have been submerged in teacher education. Most historians divide the women's movement in the United States into two waves. According to Maggie Humm (1992), "The first wave commenced in the 1840s with Elizabeth Cady Stanton's and Susan B. Anthony's anti-slavery and temperance campaigns" (p. 2). After the Civil War, the antislavery movement began to fade, but women continued their activism and carried this momentum forward to the National Woman Suffrage Association. In 1920, the 19th Amendment giving women the right to vote was passed. With its main goal accomplished, the first wave ended. The second wave of feminism was called the Women's Liberation Movement or the contemporary women's movement and began in the late 1960s (McCormick, 1994). It was based on the concept that women were oppressed and that they needed to develop a theory and a politics that would free them from this oppression. Second-wave feminists also contend that women's lives and experiences need to be acknowledged as a major source of information. By the 1990s, a powerful backlash occurred against the women's liberation movement, resulting in many of the cutbacks discussed in this section. Susan Faludi (1991) defines backlash as "an attempt to retract the handful of small and hard-won victories that the feminist movement did manage to win for women" (p. xviii). Faludi (1991) claims that: "A backlash against women's rights is nothing new in American history. Indeed, it's a recurring phenomenon: it returns every time women begin to make some headway toward equality" (p. 46). Although the Women's Liberation Movement (WLM) is believed to be ongoing, some researchers now refer to the "post-feminist culture of the United States" (Conway, 1997, p. 1).

One of the most important issues that second-wave feminists addressed was the disadvantages that females experienced in education. Although many individuals in the contemporary women's movement believed that schools reinforced the larger, gendered order of society, it also believed that these same institutions could be used to address these inequities. As Jo Anne Pagano (1990) asserts: "Knowledge is power. Those who have it are more powerful than those who do not. Those who define what counts as knowledge are the most powerful" (p. xvi). Many publications began to appear on the market about the problems that girls encountered in their educational journeys in the first half of the 1990s. The first report to receive much publicity was

the American Association of University Women's (AAUW) *How Schools Shortchange Girls* (1992). In their report, the AAUW detailed how the curriculum, especially in science and mathematics, was geared towards boys and described how chilly the educational environment was for girls. Four other popular books appeared in rapid succession: *Meeting at the Crossroads: Women's Psychology and Girls' Development* (1992) by Lyn Mikel Brown and Carol Gilligan; *Failing at Fairness: How Our Schools Cheat Girls* (1994) by Myra Sadker and David Sadker, *School Girls: Young Women, Self-Esteem, and the Confidence Gap* (1994) by Peggy Orenstein; and *Reviving Ophelia: Saving the Selves of Adolescent Girls* (1994) by Mary Pipher. All of these authors referred to the crises that adolescent girls were experiencing. They claimed that young girls have a lower sense of self-efficacy than boys, encounter overt classroom discrimination, experience a loss of voice as they grow older, have more problems with eating disorders and self-mutilation, and are underachievers in mathematics and science. Due to all of this publicity, much attention was given to the neglect of girls in the educational world. According to Weaver-Hightower (2003): "attention to these issues has led to great strides in understanding the function of gender in educational context . . . until recently" (p. 472).

By the mid 1990s, the public interest and many publications seemed to switch its focus from girls' inequalities to the problems that boys were experiencing. Once again, the issues of gender, education, and equity were being highlighted, except this time from a different perspective. This backlash may be attributed to a number of different causes, three of which will be briefly examined: the "What about the boys?" culture, the backlash against the Women's Liberation Movement, and the backlash against the real progress of women in education.[2]

First, similar to the popular literature that appeared about girls' problems in the early 1990s, a "What about the boys?" culture developed in the late 1990s. These *boy books* fall into two categories: books that expand the lessons learned from feminists to the gender role challenges boys confront, and books that blame girls for the problems that boys face suggesting that if girls advance, boys must lose. The first book to appear on the mass market was William Pollack's *Real Boys* (1998), which falls into the first category. Like the "What about the girls?" books, Pollack uses feminist research to illustrate how our modern society has a harmful psychological effect on boys. Consequently, Pollack cites statistics showing how there has been an increase in boys' drug use, violence, depression, academic failure, teen sex—to name just a few of the problems. Likewise, in *Raising Cain*, Kindlon and Thompson (1999) suggest that boys are at risk because of gender role restrictions. They advocate that teachers help boys express emotions. The misinformation campaign of Sommers (1994, 2000) went much further, and the pronouncements of Gurian (Gurian & Stevens, 2005) and Sax (2005) offer the veneer of science to the proposition of dramatic and destined sex differences. Contrary to the evidence in the Hyde and Lindberg chapter in this *Handbook*, Gurian advocates that boys and girls have brains and learning styles so biologically different that they should be educated apart. Sommers

---

[2]Some of these interpretations of the recent backlash are based analyses in Weaver-Hightower (2003).

introduces another element into the discussion as she attacks the honesty, competence, and motivation of most feminists, and many educators and researchers, claiming that they intentionally work against boys. Her books mark not only an assault on the integrity of researchers and the motivations of feminists, but also an effort to maintain traditional and historical roles and avoid modifications of the conventional male gender role (Sadker, 2000; Sadker, May, 2000, Sadker, 2002). Zittleman and Sadker (2002/2003) summarize the mood of the country during this time period: "Are attempts to level the playing field for girls harmful to boys? This polarizing political ideology blames the academic problems of boys on efforts to ensure equal educational opportunities for girls, and several textbooks now include this argument" (p. 60).

The second probable cause of this recent backlash against gender equity in education is the longstanding conservative political and religious backlash against many women's issues (Faludi, 1991; Sadker, November 2002), including education. The conservative agenda includes privatization of schools (primarily through vouchers and charter schools and the entry of for-profit companies in the public education arena) and accountability (through the form of *high-stakes* standardized student academic achievement testing and penalties for public schools not meeting test standards). Teacher education has also undergone a cultural transformation with increased testing of new teachers and a federal pressure for states to hire *highly qualified* teachers, a phrase that puts more weight behind subject matter specialization than pedagogy.

Even the highly successful Title IX, the law that prohibits sex discrimination in federally funded education, is being attacked. As discussed in the "Gender Equity in Coeducational and Single Sex Educational Environments" and "The Role of Government in Advancing Gender Equity in Education" chapters in this *Handbook*, in October 2006, the Department of Education changed the regulations, making it easier to operate separate schools and classes by sex without even showing that these sex segregated interventions would do anything to decrease sex discrimination, the sole purpose of Title IX.

The third probable cause of this backlash is that girls have been making substantial progress in many areas from sports, to college attendance, to increases in many areas of science such as biology. This progress is documented in many of the other chapters in this *Handbook*, but it is also noted that boys and men have also been making progress.

Similar to the analyses of challenges to gender equity in education, many solutions have been discussed, but only two will be mentioned. First, the discussion about quality education for our children should not come down to an either/or situation. In these days of limited resources, educators need to create curriculum and pedagogy that empowers both girls and boys. Second, the question should be asked which boys and which girls are experiencing discrimination in education, because often the heterosexual, White, middle- to upper-class boys are still scoring highest on many indicators. If one were to examine the economic and social outcomes of these privileged boys' educational journeys, research would show that their achievements are higher than ever, whereas higher literacy rates do not increase girls' marketability. Latino and Latina students, African American boys and others certainly do confront special challenges, but these have a great deal to do with race, language, and social class, major issues too often omitted by the boys as victims advocates. (See the *Handbook* chapter on the "Impact of Education on Gender Equity in Employment and its Outcomes" and the seven chapters in part V on "Gender Equity Strategies for Diverse Populations.")

The impact of the general backlash against women's educational equity has had negative implications for the optimistic advancement of gender equity in teacher education anticipated in the previous "Teacher Education" chapter in the 1985 *Handbook for Achieving Sex Equity through Education.*

RECOMMENDATIONS AND TEACHER EDUCATION SOLUTIONS

Back in 1985, when the first *Handbook* was published, a few programs were already being implemented to promote gender equity. Since that time, several have been evaluated and found to make measurable differences. In 1985, a number of recommendations appeared in the *Handbook* designed to promote gender equity in teacher education. During the ensuing decades, progress on implementing these recommendations has been sporadic and not necessarily enduring, and many of those original recommendations still merit and await implementation. Implementation of gender equity teacher education programs has also been infrequent. We shall offer recommendations in three areas: policy, practice/programs and research.

Policy

The following recommendations reflect both those originally proposed more than two decades ago, as well as new recommendations.

Teacher Education Institutions and Programs

Gender equity evaluation of teacher education programs and institutions. Involve Title IX coordinators and committees of students and staff in reviewing education policies and practices related to gender. This periodic evaluation could include curricular materials and syllabi to see if gender issues, sex differences, gender bias and discrimination, and other similar issues and topics are part of a new teacher's preparation. Are the experiences of women in education included? Is the exploitation history of teachers generally, and female teachers in particular, part of the official curriculum, or the null curriculum? What do new teachers know about such basic areas as sex differences and similarities? Are new teachers working from outdated and stereotypic gender role frameworks? Can new teachers differentiate gender issues and beliefs portrayed through the popular press contrasted with what research and best practices advise? There should be a central publication, Web site and other means to disseminate information about meritorious programs, as well as those in need of further development to serve as a consumer advisory for future teacher educators and students.

Implement already developed meritorious federal programs. Over the past few decades, programs and materials have been developed to promote gender equity in teaching. They have been primarily funded by the Department of Education and NSF and are described in the chapter on "The Role of Government in Advancing Gender Equity in Education." We support the recommendations in this chapter that these programs to support R&D-based replication of gender equity interventions should be continued and expanded. This includes the reinstitution of the Department of Education-supported Gender Equity Expert Panel (GEEP), which reviewed a number of these programs and identified several that offered promising evidence of impact, such as Succeeding at Fairness and A Women's Place in the Curriculum. (See http://www.ed.gov/offices/OERI/ORAD/KAD/expert_panel/geawards.html) Reinstating GEEP would be an important step in encouraging and recognizing future promising programs. As previously mentioned, a national dissemination center for resources and the exchange of information on gender equity education such as the WEEA Equity Resource Center should also be reinstituted.

Evaluate staffing. What is the distribution of senior administrative positions and faculty ranks between the genders? What are the race, ethnicity, and gender intersections in staffing positions? Are prestigious, higher paying, and influential positions more common among one gender, race, and ethnicity than others?

Incorporate teaching skills for gender equity. Are preservice education students being prepared in nonsexist, nonracist teaching skills? Are they being taught strategies to individualize instruction and widen student horizons, to respond to individual differences and not to sex-role expectations? Are they being taught how to confront the historical challenges that confront girls and boys? Are they being taught about their civil rights protections under such laws as Title IX? We have found no evidence to indicate that today's teacher education programs are any more successful in these areas than 1985, when the first edition of the *Handbook* was published. We recommend that the teacher education programs undergo an equity audit to assure that critical gender information and skills are seamlessly included in the teacher education program. Furthermore, we suggest that the concepts behind culturally relevant teaching, including connecting with the backgrounds of teacher education students and promoting social justice projects, become a required part of teacher education.

Professional Associations

Attend to gender in accreditation reviews. Gender equity knowledge, dispositions and skills, and related research efforts should be clearly articulated and promoted in teacher education programs and used in accreditation visits and reviews by these agencies. Visitation teams should receive training in gender equity issues, and organizations like AERA and AACTE should be leading in such efforts.

Evaluate organizational implementation. How can gender issues, in particular, and equity issues taken more broadly, become institutionalized as opposed to rising and falling with staff changes? Professional associations should institutionalize research efforts, awards, programs, presentations, and the like on an ongoing basis, rather than reflect the personal preferences of ever-changing staff and elected officers. In some cases, even institutionalized awards and activities are ignored, and a more coherent policy and consistent approach is needed.

Practice/Programs

While current teacher education textbooks and programs offer few specific resources or strategies to promote gender fairness, there are several programs that have been field tested and shown to provide evidence of effectiveness, as determined by the previously discussed Gender Equity Expert Panel. The Panel recommended these programs as "promising" in positively impacting teachers' performance in promoting gender equity. Among these are two in teacher education: Succeeding at Fairness: Effective Teaching for All Students and A Women's Place is in the Curriculum. (United States Department of Education, Gender Equity Program, 2000). These programs provide focused training on developing equitable teaching skills as well as including curricular materials that are more equitable and more balanced. The Panel evaluated evidence of these programs to assess that they had measurable behavioral impact on teachers and administrators. Beyond these two programs, a myriad of other gender equity programs have been widely used, although not evaluated by the Gender Equity Expert Panel. For example, Generating Expectations for Student Achievement, an Equitable Approach to Educational Excellence (GESA), draws from research on teacher responses to student characteristics such as how gender, race, and social class affect achievement (Grayson & Martin, 1997). It has been widely implemented in numerous school districts. Scores of other programs and materials are also available, but for the most part have not been distributed or implemented at the nation's teacher education institutions.

Publishers, Teacher Education Curriculum, Governmental Agencies and Professional Associations: Correcting Bias in Curricular and Professional Materials

Even when programs such as these are not implemented, there are steps that teachers and teacher educators can take to create more equitable and effective learning climates. In curriculum, for example, teaching students to recognize common forms of bias can pay rich learning dividends. Following is a description of a framework for assessing curricular bias developed by Shirley McCune and Martha Matthews (1978) and expanded by Myra Sadker and David Sadker (2005). Since these forms of bias exist from picture books to college texts, from brochures to official documents, and apply not only to gender but to many groups, mastering this framework offers a useful lesson to teachers and students of all educational levels (Zittleman & Sadker, 2002/2003).

Invisibility. Certain groups have been underrepresented in education, by the media and materials. The significant omission of women and people of color has become so great as to imply that these groups are of less value, importance, and significance in our society. Textbooks published prior to the 1960s largely omitted African Americans, Latinos, and Asian Americans (Sadker & Sadker, 1982), and many of today's textbooks continue to give minimal treatment to women, those with disabilities, gays and lesbians, and others (Sleeter & Grant, 1991; Zittleman & Sadker, 2002). Typically omitted or given only glancing treatment in teacher education texts are women's issues, the contributions of women to education, or the economic exploitation of women in teaching. The significance and problem with the gender segregation in teaching is infrequently included (the absence of male elementary teachers, few female superintendents, and the overwhelming gender stereotyping in career education). It is unlikely that such glaring gender issues will be addressed until our training programs and materials recognize the problems, and publishers should include such materials in their textbooks. Methods texts typically ignore gender issues, such as boys' reading challenges and girls' challenges in math, technology, and some sciences. These books lack relevant information about appropriate skills or resources teachers need to overcome these educational challenges. The texts and teaching materials produced by publishers typically omit all or most of Title IX and related civil rights information. As a result, tomorrow's teachers have little knowledge of the civil rights protections guaranteed by the law, and are unable to share such information with their students. The civil rights of educators and students in relation to gender are at risk because of such omissions.

Stereotyping. Perhaps the most familiar form of bias is the stereotype, which assigns a rigid set of characteristics to all members of a group, denying individual attributes and differences. Textbooks, pictures, and other displays often reinforce cultural stereotypes by casting males as active, assertive, and curious, while portraying females as dependable, conforming, and obedient. For examples, a 1990s study of elementary mathematics software revealed that only 12% of the characters were female. Reinforcing stereotypes, female characters were portrayed passively as mothers and princesses, while male characters were shown as active and as "heavy equipment operators, factory workers, shopkeepers, mountain climbers, hang gliders, and garage mechanics" (Hodes, 1995/1996).

Imbalance/selectivity. The media and text materials have perpetuated bias by presenting only one interpretation of an issue, situation or group of people. This imbalanced account restricts the knowledge of students regarding the varied perspectives and alternative possibilities. When math and science texts reference only male discoveries and formulas, an incomplete picture of scientific inquiry is described. What inventions have female fingerprints? The cotton gin is one example. But because women were denied patent registration, Eli Whitney is given solo credit, and few even know the name of Catherine Littlefield Greene, also a co-inventor (Sadker & Sadker, 1995).

Unreality. Materials, media and books have frequently presented an unrealistic portrayal of our history and contemporary life experience. Controversial topics have been glossed over, and discussions of discrimination, sexual harassment and prejudice have been avoided. Unrealistic coverage denies us the information we need to recognize, understand and perhaps someday conquer the problems that plague our society. In order to overcome this unreality, educational leaders and students need to be aware of their own patterns as they provide services and instruction.

Fragmentation/isolation. By separating issues related to people of color/women from the main body of schooling, instruction has implied that these issues are less important than and not a part of the cultural mainstream. Many of today's texts include special inserts or even chapters highlighting certain topics. "Ten Women Achievers in Science" and "What If He Has Two Mommies?" are examples of such fragmentation. Such isolation presents these groups and topics as peripheral, less important than the main narrative.

Linguistic bias. Language can be a powerful conveyor of bias, in both blatant and subtle forms. James Comer and Alvin Poussaint (1992), two leading American child psychologists, warn that overly harsh punishment promotes four responses from students: "It either destroys a child's spirit, has no effect at all, worsens the problem, or makes it more difficult for you to work with the child in school—he or she no longer trusts you" (p. 80). The final phrase, "he or she no longer trusts you," is gender inclusive. It is not always the way great speakers present their wise words. Sexist language from recent and not-so-recent history needs to be explained directly, or students may not understand the sexist language. Martin Luther King, Jr. closed his 1963 *I Have a Dream* speech with, "When we let freedom ring, we will be able to speed up that day when all of God's children, black men and white men, . . ." Moreover, *The Declaration of Independence*, our nation's call for freedom, begins with, "All men are created equal." The exclusive use of masculine terms and pronouns, ranging from our *forefathers*, *mankind*, and *businessman* to the generic *he*, denies the full participation and recognition of women. Further, the insistence that we live in an English-only, monolingual society can have major economic, social and political ramifications in a global community.

Cosmetic bias. Textbook publishers are aware that educators and reform movements are demanding better, fairer, and more comprehensive materials in education. To rewrite text requires thorough research and infusion. Occasionally, publishers and authors minimize the process by creating an illusion of equity. Two common short cuts are: large pictures of nontraditional people (in the beginning of the book or fronting major chapters) with little evidence of content inclusion; "special focus sections" such as a glossy pullout of female scientists, but precious little narrative of the scientific contributions of women.

Making Gender Visible in Teacher
Education Materials and Institutions

The few teacher education programs that share these strategies with their students or respond to gender issues in their teacher education programs are the exception. The same is true of many professional and government agencies, although some are better than others at working for balance and fairness in their publications. In fact, some textbooks are actually promoting ideas which are neither helpful nor accurate, as reported by Zittleman and Sadker (2002). Why do some publishers, teacher education programs and organizations promote gender equity while others ignore it or worse? Often, it comes down to one or a few faculty members, editors, or employees who, for personal or professional reasons, are committed to promoting gender equity (Sanders, 2002). Enduring, wide-spread, institutional change has yet to be sparked at the college and university level, and when we turn our attention to the relevant national associations that influence policy, a similar pattern emerges. What is needed are programs and policies that go beyond individuals and incorporate gender across the curriculum.

Teacher Education Institutions

Improve recruitment.   Institutions should work to end the gendered nature of teaching. Creative strategies need to go beyond brochures and catalogue descriptions to recruit and retain men and women in education fields where they are currently underrepresented. Recruiting more males in elementary teaching and more females in technology, physics, and school administration would be examples of such affirmative recruitment goals. Special attention should also be given to recruiting educators from greatly underrepresented minority groups such as Asian and Asian Pacific Islanders and Latina/os as described in the chapters on these populations in this *Handbook*.

Model Title IX.   Teacher education programs should be a reflection of Title IX in action, a living school of gender equitable policies and practices. Students and faculty in those programs should not only be familiar with Title IX protections, they should be implementing those protections in their own teaching. Perhaps teachers particularly interested in Title IX and gender issues could volunteer to be Title IX coordinators and be compensated for their work. Publishers should include Title IX information in textbooks, and government, universities, and professional organizations should adhere to equity laws already on the books, which is not always the case.

Teacher Accreditation Organizations

Specify gender in standards.   Gender equity knowledge, dispositions, and skills should be clearly articulated in teacher education programs and used in accreditation visits and reviews by these agencies. Visitation teams should receive training in gender equity issues including protections against sex discrimination required by Title IX and the Equal Protection Clause of the Constitution.

Institutionalize equity.   The past two decades have spotlighted the lack of institutional commitment to equity. Awards and programs have disappeared as the advocates of those efforts leave the association. A commitment beyond this is required if these issues are to remain priority issues in these organizations.

This means that equity awards, convention topics and professional journal themes, and other organizational efforts be made a continuing and integral part of the organizations.

Federal and State Education Agencies

Monitor gender civil rights.   State and federal agencies should take steps to insure that Title IX and relevant state civil rights laws are in place and in practice. It is unlikely that education students or teachers themselves are aware of Title IX and related state law. The lack of such information jeopardizes the impact of civil rights gender protections.

Fund research and development.   With the current backlash in place, there is little in the way of objective ED-sponsored research in gender issues underway or gender equity related materials as was the case decades earlier. (See governance chapter.) Many of the studies of the past few decades have been archived by the current administration and are not readily accessible. This climate of disregard of research findings is of great concern. Too often, the research gap is being filled by political posturing and pseudoscientific claims such as those of Gurian and others discussed in the backlash section of this chapter. This politicalization of research is an ominous development. We are recommending a reform in current research practices at the federal level and as much as possible in a politically-charged environment, the decoupling of research from political agendas of either the left or right. This should be a bipartisan effort, although such a prospect at the time of this writing seems remote. For instance, the federal administration in 2006 changed Title IX to allow single-sex classes and schools in the public sector despite the lack of coherent research findings to support such an effort and the possibilities that such efforts might in fact cause harm. These changes and publications are fed by a common stream: the absence of objective and fair-minded research that is accurately disseminated to the public.

Testing

The current climate of frequent, high-stakes testing promoted under *No Child Left Behind* has shed little light on gender issues. Rather, it has created much controversy concerning school failures, students held back from graduation, and the narrowing of the curriculum (Sadker & Zittleman, 2004). Certainly, a more effective assessment strategy could assess educational needs, diagnose problems, and serve to direct educational resources. But the current testing programs do not consistently disaggregate data by gender in their analysis and reporting. In effect, the current assessment system is built on *gender blindness*, and a pressing recommendation would be to construct a testing program that informs us about gender issues, and insure that teachers are able to interpret and plan based on such tests. Moreover, the reliance on standardized testing has disregarded those with skills and talents not assessed in this manner. Diversity of testing measures and approaches should be developed and implemented to help all students receive appropriate, diagnostic, and comprehensive assessment data.

Resources

Since the closing of the WEEA Resource Center, there are few materials available to promote gender equity in teacher education or staff development. The federal and state governments should fulfill their obligations to insure that teachers are educated in a way to insure that all students, regardless of gender, will be taught to broaden options, rather than limit them. Clearly, materials need to be made available to educators and students, and another dissemination center needs to be opened. Model programs and practices need to be encouraged and disseminated. The lack of resources and materials has left schools and teacher educators without the basic materials they need to build on past progress and contribute progress of their own.

Teacher Qualifications

No Child Left Behind.   Is only the most recent effort to define the skills needed for qualified, or in this case, highly qualified teachers. The current emphasis is that teachers should demonstrate content mastery, or knowledge of subject. Much less emphasis is being placed on skill development for teachers. Issues like gender differences in the classroom, or even individualization of instruction, are being relegated to a lower status. Clearly, equitable attitudes, knowledge, and teaching skills are needed for effective learning. How can different approaches to learning, differentiated instruction, cooperative learning, technology, and the like better meet the needs of all students? How can teachers instruct and manage all students, assertive and quiet, more effectively? How can cooperation and competition be honored learning styles in the classroom? What can boys and girls teach each other about learning? How can teachers acquire the critical skills they need to be more effective to all students? (See Sadker & Silber, 2007)

Research

Universities

Incorporate gender into mainstream institutional research.   Too often, university research agendas are shaped by factors that are not always logical. Dissertations or studies may be initiated by availability of subjects or materials, interests of professors or funding agencies, or other factors that neither incorporate nor consider previous work. The result is diverse studies too often without reflection or a view of the big picture. In gender equity, research seems to ebb and flow as much on whim as a plan to measure and direct forward progress. Here are some questions universities may want to consider in creating a coherent research agenda. Is gender a part of the research priorities in teacher education? In the university? How will issues of gender be investigated in institutional studies, theses, and doctoral dissertations? How do previous gender studies serve as a framework for future efforts? Are previous studies replicated to determine if there has been change?

Monitor salary figures.   It has been impossible for us to compare male and female salaries in the field of teacher ed-

ucation. It is often possible to uncover male and female salary differences by institution and sometimes salary differences by discipline. These numbers suggest that gender may well be playing a pivotal role (Umbach, April 2006). What was difficult for us to uncover in researching this chapter was official salary figures by rank within a discipline for males and females. How do male and female salaries differ within a department or school among professors, associate professors, and assistant professors? Are female teacher educators at the same rank paid less than male teacher educators? Some studies have looked at this at particular institutions and other studies depend on salary figures volunteered. But this piecemeal approach leaves much to be desired. Universities are encouraged to research these distinctions so that inequities can become visible, and hopefully, eliminated. It is puzzling to consider why such a fundamental issue as gendered salaries, so widely known and criticized in the general population, has escaped a more in depth analysis in colleges and universities.

A broader and slightly different study could examine the relationship between salary levels and the presence of female faculty. Are salaries lower as females become more numerous?

Review teacher evaluation and merit pay.   Although there exists a growing body of literature that the gender of the professor and the gender of the students influence student evaluations of teacher effectiveness, institutions typically ignore the influence of gender in student evaluations. Such gender blindness serves to institutionalize sexism, representing not only a force for continuing salary and promotion inequities, but also a lost opportunity for teaching students about the persistence and subtle nature of gender bias (Basow, 1995; Basow, 2000, Baker & Copp, 1997). Since universities are often constructed on a merit paradigm, it is critical to see if the invisible hand of gender is tipping the scales of promotion, recognition, and salary. More study needs to be undertaken about the subtle role of gender bias on the distribution of compensation, especially merit pay. What are other subtle and not-so-subtle gender biases working against one gender or the other? How is it manifested in different disciplines and institutions? Until this is done, inequities will persist and learning opportunities will be lost.

This list of recommendations can easily be much longer. But these offer a good beginning. In a *Journal of Teacher Education* editorial, Sadker, Sadker and Hicks (1980) wrote that we cannot afford "to prepare another generation of teachers who will be likely to promote rather than eliminate sex bias. The loss of human potential is too great. Sex equity in teacher preparation must be a priority for this decade" (p. 3.).

Unfortunately, that view is no less apt today than it was a quarter of a century ago.

ACKNOWLEDGMENTS

We would like to thank Donna M. Gollnick, Senior Vice President of the National Council for Accreditation of Teacher Education (NCATE) and co-author of several teacher education textbooks, including *Multicultural Education in a Pluralistic Society*, for her helpful review of this chapter.

References

Aisenberg, N., & Harrington, M. (1988). *Women of Academe—Outsiders in the Sacred Grove*. Amherst: The University of Massachusetts Press.

Altermatt, E., Jovanovic, J., & Perry, M. (1998). Bias or responsivity? Sex and achievement-level effects on teachers' classroom questioning practices. *Journal of Educational Psychology, 90*, 516–527

American Association of Colleges for Teacher Education. (2004). *Director of members 2004*. Washington, DC: AACTE.

American Association of Colleges for Teacher Education. (2006a). Governance Structure/Committee Structure. Retrieved July 1, 2006, from http://www.aacte.org/About_us/sitemap.aspx

American Association of Colleges for Teacher Education, (2006b). AACTE 2007 Awards Call for Entries. Retrieved July 1, 2006, from http://www.aacte.org/Events/Awards/index.aspx

American Association of University Women. (1992). *How schools short-change girls*. Washington, DC: AAUW.

American Educational Research Association (2006). About AERA Delegates and Representatives. Retrieved July 1, 2006, from http://www.aera.net/aboutaera/?id=264

Apple, M. (1990). *Ideology and Curriculum*. New York: Routledge.

Bailey, B., Scantlebury, K., & Letts, W. (1997). It's not my style: Using disclaimers to ignore issues in science. *Journal of Teacher Education, 48*(1), 29–35.

Baker, P., & Copp, M. (1997). Gender matters most: The interaction of gendered expectations, feminist course content, and pregnancy in student course evaluations. *Teaching Sociology, 25*(1), 29–43.

Basow, S. A. (2000). Best and worst professors: Gender patterns in students' choices. *Sex Roles, 43*(5/6), 407–417.

Basow, S. A. (1995). Student evaluations of college professors: When gender matters. *Journal of Educational Psychology, 87*(4), 656–665.

Beyer, L. (2001). The value of critical perspectives in teacher education. *Journal of Teacher Education, 52*(2), 151–163.

Blackwell, P. J., with Applegate, J., Earley, P., & Tarule, J. (2000). *The missing discourse of gender*. Washington, DC: AACTE.

Britzman, D. (1991). *Practice Makes Practice—A Critical Study of Learning to Teach*. Albany: State University of New York Press.

Brown, L. M., & Gilligan, C. (1992). *Meeting at the crossroads: Women's psychology and girls' development*. Cambridge, MA: Harvard University Press.

Campbell, P., & Sanders, J. (1997). Uninformed but interested: Findings of a national survey on gender equity in preservice teacher education. *Journal of Teacher Education, 48*, 69–75.

Caplan, P. (1995). *Lifting a ton of feathers—A woman's guide for surviving in the academic world*. Toronto: Council of Ontario Universities.

Chamberlain, L., & Meece, L. (1937, March). Women and men in the teaching profession. *Bulletin of the Bureau of School Services, 9*(3). College of Education, University of Kentucky,

Comer, J., & Poussaint, A. (1992). *Raising black children. Two leading psychiatrists confront the educational, social, and emotional problems facing black children*. New York: Penguin Books.

Conway, J. K. (1997). The education of a publisher. *The Washington Post's Book World* (January 26), p. 1.

Cooper, J., & Stevens, D. (2002). *Tenure in the sacred grove: Issues and strategies for women and minority faculty*. Albany: State University of New York.

Davis, A., & McDaniel, T. (1999). You've come a long way, baby—or have you? Research evaluating gender portrayal in recent Caldecott-winning books. *Reading Teacher, 52*, 532–536.

Eisenmann, L. (1991). Teacher professionalism: A new analytical tool for the history of teachers. *Harvard Educational Review, 61*(2), 215–224.

Evans, L., & Davies, K. (2000). No sissy boys here: A content analysis of the representation of masculinity in elementary school reading textbooks. *Sex Roles, 42*, 255–270.

Faludi, S. (1991). *Backlash: The undeclared war against American women*. New York: Anchor Books.

Farris, P. (2001). *Elementary and middle school social studies: An interdisciplinary instruction approach* (3rd ed.). New York: McGraw-Hill.

Flesch, R. (1955). *Why Johnny can't read: And what you can do about it*. New York: Harper.

Frazier, N., & Sadker, M. (1973). *Sexism in school and society*. New York: Harper and Rowe.

Gates, A. (1961). Sex differences in reading ability. *Elementary School Journal, 61*, 431–434.

Giroux, H., & McLaren, P. (1986). Teacher education and the politics of engagement: The case for democratic schooling. *Harvard Educational Review, 56*(3), 213–238.

Good, T., & Brophy, J. (2000). *Looking in Classrooms* (8th ed.). New York: Wesley Longman.

Goodlad, J., Soder, R., & Sirotnik, K. (Eds.). (1990). *Places where teachers are taught*. San Francisco: Jossey-Bass.

Grayson, D., & Martin, M. (1997). Generating expectations for student achievement: An equitable approach to educational excellence, *Teacher handbook* (3rd ed.) Tehachapi, CA: GrayMill.

Gurian, M., & Stevens, K. (2005). The minds of boys; Saving our sons from falling behind in school and life. San Francisco: Jossey-Bass.

Hall, R., & Sandler, B. (1984). *Out of the Classroom: A Chilly Campus Climate for Women?* Washington, DC: Project on the Status and Education of Women, Association of American Colleges.

Hodes, C. (1995/1996). Gender representations in mathematics software. *Journal of Educational Technology Systems, 24*, 67–73.

Howe, F. (1979.) The first decade of women's studies. *Harvard Educational Review, 49*, 413–421.

Humm, M. (Ed.). (1992). *Modern feminisms: Political, literary, cultural*. New York: Columbia University Press.

Kindlon, D., & Thompson, M. (1999). *Raising Cain: Protecting the emotional life of boys*. New York: Ballantine Books.

Jackson, P. (1968). *Life in Classrooms* New York: Holt, Rinehart, & Winston.

Johnson, J., Dupuis, V., Musial, D., Hall, G., & Gollnick, D. (1999). *Introduction to the foundations of American education* (11th ed.). Needham Heights, MA: Allyn and Bacon.

Johnson, D., & Johnson, R. (1999). Learning together and alone: Cooperations, competitive, and individualistic learning. 5th ed. Boston: Allyn & Bacon.

Jones, G., & Gerig, T. (1994). Silent sixth-grade students: Characteristics, achievement, and teacher expectations. *The Elementary School Journal, 95*, 169–182.

Lather, P. (1981). Reeducating educators: Sex equity in teacher education. *Educational Horizons, 60*(1), 38–40.

Lee, V., & Smith, J. (1990, Spring). Gender equality in teachers' salaries: A multiple approach. *Educational Evaluation and Policy Analysis, 12*, 57–81.

Lingard, R., & Douglas, P. (1999). *Men engaging feminisms: Profeminism, backlashes, and schooling*. Buckingham, UK: Open University Press.

Lockheed, M. (1985). Sex equity in classroom organization and climate. In Susan S., Klein (Ed.), *Handbook for achieving sex equity in education* (pp. 189–217). Baltimore: Johns Hopkins Press.

Mader, C. (1994). Gender equity instruction in Michigan teacher education programs. *Dissertation Abstracts International, 55*(07), 1917. (UMI No. 9431288).

Maher, F., & Ward, J. (2002). *Gender and teaching.* Mahwah, NJ: Lawrence Erlbaum Associates.

McCormick, T. (1994). *Creating the nonsexist classroom: A multicultural approach.* New York: Teachers College Press.

McCune, S., & Matthews, M. (1975). Eliminating sexism: Teacher education and change. *Journal of Teacher Education, 26,* 294–300.

McCune, S., & Matthews, M. (Eds.). (1978). *Implementing Title IX and attaining sex equity: A workshop package for postsecondary educators.* Washington, DC: U.S. Government Printing Office.

McNergney, R., & Herbert, J. (2001). *Foundations of education: The challenge of professional practice* (3rd ed.). Needham Heights, MA: Allyn and Bacon.

Montague, M., & Rinaldi, C. (2001). Classroom dynamics and children at risk. *Learning Disability Quarterly, 24,* 75–83.

Montecinos, C., & Nielsen, L. (2004). Male elementary preservice teachers' gendering of teaching. *Multicultural Perspectives* 6(2), 3–9.

Morrison, G. S. (2000). *Teaching in America* (2nd ed.). Needham Heights, MA: Allyn and Bacon.

National Council for the Accreditation of Teacher Education. (2006). *Standards.* Retrieved July 1, 2006 from http://www.ncate.org/public/standards.asp?ch=4

National Education Association. (2003). *Status of the American public school teacher, 2000–2001.* Washington, D.C.: NEA Research: 14, 78, 82. University of New Orleans, Louisiana.

National League of Teachers Associations. (1925). *The single salary scale.* Pamphlet, Special Collections, Earl Long Library, unpaged.

Orenstein, P. (1994). *School girls: Young women, self-esteem, and the confidence gap.* New York: Random House.

Pagano, J. (1990). *Exiles and communities: Teaching in the patriarchal wilderness.* Albany, NY: State University of New York.

Parkay, F., & Stanford, B. (2001). *Becoming a teacher* (5th ed.). Needham Heights, MA: Allyn and Bacon.

Pipher, M. (1994). *Reviving Ophelia: Saving the selves of adolescent girls.* New York: Ballantine Books.

Pollack, William S. (1998). *Real boys: Rescuing our sons from the myths of boyhood.* New York: Holt and Company.

Posamentier, A., & Stepelman, J. (1999). Teaching secondary mathematics: Techniques and enrichment units (5th ed.). Upper Saddle River, NJ: Merrill-Prentice Hall.

Preston, J. (2004). *Single or double salary scales?: Institutionalized gender discrimination in teachers' pay, 1900–1950.* Paper presented at the annual meeting of the AERA, San Diego, CA.

Preston, J. (2003). He lives as a master: Seventeenth-century masculinity, gendered teaching, and careers of New England schoolmasters. *History of Education Quarterly, 43*(3, Fall), 350–371.

Pryor, S., & Mader, C. (1998, April 16). *Gender equity instruction in teacher education: What do students learn? What do faculty teach? What are the influences?* Paper presented at the annual meeting of the American Educational Research Association, San Diego, California.

Riedesel, C. A., & Schwartz, J. (1999). *Essentials of elementary mathematics.* (2nd ed.). Boston: Allyn and Bacon.

Rowe, M. B. (1978). *Teaching science as continuous inquiry.* (2nd ed.) New York: McGraw-Hill.

Rowe, M. B. (1986). Wait time: Slowing down may be a way of speeding up! *Journal of Teacher Education, 37,* 43–50.

Sadker, D. (May, 2000) *The war against boys.* Retrieved from http://www.sadker.org/waragainstboys.htm (Excerpts from this letter were printed in the *Atlantic Monthly* in response to Christina Hoff Sommers' The War Against Boys (May 2000).

Sadker, D. (2000, July 30). Gender games. *Washington Post.*

Sadker, D. (2002, November). An educator's primer to the gender war. *Phi Delta Kappan, 84*(3), 235–240, 244.

Sadker, M., Bauchner, J., Sadker, D., & Hergert, L. (1984). *Promoting effectiveness in classroom instruction: Year 3: Final report ED257819.* Washington DC: National Institute of Education, United States Department of Education.

Sadker, M., & Sadker, D. (1980). Sexism in teacher education texts. *Harvard Educational Review, 50,* 36–46.

Sadker, M., Sadker, D., & Hicks, T. (1980). Sex equity in teacher preparation: A priority for the eighties. *Journal of Teacher Education, 31*(3), 3.

Sadker, M., & Sadker, D. (Eds.). (1982). *Sex equity handbook for schools.* New York: Longman.

Sadker, M. D., & Sadker, D. M. (1985). The treatment of sex equity in teacher education. In Susan S. Klein (Ed.), *The handbook for achieving sex equity through education* (pp. 145–161). Baltimore: Johns Hopkins Press.

Sadker, M., & Sadker D., (1994). *Failing at fairness: How our schools cheat girls.* New York: Touchstone.

Sadker, M., & Sadker D. (1995). Missing in interaction. In *Failing at fairness: How our schools cheat girls* (pp. 42–76). New York: Touchstone.

Sadker, M., & Sadker, D. (2005). *Teachers, schools, and society* (7th ed). New York: McGraw-Hill.

Sadker, D., & Silber, E. (Eds.). (2007). *Gender in the classroom: Foundations, skills, methods and strategies across the curriculum.* Mahwah, NJ: Lawrence Erlbaum Associates.

Sadker, D., & Zittleman, K. (2004). Test anxiety—Are students failing tests—or are tests failing students? *Phi Delta Kappan, 85*(10), 740–744, 751.

Sanders, J. (2002). Something is missing from teacher education: Two genders. *Phi Delta Kappan, 84*(3), 241–244.

Sax, L. (2005). Why gender matters: What parents and teachers need to know about the emerging science of sex differences. New York: Doubleday.

Sleeter, C., & Grant, C. (1991). Race, class, gender, and disability in current textbooks. In M. Apple & L. Christian-Smith (Eds.), *The politics of the textbook* (pp. 78–101). New York: Routledge.

Smith, J., & Vaughn, C. (2000, Summer). A conundrum: Perceptions of gender and professional educators during the nineteenth and early twentieth centuries. *Educational Foundations, 14*(3), 5–20.

Sommers, C. (1994). *Who stole feminism?: How women have betrayed women.* New York: Touchstone.

Sommers, C. (2000). *The war against boys: How misguided feminism is harming our young men.* New York: Simon & Schuster.

Tarule, J. M., Applegate, J. H., Earley, P. M., & Blackwell, P. J. (2006). Narrating Gendered leadership. In D. R. Dean, S. Bracken, & J. Allen (Eds.), *Women in academic leadership: Professional strategies, personal choices: Vol. 2, Women in academe.* Sterling, VA: Stylus Publishing LLC.

Titus, J. (1993). Gender messages in education foundations textbooks. *Journal of Teacher Education, 44,* 38–44.

Umbach, P. (April 2006). *Gender equity in the academic labor market: An analysis of academic disciplines.* Paper presented at the 2006 annual meeting of the American Educational Research Association, San Francisco, CA.

United States Department of Education. Gender Equity Panel. (2000). *Exemplary and promising gender equity programs.* Washington, DC: United States Department of Education. Retrieved on July 27, 2005, from http://www.ed.gov/pubs/genderequity/index.html

United States Department of Education . National Center for Educational Statistics. (1999). *National Study of Postsecondary Faculty Report on Faculty and Instructional Staff in 1998* (Table 30, p.46). Washington, DC: Office of Educational Research and Improvement.

United States Department of Education. National Center for Education Statistics. (2004a). *Digest of education statistics, 2003.* Washington, DC: Office of Educational Research and Improvement.

United States Department of Education. National Center for Education Statistics. (2004b). *National Study of Postsecondary Faculty Report on Faculty and Instructional Staff in Fall 2003,* Table 8, p.14. Washington DC: Office of Educational Research and Improvement.

Van De Walle, J. (2001). *Elementary and middle school mathematics: Teaching developmentally* (4th ed). New York: Addison Wesley Longman.

Weaver-Hightower, M. (2003). The "boy turn" in research on gender and education. *Review of Educational Research, 73*(Winter), 471–498.

Webb, D., Metha, A., & Jordan, F. (2000). *Foundations of American Education.* Upper Saddle River, NJ: Merrill.

Weis, L. (1986, Fall). Inequality: A sociological perspective in teacher education. *Educational Foundations, 1*, 41–50.

Wilson, R. (2004, December 3). Where the elite teach, it's still a man's world. *The Chronicle of Higher Education, LI*(15), A8–A12, A13.

Witt, S. (1996). Traditional or androgynous: An analysis to determine gender role orientation of basal readers. *Child Study Journal, 26*, 303–318.

Zittleman, K., & Sadker, D. (2002, December/2003, January). Teacher education and gender equity: The unfinished gender revolution. *Educational Leadership, 60*(4), 59–62.

Zittleman, K., & Sadker, D. (2002). Gender bias in teacher education texts: New (and old) lessons. *Journal of Teacher Education, 53*(2), 168–180.

Part

•III•

OVERVIEW: GENERAL EDUCATIONAL PRACTICES FOR PROMOTING GENDER EQUITY

Lynn H. Fox

While some aspects of gender equity in education may be specific to particular contexts, special populations, or instructional domains, some general themes cut across levels of schooling, subject matter content, and diverse populations. These are educational tools and learning environments. Thus two topics from the section on general educational practices for promoting gender equity in the original handbook in 1985 have been revisited in this volume. The learning tools chapters are chapter 8 on testing and chapter 10 on technology, and the learning environment chapters are chapter 9 on coeducation and single-sex education and the major gender equity problem of sexual harassment in chapter 11. This section in the 1985 *Handbook* contained three chapters, one on testing, one on classroom organization and climate, and one on bias in instructional materials. Since the publication of the original *Handbook*, several issues that were just emerging at that time and thus only treated in short passages in other sections have come to warrant chapters of their own in this volume. These are the topics of single-sex versus coeducational schools and classes, and uses of technology as an information-access and learning tool. The chapter on bias in instructional materials has been removed from this section in this volume, but this important topic is addressed by the chapters in section IV on "Gender equity strategies in the content areas," as well as the part II chapters related to teacher and administrator education. It is also discussed in some of the chapters addressing gender equity strategies for diverse populations.

Most discussions of sex or gender differences invariably turn to issues of measured outcomes, indicators, or predictor variables. Thus one of the most challenging tasks facing educators and psychologists in the area of individual differences is the degree to which we can obtain unbiased measures of attitudes, interests, achievement, and developed abilities. In chapter 8 the authors describe the theory and practice in detecting and eliminating bias in measurement instruments that evolved through the years as a result of the efforts of various professional soci-

eties led by the American Psychological Association and the American Educational Research Association.

Although test publishers now routinely scrutinize tests for potential sources of bias related to content validity, some questions about the possibilities of gender bias in the predictive validity of tests remain. Most of the research on bias has focused on the use of tests in what is often referred to as *high stakes* testing, where important decisions are made about individuals or institutions on the basis of either achievement or developed abilities test scores. More research is needed to examine the issues of bias in more informal assessment tools, particularly teacher-constructed instruments used in K–12 classrooms, such as performance checklists or portfolios.

This chapter identifies several areas where more research is needed as the use of tests increases for school system accountability, and as methods of assessment change due to emerging technologies. In addition, the authors make some recommendations for practice based on current research. The most critical issue at this time appears to be the need for disaggregation of test score results by sex and ethnicity. When data is not disaggregated, the patterns of achievement or developed abilities that result from inequitable treatments can be obscured. When data is not disaggregated, it is impossible to ensure equitable treatment through careful monitoring of outcomes.

In chapter 9 the author summarizes the body of research on bias within the coeducational classroom and updates the findings from the 1985 *Handbook*. Despite many efforts and increased public and teacher awareness of patterns of gender inequities in classroom interactions, there is no recent evidence to suggest that this inequity has disappeared. Though gender bias persists in the classroom, many view sexism as irrelevant or old fashioned. Research suggests that gender inequities in teacher attention impact both girls and boys in coeducational classrooms. Girls are often ignored while boys often receive more negative teacher attention generally related to their disruptive behavior. Although in the late 1980s and early 1990s there were some teacher and administrator training programs developed to combat gender inequities, due to funding issues, political climate, etc., these programs were not broadly replicated and thus did not have a wide-ranging impact.

In 1985, most instances of single-sex education were at the school level, predominantly in private schools. Today the interest in possible gender differences and in establishing public charter schools has led to a number of public school systems experimenting with same-sex classes or even schools. Advocates for single-sex education have many interesting expectations and often cite research to support their claims. Chapter 9 of this volume identifies the challenges in conducting research on single-sex education as well as in interpreting the results. For example, Title IX (which prohibits sex discrimination in education programs or activities receiving federal financial assistance) only allows single-sex education when it can contribute in the longer term to decreasing sex discrimination). Thus, research involving schools covered by Title IX or the Equal Protection Clause of the 14th Amendment to the U.S. Constitution must meet complementary legal as well as research standards such as making sure that the single-sex intervention increases gender equity, and making sure that comparisons of single-sex male and single-sex female classes or schools with each other and with coed interventions are well matched for research and legal purposes.

Readers of this chapter should greatly increase their understanding of why research findings on the value of single-sex education interventions has been so inconclusive and also what can be done to learn if specific well-planned single-sex education should be replicated and used by many others to advance gender equity both in and through education.

Using the *Trilogy for Student Success* model proposed by Jolly, Campbell, and Pearlman (2004)[1] as the theoretical framework, the authors of chapter 10, "Gender Equity in the use of Educational Technology," examine the research literature on educational uses of technology in terms of the elements of *engagement, capacity,* and *continuity*. Although the chapter concludes that gender parity has been reached in technology use or access, research findings indicate that girls and boys use technology differently in ways that can limit girls' future education and career options. For example, in elementary and middle-level grades, boys and girls are equally computer literate and equivalent in their use of computers at school. As they move into high school, however, gender differences in use patterns begin to emerge, and quality of *engagement* changes. Although girls continue to refine word processing skills, Power Point presentations and other business/clerical skills, boys dominate the computer science and programming classes. As adults, men are more likely than women to use the Internet to research financial and travel information and more likely to use spreadsheets, presentation tools, and audio/video editing tools.

Females, particularly high school girls, have negative attitudes regarding technology use and tend to think of technology use as playing violent games or primarily in terms of computer programming. This chapter reviews the research on several factors that have been described as influencing attitudes toward technology such as: (a) the male-dominated computer culture, (b) societal gender bias, and (c) gender bias in computer software design.

The authors describe a number of technology applications designed to *engage* girls. These applications also help girls develop the *capacity* for using a greater number of technology applications. Although technology education is moving in a direction that will benefit girls and should result in a greater level of equity eventually, there are issues of *continuity*, especially in terms of differential access for both girls and boys of lower socioeconomic status at school and at home. Another *continuity* issue is uses of technology by teachers. With respect to teachers, barriers that remain are primarily issues of institutional continuity such as the lack of time and incentives for teachers and higher education faculty to learn to use IT in its full capacity, and the lack of gender sensitive technology integration within teacher preparation and preprofessional development programs.

Chapter 11 concludes part III with a discussion of sexual harassment and bullying. This chapter is new to the *Handbook* although sexual harassment was briefly discussed in the original 1985 *Handbook* under the discussions of school and classroom climates and postsecondary education. One disturbing finding is that despite more schools having policy statements and offering students educational materials on sexual harassment, students continue to engage in sexual harassment and rarely tell school administrators about being victimized. It is estimated that between 11 and 50% of adolescent girls experienced behaviors at school that fit the legal definition of sexual harassment (i.e., unwelcome sexual advances, requests for sexual favors and other verbal or physical conduct that unreasonably interferes with an individual's school or work performance, creates an intimidating or hostile school or work environment, or is required in exchange for a grade or a job).

The authors of chapter 11 provide descriptions of both interventions and guidelines for policy and practice and, where possible, research evidence in support of various approaches. Many research studies on bullying and sexual harassment have focused on identifying pathology in an individual; the authors argue for more studies at the institutional level of analysis to explain the prevalence of sexual harassment and to recognize the contexts within which sexual harassment is more likely to occur.

What emerges across the four chapters is the importance of the interface of research with effective practice and public policy. Chapter 8 on testing shows how some policy and practice has been influenced by the research on gender equity since the publication of the first *Handbook*. Publishers of tests, particularly standardized tests used in many instances of high stakes assessment, have implemented many procedures to scrutinize the construction of such instruments and organizations such as the American Psychological Association and the American Educational Research Association have worked to develop standards for the equitable development and use of tests. The gap between research and practice is greatest in terms of the lack of data about teacher-constructed assessment tools and bias.

---

[1]See reference for Jolly, Campbell and Pearlman (2004) in chapter 10.

Chapter 9 on single-sex schools and classroom climate shows a clear mismatch between policy, practice, and research. While numerous studies have looked at issues of single-sex schooling, the methodological limitations of these studies leave practitioners and policy makers confused by the conflicting results. Many key questions for the proper implementation of the intent of Title IX for example are not addressed by most of the research that tries to compare single-sex and coed educational environments but ignores the intent of the law by failing to measure the impact of these environments in terms of gender equity outcomes per se.

Although many research findings reported in these four chapters indicate some improvements in terms of reduced gender gaps or lessening levels of gender bias since the time of the publication of the first *Handbook*, all four raise a cautionary note about the need for continued attention to equity issues and the importance of data-based evidence. All four chapters provide arguments for the importance of disaggregation of data by sex and often by more complex breakdowns such as sex by ethnicity, socioeconomic status, and disability status. It is impossible to detect gender bias when test scores or other outcome measures are not reported by sex. The significance of continued scrutiny of policy, practice, and outcomes is further reinforced in several other chapters in this volume, particularly those in part V, which looks at seven diverse populations and subgroups such as gifted students, people with disabilities, and members of several different minority groups.

·8·

GENDER EQUITY IN TESTING AND ASSESSMENT

Dianne Reed,* Lynn H. Fox,* *Mary Lou Andrews,*
Nancy Betz, Jan Perry Evenstad, Anthony Harris,
Carol Hightower-Parker, Judy Johnson, Shirley Johnson,
Barbara Polnick, and Phyllis Rosser

INTRODUCTION

Gender bias is so subtle that we barely recognize it. It is so ingrained as to how we define ourselves that it is essentially invisible (Koontz, 1997). In considering the concept of gender equity in testing and assessment, it is important to recognize that tests and assessments have historically served as sifters to filter out not only females, but also language-minority students, students from low socioeconomic levels, and students of color from educational opportunities.

Some educators and policymakers assume that new forms of tests and assessments will lead to more equitable outcomes. Changing the forms of tests and assessments will not solve this complex issue. As a result, educators must pay careful attention to the ways tests and assessments are used and argue for policies that ensure support for reform. Tests and assessments can be used to (a) provide teachers with practical information on student learning; (b) enable schools to engage in the process of assessing students' needs; (c) develop strategic planning based on the identified needs; and (d) implement innovative programs and practices supported by the data to positively impact the achievement of all students.

The chapter on "Sex equity in testing," written by Diamond and Tittle for the 1985 *Handbook*, addressed many of the same areas that we are still focusing on today. It appears that changes have occurred in only small increments. This chapter is a synthesis of literature addressing gender equity relating to testing and assessment and documents the small, but sig-

nificant, changes since 1985. This chapter specifically focuses on the following:

1. The definitions of gender bias and gender equity and a discussion of the standards, concepts and procedures that are used to analyze or eliminate bias.
2. The factors that may impact gender differences in performance such as anxiety and *stereotype threat*.
3. A synthesis of the literature on gender equity issues in high-stakes testing, such as the use of standardized measures of developed abilities and achievement for admissions decisions, school accountability, and federal reporting.
4. A synthesis of the literature on gender equity issues in the use of vocational aptitude and interest tests, as well as the Scholastic Aptitude Test/Scholastic Assessment Test (SAT).[1]
5. Issues of gender equity-related classroom assessments such as teacher-made tests, portfolios, and performance assessments.

DEFINING AND ELIMINATING BIAS IN TESTING

Since the mid-1980s, when there was substantial attention to test fairness and both empirical and judgmental methods to improve assessments were designed and widely implemented, the "look and feel" of tests has changed dramatically, and there is much more systematic attention to test fairness in general, and gender fairness in particular. This is true of both academic and vocational/career tests. Fairness has become a mainstream value

---

*The bold face names are the Lead Authors.

[1]The name of the SAT has been changed from Scholastic Aptitude Test to Scholastic Assessment Test, however, most of the research cited here is based on the research prior to this name change and so the older name is used throughout this paper except in explicit discussions of the newest version.

among test developers and users. It is now integral to validity theory and to the standards to which tests are held, including the AERA/APA/NCME *Standards for Educational and Psychological Testing* and the *Code of Fair Testing.*

Defining Bias

In 1985, Diamond and Tittle defined bias related to testing and assessment as a judgmental aspect referring to intrinsic test characteristics referencing question content, constructs being measured, and the context within which the constructs were set. They expanded that prevailing definition to include a stereotypical presentation of genders/subgroups within the test narrative (e.g., no minority representation within the content; pictorial depictions of only White political candidates), females portrayed in traditional female roles, or verbal representation of males as dominant in a field (e.g., males portrayed as superior to females in mathematics and science). They also distinguished bias inherent to an instrument in relation to a group and *fairness* in the interpretation or use of an instrument or data in terms of ethics.

In the ensuing years, several authors have suggested further extension of this definition, for example, discussing parity for underrepresented populations (Chilisa, 2000; Spencer, Porche, & Tolman, 2003), or gender equity, in the form of standpoint theory (Chilisa, 2000; Thompson & Gitlin, 1993). This definition supports the premise that each and every question included in an assessment process is based on and reflects the values, social constructs, and societal assumptions of the designers and/or those scoring the assessments. These issues range from social expectancy theory to standpoint theory (Gipps, 1994; Thompson & Gitlin, 1993). They also relate to providing attention to gender differences in the instructional setting (Sadker & Sadker, 1994) and even to gender ideologies (i.e., what is considered normative and acceptable within the broader society; Connell, 1993; Tolman & Porche, 2000).

Thus, the organizing framework in which the assessment processes are developed and evaluated may be inadvertently biased by the value structures and social constructs of the developers and scorers themselves. Similarly, the individual involved in the assessment process brings values, experiences, and social constructs to the process. This combination of personal and social constructs creates the potential for inequities in the testing procedures.

Bias in testing may occur when one group outperforms another on the assessment instruments, although in reality there are no differences in knowledge or ability between the groups. There are, of course, several possible explanations for differences found in test performance between groups. Some of these explanations would reflect valid differences in what is being measured; others would generate test invalidity by creating variance in test scores that is related to test takers' group membership, but not to what is intended to be measured. For example, a valid test will show differences that actually reflect current differences among people in the knowledge or developed abilities that the test is intended to measure. Such differences could be due to different experiences that test takers bring to the test, or to differential efforts that they have made. These differences are not indicative of invalidity in the test instruments, even though they may reflect the negative impact of lack of opportunity based on a more general bias in the culture, or individual characteristics that have been fostered by negative prior experiences. Another explanation is that there is bias or invalidity in the testing that could stem from either material that should be there that is lacking, or from material that should not be there but is. Sources of invalidity that are not relevant to the intended construct may come from many sources, including:

1. the content of the questions that are included in or excluded from the test instrument;
2. lack of linkage between what the test is supposed to measure, what the test specifications call for, and what the questions actually measure;
3. flaws in question writing such as unclear or confusing language, offensive language or upsetting situations described, excessive reading load in non-reading tests, or excessive calculation in mathematical reasoning tests the way the test is administered, timed, or scored; or
4. faulty assumptions about whether all of the test takers in fact have the necessary prior knowledge to answer the questions (e.g., knowledge of calculus for an advanced mathematical reasoning test).

Any of these factors could lead to mistaken interpretations of the test score, which is the core definition of test invalidity. To the extent that these factors result in misinterpretations that are specific to gender or other factors, the test can be considered unfair to the group affected, as well as invalid. Non-test factors can also create invalidity, for example test takers who experience stereotype threat in a testing situation. Likely threats to validity and fairness can and should be identified a priori, and controlled through appropriate test design, administration, and judgmental and empirical analysis of differential patterns of performance by gender and other relevant groups.

These and other principles to ensure valid and fair tests are available in *Standards for Educational and Psychological Testing* (AERA/APA/NCME, 1999), which were created by the American Educational Research Association (AERA), the American Psychological Association (APA), and the National Council for Measurement in Education (NCME), and are widely held to be the most important technical and legal standard for quality testing in all educational settings. Many other sets of standards exist for more specific purposes. For example, the Joint Committee on Testing Practices (JCTP) of the American Psychological Association (APA) has also addressed the issue of test quality and fairness, and has published a *Code of Fair Testing Practices in Education* (2004). This publication was written as a "guide for professionals in fulfilling the need to provide and use tests that are fair to all test takers regardless of age, gender, disability, race and national origin, religion, sexual orientation, linguistic background, or other personal characteristics as a primary consideration in all aspects of testing" (p. 2).

This *Code* is consistent with the AERA/APA/NCME *Standards* and emphasizes "careful standardization and administration to ensure that all test takers experience a comparable opportunity to perform in the given test area" (p. 2). The *Code* is addressed to both test consumers and test developers. The *Code* provides guidance separately for test developers and test users in four critical areas: developing and selecting appropriate tests; administering and scoring tests; reporting and interpreting test results; and informing test takers. Other standards relevant to fairness in assessment include: *Responsibilities of Users of Standardized Tests* (Association for Assessment in Counseling, 1989), *APA Test User Qualifications* (APA, 2000), *ASHA Code of Ethics* (American Speech and Hearing Association, 2001), *Ethical Principles of Psychologists and Code of Conduct* (APA, 1992), *NASP Professional Conduct Manual* (National Association of School Psychologists, 2000), *Code of Professional Responsibility* (NCME, 1995), and *Rights and Responsibilities of Test Takers: Guidelines and Expectations* (Joint Committee on Testing Practices, 2000).

Methods for Analyzing Tests for Issues of Fairness

Issues of bias center on questions about the validity in the interpretations and uses of the test for particular populations or the appropriateness of the norms of the test for use with a particular population. Three types of validity issues are described next, followed by a discussion of a statistical approach, *Differential Item Functioning* analysis (DIF). This section concludes with some discussion of the problems of fairness in the uses and interpretation of tests, particularly issues related to the representativeness of normative samples and disaggregation of data.

Content validity. Validity-related evidence based on test content is a matter of judgment rather than any statistical analysis. It has become standard procedure to evaluate tests in the developmental stages. For achievement tests and some measures of developed abilities the procedure usually involves having a panel of subject matter experts examine items for accuracy and relevance. They may be asked to also evaluate the content for possible bias or offensiveness, including male and female representation imbalances, or another panel may be convened for that sole purpose.

Predictive validity. Predictive studies ask if a test under- or overestimates performance on a later criterion such as grades for one group versus another. This type of validity-related evidence is of interest for high-stakes testing used for selection purposes such as measures of developed abilities and achievement used in college admissions. The procedure requires statistical comparisons of the correlations between the test and other later measures such as grades in courses, overall graduation rates, or grade point averages. These types of studies are somewhat difficult to do properly, in part because of the statistical limitations such as restriction of test score range because people with the full range of test scores were not admitted to an institution, or restriction of grades' range because students all received only A's or B's.

Construct validity. One change since 1985 and the first *Handbook* that has had a huge impact on testing is the expansion of the notion of construct validity. Current validity theory (construct validity; see AERA/APA/NCME, 1999, and Messick, 1989) is based on the idea that validity resides in the inferences

made from test scores, not in the test itself. These inferences should not go beyond what the test measures; inferences must acknowledge that extraneous material can weaken the validity of test scores, and that test scores should not be considered valid overall if there is some subgroup (women or underrepresented minorities, for example) for whom this is not true. Also, test scores are considered fundamentally invalid if there are negative consequences from their use that are attributable to construct underrepresentation or the presence of construct irrelevant variance. This means, in essence, that scientifically speaking, the concept of a fair test, their interpretations of scores and their uses, is a central concept used to judge test quality today. This is no longer a peripheral issue or simply a matter of racial or gender politics.

Differential item functioning. An increase in the use of comprehensive sensitivity reviews and statistical monitoring procedures, such as *differential item functioning* (DIF), led to the development of standardized tests and test revisions that have much less gender bias.

According to Willingham, Cole, Lewis, and Leung (1997), DIF focuses on identifying items that may contribute to differences in performance between groups that are matched with respect to the ability, knowledge, or skill of interest. The total score on the test being analyzed is used as the matching criterion in order to identify any individual item that functions differently for groups—that is, items that are differentially difficult for a subgroup of examinees that are equally capable of answering questions of this general type as defined by the total score on the test. This method relies on the total test score as the criterion for identifying items, not a criterion that is external to the test itself. Statistical evaluation of the differential performance of gender subgroups on test items has been incorporated by most testing organizations as part of their test development and test revision process. One of the DIF methods used at the Educational Testing Service (ETS) is the *standardization procedure* developed by Dorans and Kulick (1983, 1986). With this procedure, an item is said to exhibit DIF when the probability of correctly answering the item is lower or higher for examinees from one group, such as females, than for equally able examinees from a comparison group, such as males. Another method used at ETS is the *Mantel-Haenszel* (MH) method adapted by Holland and Thayer in 1988. DIF on test items can be performed at different points in the test development or revision process, usually at the pretest stage (Nandakumar, Glutting, & Oakland, 1993; Willingham et al., 1997).

DIF studies can indicate that some item content, format, or structure factor may to be related to the differential item performance of a gender group. DIF statistics in themselves do not address what these factors may be, but some information can be obtained by aggregating questions that have shown DIF for or against a group, and analyzing them to determine what the common theme is. For example, some studies have found that human relationships or aesthetics/philosophy content, favor female test takers, and science-related content, specialized terminology (e.g., science, industrial arts, military) favor males. Females tend to do better with antonyms and analogy items having human relationships or aesthetics or philosophy content. Performance on reading comprehension passages having content related to science appears to be easier for males. Females have been found to perform better on algebra items and on more abstract, pure mathematics items, while males appear to do better with geometry items and mathematics word problems (Donlon, 1973; Willingham et al., 1997; Zenisky, Hambleton, & Robin, 2003–2004). In addition, females perform better when mathematics problems are presented in typical textbook style or are solvable by using strategies that they have been taught in class; males appear to solve problems more intuitively ("they dislike writing down all the steps of a problem, because they have found the answer in their head"; Willingham et al., p. 185).

Not all authors would agree with the aforementioned writers. For example, Hunter and Schmidt (2000) argued that findings of biased items based on DIF can be explained by three factors, none of which is related to gender bias. They believe that statistical errors or biases exist in the following:

1. failure to control for measurement error in ability estimates;
2. violations of the unidimensionality assumption required by DIF detection methods; and
3. reliance on significance testing, causing tiny DIF effects that are artifacts, rather than true differences.

Thus, they conclude that there is no evidence that items currently used in standardized achievement testing function differently in various gender groups. These and other studies are contributing data that will continue to make test construction more fair for both genders who are required to take the examinations. However, "the key to understanding gender differences is probably at the level of the underlying constructs, not the surface features of test administration" (Bridgeman & Schmitt, 1997, p. 226; see also Buck, Kostin, & Morgan, 2002).

Development of representative normative data and data disaggregation. Although the issues of representative samples in normative data are generally raised in terms of ethnic and socioeconomic comparisons, there are related concerns in terms of gender. This issue is particularly important in the discussion of vocational interest and aptitude instruments and will be more fully developed in the vocational assessment section. In terms of achievement tests and tests of developed abilities, the biggest issue may be the lack of test data reporting disaggregated by sex, or by sex and other key variables such as ethnicity. For example, data suggest that patterns of sex differences for African American or Hispanic students on achievement tests may be different than for Whites. When data are not disaggregated, the results of gender-bias analysis could be distorted depending on the ethnic mix of the populations tested (Buck et al., 2002).

Perry Evenstad conducted a study (2003) that used data disaggregation to analyze the Colorado Student Assessment Program (CSAP) reading scores for students in grades 3 through 10. The data were from a sizable and diverse school district to determine what pattern of achievement emerged when (a) gender, (b) race/ethnicity, (c) socioeconomic status, (d) English language proficiency, and (e) grade level were considered simultaneously. The results revealed that each variable was unique in its contribution to the overall student profile and subsequent score. The disaggregation of data showed that interpreting achievement results is complicated when simultaneously considering gender and other variables. Therefore, consideration must be given to instructional methods, standards, curriculum materials, and how reading is taught in relation to the variables analyzed in the study.

POSSIBLE GENDER-LINKED FACTORS THAT INFLUENCE TEST PERFORMANCE

A considerable body of evidence suggests that an individual's test performance may be impacted by a wide range of personal, societal, and assessment factors such as personal test-taking style, internalized societal expectations, or characteristics of the test or test items themselves. Some of these factors seem to differentially impact males and females and may account for some of the observed group differences. In the following sections, factors that influence test performance have been categorized as either those that are a function of the test themselves, those that are characteristics of the test taker, and those that are linked to societal expectations and interactions.

Test Characteristics

Test format or item type has been found to relate to gender differences in test performance. Willingham et al. (1997) concentrated on a battery of 12 standardized tests of achievement that had been administered to 25 randomly drawn national samples at the end of high school. These cohorts previously had been tested at 4th and 8th grades as well, and the results were available for analysis. In addition, they secured annual test scores from major testing programs. They found in looking at gender differences in Advanced Placement (AP) tests (from more restricted samples of high-performing students), an (inconsistent) tendency for females to perform better on free-response or essay questions, while males tended to perform better on a multiple-choice format. Female students in all racial and ethnic groups outscored males on the writing section of the National Assessment of Educational Progress (NAEP) exam in 4th, 8th, and 12th grades, as well as on the SAT II exam for writing, a subject-specific test, formerly required by the nation's most selective schools (Alaimo 2004).

Males seemed to do better than females in terms of *speeded* tests such as the SAT Mathematics test where a larger percentage of females than males omitted the last 10 questions in both mathematics sections (Linn & Kessel, 1996). In their 1996 meta-analysis, Linn and Kessel concluded that the SAT's emphasis on speed required students to solve 25–30 problems in 30 minutes compared to "reformulated mathematics courses that include an emphasis on solving complex, ill-posed, and personally relevant problems [that] place an emphasis on sustained reasoning" (p. 72). Their research showed that women were able to perform as well as men on mathematics exams in other countries that required solutions to several long problems.

In a small-scale study by Benjamin-Kelly and Rosser in 1989 (Benjamin-Kelly, 2000), 40 New York City high school juniors

(20 females, 20 males, 20 Whites, 20 African Americans) were interviewed to see how they solved SAT mathematics problems, and 20 high school juniors in Seattle, Washington (10 girls, 10 boys, 10 Whites, 10 African Americans) were interviewed regarding their verbal problem-solving processes. These students were retested on the SAT and given all the time they needed to answer each question, to see whether SAT time pressure affected the sexes differently. Most of them took more time than the 40 to 60 seconds allotted per question on the actual test. In general, the females were more likely to work the mathematics problems as they had been taught in the classroom, i.e., in a step-by-step manner using formulas or knowledge of geometry. The males, on the other hand, were more likely to use test-taking strategies such as substituting answer choices in the problem to see which one worked or noticed the answer choice that was different from all the others (usually the correct one). Giving the females all the time they needed seemed to work in their favor because it allowed them to do the required mathematics. But increased time was not associated with improvements in scores for males; they answered fewer questions correctly despite the expanded time frame. The females who scored highest in the verbal study took the most time per question, more time than the males who answered correctly, more than the females who answered incorrectly, and more time than the SAT average on the verbal section of 40 seconds per question. On the other hand, African American females averaged the most time per question in the mathematics test but had the fewest correct answers; unlimited time does not always improve performance.

Test-taker Characteristics

It has been suggested that males and females have different test-taking styles. For example, females tend to leave more questions unanswered than males on tests such as the SAT (Rosser, 1989a). One theory about differential omissions postulated that females were less likely to be risk takers and therefore guess less than males largely because of their socialization and early education (deNuys & Wolfe, 1985; Sadker & Sadker, 1985). "Girls think the SAT measures their intelligence and they mustn't cheat. But, boys are more competitive and they play it like a pinball game" (Gilligan & Attanucci, 1988, p. 223).

Another possibility is that females may be more likely to follow instructions or "play by the rules" (Rosser, 1989b). Playing by the rules may also present a problem for questions where students must apply the rule learned in mathematics class to the new situations presented on the test. Mathematics grades show that females are as competent as males, but they may be more reluctant to use mathematics in an unfamiliar way. In fact, studies have found females are more likely than males to follow the mathematics procedures (algorithms) taught in the classroom (Benjamin-Kelly, 2000).

In earlier forms of the SAT, the monitor read the following instructions before each administration: "Scores on these tests are based on the number of questions answered correctly minus a fraction (1/4 point per question) of the number of questions answered incorrectly, therefore, random or haphazard guessing is unlikely to change your scores" (*Taking the SAT*, College Board, 1985, p. 10). This admonition about guessing (with the information that students are penalized for wrong answers) was possibly taken more seriously by females (Rosser, 1989c).

Anxiety may also be a factor in test performance. In a study of 1,112 students in a coaching class taking a practice SAT, two and a half times as many females as males said they were "extremely anxious," and those females who said they were "extremely anxious" scored lower on the mathematics SAT than the "somewhat anxious" females (Steele, 2004). Whether or not the anxiety lowers performance or is caused by poor performance is unclear. Some evidence suggests that expectations about one's performance might influence performance. For example, Steele (2004) found that on an AP Calculus exam, when females' stereotype threat was activated by their being told to write down their sex beforehand, they did worse than males; but, when they were told, "this is a test you will do better on even though females generally do worse in mathematics," they did better than males (p. 73). Faigel (1991) found that students suffering from unusually severe test anxiety have difficulty thinking: "An hour later they remember not only the questions but also the right answers" (p. 442).

Test sophistication may also be a factor related to gender. Of the 60 students interviewed in New York and Seattle in one study, only four received some coaching, but the males were found to be more *test wise* (Benjamin-Kelly, 2000). More than half the males, but only two females, in the verbal study asked if there was a guessing penalty. This suggested that these males had more of a gaming strategy toward the test. The females who worked the mathematics problems also showed a lack of test-wiseness by using a strategy that was too slow for the actual test. The males were more likely to know the tricks of the test, such as trying out answer choices to find the right one on the mathematics problems.

Context and Stereotype Threat

"From 'white men can't jump' to 'girls can't do mathematics,' negative images that are pervasive in the culture can make us choke during tests of ability" (Begley, 2000, p. 66). The power of stereotypes, scientists had long figured, lay in their ability to change the behavior of the person holding the stereotype (Steele, 1997). Steele (1997) stated that it is the target of a stereotype whose behavior is most powerfully affected. "Stereotypes such as 'ditzy blondes' and 'forgetful seniors' make people painfully aware of how society views them. So painfully aware, in fact, that knowledge of the stereotype can affect how well they do on intellectual and other tasks" (Begley, 2000, p. 67).

Steele (1997) and his colleagues have described *stereotype threat* as the idea that students in groups that have been negatively stereotyped are less likely to perform well in situations such as standardized tests, especially if they feel they are being evaluated through the lens of that stereotype. Steele (1997) examined the theory that a stereotype threat can be powerful enough to shape the intellectual performance and academic identities of entire groups of people. Steele (1997) further explained stereotype threat as based on a person's belief that simply by being in a situation where a negative stereotype about a group could apply, the members of the group know that they could be judged in terms of that stereotype, treated in terms of it, or inadvertently do something that would confirm the stereotype. If the members of the group care about doing well in that situation, the prospect of being treated stereotypically will be upsetting and disturbing to them. If the intellectual abilities of the group are negatively stereotyped, a stereotype threat might occur. That negative stereotype could be applicable during an important standardized test. Steele and his colleagues reasoned that this threat, the prospect of confirming a stereotype, or just being viewed in that manner, would be distracting and upsetting enough to undermine a person's performance at crucial moments in a test situation (Aronson et al., 1999).

According to Steele (1997), anyone may experience a stereotype threat when a negative stereotype exists about the group an individual feels part of, and when the person is deeply invested in succeeding in an endeavor. He studied powerfully affected groups, females in mathematics and minorities in many academic fields. Steele (1997) documented the powerful interfering effects of stereotype threats and identified the effects when pressure is alleviated, resulting in dramatically improved performance. He analyzed the nature of group identity and its roots in the perception that one is under threat because of that identity (Croizet & Claire, 1998; Steele, 1997).

It is important to stress, according to Steele (1997), that everyone experiences stereotype threat because everyone is a member of one group or another that is negatively stereotyped in society. For example, imagine a group of males talking to females about pay equity. The males might experience a sense of being threatened by the possibility of being judged in terms of the male stereotype or what they say being interpreted that way. In particular, for those who care about being seen equitably, such interpretation is upsetting and disturbing. The possibility of such stereotyping might cause avoidance of similar situations or possibly encourage embarrassing slips of the tongue. The focus of Steele's and his colleagues' research is stereotypes that target groups for whom the stereotypes impugn their abilities (Spencer, Steele, & Quinn, 1999). For example, because the world of mathematics and science tends to be male dominated, the stereotype threat for females becomes more intense on mathematics and science tests (Spencer et al., 1999).

Through research it has become vividly clear to Steele and others that the effects of the stereotype are most powerful for the students who are the strongest and the most motivated (Steele & Aronson, 1995). For example, if a female who is performing mathematics, but really does not identify with mathematics, is given a very difficult mathematics test, she will start to do it, and will do her best, but as she gets frustrated she will probably start to say, "Well, this is not me. This is not important to me," and she may withdraw. So the problem of stereotype threat impacts the female mathematics student who wants to do well in mathematics, and for whom doing well is very important (Steele & Aronson, 1995). It is for that kind of student, one who has a great deal invested in mathematics, the prospect of being stereotyped in it, of doing something that would increase the likelihood of their being stereotyped, is disturbing (Steele & Aronson, 1995). In some of Steele's research, he found that students' blood pressure was elevated in stereotyped situations. For these students, the stereotype threat was disturbing, dis-

tracting, and likely to interfere with their test performance and their interactions and behaviors (Steele & Aronson, 1995).

Steele and colleagues (Aronson et al., 1999) also studied stereotypes in White males, a group that is not negatively stereotyped in society on mathematics performance. The study addressed the question, "Can stereotype threat affect the performance of groups who are not subject to any negative stereotype about something?" The population for the study was White males who were heavily invested in mathematics, including graduate engineering students and undergraduate mathematics honor students in mathematics. The students were told just before taking the mathematics test, "Gee, this is a test on which Asians tend to do better than Whites." Now, they were under the comparative stereotype threat. Since their group was not negatively stereotyped about mathematics but rather to Asians, there may be possibility of a threat. This resulted in underperformance on the mathematics test for those students. The study made it clear that this reaction was not coming from a self-believing, self-fulfilling negative stereotype, but rather from an intense situational pressure that happens to individuals who are invested in doing well in the domain (Aronson et al., 1999).

HIGH-STAKES TESTING

There are several issues about the consequences of testing on schools and classrooms. For the purposes of this chapter, high-stakes testing will be divided into three areas: admissions testing, accountability in schools and school systems, and screening for special populations. In terms of gender equity, the most widely researched questions have focused on the uses or misuses of tests in the admissions process, but data also suggest gender issues for the other three areas as well.

Discussions of high-stakes testing need to be tempered by some important distinctions between the uses of tests and the impact that has upon those who choose or are chosen to be tested. First, in the 20 years since the last *Handbook*, there have been substantial changes in women's participation in education, and thus in testing. (The "Postsecondary" chapter documents several aspects of this, such as degree attainment and increases in women in graduate and professional schools.) Both the SAT and the Graduate Record Examination (GRE) have data, disaggregated by gender, online that show how this is reflected in the number of test takers.

A second factor is the extent to which one can differentiate among tests that can be used to generalize to the population as a whole, such as NAEP, and those that cannot, such as the ACT and the SAT. NAEP is administered to a carefully selected sample of the population, with the goal of being able to make valid inferences about a particular population such as fourth grade African American girls. Individual students do not volunteer for this testing depending on their interests and educational goals. In sharp contrast, many highly personal factors go into an individual's deciding whether or not to take a college admission test. Self-selected samples such as that of the ACT and SAT cannot be generalized to a larger population that would include individuals who did not choose to take the tests. Even more important for our purposes is that in the past 20 years there have been important changes in both men's and women's decisions to take college admission tests. More women are now taking such tests, and more women than men are now attending college (the ratio is much larger if only African American students are considered). Some of the women new to the college testing *pool* are those who are poorer than college students in the past, are the first in their families to go to college, and so represent both the upward mobility that the women's movement encouraged them (successfully) to seek, and the reality that *as a group*, the women aspiring to college now show less developed ability in school work than previously. A complicating factor is that in the same time period, boys and men of all ethnic groups have shown increasing disengagement with academic work at almost all levels, making the character of this group very different from the past, as well (Mortenson, 2005).

The third important consideration in the discussion of group and individual differences is the distinction between modern ideas of developed abilities as opposed to the older concept of aptitudes that implied a more fixed nature for abilities that were not changed by learning. Performance on tests directly reflects the quality of prior schooling and other educational experiences. Women and underrepresented minority students are especially likely to hold ideas about the nature of intelligence (fixed, innate, rather than developed by effort and strategies) that depress their achievements. They tend to attribute success and failure to things that are within themselves and not under their control (Dweck, 2000, 2002). Thus it is especially important for gender equity and fairness in test use that tests and test scores are discussed and used in terms of developed abilities. Score interpretations that suggest that tests measure an entity that is unchangeable are not appropriate and should be discouraged. At present, the term *aptitude* is still used in some published test names.

Admissions Testing/Scholarships

Considerable work has been done on the question of gender fairness in terms of assessment practices used in admissions to post-secondary education, graduate education, professional schools, and related scholarship programs. Much of the work on college admissions has focused on the role of the College Board Entrance Examination Board (CEEB) tests such as the SAT, PSAT, and AP examinations. There have also been some important legal cases and settlements, making it clear that sex discrimination related to the use of these tests is illegal under Title IX, which has specific prohibitions against sex discrimination in testing. Much of the criticism of these tests has been in their lack of predictive validity for female and male students since while the male students typically receive higher scores, such as on the SAT, the female students even with lower scores do better with their college grades. In 1996, FairTest reached a settlement with the College Board and ETS to revise the Preliminary SAT/National Merit Scholarship Qualifying Test to add a multiple-choice writing section since males had been scoring higher and receiving many more of the scholarships. An earlier 1988 settlement involved stopping sole use of the SAT for NY Regents Scholarships. By adding high school grades to the SAT test score criteria, girls' proportion of scholarships changed from 28 to 52% of the scholarships (Lee, 2006).

There have been consistent patterns of sex difference over the years in many high stakes tests favoring males. Some of these patterns are slightly different for the elementary and secondary levels and the postsecondary tests. For the postsecondary area, Grandy (1999) reported on trends of GRE scores from 1982 to 1996:

1. Verbal score averages for males over age 30 remained essentially the same as score averages for males under age 30. Both were higher than the score averages for females. Further, score averages for older female examinees were higher than score averages for younger female examinees.
2. After 1989, verbal score averages declined 23 points for females under age 30 and 25 points for females over age 30. For males, the decline was 20 points for those under age 30 and 19 points for those ages 30 and older. Quantitative score means declined the most for younger males, whose averages dropped 15 points from 603 to 588 in 7 years. Older males showed a decline of 6 points, younger females showed a decline of 4 points, and older females showed a decline of only 2 points.
3. Wilder and Powell (1989) and Carlton and Harris (1992) reported the following regarding standardized admissions tests:
   a. On all graduate admissions tests of quantitative and mathematics ability and achievement, males outperformed females, often significantly, and the differences appeared to be greater on tests of developed ability rather than achievement.
   b. On tests in specific fields, like the AP or Graduate Record Exam (GRE) subject tests, males also did better in traditionally "male" subjects like science.
   c. Validity studies, comparing admission test scores (SAT, GRE) with first year college grade point average (GPA) showed females' test scores to be under-predictive, and men's to be overpredictive. These test scores were also more predictive of performance for the females.
   d. The differences in quantitative ability were larger and better supported by the literature than the differences in verbal ability.

The SAT and gender equity. Historically, the major stated purpose of the SAT has been to predict first year college grades, but it has always under predicted for females and overpredicted for males. This underprediction diminishes women's educational opportunities by denying them admission to the most competitive colleges and millions of dollars in scholarship money (National Center for Fair and Open Testing, 2004). Since 1972, female verbal score averages have ranged from 2 to 13 points lower than males. Males' mathematics score averages range from 30 to 52 points higher than those of females (College Board, 2004). In 2004, the College Board reported that females' scores averaged 504 on the verbal section and 501 on the mathematics section. Males averaged 512 on the verbal and 537 on the mathematics. Because of the differences in math section averages, women's total score averages were 44 points lower than males' despite their higher average first year grade point average (GPA). Females were 53% of the test takers.

Wendler and Carlton (1987) conducted an item analysis for the November 1987 SAT in order to examine possible causes of the gender inequity in scores. On this test, females averaged 14 points lower than males on the verbal section and 44 points lower on the mathematics section. Six verbal questions showed substantial differences in the number of males and females who answered them correctly (females performed better on two of them and less well on four).

These differences in item performance related to context. Women scored higher on questions about relationships and men scored higher on questions about science, sports, and the stock market. Women performed better on questions that were general and abstract or set in a context characteristic of humanities questions. Men performed better on questions that were specific and concrete, as found in questions about science and practical affairs. The SAT verbal content was not balanced among areas that interest each sex (Wendler & Carlton, 1987).

The analysis of the mathematics test items was a different story. Men answered correctly more often than women on all 60 of the mathematics questions despite their historically lower classroom grades (Wendler & Carlton, 1987). The differences were smallest on the easiest questions at the beginning of each section and highest on the most difficult questions at the end of each section. Score differences indicated that females found word problems, regardless of whether the content was familiar, more difficult than other types of mathematics. They scored lower than men on 6 of the 10 word problems even though several questions were set in content more familiar to women such as food, cooking, and pottery making.

Geometry questions had the largest sex differences of all the item types on the test. Past research found that females perform less well in geometry than in algebra or arithmetic and the findings of the item analysis confirmed this. Arithmetic questions showed the smallest sex differences. Studies have shown that females in advanced high school mathematics classes have higher grades than their male classmates and the same female mathematics students receive lower SAT mathematics scores (Wendler & Carlton, 1987).

The new SAT. The SAT gender gap may close somewhat in the near future. In March 2005, a required writing test was added to the verbal and mathematics sections. This includes 35 minutes of multiple-choice, copy-editing questions and one short essay to be handwritten within a 25-minute time block. Each section is graded on a 200 to 800 point scale so that the addition of the third score will make the perfect score on the SAT a total score of 2400. The testing time was increased from 3 hours to 3 hours and 45 minutes (National Center for Fair and Open Testing, 2004).

Alaimo (2004) reported that research scientists at the College Board indicted that the revised SAT exam was not designed with the sex gap in mind. "You never think to design a test towards a particular group. You only make efforts not to exclude a particular group. If boys were more likely to get correct an item related to the military, we'd throw that question out" (p. 2). It was also noted that the old SAT often unfairly reflected on young women's potential (Alaimo, 2004). "We're really underpredicting women's performance in college when we look at SAT scores," she said (p. 2).

Results for the first-time reported scores for the new version found a small overall decline in both critical reading and mathematical section means for males and females so that males scored 505 on critical reading and 536 on mathematics, whereas females scored 502 on both whereas there was a mean score difference of 11 points in favor of females on the writing section (College Board, 2006). Thus, the overall difference was 1532 for males and 1506 for females out of the new possible total of 2400. More research is needed to see if women will continue to outscore males on the new writing section. This seems likely because females typically outperform males in writing on other standardized tests. Female students in all racial and ethnic groups outscore males on the writing section of the National Assessment of Educational Progress (NAEP) exam in 4th, 8th, and 12th grades, as well as on the SAT II exam for writing, a subject-specific test formerly required by the nation's most selective schools (Alaimo, 2004).

School Accountability and the Gender Gap in K–12 High Stakes Achievement Testing

While there are diverse opinions about establishing national tests in the U.S.,[2] the compromise in the most recent re-authorization of the federal Elementary and Secondary Education Act (ESEA) of 1965, generally known as The No Child Left Behind Act (NCLB) of 2001, required states to develop and administer a system of standards-based assessments in reading/language arts and mathematics in grades 3–11 and science in one grade level between grades 3–5, 6–9, and 10–12. Assessments in reading and mathematics were to be administered no later than the start of the 2005 academic year, and in science no later than the 2007 academic year. In addition, NCLB required states to administer an annual assessment of English proficiency to Limited English Proficiency (LEP) students in the 2002 academic year (Public Law 107-110, 2002).

Achievement gap. Historically, an achievement gap favoring males has existed in two of the three subject areas assessed under NCLB, mathematics and science. As noted previously, however, males lag behind females in performance in reading/language arts according to results on NAEP (National Center for Education Statistics, 2003). Bickel & Maynard (2004) have asserted, based on an assessment of achievement in rural Appalachia, that "as the percentage of students who are male increases, school mean scores [NAEP] in reading achievement decline. Given the accountability measures and sanctions proposed by the No Child Left Behind Act, having a large percentage of males in a school could be disastrous" (p. 24).

---

[2]However, the National Assessment of Educational Progress (NAEP) is based on a national sampling of students is well accepted, but it is not to be used as a test.

Attitudes toward and performance in these subject areas seem to suggest that historically males and females achieve at different levels and hold different attitudes about these subject areas. Due in part to a pervasive pattern of social conditioning and sex-role stereotyping, teachers, parents, and students inculcated and normalized the belief that males are smarter than females in mathematics and science and are therefore more naturally gifted on scientific and quantitative tasks. For decades, the effects of this type of social conditioning and stereotyping have gone beyond class grades and course selections into career decisions that males and females make.

Narrowing of the achievement gap. The current picture continues to be mixed regarding the performance in and attitudes towards mathematics and science by males and females. Recent NAEP (National Center for Education Statistics, 2003) data suggest that the achievement gap in mathematics is narrowing, particularly at the 4th and 8th grade levels. According to data from the National Center for Education Statistics (2003), average NAEP scores for mathematics among 4th grade males and females were virtually the same (233 for females and 236 for males). Similarly, among 8th grade males and females, the average NAEP mathematics scores were nearly identical (277 for females and 278 for males).

Adequate Yearly Progress School Accountability Requirements. An important provision of the NCLB legislation associated with achievement is the requirement that school districts be able to demonstrate adequate yearly progress of all students. Under NCLB, each state is responsible for defining and determining how to assess if a school or district is making adequate yearly progress. According to the statute, any Title I school that fails to meet AYP goals must be identified for improvement. All public schools and local education agencies (LEA) are held accountable for the achievement of individual subgroup. Subgroups for AYP accountability decisions are major ethnic/racial groups, economically disadvantaged students, limited English proficient (LEP) students, and students with disabilities [see NCLB Sec. 111(b)(2)(C)(v)]. Each subgroup of students enrolled in schools must meet annual objectives in reading and math to make their AYP goals (http://www.ed.gov/policy/elsec/guid/secletter/020724.html). But subgroup analysis by sex in general or within these other subgroups is not required for AYP decision making, although reporting of information by sex is required for most other state and local academic assessment reporting [NCLB Sec. 1111(3)(C)(xiii)] and of course, it is one of the easiest data categories for schools to analyze. In light of the gender disparities in some areas, especially within ethnic and disability subgroups, it is likely that this AYP accountability procedure would be more useful if it required an analysis of subgroups by sex. As discussed in other parts of this chapter, this disaggregation of results by gender and other subgroups is also important for learning if there is gender bias in all aspects of testing, but it is often ignored. Given the extent of differences in test performances, such as those reported elsewhere in this *Handbook*, failure to improve instruction based on achievement data disaggregated by gender alone as well as within other subgroups allows gender inequities to go undetected and unaddressed.

Testing for Special Populations

Research on sex differences in test performance for special needs populations has generally been rather limited. Many have noted the striking differences in referral and placement in special education for males and females. Research suggests that while the incidence of learning disabilities among males and females is about the same, males are about twice as likely to be referred for evaluation and placement in special programs. Thus, the inequities are not in the testing instruments but in the screening and referral system. The analysis of gifted-and-talented programs suggests that in some cases the instruments used for screening are biased in favor of males, and in some instances the referral system may lead to slightly more males than females being referred for screening. These studies and topics are detailed in the chapters on gifted students and those with disabilities in section V of this *Handbook*.

Gender equity and tests used to identify attention deficit disorder with hyperactivity (ADHD) in children. While most of the literature published to date on gender bias in standardized testing focuses on academic achievement, other studies have explored gender differences in other types of testing performed in the educational environment. One of the most prevalent questions teachers and parents ask today is, "Does my child have an attention deficit?" ADHD appears to be far more common among males than females (Lahey, Miller, Gordon, & Riley, 1999). Because the bulk of research on ADHD has been conducted on males (Hartung & Widiger, 1998; Waschbusch & King, 2006), it has been suggested that there is gender bias in the diagnostic criteria or because the behavioral checklists used by parents and teachers for screening are not based on separate norms for males and females (Elgar, Curtis, McGrath, Waschbusch, & Stewart, 2003; Keenan & Shaw, 1997); (Walton, 1996). Further research is needed to determine if ADHD is indeed more prevalent among males or merely more frequently diagnosed due to bias in the referral process or bias in the diagnostic criteria.

VOCATIONAL INTEREST AND APTITUDE TESTS AND GENDER EQUITY

Organizations (e.g., the military) use ability and interest measures for career assessment and counseling and for purposes of placement in the organization. This placement is derived from the *matching* or trait-factor approach to vocational psychology (Dawis, 1996). Simply stated, the bases of this approach are that: (a) individuals differ in their job-related abilities and interests; (b) job/occupational environments differ in requirements and in the interests to which they appeal; and (c) congruence or *fit* between an individual's characteristics and the characteristics of the job is an important consideration in making good career choices. Therefore, the purpose of assessment from the matching perspective is to assist individuals and/or organizations in finding and choosing educational or career options that represent a good person-environment fit. While the matching approach has been supported by considerable empirical research, it is evident that it oversimplifies the career choice process for some groups of people. For example, research has indicated that females tend to underutilize their abilities in selecting careers (Betz & Fitzgerald, 1987). In addition, women's overrepresentation in traditionally female careers and underrepresentation in many male-dominated careers (Betz, 2005) may be due partly to restrictions in how their vocational interests have developed.

Betz (1993) argued that one major alternative explanation for females' poorer performance on some kinds of ability and aptitude tests and their restricted patterns of vocational interests is traditionally female gender socialization—gender socialization that has led to narrowed and gender-stereotypic access to the kinds of learning opportunities that could lead to a broader range of competencies and interests. It is essential that people using tests and inventories know what these limitations can be and learn, as well, the best ways to make sure that restricted learning experiences do not over determine test and inventory scores. The next sections focus on these issues. In the sections to follow, restrictions in females' development of vocationally relevant interests and aptitudes will be described, and the implications of these for testing will be discussed.

Gender Issues in Vocational Interest Testing

Interest inventories might seem to be benign in their effects since they are usually not used for selection, but rather in career counseling. However, their use may have perpetuated occupational gender segregation through the phenomenon of gender restrictiveness. Gender restrictiveness occurs when interest inventories reinforce occupational gender stereotypes (Diamond & Tittle, 1985). The concept of gender restrictiveness in interest inventories is based on the pervasive and strong influence in our society of gender-role socialization and the continuing existence of occupational sex segregation (Betz & Fitzgerald, 1987). Vocational interest inventories have, at least until recently, unintentionally emphasized socialized sex differences. Consequently, these inventories have perpetuated occupational sex segregation and have limited the options of individual males and females. To understand the effects of gender restrictiveness, by which this has occurred, a brief discussion of the history of interest measurements may be helpful.

Historically, both the measurement of vocational interests and the interpretation of vocational interest inventories were focused on three major types of scales: (a) the Strong Interest Inventory (SII; Harmon, Hanson, Borgen, & Hammer, 1994), (b) the Kuder Occupational Interest Survey (KOI; Kuder & Zytowski, 1991), and (c) the Campbell Interest and Skill Survey (CISS; Campbell, 2000). These occupational scales were designed to assess the similarity of the person's activity preferences to those persons in specific occupations, for example, physician, psychologist, and banker. It is important to note that this comparison is usually made in reference to a specific gender, for example, female lawyers or male lawyers.

Gender restrictiveness was most pervasive in the late 1960s. The Strong Vocational Interest Blank (SVIB-M) men's profile included a preponderance of occupations in the sciences, engineering, and business management (Hanson, 1984). The Strong

Vocational Interest Blank (SVIB-W) women's profile emphasized socially oriented and *pink collar* occupations. For a woman taking the SVIB-W, the management occupation most likely suggested was "Executive Housekeeper" (Hanson, 1984). In the area of the basic interest scales, there were differences that can only be described as sexist. For example, the men's profile contained a basic interest scale for mathematics, while the analogous scale on the women's form was *numbers*. In other words, it was assumed that men do mathematics and women count.

The developers of the Strong inventories eventually did recommend that career-oriented women could be administered the SVIB-M rather than the SVIB-W because the men's inventory had greater utility in suggesting professional level careers (Campbell & Hanson, 1981). However, this was the exception rather than the rule. It should be noted that this blatant sexism was characteristic of all the interest inventories in use at the time and not just the Strong inventories. In fact, the Strong group was the first to address and rectify issues of gender restrictiveness. Another blatant type of bias was the use of sexist occupational titles in the inventory and profile, such as, policeman, repairman, and fireman.

Criticisms of bias and restrictiveness in interest inventories led to the elimination of separate forms for males and females and of sexist language, but gender restrictiveness remained because men and women continued to respond differentially to many interest inventory items. In general, females are more likely to endorse socially oriented items and males scientific, technical, and outdoor oriented items (Gottfredson & Holland, 1978).

Similar findings resulted using the Vocational Interest Inventory (VII; Lunnenborg, 1980), a measure of Roe's eight fields of occupational interest. Findings of sex differences on basic dimensions of vocational interest are most evident and durable for social and realistic (technical) interests. Social interests are far more predominant among females, whereas technical interests are found far more frequently among males (Lunnenborg, 1980; Prediger, 1980).

Although different score patterns are not by themselves a problem, these differential raw (and combined sex norm) score patterns among males and females result in occupational suggestions that reinforce the existing segregation of females and males in our society. High scores on the social and conventional themes suggest traditionally female educational, social welfare, office, and clerical occupations. In contrast, females' lower scores on the realistic, investigative, and enterprising themes result in less frequent suggestions of traditionally male professions such as, medicine, engineering, science, management, and the skilled trades. Thus, socialized patterns of interest led to interest inventory results that perpetuated females' overrepresentation in traditionally female occupations and their underrepresentation in occupations traditionally dominated by males.

The socialization experiences of most females have been gender stereotypic, limiting the range of experiential opportunities that could lead to the development of new interests or competencies. If females were not encouraged to take high school shop classes (instead of home economics), then they had less opportunity to learn skills in that area. Less encouragement toward science or computers would limit experiences in those domains.

This kind of bias has been well dealt with through the development of gender-balanced item sets in inventory scales. More specifically, same-sex normative scores compare a person's scores on basic dimensions of vocational interest, for example, the Holland themes or the basic interest scales of the Strong—to those of persons of the same sex. Thus, females are compared to other females, whereas males are compared to other males. The use of same-sex norms increases the likelihood that the background socialization experiences of the comparison sample are more similar to those of the examinee, and this in turn tends to highlight interests that have developed in spite of the limiting effects of sex-role socialization. The SII provides same-sex normative scores for both the general occupational (i.e., Holland) themes and the basic interest scales.

The second approach to reducing sex restrictiveness in interest inventories is the use of gender-balanced item sets. A gender-balanced inventory scale (for example, one of the Holland themes) would be constructed to include items more likely to characterize male sex-role socialization and others more common in female socialization with the desired end result being interest scales on which the sexes obtain similar raw scores. The Unisex Edition of the ACT-IV (UNIACT; Lamb & Prediger, 1981) and the revised version of the Vocational Interest Inventory (VII; Lunnenborg, 1980) are based on this strategy of scale construction, and both result in more equivalent distributions of scores across the six Holland themes (UNIACT) or Roe's eight fields (VII) for the two sexes. Thus, on the UNIACT for example, the Realistic scale contains items pertaining to sewing and cooking or content areas more often emphasized in the backgrounds of females, in addition to items more reflective of males' socialization experiences, such as the skills learned in high school shop courses.

While attempts to remove gender restrictiveness from interest inventories are important and useful, the more direct solution to the problem of gender stereotypic vocational interests involves increasing the range of experiences relevant to the development of those interests. Until females have the opportunity to engage in activities relevant to, for example, realistic and investigative as well as social and artistic interest areas, interests in nontraditional areas may not develop in the majority of females. It is important to both encourage a wider variety of activities and experiences for young girls and women and also to encourage involvement in jobs or job-related experiences beyond the limits of socialized interests and experiences. Women's vocational interests and, consequently, their career choices, should derive from a rich background of experience and knowledge rather than from a background exposing them only to stereotypical female areas of activity and interest.

Gender Issues in Using Tests of Developed Abilities in Vocational Counseling Settings

The use of multiple aptitude or ability batteries such as the Differential Aptitude Tests (DAT) and the Armed Services Vocational Aptitude Battery (ASVAB) is intended to help high school students who are not college bound make decisions about post-high school training (e.g., vocational schools, community colleges, and the military). The issues involved here are somewhat different than those involved in the use of tests designed for college selection, discussed earlier because multiple ability batteries are more often used to select a direction for training, rather than for collegiate selection and the awarding of scholarships.

More specifically, males have often obtained higher scores than females on tests of developed abilities representative of stereotypically male domains, such as, mechanical reasoning, spatial ability, and mathematical ability, while females have high scores on tests of clerical skills and clerical perception, typically stereotyped as female skill sets. Such score differences, when used in educational or occupational planning, may serve, like interest inventories, to perpetuate gender stereotypic career choices.

To some extent, ability test score differences, like interest test score differences, are attributable to differential patterns of male and female socialization in society. For example, males have been encouraged to take mathematics, science, technical, and shop courses, and females have been encouraged to take English, home economics, and typing. But tests originally complicated the problem through bias in item content and wording. Examples of sex-biased content occurred in the General Aptitude Test Battery (GATB), formerly used extensively in the government's employment training programs. For example, spatial aptitude was measured by the Tool Matching Test. Males are more often than females taught tool identification and use, so the content of all the test items was at the outset more familiar to boys. In the GATB Numerical Reasoning Test, male characters and objects predominated in the word problems, which focused on amounts of lumber and electrical wire rather than on fabric or recipe ingredients.

The revision of the DAT included gender balancing of test content, as well as considering an equal number of male or female pronouns in test items and equal numbers of males and females represented in pictorial content. In addition, all other things being equal, tests providing same-sex as well as opposite-sex or combined-sex norms (e.g., the DAT and the ASVAB) are preferable to tests providing only combined gender norms.

Test items could easily be written to use content such as sewing patterns to measure form perception and amounts of food or fabric in spatial test items or in mathematics word problems. This content would probably tap more into the socialization experiences of females and yet be equally appropriate in the measurement of spatial and mathematics abilities.

In an illuminating study, Betz and Hackett (1983) measured the perceived self-efficacy expectations or confidence of college women and men with respect to a variety of mathematics tasks and problems. As predicted, males reported higher expectations of self-efficacy on 49 of the 52 mathematics-related items. There were only 3 out of 52 items on which females reported higher expectations of self-efficacy than males. Those three items were:

1. figure out how much material to buy in order to make curtains,
2. estimate your grocery bill in your head as you pick up items, and
3. calculate recipe quantities for a dinner for 41, when the original recipe was for 12 people.

If the sex differences in self-efficacy expectations can be eliminated by asking questions based on content familiar to females, it seems that ability and aptitude measurement should also be revised. It should be noted that revisions of test content should not be taken as a sufficient answer to the limiting effects of sex-role socialization on the development of both males and females, and it is important that broadened childhood experiences for both boys and girls are facilitated by parents, the schools, the media, and so on. But until socialization practices change for the majority of girls and women, testing them using content underemphasized in their background experiences is unfair.

CLASSROOM ASSESSMENT AND GENDER EQUITY

Ideally, classroom assessment should be integrated with, not separate from, curriculum and instruction. The heart of assessment is a continuing process in which the teacher (in collaboration with the student) uses information to guide the next steps in learning. Instruction and assessment should not presume uniformity of experience, culture, language, and ways of knowing (Black & Wiliam, 1998; Koontz, 1997). In the context of classroom assessment, perhaps the most complex issue is whether teachers will be able to assess all their students fairly, accurately, and comprehensively. Such evaluation requires more than that teachers be unbiased; they must understand their students (Belcher, Coates, Franco, & Mayfield-Ingram, 1997).

Teachers use a variety of assessment tools and processes in the classroom. They may construct paper and pencil tests that use a variety of formats ranging from fixed response items such as true and false or multiple choice and fill-in-the-blanks to more open-ended short answer or long essay questions. Teachers often use data from cognitive-developed ability measures or achievement tests or a combination of both to establish the starting point from which progress will be measured (Bradford, Nobel, & Wragg, 2000). Teachers also tend to use performance assessments that may include a range of behavior samples such as written products, oral presentations, constructed products like dioramas, simulations, and role play skits. Some teachers use various types of portfolios to have students document their growth in knowledge and skills across time.

Little is known about gender fairness in all of these processes. Teachers typically do not do the type of analysis of their own tests that would yield information about gender differences. One could speculate that portfolios and performance assessments, especially those graded on neatness and appearances, might favor females, whereas multiple-choice teacher tests might favor males. The fact that females as a group tend to get slightly better grades in school suggests that classroom assessment is either unbiased or biased in favor of females. Alternatives to paper-and-pencil tests used in classrooms vary from those sometimes called *performance assessments* or *authentic assessments* and include oral reports, simulations, and portfolios. One study of portfolios examined the gender issue and concluded that portfolios favor females, at least in elementary school grades (Koretz, Stecher, Klein, & McCaffrey, 1994).

Whatever school improvement strategies are being developed within a school, teachers need to be able to answer the question, "Where are we now?" This must be split into, "How are our girls doing?" and, of course, "How are our boys doing?" (Bradford, Noble & Wragg, 2000). The more delving that takes place at this point, the more secure will be the knowledge about particular groups of boys and girls. How are our boys and girls doing in each subject area? How are our boys and girls from different ability groups performing? Good teaching practice is an escape route from failure; poor teaching practice is more likely to confirm it. (Bradford et al., 2000)

RECOMMENDATIONS

The following gender equity recommendations for test design and use, and for future research, are offered for consideration based the insights in this chapter.

Recommendations for Practice

1. Adhere to professional standards and guidelines for equitable use and interpretation of test scores (the *Standards for Educational and Psychological Testing* (AERA/APA/NCME, 1999 and others). Test users should consult sample tests, test manuals, and test reviews to determine the extent to which test developers have removed obvious gender biases and test content. Schools and school systems should be sure that these guidelines are known and used by appropriate school instructional staff, test evaluators, and school psychologists.
2. Use valid and fair instruments. The goal of assessment is to determine what each student knows about the subject. Teachers need more training about effective assessment practices in the classroom, such as how to do an item analysis of their own tests to evaluate for gender-biased items.
3. Teach self-assessment skills to students. Being able to assess one's own work is an essential skill for success in most future careers. Students can be given opportunities to give one another feedback in small groups, to present their strategies to the class for discussion, and to revise their work after it has been reviewed by peers and adults.
4. Because much problematic gender-biased material is no longer in tests, improvements in test content will probably show diminishing returns in decreasing gender gaps in test scores. Vigilance is needed in this area, as there is some evidence of conservative backlash against these testing improvements (e.g., labeling guidelines for fair representation of both genders in tests as *politically correct* tampering with authors' texts, or as *social engineering*.). Vigilance is also needed to keep test makers attuned to the idea that this is still an important set of concerns, even though the most of the possible marginal improvements have been accomplished.
5. More attention needs to be paid (by researchers, test makers, and test users) to test-related psychological factors, including self-theories of intelligence, stereotype threat, and possibly factors associated with anxiety in testing situations and risk taking that differ by gender. Self-selection on the basis of admission test scores is also a huge issue. Given how few colleges are truly selective, this is bigger than any admission policies based on test scores. Research has shown these to

be important factors, and their import is not always taken into account in testing practices either in the classroom or in external testing.

6. Report all test results using disaggregated data by gender and other relevant variables for the population. On vocational tests, publishers should provide same-sex as well as opposite-sex normative comparisons, not combined-sex norms (e.g., the DAT, ASVAB) are preferable to tests which provide only combined-gender norms.

7. Teach students test-taking skills and strategies to eliminate bias due to test sophistication.

8. We need to continue to encourage girls to keep their options open by taking appropriate math and science curricula and tests, and boys to improve their communications skills in the area of writing.

Recommendations for Research

1. More studies to monitor the effects of test-based accountability on gender equity outcomes.

2. Continued research on the issues of gender inequities in screening for special needs programs.

3. Further research on the use of interest inventories with minority women, special needs populations, and gifted women.

4. More research on the use of computerized tests, computer-adapted assessments, and other innovations or changes to traditional pencil-and-paper tests to ensure that these approaches to assessment are gender-fair.

5. More research on teacher classroom assessment practices in relation to student subgroups disaggregated by gender and ethnicity, and by special education status.

6. Research is needed on student demographics related to testing, especially with respect to college admissions testing and screening for special needs populations.

7. More research on the gender equity impact of including more measures of writing in critical high stakes tests.

CONCLUSIONS

Chapters in this *Handbook* and other reviews such as reports from the National Center for Education Statistics (2003) indicate that while the achievement gap between males and females is narrowing, gender equity issues still exist. Gender differences continue to be seen particularly in the ways males and females approach testing situations, their interests and motivations, expectancies and experiences. As educators prepare students for high-stakes, federally mandated assessments, vocational apti-

tude and interest tests, college admissions tests, and standardized educational assessments, they, along with other stakeholders, must level the academic playing field for all students. Teachers must be able to assess their students in ways that allow them to demonstrate their learning and that provide the information teachers need to guide their future learning with the best and most unbiased instruments possible, both published measures and teacher formal and informal assessments.

Test performance can be influenced by factors such as format, item types, time limits, and methods of administration. Most of the results show that as a group women are more negatively affected than men by these subtle factors. Women are more likely than men to also exhibit test anxiety, while men may be more test-wise or have more effective strategies for taking tests especially those where speed may be a factor. It has been suggested that individual differences in test-taking strategies or style, such as anxiety or risk taking, are linked to self-confidence and perceiving the test as an accurate measure of one's ability. This in turn relates to the research on stereotype threat.

In general, educators and others tend to think standardized test scores are impartial measures of students' potential to succeed in school. Smith and White (2002). Steele's research, however, raises at least one source of concern in that different groups in the midst of those tests may be under different degrees of pressure and that their performance reflects that (Steele, 1997). Smith and White (2002) found that nullifying stereotype threat may not be too difficult. In their study, just the suggestion that men and women perform equally well on a math test was enough to avert the effects of stereotype threat.

The purpose of gender equity is to protect the rights and privileges of males and females so that both receive equitable and correspondingly fair treatment in the educational system. Testing is an integral part of the educational process for the purposes of institutional accountability, as well as for feedback and monitoring of individual student progress. Although significant strides have been made toward developing professional guidelines to eliminate bias in test instruments and the misuse of test results, it requires continual monitoring to ensure that attention is paid to issues of equity by ethnicity, socialeconomic strata, and gender in the (a) construction of published and teacher-made tests, (b) their administration, scoring, and reporting, and (c) the uses and interpretations of data from the results.

ACKNOWLEDGMENTS

The authors thank Carol Title, City University of New York and coauthor of the 1985 *Handbook* chapter on testing and *Handbook* editors for reviewing various drafts of this chapter.

References

Alaimo, K. (2004). New SAT could shrink test's gender gap. *WeNews*. Retrieved March 21, 2005, from http://www.womensnews.org

American Educational Research Association, American Psychological Association, and National Council on Measurement in Education.

(1999). *Standards for educational and psychological testing*. Washington, DC.

Aronson, J., Lustina, M. J., Good, C., Keough, K., Steele, C. M., & Brown, J. (1999). When White men can't do mathematics: Necessary and sufficient factors in stereotype threat. *Journal of Experimental and Social Psychology, 35,* 29–46.

Begley, S. (2000). The stereotype trap. *Newsweek,* 66–68.

Belcher, T., Coates, G. D., Franco, J., & Mayfield-Ingram, K. (1997). Assessment and equity. In *Multicultural and gender equity in mathematics classrooms: The gift of diversity NCTM yearbook* (pp. 195–200). Reston VA: NCTM.

Benjamin-Kelly, K. (2000). The young women's guide to better SAT scores: Fighting the gender gap. New York, NY: Bantam Books.

Betz, N. (1993). Women's career development. In F. L. Denmark & M. A. Paludi (Eds.), *Psychology of women: A handbook of issues and theories* (pp. 625–684). Westport, CT: Greenwood.

Betz, N. E. (2005). Measuring confidence for basic domains of vocational activity in high school students. *Journal of Career Assessment, 13*(3), 251–270.

Betz, N. E., & Fitzgerald, L. (1987). *Career psychology of women.* Orlando, FL: Academic Press.

Betz, N. E., & Hackett, G. (1983). The relationship of mathematics self-efficacy expectations to the selection of science-based college majors. *Journal of Vocational Behavior, 23,* 329–345.

Bickel, R., & Maynard, A. S. (2004). Group and interaction effects with No Child Left Behind: Gender and reading in a poor, Appalachian district. *Education Policy Analysis Archives, 12*(4). Retrieved March 21, 2005, from http://epaa.asu.edu/epaa/v12n4/

Bradford, W., Noble, C., & Wragg, T. (2000). *Getting it right for boys—and girls.* London: Routledge.

Black, P., & Wiliam, D. (1998). Assessment and Classroom Learning. *Assessment in Education, 5*(1), 7–71.

Bridgeman, B., & Schmitt, A. (1997). Fairness issues in test development and administration. In W. W. Willingham & N. S. Cole (Eds.), *Gender and fair assessment* (pp. 185–226). Mahwah, NJ: Lawrence Erlbaum Associates.

Buck, G., Kostin, I., & Morgan, R. (2002). *Examining the relationship of content to gender based performance differences in advanced placement exams.* NY: College Entrance Examination Board.

Campbell, D. P. (2000). *Campbell interest and skills survey.* NCS Pearson, Inc.

Campbell, D. P., & Hansen, J. C. (1981). *Manual for the SVIB-SCII* (3rd ed.). Stanford, CA: Stanford University Press.

Carlton, S. T., & Harris, A. M. (1992). *Characteristics associated with differential item functioning on the Scholastic Aptitude Test: Gender and majority/minority group comparisons.* Princeton, NJ: Educational Testing Service.

Chilisa, B. (2000). Towards equity in assessment: Crafting gender-fair assessment. *Assessment in Education: Principles, Policy, & Practice, 7*(1), 61–81.

Code of fair testing practices in education. (2004). Washington DC: Joint Committee on Testing Practices. Retrieved May 21, 2006, from http://www.apa.org/science/jctpweb.html

College Board. (1985). *Taking the SAT: The official guide to the scholastic aptitude test and test of standard written English.* New York: College Entrance Examination Board.

College Board. (2004). College Bound Seniors. Retrieved March 30, 2005, from http://www.collegeboard.org

College Board. (2006). College Board Announces Scores for New SAT® with writing section (Press Release 08/29/06). Retrieved October 1, 2006, from http://www.collegeboard.com/press/releases/150054.html

Connell, R. W. (1993). Disruptions: Improper masculinities and schooling. In L. Weis & M. Fine (Eds.), *Beyond silenced voices: Class, race, and gender in United States school* (pp. 191–209). New York: State University of New York Press.

Croizet, J. C., & Claire, T. (1998). Extending the concept of stereotype threat to social class: The intellectual underperformance of students from low socioeconomic backgrounds. *Personality and Social Psychology Bulletin, 24,* 588–594.

Dawis, R. V. (1996). The theory of work adjustment and person-environment correspondence counseling. In D. Brown & L. Brooks (Eds.), *Career choice and development* (3rd ed., pp. 75–120). San Francisco, CA: Jossey-Bass.

deNuys, M., & Wolfe, L. R. (1985). *Learning her place—Sex bias in the elementary school classroom.* Washington, DC: Project on Equal Education Rights.

Diamond, E., & Tittle, C. K. (1985). Sex equity in testing. In S. S. Klein (Ed.), *Handbook for achieving sex equity through education.* Baltimore, MD: Johns Hopkins Press.

Donlon, T. (1973). *Content factors in sex differences on test questions.* Princeton, NJ: Educational Testing Service.

Dorans, N., & Kulick, E. (1983). *Demonstrating unexpected differential item performance of female candidates on SAT and TSWE forms administered in December 1977: An application of the standardization approach* (Research Report No. RR-83-9). Princeton, NJ: Educational Testing Service.

Dorans, N., & Kulick, E. (1986). Demonstrating the utility of the standardization approach to assessing unexpected differential item performance on the Scholastic Aptitude Test. *Journal of Educational Measurement, 23,* 355–368.

Dweck, C. S. (2000). Self-theories: Their role in motivation, personality, and development. Philadelphia: Taylor & Francis/Psychology Press.

Dweck, C. S. (2002). Messages that motivate: How praise molds students' beliefs, motivation, and performance (in surprising ways). In J. Aronson (Ed.), *Improving academic achievement: Classic and contemporary lessons from psychology.* New York: Academic Press.

Elgar, F. J., Curtis, L. J., McGrath, P. J., Waschbusch, D. A., & Stewart, S. H. (2003). Antecedent-consequence conditions in maternal mood and child behavioural problems: A four-year cross-lagged study. *Journal of Clinical Child and Adolescen Psychology, 32,* 362–374.

Faigel, H. C. (1991). The effect of beta blockade on stress-induced cognitive dysfunction in adolescents. *Clinical Pediatrics, 30,* 441–445.

Gilligan, C., & Attanucci, J. (1988). Two moral orientations: Gender differences and similarities. *Merrill-Palmer Quarterly, 34,* 223–237.

Gipps, C. (1994). *Beyond testing: Towards a new theory of educational assessment.* London: The Fulmer Press.

Gottfredson, G. D., & Holland, J. L. (1978). Toward beneficial resolution of the interest inventory controversy. In C. K. Tittle & D. G. Zytowski (Eds.), *Sex-fair interest measurement: Research and implications* (pp. 43–51). Washington, DC: National Institute of Education.

Grandy, J. (1999). *Trends and profiles: Statistics about GRE general test examinees by gender, age, and ethnicity* (2nd ed.). Princeton, NJ: Educational Testing Service.

Hansen, J. C. (1984). The measurement of vocational interests: Issues and future directions. S. D. Brown & R. L. Lent (Eds.), *Handbook of counseling psychology* (pp. 99–136). New York, NY: Wiley.

Harmon, L., Hansen, J. I., Borgen, F., & Hammer, A. (1994). *Strong interest inventory: Applications and technical manual.* Palo Alto, CA: Consulting Psychologists Press.

Hartung, C. M., & Widiger, T. A. (1998). Gender differences in the diagnosis of mental disorders: Conclusions and controversies of the *DSM–IV. Psychological Bulletin, 123,* 260–278.

Hunter, J., & Schmidt, F. L. (2000). Racial and gender bias in ability and achievement tests: Resolving the apparent paradox. *Psychology, Public Policy, & Law, 6*(1), 151–158.

Koontz, T. (1997). Know thyself: The evolution of an intervention gender-equity program. In *Multicultural and gender equity in the mathematics classroom: The gift of diversity yearbook* (pp. 186–194). Reston VA: The National Council of Teachers of Mathematics, Inc.

Koretz, D., Stecher, B., Klein, S., & McCaffrey. (1994). The Vermont portfolio assessment program: Findings and implications. *Educational Measurement: Issues and Practice, 13*(3), 5–16.

Kuder, F., & Zytowski, D. G. (1991). *Kuder occupational interest survey, general manual* (3rd ed.). Adel, IA: National Career Assessment Services, Inc. Lamb, R. R., & Prediger, D. J. (1981). *Technical report for the unisex edition of the ACT interest inventory (UNIACT)*. Iowa City, IA: American College Testing Program.

Lahey, B. B., Miller, T. I., Gordon, R. A., & Riley, A. W. (1999). Developmental epidemiology of the disruptive behavior disorders. In H. C. Quay & A. E. Hogan (Eds.), *Handbook of disruptive behavior disorders* (pp. 23–48). New York: Kluwer Academic/Plenum Publishers.

Lee, J. (2006). *Title IX infractions: Individuals' legal options and winning cases.* Paper prepared for the Education Equality web page of the Feminist Majority Foundation www.feminist.org/education.

Leo, J. (1992). Sexism in the schoolhouse. *U.S. News & World Report, 112*(9), 22–26.

Linn, M. C., & Kessel, C. (1996). Success in mathematics: Increasing talent and gender diversity among college majors. *CBMS Issues in Mathematics Education, 6*, 101–144.

Lunnenborg, P. W. (1980). Reducing sex bias in interest measurement at the item level. *Journal of Vocational Behavior, 16*, 226–234.

Merriam-Webster's collegiate dictionary (10th ed., pp. 33 & 112). (2001). Springfield, MA: Merriam-Webster.

Messick, S. (1989). Validity. In R. Linn (Ed.), *Educational measurement* (3rd ed., pp. 13–103). New York: Macmillan.

Mortenson, T. (2005, February). What's *still* wrong with the guys? *Postsecondary Education Opportunity, 152*(whole issue).

Nandakumar, R., Glutting, J., & Oakland, T. (1993). Mantel-Haenszel methodology for detecting item bias: An introduction and example using the guide to the assessment of test session behavior. *Journal of Psychoeducational Assessment, 11*(2), 108–119.

National Center for Education Statistics. (2003). *The nation's report card: Mathematics highlights 2003.* Retrieved March 21, 2005, from http://www.nces.ed.gov/nationsreportcard/mathematics/results2003/natscalescore.asp

National Center for Fair and Open Testing. (2004). New SAT: High anxiety, little change. *Fair Test Examiner, 18*(1&2; Spring-Summer).

Perry Evenstad, J. (2003). *Disaggregating Colorado student assessment program data: Implications for predicting educational equity.* Unpublished doctoral dissertation, University of Denver, Denver, CO.

Prediger, D. J. (1980). The marriage between tests and career counseling. *Vocational Guidance Quarterly, 28*(6), 217–305.

Public Law 107-110, 115 U.S.C. § 1425 (2002).

Rosser, P. (1989a). *The SAT gender gap: Identifying the causes.* Washington, DC: Center for Women Policy Studies.

Rosser, P. (1989b). *Gender and testing.* Boston, MA: National Center for Testing and Public Policy.

Rosser, P. & Staff of the National Center for Fair and Open Testing. (1989c). *Sex bias in college admissions tests: Why women lose out* (3rd ed.). Cambridge, MA: National Center for Fair and Open Testing.

Sadker, M., & Sadker, D. (1985, March). Sexism in the schoolroom of the '80s. *Psychology Today*, 54–57.

Sadker, M., & Sadker, D. (1994). Failing at fairness: How America's schools cheat girls. *Journal of Research in Science Teaching, 35*, 951–961.

Spencer, R., Porche, M., & Tolman, D. (2003). We've come a long way—maybe: New challenges for gender equity in education. *Teachers College Record, 105*(9), 1774–1807.

Spencer, S. J., Steele, C. M., & Quinn, D. M. (1999). Stereotype threat and women's mathematics performance. *Journal of Experimental and Social Psychology, 35*, 4–28.

Steele, C. M. (1997). A threat in the air: How stereotypes shape intellectual identity and performance. *American Psychologist, 52*, 613–629.

Steele, C. M. (2004). Not just a test. *The Nation*, 1–4.

Steele, C. M., & Aronson, J. (1995). Stereotype threat and the intellectual test performance of African Americans. *Journal of Personality and Social Psychology, 69*, 797–811.

Thompson, A., & Gitlin, A. (1993, April). *The reconstruction of knowledge in feminist praxis and action research.* Presentation at the annual meeting of the American Educational Research Association, Atlanta, GA.

Tolman, D. L., & Porche, M. V. (2000). The adolescent femininity ideology scale: Development and validation of a new measure for girls. *Psychology of Women Quarterly, 24*(4), 365–376.

Walton, C. D. (1996). The effect of gender on school psychologists' diagnosis of attention deficit/hyperactivity disorder. *Dissertation Abstracts International Section A: Humanities & social Sciences, 57*(3-A), 1036.

Wendler, C. L. W., & Carlton, S. T. (1987). *An examination of SAT verbal items for differential performance by women and men: An exploratory study.* Paper presented at the annual meeting of the American Educational Research Association, Washington, DC.

Wilder, G. Z., & Powell, K. (1989). *Sex differences in test performance: A survey of the literature.* Princeton, NJ: Educational Testing Service.

Willingham, W. W., Cole, N. S., Lewis, C., & Leung, S. W. (1997). Test performance. In W. W. Willingham & N. S. Cole (Eds.), *Gender and fair assessment* (pp. 55–126). Mahwah, NJ: Lawrence Erlbaum Associates.

Zenisky, A., Hambleton, R., & Robin, F. (2003–2004). DIF detection and interpretation in large scale science assessments: Informing item writing practices. *Educational Assessment, 9*(1&2), 61–78.

GENNDER EQUITY IN COEDUCATIONAL AND SINGLE-SEX ENVIRONMENTS

Emily Arms

INTRODUCTION

In the 1985 *Handbook*, this chapter was titled "Sex Equity in Classroom Organization and Climate" (Lockheed & Klein, 1985) and sought to define the elements of a sex-equitable classroom so that "both overt and hidden curriculum treat boys and girls equitably [and] that they receive equal benefits from instruction" (p. 190). It focused on three areas where classroom inequity was most prevalent: sex segregation in the classroom, inequity in teacher-student interactions, and inequities in peer interactions. Specific studies cited students' tendencies from a very young age to voluntarily segregate into single-sex groupings, teachers' "sex-differentiated expectations" of and interactions with students, and male domination of mixed-sex groups (p. 199). In brief, coeducational classrooms were found to reflect and reproduce sex inequities found in larger society. Several strategies or interventions to combat classroom inequities were proposed including teacher training in the following areas: raising teacher awareness of equitable student-teacher interactions, encouraging cross-sex student groupings, and creating collaborative, mixed-sex groups. In addition to those strategies, single-sex schooling was briefly discussed but rejected as a possible solution to remedy the gender inequities present in coeducational classrooms.

Because of the potential for single-sex schools to both reinforce stereotypes and engender further inequities, the 1975 regulations to Title IX prohibited single-sex interventions in publicly funded schools except under certain limited situations. Those circumstances included contact sports, human sexuality classes, and *remedial* or *affirmative* activities that would help reduce sex discrimination. In part because of the examples set by successful private and parochial institutions, as well as changing attitudes towards public education in general, interest in single-sex schooling has grown, prompting some public schools

to begin experiments with single-sex classes or schools. By necessity, these programs have mostly flown under the radar of federal scrutiny.

But the landscape for single-sex schools changed dramatically, as this *Handbook* went to press, when the U.S. Department of Education issued new Title IX regulations in fall of 2006. These modified regulations now allow public schools to offer single-sex classes for more broadly defined purposes such as "improving the educational achievement of students" by "providing diverse educational opportunities" or meeting the particular, identified educational needs of its students (Office for Civil Rights, October 25, 2006). The door has been potentially flung open for a radical change in public schooling, a kind of change not seen since the 1970s. This, despite the fact that research on public single-sex schooling remains mixed and inconclusive.

The purpose of this current chapter, then, is to touch briefly on gender equity research in coeducational classroom interactions since 1985, to present the emerging research on single-sex classrooms and schools, to identify solutions/interventions that impact increasing or decreasing gender equity in both coed and single-sex environments, and to make recommendations for policy, practice, and future research.

GENDER EQUITY IN EDUCATION: UP TO AND BEYOND TITLE IX

Education in the United States carries with it a legacy of separate and unequal access, resources, and attainment for women, people of color, and those with low income. For over 200 years, only White, privileged men were formally educated and admitted to the most prestigious universities. Separate girls' schools (and schools for *coloreds*) prepared students for their segregated roles in society. Well into the 1970s, even students in co-educational public secondary schools routinely received instruction along different tracks, with boys being placed in shop classes, while girls were enrolled in home economics. Male students were also more likely to be funneled into upper level mathematics and science courses. Many of the most prestigious universities were all-male. Harvard University, the oldest university in the U.S., did not formally admit female college students until 1970 (though Radcliffe women had been taking classes with Harvard men for several decades). And just as Brown v. Board of Education (1954), the subsequent Civil Rights Act (1964), and the Civil Rights Movement eventually changed the institutionalization of separate and unequal educations for racial and ethnic minorities, Title IX of the Education Amendments (1972) and the Women's Movement of the 1960s and 1970s began the march toward gender equity for women in education. Title IX states:

No person in the United States, on the basis of sex, can be excluded from participation in, be denied the benefits of, or be subjected to discrimination under any education program or activity receiving federal financial assistance.

Though Title IX provides broad protections against all types of sex discrimination in educational environments, inequities in classroom interactions are hard to capture and even more difficult to prove. These differences in teacher and student interaction patterns are often small, quick, subtle, and unintentional, and it is difficult to document the impact of these gender inequities on student outcomes. Thus, gender equity educators have advocated training and awareness programs, rather than legal challenges, to provide equitable educational environments and outcomes for all students. These training recommendations are discussed in this *Handbook's* teacher education chapter as well as later in this chapter.

As the authors noted in the 1985 edition (Lockheed & Klein 1985), studies on classroom interactions documented how boys received more attention than girls in coeducational classrooms. As evidence of gender inequities and sexual harassment mounted throughout the 1980s and 1990s (AAUW 1992, 1998a), some began to advocate single-sex education, especially for girls. Proponents saw single-sex schools as studious environments free from distractions, or as an opportunity to help women overcome sex stereotypes and succeed in areas where males traditionally had the advantage, such as science and engineering. Later, a demand for the kind of success promised by single-sex schools was seen by school choice advocates as additional justification for the need for charter schools and vouchers.

But opponents have argued that separate has never meant equal in U.S. education, and that many single-sex school curricula were not designed to address sex discrimination. Some programs were found to reinforce sex stereotypes, while others were declared illegal under Title IX or the Equal Protection clause of the 14th Amendment and were shut down. This chapter will discuss the difficulties in answering the question of whether single-sex education is worthwhile for advancing equity. The answer will always be "it depends." It depends upon the nature of and reason for the single-sex intervention, what it is compared to, and the consistent results or outcomes associated with or attributed to its use. See also Sadker (2004).

For close to 35 years, the 1975 Title IX regulations have been providing guidance on how the law should be interpreted in the many areas it covers, from athletics to vocational education. Part of this guidance relates to single-sex education. Segregation of students by sex has been accepted as a type of sex discrimination and thus a violation of Title IX, even if it is done voluntarily. Often interpreted as prohibiting all single-sex classes and single-sex public schools, the 1975 Title IX regulations in fact allow these classes and schools under certain limited circumstances.[1,2] These exceptions, as noted previously, include allowing schools to offer single-sex classes for instruction in specific areas such as contact sports or human sexuality. Additionally, they permit some single-sex schools or the separation of students in sex-segregated classes within schools if the reasons constitute "remedial or affirmative action." Remedial or affirmative action has been interpreted by gender equity advocates as being designed to decrease sex discrimination in educational outcomes, the main purpose of Title IX.

Restrictions on single-sex education were loosened in October 2006 when the new Title IX regulations—proposed in 2004—were issued by the U.S Department of Education. Despite numerous public objections to the proposed changes (over 5,000 public comments) and a lack of conclusive research on single-sex schooling, the U.S. Department of Education issued regulations that amend, but do not retract, the single-sex guidelines in the 1975 Title IX regulations. The Department did this by making it much easier to justify legally permissible K–12 nonvocational single-sex education. And while increasing the purposes and circumstances under which sex-segregated education may occur, these recent regulations do not require the educational institution to explicitly end sex discrimination. As discussed next, the 2006 regulations say that single-sex education can be used for important governmental objectives such as increasing academic achievement by offering diverse educational opportunities. Separate facilities or classes are now allowed as long as the excluded gender receives *substantially equal* educational opportunity in a single-sex or coeducational setting. Evaluations must be conducted every 2 years, at minimum.

Critics have raised a number of concerns regarding the 2006 Title IX regulation changes. First, *substantially equal* is not specifically defined nor is it the legal standard. The law demands true equality. Second, there are no instructions in the regula-

---

[1]This information applies to all recipients of federal financial assistance covered by Title IX, as well as other institutions covered by the 14th Amendment Equal Protection Clause or state laws providing for equal rights on the basis of sex or laws prohibiting sex discrimination in education. Thus, it could apply to museum and recreation department programs, as well as health education and employment training programs funded by other federal agencies.

[2]While overshadowed by the less stringent justifications for single-sex education in the 2006 modifications of the 1975 Title IX regulations, the single-sex exceptions in the 1975 regulations have not been rescinded.

tions to learn if the single-sex environment contributes to increased sex stereotyping and sex discrimination, or if it contributes to achieving any important governmental or educational objective such as increased academic achievement. There is also no expectation that this single-sex intervention provides evidence that it is any better than comparable, high-quality instruction in coeducational environments or, finally, that the selection of the single-sex option is truly completely voluntary.

An additional concern is that this shift to allowing more experimentation seems to be at odds with the Department of Education's policies and legislatively mandated standards. For example, the requirements for education innovations set forth in the No Child Left Behind (NCLB) legislation of 2002 and in the Department's Institute of Education Sciences in 2003 mandate that educators make changes in education programs only if these changes can demonstrate a positive impact based on scientific evidence. The Department of Education's wording—that "single-sex education *may* provide benefits to *some* students under *certain* circumstances" [italics added]—does not appear to be based on conclusive, scientific evidence. Indeed, later sections of this chapter will note that virtually no studies on single-sex schooling meet the Department's current definition of scientific rigor to determine effectiveness. While a descriptive study on public single-sex schooling, commissioned by the U.S. Department of Education in 2003 is currently underway, thus far, their literature review (2005) notes that research on single-sex schooling is equivocal. Critics note a shift in policy now years in the making where the federal government, traditionally the watchdog of civil rights and equal opportunity, has lowered its standard for equity in education, while at the same time raising its stake in academic achievement standards and curriculum, traditionally the domain of state and local authorities.

With so many unanswered questions remaining for this 2006 modification of the 1975 Title IX regulations, it remains to be seen whether it will withstand the certain legal challenges to its application without changes, or whether the rules might not be revised or rescinded by a future administration. Nevertheless, it is for now the law of the land and the recommendations section of this chapter and the summary chapter 31 will discuss what educators and researchers can do to continue to further gender equity.

GENDER EQUITY IN COEDUCATIONAL CLASSROOMS

Since the 1970s, numerous U.S. studies have documented gender inequities in coeducational classrooms from preschool to graduate school. This bias most often takes the form of males and females being treated differently by teachers. For example, girls often receive less teacher attention than boys. Sexism among peers, where male students dominate coeducational classes or groups, has also been found. Hall and Sandler's (1982) early work was among the first to document this chilly climate women face in college classrooms where professors call on male students more frequently than female students and female students are interrupted more often than male students. In 1985, this chapter summarized key findings from the 1970s

and early 1980s on classroom interactions that further illustrated gender inequities (see Lockheed & Klein 1985). Research on both teacher-student interactions and peer interactions brought to life the inequities girls and women and sometimes boys faced in the coeducational classroom.

This new chapter will focus on the key research studies and research reviews that kept this topic at the forefront of the national conversation. When the 1985 *Handbook* was in press, the U.S. Department of Education released studies by Lockheed and Harris (1984) as well as Sadker and Sadker (1984). Both were descriptive studies of sex equity in coed classroom interactions. They used somewhat different observation instruments, but arrived at complementary conclusions. Both studies found that teachers reacted differently to the behaviors of male and female students. In the Lockheed and Harris study, the authors reported that boys, on average, were more disruptive in the classroom and received more of the teacher's attention. This male preeminence or dominance was found uniformly across the study in all 29 classrooms observed across two school districts. Similarly, the Sadkers' study spent 3 years investigating sex bias in classroom interactions in over 100 classrooms, and developing training strategies to reduce or eliminate them. Though bias was reduced in the classrooms where teachers received training interventions, the authors found that boys participated more disproportionately in class when compared with girls. Boys also received more teacher praise, acceptance, remediation, and criticism than girls. Though both were important studies, they did not receive nearly the attention that the American Association of University Women report (1992) and the Sadkers' book on gender equity (1994) did a decade later.

How Schools Shortchange Girls (AAUW 1992) and *Failing at Fairness* (Sadker & Sadker 1994) together brought national attention to persistent gender inequitable practices present in coeducation. Both summarized numerous classroom studies that documented how male students still received the majority of the teachers' time and attention, how males called out more than females, and how males received more precise feedback and criticism from instructors. Even in preschool, boys received more "hugs, more instructional time and more teacher attention" (AAUW 1992, p. 118). When the Sadkers examined gender and race, they found that the students who were most likely to receive teacher attention were White males, followed by minority males, White females and, lastly, minority females. This imbalance of teacher attention was even more pronounced in traditionally male subject areas such as math, science, and technology (Lee, Marks, & Byrd, 1994).

Ten years later, Jones and Dindia (2004) conducted a meta-analysis of 32 studies from 1970 to 2000 on sex differences in classroom interactions. The authors concluded that females continue to be shortchanged in the coeducational classroom, and that there is sufficient evidence to support the claim that teachers treat male and female students differently. In a majority of studies reviewed—conducted in kindergarten through post-secondary classrooms—teachers interacted more with male students than female students, primarily to reprimand or critique male performance. This finding has stayed constant over time (1970–2000), though the authors note there are few empirical studies after 1985. In addition, teachers were not found to praise male students more than female students. The authors looked at how several factors such as teacher sex, student behavior, and student achievement may contribute to the dynamics of teacher-student interactions, but did not find any systematic patterns of relationships in the studies they examined. These results agree with the previously discussed national studies by Lockheed and Harris and the Sadkers that were not included in the Jones and Dindia meta-analysis. Finally, these studies found no consistent pattern for sex of the teacher in relation to their interactions with female or male students. In other words, even female teachers who considered themselves to be unbiased were found to pay more attention—albeit more negative attention—to the males in the classroom.

Despite many efforts and increased public and teacher awareness of these patterns of gender inequities in classroom interactions, there is no recent evidence to suggest that this inequity has disappeared. Though gender bias persists in the classroom, many view sexism as irrelevant or old-fashioned. Others remain oblivious to gender bias in the classroom and are, as Sadker describes, *gender blind* (see teacher education chapter in this volume) when it comes to evaluating their classroom or school climate. An example of this is seen in a study of one public middle school (Spencer, Porsche, & Tolman, 2003), which found that although teachers and students reported in surveys that their school was gender fair, classroom observations and interviews found major differences in how boys and girls behaved and were treated by teachers. In particular, as boys were more vocal and demanding of teachers' attention, teachers spent more time with boys. As in the meta-analysis by Jones and Dindia discussed previously, boys in this study appear to receive more of teachers' time, though it is often time spent in more negative interactions. This suggests that gender equity cuts both ways, and that both girls and boys may be shortchanged in coeducational classrooms. Girls are often ignored and boys often receive more negative teacher attention generally related to their disruptive behavior.

In addition to these studies and research reviews, popular books and media coverage helped make teachers and the public more aware of gender inequities in classroom interactions. As a result, teacher and administrator training programs were developed in the late 1980s and early 1990s to address gender inequity in classrooms. However, due to funding issues, political climate, etc., these programs were not broadly replicated and thus did not have a wide-ranging impact, though there is some evidence that they were helpful in promoting gender-equitable interactions in the classroom. For example, the Sadker program "Succeeding at Fairness" was recommended as a promising program by the U.S. Department of Education-sponsored Gender Equity Expert Panel (U.S. Department of Education, 2001).

As mentioned earlier, this attention to gender bias in the classroom may help explain why since the mid-1990s an increasing number of parents seek single-sex education for their children, particularly for their daughters. The next section will suggest why this movement has gained increased visibility and media attention, though it still accounts for a very small proportion of schools[3] and even a decreasing proportion of Catholic schools.[4] Though the increase in parents seeking single-sex education may be the result of some parents seeking less sexist schooling options for their daughters, there is no compelling evidence that single-sex schooling is a general remedy for the problem of gender inequity in coeducational environments (AAUW, 1998b). In fact, a closer look at the history of single-sex schools in the U.S. reveals just the opposite effect: separate is not equal.

GENDER EQUITY RELATED TO SINGLE-SEX SCHOOLING IN THE UNITED STATES

Historical Background

Sex-segregated schooling is not a new idea. From colonial times until the mid-1800s, "only a few schools were open to girls" (Tyack & Hansot, 1990) in the U.S. But the history of single-sex schools and classes in the United States has generally been one of unequal resources and sex-stereotyped curriculum with preference and resources given to the education of males. Many believed that women and men were naturally different, and thus, they needed separate educations to prepare them for their different futures. Early colonial dame schools, and later women's colleges and seminaries, had the primary mission of preparing young women for their place in society as wives and mothers and, later, teachers (Tyack & Hansot, 1990).

Even well into the 20th century, most private all-girls schools and women's colleges (with a few notable exceptions) continued to offer a less rigorous academic curriculum than their all-boys counterparts. In cities that had separate public high schools for boys and girls, the girls' schools always received less funding and fewer resources (Sadker & Sadker, 1994). Not until Title IX was enacted in 1972 did things truly begin to change in educational environments that received federal funds. While Title IX was generally interpreted as prohibiting new public single-sex schools, private schools—that did not obtain federal financial assistance—remained unaffected.

To comply with the non-sex discrimination provisions of Title IX, public schools integrated formerly gender-segregated classes like home economics and auto shop/woodworking classes. But in violation of Title IX, many continued sex-segregated physical education classes for non-contact sports. (See the physical education/athletics chapter 18 in this volume.) Girls could no longer be legally prohibited from taking traditionally male courses like physics or calculus, or be discriminated against in

---

[3]The 1987–88 NCES schools and staffing survey reported that only .1% of all students attending public schools attended single-sex schools and 7.9% of all private school students attended single-sex schools, so that the national student total in single-sex schools was only 1.0% (see Hollinger, 1993, p. 29).

[4]A recent report by the National Catholic Educational Association found that 140 Catholic schools consolidated or closed in 2002, the majority in cities. Between 1993 and 2003, 394 Catholic schools, most built to serve immigrant communities, have closed. There was also a decrease in Catholic single-sex high schools from 424 in the 2002–2003 school year to 392 in 2005–2006, while the total of coed schools remained about the same at 791 to 793 (www.ncea.org visited on 7-20-06).

admissions to public universities, or be subject to quotas in graduate schools. Despite these advances in girls' access to opportunities, research documented how gender bias and sexism persisted in coeducational classrooms throughout the 1980s and 1990s (see previous section on coeducation for specific studies). Research also documented how sexual harassment on school campuses, especially in traditionally male-dominated courses or majors, creates an unfriendly or hostile environment for females (AAUW 1993, 2002,1998a and chapter 11 on sexual harassment in this *Handbook*) thus, the renewed interest in an old idea: single-sex schooling.

Paradoxically, this rekindled interest in single-sex schooling came at a time when many single-sex colleges and religious schools had been experiencing declining enrollment. From their peak in the 1950s, the number of single-sex colleges for women and men steadily declined as many institutions became coeducational primarily for financial survival. Although previously established single-sex colleges, such as the Virginia Military Institute, had been allowed under Title IX regulation, using the Equal Protection Clause of the 14th Amendment, the Supreme Court decided in 1996 that VMI had to admit women since there were no comparable public Virginia colleges for women.

During the same time period, many single-sex Catholic high schools became coeducational in order to maintain their enrollment levels. Despite this decrease in Catholic single-sex schools, there was some increase in private single-sex schools, especially for girls. The National Coalition of Girls Schools reported a 23% increase in student enrollment from 1991 to 2005 for K–12 private girls schools (see www.ncgs.org), though these tended to be schools with extremely high tuition that serve predominantly White, upper-class girls.

Recently, there has been a small increase in public single-sex, K–12 schools. While in 1996 there were only five public single-sex schools still operating in the U.S. (among them Western High School in Baltimore, founded in 1844, and the Philadelphia High School for Girls, founded in 1846),[5] by 2005 that number had increased to over 30 public single-sex schools across the nation. Add to that figure the many public coed schools now experimenting with single-sex classes or dual academies, and the total number of public single-sex schools in the U.S. may be in the hundreds. (Prior to the 2006 Title IX regulations, it was extremely difficult to get an accurate count of public single sex-schools, as some schools feared legal challenges if they were not in compliance with Title IX.)

CHALLENGES TO CONDUCTING RESEARCH ON SINGLE-SEX SCHOOLING

Studying and making decisions about when it is likely to be helpful to try single-sex education is very complex. While most of this chapter is focused on single-sex schools, the research challenges for single-sex classes and programs are similar. For example, one issue unique to publicly funded sex segregation is that it must occur on a voluntary basis. In other words, parents and students must choose to participate in single-sex schools/classes. This makes scientific studies extremely difficult when random assignment of students is not possible. The next section discusses how this and other methodological considerations create challenges that make conducting quality research studies on single-sex education very difficult.

Research Methodology Challenges

Much of the existing research suffers from one or more methodological weaknesses making it extremely difficult to make well-supported, research-based decisions on patterns of results even from a substantial cluster of studies with similar conclusions. Some methodological challenges or problems in interpreting research results from single-sex studies will be discussed in this section in terms of: (a) issues in inferring results from one population to another (generalizability); (b) limitations associated with comparing studies using different process and outcome measures; (c) confounding treatment variables, particularly in large data base studies that make it difficult to know what might have explained the patterns of associations as well as limited knowledge of causal impact; (d) inadequate attention to many aspects of gender analysis from the simple disaggregation of information on males and females in the coed comparison to the use of indicators and analyses that focus on gender-sensitive information; and finally, (e) the pervasive issue of selection bias in studies of single-sex environments, including especially, but not limited to, private and parochial settings.

Since most of the research on single-sex education has been on schools, the following discussions will also dwell on that type of intervention. First, the four types of methodological challenges will be described in more detail, followed by a discussion of four major reviews of research on single-sex schools since the 1985 *Handbook*. Lastly, an examination of selected studies on single-sex schooling will further illustrate the challenges inherent in this type of research.

Key methodological challenges that are especially salient for research on single-sex education include:

Generalizability or making inferences from the specific study or clusters of studies to other contexts. Single-sex studies of schools, classes, or programs (or interventions) rarely attend to all the key comparisons: male-only versus female-only interventions, and male-only and female-only interventions versus well-matched coeducational interventions. Readers of individual research studies as well as of research reviews should always look for all of these comparisons. Most studies of single-sex schools compare schools for women with coeducational schools. For example, if they just examined girls schools, but stated their results in terms of single-sex versus coed schools, it would be

---

[5]In Philadelphia, the prestigious companion single-sex high school for boys became coed after a successful law suit using the state Equal Rights Amendment to allow girls equal opportunities, but there has been no parallel integration of Girls High by boys.

inappropriate since there would be no reason to assume that the positive or negative results also pertained to boys schools.[6]

In making comparisons between the single-sex and coed environments, it is important to try to have well-matched comparison groups for both legal and research purposes. In studying single-sex interventions, especially related to the allocation of public funds, it is also important to know if the same resources and support are provided for males and females. Thus, if sex-segregated academies are being established, it is important to make sure that the girls and the boys academies receive equal tangible and intangible support and benefits. If not, the schools are probably not complying with Title IX or the 14th Amendment equal protection clause of the U.S. Constitution and possibly other state laws providing for equal rights. Additionally, for research purposes when making these three-way comparisons of single-sex and coed schools, it is important to make appropriate matches among types of schools such as elite academic schools, alternative schools, dual academies, public schools, private schools, religious schools, or secular schools, urban, or rural, size of school and much more.

Another generalizability issue that is more feasible to examine in specific single-sex classes or programs than in single-sex schools is whether the intervention is documented clearly enough to be replicable for other sites. Some single-sex interventions focused on helping girls in math and science have been replicated with similar results in various sites using different instructors. (See science, engineering, and technology chapter 13 in this *Handbook*.)

Some common over generalizations in discussions of single-sex research in addition to not making clear what is being compared (schools, classes, programs) involve claims that: (a) patterns of single-sex research results from colleges apply to single-sex elementary and secondary schools in the U.S., (b) research on private and religious schools in the U.S. should explain what will happen in public U.S. schools, and (c) that studies in other countries, particularly those that have a history of single-sex education, should be equally applicable to the U.S. where the context is quite different.

1. Discussions of single-sex education often point to research on private women's colleges that report favorable outcomes for alumna when compared to their coeducational peers (Tidball et al., 1995; Astin, 1993; Tidball & Kistiakowsky, 1976). Some women's colleges have been found to positively influence student self-confidence and leadership involvement. Though coed colleges can certainly learn from the success of women's college alumna, the findings from studies on women's colleges are difficult to assess for the same reasons already discussed. For example, it is difficult to determine whether the success of women's college alumna is due to their family's socioeconomic status or the selectivity of the school. It is also problematic to generalize from studies of colleges to K–12 schooling.

   Even when women's colleges have purposeful and unique approaches to meeting needs of women, it is generally difficult to document what the key aspects of this are that may

contribute to their success, and how these supportive practices may also be used by other women's colleges or perhaps by coed colleges to better meet women's needs. Reviews by Tidball, Smith, Tidball and Wolf-Wendel (1999) and *A Closer Look at Women's Colleges*, a U.S. Department of Education report (Harwarth, 1999), shed some light on these questions, but it must be remembered that most women's colleges remain exclusive institutions that generally cater to students from middle to high socioeconomic status. The postsecondary chapter 30 in this volume contains more information on single-sex colleges.

2. Even many studies conducted within the U.S. on single-sex schooling have limited generalizability for public education because they have been primarily conducted in Catholic schools or private schools and colleges. Any findings drawn from these studies must take into account the religious orientation of the schools and the fact that their selectivity limits their student body. Because families choose these schools and students are not randomly assigned, studies that compare single-sex schools with coeducational schools are limited by the inability to fully control for differences between the student populations. Findings on student achievement are confounded by variables such as socioeconomic status, self-selection related to achievement motivation, or other idiosyncratic characteristics of particular populations.

3. Though numerous studies have been conducted internationally or in U.S. private schools or colleges, it is generally inappropriate to generalize these findings to the unique context of U.S. public schools. Most published international studies were conducted in countries with long traditions of public single-sex schools like the United Kingdom, New Zealand, or Australia, and are difficult to compare to the U.S. (Daly & Shuttleworth 1997; Harker, 2000; Jackson, 2002; Sanford & Blair, 2002; Warrington & Younger, 2003). The same holds true for international comparative studies that examine single-sex schools across countries as diverse as Nigeria or Thailand (Baker, Riordan, & Shaub, 1995; Jimenez & Lockheed, 1989; Lee & Lockheed, 1990) where there may be a history of educating only the upper classes. Indeed, as Mael (1998) notes: "until some empirical basis is devised for including or excluding research from various countries . . . resolutions cannot be properly attempted without fueling even further controversy" (p. 119). Simply put, inferences from international studies may not be appropriate for the U.S. where the context for single-sex schools is so different.

Inconsistency in comparative measures or indicators. Not all studies use the same high-quality measures as indicators of what is happening during or as a result of the single-sex or coed experience being compared, and it is likely that different measures will be used for the same type of indicator such as self-esteem, dropout rates, or even achievement test scores. Not all studies use the same test data even for the same skill such as writing. Some studies look at process indicators and short-term outcome indicators such as classroom tests, and other studies look at long-term outcomes such as career paths

---

[6]This would be like the earlier medical studies that only studied males but suggested that the results applied to both males and females.

and earnings. Some studies focus only on measures of attitudes rather than achievement. For example, one study may report girls became more positive towards mathematics, but does not indicate if that translated to higher levels of achievement. It is also common for results in one site to be positive on some outcome measures and negative on others.

Furthermore, often little attention is given to examining indicators that are especially sensitive to gender equity issues. For example, since the first part of the chapter clearly documents the importance of attending to equity in classroom interaction patterns, even single-sex studies could examine these patterns as well as attitudes and behaviors related to sex or gender stereotyping. Similarly, indicators that are likely to provide information on ending sex discrimination should be selected whenever possible. (Other aspects of challenges relating to gender analysis will be described in the last part of this section on research methodology challenges.)

Confounding variables that restrict interpretations of correlational or causal relationships. A key rationale for single-sex education is to show that the intervention is more effective for the male and female students than alternative ways of organizing instruction that are less likely to contribute to gender inequities. Thus, it is important to know that there is a fair match in what is being compared and that there is a good chance that the planned single-sex education is responsible for, or a major contributor to, some indicators of success. However, many things other than the specified intervention happen even in a fairly well matched comparison classroom or school that may contribute to the results. Studies often fail to address the possibility that any achievement or other outcome differences may result from the unplanned differences in instructional or curricular aspects of the schools being compared and not the effect of planned single-sex or coed intervention per se. These differences my be associated with differences among teachers and their expectations of male or female students in the same school, or even in something as hard to measure as whether a school has a clear vision and focus that supports its single-sex or other activities.

While some findings indicate positive outcomes for graduates of all-girls schools compared to coeducational schools, it is not known how important other factors that have been associated with school success such as small class size, quality of the education, methods of instruction, adaptations of curricular materials, novelty and focus of the school, a charismatic leader, extra resources, parental support, personal commitment to single-sex education, and so forth may be in contributing to these differences. There may also be predictable differential results for males and females that would happen with or without a single-sex intervention. For example, if grades of students in all-girls schools are higher than grades of students in coeducational schools (with equal grading policies and the same curriculum), a potential explanation would be that this would be expected anyway since females in general earn higher grades than their male peers.[7] And as mentioned earlier, the students attending single-sex schools or classes may differ from those attending coeducational schools for various reasons, but it is difficult for researchers to use the normal procedure of random assignment to help control for these potential differences when participation in single-sex interventions must be voluntary.

Lack of appropriate analysis of key gender equity process and outcome indicators. Lastly, is the issue of paying attention to gender equity per se in the processes and outcomes of instruction—a key purpose of this Handbook. This includes keeping track of what is happening to male and female students in the coed as well as the single-sex environments. It has been rare for studies to examine both gender equity process and outcome indicators in these environments. Few have asked, "Does the single-sex education decrease sex discrimination or increase gender equity in any significant way?" This can be both a legal compliance question as well as a research question. For example, it is important to compare single-sex and coed interventions to make sure that there are comparable matches to judge the impact on the research outcomes and to also make sure that the "substantially equal" legal guarantees,[8] such as those suggested in the 2006 Title IX regulations, are met. Although the 2006 Title IX regulations allow sex segregation for purposes not related to ending sex discrimination, they do mention the importance of obtaining evidence of comparability of single-sex and coeducational education. In the required two-year evaluations, schools must show evidence that the single-sex education was provided "consistent with the requirements of Title IX" and that the single-sex classes, extracurricular activities, and schools are provided in a "nondiscriminatory manner."

Therefore, it is important for both legal analyses and research studies on single-sex environments to pay careful attention to indicators of gender equity in education. This would include increased equity in classroom interactions as well as outcomes such as decreasing gender gaps in achievement. This information can provide guidance on whether or not we are returning to a "separate and unequal" world where all-girls schools had fewer resources and less rigorous curricula than all-boys schools. It can also help counteract the danger of reinforcing sex stereotypes, which can lead to long-term negative consequences for students. For example, the ACLU made a successful argument against using single-sex classes to reinforce sex stereotypes in requesting the Livingston Parish Louisiana School Board to stop its plans to change its coeducational Southside Junior High to all single-sex classes based on stereotypic notions of gender differences. (ACLU, 2006; Louisiana Girl Fights Against Sex-Segregated Classrooms, Wins, 2006).

In summary, the methodological and legal issues described in this section highlight the importance of using caution in implementing a single-sex intervention as well as the important role research can play in decreasing sex discrimination or other important outcomes such as equal improvements in academic achievement for both girls and boys. Indeed, in examining reviews of studies of single sex schooling, it is clear that method

---

[7]This weakness could be counteracted if comparative information was provided for grades of girls in each type of school, but it is rare to find this type of disaggregation.

[8]Many equity advocates point out that "substantially equal" is vague, and that the true standard should be equality.

ological weaknesses often mitigate confidence in any findings on single-sex education.

Research Reviews on Single-Sex Schooling

As of our 2006 press deadline, there were no published studies in the U.S. that compare public single-sex students with public coed students, in part, because most public single-sex schools have not been in existence long enough. And while publications such as the AAUW's *Separated by Sex* (1998b) and Salomone's *Same, Different, Equal* (2003) discuss many of the issues surrounding single-sex schooling, they are not solely literature reviews. One of the first reviews of studies on single-sex schooling since the 1985 *Handbook* was in Vol. 1: *A Special Report from the Office of Educational Research and Improvement*, U.S. Department of Education, called "Single-sex schooling: Perspectives from Practice and Research," edited by Hollinger (1993) and initiated by OERI Assistant Secretary Diane Ravich who was concerned about the disappearance of single-sex schools and colleges. This report contains a research review by contractors at Mathematica Policy Research, Inc. It reviews 20 published studies on gender policy effects at the secondary school level, and 11 more on at the postsecondary level. The questions addressed at the secondary level are about: (a) differences in academic and social/affective outcomes of students in single-sex and coeducational schools, (b) "whether the differences vary for men and women students," and (c) "whether these differences are sustained once the outcomes are controlled for family background, student and school variables and sex differences" (p. 12). They concluded that "Results of the studies are inconclusive as to whether one type of school is more effective than another in promoting higher academic achievement and psychosocial development" (p. 17).

At the postsecondary level the researchers noted problems in making comparisons because of the diversity of the schools on the basis of much more than the sex composition of the student body. While the studies showed frequent positive outcomes in the comparative longitudinal studies, the authors acknowledged the possibility that women who selected women's colleges may be different in what is being measured than women in coeducational colleges. They also noted that their data was from women who went to college in the 1970s, so the results may not even generalize to their research review that was conducted in the early 1990s.

There are, however, three more recent and comprehensive literature reviews on the efficacy of single-sex schooling, though each of these has their own distinct limitations. The first review (Mael, 1998) examines over 100 studies of single-sex and coeducational schooling in the United States and abroad. In particular, this review categorizes studies by the criterion examined: academic performance, attitudes toward academics, enjoyment of school, student aspirations, non-stereotypical coursework, self-esteem, and post school success. While the author notes the lack of generalizability of studies conducted in Catholic, private, and international schools, those institutions are included in this review. Mael concludes that though there are possible benefits of single-sex schooling, particularly for females, it should remain an "option not a norm" (p. 106).

The second review (Haag, 2002) examines over 100 articles and essays from national and international contexts. The au-

thor groups the studies according to the variables examined, including self-esteem, attitudes toward academic subjects, sex stereotypes, school environment, and achievement. This review also includes studies of private and Catholic institutions where selection bias remains a concern. Overall, the author concludes that research on single-sex schools is "inconsistent" (p. 670), though she argues that some studies point to higher achievement for females in single-sex schools (not classes).

The most recent review of literature on single-sex schools comes from the U.S. Department of Education's contracted multi-year study on single-sex schooling begun in 2003. This literature review, *Single-Sex Versus Coeducational Schooling: A Systematic Review* (U.S. Department of Education, 2005), examines 40 quantitative studies and 4 qualitative or mixed methods studies. The most sophisticated review to date, it still grapples with the methodological issues inherent in single-sex research. Initially the authors identified 2,221 potential studies, but narrowed them to 379 by excluding postsecondary studies and studies of single-sex classes. The next screening found that only 114 were actual studies. None of them met the Department of Education's What Works Clearinghouse criteria for scientific studies that provide evidence of effectiveness, such as randomized experimental studies, and quasi-experimental designs with matching or regression discontinuity designs. Thus, the authors used less rigorous criteria to select the 44 studies for the analysis. They selected correlational studies if they had statistical controls on some covariates that could have greatly influenced the results, as well as appropriate measurements of the variables used. They did note that other important covariates such as motivation or socioeconomic status or grade level were not controlled. In some cases they also didn't have information on whether the correlations were similar for boys and girls (p. 89). They discuss this as a moderator variable.

As the title of the review suggests, the only comparisons it examined were with single-sex schools and coeducational schools while looking at short-and long-term indicators of success such as academic accomplishment and socioemotional development. The authors also said they looked for information to address these two questions: "Are single-sex schools more or less effective than coeducational schools in terms of addressing issues of procedural (e.g., classroom treatment) and outcome measures of gender equity?" and "Are single-sex schools more or less effective than coeducational schools in terms of perceptual measures of the school climate or culture that may have an impact on performance?" (See their coding instrument, p. 107.)

The authors reported on over 100 process and outcome indicators ranging from student academic achievement to socioemotional indicators in the 44 studies. They found equivocal results for single-sex schooling when compared to coeducational schooling. Most of the studies compared all-girls schools with coed schools (often of unknown similarity), although the California Dual Academy study was included in the summary of qualitative studies, so some comparisons of paired male and female schools were possible.

Despite its systematic approach, the Department's literature review has methodological weaknesses. Unlike much of the research on gender differences and similarities reported in the Hyde and Lindberg chapter 2 in this *Handbook* and the Jones and Dindia research review described in the first part of this chapter, this ED review was not a review of meta-analytic studies by others or a meta-analysis in its own right. Although this ED-sponsored research review asked important questions about process and outcome variables or indicators, including some focused on gender equity, it did not include studies that used gender equity as an outcome variable at the school level (p. 85). This means that none of the studies reported on indicators related to ending sex discrimination such as decreases in pregnancy, bullying, or improved leadership performance. Another limitation was their inclusion of international studies conducted in countries with vastly different education systems compared to the U.S. Lastly, over 20 of the 44 selected studies were conducted in Catholic schools.

Selected Studies on Single-Sex Education

Bearing in mind the challenges discussed previously, some strengths and weaknesses of three types of selected studies will be discussed. These are primarily peer-reviewed scholarly studies conducted in K–12, U.S. settings between 1985 and 2005. This should show challenges in complying with both research and legal constraints to learn if the single-sex education intervention advances gender equity or even if it has other outcome benefits to warrant its implementation in U.S. public schools. The key studies on single-sex schooling can be grouped into the following three categories: (a) studies using large-size national data sets on high school students, (b) small-scale studies comparing single-sex high schools with coeducational schools, and (c) studies of public single-gender dual academies. Summary information on the studies referenced can be found in Tables 1, 2, and 3.

STUDIES ON SINGLE-SEX SCHOOLS USING LARGE NATIONAL DATA SETS

Quite a few major studies on U.S. single-sex schools are secondary analyses of large, national longitudinal databases such as the High School and Beyond Study and the National Educational Longitudinal Studies with data representing thousands of students and schools. These studies use such large samples that they can provide information on the three key types of comparisons. They can examine outcomes for male versus female schools and they can also compare male schools with coed schools and female schools with coed schools. With the large numbers of subjects (both schools and students) these studies paint broad brushstrokes of trends. However, they often do not control for confounding variables such as student background characteristics. Nor do these studies control for differences in classroom climate, student-teacher interactions, or differences in pedagogy or curriculum. With the secondary analysis data alone, they cannot paint a detailed picture of students' lived experiences in a single-sex or coeducational environment. Without this information it is impossible to know if the single sex male school was more or less sexist than the single-sex female school or the paired coeducational schools.

Although some of these studies used the same national data base (but often for different years), they did not always examine the same indicators across schools. Also, many of these studies focus on Catholic high schools and compare Catholic single-sex and Catholic coed high schools (Lee & Bryk, 1986; Lee & Marks, 1990; LePore & Warren, 1997; Marsh, 1989; Marsh, 1991). Some other studies compare Catholic and public school student achievement using a variety of different outcome indicators (Marsh, 1991; Riordan 1985; Riordan 1990). It is not surprising that even studies using large numbers of schools and students and sometimes the same data base and the same researchers find different results when comparing single-sex and coeducation schools on a wide variety of different indicators. For example, five studies (Lee & Bryk, 1986; Lee & Marks, 1990; Marsh, 1989; Marsh, 1991; Thompson, 2003) used the same High School and Beyond database, but examined different outcome measures and came to different conclusions. None of them obtained information on the extent to which the school supported gender equity. However, two other studies drawn from the large databases examined gender equity outcomes such as students' attitudes toward sex-stereotyped majors, careers, or roles. The study by Lee and Bryk (1986) examined the effect of school type on a number of outcome measures including sex-role stereotyping and described some positive relationships such as finding less stereotypical sex-role attitudes for students attending the all-girls Catholic schools. In Thompson's (2003) study of alumna from over 2,000 schools (all-girls private, coed private, and coed public), women who attended all-girls schools were found to be more likely to major in sex-integrated fields, versus highly female fields, than women who attended coed schools. However, confounding variables in these studies (even in the studies of Catholic single sex and coed schools) make it difficult to attribute findings solely to the single-sex environment. Even when controlling for student background characteristics, other variables such as class size or differences in curricular and instructional programs/resources may have been at play. Factors such as class size, parents' socioeconomic status, teacher attention, and specific curricular programs may have been more significant than whether a school was coed or single sex. In other words, though there may be a correlation between single-sex schools and the findings, it was not possible to prove causation.

The study "Sexism in Single-Sex and Coeducational Independent Secondary School Classrooms" by Lee et al. (1994) was unique in that in addition to using information from the large private schools data base, it obtained classroom observations in 20 girls, 20 boys, and 20 coed schools. Thus, unlike most large data base studies, the researchers were able to describe how the patterns of sex stereotypes varied similarly in all three types of schools; in other words, male, female, and coed schools can each be equally good or bad at perpetuating or fighting sex stereotypes. For example, in studying the classroom interactions, Lee and her colleagues found teachers initiated similar types and frequency of sexism in all three types of schools. The sexism ranged from teachers' encouragement of sex stereotyping to teachers' use of offensive, uncensored sexist language.

SMALL SCALE STUDIES COMPARING SINGLE-SEX WITH COED SCHOOLS

There are many dissertations and other small-scale studies of single-sex environments, usually private, independent high schools, or Catholic schools. These small-scale studies rarely do the full three-way comparison of matched girls and boys schools and coed schools, but may pay attention to gender analysis of both process and outcome indicators. They are usually convenience examples of no more than six single-sex schools. Studies on all-girls schools are more common than studies of boys' schools. Shmurak (1998), for example, did a longitudinal case study of students at four all-girls and coeducational schools to examine academic achievement, career aspirations, and attitudes toward gender. Streitmatter (1999) studied one all-girls private school and all-girls math and science classes in public coeducational schools where students reported being less distracted in all-girls settings, and having more positive attitudes toward math and science. Some of these studies collect information from enrolled students and may even do systematic observations of the schools, but others collect more post hoc or longitudinal information. For example, James and Richards (2003) collected information from male graduates of private male and coed schools.

Small-scale studies may look in-depth at gender issues and focus on the cultural aspects of single-sex schools and classrooms. Their generalizability is severely limited however, by their small numbers of non-representative, non-randomly selected schools and students. Often too, the selected schools are not well matched, or may be undergoing substantial transitions. For example, studies by (Signorella, Frieze, & Hershey, 1996; Steinback & Gwizdala, 1995) were conducted in all-girls schools making the transition to coeducational education. A related major study by Brody, Schmuck and other colleagues examined gender equity issues in a Catholic boys high school that became coeducational and two nearby Catholic girls high schools (Brody et al., 2000; Schmuck, Nagel, & Brody, 2002). These transition studies present a whole host of confounding variables, as well as insights on the influence of gender. Overall, small-scale studies of single-sex schools—when they are well matched with comparable male and female and coed schools—have the potential to illuminate many of the complexities of single-sex schools, as well as strategies to increase gender equity. They should also be able to document purposeful strategies used to decrease sex discrimination in outcomes and to document efforts to counteract sex stereotyping in the philosophy and practices of the school.

STUDIES OF SINGLE-GENDER DUAL ACADEMIES

Several studies of public single-sex schools examine dual academies, coeducational schools with all-girls and all-boys classes. Because these schools have both boys and girls on the same campus (sometimes with the same teachers/administrators), the pairs of girls and boys schools are well matched in facilities and resources. The largest study of public single-sex schools to date is a three-year study of 12 single-sex schools in 6 California dual academies that served low income or minority students (Datnow, Hubbard, & Woody, 2001). There are also smaller studies of some of these dual academies. These single-gender dual academies were created as a pilot program via state legislation and received $500,000 state grants. They were primarily designed to increase school choice, but little thought or teacher training was provided to attend to any gender consciousness issues raised by this overt sex segregation. The Datnow, Hubbard, and Woody study conducted over 300 interviews and classroom observations and focused on examining equity implications. They found that in most cases the main reason students attended these dual academies was because these single-gender academies had more resources than their district's coed schools. While there were active efforts to recruit at-risk students for the dual academies, in some districts the academies operated under capacity and only four academies remained after 2 years and only one after 3 years when the state funding ended. The single-sex academies also had some positive and some negative implications for the districts' coeducational schools, but no explicit comparisons with matched coed schools were studied.

This overall study generally found that the sex-segregated schools increased sex discrimination. For example, the study found that "traditional gender stereotypes were often reinforced in the single gender academies. Boys tended to be taught in more regimented, traditional, and individualistic fashion, and girls in more nurturing, cooperative and open environments." Also, "students received mixed messages about gender from their teachers." One of the findings that may be more likely to occur in dual academies than separate single-sex schools is that "the creation of separate academies for boys and girls on the same campus led to a dichotomous understanding of gender, where girls were seen as 'good' and boys were seen as 'bad'" (Study Executive Summary, p. 4).

In a substudy, Hubbard and Datnow (2005) found that the smaller classes and increased resources achieved through additional funding made a bigger difference to "at-risk students" than the single-sex classes. So, even in what may seem as a well-matched set of similar experiments with a clear focus on sex segregation, it is still challenging to attribute outcomes solely to single-sex arrangements. However, like many of the small-scale studies, the researchers were able to examine what was happening enough to learn that there was little attention to the purposes of single-sex instruction to either address common socialization related needs of the male and female students or to counteract sex stereotyping. For example, Woody (2002) found that grouping of males who were having trouble in school was not addressed with any effective strategies to help them maximize their special abilities.

Although there may be fewer confounding variables in studies of dual academies than in other comparisons of single-sex and coed schools since the girls and boys are on the same campus and the equitable distribution of resources can be monitored, unplanned and undocumented differences in pedagogy and curriculum can still be a concern. If dual academies increase in number, it may be possible to design rigorous comparisons of all-male and all-female groups such as these fairly well-matched schools, or perhaps even study matched sex-segregated classes if the nature of the treatment to decrease sex discrimination is clear. However, any future dual academies or single-sex classes need to be fully compliant with Title IX, the 2006 Title IX regulations, and the Equal Protection clause of the 14th Amendment. That means that there needs to be an accurate research based rationale for why the dual-academy option would decrease sex discrimination or improve students' achievement,

TABLE 9.1   Large Data Base Studies of Single-Sex Schools

Author	Article Title Journal Source	Sample	Measure	Findings
Riordan, C., 1985.	Public and Catholic Schooling: The Effects of Gender Context Policy *American Journal of Education*	22, 652 seniors in 1,318 schools (37 Catholic single sex schools, 37 Catholic coed schools, 20 public single sex schools, 1212 public coed schools, 1 private single sex school, and 11 private coed schools) Students from the National Longitudinal Study of High School Class of 1972.	Student questionnaire, school records, test battery taken from the NLS (National Longitudinal Study) to measure the effects of school type on academic achievement.	Both males and females at Catholic single sex schools outperformed their coed Catholic counterparts. For females in vocabulary and reading; for males in math and ultimate educational attainment.
Lee, V. E., and Bryk, A. S., 1986	Effects of Single-Sex Secondary Schools on Student Achievement and Attitudes *Journal of Educational Psychology*	1,807 students in 45 single-sex Catholic schools and 30 Catholic coed schools. Students from the High School and Beyond Study (HSB).	Survey of effects of single-sex versus coed schooling on academic achievement, achievement gains, educational aspirations, locus of control, sex- role stereotyping, and attitudes and behaviors related to academics.	Single sex schools deliver specific advantages such as a more positive attitude toward academics and homework, higher achievement in reading and science and greater locus of control and higher career aspirations, to their students in all areas, particularly female students.
Marsh, H. W., 1989	Effects of Attending Single-Sex and Coeducational High Schools on Achievement, Attitudes, Behaviors, and Sex Differences *Journal of Educational Psychology*	2, 332 Catholic high school students attending 47 single-sex Catholic schools and 33 coed Catholic schools. Students from the HSB (High School and Beyond) Study.	Effects of school type, sex, and interaction on senior year outcomes and postsecondary activities.	Changes during the period analyzed were unaffected by school type. There were changes related to sex, such as higher educational aspira-tions and likelihood of taking math and science courses, but the sex differences were unaffected by school type.
Lee, V. E., and Marks, H. M., 1990	Sustained Effects of the Single-Sex Secondary School Experience on Attitudes, Behaviors, and Values in College *Journal of Educational Psychology*	1,533 college students who attended 75 Catholic secondary schools, 45 single-sex and 30 coeducational schools. Students from the HSB (High School and Beyond) Study.	Sustained effects of single-sex and coeducational secondary schools on attitudes, values, and behaviors of both men and women, measured 2 or 4 years after graduation.	There were sustained effects of single-sex secondary schooling for both men and women, however, effects for women extended to attitudinal and behavioral outcomes. Single-sex educational experiences were found to impact young women positively in regards to academic and professional achievement.
Riordan, C., 1990.	*Girls and Boys in School: Together or Separate?*	Students from single- sex and coeducational high schools (public and private/Catholic schools)	Student academic achievement, aspirations and attitudes.	Significant differences for African- and Hispanic-American boys in single sex schools. No significant differences in math or science for both boys and girls.
Marsh, H. W., 1991	Public, Catholic Single-Sex, and Catholic Coeducational High Schools: Their Effects on Achievement, Affect, and Behaviors *American Journal of Education*	10,507 students from 853 public schools, 33 Catholic coed schools, 21 Catholic boys' schools, 26 Catholic girls' schools. Students from the High School and Beyond Study (HSB)	Three-group design using data from the HSB Study. Main effects of school type (public, Catholic coed, Catholic single sex) on growth during last two years of high school examining affective variables, academic choices, post-secondary activities, and academic achievement outcomes	Students from single- sex Catholic schools and coed Catholic schools demonstrate a similar pattern of growth in terms of locus of control, academic achievement, and self- concept during the last two years of high school.

(continued)

TABLE 9.1 *(Continued)*

Author	Article Title Journal Source	Sample	Measure	Findings
Lee, V. E., and Marks, H. M. and Byrd, T., 1994	Sexism in Single-Sex and Coeducational Independent Secondary School Classrooms *Sociology of Education*	86 classrooms from 60 private schools (20 boys' schools, 20 girls' schools, 20 coed schools) observed. Data from 3,183 students from the schools' senior class and 629 secondary math and English teachers Part of the National Study of Gender Grouping in Independent Secondary Schools.	How engenderment (socialization to gender) and sexism operates in three types of independent secondary schools. Classroom observation of interaction between teacher-student, student-student.	Teachers initiated most of the incidents in six categories of sexism. Although the frequency of incidents was similar, the forms of sexism were different at each of the three types of schools.
LePore, P. C., and Warren, J. R., 1997	A Comparison of Single-Sex and Coeducational Catholic Secondary Schooling: Evidence from the National Educational Longitudinal Study of 1988 *American Educational Research Journal*	105 male and 65 female 10th grade students from single-sex Catholic secondary schools; 79 male and 96 female 10th grade students from coed Catholic secondary schools; 95 male and 53 female 12th grade students from single- sex Catholic secondary schools; 64 males and 87 female 12th grade students from coed Catholic secondary schools. Students taken from the National Educational Longitudinal Study of 1988.	Differences between single-sex and coeducational Catholic secondary school students in academic and social psychological outcomes and whether these differences affect women more favorably.	Results indicated that single-sex schools were not especially favorable academic settings and that any advantages of attending these schools favored boys only.
Thompson, J., 2003	The Effect of Single-Sex Secondary Schooling on Women's Choice of College Major *Sociological Perspectives*	Seniors and sophomores from 36 Catholic single sex and 36 Catholic coed schools surveyed from 1980–1992, every two years. Student sample taken from the High School and Beyond study.	Effect of attending an all-girls' school on sex traditionality of women's choice of college major.	Women who attended all-girls' high schools versus coed high schools were more likely to major in sex-integrated fields such as engineering, health sciences and business, compared to highly female fields such as humanities and education.

and an evaluation to provide evidence that this happened because of the intervention that was used. Ideally, this research should also include comparison with coeducational classes using similar interventions to increase gender equity. Although it may complicate the research design, as previously mentioned, students must be able to voluntarily select either the single-sex option or a comparable coeducational option.

Gender Equity Outcomes and Single-sex Schools

Of the studies referenced in this section, 10 of the 19 include some specific aspect of gender equity in their research. This is important to note because gender bias in coeducational classrooms is one of the most popular justifications for single-sex

schooling in the United States, with proponents arguing that these schools have more gender-equitable climates in which students are free to flourish in all academic subjects. But, as these studies demonstrate, there is very little published empirical research to support the notion that single-sex schools are more gender-equitable institutions.

As detailed in the previous sections, there are mixed findings with regard to single-sex environments and gender equity. Simply put, there are no guarantees that separating boys and girls automatically creates a more equitable learning environment. Nor does it foster a climate that interrupts teachers' or students' stereotypical beliefs about gender differences. Clearly, teacher training and on-going support must accompany the implementation of any single-sex school in the public sector. The few studies that do examine gender equity demonstrate the immediate

TABLE 9.2   Small Scale Studies

Author	Article Title Journal Source	Sample	Measure	Findings
Steinback, M., and Gwizdala, J., 1995	Gender Differences in Mathematics Attitudes of Secondary Students *School Science & Mathematics*	450 students in Year 1 enrolled, 353 participants (all female); 1,000 students in Year 2 enrolled, 697 participants (323 females, 375 males). Students who attended an all-girls' Catholic school that merged with a similar all boys' school to create one Catholic coed school.	Investigator-constructed questionnaire to measure the like or dislike of mathematics, self-esteem in math, view of the importance and usefulness of math, and views of the mixed-sex school environment.	Traditional male and female differences were found in the areas of self-confidence, usefulness of mathematics, and classroom behavior. Female students' attitudes remained positive but their predictions about the mixed-sex classroom were confirmed.
Signorella, M. L. Hanson Frieze, I., and Hershey, S. W., 1996	Single-Sex Versus Mixed-Sex Classes and Gender Schemata in Children and Adolescents *Psychology of Women Quarterly*	66 students in grades 2–5 and 87 students in grades 6–12 from one private all girls' school which that has begun the transition of becoming coeducational	Pre-test and post-test at the beginning and end of the school year measured student attitudes toward sex-stereotyped activities and attitudes towards women and gender roles gender roles.	All students regardless of classroom setting were less stereotyped at the end of the school year than at the beginning.
Shmurak, C. B., 1998	*Voices of Hope: Adolescent Girls at Single Sex and Coeducational Schools*	Students at four all-girls and coeducational high schools	Longitudinal case study of students' academic achievement, career aspirations, and attitudes toward gender.	No difference in students' SAT scores, career aspirations or attitudes toward gender. Girls from single sex schools had higher AP test scores, while girls at coed schools took more science courses and were accepted at more selective colleges.
Streitmatter, J., 1999	*For Girls Only: Making a Case for Single Sex schooling*	One private all-girls school, and public middle and high schools experimenting with all-girls math and science classes	Interviews with teachers, students, administrators and parents	Students reported being more focused and less distracted in all-girls settings. Students also reported more positive attitudes towards math or science.
Schmuck, P., Nagel, N., and Brody, C., 2002; Brody, et al., 2000	Studying Gender Consciousness in Single-sex and Coeducational High Schools *Gender in Policy and Practice*	One elite, all-male Catholic high school making the transition to coeducational, and the impact on two local all-female "sister" schools	Case study with interviews of faculty, administrators, trustees and students; classroom observations; and focus groups of students and faculty	The all-female and all-male schools responded differently to the transition to coeducation. Whereas the all-female school developed new extra-curricular programs for males and changed curricula, the all-male school made no such changes in adding young women to their school.
James, A. N. and Richards, H. C., 2003	Escaping Stereotypes: Educational Attitudes of Male Alumni of Single Sex and Coed Schools *Psychology of Men and Masculinity*	412 male graduates from 12 private schools (3 all boys' boarding schools, 3 all boys' day schools, 3 coed boarding schools, 3 coed day schools).	1. Estes Attitude Scale (EAS) to assess attitudes towards English, reading, social studies, math and science and was modified to include verbal interest and quantitative interest. 2. Demographic information: College attended, major area of study, current occupation. 3. Checklist of 15 job-related skills that they perceived they learned in secondary school and which 3 that they currently use in their occupation.	Significant differences in preference towards reading and writing subjects between boys who attended single sex schools versus coed schools as well as men who chose humanities majors after high school. Significant differences between the number of men who went into science and technology fields versus humanities fields after college between single sex and coed schools.

TABLE 9.3 Dual Academy Studies

Author	Article Title Journal Source	Sample	Measure	Findings
Datnow, A., Hubbard, L., and Woody, E., 2001	Is Single Gender Schooling Viable in the Public Sector? Lessons from California's Pilot Program	Qualitative case study of 12 public single gender academies (6 all boys, 6 all girls)	Classroom observation of student-teacher interactions, student-student interactions, and pedagogical strategies. 200 interviews and observations with students, teachers, principals, parents and district officials.	Single gender schools, though started with the intention of addressing gender equity, became an avenue to serve other populations (i.e., low achieving). There was an absence of deep inquiry about gender equity among educators, and an absence of discussion about the difference in teaching styles for boys and girls.
Woody, E., 2002	Constructions of Masculinity in California's Single-Gender Academies Gender in Policy and Practice	Part of a larger qualitative case study of 12 public single gender academies (6 all boys, 6 all girls)	Student interviews and focus groups about the single-gender reform.	Separating boys and girls did little to challenge students' traditional beliefs about masculinity or how boys should act.
Herr, K., and Arms, E., 2004	Accountability and Single-Sex Schooling: A Collision of Reform Agendas American Educational Research Journal	One coeducational public middle school that created school-wide single sex classes (over 1,000 students)	Ethnographic case study including in-depth teacher, administrator, and student interviews; participant observation of classrooms; open-ended student surveys; and, document analysis.	Pressure to increase students' standardized test scores impacted curriculum and instruction, and diverted attention from gender and the single-gender reform. Study highlights the importance of instituting on-going teacher professional development on gender equity issues in tandem with single-sex classes.
Hubbard, L., and Datnow, A., 2005	Do Single-sex Schools Improve the Education of Low-iIncome and Minority Students? An investigation of California's Public Single-Gender Academies Anthropology and Education Quarterly	Six single-gender academies (three all-boys, three all-girls)	Interviews with 88 male students and 83 female students	Boys and girls reported fewer distractions and more intimate, caring relationships with teachers. Not clear if this was due to single-sex classes or smaller class sizes and increased resources

need for more research in K–12 schools, as well as clearer federal or state guidelines for implementing gender-equitable policies and practices in all school types.

DISCUSSION OF ASSUMPTIONS RELATING TO SINGLE-SEX EDUCATION

Claims Favoring Single-Sex Education

Why, in the 21st century, have we seen a return to the old-fashioned notion of sex-segregated schooling? Certainly, the rhetoric of the school choice and the voucher movement has contributed to the notion that single-sex schools should be another item on the menu of public school choices that families have for their children. In addition, the recent media attention given the emerging science of gendered brain differences has supported popular notions that boys and girls learn differently and therefore can benefit from separate learning environments.

More often, claims in favor of single-sex schooling cite what Coleman (1961) called the dating and social culture of coed schools, and the distraction from academics this poses for adolescents. Single-sex schools have been promoted as more serious and studious environments that have academic and socioemotional benefits for students. Lastly, much of the previously discussed classroom interaction research continues to document gender bias in coeducational classrooms and has fed public interest in single-sex schools. But are single-sex classrooms and schools—by their very nature—more gender equitable environments? At the heart of the single-sex schooling debate lies a set of popular assumptions that continue to drive policy in the absence of conclusive research.

Popular Assumptions about Single-Sex Education

Despite decades of progress, there remains a wide acceptance that there are simply innate differences between the sexes, a proposition supported by different camps for different reasons across the political spectrum. Are female and male brains different? Do, as Gurian (2001) suggests, girls and boys learn differently? Are boys more competitive and girls more collaborative? For those who would answer yes to these questions, single-sex education may be viewed as a preferred way to build on common strengths. Others may prefer to have single-sex schools counteract gender-socialized behavior by helping boys to work more collaboratively and girls to be more competitive.

But there is a danger to essentializing gender differences. Even those who cite brain research and other biological factors in support of single-sex education such as Sax (2005a, b) and Deak (2002) concede that there is considerable variability within the sexes themselves. As Hyde and Lindberg note in chapter 2 of this volume, there still exists no conclusive evidence that these biological differences result in different learning styles. If, in a single-sex environment, you teach to these supposed gender differences, what is the percentage of students who *don't* learn best in that way?

Also, in emphasizing gender differences in instructional practice, there is a risk of reinforcing traditional gender stereotypes. Early single-sex schools in the U.S. based their pedagogy and curriculum on the established *fact* that boys and girls are just different. How easy would it be to accept these differences and return to separate and unequal educations, especially in regions of the U.S. where local context or culture may wholeheartedly endorse sex-stereotyped separate spheres for women and men?

Research on the psychology of gender differences argues that males and females are ultimately more alike than different (Hyde 2005; Maccoby, 1998), and the small sex differences that do exist are malleable and increased or decreased by socialization and education (Sadker & Sadker, 1994). Researchers in the UK—where a more established system of sex-segregated schooling has allowed for more in-depth study—are firmly against a "gendered pedagogy that emphasizes essentialist constructions of boys' and girls' learning styles" (Younger & Warrington, 2006, p. 603).

A second assumption is that girls thrive in single-sex environments. They perform better academically (especially in math, science, and technology), participate in more leadership opportunities and pursue more prestigious careers. While a small number of studies discussed previously suggest advantages for girls in single-sex schools and women's colleges, overall, this assumption is not supported by current research on K–12 schools in the U.S. This widely accepted notion may be based in part on the small body of research on the successful careers of alumna from elite women's colleges in the U.S., research that has been improperly generalized to graduates of girls high schools. As previously noted, all U.S. women's colleges are private, and thus draw primarily from a selective pool of female applicants who can afford private college tuition or earn a scholarship. Critics of the research on private women's colleges, as well as all-girl high schools, point out that it is extremely difficult to know just how much of a role *selection bias* plays in their overall success.

A third assumption about single-sex schools is that they offer a studious environment free from the distractions of or harassment from the opposite sex. While this is a popular reason parents give for choosing single-sex schooling for their children, especially girls (Heather, 2002; Datnow et al., 2001), it completely discounts the real fact that students of the same sex are still able to distract one another from academics. This phenomenon was documented in a British study of single-sex classes that found all-boys classes had a "macho, male culture [where] boys are more distracted by each other than they are by the girls" (Jackson, 2002). Another study (Askew & Ross, 1990) points to increased bullying in all-boys schools where dominant forms of masculinity may be exacerbated. In fact, some have suggested that same-sex bullying and sexual harassment is just as prevalent in single-sex schools as in mixed sex schools, perhaps even more so (see chapter 11 by Paludi, this volume.) Furthermore, as Campbell and Sanders (2002) argue, the distraction argument makes the false assumption of heterosexuality and ignores the issues confronting lesbian, gay, bisexual, or transgender students who may be more distracted in a single-sex classroom. Finally, if these schools truly eliminated all student distractions and sexual tension, one would expect to find higher achievement in all single-sex schools, which is simply not the case. Rather than accepting bullying and sexual harassment as a fact of life in coeducational schools or decamping to single-sex schools, parents, students, community members, and teachers need to work together to eliminate these tensions from all schools. Creating schools free from harassment, bullying, and violence should be the first priority, and as Sadker (2004) argues, the central issue is "investing in the real equity needs of coeducational schools" (p. 8).

One relatively new assumption has begun to take hold in the past few years. Single-sex schools, as a matter of personal preference, should be available to public school students. This view aligns with the school choice movement that has gained momentum since the late 1980s and has rapidly expanded public school options beyond the neighborhood school to magnet and charter schools. With the free *marketizing* (Apple, 2001) of education, consumers (i.e., parents) are free to choose what they think is the most appropriate academic environment for their children. Why shouldn't public school students be offered an option previously available only to parents willing to pay for a private or religious education? Would individuals who support having a choice of a single-sex school or class also support having a public school exclusively for one race or social class?

This school choice assumption has been further fueled by the commonly held, but false, belief that NCLB provided new federal funds to pay for single-sex education. While the Local Innovative Education Programs section of NCLB (2002) states that funds can be used for same-sex schools and classrooms, this provision only allows funds to be used consistent with applicable law. With the 2006 changes to Title IX regulations, educators now have the opportunity to use all federal funding for more K–12 single-sex education purposes than previously allowed, but their single-sex activities still must be consistent with applicable laws such as Title IX and the Equal Protection Clause of the 14th Amendment.

As previously mentioned, concurrent and seemingly contradictory to this laissez-faire climate, are increasing federal education mandates such as provisions in the No Child Left Behind Act (2002) and the legislation establishing the Institute for Education Sciences that call for schools to implement only those education programs or practices that have been proven effective through "rigorous scientific research" (*www.ed.gov/nclb*). The federal government further defines reliable evidence as obtained from studies that use experimental and control groups to test the effectiveness of an intervention. Since there are currently no published studies of public single-sex schools utilizing these research methods, parents enrolling their children in these single-sex schools or classes need to be cautious. According to the federal government's own definition, public single-sex schools fall under the category of *an untried program* that could turn out to be *a fad* (www.ed.gov/nclb).

There is no convincing data on the effectiveness of public single-sex schools or classes. Many of these experiments have been just recently implemented, and few have been designed as rigorous research or evaluation experiments with a clear purposeful rationale for sex segregation or proper controls to collect appropriate data and draw any conclusions about the impact or effectiveness of the single-sex educational intervention. The U.S. Department of Education-sponsored study that is currently underway on nearly 30 public single-sex schools will be the first large-scale descriptive study of single-sex schools since the Datnow et al.'s (2001) qualitative case study of 12 single-gender academies in California. Like the California study, this national ED study of public charter schools, dual academies, and other single-sex schools has not been designed to examine whether or not single-sex schools are effective.

There is even less systematic research on the uncharted proliferation of single-sex classes, which like single-sex schools, are often implemented without any clear rationale or teacher training to counteract likely sex stereotypes that may be reinforced by this type of sex segregation.

RECOMMENDATIONS FOR POLICY, PRACTICE, AND FURTHER RESEARCH

In the 1985 version of this chapter "Sex Equity in Classroom Organization and Climate" (Lockheed & Klein, 1985) the focus fell more squarely on patterns of gender inequality in coeducational classrooms. The current chapter updates the summaries of the research on gender equity in coeducational classroom environments, but now also includes the growing body of research on single-sex schools and dual academies. While many of the recommendations in 1985 centered on improving the climate of coeducational student groupings, this chapter begins to address those issues unique to gender-segregated environments. With the 2006 Title IX regulations putting single-sex education once again in the national spotlight, there are renewed opportunities for improved policy, practice, and future research.

Policy: Putting Gender on the Agenda

While the 1975 and the 2006 Title IX regulations provide some protections against overt and institutional discrimination on the basis of sex, the problems of gender inequality in the classroom are often unintentional, subtle, and pervasive micro-inequities that are difficult to document. The research covered in this chapter suggests that explicit gender equity policies are still needed for both coeducational and single-sex environments. Policymakers at the federal, state and local levels must:

1. Maintain the goal of gender equity in coeducational schools.

Even though local districts now have more freedom to offer different kinds of single-sex schooling, this will certainly not be an option for a majority of public school students. Therefore, it is imperative that the "government's goal should be to create a successful coeducational school system free from sex discrimination" (Stone 2004, p. 21). One policy recommendation is to raise awareness as to the requirements and safeguards built into Title IX, the Equal Protection Clause of the 14th Amendment, and state laws prohibiting sex discrimination.

Title IX, now on the books for almost 35 years, is widely misunderstood and unevenly enforced. In a survey of 440 students and 84 teachers in five middle schools, Zittleman and Sadker (2005) found that the vast majority of participants did not have a basic understanding of the law. The few respondents who knew anything about the law, predictably linked it solely to issues of women's athletics.

Clearly, the federal government needs to raise awareness among all educators in all contexts as a first step, even as local Title IX coordinators and other school officials implement policies to assess and insure gender equity in all aspects of the school climate. This focus should go beyond on-campus sexual harassment and sports to include equitable academic achievement and educational opportunities for both females and males.

2. Repeal the 2006 Title IX modifications to the 1975 Title IX regulations.

This chapter's research review provides no convincing evidence that single-sex environments in general decrease sex stereotyping in instruction or significantly close the gender gap in educational outcomes. Separate education is rarely equal even if it is voluntary. The 2006 Title IX regulations, with so many questions unanswered, appear to move us no closer to these goals and very well may set back the gains that have been achieved by using single-sex education sparingly as specified in less permissive affirmative action provisions in the 1975 Title IX regulations.

A repeal of the overbroad and ill-defined 2006 regulations is the only prudent course of action at this time. A prompt repeal would forestall the many court challenges that are sure to come as students present evidence of sex discrimination from poorly crafted programs with limited oversight that yield unequal treatment. For example, new single-sex programs could end up receiving more public and nonpublic resources than the mixed sex alternatives.[9]

Prior to this repeal, educators who are concerned about advancing gender equity or even those who want to avoid lawsuits should consider using the remedial or affirmative action justifications in the 1975 Title IX regulations. This would mean allowing single-sex education primarily to decrease sex discrimination. Even using the broader justifications in the 2006 regulations, educators should not implement a single-sex program unless they have clear and convincing evidence that what they plan to do will result in attaining educationally important objectives without increasing sex discrimination. For suggestions on strategies to do this see Klein (2003) and Klein (2005).

Prior to making a decision to implement any single-sex education, educators should follow guidance from a 1996 GAO report *Issues Involving Single-Gender Schools and Programs*(U.S. Government Accounting Office, 1996). It states the need for the following justifications for single-gender classes or programs:

(1) beneficiaries of the single-gender classes or programs must have had limited opportunities to participate in a school's programs or activities due to their sex, (2) less restrictive or segregative alternatives that may have accomplished the goals of the single-gender classes or programs must have been considered and rejected, and (3) there must be evidence that comparable sex neutral means could not be reasonably expected to produce the results sought through the single-gender classrooms or programs. (U.S. GAO, 1996, pp. 22–23)

To attain our *Handbook* goal of actively increasing gender equity through education, it is important to select only single-sex education options that have a high likelihood of increasing gender equity and that are more likely to do so than using gender equity promoting strategies in a mixed-sex environment. If the evidence shows that this has been accomplished, then it would be legitimate to continue the sex segregation. But since it is easy to slide into patterns of inequity and stereotyping, we recommend that all single-sex education schools or activities be actively monitored and evaluated annually to ensure that they do not foster sex discrimination, but instead advance gender equitable outcomes.[10]

3. **Institute policies to monitor gender equity in coeducational and single-sex environments in *all* educational institutions covered by Title IX.**

Coeducational and single-sex environments in public and private coed schools receiving federal financial assistance must be monitored to ensure that they are not discriminating on the basis of sex. Most of the Title IX complaints have been in sex-segregated athletic activities that have been allowed under the 1975 Title IX regulations for contact sports. As described in chapter 18, federal policies such as the athletics disclosure act

have been useful in making educators aware of whether or not they are treating their male and female students equitably.

If the 2006 Title IX regulations are not repealed quickly, it may be necessary to develop similar monitoring and reporting requirements for single-sex education or to request special studies by GAO or others to assure full compliance with the 2006 Title IX regulations. Concurrently, publicly accessible Web-based annual evaluations should assess whether single-sex education is being implemented free of sex discrimination according to applicable laws. The evaluations can be facilitated by Title IX coordinators. If they are looking at the comparative effects of single-sex interventions, it would be best if they are conducted by qualified external evaluators who can produce evidence that will meet the standards of the What Works Clearinghouse.

Even meeting the minimal *substantially equal* requirements of the 2006 regulations in terms of curriculum, resources, faculty, and facilities will be a challenge. For example, there may be inequities in areas such as curricular pacing. One study (Herr & Arms, 2002) found that teachers who taught the same academic subject to both an all-girls class and all-boys class deliberately held back their girls' class when it became clear that the boys' class could not cover the material at the same pace.

Practice: Promoting Gender Equitable Pedagogy Among Teachers

The 1985 predecessor to this chapter highlighted the importance of awareness of strategies for promoting equitable teacher-student interactions. Yet research has continued to document gender inequality in the coeducational classroom—for both girls and boys. Clearly, equitable teaching practices have not been achieved in schools. Teachers, administrators, and the teacher education community must:

1. **Implement gender equity training in teacher education programs.**

Few teacher education programs have incorporated gender equity interventions and strategies into their courses, and yet these programs can work. Teacher certification programs must require teacher candidates, and administrators, to study high-quality research on such topics as gender similarities and differences, gender equity issues, and bias in classroom interactions. Ongoing training should be provided for both preservice and inservice teachers, helping them to recognize the various forms of gender bias in teaching as well as in curricular materials. College instructors teaching in education programs must be familiar with Title IX protections, model gender equitable practices, and incorporate gender issues into their curriculum. Finally, teachers, administrators, and entire schools should be held accountable as to whether and how they address gender equity or gender gaps at their institutions. Systems used to evaluate all types of educators should include specific criteria to ensure they advance gender equity.

---

[9]In fact, in the dual academies in CA, the promise of additional resources was a key reason parents gave for selecting these schools (Datnow et al., (2001).

[10]Some gender equity advocates believe that any single-sex education should be extremely rare and that these interventions should not be limited to one sex, although they could be designed to meet the needs that were most common for one sex such as the classes designed to overcome math anxiety that served both women and men.

2. Require accreditation bodies to evaluate teaching programs to ensure that they include appropriate instruction on gender equity.

National organizations such as the National Council for Accreditation of Teacher Education (NCATE) must establish clearer criteria for evaluating teacher education programs related to their attention to promoting gender equity and preventing gender bias. These organizations should promote best practices and heighten awareness of gender equity issues in classroom instruction. State teacher assessment and credentialing programs must also evaluate teacher candidates' knowledge and understanding of gender similarities, of Title IX, and other relevant laws that facilitate gender equity and gender equitable teaching practices whether in coeducational or single-sex classrooms.

3. Refine and develop curricula to help K–12 students learn gender equitable interactions.

Programs should be refined and, as needed, developed to help students learn to interact in nonstereotypic, gender equitable ways with their peers, teachers, and others to learn about their rights under Title IX. Already-developed promising programs, such as the ones detailed in the U.S Department of Education's report from the Gender Equity Expert Panel (2001), must be implemented at the school level.

Further Research and Evaluation on Single-sex Schooling

The following gender equity issues must be addressed in future research studies:

1. Conduct further studies on gender equitable classroom interactions.

Though Title IX mandates that both boys' and girls' classes have access to the same resources and curriculum, it cannot legislate the gendered beliefs that teachers and students bring with them to the classroom. As Lee, Marks and Byrd (1994) found, single-sex schools are often the most sexist, with teachers and students engaging in "gender reinforcement" or "sex-role stereotyping" (1994). It is important to conduct research in both coed and single-sex environments on the most effective ways to go from awareness of gender inequalities in classroom interaction to actual behavioral changes where teachers and students routinely interact in gender equitable ways.

2. Study and evaluate public single-sex schools with comparable coeducational schools.

Studies on public single-sex schools covered by Title IX must compare girls and boys schools (or dual academies), and these schools should be compared with well-matched coed schools.[11] The comparisons should examine process and outcome indicators on a number of variables such as sex stereotyping, as well as achievement, attitude, college enrollment, and career choices. Research must examine the culture of single-sex schools, including classroom interactions, curricular content, school climate, and organization. When making comparison studies on single-sex education, one must control for other factors like small class size and selection bias.

To learn about relative merits among single-sex options, researchers should examine various types of single-sex environments, such as single-sex schools, dual academies, coeducational schools with gender segregated classes, and even activities focused on meeting the common needs of girls or boys, but that allow both genders to participate. It is also necessary to examine the effectiveness of these interventions at different grade levels (e.g., elementary school, middle school, high school, college), and for diverse racial and ethnic populations.

3. Identify specific replicable single-sex schools, classes, and programs that increase gender equity.

Future studies should identify successful single-sex interventions and their characteristics, and determine whether they are replicable and effective in other contexts. A database of good-quality evaluations of single-sex interventions (schools, classes, and even after-school programs) should be developed, and patterns among related clusters of interventions should be described. If effective single-sex classes or programs such as Orientation to Nontraditional Occupations for Women (ONOW) are identified, they should be replicated in related contexts and further evaluated. Examples of gender equity results may include students' attitudes toward and achievement in nontraditional academic subjects, students' choice of majors and careers, and decreased gender gaps in desired outcomes. Wherever possible, evaluations of adaptations of these programs developed for single-sex environments, but used in mixed sex environments, should be reported. It is likely that many will be equally effective in coeducational environments.

ACKNOWLEDGMENTS

The author wishes to thank external reviewers Amanda Datnow, University of Southern California, Los Angeles; Elizabeth Woody, University of California, Berkeley; Elena Silva, Education Sector, Washington, DC; David Sadker and Karen Zittleman, American University, Washington DC; Kathryn Herr, Montclair State University, Montclair, New Jersey; Elizabeth Homer, Michigan NOW, Lansing, MI; Lory Stone, San Juan, Puerto Rico; Jocelyn Samuels, National Women's Law Center, Washington, DC; and Marlaine Lockheed, Princeton, New Jersey, author of the related 1985

---

[11]The 2006 Title IX regulations no longer require that single-sex options for both girls and boys be routinely established. Instead, in many instances all that is required is a coeducation option or comparison.

[12]See Stone, 2004 and Chapter 31 "Summary Recommendations for Achieving Gender Equity in and through Education."

Handbook chapter, for their valuable comments on drafts of this chapter. Thanks are also due to *Handbook* editors, Lynn Fox and Sue Klein for sharing information and feedback on multiple drafts of this challenging chapter.

References

American Association of University Women (AAUW). (1992). *How schools shortchange girls*. New York: Marlowe & Co.

American Association of University Women (AAUW). (1993). *Hostile hallways: The AAUW survey on sexual harassment in America's schools*. Washington, DC: AAUW Educational Foundation.

American Association of University Women (AAUW). (1998a). *Gender gaps: Where schools still fail our children*. Washington, DC: AAUW Educational Foundation.

American Association of University Women (AAUW). (1998b). *Separated by sex: A critical look at single-sex education for girls*. Washington, DC: AAUW Educational Foundation.

American Association of University Women (AAUW). (2002). *Hostile hallways. Bullying, teasing and sexual harassment in school*. Washington, DC: AAUW Educational Foundation.

American Civil Liberties Union (2006). *Memorandum of Law in support of Plaintiff's Motion for a Temporary Restraining Order/Preliminary Injunction*. Michelle Selden, Darren Selden and Rhonda Selden Plaintiffs against Livingston Parish School Board. (Aug. 2, 2006).

Apple, M. W. (2001). *Educating the "right way": Market, standards, God and inequality*. NY: RoutledgeFalmer.

Askew, S. & Ross, C. (1990). *Boys don't cry: Boys and sexism in education*. Buckingham, England: Open University Press.

Astin, A. (1993). *What matters in college: Four critical years revisited*. San Francisco: Jossey-Bass.

Baker, D. P., Riordan, C., & Schaub, M. (1995). The effects of sex-grouped schooling on achievement: The role of national context. *Comparative Education Review*, *39*, 468–482.

Brody, C., Fuller, K., Gosetti, P., Moscato, S., Nagel, N., Pace, G., et al. (2000). Gender consciousness and privilege. London: Falmer Press.

Campbell, P. B., & Sanders, J. (2002). Challenging the system: Assumptions and data behind the push for single-sex schooling. In A. Datnow & L. Hubbard (Eds.), *Gender in policy and practice: Perspectives on single-sex and coeducational schooling*. NY: Routledge Falmer. (www.feminist.org/education)

Coleman, J. S. (1961). *The adolescent society*. New York: Free Press of Glencoe.

Daly, P., & Shuttleworth, I. (1997). Determinants of public examination entry and attainment in mathematics: evidence on gender and gender-type of school from the 1980's and 1990's in northern Ireland. *Evaluation and Research in Education, 11*(2), 91-101.

Datnow, A., & Hubbard, L. (2002). Introduction. In A. Datnow & L. Hubbard (Eds.), *Gender in policy and practice: Perspectives on single-sex and coeducational schooling*. NY: RoutledgeFalmer.

Datnow, A., Hubbard, L., & Woody, E. (2001). *Is single-gender schooling viable in the public sector? Lessons from California's pilot program*. Policy report, Ford and Spencer Foundations.

Deak, J. (2002). *Girls will be girls: Raising confident and courageous daughters*. New York: Hyperion.

Gurian, M. (2001). *Boys and girls learn differently: A guide for teachers and parents*. San Francisco, CA: Jossey-Bass.

Haag, P. (2002). Single-sex education in grades K–12: What does the research tell us? In *The Jossey-Bass reader on gender in education*. San Francisco, CA: John Wiley & Sons, Inc.

Hall, R., & Sandler, B. (1982). *The classroom climate: A chilly one for women?* Washington, DC: Project on the Status and Education of Women, Association of American Colleges.

Harker, R. (2000). Achievement, gender, and the single sex/coed debate. *British Journal of Sociology of Education, 21*:203–218.

Harwarth, I. B. (Ed.). (1999). *A closer look at women's colleges*. Washington, DC: U.S. Department of Education.

Heather, B. (2002). Constructions of gender in parents' choice of a single-sex school for their daughters. In A. Datnow & L. Hubbard (Eds.), *Gender in policy and practice: Perspectives on single-sex and coeducational schooling*. New York: RoutledgeFalmer.

Herr, K., & Arms, E. (2002). The intersection of educational reforms: Single-gender academies in a public middle school. In A. Datnow & L. Hubbard (Eds.), *Gender in policy and practice: Perspectives on single-sex and coeducational schooling*. New York: RoutledgeFalmer.

Herr, K. & Arms, E. (2004). Accountability and single-sex schooling: A collision of reform agendas. *American Education Research Journal, 41*(3), 527–555.

Hollinger, D. K. (Ed.). (1993). *Single-sex schooling perspectives from practice and research* (Vol. 1). Washington DC: Office of Educational Research and Improvement, U.S. Department of Education.

Hubbard, L., & Datnow, A. (2005). Do single-sex schools improve the education of low-income minority students? An investigation of California's public single gender academies. *Anthropology and Education Quarterly, 36*(2), 115–131.

Hyde, J. S. (2005). The gender similarities hypothesis. *American Psychologist, 60*(6), 581–592.

Jackson, C. (2002). Can single-sex classes in co-educational schools enhance the learning experiences of girls and/or boys? An exploration of pupils' perceptions. *British Educational Research Journal, 28*(1), 37–48.

James, A. N., & Richards, H. C. (2003). Escaping stereotypes: Educational attitudes of male alumni of single sex and coed schools. *Psychology of Men and Masculinity, 4*(2), 136–148.

Jimenez, E., & Lockheed, M. E. (1989). Enhancing girls' learning through single-sex education: Evidence and a policy conundrum. *Educational Evaluation and Policy Analysis, 11*(2), 117–142.

Jones, S. M., & Dindia, K. (2004). A meta-analytic perspective on sex equity in the classroom. *Review of Educational Research, 74*(4), 443–471.

Klein, S. (2003, April 22). Research and evaluation options to learn about the effectiveness of single-sex education interventions. Paper presented at AERA annual meeting, Chicago, IL, as part of Symposium 26.059 "How can research and evaluation be used to learn if and how single-sex education interventions advance gender equity?"

Klein, S. (2005, October 20). Title IX and single-sex education. Presented at the AERA SIG Research on Women in Education annual meeting in Dayton, OH (www.feminist.org/education)

Lee, V. E., & Bryk, A. S. (1986). Effects of single-sex secondary schools on student achievement and attitudes. *Journal of Educational Psychology, 78*(5), 381–395.

Lee, V. E., & Lockheed, M. E. (1990). The effects of single-sex schooling on achievement and attitudes in Nigeria. *Comparative Education Review, 34*(2), 209–231.

Lee, V. E., & Marks, H. M. (1990). Sustained effects of the single-sex secondary school experience on attitudes, behaviors, and values in college. *Journal of Educational Psychology, 82*(3), 578–592.

Lee, V. E., Marks, H. M., & Byrd, T. (1994). Sexism in single-sex and coeducational independent secondary school classrooms. *Sociology of Education, 67*, 92–120.

LePore, P. C., & Warren, J. R. (1997). A comparison of single-sex and coeducational Catholic secondary schooling: Evidence from the national educational longitudinal study of 1988. *American Educational Research Journal, 34*(3), 485–511.

Lockheed, M., & Harris, A. (1984). *Final Report: A study of sex equity in classroom interaction (Volume 1 and Volume 2)*. Washington, DC: U.S. Department of Education, National Institute of Education.

Lockheed, M., & Klein, S. (1985). Sex equity in classroom organization and climate. In S. Klein (Ed.), *Handbook for achieving sex equity through education*. Baltimore: Johns Hopkins University Press.

Louisiana Girl Fights Against Sex-Segregated Classrooms, Wins. (August 8, 2006). *Feminist Daily News Wire*. Retrieved August 8, 2006. from http://www.feminist.org/news/newsbyte/uswirestory.asp?id=

Maccoby, E. (1998). *The two sexes: Growing up apart, coming together*. Cambridge, MA: Belknap Press.

Mael, F. A. (1998). Single-sex and coeducational schooling: Relationships to socioemotional and academic development. *Review of Educational Research, 68*(2), 101–129.

Marsh, H. W. (1989). Effects of attending single-sex and coeducational high schools on achievement, attitudes, behaviors, and sex differences. *Journal of Educational Psychology, 81*(1), 70–85.

Marsh, H. W. (1991). Public, Catholic single-sex and catholic coeducational high schools: Their effects on achievement, affect and behaviors. *American Journal of Education, 99*(3), 320–356.

National Coalition of Girls Schools. (www.ncgs.org/)

No Child Left Behind Act (www.ed.gov/nclb/)

Office for Civil Rights. (1975, June). *Final Title IX regulation implementing education amendments of 1972 prohibiting sex discrimination in education*. Washington, DC: U.S. Department of Health, Education and Welfare/Office for Civil Rights..

Office for Civil Rights. (2006, October 25). Final regulations nondiscrimination on the basis of sex in education programs or activities receiving federal financial assistance. Washington, DC: U.S. Department of Health, Education and Welfare/Office for Civil Rights. *Federal Register*/Vol. 71, No. 206/Wednesday, October 25, 2006 (pp. 62529–62543). Retrieved October 30, 2006, from www.ed.gov/legislation/FedRegister/finrule/2006-4/102506a.html.

Riordan, C. (1985). Public and Catholic schooling: The effects of gender context policy. *American Journal of Education, 93*(4), 518–540.

Riordan, C. (1990). *Boys and girls in school: Together or separate?* New York: Teachers College Press.

Sadker, D. (2004, November 25). *Single-sex versus coeducation: The false debate*. Paper presented at the First International Conference on Gender Equity Education in the Asia Pacific Region, Taipei, Taiwan.

Sadker, M., & Sadker, D. (1984). *Year 3 final report: Promoting effectiveness in classroom instruction*. Washington, D.C.: National Institute of Education.

Sadker, M., & Sadker, D. (1994). *Failing at fairness: How our schools cheat girls*. New York: Simon and Schuster.

Salomone, R. (2003). *Same, different, equal: Rethinking single-sex schooling*. New Haven: Yale University Press.

Sanford, K., & Blair, H. (2002). Engendering public education: Single-sex schooling in western Canada. In A. Datnow & L. Hubbard (Eds.), *Gender in policy and practice: Perspectives on single-sex and coeducational schooling*. New York: RoutledgeFalmer.

Sax, L. (2005a). The promise and peril of single-sex public education. *Education Week, 24*(25), 48.

Sax, L. (2005b). *Why gender matters: What parents and teachers need to know about the emerging science of sex differences*. New York: Doubleday.

Schmuck, P., Nagel, N., & Brody, C. (2002). Studying gender consciousness in single-sex and coeducation high schools. In A. Datnow & L. Hubbard (Eds.), *Gender in policy and practice: Perspectives on single-sex and coeducational schooling* (pp. 196–211). New York: Routledge and Falmer.

Shmurak, C. B. (1998). *Voices of hope: Adolescent girls at single sex and coeducational schools*. New York: Lang.

Signorella, M. L., Frieze, I. H., & Hershey, S. W. (1996). Single-sex versus mixed-sex classes and gender schemata in children and adolescents. *Psychology of Women Quarterly, 20*, 599–607.

Spencer, R., Porche, M., & Tolman, D. (2003). We've come a long way—maybe: New challenges for gender equity in education. *Teachers College Record, 105*(9), 1774–1807.

Steinback, M., & Gwizdala, J. (1995). Gender differences in mathematics attitudes of secondary students. *School Science and Mathematics, 95*(1), 36–41.

Stone, L. (2004). *Turning back the clock: How the Department of Education's proposed amendments to increase single-sex schools and classrooms violate the Constitution and undermine the purpose of Title IX*. Unpublished manuscript (www.feminist.org/education)

Streitmatter, J. (1999). *For girls only: Making a case for single-sex schooling*. Albany, NY: SUNY Press.

Thompson, J. (2003). The effect of single-sex secondary schooling on women's choice of college major. *Sociological Perspectives, 46*(2), 257–277.

Tidball, E., & Kistiakowsky, V. (1976). Baccalaureate origins of American scientists and scholars. *Science. 193*, 646–652.

Tidball, M. E., Smith, D. G., Tidball, C. S., & Wolf-Wendel, L. E. (1999). *Taking women seriously: Lessons and legacies for educating the majority*. New York: American Council on Education Oryx Press.

Title IX of the Education Amendments of 1972 20 U.S.C. §§ 1681–1688.

Tyack, D., & Hansot, E. (1990). *Learning together: A history of coeducation in American public schools*. New York: Sage.

U.S. Department of Education, Gender Equity Expert Panel (2001). The U.S. Department of Education's Gender Equity Expert Panel *Exemplary & promising gender equity programs* 2000. Washington, DC.

U.S. Department of Education, Office of Planning, Evaluation and Policy Development, Policy and Program Studies Service. (2005). *Single-sex versus coeducational schooling: A systematic review*, Washington, DC. Retrieved Dec. 2, 2006, from http://www.ed.gov/rschstat/eval/other/single-sex/single-sex.pdf

U.S. General Accounting Office. (1996). *Public education: Issues involving single-gender schools and programs*. Report to the Chairman, Committee on the Budget, House of Representatives, Washington, DC.

Warrington, M., & Younger, M. (2003). 'We decided to give it a twirl': Single-sex teaching in English comprehensive schools. *Gender and Education, 15*(4), 339–350.

Woody, E. (2002). Constructions of masculinity in California's single-gender academies. In A. Datnow & L. Hubbard (Eds.), *Gender in policy and practice: Perspectives on single-sex and coeducational schooling*. NY: Routledge Falmer.

Younger, M., & Warrington, M. (2006). Would Harry and Hermione have done better in single-sex classes? A review of single-sex teaching in coeducational secondary schools in the United Kingdom. *American Educational Research Journal. 43*(4), 579–620.

Zittleman, K., & Sadker, D. (2005, April). *Title IX and gender issues: A study of the knowledge and perceptions of middle school teachers and students*. Paper presented at the Annual American Educational Research Association, Montreal, Canada.

·10·

GENDER EQUITY IN THE USE
OF EDUCATIONAL TECHNOLOGY

Gypsy Abbott,* **Lisa Bievenue,*** *Suzanne Damarin, Cheris Kramarae*
with Grace Jepkemboi and Constance Strawn

INTRODUCTION

Clearly, rapid advances in information technologies have transformed nearly every aspect of our world in the last decade. This has required an immediate response from educators to adequately prepare future members of the 21st century workforce. Early responses ranged from immediate use of information technology (especially the Internet) for the sake of technology itself to thoughtful integration that supports learning and curricular goals, especially as specified by national professional organizations (e.g., the International Society for Technology in Education (ISTE; http://www.iste.org). Hastily applied uses of information technology were not without justification, since schools are expected to respond to societal and economic forces that demand new workers to be facile with new technologies. However, now that the use of information technology both in and out of schools is pervasive, the emphasis is on *who*, *how*, and *for what purpose the technologies* are used.

Gender equity in uses of, as well as interest in, information technology at each stage of the educational continuum, within the domains of teacher preparation and student education, is examined in this chapter. Specifically, the emphasis is on examination of gender equitable uses of information technology, the impact that the integration of information technology into curricula and course management has had on male and female students' interest and engagement at each stage of the educational continuum in terms of both teaching and learning, and in terms of teacher preparation and K–16 education. Thus, research findings related to gender equity in the use of educational and information technologies from both a student perspective (the first section on Student Access, Use, and Engagement) and a teacher perspective (the second section on Teacher Uses of Educational and Information Technologies) are described. The research review is followed by a discussion of ways in which inequities are being addressed through education in third section on Addressing Inequities through Education. Recommendations for improved practice are provided in the final Summary section.

Definition of Terms

A variety of terms are used to describe the use of technology in education; these include *information technology*, *instructional technology*, *educational technology*, and many related terms. Since both instructional technology and information technology are used in educational settings, there is a need to differentiate between the two, as well as describe their intersection. Consistent with current general practice, these terms are defined as follows.

Information technology: Information technology (IT) has been operationally defined as the use of computers and other emerging technologies for multiple purposes in societal contexts including education (Access IT, 2002).

Instructional technology: Today, instructional technology includes any educational materials or tools, including textbooks, testing practices, chalkboards, television, computers, calculators, white boards, smart boards, Internet, interactive simulations, and others, but the defining features of instructional technology are that it is *objective driven, systematic, and replicable*.

Educational technology: In today's usage, *educational technology* is a broader term than *instructional technology* and includes many approaches to the use of media and technology in the processes of teaching, learning, motivating, managing, practicing, extending, or otherwise contributing to educational goals, processes, and institutions.

---

*The bold face names are the Lead Authors.

Since the 1980s, there have been many advances in information technology that have resulted in multiple applications in educational technology. Discussions of educational technology have often focused on hardware and software; but many educational researchers and theorists point out that educators' concerns should not be with the information technology itself, but rather with the media associated with, and made possible by, the technologies. Because these media and their educational potentials are complex, Bruce and Levin (1997) developed a frame of reference for thinking about these technologies. They defined four categories of use of educational technology: (a) media for inquiry, (b) media for communication, (c) media for construction of knowledge, and (d) media for expression. Readers interested in the state of the knowledge on various aspects of educational technology might wish to consult the *Handbook of Research on Educational Communications and Technology* (Jonassen, 2004).

Theoretical Framework

A beginning point for thinking about equity, both in terms of assessment (i.e., is there equity?) and in terms of strategies to build and sustain equity (i.e., educational interventions), is to think in terms of what equity should look like, or what is success? Repeatedly, women have been described as saying that *we can, but choose not to* (AAUWEF, 2000). Here we ask, if women have the capability to succeed in using technology but choose not to, is that success? In *Engagement, Capacity and Continuity: A Trilogy for Student Success*, three components are identified as necessary for success: engagement, capacity, and continuity (Jolly, Campbell, & Perlman, 2004). Application of the *Trilogy* model to uses of educational technology in its broadest sense is used to frame the following review of research findings regarding gender equity and technology use. *Engagement* is described as an awareness of the science, technology, engineering and mathematics (STEM) fields, with an interest in pursuing the acquisition of more knowledge about them. *Capacity* is

described as the intellectual ability to learn the theories and precepts of the STEM fields. *Continuity* relies on institutional commitment to equity in the form of adequate funding, awareness about teaching that addresses different learning styles, and guidance for students and educators that results in valid information about the many aspects of science, engineering and technology (SET) careers. Jolly et al. suggest that we will only be successful in recruiting and retaining students in SET when three factors are present: engagement, capacity, and continuity.

The *Trilogy* model is also discussed in the "Gender Equity in Science, Engineering and Technology" chapter of this *Handbook*.

Methodology

Several recent reviews of literature describing the use of technology and gender equity have been published (Sanders, 2005; Sanders & Tescione, 2004; Linn, 2005). The goal of this chapter is to build on existing information from these reviews and to extend current knowledge by focusing on research findings and reports that have primarily been published since 1999. By focusing on the recent articles and reports, we can see that new trends in the use of many types of technology appear to be emerging.

Findings from both quantitative and qualitative studies, reports from U.S. government agencies such as the National Science Foundation (NSF) and the U.S. Department of Education, and reports from other countries were examined in preparing this literature review. Over 400 articles and reports were reviewed to determine their appropriateness for inclusion in this review. Results of individual studies are reported as findings; conclusions have been drawn only when findings from multiple studies provide valid evidence to support a conclusion.

Limitations in use of methodology. Lack of information about the specific aspects of the research design raises questions regarding how findings from some studies should be interpreted within the larger body of literature. Many studies were missing

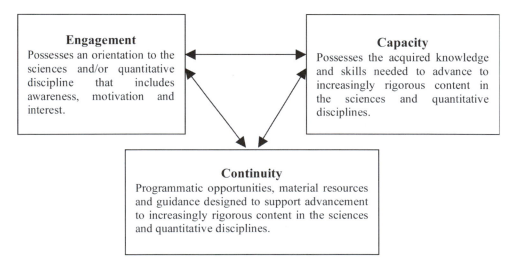

FIGURE 10.1. The Trilogy Model (Jolly, Campbell, & Perlman, 2004)

sample sizes and information describing the reliability and validity of instruments used. While there is a great deal of research on how technology is used in education, many large-scale studies do not consider gender as one of the variables to be studied, thus limiting what we might otherwise understand about how males and females use and benefit from technology differently. Furthermore, when girls and boys are compared on various dimensions related to technology, the emphasis on difference can obscure similarities and contextual variables.

STATUS OF GENDER EQUITY IN THE USE OF EDUCATIONAL AND INFORMATION TECHNOLOGIES: STUDENT ACCESS, USE, AND ENGAGEMENT

Student Access

Until recently, the focus of equitable uses of educational technology has been to provide equal *access* (continuity as described in the *Trilogy* model) to computers for all students, regardless of gender, ethnicity, socioeconomic background, and disability (Forcier & Descy, 2002; Roblyer, 2003). There has also been concern regarding equitable access to Internet use, a more frequently studied measure of technology access, which also presumes access to computers or some other technology. Previous research findings have suggested that before 1999, gender differences were present between boys and girls in both computer use and Internet use (Sanders 2005; Sanders & Tescione, 2004). According to the report by *Computer and Internet Use by Children and Adolescents in 2001* (DeBell & Chapman, 2003), however, more recent data suggests no significant differences in computer use or Internet use related to gender at either the elementary or secondary level. This report was based on supplemental data from the *2001 Current Population Survey*, which described results of telephone interviews from approximately 56,000 households in 754 primary sampling units, regarding the experiences of 28,000 students, ages 5–17. Other studies have confirmed these findings of parity in use of computer and technology as related to gender (Cooper & Weaver, 2003; Lenhart, 2003; Snyder, Tan, & Hoffman, 2004, Table 428). Additional findings suggest that gender parity in Internet use has also been noted at the postsecondary level. According to a survey by the Higher Education Research Institute (Sax, Astin, Korn, & Mahoney, 2000), an equal percentage of female and male freshman college students report that they are frequent users of computers, although one Nielsen//Netratings survey (2001) indicates that men spend more time online than women (10 hrs, 24 min vs. 8 hrs, 56 min).

Despite the parity in access to technology with respect to gender, there is compelling evidence that gaps exist for minority and low SES (Socio-Economic Status) students. Multiple studies have confirmed that a digital divide exists when examining the intersection of race/ethnicity and SES as concluded by Cooper and Weaver in 2003 and others. At the current time, minority students and students from disadvantaged backgrounds use both computers and the Internet less than do their nonminority, more affluent peers. Minority girls seem to have slightly (*very* slightly) higher use than minority boys. Indicator 10 from the U.S. Department of Education's report *Trends in Educational Equity of Girls & Women: 2004* (Freeman, 2004) provides a snapshot of the status of comparisons of gender, race, and ethnicity for use of computers as of 2001. As has been noted, computer use appears to be at parity with respect to gender, but minority students still lag behind in computer use in elementary and middle schools.

Other findings of the *Trends in Educational Equity* report were related to *where* students used computers and technology. According to a U.S. Department of Education report of 2005 data (Wells et al., 2006), the availability of the Internet access in schools has increased use by students, and nearly 100% of schools have some Internet access. According to the *Trends in Equity* report, between 1993 and 2001, the percentage of students who used a computer at school increased by 24 points, rising from 60% in 1993 to 84% in 2001. In both of the comparison years, the percentages of males and females who used computers while in school were similar. The percentage of students who reported home computer use increased by about 40 points between 1993 and 2001, rising from 25 to 66%. In both comparison years, the percentages of males and females who reported home computer use were similar. It can be concluded that availability of computers and Internet access has increased dramatically with no negative impact in use and access related to gender. The continued efforts in equity need to be focused on equity for minority and low SES students since gender access and use appears to have reached parity.

Quality and Types of Technology Use

As previously stated, gender parity has been reached in technology use and access. The more compelling issue is that girls and boys have been reported to use technology differently. This can be problematic when girls do not take the kinds of courses in secondary school that are "heavy in technology." Research findings have suggested that choices of how boys and girls at the secondary level use technology differently can limit their future education and career options.

"Despite evident parity in general access to and use of computers, however, there is evidence that males are leaving high school with greater interest in and having a higher level of specialized knowledge about computers" (Freeman, 2004). Of students who took AP exams in Computer Science in 2005, 85% were males (College Board, 2005). When AP scores in computer science are compared by gender, there is only a small difference, with boys scoring somewhat higher. The critical issue is the low number of girls who either took an AP class in computer science or who took the test.

In examining the quality and types of access, DiMaggio and Hargittai (2001) identified five dimensions of Internet use to probe "deeper than simple" access in order to measure the *quality* of access:

1. the quality of equipment used for access;
2. the user's autonomy in ability to access it;
3. the navigational skills needed to understand how to use the complex Web of information stored on the Web;

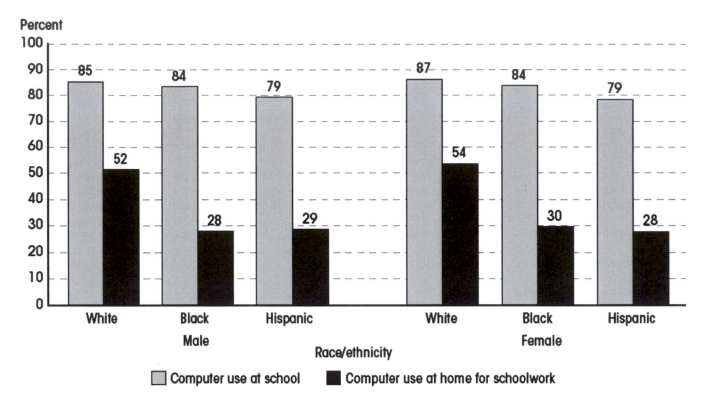

FIGURE 10.2.   Percent of elementary and secondary students using computers, by sex, race/ethnicity, and location of use: 2001. *Source:* Trends in Educational Equity of Girls & Women (2004).

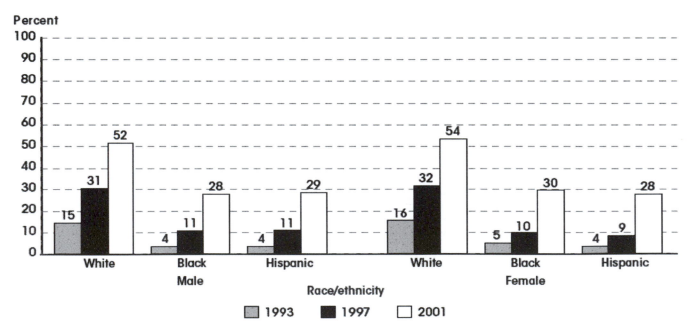

FIGURE 10.3.   Percent of elementary and secondary students using home computers for schoolwork, by sex and race/ethnicity: 1993, 1997, and 2001.
Source: Trends in Educational Equity of Girls & Women (2004).

4. the social support networks that inform some users to become more familiar with its potentials, and finally;
5. the types of sites the user visits while online.

Based on these criteria, surveys in the last few years (~2002–2005) paint a nearly equitable picture on all but the last of DiMaggio and Hargittai's dimensions. The primary difference, however, are in how males and females choose to use the Internet when online, that is, how they are, or become, engaged (the engagement component of the *Trilogy* model). Males and females were similar in their use of home computers for schoolwork in 1997 and 2001. However, girls, ages 5–17, are slightly more likely than boys to use home computers for e-mail, word processing, and completing school assignments.

As another example of a difference in how technology is used is that adult males tend to spend significantly more time online for entertainment purposes than adult females (Kvavik, & Caruso, 2005; Robinson, DiMaggio, & Hargittai, 2003; Fellows, 2004, 2005), whereas women tend to use the Internet as a communication and time-saving tool (Fellows, 2005; Shiver, 2000). Men have been reported as more likely to use the Internet to research financial and travel information (Robinson et al., 2003). Beyond the Internet, other uses of Information Technologies (IT) related to gender indicate that men are more likely to use spreadsheets, presentation tools, and audio/video editing tools (Kvavik, & Caruso, 2005, 2005).

At this time, for students in higher education, one of the fastest growing uses of the Internet is social networking using sources such as Facebook. Using these personal Web spaces, students describe daily, routine, as well as personal aspects of their lives, apparently without thinking about the fact that they are providing personal information in a nonconfidential space. To date, no reports have described gender differences in use of this new Web communication tool, but this emerging Internet tool for social networking has become so widespread in the past few years that ethical and safety uses have become part of freshmen orientation for undergraduate students. Future research is needed to examine possible issues related to gender that emerge with increasing accessibility to these technologies.

Students in the 21st Century

Students in the 21st century are much more technology savvy than even in the year 2000. According to Marc Prensky (2001), in his article *Digital Natives, Digital Immigrants,* today's students are radically different from the teachers who are teaching them: "They are not the people our educational system was designed to teach" (p.1). They are the Net Generation (Net Gens) who have grown up using multiple forms of technology for multiple purposes resulting in their ability to multitask and multiprocess. These include but are not limited to computers, Internet use for information seeking and social networking, MTV, instant messaging and cell phones (Foreman, 2003; Oblinger, 2003; Tapscott, 1998). Prensky has hypothesized that these students have developed thinking processes that are different than students in previous decades, and that their ways of processing information have fundamentally changed. Other researchers have reported that the learning preferences of this group have most certainly

changed. Net Gens have been reported to be much more comfortable in constructing their own knowledge than being instructed. In addition, they prefer that learning experiences be interactive and social. "They want to be users not just viewers or listeners" (Tapscott, 1998, p. 3). In more general terms, this group is described as preferring the Internet to television, being able to do something more than knowing something, and desiring to stay connected through multiple devices (Foreman, 2003; Prensky, 2001). The Net Gens have also been described as having shorter attention spans than previous students and being able to multitask. Brown (2000) stated that many students prefer the Internet to TV because they can control more of their world on the Net than in watching television. Being constantly *connected* as are the Net Gens, a new definition of teamwork is evolving. This generation has little tolerance for delays; they live in a 24 × 7 × 365 world. They expect instant access and instant responses. Brown (2000) reported that e-mail is "old news" to these students when instant messaging and text essaging is quicker and more efficient. Thus, in reflecting on the relevance of the *Trilogy* model as related to Net Gens, they are typically *engaged* in technology use and their prior experiences with technology have helped them to build *capacity* for technology use.

Gender differences among Net Gens have not been investigated thoroughly at this time. In a broader perspective, however, since the learning preferences of Net Gens are similar to that of best practices for equity in instruction for girls, it appears that the characteristics of the students themselves are likely to drive instruction that will be congruent with gender equitable practices in learning. The challenge, as discussed later in this chapter, is for teachers to understand and adapt teaching strategies to engage Net Gens.

The current discussion of *digital natives* or Net Gens fits well with many social scientists' and futurists' views of the overall implications of information technology, as well as with the visions of many educators who led the 1990s' efforts to implement information technology in schools (e.g., Jones, Valdez, Nowakowski, & Rasmussen, 1995; Carroll, 2000). For many current students, however, this vision bears little relation to their classroom realities. Based on his visits to 20 schools across the country, William Pflaum (2004) described classrooms with various levels of technology availability and use. While some students he observed have the technology and experiences that nurture digital natives, others in his study are deprived of the needed facilities and opportunities (i.e., continuity in the *Trilogy* model). Students from the least affluent areas are most likely to have little or no school or home access to technology. At the current time, such access is related to income level of parents and to a lesser extent to race across all income levels (NTIA, 2002).

Gender-Based Attitudes, Comfort, and Confidence

In general, girls' approach to use of IT mirrors broadly accepted research on gender-based differences, which indicates that among females, play and work are more collaborative and affiliative, whereas males tend to be competitive and hierarchical (Rajagopal & Bojin, 2003a; Tannen, 1990; Tannen, 1994). Research findings have suggested that when using technology, girls articulated preferences for same-sex collaborative activity and interactively enjoyed problem solving and critical thinking skills (Abbott, 2000; Corston & Colman, 1996; Martin, 1998; Pryor, 1995; Rajagopal & Bojin, 2003a; Selby & Ryba, 1994; Valenza, 1997). Other general findings on differences in the way males and females use technology include (Rajagopal & Bojin, 2003a):

1. More female than male students have been reported to identify with the process of learning, and indicate that use of IT improves their learning.
2. Male students have been reported to focus the outcomes of their learning, indicating that IT increases their productivity compared to females.
3. More male than female students find that IT makes learning in classes more enjoyable.
4. More female than male students emphasize using IT for research rather than in-class learning.

Information and communication technology research shows that in the elementary and middle-level grades, boys and girls are equally computer literate and tend to use the computer equally at school (Sanders, 2005). This indicates that the engagement component of the *Trilogy* model appears to be present in early elementary school. Girls and boys appear to be equally enthusiastic when it comes to using the computer, until their transition to high school. However, as they move into high school, gender differences in use patterns begin to emerge, and quality of engagement changes. Although girls continue to refine word processing skills, Power Point presentations and other business/clerical skills, boys overwhelmingly populate the computer science and programming classes (MacDonald, 2004; Parkins, 2004; Sanders, 2005). High school girls have been reported as developing negative attitudes regarding technology use due to thinking that all technology use is computer programming or playing violent games. In *Tech Savvy*, girls were described as stating that programming is boring and, while they believe they can do it, they are simply not interested (AAUWEF, 2000). Other aspects that have been described as influencing girls' attitudes toward technology are: (a) the male-dominated computer culture, (b) societal gender bias, (c) parental bias, (d) gender bias in computer software, and (e) level of self-confidence.

Male-dominated computer culture. Initial research beginning in the 1980s focused almost entirely on the male-dominated *computer culture*, which includes the use of computing in education, but is not limited to education. Technology use has been surrounded by a culture of masculinity: male-dominated discourse, competitiveness, emphasis on speed and power, exclusion, isolation, violent content/games, and violent language. Studies on perceptions of computer use also reported that most people associated images of computing as masculine (NSF, 1997; Strassman, 1999; Strawn, 1999). Sanders's review of literature on "Gender and Technology" (2005) reports findings that students in the United States, Canada, and New Zealand have historically held negative notions of the computer culture and computer enthusiasts as geeky, nerdy, social isolates who are adolescent, competitive, and exclusively focused on programming (Dryburgh, 2000; Durndell, 1990; Johnson, Johnson,

& Stanne, 1985; Klawe & Leveson, 2001; McCormick & McCormick, 1991; MIT Department of Electrical Engineering & Computer Science, 1995; Pearl, Pollack, Riskin, Thomas, Wolf, & Wu., 1990; Selby, 1997). However, several other studies have suggested that it is not necessarily computers and technology per se that females avoid, but rather the competitive, male environment that surrounds the field (Arun & Arun, 2001; Canada & Brusca, 1991; AAUWEF, 2000). While these perceptions may still exist, the computer culture is now moving beyond what was once relegated to a subset of how we use technology (mainly computation and programming). Since more applications and uses of information technology that appeal to both men and women are now being used, a more informative review, for the purposes of this chapter, will focus on how males and females use information technology differently.

Societal gender bias. Historically, societal gender bias has impacted how students view technology (i.e., engagement), how and if teachers use technology in their instructional methodology (i.e., continuity), and how teachers perceive students' abilities in technology (i.e., the intersection of continuity and capacity). Until recently, this bias was evident and significant; many studies in the 1980s and 1990s, and even as late as 2002, reported socialized gender-based preferences, attitudes, and behaviors that result in girls spending less time using computers at the high school level, often opting to not enroll in courses that require higher levels of skills in technology at both the secondary and postsecondary levels. This decision by girls takes on critical importance when they avoid gatekeeper courses that can limit their subsequent educational and career decisions at the postsecondary level. As Sanders (2005, p. 10) summarized:

Many studies and in many countries find that boys have more positive feelings about the computer than girls — boys tend to like computers more and are more interested in them. Again with some exceptions, many studies find that the level of computer experience correlates with liking and interest. Typically, studies find that computer liking and interest decrease with age for both girls and boys but more strongly for girls. (Gurer & Camp, 2002; Lage, 1991; Shashaani, 1993; Whitley, 1997)

There is reason to believe that the differences in these attitudes toward computers and the behaviors that result (i.e., engagement in the *Trilogy* model) resulted from socialization (i.e., a form of continuity), rather than ability (i.e., capacity), since many studies have found that gender differences are relatively small at younger ages but increase as students become older. Previous research has attributed these changes in attitudes to societal bias (Collis & Williams, 1987; Kirkpatrick & Cuban, 1998; McCormick & McCormick, 1991; Reece, 1986). Whitley, in his 1997 review of 82 studies, concluded that the longer students are in school, the greater the gender differences become. Only one study was found prior to 2003 that differed from the conclusions related to the importance of gender socialization in explaining differences between the attitudes of boys and girls toward computer use. In contrast, Colley, Gale, and Harris (1994) indicated that when the factors of experience and gender stereotyping were removed, girls' and boys' computer attitudes were similar. More recent findings, reported in a 2004 U.S. Department of Education report, *Trends in Educa-*

tional Equity of Girls & Women, were significantly different from those of previous research, indicating that attitudes about computer use by girls did not change from elementary to high school (Freeman, 2004). Furthermore, a recent comprehensive survey of college freshman and seniors indicated that males and females have similar experiences, attitudes toward technology, and types of technology used (Kvavik & Caruso, 2005).

The most current and critical causes for social gender bias appear to be: (a) parental attitudes and (b) the media, including computer games and software. Each is described in the following paragraphs.

Parental beliefs and attitudes. Parents' beliefs, however subtle, have had significant influence on their daughters' use of computers, potentially even overshadowing socioeconomic status (Creamer, Lee, Meszaros, Laughlin, & Burger, 2005; Cohoon & Aspray, 2006; Shashaani, 1994). Findings in the late 1990s by Shashaani (1997) found that daughters who perceived their parents believed computers were more appropriate for boys were less interested in computers. Some research findings have indicated that some parents tend to reinforce subtle stereotypes that encourage their sons' computer use, but discourage daughters' computer use (e.g., Kekelis, Ancheta, & Heber, 2005; Shashaani, 1994). More recently, in a large-scale study of 40 women enrolled in undergraduate education programs, parents were described as playing a greater role in career choices of their daughters than has been previously reported in research findings. For example, when girls who chose an IT career were asked who they discussed their decision with, overwhelmingly these girls indicated that they talked predominantly with their mothers and sometimes their fathers. This finding suggests that parents must be involved in their daughters' activities when related to technology so that they, themselves, can provide informed advice regarding IT careers to their daughters (Creamer, Lee, Maszaros, Laughlin, & Burger, 2005).

Media. Negative sterotyping in the media has played a role in promoting the streotype of technology as a male domain. On the positive side, the parity of technology use by gender is likely due to the fact that technology itself has become more pervasive in all domains, including uses that most appeal to women's interests and habits. For example, a variety of communication devices make it easier for women to stay connected to others, including cell phones, text messaging and instant messaging. Earlier studies pointed out that because teachers, parents, and girls, themselves, perceive girls to lack scientific skills and possess more social skills (i.e., capacity for technology), they had lower expectations for girls' interest and skill in technology (Norby, 2003). However, newer technologies actually support their social skills, thereby enabling girls' natural interests and giving them experience with technology. In other words, in terms of the *Trilogy* model, some technologies encourage girls to engage, which may promote the building of capacity for technology in general. In a 2003 survey conducted by the Education Development Center, men and women were asked about their technology fantasies. "Feminine expectations for technology are about small, flexible objects that can be worn or carried around easily and that allow women to communicate and connect and to share ideas and stories" (Brunner, 2003,

p. 2). Thus, while gender differences in IT use have been reported from an historical perspective, the emerging trend appears to indicate less influence of societal biases except those related to encouragement by parents. However, technology-related content choices of males and females continue to differ (see MacDonald, 2004; Parkins, 2004; Sanders, 2005).

Gender bias as portrayed computer games, software and programming. Use of computer software and games can be viewed as engagement and building capacity, the second component of the *Trilogy* model. Computer software was initially, for the most part, designed by males for males (Kiesler, Sproull, & Eccles, 1983).

Computer games. As Denner and her colleagues (Denner et al., 2005) stated, few females create games, and fewer girls than boys play games. According to the Interactive Digital Software Association's 2003 survey, 72% of all video game players are male. This is unfortunate, as early game playing not only fosters specific cognitive and motor skills, but also improves spatial and problem-solving skills (Denner et al., 2005, p.90)

Certainly this raises the question of what can be done to better attract, engage, and sustain the interests of girls in playing games. Use of the *Trilogy* as a framework for this review highlights the need for increased numbers of games that are attractive to girls (Jolly et al., 2004).

According to Denner and colleagues (2005), the most popular console games on the market today have distinct qualities:

They provide spaces for players to take initiative, are competitive, and give players the opportunity to save the world or have personal triumphs. The most popular games typically have larger-than-life settings, and the goal is to win, rather than to experience new cultures or relationships. Success comes from eliminating competitors, not making friends. Games allow players to become successful football players in the NFL, professional skateboarders, and to test their bravery as soldiers fighting an invisible enemy or in a one-on-one duel. (p. 2)

The competitiveness of many of the currently available games is for many girls a reason to NOT engage in game playing (AAUWEF, 2000). To appeal to girls, Ray (2003) has suggested that contents of games should be developed that do not result in a win-lose situation for game players. The *Children Now Report* (2001) has suggested that the games that are most popular with girls and women have positive female characters, allow them to explore relationships and roles, and take place in realistic worlds, such as the Sims and 102 Dalmatians.

According to a recent report by AAUWEF (2000), boys tend to play computer games starting at younger ages compared to girls. In addition, boys have been described as playing games for long periods of time and tend to persist in game playing as they get older; girls tend not to follow these patterns (Robinson, DiMaggio, & Hargittai, 2003; Sanders, 2005). These differences notwithstanding, there is a legitimate argument that computer games are central to the ways in which *digital natives* learn and understand their world. James Gee's book *What Video Games Have to Teach Us about Learning and Literacy* (1999) articulates this argument and has been cited widely in educational and related literatures.

Denner and Werner (2005) have developed a curriculum that engages and sustains girls' development and use of games. These researchers provided the opportunity for 90 girls, ages 10–13, to develop their own games during an after-school program. They used a "create your own adventure" plan with multiple points of entry into the adventure. Research findings of these researchers indicated that:

1. Many features of the girls' games were very different than the most popular games currently being marketed.
2. One fifth included opportunities for personal triumph, such as saving the world or other people.
3. Most games took place in a realistic rather than a fantasy world.
4. Over half the games focused on social issues that are concerns for preteen girls, such as babysitting, boys, school dance, and difficulties at school.

These researchers concluded that when given the opportunity, girls design games that challenge the current thematic trends in the gaming industry (Denner & Werner, 2005). A critical value of the results of the Denner project is that girls themselves can tell us what they like about games as well as be empowered to create their own games. These findings are congruent with those of earlier reports by Brunner and colleagues who also indicated that, when playing games, girls want opportunities to experiment with different notions of femininity (Brunner, Bennett, & Honey, 1998) and experiment with fears, as well as different identities in realistic rather than fantasy settings (Jenkins, 1997). Another conclusion by Denner and other researchers is that software developers should consider creating gender-neutral games. These can *engage* and build *capacity*, as well as sustain interests in technology for both boys and girls. Denner and her colleagues have recommended that in order to engage and sustain females' interest in technology, the gaming industry needs to create software to "highlight the human, social, and cultural dimensions and applications of computers rather than the technical advances, the speed of the machines or the entrepreneurial culture surrounding them" (AAUWEF, 2000, p. 10).

Computer software.   In Canada, the E-GEMS project (Electronic Games for Education in Math and Science) (http://www.cs.ubc.ca/nest/egems/index.html) operated from 1994 until 2002 and was widely acclaimed for its work designing and developing software to engage students in solving mathematical puzzles. The developers and researchers focused much of their attention on learning styles and gender. Their successful product, *Phoenix Quest*, is a fantasy game in which players progress by solving puzzles, has been widely used in schools and has proven to be equally popular with girls and boys in the targeted age group (9–14), though girls and boys reported enjoying different features of it (DeJean, Upitis, Koch, & Young, 1999). Other attempts to develop software, particularly games, appealing to girls were presented at a 1997 Harvard conference and in a subsequent edited book, *From Barbie to Mortal Kombat: Gender and Computer Games* (Cassell & Jenkins, 1998). Reading across the 14 chapters in this volume and related papers by chapter authors and their collaborators (among others), sev-

eral themes are apparent. Recently, there has been substantial and rigorous research into issues of gender and software design; findings of these studies have often been implemented in educational games, and the games have been successful with groups of girls. By and large, these more successful games incorporate higher levels of collaboration and communication than the games already on the market; research points to the importance of this for girls, and the popularity of many of the researchers' games among girls further supports this direction in the work.

Researchers concerned with gender and educational software have taken a more diversity-oriented and socially conscious view and approach to many aspects of software design and use. Some software research and development projects aim to address subgroups of girls and women. Nicole Pinkard (2001) has developed culturally relevant software for urban African American students; her programs, *Rappin' Reading* and *Say, Say Oh Playmate* are based on hip hop and Chicago street culture themes, including the chants young girls use in jump rope and other games. Other educational software researcher/developers take up themes of identity, specifically, gay and lesbian identities (Jenson, deCastell, & Bryson, 2003).

Since 1999, a persistent group of educational technology researchers has made serious efforts to design software that has educational value and that more girls would find appealing and engaging. For example, in the early 1990s, researchers at the Center for Children and Technology investigated what men, women, girls, and boys would like to see technology do and what they would design it to do:

Women [and girls] commonly saw technological instruments as people connectors, communication, and collaboration devices, control, tremendous speed, and unlimited knowledge. Their technological fantasies were often embedded in human relationships, and they served to integrate their public and private lives. The men [and boys], in contrast, tended to envision technology as extensions of their power over the physical universe. Their fantasies were often about absolute control, tremendous speed, and unlimited knowledge. (Honey, Moeller, Brunner, Bennett, Clements, & Hawkins, 1991, p. 3)

Computer programming.   Efforts to engage girls in computer programming have been only somewhat successful. According to Randy Pausch, a computer science professor at Carnegie Mellon University (CMU), there are fewer students enrolling in computer science programs and that only 20% of those enrolling are female (Sohn, 2006). To address this need, researchers at CMU have developed an interactive computer program, Alice, to demonstrate the exciting opportunities that computer science can offer. "Using 'Alice', a student can quickly create an animated movie in which characters move about and interact in an imagined 3-D world. Along the way, the student learns how to write a simple computer program" (Sohn, p. 2, 2006). Students can create stories and lists of actions that are required to tell the story. Thus, students are breaking a larger problem into its component parts. The students who develop the stories select the characters that they want to use and then create the scenes in which characters talk and move around in the virtual environment; they are learning programming skills without realizing that they are programming.

A primary advantage of using Alice is that, as students learn to use a mouse to select commands, they are "in control" and are actively constructing new knowledge for themselves as described in the section of this chapter that discusses learning needs of Net Gens. If the computer image is not what they wanted, they can simply change the command. Since an initial frustration for students trying to learn a programming language is the inability to know what they have not done correctly, resulting in trial and error programming, use of Alice eliminates that initial frustration. Research studies indicate that Alice is a successful tool for improving both grades and retention of freshman students in computer science. According to Moskal, Lurie and Cooper (2004), both male and female students who did not have access to Alice in their freshman year made either failing or low grades (C's and below) and only 47% took a second computer science course. This compares with students who used Alice as the initial programming language. They increased the course grade average to a B, and 88% took a second computer science course. No differences related to gender were reported in this study.

Use of Alice provides a less frustrating way to learn the process of programming and prepares students to move to other object-oriented programming languages such as Java. Alice has also been used with middle school girls and with the Girl Scouts with similar levels of success (Sohn, 2006). Sohn stated, "The beauty of Alice is that it shows students how exciting and creative computer science can be. Working with computers doesn't make you a geek . . . Computer work is an art form, only better" (Sohn, 2006, p. 4). Carnegie Mellon in conjunction with a commercial producer, Electronic Arts, is producing a new version of Alice that has more sophisticated options.

Clearly, the kinds of computer uses presented by using Alice are consistent with findings of other studies and with the Tech Savvy report (AAUWEF, 2000) regarding the kinds of things that tend to interest girls in computing. In addition, use of robotics has been described by some researchers as a tool to increase girls' interests in programming (PENNlincs, 2001; Turbak & Berg, 2002). Another example of an intervention that appears to be successful in increasing girls' interest in IT is the Computer Mania Program at the University of Maryland, Baltimore County (Morrell et al., 2004). (See "Direct and Indirect Interventions" in the final Summary section of this chapter for more programs to increase gender equity.)

Summing up issues of equity in relation to computer software, over the past decade and more, we have gained knowledge related to making computer software more appealing to girls. The lack of input by female software designers has been, and continues to be, of major concern and is driving the serious efforts to attract young women to the field of computer science (Margolis & Fisher, 2002). It is widely believed that attracting more women to professions in technology design and development is essential to making software that is available more female friendly. There is, however, an emerging trend resulting from women moving into roles of being designers and producers of software so that the end product, that is, the software, is more likely to attract the targeted females audiences. Thus, as part of the development process, it is likely that the new generation of computer software will reflect their influences (Associated Press, 2005).

Online Learning

Typical patterns of both learning and behavior described by women would suggest that based on women's enjoyment in social interaction and collaboration, they would not prefer the isolation of online learning (Hsi & Hoadley, 1997; Leong & Hawamdeh, 1999; Belenky et al., 1997). On the other hand, online collaborative learning systems might afford *more* interaction than is available in face-to-face classes. Indeed, there are conflicting reports in the literature that address gender issues in online learning. In a study published in New Zealand, women were reported to have performed better online than in a classroom environment in one Web design course (Gunn, 2003). Findings from another study indicated that online academic discussions equalized female and male contributions; in this study, contribution was measured in terms of how frequently and extensively males and females posted to online discussions (Linn, 2005). In courses that use online mixed-sex discussion groups, Wolfe (1999) found that male students contribute more turns and more words online than do the females. However, online participation has not absolutely been demonstrated to be a predictor of achievement (Kimbrough, 1999). Others found nonexistent or very small gender differences in online behavior (Atan, Sulaiman, Rahman, & Idrus, 2002; Atan, Azli, Rahman, & Idrus, 2002; Davidson-Shivers, Morris, & Sriwongkol, 2003).

Use of online learning for high school students is a relatively new phenomenon and is especially helpful for rural students (Cook, Leathwood, & Oriogon, 2001; Myers, Bennett, & Lysaght, 2004). However, gender equity issues in online secondary courses have been described as problematic. In an Australian study, the instructor declined to deal with male online hostility despite repeated requests from female students. In theory, asynchronous electronic forms of communication would better support female students: many participants can talk at once without fear of interrupting or being interrupted, students no longer have to wait for a teacher to call upon them, and students who have trouble articulating their thoughts orally can take their time to think and compose (Herring, Johnson & DiBenedetto, 1998). However, Herring has suggested that females do not often control the topics of discussion except in groups where women are a clear majority (Herring, in press; 1997). In computer-mediated discussions, females are just as likely as males to initiate disagreements, but the females tended to use more agreement terms (which can encourage and promote the participation of others) and tended to drop out of the conversations rather than to continue to defend their ideas when they are challenged (Wolfe, 1999).

The phenomenon of online learning has become increasingly more predominant in the postsecondary settings, with entire degree programs that can be completed online through virtual universities; 96% of public institutions and 89% of private institutions report that online learning is critical to their long-term strategy (Allen & Seaman, 2004). There is also a rapidly occurring move toward high school students taking online classes. Advantages of online courses reported by females include being able to attend class from home and complete assignments at times when other responsibilities related to family have been completed (Kramarae, 2003; Sullivan, 2001; Ross-Gordon & Brown-Haywood, 2000; Guri-Rosenbilt, 1999). This advantage is currently being capitalized on by a growing number of older women who wish to improve their economic situation (Kramarae, 2003). Family considerations entered in when women did their online coursework later at night than men, and when women reported they had less access to computers than men because of the need to share a computer with others in the family. Grades, however, were equal (Gunn, 2003).

The flexibility in online learning afforded both men and women has been cited as instrumental in their ability to develop new job/career options for themselves (Kramarae, 2003) and as indicated by Strawn (1999). Online courses can provide the opportunity for both men and women to *re-invent* themselves. It is more likely for women, however, who are deferring both their time for using the family computer and time for improving their educational status to that of others in their family. This specific situation was initially referred to by Kramarae as *"The Third Shift"* (2001).

Due to the rapidly increasing numbers of online professional preparation programs, gender differences in response to virtual learning environments need to be examined in a similar fashion as traditional classroom interactions have been (AAUWEF, 2000; Lucas, 2003). Some educators have suggested that gender as well as race, sexual orientation, physical abilities, and age hierarchies are not conspicuous features of online classroom interaction because physical cues are lacking online, and because traditional interruption patterns are not present online (Cohoon & Aspray, 2006). This would suggest that online environments would provide equitable learning environments. However, there is no research consensus that supports this hypothesis, and the evidence of equity in online environments is equivocal when describing males' and females' experiences with online environments. In addition, there is little evidence that a person's gender remains anonymous; often participants do not attempt to disguise their personal feelings and emotions that guide their postings, and, when they do, discussion styles and length of postings often give them away (Herring, 2000). A methodological concern in reporting online communication is that frequency, rather than quality, is reported for females as well as males. Evaluations of the quality of online experiences should be part of the criteria for assessing quality of online experiences. However, understanding that this limitation exists, the following research findings are reported.

Research on online interests related to gender indicates that girls have been described as visiting a broader range of civic and political sites (for example, 31% of girls visited a charity site compared with 22% of boys; Livingstone & Bober, 2005). In a 2002 survey of Texas college undergraduate students (Royal, 2002), women were more likely to report visiting personal/family (24.5% vs. 6.5%) and hobby (18.2% vs. 8.7%) sites, and to participate in blog sites (10.9% vs. 2.2%). Men were more likely to use the Internet for Web design (13% vs. 5.5%) and to visit sports sites. Women appeared slightly more interested in news, academic, and entertainment sites.

Online resources. An effective way to encourage all students to use IT more frequently is to require use of information or resources that are not available, are inconvenient, or are uncomfortable to obtain otherwise except when using IT. For example, many youth report valuing intimacy and privacy of mobile and online communication. Twenty-five percent of teens go online for advice (Livingstone & Bober, 2005). In fact, it may be that online communication increases one's social networks and communication with family and friends. In the UCLA Internet report *Surveying the Digital Future* (2003), 45% of teens reported that online communication had increased communication with family and 54% believed it had increased the number of people they stay in touch with. There are, however, mixed results regarding whether or not online communication has an adverse impact on face-to-face contact with family and friends; In the UCLA Internet Report—Year Three (2003), findings indicate that 84% of teens agree that time spent with family and friends remained the same, while the Pew Report suggests that 64% of U.S. teens believed that the Internet kept them from spending time with their family (Lenhart, Rainie, & Lewis, 2001). Unfortunately, this report by the Pew group did not present data disaggregated by gender, so only conclusions about the groups of teens in the sample can be drawn.

Two important recommendations from the U.K. Online survey (Livingstone & Bober, 2005), which also apply to the U.S., are to encourage more creation of online content and to shift students' thinking of online communication from "having your say" to "being listened to." To encourage children to create more content, educators need both to help students learn the necessary skills to create online content and to make it an exciting and desirable activity (i.e., not just another boring school project). Some places have put this into practice via after-school clubs, competitions, or civics-oriented community projects to encourage students to value their own input, as well as believe that others will value their input, one recommendation is to make civics sites more attractive, as well as to begin the development of a genuinely interactive environment in which young people's contributions are directly responded to in such a way that their efforts can be sustained and experienced as rewarding (Livingstone & Bober, 2005).

Issues Related to Safety and Ethics in Emerging Technologies

Emerging technologies have made available new forms of communications that have resulted in potential safety issues for students, e.g., bullying and breach of security systems, plagiarism, and viewing sexually explicit sites, thus impacting girls' potential engagement with the technology. The number of teenagers using the Internet has grown 24% in the past four years; 87% of boys and girls between the ages of 12 and 17 now describe themselves as Internet users. Compared to 4 years ago, teens' use of the Internet has intensified and broadened as they log on more often and do more things when they are online (Lenhart, Madden, & Hitlin, 2005). Emerging technologies enable a variety of methods and channels by which youth can communicate with one another as well as with their parents and other authorities. E-mail is losing its privileged place among many teens as they express preferences for instant messaging (IM) and text messaging as ways to connect with their friends (Lenhart et al., 2005). One gender difference in IT use, noted in the most recent Pew Report on Teen Internet use (Lenhart et al., 2005), was that girls are leaders in creating blogs and are more frequent bloggers than males. Both boys and girls are communicating with peers through use of social networking tools such as Facebook. Since it is clear that some students may not understand the impact of putting personal information online, it is important for teachers and parents to educate students about the possible consequences of making personal information available online.

Studies such as the UK Children Go Online project (Livingstone & Bober, 2005) address challenges related to safety in technology use based on students' self-reported practices and survey reports by teachers and IT coordinators. Samples from 444 schools noted several issues related to Internet safety, including (a) plagiarism, (b) seeking unsuitable online content, (c) cyber-bullying using mobile phones and Internet chat rooms, Web sites, or e-mail, and (d) breach of security systems. Plagiarism has been made easier since the Internet has become a provider of assistance to students in completing homework and projects and has also made convenient the sharing of information by easy transfer of documents (BECTA, 2006). Approximately half the teachers surveyed indicated that "intentional plagiarism was common in boys and in girls, although 43% reported it was predominant among boys" (p. 58). Teachers of students in grades 6–12 reported that boys are more likely to visit sites with unsuitable content than are girls (Livingstone & Bober, 2005).

A somewhat different trend emerging is cyber-bullying. Cyber-bullying involves the use of information and communication technologies such as e-mail, cell phone and pager text messages, instant messaging, potentially defamatory personal Web sites and defamatory online personal polling Web sites to support deliberate, repeated, and hostile behavior by an individual or group of individuals (Belsey, 2005). In the UK report, most instances occurred in the later years of school with bullying on mobile phones slightly more frequent among girls, as reported by 47% of teachers. However, 31% indicated that bullying incidents were common for both genders and 22% reported they were most common among boys. These differences were statistically significant, and findings from other studies also indicated that girls are more likely to bully other students using mobile phone technology. The fact that girls may be more likely to use mobile phones may be an intervening variable in this study; however, a similar pattern was also found in prevalence of bullying by chat rooms, Web sites, or e-mail. In this sample of teachers, 47% reported that bullying was equally common among both genders.

Another safety issue in which differences related to gender were reported by teachers was contact with inappropriate persons. Although in this report the contact by inappropriate persons was not frequent, when reported it was most frequently perpetuated against girls. On the other hand, 81% of teachers surveyed reported that breaching security systems was most frequently associated with boys. Thus with respect to safety and ethical issues, behaviors described are either at parity or reflect discriminative patterns related to gender.

Comfort and confidence in using technology. Findings from studies both before 1999 and since that date have consistently reported that females, of all ages, have levels of confidence (i.e., engagement and capacity) in using technology that are significantly lower than that of males, even though there is little or no difference in actual ability (i.e., capacity; BECTA, 2002; Higher Education Research Institute, 2000; Rajagopal & Bojin, 2003a; Lee, 2003; Miller & Wasburn, 2002; Sax et al., 2001). A previous examination of confidence in using technology was explored using the Bem Sex Role Inventory; results using this instrument indicated that positive computer attitudes correlated with high masculinity for both males and females, not with maleness per se (Brosnan, 1998a, b; Charlton, 1999; Colley et al.,1994; Ogletree & Williams, 1990), even when females were more successful than the males in the class (Gurer & Camp, 1998; Selby, 1997; Shashaani, 1997).

Historically, girls with lower levels of confidence in using technology have been reported to be less likely to choose courses that involve heavy or extensive computer or technology use (Kekelis, Ancheta, Heber, & Countrymanet al., 2004; National Council for Research on Women, 2001; Seymour, 1999). Issues of confidence in technology use have also been consistent across age levels. Middle-school boys were reported to have more confidence in their computer skills despite: (a) their teachers' deliberate encouragement of girls, (b) the girls' disbelief that computers were for boys, and (c) boys' feeling that teachers did not take their interest in computer careers seriously (Young, 2000).

At postsecondary levels of education, gender differences in confidence have been reported even when all students were required to have their own laptops; students used them similarly, but females still rated their skill levels lower than males (McCoy & Heafner, 2004). This lack of confidence has also been documented in online skills. In assessing Web-use skills to examine differences related to gender in learning to navigate content on the Web, Hargittai and Shafer (2006) found that women and men do not differ greatly in their actual online abilities; however, women did not perceive themselves as having skills at the same level of men. Other studies, both pre-1999 and post-1999, provide findings that women and girls report confidence in using technology that is similar to that of their male counterparts *when their level of experience is eliminated as a potential confounding variable*. Hackbarth (2004) discovered this with a group of nearly 100 fourth grade students, and Li (2004) also confirmed it in a Canadian study of 450 secondary students. Further, in a meta-analysis including 150,000 subjects, Barnett and Rivers reported no significant difference in confidence related to gender (2004). Rajagopal and Bojin (2003a) reported that after students completed a course that used IT and online discussions, women felt equally confident and adept in using IT, and even preferred online discussions to face-to-face ones. Earlier studies also found that experience is a more significant predictor of confidence than gender (Chen, 1985; Hunt & Bohlin, 1993; Levin & Gordon, 1989; Rosen, Sears, & Weil, 1987). A study by Voyles and Williams (2004) has shed some light on the seemingly conflicting results on self-confidence: self-reports via surveys and interviews indicated no difference in confidence, but the researchers observed behaviors indicating that girls (compared to boys) made fewer self assured statements and had less interest in a robotics course, which was the context of the study. Explanations for why girls might have confidence but not display it include socialization, prior experiences of failure with similar courses, and simply different interaction styles of girls vs. boys (e.g., girls are more modest and make fewer self-assured statements even when they are confident). Thus, the issue that needs to be addressed is how to ensure that girls have more experiences with technology use, or in terms of the *Trilogy* model, how to *engage* girls in order to build *capacity* both in use of computer games and in educational use in settings. The question of the extent to which girls' and women's lower self-confidence affects lack of continuity is an issue that needs to be considered in future research.

TEACHER USES OF EDUCATIONAL AND INFORMATION TECHNOLOGIES

When considering gender effects on the use of educational and information technologies in a K–12 setting, there are two issues: a) is the sex of a teacher related to how and when, or if, he or she uses technology? and b) do teachers (male or female) implement technology in gender-equitable ways? The first issue is mainly an extension of the same differences and concerns that described the use of IT for students. The second issue is primarily a discussion of how K–12 teachers and higher education faculty learn (or don't learn) to use technology within teacher preparation programs and inservice professional development. Both of these issues are mainly concerned with the continuity component of the *Trilogy* model, but are certainly impacted by the engagement and capacity of the teachers, preservice teachers, and teacher education faculty. This section of the chapter is a discussion of the status of teacher and faculty use of both information and educational technology. In addition, how preservice teacher preparation and inservice professional development impacts teachers' use of technology is discussed. Finally, some recommendations for improving both teacher preparation and professional development in order to promote gender equity are included.

21st Century K –12 Teachers and Higher Education Faculty

If today's students are *digital natives* or Net Gens, then a large percent of teachers/faculty who are trying to keep abreast with technology are the *digital immigrants* (Prensky, 2001). However, even while attempting to keep up with the natives, the digital immigrant teachers are struggling to avoid being disconnected. Many teachers appear unaware of the actual impact of growing up in the Net Generation, assuming today's students learn the same ways as students did a decade or more ago, and that the same methods used then will still work now:

Digital Immigrants don't believe their students can learn successfully while watching TV or listening to music, because they (the Immigrants) can't. Of course not—they didn't practice this skill constantly for all of their formative years. Digital Immigrants think learning can't (or shouldn't) be fun. Why should they—they didn't spend their formative years learning with Sesame Street. (Prensky, p. 3)

But today's learners are different, and they aren't responding positively to the same traditional teaching methods. To date, gender differences related to past practices for teaching the Net Generation have been suggested but few have a research base

to support the suggestions. Some students *drop out* of the learning activity, and some actively resist *powering down*, making it harder to teach them in a traditional fashion. Prensky argues that it may be impossible to ask the digital native students to "go backwards . . . their brains may already be different" (p. 3). Whether today's teachers like it or not, the issue must be confronted, and both teaching methods and content must be reconsidered. This will require a paradigm shift that has already begun in some classrooms.

K–12 Teachers

In several studies, K–12 female teachers have been described as reluctant to embrace IT due to low self-esteem, lack of time, and lack of training (e.g., Bauer, 2000; Bobis & Cusworth, 1994; Handal, 2004). Lack of time is consistently described as a primary barrier.

Time. "Women's time is a critical resource in short supply. Any systems or activities meant to improve their lives and increase their empowerment must be perceived by women to save time or increase their efficiency rather than add to the already overly long list of activities in a day" (Huyer, 1997, p. 3). Many teachers report that they lack the time to learn the technology as well as the time to use it in instruction, often due to accountability constraints imposed by the No Child Left Behind Act (2001). In a recent preliminary report of a large-scale Web-based teacher survey conducted by the Gender, Diversities & Technology Institute of the Education Development Center, 71% of K–12 teachers reported that the time required to find usable/appropriate resources online was their most pressing need in technology use and integration (Carlson & Reidy, 2003). This finding is confirmed by every survey of teachers and faculty reviewed for this chapter (e.g., Kramarae, 2003; Goulding & Spacey, 2002; Netday Speak Up Day, 2004; Resnick, 1995). Time has also consistently been found to be an obstacle to general uses of technology, not only online uses (Education Week, 1999; Fontaine, 2000; Hafkin & Taggart, 2001; NCES, 2000; Spotts, Bowman, & Mertz, 1997; Trotter, 1999).

Confidence. It is nearly self-evident that teachers' attitudes toward technology impact students' attitudes (Handal, Bobis, & Grimison, 2001; Lovat & Smith, 1995). If teachers are not confident with technology they will not use it and the students will not benefit from technology use. Since a predominance of women tend to describe themselves as "not strong in the sciences," and since math and science are often associated with the use of technology, a logical conclusion might be that female teachers may have difficulty in the successful use of technology, or, in terms of the *Trilogy* model, do not believe they have the capacity to work successfully with technology, or at least are not engaged with technology. It is also reasonable to assume that if teachers are not confident with technology use, they may unknowingly transmit that lack of confidence to their students. If the teachers are female, that is double jeopardy for girls (Sanders, 2005). Their lack of confidence can easily be noted by students, especially female students, and this limits the ability to serve as role models for their female students.

However, similar to the research findings for students, research literature suggests that while initial surveys and reports indicate less use of technology by female teachers, this is changing; the main predictor for technology use, and confidence in that use, is how much prior and personal experience the teacher has with technology, not the teacher's sex (Buck & Horton, 1996; Wozney, Venkatesh, & Abrami, 2006). Thus, the issue to address is how to encourage these female teachers to use technology (i.e., engagement) before they become teachers, specifically during the teacher preparation, or in the early stages of their teaching career through professional development. Given the changes inherent in the Net Generation, this is becoming easier and easier to accomplish simply by using the technology. Mitra (2000) has suggested that as the computer becomes an expected and standard part of the process of learning, women are likely to embrace it more readily.

Pre-service Teacher Preparation

If teachers are expected to use technology effectively and equitably, it is crucial for schools and colleges of education to include such training within the preservice teacher preparation program. In terms of the *Trilogy* model, without satisfactory preservice teacher preparation experiences, continuity is compromised and effective gender equity cannot be achieved. Unfortunately, two national surveys of mathematics, science and technology methods instructors reported that approximately 75% of the respondents, in both 1997 and 1999, said that they had been taught concepts related to gender equity, if at all, for fewer than 2 hours per semester (Campbell & Sanders, 1997; Campbell, Hoey, & Perlman, 1999). A 1999 survey of California institutions indicated that gender equity was not an integral part of the curriculum at 6 in 10 institutions (California Commission on Teacher Credentialing, 1999). Even basic integration of technology and instruction on how to integrate technology are lacking in most teacher preparation programs; studies cite barriers such as time, support, infrastructure, and culture (Adams, 2002; Brzycki & Dudt, 2005; Bunch & Broughton, 2002; Rakes & Casey, 2002). This suggests a mandate for extensive inclusion of technology and gender equity in preservice programs.

K–12 Teacher Professional Development

In the last decade, as new technologies and uses of technologies have emerged, vast financial resources have been committed for the professional preparation of teachers in the use of technology (i.e., providing continuity). Federally funded grant programs, such as the U.S. Department of Education's Preparing Tomorrow's Teachers to use Technology (PT3) and the Technology Innovation Challenge Grant programs, have provided funds both to increase the number of teachers using technology and to improve the quality of that use. In the private sector, Marco Polo, Intel's *Teach to the Future*, and Microsoft's *Anytime Anywhere Learning Program,* have also developed powerful models for teacher professional development. Unfortunately, most of the commercially produced professional development programs do not include gender as an instructional component.

After years of successes and failures in integrating technology into K–12 education, there are ample research data on the requirements to motivate (i.e., engage) and support (i.e., provide continuity) teachers to successfully integrate technology: administrative support, technical assistance, financial incentives, time, recognition, and professional development (CEO Forum, 2001; Charp, 2001; Leggett & Perischitte, 2000; Maddin, 1997; Sherry, Billig, Tavalin, & Gibson, 2000; Valdez, 2005). Unfortunately, the issues are not limited to simply how to use and integrate technology. Teachers must also consider how the Net Generation learns (e.g., by doing) and how to use and integrate technology in equitable ways. In terms of the *Trilogy* model, teachers must learn how to engage students, provide continuity within the curriculum and school, and build students' capacity for incorporating technology; teacher professional development programs that do not address all three components will not be successful in the long term.

Fortunately, since typically the Net Generation (or digital natives) has developed preferences for technology that are consistent with female preferences for technology (emphasis on social applications, technology for learning, and the use of technology to achieve other goals, i.e., not for the sake of technology itself), if teachers can adapt to teach the Net Generation, they are also moving toward the adoption of gender equitable uses of technology. Nonetheless, the focus has been on using the technology, not on gender issues related to using technology in educational settings. However, according to NCES (2000) "some studies have found that although most teachers now use computers in their classrooms, they often use them for drill-and-practice exercises rather than for more sophisticated tasks and projects such as multimedia projects and teaching" (NSF, 2004). Despite the huge infusion of financial commitment into technology professional development for teachers (e.g., NCLB federal legislation mandates that 25% of funds from technology grants must be spent on high-quality professional development on technology integration; CEO Forum on Education and Technology, 1999; Means, 1998; Rocap, Cassidy, and Connor, 1998), inadequate professional development was listed as a barrier to effective IT use by two thirds of teachers in a 1999 survey (NCES, 2000). Still, teachers who participate are more likely to increase their use of IT (Becker, 1999; Fatemi, 1999; Wenglinsky, 1998), and 78% of teachers report that professional development (more than any other category, such as colleagues, online sources, and journals) is at least one way that they find out about new educational resources (Carlson & Reidy, 2003). Also, once a female teacher becomes tech savvy, women are more likely to feel empowered than men (36% vs. 30% of men) and challenged (38% vs. 25%) (AAUWEF, 2000). Thus, *any* effective professional development in the use of emerging educational technologies may help to promote gender equity in the use of technology.

Higher Education Faculty

University faculty have been described as often slow to adopt new technologies for a variety of reasons. Most of these reasons center around the fact that university faculty may not have an understanding of the positive role that technology can have on their academic life: (a) They don't know the potential of the new technology, (b) they don't know which technologies will make their research and teaching easier or more effective, (c) they don't know which technologies are easy to use and which technologies are harder to use, and, (d) they aren't willing to keep up with rapidly changing new technologies or software versions (Strauss, 2005). This lack of knowledge about technology prevents university faculty from knowing how to push the limits of technology. Since they are unfamiliar with technology, they are unable to gauge their technological competence, making them less likely to seek out technological tools that could potentially increase their productivity as academics. While higher education faculty have readily endorsed some technology uses for instruction, namely use of PowerPoint. However, use of PowerPoint alone has been described as "power-point-less," (Panoff, 2003) and will not meet the expectations of the Net Generation.

While these concerns are valid for both male and female faculty, there are a few differences in attitudes towards IT use. Female academics have reported that they tend to feel that IT is useful in improving the quality of education and class instruction, whereas male academics emphasize that IT improves convenient access to education. According to surveys conducted by Rajagopal and Bojin (2003b), women faculty typically prioritize quality of teaching and communication with students, whereas men tend to stress communication with colleagues and students as the most important outcome of IT. These researchers also found that women faculty rated highly the importance of IT such as word processing for handouts (83% vs. 44% of men), computing labs (70% vs. 53%), and Web resources (57% vs. 41%). However, male faculty (40% vs. 21%) view IT as important for increasing students' accessibility to higher education, as well as universities' attractiveness and ability to increase student enrollments.

While male faculty seem to have greater confidence in using IT in general, a survey by Rajagopal and Bojin (2003b) found that male and female faculty showed equal confidence in some technological areas—word processing, e-mail and presentation software—but not in others; and more women (61% vs. 38%) rated their skill in searching library resources as high. Male faculty have been described as less interested in receiving IT training, especially IT specifically related to teaching and learning; rather, they learn and use the skills for the inherent advantages of learning new technologies, regardless of the context (Rajagopal & Bojin, 2003b).

Female faculty (50% vs. 33%) are more likely to cite time as a barrier to using more IT. This is a particularly significant barrier since at the postsecondary level, more time is required for online courses (Kramarae, 2003), a venue argued to make education more accessible and convenient to female students (Guri-Rosenblit, 1999; Kramarae, 2003; Ross-Gordon & Brown-Haywood, 2000; Sullivan, 2001). Some research findings have suggested the time involved in teaching an online class is double or triple the time required for face-to-face classes (Palloff & Pratt, 1999). However, the female faculty report that time is not as much of an issue if their time is acknowledged by administration and compensated for (Kramarae, 2003). Female faculty have, historically as well as in the present, emphasized lack of recognition for using IT as a barrier, reporting that release time, merit pay, monetary rewards, recognition by the university, and recognition toward promotion and tenure are important reasons to use IT, or not to use IT if those rewards are lacking (Lederman, 2005; Spotts et al., 1997).

ADDRESSING INEQUITIES THROUGH EDUCATION

"[A]lthough adults tend to rely on self-teaching . . ., for children and young people it is teachers and parents who are the primary supports for learning. [S]chools represent, potentially, the fairest and most appropriate location for such [computer] literacy training" (Livingstone & Bober, 2005, p. 15). In terms of the *Trilogy* model, the schools represent the continuity that works to engage students and build capacity to use and embrace technology.

Breaking down barriers related to the use of IT may be best accomplished by teachers designing their pedagogy to defy gender stereotypes, encourage cooperation, blur distinctions between teaching and learning, and encourage academic productivity and technical proficiency by breaking down gender barriers in the use of IT (Christie, 1997). According to NSF, as of 2002, 26 states and the District of Columbia required teachers to have one IT training or course before initial teacher licensure (NSF, 2004). This leaves 24, or almost 50%, of the states that do not have such criteria for initial teacher certification. If technology proficiency is not required, then measures of accountability will not be in place to motivate use of technology, since the processes of learning IT and learning how to integrate technology into curriculum are time consuming.

Direct Interventions for Students

A *direct intervention* is operationally defined here as a measure or program designed to specifically target girls' or women's use of technology in order to improve their skills, attitudes, or behaviors in relation to using technology. Often these interventions are designed to encourage young women to pursue science or technology careers, but in the process of that promotion also serve to dispel myths and fears about technology in general. These programs may be embedded within a formal education setting (as a course or curriculum integration), in single-sex or mixed-sex settings, or as informal, extracurricular activities such as after-school programs, summer camps, mentoring, interactive Web sites, radio programs, etc.

Extracurricular programs are most often primarily focused on only the engagement component of the *Trilogy* model and rely on other resources, such as formal education, to provide continuity and capacity building. Many such programs have been funded through a variety of federally funded grant programs, including the Department of Energy, NASA, the Department of Defense, the Department of Education, and NSF. NSF has sponsored grant programs such as Information Technology Experiences for Students and Teachers; Alliances for Broadening Participation in STEM; Informal Science Education, Science, Technology, Engineering, and Mathematics Talent Expansion Program, Program for Gender in Science and Engineering, and Gender Diversity in STEM Education. NSF funded hundreds of efforts to broaden participation in science, mathematics, engineering and technology; for a collection of brief descriptions of such programs, see *New Formulas For America's Workforce: Girls In Science And Engineering* (NSF, 2003), a collection compiled by NSF's Gender Diversity in STEM Education program. Another resource is the Diversity Institute at the Center for the Integration of Research, Teaching and Learning (http://www.cirtl.net/DiversityInstitute/), which has compiled a comprehensive list of programs and research studies.

Extracurricular programs to encourage girls— Engagement.

The majority of the programs listed in NSF's *New Formulas for America's Workforce* are extracurricular programs or informal education. One example is a new program by Boston University's Photonics Center, we developed Lia to address a lack of positive media portrayals of Hispanic females. Lia recently made her debut appearance on the National Academy of Science's http://www.iwaswondering.org Web site where she will assume the persona of an agent for a secret organization that is trying to save the planet.

Other initiatives to get more girls interested in high-tech careers include programs, such as the Sally Ride Science Clubs, to connect girls to people, information, and attitudes that nurture their relationship with science so that it will remain vibrant and relevant to them. The Center for Women & Information Technology (http://www.umbc.edu/cwit) has also developed and implemented after-school programs such as ESTEEM to help build girls' confidence in using technology.

Development of technology skills—Capacity building.

As described previously, females, at least until they gain experience, have considerably less confidence in their technology skills. Many of the studies in earlier sections of this chapter reported that males tended to overestimate their ability, and in fact, a study by Nancy O'Hanlon (2002) found that *all* students tend to overestimate their proficiency in computer skills. Other studies have reported that while men tend to use an inquiry approach to self-educate in IT, women rely on formal training to learn their IT skills. O'Hanlon suggests that IT workshops for all entry-level (college) students may help to level the playing field in IT training.

At the K–12 level, technology courses are required, especially to provide a baseline level of skill training for both males and females. This provides more equity because female students are less likely than male students to develop those skills independently or outside of the classroom. However, once girls acquire that training, their skills and abilities to integrate technology appropriately are on a par with males. One study in British Columbia recommends that more technology courses be made available and required (for both girls and boys) at the secondary level, with the caveat that access and outcomes must be redefined with a focus on equity. "Access to technologies must follow access to equities; equities must precede outcomes" (Bryson, Petrina & Braundy, 2003, p. 192). The authors also recommend accountable, gender-specific, intensive experiences in technology that promote equity, for all boys and girls, rather than chance integration. If some high schools are now offering some programming courses that include development tools for Web-based applications, working on real-life projects seems to hold an equal interest for both sexes, and the stigma of the male *computer geek* is disappearing (Schrock, 2005).

Telementoring—Engagement and capacity building.

Mentoring is consistently recommended by several projects as an important component in support of girls' exploration and use of technology (Schrock, 2005; Bennett, Brunner, & Honey, 1999). The Center for Children and Technology developed and studied the *Telementoring* program to link high school women to practicing female professionals in science and technology-related fields. Key findings suggested that a) knowledge about the "social surrounds" is necessary to support such an on-line environment, b) effective online structures are needed to support students and mentors in online conversations, and 3) skilled adult facilitators are necessary to maintain effective communication (Bennett et al., 1999).

Curricular embedded integration—Engagement, capacity building, and continuity.

Teachers need to be prepared to make use of the communicative and creative potential of computers throughout the curriculum. "The more emphasis we place on computers as useful tools for sharing ideas with others, the more attractive the medium will become to people with a feminine perspective on technology" (Brunner; 2003, p. 2). Many researchers have concluded that engaging women and girls in the use of technology should be embedded in rich, meaningful projects and classroom assignments (Brunner, 2003; Damarin, 2000).

Beyond basic technology courses, a variety of curricular resources are available to complete the component of continuity in the Trilogy model by providing additional opportunities for engagement and building capacity. Several organizations have published various recommendations, standards, and guidelines for evaluating and refining curricula to design for equity with technology; and most of those organizations call for integrating technology across the curriculum, whether their goal is to use technology effectively or to make the use of technology more equitable; interestingly, those goals often are met with the same strategies. One comprehensive guide published by The Diversity Institute is *Reaching All Students: A Resource for Teaching in Science, Technology, Engineering & Mathematics* (Sellers, Roberts, Giovanetto, & Friedrich, 2005), which provides comprehensive, research-based, recommendations for teachers to develop a gender-equitable classroom and curriculum. Also, the Northwest Regional Education Laboratory has published *Closing the Equity Gap in Technology Access and Use: A Practical Guide for K–12 Educators* (Waren-Sams, 1997) to provide guidance for practicing teachers. The Center for Women & Information Technology also makes available several teaching resources at their Web site (http://www.umbc.edu/cwit). For a discussion of additional related gender equity interventions, see this *Handbook's* chapter 13 on "Gender Equity in Science, Engineering and Technology".

Indirect Interventions for Students

An *indirect intervention* is operationally defined as a measure or program not overtly targeted at girls or women, but implemented for all students in a gender-sensitive manner with the intention that an appropriate implementation will benefit all students to better utilize information and educational technologies.

Pedagogy and gender equity in IT—Engagement.   In designing instruction that uses technology, socialized gender differences in how students approach learning should be considered. For example, girls tend to ask more questions when using technology, which does not necessarily indicate less understanding, but reflects girls' more communicative and personal learning style (Voyles & Williams, 2004; Li, 2002). Their findings also indicate that girls have been described as making fewer self-assured statements, which doesn't necessarily indicate less self-confidence but reflects girls' tendency to be modest or even self-effacing. These researchers also applied Bernard Weiner's Attribution Theory (Weiner, 1974, 1994) and have suggested that one way for teachers to address women's tendency to attribute success externally (e.g., task difficulty or luck) and failure internally (e.g., ability or effort) is to emphasize the goal of "figuring it out" as opposed to "getting it right."

Furthermore, both in recent and historical studies, several factors have been shown to be strongly correlated with not only engaging but retaining students' use of technology, such as hands-on, cooperative learning (vs. competitive applications of technology) and constructivist environments with real-world problem solving (vs. solving a problem in technology in and for itself; Norby, 2003; Oakes, 1990; Peterson & Fennema, 1985; Savard, Mitchell, Abrami, & Corso, 1995).

Recommendations for appropriate pedagogical methods to integrate technology in gender equitable ways include emphasizing aspects that women find attractive and positive, such as peer interaction (Hackbarth, 2004; Kantrowitz, 1996; Sullivan, 2001), which also happens to be a recommended pedagogical approach for all students (Bonk & Cunningham, 1998) and an approach particularly suited to online learning (Cummings, Bonk, & Jacobs, 2002; Matusov & Rogoff, 1995; Tharp & Gallimore, 1988). Other researchers, Rajagopal and Bojin (2003a), provide an in-depth pedagogical discussion of implementing gender-equitable IT that is summarized by Alley and Jansak's (2001) "five integral blocks of knowledge-building as constituent pedagogical elements for high quality electronic learning":

1. Since all new knowledge is founded on prior knowledge, it is essential to interlink already established information with the newly discovered knowledge (Jonassen, 1995).
2. Integrating IT in teaching anticipates equipping students with self-directed learning tools so that they would know how to use a technology . . . as a research tool.
3. A pedagogy integrating IT needs to inspire self-motivated learning in students, and this process should not be marred by lack of time or technical support.
4. Learning materials should provoke inquiry and reflection. IT can be used to gain knowledge through both individual learners working in isolation, and through collaborative learning from interaction with peers and academics.
5. New technologies are more conducive to non-linear thinking and teaching. Academics can use IT to guide the students through a spiral path, acquiring layers of knowledge built up

as a pyramid to achieve deeper and layered levels (Hamid, 2002).

Finally, it is important for teachers to be aware of feminist scholarship in the content of the course and also the ways that women's and men's work and interests are involved in the agenda and research of any field of study" (Kramarae, 2003, p. 265). Kramarae posits, "As Women's Studies research during the last 30 years makes very clear, every study area is influenced by gender (itself a complex concept), including the questions and methods of investigation, and the standards of 'merit,' 'rigor,' and 'impartiality'" (See for example, Feminist Periodicals; Harcourt, 1999; Hayes & Flannery, 2000; Kramarae & Spender, 2000; New Books on Women and Feminism; Paul, 2000).

"Real-World" technology courses—Capacity building. In 2000, the Gender Equity Expert Panel, U.S. Department of Education, recommended five programs related to math, science, and technology as "Promising Programs in Math, Science, and Technology for Females." The most indirect of these gender equity programs was the Alabama Supercomputing Program to Inspire [C]omputional Research in Education (ASPIRE; Abbott, 2000). In the ASPIRE program, students are engaged in the use of math models and scientific visualization, also described as computational science, to solve real-world problems (http://aspire.cs.uah.edu). The ASPIRE curriculum, an elective course for middle and high school students, requires that students develop a research question, find math algorithms that can be used to simulate an answer to the research question, and use programming skills to generate a solution to the research question. It was noteworthy that the ratio of females to males in this middle and high school elective course was approximately equal. In addition, although this might have been expected to be a traditional male-focused course, it counteracted these gender stereotypes, and girls received approximately the same number of awards as did boys in state-wide competition in Alabama (Abbott, 2000). Similar findings were reported in the evaluation of a companion program, Adventures in Supercomputing (AiS; Honey, McMillan, Tsikalas, & Grimaldi,1995). These programs, designed with an inquiry, student-centered approach, and a problem-based format based on real-world problems, provided early indicators to elements of computing that would interest young females (http://aspire.cs.uah.edu). Examples of ASPIRE projects conducted by females in the last few years are "Get the Most Out of Shipping and Handling," "To Puff or Not to Puff: Will You Cave to the Pressure?" "Mesh Book Bags: Modeling the Spread of Mononucleosis." Both males and females in the ASPIRE program have benefited from over a decade of instruction that has been "female friendly." Follow-up studies of students who have participated in the program indicate that not only do females do as well in terms of grades in the class, they also chose computer-related majors at a higher rate than do females in general (Abbott, 1997, 1998, 2000).

Technology across the curriculum—Continuity.   The AAUW Educational Foundation Commission on Technology, Gender, and Teacher Education (2000) recommends the use of technology infusion across the curriculum in which technology is not isolated in a single location (e.g., computer lab), discipline (e.g., computer science), or discrete set of skills (e.g., programming). Findings from Schrock (2005) concur that technology must be embedded in content areas in which all students are likely to be successful. Becker (2000) found when computers are used for project-based work, students are highly engaged, independent of ability and SES. Furthermore, some studies have reported that using technology to learn course content "expands the students' critical understanding of how they are learning, and who they themselves are as learners" (Palloff & Pratt, 1999; Coy, Velazquez, & Bussman, 2001). The implications of how this expanding of critical thinking as related to sex have not been thoroughly examined.

Rajagopal and Bojin (2003a) reported that female students learning new technology in the process of course learning benefited from all these advantages of IT. In a study of more than 150 fourth grade students, Hackbarth (2004) found that even though experience with technology increased the girls' confidence, more girls reported dislike for technology after a computer laboratory experience (as opposed to home use or embedded classroom use). To enable this kind of integrated use of technology, AAUWEF (2000) suggests a focus on helping students master the skills of using the computer as a tool. Schrock also recommends helping girls and boys use and hone their technology skills to support community service initiatives and participate in community-based mentoring programs.

Support for teachers and faculty. An important resource for teachers and faculty previously mentioned is the Diversity Institute at the Center for the Integration of Research, Teaching and Learning (http://www.cirtl.net/DiversityInstitute/), which has compiled a comprehensive literature review on research related to gender equitable applications of instructional technology. Another important resource is the Educational Cyberplayground K–12 Education Reference Directory of Resources and Schools, Content for Music, Teachers, Internet, Technology, Literacy, Arts and Linguistics (*http://www.edu-cyberpg.com/toc.asp*). Bonnie Bracey, a teacher agent of change is the ringleader of this cyber-playground.

Institutional support—Continuity. For 75% of women faculty, the motivating factors for learning IT are the university's investment in technical training and availability of internal and external grants. In addition, 44% of women faculty (vs. 18% of men) report that a reduction in their teaching load would allow them to have more time to learn the new technology (Rajagopal & Bojin, 2003b).

Professional development—Building capacity. While there is significant research on the development and delivery of effective professional development on IT, there is little research on how to implement either IT specifically, or educational technologies generally, in gender equitable ways. There are, however, several programs that at least claim to be successful in promoting gender equity within professional development programs (NSF, 2003). In addition, several published recommendations for more equitable access and use of technology have been identified, some of them based on research (see, e.g., Brown, Higgins & Hartley, 2001 or the Center for Children and

Technology Access and Equity projects: http://www2.edc.org/CCT/research_access.asp).

Finally, it is worth noting that recommendations for effective integration of technology into a classroom or curriculum are typically recommendations that *do* benefit girls and young women. As stated earlier in this chapter, young women respond to applications of technology in context, social interaction, and cooperative learning (Norby, 2003; Oakes, 1990; Peterson & Fennema, 1985; Savard et al., 1995); these are also approaches currently being recommended for technology integration (Valdez, 2005), whether or not the authors intended for their technology integration plan to promote more gender equitable learning environments.

Content—Continuity. "The design features educators would most like to find on a Web site for educational resources include searching capabilities, methods for submitting questions, links to related resources, and assurance that the Web site is supported by a reputable source" (Carlson & Reidy, 2003, p. 4).

SUMMARY: CONCLUSIONS AND RECOMMENDATIONS

Technology applications are rapidly changing in a way favorable to girls' and women's increased use and skills. As of 2006, access to computers, Internet, and training is reported to be gender equitable, even if women and men tend to use technology in different ways and for different goals. The current status for both teachers and students has been summarized using the *Trilogy* model, the theoretical framework for this chapter. Numerous interventions related to the three elements of the *Trilogy* model, engagement, capacity, and continuity, have been described in the third section of this chapter in Addressing Inequities through Education.

Conclusions

With respect to students, there is a rapidly growing number of technology applications designed to engage girls. These applications also help girls develop the capacity for using a greater number of technology applications. However, in terms of continuity, there is differential access for both girls and boys of lower socio-economic status at school and at home. Another continuity issue for students is related to the continuity issue for teachers: if teachers do not use technology with ease and integrate it appropriately into the curriculum, students may not develop the confidence and appreciation of various technology uses. In summary, technology education is moving in a direction that will benefit girls and should eventually result in a greater level of equity.

With respect to teachers, barriers that remain are primarily issues of institutional continuity:

1. Lack of time for teachers and higher education faculty to learn to use IT in its full capacity—both an engagement and a capacity issue.

2. Lack of institutional incentives, which can result in a deficit in all three components of the *Trilogy* model.
3. Lack of gender-sensitive technology integration within teacher preparation programs.
4. Lack of gender-sensitive professional development programs.

Findings in this review of research suggest a clear mandate for extensive inclusion of technology and gender equity in preservice programs. At the current time, even basic integration of technology and instruction on how to integrate technology appears to be lacking in most teacher preparation programs; studies cite barriers such as time, support, infrastructure, and culture (Adams, 2002; Brzycki & Dudt, 2005; Bunch & Broughton, 2002; Rakes & Casey, 2000). The very foundation of education for the 21st century requires that teachers at all levels be fluent in technology use and in their confidence in use of technology.

At the higher education level, institutions will need to make training in technology use a priority for faculty and will need to support that priority with incentives by linking it to faculty evaluation. Use of a transdisciplinary approach is suggested, that is, which technology applications would be most useful in various fields.

Recommendations for Additional Research and Educational Practice

We are beginning to understand differences between the Net Generation and their learning preferences. However, little research has been conducted to delineate gender differences that may or may not exist in this new generation of students. In addition to survey research, it is recommended that other research methods be used to increase our understanding about these issues.

We now know more about attitudes and behaviors related to gender differences in the use of technology. However, some questions still remain. For example, girls may appear less motivated and less confident, but could it be that girls simply demonstrate confidence in different ways? In what ways are levels of confidence confounded by lack of time spent using technologies and by lack of prior experiences? Some research indicated some success in involving girls in the gaming process—gaming is probably one of the primary reasons that boys spend more time with various technology applications than do many girls. Hopefully, research and development in the engagement of girls in the gaming process will move from the level of studies into the venue of commercial producers of games, using information gained from research studies. Finally, given that the digital divide still exists for students of less-privileged backgrounds, educational institutions at all levels need to provide experiences at school to increase the level of engagement and capacity for these students (Bracey, 2005). The issue of continuity needs to be addressed from an institutional perspective also. Students who attend schools with a high ratio of low SES students need to have the opportunity to use emerging technologies while at school. One researcher, O'Hanlon (2002), has suggested that IT workshops be held for students entering college to assure a level playing field with respect to knowledge of technology.

Several questions for research in equitable use of technology in the teaching/learning process include:

1. What must be done so that teachers at all levels of the educational continuum use technology in an equitable way?
2. What differences exist in use of technology in higher education related to sex of the professor?
3. What applications of technology make the largest impact on student learning? Does this differ for males and females?

ACKNOWLEDGMENTS

Much appreciation to Jo Sanders, josanders.com, Camano Island, WA, for her review and suggestions for this chapter. Thanks also to Rosalind Hale, Miles College, Birmingham, AL, who was the initial lead author for this chapter when at Xavier University, New Orleans, but was displaced by Hurricane Katrina, and to Terry Sosa, St. Joseph's University, Philadelphia, PA, who also made early contributions to this chapter.

References

Abbott, G. A. (1997). *Evaluation of the Alabama Supercomputing Program to Inspire Research in Education*. Alabama K–12 Supercomputing Program, administered by the Alabama Commission on Higher Education.

Abbott, G. A. (1998). *Evaluation of the Alabama Supercomputing Program to Inspire Research in Education*. Alabama K–12 Supercomputing Program, administered by the Alabama Commission on Higher Education.

Abbott, G. A. (2000). *Evaluation of the Alabama Supercomputing Program to Inspire Research in Education*. Alabama K–12 Supercomputing Program, administered by the Alabama Commission on Higher Education.

Abbott, G., Morrell, C., Bracey, B., Bievenue, L., & Scripa, R. (2006). Building intellectual capital in young women. Paper presented at the *Society for Information Technology in Education*, Orlando, FL.

AccessIT (2002). What is electronic and information technology? AccessIT, National Center on Accessible Information in Technology in Education, University of Washington. Retrieved August 1, 2006, from http://www.washington.edu/accessit/articles?106

Access IT. (2006). What is electronic and information technology? Fact sheet #106, National Center on Accessible Information Technology in Education, University of Washington. Retrieved June 1, 2006, from http://www.washington.edu/accessit/articles?106

Adams, N. (2002). Educational computing concerns of postsecondary faculty, *Journal of Research on Technology in Education, 34*, 285–303.

Allen, I. E., & Seaman, J. (2004). *Entering the mainstream: The quality and extent of online education in the United States, 2003 and 2004*. Needham, MA: Sloan Center for Online Education. http://www.sloanc.org/publications/books/survey04.asp

Alley, L. R., & Jansak, K. E. (2001). The ten keys to quality assurance and assessment in online learning. *Journal of Interactive Instruction Development*, *14*(3), 3–18.

American Association of University Women Educational Foundation (AAUWEF) Commission on Technology and Teacher Education. (2000). *Tech-Savvy: Educating girls in the new computer age.* Washington, D.C.: American Association of University Women Educational Foundation.

Arun, S., & Arun, T. G. (2001). Gender at work within the software industry: An Indian perspective. *Journal of Women and Minorities in Science and Engineering, 7*(3), 30–45.

Associated Press. (2005). *Programmers: Video games need a woman's touch.* Retrieved July 25, 2005, from http://www.cnn.com/2005/TECH/fun.games/07/25/game.girls.ap/index.html

Atan, H., Azli, N. A., Rahman, Z. A., & Idrus, R. M. (2002). Computers in distance education: Gender differences in self-perceived computer competencies. *Journal of Educational Media, 27*(3), 123–135.

Atan, H., Sulaiman, F., Rahman, Z. A., & Idrus, R. M. (2002). Gender differences in availability, Internet access and rate of usage of computers among distance education learners. *Educational Media International, 39*(3–4), 205–210.

Barnett, R. C., & Rivers, C. (2004). *Same difference: How gender myths are hurting our relationships, our children, and our jobs.* New York: Basic Books.

Bauer, J. (2000). *A technology gender divide: Perceived skill and frustration levels among female pre-service teachers.* Proceedings of the Twenty-Ninth Annual Meeting of the Mid-South Education Research Association.

Becker, H. J. (1999). *Internet use by teachers: Conditions of professional use and teacher-directed student use* (No. 1). Irvine, CA: Center for Research on Information Technology and Organizations.

Becker, H. J. (2000). Pedagogical motivations for student computer use that lead to student engagement, *Educational Technology, 40*(5), 5–17.

Belenky, M. F., Clinchy, B. M., Goldberger, N. R., & Tarule, J. M. (1997). *Women's ways of knowing: The development of self, voice, and mind.* New York, NY: BasicBooks.

Belsey, B. (2005). *Cyberbullying: An emerging threat to the "always on" generation.* Retrieved February 10, 2007, at http://www.cyberbullying.ca.

Bennett, D., Brunner, C., & Honey, M. (1999). *Gender and technology: Designing for diversity.* New York, NY: Education Development Center.

Bobis, J., & Cusorth, R. (1994). Changing preservice primary teachers' attitudes toward mathematics and science/technology. *Forum of Education, 49*(2), 9–20.

Bonk, C., & Cunningham, D. J. (1998). Searching for constructivist, learner-centered, and socio cultural components for collaborative educational learning tools. In C. Bonk & K. King, (Eds.), *Electronic collaborators: Learner-centered technologies for literacy, apprenticeship, and discourse* (pp. 25–50). Mahwah, NJ: Lawrence Earlbaum Associates.

Bracey, B. (2005). Online Teacher and Educator Resources for K–12 Teachers Administrators & Parents. Retrieved on July 10, 2005, from http://www.edu-cyberpg.com/Teachers/Home_Teachers.html

British Educational Communications and Technologies Agencies (BECTA). (2002). *Research: Reports and publications.* Retrieved June 1, 2006, from http://www.becta.org.uk

British Educational Communications and Technologies Agencies (BECTA). (2006). *Research: Reports and publications.* Retrieved June 1, 2006, from http://www.becta.org.uk

Brosnan, M. J. (1998a). The impact of psychological gender, gender-related perceptions, significant others, and the introducer of technology upon computer anxiety in students. *Journal of Educational Computing Research, 18*(1), 63–78.

Brosnan, M. J. (1998b). The role of psychological gender in the computer-related attainments of primary school children (aged 6–11). *Computers and Education, 30*(3–4), 203–208.

Brown, J. S. (2000). Growing up digital: How the web changes work, education and the ways people learn. *Change, 32*(2), 10–20. Retrieved June 30, 2006, from http://www.nursingworld.org/ojin/topic30/tpc30_4.htm

Brown, M. R., Higgins, K., & Hartley, K. (2001). Teacher and technology equity, *TEACHING Exceptional Children, 33*(4), 32–39.

Bruce, B. C., & Levin, J. A. (1997). Educational technology: Media for inquiry, communication, construction, and expression. *Journal of Educational Computing Research, 17*(1), 79–102.

Brunner, C., Bennett, D., & Honey, M. (1998). Girls games and technological desire. In J. Cassell & H. Jenkins (Eds.), *From Barbie To Mortal Kombat: Gender and Computer Games,* (pp. 72–88). Cambridge, MA: MIT Press, Cambridge, MA.

Brunner, C. (2003, April). Approaching Technology. *WEEA Equity Resource Center Digest.*

Bryson, M., Petrina, S., & Braundy, M. (2003). Conditions for success? Gender in technology–intensive courses in British Columbia Secondary Schools. *Canadian Journal of Science, Mathematics and Technology Education, 3*(2), 185–194.

Brzycki, D., & Dudt, K. (2005). Overcoming barriers to technology use in teacher preparation programs. *Journal of Technology and Teacher Education, 13*(4), 619–641.

Buck, H. J., & Horton, P. B. (1996). Who's using what and how often: An assessment of the use of instructional technology in the classroom. *Florida Journal of Educational Research, 36*(1).

Bunch, W., & Broughton, P. (2002). New instructional technology and faculty development: Negotiating the titanic through the North Atlantic. In C. Crawford et al. (Eds.), *Proceedings of Society for Information Technology and Teacher Education International Conference 2002* (pp. 748–751). Chesapeake, VA: AACE.

California Commission on Teacher Credentialing. (1999). *Gender equity in teacher preparation: Findings of the survey of California teacher preparation programs.* Sacramento, CA.

Campbell, P. B., & Sanders, J. (1997). Uninformed but interested: Findings of a national survey on gender equity in pre-service teacher education. *Journal of Teacher Education, 48*(1), 69–75.

Campbell, P. B., Hoey, L., & Perlman, L. (1999). *Washington State Gender Equity Project: Some preliminary findings from the survey of math and science methods instructors.* Groton, MA: Campbell-Kibler Associates, Inc.

Canada, K., & Brusca, F. (1991). The technological gender gap: Evidence and recommendations for educators and computer-based instruction designers. *Educational Technology Research and Development, 39*(2), 43–51.

Carlson, G., & Reidy, S. (2003). *Effective access: Teachers' use of digital resources.* Presented at the Merlot International Conference, Vancouver, B.C., Canada. Accessed June 1, 2006, from http://www2.edc.org/GDI/publications_SR/MERLOTpaper.doc. Gender, Diversities & Technology Institute, Education Development Center.

Carroll, T. G. (2000). If we didn't have the schools we have today, would we create the schools we have today? *Contemporary Issues in Technology and Teacher Education* [Online serial], *1*(1). Retrieved May 10, 2006, from http://www.citejournal.org/vol1/iss1/currentissues/general/article1.htm

Cassell, J., & Jenkins, H. (1998). *From Barbie to mortal combat: Gender and computer games.* Cambridge, MA: MIT Press.

CEO Forum on Education and Technology. (1999). *School technology and readiness report. Professional development: A Link to better learning.* Washington, DC. Retrieved June 1, 2006, from http://www.ceoforum.org/downloads/99report.pdf

CEO Forum on Education and Technology. (2001). *The CEO Forum school technology and readiness report: Key building blocks for student achievement in the 21st century.* Retrieved June 1, 2006, http://www.ceoforum.org/downloads/report4.pdf

Charlton, J. P. (1999). Biological sex, sex-role identity, and the spectrum of computing orientations: A re-appraisal at the end of the 90s. *Journal of Educational Computing Research, 21*(4), 393–412.

Charp, S. (2001). Professional development, *T.H.E. Journal*, *28*(11), 10, 12.

Chen, M. (1985). *Gender and computers: The beneficial effects of experience on attitudes.* Paper presented at the Conference on Computers & Children. Ann Arbor, MI.

Children Now (2001). *Fair play: Violence, gender and race in video games.* Los Angeles, CA: Children Now.

Christie, A. A. (1997). Using e-mail within a classroom based on feminist pedagogy. *Journal of Research on Computing in Education, 30*(2), 146–176.

Cohoon, J. M., & Aspray, W. (2006). *Women in information technology: Research on underrepresentation.* Cambridge, MA: The MIT Press.

College Board (2005). *AP Exam Summary Reports: National Report 2005.* Retrieved February 10, 2007 from http://www.colloegeboard.com/student/testing/ap/exgrd_sum/2005.html

Colley, A. M., Gale, M. T., & Harris, T. A. (1994). Effects of gender role identity and experience on computer attitude components. *Journal of Educational Computing Research, 10*(2), 129–137.

Collis, B. A., & Williams, R. L. (1987). Cross-cultural comparison of gender differences in adolescents' attitudes toward computers and selected school subjects. *Journal of Educational Research, 81*(1), 17–27.

Cook, J., Leathwood, C., & Oriogun, P. (2001). *Online conferencing with multimedia students: Monitoring gender participation and promoting critical debate.* Paper presented at the Higher Education Academy, Center for Information and Computer Sciences, London.

Cooper, J., & Weaver, K. D. (2003). *Gender and computers: Understanding the digital divide.* Mahwah, NJ: Lawrence Erlbaum Associates.

Corston, R., & Colman, A. M. (1996). Gender and social facilitation effects on computer competence and attitudes toward computers. *Journal of Educational Computing Research, 14*(2), 171–183.

Coy, L., Velazquez, N., & Bussman, S. (2001). A learning community of educational leaders, *Learning Technology Newsletter, 3*(4). Retrieved June 1, 2006, from http://lttf.ieee.org/learn_tech/issues/october2001/#14

Creamer, E. G., Lee, S., Meszaros, P. S., Laughlin, A., & Burger, C. J. (2005). *Predicting women's interest and choice in a career in information technology.* Paper presented at the 2005 International Conference: Crossing Cultures, Changing Lives: Integrating Research on Girls' Choices of IT Careers. Manchester College, Oxford, England.

Cummings, J. A., Bonk, C. J., & Jacobs, F. R. (2002). Twenty-first century college syllabi: Options for online communication and interactivity. *Internet and Higher Education, 5*(1), 1–19.

Damarin, S. K. (2000). The "digital divide" versus digital differences: Principles for equitable use of technology in education. *Educational Technology, 40*(4), 17–22.

Davidson-Shivers, G., Morris, S., & Sriwongkol, T. (2003). Gender differences: Are they diminished in online discussions? *International Journal on E-Learning, 2*(1), 29–36.

DeBell, M., & Chapman, C. (2003). *Computer and Internet Use by Children and Adolscents in 2001,* NCES 2004-014, Washington, DC: U.S. Department of Education, National Center for Education Statistics.

DeJean, J., Upitis, R., Koch, C., & Young, J. (1999). The story of Phoenix Quest: How girls respond to a prototype language and mathematics computer game. *Gender and Education 11*, 207–233.

Denner, J., Werner, L., Bean, & Campe, S. (2005). The girls creating games program: Strategies for engaging middle-school girls in information technology. *Journal of women studies, 26*(1), 90–98.

DiMaggio, P., & Hargattai, E. (2001). From the "Digital Divide" to "Digital Inequality": Studying Internet Use as Penetration Increases, *Working Paper #19*, Center for Arts and Cultural Policy Studies, Woodrow Wilson School, Princeton University.

Dryburgh, H. (2000). Underrepresentation of girls and women in computer science: Classification of 1990s research. *Journal of Educational Computing Research, 23*(2), 181–202.

Durndell, A. (1990). Why do female students tend to avoid computer studies? *Research in Science & Technological Education, 8*(2), 163–170.

Education Week (1999). *Technology Counts '99: Building the Digital Curriculum, Education Week,* September 23, 1999.

Fatemi, E. (1999, September 23). Building the digital curriculum: Summary. *Education Week, 19*(4). Retrieved June 1, 2006, from http://counts.edweek.org/sreports/tc99/articles/summary.htm

Fellows, D. (2004). *The Internet and daily life.* Washington, DC: Pew Internet & American Life Project. Retrieved June 1, 2006, from http://www.pewinternet.org/pdfs/PIP_Internet_and_Daily_Life.pdf

Fellows, D. (2005). *How women and men use the Internet.* Washington, DC: Pew Internet & American Life Project. Retrieved June 1, 2006, from http://www.pewinternet.org/pdfs/PIP_Women_and_Men_online.pdf

Feminist Periodicals. *A Current Listing of Contents. 1981–Present.*

Fontaine, M. (2000). A high-tech twist: IT access and the gender divide. *TechKnowLogia* (March/April). Retrieved June 1, 2006, from http://www.techknowlogia.org/TKL_active_pages2/CurrentArticles/main.asp?FileType=PDF&ArticleID=94

Forcier, R. C., & Descy, D. E. (2002). *The computer as an educational tool: Productivity and problem solving.* Columbus, OH: Merrill Prentice Hall.

Foreman, J. (2003). Next generation: educational technology versus the lecture. *Educause Review, 38,* 12–20.

Freeman, C. E. (2004). *Trends in educational equity of girls & women: 2004* (No. NCES 2005-016). Washington DC: National Center of Education Statistics, U.S. Department of Education.

Gee, J. P. (1999). *What video games have to teach us about learning and literacy.* Cambridge, MA: MIT Press.

Goulding, A., & Spacey, R. (2002). Women and the information society: Barriers and participation. *Proceedings of the 68th IFLA Council and General Conference (Glasgow, Scotland),* The Hague, Netherlands: International Federation of Library Associations and Institutions.

Gunn, C. (2003). Dominant or different? Gender issues in computer supported learning. *Journal of Asynchronous Learning Networks, 7*(1), 14–30.

Gurer, D., & Camp, T. (1998). *Investigating the incredible shrinking pipeline for women in computer science* (Final report of NSF Project).

Gurer, D., & Camp, T. (2002). An ACM-W literature review on women in computing. *ACM SIGCSE Bulletin, 34*(2), 121–127.

Guri-Rosenbilt, S. (1999). *Distance and campus universities: Tensions and interactions: A comparative study of five countries.* Oxford and New York: Elsevier Science, Inc.

Hackbarth, S. (2004). Changes in 4th-graders' computer literacy as a function of access, gender, and race. *Information Technology in Childhood Education Annual, 2004,* 187–212.

Hafkin, N., & Taggart, N. (2001). *Gender, information technology, and developing countries: An analytic study.* Washington, DC: Academy for Educational Development.

Hamid, A. A. (2002). E-Learning: Is it the "e" or the learning that matters? *Internet and Higher Education, 4,* 311–316.

Handal, B. (2004). Teachers' instructional beliefs about integrating educational technology. *E-Journal of Instructional Science and Technology, 7*(1). Retrieved May 15, 2006, http://www.usq.edu.au/electpub/e-jist/docs/Vol7_No1/content.htm

Handal, B., Bobis, J., & Grimison, L. (2001). Teachers' mathematical beliefs and practices in teaching and learning thematically. In J. Bobis, B. Perry, & M. Mitchelmore (Eds.), *Numeracy and Beyond.* Proceedings of the Twenty-Fourth Annual Conference of the Mathematics Education Research Group of Australia Inc. (pp. 265–272), Sydney: MERGA.

Harcourt, W. (1999). *Women@Internet: Creating new cultures in cyberspace.* London and New York: Zed Books.

Hargittai, E., & Shafer, S. (2006). *Social Science Quarterly, 87*(2), 432–448.

Hayes, E., Flannery, D. D., with Brooks, A. K., Tisdell, J. J., & Hugo, J. M. (2000). *Women as learners: The significance of gender in adult learning*. San Francisco: Jossey Bass.

Herring, S. C. (2000). Gender differences in CMC: Findings and implications. *The CPSR Newsletter (Computer Professionals for Social Responsibility), 18*(1). http://trout.cpsr.org/publications/newsletters/issues/2000/Winter2000/index.html

Herring, S. C. (in press). Who's got the floor in computer-mediated conversation? Edelsky's gender patterns revisited. In S. C. Herring (Ed.), *Computer-Mediated Conversation*. Cresskill, NJ: Hampton Press.

Herring, S. C., Johnson, D. A., & DiBenedetto, T. (1998). Participation in electronic discourse in a 'feminist' field. In J. Coates (Ed.), *Language and gender: A reader*. Oxford: Blackwell.

Hert, P. (1997). Social dynamics of an on-line scholarly debate. *The Information Society, 13*, 329–360.

Higher Education Research Institute. (2000). *The American freshman: National norms for Fall 2000*. Retrieved February 10, 2007, from http://www.gseis.ucla.edu/heri/norms_pr_00.html.

Honey, M., McMillan, K., Tsikalas, K., & Grimaldi, C. (1995). *Adventures in supercomputing: 1993–1994 evaluation: Final Report, CCT Reports*, Issue No. 1, Newton, MA: Education Development Center, Inc. Accessed June 1, 2006, from http://www2.edc.org/CCT/admin/publications/report/ASC-94.pdf

Honey, M., Moeller, B., Brunner, C., Bennett, D., Clements, B., & Hawkins, J. (1991). *Girls and design: Exploring the question of technological imagination*. New York: Center for Children and Technology, Technical Report 17. Accessed June 1, 2006, from http://www2.edc.org/CCT/publications_report_summary.asp?numPubId=48

Hsi, S., & Hoadley, C. M. (1997). Productive discussion in science: Gender equity through electronic discourse. *Journal of Science Education and Technology, 6*(1), 23–36.

Hunt, N. P., & Bohlin, R. M. (1993). Teacher education students' attitudes towards using computers. *Journal of Research on Computing in Education, 25*(4), 487–497.

Huyer, S. (1997). *Supporting women's use of information technologies for sustainable development*. WIGSAT submitted to the Gender and Sustainable Development Unit, IDRC.

Jenkins, E. W. (1997). Gender and science and technology education. *UNESCO international science, technology, and environmental newsletter, 1*, 1–2.

Jenson, J., deCastell, S., & Bryson, M. (2003). "Girl Talk": Gender, equity, and identity discourses in a school-based computer culture. *Women's Studies International Forum, 26*(6), 561–573.

Johnson, R. T., Johnson, D. W., & Stanne, M. B. (1985). Effects of cooperative, competitive, and individualistic goal structures on computer-assisted instruction. *Journal of Educational Psychology, 77*(6), 668–677.

Jolly, E., Campbell, P. B., & Perlman, L. K. (2004). *Engagement, capacity and continuity: A trilogy for student success*. Accessed June 1, 2006, from http://www.smm.org/ecc/

Jonassen, D. H. (1995). *Constructivism: Implication for designs and delivery of instruction*. New York: Scholastics.

Jonassen, D. H. (2004). *Handbook of research on educational communications and technology*. Mahwah, NJ : Lawrence Erlbaum Associates.

Jones, B. F., Valdez, G., Nowakowski, J., & Rasmussen, C. (1995). *Plugging in:Choosing and using education technology*. Oak Brook, IL: North Central Regional Educational Laboratory. Retrieved May 10 2006, from http://www.ncrel.org/sdrs/edtalk/toc.htm

Kantrowitz, B. (1996). Men, women, computers. In V. Vitanza (Ed.), *CyberReader* (pp. 134–140). Boston: Allyn and Bacon.

Kekelis, L. S., Ancheta, R. W., Heber, E., & Countryman, J. (2004). *Bridging differences: How social relationships and racial diversity matter in a girls' technology program*. Unpublished manuscript.

Kekelis, L. S., Ancheta, R. W., & Heber, E. (2005). Hurdles in the pipeline: Girls and technology careers. *Frontiers: A Journal of Women Studies, 26*(1), 99–109.

Kiesler, S., Sproull, L., & Eccles, J. S. (1983, March). Second class citizens? *Psychology Today*, 41–48.

Kimbrough, D. R. (1999). On-line "chat room" tutorials: An unusual gender bias in computer use. *Journal of Science Education and Technology, 8*(3), 227–234.

King, L. J. (2000). Gender issues in online communities. *CPSR Newsletter, 18*(1), http://www.cpsr.org/publications/newsletters/issues/2000/Winter2000/king.html

Kirkpatrick, H., & Cuban, L. (1998). Should be we worried? What the research says about gender differences in access, use, attitudes, and achievement with computers. *Education and Computing, 38*(4), 56–61.

Klawe, M., & Leveson, N. (2001). Refreshing the nerds. *Communications of the ACM, 44*(7), 67 ff.

Kramarae, C. (2001). *The third shift: Women learning online*. Washington, DC: American Association of University Women.

Kramarae, C. (2003). Gender equity online, when there is no door to knock on. In M.G Moore & B. Anderson (Eds.), *Handbook of Distance Education* (pp 261–272). Mahwah, NJ: Lawrence Erlbaum Associates.

Kramarae, C., & Spender, D., (Eds.). (2000). *Routledge international encyclopedia of women: Global women's issues and knowledge (4 volumes)*. New York: Routledge.

Kramer, P. E., & Lehman, S. (1990). Mismeasuring women: A critique of research on computer ability and avoidance. *Signs: Journal of Women and Culture in Society, 16*(1), 158–172.

Kvavik, R. B., & Caruso, J. B. (2005). *ECAR study of students and information technology, 2005: Convenience, connection, control, and learning*. Boulder, CO: EDUCAUSE Center for Applied Research (www.educause.edu/ecar).

Lage, E. (1991). Boys, girls, and microcomputing. *European Journal of Psychology of Women, 6*(1), 29–44.

Laurel, B. (2000). *Utopian entrepreneur*. Cambridge, MA: MIT Press.

Lederman, M. (2005). Science as a social enterprise. *The Chronicle of Higher Education*, (May 14). Accessed June 1, 2006, from http://chronicle.com/weekly/v50/i36/36b01601.htm

Lee, A. C. K. (2003). Undergraduate students' gender differences in IT skills and attitudes. *Journal of Computer Assisted Learning, 19*(4), 488 ff.

Leggett, W. P., & Persichitte, K. A. (2000). Blood, sweat, and TEARS: 50 years of technology implementation obstacles. *Tech Trends, 43*(3), 33–36.

Lenhart, A. (2003). *The ever-shifting Internet population*. Washington, DC: Pew Internet & American Life Project. Accessed June 1, 2006, from http://www.pewtrusts.org/pdf/vf_pew_internet_shifting_pop.pdf

Lenhart, A., Madden, M., & Hitlin, P. (2005). *Teens and technology: Youth are leading the transition to a fully wired and mobile nation*. Washington, DC: Pew Internet & American Life Project. Retrieved August 30, 2005, from http://www.pewinternet.org/PPF/r/162/report_display.asp

Lenhart, A. Rainie, L., & Lewis, O. (2001). *Teenage Life Online: The rise of the instant-message generation and the Internet's impact on friendships and family relationships*, Washington, DC: Pew Internet & American Life Project. Retrieved June 1, 2006, from http://www.pewinternet.org/PPF/r/36/report_display.asp

Leong, S. C., & Hawamdeh, S. (1999). Gender and learning attitudes in using web-based science lessons. *Information Research, 5*(1).

Levin, T., & Gordon, C. (1989). Effect of gender and computer experience on attitudes toward computers. *Journal of Educational Computing Research, 5*, 69–88.

Li, Q. (2002). Gender and computer-mediated communication: An exploration of elementary students' mathematics and science learning, *Journal of Computers in Mathematics and Science Teaching, 21*(4), 341–359.

Li, Q. (2004). *Mathematics, science, and technology: Do gender and race matter?* Paper presented at the E-Learn conference, Washington, DC. *Proceedings of the World Conference on E-Learning in Corporate, Government, Healthcare, & Higher Education, 2004*(1), 2379–2384.

Linn, M. C. (2005). Technology and gender equity: What works? In N. F. Russo, C. Chan, M. B. Kenkel, C. B. Travis, & M. Vasquez (Eds.), *Women in Science and Technology*. New York: American Psychological Association.

Livingstone, S., & Bober, M. (2005). *UK children go online: Final report of key project findings*. UK Children Go Online. Retrieved June 1, 2006, from http://www.lse.ac.uk/collections/children-go-online/UKCGO_Final_report.pdf

Lovat, T. J., & Smith, D. (1995). *Curriculum: Action on reflection revisited*. Australia: Social Science Press.

Lucas, S. (2003). *Relationship of gender to faculty use of online educational tools*. Tuscaloosa, AL: The University of Alabama. Retrieved May 15, 2006, from http://www.educause.edu/ir/library/pdf/EDU 03159.pdf

MacDonald, J. (2004). *Gurl tech: Net basics*. [Nortel Network Kidz Online Streaming video] Retrieved January 3, 2005, from http://www.kidzonline.com/nclb2004

Maddin, E. A. (1997). The real learning begins back in the classroom: On-the-job training and support for teachers using technology. *Tech Trends, 37*(5), 56–59.

Margolis, J., & Fisher, A. (2002). *Unlocking the clubhouse: Women in computing*. Cambridge, MA: MIT Press.

Martin, S. (1998). Internet use in the classroom: The impact of gender. *Social Science Computer Review, 16*(4), 411–418.

Matusov, E., & Rogoff, B. (1995). Evidence of development from people's participation in communities of learners. In J. Folk (Ed.), *Public institutions for personal learning: Understanding the long-term impact of museums*. Washington, DC: American Association of Museums.

McCormick, N., & McCormick, J. (1991). Not for men only: Why so few women major in computer science. *College Student Journal, 25*, 345–350.

McCoy, L. P., & Heafner, T. L. (2004). Effect of gender on computer use and attitudes of college seniors. *Journal of Women and Minorities in Science and Engineering, 10*(1), 55–66.

Means, B. (1998, April 13–17). *Models and prospects for bringing technology-supported education reform to scale*. Paper presented at American Educational Research Association meeting, San Diego, CA.

Miller, S. G., & Wasburn, M. H. (2002). *Women in technology at Purdue University: Attitudes, perceptions, and beliefs about their majors and intended careers*. Proceedings of the American Society for Engineering Educators 2002 Annual Conference. Montreal, Canada.

MIT Department of Electrical Engineering & Computer Science. (1995). *Women undergraduate enrollment in electrical engineering and computer science at MIT*. Cambridge, Massachusetts: MIT.

Mitra, A. (2000). Gender and instructional use of computers. In P. Kommers & G. Richards (Eds.), *Proceedings of World Conference on Educational Multimedia, Hypermedia and Telecommunications 2000* (pp. 758–763). Chesapeake, VA: AACE.

Morrell, C., Cotten, S., Sparks, A., & Spurgas, A., (2004). *Computer Mania Day: An effective intervention for increasing youth's interest in technology*. Center for Women & Information Technology, University of Maryland/Baltimore County.

Moskal, B., Lurie, D., & Cooper, S. (2004). Evaluating the effectiveness of a new instructional approach. *ACM SIGCSE Bulletin, 36*(1), 75–79.

Myers, W., Bennett, S., & Lysaght, P. (2004). *Asynchronous communication: Strategies for equitable e-learning*. Paper presented at the Australian Society for Computers in Learning in Tertiary Education, Perth, Australia.

National Center for Education Statistics (2000). *Teachers' tools for the 21st century: A report on teachers' use of technology*. NCES 2000-102. Washington, DC: U.S. Department of Education.

National Council for Research on Women (2001). *Balancing the equation: Where are women and girls in science, engineering, and technology?* New York: National Council for Research on Women.

National Science Foundation (NSF). (1997). *Review of instructional materials for middle school science*. Arlington, VA: Division of Elementary, Secondary, and Informal Education.

National Science Foundation (NSF). (2003). *New formulas for America's workforce: Girls in science and engineering*. Arlington, VA: Division of Education and Human Resources.

National Science Foundation (NSF). (2004). *Women, minorities, and persons with disabilities in science and engineering, 2004*. Arlington, VA: Division of Science Resources Statistics, NSF.

National Telecommunications Information Agency, (2002). *A nation online: How Americans are expanding their use of the Internet*. U.S. Department of Commerce. Retrieved June 1, 2006, from http://www.ntia.doc.gov/ntiahome/dn/html/anationonline2.htm

Netday Speak Up Day (2004). *Insights and ideas of teachers on technology national report on Netday Speak Up Day For Teachers 2004*. Retrieved on May 1, 2006, from http://www.netday.org/downloads/NetDaySUD4T2004Report.pdf

New Books on Women and Feminism. Madison, WI: University of Wisconsin, 1979–present (Semi-annual).

Nielsen//Netratings (2001). *Number of female Web surfers grow faster than overall Internet population, according to Nielsen//Netratings*. Retrieved June 1, 2006, from http://www.nielsen-netratings.com/pr/pr_020118_monthly.pdf.

No Child Left Behind Act (2001, P.L. 107-110). Washington, DC: U.S. Congress. Retrieved June 1, 2006, from http://www.ed.gov/policy/elsec/leg/esea02/index.html

Norby, R. F. (2003, March 23–26). *It is a gender issue! Changes in attitude towards science in a technology based K–8 pre-service preparation science classroom*. Paper presented at the Annual Meeting of the National Association for Research in Science Teaching, Philadelphia, PA.

O'Hanlon, N. (2002). Net knowledge: Performance of new college students on an Internet skills proficiency test, *Internet and Higher Education, 5*, 55–66.

Oakes, J. (1990). Opportunities, achievement, and choice: Women and minority students in science and mathematics. *Review of Research in Education, 16*, 153–222.

Oblinger, D. (2003). Boomers, Gen Xers, Millenials: Understanding the new students. *Educause Review, 38*, 37–47.

Ogletree, S. M., & Williams, S. W. (1990). Sex and sex-typing effects on computer attitudes and aptitude. *Sex Roles: A Journal of Research, 23*(11/12), 703–712.

Palloff, R. M., & Pratt, K. (1999). *Building learning communities in cyberspace: Effective strategies for the online classroom*. San Francisco: Jossey-Bass.

Panoff, R. (2003). Personal communication.

Parkins, K. (2004). *Gurl tech: Online collaboration*. [Nortel Network Kidz Online Streaming video] Retrieved January 3, 2005, from http://www.kidzonline.com/nclb2004/

Paul, E. (2000). *Taking sides: Clashing views on controversial issues in sex and gender*. Guilford, CT: Dushkin/McGraw-Hill.

Pearl, A., Pollack, M. E., Riskin, E., Thomas, B., Wolf, E., & Wu, A. (1990). Becoming a computer scientist: A report by the ACM Committee on the Status of Women in Computer Science. *Communications of the ACM, 33*(11), 47–57.

PENNlincs Institute for Research in Cognitive Science (2001). *Agents for change: Robotics for girls, A robotics curriculum for the mid-*

dle school years. Retrieved on August 21, 2006, from http://www.ircs .upenn.edu/pennlincs/

Peterson, P. L., & Fennema, E. (1985). Effective teaching, student engagement in classroom activities, and sex-related differences in learning mathematics. *American Educational Research Journal, 22*, 309–335.

Pflaum, W. D. (2004). *The technology fix: The promise and reality of computers in our schools.* Arlington, VA: ASCD.

Pinkard, N. D. (2001). *Lyric reader: Creating intrinsically motivating and culturally responsive reading environments.* Report #1-013. Center for the Improvement of Early Reading Ability, University of Michigan.

Prensky, M. (2001). Digital natives, digital immigrants, *On the Horizon* (NCB University Press), *9*(5).

Pryor, J. (1995). Gender issues in groupwork–a case study involving computers. *British Educational Research Journal, 21*(3), 277–284.

Rajagopal, I., & Bojin, N. (2003a). A gendered world: Students and instructional technologies, *First Monday, 8*, Accessed June 1, 2006, from http://firstmonday.org/issues/issue8_1/rajagopal/index.html

Rajagopal, I., & Bojin, N. (2003b). I don't do Windows: Gender, pedagogy, and instructional technologies, *Education & Society, 21*(1), 75–97.

Rakes, G., & Casey, H. (2002). Institutionalizing technology in schools: Resolving teacher concerns. In C. Crawford et al. (Eds.), *Proceedings of Society for Information Technology and Teacher Education International Conference 2002* (pp. 2082–2085). Chesapeake, VA: AACE.

Reece, C. C. (1986). *Gender and microcomputers: Implications for the school curriculum.* Paper presented at the Mid-South Educational Research Association, Memphis, TN.

Resnick, R. (Ed.). (1995). *IPA's Survey of Women Online.* Retrieved July 29, 2006, from http://www.netcreations.com/ipa/women

Robinson, J. P., DiMaggio, P., & Hargittai, E., (2003). New social survey perspectives on the digital divide. *IT & Society, 1*(5), 1–22.

Roblyer, M. D. (2003). *Integrating educational technology into teaching.* Columbus, OH: Merrill Prentice Hall.

Rocap, K., Cassidy, S., & Connor, C. (1998). *Fulfilling the promise of technologies for teaching and learning.* Washington, DC: U.S. Department of Education, Office of Educational Research and Improvement.

Rosen, L. D., Sears, D. C., & Weil, M. M. (1987). Computerphobia. *Behavior research methods, instrumentation, & computers, 19*(2), 167–179.

Ross-Gordon, J., & Brown-Haywood, D. (2000). Keys to college success as seen through the eyes of African American adult students. *The Journal of Continuing Higher Education, 48*(3), 14–23.

Royal, C. (2002, August). *Mind the gender gap: Gender differences in motivation to contribute online content.* Paper presented at the Association for Education in Journalism and Mass Communication Conference, Miami, FL.

Sanders, Jo., & Tescione, S. T. (2004). *Equity in the IT classroom.* Retrieved June 25, 2005, from http://www.josanders.com/portal/index.htm

Sanders, Jo. (2005). *Teaching teachers about gender equity in computing.* Paper presented at Crossing Cultures, Changing Lives: Integrating Research on Girls' Choices of IT Careers, Oxford, England.

Sanders, J. (2005). *Gender and technology: A research review.* Retrieved October 1, 2005 from www.josanders.com/resources.

Savard, M., Mitchell, S. N., Abrami, P. C., & Corso, M. (1995). Learning together at a distance. *Canadian Journal of Educational Communication, 24*(2), 117–131.

Sax, L. J., Astin, A. W., Korn, W. S., & Mahoney, K. M. (2000). *The American freshman: National norms for fall 2000.* Higher Education Research Institute, UCLA Graduate School of Education & Information Studies.

Schrock, K. B. (2005, Summer). *Closing the gender gap—schools strive to develop technologically fluent girls.* EDTECH. Retrieved May 15, 2006, from http://edtech.texterity.com/article/200505/14

Selby, L. (1997). *Increasing the participation of women in tertiary level computing courses: What works and why.* Paper presented at the Australian Society for Computers in Learning in Tertiary Education, Perth, Australia.

Selby, L., & Ryba, K. (1994). Creating gender equitable computer learning environments, *Journal of Computing in Teaching Education, 10*(2), 7–10.

Sellers, S. L., Roberts, J., Giovanetto, L., & Friedrich, K. (2005). *Reaching all students: A resource for teaching in science, technology, engineering & mathematics.* Diversity Institute of the Center for the Integration of Research, Teaching, and Learning (CIRTL). Accessed June 1, 2006, from http://cirtl.wceruw.org/diversityinstitute.

Seymour, E. (1999). The role of socialization in shaping the career-related choices of undergraduate women in science, mathematics, and engineering majors. *Annals of the New York Academy of Sciences, 869*(1), 118–126.

Shashaani, L. (1993). Gender-based differences in attitudes toward computers. *Computers and Education, 20*(2), 169–181.

Shashaani, L. (1994). Socioeconomic status, parents' sex-role stereotypes, and the gender gap in computing. *Journal of Research on Computing in Education, 26*(4), 433–451.

Shashaani, L. (1997). Gender differences in computer attitudes and use among college students. *Journal of Educational Computing Research, 16*(1), 37–51.

Sherry, L., Billig, S., Tavalin, F., & Gibson, D. (2000). New insights on technology adoption in schools, *T.H.E. Journal, 27*(7), 43–46.

Shiver, J. Jr. (2000). Internet gender gap closes in U.S., study says. *Los Angeles Times,* May 11.

Snyder, T. D., Tan, A. G., & Hoffman, C. M. (2004). *Digest of education statistics 2003.* Washington DC: U.S. Department of Education, Institute of Education Sciences.

Sohn, E. (2006). Programming with Alice. *Science News for Kids,* February 22, 2006.

Spotts, T. H., Bowman, M. A., & Mertz, C. (1997). Gender and use of instructional technologies: A study of university faculty. *Higher Education, 34*(4), 421.

Strassman, P. A. (1999, February). Women take over. *Computerworld.*

Strauss, H. (2005, June 24). Why many faculty members aren't excited about technology. *The Chronicle of Higher Education.*

Strawn, C. A. (1999). *Moving in a man's world: Three qualitative case studies illustrate how women can survive in male-dominated work environments.* Unpublished Dissertation, Ames, IA: Iowa State University.

Sullivan, P. (2001). Gender differences and the online classroom: Male and female college students evaluate their experiences. *Community College Journal of Research and Practice, 25*(10), 805–818.

Tannen, D. (1990). *You just don't understand: Women and men in conversation.* New York: Ballantine.

Tannen, D. (1994). *Gender and discourse: Featuring a new essay on talk at work.* New York: Oxford University Press.

Tapscott, D. (1998). *Growing up digital: The rise of the net generation.* New York: McGraw-Hill.

Taylor, R. P. (Ed) (1980). *The computer in the school: Tutor, tool, tutee.* New York: Teachers College Press.

Tharp, R., & Gallimore, R. (1988). *Rousing minds to life: Teaching, learning and schooling in social context.* Cambridge: Cambridge University Press.

Trotter, A. (1999). Preparing teachers for the digital age. *Technology Counts '99; Building the Digital Curriculum, Education Week* (September 23).

Turbak, F., & Berg, R. (2002). *Robotic Design Studio: Exploring the big ideas of engineering in a liberal arts environment.* Retrieved August 21, 2006, from http://www.wellesley.edu/Physics/Rberg/papers/RDS-JSET-final.pdf#search=%22robotic%20design%20studio%22

The UCLA Internet Report—Surveying the Digital Future (2003). *The UCLA Internet Report—Year Three*, UCLA Center for Communication Policy. Accessed June 1, 2006, from http://www.digitalcenter.org/pdf/InternetReportYearThree.pdf

Valdez, G. (2005). *Critical issue: Technology: A catalyst for teaching and learning in the classroom.* Naperville, IL: North Central Regional Educational Laboratory. Retrieved May 10, 2006, from http://www.ncrel.org/sdrs/areas/issues/methods/technlgy/te600.htm

Valenza, J., (1997). Girls + technology = turnoff? *Technology Connection, 3*(10), 20–21, 29.

Voyles, M., & Williams, A. (2004). Gender differences in attributions and behavior in a technology classroom. *Journal of Computers in Mathematics and Science Teaching, 23*(3), 233–256.

Waren-Sams, B. (1997). *Closing the equity gap in technology access and use: A practical guide for K–12 educators.* Portland, OR: Northwest Regional Educational Laboratory. Retrieved July 1, 2006 at http://www.nwrel.org/cnorse/booklets/equitygap/Equity_gap.pdf.

Weiner, G. (1974). Motivational psychology and educational research, *Educational Psychologist, 11*, 96–101.

Weiner, B. (1994). Integrating social and personal theories of achievement striving, *Review of Educational Research, 64*(4), 557–573.

Wenglinsky, H. (1998). *Does it compute? The relationship between education technology and student achievement in mathematics.* Princeton, NJ: Educational Testing Service. Accessed June 1, 2006, http://www.ets.org/Media/Research/pdf/PICTECHNOLOG.pdf

Whitley, B. E., Jr. (1997). Gender differences in computer-related attitudes and behavior: A meta-analysis. *Computers in Human Behavior, 13*(1), 1–22.

Wolfe, J. (1999). Why do women feel ignored? Gender differences in computer-mediated classroom interactions. *Computers and Composition, 16*(1), 153–166.

Wozney, L., Venkatesh, V., & Abrami, P. C. (2006). Implementing computer technologies: Teachers' perceptions and practices. *Journal of Technology and Teacher Education, 14*(1), 173–207.

Young, B. J. (2000). Gender differences in student attitudes toward computers. *Journal of Research on Computing in Education, 33*(2), 204–216.

·11·

SEXUAL HARASSMENT:

THE HIDDEN GENDER EQUITY PROBLEM

Michele A. Paludi, * *Jennifer Martin*
and Carmen A. Paludi, Jr.

INTRODUCTION

In 1978, the Project on the Status and Education of Women of the Association of American Colleges referred to sexual harassment as a "hidden issue." This term was coined earlier[1] to highlight the silence that surrounded sexual harassment; i.e., victims were afraid to come forth with complaints for fear of retaliation, and campus administrators didn't investigate complaints brought to their attention. A similar lack of attention to sexual harassment has also occurred in elementary, middle, and high school. For example, The American Association of University Women (AAUW) Educational Foundation's "The AAUW Report: How Schools Shortchange Girls" (1992) labeled sexual harassment as part of the "evaded curriculum" (along with body image, eating disorders, early sexuality, drugs and alcohol, and personal safety) to connote the silence that exists around this topic by administrators and teachers.

Since 1978, research, legislation, case law, policies, and investigatory procedures followed in an attempt to ease victims' fear of coming forth with their complaints of sexual harassment and assist administrators in developing an educational program on sexual harassment prevention for their school/campus community (see the 1985 edition of the *Handbook for Achieving Sex Equity through Education*, pp. 480–481 and Dziech, 2003 for a review). However, more than 25 years after the Project on the Status of Education of Women's used the term "hidden issue," sexual harassment may become hidden again, being foreshadowed by attention to "bullying." This backlash has resulted in some schools and colleges focusing on bully prevention. Although many see sexual harassment as a form of sexual bullying, when they focus on bully-prevention activities, they are not likely to remember to attend to sexual harassment because they think about bullying and sexual harassment as separate issues (Sandler & Stonehill). This is a serious omission because there are federal as well as state laws against sexual harassment (but only a few state laws against bullying) and because cases of sexual harassment are more prevalent than cases of bullying. "Thirty percent of students are involved in traditional bullying as victims, bullies, or both. In contrast, approximately 4 out of 5 students or 80 percent are sexually harassed by their peers, with some studies reporting even higher figures" (Sandler & Stonehill, 2005, p. 2).

Stein (2003, 2004) has argued that focusing on bullying is equated to "de-gendering" the concept of sexual harassment; to ignore that most victims of sexual harassment are girls and to focus on boys' experiences with being bullied instead. This focus on bullying also assumes the problem is an interpersonal one between two or more individuals and that the goal of prevention is to provide help to the pathological bully. The focus on sexual harassment demands schools and campuses intervene, since under Title VII and Title IX protections, sexual harassment is an organizational responsibility (Note: Title IX covers employees and students in organizations with educational programs and activities who are recipients of federal financial assistance. Title VII protects employees from sex and other forms of discrimination in organizations even if they are not recipients of federal financial assistance). To comply with these laws, the employer or educational institution would be wise to use an effective policy statement, investigatory procedures, and school/campus-wide training on sexual harassment awareness in general as well as the

---

*The bold face names are the Lead Authors.

[1]In the mid 1970s, Catherine MacKinnon pioneered the legal claim for sexual harassment. In 1979, she published *Sexual Harassment of Working Women*, arguing that sexual harassment is a form of sexual discrimination under Title VII of the Civil Rights Act of 1964 and of any other sex discrimination prohibition.

organization's policy and procedures (Paludi & Paludi, 2003). Finally, a focus on bullying has placed this as a way of school life or a rite of passage of childhood and adolescence. A focus on sexual harassment places this as a form of sexual victimization.

The rest of the chapter uses the term *sexual harassment* instead of *sexual bullying*. The following sections discuss the definition of and protections against sexual harassment, the incidence of sexual harassment in K–12 and college campuses, the research challenges in understanding sexual harassment, the impact of sexual harassment on students, theoretical explanations for why sexual harassment occurs, and steps schools and campuses can take to deal with and prevent sexual harassment.

This chapter does not provide an overview of the laws protecting students and employees from other types of sexual misconduct such as educator or priest misconduct, which often occurs in an educational, a recreational, or a counseling context (see Shakeshaft, 2004 for a review).

DEFINITION OF SEXUAL HARASSMENT

Sexual harassment is legally defined as "unwelcome sexual advances, requests for sexual favors, and other verbal or physical conduct of a sexual nature" when any one of the following criterion is met:

- Submission to such conduct is made either explicitly or implicitly a term or condition of the individual's employment or academic standing;
- Submission to or rejection of such conduct by an individual is used as the basis for employment or academic decisions affecting the individual;
- Such conduct has the purpose or effect of unreasonably interfering with an individual's work or learning performance or creating an intimidating, hostile or offensive work or learning environment.

There are two types of sexual harassment situations that are described by this legal definition: (a) quid pro quo sexual harassment and (b) hostile-environment sexual harassment.

Quid pro quo sexual harassment involves an individual with organizational power who either expressly or implicitly ties an academic or employment decision or action to the response of an individual to unwelcome sexual advances. Thus, a teacher may promise a reward to a student for complying with sexual requests (i.e., a better grade or a letter of recommendation for college or a job) or threaten a student for failing to comply with the sexual requests (i.e., threatening to not give the student the grade earned).

Hostile-environment sexual harassment involves a situation where an atmosphere or climate is created by staff or other students in the classroom or other area in the school that makes it difficult, if not impossible, for a student to study and learn because the atmosphere is perceived by the student to be intimidating, offensive, and hostile.

Sexual harassment includes, but is not limited to, the following:

- Unwelcome sexual advances
- Sexual innuendos, comments, and sexual remarks

- Suggestive, obscene, or insulting sounds
- Implied or expressed threat of reprisal for refusal to comply with a sexual request
- Patting, pinching, brushing up against another's body
- Sexually suggestive objects, books, magazines, poster, photographs, cartoons, e-mail, or pictures displayed in the school/work area
- Actual denial of an academic-related benefit for refusal to comply with sexual requests

Thus, sexual harassment can be physical, verbal, visual, or written. These behaviors are often committed by individuals who are in supervisory positions or peers. These behaviors also constitute sexual harassment if they occur between individuals of the same sex or between individuals of the opposite sex.

According to Title IX of the 1972 Education Amendments:

No person in the United States shall, on the basis of sex, be excluded from participation in, or denied the benefits of, or be subjected to discrimination under any educational program or activity receiving federal assistance.

Title IX is an antidiscrimination statute prohibiting discrimination on the basis of sex in any educational program or activity receiving federal financial assistance. Title IX is at the heart of efforts to create gender-equitable schools. Title IX requires educational institutions to maintain policies, procedures, and programs that do not discriminate against anyone based on sex. Title IX extends to recruitment, admissions, educational activities and programs, course offerings, counseling, financial aid, health and insurance benefits, scholarships, and athletics.

Schools must designate a Title IX Coordinator, whose responsibility is to enforce Title IX including the prevention of sexual harassment. They may also designate an additional sexual-harassment administrator or counselor. Schools can lose federal funds for noncompliance with Title IX and they can be sued if they fail to respond to and stop sexual harassment when someone has complained about it (Table 11.1).

INCIDENCE OF SEXUAL HARASSMENT AMONG STUDENTS IN K–12

Ageton (1983) reported that between 5 and 11% of adolescent girls experienced behaviors at school that fit the legal definition of sexual harassment (i.e., unwelcome sexual advances, requests for sexual favors, and other verbal or physical conduct that unreasonably interferes with an individual's school or work performance, creates an intimidating or hostile school or work environment, or is required in exchange for a grade or a job). Wellesley College's Center for Research on Women's study, with 4,000 girls in grades 2 through 12, found that 39% experienced sexual harassment every day at school. Eighty-nine percent of the girls reported experiencing sexual comments and gestures (Stein, Marshall, & Tropp, 1993).

Similar results were obtained by the first scientific national study of academic sexual harassment of children and adoles-

TABLE 11.1   Key Supreme Court Decisions Relating to Sexual Harassment and Education

1979	Cannon v. University of Chicago Individual can bring a private lawsuit directly against an educational institution for violation of Title IX
1980	Alexander v. Yale University The definition of sex discrimination under Title IX includes sexual harassment
1982	North Haven Board of Education v. Bell Title IX can protect employees of educational institutions as well as students
1983	Grove City College v. Bell Limits Title IX to program specific coverage. If sexual harassment occurs in a dorm that didn't receive federal funds, the student would not be protected.
1984	Moire v. Temple University School of Medicine Title IX extended to include hostile environment sexual Harassment
1985	Walters v. President and Fellows of Harvard College Custodial worker could not recover damages from sexual harassment under Title IX since the position held by the employee was not directly related to the delivery of an educational service
1988	Civil Rights Restoration Act of 1987 (It was signed in 1988) Overruled "program specific" requirements of Grove City College Decision; If any program of an educational institution receives federal funds, the entire operation of the institution is subject to the requirements of Title IX
1992	Franklin v. Gwinnett County Public Schools Remedies available to a Title IX plaintiff included monetary damages
1998	Gebser v. Lago Vista Independent School District Title IX requires schools to take action to prevent and stop the harassment of students by teachers or other students
1999	Davis v. Monroe County Board of Education Private damage actions are allowed against schools that act with deliberate indifference even to peer-to peer sexual harassment that is severe enough to prevent victims from enjoying educational opportunities.
2005	Jackson v. Birmingham Board of Education Title IX protects even third parties such as educators from retaliation if they are trying to protect students from sex discrimination.

cents conducted by the American Association of University Women in 1993. In this study, incidence rates of students' experiences with sexual harassment was collected from 1,632 girls and boys in grades 8 through 11 from 79 schools across the United States. Students were asked the following question, adapted from the legal definition of sexual harassment: "During your whole school life, how often, if at all, has anyone (this includes students, teachers, other school employees, or anyone else) done the following things to you when you did not want them to?"

- Made sexual comments, jokes, gestures, or looks
- Showed, gave, or left you sexual pictures, photographs, illustrations, messages, or notes
- Wrote sexual messages or graffiti about you on bathroom walls, in locker rooms, etc.
- Spread sexual rumors about you
- Said you were gay or lesbian
- Spied on you as you dressed or showered at school
- Flashed or "mooned" you
- Touched, grabbed, or pinched you in a sexual way
- Pulled at your clothing in a sexual way
- Intentionally brushed against you in a sexual way
- Pulled your clothing off or down
- Blocked your way or cornered you in a sexual way
- Forced you to kiss him or her
- Forced you to do something sexual other than kissing

Results indicated that 4 out of 5 students (81%) reported that they had been the target of some form of sexual harassment during their school lives. With respect to gender comparisons, 85% of girls and 76% of boys surveyed reported that they had experienced unwelcome sexual behavior that interfered with their ability to concentrate at school and in their personal lives. This research also analyzed the data for race comparisons. African-American boys (81%) were more likely to have experienced sexual harassment than White boys (75%) and Latinos (69%). For girls, 87% of Whites reported having experienced behaviors that constitute sexual harassment, compared with 84% of African-American girls and 82% of Latinas.

The AAUW study also found that adolescents' experiences with sexual harassment were most likely to occur in the middle-school or junior-high school years of sixth to ninth grade. The behaviors reported by students, in order from most often experienced to least often experienced, include the following:

- Sexual comments, jokes, gestures, or looks (76% of girls; 56% of boys)
- Touched, grabbed, or pinched in a sexual way (65% of girls; 42% of boys)
- Intentionally brushed against in a sexual way (57% of girls; 36% of boys)
- Flashed or "mooned" (49% of girls; 41% of boys)
- Had sexual rumors spread about them (43% of girls; 34% of boys)
- Had clothing pulled at in a sexual way (38% of girls; 28% of boys)
- Shown, given, or left sexual pictures, photographs, illustrations, messages, or notes (31% of girls; 31% of boys)
- Had their way blocked or were cornered in a sexual way (38% of girls; 17% of boys)
- Had sexual messages or graffiti written about them on bathroom walls, in locker rooms, etc. (20% of girls; 18% of boys)
- Forced to kiss someone (23% of girls; 14% of boys)
- Called gay or lesbian (10% of girls; 23% of boys)
- Had clothing pulled off or down (16% of girls; 16% of boys)
- Forced to do something sexual other than kissing (13% of girls; 9% of boys)
- Spied on as they dressed or showered at school (7% of girls; 7% of boys)

Students reported that they often experience these behaviors while in the classroom or in the hallways as they are going to class. Although the majority of harassment in schools is student-to-student or peer harassment, 25% of girls and 10% of boys reported they were harassed by teachers or other school employees.

A number of research studies subsequent to the AAUW report reinforced the AAUW findings. For example, Roscoe, Strouse, and Goodwin (1994) asked 11–16-year olds about their experiences with sexual comments, telephone calls, letters/notes, pressure for dates, physical contact, and sexual advances. Roscoe et al. reported a significant percentage of early adolescents' experiences with sexual harassment by peers. They found that 50% of girls and 37% of boys had been sexually harassed.

Similar results were obtained by Turner (1995), with students in grades six, seven, and eight. Turner's results suggested that girls were more sensitive to verbal and physically harassment than boys. Murnen and Smolak (2000) reported that girls in their sample commonly experienced having an entrance blocked and being stared at.

In their study of sexual harassment of high-school students, Houston and Hwang (1996) reported that adolescents who experienced sexual harassment during childhood experienced more sexual harassment in high school than those teens who were not sexually harassed years earlier. The 1998 World Health Organization's Health Behavior in School-aged Children's Survey found that 29% of children in grades 6 through 10 are directly involved in bullying with 10% as bullies, 13% as victims, and 6% as both. This study also reported that 52% of students experienced sexual bullying (47% of boys and 57% of girls). It defined a bully as an individual who repeatedly targets another, either directly and physically (i.e., hitting) or indirectly (i.e., shunning another student). Bullying behaviors include sexual jokes, comments, or gestures, which are referred to as "sexual bullying" (Espelage, 2003; Olewus, 1993), Table 11.2 provides accounts of the types of sexual harassment children and adolescents experience at school.

TABLE 11.2   Students' Accounts of Sexual Harassment

The print shop teacher, who was in the habit of putting his arms around the shoulders of the young women, insisted, when one young woman asked to be excused to go to the nurse to fix her broken pants' zipper, that she first show him her broken zipper. She was forced to lift her shirt to reveal her broken pants' zipper (Bogart, Simons, Stein, & Tomaszewski, 1992, p. 197).

One female in diesel shop refused to go to lunch during her last two years of shop because she was the only young woman in the lunchroom at that time. When she went to the cafeteria, she was pinched and slapped on the way in, and had to endure explicit propositions made to her while she ate lunch (Stein, 1986, cited in Bogart, Simmons, Stein, & Tomaszewski, 1992, p. 208).

A particular shop's predominantly male population designated one shop day as National Sexual Harassment Day, in honor of their only female student. They gave her non-stop harassment throughout the day, and found it to be so successful (the female student was forced to be dismissed during the day), that they later held a National Sexual Harassment Week (p. 208).

In 2001, AAUW found results similar to their earlier research. They sampled 2,064 students in public school in grades 8–11. Eighty-one percent of students experience some form of sexual harassment during their school lives, 59% occasionally, and 27% often. This study also found that girls (85%) were more likely than boys (79%) to experience sexual harassment ever or often (30% vs. 24% often). In addition, 32% of students reported being afraid of being sexually harassed, with girls more than twice as likely as boys to feel this fear (44% vs. 20%). Eighty-five percent of students reported peer sexual harassment, 38% reported being harassed by a teacher or other school employee.

We note that the differences in incidence rates may be due to methodological variations among research studies (Paludi, 2000). For example, some researchers have used retrospective data in collecting incidence rates, i.e., asking introductory college students about their experiences being sexually harassed in high school. Other researchers have asked high-school students about their more immediate experiences with sexual harassment. The AAUW study asked students to recall all of their sexual-harassment experiences during their entire school history. Students were also asked to focus on the most severe incident of sexual harassment. Asking students to remember and focus on their worst incident may yield distorted data regarding the severity of sexual harassment they frequently experienced.

In addition, direct questions about sexual harassment may elicit unreliable incidence rates since individuals do not typically understand what constitutes sexual harassment (Fitzgerald et al., 1988). Thus, random and systematic error is introduced into the procedure.

Furthermore, several measuring instruments used to collect incidence data have not been submitted to psychometric analyses, including reliability and validity. Some research studies have used the Sexual Experiences Questionnaire (Fitzgerald et al., 1988); others have used surveys designed only for their study (i.e., Roscoe, 1994). Comparing incidence rates with studies that have not used the identical measuring instrument also poses a methodological problem.

Finally, cross-cultural studies may not be using the same definition of sexual harassment as do researchers in the United States. As DeSouza and Solberg (2003) stated: "The use of different methodologies, including survey methods, instructions, wording of survey items, time frames, and sampling techniques, makes cross-cultural comparisons problematic if not impossible" (p. 16). One notable exception is Sigal et al. (2005), who ensured the methodology used in their research, which included a scenario, was comparable to all cultures.

The incidence data just reported as well as in the following section on college students' experiences with sexual harassment should be interpreted in light of these methodological issues.

INCIDENCE OF SEXUAL HARASSMENT AMONG COLLEGE STUDENTS

In one of the first books concerning sexual harassment of college students, Dziech and Weiner (1984) reported that 30% of undergraduate women experienced sexual harassment from at least one of their instructors during their four years of college.

Adams, Kottke, and Padgitt (1983) reported that 13% of the women they surveyed said they had avoided taking a class or working with a particular faculty member because of the risk of being subjected to sexual advances. In this same study, 17% of the women reported verbal sexual advances, 14% received sexual invitations, 6% had been subjected to physical advances, and 2% reported direct sexual bribes.

Similar results were obtained with female graduate students (Bailey & Richards, 1985). Of the 246 women graduate students sampled, 13% indicated they had been sexually harassed, 21% had not enrolled in a course to avoid such behavior, and 16% indicated they had been directly assaulted by a professor. Bond (1988) also studied female graduate students' experiences with sexual harassment. She reported that 75% of the 229 women who responded to her survey experienced offensive jokes with sexual themes during their graduate training, 69% were subjected to sexist comments demeaning to women, and 58% of the women reported experiencing sexist remarks about their clothing, body, or sexual activities.

In the first large-scale study with college students, Fitzgerald and colleagues (1988) investigated approximately 2,000 women at two major state universities. Half of the women respondents reported experiencing some form of sexually harassing behavior. The majority of these women reported hearing sexist comments by faculty. The next largest category of sexually harassing behavior was seductive behavior, including being invited for drinks and a backrub by faculty, being brushed up against by their professors, and having their professors show up uninvited at their hotel rooms during out-of-town academic conferences.

More recently, Hill and Silva (2005) reported findings from their nationally representative survey of 2,036 undergraduate students (1,096 women; 940 men) commissioned by the American Association of University Women Educational Foundation. Their research found that sexual harassment is experienced by the majority of college students. Approximately one third of the students reported physical harassment, including being touched, grabbed, or forced to do something sexual. Hill and Silva (2005) also reported that men and women are equally likely to experience sexual harassment although in different ways. For example, women were more likely to report experiencing sexual comments and gestures while men reported experiencing homophobic comments. Furthermore, Hill and Silva (2005) found that men are more likely than women to harass others.

For certain student groups, such as graduate students, the incidence of sexual harassment appears to be higher than others (Barickman, Paludi, & Rabinowitz, 1992; DeFour, 1996; Dziech, 2003). For example:

- Women of color, especially those with "token" status
- Students in small colleges or small academic departments, where the number of faculty available to students is quite small
- Women students in male populated fields, i.e., engineering
- Students who are economically disadvantaged and work part-time or full-time while attending classes
- Lesbian women, who may be harassed as part of homophobia
- Physically or emotionally disabled students
- Women students who work in dormitories as resident assistants

- Women who have been sexually abused
- Inexperienced, unassertive, socially isolated women, who may appear more vulnerable and appealing to those who would intimidate or coerce them into an exploitive relationship

Women of color are especially vulnerable to sexual harassment from their professors; they are subject to stereotypes about sex, are viewed as sexually mysterious and inviting, and are less sure of themselves in their careers. They also frequently experience an interface between racism and sexual harassment (Chan, Tang, & Chan, 1999; DeFour, David, Diaz, & Thompkins, 2003; DeSouza & Solberg, 2003). For example, Lombardo, Pedrabissi, and Santinello (1996) found that 48.2% of female students in Italy reported having experienced comments about their bodies, 29.3% seductive behavior, 3.4% bribery (i.e., being offered a reward for engaging in sexual activity), 4.5% coercion (i.e., coercing someone by threat of punishment), and 25.8% sexual assault. Gardner and Felicity (1996) found that, among Australian women students, 91.3% indicated that they had experienced at least once a sexually harassing behavior from a professor or a peer, but only 31.7% labeled such behavior as sexual harassment.

Peer sexual harassment is common among college students (Hill & Slava, 2005; Sandler & Shoop, 1997). The main verbal form of peer sexual harassment experienced by female students involved "lewd" comments or sexual comments. Tang, Yik, Cheung, Choi, and Au (1996) reported that peer sexual harassment of Chinese women by male college students occurred twice as frequently as faculty-student sexual harassment. Gardner and Felicity (1996) reported that 88.1% of Australian female college students indicated that they had experienced at least once a sexually harassing behavior from a peer.

Fitzgerald and Omerod (1993) concluded that:

. . . it seems reasonable (if not conservative) to estimate that one out of every two women will be harassed at some point during her academic or working life, thus indicating that sexual harassment is the most widespread of all forms of sexual victimization studied to date. (p. 559)

This estimate has been supported by countless empirical research studies, using different methodologies to collect incidence data in different parts of the world (i.e., Barak, 1997; Buchanan, 2005; DeFour, 1996; DeFour, David, Diaz, & Thompkins, 2003; Dziech, 2003; DeSouza, 2005; DeSouza & Solberg, 2003; Gruber, 1997; Sigal, Rashid, Anjum, Goodrich, & Gibbs, 2001). For a review of intercultural and intracultural research, see DeSouza and Solberg (2003) and DeFour et al. (2003).

DeFour et al. (2003) reviewed the empirical research on sexual orientation and sexual harassment. They noted that much of the behavior experienced by lesbian, gay, and bisexual individuals was both homophobic and sexist in nature. Examples of sexual harassment relating to sexual orientation include,

- Hearing derogatory or stereotypical comments about lesbian, gay, or bisexual individuals
- Accusations of being lesbian, gay, or bisexual
- Threats to expose the individual's sexual orientation
- Being forced to reveal their sexual orientation

The incidence of sexual harassment of lesbian, gay, and bisexual individuals is difficult to document. If they are out, victims worry about their sexual orientation will be exposed during the investigation process in retaliation for filing the complaint (Pryor & Whalen, 1997).

EXAMPLES OF SEXUAL HARASSMENT

Hughes and Sandler (1988) offered illustrations of sexual harassment to compliment the statistics:

- A group of men regularly sit at a table facing a cafeteria line. As women go through the line, the men loudly discuss the women's sexual attributes and hold up signs with number from 1 to 10, "rating" each woman. As a result, many women skip meals or avoid the cafeteria.
- Sexist posters and pictures are placed where women can see them. A fraternity pledge approaches a young woman he has never met and bites her on the breast—a practice called "sharking."

Similar summaries were offered by college students in Hill and Silva's research (2005, p. 20):

Types of Student-to-Student Sexual Harassment:

"There is a guy in all my classes who consistently touches me in a sexual way that I really don't appreciate."

"People who lived in the same hall as me in the dorms started spreading rumors about my sex life, which were not even close to true. They also spread condoms around my room."

"Phone harassment calling me derogatory homosexual names and leaving messages."

Research (i.e., Hughes & Sandler, 1988) has indicated that some of the most serious forms of peer harassment involve groups of men. When men outnumber women, as in fraternity houses and stadiums or at parties, group harassment is especially likely to occur. Examples of group sexual harassment include,

- Yelling, whistling, and shouting obscenities at women who walk by fraternity houses or other campus sites.
- Intimidating a woman by surrounding her, demanding that she expose her breasts, and refusing to allow her to leave until she complies.
- Vandalizing sororities

IMPACT OF SEXUAL HARASSMENT ON CHILDREN AND ADOLESCENTS

The 1993 AAUW study reported that approximately 1 in 4 students (middle-school aged) who had been sexually harassed did not want to attend school or cut a class. In addition, 1 in 4 students became silent in their classes following their experience of sexual harassment. With respect to the emotional aspects of sexual harassment, the AAUW study reported the following experiences, in rank order, among the students who were sexually harassed:

- Embarrassment
- Self-consciousness
- Being less sure of themselves or less confident
- Feeling afraid or scared
- Doubting whether they could have a happy romantic relationship
- Feeling confused about who they are
- Feeling less popular

In addition, 33% of girls who reported experiencing sexual harassment no longer wished to attend school. Thirty-two percent of girls stated that talking in class was more difficult and 20% indicated they had received lower grades. Girls further reported that they altered their behavior to decrease the likelihood of sexual harassment by avoiding people or places, including school events. Twelve percent of the boys who reported experiencing sexual harassment did not want to attend school; 13% of the boys indicated they talked less in class following incidents of sexual harassment. Roscoe et al. (1994) described girls' experiences with sexual harassment as creating an inhospitable learning experience. These researchers further reported that boys' experiences with sexual harassment did not similarly interfere with their school experiences. Murnen and Smolak (2000) found that girls were more likely to perceive sexual harassment as frightening whereas boys do not. Timmerman (2002) and Duffy, Wareham, and Walsh (2004) reported that sexual harassment of adolescents contributed to lower self-esteem and poorer psychological health.

Fineran and Gruber (2004) reviewed the impact of sexual harassment, including bullying, on children and adolescents. They noted that the outcomes of sexual harassment can be examined from three main perspectives: (a) learning-related, (b) social/emotional, and (c) health-related. Responses include depression, feeling sad, nervous, threatened and angry, loss of appetite, feelings of helplessness, nightmares or disturbed sleep, loss of interest in regular activities, isolation from friends and family, and loss of friends. Fineran and Gruber also reported long-term effects from sexual harassment: depression, loss of self-esteem, lowered grades, lost educational and job opportunities that affect students after high-school graduation, which may cause fewer career choices.

Fineran and Gruber (2004) reported both bullying and sexual harassment diminished adolescents' physical and emotional health, resulting in increased post-traumatic stress. In addition, they found that sexual harassment was correlated with adolescents' academic withdrawal and tardiness while bullying did not.

Fineran and Gruber (2004) also studied the impact of sexual orientation on experiencing sexual harassment and bullying. They noted that gay and bisexual students who were physically sexually harassed had higher levels of school avoidant behavior than did heterosexual students who were physically harassed.

Furthermore, gay and bisexual students who were verbally sexually harassed had more trauma symptoms and poorer emotional health than did heterosexual students who were verbally sexually harassed.

Fineran and Gruber (2004) as well as the AAUW studies (1993, 2001) found that sexual harassment affected girls' behavior more than boys', with girls being taught to be fearful and avoid the situation rather than taking direct action to cease the sexual harassment. The AAUW study (1993) further reported that girls were less likely than boys to feel confident about themselves after incidents of sexual harassment.

Paludi (2004) recently applied the "broken windows" theory to schools trying to prevent and deal with sexual harassment. If what is perceived by the school to be trivial isn't handled immediately, other forms of sexual harassment and sexual victimization will result. Stein (1993) has argued that such behavior on the part of schools contributes to adolescent girls believing sexual harassment is acceptable and "normal" and keeping silent about their experiences.

Phinney (1994) reported that sexual harassment is a "dynamic element" in the lives of adolescent girls since schools perpetuate male dominance through sports and pedagogical techniques in the classroom. Sheffield (1993) argued that sexual harassment and other forms of sexual violence encourage girls to feel fearful, what she described as her "sexual terrorism theory."

IMPACT OF SEXUAL HARASSMENT ON COLLEGE STUDENTS

Similar to the research findings with children and adolescents, studies with college students have documented the high cost of sexual harassment to individuals (i.e., Danksy & Kilpatrick, 1997; Hill & Silva, 2005; Lundberg-Love & Faulkner, 2005; Lundberg-Love & Marmion, 2003; Quina, 1996). Research with college students indicated that there are career-related, psychological, and physiological outcomes of sexual harassment. For example, women students have reported decreased morale, decreased satisfaction with their career goals, and lowered grades. Furthermore, women students have reported feelings of helplessness and powerlessness over their academic career, strong fear reactions, and decreased motivation. Women college students have also reported headaches, sleep disturbances, eating disorders, and gastrointestinal disorders as common physical responses to sexual harassment.

Danksy and Kilpatrick (1997) noted that these responses are influenced by disappointment and self-blame in the way others react, and the stress of sexual harassment induced life changes, such as loss of teaching or research fellowships, loss of student loans, and disrupted educational career path. Schneider's (1987) research indicated that 29% of women reported a loss of academic or professional opportunities and 13% reported lowered grades or financial support because of sexual harassment.

Ramos' (2000) research with Spanish college women attending the University of Puerto Rico found that sexual harassment had a negative impact on health, academic success, and psychological well-being. Women who had been sexually harassed reported more physical symptoms, poorer mental health, greater academic withdrawal, lower self-esteem, and lower life satisfaction than women who had not been sexually harassed. Dansky and Kilpatrick (1997) and Quina (1996) noted that symptoms are exacerbated by experiencing repeated sexual harassment and sexual harassment in front of peers. In addition, symptoms become more pronounced the longer the student has to endure the sexual harassment.

TO REPORT OR NOT REPORT

Research with college students (as well as with children and adolescents) indicated that despite the fact that they reported experiencing behaviors that fit the legal definition of sexual harassment, they did not label their experiences as such. However, as Magley, Hulin, Fitzgerald, and DeNardo (1999) noted, "whether or not a woman considers her experience to constitute sexual harassment, she experiences similar negative psychological, work, and health consequences" (p. 399).

Most students do not tell the harasser to stop. Reilly, Lott, and Gallogly (1986) found that 61% of women college students victimized by sexual harassment ignored the behavior or did nothing in response, and 16% asked or told the faculty member to stop. In addition, students' initial attempts to manage the initiator are rarely direct. Furthermore, the first or first several incidents of sexual harassment are often ignored by students, especially when the behavior is subtle (Fitzgerald, Gold, & Brock, 1990). Hill and Silva (2005) noted that 35% of the students in their sample told no one about their experiences with sexual harassment. Approximately half of the students confided in a friend; 7% reported incidents to a college employee. Students fear retaliation should they confront the harasser. They do not want their lives or careers threatened.

Malovich and Stake (1990) reported that women students who were high in performance self-esteem and who held egalitarian gender-role attitudes were more likely to report incidents of sexual harassment than women who were low in self-esteem and held traditional gender-role attitudes. Similar results were obtained by Brooks and Perot (1991), who noted that feminist students reported incidents of sexual harassment more than nonfeminists. Tang et al. (1995) noted that women victims of sexual harassment may not report their experiences out of shame and embarrassment. Thus, there is not a one-to-one correspondence between incidence and reporting of sexual harassment by students (see DeSouza & Solberg, 2004 for a distinction between legal and psychological responses in this regard).

WHY INDIVIDUALS SEXUALLY HARASS

Research has indicated that boys and men are more likely to sexually harass than girls and women (i.e., Fitzgerald et al., 1988). The incidence of female-female sexual harassment and female-male sexual harassment is small compared to male-female sexual harassment. When boys and men are sexually harassed, it is usually another male who engaged in the behavior (Stockdale, Visio, & Batra, 1999; Waldo, Berdhal, & Fitzgerald, 1998). Stockdale, et al. (1999) concluded that same-sex sexual harassment against men takes place because the "targeted men do not fit their offender's gender-role stereotype of heterosexual hyper masculinity" (p. 637). Fitzgerald and Weitzman (1990) challenged the belief in a "typical harasser." They found that men who sexually harass are found in all teaching ranks and age groups.

Hill and Silva (2005, p. 22) offered the following reasons students identified as to why they sexually harass:

- I thought it was funny.
- I thought the person liked it.
- My friends encouraged/"pushed" me into doing it.
- I wanted something from that person.
- I wanted that person to think I had some sort of power over them.

Paludi (2004) noted that while the focus had been on males' attitudes toward females, it would be more helpful to study boys' attitudes toward other boys, competition, and power. Boys and men often act out of extreme competitiveness or fear of losing their positions of power. They don't want to appear weak or less masculine in the eyes of other boys, so they engage in the "scoping of girls," (i.e., rating girls' bodies) pinching girls, making implied or overt threats, or spying on women. Girls are the objects of the game to impress other boys. When boys are encouraged to be obsessionally competitive and concerned with dominance, it is likely that they will eventually use sexual harassment to achieve dominance.

Boys are also likely to be verbally abusive and intimidating in their body language. De-individuation is common among adolescent boys, who during class changes and lunch breaks, scope girls as they walk by in the hall. They discontinue self-evaluation and adopt group norms and attitudes. Under these circumstances, group members behave more aggressively than they would as individuals. Recent research by Giladi (2005) supported this interpretation in her research with young children in Israel.

DeSouza (2004) noted that the male-as-dominant or male-as-aggressor is a theme so central to many adolescent males' self-concept that it literally carries over into their interpersonal communications, especially female peers. Lott (1993) found empirical support for sexual harassment is part of a larger and more general misogyny. This hostility toward women includes extreme stereotypes of women such as the idea that sexual harassment is a form of seduction and that women secretly need/want to be forced into sex.

In theorizing about why sexual harassment occurs, researchers have all acknowledged the power differential between sexual harassers and victims of sexual harassment (i.e., Fitzgerald, et al., 1998; Paludi, 1990; Zalk, 1990). As Zalk (1990) concluded, the "bottom line" in the relationship between professors and students is power:

The faculty member has it and the student does not. As intertwined as the faculty-student roles may be, and as much as one must exist for the other to exist, they are not equal collaborators. The student does not negotiate—indeed, has nothing to negotiate with. (p. 145)

Zalk also noted that professors' greatest power lies in their capacity to:

. . . enhance or diminish students' self-esteem. This power can motivate students to master material or convince them to give up. It is not simply a grade, but the feedback and the tone and content of the interaction. Is the student encouraged or put down? Does the faculty member use his/her knowledge to let students know how "stupid" they are or to challenge their thinking? This is real power. (p. 146)

Kenig and Ryan (1986) reported that male professors are more likely than female professors to believe individuals can handle unwanted sexual attention on their own without involving the college. Thus, male professors view sexual harassment as a personal, not an organizational issue. They attribute more responsibility to women victims of sexual harassment and minimize the responsibility of the college administration. The power differential that exists between students and professors helps to explain students' desire to remain silent about being sexually harassed.

Contrapower sexual harassment involves subordinates as harassers. Thus, students who have no formal power in the school/college harass those who have formal organizational power, i.e., students sexually harassing a teacher. Women faculty have reported experiencing sexual harassment from male students (Matchen & DeSouza, 2000; Quina, 1996). This occurs more frequently in women's-studies courses and other courses where the woman professor is identified as a feminist, which has negative connotations for some students. Most women faculty members choose to remain silent about their harassment from male students for fear of professional repercussions (i.e., not being granted tenure; having their woman-centered course cancelled). This fear on the part of adult women underscores their tenuous existence on campus (Quina, 1996).

The reality is that sexual harassment occurs anywhere once communal barriers—the sense of mutual regard and the obligations of civility—are lowered by actions that seem to signal that "no one cares." Having an effective and enforced policy, procedures, and training program will signal caring by the school and provide a strong foundation for prevention which will lead to students' rights to receive equal educational opportunities.

DEALING WITH AND PREVENTING SEXUAL HARASSMENT

One change over eight years identified in the 2001 AAUW study of sexual harassment of students was that 69% of students, compared to 26% in 1993, indicated that their schools have a sexual harassment-policy statement. In addition, in the 2001 AAUW study, 36% of students compared to 13% in 1993 reported that their schools distribute training/educational materials on sexual harassment.

A disturbing finding from the 2001 study, however, is that despite more schools having policy statements and offering students educational materials on sexual harassment, students continue to engage in sexual harassment and rarely tell school administrators about being victimized. If they do tell anyone about their experiences, it is usually a friend. Boys were twice as likely as girls not to tell anyone about being sexually harassed. There is empirical research to suggest that there are personality factors that contribute to students remaining silent or reporting sexual harassment (i.e., Craig, Pepler, Connoly, & Henderson, 2001).

In addition to personality factors related to reporting sexual harassment, there are organizational factors that are useful predictors of reporting as well. For example, Sandler and Paludi (1993) reported that adolescents are more likely to experience teacher/student sexual harassment and peer sexual harassment if they attend schools that,

- Do not have a policy prohibiting sexual harassment
- Do not disseminate the policy or report information regarding sexual harassment
- Do not have a training program for teachers, staff, and students
- Do not intervene officially when sexual harassment occurs
- Do not support sexual harassment victims
- Do not remove sexual graffiti quickly
- Do not sanction individuals who engage in sexual harassment
- Do not inform the school community about the sanctions for offenders
- Have been previously an all-male school or have a majority of male students

Paludi and Paludi (2003) suggested that schools, similar to workplaces, should exercise "reasonable care" to ensure a sexual-harassment-free environment and retaliatory-free environment for students (and employees). This "reasonable care," adapted from the Supreme Court ruling in *Faragher v. Boca Raton* (1998) includes the following at a minimum:

- Establish and disseminate an effective antisexual harassment policy
- Establish and disseminate an effective investigatory procedure
- Offer training in sexual harassment in general and in the school's policy and procedures specifically

Roscoe's findings (1994) add support to this triad perspective. He found that following a training program for seventh and eighth graders at a public middle school, reports of sexual harassment increased. In addition, 85% of the girls and 73% of the boys indicated that the training was valuable with respect to understanding definitions, impact, and resolution of sexual harassment.

This perspective supported the "Comprehensive Approach to Eliminating Harassment" identified by the Office for Civil Rights (OCR) of the U.S. Department of Education and the National Association of Attorneys General (NAAG) (1999). According to OCR and NAAG:

While building a strong program often starts with developing and enforcing written policies and procedures, all of a school district's programs and activities should support its anti-harassment efforts. The school's instructional program, calendar of events, extracurricular activities, professional development efforts, and parent involvement are key to establishing an environment in which respect for diversity can flourish. (p. 5)

RECOMMENDATIONS

Policy Statements Prohibiting Sexual Harassment

In order to promote effective and equitable resolution of sexual-harassment complaints, it is necessary to have an explicit policy adopted by the school/campus in compliance with the provision of Title IX for students (and Title VII for employees) that encourages complaints. A policy alone won't solve sexual harassment, but it is the foundation on which to build a strategy of prevention.

According to OCR:

A comprehensive approach for eliminating harassment includes developing and disseminating strong, written policies specifically prohibiting harassment. Polices should take into account the significant legal factors relevant to determining whether unlawful harassment has occurred and should be tailored to the needs of the particular school or school district.

Components of an effective policy statement that have been identified in the sexual-harassment literature (i.e., Gutek, 1997; Levy & Paludi, 2002; Paludi, 2004; Sandler & Shoop, 1997) that accomplishes OCR's recommendations are identified here:

Statement of Purpose

It is helpful to clearly establish the goal of the policy in this statement. It is necessary to make sure that everyone knows the seriousness of sexual harassment and of their responsibility in carrying out this policy.

Legal Definition

Include both quid pro quo and hostile environment forms of sexual harassment; discuss sexual bullying; include state law, if applicable.

Behavioral Examples

Explain and illustrate the concept of "unwelcome." This will assist individuals in differentiating between a socially acceptable, polite compliment and sexual harassment.

Statement Concerning Impact of Sexual Harassment

Summarize the impact on individuals' emotional and physical health and career development.

Statement of Individual's Responsibility in Filing Complaint

Ask individuals to provide information about the incident(s) (i.e., what happened who was present, what was said, done?), how the incident(s) impacted them, and what they want to have the school/campus do to resolve the behavior. Ask teachers and employees to report sexual harassment that they observe, have knowledge about, or is reported to them.

Statement of School's Responsibility in Responding to Complaint

The victim of sexual harassment must be guaranteed effective protection. Close follow-up is needed until the danger of new attempts at sexual harassment has passed. Teachers and school administrators have a special responsibility to safeguard the victim at school. Sexual-harassment victims must be able to trust that the adults are both willing and capable of providing the help that they need. If sexual harassment is taken up in a rushed or casual manner, without ensuring that the victim is given solid protection against further harassment, the situation will almost always become worse. In order to provide the bullied student with sufficient security, close cooperation and frequent exchange of information is usually needed between the school and the student's family. Discuss formal and informal resolution of complaints, including timeframe to complete the process.

Statement Concerning Confidentiality of Complaint Procedures

Statement Concerning Sanctions Available

Statement of Prohibition of Retaliation and Sanctions for Retaliation

Statement Concerning False Complaints

Identification and Background of Individual(s) Responsible for Hearing Complaints, Including Telephone Number, and Office Location

It is recommended that the policy statement be reissued each year by the senior administrator as well as placed prominently throughout the school/campus. In addition, the policy statement should be published in student, faculty, and employee handbooks. The responsibility for communicating the policy statement must be made a part of the job description of anyone with authority in the school/campus. It is also recommended that students sign a sheet that they have been given a copy of the policy and that they understand it, and have been trained on it (see the following discussion).

The names and contact information for Title IX Coordinators and sexual harassment counselors should also be publicized and easy to find on the institution's Web site. In addition, professional staff must be taught to intervene when they observe sexual harassment.

Paludi and Paludi (2003) also provided the following recommendations with respect to effective sexual harassment policy statements:

- Draft the policy in sex neutral terms.
- The policy statement must contain an alternative procedure for complaints if the investigator or supervisor is the alleged harasser.

- Have a woman and man as coinvestigators of sexual harassment complaints.
- Claims of sexual harassment should not be trivialized but treated seriously. All claims must be thoroughly investigated before any action is taken. Should an individual felt hat she/he is in physical danger, changes must be made in the classroom. Suggestions for notifying police must also be provided.
- The policy statement must be available in languages in addition to English.
- The policy statement must be revised when new case law and state law modifications deem it appropriate. Involve students, parents, school staff, teachers, and community members in the development of a sexual harassment policy statement.
- The policy must state how, when and by whom the policy will be monitored, evaluated, and reviewed.
- All those involved in the school/campus must be committed to the policy. Teachers and staff need to understand that their responses to sexual harassment makes a difference. Students cannot do it alone. Schools/campuses must develop an atmosphere of trust within which students can have the courage to report sexual harassment, including bullying, either of themselves of others. If we teach students to report sexual harassment but don't prepare teachers to respond appropriately and effectively, we will be defeating the purpose. Students will quickly learn that they will receive inconsistent or nonresponses and will no longer report sexual harassment.
- The policy must be applied consistently.
- Children's and adolescents' levels of cognitive development must be taken into consideration when developing a policy statement. Most children and adolescents need to be provided with concrete examples, not hypothetical, theoretical situations in order for them to grasp a concept accurately. Thus, the policy must include behavioral examples and language written in terms easily understandable by children and adolescents at various stages of their cognitive development.
- Engage children and adolescents in role playing in their learning about the policy statement, including how to file a complaint of sexual harassment.
- The policy must make clear how families can contact the school with concerns about sexual harassment and how they will be involved in dealing with sexual harassment.

According to OCR (1999):

A district will need to decide whether to adopt one policy covering all types of unlawful harassment or separate polices covering the different bases of harassment. Small districts may find it more practical to develop one policy. (p. 15)

EFFECTIVE INVESTIGATORY PROCEDURES

Results from the AAUW studies as well as other empirical research on individuals' experiences with sexual harassment suggest that procedures for investigating complaints of sexual harassment must take into account the psychological issues involved in the victimization process (Fitzgerald & Omerod, 1993;

Levy & Paludi, 2002). These issues include individuals' feelings of powerlessness, isolation, and changes in their social-network patterns, and their wish to gain control over their personal and career development. Research has indicated that the experience of participating in an investigative process can be as emotionally and physically stressful as the sexual harassment itself (Levy & Paludi, 2002; Paludi & Barickman, 1998). Therefore, it is important not only to build in several support systems but also to help complainants and alleged perpetrators cope with the process of the complaint procedure. Counselors may work with the investigator for this purpose. Supportive techniques for working with complainants may be found in Paludi and Paludi (2003).

While each school district and college typically establishes its own complaint procedure that fits with its unique needs, OCR and NAAG (1999) has identified several guidelines that apply to investigations of sexual harassment. According to OCR and NAAG:

The lack of a strong, immediate response by a teacher or administrator who is aware of the harassment may be perceived by a student as approval of the activity or as an indication that the student deserves the harassment. (p. 25)

These guidelines include:

- Informing the school that there is an obligation to make the environment free of sexual harassment and free of the fear of being retaliated against for filing a complaint of sexual harassment.
- Informing individuals that the school will not ignore any complaint of sexual harassment.
- Informing the school that investigations of sexual harassment complaints will be completed promptly.

Additional guidelines may be found in Paludi and Paludi (2003), Dziech, 2003, Strauss (2003), and Sandler and Stonehill (2005).

In addition to these guidelines, OCR and NAAG (1999, p. 32) offered several "practical considerations" for establishing effective grievance procedures, including:

- How many levels will the procedure have, and what will be the time frame for each level.
- Who may file complaints on behalf of the injured party
- Whether investigations should be conducted by building administrators, other building staff, or district-level officials.
- Whether an evidentiary hearing should be part of the process.
- Whether district-level administrators should review the investigator's decision in all instances or only when the decision is appealed.

TRAINING PROGRAMS

Schools and campuses are required to take reasonable steps to prevent and end the sexual harassment of its students as well as its faculty, administrators, and employees. They must facilitate training programs on sexual-harassment awareness. Training programs involve more than a recitation of individuals' rights and responsibilities and the requirements of the law and school/campus policy. Training also requires dealing with individuals' assumptions and misconceptions about power as well as the anxieties about the training itself (Levy & Paludi, 2002). Stereotypes about females, males, sex, and power often remain unchallenged unless individuals participate in effective trainer-guided intervention programs.

In addition, training programs on sexual harassment must provide all individuals with a clear understanding of their rights and responsibilities with respect to sexual harassment. Training must also enable individuals to distinguish between behavior that is sexual harassment and not sexual harassment; bullying and nonbullying behaviors. Training programs also provide individuals with information concerning the policy statement against sexual harassment and investigatory procedures set up by the school. Finally, the goal of training programs should be to help empower individuals to use their school's procedures for resolving complaints.

Relatively little empirical research exists on the impact of training programs on individuals' attitudes and behavior with respect to sexual harassment (Martin, 2005). The available research has indicated the following:

- Training increases tendency to perceive sexual harassment (i.e., Moyer & Nath, 1998; Blakely, Blakely, & Moorman, 1998)
- Training increases knowledge acquisition and reduces the inappropriate behavior of men who have a high propensity to sexually harass (i.e., Perry, Kulik, & Schmidtke, 1998)
- College students are more sensitive to incidents of sexual harassment when case analyses are used (i.e., York, Barclay, & Zajack, 1997)
- Training assists sexual harassment contact persons with listening and helping skills, and confidence (i.e., Blaxall, Parsonson, & Robertson, 1993)
- Training on sexual harassment, including legal aspects, increases knowledge and changes attitudes (i.e., Maruizio & Rogers, 1992; Roscoe, 1994)
- Training increases reporting of sexual harassment (i.e., Roscoe, 1994)

For additional suggestions on implementing "reasonable care" with middle-school students, refer to Sandler and Stonehill (2005), who offer strategies for dealing with peer-to-peer sexual harassment.

ADDITIONAL EDUCATIONAL PROGRAMS

To supplement the training programs in sexual-harassment awareness, there are additional educational programs that have been recommended in the literature. Title IX Compliance coordinators can play a prominent role in promoting "reasonable care" in their school districts by enforcing these educational interventions (AAUW, 2004; Paludi, 1997; Paludi & Barickman, 1998):

- Include information on sexual harassment in new student/employee orientation materials.

- Facilitate a "sexual-harassment awareness week" and schedule programs that include lectures, guided video discussions, and plays.
- Report annually on sexual harassment.
- Encourage teachers to incorporate discussions of sexual harassment in their classrooms.
- Encourage students to start an organization with the purpose of preventing sexual harassment.
- Provide educational sessions for parents about sexual harassment and the school district's policy and procedures.

Paludi and Paludi (2003) recommended conducting a needs assessment with the administrative staff of the school to identify additional issues they expect to be covered in the training session. Additional recommendations for education and training may be found in Strauss (2003).

An essential resource is Sjostrom and Stein's (1996)'s "Bully-proof: A Teacher's Guide on Teasing and Bullying for Use with Fourth- and Fifth-Grade Students," which contains experiential exercises to assist students understand the difference between teasing and bullying.

Interventions created to combat bullying and sexual harassment should involve students in making policies intended to alter the school climate with regard to these forms of victimization in order to promote positive interaction between students; this will serve to promote inclusion and empowerment for students (Arora, 1994; Paludi, 2004; Roffey, 2000). Interventions should also send a clear message that bullying and sexual harassment will not be tolerated. Teachers, administrators, parents, and all school staff should be included as well as students. It is only when the entire school community is included that successful change can occur (Olweus, 1993).

REMEDIES THROUGH THE OFFICE FOR CIVIL RIGHTS

The Office for Civil Rights (OCR) enforces Title IX of the 1972 Education Amendments. When their investigations indicate a violation of Title IX has occurred, OCR gives the school district/ campus a chance to voluntarily correct the problem. If the school refuses to correct the situation, OCR initiates enforcement action.

According to Herskowitz and Kallem (2003), remedies sought by OCR for harassment include,

- Corrective and preventive actions to stop the harassment and minimize the chance of its recurrence. This can include counseling and/or discipline of the harasser and age-appropriate training for students and staff on how to recognize harassment and what to do if they are harassed or observe harassment.
- Psychological or other counseling.
- Compensatory education to make up for any time lost from the educational program as a result of the harassment.
- Adjustment of any grades affected by the harassment and/or the opportunity to repeat a course (without additional cost at the postsecondary level).

- Where the complainant was forced to leave the academic program due to the harassment, reimbursement for any costs that occurred as a result and/or an opportunity to reenroll. An example would be tuition reimbursement for a public high-school student who was forced to leave the high school because of the harassment and enroll in a private school. Another example would be an opportunity for a student who was forced by the harassment to drop out of college to reenroll. (p. 207)

Herskowitz and Kallem (2003) have indicated that OCR has resolved hundreds of complaints of sexual harassment of students. These resolutions have resulted in individual relief for the students involved, as well as benefited countless other students by bringing about changes in the policies and procedures of school districts, colleges, and universities that have helped to ensure a safe and nondiscriminatory learning environment. A number of OCR decisions have been cited in Title IX court cases, and have thus helped to shape the law as it has developed (p. 208).

CONCLUSION

The focus of much, if not all, of the research on bullying is on identifying pathology in an individual. Once this person is removed from the school or campus or disciplined, all individuals will be safe. The goal in dealing with sexual harassment is to pursue an institutional level of analysis to explain the prevalence of sexual harassment and to recognize the context within which sexual harassment is more likely to occur. At the same time, it is certainly important to pay attention to individuals who have been perpetrators or recipients of sexual harassment, as Stein (1996) has argued: "If school authorities do not intervene and sanction students who sexually harass, the schools may be encouraging a continued pattern of violence in relationships: Schools may be training grounds for the insidious cycle of domestic violence" (p. 22).

Responses from students in the 2001 AAUW study (p. 17), when asked, "What could your school do to address sexual harassment," included,

- Maybe if they had an assembly about sexual harassment and expulsion for those who violate rules.
- I'd just like them to, if the matter comes up, deal with it swiftly and fairly, taking in all considerations.
- Make aware what exactly it is and what to do about it if you are offended.
- Seminars, a definite policy in the handbook.
- Have the same no-tolerance policy as knives or guns and make an example of anyone who does commit sexual harassment, so maybe it will stop others.

According to Stein (2005), "despite longstanding efforts toward gender equity and the current intense focus on school safety, the simple right of boys and girls to an equitable and safe school environment—the right to be free from the need to negotiate inequity or violence as part of their school day—has yet to be secured."

The students' responses from the AAUW study suggest the next step in dealing with sexual harassment: to value students and to empower them so they do indeed achieve and experience educational equity, and the powerful silence surrounding sexual harassment is broken, making it no longer part of an evaded curriculum.

As Hill and Silva (2005) concluded:

Sexual harassment defies a simple solution but demands action. It is unlikely to go away on its own. Talking candidly about the problem—seeking commonalities but acknowledging the inevitable conflicts—is a necessary step toward creating a harassment-free climate in which all students can reach their full potential. (p. 39)

ACKNOWLEDGMENTS

Bernice Sandler, Women's Research and Education Institute, Washington, DC, and Harriett Stonehill, University of the District of Columbia, Washington, DC, served as reviewers for this chapter. Liesl Nydegger assisted in obtaining research articles to use for this chapter

Suggested Readings and Web Sites

Dziech, B., & Hawkins M. (1998). *Sexual harassment in higher education*. New York: Garland Press.

Espelage, D., & Swearer, S. (2003). Research on school bullying and victimization: What have we learned and where do we go from here? *School Psychology Review, 32*, 365–383.

Paludi, M., & Paludi, C. (Eds.), (2003). *Academic and workplace sexual harassment: A handbook of cultural, social science, management, and legal perspectives*. Westport, CT: Praeger.

Sandler, B., & Stonehill, H. (2005). *Student-to-student sexual harassment in K12: Strategies and solutions for educations to use in the classroom, school, and community*. Lanham, MD: Rowman & Littlefield Education.

Stein, N. (1995). Sexual harassment in school: The public performance of gendered violence. *Harvard Educational Review, 65*, 145–162.

Stein, N. (1999). Bullying or sexual harassment? The missing discourse of rights in an era of zero tolerance. *University of Arizona Law Review, 45*, 783–799. Feminist Majority Foundation: http://www.feminist.org/education/title ix.asp

References

Adams, J., Kotke, J., & Padgitt, J. (1983). Sexual harassment of university students. *Journal of College Student Personnel, 24*, 484–490.

Ageton, S. (1983). *Sexual assault among adolescents*. Lexington, MA: Lexington.

American Association of University Women Educational Foundation. (1992). *The AAUW Report: How schools shortchange girls*. Washington, DC: Author.

American Association of University Women Educational Foundation. (1993). *Hostile hallways: The annual survey on sexual harassment in America's schools*. Washington, DC: Author.

American Association of University Women Educational Foundation. (2001). *Hostile hallways: Bullying, teasing, and sexual harassment in school*. Washington DC: Author.

American Association of University Women. (2004). *Harassment-free hallways: How to stop sexual harassment in schools*. Washington, DC: Author.

Arora, T. (1994). Is there any point in trying to reduce bullying in secondary schools? A two year follow-up of a whole-school anti-bullying policy in one school. *Association of Educational Psychologists Journal, 10*, 155–162.

Bailey, N., & Richards, M. (1985, August). Tarnishing the ivory tower: Sexual harassment in graduate training programs in psychology. Paper presented at the American Psychological Association, Los Angeles, CA.

Barak, A. (1997). Cross-cultural perspectives on sexual harassment: In W. O'Donohue (Ed.), *Sexual harassment: Theory, research, and treatmen, 263*–300. Needham Heights, MA: Allyn & Bacon.

Barickman, R., Paludi, M., & Rabinowitz, V. (1992). Sexual harassment of students: Victims of the college experience. In E. Viano (Ed.), *Victimization: An International perspective*, 153–165. New York: Springer.

Blakely, G., Blakely, E., & Moorman, R. (1998). The effects of training on perceptions of sexual harassment allegations. *Journal of Applied Social Psychology, 28*, 71–83.

Blaxall, M., Parsonson, B., & Robertson, N. (1993). The development and evaluation of a sexual harassment contact person training package. *Behavior Modification, 17*, 148–163.

Bogart, K., Simmons, S., Stein, N., & Tomaszewski, E. (1992). Breaking the silence: Sexual and gender-based harassment in elementary, secondary, and postsecondary education. In S. Klein (Ed.), *Sex equity and sexuality in education*, 191–221. Albany, NY: State University of New York Press.

Bond, M. (1988). Division 27 sexual-harassment survey: Definition, impact, and environmental context. *The Community Psychologist, 21*, 2–10.

Brooks, L., & Perot, A. (1991). Reporting sexual harassment: Exploring a predictive model. *Psychology of Women Quarterly, 15*, 31–47.

Buchanan, N. (2005, August). *Incorporating race and gender in sexual harassment research: The racialized sexual harassment scale*. Paper presented at the Conference of the International Coalition Against Sexual Harassment, Philadelphia.

Chan, D., Tang, C., & Chan, W. (1999). Sexual harassment: A preliminary analysis of its effects on Hong Kong Chinese women in the workplace and academia. *Psychology of Women Quarterly, 23*, 661–672.

Craig, W., Pepler, D., Connoly, J., & Henderson, K. (2001). Developmental context of peer harassment in early adolescence: The role of puberty and the peer group. In J. Juvonen & S. Graham (Eds.), *Peer harassment in school: The plight of the vulnerable and victimized*. New York: Guilford Press.

Dansky, B., & Kilpatrick, D. (1997). Effects of sexual harassment. In W. O'Donohue (Ed.), *Sexual harassment: Theory, research, and practice,* 152–174. Boston: Allyn & Bacon.

DeFour, D. C. (1996). Racism and sexual harassment. In M. Paludi (Ed)., *Sexual harassment on college campuses: Abusing the ivory power,* 49–55. Albany, NY: State University of New York Press.

DeFour, D. C., David, G., Diaz, F., & Thompkins, S. (2003). The interface of race, sex, sexual orientation and ethnicity in understanding sexual harassment. In M. Paludi & C. Paludi (Eds.), *Academic and workplace sexual harassment: A handbook of cultural, social science, management, and legal perspectives,* 31–45. Westport, CT: Praeger.

DeSouza, E. (2004, July). *Intercultural and intracultural comparisons of bullying and sexual harassment in secondary schools.* Paper presented at the Association for Gender Equity Leadership in Education, Washington, DC.

DeSouza, E. (2005, August). *Issues related to same-sex harassment in the United States and the world.* Paper presented at the Conference of the International Coalition Against Sexual Harassment, Philadelphia.

DeSouza, E., & Solberg, J. (2003). Incidence and dimensions of sexual harassment across cultures. In M. Paludi & C. Paludi (Eds.), *Academic and workplace sexual harassment: A handbook of cultural, social science, management, and legal perspective,* 3–30. Westport, CT: Praeger.

Dziech, B. (2003). Sexual harassment on college campuses. In M. Paludi & C. Paludi (Eds.), *Academic and workplace sexual harassment: A handbook of cultural, social science, management, and legal perspectives,* 147–171. Westport, CT: Praeger.

Dziech, B., & Weiner, L. (1984). *The lecherous professor.* Boston: Beacon Press.

Espelage, D. (2003). Assessment and treatment of bullying. In L. VandeCreek (Ed.), *Innovations in clinical practice: Focus on children and adolescents.* Sarasota, FL: Professional Resource Press.

Faragher v. Boca Raton, 524 U.S. 775 (1988).

Fineran, S., & Bennett, L. (1999). Gender and power issues of peer sexual harassment among teenagers. *Journal of Interpersonal Violence, 14*(6), 626–641.

Fineran, S., & Gruber, J. (2004, July). *Research on bullying and sexual harassment in secondary schools: Incidence, interrelationships and psychological implications.* Paper presented at the Association for Gender Equity Leadership in Education, Washington, DC.

Fitzgerald, L, Gold, Y., & Brock, K. (1990). Responses to victimization: Validation of an objective policy. *Journal of College Student Personnel, 27,* 34–39.

Fitzgerald, L., & Omerod, A. (1993). Sexual harassment in academia and the workplace. In F. Denmark & M. Paludi (Eds.), *Psychology of women: A handbook of issues and theories,* 551–581. Westport, CT: Greenwood.

Fitzgerald, L., Shullman, S., Bailey, N., Richards, M., Swecker J., Gold, Y., et al. (1988). The incidence and dimensions of sexual harassment in academia and the workplace. *Journal of Vocational Behavior, 32,* 152–175.

Fitzgerald, L., & Weitzman, L. (1990). Men who harass: Speculation and data. In M. Paludi (Ed.), *Ivory power,* 125–140. Albany, NY: State University of New York Press.

Gardner, J., & Felicity, A. (1996). Sexual and gender harassment at university: Experiences and perceptions of Australian women. *Australian Psychologist, 31,* 210–216.

Giladi, A. (2005, August). *Sexual harassment or play? Perceptions and observations of young children's experiences in kindergarten and early schooling in Israel.* Paper presented at the Conference of the International Coalition Against Sexual Harassment, Philadelphia.

Gruber, J. (1997). An epidemiology of sexual harassment: Evidence from North America and Europe. In W. O'Donohue (Ed.), *Sexual harassment: Theory, research and treatment,* 84–98. Needham Heights, MA: Allyn & Bacon.

Gutek, B. (1997). Sexual harassment policy initiatives. In W. O'Donohue (Ed.), *Sexual harassment: Theory, research, and practice,* 186–198. Boston: Allyn & Bacon.

Herskowitz, E., & Kallem, H. (2003). The role of the Equal Employment Opportunity Commission and Human Rights Commission in dealing with sexual harassment. In M. Paludi & C. Paludi (Ed.), *Academic and workplace sexual harassment: A handbook of cultural, social science, management and legal perspectives,* 200–215. Westport, CT: Praeger.

Hill, C., & Silva, E. (2005). *Drawing the line: Sexual harassment on campus.* Washington, DC: American Association of University Women Educational Foundation.

Houston, S., & Hwang, N. (1996). Correlates of the objective and subjective experiences of sexual harassment in high school. *Sex Roles, 34,* 189–205.

Hughes, J. O., & Sandler, B. R. (1988). *Peer harassment: Hassles for women on campus.* Washington, DC: Project on the Status and Education of Women, Association of American Colleges.

Kenig, S., & Ryan, J. (1986). Sex differences in levels of tolerance and attribution of blame for sexual harassment on a university campus. *Sex Roles, 15,* 535–549.

Levy, A., & Paludi, M. (2002). *Workplace sexual harassment* (2nd ed.). Upper Saddle River, NJ: Prentice Hall.

Lombardo, L., Pedrabissi, L., & Santinello, M. (1996). La diffusione delle molestie sessuali in un contesto lavorativo [The diffusion of sexual harassment in the workplace]. *Bolletino di Psicologi Applicata, 218,* 25–34.

Lott, B. (1993). Sexual harassment: Consequences and realities. *NEA Higher Education Journal, 8,* 89–103.

Lundberg-Love, P., & Faulkner, D. (2005, August). *The emotional sequelae of sexual harassment,* 77–101. Paper presented at the Conference of the International Coalition Against Sexual Harassment, Philadelphia.

Lundberg-Love, P., & Marmion, S. (2003). Sexual harassment in the private sector. In M. Paludi & C. Paludi (Ed.), *Academic and workplace sexual harassment: A handbook of cultural, social science, management and legal perspectives.* Westport, CT: Praeger.

MacKinnon, C. (1979). *Sexual harassment of working women: A case of sex discrimination.* New Haven, CT: Yale University Press.

Manning, A. (1993, March 24). School girls sexually harassed. *USA Today,* p. 1D.

Martin, J. (2005, April). *Peer sexual harassment: Finding voice, changing culture.* Paper presented at the American Educational Research Association, Toronto, CN.

Matchen, J., & DeSouza, E. (2000). The sexual harassment of faculty members by students. *Sex Roles, 42,* 295–306.

Maurizio, S., & Rogers, J. (1992). Sexual harassment and attitudes in rural community care workers' health values. *The Journal of Health Behavior, Education and Promotion, 16,* 40–45.

Moyer, R., & Nath, A. (1998). Some effects of brief training interventions on perceptions of sexual harassment. *Journal of Applied Social Psychology, 28,* 333–356.

Murnen, S., & Smolak, L. (2000). The experience of sexual harassment among grade-school students: Early socialization of female subordination? *Sex Roles, 24,* 319–327.

Olewus, D. (1993). *Bullying at school: What we know and what we can do.* Oxford, UK: Blackwell Publishers.

Paludi, M. (Ed.). (1990). *Ivory power.* Albany, NY: State University of New York Press.

Paludi, M. (1997). Sexual harassment in the schools. In W. O'Donohue (Ed.), *Sexual harassment: Theory, research and treatment.* Needham Heights, MA: Allyn & Bacon.

Paludi, M. (2000, August). *Contributions from the discipline of psychology to the understanding and prevention of sexual harassment in education and the workplace.* Part of panel presentation: Sexual harassment: Evolution of an issue, B. Dziech (Chair). Presented at the International Coalition Against Sexual Harassment, Washington, DC.

Paludi, M. (2004, July). *Effective policies and procedures for bullying and sexual harassment.* Paper presented at the Association for Gender Equity Leadership in Education, Washington, DC.

Paludi, M., & Barickman, R. (1998). *Sexual harassment, work, and education: A resource manual for prevention.* Albany, NY: State University of New York Press.

Paludi, M., & Paludi, C. (Eds.), (2003). *Academic and workplace sexual harassment: A handbook of cultural, social science, management and legal perspectives.* Westport, CT: Praeger.

Perry, E., Kulik, C., & Schmidtke, J. (1998). Individual differences in the effectiveness of sexual harassment awareness training. *Journal of Applied Social Psychology, 28,* 698–723.

Phinney, G. (1994). Sexual harassment: A dynamic element in the lives of middle school girls and teachers. *Equity and Excellence in Education, 27,* 5–10.

Project on the Status and Education of Women (1978). *Sexual harassment: A hidden issue.* Washington, DC: Association of American Colleges.

Pryor, J., & Whalen, N. (1997). A typology of sexual harassment: Characteristics of harassers and the social circumstances under which sexual harassment occurs. In W. O'Donohue (Ed.), *Sexual harassment: Theory, research and treatment,* 129–151. Needham Heights, MA: Allyn & Bacon.

Quina, K. (1996). Sexual harassment and rape: A continuum of exploitation. In M. Paludi (Ed.), *Sexual harassment on college campuses: Abusing the ivory power,* 184–197. Albany, NY: State University of New York Press.

Ramos, A. (2000). Sexual harassment at the University of Puerto Rico. *Dissertation Abstracts International, 60,* 5839.

Reilly, M., Lott, B., & Gallogy, S. (1986). *Sexual harassment of university students.* Paper presented to the convention of the Association for Women in Psychology, Oakland, CA.

Roffey S. (2000). Addressing bullying in schools: Organizational factors from policy to practice. *Educational and Child Psychology, 17,* 6–19.

Roscoe, B. (1994). Sexual harassment: An educational program for middle school students. *Elementary school Guidance and Counseling, 29,* 110–120.

Roscoe, B., Strouse, J., & Goodwin, M. (1994). Sexual harassment: Early adolescents' self reports of experiences and acceptance. *Adolescence, 29,* 515–523.

Sandler, B., & Paludi, M. (1993). *Educator's guide to controlling sexual harassment.* Washington, DC: Thompson.

Sandler, B., & Shoop, R. (1997). *Sexual harassment on campus: A guide for administrators, faculty and students.* Boston: Allyn & Bacon.

Sandler, B., & Stonehill, H. (2005). *Student-to-student sexual harassment in K–12: Strategies and solutions for educations to use in the classroom, school, and community.* Lanham, MD: Rowman & Littlefield Education.

Schneider, B. (1987). Graduate women, sexual harassment and university policy. *Journal of Higher Education, 58,* 46–65.

Shakeshaft, C. (2004). *Educator sexual misconduct: A synthesis of existing literature.* Washington, DC: U.S. Department of Education.

Sheffield, C. (1993). The invisible intruder: Women's experiences of obscene phone calls. In P. Bart & E. Moran (Eds.), *Violence against women: The bloody footprints, 73–78.* Newbury Park, CA: Sage.

Sigal, J., Rashid, T., Anjum, A., Goodrich, C., & Gibbs, M. (2001, April). *Cross-cultural and gender differences in response to academic sexual harassment: A comparison of Pakistan and American college students, 73–78.* Paper presented at the meeting of the Eastern Psychological Association, Washington, DC.

Sjostrom, L., & Stein, N. (1996). Bullyproof: *A teacher's guide on teasing and bullying for use with fourth and fifth grade students.* Wellesley, MA: Wellesley College Center for Research on Women.

Stein, N. (1993, August). *Secrets in full view: Sexual harassment in our K–12 schools.* Paper presented at the American Psychological Association, Toronto, CN.

Stein, N. (1995). The public performance of gendered violence. *Harvard Education Review, 65,* 145–162.

Stein, N. (1996). From the margins to the mainstream: Sexual harassment in K–12 schools. *Initiatives, 57*(3), 19–26.

Stein, N. (2003). Bullying or sexual harassment? The missing discourse of rights in an era of zero tolerance. *University of Arizona Law Review, 45*(3), 783–799.

Stein, N. (2004, November). *Gender violence and gender safety in US schools.* Paper presented at the First International Conference on Gender Equity Education in Asia-Pacific Region, Taiwan.

Stein, N. (2005, August). Gender safety in US schools. Paper presented at the Conference of the International Coalition Against Sexual Harassment, Philadelphia.

Stein, N., Marshall, N., & Tropp, L. (1993). *Secrets in public: Sexual harassment in our schools. A report on the results of a Seventeen magazine survey.* Wellesley, MA: Wellesley College Center for Research on Women.

Stockdale, M., Visio, M., & Batra, L. (1999). The sexual harassment of men: Evidence for a broader theory of sexual harassment and sex discrimination. *Psychology, Public Policy and Law, 5,* 630–664.

Strauss, S. (2003). Sexual harassment in K–12. In M. Paludi & C. Paludi (Eds.), *Academic and workplace sexual harassment: A handbook of cultural, social science, management, and legal perspectives.,* 106–145. Westport, CT: Praeger.

Tang, C., Yik, M., Cheung, F., Choi, P., & Au, K. (1995). How do Chinese college students define sexual harassment? *Journal of Interpersonal Violence, 10,* 503–515.

Tang, C., Yik, M., Cheung, F., Choi, P., & Au, K. (1996). Sexual harassment of Chinese college students. *Archives of Sexual Behavior, 25,* 201–215.

Timmerman, G. (2002). A comparison between unwanted sexual behavior by teachers and by peers in secondary schools. *Journal of Youth and Adolescence, 31,* 397–404.

Turner, P. (1995). *Sensitivity to verbally and physically harassing behaviors and incidents in junior high/middle school students.,* (thesis was not published). Master's Thesis, Fort Hays State University.

U.S. Department of Education and National Association of Attorneys General. (1999). *Protecting students from harassment and hate crime.* Washington, DC: Author.

Waldo, C., Berdahl, J., & Fitzgerald, L. (1998). Are men sexually harassed? If so, by whom? *Law and Human Behavior, 22,* 59–79.

World Health Organization. (1998). *Health behavior in school-aged children's survey.* Washington, DC.

York, K., Barclay, L., & Zajack, A. (1997). Preventing sexual harassment: The effect of multiple training methods. *Employee Responsibilities and Rights Journal, 10,* 277–289.

Zalk, S. R. (1990). Men in the academy: A psychological profile of harassment. In M. Paludi (Ed.), *Ivory power,* 141–175. Albany, NY: State University of New York Press.

Part

·IV·

OVERVIEW: GENDER EQUITY STRATEGIES IN THE CONTENT AREAS

Cheris Kramarae

When the 1985 *Handbook* was published, the interest in gender equity in education in the United States was increasing in most content areas, and many of us working in gender studies thought that, with dedicated additional committed and innovative work, we would soon see dramatic, and lasting, changes and choices in education. We *have* seen some improvements, as documented in these chapters. Some of these improvements come from the work of the many people who now agree that hierarchies such as those ascribed to gender, race, and class are damaging and unwarranted in the education system. Yet, to change the effects of long-established power differentials is a large task. In addition, the problems facing society and education continue to change, altering some primary concerns and solutions; thus, the importance of the current assessment that this book constitutes.

The authors in this section of the *Handbook* have done research and extensive literature reviews for their overviews of specific areas of study, providing new energy, information, and recommendations to all who seek more effective gender equity strategies.

As the authors point out, research into the classroom experiences of girls and women continues to reveal curriculum, expectations, and classroom interaction that make clear that girls and women are not as likely as are boys and men to be considered innately bright and deserving of attention, resources, and opportunities. In general, boys and men continue to take up more space in the classroom and in the curriculum, while girls' and women's preferences, interests, and achievements are often ignored or devalued. Studies of hiring practices and promotions document the skewed, damaging treatments that many female teachers, as well as students, receive. One of the contributions of this *Handbook* is a comparison of the conditions and issues of gender equity in disciplines in 1985 and now, an assessment critical for any plans for sustained educational reforms.

Another major contribution has been the knowledge authors have gained from the debates, leading them to rethink gender equity problems and policies. New research and perspectives can better inform us about the causes, impact, and resolutions of gender equity in each content area. For example, while in the 1980s and 1990s much of the focus in education settings was on obtaining equal educational opportunities and resources, we now see more clearly that attempts to integrate and treat women and men equally do not achieve the restructuring necessary for gender equity. "Gender-blindness" is not a prime virtue or goal in the education setting today.

While most of the following chapters include information on the theories of researchers and policy analysts in the content areas, the foci are primarily on assessment and needs of students, faculty, and administrators, and on recommendations for change. Addressed here are the benefits of increased gender equity for students, the development of each field of study, and the health of institutions and the nation. Given that education is based in community, national, and global networks of beliefs and practices, the cultural norms of masculinity and femininity that place women at a disadvantage in schools, homes, and workplaces have, of course, deep, interconnected roots. Many of the authors place the individual disciplines in (a) their context (within their institutions), (b) their national political and economic settings, and (c) changing global circumstances.

Another important contribution of the chapters is the gathering in one section the work from several subjects and fields of study. Even such interdisciplinary fields as gender studies, second-language acquisition, and communication tend to be self-referential. Reading across the chapters provides valuable links and comparisons. While there are many differences in what has happened to gender equity in fields such as, say, arts, dance, and mathematics, we can see some critical similarities.

THEMES ACROSS THE CHAPTERS IN THIS SECTION

These chapters indicate that, in reference to research of gender equity in many fields of study, we have learned the following:

- Gender is not primarily a matter of sameness or difference; gender is a social hierarchy that many use as an excuse for disparities in treatment and judgments. Therefore, correcting the effects of this hierarchy for girls and boys, and women and men, in education settings requires not so much the pinpointing of sameness and differences but, primarily, the (a) highlighting of the types of inequalities, (b) search for remedies, and (c) determination to achieve equity. Yet much research in the content areas is still rooted in the paradigm of sex-based differences. (See, for example, the discussion in Gender Equity in Social Studies.)

- Equity is often confused with equality, which deals with equal access to resources, a necessary but not sufficient condition for equity. Advocates for equity point out that what is considered equal (a) does not necessarily remove barriers to access for girls and women, (b) does not address imbalanced treatment once they are provided access, (c) does not acknowledge diversity in each category (female/male), and (d) does not establish a way of restructuring the existing education culture. Equity involves questions about gender, race, class, and sexual orientation within a system of education, including hiring practices, policies, language, curricula, and everyday practices. The action recommendations included in each chapter provide help with ways in which the needed restructuring can be assisted.

- The sex/gender system is not binary. Race, ethnicity, class, age, sexual orientation, and disabilities are other ways that women and men have been grouped. When research findings that disaggregate sex, race, and ethnic differences in education are available or can be deciphered, the authors of the following chapters have tried to include that information. Concern in these chapters about oppression, missed opportunities, and disenfranchisement, and about suggestions for change is not intended to work toward a loss for some students and teachers in order to benefit others, but toward the benefit of all. As the authors of several of the chapters in this part attest, the students' learning practices are affected by a variety of factors ranging from their learning preferences, interests, sex, age, and childhood culture.

- "Letting in" more girls and women to courses designed primarily by and for males quite clearly will not solve equity problems, or change the basic structures that have put the inequities into effect. The education curriculum and culture need to be changed in fundamental ways. For example, in engineering and science fields, this may mean (a) providing innovative summer programs for high school girls, (b) designing courses to even up experience gaps, (c) hiring more women faculty at the university level and more men at the grade school level, and (d) providing explicit training in effective classroom discussions that respect the contributions of students with differing experiences. (See "Gender Equity in Science, Engineering, and Technology.")

- In the fields where girls and women tend to receive better scores and grades, such as literacy and modern languages, their academic success does not necessarily correspond to their workforce participation, managerial positions, or salaries. The relative underachievement in these areas by boys and men does not seem to translate into inferior jobs and salaries, nor does it seem to diminish their self-confidence. Boys tend to explain their underachievement through external factors such as inadequacy of their teachers or the format of the exam, or through a perception of reading as feminine and, thus, an activity to be avoided. (See "Gender Equity in Communication Skills," and "Gender Equity in Foreign and Second Language Learning and Instruction.").

- Yet, boys' "underachievement" in communication skills (at least, according to test scores) should be a concern, since any construction of areas of learning and expression as sex-linked can lead to educational restrictions for both boys and girls. The chapters in this section investigate explanations for sex differences on test scores and grades, including a review of arguments that these are caused by biological differences. The fact that girls, once considered less skilled at learning math and science, are now doing equally well at in elementary classes seems to demonstrate how social factors have played a very important part in gender and achievement scores. (See, especially, "Gender Equity in Mathematics.")

- Equal opportunity initiatives to help correct the dominant cultural expectations and inequalities in the content areas are often small-scale, sporadic, and under-funded, even for relatively well-funded areas such as science, engineering, and technology. The authors in this section document inequalities and make many recommendations for sustained changes to raise the achievement of females and males in these highlighted disciplines. As these chapters illustrate, the disruption of conventional gender discourses and assumptions can stimulate the skills and opportunities of both females and males. Equity policies need to have built-in reviews and accountability. Each chapter provides recommendations.

- People need professional development and opportunities throughout their lives and careers. Welfare cutbacks that restrict recipients' participation in education systems make special difficulties for single parents on low incomes. The education systems of the nation must (a) attend to the needs of individuals with varying levels of work experience and education, (b) end cycles of poverty, and (c) meet the demands of the local and global job market. (See "Gender Equity in Career and Technical Education.") More research is needed on the needs of those with barriers to educational achievement, and on the effectiveness of new technologies that can be used for new methods of instruction and learning.

- Our challenge as administrators and teachers, whatever the discipline, is to create girl- and woman-friendly—indeed, student-friendly—classrooms. This includes raising awareness of the impact of gender on classroom dynamics, for example, not ignoring students' sexist and homophobic remarks made in class, but, rather, consider them as teaching moments. A variety of lesbian, gay, bisexual, and transsexual (LGBT) issues are present on every level of education, from the harassing of LGBT teachers and students, to anti- LGBT-themed classroom materials (Blount, 2006). The chapters in this section provide many specific examples of classroom interaction problems, and some possible actions to deal with them. "The Role of Women's and Gender Studies in Advancing Gender Equity" chapter on the women's and gender studies documents how Gay and Lesbian Studies scholars, especially, are examining the ways heterosexual privilege works alongside other forms of privilege and oppression in the formal education system. (Also, see "Gender Equity for Lesbian, Gay, Bisexual, and Transgendered Students" chapter in Part V.)

• Where discussions of gender and of sexuality are involved, the media often have a large impact on what is considered acceptable academic practices and research. See, for example, the discussion, in "Gender Equity in Physical Education and Athletics," of the critical impact that the media has had on problems of inequity in those fields. Dominant public discussions about sexuality have led to political battles about sexuality classes in the schools that have had detrimental impact on what information is available to students. (See "Gender Equity in Formal Sexuality Education.")

• While each discipline has its own approaches to research design, data collection, and methods of data analysis, the mixed research methods, and the analyses of different types of related evidence in the syntheses reported in these chapters, help provide more complete information than is often available in other reference works.

FIELDS OF STUDY INCLUDED IN THIS SECTION OF THE HANDBOOK

Since the 1985 edition of the *Handbook* was published, there has been a great deal of additional research on gender equity in education. Yet, while there have been many impressive, discrete projects—many of them reported here—the chapters in this current volume make clear that gender equity research has not yet been well integrated into the K–12 and postsecondary education plans. For just one example, while the authors of many of the chapters in this section and in other sections describe Title IX, and while many educators and authors of textbooks acknowledge the existence of Title IX, its breadth is seldom acknowledged and utilized by educators. The law applies not only to physical education and athletics, but also to educational programs, course offerings and access, financial aid, scholarships, and sexual harassment problems, as well as many other aspects of the public education system.

These chapters also make clear that the discussion of the costs (economic, developmental, and psychological) of discriminatory gender assumptions and treatment is not yet firmly built into policies and practices regarding teacher recruitment, administration development, textbook writing, curriculum planning, classroom interaction, and testing.

The chapters in this part on curriculum content should provide a great deal of assistance for those working on the goal of gender equity. For comparison purposes, the organization and topics of this part of the *Handbook* are related to those of the 1985 *Handbook*, with a few changes. While coverage of relevant

research is greatly expanded in this volume, not all the chapters deal with all levels of education or all related topics. For example, if the social studies chapter had also been able to deal with social sciences in postsecondary education, we might have more insights about the gender equity issues in the entire field. If the formal sexuality education chapter had also covered health education, we might have touched on more sexuality issues related to body image, mental health, and violence. What all the chapters all do accomplish, however, is to provide a great deal of information about gender equity and inequity in each content area, along with strategies to counter the gender bias still so prevalent.

Other important fields of study are not dealt with explicitly in these chapters. Here, I mention just a few examples of the many that could have been included had space allowed.

Nursing, home management, and nutrition.   For more than 150 years, women have worked to have the productive and educational value of these fields recognized by school systems and governments. Within grade schools, high schools, and universities, work associated with family and caring for others has been assumed all too often by many administrators to be primarily women's fields and, thus, in no need for gender equity assessments.

Urban planning and geography.   The work of feminists who have studied issues of housing, public policy, and economic development—including the roles of women in the study of transportation, domestic architecture, urban segregation, housing, daycare, and land use—has provided graphic illustrations of the ways in which women used to be almost invisible to planners and urban planning teachers. Seeing city planning research through gender lenses can lead to rethinking the basic methodology and questions used in the field (Fainstein & Servon, 2005), illustrating how the history of women and minorities can be restored to the urban landscape and to the urban planning and geography disciplines on all education levels. Community safety, public transport, and location of childcare facilities and shops all have (differing) implications for educational opportunities for women and men. Women in particular are identifying these issues. Yet Kathryn Anthony's (2001) study of architecture reports gender and racial discrimination still runs rampant in the architectural education system and practice.

Sociology.   For the past three decades, feminist sociologists and other social-mobility researchers have documented the dramatic changes in household and family structures and in women's economic roles, and the increases in the percentage of family households with low incomes during that time. The changes in family structure, women's economic roles, and income inequality are closely connected to inequality among U.S. children in their educational attainment and employment (Sorensen, 2005, pp. 119, 123).

With much more space, we would want to include equity assessments and recommendations in many other fields, including other medical fields, peace studies, ethnic studies, literary studies, religious studies, cultural studies, anthropology, philosophy, political science, history, law, library science, linguistics, music, and psychology. Adrienne Rich wrote in the early 1970s, "There is no discipline that does not obscure and devalue the history and experience of women as a group" (Rich, 1980, pp. 134–135). We need to keep testing her assessment, and working toward making it only an historical statement about our education system.

As the chapters in this section and the rest of the *Handbook* make clear, each of us in her or his field of study and education level is responsible, every day, for the formulation of gender equity policies and practices. Many of us might claim that we try to never differentiate on the basis of sex; however, even our attempts at "equal treatment" often impose discrimination and do not eliminate gender gaps; claims of "gender-blindness" can result in the continual marginalization of girls' and women's interests. These chapters help us understand that gender discrimination needs to be *addressed* in order for gender equity to be achieved.

References

Anthony, K. (2001). *Designing for diversity, Gender, race and ethnicity in the architectural profession*. Urbana, IL: University of Illinois Press.

Blount, J. (2006). LGBT school workers. In Cobb-Roberts, D., Dorn, S., & Shircliffe, B. J. (Eds.) *Schools as imagined communities: The creation of identity, meaning, and conflict in U.S. history* (pp. 109–124), New York: Palgrave Macmillan..

Fainstein, S. S., & Servon, L. J. (2005). *Gender and planning: A reader*. New Brunswick, N.J.: Rutgers University Press.

Rich, A. (1979). *On lies, secrets and silence: Selected prose 1966–1978*. New York: Norton.

Sorensen, A. (2005). Family structure, gender roles, and social inequality. In Svallfors, S. (Ed.) *Analyzing inequality: Life chances and social mobility in comparative perspective* (pp. 108–128). Stanford, CA: Stanford University Press.

·12·

GENDER EQUITY IN MATHEMATICS

Carole B. Lacampagne,* Patricia B. Campbell, Abbe H. Herzig, Suzanne Damarin and Christina M. Vogt

THE STATUS OF SEX EQUITY IN MATHEMATICS

In 1985 the authors of the chapter on this topic for the original *Handbook for Achieving Sex Equity through Education* concluded that data on the patterns of sex differences in mathematics participation and achievement were "inconsistent" (Stage, Kreinberg, Eccles, & Becker, 1985). In many ways, their conclusion still holds.

Course-Taking

The earlier *Handbook* reported parity in selection of mathematics courses in high school, except at the highest level of calculus. This pattern continues, although the number of mathematics courses high school graduates take has increased considerably to an average of 3.7 courses (Perkins, Kleiner, Roey, & Brown, 2004). Among high school graduates, girls were slightly more apt than boys to have taken geometry (77% vs. 74%) and algebra II (64% vs. 60%), and equally apt to have taken precalculus (23% each) and calculus (11% each; Huang, Taddese, & Walter, 2000). The primary difference in course-taking was in advanced placement calculus, where in 2002, 48% of those taking the first level advanced placement Calculus AB exam were girls, while girls represented only 39% of those taking the higher-level Calculus BC exam (College Board, 2003).

The more things change, the more they remain the same. The pattern of few differences in mathematics course-taking held for students taking SAT I. In 2005, on average, female and male students taking the SAT, took the same number of mathematics courses (3.8) and received approximately the same grades (3.11). Although 53% of the stu-

dents taking the SAT I were female, proportionately fewer students taking more than four years of high school mathematics were female (51%; College Board, 2005).

Other than SAT scores themselves, SAT data are not broken out by race and sex annually. In 2001, Coley did do such a breakdown for 1999 SAT data. He found few sex differences in the numbers of students taking four years of mathematics courses for White, African American, and Asian American students, although Hispanic boys were more apt than Hispanic girls to do so. Overall Asian American and White students were more apt than African American and Hispanic students to take at least four years of high school mathematics.

Achievement[1]

The National Assessment of Educational Progress (NAEP)

Twenty years ago, the original *Handbook for Achieving Sex Equity through Education* authors reported that the National Assessment of Educational Progress (NAEP) continued to find sex-related differences in mathematics achievement that increased from age 9 to age 13 to age 17 favoring boys, although other researchers were not finding sex-related differences in achievement in areas in which they were previously found (Stage et al., 1985). Between the 1990 and the 2005 NAEP mathematics tests, impressive gains and small sex differences in mathematics scores for 4th and 8th graders can be seen. Fourth grade mean scores increased by 25 points, from 213 to 238, with sex differences remaining between one and three points and favoring boys. For the eighth graders, the mean scores increased 16 points, from 263 to 279, again with small sex differences, one to four points, favoring boys (National Assessment of Educational Progress [NAEP], 2005).

---

*The bold face names are the Lead Authors.

[1]While it is beyond the scope of this paper to report results by state, sex differences in student mathematics achievement are now reported by school in states' on-line school report cards. See Campbell and Perlman (2005) for information on how to access these data.

During the same period, the percentage of fourth-grade boys scoring at or above the proficiency level almost tripled to 38%, while the percentage of girls at that level increased from 12% to 34%. Sex differences also increased from 1 to 4%. The percent of eighth-grade boys scoring at or above proficient almost doubled to 31% while the percentage of girls did double to 28%. Sex differences, favoring boys, remained constant.

The pattern was quite different for 12th graders where, between 1990 and 2000,[2] boys' mean scores remained the same and girls' mean scores actually decreased. Over that same period, the percentage of 12th-grade boys at proficient or above increased from 15% to 20%, while the percentage of girls increased from 9% to 14%. The 12th-grade gender gap remained at 5% (NAEP, 2001; Clewell & Campbell, 2002).

The above data were for girls and boys across race/ethnicity. In 2005, NAEP reported fourth- and eighth-grade scores by sex and by race/ethnicity.[3] As shown in the following graph, sex differences between eighth graders from different ethnic groups are very small; however, achievement differences by race/ethnicity are very large. Results are similar for fourth graders.

ACT/SAT

NAEP data are collected over national samples, while the ACT and Scholastic Achievement Tests (SAT)[4] samples only include those who are considering going to college. Similar to the NAEP data, over the past 20 years, there have been increases in both girls' and boys' scores on the ACT, while small sex differences remain, in mathematics. Sex differences in the ACT composite score were minimal (boys, 21; girls, 20.9) while sex differences were small in mathematics scores. In 2004, boys scored 1.1 points on average higher than girls (boys, 21.3; girls, 20.2), a difference of .22 of a standard deviation (ACT Inc., 2004b).

Sex differences in the other national test to predict college success, the SAT, were much larger. In 2005, boys' average SAT I scores were 1051, while girls' scores were 1009. Thirty-four of the 42-point difference was due to sex differences in the SAT I: Mathematics. Among girls, mean SAT I: Mathematics scores ranged from a high of 566 for Asian American girls to a low of 424 for African American girls. With the exception of African Americans, for whom the sex difference favoring boys was 18 points, across different racial and ethnic groups, the size of the sex difference is at least 29 points (College Board, 2005).

Variability

To provide a more complete picture of sex and mathematics achievement, it is necessary to look at the variability of scores as

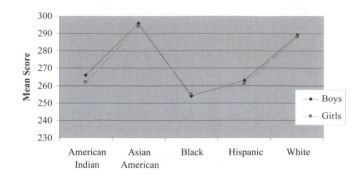

FIGURE 12.1. NAEP 2005 8th Grade Math Achievement.

well as at mean scores. There has been some indication that there is greater variability in boys' scores than in girls' (e.g., Bielinski & Davison, 1998); however, Willingham, Cole, Lewis, and Leung (1997) found little difference in the variability of scores on cognitive tests, including mathematics tests that were given in the earlier grades. By grade 12, they found very small sex differences in the variability of mathematics test scores over national samples. For every five boys in the top 10% of scores, there were more than four girls. For students in the bottom 10%, there were also more than four girls for every five boys[5] (Willingham, Cole, Lewis, & Leung, 1997; Clewell & Campbell, 2002). For White students taking the SAT, the SAT I: Mathematics standard deviation for girls was 98, while for boys it was 103 (College Board, 2005), while the standard deviation for the ACT Mathematics scores for girls was 4.8 and for boys was 5.3 (ACT Inc., 2004b).

Figure 12.2, based on 2004 ACT scores, indicates sex differences at the extreme ends of the distributions. Indeed, three times as many boys as girls scored at the highest ACT Mathematics level (3% vs. 1%) (ACT Inc., 2004b) a proportion similar to the number of boys vs. girls scoring 800 in the SAT Mathematics (College Board, 2004a). Yet even here, with the select sample of students choosing to take the ACT, there is a great overlap between girls' and boys' scores.

Careers

With few exceptions, sex differences in achievement and course-taking are minimal, yet sex differences in mathematics-related careers and in career aspirations are not. Among students taking the SAT in 2005, 5% of boys and 1% of girls were planning to major in computer science, and 10% of boys and 2% of girls were planning to major in engineering. Percentages were much

---

[2]Trend data for 12th graders were only available through 2000.

[3]We applaud this policy change, which now allows for the important examination of sex similarities and differences across different races/ethnicities.

[4]The purpose of the ACT and the SAT is to predict success in college. Overall weighted averages have found the SAT: Mathematics correlates .41 with undergraduate grade point average while high school grades correlate .42. The weighted average correlation for the combination of SAT: Mathematics, SAT: Verbal, and high-school grades with undergraduate GPA is .52 (Burton & Ramist, 2001).

[5]This assumes that the distributions are normal, an appropriate assumption with large sample sizes. If distributions are not normal, the imbalance could be smaller or larger.

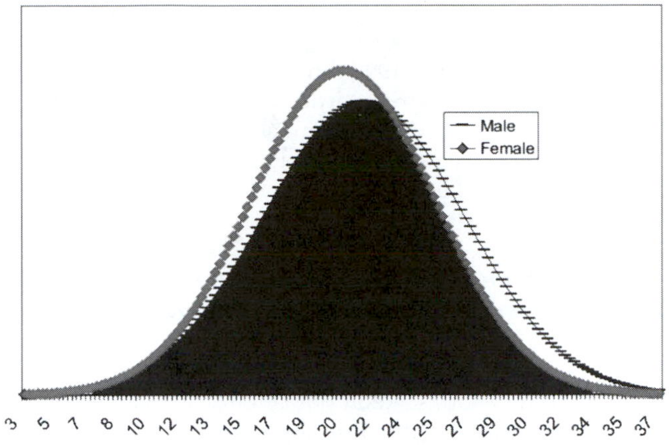

FIGURE 12.2. Female and Male ACT: Math Scores for 2004.

closer in mathematics but overall less than 1% of students were planning to major in mathematics (College Board, 2005).

In summary,

- Girls' and boys' mathematics achievement levels are increasing although small differences favoring boys still remain on standardized test scores and SAT I: Mathematics scores. The largest gender differences are among the small percent of students at very advanced levels.
- Girls are now taking the upper level mathematics in about the same numbers of boys. This increase in course taking, however, has not led to the expected increases in mathematics-related careers.
- While sex differences in mathematics achievement and course taking are small within and across such different races/ethnicities, race/ethnic group differences are large. One must look at sex and race/ethnicity in the design and implementation of policies and programs to increase participation in mathematics if efforts are to be successful.

There are a variety of possibilities that may have lead to these changes. For example between 1987 and 2000 the number of states requiring at least 2.5 mathematics courses for graduation increased from 12 to 25 (Perkins, Kleiner, Roey, & Brown, 2004). Also during that same time period, the National Council of Teachers of Mathematics (NCTM) issued two important documents on the learning and teaching of school mathematics: (a) *Curriculum and Evaluation Standards for School Mathematics* (1989) and (b) *Principles and Standards for School Mathematics* (2000). These documents, written by teachers and teacher educators, had as their first "principle" that "excellence in mathematics education requires equity, high expectations, and strong support for all students" (NCTM, 2000, p. 11). Also explicit or implied in these standards were concerns with teaching for understanding, for "real world" mathematics applications and problem solving, for teaching and learning strategies representing mathematics in multiple ways (including verbally, pictorially, and in writing), and for working in groups—strategies that have been claimed to be particularly effective in teaching mathematics to girls. The standards led to the funding of a variety of projects to "stimulate the development of exemplary educational models and materials (incorporating the most recent advances in subject matter, research in teaching and learning, and instructional technology) and facilitate their use in the schools" (National Science Foundation [NSF], 1989, p. 1). There is some debate in the mathematics community as to whether these materials or more traditional materials are more effective in the teaching and learning of mathematics; however, many of these changes have been seen as more "girl friendly" than their predecessors.

GENDER DIFFERENCES IN INVOLVEMENT IN EXTRA-CURRICULAR MATHEMATICS ACTIVITIES

There are a variety of extracurricular mathematics activities in which many of those who become mathematicians or chose mathematics intensive careers have engaged during their school and college years. Whether participation in these activities has enhanced mathematics talent and career choice is hard to establish; however, such activities may contribute to gaining knowledge, style, confidence, and enjoyment of mathematics. Further, there are gender differences in participation in these activities. Examples of two such activities—(a) mathematics competitions and (b) summer math programs—are described below. These activities are not meant to be exhaustive, but are examples of longstanding programs that have some evidence of success.

Mathematics Competitions

Mathcounts.   Begun in 1983, Mathcounts is a U.S. competition for middle- and junior-high-school students. This competition resembles a spelling bee, designed to award competitors for achievement under pressure. This competition is tiered, with school teams of four competing at a chapter level, and winning teams advancing to the state then national levels. At the national level, about 10% of the competitors are girls.

The International Mathematics Olympiad.   One of the oldest and most prestigious of these competitions is the International Mathematical Olympiad (IMO) for extraordinarily talented students, high-school age or younger. This yearly competition was first held in 1959, but the United States did not enter a team until 1974. Members of the U.S. team are chosen from results of the American Mathematics Competitions (AMC). The beginning AMC competitions are tests in multiple-choice format, while the last competition, the United States of America Mathematics Olympiad, is in a format similar to the IMO: three problems to be solved in 4 ½ hours on each of 2 days. A small group of high scorers is then sent to a summer camp from which the six U.S. IMO team members are selected. About 400,000 students participate in these competitions each year. Just as in the sports Olympiad, there are no winning nations, but individual team-member scores are tallied, and the United States usually places first, second, or third in this individual tally. U.S. participants have generally been multitalented, with interests such as science, computer science, juggling, and music, in addition to mathematics. Most go to top universities and have academic careers in mathematics or the sciences. Others use their mathematical skills as lawyers, engineers, doctors, securities analysts, or technology innovators.

By the year 2001, when the 40-second IMO was held in Washington, DC (appropriately, on days surrounding July 4), nearly 500 students from 83 countries participated in this event; 28 were girls, none from the United States (Olson, 2004). In fact, through 2001, the United States sent 119 different students to these events, only one of whom was a girl. Although girls participate in the IMO much less frequently than boys, teams from other countries have had much higher female participation than the United States.

The High School Mathematical Contest in Modeling.

Established in 1999, the High School Contest in Modeling (HSMCM) was designed to stimulate and improve high school students' problem solving and writing skills by tackling such real world problems as designing a model to program a bank of elevators in a sky scraper to transport people efficiently to and from their designated floors. HSMCM invites teams of at most four students to work over a period of 36 continuous hours to analyze one of two given problems and to write a paper discussing their analysis. Students may consult libraries and Web sources in gathering information pertinent to their analysis. Team results are judged on the basis of their (a) executive summary, (b) assumptions or hypotheses, (c) list of variables and definitions, (d) model design and justifications, (e) test of the model, (f) conclusions, (g) model's strengths and weaknesses, and (h) writing style. Over a thousand high-school students participate in this competition each year, with about the same number of girls as boys participating. Regional Team papers are judged Successful, Honorable Mention, Meritorious, and Outstanding. The regional Outstanding papers are then read by a national panel of judges from which a group of National Outstanding papers emerge (Straley, 2004).

The Mathematical Contest in Modeling.

Established in 1984, the Mathematical Contest in Modeling (MCM) is the mother of the HMCM, similar in design and structure except for the size of each team which in the MCM is two or three. In 2004, 600 teams of undergraduates for 253 institutions and 11 countries participated in MCM. Teams were asked to model one of two problems: one involving continuous variables, the other discrete variables. Data collected on the 1997 MCM indicates a gender difference in the type of problem selected. Of the 401 teams in that competition, 171 chose the discrete problem and 232 the continuous problem; however, 98 teams with at least one female member chose the discrete problem, while 101 chose the continuous problem. Seventy-three all-male teams chose the discrete problem while 131 chose the continuous problem (Donoghue, 2005). In 2004, one problem, involving the probability of the uniqueness of fingerprints, was to compare the probability of misidentifying fingerprint evidence with misidentifying DNA evidence. The other was to design and an-

alyze a "quick pass" system to reduce people's wait time in line (Giordano, 2004). Data have been collected on female/male participation in MCM from 1998 through 2004. Of the more than ten thousand students who participated in this contest during those years, 23% were female, with all male teams greatly outnumbering all female of mixed sex teams. (e-mail communication with Roland Cheyney, COMAP, Inc. Levington, MA, Jan. 30, 2005).

The William Lowell Putnam Mathematical Competition.

The Putnam Competition was first held in 1938. It was "designed to stimulate a healthful rivalry in mathematical studies in the colleges and universities of the United States and Canada" (http://math.scu.edu/putnam/historybJan.html). The competition is designed to test originality, as well as technical skills. Participants are expected to be familiar with formal theories embodied in undergraduate mathematics, but at a more sophisticated level than minimal course requirements would imply. At the present time, more than 2,000 students participate in the Putnam each year, but data are preserved only for the top 500. In this top 500, percents of participants who could be identified as female ranged from 5% to 9% during the mid 1990s (Donoghue, 2005). The Putnam is based on individual performance and is viewed as extremely challenging, with nearly half of all participants giving less than 2% correct problem solutions. Only the most talented and self-confident need participate. Nevertheless, many mathematicians of note had been Putnam winners during their undergraduate years.

Programs for Women and Girls

NSF Funded Programs.

Since 1993, the National Science Foundation (NSF) has funded Programs for Women and Girls (PWG) designed to increase access for girls and women to study mathematics and choose careers in mathematics, science, engineering, and technology.[6] Funded programs rely on several different strategies: (a) extracurricular activities, (b) mentoring/role modeling, (c) professional development for educators and leaders, (d) special in-school coursework, (e) summer camps, (f) parent activities, (g) field trips, (h) internships, (i) tutoring, and (j) discussion groups. An evaluation of this program was conducted for NSF by the Urban Institute Education Policy Center. In general, this evaluation was positive, finding that several funded programs met its criteria of promoting knowledge, social, and human capital. The evaluation noted a side benefit of several of these programs to their female principal investigators; namely, "positive personal and professional change; enhancement of networking and contacts; promotion; institutional, community, and national recognition; tenure; and awards resulting at least in part from PWG projects" (The Urban Institute Education Policy Center, 2002, p. 37)

The current program, Research on Gender in Science and Engineering, "seeks to broaden the participation of women and girls in all fields of science, technology, engineering and mathe-

---

[6]"Program for Women and Girls" was renamed "Program for Gender Equity in Science, Mathematics, Engineering and Technology" in November 1998, again renamed "Gender Diversity in STEM Education" and is currently called "Research on Gender in Science and Engineering."

matics education by supporting research, dissemination of research, and extension service in education that will lead to a larger and more diverse domestic science and engineering workforce" (NSF, 2005). Some of the following summer programs were originally funded under NSF grants.

The Tensor Foundation Grants. Since 1994, the Tensor Foundation has awarded small grants for projects that encourage women and girls to continue with the study of mathematics and science. Special attention is paid to those projects aimed at racial and ethnic minority women. Many of these grants have been awarded for one-day programs for girls, such as Expanding Your Horizons and Sonia Kovalevsky High School Mathematics Days. These programs bring together middle- and high-school-age girls—and often, their parents and mathematics teachers—to university campuses, where they engage in stimulating talks and hands-on mathematics activities with female mathematics professors and other women engaged in mathematically intensive careers. The National Security Agency and the Association for Women in Mathematics often cosponsor these events. Other Tensor grants have been awarded for (a) developing college courses involving the history of women in mathematics, (b) conducting local summer camps, (c) developing and running mentoring programs where women with mathematics-related careers mentor high school girls, and (d) bringing together Tensor awardees at meetings of the Mathematical Association of America to share their experiences, develop techniques for assessing their projects, and present poster sessions on their work (Fasanelli, 2005).

As with the NSF PWG program, the Tensor Principal Investigators often benefit from their activities in terms of campus and national prestige, as well as career advancement. Many awardees go on the participating and often securing large awards from NSF for continuation and expansion of their Tensor projects. Evaluation of these projects is often limited to questionnaires filled out by participants at the end of the program. Such questionnaires usually reveal great enthusiasm for the program.

Summer Programs in Mathematics

The Ross Program. The Ross Program is an intensive, eight-week, summer-residential mathematics program for precollege students (ages 14 to 18). Dr. Arnold Ross began the program in 1957, partly in response to the launching of Sputnik. The program continues to this day, with many spin-offs run by "graduates" of the Ross Program who are now mathematics professors at various universities. From its inception, "the central goal of the Ross Program has been to instruct and encourage bright young students in the art of abstract thinking and to inspire them to discover for themselves that abstract ideas are valuable and important" (http://www.math.ohio-state.edu/ross/introduction.html). First-year students are instructed in number theory, and many of the problems posed to them are from that branch of mathematics. Students may return a second summer. Admission decisions are made on the basis of the applicant's solutions to some challenging mathematics problems, recommendations, and an essay. Tuition and room and board are not cheap, but scholarships are available.

In the past ten years the program has admitted about 25 first-year students per year, along with a few returning students, 5 to 10 junior counselors, and 10 counselors each year. The counselors are alumni of the program who are currently undergraduate mathematics majors. Over the years, approximately 25% of the students have been female and 50% Asian. Although the program has not made an effort to keep track of alumni, anecdotal evidence indicates that many mathematicians in the field, particularly women, claim their serious interest in mathematics began at the Ross Program (4/26/05 email from Dan Shapiro, personal communication, 2005).

The Ross Program also runs a three-week program for teachers in tandem with the eight-week Ross Program for high-school students. The teacher program enables teachers to increase their mathematics content knowledge and to explore mathematical concepts using problem-based methods.

SummerMath. Originally funded in 1982 under an NSF grant, SummerMath continues to (a) strengthen young girls' mathematical, computer, and communication skills, (b) develop problem solving strategies, and (c) build their confidence in doing mathematics. This four-week residential program targets young women entering 9th through 12th grades. Mornings are spent in class, working in pairs to discover how mathematics is applied to everyday life. Afternoons are spent in recreational and sports activities on the Mount Holyoke College campus. SummerMath brings together a diverse group of high-school-aged girls. Over 50% of the girls are African-American, Latina, or Native American http://www.mtholyoke.edu/proj/summermath/about.html).

Young Scholars Program. The Young Scholars Program (YSP) was originally funded by NSF but funding was discontinued, probably because there was not sufficient evidence that bright students who attended these programs were more likely to continue with the study of mathematics and science and enter careers in these fields that equally bright students who had not attended. Mathematicians felt that this program was so important, however, that it is currently being funded, but at a lower level, by the American Mathematical Society (AMS). The current program supports summer activities that cater to talented mathematics students at the high-school level. University mathematics faculty usually runs these programs. The programs tend to emphasize number theory.

Analysis and Commentary

Mathematical competitions. Mathematics competitions may have a profound effects on student's confidence in their ability to do mathematics, both positive and negative, and in their drive to succeed in this field. These competitions give students not only a keen sense of competition, but also a sense of belonging to a rare group of talented people. Many U.S. International Mathematics Olympiad participants began such competitions in their middle-school years with Mathcounts. As Melanie Woods, who later became the first girl on a U.S. IMO team, remarked about her experiences with the Mathcounts competition, "The other students on the team thought and talked about math problems in the same way I did, and this was something I had never shared with any peers, or even teachers before. It was really exciting to be able to communicate about the problems I found so interesting to people who could understand my ideas" (Olson, 2004, p. 21). She remarked further, "My mom and I were just totally stunned by all this. I knew that I was pretty good at math, but I was pretty good at English and science and history—I was a good student. But I never would have guessed that I would win as a seventh grader in the city, much less the state. That really flipped my world around in terms of making math something important in my life and changing my view of who I was and what I was good at" (Olson, 2004, p. 20). On the other hand, Ms. Woods commented on the IMO experience, "I've always been opposed to summing up scores and saying that this is who wins and this is who loses. I like to work with people. I don't like to wonder if I can beat them. I mean, I don't mind saying, 'Oh, we're going to beat the Bulgarians or the Russians,' because I don't know them. But I have a lot of issues with not working together with someone else on your team" (Olson, 2004, p. 93). Perhaps the concept of "working with people" or teamwork that is often cited as a characteristic of female activity is related to the types of mathematics competitions that most appeal to females. It may account in part for the higher female participation in the modeling versus other types of mathematics competitions.

With the possible exception of Mathcounts, all competitions discussed in this chapter require high levels of problem solving skills, of combining previously learned mathematics with novel methods when approaching problems not previously encountered. That there may be gender-related differences in problem-solving techniques is suggested by the different types of problem type selected (discrete, continuous) among the all-male, all-female, and coed teams in the modeling competitions. Further, girls have been observed to use different problem-solving strategies than boys. For example, Gould (1996) found gender-related differences in problem-solving strategies used by high-school students when she videotaped 21 pairs of students (male, female, and mixed-gender) with similar mathematics background and analyzed their strategies in solving eight novel problems. She found that females pairs spent a larger proportion of their time on building fundamentals, while male pairs first identified the students with the greater mathematical ability, and then jumped right in, willing to make mistakes until they found a correct approach. The female pairs tended to rely on procedural, rule-bound approaches and were less comfortable with the idea of logical equivalence. Female pairs were also more concerned with issues that were only peripherally related to the problem.

Whether mathematical competitions help bring out mathematical talent or whether they appeal to already talented youth, it is important to encourage girls to participate in those competitions that match their levels of mathematical competence, confidence, competitiveness, and learning styles.

Mathematics Grants and Programs

Many people that are in mathematics or mathematics-intensive careers attribute their interest and success in mathematics to their participation in a variety of extra curricular programs; however,

causality is hard to attribute. Unless designed specifically for girls and women, many more males participate in these activities than females. Women who have designed and run such programs often find that they have gained stature in their careers from having led such programs. It is interesting to note that so many of these programs stress number theory, with some extensions to graph theory and combinatorics. It is perhaps because problems in these fields are intrinsically interesting, may be stated in layman's terms (although solutions may be extremely complex), and, at least at the elementary level, require minimal advanced mathematics. Certainly, informing parents and teachers of these programs and active recruiting of female students to participate in them should be undertaken. Long-range data on participants of the seemingly more successful of these programs needs to be collected and analyzed to determine their effectiveness and reliability in other settings. Since many of these programs are expensive to run and tuition to attend is high, funds need to be provided for students who would not be able to attend without financial help.

GENDER EQUITY IN POSTSECONDARY MATHEMATICS

Mathematics is generally regarded as an objective field of knowledge, in which mathematicians work to discover "truths" about the natural and abstract worlds (Maddy, 1990; Steen, 1999). Further, "Academic science presumes a taken-for-granted male model of social organization that takes little or no account of non-work related roles or social relationships" (Etzkowitz, Kemelgor, Neuschatz, & Uzzi, 1992, p. 161). This is particularly the case in mathematics, in which the presumed objectivity of the discipline leads to a cultural blindness to personal issues. Consequently, mathematicians have largely ignored issues of gender and race, and students who do not correspond to the cultural norm (male, White, childless, self-assured) are sometimes at a disadvantage (Hinchey & Kimmel, 2000).

Little scholarship has addressed gender issues in postsecondary education in general; even less has addressed mathematics in particular. In this section, we review issues confronting women in postsecondary graduate school mathematics. Because the largest drop in the percentage of women persisting in mathematics studies occurs at the graduate level, we place a particular emphasis on graduate education. First, we give a statistical summary of women's participation in postsecondary mathematics. While women participate in undergraduate mathematics at similar rates to men, they are underrepresented at the graduate level, and this is where we focus for the balance of this section. Next, we describe the studies that form the sources for the arguments to follow. We then argue that the training of graduate students—like the training of students at all levels—requires the acquisition of mathematical knowledge, participation in mathematical practices, and the development of a sense of belonging as a mathematician. We argue that the last of these factors is most often overlooked, and perhaps the most critical, in addressing gender inequities in postsecondary mathematics. Finally, we describe a series of obstacles to belonging faced by women in graduate mathematics.

Participation of Women in Postsecondary Mathematics

The participation of females in advanced mathematics decreases at every educational stage. In 2003, female high-school graduates were more likely than male graduates to enter college (Bureau of Labor Statistics, 2004), and 57% of all college students were female (National Center for Education Statistics, 2004). Also in 2003, women received 41% of bachelor's degrees awarded in the mathematical sciences in the United States (Kirkman, Maxwell, & Rose, 2004b).

The only comprehensive report on attrition rates among undergraduates indicates that mathematics has the highest attrition rate among all liberal arts disciplines (and among all disciplines, except for the health professions), with one of the highest differences in the attrition rates between women and men. Women are more likely to leave mathematics than men (Seymour & Hewitt, 1997). Of undergraduate students entering college in 1987 with an intention of majoring in mathematics, an estimated 71% (60% of men and 72% of women) switched to other majors by 1991 (Seymour & Hewitt, 1997). Few of these students stayed in science, mathematics, and engineering (SME) majors; instead, the majority of the students switched to education and to the humanities, with women more likely to switch to education than men. This large gender gap in attrition from the mathematics major results in 47% of mathematics bachelor's degrees being earned by women. Thus, something is happening in undergraduate mathematics to lead interested women out of mathematics.

In 2003, women comprised 35% of mathematics graduate students (30% of full-time graduate students; Kirkman et al., 2004b) and earned 30% of doctorates awarded in mathematics in the United States (Kirkman, Maxwell, & Rose, 2004a). Between 1981–82 and 2004–05, among U.S. citizens earning PhDs in the mathematical sciences, the percentage of women increased from 18% to 28% (see Fig. 12.3); similar patterns are evident for African Americans, Native Americans, and Latinos. Of graduate students enrolled in the mathematical sciences in 1999, 4% were Latino, 6% were Black, and 0.3% were Native American (NSF, 2003). Of the PhD recipients in the United States in 2004–2005, 4% were Latino, 3% were Black, and only 5 out of 1,116 were Native American (Kirkman, Maxwell, & Rose, 2006). Although these numbers represent large increases, these small percentages indicate that substantial obstacles remain for women and people of color in graduate mathematics.

Statistics on attrition from graduate study for women and for men are not generally available, in part because attrition is difficult to define and measure. For example, graduate students may stay nominally enrolled, whether or not they intend to continue their degrees, while others may take some time off to return to complete their degrees later. However, some things can be inferred about women's persistence in graduate school. In 1998, women constituted about one third of all graduate students enrolled in mathematics (Davis, Maxwell, & Remick, 1999); in that same year, they earned 38% of the graduate degrees awarded, 25% of doctorates, and 42% of master's degrees (NSF, 2002); however, it is not known if the women receiving master's degrees entered graduate school with the intent to earn that degree, or if they represent attrition from the PhD.

Women received 20% of new doctoral faculty positions filled in mathematics departments in the United States and comprised 13% of the total full-time doctoral faculty in 2003 (Kirkman et al., 2004b).

Overall, women are less likely to enter graduate school, less likely to complete PhDs, and less likely to attain faculty positions in mathematics than men—that is, at every educational and professional stage, women stay in mathematics at lower proportions than their male contemporaries. This exodus of women from mathematics has often been described as a "leaky pipeline," but this metaphor is problematic in several ways. First, the metaphor of a pipeline poses students as passive participants in their education, whose progress through their education is affected only by the global forces of fluid dynamics (and perhaps other molecular-level forces). A "leaky pipeline" does not adequately address why students of some demographic groups stay in mathematics while others leave in greater proportions, and it fails to model important features of postsecondary mathematics education that may contribute to attrition, such as its competitive and individualistic nature. By combining all students into one undifferentiated volume of "fluid," this metaphor allows researchers and policymakers to overlook the very human implications of the postsecondary educational environment in mathematics (Herzig, 2004a). Alternative views of the educational terrain are necessary to help mathematicians and policymakers construct more effective solutions to the problems of diversity and equity in mathematics. A more promising metaphor is "pathways" (Adelman, 1998), suggesting that there are or should be different pathways to advanced work in mathematics. Moreover, this metaphor puts the onus of achieving not only on the student, but also on the educational system to provide alternative pathways.

The balance of this section describes some of the inequities inherent in the structure of graduate mathematics education. First, we describe available studies about gender in graduate mathematics, and then the importance of students' development of a sense of belonging in mathematics, and use that as a model for understanding those inequities.

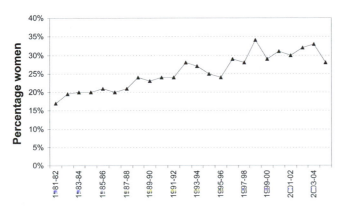

FIGURE 12.3. Females as a percentage of U.S. citizens earning the PhD in the mathematical sciences (From Kirkman, Maxwell, & Rose, 2006).

Studies about Gender in Graduate Mathematics

At the graduate level, there are few studies of gender issues in specific disciplines; instead, these issues have often been investigated in broad categories such as engineering or science (which may include mathematics). Only 13 studies were located that specifically reported on the experiences of women graduate students in mathematics. Of these 13, ten reported only on mathematics (Carlson, 1999; Committee on the Participation of Women, 2003; Cooper, 2000; Herzig, 2002, 2004c, 2004d; Manzo, 1994; Mathematical Association of America & National Association of Mathematicians, 1997; National Research Council [NRC], 1992; Stage & Maple, 1996); three others included mathematics combined with physics (Hollenshead, Younce, & Wenzel, 1994) or computer science (Becker, 1984, 1990).

Since only a small number of studies address graduate student experiences specifically in mathematics, we augment the research on gender in postsecondary mathematics with empirical studies about other disciplines. Four studies investigated women graduate students or faculty members in the sciences (Etzkowitz et al., 1992; Etzkowitz, Kemelgor, & Uzzi, 2000; Grant, Kennelly, & Ward, 2000; Sonnert & Holton, 1995). Seven additional studies addressed graduate students across a range of disciplines in the humanities, social sciences, and physical sciences (Bair & Haworth, 1999; Berg & Ferber, 1983; California Postsecondary Education Commission, 1990; Girves & Wemmerus, 1988; Golde, 1996; Lovitts, 2001; Nerad & Cerny, 1993). Finally, two studies contained helpful statistical information that provided context for the analysis presented here (Bowen & Rudenstine, 1992; Zwick, 1991). Throughout the review, we specifically analyze aspects of these findings to infer ways in which this broader literature can apply specifically to mathematics. Further research on the graduate student experience needs to focus on these experiences in particular disciplinary contexts.

The studies use a mix of qualitative, quantitative, and mixed-method analyses, drawing their data from surveys, institutional databases, and interviews; most use a combination of methodologies and data sources. Many of the studies are based on small samples of students, involving interview and focus-group methods in small numbers of departments and institutions, often sampling from only one department or several departments at one or two institutions. Because the numbers of women and students of color in doctoral mathematics are so small overall, their numbers in specific graduate programs are generally quite small as well. While these qualitative studies are very valuable for the insights they provide to the experiences of graduate students, the considerable differences among departments and institutions make it difficult to generalize from these studies to the overall population of graduate students. The consistency of findings across these studies is compelling, but future research needs to include larger scale studies to validate and extend the findings from these investigations.

Some studies focus on attrition of graduate students, while others focus on their persistence or other aspects of their experience in graduate school. Collectively, these provide important insights into the experiences of graduate students in mathematics—particularly, women and students of color.

Belonging in Mathematics

Successful study of mathematics at the graduate level—as at earlier levels—requires more than just learning the content of mathematics. According to sociocultural theories, learning entails students' appropriation of knowledge, participation in practices, and developing a sense of identity or belonging within the discipline (Boaler, 2002; Boaler, Wiliam, & Zevenbergen, 2000; Herzig, 2004a, 2004c). All three of these dimensions of students' learning are critical for students' development as mathematicians, and provide a useful framework for analyzing women's opportunities to learn mathematics.

Mathematics graduate programs in the United States are primarily structured to provide disciplinary training in the core areas of mathematical scholarship (Bass, 2003; NRC, 1992). Recently, there has been a growing emphasis on training graduate students in practices of the profession (Bass, 2003); however, little attention has been paid to a student's development of a sense that she has a place within the mathematical community.

Building students' sense of belongingness in mathematics has been proposed as a critical feature of an equitable K–12 education (Allexsaht-Snider & Hart, 2001; Ladson-Billings, 1997; National Council of Teachers of Mathematics, 2000; Tate, 1995). A similar construct has been proposed at the graduate level, with several authors arguing that students' involvement or integration into the communities of their departments is important for their persistence (Girves & Wemmerus, 1988; Golde, 1996; Herzig, 2002, 2004c; Lovitts, 2001; NRC, 1992; NSF, 1998; Tinto, 1993). Students with multiple avenues for developing a sense of belonging within mathematics (for example, through family members who were mathematicians, or involvement in mathematics outside of formal schooling) have been found to be more likely to persist in graduate school (Herzig, 2002). It seems, then, that developing an identity as a mathematician, a sense that "I belong here" is a critical component in the professional development of graduate students.

Students in several programs have described the importance of having "critical mass" of women or students of color (Cooper, 2000; Manzo, 1994). Graduate women in mathematics, computer science, and physics have reported feeling isolated or alienated in their male-dominated departments, and have described ways that they feel that they do not fit in (Becker, 1990; Etzkowitz et al., 2000; Herzig, 2004c; Hollenshead et al., 1994). Women in mathematics have few female role models to guide them; in the fall of 2003, while 30% of full-time graduate students were women, only 13% of full-time doctoral faculty were women (Kirkman, Maxwell, & Priestly, 2004). Statistics about mathematics faculty of color are not available, but so few PhDs have been earned by African Americans, Latinos, and Native Americans over the past several decades (NSF, 2004) that the number of faculty of those groups are necessarily quite small as well, making it more difficult for women and students of color to see evidence that they do belong in mathematics.

Mathematicians and mathematics students have commonly been stereotyped as lacking in social skills and without interests outside of mathematics (Campbell, 1995; Herzig, 2004d; Noddings, 1996). Suzanne Damarin (2000) analyzed discourses surrounding mathematical ability, and concluded that:

From leading journals of pubic intellectual discussion, from the analyses of sociologist of science, from the work of (genetic) scientists themselves, from the pages of daily papers, and from practices of students and adults within the wall[s] of our schools, there emerges and coalesces a discourse of mathematics ability as marking a form of deviance and the mathematically able as a category marked by the signs of this deviance. (p. 78)

In addition to being marked as women, mathematical women are further marked by the stereotypes of the mathematically talented. This double marking is not simply additive; instead, women are constructed as deviant separately within each marked category. First, their mathematical ability defines them as deviant. Second, given common stereotypes of mathematics as a male domain, mathematical women are often marked as outside the mathematical domain. For women of color, or women who are mothers, the marking is even more complex, leading them to be distanced from each of those communities to which they might otherwise belong (Herzig, 2004d). Women who choose to pursue mathematics must be willing to endure these multiple constructions of themselves as deviants, and may not have access to the mainstream community of the mathematically able, as their multiple markings as deviant marginalize them from this community.

Obstacles Women Face in Postgraduate Mathematics

While all students face some challenges to belonging, for women and people of some racial and ethnic groups, coming to belong in graduate mathematics is an even more difficult struggle. Challenges faced by women in graduate mathematics fall into two categories. In the first are aspects of graduate education that make graduate school an inhospitable environment for women: (a) negative or absent relationships with faculty, (b) ineffective styles of communication and competition, (c) unfamiliar epistemology, and (d) conflicts with family responsibilities. The second category entails ways that the discourses surrounding graduate mathematics education construct women themselves as incompetent or incapable of mathematics: (a) notions of autonomy and independence, (b) beliefs about talent and who is capable of doing mathematics, and (c) confidence.

An Inhospitable Environment for Women

Negative or absent relationships with faculty.   Encouragement from people influential in students' lives plays an important role in students' decisions to enroll and persist in graduate studies. Both men and women have acknowledged the importance of encouragement and moral support from family members (Becker, 1990; Berg & Ferber, 1983; Carlson, 1999; Hollenshead et al., 1994; Sonnert & Holton, 1995; Stage & Maple, 1996); however, more women than men report receiving moral support (Becker, 1984; Berg & Ferber, 1983; Lovitts, 2001; Sonnert & Holton, 1995). Joanne Rossi Becker (1984, 1990) found that women in mathematics and computer science recalled both support and discouragement, while men recalled little encouragement and no discouragement: "The encourage-

ment seemed really helpful to the women in their decisions to attend graduate school. The men seemed to be able to decide without ostensible support" (1990, p. 127). Women may be less likely than men to embark on graduate studies when these types of support are unavailable, or alternatively, women may be more aware of or more willing to acknowledge support (Becker, 1990; Berg & Ferber, 1983; Sonnert & Holton, 1995). Few mathematics graduate students report having received moral support or encouragement from faculty or mentors within their departments or programs, although when such encouragement was offered, it made a big difference to them (Herzig, 2002, 2004c; Mathematical Association of America & National Association of Mathematicians, 1997).

Students who are treated as "junior colleagues" are more likely to stay enrolled in graduate school and complete degrees (Berg & Ferber, 1983; Girves & Wemmerus, 1988; Nerad & Cerny, 1993), and conversely, students who feel they are treated as "adolescents" are less likely to complete degrees (Nerad & Cerny, 1993).

Relationships between faculty and doctoral students of color (both men and women) have not been reported on in the research literature, but negative interactions with faculty are pervasive for women in science. Gerhard Sonnert and Gerhard Holton (1995) documented forms of discrimination that women faced in finding mentors, ranging from professors who would not take on women students to mentors who just did not seem to tap into their professional networks as vigorously for their women students as they did for men. Women's opportunities have also been limited by being excluded from the informal social networks of their laboratories or departments, being treated as "invisible," or otherwise having had their contributions marginalized (Becker, 1990; Committee on the Participation of Women, 2003; Etzkowitz et al., 1992; Etzkowitz et al., 2000; Sonnert & Holton, 1995; Stage & Maple, 1996). The Committee on the Participation of Women of the Mathematical Association of America (2003) reported on sexist behavior experienced by women in graduate mathematics, including unwanted sexual advances from faculty, tolerance by colleagues of public sexist comments, and professors who openly state that women are not as smart, dedicated, or talented as men.

Women students in the sciences and mathematics receive less mentoring from male faculty than do men students (Berg & Ferber, 1983; Etzkowitz et al., 2000; Hollenshead et al., 1994; Sonnert & Holton, 1995). There has been a tendency reported for faculty to mentor same-sex students (Berg & Ferber, 1983); however, there are few women faculty in most STEM disciplines. This is currently true of mathematics in particular: as previously discussed, the proportion of female graduate students is almost three times the proportion of female faculty. Leone Burton (1999) interviewed 70 practicing mathematicians in the United Kingdom, however, and found that none of them had had a female advisor, yet many of the 35 women she interviewed were advising graduate students; she concluded that there may be reason to expect that women in mathematics will have increased opportunities to have women as advisors.

Thus, women and students of color have fewer opportunities to develop substantive relationships with faculty compared with their majority classmates. When students do not receive adequate guidance and advisement about the nature of graduate school, they can have unrealistic expectations, which contribute to negative experiences in graduate school (Golde, 1996; Herzig, 2004c; Lovitts, 2001; NRC, 1992). Further, students who have limited or negative relationships with faculty have fewer avenues to develop the knowledge, practices, and sense of belonging that are critical to success in graduate school.

Ineffective styles of communication and competition.

Despite the collaborative nature of much of their work, some mathematicians have described the intense competition of their work worlds, including the confrontational atmosphere at conferences (L. Burton, 1999; 2000) and relationships with their PhD supervisors in which "arrogance, bullying, favoritism, and the need for tenacity all featured" (L. Burton, 2000, p. 4). Some of the mathematicians Leone Burton interviewed described communication styles commonly used in mathematics that were meant to impress and mystify, rather than to explain and illuminate. In an essay about communication styles in mathematics, mathematician Sandra Keith (1988) described the confrontational language that is a normal part of mathematics discourse. Common terms used in mathematics such as "we claim," "the proof is trivial," "it is obvious," and "it is commonly known that," which are "a vocabulary of mathematical punctuation," (p. 5) can be intimidating. Leone Burton (2000) echoed these findings, citing mathematicians' language for describing published mathematical results using words such as "important," "significant," or "trivial." This assertive communication style may be a mode of communication that is uncomfortable for some students, particularly women:

[T]he mode in which mathematics is usually written and spoken is one of advocacy, of claims and assertions, one which generally ignores its audience. It is a language which I feel is more easily adopted by men than women, if we can believe what we are told about women using fewer declarative sentences in conversation. And it is a language, which particularly when spoken, is frequently confused with impatience, frustration, and defensiveness. Mathematical "arguments" in the rhetorical sense of the word, move easily into "argumentative" encounters. (Keith, 1988, p. 8)

Further, the forms of communication used by women and some students of color may make it particularly difficult for their attempts at mathematical communication to be accepted (Orr, 1997; Rosser, 1995). Students who do not fit faculty expectations for graduate students in a given field—those who do not master the tacit knowledge of the field—may be judged to be incompetent in the field (Etzkowitz et al., 2000).

Positive interactions with peers are important to students' experiences and persistence in graduate school (Bair & Haworth, 1999; Hollenshead et al., 1994). The perceived competition of graduate study has been cited as a factor in students' decisions to leave graduate school (Golde, 1996; Lovitts, 2001; Stage & Maple, 1996), and in enrolled students' dissatisfaction with their experiences in graduate school (Hollenshead et al., 1994).

Unfamiliar epistemology of graduate mathematics.

Students have described being attracted to mathematics because of its abstract nature (Becker, 1984, 1990; Herzig, 2002, 2004c). Other students have reported disillusionment with how far removed their studies or research in mathematics or science was from meaningful or relevant questions (Golde, 1996; Herzig, 2002, 2004c; Stage & Maple, 1996). In interviews with seven women who had left graduate programs in mathematics, Frances Stage and Sue Maple (1996) found that:

most described a growing frustration with the seeming lack of connection of mathematics with the world surrounding them. Mathematics began to seem an endless series of puzzles that could be solved if enough time or effort was invested. . . . Solutions bore little relationship to others' learning of mathematics, social issues, or the people in their own lives. (p. 32)

Biology students interviewed by Christine Golde (1996) cited the irrelevance of research to important real-world questions. Gerhard Sonnert and Gerhard Holton (1995) also found that:

a frequent cause [of leaving science] mentioned by both men and women was rooted in the culture of science: they felt their science jobs required too many hours of hard work, the work itself was too fragmented and meaningless, and the results lacked applicability and relevance. (p. 170)

Graduate study in mathematics is largely focused on traditional, theoretical mathematics (NRC, 1992). As a result, "many researchers lack the broad knowledge needed to address real-world problems . . . and the system of education is more or less self-contained, with graduates teaching what they have been taught in the same manner they have been taught" (NRC, 1992, p. 15).

Mathematics is often taught in highly abstracted ways, with little or no explicit connection to other mathematical ideas, ideas outside of mathematics, or the mathematical "big picture" (Herzig, 2002). Some authors have argued that women tend to be more interested in relationships and interaction among ideas than men (Belenky, Clinchy, Goldberger, & Tarule, 1986), and in science, women are more eager to learn how scientific ideas and facts fit together than are men, who may be more content to examine information out of context (Rosser, 1995). Some feminist writers challenge the predominance of abstraction in mathematics; for example, Betty Johnston (1995) claimed that abstraction in mathematics is a consequence of modern industrial society, based on the idea of separating things into manageable pieces, apart from their context. She further argued that this abstraction of mathematics is a masculine artifact, a way of denying the social nature of mathematics. Yet the beauty and utility of the mathematics that have developed over more than 2000 years lie in its abstraction and universality.

Conflicts with family responsibilities.

In a synthesis of 118 studies on doctoral student attrition, Carolyn Richert Bair and Jennifer Grant Haworth (1999) concluded that "the weight of evidence indicates that the number of children or dependents of doctoral students is not a significant predictor of persistence or attrition" (p. 22). This is consistent with the common finding that parenthood does not have an impact on research productivity in science (Cole & Zuckerman, 1987). Citing sociologist Dorothy Smith, researchers Linda Grant, Ivy Kennelly, and Kathryn B. Ward (2000) called this finding a "critical rift": "a point at which the world we study as sociologists diverges sharply from women's lived experiences" (p. 62).

Several authors have warned about sample selectivity and other biases in the studies of the effects of parenthood on the productivity of scientists (Grant et al., 2000; Sonnert & Holton, 1995). For example, scientists who faced the most serious obstacles to combining an academic career with family life might no longer participate in science, skewing the sample of those who remain; further, most of studies on scientific productivity focus on elite scientists (Grant et al., 2000). While much of this research studies the impacts of family responsibilities on scientific productivity, they do not study the reverse: the ways in which a career in science affects the decisions scientists make about marriage and family (Grant et al., 2000). To avoid conflicts with the demands of their careers, some scientists (particularly women) have decided not to marry or have children, to postpone having children until their careers were more established, or to have fewer children than they had originally planned (Etzkowitz et al., 2000; Grant et al., 2000; Sonnert & Holton, 1995); these decisions were made more commonly in the natural and physical sciences than in the social sciences.

Doctoral students with dependents generally take longer to complete their degrees (Nerad & Cerny, 1993), and the impact of having dependents is substantially greater on women than on men (Lovitts, 2001; Nerad & Cerny, 1993; Sonnert & Holton, 1995), particularly in the physical sciences and mathematics. Women graduate students in science who marry or have children have been described as not serious about their studies, or as unreliable and not worth the investment; men who marry or have families do not face the same biases (Etzkowitz et al., 2000).

In order to accommodate family life, women in science often choose to pursue careers in industry, and those who remain in academe tend to aspire to jobs in small teaching colleges rather than research universities (Etzkowitz et al., 1992). Christine Golde (1996) reported that both women and men graduate students in science left graduate school because of a perceived imbalance between family and work responsibilities. "The lives that were modeled for students (few children, many divorces) did not give students hope that they could lead the balanced lives they valued" (p. 209). In mathematics in particular, some women reported having left graduate mathematics altogether because of the perceived incompatibility of the life of a doctoral student in mathematics and a personal life outside of mathematics (Stage & Maple, 1996). Other women have reported the double bind of combining motherhood with graduate school, as they felt that they were not able to devote enough time or energy to either (Herzig, 2004d). These perceived conflicts for women, between life in and out of mathematics and science, may explain why women graduate students have been reported to be less likely to be married and have families than male graduate students (Berg & Ferber, 1983; California Postsecondary Education Commission, 1990; Nerad & Cerny, 1993).

Women are more likely than men to make career compromises to follow a spouse, and they are more affected by the concurrent timing of the graduate school, tenure, and childbearing clocks (Etzkowitz et al., 2000; Grant et al., 2000; Sonnert & Holton, 1995). What makes women faculty attractive as role models for women graduate students might not be their professional success as much as their ability to combine a successful career with a family life (Etzkowitz et al., 2000; Golde, 1996; Sonnert & Holton, 1995).

An additional obstacle facing students with family responsibilities is family-unfriendly scheduling, which limits the ability of some students to participate in the practices and activities of the department (Committee on the Participation of Women, 2003). Certainly, some of the effects of family life on graduate student progress could be ameliorated by appropriate institutional responses, such as (a) affordable childcare, (b) support for part-time study, (c) flexible deadlines and a slower pace for students who are also parents, (d) financial support, and (e) flexibility in scheduling (Etzkowitz et al., 2000; Manzo, 1994; Nerad & Cerny, 1993).

Constructing Women as Incompetent or Incapable

Independence and autonomy. Women graduate students in science and mathematics have been stereotyped as less capable and uncompetitive compared with men, and as a result, they may not be taken seriously by faculty (Becker, 1990; Committee on the Participation of Women, 2003; Etzkowitz et al., 2000; Stage & Maple, 1996). Starting from a young age, women's socialization leads them to look for interaction, attention, and reinforcement, rather than to be autonomous and independent learners (Etzkowitz et al., 2000; Fennema & Peterson, 1985). This pattern of socialization can work against them in the eyes of their advisors, especially in a disciplinary culture such as that found in mathematics, where work is expected to be individualistic and independent. Because of their socialization, female graduate students' styles of interaction may be different from those expected by male faculty; those behaviors may be misinterpreted as inferior, rather than different (Etzkowitz et al., 1992, p. 174).

Henry Etzkowitz et al. (2000) argued that students can only act independently if they feel safe and accepted. Students who do not feel that they fit in may have more difficulty acting autonomously. In effect, autonomy and independence are double-edged swords for women in science.

Isolated and without interpersonal connection, a woman's ability to be playfully creative is impeded. . . . A gendered 'apartheid system' exists in which many male advisors offer support to male students, but leave women to figure things out for themselves. With no support or connection with an advisor, taking risks in the lab becomes to threatening. People only take risks when they feel safe to do so. In contrast, there is sufficient support and acceptance, by way of informal interactions with male advisors and peers, for male students to enjoy the freedom to be innovative. (Etzkowitz et al., 2000, p. 86)

That is, male students have enhanced relationships with faculty (Herzig, 2004a), which provides those students with increased opportunities to develop a sense of belonging. This feeling of acceptance is a prerequisite for independent and autonomous work. Denied the same degree of relationships with faculty, female students find it more difficult to act independently.

Beliefs about talent and who can do mathematics. Faculty in mathematics graduate programs have cited the poor preparation of graduate students as a problem in their programs (Conference Board the Mathematical Sciences, 1987, as cited in Madison & Hart, 1990; Herzig, 2002; NRC, 1992). In Carolyn

Richert Bair and Jennifer Grant Haworth's (1999) review of research on doctoral student attrition, a majority of studies found that traditional measures of achievement, such as graduate and undergraduate grades and standardized test scores, are unreliable predictors of doctoral student persistence. Of the small number of studies that indicated positive correlations between achievement measures and persistence, none focused specifically on mathematics, and most were published more than two decades ago. Research consistently reports that students who leave graduate school do not have lower grades or GRE scores (Berg & Ferber, 1983; Bowen & Rudenstine, 1992; Girves & Wemmerus, 1988; Golde, 1996; Lovitts, 2001; Zwick, 1991). However, students admitted to a graduate program are already among the top performers, so the small variance they exhibit in grades and standardized test scores limits the ability of these measures to predict degree completion (Tinto, 1993).

In interviews with 10 faculty mathematicians, Abbe Herzig (2002) found that their beliefs in the importance of "talent" or "ability" led them to virtually ignore doctoral students in their first several years of the program, describing instruction as providing an opportunity for students to discover or prove if they possess that talent. Some of these faculty felt that they were doing students a favor by helping them avoid wasting time if they were unlikely to "have what it takes" to make it in graduate mathematics:

These beliefs on the part of the faculty provide an explicit obstacle to students' participation in the program, in that students are required to prove themselves *first*; only after they have proven themselves would they have opportunities to participate in meaningful ways in mathematics practice. This forms a sort of a "catch-22," since it ignores the way that meaningful participation might enhance students' abilities and skills at mathematics. (Herzig, 2002, p. 187)

This faculty belief in talent moved the focus of doctoral education from fostering students' development as mathematicians to filtering out students without the prerequisite talent or ability. In contrast, based on a review of research on children's motivation to learn, Carole Ames (1992) concluded that making ability a salient feature of an educational environment interferes with students' motivation to learn, their use of effective learning strategies, and their engagement with the content of the curriculum.

Confidence. Confidence has been described as an important feature in a graduate student's persistence toward a degree (Berg & Ferber, 1983), and as an influence on students' career plans and their persistence in pursuing them (Becker, 1984; Berg & Ferber, 1983). Science students have been reported to need confidence in their abilities in order to persevere when experiments fail; some students interpret the discouragement of a failed experiment to mean that they are ill suited to scientific work (Golde, 1996). Similarly, mathematics students may need patience and perseverance in solving mathematics problems, both in coursework and in research.

Men in science and mathematics have tended to appear more confident than women (Becker, 1984, 1990; Etzkowitz et al., 2000; Sonnert & Holton, 1995). Overall, compared to men, "women appear more timid, tend to set lower goals for themselves, and are likely to be given less encouragement" (Berg &

Ferber, 1983, p. 631). In a survey of previously enrolled graduate students in the physical and biological sciences, Helen Berg and Marianne Ferber (1983) found that significantly more women than men (63 % vs. 37%) in the physical and biological sciences indicated that the ability to handle the work was an important factor in their choice of a field of study, despite the lack of significant differences in GPAs between men and women in their samples. The authors interpreted these findings to mean that women are "less likely to take their ability to do whatever they want to do for granted" (p. 635), although it simply may be the case that women are more willing than men to express their uncertainty (L. Burton, 1999). While women have reported entering graduate school with lower self-confidence than men, their confidence is often further eroded by experiences within graduate school (Becker, 1984; Etzkowitz et al., 2000; Golde, 1996).

Confidence and ability are often intermingled in the research literature (L. Burton, 1999), as researchers describe students' confidence in their abilities and frequently its relationship to gender. However, most authors discuss confidence and ability without defining these constructs, and without problematizing their often-gendered connotations and implications (L. Burton, 1999; 2001). Some authors have equated ability with the possession of certain forms of cultural capital—that is, students are constructed as talented not because of any measurable, definable attribute such as ability, but rather because they possess particular types of cultural capital that are consistent with practices and expectations in schools (Herzig, 2004b; Zevenbergen, 2004). Similarly, students may be described as confident when they possess the cultural capital to behave in ways that are valued within the mathematical community. Students who behave differently than the ways commonly accepted—as may be the case for women and some people of color— may not fit well in the mathematical culture, which often does not welcome diversity.

WOMEN'S WAYS OF KNOWING MATHEMATICS

The idea that there might be meaning in the phrase "women's ways of knowing mathematics" and what that meaning might be has been the focus of much and varied attention among researchers and scholars interested in gender and mathematics throughout the last quarter century. Multiple possible meanings of this phrase are examined in the paragraphs below; before turning to that discussion, however, we consider briefly the late 20th-century history and controversy surrounding the general idea of women's ways of knowing.

In 1986, Mary Belenkey, Blythe Clinchy, Nancy Goldberger, and Jill Tarule published the results of an extensive qualitative study of 135 women's discussions of their own processes of knowing and understanding under the title *Women's Ways of Knowing: The Development of Self, Voice and Mind (WWK)*. The research was motivated by the failure of Harvard psychologist William Perry (1970) to include women in his influential study of knowing. *WWK* set forth five basic modes or categories (not stages) of knowing which were prevalent among the women interviewed: (a) silence, (b) received knowledge, (c) subjective knowledge, (d) procedural knowledge, and (e) constructed knowledge. In conceptualizing knowing, the authors rejected the predominant (malestream) metaphor of knowledge as seeing with the "mind's eye" and, instead, used voice as a metaphor, which, they argued, is more appropriate to women's experiences and ways of knowing (see especially pp. 16–20). This book has served several important functions related to research on gender and knowledge. First, it made a highly visible statement that gender researchers were no longer bound to models based on norms established through the study of males and would no longer be limiting their research into women's learning and cognition to studies of sex differences. Instead, women's intellect could and would be investigated and understood through the study of women in their own right, not only in relation to men. Secondly, at least within contexts of education, *WWK* was the most widely publicized of the many contemporary studies related to women's understandings. In areas related to science and mathematics, the work of Evelyn Fox Keller (1983, 1985), Sandra Harding (1986, 1987), Luce Irigaray (1983), and others addressed the relations of scientific knowledge, women's knowledge, and how *women* come to know. Extending Carol Gilligan's (1982) work on women's moral voice to epistemological voice, *WWK* provided metaphors, vocabulary, and a taxonomy with which researchers could organize, report, compare, and even combine their work. Third, *WWK* served as a springboard for new work in education generally (e.g., Goldberger et al., 1996) and mathematics education in particular (e.g., Becker, 1995). Fourth, this book served as a "lightening rod" for antifeminist backlash and criticism of sex/gender studies in general.

Criticism of *WWK* is a focused version of criticism of studies of women's ways of knowing more generally; it makes two basic complaints: (a) bias and (b) essentialism. The claims that this work is biased share a fundamental unhappiness that men have not been included in the study, and that women's ways of knowing are described without reference to men. For these critics, there can be no valid study of women except sex differences study. The ways biases of overemphasis on sex differences (and, conversely, on sex sameness) operate in research on gender are described well by Rachel Hare-Mustin and Jeanne Maracek (1988). The second area of criticism argues that *WWK* essentializes women. Essentialism is the claim that there are characteristics which all women share; theories of gender which assert the existence of such characteristics and studies which purport to find them are said to be essentializing. For example, claims that all women have a "maternal instinct" are essentializing. *WWK* has been said to be essentializing because it identifies five ways of knowing and claims that, together, these describe all women's knowing. Moreover, although the authors take pains to deny that they are laying out a stage theory, they explicate the modes of knowing in a linear order from least to most independent and sophisticated, and many readers interpret *WWK* to be a stage theory and, therefore (like all stage theories), as lending itself to essentializing. Responses, accusations, and debates over whether *WWK* is essentializing have been extensive. Jane Roland Martin (1994) argued convincingly, however, that excessive fear of essentializing can keep researchers from gaining important insights into the lives of women and the operation of gender. Some degree of generalization is necessary to conduct research, and to organize and implement findings.

Women's ways of knowing school mathematics.   The work of Belenky and colleagues (1986) has influenced the study of gender and school mathematics in at least two directions. Predating *WWK*, studies of women, girls, and mathematics through interviews, observations, and mathematics autobiographies were begun by Dorothy Buerk (1982, 1985). Because they provide insight into various women's thinking in relation to mathematics, such studies have proliferated, and many more are conducted each year. Many qualitative researchers have adopted the voice metaphor and the modes of knowing elaborated in *WWK* as a common body of terms and constructs used by researchers to organize, understand, and report on their data (papers collected in Rogers & Kaiser, 1995; Schmittau & Taylor, 1996; and elsewhere). As this body of studies has grown, the work of Foucault (1979) and of feminist theorists has led to the addition of other concepts (e.g., subject position, agency, discourse, power/knowledge) to the analytic tools used in understanding gender and mathematics (Walkerdine, 1988, 1989; Appelbaum, 1995; Walshaw, 2001). With increasing sophistication, researchers within the area of gender and mathematics have introduced concepts of their own (e.g., Erchick's [1996] space-barrier). Thus today, there is a rich literature describing the ways women experience mathematics in classrooms, both as students and as teachers, how they come to know mathematics, how mathematics operates within their lives, and related issues.

Although in a somewhat different direction, Joanne Rossi Becker and Judith Jacobs (Becker, 1995; Jacobs, 1993; Jacobs & Becker, 1997) also worked from the findings of Belenkey, Clinchy, Goldberger and Tarule (1986). These researchers examined the teaching of mathematics in light of the five modes of knowing, seeking to interpolate them with school mathematics and to identify ways in which curricula might be designed to address girls and women whose ways of knowing fit with each of these modes. Designing and testing lessons directed toward specific ways of knowing, Becker and Jacobs illustrated ways in which *WWK* could be used to change mathematics curricula. In yet a different direction, Suzanne Damarin (1996, 2000) also examined elements of classroom mathematics from a gender perspective, identifying mismatches between experiences of young women and girls and the approaches to specific curricular elements (fractions, distance problems) in textbooks and popular lessons.

Through the studies mentioned above and a great deal of related work, the decade from the mid 1980s to the mid 1990s was one of very active research in gender and mathematics, much of it qualitative in nature and contributing to conceptual change in the understanding of women's relations to mathematics. A major shift in the research literatures and educational activism of scholars engaged in mathematics-related gender work was underway. At the beginning of this period, the dominant focus was on sex-differences studies in which the mathematical abilities, accomplishments, attitudes, and behaviors of women were compared unfavorably with those of their male counterparts. Activism took the forms of remediation, recruitment to mathematical activity, and persuasion of its value. A decade later, qualitative researchers had learned a great deal about the inner strengths of girls and women, including their intellectual strengths, and about the difficulties girls and women encounter in the pursuit of mathematics and the absence of support for them as they negotiated these difficulties. In response, the gender and mathematics researcher/educational activist community made a major shift in focus, adopting the slogan "stop trying to fix the women; we have to fix the mathematics!"

This shift of allegiance, purpose, and direction, however easily stated, did not really resolve any problems, but instead introduced ambiguities, complexities, and a host of questions for researcher attention. What is the meaning of the phrase "fix the mathematics"? Are there really two fields—school mathematics and "real" mathematics? Can one of these be "fixed" without changing the other? Left to their own devices, would women create a different mathematics? Who would decide whether what they created was mathematics? What is mathematics, anyway? What about mathematics as a set of practices? As a community of workers? As the language of computing? Where should the focus of this "fixing" be directed? On the pedagogies of mathematics? On the content of mathematics curricula? The questions seem endless. In the remaining paragraphs of this section, we explore some of these issues entailed in "fixing the mathematics."

In turning to these discussions, it is important to be aware that the study of gender and mathematics is not the only area of study related to mathematics and mathematics education to undergo significant changes in the three or four decades since the 1970s. During roughly the same period, the dominant theoretical framework both for understanding students' learning of mathematics and for defining teaching practices has evolved from objectivist behaviorist and information processing theories to radical constructivism, situated cognition, and the social constructivism which undergirds much research and practice in mathematics education today. These shifts are deeply related to changes in the meanings of "knowledge" and "knowing" in ways that are often unstated (and more often unexamined); they challenge fundamental ideas of objectivity and some aspects of the logic of mathematics as taught in schools.[8] Simultaneous with these changes are changes in the conduct of mathematics per se. The use of probabilistic and computer-based methods in proof and the development and widespread use of fractals and chaos theory are but two examples. The growth of computing technology during the past quarter century has also had a substantial impact on all aspects of mathematics teaching and research. Mathematicians (e.g., Wolfram, 2002) predicted that further changes and radically new developments in mathematics will be necessary in the coming years to meet the needs of the sciences through which we understand and organize our world.

Women's ways of knowing mathematics in the (early) 21st century.

As we look toward the next several decades and the ways in which women's ways of knowing mathematics might develop and flourish, it is important to recall and respond to some concerns among women mathematicians—that is, among those women whose ways of knowing mathematics are currently most productive of new mathematical knowledge. In the view of (at least some) women mathematicians (e.g., Ruskai, 1995, 1997), current literature on gender and mathematics portrays women as mathematically incompetent and makes invisible both the contributions of women to mathematics and the practices that contribute to their success. This criticism has some validity, and it is important to celebrate successful women mathematicians. At the same time, it is important to eschew essentializing the life courses and work of today's successful women as the only way women can come to know and do mathematics in the future. At least in the United States, the practice of mathematics has not been equally open to all people (nor has the study of gender and mathematics). Full understanding of "women's ways of knowing mathematics" would require understanding of ethnomathematics (e.g., D'Ambrosio, 1979; Ascher, 1991; Eglash, 1999), as well as increasing the opportunities for Latinas and women of African and Native American (as well as Asian) descent to participate more fully in the study of mathematics. With these provisos in mind, we turn to the multiplicity of ways in which women may contribute further to and affect the knowing of mathematics in the coming years.

Some points from feminist theory and study of science.

Feminist philosophers and social scientists have been examining questions related to women and science for more than two decades. In *The Science Question in Feminism,* philosopher Sandra Harding (1986) asked why more women do not pursue careers in science (including mathematics) and posed five possible answers. Two of her answers are of interest here: (a) science and mathematics do not fit well with the way women view the world around them, and (b) women are not interested in pursuing the kinds of professions for which study of science and mathematics would prepare them. While the work of Harding and other feminist theorists has been a source of conflict between feminist theorists and scientists (see Longino & Hammonds, 1990; Gross, Levitt, & Lewis, 1997), there are reasons to believe that current and future developments will cause some of this conflict to dissipate and some convergence to occur around "women's ways of knowing mathematics." In particular, there is reason to hope that the two of Harding's observations cited above will become outdated.

The study of a field and its practices through lenses of feminist theory is not easy because it requires suspending assumptions and "unthinking"—if only temporarily—thoughts and beliefs that have become habitual. The difficulty of this unthinking is inversely related to the level of experience and other evidence that conflicts with the ideas and thus supports their unthinking. For this reason, the development and influence of feminist theory has been strongest in those areas of study closest to everyday lives (e.g., social sciences, arts, and literature). In this context, it is not surprising that there has been very little direct critique of mathematics or the ways we know it. Two exceptions are mathematician Bonnie Shulman's (1996) feminist historical

---

[8]In this short space, it is impossible to discuss these matters in detail. The point here is that the turn away from objectivity is a turn away from universal decidability and the "law of excluded middle." Without this law, proof by contradiction is impossible. In one sense, this is nothing new; there are longstanding constructivist schools within the Philosophy of Mathematics (Wilder, 1952); but nonetheless, proof by contradiction has been the curricular approach to the indefinability of a/0, irrationality of sqr(2), and the Fundamental Theorem of Arithmetic.

analysis of choices made in the development of mathematics and French feminist philosopher Luce Irigaray's (1983) challenge to psychoanalytic object-relations theory and its implications for mathematics.

There are at least two reasons to believe that we are at a point of change in the study of gender and mathematics. First, beginning with biology and medicine, and more recently, with engineering and physics, feminist thought is achieving a place in the study of the empirical sciences. It is easy to forget but important to remember that prior to 1970s feminist demand for change, little research was conducted on women's health; the very idea of "women's ways of having heart disease" would have been considered absurd. Today there are large-scale medical studies focused on women and the etiologies of disease among females. Simultaneously, an increasingly large and complex body of research and scholarship (e.g., Mayberry, Subramaniam, & Weasel, 2001) provides a broadly based investigation of science by scientists working from standpoints informed by feminist theory. Of particular interest to mathematics is the work of theoretical physicist Karen Barad (1995, 2003), who has been working with Neils Bohr's theory, linking scientific theory with concepts such as agency and objectivity as they have been developed in feminist research. Barad's work points to the inseparability of methods and constructs through which scientists investigate and understand the world. While she is speaking primarily of methods of measurement, extending her work to analysis of quantitative, spatial, or other data would link feminist theories of agency and strong objectivity with women's ways of knowing mathematics.

The second reason to anticipate the coming together of feminist theorists and mathematicians lies in the need for new mathematics on the part of researchers in a wide variety of fields, but particularly, for the study of issues related to equity and diversity across gender, race, class, and other dimensions of our social structure. Many researchers/scholars in these areas have found strict reliance on statistical methods to be insufficient for their investigations. Beyond demographic studies, feminist research methodology (e.g., Fonow & Cook, 1991) is, by and large, ethnographic or more generally qualitative in approach. The data gathered are in textual form, increasingly supplemented with digital video, and are highly complex; however, the computer-based methods of data reduction available to date are simplistic. An extensive literature (see Denzin & Lincoln, 2000) guides data analysis and reduction, but analyses are currently far from algorithmic. In addition, findings of qualitative study are currently considered to be "local" to the particular study and, in the absence of rigorous methods, synthesis of findings across studies is not supported. Whereas quantitative researchers are responsible for assuring generalizability of their findings to larger populations, qualitative researchers use rigorous methods to reveal detail and to deepen our understanding of particular situations. With regard to generalizability, the job of the qualitative researcher is to triangulate findings (assuring consistency across forms of data) and to report data and findings with sufficient fidelity and detail that educators at other sites can determine whether the findings would generalize to their settings. Thus, while quantitative studies lend themselves to brief statistical summaries and to syntheses using meta-analytic techniques (Glass, McGaw, & Smith, 1981), similar modes of presenting detailed but brief summaries are not available for qualitative work. The richness of qualitative equity studies, for example, cannot be synthesized and their findings reduced to a brief document for consideration by policy makers; therefore, in the absence of synthetic methods, a collection of rigorous qualitative studies is often viewed erroneously as simply a collection of anecdotes.

This is a particular case of the more general need for new mathematics, new ways of representing complexity. How this problem is resolved will depend on the basic assumptions, conscious or unconscious, of those devising and/or applying the mathematics in question. It is in the resolution of the complexity of data surrounding issues of interest and importance to women that women's ways of knowing mathematics must and will grow in magnitude and importance in the coming years.

SUMMARY AND RECOMMENDATIONS

In this chapter, we have explored the current status of females in mathematics, setting our findings against the backdrop of the mathematics chapter in the 1985 *Handbook for Achieving Gender Equity through Education.* We see increasing signs of gender equity in mathematics at the school and undergraduate level. Small but statistically significant sex-related differences favoring white and Asian American males do occur in some measures of mathematics ability and achievement. Despite this, a larger percentage of girls are now taking advanced placement mathematics courses at the high school level than in 1985.

Studies of gender-related attitudinal differences still report differences in confidence in one's ability to do mathematics, in perceived usefulness of mathematics, and perceived feelings of belonging in the mathematical community which "favor" males, and studies of problem solving strategies and choices of mathematics areas of comfort often show gender-related differences. Traditional attitudes of our society also play a part in gender-related differences in mathematics. As Susan Chipman stated, "It is clear that many people *do not want to believe* that girls and women can be good at mathematics. . . . Whenever a statistically significant difference is found in the way males and females tend to do mathematics is observed, the male way of doing things (faster retrieval of math facts) tends to be stated in a more positive way than the supposedly female way of doing things (reliance on rote learning)" (Chipman, 2005, p. 18) .

Nevertheless, female and male undergraduates are declaring mathematics majors in equal numbers, but females are more likely to drop out of the mathematics major than males. Similar to all sciences and engineering programs, in math it is at the graduate and postgraduate level and in academic employment where large disparities in positions or pay between males and females still exist. By contrast, women have made much more progress in the law and in medicine than in mathematics and mathematics-based sciences such as computing, physics, or engineering. "Putative sex differences in cognitive abilities continue to be advanced as the preferred explanation for sex difference in career participation, even though large sex differences in other variables would seem to be more plausible. The topic of sex differences remains far too sexy a topic" (Chipman, 2005, p. 18).

Looking at mathematics from a feminist perspective, one would say, "Don't fix the women, fix the mathematics." Indeed, mathematics has changed considerably in the last 20 years or so. Applied mathematics is taking a larger role in the community, with applications to business, biology, graphics, and computer sciences just to mention a few. Working in teams of interdisciplinary scholars, communication and writing are becoming essential skills. Even the nature of mathematical proof has expanded to incorporate extremely complex computer-generated solutions.

Undoubtedly, the need still exists to encourage girls and young women to enter the field of mathematics, not only for reasons of fairness and equity, but also because our nation is woefully short of the mathematical talent needed to keep the United States at the forefront of science and technology. To nurture young talent, many extracurricular programs exist that enhance mathematics talent and skills. Unfortunately, most of these are dominated by males, who may then continue this domination throughout their academic and career paths.

RECOMMENDATIONS

Data on sex-related differences in mathematical achievement, persistence, and attitudes should continue to be collected and analyzed; however, these data need to be disaggregated across race/ethnicity lines. We know too little about gender-related differences in mathematical achievement, persistence, or attitudes between females and males in racial and ethnic groups. Variability as well as mean scores should be contrasted.

Quantitative analysis can give a picture of current performance and, with longitudinal studies, can indicate changes in performance and persistence. It cannot, however, help determine how to enhance mathematical performance, attitudes, and per-

sistence among girls and women. Particularly missing in the research are reasons for women's lack of persistence in continuing in mathematics from the undergraduate to the graduate program. Case and ethnographic studies are needed here to present a deeper and more graphic explanation of the problems; however, many such studies in all fields lack sufficient key elements to ensure reliability or replicability. These studies need to (a) clearly stipulate under what hypotheses they are undertaken, (b) describe how claims are produced, and be backed by evidence, and (c) identify alternative explanations for the evidence presented. (NRC, 2002, 2004). Gender-related studies should be viewed from a feminist perspective to insure that the right questions are asked and that found differences are not phrased in a putative manner.

Analysis of the value of the most promising programs to encourage, recruit, and retain women in mathematics should be undertaken with wide dissemination of the design of those found to be well-researched, proven successful, and replicable. Over the past twenty years, much reinvention of the wheels has occurred without reference to past successes and failures. The time, energy, and enthusiasm of many young women in mathematics have been spent in planning programs for which there are already good models.

ACKNOWLEDGEMENTS

Carole Lacampagne was the lead author and primarily responsible for The Gender Differences in Involvement in Extra Curricular Mathematics Activities and Summary and Recommendations. Patricia Campbell contributed The Status of Sex Equity in Mathematics. Abbe H. Herzig contributed Gender Equity in Postsecondary Mathematics, Suzanne Damarin contributed Women's Ways of Knowing Mathematics. Christina M. Vogt contributed additional material and editorial suggestions to the chapter.

The authors would also like to thank Joanne Rossi Becker, San Jose State University, San Jose, CA for her helpful review.

References

ACT Inc. (2004a). ACT high school profile. Retrieved October 5, 2004, from chttp://www.act.org/news/data/04/pdf/t6-7-8.pdf

ACT Inc. (2004b). 2004 ACT national and state scores. Retrieved October 4, 2004, from http://www.act.org/news/data/04/charts/text.html#four

Adelman, C. (1998). Women and men of the engineering path: A model for analyses of undergraduate careers. Washington, DC: U. S. Department of Education.

Allexsaht-Snider, M., & Hart, L. E. (2001). "Mathematics for All": How do we get there? *Theory into Practice, 40*(2), 93–101.

Ames, C. (1992). Classrooms: Goals, structures, and student motivation. *Journal of Educational Psychology, 84*(3), 261–271.

Appelbaum, P. (1995). *Popular culture, educational discourse, and mathematics.* Albany, NY: SUNY Press.

Ascher, M. (1991). *Ethnomathematics: A multicultural view of mathematical ideas.* Belmont, CA: Brooks/Cole.

Astin, A. W. (1993). What matters in college: Four critical years revisited. San Francisco: Jossey-Bass, 1994.

Bair, C. R., & Haworth, J. G. (1999, November). *Doctoral Student Attrition and Persistence: A Meta-Synthesis of Research.* Paper presented

at the Annual Meeting of the Association for the Study of Higher Education (ASHE), San Antonio, TX.

Barad, K. (1995). A feminist approach to teaching quantum physics. In S. V. Rosser (Ed.), *Teaching the Majority: Breaking the Gender Barrier in Science, Mathematics, and Engineering* (pp. 43–75). New York: Teachers College Press.

Barad, K. (2003). Posthumanist performativity: Toward an understanding of how matter comes to matter. *Signs: Journal of Women in Culture & Society, 28*(3), 801–832.

Bass, H. (2003). The Carnegie Initiative on the Doctorate: The case of mathematics. *Notices of the American Mathematical Society, 50*(7), 767–776.

Becker, J. R. (1984). In pursuit of graduate education in mathematics: factors that influence women and men. *Journal of Educational Equity and Leadership, 4*(1), 39–53.

Becker, J. R. (1990). Graduate education in the mathematical sciences: Factors influencing women and men. In L. Burton (Ed.), *Gender and mathematics: An international perspective* (pp. 119–130). London: Cassell Educational Limited.

Becker, J. R. (1995). Women's ways of knowing mathematics. In P. Rogers & G. Kaiser (Eds.), *Equity in mathematics education: Influences of feminism and culture* (pp. 163–174). London: The Falmer Press.

Belenky, M. F., Clinchy, B. M., Goldberger, N. R., & Tarule, J. M. (1986). *Women's ways of knowing: The development of self, voice, and mind*. New York: Basic Books.

Berg, H. M., & Ferber, M. A. (1983). Men and women graduate students: Who succeeds and why? *Journal of Higher Education, 54*(6), 629–648.

Bielinski, J., & Davidson, M. J. (1998). Gender differences by item difficulty: Interactions in multiple-choice mathematics items. *American Educational Research Journal, 35*(3), 455–476.

Boaler, J. (2002). The development of disciplinary relationships: Knowledge, practice, and identity in mathematics classrooms. *For the Learning of Mathematics, 22*(1), 42–47.

Boaler, J., Wiliam, D., & Zevenbergen, R. (2000). *The construction of identity in secondary mathematics education.* Paper presented at the Mathematics and Society Conference, Montechoro, Portugal, March 2000.

Bowen, W. G., & Rudenstine, N. L. (1992). *In Pursuit of the Ph.D.* Princeton, NJ: Princeton University Press.

Buerk, D. (1982). An experience with some able women who avoid mathematics. *For the Learning of Mathematics, 3*(2), 19–24.

Buerk, D. (1985). The voices of women making meaning in mathematics. *Journal of Education, 167*(3), 59–70.

Bureau of Labor Statistics. (2004, April). *College enrollment and work activity of 2003 high school graduates.* Retrieved December 19, 2004, from http://www.bls.gov/news.release/hsgec.nr0.htm

Burton, L. (1999). Fables: The tortoise? The hare? The mathematically underachieving male? *Gender and Education, 11*(4), 413–426.

Burton, L. (2000, November). Strangers in paradise? The construction of mathematics as a male community of practice, *5th Symposium on Gender Research, The Nature of Gender—The Gender of Nature.* Kiel, Germany.

Burton, L. (2001, October). Mathematics? No thanks—choosing and then rejecting mathematics, *National Day Conference, Key Stage 3 Teachers: the current situation, initiatives, and visions.* London, England.

Burton, N. W., & Ramist, L. (2001). *Predicting success in college: SAT studies of classes graduating since 1980.* New York: College Board. Retrieved May 21, 2005, from http://www.collegeboard.com/research/pdf/rdreport200_3919.pdf.

Cahalan, C. (2000). Gender differences in advanced mathematical problem solving. *Journal of Experimental Child Psychology, 75*(3), 165–190.

California Postsecondary Education Commission. (1990). *Shortening Time to the Doctoral Degree: A report to the legislature and the University of California in Response to Senate Concurrent Resolution 66* (No. 90-29). Sacramento, CA: Author.

Campbell, P. B. (1995). Redefining the 'girl problem in mathematics'. In W. G. Secada, E. Fennema & L. Byrd Adajian (Eds.), *New directions for equity in mathematics education* (pp. 225–241). New York: Cambridge University Press.

Campbell, P. B., & Perlman, L. K. (2005). Does it work? Using web-based data in decision-making. Retrieved January 15, 2006, from http://www.pdf/ME-DoesItWork.pdf

Carlson, M. P. (1999). The mathematical behavior of six successful mathematics graduate students: Influences leading to mathematical success. *Educational Studies in Mathematics, 40,* 237–258.

Chipman, S. F. (2005). Research on the woman and mathematics issue: A personal case history. In A. M. Gallagher & J. C. Kaufman (Eds.) *Gender differences in mathematics: An integrative psychological approach* (pp. 1–24). New York: Cambridge University Press.

Clewell, B. C., & Campbell, P. B. (2002). Taking stock: Where we've been, where we are going. *Journal of Women and Minorities in Science and Engineering, 8,* 255–284.

Cole, J. R., & Zuckerman, H. (1987). Marriage, motherhood and research performance in science. *Scientific American, 256*(2), 119–125.

Coley, R. J. (2001). *Differences in the gender gap: Comparisons across racial/ethnic groups in education and work.* Princeton, NJ: Educational Testing Service.

College Board. (2003). Participation in AP: Women. Retrieved October 5, 2004 from http://apcentral.collegeboard.com/article/0,3045,150-156-0-2060,00.html

College Board. (2004a). *2004 college bound seniors: A profile of SAT program test takers.* Retrieved October 5, 2004, from http://www.collegeboard.com/prod_downloads/about/news_info/cbsenior/yr2004/2004_CBSNR_total_group.pdf

College Board. (2004b). *SAT percentile ranks for males, females and total group college-bound seniors-Mathematics.* Retrieved May 21, 2005 from http://www.collegeboard.com/prod_downloads/about/news_info/cbsenior/yr2003/pdf/2003CBSMathematics.pdf.

College Board. (2005). *2005 college bound seniors: Total group profile report.* Retrieved October 15, 2005, from http://www.collegeboard.com/prod_downloads/about/news_info/cbsenior/yr2005/2005-college-bound-seniors.pdf

Committee on the Participation of Women. (2003). Improving the persistence of women in graduate mathematics. *Joint Meeting of the American Mathematical Society and the Mathematical Association of America.* Baltimore, MD, January 2003.

Cooper, D. A. (2000). Changing the faces of mathematics Ph.D.'s: What we are learning at the University of Maryland. In M. E. Strutchens, M. L. Johnson, & W. F. Tate (Eds.), *Changing the Faces of Mathematics: Perspectives on African Americans* (pp. 179–192). Reston, VA: National Council of Teachers of Mathematics.

Damarin, S. K. (1996). Thoughts on Gender, Fractions and Toys. *Focus on Learning Problems in Mathematics, 18*(1, 2, 3), 97–105.

Damarin, S. K. (2000). Equity, experience, abstraction: Old issues, new considerations. In W. G. Secada (Ed.), *Changing Faces of Mathematics: Multiculturalism and Gender Equity* (pp. 75–83) Reston, VA: National Council of Teachers of Mathematics.

Damarin, S. K. (2000). The mathematically able as a Marked Category. *Gender and Education, 12*(1), 69–85.

D'Ambrosio, U. (1979). Mathematics and society: Some historical considerations and implications. *Philosphia Mathematica, 15/16,* 106–126.

Davis, P. W., Maxwell, J. W., & Remick, K. M. (1999). 1998 Annual Survey of the Mathematical Sciences (Second Report). *Notices of the American Mathematical Society, 46*(8), 894–909.

Denzin, N. K., & Lincoln, Y. S. (2000). Handbook of qualitative research (2nd ed.). Thousand Oaks, CA: Sage Publications.

Donoghue, E. F. (2005). Gender differences in mathematics contest performance. Unpublished raw data.

Eglash, R. (1999). *African fractals: modern computing and indigenous design.* New Brunswick, NJ: Rutgers University Press

Erchick, D. B. (1996). *Women and mathematics: Negotiating the Space/Barrier.* Unpublished doctoral dissertation, Ohio State University, Columbus.

Etzkowitz, H., Kemelgor, C., Neuschatz, M., & Uzzi, B. (1992). Athena unbound: Barriers to women in academic science and engineering. *Science and Public Policy, 19*(3), 157–179.

Etzkowitz, H., Kemelgor, C., & Uzzi, B. (2000). *Athena unbound: The advancement of women in science and technology* (Vol. 19). Cambridge: Cambridge University Press.

Faranelli, F. (2005). History of the MAA/Tensor small grant program: Ten years encouraging women in mathematics and science. *Focus: The Newsletter of the Mathematical Association of America, 25*(2), 7–8.

Fennema, E., & Peterson, P. (1985). Autonomous learning behavior: A possible explanation of gender-related differences in mathematics. In L. C. Wilkinson & C. B. Marrett (Eds.), *Gender Influences in Classroom Interaction* (pp. 17–35). Madison, WI: University of Wisconsin.

Fonow, M. M., & Cook, J. A. (1991). *Beyond methodology: feminist scholarship as lived research*. Bloomington, IN: Indiana University Press.

Foucault, M. (1979). *Discipline and punish: the birth of the prison* (A. Sheridan, Trans.). New York: Vintage Books.

Gilligan, C. (1982). *In a different voice: psychological theory and women's development*. Cambridge, MA: Harvard University Press.

Giordano, F. (2004). Modeling forum: Results of the 2004 mathematical contest in modeling. *UMAP: The Journal of Undergraduate mathematics and its Applications, 25*(3), 189–214.

Girves, J. E., & Wemmerus, V. (1988). Developing models of graduate student degree progress. *Journal of Higher Education, 59*(2), 163–189

Glass, G. V., McGaw, B., & Smith, M. L. (1981). *Meta-analysis in social research*. Beverly Hills, CA: Sage Publications.

Goldberger, N. R. et al. (Ed.). (1998). Knowledge, difference, and power: Essays inspired by Women's ways of knowing. New York: Basic Books.

Golde, C. M. (1996). *How departmental contextual factors shape doctoral student attrition*. Unpublished doctoral dissertation, Stanford University, California.

Gould, S. L. (1996). *Strategies used by secondary school students in learning new concepts which require spatial visualization*. Unpublished doctoral dissertation, Teachers College, Columbia University, New York.

Grant, L., Kennelly, I., & Ward, K. B. (2000). Revisiting the gender, marriage, and parenthood puzzle in scientific careers. *Women's Studies Quarterly, 28*(1/2), 62–85.

Gross, P. R., Levitt, N., & Lewis, M. W. (Eds.). (1997) *The flight from science and reason*. New York: New York Academy of Sciences; Baltimore: Johns Hopkins University Press.

Harding, S. (1986). *The science question in feminism*. Ithaca, NY: Cornell University Press.

Harding, S. (1987). The Method Question. *Hypatia, 2*(3), 19–36.

Hare-Mustin, R. T., & Maracek, J. (1988). The meaning of difference: Gender theory, postmodernism, and psychology. *American Psychologist, 43*(6), 455–464.

Herzig, A. H. (2002). Where have all the students gone? Participation of doctoral students in authentic mathematical activity as a necessary condition for persistence toward the Ph.D. *Educational Studies in Mathematics, 50*(2), 177–212.

Herzig, A. H. (2004a). Becoming mathematicians: Women and students of color choosing and leaving doctoral mathematics. *Review of Educational Research, 74*(2), 171–214.

Herzig, A. H. (2004b). *The Filter of Mathematics: What Does Mathematics Filter For?* Paper presented at the annual meeting of the American Educational Research Association, San Diego, CA.

Herzig, A. H. (2004c). "Slaughtering this beautiful math": Graduate women choosing and leaving mathematics. *Gender and Education, 16*(3), 379–395.

Herzig, A. H. (2004d). *Thinking, feeling, acting like a mathematician: Women and people of color in doctoral mathematics*. Paper presented at the annual meeting of the North American Chapter of the International Group for the Psychology of Mathematics Education, Toronto, Canada.

Hinchey, P. H., & Kimmel, I. W. (2000). *The graduate grind: A critical look at graduate education*. New York: Falmer Press.

Hollenshead, C., Younce, P. S., & Wenzel, S. A. (1994). Women graduate students in mathematics and physics: Reflections on Success. *Journal of Women and Minorities in Science and Engineering, 1*, 63–88.

Huang, G., Taddese, N., & Walter, E. (2000). *Entry and persistence of women and minorities in college science and engineering education* (NCES 2000-061). Washington, DC: U.S Government Printing Office.

Irigaray, L. (1983). Is the subject of science sexed? *Hypatia, 2*(3), 65–88.

Jacobs, J. (1993). *Using a feminist pedagogy to promote gender equity*. Presentation at the 1993 NCTM National Conference, Seattle, WA.

Jacobs, J. E., & Becker, J. R. (1997). Creating a gender-equitable multicultural classroom using feminist pedagogy. In J. Trentacosta & M. J. Kenney (Eds.), *Multicultural and gender equity in the mathematics classroom, 1997 Yearbook* (pp. 107–114). Reston, VA: National Council of Teachers of Mathematics.

Johnston, B. (1995). Mathematics: An abstracted discourse. In P. Rogers & G. Kaiser (Eds.), *Equity in mathematics education: Influences of feminism and culture* (pp. 226–234). London: The Falmer Press.

Keiser, L. R., Wilkins, V. M., Meier, K. J., & Holland, C. (n.d.). Lipstick and logarithms: Gender, institutional context, and representative bureaucracy. Retrieved October 16, 2005 from http://teep.tamu.edu/pubs/lipstick.pdf.

Keller, E. F. (1983). *A feeling for the organism: The life and work of Barbara McClintock*. New York: W. H. Freeman.

Keller, E. F. (1985). *Reflections on gender and science*. New Haven, CT: Yale University Press.

Kirkman, E. E., Maxwell, J. W., & Rose, C. (2004a). 2003 annual survey of the mathematical sciences (first report). *Notices of the American Mathematical Society, 51*(2), 218–233.

Kirkman, E. E., Maxwell, J. W., & Rose, C. (2004b). 2003 annual survey of the mathematical sciences (third report). *Notices of the American Mathematical Society, 51*(8), 901–912.

Kirkman, E. E., Maxwell, J. W., & Rose, C. (2006). 2005 annual survey of the mathematical sciences (first report). *Notices of the American Mathematical Society, 53*(2), 230–245.

Klopfenstein, K. (n.d.). Beyond test scores: The impact of black teacher role models on rigorous mathematics-taking. Retrieved October 16, 2005, from http://www.utdallas.edu/research/tsp/pdfpapers/newpaper2.pdf

Ladson-Billings, G. (1997). It doesn't add up: African American students' mathematics achievement. *Journal for Research in Mathematics Education, 28*(6), 697–708.

Longino, H. E., & Hammonds, E. (1990). Conflicts and tensions in the feminist study of gender and science. In M. Hirsch & E. Fox Keller (Eds.), *Conflicts in feminism* (pp. 164–183). New York: Routledge.

Lovitts, B. E. (2001). *Leaving the ivory tower: The causes and consequences of departure from doctoral study*. Lanham, MD: Rowman and Littlefield.

Maddy, P. (1990). *Realism in Mathematics*. Oxford, UK: Clarendon Press.

Madison, B. L., & Hart, T. A. (1990). A challenge of numbers: People in the mathematical sciences. Washington, DC: National Academy Press.

Manzo, K. K. (1994). American University: Success is in the numbers, African American women excel in math Ph.D. program. *Black Issues in Higher Education, 11*, 40–43.

Martin, J. R. (1994). Methodological essentialism, false difference, and other dangerous traps. *Signs, 19*(3), pp. 630–657.

Mathematical Association of America, & National Association of Mathematicians. (1997). *Survey of minority graduate students in U.S. mathematical sciences departments*. Washington, DC.: Author

Mayberry, M., Subramaniam, B., & Weasel, L. H. (Eds.). (2001). *Feminist science studies: a new generation*. New York: Routledge.

Mount Holyoke. (2005). *Summer math*. Retrieved October 10, 2004, from http://www.mtholyoke.edu/proj/summermath/about.html

National Assessment of Educational Progress. (2001). *The nation's report card mathematics*. Retrieved December 2, 2001, from http://nces.ed/gov/nationsreportcard/mathematics

National Assessment of Educational Progress. (2005). The nation's report card mathematics. Retrieved October 19, 2005, from http://nationsreportcard.gov/reading_mathematics_2005/s0018.asp

National Center for Education Statistics. (2004). *Mini-Digest of education statistics, 2003*, (NCES 2005–017). Washington, DC: Author.

National Council of Teachers of Mathematics. (1989). *Curriculum and evaluation for school mathematics.* Reston, VA: Author.

National Council of Teachers of Mathematics. (2000). *Principles and standards for school mathematics.* Reston, VA: Author.

National Research Council. (1992). *Educating mathematical scientists: Doctoral study and the postdoctoral experience in the United States.* Washington, DC: National Academy Press.

National Research Council. (2004). *On evaluating curricular effectiveness: Judging the quality of K–12 mathematics evaluations.* Committee for a Review of the Evaluation Data on the Effectiveness of NSF-Supported and Commercially Generated Mathematics Curriculum Materials. Confrey, J. & Stohl, V., Editors. Mathematical Sciences Education Board. Division of Behavioral and Social Sciences and Education. Washington, DC: The National Academy Press.

National Research Council. (2002). *Scientific research in education.* Committee on Scientific Principles for Education Research. Shavelson, R. J.,& Towne, L., Editors. Center for Education. Division of Behavioral and Social Sciences and Education. Washington, DC: National Academy Press.

National Science Foundation. (1989). *Materials for middle school mathematics instruction: Program solicitation.* Arlington, VA: Author.

National Science Foundation. (1998). *Summary of workshop on graduate student attrition* (No. NSF 99-314). Arlington, VA: Author.

National Science Foundation. (1999). *Women, Minorities, and Persons with Disabilities in Science and Engineering,* (NSF99–338) Arlington, VA: Author.

National Science Foundation. (2002). *Science and Engineering Indicators—2002,* (NSB-02-1). Arlington, VA: Author.

National Science Foundation. (2003). *Graduate students and postdoctorates in science and engineering: Fall 2001,* (NSF 03–320*).* Arlington, VA: Author.

National Science Foundation. (2004). *Science and Engineering Indicators 2004,* (NSB-04-01). Arlington, VA: Author.

Nerad, M., & Cerny, J. (1993). From facts to action: Expanding the graduate division's educational role. *New Directions for Institutional Research, 80,* 27–39.

Noddings, N. (1996). Equity and mathematics: Not a simple issue. *Journal for Research in Mathematics Education, 27*(5), 609–615

The Ohio State University. (2005). *The Ross Program.* Retrieved May 26, 2005, from http://www.math.ohio-state.edu/ross/introduction.html.

Olson, S. (2004). *Count down: Six kids vie for glory at the world's toughest math competition.* Boston, MA: Houghton Mifflin Company.

Orr, E. W. (1997). *Twice as less: Black English and the performance of black students in mathematics and science.* New York: W.W. Norton.

Perkins, R., Kleiner, B., Roey, S., & Brown, J. (2004). *The high school transcript study: A decade of change in curricula and achievement, 1990–2000,* (NCES 2004-455). Washington, DC: US Department of Education: Institute of Education Sciences

Perry, W. G. (1970). *Forms of Intellectual and Ethical Development in the College Years.* New York: Holt, Rinehart, and Winston

Rogers, P., & Kaiser, G. (Eds.). (1995). *Equity in mathematics education: Influences of feminism and culture.* London & Washington, DC: The Falmer Press.

Rosser, S. V. (1995). Reaching the majority: Retaining women in the pipeline. In S. V. Rosser (Ed.), *Teaching the majority: Breaking the gender barrier in science, mathematics, and engineering* (pp. 1–21). New York: Teachers College Press.

Ruskai, M. B. (1995). A mathematician's perspective. In B. Grevholm & G. Hanna (Eds.). *Gender and mathematics education* (pp. 385–389). Lund, Sweden: Lund University Press.

Ruskai, M. B. (1997). Are "feminist perspectives" in mathematics and science feminist? In P. R. Gross, N. Levitt, & Martin W. Lewis (Eds.), *The flight from science and reason* (pp. 437–444). New York & Baltimore: New York Academy of Sciences & Johns Hopkins University Press.

Schmittau, J., & Taylor, L. (Eds.) (1996). Focus on learning problems in mathematics [Special issue]. *Gender and Mathematics: Multiple Voices, 18*(1, 2, & 3).

Seymour, E., & Hewitt, N. M. (1997). *Talking about leaving: Why undergraduates leave the sciences.* Boulder, CO: Westview Press.

Shulman, B. (1996). What if we change our axioms? A feminist inquiry into the foundations of mathematics. *Configurations 4*(3), 427–451.

Sonnert, G., & Holton, G. (1995). *Who succeeds in science? The gender dimension.* New Brunswick, NJ: Rutgers University Press.

Stage, E. K., Kreinberg, N., Eccles, J., & Becker, J. R. (1985). Increasing the participation and achievement of girls and women in mathematics, science and engineering. In S.S. Klein (Ed.), *Handbook for achieving sex equity through education.* (pp. 237–268). Baltimore, MD: Johns Hopkins Press.

Stage, F. K., & Maple, S. A. (1996). Incompatible goals: Narratives of graduate women in the mathematics pipeline. *American Educational Research Journal, 33*(1), 23–51.

Steen, L. A. (1999). Theories that gyre and gimble in the wabe. [Review of *Mathematics Education as a Research Domain: A Search for Identity*]. *Journal for Research in Mathematics Education, 30*(2), 235–241.

Straley, H. W. (2004). Mathematical modeling in high school. *Consortium: The Newsletter of the Consortium for Mathematics and its Applications, 87,* 3–6.

Tate, W. F. (1995). Returning to the root: A culturally relevant approach to mathematics pedagogy. *Theory into Practice, 34*(3), 166–173.

Tinto, V. (1993). *Leaving College: Rethinking the Causes and Cures of Student Attrition* (2nd ed.). Chicago: University of Chicago Press.

The Urban Institute Education Policy Institute. (2002). *Summary Report on the Impact Study of the National Science Foundation's Program for Women and Girls.* Arlington, VA: National Science Foundation.

Walkerdine, V. (1988). *The mastery of reason: Cognitive development and the production of rationality.* London & New York: Routledge.

Walkerdine, V. (Compiler). (1989). *Counting girls out.* London: Virago.

Walshaw, M. (2001). A Foucauldian gaze on gender research: What do you do when confronted with the tunnel at the end of the light? *Journal for Research in Mathematics Education, 32*(5), 471–492.

Willingham, W. W., Cole, N. S., Lewis, C., & Leung, S. W. (1997). Test performance. In W. W. Willingham & N. S. Cole (Eds.), *Gender and fair assessment* (pp. 55–126). Mahwah, NJ: Lawrence Erlbaum.

Wolfram, S. (2002) *A new kind of science,* pp. 55–126. Champaign, IL: Wolfram Media.

Zevenbergen, R. (2004). *Bourdieuian framings of mathematics education practice.* Paper presented at annual Meeting of the American Educational Research Association, San Diego, CA.

Zwick, R. (1991). *Differences in Graduate School Attainment Patterns across Academic Programs and Demographic Groups.* (No. ERIC Document No. 354 852). Princeton, NJ: Educational Testing Service.

·13·

GENDER EQUITY IN SCIENCE, ENGINEERING, AND TECHNOLOGY

Carol Burger, * *Gypsy Abbott, Sheila Tobias, Janice Koch, Christine Vogt, Teri Sosa with Lisa Bievenue, Delores Carlito, and Candace Strawn*

FROM MARGIN TO MAINSTREAM: WOMEN ARE ESSENTIAL TO THE SOLUTION

In 1985, when the first *Handbook for Achieving Sex Equity through Education* (Klein, 1985) was published, there were scores of activists, scholars, and administrators concerned with the near absence of women in certain disciplines and their overall underrepresentation in the science, engineering, and technology (SET) fields. Gender equity—and its concomitant, racial equity—in SET was a women's problem, not society's. Globalization was providing opportunities—not competition—for American business, and, since the United States was able to attract as many PhD candidates and fully trained researchers from other countries as it needed, our country continued to lead the world both in scientific and engineering research and in the innovative new products and whole new industries that such research could deliver. Integrating women and minorities into science and engineering was desirable but was not an essential ingredient.[1]

This was not the case two decades later. Fallout from September 11th, a more profound understanding of the threats as well as the benefits of globalization, and continued (and embarrassing) cross-national comparisons of U.S. math and science achievement reported in the periodic *Trends in the International Mathematics and Science Study* (*TIMSS*) (Martin, Mullis, Gonzalez, & Chrostowski, 2004) moved the integration of women and girls into SET from a problem at the margin to an essential part of the solution (Association of American Universities, 2000, 2004; Committee on Science, Engineering, and Public Policy, 2006).

The United States has too few scientists and science workers to support a high-tech, innovation-driven economy without the influx of new science workers. The average age of the current scientific workforce is 54, and some of our most talented foreign born, who might have replaced these workers, are choosing instead to go back home. The National Science Foundation reported (Oliver, 2005) that there was a steady three-year drop (from 2001 to 2004) in the number of students with temporary visas who enrolled in graduate science and engineering programs at U.S. universities. Maintaining America's economic competitiveness especially in the sciences and technology, has come to be seen as more dependent on attracting and retaining American-born students in science, which, in turn, is essential to meeting America's economic and security challenges in the 21st Century (Association of American Universities, 2006; Augustine, 2005; Business Roundtable, 2005; Friedman, 2005; Committee on Science, Engineering, and Public Policy, 2006).

A majority of young people in the U.S. disengage early from science. A large (perhaps disproportionate) number of those who could do science and choose not to are women and minorities (Sztein, 2005). However, their disengagement can no longer be regarded as unique to their gender or race, but rather as symptomatic.

The enduring metaphor for women's voyages through SET is that of the leaky pipeline (Alper, 1993; Camp, Miller, & Davies, 2000; Changing America, 1989; Gurer & Camp, 2002, but this metaphor is problematic in several ways. The metaphor of a pipeline poses students as passive participants in their education, whose progress through their education is affected only by market forces. A leaky pipeline does not ade-

---

*The bold face name is the Lead Author.

[1]One scientist, Gerald Holton, saw the situation differently already in 1983. While not yet focusing on the "gender dimension in science" (this came later; viz Sonnert G. (and Holton) *Who Succeeds in Science? The Gender Dimension* 1995), Holton sounded an early alarm, calling for radical educational reform (especially in the sciences) in *A Nation at Risk* (Holton, 1983).

quately address why students of some demographic groups stay in SET while others leave in greater proportions, and it fails to model important features of postsecondary SET education that may contribute to attrition, such as its competitive and individualistic nature. By combining all students into one undifferentiated volume of "fluid," this metaphor allows researchers and policymakers to overlook the very human implications of the postsecondary educational environment in mathematics (Herzig, 2004). Using the pipeline metaphor, we see that most programs address the input end of that pipeline with the thought that even with leaks, more women into SET would have to equal more women out into the SET workplace. Not many programs have addressed plugging the leaks themselves mainly because this is rightly seen as an attempt at institutional transformation. Engendering a cultural change in physics or engineering is a much more difficult prospect than organizing a weeklong summer science camp for middle-school girls. One suggestion for slowing girls' attrition was made by Lederman (2005) who suggested that students who are exposed to the ideas about how science and society interact may be more likely to appreciate how SET is influenced by society in the way research questions are posed and how science evolved as a male pursuit. We anticipate that they will see that the scientific effort is not immutable and how it can have room for a diversity of opinions and viewpoints. As stemming the leaky pipeline becomes an urgent national priority, the analyses and interventions designed to attract and retain girls and women in science outlined in this chapter will be of greater and greater relevance to us all (Business Roundtable, 2005).

CURRENT STATUS OF WOMEN IN SCIENCE

In the 40 years since the women's movement was reenergized in 1966, discrimination on the basis of gender along with its many more subtle manifestations has been significantly reduced by federal law. The legislative history is described in the chapter on "The Role of Government in Advancing Gender Equity in Education." In addition to legislation, in the 1970s scholars embarked on a critical examination of the culture of science especially about how science and scientists are represented in the telling of the history of science, in textbooks, in teacher attitudes, and in the popular media (Noble, 1992). It was widely documented and is now generally understood that for a long time these elements had constrained the numbers and proportions of women and girls choosing science, both as a favored discipline of study and as a career.

Finally, the social science research community, supported by its private and public funders, has taken the under-representation of girls and women and minorities in the sciences as a problem to be understood and, as quickly as possible, solved (Meece & Eccles, 1993). This chapter will review that body of research and the best practices found to make a difference. However, before we begin, the numbers and proportion of women in science over the period under consideration are shown in Table 13.1.

Today, the undergraduate population in the biological sciences is over 50% female; chemistry has grown from less than 10% female bachelor's-level graduates in the 1960s to 50% in 2005; physics and engineering lag at 25% and 22%, respectively; and the percentages of women in computer science has actually declined from 28.6% in 1994 to 27.6% in 2001 (NSF, 2004). However, the lagging fields are still two or three times more as popular with women (in total numbers) than they were 30 years ago (NSF, 2000, 2004). Meanwhile, anthropology, primatology, and veterinary medicine are attracting, and most likely will continue to attract, female majorities. In high schools, more girls than ever before are taking advanced placement (AP) classes in biology, chemistry, and calculus (Linn, 2005) qualifying them for the introductory college-level science and math courses that are the prerequisites for SET majors. Unfortunately, the number of females who opt to take the AP examinations in calculus (30/1000 12th graders), computer science (1/1000 12th graders), and science (34/1000 12th graders) lags behind the number of males who take the same examinations (36, 5, and 41, respectively) (College Board, 1999)

As the millennium arrived, so did several overall assessments of both the cause of women's and girls' reluctance to pursue SET fields of study and the usefulness of some of the interventions. *Balancing the Equation: Where Are Women and Girls in Science, Engineering, and Technology?* (National Council for Research on Women, 2001), *New Formulas for America's Workforce: Girls in Science and Engineering* (National Science Foundation, 2003) and *Under the Microscope* (Dyer, 2004) together provided a sense of why large numbers of young women still don't enroll in SET classes in high school; why even many of those who do enter college intending to major in SET don't persist with the major; and why even those who do earn a degree in a SET field leave the field at a faster rate than men. The other research focus, that on programs that work, concluded that hands-on experiences with SET whether inside or outside the science classroom (in schools, museums, or with groups like the Girl Scouts and Girls Inc.) positively affect girls' longer-term commitment to science.

Not surprisingly, the disciplines that were (and remain) resistant to women entrants have received the most attention from the National Science Foundation. The reason physics, computer science, information technology (IT), and most of the engineering disciplines have seen much smaller increases in female enrollment has been attributed to the following factors: (a) the absence of a requirement to take physics or more advanced computer-science courses in high school; (b) the absence of "female-friendly science" practice in the undergraduate and graduate classrooms (AAUW, 1992; Benckert & Staberg, 2000); (c) the absence of real-world applications for what students are learning (Rosser, 1990); and (d) the very small proportion of women college faculty in these fields, particularly at Research I universities (AAUW, 1999; Benjamin, 1999; Rosser, 1997).

For all of its 30 years of activism-inspired research, the women-in-science (and minorities) movement has had two explicit goals: (a) to equalize opportunity by eliminating prejudice, discrimination, and bad practice; and (b) to add new dimensions to the science enterprise itself (that is, improve science) by bringing to science those with diverse life experiences (Selby, C.C., 2004). The first set of research questions emerged from the deepest prejudice of all among some in the

TABLE 13.1   Women as a Percentage of All Bachelors' Recipients, by Major Field Group: 1966–2001

Academic Year Ending	All Fields	Total S&E Fields	Engineering	Physical Sciences	Earth, Atmos. & Ocean Sciences	Mathematics/ Computer Sciences	Biological/ Agricultural Sciences
1966	42.6	24.8	0.4	14.0	9.4	33.2	25.0
1967	42.3	25.4	0.5	13.9	10.2	34.1	24.5
1968	43.5	27.1	0.6	14.3	10.0	36.7	24.8
1969	43.8	27.8	0.8	14.3	10.0	36.6	24.4
1970	43.2	28.0	0.8	14.5	10.2	36.1	24.1
1971	43.5	28.9	0.8	14.7	10.8	36.0	24.1
1972	43.7	29.4	1.1	15.8	12.2	35.9	24.4
1973	43.9	29.9	1.2	15.8	12.2	36.3	25.2
1974	44.4	31.4	1.6	16.8	15.9	36.6	27.0
1975	45.4	32.8	2.1	18.8	17.0	37.0	29.2
1976	45.6	33.6	3.4	19.5	18.3	35.3	31.2
1977	46.2	34.6	4.9	19.9	20.8	36.1	32.9
1978	47.2	35.5	7.4	21.5	21.6	35.7	35.2
1979	48.3	36.3	9.1	22.6	22.8	35.9	37.1
1980	49.2	37.2	10.1	24.0	23.8	36.4	39.1
1981	49.9	37.8	11.1	24.7	24.9	36.9	41.1
1982	50.5	38.5	12.3	26.2	25.6	37.9	42.3
1983	50.7	38.8	13.3	28.5	25.3	38.9	43.8
1984	50.7	38.6	14.1	29.4	24.4	39.3	44.4
1985	50.9	38.8	14.5	29.7	24.6	39.5	45.1
1986	51.0	39.0	14.5	29.8	22.3	38.8	45.5
1987	51.7	39.7	15.3	30.2	22.6	38.2	46.1
1988	52.2	40.6	15.4	32.1	23.8	36.9	47.7
1989	52.7	41.3	15.2	30.9	25.2	35.9	47.6
1990	53.3	42.5	15.4	32.2	27.9	35.8	48.2
1991	54.1	43.9	15.5	32.4	28.7	36.1	48.7
1992	54.3	44.9	15.6	33.1	32.0	35.6	49.3
1993	54.4	45.3	15.9	33.6	30.0	35.4	48.9
1994	54.6	45.8	16.5	34.6	31.1	35.2	48.9
1995	54.8	46.5	17.3	35.5	34.0	35.1	49.7
1996	55.2	47.1	17.9	37.0	33.3	33.9	50.2
1997	55.7	48.1	18.4	38.5	34.5	33.6	51.6
1998	56.2	48.7	18.6	39.2	37.0	32.9	52.7
1999	—	—	—	—	—	—	—
2000	57.2	50.4	20.5	41.1	40.0	32.7	55.8
2001	57.4	50.6	20.1	41.7	40.9	31.8	57.3

Key: Detailed national data were not released for the academic year ending 1999 by the National Center for Education Statistics.

Notes: Details may not sum to totals due to rounding.

Source: Adapted from tabulation by National Science Foundation/Division of Science Resources Statistics; data from Department of Education/National Center for Education Statistics: Integrated Postsecondary Education Data System Completions Survey.

science and education communities, namely: did women have the physical, psychological, and degree of interest and commitment to succeed in science? The argument over women's nature, a focus on what Sonnert referred to as the deficit argument, may never be settled (Sonnert, 1995). As late as January 2005, then-Harvard President Larry Summers made the claim that brain differences (deficits), together with an inability to focus single-mindedly on any career outside the family, largely explain the lower percentage of women in the top ranks in science (Bombardieri, 2005; Fogg, 2005; Summers, 2005). Determinists (like Camilla Benbow and Julian Stanley, 1982) argued that there might even be a "male math gene" to account for males' overrepresentation in science (Benbow & Stanley, 1980). In fact, sex differences on standardized test scores have declined over time, differ wildly from country to country, and cannot account for the gender gap in SET participation by themselves. A majority of researchers consistently found that differences in scores within each sex are far larger than the average difference between the sexes. (See chapter 2 on "Facts and Assumptions About the Nature of Gender Differences and the Implications for Gender Equity.")

An obvious alternative to the intrinsic differences finding is to posit gender differences in attitude, motivation, and performance in SET fields as the result of sex-role socialization (Bem, 1995). From this vantage point, their education and the culture in which they live send signals to women and girls as to the personal suitability (or unsuitability) of science as a career (Abbott, Morrell, Bievenue, Bracey, & Scripa, 2006). Longer-term studies (Zuckerman, Cole, & Bruer, 1991) documented how women's differences from male-defined norms cause accumulated disadvantage. Many early interventions derived from the sex-role socialization analysis aim to counter the "science culture" with women's-only training sessions, women-to-girls mentoring, and programs like SummerMath.

Given the role-socialization analysis, it was inevitable that, in the second stage of women-in-science research, scholars would turn to how science comes to be defined and dominated by men. Those norms express themselves in criteria for selection, training, and mentoring and predetermine what constitutes success throughout a scientific career. Sharon Traweek provided an account of dominant maleness (sexism and hazing) in the high-energy physics community (Traweek, 1988). Other researchers (Merchant, 1980; Schiebinger, 1989) went into the history of Western science to locate the origins of the notion that science is a male domain (Schiebinger). Margaret Rossiter's two-volume history of American women in science revealed the ways in which women had to cope with discrimination, isolation, antinepotism rulings, and what we would later call sexual harassment without any legal recourse or redress (Rossiter, 1982, 1995). In our generation, even with the legal elimination of discrimination, prejudice and isolation remained. As long as the women making their way through the system—especially in the physical sciences—were not yet in power positions, the subculture of a particular group of researchers in a particular setting could remain unwelcoming.

Throughout the period under review, the prize for women in science was usually a career in research. Engineering and computer science received some attention but not nearly as much as the classical research-oriented sciences. As a result (in part), engineering remained stuck at 22% women students and fewer than 20% women professionals; and computer science saw a drop in the numbers of women (McIlwee & Robinson, 1992).

It was not until the mid-1990s that a third stage of intervention research emerged with the development of alternate science-training opportunities that would, it was argued, provide a better "fit" with women's career needs and expectations (Nauta, Epperson, & Waggoner, 1999). New master's level degrees in the sciences and mathematics emerged from that analysis that are terminal, applied, practical, portable, and relevant both to business and industry and to the public and academic sectors (Tobias, Chubin, & Aylesworth, 1995). Without expressly targeting women graduates in science, the degree (now in 54 institutions) fits many of women's longer-term career aspirations and therefore attracts 43% women. Now the same national studies calling for increasing participation of U.S. citizens in science and engineering recommend professionally oriented master's degree programs as one more source to meet the nation's workforce needs.

UNDERSTANDING MOTIVATION AND PERSISTENCE

When examining outcome data, such as number of women participating in SET areas as well as the antecedents of their choices, it is beneficial to view such outcomes from a theoretical perspective or by means of a research-based model.

Bandura offered a corrective to McClelland's model (tried out incidentally only on male subjects) of some kind of intrinsic need for achievement (McClelland, 1961). Bandura and colleagues found motivation to be significantly more complicated,

and that individuals' *ability-related self-perceptions* may determine the parameters of their achievement behavior as much as raw talent (Bandura, 1986, 1989, 1997, 1998; Bong & Clark, 1999; Covington, 1984; Crandall, 1969; Dai, Moon, & Feldheusen, 1998; Eccles, 1983; Eccles & Harold, 1992; Feather, 1982, 1988; Nicholls, 1984; Schunk, 1984; Schunk & Ertmer, 2000; Weiner, 1986).

Other researchers emphasized extrinsic variables. Meszaros, Creamer, Burger, and Matheson (2005) pointed out that, as presented by parents or other outsiders, the role of a scientist or engineer may conflict with females' perceived personal fulfillment. Andre, Whigham, Hendricksen, and Chambers (1999) found that many third-grade boys and girls already have formed the idea that physical sciences are for boys and reading is a subject at which girls are superior, corresponding to the fact that the girls' parents felt that science was more interesting and much more important for boys.

Eccles and her colleagues (1984) used the Expectancy-Value Model to explain sex differences in academic achievement patterns. Simply stated, motivation to achieve is jointly determined by (a) expectation of success (Swim & Sanna, 1996) and (b) the value placed by the individual on succeeding. Thus, depending on the degree to which girls and women internalize the view that math is a male domain, they will disparage their own likelihood of succeeding and even the value of success. The Expectancy-Value Model is the result of four self-defined variables: (a) perception of task difficulty, (b) perception of likelihood of success, (c) degree of engagement, and (d) perception of ability (Eccles & Wigfield, 2002; Wigfield & Eccles, 1992; Wigfield, Eccles, & Rodriquez, 1998).

Some researchers focused on interest (as if interest were unique only to SET fields) and enjoyment as primary motivators. Margolis, Fisher, and Miller (1999, 2002) found that male computer-science students cited enjoyment of computing as their primary motivation for majoring in computer science; females were more motivated by the *usefulness* of the field (such as secure employment, flexibility, and the option to combine computing with other interests). These factors could explain why many girls eschew engineering as being neither interesting nor useful. When girls are given specific information about engineering, both their interest and their perception of the usefulness of engineering increase.

Another complicating factor in analyzing interest comes from the fact that women tend to want careers that will improve the quality of other people's lives and are not just intrinsically or financially rewarding careers. This factor sometimes accounts for why women tend to choose the social sciences over the natural sciences, except for medicine (Margolis, Fisher, & Miller, 1999).

The model proposed by Jolly et al. (2004) suggested that we will only be successful in recruiting and retaining female students in SET when three additional factors are present: (a) engagement, (b) capacity, and (c) continuity. Engagement presumes awareness of the fields and a desire to learn more about them. Capacity refers to the intellectual ability needed to master the fields. The continuity factor relies on institutional commitment to equity, adequate funding, and teaching to different learning styles, and appropriately presented information about SET careers. The missing element in engineering, computer science, and IT is engagement.

The difference/deficit model posited by Sonnert (1995a, 1995b) differentiates issues of intellectual capability (deficits) from lack of equivalent interest (difference) in SET owing to negative stereotypes and inadequate appreciation of the range of work opportunities. In his studies, Sonnert found women leaving science because of exclusion from social networks, insufficient financial support, lack of access to resources and power, and hostile work environments.[2]

Finally, Trauth (2002) incorporated most of the variables just noted in her effort to understand the particular culture for women working in IT. She discovered that in the IT world, people believe that there are fixed, unified, and opposed female and male natures; also that information technology is inherently masculine causing women to feel either that they must try to fit themselves into a male domain or change their profession. Trauth's own view was that there are many similarities among men and women as individuals, and more variation within each gender than between them.

THE SIGNIFICANCE OF ATTITUDES TOWARD SCIENCE, ENGINEERING, AND TECHNOLOGY

Land of Plenty: Diversity as America's Competitive Edge in Science, Engineering, and Technology (NSF, 2000) reported that even though eighth-grade girls have achieved equivalent academic credentials, they constitute only 25% of students who expressed an interest in an SET career and, for the most part, were only interested in the biological sciences. The American Association of University Women report *Tech-Savvy: Educating Girls in the New Computer Age* (AAUW, 2000) discussed girls' reservations about entering the computer culture. Girls have a limited concept of the career possibilities open to them in computer-related fields (Creamer & Laughlin, 2005; Creamer, Meszaros, & Burger, 2004). For example, reports from *Tech-Savvy* (2000) indicated that girls equate computers with programming and social isolation. Where do such attitudes come from? Are girls making free choices with all requisite information at hand? If not, are their "poor choices" lapses, something that making science fun could cure (Nauta, Epperson, & Kahn, 1998)?

In their discussion of the issues, the authors of *Tech-Savvy* voiced concerns that girls will end up as computer users, taking keyboarding classes instead of programming, learning word-processing and spreadsheet skills while not understanding the basics of how a computer works and, more importantly, without the problem-solving skills to troubleshoot problems that arise when using a computer or computer software.

Critics (most notably C. H. Sommers, 2000) have countered these findings by stating that if girls don't like physics, IT, or engineering, we should just leave them alone. Considering that fewer than 5% of the entering students at any broad-based college or university major in SET fields, aren't we excluding many boys, too? One problem with the attitudinal argument is that it is based on the idea that girls are making their decisions freely and with all of the information at hand.

WOMEN SCIENTISTS IN ACADEME

Women scientists in academe have two significant functions in terms of advancing women more generally in science and engineering: first, to dispel, by their own achievement, any remaining myths and prejudices about women's capacity for doing cutting-edge science; and second, to function as role models for younger women (and men). The importance of transforming the institutions of higher learning in order to support women's advancement has been widely acknowledged. NSF's ADVANCE program is a case in point where a change strategy has to involve top administrators.[3] Sonnert and others documented that both women scientists who left academe and those who stayed experienced the following kinds of problems. (Glazer-Rayumo, 1999; Henzel, 1991; Hopkins, 1999; Long, 2001; Sonnert, 1995a 1995b). Female scientists and engineers:

- were given fewer resources and smaller lab spaces for their research by their institutions than were men (Bailyn, 1999);
- published less, were recognized as leaders less often, and received fewer awards and honors for their work than their male peers (Valian, 1997);
- worked at less prestigious institutions than men (Benjamin, 1999);
- swelled the lower ranks of academia and were more likely to be nontenure track, part-time, or adjunct faculty (Mason & Goulden, 2002);
- progressed through the academic ranks (assistant, associate, and full professorships) more slowly than men and were less likely than men to become full professors, even controlling for age and year since degree (NSF, 2004);
- had salaries that were lower than men's were: In 2001, in the age group 30–39, the median annual income for female doctorate holders was $52,000, while it was $70,000 for their male counterparts. (Long, 2001; NSF, 2004); and
- were less well represented the higher up the academic ladder one goes and leaked out of the science pipeline at every successive level from high school to full professorships (NSF, 2004).

---

[2]While few of the women interviewed by Sonnert reported overt gender discrimination or harassment, the covert acts they experienced were wearing on their self-esteem and belief in themselves as successful. Women who held both faculty and post-doctoral research positions had their opinions ignored in research meetings, felt they received less respect during faculty meetings, and had less access to social networks and informal mentoring than did their male colleagues. The difference/deficit pair can also be put in terms of the personal response/institutional response to equity issues.

[3]Information about the goals of the ADVANCE: Increasing the Participation and Advancement of Women in Academic Science and Engineering Careers program can be found on the NSF Web site at: http://www.nsf.gov/funding/pgm_summ.jsp?pims_id=5383&org=NSF&from=fund

CURRENT STATUS AND OUTLOOK

The Biological Sciences

Women have made the greatest strides in the biological sciences including the disciplines of botany, ecology, immunology, microbiology, and zoology as well as in the environmental sciences. Female high school students take biology courses at a slightly higher rate than their male counterparts do, but their participation in advanced placement courses has increased over the years (Table 13.2). At most colleges and universities, women make up 50% or more of the undergraduate majors in the biological sciences. Looking only at U.S. citizens and permanent residents, the number of women earning doctorates in the biological sciences (which includes not only botany, immunology, microbiology, and zoology, but also many other fields) increased 631%, from 273 in 1966 to 1,997 in 2004. This compared with an increase of only 44% for men, from 1,519 in 1966 to 2,188 in 2004. Because of this wide variation in growth rates, women are nearing parity in the biological sciences, receiving 47.7% of the total doctorates earned in 2004 (NSF, 2006). This interest in the life sciences is also demonstrated in veterinary medicine where women now make up about 70% of all students.

In allopathic medicine, much has changed since the first U.S. woman physician, Elizabeth Blackwell, graduated medical school in 1849. Most of the change has happened within the last decade. Equality in overall numbers seems to be becoming a reality, and women are finally changing the face of medicine. Indeed, in some countries, notably, the U.K., women represent up to 70% of entering students. In 1970, women comprised just 7.6% of physicians in the U.S. By 1990, this percentage had grown to 16.9%. In 2003, women made up 26% of all working physicians (AMA, 2003). Women applying for admission to U.S. medical schools reached 49.8% of all applicants for the first time in 2003 according to a report by the Association of American Medical Colleges (AAMC, 2003).

The Physical Sciences

Physics is notable for (a) having suffered a significant decline in total numbers of undergraduate majors and in proportion of PhD graduates who are born in the U.S. (Feder, 2002), and (b) for being the least hospitable of the sciences to women (within the U.S.) (Hartline & Michelman-Ribeiro, 2005). Having said that, there has been significant support from the top for change within the physics community. From the mid-1980s un-

til the present, a Committee on the Status of Women in Physics (CSWP) has convened forums at professional physics meetings, recommended new policies to attract and accommodate women physicists, initiated women-only award competitions, and sent visiting committees to physics departments all over the country to observe and interview women faculty, women researchers, women graduate students, and women undergraduates from which reports are published. Additionally, the American Institute of Physics, the statistical research arm of the American Physical Society, has maintained detailed records of women's status in the physics community and prepared two reports (International Union of Pure and Applied Physics, 2002, 2005) on the status of women in physics internationally (Tobias & Birrer, 1999).

Part of the motivation has been a recognition that from the 1980s to the present, the number of American students graduating with the bachelor's degree in physics has hovered around 4,000 and most recently dropped to 3,457 (NSF, 2004) with men leaving the major at a greater rate than women. (While the number of men majoring in physics has declined from 3,295 to 2,701, the number of female students has actually increased from 710 to 756). Even with a brief decline from 1995–1998 (Fig. 13.1), the percentage of women receiving undergraduate and graduate degrees in physics has steadily increased from 1972 to 2003. Rationally, then, physics should look upon women as providing a significant source of new recruits. However, not all physics departments do.

In a study that included in-depth interviews with faculty, graduate students, and administrators, Fox found that physics departments registering the greatest success in recruiting and retaining female students shared a number of characteristics: they made explicit, and enforced, policies about sexual harassment; they valued and encouraged mentoring; they supported undergraduate student research even providing financial aid for that research; and they encouraged faculty members to commit themselves to gender equity in their pedagogy (Fox, 2000, 2001, 2003).

What then is the likelihood of American physics beginning to achieve the near parity of women and men that Argentina, Italy, and some developing countries display (Tobias & Birrer, 1999)? Ivie and Ray of the American Institute of Physics (2005) reported that the number of girls taking physics in high school reached an all-time high of 46% in 2001. Moreover, from 1999 to 2003, 18 university physics departments awarded 40% (or more) of their physics bachelor's degrees to women and 10 physics departments awarded more than 25% of their PhDs to women in that same period. Further, women now constitute 10% of the physics faculty overall in U.S. colleges and uni-

TABLE 13.2 Percentage of High School Students Completing Biology and AP/Honors Biology Courses, by Sex: 1990, 1994, and 1998*

Course	1990			1994			1998		
	Total	Male	Female	Total	Male	Female	Total	Male	Female
Biology	90.9	89.4	92.3	93.2	91.8	94.5	92.7	91.4	94.1
AP/Honors Biology	10.1	9.4	10.8	11.9	10.9	12.8	16.2	14.5	18.0

*Adapted from NSF (2003, p. 103).

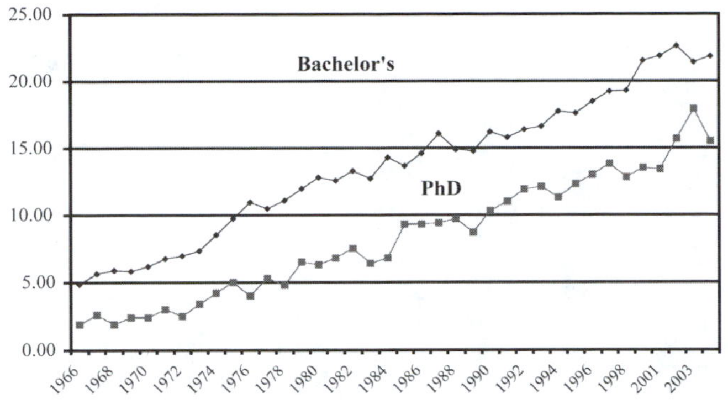

FIGURE 13.1 Percent or physics bachelor's and PhDs earned by women, 1996 to 2004. (*Source*: National Science Foundation, WebCASPAR Database).

versities. This suggests that the numbers and proportions of women undergraduates and graduate women in physics will continue to increase as long as research support for physics remains constant.

Nevertheless, physics, like the other sciences, experiences a decrease from high school where nearly half of physics enrollees are girls to college graduation where they constitute less than one fourth. The numbers of underrepresented minorities among women majoring in physics are too low to count; and, even when corrected for time since degree, the salaries of female physics professors remain lower than those for men. Ivie and Ray (2005) concluded: "Despite years of continued growth, women's participation in physics remains among the lowest of any scientific field" (p. 3).

In order to get to the roots of the problem, Ivie and Guo (2006) surveyed 1,350 female physicists from more than 70 countries. In answer to the question of how they managed to succeed in physics, most cited intrinsic drive and determination together with the support of at least one other person. In most cases, the decision to study physics was made in secondary school. (Note that in many countries, high school is sex segregated and physics is a required subject for the girls as well as the boys.) For the United States this finding is problematic, since U.S. high schools are not sex segregated and do not usually require even a single course in physics. Ivie and Guo also found that even those female physicists who succeed in physics encounter negative attitudes and outright discrimination from their colleagues (Ivie & Guo, 2005; Tobias, Urry, & Venkatesan, 2002). While physics professional organizations and physicists have been working hard to communicate the excitement of the process of discovery and research in physics, girls and young women are being bombarded with conflicting messages about the need to achieve and the need to fit in. In general, "smart" and "popular" are not synonymous during adolescence, and physics, being the least "cool" and most "nerdy," is the hardest for girls to embrace (Borg, Budil, Ducloy, & McKenna, 2005).

Borg and her colleagues identified the need for effective mentors for women seeking a foothold in physics. Girls and young women need encouragement and support from their parents, teachers, counselors, and advisers to overcome societal pressures and issues relating to discipline-specific self-esteem. When elementary school teachers, who are largely female, do not have current information about the range of careers open to physics majors, they cannot engage any of their pupils nor can they provide positive role modeling to girls' ambitions in science. College-age women appear to need even more support for their decision to major in physics, both professional (research mentor, grant writing, employment) and personal (thriving in the "chilly" physics climate, balancing work-life questions) (Borg et al., 2005).

Chemistry

While the increase in women's participation in chemistry has not been as dramatic as what has occurred in biology and in other biological sciences, there has been a steady increase in the percentage of female students at the bachelor's, master's, and Ph.D. levels. As seen in Table 13.3, the percentage of female undergraduates is now over 50%. At the master's and Ph.D. levels, both the number and percentage of women graduates has steadily increased.

The numbers and proportion of female faculty members in chemistry has lagged. The Nelson Diversity Studies survey (Nelson & Rogers, 2005) showed that in 2002 women filled only 12% of tenure and tenure-track positions in the top 50 U.S. chemistry departments. An idea put forth by Debra Rolison was to identify universities that do not have an equitable number of female faculty and then use the power of Title IX (the major U.S. law prohibiting sex discrimination in education) to compel them to increase the percentage of female faculty members (Rolison, 2004; Zare, 2006). While there were statements in 2006 indicating that the Office for Civil Rights in the U.S. Department of Education would initiate some of these investigations (Postsecondary Science and Math Departments Face Title IX Review, 2006), universities need not wait to be threatened with the enforcement of Title IX. Instead, university officials and their search committees should seek out, recruit, and hire female faculty in chemistry and other areas with similar imbalances, so they will be in full compliance with Title IX.

TABLE 13.3 Number and Percentage of Female and Male Undergraduate Chemistry Majors for Select Years

Year	Female	Male	Total	% Women
1966	1,801	7,934	9,735	18.50
1970	2,116	9,501	11,617	18.21
1980	3,277	8,169	11,446	28.63
1990	3,324	4,965	8,289	40.10
1996	4,622	6,091	10,713	43.14
2000	4,907	5,483	10,390	47.22
2001	4,775	5,047	9,822	48.61
2002	4,729	4,719	9,448	50.05
2003	4,682	4,650	9,332	50.17
2004	4,755	4,550	9,305	51.10

Adapted from National Science Foundation, 2004.

Engineering

Engineering has been particularly resistant to women both in academia and in the workforce (Sanders, 2005; Morris, 2002; National Science Board, 2004b; Ahuja, 2002; Cohoon & Aspray, 2006; Fox, Johnson, & Rosser, 2005; Gatta, 2002; Linn, 2005; Trauth, 2006; Vogt, 2002). When the first *Handbook for Achieving Sex Equity through Education* (Klein, 1985) was published, the proportion of women students in engineering programs nationwide was approximately 12%. Seven years later, in 1992, women constituted 15.7% of the bachelor's degrees awarded in engineering; and by 2004, that number had increased to 20.5%. However, when the actual student numbers were tallied, it appeared that the numbers of men choosing to major in engineering was flat. In 1992, 9,972 women and 53,681 males earned the BSE from accredited U.S. universities and engineering schools. By 2002, just five years later, women were at 14,102, (a difference of 4,130). The total number of BSE males stood at 54,546 (only 867 more than in 1992). Meanwhile, the number of American minorities in engineering has increased over the past 10 years. The largest group, Asian/Pacific Islanders, rose from 6,479 in 1992 to 8,669 in 2002; African Americans from 1,374 to 3,358; Hispanics from 2,708 to 4,298; and American Indians/Alaska natives from 163 to 315 engineering graduates (Table 13.4) (NSF, 2004).

Within engineering, perhaps the greatest growth since 1985 has been the number of women in engineering graduate programs. While women attained 20.1% of the bachelor's (in 2001) (NSF, 2004), they received 21.2% of the master's degrees (in 2001) (NSF, 2004) and 17.6% (in 2004) (NSF, 2006) of the doctoral degrees. Of those percentages, the breakdown by race and ethnicity is shown in Fig. 13.1.

Women are not moving into all subfields of engineering at the same rate (Fig. 13.2). In 1994, women earned 29% of all industrial engineering degrees awarded; in 2001, their portion was 32%. Aerospace engineering saw an increase in women's graduation rates from 13% in 1991 to 20% in 2001—again largely owing to a decline in the number of males. In addition to industrial engineering, women have made numerical and proportional gains in the fields of biomedical, chemical, environmental, and architectural engineering as compared to the more traditional electrical, mechanical, and aerospace engineering (NSF, 2004).

While attracting women into engineering remains an imperative, given that so few enroll, retaining women who do enter remains crucial. Those women who leave engineering usually attribute their departure to alternative choices rather than poor

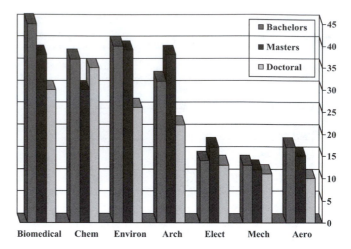

FIGURE 13.2   Contrast of the Branches of Engineering Undertaken by Women (Gibbons, 2004).

academic performance (NSF, 1998; Seymour & Hewitt, 1997). Most of these women obtain their degrees in other science majors indicating that factors unique to the engineering culture, like weed-out courses and the lack of mentors or role models, may be discouraging women (Huang, Taddese, & Walter, 2000; National Institute for Science Education [NISE], 1998; Seymour, 1995). The increased number of women completing their undergraduate engineering degrees and the increased number going on to complete graduate degree is due both to national attention paid to the issue and to the establishment of offices to support women in engineering at various engineering schools (Santiago & Einarson, 1998).

Since 1990, the Women in Engineering Program Advocates Network (WEPAN) has organized, educated, and inspired women who run engineering offices. Since the women in these positions cannot control recruitment, their focus is on retention, which is where the greatest measurable success has taken place. Once admitted, women are persisting at slightly higher levels than men are (NCES, 2000). Retention appears to derive primarily from strong family support, high self-expectations, self-confidence, and solid academic preparation. Recent research concluded that high ACT scores in math coupled with a better understanding about what engineers do contribute to persistence in the field. (Lewerke, Robbins, Sawyer, & Hovland, 2004). Nevertheless, since women are still a minority in the field, they experience interpersonal stress (NISE, 1998; NSF, 1998; Seymour, 1995; Seymour & Hewitt, 1997).

Certainly negative stereotypes exist for all SET fields, but while there are many female doctors and veterinarians, insufficient identification with women who are satisfied and successful in their engineering careers may deter young women from embarking on an engineering career path (Steele & Aronson, 1995). Strong stereotypes exist about engineers; they are sometimes labeled as nerdy, socially inept, socially isolated, and almost always male. These stereotypes do not convey positive emotional messages to women.

Furthermore, the media may not support women's participation in nontraditional fields. Sheldon (2004) found significantly

TABLE 13.4   Undergraduate Engineering Graduates by Gender and Race

Group	1992	%	2002	%
Female	9972	15.7%	14102	20.5%
Male	53681	84.3%	54546	79.5%
Asian/Pacific Islander	6479	10.2%	8669	12.6%
African American	2374	3.7%	3358	4.9%
Hispanic	2708	4.3%	4298	6.3%
American Indian/Aleut	163	0.03%	315	0.05%

Adapted from NSF, 2004.

more male characters than female characters in preschool educational software, which makes it difficult for teachers to address gender diversity. Male characters were more likely than female characters to exhibit several masculine-stereotypical traits. When Zittleman and Sadker (2002) evaluated the content of newer editions of teacher-education textbooks, they found "minimal progress" in gender-equality compared to the Sadkers' evaluations 20 years before (Sadker & Sadker, 1982). Some informational Web sites intended to encourage young women may have discouraging aspects when girls read about the complexity of occupational problems women engineers face (Steinke, 2004). Central to this discussion, engineering needs to be seen as not just acceptable for young women, but normative for them (Ketcham, Frehill, & Jeser-Cannavale, 2004)

Engineering careers must be appealing to both females and males. The underlying affective ideations of young females toward studies in engineering are crucial to their motivation and subsequent commitment to studies in those related subjects. If young females are exposed to successful models, their role-conflict anxiety is reduced while their positive attributions are increased, thus leading to fulfilling career aspirations (Nauta, Epperson, & Waggoner, 1999).

WOMEN FACULTY IN ENGINEERING

The dearth of women faculty in engineering is definitely a deterrent to potential undergraduate and graduate women. Women are 10.4% of working engineers, and constitute 5.8% of full professors, 12.4% of associate professors, and 17.9% of assistant professors in engineering. The numbers of Hispanic, African American, and Native American women are so low as to almost disappear (Fig. 13.3). The common stereotype notwithstanding, the number of Asian women is only about 20% of the total number of female engineering faculty members (NSF, 2004).

If we consider that early on, girls engage in more person-centered subjects, engineering, as compared to biological sciences, may seem cold, abstract, and unrelated to what they perceive

as real-life problems (Adamson, Foster, Roark, & Reed, 1998). Designing a lighting system does have a human dimension, but it is not as obvious as treating an illness or arguing for the rights of a plaintiff. An examination of the types of engineering degrees women pursue displays the same pattern: the greater the human or societal emphasis, the higher their enrollment.

While it was once acceptable to measure mathematics as the litmus test for women's confidence in engineering fields, more current studies reveal that women do not see themselves as having a lower ability to succeed in math than their male peers (Fredricks & Eccles, 2002; Goodman Research Group, 2002; Vogt, Hocevar, & Hagedorn, 2007). Therefore, intervention strategies must target high school computer science and physics classrooms, as these might be the new "weak link" to engineering. The efforts used by educators and activists to promote female friendly mathematics courses in the 1980s and 1990s might be applied to bolster female enrollments in computing and physics: both core components of engineering studies. (For more information about core competencies, see the chapter about mathematics in this book).

Computer Science

Course enrollment and degree completion trends in computer science have not followed typical patterns of steady increases in participation by women seen in other SET disciplines. Even though women enjoyed a substantial share (34%) of computer science bachelor's degrees in the mid-1980s, this fell sharply in 1990, and did not rebound until 1998. In Fig. 13.4, one can see that the rise and fall of computer-science degrees earned by women followed a pattern similar to that of men, and this is likely to have been caused by economic and technology-boom/bust conditions unrelated to gender bias (NSF, 2004). However, the number of women pursuing computer-science education and careers has been considerably and consistently lower than for men. Where the number of computer science degrees decreased at the same rate for both men and women, the proportion of women to men fell from 37% to 28%. Furthermore, when

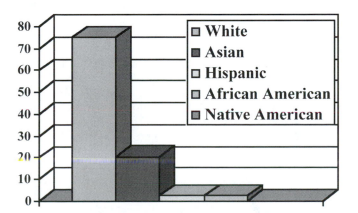

FIGURE 13.3 Percentage of Female Engineering Faculty by Race/Ethnicity (NSF, 2004).

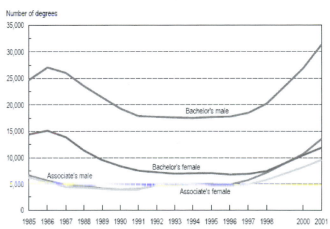

FIGURE 13.4 Bachelor's and associate's degrees awarded in computer science, by sex: 1985–2001.

the numbers started increasing for both men and women, the increase for women was at a slower rate, thus widening the gap between the male and female cohorts.

Businesses have recognized the importance of a diverse workforce as described by the Commission on the Advancement of Women and Minorities in Mathematics, Science, Engineering and Technology (CAWMSET) (NSF, 2000), but an analysis of information about workers in high tech fields reflects the continued underrepresentation of women. Aggregated data on women programmers, computer scientists, computer engineers, and software designers indicated that women are between 25%–30% of the total programming workforce (U.S. Department of Labor, 2006; Information Technology Association of America, 2003). Furthermore, women in mid- to upper-level computer engineering jobs in the United States comprise only 9% of the total population of computer engineers (Klein, 2001).

A cause for alarm is the low number of women enrolled in computer courses in high school on through college or graduate school and continuing into employment (Camp, 1997; Spertus, 1991). If one tests boy/girl interest in computers using measures suggested by Jolly, Campbell, and Perlman (2004), it appears that in the elementary and middle-level grades boys and girls are equally computer literate and tend to use the computer at the same rate, demonstrating equality in *capacity*. Girls and boys also appear to be equally enthusiastic when it comes to using the computer; that is, demonstrating equality in *engagement*. However, as they move into high school, gender differences and stereotypes begin to surface (Sandoval, 2005). Although girls continue to refine their word processing skills along with other business and clerical skills, boys overwhelmingly populate classes in computer science and especially programming (MacDonald, 2004). High school girls may develop negative attitudes about computers and programming because of overt or covert gender bias (Sanders, 2005), translating into lack of aptitude or interest in computers (Sanders & Hale, 2005). When they do, they are accepting the social stereotypes that computing is mostly a masculine activity (Sanders, 2005). One result of this divergence is the disproportion between males and females preparing for computer-science careers. In a 2004 College Entrance Examination Board survey of freshmen students who intended to major in computer science, 88% were male (MacDonald, 2004).

Engagement is the component of the Jolly et al. model that corresponds to the "we choose not to" element and poses more questions than it answers: Why are girls not as likely to spend time using technology and, more specifically, computers? Why do so many girls shy away from computer and computer-programming courses? Girls, the AAUW report *Tech Savvy* (2000) suggested, simply find programming boring. Is that because the computer is empowering mainly in fields that girls have already decided are not for them? The Carnegie Mellon University faculty was able to counter this prejudice by altering the way computer programs were assessed in class. Instead of "dazzle," students were graded on how useful, how compatible, and how easy to learn their program designs would be in a real-world setting (Margolis & Fisher, 2002, quoted in Tobias, Urry, & Venkatesan 2002). Engagement issues appear to be related to societal gender bias and the male culture of information technology. However, emerging patterns of computer use by

women suggest that when students are working in an applied field that is grounded in the contexts of real-world problems, females are more likely to experience a positive attitude toward work using computer science and computer-related disciplines (Ahuja, Herring, Ogan, & Robinson, 2004; Ogan, Herring, Ahuja, & Robinson, 2005).

Parents' attitudes also matter. Shashaani (1997) found that daughters who perceived their parents believed computers were more appropriate for boys were less interested in computers. Several studies have indicated that parents harbor stereotypes that encourage their sons' computer use but discourage daughters' computer use (e.g., Shashaani, 1994; Kekelis, Ancheta, & Heber, 2005). The work of Meszaros et al. (2005) emphasized the importance of parents, and particularly mothers, in helping girls appreciate their computer abilities and see themselves as future computer scientists.

Researchers found that teachers are quite important in engaging or failing to engage girls in use of computers. Several studies reported that a teacher's attitude and perceived self-confidence in using computers can impact girls' use of computers (Collis & Williams, 1987; Kirkpatrick & Cuban, 1998; McCormick & McCormick, 1991; Reece, 1986). A more recent study, conducted at the Center for Women in Information Technology at the Univeristy of Maryland-Baltimore, suggested that even supportive, tech-savvy teachers may have difficulty engaging girls in technology use if not supported by parents (Morrell, Cotton, Sparks, & Spurgas, 2004).

Attitudes toward and confidence in using computers continue to be studied. Many researchers reported that less time on the computer at home leads to fewer computer courses taken in high school and college and overall a less positive attitude toward computers (AAUW, 2000; Blum & Frieze, 2005; Sanders, 2005; Young, 1999). However, as early as 1994, a study by Colley, Gale, and Harris found that when the factors of experience and gender stereotyping were removed, girls' and boys' computer attitudes were similar. Unfortunately, even when females obtain the same grades as males in classes with heavy computer applications, females consistently describe themselves as less confident than do males (Sanders, 2006). In terms of the Trilogy Model, this speaks to their having capacity but not experiencing continuity.

Strawn (1999) described another key to women's work in male-dominated professions: reinvention. That is, women often need to reinvent themselves and find special areas in which they can excel. In one case study, a subject discussed how she made an excellent decision to leave the fields of physics and mathematics in the early 1970s for the world of computer science, which was when computers were just emerging as a powerful technological tool. As the subject's career progressed, she was able to work in many different areas of computers—"from programming languages and computer graphics to software engineering and information systems," which gave her the flexibility she needed to advance in her career (p. 140). Thus, flexibility allows women in computer science to have careers that change to meet their intellectual and personal demands.

A number of studies have indicated that, at least until recently, the "geek" image of computer programming was a large factor that inhibited girls' interests in pursuing these types of courses at all educational levels. In addtion, the image that males are focused entirely on a machine and on programming has been cited as a reason why girls are not interested in computers (AAUW, 2000; Dryburgh, 2000; Durndell, 1990; Johnson, Johnson & Stanne, 1985; Klawe & Leveson, 2001; McCormick & Mc-Cormick,1991; MIT Department of Electrical Engineering & Computer Science, 1995; Pearl, Pollack, Riskin, Thomas, Wolf, & Wu, 1990; Selby, 1997; Strawn, 1999). Some researchers have concluded that it is not necessarily computers or technology itself that females avoid but rather the competitive, male environment surrounding the field (Canada & Brusca, 1991; Margolis & Fisher, 2002).[4] After reviewing the literature, Cohoon and Aspray (2006) stated, "While much of the literature points to the 'nerd' sterotype as a problem for women in particular, our data suggest that it is less of a problem than getting the word out about what computer scientists actually do" (p. 261).

As regards interventions or "best practice," several studies offer suggestions about where attention should be focused to attract more females into computer science. Girls' attention should be drawn to: (1) the value and usefulness of computers and technology in our society, and (2) the use of computer science to solve real world problems (as against a focus mainly on pure programming). Setting computer use into specific contexts that appeal to girls (medical imaging, landing a rover on Mars, bioinformatics) may be more engaging. Personal self-confidence remains important. Margolis' and Fisher's much admired study of an intervention at Carnegie Mellon University found that a female student's loss of confidence in her computer abilities precipitates a drop in her interest in computers (not the reverse). (Margolis, Fisher, & Miller, 2000, p. 7)

THE INFORMATION SCIENCES

Information sciences includes, but is broader than, computer science. It will be discussed in detail because this emerging area has important potential for gender equity. Education-related aspects of these careers are discussed more in this *Handbook* chapter 10 "Gender Equity in the Use of Educational Technology." What is an information technology (IT) career? Information technology (sometimes denoted as Information and Communication Technology or ICT) is broadly defined as the technology required for information processing. In particular, the use of electronic computers and computer software to convert, store, protect, process, transmit, and retrieve information from anywhere, anytime (Labor Law Talk, 2006). IT includes all forms of technology used to create, store, exchange, and use information in its various forms: business data, voice conversations, still images, motion pictures, multimedia presentations, and other forms, including those not yet conceived (http://www.WhatIs.com, http://www.whatis.tech target.com). IT is distinguished from computer science in that it is not just concerned with hardware and software, but with using those tools to solve problems. IT schools emphasize the human element that pervades their courses: team and group problem solving, working with real-world problems, and using computers as a tool rather than an end in themselves (see, for example, the Web site for the Penn State College of Information Sciences and Technology at http://ist.psu.edu/).

The most common IT-related fields include: computer science, information science, information security, World Wide Web, digital library, pattern recognition, data management, data processing, data mining, metadata, data storage, database, data networking, technology assessment, cryptography, information technology governance, and telematics (Labor Law Talk, 2006). However, these are not fixed because the technologies are changing quickly. An IT employee may or may not be located in the technology industry. In fact, most IT jobs are located in non-IT companies such as banking, retail, insurance, transportation, and education. In other areas, like library science, the role of IT is still emerging. Any of these positions may be at the managerial, technical, or support levels and may or may not require a computer-science degree for success (Roldon et al., 2004).

Women in IT Careers

Since information technology has only recently become a discipline in its own right, there are few studies about recruitment and retention of women into IT. We do know that, as in several of the other sciences, women and minorities are significantly underrepresented in the IT fields but better represented than in other areas of science and engineering. As of 2005, women constitute 30% of the U.S. IT workforce (ITAA, 2005; Sumner & Niederman, 2002). While this does not measure those doing hands-on computer work, it does include women (one out of every three) who are in administrative job categories, such as being the manager of an IT support service or of a network maintenance team (ITAA). Further, women are overrepresented in lower-level jobs identified by Sumner and Niederman as being "pink-collar ghettos" (also as noted in Roldon, Soe, & Yakura, 2004).

The failure of women to take elective computer courses in high school might limit their career options (Crombie, Abarbanel, & Anderson, 2000). On the one hand, girls should mimic boys' trajectories beginning with advanced computer science courses in high school. On the other hand, to succeed, according to Ullman (1997) and reiterated by Leventman & Finley (2005), women are required to develop strong technical skills outside the traditional mainstream. The economic cost can be high. When young women are not aware of factors that can lead to their future earning ability, their access to higher paying career opportunities may be limited. IT careers are high paying and position young executives for even higher placement (Maria Cantwell of Microsoft, for example, who is now the U.S. Senator of the state of Washington) (Teague, 2002). Because women are in lower-level positions in IT, their perspectives and concerns may not be reflected in the design, development, implementation, and assessment of emerging technologies. Further, the lack of a balanced representation of women and minorities in IT careers may lead to new technologies reflecting male values and styles of doing IT work even more.

Given the vast number of jobs that involve IT and since the United States is outsourcing many IT jobs due to a lack of qual-

---

[4]See Tobias' review of Margolis and Fisher's book entitled, "Women.com: Are the geeks keeping the gals away from the computer?" in Literary Review of Canada, May 2002, pp. 12–14.

ified workers, questions about the underrepresentation of women have become compelling at the national as well as international level.

Why are women, who comprise 47% of the U.S. workforce, involved in fewer than 20% of the non-administrative careers in IT (ITAA, 2005)? Recent research suggested fewer females than males choose IT careers because: (a) girls are discouraged from using technology as early as elementary school (Sadker, Sadker, & Klein, 1991); (b) their self-confidence in their abilities related to technology is lower than that of men (Zeldin & Pajares, 2000); (c) technology and its applications are still perceived of as a male domain; and (d) they are not encouraged to participate in technology use (Pajares, 1996; Zeldin & Pajares, 2000). These findings suggested that the low participation of women in IT is historical and cultural and will be most effectively addressed at the K–12 level.

Other factors that appear to influence women's IT career choice are common to all professional fields and include workplace climate, actual face-to-face discrimination, sexual harassment, and family-work balancing, especially as related to business travel. The impact of the 2000 "dot.com crash" is another factor suggesting uncertainty in the profession. The rapid rate of change suggests to women that it will be difficult to get back up to speed if they take time off for work or family duties (National Research Council, 2004; Roldon, et al., 2004; Sonnert, 1995b; Xie & Shauman, 2003).

Women's IT Career Trajectory

While the proportion of women in IT careers is 25%–30 % of the U.S.-based IT workforce (U.S. Department of Labor, 2006; Information Technology Association of America, 2005), only 9% of the mid- to upper-level computer engineering jobs are held by women (Table 13.5) (Gender Advisory Board, 2000).

While there are multiple routes to an IT career, and not all paths require high-school programming courses or even undergraduate computer-science degrees and courses, women without this formal training are often at even a greater disadvantage than men without this formal training.

In a survey of IT professionals (Campbell & Perlman, 2005), 27% of men had an undergraduate IT degree[5] versus 17% of women, but, of those who had IT graduate degrees as their first degree, 48% were women and 28% were men. Forty-five percent of men had no IT degree at all, versus 35% of women. This would indicate that women are more likely to enter into, persist, and succeed in an IT career if they have some formal training. Because formal IT training has not been in existence for very long, there are no longitudinal studies from which to draw conclusions about how much value prior experience has in college and career success. However, earlier work by Taylor and Mounfield (1994) found that prior programming experience was four times more predictive of computer science success in college for women than it was for men. Moreover, there was a positive

TABLE 13.5   Job Types and Percent of Female IT Workers

Computer and information systems managers	31.0%
Computer scientists and systems analysts	29.4%
Computer programmers and software engineers	26.7%
Database administrators	33.6%
Network and computer systems administrators	20.3%
Network systems and data communication analysts	21.9%
Operations research analysts	4.3%

Adapted from the U.S. Bureau of Labor Statistics, 2005.

correlation, for both males and females, between taking programming in high school and persistence in computer science in college (Nelson, Weise, & Cooper, 1991). There are no available data to explain whether this formal training is needed to give women the necessary skills and knowledge to succeed or if it simply increases their confidence enough to persist, but if we measure success in terms of the number of women in IT careers, perhaps it is enough to recognize the correlation between formal training and the number of women in IT careers.

Two large-scale studies provide insight into the female IT workforce. The first, *Why Women Choose Information Technology Careers: Educational, Social, and Familial Influences*, examined the educational backgrounds of female IT professionals by surveying members of *Systers*, an organization for women IT professionals (http://www.systers.org). The survey response was low (275 useable responses from about 2,500 members), but the authors stated, "While their responses cannot be regarded as statistically representative of women's experiences in general, their perceptions and their stories do provide valuable insights about the issues facing women who pursue careers in the IT field. It is possible to garner valuable lessons from their stories" (p. 3). Other studies documented the idiosyncratic nature of women's progress through IT careers. Nearly one-third of the women currently working in IT fields did not enter by way of a computer science degree but chose IT jobs later because they provided emotional fulfillment and were a good fit for their skills (Turner, Bernt, & Pecora, 2002).

In the second study, *Multiple Pathways to IT Careers*, Leventman and Finley (2005) reported that the varied backgrounds of IT professionals prompted Northeastern University IT Workforce Study researchers to seek stronger indicators of IT-career pathways than formal education alone. Surveys from 432 IT professionals were obtained from two sources: (a) graduates of the Northeastern University Masters in Information Science program, a career transition program, and (b) IT professionals from four large corporations. Follow-up interviews were conducted with 44 of the survey respondents. IT professionals appear to be grouped equally into three categories: (a) Traditional, (b) Transitional, and (d) Self-Directed. The Traditional one-third decided on and pursued a technical career in high school or college. The Transitional third had nontechnical backgrounds and had to obtain a technical master's degree to enter an IT career. The Self-Directed respondents also had nontech-

---

[5]More universities are establishing information technology programs distinct from their computer science departments. For example, Pennsylvania State University admitted the first students to the new College of Information Sciences and Technology in 1999. In Spring 2006, 241 students graduated from Penn State with an IST degree.

nical backgrounds, but they honed their IT skills on the job (Leventman & Finley, 2005).

Overall, the salaries of male IT workers are somewhat higher than the salaries of women, but only among those who entered IT careers through the traditional pathway. No salary differences existed between the women and men who entered IT through the Transitional and Self-Directed pathways.

Recruitment to and Retention in IT Careers

Women who enter IT fields do so either owing to personal idiosyncrasies, external influence, or both (Trauth, 2002). Those factors account for men's recruitment, too; but, in addition, women want their IT work to be purposeful and tied to people and other areas within the organization (Margolis & Fisher, 2001). A negative for married women with children is that IT careers are primarily full-time, with considerable "after-hours work" and travel built in to the job (Webster, 1996; Ahuja et al., 2004).

Women interviewed in Sosa's study had an average of 20 years experience in computer programming. For these women, "achievement" was a key to both their motivation and their degree of satisfaction with their work. Even when the external environment did not provide formal recognition for their achievement, they took pride in and got satisfaction from their technical competence (Sosa, 2004; Turner, Bernt, & Pecora, 2002; Wolters, 1998).

In conclusion, future recruitment of women into IT careers does not look bright. Young women who are not encouraged to use and develop confidence in their abilities to use technology during their K–12 years will not be eligible or interested in IT careers. Young women may be less confident than males in their technology skills, even when it is unwarranted (Lee, 2003; Gurer & Camp, 1998; Palloff & Pratt, 2001; Sax, Astin, Korn, & Mahoney, 2000). Girls with lower levels of confidence in using technology are, of course, less likely to choose courses that involve heavy or extensive computer or technology use (Kekelis et al., 2005; National Council for Research on Women, 2001; Seymour & Hewitt, 1997). Efforts to bolster teachers' confidence in using technology are an obvious first step. (See Chapter 12, "Gender Equity in Mathematics," in this *Handbook* for more detailed information.)

GENDER ISSUES IN SCIENCE, ENGINEERING, AND TECHNOLOGY EDUCATION

In School Environments

Gender differences begin at home and are reinforced by stereotypic toys, access to organized athletics, and divisions of work inside and outside the home (Karniol & Aida, 1997). However, even children whose mothers work as scientists or engineers have stereotypic views about who could be a scientist or an engineer. By the time children enter kindergarten, they already have gendered occupations—ballerina or fireman, doctor or nurse, boss or secretary. We can only devise approaches to allow children to rethink their basic values and beliefs when teachers recognize their own gender schemas and those of their students (Jussim & Eccles, 1992).

The groundbreaking work by Sadker and Sadker (1982, 1994, 2005) and Zitteman and Sadker (2002) gave us insight into classroom dynamics as seen through a gender equity lens. (Also see Chapter 7, "The Treatment of Gender Equity in Teacher Education" in this *Handbook*.) The authors discovered that male students are privileged and female students are silenced in the classroom and that this is especially true in SET classroom settings. Gender research results are often described by attributing behaviors to aggregate groups, disregarding individual difference within groups (i.e. active girls, silent boys). This trend toward describing female groups and male groups as a whole and disregarding individual differences is changing as we explore differences within groups and understand how race and class mediate gender socialization. Studies addressing gender issues in the classroom, however, described differences between populations of girls and boys in the same classroom settings. The results indicated different patterns of classroom interactions and performance for precollege boys and girls. These patterns were not random and reflected differing social and academic expectations and opportunities for male and female students. Many of the differentiated experiences reflected the ways in which teachers in classrooms reinforce group stereotypes about student skills and opportunities (AAUW, 1998; Plucker, 1996).

Common gendered teacher behaviors are components of what researchers have termed the "hidden" curriculum: the tacit messages students receive from the daily practices, routines, and behaviors that occur in the classroom. The hidden curriculum of the school's climate refers to "things not deliberately taught or instituted, but which are the cumulative result of many unconscious or unexamined behaviors that add to a palpable style or atmosphere" (Chapman, 1997; Levine, 2004). An example of these types of behaviors can be seen in elementary-school environments when teachers assign girls the task of recording on the board during a demonstration lesson in science, for example, while boys are required to set up or assemble the accompanying materials. This fine motor/gross motor distinction is one of many types of gendered expectations that can lead to differentiated outcomes.

In high schools offering advanced placement science courses in chemistry and physics with more males enrolled than females, school administrators or teachers seldom ask, "Where are the girls?" The message is that they are not expected to enroll. When teachers focus a microscope, for example, for the female students who seek help but encourage the male students to figure it out for themselves, the hidden curriculum is implemented (Grandy, 1994; Koch, 1996; Sanders, Koch, & Urso, 1997). In short, the hidden curriculum comprises the unstated lessons that students learn in school. It is the running subtext through which teachers communicate behavioral norms and individual status in the school culture and the process of socialization that cues children into their place in the hierarchy of larger society (Orenstein, 1995).

While the deficit model emphasizes girls' inabilities to perform as well as boys on various standardized tests throughout the precollege experience, early work in gender equity challenged this deficit model because it suggested that there was something wrong with the girls that needed to be fixed or remedied.

This prompted researchers to explore learning environments for girls and boys while they were participating in the same classroom with the same teacher (Sadker & Sadker, 1982, 1994; Klein, 1985). They found that in predominantly White middle-class classrooms the problems for the girls were not internal but situated in the external-learning environment. Early studies then revealed that classroom practices routinely favor the academic development of boys and interventions were developed to provide more equitable learning environments for girls (Sadker & Sadker, 1984; Greenberg, 1985; Clewell, Anderson, & Thorpe, 1992; Logan, 2003; Sanders, Koch et al., 1997). While these interventions helped individual girls to achieve in areas in which they were lagging, this deficit model inferred that girls would be successful if they just acquired the same strengths as boys. This has shifted to conceptualize equitable learning environments as those that capitalize on the strengths of all individuals, both boys and girls, and invite each to adopt behaviors that help each gender cultivate strengths not usually developed due to socialization practices and stereotyping.

Curriculum

There is an ongoing debate about the efficacy of girls-only science classrooms. One influential report (AAUW, 1998) stated that the research performed to that point was unclear about the benefits of single sex education. In some cases, outcomes indicated that girls in single-sex classes did learn more about physics, for example, and, more importantly, had a better understanding of the field and said they were more likely to consider physics as a college major. In other cases, especially in long-term studies, there was no significant difference in the number of girls who entered college as SET majors. The research that has been done to this point has not had the funding or ability to track students for an extended period in order to assess the long-term benefits or neutral effects of single-sex education or of single-sex SET classroom instruction. Another problem is a lack of effective control groups. Many projects use the single-sex classroom to do more team projects and hands-on demonstrations while the students in mixed classrooms are subject to the same static lectures with no hands-on or active learning experiences (Crombie, Abarbanel, & Anderson, 2000). The implications from the Chapter 9, "Gender Equity in Coeducational and Single-Sex Educational Environments" in this *Handbook* are that while it is important to use a variety of effective interventions to increase the participation and valued outcomes of girls and women in SET areas, the single-sex option may not be any more effective (and may be harmful) compared to a well-planned and evaluated alternative designed to accomplish similar objectives in a coed setting.

Reports abound about transformed college courses. In Musil (2001), there were reports about the development of "unconventional" biology and evolutionary ecology courses (Kinsman, 2001) and chemistry (Wenzel, 2001) courses. Molecular biology (Spanier, 2001), ornithology (Elekonich, 2001), animal behavior (Jackson, 2001), and geology courses (Phillips & Hausbeck, 2001) have been transformed using the principles of female-friendly pedagogy. A review of research about what goes on inside of science classes provides insight and hope for creating a more equitable climate of participation and a more engaging curriculum. Research demonstrates that when high school physics teachers give appropriate attention to gender issues in their classrooms, achievement and participation improves all their students and especially for their female students (Rop, 1997). Creating a classroom culture that is emotionally safe for females and males alike and sanctioning risks and mistakes as vital to learning requires teachers to model ways to take individual risk (Kasov, as quoted by Rop, 1997). In high school chemistry and physics, assigning students research articles by women, taking a direct approach with females to actively encourage their participation in advanced science courses, and providing female mentoring are interventions that have proven successful (Wilson, 2006).

One such intervention for chemistry students includes creating electronic or face-to-face mentoring relationships with women chemists who have successful careers. High school chemistry teachers have reported that this has resulted in encouraging young women to consider science as a career (Campbell & Storo, 1994; Sanders, Koch, & Urso, 1997; Kahle & Meece, 1994; Rop, 1997). Restructuring curriculum to provide a holistic view of the subject area encourages scientific study for both males and females. Integrating the history, social context, and social implications of scientific study by making connections to contemporary issues in the scientific field brings the physical sciences to life in important and meaningful ways. Making connections to real experiences is an agenda for the National Science Education Standards (National Research Council, 1996) and could help encourage participation in the sciences.

In studies where adult women reflect on their science experiences through personal narratives, their stories reveal both a sense of estrangement from the scientific disciplines as well as their fear of making a mistake (Meyer, 1995; Koch, 1998). Incompetent pedagogy and an inability to make connections to students' lived experiences can result in feelings of incompetence in science and, for women, a sense that this is not their space (Larkin, 1994). In these studies, surveys, personal interviews, and analysis of personal narratives, sometimes called science autobiographies, it is revealed that the distance that many women feel from natural science is frequently a result of feeling like a deficient female. While males may feel deficient in science, the images of scientific heroes and their stories create a culture of entitlement to success that allows males' feelings of incompetence to be separated from gender issues. Many females feel they are part of an aggregate group that is supposedly not "good" in science.

The rigor of natural science is not seen as a deterrent to female participation; rather, the method of teaching has emphasized a false disconnection between studying the sciences and understanding their contributions to society. In a recent study (Linn, 2000), researchers and teachers created important curriculum contexts for making science relevant to students' lives. By integrating scientific controversies into the secondary science curriculum, students gained the opportunity to connect to contemporary scientific debates and began to see that scientists regularly revisit their ideas and rethink their views, empowering students to do the same:

I challenge all concerned about science education to remedy the serious declines in science interest, the disparities in male and female persistence in science, and the public resistance to scientific understandings by forming partnerships to bring to life the excitement and controversy in scientific research. (Linn, 2000, p. 16)

In this study, students were engaged in exploring a contemporary controversy about deformed frogs. By using selected Internet materials to construct their own arguments, students prepared for a classroom debate around two main hypotheses: (a) the parasite hypothesis stating that the trematode parasite explains the increase in frog deformities, or (b) the environmental hypothesis that suggests an increase in specific chemicals used to spray fields adjacent to the frog pond caused the deformities. In order to construct an argument, students examined evidence from research laboratories, discussed their ideas with peers, and searched for additional information. Using a Web-based environment, middle school students partnered with graduate students working in a laboratory at University of California Berkeley as well as with technology and assessment experts (http://wise.berkeley.edu).

In their report of this project, researchers interviewed and surveyed teachers and students prior to their participation. They designed pre- and posttests, inquiry activities, and curricular materials that ensured that curriculum and assessment were aligned. The classroom research continued to help teachers refine the materials used for instruction. Prior to this scientific controversy unit, the students often reported that science had no relevance to their lives and that science was best learned by memorizing (Linn & Hsi, 1999). In the deformed frogs study, pre- and posttest assessments revealed that over two-thirds of the students were able to use the mechanism for the parasite hypothesis that they learned from the Internet evidence. The answers often revealed the complex use of language learned from reviewing and integrating Web resources. On all assessment measures for content, females and males were equally successful.

This scientific controversy unit was carried out with diverse middle school students, where half the students qualify for free or reduced-price lunches and only 25% of students speak English at home. As a result of this scientific controversy unit, more students participated in science, more students gained scientific understanding, and students became more aware of the excitement that motivates scientists to pursue careers in science (Linn, 2000). The skills that students acquired by working in these partnerships and critically evaluating and interpreting scientific data were contextualized and situated within the real world of science, ponds, and frogs.

These studies highlight the need to develop new approaches to learning new material. These approaches would, in fact not exclude men, but would actively attract women (Rosser, 1997).

Science Teacher Education

Elementary school teachers, most of whom are women, tend to avoid teaching science because it is an area in which they are least comfortable as a result of their own gender socialization and lack of preparedness. This attitude comes across to the students and begets a spiral of disenfranchisement for females in science. However, this is changing, and elementary school teachers are becoming some of the most skilled science teachers in

their abilities to engage students in experiences that require inquiry activities—the open-ended investigation of a problem (Bianchini & Colburn, 2000; Gess-Newsome & Lederman, 1999). Elementary school science is crucial because it functions as a springboard for middle school science. Decisions about pursuing scientific study are usually made by eighth grade (AAUW, 1998).

Old habits die slowly. A marked gender gap persists in high-school physics and computer science courses, and girls' scores on the National Assessment of Education Progress (NAEP) in math and science lag behind boys'. The gender gap increases with grade level. The exception is African American girls who outscore African American boys at every assessment point (AAUW, 1998; Taddese, & Walter, 2000).

Several intervention strategies have shown promise in changing some of these patterns. Unless future teachers are informed of the problem and some of the solutions, future progress may be stymied. We have seen in Chapter 7 that gender issues have been removed from teacher education textbooks during the past 10 years. Certainly, teacher educators can raise gender and science issues in elementary methods courses, particularly as regards stereotyping scientists. Teachers can ask, "Does the type of person represented in the stereotype reflect the makeup of any class you have recently seen?" or "If the students in a typical classroom were omitted by the stereotype, how would that make them feel about science?" You may suppose that stereotypes about scientists diminish as children mature. In fact, a study of over 1,500 students in grades K–8 revealed that the students' drawings of scientists became more stereotypical as the students got older. These students drew mostly White male scientists, suggesting that the stereotype persists despite recent changes in curriculum materials (Barman, 1997; Koch, 2005).

Any discussion of the true scientific method is bound to remove other stereotypes—some of them gender related—about scientists. When students have one experience trying, as a team, to solve a problem or find an answer, they will begin to understand that "wrong answers" are very often stepping-stones to "right" ones, and that scientists are not isolated in their work, but do a lot of sharing in teams.

Research shows that many girls and women, and some males, are disenfranchised by school science, especially when it makes few connections to their real-life experiences (Meyer, 1995). Daylight savings time becomes an opportunity to explore the earth's rotation on its axis, its revolution around the sun, and the length of day and night at differing times of the year. One university science teacher takes her predominantly female class ice skating in order to help them learn more about the relationship between force, mass, and acceleration. In a local elementary school, fifth-grade students take samples of water from the school fountains to test it for acidity and contaminants.

Countering Stereotypes

Gender stereotypes have existed along career and academic lines for centuries. Vispoel and Fast (2000) noted that college students rated men as better at math with women possessing greater morality and superior English skills. In 2004, Skaalvik and Skaalvik found that middle- and high-school students' self-perceptions reflected these same prejudices: boys are better at math and girls are better at English. Women's performance in engineering classes was found to be influenced by their encounters with the stereotypic views of others (Bell, Sherman, Iserman, & Logel, 2003). However, Heyman and Legare's (2004) report on kindergartners and first graders indicated that while girls in this age group perceived themselves to be better at language arts, these young children did not reflect traditional stereotypes about mathematics. Either very young children are unaware that their interests are supposed to reflect gender stereotypes or these stereotypes may be lessening as a result of women's increased presence in once male-only fields.

Girls and boys have different science-related experiences outside school, and this contributes to a gender gap (Kahle & Lakes, 1983; Linn, 1990; Sjoberg & Imsen, 1988). In terms of the engagement, capacity, and commitment model established by Campbell, Jolly, and Perlman (2004) and mentioned earlier, the difference in informal experiences makes the idea of engagement or having an orientation to the sciences less likely for girls.

To counter stereotypes, NSF has supported the production of a series of posters about different SET fields, all of which feature female scientists. The primary goals of the Phi Delta Kappa Poster Project are to encourage scientific literacy and promote the public's awareness and appreciation of science and technology by humanizing the image of research science and scientists. (Information about the posters can be found at http://www.pdksciart.com/). Radio segments have aired on National Public Radio highlighting women who have made significant contributions to our standard of living and quality of life. Kiosks with touch screens to access scientific information and learn about women's contributions to science have been set up in malls. Scholars and researchers working in the area of gender and science have developed and produced videos (*You Can Be Anything* was produced by the Center for Women and Information Technology at the University of Maryland Baltimore County and is available for viewing and ordering at http://www.umbc.edu/be-anything/), written and distributed monographs, handbooks, and books (use your favorite Web browser to find these), and developed science kits (like the one developed for the Girl Scout science badges). Girls, Inc. (http://www.girlsinc.org) has been at the forefront in developing science education programs for inner city girls. These programs are culturally and socially significant for the girls.

Intervention Programs

The 2004 report *Under the Microscope* (Dyer, 2004) concluded that most gender equity projects were planned as extracurricular while few were integrated into the school curriculum. This means that even after decades of research, few educators have recognized that what goes on in the classroom is not gender neutral. Recently, the Congressional Commission on the Advancement of Women and Minorities in Science, Engineering, and Technology Development reiterated the need for *both* in class and extracurricular intervention programs for those underrepresented in SET (NSF, 2000).

Programs have been initiated both at the middle and high school levels to interest girls in engineering. School clubs, mentoring programs, guest speakers, summer camps, and Web sites were established to encourage girls to see engineering in the same way as they saw the biological sciences: as the path to a career with applications in the real world, as a way to help people and as a profession that valued team work and left time for a family that included children. In colleges of engineering, women in engineering programs, like Society of Women Engineers (SWE) student clubs, organize mentoring and internship opportunities and bring successful women engineers to campus.

Family Tools and Technology (FT²) is an after-school program that integrates concepts from physical science, design technology, pre-engineering, and mathematics with career information. It was developed for girls and boys in grades 4–7 and their parents. Evaluation of the program showed a reduction in students' stereotypes about "Girls who use tools . . .," "A woman should . . ." and "A man should . . ." FT² did not appear to have an impact on children's' stated career aspirations. There are also some areas in which FT² did not work as well as hoped, specifically knowledge about the training needed to enter a SET career and school-oriented problem solving. The lack of change in careers considered by the students is relatively easy to address and is now being done in the revised FT² program. Teachers, parents, and students are talking about the skills needed for different jobs and how those skills and those jobs are related to the activities students do under FT². The efficacy of FT² was recognized by the Gender Equity Expert Pane, which named it one of five programs in the SET area recommended as being promising (U.S. Department of Education, 2001). It is expected that this focus on jobs and careers will have an impact on students.

University Pilot Programs

A few significant engineering and computing pilot programs appealing to women's different motivational inducements (i.e., more humanistic and multidimensional) have shown remarkable results. Smith College's implementation of a new type of female-inspired engineering promises to redefine the profession (Riley, 2003). (The philosophy of the program can be found at http://www.science.smith.edu/departments/Engin/about_philosophy.php) An interdisciplinary curriculum has interrelated the sciences with social sciences and humanities, created a focus on quantitative literacy, and forged corporate partnerships without the corporate facade.

Other notable programs, such as those at Oklahoma University (Kolar & Sabatini, 1996), the University of Maryland Baltimore (Elliot, Oty, McArthur, & Clark, 2001), Rutgers University, Rensselaer Polytechnic Institute, and Syracuse University (Youngman & Egelhoff, 2003) have reported that conducting courses that are interdisciplinary and interactive with close proximity to professors have continued to attract and retain more of the underserved (i.e., minorities and women) into engineering programs. The Carnegie Mellon University program to actively recruit and retain more women, institute outreach programs, and make the computer science program more balanced has been a success (Blum & Frieze, 2005).

While institutions and the appeal of their courses are critical, so are teachers and what they bring to the classroom. Kleinman (1998) and the Sadkers (1994) have argued that female teachers may have different instructional preferences than males such as establishing more collaborative and interactive classrooms. These would foster girl's higher levels of engagement in the subject matter. Using the techniques of problem based and cooperative learning as well as the inclusion of examples that relate to real-life dilemmas would more fully engage the interest of girls (and some boys).

In 1986, Hidi and Baird's research in "interestingness" determined that classroom features such as personal relevance, novelty, activity level, and comprehensibility arouse situational interest. In science classes, females have been shown to prefer group learning (comprehensibility and activity) and solving relevant problems (personal relevance), and to relate to examples of females' scientific contributions in order to develop a "me too" perspective (McGinnis & Pearsall, 1998).

Both in-school activities and extracurricular activities must be organized to instill importance, utility, and interest in engineering for girls. For example, children's hobbies are extremely gendered and these are speculated to have kept the computing and engineering advantage in favor of males (Gouldner, 1985; Jackson, Fleury, Girvin, J., & Gerard, 1995). Several curricula have been launched to change girls' limited interactions in once boys-only realms.

One example, in a program by Boston University's Photonics Center, is the development of the character, "Lia," a science-savvy, teenaged Latina operative in a secret global organization dedicated to using technology to tackle the world's problems. Lia, standing for Light In Action, addresses a lack of positive media portrayals of Hispanic females. Lia made her debut appearance on the National Academy of Science's iwaswondering.org Web site where she is the science savvy host of their portal to its Women's Adventures in Science book series. (Information about the Lia project can be found at http://www.bu.edu/photonics/lia_project.htm)

Other initiatives to get more girls interested in high tech careers are student-directed UCLA outreach programs that emphasize the "coolness" of engineering to middle and high school girls. The Sally Ride Science Clubs were developed by Sally Ride in order to foster connections between girls and people, information, and attitudes that can nurture girls' relationship with science. More information about this project can be found at http://www.sallyrideclub.com.

In conclusion, having parents, teachers, and trusted others provide young females with the encouragement to undertake studies in the requisite science and math courses needed for engineering studies remains essential (Meszaros et al., 2005). These efforts must avoid gender stereotypes about who performs the job of an engineer. Although evidence suggests that parents' attitudes have been changing with respect to math, they may not be changing with respect to other branches of science (Andre et al., 1999; NSF, 1998). This may explain why currently women are receiving about half the math degrees yet continue to lag behind in many of the physical sciences, including engineering.

What Were the "Gender Effects" of the Science Education Reform Movement?

From 1985 to the present, scientists, in collaboration with teacher educators, initiated not just reforms in K–16 science education, but also a *reform movements*. While not dedicated specifically to women and minorities, these reforms were beginning to target

what Sheila Tobias has called science's "second tier" (Tobias, 1990) and Elaine Seymour and Nancy Hewitt, "the leavers" (1997). Reforms included new high school textbooks, such as Chemistry in Context, Chemistry in the Community, and, Conceptual Physics, designed to present the physical sciences as both more conceptual and more relevant to the issues (such as the environment) young people care about. such as *Chemistry in Context, Chemistry in the Community,* and, *Conceptual Physics.* Tracking positive outcomes by gender has not been done routinely, so it is not possible to prove, but it is believed that these new texts have partly contributed to the increasing numbers of girls taking high school physics and more than one year of high school chemistry (Michael Neuschatz, personal communication, July 2006).

In addition to new curricula, the reform movement introduced radical new pedagogies including peer instruction, constructivism, cognitive mapping, electronic clicker responses, and a revived appreciation of the importance of the visual in chemistry (Ealy & Hermanson, 2006). Further, the reforms exploited the many new technological assists, starting with a telephone-line connection to the University of Illinois' Plato system, and continuing with the ever more common PC: CAI (computer-assisted instruction), Web-based courses, prelab computer simulation, and more sophisticated calculators. Also, there was some experimentation with new testing strategies. Even if these reforms were not specific to gender in all (or even most) cases, further research might support the intuitive notion that, in general, improved science pedagogy is to girls what improved reading instruction is to boys.

Although it is impossible to summarize the extensive work that took place over the past 20 years, one specific information source is *The Journal of Science Education and Technology* (Springer), which was founded in 1990 specifically to track these reforms. Another excellent source is *The Journal of Research in Science Teaching.* Because many of these reforms were carried out and reported by scientists, information can also be found in the *Journal of Chemical Education, American Journal of Physics, Physics Today,* and, as a more general source, the *Journal of Women and Minorities in Science and Engineering.*

SUMMARY AND RECOMMENDATIONS

Researchers, scholars, and activists have been studying the dearth of female scientists and engineers for many years. They have suggested reasons for the situation that range from overarching theoretical frameworks to specific programs to implement inside and outside of our educational institutions. We have seen a steady, if sometimes slow, increase in the numbers of women choosing to pursue SET majors and careers over the past 30 years. Two notable scholars have made observations and suggestions that are worth noting.

Sue Rosser (1997), scientist and the first female dean at Georgia Tech, noted that there tend to be six phases in recognizing gender bias and creating gender equitable science content and teaching:

1. The absence of women in science is not noted in the course materials.

2. There is some recognition that most scientists are men and thus science may reflect a masculine perspective.
3. There is identification of the barriers that prevent women from pursuing and entering science-related fields.
4. There is a search for women scientists and inclusion of their contributions.
5. Science is done by women (particularly feminists).
6. Science is redefined and reconstructed to include everyone.

These phases can be applied to any subject and at any educational level. Some disciplines can be seen to be at several levels at once. Importantly, the presence of a large number of female students or faculty does not insure the transformation of the science, as seen in the increase of female computer science undergraduates until about 1986 and then a decline in those numbers. Our theories of a critical mass of females—usually set at about 30%—did not change the computer science culture and did not have the predicted result of seeing more women choosing to major in that discipline. The decline in the percentage of women in computer science may have been the result of institutional factors at every educational level, such as a lack of attention to transforming the curriculum or few female computer-science instructors.

When we look at the status of women in SET today, we see that, within the disciplines themselves, we may have reached phase three. Outside of SET, there is a broad literature suggesting changes that could take SET disciplines to phase six. The key is to bridge the gap between the social science literature that has identified problems and solutions and the science education literature that has only a passing interest in equity issues.

Valian and Rabinowitz (2004) have made other suggestions for institutions of higher learning about how to help women in academic science careers. These recommendations are equally valid and can be adapted for all levels of education and the SET professions:

• Take a "fix the institution," not "fix the woman" approach.
• Understand that equity will not be achieved or sustained without special effort.
• Commit to making and institutionalizing that effort.
• Teach decision makers about how gender and race work to disadvantage women and people of color in the workplace.
• Perform frequent reviews of hidden and subtle forms of bias; train oneself and other evaluators to correct errors in evaluation and decision procedures.
• Communicate information equally to men and women about the criteria for success within and outside the institution;
• Ensure equal job responsibilities, participation in public settings, and committee/service obligations of women and men.
• Understand that everyone needs professional development opportunities and support throughout their careers.
• Companies should implement consistent policies for recruitment, training, appraisal, mentoring, and development that are friendly to both males and females.

• Increase school resources so girls and boys have access to scientific and technology equipment.
• Make sure girls at all levels have access to mentors and role models.
• Use a variety of support systems like as professsional organizations both in acaemica and in workplace.

The key is for institutions and individuals who make and implement policy to commit the time and resources necessary to support underrepresented groups as they enter and seek to stay in SET fields. Before this can happen, Rosser's first phase must be engaged—we must recognize that women are underrepresented, and that their participation in SET will benefit not only the individual women but will expand and enrich SET disciplines and the products of SET research.

CONCLUSION

Over the years, gender discrimination in the U.S. has been attacked in the courts and with Title IX, and, while residual prejudices and stereotypic beliefs about women's intellectual potential remain (Summers, 2005), these beliefs are quickly countered by well researched data. This does not mean that everyone is convinced of women's innate capability to do science as well as men. For example, Charles Murray, coauthor of *The Bell Curve* in 1994, continues to argue (in 2005) that male dominance in the mathematical and theoretical fields can be explained by their larger brain mass (Murray, 2005).

Regardless of these unproven assertions, we have seen that (mostly White) girls' and women's access to SET fields of study and science careers is no longer restricted in the way they were in 1985. Tremendous strides have been made in attracting women and girls to science. Four of the major sciences (life sciences, chemistry, astronomy, and geology) are now at least half populated with women at the bachelor's level. The applied fields of medicine, veterinary, and pharmaceutical sciences show the same increases in women's participation. The three areas remaining (physics, computer science, and engineering) need work but the slope of the curve, at least in physics and engineering, is in the right direction (Lewin, 2006). Even if we cannot pinpoint which of the various educational interventions caused this to happen, U.S. educators can take pride and credit in having installed a far more fair and inviting set of pathways into science (and mathematics) for women and girls than before.

In terms of policy, however, the fact that we can't pinpoint exactly which educational interventions contributed to improved access and which did not *is* problematic. How can we extrapolate from the remarkable transformation of (mostly White) women's and girls' attitudes toward and willingness to study the SET disciplines to minority women and lower-income women, absent clear and summative evaluation?[6] In 2004, the National Research Council (of the National Academies of Science) asked this very

---

[6]Once we disaggregate the female population choosing science, we realize that certain subgroups of females haven't yet caught the science "bug" whether because of income or other variables and are still not pursuing science, math, and engineering at the college level. Low-income and minority women are still so few as to be not countable. But then so are low-income, minority men. We need new thinking and dedicated resources to meet the not yet well understood needs of that population.

question of a large quantity of mathematics interventions that had taken place in the preceding two decades. Their finding: post-hoc program evaluations do not provide the answers we are seeking (National Research Council, 2004). The same would probably be found for the sciences. The most obvious measure of change in girls' attitudes toward and willingness to study science after some intervention would be longitudinal, starting with their subsequent course-taking behavior. However, given the limited timeframes for interventions, this variable is rarely taken into consideration. All we can say with certainty is that a whole suite of actions and activities helped teachers learn how to affect girls' attitudes and improve their competencies.

Another reason is that it is hard to tease out what works and what doesn't work is that a *critical mass* of women in a previously male-dominated field causes a numerical tipping point which, in turn, alters the parameters of the problem as it has previously been defined. Thus, two methodological problems immediately reveal themselves: (a) casting about for firm determinants of cause and effect, and (b) trying to keep a moving target in sight.

Finally, to confound cause-and-effect still more, we should consider two developments contemporaneous with gender equity interventions that have affected *both* girls' motivation to succeed in science, and science educators' interest in improving their product (Linnenbrink & Pintrich, 2002). The first includes the wide-ranging changes in society's expectations of girls as the 1960s women's movement set out and then achieved many of its goals. The second, under the general rubric of *Science for All Americans* and Project: 2061 (Rutherford & Ahlgren, 1990), has been the extensive efforts by science (and math) educators since the 1980s to significantly reform and, indeed, even *transform* the teaching/learning of science in grades K–16. This movement began with the publication of *Nation at Risk* (Holton, 1983). In response to this publication, the National Science Foundation began investing more heavily in science education efforts to research and implement new curricula, teacher training and retraining, and the application of technology to science teaching and learning. Some of this federal support focused on gender equity. (See description of NSF gender equity programs in this *Handbook* Chapter 5, "The Role of Government in Advancing Gender Equity in Education.) While not all science reform programs targeted girls *per se*, many of the curricula and pedagogical improvements—particularly those that are holistic—confront misconceptions, consider alternate learning styles, and feature essay writing and personal journaling disproportionately benefited girls (Rosser, 1990; AAUW, 1999).

These ongoing efforts may result in more incremental increases in girls' participation in areas of SET where they are underrepresented. We suggest that a new, more powerful paradigm needs to be employed to revitalize research about SET curricula and cultures that continue to turn females away from these fields.

ACKNOWLEDGMENTS

We want to thank Donna Nelson, University of Oklahoma, Norman, OK, and Dale McCreedy, Franklin Institute Science Museum, Philadelphia, PA, for their review comments. Special thanks to Sheila Tobias for contributing to the chapter in its final stages. We also thank Grace Jepkemboi, graduate research assistant, University of Alabama Birmingham, who gave invaluable assistance with reference checking.

References

Abbott, G., Morrell, C., Bievenue, L., Bracey, B., & Scripa, R. (March, 2006). *Building intellectual capital in young girls*. Panel presented at the meeting of the Society for Information Technology & Teacher Education, Orlando, FL.

Adamson, L., Foster, M., Roark, M., & Reed, D. (1998). Doing a science project: Gender differences during childhood. *Journal of Research in Science Teaching, 35*(8), 845–857.

Ahuja, M. K. (2002). Women in information technology profession: A literature review, synthesis, and research agenda. *European Journal of Information Systems, 11*, 20–34.

Ahuja, M., Herring, S. C., Ogan, C., & Robinson, J. (2004, April). Exploring antecedents of gender equitable outcomes in IT higher education. *Proceedings of SIGMIS'04*, Tucson, AZ.

Alper, J. (1993). The pipeline is leaking women all the way. *Science, 260*, 409–411.

American Association of University Women (AAUW). (1992). *How schools shortchange girls*. New York: Marlowe & Company

American Association of University Women (AAUW). (1998). *Separated by sex: A critical look at a single-sex education for girls*. Washington, DC: American Association of University Women Educational Foundation.

American Association of University Women (AAUW). (1999). *Gender gaps: Where schools still fail our children*. Washington, DC: American Association of University Women Educational Foundation.

American Association of University Women Educational Foundation Commission on Technology, Gender, and Teacher Education. (2000). *Tech-savvy: Educating girls in the new computer age*. Washington, DC: American Association of University Women Educational Foundation.

American Medical Association. (2003). *Women in medicine statistics*. Retrieved December 15, 2005, from http://www.ama-assn.org/

Andre, T., Whigham, M., Hendrickson, A., & Chambers, S. (1999). Competency beliefs, positive affect, and gender stereotypes of elementary students and their parents about science versus other school projects. *Journal of Research in Science Teaching, 36*(6), 719–747.

Association of American Medical Colleges. (2003, November). *Applicants to U.S. medical schools increase women the majority for the first time*. Retrieved July 26, 2006, from http://www.aamc.org/newsroom/pressrel/2003/031104.htm

Association of American Universities. (2006, January). National Defense Education and Innovation Initiative: Meeting America's Economic and Security Challenges in the 21st Century. AAU white paper on competitiveness. Retrieved February 7, 2007, from http://www.aau.edu/reports/NDEII.pdf

Augustine, N. (Chair). (2005). *Rising above the gathering storm: Energizing and employing America for a brighter economic future*. Washington, DC: National Academies Press.

Bandura, A. (1986). *Social foundations of thought and action: A social cognitive theory*. Englewood Cliffs, NJ: Prentice Hall.

Bandura, A. (1989). Regulation of cognitive processes through perceived self-efficacy. *Developmental Psychology, 25*(5), 729–735.

Bandura, A. (1997). *Self-efficacy: The exercise of control*. New York: Freeman.

Bandura, A. (1998). Health promotion from the perspective of social cognitive theory, *Psychology and Health, 13*, 623–649.

Barman, C. (1997). Students' views of scientists and science: Results from a national study. *Science and Children, 35*(1), 18–24.

Bailyn, L. (1999). A study on the status of women faculty in science at MIT. *MIT Faculty Newsletter,* Special Edition, *11,* 1–15.

Bell, A. E., Sherman, S. J., Iserman, E., & Logel, C. (2003). Stereotype threat and women's performance in engineering. *Journal of Engineering Education, 92*(4), 307–312.

Bem, S. L. (1995). *The lenses of gender: Transforming the debate on sexual inequality*. New Haven, CT: Yale University Press.

Benbow, C. P., & Stanley, J. C. (1980). Sex differences in mathematical ability: Fact or artifact? *Science, 210*, 1262–1264.

Benbow, C. P., & Stanley, J. C. (1982). Consequences in high school and college of sex differences in mathematical reasoning ability: A longitudinal perspective. *American Educational Research Journal, 19*(4), 598–622.

Benckert, S., & Staberg, E. (2000). Women in chemistry and physics: Questions of similarities and difference. In S. V. Rosser (guest editor), *Women's Studies Quarterly: Building inclusive science: Connecting women's studies and women in science and engineering, 28*(1/2), 24–45.

Benjamin, E. (1999). Disparities in the salaries and appointments of academic women and men. *Academe, 85*(1), 60–62.

Bianchini, J. A., & Colburn, A. (2000). Teaching the nature of science through inquiry to prospective elementary teachers: A tale of two researchers. *Journal of Research in Science Teaching, 37*(2), 177–209.

Blum, L. (2001). Women in computer science: The Carnegie Mellon experience. In *The future of the university: The university of the future*. Retrieved June 5, 2006, from http://www-2.cs.cmu.edu/~lblum/PAPERS/women_in_computer_science.pdf

Blum, L., & Frieze, C. (2005). In a more balanced computer science environment, similarity is the difference and computer science is the winner. *Computing Research News, 17*(3). Retrieved June 15, 2006, from http://www.cra.org/CRN/articles/may05/blum.frieze.html

Bombardieri, M. (2005, January 17). Summers' remarks on women draw fire. *The Boston Globe*. Retrieved June 22, 2006, from http://www.boston.com/news/education/higher/articles/2005/01/17/summers_remarks_on_women_draw_fire/

Bong, M., & Clark, R. E. (1999). Comparison between self-concept and self-efficacy in academic motivation research. *Educational Psychologist, 34*(3) 139–153.

Borg, A., Budil, K., Ducloy, M., & McKenna, J. (2005). Attracting girls into physics. Women in physics: 2nd IUPAP International Conference on Women in Physics. *AIP Conference Proceedings, 795*, 7–10.

Business Roundtable. (2005, July). *Tapping America's potential: The education for innovation initiative*. Retrieved June 30, 2006, from http://www.businessroundtable.org/pdf/20050803001TAPfinalnb.pdf

Camp, T. (1997, May). A decade in the university pipeline. *Computing Research News*.

Camp, T., Miller, K., & Davies, V. (2000). *The incredible shrinking pipeline unlikely to reverse*. Retrieved June 2, 2006, from http://www.mines.edu/fs_home/tcamp/new-study/new-study.html

Campbell, P. B., Jolly, E. J., & Perlman, L. (2004). *Engagement, capacity and continuity: A trilogy for student success*. Retrieved December 2, 2005, from http://www.campbell-kibler.com

Campbell, P., & Perlman, L. (2005). *What brings workers to information and why do they stay?* Retrieved on November 30, 2005, from http://www.campbell-kibler.com

Campbell, P. B., & Storo, J. N. (1994). *Girls are . . . Boys are . . .* Retrieved November 30, 2005, from http://www.campbell-kibler.com

Canada, K., & Brusca, F. (1991). The technological gender gap: Evidence and recommendations for educators and computer-based instruction designers. *Educational Technology Research and Development, 39*(2), 43–51.

Changing America (1989). *The new face of science and engineering*. Final report of the National Science Foundation Task Force on Women, Minorities, and the Handicapped in Science and Technology, Washington, DC. ED #317386

Chapman, A. (1997). *A great balancing act: Equitable education for girls and boys*. Washington, DC: National Association of Independent Schools.

Clewell, B. C., Anderson, B. T., & Thorpe, M. E. (1992). *Breaking the barriers: Helping female and minority students succeed in mathematics and science*. San Francisco: Jossey-Bass.

Cohoon, J. M., & Aspray, W. (2006). *Women and information technology: Research on the reasons for underrepresentation*. Cambridge, MA: MIT Press.

College Board. (1999). *National Summary Reports*. New York: College Entrance Examination Board.

Colley, A. M., Gale, M. T., & Harris, T. A. (1994). Effects of gender role identity and experience on computer attitude components. *Journal of Educational Computing Research, 10*(2), 129–137.

Collis, B. A., & Williams, R. L. (1987). Cross-cultural comparison of gender differences in adolescents' attitudes toward computers and selected school subjects. *Journal of Educational Research, 81*(1), 17–27.

Committee on Science, Engineering, & Public Policy (COSEPUP). (2006). *Rising above the gathering storm: Energizing and employing America for a brighter economic future*. Washington, DC: The National Academies Press.

Covington, M. V. (1984). The self-worth theory of achievement motivation: Findings and implications. *The Elementary School Journal, 85*(1), 5–20.

Crandall, V. C. (1969). Sex differences in expectancy of intellectual and academic reinforcement. In C. P. Smith (Ed.). *Achievement-related motives in children*, (pp. 11–45). New York: Russell Sage Foundation.

Creamer, E. G., & Laughlin, A. (2005). Self-authorship and women's career decision-making. *Journal of College Student Development, 46*(1), 13–27.

Creamer, E. G., Meszaros, P. S., & Burger, C. J. (2004). Characteristics of young women with an interested in information technology. *Journal of Women and Minorities in Science and Engineering, 10*(1), 67–78.

Crombie, G., Abarbanel, T., & Anderson, C. (2000). All-female computer science. *Science Teacher, 67*(3), 40–43.

Dai, Y., Moon, S., & Feldhuesen, J. (1998). Achievement motivation and gifted students: A social cognitive perspective. *Educational Psychologist, 33*(2/3), 45–63.

Dryburgh, H. (2000). Underrepresentation of girls and women in computer science: Classification of 1990s research. *Journal of Educational Computing Research, 23*(2),181–202.

Durndell, A. (1990). Why do female students tend to avoid computer studies? *Research in Science & Technological Education, 8*(2), 163–170.

Dyer, S. K. (Ed.). 2004. *Under the microscope: A decade of gender equity projects in the sciences*. Washington, DC: American Association of University Women Educational Foundation.

Ealy, J., & Hermanson, J. (2006, March). Molecular images in organic chemistry. *Journal of Science Education and Technology, 15*(1), 59–68.

Eccles, J. (1983). Attributional processes as mediators of sex differences in achievement. *Journal of Educational Equity and Leadership, 3*(1), 19–27

Eccles, J., Adler, S., & Meece, J. L. (1984). Sex differences in achievement: A test of alternate theories. *Journal of Personality and Social Psychology, 46*(1), 26–43

Eccles, J., & Harold, R. (1992). *Gender differences in educational and occupational patterns among the gifted*. In N. Colangelo, S. G. Assouline, & D. L. Ambroson. Talent Development: Proceedings from the 1991 Henry B. and Jocelyn Wallace National Research Symposium or Talent Development (pp. 2–30). New York: Trillium Press .

Eccles, J. S., & Wigfield, A. (2002). Motivational beliefs, values, and goals. *Annual Review of Psychology, 53*, 109–132.

Elekonich, M. (2001). Contesting territories: Female-female aggression in the song sparrow. In M. Mayberry, B. Subramaniam, & L.H. Weasel, (Eds.), *Feminist Science Studies* (pp. 97–105). Oxford, UK: Routledge.

Elliot, B., Oty, K., McArthur, J., & Clark, B. (2001). The effect of an interdisciplinary algebra/science course on students' problem solving skills, critical thinking skills and attitudes towards mathematics. *International Journal of Mathematical Education in Science and Technology, 32*(6), 811–816.

Feather, N. (1982). *Expectations and actions*. Hillsdale, NJ: Erlbaum.

Feather, N. T. (1988). Values, valences, and course enrollment: Testing the role of personal values within an expectancy-valence framework. *Journal of Educational Psychology, 80*(4), 381–391.

Feder, T. (2002, May). Women and some men, ask why women don't flock to physics. *Physics Today*, 55(5), 24–26.

Fogg, P. (2005). Harvard's president wonders aloud about women in science and math. *The Chronicle of Higher Education: The Faculty, 51*(21), A12. Retrieved July, 7, 2006, from http://chronicle.com

Fox, M. F. (2000). Organizational environments and doctoral degrees awarded to women in science and engineering departments. *Women's Studies Quarterly, 28*(1/2), 47–61.

Fox, M. F. (2001). Women, science, and academia: Graduate education and careers. *Gender & Society, 15*, 654–666.

Fox, M. F. (2003). Gender, faculty, and doctoral education in science and engineering. In L. Hornig (Ed). *Equal rites, unequal outcomes: Women in American research universities* (pp. 91–109). New York: Kluwer Academic/Plenum Publishers.

Fox, M. F., Johnson, D., & Rosser, S. V. (2005*). Women, gender, and technology.* Champaign-Urbana, IL: University of Illinois Press.

Fredricks, J. A., & Eccles, J. S. (2002). Children's competence and value beliefs from childhood through adolescence: Growth trajectories in two male sex-typed domains. *Developmental Psychology, 38*(4), 519–533.

Friedman, T. (2005). *The world is flat*. New York: Farrar, Strauss, & Giroux.

Gatta, M. (2002). Women in science, engineering, and technology: Equity in the 21st century. Research in brief. *Rutgers Center for Women and Work*. Retrieved June 5, 2006, from http://www.rci .rutgers.edu/~cww/dataPages/rbwomeninset.pdf

Gender Advisory Board. (2000). Increasing the Participation of Women in Computer Science and Engineering (CSE). Recommendations to the World Summit on the Information Society. United Nations Commission on Science and Technology for Development Global Alliance for Diversifying the Science and Engineering Workforce. Retrieved on April 15, 2006, from http://gab.wigsat.org/ wsis.html

Gess-Newsome, J., & Lederman, N. G. (Eds.) (1999). *Examining Pedagogical Content Knowledge: The Construct and Its Implications for Science Education*. Boston: Kluwer Academic Publishing.

Gibbons, M. (2004). *A new look at engineering*. Washington, D.C.: American Society for Engineering Education.

Glazer-Raymo, J. (1999). *Shattering the myths: Women in academe* Baltimore: Johns Hopkins Press.

Goodman Research Group, Inc. (2002). *A comprehensive evaluation of women in engineering programs*. Retrieved June 3, 2002, from http://www.grginc.com

Gouldner, H. (1985). *Women in engineering*. Retrieved August 27, 2005 from http://www.nap.edu/books/0309035864/html/57.html

Grandy, J. (1994). *Gender and ethnic differences among science and engineering majors: Experiences, achievements, and expectations* (RR-94-30). Princeton, NJ: Educational Testing Service.

Greenberg, S. (1985). Educational equity in early education environments. In S. Klein (Ed.), *Handbook for achieving sex equity through education* (pp. 457–469). Baltimore: Johns Hopkins University Press.

Gurer, D., & Camp, T. (1998). *Investigating the incredible shrinking pipeline for women in computer science*. Retrieved June 9, 2006, from http://women.acm.org/documents/finalreport.pdf

Gurer, D., & Camp, T. (2002). An ACM-W literature review on women in computing. *AC SIGCSE Bulletin, 34*(2), 121–127.

Hale, K. V. (2005). Gender Differences in Computer Technology Achievement. *Meridian: A middle school computer technologies journal, 8*(1), 1–4.

Hartline, B. K., & Michelman-Ribeiro, A. (2005, May). *Women in Physics*. Second IUPAP International Conference on Women in Physics, AIP Conference Proceedings, Vol. 795, held 23–25 May, 2005 in Rio de Janeiro, Brazil. Melville, NY: American Institute of Physics, 2005.

Henzel, N. (1991). *Realizing Gender equality in higher education: The need to integrate work/family issues* (ASHE-EIC Higher Education Report No. 2). Washington, D C: The George Washington University School of Education and Human Development.

Herzig, A. H. (2004). Becoming mathematicians: Women and students of color choosing and leaving doctoral mathematics. *Review of educational research, 74*(2), 171–214.

Hewitt, P. G. (2005). *Conceptual Physics*. New York: Addison Wesley.

Heyman, G. D., & Legare, C. H. (2004). Children's beliefs about gender differences in academic social domains. *Sex Roles, 50*(3/4), 227–239.

Hidi, S., & Baird, W. (1986). Interestingness: A neglected variable in discourse processing. *Cognitive Science, 10*, 179–94.

Holton, G. (1983, April). *A nation at risk: The imperative education reform.*A Report to the nation and the secretary of education, United Sates department of education/by the National Commission on Excellence in Education. Retrieved February 8, 2007, from http://www.ed .gov/pubs/NatAtRisk/index.html

Hopkins, N. (1999). MIT and gender bias: Following up on victory. *The Chronicle of Higher Education, 45*(40). Retrieved June 5, 2006, from http://chronicle.com/colloquy/99/genderbias/background.htm

Huang, G., Taddese, N., Walter, E. (2000). Entry and persistence of women and minorities in college science and engineering education. Washington, D.C.: National Center for Educational Statistics. NCES 2000-601, 2000.

Information Technology Association of America (2003, May 5). *ITAA Blue Ribbon Panel on IT Diversity*. Presented at the National IT Workforce Convocation, Arlington, VA. Retrieved October 22, 2005, from http://www.itaa.org

Information Technology Association of America (ITAA) Task Force Report. (2005). *Building the 21st century information technology workforce: Groups underrepresented in the IT workforce*. Retrieved October 10, 2005, from http://www.itaa.org/workforce/studies.recruit.htm

International Union of Pure and Applied Physics. (2005, October 26–28). *Report from the Working Group on Women in Physics*. Presented at the 25th IUPAP General Assembly, Cape Town, South Africa. Retrieved June 18, 2006, from http://www.iupap.org/wg/wip/report-05.html

Ivie, R., & Guo, S. (2006). *Women physicists speak again, AIP Report* (AIP Publication Number R-441). College Park, MD: American Institute of Physics.

Ivie, R., & Ray, K. N. (2005). *Women in Physics and Astronomy, 2005, AIP Report* (AIP Publication Number R-430.02). College Park, MD: American Institute of Physics.

Jackson, J. K. (2001). Unequal partners: Rethinking gender roles in animal behavior. In M. Mayberry, B. Subramaniam, & L. H. Weasel, (Eds.), *Feminist Science Studies* (pp. 115–119). Oxford, UK: Routledge.

Jackson, L., Fleury, R., Girvin, J., & Gerard, D. (1995). The numbers game: Gender and attention to numerical information. *Sex Roles, 33*(7/8), 559–568.

Johnson, R. T., Johnson, D. W., & Stanne, M. B. (1985). Effects of cooperative, competitive, and individualistic goal structures on computer-assisted instruction. *Journal of Educational Psychology, 77*(6), 668–677.

Jolly, E. J., Campbell, P. B., & Perlman, L. (2004). *Engagement, Capacity and Continuity: A Trilogy For Student Success.* Retrieved June 1, 2006, from http://www.smm.org/ecc/

Jussim, L., & Eccles, J. E. (1992). Teacher expectations II: Construction and reflection of student achievement. *Journal of Personality and Social Psychology, 63,* 947–961.

Kahle, J. B., & Lakes, M. K. (1983). The myth of equality in science classrooms. *Journal of Research in Science Teaching, 20*(2), 131–140.

Kahle, J. B., & Meece, J. (1994). Research on girls and science: Lessons and applications. In D. Gabel (Ed.), *Handbook of research in science teaching and learning* (pp. 542–576). Washington, DC: National Science Teachers Association.

Karniol, R., & Aida, A. (1997). Judging toy breakers: Gender stereotypes have devious effects on children. *Sex Roles, 36*(3/4), 195–205.

Kekelis, L. S., Ancheta, R. W., & Heber, E. (2005). Hurdles in the pipeline: Girls and technology careers. *Frontiers: A Journal of Women Studies, 26*(1), 99–109.

Ketcham, L. M., Frehill, L. M., & Jeser-Cannavale, C. (2004). *Women in engineering: A review of the 2004 literature.* Retrieved August 20, 2005 from http://www.swe.org.

Kinsman, S. (2001). Life, sex, and cells. In C. M. Musil (Ed.), *Gender, science, & the undergraduate curriculum: Building two-way streets* (pp. 17–28). Washington, DC: Association of American Colleges & Universities.

Kirkpatrick, H., & Cuban, L. (1998). Should be we worried? What the research says about gender differences in access, use, attitudes, and achievement with computers. *Education and Computing, 38*(4), 56–61.

Klawe, M., & Leveson, N. (2001). Refreshing the nerds. *Communications of the ACM, 44*(7), 67–68.

Klein, S. (Ed.). (1985). *Handbook for achieving sex equity through education.* Baltimore: Johns Hopkins University Press.

Kleinman, S. (1998). Overview of feminist perspectives on the ideology of science. *Journal of Research in Science Teaching, 35*(3), 837–845.

Koch, J. (1996). Gender study of private school students' attitudes and beliefs about school life. *Resources in Education (RIE).* ERIC document ED 398650 http://eric.ed.gov/ERICWebPortal/Home.portal?_nfpb=true&_pageLabel=RecordDetails&ERICExtSearch_SearchValue_0=ED398650&ERICExtSearch_SearchType_0=eric_accno&objectId=0900000b8011eda6

Koch, J. (1998). Response Karen Meyer: Reflections on being female in school science. *Journal of Research in Teaching Science, 35*(4), 473–474.

Koch, J. (2005). Creating gender equitable classroom environments. In G. Kiger & D. Byrnes (Eds.). *Common Bonds: Anti-bias teaching in a diverse society* (pp. 91–104). Wheaton, MD: ACEI.

Kolar, R. L., & Sabatini, D. A. (1996). *Coupling team learning and computer technology in project-driven undergraduate engineering education.* Retrieved June 5, 2006, from http://ieeexplore.ieee.org/xpl/abs_free.jsp?arNumber=569937

Labor Law Talk. (2006). *Dictionary by Labor Law Talk.* Retrieved June 22, 2006, from http://encyclopedia.laborlawtalk.com/Information_science

Larkin, J. (1994). *Sexual harassment: High school girls speak out.* Toronto, CA: Second Story Press.

Lederman, M. (2005, May 14). Science as a social enterprise. *Chronicle of Higher Education, 50*(36). Retrieved June 5, 2006, from http://chronicle.com/weekly/v50/i36/36b01601.htm

Lee, A. C. K. (2003). Undergraduate students' gender differences in IT skills and attitudes. *Journal of Computer Assisted Learning, 19*(4), 490–503.

Leventman, P., & Finley, M. (2005). *Women in the workforce: The societal context of IT employment and feelings, attitudes and opinions of IT professionals.* Retrieved August 30, 2005, from http://www.campbell-kibler.com/SocialContextIT.doc

Levine, T. (2004). *Girls in computer-supported science classrooms: Perceived classroom climate and attitudes toward the learning of science.* Retrieved June 3, 2004, from http://www.wigset.org/gasat/36.txt

Lewerke, W. C., Robbins, S., Sawyer, R., & Hovland, M. (2004). Predicting engineering major status from mathematics achievement and congruence. *Journal of Career Assessment, 23*(2), 135–149.

Lewin, T. (2006, July 9). At colleges, women are leaving men in the dust. *The New York Times*, p. 1, section 1.

Linn, M. (1990). *Gender, mathematics and science: Trends and recommendations.* Mystic, CT: Council of Chief State Officers Summer Institute.

Linn, M. (2000). Controversy, the Internet, and deformed frogs: Making science accessible. *Who will do the science of the future?* (p. 16–27). In National Academy of Sciences, Committee on Women in Science and Engineering. *Who Will Do the Science of the Future? A Symposium on Careers of Women in Science.* Washington, D.C.: National Academy Press. Washington, DC: National Academy Press.

Linn, M. C. (2005). Technology and gender equity: What works? In N. F. Russo, C. Chan, M. B. Kenkel, C. B. Travis, & M. Vasquez (Eds.), *Women in science and technology.* New York: American Psychological Association.

Linn, M., & Hsi, S. (1999). *Computers, teachers, peers: Science learning partners.* Hillsdale, NJ: Lawrence Erlbaum Associates.

Linnenbrink, E. A., & Pintrich, P. R. (2002). Motivation as an enabler for academic success. *School Psychology Review, 31*(3), 313–327.

Logan, K. (2003). Do girls prefer a different computing learning environment to boys? An analysis of the computing learning environment of upper secondary students in Wellington, New Zealand. *Proceedings of the 2003 Australian Women in IT Conference* (pp. 29–37). Retrieved February 8, 2007, from http://www.auswit.org/2003/papers/1-4_Logan.pdf

Long, J. S. (Ed.). (2001). *From scarcity to visibility: Gender differences in the careers of doctoral scientists and engineers.* Washington DC: National Academy Press.

MacDonald, J. (2004). *Gurl tech: Net basics.* [Nortel Network Kidz Online Streaming video] Retrieved January 3, 2005 from http://www.kidzonline.com/nclb2004.

Margolis, J., & Fisher, A. (2001). *Unlocking the clubhouse: Women in computing.* Cambridge, MA: MIT Press.

Margolis, J., Fisher, A., & Miller, F. (1999). *The anatomy of interest: Women in undergraduate computer science.* Pittsburgh, PA: Carnegie Mellon University Press.

Margolis, J., Fisher, A., & Miller, F. (2000). The anatomy of interest: Women in undergraduate computer science. *Women's Studies Quarterly, 28,* 104–127.

Margolis, J., Fisher, A., & Miller, F. (2002). *Caring about connections: Gender and computing.* Pittsburgh, PA: Carnegie Mellon University Press.

Martin, M. O., Mullis, I. V. S., Gonzalez, E. J., & Chrostowski, S. J. (2004). *Findings from IEA's Trends in international mathematics and science study at the fourth and eighth grades.* Chestnut Hill, MA: TIMSS & PIRLS International Study Center, Boston College.

Mason, M. A., & Goulden, M. (2002). Do babies matter?: The effect of family formation on the life long careers of women. *Academic Search Premier, 88,* 21–28.

McClelland, D. C. (1961). *The achieving society.* Princeton, NJ: Van Nostrand.

McCormick, N., & McCormick, J. (1991). Not for men only: Why so few women major in computer science. *College Student Journal, 25,* 345–350.

McGinnis, R., & Pearsall, J. (1998). Teaching elementary science methods to females: A male professor's experience from two perspectives. *Journal of Research in Science Teaching, 35*(3), 919–949.

McIlwee, J., & Robinson, J. G. (1992). *Women in engineering: Gender, power, and workplace culture.* Albany, NY: State University of New York Press.

Meece, J., & Eccles, J. (1993). Recent trends in research on gender and education. *Educational Psychologist, 28*, 313–319.

Merchant, C. (1980). *The death of nature: Women, ecology, and the scientific revolution.* New York: Harper & Row.

Meszaros, P. S., Creamer, E. G., Burger, C. J., & Matheson, J. (2005). Mothers and millennials: Career talking across the generations. *Kappa Omicron Nu FORUM (online journal), 16*(1).

Meyer, K. (1995). Reflections on being female in school science: Toward a praxis of teaching science. *Journal of Research in Science Teaching, 35*(4), 463–371.

MIT Department of Electrical Engineering & Computer Science. (1995). *Women undergraduate enrollment in electrical engineering and computer science at MIT.* Cambridge, MA: MIT Press.

Morrell, C., Cotton, S., Sparks, A., & Spurgas, A. (2004). *Computer mania day: An effective intervention for increasing youth's interest in technology.* Baltimore: Center for Women & Information Technology, University of Maryland.

Morris, L. K. (2002). *Women in information technology literature review: Recruitment, retention and persistence factors.* Paper prepared for presentation at the 29th Annual Meeting of the Mid-South Educational Research Association, Chattanooga, TN.) (ED 477715) Retrieved February 8, 2007 from http://eric.ed.gov/ERICDocs/data/ericdocs2/content_storage_01/0000000b/80/22/42/58.pdf

Murray, C. (2005). The inequality taboo. *Commentary Magazine, 120*(2), 13–22.

Musil, C. M. (Ed.) (2001). *Gender, science, & the undergraduate curriculum: Building two-way streets.* Washington, DC: Association of American Colleges & Universities

National Council for Research on Women. (2001). *Balancing the equation: Where are women and girls in science, engineering, and technology?* Washington, DC: Author.

National Institute for Science Education. (1998). *Women and men of the engineering path: A model for analysis of undergraduate careers* (ED Publication No. PLLI 98-8055). Washington, DC: U.S. Department of Education.

National Research Council. (1996). *The national science education standards.* Washington, DC: National Academy Press.

National Research Council. (2004). *On evaluating program effectiveness: Judging the quality of K–12 mathematics evaluations.* Washington, DC: National Academy Press.

National Science Board. (2004a). Science and engineering indicators 2004 (Vols. 1–2; NSB 04-1, NSB 04-1A) Arlington, VA: National Science Foundation.

National Science Board. (2004b). *Broadening participation in science and engineering faculty* (NSB 04-41). Retrieved June 5, 2005, from http://www.nsf.gov/publications/pub_summ.jsp?ods_key=nsb0441

National Science Foundation. (1998). *Women, minorities, and persons with disabilities in science and engineering* (NSF 99-338). Arlington, VA: Author.

National Science Foundation. (2000). *Land of plenty: Diversity as America's competitive edge in science, engineering, and technology.* Arlington, VA.: Author. cawmset0409. Retrieved June 21, 2006, from http://www.nsf.gov/publications/pub_summ.jsp?ods_key=cawmset0409

National Science Foundation. (2003). *New formulas for America's workforce: Girls in science and engineering* (NSF 03-207). Arlington, VA: Author.

National Science Foundation. (2004). *Women, minorities, and persons with disabilities in science and engineering* (NSF 04-317). Arlington, VA: Author.

National Science Foundation. (2006). *First-time S&E graduate enrollment of foreign students drops for the third straight year.* Retrieved June 16, 2006, from http://www.nsf.gov/statistics/inf brief/nsf06321/

Nauta, M., Epperson, D., & Kahn, J. (1998). A multiple-groups analysis of higher-level career aspirations among females in mathematics, science and engineering majors. *Journal of Counseling Psychology, 45*(4), 483–496.

Nauta, M., Epperson, D., & Waggoner, K. (1999). Perceived causes of success and failure: Are women's attributions related to persistence in engineering majors? *Journal of Research in Science Teaching, 36*(6), 663–676.

Nelson, L. J., Weise, G. M., & Cooper, J. (1991). Getting started with computers: Experience, anxiety, and relational style. *Computers in Human Behavior, 7*, 185–202.

Nelson, D. J., & Rogers, D. C. (2005). *A national analysis of diversity in science and engineering faculties at research universities.* Retrieved July 26, 2006, from http://cheminfo.chem.ou.edu/faculty/djn/djn.html.

Nicholls J. G. (1984). Conceptions of ability and academic motivation. In R. Ames & C. Ames (Eds.), *Research on motivation in education* (pp. 39–73) (Vol. 1, Student motivation). Orlando, FL: Academic Press.].

Noble, D. F. (1992). *A world without women: The Christian clerical culture of western science.* Oxford, UK: Oxford University Press.

Ogan, C. L., Herring, S. C., Ahuja, M., & Robinson, J. (2005, May). *The more things change, the more they stay the same: Gender differences in attitudes and experiences related to computing.* Paper presented at the annual meeting of the International Communication Association, New York. Retrieved March 21, 2006 from http://ella.slis.indiana.edu/~herring/ica.pdf]

Oliver, J. (2005). Graduate enrollment in science and engineering programs up in 2003, but declines for first-time foreign students. *INFOBRIEF SRS.* National Science Foundation, 05-317. Retrieved February 8, 2007. from http://www.nsf.gov/statistics/infbrief/nsf05317/

Orenstein, P. (1995). *Schoolgirls: Young women, self-esteem, and the confidence gap.* New York: Doubleday.

Pajares, F. (1996). Self-efficacy beliefs in academic settings. *Review of Educational Research, 66*(4), 543–578.

Palloff, R., & Pratt, K. (2001). *Lessons from the cyberspace classroom.* San Francisco: Jossey- Bass.

Pearl, A., Pollack, M. E., Riskin, E., Thomas, B., Wolf, E., & Wu, A. (1990). Becoming a computer scientist: A report by the ACM Committee on the Status of Women in Computer Science. *Communications of the ACM, 33*(11), 47–57.

Phillips, J., & Hausbeck, K. (2001). Just beneath the surface: Rereading geology, rescripting the knowledge/power nexus. In M. Mayberry, B. Subramaniam, & L. H. Weasel (Eds.), *Feminist Science Studies*, (pp. 225–137). Oxford, UK: Routledge.

Plucker, J. (1996). Secondary science and mathematics teachers and gender equity: Attitudes and attempted interventions. *Journal of Research in Science Teaching, 33*(7), 737–751.

Postsecondary science and math programs face Title IX review. (2006, April 3). *Feminist Daily News Wire.* Retrieved February 8, 2007, from http://www.feminist.org/news/newsbyte/uswirestory.asp?id=9596

Reece, C. C. (1986). *Gender and microcomputers: Implications for the school curriculum.* Paper presented at the Mid-South Educational Research Association, Memphis, TN, November 19–21, 1986.

Riley, D. (2003). *Pedagogies of liberation in an engineering thermodynamics class.* Proceedings of the 2003 American Society for Engineering Education Annual Conference & Exposition. Nashville, TN. Session 2692.

Roldon, M., Soe, L., & Yakura, E. K. (2004, April, 22–24). *Perceptions of chilly IT organizational contexts and their effect on the retention and promotion of women in IT.* Presented at SIGMIS 04, Tucson, AZ. (pp. 108–13).

Rolison, D. R. (2004). Title IX as a change strategy for women in science and engineering . . . and what comes next. Retrieved February 8, 2007, from http://www.barnard.edu/bcrw/womenandwork/rolison .htm#end2. *Women, Work and the Academy: Strategies for Responding to "Post-Civil Rights Era" Gender Discrimination. New York, NY. Barnard College.*

Rop, C. (1997). Breaking the gender barrier in the physical sciences. *Educational Leadership, 55*(4), 58–60.

Rosser, S. V. (1990). *Female-friendly science: Applying women's studies methods and theories to attract students.* New York: Pergamon Press.

Rosser, S. V. (1997). *Re-engineering female friendly science.* New York: Teachers College Press.

Rossiter, M. (1982). *Women scientists in America: Struggles and strategies to 1940.* Baltimore: Johns Hopkins University Press.

Rossiter, M. (1995). *Women scientists in America: Before affirmative action 1940–1972.* Baltimore: Johns Hopkins University Press.

Rutherford, F. J., & Ahlgren, A. (1990). *Science for all Americans.* New York: Oxford University Press.

Sadker, M., & Sadker, D. (1982). *Sex equity handbook for schools.* New York: Longman.

Sadker, M., & Sadker, D. (1994). *Failing at fairness: How America's schools cheat girls.* New York: Charles Scribner's Touchstone Press.

Sadker, M., & Sadker, D. (2005). *Teachers, schools, and society* (7th ed.). New York: McGraw-Hill.

Sadker, M., Sadker, D., & Klein, S. (1991). The issue of gender in elementary and secondary education. In G. Grant (Ed.) *Review of research in education,* (pp. 269–334). Washington, DC: American Educational Research Association.

Sanders, J. (2005 July). *Teaching teachers about gender equity in computing.* Paper presented at crossing cultures, changing lives: Integrating research on girls' choices of IT Careers, Oxford, England.

Sanders, J. (2006). Gender and technology in education: A research review. In C. Skelton, B. Francis, & L. Smulyan (Eds.), *Handbook of gender in education.* London: Sage Publications.

Sanders, J., Koch, J., & Urso, P. (1997). *Right from the start: Instructional activities for teacher educators in mathematics, science and technology.* Hillsdale, NJ: Lawrence Erlbaum Associates.

Sandoval, G. (2005, July). Video-game world remains male territory. *The Associated Press.* Retrieved July 25, 2005, from http://www .azcentral.com/business/articles/0725gamegirls25.htm

Santiago, A., & Einarson, M. (1998). Background characteristics as predictors of academic self-confidence and self-efficacy among graduate science and engineering students. *Research in Higher Education, 39*(2), 163–198.

Sax, L. J., Astin, A. W., Korn, W. S., & Mahoney, K. M. (2000). *The American freshman: National norms for Fall 2000,* Higher Education Research Institute, UCLA Graduate School of Education & Information Studies. Los Angeles: Higher Education Research Institute, UCLA.

Schiebinger, L. (1989). *The mind has no sex: Women and the origins of modern science.* Cambridge, MA: Harvard University Press.

Schunk, D. H. (1984). Self-efficacy perspectives on achievement behaviour. *Educational Psychologist, 19,* 48–58.

Schunk, D. H., & Ertmer, P. A. (2000). Self-regulation and academic learning. Self-efficacy enhancing interventions. In M. Boekaerts, P. R. Pintrich, & M. Zeidner (Eds.), *Handbook of self-regulation* (pp. 631–649). San Diego, CA: Academic Press.

Selby, C. C. (2004). From the needs of women to the needs of science. *Bulletin of Science, Technology & Society, 22*(1), 46–47.

Selby, L., Young, A., & Fisher, D. (1997). Increasing the participation of women in tertiary level computing courses: what works and why. In R. Kevill, R. Oliver, & R. Phillips (Eds). *What works and why.* Proceedings of the 14th annual Australian Society for Computers in Learning in Tertiary Education '97 conference. Curtin University of Technology, Perth, 8–10 December.

Seymour, E. (1995). The loss of women from science, mathematics, and engineering undergraduate majors: An explanatory account. *Science Education, 79*(4), 437–473.

Seymour, E., & Hewitt, N. (1997). *Talking about leaving: Why undergraduates leave the sciences.* Boulder, CO: Westview Press.

Shashaani, L. (1994). Socioeconomic status, parents' sex-role stereotypes, and the gender gap in computing. *Journal of Research on Computing in Education, 26*(4), 433–451.

Shashaani, L. (1997). Gender differences in computer attitudes and use among college students. *Journal of Educational Computing Research, 16*(1), 37–51.

Sheldon, J. (2004). Gender stereotypes in educational software for young children. *Sex Roles, 51*(7–8), 433—444.

Sjoberg, S., & Imsen, G. (1988). Gender and science education I. In P. Fensham (Ed.), *Development and dilemmas in science education* (pp. 218–248). London: Falmer Press.

Skaalvik, S., & Skaalvik, E. M. (2004). Gender performance in math and verbal self-concept, performance and expectations and motivation. *Sex Roles, 50*(3/4), 241– 252.

Sommers, C. H. (2000). *The war against boys: How misguided feminism is harming our young men.* New York: Simon & Schuster

Sonnert, G. (1995a). *Gender differences in science careers: The Project Access Study.* New Brunswick, NJ: Rutgers University Press.

Sonnert, G. (1995b). *Who succeeds in science?: The gender dimension.* New Brunswick, NJ: Rutgers University Press.

Sosa, T. L. (2004). *Voices of women computer professionals: Perspectives on achievement.* Unpublished doctoral dissertation, Northern Illinois University, DeKalb, IL.

Spanier, B. (2001). Foundation for a "new biology" proposed in molecular cell biology. In M. Lederman & I. Bartsch (Eds.), *The Gender and Science Reader* (pp. 272–288). New York: Routledge.

Spertus, E. (1991). *Why are there so few female computer scientists?* Retrieved June 5, 2006, from http://www.ai.mit.edu/people/ellens/ Gender/pap/pap.html

Steele, C., & Aronson, J. (1995). Stereotype threat and the intellectual test performance of African Americans. *Journal of Personality and Social Psychology, 69*(5), 797–811.

Steinke, J. (2004). Science in cyberspace: Science and engineering World Wide Web sites for girls. *Public Understanding of Science, 13*(1), 7–30.

Strawn, C. A. (1999). *Moving in a man's world: Three qualitative case studies illustrate how women can survive in male-dominated environments.* Unpublished doctoral dissertation, Iowa State University, Ames.

Sumner, M., & Niederman, F. (2002). The impact of gender differences on job satisfaction, job turnover, and career experiences of information systems professionals. Special Interest Group on Computer Personnel Research Annual Conference archive. *Proceedings of the 2002 ACM SIGCPR conference on Computer personnel research* (pp. 154–162).

Summers, L. H. (2005). *Remarks at NBER Conference on Diversifying the Science & Engineering Workforce,* January 14–15, 2006. Cambridge, MA. Retrieved June 22, 2006, from http://www.president.harvard.edu/speeches/2005/nber.html These proceedings provide a compilation of the papers presented at the annual conference of the Association for Computing Machinery's (ACM) Special Interest Group on Computer Personnel Research (SIGCPR), in Kristiansand, Norway, May 14--16, 2002

Swim, J. K., & Sanna, L. J. (1996). He's skilled, she's lucky: A meta-analysis of observers' attributions for women and men's successes and failures. *Personality and Social Psychology Bulletin, 22*(5), 507–519.

Sztein, A. E. (2005). *Women in science: Assessing progress, promoting action.* Washington, DC: Association for Women in Science.

Taylor, H. G., & Mounfield, L. (1994). Exploration of the relationship between prior computing experience and gender on success in college computer science. *Journal of Educational Computing Research, 11*(4), 291–306.

Teague, J. (2002). Women in computing: What brings them to it, what keeps them in it? *Women and Computing, 34*(2), 147–158.

Tobias, S. (1990). *They're not dumb, they're different: Stalking the second tier.* Tucson, AZ: Research Corporation of America.

Tobias, S., & Birrer, F. A. J. (1999). Who will study physics, and why? *European Journal of Physics, 20,* 365–372.

Tobias, S., Chubin, D. E., & Aylesworth, K.(1995). *Rethinking science as a career: Perceptions and realities in physical sciences.* Washington DC: Research Corporation.

Tobias, S., Urry, M., & Venkatesan, A. (2002). Physics: For women, the last frontier. *Science, 296*(17), 1201.

Trauth, E. M. (2002). Odd girl out: An individual differences perspective on women in the IT profession. *Information Technology & People, 15*(2), 98–118.

Trauth, E. M. (Ed.). (2006). *The encyclopedia of gender and information technology.* Hershey, PA: Information Science Publishing.

Traweek, S. (1988). *Beamtimes and lifetimes: The world of high energy physicists.* Cambridge, MA: Harvard University Press.

Turner, S. V., Bernt, P. W., & Pecora, N. (2002, April). *Why women choose information technology careers: Educational, social, and familial influences.* Paper presented at the Annual Meeting of the American Educational Research Association, New Orleans, LA.

Ullman, E. (1997). *Close to the machine: Technophilia and its discontents.* San Francisco: City Lights Publishers.

U.S. Department of Education. (2001). *The U.S. Department of Education's Gender Equity Expert Panel Exemplary and Promising Gender Equity Programs 2000.* Retrieved July 14, 2005, from http://www.ed.gov/offices/OERI/ORAD/KAD/expert_panel/gender.html

U.S. Department of Labor. (2006). *Women in the labor force in 2005.* Retrieved June 5, 2006, from http://www.dol.gov/wb/factsheets/Qf-laborforce-05.htm

Valian, V. (1997). *Why So Slow? The advancement of women.* Cambridge, MA: MIT Press.

Valian, V., & Rabinowitz, V. (2004). *Hunter College Gender Equity Project.* New York: Hunter College Press.

Vispoel, W., & Fast, E. (2000). Response biases and their relation to sex differences in multiple domains of self-concept. *Applied Measurement in Education, 13*(1), 79–97.

Vogt, C. (2002). An account of women's progress in engineering: A social cognitive perspective. *Journal of Women and Minorities in Science and Engineering, 8*(3/4), 217–238.

Vogt, C., Hocevar, D., & Hagedorn, L. (2007). A social cognitive construct validation: Determining women and men's success in engineering programs. *Journal of Higher Education*, in press.

Webster, J. (1996). *Shaping women's work: Gender, employment and information technology.* London: Longman

Weiner, B. (1986). An attributional theory of emotion and motivation New York; Springer-Verlog. In P. Pintrich & D. Schunk, *Motivation in education theory: Research and applications.* Englewood Cliffs, NJ: Prentice Hall.

Wenzel, T. J. (2001). General chemistry: Expanding the goals beyond content and lab skills. In C. M. Musil (Ed.), *Gender, science, & the undergraduate curriculum: Building two-way streets* (pp. 29–46). Washington, DC: Association of American Colleges & Universities.

Wigfield, A., & Eccles, J. (1992). The development of achievement task values: A theoretical analysis. *Developmental Review, 12,* 1–46.

Wigfield, A., Eccles, J., & Rodriquez, D. (1998). The development of children's motivation in school contexts. *Review of Research in Education, 23,* 73–118.

Wilson, R. (2006, May 26). The chemistry between women & science. *Chronicle of Higher Education, 52*(38), A10. Retrieved June 21, 2006, from http://chronicle.com/weekly/v52/i38/38a01001.htm

Wolters, C. A. (1998). Self-regulated learning and college students' regulation of motivation. *Journal of Educational Psychology, 90*(2), 224–235.

Xie, Y., & Shauman, K. A. (2003). *Women in science: Career processes and outcomes.* Cambridge, MA: Harvard University Press.

Young, B. J. (1999). Gender differences in student attitude toward computers. *Journal of Research on Computing in Education, 33*(2), 204–216.

Youngman, J. A., & Egelhoff, C. J. (2003). Best practices in recruiting and persistence of underrepresented minorities in engineering: A 2002 snapshot. *Frontiers in Education, 2,* 11–16.

Zare, R. N. (2006). Sex, lies, and Title IX. *Chemical & Engineering News, 84*(20), 46–49.

Zeldin, A. L., & Pajares, F. (2000). Against the odds: Self-efficacy beliefs of women in mathematical, scientific, and technological careers. *American Educational Research Journal, 37*(1), 215–246.

Zittleman, K., & Sadker, D, (2002). Gender bias in teacher education texts. *Journal of Teacher Education, 53*(2), 168–180.

Zuckerman, H., Cole, J. J., & Bruer, J. (1991). *The outer circle: Women in the scientific community.* New York: W. W. Norton.

GENDER EQUITY IN COMMUNICATION SKILL

Anita Taylor, * Alison Bailey, Pamela Cooper, Carol Dwyer, Cheris Kramarae, and Barbara Lieb

Teaching and learning are primarily communication processes that rely on interactions of students and teachers. Any factor that inhibits effective communication in the teaching and learning process therefore adversely affects the learning process; if communication is restricted or gender biased, then learning will be different for girls and boys. Because of the foundational role of communication in all learning, this chapter focuses primarily on teaching/learning of the basic skills of listening, reading, speaking, and writing. We attend to communication as a primary subject matter only briefly.[1]

Previous research has demonstrated gender bias in language and in its use (Borisoff & Merrill, 1998; Cameron, 1990, 1998; Eckert & McConnell-Ginet, 2003; Hellinger & Bussman, 2001; Hill, 1986; Holborow, 1999; Lakoff, 1990; McConnell-Ginet, 1975; Miller & Swift, 1991, 1976; Penelope, 1990; Schulz, 1990; Spender, 1985, among many others). Other research has shown extensive sex segregation in occupations and significant associated salary differentials (Freeman, 2004; Costello & Krimgold, 1996; Costello & Stone, 2001; Costello, Wight & Stone, 2003 as well as the material in the chapters in this book "Impact of Education on Gender Equity in Employment and Its Outcomes" and "Gender Equity in Career and Technical Education"). A primary concern in this chapter is to explore whether inequities or omissions in education affect persistence of these patterns of inequities, and more specifically to what extent students' achievement of the varied communication skills reinforce these cultural patterns. Where inequities or omissions in communication education exist, we need to identify them in order to remedy some of the forces perpetuating societal patterns.

First, we discuss matters of definition. Next, we examine extant data to learn where differences in skills and competence in communication exist between girls and boys—and, when relevant, women and men—as groups. We then explore the extent to which these differences relate to educational practices and structures, thus examining the processes of teaching and assessing communicating skills in diverse populations. We look briefly at communication in social patterns and structure using the status of women in journalism/communication education as illustrative of one factor in media literacy learning. Finally, we make recommendations for achieving equity in the materials and methods used in teaching communication skills.

Overall, this chapter raises more questions than it provides answers. Readers seeking definitive information or claims about how education "shortchanges" girls/women or boys/men will be dissatisfied. The scholarship reviewed shows that previous study of equity in communication education has only partially covered communication skills and assessed only in part achievement of those skills that have been measured. We argue that previous researchers and commentators have too quickly generalized about differences between girls and boys (or women and men) as population groups and have inadequately disaggregated data to study within-population differences. The primary contribution of the chapter is to show where more study is needed, what new assessment efforts are required, and where more careful analysis should preclude facile generalizations. We conclude with recommendations for policy and other changes needed to facilitate these changes.

UNDERSTANDING GENDER EQUITY IN COMMUNICATION SKILLS LEARNING

This chapter focuses on gender issues in teaching and learning in the content areas of communication skills in English. Thus,

---

*The bold face names is the Lead Author.

[1]Other discussions related to communication education can be found in the chapters "Facts and Assumptions about the Nature of Gender Differences," and "Implications for Gender Equity; Gender Equity in Coeducational and Single-Sex Educational Environments," "Gender Equity in the Use of Educational Technologies," and "Gender Equity in Foreign and Second-Language Learning.

we use the term, communication, to refer to all its processes: listening, reading, speaking, and writing (including use electronic and print media). We begin with definitions to provide clarity, describing some of the terminologies common to each process as well as those that differentiate among them.

Communication skills are all grounded in knowledge about and use of *language* (sometimes referred to by communication theorists as a "message code.") People are not equally skilled in using a particular language in all communication processes. For example, individuals may be able to read (or decode) English quite fluently, but not be able to speak or write it as fluently. Also, the reverse is often true. Further, individuals may find themselves differently restricted in what they think they can safely say, or even if they can safely say anything, in some settings. In addition, their skills vary as the medium used changes. Measurement of communication skills achievement is complicated not only by these situational aspects of language use, but also by the variants of language codes and communication customs in diverse cultures and subcultures in various institutions and regions. Prior research often did not attend to such cultural anomalies of language use or language communities, which leads to a requirement that all reported findings be interpreted cautiously.

Within the category of "language," we must also distinguish between processes of verbal and nonverbal language. The term *verbal* refers primarily to the use of words, whether spoken or written. *Nonverbal* language relies on visual, auditory, kinesthetic, tactile, spatial, and other aspects of communication that stand in place of or complement verbal language. In interactive, spoken communication the nonverbal aspects of language are often more potent in carrying the intended message than are the verbal aspects.[2] Since English is not an overtly gendered language, nonverbal communication carries most of the gender messages among English speakers (Fivush, 1989; Gleason, 1989; Henley, 1986).

Nonverbal communication also occurs within the processes of reading and writing, although these seldom involve the message potency, constancy, and interpretive complexities of interactive spoken communication. However, for very young children, the pictures in books (a nonverbal language form), even more than the words, carry a great deal of meaning, as do the vocal tones and intensities or body language of the adults who read to them. Pictures in texts for older children also serve as nonverbal communication, as do visual images in all media; all these usually carry messages about gender, as does the verbal text. The topics we ask children to write about, the pictures we ask them to draw, or the points we award for writing neatly, provide communicative information beyond the verbal language. When any of these messages, verbal or nonverbal, vary according to the sex of the sender or the intended recipient, they constitute gender messages. The question for this chapter is to what extent such differences promote gender inequity in educational settings and desired outcomes.

Finally, it must be understood that communication, especially in oral forms, involves meanings beyond the cognitive. Communication involves affective, expressive, relational, and instrumental messages. Thus, not only do oral messages seek to accomplish goals of understanding or persuasion (cognitive and instrumental), they express feelings (affective and expressive), seek to achieve, change, or maintain relationships (relational and instrumental). The gender ramifications in such multiple interactions add complexity since messages involve gender in values, expectations, and cultural prescriptions, all usually unstated. The point here is that interest in equity in learning/teaching communication skills requires attention, at all times, to the multifaceted and interactive nature of sender skills and intentions, receiver values and expectations, as well as other factors of the situation.

The Importance of Communication Skills

Complicated as our topic is, it especially needs attention because communication skills (listening, reading, speaking, and writing via a variety of media) are arguably the most important academic skills for later success in life (Morreale, Osborn, & Pearson, 2000; Poole & Walther, 2002; Stump & Selz, 1982). The business community has for many years expressed dissatisfaction with the quality of reading, writing, and oral communication skills of both high-school and college graduates (National Alliance for Business, 1996; Rodriguez & Ruppert, 1996). Success in business and in most professions, as well as in family and social life, correlates highly with communication competence (Carnevale, 1996; Endicott, 1978; Daly, 1994; reAmaze, 2005; Van Horn, 1995). Yet, national and international test data show that a large percentage of American students do not achieve acceptable levels of reading and writing proficiency as defined by our national and local standards, and do not compare favorably with their peers from other nations. Such deficiencies not only can limit access to further education but can also affect later employment and life outcomes. For example, low literacy skills are associated with a number of other negative factors such as poverty and incarceration. Barton and Lapointe (1995), discussing findings from the National Center for Educational Statistics (NCES) National Adult Literacy Survey (NAAL), report that measured levels of document literacy strongly predict wages both across education level (high-school graduate, two-year degree, four-year degree) and within each of these levels.[3] Literacy levels also positively correlate with indicators of engaged citizenship (Barton, 1994). Clearly, acquiring competence in communication is critical to many other achievements.

---

[2]This claim is supported in a considerable recent history of research dealing with nonverbal communication. The work ranges from that completed in the 1970s by scholars such as Ekman, Friesen and Pheobe (e.g., 1969, 1972), Birdwhistell (e.g., 1968, 1970); to current scholarship exemplified by that of Peter Andersen and colleagues (e.g., 1998, 1999, 2001) as well as ongoing work by Ekman and colleagues (2005). Thousands of research studies have explored the varieties of nonverbal communication.

[3]Literacy is broadly defined as ability to read and write, and is often defined according to scaled ability levels. Document literacy as defined in the NCES survey is ability to use documents, such as short forms or graphically displayed information found in everyday life, including job applications, payroll forms, transportation schedules, maps, tables,and graphs. Measured document literacy tasks included, among many others, locating a particular intersection on a street map, using a schedule to choose the appropriate bus, or entering information on an application form (NCES, 2005). See also Venezky, Kaestle, and Sum, 1987; and Tuijanmin, 2000.

For our interests here, however, the most relevant issues are those related to gender, especially the possible interactions among gender, literacy, and wages. We need to know not only whether literacy levels vary by sex, but also if being literate makes a bigger difference in life outcomes for either women or men. Data to answer this question are hard to find, but we do know that many skilled labor jobs are still more open to men than women, that the first level of skilled work for many women is clerical, and that wages differ substantially between those two classes of employment. We also know that men's wages and salaries outstrip women's at all levels of literacy. Hence, it may be true that literacy matters more for women than for men (Rosser, 2005). In addition, if it is accurate, as research suggests, schools must do a better job of preparing girls for verbal literacy as currently defined, and then it is possible that differences in educational literacy outcomes do not present an inequitable situation for men. These differences may be, instead, a counterforce to what otherwise would be an inequity for women.[4]

It is also possible that the tools used to measure educational performance are inadequate. An analysis of the scores on both major university admissions testing tools, the SAT and the ACT, demonstrated that in spite of claims to the contrary (Alperstein, 2005) boys' average scores are higher than girls' (ACT, 2005; SAT, 2005; Rosser, 2005). These widely used tests sizably underpredict women's performance in college, where females continue to earn higher grades than males (Rosser, 2005, 1989, 1990).[5] While discussion of testing issues is elaborated in the chapter "Gender Equity in Testing and Assessment" in this *Handbook,* the issue is relevant here because we raise questions about the validity of currently used literacy outcome measures. For example, in reviewing 20 of research on composition, Chapman (2006) pointed out that while most states conduct writing exams "very few studies have been done to determine the effectiveness of these assessments" (fr. 2). Pending the thorough analysis of writing results in the National Assessment of Educational Progress (NAEP) to be conducted in 2007 and conclusions to be learned from the addition of writing samples in SAT testing, we have few concrete data about any K–12 students' learning outcomes in writing, much less knowledge about gender differences within those outcomes.

What the research reviewed in this chapter shows clearly is that analysis of data regarding equity issues in communication education supports few definitive statements about the critical questions just posed; considerable additional study is needed. The questions also show clearly that the task of assessing edu-

cational equity in communication-skills learning goes beyond identifying inequities in outcomes by broad difference categories such as sex. It encompasses questions related to class, race, ethnicity, and social attitudes toward usefulness of communication and literacy skills. It involves attending to what role schools need to play in preparing students to recognize and cope with inequities that may continue throughout their lives (AAUW, 2001).

Gender Gaps in Communication Skills: Examining the Complexity of Data Analysis

Our discussion emphasizes the multifaceted nature of gender and equity issues in communication and communication learning. Communication skills are not unitary; nor are gender or equity unidimensional concepts. Moreover, even when average differences between girls and boys or women and men are found, it is usually the case that even larger differences exist within those groups. As discussed in the chapter "Examining the Achievement of Gender Equity in and through Education" equity is not a simple matter of treating every child the same. Moreover, gender equity cannot be explored simply by identifying whether females and males are treated equally or achieve equal outcomes. Educational experiences vary widely as race, ethnicity, socioeconomic status, and degree of physical ability (among other things) vary.[6] Not only do each of these factors (communication skills, gender, equity) have much internal complexity, but the factors interact. To understand the communication competencies of students and teachers, we must recognize gendered social and cultural structures in which their communication occurs as well as the differently valued aspects of communication when enacted by or attributed to females or males.

Most common assumptions about the communication skills and competence of females and males vastly oversimplify the complex set of behaviors that constitute such competence. We grow up learning that some behaviors and attributes are male identified (hence thought of as masculine) and some behaviors and attributes that are female identified (hence considered feminine). Moreover, the male-identified and female-identified behaviors are differently valued (Bem, 1993; Blair, Brown, & Baxter, 1994; Broverman, 1970; Broverman, Vogel, Broverman, Clarkson, & Rosenkrantz, 1972). To truly achieve gender equity in communication requires, first, that female identified (associated) behaviors are valued and responded to in the same ways as male identified (associated) ones; and second, that commu-

---

[4]Given that the entry-level jobs most open to women have higher need for literacy than those jobs that are male-identified and less open to women, if schools were to treat girls and boys in ways to try to insure no differences in literacy outcomes occur, then such treatment would, in its effect, be inequitable.

[5]ACT Average scores for 2005 were 20.9 for females; 21.1 for males, with females constituting 56% of the 1.19 million test takers (ACT, ACT High-School Profile Report 2005). SAT scores for 2005 on the verbal portion of the exam were 505 for females, 513 for males, with females constituting 53% of the 1.48 million test takers. FairTest calculated averages from: College Board, College-Bound Seniors 2005: Total Group Profile Report. The College Board, in August 2006, reported that for 2006 test takers, the verbal scores (now termed critical reading) were 505 for males and 502 for females, while the new writing portion of the exam showed an 11-point advantage for females, 502 to 491 for males (http://www.collegeboard.com/press/releases/150054.htm).

[6]These subgroups are not mutually exclusive and reporting of gender differences within subgroups would provide a finer grained picture of the impact of the new elementary and secondary accountability system on student performance.

nication behaviors are similarly valued whether the person doing them is female or male. In relating education and communication skills, such equity would mean that interruptions, aggressiveness, silence, talkativeness, preferring action to talk, liking to read books, preferring violent video games to reading a book, writing, talking logically or emotionally, displaying empathy or lack of it, would each be equally valued and encouraged, or considered inappropriate and discouraged, whether engaged in by girls or boys.

To provide a concrete illustration of the disregard for complexity in interpreting the available data, we discuss one example of one widespread stereotype: that girls excel in verbal skills and boys excel in mathematics. Close analysis of research findings shows how the generalization vastly oversimplifies the reality. (See, for example, Barnett & Rivers, 2004; and the careful summary of meta-analytic reviews of empirical studies given by Hyde and Lindberg in their chapter in this book, "Assumptions about the Nature and the Implications for Gender Equity.") In sum, the data show that most of the differences between boys and girls as a group, when observed across a wide range of verbal skills, are small and that the male and female distributions overlap substantially. Small effects found across many studies can be important; if they show small but pervasive differences, the collective impact can be substantial. What is dangerous, however, is that focusing on these relatively small overall differences between girls and boys in arithmetic and verbal skills often leads to failure in attending to other variables. While boys predominate in the highest levels of math skills, many girls also score high in math; and it is also true that many boys are found in the lowest math achievement groups. Most assessments show the reverse to be true in verbal skills. Too often ignored is that even when average skills of girls and boys are found to differ, bigger differences are found within groups. To achieve equity for all will require attention to all kinds of differences, especially race, ethnicity, and socioeconomic class, and the ways in which these interact. This does, of course, vastly complicate the matter of exploring and providing educational equity, but attending to the complexity is essential if we are to avoid both replicating social stereotypes and expending effort on the least important inequities.

Another complexity in assessing communication outcomes (and hence possible inequities) is that gaps found between girls and boys differ by the subskill that is being measured. Different subskills are taught and measured at different age levels, or rarely measured at all in the case of oral communication skills and competence (with the notable exception of English language learners in U.S. schools, whose oral language and literacy performance in English and some other languages are taught and measured explicitly in schools). Specific discussion of testing issues can be found in "Gender Equity in Testing and Assessment" and, for English as a foreign language, in "Gender Equity in Foreign and Second-Language Learning and Instruction." Attention to writing occurs throughout the school levels, but typically, in the United States, direct instruction in reading comprehension is limited to the first three grades of elementary school.

For the vast majority of students, direct instruction in speaking focuses on public speaking, which is available as elective courses in most high schools. Unified instruction in interpersonal communication, use of nonverbal messages, and listening skills is minimal, and explicit attention to the ways in which all of these are gendered is slight. In their discussion of teaching to support emergent literacy, Soderman, Gregory, and O'Neill (1999) pointed out the importance of the links between oral language, the home environment, and literacy. They remarked on the irony of how usually, "as children mature . . . more emphasis is placed on reading and writing and less time and energy is spent during the school day engaged in oral language . . . [with] reduced amounts of time spent in meaningful conversation with peers and expressing ideas" (28).

Given major differences in amounts of instruction and types of measurements, up to and including virtually no systematic teaching or assessment of oral communication skills, all conclusions about gender differences in this domain must be regarded with caution and interpreted with great care. Evidence of gender gaps in reading should be considered with reference to the source of data: test results, course grades (often highly overlapping with test scores), diagnosed dysfunction (such as dyslexia), participation in remedial courses at the elementary/secondary and postsecondary levels, and life outcomes such as career success, educational attainments, earnings, etc. With respect to test results, some sources such as the NAEP, deal with carefully constructed representative samples of the population. Other indicators such as the SAT provide data based on "volunteer" self-selected samples, since students can decide (or be guided by others) to take the test or not. The resulting group data thus reflect more than what the test itself measures. They also reflect the composition of the subgroups, which may differ in significant ways regarding motivation, social, and material rewards (or lack thereof) for high achievement, quality of prior educational experiences, subject-matter interests, and so on (College Board, 2004a; also see Pennock-Roman, 1994).

Some findings seem clear, although their implications for either the existence of, or remedy for, gender inequities are far from clear. Data from the National Household Education Surveys Program (NHES), for example, show that boys are almost twice as likely as girls to be diagnosed as having learning disabilities, including dyslexia, and are more than twice as likely to be diagnosed as having speech impediments (Freeman, 2004). What we do not have are data to demonstrate that these outcomes mean there is inequity; such a conclusion would require showing that remedial services are not available or inequitably provided. We do not have such data although some discussion of related issues can be found in the chapter "Gender Equity for Populations with Disabilities."

Influences on reading and communication skills include both in-school *and* out-of school factors. For example, among three- to five-year-olds, boys are not read to or told a story at home as often as girls, and boys' families are less likely to report having taken their children to a library within the past month than are girls' families (Freeman, 2004). NCES reports that there were some gains from 1991 to 2001 in these preschool factors, and that the gains were a somewhat higher for girls than for boys. Denton and West (2002), in an analysis of an early childhood longitudinal study of students in about 1,000 kindergarten programs during 1998–99, reviewed patterns of reading skills and concluded, in part, "Children's overall reading achievement does not vary by their sex." They go on to point out how both child and family characteristics relate to achievement, noting that as early as first grade, girls are more likely to be reading and boys are more likely to be successful at mathematical operations such as multiplication and division. Such divergence in interests seems to persist. Girls' greater interest than boys in some communication subjects is reflected in the College Board's Advanced Placement (AP) Program's National Summary Report (College Board, 2004b). Of high-school students who took the AP English language and composition examination, 63% were female. Of those taking AP foreign language (French, German, Latin, Spanish) examinations, 65% were female.) These findings reinforce the point made earlier, that achieving equity may involve helping students become aware of and cope with societal expectations and prejudices.

What must be resisted as these data are explored is the tendency to oversimplify complex phenomena. Framed with that caveat, we introduce the results from one major effort in the print domain that has allowed for examination of gender differences in communication learning outcomes, the National Assessment of Educational Progress (NAEP, 2005), also known as "The Nation's Report Card," a congressionally mandated collection of national data on student attainments in grades 4, 8, and 12. Data collected at these grade levels include reading and writing. NAEP also collects data in another area related to reading and communication skills, the study of foreign languages, a discussion found in the chapter "Gender Equity in Foreign and Second Language Learning and Instruction" of this book. NAEP began its data collections in 1969, so a great deal of trend data is available.[7]

LEARNING OUTCOMES IN READING AND WRITING SKILLS (LITERACY)

Examples of NAEP testing content in reading include (grouped from highest proficiency level to lowest): compare descriptions to interpret character, explain thematic differences between poems, suggest improvements to a document, identify author's use of specific details, use text information to provide a description, explain major idea in an article, and identify character's main dilemma.

NAEP scores are especially valuable because they are also associated with out-of-school variables. For example, information from the NAEP Data Tool (2005) indicated that among 12th graders in 1998, those who reported having 0 to 2 types of reading material (newspaper, encyclopedia, magazines, more than 25 books) in their home had an average NAEP scaled reading score of 273; those who reported having all four types of material had an average NAEP scaled reading score of 298. The relevance of these data is their portion of the issue of extra-classroom influence on what happens in the classroom, a matter

previously discussed, and also forthcoming with regard to mass-media consumption and images.

The reading data from 1992 through 2003 show very little change in the size of the male/female gap during this time (NAEP, 2005). For example, the average scaled score for grade-four females in 2003 was 221.9 (standard error 0.3); for males 214.6 (standard error 0.3). The 2003 grade-four gender difference of 7.3 scaled score points in favor of females does not represent a significant difference from the 1992 data collection. In fact, in the six grade-four data collections conducted since 1992, there has not been a single one whose gap changed significantly from the previous data collection. Grade eight reading data collections from 1992 to 2003 indicate a slight narrowing of the gender gap when certain pairs of data collections are compared, but the overall grade-eight reading gender gap remains unchanged from 1992 to 2003. The grade-eight gender gap is slightly larger than the grade four gap. For example, in 2003 female students at grade-eight had an average scaled score of 268.6 (standard error 0.3); male students at grade eight had an average scaled score of 258.0 (standard error 0.3). For grade 12 students, females' average reading scaled scores in 2002 were 295.0 (standard error 0.7); males' average scaled scores were 279.0 (standard error 0.9), making a gender gap not statistically significantly different from in the 1992 grade-12 data.

Although these differences seem stable, probably because of the nature of the data set, the practical implications are unclear. Females' advantage over males is evident across NAEP levels. Fewer female than male students score Below Basic, and more female than male students score at the Proficient and Advanced levels. Coley (2003) reported that there was little difference between males and females in terms of the *growth* that they made in NAEP reading scores between fourth and eighth grades. That is, looking at data for cohorts from 1994—1998, females in the eighth grade had advanced about 51 scaled-score points since fourth grade, while males had advanced about 48 points. Taking a longer historical perspective, the National Center for Educational Statistics (2000) concluded from the NAEP data that, "For 9- and 13-year-olds, average reading scores improved slightly between 1971 and 1980 and showed little or no change between 1980 and 1996. Scores for 17-year-olds have remained relatively consistent since 1971. Females outscore males in reading performance across all age groups." Thus, while it is clear that these differences are statistically stable, alone they do not demonstrate significant gender inequities, especially when compared with contrasting outcomes on other tests. (See for example the discussions related to testing for general academic achievement, for university admission and for scholarships in the chapter "Gender Equity in Testing and Assessment.") Moreover, as we noted above, the differences are relatively small when compared to differences of race, ethnicity, and socio-economic status within each sex group (Mead, 2006).

---

[7]Data are collected according to a complex pattern of priorities, so complete data for every year, subject, and grade level are not available. A major study of writing outcomes, for example, will be conducted in 2007, to be reported in 2008 for comparison to the 2002 data now available. NAEP groups the scores on its assessments into levels, *Advanced, Proficient, Basic,* and *Below Basic.* NAEP has linked types of skills and assessment questions to these levels across the grades in which assessments are given. The broad content of the NAEP assessments is explicitly linked to school curricula at the appropriate grade levels. See http://nces.ed.gov/nationsreportcard/ndeinfo.asp for easily accessible reports of the assessment data.

In the United States, among the skills commonly designated as verbal, writing shows the largest consistent average differences between girls and boys. Gender differences in NAEP writing assessments are somewhat larger than in reading, again favoring females. In 2002, the average scaled score for grade-four females in writing was 162.7 (standard error 0.4); the average scaled score for grade-four males was 145.6 (standard error 0.6). There is not a statistically significant difference between this 2002 grade-four gender gap and the 1998 grade-four gender gap in writing. Grade eight NAEP writing data show an average female scaled score of 163.6 (standard error 0.6), and an average male scaled score of 143.1 (standard error 0.6). The grade-eight gender gap is slightly larger than the grade-four gap, but again, does not show any sign of increasing or decreasing over the time period from 1998 to 2002. At grade 12, NAEP writing scores also favor females, 160.5 (standard error 0.9) compared to 135.7 (standard error 0.8). The grade-12 gap is slightly larger than the grade-eight gap and NAEP reports show that at the grade-12 level, the gender gap widened to a degree that is statistically significant between 1998 and 2002.

These gaps also reflect the issue of complexity discussed earlier. Conceivably, much of the perceived gender gap in reading and literacy stems from too-narrow definitions of literacy. What is measured when reading scores are obtained? Some scholars argued that if reading for computer literacy (with testing for specific problem solving rather than for general comprehension) were more valued in schools, boys would be more motivated, and therefore achieve higher literacy (Coles & Hall 2001; Harste 2001). Smith and Wilhelm (2004) reported a study of middle- and high-school boys in which the students indicated they reject activities in which they believed they would not be competent. Recall the findings reported earlier about children's interests varying as early as first grade. Perhaps if the question of boys' interest in various communication media were raised, findings for literacy assessment similar to those reported by Smith and Wilhelm might well result.

The data on this issue reflect the complexity in such issues discussed earlier. First, it is important to remember that these are generalizations about all males, based on averages of the group; in some cases, differences within subgroups are striking. As noted earlier, among students taking university entrance preparation tests, the advantage to girls diminishes. The change probably results from the population being tested, as only students considering college take SAT and ACT exams. Except for the students of elite universities and of higher socioeconomic groups, more women than men enroll in undergraduate programs. Less-prepared boys and those from lower socioeconomic groups, more than other groups of boys, don't plan to do university education. Thus, they are not among those taking the PSAT, SAT, and ACT exams. Although at press time for this chapter detailed analysis by socioeconomic groups of test takers was not available, some preliminary comparisons by race, ethnicity, and English-as-a-second-language (ESL) status are intriguing. The August (2006) press release by the College Board showed that among the critical reading (formerly verbal) section of the 2006 test takers, White students scored 527, and Asian-heritage students 510. In contrast, Mexican-American and other Hispanic averages were 459 and 458 respectively, while Black students scored 434. The board reported that males

outscored females in critical reading in all ethic groups except for African American. Students for whom English is a second language increased scores compared to 2005, to an average of 467 (http://www.collegeboard.com/press/releases/150054.html). In contrast, females outscored males in the new writing section across all race and ethnic groups. Group disparities suggested in these data highlight significant problems, but the nature of those problems will be not be understood if one merely compares the scores of girls and boys on the whole.

Another possible explanation for differences between the NAEP findings and the university admission exams is in the nature of the exams. Buck, Kostin, Phelps, and Kutz (n.d.) reported a "small but consistent difference between mean scores for males and females on the PSAT Verbal which favors males." The Sentence Completion and Analogy subsections, in particular, likely impacted the scores of female test takers. Looked at PSAT verbal scores and found a difference in mean scores, with males scoring slightly (but consistently) higher than females. A content analysis of the items in these subsections revealed more items with male-identified content such as politics, economics, physical danger, etc. than female-identified content such as feelings and emotion, art and literature, personal appearance, etc. Using large sample sizes and cross-validation techniques, Buck et al. categorized the items in this manner (i.e., items of more interest to girls and of more interest to boys), and found subtle but pervasive and repeated effects for this content: girls did better on profemale content, and boys on promale content. These items had already been through Differential Item Functioning analysis and a review of gender biases, but clearly the manner in which male and female test takers respond to seemingly unbiased content can impact performance. Female-identified content resulted in about a 1% improvement in female performance with the same effects for the promale content on boys.

The overall slightly lower scores in literacy, English, and modern languages for boys raised a number of important issues. Relevant research, discussed and documented in detail in Francis and Skelton (2005), supported the following conclusions. Importantly, boys' long-standing achievement gap in these areas did not seem to have impacted significantly their future positions and economic status. The highest-status and best-paying jobs continue to go to primarily to (White, middle-class) men. Indeed, since women are still not competing evenly with men in the employment market, it could be argued that raising boys' scores would only increase the inequality in employment. Nonetheless, for the individual children involved, their tendency to score below grade level in language and literacy subjects can have clear costs and raises significant questions. Foremost of the questions is to what extent the achievement shortfalls are concentrated in specific socioeconomic groups—and therefore impact some groups of children much more than others. Moreover, it is important to note the gaps are not matters of gender alone, and therefore the problems, although they may involve some gender differences, are not limited to gender differences, which are generally smaller than those related to socioeconomic and cultural factors.

Another perspective is provided by examining the sources of inequities that may extend well beyond schools (Francis & Skelton, 2005). For example, since education was extended beyond the upper classes in the United States, reading, writing, and traditionally conceived interpersonal oral-communication skills have had lower status than, say, science and technical skills. So boys' underachievement at communication subjects, including not only reading and writing but also "emotional literacy," such as articulating feeling and emotions clearly, may have serious implications for their effective interaction with others. Two points are involved here: the need for broader-based definitions and testing as we have discussed elsewhere in the chapter; and the need to disaggregate the overall skills to locate more clearly where the shortcomings in boys' learning are. These points are hard to overemphasize because as the work on achievement throughout this *Handbook* shows, social policies and gender assumptions and expectations play a major role in the level of achievement. For example, in the United States, when French was a valued, prestigious subject of study, boys were thought better at learning French than were girls. When that language lost some of its social status, it became a subject associated with feminine skills.

Whatever its source, the disaffection of many boys from school language and literacy programs, and any related disruptive behavior by boys, negatively impacts both their own learning and that of their classmates. Contrary to the proposal of many policymakers, the solution of providing higher numbers of male teachers does not by itself appear to increase boys' attainment or result in less disruptive behavior (Thornton & Brichenco; Younger et al., 2005). Smith and Wilhelm (2002) provided in-depth cases studies of boys from 7th through 12th grade that reveal the interplay of gender and ethnicity on boys' attitudes toward and uses for their literacy skills. Identification with the lone, European or Euro-American, male protagonist in much of classic English literature may be no more attractive or achievable for many boys in U.S. schools than it is for many girls. Much more balanced scholarly attention to these complex issues of gender, racial, ethnic and socioeconomic issues is thus needed. Clearly, both girls and boys should have the opportunity to fully develop their potential, so equality in achievement is a valuable goal in all subjects. Encouraging boys to increase their communication aptitudes and making reading and writing "safe territory" for boys can help avoid the continued construction of gender difference (See also Pickering, 1977). We comment on types of encouragement to deconstruct current gender boundaries in the following recommendations section.

A Wider Lens in Assessing Literacy and Gender Differences

Another factor, which may be producing the results described in the previous section discussing literacy scores, is that current methods of assessment may be missing actual literacy on the part of many children, especially boys (Venezky, Kaestle, & Sum, 1987). To date, Western perspectives on literacy rarely consider reading and writing in a digital environment. Because they develop a different kind of literacy, and because they have potentially strong links to gender, computer games and other elements of digital communication should be taken into account, instead being thought of only as a deterrent to literacy achievement. Boys (and men) devote many hours to such activities that seem far from the language and traditional forms of reading and writing. Uses vary considerably, depending on purpose and au-

dience, but deserve attention as important new applications for communication skills. By engaging in what gets labeled as game playing, which is often considered the antithesis of school, the users of computer-based gaming may gain an important entry point to competence and confidence with some valuable communication processes. Many avenues for writing (and other communication skills) have developed in the digital environment, among them instant messaging, e-mail, chatrooms, and blogs. The Perseus Development Corporation (2003) reported that 52% of all blogs are created and maintained by 13- to 19-years-olds. Huffaker and Calvert's (2005) study of 70 Web blogs authored by teens found usual length of postings about 2,000 words, with no significant differences in the way in which girls or boys wrote. Both wrote about interpersonal issues, using emoticons similarly as well.

Many students, girls and boys though perhaps especially boys, find focusing on classroom texts and waiting for teachers to provide learning material and objectives both uninteresting and unnecessary. Many boys, who have difficulty with reading and writing in school or who are not interested in reading and writing, do excel in "home-literacy" activities such as sports, music, and video games (Smith & Wilhelm, 2002, 2004). Individual, text-based literacy activities of the classroom are unlikely to compete successfully with the more interactive, playful engagement that so many children, perhaps especially boys, experience with a variety of media, including games (Jenson, de Castell, & Bryson 2003; Jensen & de Castell 2004; de Castell & Jenson 2004).

As noted in a discussion of literacy by the National Council of Teachers of English (NCTE), "Adolescents are already reading in multiple ways when they enter secondary classrooms . . . Their texts range from clothing logos to music to specialty magazines to Web sites to popular and classical literature." The NCTE argued that teachers must learn to recognize and value the multiple literacy resources students bring to the acquisition of school literacy.

Arguably, teaching and assessments of all communication literacy should be reconceptualized to include such skills. Learning through computer gaming is unlike most school-based learning in important ways. Many of the current computer games have no age restrictions, and are not text-based; they provide players with quick access to a global mass-media industry and new structures of interactive learning. Traditional education formats, which by several measures seem to fail at gaining enthusiastic attention of many boys, perhaps should be adapted to include some aspects of the sophisticated commercial digital games being played by millions of users. In so doing, however, attention to equity will be important. What might be attractive and successful with boys could once again marginalize girls, as most extant computer games are neither attractive to nor hospitable toward girls. Jenson and de Castell (2004) outlined many gender issues in need of serious consideration when bringing an understanding of the impact of this new communication situation into the educational setting.

Computers and literacy raise complex questions. Simply providing equal access to and use of computers in school labs, while necessary, will not be sufficient to recognize or achieve major changes in literacy; many kinds of communication competence arise from increased use of many different kinds of digital programs. While recently, Western education has been basically a process of imparting print literacy focused on separating information from stories, and then presenting it as data, description, theory, and prescription (Cajete, 1994), today's environment differs dramatically. Many students have moved to more narrative modes of learning, in which they interact with accounts provided by commercial storytellers and many other information and entertainer providers other than their teachers and texts. As Gerbner has argued, widespread use of television and other forms of popular culture has now changed the entire process of learning. To assess skills of children who have grown up in a world dominated by electronic media will require an expanded way of thinking about—and testing—literacy. Some recent work in the area looking at antecedents of literacy (Soderman, Gregory, & McCarty, 2004) suggested a number of factors, in addition to gender, that need to be considered, making it "very difficult to parse out the proportional contribution of any one factor" (Backlund, 2006, personal communication).

At a minimum, the issues of validity in testing must be raised, and new measures of literacy must include communication in the digital and electronic media environments (Olsen & Torrance, 1991; Taylor, 2004, 2005). New forms of writing deserve attention as do visual messages. In one sense, this set of requirements for education to adapt to the changed communicative environment seems unrelated to gender. In another sense, that apparent irrelevance makes attention to gender issues in digital environments especially important. Since we know that gendered expectations have pervaded the environment in which communication has occurred previously, if alterations in the environment are changing gender expectations, that is important to know. Much might be learned about how we might change the existing patterns of bias. (See "Gender Equity in the Use of Educational Technologies".) While the changes in the ways we communicate will necessitate new policies and standards for gender-sensitive education systems, the necessity to work on inclusion, enhancing capabilities, and gender/social equalities won't change.

International Perspective on Reading and Gender Gaps

International data may provide an initial basis for examining how cultural differences affect communication learning. Organisation for Economic Co-operation and Development (OECD, 2001) literacy data, based on a study of 15-year-olds, indicate statistically significant differences in favor of females on the Programme for International Student Assessment (PISA) combined reading literacy scores in all 28 of the participating countries. These gaps in favor of females differ somewhat in magnitude across countries. The smallest gaps in favor of females are found in Korea (14 points of a scale of more than 300 points),[8] Mexico (20), and Spain (24). The largest gaps in this study were found in Finland (51), New Zealand (46), and Norway (43). The gender gap among American students in this study was 29 scaled score points. The PISA study also looked at mathemati-

cal and scientific literacy among the same countries, and found much smaller gender gaps in these areas than were found in reading. The mathematical literacy gender gaps tended to favor males, although many comparisons were not statistically significant; scientific literacy gaps were largely nonexistent.

In the 2001 IEA Progress in Reading Literacy Study [PIRL] done by the International Association for the Evaluation of Educational Achievement (IEA) (OECD, 2001), data from fourth graders in 16 OECD countries were collected. As with the PISA study of 15-year-olds, differences in every country favored females. The smallest differences were observed in Italy (8 score-scale points), France (11), and the Czech Republic (12). Note that the three countries listed above as having the smallest differences among 15-year-olds, Korea, Mexico, and Spain, did not participate in the PIRLS study. The largest differences were found in New Zealand (27); England and Sweden had the next largest differences (22), followed by Greece and Norway (21). Finland did not participate in the PIRLS study.

The PISA study of 15-year-olds in 28 countries also considered students' self-reports of habits and attitudes related to learning. In the United States, females reported more use of self-regulating behaviors in the areas of memorization ($d = 0.17$) and elaboration strategies ($d = 0.08$), effort and persistence ($d = 0.31$), an index of cooperative learning ($d = 0.21$), and, of particular concern to us in this chapter, interest ($d = 0.36$), and self-concept ($d = 0.36$) in reading. The patterns of gender gaps in some of these areas (indices of elaboration strategies, control strategies, and instrumental motivation) in other countries are more mixed than are the patterns of gender gaps in attainments across countries. It is also noteworthy that in this same PISA study, in the United States and elsewhere, males led, to a small degree, in self-reported interest (over all countries, $d = -0.20$; U.S. $d = -0.08$) and self-concept (over all countries, $d = -0.25$; U.S. $d = -0.13$) in mathematics. Males also led in the indices of competitive learning (over all countries, $d = -0.21$; U.S. $d = -0.13$) and self-efficacy (over all countries, $d = -0.22$; U.S. $d = -0.06$).

Wittmann (2004) provided an interesting and innovative analysis related to interpretation of national and international trends in verbal and quantitative assessments, based on Brunswik symmetry,[9] that attempts to quantify the nature of the relationships among verbal and quantitative skills at both the individual level and at a much higher level of aggregation, the country level. He noted, based on analyses of data from PISA and other studies, that "tilted profiles" of verbal and quantitative abilities are typical of countries as well as individuals and males/females as a group. In general, he found that while females exhibited a profile "tilted" toward verbal, males exhibited a profile "tilted" toward quantitative. Using PISA data, he also designated countries as having a verbal (e.g., Italy, Ireland, Mexico, Spain), or quantitative (Korea, Japan, Switzerland) tilt. The tilt of the United States is moderately verbal in Wittmann's analyses (1988; Wittmann & Süß, 1999).

---

[8]PISA uses highly sophisticated statistical techniques for its sampling, scoring, and scaling. A treatment of these is beyond the scope of this chapter, but complete technical details for PISA can be found at http://www.pisa.oecd.org/

[9]A full treatment of this complex methodology is beyond the scope of this chapter. For further details, see Wittmann, 1988 and Whittman & Süß, 1999).

Assessing Oral Communication Skills

One major problem faced when attempting to discuss gender equity in education with respect to oral communication is that no data exist comparable to those for reading and writing. Systematic, nationwide, or international assessments of students' achievement of listening and speaking competence do not exist. (One major exception to this conclusion is with English-language-learner [ELL] students whose language skills, including speaking and listening, are often measured and provide some useful information on this topic. See the discussion later in the chapter.) One reason assessments have not been conducted is that competence in oral communication cannot be measured by assessing individual skills in isolation; oral communication, wherever it happens, in school or out, is an interactive process involving relational and affective meanings as well as cognitive ones. Such interactive processes are not easily captured in standardized testing methods. One cannot simply measure a set of unidimensional skills and assume that the sum of those behaviors will be competence. Nonetheless, assessing communication competence is possible.

Acknowledging the importance of speaking and listening as school subjects, Title II of the Elementary and Secondary Education Act Amendments of 1978 altered the list of basic skills students should achieve in education. The amendments, renewed in 1987, identified these basic skills as "reading, mathematics, and effective communication, both written and oral" (Lieb-Brilhart, 1975; del Polito & Lieb-Brilhart, 1981). Given this first-ever national recognition that schools need to help students achieve oral communication competence, the National Communication Association (NCA, then known as the Speech Communication Association), supported by staff in the U.S. Department of Education, turned to identifying components of communication competence, ways of helping students learn to use them, and means for assessing their achievements. In the decades since, several national task forces have produced reports including measurement instruments, and many states have pursued a variety of efforts at identifying standards for oral communication learning and ways for implementing such instruction and assessment. These included standards for preparing teachers to help students learn communication skills. (See Backlund, 1982; Darling & Dannels, 1998; DeWitt, Bozik, Hay, Litterst, Strohkirch & Yokum, 1991; Lynn & Kleiman, 1976; Morreale, Backlund, & Dallinger, 1996; Morreale & Backlund, 2002; Peterson, 1991; Rosenthal, 2002; Rubin, 1982, 1985; Rubin, Mead, & Daly, 1984). Thus, assessment tools do exist, although the issues are not simple and the tools continue to be refined (Bergvall & Remlinger, 1996; Halliday, 1985; Morreale & Backlund, 2002; Spitzberg, 1987). The outcomes of this work are available in a number of publications available through the NCA at http://www.ncastore.com/Assessment.html.

In the education legislation known as Goals 2000 (National Educational Goals Panel, 1998), communication remained among those skills identified as essential for students' achievement and also for exit from post-secondary education (Lieb & Stacey, 1993). Still, widespread and systematic use of the assessment tools has not occurred, probably for several reasons. Reading and mathematics have had primacy of focus at the federal level; many educators think communication doesn't require the for-

mal teaching that reading and writing do; testing interactive, situationally based skills is quite costly (Lieb, 1994). Thus, with implementation of assessment programs that are sporadic at best, we can report little data driven information about gender difference in oral communication competence outcomes in education or any inequities that may exist. What we can do is draw some logical inferences from the various data that do exist.

LEARNING COMMUNICATION SKILLS THROUGH CLASSROOM TALK AND INTERACTIONS

One way in which students learn communication skills is through classroom talk and interactions (Cooper, 1988). As previously noted, virtually all education relies on communication as a medium of "delivery." Extant research suggests no reason to think students' interactions in communication classes and instructors' responses to them differ from those in other kinds of classes as discussed in earlier chapters. (See especially the following chapters in this book: "The Treatment of Gender Equity in Teacher Education"; "Gender Equity in Coeducational and Single-Sex Educational Environments"; and "Sexual Harassment.") Hence, communication that happens in other subject-matter classes probably reinforces previously learned patterns. When new patterns are "taught," the goal is rarely a focus on a communication skill but on whatever might be the "subject" of the class. Because learning about communication in such settings is usually not the focus of student lessons, it becomes part of the unstated classroom agenda, the "hidden lessons" of the curriculum (Sadker & Sadker, 1994). Precisely because these lessons do not focus overtly on communication learning, the communicative behaviors teachers model and reward as well as those peers reward or punish are likely to reify patterns preestablished in a culture. For that reason, a quick review of what is known about communicative interaction is worth our attention to the question, "How do classroom talk and interactions impact gender equity in communication learning?"

On the whole, we know that in mixed-sex groups, including classrooms, female students use and control less conversational space. (See the review of this literature in Bergvall and Remlinger 1996). Studies of classrooms have used a variety of methods: examining conversations (e.g., Schegloff, 1983) and participant structures (e.g., Fleming, 1995), and have paid attention to the nature and count of turns, words or seconds, topic control and interruptions (Canary & Dindia, 1998; Dindia, 1987; Grob, Meyers & Schuh, 1997; Hosman, 1989; Kennedy & Camden, 1983; West & Zimmerman, 1983). The concept of "linguistic space" has been explored (Mahony, 1985). Observational studies have reported both qualitative analyses and data counts (e.g., Pearson & West, 1991; Taps & Martin, 1990); students' perceptions have been surveyed and a variety of anecdotal reports have been reviewed (e.g., Donovan & MacIntyre, 2004; Edelsky, 1993); classes with different course content and in educational settings at various levels have been examined. Overall, the research indicates that female students in classrooms control less floor time and receive less attention from teachers and other students; male students talk more, are permitted to respond to more questions, and receive more praise than girls. Teachers tend to maintain more eye contact with male students and ask them more content-related questions, accept their responses, and give them more academic help (Sadker & Sadker, 1994; see also research reviewed in Stewart, Cooper, & Stewart, 2003, and in this *Handbook* the chapter "Gender Equity in Co-educational and Single-Sex Educational Environments"). On average, girls in school have fewer opportunities to practice public speech or engage orally as a way to refine their ideas. Concomitantly, males receive more overt discipline in classrooms and are subject to more overtly negative messages (Jones & Dindia, 2004; National Coalition for Women & Girls, 2002).

These findings parallel other studies (of adults) of interaction in mixed-sex groups (see the reviews of such work in Stewart, Cooper, & Stewart, 2003; Pearson, West, & Turner, 1995; Wood, 2005). When they are in groups, males talk more in classes, work settings, and experimental studies, and have more control over agendas and topics, thus determining what issues are addressed and which are dropped. Some studies have examined the gender perceptions of students and instructors. In a survey of 1,000 students in 51 university-level classes, Fassinger (1995) found that male students perceived themselves as more confident and involved in the classroom; whereas female students perceived themselves as more interested in class content and in others' comments. Condravy, Skirboll, and Taylor (1998) reported that both male and female faculty perceived that (a) male students interrupt more frequently and assume leadership roles more frequently than females, and (b) female students seek outside help and were more open to constructive criticism than male students. Male faculty perceived that female students participated more and volunteered responses more frequently than male students. In contrast, female faculty perceived that male students participated with volunteered responses more than female students. Furthermore, female faculty perceived male students as more defensive and more confident than did male faculty.

Some research about gender and communication focuses on matters that may not be taken into consideration when gender in classrooms is addressed—silence, for example. While we do not have empirical evidence of a positive correlation between how much student's talk in class and their academic achievement, in middle-class Euro-American and British schools, verbal communication is prized more highly than silent participation, listening, and observation. Since studies indicate that boys, or at least some of them (Sunderland, 1996), are apt to talk more in class than girls, conceivably evaluations are affected by that. Teachers writing references for secondary and college students applying for college admission mentioned talk far more often than silence (Jaworski & Sachdev, 2004). Male recommenders mentioned silence more often for female referees, and mentioned talk more often in the references for male students. The women recommenders did not differentiate between the amount of time the female and male applicants talked, although they did mention talk more often for both females and males than did the men. Sunderland's work, along with that of others (See chapter 25 in this book), demonstrated again the issue of how often differences within groups are ignored when the focus is comparing women and men in general. In all situations, classrooms included, some involved participants, males and females, will remain largely silent while others will be more verbal and use much more of the talk time. Culture, personality, interest, experience, and situation influence these differences within the "groups" of women and men. Relationships among silence, learning, and other communication outcomes remain largely unknown. Research is needed to connect the issues.

Insufficient scholarly attention has been devoted to other issues as well. One is the matter of making links throughout conversations. For example, consider topic transitions: By the time they reach college, females, in comparison with males, have been found more adept at "smoothing out the transitions" from one topic to another, while males seem more likely to create abrupt disjunctures in the flow of conversation (West, 1995). This communication skill is seldom considered in existing assessments of students' conversational competence. Another area that has been subject of much scholarship but has seldom been related to classroom outcomes is politeness (Ng & Bradac, 1993). While girls show themselves quite capable of using impolite, imperative forms (e.g., "Don't do that," "Get outta here!"), or even profanity, they have also shown themselves as more adept than boys at posing directives as proposals (e.g., "Let's go," "Maybe we can get some more."). Girls tend to seek agreement and avoid conflict (Andersen, 1990; Goodwin, 1988, 1980).

Much of this research relates to how students listen and observe, contribute responses, and pose their own questions without undermining the attempts of others to enter the conversation. Studies of these issues tell us much about asymmetries in conversation, and about conversational skills that are seldom (but could be) acknowledged and rewarded (Bergvall & Remlinger, 1996). Research is needed to see if there are links among such participation in the classroom and related kinds of interactions in life situations outside classrooms. What interactions might exist among gender, group interactions, and specific teaching styles is a question inadequately studied. To date, educational outcomes studies have not asked about links to gender imbalances in talk, which leads to important unanswered questions.

In contrast, for reading and writing, some aspects are measured. These findings, along with some other measures such as grades, seem to show fairly persistent superior educational outcomes for girls compared to boys, although university admissions measures do not reflect that consistently. At the same time, employment outcomes and other disparities continue to favor men. Is it possible that the actual and perceived masculine oral communication skills (styles—see the following discussion) have more value than reading and writing skills in life outside the formal educational setting? With the absence of more systematic measurement of educational outcomes for the whole array of communication skills and more attention to the links between such outcomes and post-educational successes, conclusions about equity cannot be drawn. Such research is needed.

Bullying and sexual harassment are other significant issues of classroom communication climate and gender equity, topics largely addressed in the chapter on sexual harassment in this book. Here, we note only that both harassing behaviors and the appropriate responses are communication behaviors, and that currently communication education gives little attention to these problems.

Inequities Involved in Gender-Related Communicative "Styles"

We also need to consider, at least briefly, teaching and learning about communication that occur in contexts other than formal educational settings. This is important because what happens in classroom talk and how it is interpreted relates to widespread beliefs in and expectations about the existence of gendered patterns, or "styles." Students (and teachers) sometimes engage in inequitable classroom interactions based, in part, on what they have learned as culturally sanctioned ways to communicate.

Relevant scholarship about gender and communication styles that affect learning about communication in classrooms and communication within classrooms fits into two primary categories: (a) studies that examine beliefs about how women and men (girls and boys) communicate (e.g., Thorne, Henley, & Kramarae, 1983; Henley & Kramarae 1991; Tannen, 1990, 1994); and (b) research that explores expectations about what are described as feminine or masculine patterns (e.g., Taylor & Beinstein Miller, 1994; Tannen, 1993; Turner & Sterk, 1994; Warner, Ahers, Bilmes, Oliver, Wertheim, & Chen, 1996; Wood, 2005). Studies of beliefs involve what people think girls and women (or boys and men) do as they communicate, and, on the other hand, what role (or identity) behaviors are expected. Prior to presenting what is known about these beliefs in communication patterns, we note that the behaviors expected from girls and women or from boys and men vary greatly according to time, cultural and social group, situational exigencies, and the behaviors in which they actually engage. Unfortunately, most research on these topics has not covered this wide range of variable settings. Subjects of most studies have been predominantly White, middle class and above, or upwardly mobile members of other groups in cultures dominated by the White middle class and above. And, even within these groups, none of the research described communication patterns, actual and perceived, of *all* girls and women or boys and men in the groups studied. Thus, even for people for whom the descriptions are accurate much of the time, they do not describe such persons' behavior all the time (Crawford, 1995; Aries, 1996).

Given the caveats just laid out, one might wonder why we bother describing scholarship about feminine and masculine styles at all. The answer is that although the average differences between females and males are small and the differences among females and males are wide, widespread, and persistent beliefs about female and male communication styles exist (e.g., Gray, 1992, 2002). Thus, we attend to what people believe exists, because such beliefs affect both how teachers deal with students (and vice versa) and how students deal with each other.[10] Moreover, beliefs in these styles exist alongside a strong bias against feminine style in workplace settings. Hence, when either girls or boys (and women or men) engage in behaviors thought of as feminine in settings that expect masculine style, they will likely be responded to negatively. For examples, see several of the articles in Fischer (2000), especially Brody (2000) and Jansz (2000).

In dominant U.S. culture and many other groups as well, a feminine communication style is perceived as being relationship centered. Hence, feminine style involves communication behaviors that reflect the importance of relationships (caring, sensitivity to others, and the feeling content of the communication), are characterized by responsiveness, cooperativeness, and supportiveness, have message content that is concrete and personal and often expressed tentatively. Messages involve welcoming personal exchanges and interaction. In short, feminine styles emphasize the "we" in the interaction. Masculine style in contrast centers around the communicator's autonomy (Tannen, 1990; Jansz, 2000). Hence, masculine style involves communication behaviors directed toward that goal: messages focus on content that involves problem solving or strategy, use abstract logic and principles in reasoning, are directed toward locating the individual in a status hierarchy free from control by others. Communication in masculine style is characterized by competitive interactions, assertive statements, and confidently expressed conclusions.

The behaviors called "feminine style" seem especially common to interpersonal settings, home, family, and friendship communication situations—locations often described as the "private" sphere of life (Wood & Inman, 1993; Wood, 1994). Behaviors called "masculine styles," in contrast, have been (and to a large extent still are) considered appropriate for the situations in life described as "public," such as work, business, politics, and government (Campbell & Jerry, 1988; Hanson, 1996). Because both women and men inhabit both the public and private spheres, effective communication education would stress the value of both in both settings. Scholarship available does not demonstrate that it does.

Masculine style primarily characterizes university classrooms in general (Hall & Sandler, 1985; Sandler & Hall 1986; Sandler, Silverberg, & Hall, 1996). Communication curriculum classes in journalism, mass media, public speaking, rhetoric, and many of the associated cocurricular activities reflect the same pattern (Foss & Foss, 2002; Foss & Griffin, 1995). Course materials and interaction norms in many classes reveal a strong if implicit bias toward traditional so-called masculine communication patterns (e.g., directness, linear logic, assertive, and competitive—even combative—verbal and nonverbal presentations) and a strong negative bias against so-called feminine patterns that reflect more passivity, deference to others, soft-speaking, and noncombative nonverbals (Foss, Foss, & Griffin, 1999). In contrast, in interpersonal communication skills classes, a bias may exist toward a communication style that many males do not like and are not socially rewarded for using (Wood & Inman, 1993). Conversely, in courses where masculine styles are privileged (including most university classrooms), penalties are especially severe for males who engage in feminine styles, and for elementary and secondary students these penalties are often quite overt.

Both styles carry penalties for nonconformity. A boy who doesn't enjoy the rough and tumble of typically "boy" activities

---

[10]Much recent attention has been given to the matter of gender differences that tie in some way to biology, whether it is in brain research or studies of genetics. These issues have been discussed with reference to communication, in work epitomized by that of James McCroskey (1998) and McCroskey, Michael Beatty, and Kristin Valencic (2001). This work is primarily theoretical, attempting to account for sources of difference and permanence in communication "traits." It does not present anything new with regard to the size of the differences between women and men as a group, although if such differences as can be established can be demonstrated to be trait based and dispositional (and thus not amenable to substantial alteration), the work might ultimately be useful in suggesting avenues to adapting instruction to account for such dispositions. Since, however, none of the current work suggests larger differences between females and males as groups than within each of the groups, its usefulness to examine gender equity is limited. What the work does demonstrate, as do many other approaches to communication learning that are not trait based, is the need for instruction materials, settings, and approaches to be tailored carefully to individual students, not to students as members of any group.

or who prefers to play quietly in small groups that include girls will quickly be labeled a "sissy"—among the worst epithets boys can receive. Much bullying directed toward smaller or weaker boys includes accusations of the child being a sissy or a fag. Changes in schools and the legal system are making such overt expressions of bias less common, at least in formal settings supervised by school staff; instances of sports coaches who accuse their teams of behaving like girls, as in "you throw like a girl," are now rare and these coaches could be disciplined (See the chapter "Gender Equity in Physical Education and Athletics" in this *Handbook* for the continuing difficulties of students in physical education classes). Nonetheless, gender bias remains against males who communicate in ways counter to the traditional masculine gender-role expectations. For two reasons, communicating in counter-stereotypical ways elicits fewer negative responses for girls and women in most educational settings. First, as just noted, the so-called masculine communication style is appropriate for most modes of education. Most educational settings reward logical, linear communication and styles of argument that fit well within the masculine style, so teachers tend to reward both girls and boys who use it. Girls and women who enter and succeed in these environments will have learned to adapt and use the style. Indeed, the masculine style will be thought of as how one is supposed to talk in school and won't even be perceived as being gendered. Second, when such counter-stereotypical behavior is noticed, in play and other competitive situations, it will often result in a girl being tagged as a "tomboy," a label that carries fewer negative connotations than does a sissy label for boys. For some girls, it earns a positive cachet, but many girls (and women) work hard to balance, usually nonverbally, the masculine connotations with a kind of hyper-femininity. The point here is that feminine style evokes negative outcomes in the learning climate for both girls and boys as we noted previously and as Janet Hyde and Sara Lindberg explored as well in the chapter "Facts and Assumptions about the Nature of Gender Differences and the Implications for Gender Equity."

These styles carry with them other limitations in classrooms. Sexist language, stereotypes, and communication patterns restrict students' freedom to experiment with words and ideas, and perhaps especially for males, the heterosexual norms created and replicated in classrooms exert great social pressure for conformity (Davies, 2003). Davies pointed out that if all students are to have similar opportunities to talk—and the same responsibilities to engage others in classroom discussions—teachers will need to encourage more explicit discussions of the ways conversations are shared and disrupted. Without teachers' careful structuring of talk during tasks in the classroom, students—both female and male—will experience much negative social "noise" and have more difficulty in reaching academic goals (p. 130). This issue pointed to the importance of attending to differences among girls and among boys. Inequity may not show up across whole groups of females or males, but might significantly impact those whose skills and styles do not reflect socially approved gender-appropriate behavior (see the several articles in Fischer, 2000).

A final point regarding the so-called feminine and masculine styles is that the expectations ignore what the body of research dealing with communication competence has demonstrated, that competent communicators need skill in both sets of behaviors (Morreale & Backlund, 2002). Because there is little or no systematic assessment of communication competency in educational settings, we cannot report whether boys and girls score differently on the subskills associated with each of the styles. Research conducted with adult subjects shows that while widespread perceptions exist that women are more adept than men at feminine style, the few actual observational studies that are available suggest the differences between women and men as a group are small and show wider variations within the sex groups than between them (Aries, 1996; Canary & Dinidia, 1998; Crawford, 1995). It may be reasonable to infer the differences between girls and boys in the classroom are also small and that more attention should be focused on the outliers, the less competent among both girls and boys, than on generalizations about children by sex groupings. Moreover, it is equally reasonable to conclude that discussion in classrooms of these issues of style and what kinds of competencies fit what kinds of situations would improve by the dynamics of classroom interactions and reduce inequities both within sex groups and between them.

GENDER BIAS IN COMMUNICATION CURRICULUM AND LEARNING MATERIALS

Our final area of exploration is with learning materials and the extent to which gender inequities pervade the classroom resources. Cooper (1987, 1989, 1993, 1994, 2000) identified significant degrees of sexism and role stereotyping in a variety of children's literature. Communication texts (like most texts) display gender stereotypes of many sorts (Gullocks, Pearson, Child, & Schwab, 2005; Purcell & Stewart, 1990; Tetenbaum & Pearson, 1989). Messages, mostly nonverbal, in the texts suggest that the most important writers, speakers, and theorists are men. For example, collections of literature for high-school English classes include mostly male authors (Carlson, 1989). Harmon (2000) reported similar findings about anthologies of literature for use in university English courses. Historically, collections of "great" or "representative" speeches have featured no speeches by women. To counter these imbalances, some collections of women's speaking have been created (Campbell, 1989; Kennedy & O'Shields, 1983, among others). However, until women's words appear in equitable numbers in regular anthologies and collections, the nonverbal messages to students will continue to be that women do not speak on the "important" public issues do not have the eloquence of men. More recently, some addresses by women have been included in materials specifically aimed at student audiences, but these anthologies continue to feature many more speeches by men than women (Campbell, 1991; Vonnegut, 1992). Sixteen of the 17 public-speaking texts analyzed by Hanson (1999) pictured men in power positions more frequently than women and all of the texts pictured men more frequently in photographs, a finding replicated in Gullock et al.'s (2005) examination of the 2002 ten best-selling public-speaking texts. When texts in all content areas are examined, similar gender biases are found (Hurd & Brabeck, 1997; Hogben & Waterman, 1997; Stone 1996; Feiner & Morgan, 1987; see also research reviewed in Jossey-Bass, 2002).

Hanson's (1999) investigation of public-speaking textbooks found that the mean number of pages devoted to discussing gender issues was 7.26, fewer than 5% of the pages in any of the best-selling volumes. The near-absence of women as speakers, writers, and theorists in public communication materials along with the near-absence of discussion of gender leaves intact the privileging of men's activities with very little attention to the gender implications.

Increasingly, films, videos, music, and Web pages are used as learning materials. Too rarely do the lessons call attention to the gender issues depicted. Moreover, since much of what happens in any classroom is determined by the resources brought to the room by the students as well as the instructor, the considerable amount of electronic media consumption by students becomes an issue for the communication classroom. We know from much research that students consume huge daily doses of information from music, computers, television, and movies (Swanson, 1992). A Kaiser Foundation study (Rideout, Roberts, & Foehr, 2005) found young people between the ages of 8 and 18 spent on average 6 hours per day using electronic media (compared to 43 minutes reading print materials). For an easily accessible summary of the report, go to www.kff.org/entmedia/index.cfm. Moreover, in a commercial world, students are subjected to equally massive daily doses of advertising designed to teach them how to live. A conclusion reported by the Canadian Paediatric Society (2005) was that the average Canadian child, who is exposed to watch less television than the average U.S. child, sees at least 20,000 commercials annually. Therefore, when these sources contain gender biases of many kinds, as we know they do (Borchert, 2004; Buck & Newton, 1989; Butruille & Taylor, 1987; Consalvo, 2004; Cooks, Orbe, & Bruess, 1993; Creedon, 1993; Daddario, 1992; Glascock & Ruggerio, 2004; Lovdal, 1989; among many others), students learn from these gendered messages, which form part of the context in which communication education takes place. Thus, even if all materials brought to the classroom by teachers were equitable and unbiased, the media environment still places an additional demand on teachers. Current curricula include little attention to media literacy in classrooms and, when it is present (in elective courses or literature classes), no assessments show whether students are alerted to the gender biases and distortions in popular media. Nor do we have studies that show that courses help students find ways to resist accepting those messages as prescriptions for how they should live, what they should buy, and what should consume their time and attention.

Gender Gaps in Communication Skills of English Language Learners

The field of education faces the challenge of assuring that English language learners (ELLs) attain academic standards, given the current gulf in performance between ELL and native-English or English-proficient students. The magnitude of this challenge is large and growing, with more than 5.1 million ELL students enrolled in U.S. public schools in the past year (U.S. Dept. of Ed., 2005). Addressing how to validly assess and educate students who are developing English language skills is essential to their fair and equitable treatment in education (Bailey & Butler, 2004). The chapter "Gender Equity in Foreign and Second-Language Learning and Instruction" in this book discusses these issues in detail.

In this chapter, the focus is on the learner of English communication skills and what issues of gender equity might be involved in this acquisition that impact the rest of the student's educational experience. The goal of focusing on reading and communication skills for the English-language learner is to bring these students into the mainstream of education with the necessary tools for their education. Having adequate English language skills to benefit from American public education is of concern for all students, at all levels. The issues especially related to English-language learners involve sociological and individual psychological variables such as learning style, motivation, social stratification, etc., as well as curricular concerns (what is taught and how).[11]

The No Child Left Behind Act (NCLB, 2001a) requires that achievement data for math and reading (and science by 2006) be disaggregated by student subgroups according to race, ethnicity, gender, English-language proficiency, migrant status, disability status, and low-income status.[12] Consequently, NCLB has placed the assessment of ELL students at the forefront of the educational arena in the United States. Under this law, not only must the performance of ELL students on standards-based assessments for math and reading be included in a district's calculation of Adequate Yearly Progress, but ELL students must show measurable progress each year in English-language development; namely listening, speaking, reading, writing, and comprehension (NCLB, 2001b). However, the question remains: Do male and female students who are acquiring English-language skills along with content knowledge fare comparably in performance?[13]

Why is such a question important to ask and attempt to answer? Certainly important differences in the performances of girls and boys may be masked if the ELL subgroup is treated as homogenous, without disaggregating gender (Jule, A., 2001, 2002). Gender-related differences may stem from different cultural expectations for performance by boys and girls in K–12 schooling as well as for the college-level population. Reactions to the testing situation and gender bias in test items may differentially impact the performance of boys and girls on the assessments that are at the very crux of the NCLB accountability sys-

---

[11]See the related discussions in the chapter "Gender Equity in Foreign and Second Language Learning and Instruction."

[12,13]One state that allows for the break down of English-language development scores by gender is California, with 1,598,535 ELL students (or approx. 34% of the United States total ELL enrollment) at the K–12 level (California Department of Education, 2004). Examination of scores for the 2004–2005 school year on the California Test of English Language Development (CELDT) suggested only very small gender differences and in quite similar magnitude across much of the K–12 Grade spectrum (CDE, 2005). For the combined Listening/Speaking subsection, boys trailed girls by about four mean scale score points until grades 10-12 when their performance matched that of girls. For the Reading subsection, boys trailed girls by a larger margin of approximately six-eight mean scale score points until they matched girls' performance at grades 11 and 12. Differences in the gap between boys and girls is widest on the Writing subsection of the CELDT with boys' scale scores on average remaining below girls throughout their K–12 careers (approximately 10 mean scale score points below the girls). These differences between boys and girls across most grade levels appear relatively stable over time with similar patterns of performance by gender reported each year since the CELDT's adoption in the 2001-2002 school year.

tem. It is well documented in the psychometric literature that gender-related effects on test scores exist and need to be guarded against. In a statistical examination of the result of a reading and listening assessment for college-level speakers of English-as-a-second-language (ESL), Kunnan (1990) found that 20% of items favored male test takers. More recently, using conversational analysis techniques, Brown and McNamara (2004), reported biases in a face-to-face ESL assessment of spoken English at the college level that may stem from differences in the gender of the interviewer/examiner, with female interviewers of test takers giving higher scores than a male interviewer.

Complex interactions between topic, gender of test-takers, and gender of nonpresent listeners, or audience (or nonpresent testers in the case of tape-recorded test responses) have also been recently documented (Lumley & O'Sullivan, in press) That is, when female college-level ESL students are required to talk about an unfamiliar topic to a hypothetical native English-speaking male listener, they performed less well than when they perceived the audience to be female despite the same level of unfamiliarity with the topic. Such findings with ESL students at the college level suggest that similarly complex interactions between gender and performance on reading and communicative skills are likely to also exist for the K–12 population, although fewer studies of gender and ESL have been conducted with elementary and secondary ELL students. Testing and instructional implications will follow from this kind of research. For instance, in addition to the current use of psychometric techniques and bias reviews for addressing the effects of gender biases, we need to see closer examination of the effects of interactions between gender of test takers and text examiners (both face-to-face and perceived audience gender), and closer examination of topics so that the selection of reading and listening passages on assessments captures the range of topics that are representative of both the profemale and promale categories identified by Buck et al. (n.d.) (Also see the chapter "Gender Equity in Testing and Assessment.")

Numbers, Degrees, and Salaries in Journalism/Communication Education

In this chapter, space limitations prohibit attention to education in each of the specific communication career fields (e.g., organizational communication, public address, intercultural communication, mass media). We have focused instead on communication learning that relates to all students and their achievement of communication competence. Due, however, to the ubiquity of the electronic communication discussed earlier and the necessity for mainstreaming knowledge about gender inequities in popular culture as well as in formal-learning settings, some attention to this specific area of education for a communication career is warranted. Thus, we attend briefly to the status of education in journalism and other areas of electronic communication at the college level. In these fields, throughout history employment has been heavily skewed toward men (Wooten, 2004). Relatively few women have played significant roles either as print journalists or in the media of radio, movies, television, and music. More recently, diversity in newsrooms and electronic media has increased somewhat, with demonstrable effects of more diverse programming and news coverage. For example, those newspapers with a high percentage of men in managerial positions (the majority of newspapers) tend to focus more on crime (Craft & Wanta, 2004). Newspapers with women in significant editorial positions include more coverage of women, hire more women writers, and include more women quoted as experts in stories (Bridge & Bonk, 1989; Bridge, 1989, 1994).

These facts make clear why the status of women in journalism education deserves some mention. We examined several recent surveys about the status of students and teachers in journalism and electronic media. The data show that while there has been some progress in terms of equity during the past 20 years, major inequities remain.

Women constitute the majority of the students enrolled in college and university journalism and mass communications programs. In 2001–2002, women received 64.6% of the 42,060 bachelor's degrees, 64.2% of the 3,700 master's degrees, and 50.3% of the 180 doctoral degrees in these programs. These numbers do not correspond to the numbers of women and men seeking and getting media jobs. Only 34.2% of the women graduates who sought work on a daily newspaper were offered a job, compared with 44.3% of the male graduates. In television, 33.9% of the women graduates who looked for a job received an offer, compared with the lower statistic of 35.2% of the men graduates. Women students were more likely then men to take a job in public relations (5.2% of the women, 2.6% of the males). (See Becker 2003 for a summary of several relevant surveys.) Women journalism and mass communications students are more than twice as likely as men to major in public relations, in large part because there has been historically less overt discrimination in the field (Rush, Oukrop, & Creeden, 2004). Rush et al. suggested some other explanations as well, most relating to the fact that the working conditions in public relations are more conducive to combining a family and a career than is the case in journalism or the electronic media industries. Other factors probably involve the fact that women are less likely to have an internship in the media while in college and are less likely to have worked for the campus newspaper, radio, or television station. Additionally, in that the definition of news in newsrooms primarily focuses on conflict and negativity (Becker, 2003), many women reject the climate of the work. Indeed, the situation illustrates another way in which inequities that begin early in education have a reciprocal relationship to inequities elsewhere in society.

Inequities of salary, promotion, tenure, workload, and appointment to leadership positions for teachers and administrators all continued to be major concerns of the women in journalism (Rush, Oukroup, & Creedon, 2004). According to researchers who have been surveying gender-equity issues in journalism and mass communication education, there are more women in these fields than 30 years ago, but "the same issues of discrimination in about the same amounts" (p. 104). The major, flagship research indicated that "public universities are less likely than other schools to have faculty gender and race equity in terms of numbers" (pp. 118–119). Women comprised approximately 25% of the top administrators in U.S. journalism programs in 2002; 4.5% of these female administrators were minorities. Women comprised approximately 18% of the full professors (Endres, Creedon, & Henry, 2004). The slow pace of improvement in the number and status of women and minority men in journalism and mass communication programs has lead one reviewer to give them a general grade of "D" on faculty diversity (Poindexter, 2000). A 2002 survey of journalists in newsrooms of papers with circulation of more than 50,000 found women less likely than men to be confident of promotion, less satisfied with their current jobs, and more likely to be planning to leave the field (Selzer, 2002).

CONCLUSIONS AND RECOMMENDATIONS: HOW FAR HAVE WE COME?

Over 20 years ago in the 1985 *Handbook* chapter "Sex Equity in Reading and Communication Skills," authors Scott, Dwyer, and Lieb-Brilhart recommended guidance similar to the following principles to enhance the competence of males as well as females (1985):

- Instruction should attend to students' individual differences without perpetuating sex stereotypes.
- Reading materials should portray females and males in non-stereotypical situations, including reading as something that males can do and high-level thinking as something females can do.
- Instruction should promote sex-equitable language and communication patterns for all students.
- Teacher education and materials should decrease sex-stereotyped classroom interactions and learning.

Analyzing the research available 20 years ago, writers reviewed the various explanations for girls' assumed advantage in reading comprehension, noting the need for better reading role models for boys and better intellectual role models for girls in strategies coping with inferential reading materials, as well as less culturally stereotyping classroom communication. Cultural stereotyping for gender-related communication styles and preferences was reported, and it was clear that there was a nature-nurture controversy surrounding this aspect of communication. Nationwide assessments of these skills with respect to gender were not available, and only a few studies focused on gender differences in reading interests and skill, with much of the difference assumed to reside in differences in gender acculturation. Little was reported on the impact of media on stereotyping, gender-related use of technology, especially computer usage, and the gender-related differences of interest in reading content (which might account for differences in testing outcomes).

The current chapter shows that many national- and state-level assessments of reading and writing competencies have been completed or are ongoing. In addition, much research including attention to data on gender has occurred. Most current measurements show a gender gap in favor of girls in reading and in writing, college entrance examinations being the exception. These advantages have remained relatively steady over the two-plus decades. This finding occurs also in some international assessments of reading. Yet there is no more evidence today than 25 years ago that the presumed advantages in these skills

translate into advantage in life and work situations after formal schooling. Data showing increased attention to oral communication skills in standards and curricula after the ESEA legislation of 1978 included speaking and listening as basic skills. The addition spurred professional attention to specifying speaking and listening objectives for assessment, and national associations identified assessment and implementation tools. The women's movement of the late 20th century promoted attention to the roles of women in a wide range of communication activities. However, federal interest in supporting research on assessment of oral competency has recently waned. The current iteration of ESEA (No Child Left Behind, NCLB, 2001a) focused on collecting data on reading and mathematics with little acknowledgment of their interrelationships with listening and speaking. Attention to English-language learners provides the exception to this case (NCLB, 2001b). Addition of an actual writing portion in the national college aptitude exams (ACT & SAT) will spur increased understanding of writing skill acquisition outcomes for college-bound students, but the development is too recent to permit informed analysis of any gender impacts at this time, although given the persistent writing advantage for girls shown in other measures, it is not surprising that as discussed earlier in this chapter, the 2006 SAT writing section results show that girls outscore boys. It will be important to monitor these findings over more than a single year to fully understand the outcome. It remains obvious that without nationwide assessments in speaking and listening, especially in the interactive settings that establish whether or not oral-communication competency exists, and without wider recognition of the electronic media as involving important communication processes that impact both learning and gender, few definitive claims can be made about gender inequities in learning oral communication skills among students at any level.

Data suggest that despite more attention among both scholars and teachers to the impact of gendered communication over two decades, biased communication still occurs in education as well as in the larger culture. As noted elsewhere in this volume, while there are more laws punishing overt gender discrimination now than 20 years ago, the images in media and schooling, not to mention the persistent pay gap between women and men, still communicate substantial gender inequities for women. At the same time, some inequities for boys and men in education exist as well, a pattern not explored in the earlier volume, although all evidence suggests it is not a new pattern. These are biases against femininity and feminine communication behaviors that affect boys whose behaviors do not fit the traditional masculine patterns as well as girls and women once they reach the workplace.

A flurry of recent popular attention about possible gender inequities in education for boys has occurred because overall enrollment of women at the college and university level in the United States now significantly outpaces that of men. Some commentators see these imbalances as evidence of an educational neglect of boys, although the disproportionately high enrollment by women is not found at the elite universities (Sadker, 2000) nor is it found in most of the science and technical fields of study. Nonetheless, the situation warrants attention, especially because, when the data are explored by race, class, and ethnicity, women's enrollment percentage is highest in some, though not all, minority groups, and because some claims have been made that the changes in enrollment patterns spring from changes in the schools that made them more equitable for girls (Mortenson, 2001). The charge that changes in the last 20 years have caused these problems of boys' achievements seems spurious since some of the patterns cited far predate the legislation mandating sex-equity of 1972. A higher rate of discipline problems and more diagnosed reading disabilities in boys as well as too few male teachers in elementary and primary-school classrooms have existed in U.S. schools far longer than 20 years. Moreover, the actual impact of the college and university enrollment disparities remains quite unclear. What links any of these outcomes may have to communication education is unclear. As Sara Mead (2006) wrote, the fact that girls and women surpass the boys in a few areas creates more media concern than larger equity issues (2005, accessible at www.education-sector.org). Mead pointed out that White boys score significantly better than Black and Hispanic boys in reading, at all grade levels. Closing racial and economic gaps would help the poor and minority boys more than would trying to close gender gaps, she concluded.

All reflect social patterns that deserve to be changed; what role the schools should play in creating those changes remains an issue of serious debate. Even in the field of communication, where changes in the enrollment, faculty, and career placements have changed dramatically with increasing participation of women, the salaries that college-educated women earn in the field remain considerably lower than those of men (Becker, 2003) and women have more difficulties than men in securing employment (Endres et al., 2004; Poindexter, 2000). What all of this makes most clear is how badly more research is needed—into the relationships between communication competence, gender in communication education, and employment outcomes. Especially relevant for this chapter are questions of how communication competence relates to gendered expectations in career choices and workplaces (Barnett & Rivers, 2004; see also the chapter "Gender Equity in Career and Technical Education" in this *Handbook*). With these concerns in mind, we offer summary conclusions and action recommendations grouped into five categories: (a) curriculum, (b) assessment, (c) professional development, (d) research, and (e) policy.

RECOMMENDATIONS FOR ACTION

Curriculum. Curricula involving communication must be transformed, a task important for both girls and boys because gendered expectations affect both, often negatively.

- Schools should integrate age and developmentally appropriate focus on all communication skills (listening, reading, speaking, and writing, media literacy) at all levels, K–16
- Special attention is needed to understand and respond to the impacts of ethnicity and race, socioeconomic status, and different languages spoken in the home.
- Curricula need to attend to literacy in its broadest sense. No longer should it be assumed that children enter school need-

ing only to achieve reading literacy and writing competence. Competence in listening and speaking and interactive skills, including in use of the wide variety of modern electronic media, is required to function successfully in the 21st century. On the surface, this recommendation does not seem related to gender, but it is. Education exists within a gendered culture in which all communication in some way references gender norms involving verbal and nonverbal language and interaction patterns; and popular media are structured to perpetuate those gendered patterns. Therefore, competent communicators, whatever the medium of interaction, must attend to those norms. As education is currently provided in the United States, learning how gender functions in communication is almost exclusively the province of unstated agendas within the classroom, even though it is always present and reflects often overt teaching outside the classroom through students' interactions with each other, their families, workplace, their media, and their culture.

- Curricula need to include overt attention to gender norms, patterns, and outcomes to make sure students understand and can evaluate the gendered expectations found in all sources, academic, social and cultural; and the curriculum needs to show students how these attitudes affect their communication and (hence) their lives. Curricula need to help teachers and students see that many gendered associations are problematic and can be changed. Needed curricular changes will attend to gender equity in course content, instructional materials, interaction patterns and media; and the changes will involve assignments that link to students' lived experience both as children and prospective effectively functioning adults.
- The elements just outlined, present in isolated parts and places in today's formal education system, need to become as central a part of the formal learning process as they are of students' communicative lives.
- Schools with model communication education programs should be identified, publicized, and replicated.
- Achieving the transformation described here will require examination of textbook and other formal learning materials, but it will also include attention to gendered messages found in popular culture artifacts of all types, especially in music, television, movies, computer games, and programs.

Assessment. Assessment of student learning of gender and communication needs to be significantly expanded.

- Assessment should encompass the full range of communication skills (listening, reading, speaking, writing, media literacy) and be done on a systematic basis with careful attention to technical quality and educational consequences, whether the tests are teacher-made or mandated by others, and whether they are formative or summative in nature.
- Assessment needs to attend to differences within gender groups, especially as they involve race, ethnicity, and socioeconomic class. Such reporting of gender differences within subgroups of students would not only show the impact of the new elementary and secondary accountability system on stu-

dent performance in all communication skills, it would also provide a more finely grained picture of the impacts of ethnicity, race, and class on accomplishment and equity.

- Assessment processes need to keep pace with the role of electronic communication in students' lives by incorporating a conceptualization of communication literacy that includes computer and other media literacy.

Professional development.   Significant changes in communication education will depend on changes in the professional development of teachers at all levels, curriculum and test developers, and those who teach these education practitioners. A deliberate attempt to integrate gender research and theory in the development of these professionals will help ensure a future supply of practitioners prepared for the challenges to communication education made by attending to gender.

- Knowledge about both the full range and complexity of communication processes and the central role of gender within those processes should be integrated into the formal preparation of teachers and other education practitioners such as curriculum and test developers.

- Skills of analysis and assessment of language and discourse need to be included in teacher preparation to provide the foundation for critical examination of formal learning materials such as curricula, as well as the artifacts of popular culture.

- Teachers will need knowledge of both the purpose of assessments and how to interpret a range of communication assessments for use in implementing curriculum and other instructional decisions.

- Formal, well-supported professional-development programs for acquiring the skills and knowledge just outlined should be made available to teachers currently in the classroom.

- In order to remain effective educators at the higher-education level, those responsible for the education and continued development of teachers and other education practitioners must also have the related skills and knowledge about communication processes, assessment, and curricula and the central role of gender in these areas.

Research.   An expanded research program is required to clarify the links among communication; gender; specific teaching and learning behaviors; and life experiences in the home, the public arena and the workplace.

- Much scholarship will be needed to fully understand the links among gender attitudes, teacher behaviors, school curricula, social and cultural factors and student life outcomes.

- Especially needed is longitudinal work that can examine (a) students' interactions with each other; (b) students' interactions with the wide variety of popular media in which most are immersed; and (c) how and what social/cultural influences enhance their communication and gender competency.

- In all this scholarship, careful attention is needed to within-sex-group differences, especially those of race, ethnicity, class, and any other factors likely to significantly affect both

what communicative competence means within that group and how gendered expectations may vary from the mainstream.

- To enable and support this research, more women and minorities need to be hired for university communication faculties and administrations, appointed to publication selection committees, encouraged to submit articles for publication, and nominated for awards (see Wooten, 2004).

Policy.   To implement the recommendations above, policy changes will be required.

- Education policies at the national, State, district, university, and school levels must emphasize communication proficiency requirements in the governance of the pre-K through 16 education enterprise.

- Research-based knowledge about communication must be translated into education policy. Although research from disparate fields has demonstrated the importance of communication in every area of life, this knowledge has not translated into education policy. We know that every act of teaching and learning, of administration and supervision, of linking education to communities, for example, relies on complex enactments of communication behaviors. Typical policies urge educators to communicate effectively in these contexts, but few policies at any level equip educators with the tools to do this.

- The Congress should require the U.S. Department of Education to fund a National Research and Development Center on Communication within its "education sciences" mandates. This center should encompass all of the literacy and communication skills described in this chapter, with special emphasis on promoting excellence and equity among all groups.

- At the national level, education reform legislation (for example, in reauthorizing the Elementary and Secondary Education Act), should emphasize policies that promote both student and teacher proficiencies in all aspects of communication at all levels of schooling. Attention to the powerful interactions between gender (as one aspect of diversity) and communication should be emphasized. Such legislation should support the efforts of various stakeholders (e.g., teacher-education institutions, professional organizations, licensing, certification, and assessment agencies) to implement standards, assessments, and programs for communication proficiency. Policies should support a bottom line: No teacher should enter a classroom without demonstrating the proficiency in reading, writing, speaking, listening, media, and interactive behaviors necessary for promoting student learning.

- Federal agencies should coordinate policies with the Department of Education for enhancing productive communication skills for the especially diverse citizenry of the United States. Since the Departments of Labor, Health and Human Service, Housing and Urban Development, Immigration, and other agencies all serve individuals and families, implementing communication education is in part included in their mandates.

Literacy and communication skills are crucial in promoting health, job mobility, family welfare, and other missions of these agencies. Various Inter-Agency Federal Coordinating Agencies now coordinate policies, for example for linking jobs and education, for providing free materials for teachers, for teaching adult literacy, etc. For coherent policy implementation, they need to incorporate key principles of communication that impact on gender equity in multiple contexts.

ACKNOWLEDGMENTS

The authors gratefully acknowledge the contributions of reviewers Phil Backlund, Central Washington University, Ellensburg, WA;, Shirley Brown, Consultant, Philadelphia, PA;, and Sherwyn P. Morreale, University of Colorado, Colorado Springs, CO. Authors' names, after that of lead author, are listed alphabetically.

References

Alperstein, J. F. (2005, May 16). *Commentary on girls, boys and test scores and more*. Retrieved November 4, 2005, from file:///Users/1com/Desktop/TCRecord-%20Article.webarchive.

American Association of University Women Educational Foundation. (2001). *Beyond the 'Gender Wars': A Conversation about Girls, Boys, and Education*. Washington, D.C.: Author.

American Federation of Teachers. (2003). *Setting strong standards*. Washington, DC: Author.

Andersen, E. S. (1990). *Speaking with Style: The Sociolinguistic Skills of Children*. London: Routledge, Kagan Paul.

Andersen, P. S. (1999). *Nonverbal communication: Forms and functions*. Mountain View, CA: Mayfield.

Andersen, P. S., & Guerrero, L. K. (Eds.). (1998). *Handbook of communication and emotion: Research, theory, applications, and contexts*. San Diego, CA: Academic Press.

Andersen, P. S., Guerrero, L. K., & Afifi, W. A. (Eds.) (2001). *Close encounters: Communicating in relationships*. Mountain View, CA: Mayfield.

Aries, E. (1996). Men and women in interaction: Reconsidering the differences. New York: Oxford University Press.

Backlund, P. (1982). *State practices in speaking and listening skill assessment*. Annandale, VA: Speech Communication Association.

Backlund, P. (January, 2006). Letter to author.

Bailey, A. L., & Butler, F. A. (2004). Ethical considerations in the assessment of the language and content knowledge of English language learners K–12. *Language Assessment Quarterly, 1*, 177–193.

Barnett, R. C., & Rivers, C. (2004). *Same difference: How gender myths are hurting our relationships, our children, and our jobs*. New York: Basic Books.

Barton, P. E. (1994). *Becoming literate about literacy* (ETS Policy Information Report No. ED 372 227). Princeton, NJ: Educational Testing Service.

Barton, P., & Lapointe, A. (1995) *Learning by degrees: Indicators of performance in higher education* (ETS Policy Information Report No. ED 379 323). Princeton, NJ: Educational Testing Service.

Beatty, M. J., McCroskey, J. C., & Valencic, K. M. (2001). *The biology of communication: A communibiological perspective*. Cresskill, NJ: Hampton Press.

Becker, L. B. (2003). *Gender equity elusive, surveys show*. Accessed October 20, 2005, from http://www.freedomforum.org/templates/document.asp?documentID=17784

Bem, S. L. (1993). *The lenses of gender*. New Haven, CN: Yale University Press.

Bergvall, V. L., & Remlinger, K. A. (1996). Reproduction, resistance and gender in educational discourse: The role of critical discourse analysis. *Discourse & Society, 7*(4), 453–479.

Birdwhistell, R. L. (1968). Some body motion elements accompanying spoken American English. In L. Thayer (Ed.). *Communication: Concepts and perspectives*. Washington, DC: Spartan.

Birdwhistell, R. L. (1970). *Kinesics and context; essays on body motion communication*. Philadelphia: University of Pennsylvania Press.

Blair, C., Brown, J. R., & Baxter, L. A. (1994). Disciplining the feminine. *The Quarterly Journal of Speech, 80*, 383–409.

Borchert, M. (2004). Lions, tigers & little girls: Representations of gender roles in *Power Rangers and Wild Force*. In P. M. Backlund & M. R. Williams (Eds.) *Readings in Gender Communication* (pp. 314–321). Belmont, CA: Wadsworth Thomson.

Borisoff, D., & Merrill, L. (1998). *The power to communicate: Gender differences as barriers* (3rd ed.). Prospect Heights, IL: Waveland Press.

Bridge, J. (1989). News magazines neglect females. Alexandria, VA: Unabridged Communications.

Bridge, J. (1994). *Arriving on the scene*. Alexandria VA: Unabridged Communications.

Bridge, J., & Bonk, K. (1989). *Women, men and media: A report of content analysis of newspaper and television reporting*. Alexandria, VA: Communications Consortium.

Brody, L. R. (2000). The socialization of gender differences in emotional expression: Display rules, infant temperament, and differentiation. In A. H. Fischer (Ed.) *Gender and Emotion: Social Psychological Perspectives*. (pp. 24–37). Cambridge: Cambridge University Press, UK.

Broverman, I. K. (1970). Sex-role stereotypes and clinical judgments of mental health. *Journal of Consulting & Clinical Psychology, 34*(1) 1–7.

Broverman, I. K., Vogel, S. R., Broverman, D. M., Clarkson, F. E., & Rosenkrantz, P. S. (1972). Sex-role stereotypes: A current appraisal. *Journal of Social Issues 28*, 59–78.

Brown, A., & McNamara, T. (2004). 'The devil is in the details': Researching gender issues in language assessment. *TESOL Quarterly, 38*(3), 524–538.

Buck, E. B., & Newton, B. J. (1989). Research on the study of television and gender. In B. Dervin, & M. J. Voigt (Eds.) *Progress in Communication Sciences* (Vol. 9; pp. 1–42). Norwood, NJ: Ablex.

Buck, G., Kostin, I. Phelps, M., & Kutz, D. (n.d.). *Understanding the origins of gender-based impact on the SAT Verbal: Exploring item content*. Princeton, NJ: Educational Testing Service.

Butruille, S., & Taylor, A. (1987). Women in American popular song. In L. Stewart & S. Ting-Toomey (Eds.) *Communication Gender and Sex Roles in Diverse Interaction Contexts* (pp. 179–188). Norwood, NJ: Ablex.

Cajete, G. (1994). *Look to the mountain. An ecology of indigenous education*. Durango, CO: Kivaki Press.

Calahan, C., Mandinach, E. B., & Camara, W. J. (2002). *The College Board Report No. 94-2*. New York: The College Board.

California Department of Education (COE). (2005). *California English Language Development Test (CELDT) Reports, 2001–2005*. Retrieved February 20, 2005, from http://celdt.cde.ca.gov/reports.asp

Cameron, D. (Ed.). (1990). *The feminist critique of language: A reader*. London: Routledge.

Cameron, D. (Ed.). (1998). *The feminist critique of language: A reader* (2nd ed.). London: Routledge.

Campbell, K. K. (1989). *Man cannot speak for her: A critical study of early feminist rhetoric*. New York: Praeger Publishers.

Campbell, K. K. (1991). Hearing women's voices, *Communication Education, 40*, 33–48.

Campbell, K. K., & Jerry, E. (1988). Woman and speaker: A conflict in roles. In S. Brehm (Ed.), *Seeing female: Social roles and personal lives*. New York: Greenwood.

Canadian Paediatric Society. (2005). Impact of media use on children and youth. *Paediatrics & Child Health* 2003, *8*(5), 301–306. Retrieved December 31, 2005, from http://www.cps.ca/english/statements/PP/pp03-01.htm

Canary, D. J., & Dindia, K. (Eds.). (1998). *Sex differences and similarities in communication: critical essays and empirical investigations of sex and gender in interaction*. Mahwah, NJ: Lawrence Erlbaum.

Carlson, M. (1989). Guidelines for gender-based curriculum in English, grades 7–12. *English Journal, 36*, 30–3.

Carnevale, A. P. (1996). Liberal education and the new economy. *Liberal Education* Washington, DC: American Association of College and Universities.

Chapman, C. (2006). *Review of research on composition. Multiple perspectives on two decades of change*. Retrieved June 6, 2006, from www.tcrecord.org/Content.asp?ContentID=12532.

Coles, M., & Hall, C. (2001). Boys, books and breaking boundaries: Developing literacy in and out of school. In W. Martino & B. Meyenn (Eds.), *What about the boys? Issues of masculinity in schools* (pp. 211–221). Buckingham, UK: Open University Press.

Coley, R. J. (2003). *Growth in school revisited: Achievement gains from the fourth to the eighth grade* (ETS Policy Information Report). Princeton, NJ: Educational Testing Service.

College Board. (2004a). *2004 College-bound seniors: A profile of SAT program test-takers*. New York:

College Board. (2004b). *National Summary Report*. Retrieved January 27, 2005, from http://apcentral.collegeboard.com/repository/program summaryreport_39028.pdf

College Board. (2006, August 29). College Board announces scores for new SAT® with Writing. Retrieved August 31, 2006, from http://www.collegeboard.com/press/releases/150054.html

Condravy, J., Skirboll, E., & Taylor, R. (1998). Faculty perceptions of classroom gender dynamics. *Women & Language, 21*(1), 18–27.

Consalvo, M. (2004). Borg babes, drones, and the collective: Reading gender and the body in *Star Trek. Women's Studies in Communication, 27*, 177–203.

Cooks, L. M., Orbe, M. P., & Bruess, C. S. (1993). The fairy tale theme in popular culture: A semiotic analysis of *Pretty Woman. Women's Studies in Communication, 16*, 86–104.

Cooper, P. (1987). Sex role stereotypes of stepparents in children's literature. In L. P. Stewart & S. Ting-Toomey (Eds.), *Communication, Gender, Sex Roles in Diverse Interaction Contexts* (pp. 61–82). Norwood, NJ: Ablex.

Cooper, P. J. (1988). *Speech communication for the classroom teacher*. Scottsdale, AZ: Gorsuch Scarisbruck.

Cooper, P. (1989). Children's literature: The extent of sexism. In C. M. Lont & S. A. Friedley (Eds.), *Beyond Boundaries: Sex & Gender Diversity in Communication* (pp. 233–249). Fairfax, VA: George Mason University Press.

Cooper, P. (1993). Women and power in the Caldecott and Newberry winners, 1980–1990. In C. Berryman-Fink, D. Ballard-Reisch, & L. Newman (Eds.). *Communication and sex-role socialization* (pp. 7–27). New York: Garland.

Cooper, P. (1994). The image of stepmothers in children's literature 1980–1991. In L. Turner & H. Sterk (Eds.), *Differences that make a difference*. Westport, CT: Bergin and Garvey.

Cooper, P. (2000, October). *Image of stepmothers in children's literature 1980–2000*. Paper presented at the convention of the Organization for the Study of Communication, Language, and Gender, Milwaukee, WI.

Costello, C. B., & Krimgold, B. K. (Eds.). (1996). *The American woman, 1996–97: Women and work*. NY: Norton.

Costello, C. B., & Stone, A. J. (Eds.). (2001). *The American woman, 2003–2004: Getting to the top*. NY: Norton.

Costello, C. B., Wight, V. R., & Stone, A. J. (Eds.). (2003). *The American woman: Daughters of a revolution—young women today*. NY: Palgrave Macmillan.

Craft, S., & Wanta, W. (2003, Spring). Women in the newsroom: Influences of female editors and reporters on the news agenda. *Journalism & Mass Communication Quarterly, 81*(1), 124–138.

Crawford, M. (1995). *Talking difference: On gender and language*. London: Sage.

Creedon, P. J. (1993). *Women in mass communication: Challenging gender values*. (2nd ed.). Beverly Hills, CA: Sage.

Daddario, G. (1992). Swimming against the tide: *Sports Illustrated*'s imagery of female athletes in a swimsuit world. *Women's Studies in Communication, 15*(1), 49–64.

Daly, J. A. (1994). Assessing speaking and listening: Preliminary considerations for a national assessment. In S. Morreale, & M. Brooks (Eds.), *1994 SCA summer conference proceedings and prepared remarks* (pp. 17–31). Annandale: VA: The Speech Communication Association.

Darling A. L., & Dannels, D. P. (1998, November). *Disciplinary assessment of oral communication*. Paper presented at the annual meeting of the National Communication Association, New York.

Davies, J. (2003, March). Expressions of gender: An analysis of pupils' gendered discourse styles in small group classroom discussions. *Discourse & Society, 14*(2), 115–132.

de Castell, S., & Jenson, J. (2004). Paying attention to attention: New economies for learning. *Educational Theory, 54*(4), 381–397.

delPolito, C. M., & Lieb-Brilhart, B. (1981). Implications of oral communication as a basic skill. In G. Friedrich (Ed.), *Education in the 80s*. Washington, D.C.: National Education Association.

Denton, K., & West, J. (2002). *Children's reading and mathematics achievement in kindergarten and first grade*, (NCCES 2002-125). Washington, DC: U. S. Department of Education.

deWitt, J., Bozik, M., Hay, E., Litterst, J., Strohkirch, C., & Yokum, K. (1991). Oral communication competency and teacher certification in the United States: Reality and recommendations. *Communication Education, 40*, 144–151.

Dindia, K. (1987). The effects of sex of subject and sex of partner on interruptions. *Human Communication Research, 13*, 345–371.

Donovan, L., & MacIntyre, P. D. (2004). Age and sex differences in willingness to communicate: Communication apprehension, and self-perceived competence. *Communication Research Reports, 21*, 420–427.

Dwyer, C. A., & Johnson, L. M. (1997). Grades, accomplishments, and correlates. In W. W. Willingham & N. S. Cole (Eds.), *Gender and fair assessment* (pp. 127–156). Mahwah, NJ: Lawrence Erlbaum Associates.

Eckert, P., & McConnell-Ginet, S. (2003). *Language and gender*. New York: Cambridge University Press.

Edelsky, C. (1993). Who's got the floor? In D. Tannen (Ed.), *Gender and Conversational Interaction* (pp. 189–227). New York: Oxford University Press.

Ekman, P., & Friesen. W. V. (1969). The repertoire of non-verbal behavior: Categories, origins, usage and coding, *Semiotica, 1*, 1–20.

Ekman, P., Friesen, W. V., & Phoebe P. (1972). *Emotion in the human face: Guide-lines for research and an integration of findings*. New York: Pergamon.

Ekman, P., & Rosenberg E. L. (2005). *What the face reveals: Basic and applied studies of spontaneous expression using the facial action coding system* (2nd ed.). New York: Oxford University Press.

Endicott Report. (1978). *Endicott report: 32nd annual survey of well-known business and industrial firms concerning employment trends for college graduates.* Evanston, IL: Northwestern University.

Endres, K., Creedon, P. J., & Henry S. (eds.) (2004). Timeline and vignettes: Exploring the history and status of women in journalism and mass communication education. In R. R. Rush, C. E. Oukrop, & P. J. Creedon. *Seeking equity for women in journalism and mass communication education: A 30-Year update* (pp. 33–50). Mahwah, NJ: Lawrence Erlbaum Associates.

Fassinger, P. (1995). Understanding classroom interaction: Students and professors' contributions to students' silence. *Journal of Higher Education*, 66(1), 82–97.

Feiner, S., & Morgan, B. (1987). Women and minorities in introductory economics textbooks: 1974–1984. *Journal of Economic Education, 18*, 376–392.

Fischer, A. H. (2000). *Gender and emotion: Social psychological perspectives.* Cambridge, UK: Cambridge University Press.

Fivush, R. (1989). Exploring sex differences in the emotional context of mother-child conversations about the past. *Sex Roles, 20*, 675–691.

Fleming, S. (1995). Whose stories are validated? *Language Arts, 72*, 590–596.

Foss, K. A., Foss, S. K., & Griffin, C. L. (1999). *Feminist rhetorical theories.* Thousand Oaks, CA: Sage.

Foss, S. K., & Foss, K. A. (2002). *Inviting transformation: Presentational speaking for a changing world* (2nd ed.). Prospect Heights, IL: Waveland Press.

Foss, S. K., & Griffin, C. L. (1995). Beyond persuasion: A proposal for an invitational rhetoric. *Communication Monographs, 62*, 2–18.

Francis, B., & Skelton, C. (2005). *Reassessing gender and achievement: Questioning contemporary key debates.* New York: Routledge.

Freeman, C. E. (2004). *Trends in educational equity of girls & women: 2004* (NCES 2005-016). U.S. Department of Education, National Center for Educational Statistics. Washington, DC: U.S. Government Printing Office.

Gerbner, G. (1994). Reclaiming our cultural mythology. *In Context: A Quarterly of Humane Sustainable Culture, 38*, 40. Retrieved October 30, 2005, http://www.context.org/ICLIB/IC38/Gerbner.htm.

Glascock, J., & Ruggiero, T. E. (2004). Representations of class and gender on primetime Spanish-Language television in the United States. *Communication Quarterly, 52, 390*–402.

Gleason, R. B. (1989). Sex differences in parent-child interaction. In S. Phillips, S. Steel, & C. Tang (Eds.), *Language, gender and sex in comparative perspective* (pp. 189–199). Cambridge, UK: Cambridge University Press.

Goodwin, M. H. (1980). Directive-Response Speech Sequences in Girls' and Boys' Task Activities. In S. McConnell-Ginet, R. Borker, & N. Furman (Eds.). *Women and Language in Literature and Society* (pp. 157–173). New York: Praeger.

Goodwin, M. (1988). Cooperation and competition across girls' play activities. In A. D. Todd & S. Fisher (Eds.), *Gender and discourse: The power of talk.* Norwood, NJ: Ablex.

Gray, J. (1992). *Men are from Mars, women are from Venus: A practical guide for improving communication and getting what you want in your relationships.* New York: HarperCollins.

Gray, J. (2002). *Men, women and relationships: Making peace with the opposite sex.* New York: HarperCollins.

Grob, L., Meyers, R. A., & Schuh, R. (1997). Powerful/Powerless language use in group interactions: Sex differences or similarities? *Communication Quarterly, 45*, 282–303.

Gullocks, K. A., Pearson, J. C., Child, J. T., & Schwab, C. R. (2005, May) Diversity and Power in Public Speaking Textbooks. *Communication Quarterly, 53*, 247–258.

Hall, R. M., & Sandler, B. R. (1985). A chilly climate in the classroom. In A. G. Sargent (Ed.), *Beyond Sex Roles* (2nd ed., pp. 503–510).

Halliday, M. A. K. (1985). *An introduction to functional grammar.* London: Edward Arnold. St. Paul, MN: West Publishing

Hansen C., & Hansen, R. (1988). How rock music videos can change what is seen when boy meets girl: Priming stereotypic appraisal of social interactions. *Sex Roles, 19*, 287–316.

Hanson, T. L. (1996). A comparison of leadership practices used by male and female communication department chairpersons. *Journal of the Association for Communication Administration, 1*, 40–55.

Hanson, T. L. (1999). Gender sensitivity and diversity issues in selected basic public speaking texts. *Women & Language, 22*(2), 13–19,

Harmon, M. R. (2000). Gender/language subtexts as found in literature anthologies: Mixed messages, stereotypes, silence, erasure. In M. J. Hardman & A. Taylor (Eds.), *Hearing Many Voices* (pp. 75–86). Cresskill, N.J.: Hampton Press.

Harste, J .C. (2001). What education as inquiry is and isn't. In S. Boran & B. Comber (Eds.), *Critiquing whole language and classroom inquiry* (1–17). Urbana, IL: National Council of Teachers of English.

Hellinger, M., & Bussmann. H. (2001). *Gender across languages: The linguistic representation of women and men.* Amsterdam/Philadelphia: John Benjamins. Three vol.

Henley, N. (1986). *Body politics: Power, sex, and nonverbal communication.* NY: Simon & Schuster (Original work published 1977 by Prentice-Hall).

Henley, N., & Kramarae, C. (1991). Gender, power and miscommunication. In N. Coupland, H. Giles, & J. Wiemann (Eds.), *Miscommunication and Problematic Talk* (pp. 18–43). Newbury Park, CA: Sage.

Hill, A. O. (1986). *Mother tongue, father time: A decade of linguistic revolt.* Bloomington, IN: University Press.

Hogben, M., & Waterman, C. (1997). Are all of your students represented in their textbooks? A content analysis of coverage of diversity issues in introductory psychology textbooks. *Teaching Psychology, 24*, 95–100.

Holborow, M. (1999). *The politics of English.* London: Sage, *1999.*

Hosman, L. A. (1989). The evaluative consequences of hedges, hesitations, and intensifiers: Powerful and powerless speech styles. *Human Communication Research, 15*, 383–406.

Howes, C., & Matheson, C. C. (1992). Sequences in the development of competent play with peers: Social and social pretend play. *Developmental Psychology, 28*, 961–974.

Howes, C., & Phillipsen, L. (1992). Gender and friendship: Relationships within peer groups of young children. *Social Development, 1*, 230–242.

Huffaker, D. A., & Calvert, S. L. (2005). Gender, identity, and language use in teenage blogs. *Journal of Computer-Mediated Communication, 10*(2), 1. Retrieved November 5, 2005, from http://jcmc.indiana.edu/vol10/issue2/huffaker.htm

Hurd, T., & Brabeck, M. (1997). Presentation of women and Gilligan's ethic of care in college textbooks, 1970–1990: An examination bias. *Teaching of Psychology, 24*, 159–167.

Jansz, J. (2000). Masculine identity and restrictive emotionality. In A. H. Fischer, (Ed.) *Gender and Emotion: Social Psychological Perspectives* (pp. 166–188). Cambridge, UK: Cambridge University Press.

Jaworski, A., & Sachdev, I. (2004). Teachers' beliefs about students' talk and silence: Constructing academic success and failure through metapragmatic comments. In Jaworski, A., Coupland, N., & Galasinski, D. (Eds.), *Metalanguage: Social and ideological perspectives* (pp. 227–246) Berlin, Germany: Mouton de Gruyter.

Jenson, J., & de Castell, S. (2004 July/November). 'Turn it in': Technological challenges to academic ethics. *Education Communication & Information, 4*(2/3), 311–320.

Jenson, J., de Castell, S., & Bryson, M. (2003). "Girl talk": Gender, equity, and identity discourses in a school-based computer culture. *Women's Studies International Forum, 26*(6), 561–573.

Jones, S. M., & Dindia, K. (2004). A meta-analytic perspective on sex-equity in the classroom. *Review of Educational Research, 74*(4), 443–471.

Jossey-Bass. (2002). *The Jossey-Bass Reader in Gender in Education.* San Francisco: Jossey-Bass.

Jule, A. (2001). *Speaking silence? A study of linguistic space and girls in the ESL classroom*. TESOL annual conference, Vancouver, BC, Canada.

Jule, A. (2002). *Speaking their sex: A study of gender and linguistic space in an ESL classroom*. *TESL Canada Journal, 19*(2), 37–51.

Kennedy, C. W., & Camden, C. T. (1983). A new look at interruptions. *Western Journal of Speech Communication, 47*, 45–58.

Kennedy, P. S., & O'Shields, G. H. (1983). *We shall be heard: Women speakers in America*. Dubuque, IA: Kendall/Hunt Publishing.

Kunnan, A. (1990). DIF in native language and gender groups in an ESL placement test. *TESOL Quarterly, 24*, 742–746.

Lakoff, R. T. (1990). *Talking power: The politics of language*. New York: Basic Books/HarperCollins.

Lesikin, J. (1998). Determining social prominence: A methodology for uncovering gender bias in ESL textbooks. *College ESL, 8*(1), 83–97.

Lieb, B. (1994). National contexts for developing postsecondary competency assessment. In S. Morreale & M. Brooks (eds). *1994 SCA Summer Conference Proceedings & Prepared Remarks*. Annandale, VA: Speech Communication Association.

Lieb, B., & Stacey, N. (Eds.). (1993). *Reaching the goals: Goal 5: Adult literacy and lifelong learning* (Prepared by the Goal 5 Work Group). Washington, DC: Office of Educational Research and Improvement, U.S. Department of Education.

Lieb-Brilhart, B. (1975). Speech Communication Association and American Theatre Association guidelines for speech communication and theatre in teacher education. *Speech Teacher, 24*, 343–364.

Lovdal, L. (1989). Sex role messages in television commercials: An update. *Sex Roles, 21*, 715–724.

Lumley, T., & O'Sullivan, B. (in press). The effect of test-taker gender, audience and topic on task performance in tape-mediated assessment of speaking. *Language Testing*.

Lynn, E. M., & Kleiman, D. (1976). *Improving classroom communication: Speech communication instruction for teachers* (p. 289) Falls Church, VA: Speech Communication Association.

Mahony, P. (1985). *Schools for the boys? Co-education re-assessed*. London: Hutchinson.

McConnell-Ginet, S. (1975). Our father tongue: Essays in linguistic politics. *Diacritics, 5*, 44–50.

McCroskey, J. C. (1998). *Communication and personality: Trait perspectives*. Cresskill, NJ: Hampton Press.

Mead, S. (2006). *The truth about boys and girls*. Washington, D.C.: Education Sector. Retrieved June 29, 2006, from www.educationsector.org

Miller, C., & Swift, K. (1991). *Words and Women: New language in new times, Updated*. New York: Harper Collins. (Original work published 1976 by Anchor Press/Doubleday).

Morreale, S. L., Backlund, P. M., & Dallinger, J. M. (1996). *Large scale assessment of oral communication: K–12 and higher education*. Annandale, VA: Speech Communication Association.

Morreale, S. P., & Backlund. P. M. (2002). Communication curricula: History, recommendations, resources. *Communication Education, 51*, 2–18.

Morreale, S., & Brooks, M. (Eds). (1994). *1994 SCA summer conference proceedings and prepared remarks*. Annandale: VA: The Speech Communication Association.

Morreale, S. P., Osborn, M. M., & Pearson, J. C. (2000). Why communication is important: A rationale for the centrality of the study of communication. Retrieved September 20, 2005. *Journal of the Association for Communication Administration, 29*(1), 1–25.

Mortenson, T. (2000). Fact sheet: What's wrong with the guys? Retrieved September 20, 2005, www.postsecondary.org/archives/Reports/Spreadsheets/Private.htm

Mortenson, T. (2001, February). Where the guys are not: The growing gender imbalance in college degrees awarded.Retrieved September 20, 2005. *Postsecondary Education Opportunity*. No. 104. Retrieved September 2005, from www.postsecondary.org/archives/

National Alliance for Business. (1996). *Challenge of change: Standards to make*. Washington, DC: Business Coalition for Education Reform.

National Assessment of Educational Progress (NAEP). (2005). *The nation's report card*. Retrieved January 27, 2005, from http://nces.ed.gov/nationsreportcard/

National Center for Educational Statistics (NCES). (2000, March 1). *Indicator of the month: Trends in the Reading performance of 9, 13, and 17-year-olds*. Retrieved June 3, 2004, from http://nces.ed.gov/pubsearch/pubsinfo.asp?pubid=2000006

National Center for Educational Statistics (NCES). (2002). Common Core of Data Resources. Retrieved September 23, 2003, from http://nces.ed.gov/ccd/

National Center for Educational Statistics (NCES). (2003). *National assessments of adult literacy: Defining literacy and sample items*. Retrieved November 30, 2005, from http://nces.ed.gov/naal/

National Coalition for Women and Girls in Education (NCWGE). (2002). *Title IX at 30: Report Card on Gender Equity*. Washington, DC: Author.

National Communication Association. (1998). The speaking, listening and media literacy standards and competency statements for K–12 education. Annandale, VA: Author.

National Council of Teachers of English. (2005). Retrieved January 7, 2006, from http://www.ncte.org/collections/adolescentliteracy

National Educational Goals Panel. (1998). Washington, DC: Author. Electronic publication available at http://govinfo.library.unt.edu/negp/page9-3.htm

Ng, S. H., & Bradac, J. J. (1993). *Power in language: Verbal communication and social influence*. Thousand Oaks, CA: Sage.

No Child Left Behind (NCLB). (2001a). *No Child Left Behind. Title I: Improving the academic achievement of the disadvantaged*. 107th Congress, 1st Session, December 13, 2001. (Printed version prepared by the National Clearinghouse for Bilingual Education). Washington, DC: George Washington University, National Clearinghouse for Bilingual Education.

No Child Left Behind (NCLB). (2001b). *No Child Left Behind. Title III: Language instruction for limited English proficient and immigrant students*. 107th Congress, 1st Session, December 13, 2001. (Printed version prepared by the National Clearinghouse for Bilingual Education). Washington, DC: George Washington University, National Clearinghouse for Bilingual Education.

Olsen, D., & Torrance, N. (1991). *Literacy and orality*. Cambridge, UK: Cambridge University Press.

Organization for Economic Co-operation and Development (OECD). (2001). *OECD Literacy Data*. Retrieved September 1, 2005, from http://www.oecd.org/dataoecd/0/45/14165144.xls (Tables A.11.3, A.11.5a, & A11.5b) and http://www.oecd.org/dataoecd/52/32/336699095.xls (Tables A9.5 & A9.5b).

Pearson, J. C., & West, R. L. (1991). An initial investigation of the effects of gender on student questions in the classroom: Developing a descriptive base. *Communication Education, 40*, 22–31.

Pearson, J. C., West, R. L., & Turner, L. H. (1995). *Gender and Communication*. Wm. C. Brown/Dubuque, IA.

Penelope, J. (1990), *Speaking Freely: Unlearning the lies of the fathers' tongues*. New York: Pergamon Press.

Pennock-Roman, M. (1994). *College major effects and gender differences in the prediction of college grades*. New York: College Entrance Examination Board.

Perseus Web Surveyor (2003). *The blogging iceberg*. Perseus Development Corporation. Online publication. Retrieved August 1, 2006. www.perseus.com/blogsurvey/iceberg.html

Peterson, E. E. (1991). Moving toward a gender balanced curriculum in basic speech communication courses. *Communication Education, 40*, 60–72.

Pickering, J. (1997). *Raising boys' achievement*. Stafford, CA: Network Educational Press.

Poindexter, P. M. (2000). Improving journalism education's diversity grade in the 21st century. Paper presented at the AEJMC Conference, Phoenix, AZ.

Poole, M. S., & Walther, J. (2002). Communication: Ubiquitous, complex, consequential. Washington, DC: National Communication Association.

Purcell, P., & Stewart, L. (1990). Dick and Jane in 1989. *Sex Roles, 22*, 177–185.

reAMAZE. (2005). Six factors of career success. Retrieved October 28, 2005, from http://www.rezamaze.com/PAGE-article_6_factors.html

Rideout, V., Roberts, D. F., & Foehr, U. G. (2005). *Executive Summary: Generation M Media Use in the Lives of 8–18 year olds* (A Kaiser Foundation Study). Retrieved December 30, 2005, from www.kff.org/entmedia/index.cfm

Rodriguez, E. M., & Ruppert, S. S. (1996). *Postsecondary Education and the New Workforce*. Denver: State Higher Education Executive Officers (SHEEO). (Funded by the U.S. Department of Education/OERI)

Rosenthal, A. (2002). Report of the Hope College Conference on Designing the Undergraduate Curriculum in Communication. *Communication Education, 51*, 19–25.

Rosser, P. (1989). *The SAT gender gap: Identifying the causes*. Washington DC: Center for Women Policy Studies.

Rosser, P. (1990). The SAT gender gap. *Women and Language, 13(2)*, 2–7.

Rosser, P. (2005). Too many women in college? *Ms. Magazine*. Retrieved October 30, 2005, from http://www.msmagazine.com/fall2005/college.asp

Rubin, R. B. (1982). Assessing speaking and listening competence at the college level: The communication competency assessment. *Communication Education, 52*, 19–32.

Rubin, R. B. (1985). The validity of the communication competency assessment instrument. *Communication Monographs, 52*, 171–185.

Rubin, D. L., Mead, N. A., & Daly, J. (1984). *Large scale assessment of oral communication skills: Kindergarten through grade 12*. Annandale, VA: Speech Communication Association.

Rush, R. R., Oukrop, C. E., & Creedon, P. J. (Eds.). (2004). *Seeking equity for women in journalism and mass communication education: A 30-Year update*. Mahwah, NJ: Lawrence Erlbaum Associates

Sadker, D. (2000, July 31). *The Washington Post* A19.

Sadker, M., & Sadker, D. (1994). *Failing at fairness: How America's schools cheat girls*. New York: Charles Scribner's Sons.

Sandler, B. R., & Hall, R. M. (1986). *The campus climate revisited: Chilly for women faculty, administrators, and graduate students*. Washington, DC: Association of American Colleges, Project on the Status and Education of Women.

Sandler, B. R., Silverberg, L. A., & Hall, R. M. (1996). *The chilly classroom climate: A guide to improve the education of women*. Washington, DC: The National Association for Women in Education.

Schegloff, E. A. (1982). Discourse as an interactional achievement: Some uses of 'uh huh' and other things that come between sentences. In D. Tannen (Ed). *Analyzing discourse: Text and talk*. Washington, DC: Georgetown University Press, 71–93.

Schulz, M. R. (1990). The semantic derogation of woman. In Cameron, D. (Ed.), *The Feminist Critique of Language* (pp. 134–137). London: Routledge.

Scott, K. P., Dwyer, C. A., & Lieb-Brilhart, B. (1985). Sex equity in reading and communication skills. In S. Klein (Ed.), *Handbook for Achieving Sex Equity through Education*. Baltimore, M.D: Johns Hopkins University Press.

Selzer & Co. (2002). *The great divide: Female leadership in U. S. newsrooms*. American Press Institute Pew Center for Civic Journalism. Retrieved January 7, 2006, from http://www.americanpressinstitute.org/content/745.cfm

Smith, M. W., & Wilhelm, J. D. (2002). *Reading don't fix no Chevys: Literacy in the lives of young men*. Portsmouth, NH: Heinemann.

Smith, M., & Wilhelm, J. D. (2004, March). 'I just like being good at it': The importance of competence in the literate lives of young men. *Journal of Adolescent & Adult Literacy, 47(6)*, 454–461.

Soderman, A. K., Gregory, K. M., & O'Neill, L. (1999). *Scaffolding emergent literacy: A child-centered approach for preschool through grade 5*. Boston: Allyn & Bacon.

Soderman, A. K., Gregory, K. M., & McCarty, L. I. (2004). *Scaffolding emergent literacy: C child-centered approach for preschool through grade 5* (2nd ed.). Boston: Allyn & Bacon.

Speech Communication Association. (date) *SCA Report on Sophomore Competences: Communication is life, essential college sophomore speaking and listening competencies* (Task force report). Annandale, VA: Author.

Spender, D. (1985). *Man made language*. London: Routledge & Kegan Paul, 2nd ed.

Spitzberg, B. H. (1987). Issues in the study of communicative competence. In B. Dervin & M. J. Voigt, (Eds.). *Progress in Communication Sciences* (Vol. 8, pp. 1–45). Norwood, NJ: Ablex.

Stewart, L. P., Cooper, P. J, & Stewart, A. D., with Friedley, S. (2003). *Communication and gender* (4th ed.). Boston: Allyn & Bacon.

Stone, P. (1996). Ghettoized and marginalized: The coverage of racial and ethnic groups in introductory sociology texts. *Teaching Sociology, 24*, 356–363.

Stump, R. W., & Selz, N. (1982). Basic skills for the world of work. In L. R. & S. Ward, *Basic Skills Issues and Choices: Issues in Basic Skills Planning and Instruction*. St. Louis: CEMREL, Inc.

Sunderland, J. (1996, October). *Girls and boys or just a class of individuals?: An illustration of gendered diversity*. Paper presented at annual meeting of the Organization for the Study of Communication, Language and Gender. Tempe, AZ.

Swanson, D. (1992). Review of Media Matter: TV Use in Childhood and Adolescence. [Review of the book *Media Matter: TV Use in Childhood and Adolescence*]. *Communication Theory, 2*, 87–90.

Tannen, D. (1990). *You just don't understand: Women and men in conversation*. New York: William Morrow.

Tannen, D. (Ed.). (1993). *Gender and conversational interaction*. New York: Oxford University Press.

Tannen, D. (1994). *Talking from 9 to 5: How women's and men's conversational styles affect who gets heard, who gets credit, and what gets done at work*. New York: William Morrow.

Taps, J., & Martin, P. J. (1990). Gender composition, attributional accounts and women's influence and likeability in task groups. *Small Group Research, 21*, 471–491.

Taylor, A., & Beinstein Miller, J. (1994, April). Gender diversity: Conceptions of femininity and masculinity. Paper presented at the Berkeley Women and Language Conference, Berkeley, CA.

Taylor, D. L. (2004/2005, December/January). 'Not just boring stories': Reconsidering the gender gap for boys. *Journal of Adolescent & Adult Literacy, 48(4)*, 291–298.

Tetenbaum, T., & Pearson, J. (1989). The voices in children's literature: The impact of gender on the moral decisions of storybook characters. *Sex Roles, 20*, 381–395.

Thorne, B. (1993). *Gender play: Boys and girls in school*. New Brunswick, NJ: Rutgers University Press.

Thorne, B., Henley, N., & Kramarae, C. (1983). *Language, gender and society*. Rowley, MA: Newbury House.

Thornton, M., & Brichenco, P. (2002, September). *Staff gender balance in primary schools*. Paper presented at the British Educational Research Association Annual Conference, Exeter, UK: University of Exeter.

Tuijnman, A. (2000). *Benchmarking adult literacy in America: An international comparative study*, (Statistics Canada, 2000), from: http://www.edpubs.org/

Turner, L. H., & Sterk, H. M. (Eds.). (1994). *Differences that make a difference: Examining the assumptions in gender research*. Westport, CN: Bergin & Garvey.

U.S. Department of Education. (2005). *FY 2002–2004 Biennial Report to Congress on the Implementation of NCLB, Title III, the State For-*

mula Grant Program. Washington, DC: Author. Retrieved March 31, 2005, from http://www.ncela.gwu.edu/oela/biennial05/index.htm.

Van Horn, C. (1995). *Enhancing the connection between higher education and the workplace: A survey of employers.* Denver: State Higher Education Executive Officers (SHEEO). (Funded by the U.S. Department of Education/OERI).

Venezky, R. L., Kaestle, C. F., & Sum, A. (1987). *The Subtle Danger: Reflections on the Literacy Abilities of America's Young Adults.* Princeton, NJ: Educational Testing Service.

Vonnegut, K. S. (1992). Listening for women's voices: Revisioning courses in American public address. *Communication Education, 41,* 26–40.

Warner, N., Ahlers, J., Bilmes, L., Oliver, M., Wertheim, S., & Melinda Chen, M. (Eds.). (1996). *Gender and belief systems: Proceedings of the fourth Berkeley women and language conference, April 19–20, 1996.* Berkeley, CA: Berkeley Women and Language Group.

West, C. (1995). Women's competence in conversation. *Discourse & Society, 6*(1), 107–131.

West, C., & Zimmerman, D. H. (1983). Small insults: A study of interruptions in cross-sex conversations between unacquainted persons. In B. Thorne, C. Kramarae, & N. Henley (Eds.), *Language, gender and society* (pp. 102–117). Rowley, MA: Newbury House.

Wittmann, W. W. (1988). Multivariate reliability theory. Principles of symmetry and successful validation strategies. In J. R. Nesselroade & R. B. Cattell (Eds.), *Handbook of multivariate experimental psychology* (2nd ed., pp. 505–560). New York: Plenum.

Wittmann, W. W. (2004, October). *Brunswik-symmetry: A key concept for successful assessment in education and elsewhere.* Paper presented at the Fourth Spearman Conference, Philadelphia.

Wittmann, W. W., & Süß, H.-M. (1999). Investigating the paths between working memory, intelligence, knowledge, and complex problem-solving performances via Brunswik symmetry. In P. L. Ackerman, P. C. Kyllonen, & R. D. Roberts (Eds.), *Learning and individual differences: Process, traits, and content determinants* (pp. 77–108). Washington, DC: American Psychological Association.

Wood, J. T. (1994). *Who cares: Women, care and culture.* Carbondale, IL: Southern Illinois University Press.

Wood, J. T. (2005). *Gendered lives: Communication, gender and culture.* Belmont, CA: Wadsworth.

Wood, J. T., & Inman, C. C. (1993). In a different mode: Masculine styles of communicating closeness. *Journal of Applied Communication, 21,* 279–295.

Wooten, B. (2004). Examining how masculinity affects journalism. In R. R. Rush, C. E. Oukrop, & P. Creedon (Eds.), *The Search for Equity: Women in Journalism and Mass Communication Education* (pp. 129–148). Mahwah, N.J.: Erlbaum.

Younger, M., Warrington, M., Gray, J., Rudduck, J., McLellan, R., Bearne, E., et al. (2005). *Raising Boys' Achievement.* University of Cambridge, Faculty of Education. Retrieved (June 20, 2006), from http://www.standards.dfes.gov.uk/genderandachievement/

GENDER EQUITY IN FOREIGN
AND SECOND LANGUAGE LEARNING

Cindy Brantmeier, * **Jeanne Schueller,** *
and Judith A. Wilde, * *and Celeste Kinginger*

INTRODUCTION

Learning a foreign (FL) or a second language (L2)[1] is a complex process involving a plethora of variables, and some research indicates that gender-based differences have interacted with this process. In fact, the number of FL and L2 investigations reporting gender-based differences has increased in recent years. Despite attention to gender-related research in language learning, gender continues to be seldom examined or discussed in this field. The purpose of this chapter is to showcase data related to gender and language learning, review findings of the most concentrated areas of research, and offer directions for future studies.[2]

The organization of this chapter will progress in the following manner: The first section on foreign and second language learning in adults reviews research on gender and L2 learners at the high school and university levels. We examine descriptive statistics by gender related to enrollment figures in language courses, results of advanced placement examinations, and language degrees granted as a catalyst for further exploration of gender-related issues in language learning. We also review the research on gender and adult FL/L2 reading comprehension, and then we synthesize studies involving gender and adult strategy use in L2 reading. This review is followed by the research on gender, identity, and language learning abroad.

In the second part of this chapter, the focus shifts to another group of language learners, English language learners in the K–12 setting. This section includes a historical context for the discussion and then a synthesis of the research findings for English language acquisition and content area achievement, including issues of gender and language of instruction.

---

*The bold face names are the Lead Authors.

[1]The terms "foreign language" (FL) and "second language" (L2) refer to the environment in which the language is being learned. Usually a FL is learned in a non–target language environment (such as learning Chinese in the United States), whereas an L2 is learned in a target language environment. Thus the learning of English in the United States is called English as a Second Language (ESL). Likewise, the learning of Spanish in the United States is often referred to as acquiring a second language or L2. An example of L2 is when a native English speaker is exposed to Spanish as a target language. Whereas L2 is used as a general term implying any second or foreign language being learned regardless of the target language environment, L1 refers to the native or home language.

[2]This chapter does not examine gender in the structure of languages. Rather, it focuses on language learning research. However it is important to note that in addition to the problems with uses of "false generics" (as in 'Any child can grow up to be whatever he wants to be,' which can be repaired to the gender-neutral and more inclusive plural, 'Children can grow up to be whatever they want to be'), there are other important issues. For example, some researchers point to the problem with Spanish grammar that dictates that for a mixed-gender group, people are referred to with masculine endings—even when there are one male and 20 females present (Lee, 2001, p. xiii). Hellinger and Bussmann and the many authors in their three edited volumes (2001) look at English, French, Spanish, and many other languages, assessing the grammatical, lexical, referential, and social issues involved in an analysis of gender in languages, including address forms, idiomatic and metaphorical expressions, and expected female–male discourse patterns. As linguist Suzanne Romaine (2001) writes, "If the world is constructed and given meaning through language, then our history, philosophy, government, laws and religion are the products of a male way of perceiving and organizing the world" (p. 156). She and many other researchers suggest that male actions and values become deeply embedded in linguistic structures and practices, a critical matter for all concerned about gender equity in education and all other aspects of life.

FOREIGN AND SECOND LANGUAGE LEARNING IN ADULTS[3]

The following three sections provide professionals with an examination of the relationships between gender, language learning, and instruction with adult learners. The topic of gender in language learning and instruction is approached from multiple perspectives, both inside and outside the classroom. A brief background section will provide some information on the participation of women and men in foreign and second language learning in the United States. Most research in this area has emphasized reading comprehension, strategy use, and study abroad. Each research section offers a theoretical framework, a comprehensive literature review, and empirical evidence to support assertions. Finally, the section confirms that with adults, gender does matter in foreign and second language settings (Chavez, 2001, p. xv).

Participation of Women and Men in Foreign Language Learning

Since the late 1890s, enrollment of high school students in FL courses has increased steadily. By 2000, almost 7 million students in American public secondary schools (grade 7–12) were enrolled in foreign languages (Draper & Hicks, 2002). Female high school students are completing FL courses at higher rates than their male peers. In a recent report by the National Center for Education Statistics, 36% of high school females, but only 24% of males, completed three or more years of foreign languages. Among both males and females who completed three or more years in a particular language, Asian/Pacific Islanders had the highest percent of students. Hispanics and Whites tied for second, Blacks in third place, and American Indians last (National Center for Education Statistics, 2003).

Females accounted for 70% of the examinees registered for the Advanced Placement (AP) French language exam, 49% of the test population for German, approximately 50% of those signed up for the Latin AP exam, and 65% of those registered for the Spanish exam (College Board, 2006). In both 1996 and 2005 groups of college-bound seniors who took the American Scholastic Aptitude Test (SAT), more females than males studied foreign languages for three or more years. With the exception of the German language in 1996 and 2005 and Japanese in 2005, women comprised a higher percent of students in all languages. Men were 53% and 54% of the German language students in 1996 and 2005, and 52% of the Japanese language students in 2005. In 2005 women made up 62% of the French language students, and 55% of the Spanish language students (College Board, 1996, 2005).

According to the latest results, female students appear to be performing better than their male counterparts on most national foreign language tests. (See http://collegeboard.com/student/testing/ap/exgrd_sum/2005.html). The tables show that in the five highest populated states (California, Texas, New York, Florida, and Illinois), more females than males are registering to take the AP test, but no conclusions can be drawn from the information provided regarding their relative performance. There are instances in which females perform better than males (defined as passing with a score of 4 or 5) in certain areas of the United States and on a specific test, but the results can completely conflict with results in another area of the country and in a different foreign language.

There has been a major increase in FL students at the postsecondary level. During the 1949–1950 academic year, 4,477 students at the postsecondary level were pursuing bachelor's degrees in a modern foreign language or literature. Of those students, females accounted for more than half—reaching a total of 2,731 students. During the 2002–2003 academic year, 14,843 students were pursuing bachelor's degrees in a modern foreign language or literature. Of those students, 10,641 of them were women and 4,202 men. Of the doctoral degrees granted in the 1949–1950 academic year, males earned 135 and females 33. By 2002–2003, males earned 282 doctoral degrees and females 467. These figures show the increased participation of female students compared to their male peers in foreign languages at the postsecondary level (National Center for Education Statistics, 2005).

Gender and Reading Comprehension

Before we move into an examination of research on gender, passage content, and foreign and second language reading, a brief mention of L2 reading models is essential to understand where gender fits in the reading process.[4] Interactive models of L2 reading emphasize different components involved in the process, and most models include and highlight the importance of comprehension (Bernhardt, 1991, 2005; Coady, 1979). L2 reading researchers have defined and discussed comprehension relying heavily on Bernhardt's (1991) model (Hammadou, 1990; Wolf, 1993; Young, 2000), and they concur that comprehension is a critical component of the interplay of mechanisms involved in L2 reading. Recently, Bernhardt (2005) reports that 50% of the variance in the L2 reading model is left unaccounted for. Gender may be a factor involved in the unexplained variance.

Clearly there is a bond between the reader and the text as readers experience and respond to the text. The reader's interpretation and understanding of the content of a text is grounded in personal identity. Undeniably, a characteristic of the reader's identity is gender, and a trait of a text is the topic or content. For some time now, researchers have investigated the influence of passage content, the reader's background knowledge, and topic

---

[3]This first section of the chapter was authored by Cindy Brantmeier, Jeanne Schueller, and Celeste Kinginger, respectively. The foreign language background information was identified by Sharon Barksdale, Feminist Majority Foundation intern from George Mason University during the Spring 2006 semester.

[4]As mentioned earlier in the chapter, the term L2 can refer to foreign and second languages combined or a second language learned in an environment where the target language is spoken.

familiarity[5] on L2 reading with ESL students of many different instructional levels at the university. Results have consistently revealed that a student's prior subject knowledge significantly influences the understanding of L2 reading materials (Carrell, 1981, 1983a, 1983b; Hudson, 1982; James, 1987; and Johnson, 1981). A closer look at studies with participants from only intermediate and advanced levels of ESL instruction reveals that content schemata, as seen as culturally familiar and unfamiliar content, continue to influence first and second language reading comprehension (Carrell 1987; Pritchard, 1990; Steffenson et al., 1979). When ESL students are more familiar with the reading topics, they comprehend better across all levels of language instruction. As is evidenced by the aforementioned research on passage content and background knowledge, the field of L2 reading has continuously shown great concern about the cultural contexts of the learner but has given surprisingly little attention to the culture of gender.[6] Are men and women[7] at the university level familiar with the same topics? Prior to 2000, only a few studies had considered male–female differences in L2 reading (Chavez, 2001).

We need additional research on the following questions: How does gender interact with topic familiarity and L2 reading comprehension across stages of acquisition? Does gender play other roles in L2 reading? Patterson (1995) reviewed all of the articles published in the *Reading Research Quarterly,* a leading journal of first language reading research, and reported that 45% of the research designs included a description of participants in terms of gender, but only one study included gender as part of the analysis. For the present chapter, all articles in *Reading Research Quarterly* were reviewed from 1995 to 2004. A total of 45 articles described participants in terms of gender, but it appeared that only six included gender as a factor in the analysis. This deficiency in reading investigations conducted in classroom situations may lead readers to believe that gender does not play a role in the reading process. On the contrary, researchers have examined gender and passage content on first language (L1) standardized exams and found that gender is an important factor in the reading process (Doolittle & Welch, 1989; Hyde & Linn, 1988; Silverstein, 2001). Indeed, in the communication skills chapter in this *Handbook,* the authors report that across recent studies, gender differences in reading are small. However, those authors also point out that in the United States, direct instruction in reading comprehension is generally limited to the first three elementary grades; they also note that individual, family, and societal factors need to be considered along with gender when doing reading research.

First language reading research concerning standardized exams has revealed intriguing insights that may be connected to L2 reading issues. Hyde and Lynn (1988) reported lower performance by females on the language part of the SAT (American Scholastic Attitude Test) and attributed this to the content of the readings of the test (technical material that is covered in physics and chemistry classes). Doolittle and Welch (1989) reported no overall performance differences by women on the reading sections of a standardized exam, but when they examined performance on specific passages, they found that females scored higher than males on humanities-oriented readings whereas males outperformed their female counterparts on passages with science-oriented topics. In her book on gender in the L2 classroom, Chavez (2001) suggests that topics of personal relevance on reading comprehension tests may affect male and female performance. Empirical investigations on L2 reading support the assertion that topic of text affects male and female reading achievement. Table 15.1 lists a summary of selected L2 investigations that consider readers' gender and comprehension across instructional levels with adults. The following discussion offers a brief review of relevant studies. See Brantmeier (2006) for more details.

With the national foreign language examination in the Netherlands, Bügel and Buunk (1996) found that males scored significantly better than females on the multiple choice comprehension items for essays concerning laser thermometers, volcanoes, cars, and football players, and females achieved significantly higher scores on the comprehension tests for essays on text topics such as midwives, a sad story, and a housewife's dilemma. They concluded that the topic of a text is an important factor in explaining gender-based differences in second language reading comprehension.

Contrary to Bügel and Buunk (1996), Young and Oxford (1997) reported no significant differences by gender with recall scores for all text topics (economics, presence of foreign cultures, and history), and there were no self-reported differences by gender in the familiarity ratings with passage topics or background knowledge of any of the passages. Moreover, there were no overall significant differences by gender in the use of global versus local strategies, with a few specific exceptions: males monitored their reading pace and paraphrased more often than females with the Spanish passages, and females solved vocabulary problems more often than males while reading the texts.

With students studying German, Schueller (1999) controlled for the effects of passage content and reported a higher degree of reading comprehension among females. She used readings that were equally familiar to both men and women. Her study was the first to examine gender as a variable when looking at the effects of top-down and bottom-up reading strategies instruction on the comprehension of literary texts. She found that males and females profit in similar ways from bottom-up and top-down strategy training. More specifically, every female group scored higher on comprehension than the male groups

---

[5]Researchers in applied linguistics have used the terms background knowledge and topic familiarity interchangeably. However, research by Alexander, Kulikowich, and Jetton (1995) has shown that these two factors are separate phenomena. A measure of background knowledge tests existing knowledge, and a test of topic familiarity often consists of self-reported questionnaires with rated familiarity items.

[6]Belcher (2001) offers a discussion about gender as a factor in research on L2 writing.

[7]Firth and Wagner (1997) contend that second language acquisition (SLA) research often sees participants in binary terms (male and female) and that researchers often ignore the social and contextual dimensions of language (p. 288). In the present article, gender is the label under which other forces emerge (Chavez, 2001).

TABLE 15.1   Summary of Investigations on L2 Reading, Gender, and Comprehension Across Instructional Levels with Adults

Title	Participants	Reading Passages	Results
Bügel & Buunk 1996 **Sex differences in foreign language text comprehension: The role of interests and prior knowledge**	High school students in their final year of study in the Netherlands who had 3 or more years of English as a foreign language.	11 passages: "Female" topics: (1) human relations (2) female professions (3) self care and care of others (4) home, cooking (5) art, literature, dance (6) pity (7) philosophy "Male" topics: (1) economy, money (2) politics (3) crime, war, violence (4) sports (5) machines, physics (6) automobiles	Females did significantly better on reading passages about human relations, education, care, art, and philosophy; males did significantly better on politics, sports, violence, economics, and technological topics.
Young & Oxford 1997 **A gender-related analysis of strategies used to process input in the native language and a foreign language***	Intermediate Spanish at the University level.	Passages taken from textbooks on the following topics: economics, presence of foreign cultures, and history	No significant differences by gender with recall scores for all text topics. No self-reported differences by gender in the familiarity ratings with passage topics or background knowledge of any of the passages.
Schueller 1999 **The effect of two types of strategy training on foreign language reading comprehension: An analysis by gender and proficiency**	Participants from second-year courses of German at the university level.	Passages were gender-neutral narratives (borne out by statistical analyses)	Schueller controlled for the effects of passage content and reported a higher degree of reading comprehension among females. More specifically, every female group scored higher on comprehension than the male groups regardless of strategic training and comprehension assessment task with only one exception: males with top-down (overall textual gist) strategy training did better than females on multiple choice (but not on recall).
Brantmeier 2002 **The effects of passage content on L2 reading comprehension by gender across instruction levels**	132 total; 76 Advanced Grammar (11 males; 65 females); 56 Advanced Literature (9 males; 47 females).	Cortázar passage on boxing; Poniatowska passage on housewife; topic familiarity questionnaire; written recall and multiple choice questions.	Effects of passage content on L2 reading comprehension by gender do not maintain at higher levels of instruction; significant topic familiarity differences do maintain.
Brantmeier 2003a **Does gender make a difference? Passage content and comprehension in L2 reading**	78 total (29 males, 49 females), Hispanic culture course (intermediate level; course beyond first two years of Spanish).	Cortázar passage on boxing; Poniatowska passage on housewife; topic familiarity questionnaire; written recall and multiple choice questions.	Reported significant topic familiarity differences by gender; passage content affects L2 reading comprehension by gender (for both multiple choice and recall).
Brantmeier 2003b **The role of gender and strategy use in processing authentic written input at the intermediate level**	78 total, (29 males, 49 females) from third year Hispanic culture course; fifth semester students of Spanish.	Cortázar passage on boxing; Poniatowska passage on housewife; writter recall and multiple choice questions. Questionnaire on global and local strategies.	Although findings of the present study indicated that men use more top-down strategies than women when faced with the Cortázar passage, results revealed that strategy use did not significantly correlate with performance on comprehension tasks. Type of strategy use did not predict comprehension at the intermediate level.

(continued)

308

TABLE 15.1 (*Continued*)

Title	Participants	Reading Passages	Results
Brantmeier 2003c **Language skills or passage content? A comparison of native and nonnative male and female readers of Spanish**	70 Costa Rican students studying EFL in Costa Rica, (27 males, 43 females).	Cortázar passage on boxing; Poniatowska passage on housewife; written recall and multiple choice questions; questionnaire on global and local strategies.	No gender differences in topic familiarity were reported. Results revealed significant main effects of female-oriented passage content by reader's gender on recall only. Costa Rican females outperformed their counterparts on recall for the Poniatowska passage, but they did not differ from males on recall scores for the Cortazar passage. No gender differences were found with strategy use, but results revealed a significant relationship between global strategy use and both comprehension tasks.
Brantmeier 2003d **Beyond linguistic knowledge: Individual differences in second language reading**	86 students (34 males, 52 females) enrolled in intermediate Spanish.	Cortázar passage on boxing; Poniatowska passage on housewife; written recall.	Males indicated they know more about the boxing passage, and they showed greater interest in and enjoyment of this passage. Similar results were found for the females with regard to the female passage. Males performed better than females on recall for the boxing passage, and females performed better than males on recall for the housewife passage. Lack of topic familiarity interfered with recall, but low levels of enjoyment and interest factors did not hinder performance on recalls.
Brantmeier 2004a **Gender and violence-oriented passage content in L2 reading**	68 students enrolled in advanced Spanish grammar courses.	Short stories by Horacio Quiroga, "The Decapitated Chicken" (DC), and Julio Cortázar, "Slaughter at Naptime" (SN); written recall and multiple choice questions; topic familiarity questionnaire.	Men and women reported being equally familiar with both text topics. Results revealed no significant main effects of readers' gender and topic familiarity with both passages. Performance by males and females on the recall comprehension task and multiple choice questions was significantly affected by the interaction of DC passage content and readers' gender. For the DC passage, females scored higher than the males on the recall task and multiple choice questions.

*This figure appeared in Brantmeier (2006) and is modified and reproduced here by permission of the author.

regardless of strategic training and comprehension assessment task with only one exception: males with top-down strategy training did better than females on multiple choice questions (but not on recall). Details concerning strategy use are discussed in the next section of this chapter.

Brantmeier (2002)[8] reported no significant gender differences in comprehension of two different passages with learners of Spanish at the advanced stages of acquisition. However, using the same reading passages, Brantmeier (2003a) reported significant interactions between readers' gender and passage content with comprehension among intermediate L2 learners of Spanish. Overall results indicated better performance by females on both recall scores and multiple choice questions. With participants from both the advanced grammar classes and literature courses, females achieved higher recall scores across pas-

sages than males. However, for the advanced levels, mean scores for multiple choice items across passages were the same for women and men. Brantmeier concluded that these findings may suggest that as learners advance in their language studies, differences between men and women in reading comprehension may depend on assessment tasks, such as recall and multiple choice, used to measure comprehension, rather than on passage content. Using the same reading passages but without focusing on comprehension, Brantmeier (2003b) reported that with readers at the intermediate level, there are no significant gender differences in strategy use when reading an L2, even though there are topic familiarity differences by gender. Brantmeier concluded that successful second language reading comprehension depends on a variety of factors, and with students from the intermediate courses of Spanish, important interacting

[8]Reading passages were taken from materials commonly used at these levels of Spanish language instruction. Brantmeier does not propose that male and female comprehension differences exist. Rather, the issue concerns male–female topic familiarity. Topic familiarity differences by gender were borne out statistically. There were no significant degrees of variation in topic familiarity levels within gender groups.

factors to be considered are readers' gender, passage content, topic familiarity, and assessment tasks.

With first language (L1) readers, Brantmeier (2003c) utilized the same reading passages and comprehension assessment tasks as Brantmeier (2002, 2003a) to determine whether comprehension is affected by passage content, and whether gender plays a role in native readers' strategy use. More specifically, Brantmeier (2003c) investigated whether gender differences by text topic will disappear with L1 readers of Spanish as they did with advanced L2 readers of Spanish (Brantmeier, 2002). The participants in the study were 70 adult (age 22–30) native Spanish speakers (27 men; 43 women) studying intermediate level English as a Foreign Language (EFL) in San José, Costa Rica. Results revealed no significant differences by gender for reported topic familiarity; however, with a passage about a housewife, results revealed significant main effects by gender on the recall assessment task. Females recalled more than males for this passage. No gender differences were found with strategy use. The findings echoed those in previous research that revealed higher achievement by females on L1 literacy tests with specific passage topics and with a writing task as a measure of comprehension.

To explore additional individual differences in L2 reading with learners from the intermediate levels of Spanish, Brantmeier (2003d) examined the effects of male and female self-reported levels of enjoyment, interest, and topic familiarity on written recalls. The outcome of males showing higher comprehension of a boxing passage and females showing higher comprehension of the female-oriented passage was only partially explained by the predicted variables. Enjoyment and interest mattered little at this level. Reading for meaning was hindered by a lack of topic familiarity, but not by the other individual difference variables.

More recently, Brantmeier (2004a) was interested in utilizing passages that yielded no topic familiarity differences by gender to examine male–female differences in scores with two comprehension tasks. She examined the topic familiarity levels and comprehension of advanced university-level male and female L2 readers with two different authentic violence-oriented texts of 700 words each. The results of this study showed that while male and female readers at the advanced levels of instruction indicated being equally familiar with violence-oriented content of the target culture, females outscored their male counterparts on L2 comprehension tasks (both multiple choice and recall) for the decapitated chicken (DC) text, which involved male-to-female violence. The overall results echo previous findings by Brantmeier where females may have an advantage over males in the free written recall procedure. Though the results provide support for a model of L2 reading that includes many variables (Bernhardt, 1991), one cannot assert that the apparent gender differences in the comprehension of the passage involving violence is actually due to the sex of the story's victim. Consequently, Brantmeier asserted that future research should further examine this issue.

With adults at various levels of language acquisition, some of the aforementioned L2 reading studies examined whether gender interacts with other variables to account for differences in the reading processes (strategies) and product (comprehen-

sion measured via various tasks). In the past, variations in research design and methods, especially regarding level of instruction and passage type, made it difficult to offer generalizations about L2 reading and gender (Brantmeier, 2001). For example, Bügel and Buunk (1996) utilized more advanced participants and the passages were essays; Young and Oxford's (1997) participants were from the intermediate level and the passages were essays taken from textbooks; Schueller (1999) used participants from second-year courses and the passages were gender-neutral narratives; Brantmeier's (2002; 2003a; 2003b; 2003c; 2004a) participants were from intermediate and advanced levels and the passages were authentic vignettes from short stories. Given the inconsistencies in research methods and procedures, it comes as no surprise that the results are somewhat disparate. However, the studies show how gender can be an important variable in L2 reading research.

Strategies Used in Foreign and Second Language Learning

Most recent research on gender and strategy use has focused on reading comprehension and processing of written texts. Consequently, this research should continue in order to achieve clear conclusions regarding gender and strategy use. Below we use the current body of research to:

1. provide a synthesis of previous research on learning strategies;
2. point out limitations of that research;
3. call attention to individual differences, such as the variety of proficiency levels, target languages, definitions of strategies, and research design; and
4. highlight future areas of research and pedagogical implications.

Cohen (1998) defines language learning and language use strategies as "those processes which are consciously selected by learners and which may result in action taken to enhance the learning or use of a second or foreign language, through the storage, retention, recall, and application of information about that language" (p. 4).[9] He goes on to explain that these strategies encompass both language learning and language use (p. 5). The strategies can be broken down into four categories depending on how they are used and are illustrated in Table 15.2 based on Cohen (1998, pp. 7–8).[10]

Learning styles also have been linked to L2 strategy use. One style preference that is particularly relevant in studies dealing with gender is global (or top-down) versus local (or bottom-up) processing of ideas. Global strategies focus on the "big picture" and include, for example, using background knowledge, brainstorming, skimming for an overview or gist, guessing meaning from context, and integrating new and old information. Local strategies deal with details and include focusing on linguistic elements and grammatical structures; dissecting words and phrases morphologically, syntactically, or phonetically; decoding meaning by using dictionaries, L1 cognates, or

---

[9]Cohen admits that whether or not learning strategies are consciously selected is controversial but argues that it is this element of awareness that "distinguishes *strategies* from those processes that are not strategic" (p. 4).

[10]See Cohen (1998) for a more complete description of other subsets of language learning and language use strategies.

TABLE 15.2   Types of Strategies of Adult Learners

Strategy Type	Language Learning and Language Use Strategies
Cognitive	Identification, grouping, retention, and storage of language material; retrieval, rehearsal, comprehension or production of words, phrases, and other elements of the L2
Metacognitive	Preassessment and preplanning, evaluation and postevaluation of language learning activities and language use events
Affective	Strategies that regulate emotions, motivation, and attitudes, e.g., those that reduce anxiety and promote self-encouragement
Social	Actions chosen in order to interact with other learners and native speakers, e.g., asking questions or cooperating with others on tasks

grammatical categories; and translating from the L1 into the L2 (Schueller, 2004). Some basic trends have been found in how males and females use or report using L2 strategies. First, females tend to report using more strategies overall and using them more frequently than males (Young & Oxford, 1997). Second, most, though not all, studies have found that females rely more frequently on global strategies than males, who are more likely to use local strategies (Bacon, 1992; Bacon & Finnemann, 1992; Young & Oxford, 1997). Third, female learners utilize more social strategies than males (Politzer, 1983). In their state-of-the-art review of research on gender differences in strategy use, Young and Oxford (1997) found eleven studies dealing with gender differences in strategy use of nonnative speakers of English. Their review summarized in Table 15.3, which supplies the most up-to-date summary of the research on this topic prior to 1997, appears to support the above claims.

Nearly all of the studies found that females used more strategies than males. One study showed that females make use of more global and males local strategies (in this case for listening comprehension) (Bacon & Finnemann, 1990) but none showed the reverse, i.e., that females used more local strategies. Several studies indicate that females were more often associated with social strategies than males (Bacon & Finnemann, 1990; Oxford et al., 1993; Oxford et al., 1996; Politzer, 1983). In the following section, we review studies that have appeared since Young and Oxford (1997).[11] Table 15.4 shows a summary of investigations on L2 strategy use and gender including relevant research questions, participants and procedures, and results.

The nine studies summarized in Table 15.4, all appearing between 1997 and 2005, seem to have found fewer significant differences overall in gender and strategy use than the eleven studies reported on by Young and Oxford (Table 15.3) that all appeared between 1983 and 1996. Although the findings vary, some trends emerge. When significant differences between females and males were found, females outperformed males (Schueller, 2004), and females report using certain strategies more than males (El-Dib, 2004; Khalil, 2005), including cognitive and metacognitive (Woodrow, 2005). These findings are consistent with those summarized in Fig. 15.3.

Several of these studies used an instrument called the Strategy Inventory for Language Learning (SILL) to assess strategy use. While self-report instruments such as the SILL have been used in scores of studies around the world, it is unclear whether males and females are equally able to assess their own strategy use or are even reliable in doing so. In fact, it may be the case that learners who employ more strategies may in turn be more aware of their strategy use. Barnett (1988) found a correlation between the two and states that "as strategy use increases, student perception of strategy use also increases" (p. 156).

Some researchers offer reasons why females and males differ in performance. Schueller (2004) considers several reasons why, with few exceptions, the females in her study outperformed the males. She proposes that females may have done better on the recall task because of its global nature and cites earlier research such as Oxford (1993), which suggests that females are more global learners and males more analytical learners, and Chavez (2001), who speculates that female students may be more inclined to please the teacher than are the male students. For example, females may have deliberately written more on the recall task and therefore scored higher on that reading comprehension assessment measure. El-Dib (2004), whose study took place in Kuwait, suggests that the "cultural milieu . . . determined the types of strategies used by either sex" (p. 93).

Despite obvious variability in the findings reported on here and in Young and Oxford (1997), certain pedagogical implications can be drawn based on the studies outlined above. There seems to be a consensus that promoting awareness and understanding of how strategies work and how to apply them appropriately will enhance student learning of the L2. Many of the researchers reported on here (Brantmeier, 2003b; Khalil, 2005; Kocoglu, 1997; Schmais, 2003; Schueller, 2004; Young & Oxford, 1997) suggest a similar course of action for classroom instruction: explicit strategy instruction. This sentiment is shared by Cohen (1998), who recommends that "explicitly describing, discussing, and reinforcing strategies in the classroom—and thus raising them to the level of conscious awareness—can have a direct payoff on student outcomes" (p. 19).

However, as Cohen (1998) points out, there is nothing intrinsically effective about any given strategy, and that selecting successful strategies depends on the task, individual learner differences, and language proficiency. Strategy training should "explicitly teach students how, when, and why strategies can be used to facilitate their efforts at learning and using a foreign language" (p. 69). In addition, strategy instruction should "help students explore ways that they can learn the target language more effectively, as well as to encourage students to self-evaluate and self-direct their learning" (p. 69). Learners need to first become aware of the strategies already in their repertoire and then add to these so they can pick and choose depending on what they are trying to accomplish. Cohen reports on how strategy training has been implemented in a classroom setting, workshops, peer tutoring, language textbooks, and videotaped mini courses. Table 15.5 outlines one step-by-step approach for implementing explicit in-class strategy training discussed by Cohen (1998, pp. 72–73.)

---

[11]The author does not claim that this review summary is exhaustive but rather is a representative sample of available research.

TABLE 15.3   Gender Differences in Strategy of Native Speakers of English Learning Other Languages*

Study	Languages Learned	Strategies Females Used More Than Males	Strategies Males Used More Than Females
Politzer (1983)	French, German, Spanish	Social strategies	None
Ehrman and Oxford (1989)	Many	General study strategies Strategies for meaning Self-management strategies Functional practice strategies	None
Oxford and Nyikos (1989)	French, German, Italian, Russian, Spanish	Formal rule-based strategies General study strategies Conversational input–elicitation strategies	None
Nyikos (1987)	German	After training: Color-only memory strategies	After training: Color plus picture memory strategies
Oxford, Park-Oh, Ito, and Sumrall (1993)	Japanese	Cognitive strategies Social strategies Affective strategies	None
Wildner-Bassett (1992)	German Russian Spanish	Compensation strategies Social strategies	None
Bacon and Finnemann (1990)	Spanish	Global listening strategies Making friends with Spanish speaker (social strategy)	Local listening strategies
Bacon (1992)	Spanish	Metacognitive strategies Cognitive strategies; (used formulaically)	Linear processing strategies; reference to native language
Brecht, Davidson, and Ginsberg (1990)	Russian (in Russia)	None	Social strategies Affective strategies
Zoubir-Shaw and Oxford (1995)	French	Strategy types: Learning conjugations Learning grammar Learning from context	Strategy types: Learning from various activities
		Specific strategies: Using color-coded cards for gender, using pink/blue for gender, using other colors for gender, using flash cards, using organized lists, accepting rules at face value, reviewing textbook material	Specific strategies: Concentrating more on oral communication than structures, being impeded by not knowing the meaning of a word (neg.); not comparing and accepting rules as a separate system (neg.); looking for the general meaning, idea, or theme
Oxford et al. (1996)	Spanish	Strategy types: Cognitive strategies Memory strategies Social strategies Affective strategies	Strategy types: None
		Specific strategies: Trying out new vocabulary learning strategies	Specific strategies: Thinking about my progress; judging success of a given strategy

*This figure appeared in Young and Oxford (1997, pp. 50–52) and is reproduced here by permission of the authors.

Gender, Identity, and Language Learning Abroad

The study abroad context is viewed by many U.S. foreign language professionals as the quintessential learning experience in which students have unlimited access to the kinds of activity that promote the development of communicative competence.

Confidence in the study abroad experience is such that one university recently abolished its home curriculum in foreign languages in favor of systematic sojourns abroad for students (Schneider, 2001). However, systematic research has yet to demonstrate universal effectiveness of study abroad for language learning. Rather, findings of empirical studies point to the

TABLE 15.4   Summary of investigations on L2 Strategy Use and Gender*

Study	Research Questions (Related to Gender and Strategy Use)	Participants/Procedure	Results
Young & Oxford (1997) **A gender-related analysis of strategies used to process written input in the native language and a foreign language**	1. Are there significant differences in the types of strategiees male and female learners use to process FL and L1 texts? 2. Are there significant differences in FL and L1 recall scores between males and females?	49 native-English-speaking students (26 females; 23 males) ranking from first- to fourth-year Spanish. Students read 3 passages (2 in TL; 1 in L1) based on level. Subjects participated in think-aloud protocols and a reading recall task for each passage. There were three different text types: TL-edited, TL-authentic, and L1.	**Q1: No difference in mean use of strategy by gender.** Females tended to use global strategies more often than males, though not significantly more. Some strategies were used more often by males (monitoring pace and reading behavior and paraphrasing) and some by females (solving vocabulary problems and acknowledging lack of background knowledge). **Q2: No significant differences in recall scores by gender.**
Kocoglu (1997) **The role of gender on communication strategy use**	Are there similarities and/or differences between male vs. female Turkish EFL learners in the use of communication strategies (CSs) while interacting with NS of the TL?	Turkish learners of English were paired with NS of English to form 20 dyads (10 same-sex and 10 opposite-sex pairs).	**All subjects used more CSs when interacting with female rather than male NSs of English.** Author suggests that the former were more "cooperative and more encouraging in conversations than the latter" (p. 4). Thus, the gender of the interlocutor is more important than the gender of the student in this study on CSs.
Shmais (2003) **Language learning strategy use in Palestine**	Is there a significant difference in strategy use due to gender among Arab EFL majors?	19 males and 80 females enrolled as English majors at a university in Palestine. All subjects had studied TL formally for 8 years. To measure students' self-perception of themselves as learners, students were asked to report on their actual progress in English (GPA) and to rate themselves on a scale of 1–3 to indicate how successful they thought they were at listening, reading, writing, and speaking the TL (1 = very good, 2 = good, 3 = poor). The SILL (in the L1) was used to measure strategy use.	**No main effect for gender on strategy use was found.**
Brantmeier (2003b) **The role of gender and strategy use in processing authentic written input at the intermediate level**	Are there gender differences in readers' overall global and local strategy use with two L2 authentic texts at the intermediate level of language instruction?	78 participants (29 men and 49 women) in a fifth-semester Spanish course. All were NSs of English and had not studied abroad. Subjects read two glossed passages, completed a written recall and MC task, reported their degree of familiarity with the topic, and filled out a strategy-use questionnaire.	**No significant gender differences were found in the number of global and local strategies that participants used to process the two texts.**
Schueller (2004) **Gender and foreign language reading comprehension: The effects of strategy training**	Do males and females benefit similarly in different types of prereading strategy training? And do differences in strategic benefits linked to gender vary by proficiency level?	128 university students (78 females and 50 males) enrolled in a second-year German course were divided into two treatment groups (prereading training in either top-down or bottom-up strategies) and a control group. In the treatment groups, prereading	**The interaction of treatment by gender was not significant.** There were no significant differences between males' and females' mean recall and MC scores within each treatment group. But significant gender differences in performance showed that females outperformed males on both tasks regardless of treatment except on the MC test.

(continued)

TABLE 15.4   (*Continued*)

Study	Research Questions (Related to Gender and Strategy Use)	Participants/Procedure	Results
Schueller (2004) (continued)		instruction consisted of one training session. Following the treatment, subjects read a text and completed an immediate recall protocol and a MC test.	Males with top-down training scored higher on the MC test than all other groups (male and female) and males in the control group outperformed females in the control group on the MC test.
El-Dib (2004) **Language learning strategies in Kuwait: Links to gender, language level, and culture in a hybrid context**	Is there a significant difference between gender and the factors identified (i.e., those that explain variability) on the SILL?	504 college students (260 females and 244 males) in Kuwait completed the SILL.	**Results indicate significant differences between male and female reported use of strategies for three of the factors identified.** Females used two types of strategies more than males (cognitive–compensatory and repetition and revision); males used one strategy type more than females (active naturalistic).
Khalil (2005) **Assessment of language learning strategies used by Palestinian EFL learners**	Do language proficiency level and gender affect strategy use among Palestinian EFL learners?	378 high school and university students (194 females, 184 males) completed the SILL.	**Gender has a main effect on strategy use.** Six categories of strategies were identified. Of those, two were used significantly more by females (memory and metacognitive); 16 specific strategies on the SILL were reported used significantly more by females; 2 strategies were used more by males (using flashcards and physical actions to remember new words.
Nisbet, Tindall, & Arroyo (2005) **Language learning strategies and English proficiency of Chinese university students**	Is there a difference in learning strategy preference and proficiency by gender?	168 third-year English majors (139 females, 29 males) in China completed the SILL.	**No significant gender differences were found.**
Woodrow (2005) **The challenge of measuring language learning strategies**	Is there a significant effect of gender on strategy use? (The study's main research goals were to assess the usefulness, reliability, and validity of the instrument.)	249 (137 females, 112 males) English-for-academic-purposes students in Australia completed a 20-item Likert-scale survey based on Schmidt and Watanabe (2001).	**Females are more likely to use cognitive and metacognitive strategies than males.**

*Note the following abbreviations: target language (TL), native language (L1), native speaker (NS), Strategy Inventory for Language Learning (SILL), communication strategies (CS), multiple choice (MC).

TABLE 15.5   Explicit In-Class Strategy Training

Oxford et al. (1990) Emphasizes strategy awareness and benefits of strategy use, practice, and self-evaluation	1. Ask learners to do a language activity without any strategy training. 2. Have them discuss how they did it, praise any useful strategies and self-directed attitudes they mention, and ask them to reflect on how the strategies they selected may have facilitated the learning process. 3. Suggest and demonstrate other helpful strategies, mentioning the need for greater self-direction and expected benefits, and ensure that the students are aware of the rationale for strategy use. Learners can also be asked to identify those strategies they do not currently use and consider ways they could include new strategies in their learning repertoires. 4. Allow learners plenty of time to practice the new strategies with language tasks, 5. Show how the strategies can be transferred to other tasks. 6. Provide practice using the techniques with new tasks and allow learners to make choices about the strategies they will use to complete the learning task. 7. Help students understand how to evaluate the success of their strategy use and how to gauge their progress as more responsible and self-directed learners.

significance of individual differences in a variety of contexts and learning situations (e.g., Freed, 1995; Huebner, 1995; Marriott, 1995) or suggest that language development in study abroad may be less dramatic than anticipated (Hoffman-Hicks, 2001).

Gender-related effects, while widely acknowledged, have received relatively little systematic attention. An important exception is Polanyi's (1995) narrative study of language learner journals, a study complementing the findings of a research project in which gender was determined to be a major factor predicting gain scores on the Oral Proficiency Interview (a standard test of speaking ability) by American sojourners in Russia (Brecht et al., 1995). In this statistically robust study involving 686 subjects, male gender was shown to offer a significant advantage in learning to speak Russian. Polanyi's analysis of learners' stories revealed that stories of men's experience often highlighted situations in which the participants were framed as competent participants in communicative settings well before they actually were able to participate, or situations in which their needs were anticipated and met without need of discussion. The women, on the other hand, rarely were set up to participate actively in social interaction and recounted stories of recurrent and unwanted interactions with Russians. These women perceived many of their encounters with Russians as sexist in nature or as constituting harassment; their access to language learning opportunities was limited correspondingly.

Another example is found among the earliest qualitative studies of second language acquisition (SLA) in John and Francine Schumann's inauguration of the "diary study" (Schumann & Schumann, 1977) based on narrative documentation of their experiences as language learners abroad. The focus of the initial publication of this work was the discovery of what the Schumanns then termed "personal variables," or individual characteristics that would intervene among more robust social and psychological factors such as social distance, language dominance patterns, attitude, or motivation to determine the outcomes of SLA. Subsequently, Francine Schumann published a re-analysis of her diary focusing explicitly upon the identity-related aspects of her attempts to learn Farsi in Iran as a female Peace Corps participant (Schumann, 1980). In this article, F. Schumann turns away from the neutral positivism of the earlier writing, in which the language learner is equated with a gender-neutral pinball tracing a pathway through a machine studded with variables (Schumann & Schumann, 1977, p. 248). Instead, she examines the difficulties she encountered in gaining access to language learning as a foreign woman, citing the negative attitudes of the expatriate community toward their host community and the desirability of interaction in English, her native language. Most significant is the fact that many of the interactive settings required for language learning were not available to women and that no attention to this reality was given in the Peace Corps predeparture training sessions at the time of Schumann's participation:

I've come to believe after keeping a language journal that the task of learning the language of a country like Iran is far greater an endeavor for a woman than for a man. . . . In order to learn a language, one must practice it and be immersed in it, ideally in the target culture. There the opportunities abound for the language student. No one ever informed the female language learner that in any given daily contact situation in Iran a good many of these opportunities are "off bounds." (Schumann, 1980, p. 55)

Attempts to understand the *qualities* of the study abroad experience thus have come to complement studies emphasizing its demonstrable impact on language competence. Wilkinson (1998), for example, designed an ethnographic study to investigate what kinds of interactions influenced learning of French in France. While interpreting her results, she stresses the complexity of the setting:

. . . the immersion context, far from the protective environment of a language lab, is a complex, multidimensional setting where verbal communication holds significant, yet often invisible, cultural and social meanings, in addition to the literal denotations which students are already trained in the classroom to recognize. (p. 132)

Analysis of the study abroad setting, according to Wilkinson, must take into account both the types of contact the students develop and also their reactions to and perceptions of these contacts. Given the ubiquity of gender and gendered identities in the shaping of social relations, it follows that, within the literature on study abroad, gender often emerges as a defining characteristic of the experience.

Table 15.6 summarizes seven studies investigating gender issues in study abroad programs. Two studies have focused on the effects of public displays of behavior perceived as sexist. Twombly (1995) conducted a study based on interviews and focus group discussions with students conducted upon arrival and after 4.5 months in various programs situated in Costa Rica. Interpretation of these data centers on two strongly emergent themes. First, the young American women involved in the study initially were quite perturbed by the practice of "piropoing," or catcalling in the street, because they felt targeted by this practice both for their gender and for their status as foreigners. "The results of our interviews suggest that for many of the students we interviewed and observed, at least the first four months of the sojourn in the foreign country were not an immersion experience, but an alienating experience in which gender played a major role. To compound the situation, those responsible for study abroad programs were not fully aware of this 'gender dynamic' for female students" (Twombly, 1995, p. 2). Second, women in the programs reported that it was much more difficult for them to make female friends rather than male friends, due in part to differences in university-related institutional cultures and gender roles in the United States and in Costa Rica. Although the report on the study does not detail the preparation that these students received, the author recommends explicit treatment of gender-related issues both in orientation programs and in courses taking place during the study abroad sojourn.

Talburt and Stewart (1999) undertook an ethnographic study of a summer program in Spain, exploring the relationship between students' formal and informal experiences for an entire cohort. Students in the group came prepared with a minimum of two years of Spanish study and enrolled in a course designed to guide them as observers of culture through training in ethnography and practice in focused observation. Within this context, their attention was drawn persistently to the plight of Mishiela, the only African American student on the program, whose experience was marked by "hypervisibility" in that she was subjected to continuous and humiliating emphasis on race

TABLE 15.6   Summary of Studies Investigating Gender in Study Abroad

Study	Participants	Method/Major Focus	Results
Schumann, F. (1980)	The author, learning Arabic and Farsi in Tunisia and Iran as an adult Peace Corps volunteer	Diary study attempting to pinpoint personal variables influencing second language acquisition	Access to language learning opportunities may be limited by female gender
Polanyi (1995)	Participants in a large-scale study of language development in Russia	Narrative study of learner journals, focusing on stories of gendered experience	Women report failure to achieve access to learning opportunities in social interaction, and sexual harassment
Twombly (1995)	Undergraduate participants in various study abroad programs in Costa Rica	Interviews, focus group discussions with content analysis of emergent themes	Women in the program are disturbed by the practice of "piropos," find it difficult to make female friends
Talburt and Stewart (1999)	A focal participant (Misheila) in a group of 35 under-graduate students in a short-term program in Spain	Ethnographic account of the relationship between student experiences in and out of class	Race and gender become salient to the participant and to her classmates
Siegal (1996)	One focal participant in a study of professional women learning Japanese in Japan	Case history including conversation analysis of interactions involving power imbalance	The observation of native speaking norms for the performance of gender in Japanese conflicts with the learner's core identity.
Kline (1998)	A cohort of students in a study abroad program in France	Ethnography of literacy as social practice	Following perceived sexual harassment, female participants take refuge in literacy and in the American group's hybrid subculture.
Churchill (2005)	A male focal participant, Masa, in a group of Japanese learners of English on a short-term study abroad program in the U.S.	The influence of gender as social practice on the learning of English	Masa's male gender contributed to a more favorable environment for development of oral proficiency at home and in school than that of his female classmates

and sexuality in her interactions with Spaniards. In Misheila's words (translated from her Spanish):

For me while I have been in Spain I notice that the African woman is a symbol of sexuality. When I walk in the streets I receive comments on my skin and sexual commentaries. . . . It's very difficult for me and I don't think it is something cultural, it is an ignorant mind. When they make commentaries to me I feel that they're taking advantage of me being different and not having command of the language. And I don't like it. (p. 169)

The researchers offer a close analysis of an in-class discussion where Misheila's negative appraisal of the situation is analyzed by students and their instructor, demonstrating the potential for development of critical thinking about race and gender within an embodied cultural curriculum where race and gender are problematized explicitly and used as a fulcrum for cultural understanding.

Siegal (1996) presents a case study focusing on the role of learner subjectivity in the acquisition of sociolinguistic competence by European women learning Japanese in Japan. The study, part of a longer ethnographic project, examines the conflict concerning sociolinguistic appropriateness experienced by one learner in conversation with her professor, where unequal power and positionality exert influence upon the quality of the interaction. Although she did understand the pragmatics of

appropriate demeanor for a woman in Japanese society, in attempting to craft a voice for herself as a professional woman in Japanese, the student manipulated honorifics, modality, and topic control in ways that sometimes resulted in inappropriate language use. The study emphasizes the conflict inherent in this learner's need to honor her interlocutor through appropriate behavior yet to maintain "face" as a professional woman. Siegal's study is representative of the profession's burning interest in the interface of language use and identity at advanced levels of proficiency, where second language resources for the performance of identity may conflict with learners' desired presentation of self, a conflict that can engender learner resistance to native speaking norms both within and across learning contexts (DuFon, 2000; Ishihara, 2003; Kinginger, 2004a; Ogulnick, 1998; see also Kramsch, 1997 on the "privilege of the non-native speaker" to adopt or decline native-like behaviors).

A study by Kline (1998) examined literacy practices among American students studying in France. In her study, the female participants also encountered behavior they perceived as sexist or humiliating, opting, for example, to take refuge in literacy at the expense of attempts to develop social networks outside their own American "hybrid subculture."

Finally, Churchill (2005) provides a case study examining the experience of gendered language learning by a male Japanese high school student ("Masa") in a short-term study abroad program in the United States. Masa's minority status as one of four men in a class of 47 students contributed to his isolation and academic difficulties at home, but in the study abroad context this status was turned to his advantage. Not only did he enjoy placement as the only study abroad student in his host family (in contrast to the females who were placed in groups), a situation that afforded significant opportunity to interact in English, but he also was welcomed immediately into peer group activities, such as the cross-country team, where he was able to profit from a network of peers and corresponding interactive resources. Assessment of Masa's oral proficiency at the end of the program is compared with that of a female participant with a similar predeparture profile. This assessment, along with the qualitative findings, supports the overall assessment of study abroad as a relatively favorable environment for the development of speaking skill by male learners.

Language Learning, Narrative, and Transformation of Gendered Identities in Study Abroad

The unacknowledged issue in the study abroad literature is that additional language learning *inevitably* involves exposure to new identity-related resources. New gender ideologies and performances may present conflict with the old. For adult learners, when the array of gender-related resources developed in the first language does not translate easily into the second, the adult learners must first understand the nuanced meanings invoked and then choose how to proceed and whether, or to what extent, they shall adopt these new resources as their own. Pavlenko (2001) illustrates how transformation of gendered identities is played out in the cross-cultural life writing of immigrants and sojourners abroad. Beginning with the assertion that gendered identities are social and cultural constructs, she argues the case for cross-cultural differences in normative masculinities and femininities. Gendered styles are produced in speech communities, and individuals produce themselves as gendered subjects through accommodation to these styles. Although gender performance in a particular society is not predetermined, a limited range of gendered subjectivities is validated in a given society at a given moment. Thus, "a transition to a different culture, a different society, may involve change in how one views and performs gender" (Pavlenko, 2001, p. 135). Through careful exegesis of language learning memoirs, Pavlenko illustrates how border crossers encounter, celebrate, and resist ideologies of gender. Those who choose to assimilate may experience this transition as liberation from oppressive childhood socialization or a as a painful process of self-translation in which previous closely held identities are lost.

Gender, Language Socialization, and Ideology in Study Abroad

Contemporary work on the role of gender in study abroad therefore takes a broad view of gender as one aspect in the life-

long process of language socialization and views the study abroad experience as a time of choice, when learners are exposed to the gender-related identity options and challenges associated with advanced competence in their second language, and when investment in language learning is either furthered and enhanced or withdrawn (Norton, 2000; Pavlenko, 2002).

Kinginger examined the cases of two women whose learning of French are exceptional: "Alice," who overcame extraordinary social obstacles to her learning of the language in study abroad; and Nancy Huston, who grew up in Anglophone Canada yet has become a celebrated French language writer. Alice (Kinginger, 2004a), a young working-class woman from a migrant family in the southeastern United States, initially associated learning the French language with higher class values and experiences, as reflected in the American media and textbook industry's portrayal of France as a place where consumption of rarified, elite products takes place in an ambiance of cultured gentility. In addition, however, her drive to learn was fueled by personal aspirations: to overcome fatalism and self-deprecation and to turn her past experiences of impermanence and transience on their head and make of them a virtue. After a struggle to enter a university-sponsored study abroad program, Alice was confronted with the reality of daily life in France as an American woman whose only option for practice in speaking French was "to let old, drunk French men buy her drinks." Alice suffered a severe bout of depression before aligning her motives in concert with her new surroundings, fighting for access to conversations in French, and ultimately gaining the ability to appreciate and to participate in acts of sociopolitical critique.

The case of the French–English bilingual writer Nancy Huston (Kinginger, 2004b) also offers an illustration of the ways in which foreign language learning offers an attractive potential for the performance of new and different emotional selves. Although she grew up in western Canada, Huston is now a celebrated French-language writer, with over 25 major works to her credit. In her autobiographical works, Huston repeatedly praised her second language not only for its civilizing influence upon her subjectivity but also for the feeling of unlimited exoticism she derives from self-expression in French and the access to literary creativity she derived from this medium. Huston claims to have used French as an escape route from the boredom of her childhood, a drab world of Anglo-Saxon propriety set on a backdrop of rugged western pursuits involving rodeos and cheap beer, from which she was buoyed away by French—and the French feminist movement—into an adulthood of refinement, autonomy, self-esteem, and creative satisfaction.

A more recent project examines the mediating role of identity, including gender and gender-related ideologies, in the language socialization of 23 American undergraduates spending a semester in France during the spring semester of 2003.[12] Employing a hybrid methodology, the study examines both qualitative data in the form of journals and interviews, and outcomes on formal assessments of gain in academic proficiency and awareness of sociolinguistic variation in French. In the design of assessments, the intent of the study is to discover how learners'

[12]This research is supported by CALPER (Center for Advanced Proficiency Education and Research), a National Foreign Language Resource Center (United States Department of Education, CFDA 84.229, P229A020010-03). However, the contents do not necessarily represent the policy of the Department of Education, and one should not assume endorsement by the federal government.

access to a range of social settings and networks "in the field" impacts their knowledge of both formal and informal language use.

Kinginger and Whitworth (2005) explore three individual case histories resulting from this project. These case studies reveal that gender, as a key aspect of identity, plays a significant role not only in the qualities of access to learning opportunities reported in the narrative data but also in the interpretation that learners bring to these events and, ultimately, in the development of their language competence. As in the case of the Polanyi (1995) study cited above, young men's accounts of their experience tend to be relatively gender neutral and include scenes in which their language competence is explicitly fostered through assisted performance by well-meaning others. "Bill," for example, entered the study abroad context as a beginning learner of French and reports a broad array of formal and informal encounters in which his use of French is actively assisted and encouraged. His test results show dramatic gains in both academic and informal varieties of the language. Young women's accounts, however, include numerous references to gender as embodiment (Gergen, 2001), to the objectification of women, and to sexual harassment. "Deirdre," for example, experienced an increasing sense of alienation from French society due in part to her perception of gender-based discrimination and public harassment, ultimately limiting her informal interactions in French to strictly utilitarian service encounters. Her test results show little gain in academic French (including a drop in her reading score) and only a modest improvement in her awareness of informal usage.

Neither Bill nor Deirdre appear to have questioned their own conceptions of gender or its performance during this experience; for Bill, few challenges were presented whereas for Deirdre the challenges were overwhelming. Transformation of gendered identity, in Pavlenko's sense of the term, does develop into an issue, however, in the cases of young women such as "Jada," who retain an investment in language learning and choose to craft a gendered identity appropriate for the new context. Although she initially took refuge in the hybrid subculture of American participants in the program (Kline, 1998), for Jada this process involved close observation of the strategies of female expert users of French, strategies that would permit her to seize control of interactions and thereby further her goal of engaging in learning opportunities. In other words, her socialization as a user of French passed through an initial stage of reflection and accommodation to local gendered norms. If Jada's gain scores on the tests of formal and informal French are modest, it may be because of the challenges she encountered in the initial phases of her experience.

Achieving Equity in Study Abroad Programs for Language Learning

Clearly, the study abroad context poses considerable challenges for the project of achieving gender equity in educational settings. When learners sojourn abroad, they discover different ways of understanding and performing gender, many of which may conflict with the norms of American society, including, of course, the very desirability of gender equity itself. Meanwhile, in the United States materials for language learning, tests and other assessments and programs to prepare students for the study abroad experience remain fixed on the goal of generalizability, a comfortable neutrality centered on the "one" standard learner (the white, middle-class male), critiqued in strong terms by Polanyi in the conclusion to her 1995 study:

That impersonal "one" who "needs to know" or "learns a language" is the issue. Who "one" is is a factor of one's native talent for language learning, one's educational background and motivation but it is also a product of one's gender, one's class, one's race, one's sexual orientation, one's health and degree of ableness. Ultimately, every language learner is alone with a unique experience, an experience tailored to, by and for that individual. (p. 287)

At the very least, the studies examining gendered identity and study abroad suggest that this aspect of the experience be recognized and acknowledged. Ideally, students would be informed about the norms governing performance of gender in the societies they are studying, and the gender-related challenges to language learning that their predecessors have encountered and recounted in their stories would be shared, discussed, and subjected to critical assessment.

ENGLISH LANGUAGE LEARNERS IN THE K–12 SETTING[13]

The focus of this section of the chapter is on gender differences in language acquisition and content achievement among second language learners in the K–12 school setting. These students often are referred to as learning L2 (English, usually their second language); whether, and to what extent, they maintain L1 (their first, or home, language) is more controversial. Although there is research that explores best practices for these English language learners (ELL), there is a dearth of research that includes gender as a variable of consequence.

The following sections provide an overview of the current status of research in the field of educating ELL students. To understand the challenges more fully, we first provide a brief historical context for the discussion, including a description of students now being served by bilingual English as a Second Language (ESL) programs, and then a synthesis of the research findings for English language acquisition and content area achievement, including issues of gender and language of instruction.

Historical Context

Although it is not the purpose of this section to detail the history or current practices of bilingual education in the United States, an overview of both provides a context for understanding the discussion of gender-related issues. The majority of this

---

[13]This second section of the chapter was authored by Judith A. Wilde.

section will provide a synthesis of the research that considers gender differences among ELL students and within ELL student achievement. As we will see, the area is one in great need of research. Although it is fairly common for the numbers of male and female students to be specified, it is uncommon for researchers to analyze the results by sex.

The founders of the United States chose to adopt neither "an official language nor a government-sanctioned body to regulate speech" (Crawford, 1999, p. 22). At that time, the most common languages in the United States came from northern Europe as well as from 250 to 1,000 American Indian language groups. Although some states published official documents in languages other than English, Congress refused to do so, and although some states authorized bilingual education, others mandated English-only instruction (Ovando, 2003).

During the 19th century, immigrants formed communities that actively maintained their languages, religions, and cultures. Today's remnants of these communities are in cities that have a "Little Korea" or a "Chinatown," such as South Philadelphia with its distinctly Italian flavor or Boston's Irish reputation.

In 1900, 4% of the nation's children were German-speaking, the largest non–English speaking group in the country. In addition, 9 states taught students in German, Scandinavian languages were used to teach students from those countries in eight states, and Spanish was used in southwestern states because of the large number of students from Mexico and Central America (Kloss, 1998). Still today, New Mexico is a constitutionally bilingual state, requiring Spanish-English education and translation of official documents.

The late 19th and early 20th centuries marked a distinct change in policies. Two sets of policies marked repressive changes: (a) a restrictive Indian language policy was designed to "civilize" American Indians and, for military reasons, to contain them on reservations and (b) combining anti-Catholic sentiment with a fear of "foreigners" speaking another language, English-only laws were passed and focused on the largest non-English speaking group in the country—Germans. With World War I, the hostility against Germans increased and caused the United States to push for monolingualism; even teaching German as a FL was eliminated from most school districts. As described by Ovando, the "push for homogeneity became a well-established pattern within schools during the first half of the 20th century. . . . World War II served as the first wake-up call regarding the United States' inadequacies in foreign-language instruction. Because language, math, and science skills were essential for military, commercial, and diplomatic endeavors, these subjects became a high priority in the national defense agenda during the cold war period" (2003, pp. 5, 7). While courses in foreign language, math, and science were added to many high school curricula, they had little

effect on female students, much less ELLs or female ELL students. Even with the need for individuals with a good command of a second language, ELL students still were encouraged to replace L1 with English, and native English-speakers were encouraged to add a FL to their knowledge of English. The only real exceptions were the Navajo Code Talkers of World War II, all males serving in the military.

Language education within the United States became one of "subtractive bilingualism" in which a student's home language is "removed" and replaced with English. Canadians and Europeans have maintained a standard of "additive bilingualism" in which another language or languages are added to the student's knowledge base, enhancing school achievement as well as L1 literacy skills (Gómez, 1990; Thomas & Collier, 1997).

The first federal legislation that addressed the education of native-born and immigrant ELL students was in 1968, when the Bilingual Education Act (BEA) was passed as part of President Lyndon Johnson's War on Poverty. This was the first official federal recognition of the needs of ELL students (Stewner-Manzanares, 1988). Congress knew that ELL children faced "serious learning difficulties" in English-only classrooms and believed that this created "a unique and perplexing educational situation" (PL 90-247, §701). Shortly thereafter, the *Lau v. Nichols* case was filed as a class-action suit against the San Francisco school district on behalf of 1,800 Chinese students denied an equal education because of their limited English skills. Ultimately, the Supreme Court ruled that merely offering the same facilities, textbooks, teachers, and curricula do not constitute an equal education for all children. These two events, the BEA and *Lau v. Nichols,* sparked a major and ongoing battle over the "best" way to teach students who come to school speaking a language other than English.

Instructional Approaches for ELLs

The first BEA (which was reauthorized for the sixth time within the No Child Left Behind Act of 2001) was purely experimental; research in educating ELL children[14] was just beginning. The purpose of the BEA was to provide financial assistance, on a competitive grant basis, to develop "new and imaginative elementary and secondary school programs to meet these special educational needs" (§702).

Since that time, three general approaches to teaching ELL students have been developed: (a) ESL approaches that focus on teaching students in English as they learn both academic content and English language proficiency; (b) transitional bilingual approaches that begin by teaching students academic content in L1 and gradually transition them into all-English class-

---

[14]The federal definition has changed little across the reauthorizations of the BEA. Currently, "the term 'limited English proficient,' when used with respect to an individual, means an individual (A) who is aged 3 to 21; (B) who is enrolled or preparing to enroll in an elementary school or secondary school (C)(i) who was not born in the United States or whose native language is a language other than English; (ii)(I) who is a Native American or Alaska Native, or native resident of the outlying areas; and (II) who comes from an environment where a language other than English has had a significant impact on the individual's level of English language proficiency; or (iii) who is migratory, whose native language is a language other than English, and who comes from an environment where a language other than English is dominant; and (D) whose difficulties in speaking, reading, writing, or understanding the English language may be sufficient to deny the individual (i) the ability to meet the State's proficient level of achievement on State assessments . . . ; (ii) the ability to successfully achieve in classrooms where the language of instruction is English; or (iii) the opportunity to participate fully in society" (NCLB, Title IX).

rooms; and (c) dual language immersion approaches, whose goal is to develop biliteracy (i.e., full proficiency in two languages) in two student groups—native L1 speakers and native L2 speakers learning together. Figure 15.1 more fully defines these approaches and some of their permutations, grouped into those that focus on teaching in two languages and those that focus on teaching in one language.

Research on these approaches has led to general agreement among proponents of bilingual education that the longer students remain in classes that support their home language, the greater their ultimate proficiency in English as well as their achievement in academic content areas. In this context, full two-way immersion approaches generally are the most effective for students, though most difficult to implement (c.f., Crawford, 1997a; Krashen, 1991; Lindholm-Leary, 2005a,b; Ramírez, Yuen, & Ramey, 1991; Slavin & Cheung, 2003; Thomas & Collier, 1997, 2002). Among opponents of bilingual education, true bilingual education only serves to encourage students' use of L1, does not enhance their academic achievement, and slows their learning of English (c.f., Baker, 1990, 1992; Crawford, 1997b; Krashen, 1991). However, there are caveats to some of the research on both sides of the issue—especially when viewed in light of the preference for true experimental research found within the current No Child Left Behind Act.

Some recent data indicate that there are no overall differences among these approaches but that differences are more situation- and context-specific (e.g., Parrish, Merickel, Pérez, Linquanti, Socias et al., 2006). These researchers studied student achievement in California since the passage of Proposition 227.[15] Analyzing data from about 1.5 million ELL students and 3.5 million English-fluent students, they found no overall differences in academic performance across educational approaches for ELL students but did note that "limitations in statewide data make it impossible to definitively resolve the long-standing debate underlying Proposition 227" (p. III-1). They also indicated that the probability of an ELL student gaining full English proficiency after 10 years in California schools was less than 40 percent. They did not analyze the data for gender differences.

Student Demographics

It is estimated that there are approximately 5.1 million ELL students in grades K–12 in the United States (Padolsky, 2005) who speak over 400 languages, including at least 137 American Indian languages (Crawford, 1997a; Hopstock & Stephenson, 2003). About 40% of these students are in California with Texas, Illinois, New York, and Florida also having large populations of ELLs. Spanish is the predominant language of these students, spoken by about 75% of them. Other high frequency languages include (with highest numbers first) Vietnamese, Hmong, Korean, Arabic, Haitian Creole, Cantonese, Tagalog, Russian, and Navajo (Hopstock & Stephenson, 2003).

While many people think of ELL students as immigrants, the majority are citizens, born in the United States. For instance, in Arizona, a state with many ELL students and sharing a border with Mexico, 72% of Spanish-speaking elementary school ELLs are U.S. citizens, and 94% of ELL children under the age of five are U.S. citizens (García, 2005). Nationally, it is estimated that 80% of ELL students are U.S. citizens (Urban Institute, 2006).

K–12 ELL Students' English Language Proficiency

Federal law requires that the English language proficiency of ELLs be assessed each year until they are deemed proficient in English. English language proficiency is a separate construct from English language arts achievement or English reading achievement; the assessments for each are different. All ELLs are tested for identification when they enter a school system, and all ELLs must be assessed each year to determine their progress in attaining English language proficiency. Data from California's English language proficiency test are provided here because the large number of students tested allows a more accurate view of ELL students as a whole.

In California, the assessment used is the state-developed California English Language Development Test (CELDT), an individually administered assessment that has been used since 2001–2002. The data from the first five administrations are available but only for specific groups of students, not for individual students. Thus analyzing data for significant or important differences in not possible, but looking for observable patterns in those data is possible.

The data below are for students who have been in California schools for at least 12 months and are quasi-longitudinal because there is no assurance that the same students reported upon in 2001–2 remained in California schools in 2005–6. Students are identified by 2001–2 grade level. In 2001–2 there were about 601,000 girls tested and about 657,000 boys tested; in 2005–6 the number tested had increased to about 619,000 girls and 707,000 boys.

Scaled scores are reported for the CELDT.[16] The CELDT provides separate scores for English listening/speaking, reading, and writing skills; in keeping with reading data reported for adult FL learners earlier, Figs. 15.2 and 15.3 provide reading skill scores for ELL students.

These two figures clearly show a variability in scores within a generally linear pattern. In 2001–2, girls appeared to have somewhat higher reading skills than boys, but five years later the gap across grades was somewhat less although girls maintained their advantage at each grade level—these probably would be significant due to sample size. The patterns for both girls and boys are similar for those who were in grades 3 through 8 in 2001–2. The greatest growth was in that first year (2001–2 to 2002–3) with growth decreasing with age. However, the boys who were in 2nd grade in 2001–2 appear to have had

---

[15]Proposition 227, endorsed by voters in 1998, strongly supports an English immersion model in which ELL students are taught in English with minimal L1 support. Analyses by Parrish et al., included statewide student-level data from 1997–98 to 2003–4 as well as data gathered in the Los Angeles Unified School District from 1997–98 to 2002–3.

[16]Scaled scores are a form of standardized scores that range from 200 to 800, with an average of 500.

All language instruction educational programs have as goals the development of proficiency in English and academic achievement. The differences among them lie in their linguistic goals: (a) proficiency in one language (English) or two (English and one other) and (b) whether and to what extent the native language is used to deliver content, particularly as students develop English.

Programs that focus on developing literacy in two languages include:

- *Two-way immersion or two-way bilingual*
  - The goal is to develop strong skills and proficiency in both L1 (home language) and L2 (English)
  - Includes students with an English background and students from one other language background
  - Instruction is in both languages, typically starting with smaller proportions of instruction in English and gradually moving to half in each language
  - Students typically stay in the program throughout elementary school
- *Dual language*
  - When called "dual language immersion," usually the same as two-way immersion or two-way bilingual
  - When called "dual language," may refer to students from one language group developing full literacy skills in two languages—L1 and English
- *Late exit transitional, developmental bilingual,* **or** *maintenance education*
  - The goal is to develop some skills and proficiency in L1 and strong skills and proficiency in L2 (English)
  - Instruction at lower grades is in L1, gradually transitioning to English; students typically transition into mainstream classrooms with their English-speaking peers
  - Differences among the three programs focus on the degree of literacy students develop in the home language (L1)
- *Early exit transitional*
  - The goal is to develop English skills as quickly as possible, without delaying learning of academic core content
  - Instruction begins in L1, but rapidly moves to English; students typically are transitioned into mainstream classrooms with their English-speaking peers as soon as possible
- *Heritage language* **or** *indigenous language program*
  - The goal is literacy in two languages
  - Content taught in both languages, with teachers fluent in both languages
  - Differences between the two programs: heritage language programs typically target students who are non–English speakers or who have weak literacy skills in L1; indigenous language programs support endangered minority languages in which students may have weak receptive and no productive skills—both programs often serve American Indian students

Programs that focus on developing literacy only in English include:

- *Sheltered English, Specially Designed Academic Instruction in English (SDAIE),* **or** *Content-based English as a Second Language (ESL)*
  - The goal is proficiency in English while learning content in an all-English setting
  - Students from various linguistic and cultural backgrounds can be in the same classroom
  - Instruction is adapted to students' proficiency level and supplemented by gestures, visual aids, and so on
  - May be used with other methods; e.g., early exit may use home language for some classes and SDAIE for others
- *Sheltered English, Specially Designed Academic Instruction in English (SDAIE), Content-based English as a Second Language (ESL), Sheltered Instruction Observation Protocol (SIOP)*
  - The goal is fluency in English, with only ELL students in the class
  - All instruction is in English, adjusted to the proficiency level of students so subject matter is comprehensible
  - Teachers need receptive skill in students' L1 and sheltered instructional techniques
- *English language development (ELD)* **or** *ESL Pull-out*
  - The goal is fluency in English
  - Students leave their mainstream classroom to spend part of the day receiving ESL instruction, often focused on grammar, vocabulary, and communication skills, not academic content
  - There is typically no support for students' L1

Note: Modified from work by Linguanti (1999) and Zelasko & Antunez (2000).

FIGURE 15.1. Title IX Coordinator Roles and Responsibilities for Local School Districts

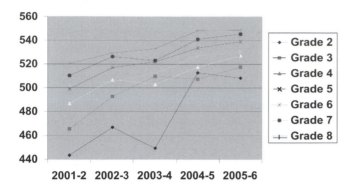

FIGURE 15.2. Boys' English language reading skills, as measured by the California English Language Development Test (CELDT), from 2001–2002 through 2005–2006

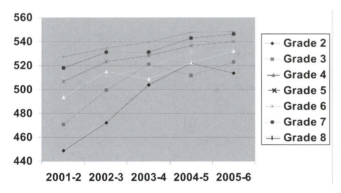

FIGURE 15.3. Girls' English language reading skills, as measured by the California English Language Development Test (CELDT), from 2001–2002 through 2005–2006

a very different pattern from their female peers. The girls' scores grew until a slight drop in 8th grade while the boys dropped greatly in 4th grade, increased more dramatically in 5th grade, and dropped slightly in 8th grade. (Note that scores are aggregated across all instructional approaches and programs.)

It is interesting to note that students' scores on the CELDT in 2001–2 match their grade levels—i.e., grade 2 has the lowest scores and grade 8 the highest—but five years later, there have been some changes, particularly focusing on those who are designated as 2nd and 3rd graders.

Taking into account achievement levels, researchers have reported gaps between the achievement of ELL students and their monolingual English-speaking peers. Indeed, Thomas and Collier reported a "typical 25 NCE[17] achievement gap between ELL and native-English speakers" (2002, p. 5). In order for the

achievement gap to close or narrow, ELL students must demonstrate more academic growth than their average English-speaking peers each year, and for several years. Proponents of bilingual education report that the strongest predictor of student achievement in L2 (English) is the amount of formal schooling in L1 (home language) (e.g., Thomas & Collier, 2002). Perhaps as a result of low achievement scores and concomitant low English proficiency skills, ELL students' reported dropout rates are well above 40% (Alva & Padilla, 1995, Padrón & Waxman, 1992). Furthermore, Hispanics born outside the United States, have dropout rates as high as 44% (Institute for Education Statistics, 2002). Boys' dropout rates usually are higher than girls' dropout rates.

K–12 ELL Student Achievement

Nearly all research on bilingual education has attempted to determine which of two or more instructional approaches has resulted in higher content area achievement or English language proficiency scores for ELL students (see, for instance, Parrish et al., 2006 or Thomas & Collier, 2002). Background variables often studied include language background, socioeconomic status (SES), schooling in the native country, and home language. If gender is mentioned, it generally is as a descriptor of students, not as a variable to be analyzed.

This section is divided into research that focuses on reading and language arts, research that focuses on math and science, and research on more generalized academic achievement as measured by standardized tests. Reviews of literature are synthesized first, then specific research studies. Unless otherwise indicated, results mentioned are either statistically significant or have large effect sizes. Unfortunately, these data point again to the paucity of research that includes gender as a variable of interest.

Reading and Language Arts Achievement

Padrón (1992) reviewed the literature to find that elementary-aged ELL students reading in their L2 (i.e., English) use fewer strategies and different types of reading strategies than English-monolingual students and that mature readers and female students are more likely to use a variety of cognitive strategies when reading. She also added that there has been little research examining the effects of cognitive strategy instruction on the strategies that ELL students use in reading text that is written in English. This finding may be because higher-level thinking skills generally are not taught until students have become proficient in English; many educators assume that students are not able to comprehend such strategies until they can use the language well. She did not report differences in cognitive strategies based on gender. Slavin and Cheung (2003) synthesized studies of beginning readers that used true experimental designs.

[17]NCEs are normal curve equivalents, a normalized score ranging from 1 to 99, with an average of 50 and a standard deviation of 21.06. When NCEs remain the same from one year to the next (growth = 0), then students have gained what they were expected to in that one year of school. When NCE's increase, then students have learned more than expected for a single school year. For more information, see Wilde & Sockey, 1995 or Wilde, 2004.b

While they did not identify gender differences, apparently because none were analyzed, they did find that the research largely supported the use of L1, particularly in two-way immersion approaches.

The following examples of individual studies that included gender analysis point out some of the complexities of this research and the inconsistencies of the results.

In a study of Spanish-speaking students in true bilingual classrooms[18] in grades 1 through 8 of a large urban school district in Arizona, Medina (1993) found that girls scored significantly higher than boys in reading, as measured by a test of reading in Spanish.

In a large ($N = 3{,}089$) two-year study of K–12 students, about 25% of whom were Southeast Asian and American Indian ELL students, Hallam (2001) did not find gender differences in reading but did find them in writing at the high school level; he also found differences with Hispanic, American Indian, and older Asian American students as well as students living in poverty scoring significantly lower in reading and writing than White and noneconomically disadvantaged students. This last finding is supported by a secondary analysis of previously published data by Krashen and Brown (2005). They found that high-SES ELL students performed about as well on tests of reading in English as did low-SES students fluent in English. We may be able to hypothesize that Hispanic and American Indian females who live in poverty have lower scores, but these data generally have not been analyzed by researchers.

Math/Science Achievement

Padrón and Waxman, in their 1992 review of the literature on math and science, also focused on linguistically and culturally diverse students and at-risk students. They pointed to much literature reporting "what is wrong" with the education of these students: (a) emphasizing basic skills only, to the exclusion of higher cognitive skills and higher-order thinking skills—for ELL students, this means that they will not be taught such skills until they master English; (b) differing teacher expectations and treatment of at-risk students—for ELL students, this means a focus on remediation, drill-and-practice content repetition, and questions related only to low-level knowledge; (c) focusing classroom order on teacher-centered instruction—for ELL students, this means less effective instruction because they tend to respond better to student-centered inquiry models; and (d) ignoring cultural differences—for ELL students this means instruction that does not meet their cultural and educational needs. Krashen and Brown (2005) also included math in their secondary analyses of previously published data. In this case, they found that high-SES ELL students clearly outperformed low-SES fluent English proficient students on tests of math achievement.

Medina's study of Spanish-speaking students in true bilingual classes also analyzed data for math and science. No gender differences were found in math or science among students in grades 2 through 8, as measured by a Spanish-language test (1993).

Academic Achievement

Wilde (2006)[19] currently is studying programs for ELL students in a large East Coast school district. Individual middle school and high school student data are available for the state-mandated annual assessments of reading, grammar, listening, and math and a state-mandated English language proficiency test that measures reading, writing, speaking, and listening, as well as a state-mandated test of achievement in reading, writing, math, and science. The results of each test are reported in different types of scores. For the years 2003–4 and 2004–5, Wilde analyzed data for over 2,000 ELL students. Factors analysed included school level (middle school or high school), English proficiency, ethnic/racial group, and gender. In no analysis of any of the test scores was gender a significant factor—neither alone nor in an interaction. There were differences in some analyses based on the English proficiency of students, on the ethnic/racial group of students, and on interactions of English proficiency and ethnic/racial group.

Davenport et al. (2002), used the Minnesota Basic Skills Test (BST) to report on the achievement of 8th grade students in years 1996–2001 (a series of cross-sectional analyses based on 51,923 to 65,913 students each year). Since 1998 the BST has been used to satisfy the high school graduation requirement; students who do not score at least 75% correct on the test in 8th grade have opportunities in grades 9 through 12 to retake the test. In secondary analyses, NAEP data were used to confirm the results of the BST. Results are disaggregated by gender, five ethnic groups, ELL/non-ELL, and SES, among others; unfortunately, the researchers do not analyze interactions (more specifically, gender by English proficiency). Davenport and his co-authors first report on an overall analysis indicating that average math scores have remained consistently around 80% correct whereas reading scores have gradually risen from about 72% correct in 1996 to 83% correct in 2001 (p. 8). The researchers found that there were consistently more males than females tested. Results of interest[20] to the current work include those listed in Fig. 15.4.

In the largest study of ELL education to date, and one of the few longitudinal studies based on archival data, Thomas and Collier (2002) reported on data collected from 1996 to 2001, with 210,054 ELL students in grades K–12, from 16 urban and rural research sites in 11 states and speaking more than 80 different languages. The dependent variables for the analyses of these data were nationally standardized tests of achievement using NCE scores. The first portion of the study looked at ELL students' long-term achievement in English total reading scores to measure academic problem solving across the curriculum, using tests such as the ITBS, CTBS, Stanford 9, and Terra Nova. These

---

[18]"True bilingual" is used here to designate any educational approach that relies, at least for some period of time, on teaching students in their L1.

[19]This study currently is in progress. At this time, the large county-wide school district wishes to remain anonymous. This request is reflected in the reference list as well. However, it can be said the district serves ELL students through a variety of methods including bilingual and ESL approaches and that the students come from a wide variety of language backgrounds and countries; nearly 75% of the students are native Spanish-speakers.

[20]All results reported are significant, but due to the large number of students in the study, the results may not represent important differences in scores.

Gender differences in reading favored females and have remained about the same across the years of the study; gender differences in math initially favored males but have decreased across time.

- Analyses of NAEP data showed larger differences favoring females in reading and males in math; these differences did not appear to change over time. No gender differences were found in any of the tests for any content area or the problem-solving total reading subtest.

ELL students do less well in both reading and math than either non-ELL students whose home language is not English (i.e., a student whose home language is not English but who is proficient enough in English to participate in mainstream classrooms) or non-ELL students whose home language is English. While the researchers report that the differences between ELL and non-ELL are narrowing, they also indicate that the rising scores appear to be "real performance gains" for reading, but for math may be an effect of changes in classifying students—regardless, the rate of decrease is small.

- ELL students scored relatively lower in reading than in math. Furthermore, there was a hierarchy to the scores of the three groups with nonELL/English home language students scoring highest, non-ELL/other home language group scoring about 7 to 8 percentage points lower, and the ELL group scoring a further 12 to 15 percentage points lower.

ELL students with individual education plans (IEPs) were compared to students who were neither ELL nor had IEPs. The differences in both reading and math were the largest reported in the study (approximately 2.5 standard deviations).

There was a hierarchy to these scores as well. English fluent students in mainstream classrooms (non-ELL/non-IEP students) scored 80% correct or better in both math and reading; ELL students in regular bilingual/ESL classrooms (ELL/non-IEP students) scored next, with English fluent students in Resource classrooms (non-ELL/IEP students) scoring third in the group, and the ELL students in Resource classrooms(ELL/IEP students) generally getting less than half of the answers correct.

Analyses based on ethnicity show that initially only white students and Asian students passed the BST in math and initially only white students passed the BST in reading although Asians began passing reading in 2000. Looking at the scores more generally, the highest scores are achieved by white students, who score consistently higher in both reading and math than (in descending order of average scores) Asians, American Indians, Hispanics, and African Americans.

- NAEP scores showed similar, though less extreme, differences among the ethnic/racial groups.

Finally, students living in poverty scored much lower in both reading and math than students who were not economically disadvantaged. Indeed, these differences appear to be increasing.

- NAEP results are consistent with these findings.

FIGURE 15.4. Summary of Analyses of the Minnesota Basic Skills Test and NAEP Data from Davenport et al., 2002.

students had entered the school district with little or no proficiency in English in grade 1 and were tested through the highest grade completed to date, including subtests for math, science, and social science.

Overall, findings indicated that there was a hierarchy to the five program-types studied. Students in English immersion classes (the lowest scores on standardized achievement tests in English) and students in the two-way immersion classes (the highest scores on standardized achievement tests in English) had the most extreme scores. There were gender differences in two subject areas: math and science. In both case, Hispanic males outperformed Hispanic females by 4 NCEs in math and 6 NCEs in science on the 11th grade tests administered in English.

The second portion of the study involved native-Spanish speakers' long-term achievement on nationally standardized tests administered in Spanish (Aprenda 2, SABE). No gender differences were found in any of the types for any content area or the problem-solving total reading subtest.

Finally, the study looked at native English-speakers' long-term achievement on nationally standardized tests in Spanish and English for those who had participated in two-way bilin-

gual immersion classes. These students maintained their English proficiency, added literacy in a second language to their skills, and achieved well above the 50th NCE in all subject areas on the test in English and equaled or outscored their monolingual English peers on all measures. There were no gender differences noted.

There are two specific instructional models that have been used with ELL students to increase their reading skills and general achievement levels. The first is Success for All (SFA), developed by Robert Slavin and his colleagues at Johns Hopkins University. The program has reading and math components and was developed primarily for students living in poverty. SFA recently has been translated into Spanish and used in two-way immersion programs

The "definitive evaluation of the reading outcomes" of SFA was a Department of Education-funded evaluation involving 41 Title I (high poverty) schools throughout the United States, many of which enrolled high numbers of ELL students (Borman et al., 2006; Slavin et al., 2006). Schools were randomly assigned to use SFA or continue with the programs they had been using in grades K–2. At the end of the 3-year study, students in the SFA schools were achieving at significantly higher levels. The final analytical samples were composed of 1,672 students from the 20 SFA treatment schools and 1,618 students from the 18 control schools, each of which included about 50% female students. However, gender was not analyzed and was reported only to demonstrate the equal distribution of students by gender, ELL status, and special education status.

The second instructional model, recently developed by the Center for Applied Linguistics (CAL), is an approach for standardizing the ESL "sheltered instruction" approach for ELL students in English-medium classrooms.[21] Over seven years, CAL collaborated with practicing teachers and researchers from the Center for Research on Education, Diversity, and Excellence (CREDE) to develop the Sheltered Instruction Observation Protocol (SIOP) and accompanying instructional model and professional development activities. Research has shown that the SIOP model is effective with both ELL and English-fluent students (Echevarria, Short, & Powers, 2006). However, again, there is no mention of the gender of the students or whether there are gender differences.

Summary

An overview of the findings from the few studies identified and reviewed for this section is presented in Table 15.7. As can be seen, the results support the oft-found findings of studies with monolingual English-speakers in the United States: There is some female advantage in reading and language arts and male advantage in math and science. However, we should not be so bold as to generalize these results to all language groups and all cultures without specifically studying reading and language arts, math, and science in more language groups and more cultures—and including those variables interacting with gender within the analyses.

In one of the few examples of a culture-gender interaction, a language arts curriculum was designed for Hawai'ian native students at the Kamehameha Early Education Program (KEEP). It was found that the students preferred to learn in same-sex dyads. When the program was moved to the Navajo Reservation, many aspects had to be tailored to Navajo culture—including that students preferred to learn in small peer groups (Tharp & Yamauchi, 1994). (Also see the chapters on gender equity among Asians and Latinos and Latinas.)

What are we to conclude from these various research studies? First, there is a distinct lack of research that looks at gender and ELL status, gender and ethnicity, gender and culture, or gender and poverty status. And, because ELL status, poverty status, culture, and ethnicity are highly related (students who speak a language other than English tend to be ethnic minorities, poor, and from minority cultures), we have little basis on which to make conclusions about any of these variable combinations. However, we can hypothesize that the female side of each interaction (the female × ELL, female × minority ethnicity, female × poverty, and female × culturally diverse status) will

have lower achievement than the female × majority status group (i.e., English speaking, White, nondisadvantaged, and majority culture). When looking at the male side of the equation, we might be able to hypothesize that females will have higher achievement than males in reading and language arts but lower achievement in math and science. Some of the few studies identified that analyzed this combination did report these findings, but there are too few studies to be conclusive.

Second, if we are to identify the "best" instructional techniques for ELL students, we also must consider the gender, language background, culture, poverty, and educational background of ELL students. Equity issues are far-ranging and often especially important for this group of students. We cannot look at ELL students only through the lens of middle-class "American" values. Rather, we must respect the culture of the students, the interaction of gender and culture, language background, and the interaction between language and culture. It is perhaps among ELL students that these issues are the most difficult to describe and the least likely to have been studied.

It is important to note, also, the effect that the No Child Left Behind Act (NCLB) is having on research about ELL students. With its focus on scientifically-based research, grants funded by the U.S. Department of Education study two-way bilingual immersion programs and ESL-type programs. Several of these grants have been awarded to the Center for Applied Linguistics and Johns Hopkins University (either together or separately) with most funded for 3 to 5 years beginning in 2001–2003. Although some papers have been presented at national conferences, little has been finalized and reviewed by the Department of Education for publication purposes. Although required scientifically-based research does suggest that gender be included and analyzed, it is unclear whether it actually is being considered within these studies. However, it is clear that students are being randomly selected and randomly assigned to treatment conditions. It will be interesting to follow these studies and see the eventual findings.

CHAPTER SUMMARY, DISCUSSION, AND RECOMMENDATIONS[22]

This section provides an overview of the research summarized in this chapter on L2 learning for both adults (primarily learning a "foreign" language) and K–12 students (learning English as a second language in American schools). In addition we provide some interpretative comments and recommendations for both researchers and practitioners. Although we have tried to stay within the confines of the research that has been presented, we also have tried to create suggestions and recommendations that are somewhat provocative and might stimulate further discussion and research ideas. Because many of the findings for adults learning a "foreign" language and K–12 students learning English are similar, we will only indicate an age group where necessary because of differences.

---

[21]For more information on the development of, and research about, SIOP, see www.cal.org/crede/si.htm.
[22]All chapter authors contributed to this section of the chapter.

TABLE 15.7   Overview of Research Findings on ELLs' Academic Achievement*

Author(s)		Language Groups	Grade Level/Age	Content Area	Findings[a]
Studies that included and analyzed gender					
Davenport et al. (2002)		Spanish-speaking Hispanic, Asian, American Indian, English-speaking	Grade 8	Reading	• **F > M*** • **ELL < non-ELL** • **Hispanic, American Indian < Asian, White** • **Poverty < nonpoverty** • F ELL > M ELL • F ELL in poverty < most others
				NAEP Reading Math	• **F > M*** • **F < M*** • **ELL < nonELL** • **Hisp, Amer Ind < Asian, white** • **Poverty < nonpoverty** • F ELL>M ELL • F ELL in poverty < most others
				NAEP Math	• **F < M***
Hallam (2001)		ELL: SE Asian, American Indian Non-ELL: Asian American, Hispanic, White Poverty and nonpoverty	K–12	Reading in English Writing in English Reading and writing	• **F = M** • **9–12 grade F > 9–12 grade M** • **Hispanic, American Indian, older Asian American, poverty < White, nonpoverty** • Hispanic, American Indian F < any others
Medina (1993)		Spanish-speaking ELLs	Grades 1–8 Grades 2–8	Spanish reading Spanish math, science	• **F > M** • **F = M**
Padrón (1992)	Her research	Unknown	Unknown, but in school	Reading in English	• Not analyzed
	Literature review	Unknown	Unknown, but in school	Reading in English	• **ELL fewer strategies** • **F more strategies than M** • F ELL strategies > M ELL strategies
Krashen and Brown (2005) (Secondary analysis of published data)		Multiple languages including English-fluent; high- and low-socioeconomic status	Multiple, in school	Reading and math	• High SES ELLs = low SES English fluent in reading • **High SES ELLs > low SES English fluent in math**
Thomas and Collier (2002)		Spanish-speaking, English-speaking, and over 80 others	K–12, longitudinal	Math in English Science in English Reading in English Math in Spanish Math in Spanish Reading in English	• **Hispanic F < Hispanic M** • **Hispanic F < Hispanic M** • **F = M** • **F = M** • **F = M** • **F = M**
Wilde (2006)		Over 100 languages, but primarily Spanish	2 years of middle school and high school students; over 2,000 students	English language proficiency (various measures of reading, writing, listening, speaking)	• **F = M** • **Higher Eng proficiency > lower Eng proficiency**
				Academic achievement: Reading, writing, math, and science in English	• **F = M** • **Higher Eng proficiency > lower Eng proficiency** • **Asian, White > Hispanic, African** • **Some race/ethnicity x Eng proficiency interactions**
Studies that did NOT analyze gender					
Echevarria, Short, & Powers (2003)		Various	Elementary and middle school	Achievement with SIOP-trained teachers	• **SIOP > not SIOP**

(continued)

326

TABLE 15.7 (*Continued*)

Author(s)	Language Groups	Grade Level/Age	Content Area	Findings[a]
Padrón and Waxman (1992) (Literature review)	Multiple	K–12	Math/Science	• Not analyzed
Parrish et al. (2006)	Multiple	2–12	Academic achievement, English proficiency	• **ELL < not ELL, gap remains about the same** • Gender not analyzed
Slavin and Cheung (2003) (Synthesis of research)	Primarily Spanish-speaking	Beginning readers	Reading in English	• Not analyzed
Slavin and colleagues (2003, 2006)	Asian, African American, and Hispanic, plus English speaking	K–2	Reading in English using SFA program	• **SFA > not SFA**
Slavin and Madden (1999)	Spanish-speaking	K–2	Reading in Spanish using SFA program	• **SFA > not SFA**

*Data were not disaggregated for gender within ELL status, but refer to the girls' average score *vs* the boys' average score
[a]Findings in bold were reported by author(s) as significant (or with large effect sizes) or not significant; findings in regular type might be hypothesized based on other analyses within the study but were not tested by the author(s). In some cases, no analyses were completed that would allow any hypotheses; these are marked as "not analyzed."

Gender and Reading Comprehension

The present review shows that second and foreign language reading performance may be affected by passage content and assessment tasks. More research needs to be conducted on matters of gender and domain-specific abilities in L2 reading before particular generalizations can be made.

Given the contradictory findings on passage content, topic familiarity, and reader's gender, it is difficult to offer practical implications for the classroom. Therefore, the suggestions below are prefaced with certain caveats: (a) this literature review is not exhaustive but rather serves as a representative sample of the research on this topic, and (b) the suggestions need further testing in classroom settings.

Prereading activities may reinforce and motivate learners to read the text, and prereading activities will help to build on the pre-existing knowledge structures. If there are gender-specific topics in the text, instructors may want to address this through prereading activities where learners interact in the classroom and learn from each other. For younger students, there is some indication that girls find a broad range of topics interesting, and boys find a narrower range of "male" topics interesting (Krashen, 1996). Reading lessons should take into account the topic familiarity and background knowledge through pre-, during-, and postreading tasks because this might motivate deeper reading and richer comprehension. Schema activation is necessary in the second and foreign language classroom. There is general agreement that every attempt should be made to allow background knowledge to facilitate performance rather than allowing its absence to inhibit performance (Alderson, 2000; Echevarria, Short, & Powers, 2003; Slavin et al., 2006).

Moreover, instructors should utilize a variety of tools to assess comprehension. Females perform better on written recalls for a text topic with which both genders are equally familiar, but male and female readers scored almost the same on multiple choice questions (Brantmeier, 2004ab). More specifically, Brantmeier's (2004b) findings indicated that with an L2 passage about boxing, readers' gender accounts for more variance than topic familiarity in recall (readers' gender = 10%; topic familiarity = 5%), but the reverse is true for multiple choice (readers' gender = 5%; topic familiarity = 11%). Likewise, with an L2 passage about a housewife, results show that readers' gender accounts for more variance than topic familiarity in recall (readers' gender = 17%; topic familiarity = 14%), and again, the reverse is true for multiple choice (readers' gender = 10%; and topic familiarity = 14%). In summary, readers' gender is more influential than topic familiarity in producing higher recall scores (with females scoring higher than males), but topic familiarity is more influential than readers' gender in producing higher multiple choice scores. These results underline the need for more research on variables that influence performance on comprehension assessment tasks. Instructors should consider this when evaluating L2 reading comprehension.

If readers are equipped with the tools to comprehend a text, then perhaps the task of writing also will be easier. As demonstrated earlier, male and female readers may associate with different topics, and if they are recreating themselves through their writing, then the topic of text should be considered when assigning compositions. Another suggestion would be to have readers choose their own texts and writing topics based on their own interests.

Finally, second and foreign language test makers also should realize the importance of topic familiarity on comprehension and examine the existing standardized instruments (both texts and tests) to make appropriate changes where warranted. Although test constructors cannot change the gender of the reader, they can be careful not to bias their tests toward either gender. Understanding how the adult reader interacts with other variables in L2 reading provides a richer and more meaningful explanation of the manner in which gender may influence successful reading comprehension.

Strategies in Foreign and Second Language Learning

Findings of recent studies vary considerably with regard to males' and females' strategic behavior as compared to the studies discussed in Young and Oxford (1997). Taken together, these studies add to the growing knowledge base of how males and females employ FL learning and use strategies, yet these studies are not enough to make generalizations about gender and strategy use. Differences in study design and objectives (for example, self-report versus treatment, no task versus task-based, cross-sectional versus longitudinal) often yield diverse results that are difficult to compare. There do appear to be salient differences in research design, target languages of the subjects, tasks (reading or speaking), and the definition of strategies. Furthermore, numerous studies before and after 1997 have *not* considered gender as a variable. In short, there simply is not enough research available to allow us to draw solid conclusions about males' and females' strategic behavior. For example, Young and Oxford (1997) and Brantmeier (2003b) lend themselves to comparisons because they employ similar instruments and ask comparable research questions. This is exactly what needs to be done to construct a theory of gender and strategy use.

It may be true, as Young and Oxford (1997) concluded, that although there may be few strategies that are "inherently male or female," future research should pay attention to strategies more commonly used by males and females, and to **how** males and females use specific strategies, and should develop approaches for helping all learners use appropriate strategies (p. 66). If researchers in all areas of second language acquisition would include gender as a variable, thereby broadly expanding the knowledge base, we can perhaps gain a clearer understanding of whether and how males and females differ in how they learn and use a second or foreign language.

Gender and Identity in Study Abroad Programs

Taken together, the studies cited in this section suggest that language learning in study abroad is a gendered experience, both at the macro level of program design and learner access to social networks, and at the micro level of interaction in specific settings and performance of identity by particular learners. This dimension of the experience is worthy of further investigation. Encounters with other cultural settings with different norms can cause serious difficulties for learners, particularly if they have been sensitized to typical American public discourses on sexism and gender equity. These norms apply not only to the more obvious, public qualities of interaction but also to the social values underlying language use. However, the story does not end with a clash of norms, nor does it involve only women.

Taken together, the studies cited here as well as earlier studies suggest that gender, as a key aspect of identity, plays a significant role in shaping the qualities of language learning experiences abroad, particularly in the cases of young women who are the majority participants in such programs (Institute for International Education, 2004). These women report that their awareness of gender is highlighted in ways that can result either in rejection of the goal of language learning or in realization that new strategies are required for the furtherance of achieving interactional communicative competence in the languages under study.

ELL Learners in the K–12 Setting

Research with regard to ELL students is still a relatively new field. It began shortly after the first BEA was passed in 1968. Since then, the research has focused on which type of educational experience (among forms of ESL, transitional bilingual, or two-way bilingual immersion) is "best" for students. Indeed, in the Development of Literacy in Spanish Speakers (DeLSS) series of studies recently funded by the U.S. Department of Education, how children learn a first language, a second language, and whether there are differences among the educational approaches still are the main focus.[23] First, of course, we must get past the idea that any one type of educational experience is "best" for all students. As August and Hakuta (1997), among others, point out, there is much evidence that true bilingualism results in students who are literate in English, have advanced cognitive skills, and are literate in a second language.

There is some evidence that variables such as educational background, home language, and home culture mediate the learning experience; these variables are just beginning to be studied—complicated by the fact that 75% of ELL students speak Spanish in the home and the second largest language group, with only 2% of the population, in Vietnamese (Hapstack & Stephenson, 1993). It should be no wonder, then, that gender is so rarely studied, even though researchers do report on gender as a demographic variable. The two problems with including gender as a variable are (1) small sample sizes which may make analyzing another variable difficult and (2) archived data which frequently maintains data for groups of students rather than student-by-student, which makes analysis impossible. The nation-wide database being developed by the U.S. Department of Education in 2006 does not collect individualized student data due to a fear that a student might be identified. However, given the types of encryption and security that can be available, as well as the need for good, in-depth data, these problems must be overcome in order to allow gender and other variables to be analyzed so they can provide further insight into how students learn.

The importance of the interaction between gender and culture is important and merits further study for language devel-

---

[23]DeLSS is a series of interrelated research projects sponsored by the National Institute of Child Health and Human Development and the Institute of Education Sciences of the U.S. Department of Education. Funding is from 2000–2005 so only interim reports and information now are available. For further information and a listing of products, see www.cal.org/delss/projects.html.

opment in both adults and K–12 students. According to the cultural compatibility hypothesis, instruction that is compatible with a student's native culture should lead to improvement in the learning processes of students. Social organization, sociolinguistics, cognition, and motivation all are psychosocial constants that vary by culture and will be determinants of culturally appropriate instruction (Tharp, 1989). This tends to be the case with most educational endeavors: curricula are developed for the majority culture, which means they are developed for the males of that culture, the "breadwinners."

Furthermore, although there often is an attempt to refer to Spanish-speaking students, Asian students, and American Indian students as three monolithic groups, they are each heterogeneous, from several different nations, cultures, and languages or dialects. It is difficult to make generalizations about American Indians because they represent at least 280 different tribal groups and vary on a number of linguistic, cultural, social, political, and economic dimensions. On the other hand, we can say that American Indians frequently are ELL students, live on or near reservations, are not succeeding in schools, have a greater likelihood than students of other ethnic groups to be identified as learning disabled and to dropout by 10th grade, and score poorly on standardized norm-referenced tests of achievement. Some of these problems may stem from a "cultural misfit" between American Indian cultures and European-American culture. For example, (a) emotional and intellectual domains are fused in informal teaching and learning processes of American Indians, and content is more important than who is teaching in the formal teaching and learning of the typical middle-class classroom; (b) the courtesies and conventions of conversation differ in cultures, such as the extended "wait time" that Pueblo Indians and Navajos (among others) expect between the time that one person speaks (or asks a question) and the other speaks (or responds to the question) and the use of verbal cues among Warm Springs and Choctaw Indians and nonverbal cues of European-American culture during the back-and-forth flow of conversation; and (c) Native Americans tend toward more holistic thought, probably due to the extent of observational learning of American Indians, than do European-Americans. (See Tharp & Yamauchi, 1994, for examples.)

SUMMARY RECOMMENDATIONS

Finally, to put a more specific focus on our comments and recommendations, we strongly suggest the following:

1. Analyze gender and report on students and teachers of FL and L2—the authors of this chapter had trouble finding this seemingly "routine" analysis during our literature searches.
2. Continue (or, in some cases, begin) to study the interactions among gender, culture, language status, and socioeconomic status—some of these are difficult to define empirically or are difficult to parse from one another, but we must begin to consider their impact on language learning.
3. Ensure that teachers, professors, and others associated with planning and implementing the education of language learners are prepared to understand differences in culture, language, and gender that may have effects on language learning and attitudes.
4. Understand issues in language that may cause problems for L2 students (whether K–12 students learning English or adults learning a foreign language)—for instance, many languages other than English assign gender to nouns (e.g., "la" versus "le" in French), and in English there are some nouns referred to as one gender or another (e.g., referring to ships as "she").
5. Encourage biliteracy so those who are learning a second language, regardless of gender, age, or purpose of learning the language, feel that their skills in both languages are valued.

ACKNOWLEDGMENTS

The authors would like to thank reviewers Dolly Young, University of Tennessee; Knoxville, Tenneseee, Richard Feldman, Cornell University, Ithaca, New York; Beverly Irby, Sam Houston State University, Huntsville, Texas; and Raphael Lara-Alecio, Texas A&M University, College Station, Texas, for their helpful suggestions.

References

Alexander, P., Kulikowich, J., & Jetton, T. (1995). The interrelationship of knowledge, interest, and recall: Assessing a model of domain learning. *Journal of Educational Psychology, 87*(4), 559–575.

Alderson, J. C. (2000). *Assessing reading*. New York: Cambridge University Press.

Alva, S. A., & Padilla, A. M. (1995). Academic invulnerability among Mexican Americans: A conceptual framework. *The Journal of Educational Issues of Language Minority Students, 15*. Retrieved July 17, 2005 from http://www.ncela.gwu.edu/pubs/jeilms/vol15/academic.htm

August, D., & Hakuta, K. (eds.) (1997). *Educating language-minority children*. Washington, DC: National Academy Press.

Bacon, S. M. (1992). The relationship between gender, comprehension, processing strategies, and cognitive and affective response in foreign language listening. *Modern Language Journal, 76*, 160–176.

Bacon, S. M., & Finnemann, M. D. (1990). A study of the attitudes, motives, and strategies of university foreign language students and their disposition to authentic oral and written input. *Modern Language Journal, 74*, 459–473.

———. (1992). Sex differences in self-reported beliefs about foreign language learning and authentic oral and written input. *Language Learning, 42*, 471–495.

Baker, K. (1990, March). *Bilingual education programs: Partial or total failure?* Paper presented at the 10th Annual Second Language Research Forum, Eugene, OR.

———. (1992). Ramírez, et al.: Misled by bad theory. *Bilingual Research Journal, 16*(1 & 2), 63–89.

Barnett, M. A. (1988). Reading through context: How real and perceived strategy use affects L2 comprehension. *Modern Language Journal, 72*, 150–162.

Bernhardt, E. B. (1991). *Reading development in a second language: Theoretical, research and classroom perspectives.* Norwood, NJ: Albex.

———. (2005). Progress and procrastination in second language reading. *Annual Review of Applied Linguistics, 25,* 133–150.

———. (2005). The national randomized field trial of Success for All: Second year outcomes. *American Educational Research Journal, 42*(4), 673–696.

Brantmeier, C. (2001). Second language reading research on passage content and gender: challenges for the intermediate level curriculum. *Foreign Language Annals, 34,* 325–333.

———. (2002). The effects of passage content on second language reading comprehension by gender across instruction levels. In J. Hammadou Sullivan. (Ed.) pp. 149–176, *Research in Second Language Learning: Literacy and the Second Language Learner.* Greenwich, CT: Information Age Publishing.

———. (2003a). Does gender make a difference? Passage content and comprehension in second language reading. *Reading in a Foreign Language, 15*(1), 1–24.

———. (2003b). The role of gender and strategy use in processing authentic written input at the intermediate level. *Hispania, 86,* 844–856.

———. (2003c). Language skills or passage content? A comparison of native and non-native male and female readers of Spanish. *Applied Language Learning, 13*(1), 183–205.

———. (2003d). Beyond linguistic knowledge: Individual differences in second language reading. *Foreign Language Annals, 36*(1), 33–44.

———. (2004a). Gender, violence-oriented passage content, and reading in a second language. *The Reading Matrix, 4*(2), 1–19.

———. (2004b). Statistical procedures for research on L2 reading comprehension: An examination of regression models and ANOVA. *Reading in a Foreign Language, Special Issue on Methods and Applications in Reading Research, 16*(2), 51–69.

Brantmeier, C. (2006). Adult second language reading in the USA: The effects of readers' gender and test method *Forum on Public Policy Online.* Fall 2006 edition. http://www.forumonpublicpolicy.com

Brecht, R., Davidson, D., & Ginsberg, R. B. (1990). The empirical study of proficiency gain in study abroad environments among American students of Russian. In D. Davidson (Ed.), *American contributions to the VII International Congress of MAPRIAL.* Washington, DC: American Council of Teachers of Russian.

———. (1995). Predictors of foreign language gain during study abroad. In B. Freed (Ed.), *Second Language Acquisition in a Study Abroad Context* (pp. 37–66). Amsterdam, The Netherlands: John Benjamins.

Bügel, K., & Buunk, B. P. (1996). Sex differences in foreign language text comprehension: The role of interests and prior knowledge. *Modern Language Journal, 80,* 15–31.

Carrell, P. L. (1981). Culture-specific schemata in L2 comprehension. In R. Orem, & J. F. Haskell, (Eds.), *Selected papers from the ninth Illinois TESOL/BE,* (pp. 123–132). Chicago: Illinois TESOL/BE.

———. (1983a). Some issues in studying the role of schemata, or background knowledge, in second language comprehension. *Reading in a Foreign Language, 1*(2), 81–92.

———. (1983b). Three components of background knowledge in reading comprehension. *Language Learning, 33*(2), 183–203.

———. (1987). Content and formal schemata in ESL reading. *TESOL Quarterly, 21,* 462–481.

Chavez, M. (2001). *Gender in the language classroom.* Boston: McGraw-Hill.

Churchill, E. (2005, July). A case study if gendered language learning at home and abroad. Paper presented at AILA (Association Internationale de Linguistique Appliquée), Madison, WI.

Coady, J. (1979). A psycholinguistic model for the ESL reader. In Mackay, R., Barhman, B., & Jordan, R. R. (eds) pp. 5–12. *Reading in a Second Language.* Rowley, MA: Newbury House.

Cohen, A. (1998). *Strategies in learning and using a second language.* London: Longman.

College Board. (1996) SAT Course Taking Patterns?

———. (2005). 2005 College-Bound Seniors: Total Group Profile Report. Retrieved July, 2006 from http://www.collegeboard.com

———. (2006) Advanced Placement Report to the Nation 2006. Retrieved July, 2006 from http://apcentral.collegeboard.com/documentlibrary

Crawford, J. (1997a). *Best evidence: Research foundations of the Bilingual Education Act.* Washington, DC: National Clearinghouse for Bilingual Education.

———. (1997b). The campaign against Proposition 227: A post mortem. *Bilingual Research Journal, 21*(1). Retrieved July 20, 2005 from http://brj.asu.edu/archives/iv21/articles/Issue1Crawford.html

———. (1999). *Bilingual education: History, politics, theory, and practice* (4th ed.). Los Angeles: Bilingual Education Services.

Davenport, E. C., Davison, M. L., Kwak, N., Peterson, K., Irish, M. L., Chan, C., et al. (2002, July). *The Minnesota Basic Skills Test: Performance Gaps for 1996–2001 on the reading and mathematics tests, by gender, ethnicity, limited English proficiency, individual education plans, and socio-economic status.* Minneapolis: The Office of Educational Accountability, University of Minnesota.

Doolittle, A., & Welch, C. (1989). *Gender differences in performance on a college-level achievement test* (ACT Research Rep. Series 89-9). Iowa City, IA: American College Testing Program.

Draper, J. B., & Hicks, J. H. (2002, May). Foreign Language Enrollments in Public Secondary Schools" American Council on the Teaching of Foreign Languages. www.actfl.org.

DuFon, M. A. (2000). The acquisition of linguistic politeness in Indonesian by sojourners in naturalistic interactions. PhD Thesis, University of Hawai'l, 1999. *Dissertation Abstracts International—A, 60*(11), 3985.

Echevarria, J., Short, D., & Powers, K. (2006). School reform and standards-based education: An instructional model for English language learners. *Journal of Educational Research, 99*(4), 195–210.

Ehrman, M. E., & Oxford, R. L. (1989). Effects of sex differences, career choice, and psychological type on adults' language learning strategies. *Modern Language Journal, 73,* 1–13.

El-Dib, M. A. B. (2004). Language learning strategies in Kuwait: Links to gender, language level, and culture in a hybrid context. *Foreign Language Annals, 37,* 85–95.

Freed, B. (1995). Language learning and study abroad. In B. Freed (Ed.), *Second Language Acquisition in a Study Abroad Context* (pp. 3–33). Amsterdam, The Netherlands: John Benjamins.

García, Eugene (2005, July). *University leadership for multilingual education.* Paper presented at the 13th Annual National Two-Way Bilingual Immersion Program Summer Conference, Monterey, CA.

Gergen, M. (2001). *Feminist Reconstructions in Psychology.* London: Sage.

Gómez, J. (1990). On being an American. *GW Forum, 37,* Spring 1990. Washington, DC: The George Washington University.

Hallam, P. J. (2001). Findings on literacy learning environment and Learning Record at combined *Learning Record* sites. San Diego, CA: Center for Language and Learning.

Hammadou, J. (1990). The impact of analogy and content knowledge on reading comprehension: What helps, what hurts. *The Modern Language Journal, 84,* 38–50.

Hopstock, P. J., & Stephenson, T. G. (2003). *Descriptive study of services to LEP students and LEP students with disabilities—Special topic report #1: Native languages of LEP students.* Contract No. ED-00-CO-0089, U.S.Department of Education. Washington, DC: Development Associates.

Hudson, T. (1982). The effects of induced schemata on the 'short circuit' in L2 reading: non-decoding factors in L2 reading performance. *Language Learning, 32*(1), 1–31.

Huebner, T. (1995). The effects of overseas language programs: Report on a case study of an intensive Japanese course. In B. Freed (Ed.),

Second Language Acquisition in a Study Abroad Context (pp. 171–193). Amsterdam, The Netherlands: John Benjamins.

Hyde, J. S., & Linn, M. C. (1988). Gender differences in verbal activity: A meta-analysis. *Psychological Bulletin, 104*, 53–69.

Institute for Education Sciences (2002). *Dropout rates in the United States: 2000*. Washington, DC: National Center for Education Statistics, U.S. Department of Education. Retrieved June 10, 2006 from http://www.nces.ed.gov/pubs2002/droppub_2000/

Institute for International Education. (2004). Open Doors 2004: Report on International Educational Exchange. Retrieved July, 2006, from http://opendoors.iienetwork.org/

Ishihara, N. (2003). Identity and pragmatic performance of foreign language speakers. Paper presented at AAAL, Arlington, VA.

James, D. (1987). Bypassing the traditional leadership: Who's minding the store? *Profession*. New York: 41–53.

Johnson, P. (1981). Effects on comprehension of building background knowledge. *TESOL Quarterly, 16*, 503–516.

Khalil, A. (2005). Assessment of language learning strategies used by Palestinian EFL learners. *Foreign Language Annals, 38*, 108–119.

Kinginger, C. (2004a). Alice doesn't live here anymore: Foreign language learning and renegotiated identity. In Aneta Pavlenko & Adrian Blackledge (Eds.), *Negotiation of Identities in Multilingual Contexts* (pp. 219–242). Clevedon, UK: Multilingual Matters.

Kinginger, C. (2004b). Bilingualism and emotion in the autobiographical works of Nancy Huston. *Journal of Multilingualism and Multicultural Development, 25*, 159–178.

Kinginger, C., & Whitworth, K. (2005). Gender and emotional investment in language learning during study abroad. CALPER Working Paper Series No. 2. The Pennsylvania State University, Center for Advanced Language Proficiency Education and Research. Retrieved July, 2006, from http://calper.la.psu.edu/publications.php

Kline, R. (1998). Literacy and language learning in a study abroad context. *Frontiers: The Interdisciplinary Journal of Study Abroad, 4*, 139–165.

Kloss, H. (1998). *The American bilingual tradition.* Rowley, MA: Newbury House.

Kocoglu, Z. (1997). The role of gender on communication strategy use. Paper presented at the Annual Meeting of the Teachers of English to Speakers of Other Languages, Orlando, FL.

Kramsch, C. (1997). The privilege of the nonnative speaker. *PMLA, 112*, 359–369.

Krashen, S. (1991, Spring). *Bilingual education: A focus on current research.* New Focus Occasional Papers in Bilingual Education, No. 3. Washington, DC: National Clearinghouse for Bilingual Education, The George Washington University.

Krashen, S. (1996). *Every person a reader: An alternative to the California Task Force on Reading.* Burlingame, CA: ALTA Book Center.

Krashen, S., & Brown, C. L. (2005). The ameliorating effects of high socioeconomic status: A secondary analysis. *Bilingual Research Journal, 29*(1), 185–196.

Lindholm-Leary, K. (2005a, July). *Promoting high quality two-way bilingual immersion in the era of NCLB.* Paper presented at the 13th Annual National Two-Way Bilingual Immersion Program Summer Conference, Monterey, CA.

———. (2005b, July). *Understanding outcomes of diverse students in two-way bilingual immersion.* Paper presented at the 13th Annual National Two-Way Bilingual Immersion Program Summer Conference, Monterey, CA.

Linquanti, R. (1999). *Fostering academic success for English language learners: What do we know?* San Francisco: WestEd. Retrieved January 29, 2005, from www.wested.org/policy/pubs/fostering/models.htm.

Marriott, H. (1995). The acquisition of politeness patterns by exchange students in Japan. In B. Freed (Ed.), *Second Language Acquisition in a Study Abroad Context,* (pp. 171–193). Amsterdam, The Netherlands: John Benjamins.

Medina, M., Jr. (1993). Spanish achievement in a maintenance bilingual education program: Language proficiency, grade, and gender comparisons. *Bilingual Research Journal, 17*(1&2), 57–81.

National Center for Education Statistics, (2003). *The Condition of Education*, U.S. Department of Education, NCES 2003-067, Washington, DC.

Nisbet, D., Tindall, E., & Arroyo, A. (2005). Language learning strategies and English proficiency of Chinese university students. *Foreign Language Annals, 38*, 100–107.

Norton, B. (2000). *Identity and Language Learning: Gender, Ethnicity, and Educational Change.* London: Longman.

Nyikos, M. (1987). *The effect of color and imagery as mnemonic strategies on learning and retention of lexical items in German.* Unpublished doctoral dissertation, Purdue University, West Lafayette, IN.

Ogulnick, K. (1998). *Onna Rashiku (Like a Woman); The Diary of a Language Learner in Japan.* SUNY Press.

Orvando, C. J. (Spring 2003). Bilingual education in the United States: Historical development and current issues. *Bilingual Research Journal, 27*(1), pp. 1–24).

Oxford, R. L. (1993). Gender differences in styles and strategies for language learning: What do they mean? Should we pay attention? In James E. Alatis (Ed.), *Strategic interaction and language acquisition: Theory, practice and research* (pp. 541–57) Georgetown University Roundtable on Languages and Linguistics. Washington DC: Georgetown University Press.

Oxford, R. L., Crookall, D., Cohen A., Lavine R., Nyikos M., & Sutter, W. (1990). Strategy training for language learners: Six situational case studies and a training model. *Foreign Language Annals, 22*, 197–216.

Oxford, R. L., Lavine, R. Z., Holloway, M. E., Felkins, G., & Saleh, A. (1996). Telling their stories: Language learners use diaries and recollective studies. In Rebecca L. Oxford (Ed.) *Language learning strategies around the world: Crosscultural perspectives.* Manoa: University of Hawaii Press.

Oxford, R. L., & Nyikos, M. (1989). Variables affecting choice of language learning strategies by university students. *Modern Language Journal, 73*, 219–300.

Oxford, R. L., Nyikos, M., & Ehrmann, M. E. (1988). Vive la difference? Reflections on sex differences in use of language learning strategies. *Foreign Language Annals, 21*, 321–329.

Oxford, R. L., Park-Oh, Y., Young Y., Ito, S., & Sumrall, M. (1993). Learning a language by satellite: What influences achievement? *System, 21*, 31–48.

Padolsky, D. (2005, March). *Ask NCELA No. 1: How many school-aged English language learners (ELLs) are there in the US?* Washington, DC: National Clearinghouse for English Language Acquisition, The George Washington University. Retrieved March 15, 2005, from www.ncela.gwu.edu/expert/faz/01leps.htm.

Padrón, Y. N. (1992). The effect of strategy instruction on bilingual students' cognitive strategy use in reading. *Bilingual Research Journal, 16*(3&4), 35–51.

Padrón, Y. N., & Waxman, H. C. (1992). Teaching and learning risks associated with limited cognitive mastery in science and mathematics for limited English proficient students. Paper presented at the Third National Research Symposium on Limited English Proficient Students: Focus on Middle and High School Issues. Retrieved July 21, 2005, from www.ncela.gwu.edu/pubs/syposia/third/padron.htm.

Parrish, T. B., Merickel, A., Pérez, M., Linquanti, R., Socias, M., Spain, A., et al. (2006). *Effects of the Implementation of Proposition 227 on the Education of English Learners, K–12: Findings from a Five Year Evaluation.* Final Report for AB 56 and AB 1116 submitted by the American Institutes for Reseach and WestEd. Retrieved June 3, 2006, from www.wested.org/online_pubs/227Reportb.pdf.

Patterson, A. (1995). Reading research methodology and the Reading Research Quarterly: A question of gender. *Reading Research Quarterly, 30*(2), 290–298.

Pavlenko, A. (2001). "How do I become a woman in an American vein?": Transformations of gender performance in second language socialization. In A. Pavlenko, A. Blackledge, I. Piller, & M. Teutsch-Dwyer (Eds.), *Multilingualism, second Language Learning, and Gender,* (pp. 133–174). Mouton De Gruyter.

———. (2002). Poststructuralist approaches to the study of social factors in second language learning and use. In V. Cook (Ed.), *Portraits of the L2 User* (pp. 277–302). Clevedon, UK: Multilingual Matters,

Polanyi, L. (1995). Language learning and living abroad: Stories from the field. In B. Freed (ed.) *Second Language Acquisition in a Study Abroad Context* (pp. 271 – 291). Philadelphia: John Benjamins.

Politzer, R. L. (1983). An exploratory study of self-reported language learning behaviors and their relation to achievement. *Studies in Second Language Acquisition, 6*, 54–68.

Pritchard, R. (1990). The effects on cultural schemata on reading processing strategies. *Reading Research Quarterly, 25*, 273–295.

Ramírez, J. D., Yuen, S. D., & Ramey, D. R. (1991). *Final report: Longitudinal study of structured immersion strategy, early-exit, and late-exit transitional bilingual education programs for language-minority children.* San Mateo, CA: Aguirre International.

Schmidt, R., & Watanabe, Y. (2001). Motivation, strategy use and pedagogical preferences. In Z. Dörnyei & R. Schmidt (eds.) *Motivation and second language acquisition* (pp. 313–352). Honolulu: University of Hawaii.

Schneider, A. (2001). A University Plans To Promote Languages by Killing Its Languages Department. *Chronicle of Higher Education, 47*(26), A14–A15.

Schueller, J. (1999). *The effect of two types of strategy training on foreign language reading comprehension. An analysis by gender and proficiency.* Unpublished doctoral dissertation. The University of Wisconsin, Madison.

———. (2004). Gender and foreign language reading comprehension: The effects of strategy training. In C. Brantmeier (Ed.) Adult foreign language reading: Theory, research, and implications (pp. 88–93). *Southern Journal of Linguistics* (special issue) 26(2).

Schumann, F. M. (1980). Diary of a language learner: A further analysis. In R. Scarcella & S. Krashen (eds.) Research in second language acquisition. Cambridge, MA: Newbury House, pp. 51–57.

Schumann, F. M., & J. H. Schumann (1977). Diary of a language learner: Introspective study of SLA. In H. Brown, C. Yorio, & R. Crymes (Eds.), On TESOL '77, (pp. 241–249). Washington, D.C.: TESOL.

Schmais, W. A. (2003). Language learning strategy use in Palestine. *Teaching English as a Second or Foreign Language, 7*(2),. Retrieved March 23, 2005, from http://www-writing.berkeley.edu/TESL-EJ/ej26/a3.html.

Siegal, M. (1996). The role of learner subjectivity in second language sociolinguistic competency: Western women learning Japanese. *Applied Linguistics, 17*(3), 356–382.

Silverstein, A. (2001). Standardized tests: The continuation of gender bias in higher education. *Hofsta Law Review, 29*, 669–700.

Slavin, R. E., & Cheung, A. (2003, December). *Synthesis of research on beginning reading programs for English language learners.* Grant No. OERI-R-117-40005. Paper presented at the OELA Celebrate Our Rising Stars II Summit, Washington, DC.

Slavin, R. E., & Madden, N. A. (1999). Effects of bilingual and English as a second language adaptations of Success for All on the reading achievement of students acquiring English. *Journal of Education for Students Placed at Risk, 4*(4), 393–416. Retrieved March 23, 2006, from http://www.successforall.org/research/index.htm.

Slavin, R. E., Madden, N. A., Cheung, A., Borman, G. D., Chamberlain, A., & Chambers, B. (2006). *A three-year randomized evaluation of Success for All: Final reading outcomes.* Baltimore, MD: Center for Data-Driven Reform in Education, Johns Hopkins University.

Steffenson, M. S., Joag-dev, C., & Anderson, R. C. (1979). A cross-cultural perspective on reading comprehension. *Reading Research Quarterly, 15*, 10–29.

Stewner-Manzanares, G. (1988, Fall). *The Bilingual Education Act: Twenty years later.* New Focus Occasional Papers in Bilingual Education, No. 6. Washington, DC: National Clearinghouse for Bilingual Education, The George Washington University.

Talburt, S., & Stewart, M. A. (1999). What's the subject of study abroad? Race, gender and 'living culture.' *Modern Language Journal, 83*(2), 163–175.

Tharp, R. G. (1989). Psychocultural variables and constants: Effects on teaching and learning in schools. *American Psychologist, 44*(2), 349–359.

Tharp, R. G., & Yamauchi, L. A. (1994). Effective instructional conversation in Native American classrooms. Educational Practice Report: 10. Santa Cruz, CA: National Center for Research on Cultural Diversity and Second Language Learning, University of California at Santa Cruz. Retrieved July 13, 2005, from www.ncela.gwu.edu/pubs/ncr-cdsll/epr10.htm.

The Urban Institute (May 2006).*Children of Immigrants: Facts and Figures.* Washington, D.C.: Author.

Thomas, W. P., & Collier, V. P. (1997). *School effectiveness for language minority students.* NCBE Resource Collection Series No. 9. Washington, DC: National Clearinghouse for Bilingual Education, The George Washington University.

———. (2002). *A national study of school effectiveness for language minority students' long-term academic achievement: Final report (Executive Summary).* Santa Cruz, CA: Center for Research on Education, Diversity, and Excellence, University of California at Santa Cruz. Retrieved July 17, 2005, from www.crede.org/research/llaa/l.les.html.

Twombly, S. B. (1995). Piropos and friendship: Gender and culture clash in study abroad. *Frontiers: The Interdisciplinary Journal of Study Abroad, 1*, 1–27.

Wilde, J. (2004a). Definitions for the *No Child Left Behind Act, 2001*: Assessment. Washington, DC: National Clearinghouse for English Language Acquisition, The George Washington University. Available at www.ncela.gwu.edu.

———. (2004b). *NCLB Definitions: Assessment.* Washington, DC: National Clearinghouse for English Language Acquisition, The George Washington University. Available at www.ncela.gwu.edu.

Wilde, J. (2006). *Evaluation of secondary ELL students' academic achievement and English language proficiency, 2003–04 and 2004–05.* (Note: as the school district has not yet determined whether they wish to be identified, no further information can be provided. Contact the author for further information.)

Wilde, J., & Sockey, S. (1995). *Evaluation Handbook.* Albuquerque: Evaluation Assistance Center–Western Region, New Mexico Highlands University.

Wildner-Bassett, M. E. (1992). The interaction of learning styles and strategies: Diversity in the foreign language classroom. Paper presented at the Annual Meeting of the American Council on the Teaching of Foreign Language, Chicago.

Wilkinson, S. (1998). On the nature of immersion during study abroad: Some participants' perspectives. *Frontiers: The Interdisciplinary Journal of Study Abroad, 4*, 121–138.

Wolf, D. (1993). A comparison of assessment tasks used to measure FL reading comprehension. *Modern Language Journal, 77*, 473–489.

Woodrow, L. (2005). The challenge of measuring language learning strategies. *Foreign Language Annals, 38*, 91–99.

Young, D. (2000). An investigation into the relationship between L2 reading anxiety and L2 reading comprehension, and self-reported level of comprehension, topic familiarity, features of an L2 text and reading ability in the L1 and L2. *Current Research on the Acquisition of Spanish,* (Eds.) R. Leow & C. Sanz. Somerville: Cascadilla Press, 15–33.

Young, D., & Oxford, R. L. (1997). A gender-related analysis of strategies used to process written input in the native language and a foreign language. *Applied Language Learning, 8,* 43–73.

Zelasko, N., & Antunez, B. (2000). *If your child learns in two languages: A parent's guide for improving educational opportunities for children acquiring English as a second language.* Washington, DC: National Clearinghouse for English Language Acquisition, The George Washington University.

Zoubir-Shaw, S., & Oxford, R. L. (1995). Gender differences in language learning strategy use in university-level introductory French classes. In C. A. Klee (Ed.) *Faces in a crowd: The individual learner in multisection courses,* (pp. 181–213). Boston: Heinle & Heinle.

·16·

GENDER EQUITY IN SOCIAL STUDIES

Carole L. Hahn, * **Jane Bernard-Powers,** * *Margaret Smith Crocco, and Christine Woyshner*

In the United States, "social studies" is the term traditionally applied to the part of the school curriculum that draws primarily on history and the social sciences for the purpose of citizenship education. At the elementary level, social studies is typically an integrated subject concerned with educating children about society and preparing them to be effective citizens. In middle and high schools, the social studies curriculum is generally enacted through separate courses in history, geography, civics/government, and economics. Curriculum standards, national assessments, and teacher education in social studies education are organized in terms of grade levels, elementary (K–5), middle (6–8), and high school (9–12). Research in social studies generally follows the same pattern, focusing on integrated subject matter at the elementary level and on discipline-based teaching and learning at the secondary level (middle and high school). There are, of course exceptions to this pattern.[1]

INTRODUCTION

Following the precedence of the chapter on social studies in the 1985 *Handbook*, we review research across the spectrum of topics in social studies education at the K–12 levels and in teacher preparation for teaching K–12 social studies (Hahn & Bernard-Powers, 1985). New scholarship in the disciplines of history, political science, sociology, psychology, and anthropology at the postsecondary level are germane to the topic but beyond the scope of this chapter.[2] We focus our review on research done in the United States, although a few studies from other countries are also included. The research synthesized here suggests that attention to gender in social studies has been partial, sporadic, and ebbing in recent years. The dramatic decline in federal funding for research and curriculum development focused on gender equity since 1985 has contributed to this pattern (American Association of University Women, 1992, p. 108). Likewise, attention to gender has proceeded somewhat unevenly across different grade levels and disciplinary emphases, with more attention given, for example, to gender and geography than to gender and economics education.

As scholars with expertise in varied social science disciplines and with commitments to social, political, and economic justice, we are cognizant of the complexity of identities in multicultural contexts. We believe that K–12 social studies should illuminate the histories, politics, economics, and narratives of the dynamics of gender in relation to race, ethnicity, class, sexual identity, and location in time and space. The complexity of gender in relation to these multiple aspects of identity and lived experiences, thus, should be evident in the K–12 social studies curriculum, such that the multiplicity and diversity of human experiences are comprehensible to young people and ultimately foster transformation in education and society.[3] However, the research that was available for review and discussion in this chapter reflects "the way things are" and "the way things have been." At the end of the chapter we recommend changes in policies, practices, programs and research that might extend and transform "what is" to "what might be" and "should be."

---

*The boldface names are the Lead Authors.

[1]Barton and Levstik (1998) studied elementary children's understanding of historical significance; several researchers studied children's understanding of geographic concepts. Some research in middle schools and, to a lesser extent, high schools treats social studies as an integrated subject.

[2]We do, however, make a few references to work on geography in higher education that has been applied to precollegiate social studies education.

[3]Critical theorists in curriculum have done much work that can inform these issues.

As with authors of other chapters in this *Handbook*, we seek to promote gender equity, in our cases, through social studies.[4] Gender equity has been defined as follows: "to be fair and just toward both men and women, to show preference to neither, and concern for both" (Klein, Ortman, & Friedman, 2002). This is a more complicated project than it may seem at first glance because defining "fairness" and "justice" regarding men and women has its own set of challenges related to whether one believes that treating people in the same fashion always promotes equitable outcomes.

We believe that if curriculum and instruction in social studies were gender equitable, the histories, narratives, and lived experiences of boys and girls, men and women, would be represented equally and accurately in social studies textbooks, supplementary curricular materials, and classroom instruction. Similarly, girls and boys, young men and young women, would be interested in all aspects of social studies—from history and geography to civics and economics—and would perform equally well (or equally poorly) on standardized tests of social studies knowledge. We also believe that social studies can foster knowledge and dispositions essential to 21st century multicultural, democratic citizenship by promoting gender equity and by developing in students of both genders attitudes and understandings supportive of men's and women's equal participation in all sectors, careers, and institutions of society, including leadership in government and business.

Such goals are rooted in our shared conviction that girls and boys, young men and women, are equally capable of understanding and using social studies subjects. However, we are not certain that curriculum, instruction, and tests satisfactorily address the reasons behind the gender differences in interest and performance that have been found in some areas within social studies, such as economics and geography. Nor do we believe that there is always a level "playing field" in particular arenas such as economics, where male dominance and longstanding positivist traditions shape the culture and its definition of important research.

The shift from the word 'sex' to 'gender' in relation to equity since 1985 is especially pertinent to the field of social studies. Over the last 20 years, adoption of the term 'gender' signals a shift from biologically-based approaches towards socially constructed, culturally, and historically imprinted views of what it means to be a man or a woman generally, and in relation to specific contexts. In other words, gender refers to the ways in which human societies have conceptualized and sorted the categories (social identities) and plans (attributes and roles) flowing from the material realities of biological differences. Because social studies content focuses on human beings in society, this shift in conceptualization is particularly relevant.

Related to this change in understanding is the increased interest and developing scholarship in several areas related to sexual identity. "Masculinity studies," the history of gays, lesbians, and transsexual/transgendered individuals, and cross-cultural and historical variations in all sexual identities constitute the terrain of this growing body of work.[5] Because these topics are part of social life, they are pertinent to social studies curriculum and instruction. However, in elementary and secondary social studies, engagement with gender and sexuality has been slow to develop, with much research still rooted in the paradigm of sex-based differences.[6]

Social studies has an important role to play in fostering notions of equity across groups divided by gender, race, religion, class, and sexual orientation, and in educating students about the sources of inequities in society. Students should learn about the histories of women's participation in American life, with attention to the intersections of ethnicity, class, gender, and sexuality; about women's involvement in voluntary organizations, the abolition and antilynching movements, varied labor movements, the worldwide peace movement, and other reform movements; about the central role diverse women have played in developing institutions such as schools, hospitals, and social welfare organizations; and about progress in advancing international human rights agreements, which affect and specifically address issues related to women and children.

In reviewing social studies research since the last *Handbook*, we have found few studies that describe solutions that have been scientifically proven to work in bringing about gender equity in K–12 classrooms. We have found that many authors have written about the need to foster gender equity across the vast field of social studies education and within society at large (e.g., Bernard-Powers, 2001; Crocco, 1997; Cruz & Groendal-Cobb, 1998; Grambs, 1976; Hahn, 1980; Levstik, 2001; Merryfield & Crocco, 2003; Woyshner, 2002). Nevertheless, despite the years of advocacy in literature and practice, we found remarkably little empirical evidence to show that social studies has become more gender equitable, has devised proven pathways to more gender-equitable practice in the field, has addressed the intersectionality of race/ethnicity, class, and gender, or has made an identifiable contribution to more gender-equitable national and global societies. In this chapter, we report key themes found in the social studies literature related to gender and then make recommendations about changes in practice, policy, and research that might contribute to a more

---

[4]Collectively, the authors have been in teacher education for 90 years, specializing in social studies education. Prior to teaching at the university level, each of us taught social studies at the elementary, middle, or high school level (collectively for 27 years). We have all written extensively on gender in social studies education, conducted in-service workshops for teachers on this subject, include gender in our teacher education courses, and conduct research on this subject. We have worked on gender equity and social studies both within the United States and internationally.

[5]For example, for masculinity studies see Lesko's (2000) edited volume, which covers a range of topics that are relevant to social studies including the relationship between coaching and teaching and the patriarchy in history books. Also for masculinity studies see Connell (2000). For lesbian, gay, bisexual, and transgender studies see the chapter on that topic in this *Handbook*.

[6]Some scholars have demonstrated that topics related to sexuality could be developed more fully if lesbian, gay, bisexual, and transgendered (LGBT) issues were central to the push for gender equity (Crocco, in press; Crocco, 2005a; Letts & Sears, 1999).

comprehensive foundation of knowledge on gender equity in social studies in the future.[7]

Since publication of the social studies chapter in the 1985 *Handbook*, a number of changes have occurred. Most prominently, the accountability or standards-based testing movement has put considerable pressure on the field. One of the effects of this movement has been to marginalize gender equity initiatives, especially in classroom practice and research. Moreover, as a consequence of the No Child Left Behind legislation, social studies is being squeezed out of the elementary school curriculum and with it, attention to gender equity in elementary social studies.

There are other phenomena that have impeded progress toward gender equity in social studies. Attention to multiculturalism has overshadowed gender even though, in theory, gender is an important component of multiculturalisms. Unfortunately, rather than doing research on the confluence of race/ethnicity, class, and gender, most scholars have tended to focus on one or another demographic variable, rather than the intersections among them. Additionally, it appears that a commonly held belief is that the major goals of the women's movement have been achieved and equity has been realized, especially for middle class American women. Thus, educators' attention has turned back to the "boy problem in education," including boys' experiences in schooling, their lower high school graduation rates, and declining proportion of enrollments in four-year colleges. Although some research we report here does indicate progress for women and girls, for example, in coverage in history textbooks and girls' performance on standardized tests in history and civics, other areas continue to show girls and young women lagging behind boys and young men in performance, especially on tests of geography and economics knowledge.

At the time the last chapter on gender equity and social studies was written, there were good reasons for optimism. The 1980s saw gains in use of inclusive language, growing attention to the gender imbalance in textbook coverage of women's lives and contributions, and budding awareness of the need to include gender as a variable in research studies. Since that time, many social studies educators have come to understand the need not to treat gender monolithically or in an essentialist fashion. Thus, many researchers are aware of the need to break down gender data by race and class and to compare the performance of U.S. students, teachers, and schools to data from other countries. Histories and historiographies of social studies education have begun to include diverse women. For example, recently published histories of the field include attention to women's contributions to "social education" more broadly conceived than earlier histories of social studies education (e.g., Crocco & Davis, 1999, 2002; Crocco, Munro, & Weiler, 1999;

Woyshner, Watras, & Crocco, 2004). For example, in their histories of social studies education, Crocco and Davis (1999, 2002) broadly defined the field of social education as citizenship education in order to include women previously overlooked in histories of mainstream social studies. Consequently, they included the important contributions of Septima Clark, Ella Baker, Marion Thompson Wright, and Deborah Partridge Wolfe. In a chapter on early American history, Crocco made the point that before there was an official school subject named 'social studies,' women like Hannah Adams and Emma Willard were "doing social studies." Other scholars have also extended the field's vision to consider the contributions of women in what might be thought of as "the prehistory" of the traditional histories, such as Sojourner Truth who worked for "citizenship education" before she was officially recognized as a citizen with the right to vote (Tyson, personal communication, January 14, 2006).

Further, some contemporary publications that are widely used in social studies teacher education include attention to gender (e.g., Adler, 2004; Bernard-Powers, 1995; Cheek & Kohut, 1992; Evans & Saxe, 1996; Ross, 1997; Stanley, 2001). Nevertheless, in many other social studies education publications, gender receives only scant attention or is subsumed under the topic of multiculturalism (e.g., Haas & Laughlin, 1999; Santora, 2001; Shaver, 1991). Finally, sexuality and sexual identity have attracted very little attention in research in the field, with the exception of a 2002 special issue of *Theory and Research in Social Education*, the field's most prominent research journal, and one chapter in a recently published history of the field (Blount, 2004).

In the section that follows, we lay out the gender-related themes that emerged across research in all subfields within social studies, K–12, since 1985. Then we describe efforts to foster gender equity in social studies. Finally, we propose a series of suggestions for enhancing gender equity in social studies that are based in published work, our collective experiences as social studies educators, and our work with practitioners who have focused on gender equity over the last 20 years.

WHAT ARE THE GENDER INEQUITIES IN SOCIAL STUDIES?

In past years, social studies education scholars noted that female students often did less well than male students on tests of social studies knowledge and that the social studies curriculum, as reflected in textbooks, tended to omit or stereotype women and did not include gender-related topics (See Hahn &

---

[7]Methodologically, for this review we identified post-1985 research from the following databases: ERIC, Dissertation Abstracts, Education Abstracts, Proquest, and JSTOR. We focused on social studies education, K–12, and teacher education. We did not look at work in the disciplines that was not explicitly concerned with education. We used the following search terms: social studies, history, geography, geography curriculum, civics/government, social studies teacher education and gender, gender differences, sex differences, woman, women, female(s), and feminism. We also included work that did not surface in this online research and consulted various experts for other nonpublished work. We focused on empirical studies, including articles that met good quality standards for research that was qualitative, quantitative, descriptive, experimental and/or historical. We excluded articles that did not use evidence. We realize that, through this process, we were not able to access reports of classroom action research, masters' theses, and other research that was not published in journals and other sources that are captured through the search engines and search strategies we used.

Bernard Powers, 1985, for a summary of the research through 1983). More recently, scholars have continued to examine gender differences in students' social studies knowledge, skills, attitudes, and experiences. In the process researchers have found that some of the earlier gender differences have disappeared. Researchers have also identified a number of areas in which gender differences remain, although the reasons for those persisting differences are not yet clear.

Over the past 20 years, researchers have also analyzed social studies curriculum guidelines, standards, and textbooks for their treatment of men and women and gender-related topics. Most of these researchers have concluded that although some improvements have been made in teaching for gender equity, problems remain. Furthermore, only a few researchers have conducted studies in social studies classrooms to shed light on how gender interacts with the instructional process.

Gender Inequities in Student Knowledge, Skills, and Attitudes

For the most part, researchers have focused on male and female students in general, rather than looking at differences within groups by ethnicity/race, social class, and other subgroup distinctions.[8] In this section, we examine first the work on gender inequities in student knowledge, skills, attitudes, and experiences. Following that, we discuss research related to gender inequities in social studies curriculum and instruction.

Girls and boys and high school age young women and men tend to be equally knowledgeable about social studies, history, and civics or government topics. The old idea that boys do better on tests of social studies knowledge can be put to rest. At the elementary level, no gender differences have been found in recent research on children's knowledge of social studies topics. For example, in the largest study of elementary social studies learning in recent years, Brophy and Alleman (1999, 2000, 2001, 2003, 2005) found no statistically significant gender differences overall in children's understanding of cultural universals, such as the need for food, housing, and shelter. In the few instances where gender differences appeared, the differences were not large and "the response patterns for boys and girls were much more similar than different" (Brophy & Alleman, 2003, p. 107). Although the researchers' main focus was not gender, they did disaggregate

their data by gender, as well as socioeconomic status and grade. In discussions of subtle gender differences that Brophy and Allemann observed, and in similar discussions by other researchers, there appears to be a tendency to look for gender differences in what Thorne (1993) has called the "well-worn grooves" of traditional expectations.[9]

The most extensive studies of students' social studies knowledge in the United States are based on results from the National Assessments of Educational Progress (NAEP) widely known as "the nation's report card." NAEP researchers assess nationally representative samples of students at grades 4, 8, and 12; through the 1970s NAEP assessments were given in social studies. However, in recent years separate assessments have been given in history, geography, and civics/government. Prior to 1995, boys and young men tended to perform better than girls and young women on NAEP history and civics tests (Anderson et al., 1990; Applebee, Langer, & Mullis, 1987; Niemi & Junn, 1998).[10] However, in recent years no significant gender differences have been found in student knowledge of history or civics and government (Lutkus, Weiss, Campbell, Mazzeo, & Lazer, 1999; National Center for Education Statistics, 2005). Similarly, in the 28-nation Civic Education Study of the International Association for the Evaluation of Educational Achievement, better known as IEA, conducted in 1999, researchers found no gender differences in civic knowledge overall or in the subscale measuring knowledge of civic content for students from the United States (Baldi, Perie, Skidmore, Greenberg, & Hahn, 2001; Torney-Purta, Lehmann, Oswald, & Schulz, 2001).[11] Interestingly, a larger percentage of students from the United States understood the concept of gender discrimination than in any of the other 27 participating countries (Torney-Purta & Barber, 2004).

In recent years male students have done less well than female students on some measures of civic skills. On the 1988 NAEP assessment in civics and government, male students scored lower than female students on items requiring students to read and interpret text material (Niemi & Junn, 1998). Ten years later, on the 1998 NAEP assessment in civics and government, male students in grades 8 and 12 had lower overall average scores than female students (Lutkus, et al., 1999). Similarly, for the United States sample in the IEA Civic Education Study on the subscale measuring civic skills, male students scored significantly lower than female students (Baldi et al., 2001). The skills subscale asked students to distinguish fact from opinion, interpret political cartoons, and comprehend in-

---

[8]Most of the researchers used tests of statistical significance to estimate the likelihood that a finding was due to chance. Unfortunately, the studies we reviewed did not report effect sizes. As a result, we are not able to report on the magnitude of the differences.

[9]For example, Brophy and Alleman noted a few patterns that might be worthy of further study: boys tended to emphasize protection as a reason for people's need for clothing whereas girls emphasized "modesty or decoration explanations in talking about the functions of clothing" (1999, p. 28); girls were more likely than boys to discuss the color(s) their ideal home would be painted and display an interest in living near certain amenities, such as restaurants, stores, and schools. In an earlier study of children's conceptions of family, researchers investigated kindergarteners' and first-graders' notions of family and found that girls were "far ahead" of boys in drawing accurate pictures of their families (Charlesworth, Burts, van-Meerveld, Stanley, & Delatte, 1989). The researchers noted the girls' "greater interest and involvement in family dramatic play, making them more conscious of their own family constellation" (p. 21).

[10]Consistent with NAEP studies conducted prior to 1995, on the National Household Education Survey conducted in 1996, male high school students in grades 9–12 were generally more likely than their female peers to correctly answer questions about political knowledge (NCES, 2000).

[11]Contrary to this general pattern of no gender differences in civic knowledge on tests administered to elementary and secondary school students, in a telephone survey of 15- to 25-year-old young people, young women consistently knew less about a number of political topics than did young men (Jenkins, 2005).

formation from political texts. The finding of male students' lower achievement on the civic skills scale appears, therefore, to be consistent with the results of the 1988 NAEP in which male students did less well than female peers in interpreting text material. These findings also appear to be consistent with much research on gender differences in reading comprehension, as reviewed in the chapter on reading and language arts in this *Handbook*. However, social studies researchers have not yet begun to explore the reasons why gender differences appear on these large-scale tests of social studies and civic skills.

Furthermore, gender differences seem to persist among the highest and lowest performing students, with male students doing better than female students on history and civics/government tests.   Despite the general finding of no gender difference in knowledge, some researchers have found that among the highest and lowest scoring students, male students tend to score higher than female students on history and civics/government tests. For example, on both the 1988 and 1998 NAEP civics assessments, male students outperformed female students at the advanced level at all three grades (Lutkus et al., 1999; Niemi & Junn, 1998). Similarly, in reviewing findings from a study of history knowledge that used a nationally representative sample of students, Chapin (1998) found more male than female students in the high scoring category for all grade levels, as well as more male than female students in the low scoring category at 8th and 10th grades.

Another "high performing" group are those high school students who take Advanced Placement (AP) tests.[12] In studies of AP test results in American and European history, researchers found that male students outperformed female students on the multiple-choice portion of the tests whereas female students did as well as or outperformed male students on the free response portion of the test (Breland, Danos, Kahn, Kubota, & Bonner, 1994; Mazzeo, Schmitt, & Bleistein, 1990, as cited in Breland et al., 1994). On the one hand, the male student advantage on the multiple choice tests appears to be consistent with other findings with respect to male students outperforming female students among high performing students. On the other hand, the finding of no gender difference or female advantage on free response items could be consistent with the findings reported above of female students doing better on tests that require mastery of literacy or interpretive skills. It is also possible that male students are more likely than their female peers to take risks and guess on multiple choice items. Those hypotheses remain to be tested with respect to AP tests and other tests that have yielded gender differences.

In another study of AP test results in urban schools, female students were more likely than male students to take the AP exam in U.S. history (Eisner, 2001). This finding corresponds with the generally stronger performance of female students than their male peers on the AP history test in urban schools. Unfortunately, other studies did not disaggregate data by gender and race/ethnicity, socio-economic status (SES), and urban/rural/suburban; consequently, we do not yet know if these differences are occurring in some, but not all, subgroups.

When gender differences have been found in student performance on history and civics/government tests, the differences are often attributable to the content of particular items on the test and/or to differential course taking patterns.   For example, using the National Education Longitudinal Study (NELS:88) data set, Le (1999) looked at Differential Item Functioning (DIF) scores on the 10th grade history test and found boys scored better on "masculine" items and girls on "feminine" ones. The differences in overall test results between boys and girls were found to "stem from differentiated historical knowledge corresponding to sex-role appropriateness" of particular items (p. 12). Based on previous research on test item construction and gender, researchers defined masculine content as themes of power, conflict, or control, and female themes as individual liberty, equality, social consequences of historical change, religion, and food. Le concluded that differences in overall test results did not stem from differing levels of historical proficiency between male and female students but from differential item functioning or item bias. Other researchers came to similar conclusions (Kneedler, 1988; Walstad & Robson, 1997; Walter & Young, 1997).

Male students tend to perform better than female students on tests of geographic and economic knowledge and skills given to elementary, high school, and college or university students; however no gender differences have been found in class performance, as indicated by grades in those subjects.   On the 1994 NAEP geography assessment at grades 4, 8, and 12, male students outperformed female students (National Center for Education Statistics, 1994). Similarly, in the Educational Testing Service Gender Study (1997), researchers analyzed data from hundreds of different tests administered to students in grades 4, 8, and 12 in the United States. They reported that in the test category 'geopolitical knowledge' male students outperformed female students.[13] The gender difference in geographic knowledge,

---

[12] In *Trends in Educational Equity of Girls and Women*, the National Center for Education Statistics (2004) reported that among the students who took social studies AP exams, 45.4% were young men and 54.6% were young women. Furthermore, the average score of male students was 3.1; and for female students, 2.8 (NCES, 2004, pp. 62–63).

[13] Spatial abilities have been an important part of discussions about sex and gender differences in geographical knowledge because they are related to map reading skills and to graphic reconstruction of environments based on experience. The preponderance of evidence on spatial abilities suggests that ". . . boys perform better than girls on certain tests of spatial ability," and that spatial ability is an aspect of sex differences in geographical knowledge (Linn & Peterson, 1985; Matthews, 1987; see also the discussion of spatial performance in chapter 2 on gender differences in this *Handbook*). The particular aspect of spatial ability phenomena that relates to geography is the ability to reconstruct three-dimensional space from memory; male students have consistently demonstrated strength in that area compared to female students. Further, in a review of research on graphicacy, Boardman (1990) found little difference between young girls' and boys' map reading abilities, but gender differences emerged as the students grew older.

which has been found repeatedly in elementary and high school students, has also been found in postsecondary populations.[14]

The one study that initially seemed to contradict this pattern was a study of geography classes in some Florida middle and high schools (LeVasseur, 1999). Although male students scored slightly higher than female students, the gender differences were not statistically significant for the total group. However, when data were compared for students scoring above average, average, and below average, gender differences were found in the above average achievement group (LeVasseur, 1999), which is consistent with the findings reported earlier on high performing students. Additionally, more male students than female students and more White students than African American students were in the above average achievement group. Among African American students, who comprised 15% of the total group, male students out performed female students in overall scores and in a geography skill subtest. This is one of the few studies that looked at gender and race/ethnicity simultaneously.

Economics, like geography, remains a subject in which young men tend to score higher on standardized tests than young women at both the high school and college levels (Amadeo, Torney-Purta, Lehmann, Husfeldt, & Nikolova, 2002; Becker, Greene, & Rosen, 1990; Hirschfeld, Moore, & Brown, 1995; Walstad & Soper, 1989). Additionally, male students tend to learn more economics than female students over the period of a semester's course, as reflected in gain scores using pretests and posttests; however, the gender difference is typically small, "on the order of a couple of multiple choice questions, when background variables are controlled" (Becker et al., 1990). There is, however, some indication that the gap may be narrowed or reversed when essay, rather than multiple choice, questions are used (Becker et al., 1990), a finding that is consistent with research on history assessments, as noted earlier.

With respect to social studies-related attitudes, the story is mixed. For some attitudes, gender differences have consistently been found, whereas for other attitudes no gender differences are apparent. First, in large-scale studies of student attitudes toward social studies, history, and economics courses at the secondary level, young men reported liking social studies, economics, and government courses better than did their female peers (Chapin, 1998; Niemi & Junn, 1998; Walstad & Soper, 1989).[15] In one small-scale study, Fouts (1990) asked: Do girls differ in their perceptions of social studies depending on the gender of the teacher? He found that the presence of a female teacher improved girl students' favorable attitudes towards social studies. Girls studying social studies with female teachers reported that they were more interested and involved in class, felt more supported by their teachers, and anticipated getting higher grades than those studying with teachers who were men. Corbin (1996) attempted to replicate Fouts' study of student attitudes toward social studies by administering questionnaires to two groups of high school seniors. Consistent with Fouts' findings, young men reported more interest in social studies than did young women. These studies need to be replicated further before we can make the claims about the reasons for differences in students' attitudes toward social studies, but the issue is certainly worth investigating further.

Second, with respect to societal attitudes that are related to the social studies area, there are no gender differences in student levels of political interest or in perceptions of conventional citizenship. In the United States young women and men are equally likely (or unlikely) to say that they are interested in politics and that a good citizen engages in conventional activities, such as voting, respecting government leaders, following political news, and discussing politics (Hahn, 1996; 1998; Torney-Purta et al., 2001).

Third, there are gender differences in attitudes toward government and citizenship. Female students in the United States are more likely than male students to report that they trust government institutions such as their local council and the courts (Baldi et al., 2001).[16] Additionally, female students are more likely than their male peers to say that the government should be responsible for society-related services, such as education and health care.[17] In a similar vein, female students are more likely than male students to associate citizenship with participation in social movement-related activities, such as helping the community and promoting human rights (Torney-Purta et al., 2001).[18]

---

[14]In studies of college and university undergraduates, male students have consistently been found to outperform female students on tests of geographic knowledge (Beatty & Trotter, 1987; Bein, 1990; Eve, Price, & Counts, 1994; Hardwick, Bean, Alexander, & Shelley, 2000; Henrie, Aron, Nelson, Poole, 1997; Nelson, Aron, & Poole, 1999). Interestingly, in two of these studies, the researchers found that the gender differences that appeared on the tests were not found in student grades; male and female students apparently performed equally well in class (Henrie et al., 1997; Nelson, Aron, & Poole, 1997).

[15]However, in other studies, which used small, nonrepresentative samples, findings were not clear cut. In one study, female students preferred social history and disliked lectures; in another study, no gender differences were found in preferences for teaching approaches; and in a third study, both genders reported liking social studies, with male students ranking it as their favorite subject and female students ranking it second, behind English/language arts (Ferguson, 1993; Lawson, 1999; Protano, 2003).

[16]That finding is similar to the results for students in Belgium (French), Denmark, and Switzerland. However, in Cyprus and Portugal, male students reported more trust in government institutions than did female students; in the other 22 countries studied, no gender differences were found (Torney-Purta et al., 2001).

[17]Similarly, in Belgium (French), England, Finland, Greece, Italy, Portugal, and Slovenia, female students were more likely than male students to say the government should be responsible for society-related activities. There were no gender differences on this scale for the other 20 countries that participated in the IEA study (Torney-Purta et al., 2001).

[18]Although no gender differences were found on the Social Movement Citizenship Scale in 19 countries, the United States was not alone in finding that female students were more likely than male students to associate social movement activities with good citizenship. Similar findings were obtained in Denmark, Finland, Germany, Greece, Italy, Norway, Sweden, and Switzerland. In no countries were male students more likely than female students to associate good citizenship with social movement activities (Torney-Purta et al., 2001).

Fourth, there are gender differences in attitudes toward rights for immigrants and women. Social studies teachers often have as one of their goals that their students will develop positive attitudes toward diverse members of society. Yet, despite the value given to this goal, few researchers have systematically studied whether female and male students are developing such attitudes. In the IEA study female students in the United States and 22 other countries were more likely than their male peers to support rights for immigrants, such as saying that immigrant children should have the same opportunities for an education as other children and immigrants should have the right to vote in elections (Baldi et al., 2001; Torney-Purta et al., 2001).

Many social studies teachers in general, and civics and government teachers in particular, want to instill in their students a belief that all citizens, regardless of gender should have equal rights to participate in civic and political life. Over the years, researchers have examined students' attitudes toward women in politics, government, and economic life, consistently concluding that female students tend to be more supportive of gender equity than male students (Hahn, 1996, 1998; Torney, Oppenheim, & Farnen, 1975; Torney-Purta, 1991). The IEA study is the most recent study that explored this topic; female students in the United States, like those in the other 27 participating countries, were more likely than their male counterparts to support political and economic rights for women (Torney-Purta et al., 2001). Despite this gender difference, however, overall, U.S. students were supportive of women having political and economic equality; 90% agreed that women should have equal rights to men to participate in politics and the economy.[19]

There are gender differences in student experiences related to social studies and participatory citizenship. It appears that today female students are more likely than male students to anticipate being politically active adults. For example, in the IEA study significantly more female students than male students anticipated that they would vote in national elections, collect money for charities, and collect signatures for a petition (Torney-Purta et al., 2001).[20] Female students in the United States were also more likely than their male peers to anticipate joining a political party, writing letters to newspapers about social or political concerns, and being a candidate for local political office (Baldi et al., 2001). In other research female high school students in the United States were more likely than their male peers to say they could make a statement at a public meeting or write a letter to a government official (NCES, 2000).[21]

In recent years researchers have been giving increased attention to young people's participation in community service activities as one indication of citizen engagement. Although community service is not necessarily linked to the social studies curriculum, often it is. Additionally, students' experiences with community service may influence their knowledge of and attitudes toward a number of issues that might be addressed in social studies classes. For this reason, social studies educators are interested in the role of community service experiences and a few researchers have begun to look at the role of gender in civic participation. In the IEA study, 50% of U.S. ninth graders said that they had participated in a group to help the community (Torney-Purta et al., 2001). In other studies, researchers have found that female students in the United States tend to engage in community service activities more than do their male counterparts (Chapin, 2001; Flanagan, Bowes, Jonson, Csapo, & Sheblanova, 1998; Independent Sector, 1996).[22] Furthermore, race/ethnicity, as well as gender, appears related to the type of group students are most likely to join. In one study African American female students were the most likely to participate in political groups; Asian female students were most likely to participate in hospital groups; White female students were most likely to participate in environmental groups; and White male students participated most in youth groups (Chapin, 2001). This is one of the few studies that considered the intersection of race/ethnicity and gender, revealing insights to young people's differing experiences. Further research is needed to ascertain why such differences occur, what these varied experiences mean to young people, and whether they have differing long-term

---

[19]Still, almost 10% of 14-year-old students disagreed and said that women should stay out of politics; 17% said that men are better qualified to be political leaders than are women (Baldi et al., 2001). Predictors of support for women's rights were: civic knowledge, confidence in participation at school, learning at school to get along with other people with diverse ideas, and an open classroom climate for discussion (Torney-Purta & Amadeo, 2004). In the IEA study of upper secondary students (grades 11, 12, or 13), young women in all 14 participating countries (which did not include the United States) expressed greater support for women's political rights than did young men (Amadeo et al., 2002). Additionally, among 14 year old, girls were more likely than boys to support rights for minorities and anti-democratic groups (Kennedy, 2006).

[20]In 24 of the 28 countries participating in the IEA study, female students were more likely than male students to say they thought they would be likely to collect money for charity as an adult and in 16 of the countries female students were more likely than their male peers to say they expected to vote in national elections (Torney-Purta et al., 2001). However, the question of whether expected voting patterns of 14 year olds become reality when the young people reach voting age has not been clearly answered. In one study of U.S. 20 to 25 year olds only about one in four men and women alike said that they had voted. In exit polls at the time of the 2004 presidential election 37% of young men reported voting, compared to 46% of young women (Jenkins, 2005). Expectations of collecting money for charity do seem to become reality; among 15 to 25 year olds in 2002, young women were more likely than young men to report that they had raised money for a charity (Jenkins, 2005).

[21]However, in the study of 15 to 25 year olds, virtually no differences separated young women from men in their rates of political voice activism; both groups were equally likely to report that they had participated in a boycott or buycott, signed a written petition, signed an email petition, contacted a public official, contacted the print or broadcast media, participated in a protest, or canvassed for a party or issue (Jenkins, 2005). Research on gender differences in news consumption has been inconsistent. In one national survey, male high school students were more likely than female peers to say they read about and watched or listened to national news daily (NCES, 2000). In the IEA study there were no significant gender differences in following national news in the newspaper or watching news broadcasts on television for U.S. students; female students in the United States were, however, more likely than male students to report listening to news on the radio (Baldi et al., 2001). Similar results were obtained in the study of 15 to 25 year olds. Young men were more likely than young women to report regularly reading the newspaper and watching the nightly news on television (Jenkins, 2005).

[22]This pattern continues into young adulthood, as more young women than young men ages 15 to 19 reported that they had volunteered for a non political group (Jenkins, 2005).

effects. It is likely that "civic action" connotes different kinds of action for students from diverse groups. For example, White middle class students of both genders may take their models from people like themselves who engaged in electoral politics or local grassroots community organizing, whereas African American students may use as their models youth who practiced civil disobedience in the Civil Rights movement or leaders like Sojourner Truth, a citizen activist without the traditional markers of citizenship.

In one other longitudinal study (which did not look at the intersection with race/ethnicity), researchers linked participation in high school extracurricular activities with women's later civic participation. Women who were active in high school activities were the most likely to become members of and leaders in community organizations as adults up to 14 years after finishing high school (Damico, Damico, & Conway, 1998). Being a leader in high school, such as a student council officer or newspaper editor, in particular, increased the likelihood of women's later civic activism.[23]

Despite the fact that numerous researchers have examined relationships between gender and social studies knowledge, skills, attitudes, and experiences in recent years, most of the research has not moved beyond identifying whether there are gender differences. Where gender differences have been consistently found, we do not yet have explanations as to why they occur. We do not yet know whether the socialization hypothesis discussed in the gender differences chapter of this *Handbook* is applicable or whether other explanations are more powerful.

Regardless of whether there are gender differences in student knowledge, skills, attitudes, and experiences, it is important that all students learn about gender-related topics if they are to acquire an accurate knowledge of the social world. In the next section we review research on gender in the social studies curriculum.

Gender Inequities in Social Studies Curriculum, Textbooks, and Instruction

Despite the presence of women's studies departments at colleges and universities since the 1970s and the creation of women's studies courses for high school students in the 1980s (Hahn, 1985), apparently few such courses exist in high schools today. In one survey of the 50 state social studies coordinators, only a few of the respondents said that school districts in their state offered separate courses in women's studies (Hahn, Dilworth, Hughes, & Sen, 1998). Rather, the coordinators said they thought that content on women and gender was infused into courses such as U.S. history. That assumption, however, is not supported if social studies curriculum standards and textbooks are any indication of the curricular content that is delivered to students. In this section we discuss studies of social studies curriculum as represented in national and state standards, textbooks, and classroom instruction in elementary and secondary social studies, history, geography, civics/government, and economics. We also consider the curriculum and instruc-

tional aspects of social studies teacher education as it relates to gender.

In recent years national curriculum standards were developed in several content areas related to social studies. The *Curriculum Standards for Social Studies* (National Council for the Social Studies, 1994), *National Standards for Civics and Government* (Center for Civic Education, 1994), *National Standards for History* (National Center for History in the Schools, 1996), *Geography for Life: National Geography Standards* (Geography Education Standards Project, 1994), and *Voluntary National Standards in Economics* (National Council on Economic Education, 1997) are relevant to an exploration of gender in the social studies curriculum. In addition, as states have been developing their own curricular standards in social studies, some researchers have analyzed state curriculum standards for their treatment of gender.

Women and gender-related topics are underrepresented in social studies curriculum standards. For the most part, curriculum standards in social studies are silent about women and gender-related topics. The only exceptions to this are references to the Seneca Falls conference for women's rights and passage of the 19th Amendment to the U.S. Constitution. Gender-related topics, such as the movements for birth control, the Equal Rights Amendment, and Title IX of the 1972 Amendments to the Higher Education Act are not mentioned. Similarly, the history of civic action through women's organizations and obstacles to women being elected to public office are omitted from curriculum documents.

Since the 1980s social studies has been greatly affected by the accountability movement and standards-based testing in American education. According to Joan Wallach Scott (1997), a member of a panel organized by the Council for Basic Education to review the *National Standards for History*, the creation of curriculum standards in American and world history had the effect of codifying a political approach that "makes the systematic inclusion of women difficult." This approach "emphasizes the growth of nation-states" (Scott, 1997, p. 173), and because women have been only marginal players in official capacities in state governance, such an approach tends to obscure women's role in history. Nevertheless, Scott noted, the national history standards did exhibit some evidence of the new knowledge generated about women's history over the last two decades.

Additionally, Symcox (2002), who took the long view in her study of the "struggle for national standards," comments that over the last century women's history gained legitimacy as a category of analysis in American classrooms. Nevertheless, the history standards and high-stakes testing movements have created new barriers to the inclusion of women's history, especially those standards adopted at the state level where the emphasis has been on political and economic history rather than social and cultural history.

In one study that analyzed elementary social studies curriculum standards, Henry (1989) examined the K–8 history—social science curriculum for one school district in California. The researcher lauded the state's framework for its "clear call for the

---

[23]Extracurricular participation in high school was not, however, predictive of men's later civic participation.

inclusion of women's history" yet pointed out that at times the "most pertinent questions" were left out. For example, the discussion of economics that espoused a global perspective neglected to "call attention to the place of women in the global economy" (Henry, 1989, p. 27). Similarly, McKenna (1989) examined the 1986 Curriculum Guide in History and Contemporary Studies for Ontario, Canada. McKenna noted the forward-thinking language of the guide on sex equity but also observed, "the guideline is riddled with unconscious bias" (p. 21). McKenna's analysis is subtle, as she points out that changes in language do not necessarily reflect gender or racial equity. For example, McKenna noted that in making the change from "common man" to "common person" when referring to the Jacksonian era, the revision did not change the fact that women and Blacks had little status or power in the period, which the text does not mention.

The National Standards for Civics and Government only mention gender twice (on pp. 95 and 111) when they suggest that women's suffrage and discrimination against women, along with similar topics related to race and ethnicity, could be used to demonstrate how citizen participation expanded over time (Center for Civic Education, 1994). One team of researchers did a content analysis of the quotations that were used as graphics in the margins of the book containing the civics and government standards (Gonzales, Riedel, Avery, & Sullivan, 2001). They found that 90% of the highlighted quotes were from men. Sixty-four of the quotations (83%) were attributed to European American men. Of the remaining 13 quotations, 7 were by European American women, 5 by African American men, and 1 by a Native American man. The researchers noted that quotes by African American women, as well as quotes by Latinos and Asians of either gender, were "conspicuously absent" (Gonzales, et al., 2001). This was particularly surprising to the researchers in light of the fact that most of the quotes that were featured were from the 20th century; clearly, the proportion of men and women in different ethnic groups that make up the country's population and the numbers of elected officials locally and in Congress were not represented.

The *Curriculum Standards for Social Studies*, developed by the National Council for the Social Studies (1994), give little explicit attention to gender; however, they are broad enough to allow teachers who are so inclined to infuse gender into teaching the subject. Nevertheless, NCSS's failure to provide curricular examples aligned with the standards that are oriented to gender resulted in a missed opportunity to facilitate the inclusion of gender in social studies courses.

Women and gender-related topics are underrepresented in social studies textbooks. The one aspect of curriculum that has been studied most frequently is the content presented in social studies textbooks. Researchers have repeatedly concluded that textbooks play a dominant role in social studies instruction (Baldi et al., 2001; Lutkus et al., 1999; Niemi & Junn, 1998). Earlier researchers concluded that textbooks for U.S. history, world history, civics/government, and economics contained few women, presented women in stereotypic roles, and gave little attention to gender-related issues (see Hahn & Bernard-Powers, 1985, for a summary of the early research). By the late 1990s, many educators assumed that publishers' non-

sexist guidelines had "taken care of the problem." Such a conclusion was premature, however, as revealed in recent studies of textbooks.

In one study of Canadian history textbooks, Light, Staton, and Bourne (1989) found that for 66 history textbooks published in the 1980s the treatment of women was inaccurate, marginal, or trivial to the main narrative in each chapter. In a recent study of 5th grade U.S. history books adopted in California, Savage (2005) found disparities in the percentages of men and women who were specifically mentioned in the books. For example, in the chapter on the Revolutionary War, 77% of the people mentioned were men compared to 23% women. In the chapters on westward expansion, 92% of the specific people mentioned were men, compared to only 8% women. Similar findings have been obtained in studies of textbooks for high school students. In a study of high school U.S. history textbooks, Clark, Allard, and Mahoney (2004) found that women were more visible than they had been in the past, although the coverage tended to be superficial. Researchers who studied world history textbooks came to a similar conclusion (Clark, Ayton, Frechette, & Keller, 2005). In a third study of high school history textbooks, Kuzmic (2000) focused on constructions of masculinity. He concluded that textbooks support notions of patriarchy and male dominance. The researchers in these and other studies concluded that although progress has been made, significant disparities in treatment of men and women in history continue to exist (American Association of University Women, 1998; Clark et al., 2004; Clark et al., 2005; Commeyras & Alverman, 1996).

Avery and Simmons (2000/2001) analyzed widely used civics, as well as U.S. history, textbooks for grades 7 through 9. They found that with only a few exceptions, such as Martin Luther King Jr., the people most frequently mentioned in the books were European American male office holders. Women received significantly less coverage than men in both the civics and history books. In the civics textbooks, women were mentioned 258 times, compared to 1,899 for men (Avery & Simmons, 2000/2001, pp. 122–123). Furthermore, several of the women who were mentioned, such as Abigail Adams and Eleanor Roosevelt, were wives of presidents and very few women of color were mentioned in either the history or civics books. The civics books, in particular, rarely highlighted women as role models in politics and government. Only one of the civics texts examined directly discussed the disparity between men and women in the political realm; the authors drew attention to a chart showing the underrepresentation of women in Congress.

In the 1980s, researchers who conducted a content analysis of high school economics textbooks concluded that there were few references to women or to gender-related topics, such as women in the work force (Hahn & Blankenship, 1983). In preparing this review of research on gender and social studies, we were unable to locate any recent studies that investigated these phenomena at the high school level. However, several researchers examined college economics textbooks for their treatment of women and minorities and gender-related topics (Feiner; 1993; Gray, 1992; Robson, 2001). They found that although the economics books had improved somewhat over earlier periods, particularly with respect to language and examples, they were still inadequate in terms of addressing issues related to gender equity. We wonder if the same might be true of the textbooks used in high school economics courses.

There is minimal research that specifically focuses on the representation of women and underrepresented groups in geography textbooks and it focuses on college level textbooks, rather than those used in elementary and high schools. For example, Mayer's (1989) study of the representation of women in eight human geography textbooks used in undergraduate courses revealed themes that might arise in middle and high school textbooks. Fewer photographs contained women than contained men (Mayer, 1989). Mayer found that women were largely invisible in the graphics and in the text material and the category of gender was not employed (Mayer, 1989, pp. 400, 405). Since this study was published, the National Council on Geographic Education proposed and acted on initiatives focusing on underrepresented groups, as discussed in the next section on what has been done to address gender inequities.

Although most textbook studies done over the last ten years report greater inclusion of women than did earlier studies, they also note that the treatment of women remains superficial and limited to sidebars (Avery & Simmons, 2000/2001; Hahn, 1996; Reese, 1994). Despite the overall gains, it is not unusual for large urban school systems to use textbooks that are 10 or 20 years old (Ginsberg, Shapiro, & Brown, 2004). To the degree that this is commonplace in American urban schools, such practice clearly undercuts the effectiveness of the progress made in gender inclusion in textbook publishing in recent years.

Women and gender-related topics tend to be absent from social studies classroom instruction.

Looking beyond textbooks, middle and high school social studies practices seem to have made only minimal adjustments related to teaching about women. Anecdotal evidence indicates that many schools mark Women's History Month in March, just as they do Black History Month in February. The greater challenge appears to be incorporating women's experience into the curriculum throughout the year. One researcher found that in 80 middle school classrooms in one state, little teaching about women's history occurred (Schmurak & Ratliff, 1993); other scholars believe that there has been "a backlash against diversity with regards to gender" (Connors, 2004). Although such a phenomenon may be difficult to confirm empirically, allegations of backlash have been widely voiced over the last 10 years.

In one case study of high school civics classes, the researcher examined the textbook in use and came to conclusions similar to those of Avery and Simmons; male "founding fathers," presidents, vice presidents, and chief justices of the Supreme Court were mentioned far more frequently than women political leaders (Hahn, 1996). Interestingly, the textbook authors had tried to portray women as activist citizens through photographs and anecdotes. Additionally, they included women in some of the special features titled Applying Skills, Solving Problems, and Citizens in Action. However, the teachers whose classes were observed over a semester did not draw attention to the special sections or to the women pictured in textbook photographs.

They also did not mention the few sentences in the textbook that noted women's participation in political life. In short, when the textbook contained the potential to explore gender-related issues, the teachers of the particular civics classes under study did not use those opportunities, nor did they supplement the textbook with additional information on gender-related issues. Moreover, despite the textbook's avoidance of male pronouns, the teachers were not as careful. The researcher concluded by saying that given this context, it was not surprising that in talking about political leaders, the students in these classes only referred to men (Hahn, 1996). Unfortunately, we do not have other case studies or surveys to shed light on how typical those civics classes are.

Apparently the women's suffrage movement, which is mentioned in the curriculum standards and the textbooks, is the one gender-related topic that students are likely to study. In focus groups for the IEA case study of civic education in the United States, both teachers and students said that in their social studies classes they had talked about the suffragists, as well as about women in colonial America.[24] A few students also mentioned learning about Rosa Parks and Eleanor Roosevelt (Hahn, 1999).

Although the evidence on what students learn about women and gender in their social studies courses is quite sparse, it does all point in one direction. Gender-related topics are rarely addressed and, with the exception of the women's suffrage movement, women's civic–political action is rarely portrayed. Given this situation, girls may choose to engage less with a subject that seems not to include people like themselves. Perhaps that is the reason that in one longitudinal study, using a nationally representative sample of students who were followed in the 8th, 10th, and 12th grades, boys reported taking more history classes and more participation in history clubs than did girls (Chapin, 1998). One researcher questions whether "females were not choosing to enroll in history at the same rate as males because of the dearth of historical female figures within the curriculum, which is thought to adversely affect girls' level of engagement" (Le, 1999). Many other scholars writing about gender balancing the curriculum have emphasized this point (Sadker & Sadker, 1994; Clark et al., 2005)

Sometimes the hidden curriculum in social studies classes conveys traditional stereotypes.

For example, in one study researchers found that in 80 middle schools visited in the state of Connecticut, only pictures of male historical figures were hung on the walls of social studies classrooms and boys dominated class discussions (Schmurak & Ratliff, 1993). Likewise, in a study of single-sex and co-educational secondary independent schools, boys dominated discussions in the majority of social studies classrooms in the co-educational schools (Lee, Marks, & Byrd, 1994). This research was notable for its attention to actual practices of teachers and its sophisticated approach to consideration of sexism in classroom contexts. However, not all researchers have observed gender differences in classroom interaction. In the case study of two ninth grade civics classes discussed earlier, for example, the researcher did

---

[24]In their studies of children's historical thinking, Barton and Levstik (1998) also found that elementary students had learned about the women's suffrage movement.

not observe any gender differences in classroom interaction patterns (Hahn, 1996).

In social studies classes male students perceive the classroom climate to be less supportive of open discussion than do their female classmates. Social studies students learn about democratic discourse and participation in society not only from the content of their textbooks and topics that are explored in lessons but also by the practices that are modeled in the classroom. The research on how young men and women perceive their social studies classroom climates in terms of support for expressing their opinions and discussing controversial issues has been quite consistent, with female secondary students reporting a more open climate than do their male peers. In the recent IEA Civic Education Study, female ninth graders in the United States were more likely than male ninth graders to report that their classes had an open climate for discussion (Baldi et al., 2001; Torney-Purta et al., 2001).[25] In the study students were asked if they felt they were encouraged to express their views and explore controversial social, economic, and political issues in their social studies classes. Items also asked if students thought that their teachers presented more than one side of an issue, and if students felt comfortable expressing their views in class even when their views differed from those of their teacher or other students. Unfortunately, despite the consistency of findings, no researchers have yet explored why male and female students report differences in the classroom climate for discussion.

In a case study of controversial issues discussion in two teachers' classes, one researcher identified a number of ways in which male and female students perceive issues related to discussion differently (Hess, 2002). At the end of the courses in which discussion skills were explicitly taught, female students were more likely to report that they spoke in discussions and less likely to say that they were afraid classmates would think their ideas unworthy of consideration than they had reported at the beginning of the course. Male students' reported enjoyment of discussions increased from the beginning of the course to the end. Additionally, male students were more likely at the end of the course than the beginning to say that all students have a responsibility to participate in discussions, at least occasionally. Although the study demonstrated students' abilities to participate effectively in controversial public issues discussions improved as a result of a course that placed primacy on such discussions, it was evident that male and female students were not affected in the same ways by the course.

For the most part social studies teacher education has been silent about gender and gender equity issues. Little research linking teacher education and gender with particular reference to the social studies has been reported. One exception to this generalization is an ethnographic study of a teacher education program at a university in western Canada.

The researcher found that preservice student teachers recognized and espoused the importance of teaching about gender and multicultural topics in the schools; however, little evidence of teaching these topics could be found within the preservice teachers' preparation program (Segall, 2002).

In another study, researchers did a content analysis of 23 major teacher education textbooks published between 1998 and 2001, including popular social studies teacher education textbooks (Zittleman & Sadker, 2003). The researchers found little attention given to gender in social studies methods books, even the most up-to-date versions. Although Zittleman and Sadker (2003) noted that social studies texts "provide more space on the topic of gender than any other methods texts," it was still only 2.5 percent of the content space.

Finally, in one study Crocco (2005b) examined gender from a global perspective in a social studies teacher education program. She questioned the use of literature in teaching about "women of the world," especially that depicting Muslim women in the post-9/11 climate of fear and stereotyping of Muslims in the West. The teacher education course, "Women of the World: Issues in Teaching," which served as the context for this research, has been described in several publications (Crocco, 2000; Crocco & Patel, 2003).

Social studies educators and social studies researchers have only recently begun to give attention to gender and sexuality. A few recent publications have linked attention to gender and sexuality to teaching social studies at the K–12 level (Blount, 2004; Crocco, 2001; 2002; Levstik & Groth, 2002; Loutzenheiser, 2006). Authors link misogyny and homophobia to violence against girls, women, gays, lesbians, transexual and transgendered individuals and call for greater attention to teaching about sexuality within the social studies curriculum as a means of helping to address social issues. Loutzenheiser (2006) explored the intersections of race, gender, and sexual orientation and reflected upon the reasons why identity and difference seem to get little attention in social education. However, so far little empirical research has been conducted on these topics in social studies classes.

Similarly, social studies educators and scholars have been largely silent about the intersection of technology, gender, and social studies. Little research linking gender, technology, and social studies has been conducted, despite the fact that considerable research outside of social studies has been done linking gender and technology. For that reason, scholars have argued that social studies teacher education needs to pay greater attention to gender when technology infusion is the goal (Crocco & Cramer, 2004a, 2004b, 2005; Goodson, Mangan, & Rhea, 1991; Owens, 1999). Although the primary professional journals in social studies and social studies research have had special issues and regular features focusing on technology and the social studies, few authors have given any atten-

---

[25]This finding was consistent with earlier small-scale studies that used nonrepresentative samples (Hahn, 1996, 1998). As with the earlier studies, the difference in perceptions by gender was statistically significant, but it was not large (Baldi et al., 2001). Nevertheless, in 23 of the 28 countries participating in the IEA study, female students perceived their classroom climates to be more open than did male students (Torney-Purta et al., 2001).

tion to gender and its possible relationship to social studies and technology.

One project that addresses this need is the GlobalEd Project, based at the University of Connecticut (www.globaled.uconn.edu). The project was designed to address perceived gender differences in leadership, decision-making styles, and values in approaches to technology. The Project uses the ICONS (International Communication and Negotiation Simulation) format, developed at the University of Maryland, to examine possible gender differences in technology use. In one study of the GlobalEd Project, Brown, Boyer, and Mayall (2003) found that male students who participated in the simulation scored higher on measures of technological self-efficacy than female students in both pretests and posttests. Nevertheless, the researchers concluded that embedding technology into academic subjects, such as was done in the GlobalEd Project, holds the potential of reducing the gender gap in technology use (Brown et al., 2003). Additional research on the use of the GlobalEd Project was reported in two dissertation studies (Johnson, 2005; Mayall, 2002). Young men exhibited higher levels of technological self-efficacy than did their female peers (Mayall, 2002), a finding commonly found in research outside social studies. In the other study, male and female students demonstrated different styles of leadership in both the on-line and face-to-face versions of the simulation (Johnson, 2005).

Several other dissertations on technology and social studies have also reported findings related to gender. In one study, Mucherah (1999) examined the use of computers in 14 social studies classrooms in three public urban middle schools. The researcher found significant gender differences, with boys more involved than girls with computers and more inclined to use computers competitively.[26] In another dissertation study, conducted in secondary schools in North Carolina, Heafner (2002) found that teacher attributes and barriers to classroom use greatly influenced the likelihood that technology would be adopted in teaching social studies. Interestingly, in this study, female social studies teachers found technology of greater value than did male social studies teachers. Men saw technology as a useful tool for classroom management and word processing. Women saw technology as a teaching tool, and favored incorporation of a greater number of applications, including spreadsheets and web publishing.

Several of these studies used small nonrepresentative samples and case studies in unique settings. Consequently, they are not generalizable. However, they do suggest hypotheses for promising research in the future using additional samples and cases.

WHAT HAS BEEN DONE TO FOSTER GENDER EQUITY IN SOCIAL STUDIES?

Although the documentation of gender inequity in K–12 social studies, addressed in the previous section, is relatively well developed, the research record on what has been done to foster gender equity is substantially less developed. There is little re-

search that documents the effects of gender-equitable social studies curricula on students' and teachers' beliefs, attitudes, and knowledge.

Nonetheless there is a considerable body of scholarship offering critiques on curricula generally and recommendations for the multiple ways that teachers and teacher educators can provide gender-inclusive content in their classrooms, schools, and curriculum documents (Bernard-Powers, 1996a, 1996b; Crocco, 1995, Levstik, 2001; Merryfield & Crocco, 2003). From this body of work we have identified what we believe are promising practices, contexts, and conditions that can foster and inform gender equity in the teaching and learning of social studies. In this section we supplement findings from empirical research with observations and commentary that are primarily descriptive, subjective, and anecdotal in an attempt to give a more complete picture than the limited view that would emerge from empirical studies alone. The aggregate suggests that there is a great deal to be gleaned from informally documented practices, as well as from research.

Curriculum and Instruction

Since the 1985 *Handbook* was published, a few researchers focused specifically on the effects of gender-inclusive and gender-sensitive social studies curriculum and instruction on students and teachers. In five studies researchers focused on teaching history to secondary students; in other studies researchers focused on teaching geography to K–12 students and teachers; and two studies focused on preservice teachers enrolled in a social studies methods course.

Revising history instruction. In one of the earliest studies Tetreault (1986) interviewed post–high school students who, when they were in the 11th grade, had participated in an elective U.S. history course on women in American society. Tetreault concluded that the students had been deeply affected by the experience of studying women's history. The young people appreciated the significance of studying women's history for understanding women's influence on society and they discussed the relevancy of history to their own lives.

A second study was a case study in one middle school class in Kentucky that studied women's history (Levstik & Groth, 2002). The researchers found that students identified women's experiences as historically significant. Additionally, the students recognized, analyzed, and expressed interest in the variety of perspectives represented by women they studied. They also worried about "reverse sexism." Students who participated in this "experiment" in teaching women's history also expressed interest in issues of gender and sexuality (Levstik & Groth, 2002).

In another case study, Doyle (1998) studied the impact of gender-balanced social studies on a group of 29 grade ten students in Canada and compared the treatment group to a comparison group of 24 students. Doyle found that students who were taught the gender-balanced curriculum showed greater ap-

---

[26]Similarly, in a study of the use of computers in sex-segregated social studies classes in Saudi Arabia, Alzamil (2003) found that young women demonstrated less knowledge, skills, and self confidence in using computers than did young men.

preciation for social studies and were more willing to take additional history courses than were students in the comparison group. Furthermore, the female students in the treatment group were "more apt to express feelings of pride and self-confidence when dealing with issues of gender . . ." (Doyle, 1998, p. iv). Doyle concluded that a gender-inclusive curriculum could be "beneficial for all those involved." Moreover, the researcher noted the importance of constructing a curriculum that was not primarily textbook-focused, but one that drew on diverse sources to teach a gender-balanced history and social studies (p. 104).

In a much larger study, conducted in The Netherlands, ten Dam and Rijkschroeff (1996) studied the effects of teaching women's history on secondary students' learning. The researchers compared 11 classes where women's history was taught with 11 classes where traditional history was taught. This study incorporated well-designed teacher materials and an orientation to the materials for the teachers involved. Students were asked to report on their instruction using a methodology known as "Learner Reports," in which they answered prompts about (a) what they learned about the subject content, and (b) how they related to the content.

The researchers in this study observed that in both the traditional and gendered- history groups, the boys reported liking women's history "slightly less" than girls did (ten Dam & Rijkschroeff, 1996, p. 81). The female students found women's history "interesting and worth studying," although they were not inclined to relate the disadvantaged positions that women occupied in the past to their own lives. According to the researchers, the female students were reluctant to identify with a group that was "lagging behind" (p. 86).

A second experimental study done in The Netherlands is closely related to the previous one. Ten Dam and Teekens (1997) compared the effects of what they called "female friendly" and "regular" methods of teaching history. They found that both male and female students did not see women's history as a body of knowledge when it was taught in a "female-friendly way" although such an approach did enhance girls' attitudes and learning of history.

Interestingly, a third study conducted in The Netherlands provides impressive evidence from a naturally occurring experiment of the effects of teaching women's experiences as part of the history curriculum. In 1990 more than 40,000 pupils in Dutch secondary schools, ranging from lower vocational schools to the most academic level of pre-university track schools, were taught by some 1,500 teachers about 20th century women's history of The Netherlands and the United States in preparation for the national history examinations (Grever, 1991). To assess the effects of this change in the national history curriculum, the Dutch Central Testing Institute examined test results from a random sample of 8,084 students who had experienced the new gender-inclusive approach to teaching history. They found that, contrary to previous years, young women's test scores were higher than the young men's scores, although the young men still achieved superior grades on the test section concerning World War II.

Although none of these studies addressed the social construction of complex identities in which ethnic identity, language, and social class interact with gender, they opened the door to a difficult question in social studies research: how do we identify, talk about, and assess the effects of gender-sensitive history and social studies instruction on students? Hopefully, these studies can serve as a base from which future researchers explore that question in more depth.

Notable developments in geography education. Of the initiatives to reform curricula and ensure more gender-equitable education, efforts in geography education stand out. In this section we discuss ways in which various geographers took steps in the late 1980s and early 1990s to address inequities in geography learning, alter the content of human geography, and make the subject more interesting to the student population generally (LeVasseur, 1993). The work involved: (a) collaboration among researchers to build a knowledge base; (b) research and scholarship focused on understanding gender differences and instructional strategies; and (c) an orchestrated and comprehensive plan to address the needs of girls and women and other underrepresented groups in geography classes.

Pioneers in gender and geography education, such as Professor Janice Monk and her colleagues in The South West Institute for Research on Women (SIROW) at the University of Arizona in Tucson, worked to alter the content of geography and disseminated the work in multiple professional settings (McDowell, 1992). Scholars who took on the challenge of understanding gender, race, and ethnic differences in geography set about creating curricula for diverse populations that have made a substantial contribution to social studies.

Wridt's (1998) project on children's experiences titled "The World of Girls and Boys: Geographic Experience and Informal Learning Opportunities" provides a good example of curriculum change that built on research. Wridt, who was a graduate student at City University of New York, designed and evaluated a lesson that built upon knowledge of gender differences in students' geographic range of experiences; that is the lesson built on the recognition that many girls tend to stay closer to home than boys who range further from their homes when playing with friends. This curriculum design and its evaluation involved 13-year-old students in Eugene, Oregon keeping diaries of their everyday travel. The results of the study ". . . suggest that males and females encounter different types of informal learning opportunities through their daily environmental interactions," and these are potentially significant for geography instruction (Wridt, 1998, p. 253).

Subsequent to the publication of Wridt's (1998) study, the researcher developed a lesson on "The Gendered Geographies of Everyday Life," which was published in the National Council for Geographic Education's Pathways project (Wridt, 2000). This project is noteworthy because researchers identified a potential barrier, a graduate student used that knowledge to create curricula, and senior researchers Rickie Sanders of Temple University and Karen Nairn of Otago University, New Zealand, worked with Wridt to revise the lesson for publication. The multigenerational approach to applying research on gender and geography to the design of specific remedies makes this project and the collaboration distinctive.

The work of geographers that focused on gender renders the field exceptional. To change geography curriculum, geography faculty at colleges and universities created a task force under the auspices of the National Council for Geographic Education. The task force designed the project "Finding a Way: Encouraging Underrepresented Groups in Geography" to enhance the achievement and motivation of young women and racial and ethnic minorities in geography classes across the United States. Additionally the task force conceived, designed, and implemented the "Pathways" project to conduct teacher workshops and to publish booklets of learning activities, bibliographies, and a synthesis of barriers to full participation and achievement for women and racial and ethnic groups. Importantly, the task force developed a comprehensive research agenda (LeVasseur, 1993; NCGE, 2000; Wridt, 2000).

Outcomes from the focused work in geography related to gender include the development of an Advanced Placement exam in human geography (notably 54% of the students who took the exam in 2004 were young women); the development of a doctoral program at Texas State University at San Marcos that focuses on diversity; and a conference on diversity in November 2006 (B. Hildebrandt, personal communication, December 15, 2005; M. LeVasseur, personal communication, November 30, 2005). The work on geography and gender can serve generally as a model for promoting gender equity in of social studies.

Teacher education. In writing this review we were unable to identify any documentation of the ratio of men to women who teach courses in social studies methods, much less in the percentages by gender and racial/ethnic group. Only at large universities do individuals specialize in social studies teacher education and have a background in social studies education at the elementary or secondary level. Although specific data were not available, it is generally understood that many people who prepare social studies teachers are not specialists in social studies teacher education. Within this broad context, in recent years only a few individuals have conducted research on gender in social studies teacher education programs. Two dissertations focused on making changes in social studies teacher education to address gender-related topics.

In one dissertation, Nelson (1990) documented the effects of a social studies methods course that explicitly addressed gender. Twenty-one preservice teachers enrolled in a social studies methods class were provided with content and specific strategies for gender-equitable teaching. The researcher found that male and female preservice teachers developed abilities to detect bias in classroom materials and created instructional units that were gender inclusive. Nelson concluded that teachers can and will create more gender-equitable curriculum when provided with appropriate instruction and support. This study suggests that explicit teaching about gender in social studies methods courses has the potential to influence teaching practices.

In another dissertation, Hill (2003) sought to determine whether more instruction about gender equity in a preservice teacher education course could alter beginning teachers' classroom behaviors and curriculum design. Hill followed 11 student teachers who had been exposed to differing levels of instruction about gender equity. She found that it was easier for beginning teachers to change curriculum content to include more women than to move teacher–student interaction patterns in more equitable directions.

In the next sections we supplement findings from empirical research with reports from participants in several reform efforts. These less formal means of assessing impact provide worthwhile evidence of change in curriculum and instruction.

Special Projects that Foster Curriculum Reform and In-Service Teacher Education

Resources and outreach have been a necessary part of the record of reform. Since 1980 the National Women's History Project (NWHP), based in Santa Rosa, California, has promoted multicultural women's history and gender equity in social studies. The project has been a hub in the wheel of disseminating ideas, curriculum materials, and bibliographies, as well as providing support for teachers, teacher educators, and community members who want to teach and learn multicultural women's history. The organization has maintained a clearinghouse of books, curriculum guides, films, posters, and other material that address gender in the social studies. Their summer conferences, consultations with schools and school districts, Website, and newsletter as well as their presence at annual conferences of the National Council for the Social Studies (NCSS) and the California Council for the Social Studies (CCSS) have been critical to the professional development of teachers and teacher educators for more than 25 years (National Women's History Project, 2005). Molly MacGregor, founding member and executive director of the project, estimates that the NWHP receives a million visits to the Web site each year (MacGregor, personal communication, July 31, 2005). Furthermore, the NWHP is the one social studies project that was recommended as "promising" by the Gender Equity Expert Panel (see Educational Equity Program available at www.feministmajority.org.).

In response to a question posed by one of the chapter authors about what is known about "what works," MacGregor, drawing on her many years of experience, responded by outlining several points relevant to classroom instruction. She emphasized: (a) The teacher is the key—his or her attitude and knowledge is pivotal; (b) content needs to be personalized and hands-on; and (c) oral history is an essential tool (M. MacGregor, personal communication, July 31, 2005). Although MacGregor said she felt certain that learning about women's history changes students' perceptions, she echoed the sentiment of this chapter that research documenting the effects is long overdue.

The Women in World History Project is another lynchpin in curriculum design, publication, and dissemination. For more than 20 years project staff members have produced carefully researched curriculum units that focus on women in world history for middle school students (Reese & Wilkinson, 1987). Lyn Reese, the project's primary author and developer, has for many years given workshops on the units and women in world history at annual meetings of NCSS, CCSS, and at history conferences in the United States, and internationally, including the United Nations' World Conferences on Women in Nairobi and Beijing.

Another example of curricular materials in which women's experiences are central is "Shaping a better world: A teaching guide on global issues/gender issues," developed by Janet Kahn and Susan Bailey at the Wellesley Centers for Women. Designed for students from middle school through college, the case studies were based on the life stories of women and girls from diverse cultures to make global issues "come alive."[27]

A large and mainly undocumented network of scholars and teachers has accomplished the dissemination of materials that promote sensitivity to and knowledge of gender issues in social studies. The efforts of the founders of the NWHP, the Women in World History Project, and the Wellesley Centers project are a few examples of the outreach that has taken place since the 1980s. It is notable that these organizations shaped their work around gender intersecting with diverse aspects of identity.

Networks for Support and Dissemination

In the 1980s one of the key factors that supported curriculum changes promoting gender-fair learning was the networking that occurred in professional organizations. The National Council for Social Studies (NCSS) had established a standing committee on Sexism and Social Justice in 1975, and in the 1980s interested social studies educators formed an NCSS sex-equity special interest group (SIG). The SIG sponsored a newsletter, a breakfast meeting at the annual meeting of NCSS, and supported a leadership structure of committed educators that generated workshops, publications, and presentations. Core participants in the network who met at conferences and retreats represented the organizations identified in the 1985 chapter on "Sex Equity in Social Studies" (Hahn & Bernard-Powers, 1985). These friendships and professional relationships sustained gender equity in social studies reforms into the 1990s. Additionally, social studies educators along with women from all over the world met at the United Nations' world conferences on women held in Nairobi and Beijing in 1985 and 1995, respectively. In addition, several social studies educators who could not attend the international conferences helped to organize the outcome activities in local communities in the months following the meetings.

Networks have been responsible for initiatives to make textbooks more gender inclusive. For example, teachers and scholars who were active in the California Council for the Social Studies joined with the Western Association of Women Historians in 1992 to review history textbooks being considered for adoption in the state. Representatives of the committee developed a Textbook Evaluation Report that was provided to the state materials adoption panel, along with oral arguments (Western Association of Women Historians, 1994, p. 2). Although there is little evidence that the initiative was successful, the example may have influenced subsequent adoptions. In 2005 the State Department of Education in California recruited scholars and practitioners to participate in the legal and social compliance review of the K–8 history—social science textbooks that were being submitted for state textbook adoption. The letter inviting people to participate specifically cited the importance of gender sensitivity and knowledge for service on the panel and for the outcome generally. However, this may have had little effect in the long run as one researcher found that the new textbooks that were adopted for 5th grade U.S. history continued to give far more attention to men than to women, as was mentioned earlier in the section on textbooks (Savage, 2005).

Several of the networks that were created in the 1970s and 1980s have since been dismantled and the energy around curriculum reforms that was evident in the 1985 *Handbook* chapter on social studies has dissipated. For example, the Upper Midwest Women's History Center, which published valuable books for students on women in various world cultures and conducted numerous workshops for a network of teachers in their region, closed due to lack of funding. Nevertheless, many professional relationships that were established in these and other networks have been sustained and the understanding that networks are a powerful way to generate and sustain reform remains (Bernard-Powers, 2001).

Mentoring and Modeling

University faculty can play key roles in the gender equity process. It is likely that faculty who work with graduate students in social studies curriculum and teacher education today have more knowledge of gender issues, are likely to include such issues in their courses, and are better able to support student theses and dissertations related to gender equity than was true in 1985.

Each of the authors of this chapter has stories of the students who have been changed by their work. For example, a seminar on gender issues at San Francisco State University, lead Esposto (2003) to conduct a study of gender in U.S. history textbooks and a successful application for funds to buy gender-fair books for her classroom.

Awele Makeba, a storyteller in the San Francisco Bay Area, used her own story-telling and research skills to create a performance that documented the hidden histories of the Montgomery Bus Boycott. The ideas, generated out of Makeba's work with a young woman in Oakland, California, and refined in graduate curriculum courses, led to a study of Claudette Colvin, one of the unsung heroines of the Montgomery Bus Boycott (Makeba, 2002a). Claudette Colvin's story, told by Awele, has since been produced as a CD (Makeba, 2002b). This is an instance of networking and mentoring ultimately leading to telling the story of a courageous young African American woman's contribution to history. Additionally, this is an example of how attending to the intersections of race/ethnicity, gender, and class can convey a more complete history than the one that has appeared in the traditional social studies curriculum.

---

[27]Susan Bailey (personal correspondence, January 25, 2006), author of the Wellesley materials, cautioned that due to lack of funding the materials were not subsequently updated. She suggested that teachers and students might use the units as starting points to research the current situation in particular countries. Bailey noted that the history of the development and dissemination of the materials illustrates the difficulty of producing new curricular materials. The initial funding was difficult to generate; the pilot testing phase was cut short due to funding constraints, and once the materials were completed, they were self published and disseminated. They are, however, still available from the Wellesley Centers for Women, 106 Central Street, Wellesley, MA 02481 or www.wcwonline.org.

These examples are illustrative of experiences of many university professors and teachers supporting students in their learning and introducing powerful ideas about gender. This is an important part of the development of preservice teachers. As Crocco's former student testified at a recent conference on women's history, the combination of courses that included gender and women's history in undergraduate study and a strong professor of curriculum who knew about women's history and supported preservice teachers prepared her to create a gender-equitable classroom. These stories of influence and change have not been formally documented, yet they constitute a valuable part of the record of what has been done to address gender equity in social studies.

RECOMMENDATIONS

Unfortunately, the momentum around the reforms in gender equity in the social studies that were begun in the 1970s and 1980s—textbook revisions, teacher preservice and in-service workshops, and the use of feminist teaching methods—has stalled at the turn of the 21st century. We believe that many educators and policy makers view the gender work as having been accomplished, possibly due to the gender equality reported on some achievement tests. We caution our readers, however, not to assume that gender parity in social studies has been reached based solely on this evidence. Moreover, with the increased emphasis on standards-based testing in mathematics and reading in recent years, teachers spend less time teaching social studies, which results in less time for gender equity in social studies. We believe these factors and others have resulted in a holding pattern for teaching, curriculum development, and research on gender and gender equity since 1985 when the first volume of *The Handbook for Achieving Sex Equity through Education* was published. This phenomenon of slowed reform has created urgency for gender equity in the social studies; we must compensate for lost momentum as much more work remains to be done. With this in mind, we make the following six sets of recommendations.

First, we recommend that social studies educators ensure that substantial attention is devoted to gender in curriculum in order to present an accurate view of gendered human experience in history and contemporary society. We maintain that the curriculum should act as both window and mirror as it enables students to see others clearly, as well as to see a reflection of themselves (Style, 1996); thus, we argue for continued development of a gender-inclusive curriculum in social studies. We recommend that changes be made in social studies textbooks and curriculum standards to accurately reflect women's contributions to society and to address gender-related issues. This recommendation echoes those made by some social studies scholars repeatedly over the years (Grambs, 1976; Hahn, 1978; Hahn & Bernard Powers, 1985; Levstik, 2001; Tetreault, 1984, 1987).

Research conducted in the last two decades has revealed a continuing need to revise textbooks and curricula. In particular, elementary social studies textbooks need attention because early, formative knowledge and experiences of a gender-balanced view could provide the scaffolding or framework for later learning. In all respects the inclusion of women in the curriculum needs to be in depth and substantial, rather than superficial. This could mean a year-long treatment of women and girls, as well as a concentrated emphasis during the March celebration of Women's History Month and keeping textbooks and curricular materials up to date both in terms of new scholarship and changes in society. Because gender is both a social category and a significant aspect of human experience, it is imperative that young people develop the knowledge and lenses to understand this fundamental principle.

In general, the textbooks in U.S. history do reflect some increased attention to gender equity in recent years. Our research revealed, however, that authors and publishers have much more work to do in the curricula for middle and high school world history, economics, and civics courses. With respect to economics texts, authors need to eliminate racial and gender stereotypes, and teachers and students need to challenge those that remain. For example, teachers can address this problem by finding alternative positions on issues such as wage gaps and comparable worth so that the experiences of women and minorities are not marginalized. Also, gender-related topics are rarely addressed and female civic-political action is rarely portrayed in civics and government courses. Overall, much of the work in civic education today reflects a broader view of citizenship than was prevalent in the past; however, it still tends not to overtly address the arguments made by feminist and womanist scholars to give attention to the diverse experiences of people who have experienced "citizenship" differently according to race and class, as well as gender (Ladson-Billings, 1996a, 1996b). In civic education, practitioners' and researchers' increased attention to community service and engagement in civil society has the potential to more fully capture the lived experiences of women and girls, as well as the majority of men and boys. However, the recent studies of civics and government textbooks and curriculum standards indicate that social studies educators will need to undertake deliberate proactive actions to change practice in the nation's classrooms.

Additionally, professional organizations that represent the interests of social studies educators, such as the National Council for the Social Studies (NCSS) and its state affiliates, need to be proactive. They need to take the lead in addressing issues germane to gender and the social studies in their annual meetings, publications, and organizational structures, such as committees and commissions. The shift of priorities that eclipsed race and gender issues in NCSS in the early 1990s led to a significant step backwards for the organization, signaling to many social studies educators that gender was not a pressing concern. Consequently, teachers and other social studies educators have had fewer opportunities to reform curriculum and instruction than they had in the 1980s.

Second, we recommend that social studies curriculum developers give more attention to the diverse experiences of women and girls by class, race, ethnicity, and sexual orientation. Gone are the days of teaching "the women's experience" or from a presumed unitary "female perspective." Scholars today emphasize that because lived experiences of women and men vary by class and race or ethnicity, gender issues need to be viewed in more subtle and complex ways than they have been in the past (Ladson-Billings, 1996a, 1996b). Critical race theory, in particular, draws attention to the need to consider whose interests are served by maintaining the status quo. These points have implications for social studies practice and research.

Several of the recent studies we reviewed point to important differences in student political knowledge, attitudes, and experiences by race, ethnicity, and socioeconomic background. Unfortunately, there are insufficient numbers of studies that look at the interaction of those factors with gender. For example, scholars do not yet know if African American female students from middle income families have similar or different political attitudes from African American male students from middle income families, nor do they know how they compare to Hispanic, Asian American, or White middle income female students or to peers from low-income or high-income families. Importantly, as increasing numbers of immigrants to the United States come from Asian and Latin American nations, scholars do not know if the civic–political socialization process differs for young men and women from particular cultural and political backgrounds. These gaps speak to the importance of research in this area, as we note there are no data sets that use large enough representative samples to make valid comparisons.[28] Until they are available, replications of small studies that use non-representative samples and qualitative studies using purposefully selected samples could shed much needed light on the interaction of gender with other variables that affect civic learning.

Third, we recommend that the notion of gender equity be expanded to include all individuals; men and boys are gendered as well as women and girls. Scholarship of recent years focuses on masculinities and education (Lesko, 2000). However, we did not locate such work applied specifically to social studies, with two exceptions—one study on the formation of gender identities in schooling and another study of masculinities in textbooks (Kuzmic, 2000; Smith, 1996). In the coming years, more attention will need to be paid to the kind of social studies that is taught and its differential impact on boys and girls as well as on gender equity as a component of social studies teacher education. For example, we need to think about how both boys and girls view particular cultural universals, which are often the focus of social studies lessons at the primary level (Brophy & Alleman, 1999, 2000, 2001, 2003, 2005). Also, a consideration of both genders speaks to what we discuss in the first recommendation, broader conceptions of citizenship and civic and political aspects of life than have been used in the past. In calling for the use of more encompassing definitions, scholars emphasize that the traditional concepts that focused narrowly on the public realm of voting and holding office overlooked important participation in civil society and the many ways that citizens take action to influence public policies

(Bernard-Powers, 1996a, 1996b; Ladson-Billings, 1996a, 1996b; Noddings, 1992a, 1992b; Stone, 1996; Woyshner, 2002).

The recent studies using nationally representative samples of students reveal substantial gender differences in civic and political attitudes and experiences, but not knowledge. Scholars now need to consider how young male and female students construct meaning about social and political issues and what in the socialization process might contribute to differences in attitudes and experiences. For example, social studies educators need to understand why young men seem to perceive the classroom climate for discussion to be less open than do young women and why male students tend to be less supportive of rights for women and immigrants than are their female peers. Gendered research in civic education speaks to the need for teachers to encourage citizens-in-the-making to think about their current and future participation as citizens of communities, the nation, and the world and to begin to develop participatory civic habits while they are still in school.

Fourth, we recommend that connections between universities and colleges and K–12 social studies educators be strengthened to support curriculum transformation based on new knowledge. Scholars in higher education generate knowledge in social science disciplines and education that should be the basis for curricular transformation in social studies teaching and learning. The critical connection between social science scholars and social studies educators has been moribund in areas that implicate social studies and gender. This holds for all the subjects that comprise the social studies, but for certain subjects in particular. For example, we were surprised to discover how little work has been done on elementary and secondary gender equity and economics in recent years, especially given the fact that state councils of economic education have been active in promoting increased attention to economics in the social studies curriculum. At the university level, feminist economists have made recommendations about how university courses in economics can more adequately address issues of gender equity (Feiner, 1994; Nelson, 1995). These developments need to find expression in the K–12 curriculum. Also, in social studies teacher preparation more attention needs to be paid to gender equity in social studies methods textbooks. While these changes are undertaken, those who prepare teachers need to think carefully about how to bring gender equity to their coursework with supplementary activities and materials.

Fifth, we recommend that policy makers, practitioners, and scholars address the need to look at structural problems in school systems and classrooms that create barriers to delivering gender-equitable social studies. For example, K–12 teachers' avoidance of controversial issues is a concern because it often results in gender-related topics being omitted from social studies. We recommend that educa-

---

[28]Although the representative sample of 2,811 9th graders that was used in the IEA study on civic education was large enough to enable researchers to report data separately by gender, race/ethnicity, and socioeconomic level, it was not large enough to report findings in terms of the interaction of these categories. The position of the National Center on Education Statistics was that the margin of error for results obtained by the small samples in each group would be unacceptable. Obtaining sufficiently large nationally representative samples is costly—but important.

tors and policy makers encourage students to investigate controversial issues, including those related to gender, in age-appropriate ways. And, as we discussed above, gender in the curriculum should appear throughout the year, not just during certain months of the school calendar or when particular historical periods are studied.

Our research revealed that there are structural implications for teacher preparation. For instance, we have observed that elementary teachers are predominately women and the majority of secondary social studies teachers are men. An irony of Title IX may be that as schools need more coaches for women's sports, in some parts of the country administrators often reserve social studies jobs for coaches, and as a result high school social studies departments appear to be more male dominated than they were 30 years ago. We were disturbed to find that no one seems to be monitoring these issues. We learned that professional organizations and state and national agencies do not regularly report data on numbers of male and female teachers in social studies. Indeed, the only figures we could find on the proportion of female to male social studies teachers were over ten years old (NCES, 1997). According to the NCES (1997) report, in 1993–94 only 37.5% of social studies teachers in public schools were women. Despite much searching and many phone calls, we were unable to locate more recent data. Yet the presence of male or female teachers may affect what is taught in social studies classes and how it is taught (Coughlin, 2003).

Particular emphasis needs to be placed on gender in K–12 teacher preparation programs, as well as in the strategies and materials available for classroom use that support the goals of gender equity. One of the major challenges is the need to teach teachers to move away from the kind of history they were taught in the way they were taught. Requiring teacher education students to have taken university courses on the history of women and/or gender studies would be one way to begin to correct this gap in the formal education of teachers. Another structural challenge lies in helping teachers supplement textbooks that do not reflect gender equity, and helping them capitalize on the gender balance in some textbooks.

Our sixth recommendation is to continue research along several lines of inquiry. Overall, compared to secondary social studies and gender, the research that examines gender in the social studies at the elementary level is scant. The most striking aspect of our literature review is that there are very few empirical studies showing the benefits or qualities of gender inclusion in social studies at the elementary level. There is a dearth of data on how elementary school children learn about gender in social studies, the effects of learning about gender in elementary school, and what elementary school students' perceptions of gender are in social studies. In order to bring about gender equity in elementary social studies, more empirical research is needed on how elementary school students develop in terms of gender socialization and how they conceptualize social studies concepts related to gender.

Other areas of research continue to be critical. For instance, research linking gender, technology, and social studies needs to be carried out. Additionally, the effects of teaching gender-equitable social studies need to be studied and documented. As one scholar noted in concluding a study of history and so-

cial studies outcomes, more research is needed on tracking, course work, and teacher practices in order to better understand gender differences that occur (Chapin, 1998). Likewise, continued research is needed on cognitive abilities, such as the relationship among spatial abilities, children's experiences of distance they typically range from home, and attitudes toward and perceptions of geography. LeVasseur (1993) outlined several research priorities in the publication, *Finding a Way: Encouraging Underrepresented Groups in Geography*. She argued for sustained and expanded data gathering on gender and geographic achievement that reaches beyond the National Assessment of Educational Progress (NAEP) scores to consider differences in knowledge of specific geographic content among and between different age groups, ethnic groups, language groups, and co-educational and single sex schools. Additional areas of research that demand attention are on classroom environment, with attention to teacher–student interactions, role models, instructional strategies, and curriculum, including textbooks and supplemental materials.

Of course, any future research conducted on gender in the social studies will have to mind the caveat of not falling into "well-worn grooves" (Thorne, 1993). That is, educators and scholars need to be careful not to simply see what they expected to find based on traditional patterns or stereotypes, whether in the classroom, curriculum, or research. Our exploration of research on gender equity in the social studies revealed that gender differences are complex, and hence require concentrated attention and continued research. Only by engaging in thoughtful and creative hypothesizing, followed by careful examination, can the phenomena of gender differences in social studies knowledge, performance, and attitudes be understood.

In summary, in light of our survey of research and experiences in social studies education we recommend that changes be made in policy, practice, and programs, and we call for more research in particular areas. Specifically,

For Policy:

- At the district level, teachers should be encouraged to plan instruction and experiences for Women's History Month in March and throughout the year (see www.nwhp.org) and include gender issues in special celebrations, such as including the long struggle for the Equal Rights Amendment to the U.S. Constitution in celebrations of Constitution Day (September 17).
- At the state level, as social studies curriculum standards and frameworks are revised, authors should give serious and sustained attention to gender-related issues.
- State competency tests in social studies should assess student learning with serious attention to gender-related issues.
- State competency tests and national assessments should be analyzed for differential item functioning; items that are determined to yield bias for male or female students should be removed. A mix of multiple choice and open-ended items should be used to avoid giving preference in answering style to either gender.
- At the national level, No Child Left Behind legislation should be revised to require that states assess social studies knowl-

edge that is gender inclusive and require that states disaggregate data on social studies tests by gender, race/ethnicity, and family income levels.

- A program like the Women's Educational Equity Act, which funded much gender equitable social studies curriculum development in the 1980s, needs to receive sufficient funding to encourage substantial curriculum development on topics that reflect a gender-inclusive perspective.
- Those individuals who administer the Teaching American History Grant program should make clear that the program's emphasis on "traditional history" does not preclude, but indeed encourages, teaching women's history in program-supported activities.
- Social studies and civics/government curriculum standards should emphasize civic engagement in ways that more fully capture the lived experiences of women and girls than past narrow conceptions of "political" activity.
- Policies affecting the treatment of gender in social studies need to take boys into account as well as girls.
- Policy makers at all levels should help support teachers' efforts to engage students in issues over which citizens disagree, including issues related to gender and sexuality.
- Teacher education programs should encourage preservice teachers to take courses in women's studies or gender studies.
- The National Council for the Social Studies (NCSS) and its state affiliates, as well as other professional organizations of social studies educators, should provide programs, publications, and committees that will help educators provide gender equitable social studies instruction.

For Practice and Programs:

- Social studies lessons, curriculum units, and textbooks need to more accurately reflect women's contributions to society and to address gender-related issues; the need is especially acute at the elementary level and in courses on economics and civics/government. For example, elementary classes should challenge gender stereotypes in the curriculum and through children's literature; economics classes should investigate wage gaps and women in the workforce; and civics classes should investigate barriers to women in political leadership.
- Teachers need to teach from multiple perspectives of gender that are inclusive of race/ethnicity, class, and sexuality.
- Teachers need to give greater attention to gender globally by teaching about issues such as those discussed in the chapter on global perspectives in this *Handbook* and in social studies publications such as the special issue of *Social Education* on Teaching about Women of the World (Merryfield & Crocco, 2003). Supplementary materials on women in diverse cultures,

such as those produced by the Upper Midwest History Center and the Wellesley Centers for Women, need to be continually revised and updated to reflect contemporary women's experiences globally in an accurate manner.

- Social studies curricula and textbooks must be in depth, up-to-date, and substantial in regard to their treatment of gender.
- Teachers need support in supplementing traditional textbooks with materials on gender. The new project Roads from Seneca Falls is one promising way of providing such support to teachers of history.[29] The New Jersey Women's History Project (www.scc.rutgers.edu/njwomenshistory) is another project that makes information available on women's history. Additionally, the Center for Women and Politics at the Eagleton Institute at Rutgers University publishes reports and provides information that would be particularly useful to civics and government teachers.
- Social studies methods textbooks and courses need to pay more attention to gender equity.

For Research: Research is needed on:

- Gender and social studies at the elementary level;
- The effects of gender-balanced social studies texts, curriculum, and instruction on elementary and secondary students;
- Masculinities in social studies education;
- Differences in student social studies–related knowledge, attitudes, and experiences by race, ethnicity, socioeconomic background and gender simultaneously;
- How young male and female students construct meaning about social and political issues;
- Treatments that overcome gender differences in economics understanding;
- The relationship between spatial abilities, children's geographic range of experiences, and attitudes toward and perceptions of geography;
- The linkages among technology, gender, and social studies;
- Preservice and in-service teachers' beliefs about gender and social studies and how those beliefs relate to their teaching practice.

The challenges are many. However, the benefits of undertaking these changes are potentially great—achieving "equality and justice for all."

ACKNOWLEDGMENTS

The authors wish to thank the reviewers Lois Christensen, University of Alabama, Birmingham; Mimi Coughlin, California State University at Sacramento; Paulette Dilworth, Indiana Uni-

---

[29]The project contains several elements: Pathways to Educational Networks (PEN) will catalogue materials by subject, grade level, and national standards; "Ask Lizzie," will be a virtual reference desk that allows students and teachers to get answers from experts to online questions; and Taking to the Road, will make connections to women's history museums and historic sites.

versity; Linda Levstik, the University of Kentucky; and Cynthia Tyson, the Ohio State University. In addition the authors wish to thank Susan Bailey, Wellesley Centers for Women, Wellesley, Massachusettes; Michal LeVasseur, National Council for Geographic Education, Jacksonville State University, Jacksonville Al-abama; Molly MacGregor, National Women's History Project, Santa Rosa, California; and Lyn Reese, Women in World History Curriculum, Berkeley, California, for their assistance in identifying "what's been done" to bring a gender equity perspective to social studies.

References

Adler, S., (Ed.) (2004). *Teacher education in social studies*. Greenwich, CT: Information Age Publishers.

Alzamil, O. A. (2003). *High school social studies teachers' attitudes and usage of instructional technology in Saudi Arabia*. (Doctoral dissertation, University of Arkansas, UMI No. 3097294).

Amadeo, J. A., Torney-Purta, J., Lehmann, R., Husfeldt, V., & Nikolova, R. (2002). *Civic knowledge and engagement: An IEA study of upper secondary students in sixteen countries*. Amsterdam: International Association for the Evaluation of Educational Achievement.

American Association of University Women. (1992). *How schools short-change women*. New York: Marlowe.

American Association of University Women. (1998). *Gender gaps: Where schools still fail our children*. New York: Marlowe.

Anderson, L., Jenkins, L., Leming, J., MacDonald, W., Mullis, I., & Turner, M. J. (1990). *The civic report card*. Washington DC: U.S. Department of Education.

Applebee, A. N., Langer, J. A., & Mullis, I. (1987). Literature and U.S. history: *The instructional experience and factual knowledge of high school juniors* [Report No. 17-HL-01]. Princeton, NJ: Educational Testing Service.

Avery, P. G., & Simmons, A. M. (2000/2001). Civic life as conveyed in U.S. civics and history textbooks. *International Journal of Social Education, 15*, 105–130.

Baldi, S., Perie, M., Skidmore, D., Greenberg, E., & Hahn, C. (2001). *What democracy means to ninth-graders: U.S. results from the international IEA civic education study*. Washington, DC: National Center for Education Statistics, U.S. Department of Education.

Barton, K., & Levstik, L. (1998). It wasn't a good part of history. *Teachers College Record, 99*, 478–513.

Beatty, W., & Trotter, A. (1987) Gender differences in geographical knowledge. *Sex Roles, 16*, 565–590.

Becker, W., Greene, W., & Rosen, S. (1990). Research on high school economic education, *AEA Papers and Proceedings, 80*, 14–22.

Bein, F. L. (1990). Baseline geography competency test: Administered in Indiana University. *Journal of Geography, 89*, 260–265.

Bernard-Powers, J. (1995). Out of the cameos and into the conversation: Gender, social studies, and curriculum transformation. In J. Gaskell & J. Willinsky (Eds.), *Gender in/forms curriculum*, (pp. 191–209). New York: Teachers College Press.

Bernard-Powers, J. (1996a). Engendering social studies: Perspectives, texts, and teaching. *Theory and Research in Social Education, 24*, 2–7.

Bernard-Powers, J. (1996b). The 'woman question' in citizenship education. In W. C. Parker (Ed.), *Educating the democratic mind* (pp. 287–308). Albany, NY: State University of New York Press.

Bernard-Powers, J. (2001). Gender in the social studies curriculum. In E. W. Ross (Ed.), *The social studies curriculum: Purposes, problems, and possibilities* (pp. 177–197). Albany, NY: State University of New York Press.

Blount, J. M. (2004). Same-sex desire, gender, and social education in the twentieth century. In C. Woyshner, J. Watras, & M. S. Crocco (Eds.). *Social education in the twentieth century: Curriculum and context for citizenship* (pp. 176–191). New York: Peter Lang.

Boardman, D. (1990). Graphicacy revisited: Mapping abilities and gender differences. *Educational Review, 42*(1), 57–64.

Breland, H., Danos, D. O., Kahn, H. D., Kubota, M. Y., & Bonner, M. W. (1994). Performance versus objective testing and gender: An exploratory study of an Advanced Placement history examination. *Journal of Educational Measurement, 31*(4), 275–293.

Brophy, J., & Alleman, J. (1999). *Primary-grade students' knowledge and thinking about clothing as a cultural universal*. Spencer Foundation Report. ERIC Document Reproduction Service ED 439 072.

———. (2000). Primary-grade students' knowledge and thinking about Native American and pioneer homes. *Theory and Research in Social Education, 28*, 96–120.

———. (2001). What primary-grade students say about their ideal future homes. *Journal of Social Studies Research, 25*(2), 23–35.

———. (2003). Primary-grade students' knowledge and thinking about the supply of utilities (water, heat, and light) to modern homes. *Cognition and Instruction, 21*, 79–112.

———. (2005). Primary grade students' knowledge and thinking about transportation. *Theory and Research in Social Education, 33*, 218–243.

Brown, S. W., Boyer, M. A., & Mayall, H. J. (2003). The GlobalEd Project: Gender differences in a problem-based learning environment of international negotiations. *Instructional Science, 31*, 255–276.

Center for Civic Education. (1994). *National standards for civics and government*. Calabasas, CA: Author.

Chapin, J. R. (1998, April). *Gender and social studies learning in the 8th, 10th, and 12th grades*. Paper presented at the annual meeting of the American Educational Research Association. San Diego, CA.

———. (2001). From eighth grade social studies to young adulthood voting and community service: National education longitudinal study of 1988 eighth graders. *The International Social Studies Forum, 1*, 33–44.

Charlesworth, R., Burts, D., van Meerveld, K., Stanley, W. B., & Delatte, J. (1989). Young children's concept of family: Cognitive developmental level, gender, and ethnic comparisons. *Journal of Social Studies Research, 13*(1), 15–27.

Cheek, D. W., & Kohut, S. (1992). *Social studies curriculum resource handbook: A practical guide for K–12 social studies curriculum*. Millwood, NY: Kraus International Publications.

Clark, R., Allard, J., & Mahoney, T. (2004). How much of the sky? Women in American high school history textbooks from the 1960s, 1980s, and 1990s. *Social Education, 68*, 57–62.

Clark, R., Ayton, K., Frechette, N., & Keller, P. J. (2005). Women of the world, rewrite! Women in world history high school textbooks from the 1960s, 1980s, and 1990s. *Social Education, 69*, 41–47.

Commeyras, M., & Alverman, D. E. (1996). Reading about women in world history textbooks from one feminist perspective. *Gender and Education, 8*, 31–48.

Connell, R. W. (2000). *The men and the boys*. Berkeley: University of California Press.

Connors, L. L. (2004). Women's roles, now writ (too?) large. *Christian Science Monitor*. March 2, 2004. Retrieved August 27, 2004 from www.csmonitor.com/2004/302/p11s02_legn.html.

Corbin, S. (1996). Gender difference and high school students' attitudes toward and achievement in social studies. *Journal of Social Studies Research, 20*(2), 18–26.

Coughlin, M. (2003, April). *Life history influences on teaching United States history*. Paper presented at the annual meeting of the American Education Research Association, Chicago.

Crocco, M. S. (1995). Bibliography on women's history related to the 19th amendment, *Social Education, 59*, 4.

——. (1997). Making time for women's history . . . when your survey course is already filled to overflowing. *Social Education, 61*, 32–37.

——. (2000). Teacher education and the study of women from a global perspective: A syllabus: Women of the world: Issues in teaching. *Women's Studies Quarterly, 28*, 347.

——. (2001). The missing discourse about gender and sexuality in the social studies. *Theory into Practice, 40*(1), 65–71.

——. (2002). Homophobic hallways: Is anyone listening? *Theory and Research in Social Education, 30*, 217–232.

——. (2005a). History, teaching of. In J. Sears (Ed.), *[Homo] sexualities education and youth: An encyclopedia*, vol. 1. (pp. 405–409). Westport, CT.: Greenwood Publishing Co.

——. (2005b). Teaching Shabanu: The challenge of using world literature in the U.S. social studies classroom. *Journal of Curriculum Studies, 37*, 561–582.

——. (In press). Gender and sexuality in the social studies. In L. Levstik & C. Tyson (Eds.), *Handbook of research on social studies*. Mahwah, NJ: Lawrence Erlbaum Associates.

Crocco, M. S., & Cramer, J. F. (2004a). Technology use, women, and global studies in social studies education. *Society for Information Technology and Teacher Education International Conference, 2004*(1), 4773–4780 (online proceedings).

——. (2004b). A virtual hall of mirrors? Confronting the digital divide in urban social studies teacher education. *Journal of Computing in Teacher Education, 20*, 133–137.

——. (2005). Women, WebQuests, and teaching controversial issues in the social studies. *Social Education, 69*, 143–148.

Crocco, M. S., & Davis, O. L. (Eds.) (1999). *Bending the future to their will: Civic women, social education, and democracy*. Lanham, MD: Rowman & Littlefield.

——. (Eds.) (2002). *Building a legacy: Women in social education 1784–1984*. Silver Spring, MD: National Council for the Social Studies.

Crocco, M. S., Munro, P., & Weiler, K. (1999). *Pedagogies of resistance: Women educator activists, 1880–1960*. New York: Teachers College Press.

Crocco, M. S., & Patel, V. (2003). Teaching about South Asian women: Getting beyond the stereotypes. *Social Education, 67*, 22–26.

Cruz, B. C., & Groendal-Cobb, J. L. (1998). Incorporating women's voices into the middle and senior high school history curriculum. *Social Studies, 89*, 271–275.

Damico, A., Damico, S., & Conway, M. (1998). The democratic education of women: High school and beyond. *Women in Politics, 19*, 1–31.

Doyle, J. L. (1998). *The effects of a gender-balanced social studies curriculum on grade ten students*. Unpublished master's thesis. Simon Fraser University, Canada.

Educational Testing Service. (1997). *The ETS gender study: How males and females perform in educational settings*. Princeton, NJ: Author.

Eisner, C. (2001). *Advancing excellence in urban schools: A report on Advanced Placement examinations in the great city schools*. Council of the Great City Schools. Washington, DC: College Board.

Esposto, A. (2003). *The representation of women in fifth grade and eighth grade recently published U.S. history textbooks*. Unpublished master's project, San Francisco State University.

Evans, R. W., & Saxe, D. W. (1996). *Handbook on teaching social issues*. Washington, DC: National Council for the Social Studies.

Eve, R. A., Price, B., & Counts, M. (1994). Geographic illiteracy among college students. *Youth and Society, 25*, 408–427.

Feiner, S. F. (1993). Introductory economics textbooks and the treatment of issues relating to women and minorities, 1984 and 1991. *Journal of Economic Education, 24*, 145–373.

——. (1994). *Race and gender in the American economy: Views from across the spectrum*. Englewood Cliffs, NJ: Prentice Hall.

Ferguson, O. W. (1993). *The effects of different instructional types on academic achievement in world history and student attitudes toward the subject*. (Doctoral dissertation, University of Southern Mississippi, AAT No. 9402529).

Flanagan, C. A., Bowes, J. M., Jonson, B., Csapo, B., & Sheblanova, E. (1998). Ties that bind: Correlates of adolescents' civic commitments in seven countries. *Journal of Social Issues, 54*, 457–475.

Fouts, J. (1990). Female students, female teachers, and perceptions of the social studies classroom. *Social Education, 54*, 418–420.

Geography Education Standards Project. (1994). *Geography for life: National geography standards, 1994*. Washington, DC: National Geographic Research and Exploration.

Ginsberg, A. E., Shapiro, J. P., & Brown, S. P. (2004). *Gender in urban education*. Portsmouth, NH: Heinemann.

Gonzales, M. H., Riedel, E., Avery, P. G., & Sullivan, J. L. (2001). Rights and obligations in civic education: A content analysis of the national standards for civics and government. *Theory and Research in Social Education, 29*, 109–128.

Goodson, I., Mangan, M., & Rhea, V. (1991). *Closing the circle: Conclusions and recommendations*, Summative Report, volume 3. Toronto: Ontario Department of Education.

Grambs, J. D. (1976) (Ed.). *Teaching about women in the social studies: Concepts, curriculum, and strategies*. Washington DC: National Council for the Social Studies.

Gray, T. (1992). Women in labor economics textbooks. *Journal of Economic Education, 23*, 362–373.

Grever, M. (1991). Pivoting the center: Women's history as a compulsory examination subject in all Dutch secondary schools in 1990 and 1991. *Gender & History, 3*, (1), 75–78.

Haas, M. E., & Laughlin, M. A. (1999, April). *Perspectives of social studies over a quarter of a century: Reflections from veteran social studies leaders*. Paper presented at the annual meeting of the American Educational Research Association, Montreal, Quebec.

Hahn, C. L. (1978). Review of research on sex roles: Implications for social studies research. *Theory and Research in Social Education, 6*(1), 73–99.

——. (1980). Social studies with equality and justice for all: Towards the elimination of sexism. *Journal of Research and Development in Education, 13*(2), 103–112.

——. (1985). The status of the social studies in the public schools of the United States: Another look. *Social Education, 49*, 220–223.

——. (1996) Gender and political learning. *Theory and Research in Social Education, 24*, 8–35.

——. (1998). *Becoming political: Comparative perspectives on citizenship education*. Albany, NY: State University of New York Press.

——. (1999). Challenges to civic education in the United States. In J. Torney-Purta, J. Schwille, & J. A. Amadeo (Eds.). *Civic education across countries: Twenty four national case studies from the IEA civic education project*, (pp. 583–607). Amsterdam: The International Association for the Evaluation of Educational Achievement. ED 431 705.

Hahn, C. L., & Bernard-Powers, J. (1985). Sex equity in social studies. In S. Klein (Ed.). *Handbook for achieving sex equity through education* (pp. 280–297). Baltimore, MD: Johns Hopkins University.

Hahn, C. L., & Blankenship, G. (1983). Women and economics textbooks. *Theory and Research in Social Education, 11*, 67–76.

Hahn, C. L., Dilworth, P. P., Hughes, M., & Sen, T. (1998). *IEA civic education project phase I: The United States—Responses to the four core international framing questions.* Volume III. Unpublished manuscript, Emory University. ERIC Document Reproduction Service ED 444 887.

Hardwick, S. W., Bean, L. L., Alexander, K. A., & Shelley, F. (2000). Gender vs. sex differences: Factors affecting performance in geographic education. *Journal of Geography, 99,* 238–244.

Heafner, T. L. (2002). *Powerful methods: A framework for effective integration of technology in secondary social studies.* Unpublished doctoral dissertation, University of North Carolina at Greensboro.

Henrie, R. L., Aron, R., Nelson, B., & Poole, D. (1997). Gender-related knowledge variations within geography. *Sex Roles, 36,* 605–623.

Henry, T. (1989). Gender and the framework. *Social Studies Review, 28*(2), 27–30.

Hess, D. (2002). How high school students experience and learn from the discussion of controversial public issues. *Journal of Curriculum and Supervision, 17,* 283–314.

Hill, C. B. (2003). *Gender equity in the classroom: A constant need to be reminded.* (Doctoral dissertation, University of Kentucky, UMI No. 3086896).

Hirschfeld, M., Moore, R. L., & Brown, E. (1995). Exploring the gender gap on the GRE subject test in economics. *Journal of Economic Education, 26,* 3–16.

Independent Sector. (1996). *Giving and volunteering in the United States.* Washington, DC: Author.

Jenkins, K. (2005, June). *Gender and civic engagement: Secondary analysis of survey data.* Silver Spring, MD: The Center for Information and Research on Civic Learning & Engagement. Retrieved January 10, 2006, from www.civicyouth.org.

Johnson, P. R. (2005). *Perceptions of leadership among high school students: Simulation versus face-to-face environments.* (Doctoral dissertation, University of Connecticut, UMI No. 3180215).

Kennedy, K. J. (2006). The gendered nature of students' attitudes to minorities. *Citizenship and Teacher Education, 2,* 1–11.

Klein, S., Ortman, B., & Friedman, B. (2002). What is the field of gender equity in education? In J. Koch & B. Irby (Eds.), *Defining and redefining gender equity in education,* (pp. 3–29). Greenwich, CT: Information Age Publishers.

Kneedler, P. E. (1988). Differences between boys and girls on California's new statewide assessments in history/social science. *Social Studies Review, 27*(3), 96–124.

Kuzmic, J. (2000). Textbooks, knowledge, and masculinity. In N. Lesko (Ed.) *Masculinities in school* (pp. 105–126). Thousand Oaks: Sage.

Ladson-Billings, G. (1996a). Lifting as we climb: The womanist tradition in multicultural education. In. J. A. Banks (Ed.) *Multicultural education, transformative knowledge and action* (pp. 179–200). New York: Teachers College Press.

———. (1996b). Multicultural issues in the classroom: Race, class, and gender. In R. W. Evans & D. W. Saxe, (Eds.) *Handbook of issues-centered social studies* (pp. 104–110). Washington, DC: National Council for the Social Studies.

Lawson, T. A. (1999). *Teaching methodologies and gender issues impact upon students' attitudes towards the social studies discipline.* Unpublished doctoral dissertation, University of Sarasota.

Le, V. N. (1999). *Identifying differential item functioning on the NELS: 88 history achievement test: CSE technical report.* California State University Center for the Study of Evaluation.

Lee, V. E., Marks, H. M., & Byrd, T. (1994). Sexism in single-sex and co-educational secondary school classrooms. *Sociology of Education, 67,* 92–120.

Letts, W. J., & Sears, J. T. (1999). *Queering elementary education. Advancing the dialogue about sexualities and schooling.* Lanham, MD: Rowman & Littlefield.

Lesko, N. (2000). *Masculinities at school.* Thousand Oaks, CA: Sage.

LeVasseur, M. (1993). *Finding a way, encouraging under-represented groups in geography: An annotated bibliography.* Pathway series. Indiana, PA: National Council for Geographic Education.

———. (1999). Students' knowledge of geography and geographic careers. *Journal of Geography, 98,* 265–271.

Levstik, L. (2001). Daily acts of ordinary courage: Gender-equitable practice in the social studies classroom. In P. O'Reilly, E. M. Penn, & K. deMarrais (Eds.) *Educating young adolescent girls.* Mahwah, NJ: Lawrence Erlbaum Associates.

Levstik, L., & Groth, J. (2002). "Scary thing, being an eighth grader": Exploring gender and sexuality in a middle school U.S. history unit. *Theory and Research in Social Education, 30,* 233–254.

Light, B., Staton, P., & Bourne, P. (1989). Sex equity content in history textbooks. *The History Social Science Teacher, 25*(1), 18–20.

Linn, M. C., & Petersen, A. C. (1985). Emergence and characterization of sex differences in spatial ability: A meta-analysis. *Child Development, 56,* 1479–1498.

Loutzenheiser, L. W. (2006). Gendering social studies, queering social education. In A. Segall, E. Heilman, & C. Cherryholmes (Eds.), *Social studies—The next generation: Researching in the postmodern* (pp. 61–75). New York: Peter Lang.

Lutkus, A. D., Weiss, A. R., Campbell, J. R., Mazzeo, J., & Lazer, S. (1999). *NAEP 1998: Civics report card for the nation.* Washington, DC: National Center for Education Statistics, U.S. Department of Education. ED 435 583.

Makeba, A. (2002a). *Performance as text: The hidden history of the Montgomery Bus Boycott.* Unpublished master's project, San Francisco State University.

———. (2002b). "The story of Claudette Colvin," on *This land is your land: Songs of unity.* Redway, CA: Music for Little People.

Matthews, M. H. (1987). Sex differences in spatial competence: The ability of young children to map "primed" unfamiliar environments. *Educational Psychology, 7,* 77–91.

Mayall, H. J. (2002). *An exploratory/descriptive look at gender differences in technology self efficacy and academic self-efficacy in the GlobalEd Project.* (Doctoral dissertation, University of Connecticut, UMI No. 3050198).

Mayer, T. (1989) Consensus and invisibility: The representation of women in human geography textbooks. *The Professional Geographer, 41,* 397–409.

Mazzeo, J., Schmitt, A., & Bleistein, C. (1990). *Exploratory analyses of some possible causes for the discrepancies in gender differences on multiple-choice and free-response sections of the Advanced Placement examinations.* Draft report. Princeton, NJ: Educational Testing Service, as cited in Breland, H. et al. (1994).

McDowell, L. (1992). Engendering change: Curriculum transformation in human geography. *Journal of Geography in Higher Education, 16,* 185–187

McKenna, K. (1989). An examination of sex equity in the 1986 Ontario curriculum guideline for history and contemporary studies. *History and Social Science Teacher, 25*(1), 21–24.

Merryfield, M., & Crocco, M. (2003). Women of the world: Special issue. *Social Education, 67,* 10–64.

Mucherah, W. M. (1999). *Dimensions of classroom climate in social studies classrooms where technology is available.* (Doctoral dissertation, University of Maryland, UMI No. 9929131).

National Center for Education Statistics. (1994). *NAEP 1994: Geography report card.* U.S. Department of Education/OERI. Washington, DC: Author.

——— (1997). *America's teachers: Profiles of a profession.* Schools and Staffing Survey 1993–94. U.S. Department of Education Statistics/OERI, NCES 97-460 document. Washington DC: Author

———. (2000). *Trends in educational equity of girls and women,* NCES 2000-30. Retrieved October, 29, 2005, from www.ed.gov.

———. (2004). *Trends in educational equity of girls & women 2004.* Washington, DC: Author.

———. (2005). *U.S. history: The nation's report card.* Retrieved September 25, 2005, from www: http: nces.ed.gov/nationsreportcard/ushistory.

National Center for History in the Schools. (1996). *National standards for history: Basic edition.* Los Angeles, CA: University of California, Author.

National Council for the Social Studies. (1994). *Curriculum standards for social studies.* Washington, DC: Author.

National Council for Geographic Education (2000). *Finding a way: Learning activities in geography for grades, 7–11,* Indiana, PA: Author.

National Council on Economic Education. (1997). *Voluntary national content standards in economics.* New York: Author.

National Women's History Project (2005). Retrieved October 3, 2005, from www.http://nwhp.org.

Nelson, B. D., Aron, R. H., & Poole, D. A. (1997). *Sex Roles, 41,* 529–40.

Nelson, C. (1990). *Gender and the social studies: Training pre-service secondary social studies teachers.* (Doctoral dissertation, University of Minnesota, ATT No. 9021339.)

Nelson, J. A. (1995). Feminism and economics. *Journal of Economic Perspectives, 9,* 131–148.

Niemi, R., & Junn, J. (1998). *Civic education: What makes students learn.* New Haven: Yale University Press.

Noddings, N. (1992a). The gender issue. *Educational Leadership, 49*(4), 65–70.

———. (1992b). Social studies and feminism. *Theory and Research in Social Education, 20,* 230–241.

Owens, W. T. (1999). Preservice feedback about the Internet and the implications for social studies educators. *The Social Studies, 90*(3), 133–140.

Protano, R. D. (2003). *Female high school students' attitude and perceptions toward the social studies discipline.* (Doctoral dissertation, Fordham University, NY, UMI No. 3101156).

Reese, L. (1994). Gender equity and texts. *Social Studies Review, 33*(2), 12–15.

Reese, L., & Wilkinson, J. (1987) *Women in the world: Annotated history resources for the secondary student.* Metuchen, NJ: Scarecrow Press, Inc.

Robson, D. (2001). Women and minorities in economics textbooks: Are they being adequately represented? *Journal of Economic Education, 32,* 186–191.

Ross, E. W. (Ed.) (1997). *The social studies curriculum: Purposes, problems, and possibilities.* Albany: State University of New York Press.

Sadker, M., & Sadker, D. (1994). *Failing at fairness.* New York: Scribners.

Santora, E. (2001). Interrogating privilege, plurality, and possibilities in a multicultural society. In W. B. Stanley (Ed.), *Critical issues in social studies research for the 21st century* (pp. 149–179). Greenwich, CT: Information Age Publishers.

Savage, S. (2005). *Gender bias in elementary level social studies textbooks.* Unpublished master's project, San Francisco State University.

Schmurak, C. B., & Ratliff, T. M. (1993, April). *Gender equity and gender bias in the middle school classroom.* Paper presented at the annual meeting of the American Educational Research Association, Atlanta.

Scott, J. W. (1997). Women's history and the National History Standards. *Journal of Women's History, 9*(3), 172–177.

Segall, A. (2002). *Disturbing practice: Reading teacher education as a text.* New York: Peter Lang.

Shaver, J. P. (Ed.) (1991). *Handbook on social studies teaching and learning.* New York: MacMillan.

Smith, R. W. (1996). Schooling and the formation of male students' gender identities. *Theory and Research in Social Education, 24,* 54–70.

Stanley, W. B., (Ed.) (2001). *Critical issues in social studies research for the 21st century.* Greenwich, CT: Information Age Publishing.

Stone, L. (1996). Feminist political theory: Contributions to a conception of citizenship. *Theory and Research in Social Education, 24,* 36–53.

Style, E. (1996). *Curriculum as window and mirror.* Wellesley Centers for Women. Retrieved January 2, 2006, from www.wcwonline.org/seed/curriulum.html.

Symcox, L. (2002). *Whose history? The struggle for national standards in American classrooms.* New York: Teachers College Press.

Ten Dam, G., & Rijkschroeff (1996). Teaching women's history in secondary education: Constructing gender identity. *Theory and Research in Social Education, 24,* 71–88.

Ten Dam, G., & Tekkens, H. F. (1997). The gender inclusiveness of a women's history curriculum in secondary education. *Women's Studies International Forum, 20*(1), 61–75.

Tetreault, M. K. (1984). Notable American women: The case of U.S. history textbooks. *Social Education, 48,* 546–550.

———. (1986). It's so opiniony. *Journal of Education, 168,* 78–95.

———. (1987). Rethinking women, gender, and the social studies. *Social Education, 51,* 170–178.

Thorne, (1993). *Gender play: Girls and boys in school.* New Brunswick, NJ: Rutgers University Press.

Torney, J., Oppenheim, A., & Farnen, R. (1975). *Civic education in ten countries.* New York: John Wiley. ERIC Document Reproduction Service ED 132 059.

Torney-Purta, J. (1991). Cross national research in social studies. In J. P. Shaver (Ed.), *Handbook on social studies teaching and learning* (pp. 591–601). New York: Macmillan.

Torney-Purta, J., & Amadeo, J. A. (2004). *Strengthening democracy in the Americas: An empirical analysis of the views of students and teachers.* Washington, DC: Organization of American States.

Torney-Purta, J., & Barber, C. (2004). *Strengths and weaknesses in U.S. students' knowledge and skills: Analysis from the IEA civic education study.* CIRCLE Fact Sheet. Retrieved August 1, 2005, from www.civicyouth.org

Torney-Purta, J., Lehmann, R., Oswald, H., & Schulz, W. (2001). *Citizenship and education in twenty eight countries: Civic knowledge and engagement at age fourteen.* Amsterdam: The International Association for the Evaluation of Educational Achievement.

Walstad, W. B., & Robson, D. (1997). Differential item functioning and male-female differences on multiple-choice tests in economics. *Journal of Economic Education, 28,* 155–171.

Walstad, W. B., & Soper, J. C. (1989). What is high school economics? Factors contributing to student achievement and attitudes. *Journal of Economic Education, 20,* 23–38.

Walter, C., & Young. B. (1994). Gender bias in Alberta social studies 30 examinations: Cause and effect. *Canadian Social Studies, 31*(2), 83–86, 89.

Western Association of Women Historians' Standing Committee on K–12 Education. (1994). *Textbook evaluation report.* An unpublished paper. Long Beach, CA: Author.

Woyshner, C. (2002). Political history as women's history: Toward a more inclusive curriculum. *Theory and Research in Social Education, 30,* 354–380.

Woyshner, C., Watras, J., & Crocco, M. S. (Eds.) (2004). *Social education in the twentieth century: Curriculum and context for citizenship.* New York: Peter Lang.

Wridt, P. (1998). The worlds of girls and boys: Geographic experience and informal learning opportunities. *Journal of Geography, 98,* 253–264.

———. (2000). *The gendered geographies of everyday life.* Indiana, PA: National Council for Geographic Education.

Zittleman, K., & Sadker, D. (2003). The unfinished gender revolution. *Educational Leadership, 40*(4), 59–63..

GENDER EQUITY IN VISUAL ARTS AND DANCE EDUCATION

Elizabeth Garber,* **Renee Sandell,*** **Mary Ann Stankiewicz,*** **Doug Risner*** with: Georgia Collins, Enid Zimmerman, Kristin Congdon, Minuette Floyd, Marla Jaksch, Peg Speirs, Stephanie Springgay, Rita Irwin

INTRODUCTION

The second wave of the women's movement has had profound effects on the visual and performing arts in U.S. society (Cameron, 2003; De Zegher, 2003; Fraser, 2003; Schor, 1999; Lovelace, 2003; Phelan, 2003). In the late 1960s, art world feminists insisted that the personal is political.[1] This holds as true in art as it does in life, initiating an intense critique of the history, practices, and teachings of the arts in mainstream Western and other cultures (Schapiro, 2001). This critique has developed over time, and has resulted in significant changes in the visual arts, dance, and other art forms (Hoban, 2007; Isaac, 1996). Understanding the impact of feminism in the arts has become central to understanding art today (Cottingham, 1994; Hoban, 2007; Lucie-Smith, 1994; Robinson, 2001).

This does not mean that problems identified by Sandell, Collins, and Sherman in their 1985 *Handbook* chapter "Sex Equity in Visual Arts Education" are resolved. One need only ask the following questions raised in 1985 to realize the persistence of gender equity problems in the arts: Are the voices and perspectives of women of all races, socioeconomic classes, and nations represented equitably in historical studies and in contemporary performances and exhibitions? Do art and dance teachers now occupy a place of respect in schools? While successes can be identified, they are often partial; furthermore, additional issues have surfaced. As in other areas of the women's movement, feminists in the arts think about equity as meaning more than equal inclusion of women's work in the arts and in what is

taught. Identity issues of multiple social locations including race, sexuality, nation citizenry, age, and religion intersect with social issues such as patriarchal institutions and systems, the body, poverty, environment, technology, and war.

Authors of the 1985 chapter considered formal and informal education and based their recommendations on the need for discipline-specific work: that teachers increase their knowledge of feminist issues and content in the arts, and develop teaching strategies to address sex equity issues in their classrooms.

Section 1 introduces gender equity issues in visual arts and dance formal education: status, curricular equity, and other issues of concern in arts making, performance, teaching, and research. Section 2 explores gender equity efforts in visual arts and dance education in terms of teaching approaches and practices, learning, leadership, and resources. Section 3 provides recommendations for gender equity in visual art and dance education.

ISSUES

Sandell, Collins, and Sherman (1985) found that the status of women in art and art education was in general secondary to that of men. Today the direction of research and scholarship has expanded in directions that extend the focus of equity to a broader view of gender intersected with a multiplicity of identities, and in directions that have created new paradigms for conceptualizing, researching, teaching, and creating or performing in the arts. This section of the chapter is divided into issues of

---

*The bold face names are the Lead Authors.

[1]Significant feminist research and practice exists in music and theater, and we hope to make this work part of any future overviews of feminist education in the arts.

status and curricular equity, as well as broader issues arising from gender equity and feminist perspectives in the arts.

Status Issues: Participation and Gender Portrayal in Visual Art and Dance

The central issues in status are who is participating in art and dance, what their status is within the disciplines and their educational and arts contexts, and how gender is represented in these disciplines.

Participation

Participation in the visual arts. In the art world, feminist artist groups such as the Guerilla Girls, The Vagina Monologues, and WAC (Women's Action Coalition), along with individual artists and performers, have increased visibility of women and other marginalized artists and often work directly to make society more equitable. However, women artists continue to be underrepresented in the art world (Cottingham, 1994; Hoban, 2007; Macadam, 2007) and women's representation in the arts often is based on traditional stereotypes of passive sexuality, objectification, and marginalized roles (Guerilla Girls, 2004; Macadam, 2007; Wilding, 1999). In 2005 in New York's Metropolitan Museum, only 3% of the artists represented in the modern and contemporary sections were women, down from 5% in 1989 (Hoban, 2007). Ninety percent of solo exhibitions at the Met during 2000–2004 featured the work of White male artists, 8.5% featured White women, and 1.5% artists of color. Statistics in three other New York museums during this period were improved, with the Whitney Museum of American Art having the best record: 50% the work of White males, 30% White females, 7% females of color, and 13% males of color (Guerrilla Girls, 2004, p. 9). Looking at the fall 2006 schedules for 125 top New York galleries, Saltz (2006) reports that only 23% of solo shows feature women, up from fall 2005's 19%. As this volume goes to press, the artworld is in a flurry about the Sackler Center for Feminist Art opening at the Brooklyn Museum. Yet despite progress, women's art overall does not garner the prices men's does and their position in powerful roles in the art world remains the exception rather than the rule (Macadam, 2007). In television, films, and music videos, men continue to perform more frequently than women (Park, 1996; Smith, 1997). There is no statistical information about women's participation in the visual arts outside the fine art world, in, for example, outsider and folk art or crafts. Traditional approaches to art making and traditional media continue to be considered "poor cousins" to New York art, suggesting that arguments made in the 1970s about the undervaluing of artmaking associated with women's traditions continue to be valid.

One of the ways of assessing equity is by looking at percentages of women and men involved in different educational aspects of the visual arts and dance. In academia, 56.5% of the art professoriate are male and 43.5% are female (Higher Education Arts Data Service [HEADS], 2004, Art/Design Chart 5),[2] with the greatest disparity occurring at the rank of full professor (see Table 17.1).

At colleges and universities, women art faculty members (generally defined as art education, art history, and studio art) holding doctorate degrees outnumber males holding doctorate degrees, although the percentage of male faculty rises in institutions offering advanced degrees (HEADS, 2004, Art/Design Chart 9) (see Table 17.2).

These figures suggest that women faculty outnumber men in art education and art history, but men still dominate studio teaching, and that in more research-oriented institutions, the ratio of male to female faculty holding a doctoral degree rises. Tenured male faculty consistently outnumber tenured females (HEADS, 2004, Art/Design Chart 13) (see Table 17.3).

An even greater disparity occurs when we consider gender *and* race, with non-White faculty composing a small percentage of art faculty members. (HEADS, 2004, Art/Design chart 60) (see Table 17.4).

In public high schools, female students' participation across the arts outweighs that of males. In 2000 males earned fewer Carnegie arts units[3] than females (National Center for Education Statistics [NCES], 2004, Table 137[4]), with White non-Hispanic students earning the most arts units and Asian/Pacific Islander and American Indian/Alaska Natives earning the fewest. Among public high school seniors, fewer males than females reported taking a music, art, or dance class outside of school at least once a week (NCES, 2004, Table 141). On 8th grade assessments of educational progress in music, visual arts, and theater, females' scores were higher in all subjects and areas tested (see Table 17.5) and Asian students' scores were higher than other groups'.

Female arts students continue to outnumber males at the tertiary level as well earning, during 2001–2002, more associate and bachelor's degrees in visual and performing arts than men (NCES, 2004, Tables 251 & 255) (see Table 17.6).

At the MFA or terminal degree level in studio, the total male population is less than the female population; however, the higher population of female students comes from non-White women (HEADS, 2004, Art/Design Charts 27-1 & 27-2) (see Table 17.7). These figures indicate that non-White women holding the MFA degree are particularly underrepresented as faculty members in higher education and that White males in studio art have a better chance of obtaining a job in higher education than does anyone else similarly educated.[5]

---

[2]HEADS Data Summaries are based on data generated from 2003–2004 Annual Reports required of member institutions of the National Association of Schools of Art and Design and on data provided voluntarily by nonmember institutions. The data is, then, not comprehensive of all tertiary education. We thank Dennis L. Jones, Director of the School of Art, University of Arizona, for making this database accessible to us.

[3]Carnegie units, developed in 1906, are a standard measure of time a student studies a subject in high school to earn a credit in that subject. Each Carnegie unit represents what is considered a year of study in that subject.

[4]Many thanks to Paula Wolfe, Arts Librarian at the University of Arizona, for helping us locate this data. Thanks also to Greta Garber-Pearson for her bibliographic research.

[5]Kiefer-Boyd notes that the gender gap of MFAs or PhDs working in the area of new media art is much greater than the statistics presented here. As new media art programs continue to grow in secondary and university art programs, women will be underrepresented if art education in K–12 does not change. Areas such as physical computing, gaming, hactivism, and other forms of mediated communication with digital technologies tend to be dominated by males (Ray, 2004).

TABLE 17.1 Comparison of Male:Female Art Faculty Ranks at Universities and Colleges*

	Male/ with MFA	Female, with MFA	Male, with Doctorate	Female, with Doctorate	Total Male at Rank of Professors	Total Female at Rank of Professors
Professor	676	302	123	122	799	424
%	69.1	30.9	50.2	49.8	65.3	34.7
					24.3	12.9
Associate Professor	449	305	113	147	562	452
%	59.5	40.5	43.5	56.4	55.4	44.6
Assistant Professor	396	389	100	164	496	553
%	50.4	49.6	37.9	62.1	47.3	52.7
Total	1,521	996	336	433	1,857	1,429
%	60.4	39.6	43.7	56.3	56.5	43.5

Based on HEADS, 2003–2004, Art/Design Charts 5 & 60.
*Percentages based on a comparison of male and female faculty with the same level of education at institutions offering similar highest degrees

TABLE 17.2 Comparison of Male:Female Art Faculty's Educational Background at Universities and Colleges Categorized by Highest Degree Granted in Art/Design*

	Male, with MFA	Female, with MFA	Male, with Doctorate	Female, with Doctorate	Total Male at Rank/of Ranked Professors	Total Female at Rank/of Ranked Professors
Highest degree offered at Institution						
Baccalaureate	462	308	60	112	522	420
%	60.0*	40.0	35.0	65.0	55.4	44.6
Masters (not MFA)	199	140	40	57	239	197
%	58.7	41.3	41.2	58.8	54.8	45.2
MFA	938	646	214	251	1,152	897
%	59.2	40.8	46.0	54.0	56.2	43.8
Doctorate	146	100	53	60	199	160
%	59.3	40.7	46.9	53.1	55.4	44.6
Totals	1,745	1,194	367	480	2,112	1,674
%	59.4	40.6	43.3	56.7	55.8	44.2

Based on HEADS 2003–2004, Chart 9.
*Percentages based on a comparison of males:females who hold the same terminal degree at the same category of institution.

TABLE 17.3 Comparison of Male:Female Arts/Design Faculty Tenure Status at Associate, Baccalaureate, Masters, MFA, and Doctoral Degree–Granting Institutions

	Tenured	Nontenured
Male	1,306	1,526
Column %	60.8	53.3
Total faculty %	26.1	30.5
Female	841	1,337
Column %	39.2	46.7
Total faculty %	16.8	26.7

Based on HEADS 2003–2004, Art/Design Chart 13.

More women than men are in doctoral programs in art education or art history and criticism (HEADS, 2004, Art/Design Chart 28-1). Among these students, twice as many non-White females were enrolled as non-White males and almost three times as many White women were enrolled as White males (HEADS, 2004, Art/Design Charts 28-1 & 28-2) (see Table 17.7).

Salaries at tertiary public institutions for male art professors averaged higher than those of females at professorial ranks with the margin of difference closing over the years. At private institutions, the disparity of male:female salaries at professorial ranks is even greater (HEADS, 2004, Art/Design Charts 14-1 & 15-1) (see Table 17.8).

In the only arts category of the U.S. Bureau of Labor Statistics that has sufficient data on male and female wages, full-time female designers earned 79% of what their male coworkers did in 2004, with men's average weekly salary $818 and women's $646 (U.S. Department of Labor, Bureau of Labor Statistics, 2005).

What these tables indicate is that while gains have been made for women in some areas of the arts, there remain gender and race differences in some hiring practices and in ranks and salaries for women at universities, despite women's greater participation in the arts at all levels of education, except for the area of technology and new media.

Participation in dance. Although women outnumber men significantly in dance, asymmetrical power relationships affect women adversely at all levels of dance training, education, and in the professional realm. As in visual arts, men have more political power in dance and are better paid. Men in dance have benefited disproportionately in the areas of funding, education,

TABLE 17.4   Comparison of Male:Female Art Faculty by Ethnicity*

	Black Non-Hispanic Latino		American Indian/ Native Alaskan		Pacific Islander		Hispanic/Latino		Asian		White Non-Hispanic		Row Totals
	M	F	M	F	M	F	M	F	M	F	M	F	
Professor	29	10	5	1	5	4	30	15	34	14	907	479	1,533
Rank %	1.9	0.6	0.3	0.07	0.3	0.3	2.0	1.0	2.2	0.9	59.2	31.2	
Total faculty %	0.6	0.2	0.1	0.02	0.1	0.08	0.6	0.3	0.7	0.3	17.8	9.4	30.0
Associate Professor	41	14	3	4	1	4	35	14	33	16	604	514	1,283
Rank %	3.2	1.1	0.2	0.3	0.08	0.3	2.7	1.1	2.6	1.2	47.1	40.1	
Total faculty %	0.8	0.3	0.06	0.08	0.02	0.08	0.7	0.3	0.6	0.3	11.8	10.1	25.1
Assistant Professor	34	27	3	3	2	1	26	24	33	51	520	546	1,270
Rank %	2.7	2.1	0.2	0.2	0.2	0.08	2.0	1.9	2.6	4.0	40.9	43.0	
Total faculty %	0.7	0.5	0.06	0.06	0.04	0.02	0.5	0.5	0.6	1.0	10.2	10.7	24.9
Instructor, Lecturer, Unranked, Visiting	22	15	2	7	1	2	25	23	22	16	474	407	1016
Faculty Rank %	2.2	1.5	0.2	0.7	0.1	0.2	2.5	2.3	2.2	1.6	46.7	40.1	
Total faculty %	0.4	0.3	0.04	0.1	0.02	0.04	0.5	0.5	0.4	0.3	9.3	8.0	19.9
Column Totals	126	66	13	15	9	11	116	76	122	97	2,505	1,946	5,102
%	2.5	1.3	0.3	0.3	0.2	0.2	2.3	1.5	2.4	1.9	49.1	38.1	

Total Non-White Males: 386
  Non-White faculty %   59.3
  Total faculty %   7.6

Total Non-White Females: 265
  Non-White faculty %   40.7
  Total faculty %   5.2

Based on HEADS 2003–2004, Art/Design Chart 60.
*Faculty whose race/ethnicity is unknown were excluded from this chart (2.4%).

TABLE 17.5   Performance of 8th Grade Students in Music, Visual Arts, and Theater, 1997, According to *The* NAEP 1997 *Arts Report Card*

	Music			Visual Arts		Theater	
Student Characteristics	Average Creating Score (%)	Average Performing Score (%)	Average Responding Score (0-300 Scale)	Average Creating Score (%)	Average Responding Score (0-300 Scale)	Average Creating/ Performing Score (%)	Average Responding Score (0-300 Scale)
Male students	32 (1.0)*	27 (1.4)	140 (1.5)	42 (0.7)	146 (1.5)	46 (2.2)	140 (6.6)
Female students	37 (1.6)	40 (1.5)	160 (1.6)	45 (0.9)	154 (1.4)	52 (2.1)	158 (5.6)
White, non-Hispanic	36 (1.2)	36 (1.4)	158 (1.4)	46 (0.9)	159 (1.3)	52 (1.9)	159 (4.4)
Black, non-Hispanic	34 (3.6)	30 (1.9)	130 (2.3)	37 (1.8)	124 (2.0)	39 (2.2)	120 (10.1)
Hispanic	29 (2.7)	24 (3.7)	127 (3.5)	38 (1.3)	128 (2.0)	44 (2.5)	139 (6.2)
Asian	31 (3.8)		152 (6.2)	45 (1.6)	153 (6.4)		

Based on NCES, 2004, Table 130.
*Standard errors appear in parentheses.

TABLE 17.6   Associate and Bachelors Degrees Awarded in Visual and Performing Arts, 2001–2002

	Associate	Bachelor
Male	9,613	27,130
%	46	40.6
Female	11,298	39,643
%	54	59.4

Source: NCES, 2004, Tables 251 & 255.

income, and employment (Van Dyke, 1996). Males hold a disproportionate number of directorial and administrative authority positions; women have less career mobility (Hanna, 1988; Samuels, 2001; Stinson, Blumenfeld-Jones, & Van Dyke, 1990; Van Dyke, 1996; Vigier, 1995). Historically, primary figures in modern dance, unlike ballet, were mostly women, but according to the latest figures available, many companies in the United States and abroad are directed by men (Adair, 1992; Hanna, 1988). Among small grants ($15,000–70,000) from the National

TABLE 17.7   MFA and Doctoral Students (Continuing and Graduating) in Visual Art, 2003–2004*

	Black Non-Hispanic Latino	American Indian/ Alaskan Native	Pacific Islander	Hispanic/ Latino	Asian	White Non-Hispanic	Total Non-White/ Non-Hispanic	Total
MFA								
Male	78	12	22	175	469	1,851	756	2,607
Total MFA student %	1.4	0.2	0.4	3.1	8.5	33.4	13.6	47.0
Female	103	12	68	341	612	1,801	1,136	2,937
Total MFA student %	1.9	0.2	1.2	6.2	11.0	32.5	20.5	53.0
Doctorate								
Male	3	0	0	4	7	49	14	63
Total doctoral student %	1.2	0	0	1.6	2.8	19.8	5.7	25.5
Female	5	0	0	9	14	156	28	184
Total doctoral student %	2.0	0	0	3.6	5.7	63.2	11.3	74.5

*This chart excludes graduates of other ethnicities that are not identified in the instrument and graduates unknown race/ethnicity.
Source: HEADS 2003–2004, Art/Design Charts 27-1, 27-2, 28-1, & 28-2.

TABLE 17.8   Salaries of Male and Female Art Professors at Public and Private Colleges and Universities

	Average Male Salary	Average Female Salary
Public institutions		
Professor	$68,900	$67,560
Associate Professor	54,155	53,201
Assistant Professor	46,541	46,151
Private institutions		
Professor	$65,631	$62,594
Associate Professor	53,661	51,871
Assistant Professor	44,395	42,347

Based on HEADS 2003–2004, Art/Design Charts 14-1 & 15-1.

Endowment from the Arts and the New York State Council on the Arts, 73% of recipients were men; grant recipients of $70,000 or more were 100% male (Hanna, 1988).

Although women outnumber men as chief administrative officers at university and college dance departments, male leadership in the last decade is on the rise (Van Dyke, 1996, *Dance Magazine College 2004 & 2005*, 2004). Listings for university and college dance departments' chief administrative officers indicated 102 female dance executives and 40 male dance executives (*Dance Magazine College 2004 & 2005*, 2004). There has been a 40% increase in male dance leadership in the last decade. Ratios of women chief executives to men in 2004 was 72% female and 28% male executives (*Dance Magazine College 2004 & 2005*, 2004). Stinson (1998a) indicates women in administration often spend large amounts of time in service and department "housekeeping" rather than managerial duties within departments, often sacrificing their own personal and professional careers to facilitate the growth and well-being of others (p. 125).

As of 2002–2003, women comprised the majority of the dance professoriate. Pursuing the MFA in Dance (terminal degree), 89% are women, and at the undergraduate level, 92.3% are female. Male faculty salaries in dance exceed female faculty salaries in public institutions across all professorial ranks by a yearly average of $3,072. Salaries for women and men at the rank of assistant professor and visiting faculty are nearly the same, as are salaries of dance faculty at private institutions. In terms of gender and ethnicity, White non-Hispanic women make up 54.9% of dance faculty; Black non-Hispanic, women 6.1%; Hispanic females, 2%; and Asian/Pacific Islander females, 1.6% (HEADS, 2003). At the undergraduate level, 76% of the dance student body is White non-Hispanic female; 7.3% is Black non-Hispanic female; 4.8% is Hispanic female; 3.7% is Asian/Pacific Islander female; and .5% is American Indian/Alaskan female (HEADS, 2003).[6]

Portrayal

The portrayal of gender in visual art.   Another way of assessing equity, and a foundational area of feminist art and film theory, is through studying representation of women in art and film, as well as mass media. Male gaze theory, which argues that spectators hold a masculine subject position and that the woman represented is positioned as an object of desire, has offered a theoretical foundation as to how women are viewed and objectified in the arts (Mulvey, 1975). Furthermore, this assumes heterosexuality as the norm. Informal surveys indicate that in 2004, 83% of the nudes in the modern and contemporary sections of New York's Metropolitan Museum of Art were women (Guerrilla Girls, 2004, p. 9). Children Now, a children's advocacy group, found that "Across a broad range of media, women are more likely to be shown preoccupied with romance and personal appearance than they are having jobs or going to school" (Smith, 1997, A17). These findings are notable in that the media plays a significant role in the way society, and in particular youth, views and constructs notions about women as well as people of non-European based cultures and ethnicities (Mander, 1991). Similar research in education and cultural studies links girls' perceptions of self and body image to ideals

---

[6]Tables are not available for the dance professoriate because of the small sample size.

presented through advertising and other venues of popular culture (e.g., Driscoll, 2002; Oliver & Lalik, 2000). Additionally, interests targeted in films, television, computer games, and music videos most often are those of teenage boys (Green, 1997; Jagodzinski, 2004; Jenkins & Cassell, 1998; Kaiser, 1999; Seger, 1996).

Portrayal of gender in dance. In dance, the body has been the basis of analyses using male gaze theory, coupled with analyses of women's lack of cultural power within dominant patriarchal structures (Kaplan, 1983; Thomas, 2003, p. 159). Dance scholars throughout the late 1980s and through the mid-1990s embraced application of male gaze theory in dance. "Feminist critics in dance were interested in the ways that women are represented generally in theatre dance and in how they might transcend or subvert the dominant modes of representation" (Daly, 1991, p. 160). Application of male gaze theory changed in the mid-1990s. Thomas notes, for example, important limitations of male gaze theory: it proposes "an ahistorical, universal structure of male, heterosexual looking, for presuming that men, unlike women, are not objectified through the gaze and for not taking account of difference, except along the lines of Freudian male/female binary divide" (p. 159).

The issue of how males are represented in dance and their gender identity is an ongoing issue in dance. Some choreographers have taken masculinity and homosexuality as their themes. Ted Shawn's all-male dance company developed "masculine movement" and his strategy for "heightened virility on stage subtly changed the message, from signs of gender inversion to a hearty flaunting of male bodily display [which provided] an example of America's potency, as a sign of essential differences between men and women, and as an ideal of homosexual love between men" (Foulkes, 2001, p. 139). Mark Morris's choreography throughout the 1980s and 1990s, especially *The Hard Nut* (an updated version of *Nutcracker*) explored gender instability and the multiplication of a variety of gender identities (Morris, 1996).

Curricular Equity Issues

Curricular Equity in Visual Art

The hierarchy of school subjects in the curriculum mirrors the traditional hierarchy of genders. Those subjects associated with men, masculine virtues, rationality, and intellectual achievements are ranked higher than subjects associated with women. In their 1985 chapter, Sandell, Collins, and Sherman showed how association of the arts with femininity contributed significantly to the low status and funding of the arts in schools and in U.S. society. Indeed, art education is "doubly feminine identified" because both the worlds of art and education have traditionally suppressed the potential of art education (Sandell, 1991, p. 183).

What is the position of the arts in today's curricula? High school graduation and college entrance policies emphasize "core" subjects such as math and science. In U.S. Department of Education data, arts and vocational requirements are grouped together as a subject area. Eighteen states require no arts/voca-

tional credits for high school graduation; 4 states require .5 credits; 16 require 1 credit; 1 state requires 1.5 credits; 5 (including the District of Columbia) require 2 credits; and 7 states reported no data (NCES 2004, Table 152). Grades in the arts often are not counted in computing high school grade point averages.

In most states, the arts are not required for college admission. Credits for Advanced Placement arts courses are not necessarily weighted equally with those of other AP courses. However, with the passage of the nationally legislated Goals 2000: Educate America Act, the arts were acknowledged as a core subject (National Art Education Association, 1994, p. 6). Title II of the Act addresses educational standards, and in anticipation of this reform legislation, some states early on adopted voluntary national art education standards and many states have followed by developing their own standards.

According to Chapman (2004, 2005), even when identified as a "core" subject, the arts are on the periphery of learning because they are not one of the subjects contributing to No Child Left Behind (NCLB) legislation that determines if schools are making "adequate yearly progress" in reading, mathematics, and science. Arts education is vulnerable to cuts not just in budgets but also in curricular time and within curriculum (Chapman, 2005).

Girls often are discouraged from taking art courses precisely because art is a feminine-identified subject. "Popular feminist educational propaganda illustrates girls claiming their rightful place in a man's world, handling heavy materials, working with sophisticated laboratory equipment or in machine workshops alongside boys, but there are few images of ideal female role models engaged in painting, drawing, or sewing" (Dalton, 2001, p. 6). Also, there are few positive role models of women working creatively with technological programming as an art form. Popular culture images, especially in films, of women knowledgeable about technology present these women as antisocial, evil, and lonely people, if they are presented at all.

Curricular Equity in Dance

Dance is largely considered a woman's art and associated with the body and physicality. Western culture has traditionally valued mind over body, associating the mind with men and the body with women (Oliver, 1994). Dance often has been housed in physical education departments at the university level, which, until relatively recently, had a strong gender divide. Influenced by legislation such as Title IX (1972) and the Equal Educational Opportunity Act (1974), physical education (and hence dance) became more co-educational. Concurrently, dance redefined itself in terms of the arts, where artistic experimentation was encouraged; in 2001, 81% of tertiary dance programs were located in fine and performing arts units. College and university dance programs, offering a major or a minor, increased 287% between 1986 and 2001 (Bonbright, 2002).

In academic environments where quantitative scholarship and publications are the standard, all the arts suffer. When faced with promotion and tenure issues, it is not uncommon for arts administrators to have to make a case for the importance of creative activity as a form of legitimate research (Clark, 1994; Stinson, 1998a).

Dance was recognized as a separate discipline of the arts by the Goals 2000: Educate America Act which led toward national and state educational standards. By 1999, 49 states had developed their own K–12 standards in dance derived from the national standards (Bonbright, 2001). Written curriculum guides supporting elementary dance instruction exist in about half of elementary schools offering dance; of these, 75% were aligned with State or National Standards for Arts Education. While most public elementary schools in the United States reported in 1999–2000 some kind of instruction in music and visual arts, only 20% provided dance instruction; dance instruction was offered by dance specialists in 7.6% of elementary schools in 1999 and 14% of public secondary schools (NCES, 2002).

Gender Equity Issues in Content and Teaching Practice

Definitions of Art and Conceptions of Feminism in Visual Art

The terms *visual culture/visual culture education* (Duncum, 2000; Freedman, 2003; Tavin, 2003) and *material culture/material culture education* (Bolin & Blandy, 2003) have recently redefined and reconceptualized art education and bear the influence of feminist theory.[7] Methods of analyzing art as visual/material culture include gender in relationship to political and cultural contexts and stress critical praxis. With an emphasis on social needs, feminist ideas such as empathy, caring, and listening (Becker, 1994; Gablik, 1991; Hicks & King, 1996; Lacy, 1995; Lippard, 1984, 1995; McRorie, 1996; Noddings, 1992) have influenced contemporary art through a process of dialogue and collective exchange between artists and communities.

Whereas the media and techniques taught in art classes often include craft media such as fibers and ceramics, most classroom discussions (such as those that take place in art criticism or art history) and most art education research emphasize painting and drawing. Because craft practice is traditionally feminine-associated, the emphasis in art classrooms reflects a gendered structure of art education (Dalton, 2001). Furthermore, the trend toward emphasizing visual culture in art education, although theoretically inclusive, emphasizes mainstream media, overemphasizing representations and interests of White males, and rarely investigates the visual culture of ethnic groups (Garber, 2005).

Today artists, writers, and youth associate feminism in art with ambivalence (Fraser, 2003), ambiguity (Nochlin, 2003; Schorr, 2003), fragmentation, pluralism, and diversity (Avgikos, 2003; Collins & Sandell, 1984). Some feminist artists find that feminism informs their work but is implied or subterranean, rather than explicit (Finkel, 2007; Schor, 1999). The generation of women artists and teachers new to art professions or currently studying often feel distanced from feminism, which is sometimes perceived as being associated with "extremism and man-hating" (Fortnum, 1998). These trends indicate that although feminist messages are alive in art and art education, the terms *feminism* and *feminist* seem to be changing. In the recommendations section, we will suggest how art educators can proactively address some of these changes.

Content Issues

Content issues in visual art. Key content issues in visual art include addressing diverse and multiple identities, the instability of gender, the representation and use of the body in art, and gender and technology. Feminists in art continue to engage in research, with sociohistoric emphases, that intersects with specific contexts (time, place, power, identity, resistance) and makes visible the lives and artistic expressions of women from diverse backgrounds and perspectives: lesbian, gay, bisexual, and transgender identities (e.g. Bradshaw, 2003;[8] Hammond, 2000; Lampela, 1995; Lampela & Check, 2003); ethnic, racial, and national identities (Desai, 2000; Dufrene, 1993; Garber, 1995, 1997; Golden, Deitcher, & Gomez-Peña, 1990; Irwin & Miller, 1997; Lippard, 1990; Stankiewicz, 2002); differing abilities (Blandy, 1996); age (Collins, 2003; Frueh, 1994; Lacy, 1986); and sexuality and the erotic (Frueh, 1996; Lorde, 1984; Meskimmon, 1998; Pollock, 1988). These identities are understood as complicated (Lucie-Smith, 1994; Schor, 1999), ambiguous (De Zegher, 2003; Macadam, 2007), partial, fragmented, contingent, and constructed (Haraway, 1991; Jaksch, 2003; Jones, 2003; Schor, 1999) and indicate one way that gender equity in art, once conceptualized as women's equal access and respect in the art world, has been reconceptualized with multiple identifiers and possibilities. As art historian Linda Nochlin has argued, there are now "feminisms . . . I see a new, more open, more critical, more inventive kind of feminism. It often works unconsciously, against the grain" (Macadam, 2007, p. 116). Further, these identities intersect with war, poverty, the environment, the local, and other life issues. An issue in approaching identity work is how to maintain forcefulness, passion, and politicization "without sliding into prescriptions" of what it means or should mean to be a feminist (Jones, 2003, p. 143).

Another content issue is the female body and its representation in art and visual culture. In the 1970s, many important

---

[7]Visual culture, a term currently gaining currency in art and art education, is eclipsing "art" or "visual art." Visual culture is currently defined in art education as art, popular culture, performing arts, film, architecture, and material culture (Duncum, 2000). While this definition includes material culture, Bolin & Blandy (2003) argue for the use of the term "material culture studies" education because it includes "all human-made and modified forms, objects, and expressions manifested in the past and in our contemporary world" (p. 249), privileges not only the visual but many senses, and is directed toward study of commonplace objects and expressions found in our daily lives, whereas the term "visual culture," although it may include all objects, signals the visual. Thus, they argue, "material culture studies" offers a broader spectrum to what is studied in art education, a "more holistic and systemic approach" (p. 247) to the practice of art education. Duncum (2000) argues that "visual culture" involves more than sight and visual images, but sounds, language, and our interactions with them. In this chapter, we will use "art" and "visual culture" and "material culture" interchangeably, generally using the term "art" as shorthand designating this broader spectrum.

[8]Because work on multicultural identity was one of the central tasks in art scholarship of the 1990s, citations represent only a small part of the work accomplished.

feminist artists turned to performance art, in which the female body was the primary art medium. Influence of postmodern theory on feminism has led to distancing of the body as material for making art (Meskimmon, 1998). In the late 1980s and 1990s, some feminist artists explored the body through abjection and flow in order to disrupt the male gaze and fetishism (Jones, 2003); for example, photographer Cindy Sherman depicted the female body as ugly, gross, or mechanically sexualized, and artist Renee Cox has used her own body, both nude and clothed, to celebrate Black womanhood and criticize a society she often views as racist and sexist.

The role of new technologies on art making practices and the arts and visual culture education raises many of the same issues found in other gender studies (Keifer-Boyd, 2005). "Though boys and girls are usually taught from the same textbooks, software, machines, and programs . . . rarely addressed are [White] masculinist cultural assumptions that are built into the very configurations of hardware and software, and naturalized in the technological environment itself" (Wilding, 1999, p. 29).

Content issues in dance. Key content issues in dance and dance education center around how ballet and modern/postmodern dance are conceptualized, homophobia, and roles assigned to dancers that are based in gender or race stereotypes. Feurer (2001) questions the culturally constructed binaries that associate modern dance with feminism and ballet with sexism because women have historically played both women's and men's roles in traditional ballet with little or no attention, but men dancing women's roles continue to garner great consideration and robust commentary. Most feminist criticism strongly suggests that dances of resistance are more likely to occur in postmodern or new dance forms than in other performance dance genres.

Dance is viewed as a predominantly feminine activity and prejudice toward male dancers and homophobia towards gay and—for that matter—straight men in dance is a recurring theme in some dance literature on gender (Foster, 1996, p. 5). Burt (1995) argues although men might certainly enjoy watching other men dance, in order to do so, males must profess an absolute repulsion toward homosexual desire or attraction.

A study of relations between race and gender indicated that Black men and especially Black women felt they were still seen as "naturally" inferior in dance (Thomas, 1996). Thus, "forced to entertain audiences receptive only to broadly stereotyped personae, African American men danced savage, hyper-masculine, aggressively heterosexual, and naïve-primitive roles which catered to traditional assumptions about the black male body" (p. 119).

Teaching Practice Issues

Teaching practice issues in visual art. In an era when feminism has been absorbed into other theories, maintaining a feminist focus in art and art education is a challenge. Feminism is naturalized into popular culture at the level of obviousness, but at the same time, the subtle and deep issues in feminism are not understood by youth or many teachers (Schor, 1999). An impor-

tant theme in gender studies in the arts is youth culture. Examples include girl culture in "zines" made by girls (Stankiewicz, 2003) and femininity in girl culture (Thomson, 1997), as well as in contemporary feminist art (Lucie-Smith, 1994; Murphy, 1997). In addressing feminist issues in visual art classrooms, teachers need strategies to convey the importance of feminist content and practice and to be willing to update their own ideas about feminist practices in today's world, so feminism remains relevant to today's students.

In the classroom, despite research indicating the effect of limited and stereotypical materials on students' learning, self-understanding, and future options, university art students continue to be inculcated into the Western canon, leaving them with minimal knowledge of women artists in historical and contemporary contexts and underprepared to address issues of gender, race, and class (Smith-Shank, 2000). Furthermore, art educators are, in practice, ambivalent toward implementing content that engages gender equity and other socially relevant issues (Keifer-Boyd & Smith-Shank, 2006). According to a study by Garber (2003), student teachers are receptive towards feminist principles but continue to conceptualize feminist practice as mastery of content rather than collaborative knowledge construction. Furthermore, demands of schools, testing, the state, and corporate interests maintain the status quo that emphasizes the formal elements and principles of design (Keifer-Boyd, 2002; Milbrandt, 2002). This ambivalence and the pressures to maintain the status quo may explain why there has been little systematic application or trickle-down of feminist art and pedagogy to elementary and secondary school art education (Amos in Schor, 1999).

Teaching practice issues in dance. Practice issues in dance center around how gender bias and homophobia are addressed, the presence of sexuality and gender identity messages in teaching and learning dance, and training regimes on dancers.

Although many dance scholars and researchers have questioned content and pedagogical methods in dance from feminist and multicultural perspectives, the profession has not substantially changed (Kahlich, 2001; Oliver, 1994). Too often dance and dance education unwittingly reproduce asymmetrical power relationships, social inequities, and sexist patriarchy (Risner, 2002a).

Risner (2002a) argues that in reproducing the status quo, the dance profession ignores vast educative opportunities for diminishing homophobia and antigay bias, a defining element in contemporary, postmodern masculinity (Kimmel & Messner, 2001). Male participation in European American dance remains a culturally suspect endeavor for male adolescents, teens, and young adults (Gard, 2003; Risner, 2002a; Sanderson, 2001). Past discourses about men in dance education have focused primarily on two questions: How can dance attract more males? and Why are gay males overrepresented in dance? In order to cultivate larger male participation in dance, strategies frequently center on bringing attention to noteworthy heterosexual male dancers (Hanna, 1988), masculinist comparisons between sports and dance (Crawford, 1994), and minimizing the influences of the significant gay male dance population (Spurgeon, 1999; Risner, 2002a). Knowing what we know now about the cultural construction of masculinity, the underpinnings of sexism, and our culture's dominant bias against gay people, Risner suggests that the focus of professionals in their daily dance practices—teaching, writing, choreographing—shift to ensure a clear affirmation of the equality of all men and women in the dance profession.

A concurrent issue in dance education is that gender and sexuality are always present, even if unacknowledged. "Do we realize," asks Kahlich (2001), "how close we are to touching our student's feelings about gender and sexuality in our role as dance educator as we routinely observe and touch [students'] bodies, probe and prod their imaginations, correct their performances, requiring them to 'present' their body to us, each other, and audience, and themselves?" (p. 46). Young women are being "hurried" to grow up too soon, exploited in a sexual way in dance that is potentially deleterious to their health. Dance education should facilitate for children and young adults an opportunity to explore, experiment, and experience a wide variety of dance possibilities without risk of exploitation or denigration (Clark, 2004).

The demands of training regimes in the professional dance world exact negative effects on dancers' health (Novack, 1990), with dancers going to extraordinary lengths to attain and maintain their "idealized" body weight. However, Green's (1999) action research found that undergraduate students were interested in challenging dominant societal constructions of the skinny, emaciated female body, and the lack of ownership of their own bodies.

PRACTICE

We begin this section with a discussion of theoretical concepts and principles used in defining feminist pedagogy as it supports classroom practice and fosters gender equity in visual art and dance education. Then we will offer examples of contemporary pedagogy, practices, and resources that promote gender equity.

How Does Feminist Pedagogy Foster Gender Equity in Arts Education?

Feminist pedagogy, involving diverse teaching approaches, seeks to empower the individual through collaboration, cooperation, and interaction directed toward the self at the same time as toward society and social justice change. In this chapter, we distinguished feminist teaching practices as a systematic and theoretically constructed idea of feminism applied to art/visual culture and dance education.

Feminist Pedagogy in the Visual Arts

Sandell (1991) notes that feminist pedagogy in art is concerned not just with gender justice but also with a transformation of teaching and learning to develop empowerment, community, and leadership for all participants, using democratic processes where learning grows from student interests and experiences, power is shared, and the teacher assumes the role

of midwife. "FAE," or "feminist art education," a term coined by Sandell (1978, 1979) and further developed 20 years later by Speirs (1998), presents feminist art pedagogy (Chicago, 1975) as an interdisciplinary location that is multiple and in continual motion, moving around practices of feminist social change. "Goals for social change are situational or positional, and determined by location, the feminist involved in the project, community, discussion, consensus, and multiple other factors that route the process" (Speirs, 1998, pp. 9–10).

Daniel (1996) suggests an educational application of Alice Walker's (1983) definition of "womanist" as the basis of principles to create a "curricular ecology." The principles include learning in great depth; utilizing emotional flexibility; commitment to the survival and wholeness of all people; the importance of the spiritual, intuition, the senses and emotions, and self-knowledge in learning and knowing; and developing a view of the world as a community, in opposition to individualism and competition that underlie much art education today. Working in the interstices between feminist ideals and institutional settings, Gaudelius (1998) suggests that feminist teaching is about building relationships between individuals and the material at hand. Such pedagogy involves exploration of subjectivity, critical self-reflection, reducing teacher–student hierarchies, developing a classroom community, hearing multiple voices, and engaging feminist issues.

Feminist art criticism is proposed by several art education scholars as a means to teach feminist principles, achieve feminist goals of social and political change, as well as to interpret art and visual culture (Congdon, 1991; Garber, 1990, 1992, 1996; Hicks, 1992). The importance of studying art in relation to social and cultural contexts as well as to women's lives and experiences, of including a variety of art works, of using narrative and conversation for discussion, of exploring multiple interpretations, and of exploring how change in art and society might occur are various underlying approaches of feminist criticism in the art classroom. Similarly, through feminist aesthetics McRorie (1996) posits philosophical discussion in art/visual culture as conversational inquiry in which students practice collaborative, context-bound inquiry that characterizes principles of feminist pedagogy.

If we define feminist pedagogy as "the fusion of feminist values into the process and methods of teaching" (Forrest & Rosenberg, 1997, p. 179), each of these theorists in art education proposes such a fusion, but we can also see different emphases, reiterating Speirs' (1998) finding that in art, feminist pedagogy is "multiplicity in action" (p. iii).

Feminist Pedagogy in Dance

A panel of dance educators at the 1992 Congress on Research in Dance recommended that educators' approach to dance be inclusive, nonhierarchical, and maintain a multicultural, multiclass, and multiage perspective. Embracing the body within a view of mind and body as a whole and incorporating questioning of gender stereotypes and roles was also recommended (Oliver, 1994). Curricula and research must incorporate a range of races, classes, and ages, as well as non-Western dance forms.

Several dance educators have proposed pedagogies for dance that systematically incorporate gender issues. Shapiro

(1998) proposes a theoretical framework for liberatory pedagogy that emerges from feminist and critical perspectives. Involving self-exploration by the teacher as well as by students, she argues for greater attention to social justice in arts education, especially focused on how we think about and value the body. Based on her struggle with dance education students (i.e., preservice teachers) as they attempt to better understand dance in the contexts of the lives of their K–12 students, Shapiro (2004) developed a pedagogy of embodiment in dance education in which young girls can celebrate sexuality and affirm pleasure and desire, and at the same time, reconnect sexuality to the responsibility and ethics of human relationships. Similarly, Marques (1998) calls for a form of dance education that is integrated into the "everyday struggles, concerns, and needs of human beings" (p. 183), rather than the discipline-based curriculum that encultures dancers into a stereotype of women as child-like.

Green (2000), in an action research project, sought to find less oppressive and more body-conscious ways to teach dance to undergraduate students and preservice teachers. Participants in the study received somatic practice experiences and body awareness exercises, as well as creative process stimulation and guidance, which expanded their definitions of choreography into a social context and led them to discover alternative structures for dance choreography and a more global approach for addressing creativity. Ross (2002) describes techniques used by dance education pioneer Margaret H'Doubler, who, through encouraging students to develop creative movement capabilities, helped them gain self-possession of their bodies and to understand themselves as integrated, unique individuals.

Daly (1994) urges dance educators to frame dance studies courses (dance history, dance appreciation) as inquiry into the cultural construction of gender because doing so enables students to reflect in more meaningful ways on their own experiences and practices in dance, their lives, and their culture. Important teaching strategies she mentions include analysis of gender as an organizing principle in dance studies courses; contrasting viewpoints; facilitated, open discussion; and regular class debates, especially focused on close readings of dance texts and choreography as analytical support for students' interpretive conclusions.

Turning to another important area in feminist pedagogy in dance, Risner (2002b) suggests that a responsive pedagogical path for confronting homophobic attitudes and social stigmatization should begin with openly discussing the fact that gay and bisexual males represent half of the male population in dance. By not only acknowledging but also acting upon the educative potential the profession holds for reducing homophobia and antigay stigmatization, dance education has an ability to play a profound leadership role in reshaping our culture's negative messages about difference and prejudice, as well as our narrow definitions of hegemonic masculinity.

Six strategies for forceful confrontation of gender bias and inequity in dance teaching and curriculum are offered by Ferdun (1994): (a) make gender a conscious topic in all aspects of dance education, (b) do not reduce dance to the "body," (c) consider and create carefully the contexts for dance performances, (d) teach a broad range of dance genres and dance from different historical and cultural contexts, (e) promote empathy in dance experience by providing opportunities to practice and imagine how it is to move and feel like another, and (f) provide dancing experiences that promote gender equality (p. 47).

Other researchers suggest dance practices to address gender equity in teaching. Pedagogical approaches to dance that overlap with feminist approaches to teaching dance include choreographic exploration of the body as a living laboratory (Arkin, 1994); use of African dance to encourage male and female students to express themselves through gender-flexible movements (Kerr-Berry, 1994); openly discussing gender identification and the experiences of dance students (Risner, 2002b); and exploring gender-bias, sexism, homophobia, elitism, and power relations (Horwitz, 1995).

What Feminist Content Is Being Taught in Arts Education to Promote Gender Equity?

It is difficult to know what feminist content is being taught in classrooms because practice isn't systematically recorded in professional publications (Saccá, 1996; Sandell, 1991), a theory–practice gap that restricts teachers in their ability to develop knowledge about gender and contribute to social consciousness. To "smell the chalk dust," we have relied on published resources for teachers and the relatively few studies that describe actual feminist classroom practice (Macdonald & Sánchez-Casal, 2002).

Feminist Content in Visual Arts

Inspired by the women's art movement, teaching about women artists and their accomplishments is a common way to incorporate gender into the art classroom. Clearly, such teaching often does not question why women artists have been excluded, does not accomplish the needed systemic changes in the structure of knowledge and inquiry, and does not promote social action in the ways that most feminist pedagogies propose (Ament, 1996, 1998; Garber, 2003; Nochlin, 1971/1988; Parker & Pollock, 1981; Sandell & Speirs, 1999; Zimmerman, 1990). Good examples of engaging students with feminist content in the visual arts might include a discussion question asking 5th graders whether they think women artists have had more difficulty in gaining recognition than men. This may lead to exploration of whether women's art is as good as men's, if women work as hard, what it takes to gain recognition in the art world and who has the power to decide, and gender stereotypes (Milbrandt, 2003). Students in grades K–12 were introduced to units of instruction designed by Kader and Tapley (2003) in which they contrasted and compared artworks created by men and women Surrealist artists in light of the historical–cultural contexts in which the artworks were created. Built environment sites designed, developed, and/or cared for by women, such as the civic memorials created by Maya Lin and a slave cemetery and memorial on Mount Vernon, are used to explore social memory and the creation of meaning (Guilfoil, 2002). Minimalist artist Ann Truitt's journals and art works were the basis for Sandell, Bell, McHugh and Wehr's (1994) curriculum for high school students to learn about, understand, and critique minimalist art as viewed through the artwork of a woman artist.

Both an issues approach (Collins & Sandell, 1987; Wyrick, 2002) and a social action approach (Zimmerman, 1990) are suggested to teach about women in art in relation to social, political, and cultural contexts. Wyrick (1996) suggests art curricular content should be developed from issues addressed by the news media interplaying these issues with students' personal experiences. For example, students create posters about local issues after studying the content and media methods of the Guerrilla Girls, an art collective that challenges with humor the sexist and racist practices in the art world. Milbrandt (2002b) suggests that the elementary curriculum should include studying contemporary women artists to engage students in critiques of society that involve gender issues. In studying the work of Maya Lin, for example, 5th graders critique historical narratives through issues of race, class, and gender. An ecofeminist "ethics of care" lays the foundation of a proposal by Hicks and King (1996) to promote a caring relationship with others and with the environment. Stankiewicz (2002) uses Lorna Simpson's photographs about race to help gifted 5th grade students learn how to make connections to world issues.

Other strategies for teaching about non-White and hidden-stream women's art include Keifer-Boyd's (1998) elementary grade art lessons about the transformative power of *arpilleras*, appliqué/embroidery wall hangings, created communally by Chilean women to enact social change. Story cloths made by Hmong women from Viet Nam about their homeland and escape from danger form the basis of Congdon's (1994) art lessons for incorporating visual story telling in 2nd and 3rd grade students' own life experiences. Irwin and Miller (1997) consider the use of oral history projects that document life experiences of First Nations women artists. Wong (1993) used Faith Ringgold's storytelling quilts and personal life stories to serve as examples for inner city middle school students to express their own vulnerabilities and responses to current social issues through their art-making.

Some art educators have used images of women created by men or mainstream culture to study historical, cultural, and political events that shaped these images. Examples are curriculum units designed by Pazienza (1992) for 5th graders about Degas's images of working women, Saunders's (1987) analysis for art teachers of Grant Wood's popular painting *American Gothic* in terms of the division of male/female labor, Garber and Pearson's (1994) lesson for middle and high school students about discussing images of women depicted in advertising, and Gaudelius and Moore's (1995/1996) article dealing with violent images of women in art. Bolin's (1995/1996) research into H. W. Janson's *History of Art*, 4th edition explores how women's art is described and interpreted in art curricula texts.

Other women art educators have used their own artwork as the basis of units of instruction to stimulate their students to take risks and express their feelings about a variety of social issues. For example, Taylor (1998) used a critical narrative approach to describe her artwork about suffering from the inability to bear children, which she shared with her students, making it possible for them to express their own personal visual narratives. Preschoolers' art-making experiences creating images from their own lives were inspired by Rahn's (1998) autobiographical drawings and photographs based on her own life journeys.

Although discussion of art by gay and lesbian artists and about queer theory exists in the art and art education literature, there is little curriculum development related to these artists or theories for art in grades Pre-K–12. Furthermore, the prevailing attitude of most teachers is, What does sexuality have to do with teaching about art? (Lampela & Check, 2003; Check, 2001; Keifer-Boyd, Fehr, Check, & Akins, 2002). Lampela (2000) proposes that when artworks are studied in context, sexuality, when relevant, can and should be discussed through clothing, body language, and surroundings. Gude (2003) has created a set of principles to queer the classroom, which include the importance of addressing expressions used by students such as "fag" and "that's so gay," encouraging students to have diverse friends, exploring homophobic attitudes, refusing to suppress difference, taking the time to research how an artist's sexuality is related to his or her art, discussing sexual imagery so students develop a comfort level, and investigating the construction of gender identities and factors that shape them through studio projects.

Helping students see how the conceptual infrastructure of the arts often excludes women and difference is a theme developed by several authors. Ament (1996) explores codes that have led to canonizing some art and artists and excluding others. In a lesson on the horse sculptures of Deborah Butterfield, students explore different representations and cultural connotations of the horse. Teaching art history as narratives about women's art worlds, argues Congdon (1996), means that the substance of art history will teach different understandings of art processes, products, languages, and experiences. She argues particularly for expanding art history to folk, popular, ethnic, and tourist arts and to women's traditional media. The practices of the museum often reinforce patriarchal values in the collection, display, and interpretation of art objects. In using museums, teachers must be willing to engage students with questions about the under-representation of women artists, how women are portrayed, what media and objects predominate, gendered language, values communicated in exhibit design, and whether multiple interpretations are encouraged (Springer, 1996).

Areas where gender is crossed with other issues include, for example, Kauppinen's (1991) look at how patriarchy, sexism, feminism, and women's liberation can be studied as part of peace education; the influence of gendered principles on art and ecology (Hicks & King, 1996), and Blandy and Congdon's (1990) investigation of pornographic type images in art.

How the content of works of art relates to learning outcomes should be closely considered, caution Sandell and Speirs (1999). This suggestion is as important to feminist art and visual culture education as it is to all education, to know how the teaching strategies employed are understood by students and what they have learned. This area of research, however, is largely lacking in feminist art and visual culture education.

Feminist Content in Dance

There is a hidden curriculum in dance that reinforces traditional gender expectations for girls including passivity, obedience, and escapism (Smith, 1998; Stinson, 1998b, 2005; Stinson, Blumenfeld-Jones, & Van Dyke, 1990; Van Dyke, 1992). Passivity is nurtured in dance when young women learn to be quiet and do as they are told, without questioning. Stinson warns that the passive role is often appealing and powerful. Traditional dance pedagogy trains for obedience by emphasizing silent conformity in which dancers reproduce what they receive, rather than critique, question, or create it.

To counteract these traditions, Arkin (1994) describes a choreographic process rooted in affirming rather than denigrating the female body in which body-deprecating societal messages about sexual organs, visual appearance, and normal body functions are resisted. Dance as a means for bodily inquiry also is studied by Thomas (2003) in respect to ways in which individuals "enact and comment on a variety of taken-for-granted social and cultural bodily relationalities" (p. 215). Undergraduate students are interested in challenging dominant societal constructions of the skinny, emaciated female body (Green, 1999, p. 97).

Another approach to counteract traditional gender expectations in dance is suggested by Kerr-Berry (1994), who recommends African dance as a way to encourage males and females to express themselves through gender-flexible movement without fear of ridicule and to discover parts of themselves that may have been unexplored. The aesthetic standards that organize West African dance differ dramatically from those that organize Western theatrical dance. Men freely participate in West African dance without being ostracized by society; how dancers use their bodies is valued over body size or appearance.

Male participation in dance remains a culturally suspect endeavor for male adolescents, teens, and young adults; changing this necessarily involves changes in attitudes about women and masculinity (Stinson, 2001). The desire to attract males into dance education often reproduces, Kahlich (2001) notes, traditionally masculine stereotypes. Dance educators must engage students in redefining terms such as "strong," "big," or "powerful" in relation to a continuum of movement dynamics and gender (p. 47).

Participation of men in the field of dance is also tied to the status men and women hold in dance. Men have traditionally fulfilled roles as choreographers and managers, whereas women have taken roles as performers or workers (Crawford, 1994). Ideas about self-discovery, exploration, self-expression, and creativity are not generally as acceptable to men (Chapman, 1974). Crawford (1994) suggests two important strategies to encourage male participation in dance and to subvert the different treatment of males and females. Movement experiences should be structured so that a sense of gender identity is created without enforcing rigid stereotypes. Movement should reflect boys' and girls' interests, and all students should be encouraged to move and dance outside their usual ways. Early exposure to dance expands boys' behavioral options and can help dispel dominant gender-role stereotyping.

Because of the particular importance situatedness the body holds in both dance and gender, dance education provides ample pedagogical space for exploring the body instrument as signifier of gender and as a personal resource that provides inspiration and ownership, and for developing a nonjudgmental process that provides alternative choices and multiple levels of expression, identification, and sharing. Male undergraduate participants' narratives reveal a deep understanding of social stigmatization as articulated through stories that lace together five important gender themes: homophobic stereotypes, nar-

row definitions of masculinity, heterosexist justifications for male participation, the absence of positive male role models [straight and gay], and internalized homophobia (Risner, 2002b). Risner argues that the dance profession might benefit greatly from knowing more about its *current* male students and their attitudes and experiences, rather than trying to increase male numbers with strategies that attempt to re-engender dance in traditionally "masculine" ways (i.e., dance as sports, competition, jumping, and turning), a theme also addressed by Kahlich (2001).

Student discussions informed by readings in queer theory, dance studies, education, and sociology can give college students a rich understanding of the complex and multiple messages the dancing body telegraphs in contemporary U.S. culture as well as alternative ways of thinking about their own sexual decision-making (Dils, 2004). Contact improvisation is proposed as a means to challenge prejudices and unequal power relations (Horwitz, 1995; Schaffman, 2001). Gender bias, sexism, homophobia, elitism, and power relations are questioned through contact improvisation and possibilities for more meaningful human interaction are broadened. In addition, Schaffman (2001) argues that contact improvisation develops partnering skills and exploration of gender identities, human touch, and weight. Bond (1994) investigated masks, ritual, and individual expression inspired by Sendak's (1964) *Where the Wild Things Are* as means for encouraging children ages 5 to 8 to experiment with flexible gender behavior and egalitarian community. Lomas (1998), through her work in community dance programs, argues that by giving value to context and intent rather than form and content, dance education has the potential to enrich, inform, and evolve in both performance and nonperformance arenas.

What Skills, Learning Differences, and Stereotypes Are Associated with Gender in the Visual Arts and Dance, and How Do Feminists Working for Equity Approach These?

Gender and Student Learning

Gender and student learning in visual art. Some studies indicate that boys and girls exhibit differences in what they depict in their art, different preferences, and different work habits. For example, Rogers (1995) notes that girls are attracted to color whereas boys like action. In a study of art teachers teaching craft subjects such as ceramics, jewelry, and fibers, Garber (unpublished manuscript) found that middle and high school girls and boys differed in their color preferences, subjects depicted, detail orientation, and willingness to experiment and make mistakes. Colbert (1996) reports that whereas young boys often include teeth and ears in their drawings of humans, young girls develop details in their drawings earlier than boys; that between the ages of 8 and 10, girls' drawings are more proportionate and realistic; and that when working in mixed gender groups, boys frequently assume leadership positions while girls often complain that boys would not cooperate because they separate themselves from the group.

At the high school level, a study of portfolio assessment in Canada, The Netherlands, and England indicates that male and female students' experiences of assessment differ according to gender (Blaikie, Schönau, & Steers, 2003). High school girls are more likely than boys to know, understand, and value the qualities a teacher is looking for in their work; value discussing their art with their teachers; and value group critiques. Although girls are more successful at the high school level in terms of grades, at the tertiary level, the trend reverses and females are less successful at these school behaviors and activities than males.

In understanding any of these studies, it is crucial to understand that interests and skills are heavily schooled (Dalton, 2001) and gender preferences and skill differences should not be understood as biological but rather as learned differences. To serve all learners through equitable instruction, teachers need to be aware of the hidden curriculum that reinforces socialization of students into gender roles. Colbert (1996) and Garber (unpublished manuscript) both caution that boys' more experimental and adventurous approaches to art can be more valued in art classrooms, resulting in boys receiving more attention, more praise for their work, and more leadership opportunities. Colbert (1996) suggests that art experiences be designed to address gender equity through teachers' careful attention to nonsexist language, messages they send girls and boys, type and amount of attention they give children of both sexes, and learning and behavior expectations they communicate to boys and girls (please see chapter 10 of this *Handbook*). She also recommends that teachers carefully review teaching content and resources to include a variety of roles for women, including leadership and artist roles.

Lessons that stereotype continue through tertiary art education, where future art teachers, as role models to their students, are either indoctrinated into continuing them or challenged to break the cycle. Many women who teach and make art quietly question their right to call themselves artists because the subtle lessons of college studio and art classes are that important artists are still usually men. Park (1996) suggests teachers take care not to overemphasize the "talented" students' work and do show women artists at work, include different roles that artists play in societies across the globe, guide students to question art historical canonical truths, and engage all students in serious dialogues about art. She also suggests that women artists and art teachers talk together about their experiences and art.

Keifer-Boyd (2003) found that students' interpretations of gender in art were influenced by gender inscriptions from visual culture and discourses about art that are normative. She suggests that feminist art educators help students examine their own processes for interpreting images using a "self-disclosure protocol" (p. 329) to expose immediate reactions to images and critique how stereotypes influence their perceptions.

Also addressing how teachers might approach augmenting changes in student learning, Daniel (1996) asks teachers to consider effects of the "neutrality factor" (p. 82), a claim by some teachers that they see no differences in people. Visible and invisible differences all play crucial roles in identity and learning. Daniel suggests that teachers utilize personal biography, which requires that the teacher know about students' different cultural backgrounds, and that they step outside their cultural comfort zone and help their students do the same, while also critically reflecting on their relationships with students and developing strategies to nurture interrelationships among dissimilar life experiences.

For intellectually or artistically gifted girls, factors such as male role models and competitiveness; images of artists as social eccentrics; and the practice of counseling academic achievers into sciences, law, or medicine have discouraged them from pursuing study of art. Zimmerman (1994/1995), in a study of talented art students in grades 6–10, found that there is cultural stereotyping in choices of subject matter made by boys and girls and that girls often did not acknowledge their art talent as did boys. One quarter of the girls but none of the boys evidenced perfection complexes and lacked self-esteem. In academic subjects, girls were more conforming than boys, who were less interested in receiving good grades. Boys also were more realistic about challenges of choosing an art career, whereas girls were more idealistic. Calvert (1996) has developed a curriculum model that involved matching gifted high school students with women artists. The students documented the artist mentors' work and lives, produced their own work, and curated a museum exhibition.

Suggesting that gender-related body ideals associated with masculinity and femininity contribute to the marginalization of persons with physical disabilities, Blandy (1996) proposes teaching about disability through analysis of images in visual culture of disabled persons based on principles developed in feminist art criticism, looking particularly at medical ideas of functional limitations, methods of image production, source of the image, context in which the image is produced, and stereotypical gender associations with the image. Through such analysis students should be able to see the limited scope within which people with disabilities are represented.

Gender and student learning in dance. In her study of 800 boys and girls in an elementary school dance program, Willis (1995) found that boys were more likely to cover large amounts of space, used more physical energy, moved quickly, took physical risks, involved others in displaying their creations, and approached their own presentations with confidence. Girls worked in limited space, moved at a slow to moderate tempo, did not take physical risks, spent considerable time standing still, and apprehensively showed their presentations. When working in mixed gender groups, boys frequently assumed leadership positions; girls often complained that boys would not cooperate because they separated themselves from the group (Willis, 1995). Cushway (1996) found that although elementary school girls follow direction and execute movement activity promptly and quietly, boys often demand and receive more attention, validation, positive feedback, and reward in dance class.

According to a 2004 study by Risner, Godfrey, and Simmons, gender differences exist in the ways teachers determine costume selections, music choices, and movement vocabulary for boys as compared to girls. Where boys often are consulted and invited to contribute in choosing music, costumes, and choreographic theme for recital dances, engaging girls' input is rare. Over time, this kind of environment for girls and young women produces passive followers rather than active leaders (Stinson, et al., 1990; Van Dyke, 1992) and may also contribute to further gender bias in dance (Cushway, 1996; Davis, 1999; Ferdun, 1994).

West (2005) explored gendered assumptions teachers hold towards Black student dancers in which Black males are connected with a hypersexuality. She cautions,

If dance teachers hope to serve diverse students equitably, then the onus to provide multiple readings of black bodies in dance pedagogy must be seriously considered, not only as a mechanism to deconstruct and correct a sordid historical legacy, but also to provide equal access to dance arts for children and young adults. (p. 66)

The call for inclusiveness embedded in multicultural dance education initiatives also extends to include those with different abilities. Numerous dance companies comprised of dancers with and without disabilities have emerged in the past two decades. Within dance education scholarship, much of the burgeoning research that addresses concerns of special needs populations in dance has its roots in the adaptive physical education movement (Boswell, 1982; DePauw, 1986; Dunn & Craft, 1985; Fitt & Riordan, 1980; Hill, 1976; Jay, 1987; Levete, 1993; Sherrill, 1976; Walberg, 1979). Recent research, informed by critical and feminist theory, focuses on social construction of disability and ways in which differently abled bodies challenge and disrupt conventional expectations of bodies in dance (Albright, 1997; Kuppers, 2000).

Curricular Resources for Achieving Gender Equity in Dance and the Visual Arts

Curricular resources for examining gender inequities in dance education remain scant. Resources in art education, however, include numerous textbooks, teaching articles, and various curriculum resources, with examples of articles previously discussed in the subsection on "Feminist Content in Visual Art." Art education resource distributors are cognizant of the need to include women; the number of resources about or including women available for educators has increased in the last 20 years. Among textbooks that offer a systematic approach to teaching art across elementary grades, some, such as Chapman's (1994) *Adventures in Art* (currently under revision) and Turner's (1987) *Art Works,* include art by women and non-White artists without altering the general approach to art education that is based on teaching children to appreciate the world through art and visual culture. Another series, *Portfolios* (Turner, 1998), spotlights one artist in each chapter; these artists are often women or women and men artists of color.

Over the last five years an instructional resource that is part of the largest circulating journal in the field, *Art Education,* includes, on average, the work of one woman artist among four artists presented. Emphasis is on the theme of the resources and not particularly on gender issues. For example, Clementine Hunter is included in a resource on teaching a sense of place in southern art (Love & Goldberg, 2003), Dorothea Lange is included in a resource on men and women at work (Zwirn, 2004), and painter Lynda Lowe is included in a resource on art and physics (Metcalf, 2004).

There are several children's books about the lives of well-known women artists such as Dorothea Lange (Partridge, 1998; Stone, 2003; Turner, 1994), Frida Kahlo (Laidlaw, 2003; Lenero, 2003; Turner, 1993a; Winter, 2002), Georgia O'Keeffe (Brooks, 1995; Bryant, 2005; Kucharcyk, 2002; Lowery, 1996; Shull, 2003; Turner, 1991; Venezia, 1993; Winter, 1998), and Faith Ringgold

(Turner, 1993b). Other books present collections of women artists (Gianturco & Tuttle, 2000; Remer, 2001; Sills, 1989). These and a few other women artists are explored over and over in children's books, falsely signaling that these are the only women artists worthy of attention. Art curriculum companies such as Crizmac, Nasco, Crystal, and Davis produce poster sets of art by well-known women artists and videos about them. Again, it is not clear if these resources are used in art classrooms to "add and stir" women and non-White artists into the traditional art curriculum or if they are part of a questioning of societal values that privilege White men. Stevie Mack (personal communication, 2004), the president of the largest U.S. multicultural arts education curriculum company, indicates that a curriculum resource guide on women produced by Crizmac, *Images of Commitment: Women Artists of the 20th Century* (Kordich, 1994), was underutilized, perhaps because it focused on big ideas associated with women artists rather than a traditional presentation of the lives and works of women artists.

As in most fields of education, there are many curriculum resources and art lessons online. For schools and teachers with the tools, any image or video on the web can be aired in the classroom. The potential exists, then, to overcome publishers' image choices, which often exclude local and lesser-known art and artists. Limitations of online curriculum and resources include their ready availability as unedited ideas, with some lessons and curricula more well thought out and teachable than others. Additionally, digital reproduction can radically change an art work—flattening 3-D work into 2-D, deleting texture, redefining color relationships, and making it hard to grasp the scale of a piece.

Critical questions, that teachers should ask when reviewing instructional materials include: are women artists from a variety of backgrounds part of the curriculum? Is a critical discussion of women as subjects of art icluded? And is non-gendered language used when discussing art? (Turner, 1996). For example, teachers are cautioned not to use "he" when referring to artists in general and not to privilege qualities associated with males such as "virility" when describing good art. In relationship to resources, however, Turner cautions, "Without a personal commitment by the art teacher to organize and present a gender-balanced art program, all other efforts—those of art coordinators, university art teachers, editors and writers of art textbooks—are to no avail" (p. 141).

What Is the Role of Feminist Leadership in Achieving Gender Equity Through Arts Education?

Feminist leadership has advanced both visual arts and dance education, initiating and sustaining progress that has been made to date. Leaders, whether they are men or women, need to direct their actions collaboratively and collegially so that everyone engaged in a project is treated equitably.

Feminist Leadership in Visual Art and Dance Education

Leadership is important to establishing feminist practice in art and art education and takes place in education in the forms of feminist role models (Thurber & Zimmerman, 1996), administrative leadership, and teacher leadership. Balancing power and authority, Irwin (1995) describes the need for "integrating professional and personal lives, acting responsibly in the world, and pursuing work which is driven by care and love" (p. 17). This leadership style emphasizes collegiality and collaboration and "'exchange of energy'" (p. 18), and fosters a sharing of power.

Noting that most art teachers are women whereas the majority of secondary school administrators are men, Thurber and Zimmerman (1997, 2002) have developed a four-stage model for developing leadership. Stage one is focused on personal voice, development of content knowledge, and reflective practice; stage two, on collaborative voice and practice in a caring community; stage three, on interaction of personal and collaborative voices for personal and social transformation; and stage four, on actions and outcomes of personal and professional empowerment.

Feminist Leadership in Dance Education

As noted earlier, men hold a disproportionate number of directorial and administrative positions in dance (Van Dyke, 1996). Women in administration appear to spend more time as caregivers (Stinson, 1998a). Samuels (2001) notes that the Gender Project, a New York-based group, sponsors presentations in university dance departments to develop awareness of gender issues and leadership concerns in the field. Lodge (2001) examined the rise of female director/choreographers in the American musical theatre, which was historically dominated by males. Lodge argues that women's success lies in their innovative approaches centered on collaboration, compassion, and vision.

"When a great many bright, articulate young women decide that there is no place in dance for them because they do not have the 'right body' or do not otherwise meet the requirements for the art as it now exists, dance leadership and vision are lost" (Stinson, Blumenfeld-Jones, & Van Dyke, 1990, p. 183). Van Dyke (1992) argues that "the obedience demanded by traditional dance pedagogy" negates possibilities for critical thought, creativity, and artistic innovation, "effectively keeping many dancers, both men and women, from seeking leadership positions" (p. 121). Recent research indicates the troubling outcome of gender inequity in dance in higher education (Warburton & Stanek, 2004) and the ways in which the status of female faculty in dance adversely affect leadership possibilities (Risner, 2006; Risner & Prioleau, 2004).

RECOMMENDATIONS FOR THE ARTS

Recommendations made by the 1985 authors for sex equity in art and art education were directed toward the need for efforts specific to the visual arts, especially given the feminine identified low status of art in the schools and of education in the art world. These recommendations for achieving gender equity in art education included changes in research, advocacy, leadership, instructional resources, curriculum development, and development of community groups as well as artist and teacher support groups. The following recommendations build on these earlier foundations. In this section, we merge our recommendations for visual art and dance into "arts." Where the recommendations are specific to one arts discipline, we name that discipline. The first two of our recommendations are conceptual premises.

Define and Identify Goals of Feminist Equity Flexibly and Inclusively

Definitions and goals of feminism and gender equity in visual art and dance are in flux, and educators and arts professionals need to remain open and responsive to these variations. We suggest that it isn't necessary to name *feminism* and *equity* in all of our varied practices leading to gender equity in arts education. Additionally, gender equity is not only about women's equity; it applies to males who are not obtaining equitable opportunities or outcomes and it involves content and practices that specifically challenge hegemony, stereotyping, and oppression. At the same time, naming feminism and talking openly about gender equity remains important.

Today's understanding of feminist equity must grow from an understanding that gendered identities are complex. Gendered identity, rather than being placed in a binary of female/male, is explored as a site of construction, directed at how gender is performed, constructed, materialized, and encountered with, in, and through the arts.

Practice Multiple Strategies Toward Equity

Feminism today builds on the work and partial successes of earlier efforts. Rather than thinking in terms of differences between "generations" of feminists, feminists must work as a diverse community on many complex issues that affect people as gendered human beings. Today's feminism, with its multiple locations and alignment with other identity, political, and social issues, means today's approaches to equity need to take into account a wide range of variables.

Embed Knowledge of Gender and Equity Issues in Arts Content

Content knowledge of the arts that crosses ethnicity, gender, race, nationality, sex, ability, and other factors continues to be circumscribed by what teachers learn in their own professional education. Teacher educators can act by:

- Developing course work and learning strategies that challenge future teachers to dig for their own knowledge, rather than providing them with lectures that tell them what content is important and the "best" strategies to teach.
- Devising situations in which future teachers and artists can question their own assumptions and learn reflective practice.
- Investigating with future teachers how inequities have developed in and been reinforced by the arts.

Disseminate to Teachers Continuing Research on Student Differences

For teachers and school administrators, understanding different behaviors among students in nonsexist ways can help alleviate continuing inequities based on preconceived and fixed notions about gender. Such understanding leads to encouraging student growth in flexible ways, giving attention and praise to diverse expressions of self, evaluating work on varied criteria, and communicating a variety of potential roles for both sexes. Dissemination must take place through multiple channels: preservice education, in-service education, workshops, professional organization venues, conferences, and publications.

Work Toward Social Change Through Political Awareness and Action in the Arts

In 1985, feminism's slogan "the personal is the political" was deeply ingrained in understanding the women's movement; the authors did not need to separately talk about feminist activism. Twenty years later, with women's studies departments entrenched in the academic hierarchy, activism must again become a distinct theme in feminist arts pedagogy. Arts education that grows from the "everyday struggles, concerns, and needs of human beings" (Marques, 1998, p. 183) has developed out of necessity and marginalization and has been among the most effective approaches.

Adopt Pedagogical Practices that Disrupt Traditional Approaches

In the classroom, a disruptive approach that engages multiple ways of learning and media that fall outside the traditional purview of arts education—for example, in art, zines, blogs, culture jamming, hacktivism, public service announcements, and public art—can help change students' and teachers' approaches to art.

Explore Self, Community, and Context Through the Arts

Visual art education has a history of encouraging identity exploration, new media, and student empowerment, but in the name of individualism. Feminist equity practice in the arts is distinct from these traditions in its process and goals. Feminist pedagogy stresses the individual and community, the individual in collaboration and cooperation with others, and reciprocity between artist/performer and viewer. Students question their own subject position and identity as part of this process, thus critically resituating the ways in which gender and body are bound together within our environments.

In extending gender studies to include diverse viewpoints created by the many cultural contexts in which people identify themselves, feminism in the arts helps us understand how to create, perform, value, and talk about the arts beyond our own identity boundaries. These explorations create vital ruptures towards critical thinking, with the goal of self knowledge and

an ethic of caring that move the learner beyond the self to act for equity through social justice.

Adopt Feminist Pedagogy as a Multiple Exemplary Practice in Arts Education

In the classroom, knowledge of feminist issues—knowing the self in relation to community and other contexts, learning to identify issues and think reflectively about them, and to take thoughtful action—are important components of feminist pedagogy discussed separately in the recommendations above. We recommend, as a democratic process and an interdisciplinary location that is multiple and in continual flux, the adoption of feminist pedagogy as a relevant and liberating approach to education that:

- involves gender as a conscious variable,
- utilizes diverse teaching approaches,
- seeks to help the individual find empowerment, collaborative learning and living strategies, and
- acts to promote social change.

Develop Leadership Capabilities among Arts Educators and Advocates

Women and men must be encouraged to aspire to positions of leadership in which they will exercise equitable and creative approaches to workers and learners they oversee. This involves finding their own voices and visions, developing a sense of agency, and adapting innovative, reflective, caring strategies for establishing a collaborative community of workers and learners. Developing an environment for girls to assume leadership roles might introduce new and innovative approaches to leadership that emphasize connected, relational leadership styles.

Work with Those Outside the Arts to Develop and Implement Equitable Policies.

All arts educators—researchers, teachers, and administrators—as well as others concerned with arts education such as parents and students can promote policy changes that recognize equity in the arts for all. Sites for enacting such equitable practices include:

- *Opportunity-to-learn standards*. At the district level, there should be equitable access to arts courses taught by qualified, certified teachers across all schools. Students who demonstrate talent or interest in the arts should have access to advanced education based on their individual needs.
- *Safe schools*. Part of making schools safe for learners can be ensuring that different student identities are respected and understood and that the arts are accessible to them to develop identity, and learn more about themselves and others. Concrete steps must be taken consistently to avoid gender, ethnic, class, or sexual preference or other bias in curriculum, staffing, and treatment of students. Bullying and dismissive language and behaviors must be confronted.

- *Teach for diversity*. Students need to engage art, visual culture, dance, and music created by diverse peoples and for diverse reasons. Community arts programs in arts centers, studios, and museums must fund scholarships to permit economically disadvantaged young people to enroll. They also should be encouraged to actively build partnerships with representatives from diverse components of their local and larger communities.

ner. We recommend that teachers, researchers, and administrators in the arts adapt these ideas and approaches into their own practices and locales and influence others to do the same so that their projects are made visible in a variety of contexts. Through feminist teaching in the arts, equity for all students and for the arts as an educational subject can become a reality.

CONCLUSION

Achieving gender equity in visual arts and dance education requires commitment, engagement, thoughtfulness, criticality, and action. There are no fixed solutions for achieving gender equity in the visual arts and dance education. Practices we have named in this chapter and our general recommendations are written as guides, not prescriptions. Furthermore, change happens across individual and collective efforts in an ongoing man-

ACKNOWLEDGMENTS

This chapter updates and expands on a chapter by Renee Sandell, Georgia Collins, and Ann Sherman (1985), "Sex equity in visual arts education," in the first edition of Susan Klein (ed.), *Handbook for Achieving Sex Equity through Education.* Baltimore: Johns Hopkins University Press.

The authors thank the reviewers for this chapter: Karen Keifer-Boyd, PhD, Professor of Art Education, Pennsylvania State University, and Julie Kerr-Berry, PhD, Professor of Dance, Minnesota State University Mankato.

References

Adair, C. (1992). *Women and dance: Sylphs and sirens.* New York: New York University.

Albright, A. (1997). *Choreographing difference: The body and identity in contemporary dance.* Middletown, CT: Wesleyan University.

Ament, E. (1996). Strategies for teaching art based on feminist aesthetics. In G. Collins & R. Sandell (Eds.), *Gender issues in art education: Content, contexts, and strategies* (pp. 104–115). Reston, VA: National Art Education Association.

Ament, E. (1998). Using feminist perspectives in art education. *Art Education, 5*(5), 56–61.

Arkin, L. (1994). Dancing the body: Women and dance performance. *Journal of Physical Education, Recreation and Dance, 65*(2), 36–38, 43.

Avgikos, J. (2003). Jan Avgikos. Feminism & art [9 views]. *Artforum, 42*(2), 146.

Becker, C. [Ed.] (1994). *The subversive imagination: Artists, society, and social responsibility.* New York: Routledge.

Blaikie, F., Schönau, D., & Steers, J. (2003). Students' gendered experiences of high school portfolio art assessment in Canada, The Netherlands, and England. *Studies in Art Education, 44*(4), 335–349.

Blandy, D. (1996). Gender reconstruction, disability images and art education. In G. Collins & R. Sandell (Eds.), *Gender issues in art education: Content, context, and strategies* (pp. 70–77). Reston, VA: National Art Education Association.

Blandy, D., & Congdon, K. G. (1990). Pornography in the classroom: Another challenge for art education. *Studies in Art Education, 32*(1), 6–16.

Bolin, P. E. (1995/1996). Discussion and depictions of women in H. W. Janson's *History of Art,* Fourth Edition. *Journal of Social Theory in Art Education, 15/16,* 146–159.

Bolin, P. E., & Blandy, D. (2003). Beyond visual culture: Seven statements of support for material culture studies in art education. *Studies in Art Education, 44*(3), 246–263.

Bonbright, J. (2001). National support for arts education. *Journal of Dance Education, 1*(1), 7–13.

———. (2002). The status of dance teacher certification in the United States. *Journal of Dance Education, 2*(2), 63–67.

Bond, K. (1994). How "wild things" tamed gender distinctions. *Journal of Physical Education, Recreation and Dance, 65*(2), 28–33.

Boswell, B. (1982). *Adapted dance for mentally retarded children: An experimental study.* (Doctoral dissertation, Texas Woman's University, 1982). *Dissertation Abstracts International, 43*(09), 2925. Abstract retrieved June 1, 2005, from Proquest UMI/Digital Dissertations database.

Bradshaw, D. (2003). The silencing effects of homophobia. In L. Lampela & E. Check (Eds.), *From our voices: Art educators and artists speak out about lesbian, gay, bisexual, and transgendered issues.* Dubuque, IA: Kendall/Hunt.

Brooks, P. (1995). *Georgia O'Keeffe: An adventurous spirit.* New York: F. Watts.

Bryant, J. (2005). *Georgia's bones.* Grand Rapids, MI: Eerdmans.

Burt, R. (1995). *The male dancer: Bodies, spectacle, sexualities.* London: Routledge.

Calvert, A. (1996). An art curriculum model for gender equity. In G. Collins & R. Sandell (Eds.), *Gender issues in art education: Content, contexts, and strategies* (pp. 154–164). Reston, VA: National Art Education Association.

Cameron, D. (2003). Dan Cameron. Feminism & art [9 views]. *Artforum, 42*(2), p. 144.

Chapman, L. H. (1994). *Adventures in art: The discover art program.* Worcester, MA: Davis.

———. (2004). No child left behind in art? *Arts Education Policy Review, 106*(2), 3–17.

———. (2005). No child left behind in art? *Art Education, 58*(1), 6–16.

Chapman, S. (1974). *Movement education in the United States.* Philadelphia, PA: Movement Education.

Check, E. (2001). In the trenches. In Y. Gaudelius & P. Speirs (Eds.), *Contemporary issues in art education* (pp. 51–60). Upper Saddle River, NJ: Prentice Hall.

Chicago, J. (1975). *Through the flower: My struggle as a woman artist.* Garden City, NJ: Doubleday.

Clark, D. (1994). Voices of women dance educators: Considering issues of hegemony and the education/performer identity. *Impulse, 2*(2), 122–130.

———. (2004). Considering the issue of sexploitation of young women in dance: K-12 perspectives. *Journal of Dance Education, 4*(1), 17–23.

Colbert, C. (1996). Issues of gender in the visual arts education of young children. G. Collins & R. Sandell (Eds.), *Gender issues in art education: Content, contexts, and strategies* (pp. 60–69). Reston, VA: National Art Education Association.

Collins, G. (2003). Retirement lessons. In K. Grauer, R.L. Irwin, & E. Zimmerman (Eds.), *Women art educators V: Conversations across time. Remembering, revisioning, reconsidering* (pp. 197–202). Reston, VA: National Art Education Association.

Collins, G., & Sandell, R. (1984). *Women, art, and education.* Reston, VA: National Art Education Association.

———. (1987). Women's achievements in art: An issues approach for the classroom. *Art Education, 40*(3), 12–21.

Congdon, K. (1991). Feminist approaches to art criticism. In D. Blandy & K. G. Congdon (Eds.), *Pluralistic approaches to art criticism* (pp. 15–23). Bowling Green, OH: Bowling Green State University Popular Press.

———. (1994). Interpreting Hmong storycloths. In T. Barrett (Ed.), *Lessons for teaching art criticism* (pp. 69–72). Bloomington, IN: ERIC.

———. (1996). Art history, traditional art, and artistic practices. In G. Collins & R. Sandell (Eds.), *Gender issues in art education: Content, contexts, and strategies* (pp. 10–19). Reston, VA: National Art Education Association.

Cottingham, L. (1994). The feminist continuum: Art after 1970. In N. Broude & M. D. Garrard (Eds.), *The power of feminist art: The American movement on the 1970s, History and impact* (pp. 276–287). New York: Abrams.

Crawford, J. (1994). Encouraging male participation in dance. *Journal of Physical Education, Recreation and Dance, 65*(2), 40–43.

Cushway, D. (1996). Changing the dance curriculum. *Women's Studies Quarterly, 24*(3/4), 118–122.

Dalton, P. (2001). *The gendering of art education: Modernism, identity and critical feminism.* Buckingham, UK & Philadelphia, PA: Open University.

Daly, A. (1991). Unlimited partnership: Dance and feminist analysis. *Dance Research Journal, 23*(1), 2–3.

———. (1994). Gender issues in dance history pedagogy. *Journal of Physical Education, Recreation and Dance, 65*(2), 34–35, 39.

Dance Magazine College 2004 & 2005. (2004). MacFadden Communications Group.

Daniel, V. A. H. (1996). Womanist influences on curricular ecology. In G. Collins & R. Sandell (Eds.) *Gender issues in art education: Content, contexts, and strategies* (pp. 78–88). Reston, VA: National Art Education Association.

Davis, K. (1999). Giving women a chance to learn: Gender equity principles for HPERD classes. *Journal of Physical Education, Recreation, & Dance, 70*(4), 13–15.

DePauw, K. (1986). Toward progressive inclusion and acceptance: Implications for physical education. *Adapted Physical Activity Quarterly, 6*(3), 1–6.

Desai, D. (2000) Imaging difference: the Politics of Representation in Multicultural Art Education, *Studies in Art Education, 41*(2), 114–129.

De Zegher, C. (2003). Catherine De Zegher. Feminism & art [9 views]. *Artforum, 42*(2), 147.

Dils, A. (2004). Sexuality and sexual identity: Critical possibilities for teaching dance appreciation and dance history. *Journal of Dance Education, 4*(1), 10–16.

Driscoll, C. (2002). *Girls: Feminine adolescence in popular culture and cultural theory.* New York: Columbia University.

Dufrene, P. (1993). Reaching in and taking out: Native American women artists in a different feminism. In K. G. Congdon & E. Zimmerman (Eds.), *Women Art Educators III* (pp. 127–138). Bloomington, IN: Indiana University.

Duncum, P. (2000). Defining visual culture for art education. *Journal of Multicultural and Crosscultural Research in Art Education, 18,* 31–36.

Dunn, J., & Craft, D. (1985). Mainstreaming theory and practice. *Adapted Physical Activity Quarterly, 2,* 273–276.

Ferdun, E. (1994). Facing gender issues across the curriculum. *Journal of Physical Education, Recreation, and Dance, 65*(2), 46–47.

Feurer, J. (2001). A mistress never a master? In J. Desmond (Ed.), *Dancing desires: Choreographing sexualities on and off stage* (pp. 385–390). Madison, WI: University of Wisconsin.

Finkel, J. (2007). Saying the f-word. *ARTnews, 106*(2), 118–119.

Fitt, S., & Riordan, A. (1980). *Focus on dance IV: Dance for the handicapped.* Reston, VA: The American Alliance for Health, Physical Education, Recreation and Dance.

Forrest, L., & Rosenberg, F. (1997). A review of the feminist pedagogy literature: The neglected child of feminist psychology. *Applied & Preventive Psychology, 6,* 179–192.

Fortnum, R. (1998). What issues are important for the upcoming generation of women artists? *Make, The Magazine of Women's Art,* 81 (September/November), p. 22.

Foster, S. (1996). *Corporealities: Dance knowledge, culture, and power.* New York: Routledge.

Foulkes, J. (2001). Dance is for American men: Ted Shawn and the intersection of gender, sexuality, and nationalism in the 1930s. In Jane Desmond (Ed.), *Dancing desires: Choreographing sexualities on and off stage,* (pp. 113–148). Madison: University of Wisconsin.

Fraser, A. (2003). Andrea Fraser. Feminism & Art [9 views]. *Artforum, 42*(2), p. 142.

Freedman, K. (2003). *Teaching visual culture: Curriculum, aesthetics, and the social life of art.* New York: Teachers College.

Frueh, J. (1994). The erotic as social security. *Art Journal, 53*(1), 66–72.

———. (1996). *Erotic faculties.* Berkeley: University of California.

Gablik, S. (1991). *The reenchantment of art.* New York: Thames & Hudson.

Garber, E. (Unpublished manuscript). Gender and craft in the art room.

———. (1990). Implications of feminist art criticism for art education. *Studies in Art Education, 32*(1), 17–26.

———. (1992). Art critics on Frida Kahlo: A comparison of feminist and non-feminist voices. *Art Education, 45*(2), 42–48.

———. (1995). Teaching art in the context of culture: A study in the borderlands. *Studies in Art Education, 36*(4), 218–232.

———. (1996). Art criticism from a feminist point of view: An approach for teachers. In G. Collins & R. Sandell (Eds.) *Gender issues in art education: Content, contexts, and strategies* (pp. 21–29). Reston, VA: National Art Education Association.

———. (1997). Multicultural art education: Chicano/a art as cultural narrative and as a dialectic. In J. Hutchens & M. Suggs (Eds.), *Art education: Content and practice in a postmodern era* (pp. 74–84). Reston VA: National Art Education Association.

———. (2003). Teaching about gender issues in the art education classroom: Myra Sadker day. *Studies in Art Education, 45*(1), 56–72.

———. (2005). Social justice and art education. *Visual Arts Research, 30*(2), 4–22.

Garber, E., & Pearson, R. (1994). Criticizing advertising: Women, ads, and art. In T. Barrett (Ed.), *Lessons for teaching art criticism* (pp. 49–52). Bloomington, IN: ERIC.

Gard, M. (2003). Moving and belonging: Dance, sport, and sexuality. *Sex Education, 3*(2), 105–118.

Gaudelius, Y. (1998). Études feminines: Hélène Cixous and an exploration of feminist pedagogy. In E. J. Saccá & E. Zimmerman (Eds.), *Women art educators IV: Herstories, ourstories, and future stories* (pp. 170–181). Boucherville, Quebec: Canadian Society for Education Through Art.

Gaudelius, Y., & Moore, J. (1995/1996). When art turns violent: Images of women, the sexualization of violence, and the implications for art education. *Journal of Social Theory in Art Education, 15/16*, 120–145.

Gianturco, P., & Tuttle, T. (2000). *With her own hands: Craftswomen changing the world.* New York: Monacelli.

Golden, T., Deitcher, D., & Gomez-Peña, G. (1990). *The decade show: Frameworks of identity in the 1980s.* New York: New Museum.

Green, G. L. (1997). Televised gender roles in children's media: Covert messages. *Journal of Social Theory in Art Education, 17*, 23–39.

Green, J. (1999). Somatic authority and the myth of the ideal body in dance education. *Dance Research Journal, 31*(2), 80–100.

———. (2000). Emancipatory pedagogy? Women's bodies and the creative process in dance. *Frontiers, 21*(3), 124–140.

Gude, O. (2003). There's something queer about this class. In L. Lampela & E. Check (Eds.), *From our voices: Art educators and artists speak out about lesbian, gay, bisexual, and transgendered issues* (pp. 73–86). Dubuque, IA: Kendall/Hunt.

Guerrilla Girls. (2004). *The Guerrilla Girls' art museum activity book.* New York: Printed Matter.

Guilfoil, J. (2002). Teaching art with historic places and civic memorials. In Y. Gaudelius & P. Speirs (Eds.), *Contemporary issues in art education* (pp. 250–262). Upper Saddle River, NJ:: Prentice Hall.

Hammond, H. (2000). *Lesbian art in America: A contemporary history.* New York: Rizzoli.

Hanna, J. L. (1988). *Dance, sex, and gender: Signs of identity, dominance, defiance, and desire.* Chicago: University of Chicago.

Haraway, D. (1991). *Simians, cyborgs, and women: The reinvention of nature.* New York: Routledge.

Hicks, L. (1992). The construction of meaning: Feminist criticism. *Art Education, 45*(2), 23–32.

Hicks, L. & King, R. (1996). Ecofeminism, care, and the environment: Towards a greening of art education. In G. Collins & R. Sandell (Eds.) *Gender issues in art education: Content, contexts, and strategies* (pp. 90–101). Reston, VA: National Art Education Association.

Higher Education Arts Data Services [HEADS]. (2003). Dance annual summary 2002–2003. Reston, VA: National Association of Schools of Dance.

———. (2004). Data Summaries 2003–2004, Art and Design. Reston, VA: Higher Education Arts Data Services.

Hill, K. (1976). *Dance for physically disabled persons: A manual for teaching ballroom, square and folk dance to users of wheelchairs and crutches.* Reston, VA: American Alliance for Health, Physical Education and Recreation.

Hoban, P. (2007). We're finally infiltrating. *ARTnews, 106*(2), 108–113.

Horwitz, C. (1995). Challenging dominant gender ideology through dance: Contact improvisation. Ph.D. Dissertation; University of Iowa.

Irwin, R. (1995). *A circle of empowerment: Women, education, and leadership.* Albany: State University of New York.

Irwin, R., & Miller, L. (1997). Oral history as community-based participatory research: Learning from the First nations women artists. *Journal of Multicultural and Cross-cultural Research in Art Education, 15*, 10–23.

Isaac, J. A. (1996). *Feminism and contemporary art: The revolutionary power of women's laughter.* London, UK: Routledge.

Jagodzinski, J. (2004). *Youth fantasies: The perverse landscape of the media.* New York: Palgrave Macmillan.

Jaksch, M. (2003). Troubling histories: Schooled identities and autobiographical explorations. In K. Grauer, R. L. Irwin, & E. Zimmerman (Eds.), *Women art educators V: Conversations across time. Remembering, revisioning, reconsidering* (pp. 144–149). Reston, VA: National Art Education Association.

Jay, D. (1987). *Effects of a dance program in the creativity and movement behavior of preschool handicapped children,* (Doctoral dissertation, Texas Woman's University, 1987) *Dissertation Abstracts International, 48*(04), 826. Abstract retrieved June 19, 2005 from Proquest UMI/Digital Dissertations database.

Jenkins, H., & Cassell, J. (Eds.). (1998). *From Barbie to Mortal Kombat: Gender and computer games.* Cambridge, MA: MIT Press.

Kader, T., & Tapley, E. (2003). Beyond the real: Comparing and contrasting student art works inspired by men and women Surrealist painters. In K. Grauer, R. Irwin, & E. Zimmerman (Eds.), *Women art educators V: Remembering, revisioning, reconsidering* (pp. 62–71). Reston, VA: National Art Education Association.

Kahlich, L. (2001). Gender and dance education. *Journal of Dance Education, 1*(2), 45–47.

Kaiser Family Foundation. (1999). *Kids and the media @ the new millennium: A comprehensive national analysis of children's media use.* Menlo Park, CA: Kaiser Family Foundation.

Kaplan, E. A. (1983). *Women and film: both sides of the camera.* New York: Methuen.

Kauppinen, H. (1991). Peace education in art: Focus on gender. (ERIC Document Reproduction Service No. ED342710).

Keifer-Boyd, K. (1998). Transformative power, controversy, and critical thinking. In E. J. Saccá & E. Zimmerman (Eds.), *Women art educators IV: Herstories, ourstories, future stories* (pp. 182–199). Boucherville, Québec: Canadian Society for Education through Art.

———. (2002). Open spaces, open minds: Art in partnership with the earth. In Y. Gaudelius & P. Speirs (Eds.), *Contemporary issues in art education* (pp. 212–224). Upper Saddle River, NJ: Prentice Hall.

———. (2003). A pedagogy to expose and critique gendered cultural stereotypes embedded in art interpretations. *Studies in Art Education, 44*(4), 315–334.

———. (2005). Children teaching children with their computer game creations. *Visual Arts Research, 60*(1), 117–128.

Keifer-Boyd, K., Fehr, D., Check, E., & Akins, F. (2002). Canceling the queers: Activism in art education conference planning. *Journal of Social Theory in Art Education, 22*, 124–143.

Keifer-Boyd, K., & Smith-Shank, D. (2006). Speculative fiction's contribution to contemporary understanding: The handmaid's art tale. *Studies in Art Education: A Journal of Issues and Research in Art Education, 47*(2), 139–154.

Kerr-Berry, J. (1994). Using the power of Western African dance to combat gender issues. *Journal of Physical Education, Recreation and Dance, 65*(2), 44–45, 48.

Kimmel, M., & Messner, M. (Eds.) (2001). *Men's lives.* Needham Heights, MA: Allyn and Bacon.

Klein, S. (Ed.). *Handbook for achieving sex equity through education* (pp. 298–318). Baltimore: Johns Hopkins University Press.

Kordich, D. (1994). *Images of commitment: 20th century women artists.* Tucson, AZ: Crizmac.

Kucharcyk, E. R. (2002). *Georgia O'Keeffe: Desert painter.* Detroit: Blackbirch.

Kuppers, P. (2000). Accessible education: Aesthetics, bodies and disability. *Research in Dance Education, 1*(2), 119–131.

Lacy, S. (1986). *Whisper, the waves, the wind: Celebrating older women.* Chicago: TerraNova Films.

Lacy, S. (Ed.) (1995). *Mapping the terrain: New genre public art.* Seattle: Bay.

Laidlaw, J. (2003). *Frida Kahlo.* Danbury, CT: Franklin Watts.

Lampela, L. (1995). A challenge for art education: Including lesbians and gays. *Studies in Art Education, 36*(4), 242–248.

———. (2000). Sexual identity in the art room. In D. Fehr, K. Fehr, & K. Keifer-Boyd (Eds.), *Real-world readings in art education: Things your professors never told you* (pp. 113–122). New York & London: Falmer.

Lampela, L., & Check, E. (2003). *From our voices: Art educators and artists speak out about lesbian, gay, bisexual, and transgendered issues.* Dubuque, IA: Kendall, Hunt.

Lenero, C. (2003). *La niñez de Frida Kahlo.* Saõ Paulo, Brazil: Callis Editora.

Levete, G. (1993). *No handicap to dance: Creative improvisation for people with and without disabilities*. London: Human Horizons.

Lippard, L. (1984). *Get the message? A decade of art for social change*. New York: E. P. Dutton.

———. (1990). *Mixed blessings: New art in a multicultural America*. New York: Pantheon. Republished by New Press, 2000.

———. (1995). *The pink glass swan: Selected essays on feminist art*. New York: The New Press.

Lodge, M. J. (2001). Dancing up the broken ladder: The rise of the female director/choreographer in the American musical theatre. PhD dissertation. Bowling Green State University. DAI-C 63/01.

Lomas, C. (1998). Art and the community: Breaking the aesthetic of disempowerment. In S. Shapiro (Ed.), *Dance, power, and difference: Critical and feminist perspectives on dance education* (pp. 149–169). Champaign, IL: Human Kinetics.

Lorde, A. (1984). *Sister outsider. Essays and speeches.* Freedom, CA: Crossing.

Love, A. R., & Goldberg, E. (2003). Instructional resources. From here to there: A sequence for introducing Southern art to young children (sense of place in art). *Art Education, 56*(4), 25–31.

Lovelace, C. (2003). Art & politics I: Feminism at 40. *Art in America, 5*(9), 67–71, 73.

Lowery, L. (1996). *Georgia O'Keeffe*. Minneapolis: Carolrhoda.

Lucie-Smith, E. (1994). *Race, sex, and gender in contemporary art*. New York, NY: Abrams.

Macadam, B. A. (2007). Where the great women artists are now. *ARTnews, 106*(2), 114–117.

Macdonald, A., & Sánchez-Casal, S. (Eds.), (2002). *Twenty-first-century feminist classrooms: Pedagogies of identity and difference*. New York: Palgrave MacMillan.

Mander, J. (1991). *In the absence of the sacred: The failure of technology and the survival of the Indian Nations*. San Francisco: Sierra Club

Marques, I. (1998). Dance education in/and the postmodern. In S. Shapiro (Ed.), *Dance, power, and difference: Critical and feminist perspectives on dance education* (pp. 171–185). Champaign, IL: Human Kinetics.

McRorie, S. H. (1996). On teaching and learning aesthetics: Gender and related issues. In G. Collins and R. Sandell (Eds.) *Gender issues in art education: Content, contexts, and strategies* (pp. 30–38). Reston, VA: National Art Education Association.

Meskimmon, M. (1998). In mind and body: Feminist criticism beyond the theory/practice divide. *Make, the Magazine of Women's Art*, no. 9 (March/May), pp. 3–8.

Metcalf, S. (2004). Instructional resource. Art and physics. *Art Education, 57*(1), 25–32.

Milbrandt, M. (2002a). Addressing contemporary social issues in art education: A survey of public school art educators in Georgia. *Studies in Art Education, 43*(2), 141–157.

———. (2002b). Elementary instruction through postmodern art. In Y. Gaudelius & P. Speirs (Eds.), *Contemporary issues in art education* (pp. 317–325). Upper Saddle River, NJ: Prentice Hall.

———. (2003). Case study: Are women just lazy? In S. Klein (Ed.), *Teaching art in context: Case studies for preservice art education* (pp. 77–81). Reston, VA: National Art Education Association.

Morris, G. (1996). "Styles of the Flesh": Gender in the dances of Mark Morris. In G. Morris (Ed.), *Moving words: Re-writing dance* (pp. 141–158). New York: Routledge.

Mulvey, L. (1975). Visual pleasure and narrative cinema. *Screen, 16*(3), 6–18.

Murphy, M. (1997). Subversity subversive pleasure: Painting's new feminine narrative. *New Art Examiner, 24*(March), 14–20.

National Art Education Association. (1994). *National visual arts standards*. Reston, VA: National Art Education Association.

National Center for Education Statistics [NCES]. (2002). *Arts education in public elementary and secondary schools: 1999–2000*. Washington, DC: U.S. Department of Education, Office of Educational Research and Improvement, NCES 2002-131.

———. (2004). *Digest of Education Statistics 2003*. Washington, DC: U.S. Department of Education. Retrieved June 5, 2006, from http://nces.ed.gov/pubs2005/2005025.pdf.

Nochlin, L. (1971/1988). Why have there been no great women artists? *Women, art, and power and other essays* (pp. 145–178). New York: Harper & Row.

———. (2003). Linda Nochlin. Feminist and Art [9 views]. *Artforum, 42*(2), p. 141.

Noddings, N. (1992). *The challenge to care in schools: An alternative approach to education*. New York: Teachers College.

Novack, C. (1990). *Sharing the dance*. Madison: University of Wisconsin.

Oliver, W. (1994). Are we feminists? How our own antifeminist bias permeates dance academe. *Impulse, 2*(3), 157–164.

Oliver, K., & Lalik, R. (2000). *Bodily knowledge: Learning about equity and justice with adolescent girls*. New York: Peter Lang.

Park, C. (1996). Learning from what women learn in the studio class. In G. Collins & R. Sandell (eds.), *Gender issues in art education: Content, context, and strategies,* (pp. 3–8). Reston, VA: The National Art Education Association.

Parker, R., & Pollock, G. (1981). *Old mistresses: Women, art, and ideology.* New York: Pantheon.

Partridge, E. (1998). *Restless spirit: The life and work of Dorothea Lange*. New York: Viking.

Pazienza, J. (1992). Edgar Degas: Images of working women. In M. Erickson (Ed.), *Lessons about art in history and history in art* (pp. 49–52). Bloomington, IN: ERIC.

Phelan, P. (2003). Peggy Phelan. Feminism & art [9 views]. *Artforum, 42*(2), p. 148.

Pollock, G. (1988). *Vision and difference: Femininity, feminism and histories of art*. New York: Routledge.

Rahn, J. (1998). Autobiography as a tool in teaching—In transformative power, controversy, and critical thinking. *Women art educators IV: Herstories, ourstories, future stories* (pp. 128–137). Boucherville, Québec: Canadian Society for Education through Art.

Ray, S. G. (2004). *Gender inclusion game design: Expanding the market*. Hingham, MA: Charles River Media.

Remer, A. (2001). *Enduring visions: Women's artistic heritage around the world*. Worcester, MA: Davis.

Risner, D. (2002a). Rehearsing heterosexuality: Unspoken truths in dance education. *Dance Research Journal, 34*(2), 63–78.

———. (2002b). Sexual orientation and male participation in dance education: Revisiting the open secret. *Journal of Dance Education, 2*(3), 84–92.

———. (2006). Critical social issues in dance education. In L. Bresler (Ed.), *International handbook of research in arts education*. Berlin, Germany: Springer.

Risner, D., Godfrey, H., & Simmons, L. (2004). The impact of sexuality in contemporary culture: An interpretive study of perceptions and choices in private sector dance education. *Journal of Dance Education, 4*(1), 23–32.

Risner, D., & Prioleau, D. (2004) Leadership and administration in dance in higher education: Challenges and responsibilities of the department chair. In D. Risner & J. Anderson (Eds.), *Conference Proceedings of the National Dance Education Organization: Merging Worlds: Dance, Education, Society and Politics,* (pp. 343–351). East Lansing, MI.

Robinson, H. (Ed.) (2001), *Feminism—art—theory: An anthology 1968–2000* (pp. 125–126). Malden, MA: Blackwell.

Rogers, P. (1995, 9 February). Girls like color, boys like action? Imagery preferences and gender. Paper presented at the National Convention of the Association for Educational Communications and Technology. Anaheim, CA. (ERIC Document Reproduction Service No. ED378956).

Ross, J. (2002). Institutional forces and the shaping of dance in the American university. *Dance Chronicle, 25*(1), 115–124.

Saccá, E. (1996). Women's full participation in art teaching and research: A proposal. In G. Collins & R. Sandell (Eds.), *Gender issues in art education: Content, contexts, and strategies* (pp. 52–59). Reston, VA: National Art Education Association.

Saltz, J. (2006). *Where the girls aren't.* Available online: http://www.villagevoice.com/art/0639,saltz,74535,13.html

Samuels, S. (2001). Study exposes dance gender gap. *Dance Magazine*, March (pp. 35–37).

Sandell, R. (1978). Feminist art education: Definition, assessment and application to contemporary art education. Unpublished dissertation, The Ohio State University. *DAI* -A 39/05, p. 2696, Nov 1978.

———. (1979). Feminist art education: An analysis of the women's art movement as an educational force. *Studies in Art Education, 20*(2), 18–28.

———. (1991). The liberating relevance of feminist pedagogy. *Studies in Art Education, 32*(3), 178–187.

Sandell, R., Bell, S., McHugh, M., & Wehr, C. (1994). Maximizing minimalism: Connecting with the art of Ann Truitt. In T. Barrett (Ed.), *Lessons for teaching art criticism* (pp. 91–95). Bloomington, IN: ERIC.

Sandell, R., Collins, G., & Sherman, A. (1985). Sex equity in visual arts education. In S. Klein (Ed.), *Handbook for achieving sex equity through education* (pp. 298–318). Baltimore: Johns Hopkins University Press.

Sandell, R., & Speirs, P. (1999). Feminist concerns and gender issues in art education. *Translations: From theory to practice, 8* (1), n.p. Reston, VA: National Art Education Association.

Sanderson, P. (2001). Age and gender issues in adolescent attitudes to dance. *European Physical Education Review, 7*(2), 117–136.

Saunders, R. (1987). "American Gothic" and the division of labor. *Art Education, 40*(3), 6–11.

Schapiro, M. (2001). The education of women as artists: ProjectWomanhouse (1972). In H. Robinson (Ed.), *Feminism—art—theory: An anthology 1968–2000* (pp. 125–126). Malden, MA: Blackwell. Originally published in Schapiro, M. (1972). *Art Journal, 31*(3), 268–270.

Schaffman, K. (2001). *From pilgrims to the mainstream: Contact improvisation and the commodification of touch.* Ph.D. dissertation, University of California at Riverside. DAI-A 62/07.

Schor, M. (1999). Contemporary feminism: Art practice, theory, and activism—An intergenerational perspective. *Art Journal, 58*(4), 8–29.

Schorr, C. (2003). Collier Schorr. Feminism & art [9 views]. *Artforum, 42*(2), 145.

Seger, L. (1996). *When women call the shots: The developing power and influence of women in television and film.* New York: Holt.

Sendak, M. (1964). *Where the wild things are.* New York, NY: Harper & Row.

Shapiro, S. (1998). Toward transformative teachers: Critical and feminist perspectives in dance education. In S. Shapiro (Ed.), *Dance, power, and difference: Critical and feminist perspectives on dance education* (pp. 7–21). Champaign, IL: Human Kinetics.

———. (2004). Recovering girlhood: A pedagogy of embodiment. *Journal of Dance Education, 4*(1), 35–36.

Sherrill, C. (1976). *Adapted physical education and recreation: A multidisciplinary approach.* Dubuque, IA: William C. Brown.

Shull, J. A. (2003). *Georgia O'Keeffe, Legendary American painter.* Berkeley Heights, NJ: Enslow.

Sills, L. (1989). *Inspirations: Stories about women artists. Georgia O'Keeffe, Frida Kahlo, Alice Neel, Faith Ringgold.* Niles, IL: A. Whitman.

Smith, C. (1998). On authoritarianism in the dance classroom. In S. Shapiro (Ed.), *Dance, power, and difference: Critical and feminist perspectives on dance education* (pp. 123–146). Champaign, IL: Human Kinetics.

Smith, D. (1997, May 1). Study looks at portrayal of women in the media. *New York Times,* p. A17.

Smith-Shank, D. (2000). Teaching and learning in Art 580: Women artists and feminist art criticism. *The Journal of Gender Issues in Art Education, 1*, 81–94.

Speirs, P. (1998). Collapsing distinctions: Feminist art education as research, art, and pedagogy. Unpublished dissertation, The Pennsylvania State University. *DAI, 59* (08A), 2823, Feb. 1999.

Springer, J. (1996). Deconstructing the art museum: Gender, power, and educational reform. In G. Collins & R. Sandell (Eds.), *Gender issues in art education: Content, contexts, and strategies* (pp. 40–50). Reston, VA: National Art Education Association.

Spurgeon, D. (1999, December). *The men's movement.* Paper presented at Congress on Research in Dance, Pomona College, Claremont, CA.

Stankiewicz, M. A. (2002). Three: Reading Lorna Simpson's art in contexts. In Y. Gaudelius & P. Speirs (Eds.), *Contemporary issues in art education* (pp. 384–394). Upper Saddle River, NJ: Prentice Hall.

———. (2003). From accomplishments to zines: Schoolgirls and visual culture. In K. Grauer, R. L. Irwin, & E. Zimmerman (Eds.), *Women art educators V: Conversations across time* (pp. 219–227). Reston, VA: NAEA.

Stinson, S. (1998a). Places I've been: Reflections on issues of gender in dance education, research, and administration. *Choreography and Dance, 5*(1), 117–127.

———. (1998b). Seeking a feminist pedagogy for children's dance. In S. Shapiro (Ed.), *Dance, power, and difference: Critical and feminist perspectives on dance education* (pp. 23–47). Champaign, IL: Human Kinetics.

———. (2001).Voices from adolescent males. *DACI in Print, 2*: November, 4–6. Dance and the Child International.

Stinson, S., Blumenfeld-Jones, D., & Van Dyke, J. (1990). Voices of young women dance students: An interpretive study of meaning in dance. *Dance Research Journal, 22*(2), 13–22.

Stone, A. (2003). *Dorothea Lange.* Chicago, IL: Raintree.

Tavin, K. (2003). Wrestling with angels, searching for ghosts: Toward a critical pedagogy of visual culture. *Studies in Art Education, 44*(3), 197–213.

Taylor, P. G. (1998). A feminist art educator's story of empowerment. In E. J. Saccá & E. Zimmerman (Eds.), *Women art educators IV: Herstories, ourstories, future stories* (pp. 141–154). Boucherville, Québec: Canadian Society for Education through Art.

Thomas, H. (1996). Dancing the difference. *Women's Studies International Forum, 19*(5), 505–511.

———. (2003). *The body, dance and cultural theory.* New York: Palgrave Macmillan.

Thomson, E. (1997). Feminism squeezed out: Reading popular teen mags. *Make, The magazine of women's art, 77*(Sept/Nov), p. 3.

Thurber, F. & Zimmerman, E. (1996). Empower not in power: Gender and leadership roles in art teacher education. In G. Collins & R. Sandell (Eds.), *Gender issues in art education: Content, contexts, and strategies* (pp. 144–153). Reston, VA: National Art Education Association.

Thurber, F., & Zimmerman, E. (1997). Voice to voice: Developing in-service teachers' personal, collaborative, and public voices. *Educational Horizons, 75*(4), 180–186.

———. (2002). An evolving feminist leadership model for art education. *Studies in Art Education, 44*(1), 5–27.

Turner, R. (1987). *Art Works.* Austin, TX: Holt, Rinehart and Winston.

———. (1991). *Georgia O'Keeffe.* Boston: Little, Brown.

———. (1993a). *Frida Kahlo.* Boston: Little, Brown.

———. (1993b). *Faith Ringgold.* Boston: Little, Brown.

———. (1994). *Dorothea Lange.* Boston: Little, Brown.

———. (1996). The development and use of instructional resources for gender balance. In G. Collins & R. Sandell (Eds.) *Gender issues in art education: Content, contexts, and strategies* (pp. 134–143). Reston, VA: National Art Education Association.

———. (1998). *State of the art program: Portfolios.* Austin, TX: Barrett Kendall.

U.S. Department of Labor. Bureau of Labor Statistics. (2005). Household Data Annual Averages. *Occupational Outlook Handbook*: Household Data Annual Averages. Retrieved June 5, 2006, from http://www.bls.gov/cps/cpsaat39.pdf

Van Dyke, J. (1992). *Modern dance in a postmodern world: An analysis of federal arts funding and its impact on the field of modern dance.* Reston, VA: American Alliance for Health, Physical Education, Recreation, and Dance.

———. (1996). Gender and success in the American dance world. *Women's Studies International Forum, 19*(5), 535–543.

Venezia, M. (1993). *Georgia O'Keeffe.* Chicago: Children's.

Vigier, R. (1995). *Gestures of genius: Women, dance and the body.* Toronto, CA: The Mercury Press.

Walberg, F. (1979). *Dancing to learn: A contemporary dance curriculum for learning and physically handicapped adolescents.* Novato, CA: Academic Therapy Publications.

Walker, A. (1983). *In search of our mothers' gardens.* New York: Harcourt, Brace, Jovanovich.

Warburton, E., & Stanek, M. (2004) The condition of dance faculty in higher education. In D. Risner & J. Anderson (Eds.), *Conference Proceedings of the National Dance Education Organization: Merging Worlds: Dance, Education, Society and Politics* (pp. 420–425). East Lansing, MI.

West, C. S. (2005). Black bodies in dance education: Charting, a pedagogical paradigm to eliminate gendered and hypersexualized assumptions. *Journal of Dance Education, 5*(2), 64–69.

Wilding, F. (1999). Contemporary feminism: Art practice, theory, and activism—An intergenerational perspective. *Art Journal, 58*(4), 27–29.

Willis, C. (1995). Factors that affect dance programs. *Journal of Physical Education, Recreation and Dance, 66*(4), 58–63.

Winter, J. (1998). *My name is Georgia: A portrait.* San Diego: Silver Whistle/Harcourt Brace.

———. (2002). *Frida.* New York: Arthur A. Levine.

Wong, F. F. O. (1993). Threading vulnerability from quilt to quilt. In K. Congdon & E. Zimmerman (Eds.), *Women art educators III* (pp. 159–184). Bloomington, IN: Mary Rouse Memorial Fund.

Wyrick, M. (1996). Teaching feminist art and social activism. In G. Collins & R. Sandell (Eds.), *Gender issues in art education: Content, contexts, and strategies* (pp. 126–133). Reston, VA: National Art Education Association.

———. (2002). Art for issues sake: A framework for the selection of art content for the elementary classroom. In Y. Gaudelius & P. Speirs (Eds.), *Contemporary issues in art education* (pp. 212–224). Upper Saddle River, NJ: Prentice Hall.

Zimmerman, E. (1990). Issues related to teaching art from a feminist point of view. *Visual Arts Research, 16*(2) (Issue 32), 1–9.

———. (1994/1995). Factors influencing the art education of artistically talented girls. *The Journal of Secondary Gifted Education, 6*(2), 103–112.

Zwirn, S. G. (2004). Instructional resource. Men and women at work: The portrayal of American workers by three artists of the 1930s and 1940s. *Art Education, 57*(2), 25–32.

·18·

GENDER EQUITY IN PHYSICAL EDUCATION AND ATHLETICS[1]

Ellen J. Staurowsky,* Nancy Hogshead-Makar, Mary Jo Kane, Emily Wughalter, Athena Yiamouyiannis and Phyllis K. Lerner

INTRODUCTION

When the Olympic Games returned to their Greek birthplace in August of 2004, the lighting of the cauldron during the opening ceremony marked a convergence of the ancient and modern worlds. No better site could be found to illustrate in such profound relief the paths human beings travel over time in their quest to attain noble goals and higher ideals. In the shadow of Mount Olympus, those poised to create history came face to face with the enduring legacies of history makers.

For Americans, games heralded for their celebration of athletic excellence symbolized the long march toward fulfillment of democratic ideals for all citizens. The ancient practice of excluding women from games where men competed was relegated to the recesses of memory, replaced by the largest contingent of women ever to participate in the Olympic Games, numbering 4,305 strong and representing 40 percent of all athletes (Rogge, 2004). With 282 men and 263 women, the U.S. team presented a nearly perfect image of gender equity to the world (Shipley, 2004).

As a measure of progress, the Olympic Games offer a showcase for understanding the fluidity of gender in various historical contexts as it is manifest in societal attitudes and expectations about females and males in sport and physical activity. With each passing generation, early 20th century prohibitions against women participating in sport have slowly faded into the background, giving way to a 21st century perspective that athleticism is not an exclusively male domain but a shared human experience. The addition of women's wrestling as an Olympic sport in 2004 vividly demonstrated this passage from ancient to modern and postmodern time (Chen, 2004; Briggs, 2004; Weiner, 2004).

Commenting on the importance of the parity within the team, U.S. Olympic Committee Executive Officer Jim Scherr stated, "Regardless of gender, socioeconomic status or race, we feel there is an opportunity for everyone to participate on our Olympic teams. We're proud of the fact that it's the ultimate meritocracy" (as quoted in Shipley, 2004, p. D01). The seamless compatibility between American values and sport values is reflected in that statement. The very foundation of our participatory democracy is built on the values of equity and fairness that serve to check discriminatory practices and beliefs so as to allow every citizen to exercise their right, and their responsibility, to contribute meaningfully to our society.

It is not surprising, given those democratic values, that Title IX of the Education Amendments Act of 1972, which prohibits

---

*The boldface name is the Lead Author.

[1]Throughout this chapter, several terms will appear as they are generally alluded to in everyday language and public policy. In a 2005 piece titled "Is it Physical Education or Physical Activity?" the National Association for Sport & Physical Education offer these definitions: "School physical education programs offer the best opportunity to provide physical activity to all children and to teach them the skills and knowledge needed to establish and sustain an active lifestyle. . . . NASPE recommends that schools provide 150 minutes of instructional physical education for elementary school children, and 224 minutes for middle and high school students per week for the entire school year. Based on sequence of learning, physical education should not be compared to or confused with other physical activity experiences such as recess, intramurals, or recreational endeavors." Physical activity as defined by NASPE is "bodily movement of any type." This may include "recreational, fitness and sport activities such as jumping rope, playing soccer, lifting weights, as well as daily activities such as walking to the store, taking the stairs or raking the leaves." NASPE recommends schools-age children accumulate at least 60 minutes and up to several hours of physical activity per day while avoiding prolonged periods of inactivity. More information on this subject can be found at http://www.aahperd.org/naspe/templace.cfm?template=difference.html. In this chapter, sport primarily refers to varsity and junior varsity athletic programs offered through schools.

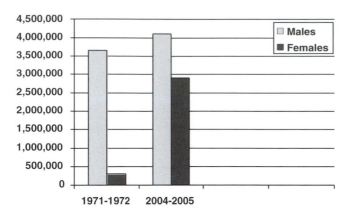

FIGURE 18.1   A comparison of female to male student participation in High School sports, 1972–2006 (Howard, 2006).

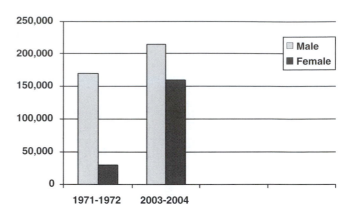

FIGURE 18.2   Intercollegiate participation rates by gender, 1971–2003 (Bray, 2004).

sex discrimination in all areas of education, has played a central role in shaping our national conversation about gender and sport in schools during the past 33 years.[2] Since its passage, the nation has witnessed profound changes for children in access and opportunity to school-based programs of sport and physical education. Nowhere are these changes seen more clearly than in the area of girls' participation in varsity sport programs.

According to the National Federation of State High School Associations (Howard, 2006), female participation has risen from fewer than 300,000 in 1972 to over 2.9 million in the academic year 2005–2006. This represents an 875% increase in the number of girls participating in high school sports over the span of three decades.

Whereas concerns have been expressed that male students in select sports have suffered a loss of access during the same period of time (Kocher, 2005), existing data show that opportunities for male students continue to increase in high school settings. In 2005–2006, boys registered rates of participation in high school sports that were the highest since 1977–1978 (Howard, 2006).[3] Although the gender composition of the student body is split almost evenly between boys and girls in high school settings, boys continue to have access to sport at a ratio of almost 2 to 1. Figure 18.1 compares female and male participation in high schools sports in 1971 and 2006. Notably, in 2005–2006, boys around the nation realized an increase of 72,066 opportunities to play high school sports compared to 43,091 for girls. When taken in their totality, these data show that male athletes have access to 1.2 million more opportunities than their female counterparts.

In a state by state analysis of the athletics gender gap, wide disparities in participation rates continue to exist (Women's Sports Foundation, 2006). Vermont, where athletic opportunities for girls are nearly equal to the percent of girls in the student population (48.0% to 48.4%), leads the way in providing equitable opportunities to female athletes in high schools. In contrast, Alabama ranks 51st with an almost 18% gap between female high school enrollment compared to females represented in the athletic population.

Although there has been little research done to examine the record of college and university compliance by state, a 2006 report compiled by the Women's Law Project in Philadelphia examining data available on the U.S. Department of Education's Office of Post-Secondary Education Equity in Athletics Disclosure Website does provide a starting point by providing information about 112 colleges and universities in Pennsylvania. In summary, evidence supported a conclusion that Pennsylvania schools were "failing to provide opportunities for female athletes in proportion to women's enrollment," with a shortfall of approximately 8,000 (Cohen, 2005).

More generally at the college level, female participation in varsity sports rose from just under 30,000 to almost 151,000 between 1971–1972 and 2003–2004, representing a more than 500% increase over that 30 year span of time (Bray, 2004; see Fig. 18.2). Even with that increase, the National Collegiate Athletic Association (Bray, 2004) reported that as of 2003–2004, there were still 44,000 more male athletes compared to female athletes. At an individual institutional level, that translates into roughly 42 more male athletes per college campus. Although male athletes still receive more access to sport than their female counterparts, between 1981–1982 to 2003–2004, there has been an increase of 150% in the number of female athletes participating and a decrease of 28.6 percent male athletes participating (Bray, 2004).

---

[2]Title IX of the Education Amendments of 1972 is the major federal statute prohibiting sex discrimination in education. It states: No person in the United States shall, on the basis of sex, be excluded from participation in, be denied the benefits of, or be subjected to discrimination under any educational program or activity receiving federal financial assistance. Other federal laws, like the 14th Amendment, have also been used to achieve gender equity in sport and physical education as have state equity laws. Due to the attention Title IX has received in relationship to athletics, the chapter references it exclusively here.

[3]In 2005–2006, 4,206,549 boys participated in high school sports compared to 2,953,355 girls (National Federation of State High School Associations, 2005).

Although the question of whether females should be permitted to participate in sport and physical activity is now settled, enduring concerns about how and in what ways females and males should participate inspire attention from educators, public policy makers, parents, and media. Addressing these concerns is no easy task. The prevailing framework for gender equity in sport and physical activity—separate but equal—is structurally anchored in a value system that not only emphasizes differences between females and males but also continues to value male experience more highly (Messner, 2002).

The now subtle, but once overt, valuing of elite male athletic experience as reflective of the societal ideal has translated into a hidden form of inequity from the standpoint that our national attention and energies have been directed toward the participation of athletes in varsity athletic programs while Title IX compliance in the area of physical education has gone comparatively unnoticed. As scholars Linda Carpenter and Vivian Acosta (2005) pointed out, "Although there are some OCR [Office of Civil Rights] complaints and law suits about Title IX violations in physical education, they are small in number compared with those that focus on athletics" (p. 46).

Prophetically, women physical educators for over half of the 20th century cautioned that the male college sport model, which emphasized sport for the few and was designed to appeal to a mass audience and generate commercial interest, would undermine the ability of educators to effectively meet the needs of citizens overall through physical education programs (Oglesby, 1990; Sack & Staurowsky, 1998). With declining fitness levels, lack of daily physical education, and obesity levels higher than ever before, their concerns have been shown to be accurate (Kluger, 2005; Weir, 2004).

This preoccupation with college and university athletic programs in particular, where the allocation and protection of monies generated from football and other designated revenue-producing sports are the primary issues (Zimbalist, 2005), has left little room for a full blown consideration of Title IX enforcement and compliance over the expanse of physical education and athletic programs nationwide (Staurowsky, 2004). This was most evident in the work of the Secretary of Education's Commission on Opportunity in Athletics, charged in 2002 to review Title IX enforcement regulations as they pertain to athletics, not physical education. "Of the 15 members on the Commission, 10 were associated with NCAA Division I-A institutions, the division with the fewest institutions and the greatest interest in obtaining exemptions for revenue-producing sports" (Staurowsky, 2003b, p. 108). Only one of the commissioners worked directly with elementary and secondary schools, which represent the most children affected by Title IX compliance and noncompliance and about whom there is the least amount of reported data.

As a consequence, our work ahead is much as it was 20 years ago, and even 100 years ago, for that matter. In the 1985 *Handbook for Achieving Sex Equity Through Education*, authors of the chapter on physical education and athletics wrote that the structural challenge to understanding gender equity in sport and physical activity was the difficulty of coming to terms "with the history of the movement toward equity in activity programs and of the ways in which fairness or lack of fairness have existed in the worlds of separateness and sameness" (Geadelmann, Bischoff, Hoferek, & McKnight, 1985, p. 319).

There are still gender stereotypes to be challenged, attitudes to be adjusted, misinformation to be countered, and visions to be forged. Although the passage of Title IX aided in creating a mass societal wave of acceptance for girls and women participating in sport that some have described as "seismic" (Lusetich, 1999), we remain largely ignorant of the full physical capability and potential of females across all age and racial groups. Furthermore, with the growth in the number of girls and women participating in "contact" or "combat" sports (wrestling, boxing, football, ice hockey) and increasing enthusiasm for girls playing team sports (Miller, 2002; Nelson, 1998; Shipley, 2004), we encounter questions about the timing and appropriateness of females and males competing with and against one another in co-ed settings. At this moment in time, when physical education programs continue to be a low priority in our public schools and a national crisis in youth fitness levels exists, seeking answers to these questions is of pressing importance (Kluger, 2005; Weir, 2004).

The remainder of this chapter is divided into five sections. The first section deals with overarching considerations that provide context for understanding issues of gender equity in physical activity and sport, including historical context, media influences, interpreting physiological differences, and benefits and negative health outcomes of participation. The second section examines the implementation of gender equity principles in physical education, specifically the compliance issues regarding co-education versus single-sex education. The third section provides an overview of gender equity issues in athletics, where separate but equal remains the guiding framework. The fourth section offers a consideration of sexual harassment in athletics. And finally, the fifth section offers recommendations for future action.

SECTION I. OVERARCHING CONSIDERATIONS

A. To what extent has the historical legacy limiting the equitable participation of women and girls in physical education and sport (compared to males) continued?

In the 1938 classic text titled *Health by Stunts*, U.S. Army captains N. H. Pearl and H. E. Brown articulated the need for lifelong physical education for males. Drawing upon the lessons from the "Great War," Pearl and Brown pointed out that the lack of physical fitness in young men of draft age in 1914 could have been avoided if public schools had devised a "more intelligent system of physical education". Notably, in a book devoted to the interests of boys, the final chapter, coincidentally numbered IX, addressed the need to adapt their plan for girls. The author, Esther Sherman, a physical educator, wrote that "all the statistical evidence gathered in the last few decades seems to bear out . . . the relative frailty of women" (p. 183). However, she continued:

That these statistics should actually be used in attempting to show that girls have not the capacity to engage in vigorous activities that boys possess, shows a deplorable lack of reasoning. These figures prove nothing at all regarding the capacity of women in physical endeavor. . . . In no way do they lead to the conclusion that girls have not the capacity for a more complete and more perfect development. (pp. 183–184)

Inasmuch as Sherman was clear in her determination that existing information about the physical capacity of girls was a reflection of the social conditions in which they were raised, by her own admission the position she took was not persuasive in the 1930s. That notwithstanding, the "physiological unfitness theory" espoused by Sherman's colleagues to justify notions of female inferiority held little persuasiveness for her. Sherman reasoned that perspectives on female physical potential should be informed by examples of women who, under "proper environmental conditions," proved to be the equal of men in work, hunting, and fighting (p. 185).

Support for this decidedly inclusionary perspective, which evidenced a consideration of female experience across class, racial, and ethnic lines, would certainly have been found in the public persona and presence of Babe Didrikson, who burst onto the national scene following the 1932 Los Angeles Olympics after winning two gold medals and the only gold-silver medal ever awarded an Olympian (Cahn, 1994; Cayleff, 1995). Of course, the woman who aspired to be "the greatest athlete that ever lived" became a contested figure herself, triggering in the society suspicions that women who competed like men were faulty or aberrant women.

The "Babe" and women athletes like her defied the theoretical assumptions of female weakness and the perceived biological naturalness of female inferiority. They also became the sites upon which social control mechanisms designed to keep females in their proper place were played out.

Thus, when biological determinism failed to adequately explain why females should be excluded or limited in their sport activities, monitoring female athletes to ensure against "mannish" behavior and "sexploitation" took over. The Gibson Girl of the 1900s was, on one hand, attractive, self-assured, and independent, and on the other, she risked acquiring a "bicycle face" (a strained, intense, unladylike appearance) if she expressed too much enthusiasm (Cahn, 1994). The liberating effects of the safety bicycle offered cheap transportation to women across social classes and considerable opportunity for adventure across town. The "bathing beauties" of the flapper era who appeared as "nymphs" on the covers of *Physical Culture* magazine, fueled societal fantasies about desirable women but toyed with prohibitions regarding female modesty and propriety, evoking the ever-present specter of "public" women being "loose women" (Cahn, 1994).

The uncertain intersections between conceptions of athleticism, female beauty, sex appeal, and commercial interests have often sparked attention and controversy during the past century. It was Annette Kellerman in the 1920s who "popularized swimming with her speed and her sleek, streamlined bathing suits—sleeveless, skirtless, form-fitting suits that replaced the bulky, full length, bloomered costumes" (Cahn, 1994, p. 46) setting the stage for the *Sports Illustrated* swim suit editions in the years ahead (Nelson, 1998) and ultimately the appearance of 2004 Olympians Amy Acuff and Haley Cope Clark in *Playboy* (Morago, 2004; Topkins, 2004).

In the 1940s, strength and femininity merged in the image of "Rosie the Riveter," prompted by economic demands posed by World War II. Activities once deemed to be appropriate for men only, such as munitions factory work, were reclassified as acceptable and necessary for women due to "manpower" shortages with the mandatory draft in effect and men called to service in the European, African, and Pacific theaters. The national necessity for the game of baseball to continue in time of war led to the creation of the short-lived All-American Girls Professional Baseball League (AAGPBL), a league whose guiding principle was to find female ball players who conformed to a predetermined "femininity principle" devised in accordance with the country's, and baseball's, worldview (Cahn, 1994; Macy, 1993). Thus, just as the "American game" had an unstated color barrier that prohibited Black players from playing in the major leagues, so too did the AAGPBL ban women of color as well.

By the 1950s, middle and upper class women would be encouraged in school to relinquish the workplace to men returning from the war for a "resurgent domesticity" that called for women to be compliant helpmates and companions. The new consumerism of the 1950s made home a place where some women could enjoy a measure of freedom as advertised in "time saving" appliances that made housework "fun" and "enjoyable" while others would balk at being tethered to the domestic sphere (Friedan, 1963; Kerber & DeHart, 1995). For poor women, especially women of color, their educational and work lives continued to reflect little privilege or entitlement.

In sport, women physical educators continued to advocate a position of what they called "moderation," a philosophy articulated in the 1920s and fostered through the 1960s, which was a negotiated compromise to allow girls and women to play sports while delicately avoiding a violation of gender role norms and expectations. The sport system women physical educators sought to achieve reflected a studied disapproval for the excesses of male sports (competition, corruption, commercialism, emphasis on winning and spectators) and a concern for female health and well-being. Thus, alternative forms of competition such as play days (where high school girls from various schools would be mixed together on teams and play games on a given day) and sports days (where high school girls would represent their own schools in day long tournaments against other schools) were organized within a model emphasizing fitness, participation, and inclusion, as articulated in the Division for Girls and Women in Sport's motto, "a sport for every girl, and a girl in every sport"[4] (Carpenter, 2001; Nelson, 1998; Sack & Staurowsky, 1998).

By the 1960s, with the emergence of the Modern Women's Movement and the Civil Rights Movement, assumptions about natural female inferiority would be challenged in significant ways (Carpenter, 2001; Durrant, 1992; Galles, 2004). The groundwork for women's championships and a greater emphasis on competition and pursuit of athletic excellence as a national agenda began to take shape upon the founding of the Commis-

---

[4]The expression "a sport for every girl, and every girl in a sport" emerged out of the 1920s as a reflection of an advocacy movement including physical educators, physicians, and sports enthusiasts. Appointed vice-president of the Women's Division of the National Amateur Athletic Federation (NAAF), Lou Henry Hoover, the wife of President Herbert Hoover, organized a conference in 1923 to discuss philosophical differences over competition versus participation, issues of facilities and space for women, and a lack of qualified women's coaches (Herbert Hoover Presidential Library and Museum, n.d.). This expression was in circulation at that time and would be maintained well into the 1950s.

sion on Intercollegiate Athletics for Women in 1966 (the precursor to what would become the female counterpart to the NCAA, the Association for Intercollegiate Athletics for Women). As was the case in previous generations, the dawning of a new age for women's sport was part and parcel of an upsurge in advocacy for women's rights in general.

Emblematic of the times, two prominent women athletes, Althea Gibson and Billie Jean King, emerged as symbols of those movements. As the nation confronted the challenges of racial discrimination in schools in the aftermath of *Brown v. Board of Education* in 1954, Althea Gibson was challenging the exclusionary practices in the all-White sports of tennis and golf. During that critical time period, Gibson became the first African American to win 11 Grand Slam titles in women's tennis, among them Wimbledon and the U.S. national tournament (what would become the U.S. Open). She went on to integrate women's golf, playing in 177 tournaments between 1963 and 1977 ("Althea's way," 2003).

Billie Jean King, a dominant women's tennis player in the 1970s, would take center stage in the gender wars in her 1973 match with Bobby Riggs. Marketed as a prime time television event pitting the "libber" versus the "lobber," the event was viewed as a "necessary spectacle" in confronting sexism not only on the tennis court but also more broadly in the society overall (Roberts, 2005). No one understood the implications of the match more than Billie Jean King herself. About the Battle of the Sexes, King said, "it wasn't about tennis. It was about social change" (HBO, 2000). King's victory in the match validated the passage of Title IX, which had happened the previous year, and offered an outright assault on prevailing notions of female frailty. Using the platform she helped create, King worked to form the first women's professional tennis tour and union, established an advocacy forum in the creation of the Women's Sports Foundation, envisioned a model for equitable and inclusionary sport in the concept of World Team Tennis, and became an outspoken advocate on behalf of women in the United States (Fleming, 1998).

The remaining four decades, from 1970 to present day, witnessed ever-expanding opportunities for girls and women in sport and physical activity, due in large measure to the passage of Title IX in 1972 and the increasing support for gender equity in athletics. Title IX's prohibitions against sex discrimination in the schools receiving federal financial assistance served as a catalyst for ongoing debates about equity in sport and physical activity (Carpenter & Acosta, 2005). The end result has been a rethinking of once seemingly intractable suppositions about the capabilities of female athletes and increasing acceptance for the nondiscrimination mandate of Title IX. The late 1990s phenomena of "girl power" and "girls rule" were inspired in significant part by the triumphs of the U.S. women's soccer team, which defeated China to win the Women's World Cup in a match played before a crowd of over 90,000 (Elliott, 2000; Miller, 2002). Entities that once vehemently opposed the application of Title IX to athletic departments, such as the National Collegiate Athletic Association, have become staunch supporters for women's sports and advocates for Title IX (Brand, 2003)

At the same time, resistance to the enforcement of Title IX has slowed progress. Unsubstantiated concerns that Title IX was being used to hurt male athletes served as the impetus for the appointment of the Secretary of Education's Commission on Opportunity in Athletics during the 30th anniversary year of the passage of Title IX in 2002 under direction of the Bush Administration (Hogshead-Makar, 2003; Staurowsky, 2005). The clear political agenda of the Commission was seen in its focus on the very narrow interests of big-time college sport programs and men's minor sport programs, specifically wrestling, to the near exclusion of the interests of children at the elementary and secondary levels. It is notable that at the time the Commission's agenda was set, the number of complaints involving sex discrimination in high school and middle school athletes exceeded those involving college athletes by five to one (Pennington, 2004).

The historical legacy of a gendered world view that conceptualizes athleticism as a male birth right and a female anomaly remains in circulation today. Steven Rhoads (2004), a professor of politics at the University of Virginia, has argued that exposure to testosterone in utero accounts for what he believes to be a "greater love of sports by males" (p. 47B).[5] Similarly, the centerpiece of assertions that Title IX has wrongly been used to cut men's sports is the argument that "women are inherently less interested in sports than men" (Samuels & Galles, 2003; Schlafly, 2004).

Just as Esther Sherman cautioned against the use of statistical data on sex differences to show that girls did not have the capacity to engage in vigorous activities in 1938, so too did the court in *Cohen v. Brown* (1996) reject the reasoning of Brown University that surveys could accurately reflect the interest of women in sport. The court wrote:

Statistical evidence purporting to reflect women's interest instead provides only a measure of the very discrimination that is and has been the basis for women's lack of opportunity to participate in sports. To allow a numbers-based lack of interest defense to become the instrument of further discrimination against the underrepresented gender would pervert the remedial purpose of Title IX.

The notion that boys and men are more naturally interested in sport persists today—after three decades of girls and women participating in sport opportunities when those opportunities have been provided—and demonstrates the degree to which present day approaches to gender equity continue to be advised by the past.

B. To what extent do mass media and conceptions of gender difference affect participation in sport and physical activity?

No one would challenge the notion that mass media play a powerful role in shaping and maintaining our most deeply held values and beliefs. As Douglas Kellner (1995) has argued, mainstream media actually create a common culture, one that, unfor-

---

[5]To refute Dr. Rhoads comment, see chapter 2 in this volume by Drs. Hyde and Lindberg addressing the facts and assumptions about the nature of gender differences and the implications for gender equity.

tunately, is far too often based on power and control. Kellner further states that one significant component of this "media culture" is the creation of spectacles on a vast public scale. Watching these spectacles we learn who has power and who does not. Sport scholars are keenly aware that in U.S. culture, sports are "media spectacles" writ large. As a result, media coverage of sport offers fertile ground for any of us who wish to understand the images, symbols, and myths that shape how we think about females and males and their participation in sport and physical activity. The purpose of this section of the chapter is to provide an overview of the research that has examined the various ways in which athletic females have been portrayed throughout mainstream media, to explore how these representations undermine and trivialize the post–Title IX sportswoman in her quest for equity, and to call on the media to reflect the reality versus the caricature of women's involvement in one of this society's most important and revered institutions—sport.

Sport Media Scholarship: An Overview

Title IX marked an unprecedented moment in the history of women's sports. Michael Messner (1988) was one of the first sport scholars to point out that this landmark federal legislation not only created a legal basis from which females (and their advocates) could pursue equity in sport, but it also reflected a cultural shift that went far beyond any legal proceedings. In short, Messner argued that the post–Title IX era could represent an unprecedented opportunity for sportswomen to challenge in a significant way the traditional ideologies and practices that assume male athletes are, by definition, the "real" athletes. But Messner also realized that such a challenge would be fiercely resisted given how much was at stake in preserving the gender-as-power dynamics that have been well established in sport. One of the most significant and all-pervasive mechanisms for resisting any and all challenges from female athletes (and their allies) is mainstream sport media. As a number of scholars have amply demonstrated, the media go well beyond the simple transmission of dominant beliefs and ideologies (Birrell & McDonald, 2000; Kane, 1998; Sabo & Jansen, 1998; Wenner, 1998). They consistently provide "frameworks of meaning" that shape, and even create, attitudes, values, and expectations about women's sports participation. Because media stories inform and legitimize unequal power relations between females and males, it is critically important that we examine the various frameworks of meaning used by the media to portray sportswomen in the post–Title IX era (Kane & Buysse, 2005).

Over the past three decades, sport media scholars have done precisely that. Through their empirical and theoretical investigations they have demonstrated how female athletes—and their bodies—are systematically portrayed in ways that undermine their accomplishments as highly skilled competitors. For example, one significant finding of sport media scholarship is that mainstream media underreport and denigrate women's athletic achievements. As a result, their ability to redefine themselves in ways that fundamentally challenge men's ideological and institutional control of sport remains an ongoing struggle (Iannotta & Kane, 2002).

Sport media scholars have made such claims in large part because of two remarkably consistent findings that make it undeniably clear that females and males are treated in remarkably different ways throughout mainstream media. First, even though young girls and women continue to increase their participation at an impressive rate 30 years and counting after Title IX, they continue to be underrepresented in terms of overall sport media coverage (Bernstein, 2002; Eastman & Billings, 2000; Fink & Kensicki, 2002; Kane & Buysse, 2005; Wann, Schrader, Allison & McGeorge, 1998).

A second pattern discovered in the research involves the type of coverage sportswomen receive. Numerous empirical investigations have shown that male athletes are presented in an endless array of visual, written, and oral texts that emphasize their physical strength, mental toughness, and athletic ability, whereas female athletes are portrayed in narratives that highlight their femininity, sexual appeal, and heterosexuality (Buysse & Embser-Herbert, 2004; Iannotta & Kane, 2002; Kane & Lenskyj, 1998; Schultz, 2004; Vincent, 2004). In short, females are significantly more likely than their male counterparts to be portrayed off the court, out of uniform, and in passive, sexualized poses.

Amount of coverage. One persistent myth perpetuated by mainstream media is that the sports landscape is predominantly occupied by men (Kane, 1996). This leaves the false impression that females represent only a small percentage of the overall athletic population. In fact, on a nationwide basis, females account for approximately 40% of all those participating in sport and physical activity (Carpenter & Acosta, 2005). Needless to say, these inaccurate assumptions perpetuate the widely-held belief that males are much more interested in participating in sports and thus deserve to be considered (and treated) as the "real," or certainly the most important, athletes.

A media study by Fink and Kensicki (2002) underscores this point. The authors wanted to replicate earlier media research studies to see whether there had been significant changes in the amount of coverage devoted to women's sports. Applying content analysis to *Sports Illustrated* (*SI*), Fink and Kensicki examined articles and photographs from 1997–1999. Their results indicated that *SI* fiercely maintained its traditional emphasis on men's sports even in the post–Title IX era. To wit: Female athletes continued to be significantly underrepresented, frequently depicted in nonsport related settings, and more often than not engaged in traditionally "feminine," individual sports. For example, only 10% of the photographs in the sample featured women's sports. How ironic that sportswomen were still being ignored by the most prestigious forum in print broadcast journalism—*Sports Illustrated*—during the same time period when U.S. sportswomen compiled an unprecedented number of athletic achievements, such as capturing gold medals in basketball, soccer, and gymnastics during the 1996 summer Olympic Games.

A recently completed study by Duncan and Messner (2005) not only highlights the lack of interest in women's sports by major media outlets but also indicates that things are actually getting worse. The authors have compiled 15 years of longitudinal data related to TV sports coverage on three local network affiliates in the Los Angeles area (NBC, CBS, and ABC). In their most recent study, they also included ESPN's "SportsCenter" and Fox's

"Southern California Sports Report." Comparing their current results with those uncovered in their earlier research, Duncan and Messner found that, quite amazingly, television coverage of women's sports has actually declined over the last five years: Female athletes received just 6.3% of total sports coverage in 2004 compared to 8.7% of total coverage in 1999. An equally alarming finding was that the percentage of coverage devoted to women's sports currently is as low as it was 15 years ago.

Unfortunately scholars and educators have done almost no research on how often women of color are represented in mainstream sport media. But what little has been done indicates that, not surprisingly, underreporting the achievements of athletic females is not confined to White women (Davis & Harris, 1998). In one of the few studies that specifically focused on sportswomen of color, Lumpkin and Williams (1991) found that between the years 1954 and 1987, African American women received the least amount of coverage in *Sports Illustrated*: Out of the approximately 3,800 feature articles appearing during that time, only 16 were devoted to African American women. In a related study, Lumpkin and Williams examined the covers of *Sports Illustrated* from 1954 to 1989. In a pattern that was quite similar to their other investigation, the authors discovered that regardless of one's racial makeup, athletic females accounted for only 6% of all the covers they sampled (114 out of 1,835), and that African American females appeared on only 5 of the 114 covers that featured sportswomen.

Type of coverage. Another myth perpetuated by mainstream sport media involves the type of coverage given to female athletes. Numerous authors have documented how sportswomen are routinely depicted off the court in "heterosexy" poses rather than in on-the-court portrayals that emphasize their athletic capabilities (Burroughs, Ashburn, & Seebohm, 1995; Daddario, 1997; Kane & Buysse, 2005). The findings from these investigations indicate that there are two interrelated (and highly persistent) media patterns—trivialization and sexualization—that deny women the respect and the status they so richly deserve (Kane, 1996). Sportswomen are trivialized, for example, when they are portrayed in visual, written, and oral texts that do not treat them, or their athletic achievements, in a serious manner. One insidious (and dangerous) way this occurs is when the media emphasize women's off-the-court physical characteristics such as their femininity and sex appeal. Sport media also routinely emphasize an athlete's personal life such as her role as wife, mother, or girlfriend. This type of coverage, by definition, removes from the radar screen any sense of female athletes as hard working, disciplined, and dedicated athletes (Kane, 1998). The second pattern of representation related to type of coverage involves sexualizing female athletes either overtly, by portraying them as sexual objects that bear alarming parallels to soft pornography, or more covertly, by overemphasizing their physical attractiveness. In both instances, their athleticism is ignored and devalued (Kane & Buysse, 2005).

An early and influential study by Margaret Carlisle Duncan (1990) revealed how these patterns of representation appear throughout mainstream media. Duncan analyzed cover and feature photographs from *Time, Newsweek, Life, Sports Illustrated*, and *Macleans* that focused on the 1984 and 1988 Olympic Games. Her findings revealed that notions of sexual difference, not to mention sexual stereotypes, dominated much of the coverage. For example, there was an overemphasis on sportswomen's physical appearance, one that highlighted their seeming heterosexuality. In addition, female athletes were frequently framed in poses that resembled soft pornography, and in body positions that emphasized their sexual submissiveness. Duncan noted that a highly accomplished and well-known American female athlete during this time period—Florence Griffith Joyner (Flo-Jo)—was a popular subject for sport photographers precisely because she fit these traditional standards of femininity: "It is no coincidence that Joyner's rapier-like, intricately painted fingernails are often visibly present in photographs. . . . Griffith Joyner's nails are an external adornment that shouts femininity" (p. 28). Duncan's findings have been replicated in numerous research studies over the past 15 years and were manifest in 2004 media coverage of Olympic athletes. For example, FHM's online magazine in its "Covergirls" section featured the "U.S. Olympic Girls," five female Olympians wearing bikinis and posing suggestively with a lead-in touting their "killer smiles, model looks and amazing bodies" (FHMUS.com, 2004).

Based on these and numerous other findings, scholars have begun to make the case that underlying much of the coverage which trivializes and sexualizes female athletes is the "image problem" that pervades women's sports. As Pat Griffin (1998) noted, media representations that frame sportswomen as pretty and heterosexy are, in reality, designed to reassure fans, coaches, corporate sponsors, parents, teammates, and even themselves that they are, or appear to be, heterosexual. And because of the long-standing and deep-seated beliefs that women's sports is a haven for lesbians, or that sports participation will turn heterosexual females gay, sportswomen have gone to great lengths to counteract these very fears (Iannotta & Kane, 2002; Kane & Buysse, 2005; Krane, 1997). A most effective way to accomplish this task is to encourage, and in many cases require, sportswomen to "engage in the protective camouflage of feminine drag" (Griffin, 1992, p. 254). There is no more effective means by which such "protective camouflage" is ensured than through the media images that dominate coverage of women's sports.

The vast sports media landscape is filled with manifestations of homophobic coverage (Kane & Lenskyj, 1998). One explicit—and powerful—manifestation of homophobic coverage is when a well-known female athlete is explicitly linked to a heterosexual role, typically as a wife or a mother. For example, Chris Evert and Nancy Lopez received a great deal more coverage than did many of their contemporaries. It is not a stretch to suggest that this was, in large measure, precisely because they occupied both roles. In fact, much of the coverage surrounding their careers emphasized these very facts. Consider the case of Evert's decision to retire from professional tennis in the late 1980s. Her retirement was deemed significant enough that *Sports Illustrated*, no friend of women's sports, decided to put Evert on its cover. But rather than emphasize her two-decade long career or her victories in Grand Slam tournaments, the caption that accompanied her posed, nonathletic photograph was: "Now I'm Going To Be a Full-Time Wife."

Some recent (and hopeful) research regarding media coverage. Learning about the results cited above may lead readers to believe that little or no progress has occurred with respect to media coverage given to women's sports. However, a just-completed investigation by Kane and Buysse (2005) indicates that in some quarters sportswomen are finally being given their due as highly skilled competitors. Kane and Buysse examined the world of intercollegiate athletics because of the enormous explosion in this particular area of women's sports since the passage of Title IX. They wanted to determine how sportswomen and sportsmen were portrayed on media guide covers in the most prestigious athletic conferences across the U.S.—the Atlantic Coast Conference (ACC), the Pacific Athletic Conference (Pac-10), the Big 10, the Big 12, the Big East, and the Southeastern Conference (SEC). Media guide covers were chosen as the unit of analysis because they are consciously constructed products by which institutions of higher education present their sports programs to members of the local and national media; corporate sponsors; and alumni, donors, and other campus and community stakeholders (Buysse & Embser-Herbert, 2004). Kane and Buysse measured how often females and males were presented on the court, in uniform, and engaged in active, athletic images. More specifically, they framed their analysis by asking two central questions: a) if images of female and male athletes were examined for the same sports (e.g., basketball, tennis and gymnastics), in the same year, at the same institution, using the same medium, would there be significant gender differences?; and b) would there be significant shifts in these images over the course of three time periods representing the 1989–1990, 1996–1997 and 2003–2004 athletic seasons? Their findings revealed two important trends. First, in the coverage of the most prestigious and influential intercollegiate athletic conferences, females were portrayed as serious, competent athletes: 97% of the sportswomen who appeared on the covers were portrayed in uniform versus out of uniform; 80% were portrayed on versus off the court; and 72% were presented in active versus passive images. Second, when making change-over-time comparisons, the authors discovered there were profound and unexpected shifts in the representations of female athletes from the early 1990s to 2004. For example, in the first media guide study (1989–1990), only 51% of sportswomen were portrayed on the court, but in the 2003–2004 season that percentage reached 80%. Obviously, these kinds of patterns are in stark contrast to much of what appears throughout print and broadcast journalism. Kane and Buysse suggest that such a dramatic departure has to do with the role of sport scholars and educators as agents of social change. These individuals not only produce and disseminate the results of their work to mainstream audiences, but they do so in a way that critiques the one-sided and unfair coverage given to female athletes. Hope, at least on college campuses, does spring eternal.

Consequences of media coverage. For the last several years, sport scholars have discussed the harmful consequences of media coverage that trivializes and denigrates female athletes (Duncan & Messner, 2005; Kane & Buysse, 2005; Kane & Lenskyj, 1998). As part of this discussion, these same scholars make two essential points. At the very least, media representations that primarily focus on a female athlete's physical attractiveness and heterosexuality undermine her athletic commitment, capabilities, and achievements. As a result, the media play no small role in ensuring that sportswomen continue to be seen (and treated) like second class citizens, a counterfeit version of the real—that is, male—athlete. At the very most, media representations, particularly those that hyper-heterosexualize female athletes, become a powerful counterforce to any gains sportswomen may accrue in the post–Title IX era. By routinely sexualizing them, the media tell us all that in the final analysis, female athletes are not (and never can or should be) comparable to male athletes.

We should not underestimate the importance of sportswomen's virtual exclusion and/or denigration in one of this society's most powerful and influential institutions. No one who advocates for better coverage is calling on the media to further a particular social or political agenda. Nor are we asking the media to exaggerate women's athletic accomplishments. We are simply asking them to turn on the camera and show us the best—and the worst—of what happens when women engage in competitive, organized activity. In short, we are calling on the media to show us the reality of women's ever-expanding involvement in sport. And when they do, we will have a more accurate and equitable sports world than the one we have today. One that is, for now, a made-up media caricature 30 years and counting after Title IX.

C. How do interpretations of the meaning of gender differences limit gender equity in physical activity and athletics?

The history of women's sport in the United States has been one of testing and overcoming perspectives that a girl's or woman's fate is determined by her biology, a biology often viewed as secondary to that of her male counterpart. Like most research, research into gender differences in athletic and sport performance is assumed to be objective particularly when it follows a rigorous scientific method.

However, in keeping with Hyde and Lindberg's discussion in chapter 2 regarding the gender-loaded assumptions that can potentially affect reporting and interpretation of data on gender differences, the literature on gender differences in athletic performance often confuses *findings of difference* with *findings of significance* and then wrongly draws *causal inferences* from *correlational data*. Vast differences occur within sex categories just as they do between sex categories. Furthermore, in sport there is a great emphasis on top achievers, both female and male. As a case in point, for the past 20 years the question of whether females will ever outpace men in running events has been a subject of great interest to sport scientists and social commentators alike.

A Case Example: Gender Differences in Running Performance

Three key moments define this ongoing discussion. In 1992 Whipp and Ward published a letter in *Nature* raising the then-provocative possibility of women outperforming men in certain running events. Examining men's and women's times in five Olympic running events, from the 200-yard dash to the marathon, from the 1920s through 1990, they found that the gender gap in performance was becoming narrower. Extrapolating from the pattern of performance they found, Whipp and Ward projected that women could be running the marathon as fast as men by 1998.

In turn, Seiler and Sailer challenged the assertion that the gender gap in physical performance was "rapidly" disappearing in articles published in the *National Review* and *SportScience News* in 1997. According to their analyses, "the absolute magnitude of the gender difference ranges from 9 to 13% across events and increases with distance" (this statistic did not include performances in the marathon) (Seiler & Sailor, 1997). In a 2004 update in *Science*, Seiler reported the gender gap was actually increasing in seven events, with the exception of the marathon, where the gap narrowed from 11.9% to 8.4% (Holden, 2004).

Notably, Seiler and Sailer (1997) concluded that elite women athletes would continue to improve their performance over time; however, the rate of improvement would be slowed due to better drug testing programs at the Olympic level. Believing they had found a connection between elite female performance and illicit performance enhancing drug use (in the 1970s and 1980s women from East Germany, the Soviet Union, and the Former Communist Bloc dominated women's running), they concluded, "The impact of masculinizing hormones on performance appears to have been far greater for women than men. The male performance data we have analyzed provides no evidence that improved drug testing since 1989 has even marginally impacted performance trends among the world's best male runners."

The discussion takes yet another turn in 2004 with the publication of Tatem, Guerra, Atkinson, and Hay's piece entitled "Athletics: Momentous Sprint at the 2156 Olympics?" in which they plotted the winning times of the men's and women's Olympic finals in the 100-meter sprint. (See Table 18.1) Contrary to Seiler and Sailer (1997) and Holden (2004), "the remarkably strong linear trends that were first highlighted over ten years ago persist for the Olympic 100-metre sprints. There is no indication that a plateau has been reached by either male or female athletes in the Olympic 100-metre sprint record" (Tatem et al., 2004).[6]

Based on these data, what are we to conclude? Is it the case, as *Science* headline writers query, that the gender gap is "everlasting" or does the possibility exist that women will one day surpass the achievements of men? Of course, this polarization of the possibilities ignores the idea of men and women running as equals; there does not seem to be a conception anywhere in these scenarios that men and women would run together, or even that men and women are running together in races now and that women are performing extremely well in those circumstances. Yes, the "momentous" moment when a woman wins one of these races has not yet arrived, but women do place well in these events. And yet there is little attention directed toward research agendas that address how women have fared within the gender-integrated pack, so to speak. As Gorman (2005) writes, ultramarathoner Ann Trason runs a 6:47-per-mile pace and she "routinely outpaces some of the best male ultrarunners in the world." What might we learn about what is really happening in the realm of athletic performance if we knew more about this phenomenon?

Given the fact that elite competition in the vast array of sports is set up as a gender binary (a rigid male–female system), one would have to concede that there is an inevitable circularity to the findings as they exist. We have a gender binary system of sport established on the basis of our understandings or assumptions about gender binaries in general (men and women must be separated when it comes to athletic competition because of their biology) and our research reflects those gender binaries. The seemingly objective question of whether females will surpass men in sport performance becomes a loaded answer in confirming once again that females are inferior to men.

The long history of women's sports has demonstrated that the existing gender binary has been encoded with messages about innate male physical superiority and female physical inferiority resulting in what effectively has been the "mismeasure" of the woman athlete. For example, it is not until the Tatem et al. (2004) article that we find female athletic performance put into perspective when they note "those who maintain that there could be a continuing decrease in [the] gender gap point out

TABLE 18.1 Winning Times of the Men's and Women's Olympic 100-Metre Sprints from 1900

Olympic Year	Men's Winning Time(s)	Women's Winning Time(s)
1900	11.00	
1904	11.00	
1908	10.80	
1912	10.80	
1916		
1920	10.80	
1924	10.60	
1928	10.80	12.20
1932	10.30	11.90
1936	10.30	11.50
1940		
1944		
1948	10.30	11.90
1952	10.40	11.50
1956	10.50	11.50
1960	10.20	11.00
1964	10.00	11.40
1968	9.95	11.08
1972	10.14	11.07
1976	10.06	11.08
1980	10.25	11.06
1984	9.99	10.97
1988	9.92	10.54
1992	9.96	10.82
1996	9.84	10.94
2000	9.87	10.75
2004	9.85	10.93

Source: Rendell, M. (ed.) (2003). *The Olympics; Athens to Athens 1896–2004* London: Weidenfeld and Nicolson. pp. 338–340.

[6]A figure illustrating the winning Olympic 100-metre sprint times for men (blue points) and women (red points), with superimposed best-fit linear regression lines (solid black lines) and coefficients of determination can be found at http://www.nature.com/nature/journal/v431/n7008/fig_tab/431525a_F1.html

that only a minority of the world's female population has been given the opportunity to compete" (n.p.).

An informed discussion about gender equity in physical activity and sport must consider the degree to which this gender binary, which has shaped our understandings about physiological differences between females and males, has been used to obscure the important similarities that exist between female and male athletes. Further, an informed discussion should also include a consideration of how a focus on gender differences to the exclusion of shared characteristics across athletes may even devalue the strength and accomplishments of female athletes. The similarities between males and females may provide the most powerful arguments for why physical education and sport, when organized and run in equitable and accessible ways, is equally important in the development of boys and girls, men and women.

The remainder of this section will avoid replicating old patterns of difference as found in the scholarship on gender differences in athletics and sport and will offer instead an exploration of the problems associated with studying physical differences between males and females. Until now research has delivered to us a generalized and rather obvious understanding that males on average are larger in size, have greater upper body strength and have greater muscle density than women (Wilmore & Costill, 2004). These differences become most pronounced after puberty when boys begin to develop their secondary sex characteristics, thus impacting strength and body weight development. However, the more illusory questions of when and if these differences matter in the pursuit of athletic health and well-being for females and under what circumstances these differences are used to limit the fulfillment of female athletic potential remain largely unanswered. To that end, two main points are considered below: how research on physical effects between males and females still affects power differences in society and why categorizing human participants by gender is problematic and may become increasingly more complicated.

Revisiting Difference As Androcentric Bias

An example can be drawn from the historical record of women's physical activity to support the notion that social order affects biology. Women's sport and physical education historians have long discussed women's physicality at the turn of the 20th century. Social mores seriously affected women's health as the advice of medical practitioners was to limit physical activity. Additionally, extreme environmental constraints such as tight corsets, heavy and imposing costumes, and poor shoe design created serious health and social consequences for women. Women lacked strength, endurance, and power for sports and recreational play because social constraints disallowed physical activity particularly for upper class White women. The physical education movement that began in the United States in colleges and universities at the turn of the 20th century was essentially developed to address some of these problems (Wughalter, 2000).

In contemporary times, the literature is not devoid of biological explanations. For example, Kimura in the *Scientific American* (2002) strongly supported a biological explanation for physical and cognitive effects when assessed by gender. She accounted for the chromosomal differences based early in development and hormonal differences as the mechanisms responsible for differences between males and females. Kimura recognized the small impact of social and environmental effects, but she attributed the major differences to biology. Although there are those who advocate primarily for biological explanations, others make clear that it is very difficult to deny the impact of social factors.

A multitude of physical differences can be examined between males and females through research in the anatomical, physiological, mechanical, and behavioral sciences. In this research males and females are studied through careful scientific measure, observation, or self-report questionnaire or survey on which they are often queried about their biological sex. In many of these measures it is difficult to remove the impact of phenomenological, historical, social, legal, and psychological effects. Toward the end of the 20th century, the Title IX era (post-1972) had a significant impact on the physical performance achievements and expectations for females, and young girls and women have turned in unparalleled physical performances. As Sparling, O'Donnell, and Snow (1998) point out, recent advances in female athlete performance are related to improved quality of training methods resulting from scholarship in the exercise sciences; equipment and uniform enhancements; advantages occurring due to new and innovative biomechanical knowledge; and the application of advanced scientific knowledge in many areas such as sport psychology and motor learning.

In their review of physical differences between males and females, Ransdell and Wells (1999) compared a variety of world class track and field, swimming, and power lifting event scores. They viewed each activity by its energy requirements. Their findings are explained in terms anatomical, physical, morphological, and cultural differences between males and females, and their data indicated the performance gap between males and females has become increasingly smaller over a 60 to 70 year period. Sparling and colleagues (1998) revealed similar percentage differences in world record running performances between males and females; however, they found the data plateaus and suggested the 11% difference is biologically determined.

In the end, the question lingers. To what extent are females still socialized to limit their physical activity and participation in sport? From a physiological and anatomical perspective the difference in running may be explained by the percentage of total body weight accounted for by body fat in women that has to be carried by the performer in a weight bearing activity such as running. On the other hand, Ransdell and Wells (1999) suggested this additional body fat might facilitate female performance in long duration swimming events to aid the body in cold water environments and the extra body fat might add to female buoyancy.

Treating sex as a dichotomous independent variable when conducting research on physical measures assumes these categories are mutually exclusive. This overly simplified approach assumes that biological differences are the same for all participants in the same category, and ignores other plausible explanations for differences (Severin & Wyer, 2000). For example, individuals' social identity, physical self-concept, or movement confidence may account for some of the measured performance differences.

Furthermore when relative measures or adjusted measures of physical characteristics are studied often the differences between the sexes are diminished and the research fails to reveal significant effects. Sparling (1979) pointed out in his meta-analysis study of maximum oxygen consumption that when expressed in absolute terms, differences were found between males and females; however, the differences were minimized when the value was expressed relative to lean body mass. Sparling argued that as females became more physically active and increased their lean body mass, their maximum oxygen consumption would improve. Thompson, Baxter-Jones, Mirwald, and Bailey (2003) found that measures of physical activity between girls and boys were not significant when measuring age at peak velocity. However, differences were found when using chronological age. These data can easily be misinterpreted to show that older females are not interested in physical activity and thus their programs do not need support or resources.

Masking the Complexity of Difference

Dynamic processes shape genetic and environmental make up and their long-term responses to movement and physical activity. By grouping individuals by sex or gender researchers collapse across the complex differences that occur within a single sex and fail to uncover similarities in the responses of males and females and the variations that occur and are important within one sex. Focusing on the mean differences between males and females provides only a superficial analysis and does not account well for this variation within a category. Also problematic are research models that include assignment of transgendered individuals to the binary categories of male and female (Severin & Wyer, 2000) and participation rates for females and males without consideration across categories of race, ethnicity, sexuality, and class.

To conclude, research designed to study differences in athletic performance is often socially constructed to marginalize the characteristics and performances of the subordinate group; therefore, information related to sex and gender differences should be carefully reviewed (Severin & Wyer, 2000). The historical record indicates that the study of performance characteristics has relied on research frameworks that valued male physical characteristics while female physical characteristics were devalued, as exemplified in the use of such value-laden terms as brute strength (male coded) versus athletic grace (female coded). Research assumptions are often guided by these values. If we are to achieve a fuller understanding of the potential of female and male athletes, we must first become more cognizant of the way in which gendered assumptions have affected our current beliefs about female and male athletic potential, moving beyond the overly simplified categories that characterize much of the work done in this area. We must also struggle to better comprehend the relative contributions of both nature and nurture as they come together in shaping male and female athletes. In the end, a reexamination of our approach to research on gender differences in sport should prompt a reevaluation of the questions we consider important and what social agenda is served by the findings. Why are some scholars so interested in whether women will ever beat men in a running race and not as interested in the question of how to foster a more accepting environment for females in sport? Why is it so off-putting for some to think that women could compete on a level playing field with men not just intellectually but physically?

D. What is the need for gender equitable participation in physical education and sport?

Since the passage of Title IX and discussion about gender equity in physical education classrooms states have been dropping quality physical education programs. As of 2005, only the state of Illinois had a requirement for daily physical education for students in kindergarten through the 12th grade, and Alabama and Washington require physical education for elementary students through the 8th grade (Weir, 2004). This illustrates the complications of determining the degree to which girls and an increasing number of boys have access to the educational opportunities and experiences they need to be healthy in later life.

The Decline of Daily Physical Education and the Rise in Childhood Obesity

The paradox of Title IX is the emphasis that has been placed on supporting programs that lead to the development of an athletic elite and cater to the needs of athletic achievers (Lerner, 2000). Whereas more boys than girls report being vigorously active (72.3% to 53.5% respectively; Kann, 1997), access to daily physical education in general has progressively declined. In 1991, 42% of students in grades 9 through 12 were enrolled in daily physical education. By 1995, that enrollment figure had dropped to 25 percent. To compound this problem, there is evidence to show that the amount of time students spend being active in physical education classes has also declined. According to the Centers for Disease Control (1997), the percent of students who were active for at least 20 minutes during an average physical education class dropped from 81 percent in 1991 to 70 percent in 1995. Across all grade levels, girls get significantly less activity than boys, yet 75% of them believe they get enough exercise (Centers for Disease Control, 1997).

In a study conducted by the Centers for Disease Control and Prevention (Lowery, Brener, Lee, & Epping, 2004), "only 55.7% of high school students were enrolled in a PE class, only 28.4% were attending PE class daily, and only 39.2% were physically active during PE." Notably, the age of the student and grade level also has a significant impact on the gender gap in activity. With a decline in girls' participation beginning in 9th grade, the average gender differences between females and males in absolute terms in vigorous physical activity is 21.7% (Ransdell, 2005).

Furthermore, female students and students in higher grades were found to be consistently more at risk for not achieving national health objectives. Although not to the degree experienced by females, male physical activity participation also decreases with increasing age during adolescence (Allison, Dwyer, & Makin, 1999; Tappe, Duda, & Ehrnwald, 1989; Tergerson & King, 2002).

Despite these trends, little sustained attention is given to the state of physical education in this country. Few schools are responding to the recommendations from the American Academy of Pediatrics and other health organizations calling for daily physical education. According to the Institute of Medicine in a report entitled "Preventing Childhood Obesity," only 8% of elementary schools, 6.4% of middle schools, and 5.8% of high schools nationwide offer daily physical education (Koplan, Liverman, & Kraak, 2004). Even in the state of Illinois where there is a daily physical education requirement, 25% of school districts provide a waiver that allows students alternatives to actually meeting the requirement. According to many physical educators, part of the problem stems from the fact that there is no recognition within the No Child Left Behind (NCLB) for physical education (Weir, 2004).

The Gender Gap in Physical Activity Among Racial Minorities & Disabled Children

Recent research on physical activity patterns across racial and ethnic groups reveals that members of racial minorities (both female and male) typically are less active than their non-Hispanic White counterparts and are at potentially greater risk for long term associated health problems (Dowda, Pate, Felton, & Saunders, 2004; Kruger, Ham, Kohl, & Sapkota, 2004; Morantz & Torrey, 2004; Unger, Reynolds, Shakib, & Spruijt-Metz, 2004).

According to Ransdell (2005), the gender difference in physical activity is more pronounced among minority students than among White students. Since 1993, the gender difference in physical activity participation has been greatest in African American and Hispanic students, with the gender differences among African American students consistently exceeding 20% (Ransdell, p. 7).

In a 2003 report done for The After School Project, a program of the Robert Wood Johnson Foundation, research by Robert Halpern focused on "what some are calling an epidemic of inactivity among low-and moderate-income children and youth" (p. 2). Elaborating further on a problem that has "multiple, intertwined roots," which include unfriendly and unhealthy physical environments, economic pressures on low-income families, damaging messages from popular culture, rampant consumerism, and an unhealthy approach to youth sport in American society, he argued for a comprehensive plan to address the needs of children.

With regard to students with disabilities, there is a dearth of information about their participation patterns. As Welch (1996) pointed out, teachers in mainstream settings have historically been exempt from teaching students with disabilities and are woefully underprepared to deal with integrating these students into physical education classes. Whereas advancements have been made in special education practice, teacher education programs have lagged behind in addressing the needs of disabled students, thus perpetuating separate systems of education for both disabled and able-bodied students. In recent works attempting to gauge physical education teachers' perspectives on creating inclusive environments, researchers have found that teacher competence and confidence is affected by exposure to teaching students with disabilities and instruction regarding

their needs (Welch, 1996; Hardin, 2005). In point of fact, Ronspies and Messerole (2005) have developed a program called PE Central Challenges that offers suggestions for how to accommodate the various skill levels and abilities of students within a class while creating challenges for all students.

Cairney, Hay, Faught, Mandigo, and Flouris (2005) reported that children with developmental coordination disorder (DCD), which results in poor motor proficiency impairing both social and academic functioning, exhibited lower self-efficacy toward physical activity and participated in fewer organized and recreational play activities than did children without the disorder. Out of all children in the study, girls with DCD (developmental coordinator disorder) generally had the lowest mean scores.

The Benefits of Physical Activity For Children

According to a report issued by the Centers for Disease Control and Prevention (CDC) in March of 2005, benefits to be derived from encouraging young people to be more physically active can decrease the risk of long-term physical and psychological issues. Because the number of overweight among children ages 6 to 11 has more than doubled during the past 20 years, a greater emphasis on getting children moving and making a commitment to healthier lifestyles early on may reduce the occurrence of weight-related illnesses, such as heart disease, high blood pressure, stroke, diabetes, some types of cancer, and gallbladder disease. Additionally, the identified long-term consequences of physical inactivity combined with overweight and obesity include an increased risk of diabetes, high blood pressure, high cholesterol, asthma, arthritis, and poor health status (U.S. Department of Health and Human Services, March, 2005).

In a study examining the health risk behaviors of athletes and non-athletes, 16,076 high school students in grades 9 through 12 were surveyed using the 1997 Youth Risk Behavior Survey (Miller, Sabo, Melnick, Farrell, & Barnes, 2000). This study indicates:

- Both female and male athletes are less likely to use illicit drugs than nonathletes.
- Male athletes were no more likely to use steroids than male nonathletes.
- Female athletes overall and highly involved male athletes were nearly one and a half times more likely to use steroids than nonathletes. Highly involved female athletes were twice as likely to use steroids.
- As a general trend, athletes (female or male) were not significantly more likely to drink alcohol or to drink to excess when compared to their nonathletic peers. However, highly involved male and female athletes were more likely to binge drink.
- In the area of tobacco use, athletes were less likely to smoke but more likely to use chewing and dipping tobacco. Highly involved female athletes were three times more likely than their female counterparts to engage in this.
- From a mental health perspective, female and male athletes were less likely to contemplate suicide or to develop a plan

to commit suicide. Male athletes were less likely than male nonathletes to attempt suicide. Highly involved athletes (both male and female) who attempt suicide, however, were nearly twice as likely to require medical treatment once they did so.

- Athletes in general were less likely to describe themselves as overweight. Female athletes, however, were more inclined to attempt to lose weight. Highly involved female athletes were more likely compared to their female counterparts to purge by vomiting or using laxatives.

- Female athletes were more likely to use seat belts. Female athletes and highly involved male athletes were also more likely to drink and drive (Miller et al., 2000, p. 4.)

In a report entitled "Her Life Depends On It" released in 2004, researchers conducted a comprehensive review of existing literature on the relationship between physical activity and girls' health (Sabo, Miller, Melnick, & Heywood, 2004). They concluded that "the current state of knowledge on the relationship of physical activity to the health and social needs of American girls warrants the serious attention of public health officials, educators and sport leaders" (p. 2) A compilation of research findings indicate that girls face what the authors describe as a "daunting array" of health risks in their youth and later life that can be reduced through physical activity and sport participation. Specifically:

- *Breast cancer risk:* One to three hours of exercise a week over a woman's reproductive lifetime (from the teens to about age 40) may bring a 20–30% reduction in the risk of breast cancer, and four or more hours of exercise a week can reduce the risk almost 60% (Bernstein et al., 1994).

- *Smoking:* Female athletes on one or two school or community sports teams were significantly less likely to smoke regularly than female nonathletes. Girls on three or more teams were even less likely to smoke regularly (Melnick et al., 2001).

- *Illicit drug use:* Two nationwide studies found that female school or community athletes were significantly less likely to use marijuana, cocaine, or most other illicit drugs, although they were no less likely to use crack or inhalants. This protective effect of sports was especially true for White girls (Miller et al., 2000; Pate et al., 2000).

- *Sexual risk:* Female athletes are less likely to be sexually active, in part because they tend to be more concerned about getting pregnant than female nonathletes (Dodge & Jaccard, 2002).

- *Depression:* Women and girls who participate in regular exercise suffer lower rates of depression (Nicoloff & Schwenk, 1995; Page & Tucker, 1994).

- *Suicide:* Female high school athletes, especially those participating on three or more teams, have lower odds of considering or planning a suicide attempt (Sabo et al., 2004).

- *Educational gains:* The positive educational impacts of school sports were just as strong for girls as for boys including self-concept, educational aspirations in the senior year, school attendance, math and science enrollment, time spent on homework, and taking honors courses (Marsh, 1993, p. 4, as reported in Sabo et al., 2004).

The Possible Health Risks Associated For Youth Sport Athletes

For all of the benefits to be realized from participation in physical activity and sport, there is another side of the coin, however. Where children have access to athletic programs and opportunities, negative health outcomes have been realized as well. According to Ewing and Seefeldt (1995), 55% of the 10–17 year olds participated in nonschool sport activity. Although the numbers of children participating in organized sport has steadily increased during the last half-century, the rate of drop out or withdraw from sport has been increasing as well. According to Petlichkoff (1996) over 65% of participants between the ages of 7 and 18 years withdraw from playing sport. Some researchers report that youth sport athletes who drop out do so mostly as a result of negative experiences whereas others report that competing interests is the primary reason (Gould, 1987; Petlichkoff, 1996). Frequently cited factors associated with youth sport athlete burn out include high training volume and time requirements, demanding performance expectations (either self- or other-imposed), continuous intense competition, excessive parental involvement, abusive coaches, lack of funding, and lack of opportunities for normal social development (Brady, 2004).

According to the Centers for Disease Control and Prevention, approximately 7 million sports-related injuries occur in the United States annually with 4.3 million requiring emergency medical attention. "Boys 10 to 14 make up the largest single segment of that injury population, followed closely by boys 15 to 19; men 25 to 44 follow this group. Girls aged 10 to 14 comprise the largest single category of females, followed by women 25 to 44" (Worrell, 2004, p. 1). Because training has become more sport-specific and occurs almost all year round even at the youth level, overuse injuries are now common among athletes aged 5 to 17 (DiFiori, 1999).

With ever increasing numbers of girls and women participating in physical activity and sport, reports of injuries among women have also increased (Ransdell, 2005). However, increased participation alone has not fully explained why women experience more knee injuries than men. In fact, in comparable sports, females have greater number of injuries to the knee compared to their male counterparts. Specifically, women incur nearly 10,000 anterior cruciate ligament (ACL) injuries in collegiate sports and 25,000 ACL injuries in high school sports (Ransdell, 2005).

In 2005, surgeons reported a five- to sixfold increase during the previous decade (1993–2003) in youth pitchers seeking surgery for elbow problems. Dr. James Andrews, an orthopedic surgeon with the American Sports Medicine Institute, notes that in addition to youth pitchers throwing year-round, risk of injury has increased because of athletes competing on more than one team (subverting playing limits imposed to reduce injuries), the effect of radar guns on pressure to perform, the existence of showcase tryouts, and poor pitching mechanics. Across sports, from gymnastics to swimming to soccer, similar factors are contributing to greater risk among youth sport participants (Pennington, 2005).

In the aftermath of U.S. House Committee on Government Reform hearings on steroid use in the spring of 2005 (Political Transcript Wire, June 15, 2005), awareness regarding the health risks associated with steroid use among youth sport athletes has grown. Data from a national survey conducted by the Centers for Disease Control released in 2004 revealed that 6.8% of boys and 5.3% of girls had used steroids without a doctor's prescription (Guregian, 2005).

In light of existing research, the challenges researchers, public policy makers, health practitioners, physical educators, and parents face moving into the 21st Century are twofold. First, school systems must be more responsiveness to the need for curricular frameworks that encourage lifelong participation in sport and physical activity because of the long term positive benefits to be realized. At the same time, there is a real need for greater steps to be taken in protecting children from the excessive physical and mental demands placed on them in youth sport settings that threaten their health and well-being.

SECTION II. EQUITY IN GENDER-INTEGRATED PHYSICAL EDUCATION CLASSES

Gender-Integrated Physical Education Under Title IX

Federal regulations offering guidance to educators regarding Title IX as it applies to any class work or curriculum, including physical education, prohibit the routine separation of boys and girls in physical education classes or using the sex of a child to require or refuse participation in certain activities. Exceptions to this prohibition in physical education include sports or activities that involve bodily contact. Even here, however, students are expected to learn about these sports in integrated settings, being separated only for class competition (Title IX Federal Regulations, Department of Education, Office for Civil Rights, 34 CFR Sec. 106.34) (also see Lirgg, 1993).

Following the passage of Title IX and the 1975 implementing regulations, physical educators and school administrators at the elementary and secondary level had to contemplate what "non-discrimination on the basis of sex" in physical education and athletics meant. The previous routine assignment of females and males into separate physical education classes that offered different activities (boys physical education curricula was typically more narrowly focused on team sports; girls curricula tended to be broader, less focused on team sports, and did not include contact sports) was no longer permissible. According to Geadelmann (1979) the necessity to comply with Title IX guidelines led to a de-emphasis on team sports, the inclusion of new activities more amenable to coeducational settings such as rappelling and orienteering, and the adoption of rules that modified team sports.

Achieving Gender-Integrated Physical Education Classes

Over time, physical educators faced the challenge of conceiving new curricular models within a discipline where activities have historically been sex stereotyped. However, the residue of thinking about specific sports as appropriate to males (contact sports, competitive team sports) or females (activities that em-phasize flexibility and grace, individual sports) continues today, among physical educators themselves and their students (Kulinna, Martin, Lai, Kliber, & Reed, 2003). Two major approaches to the shaping of physical education in light of the need to consider the equitable treatment of female and male students have emerged. Early on, attempts to integrate physical education curriculum included recommendations that heavily sex-stereotyped team sport activities, like basketball, baseball, and football, be replaced with activities organized around less competitive and more incremental skill development (Lirgg & Feltz, 1989; Steward & Corbin, 1989; Williamson, 1993). Others argued that a consideration of sex equity in physical education called for a new approach where the team sports that had been heavily associated with boys, and which inherently favored boys in areas of confidence levels and preference by virtue of exposure over time, be replaced with activities developed within an equity model, such as ropes courses, outdoor adventure activities, and long-term leisure sports (Hutchinson, 1995; Williamson, 1993).

Another common response rarely appeared in compliance reviews but was consistently evident on the floor of the gym. Departments denied the law and continued gender segregated programs, under the guise of choice, offering students options (aerobic dance or basketball) that resulted in gender segregation. The end result was often complete gender segregation. Some faculty organized programs in ways that effectively undermined the law by taking roll en masse and then allowing students to split for the rest of the instructional time without any genuine attempt to integrate their physical education classrooms. Other frequently occurring scenarios that violated the coeducation requirements of Title IX included scheduling classes such as football directly opposite aerobic dance with the intent of producing sex-segregated classes; requiring girls to pass a skill test to enroll in an advanced class or a typically males-only class such as football when boys do not have to pass such a test, and labeling classes specifically for "girls" and "boys" (Carpenter & Acosta, 2005, p. 41).

This stance on the part of physical educators to persist in gender-segregated classes in defiance of the law is not unexpected when considered in light of research conducted over the past 30 years that shows a consistent pattern of gender-bias among physical educators. In their classic work examining the gender behaviors of teachers in elementary and secondary schools, David and Myra Sadker (1994) concluded that second to vocational education, physical education was the most gender-biased subject to be found in schools. Davis (2003), in an extensive review of existing research, found that physical education teachers across all grade levels interacted both verbally and nonverbally more often with male students when compared with female students:

- asked more questions of male students,
- praised male students for good performance and female students for their effort,
- gave more corrective feedback to male students than female students,
- used gender-biased language when they interacted with students,

- expressed an expectation that male students would exhibit different behavior from female students and that male students would have better physical ability,
- selected male students to demonstrate skills more frequently than female students,
- chose not to intervene when students exhibited negative gender stereotyping toward one another,
- maintained gender-biased perceptions and explanations for student behavior,
- used teaching strategies and styles that perpetuated gender bias, and
- constructed curriculums that ignore the needs and interests of female students.

In contrast, there were only four studies Davis located that reported more gender-equitable attitudes on the part of physical educators compared to other teachers.

Whereas Geadelmann (1981) reported that effective gender integrated physical activity programs were appearing more frequently throughout elementary and secondary levels, contemporary discussions regarding physical education methodology and curriculum shows that the curriculum and approach to education has not changed as dramatically as some might have predicted. Singleton (2003), for example, wrote "Regardless of recent curriculum revisions, physical educators, faced with reduced time and/or inadequate equipment and facilities, continue to offer competitive team activities for a high percentage of their program time." In turn, Langford and Carter (2003, p. 194) pointed out that not only is physical education instruction usually limited across the life of a school child, offering essentially the same set of skill instruction from middle school through high school, but it also "invokes spectator sports or group activities" to the neglect of activities to be pursued into adulthood. When considered in light of the range of responses to Title IX, which include defiance, backsliding, "paper" compliance, "laissez-faire" co-ed classes, and enthusiastic endorsement of gender equity (Griffin, 1989, p. 30), it is clear that there is much work still to be done in conceptualizing a physical education environment that is equally beneficial to all children.

Many physical educators, like much of the rest of society, remain locked in ideological debates about the value of single-sex versus co-educational classes (Soderlund, 2005). When considering performance outcomes on skills tests, early research supported conclusions that there was little or no difference in performances when students in co-education classes were compared to students in same-sex classes (Tallman, 1970).

Notably, those who actively seek to find ways of achieving gender equity in physical education tend to be college and university professors whereas some arguing for same-sex physical education models are practitioners (Osbourne, Bauer, & Sutliff, 2002). Those who wish for a return to a pre–Title IX era when classes were separate argue that girls would experience more success in all-girl settings freed from the pressures boys place on girls in co-ed settings (Derry, 2002; Derry & Phillips, 2004) and the differences to be found in attitudes (girls are nicer, boys more aggressive) (Keinman, 1999). In turn, some physical educators have viewed the integration of physical education as the

catalyst to water down the curriculum in a way that does not challenge boys (Griffin, 1984).

The assumptions about immutable differences that serve as the departure point for arguments in support of single-sex physical education need to be refuted (see chapter 2, "Facts and Assumptions about the Nature of Gender Differences and the Implications for Gender Equity" in this volume). Research shows that although consistent patterns of gender differentiated behaviors exist, they are tied to socialization more than innate gender differences. For example, from a child development perspective, tensions between boys and girls arise and are manifest in gendered ways. Thorne's (1993) extensive work on children's interactions on the playground documented the gendered behavior of boys and girls, from taunting to invading each others' space to play. Griffin (1984) found similar evidence of those dynamics happening in co-ed physical education classes.

As Messner (2000, 2002) explains, these behaviors are not isolated but occur within a much larger system of gender performance. In his observational study of a girls and boys soccer team (ages 4 to 5 years old), he notes that it was not the numerous similarities that existed across these children as they set out on their first day of their youth soccer season but their differences that parents focused and commented upon.

Whereas the stakes are the same for all children, the access children have to physical activity, the encouragement they receive from significant adults in their lives, and the messages they receive about the value of their own physical abilities are determined in part by gender, race, and social class biases. Historically, children's involvement in physical activity has been discussed within the context of differences, reflecting the attention that difference has received in research reports. Why the dominant narrative about the sexes is one of difference is an important question to consider.

As research is conducted on the effectiveness of co-education versus single sex models of physical education, the issue of what researchers focus on—similarities or differences—becomes important to the overall understanding of what is happening in the classroom. For example, findings from one study of selected student and teacher variables for female students and female physical educators supported a conclusion that because female teachers spent less time in classroom management in single-sex classrooms, allowing for female students to be more engaged in activity, single-sex physical education is a more effective learning environment (Derry & Phillips, 2004). Apart from the fact that the findings from this study can potentially be overgeneralized given the sample (18 teachers were compared), the question of why differences or similarities may be found is as significant as the finding itself. Ryan, Fleming, and Maina (2003) found few if any significant differences in student likes and dislikes about physical education teachers across gender and racial groups, a finding that differed with other studies. Offering a rationale for why their findings differed with those of other researchers, Ryan and colleagues pointed out that the physical education teachers they studied may have played a significant role in developing the favorable attitudes students had about their experiences in class, something that transcended gender and race.

Furthermore, a compounding issue that has to be addressed in all of these studies featuring single-sex comparison groups is the fact that the samples themselves may reflect the lack of a good faith effort on the part of physical educators to sex-integrate their classrooms. As a result, the methodology behind these studies and subsequent interpretation of the findings are problematic. Are these studies measuring the effectiveness of single-sex classes in the creation of an educational climate conducive to good education, or are they measuring resistance to societal change and the required reorganization, reassessment, and reconsideration of gender-belief structures that would have to take place in order for gender-integration in physical education to occur? For example, Derry and Philipps (2004) reported that the classes they observed included traditional team sport units, including volleyball, basketball, soccer, softball, flag football, and lacrosse along with tennis. Notably, only two of those activities (basketball and lacrosse) would qualify as exempted contact sports that could be taught in single-sex rather than co-ed settings. And why would there be a necessity for tennis to be taught in a single-sex environment when the history of the sport itself has long provided for mixed doubles? If physical educators have not even been able to provide the leadership necessary to integrate their classes enough to accommodate mixed doubles, what does that say about the mindset of some physical educators in general?

Additionally, in a comparison of student activity levels in co-ed and single-sex classes, girls were found to engage in less moderate-to-vigorous physical activity (MVPA) in classes than were the boys (McKenzie, Prochaska, Sallis, & LaMaster, 2004). The authors of the study, however, point out that "some of the differences in physical activity for boys and girls in co-educational and single-gender classes were mediated by the amount of time allotted to different lesson contexts" (p. 448). In effect, girls-only classes emphasized more skill drills and less game play. Thus, the structure of the experience, rather than the gender of the participant, may help explain why girls are essentially less actively engaged in physical education classes.

This recognition for the power teachers have in creating gender equitable classroom cultures and environments needs to be explored more by physical educators. Williamson (1993) has argued that teachers who believe in gender stereotypes that assume girls and boys have different capabilities create self-fulfilling prophecies. Furthermore, merely placing girls and boys in close proximity to one another in physical education does not by itself result in gender equity. As Nilges (1998) concludes "equal access to a common curriculum may not fully eliminate gender discrimination in physical education" (p. 172). Where "we–they" dichotomies (Nilges, 1998) that pit boys against girls or situate boys and girls along the fault line of difference persist, stereotypes that undermine girls confidence in their own abilities and boys appreciation for the capabilities of girls flourish. Furthermore, there is little to challenge the persistent notion that the equity to be found in co-educational classes benefits only girls. For example, Lirgg (1993) found that "males in co-educational classes were more confident of their capability to learn basketball than males in same sex classes" (p. 324).

Although refuted earlier in this chapter, the justification of immutable differences that sustains sex discrimination in physical education and athletic settings has not disappeared from the dialogue surrounding gender and sport. For example, Rhoads (2004) wrote, "Only when we begin to take sex differences seriously enough to see that men are intrinsically more at-

tracted to sports—and need sports competition more than women do—will we be able to design public policies that are just, functional, and sensible" (p. B4). The advocacy for this position not only ignores the flawed science of biological determinism that undergirds such beliefs, but it also ignores the most basic ethical responsibility associated with teaching in a democracy. Educators are honor and duty bound to uphold a standard of excellence for students that encourages them to strive to fulfill their promise and potential as human beings and citizens. Exploring Rhoads's assertion further, what are the implications of this line of reasoning in other areas of the curriculum? Should boys, because of a stereotypical perception that they are less verbal, be evaluated using modified standards in English classes or perhaps exempted entirely? In turn, should physical educators just accept that girls will be destined for mediocrity when they enter their classrooms? It is this very logic, the logic of discrimination, that Title IX was designed to address.

There is evidence that some physical educators in secondary schools who are supposed to comply with Title IX continue to resist offering co-educational classes (Carpenter & Acosta, 2005; McKenzie et al., 2004). More importantly, explanations for why single-sex classes would better meet the needs of students in physical education include removing girls from environments where boys are threatening, aggressive, and superior (Derry, 2002; Derry & Phillips, 2004) reveal that sex discrimination is still going on in physical education classes. Derry (2002) reported that "female teachers described their less-skilled female students as being intimidated by the more athletic boys and were often the brunt of critical comments and rude remarks" (p. 24). Rather than a rationale for single-sex physical education for girls, that finding indicates that in this study, teachers were aware that girls in their mixed class settings were subjected to sexual harassment. If this is the case, removing them merely covers over the harassment and does not engage boys in meaningful ways about how they are to treat girls and women. In effect, sex segregation becomes a tool in allowing sex discrimination to continue and the patterns underlying it to go unchallenged.

It is clear from the literature that for physical educators who have the will to create more equitable classrooms and learning environments, equity can be achieved. There is evidence to show that something as simple as physical education teachers avoiding references to innate racial and gender superiority/inferiority and encouraging students to consider that performance is incremental and dependent on work and effort has an effect on how students view possibilities for themselves and for each other (Cheypator-Thomson, You, & Hardin, 2000; Li, Harrison, & Solomon, 2004). Additional steps physical educators can take include changing the culture of the classroom through their use of language and terminology, reconsidering ways in which they differentially treat students on the basis of gender, adopting different methods of class management, and altering teaching style (See Table 18.2 for more details).

The discussion about gender-integrated versus single-sex class experiences in physical education has received renewed interest in light of the Department of Education's Office for Civil Rights March 2004 proposed changes to Title IX regulations that would make it easier for schools to offer single-sex classes. Although the current Title IX regulations allow single-sex classes for affirmative or remedial purposes to decrease sex discrimination, it is not clear how this provision can be justified in phys-

TABLE 18.2 Research-Based Strategies to Achieve Gender Equity in Physical Education Classes

Steps to Achieving Gender Equity in Physical Education Classes	Physical Educators Should Consider
Changing the Culture of the Classroom (Brown et al., 1996; Napper-Owen, 1994; Parks & Roberton, 1999; Satina, 1998)	• Eliminate gender biased language and terminology (avoiding use of generic terms like "you guys") • Using parallel terms when referring to mixed groups (boys and girls, men and women) • Do not reference groups with language (girls and boys; boys and girls) • Alter activity terms (player-to-player defense instead of man-to-man)
Reconsidering Differential Treatment Based on Gender (Sprague & Engstrom, 2000; Trainor et al., 1998)	• Avoid lower expectations of girls on the basis of assumed inferiority • Consider appropriate development and learning progressions to foster mastery in all students
Class Management (Brown et al., 1996; Davis, 1999, 2001, 2003; Mitchell et al., 1995; Napper-Owen, 1994)	• Give careful consideration to arranging students in mixed-groups • Place students in groups based on ability and not gender • Avoid pitting females against males in "we–they" scenarios • Assign leadership responsibilities to males & females (squad leaders, team captains) • Use references to high profile female as well as male sports figures when instructing • Give consideration to representation of female figures on bulletin boards and in class readings • Avoid stereotyping of less proficient male students • Make class rules to avoid interruptions • Call on girls by first name
Teaching Style (Hutchinson, 1995; Lock et al., 1999; Napper-Owen, 1994)	• Reduce emphasis on winning and competition • Engage students in more critical thinking, answer open ended questions, encourage them to create their own games • Incorporate more cooperative games into the curriculum • Implement skill building approaches

ical education where the regulations prohibit sex segregation. (See also chapter 9, "Gender Equity in Coeducation and Single Sex Educational Environments," this volume.)

In a country with an education policy titled No Child Left Behind, the need to create gender equitable co-educational physical education that focuses on developing the skills and commitment for a lifetime of physical activity is critically important to our nation's health and the overall well-being of individual children.

SECTION III. GENDER EQUITY ISSUES IN SCHOOL ATHLETIC PROGRAMS

Introduction

Over the last three decades, gender equity in college athletics and secondary school athletics has been influenced significantly by government action, collegiate and scholastic leadership, and advocacy groups. Although significant progress has been made in terms of increased sport participation opportunities and increased resources for girls and women, there are still significant inequities in both participation and resources. Common inequities include inferior treatment received by many female sport participants, the low number of women as athletics directors and coaches, as well as the continued attacks against Title IX's athletics regulations.

In order to address the topic of gender equity issues in school athletic programs, we will begin by providing an overview of current statistics on girls and women in sport. Secondly, an overview of Title IX's regulations as they apply to athletics programs will be provided, including common issues about Title IX. Third, we will provide an overview of congressional and court action, educational leadership initiatives, and advocacy group action.

The Impact of Title IX on Athletics Programs

Title IX has produced a revolution in sports participation for women. It as altered the face of women's sports as well as our society's interest in and attitude toward women athletes and women's sports. It has provided the legal impetus for millions of girls and women to obtain the benefits of participating in competitive athletics. Because of the law, girls and young women are able to take advantage of superior coaching, facilities, equipment, medical treatment, travel, and publicity (for specific details regarding participation rates, see the introduction to this chapter).

Although the implementation of Title IX has led to impressive gains for women's athletics, the playing field is still far from level. Women's athletic programs continue to lag behind men's programs by almost every measurable criterion, including participation opportunities, athletic scholarships, operating budgets and recruiting expenditures. For example, in high school, 49.1% of all students are female, yet females comprise only 41% of all high school athletes and receive a total of 1.2 million fewer opportunities to play sports (NFSHA, 2005). Although women in NCAA Division I member institutions represent 54.5% of the student body, they represent less than 44% of athletes and receive only 34% of athletic department operating budgets, 33% of the recruiting budgets, and just 44% of the athletic scholarships (NCAA Gender Equity Report, 2002–2003).

Unfortunately in the athletics director's office of NCAA institutions, there has been "a loss in the presence of a female voice" (Acosta & Carpenter, 2004), particularly at the highest levels. "When Title IX was enacted in 1972, more than 90% of women's programs were directed by a female administrator" (Acosta & Carpenter, 2004, p. 4). By 2006, only 18.6% of NCAA Divisions I, II, and III institutions were headed by women whereas 14.5% of schools lacked a female administrator entirely (Acosta & Carpenter, 2006).[7] This change occurred because many separate men's and women's athletics departments merged within a few years of Title IX's enactment (Acosta & Carpenter, 1992). This leadership change and the "old boys club" valued the male applicant's experience over the female applicant's experience (Acosta & Carpenter, 1992, Hasbrook, 1988). Today, at the Division I level women have the lowest representation, with 9.3% female athletics directors and 90.7% male athletics directors. In Division II, 17.8% of the athletics directors are women, and in Division III, 26.6% of the athletics directors are women. (Acosta & Carpenter, 2006).

The percentage of women in the coaching ranks has seen a steady decline as well. Just as 90% of the administrators of women's programs were women prior to 1972, so too were 90% of the coaches of women's teams. Today, only 42.4% of women's teams are coached by females, which is the lowest representation of women coaches in history (Acosta & Carpenter, 2006). "Even though over half of women's teams are coached by males, very few females serve as head coaches of men's teams" and the percentage of females coaching men's teams "remains under 2% as it has been for the last three decades" (Acosta & Carpenter, 2006).

Title IX as Applied to Athletics

Title IX—The Legal Standard

The prohibition against sex discrimination as articulated in Title IX is very broad. It not only applies to every aspect of a federally funded education program or activity and extends to elementary schools, high schools, colleges, and universities, but it also applies to their athletics programs as well.

In 1975, the agency responsible for enforcing Title IX promulgated regulations interpreting the law as it related to athlet-

ics. These regulations require schools to provide male and female students with the following:

1. Equal opportunities to participate in sports
2. An equitable allocation of scholarships monies
3. Equitable treatment in all aspects of athletics, including coaching, facilities, equipment, medical treatment, travel, and support, among other things

The regulations required compliance in elementary schools by 1976 and in high schools and colleges by 1978.

By 1978, it became clear that schools needed further guidance on how to comply with the first requirement, equal opportunities to participate in athletics, after the agency received more than 100 complaints alleging discrimination in athletics. The central question was, How many athletic opportunities were schools required to provide? The math and reading programs could simply adopt gender-neutral admissions standards. But what did "equal opportunity" mean in the sex-segregated world of athletics? In response, the U.S. Department of Health, Education, and Welfare (HEW) issued a policy interpretation in 1979. In addition to setting forth clarification on scholarship and treatment requirements, it sets forth three wholly independent ways for schools to demonstrate that students of both genders have equal opportunities to participate in sports. Institutions could comply with the participation requirements of the provision by showing either that:

1. The percentage of male and female athletes is substantially proportionate to the percentage of male and female students enrolled in the school (the so-called proportionality test; Prong 1); or
2. The school has a history and a continuing practice of expanding opportunities for female students (Prong 2); or
3. The school is fully and effectively meeting its female students' interests and abilities to participate in sports, and competition exists within the school's competitive region (Prong 3).

If a school meets any one of these tests, it is in compliance with Title IX's participation requirements. This three-part test has been in effect for almost three decades and has been upheld by every one of the eight federal appeals courts that has considered its legality.

The first prong is fairly simple—it asks whether the female rates of participation and enrollment are "substantially proportionate." For example, if the student body is 50% female and 50% male, the gender break down among the school's athlete population should be about the same.

The second prong allows a school to defend itself by arguing that it has not achieved proportionality yet, but that it can demonstrate "a history and continued practice of program expansion which is demonstrably responsive to the developing interest and abilities of the members of [the underrepresented]

---

[7]The terms Division I, II, and III refer to NCAA designations for schools that are distinguished by the manner in which their athletic departments run. At the Division I and II levels, athletes may receive scholarships and there is considerable attention paid to "revenue-producing" sports. According to the NCAA, Division III athletic departments place "special importance on the impact of athletics on the participants rather than on the spectators". For more discussion of this, see http://www.ncaa.org/about/div_criteria.html

sex." Courts have rejected arguments from schools that teams created over ten years previously, promises to expand women's programs at some unspecified future date, smaller cuts for women than men, or improving the quality of existing programs, constitute "program expansion" within the meaning of the statute.

The third prong allows a school to defend itself by arguing that it has not achieved proportionality yet, but it can demonstrate "that the interests and abilities of the members of [the underrepresented] sex have been fully and effectively accommodated by the present [athletic] program." In essence, this prong asks whether there are girls or women who have the interest and ability to compete, but are not given the opportunity. Relative interests between men and women are not weighed. In 1996, the Office of Civil Rights (OCR) issued its Clarification of Intercollegiate Athletics Policy Guidance: The Three-Part Test.[8] It states that women athletes advocating for additional sports teams must be able to demonstrate that there is sufficient unmet interest to support an intercollegiate team, that there is sufficient ability to sustain an intercollegiate team, and that there is a reasonable expectation of competition for the team.

Enforcement of Title IX's Athletics Regulations

An aggrieved athlete or school employee may wish to resolve the inequities informally by contacting the school's Title IX coordinator, the athletic director, school board members, the school principal, or president. If an informal resolution proves to be unsatisfactory, the athlete has two other options to resolve the dispute. First, she or he can file a complaint with the Office for Civil Rights (OCR) of the U.S. Department of Education. The OCR is akin to the police; they are the governmental agency with the responsibility of enforcing Title IX in schools. The complaint can be made online[9] and does not require a lawyer. However, there are serious limitations to this process. First, inadequate resources leave the OCR unable to address all Title IX violations. For example, in 2001 the OCR initiated just two Title IX athletics reviews of schools. Additionally, athletes who file complaints with the OCR have neither the right to participate in the investigation and enforcement of their complaints nor the right to make sure their evidence or witnesses are heard. The agency is not required to help the complaining athletes. For example, the OCR may obtain a compliance agreement from the school that provides for a new soccer team, but the complaining athletes were softball players. Finally, court cases have declared schools in violation of Title IX after the OCR made a determination that it was in compliance with the law.

As a second alternative, the athlete may sue the school directly in federal court to enforce Title IX. The athlete does not need to exhaust administrative remedies prior to filing a suit. Title IX suits are generally filed as class actions to ensure that the court will not drop the case after the athlete graduates from the school.

A lawsuit will ensure that the specific remedy sought by the aggrieved athlete will be considered. While punitive damages are not available in Title IX suits, athletes may obtain injunctive relief, requiring the school to add teams or provide more resources for existing teams. They may also obtain monetary damages for losses sustained as a result of the school's discriminatory practices. Attorney's fees are also recoverable separately under the statute.

Common Issues in Title IX Disputes

Equal Numbers of Teams

Title IX's participation mandate is measured by the *overall* number of athletic opportunities offered, not by the number of teams offered. Some teams may have over 100 athletes, whereas other teams may have as few as 5. Therefore, the number of teams offered to men and women is irrelevant in analyzing whether there is discrimination in the opportunity to play sports.

Club Teams

In evaluating the number of competitive opportunities, club teams are not considered to be intercollegiate teams except in those instances where they regularly participate in varsity competition.

Exception for Football or Other "Revenue-Producing" Sport

There is no exemption for revenue-producing sports, either in calculating whether the school is providing equal opportunities or in providing equal treatment.

Per Capita Expenditures May Not Be Equivalent

Congress has recognized that some sports are inherently more expensive than others. As long as the school is providing the male and female athletes with equivalent educational programs, the school is not in violation. However, the fact finder "may consider the failure to provide necessary funds for teams for one sex in assessing equality of opportunity for members of each sex (Athletics, 106.41)." Different expenditures in required equipment may be justified—it may cost more to equip a football player than a swimmer, but different expenditures in travel, for example, may not.

Booster Clubs

A school cannot hide behind booster club contributions to men's sports as a defense explaining why its female athletes are

---

[8]Available at: http://www.ed.gov/offices/OCR/docs/clarific.html
[9]Complaints may be filed at www.ocr.gov

not treated equitably. The OCR's Title IX Investigator's Manual (Bonnette & Daniel, 1990) provides:

> Where booster clubs provide benefits or services that assist only teams of one sex, the institution shall ensure that teams of the other sex receive equivalent benefits and services. If booster clubs provide benefits and services to athletes of the other sex, then the institution shall take action to ensure that benefits and services are equivalent for both sexes. (p. 5)

Lack of Funds

A school cannot proffer the defense that it lacks the funds necessary to end the complained of discrimination.

Quotas

Attempts to argue that Title IX is a quota have consistently failed. This is true for a number of reasons. First, comparing the percentage of athletes with the percentage of the student body is only a starting point for Title IX analysis. As demonstrated by the material above, schools can still demonstrate that they have a continuing history of program expansion or that they are meeting the interests and abilities of the student athletes. Second, in the sex-segregated athletic department, it is appropriate to measure whether resources are being unfairly distributed by looking at resources provided to the other sex.

The "Athletics Arms Race" and Title IX

Title IX is often blamed when there are cuts in funding for men's athletic teams because the assumption is that the funding is going to create equity for the "less important" women's teams. However, this blame is often baseless as the bulk of the funds instead go to supporting the high-visibility men's sports that often lose more money than they gain in revenue. For example:

> Iowa State, coming off perhaps the most successful sports year in its history, cut these two programs (baseball and men's swimming) last month because its athletic department faced a $1.4 million deficit. Blame came quickly, much of it directed at the recently negotiated contracts for the school's football and basketball coaches. Football Coach Dan McCarney's compensation was doubled to $600,000 while Larry Eustachy's annual package rose to $1.1 million (from approximately $500,000), even though the basketball coach had nine years left on a 10-year deal. (NCWGE, 2002, p. 17)

The Marquette Wrestling Club was one of the plaintiffs that filed the lawsuit against the U.S. Department of Education alleging that Title IX causes discrimination against male athletes. Marquettes University' athletics director publicly blamed Title IX as the rationale for dropping the sport of wrestling, a sport that was reportedly funded at only $50,000. Institutional priorities rather than finances appear to be a motivating factor because

Marquette embarked on a venture to find new moneys to support and promote the sport of basketball:

> Marquette University, an institution that does not sponsor a football program, dropped its wrestling program following the 2000-01 season. Marquette . . . has since announced a $31 million capital campaign to build a basketball arena, in an effort to return its basketball program to national prominence. (NCWGE, 2002, p. 20)

As highlighted in the 2002 NCWGE report titled "Title IX Athletics Policies: Issues and Data for Education Decision Makers":

> A "pull-back" on the nation's commitment to civil rights cannot be precipitated by institutional decisions to emphasize one sport program, reduce the size of men's sports programs or in other ways determine the appropriate size and expense of athletics programs. Higher education should not expect the federal government to weaken its commitment to gender equity, an important civil rights law, in response to higher education's inability to control expenditures. Higher education must address budgetary issues and excess in intercollegiate athletics. (p. 14).

The 2002 NCWGE report included a number of options for exploration such as contract limitations, curtailing excessive and unnecessary expenditures in football and basketball, staff limitations, and scholarship reassessment.

Athletics Leadership and Governance

Congress

Congress has played a critical leadership role in efforts to achieve gender equity in athletics by adopting federal legislation (Title IX), restoring the application of the law when it was watered down by the courts, and instituting a monitoring mechanism to track progress.

There have been attempts over the years by members of Congress and some U. S. Department of Education political appointees to weaken Title IX as well as to support existing standards. The Tower Amendment, which attempted to exempt revenue-producing sports (e.g., football) from Title IX in 1974, was denied (Carpenter & Acosta, 2005; Hogshead-Makar, 2003; Staurowsky, 2003). Instead, the Javitz Amendment, which allows some flexibility due to the nature of certain sports without watering down the intent of the law, was adopted by Congress. And in response to *Grove City College v. Bell* in 1984, which temporarily suspended Title IX's application to athletics, Congress adopted the 1987 Civil Rights Restoration Act overturning the *Grove City College* Supreme Court decision which had placed limitations on the coverage of Title IX in all programs and activities of the institution receiving federal financial assistance (Carpenter, & Acosta, 2005; Sack & Staurowsky, 1998; Suggs, 2005a).

In an attempt to nudge schools toward equity, Congress passed the Equity in Athletics Disclosure Act (EADA) in 1994 and amended it in 1998 (Carpenter & Acosta, 2005, Sack & Staurowsky, 1998; Suggs, 2005a). The legislation requires all two- and four-year collegiate institutions to disclose participation rates and program support expenditures for male and female athletic programs.[10] Data from the survey instruments have been used by advocacy organizations to call attention to potential Title IX compliance problems. At the high school level, however, this standard information collection is not yet required by law and therefore goes largely unchecked. Proposed legislation would require high schools to engage in similar reporting practices as the EADA requires of all collegiate institutions.

U.S. Department of Education's Office for Civil Rights (OCR)

The ED Office for Civil Rights is the key federal regulatory agency responsible for administering and enforcing Title IX in educational institutions (Carpenter & Acosta, 2005). Its work is heavily influenced by the political party in power—particularly to the degree to which the regulations are enforced. In 1979, OCR produced a publication, *Intercollegiate Athletics Policy Interpretation,* that explained how Title IX applies to intercollegiate athletics and what component areas must be reviewed for compliance. In 1996, in response to some specific questions about how to determine whether men and women have equitable opportunities to play sports, the OCR provided additional compliance examples in their *Clarification of Intercollegiate Athletics Policy Guidance: The Three Part Test.*

In 2002, U.S. Secretary of Education Rod Paige, under the direction of the George W. Bush Administration, established a Secretary of Education's Commission on Opportunity in Athletics to explore whether Title IX was working as intended within athletics (see introduction, this chapter, for more details).

Due to grassroots responses of pro-Title IX advocates and the strength of the existing regulations that had been upheld in numerous court cases, the 2002–03 efforts to weaken Title IX were thwarted. In 2003, as a follow-up to the commission deliberations, the OCR sent out a *Further Clarification Letter* under Assistant Secretary for Civil Rights Gerald Reynolds's signature. In this letter the OCR stated that Title IX's athletics regulations provide sufficient flexibility, that Title IX's athletics regulations would be kept intact, and that greater education and enforcement of the law and its regulations are needed. Among the enforcement policies affirmed at that time was "the three part test."

The struggle was enjoined again in 2005 when the Department of Education issued a letter titled *Additional Clarification of Intercollegiate Athletics Policy: Three-Part Test—Part Three.* Circulated without notice or public input, this clarification alters previous approaches to enforcement of part three of the test that deals with accommodating interests and abilities (Manning, 2005). As a means of measuring female interest in sport, the OCR has stated that the administration of a web-based prototype survey, which they call a "Model Survey," would generate sufficient information to determine if schools were meeting the needs of female students in the area of athletics. Schools failing to provide proportional opportunities to female athletes or at least demonstrate a history of expanding programs could still meet the standards for compliance under this new clarification if they send out the Model Survey to female students. A provision in the methodology allows for surveys to be sent out via email. Further, the nonresponse of students to the survey would be presumed to reflect a lack of interest on the part of females.

Scholars point out that the methodology and design of the survey is flawed at a number of levels, including problems associated with potentially low response rates, the error of presuming that nonresponse is indicative of lack of interest, lack of provision for sampling errors, and the predictable misinterpretation of the purpose of the survey by students (Sabo & Grant, 2005). Those familiar with the policy also point out that the elevation of survey results as a sole indicator of interest is a major departure from previous understandings regarding the consideration of multiple factors in determining interest (National Women's Law Center, 2005b). Among those calling for the new guideline to be rescinded were a group of over 140 Democrats in the U.S. House of Representatives who sent a letter to President Bush (Suggs, 2005b), the U.S. Senate Appropriations Committee (Suggs, 2005b), and the National Collegiate Athletic Association (2005). Karr and Sanil (2005).

Action in the Courts

- *Grove City College v. Bell* (1984): The U.S. Supreme Court ruled that if a sub-unit of an educational institution did not receive federal funds, that particular sub-unit did not need to comply with Title IX. Therefore, Title IX did not apply to college athletics during the time period between 1984 and 1988. (In 1988, the Civil Rights Restoration Act of 1987 was adopted which restored the application of Title IX to athletics.)

- *Franklin v. Gwinnett County Public Schools* (1992): The Court found that monetary damages to private individuals may be awarded in Title IX cases where intentional Title IX violations occurred.

- *Cohen v. Brown* (1996): Brown University dropped two viable and existing varsity sport teams for women at a time when Brown did not meet any of the prongs for equitable participation under the Three-Part Test. The argument that women aren't as interested in sports as rationale for throwing out the Three-Part Test failed.

- Circuit Court Decisions: Eight Circuit courts have ruled in favor of the validity of the three-part test for participation opportunities.

- *National Wrestling Coaches Association et al. v. U.S. Department of Education* (2003): The NWCA challenged the legality of OCR's Three-Part Test for assessing athletics participation compliance under Title IX. In 2003, the case was dismissed because the NWCA did not have legal standing. In short, the courts said that colleges have the right to choose which sports they want to offer and the argument put forth by the wrestlers would not force colleges to add the sport of wrestling. In 2005, the District of Columbia Circuit course affirmed the ruling of the district course. The case was again dismissed.

---

[10]Participation and expenditure reports on any two- or four-year institution in the United States are available online at http://ope.ed.gov/athletics

- *Roderick Jackson v. Birmingham School District* (2005): This case involved a male high school basketball coach who alleged he had been fired as a result of pointing out the need to eliminate discrimination against his female athletes. In March of 2005, the U.S. Supreme Court ruled that individuals who are subject to retaliation as a result of their efforts to protest sex discrimination are protected under Title IX. The ruling establishes that retaliatory action directed at someone seeking to remedy sex discrimination is discrimination on the basis of sex. It further clarifies that protection against retaliation is critical to the enforcement of Title IX and that witnesses of discrimination, even when not victims themselves, have standing to challenge discrimination on behalf of others.

Collegiate and Scholastic Leadership

Despite the impressive rate of growth in female sport participation, a persistent decline in the percent of women coaches and athletic administrators has occurred since the passage of Title IX in 1972. Compared to the early 1970s, when roughly 90% of the coaches and administrators of female teams were women, in 2004 women at the college level occupied

- less than 45% of the head coaching positions for women's teams;
- less than 20% of the head coaching positions at the college level overall;
- less than 2% of the head coaches of men's teams; and
- less than 19% of athletic director positions. (Carpenter & Acosta, 2005; Drago, Hennighausen, Rogers, Vescio, & Stauffer, 2005).

From a historical perspective, the disappearance of women leaders in athletics can be traced back, in part, to the changes that happened over time in governance and administrative structures. In 1971, the Association for Intercollegiate Athletics for Women (AIAW) became "a model and a new voice in the structure of collegiate sports for women" (Carpenter & Acosta, 2005). The existence of the AIAW reflected the overall structure of college sport at that time, when women's and men's athletic programs were separate, controlled, and operated by women and men, respectively (Sack & Staurowsky, 1998; Suggs, 2005a). When the AIAW was taken over by the NCAA in 1981, which prompted the mergers and what some women of that era called "submergers" of separate athletic departments, there was a subsequent decline of women in both coaching and administration.

Research studies on the lack of women in coaching and administration focus on organizational climate and culture issues, institutional barriers, agency barriers, and strategies for inclusion/exclusion (Drago, et al., 2005; Fuchs, 2003; Galst, 2003; Martin, Kelley, & Dias, 1999; Robinson, Tedrick, & Carpenter, 2001; Sagas, Paetzold, & Ashley, 2005; Stahura & Greenwood, 2002; Stahura, Greenwood, & Dobbs, 2003; Sturm, 2003; Werthner, 2005). Studies on institutional barriers focus on access discrimination and treatment discrimination (e.g., recruitment and hiring process,

"ol' boy's network," tangible/intangible rewards). Studies on agency barriers examine the issue from an individual perspective and assess how time constraints, family obligations, support, burnout, and other personal factors may impact the number of women in coaching. Studies on agency barriers are sometimes approached from a gender difference approach, comparing male preference to female preference, which is problematic in that such studies may ignore the institutional and societal influences that may serve to impede women's "interest" levels. Clearly, more research is needed in this area and strategies for alleviating barriers and implementing inclusionary strategies to push open the door for women as coaches of men's and women's sports teams, as well as administrators, is needed.

NCAA National Leadership

The NCAA was originally viewed unfavorably by women's sports advocates as a bully during its earlier takeover of the AIAW and by its efforts to undermine Title IX (Sack & Staurowsky, 1998). But the NCAA leadership's stance on women in sport has changed over time (Brand, 2003).

Over the last several years, the NCAA leadership has demonstrated support for existing Title IX athletics regulations and support for achieving gender equity. In 1991, the NCAA undertook its first gender equity study, identified emerging sports for women in order to increase the number of female participation opportunities, adopted legislation to require NCAA institutions to undergo athletics certification, and required Division I colleges to have a gender equity plan. Furthermore, NCAA President Myles Brand spoke in support of existing Title IX athletics regulations at the Commission hearings. Most recently, the NCAA has made a commitment to pay more attention to the appointment of qualified Title IX coordinators in their institutional reviews and self-assessment guidance (Rosie Stallman, Director of Educational Outreach, NCAA, email communication, December 12, 2005).

The NCAA has also earmarked new dollars for athletics leadership and coaching education programs (e.g., NACWAA HERS Institute, the Coaching Academy, Executive Institute for Athletics Administrators, etc.), which are designed to increase the number women in athletics administration and coaching.

SECTION IV. SEXUAL HARASSMENT IN SCHOOL PHYSICAL EDUCATION AND ATHLETICS SETTINGS

In the mid-1990s, Sabo and Oglesby argued persuasively that sexual harassment in sport and in the broader society was "no longer shrouded by secrecy" but "remained clouded by controversy and confusion" (Ruder, 1995, p. 83). Their important work in this area encouraged the development of links between research and policy development (Oglesby & Sabo, 1996).

Whereas the definition and principles describing sexual harassment are found in Title VII, they apply under Title IX because of the express prohibition against discrimination based on sex (Hogshead-Makar & Steinbach, 2003; Mendelson, 2003;

Osborne & Duffy, 2005; Pinarski, 2000).[11] In 2001 the Office for Civil Rights (OCR) in the United States Department of Education issued guidance regarding sexual harassment in schools. Under their guidelines, sexual harassment is defined as "unwelcome conduct of a sexual nature . . . in each case, the issue is whether the harassment rises to a level that it denies or limits a student's ability to participate in or benefit from the school's programs based on sex"(OCR, 2001, n.p.).

As Hogshead-Makar and Steinbach (2003) pointed out, "athletics breeds special opportunities for sexual harassment" (p. 176). The situations out of which sexual harassment may emerge in athletic settings include relationships between coaches and athletes (same gender and cross gender) as well as peer-to-peer harassment. Similar situations may occur in physical education settings as well.

Carpenter and Acosta (2005) explain that courts typically categorize sexual harassment as either quid pro quo or a hostile environment. Within the context of a coach–athlete relationship, an athlete may encounter a quid pro quo scenario when his or her coach decides team- or player-related issues based on that athlete's acquiescence or refusal of sexual demands or overtures. Given the fact that coaches determine who plays on their teams, how much playing time athletes get, whether athletes will receive and retain scholarships, and what kind of opportunities athletes may have for advancement within their sport, the potential for a coercive, abusive relationship where sexual harassment can occur is clearly present.

Conversely, a hostile environment is much more general. Arising in an athletic setting, a hostile environment can be found when a coach's conduct limits or denies an athlete his or her ability to perform (Mendelson, 2003) and may also occur student-to-student (Carpenter & Acosta, 2005). Having said that, "not every crude, inappropriate, or rude remark with a sexual connotation that makes someone uncomfortable constitutes sexual harassment. Only those remarks and behaviors that are sufficiently pervasive and rise to an unreasonable level are actionable as sexual harassment. The threshold is high. Determining what meets the threshold in a specific instance is up to the court" (Carpenter & Acosta, 2005, p. 149).

The magnitude of the problem of sexual harassment in athletic and physical education settings is difficult to calculate. As is the case with all forms of interpersonal aggression and violence, the human calculus is affected by the forces that discourage or mask the occurrence. Some students or athletes who may have been sexually harassed by a coach, teacher, or student may have simply dropped out without ever reporting what had happened to them. Others may find the subject so painful or intimidating that they will not disclose information even when asked. Still, some studies suggest that female athletes who are subjected to sexual harassment do not recognize it as such (Osborne & Duffy, 2005; Toftegaard, 2001).

Since 1996, a slowly growing body of research studies, court cases, and policy statements have helped to define and recognize the magnitude of the problem in athletics and physical education in the United States and internationally, although there

is still much that remains unexamined on this topic. For example, the few studies that have been done in the United States have focused on college age athletes (Volkwein, Schnell, Sherwood, & Livezey, 1997; Volkwein-Caplan, Schnell, Devlin, Mitchell, & Sutera, 2002). Even less attention has been given to high school athletes (Hayden, 2003). Additionally, there is little information available about the degree to which male athletes are subjected to sexual harassment in athletic and physical education settings. Based on the male response to a British Broadcasting Company program titled "Secrets of the Coach" that dealt with the silence surrounding sexual abuse and coaching, where a disproportionately high number of anonymous males called in to discuss experiences they had had as athletes and had never talked about, this area warrants much more investigation as well (Brackenridge, 2001).

According to Volkwein-Caplan and colleagues (2002), who compared the experiences of college female athletes with those of female college students relative to sexual harassment from coaches and professors, female athletes were subjected to more forms of what the authors refer to as "mild sexual harassment," such as touching, questioning by coaches about personal affairs, invitations to lunch or dinner, or being called pet names, than their female student counterparts.

Anecdotal evidence over the years has offered powerful testimony to the existence of the problem, however, and to the profound affect that sexual harassment has on athletes and students in physical education settings. As a case in point, revelations that the recruitment process for top football players at the University of Colorado featured promises of sex, alcohol, and drugs in 2004 eventually prompted as many as 10 female students, one of whom was Katie Hnida, a place kicker on the football team, to publicly allege they had been sexually harassed and raped by football players (Hnida, 2006).

Two of these women, Lisa Simpson and Anne Gilmore, filed suit against the University of Colorado in the U.S. District Court for the District of Colorado (Civil Case No. 02-RB-2390). Although Robert E. Blackburn, the judge in this case found that the two women had suffered severe and objectively offensive sexual harassment, he dismissed the case on the grounds the plaintiffs had failed to prove that the university knew or was deliberately indifferent to the possibility that players and recruits would harass female students despite a history of the university being served notice of sexual violence perpetrated by players and coaches against their wives, employees at the institution, and even high school students (*Simpson & Gilmore v. University of Colorado*, 2005). In August of 2005, the plaintiffs filed an appeal based on newly released information from the University of Colorado Office of Sexual Harassment (Hartman & Vaughan, 2005).

In another high profile case, two former players at the University of North Carolina at Chapel Hill alleged that their coach had made inappropriate comments, pried into their private lives, and created a hostile environment that made them uncomfortable (*Jennings & Keller v. Dorrance*, 2002). After six years, the university settled in March of 2004 with one of the plaintiffs for $70,000. The case involving the other plaintiff was

---

[11]This section deals specifically with sexual harassment in school physical education and athletics settings. For a broader discussion of sexual harassment and bullying see chapter 11 in this volume.

subsequently dismissed. Apart from the public scrutiny directed at the coach, he was also required as part of the settlement to attend sensitivity training (Associated Press, March 25, 2004).

Whereas the most visible cases of sexual harassment appear to be those that take place between coaches and athletes, peer-to-peer harassment among athletes and students in physical education classes has also gone on. In *Snow v. Seamons* (2000), a football player was allegedly hazed and sexually harassed by his teammates with the knowledge of his coach, who rationalized the abuse by saying "boys will be boys". Similarly, in *Snelling v. Fall Mountain Regional School District* (2001), a case involving two brothers who played high school basketball, the court determined that the name-calling, taunting, and unnecessary rough treatment to which they had been subjected by teammates and their coach could constitute sexual harassment and presented issues triable under Title IX.

There have been cases, such as *Davis v. Monroe County Board of Education* (1999), illustrating the vulnerabilities children experience at the elementary school level as well. On a repeated basis, Lashonda Davis suffered the vulgar remarks and escalating inappropriate attentions of a classmate in physical education classes and at other times during the school day. Despite actions taken by both Lashonda and her mother to notify school authorities, her tormenter persisted, exacting a toll that eventually made the prospect of suicide seem a viable option to get out of the circumstances she was in. The significance of this case rests in the court's determination that in order for institutions to be held liable, notice of the sexual harassment must be given to school officials and officials must be shown to exhibit "deliberate indifference (p. 1)" after notice has been served.

Awareness in the coaching community about coaches who had been quietly dismissed from one job who would move on to sexually harass athletes on other teams came to light in a story aired on ESPN in 1993. The story focused on then coach of the University of Florida's swim program, Mitch Ivey, who had routinely pursued sexual liaisons with female athletes on his teams, some of whom were under the legal age for consent (Fish, 1998). Statements regarding sexual harassment started to appear in codes of ethics for coaches in the mid-1990s and now many organizations ranging from swim to volleyball coaches associations have ethics codes with statements regarding sexual harassment and coach conduct. As of today, there has not been a universal adoption of sexual harassment statements in coaching codes of ethics nationwide.

Addressing the issue of sexual harassment in coaching codes of ethics represent only one proactive step that should be taken to ensure that the rights of students and athletes are protected. The OCR Sexual Harassment Guidance explains the liability of educational institutions under Title IX (Osborne & Duffy, 2005). In accordance with that guidance, schools can be held liable when coaches, acting as agents on behalf of those schools, engage in sexual harassment. Thus, in circumstances where school administrators fail to act when they learn that employees are sexually harassing students or they allow behavior that continues to perpetuate a hostile environment for students, they have effectively limited student access to an education free from discrimination. Institutions are also held responsible if they knew or reasonably should have known about peer or third-party sexual harassment and did not take prompt and effective action.

Based on this, it would behoove athletic departments to have established policies in place regarding sexual harassment. However, in a recent study done by Osborne and Duffy (2005) where they surveyed 117 athletic departments of NCAA Division IA member institutions, only 77% had a written sexual harassment policy with 44% reporting the existence of a sexual harassment complaint procedure specific to athletes. Whereas it is possible that the athletic departments without express sexual harassment policies or grievance procedures may have been covered under blanket university policies, Osborne and Duffy suggest "if the department has not adopted a written policy that it advertises to its employees and student-athletes, it indicates an indifference to the issue" (p. 76).

The necessity for athletes to understand the options available to them when they have a grievance is demonstrated in the case of Jennifer Harris, a female basketball player on scholarship at Penn State University who believes she was targeted by her coach, Rene Portland, because of a Portland's perception that Harris was a lesbian. When asked why Harris did not file a complaint with officials at Penn State when she was asked not to return to the basketball program the next year, precipitating her leaving the university, she explained that she feared retaliation while the events were occurring and didn't feel safe reporting the alleged treatment to which she had been subjected (Epstein, 2005).

While there has been an awakening of sorts in the United States regarding the potential for sexual harassment in school athletic and physical education settings, there is much more work that needs to be done to ensure that children and young adults are allowed to pursue education free from this kind of abuse. To that end, there needs to be far more research and documentation regarding the problem itself and its occurrence. Furthermore, continuing efforts need to be made to encourage national sport organizations, like the National Collegiate Athletic Association (Mendelson, 2003), to provide leadership on these important issues.

SECTION V. RECOMMENDATIONS FOR FUTURE ACTION

To move forward toward the goal of achieving gender equity in physical education and athletics, the following actions are recommended:

1. *Increase Title IX Educational and Accountability Efforts.* Greater education of school administrators is needed regarding their obligations under Title IX as it relates to athletics and physical education. As an accountability mechanism, easily accessible web based information on Title IX coordinators, policies and gender and race disaggregated statistics should be developed and maintained at all levels of education and students and staff should also be informed of their rights as well as patterns of inequities.

2. *Increase Title IX Enforcement Efforts.* There is ample evidence to show that sex discrimination continues to exist in

athletic and physical education programs around the country. In its long history of application to physical education and athletics, government efforts to enforce Title IX have been inconsistent. Instead of changing existing regulations, interpretations, and policies that have been promulgated in the public domain and clarified in the courts, Title IX should be uniformly enforced (see 3c below).

3. *Keep Title IX's Regulations Strong.* When attempts are made to weaken Title IX, effort must be taken to keep Title IX's regulations intact and strong.

    a. *Rescind the OCR 2005 Additional Clarification of Intercollegiate Athletics: Three-Part Test—Part Three* on the grounds that it is based on flawed scientific methodology, irrevocably alters previous OCR policies that provided for multiple factors to be used in evaluating female student interest in sport, and that it holds the potential to reverse gains that have made for girls and women in sport.

    b. *Continue to Fight Efforts to Challenge Title IX's Single-Sex Regulations.* Proposed amendments governing single-sex classes under Title IX as outlined in 69 Fed. Reg. 11276 should be aggressively challenged on the grounds that the assumption that sex discrimination no longer goes in school settings is wrong. There is ample evidence to show that sex discrimination continues to exist in athletic and physical education programs around the country.

    c. *Advocate for the Expansion of the Equity in Athletics Disclosure Act at the High School Level.* The Equity in Athletics Disclosure Act, which requires that colleges and universities provide information regarding participation opportunities and budget allocations in athletics, has created an accountability mechanism to monitor progress at that level. A similar disclosure mechanism should be created for athletic programs for the secondary level.

    d. *Focus On Making Gender Integrated Non-Sexist Physical Education Classes A Reality.* Greater work needs to be done to create physical education environments where students can maximize their individual skills and abilities while making a positive commitment to healthy lifelong physical activity. This can be achieved through the continuing development and identification of effective teaching strategies and replicable student curriculum.

4. *Encourage Greater Focus In Sport Science Research On Gender Equity Questions.* Unlike any other area of the school curriculum, the complications of well-established sex stereotypes and traditions of sex segregated classes and athletic activities define the structure and circumstances in which children are educated in physical education and athletics within the nation's schools. Thus gender equity requires even greater scrutiny and accountability on the part of policy makers, researchers, and practitioners to regularly examine their own gendered assumptions in light of solid research in the physical activity areas as well as other aspects of the curriculum. More grant funding should be directed toward research and development designed to achieve gender equitable physical education classrooms and to understand similarities across age groups in physi-

cal performance and how to accomplish a positive commitment to lifelong physical activity to improve the health of males and females.

5. *Increase Physical Education in our Schools.* All efforts should be made to incorporate daily physical education into our nation's schools. Consideration should be given to the Model Physical Activity and Physical Education Act proposed by the Women's Sports Foundation (2006), which provides a template for implementing daily physical education or its equivalent in grades K–12.

6. *Greater Emphasis in Physical Education Teacher Education Programs On Gender Equity.* Provide greater emphasis on gender equity in physical education teacher education programs. Especially in the elementary school level, where girls are slightly ahead of boys in physical development, those efforts should be done in tandem with renewed commitment to ensuring that there is an equal playing field.

7. *More Funding Should Be Made Available For Achieving Gender Equity in Physical Education and Athletic Programs Around the Nation.* Physical educators and coaches need more training in understanding their obligations under the law. Additional federal funding should be directed through the Department of Education to create these programs.

8. *Conduct Further Research on Issues Impacting Girls and Women in Sport.* The identification of issues impacting girls and women in sport and the development of strategies to alleviate barriers and to encourage more women in coaching and athletic administration positions needs further exploration and attention.

9. *Encourage Coaches Associations, Sport Governing Bodies, and Athletic Departments to Adopt Sexual Harassment Policies and Grievance Procedures.*

10. *Create and Implement Media Awareness Initiatives.*

    a. Federal funding should be made available through the Department of Education and Department of Health and Human Services for media awareness training for teachers and sport educators.

    b. Contact local and national print and broadcast journalism organizations to insist that media representations associated with sportswomen reflect an accurate portrayal of their involvement.

ACKNOWLEDGMENTS

Ellen J. Staurowsky was lead author and assumed primary responsibility for the introduction, section I.A, section 1.D, and section IV. Staurowsky co-authored section I.C with Emily Wughalter and was assisted in the writing of section II by Phyllis Lerner. Section III was co-authored by Nancy Hogshead-Makar, Ellen Staurowsky, and Athena Yiamouyiannis; Mary Jo Kane wrote section II.

The authors wish to extend their appreciation to the reviewers of the chapter, including editors Sue Klein; Cheris Kramarae, University of Oregon; and Donna Lopiano, Executive Director, Women's Sports Foundation, East Meadow, New York.

References

Acosta, V., & Carpenter, L. J. (1992, March). As the years go by: coaching opportunities in the 1990s. *The Journal of Physical Education, Recreation & Dance, 63*(3), 36–41.

———. (2004). *Women in intercollegiate sport: A longitudinal study-27 year update 1977–2004.* Retrieved on February 7, 2007, from http://www.womenssportsfoundation.org/binary-data/WSF_ARTICLE/pdf_file/906.pdf

———. (2006). *Women in intercollegiate sport: A longitudinal study-29 year update 1977–2006.* Retrieved February 7, 2007, from http://www.aahperd.org/nagws/pdf_files/longitudinal29.pdf

"Althea's way: Tennis loses a barrier-breaking competitor." (2003, October 6). *Pittsburgh Post Gazette,* A16.

Allison, K. R., Dwyer, J. J. M., & Markin, S. (1999, February). Self-efficacy and participation in vigorous physical activity by high school students. *Health Education and Behavior, 26*(1), 12–25.

Associated Press. (2004, March 25). Soccer coach settles sexual harassment case. *Milwaukee Journal Sentinel,* p. 02C.

Athletics 106.41, *An annotated summary of the regulation for Title IX of the Education Amendments of 1972.* Washington, DC: The Mid-Atlantic Center for the Mid-Atlantic Equity Consortium. Retrieved February 4, 2007 from http://www.maec.org/annotate.html

Ballard, K., Caldwell, D., Dunn, C., Hardison, A., Newkirk, J., Sanderson, M. Thaxton Vodicka S., & Thomas, C. (2005). Is it physical education or physical activity? In *Move More, NC's Recommended Standards For Physical Activity In School.* North Carolina Department of Health and Human Services, Division of Public Health, Raleigh, NC. Retrieved January 30, 2007, from http://www.aahperd.org/naspe/template.cfm?template=difference.html

Bernstein, L., Henderson, B., Hanisch, R., Sullivan-Halley, J., & Ross, R. (1994). *Physical exercise and reduced risk of breast cancer in young women. Journal of the National Cancer Institute, 86,* 1403–1408.

Bernstein, A. M. (2002). Is it time for a victory lap? Changes in media coverage of women in sport. *International Review for the Sociology of Sport, 37,* 3–4.

Birrell, S., & McDonald, M. G. (2000). *Reading sport: Critical essays on power and representation.* Boston: Northeastern University Press.

Bleier, R. (1984). *Science and gender: A critique of biology and its theories on women.* New York: Pergamon.

———. (1988a). The cultural price of social exclusion: gender and science. *NWSA Journal, 1,* 7–19.

———. (1988b). A decade of feminist critiques in the natural sciences. *Signs: Journal of Woman in Culture and Society, 14,* 186–195.

———. (1988c). Sex differences research: science or belief? In R. Bleier (ed.), *Feminist Approaches to Science* (pp. 147–164). New York: Pergamon Press.

Bonnette, V., & Daniel, L. (1990). *Title IX Athletics Investigator's Manual,"* Washington, DC: Office for Civil Rights, Department of Education.

Brady, F. (2004, February). Children's organized sports: A developmental perspective. *Journal of Physical Education, Recreation & Dance, 75*(2), 35–43.

Brand, M. (2003, April 28). Title IX seminar keynote address. Retrieved February 7, 2007, from http://www.ncaa.org/gender_equity/general_info/20030428speech.html

Bray, C. (2004, November). *Summary of sports sponsorship and participation rates data related to the decline in sponsorship of Olympic Sports.* Indianapolis: National Collegiate Athletic Association.

Briggs, B. (2004, August 23). Miranda McMann set history American women wrestlers advance past the first two rounds in helping to break down the gender barriers on the mat. *The Denver Post,* D-08.

Brown, S., Brown, D., & Hussey, K. (1996). Promote equality in the classroom. *Strategies: A Journal for Physical Education and Sport Educators, 9*(6), 19–22.

Burroughs, A., Ashburn, L., & Seebohm, L. (1995). "Add sex and stir": Homophobic coverage of women's cricket in Australia. *Journal of Sport and Social Issues, 19*(3), 266–284.

Buysse J. M., & Embser-Herbert, M. S. (2004). Constructions of gender in sport: An analysis of intercollegiate media guide cover photographs. *Gender and Society, 18*(1), 66–81.

Cahn, S. K. (1994). *Coming on strong: Gender and sexuality in twentieth century women's sport.* New York: The Free Press.

Cairney, J., Hay, J., Faught, B., Mandigo, J., & Flouris, A. (2005, January). Developmental coordinator disorder, self-efficacy toward physical activity, and play: Does gender matter? *Adapted Physical Activity Quarterly, 22*(1), 67–83.

Carpenter, L. (2001). Letters home: My life with Title IX. In G. Cohen (Ed.), *Women in sport: Issues and controversies.* Reston, VA: NAGWS.

Carpenter, L., & Acosta, V. (2005). *Title IX.* Champaign, IL: Human Kinetics Publishers.

Cayleff, S. (1995). *Babe: The life and legend of Babe Didrikson Zaharias.* Urbana: University of Illinois Press.

Centers for Disease Control. (1997). Guidelines for school and community programs to promote lifelong physical activity among young people. Retrieved February 2, 2007, from http://www.cdc.gov/mmwR/preview/mmwrhtml/00046823.htm

Centers for Disease Control. (2006, October 20). *Physical activity: Promoting better health for young people through physical activity and sport.* Retrieved February 5, 2007, from http://www.cdc.gov/healthyyouth/physicalactivity/promoting_health/

Chen, Z. X. (2004, December 6). Your S.T.U.F.F. *The Boston Herald,* 030.

Cheyptor-Thomson, R., You, J., & Hardin, B. (2000, September 30). *Women in Sport & Physical Activity, 9*(2), 99.

Cohen, D. S. (2005, November). Gender equity in intercollegiate athletics: Where does Pennsylvania stand? A report of the Women's Law Project. Retrieved February 7, 2007, from http://www.womenslaw project.org

Daddario, G. (1997). Gendered sports programming: 1992 Summer Olympic coverage and the feminine narrative form. *Sociology of Sport Journal, 14,* 103–120.

Davis, K. L. (1999). Giving women a chance to learn: Gender equity principles for HPERD classes. *The Journal of Physical Education, Recreation and Dance, 70*(4), 13–14.

———. (2001). Gender interactions between teachers and students in selected high school physical education classes. Paper proposal submitted to SIG: Research on Learning and Instruction in Physical Education. Retrieved [supply date] from http://edtech.connect.msu.edu/Searchaera2002/viewproposaltext.asp?propID=3732

———. (2003). Teaching for gender equity in physical education: A review of the literature. *Women in Sport and Physical Activity Journal, 12*(2), 55–65.

Davis, L. R., & Harris, O. (1998). Race and ethnicity in U.S. sport media. In L. A. Wenner (Ed.), *MediaSport: Cultural sensibilities and sport in the media age* (pp. 154–169). Boston: Routledge & Kegan Paul.

Derry, J. A. (2002). Single-sex and coeducation physical education: perspectives of Adolescent girls and female physical education teachers. *Mempomene Journal, 21*(3), 21–29.

Derry, J. A., & Phillips, D. A. (2004, Winter). Comparisons of selected student and teacher variables in all-girls and coeducational physical education environments. *Physical Educator, 61*(1), 23–35.

DiFiori, J. P. (1999, January). Overuse injuries in children and adolescents. *The Physician and Sportsmedicine, 27*(1), 75.

Dodge, T., & Jaccard, J. (2002). Participation in athletics and female sexual risk behavior: The evaluation of four causal structures. *Journal of Adolescent Research, 17,* 42–67.

Dowda, M., Pate, R. R., Felton, G. M., Saunders, R., Ward, D., Dishman, R. K., & Trost, S. G. (2004, December). Physical activities and sedentary pursuits in African-American and Caucasian girls. *Research Quarterly for Exercise and Sport, 75*(4), 352–360.

Drago, R., Hennighausen, L., Rogers, J., Vescio, T., & Stauffer, K. D. (2005, August 19). *Final report for CAGE: The Coaching and Gender Equity Project.* Retrieved February 7, 2007, from http://lsir.la.psu.edu/workfam/CAGE.htm

Duncan, M. C. (1990). Sport photographs and sexual difference: Images of women and men in the 1984 and 1988 Olympic Games. *Sport Sociology Journal, 7,* 22–43.

Duncan, M. C., & Messner, M. A. (2005). Gender in televised sports: News and highlights shows, 1989–2004. Retrieved July 20, 2005, from http://www.aafla.org/9arr/ResearchReports/tv2004.pdf

Duncan, M. C., & Sayaovong, A. (1990). Photographic images and gender in *Sports Illustrated for Kids. Play & Culture, 3,* 91–116.

Durrant, S. M. (1992, March). Title IX: Its power and its limitations. *Journal of Physical Education, Recreation and Dance, 63*(3), 60–64.

Eastman, S. T., & Billings, A. (2000). Sportscasting and sports reporting: The power of gender bias. *Journal of Sport and Social Issues, 24*(2), 192–214.

Elliott, M. (2000, September 22). Girl power in full force at Olympics. *Tampa Tribune,* 1.

Epstein, D. (2005, October 13). Vendetta against lesbians? *Inside Higher Education.* Retrieved February 7, 2007, from http://www.insidehighered.com/news/2005/10/13/pennstate.

Ewing, M. E., & Seefeldt, V. (1996). Patterns of participation and attrition in American agency-sponsored youth sports. In Smoll, F. L., & Smith, R. E. (Eds). *Children and youth sport: A biopsychosocial Perspective* (pp. 31–45). Madison, WI: Brown & Benchmark.

FHMUS.com. (2004, September). *US Olympic girls.* [Electronic version]. Retrieved July 26, 2005, from http://www.fhmus.com/girls/covergirls/289/Default.asp?page=3.

Fink, J. S., & Kensicki, L. J. (2002). An imperceptible difference: Visual and textual constructions of femininity in *Sports Illustrated* and *Sports Illustrated for Women. Mass Communication & Society, 5*(3), 317–339.

Fish, M. (1998, September 23). Women in sports: growing Pains (Fourth of a seven part series). Danger zones: Some male coaches pay too much attention. *The Atlanta Journal and Constitution,* 01D.

Fleming, A. T. (1998). The battles of Billie Jean King. *Women's Sport & Fitness, 161*(173), 131–135.

Friedan, B. (1963). *The feminine mystique.* New York: Norton.

Fuchs, V. J. (2003). A comparison of the career paths of NCAA female directors of athletics at Division I, II, and III institutions, and of senior women administrators. Unpublished doctoral dissertation. Eugene, OR: Kinesiology Publications, University of Oregon. Retrieved February 7, 2007, from http://kinpubs.uoregon.edu.

Galles, K. M. (2004, Summer). Filling the gaps: Women, civil rights, and Title IX. *Human Rights, 31*(3), 16–19.

Galst, L. (2003). The sports closet. In J. Boxill (ed.), *Sports ethics: An anthology.* Malden, MA: Blackwell Publishing.

Gorman, M. O. (1995). Better in the long run. *Runner's World.* Retrieved February 4, 2007, from http://www.runnersworld.com/article/0,5033,s6-51-0-0-852,00.html

Geadelmann, P. L. (1979). Sex equality in physical education programs of selected NCA accredited Iowa high schools. *Dissertation Abstracts International 39,* 7221A (University Microfilms. No. 7913040).

———. (1981). Coeducational physical education: For better or for Worse? *NASSP Bulletin, 65*(443), 91–95.

Geadelmann, P. L. with Bischoff, J., Hoferek, M., & McKnight, D. (1985). Sex equity in physical education and athletics (pp. 319–337). In S. Klein, *Handbook for achieving sex equity through education.* Baltimore: Johns Hopkins University Press.

Gould, D. (1987). Understanding attrition in children's sport. In Gould, D. (ed.), *Advances in pediatric sport sciences behavioral issues* (vol. 2, pp. 61–85 Champaign, IL: Human Kinetics Publishers).

Griffin, G. (1989). Equity in the gym: What are the hurdles? *CAHPER Journal, 55*(2), 23–26.

———. (1984). Girls' participation styles in middle school physical education sports unit. *Journal of Teaching in Physical Education, 4*(1), 30–38.

———. (1992). Changing the game: Homophobia, sexism and lesbians in sport. *Quest, 44,* 251–265.

———. (1998). *Strong women, deep closets.* Champaign, IL: Human Kinetics.

Guregian, K. (2005, June 24). Reading, writing and 'roids: High School kids on 'roid to ruin. *The Boston Herald,* 110.

Halpern, R. (2003). *Physical (in)activity among low-income children and youth: Problem, prospect, challenge.* New York, NY: The After School Project, Robert Wood Johnson Foundation. Retrieved February 2, 2007, from http://www.theafterschoolproject.org/uploads/Physical-inActivity-Report.pdf.

Hardin, B. (2005, Winter). Physical education teachers' reflections on preparation for inclusion. *Physical Educator, 62*(1), 44–57.

Hartman, T., & Vaughan, K. (2005, August 10). New CU allegations: Two women claim football trainer was sexually assaulted. *Rocky Mountain News,* p. 4A.

Hasbrook, C. A. (1988). Female coaches—Why the declining numbers and percentages? *JOPERD: The Journal of Physical Education, Recreation, and Dance.*

Hayden, D. L. (2003). *Female and male athletic coaches' and female high school athletes' perception of sexual harassment and the incidence among female high school athletes.* Unpublished doctoral dissertation. Washington, DC: Georgetown University.

HBO (2000). *Dare to compete.* New York: Home Box Office.

Hedlund, R., Keinman, I., Davis, K. L., & Colgate, T. P. (1999, January). Should physical education classes return to teaching males and females Separately? *Journal of Physical Education, Recreation & Dance, 70* (1), 11–13.

Herbert Hoover Presidential Library and Museum. (n.d.). *Biographical sketch of Lou Henry Hoover 1874–1944.* Retrieved [supply date] from http://www.ecommcode.com/hoover/hooveronline/LHH_WEBSITE/

Hnida, K. (2006, December). *Still kicking: My dramatic journey as the first woman to play Division One football.* New York, NY: Simon and Schuster.

Hogshead-Makar, N. (2003, July). The ongoing battle over Title IX. *USA Today, 132*(2698), 64.

Hogshead-Makar, N., & Steinbach, S. E. (2003, Spring). Intercollegiate athletics' unique environments for sexual harassment claims: Balancing the realities of athletics with preventing potential claims. *Marquette Sports Law Review, 13,* 183–193.

Holden, C. (2004, July 30). An everlasting gender gap? February 4, 2007 *Science, 305,* 639–640.

Howard, B. (2006, September 18). Participation in high school sports increases again: Confirms NF.HS Commitment to stronger leadership. Press realease. national Federation of State High School Associatio. Retrieved February 2, 2007 from http://www.nfhs.org/web/2006/09/participation_in_high_school_sports_increases_again_confirms_nf.aspx

Hutchinson, G. E. (1995). Gender-fair teaching in physical education. *Journal of Physical Education, Recreation, and Dance, 66*(1), 42–47.

Iannotta, J. G., & Kane, M. J. (2002). Sexual stories as resistance narratives in women's sports: Reconceptualizing identity performance. *Sociology of Sport Journal, 19*(4), 347–369.

Kane, M. J. (1996). Media coverage of the post Title IX female athlete: A feminist analysis of sport, gender, and power. *Duke Journal of Gender, Law and Policy, 3*(1), 95–127.

———. (1998). Fictional denials of female empowerment: A feminist analysis of young adult sports fiction. *Sociology of Sport Journal, 15*(3), 231–262.

Kane, M. J., & Buysse, J. A. (2005). Intercollegiate media guides as contested terrain: A longitudinal analysis. *Sociology of Sport Journal, 22*(2), 214–238.

Kane, M. J., & Lenskyj, H. (1998). Media treatment of female athletes: Issues of gender and sexualities. In L. Wenner (Ed.), *MediaSport: Cultural sensibilities and sport in the media age* (pp. 186–201). London: Routledge.

Kann, L. (1997, June). Youth risk behavior survey. *Medicine & Science in Sports & Exercise, 29*(6), S201–S205.

Karr, A. F., & Sanil, A. P. (2005, February). Title IX data collection: Technical Manual for developing the user's guide. Technical Report Number 150. Research Triangle Park, NC: National Institute of Statistical Services.

Keinman, I. (1999). Issues. *Journal of Physical Education, 70*(1), 11–12.

Kellner, D. (1995). *Media culture.* London: Routledge & Kegan Paul.

Kerber, L. K., & DeHart, J. S. (1995). *Women's America: Refocusing the past.* New York: Oxford University Press.

Kluger, J. (2005, June 6). Couch potatoes, arise! *Time, 165*(23), 52–54.

Kocher, L. (2005). 1972: "You can't play because you're a girl"; 2004: "You can't play because you're a boy." In R. Simon (Ed.)., *Sporting equality: Title IX thirty years later*, (pp. 147–164). Piscataway, NJ: Transaction Publishers.

Koplan, J. P., Liverman, C. T., & Kraak, V. A. (2004). *Preventing childhood obesity: Health in the balance.* Washington, DC: Institute of Medicine. Retrieved February 7, 2007 from http://www.iom.edu/report.asp?id=22596.

Krane, V. (1997). Homonegativism experienced by lesbian collegiate athletes. *Women in Sport and Physical Activity Journal, 6*(2), 141–163.

Kruger, J., Ham, S. A., Kohl, H. W., & Sapkota, S. (2004, August 27). Physical activity Among Asians and Native Hawaiian or Other Pacific Islander—50 States and the District of Columbia, 2001–2003. *Morbidity and Morality Weekly Report, 53*(33), 756–761.

Kulinna, P. H., Martin, J., Lai, Q., Kliber, A., & Reed, B. (2003, April). Student physical activity patterns: grade, gender, and activity influences. *Journal of Teaching in Physical Education, 22*(3), 298–310.

Lerner, P. (2000, Spring). Winners? The girls soccer players. Losers? The rest of the kids. *Association for Gender Equity Leadership in Education (AGELE) Newsletter.* Ann Arbor, MI: AGELE.

Li, W., Harrison, L., & Solomon, M. (2004). College students' implicit theories of ability in sports: Race and gender differences. *Journal of Sport Behavior, 27*(3), 291–304.

Lirgg, C. D. (1993, September). Effects of same-sex versus coeducational physical education on the self-perceptions of middle and high school students. *Research Quarterly for Exercise and Sport, 64*(3), 324–335.

Lirgg, C. D., & Feltz, D. L. (1989). Female self-confidence in sport: Myth, realities, and enhancement strategies. *Journal of Physical Education, Recreation, and Dance, 60*(3), 49–54.

Lowery, R., Brener, N., Lee, S., Epping, J., Fulton, J., & Eaton, E. (2004). Participation in high school physical education—United States, 1991–2003. Atlanta, GA: Centers for Disease Control & Prevention. Retrieved February 4, 2007 from http://www.cdc.gov/mmwr/preview/mmwrhtml/mm5336a5.htm.

Lumpkin, A., & Williams, L. (1991). An analysis of *Sports Illustrated* feature articles, 1954–1987. *Sociology of Sport Journal, 8*, 16–32.

Lusetich, R. (1999, July 17). Girls take a giant step for womankind. *The Weekend Australian*, 53.

Macy, S. (1993). *A whole new ball game: the story of an all-American girls professional baseball league.* New York: Henry Holt.

Manning, J. F. (2005, March 17). Additional clarification of intercollegiate athletics policy: Three-part test—Part Three. Issued by the Office for Civil Rights, United States Department of Education. Retrieved February 7, 2007, from http://www.ed.gov/about/offices/list/ocr/docs/title9guidanceadditonal.html

Marsh, H. W. (1993). The effects of participation in sport during the last two years of high school. *Sociology of Sport Journal, 10*, 18–43.

Martin, J., Kelley, B., & Dias, C. (1999). Stress and burnout in female high school athletic directors. *Women in Sport & Physical Activity Journal, 8*(1), 101.

McKenzie, T. L., Prochaska, J. J., Sallis, J. F., & LaMaster, K. J. (2004). Coeducational and single-sex physical education in middle schools: Impact on physical activity. *Research Quarterly for Exercise and Sport, 75*(4), 446–449.

Melnick, M. J., Miller, K. E., Sabo, D., Farrell, M. P., & Barnes, G. M. (2001). Tobacco use among high school athletes and nonathletes: Results of the 1997 Youth Risk Behavior Survey. *Adolescence, 36*, 727–747.

Mendelson, J. (2003). Sexual harassment in intercollegiate athletics by male coaches of female athletes: What it is, what it means for the future, and what the NCAA should do. *Cardozo Women's Law Journal, 9*, 597–626.

Messner, M. (1988). Sports and male domination: The female athlete as contested ideological terrain. *Sport Sociology Journal, 5*(3), 197–211.

———. (2000). Barbie Dolls vs. Sea Monsters: Children constructing gender. *Gender & Society, 14*, 765–784.

———. (2002). *Taking the field: Women and men in sports.* Minneapolis: University of Minnesota Press.

Miller, E. (2002). *Making her mark: First and milestones in women's sports.* Chicago: Contemporary Books.

Miller, K. E., Sabo, D. F., Melnick, M. J., Farrell, M. P., & Barnes, G. M. (2000). *The Women's sports foundation report: Health risks and the teen athlete.* East Meadow, NY: Women's sports foundation.

Morago, G. (2004, August 19). The Olympian bods: Bikinis, tight uniforms, risqué cheerleaders and sexual dimension to the 2004 games. *Hartford Courant*, D1.

Morantz, C., & Torrey, B. (2004, January 14). CDC report on physical activity among children. *American Family Physician, 69*(2), 440.

Napper-Owen, G. E. (1994). Equality in the elementary gymnasium. *Strategies: A Journal for Physical and Sport Education, 8*(3), 23–26.

National Coalition for Women and Girls in Education (NCWGE). (2002, August). Title IX Athletics Policies: Issues and data for education decision makers.

National Collegiate Athletic Association (2005). NCAA leadership groups urge Department of Education to rescind additional clarification for Title IX and maintain 1996 Clarification. Press release. Retrieved February 4, 2007 at http://www.ncaa.org/wps/portal/legacysiteviewer?CONTENT_URL=http://www2.ncaa.org/portal/media_and_events/press_room/2005/april/20050428_titleix_resolution.html

National Federation of State High Schools Association. (2005). *Participation in high school sport: 2004–2005.* Retrieved November 15, 2005, from http://www.nfhs.org. On file with the author.

National Women's Law Center. (2005, March 21). Bush Administration weakens Title IX. Press release. Retrieved February 4, 2007 from http://www.nwlc.org/details.cfm?id=2198&section=newsroom

Nelson, M. B. (1998). Introduction: Who we might become. In L. Smith (Ed.) *Nike is a goddess: The history of women in sports* (pp. ix–xix). New York: Atlantic Monthly Press.

Nicoloff, G., & Schwenk, T. S. (1995). Using exercise to ward off depression. *Physician Sports Medicine, 23*(9), 44–58.

Nilges, L. M. (1998). I thought only fairy tales had supernatural powers: A radical feminist analysis of Title IX in physical education. *Journal of Teaching Physical Education, 17*, 172–194.

Oglesby, C. (1990). Epilogue. In M. A. Messner & D. Sabo (Eds.). *Sport, men, and the gender order* (pp. 241–246). Champaign, IL: Human Kinetics Publishers.

Oglesby, C., & Sabo, D. (1996, March). Sexual harassment and policy making. *Journal of Physical Education, Recreation & Dance, 67*(3), 4–6.

Osborne, K., Bauer, A., & Sutliff, M. (2002, Spring). Middle school students' perceptions of coed versus non-coed physical education, *Physical Educator, 59*(2), 83–90.

Osborne, B., & Duffy, C. (2005). Title IX, sexual harassment and policies at NCAA Division IA athletics departments. *Journal of Legal Aspects of Sport,* 59–95.

Page, R. M., & Tucker, L. A. (1994). Psychosocial discomfort and exercise frequency: An epidemiological study of adolescents. *Adolescence, 29*(113), 183–191.

Parks, J. B., & Roberton, M. A. (1999, April). *Letterman or letterwinner? Sportsmanship or sporting behavior?* Why responsible teachers encourage non-sexist language. Paper presented at the annual convention of the American Alliance for Health, Physical Education, Recreation, and Dance, Boston, MA.

Pate, R. R., Trost, S. G., Levin, S., & Dowda, M. (2000). Sports participation and health-related behaviors among U.S. youth. *Archives of Pediatric and Adolescent Medicine, 154,* 904–911.

Pearl, N. H., & Brown, H. E. (1938). *Health by stunts.* New York: The Macmillan Company.

Pennington, B. (2004, June 29). Title IX trickles down to girls in Generation Z. *The New York Times,* D1.

———. (2005, May 9). Playing too hard? *The New York Times,* 28.

Petlichkoff, L. M. (1996). The drop-out dilemma in youth sports. In Bar-Or, O. (Ed). *The child and adolescent athlete* (pp. 418–430). Blackwell Scientific Publications.

Pinarski, A. (2000, Spring). When coaches 'cross the line': Hostile athletic environment sexual harassment. *Rutgers Law Review, 52,* 911–960.

Political Transcript Wire (2005, June 15). U.S. Representative Thomas M. Davis III (R-VA) holds hearing on steroid use in young women.

Ransdell, L. B. (2005). *Ensuring the health of active and athletic girls and women.* Reston, VA: National Association for Girls and Women in Sport.

Ransdell, L. B., & Wells, C. L. (1999). Sex differences in athletic performance. *Women in Sport & Physical Activity Journal, 8,* 55–81.

Rhoads, S. (2004, July 30). Boys' "need" for sports; the fracturing ecosystem. *The Chronicle of Higher Education, 50*(47), B4.

Robbins, D. (2001, April 22). We trust our kids to them every day, but a criminal investigation reveals the relationship between secondary school coaches and students is rife with abuse: Out of bounds. *Houston Chronicle,* p. 1.

Roberts, S. (2005). *A necessary spectacle: Billie Jean King, Bobby Riggs, and the tennis match that leveled the game.* New York: Crown Publishing Group.

Robinson, M. J., Tedrick, R., & Carpenter, J. R. (2001, Winter). Job satisfaction of NCAA Division III athletic directors: A descriptive analysis and an examination of gender differences. *International Sports Journal, 5*(1), 25–32.

Rogge, J. (2004). *Athens 2004 marketing report.* Lausanne, Switzerland: International Olympic Committee.

Ronspies, S. M., & Messerole, M. J. (2005, Winter). Spicing up motor skill performances—for all! (PE Central Challenge). *Palaestra, 21*(1), 26–30.

Ryan, S., Fleming, D., & Maina, M. (2003, Spring). *Physical Educator, 60*(2), 28–43.

Ruder, K. (1995). Conference review: Women's Institute on Sport and Education Foundation. *Women in Sport and Physical Activity Journal, 3*(2), 83.

Sabo, D., & Grant, C. H. B. (2005, June). *Limitation of the Department of Education's online survey method for measuring athletic interest and ability on U.S.A. campuses.* Buffalo, NY: Center for Research on Physical Activity, Sport, & Health, D'Youville College.

Sabo, D., & Jansen, S. C. (1998). Prometheus unbound: Constructions of masculinity in sports media. In L. A. Wenner (Ed.), *MediaSport: Cultural sensibilities and sport in the media age* (pp. 202–217). Boston: Routledge Kegan Paul.

Sabo, D., Miller, K. E., Melnick, M. J., Farrell, M. P., & Barnes, G. M. (2004). High school athletic participation and adolescent suicide: A nationwide study. *International Review for the Sociology of Sport,* 103–112.

Sack, A. L., & Staurowsky, E. J. (1998). *College athletes for hire: The evolution and legacy of the NCAA amateur myth.* Westport, CT: Praeger Press.

Sadker, D., & Sadker, M. (1994). *Failing at fairness: How America's schools cheat girls.* New York: MacMillan.

Sagas, M., Paetzold, R., & Ashley, F. (2005, Spring). Relational demography in coaching dyads. *Physical Educator, 62*(2), 103–112.

Sailer, S., & Seiler, S. (1997a, December 31). Track & battlefield. *National Review.*

Samuels, J., & Galles, K. (2003, Winter). In defense of Title IX: Why current policies are required to ensure equality of opportunity. *Marquette Sports Law Review, 14*(1), 11–48.

Satina, B., Solmon, M. A., Cothran, D. J., Loftus, S. J., & Stockin-Davidson, K. (1998, April). *Patriarchal consciousness: Middle school students' and teachers' perceptives of motivational practices.* Paper presented at the annual meeting of the American Education Research Association, San Diego, CA.

Schlafly, A. L. (2004). Brief of amicus curiae Eagle Forum Education & Legal Fund in support of respondent. *Roderick Jackson v. Birmingham Board of Education.*

Schultz, J. (2004). Discipline and push-up: Female bodies, femininity, and sexuality in popular representations of sports bras. *Sociology of Sport Journal, 21*(2), 185–205.

Seiler, S., & Sailer, S. (1997, May–June). The gender gap: Elite women are running further behind. *Sportscience News.* Retrieved February 7, 2007, from http://www.sportsci.org/news/news9705/gengap.html.

Severin, L., & Wyer, M. (2000, fall). The science and politics of the search for sex differences: editorial. *NWSA Journal, 12,* vii–xvi.

Shipley, A. (2004, April 22). Female athletes continue to gain ground: Team sports, Title IX help number of women on U.S. Olympic team catch up to men, but problems still exist. *Washington Post,* D01.

Singleton, E. (2003). Rules? Relationships? A feminist analysis of competition and fair play in physical education. *Quest, 55,* 193–209.

Soderlund, K. (2005, December 18). Experts debate merits of same-sex gym classes. *The Journal Gazette,* (p. 92).

Sparling, P. (1980). A meta-analysis of studies comparing maximal oxygen uptake in men and women. *Research Quarterly in Exercise and Sport, 51,* 542–552.

Sparling, P. B., O'Donnell, E. M., & Snow, T. K. (1998). The gender difference in distance running performance has plateaued: an analysis of world rankings from *Medicine and Science in Sports and Exercise, 30,* 1725–1729.

Sprague, J., & Engstrom, D. (2000). Gender discrimination in middle school physical education programs. *Pennsylvania Journal of Health, Physical Education, Recreation, and Dance, 70*(1), 43–45.

Stahura, K. A., & Greenwood, M. (2002). Sex of head coach as a function of sport type prestige and institutional structure. *Applied Research in Coaching and Athletics Annual, 17,* 1–25.

Stahura, K. A., Greenwood, M., & Dobbs, M. E. (2003). Additional insights into occupational employment trends within women's intercollegiate athletics: Ranked program prestige. *Applied Research in Coaching and Athletics Annual, 18,* 1–36.

Staurowsky, E. J. (2003, February 14). The Title IX Commission's flawed lineup. *The Chronicle of Higher Education,* B20.

———. (2004). *On behalf of our minor daughters: Reflections on Title IX in the 21st century.* Presentation at the Marquette University National Sports Law Institute Conference, Milwaukee, WI.

———. (2005). Title IX manifesta: Reflections on the Commission on Opportunity in Athletics. In R. Simon (Ed.) (2005), *Sporting equal-*

ity: Title IX thirty years later (pp. 70–78). New Brunswick, NJ: Transaction Publishers.

Steward, M. J., & Corbin, C. B. (1989). Self-confidence of young girls in physical activity and sport. *Runner, 27*(4). 38–41

Sturm, T. J. (2003). *Gender differences in career goals of intercollegiate athletes and in perceptions of athletes and coaches about the decline in the percentage of female coaches.* Unpublished doctoral dissertation. Eugene, OR: Kinesiology Publications, University of Oregon. Retrieved February 7, 2007, from http://kinpubs.uoregon.edu/

Suggs, W. (2005a). *A place on the team: The triumph and tragedy of Title IX.* Princeton, NJ: Princeton University Press.

———. (2005b, January 14). Supporters of men's sports sue congressional agency, accusing it of anti-male bias. *The Chronicle of Higher Education*, A30.

Tallman, A. J. (1970). *Effects of coeducational and segregated classes upon selected outcomes of college physical education courses.* Unpublished doctoral dissertation. New York: New York University.

Tappe M. K., Duda J. L., & Ehmwald P. M. (1989). Perceived barriers to exercise among adolescents. *Journal of School Health, 59*(4), 153–155.

Tatem, A. J., Guerra, C. A., Atkinson, P. M., & Hay, S. I. (2004). Athletics: Momentous sprint at the 2156 Olympics?. *Nature, 431*, 525.

Tergerson, J. L., & King, K. A. (2002, November). Do perceived cues, benefits, and barriers to physical activity differ between male and female adolescents? *The Journal of School Health, 72*(9), 374–381.

Thompson, A. M., Baxter-Jones, A. D. G., Mirwald, R. L., & Bailey, D. A. (2003). Comparison of physical activity in male and female children: does maturation matter? *Medicine and Science in Sports and Exercise, 35*, 1684–1690.

Thorne, B. (1993). *Gender play: Boys and girls in school.* New Brunswick: Rutgers University Press.

Toftegaard, N. (2001). The forbidden zone: intimacy, sexual relations, and misconduct in the relationship between coaches and athletes. *International Review for the Sociology of Sport, 36*(2), 165–182.

Topkin, M. (2004, August 25). Provacative poses divide U.S. women. *St. Petersburg Times*, 9C.

Treanor, L., Graber, K., Housner, L., & Wiegand, R. (1998). Middle school students' perceptions of coeducational and same-sex physical education classes. *Journal of Teaching in Physical Education, 18*, 43–55.

Unger, J. B., Reynolds, K., Shakib, S., & Spruijt-Metz, D. (2004, December). Acculturation, physical activity, and fast-food consumption among Asian-American and Hispanic adolescents. *Journal of Community Health, 29*(6), 467.

U.S. Department of Education. (2001, January). *Revised sexual harassment guidelines: Harassment of students by employees, other students, or third parties.* Retrieved February 4, 2007, from http://www.ed.gov/about/offices/list/ocr/docs/shguide.html

——— (2005, October 7). Trends in leisure- time physical inactivity by age, sex, and race/ethnicity–United States, 1994–2004. *Morbidity and Mortality Weekly Report, 54*(39), 991–994. Retrieved February 5, 2007, from http://www.cdc.gov/mmwr/preview/mmwrhtml/mm5439a5.htm.

Vincent, J. (2004). Game, sex, and match: The construction of gender in British newspaper coverage of the 2000 Wimbledon championships. *Sociology of Sport Journal, 21*(4), 435–456.

Volkwein, K., Schnell, F., Sherwood, D., & Livezey, A. (1997). Sexual harassment in sports: Perceptions and experiences of American female student-athletes. *International Review for the Sociology of Sport, 23*(3), 283–295.

Volkwein-Caplan, K., Schnell, F., Devlin, S., Mitchell, M., & Sutera, J. (2002). Sexual Harassment of women in athletics & academia. In C. Breckenridge & K. Fasting (Ed.). *Sexual harassment and abuse in sport: International research and policy perspectives* (pp. 69–82). London: Whiting and Birch, Ltd.

Wann, D., Schrader, M., Allison, J., & McGeorge, K. (1998). The inequitable newspaper coverage of men's and women's athletics at small, medium, and large universities. *Journal of Sport & Social Issues, 22*, 79–87.

Welch, M. (1996). Teacher education and the neglected diversity: Preparing educators to teach students with disabilities. *Journal of Teacher Education, 47*, 355–366.

Wenner, L. A. (Ed.). (1998). *MediaSport: Cultural sensibilities and sport in the media age.* London: Routledge & Kegan Paul.

Weiner, J. (2004, August 22). Women's wrestling: Fifty women from 21 nations will compete in four weight classes. *Minneapolis Star Tribune*, 10.

Weir, T. (2004, 16 December). "New PE" objective: Get kids in shape. *USA Today*, 1A.

Werthner, P. (2005, May). Making the case: coaching as a viable career path for women. *Canadian Journal for Women in Coaching, 5*(3), 1–9.

Whipp, B., & Ward, S. A. (1992). Will women soon outrun men? *Nature, 355*, 25.

Williamson, K. M. (1993, October). Is your inequity showing? Ideas and strategies for creating a more equitable learning environment. *JOPERD—The journal of physical education, recreation & dance, 64*(8), 15–23

Wilmore, J., & Costill, D. L. (2004). *Physiology of sport and exercise*, 3rd ed. Champaign, IL: Human Kinetics Publishers.

Women's Sports Foundation. (2005). *Increasing youth sports & physical activity participation: A Women's Sports Foundation Public Policy Guide.*

Worrell, B. (2004, October). Hospitals are creating sport medicine centers. *Health Care Strategic Management Newsletter, 22*(10), 1, 16.

Wright, J., & King, R. C. (1991). "I say what you mean" said Alice: An analysis of gendered discourses in physical education. *Journal of Teaching in Physical Education, 10*, 210–225.

Wughalter, E. H. (2002). Transgressions and transcendence: Surpassing disciplinary boundaries. *Quest, 54*, 242–251.

Zimbalist, A. (2005). What to do about Title IX? In R. Simon (Ed.)., *Sporting equality: Title IX thirty years later* (pp. 55–60). Piscataway, NJ: Transaction Press.

·19·

GENDER EQUITY IN FORMAL
SEXUALITY EDUCATION

John DeLamater

INTRODUCTION

This chapter examines gender and gender equity issues in formal sexuality education and considers the adequacy of formal programs from several vantage points. I begin with definitions of terms that are central to the analysis. Next, attention turns to the current state of sexuality education. I will, in turn, consider formal education in K–12 schools, colleges and universities, and medical schools; the reader will note that there is more material available regarding the first than about the second or third. With this survey as background, I will discuss several gender equity issues; this section will include discussion of programs designed to address these issues. The chapter ends with conclusions and recommendations.

DEFINITIONS

To discuss formal sexuality education programs, we need a way of classifying or defining extant programs. To be sure, there are no universally accepted definitions. The following terms are widely used:

• *Sexuality education*. The lifelong process of acquiring information about sexual behavior, and of forming attitudes, beliefs, and values about identity, relationships, and intimacy (SIECUS, 1999). Notice that this broad definition includes considerations of sexual health and quality of interpersonal relationships. A program of this type for girls ages 9–17, *Preventing Adolescent Pregnancy* by Girls Incorporated (1991), consists of four age-appropriate components. Most of the available curricula are much more narrowly focused.

• *Theoretically based (comprehensive) sexuality education*. Programs that include information about sexual behavior, sexual relationships, and sexual health; they are based on em-

pirically tested theories of health promotion. These programs often teach abstinence as the best method for preventing unwanted pregnancy and sexually transmitted infections (STIs) but also provide information about condoms and contraception (Advocates for Youth, 2006). Two of the major curricula of this type are Postponing Sexual Involvement (middle school–age youth), and Reducing the Risk (high school–age youth). Such programs typically include discussion of social pressures to engage in sexual intimacy and resistance techniques. Implementation of these programs varies greatly, ranging from 10 sessions presented in a single year or grade to a more extensive program presented in multiple years or grades.

• *Abstinence plus programs*. Promote abstinence as the preferred option for adolescents but permit discussion of contraception as an effective means of reducing the risk of unwanted pregnancy and disease. These curricula may include discussion of sexual behavior, sexual relationships, and sexual health; they may be based on empirically tested theories of health promotion. Implementation of these programs also varies greatly, as indicated above.

• *Abstinence only programs*. Promote abstinence from sexual intimacy as the sole morally correct means of preventing pregnancy and STIs for persons who are not heterosexually married (includes *abstinence-only-until-marriage*). Such programs do not present positive information about condoms and contraceptives but may highlight their failure. One of the major curricula of this type is Sex Respect, which is known for the slogans that are taught as part of the program, such as "Pet your dog, not your date." These curricula often focus on negative or problematic aspects of sexual intimacy. According to the literature evaluating these programs (e.g., Minnesota Department of Health, nd), some involve 5 sessions, others 12, and others meet weekly for an academic year. Lessons may be classroom-based during the school day or after school, presented in a community services setting, or presented in a faith-based community.

- *HIV/AIDS risk education.* Refers to educational programs sharply focused on disease prevention. These curricula challenge myths about transmission and curability; they encourage delay of intercourse and condom use if sexually active. Such programs are presented in six to eight sessions. Examples include Act Smart and Choosing Health.

These programs are implemented in a variety of settings including: schools as part of a general education curriculum; afterschool programs that meet in schools, churches, community centers; and other similar settings. Both state and federal evaluations point out that the students who typically enroll in the nonclassroom programs are volunteers and therefore may be predisposed to be positively influenced by the program in which they enroll. Many nonclassroom programs are presented by volunteer teachers from the community or employees of the contractor who provides the programming. Wherever they are presented, the effectiveness of these programs depends on the training and attitudes of the instructors (de Gaston, Jensen, Weed, & Tanas, 1994).

THE CURRENT STATE OF SEXUALITY EDUCATION: K–12

How widely are these programs used in the United States? Landry, Kaeser, and Richards (1999) mailed a questionnaire to a representative sample of 1,224 U.S. school districts in 1998; 825 completed surveys were returned. Sixty-nine percent of the districts reported having a district-wide policy. Of those, 14% had a policy requiring comprehensive education. An additional 51% required an abstinence-plus program; 35% (or 23% of all districts responding) required an abstinence-only curriculum. Based on the size of the reporting districts, Landry and colleagues estimated that, of all children in grades six and higher, only 9% were in a district requiring comprehensive sex education; 45% were in districts with an abstinence-plus policy, 32% in districts requiring abstinence-only, and 14% in districts with no policy.

According to the Alan Guttmacher Institute (2006), 21 states and the District of Columbia require public schools to teach sex education. Twenty-one states, including some that do not require sex education, require that abstinence be stressed; 14 states and the District of Columbia require that programs include contraception education. Thirty-seven states and the District of Columbia require that STI/HIV education be provided, and 26 of these require that abstinence be stressed.

The data on district policies and state laws suggests that the content of sex education in K–12 schools varies a great deal. It appears that a minority of young women and men get comprehensive sex education in their public schools. Perhaps a third receives abstinence-only instruction. The most common approach, based on the data presented above, seems to be narrowly focused STI/HIV prevention education.

That sex education programs focus on the risks and dangers of sexual activity is not new. This emphasis has been present since sex education programs began in the early 20th century (Rury, 1992). The first programs grew out of fear over the spread of sexually transmitted diseases, for which there was no cure at the time. In addition, some supporters saw sex education as the way to combat the evils of promiscuity and prostitution. Classes were often taught separately to girls and boys, which allowed educators to discuss sexuality in very different terms for men and women. Thus, sex education did not challenge traditional views of gender and gendered views of sexuality, and probably reified them. These characteristics profoundly influenced the content and process of sex education.

In the past 25 years a political battle has developed over sex education. A group allied with conservative Christian churches, the Republican Party, and conservative think tanks such as the Heritage Foundation have increasingly lobbied against theoretically based (comprehensive) programs. They claim that giving information to young people about sexual intercourse, birth control to prevent unwanted pregnancy, and ways to protect themselves against STIs encourages them to engage in sexual intercourse. They argue that comprehensive programs have not been effective.

EVALUATING EFFECTIVENESS

In the context of this debate, how is effectiveness defined? To evaluate sexuality education programs, we have to establish criteria for evaluation. At the level of social policy, it is fair to say that concern about, and support for, sexuality education in the schools grows out of the recognition of two major public health problems: teen pregnancy and STIs. In 1999, there were 856,300 pregnancies involving women under age 20 in the United States (Henshaw, 2003). A significant number are terminated by abortion; Henshaw estimates that in 1999, 249,660 (29%) were terminated by abortion, accounting for 20% of the abortions in the United States. Obviously, preventing these pregnancies would reduce the number of abortions. If carried to term, many of these babies have low birth weight and suffer from health problems; this may reflect the mothers' health and lack of access to prenatal care. Most of the mothers are single and may lack social and economic resources necessary for optimal child development.

Sexually transmitted infections are epidemic in the United States. It is estimated that there are 3 million new cases of chlamydia, 5.5 million cases of HPV/genital warts, and 650,000 new cases of gonorrhea every year (CDC, 2000). The numbers of reported cases are much smaller; in 2003 there were 877,478 cases of chlamydia, 34,270 cases of syphilis, and 335,104 new cases of gonorrhea (National Center for Health Statistics, 2005). The discrepancy reflects the fact that many cases are not diagnosed or reported. These STIs have economic and emotional costs and are probably the leading cause of infertility among both men and women.

In this context, there is overwhelming public support for sexuality education programs in schools. A 1999 poll by Hickman-Brown based on interviews with a nationally representative sample of 1,050 adults found that 68% supported comprehensive sexuality education in grades 9 and 10, and at least 79% supported it in grades 11 and 12 (SIECUS, 1999). According to a 1999 survey conducted for the Kaiser Family Foundation (2000), 82% of parents of children under 18 supported comprehensive programs. Thus, there is no battle in the realm of public opinion over what should be taught in sex education programs. Note also the disconnect between public opinion and the policies of K–12 school districts reviewed earlier.

Considering these problems, it is appropriate to use some or all of five criteria to evaluate the effectiveness of sex education programs:

1. Delayed initiation of sex
2. Decreased frequency of intercourse
3. Decreased number of partners
4. Increased use of condoms if sexually active
5. Increased use of contraception if sexually active

These criteria have been employed in most of the sex-ed evaluation research to date. The second and fifth criteria presume heterosexual vaginal intercourse; to the extent that these criteria are the focus of educational programs, such programs do not speak to the concerns of lesbian, gay, bisexual, transgender, or questioning (LGBTQ) youth. The other criteria can, in principle, be applied to all forms of partnered activity.

WHAT WORKS?

There have been numerous studies of the effects of various types of formal sexuality education programs. These studies have been conducted in a variety of ways for the past 25 years. Kirby (2001, 2002) has reviewed this literature several times in the past 10 years. Many of the studies are methodologically weak. We are most interested in the results of those studies that meet the following rigorous methodological standards:

• Random assignment of youth or groups to condition, to counter "volunteer" effects
• Combined sample of at least 500, to achieve large enough subsamples to provide sufficient power for statistical analyses of the data
• Long-term follow-up, at least 12 to 18 months
• Measurement of pregnancy rates
• Measurement of sexual behavior, instead of attitudes or intention
• Proper statistical analyses
• Publication of results to allow assessment by peer review.

Based on a review of studies that meet these criteria (displayed in Table 19.1, column 1) there is no evidence that comprehensive sexuality education programs hasten the onset of intercourse, increase the frequency of sex or number of partners, or decrease use of condoms or contraceptives (Kirby, 2001). Thus, one of the major criticisms of comprehensive sexuality education programs by its opponents is not supported by empirical data.

Supporters of abstinence-only sexuality education programs argue that youth need to be encouraged to abstain from sex, and that this can be done by withholding information about sexuality, birth control, and STI prevention, as well as by inoculating youth through the use of slogans against pressure to be sexual

TABLE 19.1   The Number of Programs with Effects on Sexual and Contraceptive Behaviors by Type of Program

	Abstinence-Only Programs	Sexuality Education Programs	HIV Education Programs	Sum of Sexuality and HIV Education Programs
Initiation of Sex				
Delayed initiation	0	6	3	9
Had no significant impact	3	12	6	18
Hastened initiation	0	1	0	1
Total Number of Programs	3	19	9	28
Frequency of Sex				
Decreased frequency	0	2	3	5
Had no significant impact	2	8	5	13
Increased frequency	0	1	0	1
Total Number of Programs	2	11	8	19
Number of Sexual Partners				
Decreased number	0	0	3	3
Had no significant impact	1	4	3	7
Increased number	0	0	0	0
Total Number of Programs	1	4	6	10
Use of Condoms				
Increased use	0	2	8	10
Had no significant impact	1	5	3	8
Decreased use	0	0	0	0
Total Number of Programs	1	7	11	18
Use of Contraception				
Increased use	0	4	0	4
Had no significant impact	1	7	0	7
Decreased use	0	0	0	0
Total Number of Programs	1	11	0	11

from peers, mass media, and culture. These people assert that abstinence-only programs will be effective as measured by the criteria discussed above and will lead unmarried persons to delay the onset of intercourse. Obviously, if people don't engage in intercourse, there is no need to decrease the frequency of sex, reduce the number of partners, or increase condom and birth control use.

Again, Kirby reviewed this literature. Looking at the results of those studies that meet rigorous methodological standards displayed in Table 19.1, columns 2, 3, and 4, there is no evidence that abstinence-only educational programs delay the initiation of sexual intercourse and no evidence that they are effective on the other four criteria (Kirby 2002). In short, there is no scientific evidence that abstinence-only sex education programs work.

FEDERAL SUPPORT FOR ABSTINENCE-ONLY PROGRAMS

The debate about what kind of sex education should be taught is complicated by the involvement of the federal government in selectively funding some types of programs and not others. There are two key federal programs.

The national Personal Responsibility and Work Opportunity Act of 1996 (the so-called Welfare Reform bill) provided the states $250 million over a five-year period to support abstinence-only programs. This provision is set out in Title V of the Social Security Act. States are required to match $3 for every $4 in federal funding they receive. Recipients of these funds must agree not to provide any information that is inconsistent with the abstinence-until-marriage message. It is estimated that in 1998–2003, one half billion dollars in state and federal funds were appropriated to support the abstinence-only provision of Title V (Advocates for Youth, 2005).

Federal Definition of "Abstinence-only" Programs
(Title V Section 510 (b)(2)(A-H)

A. Have as its exclusive purpose teaching the social, psychological, and health gains to be realized by abstaining from sexual activity.

B. Teach abstinence from sexual activity outside marriage as the expected standard for all school-age children.

C. Teach that abstinence from sexual activity is the only certain way to avoid out-of-wedlock pregnancy, sexually transmitted diseases, and other associated health problems.

D. Teach that a mutually faithful, monogamous relationship in the context of marriage is the expected standard of sexual activity.

E. Teach that sexual activity outside the context of marriage is likely to have harmful psychological and physical effects.

F. Teach that bearing children out-of-wedlock is likely to have harmful consequences for the child, the child's parents, and society.

G. Teach young people how to reject sexual advances and how alcohol and drug use increases vulnerability to sexual advances.

H. Teach the importance of attaining self-sufficiency before engaging in sexual activity.

States receiving federal abstinence eduction funds must utilize the funds to support programming that meets these criteria. Typically, the federal funds are administered by state departments of health, and often subcontracted to public agencies, faith-based groups, and other contractors who provide the programming. There is wide variation both within and between states in the programming provided. Popular curricula that meet the Title V, Sec. 10 criteria include Education Now Babies Later (ENABL), Why am I tempted? (WAIT), and Family Accountability Communicating Teen Sexuality (FACTS; Advocates for Youth, 2005). Initially, every state received funds except California; California terminated its abstinence-only program in 1996 after an evaluation showed that it was not effective.

In 2001, a separate program, Community-Based Abstinence Education/Special Programs of National and Regional Significance (CBAE/SPRANS), was created to provide funds directly to individual public and private entities that present abstinence-only programming. This program is operated by the Administration for Children and Families. A dramatic increase in funding for abstinence-only programming occurred from 2002 to 2005, with funds allocated by CBAE/SPRANS increasing from $20 million in 2001 to $104 million in 2005 (American Foundation for AIDS Research, 2005).

Title V, Section 10 includes a provision requiring an evaluation of the programs funded by it. Initially, this evaluation was carried out by a technical working group, under the Assistant Secretary for Planning and Evaluation of the U.S. Department of Health and Human Services. The first report (2002) concluded that there is no evidence that abstinence-only education is effective. In 2005, a team from Mathematica Policy Research Inc. (Maynard et al, 2005) released the results of a detailed evaluation of the first-year impact of four programs funded under Title V, Section 10. The report was unable to include behavioral data. The four programs created more positive attitudes toward abstinence and increased perceptions of risks of nonmarital sex; they did not impact self-concept, refusal skills, communication with parents, or perceptions of peer pressure to have sex (Maynard et al., 2005). Given the restricted content of abstinence-only curricula, discussed above, these results are not surprising.

As we entered the seventh year of funding for abstinence-only programs, evaluations undertaken by individual states became available. These include evaluations conducted in Minnesota (Minnesota Department of Health, nd), Pennsylvania (Smith, Dariotis, & Potter, 2003), and Texas (Goodson et al., 2004). Advocates for Youth has obtained evaluation results for Arizona, Florida, Iowa, Maryland, Missouri, Nebraska, Oregon, and Washington. They summarized the results as follows:

Evaluation of these 11 programs showed few short-term benefits and no lasting positive impact. A few programs showed mild success at improving attitudes and intentions to abstain. No program was able to demonstrate a positive impact on sexual behavior over time. (Advocates for Youth, 2005, p. 2)

Abstinence-only education programs funded by state and federal dollars have not been shown to delay onset of intercourse, reduce frequency of intercourse, reduce number of partners, or prevent teen pregnancy through increased use of contraception. These programs do not accomplish the goals their supporters claim they accomplish. Based on this evidence and other considerations, Pennsylvania and Maine have joined California in refusing federal abstinence-only funds, and the Rhode Island Department of Education has banned the use of curricula by Heritage of Rhode Island.

Abstinence-only curricula are not effective because they do not provide detailed information about sexual anatomy, sexual physiology, contraception, condoms, and other methods of preventing STIs, nor do they teach teens the skills they need to make healthy decisions and choices with regard to sexuality. Worse, these programs contain misinformation and lies. For example:

- Condoms provide no proven reduction in protection against chlamydia, the most common bacterial STD (*Choosing the Best PATH*, Leader Guide, p. 18).
- AIDS can be transmitted by skin-to-skin contact (*Reasonable Reasons to Wait*, Teacher's Guide, Unit 5, p. 19).

These programs also promote gender stereotypes as facts. For example:

- "Girls need to be aware they may be able to tell when a kiss is leading to something else. The girl may need to put the brakes on first in order to help the boy." (*Reasonable Reasons to Wait*, Student Workbook, p. 96).
- "A guy who wants to respect girls is distracted by sexy clothes and remembers her for one thing. Is it fair that guys are turned on by their senses and women by their hearts?" (*Sex Respect*, Student Workbook, p. 94) (SIECUS, 2005).

The first quote reinforces the stereotypic belief that it is the girl's responsibility to manage the couple's sexual behavior. The second quote suggests that male and female sexual arousal are governed by different processes.

Congressman Henry Waxman directed the Special Investigations Division of the House Committee on Government Reform to assess federally funded abstinence-only programs. According to the report, more than 80% of the abstinence-only curricula, used by over two-thirds of SPRANS grantees in 2003, contain false, misleading, or distorted information about reproductive heath. Specifically the report finds:

- Abstinence-only curricula contain false information about the risks of abortion.
- Abstinence-only curricula blur religion and science.
- Abstinence-only curricula treat stereotypes about girls and boys as scientific fact.
- Abstinence-only curricula contain scientific errors. (Committee on Government Reform, 2004).

CHARACTERISTICS OF EFFECTIVE PROGRAMS

As described earlier, five criteria are commonly used to evaluate K–12 sex education programs: delayed initiation of sex, decreased frequency of intercourse, decreased number of part-

ners, increased use of condoms if sexually active, and increased use of contraception and protection if sexually active. Based on careful reviews of 83 evaluation studies that meet most of the methodological criteria reviewed earlier, Kirby, Laris, and Rolleri (2005) identified the characteristics of programs that are successful in achieving one or more of these goals. Successful programs:

- involved a multidisciplinary team in the development of the curriculum
- used a logical approach to specify health goals, and the risk and protective factors related to these goals
- assessed relevant needs and assets of target groups
- designed activities consistent with community values and available resources
- pilot-tested the program
- created a safe social environment for youth
- focused on specific behavioral goals
- focused narrowly on specific behaviors leading to these health goals
- addressed multiple sexual psychosocial risk and protective factors
- included multiple activities to change each of the targeted factors
- employed instructionally sound teaching methods that actively involved participants
- employed activities, methods and messages appropriate to the youths' culture, developmental age, and sexual experience
- covered topics in a logical sequence
- whenever possible, selected educators with desired characteristics and then trained them
- secured at least minimal support from authorities such as school districts and community organizations
- if needed, implemented activities to recruit youth and overcome barriers to their participation
- implemented virtually all activities with reasonable fidelity (Kirby et al., 2005, p. 27).

These authors comment that effective programs were effective among both boys and girls and across the age range from 11 to 23 years of age.

Programs that have been empirically validated and shown to delay onset of intercourse among some groups of teens include Teen Talk (12 to 15 hours), PSI/Human Sexuality and Health Screening (two years), Safer Choices (two years), and Draw the Line/Respect the Line (three years; Manlove, Papillio, & Ikramullah, 2004).

THE CURRENT STATE OF SEXUALITY EDUCATION: COLLEGE AND UNIVERSITY

There is limited published work on human sexuality courses offered at colleges and universities. Judging from the results of a Google search on "human sexuality courses," such courses are offered at many colleges and universities. The departments in which the courses are located include Anthropology, Biology, Woman's and Gender Studies, Health, Human Sexuality Studies, LGBT Programs, Psychology, Sociology, and Schools of Nursing. This list suggests that such courses are probably diverse in content and emphasis. Many are offered for three academic credits, suggesting about 40 hours, substantially more than almost any classes at the K–12 level. Therefore, college and university courses are more comprehensive.

A recent qualitative study of one such course obtained questionnaire data from 148 students at the end of the semester (Goldfarb, 2005). Asked whether the course had had an impact on their lives, students' responses fell into five categories:

- Made them better decision-makers and in some cases may affect their behaviors.
- Made them more open-minded and less judgmental, less homophobic.
- Made them more knowledgeable about themselves and their relationships, and in some cases, improved their sex lives.
- Made them into "sexuality educators" in the broadest sense, to people in their lives.
- Made them more comfortable talking about sex and sexuality in their everyday lives.

Modern college textbooks for human sexuality courses tend to be interdisciplinary, covering biological, psychological, and sociological levels of analysis. Most give balanced coverage to female and male sexuality and contain strong coverage of sexual orientation. These textbooks have been able to capitalize on the academic freedom offered by the university setting to offer accurate information about human sexuality. There are, of course, some exceptions, such as books with a heavy biological or evolutionary emphasis, and books that are heterosexist in emphasis.

This admittedly brief discussion suggests that college courses are more comprehensive and have positive impacts on the lives of students who take them. Some of the major textbooks present a more interdisciplinary and gender-equitable perspective, whereas others are characterized by a traditional view of female–male relationships and (hetero)sexual expression. There are no federal restrictions on content of college courses, but there may be state or district restrictions on courses taught in two-year college systems.

There are numerous less formal educational activities on college campuses that are relevant to sexuality education but hard to document. Some are ongoing programs such as sexual wellness peer education internship programs working out of women's centers and student centers. These programs usually focus on healthy sexual communication, and consent issues. A frequently cited campus activity is production of *Vagina Monologues* by Eve Ensler. According to Wikipedia, there are at least 23 colleges and universities that perform *Monologues* annually. Interestingly, while many feminists applaud the play, other feminists join social conservatives in criticizing it, for example, for its anti-male, pro-lesbian elements.

THE CURRENT STATE OF SEXUALITY EDUCATION: MEDICAL SCHOOLS

A recent survey of medical schools reports data on training in human sexuality (Solursh et al., 2003). Surveys were mailed to 125 medical schools in the United States and 16 schools in Canada; 101 schools responded (74% of the U.S. schools and 50% of the Canadian schools). The majority of schools reported 3 to 10 hours of instruction; most schools (83%) used a lecture format. A multidisciplinary team provided the instruction in 63% of the schools. Topics covered (in descending order by frequency) included causes of sexual dysfunction (94%); treatment of sexual dysfunction (85%); altered sexual identification (79%); and issues of sexuality in illness or disability (69%). Fifty-five percent reported providing supervision during clerkships (clinical work by third- and fourth-year students) that dealt with sexual issues, and 43% offered clinical programs, typically focused on treating patients with sexual problems. The authors concluded that an expansion of medical education may be necessary to provide the community with doctors who are knowledgeable about sexual problems.

There have been studies of the provision of abortion education in medical and allied schools. Espey and colleagues (2005) mailed questionnaires to the OB-GYN clerkship directors of 126 accredited U.S. medical schools; 78 were returned (62%). In the third-year OB-GYN rotation, 32% offered a lecture about abortion; 45% offered a clinical experience, but participation was low. In the fourth year, about half of the schools offered a reproductive health elective, but participation was low. Foster and colleagues (2006) surveyed program directors of the 486 accredited nurse practitioner, physician assistant, and certified nurse midwifery programs in the United States. They also concluded that education is limited, and that this directly affects the quality of women's health care.

In addition to content knowledge, health professionals need the ability to communicate about sexual practices and problems sensitively and without judgment. Published literature suggests that such communication skills are uncommon, indicating the need for more communication skills training in medical schools (Baraitser, Elliott, & Bigrigg, 1998).

GENDER EQUITY ISSUES IN FORMAL SEXUALITY EDUCATION

The evidence reviewed above suggests that sexuality education in K–12 programs and in medical schools is heavily focused on risk and danger, especially unwanted pregnancy and STIs in K–12 curricula, and sexual dysfunctions and issues of gender identification in medical schools. There is little, if any, discussion of sexual health and its enhancement. There is little attention to whether program outcomes differ for male and female participants. An analysis of the Ontario provincial sex education curriculum concludes that it is focused on risk and danger, that discourses of female victimization and individual morality predominate (Connell, 2005). As noted earlier, this emphasis can be traced to the roots of the sex education movement. There may be more attention to sexual health and sexual relationships in college courses in human sexuality. Some of the better college courses may provide a model for the necessary expansion of medical education.

Issue 1: Abstinence-Only Sex Education Teaches Gender Stereotypes as Fact

Formal sexuality education often neglects an examination of the ways in which gender role norms and beliefs about masculinity and femininity impact sexual expression and relationships. The critiques of K–12 education (Committee on Government Reform, 2004; SIECUS, 2005) explicitly detail ways in which these materials portray stereotypic male and female traits and behaviors as natural or biological. The result is a view of existing patterns of sexual behavior and sexual interaction as biologically determined. This view is at the root of the double standard that evaluates male nonmarital sexual activity positively, but stigmatizes women for the same behaviors (Whatley, 1992). Thus, sex education often perpetuates the male as active and female as passive view of (hetero)sexual relationships. This view disadvantages both males and females and prevents sexual interactions and relationships from moving toward equal contributions, equal responsibility, and equal pleasure.

Issue 2: Formal Sex Education Focuses on Danger and Ignores Pleasure, Especially Women's Pleasure

A well-documented equity issue in K–12 education is the failure to acknowledge and discuss female sexual desire. Fine (1988) identified the "missing discourse of desire" in sex education programs for adolescents. Based on qualitative research with adolescents, Tolman (2002) wrote about the dilemmas of desire these young women experience. They are immersed in the "'sex is risky and dangerous' discourse" in sex education and in interactions with parents. They are encouraged to view males as sexual opportunists and to fear sexual victimization. If they experience desire, therefore, it is difficult to acknowledge it. This, in turn, makes it hard for them to express sexual interest and desire, which indeed may lead to engaging in sexual activity because the male wants to and the inability to express agency in heterosexual interactions and relationships. There are also consequences for the male; his attempts to initiate sexual activity may reflect a belief that he is supposed to initiate sexual activity rather than pay attention to his own sexual desire.

Issue 3: Sex Education Teaches Heterosexuality as the Norm and Ignores the Needs of LGBT Youth

The literature suggests that penile–vaginal intercourse and heterosexual relationships are the focus of most formal sex education programs at all levels. The focus on penile–vaginal intercourse provides a severely limited view of sexual expression; there are many ways to express one's sexuality and enjoy its

pleasures. Providing a broader definition of "sex" would increase choices, probably increasing the likelihood that couples (of whatever gender and orientation) will find activities that both enjoy. It would also reduce the pressure on male–female couples to engage in penile–vaginal intercourse, thereby reducing the risks associated with that activity. A focus on heterosexual activity marginalizes the experience of LGBTQ youth. It also means that such youth will receive little benefit from formal educational programs, no matter how good they are on other criteria.

Myerson (1992) suggested that these and other gender equity issues flow from a fundamental assumption of sexual dimorphism, the state of having two distinct forms within the same species. This view is the foundation for the belief that men and women are different and that the differences are natural and inevitable. In fact, decades of research and hundreds of empirical studies provide evidence of substantial similarities between boys and girls, men and women (Hyde, 2005; Chapter 2). The distributions of men and of women on almost any characteristic overlap a great deal, and there are large variations within both genders. In the realm of sexuality specifically, there are only two consistently reported differences: men are more likely to masturbate and are more tolerant of casual sexual relations. Both of these are interpretable as outcomes of our socialization and sex education of boys and girls (Hyde & DeLamater, 2006). (The difference in masturbation may be attributed to women's reluctance to report the behavior, but this is countered by the observation that women today report oral–genital contact and anal intercourse in substantial numbers; it is unclear why they would be less willing to report masturbation.)

Issue 4: Erroneous Information in Abstinence-Only Curricula Puts Health at Risk, Especially Women's Health

Abstinence-only programs leave girls and boys without adequate information about most aspects of sexual health and sexual functioning, and, even worse, provide misinformation in some cases. This deprives youth of the ability to protect their sexual health, or to prevent pregnancy and STIs. A case can be made that the consequences are worse for women. In the event of a pregnancy, the woman will be carrying the fetus, and will experience the physical risks and consequences as well as many of the emotional ones. Also, many cases of STIs are asymptomatic, and may not be detected, leading to fertility problems later. It is estimated that there are 3 million new cases of chlamydia each year, most of them among young people ages 18 to 24. Chlamydia is asymptomatic in 75% of cases involving women and 50% of cases involving men (Hyde & DeLamater, 2006).

EFFECTIVE PROGRAMS THAT ADDRESS THE ISSUES

Several sex educators have turned their attention to the missing discourse of desire. Connell (2005) proposed an alternative curriculum. It would be based on a broad, holistic definition of sexual health, such as proposed by the World Health Organization, rather than prevention of pregnancy and disease. Such a definition would encompass a wide range of sexual activities and relationships, instead of narrowly focusing on heterosexual penile–vaginal intercourse. Discussion of risk and victimization would be balanced by discussion of the positive and pleasurable consequences of sexual activity. It would recognize the normal variability in people and their characteristics, rather than treating gender differences as a biological given. The result would be a curriculum based on a discourse of desire.

In a similar vein, Allen (2004) discussed the need for a discourse of erotics. She proposed that knowledge of the body and its role in sexual pleasure, recognition of the value of sexual pleasure throughout life, and an emphasis on the practice and enjoyment of consensual, mutually pleasurable sexual relationships would characterize such a discourse. She suggested that such an educational program should be personalized to some degree (e.g., encourage each person to identify what gives him or her sexual pleasure). She suggests that such a curriculum would empower young women and liberate young men from the strictures of hegemonic masculinity.

We reviewed above the characteristics of K–12 programs that are effective in delaying onset of sexual intercourse and reducing unwanted teen pregnancy and STIs, among other outcomes. Several such programs exist and can be purchased and implemented. However, these may not resolve some of the gender equity issues. To achieve the latter, these curricula may need to be integrated with the discourse of desire or erotics as outlined above. Further, Schaalma and colleagues (2004) suggested that in order to reorient sex education programs toward sexual health, we need to incorporate models of change from the health promotion literature. Also, they urged greater emphasis on social and relationship skills as tools in maintaining and enhancing one's sexual health. They also stated the need for well-trained educators and facilitators to implement these programs.

Turning to programming at the college level, there is a need to continue the emphasis on an interdisciplinary perspective, which is difficult in a setting that organizes instruction by disciplines. Human sexuality is one of the first areas that should be considered by initiatives to encourage interdisciplinary instruction. Another problem at the college level is the absence of opportunities for instruction for those who teach human sexuality.

Changing medical education may be more difficult. A review of data and research on women's experiences as medical students concluded that women continue to face gender harassment and stereotyping (Bickel, 2001). Furthermore, the specialty choices of women have remained stable, meaning that they are not entering all specialties in proportion to their numbers. For example, women continue to be overrepresented in dermatology, OB-GYN, pediatrics, and psychiatry, and underrepresented in emergency medicine, internal medicine, and various surgical specialties. Gender differences in values and differential encouragement by often male faculty contribute to specialty choice. A review of Canadian medical curricula with regard to gender sensitivity in content, language, and process found some progress (Zelek & Phillips, 1997).

We reviewed above survey data that suggests medical school training is almost exclusively focused on disease and dysfunction. Leiblum (2001) described the human sexuality course at Robert Wood Johnson Medical School. It is taught by an interdisciplinary team and emphasizes case-based and experiential learning. Leiblum described it as "a comprehensive and concentrated opportunity for students to become knowledgeable and comfortable" (p. 59) in dealing with human sexuality. The course is taught on five consecutive days, for a total of 40 hours. The article includes data from student evaluations. An appendix to the article provides an outline for the course.

Medical education has also been criticized for the "invisibility" of gay patients and issues in the curriculum. The course described by Leiblum includes a session devoted to these issues. A family medicine specialist at University of Western Ontario developed a gay and lesbian curriculum for postgraduate family medicine students that has been endorsed by the Canadian Medical Association (Robb, 1996). It is likely that intersex and transsexual persons are even less visible in the literature and coursework in medical and allied health schools.

CONCLUSIONS AND RECOMMENDATIONS

The biggest challenge to gender equity in formal sex education is the dominance of abstinence-only sex education in K–12 education in the United States. This dominance is largely driven by federal funding and other policies and practices that cater to a small, vocal, unduly influential minority of Americans.

The American Foundation for AIDS Research (2005) stated:

In summary, the scientific evidence does not support the U.S. government's current policy of making abstinence-only-until-marriage programs the cornerstone of its HIV prevention strategy for young people. Nor does it support the rapid scale-up of resources to promote abstinence-only-until-marriage programs in the U.S. and globally. Rather, the scientific evidence to date suggests that investing in comprehensive sex education that includes support for abstinence but also provides risk-reduction information would be a more effective HIV prevention strategy for young people.

Numerous professional organizations are calling for comprehensive sexuality education programs to deal with the public health crises associated with adolescent sexuality. These groups include the American Academy of Pediatrics (Klein, 2005), American Medical Association, National Education Association, National School Board Association, National Parent–Teachers Association, and Society for Adolescent Medicine (Santelli et al., 2006).

Under the circumstances, continued investment in abstinence-only programs can be challenged on both financial and ethical grounds:

- It is fiscally irresponsible to spend millions of dollars of taxpayer's money to support ineffective programs. This is especially true in a time when there are huge budget deficits at both federal and state levels.

- It is unethical for educators to withhold information from millions of young people that would give them the knowledge they need to make informed, responsible decisions about their bodies, and the information and means to prevent pregnancy and sexually transmitted infections.

Overall, sexuality educators, parents and everyone else concerned with the health of adolescents and adults should protest the use of another dollar to support ineffective sex education programs in our public schools and communities. Instead we should press for accurate, balanced, gender-neutral, nonheterosexist sexuality education for every adolescent—education that recognizes the spiritual and mental components as well as the physical ones.

At the college level, everyone directly or indirectly involved in sexuality and health education should encourage change in sexuality courses. We should search for and utilize materials that are interdisciplinary, focused on health as well as prevention of illness, and give appropriate attention to the social construction of gender and the similarities in women's and men's interpersonal and sexual functioning.

Finally, to meet the demand by patients (i.e., ourselves) for informed medical professionals, we should express our concern to medical school administrators and faculty about the non-existence or narrowness of existing curricula concerned with sexuality. There are models of courses that are comprehensive, focused on health, and pay appropriate attention to the variety of sexual relationships and lifestyles in the contemporary North American societies.

The barriers to accomplishing these goals were articulated by Klein (1992) as silence, confusion, and disunity. We have certainly made headway in giving voice to the problems created by the formal sexuality education practices of the early 21st century, as evidenced by many of the citations in this chapter, and the list of organizations supportive of comprehensive sex education. We have also made progress in eliminating confusion. Valid, reliable evaluation data are increasingly available showing clearly what works and what does not work, much of which are referenced in these pages. The most serious barrier today may be disunity; we still are not speaking with a unified voice to stakeholders, media representatives, policymakers, politicians, and school teachers and administrators. Too often we stand by when a sex educator working for the principles we share is attacked by those who object to providing accurate, comprehensive information to students. It can be hoped that the scrutiny given these issues by reviews such as this will increase our resolve to stand together in the face of attacks by people who seem to prefer to see young people become ill and die than to "tell it like it is."

ACKNOWLEDGMENTS

Chapter reviewers include: Heather Johnston Nicholas and Kristin A. Adams, Girls Incorporated, Indianapolis, IN; Marilyn Myerson, University of South Florida, Tampa; and Janet Hyde, University of Wisconsin, Madison.

References

Advocates for Youth. (2005). Five years of abstinence-only-until-marriage education: Assessing the impact. Retrieved on January 24, 2006, from http://www.advocatesforyouth.org/publications/stateevaluations.

———. (2006). *Sex education programs: Definitions and point-by-point comparison*. Retrieved on January 26, 2006 from http://www.advocatesforyouth.org/rrr/definitions.htm.

Alan Guttmacher Institute. (2006). *State policies in brief*. Retrieved from http://www.guttmacher.org/statecenter/spibs/spib_SE.pdf.

Allen, L. (2004). Beyond the birds and the bees: Constituting a discourse of erotics in sexuality education. *Gender and Education, 16*, 151–167.

American Foundation for AIDS Research. (2005). Assessing the efficacy of abstinence-only programs for HIV prevention among young people. Issue Brief No. 2.

Baraitser, P., Elliot, L., & Bigrigg, A. (1998). How to talk about sex and do it well: A course for medical students. *Medical Teacher, 20*, 142–159.

Bickel, J. (2001). Gender equity in undergraduate medical education: A status report. *Journal of Women's Health and Gender-based Medicine, 10*, 261–271.

Centers for Disease Control and Prevention (CDC). (2000). Tracking the Hidden Epidemics: Trends in STDs in the United States.

Committee on Government Reform. (2004). The Content of Federally-Funded Abstinence-Only Education Programs. Washington, D.C.: United States House of Representatives.

Connell, E. (2005) Desire as interruption: Young women and sexuality education in Ontario, Canada. *Sex Education, 5*, 253–268.

de Gaston, J. F., Jensen, L., Weed, S., & Tanas, R. (1994). Teacher philosophy and program implementation and the impact of sex education outcomes. *The Journal of Research and Development in Education, 27*, 265–270.

Espey, E., Ogburn, T., Chavez, A., Qualls, C., & Leyba, M. (2005). Abortion education in medical schools: A national survey. *American Journal of Obstetrics and Gynecology, 192*, 640–643.

Fine, M. (1988). Sexuality, schooling, and adolescent females: The missing discourse of desire. *Harvard Educational Review, 58*, 29–53.

Foster, A., Polis, C., Allee M. K., Simonds, K., Zurek, M., & Brown, A. (2006). Abortion education in nurse practitioner, physician assistant, and certified nurse midwifery programs: A national survey. *Contraception, 73*, 408–414.

Girls Incorporated. (1991). *Preventing adolescent pregnancy: A program development and research project*. New York.

Goldfarb, E. (2005). What is comprehensive sexuality education really all about? Perceptions of students enrolled in an undergraduate human sexuality course. *American Journal of Sexuality Education, 1*, 85–102.

Goodson, P., Pruitt, B. E., Buhi, E., Wilson, K., Raspberry, C. & Gunnels, E. (2004). *Abstinence Education Evaluation Phase 5: Technical Report*. Texas A&M University.

Henshaw, S. K. (2003). *U.S. Teenage Pregnancy Statistics with Comparative Statistics for Women Aged 20–24*. New York: Alan Guttmacher Institute.

Hyde, J. (2005). The gender similarities hypothesis. *American Psychologist, 60*, 581–592.

Hyde, J., & DeLamater, J. (2006). *Understanding Human Sexuality*, 9e. New York: McGraw-Hill.

Kaiser Family Foundation. (2000). *Sex Education in America: A View From Inside the Nation's Classrooms*. Palo Alto, CA: Kaiser Family Foundation.

Kirby, D. (2001). *Emerging answers: Research findings on programs to reduce teen pregnancy*. Washington, DC: National Campaign to Prevent Teen Pregnancy.

Kirby, D. (2002). Do abstinence-only programs delay the initiation of sex among young people and reduce teen pregnancy? Washington, DC: National Campaign to Prevent Teen Pregnancy.

Kirby, D., Laris, B. A., & Rolleri, L. (2005). Impact of sex and HIV education programs on sexual behaviors of youth in developing and developed countries. Research Triangle, NC: Family Health International, Working Paper Series No. WP05-03.

Klein, Jonathan, & The Committee on Adolescence. (2005). Adolescent pregnancy: Current trends and issues. *Pediatrics, 116,* 281–286

Klein, S. (1992). Sex equity and sexuality in education: Breaking the barriers. In S. Klein (Ed.), *Sex Equity and Sexuality in Education.* Albany, NY: SUNY Press.

Landry, D., Kaeser, L., & Richards, C. (1999). Abstinence promotion and the provision of information about contraception in public school district sexuality education policies. *Family Planning Perspectives, 31,* 280–286.

Leiblum, S. (2001). An established medical school human sexuality curriculum: Description and evaluation. *Sexual and Relationship Therapy, 16,* 59–70.

Manlove, J., Papillio, A., & Ikramullah, E. (2004). *Not yet: Programs to delay first sex among teens.* The National Campaign to Prevent Teen Pregnancy.

Maynard, R., Trenholm, C., Devaney, B., Johnson, A., Clark, M., Homrighausen, J., et al. (2005). First-year impacts of four Title V, Section 510 Abstinence Education Programs. Princeton, NJ: Mathematica Policy Research, Inc.

Minnesota Department of Health. (nd). Minnesota Education Now and Babies Later (MN ENABL): Evaluation Report (1998–2002). St. Paul, MN: author.

Myerson, M. (1992). Sex-equity and sexuality in college-level sex education. In S. Klein (Ed.), *Sex Equity and Sexuality in Education.* Albany, NY: SUNY Press.

National Center for Health Statistics. (2005). *Health, United States, 2005.* Table 51. Hyattsville, MD: National Center for Health Statistics.

Robb, N. (1996). Medical schools seek to overcome "invisibility" of gay patients, gay issues in curriculum. *Canadian Medical Association Journal, 155,* 765–770.

Rury, J. (1992). Passions and power: Sexuality, sex equity, and education in historical perspective. In S. Klein (Ed.), *Sex Equity and Sexuality in Education.* Albany, NY: SUNY Press.

Santelli, J., Ott, M., Lyon, M., Rogers, J., & Summers, D. (2006). Abstinence-only education policies and programs: A position paper of the Society for Adolescent Medicine. *Journal of Adolescent Health, 38,* 83–87

Schaalma, H., Abraham, C., Gillmore, M. R., & Kok, G. (2004). Sex education as health promotion: What does it take? *Archives of Sexual Behavior, 33,* 259–269.

SIECUS. (1999). Issues and Answers: Fact Sheet on Sexuality Education. *SIECUS Report, 27,* 29–33. Washington, DC: SIECUS.

———. (2005). In their own words: What Abstinence-only-until-marriage programs say. Fact Sheet.

Smith, E. A., Dariotis, J., & Potter, S. (2003). *Evaluation of Pennsylvania's Abstinence Initiative: Final Report.* University Park, PA: Pennsylvania State University

Solursh, D. S., Ernst, J. L., Lewis, R. W., Prisant, L. M., Mills, T. M., Solursh, L. P., et al. (2003). The human sexuality education of physicians in North American medical schools. *International Journal of Impotence Research, 15*(Suppl.), S41–45.

Tolman, D. (2002). *Dilemmas of desire: Teenage girls talk about sexuality.* Cambridge, MA: Harvard University Press.

U.S. Department of Health and Human Services. (2002). *Evaluation of Abstinence Education Programs Funded under Title V, Section 510.* Interim Report. Retrieved on February 08, 2007, from http://aspe.os.dhhs.gov/hsp/abstinence02

Whatley, M. (1992).Goals for sex-equitable sexuality education. In S. Klein (Ed.), *Sex Equity and Sexuality in Education.* Albany, NY: SUNY Press.

Zelek, B., & Phillips, S. (1997). Gender sensitivity in medical curricula. *Canadian Medical Association Journal, 156,* 1297–1300.

GENDER EQUITY IN CAREER
AND TECHNICAL EDUCATION

Mary E. Lufkin,* **Mary M. Wiberg,*** *Courtney Reed Jenkins,*
Stefanie L. Lee Berardi, Terri Boyer, Ellen Eardley, and Janet Huss

INTRODUCTION

For girls who grew up prior to 1972, it was common to be told they could not take a woodworking or auto mechanics class—simply because they were girls. And boys were not allowed to take home economics classes or to study nursing—simply because they were boys. There was a clear delineation of what the roles of men and women were to be, and public policy intended to keep it that way. Fortunately, girls and boys of today have many more options open to them. But while options are present, so are pressures.

- In 1972, the majority of women did not work outside the home while children were young. Now, it is the exception to the rule for both parents not to be employed. Today, only 20.2% of married couple families have solely the husband working (U.S. Bureau of Labor Statistics [BLS], 2006).
- Balancing work and family has become a major pressure on parents, especially for the large number of single women-headed households. In 2005, 18% of families were maintained by single women (BLS, 2006).
- While choices are present, women continue to be predominantly employed in traditionally female occupations, thus earning far less than men. The median earnings of women working full time year-round was 77% of men's median earnings in 2005, the same as the wage gap in 2002 (National Committee on Pay Equity [NCPE], 2006).
- For many years, the welfare system sought to provide educational paths to recipients, usually single parents or displaced homemakers, recognizing that education is the route to living wage jobs. Today's welfare system is designed to put people to work, discouraging them from education. While they may work, they are frequently in low-paying jobs with no upward mobility or pathway out of poverty. Nearly three million full-time, year-round workers live below the poverty line, and since the current welfare law was put in place, child poverty has increased by 12%. (Ganzglass, 2006a)

- More jobs now require some postsecondary education, but not necessarily a four-year degree (U.S. Department of Commerce et al., 1999, as cited in Brand, 2003, p. 1). Two-thirds of America's young people do not obtain a four-year college degree, and at least 25% go to work directly after high school (U.S. Department of Education [ED], 2002, p. iv).
- The world has become a global economy, one with great competitiveness and demands for high-skilled workers. While enormous efforts are being made in countries such as China and India to develop a multiskilled workforce, the United States is stagnant when it comes to assuring that American women and girls, one of our most valuable resources, are encouraged to develop their full capacity.
- In recent years, federal financial support for education, employment training, and welfare programs has been cut dramatically.

A quality career and technical education system can play a major role in better utilizing *all* of America's citizens. Gender roles continue to change and expand in contemporary America and are made more complex through the intersection of race, ethnicity, national origin, language ability, disability, age, class, and sexual orientation. The combining of work and family roles challenges young people today. Teachers, counselors, and parents are preparing students for these changes through career and technical education (CTE).

*The bold face names are the Lead Authors.

For the past 20 years, "vocational education" (as it used to be called) has been saddled with the image of being a program for non-college-bound and special education students. This has occurred despite the efforts of educators, with the assistance of active business and industry advisory committees, to continually update vocational education until it essentially evolved into tech prep[1] programs for postsecondary transition. During the implementation of the federal Perkins Act of 1984, educators made great strides in integrating academic and technical skills into the vocational education curriculum, and many vocational education courses began to fulfill academic graduation and college entrance requirements. Yet parents, academic teachers, administrators, community members, and legislators continued to define vocational education as they had experienced it. To battle this outdated image, the vocational education community began to use the term "career and technical education" during the early 1990s to name the system of secondary and postsecondary programs across the country that were preparing students for advanced training and careers.

Career and technical education (CTE) prepares both youth and adults for full participation in a spectrum of college opportunities, meaningful work, career advancement, and active citizenship (Association for Career and Technical Education [ACTE], 2006a, p. 1). CTE is offered in middle schools, high schools, two-year community and technical colleges, as well as other postsecondary schools. The subject areas most commonly associated with CTE are (a) agriculture (food and fiber production and agribusiness), (b) business (accounting, business administration, management, information technology, and entrepreneurship), (c) family and consumer sciences (culinary arts, management, and life skills), (d) health occupations (nursing, dental, and medical technicians), (e) marketing (management, entrepreneurship, merchandising, and retail), (f) technology (production, communication, and transportation systems), and (g) trade and industrial (skilled trades such as automotive technician, carpenter, and computer numerical control technician; ACTE, 2006b).

Over 95% of high school students take at least one CTE course, and about one quarter of high school students take a concentration of three or more related CTE courses before they graduate from high school (National Assessment of Vocational Education [NAVE], 2004). Participation in CTE at the postsecondary level is high as well—nearly one third of all postsecondary students are enrolled in sub-baccalaureate vocational programs (NAVE, 2004)—and as many as 40 million adults engage in short-term postsecondary occupational training (ACTE, 2006b). CTE participation rates have grown significantly in just a short period. Nationwide, over 15.1 million students were enrolled in CTE in 2004—an increase of 57% from the 9.6 million enrolled in 1999 (ED, 2005).

Students with concentration in CTE study more and higher level math (Stone & Aliaga, 2002) and increased their 12th-grade test scores on the National Assessment of Educational Progress by 4 more scale points in reading and 11 more scale points in math than students who took little or no CTE coursework (NAVE, 2004). CTE students enter postsecondary education at approximately the same rate as all high school graduates (Center on Education Policy and American Youth Policy Forum, 2000), but CTE concentrators are more likely to obtain a degree or certificate within two years, despite the fact that they are more likely to be employed while in school (National Center for Education Statistics [NCES], 2000).

This chapter is limited to addressing CTE programs from Grades 7–12 and two-year CTE associate of arts degree programs. Other programs related to gender equity in CTE are covered in greater depth elsewhere in this volume (see chapter 12, "Gender Equity in Mathematics," chapter 13, "Gender Equity in Science, Engineering, and Technology" and chapter 30 "Improving Gender Equity in Postsecondary Education")

This chapter first provides an overview of the federal public policy history related to gender equity in CTE, and then summarizes the current data on gender equity in CTE. A brief review of the root causes of gender *inequity* in CTE, both within and outside the control of educators, is followed by a discussion of strategies currently in place. The chapter continues by highlighting four excellent CTE gender-equity programs and concludes with recommendations for public policymakers, local schools and communities, and researchers.

Career, in its broadest sense, means "life path," and thus includes all the roles a person plays throughout life (Super, 1980). Career choice is, therefore, a lifelong pursuit. There is no one career choice; rather, there are multiple choices along the way. These choices are based on what people learn and what experiences they have. The best choices are those that give satisfaction and pleasure to each individual and, at the same time, allow the individual to make a contribution to society. Ideally, every person should match her or his job choice with personal talents and interests, consistent with economic opportunities and role priorities, and then strive to achieve individual career goals (Farmer, Seliger, Sidney, Bitters, & Brizius, 1985).

The key gender-equity challenge for CTE is the elimination of sex bias and stereotyping that leads to limiting students' career choices. The primary emphasis of gender equity in CTE has been to encourage men and women and boys and girls to explore nontraditional career[2] choices and to make career decisions based on their own personal interests, skills, and talents, regardless of their gender. Secondarily, this emphasis has the potential to (a) increase the diversity of the workforce, (b) improve gender equity in earnings, (c) maximize the use of an individual's talents, and (d) increase the United States' ability to compete in a global economic marketplace.

HISTORICAL BACKGROUND OF GENDER-EQUITY POLICIES AFFECTING CAREER AND TECHNICAL EDUCATION

The Federal Vocational Education Act (VEA)—1976

Without doubt, the signing of Title IX legislation in 1972 led to major policy changes in vocational education. Prior to the

---

[1]Tech prep combines at least 2 years of secondary education and 2 years of postsecondary education in a nonduplicative sequential course of study that leads to an associate's degree or certificate.

[2]Nontraditional careers are those where one gender is less that 25 percent of the individuals employed in that occupation.

nondiscrimination language of Title IX, the vocational education system was purposefully sex segregated; education institutions could, and did, legally deny girls and women entry into training deemed "inappropriate" for females, and visa versa for males. Title IX ended these restrictions and made them illegal. The 1976 amendments to the Vocational Education Act (VEA) and the Carl D. Perkins Vocational Education Act of 1984 (Perkins Act) started a new era in career and technical education, because, among other goals, they intended to dismantle sex segregation in CTE.

While Congress had provided funding for vocational education since the Smith-Hughes Act of 1917, it was only following passage of Title IX that, with the help of advocacy groups who believed it was time for gender equity to be addressed in vocational education, major changes were made in the reauthorization process. In addition to providing limited funding to address equity, the 1976 amendments to the VEA mandated a full-time sex equity coordinator (SEC) be appointed in each state to coordinate sex equity work in CTE. Ten functions were identified in the regulations that were issued in October 1977 (ED 3 C.F.R §104.73, as cited in National Alliance for Partnerships in Equity [NAPE], 2004, pp. 11–13):

- Take action necessary to create awareness of programs and activities in vocational education designed to reduce sex bias and sex stereotyping in all vocational education programs, including assisting the State Board in publicizing the public hearings on the State plan;

- Gather, analyze and disseminate data on the status of men and women students and employees in vocational education programs of the state;

- Develop and support actions to correct problems brought to the attention of the personnel, including creating awareness of the Title IX complaint process;

- Review the distribution of grants and contracts by the State board to assure that the interests and needs of women are addressed in all projects assisted under this Act;

- Review all vocational education programs (including work-study programs, cooperative vocational education programs, apprenticeship programs, and the placement of students who have successfully completed vocational education programs) in the state for sex bias;

- Monitor and implement laws prohibiting sex discrimination in all hiring, firing, and promotion procedures within the State relating to vocational education;

- Assist local education agencies and other interested parties in the State in improving vocational education opportunities for women;

- Make available to the State Board, the State Advisory Council, the National Advisory Council on Vocational Education, the State Commission on the Status of Women, and Commissioner, and the general public, including individuals and organizations in the State concerned about sex bias in vocational education, information developed under this section;

- Review the self-evaluations required by Title IX; and

- Review and submit recommendations with respect to overcoming sex bias and sex stereotyping in vocational education programs for the five-year State plan and its annual program plan prior to their submission to the Commissioner for approval.

The 1976 Act also gave special attention to the growing needs of widows and divorced women, referred to as "displaced homemakers," for programs that would help them gain marketable skills and become employed and self-sufficient. States were encouraged to provide modest funding for initial programs through the federal monies provided to them.

The Carl D. Perkins Vocational Education Act of 1984

The Perkins Act of 1984 continued the mandate for a sex equity coordinator and added a 3.5% set-aside from each state's basic CTE grant to be used for sex equity programs and services and an 8.5% set-aside for single parent and displaced homemaker programs and services. It was clear in this legislation that in addition to displaced homemakers, there were growing numbers of single parents, many of them never married, who needed help with vocational education to gain employment and success. The funding provisions amounted to more than $100 million focused on gender equity, primarily for women, a very significant change in federal legislation.

The Carl D. Perkins Career and Applied Technology Education Act of 1990

In 1990, the Perkins Act was reauthorized with continued mandates for a full-time SEC and set-asides of 3% for sex-quity programs and 7% for single parent and displaced homemaker programs (with an additional .5% at each state's discretion for either of these programs). States were required to offer a broad range of services to CTE students including career guidance and counseling, childcare, transportation, tuition assistance, mentoring, and job training, development, and placement.

During the implementation of the 1990 Perkins Act, the term "gender equity" became more commonly used than "sex equity." Between 1984 and 1998, an average of $100 million per year was spent on programs primarily serving women and girls with the goals of eliminating sex bias in vocational education and assuring that single parents and displaced homemakers had access to vocational education that led to careers with a living wage. Each state had numerous programs serving displaced homemakers and single parents (including teen parents) in place between 1985 and 1999. In addition, hundreds of programs worked to eliminate sex bias in vocational education and provided nontraditional occupational opportunities.

The Carl D. Perkins Vocational and Technical Education Act of 1998

Major changes again occurred in the 1998 reauthorization of the Perkins Act, when Congress stripped the funding for gender equity and the requirement for a state sex equity coordinator, thereby eliminating the majority of provisions encouraging gender-equity programming in CTE. Many traditional vocational educators and state officials had resented the fact that more than 10% of the state basic grant was to be spent on gender equity. Their objections, in addition to increasing political pressure from the right wing and the conservative Republican takeover of the U.S. House of Representatives, resulted in the legislative changes. In addition, the term "gender equity" became a political liability. The debate on gender-equity policy refocused on nontraditional occupations and the access of men and women to these careers. The 1998 reauthorization included few provisions that supported students pursuing nontraditional training and employment, and folded these students, as well as single parents and displaced homemakers, into the definition of "special populations." The funding that had supported gender equity (more than $100 million annually) was given to the states to use at their discretion for other CTE purposes.

In the fall of 2000, only one year after the full implementation of the 1998 Perkins Act, the Vocational Education Task Force of the National Coalition for Women and Girls in Education (NCWGE) surveyed more than 1,500 programs across the country that had received funds under the gender equity set-asides in Perkins. This was done to determine how the 1998 changes in the federal law affected the students they worked with and their own ability to provide services (National Coalition for Women and Girls in Education [NCWGE], 2001). While NCWGE experienced tremendous difficulty locating programs that were still in existence, over one third of the respondents to the survey painted a dismal picture of the effects of the 1998 Perkins policy changes. More than half of the programs reported that their funding had decreased and they predicted additional funding cuts in the future. Seventy-one percent reported services to students had significantly decreased. Nearly half reported that students' unmet needs had increased, and one third reported declining program support from State and Local Educational Agencies.

Only two sources of potential funding for former "gender-equity" programs remained in the 1998 version of the law: (a) states were required to reserve $60,000 to $150,000 of "state leadership" funds to provide services to students pursuing nontraditional training and employment, and (b) states could opt to reserve 10% of the basic state grant for local education agencies to support state-level priorities such as programs serving single parents, displaced homemakers, and students pursuing nontraditional training. The cap on state leadership funds made little sense, especially in larger states with more students to serve; for instance, $150,000 would have a greater impact on gender equity in Delaware than California. From 2000 to 2004 the average annual amount of state leadership funds spent on gender equity was $4,212,000 compared to over $100,000,000 each year prior to the 1998 reauthorization. In addition, only two states took advantage of the option to reserve 10% of local funds for single parents, displaced homemakers, and students pursuing nontraditional careers and only did so for a few years.

1998 Perkins Accountability Measures

The only other major equity initiative in the 1998 Perkins Act was an accountability measure, which required states to report student enrollment in and completion of programs that are nontraditional for both genders. State education agencies each year must report to the United States Department of Education (ED), Office of Vocational and Adult Education (OVAE) data on the performance of students in CTE on each of the four indicators of performance. These indicator include,

1. Academic and technical skill attainment.
2. Completion of a CTE program.
3. Placement in employment, military, or postsecondary education.
4. Participation in and completion of nontraditional training and employment programs.

Nontraditional training and employment is defined in the Perkins Act as "occupations or fields of work, including careers in computer science, technology, and other emerging high skill occupations, for which individuals from one gender comprise less than 25% of the individuals employed in each such occupation or field of work." Based on this definition, states had to identify CTE programs that prepare students for these occupations, and were required to set benchmarks for their performance starting in 1999. States then negotiated with the ED, Office of Vocational and Adult Education (OVAE) annual performance measures for the participation and for the completion of students in nontraditional CTE programs.

States report in their Consolidated Annual Report (CAR) the numbers and percentages of underrepresented students participating (enrolled) in nontraditional CTE programs and the numbers and percentages of underrepresented students completing nontraditional CTE programs. In addition, states are also required to disaggregate data by gender, race/ethnicity, and special population status for each of the four core indicators of performance as well as the enrollment report. (This data can be found at www.edcountability.net.) Special populations include,

- Individuals with disabilities;.
- Economically disadvantaged students, including foster children.
- Individuals preparing for nontraditional training and employment.
- Single parents, including single pregnant women.
- Displaced homemakers.
- Individuals with barriers to educational achievement, including individuals with limited English proficiency.

Although, this might sound like a rich and robust data source, the Perkins accountability system has been fraught with inconsistencies and data quality issues: states have different definitions for program participant, concentrator, and completer; different programs identified as nontraditional; and different methods of collecting the data, ranging from individual student record systems to classroom-based reporting. States have significant difficulty reporting on the numbers of single parents and displaced homemakers in CTE programs, as this data is self-reported due to federal privacy laws and there is no other proxy for the data source. Needless to say, comparing state-to-state data or trying to draw any significant or reliable national conclusions from the data is somewhat suspect or even impossible. The data, however, is extremely valuable for within-state comparisons and for use to inform local program improvement efforts. As of 2006, the OVAE was leading an initiative with the states to improve data quality and standardize definitions and measures to improve the Perkins national accountability system.

As of 2004, only two states, Massachusetts and North Dakota, have met their negotiated performance measures for nontraditional participation and completion at both the secondary and postsecondary level every year since the implementation of the 1998 Perkins Act (Peer Collaborative Resource Network [PCRN], 2006). Congress expected that this accountability tool would encourage states to take steps to improve gender equity. Without targeted funding, however, a mechanism to hold local educational agencies accountable, and stronger federal sanctions or incentives for states, progress has been at a standstill at best. On a positive note, advocates have greater access to this information, because states are now required to collect and report data about nontraditional CTE.

The Carl D. Perkins Career and Technical Education Improvement Act of 2006

In the summer of 2006, S. 250, the reauthorization of the Perkins Act (Perkins IV), was passed and signed into law. While the bill, to a large extent, replicates the 1998 Act, it adds a new requirement that use of local funds include preparation of special populations, including single parents and displaced homemakers, for high-skill, high-wage occupations that lead to self-sufficiency. The Congressional conference report defines "self-sufficiency" as "a standard of economic independence that considers a variety of demographic and geographic factors, as adopted, calculated, or commissioned by a local area or state." The term occurs in several places in Perkins III, including local plan requirements.

While some changes were made to the core indicators in the Perkins Act, the core indicators measuring gender equity were retained. The indicators continue to require both secondary and postsecondary schools receiving Perkins funds to be held accountable for increasing the participation and completion of underrepresented gender students in CTE programs that prepare for nontraditional careers. Because of the work done during Perkins III to develop valid and reliable data reporting processes and state accountability systems, states should be better equipped to set accurate benchmarks and negotiate appropriate performance measures based on historical data trends. This will be especially important for these two core indicators related to gender equity as states have had mixed success with meeting their performance measures set during Perkins III.

The new law requires continued disaggregation of data by special populations, including disparities and gaps in performance. This requirement is a means to assure that attention continues for students participating in nontraditional occupational training. National requirements include conducting an evaluation and assessment of the extent to which CTE prepares students, including special populations, for employment in high-skill, high-wage occupations (including those requiring math and science skills) or for participation in postsecondary education. Additionally, the law contains language supporting a stronger assessment of the performance of special population students and the impact of core indicators of performance on CTE in the National Assessment of Vocational Education (NAVE). This may lead to more and better evaluation of the impact of CTE on special populations, including the identification of best practices and outstanding local programs.

The most significant change from Perkins III to Perkins IV is the requirement that local recipients must negotiate performance measures on each of the core indicators with the state, increasing local accountability. Local education agencies (LEA) will be required to meet 90% of each locally adjusted performance measure annually in the first year of funding. If they fail, they must write an improvement plan to address the failing measure. If they fail to show any improvement in the second year, then the state can withhold federal funds during the third year. If they show improvement in the second year, but fail to meet the 90% threshold, they must continue to operate under the improvement plan. Should they not meet at least 90% of the measure in the third year, the state can again withhold funding.

Since there is significant data that shows states have *not* met the performance measures with the federal government, it is clear that the new accountability requirements will result in the need for greater care on the part of LEAs in negotiating performance measures and achieving them. Since the fourth core indicator relates to gender equity, there is the likelihood of more specific efforts to actually achieve the negotiated performance measures.

In order for the requirements and stronger language in Perkins IV to be effective, the equity community should encourage the U.S. Department of Education to be diligent in carrying out the intent of the law with regard to special populations. States are required to consult with representatives of special populations in development of their state plans. Because of the additional requirements in the law regarding these populations, Perkins IV may actually strengthen the manner in which CTE moves toward true gender equity.

From the 1970s on, women and girls have benefited from the strong advocacy by women's organizations especially on their behalf with regard to federal career and technical education legislation. The National Coalition for Women and Girls in Education has played a major role. The following organizations have been especially prominent in advocating for women and girls in CTE: American Association of University Women (AAUW), National Women's Law Center (NWLC), Wider Opportunities for Women (WOW), Women Work, and the National Alliance for Partnerships in Equity (NAPE).

NAPE is unique among these advocates in that it was established as a consortium of State Departments of Education in 1990 with the goal of assisting within the education community and systems in providing technical assistance to move gender equity forward. During Perkins III, NAPE worked consistently with the National Association of State Directors of Career Technical Education Consortium and the Office of Adult and Vocational Education, U.S. Department of Education, on performance measures and standards.

Title IX and the U.S. Department of Education Office for Civil Rights

Title IX of the Education Amendments of 1972 prohibits sex discrimination in any educational program or activity that receives federal financial assistance (e.g., all public middle and secondary schools, and almost all postsecondary schools and even proprietary technical training schools whose students receive federal grants or loans). In 1979, the agency that became the Department of Education implemented regulations for interpreting and enforcing Title IX. These regulations require, among other things, that each recipient of federal financial assistance

1. Designate a Title IX coordinator to ensure compliance with the law (34 CFR §106.8).
2. Adopt and publish policies and procedures for resolving complaints of discrimination (34 CFR §106.8) and harassment.[3]
3. Refrain from segregating courses by sex (34 CFR §106.34) and from discriminating on the basis of sex in guidance counseling (34 CFR §106.36).
4. Take steps to ensure that disproportionate enrollment of students of one sex in a course is not the result of discrimination (34 CFR §106.36).

These regulations also established the requirement that the ED Office for Civil Rights (OCR) undertake a compliance review or investigation of discrimination whenever a "report, complaint or any other information indicates a possible failure to comply" with Title IX (34 CFR §100.7, incorporated into the Title IX regulations by CFR §106.71).

Also in 1979, after the decision in the Adams *v.* Califano case finding continuing unlawful discrimination in vocational education programs, the ED released the "Vocational Education Guidelines for Eliminating Discrimination and Denial of Services on the Basis of Race, Color, National Origin, Sex and Handicap", hereafter referred to as the "Guidelines for Vocational Education Programs" (U.S. Department of Education, Office for Civil Rights, 1979). The guidelines emphasize that schools must offer CTE without regard to sex. Counseling activities, promotional and recruiting efforts, internships, and apprenticeships must be provided to all students without discrimination on the basis of sex.

The Title IX regulations and "Guidelines for Vocational Education Programs" impose requirements on schools that were intended to help eliminate sex discrimination against and harassment of students in nontraditional CTE. Perhaps the most important Title IX regulation for students in these highly sex-segregated CTE courses is the requirement that schools take steps to ensure that disproportionate enrollment of students of one sex in a course is not the result of discrimination. An important feature of the 1979 "Guidelines for Vocational Education Programs" is for state education agencies to have oversight responsibilities by collecting, analyzing, and reporting civil rights data, conducting compliance reviews, and providing technical assistance. The guidelines also provided that states conduct a Methods of Administration (MOA) review of school districts and postsecondary institutions receiving federal vocational education funds to assure that issues of discrimination were being addressed. The continued patterns of disproportionate enrollment demonstrated by concrete data and the evidence of discrimination suggest that schools must do a better job of complying with this regulation.

Unfortunately, lack of enforcement has limited both the MOA's and Title IX's effectiveness in eliminating sex discrimination in CTE. In recent years, rather than focusing specifically on sex discrimination in a separate MOA/Title IX review process, states have consolidated gender-equity reviews into whole school improvement reviews, often decreasing the emphasis on this issue. When the National Women's Law Center (NWLC) called on the federal government to enforce Title IX by investigating patterns of sex segregation in 2002, the OCR refused, even though federal law directs the OCR to conduct such investigations when information suggests noncompliance. The federal government's refusal to investigate patterns of sex segregation is troubling given the substantial disparities in enrollment that persist in high school CTE today, over 30 years after Title IX became law. For more information on Title IX and other federal legislation mentioned in this chapter, see chapter 5, "The Role of Government in Advancing Gender Equity in Education."

Temporary Assistance for Needy Families

Because of the focus of Perkins on single parents and displaced homemakers, Perkins-funded CTE equity programs have a long history of collaborating with the welfare system. In 1988, the Job Opportunities and Basic Skills (JOBS) Act was passed. It stressed the importance of education and training for welfare recipients. In the summer of 1996, when welfare legislation was up for reauthorization, Congress passed and President William J. Clinton signed the "Personal Responsibility and Work Opportunity Reconciliation Act of 1996" (welfare reform), radically transforming the nation's welfare system. This law reflected a "work first" philosophy, which intended to decrease welfare rolls by placing recipients in jobs—any job—as quickly as possible. Access to career and technical education, once a means to educating welfare recipients to access high-skill, high-wage occupations that might move them off assistance, became dramatically limited. The 1996 law limited a recipient's participation in CTE to 12 months and restricted 70% of a state's caseload from participating. These restrictions and the elimination of the set-asides discussed above resulted in a dramatic reduction in welfare recipients' participation in CTE (NCWGE, 2001).

Temporary Assistance for Needy Families (TANF), often referred to as "welfare," provides assistance and work opportunities to needy families by granting states the federal funds and wide flexibility to develop and implement their own welfare programs. In the Deficit Reduction Act of 2005, signed by President George W. Bush on February 8, 2006, TANF was reauthorized through 2010. The basic TANF block grant was authorized for $16.5 billion in federal funds (see www.aft.hhs.gov). TANF does not fund CTE programs directly; rather, its work requirement rules and participation rates impact the ability of single parents and displaced homemakers receiving welfare to access job training.

The 2006 TANF reauthorization did not overhaul TANF work participation standards. It maintained the "work first" philosophy, continued to restrict participation in CTE to 12 months, limited states' caseload in CTE to 30%, and maintained work participation

---

[3]Further guidance from the Department of Education in 1997 and 2001 regarding sexual harassment made clear that each school's (district's) antidiscrimination policies must include provisions for resolving complaints about sexual harassment.

rates at 50% for all families and 90% for two-parent families; however, the reauthorization made three significant changes that will make it more difficult for states to meet their participation rates:

1. Work participation standards are reduced only for caseload reductions that occur based on data from FY 2005;
2. Families in state-funded "Separate State Programs" will be counted in the work participation rate; and
3. The U.S. Department of Health and Human Services (HHS) is required to develop standards for states to define work activities and verify work participation (Congressional Research Service [CRS], 2006).

If states don't meet these participation rates, they could expect a 5% reduction in their state block grant and be required to have a higher maintenance of effort (state funding for welfare support). In FY 2004, 41 states/territories had participation rates below 50%, with the average around 32%. In addition, the Congressional Research Service's preliminary estimates indicate that in FY 2004, just over 5% of families in TANF and separate state programs participated in CTE, secondary education, or GED preparation (teen parents) (Ganzglass, 2006b). Although this could be interpreted as an incentive to purge state welfare roles even further, some advocates see this as an opportunity for states to increase their participation rates by encouraging recipients to access CTE as a work activity.

States *do* have the opportunity to maximize the use of CTE as a work activity. They can do this by making full use of their "allowance" for CTE (and teen parent school attendance), which allows them to place almost one third of all families that are counted toward the 50% rate in CTE. For states to do this, they must be willing to spend money on career and technical education. Because of severe budget cuts in many states in recent years, funding for education for welfare recipients has been significantly reduced.

Only time will tell the impact of these changes in TANF, but research shows that when welfare recipients gain employment skills, they are far more likely to achieve self-sufficiency.

Workforce Investment Act

The Workforce Investment Act (WIA), last reauthorized in 1998, is the federal investment in the U.S. Department of Labor's job training system. In FY 2006, $4.0 billion was appropriated for WIA programs. Funding for WIA is allocated to each state's Workforce Investment Board and distributed to Local Workforce Investment Boards to implement local workforce development programs. In many local workforce development areas, the provider of this job training is the CTE program at the local secondary school, area career technical center, or community college.

Despite increased need for services, from 2000–2003 there was a 14-percentage-point decline in the number of low-income, disadvantaged adults receiving training. The number of workers trained under WIA has declined significantly when compared to the preceding program, the Job Training Partnership Act (JTPA). Thirty-four percent fewer individuals received training under WIA

in Program Year 2002 than under the JTPA in Program Year 1998. The tiered system, instituted in 1998, in which job seekers had to pass sequentially through core and intensive services before receiving access to training services, resulted in many who needed training stuck in core services, like job search, rather than preparing themselves with the skills that the labor market demanded.

The United States has more than 7.3 million displaced homemakers and 13.6 million single mothers—all of whom can use training that will enable them to attain self sufficiency (Women Work!, 2005). During the reauthorization of the Perkins Act in 1998, then House Education and Workforce Committee Chairman, Representative William Goodling (R-PA), promised the gender-equity community that single parents and displaced homemakers would be better served under WIA's dislocated worker program than with gender-equity provisions to serve them in the Perkins Act. When WIA was reauthorized in 1998, displaced homemakers were included in the definition of dislocated workers, giving states the option of using dislocated worker funds to serve displaced homemakers. The reality is that Representative Goodling's promise was never fulfilled, as very few states have taken advantage of this option.

THE CURRENT STATUS OF GENDER EQUITY IN CTE

High School

The National Women's Law Center recently conducted a study of high school (Grades 9–12) CTE enrollment in 12 states[4] and found evidence of pervasive sex segregation (National Women's Law Center [NWLC], 2005a) In these states, females represent more than five out of six students enrolled in courses in traditionally female fields, but just 1 out of every 6 students in traditionally male courses (NWLC, 2005a, p. 4).

As demonstrated in Figure 20.1, girls are greatly overrepresented in courses in traditionally female fields—most noticeably in cosmetology, where 98% of students are female (NWLC, 2005a, p. 5). In both Arizona and Washington, only nine boys are enrolled in cosmetology courses in the entire state, compared to 561 and 340 girls, respectively (NWLC, 2005a, p. 5). Across the 12 states, girls also make up 87% of childcare students and 86% of students in health-related courses (70% when nutrition-related courses are included; NWLC, 2005a, p. 5). In Illinois, just 651 boys, compared to 7,731 girls, are enrolled in childcare courses (NWLC, 2005a, p. 5). In New Jersey, all 40 nursing students are female (NWLC, 2005a, p. 5).

Conversely, girls are severely underrepresented in fields that are nontraditional for their gender (NWLC, 2005a, p. 6). On average, girls represent just 14% of the total of all CTE students in the traditionally male fields of agriculture, precision production, engineering, construction and repair, and automotive service (NWLC, 2005a, p. 6). In many specific courses within these broader categories, girls are participating at even lower rates—and sometimes not at all (NWLC, 2005a, p. 6). For example, no girls are en-

---

[4]Arizona, California, Massachusetts, Michigan, Mississippi, Missouri, New Jersey, North Carolina (2003–2004 school year), Florida, Illinois, Maryland (2002–2003 school year), and Washington (2001–2002 school year).

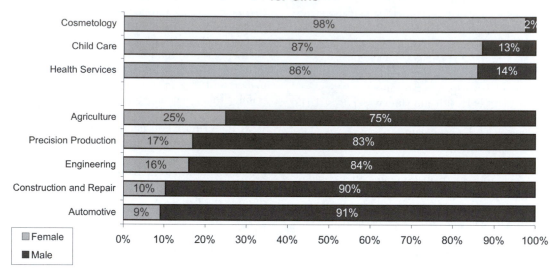

FIGURE 20.1   Sex segregation in CTE by gender.

rolled in electrician courses in Illinois, masonry courses in Missouri, or plumbing courses in North Carolina (NWLC, 2005a, p. 6). According to 2004 data, just one girl in the entire state of Florida was pursuing plumbing, and only one was learning electronic equipment installation in New Jersey (NWLC, 2005a, p. 6).

Though nontraditional courses for women represent a large percentage of CTE course options in every state (57%, on average), only a very small proportion of young women are enrolled in these courses. On average, just 1 out of every 7 girls taking CTE courses is enrolled in a nontraditional course, and in no state is more than 1 in 4 girls taking CTE courses enrolled in a nontraditional course. Conversely, girls are preparing for traditionally female occupations at a disproportionately high rate. Boys are enrolled in traditional and nontraditional programs at rates comparable to those of girls: 41% are enrolled in traditionally male courses and 9% in courses nontraditional for males. While this figure also indicates sex stereotyping, girls' enrollment patterns have especially troubling consequences, economic, and otherwise. On average, nearly 1 in 3 girls in the CTE system is concentrated in traditionally female fields—ranging from a low of 20% of girls in Michigan to a high of 38% in Maryland.

Although lack of access to educational opportunities affects both genders, it is particularly troubling for women in today's economy. Discouraging young women from pursuing nontraditional training can limit their access to nontraditional jobs, which are more likely to be high paying than traditional jobs. As Figure 20.2 shows, male-dominated fields pay a median hourly wage of $18.04, while the traditionally female fields pay just $13.80 on average. This translates into a median annual salary of $37,520 for men and $28,695 for women—a $8,825 wage gap (BLS, 2005). In local labor markets, some of the most high-demand and high-wage jobs are nontraditional for women.

In New Jersey, for example, network systems and data communications analysts are in very high demand and earn two to three times as much as those who work in the other four fastest growing occupations in the state. And among the 25 occupations with the highest percentage growth projected for 2004–2014 by the New Jersey Department of Labor, none of the five occupations with the highest hourly median wage are traditional for women (New Jersey Department of Labor, 2004).

Boys' and girls' low enrollment in nontraditional courses is neither due to low overall participation in CTE nor to a lack of nontraditional courses from which to choose. Rather, the magnitude of the enrollment disparities found in the research indicates that these patterns are not the product of unfettered choice alone, but rather that discrimination and barriers are limiting young men's and women's opportunities to pursue careers that are nontraditional to their gender. These barriers not only reinforce negative gender stereotypes, but also limit girls' opportunities to later pursue careers that often pay higher wages and offer better benefits and opportunities for advancement. As noted elsewhere, research regarding CTE and gender equity is very limited. Thus, there is more research available on the evidence of discrimination than on the mechanisms that produce it.

Additional high-school data is available on the ED Web site[5], where the Perkins accountability data is accessible by state. This accountability data includes (a) enrollment data, (b) performance measure data, including the participation and completion of underrepresented gender students in nontraditional CTE programs, and (c) summaries of the narratives from the states consolidated annual reports. Performance data is based on benchmarks set in 1999, when the accountability system was first put into place. Each year, states negotiate their annual performance measure with OVAE to set their performance goals for the year.

[5]Peer Collaborative Resource Network, available at http://edcountability.net.

Fields with a Higher Median Wage Have Fewer Female Students

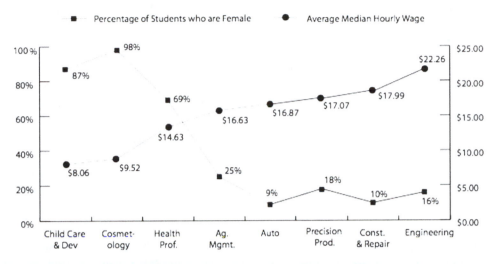

FIGURE 20.2   Female participation in CTE programs and in occupations by wage level.

High-school performance on the "fourth-core indicator" is poor at best. Only 18[6] states met their performance measure for "4s1" (secondary nontraditional participation), and only 17[7] states met their performance measure for "4s2" (secondary nontraditional completion) every year since the implementation of the 1998 Perkins Act. When disregarding the performance measure and only looking at an increase in performance over the time of implementation, however, 25[8] states increased performance on "4s1" and on "4s2" from program year 2000–01 to 2004–05.

Regardless, it is clear from both the National Women's Law Center report and the data reported to the OVAE that states and local educational agencies need assistance to increase the participation and completion of students pursuing nontraditional CTE programs.

Postsecondary

Unfortunately, data similar to that found in the NWLC study is not available for postsecondary CTE programs across the country. The most current data available to determine the status of postsecondary programs on increasing nontraditional enrollments is through the self-reported data submitted to the OVAE each year in the Perkins Consolidated Annual Reports. Mirroring secondary performance as described above, postsecondary performance on the fourth core indicator is also quite bleak. Only 13 states met their negotiated performance measure for "4p1" (postsecondary nontraditional participation) and only 10 states met their negotiated performance measure for "4p2" (postsecondary nontraditional completion) every year since the implementation of the 1998 Perkins Act. When disregarding the states-negotiated performance measure and only taking reported performance into account, however, 21 states increased their performance on "4p1" and 17 states increased their performance on "4p2" from Program Year 2000–01 to Program Year 2004–05. Needless to say, states and local education agencies are struggling with increasing the participation and completion of underrepresented gender students in nontraditional CTE programs.[9]

In a study conducted as part of the National Assessment of Vocational Education (Bailey, Alfonso, Scott, & Leinbach, 2004) researchers analyzed the educational outcomes of subpopulations who are traditionally disadvantaged in postsecondary education. These subpopulations include (a) students who are economically disadvantaged, (b) students who are academically disadvantaged, (c) single parents, (d) students of nontraditional

---

[6]FL, IA, IN, KY, LA, MA, MI, ND, NE, NJ, NV, OH, OK, SC, VA, VT, WI, WY

[7]AK, CA, FL, GA, IA, ID, KS, MA, MI, ND, NE, NJ, OK, VA, VT, WI, WY

[8]For 4s1: AL, CA, CO, DC, FL, GA, ID, IL, IN, KS, MI, MT, NC, NE, NV, NY, RI, VA, VT and for 4s2: AL, AZ, CO, DC, IN, KS, NE, NH, NV, RI, SC, SD, UT, VT

[9]The states that have met or exceeded their negotiated performance measure for postsecondary nontraditional participation for each year of the Perkins Act are Alaska, Connecticut, Delaware, Georgia, Louisiana, Massachusetts, Minnesota, North Dakota, New Mexico, Oregon, Rhode Island, South Carolina, Vermont, Washington, Wisconsin, West Virginia, and Wyoming. Those that exceeded or met their negotiated performance measure for postsecondary nontraditional completion are Alaska, Arizona, Connecticut, District of Columbia, Delaware, Georgia, Louisiana, Massachusetts, Maryland, Minnesota, North Dakota, New Mexico, Rhode Island, South Carolina, South Dakota, and Virginia. The fact that between 2000 and 2003, only 32% of states have consistently met one of their nontraditional performance measures at the postsecondary level and only 20% have met both of their nontraditional performance measures indicates that much work needs to be done at the postsecondary level as well.

age, and (e) females in nontraditional occupational major. The following are significant findings about these students:

- Special populations tend to complete degrees less often than nonspecial population groups.
- Special population students in occupational majors generally do not have significantly different completion rates than their peers in academic majors (which contrasts the findings for nonspecial population students).
- Economically disadvantaged students in occupational programs are as likely to complete their degree goals as their economically disadvantaged academic peers.
- Females in nontraditional majors are just as likely to complete their expected degrees as their counterparts who are enrolled in more traditional majors.

In this same study (Bailey et al., 2004), an analysis of the enrollments of underrepresented gender students was also completed supporting similar results as found by the National Women's Law Center for high schools.

Postsecondary CTE leads to greater employment and earnings gains, especially for women receiving public assistance. A study comparing the employment and earnings of TANF recipients who participated in the California Work Opportunity and Responsibility to Kids (CalWORKS) program and other women students who exited California community colleges in 1999 and 2000 found that CalWORKS women increased their earnings substantially after college (Mathur, Reichle, Stawn, & Wiseley, 2004). By the second year out of school, median annual earnings of CalWORKS women with vocational associate degrees were approximately 25% greater than women without AA degrees. Those who participated in certificate programs that were at least 30 units long earned more than $15,000 their second year out than women without certificates. Data such as this demonstrates the value of postsecondary CTE for low-income women, especially single parents and displaced homemakers.

The evidence given here also indicates a strong need for postsecondary institutions to continue their gender-equity efforts to ensure the success of students pursuing nontraditional careers, as well as single parents and displaced homemakers.

NEED FOR GENDER EQUITY IN CTE

Despite the years of hard work and funding, we cannot yet report that gender equity in CTE has been achieved. All significant measures of success—research on career development, data on K–12 course enrollment and postsecondary training programs, or occupational earning figures for women and men—point to the need for more work in this arena. The benefit CTE gives students in the labor market is not generally taken advantage of by females. In 2000, females earned fewer units in CTE than did their male counterparts (NCES, 2004).

Career Expectations: Gender Stereotypes and Family Responsibilities Limit Choices

Without continued efforts on the part of teachers, administrators, and parents to achieve gender equity in CTE, students will

unconsciously limit their career choices. Career selection—and elimination—based on gender-role socialization begins early. Research on human development finds that children as young as ages six to eight years begin to eliminate career choices because they are the wrong sex type (Gottfredson, 1981). By early adolescence, students already have strongly defined gender-role expectations about work (Women's Educational Equity Act [WEEA] Resource Center, 2002); however, most career exploration programs do not begin until students' adolescence, well after stereotypes are already well established. (WEEA Resource Center, 2002).

In an inequitable environment, students will make career choices based on limited factors, including family and personal demographic characteristics. Parent education and occupation, social class, and such factors as acculturation and discrimination all affect how students develop their career expectations. "Additional structural factors, including limited opportunities, immediate financial or family needs, and, for some, the mobility of living as migrant or seasonal working families, have an even greater impact" (WEEA Resource Center, 2002, p. 2).

Family and personal demographic factors often contribute to highly sex-segregated career choices. Girls with low-socioeconomic-status parents have higher sex-stereotyping scores than girls with high-socioeconomic-status parents, while boys with low-socioeconomic-status parents have lower sex-stereotyping scores than boys with high-socioeconomic-status parents (Billings, 1992). Some research shows that for African American females, "early gender-role socialization is less sex-stereotyped [than for other girls] and that African American girls often experience more crossover between traditionally male and female roles and duties in the household" and may be more open to considering nontraditional careers (Wierzbinski, 1998, p. 1).

The need for continued work to promote gender equity is just as great at the postsecondary level. Perceived and real concerns about balancing work and other life responsibilities will continue to significantly limit women's career selection. While female college students now have career expectations equal to those of males, they still perceive role conflicts and see family issues such as raising children and lacking affordable, quality childcare as potential career barriers, concerns shared by few

TABLE 20.1 Females in Majors Nontraditional for their Gender Nontraditional Occupational Majors, NELS: 88-00

Occupational Majors

Female Nontraditional Majors	Males	Females
Agriculture	80.9%	19.1%
Engineering	84.3%	15.7%
Engineering Technologies	80.9%	19.1%
Construction	88.3%	11.7%
Mechanics/Electronics	98.7%	1.3%
Precision Production	98.6%	3.2%
Male Nontraditional Majors		
Business Support/Secretarial	23.3%	76.7%
Consumer Services	8.9%	91.1%
Nursing/Nurse Assisting	17.8%	82.2%

Source: Bailey et al. (2004), Table E.1

men (American Association of University Women [AAUW] Educational Foundation, 1998; Alfeld et al., 2006). Spousal or significant-other support was found to be a major factor that differentiated the women who remained in their nontraditional occupation for more than two years from the women who left within two years or who never entered (Shanahan, Denner, Rhodes, & Anderson, 1999).

Course and Program Enrollment: Stubbornly Sex-Segregated

The need for continued efforts to achieve gender equity in CTE still exists because current data reveals persistent patterns of sex segregation in career exploration and preparation programs. The patterns, which can be dismantled at a local or state level with intense and focused attention, are consistent for high school and postsecondary CTE course and program enrollment.

In spite of the requirements of Title IX and the gender-equity provisions in the Perkins Act, pervasive sex segregation in high school CTE programs—with girls predominantly enrolled in "traditionally female" programs and boys primarily participating in "traditionally male" courses—still exists nationwide (NWLC, 2005a).

In 1980, sex segregation in vocational education was clear, with females representing 91% of students training as nursing assistants, 87% of those training as community health workers, and 92% of those training as cosmetologists and secretaries (Farmer et al., 1985). At the same time, males in vocational education were overrepresented in auto mechanics (96%), carpentry (96%), small-engine repair (96%), electrical technology (95%), welding (95%), appliance repair (94%), and electronics (90%; Farmer et al., 1985).

Twenty years later, a report conducted by the NWLC using state-level data from 12 selected states' data revealed the same pattern of sex segregation across the nation: female students make up 98% of students enrolled in cosmetology, 87% of students enrolled in childcare courses, and 86% of students enrolled in courses that prepare them to be health assistants (NWLC, 2005a, p. 5). Male students, in contrast, comprise 94% of the student body in training programs for plumbers and electricians, 90% of the students studying to be welders or carpenters, and 91% of those studying automotive technologies (NWLC, 2005a, p. 5)

In associate degree programs, women are almost four times as likely as men to major in health fields, and are also more likely to major in business and office fields (NCWGE, 2001, p. 8). In contrast, male students in associate degree programs are more than five times as likely to major in technical education and more than fourteen times as likely to major in trade and industry programs (NCWGE, 2001, p. 8).

Women and Men in the Workforce: Substantial Disparities

The need for gender-equity work within CTE continues because America's workforce remains sex-segregated and is not meeting the needs of real working men and women. For women, these needs often include salaries that allow them to support themselves and their families. Census data show there were more than 20.9 million displaced homemakers and sin-

gle parents in 2003, a 39% increase from 1994. The people in this population subset are likely to be poor, unemployed, or working in low-wage jobs. In fact, nearly 30% are working in low-paying service jobs that offer few, if any, benefits (Women Work!, 2005).

A lack of programs that help women prepare for supporting themselves and their families persists. According to a 2002 report by the NWLC, "Title IX and Equal Opportunity in Vocational and Technical Education: A Promise Still Owed to the Nation's Young Women," the pervasive sex segregation of female students into traditionally female programs has a serious adverse impact on their economic well being. For example, students entering childcare fields will earn only a median salary of $7.43 per hour, and cosmetologists will earn a median salary of $8.49 per hour (NWLC, 2002, p. 2). By contrast, the median salary for students who become plumbers and pipe fitters is $18.19 per hour, and the top 10% of workers in that field will make $30.06 per hour (NWLC, 2002, p. 3). Similarly, electricians have a median salary of $19.29, and are eligible to earn up to $31.71 while progressing in the career tracks created in their field (NWLC, 2002, p. 3). In no case, moreover, does the amount earned by the top 10% of workers in the predominantly female fields of cosmetology, childcare, or medical assistant even begin to approach the *median* wages earned by those employed in predominantly male occupations (NWLC, 2002, p. 4). For example, the top 10% of childcare workers earn $10.71 per hour, which is 41% *lower* than the median amount earned by mechanical drafters (NWLC, 2002, p. 4).

Wage earnings for men and women are significantly different within the same occupation, which raises questions of pay equity. For example, in 2005, the median weekly earnings for men and women in construction trades were $606 and $504, respectively, and the median weekly earnings for men and women as registered nurses were $1,011 and $930, respectively (BLS, 2005). Another interesting phenomenon exists: wages increase when men enter traditionally female occupations and decrease when women enter traditionally male occupations. For example, once a male-dominated profession, veterinarians are inching closer to fifty-fifty on gender with veterinary school enrollments now at 71.4% female (Veterinary Economics, 2002); however, male veterinarians earn 20.7% higher pay than their female counterparts (Veterinary Economics, 2003). As more women enter the profession, the average wages continue to decline. These data suggest that, in addition to sex segregation in CTE programs, gender bias is alive and well in the workplace. Regardless, the benefits women may gain because of careers in nontraditional occupations merit ongoing gender-equity work in CTE and with employers to overcome the challenges they face.

Men in nontraditional careers also face consequences that adversely affect their well-being. Men who work in nontraditional career fields face institutionalized challenges to their sense of masculinity (Henson & Rogers, 2001) and often face intimidating behaviors and stereotypes that prevent their full participation (Thurtle, Hammond, & Jennings, 1998). Men in nontraditional careers may also face job-placement difficulties (Thurtle et al., 1998). For more information on workforce issues, see chapter 4, "Impact of Education on Gender Equity in Employment and its Outcomes."

The most important variable affecting earnings of both genders is occupation, not education. Noble (1992) noted that women were stuck on the "sticky floor" of low-wage occupations. Mastracci (2004) described the occupational segregation among genders akin to creating a "pink collar ghetto," in which 65% of all working women are clustered into 20 of the lowest-paying occupations. Even among the women working in high-skill, high-wage, high-technology occupations (which are nontraditional by gender), women continue to cluster in the entry-level job titles. For example, five of the fastest growing occupations through 2012 are in the information technology industry (U.S. Department of Labor, 2002a). Women are making inroads into this emerging field; however, they are clustered into lower paying, lower skilled aspects of the industry, such as information processing, while the majority of the highest-paying specialties in the fastest-growing occupations, such as systems engineering, are held by men (U.S. Department of Labor, 2002b). Contrary to the "glass ceiling" phenomenon, where women are unable to rise to higher-level positions within male-dominated professions, a vastly different experience is noted for men in traditionally female occupations, such as nurses, elementary school teachers, librarians, and social workers. Hultin (2003) described an unequaled upward mobility of men in traditionally female-dominated professions as a "glass escalator," where men are quickly moved into higher-paying, more prestigious positions within the occupation.

PROBABLE CAUSES FOR THE LACK OF GENDER EQUITY IN CTE

Research shows that women and girls have made great educational progress in recent years. The gender gaps in math and science have been narrowed. Women surpass men in both bachelor and master degree achievement; however, it appears that these achievements are not being translated into nontraditional career choices that lead to high-skill, high-wage careers in science, math, engineering, and technology. What does research reveal about educational practices that are root causes for students choosing to follow a traditional or nontraditional career path? The causes are found not only in CTE itself, but also in the larger sphere of education and in societal stereotypes. They include (a) lack of early exposure to nontraditional occupations and role models; (b) student attitudes; (c) unsupportive career guidance practices and materials; (d) lack of encouragement to participate in math, science, and technology; (e) stereotyped instructional strategies and curriculum materials; (f) a chilly school/classroom climate that can result in student isolation; (g) lack of self-efficacy; and (h) limited support services (National Centers for Career and Technical Education [NCCTE], 2003).

Lack of Early Exposure to Nontraditional Occupations and Role Models

The American Counseling Association (1998) stressed the importance of early exposure to careers as a foundation for later career decisions. To be truly effective, exposure to nontraditional careers must be initiated in elementary school. Gender stereotyping regarding occupations occurs early, with children ages six to eight years beginning to eliminate careers because they were the wrong sex-type (Kerka, 2001). In fact, Billings (1992) studied perceptions of second and sixth graders and found that second graders have significantly higher sex-stereotyping scores than sixth graders. Schools have the potential to impact such stereotypes.

Nontraditional role models are a significant factor in a student's choice to pursue a nontraditional career. Many choose careers because they have been exposed to them through their interactions with others, or because they can personally identify with individuals in those fields. Interviews with women employed in the trades revealed four significant factors that influenced their career choice: (a) a perceived innate ability, (b) a strong sense of self, (c) a desire for independence, and (d) access to role models—especially family members (Greene & Stitt-Gohdes, 1997, as cited in NCCTE, 2003, p. 62). Role models can come from family, community, and the school. The lack of role models in nontraditional fields can have strong consequences in career development, particularly for minorities (Esters & Bowen, 2003).

Student Attitudes

Attitudes and biases regarding the world of school and the world of work are based on social, familial, educational, and societal experiences. Socialization has a profound impact on the ways in which males and females think about potential occupations (Welty & Puck, 2001). Further, specific courses are associated with either femininity (e.g., humanities) or masculinity (e.g., technology; Welty & Puck, 2001). These student attitudes, shaped and influenced by complex and dynamic aspects of culture and society, can be positively influenced by targeted programming, which includes early exposure to nontraditional careers and role models (Multistate Academic and Vocational Curriculum Consortium [MAVCC], 2001).

Biased Career Guidance Materials and Practices

While students often get information about career decision making through the guidance process in their schools, gender-biased career guidance practices can deter students from participating in nontraditional training programs. Guidance personnel often use interest inventories and aptitude assessments to assist students in selecting career-related coursework or majors in college, and these assessments are sometimes a means through which gender bias is propagated. For example, the Armed Services Vocational Aptitude Battery (ASVAB) assesses exposure to a subject (e.g., tests knowledge of automotive components, systems, tools, and repairs—a subject to which women have little exposure), rather than general aptitude (General Accounting Office, 1999). For more information on these assessment issues see chapter 8, "Gender Equity in Testing and Assessment."

Gender stereotyping is also evident in the CTE career counseling and recruitment system. Some counselors may not advise students on nontraditional careers because they incorrectly assume they will not be interested (NWLC, 2005a). Stereotypes and bias related to female students of color may be even greater with regards to technical and scientific fields (Ginorio & Huston, 2001). A report from the U.S. Commission on Civil Rights (2000) emphasized how important it is for teachers and counselors to encourage girls' participation in technical fields.

Lack of Encouragement to Participate in Math, Science, and Technology

Participation and success in math, science, and technology courses are gateways for participation in nontraditional careers for women, as well as in high-skill, high-demand occupations. Yet girls are still underrepresented in the preparation for these occupations. Social-psychological causes for this difference can be attributed to teachers' attitudes, beliefs, and behaviors; girls' beliefs and attitudes; current teaching practices for math and science; and the influence of parents and society (Clewell & Campbell, 2002). While significant progress has been made on closing the gap in mathematics, there still exists a perception that women are not as good as men at quantitative disciplines, and, at about middle-school age, girls tend to lose interest and confidence in math and science (National Science Foundation, 2003). While girls are taking more science and math courses at the high-school level, the gender gap in computer science advanced placement test takers has actually widened (Gavin, 2000). Relatively few girls are continuing on in engineering and other physical and quantitative disciplines at the postsecondary level, and even fewer are choosing careers in these fields (Clewell & Campbell, 2002), in spite of the fact that girls have narrowed the gap in skills and knowledge by high school graduation. The *Handbook* chapter 13, "Gender Equity in Science, Engineering, and Technology," provides more information on the progress and continued challenges in these areas.

Stereotyped Instructional Strategies and Curriculum Materials

In other chapters, the issue of instructional strategies is addressed comprehensively. These issues are magnified for teachers and students in CTE. For example, Annexstein (2003) reported that teachers often treat students differently in career and technical classrooms, including attributing boys' success in technology to talent while dismissing girls' success to luck or hard work, and having boys learn by doing while having girls sit and study their texts.

Similarly, curriculum materials with limited visual images of individuals in nontraditional careers can negatively impact student participation. Visual representation of working individuals in textbooks, displays, videos, and curricula influences students' gender stereotypes about career options (Kerka, 2001). The way nontraditional careers are advertised and perceived has a significant influence on students considering such careers. Curriculum materials should be evaluated prior to selection and distribution to ensure that they fairly represent the diversity of students (Northrop, 2002).

A Chilly School/Classroom Climate that Results in Student Isolation

Students who experience gender stereotyping, intimidating behaviors, or sexual harassment while in nontraditional CTE programs are less likely to complete the program. Often, nontraditional students have these experiences within the broader educational setting as well, giving clear messages that they do not fit the norm. Indirect messages from teachers and classmates about classroom fit with regard to physical environment (e.g., giving more physical assistance to girls, thereby conveying the assumption they are not strong enough to do the work), teacher-student interactions, and student-student interactions can create barriers to success in nontraditional programs (Sandler & Hoffman, 1992). The subtleties of the classroom environment, including the look and feel, send signals to students about how well they belong (Welty & Puck, 2001). Research suggests that a wide range of inequities in classrooms exists between student and teacher behavior; teachers, regardless of their gender, tend to ask male students three times as many questions as their female students (M. Sadker & D. Sadker, 1994). An alarming rate of student-to-student sexual harassment has been reported (American Association of University Women [AAUW], 2001). Success rates improve when efforts to create gender-equitable classrooms that engage all students are implemented (Ryan, 1999).

Women and girls engaged in nontraditional programs often have to overcome barriers in educational settings. Sanogo (1995) found that over 75% of female nontraditional students report that being the only girl in a class is difficult. Women often find male-dominated educational programs, where few women, if any, are enrolled, as competitive and unappealing. The lack of critical mass of female students is a great deterrent to completion of a nontraditional CTE program. Likewise, women tend to see the content itself as isolating. For example, women perceive use and benefit from technological pursuits when they are designed to perform a specific needed purpose, but men tend to enjoy technology as an interest independent of its application (Gurer & Camp, 2000). Programs that lack same-sex role models and/or same-sex instructors can produce feelings of isolation for men and women, even in otherwise equitable educational environments. Many nontraditional students do not want to be seen as a novelty, a pioneer, or a "token" (Milgram, 1997).

Lack of Self-Efficacy

Self-efficacy, referring to the expectation/belief that one can succeed in careers that are compatible with one's abilities, impacts the willingness of people to successfully pursue nontraditional careers. Traditionally, adult women express lower levels of self-efficacy with regard to math and science concepts (e.g., visual-spatial skills; Betsworth, 1997). Low levels of self-efficacy restrain the number of women entering and completing education and training programs in traditionally male-dominated industries. Margolis and Fisher (2003) described the difference between male and female attributions of failure. Males tend to attribute failure to external factors (e.g., the test was too hard), and females tend to attribute failure to internal factors (e.g., lack of understanding of the material) and success to external factors, such as luck, identified in the research as the imposter phenomenon or syndrome (Clance & Imes, 1978). Interventions that deal with interest and confidence in nontraditional careers can be successful in mediating the effects of lack of self-efficacy (Betz & Schifano, 2000).

Limited Support Services

Students enrolled in nontraditional CTE programs who receive individualized support services, such as tutoring, mentoring, support groups, childcare, and transportation, are more likely to succeed. Research analyzing the success rates for students in nontraditional educational programs indicated that students who are offered, and who regularly access, supplemental support services have a higher rate of program persistence (Montclair State University, 1997). For example, male nursing students are more likely to be retained if same-sex role modeling is provided (Brady & Sharrod, 2003). Programs promoting gender equity in education through the provision of a comprehensive support system have been subjected to reduced or eliminated funding (NWLC, 2004; NCWGE, 2001). When Perkins was reauthorized in 1998, many states assumed that support services were no longer an allowable use of funds. Advocacy groups worked with OVAE and convinced them to release Program Memorandum-OVAE/DVTE 99-13, clarifying the allowable use of funds for this purpose (ED, Office of Vocational and Adult Education [OVAE], 1999) The ongoing provision of support services will allow students to focus on what's important—their education (Visher & Hudis, 1999).

STRATEGIES THAT CAN MAKE A DIFFERENCE

A discussion of the probable causes of the problems, as identified by the literature, is enlightening, but does not provide guidance as to what has been tried and proven to be successful in providing more equitable opportunities in career training and choice for both men and women. Breaking down the stereotypes and opening options based upon interest and skill rather than gender role stereotypes are the goals. Participation in and completion of training for nontraditional careers is the barometer for this change. The following strategies have indicated positive movement toward this larger goal. As with all initiatives that require lasting change, the process is slow and needs to be constantly reinforced.

Review Educational and Counseling Materials Used with Students

The removal of gender bias and the presentation of positive nontraditional images is often the first step toward providing an equitable experience for men and women in CTE. School publicity and curriculum materials often carry gender-bias messages that impact student career choices. Gender-biased career guidance expectations and practices are often major barriers to student participation in nontraditional programs. Checklists, such as one developed by the Wisconsin Department of Education, have been developed to review not only the career guidance practices, but also curricula (both materials and practices) to increase awareness of these gender practices. The evaluation of equity programs in Louisiana found that programs successful at retaining students in nontraditional career technical programs evaluated their materials for gender bias and stereotyping (University of Southwestern Louisiana, 1993).

Conduct Gender-Equity Professional Development with Teachers at All Levels

While CTE teachers certainly can benefit from professional development, teachers at all levels must become better aware of gender bias and stereotyping in curriculum materials and classroom instruction that create a negative effect on student course selection. Teachers need rigorous and ongoing professional development to learn and improve instructional strategies for working with nontraditional students. Succeeding at Fairness: Effective Teaching for All Students, Generating Expectations for Student Achievement (GESA), Student Achievement Grounded in Equity (SAGE), and The Equity Principal are research-based professional development models that have been effectively used to increase teachers' and administrators' (K–16) knowledge of equitable teaching practices and leadership skills (Grayson & Martin, 2003a, 2003b; ED, 2000).

Teacher behavior that perpetuates gender bias can influence student participation in courses and selection of further study in a particular career area (Graham, 2001). To encourage participation in nontraditional programs for both men and women, collaborations should be built among teachers in feeder schools and with programs and courses that lead to participation in nontraditional CTE programs (National School-to-Work Opportunities Office, 1996; Graham, 2001).

Implement and Model Gender-Fair Institutional Strategies

Schools that value nontraditional choices for their students and model gender equity in their institutional practices are more likely to have students participate in nontraditional programs. Sound institutional strategies include (a) inviting nontraditional representatives to participate on advisory committees, (b) hiring nontraditional instructors, (c) conducting workshops on nontraditional careers with students and staff, (d) providing grant incentives in Requests for Proposals, (e) purchasing materials portraying nontraditional students, and (f) collecting data that link occupations and gender (National School-to-Work Opportunities Office, 1996). Assessments have been developed, such as the Building Level Equity Assessment by the Midwest Equity Assistance Center (MEAC), that can be used to help schools conduct institution-wide evaluations of how well they are doing to promote gender equity (Midwest Equity Assistance Center [MEAC], 2000).

Increase Competence in Diversity and Sexual Harassment Prevention

Students are not likely to persist in an instructional environment where their contributions are not valued, they are being harassed, or they feel they are being treated unfairly. The literature identifies decreasing gender bias among administrators, faculty, and staff as a common strategy for retaining female students in math and science and nontraditional students in CTE programs (Markert, 1996; National School-to-Work Opportunities Office, 1996; University of Southwestern Louisiana, 1993; Ryan, 1999; Clark, 2000; Graham, 2001). For more information, see chapter 11, "Sexual Harassment: The Hidden Gender Equity Problem."

Invite, Involve, and Educate Parents

Parents are the first to introduce a student to a career, and they have the strongest influence on student course selection and career choice (Ferris State University, 2002). Parents are often one of the strongest influences on students pursuing nontraditional careers. Greene and Stitt-Gohdes (1997) found that positive role models, especially family members, often contribute to an individual's decision to pursue a nontraditional career.

Other parents may allow a student to explore a nontraditional career, but may not support a student pursuing one as a permanent career choice. Lack of support can be somewhat attributed to misinformation about a career as well as sex bias and stereotyping. This can be overcome through parent education and exposure to accurate career information. Parents who are employed in a nontraditional occupation should be invited to serve as role models to the students and their parents.

Provide Nontraditional Role Models, Mentors, and Job Shadowing

Students need to see others like themselves participating in a career to believe they can do it, too. Ongoing exposure to nontraditional role models and mentors and job exposure with an individual in a nontraditional career are overwhelmingly presented in the nontraditional training and employment literature as a common and successful strategy for recruiting and retaining students in nontraditional careers (Montclair State College, 1991; Foster & Simonds, 1995; Florida State Dept. of Education, 1996; National School-to-Work Opportunities Office, 1996; Markert, 1996; Clark, 2000; Gavin, 2000). The use of Internet online e-mentoring has expanded the reach of mentoring relationships. The opportunity for mentor and mentee to communicate via e-mail and the Internet can expand the potential for additional communication. E-mentoring programs have been used very successfully in the STEM fields with girls and women engineers and scientists. In a 2003 evaluation of MentorNet, an online mentoring program for diversity in engineering and science, over half the students reported increased confidence that they are in the right major and can succeed in their field of study (Barsion, 2004).

Conduct Middle-School and Pretechnical Training Programs

Overwhelmingly, the research indicates that early nontraditional experiences and exposure to nontraditional careers positively affects student potential for pursuing a nontraditional career (Markert, 1996; Education Development Center, Inc., 1996; Kloosterman, 1994; Van Buren, 1993; Kerka, 2001). Many of the strategies discussed concerning parent education and student exposure in the curricula are more effective if used at the earliest grades possible, but especially at the middle-school grades.

Pretechnical training programs, at all educational levels, that introduce students to nontraditional careers (a) give them hands-on learning opportunities, (b) relieve math anxiety, (c) develop support groups, and (d) expose students to nontraditional role models, thereby encouraging participation in CTE programs. When compared to a control group, students attending a gender-equity program had significantly higher levels of career and lifestyle self-efficacy and indicated greater knowledge of nontraditional careers and training opportunities. Nontraditional students perceived greater encouragement to explore nontraditional classes and had significantly higher occupational attractiveness scores (Fox Valley Technical College, 1991; Mewhorter, 1994; Read, 1991).

Conduct Targeted Recruitment Activities

Nontraditional students must be recruited into nontraditional programs. Students do not believe they are welcome unless specifically invited to explore and supported to overcome their own gender bias and stereotyping. Successful recruitment strategies include (a) creating career-technical programs to reach all students, (b) presenting career clusters in a way that shows how career pathways can align with interests, (c) giving students multiple opportunities to explore both traditional and nontraditional careers, and (d) helping students overcome stereotypes of appropriate jobs for their gender (Clark, 2000). In the fall of 1995, 7 of 95 students in the undergraduate program in computer science at Carnegie Mellon University were women. In 2000, 54 of 130, or 42%, were women. In a research study conducted during this period, a substantial part of the success of the program was attributed to recruitment efforts to get women to apply, enroll, and persist (Margolis & Fisher, 2002). The lack of a pipeline opening (entry) is often the limiting factor to increasing the participation and completion of students in nontraditional careers.

Collaborate with Community-Based Organizations and Business

Many community-based organizations have nontraditional career exposure programs for young girls (e.g., Girls, Inc.©, American Association of University Women, YWCA, Girl Scouts, Take Our Daughters and Sons to Work). Working with community-based organizations to expose students to nontraditional careers has been identified as one successful strategy for teachers to use as a means of increasing enrollment of students in nontraditional training programs (University of Southwestern Louisiana, 1993).

Businesses have a vested interest in helping students develop the skills required for employment in their industry. Intel Corporation, in cooperation with Boston's Museum of Science and the Massachusetts Institute of Technology Media Lab, has started an after-school program, Computer Clubhouse, for female and minority students with adult mentors to learn more about computer technology (Brunner, 2000). Cisco, Inc. has started a gender initiative for recruiting women into the Cisco Networking Academies (Cisco Systems, Inc., 2000). Training programs that partner with corporations have dramatic benefits for low-income women. An example of this strategy would be the Nontraditional Employment for Women (NEW) program that places students into occupations with an average starting wage of $12/hour (National Organization for Women [NOW] Legal Defense and Education Fund, 2001).

Conduct Nontraditional Student Support Groups, Peer Counseling, and a Continuum of Support Services

Students are more likely to complete programs if they feel they are supported and are part of a peer group. These strategies are also more likely to improve a student's self-efficacy. Several studies of effective programs have identified successful retention strategies as those that include access to nontraditional student clubs and team support systems, and participation in math clubs, competitions, and after-school programs (Foster & Simonds, 1995; Silverman, 1999; Gavin, 2000). Students who participated in nontraditional support programs experienced increased self-esteem (Montclair State University, 1997). Chapter 7, "The Treatment of Gender Equity in Teacher Education," provides additional valuable information.

Students who face barriers in addition to those of gender need comprehensive support services to complete their CTE programs. Nontraditional training programs that work with populations with multiple barriers and offer a complete array of support services boast higher success rates. These support services include tutoring, childcare, transportation, and tuition assistance.

EXAMPLES OF IMPLEMENTATION OF EFFECTIVE STRATEGIES

During the years of implementation of the Perkins Act equity provisions, investment in research and development and in quality evaluation was inconsistent. Very limited research was done on effective programs. The following programs have been identified through rigorous evaluations and reviews. Each program was reviewed for evidence of success and effectiveness, a strong research base, educational significance, and the ability to be replicated in other settings. All selection criteria can be found in the references indicated for each program. These successful programs have implemented many of the strategies addressed above. Unfortunately, effective programs like these may very well no longer be used because of lack of funding.

Ohio Department of Education, Orientation to Nontraditional Occupations for Women (ONOW) Program, Ohio

The U.S. Department of Education's Gender-Equity Expert Panel selected the ONOW program as its only Exemplary Gender-Equity Program (ED, OERI, 2001). First implemented in 1987 using Perkins gender-equity set-aside funds, the ONOW program was designed to assist socioeconomically disadvantaged women and incarcerated women to explore and successfully enter high-wage careers in nontraditional fields in which they have been underrepresented, such as skilled construction (e.g., welding, carpentry), manufacturing (e.g., machine trades, production technician), transportation (e.g., automotive technology, truck driving, delivery), protective services (e.g., emergency medical services, fire fighters, highway patrol), and high-tech (e.g. Web design, drafting). The purpose of the program was to help participants overcome multiple barriers and become economically self-sufficient. It also sought to increase the numbers of women enrolled in nontraditional vocational education programs, to decrease the numbers of women on welfare in Ohio and to reduce the recidivism rate of women offenders. Participants attended eight-week training sessions, in which they received hands-on experience using applied math and science and worked with hand and power tools. The program also addressed concerns of physical fitness, employability skills, and self-esteem. Between 45 and 75 women were served at each program site per year. In addition, each ONOW coordinator participated in training designed to reduce or eliminate bias and increase sensitivity to diversity.

A five-year longitudinal study by Ohio State University showed higher wages for those who entered nontraditional employment, and confirmed that 70% of the respondents continued to be employed. At the time of the study, 76% of the participants who had been on public assistance when accepted for the program were working full time, completely off of public assistance, and earning an average of $9.38 per hour.

Minot Public Schools CTE Programs, Minot, North Dakota

Three nontraditional career exploration programs sponsored by the Minot Public Schools (MPS) received the Highest Recognition from the 2005 Programs and Practices That Work: Preparing Students for Nontraditional Careers Project (NWLC, 2005b). Over a three-year period, MPS sponsored two careers and skills awareness days (Diva Tech and Define Your Dreams) and one technology camp (Technology on the Go). Over the three years that these programs were offered at MPS High School, enrollment in classes that were nontraditional for students' gender increased by 32%.

The MPS DIVA Tech program was a daylong event targeted at girls in Grades 8–12. It provided students with hands-on opportunities to explore nontraditional areas offered in the MPS trades and technology curriculum, including auto tech, welding, and information technology. Each student selected several hour-long laboratory experiences and used the skills learned to create a take-home project. Classroom instructors and female student assistants served as helpers and role models in the labs. Professionals who hold jobs that are nontraditional for their gender gave a workshop and answered questions relating to occupational responsibilities, training requirements, salaries, benefits, and barriers in the workforce. In addition, a school career counselor described the nontraditional course available for girls in the upcoming school year and answered questions.

Define Your Dreams, targeting seventh- and eighth-grade students, brought together female professionals and students to help young women realize the importance of math, science, and problem-solving skills in daily life and careers. Students explored nontraditional careers in hands-on workshops and learned about nontraditional course options for their four-year high school plans.

Complementing the two career days, Technology on the Go took girls in grades 8–11 on a three-day field trip. Guided by female professionals, students explored local businesses, coal mines, and electrical and manufacturing plants. Throughout the tours, students were encouraged to take photographs that they used to design their own publications at the end of the program.

Illinois Center for Specialized Professional Support, Illinois State University,

The NTO Look, Illinois

Selected as the 2006 winner of the Programs and Practices That Work: Preparing Students for Nontraditional Careers Project (NWLC et al., 2006), the NTO Look is a project of the Illinois Center for Specialized Professional Support at Illinois State University and administered through funds from the Carl D. Perkins Act of 1998. The NTO Look encourages secondary and postsecondary educational institutions to partner in order to implement and strengthen their nontraditional programs. The partnerships must base their program and research on the practices that work in recruiting and retaining students in nontraditional programs; set realistic long-term and short-term goals; design and implement activities to meet those goals; and evaluate the effectiveness of the program. In the implementation phase of each site's project, the NTO Look provides each partnership with professional development, technical support, specialized resources, and financial assistance.

An important element of the NTO Look is its self-assessment requirement. Each project must complete a self-study and consider accompanying research prior to designing its activities. The NTO Look Self-Study systematically assists educational organizations in identifying strengths and challenges and leads them through a series of questions that results in the development of a strategy that has a greater potential for successfully meeting their goals. Nearly 80% of the Illinois community colleges participated in the NTO Look, and similar projects sponsored by the Illinois Center or Specialized Professional Support (ICSPS). In 2005, Illinois' postsecondary system achieved its negotiated performance level for the Perkins fourth core indicator for the first time and has credited NTO Look as one of two factors contributing to its improvement.

Minneapolis Public Schools, High Tech Girl's Society, Minnesota

Recipient of the 2006 Honorable Mention Award for the Programs and Practices That Work: Preparing Students for Nontraditional Careers Project (NWLC et al., 2006), the High Tech Girl's Society (HTG'S) was launched in 2003 to increase the representation of girls in traditionally male-dominated, high-tech courses such as aviation, engineering, and information technology. The program serves a population that is primarily low-income girls of color. Preliminary data show that 79% of the HTG'S participants are students of color, which is almost 7 percentage points higher than the district average.

The HTG'S implements a rigorous academic and technical curriculum through after-school, hands-on learning activities, tours, seminars, and other related school activities. The club works in cooperation with college, universities, and business partners to provide mentoring and counseling as well. Mentoring is essential to the program, and the HTG'S connects the girls with women who are employed in high-tech careers, and gives opportunities to meet and network with other young women with similar interests in Minneapolis high schools. The program has found that field trips to colleges and worksites, and related networking, mentoring, and teacher training activities, have helped girls to become leaders in traditionally male-dominated classes. Their presence and success and advocacy with friends have encouraged other girls to enroll in and complete programs.

The participation of girls in nontraditional classes in Minneapolis Public Schools has been increasing since the inception of the HTG'S. In 2002, male students made up 61% of students enrolled in high-tech courses, while female students made up only 39%. By 2004–05, male students comprised just over 56% of students, and female students comprised just under 44%. Moreover, female enrollment in high-tech classes increased by as many as 6 times in some cases, including increased female participation in male-dominated classes like engineering, IT, construction, and auto technology. A survey of 2005–06 "High Tech" girls indicated that they will take more math and science—and harder math and science—than is required through Minneapolis Public Schools' minimum graduation requirements.

RECOMMENDATIONS

The programs described above are examples of the effectiveness of the use of Perkins funds for gender-equity activities in improving opportunities for CTE students, especially women and girls. During the years the set-aside funds were in place, a growing number of educators and students gained an understanding of the importance of gender equity, even if they were not themselves involved in nontraditional CTE. The funding helped support change and create change, even when many traditional CTE instructors did not welcome that change. The loss of gender-equity funds has meant the loss of valuable programs, less support services for women (especially low-income women), and less emphasis on changing the status quo.

In retrospect, a major challenge to accomplishing the intent of the gender-equity provisions of the Perkins Act over its many years was the Department of Education's lack of leadership to require standardized program evaluations and data collection so that true measurement of the national impact of programs could be done. Instead, states set their own standards with the result that apples were compared to oranges on the national level. In addition, the National Center for Research in Vocational Education refused to conduct research related to gender equity under Perkins. Had more quality research been done and evaluation standards been set, the overall achievements in gender equity within CTE would have been documented and might have been much greater.

The recommendations that follow are based on the limited research available, the experience of gender-equity experts in CTE, and the effects changes in public policy, both positive and negative, have had over the past 20 years on gender equity in CTE. They are primarily based on assumptions that substantial equity can be achieved by increasing women's participation in high paying nontraditional occupations and by creating a more inclusive climate within schools and the CTE classroom. The authors of this chapter share the belief that all occupations should be valued with real availability for both men and women. See chapter 4, "Impact of Education on Gender Equity in Employment and its Outcomes."

Recommendations for Federal and State Policymakers

Federal and state policymakers should increase efforts to make the public aware of the provisions of the Title IX regulations that are directly relevant to CTE and to enforce these regulations. The public primarily associates Title IX with the progress that has been made in the participation of females in athletics, and does not realize that Title IX also affects educational programs in any educational institution that receives federal funds.

1. Federal policymakers should increase the number and frequency of OCR-conducted compliance reviews in CTE programs—utilizing Title IX and its implementing regulations, as well as the "Vocational Education Guidelines for Eliminating Discrimination and Denial of Services on the Basis of Race, Color, National Origin, Sex and Handicap"—to ensure that all CTE programs provide equal access and opportunity for all students.
2. Federal policymakers should restore the full-time sex/gender-equity coordinator position in the state departments of education, along with budgets and program responsibility to provide technical assistance and professional development to local education agencies to help them meet the core indicators of performance and succeed in serving special population students.
3. States and accrediting institutions should establish policies that mandate gender-equity training and competence for all educators involved in counseling and in CTE. Teachers and counselors should be expected to change their behaviors as well as their perceptions, attitudes, and interests as they relate to sex stereotyping.
4. Federal policymakers should use the Perkins accountability data collected by the states and reported to OVAE to in-

form practice and improve programs to advance gender equity in CTE.
5. Federal policymakers should provide support and technical assistance to states to help them improve their performance on the fourth core indicator (participation in and completion of nontraditional training and employment programs) and to evaluate disaggregated special populations data to drive program improvement efforts. In addition to working with career and technical education administrators, the federal policy makers should work with Title IX coordinators in all types and levels of institutions receiving federal financial assistance to implement this regulation.
6. States should use the flexibility given them in the Perkins Act to fund state and local gender-equity initiatives that are data driven and focused on results. This will require states to make gender equity in CTE a priority in their Perkins State Plan.
7. Federal policymakers should provide funding (via new legislation, Perkins, WEEA, Elementary and Secondary Education Act, Higher Education Act, etc.) for research and development to promote gender equity in CTE activities and implementation funding to school districts for the purpose of evaluating the effectiveness of their gender-equity activities in these areas.
8. Federal and state policymakers should strengthen programs and increase funding for programs that work with employers to improve working conditions, climate, discrimination, and pay equity for women and men in nontraditional careers (such as the U.S. Department of Labor's Women's Bureau).
9. Federal and state policymakers should pay more attention to categorical programs that are not entitlements. Programmatic funding that doesn't foster institutional change is short lived. Funding mechanisms need to be designed that have a lasting impact. The lives of hundreds of thousands of women and girls (and men in nontraditional careers) benefited from the set-aside programs.
10. Federal policymakers must include specific and clear language in a reauthorized Perkins that requires the conducting of significant and rigorous research on the elimination of sex bias and stereotyping in CTE and on the identification of practices that are proven to increase the participation and completion of students in nontraditional CTE programs.
11. Federal policymakers should recognize the intersection of Perkins, WIA, and TANF regarding the provision of support services for women in high-skill, high-wage, high-demand careers and make it a priority for funds to be used for this purpose from any federal sources.
12. Federal policymakers should recognize the value of education and training in reducing poverty and should increase access to education and training for participants in the TANF and WIA programs.

Recommendations for Researchers

1. Researchers should conduct research on how states are holding local educational agencies accountable for their compliance with state and federal civil rights laws through Title IX

reviews, OCR Memorandum of Agreement compliance reviews, and other monitoring and technical assistance efforts.

2. Researchers should conduct research on effective strategies for increasing the participation and completion of underrepresented students in nontraditional CTE programs.

3. Researchers and evaluators should compare different approaches to achieving gender-equity goals (e.g., program length, instructional presentation approaches, single-sex education, primary age of influence, types of role models) to inform local school decision makers as well as national policymakers.

4. Researchers should design longitudinal studies that follow students who participated in nontraditional CTE programs in high school to determine the impact of these experiences on postsecondary success, workforce participation, and career selection.

5. Researchers should conduct research on women in the 21st century workforce and what education reform efforts need to be supported to help reduce workplace bias.

6. Researchers should conduct research on the impact of preservice and in-service education with CTE teachers in gender equitable instructional methods on student achievement, course selection, postsecondary transition, college major selection, and career entrance.

7. Researchers should examine social security and retirement program reforms and their impact on women's long-term economic security based on career participation and career selection.

8. Researchers should continue to test theories of career development and update them to reflect the world of rapidly changing environments, personal values, and needs. Education needs a dynamic view of career development theory, one that evolves with changing environments and needs and that purposefully attends to increasing gender equity. What is true in one decade may not describe the situation in the next.

Recommendations for Educators and School Administrators

1. Educators and administrators at all levels should continue the emphasis on reducing career stereotypes. The evidence presented indicates that gender-equitable programs can change students' beliefs and attitudes, but little evidence has been provided that indicates the programs have resulted in changes in their personal interests in nontraditional careers. We recommend support for programs that provide K–12 students with experience in nontraditional careers. These experiences may provide the basis for personal interest in these careers and for more gender-free career choices at a later age.

2. Middle-school educators and administrators should take advantage of the fluid quality of this developmental stage and require both boys and girls to explore a wide array of CTE programs. Middle schools need to make a special effort to offer gender-equitable programs that allow students to explore nontraditional CTE programs in a safe and supportive environment with teachers and role models who prove that nontraditional choices are successful ones. Such experiences provide the basis for a sense of competence and self-efficacy necessary for making wise choices in high school and beyond

3. High-school students should be required to take a course in career and life planning that includes the development of an education and career development plan. Students should be encouraged to continue to explore options, pursue their interests, and develop new skills to broaden their future choices rather than narrow them.

4. High-school educators and administrators should provide students enrolled in CTE with the support services necessary for increased enrollments in nontraditional courses and programs. Such support services include orientation of students to nontraditional CTE programs, supportive behaviors by teachers and students with nontraditional students who represent a minority in these classes, and tutoring and financial support for services such as childcare, transportation, books, tuition, uniforms, tools, etc.

5. Nonsexist career guidance and counseling should be integrated into all instructional strategies so that educators can take advantage of "teachable moments" and expose students to the advantages and benefits of a particular career choice.

6. Career guidance and counseling processes must include career exploration that provides accurate and realistic information about earning potential and economic self-sufficiency based on family composition and desired residence location.

7. While a curriculum that encourages boys and girls to learn more about nontraditional careers and behaviors is essential, teachers and counselors should be careful not to discourage students from choosing the more traditional careers and behaviors. To truly expand life options is to increase students' freedom to choose based on interest rather than on gender or social class.

8. Educators should ensure that career education materials are representative of a broad range of social classes and minorities. Materials are frequently focused on white, middle-class students, to the exclusion of poor and minority students. Increasing life options for all students may require a curriculum sensitive to the person growing up in poverty or coming from an environment with different values and customs.

9. Educators and administrators should address gender equity as an institution-wide priority by making an overt effort to support students' nontraditional choices, providing career guidance and counseling that highlights the positive aspects of nontraditional career selection especially for women and girls, taking affirmative actions to hire CTE teachers that are nontraditional role models, and recognizing students of the underrepresented gender who succeed in nontraditional CTE programs.

10. Educators and administrators should take a proactive role in educating parents about nontraditional career options for their sons and daughters. With parents being the primary influencers of students' career choice, they play a key role in assuring students have all available options for their future.

Recommendations for Teacher Education and Accreditation Organizations

1. Teacher preparation institutions should include gender equity and multicultural education as part of the teacher education preservice program.
2. Teacher accreditation institutions should review gender-equity competencies for teacher educators in CTE and multicultural education, and include the competencies in the teacher certification requirements.
3. Teacher accreditation should include gender equity and multicultural education in state accreditation requirements and self-studies.
4. Teacher associations should include gender equity in their strategic goals and should develop grant programs to fund activities within the associations. Associations should develop professional support systems for teachers of nontraditional CTE courses to share best practices and exchange strategies. In addition, support systems should be put in place for those teachers who themselves are nontraditional role models in nontraditional CTE programs to provide them with a forum for personal and legal support.

ACKNOWLEDGMENTS

The authors were assisted by reviewers Helen Farmer, Professor Emerita, Univ. of Illinois, Champaign, IL and former coauthor of the related chapter in the 1985 *Handbook,* and Nancy Tuvesson, National Alliance for Partnerships in Equity, Cochranville, PA. Debra Cutler-Ortiz from Wider Opportunities for Women, Fatima Goss Graves, and Jocelyn Samuels from the National Women's Law Center in Washington, DC, assisted with federal policy information.

References

Alfeld, Corrine, Frome, P., Eccles, J., & Barber, B. (2006, March). *Why don't they want a male- dominated job? An investigation of young women who changed their occupational aspirations.* Paper presented at the biennial meeting of the Society for Research on Adolescence, San Francisco.

American Association of University Women Educational Foundation. (1998). *Gender gaps: Where schools still fail our children.* Washington, DC: Author.

American Association of University Women. (2001). *Hostile hallways: bullying, teasing and sexual harassment in schools.* Author: Washington, DC.

American Counseling Association. (1998). Developmental career programs for schools: Part one. *ACAeNews 1*(15). Retrieved October 24, 2005, from www.counseling.org/enews/volume_1/0115a.htm

Annexstein, L. (2003). Opening the door to career and technical education programs for women and girls. In M. Scott, (Ed.), *Equity issues in career and technical education* (Information Series No. 390; pp. 5–15). Columbus, OH: Center on Education and Training on Employment.

Association for Career and Technical Education. (2006a). *Reinventing the American high school for the 21st century*. Washington, DC: Author.

Association for Career and Technical Education. (2006b). *What is career and technical education?* Fact Sheet. Retrieved February 9, 2006, from www.acteonline.org/career_tech/upload/CTUFactSheet.doc

Bailey, T., Alfonso, M., Scott, M., & Leinbach, T. (2004, August). *Educational outcomes of occupational postsecondary students*. Prepared for the National Assessment of Vocational Education, U.S. Department of Education.

Barsion, S. J., (2004). *Mentor Net 2002–2003 Program evaluation highlight.* New York: SJB Research Consultants. Inc. Retrieved February 11, 2007, from http://www.mentornet.net/documents/files/Eval.0203.Highlights.pdf

Betsworth, D. B. (1997, August). *Accuracy of self-estimated abilities and the relationship between self-estimated abilities and current occupation in women.* Paper presented at the annual meeting of the American Psychological Association, Chicago.

Betz, N., & Schifano, R. (2000). Evaluation of an intervention to increase realistic self-efficacy and interest in college women. *Journal of Vocational Behavior, 56*(1), 35–52.

Billings, S. K. (1992). *Occupational sex-role stereotyping in elementary students.* Hays, KS: Fort Hays State University.

Brady, M., & Sharrod, D. (2003). Retaining men in nursing programs designed for women. *Journal of Nursing Education, 24*(4), 159–62.

Brand, B. (2003). *Rigor and relevance: A new vision for career and technical education.* Washington, DC: American Youth Policy Forum.

Brunner, R. (2000). Minority gains essential to U.S. technology future. *Electronic News, 46*(30), 10–14.

Center on Education Policy and American Youth Policy Forum. (2000). *Do you know the good news about American education?* Washington, DC: Authors. Retrieved February 8, 2007, from http://www.aypf.org/publications/good_news.pdf.

Cisco Systems, Inc. (2000). *Cisco Learning Institute Gender Initiative.* Webpage. Retrieved February 15, 2006, from http://gender.ciscolearning.org

Clance, P. R., & Imes, S. (1978, Fall). The imposter phenomenon in high achieving women: Dynamics and therapeutic interventions. *Psychotherapy Theory, Research and Practice 15*(3), 1–8. Abstract retrieved February 8, 2007 from http://www2.gsu.edu/~wwwaow/resources/ip_high_achieving_women.pdf

Clark, P. (2000). *What do we know about nontraditional Careers? (and) how can we effectively recruit and teach nontraditional students?* Columbus, OH: Ohio State University, College of Human Ecology.

Clewell, B., & Campbell, P. (2002). Taking stock: Where we've been, where we are, where we are going. *Journal of Women and Minorities in Science and Engineering, 8*(3/4), 255–84.

Congressional Research Service. (2006). *Welfare reauthorization: An overview of the issues.* Retrieved February 8, 2007, from http://www.opencrs.com/rpts/IB10140_20051222.pdf.

Education Development Center, Inc. (1996). *Exploring work: Fun activities for girls.* Newton, MA: Women's Educational Equity Act Dissemination Center.

Esters, L., & Bowen, B. (2003). Race and ethnicity equity issues. In M. Scott, (Ed.), *Equity issues in career and technical education* (Information Series No. 390; pp. 27–34). Columbus, OH: Center on Education and Training on Employment.

Farmer, H. S., Seliger, S., Sidney, J., Bitters, B. A., & Brizius, M. G. (1985). Chapter 18. In S. Klein (Ed.), *Handbook for achieving sex equity through education*. Baltimore, MD: The Johns Hopkins University Press.

Ferris State University, Career Institute for Education and Workforce Development. (2002). *Decisions without direction*. Retrieved (date), from http://www.ferris.edu/careerinstitute/research.htm.

Florida State Department of Education, Division of Workforce Development. (1996). *Career mentoring for middle- and junior-high-school girls*. Tallahassee, FL: Author.

Foster, J., & Simonds, B. (1995). *Alternative support systems for non-traditional students in vocational education*. Lansing, MI: Michigan State Department of Education, Office for Sex Equity.

Fox Valley Technical College. (1991). *A developing aptitude model—sex equity. Summary report*. Madison, WI: Wisconsin State Board of Vocational, Technical, and Adult Education.

Ganzglass, E. (2006a). *Ten years after welfare reform, its time to make work work for families*. Washington, DC: Center for Law and Social Policy. Available online at http://www.clasp.org/publications/10years afterwrpressreleasebkground08_16_06.pdf.

Ganzglass, E. (2006b). *Strategies for increasing participation in TANF education and training activities*. Washington, DC: Center for Law and Social Policy.

Gavin, M. K. (2000). *What parents need to know about . . . encouraging talented girls in mathematics: Practitioners'guide*. Storrs, CT: National Research Center on the Gifted and Talented.

General Accounting Office, National Security and International Affairs Division, GAO/NSIAD-99-212. (1999, September). *Gender issues. Trends in the occupational distribution of military women*. Report to the Ranking Minority Member, Subcommittee on Readiness and Management Support, Committee on Armed Services, U.S. Senate.

Ginorio, A., & Huston, M. (2001). *!Si Se Puede! Yes, we Can: Latinas in school*. Washington, DC: American Association of University Women Educational Foundation.

Gottfredson, L. (1981). Circumstances and compromise: A developmental theory of occupational aspirations. *Journal of Counseling Psychology, 28*, 545–79

Graham, M. (2001). *Increasing participation of female students in physical science class*. Dissertation/thesis submitted online. Retrieved August 26, 2006, ED 455 121, SE 065 092 from http://eric.ed.gov/ERICDocs/data/ericdocs2/content_storage_01/0000000b/80/26/61/e4.pdf

Grayson, D., & Martin, M. S. (2003a). *Generating expectations for student achievement: An equitable approach to educational excellence*. Tehachapi, CA: Graymill & Associates, Inc.

Grayson, D., & Martin, M. S. (2003b). *The equity principal*. Tehachapi, CA: Graymill & Associates, Inc.

Greene, C. K., & Stitt-Gohdes, W. L. (1997). Factors that influence women's choices to work in the trades. *Journal of Career Development, 23*(4), 265–278. Retrieved February 12, 2007, from http://www.springerlink.com/content/e6u47rg51361v322/

Gurer, D., & Camp, T. (2000). *Investigating the incredible shrinking pipeline for women in computer science* (Final report, National Science Foundation Project No. 9812016). Retrieved February 8, 2007, from http://women.acm.org/documents/finalreport.pdf.

Henson, K. D., & Rogers, J. K. (2001). 'Why Marcia You've Changed!': Male clerical temporary workers doing masculinity in a feminized occupation. *Gender & Society, 15*(2), 218–38.

Hultin, M. (2003, February). Some take the glass escalator, some hit the glass ceiling? Career consequences of occupational sex segregation. *Work and Occupations: An International Sociological Journal, 30*(1), 30–61.

Kerka, S. (2001). Nontraditional employment and training. *Trends and Issues Alert No. 30*. Washington, DC: Office of Educational Research and Improvement.

Kloosterman, D. M. (1994). *A program to develop awareness of non-traditional career options, gender role stereotyping, and decision-making skills in fifth and sixth grade Hispanic girls*. Ft. Lauderdale-Davie, FL: Nova Southeastern University.

Margolis, J., & Fisher, A. (2002). Unlocking the clubhouse: The Carnegie Mellon experience. *SIGCSE Bulletin, 34*(2), 79–83.

Margolis, J., & Fisher, A. (2003). *Unlocking the clubhouse: Women in computing*. Cambridge, MA: MIT Press

Markert, L. R. (1996). Gender related to success in science and technology. *Journal of Technology Studies, 22*(2), 21–29.

Mastracci, S. (2004). *Breaking out of the pink collar ghetto: Policy solutions for non-college women*. Armonk, NY: M.E. Sharpe.

Mathur, A., Reichle, J., Stawn, J., & Wiseley, C. (2004). *From jobs to careers: How California community college credentials pay off for welfare participants*. Washington, DC: Center for Law and Social Policy.

Mewhorter, V. C. (1994). *Sex equity: Recruitment and retention of non-traditional students*. Appleton, WI: Fox Valley Technical College.

Midwest Equity Assistance Center. (2000). *Building level assessment: An equity manual*. Manhattan, KS; Author

Milgram, D. (1997). *School to work: Preparing young women for technology careers, a trainer's workshop guide*. Alameda, CA: National Institute for Women in Trades, Technology & Science.

Montclair State College, Life Skills Center. (1991). *Demographic profile and needs assessment of single parents and homemakers in New Jersey vocational education programs 1990–1991*. Trenton, NJ: New Jersey State Department of Education, Division of Vocational Education.

Montclair State University, New Jersey Career Equity Assistance Center for Research and Evaluation. (1997). *Participants in New Beginnings and career equity programs gain knowledge and equitable attitudes. Evaluation Report, Program Year 1997*. Montclair, NJ: Author.

Multistate Academic and Vocational Curriculum Consortium. (2001). *Taking the road less traveled*. Stillwater, OK: Oklahoma Department of Career and Technology Education.

National Alliance for Partnerships in Equity. (2004). *Equity pioneers: The sex equity coordinators, 1976–1998*. Columbia, MO: Project SERVE/ENTER.

National Assessment of Vocational Education, U.S. Department of Education, Office of the Under Secretary, Policy and Program Studies Service. (2004). *National assessment of vocational education: Final report to congress*. Washington, DC: U.S. Department of Education.

National Centers for Career and Technical Education. (2003). *Improving performance on Perkins III core indicators: Summary of research on causes and improvement strategies*. Columbus, OH: The Ohio State University.

National Center for Education Statistics. (2000). *Vocational education in the United States: Toward the Year 2000*. Washington, DC: National Center for Education Statistics.

National Center for Education Statistics. (2004). *Trends in educational equity of girls & women: 2004*. Washington, DC: Government Printing Office.

National Coalition for Women and Girls in Education. (2001). *Invisible again: The impact of changes in federal funding on vocational programs for women and girls*. Washington, D.C.: Author.

National Committee on Pay Equity. (2006). *Wage gap remains*. Retrieved August 21, 2006 from http://www.pay-equity.org

National Science Foundation. (2003). *New formulas for America's workforce: Girls in science and engineering*. Washington, DC: Author.

National School-to-Work Opportunities Office. (1996). *Non-traditional school-to-work opportunities for young women* (Resource bulletin). Washington, DC: Author.

National Organization for Women Legal Defense and Education Fund. (2001). *Nontraditional employment for women: A guide for advocates.* Retrieved February 15, 2006 from http://www.nowldef.org (retrieved on February 15, 2006).

National Women's Law Center. (2002). *Title IX and equal opportunity in vocational and technical education: A promise still owed to the nation's young women.* Washington, DC: Author.

National Women's Law Center. (2004). *Slip sliding away: The erosion of hard-won gains for women under the Bush administration and an agenda for moving forward.* Washington, DC: Author.

National Women's Law Center. (2005a). *Tools of the trade: Using the law to address sex segregation in high school career and technical education.* Washington, DC: Author.

National Women's Law Center with the Association for Career and Technical Education, National Association of State Directors of Career Technical Education Consortium, and the National Alliance for Partnerships in Equity. (2005b). *Forging new pathways: Promising practices for recruiting and retaining students in career and technical education programs that are nontraditional for their gender.* Washington, DC: NWLC.

National Women's Law Center (A report with the Association for Career and Technical Education, National Association of State Directors of Career Technical Education Consortium, and the National Alliance for Partnerships in Equity.) (2006). *Constructing equity: Promising practices for recruiting and retaining students in career and technical education programs that are nontraditional for their gender.* Washington, D.C: NWLC.

New Jersey Department of Labor. (2004). *State of New Jersey: Occupations with the greatest percentage growth, 2004–2014.* Retrieved February 8, 2007, from http://www.wnjpin.net/OneStopCareerCenter/LaborMarketInformation/lmi04/state/pergrowocc.xls.

Noble, B. (1992, Nov. 22). And now the sticky floor. *The New York Times,* Business Section, p. 3.

Northrop, D. (2003). Introducing equity in the classroom. *WEEA Digest: Teacher Expectations.* Newton, MA: WEEA Equity Resource Center. Retrieved February 12, 2007, from http://www2.edc.org/Womens Equity/pdffiles/teacherexp.pdf, pp. 1–2.

Peer Collaborative Resource Network, U.S. Department of Education, Office of Vocational and Adult Education. (2006). Retrieved February 15, 2006, from http://www.edcountability.net

Read, B. (1991). *Women's career choices. VTAE students' selection of traditional and nontraditional programs.* Eau Claire, WI: Chippewa Valley Technical College.

Ryan, K. E. (1999). Gender bias in industrial technology at the middle school level. Unpublished dissertation/thesis submitted to Saint Xavier University and Skylight Professional Development. Abstract retrieved August 26, 2006, ED435 832 CE 079 419 from http://eric.ed.gov/ERICDocs/data/ericdocs2/content_storage_01/0000000b/80/10/93/7c.pdf

Sadker, M., & Sadker, D. (1994). *Failing at fairness: How our schools cheat girls.* New York: Touchstone.

Sandler, B., & Hoffman, E. (1992). *Teaching faculty members to be better teachers: A guide to equitable and effective classroom techniques.* Washington, D.C.: Association of American Colleges and Universities.

Sanogo, M. C .C. (1995). Facilitators and barriers to high school female participation in school-to-work: Traditional vs. nontraditional programs for females. Unpublished doctoral thesis, Graduate Program in Vocational Industrial Education, The Pennsylvania State University, State College.

Shanahan, E., Denner, P., Rhodes, T., & Anderson, D. (1999, October 13–16). *Women trained for nontraditional vocational occupations: Why do they stay or leave?* Paper presented at the 17th annual meeting of the Northern Rocky Mountain Educational Research Association in Jackson Park, Wyoming.

Silverman, S. (1999). *Gender equity and school-to-career. A guide to strengthening the links to nontraditional careers.* Hartford, CT: Connecticut Women's Education and Legal Fund.

Super, D. (1980). A life-span, life-space approach to career development. *Journal of Vocational Behavior, 16,* 282–98.

Stone, J., & Aliaga, O. (2002). *Career and technical education, career pathways and work-based learning: Changes in participation 1997–1999.* St. Paul, MN: National Center for Career and Technical Education.

Thurtle, V., Hammond, S., & Jennings, P. (1998). The experience of students in a gender minority in courses at a college of higher and further education. *Journal of Vocational Education and Training: The Vocational Aspect of Education, 50*(4), 629–46.

U.S. Bureau of Labor Statistics. (2005*). Median weekly earnings of full-time wage and salary workers by detailed occupation and sex.* Retrieved on July 25, 2006, from http://www.bls.gov/cps/cpsaat39.pdf

U.S. Bureau of Labor Statistics. (2006, May). *Employment characteristics of families in 2005.* Retrieved on August 21, 2006, from http://www.bls.gov/news.release/pdf/famee.pdf

U.S. Commission on Civil Rights. (2000). *Equal educational opportunity and nondiscrimination for girls in advanced mathematics, science, and technology education: Federal enforcement of Title IX* (Equal Educational Opportunity Project Series, 5). Washington, DC: U.S. Department of Education, Commission on Civil Rights. (ERIC Document Reproduction Service No. ED 449 580)

U.S. Department of Commerce, U.S. Department of Education, U.S. Department of Labor, National Institute of Literacy, & Small Business Administration. (1999). *21st century skills for 21st century jobs.* Washington, DC: Authors.

U.S. Department of Education, Office for Civil Rights. (March 21, 1979). Vocational Education Programs Guidelines for Eliminating Discrimination and Denial of Services on the Basis of Race, Color, National Origin, Sex And Handicap (Rules and Regulations).Washington, DC:Author. Retrieved on February 12, 2007, from www.ed.gov/about/offices/list/ocr/docs/vocre.html

U.S. Department of Education, Office of Educational Research and Improvement. (2001). *Gender equity expert panel, exemplary & promising gender equity programs 2000.* Washington, DC: U.S. Department of Education.

U.S. Department of Education, Office of the Under Secretary, Planning and Evaluation Service. (2002). *National assessment of vocational education: Interim report to Congress: Executive summary.* Washington, DC: Author.

U.S. Department of Education, Office of Vocational and Adult Education. (1999). *Program Memorandum-OVAE/DVTE 99-13.* Retrieved on August 21, 2006 from http://www.ed.gov/about/offices/list/ovae/pi/cte/vocnontrad13.html

U.S. Department of Education, Office of Vocational and Adult Education. (2005). *Carl D. Perkins Vocational and Technical Education Act report to congress on state performance, program year 2003–2004.* Washington, DC: U.S. Department of Education.

U.S. Department of Labor. (2002a). *Table 3b, The 10 fastest growing occupations, 2002–12.* Retrieved January 25, 2005, from http://www.bls.gov/news_release_ecopro.t04.htm

U.S. Department of Labor. (2002b). *Facts on working women: Women in high-tech jobs.* Washington, DC: Women's Bureau.

University of Southwestern Louisiana, Lafayette. (1993). *Strategies for increased participation of students in programs not traditional for their gender.* Baton Rouge, LA: Louisiana State Department of Education, Office of Vocational Education.

Van Buren, J. B. (1993). Modeling nontraditional career choices: Effects of gender and school location response to a brief videotape. *Journal of Counseling and Development, 71*(4), 101–4.

Veterinary Economics. (2002, August, Vol. 44, Number 4). Inching closer to fifty-fifty on gender. *Veterinary Economics*, p. 46.

Veterinary Economics. (2003, April, Vol. 43, Number 8). Women's pay: exploring checks and balance. *Veterinary Economics*, p. 34.

Visher, M., & Hudis, P. (1999). *Aiming high: Strategies to promote high standards to high schools.* Washington, DC: U.S. Department of Education, Office of Vocational and Adult Education.

Women's Educational Equity Act Resource Center. (2002). Progress and promise. *WEEA Digest: Equity and Careers.* Newton, MA: WEEA Equity Resource Center.

Welty, K., & Puck, B. (2001). *Modeling Athena, preparing young women for work and citizenship in a technological society.* Menomonie, WI: University of Wisconsin-Stout.

Wierzbinski, J. (1998, December 21). Official letter from Jean Wierzbinski, Assistant Superintendent of Curriculum and Instruction for the Vocational-Technical School System, State of Connecticut Department of Education to Elizabeth Downs, U.S. Department of Education, Office for Civil Rights, Region 1.

Women Work! (2005). *Chutes and ladders: The search for solid ground for women in the workforce.* Washington, DC: Author.

·21·

THE ROLE OF WOMEN'S AND GENDER STUDIES IN ADVANCING GENDER EQUITY

Betsy Eudey with *Scott Lukas and Elaine Correa*

INTRODUCTION

Gender equity in and through education in part requires that the curriculum includes attention to the contributions and experiences of all sexes; teaching practices are designed to engage all students; and educational opportunities are not tied to sex, gender, sexual orientation and/or gender identity. Women's studies programs and courses emerged to specifically address women's lack of inclusion in the curriculum, engage in teaching methods which valued female experiences and learning styles, and create academic experiences that embraced students of all sexes and sexual orientations. From its earliest developments in the 1970s, to its vast institutional inclusion by the beginning of the 21st Century, women's studies has played a major role in achieving gender equity through education, and advancing understanding of sex and gender. The related fields of men's/masculinity studies, gay and lesbian studies, queer studies, and sexuality studies, often combined with women's studies under the designation "gender studies," further extend attention to sex and gender within the curriculum and as the subject of research.

Women's studies is an interdisciplinary academic field that utilizes feminist theories to examine women's experiences, contributions, and roles over time, culture and geographic location, and to examine the ways in which perceptions of sex and gender influence social systems, the production of knowledge, and individual lives. Courses in women's studies address these gendered issues in the arts, humanities, social sciences, natural sciences, mathematics, technological fields, education, business, law, and health sciences. Women's studies helps to expose and eradicate inequities by examining the effects of interlocking systems of power and oppression based upon sex, gender, sexual orientation, race and ethnicity, economic class, religion, national origin and geographic location, age, ability/disability, health status, and other characteristics. The other components of gender studies draw upon a range of theoretical standpoints, including

feminist theory, to further the interdisciplinary and multicultural study of sex and gender.

When compared to other academic disciplines, women's studies and gender studies are considered relatively new fields of study whose scope and role within institutions is continually evolving. Because these are fields of study whose methods and scholarly focus often challenge the status quo, and their interdisciplinary nature disrupts the traditional disciplinary structure of academic institutions, women's and gender studies programs face many challenges, yet have continued to grow and flourish. This chapter will provide information on the development and contributions made by these fields, while also recognizing that because of their relative newness many of the impacts and outcomes have not yet been documented in longitudinal or national studies. What has been documented indicates that teachers, students, researchers and activists engaged in women's studies, and more recently men's studies, gay and lesbian studies, queer studies, and sexuality studies, are a driving force in improving knowledge about gendered experiences, promoting attention to the impacts of sex and gender in a variety of contexts, and engaging in practices to eradicate sexism and other oppressions. Women's and gender studies therefore play a vital role in the achievement of gender equity through education.

Inside the United States

Academic programs focused on Women's Studies now exist at more than 750 campuses in the United States. Additionally, campus-based women's services centers and women's research centers further the aims of women's studies outside of the classroom. Although programs vary in content and style, Zimmerman (2005) suggests that Women's Studies programs typically focus on:

woman as a category of analysis/metaphor; gender as a system of relations, power, oppression; women as concrete, material agents with lived

445

experiences; women as nodal points at which multiple systems of power and oppression intersect; feminism as historical event/process; and social changes as an essential element of education. (p. 36)

Such foci attempt to enhance understanding about, and inclusion of, women and gender, and thus support the aims of gender equity, even if equity per se is not a specific goal.

When this handbook was last written, a short chapter on "The New Scholarship on Women" provided a brief introduction to the field of women's studies to explain its role in supporting feminist scholarship. This new scholarship on women, which was seen as building from women's studies efforts, aimed "to deconstruct error about women . . .; to add to the existing body of knowledge to compensate for the absence of women in the past; and to transform consciousness through such processes" (Biklen & Shakeshaft, 1985, p. 47). The new scholarship was deemed valuable for both the subjects studied, and the methods of inquiry utilized. Women's studies was presented as somewhat ill defined and lacking in focus, yet still a growing and driving force in the quest to improve the body of knowledge about women and by extension the quality of education for all. The authors mentioned the desire that women's studies work should be consciousness raising and interdisciplinary in order to be transformative, while recognizing that such positioning also created vulnerability and appeared at times to lack rigor and coherence.

Scholarship of women has continued to expand, and academic programs dedicated to women's studies have become increasingly coherent, rigorous, focused, and entrenched in colleges and universities. Feminist scholars have furthered understanding of gender inequity, overlapping systems of oppression, and the vital relationship between theory and practice. Missing from the prior handbook was mention of women's studies' birth in and connection to feminist movements, drawing from theories generated through experience and practice, and women's studies' role in enhancing opportunities for these theories to be considered and understood in contexts broader than their original location. Although at times seeming to operate separately, feminist activism and women's studies continue to inform, influence, and support each other because of their shared aim to better understand and improve the condition of women and to eradicate inequities based on sex, sexual orientation, and gender identity.

The growth of women's studies programs and the rise of feminist scholarship, overall, has lead to greater institutional and academic support for scholarship on other aspects of gender, and the growth of men's and masculinity studies, gay and lesbian studies, queer studies, and sexuality studies (Adams & Savran, 2002; Boxer, 1998; Garber, 1994). Scholarship into the intersections of sex and gender with race, ethnicity, class, dis-

abilities, national origin, and religion also has lead to various relationships with ethnic studies,[1] area studies, American studies, disability studies, and similar fields (Brown & Chavez-Garcia, 2005; Fuchs, 2005; Guy-Sheftall & Hammonds, 2005; Kaplan & Grewal, 2002). Such fields necessarily cross disciplinary boundaries and, thus, challenge the traditional organization of knowledge and academic programs. Often labeled interdisciplinary, or transdisciplinary, such programs are enhanced by the range of subjects, theories, and research methods engaged in while examining the programmatic focus.

"Women's studies courses and scholarship draw upon feminist theories to examine the ways in which sex, gender, sexual orientation and gender identity relate to specific topics or issues. Over time, while maintaining a central focus on women, women's studies programs in the U.S. have increased their attention to and course offerings on men/masculinity, and male sexuality. A few campuses have created separate academic programs for men's studies, gay and lesbian studies, and/or queer studies, although this is not the norm. As will be discussed later, in recent years some women's studies programs have changed their name and/or focus to include greater attention to men's/masculinity and/or gay and lesbian or queer studies. By 2007, over 80% of the more than 750 programs in the United States were still called "women's studies," while an additional 72 were named some version of "women's and gender studies" to maintain attention to women studies, while indicating that men's and/or queer subjects are also included. The broad title "gender studies" is utilized by at least 26 campuses to designate attention to the full range of women's studies, men's/masculinity studies, gay and lesbian studies, and queer studies. Other program titles including feminist studies, gender and sexuality studies, and feminist and gender studies are used at an additional twenty-five campuses (Gunn, 2006). Regardless of title and focus, these are relatively new fields of study within academe, so national data is scant and often not disaggregated by program type but where possible distinctions among programs will be made. Because women's studies is the oldest, most established, and most common program form, the majority of information in this chapter will focus on this field.

The growing breadth and depth of topics and disciplines included within women's studies has fueled the growth of concentrations, minors, majors, master's degrees, and doctoral degrees. Most programs offer minors or concentrations, although by 2005, at least 302 U.S. campuses offered a major and more than 120 had master's level graduate study in women's studies and gender studies, and at least 12 offered doctoral degrees in women's studies. The first designated PhD in gender studies began at Indiana University in 2005. Table 21.1 indicates the distribution of degrees earned in women's studies (which within the National Center for

---

[1]Throughout this chapter, the term "ethnic studies" is used to refer to programs utilizing this title, as well as the variety of academic programs which focus on specific (primarily U.S.-based) ethnic groups (i.e., Asian American Studies, Chicano Studies) which are commonly grouped together under the designation "ethnic studies" within academia and U.S. government databases. The term "area studies" is typically used in academia and government databases to refer to research and scholarship tied to (especially extra-national) geographic regions (i.e., Middle Eastern Studies, African Studies). See table 21.2 for examples of government usage of these terms. The ideological, theoretical, political, and practical benefits and concerns of using the terms "ethnic studies" and "area studies" to represent such a range of interdisciplinary programs are complex, and it is beyond the scope of this chapter to address them. While recognizing the controversies, we have decided to utilize these general terms throughout this chapter because we wanted to address the relationships between sex- and gender-based programs and ethnically- and geographically-based programs, and wished to indicate that these relationships could occur amongst any and all of the possible programs without attempting to list each program title.

TABLE 21.1   Degrees Earned in Women's Studies by Degree Level and Sex of Student

Degrees Earned	Total Bachelor's Degrees	Bachelor's by Males	Bachelor's by Females	Total Master's Degrees	Master's by Males	Master's by Females	Total Doctorate Degrees	Doctorates by Males	Doctorates by Females
1991–92	330	4	326	24	0	24	0	0	0
1992–93	411	11	400	33	0	33	0	0	0
1993–94	479	11	468	52	0	52	5	0	5
1994–95	533	10	523	62	2	60	11	0	11
1995–96	602	9	593	72	3	69	0	0	0
1996–97	602	8	594	71	1	70	5	0	5
1997–98	658	4	654	67	1	66	3	0	3
1998–99	726	12	714	65	2	63	2	0	2
1999–2000	771	23	748	80	1	79	5	0	5
2000–01	763	13	750	91	3	88	4	0	4
2001–02	729	13	716	105	2	103	7	0	7
2002–03	904	11	893	118	2	116	10	0	10

Compiled from the NCES Digests of Educational Statistics 1995–2004.

TABLE 21.2   Women's Studies, American Ethnic Studies Bachelor Degree Attainment 1991–2003

Bachelor's Degrees	1991–92	1996–97	1997–98	1998–99	1999–2000	2000–01	2001–02	2002–03
Women's Studies	330	602	658	726	771	763	729	904
African American (Black) Studies	410	558	615	630	604	599	668	645
Hispanic-American Studies	87	185	243	214	256	213	234	262
Asian American Studies								125
Ethnic Studies, Other	236	278	296	309	311	360	370	
Ethnic, Cultural Minority, and Gender Studies, Other								396
Area, Ethnic, or Cultural studies, Total	5342	5839	6153	6252	6381	6317	6557	6629

Compiled from the NCES Digests of Educational Statistics 1995–2004

Education Statistics [NCES] dataset also includes gender studies programs) between 1992 and 2003. Further, nearly 40 campuses offer programs in gay and lesbian studies, with at least 9 campuses offering graduate study, and 100 housing gay and lesbian resource centers. In 2007 there were specific programs in men's and masculinity studies at only five U.S. campuses.

The data in Table 21.1 indicates that women's and gender studies graduates at the undergraduate level have nearly tripled over the past 10 years, even though there has not been a steady annual increase (NCES, 2006). The women's studies major continues to attract primarily students who identify as female, with male participation limited and sporadic. No national data is available regarding the race and ethnicity of students in these programs. It is difficult to account specifically for the decline and then exponential rise in undergraduate majors between 2000 and 2003, especially given the steady increase in master's degrees. One factor for may be the slow increase in various ethnic studies and gay and lesbian studies majors, which was acknowledged by the NCES in 2000 by the creation of a new Classification of Instruction Program (CIP) for gay and lesbian studies. Although the designation exists, this program has not yet received its own line item in the Digest of Educational Statistics, so majors are combined with other programs within either the Area, Ethnic and Cultural Studies, other or Ethnic, Cultural Minority, and Gender Studies, other categories (the latter designation replacing the former beginning with the 2004 Digest).

Given the attention that women's studies has given to queer issues, students interested in these topics prior to the creation of gay and lesbian (or queer) studies majors often chose a women's studies degree as the closest curricular option. Growth in new disciplines within ethnic, cultural, and area studies overall may also be a factor, as students with interdisciplinary interests have greater choice in majors from which to choose, especially if particular women's studies programs fail to adequately address racial and ethnic diversity. As Table 21.2 indicates, the other categories have shown almost continuous increases, while more specific majors have shown fluctuations in enrollment patterns. Additional reasons for declines in undergraduate majors may include changing student interest in the degree program, changes in the economic outlook for women's studies graduates, or institutional changes in degree offerings related to such issues as budget constraints and political climate.

Outside the United States

Women's and gender studies programs in non–United States contexts are growing as well, although comparing their development to U.S. programs is somewhat problematic. The manner in which systems of higher education are structured varies greatly, and the cultural and political contexts of states and regions greatly influence receptivity to and faculty preparation for teaching women's and gender studies topics. For example, Shymchyshyn (2005) indicated that, in the Ukraine, the loosening of central oversight of curricula has slowly allowed for women's studies topics and coursework to be incorporated into universities (including the creation of the first women's studies program in 1995). However, patriarchal cultural ideologies, lack of faculty preparation in these fields, and limited access to women's studies texts has hindered opportunities to engage in feminist teaching and scholarship. Ahfad University for Women in Sudan offered its first women's studies coursework in 1986, had an autonomous program by 1997, and now offers a required course for all students and has degree programs in women, gender and development studies at the undergraduate, master's, and doctoral levels (Ahfad University, 2002). In Thailand, the first women's studies programs began in 1986, with the first master's of arts (MAs) program, offered at Chiangmai University, enrolling students in 2000 (Liewkeat, 2001).

Australia's first women's studies course was offered in 1973 at Hinders University, and "thirty years since their beginnings, Women's Studies courses of some kind—even if under the increasingly prevalent heading of 'Gender Studies'—are to be found in almost all universities, and at least half of them have full undergraduate majors" (Magaray & Sheridan, 2002, p. 130). In areas like Australia where women's and gender studies programs have been common at the undergraduate level for decades, growth is seen particularly at the graduate level. Colleges in Australia and New Zealand offer at least 25 graduate programs in women's and gender studies, 15 are located in Canada, and nearly 50 are in the United Kingdom and Ireland.

Braidotti and de Vos (2005) indicated the European system of granting M.A.s and PhDs is rather new, and thus campuses, countries, and regions are developing new structures for coordinated graduate study. Within this framework, at least 12 women's and gender studies PhD programs now exist, including programs in Austria, England, Finland, Hungary, Italy, the Netherlands, Spain, Sweden, and Switzerland. Further, Poland, Belgium, and France include research schools on women's and gender studies that complement graduate studies in other disciplines. They also report that the Nordic Research School in Interdisciplinary Gender Studies has been developed to coordinate research on an international level, involving 30 schools spread across Denmark, Finland, Iceland, Norway, Sweden, Northwest Russia, Estonia, Latvia, and Lithuania.

It is important to note that in most locations work related to women's and gender studies does not occur only within formal women's studies academic programs. Those involved with women's studies also work in women's and gender-based services centers, women's and gender-based research centers, community and governmental agencies, activist organizations, primary and secondary schools, healthcare settings, and as independent scholars and artists. In recent years the U.S.-based National Women's Studies Association has drawn greater attention and support to the range of ways in which women's studies work is conducted by offering a standing committee for women's centers, annual pre-conferences for women's center personnel, special sessions by/for activists and K-12 teachers at annual conferences, and film and art exhibitions at its conferences.

THE DEVELOPMENT OF THE FIELDS

Women's Studies

More than 35 years after the first women's studies program in the United States was founded in 1970 at what is now San Diego State University (followed later that year by Cornell University), women's studies has many successes, yet continues to face questions of focus, disciplinary status, and vulnerability. As a field, women's studies is theoretically grounded in a variety of feminist theories and aims to enhance understanding and inclusion of women's experiences and to challenge systems which devalue and harm the female and feminine. As noted above, research and scholarship on, by, and about women can occur in research centers and in a variety academic disciplines, but not all such research is claimed as advancing the aims of women's studies. "What transforms the 'study of women' into women's studies is reflected in the terms themselves. In the '*study of women,*' women are objects; in *women's studies,* we are subjects" (Ruth, 2001, p. 5). Women's studies scholarship and activism aims to challenge gender inequities by drawing upon feminist theories to recover and reinterpret women's history, expose sex- and gender-based differences and the value judgments associated with these differences, and intentionally focus attention on the experiences of the oppressed. Ruth (2001) noted:

For women, women's studies seeks: to change our sense of ourselves— our self-image, our sense of worth and rights, our presence in the world; to change women's aspirations based on an increased sense of self-confidence and self-love, to allow women to create for ourselves new options in our own personal goals as well as in our commitments and/or contributions to society; to alter the relations between women and men, to create true friendship and respect between the sexes . . . to erase from the world all the representations of unwholesome, illegitimate power of one group over another: sexism, racism, heterosexism, classism and so on. (p. 14)

The feminist theories one advocates may influence the manner in which these ends are achieved or the priority placed on particular activities; however, the goals of justice and respect remain constant in all. Today, women's studies courses are at the forefront of challenging the ways in which the various levels of education represent women. Introductory courses pertaining specifically to women critically review the erasure, denial, silence, and invisibility of women historically. These courses raise awareness about the manner in which formal documentation of women as contributors to society has been overlooked or dismissed.

Women's studies scholars assert that women are represented stereotypically according to sex roles, or are absent from representation, and are not visually and materially represented. The invisibility of women and minority groups, or their stereotypical representations, has been the focus of extensive research on sex and gender stereotypes (Carter & Spitzack, 1989; Ferree & Hall, 1990; Kramarae, Schultz, & O'Barr, 1984). These representations indicate that when women are portrayed, they are often represented substantially fewer times than men (Purcell & Stewart, 1990), and their portrayals were frequently demeaning, distorted, or inaccurate (Streitmatter, 1994). As a corrective, women's studies scholars and other feminists seek to enhance gender equity through the critical examination of the social construction of gender, the ways in which institutions maintain unequal sexual divisions of labor and opportunities, the gendered nature of research and scholarly inquiry, the sex bias within particular disciplines, and the ways in which interdisciplinary work can further explore concepts of sex and gender. The breadth and depth of this scholarship is illustrated by the thousands of topics examined in a women's studies encyclopedia that was created to challenge and correct traditional knowledge bases (Kramarae & Spender, 2000).

Building from a U.S. feminist movement whose public face was predominantly White, middle-class, and heterosexual, the first women's studies scholars reflected this demographic because they were the most likely to have the background, means, and opportunities to pursue advanced degrees and to have their writings published by national presses (Boxer, 1998). Even so, some of the most influential founders of women's studies were women of color, working class women, and/or openly lesbian women, including Electa Arenal, Johnnetta B. Cole, Tucker Pamella Farley, Beverly Guy-Sheftall, Inez Martinez, Nellie Y. McKay, and Yolanda T. Moses. Although the inclusion of faculty and students of color has increased over time, women of color are still a marked minority. Investigating the status of women's studies, a 1996 survey completed by 276 of the 598 women's studies programs and centers existing in the United States found that 93% of administrators identified as Anglo, 1% African American, and 2% Mexican or Latin American (Scully, 1996).

However, feminist activist work has always incorporated women of all ethnicities, classes, sexual orientations, and educational backgrounds, and over time, campus faculty have become increasingly diverse as well. Women's studies faculty, feminist presses, and grassroots organizations helped to draw attention to the diversity of women's experiences, and increasingly incorporated this diversity into the core of women's studies academic programs. Indeed, the intersectionality[2] of race, class, and gender has become a key focus in women's studies, as has a transnational focus to women's studies scholarship and feminist activism (Grewal & Kaplan, 2006). Core women's studies texts are now centered on the intersectionality of race, class, gender, and nationality, yet White supremacy still requires greater attention, as it does in most other academic fields. The growth of such fields as Black women's studies (or womanist studies), Chicana studies, Jewish women's studies, and lesbian studies has helped to expand understanding of the relationships between ethnicity, sexual orientation, sexual identity, religion, and gender (Brown & Chavez-Garcia, 2005; Fuchs, 2005; Joseph, 2002; Lee, 2002).

Although the work of women's studies is conducted in a variety of locations, Orr and Lichtenstein (2004) cautioned that the scholarship and projects engaged in at the elite and research universities can often shape perceptions of the field. With high numbers of female students, students of color, working-class students, and female faculty at regional, teaching and community colleges, the field suffers when their experiences with women's studies are marginalized or minimized.

The acceptance of women's studies programs and feminist scholars within academe is affirmed by the growth of programs, and also by the success of individual scholars and faculty members. Not only are feminist teachers obtaining tenure and promotion, but they are winning campus teaching awards, fellowships, and prizes for their scholarly publications. Several former professors of women's studies have been named college deans or provosts. An accomplished teacher, scholar and administrator, the first woman president of Harvard University, Drew Gilpin Faust, directed the women's studies program at the University of Pennsylvania from 1996–2000 (Harvard University Gazette, 2007).

Men's and Masculinity Studies

While scholarly works studying masculinity can be traced to the beginning of the 20th century, most designate the 1970s as the start of the men's movement in the United States. This first movement was well informed by, and generally supportive of, the interrogations of sex, sexuality, patriarchy, and heterosexism by those involved in the women's rights and gay liberation movements of the 1960s and 1970s. A surge in attention to masculinity, and the rise of a revised focus to masculinity studies, followed the 1990 publication of Robert Bly's *Iron John* (Adams & Savran, 2002). In an abrupt shift, many entering the masculinity movement called for a return to traditional (natural) masculinity and a corrective to the reported emasculation of men because of the feminist movement. While this anti-feminist and heterosexist focus to men's studies gained popular attention and influenced many men's groups, it is not embraced by most academics studying masculinity. The majority of programs and scholars support the rejection of sex-based supremacy and draw upon aspects of feminist theories, but seek to understand the social construction of sex through a masculine/male standpoint which is seen as neglected within women's studies." Within institutions, the titles "Men's Studies" and "Masculinity Studies" are often used interchangeably, although some prefer to use *masculinity* to highlight a focus on the gendered enactment of maleness, while others prefer to use *men's* as a parallel to women's studies and potentially a more inclusive field of study than simply masculinity.

Although men, as a class, may hold patriarchal privilege in U.S. society, men's and masculinity studies examines the areas in which men as individuals and as members of groups also face challenges tied to perceptions of masculinity. Adams and Savran (2002) noted that masculinity studies are "dedicated to analyzing what has often seemed to be an implicit fact, that the vast majority of societies are patriarchal and that men have historically enjoyed more than their share of power, resources and cultural authority," and they aim to "demonstrat[e] that masculinities are historically constructed, mutable, and contingent, and analyz[e] their many and widespread effects" (p. 2). The focus

---

[2]The term "intersectionality" is commonly used within women's studies to refer to the inextricable connections among oppressions and identities. Attention to intersectionality requires one to recognize that experiences of sex and gender are tied to ethnicity, economic class, age, ablebodiedness, and a variety of other identities and characteristics.

of the scholarship continues to shift, as some claim it should specifically be on men, others on masculinity regardless of who enacts it, others on patriarchy and structures of male privilege, and others on sex and gender identity and roles (Adams & Savran, 2002; Connell, 2002; Halberstam, 1998). Much of the scholarship is informed by feminist theory and practices (Kimmel, 1997) and is conducted by feminist and masculinity scholars of all sexes. Connell (2002) suggested, "The challenge to hegemonic heterosexuality from lesbian and gay movements is logically as profound as the challenge to men's power from feminism, but has not been circulated in the same way" (p. 257). Connell suggested that this marginalization of the concerns of lesbian and gay scholars and activists could undermine the progress of men's studies by negating recognition of the interplay of masculinity, sexual orientation, and gender identity.

Coursework on masculinity issues began in the late 1970s, building to approximately 40 courses by the mid-1980s. By the mid-1990s, more than 300 men's studies courses were available, rising to over 500 at present (American Men's Studies Association, 2005). Although no centralized data is kept on minors and majors in men's studies, Hobart and William Smith Colleges are reported to have offered the first minor in men's studies, while Akamai University in Hawaii offers the first recorded major in men's studies. At least three other campuses offer men's studies minors, while others allow for concentrations within a gender studies degree. The institutionalization of men's studies has received mixed response. As noted in Adams and Savran's (2002) commentary about the inclusion of masculinity issues alongside women's studies, or the merging of the two via gender studies:

Unlike many of the fields that are its models and precursors, masculinity studies analyzes a dominant and oppressive class that has, arguably, always been the primary focus of scholarly attention. Does masculinity studies represent a beneficial extension of feminist analysis or does it represent a hijacking of feminism? In short, what is gained—and what is lost—when a field that had been defined as women's studies, understood as both a theoretical and politically activist insurgency, changes its focus to examine the construction of those subjects who historically have subjugated women? Given the limited resources in universities to support teaching and research on gender, it seems an unfortunate inevitability that masculinity studies, if it were to gain any institutional status, would enter into a competitive relationship with other related fields. (2002, p. 7)

Even while positioned as scholars within masculinity studies, Adams and Savran (2002) recognized the challenges faced by promoting the study of a dominant group. However, gender equity can only be accomplished if both the experiences of the dominant and oppressed groups are understood, evaluated, and reconceptualized. Men's Studies, when engaged in from a liberatory, social-justice standpoint, can and has been valuable in extending the interrogation of sex and gender at individual, institutional, and societal levels.

Gay, Lesbian, and Queer Studies

With groundings in a number of disciplines and interdisciplinary programs including women's studies and ethnic studies, academic programs aimed specifically at issues of sexual orientation and gender identity emerged in the United States in the 1980s. Catrone (2001) suggested that "the acceptance of Women's and Ethnic Studies programs by the academic community; the discussion of LGBT issues in mainstream society such as gays in the military and sexual discrimination; and the increased use of the Internet all helped make LGBT [lesbian, gay, bisexual, transgender] academic programs a reality" (p. 3). As of 2006, the only Department of Gay, Lesbian, and Bisexual Studies in the United States was at San Francisco City College, which was also the first campus in the United States to offer a bachelor's degree in gay and lesbian studies. Now, Cornell, Yale, Hobart and William Smith, and Sarah Lawrence also offer this major. As of 2005, more than 40 campuses in the United States offered some form of a gay and lesbian, queer, or sexuality studies concentration, minor, or major.

Gay and lesbian studies aims to examine the normativeness of sexual orientation and gender identity as these affect individuals, institutions, societies, and practices. Gay and lesbian studies scholars expose and examine the ways in which heterosexual privilege works alongside other forms of privilege and oppression; and bring a strong corrective to the perception that all men are privileged and women are oppressed within a sex/gender system. Recognizing the interrelatedness of sexuality, sex, masculinity, and femininity, gay, and lesbian scholars interrogate the experiences of gay men, lesbians, and bisexuals over time and location. In terms of gender equity, gay and lesbian studies scholars particularly seek to enhance the positive inclusion in the curriculum and as subjects of study those who identify as gay, lesbian, bisexual, and/or transgender. Further, they seek to identify means through which nonheterosexuals can be fully included and valued within institutions and societies, rather than facing marginalization, exclusion and violence.

Queer studies is a further extension of gay and lesbian studies, women's studies and men's studies, aiming to challenge entrenched binaries between men and women, heterosexuals and nonheterosexuals, masculine and feminine, and so forth. As Corber and Valocchi (2003) asserted, "'Queer' names or describes identities and practices that foreground the instability inherent in the supposedly stable relations between anatomical sex, gender and sexual desire" (p. 1). Working from positions often described as postmodern and poststructural, queer studies scholars challenge the ways in which experiences and desires are attached to human biology and socially constructed conceptions of appropriate gender-based behaviors. They aim to deconstruct categories of representation rather than examining differences between categories. They question the primacy of identifying maleness, femaleness, gay and lesbian identity, and heterosexual identity since these categories of identification are fluid, and their meanings are consistently under reevaluation. As such, rather than focusing on the differences between heterosexual and gay and lesbian experiences as might occur in gay and lesbian studies, queer studies challenges the naming of sexual desire as heterosexual and homosexual in the first place, and seeks to identify the conditions under which these labels emerged. Rather than seek gender equity, they would likely challenge why gender is the category for which equity is desired, and how sex, sexuality, and gender identity have become primary categories of difference within educational settings.

Jill Dolan (1998) noted that the rapid expansion of scholarship on gay, lesbian, and queer subjects has led to research and teaching that crosses many disciplinary boundaries, and has provided students with a greater opportunity to understand the contributions and experiences of sexual minorities. As scholars of sexual orientation and gender identity grapple with the ways in which to locate their teaching and research within educational settings, they may have the luxury of choosing from among women's studies, ethnic studies, gay and lesbian studies, men's studies, queer studies, and gender studies. Zita (1994) saw hope in "the possibility of reopening a wider discussion on gender, sexuality, class, race and other differences in the context of queer experience" (p. 268), but supports this cautiously just as feminist (and/or lesbian) women of color have often been challenged to select allegiances to either/both women's studies as it faces its historical White, heterosexist supremacy, and ethnic/area studies which have historically privileged male, heterosexual experiences. Zita noted, "As Gayle Rubin has suggested . . . lesbians are oppressed as women and as queers. While this statement has served as a springboard for lesbian participation in Queer Studies, it is the 'oppression of women' that is in danger of being overlooked by the rapid rise of male power in this new academic field" (p. 271).

For those whose scholarship on sexual and gender identity does not fit within feminist/women's studies, the need for academic programs focusing on queer studies or its various components is clearly more pressing. Recognizing the difficulties of appropriately creating gay and lesbian or queer studies and the challenges already facing women's studies and emerging men's/masculinity studies endeavors, subsuming all of this under the heading "Gender Studies" clearly proves all the more problematic, while also opening up opportunities for scholarship and coursework.

Gender Studies

Zita's (1994) commentary regarding the benefits and challenges of subsuming lesbian studies under the broader category of queer studies played out to a greater degree when considering merging women's studies, men's and masculinity studies, gay and lesbian studies, and queer studies under the umbrella of "Gender Studies." It is clear that, while at times complementary, the fields are also discrete enough to create tensions when forced together. These tensions are ideological, political, territorial, and at times personal. Because women's studies maintains the longest institutional history, has the largest number of programs, and enjoys the benefits of a large national professional association, it also has the most to lose if its title and focus is diluted to accommodate other foci. Yee (1997) suggested that desires to move from women's studies to gender studies derive from two sources, in the "recent resurgence of antifeminist and racist backlash on university campuses and in society at large and in the evolution of the study of gender in academic scholarship and teaching" (p. 55). This issue is confounded by questions as to why women's studies is being merged with sexuality and men's studies, but not ethnic/area studies, disability studies, and so forth. As will be discussed below, such questions require a greater understanding of the content of and disciplinary locations of women's and gender studies scholarship and teaching and of the influence this has on the field.

Addressing the first of these concerns, the degree to which any components of gender studies have faced backlash remains contested. As will be discussed later, there is evidence that women's studies programs and faculty have experience backlash and harassment; however, the data is not comprehensive, and this lack of data makes it difficult to affirm that a shift to "Gender Studies" from "Women's Studies" would alleviate such situations. The second of Yee's (1997) arguments for combining efforts was to respond to the evolution of writing on topics of sex and gender. This is indeed the most common claim, offering a greater possibility for interrogating issues of sex and gender in a context seemingly broader than that available through women's studies alone. Yee acknowledged the possibility of mutual support among the component parts of gender studies, but felt in the final analysis that claiming a generic heading erased the political and intellectual effectiveness of the individual programs. Speaking on behalf of women's studies remaining solitary, Yee affirmed, "As long as sexism, racism, and classism exist in all their configurations, and as long as some feminist scholars find it too risky to name their programs 'feminist studies,' 'women's studies' remains the best way to name units that promote feminist scholarship and teaching" (p. 56). From its inception, women's studies has developed as an interdisciplinary field, drawing upon scholarship and coursework from disciplines throughout the academy, as well as generating its own scholarship and coursework. Naming the diverse focus on sex and gender within women's studies alone, Zimmerman (2005) asserted:

Women's studies is both the location of new disciplinary thinking about women and gender and the point at which feminist scholarship and theorizing within [the] older disciplines intersect with those occurring within ethnic studies, area studies, sexuality studies, and cultural studies; with the work taking place in activist projects and organizations; and with the insights drawn from personal narratives and creative arts projects. As such, women's studies offers the best opportunities for productive interdisciplinary theorizing about women, gender, knowledge, and society. (p. 34)

A shift from women's studies to gender studies therefore may not substantially change a program's focus on topics of sex and gender, but may change the lenses and theoretical standpoints from which it is viewed. Regardless of focus, women's studies remains rooted in feminist theories, whereas men's and masculinity studies, gay and lesbian studies, and queer studies embrace nonfeminist standpoints as well.

An additional reason given for offering gender studies programs is tied to resources. Even if a women's studies program has proven itself viable on a particular campus, this does not ensure support for the creation of stand-alone men's studies, gay and lesbian studies, and queer studies programs. This is especially true on small campuses where there may be few faculty members with sufficient expertise to develop such programs, or at larger campuses whose disciplinary structures do not favor faculty participation in interdisciplinary programs. Waiting for the resources to develop a stand-alone program, rather than adding portions of programs to an existing sex or gender-based program, often limits opportunities for achieving equity goals. To overcome erasure, several women's studies programs have compromised by renaming themselves "Women's and Gender

Studies" or "Women's and Sexuality Studies" to maintain the focus on women while also embracing other aspects of gender studies. Gay and lesbian studies programs are struggling as well with naming, attempting to find names that are as inclusive as their scholarship and curricula permit, without erasing or deleting important categories of identification.

CONTEMPORARY CONDITIONS

Gender and Women's Studies Courses

While women's studies coursework can be found in disciplines throughout the academy, it is primarily located within the arts, humanities, and social sciences, with infrequent offerings in the natural sciences, math and computer sciences, and professional schools (Rosser, 2002). The degree to which such courses are offered depends upon faculty preparation, institutional climate, the strength of the women's studies program, and funding. Most campuses offer some set of core courses offered under a women's studies designation. These core courses often include "the introductory course; feminist theory; gender, race, and class; lesbian lives; women and health" (Zimmerman, 2002, p. ix) and increasingly, an opportunity to engage in an internship or other practical experiences. However, Zimmerman (2002) suggested that the core courses "have not always reached their full potential of smashing discrete categories of knowledge, nor do they proliferate as widely as gender-based courses within the disciplines" (p. ix). Within the disciplines, courses addressing women's literature, psychology of women, women and politics, women and the law, women's history, feminist art, feminist philosophies and ethics, and gendered communication are common. Rosser (2002) noted that, as a field that originated in the humanities and is now often located within the social sciences as well, attention to women's studies within the natural sciences has lagged far behind. Also lagging at most campuses are courses tied to the education, business, engineering, mathematics, and technology. These classes offered outside of the women's studies core are most commonly offered as an elective within a primary discipline, and serve as part of a menu of courses from which women's studies students may choose. Organizations including the National Research Council's Women in Science and Engineering group, the University of Wisconsin System's Women and Science Program, and the National Women's Studies Association provide resource materials, workshops, and conference sessions which are helping faculty to increase inclusion of these topics in women's and gender studies programs."

Unfortunately, to date, there is scant research on the exact distributions of courses across disciplines or campuses, the academic levels at which courses are offered (lower division, upper division, graduate), or the ways in which subject matter is addressed within women's studies[3] or via courses offered through other disciplines. A glimpse into these topics is found in a study, by Salley, Scott-Winkler, Celeen, and Meck (2004), about women's studies offerings in campuses in Alaska, Arizona, California, Colorado, Hawaii, Idaho, Montana, Nevada, New Mexico, Oregon, Utah, Washington, and Wyoming. Of the 38 responding schools, "21% offered between 0 and 10 classes, 32% offered between 11 and 20 Women's Studies courses, 11% between 21 and 30, 32% offered more than 30 courses" (Salley et al., 2004, p. 183). They found that most campuses offered a core that included some combination of "Introduction to Women's Studies; Feminist Theory; Psychology of Women; History of Women; Women in Literature; and Gender, Race, and Class" (Salley et al., 2004, p. 183). These courses resemble the list offered by Zimmerman (2002) above, although it may be worth noting that courses in history, psychology, and literature have become more common to the programs. The west coast research also indicates greater movement toward course foci that "allows for women to be studied across many different contexts including race, social class, ethnicity, sexual orientation, and national background" (Salley et al., 2004, p. 184), which creates a more inclusive and transnational women's studies educational experience. As expected, a majority of the courses offered were not housed solely in women's studies, but instead were either cross listed or housed fully in other academic disciplines. Additionally, the report did not find widespread course offerings outside the humanities and social sciences.

Surprisingly, although the socializing role that education plays in society has been an argument for expanding the inclusion of women's studies at the postsecondary (and even secondary) schools, few programs have developed coursework on women/gender and education, and there is limited discussion of education and schooling within introductory women's studies textbooks. Typically these introductory textbooks mention the role of education as a socializing or gatekeeping institution, or the role women's studies has played within education, but offer scant attention to the conditions of education at all levels and within U.S. and global contexts. Of the nine most popular textbooks, three had no articles or sections on education (Grewal & Kaplan, 2004; Burn, 2005; Ruth, 2001), while another included only a few paragraphs among its 86 articles (Kirk & Okazawa-Rey, 2004). Three others had two articles each on education (Richardson, 2004; Shaw 2004), and another, which included an article on gender equity in the classroom, did not consider education worthy of a chapter in its section on "Institutions That Shape Women's Lives" (Kesselman, McNair, & Schniedewind, 2003). In contrast, Sapiro's (2003) *Women in American Society,* a textbook rather than a reader, had subsections on education in two sections, and an entire chapter on education as a "gender defining institution," and Pearson Custom Publishing's popular "Reading Women's Lives" database includes, among its 400 selections, 25 selections related to education for inclusion in a customized textbook. Infusing more coursework and scholarship on women, gender, and education is certainly a recommendation for the future growth of women's studies and as a means to enhance further attention to gender equity through education.

---

[3]In 2006 the National Women's Studies Association obtained a grant from the Ford Foundation, which in part provides support for the development of a database on women's studies programs.

Other Academic Locations

Although the vast majority of women's studies programs and courses are located in four-year postsecondary institutions, these are not the only locations in which they are offered. Coursework and certificates or concentrations in women's or gender studies are becoming available in community and junior colleges throughout the United States. Community colleges enroll significant numbers of women, and especially women from backgrounds underserved by four-year institutions, and therefore are important locations for women's studies courses and programs (Roy, 2006). Karen Bojar (2006) noted that while programs do exist at community colleges, there is a lack of information about these programs because those working within them have workloads that make research and publication nearly impossible to complete. The Community College Caucus of the National Women's Studies Association is seeking funding for a study on this topic. Challenges of engaging in women's studies work at the community college level include lack of visibility and program status, poor coordination among faculty, lack of transfer relationships to four-year institutions, limited institutional support for stand-alone programs (rather than campus-wide gender inclusion), and lack of faculty expertise (Bojar, 1999; Clark & Hogan, 2003; Fisher, 2002; Roy, 2006; Tai, 2005).

Women's studies courses are also now available at a select number of high schools and middle schools. These are typically offered as electives, and are offered as literature/English courses, general introduction to women's studies courses, or as history courses. The Atlanta Semester Program for Women at Agnes Scott College and the Women's Studies Department at The Ohio State University have sponsored women's studies courses for public middle and high schools. Limited information on these programs is available beyond the local level; however, discussions about coursework at the high school and middle school levels are occurring with increasing frequency on the Women's Studies Listserv (WMST-L) and at women's studies conferences.

Faculty. The interdisciplinary nature of the field provides both opportunities and challenges for women's studies (and related fields). Reflecting the locations from which courses are taught, a significant percentage of faculty teaching courses tied to women's studies hold academic appointments in another discipline (e.g., history, sociology, English), or they receive joint appointments in both women's studies and another discipline. Burghart and Colbeck (2005) studied junior faculty doing interdisciplinary and disciplinary work in women's studies, and found that experiences varied greatly by institutional type, campus climate, and discipline; however, some generalizations were possible. They found that women's studies:

may be losing valuable feminist scholarship as some WS [women's studies] faculty contort themselves to fit into their perceptions of what their institutions, departments, and students value in order to secure tenure and promotion rewards. Others grow discouraged by the lack of resources and administrative support necessary to affirm interdisciplinary feminist work through flourishing WS programs. (Burghart & Colbeck, 2005, p. 330)

Among programs on the west coast of the United States, Salley et al. (2004) found that between 1988 and 2002, the percentage of programs with salaried faculty positions in women's studies rose from 23% to 63% (attributing some of the increase to the rise of department chairs). This increase is noteworthy, indicating greater institutional commitments to women's studies than were made a decade earlier (Scully, 1996) and serving as a reminder that data that is only a few years old may fail to adequately reflect the status of this dynamic field of study. Salley et al. also found that 42% of respondents have faculty on release time salary from another department, while 39% reported that faculty were joint appointments with women's studies and another department. Nearly 75% of the programs in the study used adjunct faculty to teach their women's studies courses. Two-thirds of the respondents noted problems "hiring qualified faculty, general lack of continuing faculty, problems funding joint appointments and release time faculty, and lack of continuing faculty development and education" (Salley et al., 2004, p. 184).

Although problems exist with joint appointments and lack of faculty lines in women's studies, faculty finds ways to support their feminist scholarship and teaching. Warhold (2002) argued that as women's studies scholars, whose work is inherently interdisciplinary, are hired into the traditional disciplines, these disciplines are themselves transformed as the scholars work both within this discipline and the interdisciplinary field of women's (and gender) studies. She claims that the intellectual and personal communities developed through the interdisciplinary project of women's studies can help to maintain a focus on feminist scholarship when colleagues interested in such issues are not available within one's disciplinary home. The challenges of location, the political nature of the women's and gender studies, and the fact that most of the involved faculty identify as women, all place special challenges on individual faculty and the program.

Annually, the College and University Professional Association for Human Resources (CUPA-HR) publishes information on faculty salaries and distribution by discipline and rank (excluding data on adjuncts and part-time faculty). The information about women's and gender studies is included in a broad category of "area, ethnic, cultural, and gender studies," but still proves rather interesting. In the most recent report (CUPA-HR, 2005), the group is ranked fourth among disciplines with the highest percentage increase in assistant professors when compared to prior years, with a growth of approximately 5.7%. Further, it indicates that the average salary for this group at four-year colleges is $65,954, compared to an all-discipline average of $66,407, with the group's salaries highest at private institutions ($69,098), followed by unionized public institutions ($65,222), with faculty at nonunionized public campuses earning the least ($63,471). Interestingly, the average salary at the private institutions is higher than the average for all disciplines ($65,784) at private institutions. Without a disaggregation, it is hard to know how the different disciplines contribute to the average, but the data is still interesting to consider. With so many women's studies faculty holding adjunct positions, or serving joint or full appointment in other departments/disciplines, the salary data for those engaged in feminist teaching and scholarship is further obscured.

Research and Scholarship

In addition to the rise in the number of faculty with graduate degrees in women's or gender studies, there is clearly a marked rise in gender-based research within the traditional disciplines. Although feminist scholars still face challenges having their research taken as seriously as more traditional work (Boxer, 1998), by 1999, more than 150 journals and scholarly publications existed in which women's studies scholars could publish their work (NWSA Task Force on Faculty Roles and Rewards, 1999). While 11 of these journals were specifically focused on women's studies, 31 fields outside of women's studies offer journals committed to feminist or women-centered scholarship, and focus on queer topics. This suggests that feminist and women's studies scholarship can influence the discourse of many academic disciplines and, by extension, can lead to greater gender inclusion and equity. In terms of the acceptance of the work of feminists and women's studies scholars, the publication of such work increased threefold in the 1970s to 1980s (DuBois, Kelly, Kennedy, Korsmeyer, & Robinson, 1987). In addition, by 2006 at least 20 scholarly journals focused specifically on queer studies or gay and lesbian topics, with at least five more on issues related to men's and masculinity studies.

Another strong sign of the growth of women's studies scholarship can be found in the increased attention to the field within doctoral dissertations. Boxer (1998) indicated that women's studies was designated as an "indexing category" by *Dissertation Abstracts International* in 1978, and by 1995 "the cumulative total of doctoral degrees under that rubric was 10,786" (p. xii). By the end of 2005, the number of dissertations with "Women's Studies" as a subject descriptor had risen to 33,317 (33,434 using "Women's Studies" as a keyword). In contrast, by 2006, "Men's Studies," "Masculinity Studies," "Queer Studies," "Gay and Lesbian Studies," and "Gender Studies" had not yet been designated as an indexing category for subject descriptors. However, when dissertations completed between 1978 and 2005 were searched by keywords, 46 contained "Men's Studies" or "Masculinity Studies" (with the former more prevalent); 60 contained "Queer Studies" or "Gay and Lesbian Studies" (equally distributed); and 234 contained "Gender Studies." As with Women's Studies, the current numbers are much higher than those from 1978–1995, with only 11 in men's/masculinity, 7 in queer/gay and lesbian, and 51 in gender studies.

These recent successes should not be interpreted as indicating that women's and gender studies scholarship is fully integrated throughout the academy, nor that its subjects adequately address the full diversity of women, men or the LGBT/queer community. For example, even though numerous reports have indicated the need to examine women's lack of inclusion in science, technology, engineering, and math (STEM), and the role women's studies could play in this regard (Bix, 2000; Goldberg, 1999; National Council for Research on Women, 2001), these areas continue to be underresearched. This may reflect both a lack of scientific interest and knowledge among women's studies scholars, and a lack of desire or opportunity among scholars within the natural sciences to focus on such topics. With women still underrepresented among STEM faculty, their focusing on issues of sex and gender may further marginalize these women within the academy. Inattention by feminist and women's studies scholars may also be a symptom and a cause of girls' lower participation in STEM courses at the secondary and postsecondary level (see Chapter 13). As expected, this lack of scholarship is also tied to the limited number of women's studies courses that address STEM content, and the limited inclusion of STEM topics within women's studies survey courses and introductory texts.

Subramaniam (2005) asserted that feminist science studies have drawn valuable attention to the ways in which women's studies scholarship can transform oppressive practices and perspectives in the sciences, and also indicates that women's studies itself is enhanced and transformed when the natural sciences are fully included. However, instead of transforming the sciences, she finds that feminist science studies are primarily focused on health-related topics, and traditionally in the form of critique. Recounting her own academic preparation and scholarship in biology and women's studies, she claimed that women's studies "provided me with the tools and methods to *deconstruct* science, not *reconstruct* it—to work *on* science, not *in* science" (Subramaniam, 2005, p. 239). Women's studies' attention to science, technology, engineering, and math cannot be limited to critique, and as Subramanian suggested, both these fields and women's studies all need to transform in order to best achieve the goals of all fields. (See Chapter 13 for expanded discussions of these issues.)

While faculty and students involved with women's and gender studies programs engage in a great deal of research on women and girls (and a variety of other gender-related issues), research on these topics is not limited to such programs. In addition to work conducted by faculty and students in other academic disciplines, there are more than 300 women's research centers located in more than 80 countries (NCRW, 2002), and more centers worldwide focusing on other gender-related issues (masculinity, sexuality, sexual orientation, etc.) that further knowledge of gender and gender equity. Within the United States, the National Council for Research on Women (NCRW) serves as "a network of more than 100 leading U.S. research, advocacy, and policy centers with a growing global reach . . . [collaborating] to ensure fully informed debate, policies, and practices to build a more inclusive and equitable world for women and girls" (NCRW, 2006). The NCRW's Women's Studies Area and International Studies Curriculum Integration Project is a valued program supporting the growth of women's studies classes and programs, and throughout their programs they have helped to develop strong data about women and have been openly critical of government misinformation. The American Association of University Women (AAUW) annually supports the work of many researchers, both faculty and students, and, in addition, initiates studies and publishes reports dealing with many issues involving equity in education. It is important to note that although they are often involved in research, NCRW, AAUW, and the related women's research centers and organizations around the world are not typically designed as women's studies research centers and organizations. There are often collaborations and partnerships, but as Beverly Guy-Sheftall is summarized as noting at an NCRW conference:

There is a growing gap in the academy between Women's Studies scholars and an increasing number of women who conduct research on women but don't associate themselves with Women's Studies; they don't necessarily identify as feminist, don't believe that interdisciplinary work is important, and don't see a need for action oriented research. (NCRW, 1998)

Individuals and the projects they work on via women's research centers and organizations do not all enact the aims of women's studies, even if engaged in work related to women and gender equity.

Co-curricular Programs: Centers and Organizations

Within academic institutions women's studies is primarily recognized as occurring within academic programs. However, women's studies scholarship and activism is also prominent within women's centers, gender and sexuality services offices, and feminist-based research institutes. Indeed, these centers and services offices support gender equity at individual levels through educational programs, counseling and advising, and challenge institutional inequities through participation in campus advocacy activities, policy development, outreach programs, and community coalitions. Feminist and women's studies-based student groups, supporting attention to the academic disciplines or aimed at activism, support, or social activities, often also support gender equity. As of 2005, more than 460 women's centers were located on college campuses in the United States, the majority serving as stand-alone centers, while a few are co-ordinated with a women's studies or gender studies academic program.

Feminist activism and scholarship is also often engaged in via student, faculty, and staff organizations on campus. While many of these activist groups are institution specific, often affiliated with either an academic program or women's center, others are local branches of national organizations. Among the most popular are the Feminist Majority Foundation's (FMF) and Feminist Majority Leadership Alliances (FMLAs). There are also chapters of the National Organization for Women (NOW) and the AAUW that serve campuses as well as the larger communities. These organizations create opportunities for those interested in feminist topics to hold educational seminars or discussions, engage in educational activities and activist work, and socialize with like-minded individuals. Such organizations provide a strong link between academic women's studies and lived experiences, and their work can often help recruit students into women's studies courses. Additional information is being provided on the FMLAs since they have many participants and have been widely mimicked by other progressive and conservative student action groups. While students and faculty participants in the FMLAs come from all types of interest areas, many take women's studies courses, and women's studies faculty members often serve as the group advisors. Launched in 1997 to train the next generation of feminist leaders, as of 2007, 196 FMLAs and their affiliates are in a wide range of public and private two- and four-year college and university campuses in 44 states. The FMLA program is built on a study and action model that defines 'choices' in its broadest sense including reproductive choices, leadership choices, career choices, and saving choices—fighting the backlash in the United States and globally. The choices manual and the organizer's binder help students learn critical skills. The campus organizers in the FMF east and west coast offices work with core groups of 15–40 active undergraduate student members on each campus. They also involve many others on their campus and typically have e-mail lists of 150–200 students. When the FMLAs engage in a wide range of frontline feminist actions such as producing *The Vagina Monologues*, spearheading the "Get Out Her Vote Campaign" and campaigns for full access to emergency contraceptives, or learning about and defending Title IX, they involve and educate many others on their campus. The exchange of information to and among the FMLAs and activists on other campuses is facilitated by a campus e-zine and Web site (http://www.feministcampus.org), which includes a Title IX action kit. Additionally, this Web site has alerts that go to over 36,000 students, 4,000 faculty and 1,400 campuses.

National Organizations

In the United States, there is no national association focused on all aspects of gender studies. Of the component parts, the flagship organization is the National Women's Studies Association (NWSA), which serves as the only U.S. based national professional organization for women's studies scholars and activists. In 2005, NWSA had more than 2,000 individual and group members. The NWSA has standing committees for Program Administrators and for Women's Centers, as well as 9 Caucuses, 9 Task Forces, and 10 Interest Groups that focus attention on particular constituents, concerns, or scholarly/activist foci. NWSA claimed that women's studies is "equipping women not only to enter society as whole, as productive human beings, but to transform the world to one that will be free of all oppression" (NWSA, 2005). As noted in the NWSA Constitution, the NWSA mission stated:

NWSA seeks to promote the creation of a just world, free from all the ideologies and structures that oppress and exploit some for the advantage of others, in which all persons can develop to their fullest potential. In pursuit of these ends, the organization supports and promotes feminist teaching, learning, research, and service, wherever these occur, that seek to understand and change oppressive structures and ideologies. (NWSA, 2005)

The term *equity* does not appear in the NWSA governance documents; however the NWSA mission clearly aims to challenge hierarchies and exclusions and to foster scholarship, teaching, and activism that enhances opportunities for all. As with most U.S. based feminist organizations, the NWSA has struggled over time to be ethnically and culturally inclusive within its structure and program, to provide attention to the range of interests of its members, and to recognize the contributions of scholars and activists in all of their locations. Through a variety of means, NWSA's Women of Color Caucus and Anti-White Supremacy Task Force have been particularly vital in drawing attention to feminist scholarship and activism which enhance inclusivity in women's studies scholarship and practices.

The first national men's studies organization developed in the U.S. in the early 1980s as a task force of the pro-feminist, gay affirming (and later explicitly anti-racist) National Organization for Men (now known as the National Organization for Men Against Sexism, or NOMAS). By the late 1980s, the task force became the Men's Studies Association (MSA) and started offering annual conferences in conjunction with NOMAS' more broadly-focused annual Men and Masculinities conferences. The American Men's Studies Association (AMSA) began in the early 1990s, under the leadership of many of the prior members of the MSA, to provide greater attention to men's studies than they felt possible within NOMAS, and to include within their association men's studies scholars who were not embraced by NOMAS' pro-feminist, gay-affirming mission. Although both organizations include pro-feminist men's studies scholars, the AMSA is more likely than the MSA to include scholars who support the maintenance of, or return to, traditional forms of masculinity, including members of the mytho-poetic movement, (Doyle & Femiano, 1998).

Unlike the fields of women's studies and men's studies, no single association in the United States attempts to serve as a primary voice for queer or gay and lesbian studies within educational settings. However, queer studies scholars are not without resources, as many professional academic organizations include Gay, Lesbian, Bisexual, Transgender, Intersex, and Queer (GLBTIQ) caucuses or groups, with foci on scholarly interests, support of those who identify as GLBTIQ, or a combination of the two. Further, the Queer Studies List (QSTUDY-L) serves as a very active international listserv for faculty, students, librarians, and researchers interested in queer studies, as members share resources, ask questions, and provide support to one another as they face personal and professional challenges.

The National Consortium of Directors of LGBT Resources in Higher Education provides support to Center Directors through a strong Web site, listserv, and meetings held at national student affairs conferences (American College Personal Association and the National Association of Student Personnel Administrators) and the annual National Gay and Lesbian Task Force's annual conference. By 2001, 56 GLBTI Centers existed on college campuses in the United States (Beemyn, 2002), while other campuses have incorporated related programs and services into women's centers, multicultural centers, or related offices. As of 2006, 100 such centers exist, extending cocurricular attention to GLBT issues and enhancing opportunities to engage in programming and activism on queer subjects (Barnett & Tubbs, 2006).

Pedagogy

Women's and gender studies serve as a challenge to disciplines that fail to incorporate explorations of gender within their coursework and research. As cutting edge academic disciplines, they have exposed gender bias and inequity at various levels of education through scholarly research. Women's studies has especially initiated and drawn considerable attention to the implication of patriarchal relations in knowledge transfer and acquisition with respect to gender bias. Courses in women's and gender studies have specifically dealt with the problematic of whose knowledge counts and to what extent gender bias is intertwined and entrenched in the educational process.

Concerns regarding revisions to course content or subject matter and pedagogical style have emerged in response to gender bias by teachers in the classroom. Less obvious and perhaps more pervasive than gender discrimination, unconscious forms of gender bias by teachers maintain rigidity in societal roles and expectations, as well as influence how women and men understand and assume positions of power (Sadker, M., & Sadker, D., 1995). Many women's studies faculty rely upon feminist pedagogies to construct classroom environments that challenge traditional classroom power relations and encourage critical thinking and application of knowledge. In a comprehensive article on feminist pedagogy, Shrewsbury (1993) claimed:

At its simplest level, feminist pedagogy is concerned with gender justice and overcoming oppressions . . . feminist pedagogy ultimately seeks a transformation of the academy and points toward steps, however small, that we can all take in each of our classrooms to facilitate that transformation. Three concepts, community, empowerment, and leadership, are central to these steps and provide a way of organizing our exploration into the meaning of feminist pedagogy. (pp. 9–10)

Seeing empowerment, a term she links to Freire, as a key concern, Shrewsbury (1993) noted:

To accomplish empowerment of all, feminist pedagogy employs classroom strategies that: 1) enhance the students' opportunities and abilities to develop their thinking about the goals and objectives they wish and need to accomplish individually and collectively, 2) develop the students' independence (from formal instructors) as learners, 3) enhance the stake that everyone has in the success of a course and thereby make clear the responsibility of all members of the class for the learning of all, 4) develop skills of planning, negotiating, and evaluating and decision making, 5) reinforce or enhance the self-esteem of class members by the implicit recognition that they are sufficiently competent to play a role in course development and are able to be change agents, 6) expand the students' understanding of the subject matter of the course and of the joy and difficulty of intense intellectual activity as they actively consider learning goals and sequences. (pp. 10–11)

Shrewsbury believed that empowering students helps them to find their own voices and develop an authentic sense of self. Scanlon (1997) highlighted the needed links between teaching and action for a pedagogy to be truly feminist. She indicates that feminist pedagogy is designed to help students get beyond mere awareness, and moves them toward action, to "go beyond providing information to empower students so that they see themselves not only as victims of injustice but as people capable of creating change in society" (Scanlon, 1997, p. 8). Further, "If what students learn in our classes does not reach outside the classroom door or stretch beyond the end of the semester, our work bears the label 'instruction' far more than it does 'feminist'" (p. 8). The utilization of feminist pedagogy while addressing subjects related to women and gender furthers the aims of gender equity and inclusion through the women's studies classroom.

CHALLENGES TO WOMEN'S AND GENDER STUDIES

Whether challenging political aims, teaching practices, or academic rigor, women's and gender studies courses and programs have faced challenges from a variety of sources. As Shrewsbury (1993) noted, "Feminist pedagogy begins with a vision of what education might be like but frequently is not" (p. 9), and as such, feminist pedagogy and women's and gender studies programs are very often construed in antagonistic and controversial terms in higher education. Such a stance can at times limit the safety faculty feel on campus or in the classroom and marginalize or threaten the stability of programs and centers within academic institutions. Scully and Currier (1997) produced for NWSA a report on backlash within women's studies. It included investigations of the types of problems faced, reviews of the instigators and tactics used, and strategies for responding to problems. In the nine years since the production of the report, challenges to women's and gender studies programs have broadened and deepened, and so have the quality of responses.

Very public attacks against the field of women's studies have been waged by conservative associations and by women claiming feminist positioning who fear feminism has gone awry. Examples include Christina Hoff Sommers' (1994; 2001) *Who Stole Feminism?: How Women have Betrayed Women* and *The War Against Boys: How Misguided Feminism is Harming our Young Men,* Daphne Patai's (2003) *Professing Feminism: Education and Indoctrination in Women's Studies,* and the Independent Women's Forum's *Room of One's Own: How Women's Studies Textbooks Miseducate Students* (Stobla, 2002). Conservative organizations also target agencies that have funded or supported women's studies, as evidenced by a Front Page Magazine article that claimed the Ford Foundation had colluded in the politicizing and liberalizing of campuses by its support of women's studies programs, scholars, and associations (Schuld, 2004). Collectively, these challenges argue that feminist teaching has become overtly anti-male, that classes distort or fabricate truth, and that courses are overly political and anti-academic. Response to these challenges have included articles, press releases, and texts that challenge the use of isolated cases as examples of widespread problems, clarify pedagogical practices and choice of curricular materials, examine the positive contributions of the fields to society and individual students, and expose the ideological nature of all aspects of education (Braithwaite, 2004; Friedman, 2002; May, 2005; Rogers & Garrett, 2002; Superson & Cudd, 2002; Wiegman, 2005).

McCaughey and Warren (2006) indicated that attacks on women's studies programs have included research reports challenging the content of women's studies programs or courses, editorials questioning taxpayer support of women's studies activities, hostile behaviors at or toward sponsored programs (e.g., *The Vagina Monologues*), calls to edit women's studies Web sites to include nonfeminist materials for balance, and calls for firing or investigating faculty for behaviors or Web site materials. They identify 15 organizations that have been "critical of women's studies, feminism, and liberal academics" (McCaughey & Warren, 2006, p. 46). The sense that one's work may be the target of conservative challenge can affect (positively and negatively) what is done in the name of women's studies.

Campus-based examples of the negative treatment given to feminist faculty, students, and staff include requirements to warn students of explicit material in classes dealing with nontraditional sexual orientations, women's studies courses not being afforded seminar status because of their content or approach, and the destruction of flyers advertising women's studies classes and events (Kolodny, 1996). Such experiences have become common among the emerging fields within gender studies as well. Research indicates that on average female professors are rated lower than male professors regardless of discipline (Basow, 1994; Senger, 2005), and Superson (2002) found that feminist professors are often rated lower than nonfeminist women or men. Very often students express negative reaction to feminist classroom topics, and such negative evaluations can be a detriment to promotion of such faculty (Bauer & Rhoades, 1996).

One of the unfortunate results of the success of political and academic feminist movements is harassment. Within all of higher education, women have experienced antifeminist intellectual harassment disproportionately. Such harassment can include death threats, physical assault, discriminatory hiring, and tenure practices, lack of administrative or institutional support, and provisions required of faculty in women's studies programs not asked of those in other disciplines (Kolodny, 1996). Students also face the harassment within the classroom, as they actively challenge the subject matter, author's viewpoints, faculty, and other students. Anecdotal reports suggest that males are the most likely perpetrators of this harassment, although formal studies are not available to confirm this perception. Gotell and Crow (2005) described the difference between antifeminist intellectual harassment and student dissent or resistance, which they claim to be "inevitable features of any process of knowledge production" (p. 287). This is an important distinction, for the former attempts to challenge feminism's aims and achievements in order to maintain or reaffirm gender inequities and can indeed be a form of backlash or a rebellion against indoctrinating behaviors. The latter is "dissent that may challenge feminist interpretations but does not seek to close down the intellectual space offered by feminism" (p. 297). Resistance can be experienced in any classroom and is a natural consequence of learning. In a women's (or gender) studies classroom that actively interrogates systems and ideologies related to race, class, and gender, it is understandable that students will be uncomfortable with interpretations that challenge the status quo. It is the responsibility of an instructor to anticipate this resistance, and to make it possible for students to express their dissent as part of the learning process.

Some of the problems come from the negative perceptions and prejudicial views of the discipline that are held by many nonwomen's studies students. Of course, students in many disciplines may be intolerant of others, but because women's studies offers a challenge to the dominant discourses, the critiques of women's studies, building upon the legitimacy given to ridicule and misrepresentation of feminist work in the larger society, seem to be more prevalent and baiting. In a survey of the views of students on an English campus, Marchbank and Letherby (2006) noted that many who have not taken women's studies courses report negative stereotypes about the courses and the students (e.g., the courses are easy, they exclude 50% of the population, they do not have real academic content, and the staff and students are lesbians who hate men). The authors concluded that many students see women's studies as in conflict with men, and thus objectionable. In this study, more men than women held these views, and students in the courses (who feel positive about what they study) did not hold them. The authors cautioned that the powerful misrepresentation of the discipline poses a danger to the political and economic stability of women's studies programs. They wrote that what is needed is the development of a counterdiscourse to dispel inaccurate stereotypes, and to make clear the continuing contributions of the women's studies programs to all the disciplines.

George (1992) and Kitch (2002) noted that some male students taking women's studies courses also felt themselves the victims of unfounded stereotypes and dehumanized. In a well-publicized case in 1999, Boston College released Mary Daly of her teaching duties after 25 years of excluding males from her women's studies courses. She afforded males the option to engage in an individual study of course topics but did not allow them in her feminist theory classroom to allow females a safe space to address patriarchy, violence against women, and a variety of other topics Daly felt could not be as adequately covered under male, patriarchal gaze. Overwhelmingly, the women's studies community supported the inclusion of males in women's studies courses, even if they appreciated Daly's position that the women-only classroom environment is different. Given that Title IX does not allow sex segregation unless it is clearly for eliminating sex discrimination, Daly's position could not be legally supported given the lack of data supporting her claims of a hostile environment caused by males. (See Chapter 9 for information on coeducational and single sex educational environments.)

Kitch (2002) recounted resistance by female students to a male student's presence in the Ohio State University women's studies master's program, concerned with, as Kitch puts it, their "refuge" being violated by the outsider or oppressor. In contrast to Daly's standpoint, Kitch suggested that males can be of value in the classroom and that faculty must work to ensure their respectful inclusion as a way to support learning for all. Gender equity demands that sex and gender do not influence one's treatment in a class, even if the subject matter is focused on specific sexes, genders, sexual orientations, and gender identities.

Kaplan and Grewal (2002) identified a variety of justifications for challenging women's studies' status within academic institutions. Some argue for the dismantling of programs because feminist scholars no longer face marginalization within the academy, and because feminist topics are well entrenched throughout the academy, thus negating the need for separate programs. Women's studies is also claimed to be more ideological and political than gender-focused work emerging from the supposedly more rigorous and apolitical disciplines where many courses are now located. Further, because feminist scholars and activists have successfully demonstrated the diversity of women's experiences and conditions, "this subject ceases to exist and thus should not be reproduced and reified as an institutional site" (Kaplan & Grewal, 2002, p. 68). Kaplan and Grewal argued that all of these standpoints are antifeminist or anti-women's studies in intent, even if on their face they appear to claim the success of the field. They suggested that the strengths of women's studies and gender studies as interdisciplinary programs must be maintained to ensure progress in destabilizing systems of oppression, yet these programs must also strive to find better entrenchment within academic institutions to ensure their long-term health.

Faculty within women's and gender studies rely upon such supports as the NWSA, the WMST-L, and the NCRW to develop strategies for addressing backlash and developing programs that can better resist institutional backlash. Strategies to address backlash may indeed require coalition building with allies whose programs may also be at risk or who benefit from the contributions of sex and gender-based scholarship and teaching. On some campuses merging women's studies, men's studies, and gay and lesbian studies may create a strong enough faculty force to withstand attacks and attempts to dismantle or discredit programs. The inclusion of all fields within one program may also limit claims that such programs fail to address men, heterosexuals, or whichever groups challengers feel are ignored by women's studies, and queer studies. However, since some attacks come from among the various parties who may be involved in the merging (for example, women's studies scholars opposed to the institutionalization of men's studies), such partnerships may reinforce strife rather than eliminate it.

Finally, it is worth noting that not all programs face the challenges listed above, and those that face them do not do so to the same degree. Orr and Lichtenstein (2004) suggested that within women's studies a "siege mentality affects feminist academics in different locations to different degrees and with very different consequences" (p. 6). At their campus, they have experienced no overt backlash, and indeed, they feel their women's studies program is quite secure within their institution. Institutional and community context plays a large role in the reception gender studies programs receive, and the degree to which their scholars are placed under scrutiny. Bell Hooks (2003) noted:

> Much antifeminist backlash, in particular the attack on Women's Studies . . . emerged not because these programs were failing to educate but rather *because* they were successfully educating students to be critical thinkers. These programs helped, and help, many students shift their ideas about learning from passively embracing education as a means of joining a professional managerial class to thinking about education as the practice of freedom. Rather than punishing students for interrogating the forms of knowledge offered them, they encouraged them to repudiate educational practices that reinforce dominant ideology, to open their minds and think critically. They learned to think in ways that reinforce self-determination. (pp. 71–72)

Hooks (2003) suggested that backlash is in fact an expected, and perhaps inevitable, outcome of the success of women's studies and related fields. The challenges of antifeminist intellectual harassment and to women's and gender studies scholarship and teaching in general, will likely continue.

IMPACTS AND USES OF WOMEN'S AND GENDER STUDIES

Women's studies and the other components of gender studies have helped to transform understanding of issues of sex and gender, institutionalize the application of feminist and gendered theories to a range of topics and disciplines, expand attention to and understanding of women's experiences and contributions, and transform the manner in which teaching and research is conducted. Women's and gender studies has therefore enhanced the achievement of gender equity by ensuring attention to sex and gender within the curriculum and pedagogical practices, and promoting the participation of all sexes as students and scholars throughout the disciplines. The rapid growth of programs, numbers of graduates at undergraduate and graduate levels, journals, and dissertations all attest to the vitality of women's and gender studies. The growth and impact of women's and gender studies is especially noteworthy given the many challenges mentioned in the previous section.

As noted by Boxer (1998), women's studies has helped to create and validate a new field of knowledge tied to feminist theory and activism, and led the way to broader inquiry into sex and gender via gay and lesbian, men's/masculinity, and queer studies. Feminist and queer research methods have changed who and what is studied, how these studies are designed and executed, and why and for whom research is conducted (Harding, 1987). Feminist pedagogical practices which gained force in women's studies courses, and are now utilized by faculty in many disciplines, have changed power relations within classes, promoted critical thinking skills, and expanded student opportunities to be engaged and active learners in the classroom (Shrewsbury, 1993). The incorporation of women's and GLBTI issues within the curriculum helps to create a campus climate in which students of all sexes and sexual orientations can feel included and validated, and increases awareness of sexism and the desire for gender equity (Catrone, 2001; Harris, Melaas, & Rodacker, 1999).

Since the emergence of these programs, it is possible to assess the effect of women's studies curricula, programs, and activities on the lives of students. One such effort is the college impact movement (Harris, Melaas, & Leckenby, 1999). In addition to acquiring important analytical, research and critical thinking skills in women's studies courses and programs, students often find that their interests, abilities, and goals are changed. A sense of competence, better self-esteem and the discovery of one's voice are examples of the profound personal ways in which students are transformed by women's studies programs (Harris et al., 1999; Macalister 1999). As Macalister (1999) explained, "Women's studies did not just educate [students], it changed them" (p. 2). Another significant impact of women's and gender studies on life enrichment is found in the example of peer education, common on many college and university campuses. Often in conjunction with campus women's centers and feminist student organizations, women's and gender studies students are involved in educating other students about important life issues, such as date rape, domestic assault, sexual orientation, gender identity, and eating disorders. Courses in all areas of gender studies commonly include off-campus internships or practical experiences to provide opportunities to apply and test information learned in classes, and to develop skills that will prepare them for postcollege employment and volunteerism. In a study of students enrolled in their first women's studies course (on Psychology of Women), the students were reported to be more aware of women's positioning in society and of gender roles, and had a greater appreciation and understanding of feminist beliefs, but also completed the course with increased anxiety related to their understanding of female oppression/devaluation (Katz, Swindell, & Farrow, 2004).

In the United States, the National Women's Studies Association has taken the lead in creating and compiling information on program administration and development, women's studies scholarly works, backlash against women's studies, graduate study in women's studies, program assessment, and student learning. For example, Musil (1992) demonstrated the range of student learning outcomes in women's studies, and the manner in which these outcomes were tied to specific elements of a course, program, or institutional location. Across the seven campuses described in Musil's book, students were found to develop stronger critical thinking skills, a greater ability to debate issues, a greater understanding of women and men, and often a sense of empowerment and feminist identity. Unfortunately, most of the reports on the outcomes of women's and gender studies academic preparation are local or anecdotal. Formal, national, and longitudinal studies are rarely available, and this lack of data proves troublesome to the growth of women's studies as well as to an assessment of its impact. This lack of data on outcomes (as well as on structure, faculty, budgets, etc.) makes it difficult for women's studies faculty and administrators to maintain or to obtain funding for programs, request new majors or graduate programs, hire new faculty, or recruit students. At the same time, given the diversity and rapid expansion of the content, focus, and structure of women's and gender studies programs and curricula, such studies are difficult to conduct and may produce data that is rapidly out of date.

As with most humanities and social sciences programs, women's and gender studies is not designed to prepare students for one particular career, but instead provides a perspective through which students can interpret their work and personal experiences while also teaching strong critical thinking skills applicable to any postcollegiate endeavor. Luebke and Reilly (1995) showed that students with women's studies degrees were able to find postcollege employment and admission into graduate and professional schools at rates typical of other liberal arts majors. Kinser (2006) identified more than 200 occupations held by women's studies graduates, based on alumni information posted on Web sites for women's studies programs. The alphabetical list did not indicate frequencies of participation in any of the occupations. While not a highly scientific study, it does suggest that women's studies graduates are obtaining employment in a variety of fields. The list was followed by 59 skills students might acquire through a women's studies program, all items culled from women's studies program Web sites in the United States. As noted before, more research is needed on these topics.

In addition to the impacts on students, the fields of women's and gender studies have had important impacts on the nature of scholarly inquiry and on society. Women's studies, and now gender studies, lead the way in addressing the intersectionality of oppressions and the structural nature of power and privilege. Scholarly and practical challenges to sexism, racism, heterosexism, and classism are particularly important contributions. Feminist and gender-focused topics, methods, and pedagogical styles have become commonplace (although clearly not the norm) on campuses across the United States and in many parts of the world. As noted earlier, the increase in gender-focused dissertations and scholarly journals indicates broader acceptance of feminist scholarship as a valuable form of academic inquiry. Gender-based research centers, service centers, and community organizations connect practical experiences with scholarly works in ways that improve conditions for individuals and communities.

RECOMMENDATIONS

The ways in which women's studies, men's and masculinity studies, gay and lesbian studies, queer studies and gender studies interrelate shall likely be the most interesting development to follow in the next decade. Tying these programs to ethnic studies, area studies, cultural studies and interdisciplinary studies may also lie in the future. Myriad factors are influencing decisions to merge or separate, including campus histories, ideological positioning, complementarity of courses, budgetary and faculty constraints, political posturing, responses to backlash, and the growth of knowledge within all areas. The fears that particular experiences of marginalized groups will become erased through the merging of fields has merit, and the challenge will be to maintain the integrity and vitality of efforts to interrogate sex, sexuality, and gender identity in an inclusive manner regardless of program structure. At the same time, there are exciting opportunities for collaboration that may enhance achievement of equity goals in all areas.

Policy Recommendations

The value of national data about academic programs cannot be understated. Statistics on program offerings, program size, graduation rates, student demographics, faculty salaries and distributions, and institutional locations can help to advance understanding of the status of a field of study, and provide the information necessary for institutions and organizations to better understand their relationship to the field. As noted throughout this chapter, the manner in which national statistics are compiled in the United States limits clear understanding of the myriad programs related to women's and gender studies. Understandably, at times, because of the diversity of program title and structure, the national data does not disaggregate the various foci of programs to support ready use of the data. For example, a broad category such as area, ethnic, cultural, and gender studies, as used by CUPA-HR, contains such a range of academic programs that salary data related to this cannot be used to directly advocate for salary ranges for any particular program within the group. Listings that combine women's studies and gender studies programs under the heading "Women's Studies" (e.g., NCES) may unintentionally limit understanding of the ways in which programs are changing over time. Therefore, the following policy recommendations are offered:

1. All research related to women's and gender studies should clearly articulate which types of programs (women's studies, gender studies, queer studies, gay and lesbian studies, men's and masculinity studies, etc.) have been included in the study and how they are being identified. They should be disaggregated by program type whenever possible.
2. Women's and gender studies data should be disaggregated from that on area, cultural, and ethnic studies. Each of these program areas has a unique intellectual and political history that affects its faculty, institutional placement, student enrollments, and budgets. By combining these programs, the nuances of each are lost, potentially obscuring useful data specific to the fields of study, and limiting the usefulness of the collected data to any program area.

3. National data should be collected on academic minors in addition to the information collected on majors. Programs like women's and gender studies that enroll many students in a minor will certainly benefit, although it seems likely that all programs and departments could find use for this information, especially if cross referenced with major field of study.

Practice/Program Recommendations

Women's and gender studies academic programs (broadly defined) have grown in number and graduates over the last 40 years, and appear to be continuing to be vital forces on college campuses. However, the interdisciplinary nature of the fields appears to offer as many challenges as it does opportunities. Although there is no template for a women's studies curriculum, over the years a set of typical core courses has emerged which has emphasized the humanities and social sciences. Gender studies, masculinity studies, queer studies, gay and lesbian studies, and related programs have less defined core courses, with offerings tied to a combination of faculty expertise, institutional politics, and curricular history. Although many disciplines are included within gender studies and its related programs, all will benefit from continued examination of ways to broaden interdisciplinary connections. Consideration of structure, faculty, and campus politics must also be considered. The following recommendations are therefore offered:

1. The naming and content of gender-related programs will certainly continue to be a challenge to all interested parties (students, faculty, administration, policy makers, employers, etc.). These parties must work together to shape the manner in which programs develop, and to articulate the ways in which program design fits within local and extra-local contexts. National academic organizations should play a vital role in this area. The continued influence of feminist theorizing and activism should be of primary focus within these programmatic discussions.
2. Attention to science, technology, engineering, mathematics, law, medicine, business, and related fields should be at the forefront in all gender-related programs, both because of women's continued underrepresentation in these fields, and because of the role these fields have played in the social construction, control, and treatment of sex, sexuality, and gender identity issues.
3. Gender issues in education should also receive greater attention within women's and gender studies academic programs. Few programs include coursework on gender and education, yet this handbook clearly demonstrates that this topic benefits from further study because of its complexity and because of the important roles that education plays within societies.
4. Women's and gender studies scholars have already identified a need to pay more attention to global/transnational issues, anti-White supremacy, ageism, able-bodiedism, and other anti-oppressive scholarship. We support this aim and encourage gender studies programs and associations to seek out partnerships with others that can assist in these aims.
5. Women's and gender studies programs need more data on such topics as program size, funding, enrollments, faculty, leadership, institutional location, curricular offerings, grad-

uation rates, and placement of graduates. Whether through the developing efforts of the NWSA or another organization, some entity must take leadership for compiling this data and making it accessible to the public. We hope that the Ford Foundation and similar agencies continue to support women's studies through grant funding of such efforts.

6. Most of the research on women's and gender studies has focused on academic programs at four-year institutions. More attention is needed on the activities and outcomes of women's and gender studies work in community colleges, secondary and middle schools, women's services centers, and women's research centers. This should also include research into the relationships among these programs and academic programs.

7. More information is needed on the curricular, programmatic, and scholarly relationships between women's studies, gender studies, queer studies, gay and lesbian studies, men's and masculinity studies, ethnic studies (and its various components), cultural studies, area studies, disability studies, religious studies, and related fields.

8. Women's and gender studies faculty, students, and activists need to expand efforts to promote the positive impacts of these interdisciplinary fields, and share strategies for building and sustaining programs. The national organizations mentioned earlier in this chapter play strategic roles in this process, but their work must be extended by individuals and local and regional entities.

Research Recommendations

The review of the status of gender studies, and its component parts, suggests that these academic programs, and their coordinate service and resource centers, have extended the ways in which all sexes, sexual orientations, and gender identities are included in classrooms and as the focus of scholarly works. However, there is little research on the structure and content of the programs, the outcomes for students and institutions, or the impact of this work on society. More research is recommended in the following areas:

1. As noted in numbers five and six above, more national (and international) data is needed on women's and gender studies academic programs—their content, structure, and outcomes; and on nonacademic ways in which women's and gender studies work is engaged.

2. There is limited data on women's and gender studies faculty preparation, salary, institutional location, and so forth. If not adequately compiled by CUPA-HR or other agencies, this must be collected by those working within gender studies.

3. There has been a great rise in the number of dissertations and published works on gender-related topics, but a systematic accounting of the trends in this scholarship and the impacts of these works is needed.

ACKNOWLEDGMENTS

We would like to thank Ann Russo, Program Director, Women's and Gender Studies, DePaul University, Chicago, IL, for her service as a reviewer of this chapter. Daquanna Harrison, Feminist Majority Foundation, Arlington, W. VA, 2006 campus organizer, helped with information on the Feminist Majority Leadership Alliances.

References

Adams, R., & Savran, D. (Eds.). (2002). *The Masculinity studies reader*. Malden, MA: Blackwell Publishing.

Ahfad University for Women's experience in introducing women and gender studies: The challenges of the 21st century. (2002). *Ahfad Journal, 19*(1), 41–50.

American Men's Studies Association (AMSA). (2005). *American Men's Studies Association*. Retrieved June 8, 2006, from http://www.mensstudies.org

Barnett, D., & Tubbs, N. (2006). *History of LBGT Centers*. Retrieved June 8, 2006, from http://www.lgbtcampus.org/resources/establishment_of_offices.htm

Basow, S. A. (1994). *Student ratings of professors are not gender blind*. Retrieved June 8, 2006, from http://feminism.eserver.org/workplace/professions/fces-not-gender-blind.txt/document_view

Bauer, D., & Rhoades, K. (1996). The meanings and metaphors of student resistance. In V. Clark, S. V. Garner, M. Higonnet, & K. H. Katrak (Eds.), *Anti-Feminism in the Academy* (pp. 95–113). New York: Routledge.

Beemyn, B. (2002). The development and administration of campus LGBT centers and offices. In R. Sanlo, B. Schoenberg, & S. R. Rankin (Eds.), *A Place of Our Own: LGBT Centers on Campus* (pp. 25–32). Westport, CT: Greenwood Press.

Biklen, S. K., & Shakeshaft, C. (1985). The new scholarship on women. In S. S. Klein (Ed.), *Handbook for achieving sex equity through education* (pp. 44–52). Baltimore: Johns Hopkins University Press.

Bix, A. S. (2000). Feminism where men predominate: The history of women's studies and engineering education. *Women's Studies Quarterly, 28*(1–2), 24–45.

Bojar, K. (1999). Conceptualizing the introduction to women's studies courses at the community college. In C. DiPalma & B. Scott-Winkler (Eds.), *Teaching Introduction to Women's Studies: Expectations and Strategies* (pp. 37–48). Westport, CT: Greenwood Press.

Bojar, K. (2006, April 28). RE: Community Colleges and WS. Message posted to WMST-L electronic mailing list, archived at https://listserv.umd.edu/cgi-bin/wa?A1=ind0604d&L=wmst-l#10

Boxer, M. J. (1998). *When women ask the questions: Creating women's studies in America*. Baltimore: Johns Hopkins University Press.

Braidotti, R., & de Vos, M. (2005). The women's studies PhD in Europe: an archive. *NWSA Journal, 17*(3), 157–173.

Braithwaite, A. (2004). Politics of/and backlash. *Journal of International Women's Studies, 5*(5), 18–33.

Brown, M., & Chavez-Garcia, M. (2005). Women's studies and Chicana studies: learning from the past, looking to the future. In E. L. Kennedy & A. Beins (Eds.), *Women's Studies for the future: Foundations, interrogations, politics* (pp. 145–155). New Brunswick, NJ: Rutgers University Press.

Burghardt, D. A., & Colbeck, C. L. (2005). Women's studies faculty at the intersection of institutional power and feminist values. *Journal of Higher Education, 76*(3), 301–331.

Burn, S. M. (2005). *Women across cultures: A global perspective* (2nd ed.). New York: McGraw-Hill.

Carter, K., & Spitzak, C. (Eds.). (1989). *Doing research on women's communication: Perspectives on theory and method.* Norwood, NJ: Ablex.

Catrone, V. (2001). New schools of thought: LGBT studies programs take their place on American college campuses. *Frontiers, 20*(3). Retrieved June 8, 2006, from http://lgbtrc.ucr.edu/studies_article .html

Clark, J. E., & Hogan, K. (2003). Doing women's studies on the sly at LaGuardia Community College. *Women's Studies Quarterly, 30*(3), 82–89.

College and University Professional Association for Human Resources. (2005). *National Faculty Salary Survey for the Academic Year 2004–2005.* Knoxville, TN: CUPA-HR Research.

Connell, R. W. (2002). The history of masculinity. In R. Adams, & D. Savran (Eds.), *The Masculinity Studies Reader* (pp. 245–261). Malden, MA: Blackwell Publishing.

Corber, R. J., & Valocchi, S. (Eds.). (2003). *Queer studies.* Malden, MA: Blackwell. Publishing.

Dolan, J. (1998). Gay and lesbian professors: Out on campus. *Academe, 84*(5), 40–45.

Doyle, J., & Femiano, S. (1998). *Reflections on the early history of the AMSA and reflections on the evolution of the field.* Retrieved June 8, 2006 from http://menstudies.org/history.htm

DuBois, E. C., Kelly G. P., Kennedy E. L., Korsmeyer, C. W., & Robinson, L. S. (Eds.). (1987). *Feminist scholarship: Kindling in the groves of academe.* Urbana: University of Illinois Press.

Ferree, M. M., & Hall, E. J. (1990). Visual images of American society: Gender and race in introductory sociology textbooks. *Gender and Society, 4*, 500–533.

Fisher, J. (2002). Women's studies without a women's studies program: The case of Hostos Community College. *Women's Studies Quarterly, 40*(3–4), 99–109.

Friedman, S. S. (2002). What should every major know? In R. Wiegman (Ed.), *Women's studies on its own* (pp. 416–437). Durham, NC: Duke University Press.

Fuchs, E. (2005). Feminism, anti-semitism, politics: Does Jewish women's studies have a future? In E. L. Kennedy & A. Beins (Eds.), *Women's studies for the future: Foundations, interrogations, politics* (pp. 159–169). New Brunswick, NJ: Rutgers University Press.

Garber, L. (Ed.). (1994). *Tilting the tower: Lesbians teaching queer subjects.* New York: Routledge.

George, D. (1992). Bridges over the gender gap: Male students in women's studies. *Radical Teacher, 42*, 28–33.

Goldberg, C. (1999, March 23). MIT acknowledges bias against female professors. *New York Times,* pp. A1, A16.

Gotell, L., & Crow, B. (2005). Antifeminism and the classroom. In E. Lapovsky Kennedy & A. Beins (Eds.), *Women's studies for the future* (pp. 287–303). New Brunswick, NJ: Rutgers University Press.

Grewal, I., & Kaplan, C. (Eds.). (2004). *An introduction to women's studies: Gender in a transnational world.* New York: McGraw-Hill.

Grewal, I., & Kaplan, C. (Eds.). (2006). *An introduction to women's studies: Gender in a transnational world* (2nd ed.). New York: McGraw-Hill.

Gunn, E. (2006). Women's Studies Programs. *PMLA, 121* (4), 1287–1292.

Guy-Sheftall, B., & Hammonds, E. (2005). Whither black women's studies: An interview, 1997 and 2004. In E. L. Kennedy & A. Beins (Eds.), *Women's Studies for the future: Foundations, interrogations, politics* (pp. 61–71). New Brunswick, NJ: Rutgers University Press.

Halberstam, J. (1998). *Female masculinity.* Durham, NC: Duke University Press.

Harding, S. (1987). *Feminism and Methodology: Social Sciences Issues.* Bloomington: Indiana University Press.

Harris, K. L., Melaas, K., & Rodacker. E. (1999). The impact of women's studies courses on college students of the 1990s. *Sex Roles, 40,* 969–977.

Harvard University Gazette. (2007). *Harvard names Drew Gilpin Faust as its 28th president.* Retrieved February 11, 2007 from http://www .news.harvard.edu/gazette/2007/02.15/99-president.html

Hooks, B. (2003). *Teaching community: A pedagogy of hope.* New York: Routledge.

Joseph, M. (2002). Analogy and complicity: Women's studies, lesbian/gay studies, and capitalism. In R. Wiegman (Ed.), *Women's Studies on its Own* (pp. 267–292). Durham, NC: Duke University Press.

Kaplan, C., & Grewal, I. (2002). Transnational practices and interdisciplinary feminist scholarship: Refiguring women's and gender studies. In R. Wiegman (Ed.), *Women's Studies on its Own* (pp. 82–105). Durhan, NC: Duke University Press.

Katz, J., Swindell, S., & Farrow, S. (2004). Effects of participation in a first women's studies course on collective self-esteem, gender-related attitudes, and emotional well-being. *Journal of Applied Social Psychology, 34*(10), 2179–2200.

Kesselman, A., McNair, L. D., & Schniedewind, N. (Eds). (2003). *Women: Images and realities, a multicultural reader* (3rd ed.). New York: McGraw Hill.

Kimmel, M. S. (1997). *Manhood in America: A cultural history.* New York: Free Press.

Kinser, A. E. (2006). What can you DO with a women's studies degree? In M. McCaughey (Ed.), *NWSA P&D Women's Studies Program Administrator's Handbook* (pp. 59–70). Washington, DC: National Women's Studies Association.

Kirk, G., & Okazawa-Rey, M. (Eds.). (2004). *Women's lives: Multicultural perspectives* (3rd ed.). NY: McGraw-Hill.

Kitch, S. L. (2002). Claiming success: From adversity to responsibility in women's studies. *NWSA Journal, 14*(1), 160–182.

Kolodny, A. (1996). Paying the price of antifeminist intellectual harassment. In V. Clark, S. V. Garner, M. Higonnet, & K. H. Katrak (Eds.), *Anti-Feminism in the Academy* (pp. 3–33). New York: Routledge.

Kramarae, C., Schulz, M, & O'Barr, W. M. (Eds.). (1984). *Language and Power.* Beverly Hills: Sage.

Kramarae, C., & Spender, D. (Eds.). (2000). *The Routledge International Encyclopedia of Women: Global Women's Knowledge and Issues* (Vol. 4). New York: Routledge.

Lee, R. (2002). Notes from the (non)field: Teaching and theorizing women of color. In R. Wiegman (Ed.), *Women's studies on its own,* (pp. 82–105). Durham, NC: Duke University Press.

Liewkeat, P. (2001). Setting up a graduate women's studies program in Thailand: The MA program in women's studies at Chiangmai University. *Women's Studies News,* 3–8.

Luebke, B. F., & Reilly, M. E. (1995). *Women's studies graduates: The first generation.* New York: Teachers College Press.

Macalister, H. E. (1999). Women's studies classes and their influence on student development. *Adolescence, 34*(134), 283–292.

Magaray, S., & Sheridan, S. (2002). Local, global, regional: Women's studies in Australia. *Feminist Studies, 28*(1), 129–152.

Marchbank, J., & Letherby, G. (2006). Views and perspectives of women's studies: A survey of women and men students. *Gender and Education. 18*(2), 157–182.

May, V. M. (2005). Disciplining feminist futures?: 'Undisciplined' reflections about the women's studies PhD. In E. L. Kennedy & A. Beins (Eds.), *Women's Studies for the future: Foundations, interrogations, politics* (pp. 185–206). New Brunswick, NJ: Rutgers University Press.

McCaughey, M., & Warren, C. (2006). Responding to right-wing attacks on women's studies programs. In M. McCaughey (Ed.), *NWSA P&D Women's studies program administrator's handbook* (pp. 43–47). Washington, DC: National Women's Studies Association.

Musil, C. M. (Ed.). (1992). *The Courage to Question: Women's Studies and Student Learning.* Washington, DC: Association of American Colleges.

National Center for Education Statistics (NCES). Digest of education statistics tables and figures. Retrieved June 8, 2006, from http://nces.ed .gov/programs/digest/

National Council for Research on Women. (1998, October 3). Perspectives on feminist theory: NCRW as an agent of transformation. *National Council for Research on Women Annual Conference.* Washington, DC. Retrieved June 8, 2006, from http://www.ncrw.org/research/98conf11.htm

National Council for Research on Women. (2001). *Balancing the equation: Where are women and girls in science, engineering, and technology.* New York: National Council for Research on Women. Washington, D. C.

National Council for Research on Women (NCRW). (2002). *International Centers for Research on Women.* Retrieved June 8, 2006, from http://www.ncrw.org/resources/intlcent.htm

National Council for Research on Women (NCRW). (2006). *About Us.* Retrieved June 8, 2006, from http://www.ncrw.org/about/about.htm

National Women's Studies Association. (2005). *Constitution of the National Women's Studies Association.* Retrieved June 8, 2006, from http://www.nwsa.org/govern/constitution.php

NWSA Task Force on Faculty Roles and Rewards. (1999). Defining women's studies scholarship: A statement of the National Women's Studies Association

Task Force on Faculty Roles and Rewards. Retrieved June 8, 2006, from http://www.nwsa.org/PAD/downloads/defining.pdf

Orr, C. M., & Lichtenstein, D. (2004). The politics of feminist locations: A materialist analysis of women's studies. *NWSA Journal, 16*(3), 1–10.

Patai, D. (2003). *Professing feminism: Education and indoctrination in women's studies.* Lanham, MD: Lexington Books.

Purcell, P., & Stewart, L. (1990). Dick and Jane in 1989. *Sex Roles, 22,* 177–185.

Richardson, L. (2004). *Feminist frontiers* (6th ed.). New York: McGraw-Hill.

Rogers, M. F., & Garrett, C.D. (2002). *Who's afraid of women's studies?: Feminisms in everyday life.* Walnut Creek, CA: Alta Mira Press.

Rosser, S. (2002). Twenty-five years of NWSA: have we built the two-way streets between women's studies and women in science and technology? *NWSA Journal, 14*(1), 103–124.

Roy, J. (2006). Two-year colleges: Century College. In M. McCaughey (Ed.), *NWSA PA&D Women's Studies Program Administrator's Handbook* (pp. 84–86). Washington, DC: National Women's Studies Association.

Ruth, S. (2001). *Issues in feminism: An introduction to women's studies.* Mountain View, CA: Mayfield Publishing.

Sadker, M., & Sadker, D. (1995). *Failing at fairness. How America's schools cheat girls.* New York: Touchstone Press.

Salley, K. L., Scott-Winkler, B., Celeen, M., & Meck, H. (2004). Women's studies in the Western United States. *NWSA Journal, 16*(2), 180–185.

Sapiro, V. (2003). *Women in American society: An introduction to women's studies* (5th ed.). New York: McGraw-Hill.

Scanlon, J. (1997). Keeping our activist selves alive in the classroom: Feminist pedagogy and political activism. *Feminist Teacher, 7*(2), 8–13.

Schuld, K. (2004, February 20). How the Ford Foundation created women's studies. *FrontPageMagazine.com.* Retrieved June 8, 2006, from http://www.frontpagemag.com/Articles/ReadArticle.asp?ID=12271

Scully, D. (1996). Overview of women's studies: Organization and institutional status in U.S. higher education. *NWSA Journal, 8*(3), 122–128.

Scully, D., & Currier, D. M. (1997). *The NWSA backlash report: Problems, instigators, and strategies.* College Park, MD: National Women's Studies Association.

Senger, E. (2005, November 25). *USRI's tainted with gender bias: Female profs get a tougher shake than male counterparts.* Gauntlet Publication Society. Retrieved June 8, 2006 from http://gauntlet.ucalgary.ca/a/story/9525

Shaw, S. (2004). *Women's voices, feminist visions: Classic and contemporary readings* (2nd ed.). NewYork: McGraw-Hill.

Shrewsbury, C. M. (1993). What is feminist pedagogy? *Women's Studies Quarterly, 3–4,* 8–15.

Shymchyshyn, M. (2005). Ideology and women's studies programs in Ukraine. *NWSA Journal, 17*(3), 173–186.

Sommers, C.H. (2001). *The war against boys: How misguided feminism is harming our young men.* New York: Simon and Schuster.

Sommers, C. H. (1994). *Who stole feminism?: How women have betrayed women.* New York: Simon and Schuster.

Stobla, C. (2002). *Room of one's own: How women's studies textbooks miseducate students.* Washington, DC: Independent Women's Forum.

Streitmatter, J. (1994). *Toward gender equity in the classroom—Everyday teachers' beliefs and practices.* Albany: State University of New York Press.

Subramanian, B. (2005). Laboratories of our own: New productions of gender and science. In E. L. Kennedy & A. Beins (Eds.), *Women's studies for the future: Foundations, interrogations, politics* (pp. 229–242). New Brunswick, NJ: Rutgers University Press.

Superson, A. (2002). Sexism in the classroom: The role of gender stereotypes in the evaluation of female faculty. In A. Superson & A. E. Cudd (Eds.). *Theorizing backlash: Philosophical reflections on the resistance to feminism* (pp. 201–216). Lanham, MD: Rowman and Littlefield.

Superson, A., & Cudd A. E. (Eds.). (2002). *Theorizing backlash: Philosophical reflections on the resistance to feminism.* Lanham, MD: Rowman and Littlefield.

Tai, E. S. (2005). Women's work: Integrating women's studies into a community college curriculum. *NWSA Journal, 17*(2), 184–191.

Warhold, R. R. (2002). Nice work if you can get it—and if you can't?: Building women's studies without tenure lines. In R. Weigman (Ed.), *Women's Studies on its Own* (pp. 224–232). Durham, NC: Duke University Press.

Wiegman, R. (2005). The possibility of women's studies. In E. L. Kennedy & A. Beins (Eds.), *Women's studies for the future: Foundations, interrogations, politics* (pp. 40–60). New Brunswick, NJ: Rutgers University Press.

Yee, S. (1997). The "women" in women's studies. *Differences—A Journal of Feminist Cultural Studies, 9*(3), 46–56.

Zimmerman. B. (2002). Women's studies, NWSA, and the future of the (inter)discipline. *NWSA Journal 14*(1), viii–xviii.

Zimmerman, B. (2005). Beyond dualisms: Some thoughts about the future of women's studies. In E. L. Kennedy and A. Beins (Eds.), *Women's studies for the future: Foundations, interrogations, politics* (pp. 31–39). New Brunswick, NJ: Rutgers University Press.

Zita, J. N. (1994). Gay and lesbian studies: Yet another unhappy marriage? In L. Garber (Ed.), *Tilting the tower: Lesbians teaching queer subjects* (pp. 258–276). New York: Routledge.

Part

·V·

ACHIEVING GENDER EQUITY
FOR DIVERSE POPULATIONS

Diane S. Pollard

For many years, researchers concerned with gender equity issues tended to ignore other important identifying characteristics, such as race, ethnicity, class, sexuality, and so on. As a result, gender equity issues tended to be portrayed as monocultural and those who were not White, middle class, heterosexual, and did not have disabilities were ignored or assumed to be assimilated into this dominant area of discourse.

Even when recognized, people from diverse populations were often marginalized by researchers studying a variety of educational issues, including gender. Thus, in the 1985 *Handbook for Achieving Sex Equity through Education*, concerns about sex equity and race, ethnicity, and so forth were confined to one chapter. It must be recognized that this type of marginalization was typical of many research studies, handbooks, and texts during this time. However, this type of treatment both reinforced the notion that diversity was not a particularly important aspect of gender or sex equity and furthered the assumption that issues of the dominant racial group could be imposed on all.

This handbook provides an important break from past practices with respect to relating gender equity to diversity in two ways. First, the section on racial and ethnic populations has been expanded from one to four chapters. In addition, new chapters have been added related to lesbian, gay, bisexual, and transgender populations and people with disabilities. This allows researchers from a variety of groups characterized by race and ethnicity, sexual orientation, and differential abilities to discuss research concerning conceptualizations of and experiences with gender equity in their own voices, as many, but not all, of the authors are from, or had close ties to some parts of, the populations covered in their respective chapters. While this expanded coverage is an important step forward in recognizing and legitimizing the realities of diversity in this country as well as the world, it also reveals an important and disturbing conundrum: the failure of educational researchers to recognize

within-group heterogeneity. As most of the authors in this section point out, there are important group differences within the broad categories of race, ethnicity, sexuality, and disability that are typically used to categorize people. Furthermore, issues around gender equity can be affected by such heterogeneity. As a result, research that focuses on these within-group differences is sorely needed. It should be noted that almost all of the handbook chapters recommend disaggregating information by gender and other population categories such as race, disability, and so on, and the authors in this section advocate the same. However, research on within-group differences would investigate issues related to subgroups within the broader categories typically used. For example, Spencer, Inoue and McField point out that research is needed that recognizes the experiences of various groups of Asian and Pacific Islanders, while Calhoun et al. note that various American Indian tribes have different cultural orientations. It appears evident from the chapters in this section that analyses of gender differences would be greatly informed if researchers explored these within-group differences further. It is likely that such explorations would require considerable use of qualitative studies along with quantitative compilations of data.

Second, this edition of the *Handbook* has attempted to reduce the marginalization of individuals who are not White, heterosexual, and without disabilities by infusing information about these diverse populations in chapters throughout the volume. This provides recognition that individuals representing diverse populations have concerns and interests in a variety of issues which may not have resonance in a Euro-American context. In this section, the primary intention is to place issues regarding gender equity within various cultural contexts. Therefore, each of the seven chapters in this section provides a unique lens on gender equity. In addition, some general themes emerge from all the chapters in this section.

In chapter 22, "Gender Equity for African Americans," Welch, Scott, Patterson, and Pollard identify four conundrums related to gender equity:

1. What are the gender differences in academic performance and educational attainment?
2. How do stereotyping, low expectations, and marginalization affect African American males' and females' experiences in K–12 and postsecondary educational environments and what are these students' strategies for coping with them?
3. What kinds of factors support academic success in African American girls/women and boys/men?
4. What underlies the sharp decline in the number of African American teachers and administrators in K–12 schools?

The authors also note that gender equity is deeply intertwined with race equity for this population.

Chapter 23 focuses on gender equity in Latina/o populations. This chapter is framed in terms of access to a "better education" for Latina/os. Ginorio, Lapayese, and Vasquez note that the term *Latina/o* encompasses several diverse groups. The authors describe the cultural advantages Latina/os bring to education and discuss how most educational institutions not only ignore these cultural assets but also denigrate, stereotype, and oppress Latinas and Latinos in school. The authors discuss the impact of these school experiences on males and females, noting that gender stereotypes intersect with ethno-racial stereotypes. As a result, Latina/o students are often subjected to forms of "gendered, classed, and linguistic segregation" that prevent access to the "better education" so strongly desired by this group.

In chapter 24, "Gender Equity for Asian and Pacific Island Americans," Spencer, Inoue, and McField identify several problems with research conducted on these populations. First, the heterogeneity among Asians and Pacific Islanders makes generalizing across this group problematic. Second, this leads to presentations of Asians and Pacific Islanders as undifferentiated, and therefore, for many, invisible in research literature. Finally, the myth that Asians and Pacific Islanders represent a "model minority" has hampered research and educational practice. In this *Handbook*, Spencer, Inoue, and McField use a "new lens of subgroup and sex category analysis (p. 502) to discuss issues related to gender equity in education. This analysis provides a rich picture of within-group differences in educational experiences and outcomes. The importance of migration and colonial histories is also discussed. As in other chapters in this section, the authors also discuss the impact of stereotyping, language issues, and other ways in which these populations' students' educational needs are not met.

Chapter 25 focuses on gender equity for American Indians. Calhoun, Goeman, and Tsethlikai discuss traditional concepts of gender which are clearly distinct from Euro-American perspectives about gender roles. They caution readers not to confuse American Indian traditional concepts of gender with European-American views of gender roles, as this tends to encourage myths about American Indian females and males.

The authors identify a number of issues that have affected gender definitions and roles among American Indians, including colonization, dysconscious racism, language, traditional indigenous educational philosophies, and so forth. A primary argument in this chapter is that Europeans' contact with and subsequent destruction of American Indian customs, practices, and institutions destroyed traditional concepts of gender, such as women's and men's roles in various Native American communities. Educational institutions were a major force in this destruction. The authors offer a number of solutions for creating gender equitable environments for American Indians involving a range of players including educational institutions, the federal government, and tribal members.

The authors of chapter 26, "Gender Equity and Lesbian, Gay, Bisexual and Transgender Issues in Education," frame their analysis of literature in terms of the relationship between sexual orientation and gender identity and expression. Kosciw, Byrd, Fischer, and Joslin explore relationships between sexism and homophobia and document gender differences in school experiences as well as educational practices that stigmatize LGBT people. The authors also review the status and experiences of LGBT educators who are subject to ongoing discrimination.

Chapter 27 focuses on gifted students. It should be noted that this was also a chapter in the 1985 *Handbook* along with chapters on rural and adult women. In this chapter, Fox and Soller provide updates on four issues around gender equity: (a) gender differences in ability, achievement, and interests; (b) bias in identifying gifted children; (c) the differential impact of equity program models on educational outcomes; and (d) barriers to educational attainment, careers, and recognition in adulthood. This chapter also provides a historical overview on giftedness and gender.

The last chapter in this section, chapter 28, focuses on achieving gender equity for people with disabilities. Mertens, Wilson, and Mounty discuss similarities and differences between feminist- and disability-rights agendas and review legislation related to educational rights of individuals with disabilities. The authors also discuss a paradigm shift from a view of a disability as a defect to a social-cultural model that emphasizes the degree to which the environment responds adequately and appropriately to a disability. These issues provide the framework for a discussion of educational and social struggles people with disabilities face, not only in this country but also internationally. A key gender concern discussed in this chapter is that many more boys than girls are placed in special education. As the authors note, this not only could indicate over-identification of boys, but under-identification of girls with needs. The chapter ends with a discussion of research needed to advance gender equity with this population.

Each of these chapters focuses on groups that have often been ignored or marginalized in discussions of gender equity. In doing so, they clearly indicate that, if discussions of gender equity are to be truly inclusive, they need to understand the various ways in which gender and gender roles are culturally informed. While each chapter provides a unique and specific orientation to gender equity, some general issues emerge across the seven chapters that comprise this section. Four overarching themes are outlined below.

1. Each of these chapters demonstrate that gender intersects with other important status markers or positions (e.g., race, ethnicity, class, sexuality, disability, etc.). All too often, writers ignore these intersections. However, more research is

needed to understand how these intersections influence the conceptualization of gender and gender roles in a diverse society.

2. The chapters in this section expand our concepts about diversity. Most of them note that the race, ethnicity, sexuality, and disability categories commonly used tend to hide the extent of within-group diversity or heterogeneity that actually exists among African Americans, Latina/os, Asians, Native Americans, LGBT people, students identified as gifted, and people with disabilities. This within-group diversity is often ignored in research, leading to inappropriate generalizations and inadequate educational practices.

3. Another common theme across these chapters concerns ongoing struggles against multiple forms of discrimination and stereotyping. Much of this is rooted in the historical oppression of these groups. However, as these chapters indicate, barriers related to achieving gender equity are deeply inter-twined with barriers related to achieving equity in the areas of race, ethnicity, sexual orientation, disability, and so on. These chapters clearly suggest that equity in one area cannot be attained without equity in the others.

4. Finally, the research cited in these chapters illustrates multiple failures by educational institutions to provide educational equity to children and adults in these groups. These failures run the gamut from biased treatment of students, to lack of inclusion of curricular material concerning these groups, to a lack of teachers and other educational staff who represent diverse groups. Under these circumstances, gender inequities are compounded by inequities related to race, ethnicity, sexuality, and other status markers. It is clear that research is needed that advances both gender equity and equity related to race, ethnicity, sexuality, giftedness, and disability. Only through such research will educational institutions contribute to a stronger society.

·22·

GENDER EQUITY FOR AFRICAN AMERICANS

Olga M. Welch, *Faye E. Patterson, Kimberly A. Scott,*
and Diane S. Pollard

INTRODUCTION

Chapter 1 in this *Handbook* suggests that gender equity means "achieving parity between males and females in the quality of life, academic, and work outcomes valued by society without limitations associated with gender stereotypes, gender roles, or prejudices" (p. 1). However, as other chapters in the *Handbook* illustrate, gender inequities for males and females in education exist. For African Americans, in particular, concerns around gender are too often entangled with or subverted to the larger issues of race and racism. This tendency to focus on race and racism when considering African Americans in education derives from two somewhat related sources.

The first has to do with the historical and contemporary contexts within which African Americans exist in the United States. African Americans' historical experiences in this country are surrounded by the unique form of slavery based on race and supported by racist notions. In addition, even after the official abolishment of slavery, African Americans have continued to cope with and resist policies and practices founded in racially oppressive attitudes and beliefs. These historical and contemporary experiences are clearly evident in the educational opportunities and experiences available to African Americans. Indeed, since the end of slavery, when one of the main thrusts of African American communities was to seek educational opportunities for their children, these efforts were met by resistance that took many forms—from denial of educational access to segregated and unequal schools (Anderson, 1998) to major resistance to integration and, currently, rapid resegregation of America's schools by race (Orfield & Eaton, 1996). Given these contexts, it is not surprising that educational equity issues for African Americans have most often been framed around race and overcoming racism.

The singular focus on race when considering African American education has also been fostered by researchers in education and the social sciences. Overwhelmingly, research on African Americans has centered on group differences comparing African Americans to Whites, with Whites most often positioned as the "normative" group. These researchers consistently have ignored within-group differences such as those that fall along the lines of gender, class, sexuality, and location, as well as the diversity of outlook, experience, and interests that exist in African American communities. More importantly, researchers have failed to investigate the intersectionalities between race, gender, class, sexuality, and disability.

Even when studies have taken account of such intersectionalities or have considered within-group variations among African Americans, research has been plagued by two additional shortcomings. First, in accounting for outcomes such as academic performance, attitudes toward education, aspirations, and so on, the tendency has been to focus on the individual, with little attention given to situational or contextual factors that may have strongly influenced such outcomes. Second, research on African Americans, similar to that conducted on some other marginalized ethnic groups, tends to take a deficit orientation. This orientation too often overemphasizes problems and failure while ignoring evidence of coping mechanisms and success. The combination of these shortcomings produces research that frequently results in a picture of African Americans as an undifferentiated group that has brought educational failure upon itself.

In this chapter, we foreground gender as a point of focus in the experiences and outcomes of African Americans in K–12 and postsecondary education. Specifically, the chapter identifies major contemporary issues related to gender equity in education for African Americans; documents where these issues are supported by strong empirical research findings and indicates where further research is needed. To accomplish these purposes, we reviewed the most current research available concerning gender and African Americans in education. While we perused research completed since the publication of the first *Handbook for Achieving Sex Equity in Education* in 1985, we have chosen to focus our discussion on research completed within the last decade.

Because of this review, we have identified four issues or conundrums in which gender equity concerns are evident. These conundrums are related to (a) gender differences in academic performance and educational attainment among African American students, (b) the experiences of African American girls/women and boys/men in educational institutions and strategies developed to cope with them, (c) factors that support academic success in African American males and females, and (d) the precipitous decline in the numbers of African American male and female teachers and administrators in K–12 schools. We shall discuss each of these issues in turn in the following pages. We will conclude the chapter with recommendations for resolving these conundrums through research, practice, and policy changes. To begin, however, we provide a brief overview of some pertinent demographic characteristics of this group.

According to the latest census, African Americans comprise approximately 12.2% of the U.S. population (12.9% if including those who identified themselves as Black along with one or more other races). Within that group, 6.4% are female and 5.8% are male (6.8% and 6.1% respectively when including those who identified themselves as Black and one or more other race) (U.S. Census Bureau 2000). Table 22.1 describes the percentage of African American females and males distributed by age.

These data indicate that a higher proportion of African Americans are younger compared to the total population. Furthermore, a higher proportion of the African American age group under 18 are males. These data have implications for the overall schooling of African Americans.

In 2000, there were approximately 53 million African American school-age children between the ages of 5 and 18, comprising 20% of the total school-age population (U.S. Census, 2000). According to Nettles and Perna (1997b), the majority of African American students (approximately 56%) lived in the South and approximately one third were in large cities. Most African American students currently attend segregrated or re-segregated schools (Orfield & Eaton, 1996). In addition, disproportionate numbers of these students are represented in alternative programs (approximately 20%) and vocational or special-education programs (approximately 30%) (Nettles & Perna, 1997b). Nettles and Perna did not provide gender breakdowns for these data.

This overview provides a context within which to view the conundrum of gender equity and academic performance and outcomes within this population. This is the next topic of consideration.

THE RACE-GENDER GAP

Academic Performance and Outcomes

Discussions about African American academic performance have focused, almost obsessively, on the "achievement gap."

This emphasis, particularly on differences in performance on standardized tests between African American and White students, has been exacerbated in recent years with the *No Child Left Behind* federal legislation that has required publication of these test results disaggregated by race with serious consequences for schools that do not show continuous improvement in their students' test scores.

The emphasis on the achievement gap is important, particularly with respect to attempts to identify strategies for helping African American students fulfill and demonstrate their academic potential and obtain the benefits of academic success. However, for the purposes of this chapter, another gap is also important and requires attention. This gap reflects differences between African American males and females in academic performance and educational attainment. These differences are evident at both the precollege and postsecondary levels.

Data from the U.S. Department of Education NCES-NAEP reports provide an overview of the performance of African American females and males in the areas of reading, writing, and mathematics at the 4th- 8th-, and 12th-grade levels. A summary of these results follows in Tables 22.2, 22.3, and 22.4. In these tables, blank cells reflect missing data.

In general, African American females outperform their male counterparts in reading and writing at all three grade levels. However, both female and male students in the 4th and 8th grades showed increases in their reading achievement in mean scores over time. For example, in 1994, the average reading score for 4th-grade African American males was 178, while in 2005 the average scale score had increased to 195. Conversely, African American females attained an average scale score of 193 in 1994, which increased in 2005 to 205. For 8th graders, the increases were smaller: 230 in 1994 to 237 in 2005 for males, and 244 to 249 respectively for females.

While both of these trends suggest improved reading scores for African Americans as they move through these grade levels, two trends worth noting emerged from the data. While the data for African American males and females in the 4th grade suggest upward progress, as do the 8th-grade data, the 12th-grade scores indicate a downward trend.

Table 22.3 shows that African American males' and females' performance in mathematics was much more similar in the 4th and 12th grades (disaggregated data were not available for 8th

TABLE 22.1 African American Population Distribution Percentage by Age Compared to Total Population Distribution Percentage by Age

	Under 18		18–64		65 and older	
	African American	Total Pop.	African American	Total Pop	African American	Total Pop.
Both Sexes	31.3	25.6	60.5	61.9	12.4	8.2
Male	33.5	26.8	59.9	62.7	6.5	10.4
Female	29.2	24.5	61.1	61.2	9.7	14.4

Source: U.S. Census Bureau, 2000.

TABLE 22.2 African American Students' Average Scale Scores for Reading

	4th grade		8th grade		12th grade	
	Male	Female	Male	Female	Male	Female
1992	185	198	231	244	268	278
1994	178	193	230	243	259	270
1998	190	195	236	251	261	276
2000	182	198				
2002	195	203	240	251	261	272
2003	193	203	293	250		
2005	195	205	237	249		

Source: U.S. Department of Education, Institute of Education Sciences, National Center for Education Statistics (NCES), National Assessment of Education Progress (NAEP).

TABLE 22.3   African American Students' Average Scale Scores for Mathematics

	4th grade		8th grade		12th grade	
	Male	Female	Male	Female	Male	Female
1990	187	188			271	265
1992	193	193			277	273
1996	199	199			279	280
2000	203	206			275	274
2003	216	216				
2005	219	220				

Source: U.S. Department of Education, Institute of Education Sciences, National Center for Education Statistics (NCES), National Assessment of Education Progress (NAEP).

TABLE 22.4   African American Students' Average Scale Scores for Writing

	4th grade		8th grade		12th grade	
	Male	Female	Male	Female	Male	Female
1998	124	137	123	138	126	140
2000						
2002	132	148	125	145	118	139

Source: U.S. Department of Education, Institute of Education Sciences, National Center for Education Statistics (NCES), National Assessment of Education Progress (NAEP).

graders). Both showed slight but steady improvements in math performance from 1990 to 2005.

Finally, Table 22.4 indicates that, similar to reading, African American females outperformed males at all three grade levels in writing.

That said, it should be noted an analysis of NAEP data conducted in 2001 found that females outperformed males in reading and writing across all ethnic groups (Coley, 2001). In mathematics, White males performed better than White females at the 4th grade level, however these differences were not found at the higher grade levels (Coley, 2001).

Another measure of academic performance is the SAT, which is taken by a smaller number of students. An analysis of trends in the SAT 1 Verbal from 1990–1999 indicated that African American females scored slightly higher than African American males. However, during this same period, African American males scored higher than African American females on the SAT 1 mathematics portion of the test (Coley, 2001).

Similarly, an analysis of the GRE exam taken during the period 1988–1998 indicated that African American males scored higher than African American females on both the GRE Verbal and GRE quantitative tests. The same pattern was found for the GRE Analytical test (Coley, 2001). These patterns were found across ethnic groups (Coley, 2001).

The data on gender differences in these measures of academic performance for African Americans indicate some interesting patterns. The NAEP data suggest a clearly demarcated gap in academic performance in the areas of reading and writing. This pattern was repeated for the SAT 1 Verbal Test, however the differences were less marked. In mathematics, NAEP data indicated males and females performed similarly. This pattern is re-

versed for the SAT 1 Mathematics test and all three portions of the GRE test. It must be noted that the SAT and GRE tests are taken by a relatively select group. In the case of the SAT, test-takers are college bound and are most probably applying for the relatively selective institutions of higher education that require the SAT. GRE test-takers are an even more select group, consisting of college students who have set their sights on graduate school. The reversal in patterns might be related to the differences in the populations taking the NAEP as opposed to the SAT and GRE. Finally, it is important to be cautious in making attributions regarding these findings because of the historical and current controversies regarding factors affecting African American students' performance on standardized tests. For example Steele's work (1997) suggested that contextual and perceptual factors may be important influences on student performance on these instruments.

Educational Attainment

Academic performance is, in many cases, a harbinger of educational attainment. Certainly, those students who demonstrate high performance levels, especially at the elementary and secondary levels, have higher probabilities of seeking and obtaining postsecondary-level attainment. However, particularly with respect to African American students, it is important to note that some have argued that performance on standardized tests may not be the most effective predictor of educational attainment, particularly at the postsecondary level (Portes, 2005; Pollard & Welch, 2003).

Despite the controversies regarding African American performance on standardized tests, educational attainment has become increasingly important in this society in which a high-school diploma is no longer sufficient to guarantee access to stable and lucrative employment opportunities. Thus it is important to understand relationships between gender and attainment for African American students. The U.S. Census provides an overview of educational attainment for African Americans and the total population, aged 25 or older, in 2000. These data are summarized in Table 22.5.

The data in Table 22.5 provide a picture of the adult populations. These data indicate that a slightly greater proportion of African American women then men, aged 25 or older, had attained at least some college education or more. It is also interesting to note that the percentages of African Americans, both male and female, that had obtained some college or an Associates Degree were quite similar to those for White men and

TABLE 22.5   Educational Attainment for African Americans

	High-School Graduate		Some College or Associates Degree		Bachelor's Degree or More	
	African American	Total Population	African American	Total Population	African American	Total Population
Both Sexes	29.8	28.6	28.2	27.4	14.3	24.4
Males	31.4	27.6	26.5	26.4	13.1	26.1
Females	28.4	29.6	29.7	28.2	15.2	22.8

Source: U.S. Census Bureau, Census 2000 Summary File 4.

women. However, at the Bachelor's level or higher, both African American women and men lagged considerably behind Whites, indicating that race was still an important predictor of post-secondary access and opportunity for this older population.

More recent data suggest that both race and gender have a dampening impact on college completion. Data compiled by the *Journal of Blacks in Higher Education* (2006) indicate that the overall college completion rate for African American students is 42%. The comparable rate for all students is 62%. However this report also indicates a widening gap between African American males and females with respect to college completion. Specifically, using data from 328 institutions of higher education, this report found that in 1990, 34% of African American women and 28% of African American men had completed college. However by 2005, 46% of African American women were completing college, compared to 35% of African American males. Although both genders had shown gains in college graduation rates, the women's gains were greater, thus widening the gap.

Coley (2001) analyzed differences between males and females aged 25–29 who completed college during the period 1974–1998. This researcher found that while more males than females completed college in 1974, by 1998 more females than males were completing college across ethnic groups. Furthermore, Coley argued that the gender patterns were somewhat similar across ethnic groups in 1998. Specifically, Coley found that "[i]n 1998, Black females held a 3 percentage point advantage, Hispanic females an advantage of 2 percentage points, and White females an advantage of 4 percentage points" (Coley, 2001, p. 41).

It is important to note that the data from the Coley and *Journal of Blacks in Higher Education* studies are from slightly different sources. For example, Coley's data came from adults, aged 25–29. This may indicate that the gender gap in college completion has widened fairly recently.

Finally, Hawkins (1996), using information obtained from the American Council on Education, reported a gender gap in graduate degree attainment among African Americans. Hawkins indicated that, as early as 1976, "African American women earned 8.5 % of Masters degrees while African American men earned 4.6%". In 1995, African American women earned more doctorates (805) than African American men (482) (http://web102.ep-net.com.ezproxy.lib.uwm.edu, April, 2006).

Implications of the Race Gender Gap for Adult Outcomes

While considerable concern has been expressed about African Americans' lower levels of academic performance and educational attainment in general, in recent years anxiety has been expressed about the widening gender gap, particularly with respect to educational attainment. For example a spring 1999 article in the *Journal of Blacks in Higher Education* was titled "The Ominous Gender Gap in African American Higher Education." In the cases of both race and gender, changes in performance and especially attainment could lead to changes in

students' life chances in the areas of employment and income. Data from the 2000 Census suggest a mixed picture with respect to employment and income. Specifically, these data indicate that African American women and men had similar rates of labor force participation in 2000 (e.g., 59.6% for women and 60.9% for men). These data were based on a sample of individuals aged 16 and older who were in the labor force. With respect to type of employment, 29.7% of African American women were in professional and managerial occupations as compared to 20.0% of African American men (U.S. Census Bureau, 2000). However, the gains by African American women in educational attainment and professional/managerial occupation did not seem to result in gains with respect to income. The 1999 census data on median earnings by sex for African Americans found that Black men who worked year-round at full-time jobs earned more than African American women with the same working patterns. This analysis indicated that African American women "who worked full-time, year round earned $85 for every $100 earned by comparable Black men" (p. 13). It was noted that this income gap was less than that for all women ($73/$100), however it is at odds with what might be expected given the race-gender gap in performance and attainment.

The discussion thus far indicates that African Americans are not achieving gender equity in key areas of education. For the larger population, NAEP data suggest gender inequities in academic performance favoring girls. The analyses of data with more narrow African American student groups (e.g., college-bound students taking the SAT and college students taking the GRE) suggested a reversal in these inequities that favors males.[1] Finally, females seem to be outpacing African American males in the area of educational attainment. While interesting, this information is not useful without some discussion of potential explanations for these gender differences.

This brings us to our second conundrum: the tendency to ignore contextual issues that shape African Americans' school experiences. We argue that much of the source for the gender differences in performance and attainment among African Americans can be explained through analyses of the experiences of these students, particularly in schools. To that end we shall review research that investigates the experiences of African American males and females in K–12 and postsecondary educational settings.

GENDER EQUITY AND THE SCHOOL EXPERIENCES OF AFRICAN AMERICANS: K–12

Many researchers who have studied African American students' school behavior and performance have identified contextual variables within the school environment as key supportive or undermining factors (Delpit, 2002; Gay, 2000; Irvine, 1990). With respect to gender issues, Kungufu (in Hawkins, 1996) argued that sources of the race gender gap begin as early as 4th grade as African American boys experience greater struggles

---

[1] A possible contributor to the change in the direction of gender gap is that more women than men take these tests and the men who take them are likely to be more committed to continuing their education than men who don't take the test.

with classroom activities, increased peer pressure, less parent involvement, and lowered teacher expectations.

Clearly, one important area to investigate involves teacher-student relationships given the important role of teachers in setting the tone or atmosphere within which children are expected to learn and develop. Here we focus on how teachers' socially charged labels of African American children reinforces intraracial gender divides and impede these youngsters' success in more ways than academic achievement.

Teachers, in general, tend to hold lower academic expectations for African-Americans than White students (Ferguson, 2003) and often express discomfort with African American students' expressive style of communication (Thompson-McMillon & Edwards, 2000; Vavrus & Cole, 2002). Equally important, many African American students are quite adept at identifying teachers' deficit thinking and modify their behaviors and academic habits to fulfill teachers' low expectations (see, for example, Ogbu (2003)).

Often perceived by teachers as "criminals in the making," Ferguson (2000) demonstrates how African American boys become the perceived uneducable students. Within an elementary school setting, she documents the ways in which Black boys' transgressions are viewed "as a sign of an inherent vicious, insubordinate nature that as a threat to order must be controlled" (p. 86). Perceived as inherently evil, moral-less culprits, Lewis (2003) revealed how such beliefs inform Black boys' self-perceptions. Believing that jail is an inevitable part of his future, one elementary-school-age Black boy explains to a teacher how "all Black men go to prison . . . and it would be more efficient to get his prison term out of the way before he went to college rather than having to do it afterwards" (p. 54).

The racially divided disciplinary actions recorded in schools do little to modify Black boys' self-perceptions. Nationwide, African American students make up 32% of all school suspensions even though they comprise only 17% of the school population (Applied Research Council, 2000). Not surprisingly, African American males receive corporal punishment and suspensions at a rate three times their percentage in the population (Townsend, 2000). They also receive corporal punishment 16 times more often than White girls (Skiba, Michael, Nardo, & Peterson, 2002). Since school suspension correlates with academic achievement, grade retention, delinquency, and school dropout rates (Mendez, Knoff, & Ferron, 2002; White-Johnson, 2001), African American boys' dropout rates are relatively high. Why would these boys want to remain in a context where disciplinary actions resemble punitive strategies for incarcerated adults (Noguera, 2003)? However, the related question becomes: Do African American girls fare any better?

Research indicates that as early as 1st grade, many teachers perceive African American girls as hypersexual beings with a "natural" proclivity for teenage motherhood (see Ferguson, 2000; Scott, 2002a, for example). Behaviors described as "precocious" for White females are often perceived as deviant when displayed by their Black counterparts (Scott, 2003). In the classroom context, African American girls' behaviors rarely gain legitimacy since the setting's "prevailing cultural framework denies her the rights for dramatic public display" (p. 180). Assertive, demonstrative behaviors earn Black girls the reputation as unfeminine and hostile among teachers and other school personnel (Fordham, 1993). Along with the hypersexual label, most teachers demonstrate more interest in African American girls' social behaviors than their academic abilities. Importantly, Grant's (1988) early work indicated that such teacher perceptions inform peer interactions. In the 1st-grade interracial classroom she studied, children of all races were more likely to interact with Black girls to resolve a social issue than approach them for an academic problem. Scott's (2002b) more recent work suggested similar behavioral patterns.

In another racially integrated school setting, Scott found that both Black and White second-grade teachers spoke more about and used more potent terms for African American girls' social behaviors than their academic achievements. Despite the fact that Scott belonged to the same race-gender category as the students, some White teachers she interviewed described Black girls as "caged animals." Importantly, teachers used such language to describe one of the most academically successful students in the class, at least according to standardized tests.

Some research indicated that as African American youngsters mature, the intraracial achievement gap widens, with the boys falling farther behind the girls (Rodcrick, 2003). Indeed, Black girls tend to have more future goals in a range of areas (e.g., education, employment, family) than Black boys (Honora, 2002) and in general perform better in school (Frederick Patterson Research Institute, 1997). However, scholastic achievement does not necessarily translate into emotional happiness.

Images of the African American woman remaining fearless and emotionally stronger than men and other women pervade society as positive representations of Black womanhood. Rather than furthering the resiliency myth of Black women, Scott argued that these images disempower the Black girl. Their societal presence allows the Black girl to assume a limited vision of her capabilities and prevents her from becoming more than a socially historicized image of the unshakeable woman. Strength masculinizes African American girls' identities. Drowning in popular images of hypersexualized, strong Black females, Black girls find little room or encouragement to critically assess and/or challenge the publicized images. Although acceptance of this myth may not impede a Black girl's academic progress, these images may jeopardize her social and emotional development.

Already, more African American females are experiencing eating disorders than previously believed (Cachelin et al., 2000; Williamson, 1998). Yet, the number of Black women receiving treatment is not commensurate with the number of diagnosed cases. While anorexia nervosa and bulimia are more common among White women than Black (Striegel-Moore et al., 2003), Black women suffer from eating disorders involving use of laxatives and diuretics at a higher rate than White women. Striegel-Moore et al.'s (2000) study confirms this assertion, finding in a community sample that 2.1% of Black women as opposed to 0.8% of White women had abused laxatives; 2.9% in contrast to 1.7% abused diuretics; and 4.1% of the Black sample had engaged in unhealthy fasting as opposed to 2.7% of White women.

Located in a society that oppresses African American females along multiple lines of intersections (e.g., race, gender, sexual orientation, social class, religion, skin complexion, etc.), navigating this hierarchical system of oppression takes an emotional toll.

Despite this, some African American girls learn to achieve and do not seem to suffer any emotional damage. O'Connor

(1997), for instance, demonstrated how some African American girls both recognize the racialized-genderized structural barriers in society and use this realization to motivate their actions towards achievement. Such a process allows Black females to develop a resilient disposition, successfully navigate the school system, and identify the institutionalized impediments they aspire to challenge. However, the long-term effects are narrowly understood. More longitudinal studies are needed to document how African American girls' resiliency in school informs their psychosocial beings as African American women.

Contextual variables require further consideration when examining African American girls' achievements. The majority of the above studies were conducted in racially integrated settings. In a predominantly African American school setting, girls' interactions with teachers provide a different image. Without condemning school desegregation, research suggests that there are some benefits for African American girls in an African American school setting. Scott's (2003, 2004) work with a cohort of 58 6th-grade African American girls in an under-resourced, predominantly Black urban district illustrates that in the school where teachers and administrators encourage female networks, girls' empowerment, and a rigorous Afrocentric curriculum, the girls incorporate many behaviors that inspire academic success. Upon exiting such classrooms, the girls develop and maintain a peer culture which encourages each individual to clearly articulate, plan, and demonstrate prosocial behaviors leading her closer to her goals. In such a setting, teachers publicly recognized the girls' achievements. Notably, the youngsters did not suffer the peer rejection or accusation of "acting white" that Ogbu and Fordham recorded (Fordham & Ogbu, 1986; Fordham, 1988, 1996; Ogbu, 1989, 1990). Instead, the girls in Scott's work received kudos and encouragement from both their female and male peers. Wattson and Smitherman's (1996) account of an Afrocentric school for boys presented similar results. In their description of the nation's first district-generated, Afrocentric, male-oriented elementary school, Malcolm X Academy, the boys (and the few attending girls) become members of a culture nurturing academic and social achievement in a district with an abysmal achievement record. While this academy is promising, Noguera (2005) noted that programs emphasizing African and African American culture and history tend to be small and nonschool-based, and often cannot "completely counter the harmful effects of attendance in unsupportive and even hostile schools because they are designed to complement learning that is supposed to take place in school" (p. 69).

The research suggested that both African American girls and African American boys are at risk of being subjected to negative experiences in the classroom. Apparently, a number of teachers still rely on stereotypical images when confronted with these children. Although the stereotypical images used are different for African American boys and girls, neither group is viewed in a positive light.

Gender Differences in Coping with Marginalization in Elementary and Secondary Schools

Several research studies suggest that African American boys and girls develop different types of strategies to cope with these negative classroom experiences. These coping strategies seem to be effective in protecting the students from the immediate situation. However, they may not have long-term protective effects. An example of such a strategy is the development of cultural mistrust (Irvine & Hudley, 2005). In a study of 75 African American high-school males, these authors found evidence of cultural mistrust. They also found that with higher levels of cultural mistrust the students placed a lower value on and held lower expectations for their academic outcomes. Kungufu (as cited in Hawkins, 1966) made a similar argument, indicating that African Americans are more likely to become disinterested in schooling as they see that they are not valued by school personnel. Hefner (2004) argued that African American boys begin to define success in terms of making money, and see education not as a route to that goal but as a barrier.

Some studies have identified strategies used by African American girls to cope with the stresses of marginalization in elementary and secondary classrooms. In a study of nine adolescent girls, six of whom were African American, who participated in a STEM project, Spatig, Parrott, Carter, Kusimo, and Keyes (2004) found that the African American girls experienced gender and racial oppression. While these students were encouraged to discuss obstacles encountered because of their gender, this was not so with respect to race. The authors suggested that the school climate discouraged acknowledgment of racial oppression. In addition, they argued that these African American girls were advised by adults to focus on survival as a coping mechanism rather than on liberation.

A study by Saunders, Davis, Williams, and Williams (2004) assessed gender differences in African American high-school students' perceptions of themselves and their academic outcomes. Their sample consisted of 243 sophomores. These researchers found that both males and females held positive self-perceptions. Furthermore, there were no gender differences in these students' intentions to complete their sophomore year of high school. However, the African American girls felt more confident about completing high school than the males. In addition they expressed stronger feelings of self-efficacy. This latter variable has been related to academic performance.

Finally, although more studies have focused on the experiences of African American females and males within the school setting, it is important to recognize that events and individuals outside of this institution may also have an impact on the development of different perspectives and coping strategies related to gender. For example, Smith and Fleming (2006) studied the role of parents in helping their African American children make choices about college. The majority of parents studied were females. The researchers found that these parents tended to provide equal levels of support for their sons and daughters in terms of helping them make choices about what colleges to consider. However, these parents expressed higher aspirations for their daughters and were more likely to encourage them to think about attending four-year colleges. Smith and Fleming speculated that parental attitudes such as these might inadvertently contribute to the race gender gap in college enrollment.

An important study by Hubbard (2005) focused on the role of gender in the academic achievement of 30 highly successful, low-income, African American high-school students. All of these students attended a public school and were involved in a program to increase academic achievement and educational and other aspirations. Hubbard found interesting gender differences in these students' orientation toward college attendance. The African American women focused on attending college to earn a degree and embark on a career. The males, on the other hand, wanted to attend college to participate in sports, and ultimately as a path to participation in professional sports. Both genders saw racial discrimination as a major problem in their school. However, the African American women were more willing to confront discrimination when it affected them. The African American males saw discrimination as inevitable and uncontrollable and, although they recognized it, they did not confront it directly. Hubbard argued that these students gendered experiences in school, with their peers, and in their families contributed to the development of their perspectives around attending college. For example, the African American men's aspirations toward sports were supported by their families and peers. In addition, although Hubbard did not discuss it, this particular pursuit is clearly fostered by larger societal institutions, such as the media, that bestow high status and celebrity on professional sports players.

Gender Equity and the Postsecondary Experiences of African American Men and Women

Data cited earlier in this chapter indicate that African American women tend to have higher enrollment and completion rates in college. This gender difference in college enrollment can be partially traced to the differential experiences and coping mechanisms of African American boys and girls in elementary and high school. Another factor that explains the gender differences in college enrollment concerns the large number of African American males who are siphoned off into the criminal justice system during their adolescence. African American males between the ages of 16 and 25 are at extremely high risk for homicide, arrest, and police brutality (Kemp, 2006; Verdugo & Henderson, 2003). Finally, there may be different expectations for African American boys and girls regarding college enrollment from significant adults in their lives, including educators and family members.

With respect to college completion, several studies indicate that, as in precollege, both African American females and African American males are subjected to attitudes and events that are marginalizing. However, gender seems to mediate these experiences to some degree.

For example, two qualitative studies of African American athletes, one of females and the other of males, found that both groups experienced challenges in spite of their status related to their participation in sports. Female African American athletes reported that they were discouraged from expressing themselves. They felt their experiences and feelings were viewed as unworthy of recognition and that this message came not only from teammates and coaches, but also from others on the college campus and even from the media (Bruening, Armstrong, & Pastore, 2005). The authors of the study of male college athletes reported that their respondents perceived that they were treated differently from their White teammates. In particular, they reported that they were prevented from taking part in decision-making opportunities and were denied access to leadership positions.

Anderson (2004) conducted a case study of African American males participating in college preparatory programs on several university campuses. He found that the programs tended to overemphasize academic achievement and did not address these young men's concerns about their feelings of alienation and concomitant concerns about safety on a White campus. In addition, the students were not provided with any support to help them cope with family and personal issues of concern.

Jackson (1998) studied African American women who were college students at three different types of institutions: a predominately White coed school, a predominately White women's school, and a predominately African American college. This researcher found that gender and ethnic identity were important for African American women in each of these three different settings. However, the school demographics had an impact on their perceptions. All of the women identified struggle as a major theme of being an African American woman. However, those at the predominately Black college emphasized the struggles of African American women in the broader society. Students at the predominately White institutions were more concerned with the struggles of African American women in their school environments. One aspect of this struggle involved coping with being perceived differently from the dominant perceptions of women in general. These women found they had to spend considerable time fighting racial stereotypes and demanding respect for their race and gender perspectives.

These three studies suggested that both African American men and women on college campuses experience race- and gender-based challenges that question their participation in these venues. Unfortunately, each of these studies focused on only one gender; therefore, they cannot comparatively address the issue of gender equity among African Americans. However, they do suggest that, for African American students, experiences around gender as well as those around race need to be taken into account, especially when pursuing efforts to improve college matriculation and graduation.

Two other studies suggest that some of the coping strategies and attitudes developed by African American males and females during their precollege years may be demonstrated as they begin their college careers. Kim and Sedlacek (1995) analyzed the responses of 212 African American students who completed a University New Student Census. They found gender differences in student attitudes and expectations. More of the African American male students indicated that college was, primarily, a route to increased income. They were less interested in pursuing graduate work and were more likely to express their intentions to work during their freshman year. More African American females emphasized involvement in campus activities and expected to pursue volunteer work. A more recent study of African Americans attending community colleges found that African American males were less likely to become involved in campus activities and interact with instructors (Bush & Bush, 2005). One could speculate that the cultural mistrust and alienation that African Americans develop in earlier years may carry over to college. However, in the absence of strong longitudinal studies, this is only speculation.

Toward Achieving Gender Equity in Education for African Americans: Focusing on African American Academic Success

The information discussed thus far indicates that issues around gender equity have implications for African American students' academic performance, educational attainment, and their experiences in both precollege and postsecondary educational institutions. Furthermore, data suggest that gender equity issues are inextricably intertwined with issues around race and class equity and racism. For example, recognition of the existence of a race-gender gap between African American males and females cannot be allowed to obscure or ignore the gap between African Americans and Whites as well as some other ethnic groups in educational performance and attainment. It seems obvious that the achievement of gender equity for African Americans cannot occur without obtaining equity in race, class, employment, and the criminal justice system.

The discussion of the problems faced by African Americans in achieving gender equity in education is extremely important. However, it highlights our third conundrum: the tendency of researchers to emphasize a deficit orientation to the exclusion of examinations of successful academic performance among African American females and males.

Fortunately, some studies have attempted to identify factors that support academic success in African American females and males. Much of this research is limited because studies have centered on single genders. However, the factors identified may prove helpful to those who are interested in supporting academic success in these groups.

Several studies have attempted to identify factors that promote academic success in African American males. Wilson-Jones (2003) studied 16 males in a rural Southern elementary school. This researcher found that the provision of academic assistance, especially in the area of early literacy activities, and encouraging parental involvement were important ingredients in school success. Grantham (2004) found that high-quality mentoring encouraged African American boys to participate in gifted programs. According to Grantham, mentors needed to encourage the development of a positive racial identity in the boys. Thompson and Lewis (2005) conducted a case study of an African American male high-school student who was highly successful in mathematics. One of their findings was that the school failed to provide high-level math courses for this young man to take and only did so after his persistent requests for them. Another finding was that this young man had access to a variety of adults who supported and encouraged his efforts.

Similarly, some studies have sought to understand the underpinnings of academic success in African American females. Brickhouse, Lowery, and Schultz (2000) conducted a qualitative study of four middle-school African American girls who were successfully engaged in science learning. They found these girls refused to accept racial and gender stereotypes. In addition, they did not report alienation from school. Bermak, Chung, and Sroskey-Sabdo (2005) argued that intervention programs involving group counseling and focusing on empowerment were effective in encouraging academic success among urban African American girls who had been labeled "at risk." Finally, Johnson-Bailey (2004) reported the results of a qualitative study of factors that supported retention among African American women who were graduate students in a college of education. Johnson-Bailey found that receptivity and respect from school faculty and administrators along with support from African American mentors and peers were important prerequisites.

Very few studies focusing on academic success included both African American males and females. The Hubbard (2005) investigation, mentioned earlier in this chapter is one. This study included children in the program AVID (Advancement Via Individual Determination). Hubbard found that this program as well as the students' families supported their academic strivings. Peers who participated in AVID were also supportive but in different ways. Hubbard reported that the females in the program supported each other in persisting with their commitments to achieve and earn a college degree. They also encouraged each other to avoid activities and involvements that might derail their academic aspirations. The males in the program, too, worked together to further academic performance, primarily through preparation for examinations. However, according to Hubbard, "for the most part, their involvement with each other revolved around athletics" (Hubbard, 2005, p. 615). Hawkins and Malkey (2005) analyzed 8th-grade data from the NELS88 study. They found that participation in athletics in school was associated with higher educational aspirations for both boys and girls.

GENDER EQUITY AMONG AFRICAN AMERICAN FACULTY AND ADMINISTRATORS

The fourth conundrum we address in this chapter focuses on gender equity among African American school staff. One factor that has been advocated as supportive of African American students' academic success involves the presence of African American faculty and administrators in schools. It has been argued that African American faculty and administrators support African American students' achievement and attainment in multiple ways. Many studies of African American women who were principals and teachers suggested that they are supportive of African American students in several ways. For example, one study found that these African American female administrators were concerned about the quality of relationships with parents (Loder, 2005). Another indicated that because of their experiences of marginalization, African American women who were teachers reported that they made efforts to be particularly inclusive and sensitive to all students, especially those from disenfranchised groups. Brown, Cervero, and Johnson-Bailey (2000). Beauboeuf-Lafontant (1997) also found that female African American teachers described themselves as committed to social justice and compared teaching to parenting.

Additionally, it has been suggested that African American males who are teachers and principals can serve as effective role models (Lewis, 2006). However, studies of African American male teachers and principals are limited.

The presence of African American male and female teachers and administrators in schools is also instructive for students who are of other races and ethnicities. These individuals provide important avenues through which students from a variety of backgrounds can learn to appreciate diversity.

During the past decade or so, considerable concern has been voiced about the decline in the numbers of African American educators in elementary and secondary schools. At the same time, postsecondary institutions are pressed to diversify their faculties. While considerable concern has focused on race, the issue of gender equity is also important in terms of the numbers of faculty and administrators in K–12 schools and colleges and universities.

In the next section we will provide an overview of the data on the prevalence of African American males and females in teaching and principalship positions. Examining gender equity in terms of faculty and administrators in K–12 schools as well as colleges and universities can furnish an important lens through which to examine African American female/male educational access and progress.

Prevalence of African American Teachers in Various School Settings

The prevalence of African American teachers in public schools varies by level; in 1993–94 women numbered an approximate 6% and men an approximate 2%. At the elementary level, African American men numbered slightly less than 1%, and African American women numbered an approximate 7%. At the secondary level, African American female public-school teachers were an approximate 5%, while African American males consisted of an approximate 2% of secondary teachers (Nettles & Perna, 1997b, p. 209).

Moreover, the percent of African American teachers in private schools was only an approximate 3% (Nettles & Perna, 1997b, p. 210). They, too, varied by level and gender. African American female teachers in elementary private schools comprised an approximate 3% versus slightly less than 0.5% for African American male private-school teachers. While at the secondary level, African American female private-school teachers comprised an approximate 1% and African American males comprised over 1% (Nettles & Perna, 1997b, p. 210).

TABLE 22.6 Prevalence of African American Teachers in Various School Settings (Percentages are Rounded)

Public School Level	Female	Male	Total
Total	6	2	8
Elementary	7	1	8
Secondary	5	2	7
Private School Level			
Total	3	1	3
Elementary	3	1	4
Secondary	1	1	2
Urban			
Urban Public School Teachers	12	3	15
Urban Private School	2	1	3
Suburban Public School	4	1	5
Suburban Private School	1	1	2
Rural Public School	3	1	4
Rural Private School	<1	<1	<2

Source: School and Staffing Survey, 1993–94; Nettles & Perna, 1997b, pp. 209–213.

In terms of urbanicity, the prevalence of African American teachers in public and private schools varied greatly. An approximate 7% of all public school teachers in the study were African Americans. An approximate 15% of African American teachers were located in urban schools (an approximate 12% were females and 3% African American males). An approximate 4% of African American female teachers and an approximate 1% of African American male teachers were in suburban schools, and an approximate 3% of females and 1% of male African American teachers were in rural schools (Nettles & Perna, 1997b, pp. 212–213).

In private urban schools, African Americans comprised an approximate 3% of teachers. African American females outnumbered African American males (an approximate 2% to an approximate 1%). Nearly 5% were located in urban areas (an approximate 4% female and slightly more than 1% male), 2% were in suburban areas (less than 2% females and almost 1% males), and less than 2% comprised African American private-school teachers in rural areas (slightly over 0.5% males and females respectively) (Nettles & Perna, 1997b, 213.)

The prevalence of African American public school teachers in urban areas (an approximate 56% total; 57% males and 55% female teachers) (Nettles & Perna, 1997b, p. 212) that are likely to educate large populations of African American students is not without its challenges. These urban settings are among the 100 largest school districts in the nation and are facing educational challenges in multiple contexts such as higher levels of poverty, diverse learners' needs, increased staffing ratios, higher salary projections, (Sable & Hoffman, 2005), reduced funding (Access, 2005; U.S. Department of Education, 2002), and attracting and maintaining highly qualified teachers and principals to meet the schools' annual academic goals.

As mentioned earlier, research on African American students' academic and other school behavior has often ignored contextual issues that may have an impact on it. One important contextual issue the prior overview of teachers and administrators underscores is the characteristics of the teachers these students encounter. It has been argued that African American teachers served as positive academic and social role models for African American students (Lewis, 2006; Tillman, 2004).

Unfortunately, as the overview also demonstrated, during the years following the historic Brown decision of 1954, a precipitous decline has occurred in the numbers of African American educators and administrators in K–12 schools. The disappearance of African American educators has resulted from a variety of factors ranging from mass firings of Black teachers and administrators as schools desegregated (Tillman, 2004), to an increase in accessibility to careers previously denied to African Americans (Lewis, 2006).

The disappearance of African American teachers from classrooms has important implications for gender equity. African American male teachers are noticeably absent. According to the National Center for Educational Statistics (2005), African Americans constitute only 8% of all teachers. However, African American males are only 1% of the teaching population. According to Lewis (2006), African American students are 20% of the total student population. These numbers indicate that not only are more African American teachers needed, but also that males are particularly needed. This situation may be exacerbated in schools heavily populated by low-income African American students, many of whom lack positive male role models in their lives.

The very small number of African American males in teaching can partially be attributed to pipeline issues related to the race-gender gap in educational attainment mentioned earlier in this chapter. It has been noted that only 4% of all males enrolled in higher education in 1998 were African Americans. However, even of the small numbers of African Americans in college, relatively few, either male or female, seem drawn to education as a career. The American Federation of Teachers indicated that only 5% of education students nationally were African American (cited in Lewis, 2006).

Presumably, both African American males and females who qualify have equal admission opportunities to colleges. Yet, more African American females are graduating from college than are African American males. African American females earned over 70% of the undergraduate education degrees awarded to Black graduates in 1996–1997 (Bae, Choy, Gedes, Sable, & Snyder, 2000). Hodgkinson (1991) and Wesson (1998) argued that minority populations will continue to increase to 38% by 2010, but fewer minorities will likely become teachers. Minorities are simply choosing more lucrative careers in other professions than teaching. Fewer minority teachers also suggest that the numbers of African American administrators may continue to decline despite increasing minority student demographics.

Prevalence of African American Administrators in Various School Settings

The National Center for Educational Statistics (NCES) has conducted School and Staffing Surveys that track the percentages of administrators in public and private elementary and secondary schools by gender and race as far back as the 1987–1988 school years. The National Opinion Research Center has produced cumulative data files from the surveys, which are made available to universities through the Inter-university Consortium for Political and Social Research (ICPSR) (Davis, Smith, & Mardsen, 2003). It is a given that not all respondents complete every item on national surveys. The missing responses become problematic if sufficient data are not available to allow researchers to make reasonable estimates from the various data cells. Through a weighting process, adjustments may be made for the missing data, which then enables researchers to produce more reliable estimates from the smaller data samples. Data based on weighted frequencies from the 1987–1988 Public Schools and Staffing Survey (SASS) indicated that 9% of all administrators in 1987–1988 were African Americans (5% males and 4% females).

The numbers of African American females in public-school administration increased from 4% in 1987–1988 to 7% in 1999–2000. Based on these data, there were a third more African American female administrators in public schools than African American male administrators (U. S. Department of Education, 2004).

Nettles and Perna (1997b) found that women comprised an approximate 73% of all teachers and only 35% of all principals in public schools in 1993–94. African American principals represented 10% of principals (6% African American female; 4% African American males (p. 298). These data might lead one to

believe that African American public school principals (an aggregate of 10%) were overrepresented when compared to the percent of African American male teachers (an approximate 7% in public schools. However, the African American principals in public schools were underrepresented compared to the percentage of African Americans comprising the school-age population of nearly 7,000,000 students .

The patterns of African American administrators in private elementary and secondary schools parallel those of public schools. Overall, data for private schools (1987–88) indicated that African Americans represented 3% of all private-school administrators (U.S. Department of Education, 2004). In 1993–1994 Nettles and Perna (Executive Summary, 1997b) found that African Americans represented 4% of private school principals. The percentage was 7% as of 1999–2000 (U.S. Department of Education, 2004).

The percent of African American teachers in private schools was only an approximate 3% (Nettles & Perna, Executive Summary, 1997b, p. 23). An approximate 4% of African American principals were located in private schools during school year 1993–94. African American female principals in private schools (3%) also outnumbered African American male principals in private schools (less than 1.5% (Nettles & Perna, 1997b, p. 298).

On the surface, it would appear that lower college enrollment of Black males, rather than a lack of equity or access to principal preparation programs, is one of the key factors that might contribute to the lower numbers of African Americans in administration, particularly males. To further exacerbate the situation, many African American college-bound students are selecting other, higher-paying careers over teaching, which is the gateway into school administration.

Although as many as two-thirds of the African Americans who earned their doctorates in 1975 had received their undergraduate degrees from HBCUs (62%), there was a sharp decline in the number of undergraduate degrees received from HBCUs between 1985 (64%) and 1995 (33%). The numbers were decreased by as much as 50% (The Graduate Record Examination General Test: 1981–1990 as cited in Nettles & Perna, 1997c, p. 322). A decline of this magnitude is bound to have lasting effects on graduate enrollments such as teacher and principal preparation programs.

In terms of gender equity, Klein (1985) stated, "The real measure of success will be seen in the number of women administrators . . ." (p. 136). Based on the aggregate data for African American administrators, it would appear that African American female administrators have achieved gender equity with African American males in public and private schools. However, a closer examination of race and gender equity through the lens of the increase in the school-age population of African Americans sheds additional light on the subject.

SUMMARY AND RECOMMENDATIONS

This chapter has examined gender equity in the education of African Americans, a topic full of complexities and conundrums. Acknowledging these complexities and conundrums, then, it has sought to use issues and trends identified in the NCES Report (2003), NAEP and Census Data on the education of Blacks as a departure point for reviewing several studies of individual, school, and societal factors in elementary and secondary schools. In addition, the chapter reviewed data on gender equity among African American teachers and administrators at the K–12 level.

Summary

Disentangling racial and gender equity, as well as other demarcations, continues to be a major complication in research on the education of African American males and females. Although this is the case, this chapter has focused on the educational experiences of African American males and females. Almost uniformly, the studies we've presented underscore the ongoing problem of access for African Americans at the elementary, secondary, and postsecondary levels, an access that has been constrained by definitions of the problem that center almost exclusively on issues of race and ethnicity.

Our review suggests that treating African Americans as a homogeneous and monolithic group without attention to, for example, the demarcations and differences that exist in gender, socioeconomic status, disabilities, and so on, contributes to an inability to identify or study the interconnectivity of these issues and the influence of that interconnectivity on the education of African American males and females.

As the research on individual, school, and societal factors that affect the academic achievement of African Americans suggests "one size does not fit all." Whether one is researching the high dropout rates of African American males at the middle- and secondary-school levels, or the gap between the admission and graduation rates of African American males and females at the postsecondary level, the assumption of a monolithic entity inhibits the ability of researchers to pose either alternative questions or to test unconventional hypotheses related to the *within-group* differences in the African American population in general, and the school and college age segment of that population in particular.

For example, in his study of the Black male crisis in America, Noguera (1997) questioned the extent to which racialized and genderized conceptions of the crisis may negate researchers' ability to discover the significance of other factors. To illustrate this complexity, he notes that the focus on the severe economic and social hardships experienced by African American males does little to advance our understanding of why some individuals, who are both African American and male, who are highly visible in public life (e.g., respected politicians, successful entertainers and celebrities, and individuals with wealth and status) do not experience the same problems. He follows this observation with some intriguing questions: "Does the notoriety of such individuals suggest that some Black males may be immune from the crisis? If so which ones? And what might this tell us about the nature of the problem?" (p. 3)

Noguera (1997) also noted that focusing on the problems of Black males introduces a troubling, if unintended, assumption sometimes made explicit in the research, that males are worse off than females and therefore more deserving and in need of attention, assistance, and intervention (p. 14). In supporting this contention, he states that, in all areas of research on African American life, "the benefits of patriarchy, like the benefits of racism, are in many ways subtle and taken-for-granted with the privileged and ubiquitous dominance of men, even Black men, going uncontested. This privileged position may help to explain why the . . . crisis of the black male receives attention, while the continued oppression of black females is accepted as the norm" (p. 15). The fact that few studies have been conducted that focus exclusively on the education of African American females at either the elementary and secondary levels underscore this point.

This summary provides an overview of the issues that emerged from our review of the research literature and national databases cited in this chapter. That review also resulted in the following policy, research, and practice recommendations.

Policy Recommendations

1. Disaggregate all standardized test score data in each subject area by gender, race, and include with-in group comparisons (i.e., disabilities categories, socio-economic status, or educational contexts such as urban, suburban, and rural). Aggregated data contribute to a perception of homogeneity for all racial and ethnic groups that does not exist.
2. Follow-up studies of the standardized test score data they collect should be conducted by states and school districts to identify possible reasons for the race-gender gap among African American students.
3. States and school districts should require schools to conduct separate studies of the rates of retention, suspension, expulsion, academic achievement, grade attainment, and participation in extracurricular activities for African American males and females. Researchers should also focus on the motivational factors for African American males and females and their possible relationship to poverty, violence, and healthcare access.
4. An accountability system should be developed to enable school districts to present and compare pupil information along race-gender divides, across grade levels, within individual schools, and across the district.

Research Recommendations

1. States and school districts should conduct follow-up studies on disaggregated standardized test data to look for gender, race, and within-group comparisons (e.g., disabilities categories, socioeconomic status, or educational contexts such as urban, suburban, and rural) and identify possible reasons for increases/decreases in performance.
2. More research should be conducted on race and gender equity among African American teachers and principals at both the preservice and in-service levels.
3. Longitudinal studies are needed documenting how gender impacts African American students' educational achievement and attainment as well as their resilience, psychosocial development and coping strategies.
4. Additional research studies are needed of the interplay with gender of contextual variables, within schools and class-

rooms (e.g., differential treatment and perceptions of African Americans) and external to them (e.g., socioeconomic status, violence, access to and quality of health care) when discussing barriers to and improvements in African American students' achievement.

5. Longitudinal studies should be conducted on the effects of Afrocentric education on the academic achievement of African American females and African American males, in both co-educational and single-sex educational settings.

6. Research is needed on the negative effects of gender role stereotyping of African Americans in education, particularly at the elementary and secondary levels.

7. Within the postsecondary context, research on gender equity and African Americans is scant. Much more information is needed, not only about African Americans in majority institutions, but also regarding the experiences of these women and men in Historically Black Colleges and Universities (HBCUs). For example, research is needed on the implications of the race gender gap at both types of institutions. In addition, research is needed on gender equity and the postsecondary experiences of African Americans who vary with respect to sexual orientation, disability, and other important demarcations.

Finally, the review resulted in the recommendations for practice that are listed below:

Practice Recommendations

1. Stories of successful African American women and men should be included in the curricula of teacher and principal preparation programs.

2. In addition to pedagogical proficiency, professors in teacher and principal preparation programs must present research studies to aspiring teachers and administrators that help them to develop initiatives to assist African American girls and boys to succeed.

3. School-based programs must be developed that encourage understanding of the roles gender has played in African American culture and history.

4. More attention must be given to developing teacher awareness of the role of teacher expectations and perceptions on the academic performance of African American males and females.

If we are to achieve gender equity for African American males and females, we must undertake systemic reforms encompassing multiple aspects of schooling. As Geneva Gay notes, such systemic reform must also "attend deliberately and conscientiously to factors of gender, social class, historical and linguistic capabilities" (Gay, 2000, as cited in Pollard & Welch, 2003, p. 381). For those desiring to unpack the conundrum of gender equity for African Americans, research and practice, informed by policies that intentionally focus on systemic reform, must be the ultimate goal.

ACKNOWLEDGMENTS

We would like to thank Beverly Guy Sheftall, Spellman College, Atlanta, GA, and Bradley Scott Intercultural Development Research Association, San Antonio, TX, for their helpful comments as reviewers of this chapter.

References

Access. (2002). Tennessee Supreme Court reaffirms its holding: Constitution requires equal educational funding and cost-based funding. Available October 3, 2005, from http://www.schoolfunding.info/states/tn/10-9-02SmallSchoolsuit.php3.

Access. (2005). *No Child Left Behind: Litigation.* Retrieved October 3, 2005, from http://www.schoolfunding.info/federal/federal.php3.

Allen, K., Jacobson, S., & Lomotey, K. (Fall, 1995). African American women in educational administration: The importance of mentors and sponsors. *The Journal of Negro Education, 64,* 409–422.

Alston, J. A. (2000). Missing from action. Where are the black female school superintendents? *Urban Education, 35*(5), 525–531.

Anderson, J. D. (1998). *The education of blacks in the South, 1860–1935.* Chapel Hill:University of North Carolina Press.

Anderson, N. (2004). A good student trapped. Urban minority males and constructions of academic achievement. *Perspectives in Education, 22(4),* 71–82.

Bae, Y., Choy, S., Geddes, C., Sable, J., & Snyder, T. (2000). Trends in educational equity of girls and women. (NCES 2000-030).

Beauboeuf-Lafontant, T. (1997, March). *I teach you the way I see us: Concepts of self and teaching of African American women teachers committed to social justice.* Paper presented at the Annual Meeting of the American Educational Research Association, Chicago, IL.

Bermak, F., Chung, R. C., & Sroskey-Sabdo, L. A. (2005). Empowerment groups for academic success: An innovative approach to prevent high school failure for at-risk urban African American girls. *Professional School Counseling, 8*(5), 377–390.

Brickhouse, N. W., Lowery, P., & Schultz, K. (2000). What kind of a girl does science? The construction of school science identities. *Journal of Research in Science Teaching, 37*(5), 441–458

Brown, A. H., Cervero, R. M., & Johnson-Bailey, J. (2000). Making the invisible visible: Race, gender and teaching in adult education. *Adult Education Quarterly, 50*(4), 273–288.

Brown, K. M. (2002). Leadership for social justice and equity: Weaving a transformative framework and pedagogy. *Educational Administration Quarterly, 40*(1), 77–108.

Bruening, J. E., Armstrong, K. L., & Pastore, D. L. (2005) Listening to the voices: The experiences of African American female student athletes. *Research Quarterly for Exercise and Sport, 76*(1), 82–101.

Bush, E. C., & Bush, L. (2005, March). Black male achievement and the community college. *Black Issues in Higher Education, 22*(2), 44.

Coley, R. J. (2001). *Differences in the gender gap: Comparisons across racial/ethnic groups in education and work.* Princeton, NJ: Educational Testing Service, Policy Information Center.

Davis, J. A., Smith, T. W., & Mardsen, P. V. (2003). GENERAL SOCIAL SURVEYS, 1972–2002: [CUMULATIVE FILE] [Computer file]. 2nd ICPSR version. Chicago, IL: National Opinion Research Center |prod|ucer], 2003. Storrs, CT: Roper Center for Public Opinion Research, University of Connecticut/Ann Arbor, MI: Inter-university Consortium for Political and Social Research, [distributors]

Delpit, L., & Dowdy, J. K. (Eds.). (2002). *The skin that we speak: thoughts of language and culture in the classroom.* New York: The New Press.

Federman, M., & Pachon, H. P. (2005). Addressing Institutional inequities in education: The case of advanced placement courses in California. In J. Petrovich & A. S. Wells (Eds.), *Bringing equity back: Research for a new era in American educational policy* (pp. 136–160). New York, NY: Teachers College, Columbia University.

Ferguson, R. F. (2003). Racial gap in teachers' perception of the achievement gap. *Urban Education, 38,* 460–507.

Fordham, S. (1993). Those loud Black girls: (Black) women, silence, and gender "passing" in the academy. *Anthropology and Education Quarterly, 24,* 3–32.

Fordham, S., & Ogbu, J. (1986). Black students, school success: Coping with the "burden of acting White." *Urban Review, 18,* 176–206.

Frederick Patterson Research Institute. (1997). *The African American education data book.* Fairfax, VA: The College Fund/The United Negro College Fund.

Funk, C. (2004). Female leaders in educational administration: Sabotage within our own ranks, *Advancing Women in Leadership Journal* (pp. 1–15). Retrieved February 2, 2005, from http://www.advancing-women.com/awl/winter2004/Funk.html.

Garibaldi, A. M. (1992). Educating and Motivating African American Males to Succeed. *Journal of Negro Education*, (Vol. 61, No. 1), Washington, D.: Howard University.

Gay, G. (2000). *Culturally Responsive Teaching: theory, research, & practice.* New York: Teachers College Press.

Gooden, M. A. (2002). Stewardship and critical leadership. Sufficient for leadership in urban schools? *Education and Urban Society*, *35*(1), 133–143.

Goodman, G. (2002). Administrator preparation programs: Do universities advance or inhibit females? In S. A. Korcheck & M. Reese (Eds.), *Women as school executives: Research and reflections on educational leadership* (pp. 126–134). (ERIC Document Reproduction Service No. ED473403).

Grantham, T. C. (2004). Multicultural mentoring to increase black male representation in gifted programs. *Gifted Children Quarterly, 48*(3), 232–246.

Gutsch, L. J. (2002). Women in elementary school leadership: Challenge and change. In S. A. Korcheck & M. Reese (Eds.), *Women as school executives: Research and reflections on educational leadership* (pp. 115–125). (ERIC Document Reproduction Service No. ED473403).

Hargreaves, B. (1996). Learning from outsiders within: Five women's discourses within the culture of the high school principal. Paper presented at the Annual Meeting of the American Educational Research Association, New York, New York. (ERIC Document Reproduction Service No. ED396437).

Harris, S. Arnold, M., Lowery, S., & Crocker, C. (2002). What factors motivate and inhibit women when deciding to become principals? In S. A. Korcheck & M. Reese (Eds.), *Women as school executives: Research and reflections on educational leadership* (pp. 252–260). (ERIC Document Reproduction Service No. ED473403).

Hart, B., & Risley, T. (1995). *Meaningful differences in everyday experiences of young American children.* Baltimore, MD: Paul Brookes Publishing Co.

Hawkins, D. (1996, July) Gender gap: Black females outpaces Black male counterparts at three degree levels. *Black Issues in Higher Education, 3*(10), 20–22.

Hawkins, R., & Malkey, L. M. (2005). Athletic investment and academic resilience in a national sample of African American females and males in the middle grades. *Education and Urban Society, 38*(1), 62–88.

Heck, R. H., & Hallinger, P. (1999). Next generation methods for the study of leadership and school improvement. In J. Murphy & K. S. Louis (Eds.), *Handbook on research on educational administration: A project of the American Educational Research Association* (2nd ed., pp. 141–158). San Francisco, CA: Jossey-Bass.

Hefner, D. (2004, June). Where the boys aren't: The decline of Black males in colleges and universities has sociologists and educators concerned about the future of the African American community. *Black Issues in Higher Education, 21*(9), 70–76.

Hodges, C.R., & Welch, O.M. (2003). Making Schools Work: Negotiating Educational Meaning and Transforming the Margins, Vol. 8 in P. DeVries & L. DeVries (Eds), Adolescents, Cultures, School and Society Series; New York: Peter Lang Publishing, Inc.

Hodgkinson, H. (1991). Reform versus reality. *Phi Delta Kappa, 73*(1), 8–16.

Honora, D. T. (2002). The relationship of gender and achievement to future outlook among African American adolescents. *Adolescence,* 3 (146), 301–316.

Hubbard, L. (2005). The role of gender in academic achievement. *International Journal of Qualitative Studies in Education, 18*(5), 605–623.

Ibid. (1999). The ominous gender gap in African American higher education, 23, 6–9. Individuals with Disabilities Education Improvement Act Statute Changes (2004). Retrieved October 3, 2005 from http://www.directionservice.org/cadre/stat_index_ideia.cfm.

Irvine, J. J. (1990). *Black students and school failure: policies, practices, and prescriptions.* Connecticut: Greenwood Press.

Irvine, M. A., & Hudley, C. (2005). Cultural mistrust, academic outcome expectations, and outcome values among African American adolescent men. *Urban Education, 40*(5), 476–496.

Jacobs, J. E. (2002). Can you be an effective principal when you don't smoke, swing a club, or ride a Harley? *Advancing women in Leadership Journal* (pp. 1–5). Retrieved February 18, 2005, from http://www.advancingwomen.com/awl/winter2004/jacobs.html.

Jackson, L. R. (1998). The influence of both race and gender on the experiences of African American college women. *Review of Higher Education, 21*(4), 359–375.

Jobe, D. A. (2003). Helping girls succeed. *Educational Leadership, 60,* 64–66.

Johnson-Bailey, J. (2004). Hitting and climbing the proverbial wall: Participation and retention issues for Black graduate women. *Race, Ethnicity and Education, 7*(4), 331–349.

Journal of Blacks in Higher Education (2006).http://www.jbhe.com/features/50_blackstudent_graduates.html

Kim, S. H., & Sedlacek, N. E. (1995, April). *Gender differences among incoming African American freshman of academic and social expectations.* Paper presented at the Annual Meeting of American Educational Research Association, San Francisco, CA.

Klein, S. S., Russo, L. N., Tittle, C. K., Schmuck, P. A., Campbell, P. B., Blackwell, P. J., et al. (1985). Summary recommendations for the continued achievement of sex equity in and through education. In S. Klein (Ed.), *Handbook for achieving sex equity through education* pp. 489–519). Baltimore, MD: The Johns-Hopkins University Press.

Kungufu Lewis, A. (2003). *Race in the schoolyard: Negotiating the color line in classrooms and communities.* New Brunswick, NJ: Rutgers University Press.

Lewis, C. W. (2006) African American males teachers in public schools: An examination of three urban school districts, *Teachers College Record, 108*(2), 224–245.

Lewis, S., Anderson, O., Cheng, L., Craig, A. F., Jackson, N., Jenkins, I., Jones, B., Murray, S. R., Rosenweig, M., Scott, P. B., & Wallace, B. (1985). Achieving sex equity for minority women. In S. Klein (Ed.), *Handbook for achieving sex equity through education* (pp. 365–390). Baltimore, MD: The Johns-Hopkins University Press.

Loder, T. L. (2005). African American principals' reflections of social change, community othermothering, and Chicago Public School reform. *Urban Education, 40,* 3, 298–320.

Major, B., & Schmader, T. (1998). Coping with Stigma Through Psychological Disengagement. In J. K. Swin & C. Stanger (Eds.) *Prejudice: The Target's Perspective,* (pp. 220–238). San Diego: Academic Press.

Mellon, E. (2005, September 30). State's school funding formula assailed. Knox mayor wants 'no logic' BEP formula changed to aid urban areas. *The Knoxville News Sentinel,* pp. A1, A9.

Mendez, L. M., Knoff, H. M., & Ferron, J. M. (2002). School demographic variables and out-of-school suspension rates: A quantitative and qualitative analysis of a large, ethnically diverse school district. *Psychology in the Schools, 39*(3), 259– 277.

National Center for Educational Statistics. (2005). *Selected characteristics: School staff.* Washington DC: U.S. Department of Education.

Nettles, M. T., & Perna, L. W. (1997a). *The African American education data book. Volume I: Higher and adult education.* Fairfax, VA: Frederick D. Patterson Research Institute of the College Fund/United Negro College Fund.

Nettles, M. T., & Perna, L. W. (1997b). *The African American education data book. Volume II: Preschool through high school education.* Fairfax, VA: Frederick D. Patterson Research Institute of the College Fund/United Negro College Fund.

Nettles, M. T., & Perna, L. W. (1997c). *The African American education data book. Volume III: The transition from school to college and college to work.* Fairfax, VA: Frederick D. Patterson Research Institute of the College Fund/United Negro College Fund.

Nettles, M. T., Perna, L. W., The Frederick Patterson Institute of UNCF, & Millett, C. M. (August 1998). Research Questions and Data Resource Needs for Examining Student Access to Higher Education, in U.S. Department of Education, National Center for Education Statistics, Reconceptualizing Access in Postsecondary Education: Report of the Policy Panel on Access, NCES 98-283) prepared for the Council of the National Postsecondary Education Cooperative, Subcommittee on the Policy Panel on Access, Washington, D.C. pp. 35–56).

Noguera, P. A. (2003). Schools, prisons, and the social implications of punishment: Rethinking disciplinary practices. *Theory Into Practice, 42*(4), 341–351 (1997). Reconsidering the "crisis" of the black male in America Reconfiguring Power: Challenges for the 21st Century-1–22), *Social Justice, 24*(2), 147(18), http://www.galegroup.com

Noguera, P. (2005). The trouble with Black boys: the role and influence of environmental and cultural factors on the academic performance of African American males. In O.S. Fashola (Ed.). *Educating African American males: Voices from the field* (pp. 51–78). Thousand Oaks, CA: Corwin Press.

O'Connor, C. (1997). Dispositions toward (collective) struggle and educational resilience in the inner city: A case analysis of six African American high school students. *American Educational Research Journal, 34,* 593–629.

Ogbu, J. (1989). The individual in collective adaptation: A framework for focusing on academic underperformance and dropping out among involuntary minorities. In L. Weis, E. Farrar, & H. G. Petrie (Eds.), *Dropouts from school* (pp. 181–204). Albany: State University of New York Press.

Ogbu, J. (1990). Overcoming racial barriers to equal access. In J. Goodlans & P. Leating (Eds.), *Access to knowledge* (pp. 59–89). New York: The College Board.

Ogbu, J. (2003). *Black American students in an affluent suburb: A study of academic disengagement.* Mahwah, NJ: Lawrence Erlbaum Associates.

Orfield, G., & Eaton, S. (1996). *Dismantling Desegregation.* New York: New Press.

Osborne, J. W. (2003). The More Things Change . . . Trends in Identification with Academics among Minority Students from 1972–1992. In C. C. Yeakey & R. D.Henderson (Eds). *Surmounting All Odds: Education, Opportunity, and Society in the New Millennium,* Vol. 1, (pp. 345–368). Greenwich, Connecticut: Information Age Publishing.

Phillips, M., Crouse, J.& Ralph, J. (1998). Does the Black-White test score gap widen after children enter school? In C. Jencks & M. Phillips (Eds.), *The Black-White test score gap* (pp. 229–272). Washington, DC: The Brookings Institution.

Pollard, D. S. (May 1996). Perspectives on gender and race. *Educational Leadership, 53,* 72–74.

Pollard, D. S., & Welch, O. M. (2003). One size does not fit all: An examination of issues in enhancing the academic achievement of African American precollege students. In C. C. Yeakey & R. D. Henderson (Eds.), *Surmounting All Odds: Education, Opportunity, and Society in the New Millenium,* Vol. 1, (pp. 369–388). Greenwich, Connecticut: Information Age Publishing.

Polleys, M. S. (1999). Mastering the maze through mentoring: Career advancement of female superintendents. Paper presented at the meeting of the American Educational Research Association, Point Clear, AL.

Polnick, B., Reed, D., Funk, C., & Edmonson, S. (2004). Groundbreaking women: Inspirations and trailblazers. *Advancing women in Leadership Journal* (pp. 1–12). Retrieved February 18, 2005, from http://www.advancingwomen.com/awl/winter2004/Polnick.html.

Portes, P. R. (2005). *Dismantling educational inequality: a cultural-historical approach to closing the achievement gap.* New York: Peter Lang Publishing.

Programs for aspiring principals: Who participates? (1997). NCES 97-591. Retrieved February 15, 2005, from http://nces.gov/pubs97/97591.pdf.

Rendon, L. R. (August 1998). Access in a Democracy: Narrowing the Opportunity Gap. U.S. Department of Education, National Center for Education Statistics. Reconceptualizing Access in Postsecondary Education: Report of the Policy Panel on Access, NCES 98-283, prepared for the Council of the National Postsecondary Education Cooperative, Subcommittee on the Policy Panel on Access, Washington, D.C.: pp. 57–70.

Reyes, P., Wagstaff, L. H., & Fusarelli. L. D. (1999). Delta forces: The changing fabric of American society and education. In J. Murphy & K. S. Louis (Eds.), *Handbook on research on educational administration: A project of the American Educational Research Association* (2nd ed., pp. 183–201). San Francisco, CA: Jossey-Bass.

Roderick, M. (2003). What's happening to boys? Early high school experiences and school outcomes among African American male adolescents in Chicago. *Urban Education, 38,* 538–607.

Sable, J., & Hoffman, L. (2005). *Characteristics of the 100 largest public elementary and secondary school districts in the United States: 2002–2003.* (NCES Publication No. 2005-312). Washington, D.C.: Author. Retrieved September 23, 2005 from: http://nces.ed.gov/pubs 2005/2005312.pdf.

Saunders, J., Davis, L. Williams, T., & Williams J. H. (2004). Gender differences in self perceptions and academic outcomes: A study of African American high school students. *Journal of Youth and Adolescence, 33*(1), 81–91.

Scott, K. A. (2002a). "You want to be a girl and not my friend": African American girls' play with and without boys. *Childhood: An International Journal of Child Research, 9,* 397–414.

Scott, K. A. (2002b, April). *"She's like an animal": Teachers' perceptions of African-American girls' academic success versus the girls' playground lives.* Paper presented at American Educational Research association, New Orleans, LA.

Scott, K. A. (2003a). In girl, out girl, and always Black: African-American girls' friendships. *Sociological Studies of Children and Youth, 9,* 179–207.

Scott, K. A. (2003b). A case study: African-American girls and their families. *State of Black America* 2003, 181–196.

Shakeshaft, C. (1999). The struggle to create a more gender-inclusive profession. In J. Murphy & K. S. Louis (Eds.), *Handbook on research on educational administration: A project of the American Educational Research Association* (2nd ed., pp. 99–118). San Francisco, CA: Jossey-Bass.

Skiba, R., Michael, R., Nardo, A., & Peterson, R. (2002). The color of discipline: Sources of racial and gender disproportionality in school punishment. *The Urban Review, 34*(4), 317–342.

Smith, M. J., & Fleming, M. K. (2006). African American parents in the search of college choice: Unintentional contributions to the female to male college enrollment gap. *Urban Education, 41*(1), 171–100.

Spatig, L., Parrott, L., Carter, C. Kusimo, P., & Keyes, M. (1998). We roll deep: Appalachian girls fight for their lives. Paper presented at the Annual Meeting of the American Education Studies Association. Philadelphia, PA: November.

Spencer, M. B., Cross, Jr., W. E., Harpalani, V., & Goss, T. N. (2003). Historical and Developmental Perspectives on Black Academic Achievement: Debunking the "Acting White" Myth and Posing New Directions for Research. In C. C. Yeakey & R. D. Henderson (Eds.). *Surmounting All Odds: Education, Opportunity, and Society in the New Millenium,* Vol. 1 (pp. 273–304)

Spencer, W. A., & Kochan, F. K. (2000). Gender related differences in career patterns of principals in Alabama: A statewide study. *Educational Policy Analysis Archives, 8*(9), pp. 1–18. Retrieved June 1, 2005, from http://epaa.asu.edu/epaa/v8n9.html

Stake, R. E. (2002). Case Studies. In N. K. Denzin & Y. S. Lincoln (Eds.). *Handbook of Qualitative Research* (2nd ed., pp. 435–454). Thousand Oaks, CA: Sage Publications, Inc.

Steele, C. M. (1997). A threat in the air: How stereotypes shape intellectual identity and performance. *American Psychologist, 52,* 613–629.

Striegel-Moore, R. H., Wilfley, D. E., Pike, K. M., Dohm, F., & Fairburn, C. G. (2000). Recurrent binge eating in Black American women. *Archives of Family Medicine, 9,* 83–87.

Striegel-Moore, R. H., Dohm, F. A., Kraemer, H. C., Taylor, C., Barr, D., Stephen, et al. (2003). Eating disorders in White and Black women. *American Journal of Psychiatry, 160,* 1326–1331.

Sykes, G. (1999). The "new professionalism" in education: An appraisal. In J. Murphy & K. S. Louis (Eds.), *Handbook on research on educational administration: A project of the American Educational Research Association* (2nd ed., pp. 227–249). San Francisco: Jossey-Bass.

Thompson, L. R., & Lewis, B. F. (2005). Shooting for the stars: A case study of the mathematics achievement and career attainment of an African American male high school student. *High School Journal, 88*(4), 6–18.

Thompson-McMillon, G., & Edwards, P. (2000). Why does Joshua "hate" school . . . but love Sunday school? *Language Arts, 78*(2), 111–120.

Tillman, L. C. (2004). (Un)intended consequences? The impact of Brown v. Board of Education Decision on the employment status of Black educators. *Education and Urban Society, 36*(3), 280–303.

Townsend, B. (2000). The disproportionate discipline of African American learners: Reducing school suspensions and expulsions. *Exceptional Children, 66*(3), 382–391. Trends in educational equity of girls and women: Transitions to postsecondary education (2004). *National Center for Educational Statistics.* U.S. Department of Education. Retrieved February 15, 2005, from http://nces.ed.gov/pubs2005/equity/Section9.asp.

Uhlenberg, J., & Brown, K. M. (2002). Teachers' perceptions and expectations and the Black-White test score gap. *Education and Urban Society, 34,* 493–530.

U.S. Census Bureau. (2004) Census 2000, Special Tabulation. Characteristics of children under 18 years by age, race, and Hispanic or Latino origin for the United States, regions, states, and Puerto Rico. Internet release date March 16, 2004. Retrieved September 16, 2005, from http://www.census.gov/population/cen2000/phc_t30/tab03.pdf.

U.S. Department of Education (2002). Retrieved October 3, 2005, from http://www.ed.gov/nclb/landing.jhtml.

U.S. Department of Education, Institute of Education Sciences. (2005). *Projections of education statistics to 2014: Thirty-third edition.* (NCES Publication No. 2005-074). Washington, D. C: Author. Retrieved September 23, 2005 from: http://nces.ed.gov/pubs2005/2005074.pdf.

U.S. Department of Education, Institute of Education Sciences. (2005). Public elementary and secondary students, staff, school, and school districts: School Year 2002–2003. (NCES Publication No. 2005-314). Washington, D. C: Author. Retrieved September 23, 2005 from: http://nces.ed.gov/pubs2005/2005314.pdf.

U.S. Department of Education, National Center for Education Statistics. (2004). 1999–2000 Schools and Staffing Survey (SASS) CD-ROM: Public-Use Data with Electronic Codebook (NCES 2004-372) [Computer file], "Public School Principal Questionnaire" and "Private School Principal Questionnaire." Washington, DC: U. S. Department of Education, Institute of Sciences.

U.S. Department of Education, National Center for Education Statistics. (2003). *Status and Trends in the Education of Blacks,* (NCES 2003–2004). By K. Hoffman & C. Llagas, Project Officer: T. D. Synder, Washington, D.C.: U.S. Department of Education..

Verdugo R. R., & Henderson, R. D. (2003). The Dropout Rate among African American Males: A Policy Perspective. In C. C. Yeakey & R. D. Henderson (Eds.) *Surmounting all odds: Education, opportunity, and society in the new millennium,* (Vol. 2) pp. 487–522. Greenwich, CT: New Information Age Publishing.

Walker, V. S. (1993). Interpersonal caring in the "good" segregated schooling of African American children: Evidence from the case of Caswell County Training School. *Urban Review, 25,* (pp. 63–77). Reprint in D. Rich & J. Van Galen, 1994, *Caring in an unjust world: Negotiating borders and barriers in schools.* New York: State University of New York. Retrieved July 27, 2005 from: http://www.netlibrary.com .proxy.lib.utk.edu:90-netlibrary-Online Reader, (pp. 129–144).

Wattson, C., & Smitherman, G. (1996). *Educating African American males: Detroit's Malcolm X academy solution.* Chicago: Third World Press.

Welch, O. M., & Hodges, C. R. (1997). Standing Outside on the Inside: Black Adolescents and the Construction of Academic Identity. New York: SUNY Press.

Wesson, L. H. (1998). Exploring the dilemmas of leadership: Voices from the field. *Advancing Women in Leadership Journal* (pp. 1–10). Retrieved February 18, 2005 from http://www.advancingwomen .com/awl/winter98/awlv2_wesson4final.html.

White-Johnson, A. F. (2001). "Peas 'N Rice" or "Rice 'N Peas"—which one are we really ordering? The plight of African American male students engaged in educational exchange process. *Urban Education, 36*(3), 343–373.

Williamson, L. (1998). Eating disorders and the cultural forces behind the drive for thinness: Are African-American women really protected? *Social Work in Health Care, 28,* 1–14.

Wilson-Jones, L. (2003, November). *Factors that promote and inhibit the academic achievement of rural African American males in a Mississippi school: A qualitative study.* Paper presented at the Annual Meeting of the Mid-South Educational Research Association, Biloxi, MS.

GENDER EQUITY FOR LATINA/OS

Angela B. Ginorio,* Yvette Lapayese,* and Melba J. T. Vásquez*

INTRODUCTION

"We want better education," read the slogan in the poster held by three Mexican American young women protesting the quality of education in Elsa, Texas (Guajardo & Guajardo, 2004, p. 509). The date of the photo is November 15, 1968, demonstrating that the struggles around schooling begun by the League of United Latin American Citizens (LULAC) in the late 1920s have been ongoing in the United States for at least 40 years (Guajardo & Guajardo, 2004; MacDonald & Monkman, 2005). The definition of "better education" in K–12 for Latina/os then and now includes bilingual education, a culturally competent staff that includes Latina/os, and school curricula that acknowledges the cultures of the students involved. In the last 40 years, the call for "better education" has also included gender equity. Then, as now, the call for equitable education extends to college at both the undergraduate and graduate levels.

Encoded in the demand for "better education" was not only a request for more access to formal education, but also for what the parents and students of Elsa, Texas, believed education would bring them. First, "better education" would end the segregated school system to which their children had access. Second, "better education" would end the structural as well as individual acts of disrespect toward the Mexican American students and parents by their teachers. And, a "better education" would substitute the existing system of education that provided Mexican Americans in the region with just enough skills to qualify them for farm work and other low-paying jobs (Guajardo & Guajardo, 2004). The first two demands addressed education in the context of community/neighborhoods and school-community relations. The third demand addressed the presumed outcome of education—social mobility through education that enhances occupation and earning potential (Urciuoli, 1996).

In our reading of "better education," we echo Valenzuela's (1999) understanding of *educación* as a "conceptually broader term than its English language cognate [that while] . . . inclu-

sive of formal academic training, *educación* additionally refers to competence in the social world (Zavella, 1997). *Educación* thus represents both means and end, such that the end state of being *bien educada/o* is accomplished through a process characterized by respectful relations (p. 23)." Valenzuela's statement articulates our understanding of the "in and through education," one of this *Handbook's* organizing themes.

In this chapter we will provide our definitions of some key terms and some numbers that reflect the current status of Latina/os in the United States as well as a review of the current status of Latina/os in education with an emphasis on K–12. Shifting the focus from the statistical to the sociocultural, we will present information on attributes Latina/os bring to their education. We will then focus on research on school-based and community-based issues *in* education and we will answer the question: What if schools provided Latina/os with "better education"? We will finish with some policy recommendations and suggestions for future research that address gender equity issues in the context of the education of Latina/os.

OVERVIEW

Definitions and Population Figures

The U.S. Census Bureau officially labeled Latinos as "Hispanic" and defines Hispanics as people whose origin is Mexican, Puerto Rican, Cuban, South or Central American, or other Hispanic/ Latino, regardless of race. In this chapter we will use the umbrella term "Latina/o" unless specific nationality-level terms are used by the author(s) we are citing or the information refers to groupings in census data. The term "Latina/o" encompasses a very diverse population that "includes new immigrants and descendants of some of the original inhabitants of this continent, undocumented residents and American citizens, English and Spanish speakers, people with different national origins, and

---

*The boldface names are the Lead Authors.

those who identity closely with their ethnic heritage and those who do not" (Ginorio, Gutiérrez, Cauce, & Acosta, 1995, p. 242).

The more than 41 million Latina/os living in the United States today constitute 14% of the U.S. population (Jelinek, 2005), with a median age for Latina/os of 26.7 years vs. 35.9 for the U.S. population (U.S. Census, 2006). In the 2000 census, 48.6% of the Hispanic population was female; a proportion that is the reverse of the majority of the U.S. population, indicating the impact of continued migration of Latinos into the United States (U.S. Census, 2006). The majority of Latina/os hail originally from Mexico (63%), 10% from Puerto Rico, 7% from Central America, 4% from Cuba, and 3% from the Dominican Republic (*Newsweek,* 2005, p. 29). This population is concentrated in 10 states, with most people of Mexican origin living in the Southwest and California, and most people of Caribbean origin living in Florida, New York, New Jersey, and Massachusetts. Some of these populations have resided in what is now U.S. territory for centuries while others are recent immigrants who are still facing the challenges of learning English. Furthermore, Latina/os were the first cultural group to arrive in the United States that was also racially heterogeneous, a fact that is recognized by the census in 2000 with its two-tiered sorting of respondents first by ethnicity (Hispanic and nonHispanic) and then for Hispanics by race. Thus, we use the term "ethno-race" to denote that both of these categorical systems may be operating in a particular context (Ginorio & Martínez 1998). Finally, class issues also divide Latina/os within and across each subnational group. Thus, any generalization about Latina/os will need to be adapted to specific populations.

Overview of Latino/a Participation in K–16+

The growth of the Latino population in the United States is reflected in the numbers of Latina/os in the U.S. public schools. In 2005, more than 10.9 million Latinos were enrolled in K–12 public schools, representing 17% of K–12 students (National Council of La Raza, 2007) compared to 6% in 1972. By 2003, Latina/os were 19% of public-school enrollment; surpassing Black enrollment for the first time in 2002 (National Center for Education Statistics, 2005). This growth in numbers is reported in spite of the high drop-out rate for Latina/os of 21% (Fry, 2003).

The proportion of Latina/os 25 years and over with at least a high-school diploma reached 55.4% in 1998. However, Latinos/as still have a long way to go before they approach the proportion achieved by all non-Hispanic Whites, which is 83.6% (Greene, 2002). Among Latina/os, Cuban Americans were the most likely to have finished at least four years of high school in 1998 (67.8%), followed by Puerto Ricans (63.8%) and Mexican Americans (48.3%) (AAAS, 2000). At the most general level of analysis these differences among Latina/o groups can be traced to the histories in the countries of origin and in their migration to what is now the U.S. territory, ethno-racial composition of the populations, and concomitant socioeconomic factors.

Latinas have a higher proportion of high-school enrollment than Latinos, but among their female peers, Latinas have a low high-school graduation rate and a low representation in gifted and talented programs and in advanced placement classes (Ginorio & Huston, 2001). One of the implications of the low levels of high-school completion among Latina/os is that the pool of Latinas/os eligible for postsecondary education is proportionately very small.

Among college students, ethnic minorities have increased from 15% in 1976 to 29% in 2002 (National Center for Education Statistics, 2003a). Much of the change can be attributed to rising numbers of Latinos and Asian American or Pacific Islander students: the numbers of Asian American or Pacific Islander students increased from 2% to 6%, and the Hispanic numbers increased from 4% to 10% during that same period. While Latinos are entering college, they are not earning four-year degrees. Among Latina/os who go to college, most Latinos choose community colleges for their post-high-school education and attend college part-time (Fry, 2002). In a 2002 study by the Pew Hispanic Center based on census data, it was reported that by age 29 only 16% of Latino high-school graduates earn a four-year college degree, compared with 37% of non-Hispanic Whites and 21% of nonHispanic African Americans (Fry, 2002).

More Latinas attend college than Latinos. As with high-school diplomas, Latinas fared better in college than Latinos, earning nearly three out of every five (57%) baccalaureates awarded to Latina/os in all fields (AAAS, 2000; Fry, 2002). The gender composition of Latino/a graduates at the bachelor's and post-baccalaureate levels is in line with that reported for all students, with more women earning degrees than males in most fields (National Center for Education Statistics, 2003a, 2003b). It is at the graduate level that the advantage in numbers of Latinas over Latinos disappears. While Latinas, following national trends (since 1984 the number of women in graduate schools has exceeded the number of men, National Center for Education Statistics, 2003a), attend graduate school in equal proportion to Latinos (4%), the number that attains the PhD is smaller than that of Latinos (0.3% vs. 0.4% for men) (Pérez Huber, Huidor, Malagón, Sánchez, & Solórzano, 2006). When broken down by different Latina/o subgroups, only Cubans exceed 1%, with 1.2% for Cubanas, and 1.3 for Cubanos obtaining a Ph.D. degree. More typical are the numbers for Salvadoreans: only 0.1% (females) and 0.2% (males) and Chicana/os: 0.2% of both Chicanos and Chicanas obtain a Ph.D. (Pérez Huber et al., 2006).

WHAT LATINAS AND LATINOS BRING TO THEIR EDUCATION

Latinas and Latinos bring many assets to their educational experience that flow from their varied and rich cultural and historical backgrounds. Research has demonstrated that they also have very high educational aspirations (Marlino & Wilson, 2006; Phinney, Dennis, & Osorio, in press) supported by, and often inspired by a sense of duty to, their families.

Cultural Factors: Ethnics, Gender, and Sexual Identity

The family serves as the basis of the early formation for all children, but especially Latinos/as (Vásquez & de las Fuentes, 1999) whose children are cared for at home as long as possible. The preference for caring for children at home and the lack of culturally appropriate pre-K services results in low levels of attendance to pre-K-level schooling (García & González, 2006).

Research has identified some of the mechanisms of development of children's ethnic identity by which behaviors significant to children's education are socialized. For example, Mexican American parents encourage in their children strong group enhancement and altruism motives while Anglo American children develop stronger competitive motives (Kagan, 1977). Other studies confirmed that the ethnic identity of the Mexican American children, inculcated by the mother's teaching about the Mexican culture, is related to the more cooperative and less competitive preferences of Mexican American students compared to Anglo American children (Knight, Cota, & Bernal, 1993). Thus, educational models based on cooperative strategies for learning may be more relevant for Mexican American students.

Identity for Latinos/as tends to be collectively and family oriented rather than individually oriented. Large extended families have been a source of strength and resilience for Latinos/as, and close friends are often considered part of this extended family network (Ginorio, Gutiérrez, Cauce, & Acosta, 1995). Several educational implications are possibly related to these tendencies. One is that Latino/a students may be more reluctant to travel far to attend college, and families prefer them to remain close to their family and community. Indeed, Latina/os tend to attend institutions in regions of the country where they are most concentrated, including California, Texas, and Puerto Rico (AAAS, 2000) even at the doctoral level (Quintana-Baker, 2002).

Identity is always gendered. For Latina/os, their gender and sexual identity is shaped in the contested terrain between the culture at home and the larger culture. While sexist and homophobic practices occur in each of these domains, the form that these practices take for Latinas respond to the cultural dictates of how a young woman should behave, whether she be Latina or not, a recent immigrant or a third-generation Latina. At home (Gallegos-Castillo, 2006) or at school (Hyams, 2006), young Latinas develop new forms of being Latina that honor the strength of the women in their lives (López, 2006) while creating what Gallegos-Castillo labeled "suspended space" and Zavella (1997) labeled "peripheral vision." Gender identity for Latinos is a less-studied area, and the results are contradictory depending on measures used, and the domain within which the research was done (for example, drug use vs. alcoholism) (Kulis, Marsiglia, & Hurdle, 2003; Polednak, 1997). In some domains gender identity rather than gender was the most predictive variable.

Cultural Factors: Linguistic Issues

Cultural and socioeconomic issues influence whether one speaks English, Spanish, or one of the many indigenous languages from Latin America; whether one is bilingual or trilingual; of at what skill level one is in language. The auditory and verbal skills necessary to perform well in school, and that a child develops through linguistic ability, are tied to an individual's socioeconomic status, migration history, and cultural commitment (Ginorio & Huston, 2001). Bilingualism, in and of itself, is not a detriment to academic performance; in fact, it is an asset to the student and actually contributes to increased cognitive flexibility and adaptability. So long as the bilingual proficiency (including vocabulary, grammar, syntax, and so forth) reflects strong skills in both languages, bilingualism constitutes strength. Evidence indicated that even after controlling for socioeconomic status, students who are bilingual tend to have larger information networks, have higher grades, and higher graduation rates than those who speak only English or Spanish (Ginorio & Huston, 2001; Rumberger & Larson, 1998). According to Children of Immigrants Longitudinal Study, a decade-long research project involving about 5,000 students of 77 nationalities in South Florida and Southern California, second-generation students who became fluent bilinguals reported better relations with their families, greater self-esteem, and higher educational aspirations than those who became English monolinguals (Portes & Hao, 2002).

GENDER EQUITY ISSUES IN K–12 SCHOOLS

Despite the educational gains described in the overview, and despite demographic trends that reveal Latina/o students are the fastest-growing minority group in the United States, their histories, experiences, cultures, and languages are often devalued within U.S. schools. The miseducation of Latina/o students can be traced to a variety of school-based issues that systematically disadvantage cultural and linguistic minorities. For Latina/o students, multiple oppressions based on gender, race, language, and social class play out in classrooms across the United States. Some of the school-based issues related to the miseducation of Latina/o students include gender and cultural bias in school curricula, educational issues raised by sexual harassment and high teen pregnancy, gendered student-teacher interactions, linguistic bias in schools, lack of minority teachers and teachers prepared to work with Latina/o students, and segregation in lower-financed schools.

Latina/o students face specific struggles in schools that discriminate against them on the basis of gender and ethnicity. The intersection of both ethno-racial and gender stereotypes and the way these stereotypes play out in the classroom challenge both the confidence and dignity of Latinas and Latinos in many secondary schools.

Gender and Cultural Bias in School Curricula and Programs

Textbooks and curricula continue to reinforce sex-role stereotypes that reduce the confidence levels of all girls (Grossman, 1998; Rogers & Gilligan, 1998); for Latina students, the gender stereotypes intersect with ethno-racial stereotypes as well. Based on her research in a hyper-segregated high school in New York City serving Dominicans, Nancy López (2006) offered a wonderful example of how the content and approaches of two different teachers offer students options that affirm or undermine their growth as students. The Latina teacher, Ms. Gutierrez provided context from the students' own lives for the examples she uses in her American History class while Mr. Hunter focused on book-based learning in his Global History course. Efforts to diversify the curriculum through multicultural education have often resulted in superficial and supplemental lessons about "other" cultures (Sleeter, 1996; Valenzuela, 1999) that continue to undermine and misrepresent Latinas/os in the school curricula.

In addition to gender and cultural bias in the curriculum, Latina/o students are tracked into different curricular programs based on their ethno-race and gender. Tracking is the practice of placing students in different classes based on perceived differences in the students' abilities. Tracking takes a variety of forms, including remedial and special education programs, as well as programs for gifted and talented students. At the high-school level, many school systems distinguish between college preparatory and vocational tracks. In general, Latina/o students are underrepresented in gifted and college-prep tracks, and overrepresented in remedial and vocational tracks (Oakes, 2005).

Gender factors into how Latina and Latino students are tracked. For instance, vocational-education enrollments clearly show Latinas being steered into gender-specific jobs with minimal career or income advancement (Romo & Falbo, 1996). Latina high-school students are frequently enrolled in cosmetology classes or tracked into noncollege preparatory general-education programs (Kozol, 2005). Latina/os, in turn, internalize those expectations; in a sample of Mexican Americans in rural areas, the number one choice of 9th-grade Latinas for a career was cosmetology and for males automobile mechanic (Ginorio & Huston, 2000). Few vocational programs encourage Latinas to enter nontraditional fields or offer them reasons to remain in school (Romo & Falbo, 1996).

Tracking of students into special-education classes affects Latina/os disproportionately at both ends of the educational spectrum. Latinos are three times more likely than Latinas to be referred to special-education programs. At the high end of the spectrum, both Latinas and Latinos have been denied access to academic enrichment programs and advanced-placement programs. In California, a state with a significant Latina population, there are disparities between Latinas and White females in "Gifted-and-Talented-Education" (GATE) programs. Though Latinas constitute 43% of girls enrolled in K–12 California public schools, they represent 21% of the females enrolled in GATE programs. Conversely, White females make up only 36% of enrolled girls but account for 52% of all girls in GATE (Solórzano, Ledesma, Pérez, Burciaga, & Ornelas, 2003). The disproportionate gender representation evident at both ends of the educational spectrum raises questions about the ways gender bias operates in school procedures (Ginorio & Huston, 2001).

The opportunities for culturally appropriate education become even slimmer for Latinas with disabilities. Census data indicates that in the age range 15–24, over 276,000 Hispanic women experience a disability, with 122,000 experiencing a severe disability (U.S. Census Bureau, 1997 data, revised August 2002). Across the country, only a few districts have programs addressing language instruction and disabilities simultaneously, and/or teachers who are adequately prepared to deliver both (Zehr, 2001). English-language learners with disabilities have even less access than mainstream English-language learners to adequate specialized intervention services (Artiles & Ortiz, 2002).

Latina students are not equally represented in Advanced Placement (AP) enrollment (Solórzano & Ornelas, 2002), although Latinas take the same number or more of AP exams than Latinos. Latinas score lower than Latinos in AP math and science exams. The underrepresentation of Latina/o students in AP enrollment negatively impacts their chances of entry into higher-education institutions.

The negative effects of tracking can be diminished by increased access to academic guidance counselors and mentors. Latina/o students have low access to academic guidance counselors, which also results in limited baccalaureate opportunities (Ceja, 2000; Oakes, 2005; Rivera & Gallimore, 2006). However, mentoring programs that provide Latina students with information and hands-on experiences have proven successful for encouraging Latinas onto the higher-education track (Ginorio & Huston, 2001). School programs specifically targeted to the Latina/o population are evident in some schools. Few programs have lasted as long as the Hispanic Mother-Daughter Program at Arizona State University, which was started in 1985 and is still ongoing, and which acknowledges the strong family bonds that are prevalent among many Latina/o families.

Issues of gender and cultural biases in both curriculum and programming serve to undermine the educational chances of Latina/o students. Through tracking, gender stereotyping, and the disparate representation of Latina/o students in both GATE and special education, many Latina/o students are being shortchanged in the classroom, either because of the outright bias inherent in the system, or the lack of knowledge and training on the part of educators on the subject of working with students of diverse backgrounds.

Sexual Harassment and Latina Teen Pregnancy

When addressing gender biases in schools, two issues are often specifically tied to girls: (a) sexual harassment and (b) teen pregnancy. We challenge the idea that sexual harassment and teen pregnancy are more gendered than the tracking discussed in the previous section or the gendered student-teacher interactions or linguistic bias we will discuss next. These two practices are tied to girls because of the sexualization of girls that is prevalent in our society, because of the conflation of traditional femininity practices in Latino culture with sexuality, and because society sees it as a female responsibility to deal with anything that requires putting limits on sexual behavior that involves males.

Sexual Harassment

As the 2001 *Hostile Hallways* documented, sexual harassment impacts Latina/o students in particular. One-quarter of Latinos fear for their personal safety in school as do almost half of Latinas (49%) (AAUW, 2001), the highest percentages reported for any of the ethno-racial groups. As a result of sexual harassment, students often stay home, miss class, or lose interest in academic learning. They may experience difficulty concentrating on schoolwork or suffer lowered self-esteem and self-confidence (Texas Civil Rights Project, 1998). Latina/os are the most likely to report that the sexual-harassment experience makes them doubt whether they "have what it takes to graduate from high school" (AAUW, 2001, p. 33). Competition and conflicts among "cliques" of girls can also result in harassment, affecting Latinas' attitudes toward school and their ability to learn (Merten, 1997).

Teen Pregnancy

Teen pregnancy can be an impediment to the educational achievement of Latinas. In 1999, the Latina teen birth rate stood at 94 per 1,000 or about twice the national average of 50 per

1,000. Nearly 3 in 5 Latinas will become pregnant between the ages of 15 and 19, and the actual pregnancy rate (as opposed to the live birth rate) for Latinas in 1997 was 165 per 1,000, nearly double the national average of 97 per 1,000 (Dickson, 2001). According to the National Center for Education Statistics, Latinas also have the highest dropout rate amongst all females (22.1% in 2001, the last year for which data were available) (Freeman, 2004).

The coupling of high teen pregnancy and high dropout rates for Latina teenagers is often interpreted as teen pregnancy causing the high dropout rate. Hyams (2006), in her study of a highly isolated school in a high-poverty neighborhood in Los Angeles, cited a formula for academic success mentioned in some form by most of the Latina teens she interviewed: "Pay attention in class . . . [and] don't get pregnant" (p. 93). While engagement in school and pregnancy have some relation, from the existing research it cannot be stated that for Latinas pregnancy causes the high dropout rate. "[T]he effect of pregnancy on Latinas' educational achievement, however, is ambiguous" as 63% of teen Latinas who got pregnant had already dropped out of school (Ginorio & Huston, 2001, p. 25).

Schools do have a role to play in issues of sexuality and pregnancy both in terms of offering services to those Latinas who do get pregnant and of prevention. As Romo (1998) noted, urban high schools offer programs to help teen parents graduate, but many provide only basic and remedial-level classes. Programs should help Latinas by giving as much assistance as needed to meet educational goals and offering training in nontraditional fields that pay higher wages than pink-collar jobs. In their study of 27 Latina teen mothers, Russell and Lee (2006) reported increases in educational aspirations and for a subset of these girls increased performance in high school.

As important as offering programs to already pregnant girls, schools should offer sex-education and pregnancy-prevention programs. Even more central to their mission, schools should ensure that young Latinas find challenges that engage them in their education in school, curricula, and staff. As López (2006) reported citing a Latina teacher in New York City: "The best birth control is education" (p. 84).

Gendered Student-Teacher Interactions

Gender plays an important role in the expectations of teachers. Positive expectations, it has been proven, can cause students to make exceptional progress in schooling (Rosenthal & Jacobson, 1974), while negative expectations can have the opposite effect. It has long been contended that teachers tend to have lower expectations for the classroom achievement of girls. Teachers call on girls less frequently, provide girls with less feedback and less-precise feedback, and reward girls for behavior traits such as docility and silence (Sadker & Zittleman, 2005; Sadker & Sadker, 1994; AAUW, 1992). Girls are reported to be rebelling against such expectations (López, 2006). In the face of girls increased performance in test based assessment, it has been argued recently that teachers are biased in favor of girls' more manageable style in school.

Gender bias, however, is not limited merely to individual teacher-student interactions. Several systemic biases also exist, including the limited access of girls to higher-level mathematics and science classes, and over-programming of girls into unchallenging and gender-biased courses of study such as traditionally female vocational coursework (Sadker & Sadker, 1994). When these lowered expectations for females intersect with similarly low expectations for Latina students, the combination can be extremely detrimental to the educational achievement and self-confidence of Latinas.

Confidence is a complex construct tied to identity, as Steele's work on stereotype threat has demonstrated (Steele, 1997). Not only are experiences of ethno-racial discrimination and sexism powerful external barriers for Latina/os, they can also erode a positive identity, and more specifically, one's educational confidence. Internalization of these experiences can result in Latinas/os feeling ignored, invisible, abused, and/or oppressed. A 1992 report from the American Association of University Women (AAUW), for example, revealed that among elementary school girls, Latina girls reported relatively high (68%) levels of being "happy as I am." By high school, all girls reported drops in such measures of self-esteem, but Hispanic girls reported the biggest percentage drop (down to 30%). Latinas/os have to struggle against internalizing negative experiences in order to be able to develop a healthy sense of self and maintain the ability to be confident.

Men of color, including Latinos, are in a different double bind in that given the social construction of masculinity, all men in general are expected to be strong, powerful and successful. For both males and females, institutional racism has resulted in continued stereotypes and deficit-thinking attitudes targeted toward Latina/o students that discourage success in school (Rosenbloom & Way, 2004; Valenzuela, 1999). For instance, Latina/os are often assumed to be gang members by teachers and counselors simply because they speak Spanish (Ginorio & Huston, 2001). Latino families are also beset by stereotypes, including that Latina/o parents do not care about their children's education (Villenas & Deyhle, 1999; Rolón-Dow, 2005), in spite of data demonstrating the opposite (NCES, 1995). School staff often overestimate the literacy skills, knowledge of the workings of the school system, and other resources Latino families have to assist their children academically (Romo & Falbo, 1996), resulting in assessments of lack of interest on the parents' part. Schools that take into consideration Latino families' levels of cultural capital and commit to responding to these needs report increased levels of parental involvement and student achievement (López, Scribner, & Mahitivanichcha, 2001).

Sexist ideologies also influence the educational experiences of Latina/o students. New research is beginning to show how Latina students in particular are subjected to hyper-sexualized identity formation, which impacts their schooling experiences (Rolon-Dow, 2005). Teachers' sexist attitudes toward Latina students as hyper-sexualized girls often lead to different educational expectations and teaching practices. Additionally, the traditional gender bias in some Latina/o cultures, where women are expected to defer to their men (fathers, brothers, etc.) and adhere to different expectations than boys (as illustrated by Hernández-Truyol, 2003) serves to perpetuate this hyper-feminine socialization that has morphed into hyper-sexualization.

Immigrant status plays an important role in the context of U.S. schooling of Latina/o students. Although the issue of gender has been relatively unexplored in the literature on immigrant youth, several scholars do identify a general pattern that is consistent with the national trend: immigrant girls outperform boys in educational settings (Brandon, 1991; Portes & Rumbaut, 2001; Rong & Brown, 2001). In their recent report on second generation Latina/o youth, Portes and Rumbaut (2001) found that boys are less engaged and have significantly lower grades, lower level of interest and work effort, and lower career and educational goals. Boys are also less likely to adhere to their parents' language compared to girls. In a study on Mexican-American adolescents, Stanton-Salazar (2001) stated that boys were less likely to be engaged with teachers and counselors. In a recent study by Suárez-Orozco and Qin-Hilliard (2004), immigrant boys tended to demonstrate lower academic achievement and encountered more challenges in schools than immigrant girls did. Boys reported feeling less support from teachers and staff and were more likely to perceive school as a negative, hostile, and racist environment. The authors suggested that immigrant boys' poor performance may be due to a combination of low social support in schools and negative teacher expectations.

Latinas are being shortchanged in the classroom because they face an institution that often judges them based upon their ethnicity and language, and disregards the cultural capital that they and their families possess. In addition to those issues of gendered interaction faced by girls of other ethnicities, Latinas must contend with the hyper-sexualization and hyper-feminization thrust upon them by societal stereotypes, both within school, and their own culture. With regards to immigration status, however, Latinas do appear to have an advantage over Latinos in their performance in schools. However, given the recent heated debates throughout the country over immigration, new research may be needed to highlight the effects of a students' immigration status on teacher expectations and interactions.

Linguistic Bias in Schools

More than 4 in 10 Latina/o students are English-language learners (ELL). Despite these numbers, language minority students of all ethno-racial groups continue to be provided curricula that dismiss and undervalue their linguistic needs. Most programs for ELLs are not based on language acquisition research for effective instruction of Spanish speakers, and are staffed by educators who lack proper training (Rumberger, Gándara, & Merino, 2006). Highly scripted lessons with a sizeable amount of decontextualized skills practice are common practice in urban classrooms. Scripted programs compounded with increased testing requirements in English, force teachers to emphasize decoding skills and abandon meaningful literacy and culturally responsive teaching for Latina/o students (Gándara, 2000; Gutiérrez et al., 2002).

Presently, the English-only movement is a language-based conflict triggered by a fear of change in the structures of power, class, and ethnicity, and not by concerns regarding language per se (Crawford, 2000; Gutierrez et al., 2002). Federal legislation, particularly the No Child Left Behind Act (2001), reaffirms the supremacy of monolingualism for language minority students. No Child Left Behind replaced the 1968 Bilingual Education Act, formerly Title VII, with the "English Language Acquisi-

tion, Language Enhancement, and Academic Achievement Act," or Title III. Although No Child Left Behind does not prohibit federal funding for bilingual education, it forcefully ends federal support for bilingual education. It emphasizes the "rapid acquisition" of English and the "quick exit" from Title III programs, which ultimately contradict strong research claims of the benefits of longer-term developmental bilingual education programs (Thomas & Collier, 2002; Slavin & Cheung, 2003; Cummins, 2000). Additionally, many states have enacted laws limiting or eliminating bilingual education, most notably Proposition 227 in California in 1998, and the recent enactment of such laws in Arizona (in 2000) and Massachusetts (in 2002) (Rethinking Schools, 2002/2003).

The relentless chipping away of bilingual education has immediate consequences for Latina/o students. Wright (2005) argued that No Child Left Behind is failing to meet the needs of Latina/o students in K–12 schools. He stated that the goals of Limited English Proficiency (LEP) programs are simply to mainstream the students as soon as possible and to teach them the content of the state standardized exam. The pressure of raising test scores discourages instruction focusing on the true needs of LEP students, such as primary-language instruction and culturally responsive curricula. In addition, the majority of LEP students are being forced to take standardized tests in a language in which they are not yet proficient. Teachers are being pressured to abandon what they recognize as good instruction for LEP students to prepare them for tests.

Equally important, the move away from bilingual education threatens the *educación* of Latina/o students. While popular with the public at large, educational policies that promote complete linguistic assimilation contain hidden costs for Latina/o students, depriving them of key social, familial, and educational resources. Bilingualism is not just an attribute of the person that can be measured by written assessments of formal language use; bilingualism is also a behavior that occurs in specific contexts. As Urciuoli (1996) argued, the practice of code switching in the formal school setting is perceived as demonstrating "bilingual" proficiency by both parents and students, but teachers consider it as monolingual use of both languages. This kind of language use is not amenable to testing and is often judged as deficient use rather than innovative application. Yet, only a few U.S. schools are encouraging Latina/o students to retain their heritage language (Alliance for the Advancement of Heritage Languages, 2006). For Latinas, bilingualism and a strong sense of ethnic identity can overcome gender barriers and enhance school success (O'Halloran, 1995).

Lack of Minority Teachers and Teachers Prepared to Work *with* Latino/a Communities

The relative dearth of Latina/o teachers, and teachers who are prepared to work in the challenging environments many Latina/o students face (i.e., high-poverty schools with few resources), serves as another strike against equity for Latina/o students in America's schools. In fact, Latinas are less likely to find support at school for high-educational achievement than other women in U.S. society (Hernández, 1995). Only 42% of Latinas reported teachers or guidance counselors (37%) as sources of career advice (Marlino & Wilson, 2006). Yet Rivera and Gallimore (2006) have shown that when that support is present, those Latinas are more likely to go to college.

According to statistics from the U.S. Department of Education (2002), 84% of all elementary and secondary teachers are European Americans (Snyder & Hoffman, 2003; Zavella, 1997). The number of Latino teachers is increasing slightly, but the percentages are still very small—approximately 5%. In California, where Latina/o students comprised about 47% of California's public school K–12 population, only 15% of the teachers were Latina/o (California Department of Finance, 2005). As a result, Latina/o students are not exposed to teachers who share their cultural or linguistic background, and when such teachers are missing, minority students land more frequently in special-education classes, have higher absentee rates, and tend to be less involved in school activities (Rueda, Gallego, & Moll, 2000; Monzo & Rueda, 2001). Moreover, a lack of minority teachers hampers the school's ability to relate to a diverse student body and boost parental involvement (Monzo & Rueda, 2001).

Not only are Latino/a teachers missing from schools, many Latina/o teachers have been taught to dismiss the value of their own cultural legacies (Quiocho & Rios, 2000). Few teachers graduating from colleges of education today have been exposed to cultural competency or antiracism training. Colleges of education do not teach skills to prospective teachers that would allow them to learn from the communities in which they teach (Grinberg, Goldfarb, & Saavedra, 2005). One of the ways colleges and schools of education can better serve the needs of Latina students is to revisit the epistemological bases of our teacher preparation courses. Nieto (2000) has argued that non-Latino/a teachers who know their student's language and are familiar with their culture can be effective with Latina/o students. As many scholars (e.g. Darling-Hammond, 1997; Moulthrop, Calegari, & Eggers, 2005; Temin, 2003) indicated, urban schools and financially disadvantaged schools and districts often experience a dearth of qualified teachers, and thus are often the proving ground for young teachers who are new to the profession. In these schools, the knowledge and skill sets needed to be an effective teacher in educational environments that put students at-risk of failing are often quite different from the knowledge and skills proffered in teacher-preparation programs and professional-development sessions (Massell, 2000). The gap between what teacher-credentialing programs teach and what is required of teachers working with at-risk populations can be staggering, and the learning curve for new teachers can be quite steep in the first few years.

The dearth of Latina/o teachers is likely to continue in spite of reports that teaching is the profession most often mentioned by high-school Latinas while at the same time those Latinas reported that they have no information about what is needed in order to pursue that degree (Rivera & Gallimore, 2006). Quiocho and Rios (2000), citing Su (1996), reported that while teaching is a respected profession among Latina/os, their own personal experiences of discrimination regarding English proficiency and race served as barriers to their pursuit of teaching. In short, colleges of education need to do a much better job of recruiting Latina/os and of preparing teacher candidates to advocate for the *educación* of Latina students.

Gendered, Classed, and Linguistic Segregation for Latina/o Students

The list of previously discussed impediments to Latina/o students in this nation's schools is significant. From ethno-racial, linguistic, and gender bias within schools to teen pregnancy to a lack of qualified Latina/o teachers to sexual harassment in schools, Latina/os face significant obstacles to higher educational attainment. However, the most significant obstacle is the *de facto* segregation that many Latina/os face when they step onto their school campuses. According to Orfield and Lee (2006), Latina/o students are the most segregated group of students, on average attending schools that are 55% Latina/o; they attend schools with the lowest proportion of White students (28% White). Additionally, the proportion of Latina/os attending schools that are more than 50% minority in composition has increased steadily since the 1991–1992 school year. This segregation is compounded by the high-risk nature of many majority Latina/o schools (i.e. high poverty, presence of gangs, etc.), as well as linguistic and class-based segregation.

Because of this segregation, most Latina/o students are educated at public high schools with different characteristics than the public schools educating White, African American, or American Indian students. Latinas/os are much more likely to attend the nation's largest public high schools. While 10% of public high schools have an enrollment of at least 1,838 students each, more than 56% of Latinas/os attend these large public high schools, in comparison with 32% of African Americans and 26% of Whites. In addition, Latinas/os are more likely to be at high schools with fewer and lesser-quality instructional resources. Nearly 37% of Latinas/os are educated at public schools with a student/teacher ratio of 22:1 in comparison to 14% of African American students and 13% of White students (Fry 2005). Schools in urban areas and with higher student-teacher ratios have higher dropout rates (Rumberger & Thomas, 2000).

Most Latina/os are also concentrated in high poverty and low-achieving schools— in fact, 45% of Latina/o students attend schools in high-poverty areas. These schools receive about $1,000 less per student than schools with fewer minority students (U.S. Senate HELP Committee, 2002). Latina/o students are concentrated in schools with a poor record of graduating students and sending them onto college. The situation is compounded since most Latina/o students live in large states with high-stakes high-school graduation tests and no affirmative action programs for college admissions (California, Texas, and Florida). In spite of *Méndez v. Westm*inster and *Brown v. Board of Education* (Jennings, 2004), what has been done to provide desegregated education for Latina/o students has failed.

Serious segregation is developing by language (Orfield, 2001). English learners are much more likely than their English-only peers to attend schools with large concentrations of English learners. In 2005, more than one third of California English learners attended just 15% of the state's public schools where they comprised more than 50% of the student body. At the elementary level, more than one half of California English learners attended 21% of the state's public schools where they comprised more than 50% of the student body. According to Rumberger, et al. (2006), this information is significant for several reasons. For one, linguistic segregation ensures that English learners are not exposed to English-language role models. In addition, schools with high concentrations of English learners are less likely to have fully certified teachers than schools with high concentrations of native English speakers, even after accounting for differences in school resources.

School segregation occurs not only by level of funding, but also other measures related to academic success. Using 2003–2004 data from public high schools in the state of California (with 6.3 million students in K–12 system), Yun and Moreno (2006) provided evidence of how concentrated disadvantage at K–12 level affected access to college. Measures of schooling disadvantage such as level of poverty, percent of English learners in a school, level of teacher certification, and number of AP courses were related to ethno-racial isolation. Not only were Latinos and Whites the most isolated from other ethno-racial groups, the isolation of Latinos was accompanied with lower access to AP courses and to certified teachers. More than 50% of all Latino students in California enrolled in isolated or hyper-isolated schools (Hidalgo, 2005).

These patterns of ethno-racial isolation can be characterized as tracking at the community level. Similarly, tracking into minimal educational development is enforced by the barriers to registration into schools and access to financial aid that exist for undocumented immigrants as well as children of immigrants with various visa statuses enforce tracking into minimal educational development.

The many facets of segregation—ethnic/racial, linguistic, financial, class—each contribute to the lowered educational achievement and attainment of Latina/o students. The high-risk, high-poverty nature of many Latina/o-dominated schools serves to separate Latina/o students even more starkly than the separation by ethno-race alone. The high-risk schools that many Latina/o students attend condemn many to a course of educational failure through their lack of resources, poor track records, and lack of both advanced courses of study and teachers qualified to teach such courses. This, perhaps, is the most distressing fact about the educational segregation faced by Latina/os. Not only is the education that a disproportionate number of Latina/os receive a separate education, it is also inherently unequal.

WHAT IF K–12 SCHOOLS PROVIDED LATINA/OS A "BETTER EDUCATION"?

The success of "better education" or *buena educación* would be measured as much by outcomes as by processes that lead to the elimination of inequalities between Latinas and Latinos, and between Latina/os and other ethno-racial groups in the United States. For example, Latina/os have made strides since 1970 in measures such as average National Assessment of Educational Progress scores in reading. However, in spite of gains in reading from fourth to eighth grade, the number of Hispanic students reading at the proficient level in eighth grade is only 17% (U.S. Dept. of Education cited in American Educational Research Association, 2004). Another measurable outcome where improvements might be noted is the proportion of Latina/os that drop out or are pushed out of school. From 1990 to 2000, the percentage of U.S. born Latina/os ages 16–19 years who did not have a high-school diploma fell from 15.2% to 14%, a barely improving situation. Unless the rate of improvement for educational attainment is increased, the educational gaps between Latina/os and other populations will continue to widen (American Association for the Advancement of Science, 2000).

The process *in* schools would center on providing skills that would guarantee the outcomes we all desire: equity in high-school graduation rates, in college attendance, and in graduation from college. These outcomes would not be obtained by the elimination of the strengths that students bring with them, including their ethnic identity and language skills. A process that increases success for Latina/o students is to be exposed to diverse school personnel who believe that all students can succeed (Lucas, Henze, & Donato, 1990).

Stories abound about the powerful impact that one person can have with otherwise impoverished and undereducated individuals and communities from Jaime Escalante, whose story was made famous in the movie "Stand and Deliver" to J. J. Guajardo, a teacher in Brownsville, Texas. In Brownsville, one of the poorest school districts in Texas, 93% of the students are designated as "economically disadvantaged" by the Texas Education Agency, and almost all (98%) are Latina/os (Gándara, 2005). Guajardo introduced chess into the Brownsville schools in 1991. The school district began to win state titles in only two years, and in 2005, a 7-year-old from Brownsville was the No. 3 player in the United States among 7-year-olds, and an 8-year-old is ranked second nationally among that age group. The 7-year-old described his chess team as "very close. We play together. We eat together. If one person loses, we all lose. We are like one heart that cannot be torn" (Gándara, 2005, p. A14). Just one person believing in the capabilities of children who otherwise would not be expected to achieve can make it possible for them to succeed.

While individuals' devotion and passion can supplement what may be lacking in time and resources enough to make a difference for individual students, an institutional commitment is needed to sustain the kind of effort that led to the Brownsville team's success. The decision of the school district to fund afternoon chess programs and to hire chess coaches is such a commitment. Without such an institutional commitment, the successful AP calculus "dynasty" that Escalante had established at Garfield High School in Los Angeles disappeared within five years of his departure (Jesness, 2002). Institutional commitments also signal that the program is structurally important and central to the mission of the school or college.

As the outcomes of the Rural Girls in Science program demonstrated, cocurricular programs that increase students' knowledge about college education and offer opportunities for participating students to experience success in college-related tasks lead to increases in Latina, American Indian, and White girls who plan to attend college, actually attend college, and even persevere in majors (Ginorio, Huston, Frevert, & Bierman, 2002). Universities and school districts working together can provide these systemic opportunities.

Systemic approaches might involve diversity training and the hiring of more Latina/o educators. The multi-ethnic classroom creates a demand for teachers who are aware of the cultural differences "that affect learning styles, behavior, mannerisms, and relationships with school and home" (Skylarz 1993, p. 22) within the student population. Teachers also need to understand differences among Latina/os and they need to move beyond stereotypes by paying more attention to generational differences and the varied histories of Latina/o groups and regional cultures (Zavella, 1997). These students need the support of teachers who have an understanding of cultural and family practices and behaviors. Students also need teachers from their cultures who can serve as role models for educational achievement and success (Quiocho & Rios, 2000).

Nowhere is the importance of well-trained personnel as evident as in bilingual education. The importance of bilingual education for students who do not speak English as their first language goes beyond language acquisition. Bilingual education is a prerequisite for establishing a school environment that welcomes all students' cultures, sends a positive message to students, and sets the groundwork for a relationship of respect and equality between schools and all families and communities. Latina/o students require bilingual and bicultural programs that maintain and affirm their cultures and languages.

Schools and colleges also need to do a better job of establishing meaningful relationships with Latina/o parents in the areas of recruitment and particularly retention. In fact, research has shown that supportive family relationships are more important than the student's family composition, income level, or intelligence scores, and that successful Latina/o students are more likely to have a teacher, coach, or other person in the school who is willing to advocate for their success (Hernández, 1995). Programs that focus on Latinas, such as the "Hispanic mother-daughter program" at the University of Texas-Austin (http://www.utexas.edu/features/archive/2002/motherdaughter.html) and Arizona State University (http://www.asu.edu/studentaffairs/mss/msc/hmpd.htm) have successfully targeted high-risk girls who come from families in which no member has graduated from college. Activities help girls and their mothers maintain interest in school and raise education and career aspirations (See Appendix C in Ginorio & Huston, 2001 and also Romo & Falbo, 1996 for lists of programs that have demonstrated academic success with Latinas).

Various factors have been identified as influencing persistence and performance for Latinas, including mother's influence (Vásquez, 1982), and a positive view of intellectual ability combined with a strong sense of responsibility for her academic future (Wycoff, 1996). In addition, the unambivalent belief in the capabilities of a student of color conveyed by teachers, mentors, and supervisors can go a long way toward encouraging confidence, persistence, performance, and motivation. Although these qualities evolve and develop by way of numerous avenues, one of the most prominent paths is the access to at least one supportive caretaker or mentor in a person's nuclear or extended family or in their social world (Levine & Niddifer, 1996, Walsh, 1996).

In a sample of high-school seniors from the West Coast, only 28% of Latina/os had educational plans for attending a four-year college, compared to 34% of African Americans and 37% of Whites in that same sample. These ethnic differences in plans for college attendance disappeared when socioeconomic status (SES) was controlled for, demonstrating that these ethno-racial differences are modulated by SES (Hirschman & Lee, 2005). While SES accounts for a large part of this difference, other structural patterns of college attendance such as going to college part-

time and attending colleges with lower graduation rates (Fry, 2002) also affect outcomes. Latina/os are also more likely to be living at home while attending college; Latinas are particularly affected by the pressure to attend college while living at home. These structural patterns are significantly related to the low percent of Latina/os graduating with four-year degrees.

Latina/os are reported to have high occupational (Farmer, Wardrop, & Rotella, 1999) and educational aspirations (Hirschman, Lee, & Emeka, 2004), but the actual expectations to achieve these educational aspirations are lower. Phinney, Dennis, and Osorio (in press) reported on the motivation to attend college in a sample of first-year students. Motivation varied significantly across four ethnic groups, with Asian Americans and Latina/os being the most motivated to attend because of family expectations. Their data shows that this expectation had been internalized so that it acts as an internal motivator. In addition, all ethnic groups examined (African Americans, Asian Americans, and Latina/os) reported a motivation to prove that one can succeed academically that we could label as "let me show you," since it is often prompted by experiences with discouragement to go beyond high school. A subset of these students were followed through their second year of study. This second study demonstrated a relation between ethnic identity, motivation for college, and self-efficacy Phinney, Dennis and Rivera (under review). reported that students with "both strong ethnic and personal motivation . . . demonstrat[ed] higher self-efficacy and life satisfaction" (p. 29).

Higher education also needs to provide "better education" for Latina/os. Ibarra (2001), in his book, *Beyond Affirmative Action*, described the importance of reframing the cultural context of the academy, including the recommendation of a new infrastructure for teaching, learning, and institutional change. Those Latina/os that make it into college discover that institutions of higher learning tend to be competitively oriented to a larger extent than K–12 school systems. The persistent family orientation of Latina/os, considered a source of strength and resiliency within the culture, is sometimes judged a deterrent to success by faculty members who value the independence, individuality, and competition more typical among Anglo-Americans (Seymour & Hewitt, 1997; Vásquez, 1994). Ibarra suggested that the focus on the Western analytical science models in higher education results in the exclusion of other legitimate learning modes and styles. He reviewed several paradigms and proposed a "Learning-and-Effectiveness" paradigm directed toward opening up new sources of knowledge—finding other ways of thinking and learning—that are derived from diverse cultural and gender perspectives. The paradigm is characterized as "connecting diversity to work," and taps fresh perspectives (Ibarra, 2001; Vásquez & Jones, 2006).

Gender Equity and Better Education for Latinas

Under present conditions of education with all of the short-comings just listed, educational outcomes for Latina/os are very low in the United States. Whether measured by attendance in school, performance in tests, access to resources in schools, participation in enrichment programs, access to college, or graduation from any level of education Latina/os are at the bottom of these scales. These measures run counter to the often-reported finding of the high motivation and interest in education by Latino/as.

Compared to Latinos, however, Latinas are doing better in many of these measures; most significantly graduation from high school and from college at the bachelor's level. Their educational experiences are still colored by stereotypic views of them as Latinas both within their communities and in the larger society. While it is important to document the pervasive inequities that continue to impact the educational experiences of Latina students, there is also a rich history of resistance aimed at dismantling racist and sexist educational policies for Latina/o students and communities (Guajardo & Guajardo, 2004; Hidalgo, 2005; Jennings, 2004; López, 2006). Chicana and other Latina feminists, for instance, have provided a gendered analysis of the ways in which traditional forms of politics and resistance have tended to make invisible the political activities that women of color engage in as part of their connection to home, family, and community (Pardo, 1998; Delgado-Bernal, 1998; Ochoa, 1999). These activists' work belies the idea that education is not important for Latina/o families.

POLICY RECOMMENDATIONS

"Better education" for all Latina/os involves policies that are instituted at every level of society, from practices within classrooms—such as curricula—to funding priorities at the state level. The following are some policy recommendations that flow from the materials presented in this chapter.

- Eliminate tracking of Latina/os into stereotypical programs or through lack of bilingual education by
  - Better utilization of middle-school and high-school guidance counselors
  - Increasing access to academic enrichment programs at K–12 levels as well as, when appropriate, to special education
  - Increasing state support for bilingual education in the form of greater number of classrooms providing quality bilingual education
  - Not discriminating against students on the basis of documentation status
- Ensure the effectiveness of instruction in K–12 for Latino/as at the staff level by
  - Requiring teachers and other academic staff to continually update their cultural competency training to include issues related to gender and diversity among Latino populations, especially in states with large numbers of ethno-racial populations
  - Retaining and supporting Latina/o teachers, counselors, and administrators
- Ensure the effectiveness of instruction in K–12 for Latino/as at the practice level by
  - Using high-stakes testing as only one of the measures of achievement and successful performance for ALL students
  - Eliminating all testing and assessment that yields differences that can be tracked by gender or ethno-race
  - Designing and using educational models based on cooperative strategies

  - Designing and using gender and ethno-racial-conscious curricula, and addressing the hidden curriculum that continues to support racist and sexist assumptions
  - Developing and using a Latina/o-appropriate sex-education curriculum
- Recognize the importance of the cultural capital that families have by
  - Developing programs that increase parents' effectiveness in supporting their children's educational aspirations
  - Encouraging students to develop recruitment and retention programs themselves
- Improve teacher preparation programs so that they come ready to be effective teachers of Latina/os by
  - Ensuring that cultural competency training acknowledges the complexities within the various Latino populations and across ethno-racial populations
  - Training more bilingually certified teachers
- Increase access of Latina/os to higher education through the
  - Establishment of recruitment and retention programs aimed at first-generation Latina/o students and their families, including mentoring programs
  - Development and implementation of better articulation agreements between community colleges and four-year universities
  - Development and implementation of connections between Latino communities and four-year colleges
- Provide Latina/o serving K–12 schools with the resources needed for the task of eliminating disparities by
  - Extending to Latina/os the benefits of smaller high schools
  - Recruiting Latina/os as school personnel through financial-aid incentives for their college education
  - Working with both public and private foundations to support innovative strategies in education for Latina/os

The implementation of all of the above policies needs to be done with attention to gender equity. Culturally sensitive training for counselors would ensure that sexist stereotypes in the larger culture or the Latino community would play no part in the advice that students receive about taking courses and careers open to them. Similarly, interventions such as pregnancy prevention or elimination of sexual harassment would not be aimed exclusively at girls.

One of the ways in which implementation of gender equity may be achieved is through the presence of a Title IX coordinator. By law, the Title IX coordinator is charged with monitoring compliance in all districts receiving federal funds. The law does not require a Title VI coordinator, but if such existed then the two coordinators could complement their efforts and prepare disaggregated data about students. Community groups or parent-teachers associations could ensure that the districts have these coordinators and that annual reports are submitted.

NEW DIRECTIONS IN RESEARCH

As we write this, in California more than 50% of the students entering kindergarten in the fall of this year (2006) will be Latina/os (Hendricks, 2003). As David Hayes-Bautista (2003, p. 1) stated about California: "To the extent we invest in this new majority, our future looks good, and to the extent we choose not to invest, our own future looks grim." Research needs to address the cutting-edge issues, such as the impact of new immigration policies on Latina enrollments, and revisit ongoing questions such as the relation of pregnancy among teen Latinas and educational achievement. We identify a few areas that need attention:

- Closely examine the impact of high-stakes testing on graduation rates for Latina/os
- Examine the impact of increasing sexualization of girls and young women on Latinas' educational outcomes
- Conduct longitudinal studies to examine the relation between school disengagement and pregnancy among Latinas
- Develop metrics to measure "gender equity" that are not based solely on numerical "gender difference"
- Examine decisions related to college attendance to institutions far from home by gender and socioeconomic status
- Examine the impact of immigration policies on educational outcomes for Latino/as, distinguishing between documented and undocumented students
- Explore how the implementation of small school impacts all aspects of the education of Latina/os, from parental involvement to college-going
- Examine the strengths and not just the weaknesses of the educational experiences of Latina/os
- Identify the kinds of work experiences in high school and college that foster graduation

We call on researchers to be attentive not only to the impact of ethno-race but also to gender in all the work they do. It is frustrating to find an excellent report on drop outs and not find a single reference to gender or girls. Disaggregation of data by gender and ethnicity is necessary for more accurate findings.

CONCLUSION

As we write this, most of the differences in educational outcomes that exist favor Latinas. Yet, Latina/os lag behind all other ethno-racial groups at all levels of educational achievement. While some may conclude that this is story of gender equity between Latinas and Latinos, as researchers, we ask whether the success of Latinas compared to Latinos indicated the elimination of gender barriers or some methodological artifact of the gender-differences approach. The higher up in the K–12 edu-

cational system students are, the more likely it is that studies will report no significant gender differences in educational outcome. This lack of reported difference may be caused by a weeding-out effect, considering that 30% to 40% of Latina/os do not finish high school. Equally plausible, an acculturation effect for the "survivors" (used in the statistical sense of the word) may be operating. Since females "survive" at a higher rate than males at all levels except in some areas of graduate education, the phenomenon is gendered; however, discrimination against females qua females may not be visible using "gender-differences" approaches. Furthermore, the conflation of ethno-race and class is so high in this country, that the main effect reported for many quantitative studies of Latina/os at the college level is attributed to SES rather than ethno-race or ethnoculture.

As we write this, the expectations of more access to quality formal education fought for by the parents and students at Elsa, Texas, are largely unrealized. While access has increased, the improvements in education have not eliminated the structural as well as individual acts of disrespect toward Latina/o students and parents by teachers and other school personnel. In many regions of the United States the miseducation of Latina/os still leaves high-school graduates with barely enough skills to qualify them for farm work and other low-paying jobs.

For far too long this country has relied on the efforts of Latina mothers who advocate for bilingual education for their children, Latina and culturally competent teachers who infuse their classrooms with culturally relevant curricula, and Latina students who transformatively overcome the educational barriers that stand in their way to get whatever measures of *buena educación* Latina/os have received. It is time to invest in the gender equitable and culturally responsive education that is needed so that Latina/os and all students succeed.

ACKNOWLEDGMENTS

The authors would like to thank Nancy Felipe Russo, Arizona State Univ., Tempe, AZ, Ellen Silber, Fordham Univ., New York, NY, & Carman DelgadoVotaw, Alliance for Children and Families, Washington, DC, for their helpful comments in an earlier version of the chapter. For discussions and reviews, we thank Rachel Chapman, Michelle Habell-Pallan, Sonnet Retman, and Shirley Yee. Jean S. Phinney, Charley Hirschman, and Nancy Felipe Russo, shared work their work-in-progress. This work could not have been completed without assistatcne with references of Martha Gamboa, Pilar Herrero Sorensen, and Sara Díaz; and the editorial guidance provided by Sue Klein and Dianne Pollard.

References

Alliance for the Advancement of Heritage Languages (2006). Retrieved August 22, 2006, from http://www.cal.org/heritage/programs/profiles/

American Association for the Advancement of Science (AAAS). (2000). *Limited progress: The status of Hispanic Americans in Science and*

Engineering. Retrieved May 20, 2005 from http://ehrweb.aaas.org/mge/Reports/Report2/Report2.html.

American Association of University Women (AAUW). (1992). *How schools shortchange girls: A study of major findings on girls and education*. New York: Marlowe.

American Association of University Women (AAUW). (2001). *Hostile hallways: Bullying, teasing, and sexual Harassment in school*. Washington, DC: American Association of University Women.

American Educational Research Association (2004). Closing the gap: High achievement for student of color. *Research Points, 2*(3), 1–4

Artiles, A. J., & Ortiz, A. A. (2002). English language learners with special education needs: Contexts and possibilities. In A. J. Artiles & A. A. Ortiz (Eds.), *English language learners with special education needs: Identification, assessment, and instruction* (pp. 3–27). McHenry, IL: Delta Systems and Center for Applied Linguistics (CAL).

Brandon, P. (1991). Gender differences in young asian americans' educational attainment. *Sex Roles, 25*, 45–61.

California Department of Finance. (2005). California Public K–12 Enrollment Projections by Ethnicity.

Ceja, M. (2000). *Making Decisions About College: Understanding the Information Sources of Chicana Students*. (ERIC Document Reproduction Service No. ED448669)

Conchas, G. Q. (2001). Structuring failure and success: Understanding the variability in Latino school engagement. *Harvard Educational Review, 71*(3), 475–504.

Crawford, J. (2000). *At war with diversity: U.S. language policy in an age of anxiety*. Clevedon, UK: Multilingual Matters Ltd.

Cummins, J. (2000). *Language, power, and pedagogy: Bilingual children in the crossfire*. Clevedon, England: Multilingual Matters.

Darling-Hammond, L. (1997, November). *Doing what matters most: Investing in quality teaching*. New York: National Commission on Teaching and America's Future.

Delgado Bernal, D. (1998). Using a Chicana feminist epistemology in educational research. *Harvard Educational Review, 68*(4), 555–582.

Delgado Bernal, D. (1998). Grassroots leadership reconceptualized: Chicana oral histories and the 1968 East Los Angeles school blowouts. *Frontiers: A Journal of Women Studies, 19*(2), 113–142.

Dickson, M.C. (2001). *Executive Summary: Latina teen pregnancy: Problems and prevention*. Retrieved May 25, 2006, from http://www.prcdc.org/summaries/latinapreg/latinapreg.html

Education Week. (2001). Bilingual students with disabilities get special help.

Farmer, H. W., Wardrop, J. L., & Rotella, S. C. (1999). Antecedent factors differentiating women and men in science/nonscience careers. *Psychology of Women Quarterly, 23*, 763–780.

Flores, B. M. (2005). The intellectual presence of the deficit view of Spanish Speaking children in the educational literature during the 20th century. In P. Pedraza & M. Rivera (Eds.). *Latino education: An agenda for community action research* (pp. 231–258). Mahwah, NJ: Lawrence Erlbaum Associates.

Flores, Y. (2006). La salud: Latina adolescents constructing identities, negotiating health decisions. In J. Denner & B. L. Guzmán (Eds.) *Latina girls: Voices of adolescent strength in the United States* (pp. 199–111). New York, NY: New York University Press.

Freeman, C. (2004, November). *Trends in educational equity of girls and women: 2004*. Washington, DC: National Center for Education Statistics.

Fry, R. (2002). Latinos in higher education: Many enroll, few graduate. *Pew Hispanic Center Web site*. Washington, DC. Retrieved April 23, 2006 from http://pewhispanic.org/reports/report.php?ReportID=11

Fry, R. (2003). Hispanic youth dropping out of U.S. schools: Measuring the challenge. *Pew Hispanic Center Report*. Washington, DC. Retrieved August 17, 2006 from http://pewhispanic.org/reports/report.php?ReportID=19

Fry, R. (2005). *The high schools Hispanics attend: Size and other key characteristics*. Washington, DC: Pew Hispanic Center.

Gallegos-Castillo, A. (2006). La casa: Negotiating family cultural practices, constructing identities. In J. Denner & B. L. Guzmán (Eds.) *Latina girls: Voices of adolescent strength in the United States* (pp. 44– 58). New York: New York University Press.

Gándara, P. (2000). In the aftermath of the storm: English learners in the post-227 era. *Bilingual Research Journal, 24*(1/2), 1–13.

Gándara, R. (2005, May 28). Valley kids master chess. *Austin American-Statesman*, A1, A14.

García, E. E., & Gonzales, D. M. (2006, July). Pre-K and Latinos: The foundation for America's future. *Pre-K Now Research Series*. Retrieved August 18, 2006, from http://www.preknow.com/documents/Pre-KandLatinos_July2006.pdf

Ginorio, A. G., Gutiérrez, L. Cauce, A. M., & Acosta, M. (1995). Psychological issues for Latinas. In H. Landrine, (Ed.), *Bringing cultural diversity to feminist psychology: Theory, research and practice* (pp. 241–264). Washington, DC: American Psychological Association.

Ginorio, A., & Martinez, J. (1998). Where are the Latinas? Ethno-race and gender in psychology Courses. *Psychology of Women Quarterly, 22*, 53–68.

Ginorio, A. B., & Huston, M. (2000). *"Road to the Future" pre-program survey: A window into social capital in the family and college aspirations of Latina and Latino students*. Unpublished manuscript, University of Washington, Seattle.

Ginorio, A. B., & Huston, M. (2001). *¡Sí, se puede! Yes, we can! Latinas in schools*. Washington, DC: American Association of University Women.

Ginorio, A. B., & Huston, M. (2001). [Pre-program survey of participants in the Rural Girls in Science's "Road to the Future" program]. Baseline data.

Ginorio, A. B., Huston, M., Frevert, K., & Bierman, J. (2002). Rural Girls in Science Project: From pipelines to affirming education. *Journal of Women and Minorities in Science and Engineering, 8*(3), 305–325.

Greene, J. P. (2002). *High school graduation rates in the United States*. Washington, DC: Black Alliance for Educational Outcomes.

Grinberg, J. G. A., Goldfarb, K. P., & Saavedra, E. (2005). Con pasión y con coraje: Schooling of Latino/a students and their teacher's education. In P. Pedraza & M. Rivera (Eds.). Latino education: *An agenda for community action research* (pp. 231–258). Mahwah, NJ: Lawrence Erlbaum Associates.

Grossman, H. (1998). *Achieving educational equality: Assuring all students an equal opportunity in school*. Springfield: Charles C. Thomas.

Guajardo, M. A., & Guajardo, F. J. (2004). The impact of Brown on the brown of South Texas: A micropolitcal perspective on the education of Mexican Americans in a South Texas Community. *American Educational Research Journal, 41*(3), 501–526.

Gutiérrez, K. D., Asato, J., Pacheco, M., Moll, L. C., Olson, K., Horng, E. L., et al. (2002). "Sounding American": The consequences of new reforms on English language learners. *Reading Research Quarterly, 37*(3), 328–343.

Hayes-Bautista, D. (2003). *Majority of babies born in california are Latino, UCLA study finds; majority of state's future students, workers, voters are latino*. Retrieved August 17, 2006, from Science Blog http://www.scienceblog.com/community/older/archives/O/c/ucl4334.shtml

Hendricks, T. (2003, February 6). State's Latino births surpass 50%, survey finds. *San Francisco Chronicle*, A17.

Hernandez, A. E. (1995). Do role models influence self efficacy and aspirations in Mexican American at-risk females? *Hispanic Journal of Behavioral Sciences, 17*(2), 256–263.

Hernandez-Truyol, B. E. (2003). Latinas-everywhere alien; Culture, gender, and sex. In A. K. Wing (Ed.), *Critical race feminism: A reader*. (pp. 57–69). New York: New York University Press.

Hidalgo, N. M. (2005). Latino/a families' epistemology. In P. Pedraza & M. Rivera (Eds.). *Latino education: An agenda for community action research* (pp. 375–402). Mahwah, NJ: Lawrence Erlbaum Associates.

Hirschman, C., & Lee, J. C. (2005). Race and ethnic inequality in educational attainment in the United States. In M. Rutter & M. Tienda

(Eds.). *Ethnicity and Causal Mechanisms* (pp. 107–138). Cambridge, U.K.: Cambridge University Press.

Hirschman, C., Lee, J. C., & Emeka, A. (2004). *Race and ethnic disparities in educational ambitions among high school seniors*. Manuscript in preparation.

Hooks, B. (1994). *Teaching to transgress. Education as the practice of freedom*. London: Routledge.

Hyams, M. (2006). *La escuela*: Young Latina women negotiating identities in school. In J. Denner & B. L. Guzmán (Eds.), *Latina girls: Voices of adolescent strength in the United States* (pp. 93–108). New York: New York University Press.

Ibarra, R. A. (2001). *Beyond affirmative action: Reframing the context of higher education*. Madison, WI: University of Wisconsin Press.

Jelinek, P. (2005, June 9). Hispanics fastest-growing minority, now one-seventh of U.S. population. *Associated Press*. Retrieved February 15, 2007, from Lexis Nexis database.

Jennings, L. (2004, May). The end of the "Mexican School." *Hispanic Business*, 26, 28.

Jesness, J. (2002, July). *Stand and Deliver revisited*. Retrieved August 7, 2006, from http://www.reason.com/0207/fe.jj.stand.shtml

Kagan, S. (1977). Social motives and behaviors of Mexican-American and Anglo-American children. In J. L. Martínez, Jr. (Ed.), *Chicano Psychology* (pp. 45–56). New York: Academic Press.

Knight, G. P., Cota, M. K., & Bernal, M. E. (1993). The socialization of cooperative, competitive, and individualistic preferences among Mexican American children: The mediating role of ethnic identity. *Hispanic Journal of Behavioral Sciences, 15*, 291–309.

Kozol, J. (2005). *The shame of the nation: The restoration of apartheid schooling in America*. New York: Crown.

Kulis, S., Marsiglia, F. F., & Hurdle, D. (2003). Gender identity, ethnicity, acculturation, and drug use: Exploring differences among adolescents in the Southwest. *Journal of Community Psychology, 31*(2), 167–188.

Ladson-Billings, G., & Tate, W. F. (1995). Toward a critical race theory of education. *Teachers College Record, 97*, 47–68.

Levine, A., & Nidiffer, J. (1996). *Beating the odds: How the poor get to college*. San Francisco: Jossey Bass Inc. Pub.

López, G. R., Scribner, J. D., & Mahitivanichcha, K. (2001). Redefining parental involvement: Lessons from high-performing migrant-impacted schools. *American Educational Research Journal, 38*(2), 253–288.

López, N. (2006). Resistance to race and gender oppression: Dominican high school girls in New York City. In J. Denner & B. L. Guzmán (Eds.) *Latina girls: Voices of adolescent strength in the United States* (pp. 79–92). New York: New York University Press.

Lucas, T., Henze, R., & Donato, R. (1990). Promoting the success of Latino language-minority students: An exploratory study of six high schools. *Harvard Educational Review, 60*(3), 315–340.

MacDonald, V-M., & Monkman, K. (2005). Setting the context: Historical perspectives on Latino/a education. In P. Pedraza & M. Rivera (Eds.). *Latino education: An agenda for community action research*. (pp. 47–73). Mahwah, NJ: Lawrence Erlbaum Associates.

Marlino, D., & Wilson, F. (2006). Career expectations and goals of Latina adolescents: Results from a nationwide study. In J. Denner & B. L. Guzmán (Eds.) *Latina girls: Voices of adolescent strength in the United States* (pp. 123–140). New York: New York University Press.

Massell, D. (2000). The district's role in building capacity: Four strategies. *CPRE Policy Briefs*. Philadelphia: University of Pennsylvania, Graduate School of Education. Retrieved February 15, 2007, from http://www.shankerinstitute.org.

Merten, D. E. (1997). The meaning of meanness: Popularity, competition, and conflict among junior high school girls. *Sociology of Education, 70*(3), 175–191.

Monzo, L., & Rueda, R. (2001). *Sociocultural factors in social relationships: Examining Latino teachers' and paraeducators' interactions with Latino students* (Research Report 9) Santa Cruz, CA and Washington, DC.

Moulthrop, D., Calegari, N.C., & Eggers, D. (2005). *Teachers have it easy: The big sacrifices and small salaries of America's teachers*. New York: The New Press.

National Center for Education Statistics, U.S. Department of Education (1995). *The educational progress of Hispanic students*. Number 4 of the findings from *The condition of education 1995* (NCES 95-767). Washington, DC: U.S. Department of Education.

National Center for Education Statistics, (2003). *Digest of Education Statistics* (Chapter 3, Postsecondary Education). U.S. Dept. of Education Institute of Education Sciences, Washington, DC. Retrieved May 20, 2005 from http://nces.ed.gov/programs/digest/d03/lt3.asp#c3.

National Center for Education Statistics, U.S. Department of Education (2003). *Postsecondary institutions in the United States: Fall 2002 and Degrees and other awards conferred: 2001–02* (NCES 2004-154). Retrieved February 16, 2006, from http://nces.ed.gov/pubsearch/pubsinfo.asp?pubid=2005154.

National Center for Education Statistics, U.S. Department of Education (2005). *Racial/Ethnic Distribution of Public School Students*. Retrieved July 30, 2005, from http://nces.ed.gov/programs/coe/2005/section1/indicator04.asp.

National Council of La Raza *Statistical Brief: Hispanic Education in the U.S.* (2007, January 8). Retrieved February 14, 2007, from http://www.nclr.org/content/publications/detail/43582/

National Council of La Raza *Statistical Brief: Hispanic Education in the U.S.* (2007, January 8). Retrieved February 14, 2007, from http://www.nclr.org/content/publications/detail/43582/No Child Left Behind Act of 2001, Pub. L. No. 107-110, § 115, Stat. 1425 (2002).

Oakes, J. (2005). *Keeping track: How schools structure inequality*. New Haven, CT: Yale University Press.

Ochoa, G. L. (1999). Everyday ways of resistance and cooperation: Mexican American women building puentes with Immigrants. *Frontiers: A Journal of Women Studies, 20*, 1–20.

O'Halloran, C. S. (1995). Mexican American female students who were successful in high school science courses. *Equity & Excellence in Education, 28*(2), 57–64.

Orfield, G. (2001). *Schools more separate: Consequences of a decade of resegregation*. Harvard University Civil Rights Project. Retrieved August 2, 2002, from http://www.civilrightsproject.harvard.edu/research/deseg/separate_schools01.php.

Orfield, G., & Lee, C. (2006). *Racial transformation and the changing nature of segregation*. Cambridge, MA: The Civil Rights Project at Harvard University.

Pardo, M. (1998). *Mexican American women activists: Identity and resistance in two Los Angeles communities*. Philadelphia: Temple University Press.

Pérez Huber, L., Huidor, O., Malagón, M. C., Sánchez, G., & Solórzano, D. G. (2006, March). *Falling through the cracks. Critical transitions in the Latina/o educational pipeline: 2006 Education Summit Report* (Chicano Studies Research Center Research Report No. 7). Retrieved April 23, 2006, from http://www.chicano.ucla.edu/center/events/Edu_Summit06/ResearchReports.html

Phinney, J., Dennis, J. M., & Osorio, N. T. (in press). Motivations to attend college among mong ethnically diverse college students. *Cultural Diversity and Ethnic Minority Psychology*.

Phinney, J. S., Dennis, J., & Rivera, W. (submitted). *Profiles of minority first-generation college students: A cluster analytic approach to studying ethnicity, motivation, and identity during the first two years of college*.

Polednak, A. P. (1997). Gender and acculturation in relation to alcohol use among Hispanic (Latino) adults in two areas of the northeastern United States. *Substance Use & Misuse, 32*(11), 1513–24.

Portes, A., & Hao, L. (2002). The price of uniformity: Language, family, and personality adjustment in the immigrant second generation. *Ethnic and Racial Studies, 25*, 889–912.

Portes, A., & Rumbaut, R. G. (2001). *Legacies: The story of the second generation*. Berkeley, C.A.: University of California Press.

Quintana-Baker, M. (2002). "A profile of Mexican American, Puerto Rican, and other Hispanic STEM doctorates: 1983-1997." *Journal of Women and Minorities in Science and Engineering, 8*, 99–121

Quiocho, A., & Rios, F. (2000). The power of their presence: Minority group teachers and schooling. *Review of Educational Research, 70*(4), 485–528.

Rethinking Schools. (2002/2003, Winter). Bilingual education is a human and civil right. *Rethinking Schools, 17*(2). Retrieved February 15, 2007, from http://www.rethinkingschools.org/archive/17_02/Bili172.shtml.

Rivera, W., & Gallimore, R. (2006). Latina adolescents' career goals: Resources for overcoming obstacles. In J. Denner & B. L. Guzmán (Eds.) *Latina girls: Voices of adolescent strength in the United States* (pp. 109–122). New York: New York University Press.

Rogers, A., & Gilligan, C. (1989). *Translating girls' voices: Two languages of development.* Cambridge: Harvard Graduate School of Education, Project on Women's Psychology and Girls' Development.

Rolón-Dow, R. (2005). Critical care: A color(full) analysis of care narratives in the schooling experiences of Puerto Rican girls. *American Educational Research Journal, 42*(1), 77–111.

Romo, H. D., & Falbo, T. (1996). *Latino high school graduation: Defying the odds.* Austin, TX: University of Texas Press.

Romo H.D. (1998). Educational opportunity in an Urban American High School: A cultural analysis. *Contemporary Sociology-A Journal of Reviews, 27,* 578–579.

Rong, X. L., & Brown, F. (2001). The effects of immigrant generation and ethnicity on educational attainment among young African and Caribbean Blacks in the United States. *Harvard Educational Review, 71,* 536–565.

Rosenbloom, S. R., & Way, N. (June 2004). Experiences of discrimination among African American, Asian American, and Latino adolescents in an urban high school. *Youth & Society, 35,* 420–451.

Rosenthal, R., & Jacobson, L. (1974). *Pygmalion in the classroom: Teacher expectations and pupils' intellectual development.* New York: Holt, Rinehart, and Winston.

Rueda, R., Gallego, M., & Moll, L. C. (2000). The least restrictive environment: A place or a context? *Remedial and Special Education Research Journal, 21*(2), 70–78.

Rumberger, R. W. & Thomas, S. L. (2000). The distribution of dropout and turnover rates among urban and suburban high schools. *Sociology of Education, 73,* 39–67.

Rumberger, R., Gándara, P., & Merino, B. (2006). Where California English Learners attend schools and why it matters. *UC Linguistic Minority Research Institute Newsletter, 15*(2), 1–3. Retrieved February 15, 2007, from http://lmri.ucb.edu/publications/newsletters/index.php

Rumberger, R. W., & Larson, K. A. (1998). Toward explaining differences in educational achievement among Mexican American Language-Minority students. *Sociology of Education, 7*(1), 69–92.

Russell, S. T., & Lee, F. C. H. (2006). Latina adolescent motherhood: A turning point? In J. Denner & B. L. Guzmán (Eds.), *Latina girls: Voices of adolescent strength in the United States* (pp. 212–225). New York: New York University Press.

Sadker, D., & Zittleman, K. (2005). Gender bias lives, for both sexes. *Education Digest, 70*(8), 27–30.

Sadker, M., & Sadker, D. (1994). *Failing at fairness: How America's schools cheat girls.* New York: Simon & Schuster.

Scott, J. (2005, May 16). Life at the top in America isn't just better, it's longer. *New York Times,* pp. A1, A18.

Seymour, E., & Hewitt, N. M. (1997). *Talking about leaving: Why undergraduates leave the sciences.* Boulder, CO: Westview Press.

Skylarz, D. P. (1993, May). Turning the promise of multicultural education into practice. *School Administrator, 50*(5), 18–20, 22.

Slavin, R. E., & Cheung, A. (2003). *Effective programs for English language learners: A best-evidence synthesis.* Baltimore: Johns Hopkins University, CRESPAR.

Sleeter, C. E. (1996). *Multicultural education as social activism.* Albany, NY: State University of New York Press.

Snyder, T. D., & Hoffman, C. M. (2003). *Digest of Educational Statistics (NCES 2003).* U.S. Department of Education, National Center for Educational Statistics. Washington DC: U.S. Government Printing Office.

Solórzano, D., & Ornelas, A. (2002). A critical race analysis of advanced placement classes: A case of educational inequalities. *Journal of Latinos and Education, 1,* 215–229.

Solórzano, D., Ledesma, M., Pérez, J., Burciaga, R., & Ornelas, A. (2003). *Latina equity in education: Gaining access to academic enrichment programs. Latino Policy & Issues Brief, 4.* Retrieved February 15, 2007, from http://www.chicano.ucla.edu/press/briefs/archive.asp

Stanton-Salazar, R. (2001). *Manufacturing hope and despair: The school and kin support networks of U.S.-Mexican youth.* New York: Teachers College Press.

Steele, C. M. (1997). A threat in the air: How stereotypes shape intellectual identity and performance. *American Psychologist 52,* 613–629.

Suárez-Orozco, C., & Qin-Hilliard, D. (2004). Immigrant boys' experiences in U.S. Schools. In N. Way & J. Chu (Eds.), *Adolescent boys in context* (pp. 256–270). New York: New York University Press.

Temin, P. (2003, Summer). Low pay, low quality. *Education Next, 3*(3), 8–13. Retrieved February 15, 2007, from http://www.hoover.org/publications/ednext/3398521.html

Texas Civil Rights Project. (1998). *Sexual Harassment in the Schools: What students suffer and what schools should do.* Austin, TX.

Thomas, W. P., & Collier, V. P. (2002). *A national study of school effectiveness for language minority students' long-term academic achievement.* Santa Cruz, CA: Center for Research on Education, Diversity and Excellence, University of California.

Urciuoli, B. (1996). *Exposing prejudice: Puerto Rican experiences of language, race, and class.* Boulder, CO: Westview Press.

U.S. Census Bureau (2002). Americans with Disabilities—Table 1. Retrieved February 14, 2007, from http://www.census.gov/hhes/www/disability/sipp/disab02/ds02t1.html.

U.S. Census Bureau (2006). Hispanic origin population. Retrieved August 22, 2006 from http://www.census.gov/Press-Release/www.releases/archives/population/006808.html

U.S. Census Bureau. (2006). PCT12. *Sex by Age in Census 2000 Summary File.* Retrieved August 22, 2006, from http://factfinder.census.gov/servlet/

U.S. Department of Health and Human Services (2001). *Mental health: Culture, race, and ethnicity—A supplement to mental health: A Report of the Surgeon General—Executive summary.* Rockville, MD: U.S. Department of Health and Human Services, Public Health Service, Office of the Surgeon General.

U.S. Senate Health, Education, Labor, and Pensions Committee. The Congressional Hispanic Caucus. The U.S. Senate Democratic Hispanic Task Force (2002). Keeping the Promise: Hispanic Education and America's Future. Washington DC: U.S. Senate.

Valenzuela, A. (1999). *Subtractive schooling: U.S.— Mexican youth and the politics of caring.* Albany, NY: State University Press.

Vásquez, M. J. T. (1994). Latinas. In L. Comas-Diaz & B. Greene (Eds.), *Women of Color: Integrating ethnic and gender identities in psychotherapy* (pp. 114–138). New York: Guilford.

Vásquez, M. J. T. (1982). Confronting barriers to the participation of Mexican-American women in higher education. *Hispanic Journal of Behavioral Sciences, 4*(2), 147–165.

Vásquez, M. J. T., & de las Fuentes, C. (1999). American-born Asian, African, Latina, and American Indian adolescent girls: Challenges and strengths. In N. G. Johnson, M. C. Roberts, & J. Worell (Eds.). *Beyond appearance: A new look at adolescent girls* (pp. 151–173). Washington, DC: American Psychological Association.

Vásquez, M. J. T., & Jones, J. M. (2006). Increasing the number of psychologists of color: Public policy issues for affirmative diversity. *American Psychologist, 61*(2) 132–142.

Villenas, S., & Deyhle, D. (1999). Critical race theory and ethnographies: Challenging the stereotypes: Latino families, schooling, resilience and resistance. *Curriculum Inquiry, 29*(4) 413–445.

Walsh, F. (1996). The concept of family resilience: Crisis and challenge. *Family Process, 35,* 261–281.

Weiler, J. D. (2000). *Codes and contradictions: Race, gender identity, and schooling.* Albany: State University of New York Press.

Wright, W. E. (2005, January). *Evolution of Federal Policy and Implications of No Child Left Behind for Language Minority Students* (EPSL-0501-101-LPRU). Tempe, AZ: Arizona State University, Education Policy Studies Laboratory, Language Policy Research Unit.

Wycoff, S. E. M. (1996). Academic performance of Mexican American Women: Sources of support. *Journal of Multicultural Counseling and Development, 24,* 146–155.

Yun, J. T., & Moreno, J. F. (2006). College access, K–12 concentrated disadvantage, and the next 25 years of education research. *Educational Researcher, 35,* 12–19.

Zavella, P. (1997). Reflections on diversity among Chicanas. In M. Romero, P. Hondagneu-Sotelo, & V. Ortiz, (Eds.), *Challenging fronteras: Structuring Latina and Latino lives in the U.S.* (pp. 187–194) New York: Routledge.

Zehr, M. (2001). Bilingual students with disabilities get special help. *Education Week, 21,* 1, 3, 2c.

ACHIEVING GENDER EQUITY FOR ASIAN AND PACIFIC ISLANDER AMERICANS

Mary L. Spencer,* Yukiko Inoue,* and Grace Park McField*

INTRODUCTION

The number of Asian and Pacific Islander Americans increased more rapidly between 1990 and 2000 than did the number of any other racial or ethnic group in the U.S. population (U.S. Census Bureau, 2001; 2002).[1] The advent of new methodologies for the 2000 U.S. Census permit our first view of some of the distinctions among the heterogeneous Asian and Pacific Islander American ethnic groups, and across females and males within each ethnic group. While census information has aided in the identification of at-risk groups and general needs, the body of educational, social, and cultural research on these groups has evolved in the past two decades, deepening understanding of the equity dynamics affecting them. Research and publication on critical questions regarding learner attributes, sociocultural influences, external conditions and forces, and the interactive effects of these factors may have been promoted by the gradual increase in the number of Asian and Pacific Islander scholars on American university faculties and in national research centers. Still, Asian and Pacific Islander American girls and boys are invisible or undifferentiated in most of the nation's large scale and longitudinal databases (e.g., the National Institute of Child Health and Human Development Study and the SAT annual results), and are infrequently represented in major research programs.

Although only a single chapter was devoted to sex equity for the collective population of "minority women" in the first handbook, *Achieving Equity Through Education* (Klein, 1985), emphasis was placed on the "myth of the monolith." The diversity of individuals identified only as minority women renders generalizations meaningless. Likewise, generalizations across the broad diversity of Asian American and Pacific Islander Americans yield little understanding of the status, needs, or relative effectiveness of pedagogical strategies for subgroups within the collective category. Many would argue with justification that ignoring the diversity across and within this label is damaging. Ignoring the dramatic statistical differences in income, frequency of poverty, and educational attainment among subgroups and between sexes buttresses barriers to resources and opportunities for those who are most in need.

Attention to a second myth, the "myth of the model minority," has unraveled misunderstandings about the extraordinary educational and economic achievements of certain subgroups of the Asian and Pacific Islander American population. Appreciation of the noteworthy accomplishments of these subgroups cannot be allowed to mask the differentiated experiences and circumstances of the others (e.g., O. Lee, 1997; D. W. Sue & D. Sue, 2003). For example, research (e.g. Talmy, 2006) has identified indicators such as socioeconomic status, achievement, educational aspirations, and home and school learning environments that are associated with greater risk for Southeast Asian (e.g., Laotian, Cambodian, Thai, & rural Vietnamese) and Pacific Islander students (e.g., Samoan & Micronesian).

Detailed analyses of the 2000 U.S. Census verify the existence of differential access to resources and educational attainment of females and males within the Asian and Pacific Islander American subgroups (Tables 24.1 and 24.4). For example, in the case of all Pacific Islander census categories and all Asian census categories, the mean earnings of full-time, year-round workers were less for women than men. Moreover, the earnings of the collective category of Asians were greater than those of the collective category of Pacific Islanders, with Asian women earn-

---

*The boldface names are the Lead Authors.

[1] While the U.S. total population grew 13% during this period, the U.S. Asian population increased from 48 to 72%, and the Pacific Islander population increased from 9 to 140%, the range depending upon the use of "Asian Alone" or "Pacific Island Alone" respondent identities versus "Asian Alone or in Combination" or "Pacific Island Alone or in Combination" identities.

TABLE 24.1 Educational Attainment of Male and Female Asian and Pacific Islander Americans,
25 Years and Older, Detailed Population Groups[a]

Population Group[b]	Percentage High School Graduate or Higher			Percentage Bachelor's Degree or Higher		
	Total	Female	Male	Total	Female	Male
United States	80.4	80.7	80.1	24.4	22.8	26.1
All Asian	80.4	77.8	83.4	44.1	40.4	48.2
Asian Indian	86.7	82.9	90.0	63.9	57.1	69.7
Bangladeshi	78.2	70.1	83.7	49.4	39.4	56.2
Cambodian	46.7	38.9	55.8	9.2	6.8	12.1
Chinese	77.0	75.1	79.1	48.1	44.0	52.6
Filipino	87.3	86.2	88.8	43.8	46.4	40.2
Hmong	40.4	28.1	53.0	7.5	4.8	10.2
Indonesian	92.6	91.2	94.2	46.6	41.7	52.3
Japanese	91.1	89.7	93.0	41.9	36.3	49.4
Korean	86.3	82.3	92.0	43.8	37.0	53.4
Laotian	50.4	45.3	55.2	7.7	6.9	8.5
Malaysian	89.1	89.2	88.8	53.5	48.2	60.7
Pakistani	82.0	75.7	86.7	54.3	46.1	60.3
Sri Lankan	86.6	83.6	89.3	51.1	42.2	59.3
Thai	79.1	73.2	90.0	38.6	32.8	49.2
Vietnamese	61.9	56.4	67.4	19.4	16.7	22.3
Other Specific Asian	84.3	81.7	86.8	51.1	47.0	55.0
All Pacific Islander	78.3	78.4	78.1	13.8	13.1	14.5
Native Hawaiian	83.2	84.4	82.0	15.2	14.6	15.8
Samoan	75.8	74.2	77.4	10.5	8.8	12.1
Tongan	65.3	67.8	63.1	8.6	9.6	7.8
Micronesian	77.2	77.7	76.8	13.2	12.8	13.6
Chamorro	77.8	79.4	76.3	14.3	14.0	14.5
Fijian	66.8	63.7	70.6	8.8	7.7	10.1
Polynesian	79.4	79.9	78.8	13.3	12.5	14.1
Melanesian	67.0	63.7	71.1	9.8	8.0	11.9

[a]U.S. Census Bureau, Census 2000 Summary File (SF 3)—Sample Data.
[b]All data is for the respective population groups *alone*; e.g., individuals reporting only one population group. Additional data is available for individuals reporting multiple population groups.

TABLE 24.2 SAT Scores by Gender in 2001

Gender	Verbal	Math	Total
Female	502	498	1000
Male	509	533	1042
All test takers	506	514	1020

Source: Haughton, 2002, http://www.fairtest.org/univ/2001SAT%20Scores.html/

ing more than Pacific Islander men. Similar differential patterns of higher education attainment are found in the collective categories of Asian and Pacific Islander American men and women; however, complex diversification of educational attainment results is revealed when subgroup achievement is examined (Table 24.1). Explanations of these differences and outlines of the trajectories of longitudinal change have been initiated by research on sociocultural characteristics, including traditional gender roles, of individual groups. Intergenerational immigration dynamics, native language and tradition maintenance and evolution within U.S. educational context, the availability and timing of economic resources to Asian and Pacific Islander American groups, and powerful globalization forces are all factors influencing educational equity for Asian and Pacific Islander Americans.

In this chapter, using the new lens of subgroup and sex category analysis, we will explore (a) educational and economic outcomes; (b) learner affective attributes such as self-concept and identity processes; (c) the influences of migration, colonial histories, and physical and psychological health factors; (d) access to resources; and (e) promising educational strategies for Asian and Pacific Islander American females and males. Recommendations for policy, practice, and research will be made.

In the following review of research on the education of Asian and Pacific Islander Americans in the United States, some learning and outcome factors can be considered sociocultural in nature. Given that 68.9% of Asian Americans in the United States are foreign-born, compared to 19.9% of Native Hawaiian/Pacific Islanders and 11.1% of all Americans (E. Lai & Arguelles, 2003), this is expected. On the other hand, there is a danger of generalizing findings that pertain to particular subgroups, to all persons who physically appear to be Asian or Pacific Islander, despite the fact that they are native-born or have lived in the United States for generations. Regardless of how many generations Asian and Pacific Islander American families and communities have resided in the United States, members of these groups are often expected to exhibit, identify with, or affiliate with particular distinguishing racial or sociocultural characteristics. Frequently, Native Hawaiians and Chamorros living on their respective islands report feeling conflicted about or outright reject identification as a Pacific Islander *American* because of the colonization of their people by the United States (e.g., C. T. Delisle, personal communication, April 26, 2005; Underwood, 2005). Thus, it is important to balance the findings and recommendations that follow with mindfulness that unique individual experiences and identity factors must be considered first and foremost, before generalizing outcomes to all Asian and Pacific Islander Americans.

An examination of equity or underrepresentation in the educational and professional realms of U.S. society brings to attention statistics for White American males. White American males constitute 33% of the U.S. population, but comprise about 80% of tenured positions in higher education; 92% of executives or similar CEO-level positions in Forbes 400 companies; 80% of the U.S. House of Representatives; 84% of the U.S. Senate; 99% of owners of sports teams; and 100% of U.S. Presidents (D. W. Sue, 2004). Some prefer to minimize the effects of race, ethnicity, color, or gender on social, educational, political, and economic opportunities, and prefer to take on "colorblind," "genderblind" perspectives. Clearly, in the past and present day United States, these perspectives are not operating with similar outcomes for particular groups of Asian and Pacific Islander Americans.

LEARNER ACADEMIC AND ECONOMIC OUTCOMES

Cognitive Testing Outcomes

Until 2005, major national databases on student achievement and aptitude failed to portray the status of male and female groups within the separate ethnic categories of Asian Americans

and Pacific Islander Americans. Since 1969, the National Assessment of Educational Progress (NAEP) conducted periodic assessments of American students' performance in various subject areas (e.g., reading, mathematics, science, writing, history, and geography) but did not report results separately for Asian and Pacific Islander female and male students, indicating that the sample size was too small (Perie & Moran, 2005). In 2005, NAEP database formats show results for combined and separated Asian girls and boys and Native Hawaiian/Other Pacific Islander girls and boys (see mathematics and communications chapters). For these groups, combined or separate fourth- and eighth-grade females outscored males in reading performance (average scaled scores differing 6 to 11 points). The converse was true for mathematics, but the difference was smaller (2 to 3 points).

The purpose of the widely used Scholastic Assessment Test (SAT) is to predict the ability of test takers to succeed in college. Unfortunately, cross tabulations of results by gender and ethnic group identity for Asian and Pacific Islander Americans are not available. Table 24.2 presents results by gender, showing a substantial gender gap in scores for ethnically undifferentiated SAT test takers. The verbal and math performance of boys was superior to that of girls. Haughton (2002) questions the validity of these results and suggests that they perpetuate the stereotype that boys are more capable in some areas of study (e.g., mathematics, science, and business) and further suggests that in many cases, girls are still being socialized away from these fields.

Reporting on SAT scores for various racial and ethnic groups, undifferentiated by sex, the National Center for Educational Statistics (Table 24.3) showed that, on average, Whites had the highest verbal scores, whereas Asian Americans had the highest math scores. The issue of bias in the SAT and its consequences for females and minorities continues to be the subject of wide debate because a significant number of institutions of

TABLE 24.3 Scholastic Assessment Test Score Averages, by Race/Ethnicity: 1986–87 to 1999–2000

Racial/Ethnic Background	1986–87	1987–88	1995–96	1996–97	1997–98	1998–99	1999–2000
SAT-Verbal							
All Students	507	505	505	505	505	505	505
White	524	522	526	526	526	527	528
Black	428	429	434	434	434	434	434
Hispanic or Latino	464	463	465	466	461	463	461
Mexican American	457	459	455	451	453	453	453
Puerto Rican	436	431	452	454	452	455	456
Asian American	479	482	496	496	498	498	499
American Indian	471	471	483	475	480	484	482
Other	480	485	511	512	511	511	508
SAT-Mathematical							
All Students	501	501	508	511	512	511	514
White	514	514	523	526	528	528	530
Black	411	418	422	423	426	422	426
Hispanic or Latino	462	463	466	468	466	464	467
Mexican American	455	460	459	458	460	456	460
Puerto Rican	432	434	445	447	447	448	451
Asian American	541	541	558	560	562	560	565
American Indian	463	466	477	475	483	481	481
Other	482	487	512	514	514	511	514

Note: Scholastic Assessment Test was formerly known as the Scholastic Aptitude Test. Possible scores on each part of the SAT range from 200 to 800.
Source: NCES (2004). Digest of Education Statistics Tables and Figures 2000. http://nces.ed.gov/programs/digest/d00/dt133.asp

higher education rely on these scores in their admission formulae. The increasing gap in scores, as well as the strong correlation of scores and income, indicate that fairness in standardized testing, and educational equity, are goals deserving continuing attention (Haughton, 2002).

High-School Drop-Out and Graduation

Nationwide, the 1999 high-school dropout rate for Asian and Pacific Islander Americans (4.8%) reached its highest level in five years (Asian American Federation Census Information Center, 2001). Of an estimated 513,000 Asian and Pacific Islander high-school students (10th–12th Grades), approximately 25,000 (4.8%) dropped out of high school in 1999, compared to the 3.8% drop out rate for nonHispanic White students. The continuing increase in the national school dropout rate for Asian and Pacific Islander American students points to the need for policymakers, education administrators, teachers, parents, and social service organizations to work together to develop effective strategies to understand and overcome this problem, addressing the dynamics of students differentiated by sex and specific Asian and Pacific Islander group.

The 2000 U.S. Census revealed that the incidence of high-school graduation for Asian Americans (80.4%) and Pacific Islander Americans (78.3%) was the same or similar to that of the total U.S. population (80.4%; Table 24.1). Asian American males (83.4%) exceeded all other Asian and Pacific Islander American sex differentiated groups, while Asian American females had the lowest high-school graduation rate (77.8%).

Closer examination of individual Asian American and Pacific Islander ethnic and sex-differentiated groups (Table 24.1) indicates important differences among ethnic groups, as well as differences between males and females within and between various ethnic groups. The most striking differences are the lower high-school graduation rates of Southeast Asian ethnic groups (Cambodian, 46.7%; Hmong, 40.4%; Laotian, 50.4%; and Vietnamese, 61.9%), relative to other Asian American groups, and the fact that for several of these groups, fewer than half of their adults have completed a high-school education. Females had substantially lower high-school graduation rates than males in each of the Southeast Asian groups, ranging from 28.1% for Hmong women to 56.4% for Vietnamese women. Women in every other Asian American ethnic group, except Malaysian, however, also lagged behind males in high-school graduation; and for some, the male-female graduation difference was considerable.

While the high-school graduation rate of the general Pacific Islander American population is similar to that of the general U.S. population, it is interesting to note that the rate of Native Hawaiians (83.2%) exceeds that of the general U.S. population. The lowest high-school graduation rates for Pacific Islander American ethnic subgroups was for Tongans (65.3%), Fijians

(66.8%), and a group given the general label of Melanesian (67%). All remaining Pacific Islander ethnic subgroups graduated at rates in the upper 70% range. While male-female graduation differences appeared for the Pacific Islander subgroups, they were smaller in magnitude than in some of the Asian subgroups, and in some groups, males had lower graduation rates than females (e.g., 4.7% fewer Tongan males graduated from high school than Tongan females).

These 2000 U.S. Census data on high-school graduation alert educators to adult education needs for a substantial segment of the Southeast Asian population, and also to the importance of promoting school persistence for elementary and secondary students in these groups. Evidence that Southeast Asian girls are at greatest risk underlines what emerging research suggests about cultural influences and an array of pressures associated with relatively recent migration (e.g., Ima & Nidorf, 1998; C. C. Park, 2001). High-school completion rates of Pacific Islanders are encouraging, yet warrant attention to various male and female groups that may be at risk. Moreover, the Compacts of Free Association[2] negotiated in the 1980s by the United States with the Federated States of Micronesia and the Republic of the Marshall Islands, and in the early 1990s with the Republic of Palau, opened special U.S. relocation and educational opportunities for Micronesians. Migration from these islands to U.S. elementary and secondary schools is likely to increase in coming years. Current Micronesian high-school completion rates in the United States are relatively high (77.2%) compared to the general U.S. population, and higher than in their countries of origin where high-school admission is not universal. Related research questions are, "What is the relative educational progress of Chamorro and Hawaiian students on the U.S. Mainland versus those attending school in their respective islands, and if there are differences, what are the factors associated with them?" The Guam Public School System has had a significant experience with Micronesian migration. Close attention to cultural and linguistic attributes of Micronesian students, and collaboration with their families and communities, has proven essential to the school persistence and success of newly arrived Micronesian and other Pacific Islander students (Smith et al., 1995; Yuen, Dowrick, & Alaimaleata, 2006).

Higher-Education Degree Attainment

Census evidence on baccalaureate degree attainment delineates three very different achievement levels across Pacific Islander Americans (13.8%), the U.S. population in general (24.4%), and Asian Americans (44.1%; Table 24.1). In each of the three groups, males have higher baccalaureate rates than women, the differential being within 1.5% to 7.8%. Among Asian American ethnic subgroups (Table 24.1), Asian Indians enjoy the highest rate of baccalaureate degree attainment (63.9%), with Asian In-

[2]The United States negotiated agreements with three Pacific political entities formed from former members of the United Nations post-World War II Trust Territory of the Pacific Islands: the Federated States of Micronesia (FSM), consisting of Chuuk, Kosrae, Pohnpei, and Yap; the Republic of the Marshall Islands; and the Republic of Palau. The agreements, which are known as Compacts of Free Association, provide for U.S. economic assistance, defense, and other benefits for the Freely Associated States, in exchange for U.S. operating rights in the entities, and denial of access to these Pacific nations by other nations. One benefit to the Freely Associated States is U.S. entry and the right to work in the United States.

dian males having the remarkable rate of 69.7% attainment at the baccalaureate or higher level, 12.6% higher than Asian Indian females (57.1%). As with high-school completion, a clear pattern of lower attainment of the Southeast Asian groups is revealed, with females of each group having attained substantially fewer baccalaureate degrees than the males of their respective groups. In only one Asian subgroup, Filipino, did a higher percentage of females (46.4%) attain baccalaureate or higher degrees than males (40.2%). Swarna (1997), reporting on the Filipino government policies designed to counter gender-role stereotypes in education, science, and technology, suggested that Filipino cultural values support improved education for both females and males.

The higher education degree attainment of Pacific Islander Americans (Table 24.1) lags far behind both the U.S. population in general and all Asian Americans, except the Southeast Asians. Native Hawaiians (15.2%), Chamorros (14.3%), and Micronesians (13.2%) lead the other Pacific Islander groups. Fijian females (7.7%) and Tongan males (7.8%) have had less success acquiring higher education credentials, relative to other Pacific Islander Americans, and at rates most resembling Southeast Asian groups.

A closer look at Asian and Pacific Islander Americans attaining doctoral or professional degrees shows that 17.4% of Asian

Americans have such degrees, compared to 4.1% for all Native Hawaiians and Pacific Islanders (4.4% for males, and 3.8% for females; E. Lai & Aguelles, 2003, p. 92). For the total U.S. population, 8.9% hold a graduate, professional, or doctoral degree. In order to ensure Asian and Pacific Islander American perspectives in higher education and research, there is an ongoing need for recruitment and retention of both groups of students at this level, with attention to the latter group, and females in particular.

Earnings

Asians and Pacific Islanders were very similar in rate of employment to the general U.S. population (Table 24.4), with approximately 80% of each group working 35 or more hours per week. As expected, the earnings of Asian and Pacific Islander Americans parallel the patterns established for high-school completion and higher education attainment. Asian Americans in general ($47,024), particularly Asian American males ($53,568), led in earned income, relative to the U.S. population ($42,707) and Pacific Islander Americans ($34,057). Male earnings in each general category were considerably higher than those of females, but the differential was less than in the U.S. general population

TABLE 24.4   Earnings and Work Status for 1999 for Male and Female Asian and Pacific Islander Americans, 16 Years and Older, Detailed Population Groups[a]

Population Group[b]	Percentage Usually Worked 35 or More Hours Per Week			Mean Earnings of Full-Time Year-Round Workers		
	Total	Female	Male	Total	Female	Male
United States	79.0	71.0	86.0	$42,707	$33,029	$49,250
All Asian	80.1	74.8	84.9	$47,024	$38,236	$53,568
Asian Indian	82.5	74.3	87.5	$59,861	$44,156	$66,995
Bangladeshi	76.9	64.9	81.4	$36,776	$25,743	$39,692
Cambodian	77.8	73.6	81.6	$29,350	$24,522	$33,205
Chinese	80.1	75.2	84.5	$50,533	$41,999	$56,993
Filipino	82.1	79.5	85.2	$39,733	$37,390	$42,341
Hmong	73.5	66.7	79.0	$26,045	$21,464	$29,034
Indonesian	75.7	68.3	82.5	$43,572	$33,842	$50,949
Japanese	78.6	71.0	85.8	$55,196	$41,671	$65,202
Korean	76.2	70.8	82.0	$45,118	$35,780	$53,119
Laotian	82.8	78.9	86.2	$27,598	$24,138	$30,086
Malaysian	69.1	68.6	69.6	$46,407	$38,968	$53,686
Pakistani	79.2	60.9	86.2	$52,278	$39,005	$55,349
Sri Lankan	78.0	67.0	86.1	$55,055	$40,425	$62,614
Thai	77.0	74.4	80.8	$36,718	$31,578	$43,327
Vietnamese	80.3	74.5	85.2	$35,183	$29,937	$38,837
Other Specific Asian	78.7	74.4	81.9	$40,962	$37,838	$43,064
Pacific Islander	79.8	74.6	84.2	$34,057	$29,619	$37,270
Native Hawaiian	78.7	74.0	82.9	$35,998	$31,755	$39,326
Samoan	81.1	76.1	85.1	$31,379	$26,918	$34,373
Tongan	80.1	75.4	83.4	$31,167	$26,004	$34,640
Micronesian	81.0	74.3	86.4	$33,114	$28,840	$33,114
Chamorro	81.4	75.1	86.6	$34,819	$29,055	$38,261
Fijian	82.6	77.7	87.9	$31,164	$27,879	$34,156
Polynesian	79.4	74.5	83.6	$34,199	$29,998	$37,292
Melanesian	82.0	77.0	87.4	$31,486	$27,942	$34,727

[a]U.S. Census Bureau, Census 2000 Summary File (SF 4, QT-P31) – Sample Data.
[b]All data is for the respective population groups *alone*; e.g., individuals reporting only one population group. Additional data are available for individuals reporting multiple population groups.

(21% higher for Asian and Pacific Islander males than females of their groups, compared to 33% higher for U.S. males relative to U.S. females). Southeast Asian groups earned less than other Asian American groups. Of Asian Americans, only Bangladeshi women ($25,743), Cambodian women ($24,522), Hmong women ($21,464), and Laotian women ($24,138) had average annual incomes at or below $25,000. Eight of the 15 Asian American subgroups exceeded the general U.S. population in annual earnings.

All Pacific Islander female and male groups had average annual earnings above $26,000. On average, Pacific Islander groups earned 20% less per year than the general U.S. population, and 28% less per year than the general Asian American population. In every Pacific Islander female-male earnings comparison, males had higher earnings than females.

When income is disaggregated by per-capita count or the number of members per household, the figures look very different. In 2000, given the median per-capita index of 3.1 family members per household for Asian and Pacific Islander Americans versus 2.45 for non-Hispanic White households, the median Asian and Pacific Islander American per-capita income was $22,352, as compared to $25,278 for Whites, $15,197 for Blacks, and $12,306 for Hispanics, and $22,199 for the total population (U.S. Census Current Population Survey, 2000, p. 227, as cited in E. Lai & Arguelles, 2003).

Poverty Rates

In 2000, poverty was defined as a family of four (two adults and two children) living with an income below $16, 895. In 2000, the poverty rate for Asian Americans as a whole was 12.6%, while the rate for Native Hawaiian/Pacific Islanders was 22.6%, both of which were much higher than the rate for nonHispanic Whites (8.1%). The rates for women living in poverty for these three groups were 12.7%, 18.7%, and 9.1%, respectively, again indicating much higher numbers of Asian American and Pacific Islander women living in poverty as compared to non-Hispanics (E. Lai & Arguelles, 2003, p. 33). Clearly, these figures break down the model minority myth and demonstrate a need to both recognize and address the significantly higher rates of poverty for Asian and Pacific Islander American women and children. A gender sensitive research agenda on these groups is warranted, and it should heed the variables Evans (2004) reviews as he points to the "cumulative rather than singular exposure of poor children to a confluence of psychosocial and physical environmental risk factors" (p. 77).

Occupational Choices

For 1994–1995, Asian and Pacific Islander Americans who are U.S. citizens ranked the field of education last as their bachelor, master, or doctorate degree choice (Table 24.5; Chan & Hune, 1997). Of the small group who selected the field of education at the bachelor and master levels, most were women (76% and 74%, respectively). Business was the most popular degree choice at the first two degree levels, when males and females were combined, with life sciences first at the doctoral level. Of these Asian and Pacific Islander survey participants, sex differ-

TABLE 24.5 Degree Proportions of Asian Pacific American (APA) Women and Others

	APA's	All Others	APA Women
Bachelor's Degrees (1994)			
Business	22.4%	21.2%	55.0%
Social Sciences	16.6%	17.4%	57.2%
Engineering	17.4%	8.8%	22.4%
Sciences	14.6%	7.2%	47.8%
Humanities	9.3%	14.2%	64.4%
Other	8.1%	11.4%	56.4%
Health	5.5%	7.2%	76.9%
Arts	4.1%	4.2%	63.8%
Education	2.0%	9.2%	76.0%
All Fields			51.6%
Master's Degrees (1995)			
Business	30.3%	24.2%	
Humanities	25.9%	10.4%	
Other	8.6%	12.4%	
Sciences	10.1%	25.7%	
Arts	6.6%	7.3%	
Health	5.9%	3.9%	
Social Sciences	5.1%	6.5%	
Engineering	5.0%	6.7%	
Education	4.1%	4.2%	
Doctoral Degrees (1995)			
Life Sciences	23.4%	18.1%	
Engineering	22.5%	8.6%	
Physical Sciences	19.6%	13.2%	
Social Sciences	14.8%	18.2%	
Humanities	14.4%	7.0%	

Source: Chan and Hune, 1997

ences were most pronounced in the low selection of engineering by women at the bachelor and master levels. In spite of the increased incidence of science and engineering degrees attained by U.S. citizens and permanent residents from all ethnic groups (except Whites) between 1990 and 1998 (National Science Foundation [NSF], 2003), Asian and Pacific Islander American and White women comprised less than half of bachelor degree recipients in their ethnic groups in these fields. Women in all other ethnic categories received more than half. Studies such as O. Lee's (1997) provide specific information and factors to consider in working with the Asian American population to reduce barriers and carry out the goal of providing quality science instruction for all students.

Expectations and aspirations. A number of studies have examined differential educational and occupational expectations and aspirations of students by race and ethnicity, and some analyze gender differences. For example, Asian-American girls have high completion levels of university preparation courses, suggesting high aspirations for acquiring a college education (California Department of Education, 2000; Grant & Rong, 1999).

In a six-year longitudinal study (Xie & Goyette, 2003) of the social mobility of Asian Americans, Asian American youth tended to choose occupations with a high incidence of Asian workers and high average earnings-to-education ratio, relative to White workers. The Asian Americans were more likely to expect to enter college and to major in fields with high financial payoffs, thus indicating that they had higher educational and occupational expectations.

Four implications may be derived from these studies: (a) parent education and perceived influence on student educational aspirations affect the pipeline of future generations of aspiring Asian and Pacific Islander American students and professionals; (b) heightening the educational and occupational aspirations of these students is best approached by addressing students and families jointly; (c) students and families with relatively short U.S. residence would benefit from information that longer residents enjoy; and (d) lower Asian American male student educational and occupational aspirations may suggest the need for counseling and student advisement attention.

Teaching. Asian American teachers represent only 1.8% of the U.S. teaching force (U.S. Census Bureau, 2006), creating a disparity relative to the number of Asian American students, which was 4.3% of the total U.S. teaching force in 2002–2003 (National Center for Educational Statistics, 2006). This denies Asian American students of the achievement, role model, and school enhancement benefits shown by researchers such as Dee, Milem, and Milner & Hoy (as cited in Torres, Santos, Peck & Cortes, 2004) when same-race teachers are available to students and able to contribute diversity to their schools. Results from these studies support inferences that greater Asian and Pacific Islander racial, ethnic, and gender diversity in the teaching force would increase essential funds of knowledge and creativity in the educational settings of both male and female students of Asian and Pacific Islander heritage. Important research questions remain to be addressed on Asian and Pacific Islander American teacher contributions to all such students and their schools.

In her study of 140 Asian American teachers in the Los Angeles area from nine ethnic groups (80% female), Chong (2002) found that the top three reasons for pursuing teaching were (a) love of children, (b) love of teaching, and (c) influence of previous teachers. Most participants were encouraged by their teachers, as well as by their parents, and almost half responded that no one had discouraged them from becoming a teacher. Chong identified four barriers to Asian American and other minority group entry into the teaching profession: (a) lack of ethnic role models representing their cultural and linguistic backgrounds; (b) difficulty in meeting admission standards and completing the teacher credential program in a timely manner due to increased testing and course requirements; (c) poor financial assistance programs for ethnic minority student teachers; and (d) lack of active recruitment of Asian American teachers. Chong recommended that teacher-training institutions offer continuing education courses to support the lifelong learning and development of Asian American teacher candidates.

Several other studies have explored factors that may discourage Asian American and Pacific Islander Americans from teaching (e.g., American Association of Colleges of Teacher Education [AACTE], 1999; Futrell, 1999; Jorgenson, 2000; Bracey, 2001; Goodwin, 1995; Gordon, 2000). Gordon (2000) identified three sources of resistance: (a) intense pressure from parents to strive for positions perceived as having higher status, greater financial rewards, and more stability than teaching; (b) a sense of personal inadequacy due to standards set by some Asian cultures for what it means to be a teacher; and (c) fear of working outside a comfort zone defined by language, diversity, responsibility for other people's children, and separation of private from public selves. C. C. Park and McField (2006), in their study of the recruitment and retention strategies of Asian and Pacific Islander teachers, indicated "lack of strong English skills" and "negative publicity about schools and education" as possible obstacles to entering the teaching profession, while Goodwin (1995) recognized the barrier of ineligibility for certain incentives such as special recruitment projects, fellowships, and state programs designed to increase the number of teachers of color. Torres, Santos, Peck, and Cortes (2004) examined factors at each point in the pipeline of teacher preparation and practice that can contribute to loss of minority teachers. Other anecdotal information from teacher retention researchers points to retention losses of scarce Asian and Southeast Asian teachers due to accented English language and other social pressures in the schools (M. F. Pacheco, personal communication, July 26, 2005). An important research strategy for improving the utility of studies on minority group inclusion in teacher preparation is adequate sampling of the different Asian and Pacific Islander American ethnic groups, differentiated by sex (e.g., AACTE, 1999).

Medicine, science, and engineering. Studies of Asian and Pacific Islander access to medical school and factors influencing their choices reveal a dramatic increase in enrollment during the 25-year period from 1974 to 1999: from 986 to 7,622, now representing a fifth of all applicants in the United States. In 1988, Asian and Pacific Islander women applicants represented 5% of all applicants, but they were 9% in 1999 (Hall, Mikesell, Cranston, Julian, & Elam, 2001). In a similar vein, the Association of American Medical Colleges (2006) reported that among 15,821 students who graduated from medical school in 2004, women comprised 46%. Since 1980, the number of women graduates from medical school has been increasing steadily, doubling from 3,497 in 1980 to 7,256 in 2004. Among the 15,821 graduates, the percentage of Asian graduates reflected a steady increase, reaching 20.5% (3,166) by 2004. Among these numbers, 46.3% are Asian American women. Given that only 6.4% of the total U.S. college population and 4.3% of the total U.S. student population in K–12 programs are Asian and Pacific Islanders (National Center for Educational Statistics, 2003, 2006b), this is proportionally much greater than the general American population. Furthermore, in 2004, 23% of the students enrolled in Harvard Medical School were Asian and Pacific Islanders, while 29% of Harvard Medical School graduates were Asian and Pacific Islanders (Harvard University, 2006). Among the Asian and Pacific Islander graduates, 48.3% (28) were women. Thus, the proportion of women in medical schools was always less than that of males. Northeastern Ohio University provides an interesting case study, where 40% of students in the College of Medicine are Asian Pacific Islander Americans, and somewhat less than half of those are women. Hall et al. (2001) and Wear (2000) both documented powerful parental influences on the educational and occupational choices of medical school students. In the first study, students reported parental desires for economic security for their children and that education was their obligation to their parents. Wear (2000) cautioned that parental pressures could "take additional emotional tolls above the ones already evoked in the excessively competitive environment of U.S. medical education" (p. 163).

As suggested by Table 24.5, Asian American participation in science and engineering education is significant. In order to investigate factors influencing these career choices for Asian American women, Chinn (2002) conducted case studies of four Chinese and Japanese college women majoring in these disciplines, and found that Confucian cultural scripts shaped gender expectations even in families living in the United States for several generations. These Asian women recognized that barriers to nontraditional behaviors, interests, and careers tended to first be imposed by the parents' Confucian-influenced cultural values, in which women and girls hold lower status; then the barriers were reinforced by gender biases of teachers and peers in mainstream institutions. Chinn concluded that especially in the case of underrepresented, racially marginalized students, teachers must be willing to learn about the lives of their students, and be willing to involve parents and community members as partners in student learning.

Business. Business is a prominent degree choice for Asian Americans. Many Asian American and Pacific Islander ethnic groups, especially Korean Americans, Japanese Americans, Chinese Americans, Indian Americans, and Vietnamese Americans, are well represented in small businesses. The Survey of Business Owners (U.S. Census Bureau, 2002) reported that as of 2002, 1.2 million businesses were operated by women of color, of which 30% were owned by Asian and Pacific Islander American women; whereas in 1997, 4.4% of businesses were owned by Asian and Pacific Islander Americans. Two out of three were independently operated without employees on payroll. Service, retail trade, finance, insurance, and real estate industries topped the types of women-owned businesses. E. Lai and Arguelles (2003, p. 226) provide an analysis of male and female race and ethnic representation among the management and executive ranks of American business and industry. Asian and Pacific Islander Americans are consistently underrepresented in management positions in all major industries, while Whites are consistently overrepresented in management positions in virtually all industries. The three industries with higher Asian and Pacific Islander American female than male representation in management positions were finance, insurance, and utilities.

Immigrant Asian American women in garment and technology industries. The majority of workers in the garment and technology industries are women, and in the United States, 20% of all garment workers are Asian Americans; Latinos comprise 70%, Whites 8%, and others 2%. Of the Asian Americans who work in this industry, Chinese comprise 44%, Koreans 25%, Vietnamese 12%, and Filipinos 7% (Sweatshop Watch and the Garment Worker Center [SWGWC], 2004). Foo (2002) cited Department of Labor estimates that more than half of the nation's 22,000 sewing shops violate federal minimum wage and overtime regulations, with many employees working 10–12 hours per day; and with about 75% of the shops violating health and safety laws. According to SWGWC surveys, only 15% of all garment workers reported speaking English very well, and only 17% had education levels beyond high school. In the "American Pacific," Saipan in the Commonwealth of the Northern Marianas Islands has a major garment industry, characterized by the same features discussed by Foo, in which most workers are low paid women guest workers from several Asian nations, without the rights of U.S. citizens. A special investigative report in *Ms. Magazine* found that the U.S. government failed to address substandard working conditions, low wages, and human rights violations (Clarren, 2006). Two successful federal class action suits in 1999 and proposed legislation in Congress have started to help remedy these inequities (Feminist Daily News Wire, June 8 & June 20, 2006).

Asian Americans are also well represented in two segments of the information technology industry: first, as the group of Asian American males (particularly Chinese and Indian Americans) to found and operate more than 3,000 companies in the Silicon Valley, California, with sales of $17 billion in the late 1990s (E. Lai & Arguelles, 2003, p. 236); and second, the group of Asian American females, mostly Filipino and Vietnamese American women, who constitute the bulk of the blue-collar labor, making chips and building computers for low pay in unhealthy environments, many without health benefits (e.g., Hossfeld, 2001; Foo, 2002, p. 84). For those in white-collar positions, the issues have to do with professional development and opportunities to advance into management positions; while for those in blue-collar positions, the issue is how to be empowered to achieve safe working conditions, fair pay, educational opportunity, and information about contracts and workers' rights.

LEARNER AFFECTIVE ATTRIBUTES AND INFLUENCES

Influence of Cultural Origins

Because Asian and Pacific Islander American students are part of a complex and differentiated minority matrix, the majority of educators, particularly in the continental United States, usually need assistance and supportive information to guide their efforts to infuse cultural competence and gender equity into the treatment of these students. What factors affect the motivations, interests, identities, aspirations, choices, outcomes, and well being of Asian and Pacific Islander American female and male students? Consideration must be given to both migration and colonial histories.

Migration. Foundational to an understanding of Asian and Pacific Islander American students is a framework for considering the influence of migration, recent or long past. The rich and growing historical and social-science scholarship on immigration and "diaspora" models of the movements of Asian and Pacific Island peoples, as well as study of the forces of "globalization," inform our understanding of Asian and Pacific Islander American students and our work to define best practices for providing educational equity for them (e.g., Chiang, Lidstone, & Stephenson, 2004; Spickard, Rondilla, & D. H. Wright, 2002).

In describing patterns of modern migration of Pacific Islanders and Asians to the United States, Spickard (2002) summarizes three models of migration: (a) immigrant assimilation, (b) transnational or diasporic, and (c) panethnicity. In the first, immigration is seen as a permanent, unidirectional move from country of origin to the United States, leaving something bad for something good, leading to rapid and substantial absorption of cultural features of the destination, with diminished adherence to indigenous cultural imperatives. In the transnational or diasporic model, which Spickard felt best describes the ancient and continuous "back and forth and around" movements of Pacific Islanders, connections with home islands endure. This is ably illustrated in the autobiographical Chamorro case study described by Perez (2004). Finally, the panethnicity model describes the process and outcome of migrant groups having certain related historical, ethnic/racial, or linguistic features, morphing into a comfortable unified whole (e.g., individual U.S. migrants from multiple distinct island populations, or from multiple and distinct Asian nations, accepting the collective identity of Pacific Islander American, or Asian American, respectively). Examples of American-born generations of Chinese, Japanese, Asian Indian, and Filipino groups addressing oppression and creating opportunity by joining forces under the collective identity of Asian American give us a glimpse of the cultural, social, and political transitions that occur across successive generations of these groups in the United States. (See Rondilla's (2002) discussion of the "brown Asian" marginalization of Filipinos for a broader understanding of the dynamics of this constructed collective ethnicity category.)

In short, the relative detailed histories of specific Asian and Pacific Islander American groups since migrating to the United States count in major ways when the goal is to understand what female and male Asian and Pacific Islander American students and their families bring to our schools and classrooms. A fourth generation (*yonsei*) female Japanese student in Seattle is likely to address her educational experiences and opportunities in a manner much less guided by traditional gendered Japanese expectations for girls than the recently arrived Japanese girl in a U.S. school. But perhaps more bewildering to educators are the unknown or unfamiliar cultural and educational experiences of students newly arrived from nonindustrialized, remote, or rural Asian and Pacific Islander origins in Micronesia or Southeast Asia, where profound adherence to cultural traditions apply. Where powerful, gendered expectations or dynamics are presented by these students or their families, possibly presenting contrasts with legal or educational standards, educators face challenges involving individual students, parents, and community groups. Among these could be traditions based in Confucian philosophy, favoring formal or higher education for male over female children; discomfort when related male and female Pacific Islander students inhabit the same learning environment, or culturally defined clothing taboos of some Asian and Pacific Islander American groups relative to physical education and sports (e.g., Ross, 2004); parental administration of harsh physical punishment, primarily by Pacific Islander fathers to sons (e.g., Dubanoski & Snyder, 1980; Fitisemanu et al., 2002); or spotty school attendance, particularly of Pacific Islander American girls, due to duty assignments at home (Spencer, 1992, p. 301).

Many materials are available on specific Asian and Pacific Islander American groups that offer educators a place to begin the integration of cultural, linguistic, and gender information and sensitivity into the schools and classrooms of Asian and Pa-

cific Islander American female and male students (e.g., Palomares, 1991; Tacheliol, 1991; William & Prasad, 1992). Educational and historical research anthologies on Asian and Pacific Islander American populations are important resources (e.g., Chu-Chang, 1983; Endo, C. C. Park, & Tsuchida, 1998; Hune & Nomura, 2003; C. C. Park, Goodwin, & S. J. Lee, 2001; C. C. Park, Goodwin, & S. J. Lee, 2003; C. C. Park, Endo, & Goodwin, 2006; Tamura, Chattergy, & Endo, 2002). The annual national conferences of the National Association for Asian and Pacific American Education (NAAPAE), the National Pacific Islander Educational Network, the Pacific Island Bilingual Bicultural Association (PIBBA), and the Pacific Resources for Education and Learning (PREL) provide opportunities to meet Asian and Pacific Islander American educators and researchers and to learn of the most current initiatives and resources. The University of Hawai'i Press, Bess Press, the Micronesian Area Research Center and the Micronesian Language Institute at the University of Guam, the College of Hawaiian Studies at the University of Hawaii, Hilo, and the Pacific Institute of the Brigham Young University, Hawai'i are key sources of scholarly publications about these populations, including women and gender studies.

Colonial history. Compared to Asian and Pacific Islander Americans who have chosen to migrate to the United States, some Pacific Islander Americans, Hawaiians and Chamorros in particular, have the profoundly different experience of the colonization of their lands and peoples (e.g., Souder, 1992). The individual and collective psyches of these people have been deeply scarred by (a) prolonged and extreme oppression of core cultural structures and tenets, (b) pressures to eliminate their native languages (e.g., Palomo, 1987; Underwood, 1987a), (c) the blanket imposition of foreign school systems with inadequate respect to local fit (Underwood, 1987b), (d) misguided health policies (Hattori, 2004), and (e) the mass takings of their native lands (e.g., Souder-Jaffrey & Underwood, 1987). Indigenous rights movements aimed at self-determination and a Hawaiian Nation movement are built upon these grievances. So, too, are the flowering Chamorro language and culture programs and the Hawaiian language immersion programs found at elementary and secondary levels of schooling, and the higher education Pacific Island Studies, Hawaiian Studies, and Micronesian Studies Programs.

Stereotypes

As Asher (2001) declared, "One phenomenon, which is particularly relevant to the marginalization of Asian Americans, is their characterization as the model minority" (p. 56). When immigration from China, Hong Kong, the Philippines, India, and Southeast Asia increased following the Immigration Reform Act of 1965, the public became more aware of academically successful Asian students (Chinn, 2002, p. 302). In a 1994 New York Times Magazine article, journalist William Peterson coined the term "model minority." The phrase has been used as a catch-all to describe Asian Americans as the hard-working, well-educated, compliant, successful minority race, succeeding in spite of racial barriers (About, Inc., 2004; Asher, 2001, p. 56). P. W. Lee and Wong (2002, pp. 86–87) have explained that this media perception has obscured the educational difficulties (e.g., high dropout rates, poverty, literacy underachievement, loss of cultural identity) confronted by the heterogeneous population of students. The label also masks the persistent racism faced by Asian Americans.

The U.S. cinema industry is responsible for other Asian and Pacific Islander American stereotypes. Mahdzan and Ziegler (2004) comment on the frequency of negative stereotypes of the Asian women as docile and quiet, working in middle-to-low economic positions, or the "dragon lady" stereotype of Asian women as seductive and desirable, but also untrustworthy. The China doll character in *The Year of the Dragon* is another common stereotype of Asian women. International tourism has been a particularly effective engine for stereotypes about Pacific Islanders. Trask (2002) expressed this powerfully in her assertion that tourism stemming from U.S. colonialism over Hawaiians has reduced Hawaiian women and men to "native artifacts" and "exotic ornaments," in the eyes of visitors and the visitor industry. Other familiar negative stereotypes of Pacific Islanders include being lazy, happy-go-lucky, unintelligent, hula dancers, bullies, football players, or gang members. Books such as J. Yung's, *Chinese Women of America: A Pictorial History* (1986), and *The Chinese of America, 1785–1980* by H. M. Lai, Huang, and Wong (1980) directly addressed Asian stereotypes by providing illustrations and text tracing the factual history of real individuals and communities. Asian and Pacific Island historical and social science scholarship by indigenous scholars has expanded rapidly in the last two decades, providing rich source materials for educators to include in a wide range of content area curricula at all levels of study.

Another line of research on early negative stereotype formation in Pacific Islander children is provocative and deserves replication and updating. Alameda's (1999) dissertation on Hawaiian elementary school students' perceptions of the academic ability of Hawaiian, Japanese, and White Americans revealed that they rated White and Japanese Americans significantly higher on this trait than Hawaiians. Moreover, neither girls nor boys rated their own sex significantly higher than the opposite sex. Babasa (1987) replicated Day's (1980) study of Hawaiian children by comparing the selections and attributions of three- to-five-year-old Chamorro children in laboratory situations requiring them to take or give presents to one of two face-like apparatuses. One apparatus was named "Liz" and spoke through a tape-recorded script in Standard English, while the other was named "Sabet" and spoke "Guamanian-dialect English." Three-year-old children evaluated Sabet as better and preferred her language; conversely, four- and five-year-olds preferred Liz's Standard English. The rapid and early switch in attitudes away from the nonstandard sociolinguistic form and the children's negative descriptions of it were interpreted as the development of negative sociolinguistic stereotypes growing out of attitudes introduced at school.

Beyond stereotypes: A case study of a traditional culture: The Hmong. Accurate information on the diversity of Asian and Pacific Islander American communities will facilitate the provision of appropriate services to these groups. Hmong Americans comprise one group that has had to reconcile many divergent sets of values and expectations between the home and school cultures. The Hmong assisted U.S. forces in the Viet-

nam War and arrived in the United States following the 1975 fall of Saigon. The Hmong culture is primarily clan-based and patriarchal in nature, and girls' education was not traditionally valued. The ideal age for marriage is between 12 and 15 for girls, and between 14 and 17 for boys, with marriages often arranged by families. The literacy background of the Hmong culture is primarily oral in nature, with the written language only having been devised by missionaries in the 1950s.

Timm (1994) studied Hmong American communities in Wisconsin and Minnesota for over two years, interviewing 26 individuals ranging from 15 to over 60 years of age. Many adults had few years of formal education upon arrival to the United States, and while education is seen as a viable means of advancement, many Hmong boys and girls dropped out of school either to work and support the family, or to get married and have children early. Public school events such as parent-teacher conferences, shaking hands at meetings, coed study groups, after-school activities, and proms and other dances were often not attended or understood. Language transfer issues, as well as different assumptions about instruction (memorization vs. constructivist learning) led to additional cross-cultural misunderstandings. Lack of previous contact and understanding between Hmong and nonHmong students led to prejudiced behavior from the non-Hmong students and social segregation and isolation for the Hmong American students. Hmong American students and families were and are in a state of adaptation, transition, and change, and educators need to be mindful of the many opposing values and conflicts that may arise, so that issues can be addressed and resolved in a positive manner that takes into account cultural aspects of goal setting and goal attainment behavior (Lese & Robbins, 1994).

Aspiration, Self-Concept, and Identity

In a study focusing on aspirations with a mixed sample of Chamorro, Filipino, and other undergraduate women on Guam, Inoue (2004) reported high educational and career expectations, as well as child and family goals, and that respondents did not perceive gender discrimination in employment. Chamorro women's influence and power in matters of home and family may contribute to this finding (e.g., Souder, 1992). These results may also reflect tenets of Chamorro and Filipino matrilineal arrangements as well as the religious beliefs of Guam's predominantly Roman Catholic society.

In a survey by J. S. Yamauchi and Tin-Mala (1998) of Chinese, Filipino, Japanese, Korean, and Vietnamese American college students, the most frequently mentioned life goal was the pursuit of career. Participants cited the advantages of being Asian American (e.g., culture, sensitivity to other cultures, language, family support), relative to the disadvantages (e.g., discrimination, language problems, success stereotypes, family pressures; Table 24.6).

Asian self-esteem and identity. Research suggests that Asian American male and female students have low self-esteem compared to other ethnic groups (e.g., Bae & Brekke, 2004).[3] In a comparison of the motivational beliefs of ninth-grade students from four Asian backgrounds and non-Asian students, Eaton and Dembo (1997) found that fear of academic failure was the great-

TABLE 24.6 Rank Order Perceptions of Advantages and Disadvantages of Being Asian American

Advantages	Disadvantages
Cultural background/values	Discrimination
Intercultural sensitivity/ appreciation	Cultural adjustment problems of other cultures
Language facility/being bilingual	Language problems/learning English
Success stereotypes	Success stereotypes
Strong familial support	Parent-family pressure to succeed
Uniqueness	Physical differences/standing out
Pride in being Asian American	Difficulty in expressing feelings
Minority program assistance	Social problems/dating non-Asians

Source: Yamauchi and Tin-Mala, 1998, p. 97

est influence for the Asian students and the least for non-Asian students. Further, Asian American students reported lower levels of self-efficacy, despite performing better than non-Asian students on the achievement task. Eaton and Dembo cited studies such as Stevenson, Chen, and Uttal (1990), in which non-Asian students' parents may have overestimated their children's performance, yet had lower academic expectations,

Based on research interviews with Japanese American women, Kim (1981) proposed that their identity process resolves initial identity conflicts, and has five stages: (a) ethnic awareness, (b) alienation from self and from other Asian Americans, (c) a feeling of alienation from Whites, (d) the gradual emergence of an Asian American identity, and (e) the women's ability to relate to different groups of people without losing their identity as Asian Americans. Respondents who grew up in predominantly non-White, racially mixed neighborhoods had less painful experiences with identity conflict than those who grew up in predominantly White neighborhoods. Vyas (2001) contended that major theoretical models of identity development (e.g., Erikson, 1980; Gergen, 1991) do not effectively explain how home and school affect the identity formation of Asian American high-school students. Her study (Vyas, 2001) indicated that Asian American students experience identity in the form of inner continuity (e.g., considering themselves "Indian," "Indian American," or "American"). She concluded that research and pedagogy could productively focus on bicultural identity concerns through supportive literacy environments (Vyas, 2001, p. 152).

Palmer (2001) explored the educational and social experiences of young Asian American women, with a focus on their experiences in schools, communities, and families and how gender bias and racism affected their ethnic/racial identity development. The study participants were Korean high-school teenagers who had been adopted by Caucasian families. They indicated that their loneliness began in their families, as they felt that their parents were not able to understand how they really felt when confronted with racism in their schools and communities. The stereotypes of Asians in the popular media had a neg-

ative impact upon these adopted Korean women, as they thought of their lives as culturally White, yet physically Korean.

In a study of gifted students, Verna and Campbell (1998) reported that Asian American students perceived more parental pressure, but less parental support and help than a comparison group of White students. Parental pressure had negative effects on the students' self-concept, while psychological support positively affected the general self-concept for Asian American students, and positively affected general, math, and science self-concepts for White students. Interestingly, students' self-concept did not significantly influence achievement in either math or science. Families with higher socioeconomic status provided more intellectual resources, assistance, support, and pressure.

Although Eaton and Dembo (1997) suggested that fear of failure can spur academic achievement and related behaviors in Asian American students, the relatively low levels of self-efficacy among Asian American students may mean that encouragement and support are critical for this population to develop a healthy psychological outlook on achievement and related goals. This is especially important, in light of studies that have found high rates of suicide attempts, planning, and execution among some Asian American student populations such as Filipinos (Lau, 1995).

Pacific Islander American identity issues. A burgeoning body of research, analysis, and commentary has emerged on Pacific Islander identity issues (e.g., Linnekin & Poyer, 1990; Spickard, Rondilla, & D. H. Wright, 2002). Because the topic is intricately associated with issues of the colonization of Pacific Islanders and their native lands, it is also a topic of considerable sensitivity. It is an important topic for any educator of Pacific Islander students. Without an understanding of the identity formation process and the cultural context of their Pacific Islander students, educators will be ill situated to provide relevant and inspiring educational environments and opportunities, nor will they be equipped to work effectively with the families of their students.

In general, Pacific Island families possess collective priorities, in contrast to the highly individualistic focus of European-American traditions, and they are frequently organized in extended families rather than small, nuclear-family arrangements. Many Pacific Island cultures are influenced by historical matrilineal patterns that may privilege certain kinds of female activity, decision-making roles, or the authority of relatives in the female line. Yet, little empirical study has been accorded the differential identity formation of Pacific Islander girls and boys.

Trask (2002), a prominent cultural commentator, educator, and one of the foremost political organizers of the Hawaiian Nation movement, forcefully rejected American feminism for its attempts to separate the concerns of Hawaiian males and Hawaiian females:

Our efforts at collective self-determination mean that we find solidarity with our own people, including our own men, more likely, indeed preferable, to solidarity with White people, including feminists.

---

[3] These results could be due to a differential item response bias, and they alert researchers that examining response bias is an important step in the interpretation of cross-cultural research protocols. Western measures of self-esteem may have limited utility when they are used with other cultural groups.

Pacific Island women, like Hawaiian women, seek a collective self-determination—want to achieve sovereignty through and with our own people, not separated from them as individuals or as splintered groups. (p. 253)

Trask's perspective is important when considering gender equity research agendas. The primacy of the collective cultural group also emerges in the writing of other Pacific Islander American scholars (e.g., Souder-Jaffrey & Underwood, 1987; Hattori, 2004); however, focus on Pacific Islander women's issues are also given serious consideration by these and other Pacific Islander scholars (e.g., Souder, 1992). Speaking from another part of the Pacific, Dominy's (1990) ethnography of New Zealand Maori women's groups described the development of radical feminist advocacy, which is at odds with Trask's attribution of collective nongender-differentiated identity for Pacific Islander women.

In tracing the colonial history of Pacific Island women, Green (2002) supplied important insights into shifts in their self-concepts and cultural identities over history, as well as into the range of traditional activities and roles played by Hawaiian women and men. Linnekin's book, *Sacred Queens and Women of Consequence: Rank, Gender, and Colonialization in the Hawaiian Islands* (1990) provides deep and detailed scholarly documentation of these gender roles, and illuminates historical changes associated with contact and colonialization. Pau'u's (2002) autobiographical description of the evolution of her Tongan identity as she grew up in four cultures vividly illustrates how Pacific Islanders often refuse to "choose one box," as Spickard (2002) has described the multiethnicity psyche of many Pacific Islander Americans. In contrast to the "melting pot" metaphor, many Pacific Islander Americans are constructing identities that combine their multiple ethnicities in a pluralistic manner, perhaps better seen through the metaphor of the "mixed salad," the specific "negotiated" form of identity that is dependent upon situational features (I. F. Funaki & L. M. Funaki, 2002, p. 211). Remembering the frequency of "back and forth and around" diasporic migration movements of Pacific Islander Americans, one can envision how the choices of negotiated identities shift from situation to situation.

Spickard (2002) enlarged our understanding of individual Pacific Islander American identity by analyzing the perceptions other Pacific Islanders have of an individual's identity and the conditions of admittance to the reference ethnic group. An individual may be accepted by a particular Pacific Island group on the basis of four elements: primarily by (a) bloodline ancestry, or (b) membership in an extended family (often including adoption and sometimes even including associations by marriage), and secondarily by (c) cultural practice, and/or (d) place (care for the land).

PHYSICAL AND PSYCHOLOGICAL HEALTH INFLUENCES

Physical Health Influences

Gender equity issues in education are linked to health (Sims & Butter, 2000). When students or their families are ill, school attendance and learning suffer. For Asian and Pacific Islander American students, the link also stems from the relation of economic status and social roles to exposure to environmental hazards, access to health care, the nature of health care, and health education. Education also holds the promise for the production of more Asian and Pacific Islander females and males in a wide range of health care and allied health careers.

Reports of the National Women's Health Information Center (2004) for 1996–2000 showing health risks more prevalent for Pacific Islander Americans include disproportionate obesity rates for Native Hawaiians and Samoans, and diabetes diagnoses for Native Hawaiians 2.5 times higher than White residents of Hawaii of similar age. Guam's death rate from diabetes is 5 times higher than that of the U.S. mainland. For Asian women, the risk of stroke is higher at ages 35–64 than for Whites.

Foo (2002, p. 103) reported that Asian American women have 1.5 to 1.7 times the rate of breast cancer in White women, and that Asian and Pacific Islander American women have the lowest rate of screening among all racial groups. Vietnamese American women have the highest incidence of cervical cancer among all women, with five times the rate for White women. Cancer screening rates are very low for Vietnamese, Hmong, and Cambodian women, with one survey revealing 21% had never been screened, compared to 5% of White women. Social and cultural traditions of some Asian American groups do not endorse some forms of physical health care, nor mental health care. This is a very significant health education and student welfare consideration. About 21% of Asian Pacific Islander women lack health insurance, compared to 16% of all Americans. Asian American women have the highest suicide rate among women 65 or older.

Sexually transmitted disease (STD) is another area of health challenge that Asian and Pacific Islander Americans face. While over two thirds of Asian and Pacific Islander American women are sexually active, approximately 40% of them, and 50% of Asian and Pacific Islander American men, do not always use protection against STDs (National Asian Women's Health Organization, 2000). According to the Centers for Disease Control and Prevention ([CDC], 1998), the rate of contraction of STD's is four times higher for Asian and Pacific Islander American women than for Asian and Pacific Islander American men, with nearly 66% of all new STDs diagnosed in Asian American women occurring with those under the age of 25.

Strategies to address these issues include integrating health care information focused on Asian Pacific Islander Americans into the school health curriculum; conducting outreach at community locations; providing translated materials; providing initial contact with medical personnel and culturally appropriate care; and promoting health related careers among female and male Asian and Pacific Islander American students.

Psychological Health Influences

The highest rate of suicide in the United States is for Asian American women over 65 years of age, and the second highest rate of suicide is for Asian American women between 15 and 24 (Foo, 2002, p. 104). Chinese American women have the highest incidence of suicide among all racial or ethnic groups, at 20 deaths per 100,000 (Foo, 2002, p. 105); however, Asian Americans as a whole seek counseling and treatment only 25% as often as Whites, and 50% as often as African Americans and Hispanics.

Culturally competent school counseling for Asian and Pacific Islander Americans on academic, cocurricular, and personal matters should stand on the shoulders of mental health and related psychological/sociological research with males and females of these groups. Although much more study is needed, an important body of research has begun to emerge.

Okazaki (2003) found that Asian Americans tend to have higher social anxiety than Whites, yet they may be no more likely to manifest dysfunctional levels or exhibit behavior that others view as social anxiety. A factor that has not received scholarly attention is the possibility that subjective social distress among Asian Americans may be heightened by their status as visible ethnic minorities, many of whom are immigrants or nonnative English speakers striving to adjust to culturally different standards. Asakawa (2001) found that parental support for autonomy and adolescents' perceived competence while studying favorably affected Asian Americans' internalization of their cultural values relevant to education and academic success, having strong positive influences on their school performance.

Depression in Asian Americans is associated with gender, age, marital status, employment status, and income. The indices of depression in Asian Americans are higher than African Americans and Latinos. Saez-Santiago and Bernal (2004) found that for Asians, poor English proficiency was associated with difficulty adjusting to American society. In another research direction, it has consistently been found that, regardless of national origin, Asian American women have relatively low rates of alcohol use and problem drinking (Collins & McNair, 2002).

Kodama, McEwen, Liang, and S. Lee (2001) proposed seven vectors of psychosocial issues influencing Asian and Pacific Islander American college students: competence, emotions, interdependence, relationships, identity, purpose, and integrity (Table 24.7). They further inferred a developmental sequence in which the first four vectors must be resolved before identity may be successfully dealt with, and some resolution of identity may be necessary before developing purpose and integrity.

Research on suicide in Micronesia, begun over 30 years ago by Jesuit priest Francis Hezel, and joined by anthropologist Donald Rubinstein (2002; Hezel, 1976, as cited in Rubinstein, 2002), provided a cautionary tale for educators working with the increasing numbers of Micronesian students in Guam, Hawaii, and Mainland U.S. schools and colleges. Rubinstein outlined the severity of the problem and its gendered incidence:

Among the age group at greatest risk—young men between 15 and 24 years old—suicide rates in Micronesia surpass reported rates from any other region within Asia and the Pacific Islands. Indeed, the youth suicide rates in Micronesia have achieved the tragic distinction of being among the highest in the world. (p. 36)

Hezel (1976, as cited in Rubinstein, 2002) and Rubinstein (2002) initially hypothesized that the genesis of these suicides was related to the rapid economic and culture contact changes that occurred from the mid-1960s onward, especially family structural change associated with shifts from subsistence to cash economies. They found that suicide was seven or eight times as prevalent among males than females, and that its inci-

TABLE 24.7   Seven Vectors of Psychosocial Issues for Asian Pacific American College Students

Competence	The emphasis on education becomes ingrained in the APA psyche at a young age, yet this emphasis can also result in a lack of attention to interpersonal competence, and social anxiety has been noted as recurring personality characteristics of APAs.
Emotions	In the college environment, expressiveness is often the norm, but APA may not be comfortable with others' openness; the strong influence of guilt and shame in many Asian cultures has a great impact on the ways in which APAs deal with emotions.
Interdependence	APAs emphasize interdependence, along with the fulfilling of mutual obligations to the family unit, and de-emphasize individual identity.
Relationships	APAs learn to conform rather than stand out, and keep quiet rather than "make waves"; developing relationships with faculty can be a particular challenge for them.
Identity	Gender identity is particularly salient for APA college-age women who may be experiencing independence for the first time, and encountering peers or role models who have a more feminist point of view and more independent experiences.
Purpose	For many APAs, purpose is often tied to the issue of academic achievement, as many APA cultures subscribe to an academic- and economic-based definition of success.
Integrity	For APAs, integrity is determined by how an individual represents the family, having respect for ancestors and upholding the family name.

Source: Adapted from Kodama, McEwen, Liang, and Lee, 2001.

dence did indeed spiral to epidemic proportions beginning in the early '60s. They identified a suicide profile of "a young man, aged 20 or so, living at home with his parents . . . normal in terms of health, mental condition, and behavior" (p. 37). Alcohol was not a significant correlate, nor were threats or warnings. "The typical triggering event for the suicide was a quarrel or argument between the young man and his parents, or occasionally an older brother or sister, or some other older relative." The suicide seemed a great overreaction to precipitating events.

Unfortunately, their later research found evidence that the phenomenon was not bounded by a one-generation cohort suddenly impacted by these changes, but rather, that suicide rates continued to increase into the 1990s. They found that the meaning of suicide had metamorphosed in the youth cultures of Micronesia, regarded by youth as more probable and acquiring "a sort of contagious power." They concluded that the epidemic was more complex than initially understood. More frightening still, Rubinstein (2002) reported that there has been an apparent increase in suicides among children aged 10–14. Hezel and Wylie (1992) reported other gendered Micronesian mental-health results from an epidemiological survey: "In Micronesia, schizophrenia and chronic mental illness were heavily weighted toward males, who constituted 77% of the total sample and outnumbered females by a ratio of 3.4/1." They also concluded that the differential use of drugs (especially marijuana and alcohol), with higher frequency use by males than females, may contribute to the greater incidence of mental illness among males. In a study in which a large sample of Asian and Pacific Islander college students at the University of Guam were assessed with an instrument measuring nine psychological symptom indices (SCL-90-R), J. K. Lee (2005) found significantly higher scores than either a U.S. nonpatient sample or a New Zealand sample including Pacific Islanders. Asian and Pacific Islander participants scored significantly higher than Caucasian students. An analysis of possible gender effects did not reveal reliable differences.

CLASSROOM AND SCHOOL CONTEXT INFLUENCES ON ASIAN AND PACIFIC ISLANDERS

Access to Asian and Pacific Islander American Educators

As described earlier, less than 1.8% of K–12 teachers are of Asian American and Pacific Islander backgrounds (U.S. Census Bureau, 2006). The odds are equally slim that Asian and Pacific Islander American students will benefit from Asian and Pacific Islander American administrators and counselors, since the numbers of such professionals in these fields are also quite scarce. The number of Asian and Pacific Islander American faculty of Education is also low. Although the growth of education doctorates awarded has risen since 1995, the growth has been minimal for those with U.S. citizenship (e.g., those most likely to work in the United States). For example, in 1995, the incidence of Asian and Pacific Islander Americans earning doctoral degrees in education was 1.4% or 80 individuals (Chan & Hune, 1997), and little progress had been made by 2002, when the figure was 1.9% or 98 of 5,265 (Doctorate recipients from U.S. Universities: Summary Report, 2002, pp. 52, 86). In 2001, Pacific Islanders were shifted to the "other" ethnic category, making it impossible to continue to trace their progress.

These data suggest that the recruitment and retention of Asian and Pacific Islander American Education faculty at both the K–12 and higher education levels continue to warrant attention and effort by universities, fellowship sources, and school districts. Given that tuition costs continue to rise and that, traditionally, graduate programs in education are minimally funded, it is especially important to expand funding sources for future Asian and Pacific Islander American teachers and professors of education. Unfortunately, major research and doctoral fellowships through entities such as the Ford Foundation continue to exclude Asian Americans from the pool of eligible applicants, perhaps due to misunderstandings about the fact that the model minority myth does not translate to large numbers of Asian and Pacific Islander American doctoral students in education or the humanities. Funding for Asian and Pacific Islander undergraduate and graduate educators would be an excellent recommendation for the recently formed Asian and Pacific Islander Scholarship Fund (www.apiasf.org), the first national scholarship fund for Asian and Pacific Islanders.

Asian and Pacific Islander American college students may find it relatively more difficult to find a faculty mentor or role model among the smaller number of Asian and Pacific Islander faculty.[4] However, emerging electronic resources may be of help to them in finding a mentor (e.g., programs such as the *Asian Pacific American Affairs* (2004) Web site; *The Mentor* Web site, published by Pennsylvania State University's Center for Excellence in Academic Advising; the National Association of Asian American Professionals; and *Project Impact,* a project dedicated to increasing the political participation of South Asian Americans).

Access to Instructional Materials Representing Asian and Pacific Islander Americans

Lu (1998) has recommended the following guidelines for selecting materials for multicultural literature, based on multicultural educators such as Pang, Colvin, Tran, and Barba (1992). With slight modification (in italics), these literature guidelines apply well to curriculum selections for and about female and male Asian and Pacific Islander American students.

1. Positive portrayals of literary characters with authentic and realistic behaviors, to avoid gender or cultural stereotyping.
2. Authentic illustrations to enhance the quality of the text, since illustrations can have a strong impact on children.
3. Pluralistic themes *with equitable inclusion of both females and males* to foster belief in cultural diversity as a national asset as well as to reflect the changing nature of this country's population.
4. Contemporary and historical fiction that captures changing trends in the roles played by *females and males of* minority groups in America.
5. High literary quality, including strong plots and well-developed characterization.
6. Historical accuracy, when appropriate.
7. Reflections of the cultural *and gendered* values of the characters.
8. Settings in the United States, *including the "American Pacific,"* that help readers build an accurate conception of the culturally diverse nature of this country and the legacy of various minority groups.

The last item on the above list is especially important. It is important to distinguish between Asian and Asian American/Pacific Islander experiences. Too often, stories and folktales from Japan or other countries are equated with the experiences of Asian Americans in the United States. Such errors perpetuate the perception of Asian and Pacific Islander Americans as perpetual foreigners, despite the fact that many Asian Ameri-

---

[4]Approximately 3% of faculty in U.S. colleges and universities in 1999 were Asian and Pacific Islanders. Compared with White faculty, Asian and Pacific Islander faculty had higher average salaries, were more likely to hold advanced degrees, and had greater representation at public doctoral, research, and medical institutions (NCES, 2004).

cans have been in this country for generations, and other Pacific Islander groups have always occupied the land of their ancestors and have been a part of U.S. territories for generations.

The previously listed recommendations apply equally and properly include and represent biracial and multiracial Asian and Pacific Islander Americans. Given that, of the total 12.5 million Asian and Pacific Islander Americans counted in the 2000 U.S. Census, nearly 15%, or 1.9 million, are multiracial, the particular experiences and complexities of multiracial identity need to be moved from the margins into the center of public school curriculum, learning, and instruction.

Language Issues

English learners from Asian-language backgrounds. Often, the language development and support services needed by Asian American students are not properly provided in American public schools. It is well known that Asian Americans are the fastest growing ethnic minority group in the United States, particularly in California, and also that the rate of growth of the English Learner (EL) population over the past decade has been rapid. At present, there are approximately six million ELs in the United States. California is home to one fourth of the nation's six million ELs. In 1992, the number of ELs in California was roughly 600,000, but by 2002, the number had tripled to roughly 1.6 million. As home to 40% of Asian Americans in the United States (2000 U.S. Census), California is a good case study of how the field of education is faring in its goals of supporting this diverse population.

In 2005–06, of the total student population in California (6,322,525), 11.3% (713,239) were Asian and Pacific Islander American, as follows: 8.2% (517,163) Asian American, 0.6% (40,363) Pacific Islander, and 2.6% (165,571) Filipino. The same year, a total of 6% (18,491) of all teachers in California (306,548) were Asian and Pacific Islander Americans, with 4.6% (14,130) Asian American, 0.2% (684) Pacific Islander, and 1.2% (3,677) Filipino teachers. About 76% of the Asian and Pacific Islander American teachers were female. The number of Asian and Pacific Islander American teachers in California has slowly but steadily increased during the last two decades (4.1% in 1983; 4.5% in 1993; 11.1% in 2003).

In 2004–05, the majority (85.3%) of California's EL population (N = 1,591,525) were students of Spanish-language backgrounds. EL students of various Asian-language backgrounds (e.g., Vietnamese, Hmong, Cantonese, Tagalog, Korean, Mandarin, Khmer, Punjabi, Japanese, Lao, Hindi, Mien, Tongan, Samoan, Thai, Ilocano, Gujarati, Indonesian, Marshallese, and Chamorro) comprised approximately 11% of the state's EL population. Primary language personnel, however, are scarce, with 5.4% (16,373) of all 306,548 California teachers certified to work with EL students, and only 2.9% (8,870) able to provide primary-language instruction to the 56 language backgrounds of California EL students. Among these, only 2.3% (173) are Asian and Pacific Islanders (California Department of Education, 2006a, 2006b, 2006c). Given the limited number of bilingual teachers of Asian and Pacific Islander backgrounds, it is useful to examine the experiences of those who are motivated to teach bilingually in Asian languages.

In her survey of teachers pursuing a Korean bilingual certificate (KBCLAD) at several California State University campuses, McField (2003) found both personal and professional motivations (e.g., to utilize their own bilingual proficiencies; to help students retain their primary-language proficiencies and assist them in developing English proficiency; to promote awareness of the Korean language and culture; to secure career stability and job opportunities). They encountered certain difficulties, such as (a) limited availability of student teaching placements; (b) difficulties inherent in language teaching in general; (c) shortage of financial aid; (d) limitations in higher education coursework in Korean and the pedagogical methods for the language; and (e) program structure and administration. All KBCLAD candidates were female. Improvements will be needed to supply the number of certified Asian-language teachers required to teach English to EL's, support English instruction in the core content areas via the primary language, and teach Asian languages as second or foreign languages at elementary and secondary levels. Recruitment could also focus on increasing the number of males certified in these areas.

Wisconsin's federally funded Project Teach and Project Forward provide a different type of case study that addresses Hmong teacher education (Root, Rudawski, Taylor, & Rochon, 2003). More than 60% of the 11,000 EL's in Wisconsin are Hmong students. Project Teach had 19 participants engaged in paraprofessional training in three universities (13 dropped out), and Project Forward had 28 participants in five universities (10 dropped out). Root and colleagues (2003) concluded that factors that may raise retention levels are forgivable loans, evening or intensive summer coursework, mentoring by school personnel, and early financial advising. Considering cultural aspects of goal setting and goal attainment behavior such as family or elder consultation in decision making (Lese & Robbins, 1994) would also be a valuable component in increasing retention of Hmong teacher candidates.

Some research is available on gender and cultural differences associated with the strategies used by Asian Americans learning English. For example, Tran's 1988 study (as cited in Chavez, 2001, p. 180) found that Vietnamese American women did not attend English as a Second Language (ESL) classes or have opportunities to practice English, with 81% reporting no opportunities with English-speaking friends; while the Vietnamese American men reported practicing strategies such as watching TV and listening to the radio more frequently. Such high levels of linguistic isolation suggest that active marketing in native community newspapers and media in support of English language learning is needed.

Pacific Islander languages. Corresponding to the essential multiethnicity of Pacific Islander Americans, the number of Pacific Island languages is large indeed. As Mugler and Lynch put it in their book on *Pacific Languages in Education* (1996):

The considerable linguistic diversity of the Pacific, combined with its recent colonial history, has contributed to making this one of the most multilingual areas of the world, in which the norm is to know at least two languages and sometimes many more (p. 4).

In public schools throughout the "American Pacific," such as Hawaii, American Samoa, the Commonwealth of the Northern Marianas, and Guam, English is usually the dominant language of instruction; while in the Freely Associated States of the Republic of Palau, the Republic of the Marshall Islands, and the Federated States of Micronesia, national languages typically dominate elementary education, giving sway to greater use of English at the secondary level. In many places, Mugler's and Lynch's (1996) description of children routinely using two or more languages, with English prominent in most school settings, is accurate. In Samoa, for example, Samoan is widely used, having been written for two centuries and possessing a large written literature; however, in Hawaii and Guam, where government and other colonial pressures to eliminate the native languages have historically been very severe (e.g., Palomo, 1987), indigenous language loss has occurred for contemporary school children through midadulthood.

Vigorous language and culture movements in these most affected areas since the 1970s continue making progress (Spencer, 1996). In Guam all public-school students have approximately 30 minutes of Chamorro-language instruction per day, and University of Guam Chamorro-language classes are so popular that they are usually overenrolled. In Hawaii, a group of Hawaiian language educators at the University of Hawaii (UH), Hilo, led language education initiatives at all levels of education (Monastersky, 2004). In addition to forging the early Hawaiian Studies Program at the University, they joined others in a nonprofit organization ('Aha Punana Leo) to initiate Hawaiian-language preschools based on the successful model of Maori-immersion schools in New Zealand, known as "language nests." Today, more than 2,000 children are enrolled in Hawaiian-immersion programs in Hawaii. There are more than a dozen private preschools and 20 Hawaiian-immersion schools. UH Hilo's College of Hawaiian Studies is the source of the curriculum materials and teacher training. It also grants master's and doctoral degrees in Hawaiian language studies. The UH, Manoa campus is also initiating a master's degree in Hawaiian studies, with the Hawaiian language playing a prominent role.

Gender differences in Pacific Island languages have not been given extensive academic study, nor have these been interpreted for use in education; however, even the most cursory study of any of these languages will reveal gender-differentiated vocabulary and sociolinguistic domains reserved for one or the other of the sexes. One interesting example is an English-based Creole spoken only by the men of Ngatic Island of Pohnpei State in the Federated States of Micronesia. Other examples pertain to culturally defined gender roles in activities such as weaving and other women's arts (e.g., Kihleng & Pacheco, 2000); the pattera (midwife), suruhana (herbal healer), and techa (prayer leader) female Chamorro roles of the Marianas Islands (e.g., Hattori, 2004); fishing, gardening, rituals, chants, or religious events. Conversely, the lexicon of star navigation is reserved almost entirely for males of the outer islands of Chuuk and Yap, where these skills developed and are maintained. Some U.S. Census studies in the Freely Associated States of Micronesia, from which significant migration to U.S. mainland states is occurring, have reported sex differences in access to education and, thus, bilingual and biliteracy educational opportunities, and school achievement. Based on these, Spencer (1992, p.

300) developed estimates of literacy for females and males that revealed lower literacy rates in a number of entities for females, as well as for all students living in remote areas. There were signs that school attendance was increasing for youth in general. Especially encouraging was the increased proportion of girls in Yap state who are now completing four or more grade levels.

Harassment and Academic Profiling

While Asian and Pacific Islander American students are often described as model students, it is imperative that different groups of Asian and Pacific Islander Americans be examined and serviced according to the different needs of each group. Often invisible or ignored are the daily incidents of harassment suffered by Asian Americans. A particularly noteworthy study (Kiang, Lan, & Sheehan, 1995) examined one elementary school comprised of one half African American and one third Asian American (mostly Vietnamese American) students. The school was noted for its mission of a "safe and caring community of learners" and for institutional responsiveness. When 26 fourth graders were asked to document incidents of harassment, however, in one month alone, students reported 84 direct incidents of harassment, 26 incidents of witnessing another Vietnamese American student being harassed, and 67 incidents of witnessing students other than Vietnamese American students being harassed. The incidents of harassment ranged from being teased and receiving verbal harassment such as being called "Chinese," to being punched or pushed.

The Vietnamese American students' own bilingual classroom was the only place in which harassment was not documented, providing perhaps the only space in which students could reflect upon the negative incidents and consider how they might respond, should they be harassed again in the future. The question that the authors ultimately pose is critical: "Who will take responsibility for race relations in the school?" One of the students' journals revealed, "I tell my teacher and see what my teach gone a do [teacher going to do] about it." Clearly, the school needed to take responsibility for the problem and address this pattern of harassment in a comprehensive manner, rather than allowing the burden to rest on one teacher. One approach that would address the harassment problem would be to implement an antibias curriculum (Derman-Sparks, 1989) throughout the entire school. An antibias curriculum would guide all students, not just the victims of harassment, to speak up about and to reduce the incidents of discrimination, harassment, and violence at the school and in the community. Gender was not explicitly discussed as a part of this study, but would be an important variable to examine, given the differential patterns of harassment by gender documented in the literature (e.g., Hand & Sanchez, 2000; Thorne, 1993; Wiseman, 2003). Studies examining harassment among Asian and Pacific Islanders are limited (e.g., Hishinuma, Chang, & Goebert, 2005; Kennedy, 1995; Mark, Revilla, Tsutsumoto, 2006). Additional research examining both gender and ethnic variables is needed.

Teranishi (2002) interviewed 80 Chinese American and 80 Filipino American students at four high schools: two schools with large Chinese American populations and two schools with large Filipino American populations. He noted that Chinese American and Filipino American students have unique racialized experiences in high school that critically influence postsecondary education and career opportunities. Despite the fact that the two groups generally share similar immigration and socioeconomic patterns in the United States, Chinese American students were perceived by schools and peers to be academic "model minority" students, while Filipino American students were perceived to be prone to gang activities and not academically inclined. Counselors steered Chinese American students into college preparatory classes and provided them with specific and timely information concerning college planning, testing, and admissions, while counselors more often recommended vocational classes and were unable to provide critical information related to college preparation for Filipino American students. Once in the college prep or vocational classes, students experienced different levels of support and information related to college admissions as well, further widening the divide in opportunities and access for the two groups of students.

Perhaps not surprisingly, given the different types of experience and resources available to the two groups of students, Chinese American students demonstrated higher levels of educational aspirations, as well as academic confidence, including certainty in completing four years of college, while more Filipino American students stated that they would be applying to vocational schools, as well as colleges. Given that the two groups of students had similar parental levels of education, and that both groups of student interviewees were selected from the top 5–10% of the students at the study schools, the discrepancies are particularly alarming. The author noted that in 2000, while 40% of the total enrollment at the University of California, Berkeley was Asian Pacific American, "Chinese Americans were nearly seven times more likely to attend UC Berkeley than Filipino Americans" (Teranishi, 2002, p. 144). The study did not note any differences by gender.

The College Experience

Sam's (2006) recent study of Asian and Pacific Islander students at the University of Hawaii at Manoa indicated that the proportionally greater representation of Asian and Pacific Islander students (60%) helped them feel comfortable and satisfied with the overall campus climate and their college experience. Based upon 785 cases collected from 267 colleges from across the country, however, Kim, J. J. Park, and Chang (2006) noted that being Asian American had a negative effect on student-faculty interaction, whether the interaction was faculty-initiated or student-initiated. Also, Asian American students were more likely than their peers to be in college environments that reduced the likelihood of interacting with faculty, as many of them (42%) tended to attend large institutions and had majors in natural sciences, which generated less frequent interactions with faculty than having majors in arts and humanities. Another recent study by Chhuon, Hudley, and Macia (2006) pointed out that the family obligations of Cambodian college students hindered their college success, although their family-oriented collectivism positively influenced their academic aspirations. These recent studies did not indicate any gender differences.

Further studies that examine contextual and environmental factors in educational outcomes are critical to building our understanding of how schools affect academic and societal out-

comes. Accordingly, more studies—or perhaps a coordinated research program—are needed that examine the interaction of gender and racial/ethnic equity with education factors among diverse Asian and Pacific Islander American populations.

PEDAGOGICAL PRACTICE WITH ASIAN AND PACIFIC ISLANDER AMERICANS

Asian American Students

C. C. Park (1997, 2000) investigated the learning style preferences of Korean, Chinese, Filipino, Vietnamese, and White American secondary students. In the first study (1997), she found that learning style preferences were influenced by ethnicity, academic achievement levels, and length of residence in the United States, but not by gender. Preference variations for learning modalities emerged for the ethnic groups. All students showed some preference for auditory learning. Relative to the group of White students, which had a negative preference for visual learning, Korean, Chinese, and Filipino American students more often preferred it. More high achievers than low achievers preferred visual learning. All groups indicated a preference for kinesthetic learning, and all indicated some preference for tactile learning, which was favored most often by Vietnamese students. In general, preferences for visual, kinesthetic, and tactile modes were not associated with gender, ESL enrollment, or length of residence in the United States, although there was some indication that students in mainstream rather than ESL classes might display kinesthetic activity preferences.

C. C. Park's (1997) examination of preferences for group versus individual learning arrangements elicited differences associated with ethnic group and achievement level, but not by gender, as might be expected because of gender segregation norms in Korean and Chinese culture. Korean, Chinese, and White American students had negative preferences for group learning, as did high achievers. Vietnamese, Filipino American, and low and middle achieving students, however, favored group learning. All groups indicated some preference for individual learning, and there were no statistically significant differences across them. Those who were foreign-born, and middle and high achievers, tended to prefer individual learning, while lower achievers tended to be negative toward this arrangement.

Another study by C. C. Park (2000) investigated learning style preferences of Southeast Asian American students. Ethnicity was the primary factor influencing learning style preferences, and no differences were found across the various learning style modalities due to gender, achievement levels, or length of residence in the United States. Relative to White students, Hmong and Vietnamese American students had a significant preference for visual learning, and Hmong students significantly preferred tactile learning. All groups of students indicated a major preference for kinesthetic learning. While White students viewed group learning negatively, all Southeast Asian American groups of students indicated either a major or minor preference for this mode. All groups indicated a minor preference for individual learning, with the exception of Cambodian American students.

Pacific Islander Students

In a remarkable 15-year research-and-development program, supported by the Kamehameha Schools/Bernice Pauahi Bishop Estate and a host of other federal and private funders, psychologists Roland Tharp and Ronald Gallimore (1988) and their respected team of collaborators designed, operated, and investigated the Kamehameha Early Education Program (KEEP). Applying psychological, anthropological, linguistic, and educational research and theory, with a special interest in Vygotsky's theory of cognitive development (e.g., Vygotsky, 1978), the KEEP team addressed the underachievement of a group of 500 at-risk Hawaiian and part-Hawaiian children at Kamehameha Schools. The team then exported a KEEP support program to another 60 public school classrooms on three Hawaiian islands that served over 2,000 students, and later, to an Arizona Navajo reservation and several schools in Los Angeles. The complex inquiry-based project designed instructional activity settings that were culturally congruent with home and community learning and communication patterns, and made teacher training and contextual support for teaching a cornerstone of the program. Evaluations of outcomes were impressive (Tharp & Gallimore, 1988): "For over a decade, the largely at-risk minority children enrolled in the Kamehameha School's KEEP system performed at national-norm levels in reading achievement" (p. 116).

Regarding gender differences, Tharp reported that the KEEP results were not disaggregated by sex—partly due to the *zeitgeist* of the times and partly because jarring gender-associated differences did not emerge in observations. However, the KEEP work in Navajo settings revealed gender separation to be a major issue (Vogt, Jordan & Tharp, 1992). "The way we construed the issue was this: Polynesia is an age-graded society; Navajo is gender-graded. We never noticed gender issues in Honolulu; in Navajo, they leapt out at us" (R. G. Tharp, personal communication March 22, 2005).

In related research, Au and Kawakami (1994) outlined five domains that facilitate cultural congruence in instruction for Hawaiian students: (a) dialect speakers, (b) participation structures, (c) ESL students, (d) narrative and questioning styles, and (e) peer groups. The concept of cultural congruence, which refers to consonance between school and the home or community, is based on three premises: (a) that learning happens in a social context, be it highly structured or relaxed, formal or informal; (b) that optimal learning occurs when learning is scaffolded or assisted by a more capable other, be it the teacher or a peer (Vygotsky, 1978); and (c) that, since learning occurs as much outside of the classroom as inside, educators need to examine features of home or community learning contexts for effectiveness and application in the classroom. The chapter authors suggest that gendered aspects of the specific Asian and Pacific Islander home and community environments need to be considered (e.g., Ross, 2004).

Based on their review of research on dialect speakers, Au and Kawakami (1994) reflected on the frequent underestimation of the abilities of these students, and the lack of opportunities provided for these students to display their skills in formal learning settings. Emphasis on conventional English usage or superficial aspects of language can silence dialect-speaking children and reduce their focus on meaning and comprehension in content areas. Effective pedagogy includes modeling high-quality oral language while scaffolding standard English learning via explicit comparison and discussion with the dialect. This should also involve creating a learning environment of trust, support, and engaged learning that allows connections between school and personal domains, opting for simple, clean sentences, avoiding slang or idioms, and providing explicit explanations of new vocabulary, concepts, or idioms.

A rich body of research and practice literature has been developed involving participation structures with minority groups such as Native American and Hawaiian students (e.g., Boggs, 1986; Philips, 1972; Watson-Gegeo & Boggs, 1977). Little has been said about differential effects associated with gender; however, since participation structure involves principles of student grouping, cultural and community perspectives on close working proximity of male and female students (especially those with familial relationships) need to be considered. Further, the collectivist versus individualist aspect of Pacific Island communities seems to inform the educational use of small group participation, and the availability of student centered rather than teacher centered instructional design. For example, Watson-Gegeo & Boggs (1977) found that incorporating the collaborative communication styles of the home and community into classroom settings, and making room for shared construction of knowledge, had positive results for the participation and learning of Hawaiian students. Students would less frequently respond with silence when called on, because they could contribute to a collaborative response. They were able to reinforce their own learning by assisting peers. Practice indications are that grouping approaches such as those described in the cooperative learning literature (e.g., Kagan, 1991; Lyman & Foyle, 1990) can contribute to culturally congruent instruction for Pacific Islander students in higher education as well as at K–12 levels (e.g., K. Skoog, personal communication, April, 2005).

In reviewing research on ESL students, Au and Kawakami (1994) pointed out effective practices such as educators who invite and incorporate the "funds of knowledge" these students bring into the classroom, and who provide students with opportunities for demonstrating their linguistic, cultural, and intellectual strengths. Clearly, these strengths include the funds of knowledge they have about gendered roles within their communities. Such educators provide tools that include concept maps, rehearsal time, opportunities for collaborative learning and inquiry, group investigation tasks (Joyce & Weil, 1986), and (the chapter authors would add) Asian and Pacific Islander male and female role models and instructional materials consistent with Lu's (1988) guidelines.

Au and Kawakami (1994) suggested that implementing an understanding of the narrative and questioning styles characteristic of Pacific Islander communication can transform the dynamics of the learning setting from an evaluative experience to a truly expressive and meaning-focused one in which teachers have more opportunity to guide student expression and understanding. In her discussion of traditional science and the transmission and use of science knowledge in Micronesia, Spencer (1994) provided an example of the elements of instruction involving familiar sociolinguistic patterns of Pacific languages (e.g., talk-story), within the context of the male domain of navigation instruction on Puluwat. Other researchers (e.g., Boggs, 1986) have illustrated the impotency of direct questioning approaches with Hawaiian students versus more integrative discussion. Cultural congruence benefiting student learning is also enhanced by longer wait times following instructional questioning.

Research on peer groups, the fifth cultural congruence domain reviewed by Au and Kawakami (1994), indicated that student learning may be mediated by perceptions of rivalry or equality among peer groups in the classroom (Pintrich & Schrauben, 1992). Challenges to teachers of diverse student groups, with complex curriculums, are great in that it is important to give voice to all students in the class, and allow them the opportunity to confront oppositional viewpoints and renegotiate premises, assumptions, and values for themselves, freeing them in the process from teacher-dominant positions. By (a) valuing students' home languages or dialects, (b) giving students time to discuss their thoughts in small and whole group structures, (c) recognizing and utilizing different narrative and questioning styles, (d) validating student abilities and providing creative opportunities to demonstrate that understanding, and (e) recognizing peer group dynamics, educators of male and female Asian and Pacific Islander American students contribute to their culturally congruent education.

SUMMARY AND RECOMMENDATIONS

Educational progress has been made for Asian and Pacific Islander female and male students, but as Fleming noted in her review (2000), differential outcomes continue to persist for females of color, English Learners, and females with disabilities. Three key policy recommendations emerged from the current review, and they apply to both females and males of the Asian and Pacific Islander American population:

1. Improved access to all levels and types of educational opportunities.
2. Continued and improved development of economic, educational, and research databases on Asian and Pacific Islander subgroups, as modeled by the 2000 U.S. Census Bureau detailed race/ethnicity reports.
3. Policy incentives and regulatory requirements to influence greater representation of Asian and Pacific Islander Americans in management positions in public and private sector organizations, where they are currently underrepresented, with earnings proportionately comparable to the higher levels of education acquired by some subgroups of this population.

Five recommendations call for new or improved practices or programs:

1. To change Asian and Pacific Islander American women's overrepresentation in low-wage, dead-end jobs, more and improved programs are needed that develop job skills, provide continuing educational opportunities (focusing especially on Southeast Asian women as the group at highest risk), information on workers rights, self-advocacy, and labor organization.

2. Accelerated recruitment and support of Asian and Pacific Islander American women in the fields of math, science and engineering where, like the general population, they are underrepresented compared to males.
3. One of the highest priorities is attracting and supporting more Asian and Pacific Islander American men and women to the full range of careers in education because of the proportionally smaller representation of these populations in the field.
4. Creation of educational environments and practices that positively address the affective development of Asian and Pacific Islander students: (a) tending to career aspirations and choice in the early years of education; (b) explicitly confronting and correcting the negative and limiting assumptions and expectations of stereotypes about the diverse Asian and Pacific Islander American subgroups; (c) actively nurturing their self-concepts, with appropriate parental involvement and input; and (d) implementing research-based, comprehensive, antibias curriculums that prevent harassment and violence at school against Asian and Pacific Islander Americans.
5. Culturally competent educational practices tied to the specific Asian and Pacific Islander subgroups, such as pedagogy based on diverse learning styles and informed by gendered cultural attitudes and traditions; textbooks reflecting these groups, with a clear distinction between U.S. communities, colonized Pacific Islands, and Asian countries, as well as nuanced representation of female and male biracial or multiracial Asian and Pacific Islander Americans; involvement of parents, with informed choice opportunities regarding primary and English language development programs.

Research on educational equity is needed for female and male students of each Asian and Pacific Islander American student subgroup.

1. Educational interventions striving for academic excellence for these students are not truly research-based until rigorous scientific research and evaluation has been conducted that includes them in adequate sample sizes on the basis of sex and ethnic group and shows what interventions are especially effective for females and males in each group.
2. The research agenda must include topics focusing on affective constructs such as self-concept, individual and group identity, resilience, and how limitations placed on the motivations, aspirations, and opportunities of Asian and Pacific Islander youth and adults can be lifted so they may achieve their potentials.
3. Along with school programs that are equally effective for females and males, basic and applied research is needed to understand and counteract the persistence of negative gender and racial stereotyping, discrimination, and harassment of Asian and Pacific Islander students in public education environments. Also needed is research on children's perceptions of discrimination, the development of healthy ways of coping with it, and supportive roles for family members and educators to prepare students to survive discrimination and harassment.

ACKNOWLEDGMENTS

The authors would like to thank Dr. Clara Park, California State University, Northridge, for her final review of the chapter; Dr. Anne Hattori, Dr. James Sellmann, and Sharleen Santos Bamba, University of Guam, and doctoral student Christine DeLisle, Women's Studies Program, University of Michigan, Ann Arbor, for their reviews of earlier drafts. These reviews provided much guidance from the perspectives of Asian and indigenous Pacific Islander American women and Asia-Pacific scholars.

References

About, Inc. (2004). *Model minority: The trouble with Asian American stereotyping.* Retrieved October, 2004, from http://racerelations.about.com/library/weekly/blmodelminority.htm

Alameda, C. K. (1999). *Hawaiian elementary school students' ratings of perceived academic ability of Hawaiian, Japanese, and White American children: A formulation from the racial identity perspective.* Unpublished doctoral dissertation, University of Nebraska, Lincoln. (UMI No. 9936751)

American Association of Colleges of Teacher Education. (1999). *Teacher education pipeline IV: Schools, colleges, and departments of education.* Washington, DC: Author.

Asakawa, K. (2001). Family socialization practices and their effects on the internationalization of educational values for Asian and White American adolescents. *Applied Developmental Science, 5*(3), 184–194.

Asher, N. (2001). Rethinking multiculturalism. In C.C. Park, A. L. Goodwin, & S. J. Lee (Eds.), *Research on the education of Asian and Pacific Americans* (pp. 55–71). Greenwich, CT: Information Age.

Asian American Federation Census Information Center (2001). *New census estimates tell two stories about Asian and Pacific Islander students.* Retrieved November, 2004, from http://www.aafny.org/proom/pr/pr20010323.asp/

Asian American identity problem (1996). *Asian American identity problems.* Retrieved November 2004 from http://www.laze.net/papers/asianamident.php/

Asian Pacific American affairs (2004). Retrieved in 2004 from http://www.odos.uiuc.edu/apaa/mentoring.asp/

Association of American Medical Colleges (2005). *Minorities in medical education: Facts & figures, 2005.* AAMC Data Warehouse.

Au, K. H., & Kawakami, A. J. (1994). Cultural congruence in instruction. In E. R. Hollins, J. E. King, & W. C. Hayman (Eds.), *Teaching diverse populations: Formulating a knowledge base* (pp. 5–24). New York: State University of New York Press.

Babasa, J. B. (1987). The development of linguistic attitudes toward Guamanian dialect English and Standard English. In M. Spencer (Ed.), *Chamorro language issues and research on Guam,* (pp. 161–173). Mangilao, GU: University of Guam.

Bae, S.-W., & Brekke, J. (2004). *The measurement of self-esteem among Korean Americans: A cross-ethnic study.* Retrieved November, 2004, from http://www.sswr.org/papers2001/073.htm

Boggs, S. T. (1986). *Speaking, relating, and learning: A study of Hawaiian children at home and at school.* Norwood, NJ: Ablex Publishing Corporation.

Bracey, G. W. (2001). Why so few Asian American teachers? *Phi Delta Kappan, 83*(1), 14–15.

California Department of Education. (2000). *Numbers of 12th grade graduates in California public schools, completing all courses required for U.C. and/or C.S.U. entrance by gender and ethnic group for the year 1998–99.* Retrieved July 12, 2006 from http://data1.cde.ca.gov/dataquest/stgradnum.asp?cChoice=StGr-dEth&cYear=1998-99&submit]=submit

California Department of Education (2006a). *State summary, number of staff by ethnicity: Teachers, 2004–2005.* Data Quest: Demographics Data files.

California Department of Education (2006b). *Statewide enrollment by ethnicity, 2005–2006.* Retrieved July 12, 2006 from http://data1.cde.ca.gov/dataquest/EnrollEthState.asp?Level=State&TheYear=2005-06&cCh

California Department of Education (2006c). *Number of English learners by language, 2004–2005.* Retrieved July 12, 2006 from http://data1.cde.ca.gov/dataquest/LEPbyLang1.asp?cChoice=LepbyLang1&cYear=2004–05&cLevel=State&cTopic=LC&myTimeFrame=S&submit1=Submit

Centers for Disease Control and Prevention. (1998). *Tracking the hidden epidemics: Trends in the STD epidemics in the U.S.* Washington, DC: Author.

Chan, K. S., & Hune, S. (1997). Special focus: Asian Pacific American demographic and educational trends. In D. Carter, & R. Wilson (Eds.), *Minorities in higher education,* Vol.15. Washington, DC: American Council on Education.

Chavez, M. (2001). *Gender in the language classroom.* New York: McGraw-Hill.

Chhuon, V., Hudley, C., & Macia, R. (2006, April). *Cambodian-American college students: Cultural values and multiple worlds.* Paper presented at the American Educational Research Association Annual Meeting, San Francisco, CA.

Chiang, L., Lidstone, J., & Stephenson, R. (2004). (Eds.). *The challenges of globalization: Cultures in transition in the Pacific-Asia region.* Lanham, MD: University Press of America.

Chinn, P. W. U. (2002). Asian and Pacific Islander women scientists and engineers: A narrative exploration of model minority, gender, and racial stereotypes. *Journal of Research in Science Teaching, 39*(4), 302–323.

Chong, S. B. (2002). Asian and American teachers and teacher candidates in California: Who are they and what they are their needs? In E. H. Tamura, V. Chattergy, & R. Endo (Eds.), *Asian and Pacific Islander American education: Social, cultural, and historical contexts* (pp. 117–131). South El Monte, CA: Pacific Asia Press.

Chu-Chang, M. (1983). *Asian- and Pacific-American perspectives in bilingual education: Comparative research.* New York: Teachers College, Columbia University.

Clarren, R. (2006). Sex and greed in a paradise lost. *Ms, 16*(2), 34–41.

Collins, R. L., & McNair, L. D. (2002). Minority women and alcohol use. *Alcohol Research & Health, 26*(4), 251–256.

Day, R. R. (1980). The development of linguistic attitudes and preferences. *TESOL Quarterly,* 27–37.

Derman-Sparks, L. (1989). *Anti-bias curriculum: Tools for empowering young children.* Washington, DC: National Association for the Education of Young Children.

Dominy, M. D. (1990). Maori sovereignty: A feminist invention of tradition. In J. Linnekin & L. Poyer (Eds.). *Cultural identity and ethnicity in the Pacific* (pp. 237–257). Honolulu: University of Hawai'i Press.

Dubanoski, R. A., & Snyder, K. (1980). Patterns of child abuse and neglect in Japanese and Samoan-Americans. *Child Abuse and Neglect, 4,* 217–225.

Eaton, M. J., & Dembo, M. H. (1997). Differences in the motivational beliefs of Asian American and non-Asian students. *Journal of Educational Psychology, 89*(3), 433–440.

Endo, R., Park, C. C., & Tsuchida, J. N. (1998). *Current issues in Asian and Pacific American education.* South El Monte, CA: Pacific Asia Press.

Erikson, E. (1980). *Identity and the life cycle.* New York: W.W. Norton & Company.

Evans, G. W. (2004). The environment of childhood poverty. *American Psychologist, 59*(2), 77–92.

Feminist Daily News Wire (2006, June 20). Kennedy adds amendment to raise minimum wage, includes Mariana Islands. Retrieved July 18, 2006 from http://www.feminist.org/news/newsbyte/uswirestory.asp?id=9717

Feminist Daily News Wire (2006, June 8). Proposed labor bill to confront human rights violations in Marianas Islands. Retrieved July 18, 2006 from http://www.feminist.org/news/newsbyte/uswirestory.asp?id=9697

Fitisemanu, D., Green, K. K., Hall, D., Hippolite Wright, D., McKenzie, B., Nauta, D., et al. (2002). Family dynamics among Pacific Islander Americans. In P. Spickard, J. L. Rondilla, & D. H. Wright (Eds.), *Pacific diaspora: Island peoples in the United States and across the Pacific* (pp. 269–278). Honolulu: University of Hawai'i Press.

Fleming, P. M. (2000). Three decades of educational progress (and continuing barriers) for women and girls. *Equity and Excellence in Education, 33*(1), 74–79.

Foo, L. J. (2002). *Asian American women: Issues, concerns and responsive human and civil rights advocacy.* New York: Ford Foundation.

Funaki, I. F., & Funaki, L. M. (2002). A compromise identity: Tongan Americans in the United States. In P. Spickard, J. L. Rondilla, & D. H. Wright (Eds.), *Pacific Diaspora, Island peoples in the United States and across the Pacific* (pp. 211–218). Honolulu: University of Hawai'i Press.

Futrell, M. H. (1999). Recruiting minority teachers. *Educational Leadership, 56*(8), 30–33.

Gergen, K. J. (1991). *The saturated self.* New York: Harper Collins Publishers.

Goodwin, A L. (1995). Asian Americans and Pacific Islanders in teaching. *ERIC Digest No. 104.*

Gordon, J. (2000). Asian American resistance to selecting teaching as a career: The power of community and tradition. *Teachers College Record, 102*(1),173–196.

Grant, L., & Rong, X. L. (1999). Gender, immigrant generation, ethnicity and the schooling progress of youth. *Journal of Research and Development in Education, 33*(1), 15–26.

Green, K. K. (2002). Colonialism's daughters: Eighteenth- and nineteenth-century western perceptions of Hawaiian women. In P. Spickard, J. L. Rondilla, & D. H.Wright. *Pacific Diaspora, Island peoples in the United States and across the Pacific* (pp. 221–252). Honolulu: University of Hawai'i Press.

Hall, F. R., Mikesell, C., Cranston, P., Julian, E., & Elam, C. (2001). Longitudinal trends in the applicant pool for U.S. medical schools, 1974–1999. *Academic Medicine, 76*(8), 829–834.

Hand, J. Z., & Sanchez, L. (2000). Badgering or bantering?: Gender differences in experience of, and reactions to, sexual harassment among U.S. high-school students. *Gender and Society, 14*(6), 718–746.

Harvard University (2006). *Degree student enrollment and degree conferred.* Cambridge, MA: Registrar Offices.

Hattori, A. P. (2004). *Colonial disease: U.S. Navy health policies and the Chamorros of Guam, 1898–1941, Pacific Islands Monograph Series 19.* Honolulu: Center for Pacific Islands Studies, University of Hawai'i, Manoa, University of Hawai'i Press.

Haughton, N. (2002). *IQ and income, race, and gender.* Retrieved November, 2004, from http://www.sq.4mg.com/Iqincome.htm/

Hezel, F. X. (1976). Micronesia's hanging spree. *Micronesian Reporter, 24*(4), 8–13.

Hezel, F. X., & Wylie, A. M. (1992). Schizophrenia and chronic mental illness in Micronesia: an epidemiological survey. *ISLA: A Journal of Micronesian Studies, 1*(2), 329–354.

Hishinuma, E. S., Chang, J. Y., & Goebert, D. A. (2005). Prevalence of victims of violence among ethnically diverse Asian/Pacific Islanders. *Violence and Victims, 58*(5), 561–575.

Hossfeld, S. (2001). *Foreign and female: Immigrant women workers in Silicon Valley.* Berkeley: University of California Press.

Hune, S. & Nomura, G. M. (2003). *Asian/Pacific Islander American women: A historical anthology.* New York: New York University Press.

Ima, K., & Nidorf, J. (1998). Troubled Southeast Asian Refugee Youth: Profile of a delinquent population. In R. Endo, C. C. Park, & J. N. Tsuchida (Eds.), *Current issues in Asian and Pacific American education* (pp. 37–63). South El Monte, CA: Pacific Asia Press.

Inoue, Y. (2004). Educational and social status aspirations among undergraduate women in Guam and Japan. *Journal of the Pacific Society, 27*(1), 51–63.

Jorgenson, O. (2000). *The need for more ethnic teachers: Addressing the critical shortage in American public schools.* (ID Number: 10551 Teachers College Record On-Line.) Retrieved November 17, 2004, from http://www.tcrecord.org/Content.asp?ContentID=10551

Joyce, B., & Weil, M. (1986). *Models of Teaching* (3rd ed). New York Prentice Hall.

Kagan, S. (1991). *Cooperative learning resources for teachers.* Riverside, CA: University of California, Resources for Teachers.

Kennedy, E. (1995). Correlates of perceived popularity among peers: A study of race and gender differences among middle school students. *The Journal of Negro Education, 64*(2), 186–195.

Kiang, P. N., Lan, N. N., & Sheehan, R. L. (1995). Don't ignore it: Documenting racial harassment in a fourth-grade Vietnamese bilingual classroom. *Equity and Excellence in Education, 28*(1), 31–35.

Kihleng, K. S., & Pacheco, N. P. (2000). *Art & culture of Micronesian women.* Unpublished manuscript, ISLA Center for the Arts, and Women & Gender Studies Program, University of Guam.

Kim, J. (1981). *Development of Asian American identity: An exploratory study of Japanese American Women.* (ERIC Document Reproduction Service No. ED216085)

Kim, Y. K., Park, J. J., & Chang, M. J. (2006, April). *Asian American students and student-faculty interaction.* Paper presented at the American Educational Research Association Annual Meeting, San Francisco, CA.

Klein, S. (Ed.). (1985). *Handbook for achieving sex equity through education.* Baltimore: The John Hopkins University Press.

Kodama, C. M., McEwen, M. K., Liang, C. T. H., & Lee, S. (2001). A theoretical examination of psychosocial issues for Asian Pacific American students. *NASPA Journal, 38*(4), 411–437.

Lai, E., & Arguelles, D. (2003). *The new face of Asian Pacific America: Numbers, diversity, and change in the 21st century.* Los Angeles: UCLA Asian American Studies Center Press.

Lai, H. M., Huang, J., & Wong, D. (1980). *The Chinese of America: 1785–1980.* San Francisco: Phelps-Schaefer.

Lau, A. (1995, February 11). Teenage suicide. *San Diego Union-Tribune,* p. A-19.

Lee, J. K. (2005). *Cross-cultural validation of the SCL-90-R with Asian/Pacific Island Populations.* Unpublished senior honors thesis, University of Guam, Mangilao.

Lee, O. (1997). Diversity and equity for Asian American students in science. *Science Education, 81,* 107–22.

Lee, P. W., & Wong, S. (2002). At-risk Asian and Pacific American Youths: Implications for teachers, psychologists, and other providers. In E. H. Tamura, V. Chattergy, & R. Endo (Eds.), *Asian and Pacific*

Islander American education: Social, cultural, and historical contexts (pp. 85–115). South El Monte, CA: Pacific Asia Press.

Lese, K., & Robbins, S. B. (1994). Relationship between goal attributes and the academic achievement of Southeast Asian adolescent refugees. *Journal of Counseling Psychology, 41*(1), 45–52.

Linnekin, J. (1990). *Sacred queens and women of consequence: Rank, gender, and colonialism in the Hawaiian Islands.* Ann Arbor, MI: The University of Michigan Press.

Linnekin, J., & Poyer, L. (Eds.) (1990). *Cultural identity and ethnicity in the Pacific.* Honolulu: University of Hawai'i Press.

Lu, M.-Y. (1998). *Multicultural children's literature in the elementary classroom.* ERIC Digest. Bloomington, IN: ERIC Clearinghouse on Reading, English, and Communication. *(ERIC Database #ED 423 552).*

Lyman, L., & Foyle, H. C. (1990). *Cooperative grouping for interactive learning: Students, teachers, and administrators.* Washington, DC: National Education Association.

Mahdzan, F., & Ziegler, N. (2004). *Asian American: An analysis of negative stereotypical characters in popular media.* Retrieved October, 2004, from http://www.mahdzen.com/fairy/papers/asian/

Mark, G. Y., Revilla, L. A., & Tsutsumoto, T. (2006). Youth violence prevention among Asian American and Pacific Islander youth. In N. G. Guerra & E. Phillips (Eds.), *Preventing Youth Violence in a Multicultural Society* (pp. 127–146). Washington, DC: American Psychological Association.

McField, G. P. (2003, February). *Asian Americans in the teacher education pipeline: the voices of Korean BCLAD candidates and teachers.* Paper presented at the annual meeting of California Association for Bilingual Education, Los Angeles, CA.

Monastersky, R. (2004, December 10). Talking a language back from the brink, Hawaiian professors band together to revive the islands' dying native tongue. *The Chronicle of Higher Education,* A8–A10.

Mugler, F., & Lynch, J. (1996). Language and Education in the Pacific. In F. Mugler & J. Lynch (Eds.), *Pacific languages in education* (pp. 1–9). Fiji: Institute of Pacific Studies, University of the South Pacific.

National Asian Women's Health Organization. (2000). *Community solutions: Meeting the challenge of STD's in Asian Americans and Pacific Islanders.* San Francisco, CA.

National Center for Education Statistics. (2003). *Higher education general information survey: Fall enrollment in colleges and universities surveys, 1976 and 1980; and integrated postsecondary education data system: Fall enrollment surveys, 1990 through 1999, spring, 2001, and spring 2002 surveys.* Author.

National Center for Education Statistics. (2004). *Digest of education statistics tables and figures 2000.* Retrieved November, 2004, from http://nces.ed.gov/programs/digest/d00/dt133.asp/

National Center for Education Statistics. (2006). *Number of Asian students in schools in regular public school districts, by region and year.* Common core data, longitudinal file. table A15a.

National Women's Health Information Center. (2004). *Health problems in Asian American/Pacific Islander and native Hawaiian women.* Retrieved October, 2004, from http://www.4woman.gov/faq/Asian_Pacific.htm

National Science Foundation. (2003). *Women, minorities and persons with disabilities in science and engineering: 2002 (*NSF 03-312*).* Arlington, VA: Author.

Okazaki, S. (2003). Expressions of social anxiety in Asian Americans. *Psychiatric Times, 20*(10). Retrieved November 2004 from www.psychiatrictimes.com/p031076.html/

Palmer, J. D. (2001). Korean adopted young women: Gender bias, racial issues, and educational implications. In C. C. Park, A. L. Goodwin, & S. J. Lee (Eds.), *Research on the education of Asian and Pacific Americans* (pp. 177–204). Greenwich, CT: Information Age.

Palomares, M. (1991). *The Tagalog-speaking child.* Mangilao, GU: BEAM Center, University of Guam.

Palomo, R. S. (1987). American Policies and practices affecting language shift on Guam: 1898–1950. In M. Spencer (Ed.) *Chamoro language*

issues and research on Guam: A book of readings (pp. 19–43. Mangilao, GU: University of Guam.

Palomo, R. S. (1989). Language policies and planning. In M. Spencer, V. Aguilar, & G. Woo (Eds.) *Vernacular language symposium on new and developing orthographies in Micronesia* (pp. 57–70). Mangilao, GU: University of Guam Press.

Pang, V. O., Colvin, C., Tran, M., & Barba, R. (1992, November). Beyond Chopsticks and Dragons: Asian-American Literature for Children. *The Reading Teacher, 46*(3), 216–224. (Reprinted in *Literacy Instruction for Culturally Diverse and Linguistically Diverse Students,* pp. 204–212, by M. F. Opitz (Ed.), 1998, Newark, DE: International Reading Association (pp. 204–212).

Park, C. C. (1997). Learning style preferences of Asian American (Chinese, Filipino, Korean and Vietnamese) students in secondary schools. *Equity and Excellence in Education, 30*(2), 68–77.

Park, C. C. (2000). Learning style preferences of Southeast Asian students. *Urban Education, 35*(3), 245–268.

Park, C. C. (2001). Educational aspirations of Southeast Asian students. In C. C. Park, A. L. Goodwin, & S. J. Lee (Eds.), *Research on the education of Asian and Pacific Americans* (pp. 1–20). Greenwich, CT: Information Age.

Park, C. C., Goodwin, A. L., & Lee, S. J. (Eds.). (2001). *Research on the education of Asian and Pacific Americans.* Greenwich, CT: Information Age.

Park, C. C., Goodwin, A. L., & Lee, S. J. (Eds.). (2003). *Asian American identities, families, and schooling.* Greenwich, CT: Information Age.

Park, C. C., Endo, R., & Goodwin, A. L. (2006). *Asian and Pacific American education: Learning, socialization, and identity.* Greenwich, CT: Information Age.

Park, C. C., & McField, G. K. (2006, January). *Addressing the shortage of Asian and Pacific American teachers.* Paper presented at the National Association for Bilingual Education Annual Conference, Phoenix, AZ.

Pau'u, T. H. (2002). My life in four cultures. In P. Spickard, J. L. Rondilla, & D. H. Wright (Eds.), *Pacific Diaspora: Island peoples in the United States and across the Pacific* (pp. 31–39). Honolulu: University of Hawai'i Press.

Perez, M. P. (2004). Insiders without, outsiders within: Chamorro ambiguity and diasporic identities on the U.S. mainland. In L.-H. N. Chiang, J. Lidstone, & R. A. Stephenson (Eds.), *The challenges of globalization: Cultures in transition in the Pacific-Asia region* (pp. 47–72). Lanham, MD: University Press of America, Inc.

Philips, S. (1972). Participant structures and communicative competence: Warm springs children in community and classroom. In C. Cazden, V. John, & D. Hymes (Eds.), *Functions of language in the classroom.* New York: Teachers College Press.

Perie, M., & Moran, R. (2005). *NAEP 2004 Trends in Academic Progress: Three Decades of Student Performance in Reading and Mathematics* (NCES 2005-464). U.S. Department of Education, Institute of Education Sciences, National Center for Education Statistics. Washington, DC: U.S. Government Printing Office.

Pintrich, P. R., & Schrauben, B. (1992). Students' motivational beliefs and their cognitive engagement in classroom academic tasks. In D. H. Schunk & J. D. Meece (Eds.), *Student perceptions in the classroom* (pp. 149–183). Hillsdale, NJ: Lawrence Erlbaum Associates, Inc., Publishers.

Rondilla, J. L. (2002). The Filipino question in Asia and the Pacific: Rethinking regional origins in diaspora. In P. Spickard, J. L. Rondilla, & D. H. Wright (Eds.), *Pacific diaspora: Island peoples in the United States and across the Pacific* (pp. 56–68). Honolulu: University of Hawai'i Press.

Root, S., Rudawski, A., Taylor, M., & Rochon, R. (2003). Hmong students in teacher education programs. *Bilingual Research Journal, 27*(1), 137–148.

Ross, T. (2004). Understanding Micronesian students in Hawai'i. *Pacific Educator, 3*(3), 17.

Rubinstein, D. (2002). Youth suicide and social change in Micronesia, *Occasional Papers. No. 36*. December 2002, 33–41. Kagoshima, Japan: Kagoshima University Center for the Pacific Islands.

Saez-Santiago, E., & Bernal, G. (2004). *Depression in ethnic minorities*. Retrieved November, 2004, from latino.rcm.upr.edu/saez.pdf/

Sam, A. A. (2006, April). *Proportional representation and Asian and Pacific Islander student perceptions of a campus climate and diversity*. Paper presented at the American Educational Research Association Annual Meeting, San Francisco, CA.

Sims, J., & Butter, M. E. (2000). Gender equity and environmental health. *Harvard Center for Population and Development Studies Working Paper Series, 10(6)*. Retrieved October 2004 from http://www.hsph.harvard.edu/hcpds/wpweb/6%20Sims-Butter%20web.htm.

Smith, K., Turk-Smith, S., Aguilar, V., Coulter, P., Woo, G., & Spencer, M. (1995). *Moderating the impact of Micronesian migrations to Guam: A multimethod study*. Paper presented at the XVIII Pacific Science Congress, Beijing, China.

Souder, L. M. T. (1992). *Daughters of the island: Contemporary Chamorro women organizers on Guam, MARC Monograph Series No. 1*. (2nd ed.). Mangilao, GU: Micronesian Area Research Center.

Souder-Jaffrey, L. & Underwood, R. A. (1987). *Chamorro self-determination: The right of a people, i derechon i taotao, MARC Education Series Publication No. 7*. Guam: Micronesian Area Research Center, University of Guam.

Spencer, M. L. (1992). Literacy in Micronesia. *ISLA: A Journal of Micronesian Studies, 1*(2), 301–327.

Spencer, M. L. (1994). Language, knowledge, and development: the Micronesian way. In J. Morrison, P. Geraghty, & L. Crowl (Eds.), *Education, language, patterns and policy: Science of Pacific Island Peoples, Volume IV* (pp. 199–212). Suva, Fiji: Institute of Pacific Studies, University of the South Pacific.

Spencer, M. L. (1996). And what of the languages of Micronesia? In F. Mugler, & J. Lynch (Eds.), *Pacific Languages in Education* (pp. 11–35). Fiji: Institute of Pacific Studies, University of the South Pacific.

Spickard, P. (2002). Pacific Islander Americans and multiethnicity: A vision of America's future? In P. Spickard, J. L. Rondilla, & D. H. Wright (Eds.), *Pacific diaspora: Island peoples in the United States and across the Pacific* (pp. 40–55). Honolulu: University of Hawai'i Press.

Spickard, P., Rondilla, J. L., & Wright, D. H. (2002). *Pacific diaspora: Island peoples in the United States and across the Pacific*. Honolulu: University of Hawai'i Press.

Stevenson, H. W., Chen, C., & Uttal, D. H. (1990). Beliefs and achievement: A study of Black, Anglo, and Hispanic children. *Child Development, 61*, 508–523.

Sue, D. W., & Sue, D. (2003). *Counseling the culturally different: Theory and practice* (4th ed.). New York: Wiley.

Sue, D. W. (2004). Whiteness and ethnocentric monoculuralism: Making the "invisible" visible. *American Psychologist, 59*(8), 761–769.

Swarna, J. (1997). Higher education and the economic and social empowerment of women: The Asian experience. *Compare, 27(3)*, 245–261.

Sweatshop Watch and the Garment Worker Center. (2004). *Crisis or opportunity? The future of Los Angeles' garment workers, the apparel industry, and the local economy*. Retrieved November 22, 2004, from www.sweatshopwatch.org

Tacheliol, R. (1991). *The Chamorro child*. Mangilao, GU: BEAM Center, University of Guam.

Talmy, S. (2006). The other *other*: Micronesians in a Hawaii High School. In C. C. Park, R. Endo, & A. L. Goodwin (Eds.), *Asian and Pacific American education: Learning, socialization, and identity* (pp. 19–49). Greenwich, CT: Information Age.

Tamura, E. H., Chattergy, V., & Endo, R. (2002). *Asian and Pacific Islander American education: Social, cultural, and historical contexts*. South El Monte, CA: Pacific Asia Press.

Tharp, R. G., & Gallimore, R. (1988). *Rousing minds to life: Teaching, learning, and schooling in social context*. New York: Cambridge University Press.

Thorne, B. (1993). *Gender play: Girls and boys in school*. New Brunswick, NJ: Rutgers University Press.

Timm, J. T. (1994). Hmong values and American education. *Equity and Excellence in Education, 27*(2), 36–44.

Teranishi, R. T. (2002). Asian Pacific Americans and critical race theory: An examination of school racial climate. *Equity and Excellence in Education, 35*(2), 144–154.

Torres, J., Santos, J., Peck, N., & Cortes, L. (2004). *Minority teacher recruitment, development, and retention*. Providence, RI: The Education Alliance at Brown University.

Tran, T. V. (1988). Sex differences in English acculturation and learning strategies among Vietnamese adults age forty and over in the United States. *Sex Roles, 19*, 747–758.

Trask, H. (2002). Pacific island women and White feminism. In P. Spickard, J. L. Rondilla, & D. H.Wright (Eds.), *Pacific diaspora: Island peoples in the United States and across the Pacific* (pp. 253–261). Honolulu: University of Hawai'i Press.

Underwood, R. A. (1987a). Language Survival. The ideology of English and Education in Guam. In M. Spencer (Ed.) *Language issues and research on Guam: A book of readings* (pp. 3–18). Mangitao, GU: University of Guam.

Underwood, R. A. (1987). *American education and the acculturation of the Chamorros of Guam*. Unpublished doctoral dissertation, University of Southern California

Underwood, R. A. (1989). Language policies and planning and the role of language commissions. In M. Spencer, V. Aguilar, & G. Woo (Eds.), *Vernacular language symposium on new and developing orthographies in Micronesia* (pp. 71–80). Mangilao, GU: University of Guam Press.

Underwood, R. A. (2005, July 3). American from Guam chokes up at national anthem, "Guam Hymn." *Pacific Daily News*, p. 3.

U.S. Census Bureau. (2001, December). The Native Hawaiian and other Pacific Islander population: 2000, *Census 2000 Brief*, (C2KBR/01-14) [Brochure]. Washington, DC: Author.

U. S. Census Bureau. (2002 February). The Asian population: 2000, *Census 2000 Brief* (C1WBR)01-16) [Brochure]. Washington, D. C.: Author.

U. S. Census Bureau. (2002). Characteristics of business owners: 2002 *Survey of Business Owners*. Washington D. C.: Author.

U.S. Census Bureau. (2004a). *Census 2000 Summary File*. (SF 3)—Sample Data.) Washington, DC: Author.

U.S. Census Bureau. (2004b). *Census 2000 Summary File*. (SF 4, QT-P31–Sample Data.) Washington, DC: Author.

U.S. Census Bureau. (2006). *Statistical abstract of the United States: Table 604. Employed civilians by occupation, sex, race, and Hispanic origin: 2004-Con*. Washington, DC: Author.

Verna, M. A., & Campbell, J. R. (1998, April). *The differential effects of family processes and SES on academic self-concepts and achievement of gifted Asian American and gifted Caucasian high school students*. Paper presented at the annual meeting of the American Educational Research Association, San Diego, CA.

Vogt, L. A., Jordan, C., & Tharp, R. G. (1992). Explaining school failure, producing school success: Two cases. In E. Jacob & C. Jordan (Eds.), *Minority education: Anthropological perspectives* (pp. 53–66). Norwood, NJ: Ablex. (Reprinted from *Anthropology & Education Quarterly, 18*, 276–286)

Vyas, S. (2001). Am I Indian, American, or Indian American? In C. C. Park, A. L. Goodwin, & S. J. Lee (Eds.), *Research on the education of Asian and Pacific Americans* (pp. 129–154). Greenwich, CT: Information Age.

Vygotsky, L. S. (1978). *Mind in society: The development of higher psychological processes*. Cambridge, MA: Harvard University Press. (Original work published in Russian in 1930)

Watson-Gegeo, K. A., & Boggs, S. T. (1977). From verbal play to talk story: The role of routines in speech events among Hawaiian children.

In S. Ervin-Tripp & C. Mitchell-Keman (Eds.), *Child discourse* (pp. 67–90). New York: Academic Press.

Wear, D. (2000). Asian/Pacific Islander women in medical education: Personal and professional challenges. *Teaching and Learning in Medicine, 12*(3), 156–163.

William, A., & Prasad, U. (1992). *The Chuukese child.* Mangilao, GU: BEAM Center, University of Guam.

Wiseman, R. (2003). *Queen bees and wannabes: Helping your daughter survive cliques, gossip, boyfriends and other realities of adolescence.* NY: Three Rivers Press.

Xie, Y., & Goyette, K. (2003). *Social mobility and the educational choices of Asian Americans. Social Science Research, 32,* 461-498.

Yamauchi, J. S., & Tin-Mala. (1998). An exploratory study of Asian American college students: An academic psycho-social profile. In R. Endo, C.C. Park & J. N. Tsuchida (Eds.), *Current issues in Asian and Pacific American education* (pp. 77-97). South El Monte, CA: Pacific Asia Press.

Yuen, J. W. L., Dowrick, P. W., & Alaimaleata, E. T. (2006). Community responsive model in literacy education. In C. C. Park, R. Endo, & A. L. Goodwin (Eds.), *Asian and Pacific American education: Learning, socialization, and identity* (pp. 121–140). Greenwich, CT: Information Age.

Yung, J. (1986). *Chinese women of America: A pictorial history.* Seattle, WA: University of Washington Press for the Chinese Cultural Foundation of San Francisco.

ACHIEVING GENDER EQUITY
FOR AMERICAN INDIANS[1]

Anne Calhoun, Mishuana Goeman, and Monica Tsethlikai*

INTRODUCTION

It is customary for many of us, most notably those of us from the Eastern tribes, to introduce our words in a good way and so we begin:

We offer these words as representative of our individual thoughts learned from our grandmothers and grandfathers and from the academy. Our words do not represent anyone other than ourselves and do not reflect any understandings of our Nations. We hope that these words are taken in a good way and that good comes from ideas presented and lessons learned. We pray that no one is unduly hurt by the words we have set down on paper.

In this chapter we discuss several issues about which educators appear to have little or no knowledge. We make this statement based on our personal experiences, observations, and our knowledge of institutional barriers in educational settings that remain for American Indian students and which continue for American Indian scholars (Mihesuah, 2003, *American Indian Quarterly, 17*, 1–2 for multiple articles). We make this statement because, unless our readers understand the importance of the values and views discussed in this chapter, there will be little hope that education may become a welcoming place for American Indian students and scholars—a place to thrive rather than merely survive. If we cannot make these accommodations, what hope is there for our American Indian students' optimal achievements toward important roles in both their nations and larger, mainstream communities? In order to help others understand issues of gender equity in education, traditional concepts of gender are first examined. In this section, we choose a few examples of historic foundations of gender conceptions and the manners in which these traditions process change of gender roles overtime. Next, we choose a representative sampling of current issues facing American Indian students in regards to gender equity in education. We continue by examining possible solutions that arise from a confluence of living traditions, innovativeness stemming from the community and native intellectuals, and organizing across communities, boundaries, and borders. Finally, we examine the implications of our findings for educational policy.

TRADITIONAL CONCEPTS OF GENDER

Our community is one family. We are interrelated and rely upon each family member to play a role in the community. We help others who are in need to ensure the ability of our community, our family, to remain strong and adapt to a continually changing environment. The survival of our community depends upon our traditional perspective [being] passed from generation to generation to help others in need. We are one family, one community. Sally Gallegos. (cited in Intertribal Friendship House & Lobo, 2002, p. 116)

While the quote at the beginning of the section may appear to be quite general, within and between the words lie concepts that we believe are basic to understanding historical gender assignment within many native nations. Even in the face of in-

---

*The boldface names are the Lead Authors.

[1]There is much discussion today about how we name ourselves, little of this based on asking tribal members. Most generally, tribal people identify themselves as a member of a nation followed in some instances by their clan relationships. Currently the "preferred" term used by the Census and Government documents is "American Indian and Alaska Natives" (Tucker, Kojetin, & Harrison, 1996). A second naming issue is based in the anti-Indian/anti-sovereignty movements whose members identify themselves as "American Indians" stating that they were born in American and are, therefore, native to America. These types of rhetorical battles are artifacts of racism, overt and dysconscious, because they are associated with Anglo's and academic discussions without reference to what tribal peoples prefer.

creased urbanization, such as Sally experiences in her work with the Pan-Indian Friendship House and United Indian nations, women and men have retained elements of gender and community practices. They have done this even though historically different American Indian tribes identified gender in various ways (a complete description of those ways would require more room than allotted in this chapter). What is necessary, however, is to understand that traditional identity is commonly imbued with both the spiritual and the everyday. Many creation stories provide a mobile structure for conceiving of gender roles within a community framework.

An anonymous Lakota manuscript stated that the beginning of the Lakota world was Spirit (Inyan). Spirit was lonely and created a disk to surround Spirit, which was called World (Maka). Everything was created from these two (Anonymous, 1963) and everything is part of and within these two. All living things both reflect and act using both aspects in developing an identity. Whether that identity becomes labeled by Euro-Americans as rock, tree, stream, mammal, mountain, bird, fish, or human, we all have Inyan and Maka creating our living identity. In return, all that is recreated by each of us also comes from and contains these two things.

Such a traditional system of thought that revolves around rituals leaves little room for Euro-American classification systems that label a living identity as "good" or "bad" or seeks to classify in hierarchical ways the usefulness of the different living identities of this world (Waters, 2004). Rather than creation being a story of recognizing difference, such as in the common Christian version of creation in Garden of Eden, this Lakota creation story provides an introduction to the creation of thought and process involved in the framing of existence, whether it be female or male, and is only one of many such creation stories that provide different perspectives in viewing the world.

Historical Foundations of Gender Roles: Myths and Realities

Much has been written about the historical realities, evolving roles, and current status of gender in the United States as defined, practiced, and recognized by native nations (Gunn-Allen, 1992, 2003; Nassaney, 1999; Shoemaker, 1995; Sleeper-Smith, 2001; Williams & Bendremer, 1997; Wishart, 1995). Because myths regarding American Indian males and females abound, it is necessary to counter such myth, by making clear that concepts about gender varied significantly among nations and the record is, at best, murky in the manner in which gender forms have been discussed in historical and contemporary documents.

Misunderstandings by anthropologists who compiled their data based on preconceived notions of the "natural" abilities of women continued long after the anthropological research was over. Ella Deloria, a Lakota scholar who worked extensively with Franz Boas, is an important figure who reframed gender practices within her tribal knowledge. Although criticized as an assimilationist by many scholars today, her writing continues to be one source that informs researchers about gender identity in historical times. She defined the equality of roles when she wrote that "a woman caring for children and doing all the work around the house thought herself no worse off than her husband who was compelled to risk his life continuously hunting and remaining ever on guard against enemy attacks on his family" (Deloria, 1944, p. 40). "The sexual division of labor was strictly upheld, women doing the work of their husbands, or men doing the work of their wives, prompted ridicule from other Lakotas" (Deloria, 1932, 63–64). Many contemporary American Indian women today continue to believe that the very act of providing life to the community signifies their equality and power in that community.

The quality of gender is frequently embedded in the languages of many native nations (Hass, 1964). For example, in some languages (e.g., Navajo, Blackfeet, Cree, and some other Plains Nations) there are specific words that define other classifications for gender (Hill, 1938; Jacobs, 1977; Jacobs, Thomas, & Lang, 1997; Lewis, 1941; Schaeffer, 1965). In other languages, notably Haudenosaunee languages and Cherokee, gender is often spatially connected to certain words (e.g., women are associated with specific places and men with other places). Perdue (2003) stated that "being a woman was intrinsically linked to growing corn, and southern Indians essentially reclassified men who farmed rather than hunted as women" (p. 64). Similarly, the Lakota assigned artistic styles by gender so the men and women were able to work side by side without overlapping one another while working on hides (Francis Waukazoo, Anonymous Lakota Manuscript, July 21, 2003). Nevertheless, there is also room to change the contextualized places and create a space for non-gender-specific description. However, just as gender is constructed historically overtime, the methods of language adaptation often correlate to the traditional. Language is a living entity in these communities and adapts to changing societal modes.

In some Ojibwe bands, boys and young adolescent males who had not made a special journey (physically and/or psychologically) were considered to be without gender until they had matured to the point where they understood the concept of interdependence and community, while, for their female relations, gender assignment was considered automatic (Waters, 2004; Wub, 1995). Among the Lakota/Dakota/Nakota, gender forms appear to have represented an identity that was a comodification of the earthly world and the spiritual world. Some Lakota youth developed alternative gender identities by means of vision quests or dreams that signified their natural condition as mediated by the Spirit world (DeMallie, 1983). DeMallie (1983) described the gender identity of Lakota/Dakota males as being zealously guarded by parents and the community. This guarding maintained the community norm that all men would eventually marry, and occasionally would have multiple wives, and have children (Medicine, 1983). If a boy engaged in pursuits assigned as feminine in nature, he might be ridiculed and shamed (DeMallie). Young boys were reminded by parents and elders to guard against such play. According to Bushotter (as cited in DeMallie), through the intersession of Spirit young men who continued to practice activities that were assigned to women took on the role of *winkte*, or "would be woman." A man following this path gained a place within the community sanctioned by Spirit, but this path was neither comfortable nor fully acceptable. However, the *winkte* held some considerable power resulting from this connection to Spirit. Hassrick (as cited in DeMallie) noted that the people believed that children labeled *winkte* would never suffer illness. The *winkte* also engaged in predicting the outcome of battles and fought in battles (Hassrick as cited in DeMallie). The postcontact, contemporary social confusion of the place of a *winkte* has been eloquently described by Deloria: "The people were faced with the problem of whether men or women should prepare the body for burial. The final decision was to request an old married couple to do the work jointly" (1932, p. 46).

For Dakota/Lakota/Nakota women, gender roles developed in more forms than for men (Medicine, 1983). Like men, women who developed a non-normative gender role did so because of intersession with Spirit usually through a series of dreams. Like the *winkte*, *ninawaki* (manly woman) developed specialized skills that included aggressive behaviors and the ability to foretell future events (Medicine, 1983). A second non-normative role for women was that of *matsaps* (crazy women), who engaged in community recognized, if not endorsed, sexual promiscuity (Medicine, 1983). *Matsaps* frequently lived in isolation and would not have been unusual for them to wander away from the protection of the community or be cast off by husbands as undesirable for their infidelities.

Fidelity in marriage was a most highly prized social norm for couples as was virginity in girls. Men were expected to have a "lack of interest" in sexual prowess while women were expected to be sexually aggressive following marriage (Medicine, 1983). A third non-normative, but highly prized and accepted role for a woman was that of *ninaki* (chief woman) (Medicine, 1983). The *ninaki* was considered a person on whom the people could depend as they might depend on a chief. She was a provider of leadership within the community. This role might also have indicated the role of favorite wife in polygamous marriages of a few Lakota/Dakota men. Such women played important sacred and ceremonial roles with their husbands. Finally, the most highly prized role of a woman was that of the Sun Dance woman, *White Buffalo Calf Woman*, whose virginity prior to marriage was unquestioned and whose abstinence from further marriage following the death of her first husband was also recognized (Medicine, 1983). Specific ceremonies honored such women and announced their status within and to the community. Medicine (1983) and DeMallie (1983) both concluded that because the normative roles for male and female in Lakota/Dakota society were so rigid in tasks, demonstration of emotion, roles, places, and relationships, the additional gender roles allowed for a more psychologically safe situation that retained the autonomy of the individual and maintained a mutual dependence upon one another within the community.

Among the Cherokee, the concept of gender roles and relationships between men and women were dramatically different being structured by clans. European political and family structure required nuclear households. Cherokee clans were the basis of social organization and clan membership was based on maternal identification. Parenting duties were dispersed in ways vastly different from today's nuclear family. Mothers' sisters were all considered to be mothers. Grandmothers had the final say and remained the most honored among women in families, a tradition that is retained today in many communities. Fathers did not have privileges or powers over their biological children but did exercise privilege and power over sisters' sons (Perdue,

2003). While Cherokee female children were expected to marry into the clan of their father's father or mother's father, they remained identified with their mother's clan (Gilbert, 1978). After marriage, new couples resided in a home built by the wife's relatives near the wife's mother's home. Strict rules governed marriage between clans. The ultimate goal of these arrangements was to maintain the balance of political and clan-based power relations, representation, and social continuity within the Nation (Gilbert, 1978). The Dawes Allotment, which characterized the communities into separate male-led nuclear households away from clan relatives, the Indian Reorganization Act, which continued to follow the patriarchal logic which preceded it, and boarding-school gender education, which revolved around ideas of the cult domesticity, are examples of the way clan systems women's roles, and women's positioning—and thus women's power within their communities—were disrupted, reshaped, or went underground.

The varieties of representation of gender among American Indian communities are evolving, recovering, and incorporating original understandings, and cognizant of the use of discreet, binary, dualist, logical categories as restrictive when talking about many American Indian precontact and to some extent postcontact views of gender (Anguksuar, 1997; House, 1997; Medicine, 1997; Tafoya, 1997; Waters, 2004). Gender subjectivity was also the place created for individuals to move between worlds (i.e., as noted in trickster stories) for all beings that from the beginning have been both spirit and earth (Vizenor, 1993). The trickster figure and the movement are necessary for the survival of the community, signifying change, adaptation, wit, perseverance, and survival. The ability of the trickster to move between gendered worlds is also one of creating a balance after the chaos. Thus, in precontact times, the term "equity" was not considered a relevant concept. All that was engendered was considered to have value necessary to the survival of traditional communities and all that was engendered was considered necessary for the survival of the people.

The misreading of "equity" and gender roles by early settler-colonialist continues in the misreading of treaty rights today. The complex constructions of government, social, and spiritual elements, which often intersected, overlapped, and supported each other, relied on complementarity in gender roles. In many native communities, women had the final say regarding important issues. For example, the Clan Mothers in the Haudenosaunee Confederation comprised of the Six Nations, traditionally and some contemporaneously, chose the representative of their clan who spoke on their behalf in longhouse councils. They also had, and in some cases still have, the power to strip the representative of power if he did not act in a proper way. The power of women emanated from their important community work as agriculturalists, mothers, distributors of food, doctors, among other roles—in other words that which enabled the healthy well being of the community as a whole. Haudenosaunee women were crucial to this system of checks and balances. Similarly, Cherokee women had the final vote over whether war would be waged because they had the most to lose from battles. The federal governments' (Individual European Nations then United States) misunderstandings of women's positions in each of the Nations has played a long-standing function in the many legal battles between tribes, especially in the

Eastern part of the United States. (Green, 1983; Hunt, 1980; Jaimes & Halsey, 1992; Kickingbird & Kickingbird, 1987).

While women of color interceded in feminism by providing theories focusing on gender construction and postulating that there are many differences, such as berdaches in the Southwest[2] or the Diné names for several gender categories based on a variety of situations, these classifications are not agreed upon by all American Indian scholars. For many current American Indian scholars the term *two-spirit people* is used to designate individuals whose gender becomes problematized by Euro-American assimilationist views (Jacobs et al., 1997). Even the differences of discussion and speculation of native scholars most likely does not capture the full precontact concepts related to the diversity of representation of gender across tribes.

Differences in what constitutes subjectivity have often made the interpretation of the division power in terms of male/female difficult, and perhaps incomprehensible to individuals and groups outside that cultural milieu. Further complicating the process of using gender as a research focus is the fact that gender, like racial identity, is not constructed within an isolated community or social context. Identities, both racialized and engendered, are informed by a multitude of cultural influences. Western forms of construction, changing work environments, and social and historical circumstances have affected the way communities have developed. The desire and necessity of racial catgorization to sustain the United States as a nation attempts to create a homogenous Indian. Gender suffers similarly, in that uncomplicated distinctions made between male/female promote a certain type of research that obscures national specificities. Ironically, the binaries of the pastoral, idealized Indian and the passive, drudge squaws are extreme, much like the binaries positioned around race (Waters, 2004). Indeed, the connection of gender binaries to racial binaries actually results in gender research that overlooks complexities of identity formation for native women. The overtones of the princess/squaw or noble warrior/enemy savage dichotomy seep into the ways that scholarship is produced and, similar to the racial dichotomies, are detrimental to native people.

We have constructed this discussion of gender to present the reader with knowledge that relates historical and contemporary concepts of gender and identity in American Indian students. Misguided conceptions of gender within native communities will not work to overcome disparities or inequities for American Indians in institutional settings. The primacy o of retaining the individual's autonomy within a complete and functional community requires the respect of each person within that community regardless of how the Euro-American world prescribes gender relations. Each living entity represents both the spiritual and the earth, and gender is embedded in that understanding regardless of biology.

WHAT ARE THE ISSUES?

Issue 1: Colonization

Gender definitions dramatically changed because of contact with European ideas and values, which were either adapted or imposed upon native people (Albers & Medicine, 1983; Briggs, 1974; Cruickshank, 1971; Green, 1983; LaFlesch, 1912; Schlegel, 1973). Prior to contact, gender identities in many tribes were envisioned as role related. Gender assignment supported the division of labor that existed for the greater good of the community or as social contracts that maintained the balance of power among clans or bands. Men and women in most tribes maintained a separate-but-equal status. With the introduction of Euro-American concepts of gender, relationships between American Indian men and women and their communities drastically changed (Anderson, 1990; Downs, 1972; Mead, 1932; Perry, 1979; Qoyawayma, 1977; Richards, 1957). Such change has resulted in the breakdown of the formerly positive interdependency of American Indian men and women (Caffrey, 2000; Lewis, 1976; Smithson, 1959; Swader & Myers, 1977) producing dire consequences for women and men.

Current American Indian gender roles appear to be primarily embedded in the colonized model of bifurcation of gender and separation of gender by biological constraints rather than by roles within the community.[3] White federal policy viewed Indian women as either debased by Indian men and tribal society or as the primary instigators for retaining culture. For example, federal policy stated:

Co-education of the sexes is the surest and perhaps only way in which the Indian women can be lifted out of that position of servility and degradation which most of them now occupy, on to a plane where their

[2]For an example of gender and sexuality construction, please see Will Roscoe's discussion of sexuality in *Changing Ones: Third and Fourth Genders in Native North America, 2000*, and Jacobs, Thomas, and Lang's edited work *Two Spirit People: Native American Gender Identity, Sexuality, and Spirituality, 1997*. Both interrogate how gender construction and sexual norms in Native communities differed from western constructions and how those constructions affected community structures. Yet, many Native scholars also feel these terms or identities have been appropriated for political purposes and individual agendas. The topic of gender and sexuality is one relatively understudied and I propose that the specificity of arguments regarding other genders is most important but needs to be done at the Tribal level. For good examples of this type of research please see Patricia Albers and Beatrice Medicine's (1983) *The Hidden Half*, one good source for Lakota understandings of gender.

[3]This is evident in the news statement that the Navajo Nation is considering a resolution that describes marriage as a union between a man and a woman. "Larry Anderson Sr. was quoted, 'Navajo Nation laws are outdated and need to be updated. That's why I'm asking for an amendment that states it is unlawful to have a marriage between two (same) sexes.' Wesley K. Thomas . . . said, same-sex relations among Navajo and other native peoples did not become an issue until Christian values were forced upon tribes 150 years ago. This (proposed) legislation is a romantic image that Anderson is trying to instill, (Associated Press, Albuquerque Journal, 1/18/2005, p. D3). The content and arguments in this discussion resonate across Indian Country as Tribes begin to consider, within their sovereign territories, issues similar to those facing state and federal governments. Deconstructing assimilationist information and colonized frameworks in order to recreate "traditional" values will become the responsibility of each of the individual Nations not necessarily of the American Indian academics who write about these issues, although, we would like to engage in the conversation.

husbands and the men generally will treat them with the same gallantry and respect which is accorded to their more favored white sisters. (Morgan, 1889)

The transition from traditional roles to colonized roles within many American Indian nations was slow but insidious (Balsam, Huang, Fieland, Simoni, & Walters, 2004). The reason that girls were equally represented at American Indian boarding schools was that policymakers knew that destroying girls' Native languages and cultures would effectively destroy the cultures and traditions of all native nations. The Canadian federal government, following the policy and practice of the federal government of the United States, likewise described the situation as:

The federal government, aware that "women embod[y] the culture and language of any nation and [that] once she is gone that Nation has no chance to survive." This calculated destruction cut to the heart of women's role as keepers of the culture. (Jamieson, as cited in Jolly, 2000; p. 101)

Colonization changed concepts of gender within American Indian Nations in many ways. Shanley (as cited in Smith, 2003) described the colonization process as one that led to the determination of American Indian Nations as a people who have a "permanent 'present' absence" within the federal, state, and social systems in North America. Contemporary America denies or narrowly categorizes the existence of American Indians in multiple ways. One of the most insidious forms of denial is the federal control of American Indian National identity. Thousands of American Indians who are not enrolled in federally recognized tribes are further marginalized (Arv Bragi, 2005). The next most dangerous form of denial of existence is the psychologically positioned colonized mindset that has been recreated within nations and American Indians as individuals through schooling and social shame—we become our own oppressors as we oppress our people and ourselves for financial gain and power. White policies, education, religion, and media have essentialized and categorized American Indians as "outsiders" within the lands that originally were given to them by Creator.

The most common myth in literature about, but sometimes not by, American Indians, portrays men as weak either because of their inability to control their personal habits (e.g., drinking, gambling, and drugs) or their psychological states (e.g., rage, anger, and depression). Portrayals of the latter can be seen in many of the sports mascots or in the use of James Earle Fraser's (1930), "The End of the Trail." Portrayals of the former are evident in the number of reports of stops and arrests of American Indians by policing forces as they "target" the illegal drug trade, the homeless, and the impaired driver (Voss, 2003). Profiling on the part of law enforcement is ubiquitous within and around American Indian communities. American Indians in Minnesota are three times more likely to be arrested than Whites, accounting for as much as 63% of arrests in one county while American Indians make up only 15% of the population (Johnson & Heilman, 2001; http://www2.mnbar.org/benchandbar/). Racial profiling has been a hot issue in Minnesota and across the nation in recent months. While certainly deserving of this attention, racial profiling is only one aspect of a much larger issue: the disproportionate number of African Americans, Latinos, American Indians, and other minorities who are arrested, convicted, and imprisoned by our criminal justice system.

Ross (1998) detailed the lives of American Indian women in Montana who represent one third of the prison population while American Indians are only 2% of the population, and American Indian men represent 18.4% of prisoners (data.opi .state.mt.us/bills/2003/billhtml/HB0026.htm n.d.). Andrea Smith (2005) reported that Indian women, like their male peers, "are overrepresented in prisons and jails" citing that Indian women in South Dakota "make up 8 percent of the women's population, but 35 percent of the state's women's prison population" (p. 149). Walker (2003) reported that American Indian males in South Dakota are 57 more times likely to be convicted than White males (http://www.dlncoalition.org/dln_issues/2003feb13 .htm n.d.), which of course affects entire communities.

These observations stand in stark contrast to research that indicated American Indian youth were less likely to commit the most severe crimes in comparison to all other ethnic groups (Bureau of Justice Statistics, 2003). Finally, Indian women endure violence from intimate partners at rates that are nearly three times that of White or Hispanic women (Bletzer & Koss, 2004; Brave Heart, 1999a; Oetzel & Duran, 2004). However, the totality of the problem of violence can only be understood in a context that acknowledges 70% of the violence perpetrated against American Indians is by non-Indian individuals or groups. Genocide and continual violence is real and a continuing reality in Indian country (Manson, Beals, Klein, Croy, & AI-SUOEROFO team, 2005; Zvolensky, McNeil, Porter, & Stewart, 2001).

Issue 2: Dysconscious Racism

The roots of dysconscious racism as a construct lie in Said's (1979) discussion of the mythical and romantic qualities of the oriental. In attempting to romanticize the *other,* European authors formulated stereotypical descriptions of members from Eurasian and Middle Eastern societies to promote western European hegemony. The need for Europeans to see through romantic eyes the value of the outsider strengthened the encoding of a stereopathic view of American Indian imagery.

King (1991) first introduced the term "dysconscious racism" in her diagnostic article regarding the lack of training that preservice teachers receive in schools and colleges of education. She defined that term as "a form of racism that tacitly accepts dominant white norms and privileges. It is not the absence of consciousness (that is, unconsciousness) but an impaired consciousness or distorted way of thinking about race as compared to, for example, critical consciousness" (1991, p. 135). King suggested that preservice teachers do not see people of color as representing individuals with unique identities and destinies but rather as groups having monolithic identities that perpetuate stereotypical outcomes. Representations of this type are frequently found in sports mascots, children's literature, and media portrayals. People are literally oblivious to racism because it is so ubiquitous. Stated explicitly, just because more people believe something and act accordingly does not make the belief or act ethical. Racism is perpetuated within schools as it is within society; those who witness acts and remain silent give tacit support for racist behavior to continue (Kailin, 1999).

Dysconscious racism exists in how institutions define individual contributions. For American Indian faculty, service to one's community is considered undesirable when it takes one away from one's work as teacher/researcher. One faculty member stated, "People ask me why I speak English so well. . . . They've already superimposed on me that I don't belong here . . . I used to think it was a harmless little question but now I feel that the message that I've received is that I don't belong, I don't look like I belong" (Turner & Myers, 2000, p. 100). Schools and colleges of education, in these descriptions, spend the most time perpetuating the stereotypy of race than other schools and colleges at the same institutions (Turner & Myers). By assenting to accept the status quo, by believing the concept that "color-blind" schooling is best, and by using "learning styles" as learning stigmas, schools and colleges continue to train teachers to make assimilative assumptions regarding race and gender (Markus, Steele, & Steele, 2001).

Steele and colleagues' work on stereotype threat indicates the detriments of dysconcious racism to the success of all students (Aronson & Steele, 2004; Aronson, Lustina, Good, Keough, Steele, & Brown, 1999; Aronson, Steele, Salina, & Lustina, 1998; Markus, Steele, & Steele, 2001; Cohen & Steele, 2002; Pronin, Steele, & Ross, 2004; Spencer, Steele, & Quinn, 1999; Steele, 1997; Steele & Aronson, 1994, 1995). According to Steele, race becomes a factor in regard to student expectations and the student's awareness of such expectations. The perception of reservation schools as ill equipped, for instance, might create in teachers a negative perception that the student in turn believes, leading to a belief that may account for lowered scores in testing that might not have been there before. We present this more benign and well-intentioned example, but more often than not, the base of the stereotype threat is embedded in much harsher racist realities that Indian students face.

Issue 3: Gender, Ontology, and Language

When I, Anne Calhoun, think about what it means to work within a philosophical ontology as an Indian woman, I focus on *ways of being*. This phrase will, understandably, make no sense to the nonindigenous reader who is thinking through western paradigms of ontology. I use this phrase as a way to fix my relationships, my place, and my actions in the community for which I bear responsibility and from which I gain autonomy. Such ways of being stand in direct juxtaposition to the Euro-American or western notions about ways of knowing (Waters, 2004) (for other views of indigenous philosophy and language please see: Turner, 2006). In an American Indian way of thinking, concepts about how we understand, learn, know, and exist overlap and interrelate with one another. Herein is the primary component of the problem that nonindigenous cultures have in understanding indigenous thought. This problem is central to understanding how gender is constructed in languages (Waters). Anishinabe-Temagami scholar, Dale Turner asserted that the conversation must happen between indigenous and nonindigenous people to reach a political understanding that fits our contemporary realities. He advocated developing an indigenous philosophy that moves away from asserting essential differences and toward developing languages upon which to gain political positioning. Turner asserted, "Aboriginal intellectuals must develop a community of practitioners within the existing dominant legal and political intellectual communities, while remaining an essential part of a thriving indigenous intellectual community" (Turner, 2006, p. 90).

Waters (2004) described Western ontology as binary, discreet, dualist logic, while American Indian ontology is a nonbinary, complementary, and nondualist logic. Western dualism requires organization within a hierarchical scheme that assigns value to each of the pairs, for example "male" stands in opposition to "female" (Waters). Because of this binary, discreet, hierarchical ordering, Western thought has never been able to escape the "–isms" that plague society today: racism (the discreet, binary, dualist contrast of skin color); sexism (the discreet, binary, dualist contrast of gender); or ageism (the discreet, binary, dualist contrast of age) as examples (Waters). Urrieta (2003) gave a good example of dualist logic when he stated that:

After a bloody invasion that decimated over 25 million people in Central Mexico (Anzaldua, 1987; Stannard, 1992; Wright, 1992), a genocide not talked about nearly as much as the Holocaust is, Spain established for New Spain a new social order Gallegos, 1992). The Spanish new social order instituted a highly structured system of castes/castas that divided people and imposed on them over two hundred hierarchical identity labels (MacLachlan & Rodriguez, 1990). Being White, Spanish, wealthy, and Roman Catholic by birth was the top caste. It was a different approach than that of the English, yet one that further divided people by Indianess. This, even today in 2003, is known as mejorando la raza, or betting the race, itself an ideological byproduct of the caste system and of cosmic race mentality. (Urrieta, 2003, p. 43)

In contrast, American Indian ontology remains strongly embedded in our individual Nations' epistemologies. Such thought requires that we understand the world by placing ourselves in direct relationship with everything else that is Maka and Inyan (world and spirit). This is the essence of the Lakota words— *mi-ta-ku-ye o-ya-sin*—or *we are all related* understood as "my relations" (Waters, 2004, p. 101). As American Indians we must think about ways of being that will connect directly to our relations as we act, think, and decide the paths that our lives take. While we have great autonomy for individual forms of expression, we also have great responsibility for *the people*. In this way there is no action, thought, or decision that does not affect all of our relations. The nature of our relations, their spiritual and earthly existence (blended identities), and their appropriate actions, states of being, and affects are embedded in many of our languages. For these reasons, languages carry cultural information necessary for community survival and sound growth. That cultural information includes equality of gender and a wider range of gender identity within many tribes even though in actuality the loss of language has allowed an assimilationist, male-dominated reality for many American Indian relationships. The current educational movement to house language immersion programs within schools and to certify American Indian language teachers grows out of the tribally recognized need to retain/regain identity, but this movement has been endangered by the recognition by the federal government of English as an official language.

Even when we use English, the philosophy of our elders informs how we behave as educators and students. Traditional Indian educational philosophies support thinking and conceptualization in a holistic manner so concepts, actions, persons, and all things in the everyday world may not have *distinct* and *separate* places and roles, but may have roles that overlap or extend into everyday practices. For example, I recall observing a Pueblo child in second grade struggling to read aloud in her classroom of all Pueblo children. Within the first few words of English, three other girls joined her reading in a unison voice so intertwined that I was not able to differentiate which individual child was speaking. These young girls demonstrated traditional understandings that no one learns alone and no one will be allowed to fail, suffer embarrassment, or be shamed. They also demonstrated the strict division of work based on gender that is commonly found among Pueblo communities and in other communities; a division that is valued equally for the survival of all the people.

The complexity of our languages illustrates these ways of being (relating). Most American Indian languages are dependent upon understanding the context (place, space, and relationships) in which a speaker makes statements. Some languages, such as Cherokee and Navajo are considered to be verb-laden. Verb forms in such languages change depending on the nature of the object to which one is referring and its distance from the subject. In other American Indian languages nouns and adjectives encode information on number, gender, and relationship, In Lakota, traditionally holding very rigid roles of separation between genders, women and men use different forms of words based on their gender and relationships. Many indigenous languages also encode information about the nature and characteristics of the object; the speaker must know whether an object is animate or engendered, or if it has a specific age or use in the community along with many other concepts attached to objects and subjects. Also, in some American Indian languages there are few indicators of gender, so comprehending the speaker's meaning requires the highest degree of contextualization. Within all Indian languages, the relationships among the people, their land, and the identities within their communities are crucial to understanding and learning the culture.

As American Indians, our community (whether community be defined as the nation, relatives from other nations, or American Indian students on one campus) defines our identities. Historically, this connectedness was sometimes less dependent on birth relatives than it was on clan or band relationships, which existed as an intensive network of clan or band and blood relatives. Consequently, family within American Indian communities can be defined in broader ways as encompassing multiple related individuals tracking back several generations (Albers & Medicine, 1983).

Issue 4: Traditional Indigenous Educational Philosophy: Non-Gendered and Community Identities

Western educational philosophy focuses on "I" as the center of importance rather than "society" or "we" in the outcome of education (Deloria, & Wildcat, 2001). The roots of the "I" reflected only males, as education was seen as wasted on women. In many Western paradigms, children's minds are described as having "blank slates" (i.e., tabula rasa, John Locke, cited in Pinker, 2002) while in contrast, many indigenous communities ascribe to their children the characteristics of having knowledge

through close contact and discourse with *spirit* who gives help to their communities. American Indian educational psychology holds that our children have knowledge from the beginning of their lives, sometimes over many generations (Cajete, 1999). So the level of respect that an American Indian adult has for children is expected to be much higher than the level of respect actually practiced in most school settings.

Oral literacy, the transmission of knowledge through stories, visual literacy, the presentation of results through visual media, and splatial literacy, the use of space and place to encode history, were the primary forms of literacy in traditional American Indian education (Calhoun & Annett, 2003). Events exemplified by pictographic, logographic, or systems of drawing/painting at a specific place are explained through story and references to space and place (Basso, 1996). Literacy forms as demonstrations of respect, ways of knowing, and formal or informal communications have been practiced within American Indian communities for millennia. Adults were teachers whose lesson planning centered primarily on observation of the natural inclinations and curiosities of individual children (Cajete, 1999; Calhoun & Annett, 2003). In historical, and some contemporary indigenous communities, learning designed to provide for the future of our communities was accomplished by skillfully matching a child's natural skills, inclinations, and curiosities with an adult whose vocation in the community most closely requires those skills, inclinations, and curiosities. The classroom is life's environment, with learning provided by older, expert practitioners to younger novice practitioners. In contemporary Western thought, Chi's research in the area of Expert-Novice knowledge construction and Vygotskian ideas of working within a child's zone of proximal development bear the most resemblance to traditional educational practice (see Chi, Farr, & Glaser, 1988; Daniels, 1996 for reviews). This approach to learning also superficially resembles some of the concepts currently employed in adult-learning theory or andragogy (Knowles, 1980; 1992). This practice did not exclude or confine children to specific tasks based on biological sex.

Issue 5: Educational Psychology, Curriculum & Public Media

American Indian Education: A Brief History

In the 18th century after contact with Europeans, a few American Indians, primarily those from tribes on or near the East Coast, were able to attend schools with their Euro-American peers. Some graduated from colleges in the East, and a few graduated with advanced or professional degrees (Mihesuah, 1998). In the 19th century as Euro-American pressures for more land coupled with federal policies developed during Jefferson's administration and continued into the era of the doctrine of Manifest Destiny, the idea of American Indians attending school took on a different, more sinister, purpose. Between 1830 and 1880, hundreds of thousands of American Indians were removed from their traditional lands and settled in reservations or camps west of the Mississippi and Missouri rivers. Many tribes from the eastern part of the new country were taken into Jackson's "Indian Territory," which later became the state of Oklahoma. Death rates on these trips were high, ranging from 25% to 70% of nations dying from accidents, disease brought on by exposure and inadequate nutrition, and murder by neglect (being left behind without help), or intentional acts.

Pratt, the founder of Carlisle Indian School, introduced the curriculum for future Indian boarding schools, which he based on the type of curriculum and boarding situation practiced within institutions for the incarceration of young males and adolescent males from other ethnic groups. Pratt described these circumstances as necessary because:

It is found that the different classes of industrial reformatories have worked upon his plan for many years and it is found to be the one salvation, not only for Indian children, but for white as well. It is impossible to train a pauper or a criminal, or a child of any kind, which has existed under evil influences, and then return him to the same low surroundings without his being drawn back to the old status of life. (Blackmar, 1892, pp. 821–822)

Prior to the development of boarding schools by the federal government, formal Western-style education was locally available to American Indian children or had been developed and run by individual tribes themselves. The Cherokee Nation created 200 K-8 day schools for students who intended to make farming or some mechanical vocation their goal and two seminary schools (grades 9–12) for students who sought to enter colleges in the East (Mihesuah, 1998). These schools offered an interesting and informative contrast with the federal Indian education policies related to the appropriate curriculum of the times.

In 1851, nearly 40 years prior to the opening of Carlisle, the first boarding school, the Cherokee Nation, then recently reorganized in Oklahoma, opened two seminary schools divided by gender. The curriculum was organized following the Mount Holyoke Seminary curriculum; a classical curriculum of college-preparatory schools of the 19th century (Mihesuah, 1998). Coursework in algebra, geometry, Greek and Latin, intellectual theology, physiology, and the reading of great European and Ancient philosophers was included. With a Western curriculum, English-only speaking student body, and students who were primarily mixed bloods from better-off families, the schools opened as the pride of the Cherokee Nation (Mihesuah, p. 1). During its existence nearly 3,000 women enrolled in the female seminary for at least one semester, and factors in their success in graduating or failure to graduate frequently were based in socioeconomic and mixed-blood politics of the nation during the last half of the 19th century (Mihesuah). The curriculum for both seminaries (male and female) was the same. The only difference between the female and male seminary life was that male seminarians were allowed considerably more freedom to pursue outside interests, such as hunting, farming, or other work with or without their families (Mihesuah). It was not until the interference of the federal government in the late 1890s that the female seminary included any classes in vocational areas such as "home management" (Mihesuah). This stands in extreme contrast with the curriculum of the newly opened boarding school on Chilocco Creek (Lomawaima, 1994). Chilocco, like many boarding schools of its time, was mired in the philosophies of the cult of domesticity, bounded in prescribed gender concepts.

The Cherokee had chosen a classical curriculum for students who had aspired to attain professional careers; whereas the Fed-

eral government assumed that American Indians were not capable of education that taught them more than a trade. "The Department of the Interior's annual report for 1899, commenting on the Seminary for females, stated that instead of 'being taught the domestic arts [girls] are given. . . . Latin and mathematics while branches of domestic economy are neglected. The dignity of work receives no attention at their hands." (Mihesuah, 1998, p. 60). Federal pressure resulted in the addition of coursework meeting these expectations, but in actuality, "the girls attending the seminary learned to make their beds and dust with only a few girls learning to be seamstresses" (Mihesuah, 1998, p. 61). Heavier housekeeping chores were allocated to hired employees or indigent students. While the seminaries did not "include any discussion of Cherokee culture the teachers did discuss the topic of Cherokee politics so that students were informed of current situations" (Mihesuah, 1998, p. 56). The seminaries operated until 1909 when, with the collusion of statehood, they were finally abandoned due to the resulting financial losses of the nation. The Cherokee Nation's educational curriculum and its application of that curriculum in Cherokee founded, funded, and staffed schools, providing the educational rigor that allowed some Cherokee youth to go on to attain professional degrees. For the majority of American Indian children, the U.S. federal policies for Indian education dehumanized and traumatized students while inculcating them into foreign traditions. This contrast between what a tribe chooses as curriculum and content (self-determination) and what occurs when self-determination is absent represented the consequences that come from the actions of an American Indian tribe's sovereignty for the good of its people.

In contrast, in the latter half of the 19th century the federal, publicly stated purpose for schooling for American Indians was "to remove the Indian and save the child" using a vocational rehabilitation curriculum that immersed students in Euro-American values systems (Pratt as cited in Adams). In 1879, the first boarding school for American Indian children, Carlisle, was opened. The opening of Carlisle came as a result of seemingly "failed" policies of education prior to this time (Adams). A series of experiments with schooling that was closer to or on reservations had been attempted, but governing bodies described these efforts as failures because of the close proximity to homes where children could retain their ties to their culture despite exposure to proper Western education (Adams). As more than 200 boarding schools opened across the United States, children, some as young as five, were taken from their parents' homes and sent to schools that were often very far away. Children were frequently taken against the parents' and child's will by systematically refusing provisions promised to members of tribes until children were handed over. Families were essentially starved into submission (Adams).

The historical conditions at boarding schools are now notorious for their cruelty to students and their families. One particular issue, at the heart of developing gender equity, was the sexual and physical abuse of both girls and boys at many of the boarding schools, which continues to affect Indian communities to this day. Under the current United Nations' definition of human rights, conditions in most boarding schools of the 19th and early 20th centuries would be in violation of basic human rights, with their practices amounting to genocide (United Nations,

1999). Children were shorn and stripped of anything that resembled a cultural remnant. They were required to only speak English, a language unfamiliar to the majority of them. The curriculum for the schools was designed to promote service-level employment and, in fact, many students at schools could expect to attend school in the morning and become a servant within a household or business for the afternoon and evening (Lomawaima, 1994). Once these students "graduated" from boarding school, they were unfit for returning to their reservations because of language loss, cultural amnesia, and training for jobs that were not available on their reservations (Lomawaima).

Although the era of boarding schools lasted only about 50 years, it left an indelible mark for two generations who passed both the abusive experiences and their maladaptive ways of coping with those experiences to their children and grandchildren. Traditional family and extended relational units were shattered because generations of children grew up without experiencing traditional parenting skills, which made it difficult for them to become competent parents in adulthood (Duran & Duran, 1995). By documenting the devastating past and demanding reparations, The Boarding School Healing Project hopes to reach those elders who were abused and to begin the intergenerational process of healing. This, hopefully will lead to making headway into the sexual-abuse epidemic that stems from this legacy (Smith, 2006). Even into the mid-20th century, families were subjected to state and federal laws that continued the destruction of family and extended relations.

Gender *inequity* for American Indian students began in boarding schools that valued men's work and devalued women's work. Girls and young women were more carefully watched, more frequently reprimanded for lapses in "lady-like" behavior or attention to work centering on cleanliness and caretaking of household and children (Lomawaima, 1994). Boys and young men were allowed more freedom in creating their own social organizations, although such organizations were based on bully-based tactics more so than on their own traditional hunting and farming skills. Males were also allowed more freedom to explore the areas surrounding their schools. At the heart of this type of curriculum and instructional framework was not only the individuation of gender roles so that women's roles became devalued, but also the direct intention to devalue the women themselves as a way to destroy the culture. Consequently, during the era of boarding schools, boys and young men were more likely to find employment in trade positions than young women were to find work in noncaretaking roles. American Indian women were more likely to become teachers, writers, or housewives living precariously from the work of husbands rather than their own work, which they previously controlled (Medicine, 1983).

Nineteenth-century federal Indian education policy won out in the continuation of a vocational rehabilitation curriculum as boarding schools became American Indian high schools and technical schools. Whether or not the adoption of assimilationist education on the part of both systems can be concluded to have been the correct one, the example of ownership of education by the Cherokee Nation clearly indicates that when Indian Nations had full control of their own schools, the outcomes were far more humane and inclusive. In the boarding schools, American Indian children were not separated by gender in academic tasks (contradicting expected norms in many tribes) but

gender assignment of learning vocational roles was aligned to the contemporary expectations of White males and females from lower classes. Learning a trade was assigned by gender and intended to devalue the work done by individuals in placing students within a hierarchical realm of work expectations. According to many accounts, the staff at boarding schools felt that American Indian children had too high a sense of self-worth, this line of thinking was especially prominent in American Indian girls.

American Indian Girls and Boys Entering Public Schools

Relocation in the 1950s resulted in many families being uprooted to major urban areas frequently severing ties with grandparents, elders, aunts, and uncles who had served as important cultural educators for young children on reservations (Intertribal Friendship House & Lobo, S., 2002). While the 1970s brought about a wave of regulations against earlier boarding school abuses, Indian students enrolled in public and private schools still endured public humiliations as classroom management, inappropriate instructional and cultural behaviors of teachers, and barrages of "lies" in textbooks, instructional materials, and classroom discussion (Council on Interracial Books for Children, 1977; Slapin & Seale, 1998; 2005). This is especially heinous because, without much effort, multiple histories could be incorporated into textbooks (i.e., for accurate biographies see, Crow, Dog, 1991; Fowler, 2002; Giese, 1974; LaFleshe, 1912; Witt, 1976). It is clear by looking at the dates for these writings that accurate and reliable information about American Indian lives and histories was readily available.

The constant media barrage, focusing on negative and disrespectful representations of historical or contemporary American Indians, denies students' recognition of positive accomplishment, discourages their achievement through media stereotypy, and lumps American Indian students into categories of deficit learners because of their culture and language styles (Benson, 2001). American Indian students' dropout rate matches that of African Americans in most urban areas, and these dropout rates are directly related to the school environment (Jeffries, Nix, & Singer, 2002; Waller, Okamoto, Hankerson, Hibbeler, Hibbeler, McIntyre, & McAllen-Walker, 2002). Parents are viewed in a manner similar to that expressed by Blackmar (1892) who stated that, "It is not to be supposed that parents of Indian children are capable of determining whether education is good for their children or not" (p. 817). We find this attitude toward parents consistently demonstrated by the manner in which they are excluded from conferences, IEP meetings, discussions about referrals to special education, as well as discussions regarding the type of curriculum and instructional methodologies that they would like to see included in their children's schools.

Contemporary school districts continue the practice of cultural genocide by admitting far more American Indian students into special-education programs than is warranted if diagnosticians understood indigenous thought and relationships (Scherba de Valenzuela, Qi, & Copeland, 2004). By continuing to track American Indian students out of advanced placement (AP) or honors courses in high school and gifted programs within elementary schools (Montgomery, 2001; Scherba de Valenzuela, et al.) American Indian youth are further marginalization and lack of social inclusion within schools (Zhang, Katsiyannis, & Herbst, 2004). There is considerable evidence that strong cultural connectedness of a student and/or programs that result in helping students and their families reconnect with their culture have positive outcomes on students' academic success (Kratochwill, McDonald, Levin, Bear-Tibbetts, & Demaray, 2004; Kulis, Napoli, & Marsiglia, 2002; Montgomery, Miville, Winterowd, Jeffries, & Baysden, 2000; Napoli, Marsiglia, & Kulis, 2003; Westby, Moore, & Roman, 2002). More research must be done to examine the question of whether the traditional role of women in carrying on culture may account for why American Indian women obtain degrees, complete school, and obtain wage employment at higher rates. Gender equity in education would work to admit more Indian students overall, but also would seek to mitigate the lack of men enrolled in higher education. This research is needed and would help tease apart the role of gender inequity and cultural expectation that exists in schools today. Faculty and administration know little about the intergenerational trauma or cultural values of American Indian families and do not understand parents' views of their roles with schools nor students' career desires (Anguiano, 2004; Brave-Heart & DrBruyn, 1998; Turner & Lapan, 2003).

Elementary and Secondary Schooling

Current Academic Achievement

Across testing years of 1992, 1998, and 2002, American Indian/Alaskan Native 8th-grade students improved their test scores from 1998 to 2002; however the 1992 scores were similar when compared to the 2002 scores (National Center for Educational Statistics, 2005). Fourth-grade American Indian/Alaskan Natives showed no significant change in test scores across all three comparisons even between genders while their White, Black, and Hispanic peers showed gains across at least two of the three years (National Center for Educational Statistics, 2005). While there are subtle differences in the relative strength of tests scores compared across ethnic groups, it is apparent that American Indian/Alaskan Native 4th- and 8th-grade students are not faring well under the current educational regime (National Center for Educational Statistics, 2005). This may point to larger differences in three areas; (a) in the quality of schools which individuals attend; (b) the quality of instruction in individual classrooms; (c) structural inequities within districts that promote structural inequities within classrooms (i.e., continually hiring non-Native administrators/teachers for all American Indian schools), and/or (d) the inability of the tests being used to adequately measure the knowledge of students in ethnic groups whose cultural values and heritage languages which stand in stark contrast to White middle-class students knowledge bases. In support of the third hypothesis, an item analysis of one standardized test administered to elementary students in all Hispanic and all American Indian schools showed that the reliability of individual subtests were far below the accepted reliability required for the creation of valid tests (Calhoun, unpublished manuscript a). It is incumbent upon test developers, in this era

of accountability, that tests have adequate psychometric properties when including students from non-White ethnic groups.

Rampey, Lutkus, and Weiner (2006) described the latest results for American Indian/Native Alaskan (AINA) fourth and eighth graders' educational rankings in reading and math. The findings are not unlike those reported above. While their report does attempt to take into account the economic context for students, using free-or reduced-lunch counts, this use of a single indicator of poverty and the decontextualization of the results limiting the report to educational rankings further problematize educational conditions for American Indian/Alaskan Native Students. For reasons that are complex and multivariate in nature, states' educational rankings are highly correlated with the number of American Indian students ($r = .378, p = .01$), and being Indian is the only ethnicity of those reported that predicts states' ranks beyond funding mechanisms ($B = 21.438, t 2, 48 = 2.69, p = 01$) (National Center for Education Statistics, 2005). The direction of this correlation is such that the more American Indian students attending schools in a state the more likely that state is to be ranked in the lower half of the academic achievement-based rankings (National Education Association, 2003).

However, this isolated fact is conflated by several factors and has little to do with the nature of American Indians becoming educated. Contributing factors are most likely poverty and its definition; American Indian land not on the tax roles therefore not in the education coffers; Bureau of Land Management land (national parks and forests) in the state and not taxed for education; and the amount of land considered rural or uninhabited versus a heavier population that increases the tax base for school appropriations. These issues that attempt to attribute low achievement in states with higher American Indian populations need to be addressed in formulae. Researcher attempts to estimate educational ranking by over-sampling in states with high AINA populations do not take into account the statistical findings regarding educational rankings. In six of the seven states used for over-sampling, the 2005 NEA educational ranking of those states was in the lower half of all states (National Education Association, Fall, 2005). This may indicate that instructional and academic settings for these students are considered less desirable than for students from more highly ranked states. In addition, those same states are ranked within the lower half of states' poverty sampling as measured by percent of families living under the poverty level (U.S. Census, 2006). Interestingly enough, the state with the largest percent of AINA students, Alaska, also has the highest education ranking and the lowest percentile of families living in poverty. Studies of the situation for students in Alaska might shed some light on practices needed in the other six states with large AINA student populations.

Finally, while this report and others attempt to gain some impression of the educational status of AINA students, even with over-sampling techniques the reported populations in both reading and math represent only .02% of the total population tested while the population of American Indians is currently at 1.5% of the total population of the United States (Census, 2000). While it is necessary for statistical theory, it is not sufficient for understanding the real educational status of AINA students. A true sampling would include AINA students who are matched on SES with White students. While this may appear to be an impossible task, it is not as impossible as our racialized stereotypes assume. Since researchers assume that income and educational ranking play a role in student outcomes, it seems obvious that these variables should be considered statistically in the analyses.

From the point of view of Western educators, the self-image of American Indian students remains problematic. Western schooling appears not to help American Indian students perform better on standardized tests of reading, mathematics, and science. Racist interpersonal relationship experiences exist within schools but are not related to academic instruction. Frequently euphemized as *school climate,* racism has been singled out as one reason for underachievement among students of color (Bulach & Malone, 1994; Cotton, 1996; Haynes, Emmons, & Ben-Avie, 1997; Saint Denis & Schick, 2003). Some research on the Euro-American concept of self-image indicated that American Indian students suffer inequitably from self-image problems (i.e., body image; weight-control) (Becker, Franko, Speck, & Herzog, 2003; Fulkerson & French, 2003; Lynch, Eppers, & Sherrodd, 2004; Parker, 2004). However, it can be argued that these conditions are the consequences of the racism expressed within academic settings as well as communities, not simply deficits of the student. Stories of the type of racism that continues are illustrated by the comments of an individual whose position within a school district was to implement the state's version of No Child Left Behind. Within the district, half of the elementary school students are made up of Indian children from local reservations. At the end of the 2005–2006 school year, the individual responsible for implementing reading programs stated semi-publicly that the children from the reservation were fine except they all belonged in special education. Rather than place the blame on the procedures of the implementation, the reading program, the law, or external and complex relationships, she chose a simplistic reason embedded in racist ideology. A second incident was witnessed by the first author while she was working within the implementation of No Child Left Behind. She observed instances of utterances to teachers and children from other school personnel that can only be considered racist in their basis. For example, in one school it appeared to be the common thread of thought that, Indian children were "angels with their wings clipped" and that the purpose of the teachers was to allow them to fly despite this deficit. Fayden (2005) detailed further incidences of dysconscious and conscious racism on the part of individuals and institutions related to these two stories.

Finally, Beauvais (2006) reported that seven young males enrolled at Rose Bud reservation have met untimely deaths prompting "council representative Marion Young-One Star to call a meeting at the tribal council chambers" to discuss the matter. These deaths are reportedly attributed to suicide or unexplained consequences—code words for murder by persons knowable but not spoken of publicly in Indian country (i.e. state-sanctioned genocide). These stories relate the instances of racism in just two areas, but there is no reason to assume that these stories and worse are not replicated daily in the lives of many Indian children. With the current climate in border towns, on reservations, and in schools, it is not surprising that some Indian scholars feel that the only solution for improving the educational of AI/NA students will be the recognition of radical cultural differences within school districts as one solution for

current problems inherent in the Euro-American educational system (Schick & St. Denis, 2005; St. Denis & Schick, 2003). The current status quo is insufficient, demoralizing, and physically threatening.

A Local Look at Barriers to College Completion

In an analysis of 10 years of undergraduate application and graduation data of American Indian students and non-Hispanic White students from one university, Calhoun (unpublished manuscript b) said that the contrast between American Indian women and non-Hispanic White women was not as extreme and both groups of women appear to consistently be graduating at higher proportions than their male counterparts. In comparisons of high-school credits taken, high-school grade performance averages, entrance-exam scores, referrals to remedial programs in English, Math, and Reading, first and second semester college GPAs and proportion of graduation completion, the means for each of these variables for American Indian men differed significantly from the means obtained by non-Hispanic White men. Although the literature is replete with evidence of resistance to remedial and special courses that are frequently required for American Indian students, American Indian students are nonetheless referred to remedial classes in reading and English at significantly higher rates than non-Hispanic White students.

Despite the barriers discussed for one institution, nationally, American Indian students are increasing their enrollment faster than the total college enrollment rate (Syverson, 2004). Additionally, not all American Indians enter remedial college courses. Many nations with stronger economic underpinnings have managed to send their students to private or more prestigious public high schools enabling their students to enter more prestigious universities. Even when American Indians attend prestigious colleges and universities, they frequently attempt to blend into the mainstream or separate themselves from activities that would allow them to enter fully into the academic and social activities at those institutions (Brayboy, 2004). Lack of such social support, whether from marginalization or self-imposition, is one of several indicators of academic persistence among college students (Gloria & Robinson, 2001; Jackson, Smith, & Hill, 2003; Williams, 2000). In addition, it appears that mainstream colleges might consider adopting some aspects of curriculum and instructional methodology from tribal colleges and universities where success rates are noticeably higher (Rousey & Longie, 2001; Shirley, 2004). American Indian women graduate in higher numbers than their male peers, and this trend continues into undergraduate degrees awarded (Census, 2005). American Indian men appear to experience racism and trauma differently than do their female peers (Brave Heart, 1999b). The affects of intergenerational trauma result in inappropriate interactions and relationships in marriages (Duran & Duran, 1995) and creates a space in the Indian social fabric for American Indian women to complete high school and attend college. Still, many American Indian female students are also burdened by obligations for being responsible parents, breadwinners, and daughters as they work through the academy (Aronson, 2004).

WHAT ARE THE SOLUTIONS?

While sovereignty is alive and invested in the reality of every living thing for Native folks, Europeans relegated sovereignty to only one realm of life and existence: authority, supremacy and dominion. In the Indigenous realm, sovereignty encompasses responsibility, reciprocity, the land, life and much more. Ingrid Washinawatok (1999) (Menominee)

Solution 1: Speaking Truth to Power

Specific institutional and individual attitudes need to change in mainstream America if the current trend toward anti-Indianism is to be halted (Cook-Lynn, 2001; Harvard Project for American Indian Economic Development, 2004). These attitudes include, but are not limited to, the following: (a) the assumption on the part of non-Indian institutions and individuals that it is ethical and right for them to claim "ownership" of stories, language, cultural knowledge, artifacts and/or assumptions of belonging that are American Indian (Brown, 2001; Cook-Lynn, 2001; Vizenor, 2000); the assumption on the part of non-Indian individuals and institutions that they have the responsibility or right to "fix" the Indian problem (Harvard Project for American Indian Economic Development, 2004; Smith, 1999); and the overwhelming use of Indian (mis)representations in the media based, first seen in the 16th century, such stereotypes assault the psychological well being of our people and may play a strong role in the unwillingness of some youth to engage in learning (Munson, 1998; Urrieta, 2003).

Myths of Indians abound in the media and academia making it is difficult for Indian scholars to publish solid evidence and empirically based studies of gender when the findings of such studies deny the greater audience their infatuation with these myths. Two myths that discourage gender studies are (a) that Indian societies are ideal in a pastoral sense—in other words, issues based on gender do not exist in egalitarian Indian societies; (b) that they are so dominated by men that women's voices are completely overridden in nationalistic endeavors (Goeman, 2003). Its opposite counterpart depicts the savagery, of the violent, drunk Indian man, which equally poses a threat to addressing the problems found in Indian communities. To Indian people who have strived for so long to be considered "human," addressing problems that result from violence, economic poverty, and intellectual tyranny are vital to survival. After all, much effort has been made to move away from the idea that Indians are "problems," a stereotype originating in the 19th century and still believed in the twentieth century. Both stances have significant negative impact in creating a gender-equitable environment. While the first may seem like a gesture toward an egalitarian society, it ends up obscuring many important factors of specific tribes' lives; gender greatly influences how tribes conceive themselves as communities. The position of relativism impacts gender studies especially where it intersects with American Indian cultures; its search for ancestral roots that posit a different trajectory of society other than the patriarchal west still romanticizes in detrimental ways. By romanticizing American Indians' communities and lives, real problems are obscured, such as sexual abuse, spousal abuse, diabetes, and substance abuse. To counter such images, educators need to think carefully about what materials they include for classroom use (Slapin & Seale, 1998, 2005).

Further societal-based issues related to racism, both overt and covert, include the need to eradicate racism demonstrated by the lack of equal opportunity to obtain housing by American Indians (U.S. Department of Housing and Urban Development, 2005); the issue of continued police-department profiling of American Indian young adults and adults; the issue of continued disregard of law on the part of social-service agencies that allow American Indian children to be adopted by non-American Indian families at rates higher than those for any other group of children; and the issue of equal access to enter businesses, both explicitly and implicitly displayed, by American Indian people (Civil Rights.org, n.d.). To this day, some businesses, agencies, and parks continue to display "No Indians or Animals Allowed" signs in their windows. Such discrimination would not be tolerated toward other groups. If readers find such conditions deplorable, perhaps their sense of decency will energize an examination of their own actions and the actions of their communities regarding American Indians.

Schools and colleges need to recognize their role in continuing racism that creates gender inequity within the classroom and curriculum of their programs. These conditions exacerbate the continuing gaps in learning, which can only be filled by highly qualified teachers. Teachers entering the profession have, for the most part, a solid and well-grounded education but little knowledge of the communities from which their students come and even less knowledge about how to teach for individual and community empowerment. Sufficient scientifically based methods courses abound in an environment that is sterilized of controversy. What is lacking are courses that require hard thinking, reflection, and sharing of historical grief and intergenerational trauma found within American Indian communities and understandings of how such trauma explicitly affects the performance of our children. Learning *methods of teaching*, scientific or not, do little to inform a teacher about how to lift the spirits of her or his students, so that the earthly realities of these students' lives may be more positively impacted (Brave Heart, 1999b).

Solution 2: The Federal Government of the United States Must Comply with Treaties of Former Presidents with the Governments of Each of the 800 + Sovereign Nations within the Boundaries of the United States.

Historical View

Tribes first and foremost recognized and asserted their sovereignty long before Europeans established a governmental system in North America. They recognized their own and each other's right to territory, cultural well being, spirituality, and composition of its citizenry. The misrecognition that men were invested with the ability to make decisions for the entire community built a treaty process that was gender biased in its earliest stages. Furthermore, although the Constitution recognized tribes as sovereign, early clashes with the Euro-American invaders resulted in the nature of that sovereignty becoming embedded in concepts related to dependency on the federal government. Johnson v. McIntosh (1823) set the present version of colonial sovereignty in 1823. These European early interpretations of tribal sovereignty defined Indian nations as having sovereignty due to the concept of "right of occupancy," which meant that if their people lived on the land first, a previous claim existed, and thus they were regarded as having legal authority over their own lands and peoples. In 1832, *Worcester v. Georgia* determined that tribes, in this case the Cherokee Nation, had the right to self-government even while retaining a dependent status on the federal government. While this was the ruling of the Supreme Court, President Jackson stated that if the Supreme Court wanted this to be law, then they would have to enforce it—because he would not. President Jackson's statement acted as a trigger that allowed the Georgia Militia to go into Cherokee land, confiscate property, round up citizens, and send 90% of the Cherokees on six different routes along what came to be known as *nu na hi du na tlo hi lu i: the Trail of Tears*. Indigenous sovereignty's standing in the courts was further weakened in 1886, by the *United States v. Kagama*, which stated that the people and lands of tribes are under the control of the Unites States. The Indian Reorganization Act of 1934 recognized and strengthened tribal sovereignty by determining that sovereignty was not granted by an act of Congress; consequently, tribes had the "inherent powers of a limited sovereignty which had never been extinguished" (Cohen, 1945, p. 122). Despite the interpretations of the U.S. Supreme Court, Indian Law had become a body of knowledge from which individual states felt at liberty to "infer" whatever they wished regarding their treatment of nations.

Self-Determination

The issue of sovereignty cannot help but become a constant legal concern for Indian people. From the time of the Constitution to the present, the remarks of the majority of Supreme Court members resolving individual cases have eroded the ability of both Indian men and women to become self-sufficient, self-developing, and self-sustaining. These cases have, in essence, developed a situation of "ghetto sovereignty" (Vicenti, 2004)—and both women and men occupy this ghetto. Some nations have developed economic stability through casinos and/or economic development. The stealing of monies from tribes by states via the arrangement of "compacts" for the state's compromise for casino operations only demonstrates the lack of knowledge on the part of state officials of the nature and status of Indian nations' sovereignty and the duplicity of federal officials who continue to assist this attack on historical rights. What is not taken into account is the educational development, language renewal, cultural revitalization, prenatal care, health care, and many other social programs implemented through economic successes. Gender equity is increased through self-determination and full recognition of sovereignty, because a return to traditional gender concepts requires balance (equity) of roles (Smith, 2006).

A second important issue for the future is a challenge: to what extent tribes can control and reverse the negative damage done and being done to their sovereignty by well-organized, special-interest groups that promote anti-Indianism? Cook-Lynn

(2001) discussed the issues related to the futures of tribes in these areas. Anti-Indian special-interest groups seek to undo the weakened but still partially intact forms of recognition of nations by attempting to overturn laws related to the sovereignty of tribes; they attempt to legally control the actions of individuals on tribal land, to control the sale and distribution of their lands, to control the use of privately owned lands within the boundaries of their reservations, and to limit the control of tribes when negotiating with states over criminal and business issues (Johasen, 2000). The inequity of women and classes in the Euro-American legal system is well researched and historically based; succumbing to this system of authority would not alleviate gender equity, but would only increase the disparity between Indian women and Indian men and especially between Indian and non-Indian (Smith, 2005).

A third important issue for the future is that American Indian nations need to consider their approach to members who no longer have residence on traditional land bases. The majority of young American Indian adults and children no longer live on their reservations even though they remain enrolled members. Many of the young people living in urban areas are the third generation to do so since their grandparents were relocated to major U.S. urban areas (American Indian Policy Review Commission, 1976; Intertribal Friendship House & Lobo, 2002). A large body of literature has been published regarding the effects of relocation and urban-American Indian life (Guillemin, 1975; Intertribal Friendship House & Lobo; Miller, 1980), yet, many nations infrequently, if ever, interact with these young adults and children. Urban Indians, young adults and children, represent a portion of the future for each nation, that nation's human capital. In return, nations represent for urban Indians a source of connection and a source for learning some of the social capital denied them by their places of residence.

One nation, among several currently addressing the issue of urban tribal members, is the Menominee who have created an official tribal office in Chicago. Many Menominee citizens reside in the city in order to find employment. The office allows both urban and reservation Indians to interact, work, and learn from one another (Harvard Project on American Indian Economic Development, 2004). The Menominee Community Center of Chicago is owned by and funded by the Menominee Nation located in Keshena, Wisconsin. Recognizing that urban Indian communities frequently struggle, the Menominee Nation sought a way in which to bring its citizens together for financial, educational, social, and physical support. Founded in 1994, the Menominee Community Center of Chicago obtained formal tribal support in 1996 (Harvard Project on American Indian Economic Development). The Menominee constitution requires that two council meetings be held at the center each year, funds the center with both financial and volunteer support, and represents the only "officially recognized off-reservation community" among the 562 federally recognized Indian nations (Harvard Project on American Indian Economic Development).

It is our hope that other nations may wish to address specific questions that focus on the responsibility of all enrolled members to develop a decolonized sense of community, which returns to concepts such as interdependency and includes tribal members living on and off reservations. Within this framework, children will receive the most benefit from such connections.

Indian girls and boys living in urban centers are more likely to learn the forms of social and cultural capital, capital that increases gender equity when based on traditional ways of relating. In this time of cyber communication, interacting with the children, who are our future, would seem an obvious response to the need for technical and professional capacity on reservations, yet little is done to overcome the lack of expertise in these areas. Access to online communication in education would increase the self-esteem of children as they learn about who they are through the eyes of their male—and female—relations.

The Constitution of the United States "recognizes three sovereigns: the United States, the states, and the tribes. Tribes have their own constitutions, associated institutions, and government-to-government relationships with the United States, state, and municipal governments. Tribal sovereignty is manifested in powers of taxation, adjudication of civil disputes and non-major crimes, management of land and resources, policing and maintenance of civil order, and provision of basic social services and infrastructure" (Harvard Project American Indian Economic Development, 2004). To change this arrangement would require a Constitutional Amendment and this is unlikely to occur. The apparent lack of knowledge and moral will on the part of governmental entities appears to lie at the heart of the contentiousness of dealing with issues involving tribal sovereignty.

Solution 3: Enacting Self-Determination and Federally-Based Sovereignty to Stem Epistemic Violence

There are mixed feelings about how to handle the problem of violence against women and children. Smith (2005) presented cogent arguments regarding the development of common violence. Violence against American Indians was prevalent in the colonization of the "new world" and was used as a tool for subjugation. Sovereignty existed at both the national and individual levels before contact with Europeans who used violence, and especially forms of abuse of human rights, as a tool to control the colonized. The intent and long-term result of colonization is to develop a colonized people who oppress themselves and it has been in this way that violence within tribal communities has become part of the colonized traditions. Smith argued that forms of violence against individuals within a community would be eliminated if tribes were allowed to function as truly sovereign nations by returning to precontact forms of gender equity. Whatever forms male/female or parent/child relationships took before contact, those forms were embedded in individual autonomy and equity of personal responsibility and rights. Recovering or implementing these forms of personal sovereignty are important in alleviating many of the problems students face. Whether a student lives on his or her reservation or off the reservation appears to have some impact on risk-taking behaviors (Gray & Winterowd, 2002). Of all the students in the United States, American Indian students score significantly lower on standardized tests, have significantly higher (alarmingly so) rates of suicide, higher rates of unemployment, and higher rates of alcohol and drug dependency (Center for Disease Control, 2001; U.S. Census, 2000; Demmert, 2005; Frank & Lester, 2002; Indian Nations at Risk, 1991). Indian women die from domestic violence at nearly three times the rate of any other group (Oetsel

& Duran, 2004; Smith, 2005). The following demonstrate main areas in which Indian people asserting their sovereignty has led to healthier, balanced communities.

Health

The lack of support on reservations for positive health outcomes is implicated in these findings (Thompson, Davis, Gittelsohn, Going, Becenti, & Metcalfe, 2001). Because most Euro-American views on these problems are rooted in a deficit (medical) model that includes a perception of an individual's culture as problematic to recovery or prevention (Connors & Donnellan, 1998; Cross, 1998), more tribes are developing programs of their own to serve tribal members within these groups (Arquette, et al., 2002; Brave Heart, 1999a; Brave Heart & De Bruyn, 1998; Brave Heart & Spicer, 1999; Dalla & Gamble, 1998; Harvard Project for American Indian Economic Development, 2004; Sixkiller, 2002; Zimmerman, Jesus-Ramirez, Washienko, Walter & Dyer, 1998). Tribes and Indian communities are beginning the long-overdue process of redefining constructs applied as deficits in order to develop programs that have positive outcomes for the people they serve (Simmons, Novins, & Allen, J., 2004). In the field of health, Indian women are doing much work to bring about gender equity. The first Indian woman to become a western medical doctor was Susan La Flesche who graduated from Women's Medical College of Pennsylvania in 1889. Indian women have been keeping their communities healthy for generations. Indian medicinal herbs and solutions have given much to the western world and yet have not had the recognition. Currently, many Indian women work in health care as nurses, elderly caretakers, community health project administrators, doctors, and administrators.

Education

Because of the Tribally Controlled Schools Act of 1988, many tribes are exercising their sovereign rights to increase control over the educational systems serving children living on reservations. Much of the effort results from a common memory of traumatic educational experiences among American Indians (Balsam et al., 2004; Brave Heart, 1999b; Duran & Duran, 1995; Oetzel, & Duran, 2004; Zvolensky, et al., 2001). Post-traumatic stress disorder is recognized by the American Psychological Association (2000) in their *Diagnostic and Statistical Manuals* and represents the disorder that is synonymous in Duran and Duran (1995), Brave Heart (1999a), and Weaver and Brave Heart (1999) to the terms *intergenerational trauma* or *historical trauma*. There are gender differences in the manner in which American Indian women and American Indian men evolve through the healing of historical trauma indicating that men may require more intense and longer sessions in which to fully recovery from carrying the grief of the nation (Brave Heart & De Bruyn, 1998). The trauma and abuse of American Indian children is well documented in historic accounts of the Federal Governments involvement and implementation of education for American Indians (Adams, 1995; Attneave & Dill, 1980; Childs, 1998; Duran & Duran, 1995; Noriega, 1992; Hunt, 1980;

Kidwell, 1979; Metcalf, 1976); Furthermore, the Federal government's programs and public school districts curricula's historically failed to meet the needs of tribes (Braudy, 1975; National Advisory Council on Indian Education, 1993). Teachers and administrators must be told this history, and the histories of other oppressed peoples, if they are to be effective educators. Currently, many tribes are choosing to open, fund, and run their own Head Start preschools and K–12 school systems. This possibility came as a result of P.L. 93-638, the Indian Self-Determination and Education Assistance Act of 1975. In addition, tribes have regained the right to determine the placements of tribal children who are in need of fostering or adopting (see also the Harvard Project on Economic Development, 2004). Since the changes that have taken place over the last 30 years in American Indian education, many tribes have developed tribally specific curriculum, standards, and content reflecting traditional belief and knowledge that align with state public-education requirements. Most notable of the earliest of these was the Rough Rock Demonstration Project (McCarty, 2002). In the beginning of this chapter, we spoke of the gender balance involved in the traditional values of Indian people, by beginning to incorporate these points of view, Indian educators are ensuring a more balanced future for both boys and girls.

In conclusion, education as a path for equity is perhaps one of the strongest American Dreams to infiltrate American Indian community values; after all, there has always been a respect for learning. Tohe (2000) told the story of how Diné women used the knowledge of their female linage to survive and overcome the imposed conditions in Indian communities "even though there is no word for feminism in the Diné language" (p. 105). Using education as a tool to help your community, rather than to further yourself as an individual, stems from the earliest historical encounters, and has been debated among Indian people for decades. Tohe wrote about crossing into the western that values women differently; this crossing demonstrates, much like the trickster crossings discussed earlier, the high value placed on the honored Diné women versus the shamed and isolated devaluing of women's roles in the Western world. In the Diné world, Tohe (2000) explained "the men in our family understood this, and we all worked together to get the work done . . . no resentment, no insecurity about male roles" (p. 109). This survival of many American Indian women has always been assured by the clan system but their economic condition has only begun to improve over the last 20 years. Many have struggled to achieve an education that allows the privilege of living in a very luxurious manner in comparison to our grandmothers. This is both an achievement and a separation, which we need to recall each day in order to remember those that gave us life.

Child Welfare

The Indian Child Welfare Act of 1978 (P.L. 85-608) assured that tribes are now empowered to direct the placement of their children. However, this fact is not well understood by many county, state, and private social-service agencies given the overrepresentation of American Indian children in the social welfare programs. American Indian children are being fostered and adopted by non-American Indian families at rates higher than those for any other ethnic group (Kreider, 2003). When raised by non-American Indian families, American Indian children have less access to traditional teachings or innovative teachings employed in new curriculums. There is irreparable psychic violence committed in these learning environments that further alienates American Indian children from cultural roots, which supports healthy development and self-image. The need to encourage the engagement of American Indian scholars and their participation in the research being conducted on American Indian education should result in findings that would clarify much of the confusion and frustration on the part of White researchers and policymakers regarding how to best improve the academic achievement of American Indian students. These words echo earlier statements by Robbins and Tippeconic (1985) and are continued into the content of Next Steps: Research and Practice to Advance Indian Education (Swisher & Tippeconnic, 1999). This proposed research agenda would insure that commonly used definitions of learning behaviors that represent learning in White children are redefined in terms of what those behaviors look like and how they vary by nation within American Indian children.

Solution 4: Activism

If there is any one theme that addresses Indian activism from the start of settler-colonialism in the 1500s to the present, it is that Indian people continue to fight to maintain their communities. Many activists have succeeded against attempted eradication of their cultural beliefs, social structures, governmental operations, and physical presence in the Americas by using education for assimilation and other federal genocidal policies. Of course, this does not mean that colonization and empire building has not affected lived experiences; rather, it means that these historical processes and struggles become all the more important in contemporary Indian life. Without ongoing activism rooted in these historical processes and arguments of resistance to imposed cultural, governmental, educational, and social norms, Indian women would be at an even higher risk for gender inequity. As mentioned in the previous section, concepts of gender are rooted and constructed in continually evolving cultures. As Lakota anthropologist Beatrice Medicine (1997) reminded those wishing to explore gender or use it as a category of study:

In examining the concept of gender in Native America, the entire range of categories and behavioral expectations should be studied within their cultural context. At the same time, one should recall that after centuries of contact with non-Indians and adaptations to repressive legal actions and genocidal intrusions . . . the relationship to human actions and gender categories has grown increasingly complex". (Medicine, 218)

Thus, if gender equity is to be achieved in Indian communities, the discussion of cultural roles and the larger milieu of external influences must be negotiated; this is rarely a simple process as Western gender conceptions have been inflicted upon already existing patterns and varying levels of equity. If accurate and valid research outcomes regarding gender equity for American Indians is to happen, than accounting for the *diversity* of American Indian gender constructions within *diverse* cultural communities is pivotal. Furthermore, spatial colonization has lead to division of many communities across national borders, such as United States/Canada and United States/Mexico. Examining differences in women's status in communities caused by relationships to distinct settler-colonial institutions is extremely important. When discussing the role of politics and activism, one voice cannot speak to all indigenous women. Rather, the voices of indigenous women, while multivocal and multiational, resound in unison. The outcomes of activism depend on the benefit to the goals of the community involved. Much activism revolves around negotiating a continuum of culture and living in an ever-changing world. Maintenance of culture and language is important for very practical reasons within Indian nations. Cultural competence has been strongly linked to academic success in schools (Bryant & LaFromboise, 2005). While school administrators may fail to recognize this, the women of our Indian nations do not. In doing so, these women remain at the center of the inclusion of culture and language programs in mainstream schools.

The breadth of Indian women's activism began early in the history of the America's invasion and continues today. From the Cherokee's Beloved Woman of the latter 18th century, Nancy Ward, to smaller rebellions reflected in the oral histories of young women at Chilocco Indian boarding school (Lomawaima, 1994), Indian women have fought to retain a sense of tribal identity and community. Lomawaima stated that the "federal practice of organizing the obedient individual whereas policy aimed to disorganize the sovereign tribe" (p. 99). Centuries of federal Indian policies were derived to complete these goals. Indian people, in particular women, were not silent and often played a larger role in the struggle for sovereignty, Indian peoplehood, and individual selfhood than has been presented in public domains of academe, media, or textual materials.

Although many Indian women do not claim feminism (though many do as well) or invest themselves in mainstream feminist organization this should not be mistaken as a reckless disregard for gender issues; in fact, the well-being, health, and value of women in Indian communities are very important. This is demonstrated in extremely significant ways in creative work, activism, and political acts (Smith, 2005). The majority of Indian women activists today focus on advocating against the violence against children and women found in many Indian families, whether in reservation or urban communities, yet many are advocating as scientist, scholars, politicians, and doctors. However, popular myths of Indian women—such as exotic and an exceptional model of gender relations that sets up a nonexistent need in relationship to feminism, the portrayal as victims in the work of a lot of feminist scholarship, or the complete lack of historicizing Indian-White *gendered* relationships—abound in ways that are detrimental to American Indian Studies theorizing about gender or participation by women. So much so that young Indian women frequently refuse to discuss issues of gender equity as a serious issue in public forums (Diane Bechtell, personal communication, September 29, 2005). Like the multiple connotations of sovereignty, feminism means different things to different women. While nation-states demonstrate sovereignty's existence by acts of power, control, and political manipulation, sovereignty as an Indian concept relies on the traditional responsibilities to the community and individual rights granted by that community in return (Smith, 2005). When Governor Mike Rounds signed into law the current ban against all abortions, accompanied by remarks about rape being a "simple

matter" by state law maker William Napoli, Cecilia Fire Thunder, elected president of Oglala Sioux Tribe on the Pine Ridge Reservation stated that, "To me, it is now a question of sovereignty. I will personally establish a Planned Parenthood clinic on my own land which is within the boundaries of the Pine Ridge Reservation where the State of South Dakota has absolutely no jurisdiction" (Giago, 2006). This act is at once indigenous and feminist activism.

Sally Roesch Wagner (1998) stated in an early article on the subject of activism and women's rights that, "knowledge of their lack of rights under English inspired law was pervasive among these early women (American Indian), as was the awareness of the prestigious position of Indian women who lived in matrilineal/matrifocal systems" (p. 224). Noted feminist historian Estelle Freedman (2002) goes so far to say that if the prominent early feminist Elizabeth Cady Stanton "had taken notice" of the 1848 constitution formed by the Seneca that granted both men and women voting rights than, "the early feminist might have couched their demands for equality in less universal terms; perhaps they would have called for a *return* [italics original] of women's power." Freedman made this statement, but does not go more in-depth as to why this constitution was formed and the fact that this "legal" issue was more a fact of documenting a system that had been in place for thousands of years.

Seneca law was not unique in the fact that it "granted" women voting power. Rather, it was a matter of course for women *to hold* power and a step toward maintaining their own laws and nationhood threatened by European settlers. Men were not in a position to *grant* power, just as the government is not in a position *to grant* sovereignty. While this statement itself has a universal and appropriating tone about it, it poses the question of the relationship of early feminist movements to Indian women, as well as other cultural sources (i.e., African American). The development of this aspect in the field of women and gender studies and in women's rights activism could greatly improve gender equity for Indian women, as richer and more complex history is divulged and understood. Indian women have had a long history of being involved with women's collaborative groups. However, with varying waves of feminist scholarship, Indian women have been addressed, often in ways that are unproductive for the indigenous communities. The *(mis)use* of Indian women to support, prove, bolster, validate, or add a multicultural component to feminist theory generates great turmoil, and a reluctance to accept research done from a feminist perspective (Smith, 2005). In other words, scholarship and organization that does not recognize Indian treaty rights and sovereignty or self-determination movements often comes with a dimension of including all the right box checking and nods. Simply adding American Indian women to the discussion is not enough; rather, a serious engagement of civil rights and how they might conflict with American Indian engagement/or refusal to engage with the state must be recognized and respected (Koyama, 2003; Richie, Tsenin, & Widom, 2002).

This example also intimates how powerful a study of gender equity could be in sovereigntist movements. If we examine presupposition about the foundations of power, then pushing toward agendas with equity for women will become a natural part of the movement for decolonization. The reality of gender equity for both women and men and their daughters and sons is rooted in the oppression of colonization that continues to be imposed by both tribal councils and federal and state entities. The negative outcomes that range from the violence against Indian women specifically and against American Indians as a group is rooted in the systemic practice of colonization by governing bodies (Brave Heart, 1999b; Duran & Duran, 1995; Manson, et al., 2005; Oetzel & Duran, 2004; Smith, 2005). The nature of feminism, while delineated in these connotations of sovereignty, needs to be clearly stated and understood through the practices that communities undertake. We as indigenous people must take it upon ourselves to remove imposed gender constructions from our minds, practices, and actions in order to reclaim a healthy balance and order and to restore our own nations. A necessary aspect of this restoration is an activism that asserts women's wellbeing in the community as necessary to asserting sovereignty.

Solution 5: Acknowledging that American Indian Scholars and Authors from Across Disciplines Should Be Given Precedence in Classroom Work on Indian People

Non-Indians generally ignored work by native men and women, virtually entirely in favor of the mythologizing found in diaries, missionary accounts, travel tales and popular folklore (songs, stories, etc.), and the mythology grew without reference to those accounts that eschewed mythology. (Green, 1983, p. 2)

Through arts and literature, politics, education, and environmentalism, Indian women have impacted their communities in order to provide a better life for their families and friends. From the beginning of contact, Indian people have picked up the pen to write against Western impositions of culture and religion and against the exploitation of Indian people. One of the earliest women writers was Sarah Winnemucca, whose book *Life among the Piautes: Their Wrongs and Claims* (1883), outlined corruption and abuses as a result of the newly forming Federal Indian policy. Across tribes, women are a vital part of this intellectual history and have used the pen as a powerful tool to assert their rights.

The works of early writers, such as, E. Pauline Johnson, Mourning Dove, Zitkala Sa (Gertrude Bonin), Ella Cara Deloria, Susan LaFlesche, Maria Campbell, are awaiting rediscovery. Literary scholars are just beginning to uncover their rich texts and intellectual histories. Research into the intellectual history of Indian women writers is increasing and a more inclusive history is unfolding. Indian people interacted in the many circles and engaged in deciding policies, social structures, and many other facets of American culture. Gender equity in educational curriculum depends on such research and examinations that provide complimentary voices to early writers.

Past writers and their contemporaries—inspired by those early works—illustrated a rich intellectual history of engagement and activism for Indian rights. Rather than draw dichotomies based on false concepts of race that have been socially constructed, it is best to discuss the historical, cultural, and contexts of early Indian activist and their relationship to each other. All American Indians did not agree on the best way to handle the onslaught of settlers and were often in disagreement based on differing social, political, cultural, *and* gender formations. Creating gender equity in the classroom depends

on basing observations, not on false dichotomies of new racial categories of White and Indian, but with a commitment to engaging with specific cultures, contexts, and histories.

Contemporary writers continue to put forth diverse ways of dealing with colonization. Joy Harjo and Gloria Bird (1998) reinvented "the Enemies Language" by presenting an anthology on diverse contemporary Indian women writings. Harjo outlined the problems and benefits of this process:

We are coming out of one or two centuries of war, a war that hasn't ended. Many of us at the end of the century are using the "enemy language" with which to tell our truths, to sing, to remember ourselves during these troubled times. Some of us speak our native languages as well as English, and/or Spanish and French. Some speak only English, Spanish, or French because of the use of tribal languages was prohibited in schools and in adoptive homes, or these languages were suppressed to near extinction by some causality of culture and selfhood. Shame outlines the loss. But to speak, at whatever the costs, is to become empowered rather than victimized by destruction. (p. 21)

Prominent authors such as Joy Harjo, Louise Erdrich, Leslie Marmon Silko, Janet Campbell Hale, Roberta Hill, Jeanette Armstrong, Wendy Rose, Laura Tohe, Luci Tapahonso, Linda Hogan, Andrea Smith and many unnamed women authors have created a greater awareness of Indian issues as much of their work becomes widely read, not only nationally, but internationally, and in many different languages. Though often fictional, the authors often conduct painstaking historical research and/or draw from oral stories, or lived experiences. Their works remain unincorporated into mainstream classroom material. Respectful teaching that contextualizes learning and uses these text to open dialogue rather than reaffirm outdated notions of Indians or reinscribe these images in new-age fantasies, would push gender equity in education forward.

Much in the same way as historical mentoring took place (as discussed in the previous sections), these Indian women have also opened up spaces of learning and success, in support of younger writers just beginning to find their voices. The burgeoning of lesser-known writers publishing means a presentation of diverse cultures, historical situations, and points of view. This diversity itself is a healthy step toward gender equity as Indian women strive to break out of monolithic categories that are inadequate for understanding gender. Many authors are also learning or relearning their own languages. Elders, whose language was once so forbidden, are teaching the language again. Organizations have been formed around this very category of language acquisition, revitalization, and retention. Respecting and encouraging a diversity of languages is important to the quest of gender equity because notions of "gender" are closely tied to the spatial and relational nature of most Indian languages.

In higher education, much work has yet to be done. Indian women make up a miniscule percent of community college faculty (even at tribal colleges), a smaller percent of tenure-track faculty, and under a half-percent (.05%) of tenured faculty. While the fact that these women are Indian does not guarantee that the subject of Indian women will be discussed at length, it would represent a view heretofore ignored. Rather than include American Indian women as a topic of the day, they need to be integral to the University and College curriculum and across fields and disciplines. Anthropology has perhaps taken up this subject more than other fields, but for the foremost the discussions are limited to detailed descriptions and an analysis that addresses cultural changes, rather than in-depth discussions regarding equity rights and issues that need to be addressed outside of and within Indian communities. Exceptions to this are Indian anthropologists such as Bea Medicine whose work examined the very foundations of a discipline based on otherness, which double binds Indian women. Medicine (1978) bared the tension between academics whose study of indigenous peoples was often self-interested and detrimental to American Indians well-being and researchers and communities who responsibly search for viable and ethical methods of engaging with academia.

Academia can be further alienating in the discussion and research on Indian women. Past feminist research causes skepticism in communities already skeptical of research endeavors, regardless of discipline, methodology, or race and gender analysis. Linda Tuhiwai Smith's (1999) effort to decolonize research methods offered insight into this relationship:

At a common sense level research was talked about in terms of its absolute worthlessness to us, the indigenous world, and its absolute usefulness to those who wielded it as an instrument. It told us things already known, suggested things that would not work, and made careers for people who already had jobs. 'We are the most researched people in the world' is a comment I have heard frequently from several indigenous communities. The truth of such a comment is unimportant, what does need to be taken seriously is the sense of weight and unspoken cynicism about research that the message conveys. (1999, p. 3).

Most Indian people, regardless of tribe, nation, or education, remain deeply aware of the devastation resulting from Euro-American scholarship and education. The history of scholarship and education as imperialist tools has had a profound impact on current communities' perceptions of research. The study of gender needs to be done in ways that would benefit Indian research agendas, which in turn benefit Indian people rather than in ways that reward the academic researcher. This is the global message on indigenous methodologies (Smith, 1998). In education research, Swisher (1998) advised that American Indians "should be the ones to write about Indian education" (p. 190). The American Indian Science and Engineering Society (AISES) (Swisher, 1998) stated that:

Just as the exploitation of American Indian land and resources is of value to corporate America, research and publishing is valuable to non-Indian scholars. As a result of racism, greed, and distorted perceptions of Native realities, Indian culture as an economic commodity has been exploited by the dominant society with considerable damage to Indian people. Tribal people need to safeguard the borders of their cultural domains against research and publishing incursions. (as cited in Swisher, 1998, p. 1991)

WHAT ARE THE INSTRUCTIONAL AND POLICY IMPLICATIONS?

Implication 1: Changes in Curriculum that Reflect the Real Diversity of Indian Nations

In today's educational settings, many American Indian communities may be described as atrisk because of quantifiable levels of poverty, unemployment, and health-related problems, yet most retain their connection to place. Many retain languages that encode ethical and moral behavior, and the very "risk factors" that non-Indian agencies ascribe to them favor the retention by the community as a mechanism for survival (Cross, 1998; Duran & Duran, 1995; Johnson, 2003). Western definitions of notatrisk that are centered on the accumulation of wealth through material goods and money are not relevant for determining the quality of Indian family life and student ability (Harvard Project on American Indian Economic Development 2004; Manson, et al., 2005). Sustainable living continues to be prevalent in Indian communities despite its implied devaluation in the poverty policies of the 1960s and 1970s. Part of this is brought about through what Tressa Berman (2003) called matrifocal women—women who sustain earlier clan obligations through a sharing of "wealth." Through reciprocal sharing of "wealth" that takes place either informally or through the ceremonial relations of production, Indian women circumvent intense poverty and, most importantly, teach ways to accommodate pubic policy federal impositions, and other such external factors by turning to their strength within the community. Children raised in subsistence life styles lead far healthier and more emotionally rich lives than children in truly impoverished circumstances. Such children have value and take part in contributing to the sustainability of the family and community. Such children are eating traditional foods rather than "fast foods" and are physically fit from the routines of sustainable living.

Colleges and schools need to be on the cutting edge of social justice rather than in the entrenched conservatism of retaining the past. There is a need to imbue educational settings with the ideal that meeting the many worldviews of our students neither diminishes quality education nor instruction. Western educators taking a note from the matri-focal women who exist within many reservations communities, even the clan mothers (Lobo, 2003) who create community in urban areas, would be a step in the right direction. This type of thinking lies at the very heart of the differences between Euro-American educational practice and American Indian educational thought. While we see the inclusion of multiple world views as both complementary and supportive of educational goals, we advocate for a transformative curriculum as envisioned by Banks (Banks & Banks, 1995; Banks, 1997, 2000) that goes beyond an additive approach and pays more than lip service to *diversity* and *multiculturism*. More to the point, within American Indian communities numerous educational projects currently address the deeper meanings for cultural relevancy beyond multicultural packaging. *The Cradleboard Teaching Project* (St. Marie, 1996), *Iroquois Corn* in a culture-based curriculum (Cornelius, 1999), Indigenous Educational Models for Contemporary Practice; In our Mother's Voice (Ah Nee-Benham & Cooper, 2000), and Indian *Science* (Cajete, 1999) stand as testimony to the potential for curriculum development within traditional values. Indian nations are beginning to see the results of reclaiming their own educational institutions. The development of survival schools, tribally run K–2 schools, and tribal colleges are beginning to produce sustainable leadership as well as a demand that sovereignty be fully and equally recognized by non-Indian individuals, agencies, and institutions (Harvard Project on American Indian Economic Development, 2004).

The final legal challenge for the future focuses on the education of American Indian children, youth, and adults. One focus of conflict revolves around the teaching of Indian language in public schools—specifically, who teaches the language and who learns the language. Whether or not tribes will regain the freedom from the Department of Interior to operate their own schools as districts within states that receive educational funding equal to that of other public-school districts in non-reservation areas is a second issue. The expression of sovereignty in educational issues will begin to be more broadly discussed as the pressures facing education produced by the effects of No Child Left Behind begin to be recognized. American Indian parents frequently teach the traditional sense of autonomy that can be said to resemble "sovereignty of the mind" in that our children, as well as every individual, have the right and responsibility to gather the knowledge that best addresses their needs and ensures their future. Many times this may be consonant with what is taught in schools but just as many times the content and curriculum clash with the beliefs and experiences of American Indian students (Fryberg & Markus, 2003). The correlation of state educational ranks with American Indian population estimates is problematic and needs to be addressed through non-punitive interventions (NCES, 2005).

Implication 2: Changes in the Curriculum that Includes the Truth of all Sides Regarding Historical, Cultural, Educational, and Linguistic Conflicts

Teachers of American Indian children and young adults need to be aware of the potential fragility of their students in terms both physical and psychological health (Brave Heart & De Bruyn, 1998; HeavyRunner & DeCelles, 1997). Teachers need to place themselves in the role of healers when working with American Indian children, a role that requires them to (a) accept limitations and work with strengths, (b) accept, learn, and interact with their students' communities; (c) encourage positive self-image by making use of appropriate instructional materials that avoiding stereotypy and mythic representation (Mitchell, & Beals, 1997; Simmons, Novins, & Allen, 2004).

American Indian children endure an educational process, whether in public or private schools, that remains primarily assimilationist in nature and monolithic in character (i.e., English is the official language, Euro-American history and social studies the accepted "facts" for their lives). This poses further negative experiences for children who may be under higher levels of stress than children from other ethnic groups due to intergenerational trauma (Balsam, et al., 2004; Brave Heart, 1999b; Duran & Duran, 1995; Oetzel & Duran, 2004; Smith, A., 2005; Zvolensky, McNeil, Porter, & Stewart, 2001). Teachers must work to form history and social-study units that equitably represent all sides of the clashes of cultures throughout the timeline from first contact to present day. Furthermore, discussing of Indian women and their roles and importance to communities must come to the forefront. Professional organizations and Indian nations must lobby to have publishers include more current research, multiple points of view, and multiple points of information (i.e., facts that represent the knowledge base of all children's ethnic groups) in order for students to construct a sense of truth that is more complex than the current simplistic view.

Teachers and administrators must create classrooms that American Indian parents feel comfortable entering. To do this requires awareness that many American Indian parents may be reliving their own experiences with school through their children's interactions at school. This movement between personalized experience and teacher experience sometimes leads teachers to believe that parents are not listening to them or may not be concerned about their child. American Indian parents care deeply for their children but recognize the assimilationist pointsofview exist within those schools. Parent and student resistance to these assimilationist mechanisms may take the form of attendance refusal, participation refusal, or passivity in the classroom. Put bluntly, American Indian parents and young adults frequently do not see the need to put energy into efforts that will not provide them equal opportunity.

Teachers and their professional organizations should take a firm stance against societal and institutional forms of racism currently confronted daily by American Indians. Most egregious of these is the use of American Indian symbols, objects, and peoples as mascots for sports groups and other school-related organizations (Durham, 1992; Munson, 1998). The constant barrage of negatively presented stereotypes must be indicted as one of those environmental pressures that are related to the physical and psychological health outcomes for American Indian children and young adults. Some of the most egregious assaults come in the textbooks and trade books that American Indian children and young adults encounter during their years of education (Council on Interracial Books for Children, 1977; Kickingbird & Kickingbird, 1987).

Additional institutional-based forms of racism need to be addressed. Non-Indian scholars, teachers, agencies and institutions need to understand the issue of sovereignty as it relates to the teaching of heritage language and cultural knowledge within schools (Sims, 2003). Second, the issue of representation of "facts" as "truth" based on Euro-American philosophical traditions and embedded in school knowledge, routines, and reading; and an awareness of emphasizing multiple "values" systems within classrooms where multiple ethnic groups are represented by the students needs to be addressed. Finally, the Harvard Project on American Indian Economic Development has urged that non-Indian entities employ the following guidelines when seeking to work with American Indian nations: (a) "Effective programs and policies are self-determined" (p. 23); (b) "Leadership can emerge from many levels of tribal society" (p. 25); (c) "'Buy-in' on the part of tribal communities and formal leadership is essential" (p. 25); (d) Effective initiatives become institutionalized within the tribal community (p. 26); (e) "Effective initiatives are spiritual in their core" (p. 26, see illustrations of how this is conceptually different from religious practice); (f) "Effective initiatives explicitly draw on and strengthen tribal cultural practices" (p. 27); (g) "Effective initiatives focus on individuals and the tribal community" (p. 28); and, (h) "Effective initiatives explicitly strengthen children's and families' social networks" (p. 28).

Teachers and administrators must know the communities, both urban and reservation, from which their students come.

They need to become involved in those communities at some meaningful level, which does not trespass on tribally recognized needs (Suina & Smolkin, 1995). Professional organizations and Indian nations must promote professional-development opportunities, which offer teachers and administrators the opportunity to interact with tribal and urban-American Indian communities.

Implication 3: Changes in Teaching Methods that Are Based on Indian Educational Psychology

Urban American Indian students frequently cite specific cultural, racial, and educational experiences as barriers to completion of high school or as reasons for dropping out. Frequently students complete their education through GED or high-school completion courses and programs offered in Urban American Indian Centers (Sally Gallegos, personal communication, August 29, 2004). Many students come to these centers with skills that are at or below the 8th -grade level (Jennifer Elk, personal communication, August 28, 2004). One West Coast American Indian male stated that the center was "a good place and they taught me well. It is a good environment and they give a lot more attention than I got in regular public school" (Zahnd, 2004; p. 7). An American Indian woman seeking to complete her high-school degree later in life stated that "it is nice to have [the center] there and feel that you can always come back. At [the center] people come together. Some who enter are lost but find their way [back]. I tell people I meet to go see Rosie at [the center] because it is a good place to be. It is like a family and it feels like home (Zahnd, 2004; p. 7). For these students the center provided a more relevant curriculum than their former high schools.

Instruction at one particular American Indian Center was differentiated from high-school instruction by several factors. Teachers emphasized critical analysis of text, which allowed students to develop their voices as they sought to interpret and comprehended text. One particular teacher makes a point of assessing students before, during, and after her course in order to better individualize the instruction. Another important aspect of these courses, cited as positive by American Indian youth and adults was the culturally relevant content. This is achieved through the materials, instructional style, and self-directed projects that produce ethnically relevant literature. Teachers who focus on the diversity among their students, allow students to describe and talk about their tribal heritage, and other important life experiences had students who reported that they were more engaged and motivated to learn as a result of these teaching styles (Zahnd, 2004).

Ceremony also plays an important role within teachers' courses. Ceremony helps remind students and teachers that each day is new and sacred, that calming one's self is an important aspect of learning, and that focusing the mind helps students do their best on assignments and exams (Zahnd, 2004). Ceremony is not religious practice, but can be equated as practices like those in public schools like saying the pledge of allegiance. Students who have had negative experiences in high schools need to be renewed and reminded of their value to their American Indian communities through these types of instructional experiences. Empower students and help them set goals that will allow them to attain jobs. Cultural empowerment is not found in the curriculum, materials, or teaching styles of most mainstream public or private high schools. Quite the opposite is true as American Indian students are assaulted by a continuous chorus of history misrepresented from what they know from their ancestor's experiences and stories, by the stereotypy in sports, not allowing traditional regalia or meaningful pieces of regalia to be worn during instruction or at high-school graduations (Martinez, 2003). Other institutional forms of racism continue to oppress American Indian students driving them to think less of themselves and their people and pushing them out the door at the earliest opportunity.

Students frequently report several experiences in high schools or mainstream programs that eventuate in their quitting or being pushed out. One student's response is somewhat representative of the problem. "I was messing up in school. I messed up and something happened, and so I didn't feel welcome there. I was kicked out so quick [even though] I was hoping to get my GED" (Zahnd, 2004; p. 13). Another student defined how s/he came to enter the courses offered at the center. "I felt it was my time and I needed to learn and be part of the new world, including the computer world. I was interested in overcoming my joblessness and having only crummy jobs, and I knew I could get more experience in creative fields. It is my responsibility and I told myself that I need to overcome barriers and to manage to make it here" (Zahnd, 2004; p. 14).

Implication 4: Changes in Research Theory and Practice

Even before Swisher's (1998) essay established the inherent right of Indians to write about Indian education, the need for truly informed research that went beyond the superficial examinations of American Indian students' learning styles, brain behaviors, and cultural competencies was apparent. European and Euro-American researchers were making very good progress in publishing research that retained the mythic views of American Indians, whether as naïve (infer incompetent) souls who needed saving by the grace of an informed teacher who would teach to a student's learning style or as carriers of a culture and language that are dying, insufficient for "intelligent" conversation of modern concepts, and representative of barriers to learning (for review see Lipka & Ilutsik, 1995) American Indian students have been as much harmed as helped by research that applies concepts defined by mainstream experience, worldview, and language to traits observed in students not raised with the same denotations for those concepts. Linda Smith's Indigenous Methodologies (1999) is an incredibly popular text used across anthropology, history, education, American Indian studies, cross-cultural studies, and women's studies courses as much for its discussion of research methodology as its commentary on indigenous world view. In setting for a series of 32 research projects that were developed by indigenous researchers using their "native" world views, Smith has created the basis for turning the hierarchical organization of mainstream research on its side . . . leveling the presumed differences between "researcher" and "researchee." Andrea Smith's Conquest (2005) also detailed projects embedded in and developed through an indigenous world view that allows for the true voice of community to meet its own needs.

There is a need for such research to continue, widen, and be supported by local communities. There is a need for American Indian scholars and citizens to work with their communities in conducting research in a respectful manner and in a way that benefits the community as much as it benefits the researcher. To this point, many Indian nations have created formal and informal Internal Review Boards (IRBs) and policies that are far more stringent than those found in most universities. Even if the IRB process is an informal one, no researcher may do research within the jurisdiction of a Indian nation without first visiting with the tribal council and verifying that the research being proposed is one that the nation sees as desirable. These processes and policies developed because European and Euro-American researchers failed to develop a sense of ethics when it came to doing research in Indian communities. That need persists today.

SUMMARY

We have addressed the historical and contemporary frames of reference used by American Indians to define identity, role, and gender. We have focused our effort in an explanation of American Indian philosophical thought and the juxtaposition of spiritual and earthly identity in life. By imposing western conceptions of race and gender onto diverse American Indian populations, researchers and educators not only undermine the strength and vitality of American Indian communities, but have much to lose by limiting their research under these colonial rubrics. We have shown that, despite tremendous difficulty in overcoming their educational backgrounds, limitations for publication, and constant disparagement on the part of Euro-American publicists, agents, and academics, American Indian women have continued a long tradition of acting up, speaking out, and resisting the constant pressures to become invisible. In doing so, we also speak for many of our American Indian male colleagues and urge them to act up, speak out, and resist as warriors for the seventh generation. We recognize that the differences between us are based on ways of thinking within the institutions in which we work, and we see these as antithetical to healthy physiological and psychological outcomes for Indian nations. The dialogue between both genders in academe is as necessary as it is in our communities.

Indian women—and increasingly men—who are concerned with gender equity issues, also focus their concerns on their fathers, uncles, and sons, as the impact of education, imprisonment, and suicide affects the entire community There is a recognition that one life is a thread in a much larger fabric necessary to each community's well being. We develop programs to meet the needs of our communities and do so even without the use of "for profit" and "not-for-profit industrial corporations" when that type of funding might undermine the work of the community (Smith, 2005). American Indian families living in urban and reservation communities and American Indian families overburdened and underemployed (Tsethlikai, 2001) are assaulted by media portrayals that obscenely demonstrate the Euro-American desire to retain the myth, continue the genocide, and divide the family from its values in community, spirituality, and education (Harvard Project on American Indian Economic Development, 2004).

The connection between their experiences in public, private, and federally run schools and these outcomes has yet to be made and represents the strong need for research that observes real situations in classrooms, analyzes texts and written materials in the school, and surveys for attitudes on the part of faculty, administration, and students regarding issues related to American Indian students. Faculty and administrators appear to act without knowledge regarding issues related to American Indian parents' expectations of the school, to assume that American Indian students are destined to remain the American underclass, and consistently work to achieve this by continuing to exclude through referral to special education or by the techniques of pushingout students whom teachers and administrators feel do not fit the institution (Anguiano, 2004; Gloria & Robinson, 2001; Jeffries, Nix, & Singer, 2002; Kratochwill et al., 2004). American Indian students desperately need institutions that will change to fit their needs so that they can succeed and thrive in the world of professional jobs, further education, and upper-income lifestyles. Our children and grandchildren require schools with teachers who see their languages and cultures as resources that strengthen their potential. They need schools with teachers who see poverty as a challenge not a deficit (Miller, Castuera, & Chao, 2003; Payne, 1996). Our children need schools with teachers who see the diversity of Indian nations' cultures as strengths on which to build curriculum units, instructional approaches, and frameworks for teaching.

ACKNOWLEDGMENTS

The authors wish to thank Dr. Andrea Smith, Michigan State University, for her thorough review of the chapter in regards to theoretical stances and educational space and Dr. Karen Schaumann, Eastern Michigan University, for her careful observations and considerations.

References

Adams, D. W. (1995). *Education for extinction: American Indians and the boarding school experience 1875–1928*. Lawrence, KS: University of Kansas Press.

Ah Nee-Benham, M. K. P., & Cooper, J. E. (2000). *Indigenous educational models for contemporary practice: In our Mother's voice*. Mahwah, NJ: Lawrence Erlbaum Associates.

Albers, P., & Medicine, B. (Eds.). (1983). *The hidden half: Studies of plains Indian women*. Washington, DC: University Press of America.

American Indian Policy Review Commission. (1976). *Report on urban and rural Non-reservations Indians*. Washington, DC: U.S. Government Printing Office.

American Psychological Association (APA). (2000). *Diagnostic and statistical manual of mental disorders* (4th ed., text revision). Arlington, VA: Author

Anderson, K. (1990). *Chain her by one foot: The subjugation of native women in Seventeenth Century New France*. New York: Routledge.

Anguiano, R. (2004). Families and schools: The effect of parental involvement on high school completion. *Journal of Family Issues, 25*(1), 61–85.

Anguksuar (Richard LaFortune). (1997). A postcolonial colonial perspective on Western misconceptions of the cosmos and the restoration of indigenous taxonomies. In S. E. Jacobs, W. Thomas, & S. Lang, (Eds.), *Two-spirit people: Native American gender identity, sexuality, and spirituality* (pp. 217–222). Urbana, IL: University of Illinois Press.

Anonymus (1963). *Inyan and Maka: Lakota Creation*. Unpublished manuscript.

Anzaldua, G. (1987). *Borderlands/La Frontera, the New Mestiza*. San Francisco: Aunt Lute Books.

Aronson, J. (2004). *Undergraduate and graduate status of women and minorities in science, technology, engineering and mathematics selected statistics from current literature*. Greater Seattle, WA: National Science Foundation Report: Puget Sound Center for Teaching, Learning, and Technology.

Aronson, J., Steele, C. M., Salinas, M. F., & Lustina, M. J. (1998). The effects of stereotype threat on the standardized test performance of college students. In E. Aronson (Ed.), *Readings about the social animal* (8th ed.). New York: Freeman.

Aronson, J., Lustina, M. J., Good, C., Keough, K., Steele, C. M., & Brown, J. (1999). When white men can't do math: Necessary and sufficient factors in stereotype threat. *Journal of Experimental Social Psychology, 35*, 29–46.

Aronson, J., & Steele, C. M. (2004). Stereotypes and the fragility of human competence, motivation, and self-concept. In C. Dweck & E. Elliot (Eds.), *Handbook of competence & motivation* (pp. 436–536). New York: Guilford.

Arquette, M., Cole, M., Cook, K., LaFrance, B., Peters, M., Ransom, J., et al. (2002). Holistic risk-based environmental decision making: A native perspective. *Environmental Health Perspectives, 110*(Suppl. 2), 259–264.

Arv Bragi, D. (2005). *Invisible Indians: Mixed-blood Native Americans who are not enrolled in federally recognized tribes*. Napa, CA: Lulu Press.

Ashley, J. S., & Jarratt-Ziemski, K. (1999). Superficiality and bias: The (mis)treatment of Native Americans in U.S. government textbooks. *American Indian Quarterly, 23*, 49–62.

Attneave, C., & Dill, A. (1980). Indian boarding schools and Indian women: Blessing or curse. *Conference on the Educational and Occupational Needs of American Indian Women, 1976*. National Institution of Education (DHEW), Washington, DC (ERIC Document Reproduction Service No. ED 194259).

Balsam, K. F., Huang, B., Fieland, K. C., Simoni, J. M., & Walters, K. L. (2004). Culture, trauma, and wellness: A comparison of heterosexual and lesbian, gay, bisexual, and Two-Spirit Native Americans. *Cultural Diversity and Ethnic Minority Psychology, 10*(3), 287–301.

Banks, C., & Banks, J. (1995). Equity pedagogy: An essential component of multicultural education. *Theory Into Practice, 34*(3), 152–158.

Banks, J. A. (1997). *Teaching Strategies for Ethnic Studies* (6th ed.). Boston: Allyn and Bacon.

Banks, J., A. (2000). *Cultural diversity and education: Foundations, curriculum, and teaching*. Boston: Allyn & Bacon.

Basso, K. H. (1996). Wisdom sits in places: Landscape and language among the Western Apache. Albuquerque, NM: University of New Mexico Press.

Beauvais, A. B. (2006, October 10). *White Buffalo Calf Woman Society holds annual awareness march*. Martin, SD: Lakota Country Times.

Becker, A. E., Franko, D. L., Speck, A., & Herzog, D. B. (2003). Ethnicity and differential access to care for eating disorder symptoms. *International Journal of Eating Disorders, 33*(2), 205–212.

Benson, R. (2001). *Children of the dragonfly: Native American voices on child custody and education*. Tuscon, AZ: University of Arizona Press.

Berman, T. (2003). *Circle of goods: Women, work, and welfare in a reservation community*. Albany, NY: State University of New York Press.

Blackmar, F. W. (1892). Indian education. *Annals of the American Academy of Political and Social Science, 2*, 813–837. ·

Bletzer, K., V., & Koss, M. P. (2004). Narrative constructions of sexual violence as told by female rape survivors in three populations of southeastern US: Scripts of coercion, scripts of consent. *Medical Anthropology, 23*, 113–156.

Braudy, S. (1975). We will remember survival school: The women and children of the American Indian Movement. *Ms. Magazine, 5*, 94–120.

Brave Heart, M. Y. H., & De Bruyn, L. (1998). The American holocaust: Historical unresolved grief among native American Indians. *National Center for American Indian and Alaska Native Mental Health Research Journal, 8*(2), 56–78.

Brave Heart, M. Y. H. (1999a). Oyate Ptayela: Rebuilding the Lakota Nation through addressing historical trauma among Lakota parents. In H. Weaver (Ed.), *Voices of First Nations People: Considerations for Human Services* (pp. 109–126). New York: Haworth Press

Brave Heart, M. Y. H. (1999b). Gender differences in the historical trauma response among the Lakota. *Journal of Health and Social Policy, 20*(4), 1–21.

Brave Heart, M. Y. H., & Spicer, P. (1999). The sociocultural context of American Indian infant mental health. In J. D. Osofsky & H. E. Fitzgerald (Eds.), *World Association of Infant Mental Health Handbook of Infant Mental Health* (Vol. 1, pp. 153–179). Hoboken, NJ: John Wiley & Sons.

Brayboy, B. M. J. (2004). Hiding in the ivy: American Indian students and visibility in elite educational settings. *Harvard Educational Review, 74*(2), 125–152.

Briggs, J. L. (1974). Eskimo women: Makers of men. In C. J. Matthiasson (Ed.), *Many sisters: Women in cross-cultural perspective* (pp. 261–304). New York: Free Press.

Brown, D. A. (2001). *Bury my heart at Wounded Knee*. New York, NY: Henry Holt & Company.

Bryant, A., & LaFromboise, T. D. (2005). The racial identity and cultural orientation of Lumbee American Indian high school students. *Cultural Diversity and Ethnic Minority Psychology, 11*(1), 82–89.

Beauvais, A. B. (2006, May 26). Recent suicides at Rosebud prompt meeting. *Lakota Times*. Retrieved May 31, 2006, from http://lakotacountrytimes.com/.

Bulach, C. R., & Malone, B. (1994). The relationship of school climate to the implementation of school reform. *ERS SPECTRUM, 12*(4), 3–8.

Bureau of Justice. (2003). *American Indians and crime*. Washington, DC: Government Printing Office.

Caffrey, M. M. (2000). Complementary power: Men and women of the Lenni Lenape. *American Indian Quarterly, 24*(1), 44–46.

Cajete, G. (1999). *Native science*. Santa Fe, NM: Clear Light Publishers.

Calhoun, J. A. (unpublished manuscript a). *American Indian educational psychology*.

Calhoun, J. A. (unpublished manuscript b). *Barriers to retention: American Indian students in college*.

Calhoun, J. A., & Annett, C. (2003). American Indian and Altai Literacies: Place as story. Available from http://ijl.cgpublisher.com/product/pub.30/prod.33). *International Journal of Learning, 10*, 2112–2124.

Center for Disease Control. (2001). *Suicide: Fact sheet*. Retrieved July 20, 2005, from http://www.cdc.gov/ncipc/factsheets/suifacts.htm/

Chi, M. T. H., Farr, M. J. & Glaser, R., (1988). *The nature of expertise*. Hillsdale, NJ: Erlbaum.

Childs, B. J. (1998). *Boarding school seasons; American Indian families 1900–1940*. Lincoln, NB: University of Nebraska Press.

Civil Rights.org. (n.d.). Civil Rights 101: Native Americans. Retrieved October 11, 2004, from http://www.civilrights.org/research_center/civilrights101/native.html. CivilRights.Org: Author.

Cohen, F. S. (1945). *Handbook of Federal Indian Law* (4th ed.). Washington, DC: Government Printing Office. Retrieved July 26, 2005, from http://thorpe.ou.edu/cohen.html.

Cohen, G. L., & Steele, C. M. (2002). A barrier of mistrust: How negative stereotypes affect cross-race mentoring. In J. Aronson (Ed.), *Improving academic achievement: Impact of psychological factors on education* (pp. 305–331). San Diego, CA: Academic Press.

Connors, J. L., &. Donnellan, A. M. (1998). Walk in beauty: Western perspectives on disability and Navajo family/cultural resilience. In H. I. McCubbin, E. A. Thompson, A. I. Thompson, & J. E. Fromer (Eds.), *Resiliency in Native American and immigrant families* (pp. 159–182). Thousand Oaks, CA: Sage

Cook-Lynn, E. (2001). Anti-Indianism and genocide: The disavowed crime lurking at the heart of America. In E. Cook-Lynn (Ed.), *Anti-Indianism in modern America: A voice from Tatekeya's Earth* (pp. 185–195). Chicago: University of Illinois Press.

Cornelius, C. (1999). *Iroquois corn in a culture-based curriculum*. Albany, NY: SUNY Press.

Cotton, K. (1996). *School size, school climate, and student performance*. Northwest Regional Educational Laboratory: School Improvement Research Series. Retrieved July 24, 2005, from http://www.nwrel.org/scpd/sirs/10/c020.html

Council on Interracial Books for Children. (1977). *Stereotypes, distortions, and omissions in US history textbooks*. New York: Author.

Cross, T. (1998). Understanding family resiliency from a relational world view. In H. I. McCubbin, E. A. Thompson, A. I. Thompson, & J. E. Fromer (Eds.), *Resiliency in Native American and immigrant families* (pp. 143–158). Thousand Oaks, CA: Sage Publications.

Crow Dog, M. (1991). *Lakota woman*. New York: Harper Perennial.

Cruickshank, J. (1971). Native women in the north. *North/Nord, 18*(6), 1–7.

D'Errico, P. (2000). Sovereignty. In *The Encyclopedia of Minorities in American Politics* (pp. 691-693). American Political Landscape Series. Phoenix, AZ: Oryx Press.

Dalla, R. L., & Gamble, W. C. (1998). Social networks and systems of support among American Indian Navajo adolescent mothers. In H. I. McCubbin, E. A. Thompson, A. I. Thompson, & J. E. Fromer (Eds.), *Resiliency in Native American and immigrant families* (pp. 183-198). Thousand Oaks, CA: Sage

Daniels, H. (Ed.). (1996). Psychology in a social world. In H. Daniels (Ed.), *An introduction to Vygotsky* (pp. 1–28). London, Routledge.

Deloria, E. C. (1932). *Dakota Texts*. New York: G.E. Stechert and Co.

Deloria, E. C. (1944). *Speaking of Indians*. New York: Friendship Press.

Deloria, V., Jr., & Wildcat, D. R. (2001). *Power and place: Indian education in America*. Golden, CO: Fulcrum.

DeMallie, R. (1983). Male and female in traditional Lakota culture. In P. Albers & B. Medicine, (Eds.), *The Hidden half: Studies of Plains Indian women* (pp. 237–266). Washington, DC: University Press of America.

Demmert, W. G. (2005). The influences of culture on learning and assessment among Native American students. *Learning Disabilities Research and Practice, 20*(1), 16–23.

D'Errico, P. (2000). Sovereignty. In *The Encyclopedia of Minorities in American Politics* (pp. 691–693). American Political Landscape Series. Phoenix, AZ: Oryx Press.

Downs, J. L. (1972). The cowboy and the lady: Models as a determinant of the rate of acculturation among the Pinon Navajo. In H. M. Bahr (Ed.), *Native Americans Today: Sociological Perspectives* (pp. 275–290). New York: Harper and Row.

Duran, E., & Duran, B. (1995). *Native American postcolonial psychology*. Albany, NY: State University of New York Press.

Durham, J. (1992). Cowboys and . . . Notes on art, literature, and American Indians in the modern American mind. In M. Annette Jaimes (Ed.), *The state of Native America: Genocide, colonization and resistance* (pp. 423–438). Boston: South End Press.

Fayden, T. (2005). *How children learn: Getting beyond the deficit myth*. Boulder, CO: Paradigm Publishers.

Fowler, C. S. (1978). Sarah Winnemucca (Hopkins), Northern Paiute. In M. Liberty (Ed.), *American Indian Intellectuals* (pp. xx–xx). St. Paul, MN: West Publishing.

Fowler, C. S. (2002). Sarah Winnemucca (Hopkins), Northern Paiute. In M. Liberty (Ed.), *American Indian Intellectuals* (pp. 38–50). Norman, OK: University of Oklahoma Press.

Frank, M. L., & Lester, D. (2002). Self-destructive behaviors in American Indian and Alaska native high school youth. *American Indian and Alaska Native Mental Health Research, 10*(3), 24–32.

Fraser, J. E. (1930). *The end of the trail*. Sculpture commissioned for the end of the Lincoln Highway in San Francisco, CA. Jersey City, NJ: The Lincoln Association.

Freedman, E. B. (2002). *No turning back: The History of feminism and the future Of women*. New York: Ballentine Books.

Fryberg, S. A., & Markus, H. (2003). On being American Indian: Current and possible selves. *Self and Identity, 2*(4), 325–344.

Fulkerson, J. A., & French, S. A. (2003). Cigarette smoking for weight loss or control among adolescents: Gender and racial/ethnic differences. *Journal of Adolescent Health, 32*(4), 306–313.

Gallegos, B. P. (1992). *Literacy, education, and society in New Mexico, 1693–1821*. Albuquerque, NM: University of New Mexico Press.

Giago, T. (2006, March 22). *Oglala Sioux Tribe on the South Dakota abortion ban*. Retrieved June 19, 2006, from http://www.indybay.org/newsitems/2006/03/22/18098591.php

Giese, P. (1974). Free Sarah Bad Heart Bull. *North Country Anvil, 13*, 64–71.

Gilbert, W. H. (1978). *The Eastern Cherokees*. Washington, DC: Smithsonian Institution.

Gloria, A. M., & Robinson, K.-S. E. (2001). Influences of self-beliefs, social support, and comfort in the university environment on the academic nonpersistence decisions of American Indian undergraduates. *Cultural Diversity and Ethnic Minority Psychology, 7*(1), 88–102.

Goeman, M. (2003). *Unconquered nations, unconquered women: Native women (re)mapping race, gender, and nation*. Unpublished doctoral dissertation, Stanford University, Palo Alto, California.

Gray, J. S., & Winterowd, C. L. (2002). Health risks in American Indian adolescents: A descriptive study of a rural, non-reservation sample. *Journal of Pediatric Psychology, 27*(8), 717–725.

Green, R. (1983). *Native American women: A contextual bibliography*. Bloomington, IN: Indiana University Press.

Guillemin, J. (1975). *Urban Renegades: The cultural strategy of American Indians*. New York: Columbia University Press.

Gunn-Allen, P. (1992). *Columbus and beyond: Views from Native Americans*. Boulder, CO: Southwest Parks & Monuments Association

Gunn-Allen, P. (2003). *Pocahontas: Medicine woman, spy, entrepreneur, diplomat*. San Francisco: Harper.

Harjo, J., & Bird, G. (1998). *Reinventing the enemy's language: Contemporary native women's writings of North America*. New York, W.W. Norton & Company.

Harvard Project on American Indian Economic Development. (2004). *The context and meaning of family strengthening in Indian America* (A report to the Annie E. Casey Foundation). Retrieved December 4, 2005, from www.aecf.org/publications/browse.php?filter=22

Hass, M. (1964). Men's and women's speech in Koasati. In D. Hymes (Ed.) *Language in culture and society* (pp. 228–234). New York: Harper & Row.

Haynes, N. M., Emmons, C., & Ben-Avie, M. (1997). School climate as a factor in student adjustment and achievement. *Journal of Educational and Psychological Consultation, 8*(3), 321.

Heavy Runner, I., & DeCelles, R. (1997). Family education model: Meeting the student retention challenge. *Journal of American Indian Education, 41*(2), 29–37.

Hill, W. W. (1938). Notes on the Pima Berdache. *American Anthropologist, 40*, 338–340.

House, C. (1997). Navajo warrior women: An ancient tradition in a modern world. In S. E. Jacobs, W. Thomas, & S. Lang, (Eds.), *Two-spirit people: Native American gender identity, sexuality, and spirituality* (pp. 223–227). Urbana, IL: University of Illinois Press.

Hunt, J. (1980). American Indian women and their relationship to the federal government. In the Department of Education/National Institute of Education's *Conference on the Educational and Occupational Needs of American Indian Women, 1976* (pp. 293–312). National Institution of Education (DHEW), Washington, DC (ERIC Document Reproduction Service No. ED 194259).

Indian Nations at Risk Task Force. (1991, October). *Indian nations at risk: An educational strategy for action* (Final report of the Indian Nations at Risk Task Force). Washington, DC: U.S. Department of Education.

Intertribal Friendship House & Lobo, S. (2002). *Urban Voices: The Bay Area American Indian Community, Community History Project, Intertribal Friendship House, Oakland, California*. Tucson, AZ: University of Arizona Press.

Jackson, A. P., Smith, S. A., & Hill, C. L. (2003). Academic Persistence Among Native American College Students. *Journal of College Student Development, 44*(4), 548–565.

Jacobs, S. E. (1977). Berdache: A brief review of the literature. *Colorado Anthropology, 1*, 25–40.

Jacobs, S. E., Thomas, W., & Lang, S., (Eds.). (1997). *Two-spirit people: Native American gender identity, sexuality, and spirituality*. Urbana, IL: University of Illinois Press.

Jaimes, M. A., & Halsey, T. (1992). American Indian women: At the center of Indigenous resistance in North America. In M. Annette Jaimes (Ed.), *The state of Native America: Genocide, colonization and resistance* (pp. 331–344). Boston: South End Press.

Jeffries, R., Nix, M., & Singer, C. (2002). Urban American Indians "dropping" out of traditional high schools: Barriers & bridges to success. *High School Journal, 85*(3), 38–46.

Johasen, B. E. (2000). The new terminators: The anti-Indian movement resurfaces. *Native Americas, 17*(3), 43.

Johnson v. M'Intosh, 21 U.S. 543, 5 L.Ed. 681, 8 Wheat. 543 (1823). Retrieved June 19, 2006 from http://www.law.nyu.edu/kingsburyb/spring03/indigenousPeoples/classmaterials/class10/.

Johnson, G. G. (2003). Resilience, a story: A postcolonial position from which to (re)view Indian education framed in "at-risk" ideology. *Educational Studies: A Journal of the American Education Studies Association, 34*(4), 510–512.

Johnson, T. L., & Heilman, C. W. (2001). Racial disparity in the criminal justice system: An embarrassment to all Minnesotans. *Bench and Bar of Minnesota, 58*(5), 28–35. Retrieved July, 16, 2005, from http://www2.mnbar.org/benchandbar/.

Jolly, M. (2000). Research framework for a review of community justice in the Yukon: Gender (Abridged version of keynote address to conference on Conflict Management and Restorative Justice in the Pacific Islands Port Vila). *Vanuatu, 19–21*. Retrieved June 14, 2005, from http://www.justice.gov.yk.ca/pdf/review/03-c_Gender.pdf.

Kailin, J. (1999). How White teachers perceive the problem of racism in their schools: A case study in "Liberal" Lakeview. *Teachers College Record, 100*(4), 724–757.

Kickingbird, K., & Kickingbird, L. S. (1987). *Indians and the United States Constitution: A forgotten legacy*. Oklahoma City,OK: Institute for the Development of Indian Law.

Kidwell, C. S. (1979). American Indian women: Problems of communicating a cultural/sexual identity. *The Creative Woman, 2*(3), 33–38.

King, J. E. (1991). Dysconscious racism: Ideology, identity, and the mis-education of teachers. *The Journal of Negro Education, 60*(2), 133–46.

Knowles, M. S. (1980). *The modern practice of adult education*. New York: Adult Education.

Knowles, M. S. (1992). *The adult learner: a neglected species* (4th ed.). Houston, TX: Gulf.

Koyama, E. (2003). *Disloyal to feminism: Abuse survivors within the domestic violence shelter system*. Portland, OR: Confluere Publications.

Kratochwill, T. R., McDonald, L., Levin, J. R., Bear-Tibbetts, H. Y., & Demaray, M. K. (2004). Families and schools together: An experimental analysis of a parent-mediated multi-family group program for American Indian children. *Journal of School Psychology, 42*(5), 359–383.

Kreider, R. M. (2003). Adopted children and stepchildren: 2000. Census 2000 Special Reports. Washington, D. C.: U. S. Department of Commerce.

Kreider, R. M. (2003). *Adopted children and stepchildren: 2000*. Census 2000 Special Reports. Washington, DC: U.S. Department of Commerce.

Kulis, S., Napoli, M., & Marsiglia, F. (2002). Ethnic pride, biculturalism, and drug use norms of urban American Indian adolescents. *Social-Work-Research, 26*(2), 101–112.

LaFleshe, F. (1912). Osage marriage customs. *American Anthropologist, 14*, 127–130.

Lewis, A. (1976). Separate yet sharing. *The Conservationist, 30*, 17.

Lewis, O. (1941). Manly-hearted women among the north Piegan. *American Anthropologist, 43*, 173–187.

Lipka, J., & Ilutsik, E. (1995). Negotiated change: Yup'ik perspectives on indigenous schooling. *The Bilingual Research Journal, 19*(1), 195–207.

Lobo, S. (2003). Urban clan mothers: Key households in cities. *The American Indian Quarterly, 27*(3/4), 305–322.

Lomawaima, T. K. (1994). *They called it prairie light: The story of Chilocco Indian school*. Lincoln, NE: University of Nebraska Press.

Lynch, W. C., Eppers, K. D., & Sherrodd, J. R. (2004). Eating attitudes of Native American and White female adolescents: A comparison of BMI- and age-matched groups. *Ethnicity and Health, 9*(3), 253–266.

MacLachlan, C. M., & Rodriguez, J. E. O. (1990). *The forging of the cosmic race, A reinterpretation of Colonial Mexico*. Berkeley, CA: University of California Press.

Manson, S. M., Beals, J., Klein, S. A., Calvin, D., Croy, C. D., & AI-SUPEROFO team. (2005). Social epidemiology of trauma among two American Indian reservation populations. *American Journal of Public Health, 95*(5), 851–859.

Markus, H., Steele, C. M., & Steele, D. M. (2001). Color-blindness as a barrier to inclusion. In R. Shweder, M. Minow, & H. Markus (Eds.), *Engaging cultural difference* (pp. 453–472). New York: Russell Sage Foundation.

Martinez, G. (2003). *How do shifts of economic, political, and social power affect the daily experiences of Indigenous youth in an urban, public high school?* Unpublished doctoral dissertation, University of Wisconsin, Madison, Wisconsin.

McCarty, T. (2002). *A place to be Navajo: Rough Rock and the struggle for self-determination in Indigenous schooling*. Mahwah, NJ: Lawrence Erlbaum.

Mead, M. (1932). *The changing culture of an Indian tribe*. New York: Columbia University Press.

Medicine, B. (1978). *The Native American woman: A perspective*. Austin, TX: National Educational Laboratory Publishers.

Medicine, B. (1983). Warrior women—Sex role alternatives for Plains Indian women. In P. Albers & B. Medicine (Eds.), *The hidden half: Studies of Plains Indian women* (pp. 123–142). Washington, DC: University Press of America.

Medicine, B. (1997). Changing Native American roles in an urban context and changing Native American sex roles in an urban contex. In S. E. Jacobs, W. Thomas, & S. Lang (Eds.), *Two-spirit people: Native American gender identity, sexuality, and spirituality* (pp. 145–155). Urbana: University of Illinois Press.

Metcalf, A. (1976). From schoolgirl to mother: The effects of education on Navajo women. *Social Problems, 23*, 535–544.

Mihesuah, D. A. (1998). *Cultivating the Rosebuds: The education of women at the Cherokee Female Seminary, 1851–1909*. Urbana, IL: University of Illinois Press.

Mihesuah, D. A. (2003). Native student, faculty, and staff experiences in the Ivory Tower. *American Indian Quarterly, 17*(1–2), 46-49.

Miller, D. I. (1980). The Native American family: The urban way. *Families Today, 1*, 441–483.

Miller, M. L., Castuera, M., & Chao, M. (2003). *Pathways out of poverty: Early lessons of the family independence initiative*. Oakland: CA: Family Independence Initiative. Retrieved November 20, 2005, from http://www.fiinet.org/.

Mitchell, C. M., & Beals, J. (1997). The structure of problem and positive behavior among American Indian adolescents: Gender and community differences. *American Journal of Community Psychology, 25*(3), 257–232.

Montgomery, D. (2001). Increasing Native American Indian involvement in gifted programs in rural schools. *Psychology in the Schools, 38*(5), 467–475.

Montgomery, D., Miville, M. L., Winterowd, C., Jeffries, B., & Baysden, M. F. (2000). American Indian college students: An exploration into resiliency factors revealed through personal stories. *Cultural Diversity and Ethnic Minority Psychology, 6*(4), 387–398.

Morgan, T. J. (1889). *Supplemental Report on Indian Education*. Retrieved July 20, 2005, from http://www.alaskool.org/native_ed/historicdocs/use_of_english/prucha.htm.

Munson, B. (1998). *Common themes And questions about the use of "Indian" logos*. Retrieved January 12, 2005, from http://www.allarm.org/articles/munson.html

Napoli, M., Marsiglia, F., & Kulis, S. (2003). Sense of belonging in school as a protective factor against drug abuse among Native American urban adolescents. *Journal of Social Work Practice in the Addictions, 3*(2), 25–41.

Nassaney, M. S. (1999). *Assessing native gender relations in Seventeenth Century Southeastern New England*. Paper presented at the annual meeting of the American Society for Ethnohistory, Ledyard, CT, October 20–23.

Nassaney, M. S. (2004). Men and women, pipes and power in native New England. In S. M. Rafferty & R. Mann (Eds.), *The culture of smoking: Recent Developments in the archaeology of smoking pipes* (pp. 334–367). Knoxville, TN: University of Tennessee Press.

National Advisory Council on Indian Education. (1993). *Keeping forgotten promises: Twentieth Annual Report to the U.S. Congress for fiscal year 1993*. Washington, DC: Government Printing Office.

National Center for Education Statistics (NCES). (2005). Build custom tables. Washington, DC: U.S. Department of Education. Retrieved September 19, 2005 from http://nces.ed.gov/.

National Education Association. (2005, Fall). *Rankings: A report of school statistics—update & estimates*. Retrieved November 2, 2005 from *http://www.nea.org/edstats/images/05rankings-update.pdf.*

Noriega, J. (1992). American Indian education in the United States: Indoctrination for subordination to colonialism. In M. Annette Jaimes (Ed.), *The state of Native America: genocide, colonization and resistance* (pp. 371–402). Boston: South End Press.

Oetzel, J., & Duran, B. (2004). Intimate partner violence in American Indian and/or Alaska Native communities: A social ecological framework of determinants and interventions. *American Indian Alaska Native Mental Health Research, 11*(3), 49–68.

Parker, T. (2004). Factors associated with American Indian teens' self-rated health. *American Indian and Alaska Native Mental Health Research, 11*(3), 1–19.

Payne, R. (1996). *A framework for understanding poverty*. Highlands, TX: Aha Process, Inc.

Perdue, T. (2003). "Mixed blood" Indians: Racial construction in the early south. Athens, GA: University of Georgia Press.

Perry, R. J. (1979). The fur trade and the status of women in the western subartic. *Ethnohistory, 26*(4), 363–376.

Pinker, S. (2002). *The blank slate: The modern denial of human nature*. New York: Viking Penguin.

Pronin, E., Steele, C. M., & Ross, L. (2004). Identity bifurcation in response to stereotype threat: Women and mathematics. *Journal of Experimental Social Psychology, 40*, 152–168.

Qoyawayma, P. (with Carlson, V. F.). (1977). *No turning back: A Hopi Indian woman's struggle to live in two worlds*. Albuquerque, NM: University of New Mexico Press.

Rampey, B. D., Lutkus, A. D., & Weiner, A. W. (2006). *National Indian education study, part I: The performance of American Indian and Alaska Native fourth and eighth-grade students on NAEP 2005 reading and mathematics assessments* (NCES 2006-463). U.S. Department of Education, Institute of Education Sciences, National Center for Education Statistics. Washington, DC: Government Printing Office.

Richards, C. E. (1957). Matriarchy or mistake: The role of Iroquois women through time. In V. F. Ray (Ed.), *Cultural stability and cultural change* (pp. 371–402). Seattle, WA: American Ethnological Society.

Richie, B., Tsenin, K., & Widom, C. S. (2000). *Research on women and girls in the justice system: Plenary papers of the 1999 conference on criminal justice research and evaluation—enhancing policy and practice through research* (Vol. 3). Washington, DC: National Institute of Justice.

Richmond, T. L. (1988). Native women as leaders in Algonkian society. *Artifacts 16*(3-4), 7–10.

Robbins, R., & J. Tippeconnic, J. (1985). *Toward a philosophy of American Indian higher education*. Tempe, AZ: Arizona State University, College of Education.

Roscoe, W. (2000). *Changing ones: Third and fourth genders in Native North America*. New York: Palgrave Macmillan.

Ross, L. (1998). *Inventing the savage: the social construction of Native American criminality*. Austin, TX: University of Texas Press.

Rousey, A., & Longie, E. (2001). The tribal college family support system. *American Behavioral Scientist, 44*(9), 1492–1504.

Said, E. (1979). *Orientalism*. New York: Vintage Press.

St. Denis, V., & Schick, C. (2003). What makes anti-racist pedagogy in teacher education difficult? Three popular ideological assumptions. *The Alberta Journal of Educational Research, 49*(1), 55–69.

St. Marie, B. (1996). *The cradleboard teaching project*. Beverly Hills, CA: Nihewan Foundation. Retrieved April, 20, 2005, from http://www.cradleboard.org/.

Schaeffer, C. E. (1965). The Kutenai female berdache: Courier, guide, prophetess and warrior. *Ethnohistory, 12*, 193–236.

Scherba de Valenzuela, J. S., Qi, C., & Copeland, S. R. (2004, June). *Unpacking the complex issue of disproportionate representation of minority students in special education*. Poster presented at the annual meeting of the American Association on Mental Retardation, Philadelphia.

Schick, C., & St. Denis, V. (2005). Troubling national discourses for anti-racist curricular planning. *Canadian Journal of Education, 28*(3), 295–317.

Schlegel, A. (1973). Male and female in Hopi thought and action. In A. Schlegel (Ed.), *Sexual stratification: A cross-cultural view* (pp. 270–291). New York: Columbia University Press.

Shirley, V. J. (2004, June 17). On the Right Path. *Black Issues in Higher Education, 21*(9), 88–91.

Shoemaker, N. (1995). *Negotiators of change: Historical perspectives on Native American women*. New York: Routledge.

Sims, C. (2003). Testimony to the senate committee on Indian affairs. Retrieved June 4, 2005, from http://www.senate.gov/~scia/2003hrgs/051503hrg/sims.PDF.

Simmons, T. M., Novins, D. K., & Allen, J. (2004). Words have power: (Re)-defining serious emotional disturbance for American Indian and Alaska Native children and their families. *American Indian Alaska Native Mental Health Research, 11*(2), 59–64.

Sixkiller Clarke, A. (2002). *Social and emotional distress among American Indian and Alaska Native students: Research findings.* Charleston, W.V.: ERIC Clearinghouse on Rural Education and Small Schools. (ERIC Document Reproduction Service No. ED459988).

Slapin, B., & Seale, D. (1998). *Through Indian eyes: The Native experience in books for children*. Berkeley, CA: Oyate Press.

Slapin, B., & Steale, D. (2005). *A broken flute: The native experience in books for children*. Berkeley, CA: Oyate Press.

Sleeper-Smith, S. (2001). *Indian women and French men: Rethinking cultural encounter in the Western Great Lakes*. Amherst, MA: University of Massachusetts Press.

Smith, A. (2003). Not an Indian Tradition: The Sexual Colonization of Native Peoples. *Hypatia, 18*(2), 70–85.

Smith, A. (2005). *Conquest: Sexual violence and American Indian genocide.* Cambridge, MA: South End Press.

Smith, A. (2006). Soul wound: The legacy of Native American schools. *Amnesty Magazine.* accessed on June 4, 2006, from http://www.amnestyusa.org/amnestynow/soulwound.html.

Smith, L. T. (1999). *Decolonizing methodologies: Research and indigenous peoples*. New York: St. Martin's Press.

Smithson, C. L. (1959). *The Havasupai woman*. New York: Johnson Reprint Corporation.

Spencer, S. J., Steele, C. M., & Quinn, D. M. (1999). Stereotype threat and women's math performance. *Journal of Experimental Social Psychology, 35*, 4–28.

St. Denis, V., & Schick, C. (2003). What makes anti-racist pedagogy in teacher education difficulty? *Alberta Journal of Educational Research, 49*(1), 55–69.

Stannard, D. E. (1992). *American holocaust: The conquest of the new world*. Oxford, U.K.: Oxford University Press.

Steele, C. M. (1997). A threat in the air: How stereotypes shape the intellectual identities and performance of women and African Americans. *American Psychologist, 52*, 613–629.

Steele, C. M., & Aronson, J. (1995). Stereotype vulnerability and the intellectual test performance of African-American. *Journal of Personality and Social Psychology, 69*(5), 795–811.

Suina, J. H., & Smolkin, L. B. (1995). The multicultural worlds of Pueblo children's celebrations. *Journal of American Indian Education, 34*(3), 18–27.

Swader, R., & Myers, A. (1977). *The Anishinabe woman*. Grand Marais, MN: Independent School District, 166.

Swisher, K. G. (1998). Why Indian people should be the ones to write about Indian education. In D. A. Mihesuah (Ed.), *Natives and Academics: Researching and Writing about American Indians* (pp. 190–199). Lincoln, NE: University of Nebraska Press.

Swisher, K. G., & Tippiconic, J. W. (1999). *Next steps: Research and practice to advance Indian education*. Charleston, WV: Eric Clearinghouse on Rural.

Syverson, P. D. (2004). *Graduate enrollment rises for second year, according to early returns from the 2001 CGS/GRE survey of graduate enrollment*. Council of Graduate Schools: Washington, DC. Retrieved July 21, 2005, from http://www.cgsnet.org/VirtualCenter Research/2001Survey.htm.

Tafoya, T. (1997). M. Dragonfly: Two-spirit and the principle of uncertainty. In S. E. Jacobs, W. Thomas, & S. Lang, (Eds.), *Two-spirit people: Native American gender identity, sexuality, and spirituality* (pp. 192–202). Urbana, IL: University of Illinois Press.

Thompson, J. L., Davis, S. M., Gittelsohn, J., Going, S., Becenti, A., & Metcalfe, L. (2001). Patterns of physical activity among American Indian children: An assessment of barriers and support. *Journal of Community Health: The Publication for Health Promotion and Disease Prevention, 26*(6), 407–421.

Tohe, L. (2000). There is no word for feminism in my language. *Wicazo Sa Review, 15*(2), 103–110.

Tsethlikai, M. (2001). *The intergenerational impact of Native American parental beliefs: An exploratory analysis.* Unpublished master's thesis, University of Kansas, Lawrence.

Turner, C. S. V., & Myers, S. L. (2000). *Faculty of color in academe: Bittersweet success.* Boston: Allyn and Bacon.

Turner, D. (2006). *This is not a peace pipe: Towards a critical indigenous philosophy.* Toronto, Canada: University of Toronto Press.

Turner, S. L., & Lapan, R. T. (2003). Native American adolescent career development. *Journal of Career Development, 30*(2), 159–172.

United Nations. (1999). *Draft declaration on the rights of indigenous peoples.* Retrieved June 19, 2006, from http://www.usask.ca/native law/ddir.html.

United States Census. (2005). *State rankings from the statistical abstract of the United States: Persons below poverty level—2003.* Retrieved May 31, 2006, from *http://www.census.gov/statab/ranks/rank34.xls*.

U.S. Department of Housing and Urban Development. (2005). *Discrimination in metropolitan housing markets: National results from phase 1, phase 2, and phase 3 of the Housing Discrimination Study (HDS)*. Retrieved February 1, 2005, from http://www.huduser.org/publications/hsgfin/hds.html

Urrieta, L. (2003). Las identidades también lloran/Identities also cry: Exploring the human side of Latina/o indigenous identities. *Educational Studies, 34*(2), 147–212.

Vicenti, C. (2004, July 30). Moving out of the "sovereignty ghetto". *Indian Country Today.* Retrieved January 2, 2006, from http://www.indiancountry.com/author.cfm?id=202.

Vizenor, G. (1993). Trickster discourse: Comic and tragic themes in Native American literature. In M. Lindquist & M. Zanger (Eds.), *Buried roots and indestructible seeds: The survival of American Indian life in story, history, and spirit* (pp. 67–83). Madison, WI: University of Wisconsin Press.

Vizenor, G. (2000). *Fugitive poses: Native American Indian scenes of absence and presence.* Lincoln, NE: University of Nebraska Press.

Voss, K. (2003). Legislative study: Eliminating racial profiling in Minnesota. *William Mitchell Law Review, 29*(3), 869–896.

Wagner, S. R. (1998). The root of oppression is the loss of memory: The Iroquois and the earliest feminist vision. In W. G. Spittal (Ed.), *Iroquois women: An anthology* (pp. 223–228). Osweken, Ontario, Canada: Iroqrafts, Ltd.

Walker, J. (2003). Study shows racial disparity: S.D. legal system needs reform, researcher says. *Argus Leader Media.* Retrieved July 21, 2005 from http://www.argusleader.com/apps/pbcs.dll/frontpage

Waller, M. A., Okamoto, S. K., Hankerson, A. A., Hibbeler, T., Hibbeler, P., McIntyre,P., et al. (2002). The hoop of learning: A holistic, multisystemic model for facilitating educational resilience among indigenous students. *Journal of Sociology and Social Welfare, 29*(1), 97–116.

Washinawatok, I. (1999). Sovereignty is more than just power. *Indigenous Women, 2*(6), 23–24.

Waters, A. (2004). *American Indian thought.* Malden, MA: Blackwell Publishing.

Weaver, H. N., & Brave Heart, M. Y. H. (1999). Examining two facets of American Indian identity: Exposure to other cultures and the influence of historical trauma. *Journal of Human Behavior in the Social Environment, 2*(1/2) 19–33.

Westby, C., Moore, C., & Roman, R. (2002).Reinventing the enemy's language: Developing narratives in Native American children. *Linguistics-and-Education, 13*(2), 235–269.

Williams, K. B. (2000). Perceptions of social support in doctoral programs among minority students. *Psychological Reports, 86,* 1003–1010.

Williams, M. B., & Bendremer, J. (1997). The archaeology of maize, pots, and seashells: Gender dynamics in late Woodland and Contact-Period New England, In C. Claassen & R. A. Joyce (Eds.), *Women in Prehistory: North America and Mesoamerica* (pp. 136–149). Philadelphia: University of Pennsylvania Press.

Wishart, D. (1995). The roles of men and women in Nineteenth Century Omaha and Pawnee societies: Postmodernist uncertainties and empirical evidence. *American Indian Quarterly, 19*(4), 509–518.

Witt, S. H. (1976). The Brave-hearted women: The struggle at Wounded Knee. *Akwasasne Notes, 8*(2), 16–17.

Wright, R. (1992). *Stolen continents, the "New World" through Indian Eyes.* Boston: Houghton Mifflin Co.

Wub, E. K. N. (1995). *We have the right to exist: A translation of aboriginal indigenous thought.* New York: Black Thistle Press.

Zahnd, E. (2004). *Program evaluation for United Indian Nations, Inc.* Oakland, CA. Unpublished manuscript.

Zhang, D., Katsiyannis,-A., & Herbst, M. (2004). Disciplinary exclusions in special education: A 4-year analysis. *Behavioral Disorders, 29*(4), 337–347.

Zimmerman, M. A., Jesús-Ramirez, K. M., Washienko, B. W., & Dyer, S. (1998). Enculturation hypothesis: Exploring direct and protective effects among Native American youth. In H. I. McCubbin, E. A. Thompson, A. I. Thompson, & J. E. Fromer (Eds.), *Resiliency in Native American and immigrant families* (pp. 199–223). Thousand Oaks, CA: Sage.

Zitkala-sa (Gertude Simmons Bonin). (1900). An Indian teacher among Indians. *Atlantic Monthly,* 85.

Zvolensky, M. J., McNeil, D. W., Porter, C. A., & Stewart, S. H. (2001). Assessment of anxiety sensitivity in young American Indians and Alaska Natives. *Behaviour Research and Therapy, 39,* 477–493.

GENDER EQUITY AND LESBIAN, GAY, BISEXUAL, AND TRANSGENDER ISSUES IN EDUCATION

Joseph G. Kosciw,* *Eliza S. Byard, Sean N. Fischer, and Courtney Joslin*

INTRODUCTION

Jesse Montgomery was subjected to frequent and continual teasing from the time he was in kindergarten. To his classmates, he was never quite enough of a "boy," so throughout his school years other students referred to him as a girl, calling him "Jessica," as well as fag, homo, freak, princess, fairy, lesbian, femme boy, bitch, queer, pansy, and queen. The harassment became physical in sixth grade, when he was punched, knocked down, and even super-glued to his seat. He was also subjected to assaults of a more sexual nature, as students grabbed his upper legs, inner thighs, chest, and crotch; or threw him to the ground and pretended to rape him anally; or sat on his lap and bounced while pretending to have intercourse with him. Over the years, officials and school staff did little to address the on-going harassment that Jesse experienced.

Jesse's experience of violence and neglect, while extreme, is far from an isolated incident. Violence, bias, and harassment directed at lesbian, gay, bisexual, and transgender[1] (LGBT) students continue to be the rule—not the exception—in America's schools. As the details of Jesse's story vividly illustrate, such victimization is not just about whether a student is, or is perceived to be, lesbian or gay, but also about deeply entrenched understandings of appropriate male and female behavior and self-presentation. Violence or threats of violence directed at gay men and lesbians play a crucial role in enforcing gender stereotypes and compulsory heterosexuality (Pharr, 1988). This dynamic plays out daily in the hallways of American schools.

This chapter examines the rising visibility of issues around sexual orientation and gender identity and expression in middle and high schools and postsecondary institutions since 1986. It also examines the responses of legislatures, courts, school districts, and advocates to the endemic problem of discrimination, violence, and harassment directed at students who are, or are perceived to be, lesbian, gay, bisexual, or transgender. It will also discuss discrimination against LGBT educators. The summary recommendations focus on what all educators and advocates can do to address the related and entwined challenges for equitable treatment of all without regard to sexual orientation and gender identity and expression with specific attention to ending sex discrimination. Throughout this chapter, we will discuss relevant findings of gender differences within the LGBT populations, particularly as patterns emerge in differences among them. However, it is our view as authors that sexism and homophobia are inextricably linked and that issues related to equity in education for all LGBT individuals, students and teachers alike, are issues of gender equity in education regardless of any one person's sex, gender, or sexual orientation.

KEY EVENTS AND DEVELOPMENTS IN LGBT ISSUES IN EDUCATION SINCE 1986

In the mid-980s, there was little discussion of sexual orientation as an issue in schools. Over the past 20 years, the increased visibility of lesbian and gay people in American society, research into student experience more generally, high-profile instances of individual tragedy, and activism and advocacy on the part of students themselves have increased awareness of the discrimi-

---

*The boldface name is the Lead Author.

[1]"Transgender" loosely refers to people who do not identify with the gender roles assigned to them by society based on their biological sex. Transgender is also used as an umbrella term for all those who do not conform to "traditional" notions of gender expression, including people who identify as transsexual, cross-dressers, or drag kings/queens.

nation, violence, and harassment that takes place in schools on the basis of sexual orientation or gender identity/expression.

From the late 1980s through the end of the 1990s, several instances of student victimization on the basis of sexual orientation began moving the issue into the public consciousness. In 1989, the U.S. Department of Health and Human Services issued a Report on Youth Suicide that included the finding that gay or lesbian youth are three times more likely to commit suicide than their peers. Although this statistic is inaccurate and inflated (for a review of suicide statistics and LGB[2] youth, see Russell, 2003), it galvanized discussions of the experiences of school-aged gay and lesbian youth that would drive them to take their own lives. In 1996, a Wisconsin student named Jamie Nabozny won a groundbreaking lawsuit against his school district for failing to protect him from years of violence and abuse. (This case is later discussed at greater length.) The court's response to Nabozny's claim put administrators and school officials on notice that they had a specific responsibility to protect gay students from violence. Then, in 1998, the murder of Matthew Shepard riveted the nation, leading many to ask where Shepard's attackers had learned to hate enough to commit brutal violence.

At the same time LGBT students were beginning to organize and advocate for improved school climates and equal access to educational opportunities for all, regardless of sexual orientation and gender identity/expression. Perhaps more than any other factor, student engagement with LGBT issues in schools has provoked greater public attention and controversy around these issues. Throughout the 1990s, the growth in the number of student clubs across the country dealing with LGBT issues, commonly known as "Gay-Straight Alliances" or GSA, has created safe spaces for students, greater visibility for these issues in schools, and an organized base for efforts to educate school communities and advocate for change. Today, nearly 3,000 such student clubs have registered with GLSEN, a conservative measure of the number of GSAs nationally. In 1986, students at the University of Virginia created an event they dubbed the "Day of Silence" during which students took a daylong vow of silence to protest the silencing of LGBT people in our society. The event

has grown in scope and visibility, and in 2005, students at nearly 4,000 K–12 schools, colleges, and universities across the country took part in the Day of Silence. GLSEN began its work on LGBT issues in schools as a national organization in 1995, and today many other national organizations, such as Parents and Friends of Lesbians and Gays (PFLAG), the Human Rights Campaign (HRC) and GenderPAC, also support efforts to create safer schools for all students. In addition, some states such as Washington and California and some major cities, such as Chicago and Seattle, have implemented policies and programs for the protection of LGBT students.

Over the years, the increased visibility of LGBT students and anti-LGBT violence and harassment in schools has led to actions in state legislatures (discussed later in this chapter) and to a number of court cases. Students in states across the country have sued their school districts for failing to protect them from assaults and abuse based on their real or perceived sexual orientation. To date, of the known cases, all of these lawsuits have resulted in a court decision and/or a resolution with the school district that were in favor of the students. School districts have paid up to $1.1 million in settlements or judgments.[3] In addition to these monetary judgments, the settlements increasingly also contain comprehensive steps that the school district must take to make these schools safer for LGBT students, including adding sexual orientation and gender identity to the school district's nondiscrimination policies and providing comprehensive training to the staff and students on the problems of harassment and discrimination of LGBT students, the obligation to respond to such discrimination, and suggestions about how to intervene.[4] Interestingly, many of these lawsuits were successfully won or settled in states that do not have state statutes prohibiting discrimination on the basis of sexual orientation, including Kentucky, Missouri, and Nevada. This is due in part to the relationship of gender and sexual orientation, as courts have found a basis for action in these cases in both the Equal Protection Clause and Title IX.

It is well established that the Equal Protection Clause prohibits the government from discriminating on the basis of gender.[5] This protection against sex discrimination includes the obliga-

---

[2]Language note: We use the expression LGBT when referring to the general population of interest in this chapter, i.e., lesbian, gay, bisexual, and transgender students. However, it is important to note that not all studies have included transgender-identified students in their sample or did not determine whether any of the participants identified as transgender. In such instances, we use LGB instead of LGBT.

[3]For example, in 2004, the Morgan Hill Unified School District in California settled a five-year-old case for over $1.1 million. The suit, *Flores v. Morgan Hill Unified School District*, 324 F.3d 1130 (9th Cir. 2003), was brought on behalf of six former students who were subjected to harassment and threats of physical violence and actual physical violence on the basis of their real or perceived sexual orientation and gender. In addition to paying the monetary award, the settlement also required the school to add sexual orientation and gender identity to their existing nondiscrimination policy, train all administrators, teachers, counselors, and other employees who monitor student behavior on harassment and discrimination on the basis of sexual orientation or gender identity, train all seventh- and ninth-grade students on preventing anti-LGBT harassment and discrimination, revise district policies and student handbooks to expressly state that harassment and discrimination based on actual or perceived sexual orientation and gender identity is prohibited under district policies and state law, and keep written records of any complaints made concerning anti-LGBT harassment or discrimination.

[4]Another recent case that settled is *Henkle v. Gregory*, 150 F. Supp.2d 1067 (D. Nev. 2001), which settled in 2002. The case was brought by a former student who endured constant harassment, discrimination and intimidation based on his sex and sexual orientation, including name-calling and assaults. In particular, during one incident, the student was punched in face. In another incident, the student was lassoed around the neck. Rather than take steps to stop the harassment, the school transferred the student and told him to keep silent about his sexual orientation. The case ultimately settled for $451,000, in addition to the requirements that the school district amend its harassment policy to include sexual orientation and train its staff and students on the policy. Information other lawsuits and their resolutions is detailed in the publication: *Fifteen Expensive Reasons Why Safe Schools Legislation Is In Your State's Best Interest*, which is available at: http://www.nclrights.org/publications/15reasons.htm

[5]See, e.g., *United States v. Virginia*, 518 U.S. 515 (1996) (exclusion of women from Virginia Military Institute violated the Equal Protection Clause; to uphold government discrimination or classifications based on gender, government has burden of demonstrating "exceedingly persuasive justification"); *Mississippi Univ. for Women v. Hogan*, 458 U.S. 718, 724 (1982).

tion of public schools to respond to sex-based harassment and discrimination of its students.[6] This includes harassment directed at a student because the student is perceived not to conform to gender stereotypes.[7] For example, if a student is subjected to severe and pervasive harassment that is targeted at him because he is a ballet dancer and the perpetrators think that it is not appropriate for a boy to be a ballet dancer, and the school is aware of the harassment and does not take steps to respond to it, the school may be found to have discriminated on the basis of sex in violation of the Equal Protection Clause. A school district also may be found to have violated the Equal Protection Clause if it takes adequate steps to respond to harassment of a girl by a boy, but fails to take similar steps in response to harassment of a boy by a boy.[8]

This was an important factor in Jamie Nabozny's case, *Nabozny v. Podlesny*,[9] the first successful appellate court decision involving school harassment of an LGBT student. Nabozny endured years of severe harassment and physical assaults, and in one particular incident, he was subjected to a mock rape while numerous students watched. When he reported this incident to the principal, she said, "boys will be boys," apparently dismissing the incident because both the perpetrators and the victim were males.[10] The court held that this response constituted discrimination on the basis of sex because the court "[found] it impossible to believe that a female lodging a similar complaint would have received the same response."[11]

In addition, refusal to treat a transgender student similarly to other students of the same gender identity may also constitute impermissible sex discrimination under the Equal Protection Clause. For example, a school may be held to be engaging in

prohibited sex discrimination if the school says that a male-to-female transgender student cannot wear the same clothes that a biological female student is permitted to wear to school.[12]

Title IX[13] of the Education Amendments of 1972 prohibits discrimination based on sex in education programs and activities receiving federal financial assistance. Although Title IX does not prohibit discrimination on the basis of sexual orientation, sexual harassment directed at an LGBT student is prohibited by Title IX if it is sufficiently severe and pervasive. For example, the 2001 Revised Sexual Harassment Guidance issued by the U.S. Department of Education's Office of Civil Rights ("OCR Revised Sexual Harassment Guidance") explains that:

> Although Title IX does not prohibit discrimination on the basis of sexual orientation, sexual harassment directed at gay or lesbian students that is sufficiently serious to limit or deny a student's ability to participate in or benefit from the school's program constitutes sexual harassment prohibited by Title IX under circumstances described in this guidance. For example, if a male student or a group of male students target a gay student for physical sexual advances, serious enough to deny or limit the victim's ability to participate in or benefit from the school's program, the school would need to respond promptly and effectively, as described in this guidance, just as it would if the victim were heterosexual.

Similarly, in 2000, a federal district court held that Jesse Montgomery may have been discriminated against on the basis of sex by relying, in part, on a pattern of assaults of a sexual nature (as described in the introduction to this chapter). The court explained that these acts were indicative of harassment based on sex.[14]

Title IX also prohibits gender-based harassment, including harassment on the basis of a student's failure to conform to

---

[6]*Nicole M. v. Martinez*, 964 F. Supp. 1369, 1383 (N.D. Cal. 1997).

[7]The Equal Protection Clause of the Fourteenth Amendment to the Constitution also imposes a duty on all public schools to protect lesbian, gay, bisexual, and transgender (LGBT) students from harassment on an equal basis with all other students. Thus, for example, if school officials failed to take action against anti-LGBT harassment because they believed that the LGBT student should have expected to be harassed, or because they believed that the LGBT student brought the harassment upon him- or herself simply by being openly LGBT, or because the school was uneducated about LGBT issues and was uncomfortable addressing the situation, the school may be found to have violated the Equal Protection Clause. See *Flores v. Morgan Hill Unified School District*, 324 F.3d 1130 (9th Cir. 2003) (holding that students could maintain claims alleging discrimination on the basis of sexual orientation under the Equal Protection Clause where school district failed to protect the students to the same extent that other students were protected from harassment and discrimination); *Nabozny v. Podlesny*, 92 F.3d 446 (7th Cir. 1996) (holding student could maintain claims alleging discrimination on the basis of gender and sexual orientation under the Equal Protection Clause where school district failed to protect the student to the same extent that other students were protected from harassment and harm by other students due to the student's gender and sexual orientation).

In *Nabozny*, after the student and his parents reported the incidents of physical violence to the appropriate school administrator, the administrator told the student and his parents that such acts should be expected because the student was openly gay. *Nabozny*, 92 F.3d at 451. See *also Montgomery v. Independent Sch. Dist. No. 709*, 109 F. Supp. 2d 1081 (D. Minn. 2000) ("We are unable to garner any rational basis for permitting one student to assault another based on the victim's sexual orientation, and the defendants do not offer us one.") (citing *Nabozny*, 92 F.3d at 458).

The school district eventually settled the *Flores* case for over $1.1 million, in addition to mandatory training for all school staff and all seventh- and ninth-grade students. The school district in *Nabozny* eventually settled the case for almost $1 million in damages. For an overview of 15 lawsuits against school districts, see *Fifteen Expensive Reasons Why Safe Schools Legislation Is In Your State's Best Interest*, available at www.nclrights.org/pubs/15reasons.pdf

[8]*Nabozny v. Podlesny*, 92 F.3d 446 (7th Cir. 1996).

[9]92 F.3d 446 (7th Cir. 1996).

[10]*Id.* at 454.

[11]*Id.* at 454–55.

[12]See e.g., *Doe v. Yunits*, 2000 WL 33162199 (Mass. Super. 2000) (holding that transgender student had a First Amendment right to wear clothing consistent with her gender identity and that treating transgender girl differently than biological girls was discrimination on the basis of sex). The court also held that failure to allow the student to wear clothing consistent with her gender identity violated her First Amendment right to free expression, as well as her liberty interests protected by the Due Process Clause.

[13]20 U.S.C. § 1681(a). Title IX provides, in relevant part: "No person in the United States shall, on the basis of sex, be excluded from participation in, be denied the benefits of, or be subjected to discrimination under any education program or activity receiving federal financial assistance."

[14]*Id.* at 1093.

stereotyped notions of masculinity and femininity. Although the OCR Revised Guidance does not go into detail about gender stereotyping, the Guidance does explain that:

Acts of verbal, nonverbal, or physical aggression, intimidation, or hostility based on sex or sex-stereotyping, but not involving conduct of a sexual nature, is also a form of sex discrimination to which a school must respond, if it rises to the level that denies or limits a student's ability to participate in or benefit from the educational program. . . .

The Montgomery case provides examples of conduct that may constitute impermissible discrimination based on gender stereotypes. As the court explained:

[The student] specifically alleges that some of the students called him "Jessica," a girl's name, indicating a belief that he exhibited feminine characteristics. Moreover, the Court finds important the fact that plaintiff's peers began harassing him as early as kindergarten. It is highly unlikely that at that tender age plaintiff would have developed any solidified sexual preference, or for that matter, that he even understood what it meant to be "homosexual" or "heterosexual." The likelihood that he openly identified himself as gay or that he engaged in any homosexual conduct at that age is quite low. It is much more plausible that the students began tormenting him based on feminine personality traits that he exhibited and the perception that he did not engage in behaviors befitting a boy. Plaintiff thus appears to plead facts that would support a claim of harassment based on the perception that he did not fit his peers' stereotypes of masculinity.

Thus, despite the absence of any federal statute that explicitly prohibits discrimination on the basis of sexual orientation in schools, students who experience anti-gay violence may be protected under laws that prohibit discrimination on the basis of sex, depending on the type of harassment and discrimination they are forced to endure.

EXPERIENCES OF A HOSTILE SCHOOL CLIMATE FOR LGBT STUDENTS IN K–12 SCHOOLS[15]

Issues of sexual orientation and gender identity/expression in our nation's schools may be increasing in visibility. Recent studies have suggested that at least half of high school students know another student who is openly gay or lesbian (Harris Interactive & GLSEN, 2005; Hamilton College, 2001; Widmeyer & GLSEN, 2004). Nearly twice as many high school students reported having a student club that addresses LGBT student issues in their school in a 2005 national survey (Harris Interactive & GLSEN) than in a similar national survey of students in 2001 (Hamilton College)—25% vs. 13%. Lastly, estimates indicated that 5% or more of secondary school students identify

themselves as LGBT (Harris Interactive & GLSEN; Massachusetts Department of Education, 2004; Widmeyer & GLSEN).

However, before children even understand what heterosexuality/homosexuality means, anti-LGBT behavior appears to be evident even in the youngest school grades. Using historical accounts of a sample of young gay adults in Australia, Plummer (2001) found that comments such as "faggot" or "poofter" were commonly used in primary school. In younger grades, use of such words did not have any sexual connotation but most often were related to characteristics that were considered not traditionally masculine, such as being timid or not athletic. Plummer found that these words became linked with homosexuality in middle school and high school. Mandel and Shakeshaft (2000) examined how heterosexism or assumptions about heterosexuality underlie adolescents' ideas of masculinity and femininity in a sample of middle school students (grades seven to nine). The authors found that although the students' definitions of femininity were diverse and often complex, masculinity was uniformly described by boys and girls as being "antifeminine" and characterized by the extent to which boys conformed to traditional conceptions of masculinity, e.g., demonstrating machismo, athleticism, or heterosexuality. For boys in particular, Mandel and Shakeshaft found that homophobic attitudes were linked to beliefs about masculinity. The authors concluded that individuals who violate traditional gender role expectations are often equated with also violating traditional heterosexual expectations. Results from a 2001 report on sexual harassment in schools by the AAUW Educational Foundation, *Hostile Hallways*, provided further evidence of this relationship between gender roles and homophobia —although the majority of both girls and boys reported that they would be very upset if someone called them gay or lesbian, it was the highest rated reason for boys.

Few studies have examined the school-related experiences of LGBT students in middle school or high school with regard to school comfort and homophobic harassment and assault, and even fewer have explored how a negative school climate affects a student's access to education, ability to learn, academic success and future educational aspirations. As Russell, Seif, and Truong (2001) stated:

there are limited empirical data available to assist concerned counselors, parents, educators and policy makers in assessing the magnitude of school-related problems for sexual minority youth, particularly the complex factors from multiple domains of adolescents' lives that may contribute to their marginalization—or resilience—within the educational system. (p. 111).

The focus of most literature has been on the experiences of homophobic victimization and its consequences such as evidence of higher rates of suicidal thoughts and attempted suicide (for a review, see McDaniel, Purcell, & D'Augelli, 2001), mental health

---

[15]As mentioned previously, we will provide information about gender differences when available. Not all research on LGBT issues in education, however, examines gender differences within this group and research that examines differences between LGBT individuals and non-LGBT individuals does not always consider gender. However, given our premise that issues related to equity in education for all LGBT individuals are issues of gender equity in education regardless of any one person's sex, gender or sexual orientation, we will discuss research regarding LGBT-related issues in education regardless of whether the research specifically includes information about gender differences.

problems (e.g., D'Augelli, 2002; Hershberger & D'Augelli, 1995), substance and alcohol use, and sexual-risk behaviors (e.g., Bontempo & D'Augelli, 2002).

In 1993, a report from the Massachusetts Governor's Commission of Gay and Lesbian Youth was a groundbreaking effort documenting and highlighting the problem for sexual-minority youth and included specific recommendations for schools to protect these students from harassment, violence, and discrimination. Since 1993, the Massachusetts Department of Education has included questions about sexual orientation in their Massachusetts Youth Risk Behavior Survey (MYRBS), a population-based survey conducted every two years by the Massachusetts Department of Education with funding from the U.S. Centers for Disease Control and Prevention (CDC) to monitor adolescent risk behaviors, including tobacco, alcohol, and other drug use, behaviors related to intentional and unintentional injuries, high-risk sexual behaviors; poor dietary patterns, and lack of physical activity. Massachusetts is the only state to examine consistently differing risk behaviors between LGB-identified and heterosexual students.

Using data from the representative sample of the MYRBS, Garofalo, Wolf, Kessel, Palfrey, and DuRant (1998) compared LGB-identified and heterosexual students and found that one quarter of the LGB youth said they had missed school in the last month because of fear, compared to 5% of the non-LGB youth. This finding reflects other differences in school-based violence experienced by the LGB youth compared to heterosexual students. One third of the LGB youth said they had been threatened with a weapon at school, compared to 7% of the other youth. More than one third (38%) of the LGB youth were involved in fights at school, in contrast to 14% of the other students. Also, half of the LGB youth reported damage to their property at school compared to 29% of the other youth.[16]

The findings from Garofalo et al. (1998) unfortunately were consistent with those from other years of the Massachusetts survey. For example, the MYRBS has consistently shown that since 1993, the year that questions about sexual orientation were first included, sexual minority students were consistently much more likely to report that they had skipped school in the past month because of feeling unsafe.[17] DuRant, Krowchuk, and Sinal (1998) found similar results in a survey of Vermont male high school students. In their study, male students with same-sex sexual experiences[18] were significantly more likely to be in fights at school, require medical attention after fights in school, be threatened with violence, and be threatened with a weapon.

In the past few years, other states and localities have begun to examine issues of sexual orientation in their population-based studies on youth risk behavior. In 2002, the California Health Kids Survey (CHKS), an annual state survey of student health risk and resilience factors, included a question about ha-

rassment based on actual or perceived sexual orientation. Nearly 10% of all students in the survey reported that they had been harassed because of their actual or perceived sexual orientation (California Safe Schools Coalition and 4-H Center for Youth Development, University of California, Davis, 2004). Those students who were harassed on this basis were more likely to report depression, drug and alcohol use, and lower grades. The CHKS did not ask participants whether they identified as lesbian, gay, or bisexual. However, a recent study by the California Safe Schools Coalition in partnership with Gay-Straight Alliance Network, the 2003 Preventing School Harassment (PSH) survey, provided a more detailed examination of school climate and harassment based on sexual orientation and gender nonconformity (see also California Safe Schools Coalition and 4-H Center for Youth Development, University of California, Davis, 2004). This study found that nearly half of LGBT students said their schools were not safe for LGBT students and two thirds reported harassment based on their actual or perceived sexual orientation.

In 2003, the Chicago Public Schools Youth Risk Behavior Survey (CYRBS), a biennial population-based survey, included questions about whether students identified as lesbian, gay, or bisexual or had had same-sex sexual activity (Coalition for Education on Sexual Orientation, 2005).[19] Students who described themselves as LGB were significantly more likely to report missing school because they felt unsafe, being involved in a physical fight at school, and being the victim of sexual assault. Researchers further found that this type of negative and hostile school environment can take its toll on students' mental and physical health—LGB students in Chicago were more likely to report being depressed, having attempted suicide, using tobacco, and engaging in other drug and alcohol use.

In addition to regional studies on LGB youth, a few studies have examined the school-related experiences of these youth nationally. D'Augelli, Pilkington, and Hershberger (2002) investigated the experiences of a geographically diverse sample of LGB youth with verbal and physical victimization in high school related to their sexual orientation. In their sample of 335 youth, the authors found that over half (59%) had experienced verbal abuse in high school, 24% had been threatened with violence, and 11% had been physically attacked. D'Augelli et al. also found that youth whose gender expression was more atypical were more likely to report being verbally and physically attacked in school.

D'Augelli et al. (2002) found significant gender differences within the LGB sample on severity of victimization experiences and their possible effects. Male students reported more experiences than female students of verbal abuse, verbal threats, and having objects thrown at them. Although female students reported lower levels of victimization, they were higher on trauma symptoms than male students. Furthermore, the authors

---

[16]Because of the small sample size of LGB youth, the authors did not examine gender differences in their examination of sexual orientation and risk behavior.

[17]Data was summarized from the Massachusetts YRBS reports from 1993 to 2003. These reports are available from the Massachusetts Department of Education website, www.doe.mass.edu

[18]As a proxy for sexual orientation, the authors categorized participants by their reported sexual behaviors, those who had multiple male partners and those who had multiple female partners.

[19]In the 2003 CYRBS, 6.3% of students identified as LGB and 8.5% reported having had same-sex sexual activity.

found that although gender (being female) was a significant predictor of post-traumatic stress symptoms, gender atypicality was not. These findings raise several questions about the relationship of gender and gender expression to students' in-school victimization. Lesbian or bisexual female students may experience harassment and victimization in school based on their gender at higher levels than male students, which could explain their higher levels of trauma symptoms. For example, although the authors asked participants about sexual assault (being attacked sexually), they did not ask participants about sexual harassment (e.g., being touched inappropriately, having comments made about one's body), which would undoubtedly be more common overall and almost certainly more common for girls than for boys. Thus, more research is needed that examines how males and females may differentially be affected by and cope with victimization, including comprehensively examining the intersection of harassment based on gender and sexual orientation.

Stephen Russell and colleagues examined the experiences of sexual-minority youth using the National Longitudinal Study of Health (Add Health), the only nationally representative study on adolescents that includes information on same-sex romantic attraction.[20] Russell, Franz, and Driscoll (2001) found that sexual-minority youth (defined as those youth who reported same-sex attraction) were at greater risk for both needing medical treatment after fights and for witnessing violence. The authors also found that sexual-minority youth were more likely to perpetrate violence, which was, however, related to the likelihood of being a victim of violent attacks. Although female youth, overall, reported fewer experiences with violence, gender was not a significant factor in their examination of sexual minority youth and experiences of violence.

Given the paucity of nationally representative data on the experiences of LGBT-identified students and the limited attention paid by federal, state, and local policymakers to LGBT youth, GLSEN (Gay, Lesbian and Straight Education Network) has conducted a biennial survey of LGBT middle and high school students about their experiences related to school climate since 1999 and, most recently, in 2005 (Kosciw & Diaz, 2006).[21] Given the difficulty in obtaining a population-based sample of LGBT students (or even adults), the National School Climate Survey (NSCS) used two methods for obtaining participants in order to create a more representative sample of LGBT youth. In the first, youth were obtained through community-based groups or service organizations serving LGBT youth. Obtaining LGBT youth solely from community-based groups could potentially lead to a biased sample—youth participating in these organizations may be more "out" or more comfortable with their sexual orientation or gender expression or conversely, may be more at risk and in need of services. Also, these groups most likely attract youth who are in close geographic vicinity, and, therefore, youth who live in areas without supports for LGBT youth would not be represented. For this reason, the NSCS was made available on the Internet via GLSEN's Web site. Notices about the online survey were posted on LGBT youth-oriented listservs and electronic bulletin boards and were also emailed to national, state, and local groups that work on issues related to LGBT-youth.

Since 1999, the National School Climate Survey has documented the incidence of hearing biased language (homophobic, racist, and sexist remarks) in school as well as students' personal experiences with harassment and assault because of their sexual orientation, gender, and gender expression. Results from the 2005 survey demonstrated that most LGBT students feel unsafe in school due to some personal characteristic—64% as a result of their sexual orientation, 41% as a result of their gender expression, and 10% as a result of their gender (Kosciw & Diaz, 2006). Male students were more likely to feel unsafe in school because of their sexual orientation and less likely because of their gender than female and transgender students. Transgender students, however, were more likely to report feeling unsafe because of their gender and gender expression than male and female students.

In examining experiences of harassment and assault, it becomes clear why so many LGBT students feel unsafe in school. In the 2005 NSCS, students were asked separate questions about their experiences with verbal and physical harassment and physical assault in the past year based on a variety of personal characteristics, including sexual orientation, race/ethnicity, gender, and gender expression. The majority of youth in the 2005 NSCS reported at least some experience of verbal harassment because of their sexual orientation with almost a quarter of the youth reporting that such harassment happened frequently (Kosciw & Diaz, 2006). The majority of youth also reported verbal harassment because of their gender expression with over 10% stating that it occurred frequently. In addition, LGBT youth reports of more severe forms of victimization such as being physical harassed (e.g., being pushed or shoved) or physically assaulted (e.g., being kicked, punched, threatened with a weapon) were not uncommon. Nearly 20% of youth, for example, reported being physically assaulted in the past year because of their sexual orientation and over 10% of youth because of their gender expression.

In the 2005 NSCS, there was a striking pattern in the differences by gender in reasons for feeling unsafe and in actual experiences of harassment and assault in school. For male students, safety issues related to their sexual orientation and gender expression were paramount. For female students, safety issues related to gender were most common. Transgender students, in contrast, frequently reported feeling unsafe and incidents of victimization due to all three characteristics: gender, gender expression, and sexual orientation. These gender differences may reflect current cultural norms for gender expression and tolerance related to sexual orientation. Male and transgender students may be more likely to become targets if they express their gender in counternormative ways, whereas female students who express their gender in what are considered to be masculine ways may be more often tolerated. It may also be these norms related to gender and gender expression that inform why female students are also less likely to be harassed for being lesbian or bisexual. Transgender students may experience the most victimization overall because they challenge the boundaries of traditional gen-

---

[20]In this study, participants were asked whether they were romantically attracted to the same-sex or opposite-sex or both. They were not asked about sexual behavior or whether they identified as lesbian, gay or bisexual.

[21]Reports from all four National School Climate Surveys are available from the GLSEN Web site, www.glsen.org

der expression further than other students. Also, transgender students, particularly those who are open about their gender identity in school, may be more likely to become targets for victimization because the challenge they pose to the established understanding of the relationship between gender and biology is so profound. Further research is needed to help us understand the school-related experiences of transgender students.

In recent years, the incidence of harassment and assault of LGBT students in their schools has remained virtually unchanged (Kosciw & Diaz, 2006). In GLSEN's climate surveys, there was a small but significant decrease from 2001 to 2003 in the number of youth who felt unsafe in school because of sexual orientation. However, no change was noted from 2003 to 2005. Similarly, the rate of physical harassment and assault declined very slightly from 2001 to 2003 but remained unchanged from 2003 to 2005. The authors did not examine whether changes over time varied by demographic categories, such as gender and race/ethnicity, and such information would be an important future contribution.

Perhaps the most insidious characteristic of a hostile school climate for LGBT students is the use of homophobic remarks in school. Three-quarters of students in the 2005 survey heard homophobic remarks, such as "fag" or "dyke," frequently or often in school (Kosciw & Diaz, 2006). Even more common is use of the expression "that's so gay" or "you're so gay," where "gay" is used to mean something that is stupid or worthless. Nearly all students reported that this expression was used frequently or often in their schools. Anecdotal reports suggested that most non-LGBT students and some school district officials and educational policymakers maintain that this expression does not directly denigrate gay or lesbian people and should not be seen as harmful or offensive. Yet two thirds of LGBT students in the 2005 survey reported that hearing this expression in school significantly bothered them.

A recent national survey of middle and high school students and teachers commissioned by GLSEN and conducted by Harris Interactive similarly found a high incidence of homophobic remarks (Harris Interactive & GLSEN, 2005). The survey found that 52% of students and 33% of teachers heard homophobic remarks often or very often in school. It is interesting to note that the incidence of homophobic remarks was quite similar to that of sexist remarks, with 50% of students and 40% of teachers hearing these remarks often or very often. However, homophobic and sexist remarks were much more commonly heard in school than were racist remarks or negative remarks about one's religion. There were no differences between male and female students in reported incidence of remarks except with regard to sexist remarks—female students were more likely to report them often or very often than were male students (58% vs. 44%).

These findings on biased remarks in school lend further evidence that homophobia and sexism are inextricably linked in that homophobic and sexist remarks are the most common in school and often most tolerated by faculty and students alike. In their report *Hatred in the Hallways*, Bochenek and Brown (2001) reminded readers that homophobia and LGBT victimization are intertwined with and inseparable from sexism. Lesbian and bisexual girls are not just victimized for their sexual orientation, but also because their sexual orientation violates a rigid gender norm that forbids girls to compete with boys. Because of this violation, many lesbian and bisexual girls are sexu-

ally harassed or threatened with sexual violence. As one female participant stated, "We'll hear things like, 'I can make you straight' or 'Why don't you get some of your girlfriends and we can have a party'" (Bochenek & Brown, 2001, p. 50). Harassment of gay and bisexual boys is also intertwined with sexism for violating rigid gender norms that forbid boys from behaving like girls. As one male participant stated, "I was expected to be misogynistic, aggressive, competitive, and homophobic. . . . To protect myself from being identified as gay, I was supposed to be sexist" (Bochenek & Brown, p. 53). Transgender youth are also subjected to extreme forms of sexism. Societal gender norms leave no room for individuals whose gender identity is at odds with their assigned sex at birth. Sexist victimization of transgender individuals is even found within the gay rights movement and among LGB youth (Bochenek & Brown, 2001).

EFFECTS OF A NEGATIVE SCHOOL CLIMATE FOR LGBT K–12 STUDENTS

It is an unfortunate reality of today's schools that homophobic remarks and anti-LGBT harassment are commonplace. It is not surprising that research has shown that in-school victimization has serious consequences for the mental health of LGBT students. Bontempo and D'Augelli (2002) have shown that high levels of at-school victimization among LGB students are associated with increased suicidality, substance use, and risky sexual behavior when compared to heterosexual students. However, those LGB students who reported low levels of at-school victimization were more similar to heterosexual youth on these outcome measures. The authors further found that males, regardless of sexual orientation, were higher on risk and victimization indicators than females, and that gay/bisexual males were higher than nongay/bisexual males. D'Augelli et al. (2002) also found that higher levels of verbal and physical victimization related to sexual orientation in high school were related to higher suicidality. They authors also found that increased victimization was related to mental health and traumatic stress symptoms.

Attitudes About School

It is a logical hypothesis that increased in-school victimization of LGBT students and their resulting poorer mental health would have severe consequences on their ability to learn in school. In recent years, several studies have examined how school climate affects how LGBT students feel about school, how they perform academically, and their educational aspirations. In their examination of the national Add Health survey, Russell, Seif, and Truong (2001) compared sexual-minority students with their heterosexual peers on attitudes about school and school troubles, which included items pertaining to peer relations, attentiveness in class, and homework activity. Among the girls in the sample, sexual minority youth, those with same-sex or both-sex attractions, reported less positive attitudes toward school and more school troubles. Among the boys, those reporting both-sex romantic attraction reported more school troubles than all other boys. Boys with other-sex attraction also reported more positive attitudes toward school than boys with same-sex and both-sex attraction.

These findings by Russell, Seif, and Truong (2001) are note-worthy in that they demonstrate how LGB students may have more problems in school and feel more disconnected than their heterosexual peers. LGBT students often struggle with how open they can and should be about their sexual orientation or gender identity in school. D'Augelli et al. (2002), for example, found that LGB students who were more open about their sexual orientation at school risked higher levels of victimization. If being less open about sexual orientation has the benefit of making one less of a target for harassment in school, it is important to examine any detriment of this behavior. In the national sample of LGBT students Kosciw and Diaz (2006) examined students' "outness," i.e., openness about their sexual orientation in school, and their psychological sense of school belonging and found that students who were either not "out" or only "out" to a few at school were much less likely to feel a sense of belonging to their school than those who were "out" to all or most of the school population. Thus, not being open about one's sexual orientation may help one avoid victimization but may also diminish one's school experience as shown by decreased belongingness. Further research is needed that examines the combined direct and indirect effects of "outness" on LGBT students' school experiences with particular attention to academic success and educational aspirations.

School Performance

For any student, in order to fully participate in school and achieve one's own academic potential, it is important to feel safe and to feel part of one's school. For LGBT students, difficulties with victimization and feeling detached from school are not uncommon and may seriously affect their achievement in high school and their aspirations for further education. Murdock and Bolch (2005), in their survey of 101 LGB-identified high school students, found that greater feelings of school exclusion were significantly related to lower grades among LGB youth. Russell, Seif, and Truong (2001) found that boys with bisexual attraction scored two tenths of a grade point lower than their peers. Kosciw and Diaz (2006) found that LGBT students who reported higher levels of harassment and assault in school related to their sexual orientation or gender expression also reported lower grades. Further, they found that LGBT youth were twice as likely to report that they did not want to continue their education than students from a general sample of secondary school students from the National Center for Education Statistics and that this difference was strongest for LGBT students reporting high levels of in-school victimization.

School Supports for LGBT K–12 Students

As previously mentioned, Massachusetts is the only state to have a comprehensive, state-wide program addressing the needs of gay and lesbian students: the Massachusetts Safe Schools Program for Gay and Lesbian Students (Massachusetts Department of Education, n.d.). The program was established to implement four components for creating safer schools: (a) school policies protecting gay and lesbian students from harassment, violence, and discrimination; (b) training for school personnel in crisis and suicide intervention; (c) support for establishing GSAs, and (d) counseling for family members of gay and lesbian students. In an evaluation of the Massachusetts program using a representative sample from the general population of high school students, Szalacha (2003) investigated students' perceptions of school climate—which was defined as the internal environment of the school regarding the level of safety, tolerance, and respect for sexual-minority individuals, based on the implementation of recommendations from the Massachusetts Department of Education—and found that there were positive differences associated with each aspect of the program. (Szalacha's analyses did not include the fourth recommendation of family counseling as no school in the state had implemented it.) Furthermore, the author concluded that regardless of sexual orientation students whose schools had implemented no components of the program were lowest overall in their perceptions of climate. In contrast, schools that had implemented all three components of the program were highest overall. Simply put, LGB students have a better educational experience if their schools provide them with any type of resource or support. Also, the more supports schools provide, the better off the students are. In this section, we will examine more specifically four types of support that LGBT students and their advocates ask for: (a) protective safe school policies, (b) student clubs commonly known as Gay-Straight Alliances, (c) educator trainings regarding LGBT student issues and (d) inclusive curriculum.

Protective Safe School Policies

Although federal sources of laws prohibiting discrimination on the basis of sex are an important source of protection for LGBT students, such as Title IX, they do not cover all harassment and discrimination that is targeted at students who are or are perceived to be LGBT. Moreover, these sex discrimination statutes do not proactively raise awareness among school officials about the disproportionate amount of harassment and discrimination that LGBT students face in schools throughout the country. Also, even when teachers or other school staff are aware of the particular problem of anti-LGBT harassment and discrimination, they may be fearful that they may not have support from their administrators to intervene effectively.

To address these concerns, a growing number of states across the country have explicitly added protections for LGBT students in their state education antidiscrimination and harassment statutes. As of 2005, nine states plus the District of Columbia prohibit discrimination or harassment on the basis of sexual orientation in schools. These states are California, Connecticut, Maine, Massachusetts, Minnesota, New Jersey, Vermont,

---

[22]Cal. Educ. Code § 200 et seq., Conn. Gen. Stat. § 10-15c; D.C. Code 1981 § 1-2520; Me. Rev. Stat. Ann., tit. 5, § 4553 (definition of sexual orientation); Me. Rev. Stat. Ann., tit. 5, § 4601-04 (prohibiting discrimination in education); Mass. Gen. Laws Chp. 76; § 5; Minn. Stat. § 363.05, subd. 5; N.J. Stat. 10:5-12f(1); N.J. Stat. 10:505(i); N.J. Stat. 18A:37-14; 16 Vt. Stat. § 11(a)(26); 16 Vt. Stat. § 565; Wash. Rev. Code §§ 28A.320; 28A.600; Wis. Stat. § 118.13.

Washington, and Wisconsin.[22] And, more recently, there has been a growing understanding that students who are perceived as gender nonconforming regardless of their sexual orientation are also targets for harassment and discrimination. In response, four of these states have added explicit protections from discrimination or harassment on the basis of gender identity in schools: California, Maine, Minnesota, and New Jersey.[23]

Nine states currently have statewide "antibullying" laws that do not explicitly define "bullying" or list categories of students who should be protected from specific and prevalent forms of bullying. These states are Arkansas, Colorado, Georgia, Louisiana, Oklahoma, Oregon, Illinois, New Hampshire, and West Virginia. However, because these laws are vague and do not provide teachers and administrators with clear legal guidance, many safe school advocates consider them to be ineffective in protecting students from harassment and discrimination. Proponents of the general bullying laws often argue that enumerated categories do not necessarily provide any extra protection and are not necessary for protective safe schools legislation. Given that many teachers do not intervene when they witness anti-LGBT bullying (Kosciw & Diaz, 2006), a clearly specified, inclusive safe schools law may provide guidance for the teachers that incidents of anti-LGBT bullying must be appropriately addressed and/or may provide sanctions for school personnel who fail to intervene. To examine any differential effects of general versus comprehensive bullying legislation, Kosciw and Diaz examined whether there were differences in students' reports of being harassed because of actual or perceived sexual orientation based on the presence and type of statewide safe schools legislation. The authors found that among students from states with comprehensive legislation, there had been a significant and consistent decrease in reported harassment based on sexual orientation from 2001 to 2005. In contrast, there were no changes over time in reports of harassment among students from states with no safe schools legislation or general antibullying laws. Further, there appeared to be no differences in frequency of harassment between states with no antibullying law and states with only a generic, noninclusive law.

Regardless of whether a statewide law exists protecting all students from harassment and victimization in school, many schools and school districts have implemented protective policies to specifically protect LGBT students. Of the 10 largest school districts in the United States, all but one has a district policy that specifically includes sexual orientation, and of those, only three also include language about gender identity or expression.[24] There is some evidence that having a school or district policy that provides protection based on sexual orientation has a positive effect on school climate for LGBT students. Kosciw and Diaz (2006) found that LGBT students who reported that their school had a comprehensive school policy about harassment were less likely than other students to hear homophobic remarks in school and reported a lower incidence of verbal harassment due to sexual orientation. Further, students who had been harassed in school were twice as likely to report the harassment to school personnel when their school had a comprehensive protective policy than students whose schools had no policy or only a generic policy (25% vs. 16% and 12%, respectively). Thus, in addition to helping create safer schools, protective school policies may instill greater confidence in students that school personnel will address incidents of victimization when they do occur.

Teachers may feel more empowered to act on behalf of LGBT students if there is an inclusive policy at the state, district, or even school level protecting these students. In the national survey of teachers conducted by Harris Interactive and GLSEN (2005), the vast majority of respondents believed that teachers and other school personnel have an obligation to ensure a safe and supportive learning environment for LGBT students. Further, when asked whether certain interventions would be helpful for creating safer schools—teacher training, safe schools policy, having GSAs in school and having the principal and/or superintendent address these safety issues openly—the largest number of teachers believed that instituting policies would be helpful.

Gay-Straight Alliances and Other School Supports

Student-run clubs known as gay-straight alliances (GSAs) have become increasingly more common in U.S. public schools. There are nearly 3,000 GSAs or other student clubs addressing LGBT student issues registered with GLSEN's Student Organizing Department, nearly double since 2001. Although narratives

---

[23]States have provided this protection in different ways. Some states have adopted a gender-identity inclusive definition of either gender or sexual orientation. Other states have added "gender identity" or "gender identity and expression" to their list of protected categories. See, e.g., Cal. Educ. Code § 220 (providing that the bases of prohibited discrimination include any basis that is included in the hate crimes statute); Cal. Penal Code § 422.56 (defining gender, for purposes of the hate crimes statute, to mean: "sex, and includes a person's gender identity and gender related appearance and behavior whether or not stereotypically associated with the person's assigned sex at birth."); Me. Rev. Stat. Ann., tit. 5, § 4553 (defining "sexual orientation," for purposes of educational nondiscrimination statute to mean "a person's actual or perceived heterosexuality, bisexuality, homosexuality, or gender identity or expression."); Minn. Stat. § 363.01, subd. 45 (defining "sexual orientation" for purposes of nondiscrimination statute, to mean "having or being perceived as having an emotional, physical, or sexual attachment to another person without regard to the sex of that person or having or being perceived as having an orientation for such attachment, or having or being perceived as having a self-image or identity not traditionally associated with one's biological maleness or femaleness. "Sexual orientation" does not include a physical or sexual attachment to children by an adult."); N.J. Stat. 18A:37-14 (including "gender identity and expression" among the categories of prohibited harassment).

[24]The following school districts have protective safe-schools policies that include protection based on both sexual orientation and gender identity and/or expression: Clark County School District, NV; Los Angeles Unified CA, and New York City Public Schools, NY.
The following school districts have protective safe schools policies that provide protective safe schools protection based on only sexual orientation: Broward County School District, FL; City of Chicago School District, IL; Dade County School District, FL; Houston Independent School District, TX, and Philadelphia City School District, PA.
The following school districts have no safe schools policy that includes sexual orientation or gender identity or expression: Hawaii Department of Education and Hillsborough County School District, FL.

have been written about the challenges and benefits of individual GSAs (e.g., Blumenfeld, 1995; Boutilier, 1993), little research actually exists on the topic. A handful of studies, however, have examined their structure and benefits.

The structure of GSAs varies from school to school since each club is individually created and managed. However, basic similarities do exist between them. Researchers have found that GSAs often include mutual support from members, a safe space for youth to meet, social activities, and education, advocacy, and visibility of LGBT issues to the entire school (Doppler, 2000; Griffin, Lee, Waugh, & Beyer, 2005). The inclusion of and emphasis placed on each activity depends on the individual GSA and the school context with which it is a part. Because school and community opposition and fear among LGBT students often accompany GSA-related efforts (Doppler, 2000), some components, such as advocacy and visibility, may be more difficult to implement within certain schools.

A handful of studies suggested that GSAs positively contribute both personally and academically to LGBT members. Szalacha (2003), in the evaluation of the Massachusetts Safe Schools Program, examined the varying contributions made by different combinations of program components and found that the presence of a GSA was the program component most strongly associated with a more positive climate for LGBT students. Doppler (2000) found that adults involved in the creation and maintenance of GSAs in Massachusetts (including state government,[25] GLSEN staff and faculty advisors of school GSAs) believed that GSAs provided many benefits, including safety, affirmation of members' LGBT identities, and opportunities to socialize with youth like themselves. Kosciw and Diaz (2006) found that LGBT students from schools with GSAs were less likely to report feeling unsafe because of their sexual orientation, less likely to miss school, and more likely to feel a sense of school belonging than students from schools without GSAs. Similarly, Bochenek and Brown (2001) reported that members of GSAs felt that the organizations gave them the chance to socialize with other LGBT students and discuss important LGBT topics such as ways to improve their school climate and issues relating to safer sex. Lee (2002) found that GSA membership may also be positively related to a number of other benefits including academic success, comfort with one's sexual orientation, and feelings of belonging to one's school, though the results of this particular study are limited by its small sample size of seven students.

Many youth who have started GSAs have confronted opposition both within the school from students, teachers, and administrative officials, as well as from the broader community (Bochenek & Brown, 2001; Doppler, 2000). In fact, probably very few students and advisors interested in creating a GSA have faced little or no opposition (Doppler). However, the right of students to form GSAs is protected by federal law. The federal Equal Access Act, (EAA)[26] requires that any public secondary school that allows at least one student-initiated non-curriculum-related club to meet on school grounds during lunch or after school *must allow* all other noncurricular student groups, including GSAs, access to the school. Thus, schools cannot otherwise discriminate against any group, even if the club represents an unpopular viewpoint. Four federal district court decisions have affirmed the right of gay-straight alliances to meet under the Equal Access Act.[27]

Even with essential governmental backing, such as in Massachusetts, supportive school administrators and advisors are needed to sustain GSA efforts and combat internal and external opposition (Griffin & Ouellett, 2002). The EAA and other governmental supports are no guarantee that a school will cooperate with students and advisors interested in starting a GSA, particularly a school administration opposes the club's formation. One example of the most extreme form of opposition came from the Salt Lake City School District in Utah in response to students at East High School who wanted to form a GSA. To circumvent the requirements imposed by the EAA, the school chose instead to ban all noncurriculum clubs, including the Human Rights Club and several ethnic clubs, in order to close the GSA (see Burrington, 1998, for a description of the East High School controversy). Fortunately, the school board reversed its decision in 2000, though the story highlights the struggle and challenges that many students endure when trying to create GSAs.

While they are becoming more popular, GSAs are not the only type of school-based support group. One alternative to the GSA model is Project 10, a program of the Los Angeles Unified School District that includes support groups for LGBT youth, student and staff education, teacher and staff training, development and enforcement of LGBT-specific, antiharassment policies, and opportunities to network with other organizations in the community for additional support (Uribe, 1995). In contrast to GSAs, Project 10 is not a student club, and the support groups are run by trained adult facilitators and counselors. Unfortunately, school-based groups like Project 10 and GSAs may be extremely difficult to create or join in areas that are extremely intolerant of LGBT individuals or where the number of LGBT students would normally be small, which may be the case in rural communities (Snively, 2004). Community-based youth programs for LGBT youth may be viable alternatives in these areas, and some offer community-wide GSAs that include members from multiple schools. Such groups may offer LGBT youth more anonymity and control over coming out while still creating opportunities for youth to connect with one another, although to our knowledge no research has examined how community-based support may benefit LGBT students' academic experience.

Teacher Support and Teacher Training

Research has found that social support from teachers, including emotional and academic support, is associated with higher aca-

---

[25]These included members of the Massachusetts Department of Education's Safe Schools for Gay and Lesbian Students Program (SSGLSP) and the Governor's Commission of Gay and Lesbian Youth.

[26]20 U.S.C. §§ 4071–4074.

[27]See *Boyd County High School Gay/Straight Alliance v. Board of Education*, 258 F. Supp.2d 667 (E.D. Ky. 2003); *Franklin Central Gay/Straight Alliance v. Franklin Township Comm. Sch. Corp.*, 2002 WL 31921332 (S.D. Ind. Dec. 23, 2002); *Colin v. Orange Unified Sch. Dist.*, 83 F. Supp. 2d 1135, 1148 (C.D. Cal. 2000); *East High Gay/Straight Alliance v. Bd. of Ed. of Salt Lake City Sch. Dist.*, 30 F. Supp. 2d 1356 (D. Utah 1998).

demic attendance and success, lower symptoms of depression, and general well-being for students in general (Felner, Ginter, & Primavera, 1982; Reddy, Rhodes, & Mulhall, 2003; Ryan, Stiller, & Lynch, 1994). Supportiveness from teachers and staff is particularly important for LGBT students, and especially for those who do not receive needed support from families and peers. Bochenek and Brown (2001) found that many LGBT students believed that having at least one supportive faculty or staff member was essential to surviving in a hostile, homophobic atmosphere. Research has shown that for LGBT students, having a supportive teacher is associated with fewer reported school troubles (Russell, Seif, & Truong, 2001), greater feelings of psychological sense of school belonging (Kosciw, 2004), and better academic outcomes (Russell, Seif, & Truong, 2001; Kosciw, 2004). Teachers may provide affirmation of an LGBT student's identity. However, in the context of a hostile school climate, they may also act in an advocacy capacity. For example, GLSEN's 2005 survey found that LGBT students were more likely to report when they had been harassed in school when there were a greater number of supportive faculty and staff.

Unfortunately, many students do not have the critical support of teachers and staff in their schools. Several studies have found that teachers and staff inconsistently or never intervene when they hear homophobic remarks or reports of harassment and assault (Bochenek & Brown, 2001; Kosciw & Diaz, 2006; Sears, 1992; Smith & Smith, 1998). While inaction to homophobic behavior can take on a variety of forms, with silence being the most common, qualitative research findings have illuminated the demeaning nature of many dismissive responses. For example, Bochenek and Brown (2001) reported that when one student approached his principal with documentation of LGBT harassment from classmates, the principal responded by telling the student he had too much time on his hands and threw the information in the trash. In GLSEN's 2005 survey, one student reported that he was told ". . . to keep my 'lifestyle' to myself and not publicize it or 'flaunt' it," and another reported that the staff in his public school told him to read the Bible (Kosciw & Diaz, 2006). Inaction and the lack of perceived support may explain why some researchers have found that most LGBT students inconsistently or never report experiences of victimization to faculty or staff (Kosciw & Diaz, 2006; Morrow & Gill, 2003).

One reason for the inaction and lack of supportiveness among teachers and staff may be the fear of a parental, student, or administrative backlash that could result in negative consequences including job loss. Two studies of teachers in the United Kingdom found that many believed their responses to homophobic bullying and harassment were limited because of a law that prohibited the "promotion of homosexuality" (Chambers, van Loon, & Tincknell, 2004; Warwick, Aggleton, & Douglas, 2001). Similar limitations are almost certainly present in many parts of the United States even if there is no formal law that inhibits addressing homophobic actions. The fear of a backlash or job loss may be especially true for LGBT teachers and staff if support of LGBT students risks revealing one's own sexual identity (Bochenek & Brown, 2001; The Governor's Commission on Gay and Lesbian

Youth, 1993). Supportive actions may be especially risky in states that do not prohibit firings based on sexual orientation.[28]

One further reason for the inaction and lack of supportiveness among many teachers is that many hold homophobic beliefs and attitudes themselves and blame LGBT students for experiences of harassment or other problems. Sears (1992), for example, surveyed a sample of prospective teachers and guidance counselors in the southern United States and found that nearly all participants expressed some degree of homophobic attitudes and beliefs. In addition, over a third of teachers and over a fifth of guidance counselors were found to be extremely homophobic. Other studies, while not directly measuring attitudes toward LGBT individuals, found that many teachers and staff overtly express homophobic attitudes and beliefs through biased comments (Kosciw, 2004; Smith & Smith, 1998).

Homophobia can be expressed by teachers in other, less obvious ways. Bochenek and Brown (2001) found that a number of students in their sample were "outed" to their parents against their will by school counselors, even though such acts clearly violate the confidentiality of the setting. Even teachers who are not overtly homophobic may still be contributing to hostile, homophobic climates by perpetuating heteronormative beliefs and attitudes, which rely on traditional notions of gender and sexuality such as strict gender roles and the idea that heterosexuality is superior and preferred over other sexual orientations. Ignorance of the seriousness of heterosexism and homophobia may prevent many teachers from responding to LGBT bullying and harassment. Teachers may structure their classes and curriculums in ways that send messages to students about acceptable norms of sexuality, oftentimes unknowingly (Ferfolja & Robinson, 2004). Perhaps one of the most common methods of perpetuating heterosexist norms is by ignoring LGBT issues altogether, thereby sending out the message that nonheterosexual individuals either do not exist or are not to be acknowledged. It is important to note that teachers' negative beliefs about LGBT students may not necessarily result in their inaction toward protecting LGBT students. For example, a teacher could believe that homosexuality is wrong but also believe that all students deserve to be protected from victimization. Further research is needed that examines the relationship between teachers' LGBT-related beliefs and their action/inaction when anti-LGBT harassment occurs in school.

One way to address issues of heteronormativity and overt homophobia may be to offer antihomophobia training during preservice teachers' education. Little research has been done that has examined the effect of inclusion of LGBT-related content in teacher education. Ferfolja and Robinson (2004), in their study of Australian educators of preservice teachers, found that most educators believed that it was important to include antihomophobia training in preservice teacher education, particularly for those going into secondary education. This type of training may help to educate preservice teachers on issues facing LGBT students and encourage them to examine their own perceptions of sexuality and gender before entering the classroom. Athanases and Larrabee (2003) found that preservice

---

[28]For more information about employment discrimination laws, refer to the Lambda Legal Web site: www.lambdalegal.org

teachers whose education classes included instruction on issues related to lesbian and gay (LG) students in schools had a positive reaction to the material. Many of the participants valued learning about lesbian and gay people, having a new opportunity to discuss LG issues and, as a result of the instruction, many understand the importance, as educators, of becoming an advocate for LG youth. Further research is needed that examines the impact of inclusive teacher education on preservice teachers, particularly as they enter the teaching profession.

Inclusive Curriculum

Research has shown that ignoring LGBT issues and topics is the norm in most classrooms. GLSEN's National School Climate Survey found that 80% of the study participants reported that LGBT issues were never mentioned in their classes (Kosciw & Diaz, 2006). Other researchers have found that less than half of secondary health teachers formally teach about LGBT issues, and of those who did mention it in class, nearly half spent less than a day on the topic (Telljohann, Price, Poureslami, & Easton, 1995). Perhaps even more disturbing, this study found that nearly a tenth of health educators who did discuss LGBT issues reported teaching that homosexuality was wrong. Of the entire sample, few teachers believed that LGBT students feel more isolated or are more likely to abuse drugs or attempt suicide, suggesting that teachers must be trained on issues affecting LGBT students (Telljohann et al.).

To counter the lack of attention to LGBT issues, several educators have suggested ways to incorporate LGBT material into classes tailored to the specific subject matter. For example, English teachers can spend more time identifying LGBT themes in famous literary works as well as allowing opportunities for writing around LGBT issues (Allan, 1999). Biology teachers can focus on the evidence for a biological basis for sexual orientation (Good, Hafner, & Peebles, 2000; Smith & Drake, 2001). Mathison (1998) suggested an even broader approach that not only encourages inclusion of LGBT material in the curriculum, but also calls for teachers to learn more about the unique culture of LGBT individuals and confront their own biases and prejudices, including assumptions that all students are heterosexual. By better understanding the culture of LGBT students, teachers can create a learning environment that is sensitive to LGBT students' needs and background. Unfortunately, many supportive teachers probably feel tension between their own goal to become more sensitive to LGBT students and their fear of reprisal from school administrators and parents. One particular article calling for biology teachers to incorporate LGBT-related material in their curriculum stated:

[Teachers must] be careful to point out that science takes no position on whether homosexual behavior is right or wrong. . . . Making sure that your instruction focuses on the scientific questions and evidence and not on personal, moral, or religious arguments is, of course, important and a solid basis for responding to any concerns that may be raised by parents or school officials. (Smith & Drake, 2001, p. 159)

One way to reduce fear and assist faculty in addressing LGBT students' needs may be through support from school and state officials. One of the best examples of governmental support for teachers in addressing LGBT curricular content is the recommendations from the Massachusetts Governor's Commission on Gay and Lesbian Youth (1993), which advised, among other things, that schools train teachers and adopt curriculums that address gay and lesbian issues. In response to these recommendations, the Massachusetts's Department of Education now provides program assistance for trainings on LGBT student issues and curriculum inclusiveness.

Most of the recent research on LGBT students has examined either the incidence and effects of in-school victimization or the benefits of school supports but few have thus far looked at the interplay between climate and supports on student outcomes. Using data from GLSEN's 2003 national survey of LGBT students, Kosciw (2005) examined the relationship between school supports and school climate as well as how school supports may mediate any negative effects of the harassment and victimization on LGBT academic achievement. The author found that a supportive school environment, e.g., having a protective policy about harassment, a GSA or an inclusive curriculum, was directly related to a less hostile school environment (i.e., fewer homophobic remarks, lower incidence of harassment and assault), which was, in turn, related to increased achievement for LGBT students. Further, he found that a supportive school population was also related to higher achievement, but indirectly by way of increased psychological attachment to school. Further research is needed examining the complex relationships among school harassment, supports, and academic achievement.

Although many of the studies examining the incidence of victimization experiences of LGBT students examined gender differences, with the exception of research from the Add Health Survey by Russell and his colleagues, few studies examined differences across genders in reporting both the presence and use of supportive resources in school and whether these resources have varying levels of effectiveness for students of different genders. Given findings that transgender students are often most at risk for in-school victimization (e.g., Kosciw & Diaz, 2006), it would be important to examine whether these students reap similar benefits from resources in school than male and female students who do not identify as transgender.

Gender Differences in the Utility of School Supports

Little research has examined any variable effects of interventions to create safer schools for LGBT students based on gender. In her evaluation of the Massachusetts Safe Schools Program, Szalacha (2003) found that sexual minority boys had the lowest ratings of their school climate and heterosexual girls had the highest ratings. Sexual minority girls' perceptions of school climate were only slightly lower than heterosexual girls and nearly the same as heterosexual boys. The author examined whether there were interactive effects between gender and the three types of school interventions and found differences in the contribution of having a GSA in one's school based on gender. Even though most of the GSAs in the study were predominately attended by girls, having a GSA was associated with a greater positive difference with boys, even if the boys did not attend the student club. Szalacha concluded that "while both teacher training and inclusive school policies are associated with positive differences in climate, a GSA disrupts the normal conversation— the assumptions of heterosexuality—and challenges the notions of 'traditional masculinity and femininity' that govern school climates" (p. 78).

EDUCATION LAWS AND POLICIES (K–12) THAT STIGMATIZE LGBT PEOPLE

In our discussions of the literature on LGBT students in K–12 schools, we have seen how a hostile school climate is negatively related to student achievement and educational aspirations and how positive school resources, such as comprehensive protective policies and supportive school personnel, are associated with a better learning environment. However, certain state and local policies and laws may act to stigmatize LGBT people, which in turn, may negatively affect LGBT students and their education.

State Legislation About the Portrayal of Homosexuality in Schools

The vast majority of students in this country may be vulnerable to in-school harassment based on their sexual orientation and/or gender identity/expression due to the inaction of most states to pass comprehensive safe school laws that protect LGBT students. In some states, the situation is more dire; these states have enacted prohibitions on the positive portrayal of homosexuality in schools, which may facilitate an even further hostile school climate for LGBT students.[29] Evidence from GLSEN's 2005 NSCS suggests that this type of negative state legislation may be related to in an increased hostile school climate for LGBT students (Kosciw & Diaz, 2006). Students who lived in states with this negative legislation were:

- More likely to report a high incidence of homophobic remarks
- More likely to report being verbally harassed in school because of their sexual orientation
- Nearly half as likely to report having a GSA in their school
- Less likely to report having Internet access to LGBT community sites from school
- Twice as likely to report that there were no faculty or staff in their school who were supportive of LGBT students.

Abstinence-Only Sexuality Education

Existing research has demonstrated that many abstinence-only curricula provide misleading and medically inaccurate information about health matters such as contraception and the prevention of sexually transmitted infections and pregnancy. Research

has also shown that the most commonly used abstinence-only curricula ignore the needs of LGBT youth, who may not receive accurate information about HIV prevention and other sexual health matters (Minority Staff, House Government Reform Committee, 2004; Santelli, Ott, Lyon, Rogers, Summers, & Schleifer, 2006; Sexuality Information and Education Council of the United States [SEICUS], 2004). Given that most commonly used abstinence-only curricula emphasize marriage (federally funded programs are, in fact, required to emphasize marriage as the only appropriate time for sexual relationships), LGBT students may also be taught that they can never have positive, intimate relationships unless they are married, which, at this time, can only happen for LGB adults in Massachusetts (Santelli et al.). Furthermore, such biased curricula may foster greater intolerance and further create a negative school environment for LGBT students.

Kosciw and Diaz (2006) found that nearly half of LGBT students reported that their school followed an abstinence-only sexuality education curriculum. For these students, having an abstinence-only curriculum was, in fact, related to negative school indicators:

- A higher incidence of missing school because they felt unsafe
- Increased harassment, particularly harassment related to sexual orientation and religion, as well as sexual harassment
- Fewer faculty or staff who were supportive of LGBT students and fewer LGBT faculty or staff who were "out" staff at their school
- Less comfort in talking one on one with school personnel about LGBT issues.

Beyond High School: LGBT Issues in Post-Secondary Education

As we have seen, high school can be a dangerous and unsafe place for many LGBT youth. For those students with the worst school experiences related to harassment and assault, college may become a remote possibility as they drop out of school or suffer in their academic achievement. For those LGBT youth who have had positive high school experiences or those who have survived their victimization experiences and graduated, what happens when they enter the halls of higher learning? In the past 20 years, attention to the experiences and needs of LGBT students has increased greatly, and some colleges and universities have enhanced the quality of life for LGBT students through changes to curricular and cocurricular programs, admissions and employment practices, and policy development. This section will highlight recent data on the experiences of LGBT college students and the practices and policies designed to provide support and decrease campus hostility and misunderstanding.

The most comprehensive study of LGBT college students and campus employees in the United States was conducted by

---

[29]States that prohibit the positive portrayal of homosexuality in schools include Alabama, Arizona, Mississippi, Oklahoma, South Carolina, Texas and Utah. Also see GLSEN's *State of the States 2004* report.

the National Gay and Lesbian Task Force (Rankin, 2003). It involved over 1,600 respondents attending 14 campuses with active centers addressing LGBT issues.[30] The report examined the pervasiveness of harassment and victimization faced by those who identify as LGBT and provided recommendations for ways in which campuses can improve the quality of life and educational and work climate for students and employees. The data indicated that:

- More than a third (36%) of LGBT undergraduate students have experienced harassment within the past year, as have 29% of all respondents.
- Those who experienced harassment reported that derogatory remarks were the most common form (89%) and that students were most often the source of harassment (79%).
- Twenty percent of all respondents feared for their physical safety because of their sexual orientation or gender identity, and 51% concealed their sexual orientation or gender identity to avoid intimidation.

The types of harassment experienced included derogatory remarks, verbal harassment or threats, graffiti, pressure to be silent/closeted, written comments, threats of physical violence, threats of exposure/outing, denial of services, and physical assault. These results compare closely with the experiences of LGBT students in secondary schools (for example, Kosciw & Diaz, 2006) and with more regional studies on college campus climate (for example, D'Augelli, 1989; D'Augelli et al., 2002; Evans & Rankin, 1998). Similar to results on secondary school students, those respondents in the NGLTF study who identified themselves as transgender were significantly more likely to report having been harassed than nontransgender men and women (41% vs. 28%). Among nontransgender participants, there were no gender differences in the number reporting harassment. The report also indicated that LGBT people of color were more likely than White LGBT respondents to report being the target of harassment, and were more likely to "conceal their sexual orientation or gender identity to avoid harassment" (p. 25).

Rankin (2003) reported that a majority of respondents believed that gay men and lesbians were likely to be harassed while on campus (61%) and that transgender people were even more likely to be targets (71%). Although these were students on campuses with active LGBT centers, over 40% of the respondents felt the campus climate was homophobic, that the university was not adequately addressing LGBT issues, and the curriculum did not include sufficient attention to the contributions of LGBT people. Perhaps not surprisingly, one study found that LGB college students perceived their campus climate more negatively than heterosexual students (Waldo, 1998).

RESOURCES AND SUPPORTS ON CAMPUS

Rankin (2003) suggested that campuses can better support the needs of LGBT people by focusing on recruitment and retention of LGBT students and employees, addressing LGBT issues within the curriculum, increasing educational programming on LGBT issues, creating policies and practices that support LGBT interests, and creating spaces for interaction. Although there is little empirical evidence demonstrating the benefits of these resources at the postsecondary level, many of these same resources have been shown to make a demonstrable difference in the lives of LGBT students in K–12 schools, as previously discussed.

Protective Policies

Only seven states and the District of Columbia have laws explicitly prohibiting discrimination or harassment based on sexual orientation and/or gender identity in higher education.[31] Thus, it is crucial that colleges and universities have policies that explicitly protect LGBT students and employees. As of 2004, over 500 colleges and universities included sexual orientation in their nondiscrimination policies, and many others have written statements that support the rights and interests of gay, lesbian, and bisexual students, faculty, and staff even if not included in the official nondiscrimination policies. The inclusion of gender identity in nondiscrimination policies is much more limited, involving fewer than 50 campuses. Further, over 275 college and universities offer domestic partnership health benefits to employees, and an increasing number are allowing student domestic partners to cohabitate in campus-owned housing. Nevertheless, when considering these numbers, it is important to remember that there are thousands of colleges and universities in the United States, and the number of institutions with protective policies for LGBT individuals are clearly the minority (Rankin, 2004).

Student Organizations

Over 1,000 campuses in the United States have at least one student organization for gay, lesbian, bisexual, transgender and/or intersex students. Some have more than one that target specific populations within the LGBT community, based on such characteristics as degree level, academic discipline, ethnicity, and national origin. Regional and national conferences for LGBT students and members of student organizations have also become popular, helping to enhance access to resources, ideas, and support.

---

[30]The survey results combine student and faculty/staff reports. Specific percentages for students are reported in this section when available and are indicated as such in the text. Otherwise, results are for the combined sample. Undergraduate or graduate/professional students comprised the majority of the sample (60%).

[31]These jurisdictions are California, the District of Columbia, Maine, Minnesota, New Jersey, Vermont, and Wisconsin. Cal. Educ. Code § 66270, Cal. Penal Code §§ 422.6, 422.55, 422.56; D.C. Code §§ 2-1402.41, § 2-1401.02; Me. Rev. Stat., Tit. 5, § 4602(4); § 4553(2-A); Minn. Stat. §§ 363A.13, 363A.03(14); N.J. Stat. 10:5-12(f), 10:5-5(1); Vt. Stat. Ann. Tit.16, § 11, Vt. Stat. Ann Tit. 16, § 11(26)(a); Vt. Stat. Ann. Tit. 16, § 140a; Wis. Stat. § 118.13; Wis. Stat. § 36.12.

Institutional Supports

Renn (2000) indicated that faculty who claim to be supportive of LGB concerns, yet remain passive when disrespectful actions occur, perpetuate unsafe environments. She noted that faculty must actively challenge homophobia on campus by providing positive attention to LGB people and issues including publicly supporting LGB staff and faculty as role models and using heterosexual privilege to advocate for the rights and needs of sexual minorities. Many institutions across the country have established resource centers or a designated staff support person for LGBT students (Barnett, 2002). The first Lesbian and Gay Resource Center was opened at the University of Michigan in 1971. By 1985, Minnesota State University, Mankato, University of Pennsylvania, and the University of Massachusetts, Amherst, had added centers. By 2005, this number has increased to over 100. Additionally, many campus women's centers and multicultural centers include staffing and programs supporting LGBT populations.

A final area that deserves particular attention is the experiences of LGBT students in campus residence halls or dormitories. Students who identify as lesbian, gay, and bisexual may face hostility from peers who are uncomfortable sharing a bedroom, living space, and/or bathroom with them out of fear of unwanted same-sex attraction or objectification. To address this issue, some college and university campuses have struggled to find ways to identify students who are comfortable sharing a living environment with LGBT peers without forcing students to document their sexual orientation or gender identity (Robison, 1998). Some campuses have also created "special-interest housing" or learning communities designed to focus on LGBT concerns, assuming that those who select such environments will be comfortable living with LGBT students, regardless of their own sexual orientation and identity. Some campuses, including the University of Southern Maine and Sarah Lawrence College, now have portions of their residence halls where students are allowed to select roommates with whom they will share bedrooms and/or suites without regard to the students' sex or gender identity. Others are providing all-gender bathrooms in residence halls (and elsewhere on campus), in addition to traditional male- and female-only bathrooms, to better serve transgender students.

Curricular Inclusion

Rankin (2003) also maintained that to combat homophobia on campus, college and university faculty must intentionally educate students about sexual minority issues, incorporate LGB materials into standard courses, create courses with a specific LGB focus, and encourage student and faculty research on LGB topics. As addressed in more detail in the chapter "The Role of Women's and Gender Studies in Advancing Gender Equity" in this *Handbook*, the past 20 years have shown a dramatic increase in curricular attention to gay, lesbian, bisexual, transgender, and/or queer issues. While women's studies, gender studies, and gay and lesbian (or queer) studies programs are the most likely programs to incorporate LGBT issues within their curriculum, LGBT-focused courses can now be found in a variety of disciplines. Undergraduate and graduate-student research

on LGBT-related topics has increased dramatically, and university library holdings on LGBT issues have increased. Several groups have been formed to support faculty engaging in the study of LGBT topics. These groups also support faculty, librarians, researchers, and sometimes students who identify as LGBT (and queer). These include the Queer Studies list (QSTUDY-L), Trans-Academics, Transecting the Academy, and Queeringtheclassroom.com. Many professional associations for faculty now include LGBT caucuses or committees, which again give attention to both research areas and personal concerns.

AND WHAT ABOUT LGBT EDUCATORS?

The bulk of this chapter has examined the experiences of LGBT students in their schools. However, discrimination in schools on the basis of sexual orientation or gender identity/expression is not confined to students. There is no federal legislation prohibiting employment discrimination based on sexual orientation or gender identity/expression, and few states have enacted such legislation. A report from the National Education Association (NEA) Task Force on Sexual Orientation noted that employment discrimination directed at LGBT education employees is commonplace:

[LGBT] employees frequently face dismissal or other adverse employment actions on the basis of their sexual orientation/gender identification, often as a result of private declarations of their sexual orientation/gender identification . . . Both the NEA Office of General Counsel and the Gay and Lesbian Rights Project of the American Civil Liberties Union inform us that they encounter a number of cases each year in which education employees have suffered employment discrimination if their sexual orientation/gender identification is disclosed. Indeed, the very nature of the problem ensures that many cases of discrimination go unreported. (National Education Association, 2002)

According to this report, there have not been any studies documenting the incidence of discrimination against LGBT educators. Yet the NEA Task Force maintained that even without statistics on employment discrimination and LGBT teachers, "the evidence suggests that such discrimination is severe and widespread" (National Education Association, 2002).

More research is clearly needed to document the prevalence with which LGBT educators face discrimination in their schools. In addition to statistics on employment discrimination, it is important to examine how school climate affects them personally and professionally. Many LGBT educators do not have protection from employment discrimination based on sexual orientation. Federal and state employment legislation is needed so to provide universal protection.

RECOMMENDATIONS FOR CREATING INCLUSIVE AND SAFE SCHOOLS AND CAMPUSES

One major goal of this chapter was to demonstrate the often hostile climate LGBT students face when entering schools. As the literature consistently shows, violence, bias, and harassment directed at LGBT students continue to be the rule—not the exception—in America's schools. Yet what may be most important is the evidence that a negative school climate for LGBT students denies their right to an education by causing them to miss school for safety reasons, by preventing their academic achievement, and by hindering their desire to learn and continue their education. The literature has also shown how school supports for LGBT students, such as a supportive faculty member or a student club that addresses LGBT issues, can potentially ameliorate the negative impact of a hostile school climate and encourage LGBT students to attend school, learn, and continue their education. Szalacha's evaluation of the Massachusetts Safe Schools program has confirmed that efforts at the school level, such as implementing teacher training or supporting GSAs, are associated with a more positive school environment for LGBT students (Szalacha, 2003). However, perhaps more importantly, this evaluation has demonstrated that efforts at the state-level can also make a positive difference in the lives of LGBT students. In order to create safer learning environments for all students and educators, we recommend the following:

- Federal, state, and local policymakers must:
  - institute and enforce policies that include "sexual orientation and gender identity" as protected classes along with existing categories such as race, religion, and ability, as such policies can dramatically reduce absenteeism among LGBT students.
  - ensure that higher-education students are protected from harassment and discrimination on campus.
  - enact nondiscrimination policies on the basis of sexual and gender orientation in matters of hiring, tenure, promotion, admissions, and financial aid.
  - enact policies of active outreach in hiring openly LGBT and/or LGBT- sensitive faculty, staff, and administrators in all segments of the school community.
  - ensure equal access and equality of all benefits and privileges granted to students and employees, including their same-sex partners.

Program/Practice

- Title IX coordinators must educate their LGBT constituents, including students, about how they can be a resource for victims of discrimination and harassment.
- Accrediting bodies for educational institutions must implement standards and policies that these institutions must follow, so that they can truly provide equal access to education and promote empowering environments for LGBT faculty, staff, and students.
- Preservice teacher education programs must include information about sexual orientation and gender identity/expression in their curriculum and prepare teachers to support LGBT students.
- School districts must:
  - provide teacher trainings on how to support LGBT students, as building the skills of teachers in supporting LGBT

students can help reduce rates of harassment and increase the future aspirations of LGBT students in terms of pursuing higher education.
  - create and support programs such as gay-straight alliances and other student clubs addressing LGBT issues, which can significantly increase students' sense of belonging at school and thereby their likelihood of furthering their educational attainment.
  - provide inclusive curriculum that includes representations of LGBT people, history, and events.
  - implement curricular programs in all K–12 aimed at reducing name-calling and bullying that are comprehensive of issues related to LGBT students, such as GLSEN's No Name-Calling Week (www.nonamecallingweek.org), a curriculum for middle schools about name-calling and bullying, or Get a Voice, a comprehensive character education program for K–8 grades (www.getavoice.net).
- Colleges and universities as well as private secondary schools must seek out openly LGBT prospective students in their recruitment and admissions processes.

Research and Evaluation

- Questions about sexual orientation (actual and perceived) and gender identity/expression should be included in all areas of educational research, particularly research aimed at school climate, and this research should take into account differences based on sexual orientation, gender, sex, gender identity/expression and other relevant characteristics.
- Education administrators must assess their own institutions with regard to school or campus climate and supportive resources for LGBT students.
- Given the general paucity of research related to LGBT issues in education, further research is needed on LGBT issues in education in general. Some specific areas for further research include:
  - the impact of including LGBT-related content in teacher-education curricula and how such curricular inclusion may affect school climate for LGBT students.
  - the effectiveness of teacher training programs addressing LGBT issues and how such training may affect the school climate for LGBT students.
  - the relationship between teachers' LGBT-related beliefs and their action/inaction when anti-LGBT harassment occurs in school.
  - further examination of the experiences of transgender-identified students in school.
  - the relationships among school harassment, supports and academic achievement for LGBT students.
  - the intersection of sexual orientation and gender with regard to access to education and educational aspirations and attainment, including examination of gender differences within the population of LGBT students, how males and females may differentially be affected by and cope with victimization, and an examination of potential differential effects by gender of interventions for creating safer schools.

By implementing these recommendations, the United States can move toward a future where schools are places where all students are free to learn, regardless of sexual orientation or gender identity/expression.

CONCLUSION

The first edition of this *Handbook,* published in 1985, did not consider issues of gender equity for LGBT students and educators. This absence perhaps reflects the relative invisibility of LGBT issues in education in the country then. Although few states now have legal protection for LGBT students, only the District of Columbia's protective legislation had been enacted prior to 1986 and Wisconsin's was enacted in 1986. In this chapter, our goal was to examine this rising visibility of issues around sexual orientation and gender identity/expression in schools since 1985 and the responses of legislatures, courts, school districts, and advocates to the endemic problem of discrimination, violence, and harassment directed at students who are, or are perceived to be, lesbian, gay, bisexual, or transgender. Twenty years after the first *Handbook*, LGBT issues in education have entered public consciousness. However, what we now see is an unsettling picture of negative school climates for many LGBT students, teachers, and educators. LGBT students like Jesse Montgomery, whose story opened this chapter, are often verbally and physically abused in school because of their sexual orientation or gender identity/expression. For some, this type of victimization continues from high school to college. LGBT teachers, who could be role models for LGBT students and are perhaps more sympathetic of their experiences with harassment in school, may not feel safe being identified as LGBT for fear of losing their jobs. This chapter was further intended to illustrate how sexism and homophobia are inextricably linked and that issues related to equity in education for LGBT individuals are issues of gender equity in education regardless of any one person's gender. Anti-LGBT victimization is not just about whether a student is or is perceived to be lesbian or gay, but is also about deeply entrenched understandings of appropriate male and female behavior and self-presentation. Violence or threats of violence directed at gay men and lesbians play a crucial role in enforcing gender stereotypes and compulsory heterosexuality. Efforts to address issues of gender equity in education must not ignore the role that this particular type of bias plays in sustaining institutionalized sexism. Educators, advocates, policymakers, and parents who wish to further equal status for all in schools, regardless of gender, must address the related and entwined questions of sexual orientation and gender identity/expression and work toward creating schools where LGBT students have equal opportunity to learn and LGBT educators have equal opportunity to educate.

ACKNOWLEDGMENTS

The authors gratefully acknowledge the editorial comments of Stacey Horn, PhD, University of Illinois at Chicago and Stephen Russell, PhD, University of Arizona.

References

AAUW Educational Foundation. (2001). *Hostile hallways: Bullying, teasing and sexual harassment in school*. Washington, DC: Author.

Allan, C. (1999). Poets of comrades: Addressing sexual orientation in the English classroom. *The English Journal, 88*, 97–101.

Athanases, S. Z., & Larrabee, T. G. (2003). Toward a consistent stance in teaching for equity: learning to advocate for lesbian- and gay-identified youth. *Teaching and Teacher Education, 19*, 237–261.

Barnett, D. (2002). *When campus LGBT centers and offices were established* (National Consortium of Directors of LGBT Resources in Higher Education). Retrieved March 14, 2005, from http://www.lgbtcampus .org/resources/establishment_of_offices.htm

Blumenfeld, W. J. (1995). "Gay/straight" alliances: Transforming pain to pride. In G. Unks (Ed.), *The gay teen: Educational practice and theory for lesbian, gay, and bisexual adolescents* (pp. 211–224). New York: Routledge.

Bochenek, M., & Brown, A. W. (2001). *Hatred in the hallways: Violence and discrimination against lesbian, gay, bisexual, and transgender students in U.S. schools.* New York: The Human Rights Watch.

Bontempo, D. E., & D'Augelli, A. R. (2002). Effects of at-school victimization and sexual orientation on lesbian, gay, or bisexual youths' health risk behavior. *Journal of Adolescent Health, 30*, 364–374.

Boutilier, N. (1993). Gay/straight: An alliance for high school activism. In S. McConnell-Celi (Ed.), *Twenty-first century challenge: Lesbians and gays in education* (pp. 39–50). Red Bank, NJ: Lavender Crystal Press.

Burrington, D. (1998). The public square and citizen queer: Toward a new political geography. *Polity, 31*, 109–131.

California Safe Schools Coalition and 4-H Center for Youth Development, University of California, Davis. (2004). *Consequences of harassment based on actual or perceived sexual orientation and gender nonconformity and steps for making schools safer.* San Francisco: Authors.

Chambers, D., van Loon, J., & Tincknell, E. (2004). Teachers' views of teenage sexual morality. *British Journal of Sociology of Education, 25*, 563–576.

Coalition for Education on Sexual Orientation. (2005). *Chicago youth risk behavior survey: Differential risks for lesbian, gay, bisexual youth*. Chicago, IL: Author

D'Augelli, A. R. (1989). Lesbians' and gay men's experiences of discrimination and harassment in a university community. *American Journal of Community Psychology, 17*, 317–321.

D'Augelli, A. R. (2002). Mental health problems among lesbian, gay, and bisexual youths ages 14 to 21. *Clinical Child Psychology and Psychiatry, 7*, 433–456.

D'Augelli, A. R., Pilkington, N. W., & Hershberger, S. L. (2002). Incidence and mental health impact of sexual orientation victimization of lesbian, gay, and bisexual youths in high school. *School Psychology Quarterly, 17*, 148–167.

Doppler, J. E. (2000). A description of gay/straight alliances in the public schools of Massachusetts. *Dissertation Abstracts International, 61* (09), 3510A. (UMI No. 9988779)

DuRant, R. H., Krowchuk, D. P., & Sinal, S. H. (1998). Victimization, use of violence, and drug use at school among male adolescents who engage in same-sex sexual behavior. *Journal of Pediatrics, 133*, 113–118.

Equal Access Act, 20 U.S.C. § 4071 (1984).

Evans, N. J., & Rankin, S. (1998). Heterosexism and campus violence. In A. Hoffman, J. Schuh, & R. Fenske (Eds.), *Violence on campus: Defining the problems, strategies for action* (pp. 169–186) Gaithersburg, MD: Aspen.

Felner, R. D., Ginter, M., & Primavera, J. (1982). Primary prevention during school transitions: Social support and environmental structure. *American Journal of Community Psychology, 10,* 277–290.

Ferfolja, T., & Robinson, K. H. (2004). Why anti-homophobia education in teacher education? Perspectives from Australian teacher educators. *Teaching Education, 15,* 9–25.

Garofalo, R., Wolf, R. C., Kessel, S., Palfrey, J., & DuRant, R. H. (1998). The association between health risk behaviors and sexual orientation among a school-based sample of adolescents. *Pediatrics, 101,* 895–902.

Good, R., Hafner, M., & Peebles, P. (2000). Scientific understanding of sexual orientation: Implications for science education. *The American Biology Teacher, 62,* 326–330.

Governor's Commission on Gay and Lesbian Youth. (1993). *Making schools safe for gay and lesbian youth: Breaking the silence in schools and in families.* Boston, MA: Author.

Griffin, P., Lee, C., Waugh, J., & Beyer, C. (2005). Describing roles that gay-straight alliances play in schools: From individual support to school change. In J. T. Sears (Ed.), *Gay, lesbian, and transgender issues in education: Programs, policies, and practices* (pp. 167–183). Binghamton, NY: Harrington Park Press.

Griffin, P., & Ouellett, M. L. (2002). Going beyond gay-straight alliances to make schools safe for lesbian, gay, bisexual, and transgender students. *Angles, 6,* 1–8.

Harris Interactive & GLSEN. (2005). *From teasing to torment: School climate in America, a survey of students and teachers.* New York: GLSEN.

Hamilton College. (2001). *The Hamilton College gay issues poll.* Retrieved July 17, 2005, from http://www.hamilton.edu/news/gay issuespoll

Hershberger, S. L., & D'Augelli, A. R. (1995). The impact of victimization on the mental health and suicidality of lesbian, gay, and bisexual youths. *Developmental Psychology, 31,* 65–74.

Kosciw, J. G. (2004). *The 2003 national school climate survey: The school-related experiences of our nation's lesbian, gay, bisexual and transgender youth.* New York: GLSEN.

Kosciw, J. G. (2005, April). *Hostile school climate, academic achievement and educational aspirations in a national sample of LGBT youth.* Paper presented at the meeting of the American Educational Research Association, Montreal, QC, Canada.

Kosciw, J. G., & Diaz, E. M. (2006). *The 2005 national school climate survey: The experiences of lesbian, gay, bisexual and transgender youth in our nation's schools.* New York: GLSEN.

Lee, C. (2002). The impact of belonging to a high school gay/straight alliance. *The High School Journal, 85,* 13–26.

Mandel, L., & Shakeshaft, C. (2000). Heterosexism in middle schools. In N. Lesko (Ed.), *Masculinities at school* (pp. 75–103). Thousand Oaks, CA: Sage.

Massachusetts Department of Education. (n.d.). *Health, safety and student support services programs: The safe schools program for gay & lesbian students.* Retrieved July 9, 2005, from http://www.doe.mass.edu/hssss/program/ssch.html

Mathison, C. (1998). The invisible minority: Preparing teachers to meet the needs of gay and lesbian youth. *Journal of Teacher Education, 49,* 151–155.

McDaniel, J. S., Purcell, D., & D'Augelli, A. R. (2001). The relationship between sexual orientation and risk for suicide: Research findings and future directions for research and prevention. *Suicide and Life-Threatening Behavior, 31,* 84–105.

Minority Staff, House Government Reform Committee. (2004). *The content of federally funded abstinence-only education programs.*

Retrieved July 1, 2006, from www.democrats.reform.house.gov/Documents/20041201102153-50247.pdf

Morrow, R. G., & Gill, D. L. (2003). Perceptions of homophobia and heterosexism in physical education. *Research Quarterly for Exercise and Sport, 74,* 205–214.

Murdock, T. B., & Bolch, M. B. (2005). Risk and protective factors for poor school adjustment in lesbian, gay, and bisexual (LGB) high school youth: Variable and person-centered analyses. *Psychology in the Schools, 42,* 159–172.

National Education Association. (2002). *Report of the NEA task force on sexual orientation.* Retrieved November 1, 2005, from http://www.nea.org/nr/02taskforce.html

Pharr, S. (1988). *Homophobia, a weapon of sexism.* Inverness, CA: Chardon Press.

Plummer, C. W. (2001). The quest for modern manhood: masculine stereotypes, peer culture and the social significance of homophobia. *Journal of Adolescence, 24,* 15–23.

Rankin, S. R. (2003). *Campus climate for gay, lesbian, bisexual, and transgender people: A national perspective.* New York: The National Gay and Lesbian Task Force Policy Institute.

Reddy, R., Rhodes, J. E., & Mulhall, P. (2003). The influence of teacher support on student adjustment in the middle school years: A latent growth curve study. *Development and Psychopathology, 15,* 119–138.

Renn, K. A. (2000). Including all voices in the classroom: Teaching lesbian, gay, and bisexual students. *College Teaching, 48*(4), 129–135.

Robison, M. W. (1998). The residence hall: A home away from home. In R. L. Sanlo (Ed.), *Working with lesbian, gay, bisexual and transgender college students: A handbook for faculty and administrators* (pp. 53–66). Westport, CT: Greenwood Press.

Russell, S. T. (2003). Sexual minority youth and suicide risk. *American Behavioral Scientist, 46,* 1241–1257.

Russell, S. T., Franz, B. T., & Driscoll, A. K. (2001). Same-sex romantic attraction and experiences of violence in adolescence. *American Journal of Public Health, 91,* 903–906.

Russell, S. T., Seif, H., & Truong, N. L. (2001). School outcomes of sexual minority youth in the United States: evidence from a national study. *Journal of Adolescence, 24,* 111–127.

Ryan, R. M., Stiller, J. D., & Lynch, J. H. (1994). Representations of relationships to teachers, parents, and friends as predictors of academic motivation and self-esteem. *Journal of Early Adolescence, 14,* 226–249.

Santelli, J., Ott, M., Lyon, M., Rogers, J., Summers, D., & Schleifer, R. (2006). Abstinence and abstinence-only education: a review of U.S. policies and programs. *Journal of Adolescence Health, 3,* 72–81.

Sears, J. T. (1992). Educators, homosexuality, and homosexual students: Are personal feelings related to professional beliefs? In K. M. Harbeck (Ed.), *Coming out of the classroom closet: Gay and lesbian students, teachers, and curricula* (pp. 29–79). Binghamton, NY: The Haworth Press.

Sexuality Information and Education Council of the United States (SEICUS). (2004). *A portrait of sexuality education and abstinence-only-until-marriage programs in the states.* Retrieved July 1, 2006, from www.seicus.org/policy/states/index.html

Smith, M. U., & Drake, M. A. (2001). Suicide and homosexual teens: What can biology teachers do to help? *The American Biology Teacher, 63,* 154–162.

Smith, G. W., & Smith, D. E. (1998). The ideology of "fag": The school experience of gay students. *The Sociological Quarterly, 39,* 309–335.

Smith, M. U., & Drake, M. A. (2001). Suicide and homosexual teens: What can biology teachers do to help? *The American Biology Teacher, 63,* 154–162.

Snively, C. A. (2004). Building community-based alliances between GLBTQQA youth and adults in rural settings. *Journal of Gay and Lesbian Youth Services, 16,* 99–112.

Szalacha, L. A. (2003). Safer sexual diversity climates: Lessons learned from an evaluation of Massachusetts Safe Schools Program for Gay and Lesbian Students. *American Journal of Education, 110,* 58–88.

Telljohann, S. K., Price, J. H., Poureslami, M., & Easton, A. (1995). Teaching about sexual orientation by secondary health teachers. *The Journal of School Health, 65,* 18–22.

Uribe, V. (1995). Project 10: A school-based outreach to gay and lesbian youth. In G. Unks (Ed.), *The gay teen: Educational practice and theory for lesbian, gay, and bisexual adolescents* (pp. 203–210).

Waldo, C. R. (1998). Out on campus: Sexual orientation and academic climate in a university context. *American Journal of Community Psychology, 26,* 745–774.

Warwick, I., Aggleton, P., & Douglas, N. (2001). Playing it safe: Addressing the emotional and physical health of lesbian and gay pupils in the U. K. *Journal of Adolescence, 24,* 129–140.

Widmeyer & GLSEN. (2004). *New poll shows at least 5% of America's high school students identify as gay or lesbian.* Retrieved May 8, 2006, from http://www.glsen.org/cgi-bin/iowa/all/news/record/1724.html

·27·

GENDER EQUITY FOR GIFTED STUDENTS

Lynn H. Fox* and Janet Soller

INTRODUCTION

Discussions of gender equity for gifted students have typically centered on the following four issues:

- The nature and extent of sex/gender differences in abilities, achievements, and interests within gifted populations.
- Bias in the process of identification of gifted children that have implications for access to programs or resources.
- The differential impact of different program models for equity in educational outcomes.
- Barriers to adult achievements in terms of educational attainment, careers, and recognition for excellence.

In the 1985 *Handbook for Achieving Sex Equity through Education,* the chapter "Gifted Girls and Women in Education" by Barbara Gordon and Linda Addison concluded that the research studies showed the following gender differences in the areas just discussed:

- No differences in general intelligence but differences in favor of males on measures of achievement and abilities in mathematics and a slight advantage for females in some verbal skills areas.
- Higher participation rates for males than females in accelerative and enrichment programs for mathematics due to differences on screening test measures.
- Different patterns of enrollment in Advanced Placement (AP) courses with more males taking advanced courses in mathematics, computers, and most areas of science except biology.
- Higher levels of adult achievement for males than females in terms of educational attainment with males receiving more post baccalaureate degrees, especially in professional programs and science and technology fields.

This chapter surveys the literature since the publication of the 1985 *Handbook* to see what has changed in terms of the four issues and to identify new trends or issues in gifted education that have consequences in terms of gender equity. The chapter will begin with a brief overview of gifted education and gender in historical perspective followed by discussions of current practices in terms of identification and program models. This will be followed by a discussion of barriers that are still relevant to gifted male and female achievement as children and adults. The chapter concludes with some recommendations for policy, practice, and future research.

HISTORICAL PERSPECTIVES ON GIFTEDNESS AND GENDER

Since he launched his longitudinal studies of gifted children in 1921, Lewis Terman has been credited as the founder of the gifted child movement in the Untied States. Terman used the Stanford-Binet intelligence test and focused on the notion of "genius" as defined by an IQ score of 140 or higher. While this work did much to dispel negative and erroneous stereotypes of gifted people, it did not seek to create an educational model but simply studied the characteristics of gifted people. While significant sex differences were found in adult outcomes for those in the study in terms of careers and accomplishments, the sex differences in documented cognitive abilities were small (Terman & Oden, 1935; see also Subonik & Arnold, 1994).

In 1957, Sputnik sparked national interest in developing programs to educate the highly able, most notably those gifted in mathematics and science. The outcomes of these efforts were largely focused on creating curriculum and instituting some scholarship competitions. Although there were significant gaps then between boys and girls in terms of mathematics and science

---

*The boldface name is the Lead Author.

participation and achievement, this sex difference received little attention.

In 1972, Sidney Marland, the U.S. Commissioner of Education, submitted a report to Congress about the status of educating gifted and talented children. The definition for "gifted" that was proposed in this report can still be found in some state legislation today:

Gifted and talented children are those identified by professionally qualified persons who by virtue of outstanding abilities are capable of high performance. These children require differentiated educational programs and services beyond those normally provided by the regular school program in order to realize their contributions to self and society.

Children capable of high performance include those with demonstrated achievement and/or potential ability in any of the following areas: (a) general intellectual aptitude, (b) specific academic aptitude, (c) creative or productive thinking, (d) leadership ability, (e) visual and performing arts, (f) psychomotor ability. (Marland, 1972, p. 2).

The *Marland Report* further stated the minimum of the school population identified as gifted would be the top 3% to 5%. It also concluded that many experts considered the top 11% to 15% "talented." In 1978, the psychomotor ability, which covered physical sports, was dropped from the definition. The *Marland Report* did not address sex differences.

Concern for the underrepresentation of gifted girls in special programs began to emerge in the writings in the gifted-education literature around 1972. This was in part a result of the dramatic findings of sex differences in mathematical talent found by the Study of Mathematically Precocious Youth at Johns Hopkins University (Fox, 1976, 1977; Fox & Cohn, 1980; Stanley, Keating, & Fox, 1974). This came at a time when there was a great deal of attention being given to sex differences in general in cognition and educational attainments.

In 1993, the definition was updated as part of a reauthorization of the Jacob K. Javits Gifted and Talented Students Education Act of 1988. Also known by the title *National Excellence: A Case for Developing America's Talent*, it serves as the most current federal guideline about gifted individuals, but it is not mandated in any way as a "legal" definition.

Children and youth with outstanding talent perform or show the potential for performing at remarkable high levels of accomplishment when compared with others of their age, experience, or environment.

The term "gifted and talented" when used in respect to students, children, or youth means students, children or youth who give evidence of high performance capability in areas such as intellectual, creative, artistic, or leadership capacity, or in specific academic fields, and who require services or activities not ordinarily provided by the school in order to fully develop such capabilities.

Outstanding talents are present in children and youth from all cultural groups, across all economic strata, and in all areas of human endeavor.

Both the *Marland Report* and the Javits' bill offered a definition of giftedness based upon performance (or potential) in a specific ability area. The *Marland Report* was more specific because it requires the identification by "professionally qualified persons" and because it listed six abilities that should be developed. The

Javits' definition provided a more flexible approach to defining giftedness. Gifted is recognized because the child has performed (or has the potential of performing) when compared to three different criteria: (a) age—their peers; (b) experience— provided by the boundaries implied by their social economic background, or (c) environment— which implied implicit and explicit value systems of societal units including family, school, and governmental units.

Current thinking on the nature and extent of sex differences seems to be divided between those who see past differences as a result of social inequities that are no longer relevant (Gallagher, 2000; Tannenbaum, 2000) and those who continue to be concerned about differences in the treatment of gifted boys and girls in educational and career settings (Freeman, 2004; Kerr, 2000; Kerr & Foley Nicpon, 2002; Schober, Reimann, & Wagner, 2004). The former group would argue that the increases in women's participation in higher education in almost every field, and reductions in sex differences in participation rates in programs such as Advanced Placement (AP) courses are proof of the elimination of gender or sex bias (Gallagher, 2000). A slight variation of this theme is the one in which any sex differences in performance or attitudes are assumed to be the inevitable result of biological differences between the sexes and not bias (Benbow & Stanley, 1983).

Those who remain concerned about gender bias see the possibilities of stereotypic views of gender-appropriate behavior as lingering and impacting gifted boys as well as gifted girls, although sometimes in different ways or differently within different contexts (Kerr & Cohn, 2001; Kerr & Foley Nicpon; 2002; Noble, Subnotik, & Arnold, 1999). This latter view will be explored in this chapter. The chapter will examine evidence of gender-related differences in the ways gifted individuals are identified and served by various program models.

DEFINING AND IDENTIFYING GIFTEDNESS

Over the past 20 years, three trends emerged that greatly impacted the education of gifted students. First, in terms of the definition of giftedness, there has been a shift away from the focus on "global intelligence" or "general intelligence" to a concept of giftedness that seeks to identify manifest or potential talent in a variety of specific subject-matter domains such as performing arts, visual arts, mathematic, leadership, and so forth (Reis, 1998; Reis & Callahan, 1989; Sternberg, 1986, 2000; Tannenbaum, 2000). A second related trend in the gifted-education field is the movement away from using standardized tests for identification and the advocacy of a variety of alternative strategies for identification, particularly informal indicators and self-report measures (Gallagher, 2000; Gardner, 1983; Renzulli, 2002). The third trend has been the advocacy of differentiating instruction within the regular classroom at the discretion of the teacher as an alternative to special programs for gifted students (Tomlinson, 1995, 1996). This latter approach does not require a formal process of screening and identification in a public manner, as was done in more traditional approaches to programs for the gifted, and relies solely on teacher judgment.

A survey of states in 1990 and 1998 found that most states use some form of the multiple talent and potential definition of giftedness suggested in federal legislative language but do not specify how this is to be measured (Stephens & Karnes, 2000). Empirical work on talent identification and related gender differences exists primarily for only two areas of special talent: mathematical and verbal abilities.

Identification of Specific Talents

Mathematical Talent

Recent National Assessment of Educational Progress (NAEP) (National Center for Education Statistics, 2003) data suggest that the achievement gap between boys and girls in mathematics is narrowing, particularly at the fourth- and eighth-grade levels. According to data from the National Center for Education Statistics (2003), average NAEP scores for math among fourth-grade boys and girls were virtually the same (233 for girls and 236 for boys). Similarly, among eighth-grade boys and girls, the average NAEP math scores were nearly identical (277 for girls and 278 for boys). Despite these generally promising results, other indicators of giftedness in mathematics continue to suggest gender differences. Hedges and Nowell (1995) analyzed test scores from six meta-analyses that spanned 35 years of data using large national samples and found huge differences within the top 10 % of the populations. Most marked are the differences found in studies of the very gifted identified through talent-search competitions.

Talent searches and competitions typically use some type of standardized test performance for identification. One of the best known and systematically researched is the series of talent searches run by universities that evolved from the Study of Mathematically Precocious Youth (SMPY) started at Johns Hopkins (Stanley, 1988; 1991; Stanley et al., 1974). This early effort to identify precocious youth, which relied on the use of the Scholastic Aptitude Test (SAT), found far more boys than girls. Indeed, through the years the ratio of high-scoring boys to girls on the mathematics part of the SAT was anywhere from to 2 to 1 to 12 to 1 depending what score was used as the cut off (Benbow, Lubinski, Shea, & Eftekhari-Sanjani, 2000; Fox & Cohn, 1980; Stanley, 1988). Furthermore, as gifted and motivated students choose to pursue graduate-level education, scores on the Graduate Record Examination (GRE) demonstrated a further increased difference in higher math scores for males (Halperin, Wai, & Saw, 2005).

Some have argued that there is an inherent genetic basis for gender differences in mathematical ability (Byrnes, 2005) while others have argued for the cultural-socialization explanation. Two studies suggested the cultural basis of gender differences among the mathematically gifted. Takihira (1995) found no gender differences on SAT I Math-type problems for gifted Japanese students. Byrnes, Hong, and Xing (1997) found no difference in mathematics performance on SAT I Math-type prob-

lems among Chinese students using samples of gifted and average. The difference between U.S. males and Chinese females in favor of the females was greater than the difference favoring the U.S. males over U.S. females.

Studies of boys and girls who are clearly talented in mathematics as measured by test performance at age 13 continue to find other differences between males and females in terms of college majors and career outcomes. In over 25 years of study, consistent differences in educational behaviors and attitudes have been found for those who were identified as mathematically gifted; girls were less likely than boys to:

- Accelerate their study of mathematics (Fox & Brody, 1980; Fox, Brody, & Tobin, 1984–85; Kolitch & Brody, 1992).
- Aspire to careers in science or technology (Benbow & Lubinski, 1994; Eccles & Harold, 1992).
- Express confidence with respect to their abilities in mathematics (Eccles & Harold, 1992; Fox, 1981; Fox, Engle, & Paek, 2001; Walters & Brown, 2005).

Some researchers have argued that the consistent performance gap on the "SAT in favor of males is less meaningful then supposed because of evidence showing that the SAT underpredicts female achievement in coursework in college, even at top-tier universities like MIT (Chipman, 2005). In addition, the gender gap in numbers of students majoring in mathematics in college has disappeared although large differences remain in computer science, physical sciences, and engineering (Astin, 1993: Halperin et al., 2005). For a more detailed discussion of gender differences and specifically mathematics and related issues in science and technology see chapters 2, 12, and 13 of this volume.

Verbal Talent

Verbal ability is not as clearly defined as mathematical talent (Fox & Durden, 1982). Verbal ability is sometimes considered reading ability, especially in the early grades and preschool years. Writing ability becomes part of the focus of interest for high-school students and adults. Gender differences on measures of verbal ability are few and slightly favor girls (Hyde & Linn, 1988; Olszewski-Kubilius & Whalen, 2000; Stanley, Benbow, Brody, Dauer, & Lupkowski, 1992). Girls tend to outperform boys in the preschool and elementary years on reading tests (Jackson, 1988, 1992) or in terms of becoming early readers.[1] By high school and beyond, results are mixed with females having moderately better scores on college-board achievement tests in French and English composition and moderate score differences in favor of males on tests in biology, American history and European history (Stumpf & Stanley, 1996). Males and females perform about the same on verbal measures such as those used for college or graduate-school admissions such as the Graduate Record Exam, Law School Admissions

---

[1]Not all early readers are gifted, but most gofted girls are early readers (Jackson, 1988, 1992).

test and Graduate Management Admissions Test (Olszewski-Kubilius & Whalen, 2000; Stanley et al., 1992). For a more in-depth discussion of verbal abilities and gender, see chapter 14 of this volume.

Alternatives to Standardized Tests

Some evidence suggests that efforts to move away from standardized testing may increase the possibilities for gender inequities. Older methods using intelligence tests tended to identify almost equal numbers of males and females if there were no bias in the referral system for being screened for giftedness (Crombie, Bouffard-Bouchard, & Schnieder, 1992). However, recent findings about gender and ethnicity further suggest test assessment alone may prohibit access to gifted students. For example, more than other females, Latina American students perceive they are uninterested in and poor achievers in mathematics; and hence, perform poorly on math test items. This performance is due to "stereotype threats" (Steele & Arronson, 1995) and "unjustified fear threats" (Cohen & Ibarra, 2005). Combined test anxieties for minority girls put girls at double risk for test only gifted identification.

Newer strategies often involve some type of teacher, parent, or self-identification or nomination and may result in more boys than girls being referred for programs or for participation to be impacted by perceptions of "gender appropriateness" of activities. However, newer strategies may put gifted girls at risk for admittance unknowingly by the girls' adult support systems. For example, girls may be less likely than boys to get parental encouragement for gifted programs in mathematics and science because some parents underestimate the abilities of their gifted daughters while they overestimate the abilities of their gifted sons (Jacobs & Eccles, 1992). Parental support may be an important factor in choices that students make in terms of participation in gifted programs. In one study of very gifted girls, those who were most likely to persist in accelerated mathematics and science programs were those who felt they had strong encouragement from both parents (Montgomery & Benbow, 1992). Parental influences have also been shown to impact gifted students' selection of science or mathematics courses in summer enrichment programs (Olszewski-Kubilius & Yasmoto, 1993). Teachers tend to refer more boys than girls for the highest levels of mathematics when ability grouping is used (Hallinan & Sorenson, 1987).

Even when traditional intelligence tests are used in screening and identifying, the process by which students are nominated for screening may be susceptible to gender-related bias. In a study of referrals for gifted programs in Canada, Daignault, Edwards, Pohlman, and McCabe (1990) found evidence of gender bias at two different stages of the referral process. First, almost twice as many boys as girls in the elementary-school grades were referred for screening by the school due to differences in teacher nominations. Once tested, of those who had borderline scores slightly below the cut off of 130 on the WISC-R, a larger percentage of males than females were admitted to the program.

The use of the Multiple Intelligences model of screening for talent and related alternative approaches to identification have been proposed, often in an attempt to find more "culturally fair" identification methods to increase the participation of underrepresented ethnic groups (Sarouphim, 2004). These instruments have received too little empirical scrutiny, especially in terms of gender fairness. If self-report by students were used on checklist, one would suspect some underreporting by girls of their talents, especially in mathematics. A study by Furnham, Wytykowska, and Petrides (2005) did find sex differences in self-report on the multiple intelligences evaluation forms but noted some cultural variation by nationality. In both Poland and Great Britain, boys rated themselves higher than girls in terms of spatial ability, but in Poland, other areas showed fewer differences between the sexes whereas the British sample showed marked differences with male rating themselves higher than females on verbal, mathematical, musical, and bodily-kinesthetic abilities.

Within Class Identification for Differentiated Instruction

The current educational climate seems to be more focused on underachievement as a result of the "No Child Left Behind" legislation by governments than on the gifted. The law offers no incentives for states to focus on "above proficient" achievers. By the early 1990s, programs for gifted seem to have declined significantly (George, 1993) and according to a report called *National Excellence: A Case for Developing America's Talent* (Ross, 1993) in terms of achievement, gifted and talented students in the United States performed poorly in terms of both national criteria and in terms of international student achievement. It is somewhat difficult to know how many children are served by programs, because there is no national reporting of participation or progress for the gifted. Only four states report that they track achievement outcomes for the gifted (Swanson, 2002).[2] Although a recent survey of the states found 32 reported mandating identification of the gifted, only 16 states actually mandated programs for them (Swanson).

One thing that is being advocated for all students is the greater use of differentiated instruction within the regular classroom by teachers in order to meet the needs of a range of abilities (Tomlinson & McTighe, 2006). Little is known about the impact of "differentiated instruction" on the identification of gifted boys and girls, since it does not necessarily result in any public acknowledgement of giftedness. While the model does indeed suggest the need to move some students through the curriculum at a faster pace or deeper level, Tomlinson (1995, 1996), an advocate overall for this approach, has acknowledged the strong possibility that differentiation is more often used for "at-risk" students rather than for the purpose of accommodating the needs of gifted students.

---

[2]They are Idaho, Kentucky, North Carolina, and Washington.

MODELS AND METHODS OF EDUCATIONAL PRACTICE FOR THE GIFTED

Although there should be roughly equal numbers of gifted boys and girls in gifted programs, a national survey in 1985–86 reported more girls overall enrolled in gifted programs, especially in the elementary-school grades. In high school there was a reversal; more boys were enrolled in programs than girls (Read, 1991). The study did not fully analyze the differences in the types of programs that were included in the survey, and did not include informal ways that gifted students might advance through grade-skipping or early admission to kindergarten. Research is scant on gender differences in participation rates for various types of programmatic models or administrative adjustments for the gifted. The following section details what is thought to be the variations in impact of program models from selected studies not conducted on a national scale.

Acceleration Opportunities

Early admission to school. Despite the evidence of the benefits of such acceleration for gifted students, the practice of early admission is rare. Studies of early identification for kindergarten or first grade have typically found more girls than boys who exhibit early readiness (Robinson & Weimer, 1991). One common practice, which is the opposite of early admission, is the practice of holding children back from starting kindergarten in order to give them a later advantage in team sports (Brent, May, & Kundert, 1996). This practice, sometimes called "redshirting," is far more likely to be invoked by parents of boys than parents of girls and does a real disservice for gifted boys who may be terribly bored by the slow pace of schooling and become "underachievers" in middle and high school (DeMeis & Stearns, 1992; Gullo & Burton, 1992).

Grade skipping. Grade skipping as a practice is rare and no evidence exists of differences in access or consequences for boys and girls. An extensive review by Koltich and Brody (1992) of all types of acceleration methods for gifted students discussed sex/gender outcomes for studies that reported them. In most cases, they found no differences in effectiveness for boys and girls. However, they did find some subtle differences in who takes advantage of options or is more often encouraged to accelerate. They also found that among the mathematically gifted of similar ability, boys were more likely to accelerate or accelerate to a greater extent than girls with similar talent. This is consistent with much older studies that found boys to be more likely to accelerate their study of mathematics, even when matched with girls on measures of mathematical aptitude (Fox & Brody, 1980; Fox & Tobin, 1988).

Advanced placement courses. In terms of high-school populations, participation and performance in Advanced Placement (AP) courses and exams are often used as the most striking and consistent indicator of gender differences among the gifted. While the size of the differences has decreased over time, there is still a gap in terms of more boys than girls taking AP examinations for chemistry, and all levels of calculus, physics, and computer science; whereas more girls are taking exams in advanced placement biology and statistics (College Board, 2005). The average scores for males were higher in all areas including biology (except for computer science, AB level, where the scores were almost equal). At the high-school level AP may be the only type of "formal" gifted program available in a school system. Of course, some students who participate in AP courses may not have been designated as "gifted" in their schools.

Radical acceleration leading to early college entrance. Radical acceleration is rare. Only a few formal programs support this and these tend to have greater male participation (Olszewski-Kubilius, 1995). One highly successfully exception is the single-sex PEG Program at Mary Baldwin College, a liberal arts college for women in Virginia. PEG (Program for the Exceptionally Gifted), which began by accepting 11 high-school age girls in 1985. The students live on campus and attend college. In 2005 with over 70 radically accelerated early college entrance women students, PEG reported that its students plan to continue their education at the nation's top medical, law, and graduate schools such as Northwestern, Columbia, and Johns Hopkins.

Enrichment. Relatively little is known about the impact of participation in enrichment programs for gifted students in general and almost nothing is known about differential outcomes by gender except in terms of gender-equity intervention programs that targeted participation in mathematics and science enrichment programs or career-awareness programs for girls. The Lake Tahoe Watershed Project, a summer enrichment program for high-achieving girls in which students work with female scientists and female teachers on projects related to environmental science in the Lake Tahoe area, found participation increased self-confidence in math and science and helped girls gain insight into the practical applications of math and science (Rohrer, 1997). Smith and Erb (1986) found that exposing middle-school students to women science career role models had a positive effect on both girls' and boys' attitudes toward women in science.

TARGETS, a NSF 1994 intervention program reaching 502 talented math and science at-risk female students, ages 11–20 had specific success (Kerr & Kurpius, 2004).

Defined by unsafe behaviors, risks of dropping out, low self-esteem, or lack of family support, girls participated in a specific intervention program based on developing their identity in the subject area and leadership skills. The girls were also supported by mentors and given guidance. The program resulted in 75% of the girls employed in careers. Almost 33% of the program participants pursued nontraditional careers in math and science.

Within Class Differentiation

Many school systems have eliminated gifted programs in favor of asking teachers to differentiate instruction within the regular classroom to accommodate a wide range of achievement levels and learning styles. Teachers are expected to prepare lessons that can be expanded to challenge the more advanced students while allowing the teacher ample opportunities to work with small groups of students at their level (Tomlinson & McTighe, 2006). Therefore, this becomes a form of grouping within the class that may shift group members daily depending on the lesson plans and the teacher's assessment of students' levels of achievement relative to the particular concept or skill. Few discussions of differentiation really address gender as a factor in thinking about instructional strategies (Tomlinson, 1995, 1996). One serious concern is that teachers will not recognize giftedness in a student, especially a quiet gifted girl. Feldhusen, J. F. and Willard-Holt, C. (1993) found that gifted boys were aware of teacher bias against gifted girls while the girls did not report awareness of the discrimination.

Of course, student outcomes may depend on the type of differentiation that is employed. Flores (1991) found that in a geometry course emphasizing the application of the material to real-life situations, girls' test performance increased and, on some measures, girls actually outperformed boys. In the traditional lecture-based control group classes, however, a gender gap remained favoring the boys. Since differentiated instruction does not require any formal identification of gifted students or special tracking of their progress, it is impossible to understand how gifted students are served or not served by this approach.

Sex Segregation for the Gifted

Some have speculated that single-sex schools or classes might be beneficial for gifted students, especially girls. Several older studies have suggested the possible power of an all-girl class in mathematics for the gifted (Fox 1976, 1977; Fox, Brody & Tobin 1984, 1985). More recently, Subotnik and Strauss (1995) found higher achievement on the BC level Calculus Advanced Placement Exam for girls in a single-sex high school as compared with girls in a coed school. It is difficult to evaluate the impact of all-girl or all-boy classes on the gifted. A discussion of the problems of interpreting single-sex research is presented in chapter 9 of this volume.

UNDERSTANDING THE BARRIERS TO THE FULFILLMENT OF PROMISE

Underacheivement is a difficult concept within gifted literature. Some approaches to the identification of the gifted focus only on manifested achievement and thus would not address the possibility of potential unrealized. Underachievement in gifted education is often described as the situation where high potential is assumed based on some measure of general intellectual ability but achievement is considered average or below (Clark, 2002) Some discussions of gifted females have focused on the concept of underachieverment in terms of adult career outcomes, which show huge differences in favor of males. Most discussions of underachievement in elementary and secondary schools focus on a discrepancy between grades and ability or dropout rates.

Underachievement in the School-Age Years

It is difficult to assess the incidence of underachievement among the gifted. It has been suggested that many students who are performing in the average range in the classroom are gifted underachievers who go unnoticed by teachers (Gallagher, 1985). Experts in the field of gifted education have suggested that between 15% and 40% of the gifted function at levels below what is expected in terms of their potential (Seely, 1993). Most studies suggested that the incidence of underachievement is higher for boys than girls (Clark, 2002; Colangelo, Kerr, Christensen, & Maxey, 1993) and one older study reported that in a program designed for underachieving gifted, 90% of those referred were male (Whitmore, 1980). Estimates of the percentages of gifted students who become school dropouts range between 18% and 25% (Robertson, 1991). Although Wolfe (1991) argued that underachievement in high school among the gifted is more of an issue for boys than girls, there is still the data suggesting a decline in girls in high school who participate in gifted programs, especially AP courses. Most educators would agree that significant numbers of gifted males and females succumb to either peer pressure against achievement or suffer from low levels of academic motivation in the high-school years (Redding, 1990).

Achievement, Eminence, and Creativity in Adulthood

Many early studies of gifted focused on eminent adults as measured by career outcomes and/or highest levels of educational attainments. Clearly the longitudinal studies of gifted students pioneered by Terman found huge sex differences in career outcomes in favor of males (Terman & Oden, 1935; see also Subotnik & Arnold, 1994, 1996). Women in Terman's study achieved as well or better than men in school, yet few had careers outside the home due to lack of opportunities or motivation (Subotnik & Arnold, 1994). More recent studies report few differences in educational attainments between gifted men and women, largely in terms of areas of study, but continue to find discrepancies in terms of career outcomes and recognition for eminence or creativity favoring men (Arnold, 1993, 1995; Kirschenbaum & Reis, 1997; List & Renzulli, 1991; Piirto, 1991; Reis, 1998, 2002; Subotnik & Arnold, 1996).

Arnold's study of high-school valedictorians, for example, showed not only higher levels of achievement in terms of pursuit of education and careers for the males as compared with their female counterparts, but also showed a decline in self-confidence for these very bright women that seemed to begin during the college years (Arnold, 1993, 1995). Piirto (1991) summarized the research on sex differences favoring males among artists, musicians, and mathematicians, particularly in terms of recognition for creativity. Female art students seemed very similar to males on many measures but lacked self-confidence and intensity of commitment to a career, some choosing to teach rather than face the challenges of being a "professional artist."

Many researchers have argued that the failure of gifted women to achieve is a result of women's dual priority of career and family relationships, while others have argued that different patterns of interests and values explain most of the differences in career outcomes (Arnold, 1993; Kerr, 1994; Lubinski, Benbow, & Morelock, 2000). Piirto (1991) suggested that the necessity to achieve early and to continue producing in creative endeavors is a problem for women who choose to have families and thus are not able to be as single-minded in the pursuit of their career. Another suggestion has been to do more in the way of career counseling for gifted girls and to provide more role models and mentors to help gifted girls and women understand their choices and opportunities (Fox, Engle, & Soller, 1999; Fox, Sadker, & Engle, 1999; Fox & Soller, 1999; Kerr, 2000; Fox & Tobin, 1988; Fox & Zimmerman, 1985).

Clues to gender differences in creative achievement and eminence are suggested in the hundreds of interviews with gifted women conducted by Reis (1998, 2002, 2003). Gifted creative women learn throughout their adult lives to balance work, family, and personal pursuits while dispersing their creative abilities thorough multiple outlets created by the various roles they play. Men tend to define an end goal and move persistently to complete that goal (Reis, 2002). Others who study lives of creative, gifted women cite both internal and external barriers but particularly the fact that childbearing occurs during peak production years as reasons for differences in productivity between creative male and female artists (Piirto, 1991; List & Renzulli, 1991). In the study of valedictorians, Arnold (1993; 1995) found that in their senior year of college, two thirds of the women valedictorians planned to reduce or interrupt their labor-force participation due to child-rearing responsibilities.

It is also true that interests and values do differ among the gifted. One study of the personalities of mathematically gifted youth found more similarities than differences between girls and boys (Benbow & Lubinski, 1994), but notable differences were found on measures of career interests and related values. Even though both males and females scored high on measures of interest in investigative careers and theoretical values, gifted girls, much more often than boys, had equally strong, competing interests and values, particularly social and artistic ones, that vie with their interest in investigative careers while males tended to have no other category of interest and values of equal strength. Presumably, individual interests and values are shaped by the values of the larger society. Freeman (2004) argued that socialization accounts for most if not all of the outcome differences as evidenced by the fact that gender gaps in outcomes vary from country to country in size and direction.

Not all experts in gifted education feel that all gifted males have an advantage over gifted females. Some argue that societal pressures for "gender-appropriate conformity" may result in gifted men faring better in the workplace in terms of prestige and money, but at a terrible price in terms of happiness or fulfillment. While gifted women may value careers that allow them to help others and do something worthwhile for society, men place more value on careers that allow them to gain prestige or earn a good salary (Jozefowicz, Barber, & Eccles, 1993). The real tragedy for some gifted men may be that they eschew work that they might truly love in the humanities, creative arts, or social-service areas and choose careers in engineering, computer science, or business because they are deemed more masculine appropriate (Colangelo & Kerr, 1991).

CONCLUSION AND RECOMMENDATIONS

Discussions of gifted education and gender must consider the issue of possible gender biases in educational settings in terms of their implications for educational practice and in terms of the complex issues of adult career and lifestyle outcomes. Clearly gifted men and women have different rates and levels of achievements at the highest levels in almost any intellectual, commercial, artistic, and athletic endeavor. These differences cannot be attributed to innate sex differences in abilities. More often, these differences in outcomes are attributed to differences in motivation, commitment, or self-confidence and subtle barriers to access. Although the study of the lives of bright and talented individuals continues to be of interest to society, there is no research to suggest ways to increase the numbers of women among the eminent except by the creation of an overall gender-fair climate at all levels of society. Thus, issues of childcare, flexible work schedules, and role models and mentors are critical for the gifted woman and may have an impact on the career choices and life satisfaction of gifted men as well.

In terms of specific educational programs and interventions, the greatest threat to gifted students may result from the lack of attention to special programs of any kind in the current educational climate in the United States. The decline of programs has resulted in less information about the educational experiences and outcomes for these students. Also, many gifted educators assume that gender inequity is a thing of the past and fail to monitor for sex differences in participation rates or achievement outcomes in gifted programs. While there are some indicators that suggest some lessoning of the achievement gaps in favor of males, overall the climate for gifted students (male or female) is viewed as less than ideal. Thus, recommendations to improve the educational experiences of gifted students in terms of policy and practice are as follows:

1. Implement more programs for the gifted and talented at every educational level.
2. Use research and examples of programs that work to develop policy that ensures programs that are gender fair.
3. Use research and examples of programs that work to develop policy ensuring equitable admissions for all with specific rubrics to evaluate access for girls and minorities or other culturally at-risk groups.
4. Use research and examples of programs that work to develop programs focusing on counseling and career education, especially for girls and minorities in gifted programs.
5. If within-class differentiation is used, provide better training for teachers in ways to work with gifted students, and track the results.

Research is still needed to address many equity issues in gifted education. While there is increased awareness of the need to identify and work with gifted students from all ethnic and socio-economic levels, there is little data collection and analysis provided by sex or by sex within ethnic groups. Thus, we know far too little about the participation and achievements of gifted students. The only consistent benchmark available is the participation in AP testing programs.

The following are some of the research questions that should be addressed:

1. What are the actual numbers of children being served by various programs for the gifted across the country broken down by sex and ethnicity and type of school and content focus?
2. What are the barriers to gifted students' participation in programs such as AP in the high-school years?
3. How extensive is underachievement among gifted boys and girls and what program models have been most effective in eliminating this problem?
4. What are the experiences at the college level that enhance effective decision making for gifted students in terms of advanced degrees and career choices?
5. How are gifted and talented boys and girls using technology in ways that foster their talents and is it the same or different by sex?
6. Do gifted students perform better in single-sex or coed environments when accelerating their knowledge in specified content areas?
7. What types of assistance do gifted men and women need in terms of childcare and flexible work schedules in order to promote career success and life satisfaction?

An examination of the state of gifted education and gender equity now finds few major changes from the results described in the *Handbook in* 1985. There appear to be subtle differences in the ways males and females are identified for programs and participation rates in gifted programs. Selection into gifted programs now appears higher for females in the early years but begins to decline in the secondary-school years. Underachievement is a problem for gifted boys and men as well as girls and women. Some evidence suggests that problems gifted boys and girls face starting in the teenage years are linked to societal expectations about gender role appropriate behaviors and interests. However, perhaps the most pressing problem facing gifted education is the need to recognize that not all gifted students will make it on their own—and that grappling with gender identity and achievement goals is a huge issue for the gifted child and adult.

ACKNOWLEDGMENTS

Reviewed by Karen Arnold, Boston College, Boston, MA, and Michael Pyryt, University of Calgary, Calgary, Canada

References

Arnold, K. (1993). Undergraduate aspirations and career outcomes of academically talented women. *Roeper Review, 15*(3), 169–74.

Arnold, K. (1995). *Lives of promise.* San Francisco: Jossey-Bass Publishers.

Astin, A. W. (1993). *What matters in college? Four critical years revisited.* San Francisco: Jossey-Bass.

Benbow, C. P., & Lubinski, D. (1994). Individual differences amongst the mathematically gifted: Their educational and vocational implications. In N. Coangelo, S. G. Assouline, & D. L. Ambroson (Eds.), *Talent development: Proceedings from the 1993 Henry B. and Jocelyn Wallace National Research Symposium on Talent Development* (pp. 83–100). Dayton, OH: Ohio Psychology Press.

Benbow, C. P., Lubinski, D., Shea, D. L., & Eftekhari-Sanjani, H. (2000). Se differences in mathematical reasoning ability at age 13: Their status 20 years later. *Psychological Science, 11*(6), 474–480.

Benbow, C. P., & Stanley, J. C. (1983). Sex differences in mathematical reasoning ability: More facts; *Science, 210*, 1262–1264.

Brent, D., May, D. C., & Kundert, D. K. (1996). The incidence of delayed school entry: A twelve year review. *Early Education and Development, 7*, 1122–1135.

Byrnes, J. P. (2005). Gender differences in math: Cognitive processes in an expanded framework. In A. M. Gallagher & J. C. Kaufman (Eds.), *Gender differences in mathematics* (pp. 73–98). Cambridge: Cambridge University Press.

Byrnes, J. P., Hong, L., & Xing, S. (1997). Gender differences on the math subtest of the Scholastic Aptitude Test may be culture-specific. *Educational Studies in Mathematics, 34*, 49–66.

Chipman, S. F. (2005). Research on the women & mathematics issue: A personal case history. In A. M. Gallagher & J. C. Kaufman (Eds.), *Gender differences in mathematics* (pp. 1–24). Cambridge: Cambridge University Press.

Clark, B. (2002*). Growing up gifted* (6th ed.). Upper Saddle River, NJ: Merrill Prentice Hall.

Cohen, A. S., & Ibarra, R. A. (2005). Examining gender-related differential item functioning using insights from psychometric & multicontext theory. In A. M. Gallagher & J. C. Kaufman (Eds.), *Gender differences in mathematics* (pp. 143–171). Cambridge: Cambridge University Press.

Colangelo, N., & Kerr, B. A. (1991). Extreme academic talent: Profiles of perfect scorers. *Journal of Educational Psychology, 82*, 404–410.

Colangelo, N., Kerr, B., Christensen, P., & Maxey, J. (1993). A comparison of gifted underachievers and gifted high achievers. *Gifted Child Quarterly, 37*, 155–160.

College Board. (2005). *Advanced placement summary reports: 2005.* Retrieved August 7, 2006, from ttp://www.collegeboard.com/students/testing/ap/exgrd_sum/2005.html

Crombie, G., Bouffard-Bouchard, T., & Schneider, B. H. (1992). Gifted programs: Gender differences in referral and enrollment. *Gifted Child Quarterly, 36*(4), 213–214.

Daignault, M., & Edwards, A., Pohlman, C., & McCabe, A. (1990). Selection for giftedness programs: Why the gender imbalance? In J. L. Ellis & J.M. Willinsky (Eds.), *Girls, women and giftedness* (pp. 61–64). New York: Trillium Press.

DeMeis, J. L., & Stearns, E. S. (1992). Relationship of school entrance age to academic and social performance. *Journal of Educational Research, 86*, 20–27.

Eccles, J. S., & Harold, R. D. (1992). Gender differences in educational and occupational patterns among the gifted. In N. Coangelo, S. G. Assouline, & D. L. Ambroson (Eds.), *Talent development: Proceedings from the 1991 Henry B. and Jocelyn Wallace National Research Symposium on Talent Development* (pp. 2–30). Unionville, NY: Trillium Press.

Feldhusen, J. F., & Willard-Holt, C. (1993). Gender differences in classroom interactions and career aspirations of gifted students. *Contemporary Educational Psychology, 18*, 355–362.

Flores, P. V. (1990, April 16-20). *How Dick and Jane perform differently in geometry: Test results on reasoning, visualization, trans-*

formation, applications, and coordinates. Paper presented at the Annual Meeting of the American Educational Research Association, Boston, MA.

Fox, L. H. (1976). Sex differences in mathematical talent: Bridging the gap. In D. P. Keating (Ed.), *Intellectual talent: Research and development* (pp. 183–214). Baltimore, MD : The Johns Hopkins University Press.

Fox, L. H. (1977). Sex differences: Implications for program planning for the academically gifted. In J. C. Stanley, W. C. George, & C. H. Solano (Eds.), *The gifted and the creative: A fifty-year perspective* (pp. 113–138). Baltimore, MD: The Johns Hopkins University Press.

Fox, L. H. (1981). *The problem of women and mathematics*. New York: The Ford Foundation.

Fox, L. H., & Brody, L. (1980). An accelerative intervention program for mathematically gifted girls. In L. H. Fox, L. Brody, & D. Tobin (Eds.), *Women and the mathematical mystique* (pp. 164–78). Baltimore, MD: The Johns Hopkins University Press.

Fox, L. H., Brody, L., & Tobin, D. (1984–5). The impact of intervention programs upon course-taking and attitudes in high school. In S. F. Chipman, L. R. Brush, & D. M. Wilson (Eds.), *Women and mathematics: Balancing the equation* (pp. 249–274). Hillsdale, NJ: Lawrence Erlbaum Associates, Inc.

Fox, L. H., & Cohn, S. (1980). Sex differences in the development of precocious mathematical talent. In L. H. Fox, L. Brody, & D. Tobin (Eds.), *Women and the mathematical mystique* (pp. 94–111). Baltimore, MD: The Johns Hopkins University Press.

Fox, L. H., & Durden, W. G. (1982). *Educating verbally gifted youth*. Bloomington, IN: Phi Delta Kappa Educational Foundation.

Fox, L. H., Engle, J., & Paek, P. (2001) An exploratory look at social factors and mathematics achievement among high-scoring students: Cross-cultural perspectives from TIMSS. *Gifted and Talented International, 16*(1), 7–15.

Fox, L. H., Engle, J., & Soller, J. (1999) Gifted girls and the math/science mystique. *Understanding Our Gifted, 11*(2), 3–7.

Fox, L. H., Sadker, D. L., & Engle, J. L. (1999). Sexism in the schools: Implications for the education of gifted girls. *Gifted and Talented International, 14*(2), 66–79.

Fox, L. H., & Soller, J. (1999). Mathematically gifted girls: Bridging the gender gap. *Gifted Education Press Quarterly, 13*(1), 2–7.

Fox, L. H., & Tobin, D. (1988). Broadening career horizons of gifted girls. *G/C/T, 11*(1), 9–13.

Fox, L. H., & Zimmerman, W. (1985). Gifted women. In J. Freeman (Ed.), *The psychology of gifted children* (pp. 219–43). London: Wiley & Sons.

Freeman J. (2004). Cultural influences on gifted gender achievement. *High Ability Studies, 15*(1), 7–23.

Furnham, A., Wytykowska, A., & Petrides, K. V. (2005). Estimates of multiple intelligences: A study in Poland. *European Psychologist, 10*(1), 51–59.

Gallagher, J. (1985). *Teaching the gifted child* (3rd ed.). Boston: Allyn and Bacon. Gallagher, J. J. (2000). Changing paradigms for gifted education in the United States. In K. A. Heller, F. J. Monks, R. J. Sternberg, & R. F. Subotnik (Eds.), *International handbook of giftedness and talent* (2nd ed., pp. 681–694). Oxford, U.K.: Elsevier Science Ltd.

Gardner, H. (1983). *Frames of mind: The theory of multiple intelligences*. New York: Basic Books.

George, D. (1993). Instructional strategies and models for gifted education. In K. A. Heller, F. J. Monks, & A. H. Passow (Eds.), *International handbook of giftedness and talent* (pp. 411–426). Oxford, U.K.: Pergamon Press Ltd.

Gullo, D. F., & Burton, C. B. (1992). Age of entry, preschool experience and sex as antecedents of academic readiness in kindergarten. *Early Childhood Research Quarterly, 7*, 175–186.

Hallinan, M. T., & Sorenson, A. B. (1987). Ability grouping and sex differences in mathematics achievement. *Sociology of Education, 60*, 63–72.

Halpern, D. F., Wai, J., & Saw, A. (2005). A psychobiosocial model: Why females are sometimes greater than and sometimes less than males in math achievement. In A. M. Gallagher & J. C. Kaufman (Eds.), *Gender differences in mathematics* (pp. 25–47). Cambridge: Cambridge University Press .

Hedges, L. V., & Nowell, A. (1995). Sex differences in mental test scores, variability and numbers of high-scoring individuals. *Science, 269*, 41–45.

Hyde, J. S., & Linn, M. C. (1988). Gender differences in verbal ability: A meta-analysis. *Psychological Bulletin, 104*(1), 53–69.

Jackson, N. (1988) Precocious reading ability: What does it mean? *Gifted Child Quarterly, 32*(1), 200–204.

Jackson, N. (1992). Understanding giftedness in young children, lessons from the study of precocious readers. In N. Colangelo, S. G. Assouline, & D. L. Ambrosen (Eds.), *Talent development: Proceedings from the 1991 Henry B. and Jocelyn Wallace National Research Symposium* (pp. 163–179). Unionville, NY: Trillium Press.

Jacobs, J. E., & Eccles, J. S. (1992). The influence of parent stereotypes on parent and child ability beliefs in three domains. *Journal of Personality and Social Psychology, 63*, 932–944.

Jozefowicz, D. M., Barber, B. L., & Eccles, J. S. (1993). *Adolescent work-related values and beliefs: Gender differences and relation to occupational aspirations*. Paper presented at the Biennial Meeting of the Society for Research on Child Development, New Orleans, LA.

Kerr, B. A. (1994). *Smart girls: a psychology of girls, women and giftedness*. Dayton, OH: Psychological Press.

Kerr, B. (2000). *Guiding gifted girls and young women*. In K. A. Heller, F. J. Monks, R. J. Sternberg, & R. F. Subotnik (Eds.), *International handbook of giftedness and talent* (2nd ed., pp. 649–658). Oxford, U.K.: Elsevier Science Ltd.

Kerr, B. A., & Cohn, S. J. (2001). *Smart boys: Talent, manhood, and the search for meaning*. Tempe, AZ: Great Potential Press.

Kerr, B., & Foley Nicpon, M. (2002). Gender and giftedness. In N. Colangelo & G. Davis (Eds.), *Handbook of gifted education* (pp. 493–505). New York: Allyn and Bacon.

Kerr, B., & Kurpius, S. E. R. (2004). Encouraging talented girls in math and science: Effects of a guidance intervention. *High Ability Studies, 15*(1), 85–102.

Kischenbaum, R. J., & Reis, S. M. (1997). Conflicts in creativity: Talented female artists. *Creativity Research Journal, 10*(2&3), 251–263.

Kolitch, E. R., & Brody, L. E. (1992). Mathematics acceleration of highly talented students: An evaluation. *Gifted Child Quarterly, 36*(2), 78–86.

List, K., & Renzulli, J. S. (1991). Creative women's development pattern through age thirty-five. *Gifted Education International 7*(3), 114–122.

Lubinski, D., Benbow, C. P., & Morelock, M. J. (2000) Gender differences in engineering and physical sciences among the gifted: An inorganic–organic distinction. In K. A. Heller, F. J. Monks, R. J. Sternberg, & R. F. Subotnik (Eds.), *International handbook of giftedness and talent* (2nd ed.; pp. 633-648). Oxford, U.K.: Elsevier Science Ltd.

Marland, S., Jr. (1972). *Education of the gifted and talented*. Report to the Congress of the United States by the U.S. Commissioner of Education. Washington, DC: U.S. Government Printing Office.

Montgomery, J. L., & Benbow, C. P. (1992). Factors that influence the career aspirations of mathematically precocious females. In N. Colangelo, S. G., Assouline, & D. L. Ambroson (Eds.), *Talent development: Proceedings from the 1991 Henry B. and Jocelyn Wallace National Research Symposium on Talent Development* (pp. 384–386). Unionville, NY: Trillium Press.

Noble, K. D., Subotnik, R. F., & Arnold, K. D. (1999). To thine own self be true: A new model of female talent develoment. *Gifted Child Quarterly, 43*, 140–149.

Olszewski-Kubilius, P. (1995). A summary of research regarding early entrance to college. *Roeper Review, 18*(2), 121–126.

Olszewski-Kubilius, P., & Whalen, S. P. (2000). The education and development of verbally talented students. In K. A. Heller, F. J. Monks, R. J. Sternberg, & R. F. Subotnik (Eds.), *International handbook of giftedness and talent* (2nd ed., pp. 397–412). Oxford, U.K.: Elsevier Science Ltd.

Olszewski-Kubilius, P., & Yasmoto, J. (1994). Factors affecting the academic choices of academically talented adolescents. In N. Coangelo, S. G. Assouline, & D. L. Ambroson (Eds.), *Talent development: Proceedings from the 1993 Henry B. and Jocelyn Wallace National Research Symposium on Talent Development* (pp. 393–398). Dayton, OH: Ohio Psychology Press.

Piirto, J. (1991). Why are there so few? Creative women: Visual artists, mathematicians, musicians. *Roeper Review, 13*(3), 142–147.

Program for the Exceptionally Gifted (PEG). (2006). Mary Baldwin College. Retrieved February 6, 2007, from http://www/mbc.edu/peg

Read, C. R.. (1991) Gender distribution in programs for the gifted. *Roeper Review, 13*(4), 188–193.

Redding, R. (1990). Learning preferences and skill patterns among underachieving gifted adolescents. *Gifted Child Quarterly, 34*(2), 72–75.

Reis, S. M. (1998). *Work left undone: Choices and compromises of talented females.* Mansfield Center, CT: Creative Learning Press.

Reis, S. M. (2002). Toward a theory of creatively in diverse creative women. *Creativity Research Journal, 14*(3&4), 305–316.

Reis, S. M. (2003). Gifted girls, twenty-five years later: Hope realized and new challenges found. *Roeper Review, 25*(4), 154–157.

Reis, S. M., & Callahan, C. M. (1989). Gifted females: They've come a long way—or have they? *Journal for the Education of the Gifted, 12,* 99–117.

Renzulli, J. (2002). Expanding the conception of giftedness to include co-cognitive traits and to promote social capital. *Phi Delta Kappan, 84*(1), 33–58.

Robinson, N., & Weimer, L. (1991). Selection of candidates for early admission to kindergarten and first grade. In W. T. Southern & E. Jones (Eds.), *The academic acceleration of gifted children* (pp. 29–50). New York: Teachers College Press.

Robertson, E. (1991). Neglected dropouts: The gifted and talented. *Equity and Excellence, 25,* 62–74.

Rohrer, J. C. (1997, July 31). *The Lake Tahoe Watershed Project: Fostering the interest of female middle school students in math and science.* Paper presented at the 12th Biennial World Council for Gifted and Talented Children, Seattle, WA.

Ross, P. O. (1993). *National excellence: A case for developing America's talent.* Washington, D.C.: U.S. Government Printing Office.

Sarouphim, K. M. (2004). Discover in middle school: Identifying gifted minority students. *The Journal of Secondary Gifted Education, 15*(2), 61–69.

Schober, B., Reimann, R., & Wagner, P. (2004). Is research on gender-specific underachievement in gifted girls an obsolete topic? New Findings on an often discussed issue. *High Ability Studies, 15*(1), 43–62.

Seely, K. R. (1993). Gifted students at risk. In L. K. Silverman (Ed.), *Counseling the gifted and talented* (pp. 263–276). Denver: Love.

Smith, W. S., & Erb, T. O. (1986). Effect of women science career role models on early adolescents' attitudes toward scientists and women in science. *Journal of Research in Science Teaching, 23*(8), 667–676.

Stanley, J. C. (1988). Some characteristics of SMPY'S 700-800 on SAT-M before the age 13 group: Youths who reason extremely well mathematically. *Gifted Child Quarterly, 32,* 205–209.

Stanley, J. C. (1991). An academic model for educating the mathematically talented. *Gifted Child Quarterly, 35,* 36–42.

Stanley, J. C., Benbow, C. P., Brody, L. E., Dauber, S., &Lupkowski, A. (1992). Gender differences on eighty-six nationally standardized achievement and aptitude tests. In N. Colangelo, S. G. Assouline, & D. L. Ambrosen (Eds.), *Talent development: Proceedings from the 1991 Henry B. and Jocelyn Wallace National Research Symposium* (pp. 42–61). Unionville, NY: Trillium Press.

Stanley, J. C., Keating, D. P., & Fox, L. H. (Eds.). (1974). *Mathematical talent: Discovery, description, and development.* Baltimore, MD: The Johns Hopkins University Press.

Steele, C. M., & Aronson, J. (1995). Stereotype threat and the intellectual test performance of African Americans. *Journal of Personality and Social Psychology, 69*(5), 797–811.

Stephens, K. R., & Karnes, F. A. (2000). State definitions for the gifted and talented revisited. *Exceptional Children, 66*(2), 219–238.

Sternberg, R. (1986). A triarchic theory of intellectual giftedness. In R. Sternberg & J. Davidson (Eds.), *Conceptions of giftedness* (pp. 223–243). Cambridge, U.K.: Cambridge University Press.

Sternberg, R. (2000). Giftedness as developing expertise. In K. A. Heller, F. J. Monks, R. J. Sternberg, & R. F. Subotnik (Eds.), *International handbook of giftedness and talent* (2nd ed., pp. 55–66). Oxford, U.K.: Elsevier Science Ltd.

Stumpf, H., & Stanley, J. C. (1996). Gender-related differences on the College Board's advanced placement and achievement tests, 1982–1992. *Journal of Educational Psychology, 88,* 353–364.

Subotnik, R. F., & Arnold, K. D. (1994). *Beyond Terman: Longitudinal studies: Contemporary longitudinal studies of giftedness and talent.* Norwood, NJ: Ablex.

Subotnik, R. F., & Arnold, K. D. (1996). Success and sacrifice: The costs of talent fulfillment for women in science. In K. D. Arnold, K. D. Noble, R. F. Subtonik (Eds.), *Remarkable women: Perspectives on female talent and development* (pp. 263–280). Cresskill, NJ: Hampton Press, Inc.

Subotnik, R., & Strauss, S. M. (1995). Gender differences in classroom participation and achievement: An experiment involving advanced placement calculus classes. *The Journal of Secondary Gifted Education, 6*(2), 77–85.

Swanson, M. (2002). *National survey on the state governance of K–12 gifted and talented education: Summary report.* Tennessee Initiative for Gifted Education Reform (TIGER). Retrieved August 18, 2006, from www.tigernetwork.org

Tannenbaum, A. J. (2000). A history of giftedness in school and society. In K. A. Heller, F. J. Monks, R. J. Sternberg, & R. F. Subotnik (Eds.), *International handbook of giftedness and talent* (2nd ed., pp. 23–54). Oxford, U.K.: Elsevier Science Ltd.

Takihira, S. (1995). *Cross-cultural study on variables influencing gender differences in mathematics performance.* Unpublished doctoral dissertation, Department of Human Development, University of Maryland, College Park.

Terman, L. M., & Oden, M. H. (1935). *Genetic studies of genius: Vol. 3. The promise of youth.* Stanford, CA: Stanford University Press.

Tomlinson, C. (1995). *How to differentiate instruction in mixed ability classrooms.* Alexandria, VA: Association for Supervision and Curriculum Development.

Tomlinson, C. A. (1996). Good teaching for one and all: Does gifted education have an instructional identity? *Journal for the Education of the Gifted, 20*(2), 155–174.

Tomlinson, C. A., & McTighe, J. (2006). *Integrating differentiated instruction and understanding by design.* Alexandria, VA: Association for Supervision and Curriculum Development.

Walters, A. M., & Brown, L. M. (2005). The role of ethnicity on the gender gap in mathematics. In A. M. Gallagher & J. C. Kaufman (Eds.), *Gender differences in mathematics* (pp. 207–219). Cambridge: Cambridge University Press.

Whitmore, J. (1980). *Giftedness, conflict and underachievement.* Boston: Allyn & Bacon.

Wolfe, J. A. (1991). Underachieving gifted males: Are we missing the boat? *Roeper Review, 13*(4), 181–183.

·28·

GENDER EQUITY FOR PEOPLE WITH DISABILITIES

Donna M. Mertens,* Amy Wilson, and Judith Mounty

INTRODUCTION

The struggle for disability rights by men and women with disabilities and their advocates shares an extensive overlap with the rights sought under the feminist banner. Disability and feminist theorists have similar goals in that both are concerned with the elimination of the exploitation and oppression of their respective constituencies (Watson et al., 2004). Specifically, females with and without disabilities have less access to appropriate educational resources and evince poorer educational and employment-related outcomes than do their male peers. Thus, Wehmeyer and Rousso and (2001) concluded that disparities on these indicators support the idea that girls and women with disabilities are in a state of double jeopardy. The combination of stereotypes about women and stereotypes about people with disabilities leads to double discrimination that is reflected in the home, school, workplace, and the larger society.

However, the focus of this chapter will not be limited to those areas of inequity in which males with disabilities are favored over females. One of the most distressing circumstances in the disability community is the over-identification of school-age boys as having a disability and the potential underrepresentation of girls of similar age. Males, especially those from minority ethnic and racial groups, are diagnosed as having disabilities in much greater numbers by a ratio of about two males for every one female (U.S. Department of Education, 2004). Minority children with disabilities all too often experience inadequate services, low-quality curriculum and instruction, and unnecessary isolation from their nondisabled peers (Losen & Orfield, 2002). Conversely, girls may be underidentified as having certain disabilities because the indicators are manifested differently for females and males, and therefore, girls are not receiving the supportive services necessary to succeed in school and life.

While the disability rights movement shares many of the same concerns with feminists, important differences between the feminist and disability rights agenda exist. As Lloyd (2001)

noted, "Women with disabilities have found themselves largely ignored by feminists and their perspective either lost by, or directly at variance with, much feminist analysis" (p. 716). For example, a point of tension exists between feminists and women with disabilities related to issues of sexuality, reproduction, and motherhood. Women with disabilities have to fight the prejudices that exclude them from fulfilling the traditional female roles relating to child bearing, motherhood, and self-presentation as a sexual human being. A second point of tension between feminists and women with disabilities arises in the reproductive rights issue around abortion. Feminists have argued for a woman's right to choose abortion, particularly when the fetus is developing abnormally. Women with disabilities include both those who favor prochoice and others who favor prolife. There is a strong sentiment expressed within that community that choices related to sustaining or ending a pregnancy should not be made based on misinformation about disability. They oppose abortion if it is based on the assumption that there is no place in this world for people who are physically and/or intellectually "abnormal". Additionally, the views of males and females with disabilities on caring and dependence are sometimes at variance with feminist views. Rather than viewing care giving as a burden, disabled men and women reframe the issue in their demands to be allowed to undertake the caring responsibilities in their personal relationships, including the right to have the practical support they may need to accomplish the tasks associated with caring.

This chapter explores gender-equity issues in the disability community, differences and similarities between the feminist and disability rights agendas, as well as potential solutions in terms of programs, legislation, and research. A review of legislation and the paradigm shift in the disability community sets the framework for understanding variables related to the identification and prevalence of people with different types of disabilities. Research is then reviewed concerning school placement, access to curriculum, technology, and after-school programs, and educational and employment outcomes, as well as issues re-

---

*The boldface name is the Lead Author.

lated to health, sexuality, sexual abuse, and the status of women with disabilities in the international community.

The intersection of type of disability with gender, race/ethnicity, and socioeconomic status is extremely complex and little research is available that adequately addresses that complexity. Quite often in research in the disability community, gender is not even included as an important dimension of diversity. Thus, this is an important limitation to acknowledge in currently available research and future research should be a priority. The chapter concludes with recommendations for a research agenda to address gender and disabilities from a transformative stance.

HISTORY AND LEGISLATION: DISABILITIES AND GENDER EQUITY IN THE UNITED STATES

The federal civil rights law protecting against discrimination on the basis of sex in education programs and activities in entities that receive federal financial assistance is Title IX of the Higher Education Act of 1972. Other civil rights laws provide protections against discrimination on the basis of disability, race, and ethnicity. Groups who brought pressure to the legislature to pass laws on civil rights issues tended to be single-issue groups. Equity professionals who fought for Title IX and related program support such as the Women's Educational Equity Act, did not press for inclusion of equity on the basis of disability or race or ethnicity. Discrimination on the basis of race and ethnicity was already included in the 1964 Civil Rights Act and the 1965 Elementary and Secondary Education Act. Similarly, advocates for access for students with disabilities did not press for equity in terms of gender and race/ethnicity. Thus, the strides made in the name of gender equity often ignored issues related to males and females with disabilities and vice versa (Lloyd, 2001; Watson, McKie, Hughes, Hopkins & Gregory, 2004).

To understand the intersection of disability and gender equity, it is necessary to consider the protections offered by federal disability rights laws, such as Individuals with Disabilities Education Act (IDEA), Section 504 of the 1973 Rehabilitation Act, and the Americans with Disabilities Act (ADA). Despite the fact that Section 504 and ADA were patterned in part on previous statutes that prohibit discrimination on other grounds in federally assisted programs or activities, such as Title VI of the Civil Rights Law of 1964 and Title IX, the disability-related legislation refers to gender in a limited way (U.S. Department of Justice, 2001a).

The Education of the Handicapped Act, passed in 1975, was changed to the Individuals with Disabilities Education Act (IDEA) in 1990, and was reauthorized in 1997 and again in 2004. IDEA allowed the U.S. Department of Education to distribute over 11 billion dollars annually since 2004. The populations included in the IDEA legislation are individuals with mental retardation, hearing impairments, speech or language impairments, visual impairments, serious emotional disturbances, orthopedic impairments, other health impairments, specific learning disabilities, multiple disabilities, deafness/blindness, autism, and traumatic brain injury. Additionally, the legislation recognizes the categories of infants and toddlers with disabilities and persons with developmental delays and those at risk.[1]

IDEA (and its predecessor legislation) resulted in fewer students with disabilities being educated in separate schools or classrooms. The 2004 version of IDEA shifted the balance of power for shaping the terms for provision of services for students with disabilities to the state and schools, while paring down the rights of parents and advocates for children with disabilities (Schemo, 2004). Supporters of the bill say it was revised to cut down on the burdensome paperwork and to lessen the adversarial role between parent and school that is sometimes associated with having a child with special needs. The law specifies the need for mediation prior to legal action, sets more specific boundaries on the conditions under which a parent can sue the school, and gives school greater latitude in removing students who misbehave and are disabled.

IDEA contains several references to gender in Section 618. Specifically, states are required to report annually to the U.S. Department of Education on the number and percentage of children with disabilities (by race, ethnicity, limited English proficiency status, gender, and disability category) who are either receiving services under IDEA or have experienced disciplinary actions, including suspensions of one day or more. The statute does not mention the need to disaggregate data by gender and disability in its other provisions, such as the number of children with developmental disabilities[2] or the section on disproportionality on the basis of race and type of disability.

Section 504 and the Americans with Disabilities Act (ADA) are both civil rights laws to prohibit discrimination on the basis of disability. ADA focuses on discrimination in employment, public services, and. Section 504 focuses on discrimination in public an private programs and activities that receive federal financial assistance. Both cover any individual with a disability who: (a) has a physical or mental accommodations impairment that substantially limits one or more life activities; or (b) has a record of such an impairment; or (c) is regarded as having such an impairment. Major life activities include walking, seeing, hearing, speaking, breathing, learning, working, caring for oneself, and performing manual tasks.

Unlike IDEA, Section 504 does not require the school to provide an individualized educational program (IEP) that is designed to meet the child's unique needs and provides the child with educational benefit (Wright & Wright, 2005). Fewer proce-

---

[1] To be protected by the ADA, one must have a disability or have a relationship or association with an individual with a disability. An individual with a disability is defined by the ADA as a person who has a physical or mental impairment that substantially limits one or more major life activities, a person who has a history or record of such an impairment, or a person who is perceived by others as having such an impairment. The ADA does not specifically name all of the impairments that are covered (U.S. Department of Justice, 2002).

[2] Developmental disabilities is defined as severe, chronic disability that results in substantial functional limitations in three or more of the following areas of major life activity: self-care, receptive and expressive language, capacity for independent living, learning, mobility, self-direction and economic self-sufficiency.

dural safeguards are available for disabled children and their parents under Section 504 than under IDEA. If the child has a disability that adversely affects educational performance, the child is eligible for special-education services under IDEA. Children who are eligible for special-education services under IDEA are protected under Section 504 (but the converse is not true). If the child has a disability that does not adversely affect educational performance, then the child will not be eligible for special education services under IDEA but will usually be entitled to nondiscrimination protections under Section 504. For example, students of average intelligence who use a wheelchair will be eligible to have access to a ramp to eliminate barriers to entering a school building. However, if such students require no additional special-education services, then they would not be included in the IDEA definition of disability. Variations in definitions of disability result in inconsistencies between coverage under IDEA and 504, as well as differences in the prevalence figures for people with disabilities. The consequences of definitions of disability rooted in biology as opposed to society are explored later in this chapter (U.S. Department of Justice, 2001b).

PARADIGM SHIFT IN THE DISABILITY COMMUNITY

People with disabilities have been viewed through various lenses throughout history. Gill (1999) summarized changes in these perceptions as shifts in paradigms in terms of the moral model, the medical model, and the sociocultural model of disability. A paradigm is a way of looking at the world. It is composed of certain philosophical assumptions that guide and direct thinking and action. The moral model suggests that the disability is a punishment for a sin or a means of inspiring or redeeming others. The medical model sees the disability as a problem or a measurable defect located in the individual that needs a cure or alleviation that can be provided by medical experts. For example, Swadner and Lubeck (1995) stated that the deficit model emphasizes "getting the child ready for school, rather than getting the school ready to serve increasingly diverse children" (p. 18). Graduate students enrolled in one of the author's courses at Gallaudet University (Mertens) were asked to reflect on the meaning of viewing deafness from a deficit model. The following comment provides insight from the perspective of one deaf student:

Deaf students being held back in school or who were just passed along to the next class because they were just too old to be held back any more . . . "graduating" with special diplomas (and often reading far below grade level) . . . being told in the classroom that their speech was fine, but then finding in the real world that people couldn't understand their speech. Being told (in school) that yes, they can do anything they want to after high school . . . then being limited to menial jobs because they are too far behind in literacy to get better jobs. They cannot even attend community college because they only have a special diploma. Elementary children are being praised for good work in the classroom . . . but being held back because they just cannot read on grade level yet. Too much focus on speech instruction and not enough on content instruction. All of this affects adult life, as I have already mentioned—limited to low-paying jobs or dependency on government hand-

outs. Many older deaf adults have given up and will not even consider trying to improve their lives, are bitter toward the world, and fiercely oppose any changes that might reduce or eliminate the monthly checks they get. (Martha Knowles, September 2004, used with permission)

In the disability community, Seelman (2000) described the change from a model that viewed a disability as a defect in the individual to a sociocultural model that focuses on the adequacy of the environmental response to the disability as a paradigmatic shift. The sociocultural paradigm is more congruent with a feminist stance in that it evolved from the efforts of people with the lived experience of having a disability, as well as those of nondisabled advocates. Within this paradigm, disability is framed from the perspective of a social, cultural minority group, such that disability is defined not as a defect, but rather as a dimension of human difference (Gill, 1999; Mertens & McLaughlin, 2004). Furthermore, the category of disability is recognized as being socially constructed with its meaning being derived from society's response to individuals who deviate from cultural standards. Furthermore, disability is viewed as one dimension of human difference. According to Gill (1999), the goal for people with disabilities is not to eradicate their sickness, but to celebrate their distinctness, pursue their equal place in American society, and acknowledge that their "differentness" is not defective but valuable.

This paradigmatic shift in the disability community serves as a basis for the transformation of the ways decisions are made about the provision of services for, and research about, people with disabilities. Previously, much of special-education research derived from a deficit perspective that located the problem in an individual and focused on their disability as the reason that they could not perform certain functions or activities. More recently, special-education researchers have shifted to a sociocultural perspective that focuses on the dynamic interaction between the individual and environment over the lifespan (Mertens & McLaughlin, 2004; Seelman, 2000). Again, a comment from one of Mertens' graduate students illustrates the contrast between disability as defect and as a cultural dimension:

It does make a huge difference whether one supports the deficit or the transformative paradigm since they are two very different and opposite paradigms. If one supports the deficit paradigm that means they are focusing on deafness as a defect and it needs to be "fixed" . . . in any way possible. It seems that those who support the deficit paradigm frown on the Deaf. One looks down upon the deaf in society as human beings with defects. If one supports the transformative paradigm, they understand that Deafness is not a defect and recognize that the Deaf have their own language and culture. One accepts the Deaf as equals among society. (Matt Laucka, September 2004)

A transformative paradigm for research has emerged in parallel with the emergence of the sociocultural view of disability (Mertens, 2004; 2005). The transformative paradigm is inclusive of feminist theory (Lloyd, 2001; Watson, McKie, Hughes, Hopkins, & Gregory, 2004), positive psychology (Seligman & Csikszentmihalyi, 2000) and resilience theory (Brown, D'Emidio-Caston, & Benard, 2001; Cooper, 2000). While feminist theory puts central importance on gender, transformative theory explicitly addresses multiple dimensions of diversity associated with discrimination and oppression. Resilience theory provides another influence in transformative research in that it focuses on the strengths of the individual and ways to modify the environment to remove barriers and increase the probability of success. It is significant that the disability community, as well as the research community, is experiencing what might be termed a paradigm shift as they reexamine the underlying assumptions that guide their theory and practice. The potential of merging paradigms between these two communities provides many possibilities. Those who drive the highways of the world know that the merge lane can be a means of accessing new frontiers, or it can also be a danger zone that must be approached carefully. The authors think this is a very apt metaphor for the state of merging paradigms in the research and disability communities. Implications for research on disability and gender within the transformative paradigm are discussed at the conclusion of this chapter.

DEFINITIONS OF DISABILITY

The definition of who has a disability, the type of disability, and the wisdom of using categories to define disabilities is contentious. It is possible to have different definitions, but some of the definitions might actually result in harm to those so labeled. Therefore, consideration must be given to issues of power in the definition of the concept of disability and types of disabilities. The IDEA and ADA legislation contain biomedical definitions of disabilities and describe disability as a consequence of impairment. A sociocultural definition of people with disabilities would characterize them as a minority group by virtue of restricted access to education, full employment, and other resources as well as being stigmatized and marginalized by others (Lipson & Rogers, 2000).

Nunkoosing (2000) provided a useful contrast between a biomedical definition and a socially constructed definition of mental retardation.[3] Under the biomedical definition, mental retardation is defined as a deficit in intelligence and adaptive behavior that is observable and measurable. It operates on the assumption that disability is a deficit, or a list of deficits in the person. This method of diagnosis is problematic for a number of reasons. First, it is based on IQ tests that are fraught with problems when used with people who are developmentally or cognitively challenged. Second, measures of adaptive behavior are usually scales with lists of poorly defined competencies. Nunkoosing suggested that a socially constructed definition would be based on the knowledge that men and women with mental retardation possess about their experience. This would lead to definitions that would support morality and justice in decisions about relationships with and provision of services for people with mental retardation.

A recognition that the definitions of disability are socially constructed in the transformative paradigm is accompanied by a conscious awareness that certain individuals occupy a position

of greater power and that individuals with other characteristics may be associated with a higher likelihood of exclusion from decisions about such definitions. For example, as one of Mertens' students wrote:

In some school systems, those who are Deaf are usually accompanied with the label communication disordered because many Deaf are in speech therapy. In the school system's view, since we can't speak clearly, we have a communication disorder. That is a strange label since there are other ways to communicate with other human beings. We could write on a paper, gesture, or use some other communication system. The hearing administrators who run the school system have a very limited view of communication. I guess it is only fair to label the hearing manually disordered since they cannot sign clearly. (Matt Laucka, September 2004, used with permission)

PREVALENCE AND DIVERSITY IN THE DISABILITY COMMUNITY

People with disabilities comprise the largest minority group in the United States. Because prevalence figures are dependent on the definition of disability that is used, it is difficult to precisely identify the number of people with disabilities. However, it is estimated that 15% to 20% of U.S. residents have a disabling condition that interferes with life activities (Davis, 1997; National Organization on Disability/Louis Harris & Associates, 1998) (from Lipson and Rogers, 2000, p. 212). In keeping with the view of people with disabilities as a cultural group, their heterogeneity is evident in terms of the many cultural dimensions that are often overlooked in research on the disability community. Gender, age, race/ethnicity, and socioeconomic status are just the beginning of the important dimensions that need to be considered in addition to the disability. Factors such as the age of onset, severity, identification with cultural groups, communication mode, and capacity for independence are other important considerations.

In the 24th Annual Report to Congress (U.S. Department of Education, 2004), comparisons of the gender and racial/ethnic distributions for people ages 3 to 21 in 1987 and 2001 indicated no significant change over time in the gender distribution of students with disabilities (69% and 67% male). At both times, males were significantly overrepresented among students receiving special education relative to students in the general population. A similar overrepresentation of males was evident even among infants and toddlers with disabilities (61%; Hebbeler, Wagner, Spiker, Scarborough, Simeonsson, & Collier, 2001).

Thompson et al. (2003) reviewed the prevalence of sex differences in two categories of disability: (a) psychopathology and (b) developmental disabilities. In the former, women experience higher rates of internalizing psychopathology, such as anxiety, eating disorders, and mood disorders, while men exhibit higher rates of externalized psychopathology such as aggres-

---

[3]Nunkoosing uses the term "learning disability" in his article. However, the definition he uses throughout conforms to the concept of mental retardation as it is used in the IDEA legislation. Perhaps this is because Nunkoosing is from the United Kingdom and terminology differs between the two countries.

TABLE 28.1 Disability Category Distribution of Youth With Disabilities, 1987 and 2000

Primary Disability Category	Federal child count (ages 12 through 17)					NLTS/NLTS2 (ages 15 through 17)		
	Cohort 1		Cohort 2		Percentage Point Change	Cohort 1	Cohort 2	Percentage Point Change
	Number	Percentage	Number	Percentage				
Learning disability	1,014,618	59.9	1,649,306	61.6	+1.7	60.4	61.4	+1.0
Speech/language impairment	104,968	6.2	129,683	4.8	−1.4	4.4	3.2	−1.2
Mental retardation	292,746	17.3	312,133	11.7	−5.6	18.0	13.0	−5.0
Emotional disturbance	196,153	11.6	286,909	10.7	−.9	11.4	11.9	+.5
Hearing impairment	17,377	1.0	32,723	1.2	+.2	1.4	1.4	.0
Visual impairment	7,905	.5	11,865	.4	−.0	.6	.6	.0
Orthopedic impairment	16,208	1.0	31,032	1.2	+.2	1.0	1.2	+.2
Other health impairment	19,572	1.2	142,853	5.3	+4.2	1.4	5.2[a]	+3.8
Multiple disabilities	23,631	1.4	52,074	1.9	+.5	1.3[b]	2.2[b]	+.9
Deaf-blindness[a]	252	.0	518	.0	+.0			
Autism[b]	NA		22,289	.8	+.8			
Traumatic brain injury[b]	NA		7,711	.3	+.3			
All disabilities	1,693,430		2,679,096					

[a]Includes students with deaf-blindness.

[b]Students with autism and traumatic brain injury have been reassigned, for comparison purposes, to other categories as described in this text, with many being included in this other health impairments category.

sion. Rates of depression are equal for boys and girls until the onset of puberty when the ratio of females to males diagnosed with depression increases to 2:1 and remains higher throughout adult life. Women also experience a higher rate of anxiety disorders, such as panic disorder, agoraphobia, and simple phobias. In actuality, it may be that men do not suffer anxiety and depressive disorders less than women, but that it is manifested differently, for example as hyperactivity, irritability, or irrational explosiveness.

In terms of developmental disabilities, boys exhibit higher rates of autism, attention deficit hyperactivity disorder, learning disabilities, and Tourette syndrome (Thompson, et al., 2003). The ratio of male to female rates of autism is 4:1 (and 10:1 in high-functioning autism and Asperger syndrome).[4] Reasons for this differential are not clear. However, Thompson et al. noted that most research in developmental disabilities has paid little attention to gender differences. Based on a review of articles that used "autism" as a keyword in PsychLit between 2000 and 2002, only 2% of the 563 studies analyzed dependent variables separately for males and females. The studies focused on prevalence, rather than on phenotypic expression of autism or treatment outcome. Thompson et al. suggested that girls may have a different phenotype than boys, and in milder cases, their autism is undiagnosed, delayed, or inaccurately diagnosed as anxiety disorder or anorexia nervosa.

The increase in the racial/ethnic diversity of the general student population is also evident among students with disabilities in comparisons of 1987 and 2001 data (U.S. Department of Education, 2002). Table 28.1 contains specific data comparing the distribution of students between the ages of 5 and 21 in terms of gender, race/ethnicity, and disability between the years of 1987 and 2001.

Hispanic students exhibited the largest increase for both groups, being half again as large in 2001 as in 1987 (14% vs. 9%, p. 05). In contrast, the proportions of students with disabilities who were White or Black declined by just over 2%. Consistent with the increase in the Hispanic population, there was more than a fourfold increase in the proportion of students with disabilities who did not use primarily English at home: the percentage grew from 3% to 14%. The reasons for the large increase in Hispanic and English-as-second-language users are not clear. Research is needed to shed light on the impact of increases for these two groups in the general school-age population and their identification as students with disabilities. Also, research could address the implications for students with disabilities increasingly facing the challenges of communicating in two languages and accommodating two cultures, in addition to the challenges posed by their disabilities. There is also a chicken-egg phenomenon to be considered. Namely, to what extent are inadequate or poorly implemented bilingual education resources contributing to learning problems, versus to what extent are learning difficulties impeding acquisition of the new/target language?

U.S. Census Bureau (2000) data are displayed in Table 28.2 for people by gender and type of disability across the age spectrum. Steelman (1999) noted great diversity within the 20% of the national population of all ages who have disabilities based on race/ethnicity and gender. In younger-age categories, men have higher rates of disability, but the balance shifts in later years, in part because women live longer. Women

[4]Tourette syndrome is an inherited disorder of the nervous system characterized by repeated involuntary movements and uncontrollable vocal (phonic) sounds called tics. In a few patients, such tics can include inappropriate words and phrases. Asperger syndrome is a pervasive developmental disability, associated with high functioning autism, repetitive behaviors, and impairments in social functioning.

TABLE 28.2 Characteristics of the Civilian Noninstitutionalized Population by Age, Disability Status and Type of Disability: 2000
(*For information on confidentiality protection, sampling error, nonsampling error, and definitions, see www.census.gov/cen2000/doc/sf3.pdf*)

Characteristic	Total		Male		Female	
	Number	Percent	Number	Percent	Number	Percent
Population 5 and older	257,167,527	100.0	124,636,825	100.0	132,530,702	100.0
With any disability	49,746,248	19.3	24,439,531	19.6	25,306,717	19.1
Population 5 to 15	45,133,667	100.0	23,125,324	100.0	22,008,343	100.0
With any disability	2,614,919	5.8	1,666,230	7.2	948,689	4.3
Sensory	442,894	1.0	242,706	1.0	200,188	0.9
Physical	455,461	1.0	251,852	1.1	203,609	0.9
Mental	2,078,502	436.0	1,387,393	6.0	691,109	3.1
Self-care	419,018	0.9	244,824	1.1	174,184	0.8
Population 16 to 64	179,697,234	100.0	87,570,583	100.0	91,116,651	100.0
With any disability	33,153,211	18.6	17,139,019	19.6	16,014,192	17.6
Sensory	4,123,902	2.3	2,388,121	2.7	1,735,781	1.9
Physical	11,150,365	6.2	5,279,731	6.0	5,870,634	6.4
Mental	9,764,439	3.8	3,434,631	3.9	3,329,808	3.7
Self-care	3,146,875	1.8	1,463,184	1.7	1,686,691	1.9
Difficulty going outside the home	11,414,509	6.4	5,569,362	6.4	5,845,146	6.4
Employment disability	21,287,570	11.9	11,373,786	13.0	9,913,784	10.9
Population 65 to older	33,346,626	100.0	13,940,918	100.0	19,405,708	100.0
With any disability	13,978,118	41.9	5,634,282	40.4	8,343,836	43.0
Sensory	4,738,479	14.2	2,177,216	15.6	2,561,263	13.2
Physical	9,545,680	28.6	3,590,139	25.8	5,955,541	30.7
Mental	3,592,912	10.8	1,380,060	9.9	2,212,852	11.4
Self-care	3,183,840	9.5	1,044,910	7.5	2,138,930	11.0
Difficulty going outside the home	6,795,517	20.4	2,339,128	16.8	4,456,389	23.0

Source: U.S. Census Bureau, Census 2000 Summary File 3

have higher rates of severe disabilities than men (9.7% vs. 7.7%), while men have slightly higher rates of nonsevere disability. Considering both sex and race, Black women have the highest rate of severe disability (14.3%), followed by Black men (12.6%). Rates of severe disability for men and women who are American Indian, Eskimo, or Aleut are nearly as high; persons who are American Indian have the highest rates of nonsevere disability.

Additional research is needed to explore the reasons for the differential rates of disability by gender and race. Researchers who undertake research with these populations need to be knowledgeable about the diversity within the community in order to be culturally sensitive in the interest of gathering valid research data and interpreting the results accurately. The U.S. monthly supplement surveys provide additional evidence concerning the variation in disabilities in the U.S. population by gender, race/ethnicity, and type of disability (U.S. Census Bureau, 2004). Latinos have statistically similar rates of severe disability when compared to Whites and non-Hispanics: 12% and 11%, respectively (Marotta & Garcia, 2003).

In older populations, ages 70–103, disaggregation by race/ethnicity and gender reveal that rates of disability are higher for women in all groups (White-62%, African American-66%, Mexican American-57%, and Other Latino-65%) (Zsembik, Peek, & Peek, 2000).

Over and Underidentification

Overrepresentation of culturally and linguistically diverse students in special education is a fact based on both legal and research findings (Mertens & McLaughlin, 2004). On the one hand, overidentification can be traced to unfair, unreliable, and invalid assessment and diagnostic practices.[5] On the other hand, disproportionality can result from a lack of cultural competency on the part of the school personnel and a consequent inability to accommodate for the diverse needs and preferences of students who are culturally and linguistically diverse. While cultural competency has many different definitions, Hanley (1999), as cited in Edgar, Patton, & Day-Vines (2002), saw it as "the ability to work effectively across cul-

---

[5]Issues related to assessment are beyond the scope of this chapter. Interested readers are referred to chapter in this Handbook, the American Educational Research Association, American Psychological Association and National Council on Measurement in Education's (1999) *Standards for educational and psychological testing,* and Mertens and McLaughlin's (2004) *Research and evaluation methods in special education.* In addition, Mounty and Martin's (2005) *Assessment of deaf and hard of hearing adults: Critical issues in testing and evaluation* addresses measurement issues specific to the deaf population.

tures in a way that acknowledges and respects the culture of the person being served" (p. 10). According to Dougherty (2001), the number of ethnic-minority group members will increase significantly in the future, and by the year 2020, the majority of school-age children in the United States will be from racial or ethnic minority groups. At the same time, the number of teachers and other service personnel who are European American comprise over 85% of the education workforce (Edgar, Patton, & Day-Vines, 2002). The resulting imbalance may lead to inappropriate referral decisions and placements in special education.

Some features in the new IDEA please advocates for people/children with disabilities. One, which is aimed at reducing the overidentification of African Americans for special education, requires the federal government to better monitor special-education enrollment and investigate racial disparities. The law (IDEA, Individuals with Disabilities Education Act) also takes aim at the disproportionate share of minority students tracked for special education.

According to the Civil Rights Project at Harvard University, Black children constitute 17% of the total school enrollment and 33% of those labeled mentally retarded—only a marginal improvement over the past 30 years (Losen & Orfield, 2002). During this same period, however, disproportionality in the area of emotional disturbance (ED) and the rate of identification for both ED and specific learning disabilities (SLD) grew significantly for Blacks. Minority students, specifically Black and Native American students, are significantly more likely than White students to be identified as having a disability. For example, in most states, African American children are identified at one and a half to four times the rate of White children in the disability categories of mental retardation and emotional disturbance.

U.S. Department of Education data from 2000–2001 reveal that in at least 13 states more than 2.75% of all Blacks enrolled were labeled mentally retarded. The prevalence of mental retardation for Whites nationally was approximately 0.75% in 2001, and in no state did the incidence among Whites ever rise above 2.32%. Moreover, nearly three quarters of the states with unusually high incidence rates (2.75%–5.41%) for Blacks were in the South. Based on national data, Latino and Asian American children are underidentified in cognitive disability categories compared to Whites, raising questions about whether the special-education needs of these children are being met. The incidence of disability reveals gross disparities between Blacks and Hispanics, and between Black boys and girls, in identification rates for the categories of mentally retarded and emotionally disturbed (Losen & Orfield, 2002). Most disturbing was that in wealthier districts, contrary to the expected trend, Black children, especially males, were more likely to be labeled mentally retarded. This raises the question: Are there real differences in prevalence by racial group or only differences in the rate of identification?

Differing risk of placement for emotional disturbance by gender and ethnicity are evident, and statistical analysis reveals that the main effect is for males (Donovan & Cross, 2002). For each racial/ethnic group, males are over three times more likely to be classified as emotionally disturbed than are females in the same racial/ethnic group except for Asian/Pacific Islander (for whom males are still more than twice as likely).

Greater identification across the high-incidence disability categories is evident for males. The greatest gender disparity in identification rates is found in the ED category (80% male), followed by LD (70% male) and MR (60% male). Flood (2001) hypothesized that the definitions of LD, ED, and MR have sufficient latitude that teachers can identify boys with behavioral problems under all three categories as a means to get them help or to move them out of the classroom.

Wehmeyer and Schwartz (2001) questioned whether the underidentification of girls is due to a lack of needed support services for them. The authors conducted a study in which they reviewed the records of every student 6 years of age and older who had been admitted to special education for the first time during a one-year span at three different school districts. Based on 695 records, the authors noted that females obtained lower scores on standardized IQ tests at the time of their admission to special education and were more likely to be placed in self-contained education settings. Boys were 10 times more likely to have behavioral factors cited in their reasons for referral. They concluded that girls with disabilities must ". . . have more significant deficits to access special educational services and supports and that when admitted, they are more likely than boys to be placed in more restrictive settings. Most of the boys referred for special-education services had genuine academic needs, yet the primary reason they were referred appeared to be behavioral. The suggestion from these findings is that girls who are not as likely to be acting out are not likely to be referred for learning problems, and thus they will have to experience more significant problems to gain the support they need" (p. 278)

SCHOOL PLACEMENT AND CURRICULA

Schools are up to three times more likely to label African American males than White males as mentally retarded, and twice as likely to label Black males as emotionally disturbed. Once identified, most minority students are significantly more likely to be removed from the general education program and be educated in a more restrictive environment (Donovan & Cross, 2002). For instance, African American and Latino students are about twice as likely as White students to be educated in a restrictive, substantially separate educational setting. Given that certain types of students with special needs may benefit most when they are educated in the least restrictive environment to the maximum extent appropriate, the data on educational settings raise serious questions about the quality of special education provided to Latino, Black, and other minority students compared to Whites, especially males. In addition, the quality of special-education services available to them is often "grossly inadequate," according to Dan Losen, a legal and policy research associate at the Civil Rights Project. The project estimates that 60% to 80% of young Black males who wind up incarcerated have learning disabilities (Schemo, 2004, p. 1).

The findings of Congress from the 1992 Amendments to the Rehabilitation Act (and in the subsequent 1998 reauthorization), state "disability is a natural part of the human experience and in no way diminishes the right of individuals to: live independently, enjoy self-determination, make choices, contribute to society, pursue meaningful careers, and, enjoy full inclusion and integration in the economic, political, social, cultural and educational mainstream of American society" (Rehabilitation Act of 1973, as amended). Educationally, the IDEA and Title II of the Higher Education Act under the No Child Left Behind Act support the Rehabilitation Act by requiring curricula and policy that support programs that result in higher academic achievement for high-school students with disabilities and prepare them to enter post-secondary programs. IDEA requires that the students have written goals and appropriate support with a plan to transition from high school to a vocational program, a two- or four-year postsecondary program, or employment.

Currently, for youth with disabilities leaving high school and transitioning to postsecondary education, there is no national data base on (a) transition success and progress made by youth with disability in postsecondary education, (b) secondary-school factors that supported success or failure in postsecondary education, and (c) extent to which persons with disabilities complete and benefit from postsecondary education programs (Burgstahler, 2002). The past and current National Longitudinal Transition Study funded through the U.S. Department of Education, Office of Special Education Programs, does not follow youth with disabilities into postsecondary education and does not address the longitudinal questions of concern for this population and setting. What information we do have comes from limited studies that rarely disaggregate data by gender and disability.

Female students in secondary schools for students with disabilities were enrolled more often in life-skills and home-economics courses whereas more males were enrolled in vocational education (Doren & Benz, 2001). The consequence of this is that women with disabilities are less likely to be employed, and if employed, they hold lower-status occupations in clerical, service, and helping occupations.

The National Science Foundation (2003) tracks participation in math and science courses for boys and girls and for people with disabilities, but it does not provide data on the intersection of gender and disability. The foundation does conclude that the majority of high-school students with disabilities are not receiving the services necessary to prepare them for career or educational placement upon their graduation. Students with disabilities were less likely to complete a full secondary-school academic curriculum, especially in math and science (National Center for the Study of Postsecondary Educational Supports, 2002) and were ranked much less likely to be minimally qualified for college admission according to an index score of their grades, class rank, National Education Longitudinal Study composite test scores, and SAT/ACT scores (NCES, 1999). Wahl (2001) believed that the incorrect societal perception that girls lack the ability to do well in math and science also negatively affects girls with disabilities. Girls with disabilities have less experiential opportunities in math and science, have few or no mentors with disabilities to act as role models, find the competitive classroom climate and teaching strategies challenging, and have limited access to standards-based math and science curricula and pedagogy.

High-school students with disabilities have not been exposed to career-option planning as have their peers without disabilities, and when career options were discussed, there were, ". . . very few options being recommended or offered; options

that reflected the low expectations of advisors; options that featured perceived needs for protection and support; and options driven primarily by community availability rather than an individual's choices" (McCain, Gill, Wills, & Larson, 2004). Shaffer and Shevitz (2001) reviewed samples of career-development texts for special-education students published between 1992 and 1997. They reported that the texts had roughly equal numbers of females and males, however, males were shown holding a wider range of careers and in more active roles. Only one text pictured individuals with disabilities and discussed the equity provisions of the ADA. The invisibility of individuals with disabilities in the curriculum and in our society is a serious omission (Rousso, 2001).

Some efforts have been made to encourage and support young disabled women in choosing careers normally denied to them. Beaverton High School in Oregon designed a curriculum specifically for their disabled female high-school students to transition smoothly from high school into the world of work (Sargent, 1999).

In order to increase the number of low-income women and girls (including those with disabilities) in the fields of mathematics, science, computer science, and in other underrepresented highly skilled careers, the U.S. Department of Education's Office of Innovation and Improvement awarded over 2 million dollars to projects through the Women's Educational Equity Act Program (Fox, 2000). Although the WEEA grants funded some programs designed to help girls with disabilities, there has been little research and development specifically focused on gender equity and disabilities. In 1995, the U.S. Department of Education created a Gender Equity Expert Panel to identify replicable programs and practices, which seemed to be high quality and to have had a positive impact on advancing gender equity. One of the six subpanels led by the Expert Panel cochair, Harilyn Rousso, focused on gender equity and disability and especially addressed issues related to body image, sexuality, violence, and lack of access to role models.

Despite an extensive national search for submissions to the panel, only a few programs were found to "specifically address the challenges faced by disabled girls, despite their relatively large numbers and the desperate need for such programs (Fox, 2000, p. VI.14)." In 1999, two of the programs reviewed by the disability subpanel were designated by the panel as good resources. They included "Disabled Women—Visions and Voices from the Fourth World Conference on Women" by Suzanne Levine, Wide Vision Productions, and "Building Community, A Manual Exploring Issues of Women and Disability" by Merle Froschl and Barbara Sprung, Educational Equity Concepts. Although no submissions to this subpanel were recommended as promising or exemplary programs with evidence showing they increased gender equity, all recommended submissions from other subpanels were reviewed to insure that they were not stereotypic or harmful in how they treated individuals with disabilities. The developers and evaluators were also asked about whether individuals with disabilities participated in and benefited from the recommended programs.

Ware (2001) described the status of curriculum and disabilities as "persistence of unexamined assumptions about disability and uninspired curriculum" (p. 108). Schools have failed to include disability other than in medical case histories. In an effort to fill in the "historical gaps" of disability in American history, Longmore and Umansky (2000) have edited a collection of essays that capture the social, cultural, and political history of disability and disability-rights activism. Because the history of the disability rights movement (DRM) has been omitted from common understanding, its reintroduction can be used to inform humanities-based disability studies and teacher education directed toward changing the status quo of discrimination based on gender and disability. Humanities-based disability studies is grounded in the desire to challenge our collective stories about disability, renarrate disability, reimagine it as an integral part of all human experience and history. The DRM has many parallels with the feminist movement and the critical theorists. Gill (1999) has established a Disabilities Studies Program at the University of Illinois at Chicago. This program, and others as described by the Society for Disability Studies,, are designed to ". . . encourage perspectives that place disability in social, cultural, and political contexts. We seek to augment understanding of disability in all cultures and historical periods, promote greater awareness of the experiences of disabled people, and contribute to social change (Society for Disability Studies, 2005).

Disabled members of the National Youth Leadership Network (American Youth Policy Forum, 2002) responded to a survey concerning the necessary experiences youth with disabilities require in order to transition successfully into adulthood. The survey questions asked what life experiences were most necessary to transition from school and work, and which of these experiences were lacking. The 200 or so participants were between the ages of 16–24 and represented diversity in terms of race/ethnicity and types of disabilities. However, the results were not disaggregated on the basis of gender. The five most important experiences follow:

1. Learn how to set goals, be assertive, and self-promote
2. Have family members that expect the youth to be a successful adult
3. Have family's encouragement and assistance
4. Learn how to stay healthy
5. Obtain health insurance

The participants responded that there were few opportunities for them to gain experiences by working in a paid job in a career of choice, learning about supports available to youth with disabilities, having access to services from vocational rehabilitation centers for independent living and other community agencies, and learning about laws like the ADA and IDEA. Thus, information was obtained concerning needs of young adults with disabilities. Unfortunately, no data concerning gender differences were included in this study.

Various programs have attempted to address the needs of youth with disabilities. For example, in the Hinsdale South High School in Darien, Illinois, mainstreamed program for deaf and hard-of-hearing youth, an elective course was created entitled, "Adult and Family Living," for high-school seniors, which includes many of these life-skill experiences. After-school clubs invited guest speakers such as adults with disabilities or experts in the various fields to make presentations and answer questions. Some programs, such as the nonprofit Massachusetts organization, Partners for Youth with Disabilities (PYD), pair youth with

mentors and role models who have disabilities (Snowden, 2003). The results of these interventions are not disaggregated by gender. Rousso (2001) also created a mentoring program for young women with disabilities that was based on the identification of successful women with disabilities serving as role models for girls with disabilities.

Struggles in High School

The National Center for the Study of Postsecondary Educational Supports (NCSPES, 2002) and the Office of Special Education and Rehabilitative Services (2000) reported that the number of students with disabilities quitting high school decreased by 4% between 1994–1998 (35% dropped out in 1994, compared to 31% in 1998) and the number of students with disabilities graduating from high school with a diploma increased (51.7% in 1994 to 55.4% in 1998). Although the numbers are improving, the dropout rate for high-school students with disabilities is double the rate of peers without disabilities (NCSPES, 2002). Adults with disabilities who completed high school reported an increase of 17% between 1986 and 2000 (61% in 1986 to 78% in 2000). Parents reported that 1% of males with disabilities drop out because of marriage or parenthood, yet 23% of females dropout for the same reasons.

After-School Programs

Including youth with disabilities in after-school activities is another area severely overlooked and lacking in most educational settings. With the passage of IDEA, more students with disabilities are being educated in their local schools, yet they are not being included in after-school activities or are segregated into their own programs (Froschl, Rousso, & Rubin, 2001). All youth need opportunities to explore their natural talents, to share and to play with others, to grow socially and emotionally, and to learn more about themselves and others. Intellectual, physical, and creative opportunities outside of the classroom offer experiences that help youth prepare for adulthood. Just as girls without disabilities suffer from a dearth of programs meant to address their needs, there are few after-school programs meeting the needs of girls with disabilities (Ms. Foundation for Women, 1999).

Froschl, Rousso, and Rubin (2001) wrote that youth agencies do not include people with disabilities in their programs because of lack of contact with the disability community, cost, lack of staff training, lack of knowledge, concerns about nondisabled youth quitting, and transportation issues. Transportation is a greater challenge for students with disabilities because of expensive special transportation or because of parents who may afraid to allow their daughter to ride alone for long distances with a male driver.

Froschl, Rubin, and Sprung (1999) believed that girls with disabilities in particular are not involved with after-school activities or their involvement is limited because of patronizing attitudes by the school and parents who believe the girl is unable to make decisions for herself or that they must protect the child from sexual or physical abuse, and, therefore, are fearful of leaving personal care of girls to others (especially if the personal-care assistant is male). Thus, a tension exists between protection of girls from sexual predators and supporting their desire for independent living. The researchers also noted that after-school programs promote sports and recreation and are often more geared toward boys than girls. False attitudes and beliefs by the school, parents, and community prevent girls with disabilities from becoming more independent, confident, and learning how to become leaders.

Special educators can raise awareness in the parents, their teaching peers, the school administrators, and the students themselves about the importance of participating in activities after school ends (Froschl, Rubin, & Sprung, 1999). In 1987, a New York City coalition of organizations and people with and without disabilities resisted the negative attitudes, fear, and ignorance of those responsible for facilitating after-school programs. Youth and adults committed to the inclusion of youth with disabilities in community-based programs created the Alliance for Mainstreaming Youth with Disabilities (AMYD). AMYD formed a Youth Leadership Training Program where disabled and nondisabled youth were trained in leadership skills, learned about disability rights and culture, and learned to recognize and understand discrimination and injustice. These young people became youth advocates in their schools and communities. The program did not report its results differentially by gender and, in 1997, the program dissolved because of a lack of funds.

Inclusion of people with disabilities in after-school programs can be increased by stipulating this as part of the children's IEPs and/or transitional plans. Parents and youth can advocate for their rights by citing disability rights laws. Creative solutions can be found for transportation issues, and community youth programs can develop leadership training to develop an advocacy strategy for promoting inclusion (Froeschl et al., 1999).

Sports

As stated earlier, discrimination on the basis of disability is illegal according to Public Law 9-112, Section 504, which states equal opportunity and equal access must be provided to persons with disabilities as to those without disabilities. Physical education, intramural activities, and athletics are provided for in this law, but as was discussed earlier, children with disabilities rarely participate in after-school activities (which often include athletics). Some authors consider participation in sports and physical activities as a basic human right promised to people with disabilities by the Universal Declaration of Human Rights (Kidd & Donnelly, 2000). Yet, when observing school athletic competition or public sporting events, people with disabilities are rarely seen. Very little research has been done in the area of disability and athletics, much less concerning gender.

Participation in sports builds competence and worth within the athlete and moves the focus away from athletes' disabilities and onto their abilities (The Feminist Majority Foundation, 2007). Young women and girls with disabilities may not be involved in sports because of their lack of exposure to sports when younger, a lack of encouragement from adults to participate in sports as they grew up, and a dearth of women with disabilities role models of women who play sports to inspire them (Sherrill, 1984; Abney & Richey, 1992). Instead of participating in mainstream sports, disabled athletes have established sports organizations based upon their disability, and that have been designed after the Olympic model such as the Athletic Association for the Disabled, Special Olympics International, and the U.S. Association for Blind Athletes.

Gender differences appear based on participation of male and female athletes. For examples, females participated in all events in the 2000 Paralympic Games in Sydney, Australia, except volleyball, football, basketball, rugby, and judo (http://www.paralympic.org/, 2005).

A six-country study done with participants of the 1995 Special Olympics reported that, relative to age and IQ, length of time in Special Olympics was the most powerful predictor of social competence. Another study found that the 1995 athletes scored higher in social competence than a non-Special Olympics group. A third study following the same athletes supported the positive effects by indicating higher scores in competence at the four-month follow-up after the Special Olympics competition (Munson, 1995). These positive results need to be tempered with the acknowledgement that they may be a result of self-selection, i.e., those people with disabilities who have greater social competence are more likely to engage in sports than those with lower levels of social competence.

These organizations serve a purpose in making sports accessible to those disabled athletes who may not have equal access otherwise, yet is exclusion rather than inclusion in sports the best way to approach physical recreation? One study of over 600 children in regular education settings showed that the majority was receptive to including children with disabilities in their recreational activities (Moon, 1991). Children are open to accepting children with disabilities playing sports with them; therefore, the responsibility lay with teachers, coaches, and parents to respond positively and proactively to adapt and modify ways that children with disabilities can participate in athletic activities. Learning and teaching approaches may need to be changed, as well as rules that will accommodate the disability (have an able-bodied peer run the bases for a disabled child who is unable to run after batting). Paralympic medalists or local athletes with disabilities could be invited to speak, coach, or attend games. Creativity and flexibility in a sport can make it accessible to all.

Cheri Blauwet, a Paralympian and the winner of the New York City, Los Angeles, and Boston Marathons, contended that sport is a human right for all people and that it is in sport that she and other disabled people can increase self-esteem and gain dignity in the eyes of themselves and others. She also felt that sport is strongly linked with education and rehabilitation (Blauwet, 2005). In September 2004, in Athens, 3,837 athletes from 136 nations participated in the opening ceremonies of the XII Paralympic Games. At the same venue, the International Paralympic Committee, as well as international disabled people's organization, Rehabilitation International, hosted the first International Paralympic Symposium on Disability Rights in order to promote the draft of the UN Convention on the Rights of Persons with a Disability, in hopes of increasing sports globally (*Disability World*, 2005).

School Climate and Discipline

Educating all children, including those with special needs, is most effective when carried out in a positive school climate.

Sexual harassment is one important determinant of school climate. Linn and Rousso (2001) lamented the paucity of research available on the prevalence and nature of sexual harassment of boys and girls with disabilities in school. While more research is needed on this topic, research findings that are available suggested that students with disabilities of both genders may experience higher rates of sexual harassment than their nondisabled peers and that young women with disabilities may experience higher rates than young men with disabilities.

According to Sugai and Horner (2001), schools are not able to provide a full continuum of effective and positive learning experiences for their students. Many schools may lack the capacity to deal effectively with defiant and disruptive behavior. An emerging trend that is demonstrating positive results is entitled positive behavior support systems (PBS) (Center on Positive Behavioral Interventions and Support, 2001). The goal of PBS is to enhance the capacity of schools to educate all students, especially students with challenging social behaviors, by establishing an effective continuum of PBS systems and practices (Sugai & Horner, 2001). This strategy was recognized in the reauthorized IDEA as a research-supported practice for use with children with behavioral issues; however, no research was reported recognizing differential gender effects with PBS.

Often the reason a student is referred for special-educational services is because the student has been disruptive. Research reported by Sugai and Horner (2001) indicated that when PBS systems are in place, then there is not only a reduction in the number of referrals, but also an increase in the quality of referrals. A positive school climate is an important piece to the puzzle of effective school practice.

TEACHER SHORTAGES FOR STUDENTS WITH DISABILITIES

Recent surveys by the National Center for Low Incidence Disabilities reported critical shortages in personnel to serve students with low-incidence disabilities[6] (Ferrell, Luckner, Jackson, Correa, Muir, Howell, et al., 2003). In both deafness and blindness, there is a severe shortage in the number of trained teachers to serve these students (Johnson, 2003; Corn & Spungin, 2003). Corn and Spungin reported that the situation is even more serious in deaf-blindness as only six programs were operating in 1999 and the percentage of the faculty time in these programs added together equals only 4 FTE faculty members. The disability-rights community is concerned not only that teachers who provide direct services are appropriately trained and of both female and male genders, but also reflective of the various disability groups. Such an important contextual variable as the training and availability of qualified teachers for low-incidence populations would be overlooked by reliance on randomized trials to determine program effectiveness.

Educators cannot and should not try to do the job alone when it comes to the education of students with special needs. They should form performance partnerships with parents aimed at achieving the shared goal of creating effective educational practices that will lead to better results for students. With the support of federal legislation, forming these partnerships is not only required but also facilitated through the direction provided by the legislation and guidelines. Parents provide a rich source of information about the strengths and needs of their children. They can be a resource to the design and delivery of special educational and related services. Parents and families are essential to the success of school-reform initiatives, yet, parental involvement remains a challenge (Davies, 1996; Lewis & Henderson, 1997).

POSTSECONDARY EDUCATION AND EMPLOYMENT

An analysis of 34 empirical studies concerning gender, disability, and employment outcomes from 1972 to 1998 show that girls with disabilities: (a) are less likely to be employed than women without disabilities or men with or without disabilities, (b) earn less than men with disabilities and the gap in wages earned increases with time, (c) are employed in positions of lower status than men with disabilities, (d) have fewer full-time positions than men with disabilities, and (e) do not stay as long in an employment position as their male counterparts (Doren & Benz, 2001).

As a result of legislative mandates, most postsecondary institutions enroll students with disabilities. Approximately 72% of the 5,040 two- and four-year postsecondary education institutions reported that they enrolled students with disabilities in academic years between 1996–97 or 1997–98 National Center for the Study of Postsecondary Educational Supports (NCSPES) (1999). Another NCSPES study (2000) showed about 6% (equal percentages for males and of all undergraduates self-reported they had a disability).

The 2000 National Organization on Disability/Harris Survey of Americans with Disabilities, a survey of approximately 1,000 adults with disabilities and 1,000 of their peers without disabilities, showed slightly more than 1 out of 10 students with disabilities graduate from college compared to slightly more than 2 out of 10 of their peers without disabilities (12% vs. 23%).

A report by the National Survey of Educational Support Provision (2000), a survey of a national sample of more than 1,500 disability-support coordinators employed in postsecondary institutions, the *Chartbook on Women and Disability in the United States,* (Stoddard, Jan, Ripples, & Krause, 1998) and Offices of Special Education and Rehabilitative Services (OSERS) (2000) reported that disabled youth are less likely to enroll in a postsecondary program or earn a degree or certificate after enrolling in a postsecondary program than their nondisabled peers. For those

---

[6]The Individuals with Disabilities Education Act (IDEA) of 1997 defines low incidence disabilities as "a visual or hearing impairment, or simultaneous visual and hearing impairments; a significant cognitive impairment; or any impairment for which a small number of personnel with highly specialized skills and knowledge are needed in order for children with that impairment to receive early intervention services or a free appropriate public education" (20 U.S.C. 1400 § 673(a)(3)). In the United States today, children with low-incidence disabilities together comprise less than one percent of the estimated resident school-age population (US Department of Education, 2002).

students with disabilities who earn a degree, 80% needed assistance to manage and/or coordinate their educational and other services. Stodden, Jones, and Chang (2002) reported that support services for people with disabilities vary in terms of type, range, and availability, and are poorly coordinated. The length of time needed to complete their degrees was significantly longer than that needed by their peers without disabilities.

Women with disabilities are five times as likely to have less than eight years of formal education when compared to women without disabilities (Traustadottir, 1997). Young women with disabilities enrolling in postsecondary programs may find they are socially and emotionally unprepared to face the challenges that lay before them. Many young women with disabilities have been raised at home and educated in a school setting where they were undervalued and overprotected, given few opportunities to participate in after-school activities, lacked a preparation for living independently, and lacked a role model or mentor to look to for guidance and advice (Educational Equity Concepts, 1993: Wagner, 1992; Sargent, 1999). The lack of preparation young women with disabilities receive to transition from high school to postsecondary programs leaves them ill-equipped to become independent adults who are able to make appropriate decisions in regards to their career choice and finances. They also do not possess the skills to advocate for their legal rights by obtaining appropriate support services.

Women with disabilities between 18 and 34 years old have lower educational attainment than women without disabilities (American Community Survey, 2003). Those who are not currently enrolled in school in this age group are more likely *not* to be a high-school graduate (26.3% vs 15.3%) and less likely to have a bachelor's degree or greater (9.2% vs 26.3%). Men with disabilities have even lower educational attainment than men without disabilities, being more likely not to be a high-school graduate (30.1% percent vs 19.1%) and less likely to have a bachelor's degree or greater (6.8% versus 21.3%).

Once accepted into a college, women with disabilities find that offices for disability services are responsive to the challenges they face; whereas women's groups and women's centers do little concerning the issues concerning women with disabilities (Traustadottir, 1997). Very few have any contact with disability services. Thus, when women with disabilities seek affirmation in their developing identities as adult women, they that find the women's centers/resources are largely inaccessible. While postsecondary institutions enroll women with disabilities and make academics and the physical environment accessible, little is done to assist with social or personal adjustment (Educational Equity Concepts, 1993). The American Institute for Research (1998) concluded that, ". . . despite the laws to the contrary, female and male students with disabilities are still not being fully integrated into their local education system, much less into the academic disciplines that are becoming essential for career growth in the 21st century."

Although many postsecondary programs are accessible for students with disabilities, data disaggregated on the basis of gender are not available. Stodden, Conway, and Chang (2003) noted several areas that need to be attended to in order for students to succeed. These include " . . . expectations of achievement, individualization, quality and intensity of support provision, self-determination and self-advocacy, full utilization of

technological advancements, and the role of the Department of Rehabilitation (p. 18).

Those youth with disabilities who have earned an undergraduate degree (both male and female) are less likely to work full-time compared with their peers without disabilities who possess a degree (U.S. Census Bureau, 2000). For both women and men with disabilities between 21 and 64 years old, only about one third are employed. For those who are employed year-round full-time, it is still only about one third (women with physical disabilities 30.7% versus 69.2% for women without disabilities; men with physical disabilities 33.7% versus 83.2% for men without disabilities). Women with physical disabilities earn a median of $25,201 per year, which is substantially less than men with physical disabilities ($32,345) or women without disabilities ($28,164); they earn only 77% of the relative U.S. median income.

Across all age groups, people with disabilities are less likely to be employed than those without disabilities and consistently earn less, working in non-professional jobs which are less secure, have few opportunities for advancement and are without sufficient medical or retirement benefits than do their peers without disabilities (NSESP, 2000; Stoddard et al., 1998; OSERS, 2000).

The presence of a disability among individuals ages 25 to 64 triples the risk of also being impoverished. One third (34%) of adults with disabilities live in a household with a poverty-level annual income of less than $15,000 in inflation-adjusted dollars, compared to about 12% of nondisabled Americans—a 22-point gap. This gap is virtually identical to the gaps reported in 1994 and 1986 (Lipson & Rogers, 2000, p. 214).

Living in a rural rather than an urban area heightens the difficulty in finding employment for women, as a study in 1995, reported that 81% of rural women with disabilities earned less than $10,000 per year (New Freedom Initiative, 2001; Szalda-Petree, Seekins, & Innes, 1999). Twenty-six percent of women with disabilities live in rural areas and are three times less likely to work (27%) compared with nondisabled rural women (38%). Szalda-Petree, Seekins, and Innes (1999) believed this discrepancy exists because ". . . women with disabilities face a wide range of obstacles to independent living, including limited employment opportunities, poverty, barriers to health care, limitation due to secondary conditions, and abuse. This may be exacerbated in rural areas due to lower levels of education, limited opportunities, and isolation."

Among people with disabilities 21 to 64 years of age, the severity of their disability makes the most significant impact on their being employed. Only 25% of women with a severe disability and 28% of men with a severe disability were employed. Less severe disabilities also negatively impacted the likelihood of employment, especially for women. Among those with a non-severe disability, 68% of women and 85% of men were working at a job or business. In comparison, 75% of women and 90% of men with no disability were working at a job or business (Stoddard, Jans, Ripple, & Kraus, 1998). Those individuals with severe disabilities are more likely to live in poverty and be covered by government insurance programs (Zsembik et al., 2000).

Unemployment rates for Latinos with disabilities remain disproportionately high when compared with the total unemployment rates of persons without disabilities (52% compared with 18%) (Zsembik, Peek, & Peek, 2000).

Use of Technology and the Digital Divide

The digital divide has sometimes been defined as the gap in technology ownership and access between those who are poor or live in rural areas with limited or no access to the Internet (Charp, 2001). The ownership and access questions are usually explored in terms of three factors: (a) race, (b) geography, and (c) economic status. Another definition expanded this concept as follows: The digital divide refers to the gap created by access or lack of access to and the manner of use of technology by members of various social-identity groups (Bolt & Crawford, 2000). Such a definition then brings in both the access to equipment, as well as the cultural issues related to economic status, race/ethnicity, gender, and disability.

The chapter "Gender Equity in Educational and Instructional Technology" in this volume reported that girls are less likely to be enrolled in advanced technology programs. Research with people with physical disabilities has not been conducted that addresses gender differences specifically for people with disabilities in this regard. However, research on people with disabilities revealed that they were less than half as likely to have computer access at home as people without physical disabilities: 24% and 52%, respectively (Kaye, 2000). People with visual impairments and conditions that restrict physical movement face some of the biggest challenges in terms of access to technology in schools. The combination of less participation in advanced technology programs for girls, as well as barriers based on disability, results in a situation of double jeopardy for girls with disabilities in this important area (Rousso, 2001).

Health, Sexuality/Sexual Identity

Sexual intimacy is as important to many persons with disability as it is to those without. Women with disabilities face major challenges getting adequate sexual healthcare and information about their bodies and sexual matters (Linn & Rousso, 2001). Parents and caregivers of individuals with more significant limitations are understandably concerned about the possibility of sexually transmitted diseases and unwanted pregnancies due to their charge's limited capacity to make sound judgments (Shepperdson, 1995). Sex-education programs are often limited, although programs have been shown to be effective in teaching persons with intellectual disability about puberty, intercourse, pregnancy, birth control, and venereal disease (Lindsay et al., 1992). The rights of women and men with developmental disabilities to marry and express sexual intimacy are ambiguous at best, and in many cases very limited. The rights of children born to mothers and fathers with intellectual disabilities and the right of those individuals to parent have been debated, generating a good deal of heat and very little light. These issues touch on deeply held moral and religious beliefs that are often manifested as provincial, state, and national legal doctrine.

However, the eugenicists' quest for the "production of fine offspring," its rhetoric and rationale are still being used to justify the death of unborn babies with disabilities. This discourse is about the birth of the disabled infant who will constitute a burden to his or her family and the state. Social problems are socially constructed from the claims of those who are legitimized by society to make such claims, often as labels and definitions. The person seen as a burden becomes a member of an "outgroup," constructed as "other." Such "others" are often despised. Therefore, it becomes easier to accept the argument that by aborting a baby with a disability; both the baby and his or her parents are being saved from future pains" (Nunkoosing, 2000, p. 57).

It appears that many women with developmental disabilities do not receive the health services that typically developing women do (Thompson et al., 2003). Routine mammograms and routine gynecologic care are often lacking or insufficient (Davies & Duff, 2001; Messinger-Rapport & Rapport, 1997). Females with disabilities, like females without, appear to be more likely to manifest mental health and behavioral distress as anxiety or depression (Heiman, 2001; Reynolds & Miller, 1985; van Os et al., 1997), while males are more likely to display aggressive behaviors and other forms of acting out (Edelstein & Glenwick, 1997). The mental-health needs of males with developmental disabilities are often seen as more pressing, since caregivers are more likely to have difficulty managing outwardly directed behavioral challenges. There may be sex differences in the responses to pharmacological agents and educational interventions as well.

Sexual Abuse of Individuals with Disabilities

For individuals with disabilities, the reported rates of sexual abuse are much higher than in the general population. Both males and females are at increased risk. In one study, children and youth with intellectual disabilities were abused at the rates of 39–68% for girls and 16–30% of boys (Province of Nova Scotia, 2002). Males with disabilities are twice as likely as males without disabilities to be sexually abused in their lifetime (Province of Nova Scotia, 2002). The higher rate for boys as well as girls was also noted in a study of the deaf school-aged population, which indicated that more than 50% of both girls and boys had experienced some kind of sexual abuse (Sullivan, Vernon, & Scanlon, 1987).

These rates are so high for a number of reasons. Individuals with disabilities often do not have equitable access to education and information on the whole. Instruction about sexuality and socially appropriate sexual conduct may not be provided, on the assumption that the students are incapable of understanding (Reynolds, 1997). In the case of deaf and hard of hearing students, teachers may not be sufficiently competent in the students' optimal language or communication system to provide clear instruction and discussion on the topic. Without this knowledge, individuals with disabilities may not realize that it is wrong for an adult (or adolescent) to be sexual with a child, or that they have the right to say "no" and not be touched or forced to participate in an activity with which they are not comfortable. Children and other victims of sexual abuse who lack this kind of education may blame themselves or feel guilty if they are physically responsive to unwanted stimulation (Potts & Lewis, 1989). If the perpetrator is someone who has been affectionate and kind to them, or who is a caretaker, the individual may be confused about what has happened even though something feels "wrong" or they may think this is something that happens to everybody (Reynolds, 1997; Mounty, 1988; Mounty & Fetterman, 1989; Westerlund, 1990, 1993).

Other factors that may increase susceptibility to victimization include dependency, poor self-esteem, shame, powerlessness (or the perception or belief thereof), isolation, depersonalization, dehumanization, and infantalization by the nondisabled majority. In some cultures and some parts of the world, persons infected with HIV have sex with individuals with disabilities because they erroneously presume such individuals are virgins and believe that sexual intercourse with virgins will "cleanse" and cure them (http://www.speakout.org.za/medical/hiv/hiv_commentary_rape_of_individuals%20.htm). Women who are blind may be especially at risk for sexual abuse because they miss visual cues that may alert others to potential danger. Blind women also may be less likely to report sexual crimes because they are not familiar with the system for doing so (http://www.ebudaphne.org/These%20Neeti%20Aryal%202%20Executive%20Summary.doc). Individuals with mobility challenges who depend on assistants for personal care may not have the means by which to report molestation or abuse or may risk losing assistance essential to their survival or retaliation by the perpetrator if they do so (Nosek & Howland, 1998). Deaf children and youth abused by an interpreter, aide, family member, or acquaintance who can sign may risk being cut off from communication and access if they report the abuse.

Individuals who are blind and those with other disabilities are more likely to be abused because they may be perceived as less human, less adult, less capable, as not having equal needs or rights, or as less likely to be believed if they report the abuse (http://www.cnib.ca/eng/national/wbu/wbu_fifth_assembly/speeches/women_face_abuse.htm June 21, 2005). Abusers may minimize or justify inappropriate behavior by saying or thinking, "He does not know what is going on," "She can't see what I am doing or hear what I am saying, anyway" or "She should be grateful for my attention because nobody else would want her." A disabled person who feels shame or low self-esteem or who has a poor body image may deny the occurrence of nonconsensual sexual activity, blame him- or herself, or be confused by the attention. Because many individuals with disabilities have restricted access to resources for education and treatment and are perceived as or perceive themselves to be less powerful than persons without disabilities, once molestation or assault occurs, the person is at greater risk of being retraumatized (Westerlund, 1990, 1993; Mounty & Fetterman, 1989). To some extent, and in some cases, this heightens the possibility that victims may become perpetrators themselves (Vernon & Rich, 1997; Vernon & Miller, 2002).

In the deaf and hard-of-hearing population, sexual abuse occurs in all settings: at home, in mainstream school programs, and in residential schools. Yet, in the 1980s and 1990s when a number of cases of sexual abuse came to light, the very survival of residential schools in particular was threatened. Federal laws regarding the education of students with disabilities promoted inclusion in regular education settings with non-disabled students. However, because of unique language and communication needs, residential schools or center programs often can best provide deaf and hard-of-hearing students with full access to language acquisition and social-emotional development. Within residential schools, the language and culture of deaf people has been passed down and preserved. For generations, sex-

ual abuse in these settings was kept quiet for fear that the schools would be closed and the close-knit fabric of the deaf community would be torn apart (Elder, 1993; Mertens, 1996).

It is very important to make clear that the fact of having a disability does not automatically translate to someone having to be or become a victim. It is not the disability itself, but rather society's perceptions of individuals with disabilities as being vulnerable, incapable of making decisions, managing their own affairs, or participating fully in family and social contexts, that puts them at great risk for victimization.

Of paramount importance in treating any kind of sexual abuse is the empowerment of the survivors. They need to be believed and validated and assured that they were not at fault. It is critical that the therapeutic relationship provide an opportunity for the survivors to develop or restore the capacity for trust. In order not to retraumatize, discussion and exploration of the abuse must proceed at their pace and in their own time. Suvivors must feel that they are in control. They must see the therapist or helping professional as someone who respects them and can relate to their reality, experience, and place in the world (Walker, 2000; Goldstein, 1995). This process may be complicated when the survivor is a member of an oppressed or disenfranchised group or there are other inequities between the survivor and helping professional related to race/ethnicity class, status, gender, or disability (Westerlund, 1990, 1993; Burke et al., 1999).

Because of oppression or lack of access to information and resources, even more than others, disabled persons may not seek treatment or may delay in doing so for many reasons. At first, they may not realize that what they have experienced is wrong, or they may be in denial, feel ashamed, or feel that they are to blame for the incident(s). Facilities may be difficult to get to, and therapists' offices may not be fully accessible. Not all mental-health professionals are equally skilled in working with survivors of sexual abuse and, of those who are, even fewer are experienced in working with individuals with various disabilities.

Deaf individuals who are sexual-abuse survivors or have issues stemming from a history of abuse, such as sexual addiction or misconduct, may have difficulty finding a therapist who is a good language and communication match and is also skilled at working with survivors. In situations where an interpreter is present, deaf individuals may be uncomfortable working with an interpreter whom they know because of the personal and sensitive nature of the issues. Similarly, they may avoid seeing a therapist who is also deaf because of the small, insular deaf community (Burke et al., 1999).

Over the past 25 years, a number of programs have been implemented in an effort to stop sexual abuse before it happens or reoccurs. Models for prevention have alternately focused on educating and empowering women and children, conducting more rigorous background checks on personnel hired to work in schools and social service agencies, and harsher punishment for offenders (Vernon & Rich, 1997; Mounty & Fetterman, 1989). In order for prevention to be effective with disabled individuals, professionals and community leaders with specific disabilities must have a role in the implementation of such programs. Unfortunately, as one of the authors (Mounty) learned, this is a challenge because of the high numbers of survivors who have not had access to treatment services and are not yet in recovery.

INTERNATIONAL DEVELOPMENT AND WOMEN

Many women throughout the world are discriminated against, either because of law, culture, or custom, and have no rights to own or inherit land, to attend school, to have access to healthcare concerning their sexual and reproductive needs, to earn a fair wage, be promoted, or work without job discrimination United Nations Population Fund (2004). (See the chapter in this volume "Gender Equity Education Globally.") Approximately 300 million women and girls with disabilities around the world suffer double discrimination because they live not only as females, but also as females with disabilities. The majority of women with disabilities lives in developing countries (80%) and face discrimination from birth (World Health Organization, 2000). If a baby girl is born with a disability and is allowed to live, she must contend with negative attitudes and beliefs about disability from her family and community. Often girls with disabilities are hidden within their homes, have less access to healthcare services, will not attend school or work, will be subject to physical and sexual abuse, will be at higher risk for HIV infection, will not receive rehabilitation services or HIV/AIDS education, testing, or access to clinical programs, and will receive less care and food in the home than her siblings (Granich & Mermin, 2006; International Labour Organization, 2004; Niemann, Greenstein, & David, 2004; United Nations, 2003–04; World Bank, 2004a).

The responsibilities and roles traditionally assigned to women for the care of children and other family members mean that the experience of disability is different for women than men. Negative attitudes and beliefs about disabilities lead many to believe girls with disabilities are unable to fulfill the roles of being a student, wife, mother, or wage earner. Only 1% of girls in developing countries with disabilities attend school. The literacy rate for girls with disabilities is under 5%. Girls who do attend school attend for a shorter amount of time than boys (United Nations, 1992). Women with disabilities do not have equal access to paid employment and are twice as unlikely to find work as men. Most girls are kept at home where they care for children and relatives, cook, clean, and do daily chores.

Little research has been done in the area of gender development and disability other than gathering statistics although international agencies are now beginning to tackle the issue (InterAction, 2002; Singleton, Beslin, & Lewis, 2001; United States Agency for International Development, 2006; United Nations Enable, 2004; World Bank, 2004b). Development agencies are looking at poverty-reduction programs, the human rights of women with disabilities, and long-term strategies to empower women with disabilities. These agencies must be aware that the resources and opportunities afforded to men are not granted to women and that these inequalities must be balanced out. Not until women are represented in government institutions and can participate in the creation of public policy will their economic, educational, and legal rights be achieved. Only recently, the Investing in Women in Development (IWID) Fellowship program, made possible by the support of the United States Agency for International Development (USAID), completed the initial recruitment for a new gender & disability specialist position to serve at USAID/Washington. The IWID Fellow develops a sex-disaggregated monitoring and evaluation system to track the progress made on the inclusion of people with disabilities in US-AID programs and activities, and oversees the implementation of the USAID disability policy with a special emphasis on gender.

The 1995, the First International Symposium on Issues of Women with Disabilities at the U.N. Fourth World Conference on Women and NGO Forum held in Beijing, China, saw the emergence of the power of women with disabilities from around the world. Their participation and collective voice empowered the participants with disabilities as well as informed other women leaders and the world about their strength, force, and determination to improve their life situation. As a result of the Beijing Conference, in 1997, disabled women from around the world organized the International Leadership Forum where women from 80 countries met in Washington, DC, as a follow up to the 1995 United Nations Fourth World Conference on Women in Beijing. The purpose of the 1997 Forum was to monitor progress on the implementation of the Beijing Platform for Action. Also, 10,000 women met at the United Nations "Beijing+5: Women 2000—Gender Equality, Development and Peace for the 21st Century." Among the participants were 65 women with disabilities from 31 countries who participated in the overall activities and in a training program. The nonprofit group, Mobility International—USA, holds Women's Institutes on Leadership and Disability and has published materials which document the many successes of women with disabilities from around the world (Mobility Internatinal-USA, 2007).

International Disabled People's Organizations in cooperation with the Special Rapporteur on the Disability of the Commission for Social Development of the United Nations are examining a new Convention, which would protect and monitor the human rights of all persons with disabilities (United Nations Enable, 2004). Since there is no international binding agreement signed by UN Member States concerning the rights of women with disabilities, it is essential gender issues are included in the proposed "Comprehensive and Integral International Convention on the Protection of the Rights and Dignity of Persons with Disabilities." Arnade and Häfner (2005) suggested that:

1. The principles of gender mainstreaming, the principle of equality between men and women and the need for particular actions to eliminate the discriminations of women with disabilities must be mentioned in the beginning of the Convention either in a separate article or integrated in the articles 2 and 4.
2. All draft articles of the Convention having a key position for women with disabilities must be complemented by the gender perspective. To identify and address the needs of women with disabilities, the Convention must include the gender aspect as intended in UN Resolution 52/100 from 1997/98. It is the only way to motivate States Parties to consider gender issues, and specifically women's issues while taking action and reporting. (p. 1)

SPECIAL RESEARCH AND EVALUATION CHALLENGES TO ADVANCE GENDER EQUITY

One of the potentially positive aspects of No Child Left Behind (NCLB) is the accountability requirement and the report card.

Within the report card, it shows how minority groups are faring, and we are finding, not surprisingly, that the scores are really low. Such data force all of us—educators, parents, researchers, evaluators, and others— to find out why these children are not succeeding and implement changes to make sure no child is left behind. In order to do this, we need to conduct research about effective practices and evaluate the programs. We need to be specific on what it is we need to research, not just the program as a whole (Mertens, 2005). With so much visibility given to research and evaluation in the NCLB, this is a propitious moment for those in the feminist and disability communities to raise the issue of gender differences and minority/disabled groups' experiences in the school system and appropriate ways to capture the complexity of this experience. While NCLB does require some disaggregation of reported data, it does not require that the data provided by states allow for scrutiny of the intersection of type of disability, gender, and race/ethnicity.

The requirements of the No Child Left Behind legislation stresses that researchers use the scientific method, along with standardized tests and randomized designs as the desired approach to demonstrate a program's effectiveness. (http://www.ed.gov/nclb/methods/whatworks/whatworks.html).[7] With specific reference to individuals with disabilities and gender equity, the effect of changes in the IDEA legislation that resulted in distributing children with disabilities across a larger number of neighborhood schools has at least two methodological implications that complicate the possible application of randomized control designs. First, identification of research subjects became more complicated, and second, placement in many schools resulted in an increase in the variability of contextual factors. The identification of the independent variable in studying the effects of educating students with disabilities in inclusive settings becomes a more complex issue, which is not satisfactorily resolved in most special education research (Gallagher, 1990; Wang et al., 1990).

Ferrell et al. (2004) identified a number of complexities in such an undertaking, including a lack of systematic empirical methods that are tailored to address the needs of those with disabilities. Particular problems are associated with the use of control groups determined by random assignment as this strategy appears to contradict the underlying logic of the Individual Education Plan (IEP), one of the legislatively mandated tools designed to identify appropriate accommodations and educational strategies for people with disabilities. The IEP has in its name the term "individual," thus indicating that this person requires a unique program in order to receive early intervention services or a free appropriate public education. Given the individual nature of such a person's needs, how can his or her "treatment" be determined by random assignment? How can the person be placed in a control group, which means that he or she will be denied the carefully identified services that constitute the IEP? What are the ethical implications of random assignment when

a child's case has been carefully studied to determine strengths and areas in need of improvement and a small number of personnel with highly specialized skills and knowledge determined were appropriate for this child?

The highly idiosyncratic nature of populations with disabilities (which is compounded for those with low incidence disabilities), also introduces challenges related to rigorous data analysis because of the possibility of small samples and restricted or highly variable ranges. The uniqueness of the population also creates problems with attempts to replicate findings. Replication makes an assumption that similar people in similar circumstances can be used to demonstrate the generalizability of results. The assumption may not be met in such a population.

The context surrounding research with people with disabilities adds another layer of challenges. For example, the low-incidence population is one in which by definition is heterogeneous. People who are deaf, blind, or have severe disabilities differ on those dimensions as well as many others, including sex, race/ethnicity, home language, communication preferences, presence of additional disabilities, to name a few. The fact that these are by definition low-incidence disabilities means that there are small numbers of people across large geographic area.

Finally, small numbers of children with disabilities means that only a small number of professionals are available to serve them. Of this small number, much is asked. Adding the conduct of research may seem an impossible additional task. In addition, the small numbers are also associated with fewer dollars to support research with such populations. The strengthened federal role that the new law details, which permits Washington to withhold money from districts that come up short, has infuriated some state officials. They say Congress, since it first passed the law in 1975, has consistently failed to sufficiently finance special education (Schemo, 2004, p. 1).

THE TRANSFORMATIVE RESEARCH PARADIGM

The world of research is operating at the moment with several competing paradigms. A *paradigm* is a theoretical construct associated with specific philosophical assumptions that describes your view of the world. Currently, four paradigms are framing theoretical discussion: (a) the post-positivist, (b) the constructivist, (c) the transformative, and (d) the pragmatic paradigms (Mertens, 2005). Each paradigm is associated with its own philosophical assumptions about reality, relationships between researcher and participants, and methodological choices. The world of research can be seen as trying to understand the reality of educational or social programs as through a prism. The prism refracts the differences of experiences into an ever-changing pattern of different lights, while we seek ways to understand the use of culturally ap-

---

[7]In response to USDOE's requirement for the scientific method, the American Evaluation Association (AEA) stated, "While we agree with the intent of ensuring that federally sponsored programs be "evaluated using scientifically based research . . . to determine the effectiveness of a project intervention," we do not agree that "evaluation methods using an experimental design are best for determining project effectiveness." (http://www.eval.org/doestatement.htm). AEA takes the position that there is not one right way to research the effectiveness of a program. Our research paradigm, philosophies, and assumptions guide us in the questions we ask, what we want to know, methodological choices, and interpretations of our data AEA is joined by other organizations such as the American Educational Research Association, the American Psychological Association and the National Education Association (NEA) in providing commentary on NCLB.

propriate, multiple methods in understanding the pattern of diverging and converging results of the research.

The transformative paradigm provides a useful theoretical umbrella to explore the philosophical assumptions and guide methodological choices for the approaches to research that have been labeled inclusive, human-rights based, democratic, empowerment, or responsive. The transformative paradigm extends the thinking of democracy and responsiveness by consciously including the identification of important dimensions of diversity in research work and their accompanying relation to discrimination and oppression in the world (Mertens, 2005). It prompts the researcher to ask such questions as, What is hidden in the mandate of scientifically based research and use of "reliable" and "valid" standardized tests when applied to populations that are extremely diverse and not found in large groups that can be ethically or logistically randomly assigned to conditions? What is the researcher's role in uncovering that which has not been stated explicitly within the context of the danger that lurks in applying the conceptualization of scientifically based research without consideration of important dimensions of diversity?

Reliance on randomized control trials alone makes these layers of diversity less visible and less able to shed light on program effectiveness. To understand the context around the experiences in schooling for groups that differ on important dimensions means that a researcher needs to understand the dimensions of diversity that are important in the study and how those dimensions of diversity play out in terms of engagement in the process, choices about research questions, and data-collection methods.

Finally, methodologically, the transformative paradigm leads us to reframe not only the understanding of our iews, but also to understand that subsequent methodological decisions need to be reframed as well (Mertens, 2005). Sampling needs to be reframed to reveal the dangers of the myth of homogeneity, to understand which dimensions of diversity are important in a specific context, to avoid additional damage to populations by using labels such as "at risk" that can be demeaning and self-defeating. Invitations to participate in research need to be made in a way that is truly inviting, considering the support needs and demands put on participants. The transformative paradigm also leads us to reframe data-collection decisions to be more inclined to use mixed methods, and to be consciously aware of the benefits of involving community members in the data collection decisions and the appropriateness of methods with a depth of understanding of the cultural issues involved. Researchers need to be aware of the necessity and process for building trust to obtain valid data and modifications that may be necessary to collect valid data from various groups. Finally, researchers need to design their studies with an eye to tying the results to social action by meaningful involvement of people with disabilities and their advocates in the research from planning to dissemination.

NEED FOR RESEARCH ON GENDER AND DISABILITY

By studying gender and disability variations in the presentation and incidence of disabilities, we may gain insights into gender differences in the neural circuitry and neurochemistry of the brain for both people with and those without disabilities (Thompson, Caruso, & Ellerbeck, 2003). In the past, many studies of disability were conducted with only one sex and the findings were extrapolated across genders. However, disability may look different depending on sex. Because there are hormonal and brain developmental differences between typically developing children, adolescents, and adults, these differences might also occur among girls and boys with developmental disabilities. Disability may look different in girls than it does in boys because of different backgrounds and neural substrate. Research questions include (a) Do disabilities look so different in males and females that it affects diagnosis and thus prevalence? (b) Do sex differences in the brain mediate the development of the disability or do they simply moderate the presentation of the disability?

These issues and those in the subsequent sections need to be systematically studied.

Over and Underidentification
(adapted from Mertens & McLaughlin, 2004):

- How can research in special education lead to the development of more culturally and ethically valid assessment instruments and processes with full cognizance of differences based on types of disability, gender, race/ethnicity, socioeconomic status, and other relevant dimensions of diversity?
- What role does cultural competency play in the decision to refer students for special education? How is cultural competency related to sex-stereotyping when gender is not explicitly considered as a factor?
- How can teachers differentiate instruction so that male and female students from the full diversity spectrum, including those who are ethnically and linguistically diverse, can benefit form their educational experiences?
- What role should families play in the design, implementation, and research of educational programs for these students? What are the gender-equity implications for such research in culturally complex communities?
- What are the implications of the possible overidentification of boys and racial/ethnic minorities in special education? What are the implications of the possible underidentification of girls in special education?

Family Involvement

- What factors drive and restrain successful parental involvement? Are there differences by children who share different dimensions of diversity, including differences by type of disability and gender?
- What strategies work best to modify parental, teacher, and administrator attitudes to enhance functional family involvement? What are the gender equity implications of these strategies?
- What new skills do parents, teachers, and administrators need to enable a positive working relationship that benefits all children, males and females?

- What strategies work best to enable schools to reach and involve traditionally underrepresented families? What gender-equity issues arise in the involvement of culturally diverse families?

School Climate and Discipline

- What specific practices will result in the development of a positive school climate and also have positive effects on teacher, parent, and student behavior? What specific gender-equity issues arise in terms of effective disciplinary practices?
- What state and local policies are needed to support the systematic application of research-based practices that yield a positive school climate?
- What is the role of after-school activities and extracurricular activities for both males and females with disabilities?
- What factors affect sexual harassment for people with disabilities? How is it similar or different for males and females?
- What is the potential of positive behavior support systems (Center on Positive Behavioral Interventions and Support, 2001) to enhance the capacity of schools to educate all students, especially those with challenging social behaviors? What is its differential effectiveness by gender?

DIVERSITY IN THE POPULATION WITH DISABILITIES

- What are effective instructional practices for students with disabilities whose native language is not English? What gender equity issues need to be addressed in terms of instructional practices?
- What are the cultural factors that contribute to success for students from diverse ethnic/racial backgrounds?

Educational Experience and Effects of Education

- To what extent do males and females with different types of disabilities have access to various types of curricula, e.g., math, science, vocational education?
- What pedagogical strategies are effective in teaching males and females with different types of disabilities?
- What variables explain differences in postsecondary outcomes for males and females with different types of disabilities?
- What strategies are effective in leading to improved postsecondary outcomes for males and females with disabilities?
- What is the role of the U.S. government in addressing these issues related to gender and disability?

- What can the government do to create more gender equitable education for students with disabilities that qualify for service under IDEA? The role of the government can be to:
  1. Provide access to data that disaggregates information on students by sex, race, and disability under NCLB and IDEA.
  2. Support more replicable programs focused on helping students with disabilities and sensitive evaluations that do not rely only on RTC designs, which are often inappropriate for diversity in terms of disability.
  3. Continue funding and evaluation of programs that seem promising, such as mentoring programs.

Based on the research reviewed in this chapter, additional research, policy changes, and improved practices are needed to address the myriad of challenges that are associated with the provision of services for both males and females with disabilities. A lengthy research agenda is identified in the last section of this chapter. The most important questions that require additional research include,

- What should be done regarding the over and underrepresentation of males and females in special education?
- What is the potential of the behavioral programs when used with people with disabilities and what are the gender differences that influence their effectiveness?
- What is it about the selection criteria and decision making that results in gender differences on so many indicators of access to and effectiveness of services for people with disabilities?

To obtain answers to these and the other questions included in this chapter requires a policy change that calls for the design of research based on a transformative model that incorporates the full spectrum of cultural diversity found in the disability community, including types of disabilities, gender, and race/ethnicity. Reporting requirements should be modified to allow for an understanding of the effects of interventions on the basis of the intersection of these characteristics. Improved practices can be derived from the limited research base that exists; additional improvements can be empirically assessed as they are implemented to determine their effectiveness.

ACKNOWLEDGMENTS

The authors, faculty and staff from Gallaudet University, wish to thank Harilyn Rousso, Disabilities Unlimited, NY, NY for her helpful review comments.

References

Abney, R., & Richey, D. (1992). Opportunities for minority women in sports—The impact of Title IX. *Journal of Physical Education, Recreation & Dance, 63*(3), 56.

American Youth Policy Forum. (2002). Youth with Disabilities and Transition to Employment. What Youth with Disabilities Say is Important For Building A Successful Adult Life? A Forum—July 29, 2002.

Retrieved February 7, 2007 from http://www.aypf.org/forum-briefs/2002/fb072902.htm

American Research Association. (2003). American Research Association response to U. S. Department of Education, Notice of proposed priority, Federal Register RIN 1890-ZA00, November 4, 2003, Scientifically Based Research Methods. Retrieved October 25, 2004, from http://www.eval.org/doestatement.htm

American Community Survey. (2003). Sex by disability status by school enrollment by educational attainment for the civilian noninstitutionalized population 18 to 34 years, 2003 Summary Tables. Retrieved May 25, 2005, from http://factfinder.census.gov/servlet/DTTable?_bm=y&geo_id=04000US03&ds_name=ACS_2003_EST_G00_&-redoLog=false&-mt_name=ACS_2003_EST_G2000_PCT046

Arnade, S., & Häfner, S. (2005, July). Towards visibility of women with disabilities in the UN Convention. *Disabled Peoples' International.* Retrieved February 7, 2007, from http://v1.dpi.org/lang-en/resources/details.php?page=278

Blauwat, C. (2005). Why sports should be included in disability rights convention, disability information dissemination network. Retrieved May 24, 2005, from http://www.disabilityworld.org/12-02_05/news/sports.shtml

Bolt, D. B., & Crawford, R. A. K. (2000). *Digital divide: Computers and our children's future.* New York, NY: Bantam Books.

Brown, J. H., D'Emidio-Caston, M., & Benard, B. (2001). *Resilience education.* Thousand Oaks, CA: Corwin Press.

Brown, D. (2005, January 14). For small survivors, a cruel new world. *The Washington Post,* p. C1.

Burgstahler, S. (2002). Bridging the digital divide in postsecondary education: Technology access for youth with disabilities. *Addressing Trends and Developments in Secondary Education and Transition, 1*(2). Minneapolis, MN: National Center on Secondary Education and Transition. Retrieved February 6, 2007, http://www.ncset.org/publications/viewdesc.asp?id=718

Burke, F., Gutman, V., & Dobosh, P. K. (1999). Treatment of deaf survivors of sexual abuse: A process of healing. In I. W. Leigh (Ed.), *Psychotherapy with deaf clients from diverse groups* (pp. 279–305). Washington, DC: Gallaudet University Press.

Center on Positive Behavioral Interventions and Support. (2001). http://www.pbis.org/main.htm Retrieved February 6, 2007.

Charp, S. (2001). Bridging the digital divide. *THE Journal, 28*(10), 10–12.

Cooper, R. (2000). Preparing students of the new millennium. *Journal of Negro Education, 68*(1), 1–3.

Corn, A. L., & Spungin, S. J. (2003). *Free and appropriate public education and the personnel crisis for students with visual impairments and blindness.* Gainesville, FL: Center on Personnel studies in Special Education. Retrieved September 21, 2004, from www.copsse.org

Crawford, J., Lewis, C., & Sygall, S. (2002). Loud, proud, and passionate: Including women with disabilities in international development programs. Eugene, Oregon: Mobility International USA.

Davies, D. (1996). Partnerships for student success. *New Schools, New Communities, 12*(3), 14–21.

Davies, N., & Duff, M. (2001). Breast cancer screening for older women with intellectual disability. *Journal of Intellectual Disability Research, 45*(3), 253–257.

Davis, M., & Marshall, D. (1987). Female and disabled: Challenged women in education. *Perspective, 5*(3).

Disability World. (2005). Summary of Rehabilitation/International Paralympic Committee Symposium. Retrieved February 7, 2007, from http://www.disabilityworld.org/1202_05/news/paralympic.shtml

Donovan, M. S., & Cross, C. T. (2002). *Minority students in special and gifted education.* Washington, DC: National Academy Press.

Dougherty, K. (2001). *The contradictory college: The conflicting origins, impacts, and futures of the community college.* Ithaca: State University of New York Press.

Doren, B., & Benz, M. (2001). Gender equity issues in the vocational and transition services and employment outcomes experienced by young women with disabilities. In H. Rousso, & M. L. Wehmeyer, (Eds.), *Double jeopardy* (pp. 271–312). Albany: State University of New York Press.

Edelstein, T. M., & Glenwick, D. S. (1997). Referral reasons for psychological services for adults with mental retardation. *Research in Developmental Disabilities, 18*, 45–59.

Edgar, E., Patton, J. M., & Day-Vines, N. (2002). Democratic dispositions and cultural competency. *Remedial and Special Education, 23*(4), 241–251.

Educational Equity Concepts, Inc. (April, 1993). *A Report on Women with Disabilities in Postsecondary Education,* Issue Paper Number 1.

Elder, M. (1993, September). Abuse because of deafness? *Moving Forward, 2*(5). Retrieved January 17, 2005, from http://www.moving-forward.org/v2n5-coverside.html

Feminist Majority Foundation. (2007). *Women with disabilities in Sport.* Retrieved January 24, 2004, from http://www.feminist.org/sports/disability.html

Ferrell, K. A., Luckner, J. L., Jackson, L., Correa, S. M., Muir, S. G., Howell, J. J., et al. (2004). All learners, all the time: Including students with low-incidence disabilities. Presentation at the 2004 Council for Exceptional Children Annual Convention, New Orleans. Retrieved September 21, 2004, from www.nclid.unco.edu/Presentations/CEC/index.html

Flood, C. (2001). Schools fail boys too: Exposing the con of traditional masculinity. In H. Rousso & M. L. Wehmeyer, (Eds.), *Double jeopardy* (pp. 207–236). Albany: State University of New York Press.

Fox, L. H. (2000). The gender equity expert panel: History and rationale report submitted to the Office of Educational Research and Improvement, U.S. Department of Education.

Froschl, M., Rubin, E., & Sprung, B. (1999, November). Connecting gender and disability. *WEEA Digest.* Retrieved on February 7, 2007, from http://www2.edc.org/gdi/publications_SR/disabdig.pdf

Gallagher, J. J. (1990). New patterns in special education. *Educational Researcher, 19*(5), 34–36.

Gerner de Garcia, B. (2004, Spring 2004). Literacy for Latino deaf students: A socio-cultural approach.*Research at Gallaudet Newsletter.* Washington, DC: Gallaudet University.

Gill, C. (1999). Invisible ubiquity: The surprising relevance of disability issues in evaluation. *American Journal of Evaluation, 29*(2), 279–287.

Goldstein, E. (1995). *Ego psychology and social work practice* (2nd ed.). New York: The Free Press.

Granich, R., & Mermin, J. (2006). *HIV health and your community: A guide for action.* Berkeley, CA: Hesperian Foundation.

Henderson, K. (2005). Overview of ADA, IDEA, and Section 504. Reston, VA: ERIC

Hanley, J. H. (1999). Beyond the tip of the iceberg: Five stages toward cultural competence: Reading today's youth. *The Community Circle of Caring Journal, 3*(2), 9–12.

Hebbeler, K., Wagner, M., Spiker, D., Scarborough, A., Simeonsson, R., & Collier, M. (2001). A first look at the characteristics of children and families entering early intervention services. Menlo Park, CA: SRI International.

Heiman, T. (2004). Depressive mood in students with mild intellectual disability: Students' reports and teachers' evaluation. *Journal of Intellectual Disability Research, 45*(6), 526–43.

Heinicke-Motsch, K., & Sygall, S. (2004). *Building an inclusive development community: A manual on including people with disabilities in international development programs.* Berkley, CA: Mobility International.

InterAction. (2002). PVO standards. Retrieved on February 7, 2007, from http://www.interaction.org/pvostandards/index.html#InterAction%20PVO%20Standards

International Labour Organization (2004). Community based rehabilitation (CBR): A strategy for rehabilitation, equalization of opportunities, poverty reduction and social inclusion of people with disabilities: *Joint Position Paper—ILO-WHO-UNESCO*. Retrieved February 7, 2007, from http://www.ilo.org/public/english/employment/skills/download/jointpaper.pdf

Kaye, S. H. (2000). Computer and Internet Use Among People with Disabilities. Disability Statistics Report No. 13. Washington DC: National Institute on Disability and Rehabilitation Research, U.S. Department of Education. Retrieved from February 6, 2007, http://dsc.ucsf.edu/pdf/report13.pdf

Kidd, B. & Donnelly, P. (2000). Human rights in sports. *International Review for the Sociology of Sport, 35*(2), 131–148.

Lewis, A. C., & Henderson, A. T. (1997). *Families crucial to school reform.* Washington, DC: Center for Law and Education. (ERIC Document Reproduction No. ED 418480.)

Lindsay, W. R., Bellshaw, E., Culross, G., Staines, C., & Michie, A. (1992). Increases in knowledge following a course of sex education for people with intellectual disabilities. *Journal of Intellectual Disabilities, 26*(6), 531–539.

Linn, E., & Rousso, H. (2000). Stopping sexual harassment in schools. In H. Rousso & M. Wehymeyer (Eds,). *Double Jeopardy: Addressing gender equity in special education supports and services.* Albany: State University of New York Press.

Lipson, J. G., & Rogers, J. G. (2000). Cultural aspects of disability. *Journal of Transcultural Nursing, 11*(3), 212–219.

Lloyd, M. (2001). The politics of disability and feminism: Discord or synthesis? *Sociology, 35*(3), 715–728.

Longmore, P., & Umansky, L. (Eds.) (1991). *The New Disability History: American Perspectives.* New York: New York University Press.

Losen, D. J., & Orfield, G. (Eds.). (2002). *Racial inequity in special education.* Boston: Harvard Education Press.

Marotta, S. A., & Garcia, J. G. (2003). Latinos in the United States in 2000. *Hispanic Journal of Behavioral Sciences, 25*(1), 13–34.

McCain, M., Gill, P., Wills, J., & Larson, M. (May, 2004). Knowledge, Skills, and Abilities of Youth Service Practitioners: *The Centerpiece of a Successful Workforce Development System.* The National Collaborative on Workforce and Disability for Youth, Washington, DC. U. S. Department of Labor, grant # E-9-4-1-0070. Retrieved February 7, 2007, from www.ncwd-youth.info

Messinger-Rapport, B. J., & Rapport, D. J. (1997). Primary care for the developmentally disabled adult. *Journal of General Internal Medicine, 12,* 629–636.

Mertens, D. M. (1996). Breaking the silence about sexual abuse of deaf youth. *American Annals of the Deaf, 141*(5), 352–258.

Mertens, D. M. (2001, August 2–5). *PT3 evaluations: Are we closing or widening the digital divide.* Paper presented at the Preparing Tomorrow's Teachers to Use Technology Annual Grantees' Meeting, Washington, DC.

Mertens, D. M. (2003). Mixed methods and the politics of human research: The transformative-emancipatory perspective. In A. Tashakkori, & Teddlie, C. (Eds.), *Handbook of mixed methods in social and behavioral research.* Thousand Oaks, CA: Sage.

Mertens, D. M., & McLaughlin, J. (2004). *Research and evaluation methods in special education.* Thousand Oaks, CA: Corwin Press.

Mertens, D. M. (2005). *Research and evaluation in education and psychology: Integrating diversity with quantitative, qualitative and mixed methods* (2nd ed.) Thousand Oaks, CA: Sage.

Mobility International-USA. (2007). *Women's Institute on Leadership and Disability (WILD).* Retrieved February 7, 2007, from http://www.miusa.org/wild

Moon, M. (1991). *Having fun: What's in and what's not.* Project REC. 38. (ERIC Document Reproduction Service No. ED369202)

Mounty, J. L. (1988, June). *Deaf CAP and diversity.* Panel presented at the New England Child Assault Prevention Conference, Worcester, MA.

Ms. Foundation for Women. (October, 1993). *Programmed neglect: Not seen, not heard.* National Girls Initiative. New York: Author.

Munson, D. (1995). *The current research efforts of Special Olympics International.* (ERIC Document Reproduction Service No. ED406098)

National Center for Educational Statistics. (2000). *Internet access in U.S. public schools and classrooms, 1994-1999.* Washington, DC: U.S. Department of Education.

National Center for the Study of Postsecondary Educational Supports (1999). *Students with disabilities in postsecondary education: A profile of preparation, participation, and outcomes.* Washington, D.C.: NCES. U.S. Department of Education, National Center for Educational Statistics. Retrieved February 7, 2007, from http://nces.ed.gov/pubsearch/pubsinfo.asp?pubid=1999187

National Center for the Study of Postsecondary Educational Supports (2000, June). *Postsecondary students with disabilities: Enrollment, services and persistence.* Washington, DC. Retrieved February 7, 2007 from http://nces.ed.gov/pubsearch/pubsinfo.asp?pubid=2000092

National Center for the Study of Postsecondary Educational Supports (2002, July). Preparation for and support of youth with disabilities in postsecondary education & employment: Implications for policy, priorities and practice. *Proceedings and briefing book for the National Summit on Postsecondary Education for People with Disabilities,* presented in Washington, DC, July 8, 2002. Retrieved February 7, 2007, from http://www.ncset.hawaii.edu/summits/july2002/default.htm

National Organization on Disability/Louis Harris and Associates. (1998). *NOD/Harris 1998 survey of Americans with disabilities* [On-line]. Available from National Organization on Disability/Louis Harris and Associates Web site, http://www.nod.org

National Science Foundation. (2003). *Women, minorities, and people with disabilities in science and engineering*—2002. Author: Arlington VA. Retrieved February 23, 2007, www.nsf.gov/statistics/nsf03312/pdf/women02.pdf−2005-04-12

New Freedom Initiative. (Februrary 1, 2001). Executive summary: Fulfilling America's promise to Americans with disabilities. Retrieved February 7, 2007, from http://www.whitehouse.gov/news/freedominitiative/freedominitiative.html

Niemann, S., Greenstein, & D. David, D. (2004). *Helping children who are deaf: Family and community support for children who do not hear well.* Berkeley, CA: Hesperian Foundation.

Nosek, M. A., & Howland, C. A. (1998, February). *Abuse and women with disabilities.* Violence Against Women Online Resources, Applied Research Forum. Retrieved January 17, 2005, from http://www.vaw.umn.edu/documents/vawnet/disab/disab.html

NSESP. (2000). *National survey of education support provision to students with disabilities in postsecondary education settings.* (Tech. Rep., June 2000). University of Hawai`i at Manoa, Rehabilitation Research and Training Center. Retrieved February 7, 2007, from http://www.rrtc.hawaii.edu/documents/products/phase1/037-H01.pdf

Nunkoosing, K. (2000). Constructing learning disability. *Journal of Learning Disabilites, 4*(1), 49–62.

Office of Special Education and Rehabilitative Services (2000). *IDEA Lessons for All!* Retrieved February 7, 2007, from http://www.ed.gov/inits/commissionsboards/whspecialeducation/reports/pcesefinalreport.doc

Center on Positive Behavioral Interventions and Support. (2001). *Positive behavior support project.* University of Delaware. Delaware Department of Education. Retrieved February 7, 2007, at http://www.udel.edu/cds/pbs/

Potts, S., & Lewis, D. (1989, Spring). Preventing childhood sexual abuse. *Independent School,* 21–29.

Province of Nova Scotia. (2002). *Fact Sheet 5,* Province of Nova Scotia. http://www.gov.ns.ca/coms/files/facts5.asp Retrieved January 20, 2004.

Reynolds, L. A. (1997). People with mental retardation & sexual abuse. *The Arc.* Retrieved January 14, 2005, from http://www.thearc.org/faqs/Sexabuse.html

Reynolds, W. M., & Miller, K. L. (1985). Depression and learned helplessness in mentally retarded and nonmentally retarded adolescents: An initial investigation. *Applied Research in Mental Retardation, 6,* 295–306.

Rousso, H. (2001). What do Frida Kahlo, Wilma Mankiller, and Harriet Tubman have in common? Providing role models for girls with (and without) disabilities. In H. Rousso & M. L. Wehmeyer, (Eds.), *Double jeopardy* (pp. 337–360). Albany: State University of New York Press.

Rousso, H., & Wehmeyer, M. L. (2001). Introduction. In Rousso, H., & Wehmeyer, M. L. (Eds.), *Double jeopardy* (pp. 1–11). Albany: State University of New York Press.

Ryan, K. (2004, November 4). *Democracy, education, and methodology, part I.* Panel proposal for the American Evaluation Association annual meeting, Atlanta, GA. Retrieved October 25, 2004, from http://www.kistcon.com/search04/session.asp?sessionid=1387&presenterid=873

Sargent, C. (1999). Preparing young women for the workplace. *Gender and Disability Digest.* WEEA Equity Resource Center. [On-line]. site, Retrieved February 7, 2007, from http://www2.edc.org/WomensEquity/pdffiles/disabdig.pdf

Schemo, D. J. (2004). Parts of special-ed bill would shift more power to states and school districts. *The New York Times,* p. A22. Retrieved from http://www.nytimes.com/2004/11/22/education/22special.html Retrieved November 22, 2004.

Seelman, K. D. (2000). *The new paradigm on disability: Research issues and approaches.* Washington, DC: National Institute for Disability and Rehabilitative Research.

Seligman, M. E. P., & Csikszentmihalyi, M. (2000). Positive psychology: An introduction. *American Psychologist, 55*(1), 5–14.

Shaffer, S., & Shevitz, L. (2001). She bakes and he builds: Gender bias in the curriculum. In H. Rousso, & M. L. Wehmeyer, (Eds.), *Double jeopardy* (pp. 115–132). Albany: State University of New York Press.

Shepperdson, B. (1995). The control of sexuality in young people with Down's Syndrome. *Child Care, Health and Development, 21,* 333–349.

Singleton, T., Breslin, M., & Lewis, C. (2001). *Gender and disability: A survey of Interaction member agencies: Findings and recommendations on inclusion of women and men with disabilities in international development programs.* Eugene, OR: Mobility International USA.

Society for Disability Studies. (2005). *General information.* [On-line]. Retrieved February 7, 2007, from http://www.uic.edu/orgs/sds/generalinfo.html

Snowden, R. (2003, Autumn). Partners for Youth with Disability. *American Rehabilitation, 27*(1), 36.

Stoddard, S., Jans, L., Ripple, J., & Kraus, L. (1998). *Chartbook on Work and Disability in the United States, 1998.* An InfoUse Report. Washington, D.C.: U.S. National Institute on Disability and Rehabilitation Research.

Stodden, R. A., Conway, M. A., Chang, K. (2003). Findings from the study of postsecondary educational supports for individuals with disabilities: Implications for the application of technology in secondary schools. *Journal of Special Education Technology, 18*(4), 29–44.

Sullivan, P. M., Vernon, M., & Scanlan, J. M. (1987). Sexual abuse of deaf youth. *American Annals of the Deaf, 132*(4), 256–262.

Sugai, G., & Horner, R. (2001). *School climate and discipline: Going to scale.* A framing paper for the National Summit on the Shared Implementation of IDEA. Arlington, VA: IDEA Partnerships. Retrieved from http://www.ideainfo.org/summit

Swadner, B. B., & Lubeck, S. (Eds.). (1995). *Children and families "at promise": Deconstructing the discourse on risk.* Albany, NY: State University of New York Press.

Szalda-Petree, A., Seekins, T., & Innes, B. (June, 1999). *Women with disabilities: Employment, income, and health.* National Institute on Disability and Rehabilitation Research, U.S. Department of Education .Research and Training Center on Disability in Rural Communities. Retrieved February 7, 2007, from http://rtc.ruralinstitute.umt.edu/RuDis/DisWomenFact.htm

Thompson, T., Caruso, M., & Ellerbeck, K. (2003). Sex matters in autism and other developmental disabilities. *Journal of Learning Disabilities, 7*(4), 345–362.

Traustadottir, R. (1997). *Women with disabilities: Issues, resources, connections revised.* The Center on Human Policy, Syracuse University.

Trochim, W. (2004, November 4). Democracy as a structured mixed methodology. Paper presented at the panel of Democracy, Education, and Methodology Part I, American Evaluation Association annual meeting, Atlanta, GA.

United Nations (2003–04). *The United Nations and Disabled Persons— The First Fifty Years.* Retrieved February 7, 2007, from http://www.un.org/esa/socdev/enable/dis50y00.htm

United Nations Enable. (2004). *Ad Hoc committee on a comprehensive and integral international convention on the protection and promotion of the rights and dignity of persons with disabilities.* Retrieved January 23, 2004, from http://www.un.org/esa/socdev/enable/rights/adhoccom.htm

United Nations Office. (1990, August). *Report on the Seminar of Women with disabilities.* Centre for Social Development and Humanitarian Affairs. Division for the Advancement of Women. Retrieved January 23, 2004, from http://www.un.org/esa/socdev/enable/women/wwdsem0.htm

United Nations Population Fund (2004). *Working from within: Culturally sensitive approaches in UNFPA programming.* New York. UNFPA.

United States Agency for International Development (2006). *Disability and Development.* Retrieved February 7, 2007 from http://www.usaid.gov/about_usaid/disability/

U.S. Census Bureau. (2000). *Employment and earnings by disability status for civilian noninstitutionalized women 21 to 64 Years: 2000.* Retrieved February 7, 2007, from. http://www.census.gov/hhes/www/disability/cps/cps104.html

U.S. Census Bureau. (2000). *Disability status of the civilian noninstitutionalized population by sex and selected characteristic for the United States and Puerto Rico, 2000.* Retrieved February 23, 2007, www.census.gov/prod/cen2000/doc/sf3.pdf

U.S. Census Bureau. (2003). *Disability Status 2000.* Washington, DC: Author.

U.S. Department of Education. (2002). *Twenty-fourth annual report to congress on the implementation of the individuals with disabilities education act.* Retrieved June 17, 2005, from http://www.ed.gov/about/reports/annual/osep/2002/index.html

U.S. Department of Education. (2004). *The facts about . . . investing in what works.* Retrieved October 24, 2005 from http://www.ed.gov/nclb/methods/whatworks/whatworks.html

U.S. Department of Justice. (2001a). *Title IV legal manual.* Washington DC: Civil Rights Division. Retrieved June 16, 2005, from http://www.usdoj.gov/crt/cor/coord/vimanual.htm

U.S. Department of Justice. (2001b). *Title IX legal manual.* Washington, DC: Civil Rights Division. Retrieved June 16, 2005, from http://www.usdoj.gov/crt/cor/coord/ixlegal.pdf

U.S. Department of Justice. (2002). *A guide to disability rights laws.* Retrieved February 10, 2005, from http://www.usdoj.gov/crt/ada/cguide.htm

Van Os, J., Jones, P., Lewis, G., Wadsworth, M., & Murray, R. (1997). Developmental precursors of affective illness in a general population birth cohort. *Archives of General Psychiatry, 54,* 625–631.

Vernon, M., & Rich, S. (1997) Pedophilia and deafness. *American Annals of the Deaf, 142*(4), 300–311.

Vernon, M., & Miller, K. R. (2002). Issues in the sexual molestation of deaf youth. *American Annals of the Deaf, 147*(5), 28–35.

Wagner, M. (1992, April). *Being female—A secondary disability? Gender differences in the transition experiences of young people with disabilities.* Paper presented at the annual meeting of the American Educational Research Association, San Francisco.

Wahl, E. (2001). Can she really do science? Gender disparities in math and science education. In H. Rousso, & M. L. Wehmeyer, (Eds.), *Double jeopardy* (pp. 133–154). Albany: State University of New York Press.

Waldrop, J., & Stern, S. (March, 2003). *Disability Status 2000.* Retrieved May 23, 2005, from www.census.gov/prod/2003pubs/c2kbr-17.pdf

Walker, L. E. A. (1984). *Abused women and survivor therapy: A practical guide for the psychotherapist.* Washington, DC: American Psychological Association.

Wang, M. C., Reynolds, M. C., & Walberg, H. J. (Eds.). (1990). *Special education research and practice.* Oxford, England: Pergamon.

Watson, N., McKie, L., Hughes, B., Hopkins, D., & Gregory, S. (2004). (Inter)Dependence, needs, and care: The potential for disability and feminist theorists to develop an emancipatory model. *Sociology, 38*(2), 331–350.

Westerlund, E. (1990). Thinking about incest, deafness, and counseling. *Journal of the American Deafness and Rehabilitation Association, 23*, 105–107.

Westerlund, E. (1993). Thinking about incest, deafness, and counseling. In M. Nagler (Ed.), *Perspectives on disability* (pp. 341–344). Palo Alto, CA: Health Markets Research.

Whelan, J. (2003, May 14). *Child sexual abuse, A National Center for PTSD fact sheet.* Retrieved June 17, 2005, from http://www.ncptsd.org/facts/specific/fs_child_sexual_abuse.html

Wehmeyer, M. L., & Rousso, H. (2001). Addressing gender equity in special education services: An agenda for the twenty-first century. In H. Rousso, & M. L. Wehmeyer, (Eds.), *Double jeopardy* (pp. 375–386). Albany: State University of New York Press.

Wehmeyer, M. L., & Schwartz, M. (2001). Research on gender bias in special education services. In H. Rousso, & M. L. Wehmeyer, (Eds.), *Double jeopardy* (pp. 271–288). Albany: State University of New York Press.

World Bank. (2004). *Impact of HIV/AIDS on disabled community largely overlooked.* Retrieved January 23, 2004, from http://web.worldbank.org/WBSITE/EXTERNAL/TOPICS/EXTSOCIALPROTECTION/EXTDISABILITY/0,,contentMDK:20287490~menuPK:282704~pagePK:64020865~piPK:149114~theSitePK:282699,00.html

World Bank and Disability. (2004). *The World Bank and Disability.* Retrieved February 7, 2007, from http://web.worldbank.org/WBSITE/EXTERNAL/TOPICS/EXTSOCIALPROTECTION/EXTDISABILITY/0,,menuPK:282704~pagePK:149018~piPK:149093~theSitePK:282699,00.html

World Health Organization. (2000, December 1) *Is there equality of opportunities for people with disabilities? A recent WHO report sums up the situation. Press Release. No 16..* Retrieved January 23, 2004, from http://www.who.int/inf-pr-2000/en/note2000-16.html

Wright, P. W. D., & Wright, P. D. (2005). *Section 504.* Retrieved February 10, 2005, from http://www.wrightslaw.com/info/sec504.index.htm

Zsembik, B. A., Peek, M. K., & Peek, C. W. (2000). Race and ethnic variation in the disablement process. *Journal of Aging and Health, 12*(2), 229–249.

OVERVIEW: GENDER EQUITY
FROM EARLY CHILDHOOD THROUGH
POSTSECONDARY EDUCATION

Carol Anne Dwyer

Throughout this *Handbook,* fundamental issues of gender equity have been addressed from the perspectives of a broad set of participants in education. These participants include students and teachers, young children's caregivers, families and peers, school administrators, and researchers, all of whom come from a diversity of demographic backgrounds. In this volume, we have also viewed education through the lens of specific disciplines that are being taught and of special educational topics such as technology and testing. Despite this panoramic view, however, there remains much to say that concerns both ends of the age spectrum. It is important to remember that many important gender-equity issues have their roots in early-childhood experiences; and that those who are being educated are increasingly people of all ages, from very young children to mature adults. It is essentially for these reasons that we have once again included separate chapters on the settings and issues that affect early-learning environments and postsecondary education. In both cases, the authors view issues related to a wide diversity of participants and the external influences that act upon them.

In my introduction to the chapters on these same topics in the original 1985 *Handbook,* I observed that there is a cycle, with respect to gender equity, in which "the seeds of change are being sown in individual preschool experiences . . . while at the same time postsecondary experiences are shaping the content of the next generation's early education" (p. 455). As the two current chapters show, to the extent that this remains an accurate observation on the life cycle of change, we are not only experiencing a significant stall in many areas of gender equity today, but will continue to experience these same problems in the future. Although early childhood-learning environments remain the focus of considerable research and policy attention, the issue of gender is markedly lacking from scholarly discourse in this arena. In addition, such public discourse as occurs on gender issues in early childhood seems too often to draw on sources of dubious scientific merit. Similarly, those who provide the educational experiences for young children continue to experience working conditions that indicate that an unrealistically low value continues to be attached to their work, to the detriment of today's students and those in future generations. In the postsecondary realm, since the 1985 *Handbook,* women have continued to make enormous progress pursuing a college education and in increasing the numbers obtaining degrees in many fields at the undergraduate, graduate, and postgraduate levels. Today's young women seem to have taken to heart the message that was a large part of the women's movement of the 1960s and 1970s, that a college education will enhance their quality of life, not only for themselves in the short run, but also for their families and their children in future generations.

As we will see in Chapter 30, however, there remain serious gender-equity issues in the postsecondary education realm for both students and faculty. In this same two decades of progress for women, men have not made similar progress in postsecondary education, a phenomenon that the popular press seems all to eager to attribute to women's successes, rather than exploring men's and women's issues in a more rigorous manner.

EARLY CHILDHOOD LEARNING ENVIRONMENTS

In chapter 29, "Gender Equity in Early Learning Environments," by Barbara Polnick, Carol Anne Dwyer, Carole Funk Haynie, Merle Froschl, Barbara Sprung, and Doris Fromberg, the authors attempt to provide us with a sense of the many factors bearing on our ability to provide young children (defined as from birth through age eight) with the education (occurring at home, in childcare settings, in schools, and elsewhere) that is optimal for them by encouraging gender equity. The authors begin by giving us an overview of modern psychological, sociological, and educational perspectives on early-childhood education, which include focusing on the development of the whole child. They note, surprisingly, that early childhood education, relative to other educational sectors, remains largely unresearched, despite widespread recognition that the developmental experiences of young children have lifelong ramifications for their later education. The need for such research was spelled out clearly, for example, by Selma Greenberg, who wrote on this topic in the first edition of this *Handbook*. Sadly, this is a theme that runs throughout this chapter: too little has changed over the past two decades regarding gender equity in early childhood, especially given that we have a good understanding of the consequences of inaction in this realm.

Polnick and her coauthors remind us that very significant aspects of gender formation take place during early childhood, and that it is not only the explicit policies and actions related to gender equity that influence gender formation, but many influences that continue to go unremarked or under researched. Polnick et al. provide us with several interesting analyses of the effects of various types of media images and commercial practices on young children, their gender formation, and their education. These include greeting cards, television, games, and toys. The authors point out the strong start that was made in the 1970s toward gender-neutral toys, books, and other media for young children, some of which has persisted until now, but some of which has fallen by the wayside with little positive to replace it.

They also address issues of gender and physical activity, so important to understanding the dynamics of young children's interactions with the world. They provide an overview of gender similarities and differences in this area, drawing on information about physical activity and aggression from Hyde and Lindberg's chapter in this volume. Polnick et al.'s treatment of this subject will be of particular interest for its exploration of the complex interconnections among play, fighting, assertiveness, aggression, teasing, and bullying. Again, a topic which arises for the first time in early childhood resonates through later life, for example in understanding phenomena such as sexual harassment and sexual violence.

Polnick et al. give us an extended view of gender and early childhood education, which is augmented by brief treatments of international issues and research, and of diverse family structures in the United States and elsewhere. In closing their chapter, the authors returns to Selma Greenberg's 1985 chapter for both the structure of the recommendations and, strikingly, for content as well. Two decades after Greenberg, it is unfortunately still necessary, for example, to address the issue of using inclusive, nonsexist language with young children.

IMPROVING GENDER EQUITY IN POSTSECONDARY EDUCATION

Chapter 30, "Improving Gender Equity in Postsecondary Education," by Joanne Cooper, Pamela Eddy, Jennifer Hart, Jaime Lester, Scott Lukas, Betsy Eudey, Judith Glazer-Raymo, and Mary Madden,

addresses gender-equity issues in higher education from the perspectives of both the student and the institution's faculty and staff. Importantly, they carve out special analyses of community (two-year) and four-year colleges, historically Black colleges and universities, and single-sex institutions, as well as the participation of older women in higher education. This chapter is also comprehensive in the sense of starting us out with a historical overview of higher education and related gender issues and keeping this historical perspective as contemporary issues are discussed.

As noted above, by almost any criterion, women have made great strides in postsecondary education, attaining bachelors and advanced degrees in many fields formerly virtually closed to them, and that trend continues until the present time. During this same time, however, men have not made comparable gains, and there are a number of disturbing trends related to men's engagement with higher education.

Cooper et al. told us that two thirds of America's colleges and universities today reported that they receive more female than male applicants, making males the more valued applicants. Institutions, as well as the students who attend them, strongly prefer "gender balance," however, they might define it. This creates concerns about admission preferences as more highly qualified females make up the applicant pool at many selective institutions.

Overall, however, men still earn more doctorates and professional degrees than women do, and men are still are more likely than women to be enrolled in the nation's most prestigious undergraduate universities. However, these trends continue to change in many fields, particularly those related to the life sciences. In the 1985 *Handbook*, Bogart et al. reported that women at that time earned half of all bachelor's degrees, 25% of professional degrees, and 30% of all doctoral degrees (p. 470), noting that this was a huge increase since 1971, near the inception of the modern women's movement. Today, Cooper et al. note, at the undergraduate level women are not only more likely than men to finish their degrees, but also more likely to have done so with honors (43% vs. 33%). Women today earn 60% of the associate degrees, 57% of the bachelor's degrees, and 59% of the master's degrees. In 2001–2002 men still earned more doctoral and first-time professional degrees (54% and 53% respectively) than did women, although there are some striking exceptions such as medicine, where women are now in a slight majority, and veterinary medicine, where women are now 80% of all students.

Although these gains for women are very large and positive, there are some disturbing trends as well. For both men and women, time to degree has been increasing, although more so for men than for women. Reasons for leaving college are gender-differentiated among very traditional lines—women who left college were more likely than men to leave school because of "change in family status, conflicts at home, or personal problems" (Bradburn, 2002; p. vii). The men who left were more likely than women to report that they left school early because of problems with grades or for immediate employment possibilities. There are also disturbing disparities in the number of degrees earned by men and women across racial-ethnic groups. The largest gap exists between Black men and women; Cooper et al. reported that in 1999–2000, Black women earned 188 associate degrees, 192 bachelor's degrees, and 221 master's degrees for every 100 earned by Black men. Furthermore, although women continue to earn a higher percentage of bachelor's and master's degrees, the 2000 annual median income for a man with a bachelor's degree was $56,334, compared to $40,415 for women. The annual median income for a man with a master's degree was $68,322, compared to $58,957 for a woman with a master's degree (Bureau of the Census, 2003). In addition, the notion of "traditionally male" and "traditionally female" fields still prevails. For example, men earned a larger percentage of the degrees awarded in business and marketing, computer and information sciences, engineering, and physical sciences.

Cooper et al. note both progress and disturbing trends among higher-educational faculty as well. Among all new faculty hires (on or off the tenure track), women slightly outnumber men at liberal arts colleges and community colleges. At doctoral-granting universities, however, women represent only one third of the newly hired faculty members (Finkelstein, Seal, & Schuster, 1998). Although the numbers of women holding faculty positions are growing, women are more often found in less-competitive institutions. For example, women are 4% of the full-time faculty at private research universities. Much larger percentages of women at these institutions are part-time employees.

CONCLUSION

It is evident from a wide variety of sources that in the United States today we are far from an ideal state of gender equity in either early childhood environments or in higher education. As these two chapters make abundantly clear, as a society we need a renewed focus, bolstered by scientific research, on our collective responsiveness to the needs of both girls and boys in their formative years, laying the groundwork for later education and life experiences that challenge each individual to do his or her best work, within a context of gender equity. Similarly, in the world of higher education, we need to be concerned with "chilly climates" that persist for women, especially in traditionally male fields of study; and with men's seemingly increasing alienation from higher education as a viable path to personal and economic wellbeing. Until we have the will to look at these issues carefully and dispassionately, with all due respect for hard evidence, we will not make the progress toward gender equity in education that was promised to us a generation ago.

References

Bradburn, E. (2002). *Short-term enrollment in postsecondary education: Student background and institutional differences in reasons for early departure, 1996–98* (U.S. Department of Education Report No. NCES 2003-153). Washington, DC: U.S. Government Printing Office.

Bureau of the Census. (2003). *Money income of households, families and persons in the U.S.* (Department of Commerce, Current Population Reports, Series P-60). Washington, DC: U.S. Government Printing Office.

Finkelstein, M. J., Seal, R. K., & Schuster, J. H. (1998). *The new academic generation: A profession in transformation.* Baltimore: Johns Hopkins University Press.

GENDER EQUITY IN EARLY LEARNING ENVIRONMENTS

Barbara Polnick, Carol Anne Dwyer, * Carole Funk Haynie,
Merle Froschl, Barbara Sprung, and Doris Fromberg

What are little boys made of, made of?
What are little boys made of?
Frogs and snails
And puppy-dogs' tails,
That's what little boys are made of.

What are little girls made of, made of?
What are little girls made of?
Sugar and spice
And all things nice,
That's what little girls are made of.

Author Unknown (Halliwell, 1842)

INTRODUCTION

Over a hundred years ago, this familiar nursery rhyme was chanted throughout the homes of America, and since that time, many girls have lived under a "sugar and spice" role expectation. Boys, too, have had their roles defined for them in terms of what they should do and be. For both genders, this stereotyping began as soon as they were wrapped in their pink or blue blankets (Basow, 1992). As traditional and natural as gender role assignments appear, gender stereotyping during the early years can define and shape the future for children.

After reviewing many studies in the area, Sanders, Koch, and Urso (1997) concluded, "As early as nursery school, boys and girls sitting in the same classroom, with the same teacher, using the same materials, have different learning experiences" (p. 3). Some of these learning experiences, planned and unplanned, happen because of a child being born male or female. Even a

focus on individual's development, as promoted in many early childhood education environments, does not always produce gender equity in terms of outcomes for children (MacNaughton, 2000). Everyday teaching practices can influence the gendering of young children's identities through both formal and informal interactions. Throughout this chapter, we explore how these different gender-based interactions can influence educational outcomes differently for girls and boys. In addition, the authors share ideas on how educators and other interested persons might structure early learning environments to promote fair gender practices. Recommendations to parents and other caregivers, educators, policy makers, and researchers regarding gender equity in early childhood are also included. To this end, the remainder of this chapter is organized into the following parts:

- Part I—Background and assumptions
- Part II—Early childhood influences on gender and the development of the whole child
- Part III—Gender and education issues
- Part IV—New and emerging issues related to gender equity in early learning environments
- Part V—Strategies and recommendations for creating gender-equitable early learning environments
- Part VI—Conclusion

BACKGROUND AND ASSUMPTIONS

Early childhood education has traditionally embraced a child-centered view of pedagogy. In today's educational climate with its focus on learning outcomes and accountability, and with its increasing emphasis on alignment of early childhood edu-

*The boldface names are the Lead Authors.

cation with later grade levels, a tension has arisen that creates a distinctive context for children's gender development and for promoting gender equity (S. Goffin, personal communication, July 31, 2006). Because early childhood is a time of tremendous change in physical, social, and cognitive development, early educational settings present a rich context for the study of gender issues, one that differs in significant ways from later school years.

Despite considerable efforts over the last 25 years to address gender equity issues in educational settings, gender inequities in early childhood education are relatively understudied, and inequities continue to exist in many early childhood learning environments (American Association of University Women [AAUW], 1991, 1992; Beaty, 2002; O'Reilly, Penn, & Demarrais, 2001; Sadker, D., 2002). Although there are many different ways to consider children's ages, for purposes of this discussion we have taken a broad view, and we define *early childhood* as extending from birth through age eight. We define *learning environments* broadly as well, including but not limited to the following settings: home (including foster homes), family (including extended family), public and private schools, child care programs, religious education centers, parks and playgrounds, and other settings where children interact frequently with adults and other children (National Association of Education of Young Children [NAEYC] 1997). Thus, providing access to gender equitable learning environments involves working with parents, caregivers, teachers, child care workers, researchers, policy makers, and others who influence the learning environments of young children. These influences include actions, behaviors, beliefs, and other expectations that encourage young boys and girls to become fully engaged learners. The degree to which children become engaged in reaching their full potentials, regardless of race, ethnicity, socioeconomic background, disability, or gender is a measure of a larger set of principles identified as "educational equity" (e.g., Women's Equity Resource Center, 2006). Those who act in a manner consistent with educational equity principles guide and encourage all children to believe in their own abilities, to be successful, and to set high expectations for themselves in order to seize the opportunities and benefits that our society offers. In this chapter, we discuss gender equity within the broader context of educational equity for all individuals. In a broad sense, gender equity is about basic fairness and justice (Koch & Irby, 2002).

EARLY CHILDHOOD INFLUENCES ON GENDER AND THE DEVELOPMENT OF THE WHOLE CHILD

"It's not just the big things, it's also the little, seemingly insignificant things that happen over and over again that make growing up different for boys and girls" (Horgan, 1995, p. 27). Both past and current research in early childhood development validates the need for examining early environmental experiences as they relate to gender issues (Beaty, 2002; Edgerton, 1979; MacNaughton, 2000; Pan American Health Organization, 1994; O'Reilly et al., 2001). Grieshaber (1998) asserted that what is necessary is a "change of mind set about the construction of gender, so that, from the beginning of their lives, children are exposed to social contexts that enable them to develop as human beings irrespective of their sex" (p. 7). According to C. West and Zimmerman (1987), gender is not something one passively is or has; instead, we "do" gender. The following sections examine the research related to the construction of gender and the role that gender equity plays in the development of the whole child.

Eight Is Too Late—Origins of Gender Formation

Witt (1997) clarified when best to begin addressing gender equity issues in educational settings. Witt emphasized that children as early as two and a half years of age use gender stereotypes and then generalize these stereotypes when playing. According to Witt, children internalize messages from their parents regarding gender and gender roles early in their lives to the point that they will deny the reality of their own lives when they see things that do not apply to already learned stereotypes. For example, the stereotype that boys grow up to be physicians and construction workers and girls grow up to be nurses and teachers may elicit responses from very young children (boys and girls alike) such as "You're a girl—you be the nurse!" even when they have seen numerous counterexamples in their own lives. Because the foundations of learning, communication, social behavior, and important metacognitive skills such as self-regulation occur in early childhood (Bransford, Brown, & Cocking, 1999), there is a critical need to examine and develop appropriate gender-equitable experiences for young children during this key developmental period (Shonkoff & Phillips, 2000).

Explanations of gender and gender formation have primarily shifted the biological perspectives that dominated up until the 1960s, to views that include the understanding of gender as a sociocultural process in which what it means to be a girl or boy is socially constructed (Alloway, 1995; Gallas, 1998; MacNaughton, 2000). Although biology determines whether a child's sex is male or female, it is the images, hopes, and child-rearing practices of mothers, fathers, and other relatives that set the stage for gender identity and gender role expectations, as do interactions with peers (Marshall, Robeson, & Keefe, 1999). The flexibility with which very young children view their roles in terms of what sex they are has also been studied in terms of gender stability or gender constancy, a child's understanding that one's gender is a fixed attribute. Some toddlers may believe that their biological sex can change, that is, that boys can grow up to be women and girls can grow up to be men (see, e.g., Puckett & Black, 2005). Children who hold these views do not have the realization that one's gender remains the same regardless of age or changes in clothing, hairstyles, or other outward characteristics.

Culture, socioeconomic status, religion, region, and ethnicity all play an important role in gender socialization. As we will see in a following section of this chapter, the media play a role as well. All societies have implicit conceptions of gender, or stereotypes that they use to differentiate the treatment of girls and boys (Pan American Health Organization, 1994). How such social interactions affect the development of gender identity is complex and can be viewed from many perspectives. Thus, teachers, parents, other caregivers, and peers influence children's sets of expectations about how children should think, act, and feel with respect to what is gender-appropriate (Robinson & Diaz, 2006).

Socialization, Gender Roles, and Gender Identity

Although a child may be born genetically and hormonally male or female, one learns to be a boy or a girl. Gender is a learned attribute. Salient issues related to gender and child development may include but are not limited to the following: socialization, gender roles, gender identity, societal expectations, gender stereotyping, and gender-based learning experiences.

As children grow and develop, boys and girls may feel pressured to conform to somewhat limited definitions of what boys do or girls do. These pressures may come from a variety of sources, including parents who have less tolerance for a crying boy than a crying girl, teachers who may favor girls because they are less boisterous and disruptive in class, and peers who are quick to pounce on any sign of weakness or unconventional behavior in either sex. The media also play a strong role in defining gender appropriateness through the images they present to young children in commercial enterprises. Through this complex set of forces, children then internalize gender-role expectations early in life, a process commonly referred to as "socialization."

Socialization and role identification begin from birth and, some argue, before birth, with the expectations others who themselves have been socialized from birth. Early studies have documented the different reactions and behaviors of parents toward their newborn babies based on the sex of their child. In one study, first-time parents were asked to describe their babies 24 hours after birth (Rubin, Provenzano, & Luria, 1974). Parents of daughters described them as delicate, weak, and inattentive; in contrast, parents of boys described them as large, coordinated, and alert. In a similar study (Fagot, 1978), parents were shown an infant dressed in girls' clothing and boys' clothing, and their initial reactions were recorded. The "girl" baby was described as tiny, delicate, and precious; while the "boy" baby was big and a bruiser and future football player. In fact, there was only one infant—only the clothing was different.

Some researchers believe that self-esteem can be related to gender-role expectations and that these feelings can be traced back to how parents dress young boys and girls from birth. For example, according to O'Reilly et al. (2001), boys, including infants, are often dressed in jeans and overalls with pockets, sending a strong message that what they do is practical and important. In contrast, girls are often dressed to be pretty or cute in delicate dresses or in underpants and socks that have lace on them, which may send the message that how they look is more important than what they do.

The social climate of early childhood environments is highly complex for both boys and girls. Gender messages received through play and other social interactions define what girls are allowed and supposed to do (e.g., girls don't push) versus what boys are allowed and supposed to do (e.g., boys will be boys). These messages serve to define the boundaries of an accepted, gender equitable, early learning environment. "The messages girls receive about femininity, and the expectations for them as adult women, still focus on becoming wives and mothers as well as having a career" (O'Reilly et al., 2001, p. 13). Greenberg (1985) wrote, "It is learning the prescribed sex role rather than learning of one's gender identity that often has limiting and damaging effects on subsequent development" (p. 457). Evidence in this present chapter supports that learning what soci-

ety expects in terms of gender roles and behaviors can affect young boys and girls in every area of development.

Media Influences on Children's Gender-Related Development

Greeting cards. Greeting cards, which are closely reflective of cultural norms and expectations (Meister & Japp, 2002; West, E., 2004), are one widespread source of insight into the use of gender-based language and imagery related to early gender socialization. Bridges (1993) analyzed cards to congratulate parents on the birth of a baby to document the role that societal expectations play in gender stereotyping from the moment of birth (or before). Greeting cards to welcome the birth of a child conveyed their messages through consistent color-coding—pink for girls, blue for boys. Baby-boy cards showed boys (usually older than an infant) engaged with balls, sports equipment, vehicles, and other objects suggesting action. Illustrations on baby-girl cards typically showed infant girls immobile in cribs or baskets, surrounded by rattles, flowers, and mobiles. The written messages were as stereotyped as the illustrations. Boys could be anything, but girls were forever little girls: small, precious, and inactive. A more recent study conducted by B. Polnick and G. Polnick (2006) yielded similar findings. In this study, researchers analyzed over 190 cards from the two leading greeting card companies for themes, language, and illustrations. Greeting cards that were analyzed included three different types of child-related cards: congratulations to parents on the birth of a baby; birthday greetings to child from parents; and birthday greetings to child from grandparents. It should be noted that the importance of having specific cards for each gender is clearly reflected in how these cards are organized on store shelves. There are separate sections for girl cards and boy cards in each of the three types. In all three types of greeting cards, those intended for girls included language that described girls' physical appearances (e.g., *cute*), their emotional relationships (e.g., *stealing hearts*), or their fantasies (e.g., *dream, wish*). Young boys were typically described in terms of their potentials (e.g., *opportunity, success*), their strong, active characters (e.g., *determined, winner*), or their behaviors (e.g., *proud of, energy*). B. Polnick and G. Polnick concluded that the content and the classification of the cards reflect a clear set of differentiated cultural expectations for boys and girls and that these expectations are communicated in subtle and not so subtle, intentional and nonintentional, messages from friends and family members over time, beginning at birth.

Television, film, and gender roles. By the time children are 16 years old, they have spent more time watching television than going to school (Basow, 1992). Research on television viewing and children's socialization indicates that television has a great impact on children's lives (Witt, 2000). Television influences children's prosocial and antisocial behaviors (Bandura, 1986; Comstock & Paik, 1991; Strasburger, 1995), as well as their attitudes about race and gender (Liebert & Sprafkin, 1988). Of the various factors that help shape gender-typed behaviors, role models, and imitation are extremely influential (Basow, 1992; Beal, 1994; Hargreaves & Colley, 1986). Aubrey and Harrison (2004) found that male characters in the favorite television shows of first and second grade students were more likely than female characters to answer questions, boss or order others, show ingenuity, and achieve a goal; and that boys' and girls' preferences were related to important learning outcomes such as valuing hard work. Smith (2004) demonstrates that television advertising is strongly gender-differentiated as well, and cites research showing that children between the ages of two and eleven see 150 to 200 hours of television advertising *per year*. Thus, although there are a number of important exceptions (e.g., a television series showing a female president of the United States), gender stereotypes are still abound on television and can have an important effect on children's beliefs about gender-appropriate behavior. For example, children who witness female characters on television programs who are passive, indecisive, and subordinate to men, and who see these characteristics reinforced in their environments, will likely believe that this is the appropriate way for females to behave (Witt, 2000). It is less likely, therefore, that female children will develop autonomy, initiative, and industriousness if they rarely see those traits modeled. Similarly, because male characters on television programs are more likely to be shown in leadership roles and exhibiting assertive, decisive behavior (e.g., presidents, generals, pilots, and executives), children learn that this is the appropriate way for males to behave (Carter, 1991; Seidman, 1999). A research study of the 101 top-grossing G-rated films released from 1990 through 2004 (Kelly & Smith, 2006) demonstrated the profound imbalance of male and female characters. Overall (major characters, characters in groups, films released in the 1990s vs. those released in the 2000s), 75 percent of the over 4,249 speaking characters analyzed were male; 83 percent of the films' narrators were male. The report notes that "gender equity has progressed in many ways. But male characters still dominate television, movies, and other media for young children" (p. 10). The authors also note that the presence of female characters in children's earliest media experiences are essential for both boys' and girls' development.

Games and toys. Games and toys are serious business for young children and can have both positive and negative effects on their developments. "Games differ in the level of competition and often contain elements of cooperation, [yet] nearly all modern games involve some form of contest, which by itself is a symbolic expression of aggression" (Reid, 1993, p. 327). Games can also reflect a form of aggression that is socially acceptable for both boys and girls. Children can experience feelings of power while playing games and tend to use games for gender exploration and gender identification. Boys tend to engage more in competitive games and imaginative play (Hasse, 2002).

Toys and games are also serious business socially and economically. Children are increasingly targeted as consumers by global corporations that produce entertainment, food, clothing, toys, books, video games, and so on, making early childhood a profitable market sector (Kasturi, 2002). Therefore, these industries have a large influence on the construction of what a particular society construes as feminine or masculine (e.g., dress, character images, human representations in dolls, style, colors, and designs). Although the specifics of what constitutes gender-appropriate differs somewhat from culture to culture, the influence of toys and games remains strong and heavily gender differentiated.

It has long been noted that toys are often heavily promoted as either girls' toys or boys' toys (Andersen, 1993; CHOICE, 1991; Richardson, L., 1988; Thorne, 1993; Unger & Crawford, 1992). This labeling has a direct effect on children's toy preferences. Martin, Eisenbud, and Rose (1995) found that children's preference for toys was negatively affected if those toys were labeled as appropriate for the opposite sex.

As is the case with greeting cards, the wide acceptability of this gender differentiation is apparent in how commercial offerings are marketed and displayed in retail outlets. Smith (1994), in a content analysis of television advertising aimed at young children, found that toys were clearly differentiated in terms of traditional gender roles, and that more toy advertising was directed toward boys (67 percent) than toward girls (33 percent). Toy manufacturers and retailers piggyback on the acceptability of some occupations' being designated as male or female in their displays and organization of products.

One of the authors of this chapter confirmed this in an informal experiment in a recent trip to a local major toy outlet. The task was to find four kinds of toys: a doctor's kit, a tool kit, baby doll supplies, and building blocks. The doctor's kit and tool kit were located in what was clearly the boys' department and the baby doll supplies were located in the girls' department. Only the building blocks were located in a gender-neutral zone.

Toy and game selection also appears to reflect broader gender attitudes that children hold. For example, children often correlate gender-linked toys with actual occupations (Singer, 1994). Researchers have found that toddlers and preschoolers display a preference for gender-typed toys matched to their own genders (Goldstein, 1994; O'Brien, Huston, & Risley, 1983). There is evidence that this is true across cultures. As noted in a study of Taiwanese families, the parents of primary-school-age children who hold strong gender-stereotyped attitudes also select traditionally gender-linked toys for their children (Pan, 1994). Interestingly enough, even among middle-class mothers of kindergarten-age children in Taiwan, more than half the sample reported that boys were allowed to engage in girl's play or gender-specific activities, and vice versa. This, of course, implies that almost half of the mothers either did forbid boys to engage in girl's play, or simply did not deal with the question. The results also imply that the meaning of the term *girl's play* as a familiar type of playing was understood by the participants.

Fromberg (1999) found that differences existed in the types of toys with which children engaged in play. In her analysis of the research on play behaviors, she found studies supporting observable differences in the way boys and girls interact with toys and games, including selection and engagement. The degree to which consumerism, advertising, parental approval and selection, and children's choices affect their engagement in play with some toys and games rather than others remains an underresearched area.

Researchers studying computer games conclude that there are no gender differences among preschool children in their interests in games on the computer, but that girls' interests, as reflected in time spent with such games, decreases with age (Comber, Colley, Hargreaves, & Dorn, 1997; Dorman, 1998). Girls Tech: Girls, Science, and Technology (Agosto, 2006) thoroughly documented the factors that contribute to this decline in girls' interest with age. These factors include representations of females in computer games, effects of violence depicted in games, and girls' preferences for content. These preferences include content that emphasizes storylines, character development, strong female characters, human relationships, educational themes, real-life locales, and nonviolent action. Girls Tech also reports that girls dislike depictions of violence, conflicts between good and evil, and games that are competitive in nature or that must be played solo.

TABLE 29.1   Summary of Conclusions About Young Males' and Females' Engagements with Toys and Games

Male	Female	Research Sources
Larger variety of toys More toys educationally oriented Toys oriented away from home More rough-and-tumble play, and play fighting	Narrower range of toys Domestic themes in toys and miniatures	Hughes, 1999; Pellegrini & Kato, 2002; Tracy, 1987
Did not receive nonrequested stereotypically girls' toys	Received nonrequested toys that were stereotypically boys' toys	Hughes, 1999
Used toys to mark gender differences at four years of age	Willing to play across stereotypical toys with a greater variety of materials Willing to play with stereotypical boys' toys	Pan, 1994 (Taiwan)
Preferred transportation toys	Preferred storybooks and drawing	Duveen & Lloyd, 1990; Garner, 1998
More group sports and games in larger groups that require strategic planning, and competition; longer-lasting play requiring more skill	More "chumships" beginning at age four; more variety of shifting alliances and some large groups, depending on context	Hughes, 1999; Maccoby & Jacklin, 1974; Thorne, 1993; Whiting & Edwards, 1988
Games more competitive, active, and adventuresome	Games more passive and consumerist	Freitag, 1998; Pinker, 2002

A consideration of the relationship between gender and toys and games suggests that most authors view gender as a simple dichotomy. However, scholars also consistently find a wide range of with gender variation (Hyde & Lindberg, 2007; Maccoby, 1998; Thorne, 1993). A further complexity, as noted above, is that very young children may be demonstrating a fluid experience of gender-based characteristics (lack of gender constancy), rather than merely reflecting culturally-sanctioned gender stereotypes (Fromberg, 2005). With these cautions to consider behavior as a range of possible experiences with a number of possible causes, the research literature summarized in Table 29.1 provides conclusions about young males' and females' preferences for and engagement with toys and games.

It is not clear that there has been a net improvement over the past 20 years in encouraging the development and use of the gender-neutral toys and games. In the 1970s, there was a strong attempt to create and market toys in a nonsexist manner and to downplay the gender differentiation in toy selection and use. However, there appears to have been much retreat from this goal during the 1980s and 1990s.

Gender and Child Development: Physical Issues

Gender issues are not isolated issues, but instead relate to the overall development of young children. The cognitive, sociological, physical, and emotional domains are all part of the development of the whole child. Recognizing that although each of the domains may usefully be considered separately for some purposes, development across the domains actually overlaps, with development in one domain affecting development in the others (Catron & Allen, 2003; Marion, 2003; Morrison, 2004). For example, by the time they are five years old, girls may be 18 months ahead of boys in their physical, social, and emotional

development. As we will discuss in a later section of this chapter, this difference in rate of development raises questions about the academic expectations for young boys and the age at which they are deemed ready to enter school.

We will first consider a number of aspects of gender-differentiated factors related to physical development in early childhood, then return to an exploration of the complex and overlapping links among the emotional, social, physical, and academic domains.

Gender, Activity Level, and Aggression

Hyde and Lindberg, chapter 2 in this volume addresses, through extensive meta-analytic work, two topics that are of significance to our consideration of physical issues with young children: activity level and aggression. Both of these factors are frequently cited by both researchers and practitioners, as reasons for young children's gender-differentiated behavior.

Hyde and Lindberg found that, over all ages, boys are more active than girls are by half a standard deviation. Among very young children, the gender differences are smaller than at older ages ($d = .29$ among infants and $d = .44$ among preschool-age children). They also noted an interaction between the physical and social domains. Gender differences increased when peers were present ($d = .62$ *with peers, d = .44* without peers present). Hyde and Lindberg concluded that the gender difference in activity level "appears early and is robust across situations and studies"(p.).

In the present chapter, we define *aggression* as acting with the intent of imposing one's will on an unwilling other. Psychologists often distinguish between prosocial aggression, which concerns enforcing society's rules, and antisocial aggression, which concerns violations of them. Most discussions of gender and early childhood education concern antisocial aggression. A further distinction is made between aggression that is physical in nature and that which is verbal. Hyde and Lindberg reported that boys are somewhat more aggressive than girls are. They cited important earlier work by Hyde, considered definitive by many, which reported an overall effect size of .50, a moderate effect, across 143 studies, with the gender differences in both physical and verbal aggression peaking during preschool and declining thereafter.

Recent research in the field of physical aggression has examined the roles that hormones, neurotransmitters, and proteins known as growth factors, play in influencing activity related to social play behaviors (Bowman et al., 2004). It should be noted, however, that research in the area of biology and its effects on human gender-related behavior is relatively new and the longitudinal impact on gender development in early childhood remains unexplored at this time.

Gender and Play

Children's interactions with each other and with caregivers during play are critical in the development of socialization skills, gender roles, and gender identity. As children approach the toddler years, their behaviors begin to reveal gender differences in the way they play, including their toy preferences and the role-playing in which they engage in. Preschoolers extend their concepts of gender identity through socialization processes that involve taking on a variety of roles during pretend play with peers, and responding to cues from peers and adults (Catron & Allen, 2003). Catron and Allen believe, and we concur, that teachers of young children need to encourage them to explore a range of roles and classroom activities to facilitate the development of a healthy and balanced view of gender identity.

As noted previously with respect to Table 29.1, it is probably more useful to consider gender as characterized as much by similarities as by differences when evaluating gender research findings, and to consider behavior as a continuum of possible experiences with a number of possible causes. With these caveats, the research literature summarized in Table 29.2 provides conclusions about young males' and females' styles of play.

Rough-and-Tumble Play

Researchers in general have found that rough-and-tumble play—playing at fighting—is one area where consistent gender differences can be observed. Boys participate in this type of play

TABLE 29.2 Summary of Conclusions About Young Males' and Females' Styles of Play.

Male	Female	Research Sources
Engage in shorter play episodes that focus on acceptance of their suggestions	Engage in longer play episodes that value focus on interaction; balance their perspective with others	Black, 1989; Gilligan, 1982; Sheldon, 1992
Distractible and competitive during problem solving projects Value autonomy and individual control	Oblivious to distractions, even when engaged in collaborative problem solving projects Expectation of group development	Hattie, Marsh, Neill, & Richards, 1997; Rankin, 1998
Object/power orientation Third person stance	Internal experience; relational Speak through a character	Rabbie, Goldenbled, & Lodewijkx, 1992; Wolf, Rygh, & Altshuler, 1984
More fluent play	More flexible, original, and collaborative	Gonen, Uzmen, Akcin, & Ozdemir, 1993
Receive less adult proximity and more corrections; Punished more harshly; receive more adult attention for assertive behavior Outdoor play away from school building	Receive more adult physical proximity, comments, and questions Tend to follow the teacher Play is closer to school building and adults	Bradley & Gobbart, 1989; Caldera, Huston, & O'Brien, 1989; Carpenter, Huston & Spera, 1989; Eron, 1992; Fagot, 1988; Golomb, Gowing, & Friedman, 1982; Hughes, 1999; Roggman & Peery; 1989; Sadker, M., Sadker, D., & Klein, 1991; Thorne, 1993
Block play, superhero, adventure, and transportation themes predominate	Housekeeping themes, art, and dress up predominate	Elgas, Klein, Kantor & Fernie, 1988; Fagot, & Leve, 1998; Garner, 1998; Paley, 1984; Polnick, B., & Funk, 2005; Trawick-Smith, 1994
Roles had more status, and boys were less willing to play stereotypical female roles after 4 years of age Older boys played less with younger sisters	Engaged in more sophisticated constructive play when playing with boys; girls were willing to play with stereotypical boys' toys Older girls played more than boys with younger brothers	Goldstein, 1995; Greif, 1976; Honig, 1998; Oden & Hall, 1998; Pellegrini & Perlmutter, 1989; Ramsey, 1998; Thorne, 1993
Primary age boys treated girls as "contaminated" and mocked boys who engaged in cross-gender friendship	Exempted boys from ridicule and viewed them as tough	Thorne, 1993
Humor more expressive More exuberant teasing, clowning	Humor more receptive and verbally aggressive	Bergen, 1998; Honig, 1998

more often than girls do, which is consistent with the findings of Hyde and Lindberg (2007) about gender and aggression.

When children play at fighting, they demonstrate an understanding of the unacceptable nature of uncontrolled aggression. Rough-and-tumble play entails aggressive themes without aggression, violence, or malicious intent. Children signal their playful intents by smiling, teasing, and relaxed body language and gestures. Although not dangerous in itself, play fighting has the potential to escalate into true aggression on rare occasions (Pellegrini, 1998). Posture, gesture, facial expression, hostile verbiage, and body tension signal the rare transformation of rough-and-tumble play into intentional aggression. Researchers found , however, that aggression on playgrounds during recess (when children are able to self-select their pastimes) occurs less than two to three percent of the time (Pellegrini & Smith, 1993).

Although rough-and-tumble play gives children the chance to explore aggression safely, female teachers tend to feel uncomfortable with the boisterous nature of rough-and-tumble play and its physical closeness, however lacking in actual danger of injury. This may be a response related to their professional responsibilities and the possibility of injury, or it may also reflect their conceptions of what is appropriate play for boys and for girls.

However adults may feel about rough-and-tumble play, learning to engage in self-organization, self-motivation, building autonomy, and resolving conflicts are important aspects of early learning that can take place during such play. During rough-and-tumble play, young children have the chance to build their own approaches to ethical, fair, and peaceful resolution of conflicts, differences, and interpersonal problems. Researchers have concluded that primary-school-age boys still demonstrate appropriate ways to express care and intimacy even during their rough-and-tumble play (Reed & Brown, 2000). When teachers or other adults categorically forbid rough-and-tumble play or exploration of aggressive themes, whether for practical reasons or in support of gender-related norms, children often move their antisocial feelings underground. For example, they may substitute a wooden block or a finger for a toy gun.

Some educators and researchers who observed war-themed play (Carlsson-Paige & Levin, 1987), extensive superhero play (Newkirk, 2002; Paley, 1984), and a variety of conflicts among preschool children (Vaughn, Vollenwelder, & Bost, 2003), all construed these episodes as learning opportunities. For example, researchers have observed some teachers role-playing and discussing alternative, mutually satisfying ways to resolve disagreements during rough-and-tumble play (Carlsson-Paige & Levin, 1987; Paley, 1984).

Other teachers view such occasions as opportunities to build on children's choices of play themes as the basis for developing literacy activities, thus bringing reluctant-to-read boys into the mainstream of literacy learning (Newkirk, 2002). It is important that caregivers and teachers distinguish between acceptable and useful rough-and-tumble play and antisocial aggression, which sometimes manifests itself as bullying. Bullying, characterized by unequal power dynamics and aggressive intent, is a very different matter from rough-and-tumble play.

Teasing and Bullying

Teasing and bullying can be acts that occur over time or a single unprovoked act in which physical, verbal, or exclusionary behavior is used by one or more children to intimidate, humili-

ate, or otherwise interfere with what another child or children are doing (Sprung, Froschl, & Hinitz, 2005). Some people believe that there is a form of teasing that can be playful, even helpful, in terms of preparing children to cope. Sprung, Froschl, and Hinitz argue that this distinction does not hold with children as young as three and four, and that a better approach in preschool is to create a teasing-free environment (p. 11), viewing teasing and bullying as a continuum of intentionally hurtful behavior (Froschl, Sprung, & Mullin-Rindler, 1998).

At one end of this continuum, there might be annoying teasing behavior, and at the other, abusive bullying. Bullying is an attempt to establish dominance and can be an aggressive strategy that both boys and girls use to attain entry into a group or to gain some form of power over an individual or group. Bullying takes a number of forms and is not always physical. Researchers note that in school settings, boys tend to dominate and thus effectively silence girls if no intervention takes place (Hegland & Ricks, 1990; Koch & Irby, 2002). Although bullying is by no means always part of this ubiquitous dynamic, one consequence of teachers' allowing boys to dominate can be teasing and bullying. In fact, teachers sometimes, consciously or unconsciously, support bullying and teasing behavior through their lack of intervention or attention (Gropper & Froschl, 2000; Kindlon & Thompson, 2000; Koch & Irby, 2002).

In one study of bullying in kindergarten through grade 3, boys initiated incidents three times as often as did girls; girls and boys were equally likely to be targets of bullying; and, strikingly, in over 70% of observed incidents, adults did not intervene (Gropper & Froschl, 2000). Children in this study were well aware of the fact that teachers usually did nothing to stop the aggressive teasing. In interviews, these children remarked, "Boys usually chase girls because that's what boys do—boys chase," "Teachers don't do anything," and "Kids won't stop until the teacher makes them" (Froschl & Gropper, 1999, p. 1). Girls' bullying often takes a more subtle approach that is more social than physical. Girls, in contrast to boys, tend to use verbal and relationship strategies such as rumor and social ostracism as their preferred forms of bullying (Ma, 2001; Pellegrini & Bartini, 2000).

The good news is that teachers, in concert with other adult members of the school community, can make a big difference in the incidence of bullying. Research supports the effectiveness of whole-school intervention strategies, which can reduce teasing and bullying behavior by as much as 35% and increase the involvement of staff by more than 100% (Gropper, 2000; Olweus, 1993). In one study, there was an increase in verbal responses over physical responses by male recipients of teasing and bullying. Other results included greater recognition among staff that adult mediation is an effective intervention strategy, and an increase in the number of staff who perceived that students are aware of bullying issues and have acquired effective strategies to deal with them (Gropper, 2000).

Gender and Child Development: Links Among Emotional, Social, Physical, and Academic Factors

Although emotional, social, physical, and academic aspects of child development can usefully be considered in isolation, research has demonstrated that there are many links among these domains that pertain to gender and early childhood education.

Emotional–Social Development Influences

Experiences affecting the emotional development of young girls and boys, be it self-esteem, self-confidence, or self-efficacy, can impact social development through expressed and assumed role expectations communicated to children by others (Bandura, 2000; Pajares, 1996; Puckett & Black, 2005). Just as children's emotional development can affect their social development, the social development of young children can affect their academic or cognitive development. Research by B. J. Taylor (2002) illustrated how social experiences can affect cognitive development. She found that children as young as three and four years of age begin to self-limit their choices of learning experiences because of the gender norms they adopt. Girls are also more likely than boys to hold self-theories or beliefs about themselves (e.g., believing that their intelligence is a fixed entity to which they attribute their school difficulties and failures), that can interfere with their academic performance in later learning environments (Dweck, 1999, 2000, 2006; Pajares, 1996). According to Dweck and Pajares, people develop beliefs that organize their world and give meaning to their experiences; these beliefs about themselves can then create different psychological worlds, leading them to think, feel, and act differently in identical situations. Special attention should be given to girls' greater tendency, relative to boys, to attribute their failures to their lack of ability rather than to circumstances under which they have control, such as increased effort. It is important, therefore, for both girls and boys to have experiences that build positive images of their abilities, so as not to create worlds filled with inappropriate self-limitation.

Physical–Social Development Influences

Expectations for social and physical activity may impact the way girls and boys are treated in early education environments, thus impacting opportunities for social growth. Children's interactions with each other through play and other school activities are critical to both their development of social skills and the development of their gender identity. For example, Pollack (1998) coined the phrase "the boy code" (p. 257) to express the constraints on boys' emotional development and the resulting inner emotional pain that many boys carry around under the façade of being normal and fine. Kindlon and Thompson (2000) called these learned behaviors "emotional illiteracy." These researchers highlight the negative outcomes of the ways boys are socialized from early childhood to conform to a societal conception of what it means to be a man.

As noted above, early childhood researchers have observed that social play behaviors in groups differ greatly between boys and girls, and that young boys as a social group play rougher than do young girls (Bowman et al., 2004). Boys are often viewed as being more active than girls because they exhibit behaviors that are more aggressive (Archer, 2004; Eaton & Enns, 1986; Geary, 1998; Hyde, 1984, 1986, 2005; Hyde & Lindberg, 2007; Knight, Guthrie, Page, & Fabes, 2002). In the Early Childhood Longitudinal Study, Kindergarten Cohort (ECLS-K), Zill and West (2001) found that girls had better prosocial skills than did boys, and they were less likely to engage in problem behaviors than were boys at the beginning of kindergarten. When problem behaviors occur, the consequences may be more physical for boys than for girls. Evidence exists that boys are punished more harshly for their transgressive behavior than are girls. The U.S. Department of Health and Human Services Administration for Children and Families (2005) released its preliminary findings of the Head Start Impact Study, which followed approximately 5,000 three- and four-year old children from fall 2002 through 2006. They found that parents of four-year-olds are less likely to use spanking to discipline girls than to discipline boys (U.S. Department of Health and Human Services, 2005). Other studies connecting stress, socioeconomic, and ethnic factors to corporal punishment, found that in low socioeconomic families, parents reported using harsher and more frequent physical punishment with boys than with girls (Pinderhughes, Dodge, Bates, Pettit, & Zelli, 2000).

Researchers have also studied biological differences as they relate to gender differences in social functioning. Scientists at the University of Wisconsin-Madison are studying disorders such as autism, which constitutes one area where gender differences in social behavior come to the forefront (Basu, 2005). These researchers have found that approximately 80% of all autism cases occur in males.

Physical–Academic Development Influences

Limiting physical activities can sometimes limit academic performance. Huston and Carpenter (1985), in their study of the interactions of preschool teachers with their students, found that although both girls and boys participated in activities structured by explicit rules and clear teacher expectations (e.g., completing a specific craft activity, taking responsibility for watering the plants in the classroom), boys were allowed and expected to participate in significantly more unstructured play than were girls. Preschool boys are encouraged to take risks; girls learn early to be cautious (O'Reilly et al., 2001). Boys are allowed to explore farther away from their parents, giving the message that taking risks and attempting difficult physical tasks are challenges that are acceptable or even encouraged for boys. In this case, restricting girls' natural desires to take risks may inhibit their future risk-taking behaviors in academic and other domains (Polnick, B., 2002; Sadker, D., & Sadker, M., 1994). Risk taking is an important characteristic of good problem solvers and is important for successful performance in science, technology, engineering, and mathematics. Parents often treat girls more protectively than they treat boys because of preconceived ideas about gender, such as keeping girl babies and toddlers closer to them and cuddling them more often than they do boy babies.

Young girls begin school knowing that when an adult authority speaks, they are supposed to sit quietly, to listen, and to do what he or she asks you to do (Basow, 1992; Sadker, D., & Sadker, M., 1994). They appear to be physically ready for such engagements (or lack of engagement). Research has long indicated that girls are born physically and developmentally more mature than boys, which may explain girls' edge in academic performance in early grades. For example, the need (and desire) to be physically active can interfere with children's responsiveness to sitting in their seats, paying attention, and completing an educational task, such as reading silently or writing. Four-to five-year-old children's interests and physical participation in real-world events can affect cognitive growth and academic performance. Most young girls, having been socialized from early on to behave like ladies and to get along equably with others, begin school knowing that when an adult authority speaks, you listen and do what is asked of you. In contrast, freer from many societal expectations for the social skills needed to live in a group, many young American boys arrive at kindergarten ready to talk and play with friends, wondering why the man or woman at the front of the room keeps interrupting them (Basow, 1992; Sadker, D., & Sadker, M., 1994).

Academic–Emotional Influences

Gender differences in academic experiences can play a part in the way children cope with school, including relationships with teachers and peers. Frustration resulting from the inability to meet academic expectations might explain some emotional and physical outbursts. Girls can develop diminished academic expectations for themselves when they are given only minimal praise for their good behaviors or for completing tasks, when boys are given multiple kudos for completing a task or behaving "properly" (Sadker, M., & Sadker, D., 1985). Lack of praise can, over time, negatively affect the emotional development of children. Dweck (2002), in a series of studies over more than 25 years, concluded that self-theories of intelligence that have a direct influence on children's learning and resilience in academic and other domains can be modified by the *type* of praise that is offered to children. Dweck (1999) showed that holding the belief that intelligence is unchangeable (called the "entity theory" of self) leads to withdrawal of effort and avoidance of challenges. Entity theories lead to increased probability of academic withdrawal and alienation, and decreased engagement with learning—all of which lead to lower achievement. In contrast, holding the belief that ability can be increased through one's own efforts (called the "incremental theory" of self) leads to increased effort and seeking out challenging materials. Fortunately, Dweck and her colleagues also found that entity theories are susceptible to change with relatively simple interventions related to how praise is given for learning outcomes (e.g., Dweck, 2000; Mueller & Dweck, 1998): Feedback for intelligence increases entity thinking; feedback for effort and strategies decreases it. An important finding of this line of research has been that entity theories of intelligence, in addition to being disruptive of the ability to seek out academic challenges, and persist in the face of difficult material, are more prevalent among females, so great care needs to be taken with how girls are praised for their good schoolwork.

GENDER AND EDUCATION ISSUES

Child Care and Preschool Environments

For many parents of young children, finding high quality, dependable, and affordable child care is one of life's greatest challenges. One reason for this is that pay and prestige for child care workers are low (e.g., Gormley, 1995), often paid at the minimum wage. Child care is also a highly feminized occupation, and one that is populated by a large number of workers without documentation, sometimes working under exploitative conditions. This adds an ethical dimension to parents' search for good child care, avoidance of employment practices that foster sexism and racism. Although this bleak picture is mitigated to some extent by such regulatory efforts as licensing and credentialing requirements, these efforts are often weak and sporadically enforced (National Center for Early Development and Learning [NCEDL], 2002). For example, NCEDL reports that most state child care licensing regulations have no or very low educational requirements for teachers or directors of child care facilities. Thus, there remain many practical and ethical obstacles to achieving the goal of finding high quality and affordable child care for all families.

According to Helburn, in *Cost, quality and child outcomes in child care centers* (1995), surveyed 401 child care centers, and found that the single largest expenditure for centers is personnel cost. The labor average was 70% of all costs per month. Improving quality to include gender equitable environments requires more investment in personnel through training, materials, and follow-up support. Studies find higher quality of care associated with specific staffing patterns such as low staff-child ratios, higher levels of staff education and specialized training, better staff wages, and lower staff turnover (Helburn, 1995; NCEDL, 2002; Phillips, Howes, & Whitebook, 1991; Whitebook, Howes, & Phillips, 1990).

Early childhood educators also need to be sensitive to another economic issue in child care—the increasing costs of education that are passed along to families. Child care programs that include curriculum enhancements such as field trips, guest speakers, book fairs, and other fee paid activities within regular school days either impose additional economic hardships on low-income families or perpetuate the separation of children into those who can go on the field trip and those who cannot. Costs associated with purchasing supplies and materials that almost everyone should be able to afford can place a financial burden on some families. Because the low-wage structure of child care providers (Gormley, 1995) can create higher turnover and other obstacles to high-quality care, scarce funds may be better directed toward providing a living wage for caregivers.

The feminized nature of any profession usually implies problematic wage structures, and this is clearly the case with child care. Cunningham and Watson (2002) pointed out, however, that the dearth of men in child care settings, as at later educational levels, may disadvantage boys by failing to provide them with role models for men as learners. Although the working conditions of those in the child care industry are thus deeply entwined with gender issues, perhaps the most important equity issue for children of both genders is simply access to care sufficient to their needs (NAEYC, 1997). NAEYC concluded, "High-quality [child care] experiences are not the norm" (p. 3), putting the figure for high-quality programs at about 15%.

To develop their full potentials intellectually, physically, socially, and emotionally, all children need quality care and early stimulation. In a study conducted by the National Institute of Child Health and Human Development (NICHD) with more than 1000 U.S. children, from birth to 54 months, researchers found that many individual children experience a wide variety of different types of child care, including center care, relative care, and child care homes (NICHD, 2004). Among their findings

- Hours spent in center care were higher in the preschool period than earlier
- Mothers who were single, those with more education and less-traditional beliefs about child rearing, and families with higher incomes and fewer children in the household used more hours of center care than other families
- Single mothers and those with fewer children used more hours in child care homes
- Minority families, those with low income, and mothers with less education and fewer children used more hours of relative care

Children who had been in center care experienced the following outcomes: Children four and a half years old who had been in center care exhibited higher externalizing behavior problems (such as physical aggression) than did other children; children who were in center care longer as infants had lower preacademic test scores; but children who had more hours in center care during their toddler years had higher language scores (Halle, Calkins, Berry, & Johnson, 2003; NICHD, 2004).

More recently, the Zero to Three Press conducted a web-based survey of people in the infant-toddler child care community and others who concerned about children's experiences in their earliest years. The top characteristics of high-quality group care settings for infants and toddlers and the essential ingredients of quality care giving were generated from 1,700 completed surveys (Goosen & Lindeman, 2004). These characteristics are broad in scope and are included in the recommendations section of this chapter. They reflect a comprehensive view of the nature of child care, including physical, emotional, and cognitive development.

Planned child care and preschool activities can also reflect gender biases through different expectations for boys and girls. For example, in child care centers and preschool programs where boys and girls are sometimes purposely divided into groups by sex, one might observe boys playing on the jungle gym or in the sandbox for a longer period of time than girls, particularly if the child care workers believe that boys need more activity than girls do. If child care instructors believe that boys are more aggressive and violent than girls, fewer opportunities may be provided for boys to share materials and work together than for girls. Through subtle and not so subtle messages such as, "Don't run, you might hurt yourself" (teacher to girl) and "Slow down, you might run into someone" (teacher to boy), child care instructors and caregivers share their different expectations for girls and boys in school.

Are girls so fragile that they are expected to fall and hurt themselves if they run? Are boys so impulsive or aggressive that they are expected not to look where they are going and therefore to run into someone? Are girls expected to sit quietly and look at books or play with dolls, and so they do? And what if they don't? Does that mean they are odd or different from other girls? How do adult caregivers respond to girls who run around, climb, or grab at things? For either girls or boys, gender stereotyping in preschool environments may result in increased criticism or less attention to the specific behavior and needs of the child by viewing children as a group, rather than as individuals. Clearly, preschool activities that encourage both sexes to participate in a variety of activities that enhance their full developments are needed.

School and Gender

With almost two thirds of today's kindergartners in school five to six hours a day, nearly double the percentage of two decades ago (Associated Press, 2005), it is imperative that we think of this time as a vital influential period in the early learning settings for young children. The academic demands of kindergarten have escalated for this generation of students, as kindergarten is increasingly seen not as a baby step into first grade, but rather as a time of rigorous work toward meeting the beginning reading and mathematics skills outlined by national organizations' academic standards (National Center for Education Statistics, NCES, 2000; Stipek, 2002). The need for young children to be exposed to a knowledge-rich environment as early as possible in order to ensure later success in school has become widely accepted over the last 20 years (Fletcher & Lyon, 1998; NICHD, 2004; Thorne, 1993).

Maturation differences in boys and girls have been explored as they relate to academic success. The relationships that children build with peers and teachers during early schooling are affected by children's abilities to regulate emotions that then either help or hurt their chances of doing well academically in later years. As noted above, children's early academic skills and emotional adjustments may be related, so that young children who struggle with early reading and have learning difficulties may grow increasingly frustrated and more disruptive (Francis, Shaywitz, S., Stuebing, Shaywitz, B., & Fletcher, 1996; Raver, 2003).

In the past 30 years, early childhood educators have paid attention to what Greenberg (1985) referred to as the "differing learning profile of the young girl from that of the young boy" (p. 459). In the 1970s, the Non-Sexist Child Development Project provided staff development, parent workshops, and curriculum to help the adults who work with children to free both girls and boys from the limits imposed by rigid sex-role expectations (Sprung, 1975). Girls were encouraged to play in the block area, boys in the dramatic play area. Activities that incorporated large movements in girls' play (e.g., running, throwing a ball, hopping, skipping rope) and fine motor movements for boys (e.g., writing, drawing, puzzles) were emphasized (Greenberg, 1985). This remains sound advice today.

Delayed Entry Into School

Delaying entry into school, sometimes referred to as "academic redshirting," is an increasingly common practice (Brent, May, & Kundert, 1996) and is linked to race and class, with about 9% to 10% of parents nationally delaying their children's entry into kindergarten (Byrd, Weitzman, & Auinger, 1997; NCES, 2000). Boys are twice as likely as girls to be held out from entering school (Brent et al., 1996; Cosden, Zimmer, & Tuss, 1993; May, Kundert, & Brent, 1995). Voluntary delayed entry for boys is closely related to parents' beliefs that boys mature more slowly than girls do (Stipek, 2002). Shepard and Smith (1986, 1988) cite demands for acceleration by middle-class parents as a cause. Boys' immediate school readiness issues are prominent in these decisions, of course, but so may perceived later consequences of boys' being older, such as increased size and physical maturity as an advantage in playing sports, and the social advantages of being a more mature teen with greater privileges (such as work opportunities, driving, etc.) than younger classmates. Shepard and others (e.g., Gilliam & Zigler, 2004; Shepard, 1991, 1992; Shepard & Smith 1986, 1988) noted that academic demands in kindergarten and first grade have increased greatly due to both educational accountability movements and the universality of kindergarten. An emphasis on school accountability based primarily on students' performance on achievement tests is likely to encourage more states and districts to consider increasing the age of school entry. The pressure to increase test scores may also encourage teachers to advise more parents to hold out relatively young children, especially boys, whom they consider to be at risk of poor achievement. Early childhood education experts who oppose the trend toward later school entry argue that time in an appropriate instructional context is more valuable and promotes academic success better than additional biological maturation, and better than general experience out of school. Shepard and Smith (1988) found that policies intended to control mismatches between children and the accelerated curriculum (e.g., raising the entrance age, readiness screening, and kindergarten retention) are ineffective and create even greater curricular escalation. Such policy interventions, they argued, are too broad to be reliable at the individual student level and do not accomplish a good match between students and instruction. This analysis is equally true of boys and girls, of course, but because boys are held out of school much more often than are girls, a gender dimension is salient to this set of issues.

Goosen and Lindeman (2004) offered the following alternatives to redshirting and retention as strategies for providing a more gender equitable learning environment in schools:

- Mixed age classes that allow children to progress at their own paces
- A curriculum that is both age and individually appropriate for each child
- All day kindergarten that is developmentally and individually appropriate and that provides children additional time in school without adding an extra year to normal school progression
- Individualized instruction that is tailored to meet the needs of individual children
- Recognizing and valuing differences among children, rather than striving for homogeneity in classroom placements
- Using tests appropriately to design and evaluate curriculum that meets the needs of each child in his or her classroom, rather than to make placement decisions that involve removing children from the regular classroom

All children, regardless of skill level, achievement, culture, social class, and background, deserve to be educated with their age peers and to follow normal school progression. Schools must begin concentrating on meeting individual children's needs in the classroom, rather than penalizing children with ineffective programming that isolates them from interactions with their higher achieving and more socially mature peers and that may add an additional year to their normal school progression (Carlson & Galle, 2000).

We would not conclude that delaying school entry has negative consequences for every child. Developmental differences may account for cases in which such an action is simply an accurate reflection of the facts for a particular individual. Where large numbers of individuals are concerned, however, the more appropriate question may be, "Why is the learning environment not ready for these students?" rather than, "Why are students not ready for the learning environment?" The authors of this chapter support the belief that no girl or boy should be limited in terms of his or her access to early learning experiences, when such experiences would enrich their lives and increase their full potential to be happy and productive members of society.

Gender and Academic Performance

The application of meta-analytic techniques has demonstrated reliable gender differences among adolescents and adults on some measures of mental rotation, spatial perception, mathematical problem solving, and science achievement, with males tending to outperform females (Halpern, 1992; Hyde, 1984, 1986, 2005; Hyde & Lindberg, 2007; Richardson, J. T., 1997). Interestingly, however, gender differences in mathematical problem solving or spatial relations are typically absent in young children. Significant differences in performance on assessments in these areas do not appear until high school and postsecondary schooling (Richardson, J. T., Caplan, Crawford, & Hyde, 1997). A number of hypotheses have been developed as to why these differences in performance appear as children progress through the education system, but most would agree the differences are related to learned behavior, not innate abilities. When students have not taken the necessary coursework to prepare them adequately for higher mathematics, they tend not to perform well on mathematics assessments (Fausto-Sterling, 1992). Because it is through our early learning experiences that some of our first concepts about mathematics form, these experiences have the potential to affect later success or failure in this subject (Polnick, B., & Funk, 2005, Sanders & Rocco, 1994). A diminished interest in mathematics, along with self-limiting behaviors, can impact mathematics performance (Hyde & Lindberg, 2007; Polnick, B., & Funk, 2005). Although this is often considered an issue for middle- and high-school girls, declining interest in some school subjects has been found as early as the first year of elementary school (Fölling-Albers & Hartinger, 1998; Gipps, 1996).

What Are Little Girls Made of, Made of?

Girls take the developmental lead in terms of school readiness. Young girls appear to be more ready for school, because they tend to sit and listen more attentively than do young boys when in large, whole group, structured activities (Women's College Coalition, 1996). The Women's College Coalition notes that girls talk earlier, read earlier, and count earlier and, in preschool, they score higher on intelligence tests than do their male peers. Although girls usually receive better grades in elementary school than boys receive, far more boys than girls are identified as gifted by fifth grade in public schools. It has been noted that girls exhibit tendencies to refrain from assertive behaviors, such as being first or being in charge. In the extreme sense, adolescent girls can be seen as going underground with their feelings, which can sometimes lead to disengagement with school (e.g., Taylor, J. M., Gilligan, & Sullivan, 1995). Emotionally, girls tend to express their frustrations with school by acting in, that is, by becoming silent, withdrawn, and nonparticipative, rather than by acting out, which is more characteristic of boys. Indirectly, girls receive messages regarding the teacher's expectations for their behavior that can cause them to become discouraged from taking risks or demonstrating signs of aggression because that has been defined for them as something only boys do. This is not to the advantage of girls, in light of the fact that taking risks is an important characteristic in many aspects of life, including problem solving.

What Are Little Boys Made of, Made of?

Researchers have examined what happens when boys repeatedly get into trouble in the early years of schooling. According to Kindlon and Thompson (2000), boys are as emotionally expressive as girls are when they are born, and in fact, boy babies cry more. Somewhere along the way, however, boys lose expressivity. Interestingly enough, by kindergarten age, boys are six times less likely than girls are to use the word *love*. Boys begin to define themselves as not emotional in an attempt to be masculine, and by doing so, start constricting parts of their emotional life (Froschl & Sprung, 2005; Kindlon & Thompson, 2000). Although acceptable boundaries for girls' choices and behaviors regarding gender have greatly expanded over the past several decades, some researchers believe that boys have remained in a "box", an ideal of masculinity that limits their emotional and relational development (Flood, 2000; Gropper, 2004; Kindlon & Thompson, 2000). In a recent series of focus groups with prekindergarten through grade 3 teachers and parents (Grooper, 2004), adults were asked to fill two boxes: Box One—What does it mean to be male in our society? Box Two—What happens to boys who do not fit into the Box One? Participants in the focus groups had no trouble identifying characteristics for the ideal male—instrumental competence, physical power, moral principles, and character. They also were well aware of the pain and suffering that result from not fitting in at school, for example, antisocial behavior, hardships, pressures, and impact on sexuality and gender identity (Gropper, 2004; Thorne, 1993). The consequences of operating outside the box are severe. Boys who do so are labeled in ways that leave them feeling isolated and shamed. Consequently, boys might develop negative attitudes in school, particularly towards the areas in which they are weakest. This may result in a disassociation with school and their teachers, especially if their learning environment is lacking in rewards and praise. Boys more often than girls express their frustrations with learning by acting out, that is, by disrupting the classroom in a variety of ways. They often appear to be more oppositional and less attentive or interested in school due to their more active behavior. Teachers have traditionally called on boys more often than on girls; on the other hand, boys may receive more criticism or disciplinary action than girls may when in a school setting. Repeated criticism can affect how boys feel about themselves, about school, and about learning in general (Glazer, 2005).

The many negative statistics about boys' emotional well being and academic achievement and the implications for their future education and careers are a clarion call for educators and parents to realize that boys issues must be addressed beginning in preschool (Best, 1983; Gallas, 1998; Koch & Irby, 2002; Paley, 1984). Although boys may be dominating the classroom, they are too often lost to the community of learning. Beginning in the late 1990s, books, such as *Real boys: Rescuing our sons from the myths of masculinity* (Pollack, 1998), *Raising Cain: Protecting the emotional life of boys* (Kindlon & Thompson, 2000), and *Bad boys: Public schools in the making of Black masculinity* (Ferguson, 2000), began to appear on the market, illuminating the public's concerns about boys' social/emotional developments and school performances. These books raise questions about the impact gender expectations have on boys' social and academic well beings. This increased attention to boys' needs should not, however, detract from attention to girls' needs; rather, it means that gender issues in the preschool years, as always, need to be addressed for the benefit of all children.

NEW AND EMERGING ISSUES RELATED TO GENDER IN EARLY LEARNING ENVIRONMENTS

International Early Childhood Education and Health Care Issues Related to Gender Roles

Only in recent years has it become seen as a legitimate position that the basic need of young children for food, healthcare, and protection are not just needs but rights (implying duties and obligations on the part of others), and that, in addition, the rights to affection, interaction, security, stimulation, and opportunities for learning are just as fundamental (Evans, 1997). In some cultures, preference for male over female children leads to the survival of many more boys than girls, creating a demographic situation that is fraught with the potential for significant social disruption (Agarwal, 1997; Megawangi, 1997). In many cultures, parents' and caretakers' preferences for boys lead to better nutritional status, better health care, and more attention to and stimulation of boys than of girls (Agarwal, 1997; Megawangi, 1997; Sadker, M., Sadker, D., & Klein, 1991). Thus, these girls and boys come to primary school with very different experiences that affect their capacity to learn and that need to be taken into account by teachers as well as curriculum developers (Agarwal, 1997; Megawangi, 1997). In most countries, girls and boys are raised from the beginning to take on very different roles and to exhibit different characteristics.

By the time a child reaches school age, he or she is firmly rooted in a gender identity, which brings with it a whole set of expectations about behavior and character (Evans, 1997). Yet much of the research on gender socialization does not look at this early, preschooling development, nor does childrearing research focus much on the development of gender traits. The Consultative Group on Early Childhood Care and Development (see Evans, 1997) conducted a set of studies that looked at gender socialization of young children in six countries: Morocco, Mali, Bolivia, India, Indonesia, and Jamaica. The purpose of these studies was to provide a preliminary understanding of how cultures socialize their children into gender roles. A review of these studies, although limited to research in third-world countries, is instructive regarding the impact that gender roles have on the development of young children.

The researchers in each of the six countries observed that when the balance of power shifts within a culture, people become uneasy, and this unease often has implications for gender roles. Gender socialization pertains not only to the differences between the expectations of girls and boys, but also to the larger conflict people are facing all over the world: how to reconcile traditional values and practices with contemporary pressures, demands, and settings (Evans, 1997). A synopsis of these studies as they relate to gender socialization is given in Table 29.3.

Early Childhood Curriculum and Diverse Family Structures

Families can feel alienated, silenced, and marginalized when their experiences and perceptions of the world are not included and represented in their children's educations. Dominant discourse of the traditional Western nuclear family (White, heterosexual, middle class) continues to inform the curriculum and practices in many early childhood settings to the exclusion of other families (Robinson & Diaz, 2006). For example, traditional discussions in preschool and kindergarten programs often include dialogue and stories about "What is a family?" This can be confusing to children who live in family units that do not follow the traditional "Daddy and Mommy" structure. These include, but are not limited to, stepfamilies, blended families, single mothers, single fathers, cohabiting families, teenage parents, gay/lesbian parents, foster and group home families, and kinship-care families (Hare & Gray, 1994). Children and family members from a growing number of these settings can be totally neglected when educators may not be knowledgeable about them or may not understand that some families differ from their own family settings. It is important that educators and child care curriculum developers become informed about the wide range of family settings to better plan and develop programs that are more inclusive, as well as to communicate effectively with all children and their caregivers.

STRATEGIES AND RECOMMENDATIONS FOR CREATING GENDER-EQUITABLE EARLY LEARNING ENVIRONMENTS

We have modified some of the recommendations from Greenberg (1985) and have included additional recommendations for meeting the emerging issues discussed earlier in this chapter.

Teachers, program planners, curriculum developers, and professional organizations have the capacity to change the learning environment for young children through their student interactions and communications, as well as their use and

TABLE 29.3   Synopsis of Six International Studies on Gender Socialization of Young Children

Focus of Study	Synopsis
Preferences for a boy or girl	Parents in all the countries studied desire sons. The degree of preference for having a son over having a daughter differed across the countries. The birth of a son is considered a positive event; this is not necessarily true for the birth of a daughter.
Behaviors	Parents have different values and attitudes regarding male and female children. As a result, children behave differently based on gender, with certain behaviors typical of girls and others typical of boys.
Development	Girls tend to achieve developmental milestone earlier than do boys.
Socialization	Socialization of children (through childrearing techniques and educational practices) reproduces and reinforces social gender differences. Women play a primary role in socializing young children; men are not significantly involved with children under the age of five.
Complementary roles	Male and female roles within the traditional culture seem to have remained in balance as long as the traditional culture was intact. Traditional culture is used as justification for differential treatment of boys and girls, even when the traditional culture is no longer fully in place.
Well-being	The community's definition of well-being included a variety of dimensions; formal education is not always among them. Formal education is not necessarily seen as crucial for either boys or girls.
Urbanization	Culture and degree of urbanization are stronger determinants of gender socialization than is socioeconomic status. Better-off rural families are usually the most hostile to girls, and tend to have a contemptuous attitude towards the life of a girl child. Better-off urban families hold more equitable perceptions about their daughters' lives.
Changing roles	As the society changes, what used to be experienced as a balance is now experienced as an imbalance between male and female roles. Under these conditions, traditional socialization practices are detrimental to both males and females within the culture.

Source: Evans, 1997.

selection of materials and implementation of activities. Achieving gender equity in early learning environments requires careful analysis of what we teach, how we teach, and how we assess outcomes.

Strategies for Caregivers and Teachers for Promoting Gender Fairness

National organizations like the National Council of Teachers of English (NCTE), the American Psychological Association (APA, 2001), and the NAEYC have developed guidelines for gender-fair practices, particularly language usage practices.[1] A few of those practices that are particularly relevant to early learning environments are included below (in slightly modified form):

1. Use Gender-Fair Language
   a. Include a careful selection of materials, such as literature that represents women and men in a variety of roles—traditional and nontraditional; search for and use nonsexist nursery rhymes (e.g., Gander, 1986), stories, songs (e.g., Thomas, 2002), games and, of course, locally-approved course materials (National Council of Teachers of English, [NCTE], 2002)
   b. Read books written by and about both men and women (NCTE, 2002)
   c. Select books that show females and males participating in a variety of settings, such as home, work, and play (NCTE, 2002)
   d. Use noninclusive text and classic sexist works as tools for discussing gender roles and gender equity, because many of these pieces of literature portray men and women in very stereotyped roles; balance these with other texts that show gender-fair roles (NCTE, 2002)
   e. Choose and use headings and activities that do not assume stereotypic male and female interests. For example, do not label materials as "toys for girls" or "books for boys" (NCTE, 2002)
2. Encourage children to read children's books that break gender role stereotypes, such as *Amazing grace* by Mary Hoffman (1991) and *Boy, can he dance!* by Eileen Spinelli (1993). These and 23 other recommended books are listed in a publication available through the NAEYC (Roberts & Hill, 2003).
3. Promote gender-fair interactions between teachers and children, such as the following (NCTE, 2002):
   a. Praise, encourage, and respond to contributions of girls and boys equally. Actively avoid sex segregation, while attending to individual needs.
   b. Call on girls as often as boys to answer both factual and complex questions.
   c. Create a classroom atmosphere where girls are not interrupted by others more often than are boys.
   d. Establish collaborative groups composed of both boys and girls to provide opportunities for all voices to be heard.

   e. Value intellect; avoid references to appearance and physical attributes
4. Avoid stereotyping jobs or roles when communicating with parents and community members. Use inclusionary alternatives, such as "Dear Families" instead of "Dear Mothers" (APA, 2001; NCTE, 2002).
5. Include examples of females in roles traditionally held by males (e.g., doctor, construction worker, engineer), and use examples of males in roles traditionally held by females (e.g., nurse, secretary, interior decorator) (NCTE, 2002).
6. Do not represent girls and boys as possessing stereotypic gendered attributes. For example, avoid saying, "Girls are quiet" or "Boys are strong," or "Boys, can you put this together for me?" or "Girls, let the boys do that, you'll get your dress dirty!" (NCTE, 2002).
7. Avoid pitting boys against girls in competitive activities, such as word games, races, and the notorious quiet game (a game in which children are often admonished for being the first person to make a sound after an extended period). Do not line up by gender. Create opportunities for nurturing and caring activities that are in a problem-solving mode and that invite all children's involvement. Choose girls for leadership positions as often as boys (NCTE, 2002).
8. Present gender-equitable contributions from the class by alternating male and female names when calling on students (NCTE, 2002).
9. Use strategies such as teacher proximity and structured playtime to involve children in activities they may otherwise avoid such as girls in large-muscle physical activities and boys in small-muscle activities such as handwriting (Greenberg, 1985; NCTE, 2002).
10. Develop verbal and physical interaction patterns that make all children equal participants in non-sex-segregated activities (NCTE, 2002), such as the following:
    a. Provide activities for practice using large-muscle coordination and development of large-motor skills
    b. Provide tasks that require cooperative girl-boy groups of three or more children for their accomplishments
    c. Provide activities that encourage listening, speaking, and conversing so that there is an equitable distribution of participation by boys and girls
    d. Provide opportunities that encourage responsibility for others in a variety of gender structures, such as girls for boys, boys for girls, girls for girls, and boys for boys.

Recommendations for Creating Educational Equity in Early Education Environments

Many types of organizations and individuals can contribute to enhancing educational equity in early education environments. The following are specific recommendations from the research literature for educators, scholars, policy makers, and families.

---

[1]The 2002 NCTE document, *Guidelines for Gender-Fair Use of Language*, were revised from the 1985 NCTE Publication *Guidelines for Nonsexist Use of Language* in NCTE publications developed by the Women in Literacy and Life Assembly (WILLA) in 1985. This latter document was based on a *Committee on the Status of Women in the Professions'* document, which was created in 1975. The *2001 APA Guidelines* for gender fair language use were developed by the Committee on Lesbian and Gay concerns (CLGC) and approved by APA's Board of Social and Ethical Responsibility in Psychology (BSERP), as well as its Publications and Communications Board.

Political/Governmental Agencies

1. The push for quality child care needs to be accompanied by specific attention to adequate implementation of gender equity strategies as recommended in the earlier section of this chapter.
2. The 1997 White House conferences examined the public policy implications of new findings from brain research literature and the role of child care as more women are employed as full-time workers (Halfon, McLearn, & Schuster, 2002). Several federal agencies have focused new attention on the development of young children, collecting new data, launching new programs, and expanding oversight and support for states and local communities that are trying to make a difference in the lives of young children. Over the past 15 years, federal legislation has formed the basis for a more defined set of social policies on young children. Head Start has grown and expanded during the 1990s, and the federal government created Early Head Start for children birth to age three in 1996, which also employs early intervention strategies to build family capacity, drawing on home visiting techniques that have been developed and tested over the past two decades. The 1992 Family and Medical Leave Act was a major boost for the children of mothers and fathers employed in workplaces of 50 or more. The Act allows mothers and fathers to take an unpaid leave of up to 12 weeks in a 12-month period without penalty in the workplace after the birth, adoption, or foster placement of a child, as well as when they need to care for a sick child. Unfortunately, however, many U.S. businesses are too small to be covered by this Act. Nevertheless, although political and governmental activities such as these are steps in the right direction, we recommend increased funding for agencies and other gender equity groups, to work together to provide resources for young children.
3. Coordination of resources that address the needs of the whole child will be even more critical in the future. Recent efforts by different institutions to address the needs of children in poverty have resulted in collaboration among agencies and care giving units. It is imperative that early childhood educators work with other cultural-responsive support agencies in the community to provide support for families.

Research/Universities/Gender Equity Organizations

1. Publish and disseminate information relating to gender-fair practices, activities, books, and interactions for parents and other caregivers. Develop online accessible links to these materials at gender equity organization, governmental and early childhood organization Web sites.
2. Research and follow up on popular books on young children, gender, and learning. These books are being widely read by today's parents and grandparents and may be accepted as fact by many readers, whether they are actually research based or not. We recommend writing to the authors and requesting the research evidence that was used to support statements made about the learning differences between boys and girls. Note the qualifications of the authors, and see if their work is supported or recognized in the professional literature from the mainstream organizations of their profession, such as neuroscience. If sufficient evidence of misrepresentation of research findings is found, position papers may need to be written by gender equity and early childhood education organizations. Examine how conclusions and findings were reached—opinions of authors versus empirical research.
3. Encourage publishers of early childhood textbooks on teaching methods to include gender-fair practices and research on the effects of gender-bias activities in the classroom. Public and private school teachers need access to this information as they develop their own beliefs while learning the management skills that are needed to create learning experiences for young children. Universities and child care training certification entities need to include gender-fair language practices, including language usage, as recommended in the strategies section of this chapter. Interventions that are more specific are needed to counteract sex socialization in society, including: eliminating educators' stereotypical behavior; correcting students' restricted gender-stereotypical learning styles; discouraging gender-stereotypical relations and communication patterns between the genders; and increasing cross-gender interactions (Grossman & Grossman, 1994).
4. We recommend that further studies be conducted regarding how child care and preschool workers plan (or do not plan) activities for children in early childhood settings. Social behaviors, physical activity, and emotional development relate to academic performance as young boys and girls begin school for the first time. Researchers agree that gender stereotypes in these areas interfere with children's learning and academic performance (Byrd et al., 1997; Koch & Irby, 2002; May et al., 1995).

Parents and Teachers

1. The authors recommend teacher and administrator training that includes some or all of the following activities and strategies for achieving gender equity in early learning environments through curricular change:
   a. Adopt and/or participate in exemplary and promising programs used in early childhood programs as recommended by the Gender Equity Expert Panel (2000):
      i. Playtime Is Science: An Equity-Based Parent/Child Science Program[2]
      ii. National Science Partnership for Girl Scouts and Science Museums[3]

[2]Developed by Educational Equity Concepts, Inc., New York, NY. An intensive three-day program implementer training package is supplemented by follow-up training to help individual schools or districts and by materials to be used with the children. It uses inquiry-based activities in the physical sciences. It has increased teacher and parent use of science activities associated with increased positive attitudes among underserved groups, especially girls. Contact: Merle Froschl and Barbara Sprung.

[3]Developed by The Franklin Institute Science Museum in Philadelphia, PA and the Girl Scouts of the USA, New York, NY. This program provides two-hour leader training for each of seven student activity kits. Each kit contains 12–25 hands-on science activities for girls, ages 6–11. It has been effective in increasing interest in science among both the girls and their Girl Scout leaders. It also provides a model for partnerships between museums and other youth-serving organizations.

iii. EQUALS[4]

iv. Succeeding at Fairness: Effective Teaching for All Students[5]

v. A Woman's Place . . . Is in the Curriculum[6]

b. In addition to these specific programs and practices, the authors recommend including the following strategies for professional development for teachers, administrators, preservice teachers and instructional support personnel:

i. Have teachers and administrators discuss and reflect on ways that gender discrimination is evidenced in classroom interactions, curricula, and physical environments, as well as in online communities

ii. Discuss in small problem-solving groups gender issues as they are observed and experienced in the classroom as well as outside of the classroom in a variety of real-world experiences boys and girls encounter

iii. Discuss issues found in single-sex schools for teachers and parents in all-girl or all-boy schools

iv. Collaboratively develop an action plan to organize and focus implementation activities, such as the diverse forms of sexism found in schools or sponsoring student-led discussions and demonstrations

v. Engage in meaningful dialogue with parents about the dangers of gender inequity and why achieving a gender balance is critical to overall student success

2. Changing key attitudes and beliefs of the teachers in the early childhood classroom is a critical step in creating gender equitable learning environments. Consequently, training is needed for early childhood educators, including both certified and noncertified personnel. However, training and materials alone may not be enough to convince teachers of the need to implement gender equity strategies in early learning environments. Early childhood teachers' understandings of many aspects of gender and gender equity are heavily grounded in their own socialization into gender roles (Lee-Thomas, Sumsion, & Roberts, 2005). Teacher education should include strategies that promote self-awareness as a core element. Involving teachers in action research combines theory and practice in ways that can challenge our existing theories and shows us ways in which we can rethink practice (MacNaughton, Rolfe, & Siraj-Blatchford, 2001). Unless teachers believe in what they are being asked to do, full support will be difficult and change will be minimal. State departments of education, universities, and gender equity and early childhood organizations should support collaborative action research projects, in which teams of teachers collect data on the challenges of practicing gender equity in early childhood classrooms. "Collaborative action research offers a powerful tool for improving our understandings about how to produce change in early childhood settings" (MacNaughton et al., 2001, p. 223). Given the limited qualifications of many child care personnel, and the lack of a coherent, nation-wide process for the professional socialization of early childhood teachers and caregivers, this will be a formidable challenge.

3. The NAEYC recommends that parents and teachers help children build a healthy self-identity by teaching them to resist bias and to value the differences between people as much as the similarities. Specific strategies for achieving this goal include the following (Derman-Sparks & ABC Task Force, 1989; Derman-Sparks, Gutierrez, & Day, 1989, 2004):

• Recognize that because we live in a society where many biases exist, we must counteract them—or else we will support them through our silence.

• At home or at school, give children messages that deliberately contrast stereotypes by providing books, dolls, toys, wall decorations, TV programs, and records that show:

– men and women in nontraditional roles

– people of color in leadership positions

– people with disabilities doing activities familiar to children

– various types of families and family activities

• Show no bias in the friends, doctors, teachers, and other service providers that you choose, or in the stores where you shop. Remember what you do is as important as what you say.

• Make it a firm rule that a person's appearance is never an acceptable reason for teasing or rejecting them. Immediately step in if you hear or see your child behave in such a way.

• Talk positively about each child's physical characteristics and cultural heritage. Help children learn the differences between feelings of superiority and those of self-esteem and pride in their own heritage.

• Provide opportunities for children to interact with other children who are racially/culturally different from themselves and with people who have various disabilities.

---

[4]Developed by the Lawrence Hall of Science, University of California, Berkeley. The EQUALS mathematics program is 30 hours of in-service workshops focusing on hands-on problem solving, equity awareness, and co-operative teamwork for teachers, parents, and community leaders who work with K–12 students. Teachers reported that EQUALS helped them address the needs of their female and language minority students and noted improvements in students' attitudes and scores in some aspects of mathematics.

[5]Developed by Myra and David Sadker, School of Education, American University, Washington, DC. This flexible three-day tiered teacher in-service training program increases the effectiveness and equity of classroom teaching. It does so by helping participants understand gender-related research and increase their own gender equitable classroom interactions. Many participants also become empowered through their own experiences in peer coaching and replicating this training program.

[6]Developed by the National Women's History Project, Windsor, CA. This five-day teacher training conference on women's history is for K–12 educators to help them incorporate multicultural women's history into all subjects from elementary school to college. The participants who come from across the nation as well as other countries bring the multicultural roles of women in US history into their schools by using existing resources and developing their own activities and courses.

- Respectfully listen to and answer children's questions about themselves and others. Do not ignore, change the subject, or in any way make the child think he or she is bad for asking such a question.
- Teach children how to challenge biases about who they are. Give them tools to confront those who act biased against them.
- Use accurate and fair images in contrast to stereotypes, and encourage children to talk about the differences. Help them to think critically about what they see in books, in movies, in greeting cards, in comics, and on TV.

  Let children know that unjust things can be changed. Encourage children to challenge bias, and involve children in taking action on issues relevant to their lives.

3. Develop and activate campaigns to support children's media and toys that promote images of girls and minorities with a positive, gender-fair view (e.g., *Dora the Explorer*). Images today are powerful tools that influence the minds (language and actions) of young children before they are old enough to walk. These influences include television shows and videos (cartoons and children's shows), video games, and toys. On the flip side, activity against violent, racial- and gender-biased media and toys needs to occur at all levels: parents, commercial marketing, screening and rating agencies, universities, training and certification centers, and gender equity organizations. Scripts using the different media to illustrate points of gender-limiting and dehumanizing practices, as well as those that do demonstrate equity for all, could be developed as tools for educators, parents, and other caregivers and commercial entities.

4. For inspiring young girls to be strong, smart, and bold, we recommend taking the following actions as supported in the doctrines and publications of both The Women's College Coalition (1996) and Girls, Incorporated (2006).

   - Encourage girls to participate in activities and experiences that may be traditionally reserved for boys. For example, girls may not ask for the chance to participate in such activities, but they are enthusiastic participants when given the opportunity. Praise demonstrations of daring and curiosity.
   - Praise your daughter for her skills and ideas rather than for her appearance and neatness. Girls have the right to accept and appreciate their bodies they way they are.
   - Encourage girls to ask questions and not always accept the answers that are given, take risks, and seek challenges. Girls have the right to take risks, to strive freely, and to take pride in success. Resist rescuing girls or providing ready answers for them. Research shows that this kind of help undermines girls' confidence in their abilities.
   - Encourage new, nontraditional thinking and methods of problem solving. Help foster an environment where girls know it is acceptable to get sweaty and dirty in pursuit of a goal. Girls have the right to express themselves with originality and enthusiasm. Girls should be encouraged to speak up and speak out, making sure their voices are heard.
   - Become a media critic and encourage that approach in girls. Discuss the portrayals of girls and women on television, in movies, in magazines, and in popular music. Do the media offer positive or negative role models for girls? Explore the messages and assumptions that the media are sending. These discussions provide ideal opportunities to explore the roles of girls and women in society.
   - Try and try again (it is okay to make mistakes); take on leadership positions in student government, sports or extracurricular activities; stick with mathematics and science classes even if these are not their strong suit; play organized sports; participate in physical activities.
   - Read what your daughter or your students are reading.
   - Check out the textbooks. Are there women represented in all disciplines, including science and history?
   - Ask teachers, principals, and counselors to provide information on careers even to elementary school students.
   - Find out if girls have equal access to computers and other equipment. Where are the computers located? What kind of rules apply for taking turns?
   - Share information about classroom climate and gender equity with faculty and staff. Encourage parent teacher organizations to identify these issues for discussion.
   - Find out if there are organized, funded, team sports for girls. If not, talk to the principal and coaches.

CONCLUSION

Greenberg (1985) reminded us in her earlier *Handbook* chapter on gender and early childhood, "If we accept the verdict of both lay and professional persons that the early childhood years are not only important in themselves but that their effects have a lifelong impact, we must view seriously what children do during these years and perhaps view even more seriously what they do not do or avoid doing" (p. 457). It is critical, therefore, to recognize the need for both knowledge and expertise in making the learning environments of young children gender equitable. Creating gender-equitable environments requires not only allowing participation but encouraging it, not only providing opportunities but creating them, and not only recognizing success but expecting it in all children, regardless of their gender. Giving all children an equal chance to develop to their fullest potential as well as succeed in school is the essence of this decade's mantra, to leave no child behind.

ACKNOWLEDGMENTS

The authors wish to thank the following reviewers for their comments on earlier versions of this chapter: Dr. Stacie G. Goffin, Goffin Strategy Group, Washington, DC; Dr. Louise Derman-Sparks, Professor Emeritus, Pacific Oaks College, Pacific Oaks, CA; and Dr. Laverne Warner, Sam Houston State University, Huntsville, TX. We are also grateful to Ms. Evelyn Fisch of ETS for her expert editorial assistance.

References

Agarwal, S. (1997). *Children of a lesser god: Differences in the treatment and perception of children 0–6 years of age by gender in India.* (Report of a study conducted with support from the Consultative Group on Early Childhood Care and Development). Retrieved May 10, 2006, from http://www.ecdgroup.com/issue_20_Gender_socialization_early_years.asp

Agosto, D. E. (2006). *A study of girls' and young women's electronic information design and content preferences.* Retrieved August 29, 2006, from http://www.girlstech.douglass.rutgers.edu/gt_summary.html

Alloway, N. (1995). *Foundation stones: The construction of gender equity in early childhood.* Melbourne, Australia: Curriculum Corporation.

American Association of University Women. (1991). *Shortchanging girls, shortchanging America.* Washington, DC: Author.

American Association of University Women. (1992). *How schools shortchange girls.* Washington, DC: Author.

American Psychological Association. (2001). *Publication manual of the American Psychological Association* (5th ed.). Washington, DC: Author.

Andersen, M. L. (1993). *Thinking about women: Sociological perspectives on sex and gender.* New York: Macmillan.

Archer, J. (2004). Sex differences in aggression in real-world setting: A meta-analytic review. *Review of General Psychology, 8,* 291–322.

Associated Press. (2005). More kindergartners in for a full day. *CNN Education for Student News.* Retrieved August 31, 2005, from http://www.cnn.com/2005/EDUCATION/08/31/full.day.kindergarten.ap/index.html

Aubrey, J. S., & Harrison, K. (2004). The gender-role content of children's favorite television programs and its links to their gender-related perceptions. *Media Psychology, 6*(2), 111–146.

Bandura, A. (1986). *Social foundations of thought and action: A social cognitive theory.* Englewood Cliffs, NJ: Prentice Hall.

Bandura, A. (2000). Self-efficacy. In E. W. Craighead & C. B. Nemeroff (Eds.), *Encyclopedia of psychology and neuroscience* (3rd ed., pp. 1474–1476). New York: Wiley.

Basow, S. A. (1992). *Gender stereotypes and roles* (3rd ed.). Pacific Grove, CA: Brooks/Cole Publishing.

Basu, P. (2005). Gender hormones may lend to social disorder therapies. *University of Wisconsin-Madison Web site.* Retrieved March 20, 2006, from http://www.news.wisc.edu/11455.html

Beal, C. (1994). *Boys and girls: The development of gender roles.* New York: McGraw-Hill.

Beaty, J. J. (2002). *Observing development of the young child,* (5th ed.). Upper Saddle River, NJ: Merrill Prentice Hall.

Bergen, D. (1998). Play as a context for humor development. In D. P. Fromberg & D. Bergen (Eds.), *Play from birth to twelve and beyond: Contexts, perspectives, and meanings* (pp. 324–337). New York: Garland.

Best, R. (1983). *We've all got scars: What boys and girls learn in elementary school.* Indianapolis, IN: University of Indiana Press.

Black, H. (1989). Interactive pretense: Social and symbolic skills in preschool play groups. *Merrill-Palmer Quarterly, 35*(4), 379–397.

Bowman, R. E., MacLusky, N. J., Sarmiento, Y., Frankfurt, M., Gordon, M., & Luine, V. N. (2004). Sexually dimorphic effects of prenatal stress on cognition, hormonal responses, and central neurotransmitters. *Endocrinology, 145,* 3778–3787.

Bradley, B. S., & Gobbart, S. K. (1989). Determinants of gender-typed play in toddlers. *Journal of Genetic Psychology, 150*(4), 453–455.

Bransford, J. D., Brown, A. L., & Cocking, R. R. (Eds.). (1999). *How people learn: Brain, mind, experience, and school.* Washington, DC: National Academy Press.

Brent, D., May, D. C., & Kundert, D. K. (1996). The incidence of delayed school entry: A twelve-year review. *Early Education and Development, 7*(2), 121–135.

Bridges, S. B. (1993). Pink or blue: Gender stereotyped perceptions on infants as conveyed by birth congratulations cards. *Psychology of Women Quarterly, 17,* 193–205.

Byrd, R., Weitzman, M., & Auinger, P. (1997). Increased behavior problems associated with delayed school entry and delayed school progress. *Pediatrics, 100,* 654–661.

Caldera, Y. M., Huston, A. C., & O'Brien, M. (1989). Social interactions and play patterns of parents and toddlers with feminine, masculine, and neutral toys. *Child Development, 60,* 70–76.

Carlson, L., & Galle, L. (2000). Alternatives to kindergarten retention and transition placement. *Fact Find.* Minneapolis, MN: Center for Early Education and Development. Retrieved June 16, 2004, from http://education.umn.edu/CEED/publications/factfind/ff2000.htm

Carlsson-Paige, N., & Levin, D. E. (1987). *The war play dilemma: Balancing needs and values in the early childhood classroom.* New York: Teachers College Press.

Carpenter, C. J., Huston, A. C., & Spera, L. (1989). Children's use of time in their everyday activities during middle childhood. In M. N. Bloch & A. D. Pellegrini (Eds.), *The ecological context of children's play* (pp. 165–190). Norwood, NJ: Ablex.

Carter, B. (1991, May 1). Children's TV, where boys are king. *New York Times,* pp. A1, C18.

Catron, C. E., & Allen, J. (2003). *Early childhood curriculum: A creative play model* (3rd ed.). Upper Saddle River, NJ: Pearson Education.

CHOICE. (1991). *Creating sex-fair family day care: A guide for trainers.* Newton, MA: WEEA Publishing Center.

Comber, C., Colley, A., Hargreaves, D. J., & Dorn, L. (1997). The effects of age, gender, and computer experience on computer attitudes. *Educational Research, 39,* 123–133.

Comstock, G., & Paik, H. (1991). *Television and the American child.* San Diego, CA: Academic Press.

Consultative Group on Early Childhood Care and Development. (1997). Rerieved February 6, 2007, from http://www.ecdgroup.com/issue_20_Gender_socialization_early_years.asp

Cosden, M., Zimmer, J., & Tuss, P. (1993). The impact of age, sex, and ethnicity on kindergarten entry and retention decisions. *Educational Evaluation and Policy Analysis, 15,* 209–222.

Cunningham, B., & Watson, L. W. (2002). Recruiting male teachers. *Young Children, 57*(6), 10–15.

Derman-Sparks, L., & The ABC Task Force. (1989). *Anti-bias curriculum: Tools for empowering young children.* Washington, DC: National Association for the Education of Young Children.

Derman-Sparks, L., Gutierrez, M., & Day, C.B. (1989). *Teaching young children to resist bias: What parents can do* [Brochure]. Washington, DC: National Association for the Education of Young Children.

Derman-Sparks, L., Gutierrez, M., & Day, C. B. (2004). *Teaching young children to resist bias: What parents can do* [Brochure]. Washington, DC: National Association for the Education of Young Children.

Dorman, S. M. (1998). Technology and the gender gap. *Journal of School Health, 68,* 165–166.

Duveen, G., & Lloyd, B. (1990). A semiotic analysis of the development of social representations and the development of knowledge. In G. Duveen & B. Lloyd (Eds.), *Social representations and the development of knowledge* (pp. 27–46). New York: Cambridge University Press.

Dweck, C. S. (1999). Caution—Praise can be dangerous. *American Educator, 23*(1), 4–9.

Dweck, C. S. (2000). *Self-theories: Their role in motivation, personality, and development*. Philadelphia: Taylor & Francis/Psychology Press.

Dweck, C. S. (2002). Messages that motivate: How praise molds students' beliefs, motivation, and performance (in surprising ways). In J. Aronson (Ed.), *Improving academic achievement: Classic and contemporary lessons from psychology*. New York: Academic Press.

Dweck, C. S. (2006). *Mindset: The psychology of success*. New York: Random House.

Eaton, W. O., & Enns, L. R. (1986). Sex differences in human motor activity level. *Psychological Bulletin, 100*, 19–28.

Edgerton, R. B. (1979). *Mental retardation: The developing child*. Cambridge, MA: Harvard University Press.

Elgas, P. M., Klein, I., Kantor, R., & Fernie, D. E. (1988). Play and the peer culture: Play styles and object use. *Journal of Research in Childhood Education, 3*(2), 142–153.

Eron, L. D. (1992). Gender differences in violence: Biology and/or socialization? In K. Bjorkqvist & P. Niemela (Eds.), *Of mice and women: Aspects of female aggression* (pp. 89–97). New York: Academic Press.

Evans, J. L. (1997). *Both halves of the sky: Gender socialization in the early years.* (Report of a study conducted with support from the Consultative Group on Early Childhood Care and Development). Retrieved May 10, 2006, from http://www.ecdgroup.com/download/cc120abi.pdf

Fagot, B. I. (1978). The influence of sex of child on parental reactions to toddler children. *Child Development, 49*, 459–465.

Fagot, B. I. (1988). Toddlers; play and sex stereotyping. In D. Bergen (Ed.), *Play: A medium for learning and development* (pp. 133–135). Portsmouth, NH: Heinemann.

Fagot, B. I., & Leve, L. (1998). Gender identity and play. In D. P. Fromberg & D. Bergen (Eds.), *Play from birth to twelve and beyond: Contexts, perspectives, and meanings* (pp. 187–192). New York: Garland.

Fausto-Sterling, A. (1992). *Myths of gender: Biological theories about women and men* (Electronic version, 2nd ed.). New York: Basic Books.

Ferguson, A. (2000). *Bad boys: Public school in the making of Black masculinity.* Ann Arbor, MI: University of Michigan Press.

Fletcher, J. M., & Lyon, G. R. (1998). Reading: A research-based approach. In W. Evers (Ed.), *What's gone wrong in America's classrooms* (pp. 50–77). Retrieved February 24, 2005, from http://www.nichd.nih.gov/crmc/cdb/approach.pdf

Flood, C. (2000). *Raising and educating healthy boys* (Concept paper). New York: Educational Equity Concepts.

Fölling-Albers, M., & Hartinger, A. (1998). Interest of girls and boys in elementary school. In L. Hoffmann, A. Krapp, K. A. Renninger, & J. Baumert (Eds.), *Interest and learning: Proceedings of the Seeon Conference on interest and gender* (pp. 175–183). Kiel, Germany: IPN.

Francis, D. J., Shaywitz, S. E., Stuebing, K. K., Shaywitz, B. A., & Fletcher, J. M. (1996). Developmental lag versus deficit models of reading disability: A longitudinal, individual growth curves analysis. *Journal of Educational Psychology, 88*, 3–17.

Freitag, P. J. (1998). Games, achievement, and the mastery of social skills. In D. P. Fromberg & D. Bergen (Eds.), *Play from birth to twelve and beyond: Contexts, perspectives, and meanings* (pp. 303–312). New York: Garland.

Fromberg, D. P. (1999). A review of research on play. In C. Seefeldt (Ed.), *The early childhood curriculum: Current findings in theory and practice* (3rd ed., pp. 27–53). New York: Teachers College Press.

Fromberg, D. P. (2005). The power of play: Gender issues in early childhood education. In B. Irby & J. Koch (Eds.), *Gender and schooling in the early years* (pp. 29–39). Greenwich, CT: Information Age Publishing.

Froschl, M., & Gropper, N. (1999). *Fostering friendships, curbing bullying*. Retrieved on July 7, 2006 from http://www.ade.state.az.us/ess/pinspals/documents/Behavioral/BR10.doc

Froschl, M., & Sprung, B. (2005). *The Anti-Bullying and Teasing Book: For Preschool Classrooms.* Beltsville, MD: Gryphon House.

Froschl, M., Sprung, B., & Mullin-Rindler, N. (1998). *Quit it! A teacher's guide on teasing and bullying for use with students in grades K–3.* New York: Educational Equity Concepts.

Gallas, K. (1998). *Sometimes I can be anything: Power, gender, and identify in a primary classroom.* New York: Teachers College Press.

Gander, F. (1986). *Father Gander nursery rhymes: The equal rhymes amendment*. Santa Barbara, CA: Advocacy Press.

Garner, B. P. (1998). Play development from birth to age four. In D. P. Fromberg & D. Bergen (Eds.), *Play from birth to twelve and beyond: Contexts, perspectives, and meanings* (pp. 137–145). New York: Garland.

Geary, D. C. (1998). *Male, female: The evolution of human sex differences.* Washington, DC: American Psychological Association.

Gender Equity Expert Panel. (2000). *Exemplary and promising programs*. Retrieved on August 5, 2006, from http://www.ed.gov/offices/OERI/ORAD/KAD/expert_panel/geawards.html

Gilliam, W. S., & Zigler, E. F. (2004). *State efforts to evaluate the effects of prekindergarten*. New Haven, CT: Yale University Child Study Center.

Gilligan, C. (1982). *In a different voice: Psychological theory and women's development*. Cambridge, MA: Harvard University Press.

Gipps, C. (1996). Introduction. In P. F. Murphy & C. V. Gipps (Eds.), *Equity in the classroom: Towards effective pedagogy for girls and boys*, (Electronic version, pp. 1–5). London: Falmer Press.

Girls, Incorporated. (2006). *Girls' bill of rights*. Washington, DC: Author. Retrieved on July 18, 2006 from http://www.girlsinc.org/ic/page.php?id=1.7

Glazer, S. (2005). Is growing up tougher for boys than for girls? *The CQ Researcher, 9*(23). Retrieved October 5, 2005, from http://library2.cqpress.com/cqresearcher/ppv.php?id=cqresrre1999061800

Goldstein, J. (Ed.). (1994). *Toys, play and child development* (pp. 6-26). New York: Cambridge University Press.

Goldstein, J. (1995). Aggressive toy play. In A. D. Pellegrini (Ed.), *The future of play theory* (pp. 127–147). Albany, NY: State University of New York Press.

Golomb, C., Gowing, E. D. G., & Friedman, L. (1982). Play and cognition: Studies of pretense play and conservation of quantity. *Journal of Experimental Child Psychology, 33*, 257–279.

Gonen, M., Uzmen, S., Akcin, N., & Ozdemir, N. (1993). *Creative thinking as 5–6 year old [sic] kindergarten children*. Paper presented at the Building bridges: International collaboration in the 1990s: The Warwick International Early Years Conference. (ERIC Document Reproduction Service No. ED392 516)

Goosen, M., & Lindeman, D. P. (2004). *Are they ready for kindergarten? The pros and cons of redshirting young children.* Parsons, KS: Kansas University Center on Developmental Disabilities. Retrieved May 20, 2006, from http://www.zerotothree.org/

Gormley, W. T. (1995). *Everybody's children: Child care as a public problem.* [Electronic version]. Washington, DC: Brookings Institution.

Greenberg, S. (1985). Educational equity in early childhood environments. In S. Klein (Ed.), *Handbook for achieving sex equity through education* (pp. 457–469). Baltimore: Johns Hopkins University Press.

Greif, E. B. (1976). Sex role playing in pre-school children. In J. S. Bruner, A. Jolly, & K. Sylva (Eds.), *Play—its role in development and evolution* (pp. 385–391). New York: Basic Books.

Grieshaber, S. (1998). Constructing the gendered infant. In N. Yelland (Ed.), *Gender in early childhood* (pp. 16–35). London: Routledge.

Gropper, N. (2000, September). *Addressing teasing and bullying: A collaboration between Educational Equity Concepts and P.S. 75* (Evaluation Report). New York: Educational Equity Concepts.

Gropper, N. (2001, July). *A collaboration between Educational Equity Concepts and Jefferson School to address teasing and bullying in grades K–3* (Evaluation Report). New York: Educational Equity Concepts.

Gropper, N. (2004). *Raising and educating healthy boys: Analysis of focus groups held with teachers and parents in urban and suburban settings.* New York: Educational Equity Concepts, Inc.

Gropper, N., & Froschl, M. (2000). The role of gender in young children's teasing and bullying behavior. *Equity and Excellence in Education, 33*(1), 48–56.

Grossman, H., & Grossman, S. (1994). *Gender issues in education.* Needham Heights, MA: Allyn and Bacon.

Halfon, N., McLearn, K. T., & Schuster, M. A. (Eds.). (2002). *Child rearing in America: Challenges facing parents with young children.* [Electronic verizon]. Cambridge, England: Cambridge University Press.

Halle, T., Calkins, J., Berry, D., & Johnson, R. (2003). *Promoting language and literacy in early childhood care and education settings* (pp. 1–17). New York: Child Care & Early Education Research Connections. Retrieved August 12, 2005, from http://www.childcareresearch.org/PDFDocs/rc2796.pdf

Halliwell, J. O. (1842). *The nursery rhymes of England, collected principally from oral tradition.* James Orchard Halliwell (Ed.) London, England: Printed for the Percy Society by T. Richards.

Halpern, D. F. (1992). Sex differences in cognitive abilities (2nd ed.). Hillsdale, NJ: Lawrence Erlbaum Associates.

Hare, J., & Gray, L. A. (1994). Nontraditional families: A guide for parents. The *Children, Youth and Families Education & Research Network (CYFERNET) Web site.* Retrieved January 5, 2006, from http://www.cyfernet.org/parent/nontradfam.html

Hargreaves, D., & Colley, A. (1986). *The psychology of sex roles.* London: Harper & Row.

Hasse, C. (2002). Gender diversity in play with physics: The problem of premises for participation in activities. *Mind, Culture, and Activity, 9*(4), 250–269.

Hattie, J., Marsh, H. W., Neill, J. T., & Richards, G. E. (1997). Adventure education and outward bound: Out-of-class experiences that make a difference. *Review of Educational, Research, 87*(1), 43–87.

Hegland, S., & Ricks, M. (1990). Aggression and assertiveness in kindergarten children differing in day-care experiences. *Early Research Quarterly, 5,* 105–116.

Helburn, S. W. (Ed.). (1995). *Cost, quality and child outcomes in child care centers* (Technical report). Denver, CO: Economics Department, University of Colorado at Denver.

Hoffman, M. (1991). *Amazing grace.* New York: Dial.

Honig, A. S. (1998). Sociocultural influences on gender-role behaviors in children's play. In D. P. Fromberg & D. Bergen (Eds.), *Play from birth to twelve and beyond: Contexts, perspectives, and meanings* (pp. 338–347). New York: Garland.

Horgan, D. (1995). *Achieving gender equity: Strategies for the classroom.* Boston: Allyn & Bacon.

Hughes, F. P. (1999). *Children, play, and development* (3rd ed). Boston: Allyn & Bacon.

Huston, A. C., & Carpenter, C. J. (1985). Gender differences in preschool classrooms: The effects of sex-typed activity choices. In L. C. Wilkinson & C. B. Marrett (Eds.), *Gender differences in classroom interactions* (pp. 143–165). New York: Academic Press.

Hyde, J. S. (1984). How large are gender differences in aggression? A developmental meta-analysis. *Developmental Psychology, 20,* 722–736.

Hyde, J. S. (1986). Gender differences in aggression. In J. S. Hyde & M. C. Linn (Eds.), *The psychology of gender: Advances through meta-analysis* (pp. 51–66). Baltimore: Johns Hopkins University Press.

Hyde, J. S. (2005). The gender similarities hypothesis. *American Psychologist, 60*(6), 581–592.

Hyde, J. S., & Lindberg, S. M. (2007). Facts and assumptions about the nature of gender differences and the implications for gender equity. In S. Klein (Ed.), *Handbook for achieving gender equity through education.* Mahwah, NJ: Lawrence Erlbaum Associates.

Kasturi, S. (2002). Constructing childhood in a corporate world: Cultural studies, childhood and Disney. In G. S. Cannella & J. L. Kincheloe (Eds.), *Kidworld: Childhood studies, global perspectives, and education.* New York: Peter Lang.

Kelly, J., & Smith, S. L. (2006). *Where the girls aren't: Gender disparity saturates G-rated films.* Retrieved September 1, 2006, from http://www.seejane.org/pdfs/g.movies give.boys.a.d.pdf

Kindlon, D., & Thompson, M. (2000). *Raising Cain: Protecting the emotional life of boys.* New York: Ballantine Book Company.

Koch, J., & Irby, B. (Eds.). (2002). *Defining and redefining gender equity in education.* Greenwich, CT: Infoage Publishing.

Knight, G. P., Guthrie, I. K., Page, M. C., & Fabes, R. A. (2002). Emotional arousal and gender differences in aggression: A meta-analysis. *Aggressive Behavior, 28,* 366–393.

Lee-Thomas, K., Sumsion, J., & Roberts, S. (2005). Teacher understandings of and commitment to gender equity in the early childhood setting. *Australian Journal of Early Childhood, 30*(1), 21–27.

Liebert, R. M., & Sprafkin, J. (1988). *The early window: Effects of television on children and youth* (3rd ed.). New York: Pergamon Press.

Ma, X. (2001). Bullying and being bullied: To what extent are bullies also victims? *American Educational Research Journal, 38*(2), 251–370.

MacNaughton, G. (2000). *Rethinking gender in early childhood education.* London: Paul Chapman Educational Publishing.

MacNaughton, G., Rolfe, S. A., & Siraj-Blatchford, I. (2001). *Doing early childhood research: International perspectives on theory and practice.* Crows Nest, Australia: Allen & Unwin.

Maccoby, E. E. (1998). *The two sexes: Growing up apart, coming together.* Cambridge, MA: Harvard University Press.

Maccoby, E. E., & Jacklin, C. T. (1974). *The psychology of sex differences.* Stanford, CA: Stanford University Press.

Marion, M. (2003). *Guidance of young children* (6th ed.). Upper Saddle River, NJ: Pearson Education.

Marshall, N. L., Robeson, W. W., & Keefe, N. (1999). Gender equity in early childhood education. *Young Children, 54*(4), 9–13.

Martin, C. L., Eisenbud, L., & Rose, H. (1995). Children's gender-based reasoning about toys. *Child Development, 66,* 1453–1471.

May, D. C., Kundert, D., & Brent, D. (1995). Does delayed school entry reduce later grade retentions and use of special education services? *Remedial and Special Education, 16,* 288–294.

Megawangi, R. (1997). *Gender perspectives in early childhood care and development in Indonesia.* (Report of a study conducted with support from the Consultative Group on Early Childhood Care and Development). Retrieved May 10, 2006, from http://www.ecdgroup.com/download/ca120fgs.pdf

Meister, M., & Japp, P. M. (Eds.). (2002). *Enviropop: Studies in environmental rhetoric and popular culture.* [Electronic version]. Westport, CT: Praeger.

Morrison, G. S. (2004). *Early childhood education today* (9th ed.). Upper Saddle River, NJ: Pearson Merrill Prentice Hall.

Mueller, C. M., & Dweck, C. S. (1998). Intelligence praise can undermine motivation and performance. *Journal of Personality and Social Psychology, 75*(1), 33–52.

National Association for the Education of Young Children. (1997). *NAEYC position statement on developmentally appropriate practice in early childhood programs serving children from birth through age eight.* Washington, DC: Author. Retrieved November 12, 2004, from http://www.naeyc.org/about/positions/pdf/PSDAP98.PDF

National Center for Early Development and Learning. (2002). Regulation of child care. *Early Childhood Research and Policy Briefs, 2*(1). Retrieved August 26, 2006 from http://www.ncedl.org

National Center for Education Statistics. (2000). *Trends in educational equity for girls and women.* Washington, DC: U.S. Department of Education, Office of Educational Research Improvement.

National Council of Teachers of English. (2002). *Guidelines for gender-fair use of language.* Retrieved August 1, 2003, from http://www.ncte.org/about/over/positions/category/lang/107647.htm?source=gs

National Institute of Child Health and Human Development Early Child Care Research Network. (2004). Type of child care and children's development at 54 months. *Early Childhood Research Quarterly, 19*(2), 203–230.

Newkirk, T. (2002). *Misreading masculinity: Boys, literacy, and popular culture*. Portsmouth, NH: Heinemann.

Olweus, D. (1993). *Bullying at school: What we know and what we can do*. Malden, MA: Blackwell.

O'Brien, M., Huston, A. C., & Risley, T. R. (1983). Sex-typed play of toddlers in a day care center. *Journal of Applied Developmental Psychology, 4*, 1–10.

Oden, S., & Hall, J. A. (1998). Peer and sibling influences on play. In D. P. Fromberg & D. Bergen (Eds.), *Play from birth to twelve and beyond: Contexts, perspectives, and meanings* (pp. 266–276). New York: Garland.

O'Reilly, P., Penn, E. M., & Demarrais, K. (Eds.). (2001). *Educating young adolescent girls*. [Electronic version]. Mahwah, NJ: Lawrence Erlbaum Associates.

Pajares, F. (1996). Self-efficacy beliefs in academic settings. *Review of Educational Research, 66*(4), 543–578.

Paley, V. G. (1984). *Boys and girls: Superheroes in the doll corner*. Chicago: University of Chicago Press.

Pan, H-L. W. (1994). Children's play in Taiwan. In J. L. Roopnarine, J. E. Johnson, & F. H. Hooper (Eds.), *Children's play in diverse cultures* (pp. 31–50). Albany, NY: State University of New York Press.

Pan American Health Organization. (1994). Gender and child development. *Fact sheet: Women, health & development program*. Retrieved June 14, 2004, from http://www.paho.org/English/HDP/HDW/child development.pdf

Pellegrini, A. D. (1998). Rough-and-tumble play from childhood to adolescence. In D. P. Fromberg & D. Bergen (Eds.), *Play from birth to twelve and beyond: Contexts, perspectives, and meanings* (pp. 401–408). New York: Garland.

Pellegrini, A. D., & Bartini, M. (2000). A longitudinal study of bullying, victimization, and peer group affiliation during the transition from primary school to middle school. *American Educational Research Journal, 37*(3), 699–725.

Pellegrini, A. D., & Kato, K. (2002). A short-term longitudinal study of children's playground games across the first year of school: Implications for social competence and adjustment to school. *American Educational Research Journal, 39*(4), 991–1015.

Pellegrini, A. D., & Perlmutter, J. C. (1989). Classroom effects on children's play. *Developmental Psychology, 25*(2), 289–296.

Pellegrini, A. D., & Smith, P. K. (1993). School recess: Implications for education and development. *Journal of Research in Childhood Education, 63*(1), 51–67.

Phillips, D., Howes, C., & Whitebook, M. (1991). Child care as an adult work environment. *Journal of Social Issues, 47*, 49–70.

Pinderhughes, E. E., Dodge, K., Bates, J., Pettit, G., & Zelli, A. (2000). Discipline responses influences of parents' socioeconomic status, ethnicity, beliefs about parenting, stress, and cognitive-emotional process. *Journal of Family Psychology, 14*(3), 380–400.

Pinker, S. (2002). *The blank slate: The modern denial of human nature*. New York: Viking.

Pollack, W. (1998). *Real boys: Rescuing our sons from the myths of boyhood*. New York: Random House.

Polnick, B. (2002). Crossing the great divide: Changing the culture of women through gender equity in mathematics teaching and learning. *Advancing Women in Leadership*. Retrieved March 20, 2004, from www.advancingwomen.com

Polnick, B., & Funk, C. (2005) Early mathematics: Learning in the block center. In J. Koch & B. Irby (Eds.) *Gender and schooling in the early years* (pp. 99–112). Greenwich, CT: Information Age Publishing.

Polnick, B., & Polnick, G. (2006). *An investigation of children's greeting cards related to gender*. Unpublished manuscript.

Puckett, M. B., & Black, J. K. (2005). *The young child: Development from prebirth through age eight* (4th ed.). Upper Saddle River, NJ: Pearson Education.

Rabbie, J. M., Goldenbled, C., & Lodewijkx, H. F. M. (1992). Sex differences in conflict and aggression in individual and group settings. In K. Bjorkqvist & P. Niemala (Eds.), *Of mice and women: Aspects of female aggression* (pp. 217–228). New York: Academic Press.

Ramsey, P. G. (1998). Diversity and play: Influences of race, culture, class, and gender. In D. P. Fromberg & D. Bergen (Eds.), *Play from birth to twelve and beyond: Contexts, perspectives, and meanings* (pp. 23–33). New York: Garland.

Rankin, B. (1998). Curriculum development in Regio Emilia: A long-term curriculum project about dinosaurs. In C. P. Edwards, L. Gandini, & G. Forman (Eds.), *The hundred language of children* (2nd ed., pp. 213–237). Norwood, NJ: Ablex.

Raver, C. (2003). Young children's emotional development and school readiness. (Report No. EDO-PS-03-8) Washington, DC: Department of Education (ERIC Clearinghouse on Elementary and Early Childhood Education No. EDD00001). Retrieved June 1, 2005, from http://ceep.crc.uiuc.edu/eecearchive/digests/2003/raver03.html

Reed, T., & Brown, M. (2000). The expression of care in rough and tumble play of boys. *Journal of Research in Childhood Education, 15*(1), 104–116.

Reid, S. (1993). Game play. In C. E. Schaefer (Ed.), *The therapeutic powers of play* (pp. 323–328). Northvale, NJ: Jason Aronson.

Richardson, L. (1988). *The dynamics of sex and gender: A sociological perspective* (3rd ed.). New York: Harper & Row.

Richardson, J. T. (1997). *Conclusions from the study of gender differences. Gender differences in human cognition* (pp. 131–162). New York: Oxford University Press.

Richardson, J. T., Caplan, P. J., Crawford, M., & Hyde, J. S., (with McKinley, N. M.). (1997). *Gender differences in human cognition*. [Electronic version] New York: Oxford University Press.

Roberts, L. C., & Hill, H. T. (2003). Come and listen to a story about a girl named Rex: Using children's literature to debunk gender stereotypes. *Young Children, 58*(2), 39–42.

Robinson, K., & Diaz, C. (2006). *Diversity and difference in early childhood education: Issues for theory and practice*. New York: Open University Press.

Roggman, L. A., & Peery, J. C. (1989). Parent-infant social play in brief encounters: Early gender differences. *Child Study Journal, 19*(1), 65–79.

Rubin, J. Z., Provenzano, F. J., & Luria, Z. (1974). The eye of the beholder: Parents' views on sex of newborns. *American Journal of Orthopsychiatry, 44*, 512–519.

Sadker, D. (2002). An educator's primer on the gender war. *Phi Delta Kappan, 84*(3), 235–240, 244.

Sadker, D., & Sadker, M. (1994). *Failing at fairness: How America's schools cheat girls*. New York: MacMillan.

Sadker, M. & Sadker, D. (1985, March). Sexism in the schoolroom of the 80s. *Psychology Today, 19*(3), 54–57.

Sadker, M., Sadker, D., & Klein, S. (1991). The issue of gender in elementary and secondary education. In G. Grant (Ed.), *Review of research in education* (Vol. 17, pp. 269–334). Washington, DC: American Educational Research Association.

Sanders, J., Koch, J., & Urso, J. (1997). *Gender equity right from the start*. Mahwah, NJ: Lawrence Erlbaum Associates.

Sanders, J., & Rocco, S. (1994). *Bibliography on gender equity in mathematics, science and technology: Resources for classroom teachers*. Seattle, WA: Jo Sanders Publications.

Seidman, S. A. (1999). Revisiting sex role stereotyping in MTV videos. *International Journal of Instructional Media, 26*, 11–22.

Sheldon, A. (1992). Conflict talk: Sociolinguistic challenges to self-assertion and how young girls meet them. *Merrill-Palmer Quarterly, 38*(1), 95–117.

Shepard, L. A. (1991). Readiness testing in local school districts: An analysis of backdoor policies. In S. H. Fuhrman & B. Malen (Eds.), *The politics of curriculum and testing: 1990 Yearbook of the Politics of Education Association* (pp. 159–179). New York: Falmer.

Shepard, L. A. (1992). Retention and redshirting of kindergarten children. In L. R. Williams & D. P. Fromberg (Eds.), *Encyclopedia of early childhood education*. New York: Garland.

Shepard, L. A., & Smith, M. L. (1986). Synthesis of research on school readiness and kindergarten retention. *Educational Leadership, 44*(3), 78–86.

Shepard, L. A., & Smith, M. L. (1988). Escalating academic demand in kindergarten: Counterproductive policies. *Elementary School Journal, 89*, 135–145.

Shonkoff, J. P., & Phillips, D. A. (Eds.). (2000). *From neurons to neighborhoods: The science of early childhood development.* Washington, DC: National Academies Press.

Singer, J. L. (1994). Imaginative play and adaptive development. In J. H. Goldstein (Eds.), *Toys, play and child development* (pp. 6–26). New York: Cambridge University Press.

Smith, L. J. (1994). A content analysis of gender differences in children's advertising. *Journal of Broadcasting and Electronic Media, 38*(3), 323–337.

Spinelli, E. (1993). *Boy, can he dance!* New York: Four Winds Press.

Sprung, B. (1975). *Non-sexist education for young children: A practical guide.* New York: Citation Press.

Sprung, B., Froschl, M., & Hinitz, B. (2005). *The anti-bullying and teasing book.* Beltsville, MD: Gryphon House.

Strasburger, V. C. (1995). *Adolescents and the media.* Newbury Park, CA: Sage.

Stipek, D. J. (2002). *Motivation to learn: Integrating theory and practice* (4th ed.). Boston: Allyn & Bacon.

Taylor, B. J. (2002). *Early childhood program management: People and procedures.* Columbus, OH: Merrill Prentice Hall.

Taylor, J. M., Gilligan, C., & Sullivan, A. M. (1995). *Between voice and silence.* Cambridge, MA: Harvard University Press.

Thomas, M. (2002). *Free to be you and me.* Philadelphia: Running Press Book Publishers.

Thorne, B. (1993). *Gender play: Girls and boys in school.* New Brunswick, NJ: Rutgers University Press.

Tracy, D. M. (1987). Toys, spatial ability, and science and mathematics achievement: Are they related? *Sex Roles, 17*(3/4), 115–138.

Trawick-Smith, J. (1994). *Interactions in the classroom: Facilitating play in the early years.* New York: Merrill Macmillan.

Unger, R., & Crawford, M. (1992). *Women and gender: A feminist psychology.* New York: McGraw-Hill.

U.S. Department of Health and Human Services, Administration for Children and Families. (2005, May). *Head Start impact study: First year findings.* Washington, DC: Author.

Vaughn, B. E., Vollenweider, M., & Bost, K. K. (2003). Negative interactions and social competence of preschool children in two samples: Reconsidering the interpretation of aggressive behavior in young children. *Merrill-Palmer Research Quarterly, 49*(3), 247–278.

West, E. (2004). *Greeting cards: Individuality and authenticity in mass culture* [Abstract]. Retrieved May 20, 2006, from http://repository.upenn.edu/dissertations/AAI3152125/

West, C., & Zimmerman, D. H. (1987). Doing gender. *Gender & Society, 1,* 125–151.

Whitebook, M., Howes, C., & Phillips, D. (1990). *Who cares? Child care teachers and the quality of care in America: Executive summary National Child Care Staffing Study.* Oakland, CA: Child Care Employee Project.

Whiting, B. B., & Edwards, C. P. (1988). *Children from different worlds: The formation of social behavior.* Cambridge, MA: Harvard University Press.

Witt, S. D. (1997). Parental influence on children's socialization to gender roles. *Adolescence.* Retrieved August 10, 2003, from http://GoZips.uakron.edu/~susan8/parinf.htm

Witt, S. D. (2000). The influence of television on children's gender role socialization. *Childhood Education, 76*(5), 322–324.

Wolf, D. H., Rygh, J., & Altshuler, J. (1984). Agency and experience: Actions and states in play narratives. In I. Bretherton (Ed.), *Symbolic play: The development of social understanding* (pp. 195–217). New York: Academic Press.

Women's College Coalition. (1996). *Expect the best from a girl: That's what you'll get.* Washington, DC: Author. Retrieved May 23, 2006, from http://www.academic.org

Women's Equity Resource Center. (2006). *What is gender equity?* Retrieved August 2, 2006, from http://www2.edc.org/WomensEquity/about.htm

Zill, N., & West, J. (2001). *Entering kindergarten: Findings from the Condition of Education 2000* (NCES 2001-035) Washington, DC: U.S. Government Printing Office.

·30·

IMPROVING GENDER EQUITY
IN POSTSECONDARY EDUCATION

Joanne Cooper, Pamela Eddy, * *Jeni Hart, Jaime Lester, Scott Lukas, Betsy Eudey, Judith Glazer-Raymo, and Mary Madden*

INTRODUCTION

As we begin the 21st century, women still long for what Jane Rowland Martin (2000) called a "global campaign for a woman-friendly academy" (p. 182). A woman-friendly academy would not only embrace the needs of women students, faculty members, staff, and administrators today, but also create a future filled with greater possibilities for women and men in higher education today. This chapter will explore the present state of gender equity in the academy, examining why calls for reform persist, as well as what current efforts are under way to change the situation for all participants in higher education.

This chapter begins with a short history of gender equity in the academy. We then examine the experiences of women in college and university settings from a variety of contexts: as students, both undergraduate and graduate; as faculty members, both tenured and untenured, as well as those working in part-time and adjunct positions; as staff; and as administrators, those holding both mid-level and top administrative positions. Gender-equity issues may also vary across institutional type. Thus, this work includes an examination of conditions in four-year colleges, community colleges, single-sex colleges, and historically Black colleges and universities (HBCUs). The view of the academy also depends on issues of race, class, and sexual orientation. A fuller exploration of the impact of the intersection of race, class, and sexual orientation with gender will be covered in chapters 22–26. We will, however, touch briefly on these issues in our discussions, since the academy may look quite different to women from varying positions of race and sexual preference (Cooper, Benham, Collay, Martinez-Aleman, & Scherr, 1999; Cooper, Ortiz, Benham, & Scherr, 2002; Cooper & Stevens, 2002; Ideta & Cooper, 2000; McDonough, 2002). By including the multiple contexts for women within higher educational settings, we hope to create a more complete picture of the state

of gender equity within academe. We close the chapter by considering the impact of current forces at work on issues of gender equity in academe, what this might mean for the future, and a set of recommendations gleaned from our discussion.

HISTORICAL PERSPECTIVES

The history of women's participation in American higher education reveals the difficulties of achieving gender equity in American society. It was not until the mid-19th century that women succeeded in gaining entry as students in male-dominated institutions. This was due in part to the Civil War and ensuing Reconstruction, and in part to the realities of the economy—that is, the need to train teachers, earn tuition revenues, and fill the seats of the land-grant universities that were established under the Morrill Act of 1862. Several models of higher education evolved between 1850 and 1880: denominational coeducational colleges, coordinate single-sex colleges, secular coeducational public and private universities, and public single-sex vocational schools. The advent of the research university increased the inequities experienced by women seeking access to doctoral programs and the professoriate. Access to professional schools was also limited for women. "The professional schools of law and medicine, business, and divinity were dominated by male students and fostered a social ethos that women did not belong" (Nidiffer, 2001a, p. 26). In fact, many did not admit women at all and those that did often had fewer than 10%. Some of these inequities began to be addressed with the campaign for universal suffrage, which mobilized women in support of their economic and political rights. However, following passage of the 19th amendment in 1920, which gave women the right to participate in the electoral process, women made only limited progress in higher education until World

War II, when they began to fill the college seats vacated by men in the armed forces.

Federal aid, in the form of the 1958 National Defense Education Act, made it possible for men and women veterans to enroll in postsecondary institutions in greater numbers by providing them with student loans, and they often received preference in admissions as well. Since there were more male veterans, this often made it harder for nonveteran women to gain admission. Quotas for women students at the undergraduate and graduate level remained common. Although their presence in the labor force was more readily accepted, women continued to be segregated into feminized professions including nursing, social services, clerical jobs, teaching, home economics, and librarianship. Women seeking professional degrees in law, medicine, engineering, and science entered a highly competitive environment that gave priority to males and to veterans (who were predominantly males). Women thus had only limited access to advanced degrees and professional employment. The quotas, particularly at the graduate level, persisted until the passage of Title IX in 1972.

Although much progress in addressing race discrimination occurred during the 1960s, women and girls as students and as faculty members or administrators were largely exempt in the new wave of legislation protecting persons from discrimination on the basis of race, color, religion, and national origin. Until the passage of Title IX of the Education Amendments of 1972 and other legislation passed that year, women and students were exempted or not covered by all the antidiscrimination laws passed by the Congress. Title VII of the Civil Rights Act of 1964 prohibited discrimination in all federally funded programs, but only on the basis of race, color, and national origin. Discrimination on the basis of sex was not prohibited. Even the 1963 Equal Pay Act which prohibited salary discrimination in employment on the basis of sex exempted executives, administrators, and professionals, so that women teachers and administrators at all levels were not covered.

Only a little-known Executive Order 11246, issued by Lyndon Johnson in 1964 to prohibit federal contractors from discriminating in employment on the basis of race, color, religion, and national origin, and amended in 1967 to cover sex discrimination, covered women in education. The Order only applied to colleges and universities that held federal contracts. In 1969, the Women's Equity Action League (WEAL) initiated a national campaign to use this Executive Order to end sex discrimination in colleges and universities by filing a class-action administrative charge with the U.S. Department of Labor against every college and university that held a federal contract. The National Organization for Women (established in 1966) and the WEAL (established in 1968) led a new wave of the women's movement to gain gender equity for women in all spheres of life.

Commissions on the status of women, professional women's caucuses, class-action challenges, and other forms of advocacy proved to be effective strategies in increasing public and institutional awareness and support for women's equity in higher education (see chapter 5 on the "Role of Government in Advancing Gender Equity in Education" in this volume, and Glazer-Raymo (1999) for analyses of equity laws, judicial decisions, and commission strategies). In the ensuing years, the Pregnancy Discrimination Act (1978); Age Discrimination in Employment Act

(1967); Title IX of the Education Amendments of 1972; Civil Rights Act of 1964; and the Equity in Athletics Disclosure Act (1994) strengthened protection for women, as did Supreme Court decisions on pension equity, sexual harassment, hostile environment, tenure reviews, and affirmative action. Working through the judicial system, women have made significant strides on a number of levels. Although they are the majority of students overall, women still lag behind as faculty members and senior administrators, particularly in male-dominated disciplines. Their gains in salaries, benefits, publications, and tenured positions often do not match those of men and continue to mask gender stratification in the allocation of resources for women's programs; the disposition of cases regarding salary and tenure inequities; and cultural, attitudinal, and structural constraints that inhibit their progress.

STUDENTS IN HIGHER EDUCATION

The passage of Title IX of the Education Amendments in 1972 prohibited institutions of higher education that received federal funds from discriminating against anyone on the basis of sex (see "The Role of Government in Advancing Gender Equity in Education" in this volume for further discussion of the passage of Title IX and efforts to weaken its civil rights protections). An exception to Title IX's protections relates to admissions to private undergraduate colleges and single-sex colleges. The impact of Title IX in postsecondary education can be measured in many ways, including the increase in the number of women attending college and earning degrees. However, this increase has also created dilemmas for those who believe that it is important to have gender parity on campuses. For example, in some cases regarding admissions to private undergraduate postsecondary institutions in the United States, less qualified males are being admitted instead of their more qualified female peers.

Enrollment

In the past 30 years, overall enrollment in undergraduate programs has risen for both male and female students. Yet the numbers and percentage of women enrolled have increased at a faster pace than for men at both the undergraduate and the graduate levels. Between 1990 and 2000, for example, the increase in the percentage of women who enrolled as undergraduates was double that of men: 14% versus 7% (National Center for Education Statistics [NCES], 2002). During that same decade there was a 57% increase in women's enrollment in full-time graduate education, compared to a 17% increase for men. Women now account for 58% of undergraduates. Table 30.1 provides a review of the distribution of the percentage of women and men attending two-year and four-year institutions. Compared to males, female undergraduates as a group have lower family incomes and are more likely to be the first in their family to attend college.

Increases in undergraduate enrollment have varied among women and men of different racial backgrounds (see Table 30.2). The percentage of White women attending college in-

TABLE 30.1   College Students—Gender/Attendance Status*

Institutional Type	Total Enrollment	Women	Men	Part-Time
2-year—Public	6,243,576	3,660,615 (59%)	2,582,961 (41%)	3,817,955 (61%)
2-year—Private	302,287	187,652 (62%)	114,635 (38%)	44,370 (12%)
4-year—Public	6,736,536	3,760,021 (56%)	2,976,515 (44%)	1,792,725 (27%)
4-year—Private	3,989,645	2,276,494 (57%)	1,713,151 (43%)	1,006,817 (25%)

*2004 figures.
Source: NCES. (2005).

TABLE 30.2   College Students—Ethnicity*

Institutional Type	Total Enrollment	Black/ Non-Hispanic	Hispanic	Asian/ Pacific Islander	Am. Indian/ Alaska Native
2-year—Public	6,243,600	833,400 (13%)	921,600 (15%)	418,600 (7%)	77,400 (1%)
2-year—Private	302,300	72,500 (24%)	50,800 (17%)	12,100 (4%)	4,900 (2%)
4-year—Public	6,736,500	741,200 (11%)	555,800 (8%)	447,400 (7%)	67,000 (1%)
4-year—Private	3,989,600	517,700 (13%)	281,300 (7%)	230,600 (6%)	26,900 (1%)

*2004 figures (rounded to nearest 100).
Source: NCES (2005).

creased 3% between 1990 and 2001, while during that same period the percentage of White men in the college population declined 2%. In 2001, White women outnumbered White men on college campuses by approximately 1,250,000. During this same time, the number of American Indian, Asian, African American, and Hispanic women and men attending college also increased (Almanac of Higher Education, 2004). Although these increases are encouraging, it is important to note that African Americans and Hispanics constitute 31% of the American population, yet represent only 17% of the students enrolled at four-year colleges and universities (State of College Admission Report, 2002).

Despite certain reversals, women have generally continued to enroll in two-year institutions at rates greater than those of men. Between 1975 and 1978, the number of women over the age of 25 in two-year colleges nearly tripled (Glazer-Raymo, 1999). By the new millennium, in all states except for South Dakota and Utah, women represented the majority of students enrolled in the community colleges (American Association of Community Colleges [AACC], 2003); 58% of all community students are women (NCES, 2004). In terms of the part-time student population, approximately 60% of all such students are women.

Research indicates that many women enter community colleges because of a life-changing event (White, 2001). Three quarters of the women in community colleges are enrolled part-time. Women's part-time status is often a consequence of familial obligations, and some studies have indicated that women experience role conflict because of familial, career, and personal goals that differ from men's. Researchers have called on colleges and universities to expand existing support services such as career development and child-care resources (White, 2001).

The admissions decisions made by today's colleges and universities are complicated by both the current rulings of the Supreme Court related to affirmative action based on race as well as by the current demographics of college applicants. Today, more women than men are applying to America's colleges and universities, causing admissions officers at private undergraduate institutions to agonize over the rejection or wait-listing of many well-qualified female applicants (Britz, 2006).

Two thirds of America's colleges and universities today report that they receive more female than male applicants, making males the more valued applicants as institutions seek "gender balance," and creating increased competition among females for prized admissions slots on campus (Britz, 2006; Rosser, 2005). As previously mentioned under Title IX, sex discrimination in admissions is allowed for private undergraduate institutions.[1] However, sex discrimination is not allowed for public postsecondary institutions or for private graduate school admissions. Additionally, except for Grove City College in Pennsylvania and Hillsdale College in Michigan which don't receive federal financial assistance, all public and private colleges in the United States are covered by all other provisions of Title IX.

However, men still earn more doctorates and professional degrees than women earn, and are more likely to be enrolled in the nation's most prestigious universities. In 2005, for example, men still outnumbered women at all the Ivy League schools except Brown and Columbia (Rosser, 2005). Thus, while there has been substantial progress, women still suffer from many disadvantages and even some legal sex discrimination in undergraduate admissions in private postsecondary institutions.

Persistence

A longitudinal national study of more than 9,000 students who first attended a postsecondary school in 1995–1996 (Berkner, He, & Cataldi, 2002) showed that after six years, one third of

[1]It is quite possible that sex discrimination in admissions, while allowed under Title IX, may be prohibited under the Equal Protection Clause of the 14th Amendment to the U.S. Constitution, as it was in the VMI Decision. It may also be prohibited under state nondiscrimination laws.

both men and women had left postsecondary institutions without attaining a degree. Among students who began their college career with the goal of obtaining a bachelor's degree, women were more likely than men to have earned a degree within six years (66% vs. 59%), more likely to have done so within four years (41% vs. 31%), and more likely to have graduated with honors (43% vs. 33%).

A study of the students who left college within three years of first enrolling (Bradburn, 2002) showed that the women who left were more likely than men to leave school because of "change in family status, conflicts at home, or personal problems" (p. vii). The men who left were more likely than women to report that they left school early because of problems with grades or for employment possibilities.

Degree Attainment

During the last 30 years, women have made substantial gains in the number and proportion of degrees attained. Although women earned only 43% of all bachelor's degrees in 1970–1971, they have earned at least 50% of the bachelor's degrees in every year since 1981–1982 (Wirt et al., 2004). In the 2001–2002 academic year for example, women earned a larger proportion of college degrees than did men, including 60% of the associate's degrees, 57% of the bachelor's degrees, and 59% of the master's degrees. In 2001–2002 men earned more doctoral and first-time professional degrees (54% and 53% respectively) than did women. Still, women have made tremendous strides in attaining doctorates since 1970–1971 when they earned only 14% of all doctorates awarded.

There are disparities in the number of degrees earned by men and women across racial-ethnic groups. The largest gap exists between Black men and women; Black women have increasingly earned more college degrees than Black men have since 1978–1979. In 1999–2000, Black women earned 188 associate's degrees, 192 bachelor's degrees, and 221 master's degrees for every 100 earned by Black men. Hispanic, White, and Asian women also earned more degrees than did their male counterparts in 1999–2000. For every 100 degrees earned by Hispanic men, Hispanic women earned 146 associate's degrees, 148 bachelor's degrees, and 153 master's degrees. White women earned 149 associate's degrees, 131 bachelor's degrees, and 151 master's degrees for every 100 degrees earned by White men. And finally, Asian women earned 131 associate's degrees, 117 bachelor's degrees, and 111 master's degrees for 100 degrees earned by Asian men (Sum, Fogg, & Harrington, 2003).

Although women continue to earn a higher percentage of bachelor's and master's degrees, the 2000 annual median income for a man with a bachelor's degree was $56,334, compared to $40,415 for women. The annual median income for a man with a master's degree was $68,322, compared to $58,957 for a woman with a master's degree (Bureau of the Census, 2003). This difference may be attributable in part to the fields in which men and women earn their degrees (Bellas, 1994, 1997a, 1997b; Bellas & Toutkoushian, 1999), but even in the same fields, women generally earn less than men with similar education and experience earn. (*Handbook* Chapter 4, "The Impact of Education on Gender Equity and Employment and its

Outcomes," and Chapter 7, "The Treatment of Gender Equity in Teacher Education" provide more examples).

In 2002, the areas in which degrees were awarded remained closely aligned with "traditionally gendered" fields. Men earned a larger percentage of the degrees awarded in business and marketing, computer and information sciences, engineering, and physical sciences. In each of these areas of study, men's proportion of the degrees earned increased or remained stable as the level of the degree increased. In business and marketing, for example, men and women each earned 50% of the bachelor's degrees; men earned 59% of the master's degrees, and 65% of the doctorates. In computer and information sciences, men earned 72% of the undergraduate degrees, 67% of the master's degrees, and 77% of the doctorates awarded. In engineering, men earned 79% of the undergraduate, 79% of the master's degrees, and 83% of the doctorates awarded. In physical sciences, men earned 58% of the bachelor's degrees, 62% of the master's degrees, and 72% of the doctorates (Almanac of Higher Education, 2004).

In 2002, women earned more degrees than men in biological sciences, education, health professions, and psychology. Unlike their male counterparts in male-dominated fields, however, the proportion of the degrees that women earned in these fields decreased as the level of the degree increased. In biological sciences, women earned 61% of the bachelor's degrees, 58% of the master's degrees, and 56% of the doctorates. In education, women earned 77% of the bachelor's degrees, 67% of the master's degrees, and 65% of the doctorates. In the health professions, women earned 85% of the bachelor's degrees, 78% of the master's degrees, and 63% of the doctorates. In psychology, women earned 77% of the bachelors' degrees, 76% of the master's, and 68% of the doctorates (Almanac of Higher Education, 2004).

Classroom Climate

Despite these very significant advances for women, research points to obstacles for them in postsecondary education. The environment that students must navigate in pursuit of a degree is as important as who enrolls, who persists, and who earns a college degree. In 1982, Hall and Sandler concluded that women face a "chilly climate" in postsecondary classrooms. More recent investigations (Allan & Madden, 2003; Brady & Eisler, 1995; Sandler, Silverberg, & Hall, 1996) have corroborated this fact and documented the persistence of a chilly climate for women in the 21st century. Chilly climates include overt and subtle gendered communication patterns and behaviors by faculty members and students that disadvantage women. Examples of male and female faculty behaviors that create a chilly climate include acknowledging, calling on, and encouraging men more often than women; using examples that reflect gender stereotypes; focusing on women's appearance rather than accomplishments; attributing women's achievements to something other than their competence; and discounting women's concerns about "women's issues." Examples of male and female behaviors that create a chilly climate include: ignoring women's contributions, controlling discussions, interrupting women, making sexual comments, and sexually harassing female students (Allan, 2002). Classroom structures such as the absence of female role models and women's contributions and perspectives in course materials also disadvantage women (Hall & Sandler, 1982; Sandler, Silverberg, & Hall, 1996). Chilly climates have been shown to be especially prevalent for women pursuing degrees in traditionally male-dominated fields such as engineering, sciences, mathematics, and computer technology (Frantz, 1995; Madden, 2000). The concept of chilly classroom climates has also been shown to apply to students based on other attributes such race, ethnicity, disability status, social class, and sexual orientation (Allen & Niss, 1990; Sandler, Silverberg, & Hall, 1996).

Strategies to improve gender equity on college campuses include the establishment of women's centers, campus child-care centers, commissions or task forces on women's issues, support of student groups such as Feminist Campus alliances or the Society for Women Engineers, enhanced campus security for safety, and women-centered consciousness-raising programs, such as the *Vagina Monologues*. (See Chapter 21, "The Role of Women's and Gender Studies in Advancing Gender Equity" in this volume for more information.)

Students/Sex Discrimination

Sexual harassment is an important issue for college students. A survey conducted by the American Association of University Women Educational Foundation concluded that nearly two thirds of all male and female college students were sexually harassed during their college years (Rainey, 2006). Sexual harassment was broadly defined to include any unwanted sexual advances that had an impact on the student's life. Harassment might be peer-to-peer or superior-to-subordinate. Although both sexes experienced harassment, women were more likely to indicate that the unwelcome advances caused negative behavioral or emotional fallout. Moreover, almost 20% of females indicated disappointment with the handling of the incident by their college.

Research on differential treatment based on gender or race highlights the fact that African Americans experience more incidents of unequal treatment in peer-faculty situations than do other students (Suarez-Balcazar, Orellana-Damacela, Portillo, Rowan, & Andrews-Guillen, 2003). Female African American students rated higher both the degree of offensiveness and the degree of discrimination they experienced. Issues of unequal power are at the root of harassment and discrimination of all students, with professors and administrators holding the power advantage. For further information, see the Chapter 11, "Sexual Harrassment: The Hidden Gender Equity Problem."

Male Gender Equity Issues

Recent research points to increased attention to male gender equity issues (Bleuer & Walz, 2003). Specifically, women have surpassed men with respect to college enrollment and now represent 58% of college students (NCES, 2004). African American men attend college at the lowest levels of participation. Men instead more often seek employment directly out of high school. As noted earlier, there are many indicators showing both male progress and lack of progress in higher education, and the overall picture cannot be reduced to the simplistic views of "winners and losers" that dominate much of the discussion of males in higher education today. For example, in a closer examination of the student data, King (2000) refuted the assertion that White, male, middle-class college students are falling behind. Instead, King concluded that the gender gap for men in higher education is overshadowed by issues related to race/ethnicity and social-economic status. A long-term look at the evidence compiled by the National Assessment of Educational Progress indicates that some reports of U.S. boys being in crisis are greatly overstated and that young males in elementary and high school are in many ways doing better than ever (Mathews, 2006). The report indicates that "much of the pessimism about young males seems to derive from inadequate research, sloppy analysis and discomfort with the fact that although the average boy is doing better, the average girl has gotten ahead of him" (p. A01). Although there are large gender gaps disfavoring male Black and Hispanic students, and two thirds of the students in special education classes are boys, in terms of absolute numbers, more men are enrolling in college now than previously (and are in the majority at the nation's most prestigious universities), and men still earn more doctorates and professional degrees than do women. A critical factor impacting college decisions is financial aid. A smaller percentage of men attending undergraduate colleges are receiving aid relative to the percentage of all women (61% of men; 65% of women). These data reflect shifts in the funding of higher education from governmental support to more individual funding. Even given this shift in funding patterns, however, is the notable difference in aid for Black, Non-Hispanic students. A full 76% of Blacks receive financial aid, with this group taking out the largest percentage of loans of all subgroups of students (43%, relative to a low of 25% of Asian/Pacific Islanders taking out loans). See Table 30.3.

In summary, although the numbers of women students in higher education have been increasing in the last 30 years, gender disparities remain by discipline, as well as in doctoral and professional degree programs. In addition, the chilly climate

TABLE 30.3   Student Financial Aid—Percentage of Undergraduates Receiving Aid*

Students	Total	Grants	Loans	Work Study	Other
Men	61%	47%	34%	7%	5%
Women	65%	54%	36%	8%	2%
White, Non-Hispanic	62%	48%	36%	7%	4%
Black, Non-Hispanic	76%	64%	43%	9%	5%
Hispanic	53%	50%	30%	9%	3%
Asian American/ Pacific Islander	63%	53%	25%	5%	2%
American Indian/ Alaska Native	67%	59%	33%	5%	3%

*2003–2004 figures
Source: NCES. (2005).

for women persists and is experienced most heavily in fields still dominated by men. Although women students outnumber men at the bachelor's and master's levels, men still earn the majority of doctoral degrees across the country and continue to earn higher salaries than women at all degree levels. There is some disagreement about whether White, male, middle-class college students are falling behind in college enrollment.

Older Women in Higher Education

In 1999–2000, the average age of a female college undergraduate was 27 (NCES, 2001). Women are 62% of undergraduates age 40 or older. Although adult women enter or return to college for many reasons, they often make this decision because of job requirements, career changes, or family life transitions (such as divorce or the death of a spouse) that require new knowledge, skills, or credentials. Clayton and Smith (1987) identified primary motivations for older women students to pursue an undergraduate degree. These include self-improvement or self-actualization; vocational requirements; humanitarian concerns; and a quest for knowledge. More than half (56%) of the women said they had multiple reasons for reentry to college.

But for many adult women the return to school raises concerns about how to cope with the multiple roles of student, family member, and worker. Terrell (1990) identified several issues faced by adult women who return to college. These include feeling guilty about not "being there" for their children, concerns about quality and expense of childcare, feelings of responsibility for maintaining their role within the family, making compromises in careers due to family considerations, minimal individual free time, perceived lack of credibility when returning to college, and insufficient support from family for returning to college.

Retention in postsecondary education of adult students is a serious concern, especially for students over age 40. This is due, in part, to traditional views of persistence that see degree completion as the goal. As noted earlier, attainment of the desired knowledge or skills may be sufficient for many adult learners. It is important to understand adult students' objectives for their education and to evaluate their success in terms of those objectives. Tinto's (1987) model, which emphasized academic performance and participation in college life as important predictors of student retention, may not always be appropriate for all adult learners. For example, Starks (1987) found that for returning women in community colleges, intellectual development was more important than grades, and contact with fellow students was more important than taking part in activities on campus. In order to retain adult students, institutions should (a) recognize that the persistence of diverse groups is affected by different factors and target retention efforts appropriately; (b) prior to or after enrollment, help adults clarify their academic and career goals; and (c) recognize that students' objectives are not necessarily degree-oriented, and measure retention success accordingly (Kerka, 1989).

An effective college program for adult students needs to include active recruitment of adults, appropriate delivery systems (including flexible scheduling and locations as well as the possibility of distance learning), flexible services, and providing credit for prior learning. Special attention needs to be given to financial aid programs. Some programs will not award financial aid to students who attend less than full time or less than half-time, an enrollment pattern that is more common among adult learners. Other programs place limits on the use of aid funds for child care, which is most likely to create an obstacle for adult learners. The Federal government has become concerned about the complexity and inconsistencies in its financial aid programs (Burgdorf & Kostka, 2005). A change could benefit all of higher education.

FACULTY IN HIGHER EDUCATION

"Substantial disparities in salary, rank, and tenure between male and female faculty members persist despite the increasing proportion of women in the academic profession" (Benjamin, 1999, p. 60). The numbers of women in higher education, including those holding faculty positions, are growing. However, women are most heavily clustered at one end of the academic pipeline (e.g., as students, and as non-tenure-track or untenured faculty members) and in less-prestigious institutions (Benjamin, 1999; Breneman & Youn, 1988; Finkelstein, Seal, & Schuster, 1998; Hensel, 1991; Park, 1994, 1996; Simeone, 1987; Stephan & Kassis, 1997; West & Curtis, 2006). As noted earlier, women have constituted the majority of students at undergraduate degree levels since 1982. Men, however, still dominate at the doctoral level and in many professional degrees programs. Even at these levels, women are now approaching 50% (Snyder, Hoffman, & Geddes, 1998). Further, women do comprise the majority of doctoral recipients in several fields, specifically anthropology, education, health, psychology, and sociology (Glazer-Raymo, 2000). In the academic year 2002–2003, men earned 51.8% and women earned 48.2% of professional degrees (NCES, 2006). Engineering had the lowest percentage of doctoral degrees awarded to women, 14% (Glazer-Raymo, 2000). It has thus become increasingly difficult to argue that the disparate numbers of academic women relative to men is due to a lack of qualified women in the pipeline or candidate pool.

Despite the presence of qualified women in the pipeline, the numbers of female full-time faculty members have increased just 10.6% in the 20-year period between 1975 and 1995 (Glazer-Raymo, 1999, 2000). Further, according to the 1998–99 American Association of University Professors (AAUP) faculty survey, women faculty members are clustered in the lower ranks—as instructors (50.4%), lecturers (54.2%), and as assistant professors (43.6%). Of those at the higher ranks, 31.8% of associate professors and only 24% of full professors are women (Bell, 1999; Glazer-Raymo, 2000; NCES, 2003; Perna, 2001a; West & Curtis, 2006). Moreover, only one third of untenured women are on the tenure track, evidence of the increased popularity of hiring faculty off the tenure-track and in part-time positions. In fact, just over one-half of all new full-time faculty hires were not in tenure-track appointments (Glazer-Raymo, 2000). Thus, overall, the increase in the proportion of female part-time and non-tenure-track faculty members is greater than the female proportion of full-time and tenure-track positions (Benjamin, 1999). While this demonstrates that the face of academic work is clearly changing, this trend highlights that the power structure is not. Although there are some important exceptions, such as Dr. Ruth Simmons, the president of Brown University, who is African American, those who hold the most decision-making authority within an institution (senior faculty members and administrators) continue to be predominantly male and White (Glazer-Raymo, 1999; Simeone, 1987; Theodore, 1986; Twale & Shannon, 1996), and women are overrepresented among those who continue to struggle for both tenure and promotions. Women and minorities must employ a number of strategies in order to overcome this prevailing power structure and attain the tenure prize (Cooper & Stevens, 2002). Table 30.4 provides a breakdown of women and men by faculty rank, and showcases the distribution of minority members by rank. White men continue to make up the majority of full professor positions.

Among all new faculty hires, whether on or off the tenure track, women slightly outnumber men at liberal arts colleges and community colleges. At doctoral-granting universities, however, women represent only one third of the newly hired faculty members (Finkelstein et al., 1998). Although the numbers of women holding faculty positions are growing, women are more often found in less-competitive institutions (Benjamin, 1999; Breneman & Youn, 1988; Finkelstein et al., 1998; Hensel, 1991; Park, 1994, 1996; Simeone, 1987; Stephan & Kassis, 1997). Table 30.5 provides a review of the percentage of women faculty at each institutional type. Juxtaposed with the low representation of women at the prestigious research universities (30% of full-time faculty at public research universities are women) are the high percentages of women holding part-time positions (50%).

From a disciplinary perspective, women have been hired in substantial numbers in education, health sciences, humanities, and the law (Finkelstein et al., 1998), which is not surprising given that women now comprise over half of the PhD recipients in most of these fields. However, women continue to occupy far fewer faculty positions in fields like engineering and mathematics (Finkelstein et al., 1998), fields which are more highly paid and have more access to resources, such as laboratories and grant funding (Volk, Slaughter, & Thomas, 2001). Table 30.6 highlights the distribution of men and women in a variety of disciplinary areas, providing further breakdowns between full-time and part-time faculty positions within each category. Patterns of feminized fields are apparent.

Not only do fewer women than men fill the highest ranks within academe, but there is also a gender gap in pay within rank. Data continue to show that academic women are paid less than their comparable male counterparts at both the departmental and institutional level (Barbczat, 1988; Bellas, 1993, 1994, 1997a, 1997b, 1999; Bellas & Reskin, 1994; Benjamin, 1999; Ferber & Loeb, 1997; Hensel, 1991). As of 2005, an AAUP study of gender equity in faculty salaries (Curtis, 2005) found that salaries for full-time faculty members at associate-degree-granting colleges are now approaching gender parity. In contrast, women's salaries at doctoral universities remain significantly lower than men's, and they do not seem to be increasing. Because women are disproportionately found in part-time positions, however, the figures actually understate the inequities in faculty pay status. If both full-time and part-time faculty positions are considered, the salaries awarded to women would be considerably lower than their male counterparts.

Full-Time Women Faculty Members in Community Colleges

Research indicates that women faculty members face unique challenges in the community college (Townsend, 1995). Women in general make up 38% of faculty members in community colleges and 53% of tenure-track positions (West & Curtis, 2006);

TABLE 30.4   College Faculty—Percentages by Academic Rank*

Faculty Characteristic	Professor	Associate	Assistant	Instructor	Lecturer
Women	24%	38%	45%	52%	52%
Men	76%	62%	55%	48%	48%
White	87%	82%	74%	79%	79%
Black	3%	5%	6%	7%	5%
Hispanic	2%	3%	3%	5%	5%
Asian American Pacific Islander	6%	7%	9%	5%	5%
American Indian Alaskan Native	0.3%	0.4%	0.4%	9%	0.4%

*2003 figures

Source: NCES (2004).

TABLE 30.5   College Faculty—Percentages by Institutional Type*

Institutional Type	Full-Time Women	Full-Time Men	Part-Time % of Total Faculty	Part-Time Women	Part-Time Men
Research-Public	30%	70%	20%	50%	50%
Research-Private	31%	69%	27%	40%	60%
Doctoral-Public	37%	63%	29%	50%	50%
Doctoral-Private	33%	67%	42%	42%	58%
Comprehensive-Public	41%	59%	36%	50%	50%
Comprehensive-Private	42%	58%	56%	46%	54%
Liberal Arts-Private	40%	60%	36%	50%	50%
2-year Public	48%	52%	63%	49%	51%

*2003 figures

Source: NCES (2005).

TABLE 30.6   College Faculty—Percentages by Academic Area*

Academic Area	Full-Time Women	Full-Time Men	Part-Time Women	Part-Time Men
Agriculture/Home Ed	35%	65%	68%	32%
Business	31%	69%	30%	70%
Education	60%	40%	71%	29%
Engineering	9%	91%	9%	91%
Fine Arts	38%	62%	49%	51%
Health	53%	47%	65%	35%
Humanities	55%	45%	68%	32%
Natural Science	25%	75%	42%	58%
Social Science	36%	64%	40%	60%

*2003 figures

Source: NCES (2005).

minority female faculty members represent only 3.6% of faculty members in community colleges (Clark, 1998). Demographic studies of faculty members in higher education indicate that more women work at community colleges than at four-year institutions of education (Clark, 1998). Within the last 20 years, the number of women faculty members employed at two-year colleges has increased an estimated 13% (CPEC, 1998). Clark (1998) argues that "the high numbers of women faculty at community colleges provide evidence that women are marginalized in the professorate as a whole" (p. 3).

Contrary to the assumption that community colleges are "perceived to be more open and friendly to women and their interests" (Clark, 1998, p. 3), the environmental climates of these institutions are often hierarchical and militaristic (Seidman, 1985; Townsend, 1995). Professional isolation has been found (Seidman, 1985) to impact women and minority community college faculty members more than other faculty members. The student-centered curriculum of community colleges also leads to heavier demands on faculty members. This is particularly true of women, given their traditional caretaker role, as they work to meet the pressing and varied needs of their diverse student bodies.

Additionally, the socialization of new faculty members, especially women, is often a tenuous process at community colleges (Clark, 1998). Some female community college faculty members report that the mere fact of teaching at a community college leads to professional stigmatization by faculty in four-year institutions (Townsend, 1998). Without proper access to professional networks, women faculty members in community colleges, as in four-year institutions, are often unaware of the true nature of the requirements for promotion and tenure at their institutions, which results in lower numbers of women in higher level and tenured faculty roles (Clark, 1998). For female part-time instructors, isolation from formal and informal networks that aid in career advancement is an unfortunate fact of their temporary and often itinerant teaching status.

Another unfortunate pattern in the community colleges is the difficult politics of tenure. In some institutions, tenure is denied to all faculty (Baldwin & Chronister, 2001); in others tenure is denied to women disproportionately (Kolodny, 1996). Clark (1998) indicated that female community college faculty members more typically work in instructor and lecturer positions that are non-tenure-track than do men. Hagedorn and Laden (2002) reviewed a national database to understand female community college faculty members' perception of the organizational climate. They found that, in fact, women at community colleges did perceive the climate as less "chilly" than at four-year institutions.

Faculty Salaries

In terms of salary, in 2006, women faculty members' salaries as a percentage of men's averaged 80.9% in all public institutions and 95.4% in public two-year colleges (West & Curtis, 2006). As of 2003–2004, the salaries at associate degree institutions had almost reached parity, with women making 96% of what comparable men earn. But the salaries of women faculty members at doctoral institutions remain below 80% of men's and do not seem to be increasing (West & Curtis, 2006).

Women's salaries in private institutions were 79.3% of men's on average, and only slightly higher at 89.6% in four-year and 95.5% in two-year colleges (West & Curtis, 2006). In some states, it appears that community colleges have more equitable salary structures than do four-year institutions; it must be noted however, that the data are only for full-time faculty members who are typically represented by unions that advocate for equitable salaries for all faculty members. According to a 2006 study conducted by the AAUP, the average salary of community college faculty across all ranks was only $52,584, compared to $77,829, $61,533, and $59,021 for doctoral-granting, master's-granting, and baccalaureate-granting institutions respectively (West & Curtis, 2006).

One comprehensive recent study found that human capital, structural, and market characteristics appear to explain gender and ethnic differences in salary and tenure within community colleges (Perna, 2003). Other research has noted that women and men appear to have almost equal representation in the tenure track faculty ranks but that women populate the non-tenured, adjunct positions at a disproportionately greater rate (Clark, 1998; Townsend, 1995). LaPaglia (1994) found that female faculty members feel that they are in a marginal culture in the overall higher-education context. Researchers have also postulated that women enter the faculty ranks at community colleges for several reasons: larger representation of women in power (e.g., in administrative positions); the egalitarian missions of the community colleges; and the presence of more female role models (Townsend, 1995).

Barriers to Success

Barriers to success in the faculty ranks vary across institutional type and individual discipline. Some barriers are common to all institutional types, such as the feminization of certain disciplines and family care issues, whereas other barriers are specific to the category of colleges, such as the role of research at research-oriented institutions and within striving institutions.

Differential rewards for teaching and research. One example of the imbalance in reward structure for academic work is the high value placed upon research, and more specifically the production of juried publications, in awarding salary increases, tenure, and promotion. Fairweather (1996) found that faculty members, regardless of discipline or institutional type, who spend more time on research and who publish more, are paid higher salaries than are those who focus on teaching. Moreover, when looking solely at teaching and salary, his findings showed that salary was inversely proportional to the number of students taught. This raises questions about the institutional value of quality instruction (Fairweather, 1996). A greater emphasis on research contributes to an institutional culture that values male interests and work habits over females' (Carlson, 1994), as men tend to spend less time focused on teaching and service than do women (Astin & Cress, 1999; Cooper & Stevens, 2002; Dickens & Sagaria, 1997; Hensel, 1991; Park, 1996; Riger, Stokes, Raja, & Sullivan, 1997; Twale & Shannon, 1996).

Bellas and Toutkoushian (1999) analyzed a data set of full-time faculty members (lecturer/instructor, assistant, associate, full professor) at two- and four-year institutions. Their data show that women spent 7.2% more time teaching than men did. In addition, women spent 6.3% less time engaged in research than their male counterparts. The reasons for these differences are unclear. Unfortunately, the data do not describe class size, number of courses taught, and whether courses (and course preparations) are new. Such information would give readers a clearer sense of the type and intensity of work that is required and help to determine whether the effort inputs of males and females are comparable. Nonetheless, the findings, based on a large national sample, do suggest that women are spending more time than men doing the types of scholarly work that are less rewarded by the academy.

"Women's work." In the nature of many organizations, each player has a specific role, a role that cannot to be altered by the individual. For example, a woman is expected by many male colleagues and by the culture of many institutions to focus on work that is seen as "metaphoric parenting" (Ferber & Loeb, 1997, p. 10). To perform such "mothering" activities, women are channeled into teaching, advising, and committee work. They are often assigned by the administration to advise more students, and to serve on more committees than are their male peers (Bellas, 1999; Park, 1994, 1996; Riger et al., 1997; Twale & Shannon, 1996). Because teaching and service are seen as caretaking activities, and women are often assumed "naturally" able to perform these roles, female faculty members dedicate significant time to these less-valued and less-rewarded roles (Simeone, 1987). Further complicating this situation, both tenured and nontenured women are at risk if they fail to conform to these gendered roles (Cooper, Kane, & Gisselquist, 2001). Tenure, promotion, and salary increases require review by department heads and colleagues who, while valuing and rewarding research, may penalize women faculty members for not fulfilling their prescribed teaching and service roles (Bellas, 1999; Ferber & Loeb, 1997).

The energy directed toward teaching and service does not mean that research is not important to women in any field of higher education. Unfortunately, however, research by or about women is often undervalued by male faculty members and the academic reward structure (Dickens & Sagaria, 1997; Glazer-Raymo, 1999; Hensel, 1991; Sandler & Hall, 1986; Simeone, 1987). Such undervaluing has direct implications for tenure, promotion, and salary. Some women are being penalized for their work specifically because of its gendered nature. The expectations of colleagues and the institution, coupled with the current academic reward system, often leave women faculty members in a double bind (Carlson, 1994; Park, 1996). If women meet their sex role expectations by emphasizing teaching and service, they are less likely to be promoted or to see a salary increase; if women diverge from the sex role expectations by emphasizing research, they are penalized for acting contrary to their sex role expectations.

This double bind experienced by female faculty members as they perform research, teaching, and service is fraught with mixed messages. All faculty members must publish, but many women feel that they are penalized if teaching and service are compromised in order to focus on research. Additionally, if they focus less on research, their tenure, rank, and promotion aspi-

rations may be jeopardized. Certainly, not all female academics experience the negative consequences attached to fulfilling or not fulfilling their prescribed gender roles, but many do. Often, women faculty members feel they need to publish, teach, and serve more than their male counterparts do, just to be considered equal to them. To compete for a higher salary, tenure, or promotion, the standards thus appear much more stringent for women than for men.

Feminized disciplines. Another circumstance many women face that has a direct impact on salary and other resources has to do with their disciplinary choices. Jacobs (1995) found that earnings in female-dominated fields declined in the early 1980s, while earnings in male-dominated fields increased, showing the relationships among disciplinary choice, gender participation, and salary. Bellas (1993) defined fields that employ 30% or more women as "feminized." "Feminized" fields have lower salaries for both genders than do other fields, but they differentially affect academic women, since by definition women are more heavily clustered in those disciplines. Current examples of "feminized" disciplines are English, education, anthropology, and psychology (Bellas, 1994, 1997a, 1997b; Bellas & Reskin, 1994; Finkelstein et al., 1998; Glazer-Raymo, 2000). Interestingly, although men and women in feminized fields both suffer, the women's salaries are slightly lower than those of comparable men within the discipline (Bellas, 1994).

Simeone (1987) suggested that women have been encouraged to enter certain fields and discouraged from others because some fields are viewed as women's work. Such socialization surely contributes to an individual's selecting one discipline over another, but comparable worth scholars ask whether it should contribute to women's earning lower salaries when faculty work requires comparable abilities across both male- and female-dominated disciplines (England, 1992). Moreover, feminized fields tend to attract fewer resources (such as internal and external research funding, computers, and graduate-student support), which translates into less support for women to participate in the more highly rewarded activity of research (Volk et al., 2001; Winsten-Bartlett, 2006).

Family care issues. Family care issues are often considered a reason why women faculty members leave academe or why they show decreased productivity relative to men. The research literature shows, however, that family caregiving may not be quite as powerful a factor as one might think (Astin & Cress, 1999; Benjamin, 1999; Park, 1996; Riger et al., 1997). In a recent survey of 6,000 faculty members, at a statistically significant level, more men than women listed raising a family as an important personal goal (Astin & Cress, 1999). Additionally, nearly half of the women who remain in academe are either single or childless (Astin & Cress, 1999), relative to 26% of men (Mason & Goulden, 2004). Researchers thus need to ask whether the academic climate has a differential impact on men's and women's choices to be with partners and to have a family.

For those who have family-care responsibilities, child rearing and eldercare can result in time away from higher education, or can contribute to a decision to choose what they may consider a more family-friendly career. The public often has the misperception that faculty roles are inherently more flexible, given the lack of a strict nine-to-five workday. In reality, faculty members often work at home on class preparation and research, making the work seem endless and providing no clear boundaries between work and personal life. Common reports of work hours for faculty members indicate an average workweek of 55 hours (Fairweather, 1996). Moreover, family-care issues do have a negative effect on salary, promotion, and tenure, and this occurs more often for women than for men (Coiner & George, 1998; Hensel, 1991; McElrath, 1992; Riger et al., 1997; Tolbert, 1986). The reasons for this are complex, however. For women, having children may be seen by their male peers and administrators as evidence of a lack of professional commitment. For men, an assumption exists that they will not be the primary caregiver if they have children, and thus, that their productivity will not be compromised. Despite some evidence to the contrary, institutions expect family care to be a women's issue. Perhaps the gendered assumption (and implicit message of the value of life outside of work) vis-à-vis family care contributes to the fact that only 36% of all institutions provide flexible scheduling to address family needs (Raabe, 1997). Despite some progress, Williams (2001) still concluded that academe has a long way to go regarding these issues.

Gendered networks.   Another factor that may contribute to the disparities between female and male faculty members' advancement is networking and mentoring. The networks in which female faculty members find themselves may limit the information to which they are privy, placing them at a disadvantage. Women academics tend to develop networks comprised of other women (Carlson, 1994; Collins, 1998; Hensel, 1991). In a male-dominated environment of faculty work, such networks can limit access to information and connections that can improve a female's position within the academy, further contributing to the disparities between men and women. Women often lack access to high-powered networks, making women's networks the only ones which they are able to join. As more women enter leadership positions, these women centered networks may take on similar high-powered status.

In addition, a benefit that often results from networks is the establishment of material resources and cultural capital. Cultural capital is a concept that has been adapted from Bourdieu (1977). It refers to the varied set of skills, knowledge, tastes, and lifestyles that individuals acquire from socialization (England, 1992; Lareau, 1987; Valadez, 1996). Knowing how to secure the "right" credentials, to interact with the "right" people, and to navigate the system within academe are examples of valuable cultural capital that can improve one's access to rewards (Glazer-Raymo, 1999; Kirkland, 1997). Knowledge, at least in this case, is clearly power, and it appears that women may not have ready access to this particular form of power. Because significantly more men than women already occupy higher-level positions within academe, material and cultural capital can be difficult for many women to acquire if they are excluded from male networks. As a result, women's salary, tenure, and promotion may be negatively affected.

Tenure denied.   All these barriers work to the disadvantage of women faculty members who apply for tenure. Tenure brings with it the approval of the academic community, as well as the promise of lifetime employment. More importantly, women who are denied tenure most often must leave the university within a short period. Because most colleges stress the permanent nature of tenure, the fact that a negative decision terminates faculty employment and sometimes ends a faculty career is often glossed over (Dyer, 2004).

Since the early 1980s, the American Association of University Women Legal Advocacy Fund has supported women faculty members in more than 60 cases of sex discrimination in higher education. Unfortunately, biased behavior and sex discrimination remain serious problems in the promotion and tenure processes of many universities today. The confidential nature of the tenure process and the lack of clear standards and guidelines for tenure are but two of the characteristics of the process that make it likely that cases of denied tenure may end up in court. Sex discrimination against women in these cases ranges from the disparate treatment of male and female faculty members, to the discounting of women's studies, to charges of a "chilly climate" for women faculty members that hinders their efforts toward career advancement (AAUW Educational Foundation and Legal Advocacy Fund, 2004). Universities often counter these charges with delaying strategies and the withholding of evidence.

While there are rewards for prevailing in a sex-discrimination lawsuit, not the least of which is fighting for what one feels is right, there are also substantial costs, both monetary and personal. Many plaintiffs who win their cases are never reinstated to their former jobs and most compensation packages that are awarded do not cover the enormous time and expense of a lawsuit. It is thus best for all concerned if the university can establish good employment policies which, when consistently applied, can prevent discriminatory practices and the lawsuits they foster (AAUW Educational Foundation and Legal Advocacy Fund, 2004). Universities should establish annual written evaluation policies for faculty members with explicit performance measures to address a candidate's yearly progress toward tenure, actively watch for and monitor abuses, and adopt policies that allow for time off the tenure clock for childbirth or parenting. In order to increase their chances of getting tenure, women faculty members can obtain clear, written information about a department's tenure and promotion policies; ask colleagues how their research, teaching, and service will be evaluated; be alert to the culture and politics of the department; and cultivate a strong network of supportive colleagues both within the department, across campus, and in the community. If necessary, they should consider cutting their losses early in the process by seeking another position.

Given the potential barriers that faculty women face, which are often further complicated by the intersection of race, ethnicity, and sexual orientation (Cooper, 2002), it is important to reiterate that the numbers of women faculty members overall have grown. Laws such as Title VII of the Civil Rights Act of 1964, the Equal Pay Act, and individual campus efforts to improve their institutional climates have led to many improvements for women in the academy. However, gender equity among faculty members in postsecondary education is far from a reality today. The title of Virginia Valian's book, *Why So Slow: The Advancement of Women* (1999) remains pertinent and serves as a call for all who are invested in higher education to accelerate their efforts toward gender equity.

NON-TENURE TRACK FACULTY

Women assume a disproportionate number of nontenure track positions in higher education, including part-time appointments. When the numbers of full-time faculty members are disaggregated, women make up nearly half (47.8%) of faculty members who are full-time, but who are ineligible for tenure (Clery, 2001; Harper, Baldwin, Gansneder, & Chronister, 2001). Although this distribution suggests gender equity, women make up only about one third of all full-time faculty members, again reflecting the fact the women are concentrated in less prestigious, lower-paying, part-time positions. In many cases, these positions have been justified as a creative way to allow women faculty members to combine family and work (Glazer-Raymo, 1999). Clark (1998) challenged this rationale by pointing out that there is no evidence to suggest that women as a group desire nontenure track positions, either part-time or full-time.

The justification for the growth in these positions since the late 1980s has been related to budgetary constraints in academe (Wilson, 2001). Although the numbers of part-time faculty have reached a plateau at 43%, according to the U.S. Department of Education, the number of faculty members working full-time who are not on a tenure track has increased to 18% (Wilson, 2001). In fact, "[b]etween 1976 and 1993, the number of nontenure track full-time faculty increased by 142% for women and 54% for men" (Perna, 2001a, p. 585). Finkelstein (2003) likened these numbers, along with the fact that in 2001, three fourths of new faculty appointments were contingent (that is, nontenure track, including part-time faculty members), to a "silent faculty revolution" (p. 1). To consider these faculty members as marginal or insignificant would be erroneous; yet research on nontenure track faculty members remains somewhat limited (Antony & Valadez, 2002; Harper et al., 2001). Given the clustering of women in these positions and the degree to which they have become a significant portion of the instructional workforce in academe, it is critical that the work-life experiences of these women and men be better understood in order to create and maintain a gender equitable climate for academic success.

Understanding the experiences of nontenure track academic women becomes increasingly more important when one considers the research literature related to these faculty members (e.g., Berger & Kirshstein, 2001, 2003; German, 1996; Glazer-Raymo, 1999; Harper et al., 2001; Leslie & Walke, 2001; Perna, 2001b). Moreover, the research that does focus on nontenure track faculty members often shows that while they feel satisfied in their jobs, they also feel marginalized (Chronister & Baldwin, 1999; Gappa, 2000; German, 1996; Harper et al., 2001; Tolbert, 1998). Indeed, the movement among many nontenure track faculty members to unionize suggests that they have real concerns, including low pay, poor treatment, and lack of benefits (Leatherman, 2001; Smallwood, 2003).

Contemporary discourse on community college part-time faculty commonly refers to "freeway flyers"—dissatisfied individuals working at several colleges in order to create the equivalent of a full-time position (generally without health and tenure benefits). Images are conjured of women running through parking lots, driving long hours to reach each college, teaching one course for a few hours, then moving on to the next. Some research, however, questions this stereotype. Although it is true that the majority of part-time faculty members are women, they are not "freeway flyers," nor are they desperate to find full-time employment in the community colleges. In fact, many of the part-timers (men and women) have full-time jobs elsewhere and are teaching at the community college for reasons related to personal intrinsic value (Gappa & Leslie, 1997). There is some evidence, however, that women part-time faculty members are not fully satisfied with their positions. Among those women who teach part-time, many indicate that they would be more likely to teach full-time if a position were available (Leslie & Gappa, 2002).

The proportion of part-time faculty members in community colleges has grown steadily over the last 30 years. In 1962, 38% of the faculty members were part-timers compared to 64% in 1995 (Conley & Leslie, 2002). Community colleges with larger enrollments hire more part-timers than do smaller community colleges. Part-time faculty members tend to be female and younger than full-time faculty members (Conley & Leslie, 2002; Palmer, 1999). Part-time faculty members perceived lower levels of support from their institution (Conley & Leslie, 2002).

Regardless of the seemingly dismal situation of part-time faculty members in community colleges, most faculty members choose to teach in the community colleges because of the emphasis on teaching. Most community college part-time faculty members report that they are satisfied with their jobs in terms of salary, benefits, and job security (Fugate & Amey, 2000). In a study that isolated only those part-time faculty members at two-year colleges who reluctantly took part-time jobs, the majority of those individuals had lower levels of job satisfaction (Palmer, 1999). It must be noted that research on part-time faculty members indicates mixed results. While some research (Fugate & Amey, 2000) indicated that faculty members are satisfied with working in part-time positions for intrinsic reasons, other studies (Palmer, 1999) found that part-timers would rather teach full-time and have lower levels of satisfaction than do other faculty members.

The greater numbers of women in part-time community college faculty positions, which occupy one of the lowest rungs in the academic hierarchy, mirrors the general condition of women in all colleges. Here, at the bottom of the institutional hierarchy, in colleges that are dedicated to issues of student access and equity, we find the greatest number of women in the student, faculty members, and administrative ranks. Yet even here matters of gender, race, and class impact the opportunities that are open to both women and men staff and faculty members.

ADMINISTRATORS IN HIGHER EDUCATION

Administrative positions cover a broad spectrum of the organizational hierarchy in postsecondary education, ranging from entry-level staff positions to the college president. Understanding the historical context of women in administrative roles can provide a perspective to these leadership positions. Women's leadership attributes may differ from those of men. A valid framework for leading institutions of higher education into the future requires consideration of what both women and men bring to their institutions.

The History of Women Administrators in Higher Education

Deans of women were at the forefront of the early move to include women in the administrative ranks of higher education. For example, conferences of deans of women began as early as 1903 in the American Midwest (Nidiffer & Bashaw, 2001). These early women leaders "sought both increasing respect for themselves and for their colleagues and an expansion of employment opportunities for women in the administrative ranks of higher education" (p. 272). They also worked to create opportunities for women faculty members and women students in their institutions. In addition to their activism, these women were capable of shrewd pragmatism in the pursuit of their goals. Rather than abandoning an initiative, women administrators were often willing to pursue such strategies as changing course, forging alliances with supportive men, or soliciting financial support from other women in order to achieve their goals. They were persistent and clever in pursuing their unwavering goal: to attain "for women 'genuine access' to the full range of college life and opportunity" (p. 276). Women now comprise over half the undergraduate population and are increasing in the ranks of senior faculty members and administrators. Although the battle for gender equity is not over, great strides have been made in the last century.

In the community colleges, opportunities given to female faculty members have also been afforded women unique administrative opportunities (Nidiffer, 2003). Beginning in the 1970s, women entered administrative positions in community colleges at increased rates (Frye, 1995). In 1970, approximately 5% of all community colleges were headed by women (Ferrori & Berte, 1970). By the 1990s, trends indicated that the number had increased to 10 % (Burgos-Sasscer, 1990; Phillippe, 2000). Several comprehensive analyses report the relative success of female presidents in the community college environment, suggesting that some women may have received benefits from affirmative action (DiCroce, 2000; Jablonski, 1996; Mott, 1997). For some faculty members, moving into the administrative realm is seen as the only opportunity for professional advancement (Seidman, 1985).

Women's Administrative Experience

Administrators in higher education can be categorized in three distinct ways: by their position in the organization (executive, midlevel, or entry-level); whether they are in academic or non-academic positions; and according to their unit of employment (Twombly & Rosser, 2002). While men are overrepresented in executive positions within higher education, women are most highly represented in positions described as entry-level (sometimes referred to as "professional"). Positions such as admissions counselor or residence-hall coordinators are typical of this category. In 1997, 60% of these positions were held by women (NCES, 2003).

Beyond the entry-level, women are increasingly ascending to executive positions in higher education, in particular to the position of college president. As of 2001, women represented 21.1% of all college presidents, up from 9.5% in 1986 (Corrigan, 2002). Even more telling is that in 2001, 24% of all appointees to the college presidency were women (Corrigan, 2002); however, most of these women leaders are found in community colleges, and particularly in colleges with enrollments of fewer than 3,000 students (Chliwniak, 1997). Fifty-six percent of college presidents hold their highest earned degree in the field of education, the largest percentage from any discipline (Corrigan, 2002); however, the relationship of highest degree in education (including higher education) and Carnegie classification is inversely related. Thus, more sitting presidents come from a background in education if they lead a public community college (76%), compared to those leading doctoral granting universities (9%). When one considers that education is a "feminized" profession, one in which women comprise over 50%, it is surprising to many that more women are not reaching top administrative positions, such as dean, provost, or chancellor, in the nation's colleges and universities. There are plenty of women in the pipeline to ascend to upper level administration, but they are not reaching these positions (Glazer-Raymo, 1999).

The path to the presidency also looks different for women compared to men. More men (22%) than women (16%) come to their presidency directly from another college presidency. More women (35%) than men (26%) ascended to their presidency from a Chief Academic Officer (CAO) or provost slot. Getting to the provost slot, however, is no easy task. The "glass ceiling," a phrase introduced in the literature of the mid-1980s to describe the limits of women's career ascension, continues to remain hard to shatter, despite the growing number of women in senior positions. "Women moving into [institutions] are generally seen as interlopers, and are at greater pains to prove that they belong" (Eckert, 1998, p. 67). Women remain clustered in mid-level administrative positions (deans and directors), in lower-level positions, or in positions more peripheral to promotion into central administration such as librarians and student services staff (Amey, VanDerLinden, & Brown, 2002). A traditional pathway through the academic ranks and the provost's office, particularly at four-year and research-intensive universities, continues as the dominant route to senior leadership. The requisite stop of a full professorship occurs less quickly (if at all) for women, however, slowing the ascension into more formal leadership roles or potential promotions. Women currently comprise only 24% of full professors (NCES, 2003), which contributes to the narrowing of the pipeline to upper management. Table 30.7 provides a breakdown by institutional type of the men and women leading these institutions. This table provides information regarding gender, race, and position held prior to the individual's current presidency.

Women in administrative roles have been historically underrepresented at all levels of higher education; however, women of color have made significant gains in the administrative ranks at community colleges. In the late 1990s, 104 women of color served as president in institutions of higher education; 61 of these were at community colleges (Chenoweth, Stephens, & Evelyn, 1998). Harvey and Anderson (2005) reported increases in women of color now leading the 3,847 public and private colleges and universities in the United States. Women of color represent 4.3% of college presidents (165 women), with almost half (48%) of these women leading two-year colleges (See Table 30.7). Clearly, these numbers are low, but consider that just a

TABLE 30.7   College Leaders—Gender/Ethnicity;
Previous Position*

	2-year	Baccalaureate	Master's	Doctorate Granting
Men	73%	81%	80%	87%
Women	27%	19%	20%	13%
White	86%	88%	87%	91%
African American	7%	7%	7%	5%
Hispanic	5%	3%	3%	1%
Asian American	1%	0.5%	2%	0.5%
Other	1%	1%	1%	1%
Prior Position				
President	25%	18%	18%	28%
CAO/Provost	31%	28%	18%	32%
Sr. Executive in Academic Affairs	11%	13%	10%	18%

*2001

Source: Corrigan, M. (2002).

few decades earlier it was difficult to find even one woman of color in a presidential role.

Women and Leadership

How women approach leadership is an important consideration in light of the increase in women college presidents and as administrators. Astin and Leland (1991) discussed the importance of empowerment of women as they develop into leaders and how women leaders use empowerment to deal with their followers. They stress the importance of communication in achieving empowerment for both leaders and followers (see Chapter 6, "Increasing Gender Equity in Leadership" in this *Handbook* for additional discussion of leadership theories).

Women's leadership style is often described as being generative, that is, a process that encourages participation, creativity, empowerment, and open communications (Chliwniak, 1997; Jablonski, 1996). Although both men and women can exhibit generative leadership styles, this style is used to characterize women's leadership style more often than their male colleagues' style. Previous research dichotomized men's and women's leadership styles, with men typically described as being hero-like, in contrast to women being described as generative leaders (Chliwniak, 1997). Research on how male and female leaders are perceived reinforces gendered stereotypes of leaders, specifically pointing out that "leaders were viewed more positively when they used a leadership style that was typical of and consistent with their gender" (Griffin, 1992, p. 14). Thus, similar to promotion within the faculty ranks, there are sex role expectations in administrative positions as well.

Descriptions of administrators often provide clues about the perception of these individuals on campus. Amey and Twombly (1992) used deconstruction of language to study leadership at community colleges. They discovered that the language used to describe the organizational development of the community college sector continuously reinforced White male norms for leadership. This reinforcement of what college leaders look and

act like may present a limitation for women and people of color. The male model of leadership may be one contributing reason that only 16% of public research universities are led by women (Corrigan, 2002).

Maintaining limited definitions and images of leaders leaves women with a narrow band of acceptable leadership behavior (Amey & Twombly, 1992). Women administrators report feelings of marginalization and an inability to represent their individuality authentically, because they are trying to fit into a model that more often represents men. A bind for women, then, involves the choice they make between adhering to traditional norms and expectations or enacting a more personally genuine, and therefore, a perhaps more female construction of leadership (Amey, 1999). Glazer-Raymo (1999) characterized women who opted to adapt as they move through the male-normed system as "playing by the rules" (p. 157). A danger for women leaders choosing to engage in the "playing by the rules" option is the reification of strict male-female conceptions of leadership. Tedrow and Rhoads (1999) suggested two positive options for women: reconciliation and resistance. Reconciliation involves the striking of a Faustian bargain, in which women recognize the limitations of the male norms, but work within the system for change. Resistors, on the other hand, strike out with active opposition to the boundaries that male norms establish.

Research on women's leadership clearly documents that women are judged against male norms (Chliwniak, 1997; Monroehurst, 1997), despite some findings that highlight that women deans are more effective leaders (Rosser, 2001) and communicators (Moskal, 1997). As they assume more positions of leadership in colleges and universities, women administrators face different constraints than do their male counterparts (Glazer-Raymo, 1999). Strongly held cultural beliefs about leaders and leadership prevail in colleges and universities:

Workplaces are gendered both by the numerical predominance of one sex within them and by the cultural interpretations of given types of work which, in conjunction with cultural norms and interpretations of gender, dictate who is understood as best suited for different sorts of employment. (McElhinny, 1998, p. 309)

Although the majority of research on college leaders has centered on men, a few studies do exist that focus on women as leaders or that offer findings based on both male and female participants. Both Helgesen (1995) and Rosener (1990) found differences in the ways women and men lead. Helgesen conducted an in-depth study of four women college executives and concluded that their success was based on not following what some might call the more traditional (male) model of management. These four women tended to form webs rather than pyramids in their organizations, avoiding traditional hierarchies. Rosener asserts that men lead through a series of transactions, rewarding employees for a job well done and punishing them for poor work. The women in her study were more interested in transforming people's self-interest into organizational goals, and were quick to encourage participation, share power and information, enhance other people's self-worth, and get others excited about their work.

Juxtaposed with this perspective is research conducted by Gillett-Karam (1997), which studied both men and women presidents at community colleges. Her findings mirror the experience data outlined earlier (age differentials between male and female presidents, experience differentials, etc.), but concluded that rather than gendered differences, leadership actions are strongly tied to situations—namely, directed leadership resulted in situations requiring decisive actions and participatory leadership occurred when decision-making allowed for this option. Eddy (2003) also found that while campus members spoke about their presidents in gendered terms, the leadership of the presidents was not in fact stereotypically gendered with men exhibiting authoritative leadership and women generative leadership.

In a study of women college presidents, Jablonski (1996) expected to find that women college presidents successfully employed alternative, participatory leadership styles, such as those described in earlier gender studies by Shakeshaft (1987) and Haring-Hidore, Freeman, Phelps, Spann, and Wooten (1990). Her analysis found, however, that while women presidents believed they were using participatory and empowering forms of leadership, the perceptions of their faculties often differed in important ways. Jablonski (1996) pointed out that although these presidents espoused generative leadership processes, their colleges' governance structures, committees, and boards of trustees did not represent such a model. She also found conflict in the desires and expectations of both male and female faculty members; while the faculty hoped for a more participatory leadership style, they also wanted strong, aggressive leaders—characteristics traditionally associated with men. Thus, although faculty members may have expected nurturing and caring from a female president, they also had conflicting expectations for strong leadership. These expectations, as well as the structure and processes of their institutions often pressured women presidents into more aggressive roles.

Jablonski's (1996) work underscored a reality for women leaders: although they occupy positions of power from which they might make a difference, they also suffer from both sexist and racist attitudes among their constituencies that reifies the double bind often faced by women—namely being authentic leaders, but being asked to live up to male-constructed norms of acceptable leadership. Ideta and Cooper (2000) for example, found that, nationally, Asian American women academic leaders in senior-level positions encountered discriminatory attitudes that often hampered their work. First, their experiences refuted the common misperception that Asian Americans do not experience discrimination in institutions of higher education. Secondly, the authors stated that:

the manner in which these women leaders were able to transform these sexist and racist encounters into catalysts for greater strength, determination, and advocacy stands as evidence to contradict the misconception that Asian Americans would be more apt to passively walk away from such problems. (Ideta & Cooper, 2000, p. 267)

A Framework for Action

Given these current discrepancies involving the lack of women in senior administrative positions, DiCroce (2000) has outlined a framework for action in her examination of women community college presidents. She suggested that women stepping into the presidency need initially to break down institutional gender stereotypes. Women presidents can model and create organizational structures based less on the traditional hierarchy and more on relations. DiCroce posits that women community college presidents can promote diversity, create and enforce policies on harassment, and encourage collegial engagement and dialogue via focus groups, brown-bag lunches, discussion sessions, and guest speakers. Next, women presidents need to penetrate their institution's power structures and create a collective redefinition of power, one that encompasses not only the entrenched systems of power but also those who feel powerless within their organization (regardless of their gender). This power redistribution can be accomplished by attending to the institution's governance structures, its committee appointment procedures, its promotion and tenure policies and practices, its recruitment and hiring practices, and its salary structures. What remains unknown is if women who have succeeded by the male norms can easily adjust to these more feminine ways of leading that involve collaboration versus directives, participation versus reliance on the hierarchy, and so on.

Women presidents are often able to utilize the power of their office to alter gender-related institutional policies. They can and should respond to the ways in which the institution may inadvertently be ignoring acts of sexual assault; harassment, and so forth. They can use the power of their office to appoint and support strong and helpful Title IX Coordinators, build a strong sense of a gender-equitable community, one that does not tolerate violence or discrimination in any form, including equal pay for comparable work. These presidents should raise the consciousness of their colleagues by initiating dialogue on gender and related issues. They need to become active players for public policy development and debate beyond the college level.

Women leaders face immense challenges from both inside and outside the organization. Their institutions often mirror the gender stereotypes and abusive practices of the larger society. Kolodny (1998) wrote candidly about the difficulties, the ambiguities, and the blunders that have been involved in women's leadership efforts. She underscores that while the challenges may be daunting, the efforts of women leaders are both necessary and exhilarating.

In framing change for the future, Nidiffer (2001b) posited a model for leadership that affords a broader range of attributes recognized as necessary for leading modern-day, complex institutions. An expanded, integrated definition of what it means to be a successful leader would then encompass leadership competencies traditionally attributed to either men or women. Eventually, as more women obtain positions of leadership, their voices will no longer be isolated, but rather will represent a new norm.

Bensimon (1991) argued that looking at women's leadership using perspectives based on male norms shortchanges women. Instead, she argued for using a feminist standpoint which places women in the center of the question versus on the margins. In this case, a more complete understanding of female leadership is allowed since androcentric norms are expanded to account for a wider conception of leadership. As noted earlier, much of historic leadership was based only on male leaders, leaving out the voice and experiences of women and ultimately making the research findings exclusionary of women's lived experiences.

Women are often shortchanged when judged by the male-dominated frameworks that abound in higher education.

Inherent in new thinking on leadership is the role of the institution. Individuals are shaped by and dependent on the organizational structure of the college (Brown, 2000), thus regardless of how individuals may prepare themselves for leadership; contextual elements provide either constraints or support for advancement. When Gillett-Karam (1997) surveyed administrators to determine experiences relative to obstacles, 52.2% of the women viewed their gender as a barrier to advancement, whereas 80% of men disagreed with this assessment. The differences highlighted in the perceptions of these men and women point to the need to alter organizational structures to remove obstacles and to level the playing field. The fact that the male participants generally did not perceive any barriers for women and that the majority of college presidents are men highlights the need for women's voices and experiences in these top-level positions in order to bring change.

Future Implications

What does the future hold? Although we can be encouraged by the increases women are making in ascending to top leadership positions in colleges and universities, it is important to consider why more women are not already in these top slots. According to Sagaria and Rychener (2002), two features affect the mobility of women administrators in higher education: "(1) the core elements of mobility, such as job changes, opportunity structures, networks and sponsoring and mentoring; and (2) characteristics and dynamics of higher education institutions" (p. 495). Because women are more likely to build their careers in a single institution, career mobility within that institution is especially important for them.

Women working as mid-level administrators, a little-studied area of leadership, may be most greatly affected by mobility factors within a single institution. In Amey and VanDerLinden's (2002) work on mid-level leadership in community colleges, they reviewed the aspects of career paths, mentoring, and professional development on advancement. They found that 22% of the current community college presidents came from within the institution, 56% of the participants had a mentor, and the career trajectory of presidents followed a traditional academic pathway of promotion through the hierarchy. In subsequent research, VanDerLinden (2003) concluded that two main barriers to women's advancement were the lack of leadership opportunities within the current institution and unwillingness to relocate for employment. This finding runs contrary to research that indicates four-year administrators are willing to move for promotions (Sagaria, 1988). One implication for those women administrators, especially mid-level administrators, who are place-bound is the need to provide additional leadership opportunities within institutions so that women can (a) obtain more experience, and (b) lead from where they are without a geographical move. Since women may not measure success by the same criteria as men do (Blackmore, 1989), a larger question is raised: Are measures of sheer numbers of college presidents a true measure of what women perceive as marking success? Inherent in this proposition is a dilemma. It would be easy to say that women are not ob-

taining leadership positions because they reject the idea that obtaining a leadership position is the only measure of their career success and are satisfied to lead from their present locations. This perspective does not account for the barriers present that prevent women from ascending to these positions nor does it account for the discrepancies between the salaries of men and women in these positions.

Recent theories of organizational leadership refer to team leadership (Bensimon & Neumann, 1993), leadership throughout the organization (Peterson & Dill, 1997), and eliminating the concept of the "hero" leader (Green, 1997). These theories broaden the concept of leadership, indicating a need to support women who are advancing to higher levels of leadership, but also to provide support for women as they lead from where they are. Issues of changing organizational structures, recognizing and valuing different forms of work, and the opening up of career advancement options must also be addressed by both male and female leaders.

The intersection of gender and race is also important to consider. Women of color face the additional burden of not representing the majority color of leaders—namely White. With the increase in diversity of college students, it becomes more critical to have the voices of leaders of color in positions of authority within institutions. It is important to keep questioning historical conceptions of leadership so that new leaders can move past these restrictive constructs into more innovative forms of leadership.

Finally, to change and expand the composition of college administrators it is important to focus on the individuals who make hiring decisions. People prefer to hire people like themselves (Glazer-Raymo, 1999), which presents a problem for women and minorities if search-and-selection committees, "Boards of Trustees," and the like are composed primarily of White men. A recent report by the American Council on Education (Hill, Green, & Eckel, 2001) pointed out that although the number of community college female presidents is on the rise, these decision-makers are often still uncomfortable with women presidents. One issue that women presidents face is that of working with male-dominated boards. Communication is often more difficult, with women receiving less feedback than their male counterparts (Glazer-Raymo, 1999). Most distressing is the comment made by Claire Van Ummersen, vice president of the American Council on Education (ACE): "They have this thing in their heads: 'We had our woman president. We've done it. It's somebody else's turn now'" (Jacobson, 2002, p. 3). As more and more women obtain leadership positions that can impact both policy and structure, they will become part of decision-making processes that will hopefully open more opportunities for women. In the meantime it is necessary for women to become prepared to take on these roles and to support policy changes, both within the institution and beyond the campus, that redefine the power structure (Getskow, 1996).

INSTITUTIONAL CONTEXT

Women may find a more welcoming home in certain types of colleges and universities, namely at community colleges, single-sex colleges, and historically Black colleges and universities

(HBCUs). Although all of these types of colleges may be more welcoming to women, they each represent distinctively different cultures. Table 30.8 provides an enrollment breakdown based on institutional context. Community colleges serve the largest population by far of students in this subpopulation of institutions.

Community Colleges

As noted earlier, community colleges have been on the forefront of issues of gender in education since their inception. Beginning as institutions that educated a disproportionate number of women, community colleges have continued to offer opportunities for women faculty members to advance their professional status through educational training and employment in administrative and teaching careers. Women have changed the focus of community colleges by resisting traditional feminine roles and curriculum, finding ways to move eventually into administrative and faculty positions. The presence of large numbers of women in two-year institutions as students, faculty members, and staff has not always led to equity. As in four-year colleges, women administrators have felt relegated to certain lower-status positions, and are overrepresented in part-time positions. Much of the discussion of community college issues has been woven into the other sections of this chapter.

"In reality, the story of women in community colleges is an account of success and failure, of hope and despair" (Dziech, 1983, p. 55). The open access policy, the nonresidential and nearby location of colleges, as well as the plethora of courses at community colleges made it possible for many women to enroll in higher-educational institutions. The response of community colleges to the "women question"—or the appropriate curricular decisions for women—has historically attempted to sustain the social norm of women as homemakers (Frye, 1995). Over time, these specifically women-centered curricula were cut, due to expanded opportunities for women. The proportion of women enrolled in community colleges has not been completely stable over time, given the "veteran's preferences" enacted in higher education that gave admission preference to men who participated in World War II, leading to a greater proportion of men than women in four-year colleges and universities (Clifford, 1983). In this period, the community college became one of the few higher-education options open

to women. Frye (1995) contended that the open-access history of the community colleges has allowed for greater female representation in the student, faculty members, and administrative ranks.

Single-Sex Colleges

In the past, women's colleges were dedicated to admitting and enrolling only female undergraduates. While these colleges numbered 214 in 1960, today their numbers have declined to around 80 institutions. They provided higher education to women when access was severely limited and thus have played a central role in the education of women. By the turn of the 20th century, coeducation had become the norm for women. Although many women's colleges held their enrollments, others suffered enrollment losses in the 1950s, 1960s, and 1970s (Wolf-Wendel, 2002). Although some saw the replacement of single-sex education with coeducation as part of women's attainment of equality with men, many women's colleges reframed their mission, transforming themselves from a focus on access in their early years, to their current focus on equitable education for women (Langdon, 2001).

Women's colleges today serve less than 1% of all women attending higher education, are all private institutions, they are often religiously affiliated (33% of all women's colleges are Catholic), and they have higher percentages of women faculty and leaders than coeducational institutions. These colleges and universities serve women of color and nontraditional-age women in higher proportions than do comparable coeducational institutions. Thus, although their numbers are small, they serve women students in important ways. Research indicates that students at women's colleges, in comparison to their counterparts at coeducational institutions, are more satisfied with their overall college experience, are more likely to enter nontraditional fields for women, and express higher levels of self-esteem and leadership skills (Wolf-Wendel, 2002). The recent research also indicates that women's colleges are more effective in fostering a sense of civic responsibility in their students (Kim, 2001). In a recent national survey of 276 colleges, women's colleges received high marks for learning effectiveness, as well as for providing enriching educational experiences and a supportive campus environment (Yates, 2001).

Women's colleges can serve as models for coeducational institutions, given the positive outcomes of their efforts. These institutions facilitate the success of their students in major ways such as putting women at the center of their mission; believing women can achieve and hold them to high expectations; making students feel like they matter; providing strong, positive role models for women; providing opportunities for women to engage in leadership, including women in the curriculum; and creating safe spaces where women can form a critical mass. In short, many women's colleges and universities create environments in which women feel empowered, nurtured, and challenged. As Wolf-Wendel (2002) stated, "What sets women's colleges apart from other campuses is that they are purposeful in their adoption of structures, policies, practices, and curricula that are sensitive to the needs of women" (p. 67).

TABLE 30.8   Institutional Context*

| Institutional Type | Enrollment | Degrees Conferred | | | |
		AA	BA/BS	MA	Ed.D./Ph.D.
Single Sex	86,239**	805***	13,141***	4,455***	103***
HBCU	306,727	3,556	30,194	6,900	351
Tribal	17,787	1,309	160	—	—
Community Colleges	6,545,900	665,301			

*2003–2004 figures.
Source: NCES (2005).
**Women represent 94.2% of total enrollment.
***Women graduates.

Historically Black Colleges and Universities

Historically Black colleges and universities (HBCUs) have existed since the 1830s and hold a common mission to provide higher education to Black Americans. Just over 100 of these institutions currently award almost one third of all baccalaureate degrees earned by Black Americans. In 1998, total enrollment for HBCUs was approximately 300,000 students, of which 55% were women (Brown & Freeman, 2002). Spelman College, established in 1881, was the first HBCU dedicated solely to the education of women. Spelman has remained one of the top HBCUs academically and produces many African American women in leadership positions today. Both Spelman and Bennett College continue to serve their original mission of educating Black women. Bejar (2002) stated, "At times when higher education was barely accessible to women, historically Black colleges and universities, some established solely for women, remained open and accessible to a minority group within a minority: female Black Americans" (p. 43).

THE IMPACT OF CURRENT FORCES ON GENDER EQUITY[2]

Despite the good intentions of many universities that are committed to gender equity, these institutions must grapple with many other forces that impinge on the governance of the modern university. These forces include the rise of business values in academe, the rethinking of affirmative action policies, and the continued "chilly climate" (Hall & Sandler, 1982) that the academy often creates for women.

First in our discussion is one of the most powerful forces at work today in the governing of the university: the rise of business values and the belief that efficiency and the marketplace are among the best measures of a university's success. As state legislatures reduce their allocations to their public institutions, and for-profit universities such as the University of Phoenix continue to grow, Kirp (2003) compared university presidents to Sisyphus, endlessly rolling a rock up a hill in their efforts to raise funds and placate multiple constituencies in the university community. In addition to university presidents, faculty members at both community colleges and four-year colleges are encouraged to be more entrepreneurial and to focus on how to bring more funding into higher education. Yet some scholars, such as Readings (1996) and Kirp (2003), have convincingly argued that when the values of the market and those of the public come into conflict, higher education's commitment to access may be weakened, and its promise to function as an engine of mobility for women and minorities may be neglected (Kirp, 2003).

A second force is the continued attention to equity laws and policies and their implementation. There are more detailed discussions of Title IX and other civil rights laws in earlier parts of this chapter as well as many other chapters in this *Handbook*. Most agree that Title IX has contributed to a marked increase in the participation of women in college and in college athletic programs in particular, but that it hasn't been applied vigorously to many other continued areas of disparity such as the low proportion of women faculty in areas like chemistry compared to the number of qualified women with doctorates in chemistry. This application of Title IX is discussed in this *Handbook's* Chapter 13, "Gender Equity in Science, Engineering and Technology."

A third force at work in the academy is the continued chilly climate for women in academe, a force that contributes to the glass ceiling women frequently encounter. Additionally, the gender and power relations and continued sex stereotyping and discrimination in the academy often make it especially difficult for women to meet "publish or perish" criteria. They often get fewer grants and are asked to perform service activities rather than conducting research and publishing. For women of color who wish to serve their ethnic communities, the pull of service in contrast to research and publishing may be doubly enticing.

This chilly climate is exacerbated by the fact that women often struggle to juggle the dual roles of mother and professor. A recent study of academic motherhood found that grappling with these two roles is likely to produce stress and guilt. Women must contend with society's expectations that they be married to their careers. Women who are both mothers and professors often find that "both family and academia are 'greedy' and 'all-consuming' of one's time (Ward & Wolf-Wendel, 2004, p. 253), leaving women in academe with a delicate balancing act.

Glazer (1997) has asserted that instead of simply stating that women professors are more likely to be single or childless, to work part-time, to leave the university, and to hold low-level leadership positions, "it would be appropriate to determine what it is about institutional structures that make them more compatible with men's lives" (pp. 177–178).

RECOMMENDATIONS

Policy Recommendations

This section offers policy recommendations for students and educators in higher education. As indicated in the reports of Britz (2006) and Rosser (2005), admissions policies are morphing informally before our very eyes as more women apply to college. A kind of de facto policy is in place in the struggle for colleges to keep at least a 60/40 ratio of women to men on their campuses. Beyond that point college admissions officers at private undergraduate institutions begin to bend the requirements for admissions to maintain a gender balance in their incoming freshman classes, acting on the perceived wishes of students as well as the institution itself. Some colleges also try to develop activities such as football teams to help recruit more male students. Clear policies that meet all aspects of Title IX and other civil rights laws need to be discussed and put in place, policies that are based on solid research about the impact of the changing numbers of women and men on today's campuses.

---

[2]Portions of this section were drawn from Cooper, J. (2006) Glass slippers and glass ceilings: Gender equity, governance and transformation in higher education. In Anderson, W., Dator, J., & Tehranian, M. (Eds.), Learning to seek: Globalization and governance in higher education (pp. 69–81). Somerset, NJ: Transaction Publishing.

There is solid evidence of a continued chilly climate on today's campuses, both for women students in particular disciplines and for women faculty members who are still clustered at the lower ranks of the academic career ladder. Once students and faculty members have gained entrance into the ivory tower, they must contend with the chilly climate encountered by both women and male minorities. Tierney and Bensimon (1996) asserted that institutional cultures need to "change seemingly innocent and natural practices that have the effect of placing women at a disadvantage and silencing them" (p. 101). While organizational cultures do not change easily, progress is being made, as more women reach higher positions in the organization and are able to function as role models for those who follow.

Creating policies explicit to the needs of women will also help to change campus climates. Campuses today need to consider parental leave policies and tenure-clock modifications to accommodate productivity gaps associated with childbirth. These modifications will serve both women and men as the demographics of faculty change and concerns about balancing work and family become more public. Ward and Wolf-Wendel (2004) asserted that in the long run, these policy modifications "will also encourage more high-quality individuals to consider academic careers" (p. 255).

The elimination of the chilly climate for women and the development of a more women-friendly university are still necessary and "would involve major attitudinal and behavioral changes" for universities, according to Armenti (2004, p. 226). Policies currently considered gender-neutral often reinforce the male-defined culture of higher education and force women to adapt to institutional norms rather than the campus accommodating their differences. One way of addressing this is renewed attention to the use of a gender equity institutional self-assessment with the assistance of Title IX Campus Coordinators and the President's Office. Campuses often have president-appointed committees on the role and status of women that might take part in such an assessment. Explicit policies and most importantly implementation procedures and budgets should then be recommended to address gender inequities on individual campuses.

Given the progress in the past, the goal of an equitable campus is still possible. But various forces at work in our society, such as the rethinking of affirmative action by the Supreme Court, threats to tenure, and the dominance of business values, may well distract U.S. colleges and universities from the goal of equitable educational opportunities for all. A first step is to be aware of the possibilities or dangers these forces hold as America moves through the 21st century.

Practice/Program Recommendations

This chapter also indicates the need for changes at the programmatic level. For example, Kirp (2003) asserted that higher education could do much to remedy the problem of discrimination at the level of admissions for students in higher education. One example is the marketing strategies adopted by MIT's Michael Behnke, who made a point, with the administration's backing, of searching out able female high-school students in order to change the strong male culture of MIT. He succeeded in significantly increasing the number of undergraduate females, only to be faced with a barrage of faculty complaints that he was giving preferential treatment to women. An evaluation by the faculty senate ultimately concluded that the female students were just as qualified as the males. Behnke had simply changed his recruiting tactics (Kirp, 2003). Given the current situation in which women outnumber men at the undergraduate and master's level, care needs to be taken to recruit both women and men using methods similar to Michael Behnke's. Attention needs to be paid to inequities related to race/ethnicity and socioeconomic status given the reality that the gender gap for men in higher education is overshadowed by issues related to race/ethnicity and social-economic status. One potential practice for increasing the number of males and students of lower socioeconomic levels enrolling in higher education who might normally seek employment right out of high school is the dual enrollment of high-school students in colleges and universities, which allows students to attend college classes while still in high school (Cohen & Brawer, 2003).

What is required here is the long-term commitment of institutions of higher education to ensure equity at all levels for women of all colors in all positions within academe. As Eugene Lowe, Associate Provost of Northwestern University, observed in 1999, at the dawn of the new century:

> While the present time is unquestionably a period of opportunity, we who are stewards of educational institutions have a responsibility to future generations to put in place a foundation for a more encompassing equity and a vision of excellence that does not embody or revive the stigmas of past policies and habits of discrimination. (p. 201)

This vision must include better hiring practices and more equitable pay, as well as changes in the promotion and tenure system now in place. Tierney and Bensimon (1996) held that the problem lies not with individuals, but with the processes and governing structures of the academy. Such strategies as mentoring and the clarification of expectations for tenure and promotion are recommended for all new faculty members. Beyond these individual strategies, Tierney and Bensimon call for a turn to more self-reflective organizations: "Indeed, at a time when academic institutions are beset with criticism about their nature and function, it is incumbent on all of us to be more self-reflective about the kind of institution we want to have" (p. 139). Self-reflection at the institutional level calls for conversations among colleagues about current practices and policies, as well as a vision of possible futures. These conversations can only be enriched when they include the voices of women and minorities, as they join the academic ranks. Cooper and Stevens (2002) stated that "the university may not always like what it hears from these others, but it is imperative that it listen" (p. 231).

One powerful long-standing suggestion is reinforced by researchers (e.g., Bensimon, 2005) who recommend that institutions disaggregate student outcome data by race/ethnicity and by gender within racial and ethnic categories in order to facilitate organizational learning and foster new more equitable educational practices on today's campuses. Bensimon suggests a new way of thinking about existing inequities, one that is grounded in organizational learning and is fostered by a realistic look at campus data. She asserted that:

disaggregated data serve as the medium through which individuals learn about unequal outcomes on behalf of their campuses. The way in which data are displayed and discussed can intensify learning, confirm or refute untested hypotheses, challenge preconceived ideas, motivate further inquiry, and provide the impetus for change. (p. 106)

Bensimon suggests the use of an Equity Scorecard which provides useful feedback to campuses about the outcomes of their current practices and fosters organizational learning which can then be translated into new more powerful equity practices on today's campuses.

SUMMARY

This chapter provides the reader with an overview of the gender equity issues in higher education both in the past and in today's institutions. This view encompasses the experiences of women as students, as faculty members, and as administrators or leaders in academe. It also discusses a perspective on conditions in various institutional types, such as four-year institutions and community colleges, as well as single-sex colleges and historically Black institutions.

Women have made great strides in their search for welcome ground in higher education, from their initial struggles to gain entry to male-dominated institutions, to their current position as over half the student body at the undergraduate and master's levels. Women are more strongly represented in community colleges, both as faculty members and as educational leaders, than at four-year institutions or in graduate schools. Gender, race,

sexual preference, and disability status still impact the experiences of women in today's institutions of higher education, although progress has been made on all these fronts.

The future, however, is still uncertain. Some policies that have served the cause of gender equity in postsecondary education are being weakened. For example, in March, 2005 the Department of Education released a letter weakening the Title IX compliance standards for college athletics. In contrast, there have been positive policies. For example, women faculty members at Harvard University claimed that the university was not granting tenure equitably. The response from Harvard was to commit $50 million over the next 10 years to implement recommendations made by two taskforces on Women Faculty and Women in Science and Engineering (Feminist Daily News Wire, 2005). Thus, the picture for the future of gender equity in higher education may be filled with both setbacks and advances. Most of us still long for an academy that would create a future with greater possibilities for women and men, regardless of gender, race, class, disability, or sexual preference. It is the sincere hope of all the authors of this chapter that this work can lead us closer to that goal.

ACKNOWLEDGMENTS

The authors would like to thank Bernice Sandler, Women's Research and Education Institute, Washington, DC, for her helpful review and suggestions on two previous versions of this chapter. We would also like to thank Ruth B. Ekstrom of ETS for her contribution of material on older women in higher education. Dr. Ekstrom was the co-author of the chapter "Educational Programs for Adult Women" in the first *Handbook*. We are also grateful to Evelyn Fisch of ETS for her expert editorial assistance.

References

Allan, E. J. (2002). Classroom climates in postsecondary education. In A. M. Aleman, & K. A. Renn (Eds.), *Women in higher education: An encyclopedia* (pp. 282–287). Santa Barbara, CA: ABC-CLIO Press.

Allan, E. J., & Madden, M. (2003, April). *Chilly classrooms for female undergraduate students at a research university: A question of method?* Paper presented at the annual meeting of the American Educational Research Association, Chicago, IL.

Allen, B. P., & Niss, J. F. (1990). A chill in the college classroom? *Phi Delta Kappan, 71*(8), 607–609.

The Almanac of Higher Education, 2004–2005. (2004). [Special issue]. *The Chronicle of Higher Education, 51*(1).

American Association of Community Colleges. (2003). *State-by-state profile of community colleges* (6th ed.). Washington, DC: Community College Press.

American Association of University Professors. (1999, April). 1998–99 AAUP faculty salaries. *Chronicle of Higher Education, 45*(33), A16. Retrieved August 16, 2006, from http://chronicle.com/weekly/v45/i33/stats/4533aaup.htm

American Association of University Professors. (2004). The annual report on the economic status of the profession, 2003–2004, *Academe, 90*(2), 20–103.

American Association of University Women. (2004). *Education and legal advocacy fund.* Retrieved August 16, 2006, from http://www.aauw.org/laf/index.cfm

Amey, M. J. (1999). Navigating the raging river: Reconciling issues of identity, inclusion, and administrative practice. In K. Shaw, R. A. Rhoads, & J. Valadez (Eds.), *Community colleges as cultural texts: Qualitative explorations of organizational and student cultures* (pp. 59–82). Albany: State University of New York Press.

Amey M. J., & Twombly, S. B. (1992). Re-visioning leadership in community colleges. *The Review of Higher Education, 15*(2), 125–150.

Amey, M. J., & VanDerLinden, K. (2002). *Career paths for community college leaders* (AACC Research Brief. Leadership Series). Washington, DC: American Association of Community Colleges.

Amey, M. J., VanDerLinden, K., & Brown, D. (2002). Perspectives on community college leadership: Twenty years in the making. *Community College Journal of Research and Practice, 26*(7), 573–589.

Antony, J. S., & Valadez, J. R. (2002). Exploring the satisfaction of part-time college faculty in the United States. *Review of Higher Education, 26*(1), 41–56.

Armenti, C. (2004). May babies and post tenure babies: Maternal decisions of women professors. *The Review of Higher Education, 27*(2), 211–231.

Astin, H., & Cress, C. (1999, January). Women faculty model new values for research universities. *Women in Higher Education*, p. 35.

Astin, H. S., & Leland, C. (1991). *Women of influence, women of vision: A cross-generational study of leaders and change.* San Francisco: Jossey-Bass.

Baldwin, R. G., & Chronister, J. L. (2001). *Teaching without tenure: Policies and practices for a new era.* Baltimore: Johns Hopkins University Press.

Barbezat, D. (1988). Gender differences in academic reward system. In D. W. Breneman & T. I. K. Youn (Eds.), *Academic labor markets and careers* (pp. 138–164). Philadelphia: Falmer Press.

Bejar, E. M. (2002). Historically Black colleges and universities. In A. M. Martinez & K. A. Renn (Eds.), *Women in higher education: An encyclopedia* (pp. 40–44). Santa Barbara, CA: ABC-CLIO Press.

Bell, L. (1999). Ups and downs: Academic salaries since the early 70s. *Academe*, *85*(2), 12–20.

Bellas, M. L. (1993). Faculty salaries: Still a cost of being female? *Social Science Quarterly*, *74*(1), 62–75.

Bellas, M. L. (1994). Comparable worth in academia: The effects of faculty salaries on the sex composition and labor market conditions of academic disciplines. *American Sociology Review*, *59*, 807–821.

Bellas, M. L. (1997a). Disciplinary differences in faculty salaries: Does gender bias play a role? *Journal of Higher Education*, *68*(3), 299–321.

Bellas, M. L. (1997b). The scholarly productivity of academic couples. In M. A. Ferber & J. W. Loeb (Eds.), *Academic couples: Problems and promises* (pp. 156–181). Chicago: University of Illinois Press.

Bellas, M. L. (1999). Emotional labor in academia: The case of professors. *Annals of the American Academy of Political and Social Science*, *56*(1), 96–110.

Bellas, M. L., & Reskin, B. F. (1994). On comparable worth. *Academe*, *70*(5), 83–85.

Bellas, M. L., & Toutkoushian, R. K. (1999). Faculty time allocations and research productivity: Gender, race, and family effects. *The Review of Higher Education*, *22*(4), 367–390.

Benjamin, E. (1999). Disparities in the salaries and appointments of academic women and men: An update of a 1988 report of Committee on the status of women in the academic profession. *Academe*, *85*(1), 60–62.

Bensimon, E. M. (1991). A feminist reinterpretation of president's definitions of leadership. In M. Peterson (Ed.), *Organization and governance in higher education* (4th ed., pp. 465–473). Needham Heights, MA: Simon and Schuster Custom Publishing.

Bensimon, E. M., & Neumann, A. (1993). *Redesigning collegiate leadership: Teams and teamwork in higher education.* Baltimore: The Johns Hopkins University Press.

Bensimon, E. M. (2005). Closing the achievement gap in higher education: An organizational learning perspective. In A. Kezar (Ed.), *Organizational learning in higher education.* San Francisco: Jossey-Bass.

Berger, A. R., & Kirshstein, R. J. (2001, November). *"Careerists" and "moonlighters": Recognizing the diversity of part-time faculty.* Paper presented at the annual meeting of the Association for the Study of Higher Education, Richmond, VA.

Berger, A. R., & Kirshstein, R. J. (2003, April). *The many faces of part-time faculty.* Paper presented at the annual meeting of the American Educational Research Association, Chicago, IL.

Berkner, L., He, S., & Cataldi, E. F. (2002). *Descriptive summary of 1995–96 beginning postsecondary students: Six years later* (NCES No. 2003–151). U.S. Department of Education, National Center for Education Statistics. Washington, DC: U.S. Government Printing Office.

Blackmore, J. (1989). Educational leadership: A feminist critique and reconstruction. In J. Smyth (Ed.), *Critical perspectives on educational leadership* (pp. 93–130). New York: Falmer Press.

Bleuer, J. C., & Walz, G. R. (2003). *Are boys falling behind?* Washington, DC: U.S. Department of Education. (ERIC Document Reproduction Service No. ED470-601)

Bourdieu, P. (1977). *Outline of a theory of practice.* Cambridge, MA: Cambridge University Press.

Bradburn, E. (2002). *Short-term enrollment in postsecondary education: Student background and institutional differences in reasons for early departure, 1996–98* (NCES 2003-153). U.S. Department of Education, National Center for Education Statistics. Washington, DC: U.S. Government Printing Office.

Brady, K. L., & Eisler, R. M. (1995). Gender bias in the college classroom: A critical review of the literature and implications for future research. *Journal of Research and Development in Education*, *29*(1), 9–19.

Breneman, D. W., & Youn, T. I. K. (Eds.). (1988). *Academic labor markets and careers.* Philadelphia: Falmer Press.

Britz, J. D. (2006, March 23). To all the girls I've rejected. *New York Times.* Retrieved July 10, 2006, from http://www.nytimes.com/2006/03/23/opinion/23britz.html?ex=1152676800&en=f37980f105108f2a&ei=5070

Brown, T. (2000). *Female presidents of selected independent colleges.* Unpublished doctoral dissertation, North Carolina State University, Raleigh, NC. (ERIC Document Reproduction Service No. ED442346)

Brown, M., & Freeman, K. (2002). Introduction. *Review of Higher Education*, *25*(3), 237–240.

Bureau of the Census. (2003). *Money income of households, families and persons in the U.S.* (Department of Commerce, Current Population Reports, Series P-60). Washington, DC: U.S. Government Printing Office.

Burgdorf, B. D., & Kostka, K. (2005). *Eliminating complexity and inconsistency in Federal financial aid programs for higher education students: Towards a more strategic approach.* Paper prepared for the Secretary of Education's Commission on the Future of Higher Education. Washington, DC: U.S. Department of Education.

Burgos-Sasscer, R. (1990, July 8–11). *The changing face of leadership: The role of Hispanics.* Paper presented at the International Conference on Leadership Development for the League for Innovation in the Community College, "Leadership 2000", San Francisco, CA.

Carlson, L. G. (1994). Women faculty in higher education: Strategies for influence. In *Proceedings of the Seventh Annual International Conference on Women in Higher Education* (pp. 77–87). El Paso: University of Texas.

Chenoweth, K., Stephens, A., & Evelyn, J. (1998). Powerful sisters: Profile of five women of color who head community colleges. *Black Issues in Higher Education*, *15*(7), 12–14.

Chliwniak, L. (1997). Higher education leadership: Analyzing the gender gap. (ERIC digest). Washington DC: ERIC Clearinghouse on Higher Education. (ERIC Identifier No. ED410846)

Chronister, J. L., & Baldwin, R. G. (1999). Marginal or mainstream? Full-time faculty off the tenure track. *Liberal Education*, *85*(4), 16–23.

Clark, S. L. (1998). Women faculty in community colleges: Investigating the mystery. *Community College Review*, *26*(3), 77–88.

Clayton, D. E., & Smith, M. M. (1987). Motivational typology of reentry women. *Adult Education Quarterly*, *37*, 90–104.

Clery, S. B. (2001). Part-time faculty. *NEA Higher Education Research Center Update*, *7*(4), 1–8.

Clifford, G. J. (1983). Shaking dangerous questions from the crease: Gender and American higher education. *Feminist Issues*, *34*(2), 3–62.

Cohen, A., & Brawer, F. (2003). *The American community college* (4th ed.). San Francisco: Jossey Bass.

Coiner, C., & George, D. H. (Eds.). (1998). *The family track: Keeping your faculties while you mentor, nurture, teach, and serve.* Chicago: University of Illinois Press.

Collins, L. H. (1998). Competition and contract: The dynamics behind resistance to affirmative action in academe. In L. H. Collins, J. C. Chrisler, & K. Quina (Eds.), *Career strategies for women in academe: Arming Athena* (pp. 45–74). Thousand Oaks, CA: Sage.

Conley, V. M., & Leslie, D. W. (2002). Part-time instructional faculty and staff: Who they are, what they do and what they think. *Education Statistics Quarterly*, *4*(2), 97–103.

Cooper, J. E. (2002). Overview. In A. Martinez & K. A. Renn (Eds.), *Women in higher education* (pp. 373–380). Santa Barbara, CA: ABC-CLIO Press.

Cooper, J., Benham, M., Collay, M., Martinez-Aleman, A., & Scherr, M. (1999). A famine of stories: Finding a home in the academy. *Initiatives, 59*(1), 1–18.

Cooper, J., Kane, K., & Gisselquist, J. (2001). Forces eroding affirmative action in higher education: The California-Hawai'i distinction. In B. Lindsay & M. J. Justiz (Eds.), *The quest for equity in higher education: Towards new paradigms in an evolving affirmative action era* (pp. 163–181). Albany: State University of New York Press.

Cooper, J., Ortiz, A., Benham, M., & Scherr, M. (2002). Finding a home in the academy: Resisting racism and ageism. In J. Cooper & D. Stevens (Eds.), *Tenure in the sacred grove: Issues and strategies for women and minority faculty* (pp. 71–89). Albany: State University of New York Press.

Cooper, J., & Stevens, D. (Eds.). (2002). *Tenure in the sacred grove: Issues and strategies for women and minority faculty*. Albany: State University of New York Press.

Corrigan, M. (2002). *The American college president 2002 Edition*. Washington, DC: American Council on Education Center for Policy Analysis.

Curtis, J. W. (2005). Inequities persist for women and non-tenure-track faculty. *Academe, 91*(2), 21–45.

Dickens, C. S., & Sagaria, M. A. D. (1997). Feminists at work: Collaborative relationships among women faculty. *Review of Higher Education, 21*(1), 79–101.

DiCroce, D. M. (2000). Women and the community college presidency: Challenges and possibilities. In J. Glazer-Raymo, B. Townsend, & B. Ropers-Huilman (Eds.), *Women in higher education: A feminist perspective* (pp. 252–259). Boston: Pearson Custom Publishing.

Dyer, S. K. (Ed.). (2004). *Tenure denied: Cases of sex of discrimination in academia*. Washington, DC: American Association of University Women.

Dziech, B. W. (1983). Changing status of women. In G. Vaughan (Ed.), *Issues for community college leaders in a new era* (pp. 55–75). San Francisco: Jossey Bass.

Eckert, P. (1998). Gender and sociolinguistic variation. In J. Coates (Ed.), *Language and gender: A reader* (pp. 64–75). Oxford: Blackwell.

Eddy, P. L. (2003). Views of gender in the community college presidency. *Community College Enterprise, 9*(2), 49–64.

England, P. (1992). *Comparable worth: Theories and evidence*. New York: Aldine de Gruyter.

Fairweather, J. S. (1996). *Faculty work and public trust: Restoring the value of teaching and public service in American academic life*. Boston: Allyn and Bacon.

Feminist Daily News Wire. (2005). *Harvard president pledges $50 million for women's programs*. Retrieved July 10, 2006, from http://www.feminist.org/news/newsbyte/uswirestory.asp?id=9045

Ferber, M. A., & Loeb, J. W. (Eds.). (1997). *Academic couples: Problems and promises*. Chicago: University of Illinois Press.

Ferrori, M., & Berte, N. (1970). *American junior colleges: Leadership and crucial issues for the 1970's*. Washington, DC: U.S. Department of Health, Education, and Welfare, Office of Education.

Finkelstein, M. J. (2003). The morphing of the American academic profession. *Liberal Education, 89*(4), 6–15.

Finkelstein, M. J., Seal, R. K., & Schuster, J. H. (1998). *The new academic generation: A profession in transformation*. Baltimore: Johns Hopkins University Press.

Frantz, C. (1995). An electronic storage and access system for special education legislation. *Dissertation Abstracts International, 56*(11), 4290A. (UMI No. DA 9608-530)

Frye, J. H. (1995). Women in the two-year college, 1990 to 1970. *New Directions for Community Colleges, 89*, 5–13.

Fugate, A. L., & Amey, M. J. (2000). Career stages of community college faculty: A qualitative analysis of their career paths, roles, and development. *Community College Review, 28*(1), 1–22.

Gappa, J. M. (2000). The new faculty majority: Somewhat satisfied but not eligible for tenure. *New Directions for Institutional Research, 27*(1), 77–86.

Gappa, J. M., & Leslie, D. W. (1997). *Two faculties or one? The conundrum of part-timers in a bifurcated work force* (Inquiry #6, New Pathways Working Paper Series). Washington, DC: American Association for Higher Education.

German, K. M. (1996). Part-time faculty: Identifying the trends and challenges. *Journal of the Association for Communication, 3*, 231–241.

Getskow, V. (1996). Women in community college leadership roles. (ERIC digest). Los Angeles: ERIC Clearinghouse for Community Colleges. (ERIC Identifier No. ED400025)

Gillett-Karam, R. (1997). *Administrators in North Carolina community colleges: A comparative study by gender. Preliminary report*. North Carolina: American Council on Education, Women Administrators on North Carolina Higher Education. (ERIC Identifier No. ED409073)

Glazer, J. S. (2000). Affirmative action and the status of women in the academy. In J. Glazer-Raymo, B. Townsend, & B. Ropers-Huilman (Eds.), *Women in higher education: A feminist perspective* (pp. 170–180). Boston: Pearson Custom Publishing.

Glazer-Raymo, J. (1999). *Shattering the myths: Women in academe*. Baltimore: Johns Hopkins University Press.

Glazer-Raymo, J. (2000). The unfinished agenda for women in American higher education. In R. Bohr & J. Longnion (Eds.), *Women's lives, women's voices, women's solutions: Shaping a national agenda for women in higher education*. Minneapolis: University of Minnesota.

Griffin, B. Q. (1992, March). *Perceptions of managers: Effects of leadership style and gender*. Paper presented at the annual meeting of the Southeastern Psychological Association, Knoxville, TN.

Green, M. F. (1997). No time for heroes. *Trusteeship, 5*(2), 6–11.

Hagedorn, L. S., & Laden, B. V. (2002). Exploring the climate for women as community college faculty. In C. L. Outcalt (Ed.), *Community college faculty: Characteristics, practices and challenges: New directions in community colleges, No. 118* (pp. 69–78). San Francisco: Jossey-Bass.

Hall, R., & Sandler, B. (1982). *The classroom climate: A chilly one for women?* Washington, DC: Project on the Status and Education of Women, Association of American Colleges.

Haring-Hidore, M., Freeman, S., Phelps, S., Spann, N.G., & Wooten, H. R., Jr. (1990). Women administrators' ways of knowing. *Education and Urban Society, 22*(2), 170–181.

Harper, E. P., Baldwin, R. G., Gansneder, B. G., & Chronister, J. L. (2001). Full-time women faculty off the tenure track: Profile and practice. *Review of Higher Education, 24*(3), 237–257.

Harvey, W. B., & Anderson, E. L. (2005). *Minorities in higher education 2003–2004: Twenty-first annual status report*. Washington, DC: American Council on Education.

Helgesen, S. (1995). *The web of inclusion: A new architecture for building great organizations*. New York: Currency/Doubleday.

Hensel, N. (1991). *Realizing gender equality in higher education: The need to integrate work/family issues* (ASHE-ERIC Higher Education Report No. 2). Washington, DC: The George Washington University, School of Education and Human Development.

Hill, B., Green, M., & Eckel, P. (2001). *What governing boards need to know and do about organizational change*. Washington, DC: American Council on Education.

Ideta, L., & Cooper, J. (2000). Asian women leaders of higher education. In J. Glazer-Raymo, B. Townsend, & B. Ropers-Huilman (Eds.), *Women in higher education: A feminist perspective* (ASHE reader series; pp. 259–270). Boston: Pearson Custom Publishing.

Jablonski, M. (1996). The leadership challenge for women college presidents. *Initiatives, 57*(4), 1–10.

Jacobs, J. A. (1995). Gender and academic specialties: Trends among recipients of college degrees in the 1980s. *Sociology of Education, 68*(2), 81–98.

Jacobson, J. (2002, June 27). Parity and the presidency. *The Chronicle of Higher Education.* Retrieved November 13, 2004, from http://chronicle.com/jobs/2002/06/2002062701c.htm

Kerka, S. (1989). *Retaining adult students in higher education* (ERIC digest No. 88). Columbus OH: ERIC Clearinghouse on Adult Career and Vocational Education. (ERIC Identifier No. ED308401)

Kim, M. (2001). Institutional effectiveness of women-only colleges. *Journal of Higher Education, 72*(3), 287–321.

King, J. (2000). *Gender equity in higher education: Are male students at a disadvantage?* Washington, DC: American Council on Education.

Kirkland, J. J. (1997). Role models for the student majority. *Thought and Action, 13*(1), 93–101.

Kirp, D. L. (2003). *Shakespeare, Einstein, and the bottom line: The marketing of higher education.* Cambridge, MA: Harvard University Press.

Kolodny, A. (1996). Paying the price of antifeminist intellectual harassment. In V. Clark, S. N. Garner, M. Higonnet, & K. Katrak (Eds.), *Antifeminism in the academy* (pp. 3–33). New York: Routledge.

Kolodny, A. (1998). *Failing the future: A dean looks at higher education in the twenty-first century.* Durham, NC: Duke University Press.

Langdon, E. A. (2001). Women's colleges then and now: Access then, equity now. *Peabody Journal of Education, 76*(1), 5–30.

LaPaglia, N. (1994) *Storytellers: The image of the two-year college in American fiction and in women's journals.* DeKalb: LEPS Press, Northern Illinois University.

Lareau, A. (1987). Social class differences in family-school relationships: The importance of cultural capital. *Sociology of Education, 60,* 73–85.

Leatherman, C. (2001). Part-time faculty members try to organize nationally. *The Chronicle of Higher Education, 47*(20), A12.

Leslie, D. W., & Gappa. J. M. (2002). Part-time faculty: Competent and committed. *New Directions for Community College, 118,* 59–67.

Leslie, D. W., & Walke, J. T. (2001). *Out of the ordinary: The anomalous academic* (Alfred P. Sloan Foundation Report). Williamsburg, VA: The College of William and Mary.

Lowe, E. (1999). *Promise and dilemma: Perspectives on racial diversity and higher education.* Princeton, NJ: Princeton University Press.

Madden, M. (2000, April). *Gender doesn't matter! Or does it? Women engineering students speak.* Paper presented at New England Education Research Organization Annual Conference, Portsmouth, NH.

Mason, M. A., & Goulden, M. (2004). Do babies matter (Part II)? Closing the baby gap. *Academe, 90*(6), 10–15.

Martin, J. R. (2000). *Coming of age in academe.* New York: Routledge.

Mathews, J. (2006, June 26). Study casts doubt on the "boy crisis": Improving test scores cut into girls' lead. *Washington Post,* p. A01.

McDonough, P. (2002). Resisting common injustice: Tenure politics, department politics, gay and lesbian politics. In J. Cooper & D. Stevens (Eds.), *Tenure in the sacred grove: Issues and strategies for women and minority faculty* (pp. 127–146). Albany: State University of New York Press.

McElhinny, B. S. (1998). "I don't smile much anymore": Affect, gender & the discourse of Pittsburgh police officers. In J. Coates (Ed.), *Language and gender: A reader* (pp. 309–327). Oxford, UK: Blackwell.

McElrath, K. (1992). Gender, career disruption and academic rewards. *Journal of Higher Education, 63*(3), 269–281.

Monroehurst, R. (1997). Leadership, women and higher education. In H. Eggins (Ed.), *Women as leaders and managers in higher education* (pp. 3–16). Bristol, PA: The Society for Research into Higher Education & Open University Press.

Moskal, B. (1997, February 3). Women make better managers. *The Management Magazine, 24,* 17–19.

Mott, M. C. (1997). *Women community college presidents' leadership agendas.* Unpublished doctoral dissertation, Center for the Study of Higher Education, University of Arizona, Tucson.

National Center for Education Statistics. (2001). *National postsecondary financial aid study 1999–2000* (NPSAS 2000) (NCES No.2001-209). Washington, DC: U.S. Government Printing Office.

National Center for Education Statistics. (2002). *The condition of education 2002* (NCES No. 2002-025). Washington, DC: U.S. Government Printing Office.

National Center for Education Statistics. (2003). *Digest of education statistics, 2002* (NCES No. 2003-060). Washington, DC: U.S. Government Printing Office.

National Center for Education Statistics. (2004). *Digest of Education Statistics, 2004* (NCES No. 2006-005). Washington, DC: US Department of Education.

National Center for Education Statistics. (2005). *Digest of Education Statistics, 2005.* Washington, DC: US Department of Education. Retrieved September 13, 2006, from http://nces.ed.gov/programs/digest/d05/lt3.asp#16

National Center for Education Statistics. (2006). Programs and plans of the National Center for Education Statistics, 2005 Edition. *Education Statistics Quarterly, 7*(1 & 2). Retrieved July 10, 2006, from http://nces.ed.gov/programs/quarterly/vol_7/1_2/2_1.asp

Nidiffer, J. (2001a). Crumbs from the boy's table: The first generation of coeducation. In J. Nidiffer & C. T. Bashaw (Eds.), *Women administrators in higher education: Historical and contemporary perspectives* (pp. 13–34). Albany: State University of New York Press.

Nidiffer, J. (2001b). New leadership for a new century: Women's contribution to leadership in higher education. In J. Nidiffer & C. T. Bashaw (Eds.), *Women administrators in higher education: Historical and contemporary perspectives* (pp. 101–134). Albany: State University of New York Press.

Nidiffer, J. (2003). From whence they came: The contexts, challenges, and courage of early women administrators in higher education. In B. Ropers-Huilman (Ed.), *Gendered futures in higher education* (pp. 15–34). Albany: State University of New York Press.

Nidiffer, J., & Bashaw, C. (2001). *Women administrators in higher education.* Albany: State University of New York Press.

Palmer, J. C. (1999). Part-time faculty at community colleges: A national profile. *The NEA 1999 Almanac of Higher Education.* Washington, DC: National Education Association.

Park, S. M. (1994). Am I qualified? Gender bias in university tenure and promotion criteria. In *Proceedings of the 7th Annual International Conference on Women in Higher Education,* (pp. 329–332). Minneapolis: University of Minnesota.

Park, S. M. (1996). Research, teaching, and service: Why shouldn't women's work count? *Journal of Higher Education, 67*(1), 46–84.

Perna, L. W. (2001a). Sex and race differences in faculty tenure and promotion. *Research in Higher Education, 42*(5), 584–611.

Perna, L. W. (2001b). The relationship between faculty responsibilities and employment status among college and university faculty. *Journal of Higher Education, 72*(5), 584–611.

Perna, L. W. (2003). The status of women and minorities among community college faculty. *Research in Higher Education, 44*(2), 205–240.

Peterson, M. W., & Dill, D. D. (1997). Understanding the competitive environment of the postsecondary knowledge industry. In M. W. Peterson, D. D. Dill, & L. A. Mets (Eds.), *Planning and management for a changing environment: A handbook on redesigning postsecondary institutions,* (pp. 3–29). San Francisco: Jossey-Bass.

Phillippe, K. A. (Ed.). (2000). *National profile of community colleges: Trends and statistics.* Washington, DC: Community College Press.

Raabe, P. H. (1997). Work-family policies for faculty: How "career- and family friendly" is academe? In M. A. Ferber & J. W. Loeb (Eds.), *Academic couples: Problems and promises* (pp. 208–225). Chicago: University of Illinois Press.

Rainey, A. (2006). Sexual harassment pervades college campuses and injures men as well as women, survey finds. *The Chronicle of Higher Education, 52*(22), A38.

Readings, B. (1996). *The university in ruins.* Cambridge, MA: Harvard University Press.

Riger, S., Stokes, J., Raja, S., & Sullivan, M. (1997). Measuring perceptions of the work environment for female faculty. *Review of Higher Education, 21*(1), 63–78.

Rosener, J. B. (1990). Ways women lead. *Harvard Business Review, 68,* 119–125.

Rosser, P. (2005). Too many women in college? *Ms. Magazine.* Retrieved July 12, 2006, from http://www.msmagazine.com/fall2005/college.asp

Rosser, V. J. (2001, April). *Women and their effectiveness as leaders: What makes the difference among deans?* Paper presented at the American Educational Research Association Annual Meeting, Seattle, WA.

Sagaria, M. A. D. (1988). Administrative mobility and gender: Patterns and processes in higher education. *Journal of Higher Education, 59*(3), 305–326.

Sagaria, M. A. D., & Rychener, M. A. (2002). Women administrators: Mobility. In A. M. Martinez Aleman & K. A. Renn (Eds.), *Women in higher education: An encyclopedia* (pp. 495–497). Santa Barbara, CA: ABC-CLIO Press.

Sandler, B. R., & Hall, R. (1986). *The campus climate revisited: Chilly for women faculty, administrators, and graduate students.* Washington, DC: Association of American Colleges and Universities.

Sandler, B. R., Silverberg, L., & Hall, R. M. (1996). *The chilly classroom climate: A guide to improve the education of women.* Washington, DC: National Association of Women in Education.

Seidman, E. (1985). *In the words of the faculty: Perspectives on improving teaching and educational quality in community colleges.* San Francisco: Jossey-Bass.

Shakeshaft, C. (1987). Theory in a changing reality. *Journal of Educational Equity and Leadership, 7*(1), 4–20.

Simeone, A. (1987). *Academic women: Working towards equality.* South Hadley, MA: Bergin & Garvey.

Smallwood, S. (2003). United we stand? Part-time professors are forming unions, but many wonder if teaming up with full-timers would be better. *The Chronicle of Higher Education, 49*(24), A10.

Snyder, T., Hoffman, C., & Geddes, C. (1998). *Digest of educational statistics.* Washington, DC: National Center for Educational Statistics, Office of Educational Research and Improvement.

State of College Admission Report. (2002). *National association for college admission counseling.* Alexandria, VA.: NACAC.

Starks, G. (1987, April). *Retention of adult students in the community college.* Paper presented at the annual meeting of the American Educational Research Association, Washington, DC. (ERIC Document Reproduction Service No. ED 281 592)

Stephan, P. E., & Kassis, M. M. (1997). The history of women & couples in academe. In M. A. Ferber & J. W. Loeb (Eds.), *Academic couples: Problems and promises* (pp. 44–79). Chicago: University of Illinois Press.

Suarez-Balcazar, Y., Orellana-Damacela, L., Portillo, N., Rowan, J. M., & Andrews-Guillen, C. (2003). Experiences of differential treatment among college students of color. *Journal of Higher Education, 74*(4), 428–444.

Sum, A., Fogg, N., & Harrington, P. (with Khatiwada, I., Palma, S., Pond, N., & Tobar, P.). (2003). *The growing gender gap in college enrollment and degree attainment in the U.S. and their potential economic and social consequences.* Boston: Northeastern University, Center for Labor Market Studies.

Tedrow, B., & Rhoads, R. A. (1999). A qualitative study of women's experiences in community college leadership positions. *Community College Review, 27*(3), 1–18.

Terrell, P. S. (1990). Adapting institutions of higher education to serve adult students' needs. *NASPA Journal, 27,* 241–247.

Theodore, A. (1986). *The campus troublemakers: Academic women in protest.* Houston: Cap and Gown Press.

Tierney, W. G., & Bensimon, E. M. (1996). *Promotion and tenure: Community and socialization in academe.* Albany: State University of New York Press.

Tinto, V. (1987). *Leaving college.* Chicago: University of Chicago Press.

Tolbert, P. S. (1998). Two-tiered faculty systems and organizational outcomes. In D. W. Leslie (Vol. Ed.), *New directions for higher education, 104* (pp. 71–80). San Francisco: Jossey-Bass.

Townsend, B. K. (1995). Women community college faculty: On the margins or in the mainstream? In B. K. Townsend (Ed.), *New directions for community colleges. Gender and power in the community college, No. 89* (pp. 39–46). San Francisco: Jossey-Bass.

Townsend, B. K. (1998). Women faculty's satisfaction with employment in the community colleges. *Community College Journal of Research and Practice, 22*(7), 655–661.

Twale, D. J., & Shannon, D. M. (1996). Gender differences among faculty in campus governance: Nature of involvement, satisfaction, and power. *Initiatives, 57*(4), 11–19.

Twombly, S. B., & Rosser, V. J. (2002). Women administrators: Introduction. In A. M. Martinez Aleman & K. A. Renn (Eds.), *Women in higher education: An encyclopedia* (pp. 459–465). Santa Barbara, CA: ABC-CLIO Press.

Valadez, J. R. (1996). Educational access and social mobility in a rural community college. *The Review of Higher Education, 19*(4), 391–409.

Valian, V. (1999). *Why so slow? The advancement of women.* Cambridge, MA: MIT Press.

VanDerLinden, K. (2003, April). *Career advancement and leadership development of community college administrators.* Paper presented at the American Educational Research Association, Chicago, IL.

Volk, C., Slaughter, S., & Thomas, S. (2001). Models of institutional resource allocation: Mission, market, and gender. *Journal of Higher Education, 72*(4), 387–413.

Ward, K., & Wolf-Wendel, L. (2004). Academic motherhood: Managing complex roles in research universities. *Review of Higher Education, 27*(2), 233–257.

West, M. S., & Curtis, J. W. (2006). *AAUP faculty gender equity indicators 2006.* Washington, DC: AAUP.

White, J. (2001). *Adult women in community colleges.* (ERIC digest). Los Angeles: ERIC Clearinghouse for Community Colleges. (ERIC Identifier No. ED451860)

Williams, W. M. (2001, July 20). Women in academe, and the men who derail them [The Chronicle Review]. *Chronicle of Higher Education,* B19-20.

Wilson, R. (2001, May 4). Proportion of part-time faculty members leveled off from 1992 to 1998, data show. *The Chronicle of Higher Education, 47*(34), A14.

Winsten-Bartlett, C. (2006). Gendered patterns of resource deprivation in higher education. *Higher Education Perspectives, 2*(1). Retrieved July 12, 2006, from http://hep.oise.utoronto.ca/viewarticle.php?id=87

Wirt, J., Choy, S., Rooney, P., Provasnik, S., Sen, A., & Tobin, R. (2004). *The condition of education 2004* (NCES No. 2004-077). U.S. Department of Education, National Center for Education Statistics. Washington, DC: U.S. Government Printing Office.

Wolf-Wendel, L. (2002). Women's colleges. In A. M. Martinez Aleman & K. A. Renn (Eds.), *Women in higher education: An encyclopedia* (pp. 61–67). Santa Barbara, CA: ABC-CLIO Press.

Yates, E. (2001). Women's colleges receive high marks for learning effectiveness. *Black Issues in Higher Education, 17*(24), 22–24.

·31·

SUMMARY AND RECOMMENDATIONS
FOR ACHIEVING GENDER EQUITY
IN AND THROUGH EDUCATION

Susan S. Klein* *and Elizabeth Ann Homer,** *with Cheris Kramarae,*
Margaret A. Nash, Carol J. Burger, and Linda Shevitz

INTRODUCTION

The authors of these 2007 *Handbook* chapters documented some gains in advancing the gender-equity process and outcome goals since the publication of the 1985 *Handbook for Achieving Sex Equity through Education.* The process goals focus on what happens in education settings to eliminate sex discrimination and reduce sex and gender stereotyping. The outcome goals focus on what education can do to create a more gender equitable society.[1] However, none of the 2007 *Handbook* authors report that these goals of attaining gender equity in education contexts or because of education have been fully accomplished. Both subtle and complex sex discrimination continues although some of the overt types of clearly illegal sex discrimination (in education processes) such as not allowing women into engineering programs have stopped.[2]

Many authors have made it clear that hierarchies related to gender, race, economic, religious, or other societal stratifications and stereotyping are persistent and intertwined barriers that need to be removed to attain full equality in education and society. They point out that while there are some areas where attention to equity is important for men and boys, it is especially important to focus on equity goals for women and girls as they have generally faced most negative discrimination as frequent occupants of the lower- or less-valued parts of this societal hierarchy.

The chapters provide insights into how both formal and informal education can be transformed to play a major role in creating gender equitable schools, programs and activities as well as insights into longer-term strategies for a more gender equitable society. This summary chapter provides recommendations for policy, practice/programs, and research for achieving gender equity both in education and through education. In doing so, it highlights some context changes over the past two decades, provides examples of gains as well as continued inequities, and discusses conundrums in the quest for gender equity.

KEY CHANGES IN CONTEXT SINCE 1985

Chapter 1 of this *Handbook* discusses how changes in U.S. society such as the continued growth of the field of gender-equity education, increased use of technology, a greater focus on global gender equity, and more attention to the intersections of gender and other education equity concerns have influenced some gains since the 1985 *Handbook for Achieving Sex Equity through Education.* After discussing some additional contextual

---

*The bold face names are the Lead Authors.

[1]Gender equity process goals focus on eliminating sex stereotyping and sex differential (discriminatory) treatment in classrooms, school policies, testing, and much more. Gender-equity outcome goals include education attainment, career choices, and basic indicators of quality of life such as health, productivity, knowledge, happiness, freedom, safety, economic self-sufficiency, etc. *Handbook* authors present some evidence of positive relationships between gender-equitable processes and gender-equitable outcomes.

[2]As discussed in many other chapters Title IX of the 1972 Education Amendments and other federal and state laws make sex discrimination in education programs and activities covered by these laws illegal.

influences, this part of the chapter will discuss the barriers and continued challenges to achieving gender equity. Contextual influences include:

Increased attention to boys and men

Over the past 20 years, there has been more attention to the role of gender equity in helping boys and men. For example, in the 1985 Handbook, 6 of the 25 chapter titles specified girls or women such as "Strategies for Overcoming the Barriers to Women in Educational Administration," "Achieving Sex Equity for Minority Women," and "Gifted Girls and Women in Education." In this 2007 *Handbook*, no chapter titles address only women or only men. Authors of all chapters pay attention to equity issues for both males and females. In giving more attention to male gender-equity issues, some authors focus on the needs of minority boys and men since they have not been achieving equity with respect to minority girls and women or with respect to their nonminority male peers related to their academic achievement, safety, and freedom from negative involvement with the criminal justice system. Other authors discuss the study of maleness and masculinity within the field of gender studies and how gender-role stereotypes can be as damaging and limiting to men as to women.

Sometimes increased attention to boys and men has been related to backlash against the progress of girls and women such as concerns that women are overrepresented in the student bodies of many colleges. Some authors have provided evidence to counteract proponents of "gender wars" who believe achieving gender equity is a zero-sum game—if girls gain, boys must lose.

More attention to Title IX and other gender-equity laws

Over the past 20 years, there have been indicators of continued ignorance and neglect by educators about their gender-equity responsibilities and knowledge of Title IX. This lack of attention is associated with decreased federal funding and leadership in implementing gender-equity education policies and laws especially since the late 1990s. Chapter 5, "The Role of Government in Advancing Gender Equity in Education," and chapter 9 "Gender Equity in Coeducational and Single-Sex Educational Environments" document how the federal government has weakened Title IX. For example, the October 25, 2006, changes in the Title IX Regulations allow such flexible use of single-sex education that it is more likely to increase than reduce sex discrimination, which is the sole purpose of Title IX (OCR, 2006). This is especially perplexing because the Department of Education requires more rigorous evidence of effectiveness for curriculum improvements such as reading programs than it does in its uniquely federal area of responsibility: providing protection against sex discrimination under Title IX.[3]

More governmental accountability in general, but less for gender equity

Over the past two decades, governmental education accountability policies have exerted more systematic control on many aspects of education. However, gender equity is often omitted from these policies even in reports and discussions of progress toward education equity, which require information on race but often not race and sex. Many authors recommend that federal and state governments include specific provisions to collect gender information for accountability purposes such as the Athletics Disclosure Act discussed in chapter 18 on "Gender Equity in Physical Education and Athletics." The authors also encourage using the Internet to collect and exchange information such as data disaggregated by sex, race, and poverty as well as contact information on the legislatively required Title IX coordinators.

More attention to gender equity needs of diverse populations

The diverse populations examined in this Handbook include high poverty countries around the world as well as increased U.S. focus on the education needs of populations ranging from key groups to individuals with disabilities. A more recent societal, but not a federal, focus has been on lesbian, gay, bisexual, and transgender issues in education. Despite increased societal interest, little research or funding has focused on gender-equity issues within and for these populations.

INDICATORS OF PROGRESS IN ATTAINING GENDER EQUITY

Since the 1985 *Handbook*, many gaps in education achievements between female and male students have decreased. In some cases, both men and women improved on education achievement indicators and the women improved more, sometimes surpassing their male peers. However, in many other areas the gaps favoring males continued or increased and obstacles to attaining gender equity are still formidable.

Some examples of gains with caveats include:

1. There has been increased public understanding and media attention related to gender equity in education.

   - Studies around the world show that the health, education, welfare and economies of countries are positively associated with educating girls and their mothers. However, there is a need for boys and men to understand the value of gender equity in education and in society and the ways equity frees men for a greater variety of choices in careers and avocations, opens up new household and parenting roles, and allows for more healthy lifestyle choices (by, for instance, reducing high-risk behaviors.)

   - Popular media and popular book coverage of gender-equity education issues has increased. Much of this information is fair and helpful. However, some such as discussions of "gender wars" and improper characterizations of sex dif-

---

[3]This will be discussed later in this chapter under the last conundrum.

ferences and gender-equity provisions of federal laws are inaccurate and misleading. This *Handbook* provides a definitive source of summary information on these complicated issues based on patterns of evidence from multiple studies.

Media coverage of the controversy generated by former Harvard University President Lawrence Summers' remarks claiming that innate differences between the sexes might help explain the dearth of women in the top science jobs has helped educate the public about the falcity of this claim and the importance of efforts to stop sex discrimination and advance women in scientific and other leadership positions. The media and public reaction encouraged Harvard to show that it valued the full participation of women. It allocated $50 million to counteract discrimination against women and minorities on campus and in 2007 selected Drew Gilpin Faust as its first women president. Media coverage of her appointment has helped advance gender equality by highlighting her leadership of the faculty Task Forces which requested the $50 million, her scholarship on women, and her collaborative leadership style as director of Women's Studies at the University of Pennsylvania and Dean of the Radcliffe Institute for Advanced Study. This Institute, focuses on gender issues and interdisciplinary research, important aspects of Harvard's reform efforts. Media attention related to Dr. Faust's presidency has also helped educate the public about progress and challenges of women as academic leaders.

Despite the generally insightful media coverage of these influential Harvard activities, what the media covers and how it does so might be misleading and inaccurate. For example, there was substantial September 2006 coverage of the Dee (2006) study that found that students learn best with same-sex teachers. These findings were not substantiated by other studies completed over the past two decades. Instead, they were based on a secondary analysis of 1988 data with no classroom observations to support or refute the reported findings.[4] Rather than refuting popular misconceptions, most of the *Handbook* authors focus on what is known from a variety of well-documented research perspectives as seen by extensive reference lists in each chapter.

- With more women in the paid workforce in the United States and many other countries, there is a fuller understanding of the relationship of gender equity in education, the workforce, and the home, but education has not provided much leadership to other professions in developing comprehensive policies to increase gender equity such as for flexible work hours, job sharing, or child care.

2. The U.S. gender-equity laws and policies, especially Title IX and the Equal Protection Clause of the 14th Amendment to the U.S. Constitution as well as state ERAs and other laws and policies, have been used to protect women and men from sex discrimination in education.

- This 2007 *Handbook* focuses more on Title IX and its enforcement than did the 1985 *Handbook*, which had more emphasis on positive government support for women's educational equity programs than on using Title IX to prohibit discrimination. This shift in emphasis probably was related to the 1984 Supreme Court decision on Grove City College that temporarily limited Title IX's coverage to specific federally funded programs rather than to the discriminatory actions of the whole education organization that received federal financial assistance. Due to the hard work of women's rights and civil rights organizations, especially the National Organization for Women, the Grove City College decision limiting Title IX coverage was overturned by the Civil Rights Restoration Act of 1987. Title IX and Title VII of the 1964 Civil Rights Act have been used to protect both women and men from sexual harassment, a topic that was barely mentioned in the 1985 *Handbook*.

- There have been gains but not parity in areas like athletics where more women have learned skills and participated in competitive teams due to attention to Title IX. There has been an increase in the number of women students and faculty in some areas of science, but decreases in areas such as computer science.

3. There have been decreases in gender gaps in education achievement tests formerly favoring men and boys and in educational attainment. In some cases, the gaps have been reversed to favor women and girls.

- Patterns of results from meta-analyses of multiple studies show few large sex differences in key subject areas such as verbal and mathematical performance, which had often been characterized as having large gender differences. An increased understanding of gender similarities is reflected in chapter 2 on "Facts and Assumptions About the Nature of Gender Differences and the Implications for Gender Equity," chapter 8 on testing, in many of the content area chapters in Part IV, and in Hyde and Linn (2006). Decreased gender gaps are especially clear in many mathematics tests and in the increased participation and achievement in science areas, such as biology and chemistry, and in foreign language learning. The gaps favoring girls in verbal-skills tests have remained fairly consistent and small. Men are still doing slightly better than women are in the SAT critical-reading scores, but women in all ethnic groups scored higher than men in the new 2006 writing test (College Board, 2006). International data show patterns similar to the United States with most gender differences in achievement in the higher grade levels.

- There is substantial evidence that the few gender gaps in academic indicators that continue are related to socialization and experiences and sometimes due to differences

---

[4]The accompanying web page to be developed for each chapter may be able to refute some key misinformation as it appears in the popular press. The 2006 study by Thomas Dee was disseminated in the *Education Next* journal and Web site (www.educationnext.org) of the conservative Hoover Institution.

in the female and male populations that take the test rather than to any innate physiological or biological differences. For example, this applies to the learning of spatial skills where men and boys have traditionally scored higher than women and girls. It is also clear that experiences, expectations, and stereotypes may contribute to preferences in learning styles. Educators should not reinforce these stereotypes, but should instead help students use diverse learning strategies.

- Some chapters report that in general, girls and women try harder in school and often receive better grades than their male peers. In many countries, boys tend to repeat school more than girls, but they also complete primary and secondary school at higher rates than girls. It is likely that parents keep their sons in school longer than their daughters and that girls take their studies more seriously. In the mathematics and science areas, some of the progress of girls can be associated with increased state and local course-taking requirements for all. An additional explanation may be that girls see the value of doing well academically and getting more education to prepare them for a successful life. In most cases, this means that they will be expected to bring in an income to help the family and that they are unlikely to be an unemployed, stay-at-home full-time mother for long or at all. The authors of chapter 4 also show that women need more formal education to approach the salaries of men with less education.

- There have been increases of women in many areas of postsecondary education, especially as students in the United States. Compared to men, women are now earning more bachelors and masters degrees in many disciplines and they apply for and receive more financial assistance to attend postsecondary institutions. (See chapter 30 on "Improving Gender Equity in Postsecondary Education").

- More women now work in prestigious previously male-dominated occupations, such as law, business, medicine, but not necessarily in as many high-level or high-salary jobs that would be expected based on the higher percent of degrees and credentials earned by women. (See the chapter 6 on "Increasing Gender Equity in Educational Leadership" and chapter 4 on "The Impact of Education on Gender Equity in Employment and its Outcomes.")

- In the past 20 years, more girls have been educated in low-income countries with related improvements in gender parity and literacy. However, the millennium development goals for gender parity in primary and secondary education have not been achieved. (See chapter 3, "Gender-Equity Education Globally.")

4. There is some indication that women's internalized barriers to success such as low self-esteem, attributions of success to luck, and "women's posited fear of success" have decreased since the 1985 *Handbook* findings. (See chapter 4 on "Employment and its Outcomes" and chapter 6 on "Edu-

cational Leadership.") Teaching people skills and conveying positive expectations is more likely to have a positive impact on self-esteem than trying to teach people to feel good about themselves.

PERSISTENT OBSTACLES TO ACHIEVING GENDER EQUITY

Even in areas where there has been some progress in increasing gender equity, there have been related patterns of gender inequities. For example, while there is more gender parity in athletics and greater success of women at the Olympics and in some occupations, many education-related gender inequities persist.

1. Women still suffer negative effects of discrimination in quality of life outcomes related to their safety and employment and leadership of government and business organizations. Females, more than males, are victims of sexual harassment and school shootings. There are few women leaders or top officials especially in national politics even though their stereotyped strengths for being less likely to be influenced by corruption and more likely to advance peace and cooperation are desired by all. The authors have noted that,

   - In the labor force "Although there are racial and age inequities, the most continuous and startling inequities are between men and women" (chapter 4 p. 54).

   - Gender inequities and employment discrimination continue in education, politics, law enforcement, business, medicine, media, the military, and religion.

   - Creative contributions of women are less encouraged and recognized than are those of men in many areas such as the arts and sciences (chapters 12, 13, 17).

   - Often occupations that switch from more men to more women find decreases in prestige and even in the relative pay of both men and women compared to more male dominated occupations. Chapter 7 on "The Treatment of Gender Equity in Teacher Education" provides evidence on this trend for education professionals, which is a similar persistent challenge for psychologists and social workers.

2. Men and boys still face barriers to gender equity. These barriers are most severe among African American and Hispanic men and boys from low-income families in the United States. Many of the barriers are related to patterns of stereotyped low expectations such as being identified for special-education services or for incarceration. There is the expectation that they might be able to succeed in earning money based on attributes and skills that are often not associated with educational attainment (e.g., sports, entertainment, manual labor, or substantial technical computer abilities.)

3. There has been little recent federal attention to implementing and enforcing gender equity. In some cases, policies such as federal funding of abstinence-only education reinforce sex

stereotypes and even provide inaccurate information, which may contribute to unintended pregnancies and sexually transmitted diseases.

- Federal research, development, and dissemination support for gender equity is limited compared to other education areas where there has been higher-priority national attention, such as special education or reading. Even within these priority areas, attention to gender equity has been minimal. The story is more positive in the priority areas of science, technology, engineering, and mathematics (STEM), where there has been some increase in federal funding for an array of projects to increase equity for all groups underrepresented in STEM.

4. Most recent research related to gender equity is limited to small isolated studies or some secondary analysis of older databases. The authors of chapter 6 on increasing gender equity in educational leadership indicate that most of the gender research in their area is by women doctoral students for their dissertations, which are usually small-scale studies. Chapter 5 on "The Role of Government in Advancing Gender Equity" documents minimal federal funding especially for the development and evaluation of interventions designed to advance gender equity. Even when federal funding was available for research-based replicable gender-equity programs, it has often been discontinued and the programs were not disseminated nationally. The Women's Educational Equity Act Program had a strong focus on developing effective models that could be used by others and good dissemination contracts with the Education Development Center, but the full promise of this strategy has yet to be met because of severely limited funding. The U.S. Department of Education refused to continue funding the dissemination contract and the related Gender Equity Expert Panel, which was designed to identify and provide incentives for evaluations of model programs to learn about their impact on increasing gender equity.

- Subtle barriers persist in the form of micro-inequities in classroom interactions, counseling, student ratings of teachers and low expectations. These subtle but cumulative gender inequities are often hard or expensive to measure. Thus, it is difficult to use them to document violations of Title IX and other nondiscrimination laws based not only on sex, but also on race, ethnicity, national origin, disability, sexual orientation, and social and economic status.

CONUNDRUMS IN OUR QUEST TO ACHIEVE GENDER EQUITY

Since this *Handbook for Achieving Gender Equity through Education* focuses on change and action, the authors have been asked to do much more than synthesize research addressing women's or gender issues in education. Education equity involves comparisons of diverse groups (e.g., females and males, rich and poor, majority and minority) related to values and goals. In our complex democratic society, not all paths to achieving equity are clear and unambiguous. In their analyses of these paths,

many authors identified conundrums, which are difficult problems that they have encountered in analyzing the situation and making recommendations for achieving gender equity. Where feasible, they have suggested solutions to these conundrums. The following questions and answers describe some conundrums that interfere with achieving gender-equity goals in education and provide suggestions on ways that they might be resolved.

Conundrums Related to Gender Differences and Gender Similarities

Why focus on gender differences when we are interested in increasing gender similarities or gender equality? Should gender differences be valued and reinforced or devalued and decreased?

The *Handbook* provides evidence that there are both gender differences and similarities. Most people are aware of general physiological and reproductive sex differences between most women and men as well as sociocultural differences such as masculinity and femininity.

A key concern is that, if not handled carefully, a focus on gender differences and related gender stereotypes will reinforce the differences and make it harder to advance gender equality. One of the equity concerns related to a focus on differences is that attributes associated with women are often not valued as highly as those associated with men. For example, many social and religious traditions reinforce different gender roles and usually value what the men frequently do more than what the women do. Similar stereotypes apply to the study of race differences and similarities.

This gender-difference conundrum, which is a possible impediment to advancing gender equality and increasing gender similarities, can be overcome by:

- When educators learn about patterns of gender differences and similarities, they are better able to gage the effectiveness of their teaching strategies. This is especially important when gender disparities reveal patterns of sex discrimination that violate laws such as Title IX. Statistically significant differences between males and females may be found on a wide range of meaningful measures. While these differences may not apply directly to an individual student simply based on their gender, they can help educators anticipate the numbers of males or females likely to have particular strengths and weaknesses and devise strategies to insure that students that need assistance are not being overlooked either because their needs do not fit the stereotype for their gender or, in some cases, because they do and are therefore accepted weaknesses for their gender. An example might be a reading program for students with dyslexia. Dyslexia occurs about 3.5 times more often in males than females. Knowing the pattern of gender differences for dyslexia in the population could be a guide for how many males and females would be likely to be in the program and if there was a deviation from this pattern, educators might need to look at their admission process for this program.

- Ensuring that goals valued by society are equally valued for women and men and girls and boys. For example, goals should reinforce values often associated with women such as caring for others, and encourage men to assume more of these responsibilities. (See *Handbook* chapter 1 for this goal's framework.) Also, goals should continue to encourage women to attain equal mastery of what has traditionally been valued for men such as physical and business prowess and political leadership. Despite persistent hierarchies in many aspects of U.S. society,[5] chapter authors have indicated that male roles or stereotypes should not be assumed as more valuable than attributes usually associated with females. Additionally they provide evidence that the frequent valueing of men more than women is associated with decreases in prestige and compensation in occupations such as education or psychology as these occupations attract a higher percentage of females than males. Similarly, a major report by The National Academies (2006), "Beyond Bias and Barriers: Fulfilling the Potential of Women in Academic Science and Engineering," found that women science faculty felt that they and their work were devalued compared to their men peers. Additionally, compared to equally productive men, women faculty members were paid less, promoted more slowly, and were less likely to be recognized for leadership or honors. This report and the *Handbook* have numerous recommendations on ways to value and equally reward contributions of women and girls and men and boys. In some cases, this even involves changing the criteria and measures of what is valued as seen in the addition of the writing sample to the SAT (College Board 2006).[6]

- Counteracting the bias of researchers, the media, and educators to focus on gender differences rather than similarities. The authors point out that there is a media bias to look for and publicize gender differences, and that this is often inaccurate or misleading. Many discussions of gender differences tend to omit any mention that there is more variation within the male and female populations than between them. In addition, there are compounding variations related to race, ethnicity, disability, sexual orientation, age, and social economic status that should be examined. Many of the popular discussions exaggerate gender differences and their implications for learning and often attribute them to innate differences that are unlikely to be altered by education or socialization.

- Taking care to ensure that those being studied aren't encouraged to respond according to expected gender stereotypes reinforcing sex differences. Educators sometimes face this challenge related to their own beliefs about gender roles and even more often when they address the expectations of their students and communities. A key theme of this *Handbook* is that both women and men should be assisted in attaining common societal goals. Thus, the refrain "Long live the differences" should be changed to "Celebrate individual uniqueness" and "Create a gender equitable society" by eliminating or at least decreasing the stereotyped and learned sex differences to open opportunities and benefits for all.

Is it useful to compare females and males, or should they be studied separately?

Many who study gender would prefer to focus on either women or men. However, since this *Handbook* is on achieving gender equity, it is often important to compare women and men. The following show how some of the chapter authors addressed this challenge to learn about achieving gender equity.

- The authors of chapter 6 on "Increasing Gender equity in Educational Leadership" emphasized studying women and girls in depth, often without comparing them to men and boys. They explained that past research focused mainly on men who dominate education leadership. They argued that it is important to independently study the attributes of women in these positions from their own perspectives and noted that effective women leaders may do some things differently than the effective leadership styles developed by men. They also documented increases in education administration leadership studies focusing only on women since 1985. However, in some cases, they also made relevant comparisons with men in K–12 education administration such as when they showed that a higher percentage of women are earning degrees in this area, but a higher percent of men still occupy the education administration positions.

- Although most of chapter 8 on testing and assessment focused on sex differences, the authors also explained when it was useful to develop separately normed interest tests for females and males.

- Other chapters noted problems comparing men and women in some instances. Chapter 21 on "The Role of Women's and Gender Studies in Advancing Gender Equity" suggests that rather than comparing men and women students or faculty, the key questions should focus on the attainment of gender-equity goals for both female and male students. Comparisons of women and men did not come easily to the authors of chapters 25 and 26 on "Gender Equity for American Indians" and "Gender Equity and Lesbian, Gay, Bisexual and Transgender Issues in Education" (LGBT). The authors of the chapter about American Indians point out that sex differentiation of roles for many tribes does not mean that the roles of women and men are valued differently. Also, some traditional Native American groups may be more likely to refer to three or more sexes, not just males and females. Thus, the goal of equity for men and women is not a part of the culture of most tribes and comparing females and males on various indicators is not of much interest from many perspectives. Similarly, the authors of the LGBT chapter see the issues and comparisons

---

[5]The authors of chapter 25. *Gender equity for American Indians* point out that while American Indian women and men may have different roles they are often valued equally.

[6]An early report indicates that some major universities do not plan to use this writing sample, perhaps because they are concerned that it would lower chances of accepting the sometimes scarce male students (Hass, 2006).

being related to sexual orientation/identity, rather than male and female biological designations and they see gender inequity as discrimination related to LGBT issues. Thus, they rarely have data on the sex of students, including the membership in student clubs to support LGBT students such as the Gay, Lesbian, Straight Education Network (GLSEN) and Gay-Straight Alliances.

These perspectives show that achieving gender equity can be much more nuanced than reducing gender gaps in what is desired by society. In addition to comparing females and males and studying each in depth, achieving gender equity may be measured by decreased sex segregation and gender stereotypes for both women and men.

What are appropriate and inappropriate strategies to address gender differences?

While it garners peoples' attention, an overemphasis on gender differences perpetuates gender stereotypes and often leads to inappropriate strategies to address these inequities. On the other hand, gender blindness or ignoring gender comparisons (of differences, similarities, or stereotypes) is undesirable because it does not identify or address common gender-related needs or illegal sex discrimination. Educators need to learn to identify and address gender differences appropriately. For example:

- The evidence is strong that on the average groups of women and girls do not perform as well as groups of men and boys on tests of spatial abilities, but there is also evidence that spatial abilities are learned and that often men have more experiences that helped them learn these skills. Instruction should be provided to both males and females who have not performed well on these tests. (See Chapter 2.) It is unlikely that this instruction should be provided in a single-sex setting, unless there are no men in that location who need this instruction or unless there is evidence that the type of instruction provided is only effective with either women or men.

- Even if boys and girls say they prefer different learning styles, it is important to avoid gender-differentiated instruction that can perpetuate stereotypes such as teaching girls and boys differently when there is no evidence that it will be beneficial. For example, research results do not show that teaching boys with a competitive style and girls with a cooperative style will have a desired effect on any type of learning. (See Chapters 2 and 9.)

- Research shows that making educators and students aware of gender differences and stereotypes can work in two ways. It can sometimes reinforce or increase gender differences or it can be used to encourage students to counteract these differences and stereotypes. (These issues are covered in Chapters 1, 7, and 14). The authors of the communications skills chapter 14 note that the continued reinforcement of gender stereotypes "will require examination of textbook and other formal learning materials, but it will also include attention to gendered messages found in popular culture artifacts of all types, especially in music, television, movies, computer games and programs." (p. 46)

Conundrums Related to Changing Education and Society to Create Gender Equality for All

To what extent can and should governments in the United States try to change education to eliminate sex stereotyping and sex discrimination and stratification in our pluralistic diverse society?

Global and other evidence shows that most gender roles are learned and the "Gender Equity Education Globally" reinforced by society but they can be changed. For example, chapter 3 points out that "Nordic countries have been successful in decreasing male stereotypes and improving male parenting skills through various schools interventions" (Chapter 3, p. 36). The *Handbook* authors' answer to this challenge is that federal, state, and local governments should not only ensure nondiscrimination on the basis of sex, but also should actively increase educational opportunities and gender equitable outcomes by using their resources to create a more equitable and productive society with a high quality of life for all. Many chapters especially Chapter 5 on "The Role of Government in Advancing Gender Equity in Education and Chapter 20 on "Gender Equity in Career and Technical Education" suggest ways to start this transformation in the United States. They urge the development of comprehensive strategies to prioritize and implement needed changes outside of what is covered under current laws.

What is the role of education in changing learning experiences to foster gender equity in desired outcomes?

The 1985 *Handbook* summary chapter noted, "The pattern is quite clear: there are larger sex differences in outcomes in areas that are most influenced by socialization. Another related pattern is that as sex roles in society become less differentiated and as female and male students receive more similar learning experiences, the sex differences in education-related outcomes decrease" (p. 492). The current 2007 *Handbook* chapters reinforce this conclusion, but what should educators do when society or specific population groups have strong views that value certain gender-role stereotypes or when the relationship of some stereotypes to desired outcomes is confusing?

Chapter 22, "Gender Equity for African Americans" reports on common teacher and societal stereotypes. It points out that some stereotypes of African American girls as "fearless and emotionally stronger than men" (p. 17) may not have a positive impact. Just as negative stereotypes and expectations are likely to have detrimental impact on educational attainment, the authors suggest that this positive stereotype may jeopardize the Black girl's social and emotional development (p. 471). The chapter also highlights Noguera's contention that "the benefits of patriarchy, like the benefits of racism, are in many ways subtle and taken for granted with the privileged and ubiquitous dominance of men, even Black men, going uncontested. This privileged position may help to explain why the crisis of the Black male receives attention, while the continued oppression of Black females is accepted as the norm" (Noguera, 1997, p. 15 in Chapter 4 on "The Impact of Education on Gender Equity in Employment and Its Outcomes").

Points out that education achievement has little to do with the gender-wage gap, *Handbook* authors suggest that this conundrum can be resolved by learning what works to ensure educational opportunity and achievement without regard to sex-role stereotyping and bias. The authors would not approve reinforcing cultural bias and gender inequality by groups such as those advocating sex segregating African American males. Such groups must avoid discriminating even if they think it will help them. Research and legal opinions regarding the 14th Amendment and Title IX do not support their beliefs. The Handbook authors argue sex segregated programs should be restricted to educational approaches that meet the standards in the 1975 Title IX regulations.

How can education change values and rewards in society to promote gender equality?

Chapters 3, 4, 7, 17, 20, and 29 provide evidence that in the United States and globally, activities associated with women receive less pay and prestige compared with similar activities by men. These chapters also note that when women become a majority in occupations such as psychology, child care and elementary-school teaching, the autonomy, pay, and prestige of the occupation is likely to decrease.

Educators working with nontraditional occupations face a values conundrum. Should they encourage more women to go into higher-paying and prestigious occupations that have been traditional for men? Should they encourage men to go into low-paying occupations that are traditional for women? Or for the more ideal solution, can education help change society so that occupations requiring comparable educational preparation, skill, and risk become similarly valued and rewarded? Should education try to eliminate gender-based differential education aspirations and career choices?

Chapter 4 authors Richardson and Sandoval suggest that society would be more gender equitable if:

- There was an increase in the value of female-stereotyped roles. Now, "the closer the job is to mothering young children, the lower the pay" (chapter 4, p. 46). And, "When we look at how jobs are valued, it seems clear that technology is valued more than caring" (chapter 4, p. 54).
- And if there is widespread use of men assume more of the family-care responsibilities, but also implement family-friendly policies to help women and men who assume caring responsibilities (pp.12–13). For example, increased flexibility in hiring, tenure, and promotion policies to account for needs of faculty members as they go through various life stages was a key recommendation in the 2006 report of the Committee on Maximizing the Potential of Women in Academic Science and Engineering (National Academies, 2006).

The *Handbook* authors realize this is an area where gender-equity advocates in education need to develop consensus strategies in conjunction with their peers working on gender equity in employment.

Conundrums Related to Defining Desired Gender Equity Outcomes

What is Parity/Equality/Equity? Should close to 50/50 female and male distribution of all that is valued be the goal for most education process and outcome statistics?

The authors of the *Handbook* raise more questions than answers about tipping points to guide the use of specific remedies to increase gender equity or equality in outcomes. A key consideration is to cause no harm to the achieving group while enhancing the outcomes of the group in need. Generally, the authors discuss, but don't recommend, when to declare gender equity achieved or even at what point a gender disparity is illegal.[7] The exceptions to this lack of specificity occur when there are governmental standards such as the three-prong test of compliance related to athletics under Title IX (See chapter 18) and federal definitions of nontraditional occupations as having "individuals from one gender comprise less than 25 percent of the individuals employed in each such occupation" (chapter 20, p. 424). The following are some questions related to gender-parity goals that the *Handbook* authors have discussed:

- Should the current slight dominance of women students in U.S. postsecondary education be valued and purposefully retained because women need the postsecondary credentials more to compete in the biased job market that still favors men? Or should affirmative action for undergraduate men prevail along with affirmative action to get women and men in specific programs such as engineering where women are underrepresented or nursing where men are underrepresented?

Chapter 30 on postsecondary education noted that some private undergraduate colleges try "to keep at least a 60/40 ratio of women to men on their campuses" (p. 641). However, attention to admissions ratios should not result in quotas that block the aspirations of either women or men. Sex discrimination in undergraduate admissions is allowed under Title IX for private colleges even if they are prohibited from sex discrimination in all other areas of Title IX coverage, but it is not allowed for public institutions or graduate programs in private colleges. The following example describes how knowledge about patterns of gender differences have been used to help create a gender-balanced student body.

Admissions criteria have been developed to use knowledge about typical sex differences such as that women receive better grades and men receive better test scores. Instead of following the trend to give preference to good grades more than high SAT scores because grades are more predictive of college success, Towson University, a public institution in Maryland, has a program to admit some students if they have SAT scores

---

[7]While true gender equality in achieving what is desired by society would be a 50/50 distribution related to the proportion of girls and women or boys and men in the population, society's tolerance for reaching the final equitable outcome goals may differ for different outcomes and these may even change over time as progress is made. As some of the authors suggest, an analysis of needs and costs and benefits can also be included in determining acceptable gender ratios in attaining specific goals at any given time in any part of society.

that are better than the university average, but high-school grades below the University average. In "Affirmative action for white C+ guys," Jaschik (2006) raised questions about both the effectiveness and legality of this type of affirmative action.

What does gender equity mean in these cases? Should there be full gender parity (affirmative action for males) in college admissions even if women meet the criteria more fully than men? To what extent is it legal or wise to put more efforts into the recruitment of the less-represented group or provide incentives or activities that might be especially attractive to the underrepresented group such as starting a football team at a formerly women's college to attract men students? Supreme Court decisions related to affirmative action such as the 2003 University of Michigan cases (*Grutter v. Bollinger* and *Gratz v. Bollinger*) can also provide some guidance on these goals and fair ways to achieve them.

- Does decreasing the gender gap in writing mean that fewer women will excell in writing? In addressing this conundrum, all must remember that reducing gender gaps is not a zero-sum game—the goal should be to help all boys and girls improve to the full extent possible. The authors of the "Gender Equity in Communication Skills" chapter 14 explain "Given that the entry-level jobs most open to women have higher need for literacy than those jobs that are male identified and less open to women, if schools were to treat girls and boys in ways to try to insure no differences in literacy outcomes, then such treatment would, in its effect, be inequitable" (chapter 14, note 4, p. 283). This potential "remedy" is raised to stimulate thought about long-term outcomes, but in the authors would agree that when boys are underachieving in writing, they along with all the girls who are underachieving in writing should have their educational needs met. It may be that a remedial writing class may have more males than females, but females should not be neglected. The same process should be followed in math or physics where strategies are developed to decrease gender stereotyping in content and improve the performance of ALL underachievers.

- Should women continue to invest in schooling more than men even if there is less economic payoff for them to attend school? This is related to stereotypical career choices and continued sex discrimination in employment especially when employers do not provide more equitable rewards for individuals with more education. The chapter 4 authors do not suggest simplistic responses to this question. Instead, they more often suggest structural changes as described in Homer's recommendations to change the nature of many vocational courses so they are more likely to be a good solution for both girls and boys. This was done with the reorientation of "the office training program that used to be 90 percent female, with the girls training to be secretaries and the boys in accounting and computing," to "one comprehensive Business Services Program that all office students take, and 35 percent of these students are male" (Homer, 1997, p. 13). Similarly, job descriptions and classifications can be based on education levels, experience, abilities, and knowledge in ways that value the relevant typical strengths of both women and men, so that they can be selected in non-sex-discriminatory ways. No one should

be recruited into programs that do not provide a living wage and they should also realize the high likelihood of having multiple careeers over time.

- To what extent should United States societal goals include gender parity in athletics, military, law enforcement, nontraditional occupations, political leadership, etc? How should societal needs and goals to overcome barriers related to discrimination, sex bias, and stereotyping be factored into establishing specific gender-equitable outcome goals?

Many argue that determining what is equitable is difficult to establish as long as barriers related to discrimination, bias, and stereotyping exist. Each woman and man should have an equal opportunity to reach their potential without facing these barriers. Gender-equitable outcome goals need to be developed based on knowledge about discrimination, stereotyping, and effective strategies to meet societal needs.

Conundrums Related to Inequities in Educational Processes that May Lead to the Creation of Gender-Equitable Outcomes

The process and outcome conceptual framework for examining gender equity in and through education is detailed in chapter 1, "Examining the Achievement of Gender Equity in and Through Education" and referenced in numerous other chapters. It is useful in addressing many of the issues raised by these conundrums.

Should special recruitment activities be provided to encourage men to enter lower prestige traditional women's occupations such as education of young children or nursing? Similarly, should women be recruited to enter fields where they are underrepresented such as engineering, the military, police work, etc?

The relationship of the laws and research and evaluation to address the issues related to this process and outcome conundrum are discussed in chapter 4, "Impact of Education on Gender Equity in Employment and Its Outcomes," and in chapter 20, "Gender Equity in Career and Technical Education." Special incentives and bonus offers for entering a field are illegal under Title IX and Title VII.

Is sex discrimination in educational processes allowed for some purposes if it is not exclusionary?

Aside from privacy reasons (such as contact sports and discussions of human sexuality or other exceptions in the Title IX Regulations), is it sometimes okay to treat girls and boys differently in the same coed class or in a single-sex class? (They should not be treated differently on the basis of their sex, but individuals can be treated differently for other reasons such as ability.) Is it fair to have special facilities or resources (such as women's centers) primarily for girls or boys or for women or men? (Yes, this is okay, but both women and men must also be allowed to use the single-sex-focused facilities and services.) A common solution is to provide education that meets the needs of women or men such as women's studies courses all of which are also available to men who want to participate although they may be a minority group in the class. (See chapter 21, "The Role of Women's and Gender Studies in Advancing Gender Equity.) Sheila Tobias, whose early work identified and addressed math anxiety, said it was common to allow men as well as women who felt they needed help with math anxiety to come to the math-anxiety clinics.

In some cases are risks of sex discrimination in educational processes worth taking to decrease sex differences in outcomes valued by society?

This justification has been made to allow experiments with sex-segregated programs for girls or boys under the 1975 Title IX Regulations. In the following discussion, sex-segregated educational processes, such as schools, classes, or extracurricular activities, will often be referred to collectively as single-sex or sex-segregated education interventions. The conundrums here are especially challenging because of the new controversial October 25, 2006, Regulations implementing Title IX, (Office for Civil Rights, 2006). These 2006 Title IX Regulations weaken the legal protections against sex discrimination in single-sex classes, schools, and extracurricular activities in nonvocational K–12 education institutions receiving federal financial assistance.[8]

The following four questions and answers related to this conundrum are discussed in detail because they are important to the future of gender equity in the United States and because they address important conceptual and practical issues relevant to many of the *Handbook* chapters.

1. Is sex segregation in education a risk?
    Yes, single-sex interventions are generally a risk to gender equity and many other education improvement goals. The *Handbook* authors provide much evidence that single-sex education or sex segregation[9] even if it is voluntary is likely to be associated with increased sex discrimination in educational processes and outcomes. In fact, goals of this *Handbook,* which are outlined in chapter 1 and elsewhere, specify the importance of decreasing both sex stereotyping and sex segregation to achieve gender equity. The research reviewed in this *Handbook* reinforces the conclusions in the 1954 Supreme Court *Brown v. Board of Education* decision that separate segregated education is not equal. This applies to sex as well as race segregation. There is substantial evidence that sex segregation is more likely to reinforce than combat stereotypes and that the lower-prestige or lower-valued group almost always gets fewer resources than the dominant group.
    Single-sex education is only permitted in some specific cases such as for remedial or affirmative purposes according to the 1975 Title IX Regulations. Part of the conundrum re-

lated to determining the risks associated with sex-segregated education for specific purposes is that some single-sex groupings may be used to decrease sex discrimination and sex stereotyping in education processes and in the outcomes. For example, there is some evidence that specific model single-sex programs that address inequities in the experiences and expectations related to girls and women in some areas of science where they have been underrepresented may contribute to decreased gender gaps in science achievement. There is also evidence that the gender gap in science achievement is closing without the use of single-sex programs or schools. Additionally, there is little information on the effectiveness of single-sex compared to coeducational or nonexclusionary programs (such as women's studies programs) that are designed to address the needs of the less-represented group but are open to all qualified participants. It is even harder to find examples of equally effective single-sex interventions to help boys increase gender-equitable outcomes.

As just discussed, educators contemplating single-sex instruction should first look for information on coeducation programs or policies associated with closing the gender gap. They also may find that specific aspects of an effective single-sex program can be effectively included in a coeducational program. Finally, if they have evidence that it is best to have a program focused on the frequent needs of women (or men) can it be modeled on the nonexclusionary strategies used in many math-anxiety programs that also allow men with similar needs?

2. Are educational processes in sex-segregated environments more likely to perpetuate sex discrimination than if they are provided in a coeducational environment?
    As documented in chapter 9 "Gender Equity in Coeducational and Single-Sex Educational Environments," there is plenty of evidence that there is sex discrimination in coeducational classes, but little evidence that single-sex classes are better at eliminating any types of sex discrimination and stereotyping than coed classes. The research shows that teachers and classes in either environment may be perpetuating or, in some cases, doing a good job at eliminating sex stereotyping and discrimination. However, it is often easier to identify inequities in all types of education-process indicators or resources when schools or classes are sex segregated. For example, even in the California Dual Academy study described in chapter 9, the researchers found that the qualifications and expectations of the teachers for the girls and boys academies were different and inequitable even though the facilities in the same campus were usually comparable. Similarly, when the Brighter Choice Charter Schools for boys and girls Albany, NY, had to split into two buildings in 2006, the boys were moved to the new school down the block from the old school (Office of Innovation and Im-

---

[8]The October 2006 Title IX regulations are discussed in more detail in chapter 9.

[9]As discussed later some well-designed single-sex interventions might be desirable in some circumstances because they are effective in increasing gender-quitable outcomes. However they are most likely to be a good strategy to advance gender equity if they are operated in a nonexclusionary way like college women's studies programs that always are open to men.

provement, 2006). With the focus on increased educational accountability, it should be easier to document and use Web sites to distribute information on gender inequities in single-sex environments than in mixed-sex environments where it is often essential to have observers to document the subtle micro-inequities in the treatment of girls and boys in the co-educational classroom.

3. Are single-sex intervention programs aimed at increasing gender equity being effectively monitored and evaluated to show that they advance gender equity?

No, the U.S. Department of Education (ED) has not included adequate accountability and evaluation requirements in the 2006 regulation changes. And it has failed to provide any other assistance or guidance to assure that risky sex segregation would be limited in accordance with the exceptions allowed in the 1975 Title IX Regulations.

Although sex segregation is allowed under the 1975 Title IX regulations if it results in decreasing sex discrimination in the outcomes, ED provides no guidance on identifying programs that do this. In fact, ED discontinued its Gender Equity Expert Panel which had criteria and procedures to identify promising and exemplary programs that were effective in increasing gender equity.[10] (Also see in Chapter 5, "The Role of Government in Advancing Gender Equity in Education")

4. Why are organizations that support gender equity concerned that the October 25, 2006, Title IX Regulations will increase rather than decrease sex discrimination in education?[11]

Organizations that support gender equity see many problems with the U.S. Department of Education's inappropriate weakening of Title IX protections against sex discrimination to allow for increased risky sex-segregated schools, classes, and extracurricular activities. In addition to lack of evidence that single-sex education is more effective than comparable coeducational education, there are important legal, technical, and practical criticisms of the October 2006 Regulations.

Legal objections. The new regulations violate the regulations they are replacing and do not further any government interest that is more important than ending sex discrimination, the sole purpose of Title IX. There is no exceedingly persuasive legal justification for allowing more than the remedial or affirmative single-sex education exceptions already allowed under the 1975 Title IX Regulations (Office for Civil Rights, 1975).[12] The justification by Secretary Spellings in announcing the October 2006 Regulations that "Research shows that some students may learn better in single-sex education environments" (Secretary Spellings, October 24, 2006) falls extremely short of meeting the exceedingly persuasive standard used in the Supreme Court Virginia Military Institute (VMI) decision and would be in violation of the Equal Protection Clause of the Fourteenth Amendment. (See Stone, 2004 for the legal reasoning and chapter 9 for a review of the inconclusive research findings on the value of single-sex education.)

Technical objections. Compared to the 1975 Title IX Regulations these confusing 2006 Regulations pay less attention to the risks of sex discrimination in both the education process related to the use of the single-sex interventions and in the types of outcomes that are sufficiently worthwhile to justify taking this risk. The 1975 Title IX Regulations contain a few exceptions to allow some types of single-sex education in classrooms and schools such as if there is evidence that this sex segregation is being used for affirmative or remedial purposes to end sex discrimination in the desired outcomes. The 2006 Title IX Regulations did not remove this "affirmative" justification language, but they also allow risky single-sex education for purposes that are not related to ending sex discrimination.

The 2006 Title IX Regulations also have no active accountability provisions to determine if there is sex discrimination or even if they accomplish "important governmental or educational objectives" such as improving educational achievement. The Regulation's guidance on evaluation is passive since organizations implementing single-sex education are only supposed to keep a two-year evaluation on file in case they are investigated instead of actively publicly sharing their evaluation design, plan, and results for public scrutiny.

While the 2006 Title IX Regulations contain vague suggestions of compliance with nondiscrimination provisions of Title IX and the Equal Protection Clause of the 14th Amendment, there is no clear procedural or substantive guidance on how potential implementers of single-sex education should provide evidence to show that they are not discriminating in education processes or outcomes. The 2006 Title IX Regulations fail to help educators know what indicators should be compared to show nondiscrimination and also what *substantially equal* process activities and resources mean. A key concern is that substantially equal is not equal and that this change does not maintain the equality standards that were established in the Brown decision and that can be used to show that separate is not equal. The 2006 Title IX Regulations also eliminate the need to justify the single-sex intervention on the grounds that it will be likely to decrease sex discrimination in the outcomes. In summary, although the 2006 Title Regulations suggest that segregated instructional activities for girls or boys should be as equal as possible to conform to the standards[13] in the VMI decision with the exception of re-

---

[10]Of the 11 programs recommended by the Gender Equity Expert Panel as promising or exemplary, only two were single sex and they were both developed for single-sex environments such as a program on orientation to nontraditional careers for women in correctional institutions and a program for Girl Scouts in science museums.

[11]The following reasons relate to this conundrum. There are also many more reasons outlined on the Web sites of organizations such as www.feminist.org/education and www.ncwge.org.

[12]Many also note that these 1975 Title IX Regulations have greatly contributed to advancing gender equity for the past 30 years and see no reason why they should be reversed at this time.

[13]This means that schools or classes for boys and girls or the comparison coed class or school should have equitable tangible and intangible resources such as facilities, endowments, qualified teachers and career networks for their graduates.

questing that evaluation information be on file, there are no on-going requirements to insure accountability for equality.

Practical and logical education resource allocation objections.

The gender-equity organizations believe that the highest standards of evidence of effectiveness should be used to determine the risks of any single-sex interventions since all single-sex programs, especially those that are exclusively for girls or boys, require some sex discrimination in the education process.

The gender-equity organizations argue that it is unwise to view sex segregation as a potentially important tool in improving any aspect of education when there is no evidence that it is anything more than a potentially damaging fad. For example, even the few programs that have some evidence that they help girls attain desired outcomes in science rarely have evidence that they are more effective than coeducational programs addressing these same needs. Since there is limited funding for gender equity and education in general, gender equity organizations often remind those who may want to try sex segregation with the expectation that it will help either boys or girls that sex-segregated education is generally more expensive than a high-quality coeducational alternative. Most of the single-sex charter schools, for example, receive additional resources. The same is also true for even dual-academy-type schools as shown by the California experiment described in chapter 9. The dual schools for girls and boys received extra money from the state and, even though they were in the same school campus or building, dual academies incurred additional expenses such as paying for two sets of school administrators. The next section describes the additional expenses needed for an adequate evaluation of single-sex interventions and the possibility of high legal fees from litigation when students find that they are being discriminated against.

5. How can research and evaluation be used to resolve this conundrum?

Most educators want to do what will most likely help all students, and they do not want to follow fads that might help some students if there is evidence that the risks of helping some students will likely harm others. They also do not want to waste their valuable education resources on legal defenses for their actions and, in many cases, they would rather not spend their funds for expensive high-quality evaluations to prove that their risky single-sex intervention has positive results even if these positive results are not related to *decreasing* sex discrimination. However, they will still have to prove that their process indicators and their outcomes/results do not *increase* sex discrimination. Since the 2006 Regulation says that the single-sex intervention still has to comply with Title IX, educators still might lose a lawsuit if there is any evidence that the process indicators in the interventions for girls and boys are unequal. For example, the VMI Supreme Court decision found inequities in many types of resources available for men at VMI compared to what was available for women in the supposedly comparable single-sex college).

Researchers and evaluators can play important roles in addressing this conundrum and providing guidance to educators.

- They can help the education decision makers obtain and examine evidence related to the likely success or failure of the proposed single-sex intervention for students in attaining important goals by comparing what happened to the participants in the single-sex intervention with comparable students who received similar instruction in a coeducational setting or in a three-way comparison with (boys only, girls only and coeducational). Researchers and evaluators can also help the decision makers learn if the previous use of the single-sex intervention was associated with increased sex discrimination in the education process and in the outcomes.

- If the organization decides to proceed with the single-sex interventions, the researchers and evaluators can help design and implement an evaluation that will meet the criteria of effectiveness established by the U.S. Department of Education's What Works Clearinghouse to determine if the intervention is responsible for the outcomes. They should also work with the institution's Title IX Coordinator and federal program accountability staff to make sure that there are no aspects of sex discrimination or sex stereotyping in the implementation of the single-sex intervention that would discriminate against students who are participating in the intervention or who are participating in other alternatives. If there are separate interventions for boys and girls, it would be necessary to keep records on the resources and activities for each compared with students who choose a coeducational alternative. (See chapter 9 for descriptions of challenges in related comparative research on single-sex schools.)

- The researchers and evaluators should prepare annual reports that should be posted on the institution's Web sites to allow all constituents to learn about the success and problems in the single-sex intervention as it relates to all the process and outcome indicators and any instances of sex discrimination. As with all other research and evaluation, short- and long-term results should be provided and disaggregated not only on the sex of the students, but also on other key characteristics such as race, ethnicity, parental income, age, and ability.

- Researchers and evaluators should help interpret the findings from the annual report and, at least every two years, make recommendations about the cancellation or continuation of the single-sex intervention based on the results and evidence of patterns of sex discrimination. Part of this information should examine relative costs of the program and the evaluation compared to the benefits. These recommendations and related information should be posted on the institution's Web site and compliance with the recommendations should be checked by the U.S. Department of Education every two years to justify the continuation of this risky type of sex discrimination.

The reviews of research and evaluation in various chapters in this Handbook,[14] have helped develop some answers especially

---

[14]Chapters 1, 5, 7 and 9 have provided us with substantial insights to address this conundrum.

related to this conundrum about whether risks of sex discrimination in educational processes are worth taking to decrease sex discrimination in outcomes valued by society.

> However, we would also like to point out a related disturbing conundrum that is broader than gender equity. Department of Education would promulgate policies such as the 2006 Title IX Regulations that counteract research evidence and that fail to apply their own research and evaluation standards to an area where they have unique responsibility—protecting civil rights in education throughout the nation. This is especially disturbing since the Department applies these standards of effectiveness to other curriculum subject areas where states typically have more responsibility than the federal government, such as programs to improve student achievement in reading

The *Handbook* authors hope these last conundrums will be resolved soon by withdrawing these harmful 2006 Title IX Regulations and by educating decision makers covered by Title IX to avoid single-sex education unless they have evidence that the specific intervention they plan to use works to increase gender-equity outcomes and that it works much better than a coeducational option. The limited allowance of sex segregation under the 1975 Title IX Regulations as one means to achieve gender equitable outcomes can be maintained only when it decreases sex discrimination in outcomes. However, if educators focus on high-quality gender-equitable coeducation for all, they will avoid obvious threats to equity as well as the loss of valuable resources since single-sex fads are more costly in terms of operation, evaluation, and litigation than high-quality gender-equitable coeducation.

SOLUTIONS OR SELECTED RECOMMENDATIONS TO ADVANCE GENDER EQUITY

Authors of each chapter developed recommendations for policy, practice, and research to advance gender equity. Table 31.1 "Key Chapter Recommendations" shows chapter numbers to indicate chapters containing the recommendations. The rows are organized according to the six parts of the *Handbook*. In general, the chapter recommendations are in numerical order from the top to the bottom of the table—with chapter 30 on postsecondary education in the bottom row. The recommendations for more gender-equitable practice have been separated into two columns to indicate the practices and programs that are primarily focused on helping students and those that are focused on educators. Authors of chapters have noted that many of the recommendations from the 1985 *Handbook* still merit implementation and that as in 1985 "progress on implementing these recommendations has been sporadic and not necessarily enduring" (chapter 7, p. 43). Recommendations have been shortened and consolidated if they were similar in multiple chapters. For example, many chapters recommended that Title IX be specifically applied to their focus area. We consolidated these recommendations in Part II

on administrative strategies but indicated multiple-chapter numbers, so that readers can obtain increased understanding of the importance of these recommendations in different contexts. On the other hand, if the recommendation was related to chapter 19 on formal sexuality education, but also mentioned in chapter 5 on the role of government, we put it with the sexuality education chapter. Often recommendations specified for one chapter would be equally worthwhile in many other chapters even if they were not mentioned by all the authors.

CONCLUSION

We hope that this updated *Handbook for Achieving Gender Equity through Education* will help readers understand the importance of this area of inquiry and action for students, educators, and the public, and will help create a more equitable global society. We have learned that key gender gaps and overt discrimination can be diminished especially in educational processes identified as having negative consequences for specific populations such as women or men and that are covered by civil rights laws. However, we have also been disappointed that many of the promising efforts to systematically eliminate gender inequities via educational programs and federal support for research, development, evaluation, and dissemination have greatly diminished. We recommend that the community of gender equity advocates use what has been learned in this *Handbook* to obtain federal and other resources to make much more systematic progress in purposefully using education to create a more gender-equitable society.

We hope that the authoritative information from over 200 authors and reviewers will help readers address their own goal-related conundrums or specific practical questions about achieving gender equity both in and through education. Finally, we invite you to work with colleagues on implementing some of the many recommendations in Table 31.1 as well as others stated implicitly or explicitly in the chapters. As you do so, we encourage you to visit and contribute to the Web page that is being designed to accompany this *Handbook* and keep the ever-changing research-based information on achieving gender equity education as current, accurate, and useful as possible to a wide range of *Handbook* users.

ACKNOWLEDGMENTS

Special thanks to Feminist Majority Foundation summer 2006 interns Kamaria Campbell from Duke University and Jennifer Lee from the University of Virginia who helped prepare the initial version of Table 31.1 "Key Chapter Recommendations" and to the Feminist Majority Foundation's Shana Carignan for improving the Table format. Also, thanks to reviewers Eleanor Smeal, Feminist Majority Foundation, Arlington, VA and Bernice Sandler, Women's Research and Education Institute, Washington, DC for their helpful suggestions.

TABLE 31.1 Key Chapter Recommendations

	Policy Recommendations As They Relate to Organizational Improvement	Educational Practice Recommendations As They Relate to Learners	Educational Practice Recommendations as They Relate to Educators (teachers, administrators, parents)	Recommendations for Research, Development, Dissemination and Evaluation
I. Facts & Assumptions about the Nature & Value of Gender Equity (chs. 1, 2, 3, 4)	Identify & enforce international as well as national, state, and local policies that are likely to advance gender equity education. This includes funding and support for gender equity provisions in Education for All & the UN Millennium Development Goals. (ch. 1, 3, 5) Work with NGOs that promote women's rights and support education programs that foster empowerment (ch. 3, 5, others) Support comparable worth policies to decrease gender-related pay gaps in traditionally gendered occupations with equal educational requirements. Don't continue to value technology more than caring. (ch. 4, 20) Change U.S. policies to allow women and others receiving public assistance to obtain education and job training to improve their status in the labor force. Increase support for education and training in TANF and WIA programs (ch 4–5, 20)	Teachers should not use gender or other stereotypes in expectations for student achievement or in advising students. (chs. 2, 7, 9-10, 14, 20, 22–30) Educators should use nonsexist materials and challenge cultural stereotypes such as those that heighten the perceived conflict between family and workplace roles for both sexes. (chs. 3–4, 7, 9, 11, 20, others) Teachers should teach in gender-free ways to expose both sexes to a wide range of instructional styles and careers. (chs. 2, 4, 7, 9) Teachers should teach an "explicit curriculum in spatial skills" to help all the girls and boys that need them. (chs. 2, 12–13) Teachers should teach self-efficacy and "the how/why of political action. (ch. 2, others) Teachers should teach students to recognize common forms of bias including bias in the media (chs. 7, 14, 29)	Educators should change from beliefs that ability is innate to beliefs that hard work and perseverance will help eliminate gender inequities. (ch. 2, 3, 4, others) Educators should convey to parents that most gender differences, especially in math, are small or nonexistent and thus they should be wary of and resist single-sex education arguments based on this premise. (chs. 2, 9, 12) Encourage educators at all levels and in all countries to understand their responsibilities to advance gender equity using national and international laws. (ch. 3, others) Educate students, educators, & the public about gender-equity rights & responsibilities. (chs. 1, 3–5, others) Provide financial support and training to Title IX coordinators so they can participate in national meetings on gender-equity education and learn from each other.	Encourage the use of specific gender equity definitions ; use the process & outcome framework in research and legislation. (chs. 1, 9) "Researchers should be aware of the bias toward finding gender differences and ignoring gender similarities. They should strive for balanced reporting of differences and similarities." (ch. 2, p. 33) Collect and report higher quality and more sex-disaggregated statistics. Information should cover : –student attendance, retention, and progress over time for a wide variety of populations. –large-scale longitudinal data sets to track historical and demographic changes in women's status in the labor force and subgroup populations. (chs. 4, 6–all chapters) Sample topics for global and U.S. research include: –children's perceptions of discrimination and the development of healthy ways of coping with it –supportive roles for family members & educators to prepare students to address discrimination and harassment. –career aspirations vs. actual choices –entry into and success in non-traditional jobs for both women and men –links between educational achievement and status in the labor force by gender, race, etc. (chs. 4, 20, 26, others)
II. Administrative Strategies for Implementing Gender Equity (chs. 5, 6, 7)	Maintain full strength of Title IX/other federal and state civil rights laws and regulations & fully implement them. (chs. 5–11, 13, 18, 30) Increase proactive activities, funding and technical assistance, and enforcement of federal and state civil rights laws. (ch. 5)	Teach all to recognize and combat common forms of gender bias ranging from invisibility to stereotyping. (ch. 7) Raise awareness of Title IX protections for students, parents, & educators. (chs. 5–7, 9)	Education leaders at all levels need to be thoughtful about social justice & strategic in promoting equity. They should ensure the full implementation of Title IX & appoint & support active, effective Title IX coordinators to institutionalize and monitor gender equity in their schools. (chs. 5, 6)	Restore and expand federal support for the research, development, evaluation, dissemination and implementation of effective high-quality replicable gender equity programs, practices, and resources. (chs. 5–7) –Conduct research on the implementation of civil rights laws (chs. 7.9). –Conduct and report on equity audits that focus on gender.

Increase efforts to make the public aware of compliance with the provisions of the Title IX regulations: Have GAO study national awareness and compliance with the Title IX coordinator regulations by:

—Extensive use of monitoring/accountability practices to judge progress in decreasing sex discrimination in athletics, career and technical education, and many other areas at state, local, and institutional levels.

—Supporting the development of a vigorous NGO led network of Title IX coordinators and their gender-equity allies.

—Requiring Title IX coordinators to use Web sites to post information on their services & provide annual reports with disaggregated data on students' and employees' challenges and progress in achieving gender equity. (chs. 3, 5, 8–9, 13, 18, 20, 30, others)

Expand coverage, guidance, and support for gender equity (for example: pass ERA, stronger state laws, appoint and support Title IX Coordinators, U.S. ED Special Assistant for Gender Equity, Commissions on gender equity; gender, equity counselors, etc.) (chs. 5, 18, 20, 23)

Restore and expand federal-gender equity programs such as WEEA, Equity Assistance Centers, State CRA Title IV funding, Gender-Equity Research, Gender-Equity Expert Panel, Vocational Education Sex-Equity Coordinators and program funds, NSF Gender-Equity Programs, WID gender-equity education work, etc, (chs. 5, 7, 9, 18, 20)

Strengthen and attend to gender-equity provisions in administrator, teacher certification and institutional accreditation requirements. (chs. 5–7)

Use programs to help students learn to interact in nonsterectypic, gender equitable ways with their peers, teachers, and others.

Every school should have at least one highly qualified Title IX coordinator with sufficient resources and support to implement the law. Interested teachers should also volunteer to become Title IX coordinators in their schools and serve on Title IX Committees. (chs. 5, 7, 9)

Involve Title IX coordinators and committees of students and staff in reviewing education policies and practices related to gender. This periodic evaluat on could include curricular materials and syllabi to see if gender issues, sex differences, gender bias, and discrimination and other similar issues and topics are part of a new teacher's preparation. (chs. 5, 7)

Develop, improve, share and evaluate gender-equity resources and models to help Title IX coordinators and other educators work with each other as well as other gender equity advocates (chs. 5, 7)

Education students, administrators, and faculty should be familiar with Title IX protections, and implement those protections in their own teaching, coaching, etc. This should just be one part of gender-equity training in teacher and administrator education programs. They should also ensure that teacher and administrator education texts and resources provide substantial information on Title IX as well as strategies to combat sex stereotyping. Examples of pre- and in-service programs that address gender equity include: "Succeeding at Fairness: Effective Teaching for All Students" and "A Women's Place Is in the Curriculum" and a new text *Gender in the Classroom*, Sadker and Silber 2006. (ch. 5–7, 9)

—Collect baseline & then periodic information on Title IX implementation & activities of Title IX coordinators.

—Ensure that NCLB & other federal programs & activities include gender analysis in all data reporting as well as the AYP calculations, the work of the What Works Clearinghouse, etc. (chs. 5, 8).

—Continue & expand NCES reports on education equity for girls & women.

Conduct research on:

—how to "build the gender equity education infrastructure with a focus on Title IX Gender Equity Coordinators"

—how states are holding local educational agencies accountable for state and federal civil rights laws through Title IX reviews, Office of Civil Rights Memorandum of Agreement Compliance reviews and other monitoring and technical assistance efforts.

—successful women and minority administrators to provide models for career choices"

—the challenges minority women face and the "intersection of race, culture and gender"

—the relation of leadership and family responsibilities on men and women

—the distribution of senior administrative positions in relation to gender

—gender differences in teacher evaluations of students and student evaluations of teachers (chs. 5–8, 22–25)

Require accreditation bodies to evaluate teaching programs on gender equity (chs. 7, 9)

(continued)

TABLE 31.1   Key Chapter Recommendations

	Policy Recommendations As They Relate to Organizational Improvement	Educational Practice Recommendations As They Relate to Learners	Educational Practice Recommendations as They Relate to Educators (teachers, administrators, parents)	Recommendations for Research, Development, Dissemination and Evaluation
	Institutionalize attention to gender equity in education associations via programs, awards, and organizational policies and activities. (chs. 5–7)		School of Education accreditation visitation teams should review gender-equity protections to ensure compliance with Title IX and the 14th amendment. (chs. 7, 9)	
			Work to end the gendered nature of teaching. Recruit underrepresented men and women into education fields. (ch. 7)	
			Women and men in positions of power in educational systems must deliberately mentor more women and especially more women of color. Additionally they must help all successfully balance family responsibilities and job demands. (chs. 4, 6)	
III. General Educational Practices for Promoting Gender Equity (chs. 8, 9, 10, 11)	Maintain the goal of gender equity in coeducational schools (ch. 9)	Use exemplary and promising programs that have some indicators that they advance gender equity. (Most chapters)	Use professional standards and guidelines for equitable use and interpretation of test scores. (ch. 8)	More attention needs to be paid (by researchers, test makers, and test users) to test-related psychological factors including, stereotype threat, and possibly factors associated with anxiety in testing situations and risk taking that differ by gender. (ch. 8)
	Enforce the 1975 Title IX regulations that limit single-sex schooling and rescind the 2006 Title IX Regulations because they weaken protections against sex discrimination. Require adequate evidence to ensure that single-sex education does not increase any aspect of sex discrimination including the outcomes (ch. 9)	To create more gender-equitable assessment –administer tests in environments that are familiar or friendly –teach self-assessment skills to students. –teach students test-taking skills & teachers to use strategies to eliminate bias in tests. (ch. 8)	Teacher education and materials should decrease sex-stereotyped classroom interactions and learning. (chs. 7, 9,14) Publicize protections against sexual harassment under Titles VII & IX so that parents, teachers & administrators will use them as needed.	Research the new technological approaches to assessment to ensure that they are gender-fair (ch. 8) Research on teacher classroom assessment practices in relation to student subgroups such as gender, ethnicity, and special education status. (ch. 8)
	Continue federal grant programs for gender equity such as the NSF programs in science, mathematics, engineering & technology. (chs. 5, 10, 12, 13).	Use direct interventions to encourage girls to use/like technology and to dispel myths and fears about technology in general. Use peer interaction and embed technology in	In addition to taking courses on preventing sexual harassment, administrators, teachers, & parents should work with Title IX coordinators & sexual harassment counselors to ensure that this behavior is not tolerated (ch 11)	

10

(continued)

IV Gender Equity Strategies in the Content Areas (chs.. 12, 13, 14, 15, 16, 17, 18, 19, 20, 21)

11

Follow OCR guidelines and other recommendations for effective sexual-harassment policy statements and apply these policies consistently. Also ensure policy is written in sex-neutral terms. (ch. 11)

Have effective investigatory procedures for Title IX violations (ch. 11)

15

Continue to require key mathematics and science courses for all in K–12 so that girls and boys will obtain needed skills and credentials. (chs. 12–13)

Continue to identify underrepresented groups and barriers they face in science areas such as physics, engineering, and computer science and use multiple strategies to increase gender parity. Transform science so that it is appealing to and includes everyone. (ch. 13)

Continue to increase federal funding for gender-equity efforts in science and technology areas where women and minorities are underrepresented. (chs. 5, 10, 13)

Provide periodic national gender analyses of foreign language and English-as a second language students and teachers at all educational levels. (ch. 15)

Encourage bi-literacy for girls and boys so that skills in both languages are valued. (ch. 15)

11

the curriculum content areas in which all students are likely to be successful. (ch. 10)

Use comprehensive effective sexual-harassment prevention training programs appropriate for the assigned students. (ch. 11)

Victims of sexual harassment must be guaranteed effective protection by teachers and administrators including protection from retaliation. (ch. 11)

14

Identify, disseminate, and replicate successful effective programs to encourage, recruit and retain women in mathematics, science, engineering, and technology. (chs. 12–13)

14

Instruction should attend to students' individual differences without perpetuating sex stereotypes. (chs. 14 and others)

Curricula need to include overt attention to gender norms, attitudes, patterns, and outcomes to make sure students understand and can evaluate and counteract the gendered expectations found in all sources, academic, social, and cultural. (ch. 14)

Reading materials should portray females and males in nonstereotypical situations, including reading as something that boys do and leadership as something girls do. (ch. 14)

Instruction should promote sex-equitable language and communication patterns for all students. (chs. 7, 9, 14)

9

Conduct further studies on gender equitable classroom interactions. (ch. 9)

Use clear research based guidelines for implementing and evaluating single sex interventions to optimize the likelihood that they will decrease sex discrimination. (ch. 9)

Examine all education institutions covered by Title IX to determine their compliance with the 1975 Title IX regulations relating to single sex schools and classrooms. (ch. 9)

10

Perform frequent reviews of hidden and subtle forms of bias. (ch. 13 and others)

Communicate equally to women and men about the criteria for success and as needed change the institutional criteria to ensure that it accommodates needs of women and men. (chs. 13, 30)

Use consistent policies to recruit, train, appraise, and mentor that are friendly to both males and females especially in science areas where they are underrepresented.

14

Knowledge of the central role of gender in complex communications processes should be integrated into the preparation of educators. Skills to analyze language and discourse will help educators critically examine curricula as well as the artifacts of popular culture. (ch. 14)

Educators should make sure they do not reinforce biases against femininity and feminine communication behaviors for either girls or boys. (ch. 14)

10

Conduct research on the Net Generation of students to learn about gender differences and similarities. (ch. 10, 53)

Learn what applications of technology make the largest impact on student learning and if there are gender differences. (ch. 10)

Continue to collect and analyze data on sex, race and ethnic differences in mathematical, science, engineering and technology achievement, persistence, and attitudes and contrast variability and mean scores as they relate to differences in achievement, persistence, and attitudes between females and males and in racial and ethnic groups (chs. 12–13)

14

Conduct research using gender analysis to learn about barriers as well as likely causes of progress for women. Use case and ethnographic studies to increase understanding of challenges such as women's lower persistence in continuing in mathematics, physics, engineering and computer science (chs. 12–13, others)

Assessment related to communication skills needs to attend to differences within gender

TABLE 31.1   Key Chapter Recommendations

Policy Recommendations As They Relate to Organizational Improvement	Educational Practice Recommendations As They Relate to Learners	Educational Practice Recommendations as They Relate to Educators (teachers, administrators, parents)	Recommendations for Research, Development, Dissemination and Evaluation
16 At the national level, No Child Left Behind legislation should be revised to require that states assess social studies knowledge that is gender inclusive and require that states disaggregate data on social studies tests by gender, race/ethnicity, and family-income levels. (ch. 16) A program like the Women's Educational Equity Act, which funded much gender equitable social studies curriculum development in the 1980s, needs to receive sufficient funding to encourage substantial curriculum development on topics that reflect a gender-inclusive perspective. (ch. 16) At the state level, as social studies curriculum standards, frameworks & tests are revised, authors should give serious and sustained attention to gender-related issues. (ch. 16) Professional organizations such as the National Council for the Social Studies need to take the lead in addressing issues germane to gender and the social studies in their annual meetings, publications, and organizational structures, such as committees and commissions. (ch. 16) Connections between universities and colleges and K–12 social studies educators should be strengthened to support curriculum transformation based on new knowledge. For example, at the university level, feminist economists have made recommendations about how university courses in economics can more adequately address issues of gender equity. (ch. 16)	**15** Understand issues in language that may cause problems for K–12 students learning English or adults learning a foreign language. For instance, many languages other than English assign gender to nouns. (ch. 15) **16** Social studies lessons, curriculum units, and textbooks, and curriculum standards need to more accurately reflect women's contributions to society and to address gender-related issues. The need is especially acute at the elementary level and in courses on economics and civics/government. For example, civics classes should investigate overcoming barriers to women in political leadership. (ch. 16) Materials on women in diverse cultures, such as those produced by the Upper Midwest History Center and the Wellesley Centers for Women, need to be continually revised and updated to reflect contemporary women's experiences globally in an accurate manner. (ch. 16) **17** Explore self, community, and context through the arts. (ch. 17) Concrete steps must be taken consistently to avoid gender, ethnic, class, sexual preference, or other bias in curriculum, staffing, and treatment of arts and dance students. (ch. 17) Adopt feminist pedagogy stressing the individual and community and reciprocity between the artist and the viewer. It also involves gender as a conscious variable, uses diverse teaching approaches,	More women and minorities need to be hired for university communication faculties and administrations, appointed to publication selection committees, encouraged to submit articles for publication, and nominated for awards. (ch. 14, others) **15** Help language teachers understand differences in culture, language, and gender that may impact language learning and attitudes. (ch. 15) **16** Social studies curriculum developers should give more attention to the diverse experiences of women and girls by class, race, ethnicity, and sexual orientation. (ch. 16) Increase attention to the impact of social studies curriculum on gender equity for girls as well as boys and how it can decrease gender gaps in attitudes and experiences. (ch. 16) Increase teachers' knowledge of gender-equity issues by requiring teacher-education students to take courses on the history of women or gender studies. Teachers should also learn how to include this information in their courses especially if it is not adequately included in their textbooks. (ch. 16) Help pre- and in-service teachers learn about beliefs related to gender and social studies. (ch. 17) At the district level, teachers should be encouraged to plan instruction and experiences for Women's History Month in March and throughout the year (see www.nwhp.org) and include gender issues	groups, and it should encompass the full range of communication skills (listening, reading, speaking, writing, computer, and media literacy). It is important to attend to within-sex group differences, especially those of race, ethnicity, class, culture and any other factors likely to significantly affect both what communicative competence means within that group and how gendered expectations may vary from the mainstream. (chs. 14–15) Much scholarship will be needed to fully understand the links among gender attitudes, teacher behaviors, school curricula, social and cultural factors and student life outcomes. (ch. 14, others) Especially needed is longitudinal work that can examine 1) students' interactions with each other; 2) students' interactions with the wide variety of popular media in which most are immersed; and 3) how and what social/cultural influences enhance their communication and gender competency. (chs. 9, 14, 16, others) **15** Routinely analyze and report on gender of students and teachers of Foreign language and English as a second language in the U.S. (ch. 15) Although the research on gender differences in learning second languages is inconclusive, additional efforts to regularly use gender analysis might provide insights on how to better help girls and boys improve their language skills. (ch. 15) Learn more about how to promote gender equity in language learning in study abroad programs which is often a gendered experience that may be especially discriminatory for women. (ch. 15) Data on gender, race and ethnicity of teachers at all levels in all content areas should be collected and reported at the local, state and national

Policy makers, practitioners, and scholars need to eliminate structural problems in school systems and classrooms that create barriers to gender-equitable social studies. For example, K–12 teachers' avoidance of controversial issues it often results in gender-related topics being omitted from social studies. (ch. 16)

17

Work toward social change through political awareness and action in the arts (ch. 17)

18

Centralize free public web access to accurate data on high school athletics similar to provisions of the Athletics Disclosure Act for collegiate data.

Increase physical education and make gender-integrated nonsexist physical education classes a reality. (ch. 18)

19

Provide government support for effective, accurate comprehensive sexuality-education programs, but eliminate all requirements & federal funding for abstinence only programs. (ch. 19)

20

Increase the number and frequency of compliance reviews that the U.S. Department of Education's Office for Civil Rights conducts in CTE programs, using Title IX and its implementing regulations, as well as the Department's Vocational Education guidelines for eliminating discrimination and denial of services on the basis of race, color, national origin, sex, and handicap, to ensure that all CTE programs provide equal access and opportunity for all students. (ch. 20)

---

encourages empowerment and collaboration, and promotes social change. (ch. 17)

18

Continue work toward increased parity of girls and boys in sports and increase appealing daily coeducational physical education activities for all students.

Ensure that there is equity in this health-promoting physical activity by gender and race. (ch. 18)

19

Make sure that sexuality education is accurate and effective and that it does not teach stereotypes as a fact, that it focuses on pleasure as well as dangers, and that it attends to the needs of LGBT individuals. (ch. 19)

Encourage a focus on health as well as prevention of illness and give attention to the social construction of gender. (ch. 19)

20

Support programs that provide students with experience in nontraditional careers. (ch. 20)

At the middle-school level, educators should take advantage of the fluid quality of this developmental stage and require both boys and girls to explore a wide array of nontraditional career- and technical-education programs in a safe and supportive environment. (ch. 20)

At the high-school level, all courses in career & life planning should include accurate & realistic information about wage-earning potential and economic self-sufficiency based on desired family composition and residence location. (ch. 20)

---

in special celebrations, such as including the long struggle for the Equal Rights Amendment to the U.S. Constitution in celebrations of "Constitution Day" (September 17). (ch. 16)

17

Help future teachers learn how gender inequities are developed and reinforced by the arts. (ch. 17)

Encourage art-education leaders to use gender-equitable practices and to correct gender inequities related to their faculty. (ch. 17)

18

Educate school administrators, physical educators, and coaches about their obligations under Title IX. (ch. 18)

Emphasize gender equity in physical-education teacher-education programs. (ch. 18)

19

Encourage coaches associations, sport governing bodies, and athletic departments to adopt grievance procedures related to sexual harassment. (chs. 11, 18)

20

Encourage medical school administrators and faculty to broaden existing sexuality curricula. (ch. 19)

Review gender-equity competencies for teacher educators in CTE and multicultural education and include as part of the teacher certification and accreditation requirements. (ch. 20)

Teacher associations need to include gender equity as part of their strategic goals and should develop grant programs to fund these activities within the association. (chs. 7, 20)

---

levels for pre K and postsecondary education. (chs. 15–16, others)

Study on how K–12 children learn about gender in social studies as it relates to how they construct meaning about social and political issues (ch. 16)

18

Encourage greater focus in sport science research on gender equity questions relating to physical education and sports. (ch. 18)

19

Prepare consumer information on effective comprehensive sexuality education programs and their impact on girls and boys. (chs. 5, 19)

20

Conduct research on effective strategies for increasing the participation and completion of underrepresented students in nontraditional CTE programs.

–Design research to compare different approaches to achieving gender equity goals. For example, program length, instructional presentation approaches, single sex education, primary age of influence, types of role models.

–Design longitudinal research studies that follow students who participated in nontraditional CTE programs in high school to determine the impact of these experiences on postsecondary success, workforce participation and career selection. (ch. 20)

Conduct research on women in the 21st century workforce and what education reform efforts need to be supported to help reduce workplace bias. (ch. 20)

Conduct research on the impact of pre-service and in-service education with CTE teachers in gender equitable instructional methods on student achievement, course selection, postsecondary transition, college major selection and career entrance. (ch. 20)

(continued)

TABLE 31.1   Key Chapter Recommendations

Policy Recommendations As They Relate to Organizational Improvement	Educational Practice Recommendations As They Relate to Learners	Educational Practice Recommendations as They Relate to Educators (teachers, administrators, parents)	Recommendations for Research, Development, Dissemination and Evaluation
Restore the full-time gender-equity coordinator position in the State Departments of Education to provide technical assistance and professional development to local education agencies to help them meet the core CTE performance indicators & succeed in serving special population students. (ch. 20)	Career guidance and counseling should be integrated into all instructional strategies throughout the school taking advantage of teachable moments when a student can be exposed to the advantages and benefits of a particular career choice. (ch. 20)	Associations should develop professional support systems for teachers of nontraditional CTE courses to share best practices and exchange strategies. (ch. 20)	Conduct research on social security and retirement program reform and its impact on women's long term economic security based on career participation and career selection. (ch. 20)
States and accrediting institutions should establish policies that mandate gender-equity training and competence for all educators involved in counseling and in career and technical education. (ch. 20)	Career guidance and counseling processes must include career exploration that encourages boys and girls to learn more about nontraditional careers and behaviors, but teachers and counselors should be careful not to discourage students from choosing the more traditional careers and behaviors. (ch. 20)	Support systems should be put in place for those teachers who themselves are nontraditional role models in nontraditional CTE programs to provide them with a forum for personal and legal support. (ch. 20)	Continue to test theories of career development and update them to reflect the world of rapidly changing environments, personal values, and needs. (ch. 20)

Implementation of the 2006 Perkins law must include significant and rigorous research on the elimination of sex bias and stereotyping in CTE and on identification of proven practices to positively impact performance on increasing the participation and completion of students in nontraditional CTE programs. (ch. 20) |
States should strategically use the Perkins accountability data that they collect on the participation and completion of students in career- and technical-education programs nontraditional for their gender. (ch. 20)	Educators should make sure career-education materials are representative of a broad range of social classes and minorities. (ch. 20)		**21**
States should use the flexibility given them in the Perkins Act to fund state and local gender-equity initiatives that are data driven and focused on results. (ch. 20)	Schools need to address gender equity as an institution wide priority by making an overt effort to support students nontraditional choices, providing career guidance and counseling that highlights the positive aspects of nontraditional		Women's and Gender Studies programs need more data on such topics as program size, funding, enrollments, faculty, leadership, institutional location, curricular offerings, graduation rates, and placement of graduates and on programs in middle schools, high schools, community colleges, women's service centers and research centers. (ch. 21)
Federal funding (i.e. new legislation, Perkins, WEEA, Elementary and Secondary Education Act, Higher Education Act, etc.) should be provided for research and development to promote gender equity in career and technical education activities and funds should be provided to evaluate the effectiveness of their gender-equity activities in these areas. (ch. 20)	career selection especially for women and girls, taking affirmative actions to hire CTE teachers that are nontraditional role models, and recognizing students of the underrepresented gender who succeed in nontraditional CTE programs. (ch. 20)		Increase research on the structure and content of the programs, the outcomes for students and institutions, & the impact of this work on society at large. (ch. 21)
Strengthen programs and increase funding for the Women's Bureau and other programs to improve working conditions, climate, discrimination, and pay equity for women and men in nontraditional careers. (ch. 20, 5)	Schools must take a proactive role in educating parents about nontraditional career options for their sons and daughters. (ch. 20)

Students should be aware that the interdisciplinary nature of the fields related to women's studies present both challenges and opportunities. The typical | | This research should document the growth, positive contributions, and effective strategies used at all levels from high school women's studies courses to community colleges & adult education. |

674

V. Gender Equity Strategies for Diverse Population (chs. 22, 23, 24, 25, 26, 27, 28)

21

Increase disaggregated national U.S. data on women's and gender studies and related programs. (ch. 21)

Gender issues in education should receive greater attention within Women's and Gender Studies academic programs. (ch. 21)

22

Improve access to all levels and types of educational opportunities for the multiple population groups. (chs. 22–25)

States and school districts should require schools to conduct separate studies of the rates of retention, suspension, expulsion, academic achievement, grade attainment, and participation in extra-curricular activities for African American girls and boys well as other racial and ethnic groups in the U.S. (chs. 22–25)

An accountability system should be developed to enable school districts to present and compare pupil information along race-gender divides, across grade levels, within individual schools, and across the district. (chs. 22–25)

23

Eliminate tracking of Latina/os into stereotypical programs by:
–providing more high-quality bilingual education—not discriminating on the basis of documentation status,
–improving guidance counseling, and access to academic enrichment and special education. (ch. 23)
–increasing access of Latina/os to higher education (ch. 23)

---

set of core women's studies courses focuses on the humanities and social sciences. Gender Studies, Masculinity Studies, Queer Studies, Gay and Lesbian Studies, and related programs have less defined core courses. As they select their courses and activities, students should consider how the options will help them benefit from interdisciplinary perspectives. (Ch. 21).

School-based programs must be developed that encourage understanding of the roles gender has played in African American culture and history. (ch. 22)

23

Support Latina students by cultivating gender and ethnoracial conscious curricula, and address the hidden curriculum that continues to support racist and sexist assumptions. (ch. 23)

Develop programs to increase parents' effectiveness in supporting their children's educational aspirations and use a Latina/o appropriate sex education curriculum. (ch. 23)

24

To change Asian and Pacific Islander American women's overrepresentation in low-wage, dead-end jobs, more and improved programs are needed that develop job skills, provide continuing educational opportunities (focusing especially on Southeast Asian women as the group at highest after risk), and that provide information on workers rights, self-advocacy, and labor organization. (ch. 24)

Accelerate recruitment and support of Asian and Pacific Islander American women in the fields of math, science,

---

Women's & gender studies faculty, students, & activists need to expand efforts to promote the positive impacts of these interdisciplinary fields, & share strategies for building and sustaining programs. National organizations and publications such as Ms. Magazine can play a role in doing this. (ch. 21)

22

More attention must be given to developing teacher awareness of the role of teacher expectations and perceptions on the academic performance of African American males and females.
(ch. 22, pp. 39–41)

Stories of successful African American women and men should be included in the curricula of teacher and principal preparation programs. (ch. 22)

In addition to pedagogical proficiency, professors in teacher and principal preparation programs must present research results to aspiring teachers and administrators that help them to develop initiatives to help African American girls and boys succeed. (ch. 22)

23

Require educators to have updated cultural competency training that includes issues related to gender and diversity among Latino populations. (ch. 23)

24

Attract and support more Asian and Pacific Islander American men and women to the full range of careers in education because of the proportionally smaller representation of these populations in education. (ch. 24)

Educational interventions striving for academic excellence for these diverse students are not truly research-based until rigorous evaluations show what interventions are especially effective for girls and boys in each group. (chs. 24–28)

22

Research is needed to identify possible reasons for the race-gender gap among African American students. For example,
–Study motivational factors for African American girls and boys and their possible relationship to poverty, violence, and health care access.
–Conduct follow-up studies on disaggregated standardized test data to look for gender, race, and within-group comparisons (i.e., disabilities categories, socio-economic status, or educational contexts such as urban, suburban, and rural) and identify possible reasons for increases or decreases in performance.
–More research should be conducted on race and gender equity among African American teachers and principals at both the pre-service and in-service levels.
–Longitudinal studies are needed documenting how gender impacts African American students' educational achievement and attainment as well as their resilience, psycho-social development and coping strategies.
–Evaluate the effects of Afro-centric education on the academic achievement of African American girls and African American boys.
–Study the negative effects of gender role stereotyping of African Americans in education,

(continued)

TABLE 31.1 Key Chapter Recommendations

Policy Recommendations As They Relate to Organizational Improvement	Educational Practice Recommendations As They Relate to Learners	Educational Practice Recommendations as They Relate to Educators (teachers, administrators, parents)	Recommendations for Research, Development, Dissemination and Evaluation
Provide financial incentives to recruit Latina/os educators. (ch. 23)	and engineering where, like the general population, they are underrepresented compared to males. (ch. 24)		particularly at the elementary and secondary levels. (ch. 22)
			At the postsecondary level it is important to learn more about African Americans in majority and HBCU institutions. Examine the implications of the race gender gap at both types of institutions related to race, gender, sexual orientation, disability and other important demarcations. (ch. 22)
			23
			Examine the impact of new immigration policies on Latina/os enrollments, the impact of high stakes testing on graduation rates for Latina/os, the impact of increasing sexualization of girls and young women on Latinas' educational outcomes, and conduct longitudinal studies to examine the relation between school disengagement and pregnancy among Latinas. (ch. 23)
24		**25**	**24**
Federal policy should continue and improve development of economic, educational, and research databases on Asian and Pacific Islander subgroups, as modeled by the 2000 U.S. Census Bureau detailed race/ethnicity reports. (ch. 24)	Create educational environments and practices that positively address the affective development of Asian and Pacific Islander students: tending to career aspirations and choice in the early years of education: explicitly confronting and correcting the negative and limiting assumptions and expectations of stereotypes about the diverse Asian and Pacific Islander American subgroups; actively nurturing their self-concepts, with appropriate parental involvement and input; implementing research-based, comprehensive, antibias curriculums that prevent harassment and violence at school against Asian and Pacific Islander Americans. (ch. 24)	Professional organizations and Indian Nations must promote professional development opportunities, which offer teachers and administrators the opportunity to interact with tribal and urban American Indian communities. (ch. 25)	The research agenda must include topics focusing on affective constructs such as self-concept, individual and group identity, resilience, and how limitations placed on the motivations, aspirations, and opportunities of Asian and Pacific Islander girls and women can be lifted so they may achieve their potential. (ch. 24)
Use policy incentives and regulatory requirements to influence greater representation and equitable treatment of Asian and Pacific Islander Americans in management positions in public- and private-sector organizations, where they are currently underrepresented. (ch. 24)		Non-Indian scholars, teachers, agencies, and institutions need to understand the issue of sovereignty as it relates to the teaching of heritage language and cultural knowledge within schools. (ch. 25)	**25**
25	**25**	Teachers and administrators must know the American Indian communities, both urban and reservation, from which their students come and use teaching methods that are especially effective for their students. (ch. 25)	American Indian scholars and citizens need to work with their communities in conducting research in a respectful manner and in a way that benefits the community as much as it benefits the researcher and results in increased knowledge. (ch. 25)
Change curriculum to reflect the real diversity of Indian Nations and to include historical, cultural, educational, and linguistic conflicts regarding Native Americans. (ch. 25)	Use culturally appropriate educational practices tied to the specific Asian and Pacific Islander subgroups, such as pedagogy that is aware of gendered cultural attitudes and traditions. Textbooks should make a clear distinction between U.S. communities, colonized Pacific Islands, and Asian countries, as well as nuanced representation of female and male biracial or multiracial Asian and Pacific Islander Americans. (ch. 24)	**26**	
26		Title IX coordinators must educate their LGBT constituents, including students, about how they can be a resource for victims of discrimination and harassment. (ch. 26)	
Federal, state, and local policymakers must institute and enforce policies that include "sexual orientation and gender identity" as protected classes along with existing categories such as race, religion, and ability, at all education levels as such policies can improve the climate and chances of success for LGBT students. (ch. 26)	**26**	Accrediting bodies for educational institutions must implement standards and policies to provide equal access to education and promote empowering environments for LGBT faculty, staff, and students. (ch. 26)	
Federal, state, and local policymakers must enact nondiscrimination policies on the basis of sexual and gender orientation in matters of hiring, tenure, promotion, admissions, and financial aid as well as hiring openly LGBT and/or LGBT-sensitive faculty, staff, and	Teachers and administrators must create classrooms that American Indian parents feel comfortable entering (ch. 25)	Preservice teacher education programs and school districts must include information about sexual orientation and gender identity/expression in their curriculum and prepare teachers and others on ways to support LGBT students. (ch. 26)	
	Teachers and their professional organizations should take a firm stance against societal and institutional forms of racism confronted daily by American		

676

administrators in all segments of the school community. (ch. 26)

Federal, state, and local policymakers must ensure equal access and equality of all benefits and privileges granted to students and employees, including their same-sex partners. (ch. 26)

27

Implement more programs for the gifted and talented at every educational level and ensure that they pay attention to gender equity not only in the selection of participants, but also in the content of the programs. (ch. 27)

28**

Include strong provisions for equality between men and women in the proposed UN Convention on the Protection of the Rights and Dignity of Persons with Disabilities. (ch. 28)

Provide access to better disaggregated information on students by sex, race, and disability under NCLB and other legislation designed to help individuals with disabilities. (ch. 28)

Provide federal support for :ms more replicable programs focused on helping students with disabilities and –sensitive evaluations that do not rely only on RTC designs, which are often inappropriate for diversity in terms of disability. (ch. 28)

Continue funding and evaluation of programs that seem promising for students with disabilities such as mentoring programs. (ch. 28)

Indians. This includes stopping the use of American Indian symbols, objects, and peoples as mascots for sports groups and other school-related organizations. It also includes not representing facts based on Euro-American philosophical traditions as "truth" and instead emphasizing multiple "values" systems within classrooms where multiple ethnic groups are represented 25. (ch. 25)

26

Create and support programs such as gay-straight alliances and other student clubs addressing LGBT issues, which can significantly increase students' sense of belonging at school and thereby their likelihood of furthering their educational attainment. (ch. 26)

Provide inclusive curriculum that includes representations of LGBT people, history, and events. (ch. 26)

Implement curricular programs in all K–12 aimed at reducing name-calling and bullying such as GLSEN's No Name-Calling Week (www.nonamecallingweek.org), a curriculum for middle schools or Get a Voice, a comprehensive character education program for K–8 grades (www.getavoice.net). (ch. 26)

Colleges and university as well as private K–12 institutions must actively recruit openly LGBT prospective students and staff.

Use research and examples of programs which work to develop policy which ensures programs that are gender fair. In doing so, develop specific rubrics to evaluate access for girls and minorities or other culturally at risk groups that provide equitable admissions for all. Use

Education administrators must assess their own institutions with regard to school or campus climate and supportive resources for LCBT students. (ch. 26)

27

If within class differentiation of students by ability is used, provide better training for teachers in ways to work with gifted students, and track, report, and compare the results for girls and boys. (ch. 27)

Publicly criticize "popular" books on young children, gender, and learning if they find misrep-esentation of research findings. (ch. 29)

Use informal Internal Review Boards of Indian Nations to maintain quality research (ch. 25)

26

Research on LGBT issues in education should focus on examining:
–the role of sexual orientation (actual and perceived) and gender identity/expression especially in studies of school climate.
–the effectiveness of teacher training programs that address LGBT issues and how such training may affect the school climate for LGBT students,
–the relationship between teachers' LGBT-related beliefs and their action/inaction when anti-LGBT harassment occurs in school,
–the experiences of transgender-identified students in school,
–the relationships among school harassment, supports and academic achievement for LGBT students
–the intersection of sexual orientation and gender with regard to access to education, educational aspirations, and attainment, including examination of gender differences within the population of LGBT students, how males and females may differentially be affected by and cope with victimization experiences, and an examination of potential differential effects by gender of interventions for creating safer schools. (ch. 26)

27

Since research on gender equity and gifted students is minimal. It is important to provide national data on students being served in the various programs, the criteria for their selection, their outcomes, etc. All this information should be broken down by sex and ethnicity, education level, and type of school;
Research should also examine:
–barriers to gifted students participation in programs such as AP related to sex, race, SES;
–underachievement among gifted boys and girls and what program models have been most effective in eliminating this problem?

(continued)

TABLE 31.1   Key Chapter Recommendations

Policy Recommendations As They Relate to Organizational Improvement	Educational Practice Recommendations As They Relate to Learners	Educational Practice Recommendations as They Relate to Educators (teachers, administrators, parents)	Recommendations for Research, Development, Dissemination and Evaluation
	this approach to develop programs which focus on counseling and career education, especially for girls and minorities in gifted programs. (ch. 27)		–experiences at the college level that enhance effective decision-making for gifted students in terms of advanced degrees and career choices? –How gifted and talented students are using technology in ways that foster their talents and is it the same or different by sex? –What types of assistance do gifted men and women need in terms of child care and flexible work schedules in order to promote career success and life satisfaction? (ch. 27)

28

These research questions relate to disabilities:

–What are the implications of the possible over-identification of boys and racial/ethnic minorities in special education?

–What are the implications of the possible under-identification of girls in special education?

–To what extent do girls and boys with different types of disabilities have access to various types of curricula, e.g., math, science, vocational education? (ch. 28)

–For all education levels, what pedagogical strategies are effective in teaching girls and boys with different types of disabilities (ch. 28)

–What factors affect sexual harassment for people with disabilities? How is it similar or different for girls and boys? (ch. 28)

–What is the potential of programs like Positive Behavior Support systems to enhance the capacity of schools to educate all students, especially those with challenging social behaviors? What is its differential effectiveness by gender?

–What are effective instructional practices for students with disabilities whose native language is not English?

–What gender equity issues need to be addressed in terms of instructional practices? (ch. 28)

678

VI. Gender Equity From Early Through Post-secondary Education (chs. 29, 30)

Use association and other guidelines for gender-fair practices and language, since there is agreement that gender stereotypes interfere with children's learning. (chs. 29)

Implement policies to increase equitable salaries for educators working with young children and make it a more desirable activity for men. (ch. 4, 20, 29)

30

Make explicit policies to address individual campus inequities related to race/ethnicity and socio-economic status and gender related to for students, staff, and faculty. (ch. 30)

Since all but two colleges in the U.S. are covered by Title IX, ensure the appointment and support of Title IX coordinators and publicize their roles and responsibilities as well as gender-equity policies on the school's Web site. (ch. 30)

Develop and use a gender-equity institutional self-assessment with the assistance of Title IX campus coordinators, and other offices with accountability responsibilities. It should cover faculty, staff, and students. Also use an equity scorecard that provides useful feedback to campuses about the outcomes of their current practices and fosters organizational learning. (ch. 30)

Improve campus climates by creating policies that are explicit and effective in helping women where they often face discrimination such as parental leave and tenure-clock modifications associated with childbirth. (ch. 30)

Provide more gender-equitable resources for young children and their parents. (ch. 29)

Use activities and experiences for girls and boys that counteract gender stereotypes. For example,

–encourage children to read children's books that break gender-role stereotypes

–encourage children to explore nontraditional areas of interest. encourage girls, as well as boys, to question stereotypes,

–praise demonstrations of daring and curiosity. Resist rescuing girls or providing ready answers for them. Help foster an environment where girls know it is acceptable to get sweaty and dirty in pursuit of a goal.

–suggest activities for girls such as practice in large muscle coordination that may have been more emphasized for boys.

–avoid pitting boys against girls in competitive activities, such as word games, races, and the notorious "quiet game" (a game in which children are often admonished for being the first person to make a sound after an extended period of time).

–do not line up by gender.

–create opportunities for nurturing and caring activities that are in a problem-solving mode and that invite all children's involvement.

–choose girls for leadership positions as often as boys

–present gender-equitable examples by alternating girls and boys names when calling on students. (ch. 29)

30

Attend to special needs of students especially related to their gender such as

---

Individuals working to improve education should rely on research based evidence from this *Handbook* and carefully question contradictory messages and assumptions that come from the media and other sources. (chs. 1, 7, 29)

Become a media critic and encourage others to do so as well. Discuss the portrayals of girls and women on television, in movies, in magazines, and in popular music. (chs. 14, 29)

Visionary leadership in early education environments is needed to structure discourse around the social justice issues that include gender inequities facing children, parents, and other caregivers as well as educators. (ch. 29)

Gender-equity training for early childhood educators, including both certified and noncertified personnel is critical. It should be part of the credentialing and selection criteria. (ch. 29)

Insist that early childhood textbooks on teaching methods include gender-fair practices and research on the effects of gender-bias activities in the classroom. (ch. 29)

Develop and use exemplary and promising programs with gender-fair language that have evidence that they promote gender-fair interactions between teachers and children and increase gender-equity outcomes. (ch. 29)

Gender-equity teacher/caregiver training should

–provide guidance on avoiding treating girls and boys as possessing stereotypic gendered attributes and as needing to be prepared for stereotypic jobs or roles.

Publish and disseminate authoritative information relating to gender-fair practices, activities, books, and interactions for parents and other caregivers. Develop online accessible links to these materials at gender equity organizations, governmental and early childhood organization websites. (ch. 29)

U.S. and other governmental organizations should work collaboratively on supporting programmatic longitudinal research to learn how early education can be used to reduce gender stereotyping and also on ways to reinforce this outcome over the years. (ch. 29)

The fragmented global research on gender equity in early childhood education and developmental issues of young children may be ripe for meta-analyses. (ch. 29)

Develop and activate campaigns to support children's media and toys that promote images of girls and minorities with a positive, gender-fair view that push for the elimination of violent, racist or sexist media and toys. (ch. 29)

30

Learn more about the effectiveness of various types of strategies (women's centers, child care, student support groups, recruitment efforts, etc. to improve the climate and advance gender equity in various types of campuses and in non traditional areas of study. (ch. 30)

Learn about fair ways to increase gender parity in administrative and tenured faculty positions especially in areas where there have been unequal proportions of men and women such as in engineering or nursing. (ch. 30)

Learn what strategies are feasible to not only create more gender equitable employee hiring and promotion but to create more equitable compensation for faculty in women dominated

(continued)

TABLE 31.1   Key Chapter Recommendations

Policy Recommendations As They Relate to Organizational Improvement	Educational Practice Recommendations As They Relate to Learners	Educational Practice Recommendations as They Relate to Educators (teachers, administrators, parents)	Recommendations for Research, Development, Dissemination and Evaluation
Develop fair legal policies on the gender balance on campuses. For example, should institutions be allowed to ensure that there is no more than a 60/40 ratio of women to men students? (ch. 30)	need for child care facilities, security, freedom from sexual harassment, equal pay, equitable participation in sports, athletics, campus leadership and make sure that they know their legal rights. (chs. 4, 11, 18, 30)	–increase the use of strategies such as teacher proximity and structured play time to involve children in activities they may otherwise avoid. –develop verbal and physical interaction patterns that make all children equal participants in non-sex-segregated activities (ch. 29)	specialties such as education versus engineering or even community colleges. (chs. 7, 30) Research is needed on increasing feminist leaders in postsecondary education who will actively advance gender equity for their entire communities. (ch. 30)
		Postsecondary institutions and orga- nizations should educate faculty members civil rights. They should also provide mentoring for faculty & clear & reasonable expectations for success. (chs. 13, 30)	

30

References

College Board. (2006). *College Board announces scores for new SAT(r) with writing section* (Press Release Aug. 29, 2006). Retrieved October 1, 2006, from http://www.collegeboard.com/press/releases/150054.html

Dee, T. S. (2006). The why chromosome: How a teacher's gender affects boys and girls. *Education Next. 2006 No. 4*, 69–75. Palo Alto, CA: Hoover Institution. Retrieved September 20, 2006, from www.educationnext.org.html

Hass, N. (2006, November 5). Revisiting SAT essay: The writing section? Relax. *New York Times*, p. 14.

Homer, E.A. (1997). *Title IX in Michigan 1972–1997*. Michigan NOW Education Task Force.

Hyde, J. S., & Linn, M. C. (2006, October 27). Gender similarities in mathematics and science. *Science, 314*, 599–600.

Jaschik, S. (2006, November 2). Affirmative Action for White C+ Guys. *Inside Higher Ed.* Retrieved November 2, 2006, from http://inside highered.com.

Klein, S., Blackwell, P.J., Campbell, P. B., Dwyer, C. A, Murray, S. R, Russo, L. N., et al. (Eds.). (1985). *Handbook for achieving sex equity through education.* Baltimore: Johns Hopkins University Press.

Klein, S., Dwyer C. A., Fox, L., Grayson, D., Kramarae, C., Pollard, D., et al. (Eds.). (2007). *Handbook for achieving gender equity through education.* Mahwah, NJ: Lawrence Erlbaum Associates.

National Academies (2006) *Beyond Bias and Barriers: Fulfilling the Potential of Women in Academic Science and Engineering.* Washington, DC: National Academies Press.

Office for Civil Rights (1975). *Final Title IX regulation implementing education amendments of 1972 prohibiting sex discrimination in education.* Washington, DC: U.S. Department of Health, Education and Welfare (1975, June).

Office for Civil Rights (2006). *Final regulations non discrimination on the basis of sex in education programs or activities receiving federal financial assistance.* U.S. Department of Education, Washington, DC: Retrieved October 30, 2006, from www.ed.gov/legislation/FedRegister/finrule/2006-4/102506a.html

Sadker, D., & Silber E. S. (Eds.). (2006). *Gender in the classroom: Foundations, skills, methods, and strategies across the curriculum.* Mahwah, NJ: Lawrence Erlbaum Associates.

Secretary Spellings announces more choices in single sex education Amended regulations give communities more flexibility to offer single sex schools and classes. (Press Release. U.S. Department of Education, Washington, DC, October 24, 2006). Retrieved October 24, 2006, from www.ed.gov/news/pressreleases/2006/10/10242006html

Stone, L. (2004). *Turning back the clock: How the Department of Education's proposed amendments to increase single-sex schools and classrooms violate the Constitution and undermine the purpose of Title IX.* Retrieved November 14, 2006, from http://www.feminist.org/education/SexSegregation.asp

U.S. Department of Education. (2006, August 14). "Companion Charter Schools Bring Brighter Choices to Students and Families in New York." *The Education Innovator Number 9* [Electronic Newsletter]. Washington, DC: Office of Innovation and Improvement. Retrieved November 5, 2006, from http://www.ed.gov/news/newsletters/innovator/2006/0814.html

AUTHOR INDEX

Numbers in *italics* indicate pages with complete bibliographic information.

X

Y

Z

SUBJECT INDEX

Page references followed by *f* indicate figure.
Page references followed by *t* indicate table.
Page references followed by *n* indicate footnote.